Computer and Information Security Handbook

Second Edition

Edited by

John R. Vacca

AMSTERDAM • BOSTON • HEIDELBERG • LONDON • NEW YORK • OXFORD • PARIS
SAN DIEGO • SAN FRANCISCO • SINGAPORE • SYDNEY • TOKYO

Morgan Kaufmann Publishers is an imprint of Elsevier

ELSEVIER

Publisher: Steve Elliot
Senior Developmental Editor: Nathaniel McFadden
Project Manager: Mohanambal Natarajan
Cover Designer: Russell Purdy

Morgan Kaufmann Publishers is an imprint of Elsevier.
225 Wyman Street, Waltham, MA 02451, USA

Library of Congress Cataloging-in-Publication Data
Computer and information security handbook / edited by John R. Vacca.--Second edition.
    pages cm
  Includes bibliographical references and index.
  ISBN 978-0-12-394397-2 (alk. paper)
 1. Computer networks--Security measures.   2. Penetration testing (Computer security) I. Vacca, John. R.
  QA76.9.A25C627 2013
  005.8--dc23

                                                                    2013020996

British Library Cataloguing-in-Publication Data
A catalogue record for this book is available from the British Library.

ISBN: 978-0-12-394397-2

For information on all Morgan Kaufmann publications,
visit our Web site at *www.mkp.com*

Printed in the United States of America

14 15 16 17   10 9 8 7 6 5 4 3 2

This book is dedicated to my wife, Bee.

Contents

Contents

Online Chapters and Appendices

The second edition of the *Computer and Information Security Handbook* goes well beyond the classic reference status of the first edition. The second edition provides expanded coverage of security for new technologies and textbook elements including review questions, exercises, hands-on projects, and case projects for individual students and for groups of students studying in a cohort environment.

The expanded technology coverage includes cloud computing, optical networks, cryptography, and intrusion detection and prevention. The expanded security practices covered includes ethical hacking, cyber and systems forensics, cyber attack and cyber warfare countermeasures.

The expansion of technology and methods in the second edition of the *Computer and Information Security Handbook* provides the security professional and security students with a more comprehensive reference. The second edition is an essential addition to the security libraries or corporations, universities and colleges, as well as all security practitioners regardless of their level of expertise.

The inclusion of textbook elements makes the second edition of the *Computer and Information Security Handbook* a viable and attractive textbook for technical schools, colleges, and university courses at all levels. In that security issues and technology are virtually universal, the second edition will be usable in classrooms around the world.

John Vacca, and his team of computer and information security experts have assembled a wealth of knowledge along with practical actionable methods to address a wide range of security issues. The second edition of the *Computer and Information Security Handbook* will be a powerful tool in the hands of those who are working to protect and defend computer and information assets around the world.

Michael Erbschloe
Information Security Consultant
Michael Erbschloe teaches information security courses at Webster University in St. Louis, Missouri.

The second edition of this comprehensive handbook serves as a professional reference to provide today's most complete and concise view of computer security and privacy available in one volume. It offers in-depth coverage of computer security theory, technology, and practice as they relate to established technologies as well as recent advancements. It explores practical solutions to a wide range of security issues. Individual chapters are authored by leading experts in the field and address the immediate and long-term challenges in the authors' respective areas of expertise.

The primary audience for this handbook consists of researchers and practitioners in industry and academia as well as security technologists and engineers working with or interested in computer security. This comprehensive reference will also be of value to students in upper-division undergraduate and graduate-level courses in computer security.

ORGANIZATION OF THIS BOOK

The book is organized into ten parts composed of 70 contributed chapters by leading experts in their fields, as well as 12 appendices, including an extensive glossary (available online) of computer security terms and acronyms.

Part 1: Overview of System and Network Security: A Comprehensive Introduction

Part 1 discusses how to build a secure organization; generate cryptography; how to detect system intrusions; how to prevent system intrusions; secure cloud computing systems; fault tolerance and resilience in cloud computing environments; how to secure web applications, services and servers; UNIX and Linux security; eliminate the security weakness of Linux and UNIX Operating systems; Internet and intranet security; the botnet problem; LAN security; wireless network security; wireless sensor network security; cellular network security, RFID security; optical network security; and, optical wireless network security. For instance:

Chapter 1, "Building a Secure Organization," sets the stage for the rest of the book by presenting insight into where to start building a secure organization.

Chapter 2, "A Cryptography Primer," provides an overview of cryptography. It shows how communications may be encrypted and transmitted.

Chapter 3, "Detecting System Intrusions," describes the characteristics of the DSI technologies and provides recommendations for designing, implementing, configuring, securing, monitoring, and maintaining them.

Chapter 4, "Preventing System Intrusions," discusses how to prevent system intrusions and where an unauthorized penetration of a computer in your enterprise or an address in your assigned domain can occur.

Chapter 5, "Guarding Against Network Intrusions," shows how to guard against network intrusions by understanding the variety of attacks, from exploits to malware and social engineering.

Chapter 6, "Securing Cloud Computing Systems," discusses various cloud computing environments and methods to make them more secure for hosting companies and their customers.

Chapter 7, "Fault Tolerance and Resilience in Cloud Computing Environments," focuses on characterizing the recurrent failures in a typical Cloud computing environment, analyzing the effects of failures on user's applications, and surveying fault tolerance solutions corresponding to each class of failures.

Chapter 8, "Securing Web Applications, Services and Servers," provides a general overview of the breadth of web service security, an introduction to the subject area, and guides the reader to sources with deeper information.

Chapter 9, "UNIX and Linux Security," discusses how to scan for vulnerabilities; reduce denial-of-service (DoS) attacks; deploy firewalls to control network traffic; and build network firewalls.

Chapter 10, "Eliminating the Security Weakness of Linux and UNIX Operating Systems," presents an introduction to securing UNIX in general and Linux in particular, providing some historical context and describing some fundamental aspects of the secure operating system architecture.

Chapter 11, "Internet Security," shows you how cryptography can be used to address some of the security issues besetting communications protocols.

Chapter 12, "The Botnet Problem," describes the botnet threat and the countermeasures available to network security professionals.

Chapter 13, "Intranet Security," covers internal security strategies and tactics; external security strategies and tactics; network access security; and Kerberos.

Chapter 14, "Local Area Network Security," discusses network design and security deployment as well as ongoing management and auditing.

Chapter 15, "Wireless Network Security," presents an overview of wireless network security technology; how to design wireless network security and plan for wireless network security; how to install, deploy, and maintain wireless network security; information warfare countermeasures: the wireless network security solution; and wireless network security solutions and future directions.

Chapter 16, "Wireless Sensor Network Security," helps organizations design, implement and evaluate wireless sensor intrusion detection systems, which aim at transferring the computational load of the operation from the sensors to the base station.

Chapter 17, "Cellular Network Security," addresses the security of the cellular network; educates readers on the current state of security of the network and its vulnerabilities; outlines the cellular network specific attack taxonomy, also called *three-dimensional attack taxonomy*; discusses the vulnerability assessment tools for cellular networks; and provides insights into why the network is so vulnerable and why securing it can prevent communication outages during emergencies.

Chapter 18, "RFID Security," describes the RFID tags and RFID reader and back-end database in detail.

Chapter 19, *"Optical Network Security,"* presents an analysis of attack and protection problems in optical networks. It also proposes a conceptual framework for modeling attack problems and protection schemes for optical networks.

Chapter 20, *"Optical Wireless Network Security,"* focuses on free space optics (FSO) and the security that has been developed to protect its transmissions, as well as an overview of the basic technology.

Part 2: Managing Information Security

Part 2 discusses how to protect mission-critical systems; deploy security management systems, policy-driven system management, IT security management, online identity and user management services, intrusion detection and prevention systems, TCP/IP packet analysis, intruder's genesis, firewalls, penetration testing; conduct vulnerability assessments and security metrics. For instance:

Chapter 21, "Information Security Essentials for IT Managers: Protecting Mission-Critical Systems," discusses how security goes beyond technical controls and encompasses people, technology, policy, and operations in a way that few other business objectives do.

Chapter 22, "Security Management Systems," examines documentation requirements and maintaining an effective security system as well as conducting assessments.

Chapter 23, "Policy-driven System Management," focuses particularly on PBM's use for securing computing systems according to high-level security goals.

Chapter 24, "Information Technology Security Management," discusses the processes that are supported with enabling organizational structure and technology to protect an organization's information technology operations and IT assets against internal and external threats, intentional or otherwise.

Chapter 25, "Online Identity and User Management Services," presents the evolution of identity management requirements. It also surveys how the most advanced identity management technologies fulfill present-day requirements. It discusses how mobility can be achieved in the field of identity management in an ambient intelligent/ubiquitous computing world.

Chapter 26, "Intrusion Detection and Prevention Systems," discusses the nature of computer system intrusions, the people who commit these attacks, and the various technologies that can be utilized to detect and prevent them.

Chapter 27, "TCP/IP Packet Analysis," discusses how TCP/IP packets are constructed, and analyzed to interpret the applications that use the TCP/IP stack.

Chapter 28, "The Enemy (The Intruder's Genesis)," discusses process of creating a formal set of governance to define the CYBERSECURITY, and course of actions to be taken to defend against the CYBERATTACKS.

Chapter 29, "Firewalls," provides an overview of firewalls: policies, designs, features, and configurations. Of course, technology is always changing, and network firewalls are no exception. However, the intent of this chapter is to describe aspects of network firewalls that tend to endure over time.

Chapter 30, "Penetration Testing," describes how testing differs from an actual "hacker attack" as well as some of the ways penetration tests are conducted, how they're controlled, and what organizations might look for when choosing a company to conduct a penetration test for them.

Chapter 31, "What Is Vulnerability Assessment?" covers the fundamentals: defining vulnerability, exploit, threat, and risk; analyzing vulnerabilities and exploits; and configuring scanners. It also shows you how to generate reports, assess risks in a changing environment, and manage vulnerabilities.

Chapter 32, "Security Metrics: An Introduction and Literature Review" describes the need for security metrics, followed by a discussion of the nature of security metrics, including what makes a good security metric, what security metrics have been used in the past, and how security metrics can be scientifically based.

Part 3: Cyber, Network, and Systems Forensics Security and Assurance

Part 3 discusses how to implement cyber forensics; cyber forensics and incidence response; how to secure e-discovery, and network forensics. For instance:

Chapter 33, "Cyber Forensics," is intended to provide an in-depth familiarization with computer forensics as a career, a job, and a science. It will help you avoid mistakes and find your way through the many aspects of this diverse and rewarding field.

Chapter 34, "Cyber Forensics And Incidence Response," discusses the steps and methods to respond to incidents and conduct cyber forensics investigations.

Chapter 35, "Securing e-Discovery," explains EDRM from an industry insider perspective; collates issues of performance, urgency, accuracy, risk, and security to a zoned model that underpins the EDRM; explains the very real need for organizations to secure certain operations internally; provides examples through real-world experiences of flawed discovery, and what should have been done differently; and, discusses how security *from* the information as well as security *of* it, plays a critical role throughout much of the EDRM.

Chapter 36, "Network Forensics," helps you determine the path from a victimized network or system through any intermediate systems and communication pathways, back to the point of attack origination or the person who should be held accountable.

Part 4: Encryption Technology

Part 4 discusses how to implement data encryption, satellite encryption, public key infrastructure, and instant-messaging security. For instance:

Chapter 37, "Data Encryption," is about the role played by cryptographic technology in data security.

Chapter 38, "Satellite Encryption," proposes a method that enhances and complements satellite encryption's role in securing the information society. It also covers satellite encryption policy instruments; implementing satellite encryption; misuse of satellite encryption technology; and results and future directions.

Chapter 39, "Public Key Infrastructure," explains the cryptographic background that forms the foundation of PKI systems; the mechanics of the X.509 PKI system (as elaborated by the Internet Engineering Task Force);

the practical issues surrounding the implementation of PKI systems; a number of alternative PKI standards; and alternative cryptographic strategies for solving the problem of secure public key distribution.

Chapter 40, "Instant-Messaging Security," helps you develop an IM security plan, keep it current, and make sure it makes a difference.

Part 5: Privacy and Access Management

Part 5 discusses Internet privacy, personal privacy policies, virtual private networks, identity theft, and VoIP security. For instance:

Chapter 42, "Privacy On The Internet," addresses the privacy issues in the digital society from various points of view, investigating the different aspects related to the notion of privacy and the debate that the intricate essence of privacy has stimulated; the most common privacy threats and the possible economic aspects that may influence the way privacy is (and especially is not currently) managed in most firms; the efforts in the computer science community to face privacy threats, especially in the context of mobile and database systems; and the network-based technologies available to date to provide anonymity when communicating over a private network.

Chapter 43, "Privacy-enhancing Technologies," provides an overview to the area of Privacy-enhancing Technologies (PETs), which help to protect privacy by technically enforcing legal privacy principles.

Chapter 44, "Personal Privacy Policies," begins with the derivation of policy content based on privacy legislation, followed by a description of how a personal privacy policy may be constructed semiautomatically. It then shows how to additionally specify policies so that negative unexpected outcomes can be avoided. Finally, it describes the author's Privacy Management Model, which explains how to use personal privacy policies to protect privacy, including what is meant by a "match" of consumer and service provider policies and how nonmatches can be resolved through negotiation.

Chapter 45, "Detection Of Conflicts In Security Policies," identifies the common approaches to the identification of security conflicts considering three relevant scenarios: access control policies, policy execution, and network protection. The chapter focuses on the detection of the conflicts.

Chapter 46, "Supporting User Privacy Preferences in Digital Interactions," describes solutions supporting both client privacy preferences, and server disclosure policies.

Chapter 47, "Privacy and Security in Environmental Monitoring Systems: Issues and Solutions," identifies the main security and privacy issues characterizing the environmental data as well as the environmental monitoring infrastructures

Chapter 48, "Virtual Private Networks," covers VPN scenarios, VPN comparisons, and information assurance requirements. It also covers building VPN tunnels; applying cryptographic protection; implementing IP security; and deploying virtual private networks.

Chapter 49, "Identity Theft," describes the importance of understanding the human factor of ID theft security and details the findings from a study on deceit.

Chapter 50, "VoIP Security," deals with the attacks targeted toward a specific host and issues related to social engineering.

Part 6: Storage Security

Part 6 covers storage area network (SAN) security and risk management. For instance:

Chapter 51, "SAN Security," describes the following components: protection rings; security and protection; restricting access to storage; access control lists (ACLs) and policies; port blocks and port prohibits; and zoning and isolating resources.

Chapter 52, "Storage Area Networking Security Devices," covers all the issues and security concerns related to SAN security.

Chapter 53, "Risk Management," discusses physical security threats, environmental threats, and incident response.

Part 7: Physical Security

Part 7 discusses physical security essentials, disaster recovery, biometrics, homeland security, and Cyber warfare. For instance:

Chapter 54, "Physical Security Essentials," is concerned with physical security and some overlapping areas of premises security. It also looks at physical security threats and then considers physical security prevention measures.

Chapter 55, "Disaster Recovery," provides insight to the job of DR, and provide a framework of what is necessary to achieve a successful Disaster Recovery plan.

Chapter 56, "Biometrics," discusses the different types of biometrics technology and verification systems and how the following work: biometrics eye analysis technology; biometrics facial recognition technology; facial thermal imaging; biometrics finger-scanning analysis technology; biometrics geometry analysis technology; biometrics verification technology; and privacy-enhanced, biometrics-based verification/authentication as well as biometrics solutions and future directions.

Chapter 57, "Homeland Security," describes some principle provisions of U.S. homeland security-related laws and Presidential directives. It gives the organizational changes that were initiated to support homeland security in the United States. The chapter highlights the 9/11 Commission that Congress charted to provide a full account of the circumstances surrounding the 2001 terrorist attacks and to develop recommendations for corrective measures that could be taken to prevent future acts of terrorism. It also details the Intelligence Reform and Terrorism Prevention Act of 2004 and the Implementation of the 9/11 Commission Recommendations Act of 2007.

Chapter 58, "Cyber Warfare," defines cyber warfare (CW) and discusses its most common tactics, weapons, and tools as well as comparing CW terrorism with conventional warfare and addressing the issues of liability and the available legal remedies under international law.

Part 8: Practical Security

Part 8 discusses *system security*, how to secure *the infrastructure*, *access controls*, assessments and audits and fundamentals of cryptography. For instance:

Chapter 59, "System Security," shows you how to protect your information from harm, and also ways to make your data readily available for access to an intended audience of users.

Chapter 60, "Securing the Infrastructure," focuses on how security is presented to protect the infrastructure. Smart grid cybersecurity in this chapter, also addresses not only deliberate attacks, such as from disgruntled employees, industrial espionage, and terrorists; but, also inadvertent compromises of the information infrastructure due to user errors, equipment failures, and natural disasters.

Chapter 61, "Access Controls," endeavours to inform the reader about the different types of access controls that are being used, and describes the pros and cons they might have.

Chapter 62, "Assessments and Audits," presents the basic technical aspects of conducting information security assessments and audits. It presents technical testing and examination methods and techniques that an organization might use as part of an assessment and audit, and offers insights to assessors on their execution and the potential impact they may have on systems and networks.

Chapter 63, "Fundamentals of Cryptography," discusses how information security is the discipline that provides protection of information from intrusion and accidental or incidental loss. It also provides a framework for the protection of information from unauthorized use, copying, distribution, or destruction of data.

Part 9: Advanced Security

Part 9 discusses security through diversity, online reputation, content filtering, and data loss protection. For instance:

Chapter 64, "Security Through Diversity," covers some of the industry trends in adopting diversity in hardware, software, and application deployments. This chapter also covers the risks of uniformity, conformity, and the ubiquitous impact of adopting standard organizational principals without the consideration of security.

Chapter 65, "Online e-Reputation Management Services," discusses the general understanding of the human notion of reputation. It explains how this concept of reputation fits into computer security. The chapter presents the state of the art of attack-resistant reputation computation. It also gives an overview of the current market of online reputation services. The chapter concludes by underlining the need to standardize online reputation for increased adoption and robustness.

Chapter 66, "Content Filtering," examines the many benefits and justifications of Web-based content filtering such as legal liability risk reduction, productivity gains, and bandwidth usage. It also explores the downside and unintended consequences and risks that improperly deployed or misconfigured systems create. The chapter also looks into methods to subvert and bypass these systems and the reasons behind them.

Chapter 67, "Data Loss Protection," introduces the reader to a baseline understanding of how to investigate and evaluate DLP applications in the market today.

Chapter 68, "Satellite Cyber Attack Search and Destroy," discusses satellite cyber attacks with regards to hacking, interference and jamming.

Chapter 69, "Verifiable Voting Systems," emphasizes the challenge to reconcile the secrecy of the ballot, with demonstrable correctness of the result.

Chapter 70, "Advanced Data Encryption," explores advanced data encryption algorithms.

SUPPLEMENTAL MATERIALS

Instructor materials including a glossary, lecture slides, figures from the text, exercise solutions, and sample syllabi are available at: store.elsevier.com/product.jsp?isbn=9780123943972 (click the "Resources" tab at the bottom of the page)

John R. Vacca
Editor-in-Chief
john2164@windstream.net
www.johnvacca.com

Acknowledgments

There are many people whose efforts on this book have contributed to its successful completion. I owe each a debt of gratitude and want to take this opportunity to offer my sincere thanks.

A very special thanks to my publisher, Steve Elliot, without whose continued interest and support this book would not have been possible. Senior development editor Nate McFadden provided staunch support and encouragement when it was most needed. Thanks to my production project manager, Mohanambal Natarajan, whose fine work and attention to detail has been invaluable. Thanks also to my marketing manager, Todd Conly, whose efforts on this book have been greatly appreciated. Finally, thanks to all the other people at Morgan Kaufmann Publishers/Elsevier Science & Technology Books, whose many talents and skills are essential to a finished book.

Thanks to my wife, Bee Vacca, for her love, her help, and her understanding of my long work hours. Also, a very, very special thanks to Michael Erbschloe for writing the Foreword. Finally, I wish to thank all the following authors who contributed chapters that were necessary for the completion of this book: Claudio Agostino Ardagna, Jeffrey S. Bardin , Sanjay Bavisi, Stefan Berthold, Gerald Beuchelt, Rahul Bhaskar, Chiara Braghin, Albert Caballero, Professor Erdal Cayirci, Tom Chen, Hongbing Cheng, Lauren Collins, Marco Cremonini, Sam Curry, Christopher Day, Sabrina De Capitani Di Vimercati, Scott R. Ellis, Michael Erbschloe, Simone Fischer-Hbner, Sara Foresti, Errin W. Fulp, Anna Granova, Yong Guan, Cem Gurkok, Feng Hao, James T. Harmening, Markus Jakobsson, Ravi Jhawar, Almantas Kakareka, Bhushan Kapoor, Sokratis K. Katsikas, Dalia Khader, Larry Korba, Kameswari Kotapati, Thomas F. LaPorta, Jean Lencrenon, Peng Liu, Tewfiq El Maliki, John R. Mallery, Bill Mansoor, Luther Martin, John McDonald, John McGowan, Peter F. Nicoletti, Kevin Noble, Pramod Pandya, Harsh Kupwade Patil, Stefano Paraboschi, Thea Peacock, Ken Perkins, Vincenzo Piuri, Henrik Plate, Daniel Ramsbrock, Chunming Rong, Robert Rounsavall, Peter Ryan, Marco Santambrogio, Mario Santana, Steve Schneider, Jean-Marc Seigneur, Marco Slaviero, Daniel S. Soper, Terence Spies, William Stallings, Alex Tsow, Jesse Walker, Patrick J. Walsh, Xinyuan Wang, Michael A. West, Dan Wing, Zhe Zia, George O.M. Yee, Liang Yan, Gansen Zhao.

John Vacca is an information technology consultant, professional writer, editor, reviewer and internationally-known, best-selling author based in Pomeroy, Ohio. Since 1982, John has authored 72 *books* (some of his most recent books include):

- Identity Theft (Cybersafety) (*Publisher:* Chelsea House Pub (April 1, 2012)
- System Forensics, Investigation, And Response (*Publisher:* Jones & Bartlett Learning (September 24, 2010)
- Managing Information Security (*Publisher:* Syngress (an imprint of Elsevier Inc.) (March 29, 2010))
- Network and Systems Security (*Publisher:* Syngress (an imprint of Elsevier Inc.) (March 29, 2010))
- Computer and Information Security Handbook (*Publisher:* Morgan Kaufmann (an imprint of Elsevier Inc.) (June 2, 2009))
- Biometric Technologies and Verification Systems (*Publisher:* Elsevier Science & Technology Books (March 16, 2007))
- Practical Internet Security (Hardcover): (*Publisher:* Springer (October 18, 2006))
- Optical Networking Best Practices Handbook (Hardcover): (*Publisher*: Wiley-Interscience (November 28, 2006))
- Guide to Wireless Network Security (*Publisher:* Springer (August 19, 2006)
- Computer Forensics: Computer Crime Scene Investigation (With CD-ROM), 2nd Edition (*Publisher:* Charles River Media (May 26, 2005)

and, more than 600 articles in the *areas* of advanced storage, computer security and aerospace technology (copies of articles and books are available upon request). John was also a configuration management specialist, computer specialist, and the computer security official (CSO) for NASA's space station program (Freedom) and the International Space Station Program, from 1988 until his retirement from NASA in 1995. In addition, John is also an *independent online book reviewer*. Finally, John was one of the security consultants for the MGM movie titled: "AntiTrust," which was released on January 12, 2001. A detailed copy of my author bio can be viewed at URL: http://www.johnvacca.com. John can be reached at: john2164@windstream.net.

Claudio Agostino Ardagna (Chapter 42), Professor, Dept. of Information Technology, University of Milan, Crema, Italy

Jeffrey Bardin (Chapter 51, 68), Chief Intelligence Strategist, Treadstone 71 LLC, Barre, MA 01005

Sanjay Bavisi (Chapter 30), President, EC-Council, Selangor, Malaysia

Stefan Berthold (Chapter 43), Tek. Lic., Karlstad University, Karlstad/Sweden

Gerald Beuchelt (Chapters 8, 9), Principal Software Systems Engineer, Bedford, MA 01803

Rahul Bhaskar (Chapter 24, 57), Professor, Department of Information Systems and Decision Sciences, California State University, Fullerton, California 92834

Chiara Braghin (Chapter 42), Professor, Dept. of Information Technology, University of Milan, Crema, Italy

Albert Caballero CISSP, GSEC (Chapter 21), Chief Technology Officer—CTO, Digital Era Group, LLC, Surfside, Fl. 33154

Professor Erdal Cayirci (Chapters 15, 18), Professor, University of Stavanger, N-4036 Stavanger, Norway

Thomas M. Chen (Chapter 5, 16, 50), Professor, Swansea University, Singleton Park, SA2 8PP, Wales, United Kingdom

Hongbing Cheng (Chapter 15, 18), Professor, University of Stavanger, Norway

Lauren Collins (Chapters 19, 55, 59, 60, 61, 62), Senior Systems Engineer, kCura Corporation, Chicago, IL 60604

Marco Cremonini (Chapter 42), Professor, Dept. of Information Technology, University of Milan, Crema, Italy

Samuel J.J. Curry (Chapter 41), VP Product Management, RSA, the Security Division of EMC, Bedford, Massachusetts 01730

Christopher Day, CISSP, NSA:IEM (Chapter 26), Senior Vice President, Secure Information Systems, Terremark Worldwide, Inc., Miami, Florida 33131

Sabrina De Capitani Di Vimercati (Chapter 47), Professor, Università degli Studi di Milano, Crema — Italy

Scott R. Ellis EnCE, RCA (Chapters 2, 20, 33, 35, 55, 63), Manager, Infrastructure Engineering Team, kCura, Chicago, IL 60604

Michael Erbschloe (Foreword), Teaches Information Security courses at Webster University, St. Louis, Missouri 63119

Simone Fischer-Hbner (Chapter 43), Professor, Karlstad University, Karlstad/Sweden

Sara Foresti (Chapter 46), Professor, Università degli Studi di Milano, Crema (CR), Italy

Errin W. Fulp (Chapter 29), Professor, Department of Computer Science, Wake Forest University, Winston-Salem, North Carolina 27109

Anna Granova (Chapter 58), Advocate of the High Court of South Africa, Member of the Pretoria Society of Advocates, University of Pretoria, Computer Science Department, Hillcrest, Pretoria, South Africa, 0002

Yong Guan (Chapter 36), Litton Assistant Professor, Department of Electrical and Computer Engineering, Iowa State University, Ames, Iowa 50011

Cem Gurkok (Chapter 6, 34), Threat Intelligence Development Manager, Terremark, Worldwide, Inc., Miami, Florida 33131

Feng Hao (Chapters 40), Professor, Newcastle University, Newcastle Upon Tyne NE1 7RU

James T. Harmening (Chapters 22, 48), President, Computer Bits, Inc., Chicago, Illinois 60602

Markus Jakobsson (Chapter 49), Associate Professor of Informatics at IUB and Associate Director of CACR, Indiana University, Bloomington, IN 47408

Ravi Jhawar (Chapter 7), Professor, Universita' degli Studi di Milano, Crema (CR), Italy

Almantas Kakareka CISSP, GSNA, GSEC, CEH (Chapter 3, 31), CTO, Demyo, Inc., Sunny Isles Beach, Florida 33160

Bhushan Kapoor (Chapters 24, 37, 57), Chair, Department of Information Systems and Decision Sciences, California State University, Fullerton, California 92834

Sokratis K. Katsikas (Chapter 53), Department of Technology Education & Digital Systems, University of Piraeus, Piraeus 18532, Greece

Dalia Khader (Chapter 40), Collaborateur scientifique, University of Luxemburg, Coudenhove-Kalergi, L-1359 Luxembourg

Larry Korba **(Chapter 44),** Ottawa, Ontario, Canada K1G 5N7.

Kameswari Kotapati **(Chapter 17),** Department of Computer Science and Engineering, The Pennsylvania State University, University Park, Pennsylvania 16802

Thomas F. LaPorta **(Chapter 17),** Department of Computer Science and Engineering, The Pennsylvania State University, University Park, Pennsylvania 16802

Jean Lancrenon **(Chapter 40),** Interdisciplinary Centre for Security, Reliability and Trust, Luxembourg-Kirchberg, Luxembourg

Peng Liu **(Chapter 17),** Director, Cyber Security Lab, College of Information Sciences and Technology, The Pennsylvania State University, University Park, Pennsylvania 16802

Tewfiq El Maliki **(Chapter 25),** Telecommunications labs, University of Applied Sciences of Geneva, Geneva, Switzerland

John Mallery **(Chapter 1),** President, Mallery Technical Training and Consulting, Inc., Overland Park, KS 66223

Bill Mansoor **(Chapter 13),** Information Security Analyst III, Information Security Office County of Riverside, Viejo, California 92692

Luther Martin **(Chapter 56),** Chief Security Architect, Voltage Security, Palo Alto, California 94304

John McDonald **(Chapter 51),** EMC Corporation, Hopkinton, Massachusetts 01748

John McGowan **(Chapter 51),** EMC Corporation, Hopkinton, Massachusetts 01748

Peter F. Nicoletti **(Chapter 66),** Miami, Florida, Tavernier, FL 33070

Kevin Noble CISSP GSEC **(Chapter 64),** Director, Secure Information Services, Terremark Worldwide Inc., Miami, Florida 33132

Pramod Pandya **(Chapters 14, 27, 28, 37, 70),** Professor, Department of Information Systems and Decision Sciences, California State University, Fullerton, California 92834

Harsh Kupwade Patil **(Chapter 16, 50),** Professor, Southern Methodist University, Dallas, Texas

Stefano Paraboschi **(Chapter 23, 45),** Professor, Universita degli studi di Bergamo, Bergamo Italy

Thea Peacock **(Chapter 69),** Professor, University of Luxemburg, Coudenhove-Kalergi L-1359 Luxembourg

Ken Perkins **(Chapter 67),** CIPP (Certified Information Privacy Professional), Sr. Systems Engineer, Blazent Incorporated, Denver, Colorado 80206

Vincenzo Piuri **(Chapter 7, 47),** Professor, Universita' degli Studi di Milano, 26013 Crema (CR), Italy

Henrik Plate **(Chapter 23),** Senior Researcher, CISSP, SAP Research Security & Trust, Mougins, France

Daniel Ramsbrock **(Chapter 12),** Senior Consultant, CapTech Consulting, Richmond, VA 23220

Chunming Rong **(Chapters 15, 18),** Professor, Ph.D., Chair of Computer Science Section, Faculty of Science and Technology, University of Stavanger, N-4036 Stavanger, Norway

Robert Rounsavall **(Chapter 52),** CEO, Digital Era Group, LLC, Miami, Florida 33155

Peter Y.A. Ryan **(Chapter 40, 69),** Professor, GCWN, University of Luxemburg, Coudenhove-Kalergi, L-1359 Luxembourg

Mario Santana **(Chapter 10),** Consultant, Terremark, Miami, Florida 33131

Steve Schneider **(Chapter 69),** Profesor, University of Surrey, Guildford, Surrey, GU2 7XH

Jean-Marc Seigneur **(Chapters 25, 65),** Advanced Systems Group, University of Geneva, Switzerland

Marco Slaviero **(Chapters 58),** Security Analyst, SensePost Pty Ltd, Pretoria, South Africa

Daniel S. Soper **(Chapter 38),** Professor, Information and Decision Sciences Department, Mihaylo College of Business and Economics, California State University, Fullerton, California 92834-6848

Terence Spies **(Chapter 39),** Chief Technology Officer// vice president of engineering, Voltage Security, Inc., Palo Alto, California 94304

William Stallings **(Chapter 54),** Independent consultant, Brewster Massachusetts 02631

Alex Tsow **(Chapter 49),** The MITRE Corporation, Mclean, Virginia 22102

Jesse Walker **(Chapter 11),** Principal Engineer, Intel Corporation, Hillsboro, Oregon 97124

Patrick J. Walsh **(Chapter 5),** eSoft Inc., Broomfield, Colorado 80021

Xinyuan Wang **(Chapter 12),** Professor, Department of Computer Science, George Mason University, Fairfax, Virginia 22030

Michael West **(Chapter 4),** Senior technical writer, Truestone Maritime Operations Martinez, California 94553

Dan Wing **(Chapter 50),** Distinguished Engineer, Cisco Systems, Inc., San Jose, CA 95123

Zhe Xia **(Chapters 69),** Professor, University of Surrey, Guildford, Surrey, GU2 7XH

George O.M. Yee **(Chapter 32, 44),** Adjunct Research Professor, Carleton University, Ottawa, ON, Canada K1G 5N7

Liang Yan **(Chapter 15, 18),** Professor, University of Stavanger, Norway

Gansen Zhao **(Chapter 15, 18),** Professor, South China Normal University, Guangzhou 510631, P.R.China

## Part I

Overview of System and Network Security: A Comprehensive Introduction

## Chapter 1

Building a Secure Organization

John Mallery

Mallery Technical Training and Consulting, Inc.

It seems logical that any business, whether a commercial enterprise or a not-for-profit business, would understand that building a secure organization is important to long-term success. When a business implements and maintains a strong security posture, it can take advantage of numerous benefits. An organization that can demonstrate an infra-structure protected by robust security mechanisms can potentially see a reduction in insurance premiums. A secure organization can use its security program as a marketing tool, demonstrating to clients that it values their business so much that it takes a very aggressive stance on protecting their information. But most importantly, a secure organization will not have to spend time and money identifying security breaches and responding to the results of those breaches.

As of December 2011, according to the National Conference of State Legislatures, 46 states, the District of Columbia, Puerto Rico and the Virgin Islands had enacted legislation requiring notification of security breaches involving personal information. In 2011, 14 states expanded the scope of this legislation.[1] Security breaches can cost an organization significantly through a tarnished reputation, lost business, and legal fees. And numerous regulations, such as the Health Insurance Portability and Accountability Act (HIPAA), the Gramm-Leach-Bliley Act (GLBA), and the Sarbanes-Oxley Act, require businesses to maintain the security of information. Despite the benefits of maintaining a secure organization and the potentially devastating consequences of not doing so, many organizations have poor security mechanisms, implementations, policies, and culture.

1. OBSTACLES TO SECURITY

In attempting to build a secure organization, we should take a close look at the obstacles that make it challenging to build a totally secure organization.

---

1. http://www.ncsl.org/issues-research/telecommunications-information-technology/security-breach-legislation-2011.aspx (February 2, 2012).

Security Is Inconvenient

Security, by its very nature, is inconvenient, and the more robust the security mechanisms, the more inconvenient the process becomes. Employees in an organization have a job to do; they want to get to work right away. Most security mechanisms, from passwords to multifactor authentication, are seen as roadblocks to productivity. One of the current trends in security is to add whole disk encryption to laptop computers. Although this is a highly recommended security process, it adds a second login step before a computer user can actually start working. Even if the step adds only one minute to the login process, over the course of a year this results in four hours of lost productivity. Some would argue that this lost productivity is balanced by the added level of security. But across a large organization, this lost productivity could prove significant.

To gain a full appreciation of the frustration caused by security measures, we have only to watch the Transportation Security Administration (TSA) security lines at any airport. Simply watch the frustration build as a particular item is run through the scanner for a third time while a passenger is running late to board his flight. Security implementations are based on a sliding scale; one end of the scale is total security and total inconvenience, the other is total insecurity and complete ease of use. When we implement any security mechanism, it should be placed on the scale where the level of security and ease of use match the acceptable level of risk for the organization.

2. COMPUTERS ARE POWERFUL AND COMPLEX

Home computers have become storehouses of personal materials. Our computers now contain wedding videos, scanned family photos, music libraries, movie collections, and financial and medical records. Because computers contain such familiar objects, we have forgotten that computers are very powerful and complex devices. It wasn't that long ago that computers as powerful as our desktop and laptop computers would have filled one or more very large rooms. In addition, today's computers present a "user-friendly" face to the world. Most people are unfamiliar with the way computers truly function and what goes on "behind the scenes." Things such as the Windows Registry, ports, and services are completely unknown to most users and poorly understood by many computer industry professionals. For example, many individuals still believe that a Windows login password protects data on a computer. On the contrary—someone can simply take the hard drive out of the computer, install it as a slave drive in another computer, or place it in a USB drive enclosure, and all the data will be readily accessible.

Computer Users Are Unsophisticated

Many computer users believe that because they are skilled at generating spreadsheets, word processing documents, and presentations, they know everything about computers. These "power users" have moved beyond application basics, but many still do not understand even basic security concepts. Many users will indiscriminately install software and visit questionable Web sites despite the fact that these actions could violate company policies. The "bad guys"—people who want to steal information from or wreak havoc on computers systems—have also identified the average user as a weak link in the security chain. As companies began investing more money in perimeter defenses, attackers look to the path of least resistance. They send malware as attachments to email, asking recipients to open the attachment. Despite being told not to open attachments from unknown senders or simply not to open attachments at all, employees consistently violate this policy, wreaking havoc on their networks. The "I Love You Virus" spread very rapidly in this manner. More recently, phishing scams have been very effective in convincing individuals to provide their personal online banking and credit-card information. Why would an attacker struggle to break through an organization's defenses when end users are more than willing to provide the keys to bank accounts? Addressing the threat caused by untrained and unwary end users is a significant part of any security program.

Computers Created Without a Thought to Security

During the development of personal computers (PCs), no thought was given to security. Early PCs were very simple affairs that had limited computing power and no keyboards and were programmed by flipping a series of switches. They were developed almost as curiosities. Even as they became more advanced and complex, all effort was focused on developing greater sophistication and capabilities; no one thought they would have security issues. We only have to look at some of the early computers, such as the Berkeley Enterprises Geniac, the Heathkit EC-1, or the MITS Altair 8800, to understand why security was not an issue back then.[2] The development of computers was focused on what they could do, not how they could be attacked.

As computers began to be interconnected, the driving force was providing the ability to share information, certainly not to protect it. Initially, the Internet was designed for military applications, but eventually it migrated to colleges and universities, the principal tenet of which is the sharing of knowledge.

3. CURRENT TREND IS TO SHARE, NOT PROTECT

Even now, despite the stories of compromised data, people still want to share their data with everyone. Web-based applications are making this easier to do than simply attaching a file to an email. Social networking sites such as Omemo provide the ability to share material: "Store your files online, share your stuff and browse what other users store in the world's largest multimedia library: The Omemo peer-to-peer virtual hard-drive."[3] In addition, many online data storage sites such as DropSend[4] and FilesAnywhere[5] provide the ability to share files. These sites can allow proprietary data to leave an organization by bypassing security mechanisms, exposing them to the possibility of unwanted review and distribution.

Data Accessible from Anywhere

As though employees' desire to share data is not enough of a threat to proprietary information, many business professionals want access to data from anywhere they work, on a variety of devices. To be productive, employees now request access to data and contact information on their laptops, desktops, home computers, and mobile devices. Therefore, IT departments must now provide the ability to sync data with numerous systems. And if the IT department can't or won't provide this capability, employees now have the power to take matters into their own hands by utilizing online services.

In addition to the previously mentioned online file sharing sites, there exist numerous online file storage sites (some sites offer both services). These storage

---

2. "Pop quiz: What was the first personal computer?" www.blinkenlights. com/pc.shtml (February 2, 2012).
3. www.omemo.com (February 2, 2012).
4. www.dropsend.com (February 2, 2012).
5. www.filesanywhere.com (February 2, 2012).

sites are "springing up" everywhere, based on the desire to have access to data from absolutely everywhere. The latest operating systems from Microsoft and Apple support this concept on a home network level when they created Homegroups[6] and AirDrop, respectively. Homegroups allow users to share specific volumes or folders across a network, while AirDrop allows users to share files between Mac's, without using an established network.

"Looking for a fast way to share files with people nearby? With AirDrop, you can send files to anyone around you wirelessly—no Wi-Fi network required. And no complicated setup or special settings. Just click the AirDrop icon in the Finder sidebar, and your Mac automatically discovers other AirDrop users within about 30 feet of you. To share a file, simply drag it to someone's name. Once accepted, the fully encrypted file transfers directly to that person's Downloads folder."[7]

Employees always seem to want the same capabilities they have at home while in the workplace. This desire stems from the desire to work quickly and efficiently, with as few impediments in place as possible. Many computer users appreciate the simplicity with which they can access files while at home; they expect the same capabilities in the workplace.

Currently, the best known file storage site is Dropbox.[8] Currently, Dropbox provides 2 GB of free storage and software for Windows, Mac, Linux, and mobile devices, including iPhone, iPad, Blackberry and Android. This matches with their slogan, "Your files everywhere you are." However, you do not need to install the application on your computer; there is a web interface that allows you to upload new files and access stored files. From an accessibility perspective, this is truly amazing. From a security perspective, it is a little unnerving. Some security professionals will not consider this an issue because they can simply "blacklist" the Dropbox Web site and prevent users from installing software. However, if one thinks about this, what is to stop someone from storing material on one of these sites while using a home or library computer? Additionally, Dropbox is not the only "game in town." There are dozens of these sites; some of them are rather obscure, and new ones are created periodically. Table 1.1 identifies sites that have been identified as of this writing (and there are likely more in existence).

Some familiar tools also offer file storage capabilities. Google's free email service, Gmail is a great tool that provides a very robust service for free. What few people realize is that Gmail provides more than 7 GB of storage

---

6. http://windows.microsoft.com/en-US/windows7/Create-a-homegroup (February 23, 2012).
7. http://www.apple.com/macosx/whats-new/ (February 23, 2012).
8. http://www.dropbox.com.

TABLE 1.1 Current Sites.

4Shared	www.4shared.com
Adrive	www.adrive.com
Amazon S3 (Simple Storage Service)	www.amazon.com/s3
Box	www.box.net
Carbonite	www.carbonite.com
DocLocker	www.doclocker.com
Drive Headquarters	www.drivehq.com
DropBox	www.dropbox.com
Egnyte	www.egnyte.com
ElephantDrive	www.elephantdrive.com
fileden	www.fileden.com
Filegenie	www.filegenie.com
filesanywhere	www.filesanywhere.com
filocity.com	www.filocity.com
FirstBackup	www.firstbackup.com
FlipDrive	www.flipdrive.com
FreeDrive	www.freedrive.com
Google Docs	docs.google.com
iBackup	www.ibackup.com
iDrive	www.idrive.com
justcloud	www.justcloud.com
KeepVault	www.keepvault.com
kineticD	www.kineticd.com
LiveDrive	www.livedrive.com
lockmydrive	lockmydrive.com
MediaFire	www.mediafire.com
Minus	www.minus.com
Mozy	www.mozy.com
MyDocsOnline	www.mydocsonline.com
MyOtherDrive	www.myotherdrive.com
MyPCBackup	www.mypcbackup.com
OffsiteBox	offsitebox.com
OLSEX	www.onilinestoragesolution.com
Omemo	www.omemo.com
online file folder	www.onlinefilefolder.com
OpenDrive	www.opendrive.com
orbitfiles.com	www.orbitfiles.com

(Continued)

TABLE 1.1 (Continued)

4Shared	www.4shared.com
ourdisk	www.ourdisk.com
SafeCopy	www.safecopybackup.com
SafeSync	www.safesync.com
SnapDrive.net	snapdrive.net
SPIDEROAK	www.spideroak.com
SugarSync	www.sugarsync.com
TrueShare	www.trueshare.com
Windows Live SkyDrive	skydrive.live.com
Wuala	www.wuala.com
zipcloud	www.zipcloud.com
zohodocs	www.zoho.com

```
▲ USBSTOR
    ▷ Disk&Ven_&Prod_Flash_Disk&Rev_8.00
    ▷ Disk&Ven_Generic&Prod_USB_CF_Reader&Rev_1.01
    ▷ Disk&Ven_Generic&Prod_USB_MS_Reader&Rev_1.03
    ▷ Disk&Ven_Generic&Prod_USB_SD_Reader&Rev_1.00
    ▷ Disk&Ven_Generic&Prod_USB_xD/SM_Reader&Rev_1.02
    ▷ Disk&Ven_HTC&Prod_Android_Phone&Rev_0100
    ▷ Disk&Ven_LaCie&Prod_d2_Quadra_v3&Rev_223X
    ▷ Disk&Ven_LG&Prod_USB_Drive&Rev_2.00
    ▷ Disk&Ven_Seagate&Prod_FreeAgent_GoFlex&Rev_0148
    ▷ Disk&Ven_ST310005&Prod_28AS&Rev_0041
    ▷ Disk&Ven_ST310005&Prod_28AS&Rev_CC3E
    ▷ Disk&Ven_ST320006&Prod_41AS&Rev_0041
    ▷ Disk&Ven_ST320006&Prod_41AS&Rev_CC13
    ▷ Disk&Ven_ST350041&Prod_8AS&Rev_0041
    ▷ Disk&Ven_ST500DM0&Prod_02-1BD142&Rev_0041
    ▷ Disk&Ven_TOSHIBA&Prod_MK2576GSX&Rev_
    ▷ Disk&Ven_TOSHIBA&Prod_TransMemory&Rev_PMAP
    ▷ Disk&Ven_USB&Prod_Flash_Disk&Rev_1100
    ▷ Disk&Ven_USB_TO_I&Prod_DE/SATA_Device&Rev_0041
    ▷ Disk&Ven_USB007&Prod_mini-USB2BU&Rev_0.00
    ▷ Disk&Ven_WIBU_-&Prod_CodeMeter-Stick&Rev_v1.0
```

FIGURE 1.1 Identifying connected USB devices in the USBStor Registry key.

that can also be used to store files, not just email. The shell extension, Gmail Drive[9] provides access to your Gmail storage by means of a "drive" on your desktop. Figure 1.1 shows the Gmail Drive login screen. This

---

9. http://www.viksoe.dk/gmail/ (February 22, 2012).

ability to easily transfer data outside the control of a company makes securing an organization's data that much more difficult. There is more to these sites than simply losing control of data. These are third-party sites and anything can happen. As an example in the summer of 2011, Dropbox had a security issue that allowed people to log in to any account without the use of a password. Another issue is that the longevity of these sites is not guaranteed. For example, Xdrive, a popular online storage service created in 1999 and purchased by AOL in 2005 (allegedly for US$30 million), shut down on January 12, 2009. What happens to the data that is on systems that are no longer in service?

4. SECURITY ISN'T ABOUT HARDWARE AND SOFTWARE

Many businesses believe that if they purchase enough equipment, they can create a secure infrastructure. Firewalls, intrusion detection systems, antivirus programs, and two-factor authentication products are just some of the tools available to assist in protecting a network and its data. It is important to keep in mind that no product or combination of products will create a secure organization by itself. Security is a process; there is no tool that you can "set and forget." All security products are only as secure as the people who configure and maintain them. The purchasing and implementation of security products should be only a percentage of the security budget. The employees tasked with maintaining the security devices should be provided with enough time, training, and equipment to properly support the products. Unfortunately, in many organizations security activities take a back seat to support activities. Highly skilled security professionals are often tasked with help-desk requests such as resetting forgotten passwords, fixing jammed printers, and setting up new employee workstations.

The Bad Guys Are Very Sophisticated

At one time the computer hacker was portrayed as a lone teenager with poor social skills who would break into systems, often for nothing more than bragging rights. As ecommerce has evolved, however, so has the profile of the hacker.

Now that vast collections of credit-card numbers and intellectual property can be harvested, organized hacker groups like Anonymous have been formed to operate as businesses. A document released in 2008 spells it out clearly: "Cybercrime companies that work much like real-world companies are starting to appear and are steadily growing, thanks to the profits they turn. Forget individual hackers or groups of hackers with common goals. Hierarchical cybercrime organizations where each cybercriminal has his or her own role and reward system is what you and your company should be worried about."[10]

State-sponsored hacking, while discussed in security circles for years, received mainstream attention when a Chinese "how-to" hacking video was identified and discussed in the media.[11]

Now that organizations are being attacked by highly motivated and skilled groups of hackers, creating a secure infrastructure is mandatory.

Management Sees Security as a Drain on the Bottom Line

For most organizations, the cost of creating a strong security posture is seen as a necessary evil, similar to purchasing insurance. Organizations don't want to spend the money on it, but the risks of not making the purchase outweigh the costs. Because of this attitude, it is extremely challenging to create a secure organization. The attitude is enforced because requests for security tools are often supported by documents providing the average cost of a security incident instead of showing more concrete benefits of a strong security posture. The problem is exacerbated by the fact that IT professionals speak a different language than management. IT professionals are generally focused on technology, period. Management is focused on revenue. Concepts such as profitability, asset depreciation, return on investment, realization, and total cost of ownership are the mainstays of management. These are alien concepts to most IT professionals.

Realistically speaking, though, it would be helpful if management would take steps to learn some fundamentals of information technology and IT professionals should take the initiative and learn some fundamental business concepts. Learning these concepts is beneficial to the organization because the technical infrastructure can then be implemented in a cost-effective manner, and they are beneficial from a career development perspective for IT professionals.

A Google search on "business skills for IT professionals" will identify numerous educational programs that might prove helpful. For those who do not have the time or the inclination to attend a class, some very useful materials can be found online. One such document provided by the Government Chief Information Office of New South Wales is *A Guide for Government Agencies*

Calculating Return on Security Investment.[12] Though extremely technical, another often cited document is *Cost-Benefit Analysis for Network Intrusion Detection Systems*, by Huaqiang Wei, Deb Frinke, Olivia Carter, and Chris Ritter.[13]

Regardless of the approach that is taken, it is important to remember that any tangible cost savings or revenue generation should be utilized when requesting new security products, tools, or policies. Security professionals often overlook the value of keeping Web portals open for employees. A database that is used by a sales staff to enter contracts or purchases or check inventory will help generate more revenue if it has no downtime. A database that is not accessible or has been hacked is useless for generating revenue.

Strong security can be used to gain a competitive advantage in the marketplace. Having secured systems that are accessible 24 hours a day, seven days a week, means that an organization can reach and communicate with its clients and prospective clients more efficiently. An organization that becomes recognized as a good custodian of client records and information can incorporate its security record as part of its branding. This is no different than a car company being recognized for its safety record. In discussions of cars and safety, for example, Volvo is always the first manufacturer mentioned.[14]

What must be avoided is the "sky is falling" mentality. There are indeed numerous threats to a network, but we need to be realistic in allocating resources to protect against these threats. As of this writing, the National Vulnerability Database sponsored by the National Institute of Standards and Technology (NIST) lists 49,679 common vulnerabilities and exposures and publishes 14 new vulnerabilities per day.[15] In addition, the media is filled with stories of stolen laptops, credit-card numbers, and identities. The volume of threats to a network can be mind numbing. It is important to approach management with "probable threats" as opposed to "describable threats." Probable threats are those that are most likely to have an impact on your business and the ones most likely to get the attention of management.

Perhaps the best approach is to recognize that management, including the board of directors, is required to exhibit a duty of care in protecting their assets that is comparable to that of other organizations in their industry. When a security breach or incident occurs, being

10. "Report: cybercrime groups starting to operate like the Mafia" http://arstechnica.com/business/news/2008/07/report-cybercrime-groups-starting-to-operate-like-the-mafia.ars (February 22, 2012).

11. http://www.pcworld.com/businesscenter/article/238655/china_hacking_video_shows_glimpse_of_falun_gong_attack_tool.html (March 4, 2012).

12. http://services.nsw.gov.au/sites/default/files/ROSI%20Guideline%20SGW%20%282.2%29%20Lockstep.pdf (February 22, 2012).

13. http://citeseerx.ist.psu.edu/viewdoc/summary?doi=10.1.1.20.5607 (February 22, 2012).

14. "Why leaders should care about security" podcast, transcript October 17, 2006, Julia Allen and William Pollak, http://www.cert.org/podcast/transcripts/1leaders_care.pdf (February 22, 2012).

15. http://nvd.nist.gov/home.cfm (February 22, 2012).

able to demonstrate the high level of security within the organization can significantly reduce exposure to lawsuits, fines, and bad press.

The goal of any discussion with management is to convince them that in the highly technical and interconnected world we live in, having a secure network and infrastructure is a "nonnegotiable requirement of doing business."[16] An excellent resource for both IT professionals and executives that can provide insight into these issues is CERT's technical report, *Governing for Enterprise Security*.[17]

5. TEN STEPS TO BUILDING A SECURE ORGANIZATION

Having identified some of the challenges to building a secure organization, let's now look at 10 ways to successfully build a secure organization. The following steps will put a business in a robust security posture.

Evaluate the Risks and Threats

In attempting to build a secure organization, where should you start? One commonly held belief is that you should initially identify your assets and allocate security resources based on the value of each asset. Although this approach might prove effective, it can lead to some significant vulnerabilities. An infrastructure asset might not hold a high value, for example, but it should be protected with the same effort as a high-value asset. If not, it could be an entry point into your network and provide access to valuable data.

Another approach is to begin by evaluating the threats posed to your organization and your data.

Threats Based on the Infrastructure Model

The first place to start is to identify risks based on an organization's infrastructure model. What infrastructure is in place that is necessary to support the operational needs of the business? A small business that operates out of one office has reduced risks as opposed to an organization that operates out of numerous facilities, includes a mobile workforce utilizing a variety of handheld devices, and offers products or services through a Web-based interface. An organization that has a large number of telecommuters must take steps to protect its proprietary information that could potentially reside on personally owned computers outside company control. An organization that has widely

dispersed and disparate systems will have more risk potential than a centrally located one that utilizes uniform systems.

Threats Based on the Business Itself

Are there any specific threats for your particular business? Have high-level executives been accused of inappropriate activities whereby stockholders or employees would have incentive to attack the business? Are there any individuals who have a vendetta against the company for real or imagined slights or accidents? Does the community have a history of antagonism against the organization? A risk management or security team should be asking these questions on a regular basis to evaluate the risks in real time. This part of the security process is often overlooked due to the focus on daily workload.

Threats Based on Industry

Businesses belonging to particular industries are targeted more frequently and more aggressively than those in other industries. Financial institutions and online retailers are targeted because "that's where the money is." Pharmaceutical manufacturers could be targeted to steal intellectual property, but they also could be targeted by special interest groups, such as those that do not believe in testing drugs on live animals or have spiritual beliefs opposing a particular product.

Identifying some of these threats requires active involvement in industry-specific trade groups in which businesses share information regarding recent attacks or threats they have identified.

Global Threats

Businesses are often so narrowly focused on their local sphere of influence that they forget that by having a network connected to the Internet, they are now connected to the rest of the world. If a piece of malware identified on the other side of the globe targets the identical software used in your organization, you can be sure that you will eventually be impacted by this malware. Additionally, if extremist groups in other countries are targeting your specific industry, you will also be targeted.

Once threats and risks are identified, you can take one of four steps:

- *Ignore the risk.* This is never an acceptable response. This is simply burying your head in the sand and hoping the problem will go away—the business equivalent of not wearing a helmet when riding a motorcycle.

16. "Why leaders should care about security" podcast transcript, October 17, 2006, Julia Allen and William Pollak, http://www.cert.org/podcast/transcripts/1leaders_care.pdf (February 22, 2012).

17. www.cert.org/archive/pdf/05tn023.pdf.

- *Accept the risk.* When the cost to remove the risk is greater than the risk itself, an organization will often decide to simply accept the risk. This is a viable option as long as the organization has spent the time required to evaluate the risk.
- *Transfer the risk.* Organizations with limited staff or other resources could decide to transfer the risk. One method of transferring the risk is to purchase specialized insurance targeted at a specific risk.
- *Mitigate the risk.* Most organizations mitigate risk by applying the appropriate resources to minimize the risks posed to their network and systems.

For organizations that would like to identify and quantify the risks to their network and information assets, CERT provides a free suite of tools to assist with the project. Operationally, Critical Threat, Asset, and Vulnerability Evaluation (OCTAVE) provides risk-based assessment for security assessments and planning.[18] There are three versions of OCTAVE: the original OCTAVE, designed for large organizations (more than 300 employees); OCTAVE-S (100 people or fewer); and OCTAVE-Allegro, which is a streamlined version of the tools and focuses specifically on information assets.

Another risk assessment tool that might prove helpful is the Risk Management Framework developed by Educause/Internet 2.[19] Targeted at institutions of higher learning, the approach could be applied to other industries. Another framework that might prove helpful was developed by the National Institute of Standards and Technology (NIST). This is also referred to as the Risk Management Framework (RMF) and includes six steps as part of the process.[20]

Tracking specific threats to specific operating systems, products, and applications can be time consuming. Visiting the National Vulnerability Database and manually searching for specific issues would not necessarily be an effective use of time. Fortunately, the Center for Education and Research in Information Assurance and Security (CERIAS) at Purdue University has a tool called Cassandra that can be configured to notify you of specific threats to your particular products and applications.[17]

Beware of Common Misconceptions

In addressing the security needs of an organization, it is common for professionals to succumb to some very common misconceptions. Perhaps the most common

misconception is that the business is obscure, unsophisticated, or boring—simply not a target for malicious activity. Businesses must understand that any network that is connected to the Internet is a potential target, regardless of the type of business.

Attackers will attempt to gain access to a network and its systems for several reasons. The first reason is to look around to see what they can find. Regardless of the type of business, personnel information will more than likely be stored on one of the systems. This includes Social Security numbers and other personal information. This type of information is a target—always.

Another possibility is that the attacker will modify the information he or she finds or simply reconfigure the systems to behave abnormally. This type of attacker is not interested in financial gain; he is simply the technology version of teenagers who soaps windows, eggs cars, and covers property with toilet paper. He attacks because he finds it entertaining to do so. Additionally, these attackers could use the systems to store stolen "property" such as child pornography or credit-card numbers. If a system is not secure, attackers can store these types of materials on your system and gain access to them at their leisure.

The final possibility is that an attacker will use the hacked systems to mount attacks on other unprotected networks and systems. Computers can be used to mount denial-of-service (DoS) attacks, operate as "command and control systems" for a bot network, relay spam, or spread malicious software. To put it simply, no computer or network is immune from attack.

Another common misconception is that an organization is immune from problems caused by employees, essentially saying, "We trust all our employees, so we don't have to focus our energies on protecting our assets from them." Though this is common for small businesses in which the owners know everyone, it also occurs in larger organizations where companies believe that they only hire "professionals." It is important to remember that no matter how well job candidates present themselves, a business can never know everything about an employee's past. For this reason it is important for businesses to conduct preemployment background checks of all employees. Furthermore, it is important to conduct these background checks properly and completely.

Many employers trust this task to an online solution that promises to conduct a complete background check on an individual for a minimal fee. Many of these sites play on individuals' lack of understanding of how some of these online databases are generated. These sites might not have access to the records of all jurisdictions, since many jurisdictions either do not make their records available online or do not provide them to these

18. OCTAVE, www.cert.org/octave/ (February 22, 2012).
19. Risk Management Framework, https://wiki.internet2.edu/confluence/display/itsg2/Risk+Management+Framework. (February 22, 2012).
20. Risk Management Framework (RMF), http://csrc.nist.gov/groups/SMA/fisma/framework.html (March 4, 2012).

databases. In addition, many of the records are entered by minimum wage data-entry clerks whose accuracy is not always 100 percent.

Background checks should be conducted by organizations that have the resources at their disposal to get court records directly from the courthouses where the records are generated and stored. Some firms have a team of "runners" who visit the courthouses daily to pull records; others have a network of contacts who can visit the courts for them. Look for organizations that are active members of the National Association of Professional Background Screeners.[21] Members of this organization are committed to providing accurate and professional results. And perhaps more importantly, they can provide counseling regarding the proper approach to take as well as interpreting the results of a background check.

If your organization does not conduct background checks, there are several firms that might be of assistance: Accurate Background, Inc., of Lake Forest, California[22]; Credential Check, Inc., of Troy, Michigan[23]; and Validity Screening Solutions in Overland Park, Kansas.[24] The Web sites of these companies all provide informational resources to guide you in the process. (*Note:* For businesses outside the United States or for U.S. businesses with locations overseas, the process might be more difficult because privacy laws could prevent conducting a complete background check. The firms we've mentioned should be able to provide guidance regarding international privacy laws.)

Another misconception is that a preemployment background check is all that is needed. Some erroneously believe that once a person is employed, he or she is "safe" and can no longer pose a threat. However, people's lives and fortunes can change during the course of employment. Financial pressures can cause otherwise law-abiding citizens to take risks they never would have thought possible. Drug and alcohol dependency can alter people's behavior as well. For these and other reasons it is a good idea to do an additional background check when an employee is promoted to a position of higher responsibility and trust. If this new position involves handling financial responsibilities, the background check should also include a credit check.

Although these steps might sound intrusive, which is sometimes a reason cited not to conduct these types of checks, they can also be very beneficial to the employee as well as the employer. If a problem is identified during the check, the employer can often offer assistance to help the employee get through a tough time. Financial counseling and substance abuse counseling can often turn a potentially problematic employee into a very loyal and dedicated one.

Yet another common misconception involves information technology (IT) professionals. Many businesses pay their IT staff fairly high salaries because they understand that having a properly functioning technical infrastructure is important for the continued success of the company. Since the staff is adept at setting up and maintaining systems and networks, there is a general assumption that they know "everything there is to know about computers. It is important to recognize that although an individual might be very knowledgeable and technologically sophisticated, no one knows *everything* about computers. Because management does not understand technology, they are not in a very good position to judge a person's depth of knowledge and experience in the field. Decisions are often based on the certifications a person has achieved during his or her career. Although certifications can be used to determine a person's level of competency, too much weight is given to them. Many certifications require nothing more than some time and dedication to study and pass a certification test. Some training companies also offer boot camps that guarantee a person will pass the certification test. It is possible for people to become certified without having any real-world experience with the operating systems, applications, or hardware addressed by the certification. When judging a person's competency, look at his or her experience level and background first, and if the person has achieved certifications in addition to having significant real-world experience, the certification is probably a reflection of the employee's true capabilities.

The IT staff does a great deal to perpetuate the image that they know everything about computers. One of the reasons people get involved with the IT field in the first place is because they have an opportunity to try new things and overcome new challenges. This is why when an IT professional is asked if she knows how to do something, she will always respond "Yes." But in reality the real answer should be, "No, but I'll figure it out." Although they frequently can figure things out, when it comes to security we must keep in mind that it is a specialized area, and implementing a strong security posture requires significant training and experience.

Provide Security Training for IT Staff— Now and Forever

Just as implementing a robust, secure environment is a dynamic process, creating a highly skilled staff of security

21. National Association of Professional Background Screeners, www. napbs.com.
22. www.accuratebackground.com.
23. www.credentialcheck.com.
24. www.validityscreening.com.

professionals is also a dynamic process. It is important to keep in mind that even though an organization's technical infrastructure might not change that frequently, new vulnerabilities are being discovered and new attacks are being launched on a regular basis. In addition, very few organizations have a stagnant infrastructure; employees are constantly requesting new software, and more technologies are added in an effort to improve efficiencies. Each new addition likely adds additional security vulnerabilities.

It is important for the IT staff to be prepared to identify and respond to new threats and vulnerabilities. It is recommended that those interested in gaining a deep security understanding start with a vendor-neutral program. A vendor-neutral program is one that focuses on concepts rather than specific products. The SANS (SysAdmin, Audit, Network, Security) Institute offers two introductory programs: Intro to Information Security (Security 301),[25] a five-day class designed for people just starting out in the security field, and the SANS Security Essentials Bootcamp (Security 401),[26] a six-day class designed for people with some security experience. Each class is also available as a self-study program, and each can be used to prepare for a specific certification.

Another option is to start with a program that follows the CompTia Security + certification requirements, such as the Global Knowledge Essentials of Information Security.[27] Some colleges offer similar programs.

Once a person has a good fundamental background in security, he should then undergo vendor-specific training to apply the concepts learned to specific applications and security devices utilized in the work environment.

A great resource for keeping up with current trends in security is to become actively involved in a security-related trade organization. The key concept here is *actively involved*. Many professionals join organizations so that they can add an item to the "professional affiliations" section of their résumé. Becoming actively involved means attending meetings on a regular basis and serving on a committee or in a position on the executive board. Although this seems like a daunting time commitment, the benefit is that the professional develops a network of resources that can be available to provide insight, serve as a sounding board, or provide assistance when a problem arises. Participating in these associations is a very cost-effective way to get up to speed with current security

trends and issues. Here are some organizations[28] that can prove helpful:

- ASIS International, the largest security-related organization in the world, focuses primarily on physical security but has more recently started addressing computer security as well.
- ISACA, formerly the Information Systems Audit and Control Association.
- High Technology Crime Investigation Association (HTCIA).
- Information Systems Security Association (ISSA).
- InfraGard, a joint public and private organization sponsored by the Federal Bureau of Investigation (FBI).

In addition to monthly meetings, many local chapters of these organizations sponsor regional conferences that are usually very reasonably priced and attract nationally recognized experts.

Arguably one of the best ways to determine whether an employee has a strong grasp of information security concepts is if she can achieve the Certified Information Systems Security Professional (CISSP) certification. Candidates for this certification are tested on their understanding of the following 10 knowledge domains:

- Access control
- Application security
- Business continuity and disaster recovery planning
- Cryptography
- Information security and risk management
- Legal regulations, compliance, and investigations
- Operations security
- Physical (environmental) security
- Security architecture and design
- Telecommunications and network security

What makes this certification so valuable is that the candidate must have a minimum of five years of professional experience in the information security field or four years of experience and a college degree. To maintain certification, a certified individual is required to attend 120 hours of continuing professional education during the three-year certification cycle. This ensures that those holding the CISSP credential are staying up to date with current trends in security. The CISSP certification is maintained by internet systems consortium (ISC).[29]

Think "Outside the Box"

For most businesses, the threat to their intellectual assets and technical infrastructure comes from the "bad guys"

---

25. https://www.sans.org/security-training/intro-information-security-106-mid.

26. https://www.sans.org/security-training/security-essentials-bootcamp-style-61-mid.

27. http://www.globalknowledge.com/training/course.asp?pageid=1&courseid=16259&catid=191&country=United+States.

28. ASIS International, www.asisonline.org; ISACA, www.isaca.org; HTCIA, www.htcia.org; ISSA, www.issa.org; InfraGard, www.infragard.net.

29. (ISC)[2], www.isc2.org.

sitting outside their organizations, trying to break in. These organizations establish strong perimeter defenses, essentially "boxing in" their assets. However, internal employees have access to proprietary information to do their jobs, and they often disseminate this information to areas where it is no longer under the control of the employer. This dissemination of data is generally not performed with any malicious intent, but simply for employees to have access to data so that they can perform their job responsibilities more efficiently. However, this becomes a problem when an employee leaves and the organization takes no steps to collect or control their proprietary information in the possession of their now ex-employee.

One of the most overlooked threats to intellectual property is the innocuous and now ubiquitous USB Flash drive. These devices, the size of a tube of lipstick, are the modern-day floppy disk in terms of portable data storage. They are a very convenient way to transfer data between computers. But the difference between these devices and a floppy disk is that USB Flash drives can store a very large amount of data. A 16 GB USB Flash drive has the same storage capacity as more than 10,000 floppy disks! As of this writing, a 16 GB USB Flash drive can be purchased for less than $15. Businesses should keep in mind that as time goes by, the capacity of these devices will increase and the price will decrease, making them very attractive to employees.

These devices are not the only threat to data. Because other devices can be connected to the computer through the USB port, digital cameras, MP3 players, and external hard drives can now be used to remove data from a computer and the network to which it is connected. Most people would recognize that external hard drives pose a threat, but they would not recognize other devices as a threat. Cameras and music players are designed to store images and music, but to a computer they are simply additional mass storage devices. It is difficult for people to understand that an iPod can carry word processing documents, databases, and spreadsheets as well as music. Fortunately, Microsoft Windows tracks the devices that are connected to a system in a Registry key, HKEY_Local_Machine\System \ControlSet00x\Enum\USBStor. It might prove interesting to look in this key on your own computer to see what types of devices have been connected. Figure 1.2 shows a wide array of devices that have been connected to a system that includes USB Flash drives, a digital camera, and several external hard drives.

Windows Vista has an additional key that tracks connected devices: HKEY_Local_Machine\Software\Microsoft \Windows Portable Devices\Devices.[30] (*Note:* Analyzing

FIGURE 1.2 Gmail Drive login screen.

the Registry is a great way to investigate the activities of computer users. For many, however, the Registry is tough to navigate and interpret. If you are interested in understanding more about the Registry, you might want to download and play with Harlan Carvey's RegRipper.[31])

Another threat to information that carries data outside the walls of the organization is the plethora of handheld devices currently in use. Many of these devices have the ability to send and receive email as well as create, store, and transmit word processing, spreadsheet, and PDF files. Though most employers will not purchase these devices for their employees, they are more than happy to allow their employees to sync their personally owned devices with their corporate computers. Client contact information, business plans, and other materials can easily be copied from a system. Some businesses feel that they have this threat under control because they provide their employees with corporate-owned devices and they can collect these devices when employees leave their employment. The only problem with this attitude is that employees can easily copy data from the devices to their home computers before the devices are returned.

Because of the threat of portable data storage devices and handheld devices, it is important for an organization to establish policies outlining the acceptable use of these devices as well as implement an enterprise-grade solution to control how, when, or if data can be copied to them. Filling all USB ports with epoxy is a cheap solution, but it is not really effective. Fortunately, there are several products that can protect against this type of data leak. DeviceWall from Frontrange Solutions[32] and GFI Endpoint Security[33] are two popular ones.

30. http://windowsir.blogspot.com/2008/06/portable-devices-on-vista.html (February 29, 2012).

31. RegRipper, www.regripper.net.
32. DeviceWall, http://www.frontrange.com/software/it-asset-management/ endpoint-security.
33. http://www.gfi.com/usb-device-control.

DOXing

With the interest and ability to store data on third-party systems, it becomes increasingly necessary for the security professional to make "thinking outside the box" a part of their set of skills. While it does not seem that a security professional should be concerned with data being stored on systems other than their own, the fact that business critical and confidential materials are stored on third-party systems means that the success or profitability of a business requires that this information be secured.

In addition to data leaving an organization on thumb drives or to an external storage site, seemingly innocuous data can be collected from a variety of sources and can be used in a negative manner against an individual or organization. This process is called DOXing and is defined by the ProHackingTricks:

Doxing is a way of tracing someone or getting information about an individual using sources on the internet and social engineering techniques. Its term was derived from—Documents—as a matter of fact it's the retrieval of Documents on a person or an organization.[34]

DOXing is essentially high-tech dumpster diving, where information is gathered from the Internet as opposed to a waste bin. Initially developed by the hacker group Anonymous to harass law enforcement, the tactic was also utilized by the Occupy Wall Street protesters. This technique is possible because individuals and organizations do not understand the significance of data posted on social networking sites, blogs, corporate Web sites, and other online repositories. A single piece of information posted on a Web site may not in and of itself have significance, but when combined with materials collected from a variety of sites, that small piece of information may help fill in a complete (and possibly uncomplimentary) picture of a person or business. While this process has been targeted at law enforcement, it is just a matter of time before it will be used against executives and corporations. Being aware of this threat and educating others are now a part of the security process.

Train Employees: Develop a Culture of Security

One of the greatest security assets is a business's own employees, but only if they have been properly trained to comply with security policies and to identify potential security problems.

Many employees don't understand the significance of various security policies and implementations. As mentioned

previously, they consider these policies nothing more than an inconvenience. Gaining the support and allegiance of employees takes time, but it is time well spent. Begin by carefully explaining the reasons behind any security implementation. One of the reasons could be ensuring employee productivity, but focus primarily on the security issues. File sharing using LimeWire and Shareazza might keep employees away from work, but they can also open up holes in a firewall. Downloading and installing unapproved software can install malicious software that can infect user systems, causing their computers to function slowly or not at all. While most employees understand that opening unknown or unexpected email attachments can lead to a malware infection, most are unaware of the advanced capabilities of recent malicious code. "Advanced Persistent Threat" or the ability for a system to remain infected despite the diligent use antivirus programs has become a major problem. Employees now need to understand that indiscriminate Web surfing can result in "drive-by" installs of malware.

Perhaps the most direct way to gain employee support is to let employees know that the money needed to respond to attacks and fix problems initiated by users is money that is then not available for raises and promotions. Letting employees know that they now have some "skin in the game" is one way to get them involved in security efforts. If a budget is set aside for responding to security problems and employees help stay well within the budget, the difference between the money spent and the actual budget could be divided among employees as a bonus. Not only would employees be more likely to speak up if they noticed network or system slowdowns, they would probably be more likely to confront strangers wandering through the facility.

Another mechanism that can be used to gain security allies is to provide advice regarding the proper security mechanisms for securing home computers. Although some might not see this as directly benefiting the company, keep in mind that many employees have corporate data on their home computers. This advice can come from periodic, live presentations (offer refreshments and attendance will be higher) or from a periodic newsletter that is either mailed or emailed to employees' personal addresses.

The goal of these activities is to encourage employees to approach management or the security team voluntarily. When this begins to happen on a regular basis, you will have expanded the capabilities of your security team and created a much more secure organization.

The security expert Roberta Bragg used to tell a story of one of her clients who took this concept to a high level. The client provided the company mail clerk with a WiFi hotspot detector and promised him a free steak dinner for every unauthorized wireless access point he

---

34. http://prohackingtricks.blogspot.com/2011/06/doxing-way-of-tracing-anonymous-people.html (February 29, 2012).

FIGURE 1.3 Microsoft Security Compliance Manager.

could find on the premises. The mail clerk was very happy to have the opportunity to earn three free steak dinners.

Identify and Utilize Built-in Security Features of the Operating System and Applications

Many organizations and systems administrators state that they cannot create a secure organization because they have limited resources and simply do not have the funds to purchase robust security tools. This is a ridiculous approach to security because all operating systems and many applications include security mechanisms that require no organizational resources other than time to identify and configure these tools. For Microsoft Windows operating systems, a terrific resource is the online Microsoft TechNet Library.[35] Under the Solutions Accelerators link you can find security resources for all recent Microsoft products. An example of the tools available is the Microsoft Security Compliance Manager. Figure 1.3 shows the initial screen for this product.

TechNet is a great resource and can provide insight into managing numerous security issues, from Microsoft Office 2007 to security risk management. These documents can assist in implementing the built-in security features of Microsoft Windows products. Assistance is needed in identifying many of these capabilities because they are often hidden from view and turned off by default.

One of the biggest concerns in an organization today is data leaks, which are ways that confidential information can leave an organization despite robust perimeter security. As mentioned previously, USB Flash drives are one cause of data leaks; another is the recovery of data found in the unallocated clusters of a computer's hard drive. Unallocated clusters, or *free space*, as it is commonly called, is the area of a hard drive where the operating system and applications dump their artifacts or residual data. Although this data is not viewable through the graphical user interface, the data can easily be identified (and sometimes recovered) using a hex editor such as WinHex[36] or one of the several commercially available computer forensics programs. Figure 1.4 shows the contents of unallocated clusters being displayed by EnCase Forensic.

---

35. Microsoft TechNet Library, http://technet.microsoft.com.

36. WinHex, www.x-ways.net/winhex/index-m.html.

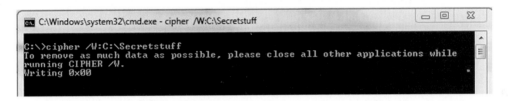

FIGURE 1.4   A view of unallocated clusters showing a Google query.

FIGURE 1.5   Cipher wiping a folder called Secretstuff.

Should a computer be stolen or donated, it is very possible that someone could access the data located in unallocated clusters. For this reason, many people struggle to find an appropriate "disk-scrubbing" utility. Many such commercial utilities exist, but there is one built into Microsoft Windows operating systems. The command-line program cipher.exe is designed to display or alter the encryption of directories (files) stored on new technology file system (NTFS) partitions. Few people even know about this command; even fewer are familiar with the /w switch. Here is a description of the switch from the program's Help file:

Removes data from available unused disk space on the entire volume. If this option is chosen, all other options are ignored. The directory specified can be anywhere in a local volume. If it is a mount point or points to a directory in another volume, the data on that volume will be removed.

To use Cipher, click **Start |** and type **cmd** in the "**Search Programs and Files**" Bod. When the cmd.exe window opens, type **cipher /w:***folder,* where *folder* is any folder in the volume that you want to clean, and then press **Enter**. Figure 1.5 shows Cipher wiping a folder.

For more on secure file deletion issues, see the author's white paper in the SANS reading room, "Secure file deletion: Fact or fiction?"[37]

Another source of data leaks is the personal and editing information that can be associated with Microsoft Office files. In Microsoft Word 2003 you can configure the application to remove personal information on save and to warn you when you are about to print, share, or send a document containing tracked changes or comments.

To access this feature, within Word click **Tools | Options** and then click the **Security** tab. Toward the bottom of the security window you will notice the two options described previously. Simply select the options you want to use. Figure 1.9 shows these options. Microsoft Office 2007 made this tool more robust and more accessible. A separate tool called Document Inspector can be accessed by clicking the **Microsoft Office** button, pointing to **Prepare Document**, then clicking **Inspect Document**. Then select the items you want to remove.

In Microsoft Office 2010, click on **File, Info,** and **Check for Issues,** to open the "Document Inspector" Window.

Implementing a strong security posture often begins by making the login process more robust. This includes increasing the complexity of the login password. All passwords can be cracked, given enough time and resources, but the more difficult you make cracking a password, the greater the possibility the asset the password protects will stay protected.

All operating systems have some mechanism to increase the complexity of passwords. In Microsoft Windows 7 the preceeding can be accomplished by:

1. Open Local Security Policy by clicking the Start button, typing secpol.msc into the Search box, and

---

37. "Secure file deletion: Fact or fiction?" www.sans.org/reading_room/whitepapers/incident/631.php (February 29, 2012).

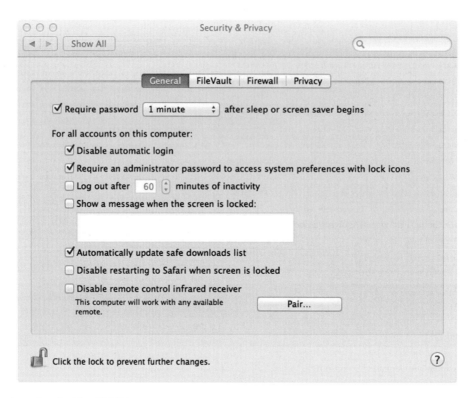

FIGURE 1.6 Security options for Mac OS X Lion.

then clicking secpol. If you are prompted for an administrator password or confirmation, type the password or provide confirmation.

2. In the Navigation pane, double-click Account Policies, and then click Password Policy.

3. Double-click the item in the Policy list that you want to change.[38]

In the right-hand panel you can enable password complexity. Once this is enabled, passwords must contain at least three of the four following password groups[36]:

- English uppercase characters (A through Z)
- English lowercase characters (a through z)
- Numerals (0 through 9)
- Nonalphabetic characters (such as !, $, #, %)

It is important to recognize that all operating systems have embedded tools to assist with security. They often require a little research to find, but the time spent in identifying them is less than the money spent on purchasing additional security products or recovering from a security breach.

Though not yet used by many corporations, Mac OS X has some very robust security features, including FileVault, which provides the ability to create an encrypted disk,

including external drives. Figure 1.6 shows the security options for Mac OS X Lion.

Monitor Systems

Even with the most robust security tools in place, it is important to monitor your systems. All security products are manmade and can fail or be compromised. As with any other aspect of technology, one should never rely on simply one product or tool. Enabling logging on your systems is one way to put your organization in a position to identify problem areas. The problem is, what should be logged? There are some security standards that can help with this determination. One of these standards is the Payment Card Industry Data Security Standard (PCI DSS).[39] Requirement 10 of the PCI DSS states that organizations must "track and monitor access to network resources and cardholder data." If you simply substitute *confidential information* for the phrase *cardholder data*, this requirement is an excellent approach to a log management program. Requirement 10 is reproduced here:

Logging mechanisms and the ability to track user activities are critical. The presence of logs in all environments allows thorough

---

38. http://windows.microsoft.com/en-US/windows-vista/Change-password-policy-settings (February 29, 2012).

39. PCI DSS, www.pcisecuritystandards.org.

tracking and analysis if something does go wrong. Determining the cause of a compromise is very difficult without system activity logs:

1. Establish a process for linking all access to system components (especially access done with administrative privileges such as root) to each individual user.
2. Implement automated audit trails for all system components to reconstruct the following events:
   - All individual user accesses to cardholder data
   - All actions taken by any individual with root or administrative privileges
   - Access to all audit trails
   - Invalid logical access attempts
   - Use of identification and authentication mechanisms
   - Initialization of the audit logs
   - Creation and deletion of system-level objects
3. Record at least the following audit trail entries for all system components for each event:
   - User identification
   - Type of event
   - Date and time
   - Success or failure indication
   - Origination of event
   - Identity or name of affected data, system component, or resource
4. Synchronize all critical system clocks and times.
5. Secure audit trails so that they cannot be altered:
   - Limit viewing of audit trails to those with a job-related need.
   - Protect audit trail files from unauthorized modifications.
   - Promptly back up audit trail files to a centralized log server or media that is difficult to alter.
   - Copy logs for wireless networks onto a log server on the internal LAN.
   - Use file integrity monitoring and change detection software on logs to ensure that existing log data cannot be changed without generating alerts (although new data being added should not cause an alert).
6. Review logs for all system components at least daily. Log reviews must include those servers that perform security functions like intrusion detection system (IDS) and authentication, authorization, and accounting protocol (AAA) servers (for example, RADIUS).

   Note: Log harvesting, parsing, and alerting tools may be used to achieve compliance.
7. Retain audit trail history for at least one year, with a minimum of three months online availability.

Item 6 looks a little overwhelming, since few organizations have the time to manually review log files. Fortunately, there are tools that will collect and parse log files from a variety of sources. All these tools have the ability to notify individuals of a particular event. One simple tool is the Kiwi Syslog Server[40] for Microsoft Windows. Figure 1.7 shows the configuration screen for setting up email alerts in Kiwi.

Additional log parsing tools include Microsoft's Log Parser[41] and, for Unix, Swatch.[42] Commercial tools include ArcSight Logger,[43] GFI EventsManager,[44] and LogRhythm.[45]

An even more detailed approach to monitoring your systems is to install a packet-capturing tool on your network so that you can analyze and capture traffic in real time. One tool that can be very helpful is Wireshark, which is "an award-winning network protocol analyzer developed by an international team of networking experts."[46] Wireshark is based on the original packet capture tool, Ethereal. Analyzing network traffic is not a trivial task and requires some training, but it is perhaps the most accurate way to determine what is happening on your network. Figure 1.8 shows Wireshark monitoring the traffic on a wireless interface.

Hire a Third Party to Audit Security

Regardless of how talented your staff is, there is always the possibility that they overlooked something or inadvertently misconfigured a device or setting. For this reason it is very important to bring in an extra set of "eyes, ears, and hands" to review your organization's security posture.

Although some IT professionals will become paranoid having a third party review their work, intelligent staff members will recognize that a security review by outsiders can be a great learning opportunity. The advantage of having a third party review your systems is that the outsiders have experience reviewing a wide range of systems, applications, and devices in a variety of industries. They will know what works well and what might work but cause problems in the future. They are also more likely to be up to speed on new vulnerabilities and the latest product updates. Why? Because this is all they do.

They are not encumbered by administrative duties, internal politics, and help desk requests. They will be more objective than in-house staff, and they will be in a position to make recommendations after their analysis.

The third-party analysis should involve a two-pronged approach: They should identify how the network appears to attackers and how secure the system is, should

---

40. Kiwi Syslog Server, www.kiwisyslog.com.
41. Log Parser 2.2, http://www.microsoft.com/download/en/details.aspx?id=24659.
42. Swatch, http://sourceforge.net/projects/swatch.
43. ArcSight Logger, http://www.arcsight.com/products/products-logger.
44. GFI EventsManager, www.gfi.com/eventsmanager.
45. LogRhythm, http://www.logrhythm.com.
46. Wireshark, www.wireshark.org.

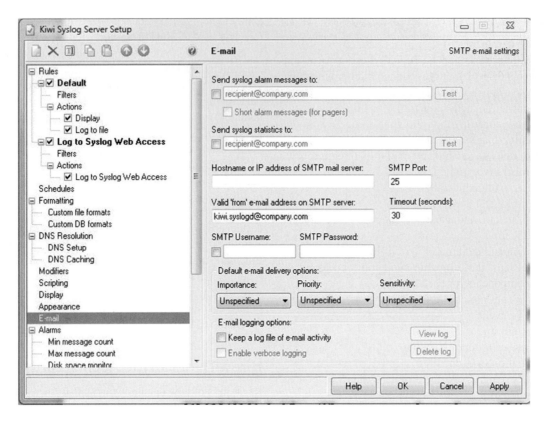

FIGURE 1.7   Kiwi Syslog Se4ver Email Alert Configuration screen.

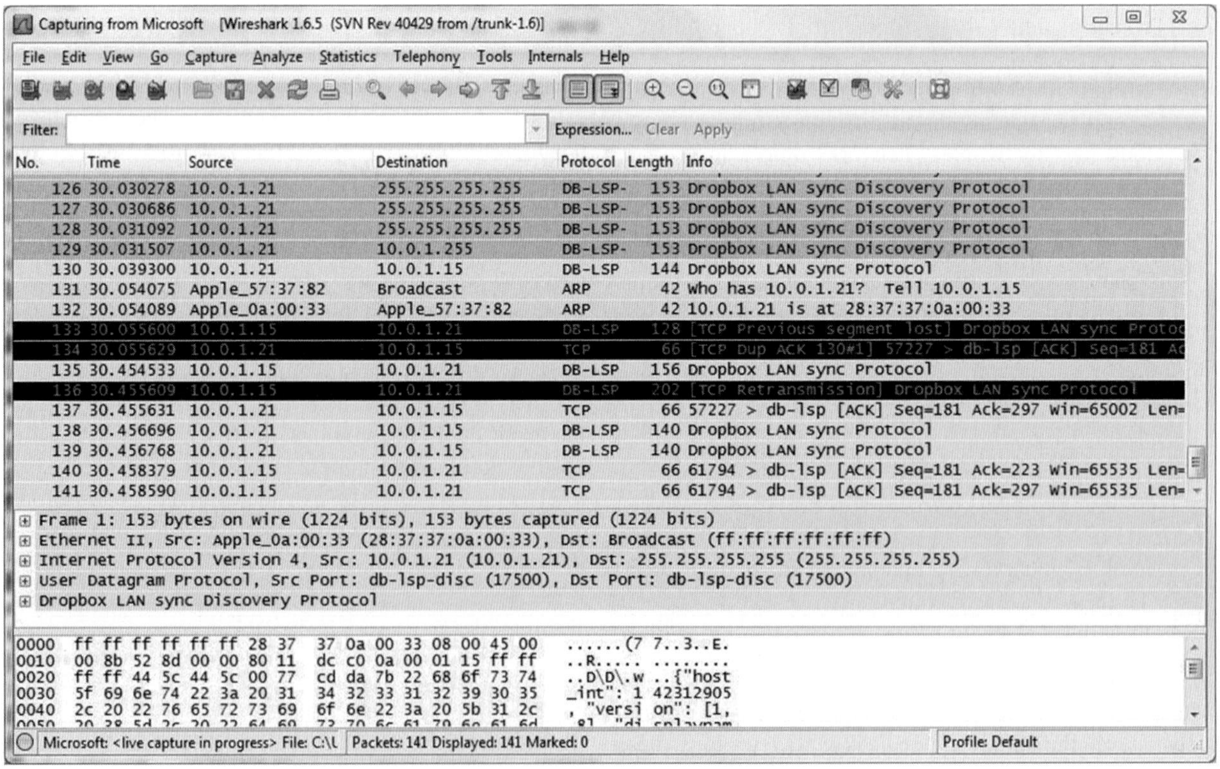

FIGURE 1.8   The protocol analyzer Wireshark monitoring a wireless interface.

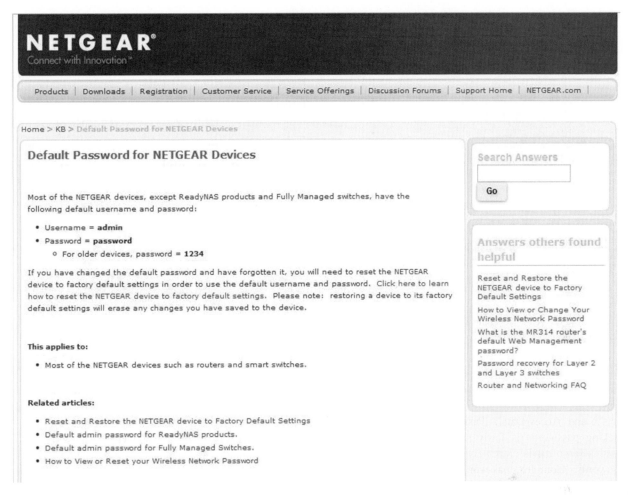

FIGURE 1.9   Default username and password for Netgear devices.

attackers make it past the perimeter defenses. You don't want to have "Tootsie Pop security"—a hard crunchy shell with a soft center. The external review, often called a *penetration test*, can be accomplished in several ways; the first is a *no knowledge* approach, whereby the consultants are provided with absolutely no information regarding the network and systems prior to their analysis. Although this is a very realistic approach, it can be time consuming and very expensive. Using this approach, consultants must use publicly available information to start enumerating systems for testing. This is a realistic approach, but a *partial knowledge* analysis is more efficient and less expensive. If provided with a network topology diagram and a list of registered IP addresses, the third-party reviewers can complete the review faster and the results can be addressed in a much more timely fashion. Once the penetration test is complete, a review of the internal network can be initiated. The audit of the internal network will identify open shares, unpatched systems, open ports, weak passwords, rogue systems, and many other issues.

Don't Forget the Basics

Many organizations spend a great deal of time and money addressing perimeter defenses and overlook some fundamental security mechanisms, as described here.

Change Default Account Passwords

Nearly all network devices come preconfigured with a password/username combination. This combination is included with the setup materials and is documented in numerous locations. Very often these devices are the gateways to the Internet or other internal networks. If these default passwords are not changed upon configuration, it becomes a trivial matter for an attacker to get into these systems. Hackers can find password lists on the Internet,[47] and vendors include default passwords in their online manuals. For example, Figure 1.9 shows the default username and password for Netgear devices.

---

47. http://cirt.net/passwords.

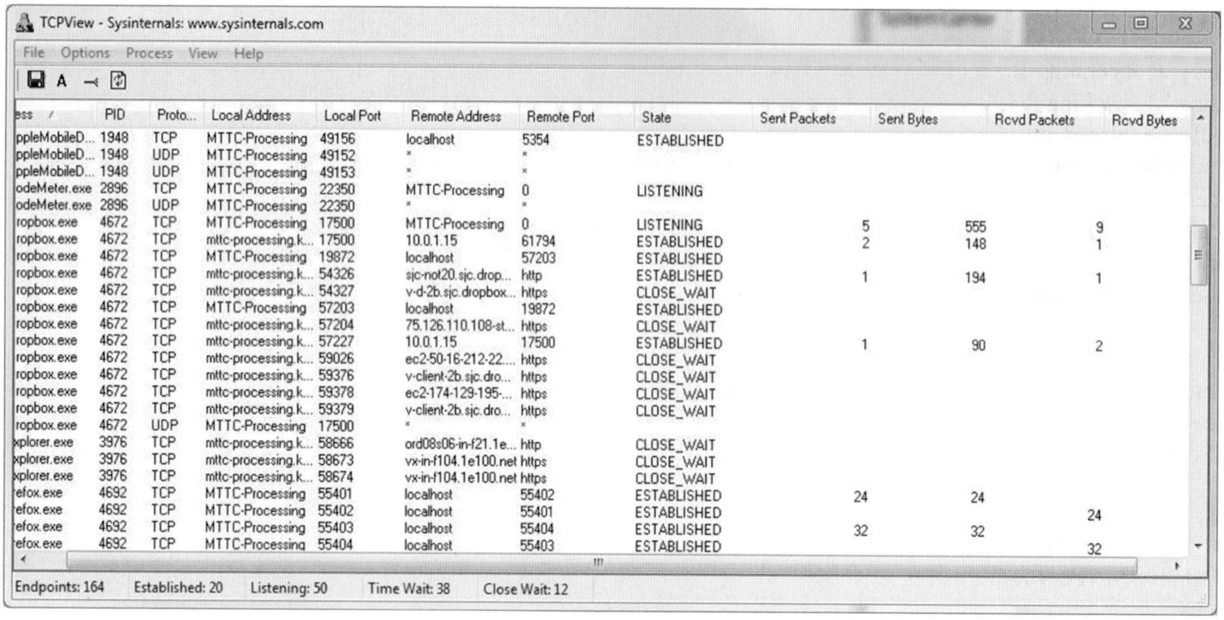

ess	PID	Proto...	Local Address	Local Port	Remote Address	Remote Port	State	Sent Packets	Sent Bytes	Rcvd Packets	Rcvd Bytes
ppleMobileD...	1948	TCP	MTTC-Processing	49156	localhost	5354	ESTABLISHED				
ppleMobileD...	1948	UDP	MTTC-Processing	49152	*	*					
ppleMobileD...	1948	UDP	MTTC-Processing	49153	*	*					
odeMeter.exe	2896	TCP	MTTC-Processing	22350	MTTC-Processing	0	LISTENING				
odeMeter.exe	2896	UDP	MTTC-Processing	22350	*	*					
ropbox.exe	4672	TCP	MTTC-Processing	17500	MTTC-Processing	0	LISTENING	5	555	9	
ropbox.exe	4672	TCP	mttc-processing.k...	17500	10.0.1.15	61794	ESTABLISHED	2	148	1	
ropbox.exe	4672	TCP	MTTC-Processing	19872	localhost	57203	ESTABLISHED				
ropbox.exe	4672	TCP	mttc-processing.k...	54326	sjc-not20.sjc.drop...	http	ESTABLISHED	1	194	1	
ropbox.exe	4672	TCP	mttc-processing.k...	54327	v-d-2b.sjc.dropbox...	https	CLOSE_WAIT				
ropbox.exe	4672	TCP	MTTC-Processing	57203	localhost	19872	ESTABLISHED				
ropbox.exe	4672	TCP	mttc-processing.k...	57204	75.126.110.108-st...	https	CLOSE_WAIT				
ropbox.exe	4672	TCP	mttc-processing.k...	57227	10.0.1.15	17500	ESTABLISHED	1	90	2	
ropbox.exe	4672	TCP	mttc-processing.k...	59026	ec2-50-16-212-22....	https	CLOSE_WAIT				
ropbox.exe	4672	TCP	mttc-processing.k...	59376	v-client-2b.sjc.dro...	https	CLOSE_WAIT				
ropbox.exe	4672	TCP	mttc-processing.k...	59378	ec2-174-129-195-...	https	CLOSE_WAIT				
ropbox.exe	4672	TCP	mttc-processing.k...	59379	v-client-2b.sjc.dro...	https	CLOSE_WAIT				
ropbox.exe	4672	UDP	MTTC-Processing	17500	*	*					
xplorer.exe	3976	TCP	mttc-processing.k...	58666	ord08s06-in-f21.1e...	http	CLOSE_WAIT				
xplorer.exe	3976	TCP	mttc-processing.k...	58673	vx-in-f104.1e100.net	https	CLOSE_WAIT				
xplorer.exe	3976	TCP	mttc-processing.k...	58674	vx-in-f104.1e100.net	https	CLOSE_WAIT				
efox.exe	4692	TCP	MTTC-Processing	55401	localhost	55402	ESTABLISHED	24	24		
efox.exe	4692	TCP	MTTC-Processing	55402	localhost	55401	ESTABLISHED			24	
efox.exe	4692	TCP	MTTC-Processing	55403	localhost	55404	ESTABLISHED	32	32		
efox.exe	4692	TCP	MTTC-Processing	55404	localhost	55403	ESTABLISHED			32	

FIGURE 1.10 Sample output from Fport.

Use Robust Passwords

With the increased processing power of our computers and password-cracking software such as the Passware products[48] and AccessData's Password Recovery Toolkit,[49] cracking passwords is fairly simple and straightforward. For this reason it is extremely important to create robust passwords. Complex passwords are hard for users to remember, though, so it is a challenge to create passwords that can be remembered without writing them down. One solution is to use the first letter of each word in a phrase, such as "**I** **l**ike **t**o **e**at **i**mported **c**heese **f**rom **H**olland." This becomes *IlteicfH*, which is an eight-character password using upper- and lowercase letters. This can be made even more complex by substituting an exclamation point for the letter *I* and substituting the number 3 for the letter *e*, so that the password becomes*!lt3icfH*. This is a fairly robust password that can be remembered easily.

Close Unnecessary Ports

Ports on a computer are logical access points for communication over a network. Knowing what ports are open on your computers will allow you to understand the types of access points that exist. The well-known port numbers are 0 through 1023. Some easily recognized ports and what they are used for are listed here:

- Port 21: FTP
- Port 23: Telnet
- Port 25: SMTP
- Port 53: DNS
- Port 80: HTTP
- Port 110: POP
- Port 119: NNTP

Since open ports that are not needed can be an entrance into your systems, and open ports that are open unexpectedly could be a sign of malicious software, identifying open ports is an important security process. There are several tools that will allow you to identify open ports. The built-in command-line tool *netstat* will allow you to identify open ports and process IDs by using the following switches:

– *a* Displays all connections and listening ports
– *n* Displays addresses and port numbers in numerical form
– *o* Displays the owning process ID associated with each connection

(*Note:* In Unix, netstat is also available but utilizes the following switches: *–atvp.*)

Other tools that can prove helpful are CurrPorts,[50] a graphical user interface (GUI) tool that allows you to export the results in delimited format, and TCPView[51] is a tool provided by Microsoft. Sample results are shown in Figure 1.10.

48. Passware, www.lostpassword.com.
49. Password Recovery Toolkit, http://accessdata.com/products/computer-forensics/decryption.
50. CurrPorts, http://www.nirsoft.net/utils/cports.html.
51. TCPView, http://technet.microsoft.com/en-us/sysinternals/bb897437.

Patch, Patch, Patch

Nearly all operating systems have a mechanism for automatically checking for updates. This notification system should be turned on. Although there is some debate as to whether updates should be installed automatically, systems administrators should at least be notified of updates. They might not want to have them installed automatically, since patches and updates have been known to cause more problems than they solve. However, administrators should not wait too long before installing updates because this can unnecessarily expose systems to attack. A simple tool that can help keep track of system updates is the Microsoft Baseline Security Analyzer,[52] which also will examine other fundamental security configurations.

Use Administrator Accounts for Administrative Tasks

A common security vulnerability is created when systems administrators conduct administrative or personal tasks while logged into their computers with administrator rights. Tasks such as checking email, surfing the Internet, and testing questionable software can expose the computer to malicious software. This means that the malicious software can run with administrator privileges, which can create serious problems. Administrators should log into their systems using a standard user account to prevent malicious software from gaining control of their computers.

Restrict Physical Access

With a focus on technology, it is often easy to overlook nontechnical security mechanisms. If an intruder can gain physical access to a server or other infrastructure asset, the intruder will own the organization. Critical systems should be kept in secure areas. A secure area is one that provides the ability to control access to only those who need access to the systems as part of their job responsibilities. A room that is kept locked using a key that is only provided to the systems administrator, with the only duplicate stored in a safe in the office manager's office, is a good start. The room should not have any windows that can open. In addition, the room should have no labels or signs identifying it as a server room or network operations center. The equipment should not be stored in a closet where other employees, custodians, or contractors can gain access. The validity of your security mechanisms should be reviewed during a third-party vulnerability assessment.

Don't Forget Paper!

With the advent of advanced technology, people have forgotten how information was stolen in the past—on paper. Managing paper documents is fairly straightforward. Locking file cabinets should be used—and locked consistently. Extra copies of proprietary documents, document drafts, and expired internal communications are some of the materials that should be shredded. A policy should be created to tell employees what they should and should not do with printed documents. The following example of the theft of trade secrets underscores the importance of protecting paper documents:

A company surveillance camera caught Coca-Cola employee Joya Williams at her desk looking through files and "stuffing documents into bags," Nahmias and FBI officials said. Then in June, an undercover FBI agent met at the Atlanta airport with another of the defendants, handing him $30,000 in a yellow Girl Scout Cookie box in exchange for an Armani bag containing confidential Coca-Cola documents and a sample of a product the company was developing, officials said.[53]

The steps to achieving security mentioned in this chapter are only the beginning. They should provide some insight into where to start building a secure organization.

Finally, let's briefly look at the process of building and assessing the security controls in organizational information systems including: the activities carried out by organizations and assessors to prepare for security control assessments; the development of security assessment plans; the conduct of security control assessments and the analysis, documentation, and reporting of assessment results; and postassessment report analysis and follow-on activities carried out by organizations.

6. PREPARING FOR THE BUILDING OF SECURITY CONTROL ASSESSMENTS

Conducting security control assessments in today's complex environment of sophisticated information technology infrastructures and high-visibility, mission-critical applications can be difficult, challenging, and resource-intensive. Success requires the cooperation and collaboration among all parties having a vested interest in the organization's information security posture, including information system owners, common control providers, authorizing officials, chief information officers, senior information security officers, and chief executive officers/heads of departments. Establishing an appropriate set of expectations before, during, and

---

52. Microsoft Baseline Security Analyzer, http://technet.microsoft.com/en-us/security/cc184923.

53. Accused in theft of Coke secrets," *The Washington Post*, July 26, 2006, www.washingtonpost.com/wp-dyn/content/article/2006/07/05/AR2006070501717.html (February 29, 2012).

after the assessment is paramount to achieving an acceptable outcome—that is, producing information necessary to help the authorizing official make a credible, risk-based decision on whether to place the information system into operation or continue its operation.

Thorough preparation by the organization and the assessors is an important aspect of conducting effective security control assessments. Preparatory activities address a range of issues relating to the cost, schedule, and performance of the assessment (see checklist: "An Agenda for Action for Preparatory Activities").

7. SUMMARY

In preparation for the assessment of security controls, this chapter covered how necessary background information is assembled and made available to the assessors or assessment team in order to build a secure organization. To the extent necessary to support the specific assessment, the organization identifies and arranges access to:

- Elements of the organization responsible for developing, documenting, disseminating, reviewing, and updating

---

An Agenda for Action for Preparatory Activities

From the organizational perspective, preparing for the building of a security control assessment includes the following key activities (check all tasks completed):

_____1. Ensuring that appropriate policies covering security control assessments are in place and understood by all affected organizational elements.

_____2. Ensuring that all steps in the Risk Management Framework (RMF) prior to the security control assessment step have been successfully completed and received appropriate management oversight.

_____3. Ensuring that security controls identified as common controls (and the common portion of hybrid controls) have been assigned to appropriate organizational entities (common control providers) for development and implementation.

_____4. Establishing the objective and scope of the security control assessment (the purpose of the assessment and what is being assessed).

_____5. Notifying key organizational officials of the impending security control assessment and allocating necessary resources to carry out the assessment.

_____6. Establishing appropriate communication channels among organizational officials having an interest in the security control assessment.

_____7. Establishing time frames for completing the security control assessment and key milestone decision points required by the organization to effectively manage the assessment.

_____8. Identifying and selecting a competent assessor/ assessment team that will be responsible for conducting the security control assessment, considering issues of assessor independence.

_____9. Collecting artifacts to provide to the assessor/ assessment team (policies, procedures, plans, specifications, designs, records, administrator/ operator manuals, information system documentation, interconnection agreements, previous assessment results).

_____10. Establishing a mechanism between the organization and the assessor and/or assessment team to minimize ambiguities or misunderstandings about

security control implementation or security control weaknesses/deficiencies identified during the assessment.

Security control assessors/assessment teams begin preparing for the assessment by:

_____11. Obtaining a general understanding of the organization's operations (including mission, functions, and business processes) and how the information system that is the subject of the security control assessment supports those organizational operations.

_____12. Obtaining an understanding of the structure of the information system (system architecture).

_____13. Identifying the organizational entities responsible for the development and implementation of the common controls (or the common portion of hybrid controls) supporting the information system.

_____14. Establishing appropriate organizational points of contact needed to carry out the security control assessment.

_____15. Obtaining artifacts needed for the security control assessment (policies, procedures, plans, specifications, designs, records, administrator/operator manuals, information system documentation, interconnection agreements, previous assessment results).

_____16. Obtaining previous assessment results that may be appropriately reused for the security control assessment (reports, audits, vulnerability scans, physical security inspections, prior assessments, developmental testing and evaluation, vendor flaw remediation activities, International Organization for Standardization/ International Electrotechnical Commission (ISO/IEC) 15408 (Common Criteria) evaluations).

_____17. Meeting with appropriate organizational officials to ensure common understanding for assessment objectives and the proposed rigor and scope of the assessment.

_____18. Developing a security assessment plan.

all security policies and associated procedures for implementing policy-compliant controls.

- The security policies for the information system and any associated implementing procedures.
- Individuals or groups responsible for the development, implementation, operation, and maintenance of security controls.
- Any materials (security plans, records, schedules, assessment reports, after-action reports, agreements, authorization packages) associated with the implementation and operation of security controls.
- The objects to be assessed.

The availability of essential documentation; as well as, access to key organizational personnel and the information system being assessed, are paramount to a successful assessment of the security controls.

When building secure organizations, one must consider both the technical expertise and the level of independence required in selecting security control assessors. Organizations must ensure that security control assessors possess the required skills and technical expertise to successfully carry out assessments of system-specific, hybrid, and common controls. This includes knowledge of and experience with the specific hardware, software, and firmware components employed by the organization. An independent assessor is any individual or group capable of conducting an impartial assessment of security controls employed within or inherited by an information system.

Impartiality implies that assessors are free from any perceived or actual conflicts of interest with respect to the development, operation, and/or management of the information system or the determination of security control effectiveness. The authorizing official or designated representative determines the required level of independence for security control assessors based on the results of the security categorization process for the information system and the ultimate risk to organizational operations and assets, individuals, other organizations. The authorizing official determines if the level of assessor independence is sufficient to provide confidence that the assessment results produced are sound and can be used to make a risk-based decision on whether to place the information system into operation or continue its operation.

Independent security control assessment services can be obtained from other elements within the organization or can be contracted to a public- or private-sector entity outside of the organization. In special situations—for example, when the organization that owns the information system is small or the organizational structure requires that the security control assessment be accomplished by individuals that are in the developmental, operational, and/or management chain of the system owner—independence in the assessment process can be achieved by ensuring that the assessment results are carefully reviewed and analyzed by an independent team of experts to validate the completeness, consistency, and veracity of the results.

Finally, let's move on to the real interactive part of this Chapter: review questions/exercises, hands-on projects, case projects and optional team case project. The answers and/or solutions by chapter can be found in the Online Instructor's Solutions Manual.

CHAPTER REVIEW QUESTIONS/EXERCISES

True/False

1. True or False? Security, by its very nature, is inconvenient, and the more robust the security mechanisms, the more inconvenient the process becomes.
2. True or False? As though employees' desire to share data is enough of a threat to proprietary information, many business professionals want access to data from anywhere they work, on a variety of devices.
3. True or False? Many businesses believe that if they purchase enough equipment, they can create a secure infrastructure.
4. True or False? For most organizations, the cost of creating a weak security posture is seen as a necessary evil, similar to purchasing insurance.
5. True or False? In addressing the security needs of an organization, it is common for professionals to succumb to some very common misconceptions.

Multiple Choice

1. Many businesses believe that if they purchase enough equipment, they can create a secure:
   A. Firewall
   B. Workstation
   C. Ecommerce
   D. Organization
   E. Infrastructure
2. Once threats and risks are identified, you can take one of four steps, except which of the following?
   A. Ignore the risk.
   B. Accept the risk.
   C. Transfer the risk.
   D. Identify the risk.
   E. Mitigate the risk.
3. Just as implementing a robust, secure environment is a dynamic process; creating a highly skilled staff of security professionals is a:
   A. dynamic process.
   B. technical infrastructure.
   C. vendor-neutral program.
   D. work environment.
   E. professional affiliation.

4. What is the largest security-related organization in the world that focuses primarily on physical security, but has more recently started addressing computer security as well?

   A. ISACA
   B. HTCIA
   C. ISSA
   D. ASIS
   E. InfraGard

5. Arguably one of the best ways to determine whether an employee has a strong grasp of information security concepts is if she or he can achieve the Certified Information Systems Security Professional (CISSP) certification. Candidates for this certification are tested on their understanding of the following knowledge domains, except which one:

   A. Proprietary information
   B. Access Control
   C. Cryptography
   D. Operations security
   E. Security architecture

EXERCISE

Problem

With regards to building a secure organization, the security assessment team (SAT) should determine organizational policies and procedures, the privileged commands for which dual authorization is to be enforced; and the information system which enforces dual authorization based on organizational policies and procedures for organization-defined privileged commands. What should the SAT examine with regards to access enforcement potential assessment methods and objects?

Hands-On Projects

Project

With regards to building a secure organization, the security assessment team (SAT) should determine how the organization: defines applicable policy for controlling the flow of information within the system and between interconnected systems; defines approved authorizations for controlling the flow of information within the system and between interconnected systems in accordance with applicable policy; and the information system enforces approved authorizations for controlling the flow of information within the system and between interconnected systems in accordance with applicable policy. What should the SAT examine with regards to information flow enforcement potential assessment methods and objects?

Case Projects

Problem

With regards to building a secure organization, what should the security assessment team (SAT) examine with regards to security assessment and authorization?

Optional Team Case Project

Problem

With regards to building a secure organization, the security assessment team (SAT) should determine how the organization: develops a contingency plan for the information system that: identifies essential missions and business functions and associated contingency.

Requirements: provides recovery objectives, restoration priorities, and metrics; addresses contingency roles, responsibilities, assigned individuals with contact information; addresses maintaining essential missions and business functions despite an information system disruption, compromise, or failure; addresses eventual, full information system restoration without deterioration of the security measures originally planned and implemented; and is reviewed and approved by designated officials within the organization. The SAT should also determine how the organization: defines key contingency personnel (identified by name and/or by role) and organizational elements designated to receive copies of the contingency plan; and distributes copies of the contingency plan to organization-defined key contingency personnel and organizational elements. What should the SAT examine with regards to contingency planning?

## Chapter 2

A Cryptography Primer

Scott R. Ellis, EnCE, RCA

kCura — Relativity Infrastructure Engineering, Manager

Cryptography, as a word, literally means the "study of hidden writing." It comes from the Greek κρυπτός, "hidden, secret"; and from γράφειν, graphein, "writing," or -λογία, -logia, "study."[1] In practice, it is so much more than that. The 0s and 1s of compiled software binary, something that frequently requires encryption, can hardly be considered "writing." Were a new word for cryptography to be invented today, it would probably be "secret communications." It follows then that, rather than point to the first altered writing as the origins of cryptography, we must look to the origins of communication and to the first known alterations of it in any form. Historically, then, you might say that cryptography is a built-in defense mechanism, as a property of language. As you'll see in this chapter, ultimately this dependency is also the final, greatest weakness of any cryptographic system, even the perceivably unbreakable AES system. From unique, cultural body language to language itself, to our every means of communication, it is in our nature to want to prevent others who would do us harm from intercepting private communications (which could be about them!). Perhaps nothing so perfectly illustrates this fact as the art of cryptography. It is, in its purpose, an art form entirely devoted to the methods whereby we can prevent information from falling into the hands of those who would use it against us—our enemies.

Since the beginning of sentient language, cryptography has been a part of communication. It is as old as language itself. In fact, one could make the argument that the desire and ability to encrypt communication, to alter a missive in such a way so that only the intended recipient may understand it, is an innate ability hard-wired into the human genome. Aside from the necessity to communicate, it could very well be what led to the development of language itself. Over time, languages and dialects evolved, as we can see with Spanish, French, Portuguese, and Italian—all of which derived from Latin. People who speak French have a great deal of trouble understanding people who speak Spanish, and vice versa. The profusion of Latin cognates in these languages is undisputed, but generally speaking, the two languages are so far removed that they are not dialects but rather separate languages. But why is this? Certain abilities, such as walking, are built into our nervous systems; other abilities, such as language, are not. From pig Latin to whispering circles to word jumbles, to languages so foreign that only the native speakers understand them, to diverse languages and finally modern cryptography, it is in our nature to keep our communications secret.

So why isn't language hard-wired into our nervous system, as it is with bees, who are born knowing how to tell another bee how far away a flower is, as well as the quantity of pollen and whether there is danger present? Why don't we humans all speak the exact same language? The reason is undoubtedly because humans, unlike bees, understand that knowledge is power, and knowledge is communicated via spoken and written words. Plus we weren't born with giant stingers with which to sting people we don't like. With the development of evolving languages innate in our genetic wiring, the inception of cryptography was inevitable.

In essence, computer-based cryptography is the art of creating a form of communication that embraces the following precepts:

- It can be readily understood by the intended recipients.
- It cannot be understood by unintended recipients
- It can be adapted and changed easily with relatively small modifications, such as a changed passphrase or word.

Any artificially created lexicon, such as the Pig Latin of children, pictograph codes, gang-speak, or corporate lingo—and even the names of music albums, such as *Four Flicks*—are all manners of cryptography where real text, sometimes not so ciphered, is hidden in what

1. Henry Liddell and Robert Scott, *Greek-English Lexicon*, Oxford University Press (1984).

appears to be plain text. They are attempts at hidden communications.

1. WHAT IS CRYPTOGRAPHY? WHAT IS ENCRYPTION?

Ask any ancient Egyptian and he'll undoubtedly define *cryptography* as the practice of burying the dead so that they cannot be found again. The Egyptians were very good at it; thousands of years later, new crypts are still being discovered. The Greek root *krypt* literally means "a hidden place," and as such it is an appropriate base for any term involving cryptology. According to the Online Etymology Dictionary, *crypto-* as a prefix, meaning "concealed, secret," has been used since 1760, and from the Greek *graphikos*, "of or for writing, belonging to drawing, picturesque." Together, *crypto + graphy* would then mean "hiding place for ideas, sounds, pictures, or words." *Graph*, technically from its Greek root, is "the art of writing." *Encryption*, in contrast, merely means the act of carrying out some aspect of cryptography. *Cryptology*, with its *-ology* ending, is the study of cryptography. Encryption is subsumed by cryptography.

How Is Cryptography Done?

For most information technology occupations, knowledge of cryptography is a very small part of a broader skill set and is generally limited to relevant applications. The argument could be made that this is why the Internet is so extraordinarily plagued with security breaches. The majority of IT administrators, software programmers, and hardware developers are barely cognizant of the power of true cryptography. Overburdened with battling the plague that they inherited, they can't afford to devote the time or resources needed to implement a truly secure strategy. And the reason, as we shall see, is that, as good as cryptographers can be, for every cryptographer there is a decryptographer working just as diligently to decipher a new encryption algorithm.

Traditionally, cryptography has consisted of any means possible whereby communications may be encrypted and transmitted. This could be as simple as using a language with which the opposition is not familiar. Who hasn't been in a place where everyone around them was speaking a language they didn't understand? There are thousands of languages in the world; nobody can know them all. As was shown in World War II, when the Allied forces used Navajo as a means of communicating freely, some languages are so obscure that an entire nation may not contain one person who speaks it! All true cryptography is composed of three parts: a cipher, an original message, and the resultant encryption. The *cipher* is the method of encryption used. Original messages are referred to as *plain text* or as *clear text*. A message that is transmitted without encryption is said to be sent "in the clear." The resultant message is called *ciphertext* or *cryptogram*. This part of the chapter begins with a simple review of cryptography procedures and carries them through; each section builds on the next to illustrate the principles of cryptography.

2. FAMOUS CRYPTOGRAPHIC DEVICES

The past few hundred years of technical development and advances have brought greater and greater means to decrypt, encode, and transmit information. With the advent of the most modern warfare techniques and the increase in communication and ease of reception, the need for encryption has never been greater.

World War II publicized and popularized cryptography in modern culture. The Allied forces' ability to capture, decrypt, and intercept Axis communications is said to have hastened the end of the war by several years. Next we take a quick look at some famous cryptographic devices from that era.

The Lorenz Cipher

The Lorenz cipher machine was an industrial-strength ciphering machine used in teleprinter circuits by the Germans during World War II. Not to be confused with its smaller cousin, the Enigma machine, the Lorenz cipher could possibly be best compared to a virtual private network tunnel for a telegraph line—only it wasn't sending Morse code, it was using a code not unlike a sort of American Standard Code for Information Interchange (ASCII) format. A grand-daddy of sorts, called the Baudot code, was used to send alphanumeric communications across telegraph lines. Each character was represented by a series of 5 bits.

The Lorenz cipher is often confused with the famous Enigma, but unlike the Enigma (which was a portable field unit), the Lorenz cipher could receive typed messages, encrypt them, and send them to another distant Lorenz cipher, which would then decrypt the signal. It used a pseudorandom cipher XOR'd (an encryption algorithm) with plaintext. The machine would be inserted inline as an attachment to a Lorenz teleprinter. Figure 2.1 is a rendered drawing from a photograph of a Lorenz cipher machine.

Enigma

The Enigma machine was a field unit used in World War II by German field agents to encrypt and decrypt

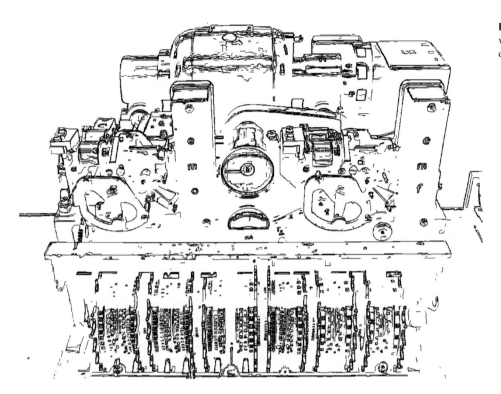

FIGURE 2.1 The Lorenz machine was set inline with a teletype to produce encrypted telegraphic signals.

messages and communications. Similar to the Feistel function of the 1970s, the Enigma machine was one of the first mechanized methods of encrypting text using an iterative cipher. It employed a series of rotors that, with some electricity, a light bulb, and a reflector, allowed the operator to either encrypt or decrypt a message. The original position of the rotors, set with each encryption and based on a prearranged pattern that in turn was based on the calendar, allowed the machine to be used, even if it was compromised.

When the Enigma was in use, with each subsequent key press, the rotors would change in alignment from their set positions in such a way that a different letter was produced each time. The operator, with a message in hand, would enter each character into the machine by pressing a typewriter-like key. The rotors would align, and a letter would then illuminate, telling the operator what the letter *really* was. Likewise, when enciphering, the operator would press the key and the illuminated letter would be the cipher text. The continually changing internal flow of electricity that caused the rotors to change was not random, but it did create a polyalphabetic cipher that could be different each time it was used.

3. CIPHERS

Cryptography is built on one overarching premise: the need for a cipher that can reliably, and portably, be used to encrypt text so that, through any means of cryptanalysis—

differential, deductive, algebraic, or the like—the ciphertext cannot be undone with any available technology. Throughout the centuries, there have been many attempts to create simple ciphers that can achieve this goal. With the exception of the One Time Pad, which is not particularly portable, success has been limited. Let's look at a few of these methods now.

The Substitution Cipher

In this method, each letter of the message is replaced with a single character. See Table 2.1 for an example of a substitution cipher. Because some letters appear more often and certain words are used more than others, some ciphers are extremely easy to decrypt and can be deciphered at a glance by more practiced cryptologists.

By simply understanding probability and with some applied statistics, certain metadata about a language can be derived and used to decrypt any simple, one-for-one substitution cipher. Decryption methods often rely on understanding the context of the *ciphertext*. What was encrypted—business communication? Spreadsheets? Technical data? Coordinates? For example, using a hex editor and an access database to conduct some statistics, we can use the information in Table 2.2 to gain highly specialized knowledge about the data in Chapter 33, "Computer Forensics," by Scott R. Ellis, in this book. A long chapter at nearly 25,000 words, it provides a

TABLE 2.1 A Simple Substitution Cipher. Letters are Numbered by their Order in the Alphabet, to Provide a Numeric Reference Key. To Encrypt a Message, the Letters are Replaced, or Substituted, by the Numbers. This is a Particularly Easy Cipher to Reverse.

A	B	C	D	E	F	G	H	I	J	K	L	M	N	O	P	Q	R	S	T	U	V	W	X	Y	Z
1	2	3	4	5	6	7	8	9	10	11	12	13	14	15	16	17	18	19	20	21	22	23	24	25	26
O	C	Q	W	B	X	Y	E	I	L	Z	A	D	R	J	S	P	F	G	K	H	N	T	U	M	V
15	3	17	23	2	24	25	5	9	12	26	1	4	18	10	19	16	6	7	11	8	14	20	21	13	22

TABLE 2.2 Statistical Data of Interest in Encryption. An Analysis of a Selection of a Manuscript (in this case, the preedited version of Chapter 33 of this book) can Provide Insight into the Reasons that Good Ciphers Need to be Developed.

Character Analysis	Count
Number of distinct alphanumeric combinations	1958
Distinct characters	68
Number of four-letter words	984
Number of five-letter words	1375

TABLE 2.3 Five-letter Word Recurrences in Chapter 33: A Glimpse of the Leading Five-letter Words found in the Preedited Manuscript. Once Unique Letter Groupings have been Identified, Substitution, Often by Trial and Error, can Result in a Meaningful Reconstruction that Allows the Entire Cipher to be Revealed.

Words Field	Number of Recurrences
files	125
drive	75
there	67
email	46
these	43
other	42
about	41
where	36
would	33
every	31
court	30
their	30
first	28
using	28
which	24
could	22
table	22
after	21
image	21
don't	19
tools	19
being	18
entry	18

sufficiently large statistical pool to draw some meaningful analyses.

Table 2.3 gives additional data about the occurrence of specific words in Chapter 33. Note that because it is a technical text, words such as *computer, files, email*, and *drive* emerge as leaders. Analysis of these leaders can reveal individual and paired alpha frequencies. Being armed with knowledge about the type of communication can be very beneficial in decrypting it.

Further information about types of data being encrypted includes word counts by length of the word. Table 2.4 contains such a list for Chapter 33. This information can be used to begin to piece together useful and meaningful short sentences, which can provide cues to longer and more complex structures. It is exactly this sort of activity that good cryptography attempts to defeat.

Were it encrypted using a simple substitution cipher, a good start to deciphering Chapter 33 could be made using the information we've gathered. As a learning exercise, game, or logic puzzle, substitution ciphers are quite useful. Some substitution ciphers that are more elaborate can be just as difficult to crack. Ultimately, though, the weakness behind a substitution cipher is the fact that the

TABLE 2.4 Leaders by Word Length in the Preedited Manuscript for Chapter 33. The Context of the Clear Text can make the Cipher Less Secure. There are, after all, only a Finite Number of Words. Fewer of them are Long.

Words Field	Number of Dupes	Word Length
XOriginalArrivalTime:	2	21
interpretations	2	15
XOriginatingIP:	2	15
electronically	4	14
investigations	5	14
interpretation	6	14
reconstructing	3	14
irreproducible	2	14
professionally	2	14
inexperienced	2	13
demonstrative	2	13
XAnalysisOut:	8	13
steganography	7	13
understanding	8	13
certification	2	13
circumstances	8	13
unrecoverable	4	13
investigation	15	13
automatically	2	13
admissibility	2	13
XProcessedBy:	2	13
administrator	4	13
determination	3	13
investigative	3	13
practitioners	2	13
preponderance	2	13
intentionally	2	13
consideration	2	13
interestingly	2	13

ciphertext remains a one-to-one, directly corresponding substitution; ultimately, anyone with a pen and paper and a large enough sample of the ciphertext can defeat it. Through use of a computer, deciphering a simple substitution cipher becomes child's play.

Example 2.1 A Sample Cryptogram. Try this Out: Gv Vw, Dtwvg?

Hint: Caesar said it, and it is in Latin.[2]

The Shift Cipher

Also known as the Caesar cipher, the shift cipher is one that anyone can readily understand and remember for decoding. It is a form of the substitution cipher. By shifting the alphabet a few positions in either direction, a simple sentence can become unreadable to casual inspection. Example 2.1 is an example of such a shift.

Interestingly, for cryptogram word games, the spaces are always included. Often puzzles use numbers instead of letters for the substitution. Removing the spaces in this particular example can make the ciphertext somewhat more secure. The possibility for multiple solutions becomes an issue; any number of words might fit the pattern.

Today many software tools are available to quickly and easily decode most cryptograms (at least, those that are not written in a dead language). You can have some fun with these tools; for example, the name Scott Ellis, when decrypted, turns into Still Books. The name of a friend of the author's decrypts to "His Sinless." It is apparent, then, that smaller-sample simple substitution ciphers can have more than one solution.

Much has been written and stated about frequency analysis; it is considered the "end-all and be-all" with respect to cipher decryption. Frequency analysis is not to be confused with cipher breaking, which is a modern attack against the actual cryptographic algorithms themselves. However, to think of simply plugging in some numbers generated from a Google search is a bit naïve. The frequency chart in Table 2.5 is commonplace on the Web.

It is beyond the scope of this chapter to delve into the accuracy of the table, but suffice it to say that our own analysis of Chapter 33's 118,000 characters, a technical text, yielded a much different result; see Table 2.6. Perhaps it is the significantly larger sample and the fact that it is a technical text that makes the results different after the top two. Additionally, where computers are concerned, an actual frequency analysis would take into consideration all ASCII characters, as shown in Table 2.6.

Frequency analysis is not difficult; once all the letters of a text are pulled into a database program, it is fairly straightforward to do a count of all the duplicate values. The snippet of code in Example 2.2 demonstrates one

---

2. Et tu, Brute?

TABLE 2.5 "In a Random Sampling of 1000 Letters," this Pattern Emerges.

Letter	Frequency
E	130
T	93
N	78
R	77
I	74
O	74
A	73
S	63
D	44
H	35
L	35
C	30
F	28
P	27
U	27
M	25
Y	19
G	16
W	16
V	13
B	9
X	5
K	3
Q	3
J	2
Z	1
Total	**1000**

TABLE 2.6 Using MS Access to Perform some Frequency Analysis of Chapter 33 in this Book. Characters with Fewer Repetitions than z were Excluded from the Return. Character Frequency Analysis of Different Types of Communications Yield Slightly Different Results.

Chapter 33 Letters	Frequency
e	14,467
t	10,945
a	9239
i	8385
o	7962
s	7681
n	7342
r	6872
h	4882
l	4646
d	4104
c	4066
u	2941
m	2929
f	2759
p	2402
y	2155
g	1902
w	1881
b	1622
v	1391
.	1334
,	1110
k	698
0	490
x	490
q	166
7	160
*	149
5	147
)	147
(	146
j	145

(Continued)

way in which text can be transformed into a single column and imported into a database.

The cryptograms that use formatting (every word becomes the same length) are considerably more difficult for basic online decryption programs to crack. They must take into consideration spacing and word lengths when considering whether or not a string matches a word. It stands to reason, then, that the formulation of the cipher—where a substitution that is based partially on frequency similarities and with a whole lot of

TABLE 2.6 (Continued)

Chapter 33 Letters	Frequency
3	142
6	140
Æ	134
ò	134
ô	129
ö	129
4	119
z	116
Total	**116,798**

obfuscation so that when messages are decrypted they have ambiguous or multiple meanings—would be desirable for simple ciphers. However, this would only be true for very short and very obscure messages that could be code words to decrypt other messages or could simply be sent to misdirect the opponent. The amount of ciphertext needed to successfully break a cipher is called *unicity distance*. Ciphers with small unicity distances are weaker than those with large ones.

Example 2.2

```
 1: Sub Letters2column ()
 2: Dim bytText () As Byte
 3: Dim bytNew() As Byte
 4: Dim lngCount As Long
 5: With ActiveDocument.Content
 6:    bytText = .Text
 7:    ReDim bytNew((((UBound(bytText()) + 1) * 2) − 5))
 8:    For lngCount = 0 To (UBound(bytText()) − 2) Step 2
 9:       bytNew((lngCount * 2)) = bytText(lngCount)
10:       bytNew(((lngCount * 2) + 2)) = 13
11:    Next lngCount
12:    .Text = bytNew()
13: End With
14: End Sub
```

Ultimately, substitution ciphers are vulnerable to either word-pattern analysis, letter-frequency analysis, or some combination of both. Where numerical information is encrypted, tools such as Benford's Law can be used to elicit patterns of numbers that *should* be occurring. Forensic techniques incorporate such tools to uncover accounting fraud. So, though this particular cipher is a child's game, it is useful in that it is an underlying

principle of cryptography and should be well understood before continuing. The primary purpose of discussing it here is as an introduction to ciphers.

Further topics of interest and places to find information involving substitution ciphers are the chi-square statistic, Edgar Allan Poe, Sherlock Holmes, Benford's Law, Google, and Wikipedia. For example, an Internet search for Edgar Allan Poe + cryptography will lead you to articles that detail how Poe's interest in the subject, and his use of it in stories such as "The Gold-Bug," served to popularize and raise awareness of cryptography in the general public.

The Polyalphabetic Cipher

The preceding clearly demonstrated that though the substitution cipher is fun and easy, it is also vulnerable and weak. It is especially susceptible to frequency analysis. Given a large enough sample, a cipher can easily be broken by mapping the frequency of the letters in the ciphertext to the frequency of letters in the language or dialect of the ciphertext (if it is known). To make ciphers more difficult to crack, Blaise de Vigenère from the sixteenth-century court of Henry III of France proposed a polyalphabetic substitution. In this cipher, instead of a one-to-one relationship, there is a one-to-many. A single letter can have multiple substitutes. The Vigenère solution was the first known cipher to use a keyword.

It works like this: First, a *tableau* is developed, as in Table 2.7. This tableau is a series of shift ciphers. In fact, since there can be only 26 additive shift ciphers, it is all of them.

In Table 2.7, a table in combination with a keyword is used to create the cipher. For example, if we choose the keyword *rockerrooks*, overlay it over the plaintext, and cross-index it to Table 2.7, we can produce the ciphertext. In this example, the top row is used to look up the plaintext, and the leftmost column is used to reference the keyword.

For example, we lay the word *rockerrooks* over the sentence, "Ask not what your country can do for you." Line 1 is the keyword, line 2 is the plain text, and line 3 is the ciphertext.

Keyword: ROC KER ROOK SROC KERROOK SRO CK ERR OOK
Plaintext: ASK NOT WHAT YOUR COUNTRY CAN DO FOR YOU
Ciphertext: RGM XSK NVOD QFIT MSLEHFI URB FY JFI MCE

The similarity of this tableau to a mathematical table like the one shown in Table 2.8 becomes apparent. Just think letters instead of numbers, and it becomes clear how this works. The top row is used to "look up" a letter from the plaintext, the leftmost column is used to locate the overlaying keyword letter, and where the column and the row intersect is the ciphertext.

TABLE 2.7 Vigenère's Tableau Arranges all of the Shift Ciphers in a Single Table. It then Implements a Keyword to Create a more Complex Cipher than the Simple Substitution or Shift Ciphers. The Number *of spurious keys*, that is, Bogus Decryptions that result from Attempting to Decrypt a Polyalphabetic Encryption, is Greater than those Created during the Decryption of a Single Shift Cipher.

Letter	A	B	C	D	E	F	G	H	I	J	K	L	M	N	O	P	Q	R	S	T	U	V	W	X	Y	Z
A	A	B	C	D	E	F	G	H	I	J	K	L	M	N	O	P	Q	R	S	T	U	V	W	X	Y	Z
B	B	C	D	E	F	G	H	I	J	K	L	M	N	O	P	Q	R	S	T	U	V	W	X	Y	Z	A
C	C	D	E	F	G	H	I	J	K	L	M	N	O	P	Q	R	S	T	U	V	W	X	Y	Z	A	B
D	D	E	F	G	H	I	J	K	L	M	N	O	P	Q	R	S	T	U	V	W	X	Y	Z	A	B	C
E	E	F	G	H	I	J	K	L	M	N	O	P	Q	R	S	T	U	V	W	X	Y	Z	A	B	C	D
F	F	G	H	I	J	K	L	M	N	O	P	Q	R	S	T	U	V	W	X	Y	Z	A	B	C	D	E
G	G	H	I	J	K	L	M	N	O	P	Q	R	S	T	U	V	W	X	Y	Z	A	B	C	D	E	F
H	H	I	J	K	L	M	N	O	P	Q	R	S	T	U	V	W	X	Y	Z	A	B	C	D	E	F	G
I	I	J	K	L	M	N	O	P	Q	R	S	T	U	V	W	X	Y	Z	A	B	C	D	E	F	G	H
J	J	K	L	M	N	O	P	Q	R	S	T	U	V	W	X	Y	Z	A	B	C	D	E	F	G	H	I
K	K	L	M	N	O	P	Q	R	S	T	U	V	W	X	Y	Z	A	B	C	D	E	F	G	H	I	J
L	L	M	N	O	P	Q	R	S	T	U	V	W	X	Y	Z	A	B	C	D	E	F	G	H	I	J	K
M	M	N	O	P	Q	R	S	T	U	V	W	X	Y	Z	A	B	C	D	E	F	G	H	I	J	K	L
N	N	O	P	Q	R	S	T	U	V	W	X	Y	Z	A	B	C	D	E	F	G	H	I	J	K	L	M
O	O	P	Q	R	S	T	U	V	W	X	Y	Z	A	B	C	D	E	F	G	H	I	J	K	L	M	N
P	P	Q	R	S	T	U	V	W	X	Y	Z	A	B	C	D	E	F	G	H	I	J	K	L	M	N	O
Q	Q	R	S	T	U	V	W	X	Y	Z	A	B	C	D	E	F	G	H	I	J	K	L	M	N	O	P
R	R	S	T	U	V	W	X	Y	Z	A	B	C	D	E	F	G	H	I	J	K	L	M	N	O	P	Q
S	S	T	U	V	W	X	Y	Z	A	B	C	D	E	F	G	H	I	J	K	L	M	N	O	P	Q	R
T	T	U	V	W	X	Y	Z	A	B	C	D	E	F	G	H	I	J	K	L	M	N	O	P	Q	R	S
U	U	V	W	X	Y	Z	A	B	C	D	E	F	G	H	I	J	K	L	M	N	O	P	Q	R	S	T
V	V	W	X	Y	Z	A	B	C	D	E	F	G	H	I	J	K	L	M	N	O	P	Q	R	S	T	U
W	W	X	Y	Z	A	B	C	D	E	F	G	H	I	J	K	L	M	N	O	P	Q	R	S	T	U	V
X	X	Y	Z	A	B	C	D	E	F	G	H	I	J	K	L	M	N	O	P	Q	R	S	T	U	V	W
Y	Y	Z	A	B	C	D	E	F	G	H	I	J	K	L	M	N	O	P	Q	R	S	T	U	V	W	X
Z	Z	A	B	C	D	E	F	G	H	I	J	K	L	M	N	O	P	Q	R	S	T	U	V	W	X	Y

This similarity is, in fact, the weakness of the cipher. Through some creative "factoring," the length of the keyword can be determined. Since the tableau is, in practice, a series of shift ciphers, the length of the keyword determines how many ciphers are used. The keyword *rockerrook*, with only six distinct letters, uses only six ciphers. Regardless, for nearly 300 years many people believed the cipher to be unbreakable.

The Kasiski/Kerckhoff Method

Now let's look at Kerckhoff's principle—"only secrecy of the key provides security." (This principle is not to be confused with Kirchhoff's law, a totally different man and rule.) In the nineteenth century, Auguste Kerckhoff stated that essentially, a system should still be secure, even when everyone knows everything about the system (except the password). Basically, his feeling was that if

TABLE 2.8 The Multiplication Table is the Inspiration for the Vigenère Tableau.

Multiplier	1	2	3	4	5	6	7	8	9	10
1	1	2	3	4	5	6	7	8	9	10
2	2	4	6	8	10	12	14	16	18	20
3	3	6	9	12	15	18	21	24	27	30
4	4	8	12	16	20	24	28	32	36	40
5	5	10	15	20	25	30	35	40	45	50
6	6	12	18	24	30	36	42	48	54	60
7	7	14	21	28	35	42	49	56	63	70
8	8	16	24	32	40	48	56	64	72	80
9	9	18	27	36	45	54	63	72	81	90
10	10	20	30	40	50	60	70	80	90	100

more than one person knows something, it's no longer a secret. Throughout modern cryptography, the inner workings of cryptographic techniques have been well known and published. Creating a portable, secure, unbreakable code is easy if nobody knows how it works. The problem lies in the fact that we people just can't keep a secret!

Example 2.3 A Repetitious, Weak Keyword Combines with Plaintext to Produce an Easily Deciphered Ciphertext

I		to	to	toto	to	to	toto	to
Plaintext	It	is	what	it	is,	isn't	it?
Ciphertext	BH	BG	PVTH	BH	BG	BGGH	BH

In 1863 Friedrich Kasiski, a Prussian major, proposed a method to crack the Vigenère cipher.[3] Briefly, his method required that the cryptographer deduce the length of the keyword used and then dissect the cryptogram into a corresponding number of ciphers. This is accomplished by simply examining the distance between repeated strings in the ciphertext. Each cipher would then be solved independently. The method required that a suitable number of bigrams be located. A *bigram* is a portion of the ciphertext, two characters long, that repeats itself in a discernible pattern. In Example 2.3, a repetition has been deliberately made simple with a short keyword (*toto*) and engineered by crafting a harmonic between the keyword and the plaintext.

3. David Kahn, *The Codebreakers —The Story of Secret Writing* (ISBN 0684831309), 1996, Scribner, New York, NY.

This might seem an oversimplification, but it effectively demonstrates the weakness of the polyalphabetic cipher. Similarly, the polyalphanumeric ciphers, such as the Gronsfeld cipher, are even weaker since they use 26 letters and 10 digits. This one also happens to decrypt to "On of when on of," but a larger sample with such a weak keyword would easily be cracked by even the least intelligent Web-based cryptogram solvers. The harmonic is created by the overlaying keyword with the underlying text; when the bigrams "line up" and repeat themselves, the highest frequency will be the length of the password. The distance between the two occurrences will be the length of the password. In Example 2.3, we see BH and BG repeating, and then we see BG repeating at a very tight interval of 2, which tells us the password might be two characters long and based on two shift ciphers that, when decrypted side by side, will make a real word. Not all bigrams will be indicators of this, so some care must be taken. As can be seen, BH repeats with an interval of 8, but the password is not eight digits long (but it is a factor of 8!). By locating the distance of all the repeating bigrams and factoring them, we can deduce the length of the keyword.

4. MODERN CRYPTOGRAPHY

Some of cryptography's greatest stars emerged in World War II. For the first time during modern warfare, vast resources were devoted to enciphering and deciphering communications. Both sides made groundbreaking advances in cryptography. Understanding the need for massive calculations (for the time—more is probably happening in the RAM of this author's PC over a period of five minutes than happened in all of the war), both sides developed new machinery—predecessors to the modern solid-state computers—that could be coordinated to perform the calculations and procedures needed to crack enemy ciphers.

The Vernam Cipher (Stream Cipher)

Gilbert Sandford Vernam (1890−1960) invented the stream cipher in 1917; a patent was issued on July 22, 1919. Vernam worked for Bell Labs, and his patent described a cipher in which a prepared key, on a paper tape, combined with plaintext to produce a transmitted ciphertext message. He did not use the term *d'art* "XOR" but did implement the exact same logic at the relay layer. The credit for automating cryptography goes to Vernam. He introduced the Baudot system, which is the Morse code of the teletype, to cryptography. In it, each character is represented by five units, or pulses. With the expectation that a set number of "pulses" would be transmitted over a given period of time, the pulse, or absence thereof, creates a system of zeroes and ones

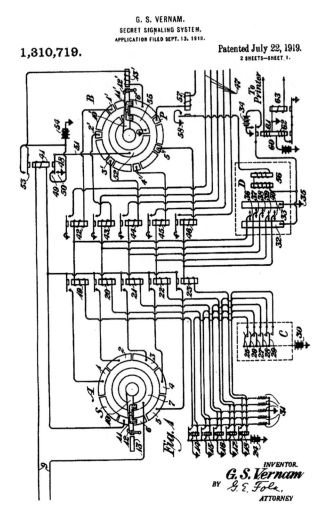

G. S. VERNAM.
SECRET SIGNALING SYSTEM.
APPLICATION FILED SEPT. 13, 1918.

1,310,719.   Patented July 22, 1919.
2 SHEETS—SHEET 1.

INVENTOR.
G. S. Vernam
BY *G. E. Fole*,
ATTORNEY

FIGURE 2.2   G. S. Vernam's Secret Signaling System introduced bit-by-bit enciphering using XOR technology to the world of cryptography for the first time.

that flesh out a binary system. Vernam was the first to suggest that a prepunched tape (cipher) could *combine* with the plaintext and yield difficult to crack ciphertext. The same tape would then be used to decrypt the ciphertext. Through testing and development, it became apparent that two tapes could be used and offset against one another to produce many different ciphers. Later, methods were derived for using a single stream of random numbers to create an unbreakable cipher. Physical problems barred this from gaining wide implementation; the logisitics of managing or transmitting the random cipher, and then knowing which message to which it applied, were simply insurmountable in wartime, where messaging increases dramatically. Regardless, Vernam's accomplishment of employing a method of automation to encryption cannot be underestimated. He developed a way whereby, using a series of magnets and relays, the cipher and plaintext pulses could be combined

electrically.[4] Figure 2.2 is a page from the actual patent papers, Patent No. 1,310,719.[5]

In effect, the Vernam stream cipher and "one-time pad" ciphers are very similar; in fact, Vernam later co-invented it. The primary difference is that the "one-time pad" cipher dictates that a truly random stream cipher be used for the encryption. The stream cipher had no such requirement and used a different method of relay logic to combine a pseudorandom stream of bits with the plaintext bits. (The XOR process is discussed in more detail in the section on XOR ciphering.) In practice today, the Vernam cipher is any stream cipher in which pseudorandom or random text is combined with plaintext to produce cipher text that is the same length as the cipher. RC4 is a modern example of a Vernam cipher.

The One-Time Pad

The "one-time pad" cipher, attributed to Joseph Mauborgne, is perhaps one of the most secure forms of cryptography. It is very difficult to break if used properly, and if the key stream is perfectly random, the ciphertext gives away absolutely no details about the plaintext, which renders it unbreakable. And, just as the name suggests, it uses a single random key that is the same length as the entire message, and it uses the key only once. The word *pad* is derived from the fact that the key would be distributed in pads of paper, with each sheet torn off and destroyed as it was used.

There are several weaknesses to this cipher. We begin to see that the more secure the encryption, the more it will rely on other means of key transmission. The more a key has to be moved around, the more likely it is that someone who shouldn't have it will have it. The following weaknesses are apparent in this "bulletproof" style of cryptography:

- Key length has to equal plaintext length.
- It is susceptible to key interception; the key must be transmitted to the recipient, and the key is as long as the message!
- It's cumbersome, since it doubles the traffic on the line.
- The cipher must be perfectly random.
- One-time use is absolutely essential. As soon as two separate messages are available, the messages can be decrypted. Example 2.4 demonstrates this.

Since most people don't use binary, the author takes the liberty in Example 2.4 of using decimal numbers modulus 26 to represent the XOR that would take place in a bitstream encryption (see the section on the XOR cipher) that uses the method of the one-time pad.

4. David Kahn, *The Codebreakers—The Story of Secret Writing* (394–403), (Scribner, 1996).
5. U.S. Patent 1,310,719.

Example 2.4 Using the Random Cipher, a Modulus Shift Instead of an XOR, and Plaintext to Produce Ciphertext

Plaintext 1

t h i s w i l l b e s o e a s y t o b r e a k i t w i l l b e f u n n y

20 8 9 19 23 9 12 12 2 5 19 15 5 1 19 25 20 15 2 18 5 1 11 9 20 23 9 12 12 2 5 6 21 14 14 25

Cipher One

q e r t y u i o p a s d f g h j k l z x c v b n m q a z w s x e r f v t

17 5 18 20 25 21 9 15 16 1 19 4 6 7 8 10 11 12 26 24 3 22 2 14 13 17 1 26 23 19 24 5 18 6 22 20

CipherText 1

11 13 1 13 22 4 21 1 18 6 12 19 11 8 1 9 5 1 2 16 8 23 13 23 7 14 10 12 9 21 3 11 13 20 10 19

k m a m v d u a r f l s k h a i e a b p h w m w g n j l w u c k m t j s

Plaintext 2

T h i s w i l l n o t b e e a s y t o b r e a k o r b e t o o f u n n y

20 8 9 19 23 9 12 12 14 15 20 2 5 5 1 19 25 20 15 2 18 5 1 11 15 18 2 5 20 15 15 6 21 14 14 25

Ciphertext 2, also using Cipher One.

11 13 1 13 22 4 21 1 4 16 13 6 11 12 9 3 10 6 15 0 21 1 3 25 2 9 3 5 17 8 13 11 13 20 10 19

k m a m v d u a e p m f k l i f j f o z u a c y b i c e q h m k m t j s

---

A numeric value is assigned to each letter, as seen in Table 2.9. By assigning a numeric value to each letter, adding the plaintext value to the ciphertext value, modulus 26, yields a pseudo-XOR, or a wraparound Caesar shift that has a different shift for each letter in the entire message.

As this example demonstrates, by using the same cipher twice, a dimension is introduced that allows for the introduction of frequency analysis. By placing the two streams side by side, we can identify letters that are the same. In a large enough sample, where the ciphertext is sufficiently randomized, frequency analysis of the aligned values will begin to crack the cipher wide open because we know that they are streaming in a logical order—the order in which they were written. One of the chief advantages of twenty-first-century cryptography is that the "eggs" are scrambled and descrambled during decryption based on the key, which you don't, in fact, want people to know. If the same cipher is used repeatedly, multiple inferences can be made, and eventually the entire key can be deconstructed. Because plaintext 1 and plaintext 2 are so similar, this sample yields the following harmonics (in bold and boxed) as shown in Example 2.5.

TABLE 2.9 A Simple Key is Created so that Random Characters and Regular Characters May be Combined with a Modulus Function. Without the Original Cipher, this Key is Meaningless Intelligence. It is used here in a Similar Capacity as an XOR, which is also a Function that Everyone Knows how to do.

										Key															
a	b	e	d	e	f	g	h	i	j	k	l	m	n	o	p	q	r	s	t	u	v	w	x	y	z
1	2	3	4	5	6	7	8	9	10	11	12	13	14	15	16	17	18	19	20	21	22	23	24	25	26

Example 2.5

The two ciphertexts, side by side, show a high level of harmonics. This indicates that two different ciphertexts actually have the same cipher. Where letters are different, since XOR is a known process and our encryption technique is also publicly known, it's a simple matter to say that $r = 18$, $e = 5$ (see Table 2.9) and thus construct an algorithm that can tease apart the cipher and ciphertext to produce plaintext.

k m a m v d u a r f l s **k** h a i e a b p h w m w g n j l w u c **k m t j s** (ciphertext 1)
k m a m v d u a e p m f **k** l i f j f o z u a c y b i c e q h m **k m t j s** (ciphertext 2)

Some Statistical Tests for Cryptographic Applications By Adrian Fleissig

In many applications, it is often important to determine if a sequence is random. For example, a random sequence provides little or no information in cryptographic analysis. When estimating economic and financial models, it is important for the residuals from the estimated model to be random. Various statistical tests can be used to evaluate whether or not a sequence is actually a random sequence. For a truly random sequence, it is assumed that each element is generated independently of any prior and/or future elements. A statistical test is used to compute the probability that the observed sequence is random compared to a truly random sequence. The procedures have test statistics that are used to evaluate the null hypothesis, which typically assumes that the observed sequence is random. The alternative hypothesis is that the sequence is nonrandom. Thus failing to accept the null hypothesis, at some critical level selected by the researcher, suggests that the sequence may be nonrandom.

There are many statistical tests to evaluate for randomness in a sequence, including Frequency Tests, Runs Tests, Discrete Fourier Transforms, and Serial Tests. The tests statistics often have chi-square or standard normal distributions that are used to evaluate the hypothesis. While no test is overall superior to the other tests, a Frequency or Runs Test is a good starting point to examine for nonrandomness in a sequence. As an example, a Frequency or Runs Test typically evaluates if the number of zeros and ones in a sequence are about the same, as would be the case if the sequence was truly random.

It is important to examine the results carefully. For example, the researcher may incorrectly fail to accept the null hypothesis that the sequence is random and thereby makes a Type I Error. Incorrectly accepting the null of randomness when the sequence is actually nonrandom results in committing a Type II Error. The reliability of the results depends on having a sufficiently large number of elements in a sequence. In addition, it is important to perform alternative tests to evaluate if a sequence is random.[6]

Cracking Ciphers

One method of teasing out the frequency patterns is through the application of some sort of mathematical formula to test a hypothesis against reality. The chi-square test is perhaps one of the most commonly used; it allows someone to use what is called *inferential statistics* to draw certain inferences about the data by testing it against known statistical distributions.

Using the chi-square test against an encrypted text would allow certain inferences to be made, but only where the contents, or the type of contents (random or of an expected distribution), of the text were known. For example, someone may use a program that encrypts files. By creating the null hypothesis that the text is completely random and by reversing the encryption steps, a block cipher may emerge as the null hypothesis is disproved through the chi-square test. This would be done by reversing the encryption method and XORing against the bytes with a block created from the known text. At the point where the nonencrypted text matches the positioning of the encrypted text, chi-square would reveal that the output is not random and the block cipher would be revealed.

Chi-squared = . . . (observed-expected)2/(expected)

Observed would be the actual zero/one ratio produced by XORing the data streams together, and expected would be the randomness of zeroes and ones (50/50) in a body of pseudorandom text.

Independent of having a portion of the text, a large body of encrypted text could be reverse encrypted using a block size of all zeroes. In this manner it may be possible to tease out a block cipher by searching for nonrandom block-sized strings. Modern encryption techniques generate many, many block cipher permutations that are layered against previous iterations $(n - 1)$ of permutated blocks. The feasibility of running such decryption techniques would require both a heavy-duty programmer and a statistician, an incredible amount of processing power, and in-depth knowledge of the encryption algorithm used. An unpublished algorithm would render such testing worthless.

The methods and procedures used in breaking encryption algorithms are used throughout society in many applications where a null hypothesis needs to be tested. Forensic consultants use pattern matching and similar decryption techniques to combat fraud on a daily basis. Adrian Fleissig, a seasoned economist, makes use of many statistical tests to examine corporate data (see the sidebar, "Some Statistical Tests for Cryptographic Applications").

The XOR Cipher and Logical Operands

In practice, the XOR cipher is not so much a cipher as it is a mechanism whereby ciphertext is produced. *Random binary stream cipher* would be a better term. The terms *XOR, logical disjunction*, and *inclusive* may be used interchangeably. Most people are familiar with the logical functions of speech, which are words such as *and, or, nor*, and *not*. A girl can tell her brother, "Mother is either upstairs or at the neighbor's," which means she could be in either state, but you have no way of knowing which

---

6. Adrian Fleissig is the Senior Economist of Counsel for RGL Forensics, 2006–present. He is also a full professor, California State University Fullerton (CSUF) with a joint Ph.D. in Economics and Statistics from North Carolina State University in 1993.

one it is. The mother could be in either place, and you can't infer from the statement the greater likelihood of either. The outcome is undecided.

Alternatively, if a salesman offers a customer either a blue car or a red car, the customer knows that he can have red or he can have blue. Both statements are true. Blue cars and red cars exist simultaneously in the world. A person can own both a blue car and a red car. But Mother will never be in more than one place at a time. Purportedly, there is widespread belief that no author has produced an example of an English *or* sentence that appears to be false because both of its inputs are true.[7] Quantum physics takes considerable exception to this statement (which explains quantum physicists) at the quantum-mechanical level. In the Schrodinger cat experiment, the sentence "The cat is alive or dead" or the statement "The photon is a particle and a wave until you look at it, then it is a particle or a wave, depending on how you observed it" both create a quandary for logical operations, and there are no Venn diagrams or words that are dependent on time or quantum properties of the physical universe. Regardless of this exception, when speaking of things in the world in a more rigorously descriptive fashion (in the macroscopically non-phenomenological sense), greater accuracy is needed.

To create a greater sense of accuracy in discussions of logic, the operands as listed in Figure 2.3 were created. When attempting to understand this chart, the best thing to do is to assign a word to the A and B values and think of each Venn diagram as a universe of documents, perhaps in

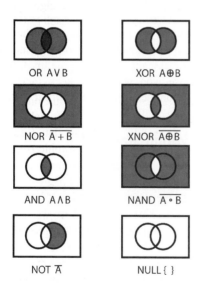

RELATI⊕NSHIPS

FIGURE 2.3 In each Venn diagram, the possible outcome of two inputs is decided.

7. Barrett and Stenner, "The Myth of the Exclusive 'Or,'" *Mind*, 80 (317), 116–121, 1971. [First names or initials needed for authors]

Example 2.6 Line 1 and Line 2 are Combined with an XOR Operand to Produce Line 3

Line 1, plaintext :   1 0 0 1 1 1 0 1 0 1 1 0 1 1 1 1
Line 2, random cipher "": 1 0 0 0 1 1 0 1 0 1 0 0 1 0 0 1
Line 3, XOR ciphertext: 0 0 0 1 0 0 0 0 0 0 1 0 0 1 0 0

---

a document database or just on a computer being searched. If A stands for the word *tree* and B for *frog*, then each letter simply takes on a very significant and distinct meaning.

In computing, it is traditional that a value of 0 is false and a value of 1 is true. An XOR operation, then, is the determination of whether two possibilities can be combined to produce a value of true or false, based on whether both operations are true, both are false, or one of the values is true.

1 XOR 1 = 0
0 XOR 0 = 0
1 XOR 0 = 1
0 XOR 1 = 1

In an XOR operation, if the two inputs are different, the resultant is TRUE, or 1. If the two inputs are the same, the resultant value is FALSE, or 0.

In Example 2.6, the first string represents the plaintext and the second line represents the cipher. The third line represents the ciphertext. If, and only exactly if, just one of the items has a value of TRUE, the results of the XOR operation will be true.

Without the cipher, and if the cipher is truly random, decoding the string becomes impossible. However, as in the one-time pad, if the same cipher is used, then (1) the cryptography becomes vulnerable to a known text attack, and (2) it becomes vulnerable to statistical analysis. Example 2.7 demonstrates this by showing exactly where the statistical aberration can be culled in the stream. If we know they both used the same cipher, can anyone solve for Plaintext A and Plaintext B?

Block Ciphers

Block ciphers work similarly to the polyalphabetic cipher, with the exception that a block cipher pairs together two algorithms for the creation of ciphertext and its decryption. It is also somewhat similar in that, where the polyalphabetic cipher used a repeating key, the block cipher uses a permutating, yet repeating, cipher block. Each algorithm uses two inputs: a key and a "block" of bits, each of a set size. Each output block is the same size as the input block, the block being transformed by the key. The key, which is algorithm based, is able to select the permutation of its bijective mapping from 2^n, where n is equal to the number of bits in the *input* block. Often, when 128-bit encryption is discussed, it is referring to the size of the *input* block.

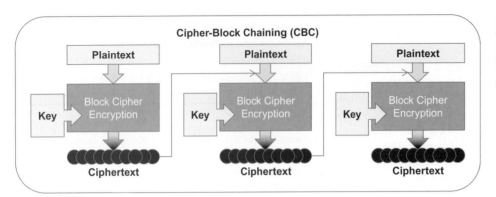

FIGURE 2.4 XOR chaining, or cipher-block chaining (CBC), is a method whereby the next block of plaintext to be encrypted is XOR'd with the previous block of cipher-text before being encrypted.

Typical encryption methods involve use of XOR chaining or some similar operation; see Figure 2.4.

Block ciphers have been very widely used since 1976 in many encryption standards. As such, cracking these ciphers became, for a long time, the top priority of cipher crackers everywhere. Block ciphers provide the backbone algorithmic technology behind most modern-era ciphers.

Example 2.7

To reconstruct the cipher if the plaintext is known, PlaintextA can be XOR'd to ciphertextB to produce cipherA! Clearly, in a situation where plaintext may be captured, using the same cipher key twice could completely expose the message. By using statistical analysis, the unique possibilities for PlaintextA and PlaintextB will emerge; *unique possibilities* means that for ciphertext = *x*, where the cipher is truly random, this should be at about 50 percent of the sample. Additions of ciphertext *n* + 1 will increase the possibilities for unique combinations because, after all, these binary streams must be converted to text and the set of binary stream possibilities that will combine into ASCII characters is relatively small. Using basic programming skills, you can develop algorithms that will quickly and easily sort through this data to produce a deciphered result. An intelligent person with some time on her hands could sort it out on paper or in an Excel spreadsheet. When the choice is "The red house down the street from the green house is where we will meet" or a bunch of garbage, it begins to become apparent how to decode the cipher.

CipherA and PlaintextA are XOR'd to produce ciphertextA:

PlaintextA: 0 0 0 0 0 0 0 1 1 1 1 1 1 1 1
cipherA: 1 1 1 1 1 1 1 1 0 0 0 0 0 0 0 0
ciphertextA: 1 1 1 1 1 1 1 1 1 1 1 1 1 1 1 1
PlaintextB and cipherA are XOR'd to produce ciphertextB:
ciphertextB: 0 0 0 0 0 0 0 1 1 1 1 1 1 1 1
cipherA: 1 1 1 1 1 1 1 1 0 0 0 0 0 0 0 0
PlaintextB: 1 1 1 1 1 1 1 1 0 0 0 0 0 0 0 0
| <——— Column 1 ———> || < ———Column 2 ——— |
Note: Compare ciphertextA to ciphertextB!

---

5. THE COMPUTER AGE

Many people consider January 1, 1970, as the dawn of the computer age. That's when Palo Alto Research Center (PARC) in California introduced modern computing; the graphical user interface (no more command line and punch cards), networking on an Ethernet, and object-oriented programming have all been attributed to PARC. The 1970s also featured the Unix clock, Alan Shepard on the moon, the U.S. Bicentennial, the civil rights movement, women's liberation, Robert Heinlein's sci-fi classic, *Stranger in a Strange Land*, the birth of my wife, and, most important to this chapter, modern cryptography. The late 1960s and early 1970s changed the face of the modern world at breakneck speed. Modern warfare reached tentative heights with radio-guided missiles, and warfare needed a new hero. And then there was the Data Encryption Standard, or DES; in a sense DES was the turning point for cryptography in that, for the first time, it fully leveraged the power of modern computing in its algorithms. The sky appeared to be the limit, but, unfortunately for those who wanted to keep their information secure, decryption techniques were not far behind.

Data Encryption Standard

In the mid-1970s, the U.S. government issued a public specification, through its National Bureau of Standards (NBS), called the Data Encryption Standard or, most commonly, DES. This could perhaps be considered the dawn of modern cryptography because it was very likely the first block cipher, or at least its first widespread implementation. But the 1970s were a relatively untrusting time. "Big Brother" loomed right around the corner (as per George Orwell's *1984*), and the majority of people didn't understand or necessarily trust DES. Issued under the NBS, now called the National Institute of Standards and Technology (NIST), hand in hand with the National Security Agency (NSA), DES led to tremendous interest in the reliability of the standard among academia's ivory towers. A shortened key length and the implementation of

Feistel Structure of DES (Simplified)

FIGURE 2.5   The Feistel function with a smaller key size.

1. Plaintext	0	0	0	0	0	0	0	0
2. Expanded plaintext A)*	0	0	0	0	0	0	>	>
3. Cipher	1	0	1	0	0	1		
4. Ciphertext A	1	0	1	0	0	1		
5. Expanded Plaintext B)	0	0	1	1	1	1		
6. Cipher from Step 1:	1	0	1	0	0	0		
7. Ciphertext B	1	0	0	1	1	1		

Expanded Plaintext B:

>> 0 0 1 1 1 1

Key Schedule
1. 101000
2. 100101
   .
   .
   .
15. 010100
16. 101101

8. Cipher (B,A)   1 0 0 1 1 1   1 0 1 0 0 0
9. Substitution (S-box)   0 0 0 1   1 0 0 1
10. Permutation P-Box   0 1 0 0   0 1 1 0

Key (16 parts): 101000 010101 101011 . . . 010100 100101 101010 101101

S – Box**	0011	0100
10	0101	1001
11	0001	1100

Permutation Box (P-Box)

*A bijective function is applied to expand from 32 bits (represented here by 8 bits) to 48 bits. A function is bijective if inverse relation f⁻¹(x) is also a function. Reduction is achieved through the S-box operation.

** This S-box is reduced to include only the four bits that are in our cipher. Typical S-boxes are as large as needed and may be based partially on the key.

substitution boxes, or "S-boxes," in the algorithm led many to think that the NSA had deliberately weakened the algorithms and left a security "back door" of sorts.

The use of S-boxes in the standard was not generally understood until the design was published in 1994 by Don Coppersmith. The S-boxes, it turned out, had been deliberately designed to prevent a sort of cryptanalysis attack called *differential cryptanalysis*, as was discovered by IBM researchers in the early 1970s; the NSA had asked IBM to keep quiet about it. In 1990 the method was "re"-discovered independently and, when used against DES, the usefulness of the S-boxes became readily apparent.

Theory of Operation

DES used a 64-bit block cipher combined with a mode of operation based on cipher-block chaining (CBC) called the *Feistel function*. This consisted of an initial expansion permutation followed by 16 rounds of XOR key mixing via subkeys and a key schedule, substitution (S-boxes), and permutation.[8] In this strategy, a block is increased from 32 bits to 48 bits (expansion permutation). Then the 48-bit block is divided in half. The first half is XORs, with parts of the key according to a key schedule. These

8. A. Sorkin, "LUCIFER: A Cryptographic Algorithm," *Cryptologia*, 8(1), 22–35, 1984.

are called subkeys. Figure 2.5 shows this concept in a simplified format.

The resulting cipher is then XOR'd with the half of the cipher that was not used in step 1. The two halves switch sides. Substitution boxes reduce the 48 bits down to 32 bits via a nonlinear function and then a permutation, according to a permutation table, takes place. Then the entire process is repeated again, 16 times, except in the last step the two halves are not flipped. Finally, this diffusive strategy produced via substitution, permutation, and key schedules creates an effective ciphertext. Because a fixed-length cipher, a block cipher, is used, the permutations and the S-box introduce enough confusion that the cipher cannot be deduced through brute-force methods without extensive computing power.

With the increase in size of hard drives and computer memory, the need for disk space and bandwidth still demands that a block-cipher algorithm be portable. DES, Triple DES, and the Advanced Encryption Standard (AES) all provide or have provided solutions that are secure and practical.

Implementation

Despite the controversy at the time, DES was implemented. It became the encryption standard of choice until the late 1990s, when it was broken when Deep Crack and distributed.net broke a DES key in 22 hours and 15 minutes.

Later that year, a new form of DES called Triple DES, which encrypted the plaintext in three iterations, was published. It remained in effect until 2002, when it was superseded by AES.

Rivest, Shamir, and Adleman (RSA)

The release of DES also included the creation and release of Ron Rivest, Adi Shamir, and Leonard Adleman's encryption algorithm (RSA). Rivest, Shamir, and Adleman, based at the Massachusetts Institute of Technology (MIT), publicly described the algorithm in 1977. RSA is the first encryption standard to introduce (to public knowledge) the new concept of digital signing. In 1997 it was revealed through declassification of papers that Clifford Cocks, a British mathematician working for the U.K. Government Communications Headquarters (GCHQ), had, in 1973, written a paper describing this process. Assigned a status of top secret, the work had previously never seen the light of day. Because it was submitted in 1973, the method had been considered unattainable, since computing power at the time could not handle its methods.

Advanced Encryption Standard (AES or Rijndael)

AES represents one of the latest chapters in the history of cryptography. Once it became clear that neither DES nor its answer to its weaknesses, "Triple-DES," could carry encryption through to the twenty-first century, a decree went out from the National Institute of Standards and Technology (NIST) so that a new standard might be achieved. AES won out over the other standards for several reasons, and it is currently one of the most popular encryption standards. For people involved in any security work, its occurrence on the desktop is frequent. It also enjoys the free marketing and acceptance that it received when it was awarded the title of official cryptography standard in 2001.[9] This designation went into effect in May of the following year.

To a large degree, this part of the chapter is merely a rehashing/book report on the FIPS 197 standard, as this appears to be one of the more authoritative guides available, short of the authors themselves. It provides a few original examples, and some observations made by the author during his examination of the standard.

Similarly to DES, AES encrypts plaintext in a series of rounds, involves the use of a key and block sizes, and leverages substitution and permutation boxes. It differs from DES in the following respects:

- It supports 128-bit block sizes.
- The key schedule is based on the S-box.
- It expands the key, not the plaintext.
- It is not based on a Feistel cipher.
- It is extremely complex.

The AES algorithms are to symmetric ciphers what a bowl of spaghetti is to the shortest distance between two points. Through a series of networked XOR operations, key substitutions, temporary variable transformations, increments, iterations, expansions, value swapping, S-boxing, and the like, a very strong encryption is created that, with modern computing, creates a cipher that itself is impossible to break. Like all ciphers, though, AES is only as strong as its weakest link, which is the password routine. This weakness will be explored toward the end of this part of the chapter.

Overview

Simply put, it works like this: First, the idea is to confuse the real message and the encrypted message. Like other encryption methods, it uses the XOR to do this. AES requires either 128, 192, or 256 bits to work; however, one must have a "key" with which to start. This might be a password, or a string of random numbers stored on a card, or any input derived from an unchanging, but unique thing, such as your retina. From there, the "key" needs to be both obfuscated and expanded to match the correct block size, and to be parceled up into the little packages, or blocks, that will be used in later operations of the encryption sequence. To accomplish this, a procedure called Password-Based Key Derivation Function (PBKDF2) is used.[10] Enciphering is achieved by then using an XOR and hashing the bits together again and again and again through a shift row offset. This effectively "shuffles the deck."

Second: Introduce diffusion by using a simple column transposition to rearrange the bits until they are no longer sensible as letters, and then hashing the bits using substitution (XOR). Furthermore, AES employs a key expansion and multiple rounds. For example, if you XOR a string and produce ciphertext, you have successfully obfuscated the message. If you want anyone to read it, just give them the key and they can reverse the XOR to get the correct text. The problem arises in portability: We want people to be able to decrypt our messages, but only if they have the pass key. This is where things get tricky, because we have to have a key that is long (128 or 256

---

9. U.S. FIPS PUB 197 (FIPS 197), November 26, 2001.

10. RSA Laboratories Public-Key Cryptography Standards (PKCS) #5: Password-Based Cryptography Specification, Version 2.0. Network Working Group, B. Kaliski.

FIGURE 2.6 A handwritten example of polynomial expansion using the Rjindael/AES encryption algorithm.

bits) but that can be generated from a password that is reasonably short, so that we can remember it. Ultimately, this is the weakness of AES or actually the gateway into it, that is, the weak link.

The FIPS 197 standard canonicalizes the Rijndael algorithm Figure 2.6 [3,4], which is a symmetric block cipher with the capability to process blocks of 128 bits. To do this, it employs a multistep operation, enciphering the plaintext blocks using cipher keys with lengths of 128, 192, and 256 bits. The Rjindael algorithm possesses the ability to handle additional block sizes and key lengths, so while the capability exists, it is not part of the published FIPS 197 standard. This part of the chapter will cover the following topics

1. Some definitions that haven't been covered yet
2. A brief discussion about the notation and conventions used
3. Some mathematical properties of the algorithm
4. A brief discussion of how a password becomes a 128 (or longer) cipher key
5. A summary of the algorithm specification, including the key expansion, encryption, and decryption routines
6. Implementation issues
7. A step-by-step example from FIPS 197

The Basics of AES

The basic unit of encryption is the byte. If you read the beginning of this part of the chapter, then you already know that the cipher key must be in the form of 128, 192, or 256 bits, which is 16, 24, or 32 bytes, respectively. All bit values are 0 or 1; NULL values are disallowed. This of course may spark the question, "how then do NULL values get encrypted in BIT columns in a database?" In Microsoft SQL Server, an additional "hidden" column called a NULLmap exists; if a value is NULL, then it will be set to 1, otherwise, 0.[11]

AES encryption operates at the byte level, with each four bits represented (for convenience here) hexidecimally so that the following is true:

Binary value.hexidecimal value

For example, the value 1100 1101 would be represented as /xCD. XOR'd, with 0111 0110 /x76, would result in 1011 1011, or /xBB. (Note how obfuscating it is that two completely different pairs can XOR to the same value.)

6. HOW AES WORKS

The following describes each step of the cipher. It is a simplification, intended to provide a solid foundation for future study of the standard.

Bytes

Programmatically, in order to encipher the plaintext bits, the AES procedure requires that all of the bits be loaded and arranged into a two-dimensional array called the State. The State has four rows in it, and each row contains 4 bytes. This is a total of 16 bytes, or 128 bits.

NOTE: You might ask, "128 bits is great, but how did we go from a 32-bit password typed by a user to a 128-bit cipher key?" This can be done in a number of ways, and an industrious engineer may certainly write his own method for it, but for the readers of this book, check out the Password-Based Key Derivation Function (PBKDF2). This is a key derivation function that is part of RSA Laboratories Public Key Cryptography Standards. It replaces an earlier standard, PBKDF1, which could only produce derived keys up to 160 bits long.

The bytes are arranged in columns, so that the first column, first row (let's call it A1) has, right "beneath" it, A2, which would the second byte of the string to be encrypted. The actual FIPS standard has more dramatic

11. Paul S. Randall, Misconceptions around Null Bitmap Size. [http://www.sqlskills.com/BLOGS/PAUL/post/Misconceptions-around-null-bit-map-size.aspx], 2012.

notations for this, but essentially, what is happening is that in the State, bytes are referred to by row and by column, and they are loaded top to bottom, left to right. Each column of 4 bytes in the State is referred to as Word. Then it starts to do some math.

Math

The AES standard employs the mathematical operations of both addition and multiplication. Addition using the XOR has already been heavily covered in this chapter. For examples see Table 2.6. This standard also relies heavily on prime, or irreducible, polynomials to allow for the enciphering of the bits and to keep things nice and tidy in 128-bit buckets. It is important that, for reversibility, all of the multiplication operations, where strings of bits are represented as polynomials which can then be manipulated, allowing for the shifting of bits, remain irreducible.

For example, multiply together the primes 3, 7, and 17, and the resulting number is easily calculated as 357. By factoring it, you can easily derive the exact three numbers used in the original equation. Now multiply together 2, 8, and 16 and you get 256. Unfortunately, if you try to invert the operation, with the requirement that you want only three factors, you can arrive at 4, 4, and 16. Perhaps this is fine if you are writing a data-scrambling application, but an encryption utility is only as good as its ability to invert the cipher and decrypt the string. The AES standard outlines the mathematical polynomials used in the multiplication operations, and it defines them as being irreducible. For example, the purpose of one of the polynomial expressions in AES is to simply rotate the word, so that [b0, b1, b2, b3] is transformed into [b1, b2, b3, b0]. An irreducible polynomial is used so that, no matter what the input produces, the inverse operation performed against the output ciphertext yields the correct input. The cipher key becomes the *solution* for an extremely long equation, a solution that has such great uniqueness that it cannot be easily or quickly guessed.

Figure 2.5 provides an example of the actual mathematics behind the first expansion of the FIPS 197 standard. In it, each power of x takes a bit position, numbered as follows: 7654 3210. So, x^7 turns on the bit in position 7, x^6 in position 6, and x^0 (i.e., 1) takes the zeroth position. Hence, $x^7 + x^6 + 1 = 1100\ 0001$. This is why the remainder has to have x to the power of 7 or less, so it can be expressed in 8 bits. According to the standard, "these bytes are interpreted as finite field elements using a polynomial representation." Frequently, to conserve space or just to make things look less ridiculously *binary*, a hexadecimal value may be used. Table 2.10 demonstrates the conversion of binary to base 16, AKA "hexidecimal."

TABLE 2.10 Binary and its Hexadecimal Equivalents.

Binary	HEX
0000	0
0001	1
0010	2
0011	3
0100	4
0101	5
0110	6
0111	7
1000	8
1001	9
1010	a
1011	b
1100	c
1101	d
1110	e
1111	f

In the Beginning

In the beginning, there are bits, and the bits have a physicality that is linear. That is, they are all lined up in one continuous string on the disk, unless the disk is fragmented, but that's another story. You should always keep your disks defragmented. Fragmentation is bad and will impact the performance of processing data for encryption. If, for example, you are encrypting thousands of files in a particular folder on the disk, and the files are all over the place, it will perform poorly. I digress. When a program that executes AES encryption gets its byte on your bits, the first thing it does is load them into a series of arrays called the State. This particular state is good because it will not take all of your money or tell you that you didn't pay enough taxes last year. What it will do is provide a place where many different operations can be executed to better encrypt your data using a 128-bit cipher key. For the purpose of convenience, though AES can handle 192- and 256-bit encryption as well, the author simply refers to the 128-bit model. All operations are performed against this two-dimensional array of bytes called the State, which contains four rows of bytes; each row holds Nb bytes, where Nb is the block length (128, 192,256) divided by 32.

The State array, s, has two indices. Denoted by the symbol s, each individual byte has two indices, with its row number r in the range $0 \leq r < 4$ and its column number c in the range $0 \leq c < Nb$. This allows an individual byte of the State to be referred to as either $s_{r,c}$ or $s[r,c]$. AES requires $Nb = 4$, so that $0 \leq c < 4$. In other words, if you think of an input, a state, and an output array as being the program product line, each array will be the exact same size. AES does explode the size of the output file.

Rounds

The number of rounds to be executed by the algorithm depends on the key size. $Nr = 10$ when $Nk = 4$, $Nr = 12$ when $Nk = 6$, and $Nr = 14$ when $Nk = 8$. AES, for encipherment, uses a "round" methodology where each round consists of four steps:

1. byte substitution driven by a substitution table (S-box)
2. the shifting of rows in the State array by an offset
3. bit and byte shuffling within each column of the State
4. adding a Round Key to the State

These transformations (and their inverses) are explained in detail in Sections 5.1.1–5.1.4 and 5.3.1–5.3.4 of FIPS 197. Details, and even code samples, can be found in the standard. This example is drawn directly from the standard and details the operations of the cipher itself. Essentially, the following functions are described in the standard and can be understood to be the steps taken in each encryption round. The number of rounds depends on the size of the encryption key:

1. SubBytes(state)
2. ShiftRows(state)
3. MixColumns(state)
4. AddRoundKey(state, w[round*Nb, (round + 1)*Nb-1])

By now, the reader of this text should realize that public standards such as FIPS-197 contain a wealth of information and that the chapters in this book can merely provide (hopefully) the background needed to lend clarity to the material. This part of the chapter is, of course, no substitution for actually reading and adhering to the standard as published.

Finally, it is conceivable that, with so complex a series of operations, a computer file and block could be combined in such a way as to produce all zeroes. Theoretically, the AES cipher could be broken by solving massive quadratic equations that take into consideration every possible vector and solve 8000 quadratic equations with 1600 binary unknowns. This sort of an attack is called an *algebraic attack*, and, where traditional methods such as differential or differential cryptanalysis fail, it is suggested that the strength in AES lies in the current inability to solve supermultivariate quadratic equations with any sort of efficiency.

Reports that AES is not as strong as it should be are at this time likely to be overstated and inaccurate because anyone can present a paper that is dense and difficult to understand and claims to achieve the incredible. It is unlikely that, any time in the near or maybe not-so-near future (this author hedges his bets), AES will be broken using multivariate quadratic polynomials in thousands of dimensions. Mathematica is very likely one of the most powerful tools that can solve quadratic equations, and it is still many years away from being able to perform this feat.

Ultimately, AES's biggest drawback is that a user can trigger an encryption using a password of his or her choice. Unfortunately, most people choose passwords that are not very strong—they want something they will *remember*. Many is the IT tech who lost his password and rendered systems inalterable. Many, too, is the sinister communication that may pass from an employee to a future employer, or a competitor with whom he has become friendly, and has decided to pass secrets. Intellectual property (IP) tort is a very real facet of litigation, and to this end, large consultancies that deal in computer forensics and e-discovery host rack upon rack of devices that are designed specifically to decrypt files that have been encrypted using AES encryption. They do this not by attacking the algorithm, but by attacking using brute force. *Hash tables*, or rainbow tables, are basically a list of all the known hash values of common (and not so common) passwords. For example, one might take every known phone number in the United States and create a table of all of their known hashes. One might also create one of every known child's name and parse that into the hash tables. For example, a phone number of 847-555-5555 might be combined with the name "Ethan" (who is known to live at a certain address, 233 TreeView), into a password of 233Ethan5555tree! (I added the exclamation point to be even more "secure"...). In fact, some of the largest consultancy firms who manage large litigations have constructed exactly this sort of database of rainbow tables, and they are generating more and more hashes each day. Programs that provide entire disk encryption are the bane of both law enforcement and litigation.

Brute force attacks are the only way to crack in when no key can (or will) be produced. Why do rainbow tables work? The spectrum of possible passwords that people may choose to use *because they can remember* them is much smaller than the total number of possible passwords that exist. By leveraging as much as 7 terabytes of rainbow tables against an encrypted body, the estimated success rate of cracking files, specutively, could be as high as 60 to 70 percent. This is a quite horrible statistic for an encryption algorithm that is supposedly "unbreakable." So perhaps the one take-away from this

---

An Agenda for Action for Selecting the Cryptographic Process Activities

The following high-level checklist questions should be addressed in determining the appropriate cryptographic mechanisms, policies, and procedures for a system (check all tasks completed):

_____1. How critical is the system to the organization's mission, and what is the impact level?

_____2. What are the performance requirements for cryptographic mechanisms (communications throughput, processing latency)?

_____3. What intersystem and intrasystem compatibility and interoperability requirements need to be met by the system (algorithm, key establishment, and cryptographic and communications protocols)?

_____4. What are the security/cryptographic objectives required by the system (content integrity protection, source authentication required, confidentiality, availability)?

_____5. For what period of time will the information need to be protected?

_____6. What regulations and policies are applicable in determining what is to be protected?

_____7. Who selects the protection mechanisms that are to be implemented in the system?

_____8. Are the users knowledgeable about cryptography, and how much training will they receive?

_____9. What is the nature of the physical and procedural infrastructure for the protection of cryptographic material and information (storage, accounting and audit, logistics support)?

_____10. What is the nature of the physical and procedural infrastructure for the protection of cryptographic material and information at the facilities of outside organizations with which cryptographically protected communications are required (facilities and procedures for protection of physical keying material)?

---

writing is that there is still room for improvement; a truly unbreakable system still does not exist, and while the algorithm of AES cannot be successfully attacked through decomposition of the cipher text, any system that fails to take into account EVERY attack vector will, ultimately, be no stronger than its weakest link.

Finally, let's briefly look at the process that is used to select cryptographic mechanisms. This is similar to the process used to select any IT mechanism.

7. SELECTING CRYPTOGRAPHY: THE PROCESS

The cryptography selection process is documented in the system development life cycle (SDLC) model. An organization can use many SDLC models to effectively develop an information system. A traditional SDLC is a linear sequential model. This model assumes that the system will be delivered near the end of its development life cycle. Another SDLC model uses prototyping, which is often used to develop an understanding of system requirements without developing a final operational system. More complex models have been developed to address the evolving complexity of advanced and large information system designs. The SDLC model is embedded in any of the major system developmental approaches:

- Waterfall: The phases are executed sequentially.
- Spiral: The phases are executed sequentially, with feedback loops to previous phases.

- Incremental development: Several partial deliverables are constructed, and each deliverable has incrementally more functionality. Builds are constructed in parallel, using available information from previous builds. The product is designed, implemented, integrated, and tested as a series of incremental builds.
- Evolutionary: There is re-planning at each phase in the life cycle, based on feedback. Each phase is divided into multiple project cycles with deliverable measurable results at the completion of each cycle.

Security should be incorporated into all phases, from initiation to disposition, of an SDLC model. The goal of the selection process is to specify and implement cryptographic methods that address specific agency/organization needs.

Prior to selecting a cryptographic method, an organization should consider the operational environment, the application requirements, the types of services that can be provided by each type of cryptography, and the cryptographic objectives that must be met when selecting applicable products. Based on the requirements, several cryptographic methods may be required. For example, both symmetric and asymmetric cryptography may be needed in one system, each performing different functions (symmetric encryption, and asymmetric digital signature and key establishment). In addition, high-level checklist questions should be addressed in determining the appropriate cryptographic mechanisms, policies, and procedures for a system (see checklist: An Agenda for Action for Selecting the Cryptographic Process Activities).

8. SUMMARY

Today's information technology security environment consists of highly interactive and powerful computing devices and interconnected systems of systems across global networks where organizations routinely interact with industry, private citizens, state and local governments, and the governments of other nations. Consequently, both private and public sectors depend on information systems to perform essential and mission-critical functions. In this environment of increasingly open and interconnected systems and networks, network and data security are essential for the optimum use of this information technology. For example, systems that carry out electronic financial transactions and electronic commerce (e-commerce) must protect against unauthorized access to confidential records and the unauthorized modification of data.

Thus, in keeping with the preceding, this chapter provided guidance to organizations on how to select cryptographic controls for protecting sensitive information. However, to provide additional information, products of other standards organizations (the American National Standards Institute and International Organization for Standardization) were briefly discussed.

This chapter was also intended for security individuals responsible for designing systems, and for procuring, installing, and operating security products to meet identified security requirements. This chapter may be used by:

- A manager responsible for evaluating an existing system and determining whether cryptographic methods are necessary.
- Program managers responsible for selecting and integrating cryptographic mechanisms into a system.
- A technical specialist requested to select one or more cryptographic methods/techniques to meet a specified requirement.
- A procurement specialist developing a solicitation for a system or network that will require cryptographic methods to perform security functionality.

In other words, this chapter provided the preceding individuals with sufficient information that allowed them to make informed decisions about the cryptographic methods that met their specific needs to protect the confidentiality, authentication, and integrity of data that is transmitted and/or stored in a system or network. In addition, this primer also provided information on selecting cryptographic controls and implementing the controls in new or existing systems.

Finally, let's move on to the real interactive part of this chapter: review questions/exercises, hands-on projects, case projects, and the optional team case project. The answers and/or solutions by chapter can be found in the Online Instructor's Solutions Manual.

CHAPTER REVIEW QUESTIONS/EXERCISES

True/False

1. True or False? For most information technology occupations, knowledge of cryptography is a very large part of a broader skill set, and is generally limited to relevant application.
2. True or False? Cryptography is built on one overarching premise: the need for a cipher that can reliably, and portably, be used to encrypt text so that, through any means of cryptanalysis—differential, deductive, algebraic, or the like—the ciphertext can be undone with any available technology.
3. True or False? In effect, the Vernam stream cipher and "one-time pad" ciphers are very different − in fact, Vernam later co-invented it.
4. True or False? DES used a 64-bit block cipher combined with a mode of operation based on cipher-block chaining (CBC) called the *Feistel function*.
5. True or False? The cryptography selection process is documented in the system development life cycle (SDLC) model.

Multiple Choice

1. In essence, computer-based cryptography is the art of creating a form of communication that embraces the following precepts, except which two?
   A. Can be readily misunderstood by the intended recipients
   B. Cannot be understood by unintended recipients
   C. Can be understood by unintended recipients
   D. Can be readily understood by the intended recipients
   E. Can be adapted and changed easily with relatively small modifications, such as a changed pass phrase or word
2. What is known as the method of encryption?
   A. Plaintext
   B. Clear text
   C. Ciphertext
   D. Cryptogram
   E. Cipher
3. Decryption methods often rely on understanding the context of the:
   A. cipher
   B. ciphertext
   C. shift cipher
   D. cryptogram
   E. cryptographic algorithms
4. The amount of ciphertext needed to successfully break a cipher is known as:
   A. Benford's Law.
   B. chi-square statistic.

    C. polyalphabetic cipher.

    D. Kerckhoff's principle.

    E. unicity distance.

5. One method of teasing out the frequency patterns is through the application of some sort of mathematical formula to test a hypothesis against reality. What test is perhaps one of the most commonly used:?

    A. Inferential statistics test

    B. Chi-square test

    C. Statistical test

    D. Random binary stream cipher test

    E. Block cipher test

EXERCISE

Problem

OpenSSL has a trick in it that mixes uninitialized memory with the randomness generated by the OS's formal generator. The standard idea here is that it is good practice to mix different sources of randomness into your own source. Modern operating systems take several random things like disk drive activity and net activity and mix the measurements into one pool, and then run it through a fast hash to filter it. Cryptoplumbing on the other hand, of necessity involves lots of errors and fixes and patches. Bug-reporting channels are very important, and apparently this was used. A security team found the bug with an analysis tool. It was duly reported up to OpenSSL, but the handover was muffed. The reason it was muffed was that it wasn't obvious what was going on. And the reason it wasn't obvious is that code was too clever for its own good. It tripped up the analysis tool; the programmers; and, the fix did not alert the OpenSSL programmers. Complexity is always the enemy in security code. So, with the preceding in mind, what would you do as a risk manager to fix the problem?

Hands-On Projects

Project

What is the basic method for using the output of a random bit generator?

Case Projects

Problem

How would an organization go about generating key pairs for asymmetric key algorithms?

Optional Team Case Project

Problem

How would an organization go about generating keys for symmetric key algorithms?

## Chapter 3

Detecting System Intrusions

Almantas Kakareka, CISSP, GSNA, GSEC, CEH
Demyo, Inc.

1. INTRODUCTION

First things first: Detecting system intrusion is not the same as Intrusion Detection System/Intrusion Prevention System (IDS/IPS). We want to detect system intrusion once attackers pass all defensive technologies in the company (such as IDS/IPS mentioned above), full-packet capture devices with analysts behind them, firewalls, physical security guards, and all other preventive technologies and techniques. Many preventative technologies are using blacklisting [1] most of the time, and thus that's why they fail. Blacklisting is allowing everything by default and forbidding something that is considered to be malicious. So, for the attacker, it is a challenge to find yet another way to bypass the filter. It is so much harder to circumvent a whitelisting system.

2. MONITORING KEY FILES IN THE SYSTEM

What are key files on the server? In the Linux machine it will be /etc/passwd, /etc/shadow, just to mention a few. Let's take a look at an example of /etc/shadow file below:

```
# cat /etc/shadow
root:$6$OFny79f/$LC5hcqZXNYKachPKheRh5WkeTpa/
zO3y8OX3EUHrFkrFQAdLUTKwGjLPSdZ9uhwJQ9GmChLvbh
PRbPw71DTg90:15231:0:99999:7:::
daemon:x:15204:0:99999:7:::
bin:x:15204:0:99999:7:::
sys:x:15204:0:99999:7:::
www-data:15204:0:99999:7:::
<snip>
pulse:j:15204:0:99999:7:::
rtkit:j:15204:0:99999:7:::
festival:j:15204:0:99999:7:::
postgres:!:15204:0:99999:7:::
apache:$6$LqrWIgqp
$jdq1exB2GiBFgLL9kDlDkks30azWBJl/mDU.
to84mHn6nmzUzV7iHiMXK7rVm8.
plMmaNKg9Yyu7ryw0Or5VX.:15452:0:99999:7:::
```

What is wrong with the preceding file? If you take a look at users listed in this file, you will notice that an apache user has a hash value attached to it. Typically, apache service never has any hash associated with it. If there is a hash for a use in this file, that means this user has a password associated with it and is able to log in via Secure Shell (SSH). What happens here is that a hacker made a brand-new account and is trying to camouflage it with a valid system user/process.

One of the ways to monitor changes in the file system is to implement LoggedFS. This particular file system logs everything that happens inside the file system. It is easily configurable via Extensible Markup Language (XML) files to fit your needs [2]. An example of a LoggedFS configuration file is as follows:

```
<?xml version="1.0" encoding="UTF-8"?>
<loggedFS logEnabled="true"
printProcessName="true">
<includes>
<include extension=".j" uid="j" action=".j"
retname=".j"/>
</includes>
<excludes>
<exclude extension=".j\.bak$" uid="j" action=".
j" retname="SUCCESS"/>
<exclude extension=".j" uid="1000" action=".j"
retname="FAILURE"/>
<exclude extension=".j" uid="j"
action="getattr" retname=".j"/>
</excludes>
</loggedFS>
```

The preceding configuration can be used to log everything except if it concerns a *.bak file, or if the uid is 1000, or if the operation is getattr.

Files Integrity

File integrity monitoring (FIM) is an internal control or process that performs the act of validating the integrity of the operating system and application software files using a verification method between the current file state and the known, good baseline. This comparison method often involves calculating a known cryptographic checksum of the file's original baseline and comparing that with the calculated checksum of the current state of the file. Other file attributes can also be used to monitor integrity.

Generally, the act of performing file integrity monitoring is automated, using internal controls such as an application or a process. Such monitoring can be performed randomly, at a defined polling interval, or in real time.

3. SECURITY OBJECTIVES

Changes to configurations, files, and file attributes across the IT infrastructure are common; but hidden within a large volume of daily changes can be the few that impact the file or configuration integrity. These changes can also reduce security posture and in some cases may be leading indicators of a breach in progress. Values monitored for unexpected changes to files or configuration items include:

- Credentials
- Privileges and security settings
- Content
- Core attributes and size
- Hash values
- Configuration values

Many open-source and commercial software products are available that perform file integrity monitoring:

- CimTrak
- OSSEC
- Samhain
- Tripwire
- Qualys
- nCircle
- Verisys
- AIDE [3]

An nCircle file integrity monitor panel is shown in Figure 3.1.

There Is Something Very Wrong Here

One bit or one symbol in the output may make the difference between war and peace, friend and foe, compromised and clean system. Let's take a look at the example

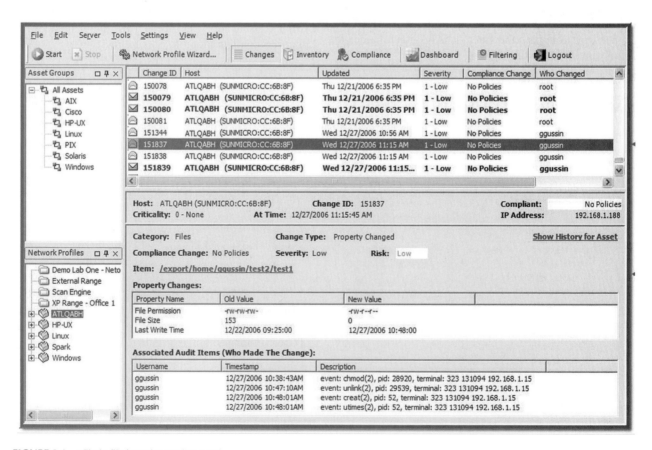

FIGURE 3.1   nCircle file integrity monitor panel.

that is shown in Figure 3.2: What appears to be wrong with this screenshot?

For those who don't see the wrong symbol here, I will give you a hint. It is a command to list files in the directory; switch −h is for listing output in human readable format (megabytes will be megabytes and gigabytes will be gigabytes, not 1 073 741 824 bytes). Switch −l makes a list of files, once again to be easily readable by humans. Now, we are coming to the main piece of information here: Switch −a output will include directory entries whose names begin with a dot (.). A common hacker's technique is to hide within legitimate file names or within somewhat legitimate names. In this case, the hacker has a directory on the system, which is named '. ' ; this is the main issue here. In normal output, you should see one single dotted directory; in this case, we see two single dotted directories, which should raise big red flags for you. A change to this hidden directory is made by issuing command cd '. '. Just make sure there is a space after dot.

```
[root@vps www]# ls -hal
total 32K
drwxr-xr-x  8 root root 4.0K Feb 27 16:51 .
drwxr-xr-x  2 root root 4.0K Feb 27 16:51 .
drwxr-xr-x 18 root root 4.0K Feb 17 13:25 ..
drwxr-xr-x  2 root root 4.0K Feb 13 17:33 cgi-bin
drwxr-xr-x  2 root root 4.0K Feb 27 16:51 demyo.com
drwxr-xr-x  3 root root 4.0K Feb 17 13:25 error
drwxr-xr-x  5 root root 4.0K Feb 17 13:47 html
drwxr-xr-x  3 root root 4.0K Feb 17 13:25 icons
[root@vps www]#
```

FIGURE 3.2   The wrong symbol.

So, that's why we want to use ls −hal with switch 'a' all the time: because we want to see hidden directories and hidden files. It is pretty common to have these hidden directories in common places, such as: /root, /var/www, /home, and others.

Additional Accounts on the System

Every account on the system should be accounted for. If there are accounts whose source nobody knows, that may mean the system is compromised. Sometimes, IT administrators forget to disable old accounts for people who have left the company; some of these accounts may be active for months and even years. This is an unnecessary risk that is introduced by poor IT administrators' management. A good practice is to disable an employee's account before the exit interview. After a compromise, hackers may create a new account on the server and try to mimic some legitimate accounts that should exist. An example of additional account Distributed Brokered Networking (DBNET) is shown in Figure 3.3.

Timestamps

A timestamp is a sequence of characters or encoded information that identifies when a certain event occurred, usually giving date and time of day; it is sometimes accurate to a small fraction of a second. The term is derived from the rubber stamps that were used in nineteenth-century offices to stamp the current date and time (in ink) on paper documents and to record when the document was received. A common example of this type of timestamp is a postmark on a letter. However, in modern times, usage

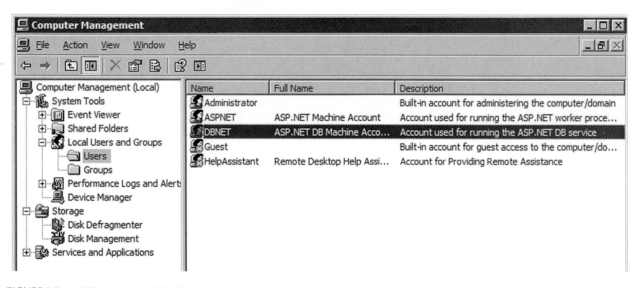

FIGURE 3.3   Additional account DBNET.

of the term has expanded to refer to the digital date and time the information was attached to digital data. For example, computer files contain timestamps that tell when the file was last modified; digital cameras add timestamps to the pictures they take, recording the date and time the picture was taken.

A timestamp is the time an event is recorded by a computer, not the time of the event itself. In many cases, the difference may be inconsequential: The time at which an event is recorded by a timestamp (entered into a log file) should be close to the time of the event.

The sequential numbering of events is sometimes called timestamping. The practice of recording timestamps in a consistent manner along with the actual data is called timestamping. This data is usually presented in a consistent format, allowing for the easy comparison of two different records and tracking progress over time.

Timestamps are typically used for logging events or in a sequence of events (SOE), in which case each event in the log or SOE is marked with a timestamp. In file systems, the timestamp may mean the stored date/time when a file is created or modified.

Let's say you have a lot of folders and executable files in the C:/Windows/System32 directory. All of them pretty much match operating system (OS) installation date and time, but there is one folder that does not match OS installation time. Could there be a problem? This executable might be just some additional software that was installed later on the system, or it also

might be malware hiding in this directory. Windows malware just loves this folder! The folder shown in Figure 3.4 was modified in a different month from all the others.

Hidden Files and Directories

A hidden file is not normally visible when examining the contents of the directory in which it resides. Likewise, a hidden directory is normally invisible when examining the contents of the directory in which it resides.

A file is a named collection of related information that appears to the user as a single, contiguous block of data and that is retained in storage. Storage refers to computer devices or media that can retain data for relatively long periods of time (years or decades), such as hard disk drives (HDDs), Compact Disk—Read Only Memory (CDROMs), and magnetic tape; this contrasts with memory, which retains data only as long as the data is in use or the memory is connected to a power supply.

A directory (also sometimes referred to as a folder) can be conveniently viewed as a container for files and other directories. In Linux and other Unix-like operating systems, a directory is merely a special type of file that associates file names with a collection of metadata (data about the files). Likewise, a link is a special type of file that points to another file (which can be a directory). Thus, it is somewhat redundant to use phrases such as hidden files and directories; however, they are descriptive

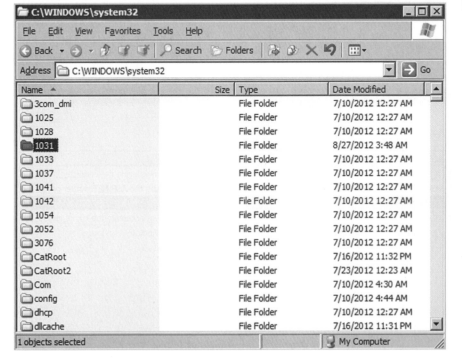

FIGURE 3.4 Folder modification.

and convenient, and thus they are frequently used. More precise terms are hidden file system objects and hidden items.

Hidden items on Unix-like operating systems are easily distinguishable from regular (nonhidden) items because their names are prefixed by a period (a dot). In Unix-like operating systems, periods can appear anywhere within the name of a file, directory, or link, and they can appear as many times as desired. However, usually, the only time that they have special significance is when they are used to indicate a hidden file or directory.

In the Microsoft Windows operating systems, whether or not a file system object is hidden is an attribute of the item, along with such things as whether the file is read-only and a system file (a file that is critical to the operation of the operating system). Changing the visibility of such items is accomplished using a multistep procedure.

Unix-like operating systems provide a larger set of attributes for file system objects than do the Microsoft Windows operating systems, including a system of permissions, which control which user(s) have access to each such object for reading, writing and executing. However, whether or not objects are hidden is not among the attributes. Rather, it is merely a superficial property that is easily changed by adding or removing a period from the beginning of the object name.

Many operating systems and application programs routinely hide objects in order to reduce the chances of users accidentally damaging or deleting critical system and configuration files. Hiding objects can also be useful for reducing visual clutter in directories, thereby making it easier for users to locate desired files and subdirectories.

Another reason to hide file system objects is to make them invisible to casual snoopers. Although it is very easy to make hidden files and directories visible, the great majority of computer users are not even aware that such files and directories exist (nor need they be) [4].

4. 0DAY ATTACKS

About 90 percent of all successful compromises are made via known flaws, so 0day attacks are not that common. A zero-day attack or threat is an attack that exploits a previously unknown vulnerability in a computer application, meaning that the attack occurs on "day zero" of awareness of the vulnerability. This means that the developers have had zero days to address and patch the vulnerability. 0day exploits (actual software that uses a security hole to carry out an attack) are used or shared by attackers before the developer of the target software knows about the vulnerability.

Attack Vectors

Malware writers are able to exploit zero-day vulnerabilities through several different attack vectors. Web browsers are a particular target because of their widespread distribution and usage. Attackers can also send email attachments, which exploit vulnerabilities in the application opening the attachment. Exploits that take advantage of common file types are listed in databases such as United States Computer Emergency Readiness (US-CERT). Malware can be engineered to take advantage of these file-type exploits to compromise attacked systems or steal confidential data such as banking passwords and personal identity information.

Vulnerability Window

Zero-day attacks occur during the vulnerability window that exists in the time between when vulnerability is first exploited and when software developers start to develop and publish a counter to that threat. For viruses, Trojans, and other zero-day attacks, the vulnerability window typically follows this time line:

- The developer creates software containing an unknown vulnerability.
- The attacker finds the vulnerability before the developer does.
- The attacker writes and distributes an exploit while the vulnerability is not known to the developer.
- The developer becomes aware of the vulnerability and starts developing a fix.

Measuring the length of the vulnerability window can be difficult, as attackers do not announce when the vulnerability was first discovered. Developers may not want to distribute data for commercial or security reasons. They also may not know if the vulnerability is being exploited when they fix it, and so they may not record the vulnerability as a zero-day attack. However, it can be easily shown that this window can be several years long. For example, in 2008, Microsoft confirmed vulnerability in Internet Explorer, which affected some versions that were released in 2001. The date the vulnerability was first found by an attacker is not known; however, the vulnerability window in this case could have been up to seven years.

Discovery

A special type of vulnerability management process focuses on finding and eliminating zero-day weaknesses. This unknown vulnerability management life cycle is a security and quality assurance process that aims to ensure the security and robustness of both in-house and third-party software products by finding and fixing unknown (zero-day) vulnerabilities. The unknown vulnerability management process consists of four phases: analyze, test, report, and mitigate.

- Analyze: This phase focuses on attack surface analysis.
- Test: This phase focuses on fuzz testing the identified attack vectors.
- Report: This phase focuses on reproduction of the found issues to developers.
- Mitigate: This phase looks at the protective measures explained below.

Protection

Zero-day protection is the ability to provide protection against zero-day exploits. Zero-day attacks can also remain undetected after they are launched.

Many techniques exist to limit the effectiveness of zero-day memory corruption vulnerabilities, such as buffer overflows. These protection mechanisms exist in contemporary operating systems such as Windows 7, Microsoft Windows Vista, Apple's Mac OS X, recent Oracle Solaris, Linux and possibly other Unix and Unix-like environments; Microsoft Windows XP Service Pack 2 includes limited protection against generic memory corruption vulnerabilities. Desktop and server protection software also exists to mitigate zero-day buffer overflow vulnerabilities.

"Multiple layers" provides service-agnostic protection and is the first line of defense should an exploit in any one layer be discovered. An example of this for a particular service is implementing access control lists in the service itself, restricting network access to it via local server firewalling (IP tables), and then protecting the entire network with a hardware firewall. All three layers provide redundant protection in case a compromise in any one of them occurs.

The use of port knocking or single-packet authorization daemons may provide effective protection against zero-day exploits in network services. However, these techniques are not suitable for environments with a large number of users.

Whitelisting effectively protects against zeroday threats. Whitelisting will only allow known good applications to access a system, and so, any new or unknown exploits are not allowed access. Although whitelisting is effective against zero-day attacks, an application "known" to be good can in fact have vulnerabilities that were missed in testing. To bolster its protection capability, it is often combined with other methods of protection such as a host-based intrusion-prevention system or a blacklist of virus definitions, and it can sometimes be quite restrictive to the user. Also, keeping the computer's software up to date is very important, and it does help.

Users need to be careful when clicking on links or opening email attachments with images or PDF files from unknown users. This is how many cyber criminals deceive users, by pretending they are something they are not and gaining the user's trust. In addition, sites should be utilized with Secure Socket Layer (SSL), which secures the information being passed between the user and the visited site.

Ethics

Differing views surround the collection and use of zero-day vulnerability information. Many computer security vendors perform research on zero-day vulnerabilities in order to better understand the nature of vulnerabilities and their exploitation by individuals, computer worms, and viruses. Alternatively, some vendors purchase vulnerabilities to augment their research capacity. While selling and buying these vulnerabilities is not technically illegal in most parts of the world, there is much controversy over the method of disclosure. A recent German decision to include Article 6 of the Convention on Cybercrime and the European Union (EU) Framework Decision on Attacks against Information Systems may make selling or even manufacturing vulnerabilities illegal.

Most formal efforts follow some form of disclosure guidelines or the more recent Office of Information Systems (OIS) Guidelines for Security Vulnerability Reporting and Response. In general, these rules forbid the public disclosure of vulnerabilities without notification to the developer and adequate time to produce a patch.

5. GOOD KNOWN STATE

When attackers compromise a system, what is the very first thing they do? They install different backdoors and as many as possible. So, if some backdoor was found on the system and it was deleted, it does not mean the system is clean. It is much safer to restore the system to a good known state; typically it is done via OS reinstallation. Big companies typically have a gold image for their systems. They use a gold image to quickly wipe any infected machine and reinstall OS with all of its updates, and software at once. On Linux systems, the software called System Imager is capable of doing many Linux installations at once.

System Imager is software that makes the installation of Linux to numerous similar machines relatively easy.

```
root@bt:~/. # ps aux
USER    PID %CPU %MEM  VSZ  RSS TTY    STAT START  TIME COMMAND
root      1 0.0 0.3 2844 1604 ?     Ss  Apr15  0:01 /sbin/init
root      2 0.0 0.0    0    0 ?     S   Apr15  0:00 [kthreadd]
<snip>
root  10962 0.0 0.0 2740  476 ?     S<  09:33  0:00 udevd --daemon
root  11550 0.0 0.0    0    0 ?     S   11:13  0:00 [kworker/0:2]
root  11567 0.0 0.0    0    0 ?     S<  11:15  0:00 [hci0]
root  11619 0.0 0.0    0    0 ?     S   11:18  0:00 [kworker/0:1]
root  11654 0.0 0.0    0    0 ?     S   11:23  0:00 [kworker/0:0]
root  11664 5.3 6.1 36092 31360 pts/1 S  11:24  0:00 ./httpd
root  11665 0.0 0.2 2764 1052 pts/1 R+  11:24  0:00 ps aux
root  12015 0.0 1.7 34800 8736 ?    S   Apr16  0:00 /usr/lib/notification-daemon/notification-daemon
```

FIGURE 3.5 The running process list.

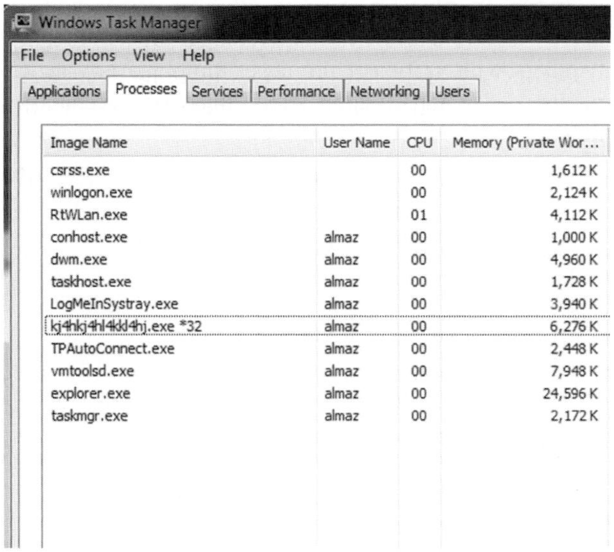

FIGURE 3.6 Strange file names.

It makes software distribution, configuration, and operating system updates easy, and it can also be used for content distribution [5].

Monitoring Running Processes in the System

What is wrong with the running process list in the following Linux system, as shown in Figure 3.5?

The process ./httpd should catch a security professional's eye. Dot slash at the beginning indicates it was launched locally from the directory. Processes on the servers typically are not launched locally from their directories. The attacker has launched a process and is trying to hide by renaming his software to legitimate-looking software typically found on the server.

Files with Weird Names

Malware frequently makes weird-looking file names. An example of this is shown in the Windows Task Manager screen in Figure 3.6.

The file: kj4hkj4hl4kkl4hj.exe shown in Figure 3.6 is running in memory. This should be a first indicator that something funky is going on in the system. Windows updates create random named temporary folders and should not be confused with malware.

6. ROOTKITS

A rootkit is a stealthy type of malicious software designed to hide the existence of certain processes or programs from normal methods of detection, and enables continued privileged access to a computer. The term *rootkit* is a concatenation of the word "root" (the traditional name of the privileged account on Unix operating systems) and the word "kit" (which refers to the software components that implement the tool). The term *rootkit* has negative connotations through its association with malware.

Rootkit installation can be automated, or an attacker can install it once they've obtained root or Administrator access. Obtaining this access is either a result of a direct attack on a system (exploiting a known vulnerability), or by having obtained a password (either by cracking, privilege escalation, or through social engineering). Once installed, it becomes possible to hide the intrusion as well as to maintain privileged access. Like any software, they can have a good purpose or a malicious purpose. The key is the root/administrator access. Full control over a system means that existing software can be modified, including software that might otherwise be used to detect or circumvent it.

Rootkit detection is difficult because a rootkit may be able to subvert the software that is intended to find it. Detection methods include using an alternative and trusted operating system, behavioral-based methods, signature scanning, difference scanning, and memory dump analysis. Removal can be complicated or practically impossible, especially in cases where the rootkit resides in the kernel; reinstallation of the operating system may be the only available solution to the problem. When dealing with firmware rootkits, removal may require hardware replacement or specialized equipment.

Kernel-Level Rootkits

Kernel-mode rootkits run with the highest operating system privileges (Ring 0) by adding code or replacing portions of the core operating system, including both the kernel and associated device drivers. Most operating systems support kernel-mode device drivers, which execute with the same privileges as the operating system itself. As such, many kernel-mode rootkits are developed as device drivers or loadable modules, such as loadable kernel modules in Linux or device drivers in Microsoft Windows. This class of rootkit has unrestricted security access but is more difficult to write. The complexity makes bugs common, and any bugs in code operating at the kernel level may seriously impact system stability, leading to the discovery of the rootkit. One of the first widely known kernel rootkits was developed for Windows NT 4.0 and released in the *Phrack* magazine in 1999 [6].

Kernel rootkits can be especially difficult to detect and remove because they operate at the same security level as the operating system itself and are thus able to intercept or subvert the most trusted operating system operations. Any software, such as antivirus software, running on the compromised system is equally vulnerable. In this situation, no part of the system can be trusted.

A rootkit can modify data structures in the Windows kernel using a method known as direct kernel object modification (DKOM). This method can hook kernel functions in the System Service Descriptor Table (SSDT), or modify the gates between user mode and kernel mode, in order to cloak itself. Similarly for the Linux operating system, a rootkit can modify the system call table to sub-

vert kernel functionality. It's not uncommon for a rootkit to create a hidden, encrypted file system in which it can hide other malware or original copies of files it has infected.

Operating systems are evolving to counter the threat of kernel-mode rootkits. For example, 64-bit editions of Microsoft Windows now implement mandatory signing of all kernel-level drivers in order to make it more difficult for untrusted code to execute with the highest privileges in a system.

Userland Rootkits

User-mode rootkits run in ring 3, along with other applications as user, rather than low-level system processes. They have a number of possible installation vectors to intercept and modify the standard behavior of application programming interfaces (APIs). Some inject a dynamically linked library (such as a .dll file on Windows, or a .dylib file on Mac OS X) into other processes and are thereby able to execute inside any target process to spoof it; others with sufficient privileges simply overwrite the memory of a target application. Injection mechanisms include:

- Use of vendor-supplied application extensions. For example, Windows Explorer has public interfaces that allow third parties to extend its functionality.
- Interception of messages
- Debuggers
- Exploitation of security vulnerabilities
- Function hooking or patching of commonly used APIs, for example, to mask a running process or file that resides on a file system

Rootkit Detection

There are a lot of software for rootkit searches that are meant to be run on a live system. One of many examples would be the software "rootkit hunter".

7. LOW HANGING FRUIT

Do you have to run faster than a cheetah? Not necessarily. You just have to be running faster than your friend, so he will be eaten and not you. Do your systems have to be as secure as Pentagon computers with a myriad of controls? Not necessarily. Your system has to be more secure than your neighbor's, and hopefully you will avoid trouble. Here are some other techniques to deter intrusions:

- Deterring intrusions by snow flaking (no two snowflakes are the same, so it takes more time to analyze a particular system in order to gain access, making them useless to be scanned with automatic tools). An example would be to move an SSH port from default TCP/22 to TCP/31234. Some determined hacker will find out pretty soon, but it will be an extra step for a script kiddie.

- Low hanging fruit is attacked most of the time by simply ignoring the pings to the host. This will deter some hackers (as there are many more systems that reply to ping), and it takes less time to detect those live IPs and scan them for vulnerabilities [7].

8. ANTIVIRUS SOFTWARE

The biggest fear for malware is the antivirus (AV) engine on the system. An antivirus can detect attack, but it might be too late already. AV is based on signatures in the files. Hackers bypass signature detection by encrypting their executables in unique ways. Every executable is encrypted in a unique way; AV engines are always losing ground because they are late arrivals in the detection game. If your AV engine fires, that means that the malware managed to slip by your IDS/IPS solution into the network and/or system.

9. HOMEGROWN INTRUSION DETECTION

In order to defeat a hacker, you have to think like a hacker. Let's take a look at what a robots.txt file looks like in a Web server. This file sits in the root of a Web page (for example, www.mywebpage.com/robots.txt); provides information to search engines of what should be cached and what should be skipped; shows how frequent crawling has to be done, and so on. Let's say you have sensitive files in a directory called "reports." This directory can be excluded from search engine crawlers and will not end up in search results. Other files and directories such as /private/, /adminpanel/, /phpmyadmin/ should be excluded from the search engine results. This technique looks great so far, but an experienced attacker will take a look at robots.txt file below and see what you don't want him to know!

Incorrect robots.txt implementation	Correct robots.txt implementation
Disallow: /adminpanel/ Disallow: /phpmyadmin/ Disallow: /backup/ Disallow: /uploads/	Move all sensitive directories into one directory called for example /private/ and disallow this directory: Disallow: /private/

A little customized robots.txt file would look like the following:

```
User-Agent: *

Disallow: /private/
Allow: /
User-Agent: hacker
Disallow: /please/go/to/an/easier/target/
```

It would give the attacker some clue that this is probably not the easiest target, and hopefully he or she will move to an easier one. Needless to say, it will not prevent a targeted attack [8]. So, if you have somebody trying to access a nonexisting directory "/please/go/to/an/easier/target/" on the server, it should give you a clue as to who is interested in your Web site.

10. FULL-PACKET CAPTURE DEVICES

Sometimes it is easier to detect intrusion on the wire by monitoring ingress and egress traffic. We have to be aware of out-of-band communications—for example, communication that comes to the corporate network via Global System for Mobile Communications (GSM) signals. These communications do not go through border routers of the company and thus cannot be inspected via this technology.

Packet capture appliance is a standalone device that performs packet capture. Although packet capture appliances may be deployed anywhere on a network, most are commonly placed at the entrances to the network (the Internet connections) and in front of critical equipment, such as servers containing sensitive information.

In general, packet capture appliances capture and record all network packets in full (both header and payload); however, some appliances may be configured to capture a subset of a network's traffic based on user-definable filters. For many applications, especially network forensics and incident response, it is critical to conduct full-packet capture, though filtered packet capture may be used at times for specific, limited information-gathering purposes.

Deployment

The network data that a packet capture appliance captures depends on where and how the appliance is installed on a network. There are two options for deploying packet capture appliances on a network. One option is to connect the appliance to the Switch Port Analyzer (SPAN) port (port mirroring) on a network switch or router. A second option is to connect the appliance inline, so that network activity along a network route traverses the appliance (similar in configuration to a network tap, but the information is captured and stored by the packet capture appliance rather than passing on to another device). When connected via a SPAN port, the packet capture appliance may receive and record all Ethernet/IP activity for all of the ports of the switch or router.

When connected inline, the packet capture appliance captures only the network traffic traveling between two points—that is, traffic that passes through the cable to which the packet capture appliance is connected. There are also two general approaches to deploying packet capture appliances: centralized and decentralized.

Centralized

With a centralized approach, one high-capacity, high-speed packet capture appliance connects to the data-aggregation point. The advantage of a centralized approach is that with one appliance, you gain visibility over the network's entire traffic. This approach, however, creates a single point of failure that is a very attractive target for hackers; additionally, one would have to reengineer the network to bring traffic to the appliance, and this approach typically involves high costs.

Decentralized

With a decentralized approach, you place multiple appliances around the network, starting at the point(s) of entry and proceeding downstream to deeper network segments, such as workgroups. The advantages include: no network reconfiguration required; ease of deployment; multiple vantage points for incident response investigations; scalability; no single point of failure—if one fails, you have the others; if combined with electronic invisibility, this approach practically eliminates the danger of unauthorized access by hackers; and low cost. The disadvantage is the potential increased maintenance of multiple appliances.

In the past, packet capture appliances were sparingly deployed, oftenonly at the point of entry into a network. Packet capture appliances can now be deployed more effectively at various points around the network. When conducting incident response, the ability to see the network data flow from various vantage points is indispensable in reducing the time to resolution and narrowing down which parts of the network ultimately were affected. By placing packet capture appliances at the entry point and in front of each workgroup, following the path of a particular transmission deeper into the network would be simplified and much quicker.

Additionally, the appliances placed in front of the workgroups would show intranet transmissions that the appliance located at the entry point would not be able to capture.

Capacity

Packet capture appliances come with capacities ranging from 500 Gigabytes (GB) to 32 Terabytes (TB) and more. Only a few organizations with extremely high network usage would have use for the upper ranges of capacities. Most organizations would be well served with capacities from 1 TB to 4 TB.

A good rule of thumb when choosing capacity is to allow 1 GB per day for heavy users, down to 1 GB per month for regular users. For a typical office of 20 people with average usage, 1 TB would be sufficient for about one to four years.

Features: Filtered versus Full-Packet Capture

Full-packet capture appliances capture and record all Ethernet/IP activity, while filtered packet capture appliances capture only a subset of traffic, based on a set of user-definable filters, such as IP address, MAC address, or protocol. Unless you use the packet capture appliance for a very specific purpose (narrow purpose covered by the filter parameters), it is generally best to use full-packet capture appliances or otherwise risk missing the vital data. Particularly, when using a packet capture for network forensics or cyber security purposes, it is paramount to capture everything because any packet not captured on the spot is a packet that is gone forever. It is impossible to know ahead of time the specific characteristics of the packets or transmissions needed, especially in the case of an advanced persistent threat (APT). APTs and other hacking techniques rely on the success of network administrators not knowing how they work and thus not having solutions in place to counteract them. Most APT attacks originate from Russia and China.

Encrypted versus Unencrypted Storage

Some packet capture appliances encrypt the captured data before saving it to disk, while others do not. Considering the breadth of information that travels on a network or Internet connection (and that at least a portion of it could be considered sensitive), encryption is a good idea for most situations as a measure to keep the captured data secure. Encryption is also a critical element of authentication of data for the purposes of data/network forensics.

Sustained Capture Speed versus Peak Capture Speed

The sustained captured speed is the rate at which a packet capture appliance can capture and record packets without interruption or error over a long period of time. This is different from the peak capture rate, which is the highest speed at which a packet capture appliance can capture and record packets. The peak capture speed can only be maintained for a short period of time, until the appliance's buffers fill up and it starts losing packets. Many packet capture appliances share the same peak capture speed of 1 Gigabytes per Second (Gbps), but actual sustained speeds vary significantly from model to model.

Permanent versus Overwritable Storage

A packet capture appliance with permanent storage is ideal for network forensics and permanent record-keeping purposes because the data captured cannot be overwritten, altered, or deleted. The only drawback of permanent storage is that eventually the appliance becomes full and requires replacement. Packet capture appliances with overwritable storage are easier to manage because once they reach capacity, they will start overwriting the oldest captured data with the new; however, network administrators run the risk of losing important capture data when it gets overwritten. In general, packet capture appliances with overwrite capabilities are useful for simple monitoring or testing purposes, for which a permanent record is not necessary. Permanent recording is a must for network forensics information gathering.

Data Security

Since packet capture appliances capture and store a large amount of data on network activity (including files, emails, and other communications), they could, in themselves, become attractive targets for hacking. A packet capture appliance deployed for any length of time should incorporate security features to protect the recorded network data from access by unauthorized parties. If deploying a packet capture appliance introduces too many additional concerns about security, the cost of securing it may outweigh the benefits. The best approach would be for the packet capture appliance to have built-in security features. These security features may include encryption, or methods to "hide" the appliance's presence on the network. For example, some packet capture appliances feature "electronic invisibility," that is, having a stealthy network profile by not requiring or using IP or MAC addresses.

Although on the face of it, connecting a packet capture appliance via a SPAN port appears to make it more secure, the packet capture appliance would ultimately still have to be connected to the network in order to allow management and data retrieval. Though not accessible via the SPAN link, the appliance would be accessible via the management link.

Despite the benefits, a packet capture appliance's remote access feature presents a security issue that could make the appliance vulnerable. Packet capture appliances that allow remote access should have a robust system in place to protect it against unauthorized access. One way to accomplish this is to incorporate a manual disable, such as a switch or toggle that allows the user to physically disable remote access. This simple solution is very effective, as it is doubtful that a hacker would have an easy time gaining physical access to the appliance in order to flip a switch.

A final consideration is physical security. All the network security features in the world are moot if someone is simply able to steal the packet capture appliance or make a copy of it and have ready access to the data stored on it. Encryption is one of the best ways to address this concern, though some packet capture appliances also feature tamperproof enclosures.

11. OUT-OF-BAND ATTACK VECTORS

What is the weakest link in any corporation? The answer is people. People fall into social engineering attacks; people bring "forgotten" Universal Serial Bus (USB) sticks and CDs from bathrooms/parking lots and plug them into their computers just out of curiosity. People bring their own devices from home and connect to corporate networks. BYOD or Bring Your Own Device is a big pain for IT administrators to manage. It also introduces additional risk because an employee's own devices might already be backdoored or infected, and by connecting these devices to the corporate network, employees are introducing a new risk. A social engineering attack with a lost CD is shown in Figure 3.7.

A Demyo plug is a full-blown Linux-based OS with many penetration testing tools preinstalled. It looks like an innocent power surge/split, but it has a Wireless Fidelity (Wi-Fi), Bluetooth, and GSM 3 g modem installed inside. Once connected to the power outlet, it immediately calls back home via GSM 3 g modem and establishes a connection. Once connected, penetration testers can use it as a jump box to do further penetration testing inside the local area network (LAN) of the corporation [9]. The Demyo plug is shown in Figure 3.8.

How do you prevent employees from bringing their "lost CDs" and "lost USB sticks" from parking lots and plugging them into their machines? A strong policy should be in place that disallows connecting nonapproved

FIGURE 3.7   A social engineering attack with a lost CD.

FIGURE 3.8   The Demyo plug.

hardware to workstations. It is not enough to just write a policy and consider the job done. Policy has to be enforced, and most importantly, policy has to be understood by employees. There is no way that rules can be followed if they are not understood. Another way to minimize risk is to provide security awareness training to employees, explaining typical social engineering attacks and how not to fall for them.

12. SECURITY AWARENESS TRAINING

Security awareness is the knowledge and attitude members of an organization possess regarding the protection of the physical and, especially, information assets of that organization. Many organizations require formal security awareness training for all workers when they join the organization and periodically thereafter (usually annually). Topics covered in security awareness training include the following:

- The nature of sensitive material and physical assets that they may come in contact with, such as trade secrets, privacy concerns, and government classified information

- Employee and contractor responsibilities in handling sensitive information, including the review of employee nondisclosure agreements

- Requirements for proper handling of sensitive material in physical form, which includes marking, transmission, storage, and destruction

- Proper methods for protecting sensitive information on computer systems, including password policy and use of the two-factor authentication

- Other computer security concerns, including malware, phishing, and social engineering

- Workplace security, including building access, wearing of security badges, reporting of incidents, and forbidden articles

- Consequences of failure to properly protect information, including the potential loss of employment, economic consequences to the firm, damage to individuals whose private records are divulged, and possible civil and criminal penalties

Being security aware means that you understand that there is the potential for some people to deliberately or accidentally steal, damage, or misuse the data that is stored within a company's computer system and throughout its organization. Therefore, it would be prudent to support the assets of the institution (information, physical, and personal) by trying to stop that from happening.

According to the European Network and Information Security Agency, "Awareness of the risks and available safeguards is the first line of defense for the security of information systems and networks." The focus of Security Awareness consultancy should be to achieve a long-term shift in the attitude of employees towards security, while promoting a cultural and behavioral change within an organization. Security policies should be viewed as key enablers for the organization, not as a series of rules restricting the efficient working of your business.

13. DATA CORRELATION

Data correlation is a technique used in information security to put all the pieces together and come up with some meaningful information. For example, if you see Linux system SSH connections coming in all day long, and after watching someone log in 200 times there is a successful login: What does it tell you? It should be a good starting point to suggest that a brute force attack is going on. All technologies help to find out intrusions; however, technologies do not find intrusions, people do. Appliances and sensors are typically good about finding bad events, but good events can combine into bad ones as well. Let's

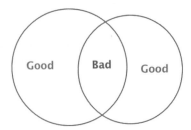

FIGURE 3.9 The combination of two good things can create one bad thing.

look at a simple scenario in which a human makes a determination about compromise:

Let's say there is a company with many employees who travel a lot around the globe. The company is doing a good job by implementing various control systems and logging systems; this company also uses Radio Frequency Identification (RFID) enabled cards for its employees in order to track who is coming and leaving its offices. All data is collected and pushed to the Security Information and Event Management (SIEM) engine to correlate events and logs. One morning two seemingly good events come into SIEM. The first event is user John's virtual private network (VPN) connection being established from overseas to the corporate office. The second event is user John's RFID badge being scanned at the entrance to the corporate office. Well, both events are pretty standard and are harmless when taken separately, but when combined, they reveal something weird. How can user John VPN in from overseas and get a physical entrance to the office at the same time? The answer is one of two: Either the VPN credentials have been compromised, or his employee card is being used by someone else to enter the office. Figure 3.9 shows how two good things can create one bad thing when combined.

14. SIEM

Security Information and Event Management (SIEM) solutions are a combination of the formerly disparate product categories of SIM (security information management) and SEM (security event manager). SIEM technology provides real-time analysis of security alerts generated by network hardware and applications. SIEM solutions come as software, appliances, or managed services, and they are also used to log security data and generate reports for compliance purposes.

The acronyms SEM, SIM, and SIEM have been used interchangeably, though there are differences in meaning and product capabilities. The segment of security management that deals with real-time monitoring, correlation of events, notifications, and console views is commonly known as Security Event Management (SEM).

The second area provides long-term storage, analysis, and reporting of log data and is known as Security Information Management (SIM).

The term *Security Information Event Management (SIEM)* describes the product capabilities of gathering, analyzing, and presenting information from network and security devices; identity and access management applications; vulnerability management and policy compliance tools; operating system, database and application logs; and external threat data. A key focus is to monitor and help manage user and service privileges, directory services, and other system configuration changes, as well as providing log auditing and review and incident response. The following are a list of SIEM capabilities:

- *Data Aggregation*: SIEM/LM (log management) solutions aggregate data from many sources, including network, security, servers, databases, and applications, providing the ability to consolidate monitored data to help avoid missing crucial events.
- *Correlation*: Looks for common attributes and links events together into meaningful bundles. This technology provides the ability to perform a variety of correlation techniques to integrate different sources, in order to turn data into useful information.
- *Alerting*: The automated analysis of correlated events and production of alerts, to notify recipients of immediate issues.
- *Dashboards*: SIEM/LM tools take event data and turn it into informational charts to assist in seeing patterns or identifying activity that is not forming a standard pattern.
- *Compliance*: SIEM applications can be employed to automate the gathering of compliance data, producing reports that adapt to existing security, governance, and auditing processes.
- *Retention*: SIEM/SIM solutions employ long-term storage of historical data to facilitate the correlation of data over time and to provide the retention necessary for compliance requirements.

15. OTHER WEIRD STUFF ON THE SYSTEM

What are the other symptoms of possible system compromises? Following are some examples:

- Log files are missing completely. Why are there no log files? Script kiddies delete logs, whereas hackers modify them by taking out only their IP addresses, their commands, and manipulations with the system.
- Network interface is in a promiscuous mode: In computer networking, promiscuous mode is a mode for a wired network interface controller (NIC) or wireless network interface controller (WNIC) that causes the controller to pass all traffic it receives to the central

processing unit (CPU), rather than passing only the frames that the controller is intended to receive. This mode is normally used for packet sniffing that takes place on a router or on a computer connected to a hub (instead of a switch) or that is part of a wireless local area network (WLAN). The mode is also required for bridged networking for hardware virtualization.

In IEEE 802 networks such as Ethernet, token ring, IEEE 802.11, and FDDI, each frame includes a destination Media Access Control address (MAC address). In nonpromiscuous mode, when an NIC receives a frame, it normally drops it unless the frame is addressed to that NIC's MAC address or is a broadcast or multicast frame. In promiscuous mode, however, the card allows all frames through, thus allowing the computer to read frames intended for other machines or network devices.

Many operating systems require super user privileges to enable promiscuous mode. In a nonrouting node, promiscuous mode can generally only monitor traffic to and from other nodes within the same broadcast domain (for Ethernet and IEEE 802.11) or ring (for token ring or Fiber-Optic Data Distribution Interface (FDDI)). Computers attached to the same network hub satisfy this requirement, which is why network switches are used to combat malicious use of promiscuous mode. A router may monitor all traffic that it routes.

Promiscuous mode is often used to diagnose network connectivity issues. There are programs that make use of this feature to show the user all the data being transferred over the network. Some protocols like File Transfer Protocol (FTP), Telnet transfer data, passwords in clear text without encryption, and network scanners can see this data. Therefore, computer users are encouraged to stay away from insecure protocols like Telnet and use more secure ones such as secure shell (SSH).

16. DETECTION

As promiscuous mode can be used in a malicious way to sniff on a network, one might be interested in detecting network devices that are in a promiscuous mode. In promiscuous mode, some software might send responses to frames, even though they were addressed to another machine. However, experienced sniffers can prevent this (using carefully designed firewall settings).

An example of the preceding is sending a ping (Internet Control Message Protocol (ICMP) echo request) with the wrong Media Access Control (MAC) address, but the right IP address. If an adapter is operating in normal mode, it will drop this frame, and the IP stack never sees or responds to it. If the adapter is in promiscuous mode,

the frame will be passed on, and the IP stack on the machine (to which a MAC address has no meaning) will respond, as it would to any other ping. The sniffer can prevent this by configuring his firewall to block ICMP traffic:

- Immutable files on the system that cannot be deleted can be found with the lsattr command. lsattr is a command-line program for listing the attributes on a Linux second extended file system. It is also a command to display attributes of devices on an Advanced Interactive eXecutive (AIX) operating system. Some malware puts a + i flag on its own executable, so you cannot delete it, even if you are a root.
- Mysterious open ports and services: All open ports and running services should be accounted for. For example, if there is a service running, but it's not clear what it does or why it is running, an investigation should be launched [10].

Finally, let's briefly look at the most common way to classify the detection of system intrusions (DSIs). Classification of the DSIs is to group them by information source. Some of the DSIs analyze network packets, captured from network backbones or LAN segments, in order to find attackers. Other DSIs analyze information sources generated by the operating system or application software for signs of intrusion.

17. NETWORK-BASED DETECTION OF SYSTEM INTRUSIONS (DSIS)

The majority of the commercial detection of system intrusions are network-based. These DSIs detect attacks by capturing and analyzing network packets. By listening on a network segment or switch, one network-based DSI can monitor the network traffic that is affecting multiple hosts connected to the network segment, thereby protecting those hosts.

Network-based DSIs often consist of a set of single-purpose sensors or hosts placed at various points in a network. These units monitor network traffic, performing local analysis of that traffic and reporting attacks to a central management console. As the sensors are limited to running the DSIs, they can be more easily secured against attack. Many of these sensors are designed to run in stealth mode, in order to make it more difficult for an attacker to determine their presence and location.

In addition, the following high-level checklist (see checklist: An Agenda for Action of the Advantages and Disadvantages of Network-Based DSIs) addresses the advantages and disadvantages of how the network-based DSIs monitor network traffic for particular network

---

An Agenda for Action of the Advantages and Disadvantages of Network-Based DSIs Activities

The following high-level checklist displays the advantages and disadvantages of how the network-based DSIs monitor network traffic for particular network segments (check all tasks completed):

Advantages

_____**1.** Install network-based DSIs so that they can monitor a large network.

_____**2.** Deploy network-based DSIs so that they have little impact on an existing network.

_____**3.** Make sure that the network-based DSIs listen in on a network wire without interfering with the normal operation of a network.

_____**4.** Retrofit a network to include network-based DSIs with minimal effort.

_____**5.** Make the network-based DSIs very secure against attack and invisible to attackers.

Disadvantages

_____**6.** Do your network-based DSIs have difficulty processing all packets in a large or busy network and, therefore, fail to recognize an attack launched during periods of high traffic?

_____**7.** Do your vendors implement DSIs completely in hardware, which is much faster?

_____**8.** Do your vendors analyze packets quickly, which forces them to both detect fewer attacks and also detect attacks with as little computing resource as possible, which can reduce detection effectiveness?

_____**9.** Is it true that many of the advantages of network-based DSIs don't apply to more modern switch-based networks?

_____**10.** Do switches subdivide networks into many small segments (usually one fast Ethernet wire per host) and provide dedicated links between hosts serviced by the same switch?

_____**11.** Do most switches that do not provide universal monitoring ports limit the monitoring range of a network-based DSIs sensor to a single host?

_____**12.** Do most switches that provide monitoring ports cause the single port to not mirror all traffic traversing the switch?

_____**13.** Is it true that network-based DSIs cannot analyze encrypted information?

_____**14.** Is the problem of not being able to analyze encrypted information increasing, as more organizations (and attackers) use virtual private networks?

_____**15.** Is it true that most network-based DSIs cannot tell whether or not an attack was successful, and that they can only discern that an attack was initiated?

_____**16.** Is it true that after a network-based DSIs detects an attack administrators must manually investigate each attacked host to determine whether it was indeed penetrated?

_____**17.** Do some network-based DSIs have problems dealing with network-based attacks that involve fragmenting packets?

_____**18.** Do malformed packets cause the DSIs to become unstable and crash?

---

segments or devices, and analyzes network, transport, and application protocols to identify suspicious activity. The network-based DSI components are similar to other types of DSI technologies, except for the sensors. A network-based DSI sensor monitors and analyzes network activity on one or more network segments. Sensors are available in two formats: appliance-based sensors, which are comprised of specialized hardware and software optimized for DSI sensor use; and software-only sensors, which can be installed onto hosts that meet certain specifications.

18. SUMMARY

As we outlined earlier, there are many ways to detect system intrusions and many ways to hide them. What is the proper way to analyze suspect systems then? The proper sequence is as follows:

1. Memory dump and analysis: Hackers are getting smart these days; they stay in the memory as long as possible. Why? Because they know forensics will be done on the HDD itself; but if they stay in memory, it requires a better skill to do memory analysis. Some companies just pull the plug from the power and network, and do HDD forensics analysis. This is wrong because as soon as you pull the power plug, half of the goodies are gone.

2. Selective HDD files analysis (we make the HDD image first, and work from the copy). Depending on the machine role on the network, doing a full-blown forensic analysis might be an overkill. In some situations, a partial forensic examination is enough.

3. A full HDD analysis is needed (we make the HDD image first and work from the copy).

Finally, let's move on to the real interactive part of this chapter: review questions/exercises, hands-on projects, case projects, and optional team case project. The answers and/or solutions by chapter can be found in the Online Instructor's Solutions Manual.

CHAPTER REVIEW QUESTIONS/EXERCISES

True/False

1. True or False? One of the ways to monitor changes in the file system is to implement LoggedFS.
2. True or False? File integrity monitoring (FIM) is an internal control or process that performs the act of validating the integrity of the operating system and application software files using a verification method between the current file state and the known, good baseline.
3. True or False? A timestamp is a sequence of characters or encoded information identifying when a certain event occurred, usually giving date and time of day, sometimes accurate to a small fraction of a second.
4. True or False? A hidden file is normally visible when examining the contents of the directory in which it resides.
5. True or False? About 90 percent of all successful compromises are made via known flaws, so 0day attacks are common.

Multiple Choice

1. Values monitored for unexpected changes to files or configuration items include the following, except which one?
   A. Credentials
   B. Cannot be understood
   C. Privileges and security settings
   D. Content
   E. Core attributes and size
2. What phase focuses on attack surface analysis?
   A. Analyze
   B. Test
   C. Report
   D. Mitigate
   E. Cipher
3. Injection mechanisms include the following, except which one:
   A. Use of vendor-supplied application extensions
   B. Interception of messages
   C. Buggers
   D. Exploitation of security vulnerabilities
   E. Function hooking or patching of commonly used APIs
4. What describes the product capabilities of gathering, analyzing, and presenting information from network and security devices; identity and access management applications; vulnerability management and policy compliance tools; operating system, database, and application logs; and external threat data?
   A. Security Information Event Management
   B. Security Information Management
   C. Security Event Management
   D. Security Management Information
   E. Security Event Information
5. What is it called when SIEM/LM tools take event data and turn it into informational charts to assist in seeing patterns, or identifying activity that is not forming a standard pattern?
   A. Compliance
   B. Retention
   C. Dashboards
   D. Alerting
   E. Correlation

EXERCISE

Problem

Which of the following attributes suggests that the packets below have been crafted?

```
00:03:21.680333          216.164.222.250.1186 > us.us.
us.44.8080: S 2410044679:2410044679 (0) win 512
00:03:21.810732          216.164.222.250.1189 > us.us.
us.50.8080: S 2410044679:2410044679 (0) win 512
```

Hands-On Projects

Project

What is the most likely reason for choosing to use HEAD requests instead of GET requests when scanning for the presence of vulnerable Web-based applications?

Case Projects

Problem

What is the LEAST effective indicator that the attacker's source address is not spoofed?

Optional Team Case Project

Problem

What is the most likely explanation for "arp info overwritten" messages on a BSD-based system?

REFERENCES

[1] B. Schneier, Whitelisting vs. Blacklisting. <https://www.schneier.com/blog/archives/2011/01/whitelisting_vs.html>, January 28, 2011.
[2] LoggedFS. <http://loggedfs.sourceforge.net/>.
[3] AIDE. <http://aide.sourceforge.net/>.
[4] Hidden files. <http://www.linfo.org/hidden_file.html>.
[5] SystemImager. <http://sourceforge.net/projects/systemimager/>.
[6] Phrack. <http://phrack.org/>.
[7] What is vulnerability. <http://bit.ly/PFCWCh>.
[8] Targeted attack. <http://bit.ly/MTjLVv>.
[9] Demyo plug. <http://www.demyo.com>.
[10] Intrusion Detection. <http://bit.ly/OCB7UU>.

## Chapter 4

Preventing System Intrusions

Michael West

Senior Technical Writer, Truestone Maritime Operations

There's a war raging across the globe, and you're right in the middle of it. But while this war doesn't include gunfire and mass carnage, its effects can be thoroughly devastating nonetheless. This war is being waged in cyberspace by people bent on stealing the heart and soul of your business, your company's plans and secrets, or worse, your client names and their financial information.

So how bad is it? Just what are you up against?

Imagine this: You're in charge of security for an advanced movie screening. You've been hired and assigned the daunting task of keeping the advanced screening from being copied and turned into a bootleg version available overseas or on the Web. So how do you make sure that doesn't happen (how many times have we heard about this scenario or seen it in the movies)?

First, you might start by controlling access to the theater itself, allowing only the holders of very tightly controlled tickets into the screening. You post a couple of personnel at the door who carefully check every ticket against a list to verify the identity of both the ticket holder and their numbered ticket. Your goal is clear: restrict the viewers and, hopefully, reduce the possibility of someone entering with a counterfeit ticket. But what about the back stage door? While you're busy watching the front door, someone could simply sneak in the back. So, you secure that door and post a guard. But what about the ventilation system (the ventilation system is a favorite Hollywood scenario—remember Tom Cruise in *Mission Impossible*)? So, you secure that too. You also secure the projection room.

Did you think about a ticket holder coming into the theater with a digital recording device? Or a recording device surreptitiously planted just outside the projection room before anyone even entered. Or, worse, someone who rigged up a digital recording system that captures the movie from *inside* the projector and feeds it directly to their computer?

The point is this: No matter how diligent you are at securing your network, there are always people waiting just outside who are just as motivated to steal what you're trying to protect as you are trying to keep them from stealing it. You put up a wall; they use a back door. You secure the back door; they come in through a window. You secure the windows; they sneak in through the ventilation system. You secure the ventilation system; they simply bypass the physical security measures and go straight for your users, turning them into unwitting thieves. And so on and so on.

There's a very delicate balance between the need to keep your network secured and allowing user access. Users may be your company's lifeblood, but they are simultaneously your greatest and most necessary asset, and your weakest link.

It almost sounds like an impossible task, doesn't it? It's easy to see how it might seem that way when a casual Internet search reveals no shortage of sites selling hacking tools. In some cases, the hacking tools were written for—and marketed to—those not schooled in programming languages.

When I wrote this chapter three years ago, the cyber world was a very different place. Back then, crackers were simply stealing credit card numbers and financial data (for example, in January, hackers penetrated the customer database for online shoe store giant Zappos and stole names, email addresses, shipping addresses, phone numbers, and the last four digits of credit card numbers for over 24 million customers), siphoning corporate proprietary information (also known as industrial espionage), and defacing Web sites.

In today's world, crackers twice took control of an American satellite called Terra Eos, not just interrupting data flow, but taking full control of the satellite's guidance systems. They literally could have given the satellite commands to start a de-orbit burn.[1] And there's no shortage of some very simple and readily accessible software tools that allow crackers to sit nearby, say, in a coffee shop and wirelessly follow your Web browsing, steal your passwords, or even assume your identity.

Now, who do you think could pull off a feat like that? Most likely, it's not your neighbor's kid or the cyberpunk with just enough skill to randomly deface Web sites.

---

1. ABC News, November 16, 2011.

Many experts believe this effort was well funded, most likely with government sponsorship. The Chinese military believes that attacking the communications links between ground stations and orbiting satellites is a legitimate strategy at the outset of any conflict. If that's the case, then a government-sponsored attack is a frightening prospect.

The moment you established an active Web presence, you put a target on your company's back. And like the hapless insect that lands in the spider's web, your company's size determines the size of the disturbance you create on the Web—and how quickly you're noticed by the bad guys. How attractive you are as prey is usually directly proportionate to what you have to offer a predator. If yours is an e-commerce site whose business thrives on credit card or other financial information or a company with valuable secrets to steal, your "juiciness" quotient goes up; you have more of value there to steal. And if your business is new and your Web presence is recent, the assumption could be made that perhaps you're not yet a seasoned veteran in the nuances of cyber warfare and, thus, are more vulnerable to an intrusion.

Unfortunately for you, many of those who seek to penetrate your network defenses are educated, highly motivated, and quite brilliant at developing faster and more efficient methods of quietly sneaking around your perimeter, checking for the smallest of openings. Most IT professionals know that an enterprise's firewall is relentlessly being probed for weaknesses and vulnerabilities by crackers from every corner of the globe. Anyone who follows news about software understands that seemingly every few months, word comes out about a new, exploitable opening in an operating system or application. It's widely understood that no one—not the most savvy network administrator, or the programmer who wrote the software—can possibly find and close all the holes in today's increasingly complex software.

Despite the increased sophistication of today's software applications, bugs and holes exist in those applications, as well as in operating systems, server processes (daemons), and client applications. System configurations can be easily exploited, especially if you don't change the default administrator's password, or if you simply accept default system settings, or unintentionally leave a gaping hole open by configuring the machine to run in a nonsecure mode. Even Transmission Control Protocol/Internet Protocol (TCP/IP), the foundation on which all Internet traffic operates, can be exploited, since the protocol was designed before the threat of hacking was really widespread. Therefore it contains design flaws that can allow, for example, a cracker to easily alter IP data.

Once the word gets out that a new and exploitable opening exists in an application (and word *will* get out), crackers around the world start scanning sites on the Internet searching for any and all sites that have that particular opening.

Making your job even harder is the fact that many of the openings into your network are caused by your employees. Casual surfing of online shopping sites, porn sites, and even banking sites can expose your network to all kinds of nasty bugs and malicious code, simply because an employee visited the site. The problem is that, to users, it might not seem like such a big deal. They either don't realize that they're leaving the network wide open to intrusion, or they don't care.

1. SO, WHAT IS AN INTRUSION?

A network intrusion is an unauthorized penetration of your enterprise's network, or an individual machine address in your assigned domain. Intrusions can be passive (in which the penetration is gained stealthily and without detection) or active (in which changes to network resources are effected). Intrusions can come from outside your network structure or inside (an employee, a customer, or business partner). Some intrusions are simply meant to let you know the intruder was there by defacing your Web site with various kinds of messages or crude images. Others are more malicious, seeking to extract critical information on either a one-time basis or as an ongoing parasitic relationship that continues to siphon off data until it's discovered. Some intruders implant carefully crafted code, such as Trojan-type malicious software (malware), designed to steal passwords, record keystrokes, or open an application's "back door."

Still worse, some high-end crackers can set up phony Web sites that exactly mimic your company's site, and surreptitiously redirect your unaware users away from your site to theirs (known as a "man in the browser attack"). Others will embed themselves into your network like a tick, quietly siphoning off data until found and rendered inert.

An attacker can get into your system physically (by gaining physical access to a restricted machine's hard drive and/or BIOS), externally (by attacking your Web servers or finding a way to bypass your firewall), or internally (your own users, customers, or partners).

2. SOBERING NUMBERS

So how often do these intrusions and data thefts occur? The estimates are staggering: In August of 2009, InfoTech Spotlight reported that "cybercrime costs organizations an average of \$3.8 million per year,"[2] and there are thousands of new, fake phishing[3] Web sites set up

---

2. Bright Hub, "Cyber Crime Costs / Cyber Crime Losses," September 13, 2010.
3. Phishing is an attempt to steal user information (e.g., usernames, passwords, credit-card information, etc.) by disguising phony Web sites as legitimate ones the user may be accustomed to accessing.

online every day. The *APWG Phishing Activity Trends Report* for the first half of 2011 shows that even though unique phishing reports are down 35 percent (from an all-time high of 40,621 in August of 2009), data-stealing Trojan malware reached an all-time high in the first half of 2011 and comprised almost *half* of all detected malware. And from January to June of 2011, the number of new malware samples hit a whopping 11,777,775—an increase of 13 percent from the second half of 2010![4]

A March 2010 report by Security Management revealed that the most common Internet fraud complaints are from people whose identities have been compromised.[5] On two occasions, I myself have been the victim of a stolen credit-card number. In one case, a purchase was made at a jewelry store in Texas, and in the other, the purchases were made at a grocery store in the Philippines.

The Federal Bureau of Investigation (FBI) reports receiving over 330,000 identity theft reports, with losses estimated at over $560 million. And McAfee reports estimate business losses topped $1 trillion!Sadly, this number is likely to climb; 72 percent of newly detected malware are Trojans capable of stealing user information.

Not surprisingly, financial services are still the hardest hit and most frequently targeted sector, and account for almost half of all industry attacks. In the first half of 2011, new and more malevolent types of "Crimeware" (software specifically designed to steal customer information such as credit-card data, Social Security numbers, and customers' financial Web site credentials) appeared. Patrik Runald, senior manager of Security Research at Websense, has stated: "With cybercrime being an industry generating hundreds of millions of dollars for the bad guys, it's clear that this is a trend we will see for a long time."[6]

Unfortunately, the United States continues to host the highest number of infected phishing sites: Nearly 60 percent of all malware-infected URLs comes from the United States.

In today's cyber battlefield, attacks are specifically targeting one organization as a prelude to attacking and penetrating others. And if you're an enterprise's IT professional, you need to make a fundamental shift in mindset away from trying to build the most impressive defenses that money can buy to thinking seriously about defense and detection. The reality is, you have to assume you have been or soon will be compromised.

Even the big boys in cybersecurity aren't immune. In March of 2010, RSA was among hundreds of major companies compromised in a massive, coordinated cyber attack. The attackers penetrated RSA's formidable defenses and made off with information that RSA said could "reduce the effectiveness" of its widely used SecurID authentication system. In what the cyber security industry refers to as an "advanced persistent threat," the crackers used the information they stole from RSA to attack defense contractor Lockheed Martin.[7]

Whatever the goal of the intrusion—fun, greed, bragging rights, or data theft — the end result will be the same: Someone discovered and exploited a weakness in your network security, and until you discover that weakness—the intrusion entry point—it will continue to be an open door into your environment.

So, just who's out there looking to break into your network?

3. KNOW YOUR ENEMY: HACKERS VERSUS CRACKERS

An entire community of people—experts in programming and computer networking and those who thrive on solving complex problems—have been around since the earliest days of computing. The term *hacker* originated from the members of this culture, and they are quick to point out that it was hackers who built and make the Internet run, and hackers who created the Unix operating system. Hackers see themselves as members of a community that builds things and makes them work. And to those in their culture, the term *cracker* is a badge of honor.

Ask a traditional hacker about people who sneak into computer systems to steal data or cause havoc, and he'll most likely correct you by telling you those people aren't true hackers. (In the cracker community, the term for these types is *cracker*, and the two labels aren't synonymous.) So, to not offend traditional hackers, I'll use the term *crackers* and focus on them and their efforts.

From the lone-wolf cracker seeking peer recognition to the disgruntled former employee out for revenge or the deep pockets and seemingly unlimited resources of a hostile government bent on taking down wealthy capitalists, crackers are out there in force, looking to find the chink in your system's defensive armor.

The crackers' specialty—or in some cases, their mission in life—is to seek out and exploit the vulnerabilities of an individual computer or network for their own purposes. Crackers' intentions are normally malicious and/or criminal in nature. They have, at their disposal, a vast library of information designed to help them hone their tactics, skills, and knowledge, and they can tap into the almost unlimited experience of other crackers through a

4. Panda Security, PandaLabs.
5. "Uptick in Cybercrime Cost Victims Big in 2009, FBI Report Says," *Security Management*, March 15, 2010.
6. APWG Phishing Activity Trends Report.

7. CNNMoney, February 28, 2012.

community of like-minded individuals sharing information across underground networks.

They usually begin this life learning the most basic of skills: software programming. The ability to write code that can make a computer do what they want is seductive in and of itself. As they learn more and more about programming, they also expand their knowledge of operating systems and, as a natural course of progression, operating systems' weaknesses. They also quickly learn that, to expand the scope and type of their illicit handiwork, they need to learn HTML—the code that allows them to create phony Web pages that lure unsuspecting users into revealing important financial or personal data.

There are vast underground organizations to which these new crackers can turn for information. They hold meetings, write papers, and develop tools that they pass along to each other. Each new acquaintance they meet fortifies their skill set and gives them the training to branch out to more and more sophisticated techniques. Once they gain a certain level of proficiency, they begin their trade in earnest.

They start off simply by researching potential target firms on the Internet (an invaluable source for all kinds of corporate network related information). Once a target has been identified, they might quietly tiptoe around, probing for old forgotten back doors and operating system vulnerabilities. As starting points for launching an attack, they can simply and innocuously run basic DNS queries that can provide IP addresses (or ranges of IP addresses). They might sit back and listen to inbound and/or outbound traffic, record IP addresses, and test for weaknesses by pinging various devices or users.

To breach your network, a cracker starts by creating a chain of exploited systems in which each successful takeover sets the stage for the next. The easiest systems to exploit are those in our homes: Most home users do little to secure their systems from outside intrusions. And a good cracker can implant malware so deeply in a home computer that the owner never knows it's there. Then, when they're asleep or away, the malware takes control of the home computer and starts sending out newly mutated versions to another compromised system. In this way, there are so many compromised systems between them and the intrusion that it sends investigators down long, twisted paths that can include dozens, if not hundreds, of unwittingly compromised systems. Once your network is breached, they can surreptitiously implant password cracking or recording applications, keystroke recorders, or other malware designed to keep their unauthorized connection alive—and profitable. From there, they sit back and siphon off whatever they deem most valuable.

The cracker wants to act like a cyber-ninja, sneaking up to and penetrating your network without leaving any trace of the incursion. Some more seasoned crackers can put multiple layers of machines, many hijacked, between them and your network to hide their activity. Like standing in a room full of mirrors, the attack appears to be coming from so many locations you can't pick out the real from the ghost. And before you realize what they've done, they've up and disappeared like smoke in the wind.

4. MOTIVES

Though the goal is the same—to penetrate your network defenses—crackers' motives are often different. In some cases, a network intrusion could be done from the inside by a disgruntled employee looking to hurt the organization or steal company secrets for profit.

There are large groups of crackers working diligently to steal credit-card information that they then turn around and make available for sale. They want a quick grab and dash—take what they want and leave. Their cousins are the network parasites—those who quietly breach your network, then sit there siphoning off data.

A new and very disturbing trend is the discovery that certain governments have been funding digital attacks on network resources of both federal and corporate systems. Various agencies from the U.S. Department of Defense to the governments of New Zealand, France, and Germany have reported attacks originating from unidentified Chinese hacking groups. It should be noted that the Chinese government denies any involvement, and there is no evidence that it is or was involved.

5. THE CRACKERS' TOOLS OF THE TRADE

Over the years, the tools available to crackers have become increasingly more sophisticated. How sophisticated?

Most security software products available today have three basic methods of spotting malicious software. First, it scans all incoming data traffic for traces of known malware (pulling malware characteristics from a source database). Then, it looks for any kind of suspicious activity (e.g., vulnerable processes unexpectedly activating or running too long, unusual activity during normally dormant periods, etc.). And finally, the security software checks for indications of information leaving from abnormal paths or processes.

Recently, however, a relatively new and extremely malicious malware program called Zeus has appeared. Designed specifically to steal financial information, Zeus can defeat the above methods by not only sitting discreetly and quietly—not drawing attention to itself but also by changing its appearance tens of thousands of times per day. But its most insidious characteristic is that it siphons data off from an infected system using your browser. Called a "man in the browser attack," Zeus implants itself in your browser, settling in between you and a legitimate Web site (say, the site for the financial institution that manages your IRA), and very capably altering what you see to the point at which you really can't tell the difference. Not knowing the difference, you confidently enter your most important financial details, which Zeus siphons off and sends to someone else. New Zeus updates come out regularly, and, once released, it can take weeks for its new characteristics to become known by security software companies.

Our "Unsecured" Wireless World

Do you think much about the time you spend using a coffee shop's free Wi-Fi signal to surf, check your email, or update your Facebook page? Probably not. But today, the person sitting next to you quietly sipping her coffee and working away on her laptop can now sit back and watch what Web sites you've visited, then assume your identity and log on to the sites you visited. How? A free program called Firesheep can grab from your Web browser the cookies[8] for each site you visit. That cookie contains identifying information about your computer, and site settings for each site you visit plus your customized private information for that site. Once Firesheep grabs that cookie, a malicious user can use it to log on to sites as you, and can, in some cases, gain full access to your account.

You may be asking yourself "So what does this have to do with my network?" If the unsuspecting user is wirelessly completing a sales transaction or bank transfer when software like Firesheep snatches the browser cookie, the cracker can log back into your site as the compromised user and drain your account.

In years past, only the most experienced and savvy crackers with expensive tools and plenty of time could do much damage to secured networks. But like a professional thief with custom-made lock picks, crackers today can obtain a frightening array of tools to covertly test your network for weak spots. Their tools range from simple password-stealing malware and keystroke recorders (loggers) to methods of implanting sophisticated parasitic software strings that copy data streams coming in from customers who want to perform an e-commerce transaction with your company. Some of the more widely used tools include these:

- *Wireless sniffers.* Not only can these devices locate wireless signals within a certain range, they can siphon off the data being transmitted over the signals. With the rise in popularity and use of remote wireless devices, this practice is increasingly responsible for the loss of critical data and represents a significant headache for IT departments.
- *Packet sniffers.* Once implanted in a network data stream, these tools passively analyze data packets moving into and out of a network interface, and utilities capture data packets passing through a network interface.
- *Port scanners.* A good analogy for these utilities is a thief casing a neighborhood, looking for an open or unlocked door. These utilities send out successive, sequential connection requests to a target system's ports to see which one responds or is open to the request. Some port scanners allow the cracker to slow the rate of port scanning—sending connection requests over a longer period of time—so the intrusion attempt is less likely to be noticed. The usual targets of these devices are old, forgotten "back doors," or ports inadvertently left unguarded after network modifications.
- *Port knocking.* Sometimes network administrators create a secret backdoor method of getting through firewall-protected ports—a secret knock that enables them to quickly access the network. Port-knocking tools find these unprotected entries and implant a Trojan horse that listens to network traffic for evidence of that secret knock.
- *Keystroke loggers.* These are spyware utilities planted on vulnerable systems that record a user's keystrokes. Obviously, when someone can sit back and record every keystroke a user makes, it doesn't take long to obtain things like usernames, passwords, and ID numbers.
- *Remote administration tools.* Programs embedded on an unsuspecting user's system that allow the cracker to take control of that system.
- *Network scanners.* Explore networks to see the number and kind of host systems on a network, the services available, the host's operating system, and the type of packet filtering or firewalls being used.
- *Password crackers.* These sniff networks for data streams associated with passwords, then employ a brute-force method of peeling away any encryption layers protecting those passwords.

6. BOTS

Three years ago, bots were an emerging threat. Now , organized cyber criminals have begun to create and sell kits on the open market that inexperienced nonprogramming crackers can use to create their own botnets. It offers a wide variety of easy to use (or pre-programmed) modules that specifically target the most lucrative

---

8. Cookies are bits of software code sent to your browser by Web sites. They can be used for authentication, session identification, preferences, shopping cart contents, and so on.

technologies. It includes a management console that can control every infected system and interrogate bot-infected machines. If desired, Zeus kit modules are available that can allow the user to create viruses that mutate every time they're implanted in a new host system.

So what are bots? Bots, also known as an Internet bots, Web robots, or WWW robots, are small software applications running automated tasks over the Internet. Usually, they run simple tasks that a human would otherwise have to perform, but at a much faster rate. When used maliciously, they are a virus, surreptitiously implanted in large numbers of unprotected computers (usually those found in homes), hijacking them (without the owners' knowledge) and turning them into slaves to do the cracker's bidding. These compromised computers, known as *bots*, are linked in vast and usually untraceable networks called *botnets*. Botnets are designed to operate in such a way that instructions come from a central PC and are rapidly shared among other botted computers in the network. Newer botnets are now using a "peer-to-peer" method that, because they lack a central identifiable point of control, makes it difficult if not impossible for law enforcement agencies to pinpoint. And because they often cross international boundaries into countries without the means (or will) to investigate and shut them down, they can grow with alarming speed. They can be so lucrative that they've now become the cracker's tool of choice.

There are all kinds of bots; there are bots that harvest email addresses (spambots), viruses and worms, filename modifiers, bots to buy up large numbers of concert seats, and bots that work together in botnets, or coordinated attacks on networked computers.

Botnets exist largely because of the number of users who fail to observe basic principles of computer security—installed and/or up-to-date antivirus software, regular scans for suspicious code, and so on—and thereby become unwitting accomplices. Once taken over and "botted," their machines are turned into channels through which large volumes of unwanted spam or malicious code can be quickly distributed. Current estimates are that, of the 800 million computers on the Internet, up to 40 percent are bots controlled by cyber thieves who are using them to spread new viruses, send out unwanted spam email, overwhelm Web sites in denial-of-service (DoS) attacks, or siphon off sensitive user data from banking or shopping Web sites that look and act like legitimate sites with which customers have previously done business.

Bot controllers, also called *herders*, can also make money by leasing their networks to others who need a large and untraceable means of sending out massive amounts of advertisements but don't have the financial or technical resources to create their own networks. Making matters worse is the fact that botnet technology is available on the Internet for less than $100, which makes it relatively easy to get started in what can be a very lucrative business.

7. SYMPTOMS OF INTRUSIONS

As stated earlier, merely being on the Web puts a target on your back. It's only a matter of time before you experience your first attack. It could be something as innocent looking as several failed login attempts or as obvious as an attacker having defaced your Web site or crippled your network. It's important that you go into this knowing you're vulnerable.

Crackers are going to first look for known weaknesses in the operating system (OS) or any applications you are using. Next, they would start probing, looking for holes, open ports, or forgotten back doors—faults in your security posture that can quickly or easily be exploited.

Arguably one of the most common symptoms of an intrusion—either attempted or successful—is repeated signs that someone is trying to take advantage of your organization's own security systems, and the tools you use to keep watch for suspicious network activity may actually be used against you quite effectively. Tools such as network security and file integrity scanners, which can be invaluable in helping you conduct ongoing assessments of your network's vulnerability, are also available and can be used by crackers looking for a way in.

Large numbers of unsuccessful login attempts are also a good indicator that your system has been targeted. The best penetration-testing tools can be configured with attempt thresholds that, when exceeded, will trigger an alert. They can passively distinguish between legitimate and suspicious activity of a repetitive nature, monitor the time intervals between activities (alerting when the number exceeds the threshold you set), and build a database of signatures seen multiple times over a given period.

The "human element" (your users) is a constant factor in your network operations. Users will frequently enter a mistyped response but usually correct the error on the next try. However, a sequence of mistyped commands or incorrect login responses (with attempts to recover or reuse them) can be a signs of brute-force intrusion attempts.

Packet inconsistencies—direction (inbound or outbound), originating address or location, and session characteristics (ingoing sessions vs. outgoing sessions)—can also be good indicators of an attack. If a packet has an unusual source or has been addressed to an abnormal port—say, an inconsistent service request—it could be a sign of random system scanning. Packets coming from the outside that have local network addresses that request services on the inside can be a sign that IP spoofing is being attempted.

Sometimes odd or unexpected system behavior is itself a sign. Though this is sometimes difficult to track, you should be aware of activity such as changes to system clocks, servers going down or server processes inexplicably stopping (with system restart attempts), system resource issues (such as unusually high CPU activity or overflows in file systems), audit logs behaving in strange ways (decreasing in size without administrator intervention), or unexpected user access to resources. You should investigate any and all unusual activity at regular times on given days, heavy system use (possible denial of service (DoS) attack) or CPU use (brute-force password-cracking attempts).

8. WHAT CAN YOU DO?

It goes without saying that the most secure network—the one that has the least chance of being compromised—is the one that has no direct connection to the outside world. But that's hardly a practical solution, since the whole reason you have a Web presence is to do business. And in the game of Internet commerce, your biggest concern isn't the sheep coming in but the wolves dressed like sheep coming in with them. So, how do you strike an acceptable balance between keeping your network intrusion free and keeping it accessible at the same time?

As your company's network administrator, you walk a fine line between network security and user needs. You have to have a good defensive posture that still allows for access. Users and customers can be both the lifeblood of your business and its greatest potential source of infection. Furthermore, if your business thrives on allowing users access, you have no choice but to let them in. It seems like a monumentally difficult task at best.

Like a castle, imposing but stationary, every defensive measure you put up will eventually be compromised by the legions of very motivated thieves looking to get in. It's a game of move/countermove: You adjust, they adapt. So you have to start with defenses that can quickly and effectively adapt and change as the outside threats adapt.

First and foremost, you need to make sure that your perimeter defenses are as strong as they can be, and that means keeping up with the rapidly evolving threats around you. The days of relying solely on a firewall that simply does firewall functions are gone; today's crackers have figured out how to bypass the firewall by exploiting weaknesses in applications themselves. Simply being reactive to hits and intrusions isn't a very good option either; that's like standing there waiting for someone to hit you before deciding what to do rather than seeing the oncoming punch and moving out of its way or blocking it. You need to be flexible in your approach to the newest technologies, constantly auditing your defenses to ensure that your network's defensive armor can meet the latest threat. You have to have a very dynamic and effective policy of constantly monitoring for suspicious activities that, when discovered, can be quickly dealt with so that someone doesn't slip something past without your noticing it. Once that happens, it's too late.

Next, and this is also a crucial ingredient for network administrators: You have to educate your users. No matter how good a job you've done at tightening up your network security processes and systems, you still have to deal with the weakest link in your armor—your users. It doesn't do any good to have bulletproof processes in place if they're so difficult to manage that users work around them to avoid the difficulty, or if they're so loosely configured that a casually surfing user who visits an infected site will pass that infection along to your network. The degree of difficulty in securing your network increases dramatically as the number of users goes up.

User education becomes particularly important where mobile computing is concerned. Losing a device, using it in a place (or manner) in which prying eyes can see passwords or data, awareness of hacking tools specifically designed to sniff wireless signals for data, and logging on to unsecured networks are all potential problem areas with which users need to be familiar.

A relatively new tool is the intrusion detection system, or IDS. IDSs merge their deep packet scanning with a firewall's blocking can filtering capabilities. A good IDS and not only detect intrusion attempts, but also stop the attack before it does any damage.

One type of IDS, known as an inline IDS, can sit between your network's outside interface and your most critical systems. They essentially inspect every data packet headed for those critical systems, sniffing and "tasting" them, then scrubbing out the ones that have suspicious characteristics.

Another type of IDS is based on an application firewall scheme. These types of IDSs sit on all protected servers and are configured to protect specific applications. They are designed to "learn" every aspect of an application—how it interacts with users and the Internet, how the application's features play with each other, and what "customizable" features the application has that may require more detailed configuration—then create a rule for dealing with those aspects. This last point reveals a drawback of application-based IDSs: In order for them to protect all aspects of the application, it has to "know" every aspect of the application. The only way you can configure the IDS to protect every one of the application's functions is to let it "learn" the functions by exercising them. It can't develop a protection rule for a feature with which it's unfamiliar. So thorough testing is needed, or the IDS may miss a particular vulnerability. And if you update the protected application, you'll need to exercise its features again to ensure the IDS knows what it's supposed to protect.

You can also set up a decoy—sort of the "sacrificial lamb"—as bait. Also known as "honey pots," these userless networks are specifically set up to draw in an attacker and gain valuable data on the methods, tools, and any new malware they might be using.

Know Today's Network Needs

The traditional approach to network security engineering has been to try to erect preventative measures—firewalls—to protect the infrastructure from intrusion. The firewall acts like a filter, catching anything that seems suspicious and keeping everything behind it as sterile as possible. However, though firewalls are good, they typically don't do much in the way of identifying compromised applications that use network resources. And with the speed of evolution seen in the area of penetration tools, an approach designed simply to prevent attacks will be less and less effective.

Today's computing environment is no longer confined to the office, as it used to be. Though there are still fixed systems inside the firewall, ever more sophisticated remote and mobile devices are making their way into the workforce. This influx of mobile computing has expanded the traditional boundaries of the network to farther and farther reaches and requires a different way of thinking about network security requirements.

Your network's endpoint or perimeter is mutating—expanding beyond its historical boundaries. Until recently, that endpoint was the user, either a desktop system or laptop, and it was relatively easy to secure those devices. To use a metaphor: The difference between endpoints of early network design and those of today is like the difference between the battles of World War II and the current war on terror. In the World War II battles there were very clearly defined "front lines"—one side controlled by the Allied powers, the other by the Axis. Today, the war on terror has no such front lines and is fought in multiple areas with different techniques and strategies that are customized for each combat theater.

With today's explosion of remote users and mobile computing, your network's endpoint is no longer as clearly defined as it once was, and it is evolving at a very rapid pace. For this reason, your network's physical perimeter can no longer be seen as your best "last line of defense," even though having a robust perimeter security system is still a critical part of your overall security policy.

Any policy you develop should be organized in such a way as to take advantage of the strength of your unified threat management (UTM) system. Firewalls, antivirus, and intrusion detection systems (IDSs), for example,

work by trying to block all currently known threats—the "blacklist" approach. But the threats evolve more quickly than the UTM systems can, so it almost always ends up being an "after the fact" game of catch-up. Perhaps a better, and more easily managed, policy is to specifically state which devices are allowed access and which applications are allowed to run in your network's applications. This "whitelist" approach helps reduce the amount of time and energy needed to keep up with the rapidly evolving pace of threat sophistication, because you're specifying what gets in versus what you have to keep out.

Any UTM system you employ should provide the means of doing two things: specify which applications and devices are allowed and offer a policy-based approach to managing those applications and devices. It should allow you to secure your critical resources against unauthorized data extraction (or data leakage), offer protection from the most persistent threats (viruses, malware, and spyware), and evolve with the ever-changing spectrum of devices and applications designed to penetrate your outer defenses.

So, what's the best strategy for integrating these new remote endpoints? First, you have to realize that these new remote, mobile technologies are becoming increasingly ubiquitous and aren't going away anytime soon. In fact, they most likely represent the future of computing. As these devices gain in sophistication and function, they are unchaining end users from their desks and, for some businesses, are indispensable tools. iPhones, Blackberries, Palm Treos, and other smart phones and devices now have the capability to interface with corporate email systems, access networks, run enterprise-level applications, and do full-featured remote computing. As such, they also now carry an increased risk for network administrators due to loss or theft (especially if the device is unprotected by a robust authentication method) and unauthorized interception of their wireless signals from which data can be siphoned off.

To cope with the inherent risks, you engage an effective security policy for dealing with these devices: Under what conditions can they be used, how many of your users need to employ them, what levels and types of access will they have, and how will they be authenticated?

Solutions are available for adding strong authentication to users seeking access via wireless LANs. Tokens, either of the hardware or software variety, are used to identify the user to an authentication server for verification of their credentials. For example, SafeNet's SafeWord can handle incoming access requests from a wireless access point and, if the user is authenticated, pass them into the network.

Key among the steps you take to secure your network while allowing mobile computing is to fully educate the users of such technology. They need to understand, in no uncertain terms, the risks to your network (and ultimately to the company in general) represented by their mobile devices, and they also need to be aware that their mindfulness of both the device's physical and electronic security is an absolute necessity.

Network Security Best Practices

So, how do you either clean and tighten up your existing network, or design a new one that can stand up to the inevitable onslaught of attacks? Let's look at some basics. Consider the diagram shown in Figure 4.1.

Figure 4.1 shows what could be a typical network layout. Users outside the DMZ approach the network via a secure (HTTPS) Web or VPN connection. They are authenticated by the perimeter firewall and handed off to either a Web server or a virtual private network (VPN) gateway. If allowed to pass, they can then access resources inside the network.

If you're the administrator of an organization that has only, say, a couple dozen users with whom to contend, your task (and the illustration layout) will be relatively easy to manage. But if you have to manage several hundred (or several thousand) users, the complexity of your task increases by an order of magnitude. That makes a good security policy an absolute necessity.

9. SECURITY POLICIES

Like the tedious prep work before painting a room, organizations need a good, detailed, and well-written security policy. Not something that should be rushed through "just to get it done," your security policy should be well thought out; in other words, the "devil is in the details." Your security policy is designed to get everyone involved with your network "thinking along the same lines."

The policy is almost always a work in progress. It must evolve with technology, especially those technologies aimed at surreptitiously getting into your system. The threats will continue to evolve, as will the systems designed to hold them at bay.

A good security policy isn't always a single document; rather, it is a conglomeration of policies that address specific areas, such as computer and network use, forms of authentication, email policies, remote/mobile technology use, and Web surfing policies. It should be written in such a way that, while comprehensive, it can be easily understood by those it affects. Along those lines, your policy doesn't have to be overly complex. If you hand new employees something that resembles *War and Peace* in size and tell them they're responsible for knowing its content, you can expect to have continued problems maintaining good network security awareness. Keep it simple.

First, you need to draft some policies that define your network and its basic architecture. A good place to start is by asking the following questions:

- What kinds of resources need to be protected (user financial or medical data, credit-card information, etc.)?
- How many users will be accessing the network on the inside (employees, contractors, etc.)?

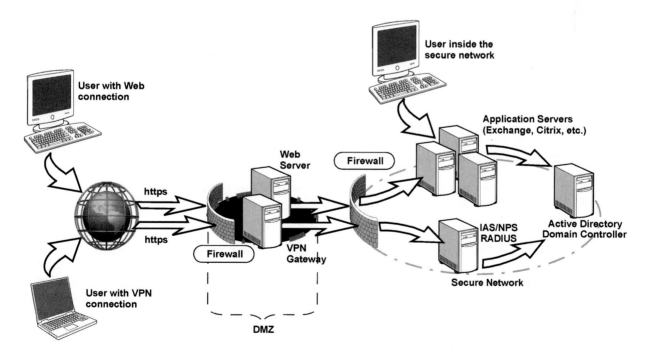

FIGURE 4.1 Network diagram.

- Will there need to be access only at certain times or on a 24/7 basis (and across multiple time zones and/or internationally)?
- What kind of budget do I have?
- Will remote users be accessing the network, and if so, how many?
- Will there be remote sites in geographically distant locations (requiring a failsafe mechanism, such as replication, to keep data synched across the network)?

Next, you should spell out responsibilities for security requirements, communicate your expectations to your users (one of the weakest links in any security policy), and lay out the role(s) for your network administrator. It should list policies for activities such as Web surfing, downloading, local and remote access, and types of authentication. You should address issues such as adding users, assigning privileges, dealing with lost tokens or compromised passwords, and under what circumstances you will remove users from the access database.

You should establish a security team (sometimes referred to as a "tiger team") whose responsibility it will be to create security policies that are practical, workable, and sustainable. They should come up with the best plan for implementing these policies in a way that addresses both network resource protection and user friendliness. They should develop plans for responding to threats as well as schedules for updating equipment and software. And there should be a very clear policy for handling changes to overall network security—the types of connections through your firewall that will and will not be allowed. This is especially important because you don't want an unauthorized user gaining access, reaching into your network, and simply taking files or data.

10. RISK ANALYSIS

You should have some kind of risk analysis done to determine, as near as possible, the risks you face with the kind of operations you conduct (e-commerce, classified/proprietary information handling, partner access, or the like). Depending on the determined risk, you might need to rethink your original network design. Although a simple extranet/intranet setup with mid-level firewall protection might be okay for a small business that doesn't have much to steal, that obviously won't work for a company that deals with user financial data or proprietary/classified information. In that case, what might be needed is a tiered system in which you have a "corporate side" (on which things such as email, intranet access, and regular Internet access are handled) and a separate, secure network not connected to the Internet or corporate side. These networks can only be accessed by a user on a physical machine, and data can only be moved to them by

"sneaker-net" physical media (scanned for viruses before opening). These networks can be used for data systems such as test or lab machines (on which, for example, new software builds are done and must be more tightly controlled, to prevent inadvertent corruption of the corporate side), or networks on which the storage or processing of proprietary, business-critical, or classified information are handled. In Department of Defense parlance, these are sometimes referred to as *red nets* or *black nets.*

Vulnerability Testing

Your security policy should include regular vulnerability testing. Some very good vulnerability testing tools, such as WebInspect, Acunetix, GFI LANguard, Nessus, HFNetChk, and Tripwire, allow you to conduct your own security testing. Furthermore, there are third-party companies with the most advanced suite of testing tools available that can be contracted to scan your network for open and/or accessible ports, weaknesses in firewalls, and Web site vulnerability.

Audits

You should also factor in regular, detailed audits of all activities, with emphasis on those that seem to be near or outside established norms. For example, audits that reveal high rates of data exchanges after normal business hours, when that kind of traffic would not normally be expected, is something that should be investigated. Perhaps, after checking, you'll find that it's nothing more than an employee downloading music or video files. But the point is that your audit system saw the increase in traffic and determined it to be a simple Internet use policy violation rather than someone siphoning off more critical data.

There should be clearly established rules for dealing with security, use, and/or policy violations as well as attempted or actual intrusions. Trying to figure out what to do after the intrusion is too late. And if an intrusion does occur, there should be a clear-cut system for determining the extent of damage; isolation of the exploited application, port, or machine; and a rapid response to closing the hole against further incursions.

Recovery

Your plan should also address the issue of recovery after an attack has occurred. You need to address issues such as how the network will be reconfigured to close off the exploited opening. This might take some time, since the entry point might not be immediately discernible. There has to be an estimate of damage—what was taken or compromised, was malicious code implanted somewhere, and, if so, how to most efficiently extract it and clean the affected system. In the case of a virus in a company's email system, the ability to send and receive email could be halted for days while infected systems are rebuilt. And there will have to be discussions about how to reconstruct the network if the attack decimated files and systems.

This will most likely involve more than simply reinstalling machines from archived backups. Because the compromise will most likely affect normal business operations, the need to expedite the recovery will hamper efforts to fully analyze just what happened.

This is the main reason for preemptively writing a disaster recovery plan and making sure that all departments are represented in its drafting. However, like the network security policy itself, the disaster recovery plan will also be a work in progress that should be reviewed regularly to ensure that it meets the current needs. Things such as new threat notifications, software patches and updates, vulnerability assessments, new application roll-outs, and employee turnover all have to be addressed.

11. TOOLS OF YOUR TRADE

Although the tools available to people seeking unauthorized entry into your domain are impressive, you also have a wide variety of tools to help keep them out. Before implementing a network security strategy, however, you must be acutely aware of the specific needs of those who will be using your resources.

Simple antispyware and antispam tools aren't enough. In today's rapidly changing software environment, strong security requires penetration shielding, threat signature recognition, autonomous reaction to identified threats, and the ability to upgrade your tools as the need arises.

The following section describes some of the more common tools you should consider adding to your arsenal.

Intrusion Detection Systems (IDSs)

As discussed earlier in the chapter, it's no longer good enough to have solid defenses. You also need to know when you've been penetrated—and the sooner, the better. Statistics paint a dismal picture. According to Verizon's threat report, less than 5 percent of cybersecurity breaches are detected within hours of the assault, and 80 percent weren't found for weeks, or months.[9] Bret Hartman, RSA's chief technology officer said, in a recent interview, that there's a new "shift in the level of paranoia to assume that you're always in a state of partial compromise."

A good IDS detects unauthorized intrusions using one of three types of models: anomaly-based, signature-based, and hybrid detection.

9. CNNMoney Tech, February 28, 2012.

- Anomaly-based systems learn what's "normal" for a given network environment, so that they can quickly detect the "abnormal."
- Signature-based systems look for slight variations, or signatures, of suspicious network activity;
- Hybrid detection systems are currently in development which compensate for weaknesses of both anomaly and signature-based systems by combining the best of both.

Firewalls

Your first line of defense should be a good firewall, or better yet, a system that effectively incorporates several security features in one. Secure Firewall (formerly Sidewinder) from Secure Computing is one of the strongest and most secure firewall products available, and as of this writing it has never been successfully hacked. It is trusted and used by government and defense agencies. Secure Firewall combines the five most necessary security systems—firewall, antivirus/spyware/spam, VPN, application filtering, and intrusion prevention/detection systems—into a single appliance.

Intrusion Prevention Systems

A good *intrusion prevention system* (IPS) is a vast improvement over a basic firewall in that it can, among other things, be configured with policies that allow it to make autonomous decisions as to how to deal with application-level threats as well as simple IP address or port-level attacks.

IPS products respond directly to incoming threats in a variety of ways, from automatically dropping (extracting) suspicious packets (while still allowing legitimate ones to pass) to, in some cases, placing an intruder into a "quarantine" file. IPS, like an application layer firewall, can be considered another form of access control in that it can make pass/fail decisions on application content.

For an IPS to be effective, it must also be very good at discriminating between a real threat signature and one that looks like but isn't one (false positive). Once a signature interpreted to be an intrusion is detected, the system must quickly notify the administrator so that the appropriate evasive action can be taken. The following are types of IPS.

- *Network-based.* Network-based IPSs create a series of choke points in the enterprise that detect suspected intrusion attempt activity. Placed inline at their needed locations, they invisibly monitor network traffic for known attack signatures that they then block.
- *Host-based.* These systems don't reside on the network per se but rather on servers and individual

machines. They quietly monitor activities and requests from applications, weeding out actions deemed prohibited in nature. These systems are often very good at identifying post-decryption entry attempts.

- *Content-based.* These IPSs scan network packets, looking for signatures of content that is unknown or unrecognized or that has been explicitly labeled threatening in nature.
- *Rate-based.* These IPSs look for activity that falls outside the range of normal levels, such as activity that seems to be related to password cracking and brute-force penetration attempts, for example.

When searching for a good IPS, look for one that provides, at minimum:

- Robust protection for your applications, host systems, and individual network elements against exploitation of vulnerability-based threats as "single-bullet attacks," Trojan horses, worms, botnets, and surreptitious creation of "back doors" in your network.
- Protection against threats that exploit vulnerabilities in specific applications such as Web services, mail, DNS, SQL, and any Voice over IP (VoIP) services.
- Detection and elimination of spyware, phishing, and anonymizers (tools that hide a source computer's identifying information so that Internet activity can be undertaken surreptitiously).
- Protection against brute-force and DoS attacks, application scanning, and flooding.
- A regular method of updating threat lists and signatures.

Application Firewalls

Application firewalls (AFs) are sometimes confused with IPSs in that they can perform IPS-like functions. But an AF is specifically designed to limit or deny an application's level of access to a system's OS—in other words, closing any openings into a computer's OS to deny the execution of harmful code within an OS's structure. AFs work by looking at applications themselves, monitoring the kind of data flow from an application for suspicious or administrator-blocked content from specific Web sites, application-specific viruses, and any attempt to exploit an identified weakness in an application's architecture. Though AF systems can conduct intrusion prevention duties, they typically employ proxies to handle firewall access control and focus on traditional firewall-type functions. Application firewalls can detect the signatures of recognized threats and block them before they can infect the network.

Windows' version of an application firewall, called Data Execution Prevention (DEP), prevents the execution of any code that uses system services in such a way that could be deemed harmful to data or virtual memory (VM). It does this by considering RAM data as nonexecutable—in essence, refusing to run new code coming from the data-only area of RAM, since any harmful or malicious code seeking to damage existing data would have to run from this area.

The Macintosh Operating System (MacOS) also includes a built-in application firewall as a standard feature. The user can configure it to employ two-layer protection in which installing network-aware applications will result in an OS-generated warning that prompts for user authorization of network access. If authorized, MacOS will digitally sign the application in such a way that subsequent application activity will not prompt for further authorization. Updates invalidate the original certificate, and the user will have to revalidate before the application can run again.

The Linux OS has, for example, an application firewall called AppArmor that allows the administrator to create and link to every application a security policy that restricts its access capabilities.

Access Control Systems

Access control systems (ACSs) rely on administrator-defined rules that allow or restrict user access to protected network resources. These access rules can, for example, require strong user authentication such as tokens or biometric devices to prove the identity of users requesting access. They can also restrict access to various network services based on time of day or group need.

Some ACS products allow for the creation of an *access control list* (ACL), which is a set of rules that define security policy. These ACLs contain one or more *access control entries* (ACEs), which are the actual rule definitions themselves. These rules can restrict access by specific user, time of day, IP address, function (department, management level, etc.), or specific system from which a logon or access attempt is being made.

A good example of an ACS is SafeWord by Aladdin Knowledge Systems. SafeWord is considered a two-factor authentication system in that it uses what the user knows (such as a personal identification number, or PIN) and what the user has (such as a one-time passcode, or OTP, token) to strongly authenticate users requesting network access. SafeWord allows administrators to design customized access rules and restrictions to network resources, applications, and information.

In this scheme, the tokens are a key component. The token's internal cryptographic key algorithm is made "known" to an authentication server when the token's file is imported into a central database.

When the token is assigned to a user, its serial number is linked to that user in the user's record. On making an access request, the authentication server prompts the user to enter a username and the OTP generated by the token. If a PIN was also assigned to that user, she must either prepend or append that PIN to the token-generated passcode. As long as the authentication server receives what it expects, the user is granted whatever access privileges she was assigned.

Unified Threat Management

The latest trend to emerge in the network intrusion prevention arena is referred to as *unified threat management*, or UTM. UTM systems are multilayered and incorporate several security technologies into a single platform, often in the form of a plug-in appliance. UTM products can provide such diverse capabilities as antivirus, VPN, firewall services, and antispam as well as intrusion prevention.

The biggest advantages of a UTM system are its ease of operation and configuration and the fact that its security features can be quickly updated to meet rapidly evolving threats.

Sidewinder by Secure Computing is a UTM system that was designed to be flexible, easily and quickly adaptable, and easy to manage. It incorporates firewall, VPN, trusted source, IPS, antispam and antivirus, URL filtering, SSL decryption, and auditing/reporting.

Other UTM systems include Symantec's Enterprise Firewall and Gateway Security Enterprise Firewall Appliance, Fortinet, LokTek's AIRlok Firewall Appliance, and SonicWall's NSA 240 UTM Appliance, to name a few.

12. CONTROLLING USER ACCESS

Traditionally users—also known as employees—have been the weakest link in a company's defensive armor. Though necessary to the organization, they can be a nightmare waiting to happen to your network. How do you let them work within the network while controlling their access to resources? You have to make sure your system of user authentication knows who your users are.

Authentication, Authorization, and Accounting

Authentication is simply proving that a user's identity claim is valid and authentic. Authentication requires some form of "proof of identity." In network technologies, physical proof (such as a driver's license or other photo ID) cannot be employed, so you have to get something else from a user. That typically means having the user respond to a challenge to provide genuine credentials at the time he or she requests access.

For our purposes, credentials can be something the user knows, something the user has, or something they are. Once they provide authentication, there also has to be authorization, or permission to enter. Finally, you want to have some record of users' entry into your network—username, time of entry, and resources. That is the accounting side of the process.

What the User Knows

Users know a great many details about their own lives—birthdays, anniversaries, first cars, their spouse's name—and many will try to use these nuggets of information as a simple form of authentication. What they don't realize is just how insecure those pieces of information are.

In network technologies, these pieces of information are often used as fixed passwords and PINs because they're easy to remember. Unless some strict guidelines are established on what form a password or PIN can take (for example, a minimum number of characters or a mixture of letters and numbers), a password will offer little to no real security.

Unfortunately, to hold down costs, some organizations allow users to set their own passwords and PINs as credentials, then rely on a simple challenge-response mechanism in which these weak credentials are provided to gain access. Adding to the loss of security is the fact that not only are the fixed passwords far too easy to guess, but because the user already has too much to remember, she writes them down somewhere near the computer she uses (often in some "cryptic" scheme to make it more difficult to guess). To increase the effectiveness of any security system, that system needs to require a much stronger form of authentication.

What the User Has

The most secure means of identifying users is by a combination of (1) a hardware device in their possession that is "known" to an authentication server in your network, coupled with (2) what they know. A whole host of devices available today—tokens, smart cards, biometric devices—are designed to more positively identify a user. Since a good token is the most secure of these options, let us focus on them here.

Tokens

A *token* is a device that employs an encrypted key for which the encryption algorithm—the method of generating an encrypted password—is known to a network's authentication server. There are both software and hardware tokens. The software tokens can be installed on a user's desktop system, in the cellular phone, or on the smart phone. The hardware tokens come in a variety of form factors, some with a single button that both turns the token on and displays its internally generated passcode; others have a more elaborate numerical keypad for PIN input. If lost or stolen, tokens can easily be removed from the system, quickly rendering them completely ineffective. And the passcodes they generate are of the "one-time-passcode," or OTP, variety, meaning that a generated passcode expires once it's been used and cannot be used again for a subsequent logon attempt.

Tokens are either programmed onsite with token programming software or offsite at the time they are ordered from their vendor. During programming, functions such as a token's cryptographic key, password length, whether a PIN is required, and whether it generates passwords based on internal clock timing or user PIN input are written into the token's memory. When programming is complete, a file containing this information and the token's serial number are imported into the authentication server so that the token's characteristics are known.

A token is assigned to a user by linking its serial number to the user's record, stored in the system database. When a user logs onto the network and needs access to, say, her email, she is presented with some challenge that she must answer using her assigned token.

Tokens operate in one of three ways: time synchronous, event synchronous, or challenge-response (also known as asynchronous).

Time Synchronous

In time synchronous operations, the token's internal clock is synched with the network's clock. Each time the token's button is pressed, it generates a passcode in hash form, based on its internal timekeeping. As long as the token's clock is synched with the network clock, the passcodes are accepted. In some cases (for example, when the token hasn't been used for some time or its battery dies), the token gets out of synch with the system and needs to be resynched before it can be used again.

Event Synchronous

In event synchronous operations, the server maintains an ordered passcode sequence and determines which passcode is valid based on the current location in that sequence.

Challenge-Response

In challenge-response, a challenge, prompting for username, is issued to the user by the authentication server at the time of access request. Once the user's name is entered, the authentication server checks to see what form of authentication is assigned to that user and issues a challenge back to the user. The user inputs the challenge into the token, then enters the token's generated response to the challenge. As long as the authentication server receives what it expected, authentication is successful and access is granted.

The User is Authenticated, but is She/He Authorized?

Authorization is independent of authentication. A user can be permitted entry into the network but not be authorized to access a resource. You don't want an employee having access to HR information or a corporate partner getting access to confidential or proprietary information.

Authorization requires a set of rules that dictate the resources to which a user will have access. These permissions are established in your security policy.

Accounting

Say that our user has been granted access to the requested resource. But you want (or in some cases are required to have) the ability to call up and view activity logs to see who got into what resource. This information is mandated for organizations that deal with user financial or medical information or DoD classified information or that go through annual inspections to maintain certification for international operations.

Accounting refers to the recording, logging, and archiving of all server activity, especially activity related to access attempts and whether they were successful. This information should be written into audit logs that are stored and available any time you want or need to view them. The audit logs should contain, at minimum, the following information:

- The user's identity
- The date and time of the request
- Whether the request passed authentication and was granted

Any network security system you put into place should store, or archive, these logs for a specified period of time and allow you to determine for how long these archives will be maintained before they start to age out of the system.

Keeping Current

One of the best ways to stay ahead is to not fall behind in the first place. New systems with increasing sophistication are being developed all the time. They can incorporate a more intelligent and autonomous process in the way the system handles a detected threat, a faster and more easily accomplished method for updating threat files, and configuration flexibility that allows for very precise customization of access rules, authentication requirements, user role assignment, and how tightly it can protect specific applications.

Register for newsletters, attend seminars and network security shows, read white papers, and, if needed, contract the services of network security specialists. The point is, you shouldn't go cheap on network security. The price you pay to keep ahead will be far less than the price you pay to recover from a security breach or attack.

Finally, let's briefly look at how host-based IPS agents offer various intrusion prevention capabilities. The following describes common intrusion prevention capabilities.

13. INTRUSION PREVENTION CAPABILITIES

As previously mentioned, host-based IPS agents offer various intrusion prevention capabilities. Because the capabilities vary based on the detection techniques used by each product, the following activities (see checklist: An Agenda for Action for Intrusion Prevention Activities") describe the capabilities by detection technique.

14. SUMMARY

This chapter has made it very apparent that preventing network intrusions is no easy task. Like cops on the street—usually outnumbered and underequipped compared to the bad guys—you face enemies with determination, skill, training, and a frightening array of increasingly sophisticated tools for hacking their way through your best defenses. And no matter how good your defenses are today, it's only a matter of time before a tool is developed that can penetrate them. If you know that ahead of time, you'll be much more inclined to keep a watchful eye for what "they" have and what you can use to defeat them.

Your best weapon is a logical, thoughtful, and nimble approach to network security. You have to be nimble—to evolve and grow with changes in technology, never being content to keep things as they are because "Hey, they're working just fine." Well, today's "just fine" will be tomorrow's "What the hell happened?"

Stay informed. There is no shortage of information available to you in the form of white papers, seminars, contract security specialists, and online resources, all dealing with various aspects of network security.

Invest in a good intrusion detection system. You want to know, as soon as possible, that a breach has occurred, what was stolen, and, if possible, where it went.

An Agenda for Action for Intrusion Prevention Activities

From the organizational perspective, preventing intrusions includes the following key activities (check all tasks completed):

_____1. **Code Analysis:** The code analysis techniques can prevent code from being executed, including malware and unauthorized applications.

_____2. **Network Traffic Analysis:** This can stop incoming network traffic from being processed by the host and outgoing network traffic from exiting it.

_____3. **Network Traffic Filtering:** Working as a host-based firewall, this can stop unauthorized access and acceptable use policy violations (use of inappropriate external services).

_____4. **Filesystem Monitoring:** This can prevent files from being accessed, modified, replaced, or deleted, which could stop malware installation, including Trojan horses and rootkits, as well as other attacks involving inappropriate file access.

_____5. **Removable Media Restriction:** Some products can enforce restrictions on the use of removable media, both Universal Serial Bus (USB-based (flash drive)) and traditional (CD). This can prevent malware or other unwanted files from being transferred to a host and can also stop sensitive files from being copied from the host to removable media.

_____6. **Audiovisual Device Monitoring**: A few host-based IPS products can detect when a host's audiovisual devices, such as microphones, cameras, or IP-based phones, are activated or used. This could indicate that the host has been compromised by an attacker.

_____7. **Host Hardening**: Some host-based intrusion detection and prevention systems (IDPSs) can automatically harden hosts on an ongoing basis. For example, if an application is reconfigured, causing a particular security function to be disabled, the IDPS could detect this and enable the security function.

_____8. **Process Status Monitoring**: Some products monitor the status of processes or services running on a host, and if they detect that one has stopped, they restart it automatically. Some products can also monitor the status of security programs such as antivirus software.

_____9. **Network Traffic Sanitization**: Some agents, particularly those deployed on appliances, can sanitize the network traffic that they monitor. For example, an appliance-based agent could act as a proxy and rebuild each request and response that is directed through it. This can be effective at neutralizing certain unusual activity, particularly in packet headers and application protocol headers.

Have a good, solid, comprehensive, yet easy-to-understand network security policy in place. The very process of developing one will get all involved parties thinking about how to best secure your network while addressing user needs. When it comes to your users, you simply can't overeducate them where network security awareness is concerned. The more they know, the better equipped they'll be to act as allies against, rather than accomplices of, the hordes of crackers looking to steal, damage, hobble, or completely cripple your network.

Do your research and invest in good, multipurpose network security systems. Select systems that are easy to install and implement, are adaptable and quickly configurable, can be customized to suit your needs of today as well as tomorrow, and are supported by companies that keep pace with current trends in cracker technology.

Finally, let's move on to the real interactive part of this chapter: review questions/exercises, hands-on projects, case projects and optional team case project. The answers and/or solutions by chapter can be found in the Online Instructor's Solutions Manual.

CHAPTER REVIEW QUESTIONS/EXERCISES

True/False

1. True or False? A network intrusion is an authorized penetration of your enterprise's network, or an individual machine address in your assigned domain.
2. True or False? In some cases, a network intrusion could be done from the inside by a disgruntled employee looking to hurt the organization or steal company secrets for profit.
3. True or False? Most security software products available today have two basic methods of spotting malicious software.
4. True or False? Crackers are going to first look for known strengths in the operating system (OS) or any applications you are using.
5. True or False? Finding a device, using it in a place (or manner) in which prying eyes can see passwords or data, awareness of hacking tools specifically designed to sniff wireless signals for data, and logging on to unsecured networks, are all potential problem areas with which users need to be familiar.

Multiple Choice

1. Which devices can locate wireless signals within a certain range, where they can siphon off the data being transmitted over the signals?
   A. Wireless sniffers
   B. Packet sniffers
   C. Port scanners
   D. Port knocking
   E. Keystroke loggers
2. You can expect to have continued problems maintaining good network security awareness. Keep it simple. You need to draft some policies that define your network and its basic architecture. A good place to start is by asking the following questions, except which one?
   A. What kinds of resources need to be protected (user financial or medical data, credit-card information, etc.)?
   B. How many users will be accessing the network on the inside (employees, contractors, etc.)?
   C. Will there need to be access only at certain times or on a 24/7 basis (and across multiple time zones and/or internationally)?
   D. What kind of budget do I have?
   E. Will internal users be accessing the network, and if so, how many?
3. A good IDS detects unauthorized intrusions using three types of models:
   A. Anomaly-based
   B. Signature-based
   C. Network-based
   D. Hybrid detection
   E. Host-based
4. For an IPS to be effective, it must also be very good at discriminating between a real threat signature and one that looks like but isn't one (false positive). Once a signature interpreted to be an intrusion is detected, the system must quickly notify the administrator so that the appropriate evasive action can be taken. The following are types of IPS, except one:
   A. Network-based
   B. Rate-based
   C. Host-based
   D. Backdoor-based
   E. Content-based
5. The latest trend to emerge in the network intrusion prevention arena is referred to as:
   A. antivirus.
   B. unified threat management.
   C. VPN.
   D. firewall services.
   E. antispam.

EXERCISE

Problem

Determine how an information system could prevent non-privileged users from circumventing intrusion prevention capabilities.

Hands-On Projects

Project

To safeguard its intellectual property and business, a pharmaceutical company had to keep pace with an increasingly sophisticated threat landscape of malware and viruses, as well as complex security legislation across its multiple sites. Please describe what type of intrusion prevention capabilities/services the company implemented.

Case Projects

Problem

A large medical center sought a powerful security solution that could continuously protect its high-throughput network without compromising network performance. It also required a healthy network: one that is safe from hackers, worms, viruses, and spyware, that can compromise the performance of the medical's life-critical applications or the federally mandated confidentiality of its medical records. In addition, the security system needed to be cost-effective and interoperate transparently with the medical center's multivendor infrastructure. In this case project, how would an intrusion prevention system (IPS) provide the pervasive and proactive protection that the medical center required?

Optional Team Case Project

Problem

With so much at stake, companies of all sizes are taking a closer look at intrusion prevention systems (IPSs) security solutions. In order to sift through the claims and separate the intrusion prevention contenders from the pretenders, the companies need to ask potential vendors a number of obvious basic questions first. Please list the basic IPS questions that a company might ask their vendors?

## Chapter 5

Guarding Against Network Intrusions

Thomas M. Chen
Swansea University

Patrick J. Walsh
eSoft Inc.

Virtually all computers today are connected to the Internet through dialup, broadband, Ethernet, or wireless technologies. The reason for ubiquitous Internet connectivity is simple: Applications depending on the network, such as email, Web, remote login, instant messaging, social networking, and VoIP, have become essential to everyday computing. Unfortunately, the Internet exposes computer users to risks from a wide variety of possible threats. Users have much to lose—their privacy, valuable data, control of their computers, and possibly theft of their identities. The network enables attacks to be carried out remotely from anywhere in the world, with relative anonymity and low risk of traceability.

The nature of network intrusions has evolved over the years. A few years ago, a major concern was fast worms such as Code Red, Nimda, Slammer, and Sobig. More recently, concerns have shifted to spyware, Trojan horses, and botnets. Although these other threats = continue to be major problems, the Web has become the primary vector for stealthy attacks today.[1]

1. TRADITIONAL RECONNAISSANCE AND ATTACKS

Traditionally, attack methods follow sequential steps analogous to physical attacks, as shown in Figure 5.1: reconnaissance; compromise; and cover-up.[2] Here we are only addressing attacks directed at a specific target host. Some other types of attacks, such as worms or malicious Web sites, are not directed at specific targets. Instead, they attempt to hit as many targets as quickly as possible without caring about who or what the targets are.

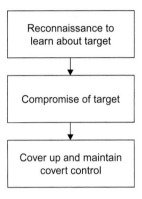

FIGURE 5.1 Steps in directed attacks.

In the first step of a directed attack, the attacker performs reconnaissance to learn as much as possible about the chosen target before carrying out an actual attack. A thorough reconnaissance can lead to a more effective attack because the target's weaknesses can be discovered. One might expect the reconnaissance phase to possibly tip off the target about an impending attack, but scans and probes are going on constantly in the "background noise" of Internet traffic, so systems administrators might ignore attack probes as too troublesome to investigate.

Through pings and traceroutes, an attacker can discover IP addresses and map the network around the target. Pings are ICMP echo request and echo reply messages that verify a host's IP address and availability. Traceroute is a network mapping utility that takes advantage of the time-to-live (TTL) field in IP packets. It sends out packets with TTL = 1, then TTL = 2, and so on. When the packets expire, the routers along the packets' path report that the packets have been discarded, returning ICMP "time exceeded" messages and thereby allowing the traceroute utility to learn the IP addresses of routers at a distance of one hop, two hops, and so on.

1. Marc Fossi et al., *Symantec Global Internet Security Threat Report*, Volume 16, 2010, available at www.symantec.com (date of access: March 1, 2012).
2. Ed Skoudis, *Counter Hack Reloaded: A Step-by-Step Guide to Computer Attacks and Effective Defenses*, 2nd ed., Prentice Hall, 2006.

Port scans can reveal open ports. Normally, a host might be expected to have certain well-known ports open, such as TCP port 80 (HTTP), TCP port 21 (FTP), TCP port 23 (Telnet), or TCP port 25 (SMTP). A host might also happen to have open ports in the higher range. For example, port 12345 is the default port used by the Netbus remote access Trojan horse, or port 31337 is the default port used by the Back Orifice remote access Trojan horse. Discovery of ports indicating previous malware infections could obviously help an attacker considerably.

In addition to discovering open ports, the popular NMAP scanner (www.insecure.org/nmap) can discover the operating system running on a target. NMAP uses a large set of heuristic rules to identify an operating system based on a target's responses to carefully crafted TCP/IP probes. The basic idea is that different operating systems will make different responses to probes to open TCP/UDP ports and malformed TCP/IP packets. Knowledge of a target's operating system can help an attacker identify vulnerabilities and find effective exploits.

Vulnerability scanning tests a target for the presence of vulnerabilities. Vulnerability scanners such as SATAN, SARA, SAINT, and Nessus typically contain a database of known vulnerabilities that is used to craft probes to a chosen target. The popular Nessus tool (www.nessus.org) has an extensible plug-in architecture to add checks for backdoors, misconfiguration errors, default accounts and passwords, and other types of vulnerabilities.

In the second step of a directed attack, the attacker attempts to compromise the target through one or more methods. Password attacks are common because passwords might be based on common words or names and are guessable by a dictionary attack, although computer systems today have better password policies that forbid easily guessable passwords. If an attacker can obtain the password file from the target, numerous password-cracking tools are available to carry out a brute-force password attack. In addition, computers and networking equipment often ship with default accounts and passwords intended to help systems administrators set up the equipment. These default accounts and passwords are easy to find on the Web (for example, www.phenoelit-us.org/dpl/dpl.html). Occasionally, users might neglect to change or delete the default accounts, offering intruders an easy way to access the target.

Another common attack method is an exploit attack code written to take advantage of a specific vulnerability.[3] Many types of software, including operating systems and applications, have vulnerabilities. Symantec discovered 6253 vulnerabilities in 2010, or 17 vulnerabilities per day on average.[4] Vulnerabilities are published by several organizations such as CERT and MITRE, as well as vendors such as Microsoft, through security bulletins. MITRE maintains a database of publicly known vulnerabilities identified by common vulnerabilities and exposures (CVE) numbers. The severity of vulnerabilities is reflected in the industry-standard common vulnerability scoring system (CVSS). In the first half of 2011, Microsoft observed that 44 percent of vulnerabilities were highly severe, 49 percent were medium-severe, and 7 percent were low-severe.[5] Furthermore, about 45 percent of vulnerabilities were easily exploitable.

Historically, buffer overflows have been the most common type of vulnerability.[6] They have been popular because buffer overflow exploits can often be carried out remotely and lead to complete compromise of a target. The problem arises when a program has allocated a fixed amount of memory space (such as in the stack) for storing data but receives more data than expected. If the vulnerability exists, the extra data will overwrite adjacent parts of memory, which could mess up other variables or pointers. If the extra data is random, the computer might crash or act unpredictably. However, if an attacker crafts the extra data carefully, the buffer overflow could overwrite adjacent memory in a way that benefits the attacker. For instance, an attacker might overwrite the return pointer in a stack, causing the program control to jump to malicious code inserted by the attacker.

An effective buffer overflow exploit requires technical knowledge of the computer architecture and operating system, but once the exploit code is written, it can be reused. Buffer overflows can be prevented by the programmer or compiler performing bounds checking or during runtime. Although C/C++ has received a good deal of blame as a programming language for not having built-in checking that data written to arrays stays within bounds, buffer overflow vulnerabilities appear in a wide variety of other programs, too.

Structured Query Language (SQL) injection is a type of vulnerability relevant to Web servers with a database backend.[7] SQL is an internationally standardized interactive and programming language for querying data and managing databases. Many commercial database products support SQL, sometimes with proprietary extensions. Web applications often take user input (usually from a Web form) and pass the input into an SQL statement. An

3. S. McClure, J. Scambray, and G. Kutz, *Hacking Exposed*, 3rd ed., McGraw-Hill, 2001.

4. Marc Fossi et al., *Symantec Global Internet Security Threat Report*, Volume 16, 2010, available at www.symantec.com (date of access: March 1, 2012).

5. Joe Faulhaber et al., *Microsoft Security Intelligence Report*, Volume 11, available at www.microsoft.com (date of access: March 1, 2012).

6. J. Foster, V. Osipov, and N. Bhalla, *Buffer Overflow Attacks: Detect, Exploit, Prevent*, Syngress Publishing, 2005.

7 D. Litchfield, *SQL Server Security*, McGraw-Hill Osborne, 2003.

SQL injection vulnerability can arise if user input is not properly filtered for string literal escape characters, which can allow an attacker to craft input that is interpreted as embedded SQL statements and thereby manipulate the application running on the database.

Servers have been attacked and compromised by toolkits designed to automate customized attacks. For example, the MPack toolkit emerged in early 2007 and is sold commercially in Russia, along with technical support and regular software updates. It is loaded into a malicious or compromised Web site. When a visitor goes to the site, a malicious code is launched through an iframe (inline frame) within the HTML code. It can launch various exploits, expandable through modules, for vulnerabilities in Web browsers and client software.

Metasploit (www.metasploit.com) is a popular Perl-based tool for developing and using exploits with an easy-to-use Web or command-line interface. Different exploits can be written and loaded into Metasploit and then directed at a chosen target. Exploits can be bundled with a payload (the code to run on a compromised target) selected from a collection of payloads. The tool also contains utilities to experiment with new vulnerabilities and help automate the development of new exploits.

Although exploits are commonplace, not all attacks require an exploit. *Social engineering* refers to types of attacks that take advantage of human nature to compromise a target, typically through deceit. A common social engineering attack is *phishing*, used in identity theft.[8] Phishing starts with a lure, usually a spam message that appears to be from a legitimate bank or e-commerce business. The message attempts to provoke the reader into visiting a fraudulent Web site pretending to be a legitimate business. These fraudulent sites are often set up by automated phishing toolkits that spoof legitimate sites of various brands, including the graphics of those brands. The fraudulent site might even have links to the legitimate Web site, to appear more valid. Victims are thus tricked into submitting valuable personal information such as account numbers, passwords, and Social Security numbers.

Other common examples of social engineering are spam messages that entice the reader into opening an email attachment. Most people know by now that attachments could be dangerous, perhaps containing a virus or spyware, even if they appear to be innocent at first glance. But if the message is sufficiently convincing, such as appearing to originate from an acquaintance, even wary users might be tricked into opening an attachment. Social engineering attacks can be simple but effective because they target people and bypass technological defenses.

The third step of traditional directed attacks involves cover-up of evidence of the compromise and establishment of covert control. After a successful attack, intruders want to maintain remote control and evade detection. Remote control can be maintained if the attacker has managed to install any of a number of types of malicious software: a backdoor such as Netcat; a remote access Trojan such as BO2K or SubSeven; or a bot, usually listening for remote instructions on an Internet relay chat (IRC) channel, such as phatbot.

Intruders obviously prefer to evade detection after a successful compromise, because detection will lead the victim to take remedial actions to harden or disinfect the target. Intruders might change the system logs on the target, which will likely contain evidence of their attack. In Windows, the main event logs are secevent.evt, sysevent.evt, and appevent.evt. A systems administrator looking for evidence of intrusions would look in these files with the built-in Windows Event Viewer or a third-party log viewer. An intelligent intruder would not delete the logs but would selectively delete information in the logs to hide signs of malicious actions.

A *rootkit* is a stealthy type of malicious software (*malware*) designed to hide the existence of certain processes or programs from normal methods of detection.[9] Rootkits essentially alter the target's operating system, perhaps by changing drivers or dynamic link libraries (DLLs) and possibly at the kernel level. An example is the kernel-mode FU rootkit that manipulates kernel memory in Windows 2000, XP, and 2003. It consists of a device driver, msdirectx.sys, that might be mistaken for Microsoft's DirectX tool. The rootkit can hide certain events and processes and change the privileges of running processes.

If an intruder has installed malware for covert control, he will want to conceal the communications between himself and the compromised target from discovery by network-based *intrusion detection systems* (IDSs). Intrusion detection systems are designed to listen to network traffic and look for signs of suspicious activities. Several concealment methods are used in practice. *Tunneling* is a commonly used method to place packets of one protocol into the payload of another packet. The "exterior" packet serves a vehicle to carry and deliver the "interior" packet intact. Though the protocol of the exterior packet is easily understood by an IDS, the interior protocol can be any number of possibilities and hence difficult to interpret.

Encryption is another obvious concealment method. Encryption relies on the secrecy of an encryption key

8. Markus Jakobsson and Steven Meyers, eds., *Phishing and Countermeasures: Understanding the Increasing Problem of Electronic Identity Theft*, Wiley-Interscience, 2006.

9. Greg Hoglund and Jamie Butler, *Rootkits: Subverting the Windows Kernel*, Addison-Wesley Professional, 2005.

shared between the intruder and the compromised target. The encryption key is used to mathematically scramble the communications into a form that is unreadable without the key to decrypt it. Encryption ensures secrecy in practical terms but does not guarantee perfect security. Encryption keys can be guessed, but the time to guess the correct key increases exponentially with the key length. Long keys combined with an algorithm for periodically changing keys can ensure that encrypted communications will be difficult to break within a reasonable time.

Fragmentation of IP packets is another means to conceal the contents of messages from IDSs, which often do not bother to reassemble fragments. IP packets may normally be fragmented into smaller packets anywhere along a route and reassembled at the destination. An IDS can become confused with a flood of fragments, bogus fragments, or deliberately overlapping fragments.

2. MALICIOUS SOFTWARE

Malicious software, or malware, continues to be an enormous problem for Internet users because of its variety and prevalence and the level of danger it presents.[10,11,12] It is important to realize that malware can take many forms. A large class of malware is *infectious*, which includes viruses and worms. Viruses and worms are self-replicating, meaning that they spread from host to host by making copies of themselves. Viruses are pieces of code attached to a normal file or program. When the program is run, the virus code is executed and copies itself to (or infects) another file or program. It is often said that viruses need a human action to spread, whereas worms are standalone automated programs. Worms look for vulnerable targets across the network and transfer a copy of themselves if a target is successfully compromised.

Historically, several worms have become well known and stimulated concerns over the possibility of a fast epidemic infecting Internet-connected hosts before defenses could stop it. The 1988 Robert Morris Jr. worm infected thousands of Unix hosts, at the time a significant portion of the Arpanet (the predecessor to the Internet). The 1999 Melissa worm infected Microsoft Word documents and emailed itself to addresses found in a victim's Outlook address book. Melissa demonstrated that email could be a very effective vector for malware distribution, and many subsequent worms have continued to use email, such as the 2000 Love Letter worm. In the 2001–2004 interval,

several fast worms appeared, notably Code Red, Nimda, Klez, SQL Slammer/Sapphire, Blaster, Sobig, and MyDoom.

An important feature of viruses and worms is their capability to carry a *payload*—malicious code that is executed on a compromised host. The payload can be virtually anything. For instance, SQL Slammer/Sapphire had no payload, whereas Code Red carried an agent to perform a denial-of-service (DoS) attack on certain fixed addresses. The Chernobyl or CIH virus had one of the most destructive payloads, attempting to overwrite critical system files and the system BIOS that is needed for a computer to boot up. Worms are sometimes used to deliver other malware, such as bots, in their payload. They are popular delivery vehicles because of their ability to spread by themselves and carry anything in their payload.

Members of a second large class of malware are characterized by attempts to conceal themselves. This class includes Trojan horses and rootkits. Worms are not particularly stealthy (unless they are designed to be) because they are typically indiscriminate in their attacks. They probe potential targets in the hope of compromising many targets quickly. Indeed, fast-spreading worms are relatively easy to detect because of the network congestion caused by their probes.

Stealth is an important feature for malware because the critical problem for antivirus software is obviously detection of malware. Trojan horses are a type of malware that appears to perform a useful function but hides a malicious function. Thus, the presence of the Trojan horse might not be concealed, but functionality is not fully revealed. For example, a video codec could offer to play certain types of video but also covertly steal the user's data in the background. In the second half of 2007, Microsoft reported a dramatic increase of 300 percent% in the number of Trojan downloaders and droppers, small programs to facilitate downloading more malware later.[4]

Rootkits are essentially modifications to the operating system to hide the presence of files or processes from normal means of detection. Rootkits are often installed as drivers or kernel modules. A highly publicized example was the extended copy protection (XCP) software included in some Sony BMG audio CDs in 2005, to prevent music copying. The software was installed automatically on Windows PCs when a CD was played. Made by a company called First 4 Internet, XCP unfortunately contained a hidden rootkit component that patched the operating system to prevent it from displaying any processes, Registry entries, or files with names beginning with sys. Although the intention of XCP was not malicious, there was concern that the rootkit could be used by malware writers to conceal malware.

A third important class of malware is designed for remote control. This class includes remote access Trojans

10. David Harley and David Slade, *Viruses Revealed*, McGraw-Hill, 2001.

11. Ed Skoudis, *Malware: Fighting Malicious Code*, Prentice Hall PTR, 2004.

12. Peter Szor, *The Art of Computer Virus Research and Defense*, Addison-Wesley, 2005.

(RATs) and bots. Instead of *remote access Trojan*, RAT is sometimes interpreted as *remote administration tool* because it can be used for legitimate purposes by systems administrators. Either way, RAT refers to a type of software usually consisting of server and client parts designed to enable covert communications with a remote controller. The client part is installed on a victim host and mainly listens for instructions from the server part, located at the controller. Notorious examples include Back Orifice, Netbus, and Sub7.

Bots are remote-control programs installed covertly on innocent hosts.[13] Bots are typically programmed to listen to IRC channels for instructions from a "bot herder." All bots under control of the same bot herder form a botnet. Botnets have been known to be rented out for purposes of sending spam or launching a distributed DoS (DDoS) attack.[14] The power of a botnet is proportional to its size, but exact sizes have been difficult to discover.

One of the most publicized bots is the Storm worm, which has various aliases. Storm was launched in January 2007 as spam with a Trojan horse attachment. As a botnet, Storm has shown unusual resilience by working in a distributed peer-to-peer manner without centralized control. Each compromised host connects to a small subset of the entire botnet. Each infected host shares lists of other infected hosts, but no single host has a full list of the entire botnet. The size of the Storm botnet has been estimated at more than 1 million compromised hosts, but an exact size has been impossible to determine because of the many bot variants and active measures to avoid detection. Its creators have been persistent in continually updating its lures with current events and evolving tactics to spread and avoid detection.

Another major class of malware is designed for data theft. This class includes keyloggers and spyware. A keylogger can be a Trojan horse or other form of malware. It is designed to record a user's keystrokes and perhaps report them to a remote attacker. Keyloggers are planted by criminals on unsuspecting hosts to steal passwords and other valuable personal information. It has also been rumored that the Federal Bureau of Investigation (FBI) has used a keylogger called Magic Lantern.

As the name implies, *spyware* is stealthy software designed to monitor and report user activities for the purposes of learning personal information without the user's knowledge or consent. Surveys have found that spyware is widely prevalent on consumer PCs, usually without knowledge of the owners. Adware is viewed by some as a mildly objectionable form of spyware that spies on Web browsing behavior to target online advertisements to a user's apparent interests. More objectionable forms of spyware are more invasive of privacy and raise other objections related to stealthy installation, interference with normal Web browsing, and difficulty of removal.

Spyware can be installed in a number of stealthy ways: disguised as a Trojan horse, bundled with a legitimate software program, delivered in the payload of a worm or virus, or downloaded through deception. For instance, a deceptive Web site might pop up a window appearing to be a standard Windows dialog box, but clicking any button will cause spyware to be downloaded. Another issue is that spyware might or might not display an end-user license agreement (EULA) before installation. If an EULA is displayed, the mention of spyware is typically unnoticeable or difficult to find.

More pernicious forms of spyware can change computer settings, reset homepages, and redirect the browser to unwanted sites. For example, the notorious CoolWebSearch changed homepages to Coolwebsearch.com, rewrote search engine results, and altered host files, and some variants added links to pornographic and gambling sites to the browser's bookmarks.

Lures and "Pull" Attacks

Traditional network attacks can be viewed as an "active" approach in which the attacker takes the initiative of a series of actions directed at a target. Attackers face the risk of revealing their malicious intentions through these actions. For instance, port scanning, password guessing, or exploit attempts can be readily detected by an IDS as suspicious activities. Sending malware through email can only be seen as an attempted attack.

Security researchers have observed a trend away from direct attacks toward stealthier attacks that wait for victims to visit malicious Web sites, as shown in Figure 5.2.[15] The Web has become the primary vector for infecting computers, in large part because email has become better secured. Sophos discovers a new malicious Webpage every 14 seconds, on average.[16]

Web-based attacks have significant advantages for attackers. First, they are stealthier and not as "noisy" as active attacks, making it easier to continue undetected for a longer time. Second, Web servers have the intelligence to be stealthy. For instance, Web servers have been found that serve up an attack only once per IP address and

13. Craig Schiller et al., *Botnets: The Killer Web App*, Syngress Publishing, 2007.
14. David Dittrich, "Distributed Denial of Service (DDoS) Attacks/Tools," available at http://staff.washington.edu/dittrich/misc/ddos/ (date of access: July 1, 2008).
15. Joel Scambray, Mike Shema, and Caleb Sima, *Hacking Exposed Web Applications*, 2nd ed., McGraw-Hill, 2006.
16. Sophos, "Security Threat Report 2012," available at http://www.sophos.com/medialibrary/PDFs/other/SophosSecurityThreatReport2012.pdf (date of access: March 1, 2012).

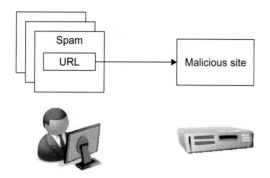

FIGURE 5.2 Stealthy attacks lure victims to malicious servers.

otherwise serve up legitimate content. The malicious server remembers the IP addresses of visitors. Thus, a visitor will be attacked only once, which makes the attack harder to detect. Third, a Web server can serve up different attacks, depending on the visitor's operating system and browser.

As mentioned earlier, a common type of attack carried out through the Web is phishing. A phishing site is typically disguised as a legitimate financial organization or e-commerce business. During the month of June 2011, the Anti-Phishing Working Group found 28,148 new unique phishing sites hijacking 310 brands (www.anti-phishing.org).

Another type of Web-based attack is a malicious site that attempts to download malware through a visitor's browser, called a *drive-by download*. A Web page usually loads a malicious script by means of an iframe (inline frame). It has been reported that most drive-by downloads are hosted on legitimate sites that have been compromised. For example, in June 2007 more than 10,000 legitimate Italian Web sites were discovered to be compromised with malicious code loaded through iframes. Many other legitimate sites are regularly compromised.

Drive-by downloading through a legitimate site holds certain appeal for attackers. First, most users will be reluctant to visit suspicious and potentially malicious sites but will not hesitate to visit legitimate sites in the belief that they are always safe. Even wary Web surfers may be caught off-guard. Second, the vast majority of Web servers run Apache (approximately 50 percent) or Microsoft IIS (approximately 40 percent), both of which have vulnerabilities that can be exploited by attackers. Moreover, servers with database applications could be vulnerable to SQL injection attacks. Third, if a legitimate site is compromised with an iframe, the malicious code might go unnoticed by the site owner for some time.

Pull-based attacks pose one challenge to attackers: They must somehow attract visitors to the malicious site, while avoiding detection by security researchers. One

obvious option is to send out lures in spam. Lures have been disguised as email from the Internal Revenue Service, a security update from Microsoft, or a greeting card. The email attempts to entice the reader to visit a link. On one hand, lures are easier to get through spam filters because they only contain links and not attachments. It is easier for spam filters to detect malware attachments than to determine whether links in email are malicious. On the other hand, spam filters are easily capable of extracting and following links from spam. The greater challenge is to determine whether the linked site is malicious.

3. DEFENSE IN DEPTH

Most security experts would agree that perfect network security is impossible to achieve and that any single defense can always be overcome by an attacker with sufficient resources and motivation. The basic idea behind the *defense-in-depth strategy* is to hinder the attacker as much as possible with multiple layers of defense, even though each layer might be surmountable. More valuable assets should be protected behind more layers of defense. The combination of multiple layers increases the cost for the attacker to be successful, and the cost is proportional to the value of the protected assets. Moreover, a combination of multiple layers will be more effective against unpredictable attacks than will a single defense optimized for a particular type of attack.

The cost for the attacker could be in terms of additional time, effort, or equipment. For instance, by delaying an attacker, an organization would increase the chances of detecting and reacting to an attack in progress. The increased costs to an attacker could deter some attempts if the costs are believed to outweigh the possible gain from a successful attack.

Defense in depth is sometimes said to involve people, technology, and operations. Trained security people should be responsible for securing facilities and information assurance. However, every computer user in an organization should be made aware of security policies and practices. Every Internet user at home should be aware of safe practices (such as avoiding opening email attachments or clicking suspicious links) and the benefits of appropriate protection (antivirus software, firewalls).

A variety of technological measures can be used for layers of protection. These should include firewalls, IDSs, routers with ACLs, antivirus software, access control, spam filters, and so on. These topics are discussed in more depth later in this chapter.

The term *operations* refers to all preventive and reactive activities required to maintain security. Preventive activities include vulnerability assessments, software patching, system hardening (closing unnecessary ports), and access controls. Reactive activities should detect malicious activities and react by blocking attacks, isolating valuable resources, or tracing the intruder.

Protection of valuable assets can be a more complicated decision than simply considering the value of the assets. Organizations often perform a risk assessment to determine the value of assets, possible threats, likelihood of threats, and possible impact of threats. Valuable assets facing unlikely threats or threats with low impact might not need much protection. Clearly, assets of high value facing likely threats or high-impact threats merit the strongest defenses. Organizations usually have their own risk management process for identifying risks and deciding how to allocate a security budget to protect valuable assets under risk.

4. PREVENTIVE MEASURES

Most computer users are aware that Internet connectivity comes with security risks. It would be reasonable to take precautions to minimize exposure to attacks. Fortunately, several options are available to computer users to fortify their systems to reduce risks.

Access Control

In computer security, *access control* refers to mechanisms to allow users to perform functions up to their authorized level and restrict users from performing unauthorized functions.[17] Access control includes:

- Authentication of users
- Authorization of their privileges
- Auditing to monitor and record user actions

All computer users will be familiar with some type of access control.

Authentication, the process of verifying a user's identity, is typically based on one or more of these factors:

- Something the user knows, such as a password or PIN
- Something the user has, such as a smart card or token
- Something personal about the user, such as a fingerprint, retinal pattern, or other biometric identifier

Use of a single factor, even if multiple pieces of evidence are offered, is considered weak authentication. A combination of two factors, such as a password and a fingerprint, called *two-factor* (or *multifactor*) *authentication*, is considered strong authentication.

Authorization is the process of determining what an authenticated user can do. Most operating systems have an established set of permissions related to read, write, or execute access. For example, an ordinary user might have permission to read a certain file but not write to it, whereas a root or superuser will have full privileges to do anything.

Auditing is necessary to ensure that users are accountable. Computer systems record actions in the system in audit trails and logs. For security purposes, they are invaluable forensic tools to re-create and analyze incidents. For instance, a user attempting numerous failed logins might be seen as an intruder.

Vulnerability Testing and Patching

As mentioned earlier, vulnerabilities are weaknesses in software that might be used to compromise a computer. Vulnerable software includes all types of operating systems and application programs. New vulnerabilities are being discovered constantly in different ways. New vulnerabilities discovered by security researchers are usually reported confidentially to the vendor, which is given time to study the vulnerability and develop a path. Of all vulnerabilities disclosed in 2007, 50 percent could be corrected through vendor patches.[18] When ready, the vendor will publish the vulnerability, hopefully along with a patch.

It has been argued that publication of vulnerabilities will help attackers. Although this might be true, publication also fosters awareness within the entire community. Systems administrators will be able to evaluate their systems and take appropriate precautions. One might expect systems administrators to know the configuration of computers on their network, but in large organizations, it would be difficult to keep track of possible configuration changes made by users. Vulnerability testing offers a simple way to learn about the configuration of computers on a network.

Vulnerability testing is an exercise to probe systems for known vulnerabilities. It requires a database of known vulnerabilities, a packet generator, and test routines to generate a sequence of packets to test for a particular vulnerability. If a vulnerability is found and a software patch is available, that host should be patched.

Penetration testing is a closely related idea but takes it further. Penetration testing simulates the actions of a hypothetical attacker to attempt to compromise hosts. The goal is, again, to learn about weaknesses in the network so that they can be remedied.

Closing Ports

Transport layer protocols, namely, Transmission Control Protocol (TCP) and User Datagram Protocol (UDP),

---

17. B. Carroll, Cisco Access Control Security: AAA Administration Services, Cisco Press, 2004.

18. IBM Internet Security Systems, *X-Force 2007 Trend Statistics*, January 2008 (date of access: July 1, 2008).

identify applications communicating with each other by means of port numbers. Port numbers 1 to 1023 are well known and assigned by the Internet Assigned Numbers Authority (IANA) to standardized services running with root privileges. For example, Web servers listen on TCP port 80 for client requests. Port numbers 1024 to 49151 are used by various applications with ordinary user privileges. Port numbers above 49151 are used dynamically by applications.

It is good practice to close ports that are unnecessary, because attackers can use open ports, particularly those in the higher range. For instance, the Sub7 Trojan horse is known to use port 27374 by default, and Netbus uses port 12345. Closing ports does not by itself guarantee the safety of a host, however. Some hosts need to keep TCP port 80 open for HyperText Transfer Protocol (HTTP), but attacks can still be carried out through that port.

Firewalls

When most people think of network security, firewalls are one of the first things to come to mind. Firewalls are a means of perimeter security protecting an internal network from external threats. A firewall selectively allows or blocks incoming and outgoing traffic. Firewalls can be standalone network devices located at the entry to a private network or personal firewall programs running on PCs. An organization's firewall protects the internal community; a personal firewall can be customized to an individual's needs.

Firewalls can provide separation and isolation among various network zones, namely, the public Internet, private intranets, and a demilitarized zone (DMZ), as shown in Figure 5.3. The semiprotected DMZ typically includes public services provided by a private organization. Public servers need some protection from the public Internet, so they usually sit behind a firewall. This firewall cannot be completely restrictive because the public servers must be externally accessible. Another firewall typically sits between the DMZ and private internal network because the internal network needs additional protection.

There are various types of firewalls: packet-filtering firewalls, stateful firewalls, and proxy firewalls. In any case, the effectiveness of a firewall depends on the configuration of its rules. Properly written rules require detailed knowledge of network protocols. Unfortunately, some firewalls are improperly configured through neglect or lack of training.

Packet-filtering firewalls analyze packets in both directions and either permit or deny passage based on a set of rules. Rules typically examine port numbers, protocols, IP addresses, and other attributes of packet headers. There is no attempt to relate multiple packets with a flow or stream. The firewall is stateless, retaining no memory of one packet to the next.

Stateful firewalls overcome the limitation of packet-filtering firewalls by recognizing packets belonging to the same flow or connection and keeping track of the connection state. They work at the network layer and recognize the legitimacy of sessions.

Proxy firewalls are also called application-level firewalls because they process up to the application layer. They recognize certain applications and can detect whether an undesirable protocol is using a nonstandard port or an application layer protocol is being abused. They protect an internal network by serving as primary gateways to proxy connections from the internal network to the public Internet. They could have some impact on network performance due to the nature of the analysis.

Firewalls are essential elements of an overall defensive strategy but have the drawback that they only protect the perimeter. They are useless if an intruder has a way to bypass the perimeter. They are also useless against insider threats originating within a private network.

Antivirus and Antispyware Tools

The proliferation of malware prompts the need for antivirus software.[19] Antivirus software is developed to detect the presence of malware, identify its nature, remove the malware (disinfect the host), and protect a host from future infections. Detection should ideally minimize false positives (false alarms) and false negatives (missed malware) at the same time. Antivirus software faces a number of difficult challenges:

- Malware tactics are sophisticated and constantly evolving.
- Even the operating system on infected hosts cannot be trusted.
- Malware can exist entirely in memory without affecting files.

DMZ

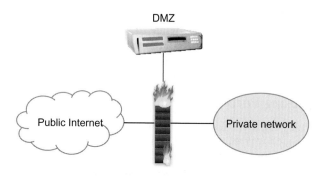

FIGURE 5.3   A firewall isolating various network zones.

19. Peter Szor, *The Art of Computer Virus Research and Defense*, Addison-Wesley, 2005.

- Malware can attack antivirus processes.
- The processing load for antivirus software cannot degrade computer performance such that users become annoyed and turn the antivirus software off.

One of the simplest tasks performed by antivirus software is file scanning. This process compares the bytes in files with known signatures that are byte patterns indicative of a known malware. It represents the general approach of signature-based detection. When new malware is captured, it is analyzed for unique characteristics that can be described in a signature. The new signature is distributed as updates to antivirus programs. Antivirus looks for the signature during file scanning, and if a match is found, the signature identifies the malware specifically. There are major drawbacks to this method, however: New signatures require time to develop and test; users must keep their signature files up to date; and new malware without a known signature may escape detection.

Behavior-based detection is a complementary approach. Instead of addressing what malware is, behavior-based detection looks at what malware tries to do. In other words, anything attempting a risky action will come under suspicion. This approach overcomes the limitations of signature-based detection and could find new malware without a signature, just from its behavior. However, the approach can be difficult in practice. First, we must define what is suspicious behavior, or conversely, what is normal behavior. This definition often relies on heuristic rules developed by security experts, because normal behavior is difficult to define precisely. Second, it might be possible to *discern* suspicious behavior, but it is much more difficult to *determine* malicious behavior, because malicious intention must be inferred. When behavior-based detection flags suspicious behavior, more follow-up investigation is usually needed to better understand the threat risk.

The ability of malware to change or disguise appearances can defeat file scanning. However, regardless of its form, malware must ultimately perform its mission. Thus, an opportunity will always arise to detect malware from its behavior if it is given a chance to execute. Antivirus software will monitor system events, such as hard-disk access, to look for actions that might pose a threat to the host. Events are monitored by intercepting calls to operating system functions.

Although monitoring system events is a step beyond file scanning, malicious programs are running in the host execution environment and could pose a risk to the host. The idea of emulation is to execute suspected code within an isolated environment, presenting the appearance of the computer resources to the code, and to look for actions symptomatic of malware.

Virtualization takes emulation a step further and executes suspected code within a real operating system. A number of virtual operating systems can run above the host operating system. Malware can corrupt a virtual operating system, but for safety reasons a virtual operating system has limited access to the host operating system. A "sandbox" isolates the virtual environment from tampering with the host environment, unless a specific action is requested and permitted. In contrast, emulation does not offer an operating system to suspected code; the code is allowed to execute step by step, but in a controlled and restricted way, just to discover what it will attempt to do.

Antispyware software can be viewed as a specialized class of antivirus software. Somewhat unlike traditional viruses, spyware can be particularly pernicious in making a vast number of changes throughout the hard drive and system files. Infected systems tend to have a large number of installed spyware programs, possibly including certain cookies (pieces of text planted by Web sites in the browser as a means of keeping them in memory).

Spam Filtering

Every Internet user is familiar with spam email. There is no consensus on an exact definition of spam, but most people would agree that spam is unsolicited, sent in bulk, and commercial in nature. There is also consensus that the vast majority of email is spam. Spam continues to be a problem because a small fraction of recipients do respond to these messages. Even though the fraction is small, the revenue generated is enough to make spam profitable because it costs little to send spam in bulk. In particular, a large botnet can generate an enormous amount of spam quickly.

Users of popular Webmail services such as Yahoo! and Hotmail are attractive targets for spam because their addresses might be easy to guess. In addition, spammers harvest email addresses from various sources: Web sites, newsgroups, online directories, data-stealing viruses, and so on. Spammers might also purchase lists of addresses from companies that are willing to sell customer information.

Spam is more than an inconvenience for users and a waste of network resources. Spam is a popular vehicle to distribute malware and lures to malicious Web sites. It is the first step in phishing attacks.

Spam filters work at an enterprise level and a personal level. At the enterprise level, mail gateways can protect an entire organization by scanning incoming messages for malware and blocking messages from suspicious or fake senders. A concern at the enterprise level is the rate of false positives, which are legitimate messages mistaken for spam. Users may become upset if their legitimate mail is blocked. Fortunately, spam filters are typically customizable, and the rate of false positives can be made very low. Additional spam filtering at the personal level can customize filtering even further, to account for individual preferences.

Various spam-filtering techniques are embodied in many commercial and free spam filters, such as DSPAM and SpamAssassin, to name two. Bayesian filtering is one of the more popular techniques.[20] First, an incoming message is parsed into tokens, which are single words or word combinations from the message's header and body. Second, probabilities are assigned to tokens through a training process. The filter looks at a set of known spam messages compared to a set of known legitimate messages and calculates token probabilities based on Bayes' theorem (from probability theory). Intuitively, a word such as *Viagra* would appear more often in spam, and therefore the appearance of a Viagra token would increase the probability of that message being classified as spam.

The probability calculated for a message is compared to a chosen threshold; if the probability is higher, the message is classified as spam. The threshold is chosen to balance the rates of false positives and false negatives (missed spam) in some desired way. An attractive feature of Bayesian filtering is that its probabilities will adapt to new spam tactics, given continual feedback, that is, correction of false positives and false negatives by the user.

It is easy to see why spammers have attacked Bayesian filters by attempting to influence the probabilities of tokens. For example, spammers have tried filling messages with large amounts of legitimate text (e.g., drawn from classic literature) or random innocuous words. The presence of legitimate tokens tends to decrease a message's score because they are evidence counted toward the legitimacy of the message.

Spammers are continually trying new ways to get through spam filters. At the same time, security companies respond by adapting their technologies.

Honeypots

The basic idea of a *honeypot* is to learn about attacker techniques by attracting attacks to a seemingly vulnerable host.[21] It is essentially a forensics tool rather than a line of defense. A honeypot could be used to gain valuable information about attack methods used elsewhere or imminent attacks before they happen. Honeypots are used routinely in research and production environments.

A honeypot has more special requirements than a regular PC. First, a honeypot should not be used for legitimate services or traffic. Consequently, every activity seen by the honeypot will be illegitimate. Even though honeypots typically record little data compared to IDS, for instance, their data has little "noise," whereas the bulk of IDS data is typically uninteresting from a security point of view.

Second, a honeypot should have comprehensive and reliable capabilities for monitoring and logging all activities. The forensic value of a honeypot depends on the detailed information it can capture about attacks.

Third, a honeypot should be isolated from the real network. Since honeypots are intended to attract attacks, there is a real risk that the honeypot could be compromised and used as a launching pad to attack more hosts in the network.

Honeypots are often classified according to their level of interaction, ranging from low to high. Low-interaction honeypots, such as Honeyd, offer the appearance of simple services. An attacker could try to compromise the honeypot but would not have much to gain. The limited interactions pose a risk that an attacker could discover that the host is a honeypot. At the other end of the range, high-interaction honeypots behave more like real systems. They have more capabilities to interact with an attacker and log activities, but they offer more to gain if they are compromised.

Honeypots are related to the concepts of black holes or network telescopes, which are monitored blocks of unused IP addresses. Since the addresses are unused, any traffic seen at those addresses is naturally suspicious (though not necessarily malicious).

Traditional honeypots suffer a drawback in that they are passive and wait to see malicious activity. The idea of honeypots has been extended to active clients that search for malicious servers and interact with them. The active version of a honeypot has been called a *honey-monkey* or *client honeypot*.

Network Access Control

A vulnerable host might place not only itself but an entire community at risk. For one thing, a vulnerable host might attract attacks. If compromised, the host could be used to launch attacks on other hosts. The compromised host might give information to the attacker, or there might be trust relationships between hosts that could help the attacker. In any case, it is not desirable to have a weakly protected host on your network.

The general idea of *network access control* (NAC) is to restrict a host from accessing a network unless the host can provide evidence of a strong security posture. The NAC process involves the host, the network (usually

20. J. Zdziarski, *Ending Spam: Bayesian Content Filtering and the Art of Statistical Language Classification*, No Starch Press, 2005.
21. The Honeynet Project, *Know Your Enemy: Learning about Security Threats*, 2nd ed., Addison-Wesley, 2004.

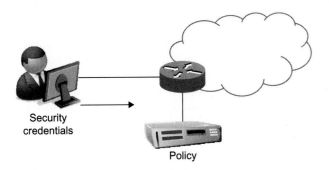

FIGURE 5.4   Network access control.

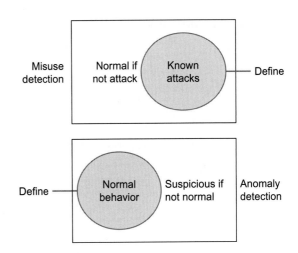

FIGURE 5.5   Misuse detection and anomaly detection.

routers or switches, and servers), and a security policy, as shown in Figure 5.4.

The details of the NAC process vary with various implementations, which unfortunately currently lack standards for interoperability. A host's security posture includes its IP address, operating system, antivirus software, personal firewall, and host intrusion detection system. In some implementations, a software agent runs on the host, collects information about the host's security posture, and reports it to the network as part of a request for admission to the network. The network refers to a policy server to compare the host's security posture to the security policy, to make an admission decision.

The admission decision could be anything from rejection to partial admission or full admission. Rejection might be prompted by out-of-date antivirus software, an operating system needing patches, or firewall misconfiguration. Rejection might lead to quarantine (routing to an isolated network) or forced remediation.

5. INTRUSION MONITORING AND DETECTION

Preventive measures are necessary and help reduce the risk of attacks, but it is practically impossible to prevent all attacks. Intrusion detection is also necessary to detect and diagnose malicious activities, analogous to a burglar alarm. Intrusion detection is essentially a combination of monitoring, analysis, and response.[22] Typically, an IDS supports a console for human interface and display. Monitoring and analysis are usually viewed as passive techniques because they do not interfere with ongoing activities. The typical IDS response is an alert to systems administrators, who may or may not choose to pursue further investigation. In other words, traditional IDSs do not offer much response beyond alerts, under the presumption that security incidents need human expertise and judgment for follow-up.

Detection accuracy is the critical problem for intrusion detection. Intrusion detection should ideally minimize false positives (normal incidents mistaken for suspicious ones) and false negatives (malicious incidents escaping detection). Naturally, false negatives are contrary to the essential purpose of intrusion detection. False positives are also harmful because they are troublesome for systems administrators who must waste time investigating false alarms. Intrusion detection should also seek to more than identify security incidents. In addition to relating the facts of an incident, intrusion detection should ascertain the nature of the incident, the perpetrator, the seriousness (malicious vs. suspicious), scope, and potential consequences (such as stepping from one target to more targets).

IDS approaches can be categorized in at least two ways. One way is to differentiate host-based and network-based IDS, depending on where sensing is done. A host-based IDS monitors an individual host, whereas a network-based IDS works on network packets. Another way to view IDS is by their approach to analysis. Traditionally, the two analysis approaches are misuse (signature-based) detection and anomaly (behavior-based) detection. As shown in Figure 5.5, these two views are complementary and are often used in combination.

In practice, intrusion detection faces several difficult challenges: Signature-based detection can recognize only incidents matching a known signature; behavior-based detection relies on an understanding of normal behavior, but "normal" can vary widely. Attackers are intelligent and evasive; attackers might try to confuse IDS with fragmented, encrypted, tunneled, or junk packets; an IDS might not react to an incident in real time or quickly enough to stop an attack; and incidents can occur anywhere at any time, which necessitates continual and extensive monitoring, with correlation of multiple distributed sensors.

---

22. Richard Bejtlich, *The Tao of Network Security Monitoring: Beyond Intrusion Detection*, Addison-Wesley, 2005.

Host-Based Monitoring

Host-based IDS runs on a host and monitors system activities for signs of suspicious behavior. Examples could be changes to the system Registry, repeated failed login attempts, or installation of a backdoor. Host-based IDSs usually monitor system objects, processes, and regions of memory. For each system object, the IDS will usually keep track of attributes such as permissions, size, modification dates, and hashed contents, to recognize changes.

A concern for a host-based IDS is possible tampering by an attacker. If an attacker gains control of a system, the IDS cannot be trusted. Hence, special protection of the IDS against tampering should be architected into a host.

A host-based IDS is not a complete solution by itself. Although monitoring the host is logical, it has three significant drawbacks: Visibility is limited to a single host; the IDS process consumes resources, possibly impacting performance on the host; and attacks will not be seen until they have already reached the host. Host-based and network-based IDS are often used together to combine strengths.

Traffic Monitoring

Network-based IDSs typically monitor network packets for signs of reconnaissance, exploits, DoS attacks, and malware. They have strengths to complement host-based IDSs: Network-based IDSs can see traffic for a population of hosts; they can recognize patterns shared by multiple hosts; and they have the potential to see attacks before they reach the hosts.

IDSs are placed in various locations for different views, as shown in Figure 5.6. An IDS outside a firewall is useful for learning about malicious activities on the Internet. An IDS in the DMZ will see attacks originating from the Internet that are able to get through the outer firewall to public servers. Lastly, an IDS in the private network is necessary to detect any attacks that are able to successfully penetrate perimeter security.

Signature-Based Detection

Signature-based intrusion detection depends on patterns that uniquely identify an attack. If an incident matches a known signature, the signature identifies the specific attack. The central issue is how to define signatures or model attacks. If signatures are too specific, a change in an attack tactic could result in a false negative (missed alarm). An attack signature should be broad enough to cover an entire class of attacks. On the other hand, if signatures are too general, it can result in false positives.

Signature-based approaches have three inherent drawbacks: New attacks can be missed if a matching signature is not known; signatures require time to develop for new attacks; and new signatures must be distributed continually.

Snort is a popular example of a signature-based IDS (www.snort.org). Snort signatures are rules that define fields that match packets of information about the represented attack. Snort is packaged with more than 1800 rules covering a broad range of attacks, and new rules are constantly being written.

Behavior Anomalies

A behavior-based IDS is appealing for its potential to recognize new attacks without a known signature. It presumes that attacks will be different from normal behavior. Hence the critical issue is how to define normal behavior, and anything outside of normal (anomalous) is classified as suspicious. A common approach is to define normal behavior in statistical terms, which allows for deviations within a range.

Behavior-based approaches have considerable challenges. First, normal behavior is based on past behavior. Thus, data about past behavior must be available for training the IDS. Second, behavior can and does change over time, so any IDS approach must be adaptive. Third, anomalies are just unusual events, not necessarily malicious ones. A behavior-based IDS might point out

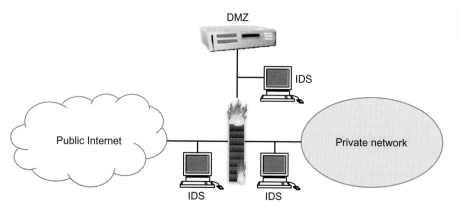

FIGURE 5.6 IDSs monitoring various network zones.

incidents to investigate further, but it is not good at discerning the exact nature of attacks.

Intrusion Prevention Systems

IDSs are passive techniques. They typically notify the systems administrator to investigate further and take the appropriate action. The response might be slow if the systems administrator is busy or the incident is time consuming to investigate.

A variation called an *intrusion prevention system* (IPS) seeks to combine the traditional monitoring and analysis functions of an IDS with more active automated responses, such as automatically reconfiguring firewalls to block an attack. An IPS aims for a faster response than humans can achieve, but its accuracy depends on the same techniques as the traditional IDS. The response should not harm legitimate traffic, so accuracy is critical.

6. REACTIVE MEASURES

When an attack is detected and analyzed, systems administrators must exercise an appropriate response to the attack. One of the principles in security is that the response should be proportional to the threat. Obviously, the response will depend on the circumstances, but various options are available. Generally, it is possible to block, slow, modify, or redirect any malicious traffic. It is not possible to delineate every possible response. Here we describe only two responses: quarantine and traceback.

Quarantine

Dynamic quarantine in computer security is analogous to quarantine for infectious diseases. It is an appropriate response, particularly in the context of malware, to prevent an infected host from contaminating other hosts.

Infectious malware requires connectivity between an infected host and a new target, so it is logical to disrupt the connectivity between hosts or networks as a means to impede the malware from spreading further.

Within the network, traffic can be blocked by firewalls or routers with access control lists (ACLs). ACLs are similar to firewall rules, allowing routers to selectively drop packets.

Traceback

One of the critical aspects of an attack is the identity or location of the perpetrator. Unfortunately, discovery of an attacker in IP networks is almost impossible because:

- The source address in IP packets can be easily spoofed (forged).
- Routers are stateless by design and do not keep records of forwarded packets.
- Attackers can use a series of intermediary hosts (called *stepping stones* or *zombies*) to carry out their attacks.

Intermediaries are usually innocent computers taken over by an exploit or malware and put under control of the attacker. In practice, it might be possible to trace an attack back to the closest intermediary, but it might be too much to expect to trace an attack all the way back to the real attacker.

To trace a packet's route, some tracking information must be either stored at routers when the packet is forwarded or carried in the packet, as shown in Figure 5.7. An example of the first approach is to store a hash of a packet for some amount of time. If an attack occurs, the target host will query routers for a hash of the attack packet. If a router has the hash, it is evidence that the packet had been forwarded by that router. To reduce memory consumption, the hash is stored instead of storing

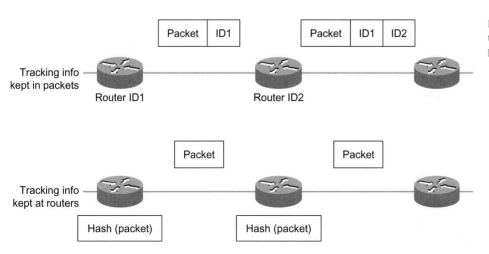

FIGURE 5.7 Tracking information stored at routers or carried in packets to enable packet traceback.

An Agenda for Action for Logging Capabilities Activities

As previously stated, network-based IPSs typically perform extensive logging of data related to detected events. This data can be used to confirm the validity of alerts, to investigate incidents, and to correlate events between the IPS and other logging sources. Data fields commonly logged by network-based IPSs include the following key activities (check all tasks completed):

_____1. Timestamp (usually date and time).

_____2. Connection or session ID (typically a consecutive or unique number assigned to each TCP connection or to like groups of packets for connectionless protocols).

_____3. Event or alert type. In the console, the event or alert type often links to supporting information for the specific vulnerability or exploit, such as references for additional information and associated Common Vulnerabilities and Exposures (CVE) numbers.

_____4. Rating (priority, severity, impact, confidence).

_____5. Network, transport, and application layer protocols.

_____6. Source and destination IP addresses.

_____7. Source and destination TCP or UDP ports, or ICMP types and codes.

_____8. Number of bytes transmitted over the connection.

_____9. Decoded payload data, such as application requests and responses.

_____10. State-related information (authenticated username).

_____11. Prevention action performed (if any).

---

the entire packet. The storage is temporary instead of permanent so that routers will not run out of memory.

An example of the second approach is to stamp packets with a unique router identifier, such as an IP address. Thus the packet carries a record of its route. The main advantage here is that routers can remain stateless. The problem is that there is no space in the IP packet header for this scheme.

Finally, let's briefly look at how a network-based intrusion protection system (IPS) monitors network traffic for particular network segments or devices and analyzes network, transport, and application protocols to identify suspicious activity. The following section describes common intrusion protection components.

7. NETWORK-BASED INTRUSION PROTECTION

Network-based IPS components are similar to other types of IPS technologies, except for the sensors. A network-based IPS sensor monitors and analyzes network activity on one or more network segments. Sensors are available in two formats: appliance-based sensors, which are comprised of specialized hardware and software optimized for IPS sensor use, and software-only sensors, which can be installed onto hosts that meet certain specifications.

Network-based IPSs also provide a wide variety of security capabilities. Some products can collect information on hosts such as which OSs they use and which application versions they use that communicate over networks. Network-based IPSs can also perform extensive logging of data related to detected events (see checklist: An Agenda for Action for Logging Capabilities Activities); most can also perform packet captures.

8. SUMMARY

This chapter made it perfectly clear that, to guard against network intrusions, we must understand the variety of attacks, from exploits to malware to social engineering. Direct attacks are prevalent, but a class of *pull attacks* has emerged, relying on lures to bring victims to a malicious Web site. Pull attacks are much more difficult to uncover and in a way defend against. Just about anyone can become victimized.

Much can be done to fortify hosts and reduce their risk exposure, but some attacks are unavoidable. Defense in depth is a most practical defense strategy, combining layers of defenses. Although each defensive layer is imperfect, the cost becomes harder to surmount for intruders.

One of the essential defenses is *intrusion detection*. Host-based and network-based intrusion detection systems have their respective strengths and weaknesses. Research continues to be needed to improve intrusion detection, particularly behavior-based techniques. As more attacks are invented, signature-based techniques will have more difficulty keeping up.

Finally, let's move on to the real interactive part of this chapter: review questions/exercises, hands-on projects, case projects and optional team case project. The answers and/or solutions by chapter can be found in the Online Instructor's Solutions Manual.

CHAPTER REVIEW QUESTIONS/EXERCISES

True/False

1. True or False? Traditionally, attack methods do not follow sequential steps analogous to physical attacks.

2. True or False? Malicious software, or malware, is not an enormous problem for Internet users because of its

variety and prevalence and the level of danger it presents.

3. True or False? Traditional network attacks can be viewed as an "active" approach in which the attacker takes the initiative of a series of actions directed at a target.

4. True or False? The basic idea behind the *defense-in-depth strategy* is to hinder the attacker as much as possible with multiple layers of defense, even though each layer might be surmountable.

5. True or False? In computer security, *access control* refers to mechanisms to allow users to perform functions up to their unauthorized level and restrict users from performing authorized functions.

Multiple Choice

1. A stealthy type of malicious software (*malware*) designed to hide the existence of certain processes or programs from normal methods of detection is known as a:
   A. wireless sniffer.
   B. rootkit.
   C. port scanner.
   D. port knocker.
   E. keystroke logger.

2. If an intruder has installed malware for covert control, he or she will want to conceal the communications between him- or herself and the compromised target from discovery by:
   A. network-based intrusion detection systems (IDSs).
   B. tunneling.
   C. multiple time zones.
   D. budgets.
   E. networks.

3. What is a commonly used method to place packets of one protocol into the payload of another packet?
   A. Encryption
   B. Signature-based
   C. Tunneling
   D. Hybrid detection
   E. Host-based

4. What is another obvious concealment method?
   A. Infection
   B. Rate
   C. Host
   D. Back door
   E. Encryption

5. What can be a Trojan horse or other form of malware?
   A. Antivirus
   B. Unified threat management
   C. Keylogger
   D. Firewall
   E. Antispam

EXERCISE

Problem

A physical security company has an innovative, patented product and critical secrets to protect. For this company, protecting physical security and safeguarding network security go hand-in-hand. A Web application in the data center tracks the serialized keycodes and allows customers to manage their key sets. The customers include everyone from theft-conscious retail chains to security-sensitive government agencies. In this case project, how would the security company go about establishing solid network security to protect them against intrusions?

Hands-On Projects

Project

A solution services company is also a managed service provider specializing in IT infrastructure, Voice over Internet Protocol (VoIP), wireless broadband, data centers, and procurement. As part of a customer network security upgrade, how would the company go about establishing a solid network to protect a school district's network from external threats; as well as the risk of unauthorized intrusions by users within the network?

Case Projects

Problem

For a international town's 10-person IT staff, upgrading its network security initiative meant expanding its multi-vendor Gigabit and Fast Ethernet network and ensuring that its growing volume of e-government services, including online tax payments, license application filings, and housing services, function without network intrusions. To accomplish this purpose, how would the town go about guarding against increasing waves of computer viruses, malware, and denial-of-service (DoS) attacks?

Optional Team Case Project

Problem

Intrusion types of systems are put in place to serve business needs for meeting an objective of network security; IDSs and IPSs provide a foundation of technology needs and for tracking; and, identifying network attacks which detect intrusions through logs of IDS systems and preventing an action through IPS systems. If a company hosts critical systems, confidential data, and strict compliance regulations, then it's great to use IDS or IPS or both in guarding network environments. So, what are the basic benefits of IDS and IPS systems?

## Chapter 6

Securing Cloud Computing Systems

Cem Gurkok

Verizon Terremark

1. CLOUD COMPUTING ESSENTIALS: EXAMINING THE CLOUD LAYERS

Cloud computing is composed of several layers, such as public, private, hybrid, and community deployment models: SaaS, PaaS, IaaS (service, platform, infrastructure as a service or SPI) service models. The NIST Model of Cloud Computing is shown in Figure 6.1.

Infrastructure as a service (IaaS) provides online processing, data storage capacity, or network capacity on a virtualized environment. It offers the ability to provision processing, storage, networks, and other basic computing resources, allowing the customer to install and run their software, which can involve operating systems (OSs) and applications. IaaS customers buy these resources as a fully outsourced service. IaaS provides a set of application programming interfaces, which allows management and other forms of interaction with the infrastructure by consumers. Amazon, Terremark, and Rackspace are typical IaaS providers.

Platform as a service (PaaS) sits on top of IaaS. It provides an application development and deployment environment in the cloud. PaaS offers the ability to deploy applications by utilizing computer programming languages and tools available from the service provider. The service provider offers developers application building blocks to configure a new business application. This provides all of the facilities required to support the complete life cycle of building and delivering Web applications and services entirely available from the Internet. Google App Engine, Microsoft Azure, Engine Yard and Collabnet are some PaaS providers.

Service as a service (SaaS) is built on IaaS and PaaS. It serves business applications utilized by individuals or enterprises, and it can also be referred to as on-demand software. SaaS offers the most popular cloud applications to almost everyone that is online. Salesforce.com, Google Docs, and Microsoft Online Services are all popular consumer and enterprise-directed SaaS applications. The applications are accessible from various client devices through a thin client interface such as a Web browser.

Analyzing Cloud Options in Depth

Table 6.1 shows us that different cloud deployment models have varying management, ownership, locations, and access levels.

Public

Public cloud is an offering from one service provider to many clients who share the cloud-processing resources concurrently. Public cloud clients share applications,

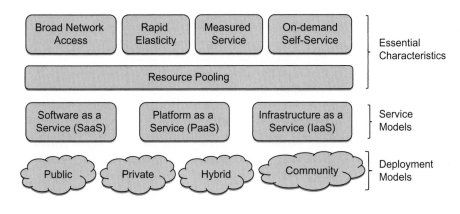

FIGURE 6.1 NIST model of cloud computing [1].

TABLE 6.1 Deployment Model's Responsibilities.

Model/Infrastructure	Managed by	Owned by	Location	Used by
Public	External CSP	External CSP	Off-Site	Untrusted
Private	Customer or external CSP	Customer or external CSP	On-site or off-site	Trusted
Hybrid	Customer and external CSP	Customer and external CSP	On-site and off-site	Trusted and untrusted

Note: CSP, Cloud Service Provider.

processing power, network resources, and data storage space. Differing levels of segregation are provided depending on the resource.

Private

A private cloud hosts one enterprise as a user. Various departments may be present in the cloud, but all are in the same enterprise. Private clouds often employ virtualization within an enterprise's existing computer servers to improve computer utilization. A private cloud also includes provisioning and metering facilities that enable fast deployment and removal where applicable. This model is similar to the conventional IT outsourcing models, but can also exist as an enterprise's internal delivery model. A variety of private cloud implementations have emerged:

- *Dedicated private cloud*: These are hosted within a customer-owned data center or at a collocation facility, and are operated by internal IT departments.
- *Community private cloud*: These are located at the premises of a third party and are owned, managed, and operated by a vendor who is bound by customized service-level agreements (SLAs) and contractual clauses with security and compliance requirements.
- *Managed private cloud*: In this implementation, the infrastructure is owned by the customer and management is performed by a third party.

Virtual Private

A virtual private cloud is a private cloud that exists within a shared or public cloud also called the Intercloud. The Intercloud comprises several interconnected clouds and legacy infrastructure. Amazon Web Services provides Amazon Virtual Private Cloud, which allows the Amazon Elastic Compute Cloud service to be connected to legacy infrastructure over an IPsec virtual private network connection. Google App Engine provides similar functionality via their Secure Data Connector product.

Hybrid

A hybrid cloud is a combination of two or more of the previously mentioned deployment models. Each of the three cloud deployment models has specific advantages and disadvantages relative to the other deployment models. A hybrid cloud leverages the advantage of the other cloud models, providing a more optimal user experience. By utilizing the hybrid cloud architecture, users are able to obtain degrees of fault tolerance combined with locally immediate usability without dependency on Internet connectivity.

Establishing Cloud Security Fundamentals

Security in cloud computing, for the most part, is no different than security in a regular IT environment. However, due to the different deployment models as described above, cloud environments present different risks to an organization. The European Network and Information Security Agency (ENISA) generally groups the risks into policy and organizational, technical, legal, and general risks and describes them as follows [2]:

Policy and Organizational Risks

Let's look at the following policy and organizational risks:

- Lock-in
- Loss of governance
- Compliance challenges
- Loss of business reputation due to co-tenant activities
- Cloud service termination or failure
- Cloud provider acquisition
- Supply chain failure

Lock-in

The potential dependency on a particular cloud provider, depending on the provider's commitments, may lead to a catastrophic business failure, should the cloud provider go bankrupt or the content and application migration path to another provider become too costly. There is little or no incentive for cloud providers to make migrating to another provider easy if they are not contractually bound to do so.

Loss of Governance

By using cloud infrastructures, the client necessarily cedes control to the cloud provider on a number of issues that may affect security. This could have a severe impact on the organization's strategy and therefore on the capacity to meet its mission and goals. The loss of control and governance could lead to the impossibility of complying with the security requirements, a lack of confidentiality, integrity and availability of data, and a deterioration of performance and quality of service, not to mention the introduction of compliance challenges.

Compliance Challenges

Certain companies migrating to the cloud might need to meet certain industry standards or regulatory requirements, such as Payment Card Industry (PCI) Data Security Standard (DSS). Migrating to the cloud could compromise these business needs if the cloud provider cannot furnish evidence of its own compliance to the relevant requirements or if the provider does not permit audits by the customer.

Loss of Business Reputation Due to Co-tenant Activities

Resource sharing can give rise to problems when the shared resources' reputation becomes tainted by a bad neighbor's activities. This would also include that certain measures be taken to mitigate, such as IP address blocking and equipment confiscation.

Cloud Service Termination or Failure

If the cloud provider faces the risk of going out of business due to financial, legal, or other reasons, the customer could suffer from loss or deterioration of service delivery performance and quality of service; as well as loss of investment.

Cloud Provider Acquisition

The acquisition of the cloud provider could increase the possibility of a strategic change and could put previous agreements at risk. This could make it impossible to comply with existing security requirements. The final impact could be damaging for crucial assets, such as the organization's reputation, customer or patient trust, and employee loyalty and experience.

Supply Chain Failure

A cloud computing provider can outsource certain specialized tasks of its infrastructure to third parties. In such a situation, the cloud provider's level of security may depend on the level of security of each one of the links and the level of dependency of the cloud provider on the third party. In general, lack of transparency in the contract can be a problem for the whole system.

Technical Risks

Let's continue now by taking a look at the following technical risks:

- Resource exhaustion
- Resource segregation failure
- Abuse of high-privilege roles
- Management interface compromise
- Intercepting data in transit, data leakage
- Insecure deletion of data
- Distributed denial of service (DDoS)
- Economic denial of service (EDoS)
- Encryption and key management (loss of encryption keys)
- Undertaking malicious probes or scans
- Compromise of the service engine
- Customer requirements and cloud environment conflicts

Resource Exhaustion

Inaccurate modeling of customer demands by the cloud provider can lead to service unavailability, access control compromise, and economic and reputation losses due to resource exhaustion. The customer takes a level of calculated risk in allocating all the resources of a cloud service because resources are allocated according to statistical projections.

Resource Segregation Failure

This class of risks includes the failure of mechanisms separating storage, memory, routing, and even reputation between different tenants of the shared infrastructure (guest-hopping attacks, SQL injection attacks exposing multiple customers' data, and side-channel attacks). The likelihood of this incident scenario depends on the cloud model adopted by the customer. It is less likely to occur for private cloud customers compared to public cloud customers.

Abuse of High Privilege Roles

The malicious activities of an insider could potentially have an impact on the confidentiality, integrity, and availability of all kinds of data, on all kinds of services, and therefore indirectly on the organization's reputation, customer trust, and employee experiences. This can be considered especially important in the case of cloud computing due to the fact that cloud architectures necessitate certain roles, which are extremely high risk. Examples of such roles include the cloud provider's system administrators and auditors and managed security service providers dealing with intrusion detection reports and incident response.

Management Interface Compromise

The customer management interfaces of public cloud providers are Internet accessible and mediate access to larger sets of resources (than traditional hosting providers). They also pose an increased risk, especially when combined with remote access and Web browser vulnerabilities.

Intercepting Data in Transit, Data Leakage

Cloud computing, being a distributed architecture, implies more data is in transit than with traditional infrastructures. Sniffing, spoofing, man-in−the-middle attacks, side channel, and replay attacks should be considered as possible threat sources.

Insecure Deletion of Data

Whenever a provider is changed, resources are scaled down, physical hardware is reallocated, and data may be available beyond the lifetime specified in the security policy. Where true data wiping is required, special procedures must be followed, and this may not be supported by the cloud provider.

Distributed Denial of Dervice (DDoS)

A common method of attack involves saturating the target environment with external communications requests, such that it cannot respond to legitimate traffic, or responds so slowly as to be rendered effectively unavailable. This can result in financial and economic losses.

Economic Denial of Service (EDoS)

EDoS destroys economic resources; the worst-case scenario would be the bankruptcy of the customer or a serious economic impact. The following scenarios are possible: An attacker can use an account and the customer's resources for his own gain or in order to damage the customer economically. The customer has not set effective limits on the use of paid resources and experiences unexpected loads on these resources. An attacker can use a public channel to deplete the customer's metered resources. For example, where the customer pays per HTTP request, a DDoS attack can have this effect.

Encryption and Key Management (Loss of Encryption Keys)

This risk includes the disclosure of secret keys (Secure Socket Layer [SSL], file encryption, customer private keys) or passwords to malicious parties. It also includes the loss or corruption of those keys, or their unauthorized use for authentication and no-repudiation (digital signature).

Undertaking Malicious Probes or Scans

Malicious probes or scanning, as well as network mapping, are indirect threats to the assets being considered. They can be used to collect information in the context of a hacking attempt. A possible impact could be a loss of confidentiality, integrity, and availability of service and data.

Compromise of the Service Engine

Each cloud architecture relies on a highly specialized platform and the service engine. The service engine sits above the physical hardware resources and manages customer resources at different levels of abstraction. For example, in IaaS clouds this software component can be the hypervisor. Like any other software layer, the service engine code can have vulnerabilities and is prone to attacks or unexpected failure. Cloud providers must set out a clear segregation of responsibilities that articulate the minimum actions customers must undertake.

Customer Requirements and Cloud Environment Conflicts

Cloud providers must set out a clear segregation of responsibilities that specify the minimum actions customers must undertake. The failure of the customers to properly secure their environments may pose a vulnerability to the cloud platform if the cloud provider has not taken the necessary steps to provide isolation. Cloud providers should further articulate their isolation mechanisms and provide best practice guidelines to assist customers in securing their resources.

Legal Risks

Now, let's look at the following legal risks:

- Subpoena and e-discovery
- Varying jurisdiction
- Data protection
- Licensing

Subpoena and e-discovery

In the event of the confiscation of physical hardware as a result of subpoena by law enforcement agencies or civil suits, the centralization of storage as well as shared tenancy of physical hardware means that many more clients are at risk of the disclosure of their data to unwanted parties. At the same time, it may become impossible for the agency of a single nation to confiscate "a cloud," given pending advances around long-distance hypervisor migration.

Varying Jurisdiction

Customer data may be held in multiple jurisdictions, some of which may be high risk or subject to higher restrictions. Certain countries are regarded as high risk because of their unpredictable legal frameworks and disrespect of international agreements. In these cases customer data can be accessed by various parties without the customer's consent. On the other hand, other countries can have stricter privacy laws and might require that certain data cannot be stored or tracked.

Data Protection

It has to be clear that the cloud customer will be the main person responsible for processing personal data, even when such processing is carried out by the cloud provider in its role of external processor. While some cloud providers, such as SAS 70-compliant ones, provide information about their data processing and security activities, others are opaque about these activities and can cause legal problems for the customer. There may also be data security breaches that are not notified to the controller by the cloud provider. In some cases, customers might be storing illegal or illegally obtained data, which might put the cloud provider and other customers at risk.

Licensing

Licensing conditions, such as per-seat agreements, and online licensing checks may become unworkable in a cloud environment. For example, if software is charged on a per-instance basis every time a new machine is instantiated, then the cloud customer's licensing costs may increase exponentially, even though they are using the same number of machine instances for the same duration.

General Risks

Let's continue by looking at the following general risks:

- Network failures
- Privilege escalation
- Social engineering
- Loss or compromise of operational and security logs or audit trails
- Backup loss
- Unauthorized physical access and theft of equipment
- Natural disasters

Network Failures

Network failure is one of the highest risks since it directly affects service delivery. It exists due to network misconfiguration, system vulnerabilities, lack of resource isolation, and poor or untested business continuity and disaster recovery plans. Network traffic modification can also be a risk for a customer and cloud provider; if provisioning isn't done properly, there is no traffic encryption or vulnerability assessment.

Privilege Escalation

Although this risk has a low probability of exploitation, it can cause loss of customer data and access control. A malicious entity can therefore take control of large portions of the cloud platform. The risk manifests itself owing to authentication, authorization, and other access control vulnerabilities, hypervisor vulnerabilities (cloud bursting), and misconfiguration.

Social Engineering

This risk is one of the most disregarded risks since most technical staff focuses on the nonhuman aspects of their platforms. The exploitation of this risk has caused loss of reputation for cloud service providers, such as Amazon and Apple due to the publicity of the events. This risk can be easily minimized by security awareness training, proper user provisioning, resource isolation, data encryption, and proper physical security procedures.

Loss or Compromise of Operational and Security Logs or Audit Trails

Operational logs can be vulnerable due to lack of policy or poor procedures for log collection. This would also include retention, access management vulnerabilities, user deprovisioning vulnerabilities, lack of forensic readiness, and operating system vulnerabilities.

Backup Loss

This high-impact risk affects company reputation, all backed up data, and service delivery. It also occurs owing to inadequate physical security procedures, access management vulnerabilities, and user deprovisioning vulnerabilities.

Unauthorized Physical Access and Theft of Equipment

The probability of malicious actors gaining access to a physical location is very low, but in the event of such an occurrence, the impact to the cloud provider and its customers is very high. It can affect company reputation and data hosted on premises; the risk is due to inadequate physical security procedures.

Natural Disasters

This risk is another ignored risk that can have a high impact on the businesses involved in the event of its occurrence. If a business has a poor or an untested business continuity and disaster recovery plan or lacks one, its reputation, data, and service delivery can be severely compromised.

Other Cloud Security Concepts

Finally, let's look at the following cloud security concepts:

- Incident response (IR), notification, and remediation
- Virtualization
- External accreditations

Incident Response (IR), Notification and Remediation

Incident response comprises a set of procedures for an investigator to examine a computer security incident. Although cloud computing brings change on many levels, certain characteristics of cloud computing pose more direct challenges to IR activities than others. The on-demand self-service nature of cloud computing environments makes it hard or even impossible to receive cooperation from the cloud service provider when handling a security incident. Also, the resource pooling practiced by cloud services, in addition to the rapid elasticity offered by cloud infrastructures, may dramatically complicate the IR process, especially the forensic activities carried out as part of the incident analysis. Resource pooling as practiced by cloud services causes privacy concerns for co-tenants regarding the collection and analysis of telemetry and artifacts associated with an incident (e. g., logging, netflow data, memory, machine images) without compromising the privacy of co-tenants. The cross-border nature of cloud computing might cause the IR team to run into legal and regulatory hurdles due to limitations placed on what data can be accessed and used in investigations.

Virtualization

Virtualization brings with it all the security concerns of the guest operating system, along with new virtualization-specific threats. A cloud service provider and customers would need to address virtual device hardening, hypervisor security, intervirtual device attacks, performance concerns, encryption, data commingling, data destruction, virtual device image tampering, and in-motion virtual devices.

External Accreditations

Rather than have a cloud service provider respond to numerous contract requests to ensure that all risks are covered, providers can obtain a number of external accreditations that will present evidence that they have both implemented appropriate security controls and follow sound security practices. One of these is the Statement on Auditing Standards (SAS) number 70, commonly known as an SAS 70 audit, which was originally published by the American Institute of Certified Public Accountants (AICPA). The audit is for service organizations and is designed to ensure that the company has sufficient controls and defenses when it is hosting or processing data belonging to one of its customers. A company that has a SAS 70 certificate has been audited by an external auditor, and the control objectives and activities have been found to be acceptable per SAS 70 requirements. When considering cloud providers, customers should look for not only SAS 70, but SAS 70 Type II. Type I certification only states that policies and procedures exist, although there is no audit to ensure that the organization adheres to these procedures. Type II certification comes only after a lengthy and rigorous in-person audit that ensures the service provider adheres to their procedures. Cloud providers, such as Terremark, Rackspace, and Amazon, are SAS 70 Type II certified.

Determining When Security Goals Require a Private Cloud

While the low cost and elastic nature of cloud computing can be beneficial for customers, due to security concerns the deployment method needs to be carefully selected. The security concerns that a potential customer needs to pay attention to are as follows:

- *Data protection (network and storage):* Sensitive and personal data, such as medical, human resources, e-mail, and government communications, will traverse the cloud environment. Securing this data in transit and storage will be important from contractual, legal, and regulatory perspectives.
- *Confidentiality:* Business processes and related information that are crucial to a company's survival may be utilized in a cloud environment. Any leakage of that information caused by voluntary communication by the cloud service provider or the cloud environment's security breach may jeopardize the customer's business and services.
- *Intellectual property:* It is important to determine who will own the intellectual property rights deployed in a cloud environment prior to engaging in cloud

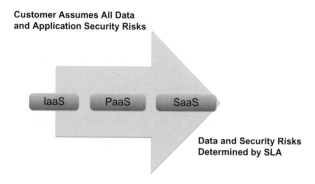

Customer Assumes All Data
and Application Security Risks

Data and Security Risks
Determined by SLA

FIGURE 6.2   Risk assumption in cloud service models.

computing activities, and further determine the use that the parties can make of the objects of such rights.

- *Professional negligence:* The customer may be exposed to contractual and tortuous liability to its customers based on negligence due to functions outsourced to the cloud service provider.
- *Outsourcing services and changes in operational control:* A customer may select working with a cloud service provider due to its perceived qualities. If the cloud service provider decides to outsource these services, security concerns could arise owing to the lack of information regarding the processes and their qualities that are adopted by the third parties.

A private cloud deployment model would address all of these concerns by providing an environment owned and managed by the customer or trusted third party, located on-premise or at a trusted location and accessible only by trusted resources. Certain government entities and financial institutions prefer private cloud deployments because of the level of control and physical separation they provide. The progression of risk assumption in cloud service models is shown in Figure 6.2.

2. SOFTWARE AS A SERVICE (SAAS): MANAGING RISKS IN THE CLOUD

In SaaS environments the service levels, privacy, compliance, security controls, and their scope are negotiated into the contracts for service. Therefore, a SaaS customer has the least tactical responsibility compared to the other cloud service models for implementing and managing security solutions.

Centralizing Information with SaaS to Increase Data Security

SaaS storage is always accessed via a Web-based user interface or a client/server application. Data is entered into the system via the Web interface and stored within the SaaS application. SaaS may consume database systems, object and file storage, or dedicated IaaS storage volumes. Data is tagged and encrypted in the SaaS application and generally managed by the provider if natively supported. Data passes through an encryption proxy before being sent to the SaaS application. This proxy can be implemented by the customer or the cloud service provider. This single point of exit and entry provides the means to easily monitor and control data being processed. Since data will be residing in a heterogeneous environment, the provider will need to encrypt data at a customer level and use separate database instances.

Implementing and Managing User Authentication and Authorization

In a SaaS environment, authentication and authorization is managed with a federated ID management solution (also known as a single sign on (SSO)). Federation is the use of Security Assertion Markup Language (SAML) to offer portability to disparate and independent security domains, with some organizations extending their DS (Directory Service) environment via a gateway product that will handle SAML assertions. Other organizations will consume native SAML assertions from an identity service. The following steps will be taken in a simplified SSO approach:

1. The user attempts to access the SaaS provider and will need to do so with some form of identifying information. For example, in the event the SaaS platform is Web based, the identifying information may be in the form of encrypted data in the URL or a cookie.
2. That information will be authenticated against the customer's user directory via a direct Web service call.
3. The customer's user directory will then reply with an assertion containing authorization and authentication information.
4. The resulting request is either fulfilled or denied based on the authentication and authorization of the assertion.

Permission and Password Protection

In a SaaS environment, the provider will offer a comprehensive password protection and permissions system. Password granting and password management (including read, write, delete options) should be clear and straightforward. Passwords will be required to change periodically to random values and will be stored in an encrypted and replicated manner.

Permissions will be assignable at different levels (workgroup, folder, subfolder), depending on the data the employee needs to access, and requestor's permissions will be validated with every access request as described in the authorization steps. The SaaS platform will capture event logs to track what data was accessed by whom at a given time.

Negotiating Security Requirements with Vendors

Service levels, security, governance, compliance, and liability expectations of the service and provider are contractually stipulated, managed to, and enforced, when the cloud provider offers a service level agreement (SLA) to the consumer. There are two types of SLAs: negotiable and nonnegotiable. When a nonnegotiable SLA is offered, the provider administers those portions stipulated in the agreement. An SLA generally comprises the parties involved, dates, scope of agreement, service hours, security, availability, reliability, support, performance metrics, and penalties.

Identifying Needed Security Measures

The security risks that were previously mentioned need to be identified and addressed by the consumer and stipulated in the SLA. Security departments should be engaged during the establishment of SLAs and contractual obligations to ensure that security requirements are contractually enforceable. SaaS providers that generate extensive customer-specific application logs and provide secure storage as well as analysis facilities will ease the burden on the customer. SLAs should cover data protection, business continuity and recovery, incident response, e-discovery, data retention, and removal [3].

Establishing a Service Level Agreement

Since multiple organizations are involved, SLAs and contracts between the parties become the primary means of communicating and enforcing expectations for responsibilities. It is important to note that the SLAs must be such that the cloud provider informs customers in a timely and reliable manner to allow for agreed actions to be taken. The customer should make sure that SLA clauses are not in conflict with promises made by other clauses or clauses from other providers [3].

SLAs may carry too much business risk for a provider, given the actual risk of technical failures. From the customer's point of view, SLAs may contain clauses that turn out to be detrimental; for example, in the area of intellectual property, an SLA might specify that the cloud provider has the rights to any content stored on the cloud infrastructure.

Ensuring SLAs Meet Organizational Security Requirements

Contracts should provide for third-party review of SLA metrics and compliance (e.g., by a mutually selected mediator). The need to quantify penalties for various risk scenarios in SLAs and the possible impact of security breaches on reputation motivate more rigorous internal audit and risk assessment procedures than would otherwise exist. The frequent audits imposed on cloud providers tend to expose risks that would not otherwise have been discovered, having therefore the same positive effect.

3. PLATFORM AS A SERVICE (PAAS): SECURING THE PLATFORM

A customer's administrator has limited control and accountability in a PaaS environment. With PaaS, securing the platform falls onto the provider, but both securing the applications developed against the platform and developing them securely belong to the customer. Customers need to trust the provider to offer sufficient control, while realizing that they will need to adjust their expectations for the amount of control that is reasonable within PaaS.

PaaS should provide functionality to allow customers to implement intrusion or anomaly detection and should permit the customers to send select events or alerts to the cloud provider's security monitoring platform. PaaS should provide encryption in the application, between client and application, in the database and proxies, as well as any application programming interface (API) that deals with the hosted data. PaaS providers generally permit their customers to perform vulnerability assessments and penetration tests on their systems.

Restricting Network Access Through Security Groups

Segregation through security groups is illustrated in Figure 6.3.

By isolating the network into physically separate parts, the cloud provider can limit traffic between public subnets and infrastructure control subnets. The network can be isolated up to a degree by utilizing network virtualization, but this can suffer from vulnerabilities and misconfiguration. Physical separation is also open to error, but this problem can be minimized by the use of process controls. Network isolation can be achieved by having physically separate networks for administrative and operational traffic, for security and network operations traffic, for storage networks, and for publicly accessible components.

Firewalls are traditionally used for network separation, and when used together with network controls, a firewall can become an extra supporting layer. This is particularly

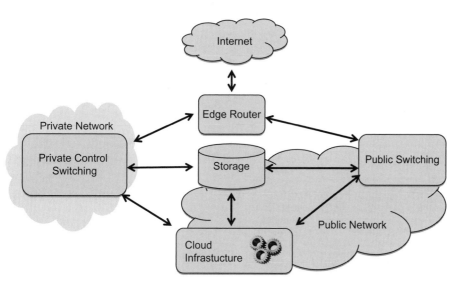

FIGURE 6.3   Segregation through security groups.

helpful when multiple subnets profit from a shared service, such as a directory.

In a PaaS environment, security groups (SGs) can act as a firewall, allowing the customer to choose which protocols and ports are open to computers over the Internet. In Amazon EC2, a security group is a set of ACCEPT firewall rules for *incoming* transmission control protocol (TCP), user datagram protocol (UDP), or internet control message protocol (ICMP). When an instance is launched with a given SG, firewall rules from this group are activated for this instance in EC2's internal distributed firewall [4].

Configuring Platform-Specific User Access Control

The cloud service provider is responsible for handling access to the network, servers, and application platforms in the PaaS model. On the other hand, the customer is responsible for access control of the applications they deploy. Application access control includes user access management, such as user provisioning and authentication. Amazon identity and access management let customers define users and their access levels, entity roles, and permissions, and provides access to federated users within the customer's existing enterprise systems. An example of user access control in PaaS is shown in Figure 6.4.

Integrating with Cloud Authentication and Authorization Systems

User access control support is not uniform across cloud providers, and offered features may differ. A PaaS provider may provide a standard API like OAuth (an open standard for authorization) to manage authentication and access control to applications. Google supports a hybrid

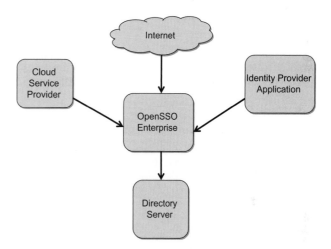

FIGURE 6.4   User access control in PaaS.

version of an OpenID (an open, decentralized standard for user authentication and access control) and OAuth protocol that combines the authorization and authentication flow in fewer steps to enhance usability. The customer could also delegate authentication to the customer's identity provider if the cloud provider supports federation standards, such as SAML. Microsoft announced the "Geneva" Claims-Based Access Platform that is compliant with SAML 2.0 standards. The platform's objective is to help developers delegate authentication, authorization, and personalization so that they don't have to implement these futures themselves.

Compartmentalizing Access to Protect Data Confidentiality

When data is stored with a PaaS provider, the provider assumes partial responsibility as the data custodian.

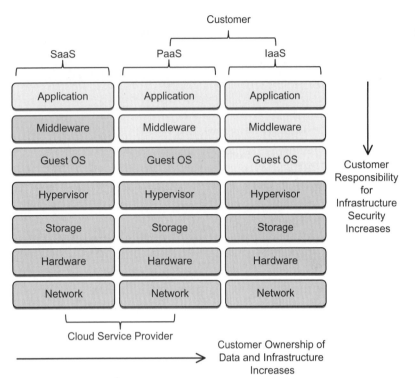

FIGURE 6.5 Ownership in different service models.

Although the responsibilities for data ownership and data custodianship are segregated, the data owner is still accountable for ensuring that data is suitably safeguarded by the custodian, as seen in Figure 6.5. In a PaaS environment, compartmentalizing access provides data confidentiality since users are prevented from being able to access certain information because they do not need access to it to perform their job functions and they have not been given formal approval to access this data (least privilege design).

Securing Data in Motion and Data at Rest

Data at rest denotes data stored in computer systems, including files on an employee's laptop, company files on a server, or copies of these files on an off-site tape backup. Securing data at rest in a cloud is not drastically different than securing it outside a cloud environment. A customer deploying in a PaaS environment needs to find the risk level acceptable and to make sure that the cloud provider is the primary custodian of the data.

Data in motion indicates data that is transitioning from storage, such as a file or database entry, to another storage format in the same or to a different system. Data in motion can also include data that is not permanently stored. Because data in motion only exists in transition (e.g., computer memory, between end points), its integrity and confidentiality must be ensured. The risk of third party observation of the data in motion exists. Data may

be cached on intermediate systems, or temporary files may be created at either endpoint. The best method to protect data in in motion is to apply encryption.

Identifying Your Security Perimeter

With the acceptance of cloud services, an organization's security perimeter has evolved to become more dynamic and has moved beyond the control of the traditional IT department. Cloud computing has extended an organization's network, system, and application realms into the cloud service provider's domain.

The Jericho Forum, an open-group consortium of IT security officers, has addressed deperimeterization. In the view of the Jericho Forum, it is essential to pinpoint the components that are critical to the customer's operation and to ensure that those are sufficiently secured, regardless of the source of the threat. In a completely deperimeterized environment, every component will be sufficiently secured to ensure that confidentiality, integrity, and availability of the data are maintained.

Techniques for Recovering Critical Data

A PaaS customer should review the available options for backup and recovery of their critical data and understand the different options available to secure the data transfer in case of an emergency. The customer should also ensure that backups and other copies of logs, access records, and any other pertinent information that may be required for legal and compliance reasons can be migrated. Data validation should be an automated or user-initiated validation protocol that allows the customer to check its data at any time to ensure the data's integrity. The cloud provider should implement fast SLA-based data recovery. The SLA should be negotiated upfront, and the customer should pay for the SLA required to ensure that there is no conflict of interest. No data, no file, or no system disk, should take more than 30 minutes to recover. PaaS providers can offer one or more of the following options:

- Basic backup and restore
- Pilot light
- Warm standby
- Multisite

Basic Backup and Restore

PaaS providers can offer storage space on their own platform where the transfer of data is performed over the network. The storage service enables snapshots of the data to be transparently copied into the storage systems. Some providers permit the transfer of large data sets by shipping the storage devices directly.

Pilot Light

The notion of the pilot light is an analogy that originates from the gas heater. In a gas heater, a small flame that is always burning can rapidly kindle the entire heater to warm up a house when desired. This situation is comparable to a backup and restore scenario; nevertheless, the customer must make sure that the critical core components of the system are already configured and running in a PaaS environment (the pilot light). When it's time for recovery, the customer would quickly provision a full-scale production environment based on the critical core components. The pilot light method will provide the customer with a shorter recovery time than the backup and restore option, because the core components of the system already exist, are running, and are continuously updated. There remains some installation and configuration tasks that need to be performed by the customer to fully recover the applications. The PaaS environment allows customers to automate the provisioning and configuration of the resources, which can save time and minimize human errors.

Warm Standby

The warm standby option extends the pilot light components and preparation. The recovery time decreases further because some services are always operating. After identifying the business-critical components, the customer would duplicate these systems in the PaaS environment

and configure them to be always running. This solution is not configured to handle a maximum production load, but it provides all of the available functions. This option may be utilized for testing, quality assurance, and internal use. In case of a catastrophe, additional resources are rapidly added to handle the production load.

Multisite

The multisite option exists in the PaaS environment as well as on the customer's on-site infrastructure where both are running. The recovery point selected will determine the data replication method that the customer employs. Various replication methods exist, such as synchronous or asynchronous. A Domain Naming Service (DNS) load balancing service can be used to direct production traffic to the backup and production sites. Part of the traffic will go to the infrastructure in PaaS, and the rest will go to the on-site infrastructure. In case of a catastrophe, the customer can adjust the DNS configuration and send all traffic to the PaaS environment. The capacity of the PaaS service can be rapidly increased to handle the full production load. PaaS resource bursting can be used to automate this process if available from the provider. The customer may need to deploy application logic to detect the failure of the primary site and divert the traffic to the parallel site running in PaaS. The cost of this option is determined by resource consumption.

4. INFRASTRUCTURE AS A SERVICE (IAAS)

Unlike PaaS and SaaS, IaaS customers are primarily responsible for securing the hosts provisioned in the cloud.

Locking Down Cloud Servers

Unlike PaaS and SaaS, IaaS customers are accountable for securing the systems provisioned in the cloud environment. Knowing that most IaaS services available today implement virtualization at the host level, host security in IaaS could be classified as follows.

Virtualization Software Security

Virtualization software is the software that exists on top of hardware and provides customers the capability to create and delete virtual instances. Virtualization at the host level can be achieved by utilizing virtualization models, such as paravirtualization (specialized host-operating system, hardware and hypervisor), operating system-level virtualization (FreeBSD jails, Solaris Containers, Linux-VServer), or hardware-based virtualization (VMware, Xen). In a public IaaS environment, customers cannot access the hypervisor because it is

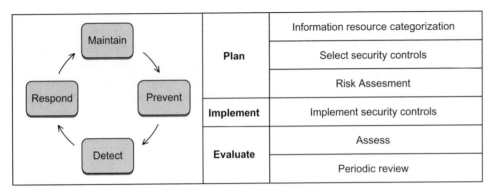

FIGURE 6.6 Cloud computing key best practices.

administered solely by the cloud services provider. Cloud services providers should implement the essential security controls, including limiting physical and logical access to the hypervisor and the other virtualization layers. IaaS customers need to comprehend the technology and access controls implemented by the cloud services provider to guard the hypervisor. This will aid the customer to recognize the compliance needs and gaps in relation to the host security standards, policies, and regulations. To show the weakness of the virtualization layer, during Black Hat 2008 and Black Hat DC 2009 Joanna Rutkowska, Alexander Tereshkin, and Rafal Wojtczuk from Invisible Things Lab showed various methods to compromise the Xen hypervisor's virtualization, including the "Blue Pill" attack.

Customer Guest Operating System (OS) or Virtual Instance Security

The virtual incarnation of an operating system is created over the virtualization layer, and it is usually configured to be exposed to the Internet. Customers have complete access to their virtual machines. Public IaaS systems can be exposed to security threats, such as the theft of keys used to access hosts (e.g., SSH private keys), the attack of exposed vulnerable services (e.g., FTP, NetBIOS, SSH), the hijacking of insecure accounts (i.e., weak or no passwords), and the deployment of malware as software or embedded in the operating system.

Ensuring the Cloud is Configured According to Best Practices

Cloud computing is still subject to conventional security best practices, but cloud services providers and their customers may find it difficult to adopt these practices since they are not tailored to the cloud space. The security best practices for cloud computing has been maturing rapidly through the contribution of the players involved in cloud

computing, such as hardware manufacturers, software providers, cloud providers, and customers. The key best practices are as follows and can be seen in Figure 6.6:

- Policy
- Risk management
- Configuration management and change control
- Auditing
- Vulnerability scanning
- Segregation of duties
- Security monitoring

Policy

It is a best practice for cloud services providers and their customers to define a solid policy for cloud security. This policy should include all security-related aspects of information security, including staff, information, infrastructure, hardware, and software. Policies are crucial to provide organizational direction. To succeed, they must be available and visible across the organization, they must have the backing of management, and they must assign responsibilities. Policies should be updated continuously, and they should be accompanied by the use of standards, procedures, and guidelines that enable the implementation of policy.

Risk Management

The goals of risk management best practices are to assess, address, and mitigate security risks in a cloud environment. This should be done in the context of determining the risks from a business standpoint. Choosing security controls and monitoring their efficacy are part of risk management. Basically, a best practice for risk management is to begin with an understanding and assessment of the risks one faces (risk analysis) and orient the selection of security controls along with appropriate security practices and procedures toward managing risks.

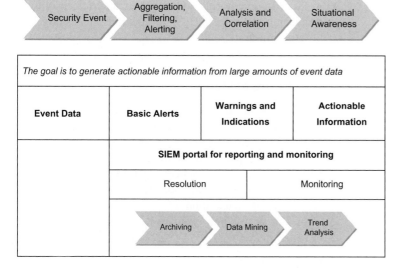

FIGURE 6.7 Security monitoring life cycle.

Configuration Management and Change Control

It is a best practice to have a configuration and change management process that can govern proposed changes. This would also include identifying possible security consequences, and providing assurance that the current operational system is correct in version and configuration.

Auditing

In auditing, the customer should seek to verify compliance, review the efficacy of controls, and validate security processes. The customer should follow a schedule in auditing, regularly evaluate security controls, use automated and manual processes to validate compliance to a policy, regularly use third-party vulnerability assessment services, and manually examine system logs to validate the effectiveness of the security monitoring systems.

Vulnerability Scanning

It is a best practice to perform periodic cloud infrastructure vulnerability scanning. This should encompass all cloud management systems, servers, and network devices. The purpose of vulnerability scanning is to locate any new or existing vulnerability so that the related risk may be reduced or eliminated.

Segregation of Duties

It is a best practice to limit the user's privileges to the level necessary for them to perform their duties. This comes from the idea of separation of duties, which in turn originates from the principle of least privilege.

Security Monitoring

It is a best practice to automate the collection of security logs from all network devices, servers, and applications. These logs should be kept in their original formats in order to preserve a legal record of all activity and so that they can be queried in an event of an alert. The purposes of security monitoring are to detect threats, expose bugs, keep a legal record of activity, and enable forensics. The most likely sources of security events are operating system logs (event logs and syslogs), application logs, intrusion detection and prevention logs, anti-virus logs, netflow logs, network device logs, and storage equipment logs. These security events are aggregated in streams and redirected via the network to a central collection service, usually a Security Information and Event Management (SIEM) system. Once these events are collected, they should be subject to an ongoing correlation and analysis process, usually performed by a Security Operation Center (SOC). The events get escalated as they are evaluated and assigned alert levels and priorities. The security monitoring life cycle is shown in Figure 6.7.

Confirming Safeguards have been Implemented

Once the IaaS environment has been implemented, it should undergo a continuous evaluation in the form of change management and periodic evaluation in the form of control review. The outcome of these evaluations would be to remedy the issues and to continue the evaluation the process. The following can be used as a generalized checklist to evaluate the IaaS environment:

- Foundations of Security
  - Policies, standards, and guidelines

- Transparency
- Employee security
- External providers
- Business Concerns
  - Business continuity
  - Disaster recovery
  - Legal considerations
  - Resource planning
- Layers of Defense
  - Software assurance
  - Authentication
  - Key management
  - Cryptography
  - Network security
  - Hypervisor and virtual machine security
  - Identity and access management
- Operational Security
  - Operational practices
  - Incident response management
  - Data center: Physical security, power and networking, asset management

Networking

The primary factor in determining whether to use private, public, or hybrid cloud deployments is the risk level an organization can tolerate. Although various IaaS providers implement virtual network zoning, they may not be the same as an internal private cloud that employs stateful inspection and other network security services. If customers have the budget to afford the services of a private cloud, their risks will decline, given they have a private cloud that is internal to their network. In some instances, a private cloud located at a cloud provider's facility can help satisfy security requirements, but will be dependent on the provider's capabilities and maturity. Confidentiality risk can be reduced by using encryption for data in transit. Secure digital signatures can make it more difficult for malicious players to tamper with data and therefore, ensure the integrity of data. The cloud service provider should provide the following information to the customer:

- Data and access control threats
- Access and authentication controls
- Information about security gateways (firewalls, Web application firewalls, service-oriented architecture, and application programming interface)
- Secure services like DNSSEC, NTP, OAuth, SNMP, and management network segmentation
- Traffic and network flow monitoring capabilities
- Hypervisor integration availability
- Security products (IDS/IPS, Server Tier Firewall, File Integrity Monitoring, DLP, Anti-Virus, Anti-Spam)

- Security monitoring and incident response capabilities
- Denial-of-service (DoS) protection and mitigation capabilities

Operating Systems

The ease of self-provisioning new virtual instances on an IaaS platform creates a possibility that insecure virtual servers may be created. Secure-by-default configuration should be implemented by default by mirroring or surpassing industry best practices. Securing a virtual instance in the cloud requires solid operational security procedures supported by automation of procedures. The following steps can be used to evaluate host and virtual machine (VM) security:

- Use a hardened system configuration. A best practice for cloud applications is to build hardened virtual machine images that have only the configuration sufficient to support the application stack. Limiting the abilities of the basic application stack not only limits the server's attack surface, but also greatly decreases the number of updates needed to maintain a secure application stack.
- Keep track of the available virtual machine images and operating system versions that are offered for cloud hosting. The IaaS provider offers some of these VM images through their infrastructure. If a virtual machine image from the IaaS provider is utilized, it should go through the same security verification and hardening process for systems within the enterprise infrastructure. The best substitute for the customer is to build its image that matches the security standards of the internal trusted systems.
- Maintain the integrity of the hardened image.
- Secure the private keys required to access hosts in the cloud.
- Separate the cryptographic keys from the cloud where the data is hosted. The exception to this would be when the keys are necessary for decryption, and this would be limited to the duration of the decryption activity. If the application needs a key to continuously encrypt and decrypt, it may not be feasible to protect the key since it will be hosted with the application.
- Do not place credentials in the virtual machine images except for a key to decrypt the file system.
- Do not permit password-based authentication for remote access.
- Require passwords to execute administrative functions.
- Install a host firewall and open to the public only the minimum ports necessary to support the services.
- Run only the needed services, and turn off the unused services (e.g., turn off FTP, print services, network

file services, and database services if they are not required).

- Install a host-based intrusion detection system (IDS).
- Log system and event logs to a dedicated log aggregator. Isolate the log server with strong access controls.
- Ensure a system to provide patching images in the cloud; both online and offline is available.
- Ensure that isolation between different customers (network and data) is provided.

Applications

The integrity and security of a cloud environment is dependent on the integrity of its components. Software is a primary route for vulnerabilities and exploits. IaaS providers, such as Amazon EC2 and Terremark, handle the applications on customer virtual machines as black boxes. This makes the providers completely independent of the operations and management of the customer's applications. Therefore, customers bear the full responsibility for securing their applications deployed in the cloud.

Web applications installed on a public cloud should be designed with an Internet facing threat model and protected with typical security measures against Web application vulnerabilities, such as those listed in the the Open Web Application Security Project (OWASP) Top 10 Web application security risks. Following common security development practices, they should also be periodically audited for vulnerabilities. Security should be embedded into the software development life cycle. It's the customers' responsibility to keep their applications and runtime platform up to date to protect their systems from a compromise. It is in the customer's best interest to designs and implement applications with the least-privileged access model.

Developers creating applications for IaaS clouds should develop their own mechanisms for authentication and authorization. Similar to traditional identity management implementations, cloud applications should also be designed to use delegated authentication services offered by an enterprise identity provider. If in-house implementations of authentication, authorization, and accounting are not properly designed, they can become a weakness. Cloud customers should avoid using in-house authentication, authorization, and accounting solutions when possible.

Scanning for and Patching Vulnerabilities

Penetration testing and vulnerability assessments of cloud infrastructure should be carried out on a periodic basis. Usually, the customer may not have the specialized skills and expertise to perform these tests; therefore, the customer should work with a third party that is professional and has the necessary skills and certifications. Penetration testing should be geared toward the entire cloud infrastructure and not just individual components. Security is only as good as the weakest link.

A penetration test and vulnerability assessment can uncover multiple vulnerabilities, not all of which can or should be fixed. Newly found vulnerabilities need to be classified by their severity. Generally, a vulnerability that is categorized as critical should be addressed to safeguard the entire cloud. Vulnerabilities categorized as having low and medium severity may be accepted as reasonable risks. Vulnerabilities that are not addressed need to have their residual risk evaluated and then accepted by the customer. If it is found that the same vulnerability exists across all servers with the virtual machine image, then this should be fixed in the golden virtual machine image.

Vulnerability scanning has additional benefits. If one collects scan data against the same targets and stores the scan results in a database, configuration errors and attack trends can be detected by analysis of this data over time. Likewise, use of a database to store scanning results, makes these immediately available to auditors and automated tools for compliance and other security checking.

Controlling and Verifying Configuration Management

The relationship between configuration management and security control procedures is an often-neglected one in commercial implementations of Internet-facing systems. The root cause is typically a process failure in configuration management or change control (CC). A recognition of this problem is found in NIST SP 800−64, Security Considerations in the Information System Development Life Cycle, which states: "Changes to the hardware, software, or firmware of a system can have a significant impact on the security of the system . . . changes should be documented, and their potential impact on security should be assessed regularly." Configuration management and change management should be well defined and provide a structured method for causing technical and administrative changes. They should also provide assurances that the information technology resources in operation are correct in their version and configuration. Configuration management and change management are essential to controlling and managing an accurate inventory of components and changes.

Vulnerability assessments can be used to confirm the configuration management data. When issues that have not been previously identified are discovered, more thorough investigation becomes necessary.

Most of the time cloud providers are responsible for the vulnerability, patch, and configuration administration of the infrastructure (hosts, storage, networks, and applications). Cloud providers should assure their customers of their technical vulnerability management program using ISO/IEC 27002 type control and assurance frameworks.

IaaS configuration management and change control focuses on infrastructure managed by the cloud provider, as well as the customer infrastructure interfacing with the IaaS environment. Therefore, the provider should be responsible for systems, networks, hypervisors, employee systems, and storage and management applications owned and operated by the provider and third parties. Instead, IaaS customers are responsible for their virtual servers, image standardization, configuration standardization, configuration management of the customer environment, and network access policies.

5. LEVERAGING PROVIDER-SPECIFIC SECURITY OPTIONS

Due to the elastic model of services delivered via the cloud, customers need only pay for the amount of security they require, such as the number of workstations to be protected or the amount of network traffic monitored, and not for the supporting infrastructure and staffing to support the various security services. A security-focused provider offers greater security expertise than is typically available within an organization. Finally, outsourcing administrative tasks, such as log management, can save time and money, allowing an organization to devote more resources to its core competencies. The security options that are provided by various cloud providers are as follows:

- Network security
- Multifactor authentication
- Identity and access management
- Data loss prevention
- Encryption
- Business continuity and disaster recovery
- Web security
- Email security
- Security assessments
- Intrusion management, detection, and prevention
- Security information and event management

Defining Security Groups to Control Access

The conventional model of network zones and tiers has been supplanted in public clouds with security groups, security domains, or virtual data centers that have logical boundaries between tiers but are less exact and offer less protection than the earlier model. A security group acts as a firewall that controls the traffic allowed into a group of instances. When the customer launches a virtual instance,

it can assign the instance to one or more security groups. For each security group, the customer adds rules that govern the allowed inbound traffic to instances in the group. All other inbound traffic is discarded. The customer can modify rules for a security group at any time. The new rules are automatically enforced for all existing and future instances in the group. The default security group usually allows no inbound traffic and permits all outbound traffic. A virtual instance can have as many security groups as needed.

Filtering Traffic by Port Number

Each security group rule enables a specific source to access the instances in the group using a certain protocol (TCP, UDP, ICMP) and destination port or ports. For example, a rule could allow a source IP address 1.1.1.1 to access the instances in the group on TCP port 80 (the protocol and destination port).

Discovering and Benefiting from the Provider's Built-in Security

Some IaaS providers have the mentioned security options built into their systems. Amazon EC2 provides its customers with identity and access management (IAM) policies and security groups (SGs). Other providers such as Terremark have multifactor authentication built into their Enterprise Cloud solutions besides IAM and SG. These built-in features decrease the time needed to launch a secure environment and reduce the cost further.

Protecting Archived Data

The same three information security principles are associated with data stored in the cloud as with data stored elsewhere: confidentiality, integrity, and availability.

Confidentiality

Confidentiality is usually provided by encrypting customer data. Data can be at the volume storage level or object storage level.

Volume storage encryption prevents snapshot cloning or exposure, exploration by the cloud provider, and exposure due to physical loss of drives. IaaS volumes can be encrypted using instance-managed encryption (instance managed, keys stored in volume and protected by a secret or key pair), externally managed encryption (instance managed, keys are managed externally, provided on request), or proxy encryption (external software or appliance managed).

Object or file storage encryption allows the user to implement virtual private storage (VPS). Like a virtual private network, VPS allows the use of a public shared infrastructure while still protecting data, since only those with encryption keys can read the data. The objects can be encrypted by standard tools, by the application using the data, or by a proxy before being placed in storage.

IaaS providers can also offer IAM policies and access control lists (ACLs) to further protect stored data. The transfer of data is also protected by provider-implemented SSL or VPN connections.

Integrity

Besides the confidentiality of data, the customer also needs to consider the integrity of their data. Confidentiality does not mean integrity. Data can be encrypted for confidentiality reasons, but the customer might not have a method to validate the integrity of that data. IaaS providers should regularly check for integrity by keeping track of data checksums and repair data if corruptions are detected by using redundant data. Data in transfer should also be checksum validated to detect corruption.

Availability

Supposing that customers' data has preserved its confidentiality and integrity, the customers should also be worried about the availability of their data. They should be concerned about three main threats: network-based attacks; the cloud service provider's own availability; and backups or redundancy. Availability is usually stated in the SLA, and customers pay for varying levels of availability based on their risk tolerances. IaaS providers may provide redundant storage (geographic and systemic), versioning, and high-bandwidth connectivity to prevent problems arising from availability issues.

6. ACHIEVING SECURITY IN A PRIVATE CLOUD

In private clouds, computing and storage infrastructure are dedicated to a single organization and are not shared with any other organization. However, just because they are private does not mean that they are more secure.

Taking Full Responsibility for Security

The security management and day-to-day operation of the environment are relegated to internal IT or to a third party with contractual SLAs. The risks faced by internal IT departments still remain. Private cloud security should be considered from different perspectives:

- *Infrastructure security:* This perspective includes physical access and data leakage concerns (loss of

hard drives), energy supply security, facility security, network security, hardware security (hardware cryptography modules, trusted protection modules), compute security (process, memory isolation), storage security, operation system security, virtualization security, and update security (hypervisor, virtual machines).
- *Platform security:* This perspective includes user experience security, application framework security, data security, development environment security, and update security.
- *Software security:* This perspective includes application security (multi-tenant partitioning, and user permissions) and update security.
- *Service delivery security:* This perspective includes connection security (SSL, authentication), and service endpoint security (traditional network security).
- *User security:* This perspective includes making sure that the users and the systems they are using to access the private cloud are trusted and secured.
- *Legal concerns:* This perspective includes governance issues, compliance issues (PCI DSS, HIPPA), data protection (personally identifiable information), and legal agreements (SLA, terms of use, user license agreements).

The advantages of a private cloud in the context of security become apparent mostly when compared to a public cloud implementation.

Managing the Risks of Public Clouds

Although a public cloud deployment is suitable for most uses that are nonsensitive, migrating sensitive, mission-critical, or proprietary data into any cloud environment that is not certified and designed for handling such data introduces high risk. A customer should first select a cloud deployment model and then make sure that sufficient security controls are in place. These actions should be followed by a reasonable risk assessment:

- *Data and encryption*: If the data is stored unencrypted in the cloud, data privacy is at risk. There is the risk for unauthorized access either by a malicious employee on the cloud service provider side or an intruder gaining access to the infrastructure from the outside.
- *Data retention*: When the data is migrated or removed by the cloud provider or customer, there may be data residues that might expose sensitive data to unauthorized parties.
- *Compliance requirements*: Various countries have varying regulations for data privacy. Because some public cloud providers don't offer information about the location of the data, it is crucial to consider the

legal and regulatory requirements about where data can be stored.

- *Multi-tenancy risks*: The shared nature of public cloud environments increases security risks, such as unauthorized viewing of data by other customers using the same hardware platform. A shared environment also presents resource competition problems whenever one of the customers uses most of the resources due either to need or to being exposed to targeted attacks, such as DDoS (distributed denial of service).
- *Control and visibility*: Customers have restricted control and visibility over the cloud resources because the cloud provider is responsible for administering the infrastructure. This introduces additional security concerns that originate from the lack of transparency. Customers need to rethink the way they operate as they surrender the control of their IT infrastructure to an external party while utilizing public cloud services.
- *Security responsibility*: In a cloud the vendor and the user share responsibility forsecuring the environment. The amount of responsibility shouldered by each party can change depending on the cloud model adopted.

Identifying and Assigning Security Tasks in Each SPI Service Model: SaaS, PaaS, IaaS

Security-related tasks tend to be the highest for the cloud provider in an SaaS environment, whereas an IaaS environment shifts most of the tasks to the customer.

- SaaS
  - *Attack types:* Elevation of privilege, cross-site scripting attack (XSS), cross-site request forgery (CSRF), SQL injection, encryption, open redirect, buffer overflows, connection polling, canonicalization attacks, brute force attacks, dictionary attacks, token stealing.
  - *Provider security responsibilities:* Identity and access management, data protection, security monitoring, security management, authentication, authorization, role-based access control, auditing, intrusion detection, incident response, forensics.
  - *Consumer security responsibilities:* Other than assessing the risk of being in a cloud environment, the customer has little to do in SaaS environment.
- PaaS
  - *Attack types:* Data tampering, buffer overflows, canonicalization attacks, Structured Query Language (SQL) injection, encryption, disclosure of confidential data, elevation of privilege, side-channel attacks (VM-to-VM)
  - *Provider security responsibilities:* Security monitoring, security management, authentication, authorization, role-based access control, auditing, intrusion detection, incident response, forensics
  - *Customer security responsibilities:* Identity and access management, data protection
- IaaS
  - *Attack types:* Data tampering, side-channel attacks (VM-to-VM , VM-to-host or host-to-VM), encryption, network traffic sniffing, physical access, brute force attacks, dictionary attacks
  - *Provider security responsibilities:* Role-based access control, auditing, intrusion detection, incident response, forensics
  - *Customer security responsibilities:* Identity and access management, data protection, security monitoring, security management, authentication, authorization

Selecting the Appropriate Product

While evaluating cloud computing products, customers usually want to know about how secure the implementation is, if the cloud provider is meeting best practices for security, how well the cloud provider is meeting discrete controls and requirements, and how the product compares with other similar services.

Comparing Product-Specific Security Features

To be able to compare cloud providers, we need to define a set of metrics and standards. Based on the previous discussions of risk and cloud security coverage, we can use the following set:

- *Organizational security:* Staff security, third-party management, SLAs
- *Physical security:* Physical access controls; access to secure areas, environmental controls
- *Identity and access management:* Key management, authorization, authentication
- *Encryption:* Connection encryption (SSL, VPN), stored data encryption
- *Asset management and security:* Asset inventory, classification, destruction of used media
- *Business continuity (BC) and disaster recovery (DR) management:* Recovery point objective and recovery time objective information, information security during DR and BC, recovery priority, dependencies
- *Incident management:* Existence of a formal process, detection capabilities, real-time security monitoring, escalation procedures, statistics
- *Legal concerns and privacy:* Audits, certifications, location of data, jurisdiction, subcontracting, outsourcing, data processing, privacy, intellectual property

The vendors that provide the highest transparency into their services will have higher coverage of metrics and a possibly higher score than the vendor with less documentation. Some vendors will lack the specific feature or will not document it properly and therefore, will not have a score for the specific metric.

Considering Organizational Implementation Requirements

Besides comparing the cloud provider's products, the customers also need to be well aware of their organization's security requirements and how they align with the cloud provider's offerings. The customers should check for the following organizational requirements to see if they apply:

- Data
  - Separation of sensitive and nonsensitive data: Segregate sensitive data from nonsensitive data into separate databases in separate security groups when hosting an application that handles highly sensitive data.
  - Encryption of non-root file systems: Use only encrypted file systems for block devices and non-root local devices.
  - Encryption of file system key: Pass the file system key encrypted at start-up.
  - Signing of content in storage.
  - Secure handling of decryption keys and forced removal after use: Decryption keys should be in the cloud only for the duration of use.
- Applications
  - No dependence on a specific virtual machine system (operating system or other cloud services).
  - Source address filtering of network traffic: Only allow needed traffic, such as HTTP and HTTPS.
  - Encryption of network traffic.
  - Strong authentication of network-based access: Authentication should preferably be performed using keys by performing mutual authentication.
  - Use of host-based firewall.
  - Installation of a network-based intrusion detection system (NIDS).
  - Installation of a host-based intrusion detection system (HIDS).
  - Usage of hardening tools: Usage of hardening tools, such as Bastille Linux, and SELinux should be possible.
  - System design for patch roll-out: System should be designed to easily patch and relaunch instances.
  - Support of SAML or other identity and access management systems.
- Other
  - Compliance support: Presence of SAS 70 Type II, PCI DSS, and other compliance certifications.

- Regular full backups stored in remote secure locations.
- Instance snapshots in case of a security breach.
- Role segregation: The infrastructure should be segmented based on roles (development, production).
- Regular verification of cloud resources configuration: This is especially important since cloud resources can be managed via different channels (Web console and APIs). Thus, if, for example, the Web console access has been hacked, this might not be immediately visible to the customer if normally management is only done via APIs. Therefore, some type of intrusion detection for the cloud resource management is needed.
- No credentials in end-user devices.
- Secure storage and generation of credentials.
- Security groups: Security groups (i.e., named set of firewall rules) should be used to configure IP traffic to and from instances completely in order to isolate every tier, even internally to the cloud.

Virtual Private Cloud (VPC)

VPC can offer public cloud users the privacy of a private cloud environment. In a VPC, while the infrastructure remains public, the cloud provider lets the customers define a virtual network by letting them select their own subnets, IP address ranges, route tables, and network gateways. Optionally virtual private networks (VPNs) are provided to further secure the virtual networks. Stored data can also be protected by assigning ACLs.

Simulating a Private Cloud in a Public Environment

VPCs utilize VPNs to secure communication channels by creating protected, virtually dedicated conduits within the cloud provider network. This eradicates the necessity to specify intricate firewall rules between the application in the cloud and the enterprise, because all locations would be linked by a private network isolated from the public Internet. VPNs form the construct of a private network and address space used by all VPN endpoints. Because VPNs can use specific IP addresses, the cloud provider can permit customers to utilize any IP address ranges without conflicting with other cloud customers. A VPC can contain many cloud data centers, but it appears as a single collection of resources to the customer.

Google Secure Data Connector (SDC)

SDC provides data connectivity and allows IT administrators to control the services and data that are available in Google Apps (Web-based office suite). SDC builds a secure link by encrypting connections between Google Apps and customer networks. Google Apps is the only external service that can make requests over the secured connection. SDC can filter the types of requests that can be routed. The filters can limit which gadgets, spreadsheets, and App Engine applications may access which internal systems. Filters can also be used to limit user access to resources. SDC implements OAuth Signed Fetch that adds authentication information to requests that are made through SDC. The customer can use OAuth to validate requests from Google and provide an additional layer of security to the SDC filters.

Amazon VPC

Amazon VPC lets their customers cut out a private section of their public cloud where they can launch services in a virtual network. Using the Amazon VPC, the customer can delineate a virtual network topology that is similar to a traditional network where the customer can specify its own private IP address range, segregate the IP address range into private and public subnets, administer inbound and outbound access using network access control lists, store data in the Amazon S3 storage service and set access permissions, attach multiple virtual network interfaces, and bridge the VPC with on-site IT infrastructure with a VPN to extend existing security and management policies.

Industry-Standard, VPN-Encrypted Connections

A customer might simply want to extend its organization's perimeter into the external cloud computing environment by using a site-to-site VPN and operating the cloud environment making use of its own directory services to control access. Companies such as Terremark and Rackspace offer site-to-site VPN solutions to extend the existing IT infrastructure into their clouds so that customers can securely use solutions deployed in the cloud (e.g., collaboration solutions, testing and development, data replication, DR).

The Hybrid Cloud Alternative

A hybrid cloud can be created by combining any of the three cloud types: public, private, and virtual private. Hybrid clouds are formed when an organization builds a private cloud and wants to leverage its public and virtual private clouds in conjunction with its private cloud for a particular purpose. An example of a hybrid cloud would be a Web site where its core infrastructure is only accessible by the company, but specific components of the Web site are hosted externally, such as high-bandwidth media (video streaming or image caching). Nevertheless, some

requirements can thwart hybrid cloud acceptance. For example, financial services companies, such as banks, might not be able to comply with regulations if customer data is hosted at a third-party site or location, regardless of the security controls. Governments also might not be able to take the risk of being compromised in case of a hybrid cloud breach.

Connecting On-Premises Data with Cloud Applications

Data transferred to the cloud should be encrypted both when on the cloud and during transfer (e.g., with SSL, VPN). The employed encryption service should provide well-thought-out encryption key management policies to guarantee data integrity. Also, the customer should retain encryption key ownership to maintain separation of duties between their business and the other cloud service providers. This permits the customers to use their encryption throughout their private and public clouds and therefore, lets them avoid vendor lock-in and to move between cloud providers.

Securely Bridging with VPC

As the name suggests, a VPC does not deliver a fully private infrastructure, but a virtually private infrastructure. Servers created in the customer's VPC are allocated from the same shared resources that are used by all other provider customers. Hence, the customer still has to consider extra security measures in the cloud, both for networking (interserver traffic) and data in shared storage.

To be able to securely bridge existing infrastructure with VPCs, the customer would need to employ tools such as CloudSwitch or Vyatta. These tools provide data isolation for the data circulating between the in-house data center and the VPCs using data encryption and therefore, applying an additional layer of security. For example, CloudSwitch isolates all network and storage access to data at the device level with AES-256 encryption. It also utilizes roles and permissions-based access to enforce corporate policies.

Dynamically Expanding Capacity to Meet Business Surges

Cloudbursting is the dynamic arrangement of an application operating on a private cloud to use public clouds to meet sudden, unforeseen demand, such as a tax services company's need to meet increasing traffic associated with tax-filing deadlines. The benefit of this type of hybrid cloud usage is that the customer only pays for the additional computing resources when they are in demand. To utilize cloudbursting, a customer would need to address workload migration (ability to clone the application environment with tools such as Chef, Puppet, CFEngine,

Cloudify), data synchronization (maintaining real-time data copies), and network connectivity.

7. MEETING COMPLIANCE REQUIREMENTS

Cloud providers recognize the difficulty of meeting a wide range of customer requirements. To build a model that can scale, the cloud provider needs to have solid set of controls that can benefit all of its customers. To achieve this goal, the cloud provider can use the model of governance, risk, and compliance (GRC). GRC acknowledges that compliance is an ongoing activity requiring a formal written compliance program. The cloud provider should undergo a continuous cycle of risk assessment, identifying the key controls, monitoring, and testing to identify gaps in controls (Security Content Automation Protocol or SCAP, Cybersecurity Information Exchange Framework or CYBEX, GRC-XML), reporting, and improving on the reported issues. The cycle of compliance evaluation is shown in Figure 6.8.

Managing Cloud Governance

Governance is the set of processes, technologies, customs, policies, laws, and institutions affecting the way an enterprise is directed, administered, or controlled. Governance also comprises the relationship betwen the stakeholders and the goals of the company. Governance includes auditing supply chains, board and management structure and process, corporate responsibility and compliance, financial transparency and information disclosure, and ownership structure and exercise of control rights. A key factor in a customer's decision to engage a corporation is the confidence that expectations will be met. For cloud services, the interdependencies of services should not hinder the customer from clearly identifying the responsible parties. Stakeholders should carefully consider the monitoring mechanisms that are appropriate and necessary for the company's consistent performance and growth.

Customers should review the specific information security governance structure and processes, as well as specific security controls, as part of their due diligence for future cloud providers. The provider's security governance processes and capabilities should be evaluated to see if they are consistent with the customer's information security management processes. The cloud provider's information security controls should be risk-based and clearly support the customer's management processes. The loss of control and governance could cause noncompliance with the security requirements, a lack of confidentiality, integrity and availability of data, and a worsening of performance and quality of service.

Retaining Responsibility for the Accuracy of the Data

Laws and regulations will usually determine who in an organization should be responsible and held accountable for the accuracy and security of the data. If the customer is storing HIPAA (Health Insurance Portability and Accountability Act) data, then the customer must have a security-related post created to ensure compliance. The Sarbanes–Oxley Act assigns the Chief Financial Officer (CFO) and Chief Executive Officer (CEO) joint responsibility for the financial data. The Gramm-Leach-Bliley Act (GLBA) casts a wider net, making the entire board of directors responsible for security. The Federal Trade Commission (FTC) is less specific by only requiring a certain individual to be responsible for information security in a company.

Verifying Integrity in Stored and Transmitted Data

One of the main difficulties in cloud computing is tracking the location of data during processing. Having control over the data's creation, transfer, storage, use, and destruction becomes crucial. Using data-mining tools and solid IT operational practices will be key to managing data. Although host-level security can be tackled, host-to-host communication and its integrity are harder to secure due to the volume and dynamic nature of data in transition. Although traditional security scanners can be used, real-time reporting provides a better assessment. Thus, an IT GRC solution would display a general view of important metrics to provide a summary of site security and reliability. This solution can keep track of version management and integrity verification of backed-up and in-transit data.

Demonstrating Due Care and Due Diligence

Before signing a contract with a cloud provider, a customer should assess its specific requirements. The range of the services, along with any limitations, regulations, or compliance requirements, should be identified. Any

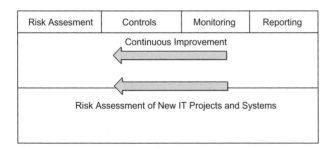

FIGURE 6.8 Cycle of compliance evaluation.

services that will be deployed to the cloud should also be graded as to their importance to the business. A customer should consider if cloud computing is a true core business of the provider, if the provider is financially sound, if the provider is outsourcing, if the physical security of the facilities meet customer needs, if the provider's BC and DR plans are consistent with the customer's needs, if the operations team is technically competent, if they have a verifiable track record, and if the provider offers any indemnifications. Performing due diligence will reduce the negotiation time and make sure that the correct level of security is in place for the customer.

Supporting Electronic Discovery

Electronic discovery (e-discovery) refers to discovery in civil litigation of information in an electronic format. Due to the nature of a cloud environment, a customer might not be able to apply or use e-discovery tools regularly used. The customer also might not have the capability or administrative permissions to search or access all of the data existing in the cloud. Therefore, the customer will need to take into consideration the additional time and expense that will result from performing e-discovery in a cloud environment.

The customers must make clear in the contractual agreement what the cloud provider needs to do if they are contacted to provide data to a third party, such as law enforcement. The customers might want to contest the request due to the confidentiality of the data or due to an unreasonable request.

Preserving a Chain of Evidence

Chain of evidence or chain of custody refers to the chronological documentation showing seizure, custody, control, transfer, analysis, and disposition of evidence. Several issues touch on the responsibilities and limits that affect customers and providers with regard to collecting legally admissible evidence for prosecution. Identifying the actors is difficult enough with an evidence chain where responsibility for collecting data is shared between the provider and tenant. One party may be the custodian of the data, while the other is the legal owner. Maintaining a chain of evidence can be difficult due to the possibility of compromising the privacy of other cloud customers, unsynchronized log times, and data tampering in open environments, such as public clouds.

Assuring Compliance with Government Certification and Accreditation Regulations

Cloud providers face an increasingly complex variety of compliance requirements from their customers, such as industry standards, regulations, and customer frameworks. Relevant audit frameworks should be used when designing the cloud provider's security control set, and periodic external audits should address the most relevant aspects of these controls.

HIPAA

Cloud providers and customers that handle protected health information (PHI) are required to comply with the security and privacy requirements established in support of HIPAA. The HIPAA security and privacy rules focus on health plans, health care clearinghouses, health care providers, and system vendors. HIPAA requires that PHI is sufficiently protected when entrusted to third parties, such as cloud providers. The level of security should be kept up to standard across all environments. HIPAA addresses administrative safeguards, workforce security, information access management, security awareness and training, security incident procedures, contingency plans, evaluations, physical safeguards (facility and user devices), and technical safeguards (access control, audit control and integrity, authentication, and encryption).

Sarbanes–Oxley

As a reaction to substantial financial reporting fraud in the early 2000s, the Sarbanes–Oxley Act of 2002 (SOX) was passed and signed into law. As a result of SOX, public company CFOs and CEOs are required to certify the efficacy of their internal controls over financial reporting (ICOFR) on a quarterly and annual basis. Management is required to do a yearly assessment of its ICOFR. Third-party auditors are required to provide an opinion about the efficacy of the management's ICOFR at the company's fiscal year end. SOX also influenced the creation of the Public Company Accounting Oversight Board (PCAOB), which was tasked with instituting audit standards. PCAOB Auditing Standard No. 2 pointed to the significance of information technology general controls (ITGCs).

SOX emphasizes the efficacy of an organization's financial reporting process, accounting and finance processes, other vital business, and controls over IT systems that have a material influence on financial reporting. SOX includes internally administered and outsourced systems that can substantially affect financial reporting. A customer using a SaaS environment might make the cloud provider relevant to their SOX scope if financial information is processed in the cloud. Cloud providers need to be clear about their own and the customer's responsibilities about processing information and ensure robust processes for user management/segregation of duties, systems development, program and infrastructure change

---

An Agenda for Action for Complying with the Data Protection Act Activities

All UK businesses holding personal data about third parties (customers) must comply with the Data Protection Act. The act's principles are as follows (check all tasks completed):

_____1. Personal data shall be processed fairly and lawfully and, in particular, shall not be processed unless:

  _____**a.** at least one of the conditions in Schedule 2 is met, and

  _____**b.** in the case of sensitive personal data, at least one of the conditions in Schedule 3 is also met.

_____**2.** Personal data shall be obtained only for one or more specified and lawful purposes, and shall not be further processed in any manner incompatible with that purpose or those purposes.

_____**3.** Personal data shall be adequate, relevant, and not excessive in relation to the purpose or purposes for which they are processed.

_____**4.** Personal data shall be accurate and, where necessary, kept up to date.

_____**5.** Personal data processed for any purpose or purposes shall not be kept longer than is necessary for that purpose or those purposes.

_____**6.** Personal data shall be processed in accordance with the rights of data subjects under this Act.

_____**7.** Appropriate technical and organizational measures shall be taken against unauthorized or unlawful processing of personal data and against accidental loss or destruction of, or damage to, personal data.

_____**8.** Personal data shall not be transferred to a country or territory outside the European Economic Area unless that country or territory ensures an adequate level of protection for the rights and freedoms of data subjects in relation to the processing of personal data.

---

management, and computer operations. Cloud providers also need to be concerned about physical security; stored and in-transit data; passwords; remote access; provider access to data; data disclosure; other customers accessing the data; data location (data centers, replicas, backups); shared resources; loss of governance; and isolation failures.

Data Protection Act

The Data Protection Act of 1998 is a United Kingdom (UK) Act of Parliament. The Act, defines UK law on the processing of data on identifiable living people (see the checklist: An Agenda for Action for Complying with the Data Protection Act Activities).

PCI DSS

Organizations that deal with credit-card transactions are required to comply with the Payment Card Industry (PCI) Data Security Standard (DSS). The compliance is ensured by third-party assessments and self-assessments, depending on the volume of credit-card processing transactions. PCI DSS contains 12 high-level requirements:

1. Install and maintain a firewall configuration to protect cardholder data.
2. Do not use vendor-supplied defaults for system passwords and other security parameters.
3. Protect stored cardholder data.
4. Encrypt transmission of cardholder data across open, public networks.
5. Use and regularly update antivirus software.
6. Develop and maintain secure systems and applications.
7. Restrict access to cardholder data based on the business's need to know.
8. Assign a unique ID to each person with computer access.
9. Restrict physical access to cardholder data.
10. Track and monitor all access to network resources and cardholder data.
11. Regularly test security systems and processes.
12. Maintain a policy that addresses information security.

Customers processing or storing cardholder data in a cloud provider need to ensure that the cloud provider and other third parties comply with PCI DSS as well. If the cloud provider has services including processing of credit-card transactions, it is crucial that the cloud provider transparently explains its information flows and how it segregates its credit-card processing and storage activities from others. This approach would limit the extent of the infrastructure that would be subject to PCI DSS. The main objectives of PCI DSS are to ensure the protection of cardholder data, avert breaches, and rapidly contain a breach. These objectives are valid for cloud computing environments as well.

Limiting the Geographic Location of Data

Cloud customers need to ensure that the providers employed outside of their country of residence and jurisdiction have sufficient security controls in place, including their primary and backup sites as well as any intermediate sites that the data crosses. The data protection laws of the European Union (EU) states and other countries are complex and have numerous requirements. The EU stipulates that the data controller and processor must notify entities that the data will be sent and processed in a country other than a member state. They must also have contracts approved by the Data Protection Authority before these activities can be performed. The customer also needs to be aware of the cloud provider subcontracting any data-related functionality since the third parties involved might host or transfer data outside of the customer's jurisdiction.

Following Standards for Auditing Information Systems

Due to multi-tenancy and shared environments, it becomes difficult to conduct an audit without the cloud provider breaching the confidentiality of other customers sharing the infrastructure. In such cases, the cloud provider should adopt a compliance program based on standards such as ISO27001 and provide assurance via SysTrust or ISO certification to its customers. Some audit frameworks are as follows:

- *SAS 70*: This framework involves the audit of controls based on control objectives and control activities (defined by the cloud provider). The auditor provides opinion on the design, operational status, and operating effectiveness of controls. SAS 70 intends to cover services that are relevant for purposes of customers' financial statement audits.
- *SysTrust*: This framework involves the audit of controls based on defined principles and criteria for security, availability, confidentiality, and processing integrity. SysTrust applies to the reliability of any system.
- *WebTrust*: This framework involves the audit of controls based on defined principles and criteria for security, availability, confidentiality, processing integrity, and privacy. WebTrust applies to online or e-commerce systems.
- *ISO 27001*: This framework involves the audit of an organization's Information Security Management System (ISMS).

Negotiating Third-party Provider Audits

When customers engage an audit provider, they should involve proper legal, procurement, and contract teams within their organization. The customer should consider specific compliance requirements and when negotiating must agree on how to collect, store, and share compliance evidence (e.g., audit logs, activity reports, system configurations). If the standard terms of services do not address the customer's compliance needs, they will need to be negotiated. Contracts should include the involvement of a third party for the review of SLA metrics and compliance (e.g., by a mutually selected mediator). Customers should prefer auditors with expertise in cloud computing who are familiar with the assurance challenges of cloud computing environments. Customers should request the cloud provider's SSAE 16 SOC2 (Statements on Standards for Attestation Engagements No. 16 Service Organization Control 2) or ISAE 3402 Type 2 (International Standard on Assurance Engagements 3402 Type 2) reports to provide a starting point of reference for auditors. SSAE 16 SOC2 provides a standard benchmark by which two data center audit reports can be compared and the customer can be assured that the same set of criteria was used to evaluate each. An ISAE 3402 Type 2 Report is known as the report on the description, design, and operating effectiveness of controls at a service organization.

8. PREPARING FOR DISASTER RECOVERY

To make sure the availability of cloud services, business continuity, and disaster recovery address a broad set of activities that are performed. Business continuity is based on standards, policies, guidelines, and procedures that facilitate continuous operation regardless of the incidents. Disaster recovery (DR) is a subsection of business continuity and is concerned with data and IT systems.

Implementing a Plan to Sustain Availability

A cloud service provider (CSP) should have a formal disaster recovery plan in place to assure the provider's viability against natural disasters, human errors, and malicious behavior. This plan should be continuously tested to ensure preparedness and should not compromise the security of the cloud in the event of a disaster.

Customers should review their contracts with the cloud provider and third parties to confirm and verify that the disaster recovery controls and certifications are in place. Customers could also conduct on-site assessments if found necessary. The cloud provider should inform the customer in advance about any disaster recovery tests.

Reliably Connecting to the Cloud across the Public Internet

There may be a substantial amount of latency between the customer's processing and the data stored in the cloud. Contingent on the amount of data being handled, this can result in unacceptable performance. If users access the data in the cloud, the latency may also cause an intolerable user experience. Wide area network optimization between the customer and the cloud provider should be in place so that the cloud enables full data mobility at reduced bandwidth, storage utilization, and cost. These performance issues might be managed with a combination of increased bandwidth or by traffic management. An alternative method is to utilize a cloud storage gateway. An issue to contemplate with a cloud storage gateway is the difference between tiering and caching. The gateways that use the caching method use cloud storage as their primary storage location. On the other hand, the gateways that utilize the tiering method use on-site storage as their primary storage and cloud storage as their secondary storage.

Anticipating a Sudden Provider Change or Loss

Some CSPs will unavoidably cease operating, therefore, making access to the data in the cloud an issue. Access to data might also be jeopardized if the provider or third party dealing with data breaches the contract and does not provide the promised services. When this happens, the customer's efforts should be directed toward finding a replacement cloud provider and confidentially removing and transferring the data from the defunct provider. It is important to clearly state the handling of data in case of bankruptcy or breach of contract in the SLA. Confidential data should be removed properly without leaving any trace.

Archiving SaaS Data Locally

Customers should perform regular extractions and backups to a format that is provider agnostic and make sure metadata can be preserved and migrated. It is also important to understand if any custom tools will have to be developed or if the provider will provide the migration tools. For legal and compliance reasons, the customer should ensure that backups and copies of logs, access records, and any other pertinent information are included in the archive as well.

Addressing Data Portability and Interoperability in Preparation for a Change in Cloud Providers

Depending on the application, it is important to integrate with applications that may be present in other clouds or on traditional infrastructure. Interoperability standards either enable or become a barrier to interoperability, and permit maintenance of the integrity and consistency of an organization's information and processes. SLAs should address the steps to change providers from a portability perspective. The customer should have a good understanding of the cloud provider's APIs, hypervisors, application logic, and other restrictions and build processes to migrate to and handle different cloud architectures. Security should be maintained across migrations. Authentication and IAM

mechanisms for user or process access to systems now must operate across all components of a cloud system. Using open standards for identity such as SAML will help to ensure portability. Encryption keys should be stored locally. When moving files and their metadata to new cloud environments, the customer should ensure that copies of file metadata are securely removed to prevent this information from remaining behind and opening a possible opportunity for compromise.

Exploiting the Cloud for Efficient Disaster Recovery Options

Besides providing all the advantages discussed in this chapter, cloud computing has brought advantages in the form of online storage. This feature can be leveraged for backup and disaster recovery and can reduce the cost of infrastructure, applications, and overall business processes. Many cloud storage providers guarantee the reliability and availability of their service. The challenges to cloud storage, cloud backup, and DR in particular involve mobility, information transfer, and availability, assuring business continuity, scalability, and metered payment. Cloud disaster recovery solutions are built on the foundation of three fundamentals: a virtualized storage infrastructure, a scalable file system, and a self-service disaster recovery application that responds to customers' urgent business needs. Some vendors that provide cloud storage services are Amazon, Google, Terremark, and Rackspace.

Achieving Cost-effective Recovery Time Objectives

Recovery Time Objective (RTO) is the maximum amount of time that is acceptable for restoring and regaining access to data after a disruption. To keep RTO low, cloud-based DR requires ongoing server replication, making network bandwidth an important consideration when adopting this approach. To keep bandwidth requirements and related costs low, customers need to identify their critical systems and prioritize them in their DR plan. Focusing on a narrower set of systems will make DR more efficient and more cost effective by keeping complexity and network bandwidth low.

Employing a Strategy of Redundancy to Better Resist DoS

Denial-of-service (DoS), or distributed-denial-of-service (DDoS) attack, is a type of network-based attack that attempts to make computer or network resources unavailable to their intended users. Customers and cloud providers should ensure that their systems have effective security processes and controls in place so that they can withstand DoS attacks. The controls and processes should have the ability to recognize a DoS attack and utilize the provider's local capacity and geographical redundancies to counter the attack's excessive use of network bandwidth (SYN or UDP floods), CPU, memory, and storage resources (application attacks).

Techniques such as cloudbursting can be used to mitigate the unexpected increase in resource consumption. Third-party cloud-based DDoS mitigation services (e.g., Akamai, Verisign) can be used to offload server functionality, defend the application layer, offload infrastructure functions, obfuscate infrastructure, protect DNS services, and failover gracefully when an attack is overwhelming.

9. SUMMARY

We have seen that cloud computing offers a service or deployment model for almost every type of customer and that each flavor comes with its own security concerns. Advantages offered by cloud solutions need to be weighed with the risks they entail. While public clouds are great for commercial customers, federal customers or other customers dealing with sensitive data need to consider private or hybrid cloud solutions. We have also seen the importance of embodying customer security requirements in SLAs to protect interests for compliance, DR, and other concerns. While delegation of resource management and procurement is a great advantage of cloud computing, customers are still accountable for the security and privacy of the deployed systems and data.

Cloud computing is a new technology that is still emerging. The challenges that appear in the realm of security are being addressed by security experts. If an organization plans to move to a cloud environment, it should do so with caution and weigh the risks to be able to enjoy the low-cost flexibility offered by this empowering technology.

Finally, let's move on to the real interactive part of this chapter: review questions/exercises, hands-on projects, case projects, and optional team case project. The answers and/or solutions by chapter can be found in the Online Instructor's Solutions Manual.

CHAPTER REVIEW QUESTIONS/EXERCISES

True/False

1. True or False? SaaS, PaaS, and IaaS are SPI models.
2. True or False? The risk-based approach is recommended for organizations considering the cloud.
3. True or False? The data and resources asset(s) is supported by the cloud.
4. True or False? A customer hosts its own application and data, while hosting a part of the functionality in the cloud. This service model is referred to as SaaS.
5. True or False? A customer's first step in evaluating its risks while considering a cloud deployment would be to select the data or function that's going to be hosted in the cloud.

Multiple Choice

1. In the criteria to evaluate a potential cloud service model or provider, a customer should consider:
   A. Comfort level for moving to the cloud
   B. Level of control at each SPI cloud model
   C. Importance of assets to move to the cloud
   D. Type of assets to move to the cloud
   E. All of the above
2. Which attack type can affect an IaaS environment?
   A. Cross-site-request-forgery attacks
   B. Side-channel attacks (VM-to-VM)
   C. Token stealing
   D. Canonicalization attacks
   E. All of the above
3. What should a cloud customer prefer for DR?
   A. High RTO, low cost
   B. Low RTO, high cost
   C. Low RTO, low cost, all data
   D. Backup critical data with a low RTO and cost
   E. All of the above
4. Which deployment model is suitable for a customer that needs the flexibility and resources of a public cloud, but needs to secure and define its networks?
   A. Hybrid
   B. Private
   C. Secured
   D. Virtual Private
   E. All of the above
5. What does an SLA cover?
   A. Service levels
   B. Security
   C. Governance
   D. Compliance
   E. All of the above

EXERCISE

Problem

Does the cloud solution offer equal or greater data security capabilities than those provided by your organization's data center?

Hands-On Projects

Project

Have you taken into account the vulnerabilities of the cloud solution?

Case Projects

Problem

As a project to build a small cloud environment, how do you set up a VPC environment on the Amazon EC2 platform ?

Optional Team Case Project

Problem

Have you considered that incident detection and response can be more complicated in a cloud-based environment?

REFERENCES

[1] Guidelines on Security and Privacy in Public Cloud Computing, NIST Special Publication, pp. 800−144.

[2] Cloud Computing: Benefits, Risks and Recommendations for Information Security, The European Network and Information Security Agency, 2009.

[3] Security Guidance for Critical Areas of Focus in Cloud Computing v3.0, Cloud Security Alliance, 2011.

[4] Amazon Virtual Private Cloud. <http://aws.amazon.com/vpc>.

## Chapter 7

Fault Tolerance and Resilience in Cloud Computing Environments

Ravi Jhawar
Universita' degli Studi di Milano

Vincenzo Piuri
Universita' degli Studi di Milano

1. INTRODUCTION

Cloud computing is gaining an increasing popularity over traditional information processing systems. Service providers have been building massive data centers that are distributed over several geographical regions to efficiently meet the demand for their Cloud-based services [1−3]. In general, these data centers are built using hundreds of thousands of commodity servers, and virtualization technology is used to provision computing resources (by delivering Virtual Machines—VMs—with a given amount of CPU, memory, and storage capacity) over the Internet by following the pay-per-use business model [4]. Leveraging the economies of scale, a single physical host is often used as a set of several virtual hosts by the service provider, and benefits such as the semblance of an inexhaustible set of available computing resources are provided to the users. As a consequence, an increasing number of users are moving to cloud-based services for realizing their applications and business processes.

The use of commodity components, however, exposes the hardware to conditions for which it was not originally designed [5,6]. Moreover, due to the highly complex nature of the underlying infrastructure, even carefully engineered data centers are subject to a large number of failures [7]. These failures evidently reduce the overall reliability and availability of the cloud computing service. As a result, fault tolerance becomes of paramount importance to the users as well as the service providers to ensure correct and continuous system operation even in the presence of an unknown and unpredictable number of failures.

The dimension of risks in the user's applications deployed in the virtual machine instances in a cloud has also changed since the failures in data centers are normally outside the scope of the user's organization. Moreover, traditional ways of achieving fault tolerance require users to have an in-depth knowledge of the underlying mechanisms, whereas, due to the abstraction layers and business model of cloud computing, a system's architectural details are not widely available to the users. This implies that traditional methods of introducing fault tolerance may not be very effective in the cloud computing context, and there is an increasing need to address users' reliability and availability concerns.

The goal of this chapter is to develop an understanding of the nature, numbers, and kind of faults that appear in typical cloud computing infrastructures, how these faults impact users' applications, and how faults can be handled in an efficient and cost-effective manner. To this aim, we first describe the fault model of typical cloud computing environments on the basis of system architecture, failure characteristics of widely used server and network components, and analytical models. An overall understanding of the fault model may help researchers and developers to build more reliable cloud computing services. In this chapter, we also introduce some basic and general concepts on fault tolerance and summarize the parameters that must be taken into account when building a fault tolerant system. This discussion is followed by a scheme in which different levels of fault tolerance can be achieved by users' applications by exploiting the properties of the cloud computing architecture.

In this chapter, we discuss a solution that can function in users' applications in a general and transparent manner to tolerate one of the two most frequent classes of faults that appear in the cloud computing environment. We also present a scheme that can tolerate the other class of frequent faults while reducing the overall resource costs by half when compared to existing solutions in the literature. These two techniques, along with the concept of different fault tolerance levels, are used as the basis for developing a methodology and framework that offers fault tolerance as an additional service to the user's applications. We believe that the notion of offering fault tolerance as a service may serve as an efficient alternative to traditional approaches in addressing user's reliability and availability concerns.

2. CLOUD COMPUTING FAULT MODEL

In general, a failure represents the condition in which the system deviates from fulfilling its intended functionality or the expected behavior. A failure happens due to an error, that is, due to reaching an invalid system state. The hypothesized cause for an error is a fault, which represents a fundamental impairment in the system. The notion of faults, errors, and failures can be represented using the following chain [8,9]:

$$\ldots Fault \rightarrow Error \rightarrow Failure \rightarrow Fault \rightarrow Error \rightarrow Failure \ldots$$

Fault tolerance is the ability of the system to perform its function even in the presence of failures. This implies that it is utmost important to clearly understand and define what constitutes the correct system behavior so that specifications on its failure characteristics can be provided and consequently a fault tolerant system can be developed. In this section, we discuss the fault model of typical cloud computing environments to develop an understanding of the numbers as well as the causes behind recurrent system failures. In order to analyze the distribution and impact of faults, we first describe the generic cloud computing architecture.

Cloud Computing Architecture

Cloud computing architecture comprises four distinct layers as illustrated in Figure 7.1 [10]. Physical resources (blade servers and network switches) are considered the lowest-layer in the stack, on top of which virtualization and system management tools are embedded to form the infrastructure-as-a-service (IaaS) layer. Note that the infrastructure supporting large-scale cloud deployments is typically the data centers, and virtualization technology is used to maximize the use of physical resources, application isolation, and

quality of service. Services offered by IaaS are normally accessed through a set of user-level middleware services that provide an environment to simplify application development and deployment (Web 2.0 or higher interfaces, libraries, and programming languages). The layer above the IaaS that binds all user-level middleware tools is referred to as platform-as-a-service (PaaS). User-level applications (social networks and scientific models) that are built and hosted on top of the PaaS layer comprise the software-as-a-service (SaaS) layer.

Failure in a given layer normally has an impact on the services offered by the layers above it. For example, failure in a user-level middleware (PaaS) may produce errors in the software services built on top of it (SaaS applications). Similarly, failures in the physical hardware or the IaaS layer will have an impact on most PaaS and SaaS services. This implies that the impact of failures in the IaaS layer or the physical hardware is significantly high; hence, it is important to characterize typical hardware faults and develop corresponding fault tolerance techniques.

We describe the failure behavior of various server components based on the statistical information obtained from large-scale studies on data center failures using data mining techniques [6,11] and analyze the impact of component failures on users' applications by means of analytical models such as fault trees and Markov chains [12]. Similar to server components, we also present the failure behavior of network component failures.

Failure Behavior of Servers

Each server in the data center typically contains multiple processors, storage disks, memory modules, and network interfaces. The study about server failure and hardware repair behavior is to be performed using a large collection of servers (approximately 100,000 servers) and corresponding data on part replacement such as details about server configuration, when a hard disk was issued a ticked for replacement, and when it was actually replaced. Such a data repository, which included server collection spanning multiple data

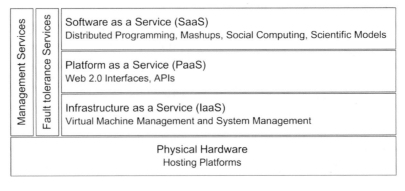

FIGURE 7.1   Layered architecture of cloud computing.

centers distributed across different countries, is gathered [6]. Key observations derived from this study are as follows:

- 92 percent of the machines do not see any repair events, but the average number of repairs for the remaining 8 percent is 2 per machine (20 repair/replacement events contained in nine machines were identified over a 14-month period). The annual failure rate (AFR) is therefore around 8 percent.
- For an 8 percent AFR, repair costs that amounted to $2.5 million are approximately spent for 100,000 servers.
- About 78 percent of total faults/replacements were detected on hard disks, 5 percent on RAID controllers, and 3 percent due to memory failures. Thirteen percent of replacements were due to a collection of components (not particularly dominated by a single component failure). Hard disks are clearly the most failure-prone hardware components and the most significant reason behind server failures.
- About 5 percent of servers experience a disk failure in less than one year from the date when it is commissioned (young servers), 12 percent when the machines are one year old, and 25 percent when they are two years old.
- Interestingly, based on the chi-squared automatic interaction detector methodology, none of the following factors—age of the server, its configuration, location within the rack, and workload run on the machine—were found to be a significant indicator for failures.
- Comparison between the number of repairs per machine (RPM) to the number of disks per server in a group of servers (clusters) indicates that (i) there is a relationship in the failure characteristics of servers that have already experienced a failure, and (ii) the number of RPM has a correspondence to the total number of disks on that machine.

Based on these statistics, it can be inferred that robust fault tolerance mechanisms must be applied to improve the reliability of hard disks (assuming independent component failures) to substantially reduce the number of failures. Furthermore, to meet the high availability and reliability requirements, applications must reduce utilization of hard disks that have already experienced a failure (since the probability of seeing another failure on that hard disk is higher).

The failure behavior of servers can also be analyzed based on the models defined using fault trees and Markov chains [12,13]. The rationale behind the modeling is two-fold: (1) to capture the user's perspective on component failures, that is, to understand the behavior of users' applications that are deployed in the VM instances under server component failures and (2) to define the correlation between individual component failures and the boundaries on the impact of each failure. An application may have an impact when there is a failure/error either in the

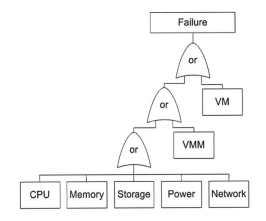

FIGURE 7.2A   Fault tree characterizing server failures [12].

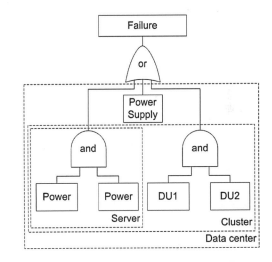

FIGURE 7.2B   Fault tree characterizing power failures [12].

processor, memory modules, storage disks, power supply (see Figure 7.2b) or network interfaces of the server, or the hypervisor, or the VM instance itself. Figure 7.2a illustrates this behavior as a fault tree where the top-event represents a failure in the user's application. The reliability and availability of each server component must be derived using Markov models that are populated using long-term failure behavior information [6].

Failure Behavior of the Network

It is important to understand the overall network topology and various network components involved in constructing a data center so as to characterize the network failure behavior (see Figure 7.3b). Figure 7.3a illustrates an example of partial data center network architecture [11,14]. Servers are connected using a set of network switches and routers. In particular, all rack-mounted servers are first connected via a 1 Gbps link to a top-of-rack switch (ToR), which is in turn connected to two (primary

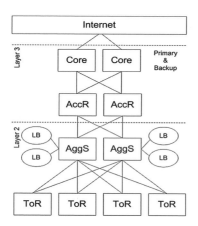

FIGURE 7.3A   Partial network architecture of a data center [11].

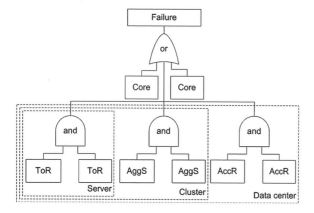

FIGURE 7.3B   Fault tree characterizing network failures [12].

and backup) aggregation switches (AggS). An AggS connects tens of switches (ToR) to redundant access routers (AccR). This implies that each AccR handles traffic from thousands of servers and routes it to core routers that connect different data centers to the Internet [11,12]. All links in the data centers commonly use Ethernet as the link layer protocol, and redundancy is applied to all network components at each layer in the network topology (except for ToRs). In addition, redundant pairs of load balancers (LBs) are connected to each AggS, and mapping between static IP address presented to the users and dynamic IP addresses of internal servers that process user's requests is performed. Similar to the study on failure behavior of servers, a large-scale study on network failures in data centers is performed [11]. A link failure happens when the connection between two devices on a specific interface is down, and a device failure happens when the device is not routing/forwarding packets correctly (due to power outage or hardware crash). Key observations derived from this study are as follows:

- Among all the network devices, load balancers are least reliable (with failure probability of 1 in 5) and ToRs

are most reliable (with a failure rate of less than 5 percent). The root causes for failures in LBs are mainly the software bugs and configuration errors (as opposed to the hardware errors for other devices). Moreover, LBs tend to experience short but frequent failures. This observation indicates that low-cost commodity switches (ToRs and AggS) provide sufficient reliability.

- The links forwarding traffic from LBs have the highest failure rates; links higher in the topology (connecting AccRs) and links connecting redundant devices have the second highest failure rates.

- The estimated median number of packets lost during a failure is 59 K, and the median number of bytes is 25 MB (the average size of lost packets is 423 Bytes). Based on prior measurement studies (that observe packet sizes to be bimodal with modes around 200 Bytes and 1400 Bytes), it is estimated that most lost packets belong to the lower part (ping messages or ACKs).

- Network redundancy reduces the median impact of failures (in terms of number of lost bytes) by only 40 percent. This observation is against the common belief that network redundancy completely masks failures from applications.

Therefore, the overall data center network reliability is about 99.99 percent for 80 percent of the links and 60 percent of the devices. Similar to servers, Figure 7.3b represents the fault tree for the user's application failure with respect to network failures in the data center. A failure occurs when there is an error in all redundant switches ToRs, AggS, AccR, or core routers, or the network links connecting physical hosts. Since the model is designed in the user's perspective, a failure in this context implies that the application is not connected to the rest of the network or gives errors during data transmission. Through use of this modeling technique, the boundaries on the impact of each network failure can be represented (using server, cluster, and data center level blocks) and can further be used to increase the fault tolerance of the user's application (by placing replicas of an application in different failure zones).

3. BASIC CONCEPTS ON FAULT TOLERANCE

In general, the faults we analyzed in the last section can be classified in different ways depending on the nature of the system. Since, in this chapter, we are interested in typical cloud computing environment faults that appear as failures to the end users, we classify the faults into two types similarly to other distributed systems:

- *Crash faults* that cause the system components to completely stop functioning or remain inactive during failures (power outage, hard disk crash).

- *Byzantine faults* that lead the system components to behave arbitrarily or maliciously during failure, causing the system to behave unpredictably incorrect.

As observed previously, fault tolerance is the ability of the system to perform its function even in the presence of failures. It serves as one of the means to improve the overall system's dependability. In particular, it contributes significantly to increasing the system's reliability and availability.

The most widely adopted methods to achieve fault tolerance against crash faults and byzantine faults are as follows:

- *Checking and monitoring*: The system is constantly monitored at runtime to validate, verify, and ensure that correct system specifications are being met. This technique, though very simple, plays a key role in failure detection and subsequent reconfiguration.
- *Checkpoint and restart*: The system state is captured and saved based on predefined parameters (after every 1024 instructions or every 60 seconds). When the system undergoes a failure, it is restored to the previously known correct state using the latest checkpoint information (instead of restarting the system from start).
- *Replication*: Critical system components are duplicated using additional hardware, software, and network resources in such a way that a copy of the critical components is available even after a failure happens. Replication mechanisms are mainly used in two formats: active and passive. In active replication, all the replicas are simultaneously invoked and each replica processes the same request at the same time. This implies that all the replicas have the same system state at any given point of time (unless designed to function in an asynchronous manner) and it can continue to deliver its service even in case of a single replica failure. In passive replication, only one processing unit (the primary replica) processes the requests, while the backup replicas only save the system state during normal execution periods. Backup replicas take over the execution process only when the primary replica fails.

Variants of traditional replication mechanisms (active and passive) are often applied on modern distributed systems. For example, the semiactive replication technique is derived from traditional approaches wherein primary and backup replicas execute all the instructions but only the output generated by the primary replica is made available to the user. Output generated by the backup replicas is logged and suppressed within the system so that it can readily resume the execution process when the primary replica failure happens. Figure 7.4a depicts the Markov model of a system that uses an active/semiactive

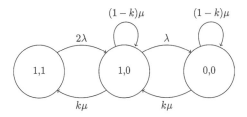

FIGURE 7.4A   Markov model of a system with two replicas in active/semiactive replication scheme [12].

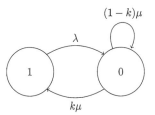

FIGURE 7.4B   Markov model of a system with two replicas in passive replication scheme [12].

replication scheme with two replicas [12]. This model serves as an effective means of deriving the reliability and availability of the system because the failure behavior of both replicas can be taken into account. Moreover, as described earlier, the results of the Markov model analysis can be used to support the fault trees in characterizing the impact of failures in the system. Each state in the model is represented by a pair (x, y) where $x = 1$ denotes that the primary replica is working and $x = 0$ implies that it failed. Similarly, y represents the working condition of the backup replica. The system starts and remains in state $(1,1)$ during normal execution, that is, when both the replicas are available and working correctly. A failure either in the primary or the backup replica moves the system to state $(0,1)$ or $(1,0)$ where the other replica takes over the execution process. A single state is sufficient to represent this condition in the model since both replicas are consistent with each other. The system typically initiates its recovery mechanism in state $(0,1)$ or $(1,0)$, and moves to state $(1,1)$ if the recovery of the failed replica is successful; otherwise it transits to state $(0,0)$ and becomes completely unavailable. Similarly, Figure 7.4b illustrates the Markov model of the system for which a passive replication scheme is applied. λ denotes the failure rate, μ denotes the recovery rate, and k is a constant.

Fault tolerance mechanisms are varyingly successful in tolerating faults [15]. For example, a passively replicated system can tolerate only crash faults, whereas actively replicated system using $3f + 1$ replicas are capable of tolerating byzantine faults. In general, mechanisms that handle failures at a finer granularity, offering higher performance guarantees, also consume higher amounts of resources [16]. Therefore, the design of fault tolerance mechanisms must take into account a number of factors such as implementation complexity, resource costs, resilience, and performance metrics, and achieve a fine balance of the following parameters:

- *Fault tolerance model*: Measures the strength of the fault tolerance mechanism in terms of the granularity at which it can handle errors and failures in the system. This factor is characterized by the robustness of failure detection protocols, state synchronization methods, and strength of the fail-over granularity.
- *Resource consumption*: Measures the amount and cost of resources that are required to realize a fault tolerance mechanism. This factor is normally inherent with the granularity of the failure detection and recovery mechanisms in terms of CPU, memory, bandwidth, I/O, and so on.
- *Performance*: Deals with the impact of the fault tolerance procedure on the end-to-end quality of service (QoS) both during failure and failure-free periods. This impact is often characterized using fault detection latency, replica launch latency, failure recovery latency, and other application-dependent metrics such as bandwidth, latency, and loss rate.

We build on the basic concepts discussed in this section to analyze the fault tolerance properties of various schemes designed for cloud computing environment.

4. DIFFERENT LEVELS OF FAULT TOLERANCE IN CLOUD COMPUTING

As discussed earlier, server components in a cloud computing environment are subject to failures, affecting users' applications, and each failure has an impact within a given boundary in the system. For example, a crash in the pair of aggregate switches may result in the loss of communication among all the servers in a cluster; in this context, the boundary of failure is the cluster since applications in other clusters can continue functioning normally. Therefore, while applying a fault tolerance mechanism such as a replication scheme, at least one replica of the application must be placed in a different cluster to ensure that aggregate switch failure does not result in a complete failure of the application. Furthermore, this implies that deployment scenarios (location of each replica) are critical to correctly realize the fault tolerance mechanisms. In this section, we discuss possible deployment scenarios in a cloud computing infrastructure, and the advantages and limitations of each scenario.

Based on the architecture of the cloud computing infrastructure, different levels of failure independence can

be derived for cloud computing services [17,18]. Moreover, assuming that the failures in individual resource components are independent of each other, fault tolerance and resource costs of an application can be balanced based on the location of its replicas. Possible deployment scenarios and their properties are as follows.

- *Multiple machines within the same cluster*. Two replicas of an application can be placed on the hosts that are connected by a ToR switch (within a LAN). Replicas deployed in this configuration can benefit in terms of low latency and high bandwidth but obtain very limited failure independence. A single switch or power distribution failure may result in an outage of the entire application, and both replicas cannot communicate to complete the fault tolerance protocol. Cluster-level blocks in the fault trees of each resource component (network failures as shown in Figure 7.3b) must be combined using a logical AND operator to analyze the overall impact of failures in the system. Note that reliability and availability values for each fault tolerance mechanism with respect to server faults must be calculated using a Markov model.
- *Multiple clusters within a data center*. Two replicas of an application can be placed on the hosts belonging to different clusters in the same data center (on the hosts that are connected via a ToR switch and AggS). Failure independence of the application in this deployment context remains moderate since the replicas are not bound to an outage with a single power distribution or switch failure. The overall availability of an application can be calculated using cluster-level blocks from fault trees combined with a logical OR operator in conjunction with power and network using AND operator.
- *Multiple data centers*. Two replicas of an application can be placed on the hosts belonging to different data centers (connected via a switch), AggS and AccR. This deployment has a drawback with respect to high latency and low bandwidth, but offers a very high level of failure independence. A single power failure has the least effect on the availability of the application. The data center level blocks from the fault trees may be connected with a logical OR operator in conjunction with the network in the AND logic.

As an example [13,19], the overall availability of each representative replication scheme with respect to different deployment levels is obtained as shown in Table 7.1. Availability of the system is highest when the replicas are placed in two different data centers. The value declines when replicas are placed in two different clusters within the same data center, and it is lowest when replicas are placed inside the same LAN. The overall availability obtained by semiactive replication is higher than

TABLE 7.1 Availability Values (normalized to 1) for Replication Techniques at Different Deployment Scenarios [12].

	Same Cluster	Same Data Center, diff. Clusters	Diff. Data Centers
Semiactive	0.9871	0.9913	0.9985
Semipassive	0.9826	0.9840	0.9912
Passive	0.9542	0.9723	0.9766

semipassive replication and lowest for the simple passive replication scheme.

As described earlier, effective implementation of fault tolerance mechanisms requires consideration of the strength of the fault tolerance model, resource costs, and performance. While traditional fault tolerance methods require tailoring of each application having an in-depth knowledge of the underlying infrastructure, in the cloud computing scenario, it would also be beneficial to develop methodologies that can generically function on users' applications so that a large number of applications can be protected using the same protocol. In addition to generality, agility in managing replicas and checkpoints to improve the performance, and reduction in the resource consumption costs while not limiting the strength of fault tolerance mechanisms are required.

Although several fault tolerance approaches are being proposed for cloud computing services, most solutions that achieve at least one of the required properties described above are based on virtualization technology. By using virtualization-based approaches, it is also possible to deal with both classes of faults. In particular, in a later section of this chapter we present a virtualization-based solution that provides fault tolerance against crash failures using a checkpointing mechanism. We discuss this solution because it offers two additional, significantly useful, properties: (1) Fault tolerance is induced independent to the applications and hardware on which it runs. In other words, an increased level of generality is achieved since any application can be protected using the same protocol as long as it is deployed in a VM, and (2) mechanisms such as replication, failure detection, and recovery are applied transparently—not modifying the OS or application's source code. Then, we present a virtualization-based solution that uses typical properties of a cloud computing environment to tolerate byzantine faults using a combination of replication and checkpointing techniques. We discuss this solution because it reduces the resource consumption costs incurred by typical byzantine fault tolerance schemes during fail-free periods nearly by half.

5. FAULT TOLERANCE AGAINST CRASH FAILURES IN CLOUD COMPUTING

A scheme that leverages the virtualization technology to tolerate crash faults in the cloud in a transparent manner is discussed in this section. The system or user application that must be protected from failures is first encapsulated in a VM (say active VM or the primary), and operations are performed at the VM level (in contrast to the traditional approach of operating at the application level) to obtain paired servers that run in active—passive configuration. Since the protocol is applied at the VM level, this scheme can be used independent of the application and underlying hardware, offering an increased level of generality. In particular, we discuss the design of *Remus* as an example system that offers the preceding mentioned properties [20]. Remus aims to provide high availability to the applications, and to achieve this, it works in four phases:

1. Checkpoint the changed memory state at the primary, and continue to the next epoch of network and disk request streams.
2. Replicate system state on the backup.
3. Send checkpoint acknowledgment from the backup when complete memory checkpoint and corresponding disk requests have been received.
4. Release outbound network packets queued during the previous epoch upon receiving the acknowledgment.

Remus achieves high availability by frequently checkpointing and transmitting the state of the active VM on to a backup physical host. The VM image on the backup is resident in the memory and may begin execution immediately after a failure in the active VM is detected. The backup only acts like a receptor since the VM in the backup host is not actually executed during fail-free periods. This allows the backup to concurrently receive checkpoints from VMs running on multiple physical hosts (in an N-to-1 style configuration), providing a higher degree of freedom in balancing resource costs due to redundancy.

In addition to generality and transparency, seamless failure recovery can be achieved; that is, no externally visible state is lost in the event of a single host failure and recovery happens rapidly enough that it appears only like a temporary packet loss. Since the backup is only periodically consistent with the primary replica using the checkpoint-transmission procedure, all network output is buffered until a consistent image of the host is received by the backup, and the buffer is released only when the backup is completely synchronized with the primary. Unlike network traffic, the disk state is not externally visible, but it has to be transmitted to the backup as part of a complete cycle. To address this issue, Remus asynchronously sends the disk state to the backup where it is initially buffered in the RAM. When the corresponding memory state is received, complete checkpoint is acknowledged, output is made visible to the user, and buffered disk state is applied to the backup disk.

Remus is built on Xen hypervisor's live migration machinery [21]. Live migration is a technique through which a complete VM can be relocated onto another physical host in the network (typically a LAN) with a minor interruption to the VM. Xen provides an ability to track guest writes to memory using a technique called shadow page tables. During live migration, memory of the VM is copied to the new location while the VM continues to run normally at the old location. The writes to the memory are then tracked, and the dirtied pages are transferred to the new location periodically. After a sufficient number of iterations, or when no progress in copying the memory is being made (i.e., when the VM is writing to the memory as fast as the migration process), the guest VM is suspended, remaining dirtied memory along with the CPU state is copied, and the VM image in the new location is activated. The total migration time depends on the amount of dirtied memory during guest execution, and total downtime depends on the amount of memory remaining to be copied when the guest is suspended. The protocol design of the system, particularly each checkpoint, can be viewed as the final stop-and-copy phase of live migration. The guest memory in live migration is iteratively copied, incurring several minutes of execution time. The singular stop-and-copy (the final step) operation incurs a very limited overhead—typically in the order of a few milliseconds.

While Remus provides an efficient replication mechanism, it employs a simple failure detection technique that is directly integrated within the checkpoint stream. A timeout of the backup in responding to commit requests made by the primary will result in the primary suspecting a failure (crash and disabled protection) in the backup. Similarly, a timeout of the new checkpoints being transmitted from the primary will result in the backup assuming a failure in the primary. At this point, the backup begins execution from the latest checkpoint. The protocol is evaluated (i) to understand whether or not the overall approach is practically deployable and (ii) to analyze the kind of workloads that are most amenable to this approach.

Correctness evaluation is performed by deliberatively injecting network failures at each phase of the protocol. The application (or the protected system) runs a kernel compilation process to generate CPU, memory, and disk load, and a graphics-intensive client (glxgears) attached to X11 server is simultaneously executed to generate the network traffic. Checkpoint frequency is configured to 25 milliseconds, and each test is performed two times. It is reported that the backup successfully took over the execution for each failure with a network delay of about 1 second when the backup detected the failure and activated the replicated system. The kernel compilation task continued to completion, and glxgears client resumed after a brief pause. The disk image showed no inconsistencies when the VM was gracefully shut down.

Performance evaluation is performed using the SPECweb benchmark that is composed of a Web server, an application server, and one or more Web client simulators. Each tier (server) was deployed in a different VM. The observed scores decrease up to five times the native score (305) when the checkpointing system is active. This behavior is mainly due to network buffering; the observed scores are much higher when network buffering is disabled. Furthermore, it is reported that at configuration rates of 10, 20, 30, and 40 checkpoints per second, the average checkpoint rates achieved are 9.98, 16.38, 20.25, and 23.34, respectively. This behavior can be explained with SPECweb's very fast memory dirtying, resulting in slower checkpoints than desired. The realistic workload therefore illustrates that the amount of network traffic generated by the checkpointing protocol is very large, and as a consequence, this system is not well suited for applications that are very sensitive to network latencies. Therefore, virtualization technology can largely be exploited to develop general-purpose fault tolerance schemes that can be applied to handle crash faults in a transparent manner.

6. FAULT TOLERANCE AGAINST BYZANTINE FAILURES IN CLOUD COMPUTING

Byzantine fault tolerance (BFT) protocols are powerful approaches to obtain highly reliable and available systems. Despite numerous efforts, most BFT systems have been too expensive for practical use; so far, no commercial data centers have employed BFT techniques. For example, the BFT algorithm [22] for asynchronous, distributed, client-server systems requires at least $3f + 1$ replica (one primary and remaining backup) to execute a three-phase protocol that can tolerate f byzantine faults. Note that, as described earlier, systems that tolerate faults at a finer granularity such as the byzantine faults also consume very high amounts of resources, and as already noted, it is critical to consider the resource costs while implementing a fault tolerance solution.

The high resource consumption cost (see Table 7.2) in BFT protocols is most likely due to the way faults are normally handled. BFT approaches typically replicate the server (state machine replication—SMR), and each replica is forced to execute the same request in the same order. This enforcement requirement demands that the server replicas reach an agreement on the ordering of a given set of requests even in the presence of byzantine

TABLE 7.2 Resource Consumption Costs Incurred by Well-Known Byzantine Fault Tolerance Protocols [23].

	PBFT [22]	SEP [25]	Zyzzyva [24]	ZZ [23]
Agreement replicas	$3f+1$	$3f+1$	$3f+1$	$3f+1$
Execution replicas	$3f+1$	$2f+1$	$2f+1$	$(1+r)$ $f+1$

faulty servers and clients. For this purpose, an agreement protocol that is referred to as the *Byzantine Agreement* is used. When an agreement on the ordering is reached, service execution is performed, and majority voting scheme is devised to choose the correct output (and to detect the faulty server). This implies that two clusters of replicas are necessary to realize BFT protocols.

When realistic data center services implement BFT protocols, the dominant costs are due to the hardware performing service execution and not due to running the agreement protocol [23]. For instance, a toy application running *null* requests with the Zyzzyva BFT approach [24] exhibits a peak throughput of 80 K requests/second, while a database service running the same protocol on comparable hardware exhibits almost three times lower throughput. Based on this observation, ZZ, an execution approach that can be integrated with existing BFT SMR and agreement protocols, is presented [23]. The prototype of ZZ is built on the BASE implementation [22] and guarantees BFT, while significantly reducing resource consumption costs during fail-free periods. Table 7.2 compares the resource costs of well-known BFT techniques. Since ZZ provides an effective balance between resource consumption costs and the fault tolerance model, later in this section we discuss its system design in detail.

The design of ZZ is based on the virtualization technology and is targeted to tolerate byzantine faults while reducing the resource provisioning costs incurred by BFT protocols during fail-free periods. The cost reduction benefits of ZZ can be obtained only when BFT is used in the data center running multiple applications, so that sleeping replicas can be distributed across the pool of servers and higher peak throughput can be achieved when execution dominates the request processing cost and resources are constrained. These assumptions make ZZ a suitable scheme to be applied in a cloud computing environment. The system model of ZZ makes the following assumptions similar to most existing BFT systems:

- The service is either deterministic, or nondeterministic operations in the service can be transformed to

deterministic ones using an agreement protocol (ZZ assumes a SMR-based BFT system).

- The system involves two kinds of replicas: (1) *agreement replicas* that assign an order to the client's requests and (2) *execution replicas* that execute each client's request in the same order and maintain the application state.

- Each replica fails independently and exhibits byzantine behavior (faulty replicas and clients may behave arbitrarily).

- An adversary can coordinate faulty nodes in an arbitrary manner, but it cannot circumvent standard cryptographic measures (collision-resistant hash functions, encryption scheme, and digital signatures).

  An upper bound g on a number of faulty agreement replicas and f execution replicas is assumed for a given window of vulnerability.

- The system can ensure safety in an asynchronous network, but liveness is guaranteed only during periods of synchrony.

Since the system runs replicas inside virtual machines, to maintain failure independence, it requires that a physical host can deploy at most one agreement and one execution replicas of the service simultaneously. The novelty in the system model is that it considers a byzantine hypervisor. Note that, as a consequence of the above replica placement constraint, a malicious hypervisor can be treated by simply considering a single fault in all the replicas deployed on that physical host. Similarly, an upper bound f on the number of faulty hypervisors is assumed. The BFT execution protocol reduces the replication cost from $2f+1$ to $f+1$ based on the following principle:

- A system that is designed to function correctly in an asynchronous environment will provide correct results even if some of the replicas are outdated.

- A system that is designed to function correctly in the presence of f byzantine faults will, during a fault-free period, remain unaffected even if up to f replicas are turned off.

The second observation is used to commission only an $f+1$ replica to actively execute requests. The system is in a correct state if the response obtained from all $f+1$ replicas is the same. In case of failure (when responses do not match), the first observation is used to continue system operation as if the f standby replicas were slow but correct replicas.

To correctly realize this design, the system requires an agile replica wake-up mechanism. To achieve this mechanism, the system exploits virtualization technology by maintaining additional replicas (VMs) in a "dormant" state, which are either pre-spawned but paused VMs or the VM that is hibernated to a disk. There is a trade-off in adopting either method. Pre-spawned VM can resume execution in a very short span (in the order of few milliseconds) but consumes higher memory resources, whereas VMs hibernated to disks incur greater recovery times but occupy only storage space. This design also raises several interesting challenges such as *how can a restored replica obtain the necessary application state that is required to execute the current request? How can the replication cost be made robust to faulty replica or client behavior? Does the transfer of an entire application state take an unacceptably long time?*

The system builds on the BFT protocol that uses independent agreement and execution clusters [25]). Let A represent the set of replicas in the agreement cluster, $|A| = 2g + 1$, that runs the three-phase agreement protocol [22]. When a client c sends its request Q to the agreement cluster to process an operation o with timestamp t, the agreement cluster assigns a sequence number n to the request. The timestamp is used to ensure that each client request is executed only once and a faulty client behavior does not affect other clients' requests. When an agreement replica j learns of the sequence number n committed to Q, it sends a commit message C to all execution replicas.

Let E represent the set of replicas in the execution cluster where $|E| = f + 1$ during fail-free periods. When an execution replica i receives $2g + 1$ valid and matching commit messages from A, in the form of a commit certificate $\{C_i\}$, $i \in A|2g + 1$, and if it has already processed all the requests with lower sequence than n, it produces a reply R and sends it to the client. The execution cluster also generates an execution report ER for the agreement cluster.

During normal execution, the response certificate $\{R_i\}$, $i \in E|f + 1$ obtained by the client matches replies from all $f + 1$ execution nodes. To avoid unnecessary wake-ups due to a partially faulty execution replica that replies correctly to the agreement cluster but delivers a wrong response to the client, ZZ introduces an additional check as follows: When the replies are not matching, the client resends the same request to the agreement cluster. The agreement cluster sends a reply affirmation RA to the client if it has $f + 1$ valid responses for the retransmitted request. In this context, the client accepts the reply if it receives $g + 1$ messages containing a response digest $\bar{R}$ that matches one of the replies already received. Finally, if the agreement cluster does not generate an affirmation for the client, additional nodes are started.

ZZ uses periodic checkpoints to update the state of newly commissioned replicas and to perform garbage collection on a replica's logs. Execution nodes create checkpoints of the application state and reply logs, generate a checkpoint proof CP, and send it all execution and agreement nodes. The checkpoint proof is in the form of a digest that allows recovering nodes in identifying the checkpoint data they obtain from potentially faulty nodes, and the checkpoint certificate $\{CP_i\}$, $i \in E|f + 1$ is a set of $f + 1$ CP messages with matching digests.

Fault detection in the execution replicas is based on timeouts. Both lower and higher values of timeouts may impact the system's performance. The lower may falsely detect failures, and the higher may provide a window to the faulty replicas to degrade the system's performance. To set appropriate timeouts, ZZ suggests the following procedure: The agreement replica sets the timeout τ_n to Kt_1 upon receiving the first response to the request with sequence number n; t_1 is the response time and K is a preconfigured variance bound. Based on this trivial theory, ZZ proves that a replica faulty with a given probability p can inflate average response time by a factor of:

$$\max\left(1, \sum_{0 \le m \le f} P(m)I(m)\right)$$

where:

$$P(m) = \binom{f}{m} p^m (1-p)^{f-m}$$

$$I(m) = max\left(1, \frac{K.E[MIN_{f+1-m}]}{E[MAX_{f+1}]}\right)$$

$P(m)$ represents the probability of m simultaneous failures, and $I(m)$ is the response time inflation that m faulty nodes can inflict. Assuming identically distributed response times for a given distribution, $E[MIN_{f+1-m}]$ is the expected minimum time for a set of $f + 1 - m$ replicas, and $E[MAX_{f+1}]$ is the expected maximum response time of all $f + 1$ replicas [23]. Replication costs vary from $f + 1$ to $2f + 1$, depending on the probability of replicas being faulty p and the likelihood of false timeouts π_1. Formally, the expected replication cost is less than $(1 + r)$ $f + 1$, where $r = 1 - (1 - p)^{f+1} + (1 - p)^{f+1}\pi_1$. Therefore, virtualization technology can be effectively used to realize byzantine fault tolerance mechanisms at a significantly lower resource consumption costs.

7. FAULT TOLERANCE AS A SERVICE IN CLOUD COMPUTING

The drawback of the solutions discussed earlier is that the user must either tailor its application using a specific protocol (ZZ) by taking into account the system architecture details, or require the service provider to implement a solution for its applications (Remus). Note that the (i) fault tolerance properties of the application remain constant throughout its life cycle using this methodology and (ii) users may not have all the architectural details of the service provider's system. However, the availability of a pool of fault tolerance mechanisms that provide transparency and generality can allow realization of the notion of fault tolerance as a service. The latter perspective on fault tolerance intuitively provides immense benefits.

As a motivating example, consider a user that offers a Web-based e-commerce service to its customers that allows them to pay their bills and manage fund transfers over the Internet. The user implements the e-commerce service as a multitier application that uses the storage service of the service provider to store and retrieve its customer data, and compute service to process its operations and respond to customer queries. In this context, a failure in the service provider's system can impact the reliability and availability of the e-commerce service. The implications of storage server failure may be much higher than a failure in one of the compute nodes. This implies that each tier of the e-commerce application must possess different levels of fault tolerance, and the reliability and availability goals may change over time based on the business demands. Using traditional methods, fault tolerance properties of the e-commerce application remains constant throughout its life cycle, and hence, in the user's perspective, it is complementary to engage with a third party (the fault tolerance service provider—ftSP), specify its requirements based on the business needs, and transparently possess desired fault tolerance properties without studying the low-level fault tolerance mechanisms.

The ftSP must realize a range of fault tolerance techniques as individual modules (separate agreement and execution protocols, and heartbeat-based fault detection technique as an independent module) to benefit from the economies of scale. For example, since the failure detection techniques in Remus and ZZ are based on the same principle, instead of integrating the liveness requests within the checkpointing stream, the heartbeat test module can be reused in both solutions. However, realization of this notion requires a technique for selecting appropriate fault tolerance mechanisms based on users' requirements and a general-purpose framework that can integrate with the cloud computing environment. Without such a framework, individual applications must implement its own solution, resulting in a highly complex system environment. Further in this section, we present a solution that supports ftSP to realize its service effectively.

In order to abstract low-level system procedures from the users, a new dimension to fault tolerance is presented in [26] wherein applications deployed in the VM instances in a cloud computing environment can obtain desired fault tolerance properties from a third party as a service. The new dimension realizes a range of fault tolerance mechanisms that can transparently function on user's

applications as independent modules, and a set of metadata is associated with each module to characterize its fault tolerance properties. The metadata is used to select appropriate mechanisms based on users' requirements. A complete fault tolerance solution is then composed using selected fault tolerance modules and delivered to the user's application.

Consider ft_unit to be the fundamental module that applies a coherent fault tolerance mechanism, in a transparent manner, to a recurrent system failure at the granularity of a VM instance. An ft_unit handles the impact of hardware failures by applying fault tolerance mechanisms at the virtualization layer rather than the user's application. Examples of ft_units include the replication scheme for the e-commerce application that uses a checkpointing technique such as Remus (ft_unit1), and the node failures detection technique using the heartbeat test (ft_sol2). Assuming that the ftSP realizes a range of fault tolerance mechanisms as ft_units, a two-stage delivery scheme that can deliver fault tolerance as a service is as follows:

The *design stage* starts when a user requests the ftSP to deliver a solution with a given set of fault tolerance properties to its application. Each ft_unit provides a unique set of properties; the ftSP banks on this observation and defines the fault tolerance property p corresponding to each ft_unit as $p = (u, \hat{p}, A)$, where u represents the ft_unit, $\hat{p}$ denotes the high-level abstract properties such as reliability and availability, and A denotes the set of functional, structural, and operational attributes that characterize the ft_unit u. The set A sufficiently refers to the granularity at which the ft_unit can handle failures, its limitations and advantages, resource consumption costs, and quality of service parameters. Each attribute $a \in A$ takes a value $v(a)$ from a domain D_a, and a partial (or total) ordered relationship is defined on the domain D_a. The values for the abstract properties are derived using the notion of fault trees and the Markov model as described for the availability property in Table 7.1. An example of fault tolerance property for the ft_unit u_1 is $p = (u_1, \hat{p} = \{reliability = 98.9\%, availability = 99.95\%\}$, $A = \{mechanism = semiactive\_replication, fault\_model = server\_crashes, power\_outage, number\_of\_replicas = 4\})$.

Similar to the domain of attribute values, a hierarchy of fault tolerance properties $\leq_p$ is also defined: If P is the set of properties, and given two properties $p_i, p_j \in P$, $p_i \leq_p p_j$ if $p_i \cdot p = p_j \cdot p$ and for all $a \in A$, $v_i(a) \leq v_j(a)$. This hierarchy suggests that all ft_units that hold the property p_j also satisfy the property p_i. The fault tolerance requirements of the users are assumed to be specified as desired properties p_c, and for each user request, the ftSP first generates a shortlisted set S of ft_units that match p_c. Each ft_unit within the set S is then compared, and an ordered list based on user's requirements is created. An example of the matching, comparison, and selection process is as follows:

As an example, assume that the ftSP realizes three ft_units with properties

$p_1 = (u_1,$ A = {mechanism = heartbeat_test, timeout_period = 50 ms, number_of_replicas = 3, fault_model = node_crashes})

$p_2 = (u_2,$ A = {mechanism = majority_voting, fault_model = programming_errors})

$p_3 = (u_3,$ A = {mechanism = heartbeat_test, timeout_period = 25 ms, number_of_replicas = 5, fault_model = node_crashes})

respectively. If the user requests fault tolerance support with a robust crash failure detection scheme, the set S = (u_1, u_3) is first generated (u_2 is not included in the set because it doesn't target server crash failures alone, and its attribute values that contribute to robustness are not defined) and finally after comparing each ft_unit within S, ftSP leverages u_3 since it is more robust than u_1.

Note that each ft_unit serves only as a single fundamental fault tolerance module. This implies that the overall solution ft_sol that must be delivered to the user's application can be obtained by combining a set of ft_units as per specific execution logic. For instance, a heartbeat test-based fault detection module must be applied only after performing replication, and the recovery mechanism must be applied after a failure is detected. In other words, ft_units must be used to realize a process that provides a complete fault tolerance solution, such as:

```
ft sol[
invoke:ft unit(VM-instances replication)
invoke:ft unit(failure detection)
do{
execute(failure detection ft unit)
}while(no failures)
if(failure detected)
invoke:ft unit(recovery mechanism)
]
```

By composing ft_sol using a set of modules on the fly, the dimension and intensity of the fault tolerance support can be changed dynamically. For example, the more robust fault detection mechanism can be replaced with a less robust one in the ft_sol based on the user's business demands. Similarly, by realizing each ft_unit as a configurable module, resource consumption costs can also be made limited. For example, a replication scheme using five replicas can be replaced with one having three replicas if desired by the user.

The *runtime stage* starts immediately after ft_sol is delivered to the user. This stage is essential to maintain a high level of service because the context of the cloud computing environment may change at runtime, resulting in mutable behavior of the attributes. To this aim, the ftSP defines a set of rules R over attributes $a \in A$ and their values $v(a)$ such that the validity of all the rules $r \in R$ establishes that the property p is supported by ft_sol (violation of a rule indicates that the property is not satisfied). Therefore, in this stage, the attribute values of each ft_sol delivered to users' applications is continuously monitored at runtime, and a corresponding set of rules are verified using a validation function $f(s, R)$. The function returns true if all the rules are satisfied; otherwise, it returns false. The matching and comparison process defined for the design stage is used to generate a new ft_sol in case of a rule violation. By continuously monitoring and updating the attribute values, note that the fault tolerance service offers support that is valid throughout the life cycle of the application (both initially during design time and runtime).

As an example, for a comprehensive fault tolerance solution ft_sol s_1 with property

$p_1 =$ ($s_1,$ $\hat{p}$ = {reliability = 98.9%, availability = 99.95%}, A = {mechanism = active_replication, fault_detection = heartbeat_test, number_of_replicas = 4, recovery_time = 25 ms}), a set of rules R that can sufficiently test the validity of p_1 can be defined as:

r_1: number_of_server_instances ≥ 3
r_2: heartbeat_frequency = 5 ms
r_3: recovery_time ≤ 25 ms

These rules ensure that end reliability and availability are always greater than or equal to 98.9 percent and 99.95 percent, respectively.

A conceptual architectural framework, the *Fault Tolerance Manager* (FTM), provides the basis to realize the design stage and runtime stage of the delivery scheme, and serves as the basis for offering fault tolerance as a service (see Figure 7.5). FTM is inserted as a dedicated service layer between the physical hardware and user applications along the virtualization layer. FTM is built using the principles of service-oriented architectures, where each ft_unit is realized as an individual Web service and ft_sol is created by orchestrating a set of ft_units (Web services) using the business process execution language (BPEL) constructs. This allows the ftSP to satisfy its scalability and interoperability goals. The central computing component, denoted as the FTMKernel, has three main components:

- *Service Directory*: It is the registry of all ft_units realized by the service provider in the form of Web services that (i) describes its operations and input/output data structures (WSDL and WSCL), and(ii) allows other ft_units to coordinate and assemble with it. This component also registers the metadata representing the fault tolerance property of each ft_unit. Service

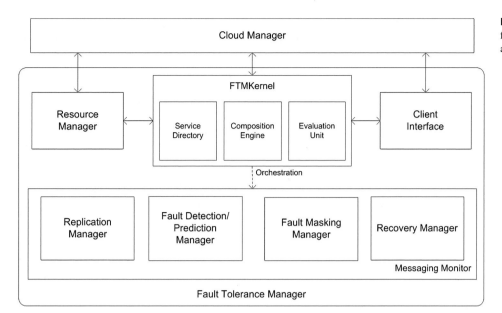

FIGURE 7.5 Architecture of the fault tolerance manager showing all the components.

Directory matches user's preferences and generates the set *S* of ft_units that satisfy p_c.

- *Composition Engine*: It receives an ordered set of ft_units from the service directory as input and generates a comprehensive fault tolerance solution ft_sol as output. In terms of service-oriented architectures, the composition engine is a Web service orchestration engine that exploits BPEL constructs to build a fault tolerance solution.

- *Evaluation Unit*: It monitors the composed fault tolerance solutions at runtime using the validation function and the set of rules defined corresponding to each ft_sol. The interface exposed by Web services (WSDL and WSCL) allows the evaluation unit to validate the rules. If a violation is detected, the evaluation unit updates the present attribute values in the metadata; otherwise, the service continues uninterrupted.

Finally, let's take a brief look at a set of components that provide complementary support to fault tolerance mechanisms that are included in the FTM. These components affect the quality of service and support ftSP in satisfying user's requirements and constraints (see checklist: "An Agenda for Action for Satisfying Users' Requirements and Constraints Activities").

For example, consider that at the start of the service, the resource manager generates a profile of all computing resources in the cloud and identifies five processing nodes $\{n_1, \ldots ,n_5\} \in N$ with the network topology represented in Figure 7.6a. Further, consider that the FTMKernel, upon gathering the user's requirements from the Client Interface, chooses a passive replication mechanism for the e-commerce service. Based on the chosen fault tolerance mechanism (the set of ft_units that realize the

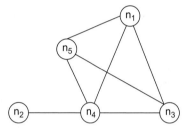

FIGURE 7.6A   Resource graph.

envisioned passive replication scheme), FTMKernel requires that the following conditions be satisfied: (i) the replica group must contain one primary and two backup nodes, (ii) the node on which the primary replica executes must not be shared with any other VM instances, (iii) all the replicas must be located on different nodes at all times, and (iv) node n_5 must not allow any user-level VM instance (rather, it should be used only to run system-level services such as monitoring unit). An overview of the activities performed by each supporting component in the FTM is as follows:

- The replication manager (RM) selects the node n_1 for the primary replica and nodes n_3 and n_4, respectively, for two backup replicas so that a replica group can be formed (see Figure 7.6b). Assume that the replication manager synchronizes the state between the replicas by frequently checkpointing the primary and updating the state of backup replicas.

- The messaging manager establishes the infrastructure required for carrying out the checkpointing protocol and forms the replica group for the e-commerce service (see Figure 7.6c).

An Agenda for Action for Satisfying Users' Requirements and Constraints Activities

Figure 7.5 illustrates the overall architecture of the Fault Tolerance Manager (FTM). Satisfying the user's requirements and constraints on the functionality of each component is as follows (check all tasks completed):

_____1. *Client Interface*: This component provides a specification language, which allows clients to specify and define their requirements.

_____2. *Resource Manager*: This component maintains a consistent view of all computing resources in the cloud to:

　　_____(i) Efficiently perform resource allocation during each user request.

　　_____(ii) Avoid over provisioning during failures.

The resource manager monitors the working state of physical and virtual resources, maintains a database of inventory and log information, and a graph representing the topology and working state of all the resources in the cloud.

_____3. *Replication Manager*: This component supports the replication mechanisms by invoking the replicas and managing their execution as defined in the ft_unit. The set of replicas that are controlled by a single replication mechanism is denoted as a replica group. The task of the replication manager is to make the user perceive a replica group as a single service and to ensure that each replica exhibits correct behavior in the fail-free periods.

_____4. *Fault Detection/Prediction Manager*: This component provides FTM with failure detection support at two different levels. The first level offers failure detection globally, to all the nodes in the cloud (infrastructure-centric), and the second level provides support only to detect failures among individual replicas in each replica group (user application-centric). This component supports several well-known failure detection algorithms (gossip-based protocols, heartbeat protocol) that are configured at runtime according to user's preferences. When a failure is detected in a replica, a notification is sent to the fault masking manager and recovery manager.

_____5. *Fault Masking Manager*: The goal of this component is to support ft_units that realize fault masking mechanisms so that the occurrence of faults in the system can be hidden from users. This component applies masking procedures immediately after a failure is detected so as to prevent faults from resulting into errors.

_____6. *Recovery Manager*: The goal of this component is to achieve system-level resilience by minimizing the downtime of the system during failures. It supports ft_units that realize recovery mechanisms so that an error-prone node can be resumed back to a normal operational mode. The support offered by this component is complementary to that of the failure detection/prediction manager and fault masking manager, when an error is detected in the system. FTM maximizes the lifetime of the cloud infrastructure by continuously checking for occurrence of faults and by recovering from failures.

_____7. *Messaging monitor*: This component extends through all the components of FTM and offers the communication infrastructure in two different forms: message exchange within a replica group and intercomponent communication within the framework. The messaging monitor integrates WS-RM standard with other application protocols to ensure correct messaging infrastructure even in the presence of failures. This component is therefore critical in providing maximum interoperability and serves as a key QoS factor.

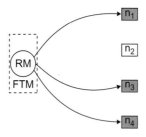

FIGURE 7.6B Nodes selected by replication manager.

FIGURE 7.6C Messaging Infrastructure created (forms a replica group).

- Assume that the service directory selects a proactive fault tolerance mechanism. As a consequence, the failure detection/prediction manager continuously gathers the state information of nodes n_1, n_3, and n_4, and verifies if all system parameter values satisfy threshold values (physical memory usage of a node allocated to a VM instance must be less than 70 percent of its total capacity).

- When the failure detection/prediction manager predicts a failure in node n_1 (see Figure 7.6d), it invokes the fault masking ft_unit that performs a live migration of the VM instance. The entire OS at node n_1 is

Replica Group

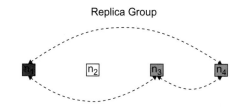

FIGURE 7.6D   Failure detected at node n_1.

New Replica Group

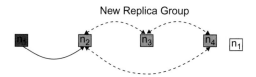

FIGURE 7.6E   Fault masking performed — VM instance migrated to node n_2.

Replica Group

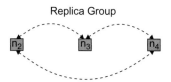

FIGURE 7.6F   Recovery Manager brings back node n_1 to working state.

moved to another location (node n_2) so that e-commerce customers do not experience any impact of the failure.

- Although the high availability goals are satisfied using the fault masking manager (see Figure 7.6e), the IaaS may be affected since the system now consists of four working nodes only. Therefore, FTM applies robust recovery mechanisms at node n_1 to resume it to a normal working state, increasing the system's overall lifetime (see Figure 7.6f).

Within the FTM framework, the notion of providing fault tolerance as a service can therefore be effectively realized for the cloud computing environment. Based on FTM's delivery scheme, users can achieve high levels of reliability and availability for their applications without having any knowledge about the low-level mechanisms, and dynamically change the fault tolerance properties of its applications (based on the business needs) at runtime.

8. SUMMARY

Fault tolerance and resilience in cloud computing are critical to ensure correct and continuous system operation. We discussed the failure characteristics of typical cloud-based services and analyzed the impact of each failure type on user's applications. Since failures in the cloud computing environment arise mainly due to crash faults and byzantine faults, we discussed two fault tolerance solutions, each corresponding to one of these two classes of faults. The choice of the fault tolerance solutions was also driven by the large set of additional properties that they offer (generality, agility, transparency, and reduced resource consumption costs).

We also presented an innovative delivery scheme that leverages existing solutions and their properties to deliver high levels of fault tolerance based on a given set of desired properties. The delivery scheme was supported by a conceptual framework, which realized the notion of offering fault tolerance as a service to user's applications. Due to the complex nature of cloud computing architecture and difficulties in realizing fault tolerance using traditional methods, we advocate fault tolerance as a service to be an effective alternative to address users' reliability and availability concerns.

Finally, let's move on to the real interactive part of this chapter: review questions/exercises, hands-on projects, case projects, and optional team case project. The answers and/or solutions by chapter can be found in the Online Instructor's Solutions Manual.

CHAPTER REVIEW QUESTIONS/EXERCISES

True/False

1. True or False? Crash faults do not cause the system components to completely stop functioning or remain inactive during failures (power outage, hard disk crash).
2. True or False? Byzantine faults do not lead the system components to behave arbitrarily or maliciously during failure, causing the system to behave unpredictably incorrect.
3. True or False? The system is rarely monitored at runtime to validate, verify, and ensure that correct system specifications are being met.
4. True or False? The system state is captured and saved based on undefined parameters (after every 1024 instructions or every 60 seconds).
5. True or False? Critical system components are duplicated using additional hardware, software, and network resources in such a way that a copy of the critical components is available even before a failure happens.

Multiple Choice

1. What measures the strength of the fault tolerance mechanism in terms of the granularity at which it can handle errors and failures in the system:
   A. Resource consumption
   B. Performance

    C. Fault tolerance model

    D. Multiple machines within the same cluster

    E. All of the above

2. What factor deals with the impact of the fault tolerance procedure on the end-to-end quality of service (QoS) both during failure and failure-free periods?

    A. Resource consumption

    B. Fault tolerance model

    C. Performance

    D. Multiple machines within the same cluster

    E. All of the above

3. How many replicas of an application can be placed on the hosts that are connected by a ToR switch (within a LAN)?

    A. One

    B. Three

    C. Five

    D. Four

    E. Two

4. How many replicas of an application can be placed on the hosts belonging to different clusters in the same data center (on the hosts that are connected via a ToR switch and AggS)?

    A. One

    B. Three

    C. Five

    D. Four

    E. Two

5. How many replicas of an application can be placed on the hosts belonging to different data centers (connected via a switch), AggS and AccR?

    A. Two

    B. Four

    C. One

    D. Three

    E. Five

EXERCISE

Problem

How secure is a cloud-based platform?

Hands-On Projects

Project

What components go into a cloud architecture?

Case Projects

Problem

How does cloud architecture scale?

Optional Team Case Project

Problem

How do you achieve fault tolerance in a cloud?

ACKNOWLEDGMENTS

This work was supported in part by the Italian Ministry of Research within the PRIN 2008 project "PEPPER" (2008SY2PH4).

REFERENCES

[1] Amazon Elastic Compute Cloud, © 2012, Amazon Web Services, Inc. or its affiliates. All rights reserved. <http://aws.amazon.com/ec2>, 2012.

[2] Azure, © 2012 Microsoft. <http://www.windowsazure.com/en-us/>, 2012.

[3] Build your business on Google Cloud Platform. <https://cloud.google.com/>, 2012.

[4] Amazon Elastic Compute Cloud, © 2012, Amazon Web Services, Inc. or its affiliates. All rights reserved. <http://aws.amazon.com/ec2>, 2012.

[5] E. Feller, L. Rilling, C. Morin, Snooze: a scalable and autonomic virtual machine management framework for private clouds, in: Proc. of CCGrid'12, Ottawa, Canada, 2012, pp. 482−489.

[6] K. Vishwanath, N. Nagappan, Characterizing cloud computing hardware reliability, in: Proc. of SoCC'10, Indianapolis, IN, USA, 2010, pp. 193−204.

[7] U. Helzle, L.A. Barroso, The Datacenter as a Computer: An Introduction to the Design of Warehouse-Scale Machines, first ed., Morgan and Claypool Publishers, 2009.

[8] B. Selic, Fault tolerance techniques for distributed systems, <http://www.ibm.com/developerworks/rational/library/114.html>, 2012.

[9] A. Heddaya, A. Helal, Reliability, Availability, Dependability and Performability: A User-Centered View, Boston, MA, USA, Tech. Rep., 1997.

[10] M. Armbrust, A. Fox, R. Griffith, A.D. Joseph, R.H. Katz, A. Konwinski, et al., Tech. Rep. UCB/EECS-2009-28 Above the Clouds: A Berkeley View of Cloud Computing, EECS Department, University of California, Berkeley, 2009

[11] P. Gill, N. Jain, N. Nagappan, Understanding network failures in data centers: measurement, analysis and implications, ACM Comp. Commun. Rev. 41 (4) (2011) 350−361.

[12] R. Jhawar, V. Piuri, Fault tolerance management in IaaS clouds, in: Proc. of ESTEL'12, Rome, Italy, October 20, 2012.

[13] W.E. Smith, K.S. Trivedi, L.A. Tomek, J. Ackaret, Availability analysis of blade server systems, IBM Syst. J. 47 (4) (2008) 621−640.

[14] Load Balancing Data Center Services SRND: Solutions Reference Nework Design, Cisco Systems, Inc., 170 West Tasman Drive, San Jose, CA 95134-1706, Copyright © 2004, Cisco Systems, Inc. All rights reserved. <https://learningnetwork.cisco.com/servlet/JiveServlet/previewBody/3438-102-1-9467/cdccont_0900aecd800eb95a.pdf> March 2004.

[15] N. Ayari, D. Barbaron, L. Lefevre, P. Primet, Fault tolerance for highly available internet services: concepts, approaches and issues, IEEE Commun. Surv. Tutor. 10 (2) (2008) 34−46.

[16] R. Jhawar, V. Piuri, M. Santambrogio, A comprehensive conceptual system-level approach to fault tolerance in cloud computing, in: Proc. of IEEE SysCon'12, Vancouver, BA, Canada, 2012, pp. 1–5.

[17] R. Guerraoui, M. Yabandeh, Independent faults in the cloud, in: Proc. of LADIS'10, Zurich, Switzerland, 2010, pp. 12–17.

[18] A. Undheim, A. Chilwan, P. Heegaard, Differentiated availability in cloud computing SLAs, in: Proc. of Grid'11, Lyon, France, 2011, pp. 129–136.

[19] S. Kim, F. Machinda, K. Trivedi, Availability modeling and analysis of virtualized system, in: Proc. of PRDC'09, Shanghai, China, 2009, pp. 365–371.

[20] B. Cully, G. Lefebvre, D. Meyer, M. Feeley, N. Hutchinson, A. Warfield, Remus: high availability via asynchronous virtual machine replication, in: Proc. of NSDI'08, San Francisco, CA, USA, pp. 161–174.

[21] C. Clark, K. Fraser, S. Hand, J.G. Hansen, E. Jul, C. Limpach, et al., Live migration of virtual machines, in: Proc. NSDI'05, Boston, MA, USA, pp. 273–286.

[22] M. Castro, B. Liskov, Practical byzantine fault tolerance, in: Proc. of OSDI'99, New Orleans, LA, USA, 1999, pp. 173–186.

[23] T. Wood, R. Singh, A. Venkataramani, P. Shenoy, E. Cecchet, ZZ and the art of practical BFT execution, in: Proc. of EuroSys'11, Salzburg, Austria, 2011, pp. 123–138.

[24] R. Kotla, L. Alvisi, M. Dahlin, A. Clement, E. Wong, Zyzzyva: speculative byzantine fault tolerance, ACM Trans. Comput. Syst. 27 (4) (2009) 7.1–7.39.

[25] J. Yin, J.P. Martin, A. Venkataramani, L. Alvisi, M. Dahlin, Separating agreement from execution for byzantine fault tolerant services, in: Proc. of SOSP'03, New York, NY, USA, 2003, pp. 253–267.

[26] R. Jhawar, V. Piuri, M. Santambrogio, Fault tolerance management in cloud computing: a system-level perspective, IEEE Syst. J. (2012).

## Chapter 8

Securing Web Applications, Services, and Servers

Gerald Beuchelt

The MITRE Corporation[1], Bedford, MA, U.S.A.

1. SETTING THE STAGE

The development of a distributed hypertext system in the early 1990s at the CERN in Switzerland was one of the defining moments in making the Internet available to an audience beyond academia and specialized communities. The combination of a simple, yet powerful, transport protocol—HTTP—with a specialization of the Standard Generic Markup Language (SGML) made it possible to render complex content on the fly and link related information, even if it was distributed.

As with many other information systems technologies, the early implementation of the Web included only very limited built-in security, especially since the system was initially designed for use within a research facility. However, the growth of the hypertext system at CERN into the World Wide Web required much more advanced security controls.

Defining Threats to Your Web Assets

Initially, there were only very few real threats to the WWW: early on, hackers proved their ability and highlighted potential threats to the new environment by defacing Web sites. Once commercial transactions (such as online shopping) and other high-value information exchanges were starting to use the Web, the number of potential threat actors and threats grew quickly. Today, any public or private Web application or service operator will need to perform at least a cursory threat and vulnerability assessment to determine appropriate risk mitigation strategy for their Web assets.

Depending on the use cases, the data, and the audience of a Web asset, a variety of threat actors should be considered when performing a threat assessment. Among these threat actors one may find a diverse crowd: script kiddies, disgruntled employees, organized crime, hacktivists, terrorists, or foreign intelligence agencies. While their capabilities and credibility as threat actors may vary significantly, they are all credible sources of attacks against simple Web sites such as nonprofit club home pages, or highly secured commercial targets such as banks or e-commerce sites.

While Web assets are typically more accessible than other services (such as file servers or databases), the general approach to performing risk assessment and management is very similar. One useful approach is described in the Special Publication (SP) series of the National Institute for Standards and Technologies (NIST) of the United States. Specifically, SP 800-30 rev. 1 and SP 800-39 describe a comprehensive approach to ensuring threat and risk assessment and mitigation. The reader is strongly encouraged to review these documents for further guidance on implementing their own risk management strategy.

Surveying the Legal Landscape and Privacy Issues

In addition to the embarrassment and potential liability for monetary damage to third parties after exposure to hackers, Web operators are often also subject to other regulatory requirements. For example, Web sites that store or process personally identifiable information (PII) may be required to disclose their data handling policies, and may have to restrict access for young children. The legal requirements for Web site operators vary from country to country, and lack of clearly defined "borders" on the Internet may require compliance with differing, sometimes contradictory, regulatory regimes.

All Web operators will minimally need to comply with the terms of service of their service provider and the laws applying to them. For example, U.S.-based providers

---

1. The opinions and guidance presented here are those of the author and do not necessarily reflect the positions of The MITRE Corporation, its customers or sponsors, or any part of the U.S. federal government.

will need to review their Web sites in the light of very diverse laws, including (but not limited to) the Children's Online Privacy Protection Act (COPPA), Sarbanes-Oxley Act (SOX), Health Insurance Portability and Accountability Act (HIPAA), and the Privacy Act. European operators will need to address not only the requirements of their respective local countries, but also the European Union Data Protection Directive.

In general, any Web site operator handling information from their employees or customers, visitors, or third parties is well advised to consult with a local law firm that specializes in Internet, compliance, and privacy law.

Web Services Overview

Web services have become a widely used technology in both corporate and Internet applications. IT practitioners such as architects, developers, and administrators have been moving away from traditional client-server architectures to loosely coupled service environments to a number of issues. Service architectures rely on clearly defined interfaces so that service clients and service providers can change their internal architectures independently from each other, allowing decoupling the development processes for different systems components. This process started in the late 1980s and has been implemented in specialized distributed architectures such as CORBA, COM+, or Java RMI. The success of Web technologies in the mid-1990s inspired system architects to profile these new platform agnostic technologies to build distributed systems that can interoperate across vendors and run-time architectures. Web services have been defined in different ways; in this chapter we will focus on the following two principal realizations of distributed services that typically use the Hyper Text Transfer Protocol (HTTP) for exchanging information:

- SOAP Web services were popularized in the early 2000s by Microsoft and IBM, and have seen broad adoption across very different platforms. SOAP services are built around the concept of a SOAP envelope, an XML document that contains a SOAP header, and a SOAP body. The header defines the necessary metadata for the SOAP message, including processing instructions and security elements. The SOAP body can—in principal—transport any media type, although the core protocol was originally formulated around XML documents.
- HTTP services have been in use since the early days of the worldwide Web. The original design of the HTTP protocol included not only the well-known operations such as GET (to retrieve data) or POST (to modify data), which are commonly used by Web browsers, but also PUT (to create data) and DELETE

(to delete data). In addition, HTTP also supports other operations that allow comprehensive management of the service and the interaction. Roy Fielding formalized the common best practices around creating HTTP services in his dissertation and coined the term *Representational State Transfer (REST)* to describe the architectural style of well-designed HTTP systems.

The protocols, architecture, and design of Web services alone are fairly complex. The reader is expected to have a basic understanding of how HTTP and SOAP work, how they are currently being used, and how they can be created. The goals of this chapter are to provide a general overview of the breadth of Web service security, give an introduction to the subject area, and guide the reader to sources with deeper information.

This chapter addresses both REST HTTP service and SOAP-based Web services. Each technology has its strengths and weaknesses, and users should clearly enumerate the requirements they have for their Web service environment before deciding to implement one or the other. In many complex cases, a hybrid environment will prove to be the best approach (See Sidebar: Protocol Versions).

Protocol Versions

Within this chapter, we will always reference the latest versions of the protocols referenced. Some of the protocols are backward compatible, since they only add features to the overall specification, but in many instances the protocols break backward compatibility to fix significant security holes. Existing implementations of these security protocols sometimes lag behind the latest standardized version (TLS being one example), but increasingly the standards community works in a much more agile way, where implementation of draft specifications are available and fully supported by vendors (OAuth 2.0 or higher). Depending on the application of Web services, the user will need to make a business-requirements and risk-based determination of which version of the protocol should be used.

---

2. BASIC SECURITY FOR HTTP APPLICATIONS AND SERVICES

Since HTTP services implementing a REST architectural style (often called REST Services) are simply using the HTTP stack, all security aspects of HTTP apply. At the same time, there is a critical distinction to Web applications: For the latter, the user agent (the software making the HTTP requests) is a Web browser, which is event-driven and operated by a human. Operations such as providing username and password credentials, selecting PKI certificates, or making choices about how to interact with the Web server are not complicated for the client. This is all very different if the client user is an agent.

Basic authentication and some other authentication and authorization mechanisms are built into the HTTP stack and the layered protocols supported by most operating systems and clients. At the same time, many of these security mechanisms were created to support end-user facing agents such as Web browsers, and they often require considerable human interaction in order to work as designed. For example, HTTP Basic Authentication or HTML forms-based authentication with clear text passwords works well for an end user that needs to access a Web site (or Web application), but username/password tokens are less ideal for machine-to-machine interactions, since they (i) require a secure store of the secret, but (ii) do not offer a particularly high level of security.

This part of the chapter introduces a number of widely available and deployed HTTP mechanisms that may be used to build interoperable, secure machine-to-machine HTTP services. In general, most security mechanism supported by the HTTP specification itself are typically the most interoperable, while layered protocols and mechanisms (such as those provided by the GSS-API and SASL) tend to be less interoperable out of the box.

Basic Authentication

HTTP[2] provides Basic Authentication[3] as part of the standard HTTP stack, where the exchange of the credential is performed. For typical Web applications, the server denies access to the resources that was requested at the URI, and returns an HTTP status code of 401, including a WWW-Authenticate header, which needs to be set to the "Basic" authentication mechanism. The client then responds with another request to the same resource, but adds a WWW-Authorization header with the Base 64 encoding of the username and password. The server can then decode the username and password and verify the credential. While this authentication mechanism is straightforward and very easy to implement, it is of limited use in environments where HTTP is used for the following machine-to-machine communication:

1. This mechanism transmits the username and password unencrypted. The simple Base64 encoding can be decoded by anyone and must be treated as clear text. As such, this authentication mechanism can only be used in conjunction with a channel protection mechanism (such as TLS) that provides for the confidentiality of the channel.

2. Assigning username/password accounts to machines tends to lead to bad code. Often, developers will hard-code the credential into the code, making changes much harder. Even if a configuration file is used, the username and password are very often not cryptographically protected on disk.

Overall it is not recommended that one rely on username/password credentials (HTTP Basic Authentication) when implementing HTTP services, especially in production environments. Note that other browser-centric authentication mechanisms (such as HTML forms-based authentication) are not usable for client-server authentication in REST architectures.

Transport Layer Security

Transport Layer Security (TLS)[4] is based on the Secure Socket Layer (SSL) protocol that was developed in the 1990s by the Netscape Corporation. The basic design requires a X.503 V3-based Public Key Infrastructure (PKI) at least for the server and requires client and server to maintain a session state. Both use PKI to negotiate a session master key: This approach ensures that the asymmetric cryptography is used to introduce client and server and establish a secure channel between the two communication partners. The establishment of the secure session key using symmetric cryptography allows leveraging the efficiency of these mechanisms in bulk encryption transactions. While most clients and servers today still support SSL 3.0 and TLS 1.0, a move to TLS 1.1 is recommended to avoid potential security holes.

Server Authentication

Every TLS transaction requires the server to authenticate itself to the client. This is typically initiated by the client sending the server a list of supported TLS versions, supported cipher-suites, and other connection information (such as the time or random parameters). Note that this initial request typically requires the client to connect to a port different from the usual port for the protocol. For example, HTTP usually operates on TCP port 80, but the TLS/SSL version of HTTP (called HTTPS) is defined to operate on port 443. The server responds with a list including the same information and also the server PKI certificate. The subject identifier of the certificate is the Web address of the server (such as https://www.example.com). The client can then use the server certificate to authenticate the server, and responds with a message that

2. RFC 2616, "Hyper Text Transfer Protocol—HTTP 1.1," R. Fielding et al., Internet Engineering Task Force, June 1999.

3. RFC 2617, "HTTP Authentication: Basic and Digest Authentication," J. Franks et al., Internet Engineering Task Force, June 1999.

4. RFC 5246, "The Transport Layer Security (TLS) Protocol Version 1.2," T. Dierks et al., Internet Engineering Task Force, August 2008.

includes a master secret, which is used to generate the session keys. Once the keys are available, the TLS handshake completes, with the client and the server starting to use the session keys and shifting to an encrypted communication channel.

Mutual Authentication

Mutual authentication means that both client and server are authenticated to each other; that is, the client needs to authenticate to the server as well. This is achieved by the server sending a Certificate Request message to the client as part of the handshake. The client will then provide a user certificate to the server. This establishes the identity of the client to the server. While subject identifiers in client certificates can vary, most often they are bound to the user's email address.

Application to REST Services

TLS channel protection adds a number of security features to the communication between a REST client and service, as follows:

1. Server authentication using strong cryptographic methods. The server certificate is bound to the server's DNS name itself by the subject identifier, thus providing additional protection against DNS attacks.
2. Channel protection. Once the secure channel handshake is complete, the secure channel provides confidentiality to the communication path between client and server. This allows the exchanges of sensitive information, including additional authentication and authorization data.
3. REST client libraries can usually make use of operating or runtime systems certificate stores in a very efficient way. Certificate stores typically provide built-in protections of the cryptographic material. Additionally, both client and server systems usually allow fairly simple updates of the certificates when needed.
4. TLS can provide a Message Authentication Code (MAC) for each packet, allowing full integrity protection of the connection.

The only significant drawback of using simple or client-authenticated TLS is the high cost of using a PKI: For cross-enterprise transactions, PKI certificates must be obtained through common trust anchors that may be too expensive in low-value transactions (such as social network interactions). For intra-enterprise connections, a custom PKI may be used, but the cost of maintaining this can also be substantial, especially for large enterprises.

GSS-API Negotiated Security

Another way to perform authentication for HTTP-based service and application is through use of the GSS-API and its security mechanisms. The GSS-API has been defined for C and the Java runtime[5] and provides a number of standard features:

- Authentication of client-server relationship through a complete handshake protocol between client and server.
- Confidentiality and integrity for the payload of the connection, independent of the protocols encapsulated. This is achieved by wrapping the payload within the structure needed for the GSS-API protected traffic. Note that the capabilities of this feature are strongly dependent on the underlying security mechanism.
- Extensibility and mechanism negotiation through the SPNego pseudomechanism. Microsoft uses this to integrate Kerberos with the HTTP protocol for authentication and provide a smooth browsing experience.

The preceding technology was initially developed in the early 1990s and has a high level of implementation maturity. At the same time, it is very focused on traditional client-server environments and encourages a much stronger coupling of the participants than is desired for typical Web services. For example, when using Kerberos over SPNego as the underlying security mechanism, the administrator will need to ensure that either client and server are part of the same Kerberos realm or there is an established trust relationship between the two realms. Since this trust and deployment model does not scale to cross-organizational deployments, this approach can only be used effectively within a single administrative domain.

3. BASIC SECURITY FOR SOAP SERVICES

The situation for SOAP-based Web services (see Sidebar: SOAP-based Web Services) is significantly different from basic HTTP services: While SOAP may use the HTTP protocol for transport, it was designed to be transport independent, and as such it needs to re-create the entire security stack in a self-contained way. This is achieved by extending the SOAP headers to support security-related information in the WS-Security protocol, and other profiles and protocols that build on top of it.

---

5. The C binding is defined in the IETF RFC 2744, and the Java binding is standardized in JSR-72. See http://tools.ietf.org/html/rfc2744 and http://jcp.org/aboutJava/communityprocess/review/jsr072/index.html for more information.

SOAP-based Web Services

SOAP version 1.2[6] or higher is a flexible XML-based protocol to exchange information. Originally developed by Microsoft, IBM, and others, SOAP is available today on most Web-enabled platforms. Conceptually, SOAP defines an Envelope as the root node of the XML document. The Envelope contains two child elements: the Header and the Body of the SOAP message. The Body typically contains the main payload of the message, which is intended to be an XML-serialized representation of a data model. The Header section of the Envelope may contain metadata about the message, sender and receiver, and about the transaction itself. The Header is highly customizable and extensible.

SOAP was originally developed as a Web service protocol, with an HTTP transport binding. At the same time, the designers of the protocol made sure that the SOAP specification was not dependent on any features of the underlying transport. As a result, SOAP can be used over a large number of transport protocols today, thus providing a consistent way of creating services over a number of different platforms. Such platforms include SMTP, FTP, and message queuing protocols. This flexibility does not come for free though, since many transport semantics (such as session security, routing, and acknowledgments that are provided by the underlying transport protocols need to be replicated within the SOAP stack. This can lead to significant performance issues and replication of functionality at different layers.

For this chapter, it is assumed that the reader has a good understanding of the basic SOAP protocol structures.

WS-Security Overview

WS-Security[7] (often abbreviated WSS) defines a Header extension to provide a number of features for SOAP-based messages, as follows:

- Signing the message to provide integrity protection and nonrepudiation
- Encrypting the message to provide message-level confidentiality
- Attaching arbitrary security tokens to the messages to provide the identity of the sender

It should be noted that since WS-Security is only tied to the SOAP messaging structures, it is completely transport independent and can therefore be used over the SOAP HTTP binding, but also with any other form of SOAP transport. At the same time due to its independence, WS-Security can be combined with the security mechanisms of the underlying transport security.

To provide the various features mentioned above, WS-Security leverages the XML Encryption and Signature standards. Users of WS-Security should have a robust understanding of how these standards work, minimally from an API perspective, but ideally also from a protocol point of view. The WSS headers directly use the <Signature>, <KeyInfo>, and <EncryptedData> elements of the XML Signature and Encryption standards, repectively.

For example, a SOAP message may be signed and encrypted at the message level using WS-Security and transported over an encrypted HTTPS connection as well. For complex situations, where the SOAP message is routed by SOAP intermediaries that sit between the sender and the server, this feature can be used to provide both: (i) secure point-to-point connections between the sender, receiver, and their respective intermediaries using HTTP over TLS, and (ii) end-to-end security from the sender to the receiver using message-level encryption.

Protocol Design

As discussed, WS-Security injects a security header as an XML child node into the SOAP Header (see Figure 8.1). This security header can contain a number of different elements that enable the various features of WSS. Note that the following examples reference the usage of WS-Security with SOAP 1.2 or higher only. The WS-Security specification also defines the use of SOAP 1.1 or higher, but this will be omitted here. The namespace prefixes below are identical to the ones used in the WSS 1.1 or higher specification. For real implementations they may be different, as long as the XML namespace rules are followed.

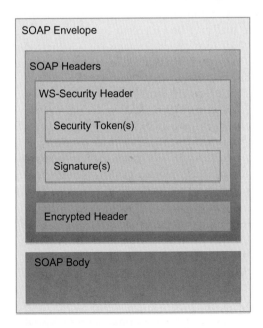

FIGURE 8.1   SOAP and WS-Security message layout.

---

6. "SOAP Version 1.2," M. Gudgin et al., W3C Recommendation, April 2007.

7. "Web Service Security: SOAP Messaging Framework 1.1," A. Nadlin et al., OASIS Open, November 2006.

The <wsse:Security> is the base WS-Security header element within the <S12:Header> element of the SOAP message. It may contain a number of typical attributes from the SOAP headers, such as mustUnderstand, to indicate that the receiver or intermediary must understand the WSS header in order to correctly process the SOAP message. Also, the <Security> header can be extended with any additional attribute or child element, effectively providing a very flexible extension point. It should be noted that open-ended extension points like this—while desirable to protocol implementers and vendors—may introduce significant interoperability issues when being deployed: If vendor-specific extensions are required for operation, environments that require cross-platform interoperability may run into significant difficulties.

In order to enable signature and encryption of arbitrary parts of the SOAP message, the WSS specification introduces the ability to reference nodes of the entire SOAP Envelope using the wsu:Id attribute. Similar to an anchor in an HTML page, an XML element within the message can be tagged with this attribute and then be referenced within the WSS header structures that are used for providing signature and encryption.

Signature is provided through the <ds:Signature> element that may contain the crypto material (such as a <ds:KeyInfo> element) and additional information to provide identification of the type of signer, the signature and canonicalization[8] algorithm, and references to the signed elements.

For encryption of elements, WSS differentiates between header elements that need to be encrypted and the main SOAP Body (or portions of the body). For the headers, WSS introduces the <wsse:EncryptedHeader> element that may be processed by SOAP intermediaries or the final receiver of the messages. If the SOAP handling system cannot decode the encrypted header, it needs to leave it in place. Within the SOAP body, the <xenc:EncryptedData> element is used to wrap encrypted parts of the XML infoset within the overall message structure.

In either case, the WSS header will contain the necessary key information to decrypt the data, similar to how this is handled for signatures. When decrypting, the decrypted elements replace the <xenc:EncryptedData> and <wsse:EncryptedHeader> elements, respectively.

Usage of WS-Security

By itself, WS-Security is of limited use: It describes how security elements such as tokens and signatures can be

incorporated into a SOAP message. It also provides limited instructions on how to protect portions of the message using these security elements.

Authentication with WSS

A common use of WS-Security is for authentication of the incoming request. In order to process (such as an update to an account using a SOAP request), the bank service will need to verify the identity of the invoker (authentication) so that it can apply its authorization policies. For this, the clients will need to attach one or more security tokens to the WS-Security header that prove their users' identity. WS-Security provides for a number of built-in tokens such as <wsse:UsernameToken> or the more generic <wsse:BinarySecurityToken>, but it can also be extended to support other token types as well. Common stacks such as Apache Axis or .NET WCF support these and others such as SAML or vendor-specific tokens as well (see Sidebar: Attaching Policies to Web Services).

Attaching Policies to Web Services

Authentication of a single request is achieved by providing the token within the security header. Since there are countless ways of doing this, the service needs to communicate to the client the type of acceptable tokens, acceptable configurations of these tokens, and how to protect them. This is typically done by adding the WS-SecurityPolicy elements: WS-SecurityPolicy is another OASIS Open standard, available at http://docs.oasis-open.org/ws-sx/ws-securitypolicy/v1.3/os/ws-security-policy-1.3-spec-os.pdf. It can prescribe the required configuration for a number of WS-Security related parameters.

WS-Security Policy is written within the WS-Policy framework, which is for describing policies associated with a Web service. In order to make WS-Policy statements available to clients, most stacks use WS-Policy Attachments, a W3C Recommendation (available at http://www.w3.org/TR/ws-policy-attach/) that describes how WS-Policy elements map to WSDL elements.

In the easiest case, a simple UsernameToken is used, which can include the password in clear text. Obviously, such a token would typically not be used without protecting the message for confidentiality. Alternatively, a trusted authentication server could sign a UsernameToken or a SAML statement. The service could then decide to trust the authentication server and not require additional credentials. If a SAML statement is used for authentication, the SAML Token Profile for WS-Security will describe the possible configurations that the server can request from the client.

---

8. WSS supports both W3C XML Canonicalization and W3C Exclusive XML Canonicalization. The latter provides a better support for XML namespaces and is recommended in most situations.

WS-I Security Profile

As seen above, the configuration parameters to simply perform authentication can be very complex. While WS-SecurityPolicy is capable of describing the server's requirements, it is impossible even within a fairly rich policy framework to describe all possible parameters for the WS-Security stack. Even though placement of individual XML elements should not matter from an infoset perspective, and most crypto parameters such as algorithms are described in the core specification, tests between different vendors have shown that acceptable interoperability cannot be achieved without a very narrow profile. The WS-I organization (now a subgroup of OASIS Open) created a number of such profiles. The WS-I Basic Security Profile includes very detailed implementation guidance for WS-Security, WS-SecurityPolicy, the various token profiles (username, SAML, X.509 certificate, Kerberos), and SOAP with Attachments. While users of WS-Security are typically not expected to implement these specifications and their profiles, it is important to understand their relevance when creating cross-platform services.

Example for a WSDL for WS-Security

Figure 8.2 contains a sample WSDL[9] for a very simple SOAP Web service with a single operation. The service requires authentication using a SAML 2.0 or higher Security token using the SAML Token Profile version 1.1 or higher. Note that within this WSDL there is no directive on how to utilize the information found within the SAML token for authorization. The SAML statement will contain information that is used for authentication and authorization. How this is used by the application server runtime and the service itself depends on the application server vendor and the service developer, respectively.

4. IDENTITY MANAGEMENT AND WEB SERVICES

Background

Since Web services are intended to implement a distributed architecture, it becomes very important to manage the identities of the participating actors: Different systems implementing the services or the clients need to fully understand who they are interacting with in order to make access control decisions that are consistent with the security policies for the systems. While this has always been the case for complex systems, the loosely coupled design of Web services exacerbates this problem and requires a number of new patterns to address this issue in a reliable

way. The identity management community created a number of patterns that allow not only simple authentication, but also advanced patterns including:

- *Single Sign On (SSO) using mutually trusted identity servers.* This idea is based on the SSO mechanisms used for Web applications: A user (or machine entity) authenticates once to a trusted identity server, which issues security tokens that can be used to sign into relying parties (sometimes also called service providers). This pattern decouples the process of identification and authentication itself from the use of the authentication and authorization.
- *Federations of identity providers.* In order to allow cross-organizational access to Web services, the concept of an identity federation was introduced. In this pattern the operators of two separate identity servers (such as in Company A and Company B) decide to trust each other's authentication process. This is realized by allowing a client to exchange a security token from the identity server of Company A with a security token from Company B. This allows the client to access services that trust Company B's identity server.
- *Complex, distributed authorization.* By fully decoupling the authentication process from the authorization to access a resource, Web services can allow very flexible authorization mechanisms such as Attribute Based Access Control (ABAC).

Other patterns, such as privacy preserving authentication and authorization, have also been demonstrated and implemented using Web services-based identity management technologies. While many of these patterns were pioneered for the SOAP stack, recent developments have brought most them to REST-styled HTTP services. Due to its expressiveness and top-down design, SOAP-based identity management is quite achievable. In real-world implementations, some of the performance issues of XML processing have limited the broad adoption of SOAP-based identity management technologies. The initially less feature-rich REST designs have always leveraged the efficiency of the underlying transport protocols, resulting in a much slower availability of useful patterns, but providing a much better price/performance ratio.

Security Assertion Markup Language

The Security Assertion Markup Language (SAML)[10] was created to provide a means for exchanging information

---

9. For readability, XML namespaces have been removed from the listing.

10. SAML Technology Overview: N. Ragouzis et al., "Security Assertion Markup Language (SAML) V2.0 Technical Overview," OASIS Committee Draft, March 2008.SAML 2.0 Core: S. Cantor et al., "Assertions and Protocols for the OASIS Security Assertion Markup Language (SAML) V2.0," OASIS Standard, March 2005.

```
<?xml version="1.0" encoding="UTF-8" standalone="yes"?>
<definitions targetNamespace="http://ws.example.com/" name="SampleService" >
  <wsp:Policy wsu:Id="SampleServicePortBindingPolicy" >
    <sp:SignedSupportingTokens>
      <wsp:Policy>
        <sp:SamlToken sp:IncludeToken="http://docs.oasis-open.org/ws-sx/ws-
securitypolicy/200702/IncludeToken/AlwaysToRecipient">
          <wsp:Policy>
            <sp:WssSamlV20Token11/>                    Using a SAML 2.0 Token with SAML
          </wsp:Policy>                                      Token Profile 1.1
        </sp:SamlToken>
      </wsp:Policy>
    </sp:SignedSupportingTokens>
    <sp:TransportBinding>                             Specifying the parameters for the HTTPS
      <wsp:Policy>                                             security parameters
        <sp:AlgorithmSuite>
          <wsp:Policy>
            <sp:Basic256Sha256/>                          Use AES 256bit with SHA-256
          </wsp:Policy>
        </sp:AlgorithmSuite>
        <sp:IncludeTimestamp/>
        <sp:Layout>
          <wsp:Policy>                                 Require HTTPS, but client certificates
            <sp:Lax/>                                            are no needed
          </wsp:Policy>
        </sp:Layout>
        <sp:TransportToken>
          <wsp:Policy>
            <sp:HttpsToken RequireClientCertificate="false"/>
          </wsp:Policy>
        </sp:TransportToken>
      </wsp:Policy>
    </sp:TransportBinding>
    <sp:Wss11/>                                          Use WS-Security 1.1
    <wsam:Addressing/>
  </wsp:Policy>
  <types>
    (omitted)
  </types>
  <message name="hello">
    (omitted)
  </message>
  <portType name="SampleService">
    <operation name="hello">                          Directive to use policy above
      (omitted)
    </operation>
  </portType>
  <binding name="SampleServicePortBinding" type="tns:SampleService">
    <wsp:PolicyReference URI="#SampleServicePortBindingPolicy"/>
    <soap:binding transport="http://schemas.xmlsoap.org/soap/http" style="document"/>
    <operation name="hello">
      (omitted)
    </operation>
  </binding>
  <service name="SampleService">
    <port name="SampleServicePort" binding="tns:SampleServicePortBinding">
      (omitted)
    </port>
  </service>
</definitions>
```

FIGURE 8.2   Example WSDL for WSS protected service.

about authenticated entities and their attributes between a client (also called service consumer) and a service. Fundamentally, SAML defines a set of security tokens that can hold information about an entity's authentication, its attributes, or its authorization status.[11] In addition, SAML defines a request/response protocol that allows

exchanging SAML security tokens in remote procedure call (RPC)-style exchanges.

The SAML protocol stack (see Figure 8.3) extends from the basic tokens and protocol to include SAML Bindings, which describe how the SAML protocol can be used with the appropriate token types over different transport mechanisms. The Bindings are then used to build profiles for different SAML system participants such as Web browser SSO clients, identity providers, or attribute providers.

---

11. In SAML 2.0, the authorization token has been deprecated by the XACML protocol.

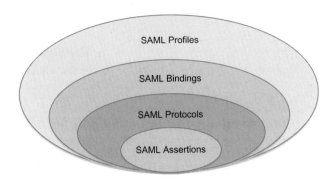

FIGURE 8.3   SAML protocol stack.

SAML Token Types

The SAML tokens are supported by many different vendors and can be used with many different protocols, even those that compete with the SAML request/response protocol. The SAML 2.0 or higher specification identifies the following three token types (called "Statements" in the specification):

- SAML Authentication Token. This statement describes how a user (or machine entity) authenticated to a given service. It can contain detailed information about the authentication act, including the time, the subject, and the authentication context.
- SAML Attribute Token. This statement can contain an arbitrary number of clear-text and encrypted attributes about a given subject, as asserted by the identity provider. This statement is the foundation for may ABAC-based authorization schemes.
- SAML Authorization Decision Token. This statement was deprecated by the XACML protocol at the time of publication of the SAML 2.0 or higher standard. It has been kept within the specification text, but should not be used unless for legacy interoperability purposes.

All tokens require a Subject element to identify the principle of the assertion. This Subject can contain identifiers (such as email addresses or distinguished names) and SubjectConfirmation elements. The use of these fields is specific to the protocols for which the tokens are used. For example, the WS-Security SAML token profile[12] defines two common SubjectConfirmation methods: Holder-of-Key (HOK) and Sender-Vouches.

Holder-of-Key ensures that the sender of the SOAP message has access to the private key of the Subject by requiring a signature over parts of the message block. This authenticates the subjects and confirms to the Web service the identity of the sender. In the Sender-Vouches method, the Web service trusts an authentication server to authenticate the client for them and requires only a signature by that authentication server over the message block.

SAML Protocol

The SAML protocol (sometimes called SAML-P to distinguish it from the SAML token format) is an XML-based protocol that implements a request/response patterns for exchanging information. It is completely transport independent and can therefore be used with a wide variety of system participants. The basic exchange implements a Request message by a client that is answered by a Response. The SAML protocol is self-contained and uses its own mechanism to indicate response status, failures, and other interaction metadata. Similar to SOAP, this independence from the underlying transport results in less effective architecture, since underlying functions such as status codes have to be replicated at the application level. The basic SAML specification defines a number of interactions, as follows:

- *SAML Assertion Query.* This protocol is used to request specific assertions about subjects from an authoritative source. This can include authentication, attribute, and authorization decision statements. The response then includes a token for the requested information about the Subject.
- *Authentication Request Protocol.* An entity can use this protocol when it wishes to obtain a statement for establishing a security context for a principal. Typically, a requester asks to obtain a SAML authentication assertion from an Identity Provider (IdP) during a Web service invocation.
- *Artifact Resolution.* A SAML Artifact is a reference to a SAML statement instead of the statement itself. This protocol is used to resolve a SAML Artifact into an actual SAML assertion.
- *Single Logout.* While Single Sign On is very desirable from a user experience perspective, single logout is critical from a security perspective. Within the SAML specification stack, this protocol ensures that assertions can be identified as invalidated once a logout was requested. It should be noted that this protocol does not guarantee logout but requires the cooperation of all relying parties.
- *Name Identifier Management and Name Identifier Mapping.* These protocols are used to create reliable, pseudonymous federations between IdPs in different administrative domains.

These protocols can then be used with different transports. The use of specific transport protocols with the SAML protocol is called a Binding and is specified in a separate document. SOAP is one of the standards transports, but other browser-centric transport bindings are

---

12. R. Monzillo et al., "Web Service Security: SAML Token Profile 1.1," OASIS Standard, February 2006.

available as well. The Bindings are use to define "Profiles," which describe complex function systems such as Identity Providers.

Although the SAML protocol is standardized in the core SAML specification, it is not implemented by all vendors: While SAML tokens have been popular across the entire identity management landscape, early adopters of the WS-* specifications such as IBM and Microsoft have been using these tokens with WS-Security, WS-Trust, and WS-Federation. Users will need to make sure what parts of the SAML specification stack (tokens, protocol, bindings, profiles) the vendors support.

Using SAML Tokens with WS-*

SAML tokens have been used with other exchange protocols as well. The term *WS-* stack* commonly refers to a set of protocols that build on top of the SOAP platform and enable additional functionality for SOAP-based Web services. This includes features such as complex transactions support (WS-AtomicTransactions), reliable delivery (WS-ReliableTransport), and service discovery (UDDI). Since these features are intended to be used in a transport agnostic way, underlying features of message queuing systems cannot be relied on for guaranteed delivery, but have to be created within the SOAP envelope through SOAP header extensions.

For security, WS-Security defines the most fundamental extension, and many of the other WS-* protocols implementing security functions rely on the WS-Security framework. The use of SAML Tokens with WS-Security is standardized in the SAML Token Profile 1.1 or higher (see footnote 9).

WS-Trust Architecture

WS-Trust is an alternative to using some portions of the SAML protocol for creating an environment with a mutually trusted authentication server, a client, and a service. WS-Trust uses WS-Security for wrapping security elements such as security tokens, signatures, and encrypted data blocks.

The mutually trusted entity is in the WS-Trust environment called a Secure Token Service (STS), which responds to token requests (see Figure 8.4). At a high level, the client (called a requestor) contacts the service (called a relying party) and obtains the token requirements through the WS-SecurityPolicy of the relying party service. These requirements include the acceptable origin of the token (the STS or list of STS that are acceptable sources for tokens).

The requestor then proceeds to request such a token from a STS by sending a RequestSecurityToken (RST) message to the STS service endpoint. This request will

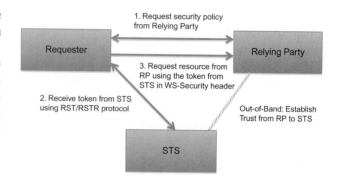

FIGURE 8.4   WS-Trust Architecture.

typically include appropriate forms of authentication (from the requestor to the STS) by providing a security token within the WS-Security headers of the WS-Trust RST message.

The STS builds a token to the specification of the requestor and wraps this in the WS-Security header of the RequestSecurityTokenResponse (RSTR) message. The requestor can then proceed to interact with the relying party using the new token.

Building Federations with WS-Federation

Since WS-Trust is only used for building a distributed authorization system, OASIS has created a number of other protocols for the WS-* stack, focusing on different functionalities. One of these is the WS-Federation specification, which is used to enable the leveraging of security tokens issued by STS from different administrative domains. This means that a client can obtain a token from "their" STS and use this to access relying parties that usually trust only tokens issued by another STS. The prerequisite for this to work is setting up a federation.

It should be noted that the most significant amount of work for creating a federation is typically not the technical configuration: The process of creating and maintaining the necessary business agreement between two organizations is complex and requires collaboration with legal, financial, and potentially human resources subject matter experts.

Advanced HTTP Security

The basic security functions of HTTP described earlier are sufficient for simple client-server systems, but are hard to manage for complex multiparty interactions. In addition, the most common security transport—TLS—typically requires a comprehensive PKI roll-out, especially when using user certificates for mutual authentication.

Typical applications of HTTP applications and services in social networking or cloud environments have use cases that cannot be easily addressed with basic HTTP authentication schemes. Furthermore, the deployment of PKI in such environments is too expensive or extremely complex: PKI implies a fairly high level of trust in the binding of the credential to a system or the user, which is hard to control in highly dynamic environments.

Based on these constraints, in 2004 a number of large Web 2.0 or higher providers (including Google, Twitter, and AOL), as well as smaller companies with deep insight into the architectures of dynamic Web applications and REST-style HTTP services, started developing technologies that are complementary to the "heavyweight" SOAP-centric identity management technologies. While initially focused on simple data sharing use cases with limited risk (such as a single sign on for blog commenting), these technologies have matured to the point where they can be used to secure commercial services and provide a simplified experience for users of social media and other Web applications.

OAuth Overview and Use Cases

The OAuth protocol dates back to the early days of social networking sites. The standard use case is for safely sharing user data held at one site with another site. This would occur when site A is a photo hosting site and site B is a site that makes prints from photos (see Figure 8.5). In this use case, users have an account at both sites and store their photos at site A. For creating a new set of prints, users will not upload or transfer their photos to site B, but instead will authorize site B to access their photo stream (or a portion thereof) on site A. This is effectively achieved by initially logging into site B and indicating the location of their photo stream (through a dropdown menu) at site A. When site B now tries to access the photo stream, the users are redirected to the login screen for site A where they need to provide their credentials. Once logged in, site A will create a token that site B can use for accessing the users' photo stream and attach this token to the HTTP redirect back to site B. The end state is now that site B has a token that it can use to attach to the HTTP request when obtaining the photos.

The exchange is somewhat more complicated than depicted in the illustration, since the Printer service initially obtains an unauthorized request token in the initial exchange between the Printer and the Photo Host service. The request token is then authorized by the user and provided to the Printer, which exchanges it into an access token. The goal for this use case is to keep the accounts at the two services separate while still allowing authorized information sharing between the two sites.

OAuth 2.0 or higher is at the time of writing in its final stages of standardization at the Internet Engineering Task Force (IETF). It is expected that the final protocol will be available very soon. Most implementations already support OAuth 2.0 or higher, and updates to implementations for transitioning from the draft versions to the final version will be minor, if any.

OpenID Connect

The original OpenID protocol was built on the concept of using URLs as identifiers for users; that is, a user would use something like "https://example.com/user" for the username. This was intended to solve the problem of discovery in identity management: Any dynamic interaction between a user and a service would only be able to leverage identity management protocols, if the relying party and the identity provider had an existing relationship. For well-defined cross-organizational interactions this is quite achievable, but to configure the respective IdPs (or

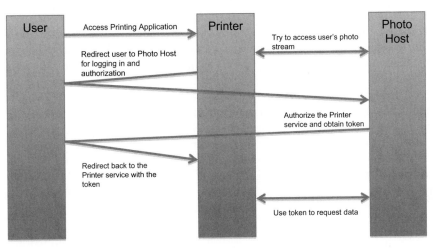

FIGURE 8.5 OAuth basic use case.

STSs), it requires relying parties and requestors to use the acceptable services for identity management and authorization services.

While the OpenID protocol did solve this problem with the URL identifier, users typically did not accept this scheme, so the large Web 2.0 or higher providers such as Google, Twitter, Facebook, and AOLsolved this by creating specialized buttons to use for OpenID login. Since most sites desired to support at least the big social networks and identity providers, the login sites often featured more than five specialized login buttons, leading to the term the *NASCAR problem*: Similar to racing cars in NASCAR, login sites would be littered with banners from all major login providers.

Additionally, the initial versions of OpenID had a number of significant security issues, leading to the realization that it would be helpful to design a new version of OpenID that could leverage a secure HTTP-based identity transport protocol. The natural choice was OAuth, and OpenID Connect now uses OAuth as its underlying security protocol. Simplified, OpenID Connect creates an identity provider Web service and uses OAuth to protect access from relying parties to it.

5. AUTHORIZATION PATTERNS

Access Control Models

Early systems implemented fairly simple access control models that rely mostly on the identity of the user and define access control lists (ACLs) that are stored with the resource that is subject to that access control list. This model has sometimes been called identity-based access control (IBAC) and has proven to be very efficient and easy to implement. Most modern operating systems support IBAC for file systems access and other security-related functions. While fast for small ACLs, very large ACLs are inefficient to evaluate, and the need to store the ACL (which is effectively a security policy for the resource) decentralized with the resources can cause significant life-cycle management problems. Some solutions such as user groups or ACL inheritance have been implemented to mitigate these shortcomings, but overall the limitations of IBAC limit its use for large-scale applications. Other access control models include role-based access control (RBAC)[13] and attribute-based access control (ABAC). Central to these models is a better separation of resources and applicable access control policies.

Web services have been pioneering technologies for implementing ABAC models especially through the

introduction of the eXtensible Access Control Markup Language (XACML).[14] Since XACML was developed to complement SAML with a flexible authorization system, it shared some architectural similarities. In fact, the XACML replaces the SAML 2.0 or higher authorization decision statement with its own request response protocol.

XACML Overview

Within the XACML model, there are a number of actors that enable the distributed authorization environment. Note that some of these actors can be co-located: Certain appliances or access managers allow configurations where PEP, PDP, and PAP are c-located, as discussed in the following components:

- *Access requester (or client).* This is the entity that initiates a request.
- *Policy Enforcement Point (PEP).* The PEP intercepts the request from the client to the resources and performs an authorization check. This actor is sometimes integrated with a reverse proxy (a façade service that wraps the resource and replicates the resource's interface to the clients).
- *Policy Decision Point (PDP).* The PDP performs the actual policy evaluation, based on the information in the request from the PEP, a policy set (i.e., the merged set of applicable policies, based on policy-merging systems), configured attribute sources, and other environmental factors (such as time of day, origin or destination of request).
- *Policy Administration Point (PAP).* The policy administration point allows the configuration and administration of applicable access control policies. The PDP is configured through the PAP to use a specific set of policies.
- *Policy Information Point (PIP).* The PIP provides contextual information input into the policies, based on a request from the PDP. If the PIP provides specific attributes for identities, for example, in the form of a Directory Server, the PIP is sometimes also called an Attribute Source (AS).
- *Resource.* The resource itself provides the service for the client. While XACML is typically used for SOAP services, the resource is not required to be implemented as a SOAP service. For example, a combined PEP/service façade can be used to expose the functionality of a legacy application to SOAP-enabled clients.

---

13. The U.S. National Institute of Standards and Technology (NIST) has published a number of documents on RBAC and how it can be implemented. See http://csrc.nist.gov/groups/SNS/rbac/ for more information.

14. XACML is standardized at OASIS Open in the XACML Technical Committee. See here: https://www.oasis-open.org/committees/tc_home.php?wg_abbrev=xacml.

FIGURE 8.6 XACML actors overview.

The preceding components and their relation to each other are shown in Figure 8.6. Conceptually, the Requestor tries to access the Resource (typically, a SOAP-based Web service, but this is not a requirement within XACML) and is intercepted by the PEP. The PEP itself formulates a decision request to the PDP with the information that is available to it, namely, metadata from the request and the resource.

With the PDP, the applicable access policies are identified, evaluated, and—if necessary—combined into a single policy decision. Note that XACML defines a rich policy language for describing access control policies in terms of Targets, Rules, and Constraints.

The PDP responds to the PEP in a Result Response with one of the following four possible decisions: Permit, Deny, Indeterminate (no decision was possible, based on the available policies and information), or NotApplicable (the request was not applicable in this context). The response may include additional obligations that need to be abided by. The complete XACML protocol, policy language, result definition, and combination algorithms can be used for very complex situations, but it is beyond the scope of this chapter to describe the details of the XACML protocol.

XACML and SAML for ABAC and RBAC

The core XACML protocol architecture is modeled on the concepts of ABAC: attributes (either provided by an Attribute Source or other PIPs providing environmental attributes) are evaluated in the context of a specific request. Although most situations will require the identity of the requestor, ABAC can even allow pseudonymous access to resources, as long as the PDP can obtain sufficient information to arrive at a "permit" authorization decision.

The core set of XACML specifications also includes guidance on how an RBAC model can be implemented using XACML. The basic idea is to model role membership through a multivalued attribute. This attribute is then evaluated in the context of access control policies designed to reflect the role-based approach.

At the same time, the technology used to implement the access control model should not be confused with the access control model itself. This means that while

XACML is currently the predominant technology to implement ABAC in distributed systems, they should not be equated.

6. SECURITY CONSIDERATIONS

Avoiding Common Errors

The flexibility of Web-based systems and the ease of implementing new services led to an early proliferation of Web applications and Web services. It became obvious pretty quickly that these new technologies resulted in a number of mistakes that were independently made by many developers. Security research groups and organizations started to look into this problem and identified a number of anti-patterns and mistakes that were particularly common, and identified measures to counter them. The following gives an overview of two well-known lists of common mistakes and useful controls, respectively.

OWASP Top 10

The OWASP Top 10 list[15] was developed by the Open Web Application Security Project (OWASP) community to enumerate common problems with Web applications. This list focuses specifically on Web application risks and deals with both transport issues (HTTP) and content problems (HTML) and how content is rendered within browsers. The latter issues are less interesting for developers of Web services, since the user agent is typically not a browser, and the data may be represented as HTML but most often is not. It is updated occasionally to reflect the changing security environment.

Figure 8.7 shows the 2010 version of the OWASP Top 10. Out of this list only A3, A4, A6, A7, A8, and A9 are highly relevant to Web service developers. Since REST-style HTTP service leverages the features of HTTP more heavily than SOAP-service using the HTTP transport binding, REST-style services will likely have to pay more attention to avoiding mistakes identified in the list. At the same time, SOAP-style services operating within standard runtime environments can suffer from issues such as security misconfigurations (A6) or problems with the transport layer protection (A9) just as easily. In the following, the more pertinent elements from the OWASP Top 10 are briefly discussed.

- A3—Broken Authentication and Session Management. If access to the HTTP resources where the service is host is not protected properly, arbitrary users may invoke the service and cause confidentiality and integrity problems. Authentication issues can arise

---

15. The document is available from https://www.owasp.org. The list was last updated in 2010.

A1 – Injection
A2 – Cross-Site Scripting (XSS)
A3 – Broken Authentication and Session Management
A4 – Insecure Direct Object References
A5 – Cross-Site Request Forgery (CSRF)
A6 – Security Misconfiguration
A7 – Insecure Cryptographic Storage
A8 – Failure to Restrict URL Access
A9 – Insufficient Transport Layer Protection
A10 – Unvalidated Redirects and Forwards

FIGURE 8.7   OWASP Top 10 (2010)

when the verification of accounts with the user database is compromised, user information is leaked through other channels, or the authentication session parameters are not set properly.

- A4—Insecure Direct Object References. If input of the access URL (for REST-style services) or the content of the SOAP request is not verified through input validation techniques, a malicious user may replace legitimate data references with improper data. For example, if a service call should reference Alice's account for receiving a money transfer, a malicious attacker could try to replace Alice's account number with Eve's, thus redirecting the transfer to a wrong account.

- A6—Security Misconfiguration. This can include default account, unpatched or unmaintained server code, references to old versions of services, and so on. Any security misconfiguration can be exploited by attackers to gain access, elevate privileges, or violate the confidentiality or integrity of the data.

- A7—Insecure Cryptographic Storage. Sensitive information such as personally identifiable information, financial data, user account or system security information, or any other regulated data should be encrypted, and the cryptographic keys should be properly protected.

- A8—Failure to Restrict URL Access. When URLs are accessible to users not authorized for access, attackers can exploit such holes and gain access to the service. All URLs—either those used for REST-style resources or SOAP HTTP endpoints—must be protected from unauthorized accessed and should ideally require at least one form of authentication. REST-style services can use the authentication and authorization mechanisms described earlier in the chapter; SOAP services can also use the application protocol-specific authentication mechanism.

- A9—Insufficient Transport Layer Protection. Lack of TLS protection, use of expired or revoked PKI certificates, or bad configuration leads potentially to violations of confidentiality and integrity. Both client and service should verify the validity of certificates and cancel transactions if they do not match.

SANS Top 20

The SANS Top 20 list of critical security controls[16] enumerates the most important technical and administrative controls for preventing or limiting attacks on computer systems. The list was developed by a number of experts from the U.S. government and the commercial sector and condenses a lot of best practices of good systems management. They provide not only a description of implementable countermeasures and system configurations, but also metrics to measure the effectiveness of the controls within a given environment. Additionally, the SANS Top 20 control description include references to the NIST SP 800-53[17] control set, which is mandatory for many systems operated by the U.S. federal government.

The controls themselves are very generic and not specific to Web services. At the same time, they can be applied to the architectural concepts, technologies, and deployed systems implementing Web services. The complete list is an excellent starting point for any secure system design, but we will focus here on the most applicable controls for securing Web service deployments.

Critical Control 3: Secure Configurations for Hardware and Software on Laptops, Workstations, and Servers

This control requires a secure configuration of all system components. It can be implemented by creating standard system images that are hardened against attacks. Such hardening may include disabling nonessential system services, limiting the visibility to network probes, configuring kernel-level security enforcement rules, and the like. A secure baseline operating system limits the potential damage that a misconfigured or compromised Web service or client can cause.

Critical Control 4: Continuous Vulnerability Assessment and Remediation

The window for attacking weak systems is significantly reduced by continuously monitoring and assessing the vulnerability profile of all deployed systems. With a comprehensive program in place, which should ideally consist of automated and human components, potential weaknesses in the Web service application runtime or the implementing code itself can be detected and fixed in near real time. This minimizes the attack window for threat actors significantly.

---

16. The list is available at http://www.sans.org/critical-security-controls.
17. NIST Special Publication (SP) 800-53 is a comprehensive list of information security controls and verification procedures.

Critical Control 6: Application Software Security

In the context of the SANS Top 20, this control focuses on the security of the code implementing the service itself. While other frameworks are available, the OWASP Top 10 list (see Figure 8.7) is a good starting point for assessing the security of the service and the quality of client software.

Critical Control 9: Security Skills Assessment and Appropriate Training to Fill Gaps

All personnel involved in the creation and maintenance of the Web service must be qualified to perform their job functions. While this seems like an ancient IT adage, many IT architects, developers, and administrators have a hard time staying on top of their field both from an application and a security perspective. Security training and evaluations should be part of everyone's responsibility. Exploring the usefulness of relevant security certifications for key staff members may augment this. Overall, only senior-level management sponsorship can ensure the successful implementation of this control.

Critical Control 10: Secure Configurations for Network Devices such as Firewalls, Routers, and Switches

Not only the actual business systems such as servers and client, but also the supporting network infrastructure components, need to be configured in the most secure way. This control is complementary to Critical Control 3 and should be implemented equivalently.

Critical Control 11: Limitation and Control of Network Ports, Protocols, and Services

It is crucial to have a comprehensive list of allowed ports, protocols, and system services for all active and passive network devices. Each individual component must only be allowed to perform its designated function and use the appropriate set of network resources to do so. This way compromised devices can be identified much more easily: If a server designated to provide Web service over HTTPS suddenly starts to send out border gateway protocol (BGP) messages, network monitors and intrusion detection and prevention systems can react immediately and take that system off the network to prevent unauthorized routing of data.

Critical Control 13: Boundary Defense

Firewalls and other boundary defense technologies have been available for a long time and despite their bad reputation for preventing advanced attacks, they are very useful in preventing certain classes of vulnerabilities. A solid boundary defense also enables close monitoring of data ingress and egress, and allows inspection and control of information flow from the Web service to the client and vice versa. Separating the rest of the world from the internal networks also makes monitoring of the use of ports, protocols, and service (Critical Control 11) much easier.

Critical Control 19: Secure Network Engineering

This control effectively augments and extends the concept of boundary defense (Critical Control 13) and takes a holistic approach to secure network design and monitoring. Proper network engineering includes a number of best practices, including grouping of similar systems and components (such as Web services or application servers) into groups and separating them from the rest of the network. This helps control clients' communication with the Web service and prevents clients from trying to scan the servers hosting the Web services for vulnerabilities.

Critical Control 20: Penetration Tests and Red Team Exercises

Even the best security engineering teams will make mistakes or miss possible attack vectors when protecting critical resources such as Web services. Only a comprehensive penetration test and recurring exercises can expose potential security flaws. More details on creating a test program for Web services are presented later in the chapter.

Other Resources

There are many other, often industry-specific sets of security controls that can handle Web service security. Examples include the American Institute of Certified Public Accountants (AICPA) Service Organization Controls (SOC) 2 or higher: "Controls at a Service Organizations Relevant to Security, Availability, Processing Integrity, Confidentiality, or Privacy,"[18] which specify requirements for cloud providers and can have relevance in the context of operating Web service on behalf of customers. Another set of applicable security controls includes the NIST SP 800-53 controls,[19] which include the latest revision of SOA controls.

There are other resources that address SOA-specific issues. One example is the Common Attack Pattern Enumeration and Classification (CAPEC),[20] which features a catalog of techniques used by attackers to break into systems. While this database is intended to cover

18. See http://www.aicpa.org/soc for more information on the SOC reports.
19. All NIST SPs can be found at http://csrc.nist.gov/publications/PubsSPs.html.
20. The CAPEC catalog can be found at http://capec.mitre.org.

all typical attack vectors against systems, it has a specialization for service-oriented issues. Typically, the information within the database is fairly comprehensive and not only addresses specific attack methodologies, but also defines a framework for classifying these approaches.

Figure 8.8 provides a sample CAPEC pattern that applies to SOA, in this case on WSDL scanning. It provides a fairly comprehensive set of attributes of this particular attack, and suggests possible mitigation strategies to counter this attack pattern. To use this catalog efficiently, it is recommended that one search the site on specific technologies and develop a list of countermeasures for mitigation.

Testing and Vulnerability Assessment

Testing Strategy

As identified in the SANS Top 20 list for Critical Controls, many other documentations of security best practices, testing, and continuous monitoring are central to maintaining a secure environment. While tests during the design of a software package such as a service are standard development practices,[21] the deployed service itself should be evaluated in context as well.

Such tests can include simple functional tests that verify the invocation of a service call in the deployed environment (or a mockup of that environment), but they may also include performance tests to ensure that the service behaves correctly under heavy load. A number of commercial and open source tools are available for performing such tests, including the popular soapUI framework[22] or WebInject[23] open source projects.

Vulnerability Assessment Tools

In addition to functional testing at development and deploy time, Web services should undergo at least a vulnerability assessment to determine their actual vulnerabilities (see Sidebar: Vulnerability Assessment versus Penetration Testing). Such a vulnerability assessment focuses on determining the problems with the exposed service, from a number of different angles.

Vulnerability Assessment versus Penetration Testing

In the past, Vulnerability Assessment and Penetration Testing have sometimes been used synonymously. While their goals and sometimes the techniques are similar, there is a fundamental difference between the two:

- Vulnerability Assessments are cooperative engagements, where the security expert, the developers, and the administrators are working hand in hand to understand, document, and eliminate the vulnerabilities of the exposed services. The assessors should have full access to the source code, the interface definition (such as the WSDL for SOAP services), security documentation, and privileged access to the servers hosting the services. The end goal is a plan to improve the security posture of the deployed service.
- Penetration Tests, on the other hand, are noncooperative exercises, where the owners of the Web service are not necessarily aware of the fact that a penetration test is underway. Depending on the rules of engagement, the penetration testers (sometimes called the red team) may use a large variety of techniques to gain access or subvert a deployed service, including trying to get physical access to the hosting servers. Furthermore, the red team may operate under rules that allow them to permanently damage the deployed service in order to better understand the potential security impact of a real attack.

While penetration tests often result in more in-depth analysis of the security posture, most companies will not allow the red team to perform a full-scale attack on production systems.

To perform a comprehensive vulnerability assessment of a service installation, the analyst should be familiar with the base techniques of vulnerability assessments for servers. Many tools are available for performing such an assessment, both commercial and open source-based solutions. Specialized Linux distributions such as BackTrack Linux[24] are specifically designed for vulnerability assessments and testing, and have many of the best tools preinstalled. For HTTP-based systems, testers should minimally employ w3af, MetaSploit, openVAS, and Nessus in addition to other standard tools.

Finally, let's take a brief look at the Web applications, services, and servers challenges that still need to be addressed. The following checklist (see checklist: An Agenda for Action for Security Actions That Web Applications, Services, and Servers Need to Consider) discusses in detail the security challenges of several Web applications, services, and servers , including Web services discovery, quality of service, quality of protection, and protection from denial-of-service attacks.

---

21. This may include Unit testing, continuous builds, and other functional tests to verify the correct functioning of the service. For services, Unit tests may include not only API invocations of the implementing classes, but also explicit calls to the service interfaces exposed on the network. Note that configuring such tests with services that implement security functionality directly (e.g., in-code authorization) may be very complex and not necessarily feasible.

22. See http://www.soapui.org/ for information on using soapUI.
23. WebInject is available from http://www.webinject.org.

24. See http://www.backtrack-linux.org/ for more information on BackTrack.

WSDL Scanning

Attack Pattern ID: 95   **Typical Severity:** High   **Status:** Draft

 Description

Summary

This attack targets the WSDL interface made available by a web service. The attacker may scan the WSDL interface to reveal sensitive information about invocation patterns, underlying technology implementations and associated vulnerabilities. This type of probing is carried out to perform more serious attacks (e.g. parameter tampering, malicious content injection, command injection, etc.). WSDL files provide detailed information about the services ports and bindings available to consumers. For instance, the attacker can submit special characters or malicious content to the Web service and can cause a denial of service condition or illegal access to database records. In addition, the attacker may try to guess other private methods by using the information provided in the WSDL files.

Attack Execution Flow

    1. The first step is exploratory meaning the attacker scans for WSDL documents. The WDSL document written in XML is like a handbook on how to communicate with the web services provided by the target host. It provides an open view of the application (function details, purpose, functional break down, entry points, message types, etc.). This is very useful information for the attacker.

    2. The second step that a attacker would undertake is to analyse the WSDL files and try to find potential weaknesses by sending messages matching the pattern described in the WSDL file. The attacker could run through all of the operations with different message request patterns until a breach is identified.

    3. Once an attacker finds a potential weakness, they can craft malicious content to be sent to the system. For instance the attacker may try to submit special characters and observe how the system reacts to an invalid request. The message sent by the attacker may not be XML validated and cause unexpected behavior.

 Attack Prerequisites

A client program connecting to a web service can read the WSDL to determine what functions are available on the server.

The target host exposes vulnerable functions within its WSDL interface.

 Typical Likelihood of Exploit

Likelihood: High

 Methods of Attack

- Analysis
- API Abuse

 Examples-Instances

Description

A WSDL interface may expose a function vulnerable to SQL Injection.

Description

The Web Services Description Language (WSDL) allows a web service to advertise its capabilities by describing operations and parameters needed to access the service. As discussed in step 5 of this series, WSDL is often generated automatically, using utilities such as Java2WSDL, which takes a class or interface and builds a WSDL file in which interface methods are exposed as web services.

Because WSDL generation often is automated, enterprising hackers can use WSDL to gain insight into the both public and private services. For example, an organization converting legacy application functionality to a web services framework may inadvertently pass interfaces not intended for public consumption to a WSDL generation tool. The result will be SOAP interfaces that give access to private methods.

Another, more subtle WSDL attack occurs when an enterprising attacker uses naming conventions to guess the names of unpublished methods that may be available on the server. For example, a service that offers a stock quote and trading service may publish query methods such as requestStockQuote in its WSDL. However, similar unpublished methods may be available on the server but not listed in the WSDL, such as executeStockQuote. A persistent hacker with time and a library of words and phrases can cycle thru common naming conventions (get, set, update, modify, and so on) to discover unpublished application programming interfaces that open doors into private data and functionality.

Source : "Seven Steps to XML Mastery, Step 7: Ensure XML Security", Frank Coyle. See reference section.

 Attacker Skills or Knowledge Required

Skill or Knowledge Level: Low

This attack can be as simple as reading WSDL and starting sending invalid request.

Skill or Knowledge Level: Medium

This attack can be used to perform more sophisticated attacks (SQL injection, etc.)

Probing Techniques

Description

An attacker can request the WSDL file from the target host by sending a SOAP message.

Description

There are free Vulnerability testing tool, such as WSDigger to perform WSDL scanning - Foundstone's free Web services security tool performs WSDL scanning, SQL injection and XSS attacks on Web Services.

FIGURE 8.8 Sample CAPEC for WSDL scanning.

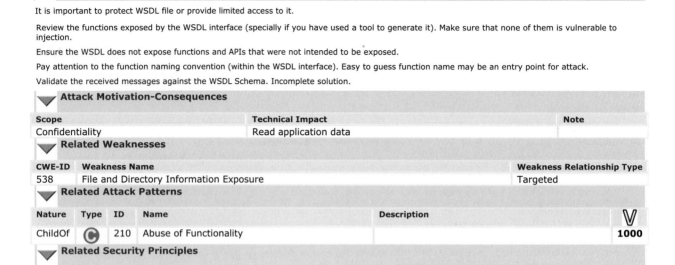

▼ **Solutions and Mitigations**

It is important to protect WSDL file or provide limited access to it.

Review the functions exposed by the WSDL interface (specially if you have used a tool to generate it). Make sure that none of them is vulnerable to injection.

Ensure the WSDL does not expose functions and APIs that were not intended to be exposed.

Pay attention to the function naming convention (within the WSDL interface). Easy to guess function name may be an entry point for attack.

Validate the received messages against the WSDL Schema. Incomplete solution.

▼ **Attack Motivation-Consequences**

Scope	Technical Impact	Note
Confidentiality	Read application data	

▼ **Related Weaknesses**

CWE-ID	Weakness Name	Weakness Relationship Type
538	File and Directory Information Exposure	Targeted

▼ **Related Attack Patterns**

Nature	Type	ID	Name	Description	
ChildOf	Ⓒ	210	Abuse of Functionality		Ⅴ 1000

▼ **Related Security Principles**

- Defense in Depth
- Never Assuming that Your Secrets Are Safe
- Securing the Weakest Link

▼ **Purposes**

- Reconnaissance

▼ **CIA Impact**

Confidentiality Impact: Medium	Integrity Impact: Medium	Availability Impact: High

▼ **Technical Context**

Architectural Paradigms	SOA
Frameworks	All
Platforms	All
Languages	All

▼ **References**

CWE - Input Validation

"Anatomy of a Web Services Attack", ForumSystems - http://forumsystems.com/papers/Anatomy_of_Attack_wp.pdf

"Seven Steps to XML Mastery, Step 7: Ensure XML Security", Frank Coyle - http://www.awprofessional.com/articles/article.asp?p=601349&seqNum=5&rl=1

FIGURE 8.8   (Continued)

7. CHALLENGES

While many of the Web applications, services, and server challenges have been met with existing standards, standards organizations are addressing a number of challenges, particularly in the area of Web services discovery and reliability. The Web Services Interoperability Organization (WS-I) acknowledges that many challenges remain to be addressed. Some examples of these challenges are as follows:

- Repudiation of transactions
- Secure issuance of credentials
- Exploitation of covert channels
- Compromised services
- Spread of malware, such as viruses and Trojan horses via SOAP messages
- Denial-of-service attacks
- Incorrect service implementations

8. SUMMARY

The practices recommended in this chapter are designed to help mitigate the risks associated with Web applications, services, and servers. Web applications, services, and

An Agenda for Action for Security Actions That Web Applications, Services, and Servers Need to Consider

The following items are possible actions that organizations should consider; some of the items may not apply to all organizations. In particular, it is necessary to balance these actions against budget requirements and the potential risks an organization's Web applications, services and servers may face (check all tasks completed):

_____1. **Replicate Data and Services to Improve Availability.** Since Web applications, services, and servers are susceptible to DoS attacks, it is important to replicate data and applications in a robust manner. Replication and redundancy can ensure access to critical data in the event of a fault. It will also enable the system to react in a coordinated way to deal with disruptions.

_____2. **Use Logging of Transactions to Improve Nonrepudiation and Accountability.** Nonrepudiation and accountability require logging mechanisms involved in the entire Web applications, services, and server transaction. In particular, the level of logging provided by various UDDI registries, identity providers, and individual Web services varies greatly. Where the provided information is not sufficient to maintain accountability and nonrepudiation, it may be necessary to introduce additional software or services into the SOA to support these security requirements.

_____3. **Use Threat Modeling and Secure Software Design Techniques to Protect from Attacks.** The objective of secure software design techniques is to ensure that the design and implementation of Web applications, services, and server software does not contain defects that can be exploited. Threat modeling and risk analysis techniques should be used to protect the Web services application from attacks. Used effectively, threat modeling can find security strengths and weaknesses, discover vulnerabilities, and provide feedback into the security life cycle of the application. Software security testing should include security-oriented code reviews and penetration testing. By using threat modeling and secure software design techniques, Web applications,

services, and servers can be implemented to withstand a variety of attacks.

_____4. **Use Performance Analysis and Simulation Techniques for End-to-End Quality of Service and Quality of Protection.** Queuing networks and simulation techniques have long played critical roles in designing, developing, and managing complex information systems. Similar techniques can be used for quality assured and highly available Web applications, services, and servers. In addition to QoS of a single service, end-to-end QoS is critical for most composite services. For example, enterprise systems with several business partners must complete business processes in a timely manner to meet real-time market conditions. The dynamic and compositional nature of Web applications, services, and servers makes end-to-end QoS management a major challenge for service-oriented distributed systems.

_____5. **Digitally Sign UDDI Entries to Verify the Author of Registered Entries.** UDDI registries openly provide details about the purpose of a Web service as well as how to access it. Web applications, services, and servers use UDDI registries to discover and dynamically bind to Web applications, services, and servers at runtime. Should an attacker compromise a UDDI entry, it would be possible for requesters to bind to a malicious provider. Therefore, it is important to digitally sign UDDI entries so as to verify the publisher of these entries.

_____6. **Enhance Existing Security Mechanisms and Infrastructure.** Web applications, services, and servers rely on many existing Internet protocols and often coexist with other network applications on an organization's network. As such, many Web applications, services, and server security standards, tools, and techniques require that traditional security mechanisms, such as firewalls, intrusion detection systems (IDS), and secured operating systems, are in effect before implementation or deployment of Web services applications.

servers are important drivers for the software industry. The primary goal of service-oriented computing is to make a collection of software services accessible via standardized protocols whose functionality can be automatically discovered and integrated into applications. While several standards bodies (such as W3C and OASIS) are laying the foundation for Web applications, services, and servers, several research problems must be solved to make secure Web applications, services, and servers a reality. Service description, automatic service discovery, as well as QoS, are some of the important problems that need to be solved.

Web applications, services, and servers are increasingly becoming an integral part of organizational information technology (IT) infrastructures—even though there are still unmet security challenges. To this end, the development and deployment of secure Web applications, services, and servers are essential to many organizations' IT infrastructures. However, the security standards of Web applications, services, and servers do not provide all of the required properties to develop robust, secure, and reliable Web applications, services, and servers. To adequately support the needs of the Web applications, services, and servers-based applications, effective risk management and appropriate deployment of alternate countermeasures are essential. Defense-in-depth through security engineering, secure software development, and risk management can provide much of the robustness and reliability required by these applications.

Finally, let's move on to the real interactive part of this chapter: review questions/exercises, hands-on projects, case projects, and optional team case project. The answers and/or solutions by chapter can be found in the Online Instructor's Solutions Manual.

CHAPTER REVIEW QUESTIONS/EXERCISES

True/False

1. True or False? The development of a distributed hypertext system in the early 1990s at the CERN in Switzerland was one of the defining moments in making the Internet available to an audience beyond academia and specialized communities.

2. True or False? Since HTTP services implementing a REST architectural style (often called REST Services) are simply using the HTTP stack, all security aspects of HTTP apply.

3. True or False? It should be noted that since WS-Security is only tied to the SOAP messaging structures, it is completely transport independent and can therefore be used not only over the SOAP HTTP binding, but also with any other form of SOAP transport.

4. True or False? Since Web services are intended to implement a distributed architecture, it becomes very important to manage the identities of the participating actors: Different systems implementing the services or the clients need to fully understand who they are interacting with in order to make access control decisions that are consistent with the security policies for the systems.

5. True or False? Most modern operating systems support IBAC-based access control for file systems access and other security-related functions.

Multiple Choice

1. SOAP services are built around the concept of a:
   A. SOAP header.
   B. SOAP body.
   C. SOAP envelope.
   D. SOAP message.
   E. All of the above.

2. The simple Base64 encoding can be decoded by anyone and must be treated as:
   A. bad code.
   B. clear text.

   C. basic authentication.
   D. server authentication.
   E. All of the above.

3. What can usually make use of operating or runtime systems certificate stores in a very efficient way?
   A. TLS
   B. PKI
   C. MAC
   D. REST client libraries
   E. Two

4. WS-Security[25] (often abbreviated WSS) defines a Header extension to provide a number of features for SOAP-based messages, except which two?
   A. Signing the message to provide integrity protection and nonrepudiation
   B. Combining WS-Security with the security mechanisms of the underlying transport security
   C. Encrypting the message to provide message-level confidentiality
   D. Attaching arbitrary security tokens to the messages to provide identity of the sender
   E. WS-Security leveragings the XML Encryption and Signature standards.

5. The identity management community created a number of patterns that allow not only simple authentication, but also advanced patterns including the following, except which two?
   A. Other patterns, such as privacy preserving authentication and authorization
   B. Single Sign On (SSO) using mutually trusted identity servers
   C. Federations of identity providers
   D. SAML Authentication Token
   E. Complex, distributed authorization

EXERCISE

Problem

When multiple requesters, providers, and intermediaries are participating in a Web service transaction, it may be necessary to coordinate them. What are the two different types of mechanisms for coordinating Web services?

Hands-On Projects

Project

Because a Web service relies on some of the same underlying HTTP and Web-based architecture as common Web applications, it is susceptible to similar threats and

---

25. "Web Service Security: SOAP Messaging Framework 1.1," A. Nadlin et al., OASIS Open, November 2006.

vulnerabilities. Web services security is based on what important concepts?

Case Projects

Problem

Web services rely on the Internet for communication. Because SOAP was not designed with security in mind, SOAP messages can be viewed or modified by attackers as the messages traverse the Internet. What options are available for securing Web service messages?

Optional Team Case Project

Problem

Security decisions must always be made with an understanding of the threats facing the system to be secured. While a wealth of security standards and technologies are available for securing Web services, they may not be adequate or necessary for a particular organization or an individual service. For that reason, it is important to understand the threats that face Web services so that organizations can determine which threats their Web services must be secured against. What are the top threats facing Web services today?

## Chapter 9

Unix and Linux Security

Gerald Beuchelt

The MITRE Corporation[1], Bedford, MA, U.S.A.

When Unix was first booted on a PDP-8 computer at Bell Labs, it already had a basic notion of user isolation, separation of kernel and user memory space, and process security. It was originally conceived as a multiuser system, and as such, security could not be added on as an afterthought. In this respect, Unix was different from a whole class of computing machinery that had been targeted at single-user environments.

Linux is mostly a GNU software-based operating system with a kernel originally written by Linus Torvalds and many of the popular utilities from the GNU Software Foundation and other open source organizations added. GNU/Linux implements the same interfaces as most current Unix systems, including the Portable Operating System Interface (POSIX) standards. As such, Linux is a Unix-style operating system, despite the fact that it was not derived from the original AT&T/Bell Labs Unix code base.

Debian is a distribution originally developed by Ian Murdock of Purdue University. Debian's express goal is to use only open and free software, as defined by its guidelines. Ubuntu is a derivative Linux distribution that is based on the Debian system. It emphasizes ease of use and allows beginning users easy access to a comprehensive Linux distribution.

All versions of MacOS X are built on top of Unix operating systems, namely, the Mach microkernel and the University of California's FreeBSD code. While the graphical user interface and some other system enhancements are proprietary, MacOS has a XNU kernel and includes most of the command-line utilities commonly found in Unix operating systems.

The examples in this chapter refer to the Solaris, MacOS, and Ubuntu Linux, a distribution by Canonical Inc., built on the popular Debian distribution.

---

1. The opinions and guidance presented here are those of the author and do not necessarily reflect the positions of The MITRE Corporation, its customers or sponsors, or any part of the U.S. federal government.

1. UNIX AND SECURITY

As already indicated, Unix was originally created as a multiuser system. Initially, systems were not necessarily networked, but with the integration of the Berkley Software Distribution (BSD) TCP/IP V4 stack in 1984, Unix-based systems quickly became the backbone of the quickly growing Internet. As such, Unix servers started to provide critical services to network users as well.

The Aims of System Security

In general, secure computing systems must guarantee the confidentiality, integrity, and availability of resources. This is achieved through a combination of different security mechanisms and safeguards, including policy-driven access control and process separation.

Authentication

When a user is granted access to resources on a computing system, it is of vital importance to establish and verify the identity of the requesting entity. This process is commonly referred to as *authentication* (sometimes abbreviated *AuthN*).

Authorization

As a multiuser system, Unix must protect resources from unauthorized access. To protect user data from other users and nonusers, the operating system has to put up safeguards against unauthorized access. Determining the eligibility of an authenticated (or anonymous) user to access or modify a resource is usually called *authorization* (*AuthZ*).

Availability

Guarding a system (including all its subsystems, such as the network) against security breaches is vital to keep the system available for its intended use. *Availability* of a system must be properly defined: Any system is

The term POSIX stands (loosely) for "Portable Operating System Interface for uniX". From the IEEE 1003.1 Standard, 2004 Edition:

"This standard defines a standard operating system interface and environment, including a command interpreter (or "shell"), and common utility programs to support applications portability at the source code level. This standard is the single common revision to IEEE Std 1003.1-1996, IEEE Std 1003.2-1992, and the Base Specifications of The Open Group Single UNIX Specification, Version 2." Partial or full POSIX compliance is often required for government contracts.

FIGURE 9.1 Various Unix and POSIX standards.

physically available, even if it is turned off; however, a shutdown system would not be too useful. In the same way, a system that has only the core operating system running but not the services that are supposed to run on the system is considered not available.

Integrity

Similar to availability, a system that is compromised cannot be considered available for regular service. Ensuring that the Unix system is running in the intended way is most crucial, especially since the system might otherwise be used by a third party for malicious uses, such as a relay or member in a botnet.

Confidentiality

Protecting resources from unauthorized access and safeguarding the content is referred to as confidentiality. As long as it is not compromised, a Unix system will maintain the confidentiality of system user data by enforcing access control policies and separating processes from each other. There are two fundamentally different types of access control: discretionary and mandatory access control. Users themselves manage the discretionary segment, while the system owner sets the mandatory. We will discuss the differences later in this chapter.

2. BASIC UNIX SECURITY OVERVIEW

Unix security has a long tradition, and though many concepts of the earliest Unix systems still apply, there have been a large number of changes that fundamentally altered the way the operating system implements these security principles.

One of the reasons that it's complicated to talk about Unix security is that there are a lot of variants of Unix and Unix-like operating systems on the market. In fact, if you only look at some of the core Portable Operating System Interface (POSIX) standards that have been set forth to guarantee minimal consistency across different Unix flavors (see Figure 9.1), almost every operating system on the market qualifies as Unix (or, more precisely, as POSIX compliant). Examples include not only the traditional Unix operating systems such as Solaris,

HP-UX, or AIX but also Windows NT-based operating systems (such as Windows XP, either through the native POSIX subsystem or the Services for Windows extensions) or even z/OS.

Traditional Unix Systems

Most Unix systems do share some internal features, though: Their authentication and authorization approaches are similar, their delineation between kernel space and user space goes along the same lines, and their security-related kernel structures are roughly comparable. In the last few years, however, major advancements have been made in extending the original security model by adding role-based access control[2] (RBAC) models to some operating systems.

Kernel Space versus User Land

Unix systems typically execute instructions in one of two general contexts: the kernel or the user space. Code executed in a kernel context has (at least in traditional systems) full access to the entire hardware and software capabilities of the computing environment. Although there are some systems that extend security safeguards into the kernel, in most cases, not only can a rogue kernel execution thread cause massive data corruption, but it can effectively bring down the entire operating system.

Obviously, a normal user of an operating system should not wield so much power. To prevent this, user execution threads in Unix systems are not executed in the context of the kernel but in a less privileged context, the user space—sometimes also facetiously called user land. The Unix kernel defines a structure called *process* (see Figure 9.2) that associates metadata about the user as well as, potentially, other environmental factors with the execution thread and its data. Access to computing resources such as memory and I/O subsystems is safeguarded by

---

2. RBAC was developed in the 1990s as a new approach to access control for computing resources. Authorization to access resources is granted based on role membership, and often allows more fine-grained resource control since specific operations (such as "modify file" or "add printer") can be granted to role members. In 2004, the RBAC model was standardized in American National Standard 359-2004 (see also http://csrc.nist.gov/rbac/ for more information).

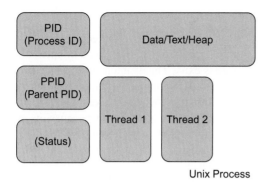

FIGURE 9.2 Kernel structure of a typical Unix process.

the kernel; if a user process wants to allocate a segment of memory or access a device, it has to make a system call, passing some of its metadata as parameters to the kernel. The kernel then performs an authorization decision and either grants the request or returns an error. It is then the process's responsibility to properly react to either the results of the access or the error.

If this model of user space process security is so effective, why not implement it for all operating system functions, including the majority of kernel operations? The answer to this question is that to a large extent the overhead of evaluating authorization metadata is very compute expensive. If most or all operations (that are, in the classical kernel space, often hardware-related device access operations) are run in user space or a comparable way, the performance of the OS would severely suffer. There is a class of operating system with a microkernel that implements this approach; the kernel contains only the most rudimentary functions (processes, scheduling, basic security), and all other operations, including device access and other operations that are typically carried out by the kernel, run in separate user processes. The advantage is a higher level of security and better safeguards against rogue device drivers. Furthermore, new device drivers or other operating system functionality can be added or removed without having to reboot the kernel. The performance penalties are so severe, however, that no major commercial operating system implements a microkernel architecture.

Many modern Unix-based systems operate in a mixed mode: While many device drivers such as hard drives, video, and I/O systems are operating in the kernel space, they also provide a framework for user space drivers. For example, the Filesystems in User Space (FUSE) allows loading additional drivers for file systems. This permits the mounting of devices that are not formatted with the default file system types that the OS supports, without having to execute with elevated privileges. It also allows the use of file systems in situations, where license conflict prevents the integration of a file system driver into the

kernel (for example, the CDDL licensed ZFS file system into the GPL licensed Linux kernel).

Semantics of User Space Security

In most Unix systems, security starts with access control to resources. Since users interact with the systems through processes and files, it is important to know that every user space process structure has two important security fields: the user identifier, or UID, and the group identifier, or GID. These identifiers are typically positive integers, which are unique for each user.[3] Every process that is started[4] by or on behalf of a user inherits the UID and GID values for that user account. These values are usually immutable for the live time of the process.

Access to system resources must go through the kernel by calling the appropriate function that is accessible to user processes. For example, a process that wants to reserve some system memory for data access will use the malloc() system call and pass the requested size and an (uninitialized) pointer as parameters. The kernel then evaluates this request, determines whether enough virtual memory (physical memory plus swap space) is available, reserves a section of memory, and sets the pointer to the address where the block starts.

Users who have the UID zero have special privileges: They are considered *superusers*, able to override many of the security guards that the kernel sets up. The default Unix superuser is named *root*.

Standard File and Device Access Semantics

File access is a very fundamental task, and it is important that only authorized users get read or write access to a given file. If any user was able to access any file, there would be no privacy at all, and security could not be maintained, since the operating system would not be able to protect its own permanent records, such as configuration information or user credentials. Most Unix operating systems use an identity-based access control (IBAC) model, in which access policies are expressed in terms of the user's identity.

The most common IBAC policy describing who may access or modify files and directories is commonly referred to as an *access control list* (ACL). Note that there is more than just one type of ACL; the standard Unix ACLs are very well known, but different Unix

---

3. If two usernames are associated with the same UID, the operating system will treat them as the same user. Their authentication credentials (username and password) are different, but their authorization with respect to system resources is the same.

4. Processes can be "started" or created in a variety of ways, for example, by calling the fork() system call or by calling the execve() system call to load a new executable file and start it.

variants or POSIX-like operating systems might implement different ACLs and only define a mapping to the simple POSIX 1003 semantics. A good example is the Windows NTFS ACL or the NFS v4 ACLs. ACLs for files and devices represented though device files are stored within the filesystem as meta data for the file information itself. This is different from other access control models where policies may be stored in a central repository.

Read, Write, Execute

From its earliest days, Unix implemented a simple but effective way to set access rights for users. Normal files can be accessed in three fundamental ways: read, write, and execute. The first two ways are obvious; the execution requires a little more explanation. A file on disk may only be executed as either a binary program or a script if the user has the right to execute this file. If the execute permission is not set, the system call exec() or execve() to execute a file image will fail. In addition to a user's permissions, there must be a notion of ownership of files and sometimes other resources. In fact, each file on a traditional Unix file system is associated with a user and a group. The user and group are not identified by their name but by UID and GID instead.

In addition to setting permissions for the user owning the file, two other sets of permissions are set for files: for the group and for all others. Similar to being owned by a user, a file is also associated with one group. All members of this group[5] can access the file with the permissions set for the group. In the same way, the other set of permissions applies to all users of the system.

Special Permissions

In addition to the standard permissions, there are a few special permissions, discussed here.

Set-ID Bit

This permission only applies to executable files, and it can only be set for the user or the group. If this bit is set, the process for this program is not set to the UID or GID of the invoking user but instead to the UID or GID of the file. For example, a program owned by the superuser can have the Set-ID bit set and execution allowed for all users. This way a normal user can execute a specific program with elevated privileges.

Sticky Bit

When the sticky bit is set on an executable file, its data (specifically the text segment) is kept in memory, even after the process exits. This is intended to speed execution of commonly used programs. A major drawback of setting the sticky bit is that when the executable file changes (for example, through a patch), the permission must be unset and the program started once more. When this process exits, the executable is unloaded from memory and the file can be changed.

Mandatory Locking

Mandatory file and record locking refers to a file's ability to have its reading or writing permissions locked while a program is accessing that file.

There might be additional implementation-specific permissions. These depend not only on the capabilities of the core operating facilities, including the kernel, but also on the type of file system. For example, most Unix operating systems can mount FAT-based file systems, which do not support any permissions or user and group ownership. Since the internal semantics require some values for ownership and permissions, these are typically set for the entire file system.

Permissions on Directories

The semantics of permissions on directories (see Figure 9.3) are different from those on files.

Read and Write

Mapping these permissions to directories is fairly straightforward: The read permission allows listing files in the directory, and the write permission allows us to create files. For some applications it can be useful to allow writing but not reading.

Execute

With this permission, a process can set its working directory to this directory. Note that with the basic permissions, there is no limitation on traversing directories, so a process might change its working directory to a child of a directory, even if it cannot do so for the directory itself.

SetID

Semantics may differ here. For example, on Solaris this changes the behavior for default ownership of newly created files from the System V to the BSD semantics.

Other File Systems

As mentioned, the set of available permissions and authorization policies depends on the underlying operating

---

5. It should be noted that users belong to one primary group, identified by the GID set in the password database. However, group membership is actually determined separately through the /etc/group file. As such, the user can be (and often is) a member of more than one group.

```
Making a directory readable for everyone:

# chmod o+r /tmp/mydir
# ls -ld /tmp/mydir

drwxr-xr-x   2 root      root           117 Aug  9 12:12 /tmp/mydir


Setting the SetID bit on an executable, thus enabling it to be run with super-user privileges:



# chmod u+s specialprivs
# ls -ld specialprivs

-rwsr-xr-x   2 root      root           117 Aug  9 12:12 specialprivs
```

FIGURE 9.3 Examples of chmod for files and directories.

system capabilities, including the file system. For example, the UFS file system in Solaris since version 2.5 allows additional ACLs on a per-user basis. Furthermore, NFS version 4 or higher defines additional ACLs for file access; it is obvious that the NFS server must have an underlying files system capable of recording this additional metadata.

Discretionary Versus Mandatory Access Control

The access control semantics described so far establish a "discretionary" access control (DAC) model: Any user may determine what type of access he or she wants to give to other specific users, groups, or anybody else. For many applications this is sufficient: For example, for systems that deliver a single network service and do not allow interactive login, the service's ability to determine what data will be shared with network users may be sufficient.

In systems that need to enforce access to data based on centralized, system operator- administered policies, DAC may not be sufficient. For example, for systems that need to operate in Multi-Level Security (MLS) environments, confidentiality of data can only be achieved through a mandatory access control (MAC) model. A number of MAC implementations for Unix-based systems are currently available, including Solaris Trusted Extensions for Solaris 10, SELinux for Linux-based operating systems, and TrustedBSD for BSD-based distributions.

Mandatory access control can be designed and implemented in many different ways. A common approach is to label operating system objects both in user and kernel space with a classification level and enforce appropriate MAC policies, such as the Bell-LaPadua (BLP) model for data confidentiality or the Biba model for data integrity.

Many Unix operating systems today provide a rudimentary set of MAC options by default: The SELinux based Linux Security Module (LSM) interface is now part of the core kernel, and some operating system vendors such as Red Hat ship their OSes with a minimal set of MAC policies enabled. To operate in a true Multi-Level Security environment, further configuration and often additional software modules are necessary to enable a BLP or Biba compliant set of MAC policies.

While MAC-based systems have traditionally been employed in government environments, modern enterprise architectures have a growing need for enforced access control around confidentiality or integrity. For example, data leakage protection (DLP) systems or auditing systems will benefit from certain types of centralized MAC policies.

3. ACHIEVING UNIX SECURITY

Achieving a high level of system security for the Unix system is a complex process that involves technical, operational, and managerial aspects of system operation. Next is a very cursory overview of some of the most important aspects of securing a Unix system.

System Patching

Prior to anything else, it is vitally important to emphasize the need to keep Unix systems up to date. No operating system or other program can be considered safe without being patched up; this point cannot be stressed enough. Having a system with the latest security patches is the first and most often the best line of defense against intruders and other cyber security threats.

All major Unix systems have a patching mechanism; this is a way to get the system up to date. Depending on the vendor and the mechanism used, it is possible to "back out" the patches. For example, on Solaris it is usually possible to remove a patch through the patchrm (1 m) command. On Debian-based systems this is not quite as easy, since in a patch the software package to be updated is replaced by a new version. Undoing this is only possible by installing the earlier package.

Locking Down the System

In general, all system services and facilities that are not needed for regular operation should be disabled or even uninstalled. Since any software package increases the attack surface of the system, removing unnecessary software ensures a better security posture.

Minimizing User Privileges

User accounts that have far-reaching access rights within a system have the ability to affect or damage a large number of resources, potentially including system management or system service resources. As such, user access rights should be minimized by default, in line with the security principle of "least privilege." For example, unless interactive access to the system is absolutely required, users should not be permitted to login.

Detecting Intrusions with Audits and Logs

By default, most Unix systems log kernel messages and important system events from core services. The most common logging tool is the syslog facility, which is controlled from the /etc/syslog.conf file.

4. PROTECTING USER ACCOUNTS AND STRENGTHENING AUTHENTICATION

In general, a clear distinction must be made between users obtaining a command shell for a Unix system ("interactive users") and consumers of Unix network services ("noninteractive users"). The interactive users should in most instances be limited to administrators that need to configure and monitor the system, especially since interactive access is almost always a necessary first step to obtain administrative access.

Establishing Secure Account Use

For any interactive session, Unix systems require the user to log into the system. To do so, the user must present a valid credential that identifies him (he or she must authenticate to the system). The type of credentials a Unix system uses depends on the capabilities of the OS software itself and on the configuration set forth by the systems administrator. The most traditional user credential is a username and a text password, but there are many other ways to authenticate to the operating system, including Kerberos, SSH, or security certificates.

The Unix Login Process

Depending on the desired authentication mechanism (see Figure 9.4), the user will have to use different access protocols or processes. For example, console or directly attached terminal sessions usually support only password credentials or smart card logins, whereas a secure shell connection supports only RSA- or DSA-based cryptographic tokens over the SSH protocol.

The login process is a system daemon that is responsible for coordinating authentication and process setup for interactive users. To do this, the login process does the following:

1. Draw or display the login screen.
2. Collect the credential.
3. Present the user credential to any of the configured user databases (typically, these can be files, NIS, Kerberos servers, or LDAP directories) for authentication.
4. Create a process with the user's default command-line shell, with the home directory as working directory.
5. Execute systemwide, user, and shell-specific start-up scripts.

The commonly available X11 windowing system does not use the text-oriented login process but instead provides its own facility to perform roughly the same kind of login sequence.

Overview of Unix authentication methods

- Simple: a username and a password are used to login to the operating system. The login process must receive both in cleartext. For the password, the Unix crypt hash is calculated and compared to the value in the password or shadow file.

- Kerberos: The user is supposed to have a ticket-granting ticket from the Kerberos Key Distribution Server (KDC). Using the ticket-granting ticket, he obtains a service ticket for an interactive login to the Unix host. This service ticket (encrypted, time limited) is then presented to the login process, and the Unix host validates it with the KDC.

- PKI based Smartcard: the private key on the smart card is used to authenticate with the system.

FIGURE 9.4 Various authentication mechanisms for Unix systems.

Access to interactive sessions using the SSH protocol follows a similar general pattern, but the authentication is significantly different from the traditional login process.

Controlling Account Access

Simple files were the first method available to store user account data. Over the course of years many other user databases have been implemented. We examine these here.

The Local Files

Originally, Unix only supported a simple password file for storing account information. The username and the information required for the login process (UID, GID, shell, home directory, and GECOS information) are stored in this file, which is typically at /etc/passwd. This approach is highly insecure, since this file needs to be readable by all for a number of different services, thus exposing the password hashes to potential hackers. In fact, a simple dictionary or even brute-force attack can reveal simple or even more complex passwords.

To protect against an attack like this, most Unix variants use a separate file for storing the password hashes (/etc/shadow) that is only readable and writable by the system.

Network Information System

The Network Information System (NIS) was introduced to simplify the administration of small groups of computers. Originally, Sun Microsystems called this service Yellow Pages, but the courts decided that this name constituted a trademark infringement on the British Telecom Yellow Pages. However, most commands that are used to administer the NIS still start with the yp prefix (such as ypbind and ypcat).

Systems within the NIS are said to belong to a NIS domain. Although there is absolutely no correlation between the NIS domain and the DNS domain of the system, it is quite common to use DNS-style domain names for naming NIS domains. For example, a system with DNS name system1.sales.example.com might be a member of the NIS domain nis.sales.Example.COM. Note that NIS domains—other than DNS domains—are case sensitive.

The NIS uses a simple master/slave server system: The master NIS server holds all authoritative data and uses an ONC-RPC-based protocol to communicate with the slave servers and clients. Slave servers cannot be easily upgraded to a master server, so careful planning of the infrastructure is highly recommended.

Client systems are bound to one NIS server (master or slave) during runtime. The addresses for the NIS master and the slaves must be provided when joining a system to the NIS domain. Clients (and servers) can always be members of only one NIS domain. To use the NIS user database (and other NIS resources, such as auto-mount maps, netgroups, and host tables) after the system is bound, use the name service configuration file (/etc/nsswitch.conf), as shown in Figure 9.5.

Using PAMs to Modify AuthN

These user databases can easily be configured for use on a given system through the /etc/nsswitch.conf file. However, in more complex situations, the administrator might want to fine-tune the types of acceptable authentication methods, such as Kerberos, or even configure multifactor authentication. Traditionally, the PAM is configured through the /etc/pam.conf file, but more modern implementations use a directory structure, similar to the System V init scripts. For these systems, the administrator needs to modify the configuration files in the /etc/pam.d/ directory.

FIGURE 9.5 Sample nsswitch.conf for a Debian system.

```
# /etc/nsswitch.conf

#
# Example configuration of GNU Name Service Switch functionality.
#
passwd:         files nis

group:          files nis
shadow:         files nis

hosts:          files nis dns
networks:       files

protocols:      db files
services:       db files
ethers:         db files
rpc:            db files
netgroup:       nis
```

```
# /etc/pam.d/common-password - password-related modules common to all services
#

# This file is included from other service-specific PAM config files,
# and should contain a list of modules that define the services to be
# used to change user passwords.  The default is pam_unix.

# Explanation of pam_unix options:
#
# The "nullok" option allows users to change an empty password, else
# empty passwords are treated as locked accounts.
#

# The "md5" option enables MD5 passwords.  Without this option, the
# default is Unix crypt.
#

# The "obscure" option replaces the old `OBSCURE_CHECKS_ENAB' option in
# login.defs.
#

# You can also use the "min" option to enforce the length of the new
# password.
#
# See the pam_unix manpage for other options.

password    requisite    pam_unix.so nullok obscure md5

# Alternate strength checking for password. Note that this
# requires the libpam-cracklib package to be installed.
# You will need to comment out the password line above and
# uncomment the next two in order to use this.
# (Replaces the `OBSCURE_CHECKS_ENAB', `CRACKLIB_DICTPATH')
#

password required    pam_cracklib.so retry=3 minlen=6 difok=3

password required    pam_unix.so use_authtok nullok md5
```

FIGURE 9.6 Setting the password strength on a Debian-based system through the PAM system.

Using the systemauth PAM, administrators can also enforce users to create and maintain complex passwords, including the setting of specific lengths, minimal number or numeric or nonletter characters, and so on. Figure 9.6 illustrates a typical systemauth PAM configuration.

Noninteractive Access

The security configuration of noninteractive services can vary quite significantly. Especially popular network services, such as LDAP, HTTP, or Windows File Shares (CIFS), can use a wide variety of authentication and authorization mechanisms that do not even need to be provided by the operating system. For example, an Apache Web server or a MySQL database server might use its own user database, without relying on any operating system services such as passwd files or LDAP directory authentication.

Monitoring how noninteractive authentication and authorization are performed is critically important since most users of Unix systems will only utilize them in noninteractive ways. To ensure the most comprehensive control over the system, it is highly recommended that the suggestions presented in this chapter be followed to minimize the attack surface and verify that the system makes only a clearly defined set of services available on the network.

Other Network Authentication Mechanisms

In 1983, BSD introduced the rlogin service. Unix administrators have been using RSH, RCP, and other tools from this package for a long time; they are very easy to use and configure and provide simple access across a small network of computers. The login was facilitated through a very simple trust model: Any user could create a .rhosts file in her home directory and specify foreign hosts and users from which to accept logins without proper credential checking. Over the rlogin protocol (TCP 513), the username of the rlogin client would be transmitted to the host system, and in lieu of an authentication, the rshd daemon would simply verify the preconfigured values. To prevent access from untrusted hosts, the administrator could use the /etc/hosts.equiv file to allow or deny individual hosts or groups of hosts (the latter through the use of NIS netgroups).

Risks of Trusted Hosts and Networks

Since no authentication ever takes place, this trust mechanism should not be used. Not only does this system rely entirely on the correct functioning of the hostname resolution system, but in addition, there is no way to determine whether a host was actually replaced.[6] Also, although rlogin-based trust systems might work for very small deployments, they become extremely hard to set up and operate with large numbers of machines.

Replacing Telnet, Rlogin, and FTP Servers and Clients with SSH

The most sensible alternative to the traditional interactive session protocols such as Telnet is the Secure Shell (SSH) system. It is very popular on Unix systems, and pretty much all versions ship with a version of SSH. Where SSH is not available, the open source package OpenSSH can easily be used instead.[7]

SSH combines the ease-of-use features of the rlogin tools with a strong cryptographic authentication system. On one hand, it is fairly easy for users to enable access from other systems; on the other hand, the secure shell protocol uses strong cryptography to:

- Authenticate the connection, that is, establish the authenticity of the user
- Protect the privacy of the connection through encryption
- Guarantee the integrity of the channel through signatures

This is done using either the RSA or DSA security algorithm, which are both available for the SSH v2[8] protocol. The cipher (see Figure 9.7) used for encryption can be explicitly selected.

```
$ ssh host -luser1 -c aes192-cbc
```

FIGURE 9.7   Create an interactive session on Solaris to host for user1 using the AES cipher with 192 bits.

The user must first create a public/private key pair through the ssh-keygen(1) tool. The output of the key generator is placed in the .ssh subdirectory of the user's home directory. This output consists of a private key file called id_dsa or id_rsa. This file must be owned by the user and can only be readable by the user. In addition, a file containing the public key is created, named in the same way, with the extension .pub appended. The public key file is then placed into the .ssh subdirectory of the user's home directory on the target system.

Once the public and private keys are in place and the SSH daemon is enabled on the host system, all clients that implement the SSH protocol can create connections. There are four common applications using SSH:

- Interactive session is the replacement for Telnet and rlogin. Using the ssh(1) command line, the sshd daemon creates a new shell and transfers control to the user.
- In a remotely executed script/command, ssh(1) allows a single command with arguments to pass. This way, a single remote command (such as a backup script) can be executed on the remote system as long as this command is in the default path for the user.
- An SSH-enabled file transfer program can be used to replace the standard FTP or FTP over SSL protocol.
- Finally, the SSH protocol is able to tunnel arbitrary protocols. This means that any client can use the privacy and integrity protection offered by SSH. In particular, the X-Window system protocol can tunnel through an existing SSH connection by using the -X command-line switch.

5. LIMITING SUPERUSER PRIVILEGES

The superuser[9] has almost unlimited power on a Unix system, which can be a significant problem. On systems that implement mandatory access controls, the superuser account can be configured to not affect user data, but the problem of overly powerful root accounts for standard, DAC-only systems remains. For an organizational and managerial perspective, access to privileged functions on a Unix operating system should be tightly controlled. For example, operators that have access to privileged functions on a Unix system should not only undergo special

---

6. This could actually be addressed through host authentication, but it is not a feature of the rlogin protocol.

7. "The Open Group Base Specifications Issue 6 IEEE Std 1003.1, 2004 Edition." See [IEEE04]. Copyright © 2001−2004 The IEEE and The Open Group, All Rights Reserved [www.opengroup.org/onlinepubs/009695399/], 2004.

8. T. Ylonen and C. Lonvick, Eds., "The Secure Shell (SSH) Authentication Protocol," Network Working Group, Request for Comments: 4252, SSH Communications Security Corp., Category: Standards Track, Cisco Systems, Inc., See [IETF4252]. Copyright © The Internet Society (2006). [http://tools.ietf.org/html/rfc4252], 2006.

9. In all Unix systems "root" is the default name for the superuser. Access to the superuser account may be disabled by default, and administrative access is only granted temporarily to users through the sudo(1) facility.

training, but also have be investigated for their personal background. Finally, it may be advisable to enforce a policy where operators of critical systems can only access privileged functions with at least two operators present (through multifactor authentication technologies).

There are a number of technical ways to limit access for the root user:

Configuring Secure Terminals

Most Unix systems allow us to restrict root logins to special terminals, typically the system console. This approach is quite effective, especially if the console or the allowed terminals are under strict physical access control. The obvious downside of this approach is that remote access to the system can be very limited: using this approach, access through any TCP/IP-based connection cannot be configured, thus requiring a direct connection, such as a directly attached terminal or a modem.

Configuration is quite different for the various Unix systems. Figure 9.8 shows the comparison between Solaris and Debian.

Gaining Root Privileges with su

The su(1) utility allows changing the identity of an interactive session. This is an effective mediation of the issues that come with restricting root access to secure terminals: Although only normal users can get access to the machine through the network (ideally by limiting the access protocols to those that protect the privacy of the communication, such as SSH), they can change their interactive session to a superuser session.

Using Groups Instead of Root

If users should be limited to executing certain commands with superuser privileges, it is possible and common to create special groups of users. For these groups, we can set the execution bit on programs (while disabling execution for all others) and the SetID bit for the owner, in this case the superuser. Therefore, only users of such a special group can execute the given utility with superuser privileges.

Using the sudo(1) Mechanism

By far more flexible and easier to manage than the approach for enabling privileged execution based on groups is the sudo(1) mechanism. Originally an open source program, sudo(1) is available for most Unix distributions. The detailed configuration is quite complex, and the manual page is quite informative.

6. SECURING LOCAL AND NETWORK FILE SYSTEMS

For production systems, there is a very effective way of preventing the modification of system-critical resources by unauthorized users or malicious software. Critical portions of the file systems (such as the locations of binary files, system libraries, and some configuration files) do not necessarily change very often.

Directory Structure and Partitioning for Security

In fact, any systemwide binary code should probably only be modified by the systems administrators. In these cases, it is very effective to properly partition the file system.

Employing Read-Only Partitions

The reason to properly partition the file system (see Figure 9.9) is so that only frequently changing files (such as user data, log files, and the like) are hosted on readable file systems. All other storage can then be mounted on read-only partitions.

Finding Special Files

To prevent inadvertent or malicious access to critical data, it is vitally important to verify the correct ownership and permission set for all critical files in the file system.

Ownership and Access Permissions

The Unix find(1) command is an effective way to locate files with certain characteristics. In the following, a number of sample command-line options for this utility are given to locate files.

Locate SetID Files

Since executables with the SetID bit set are often used to allow the execution of a program with superuser privileges, it is vitally important to monitor these files on a regular basis.

Another critical permission set is that of world-writable files; there should be no system-critical files in this list, and users should be aware of any files in their home directories that are world-writable (see Figure 9.10). Finally, files and directories that are not owned by current users can be found by the code shown in Figure 9.11. For groups, just use -nogroup instead.

On Solaris simply edit the file /etc/default/login:

FIGURE 9.8 Restricting root access.

```
# Copyright 2004 Sun Microsystems, Inc.  All rights reserved.
# Use is subject to license terms.

# If CONSOLE is set, root can only login on that device.
# Comment this line out to allow remote login by root.
#

CONSOLE=/dev/console

# PASSREQ determines if login requires a password.
#

PASSREQ=YES

# SUPATH sets the initial shell PATH variable for root
#

SUPATH=/usr/sbin:/usr/bin



# SYSLOG determines whether the syslog(3) LOG_AUTH facility should be used
# to log all root logins at level LOG_NOTICE and multiple failed login
# attempts at LOG_CRIT.
#

SYSLOG=YES

# The SYSLOG_FAILED_LOGINS variable is used to determine how many failed
# login attempts will be allowed by the system before a failed login
# message is logged, using the syslog(3) LOG_NOTICE facility.  For
example,
# if the variable is set to 0, login will log -all- failed login attempts.
#

SYSLOG_FAILED_LOGINS=5
```

On Debian:

```
# The PAM configuration file for the Shadow `login' service
#


# Disallows root logins except on tty's listed in /etc/securetty
# (Replaces the `CONSOLE' setting from login.defs)

auth       requisite  pam_securetty.so
# Disallows other than root logins when /etc/nologin exists
# (Replaces the `NOLOGINS_FILE' option from login.defs)

auth       requisite  pam_nologin.so

# Standard Un*x authentication.

@include common-auth

# This allows certain extra groups to be granted to a user
# based on things like time of day, tty, service, and user.
# Please edit /etc/security/group.conf to fit your needs
# (Replaces the `CONSOLE_GROUPS' option in login.defs)
```

FIGURE 9.8   (Continued).

```
auth      optional    pam_group.so

# Uncomment and edit /etc/security/time.conf if you need to set
# time restrainst on logins.
# (Replaces the `PORTTIME_CHECKS_ENAB' option from login.defs
# as well as /etc/porttime)

account    requisite  pam_time.so


# Uncomment and edit /etc/security/access.conf if you need to
# set access limits.
# (Replaces /etc/login.access file)

account  required       pam_access.so

# Sets up user limits according to /etc/security/limits.conf
# (Replaces the use of /etc/limits in old login)

session    required    pam_limits.so

# Prints the last login info upon succesful login
# (Replaces the `LASTLOG_ENAB' option from login.defs)

session    optional    pam_lastlog.so

# Standard Un*x account and session

@include common-account
@include common-session
@include common-password
```

The following scheme is a good start for partitioning with read-only partitions:

- Binaries and Libraries: /bin, /lib, /sbin, /usr - read-only
- Logs and frequently changing system data: /var, /usr/var - writable
- User home directories: /home, /export/home - writable
- Additional software packages: /opt, /usr/local - read-only
- System configuration: /etc, /usr/local/etc - writable
- Everything else: Root (/) - read-only

Obviously, this can only be a start and should be evaluated for each system and application. Updating operating system files, including those on the root file system, should be performed in single-user mode with all partitions mounted writable.

FIGURE 9.9   Secure partitioning.

Locate Suspicious Files and Directories

Malicious software is sometimes stored in nonstarted directories such as subdirectories named "..." that will not immediately be noticed. Administrators should pay special attention to such files and verify if the content is part of a legitimate software package.

7. NETWORK CONFIGURATION

Since many Unix systems today are used as network servers, most users will never log in these systems interactively. Consequently, the most significant threat sources for Unix- based systems are initially defective or badly configured network services. However, such initial attacks are often only used to get initial interactive access to the system; once an attacker can access a command-line shell, other layers of security must be in place to prevent an elevation of privileges (superuser access).

Basic Network Setup

Unix user space processes can access networks by calling a variety of functions from the system libraries, namely, the socket() system call and related functions. While other network protocols such as DECNet or IPX may still be supported, the TCP/IP family of protocols plays by far the most important role in today's networks. As such, we will focus on these protocols alone. A number of files are relevant for configuring access to networks, with some of the most important listed here:

```
$ find /  \( -perm -04000 -o -perm -02000\) -type f -xdev -print
```

FIGURE 9.10 Finding files with SUID and SGID set.

```
$ find / -nouser
```

FIGURE 9.11 Finding files without users.

1. /etc/hostname (and sometimes also /etc/nodename) set the name under which the system identifies itself. This name is also often used to determine its own IP address, based on hostname resolution.
2. /etc/protocols defines the available list of protocols such as IP, TCP, ICMP, and UDP.
3. /etc/hosts and /etc/networks files define what IP hosts and networks are locally known to the system. They typically include the localhost definition (which is always 127.0.0.1 for IPv4 networks) and the loopback network (defined to be 127.0.0.0/24), respectively.
4. /etc/nsswitch.conf is available on many Unix systems and allows fine-grained setting of name resolution for a number of network and other resources, including the UIDs and GIDs. Typical settings include purely local resolution (i.e., through the files in the /etc directory), resolution through NIS, host resolution through DNS, user and group resolution through LDAP, and so on.
5. /etc/resolv.conf is the main configuration file for the DNS resolver libraries used in most Unix systems. It points to the IP addresses of the default DNS nameservers and may include the local domainname and any other search domains.
6. /etc/services (and/or /etc/protocols) contains a list of well-known services and the port numbers and protocol types they are bound to. Some system commands (such as netstat) use this database to resolve ports and protocols into user-friendly names.

Depending on the Unix flavor and the version, many other network configuration files apply to the base operating system. In addition, many other services that are commonly used on Unix systems such as HTTP servers, application servers, and databases have their own configuration files that will need to be configured and monitored in deployed systems.

Detecting and Disabling Standard UNIX Services

To protect systems against outside attackers and remove the overall attack surface, it is highly recommended to disable any service not needed for providing the intended functionality. The following simple process will likely turn off most system services that are not needed:

1. Examine the start-up scripts for your system. Start-up procedures have been changing for Unix systems quite significantly over time. Early systems used the /etc/inittab to determine runlevels and start-up scripts. Unix System V introduced the /etc/init.d scripts and the symbolic links from the /etc/rc*.d/ directories. Most current Unix systems either still use this technology or implement an interface to start and stop services (like Solaris). Debian-based distributions have a System V backward compatibility facility. Administrators should determine their start-up system and disable any services and feature not required for the function of that system. Ideally, facilities and services not needed should be uninstalled to minimize the potential attack surface for both external attacks, as well as privilege escalation attacks by running potentially harmful binaries.
2. Additionally, administrator can examine the processes that are currently running on a given system (e.g., through running the ps(1) command). Processes that cannot be traced to a particular software package or functionality should be killed and their file images ideally uninstalled or deleted.
3. The netstat(1) command can be used to display currently open network sockets, specifically for TCP and UDP connections. By default, netstat(1) will use the /etc/services and /etc/protocols databases to map numeric values to well-known services. Administrators should verify that there are only those ports open that are expected to be used by the software installed on the system.

Host-Based Firewall

One of the best ways to limit the attack surface for external attackers is to close down all network sockets that are not being actively used by network clients. This is true for systems attached directly to the Internet as well as for systems on private networks. The IP stacks of most Unix systems can be configured to only accept specific protocols (such as TCP) and connections on specific ports (such as port 80). Figure 9.12 shows how to limit ssh(1) access to systems on a specific IP subnet. Depending on the network stack, this can be achieved with a setting in the System Preferences for MacOS, or the iptables(1) command for Linux systems.

Restricting Remote Administrative Access

If possible, interactive access to Unix-based systems should be limited to dedicated administrative terminals.

```
iptables -A INPUT -i eth0 -p tcp -s 192.168.1.0/24 --dport 22 -m state --state
NEW,ESTABLISHED -j ACCEPT
iptables -A OUTPUT -o eth0 -p tcp --sport 22 -m state --state ESTABLISHED -j ACCEPT
```

FIGURE 9.12   Configuration for iptables(1) for allowing ssh(1) connections from IP address range 192.168.1.1—192.168.1.254. This can be used to limit interactive access, as described in Chapter 8.

This may be achieved by limiting root access to directly attached consoles and terminals, or by creating dedicated private networks for the express purpose of allowing remote access through ssh(1), SNMP, or Web administration utilities.

Consoles and Terminals on Restricted Networks

As described earlier, root access to terminals can be limited to specific devices such as terminals or consoles. If the terminals or consoles are provided through TCP/IP-capable terminal concentrators or KVM-switches, interactive network access can be achieved by connecting these console devices through restricted networks to dedicated administrative workstations.

Dedicated Administrative Networks

Similarly, interactive access can be restricted to a small number of workstation and access points through the following technologies:

- Dedicated physical interface or VLAN segmentation—If any interactive or administrative access is limited to separate networks, preferably disconnected from operational networks, the potential attack surface is significantly reduced.
- Logical interface—If no physical or VLAN infrastructure is available, Unix networking stacks typically allow the assignment of additional IP addresses to a single physical networking interface. While more susceptible to lower-level attacks, this approach may still be sufficient for effective separation of networks.
- Routing and firewall table design—As a fairly high-level approach, administrators may limit access to specific services from preconfigured IP addresses or networks through careful design of the host-based firewall and the routing tables of the IP stack.
- Yale University has a somewhat old, but still useful, Unix networking checklist at http://security.yale.edu/network/unix.html that describes a number of general security settings for Unix systems in general, and Solaris specifically. A similar older checklist is also available from the Carnegie Mellon University's Software Engineering Institute CERT at https://www.cert.org/tech_tips/unix_configuration_guidelines.html.

- Special topics in system administration that also address security topics such as auditing, configuration management, and recovery can be found on the Usenix Web site at https://www.usenix.org/lisa/books.
- Apple provides a detailed document on locking down MacOS X 10.6 Server: http://images.apple.com/support/security/guides/docs/SnowLeopard_Server_Security_Config_v10.6.pdf.
- The U.S. federal government operates a Computer Emergency Readiness Team (US-CERT) at https://www.us-cert.gov, targeted at technical and nontechnical users for both the government and the private sector. In addition to general information, the US-CERT provides information from the National Vulnerability Database (NVD), security bulletins, and current threat information.

Finally, let's briefly look at how to improve the security of Linux and Unix systems. The following part of the chapter, describes how to modify Linus and Unix systems and fix their potential security weaknesses.

8. IMPROVING THE SECURITY OF LINUX AND UNIX SYSTEMS

A security checklist should be structured to follow the life cycle of Linus and Unix systems, from planning and installation to recovery and maintenance. The checklist is best applied to a system before it is connected to the network for the first time. In addition, the checklist can be reapplied on a regular basis, to audit conformance (see checklist: An Agenda for Action for Linux and Unix Security Activities).

9. ADDITIONAL RESOURCES

There is a large number of very useful tools to assist administrators in managing Unix systems. This also includes verifying their security.

Useful Tools

The following discussion of useful tools should not be regarded as exhaustive. Rather, it should be seen as a simple starting point.

An Agenda for Action for Linux and Unix Security Activities

No two organizations are the same, so in applying the checklist, consideration should be given to the appropriateness of each action to your particular situation. Rather than enforcing a single configuration, the following checklist will identify the specific choices and possible security controls that should be considered at each stage, which includes the following key activities (check all tasks completed):

Determine Appropriate Security

_____1. Computer role.
_____2. Assess security needs of each kind of data handled.
_____3. Trust relationships.
_____4. Uptime requirements and impact if these are not met.
_____5. Determine minimal software packages required for role.
_____6. Determine minimal net access required for role.

Installation

_____7. Install from trusted media.
_____8. Install while not connected to the Internet.
_____9. Use separate partitions.
_____10. Install minimal software.

Apply All Patches and Updates

_____11. Initially apply patches while offline.
_____12. Verify integrity of all patches and updates.
_____13. Subscribe to mailing lists to keep up to date.

Minimize

_____14. Minimize network services.
_____15. Disable all unnecessary start-up scripts.
_____16. Minimize SetUID/SetGID programs.
_____17. Other minimization.

Secure Base OS

_____18. Physical, console, and boot security.
_____19. User logons.
_____20. Authentication.
_____21. Access control.
_____22. Other.

Secure Major Services

_____23. Confinement.

_____24. tcp_wrappers.
_____25. Other general advice for services.
_____26. SSH.
_____27. Printing.
_____28. RPC/portmapper.
_____29. File services NFS/AFS/Samba.
_____30. The X Window System.
_____31. DNS service.
_____32. WWW service.
_____33. Squid proxy.
_____34. CVS.
_____35. Web browsers.
_____36. FTP service.

Add Monitoring Capability

_____37. syslog configuration.
_____38. Monitoring of logs.
_____39. Enable trusted audit subsystem if available.
_____40. Monitor running processes.
_____41. Host-based intrusion detection.
_____42. Network intrusion detection.

Connect to the Net

_____43. First put in place a host firewall.
_____44. Position the computer behind a border firewall.
_____45. Network stack hardening/sysctls.
_____46. Connect to network for the first time.

Test Backup/Rebuild Strategy

_____47. Backup/rebuild strategy.
_____48. TEST backup and restore.
_____49. Allow separate restore of software and data.
_____50. Repatch after restoring.
_____51. Process for intrusion response.

Maintain

_____52. Mailing lists.
_____53. Software inventory.
_____54. Rapid patching.
_____55. Secure administrative access.
_____56. Log book for all sysadmin work.
_____57. Configuration change control with.
_____58. Regular audit.

Webmin

Webmin is a useful general-purpose graphical system management interface that is available for a large number of Unix systems. It is implemented as a Web application running on port 10,000 by default. Webmin allows management of basic Unix functionality such as user and group management, network and printer configuration, file system management, and many more. It also comes with a module for managing commonly used services such as the OpenLDAP directory server, the BIND DNS server, a number of different mail transfer agents, and databases.

Webmin is particularly useful for casually maintained systems that do not require tight configuration management and may expose a Web application interface. It is not recommended to use Webmin on mission-critical systems or in environments where systems are exposed to unknown external users (such as on the Internet or on large private networks). Even for systems where Webmin is an acceptable risk, it is recommended to ensure that the web interface is protected by transport-level security

(HTTP with SSL), and preferably restricted to dedicated administration networks or stations.

nmap

For testing the open ports on a given host or subnet, nmap is an excellent tool. It allows scanning a given IP address or IP address range and testing what TCP and UDP ports are accessible. It is very flexible and can easily be extended, but it comes with a number of modules that allow determining the operating systems of an IP responder based on the fingerprint of the TCP/IP stack responses.

LCFG

Local ConFiGiguration System (LCFG) is an effective configuration management system for complex Unix deployments. It compiles machine-specific and default configurations for all aspects of a given Unix system into an XML file and distributes these files to the client machines. More information on LCFG can be found at http://www.lcfg.org/.

Further Information

Since this chapter can only provide an introduction to fully securing Unix-based systems, the following list of resources is recommended for a more in-depth treatment of this topic. Users are also advised to consult vendor-specific information about secure configuration of their products.

By far the most comprehensive guidance on security configuration for Unix systems is available through the U.S. Defense Information Systems Agency (DISA). DISA and the National Institutes for Standards and Technology (NIST) create, publish, and update Security Technical Implementation Guides (STIGs) for a number of operating systems at http://iase.disa.mil/stigs/os/. Beyond the general STIG for Unix security, there are vendor- specific STIGs for Red Hat Linux, Solaris, HP-UX, and AIX.

10. SUMMARY

This chapter covered communications interfaces between HP-UX, Solaris, Linux, and AIX servers and the communications infrastructure (firewalls, routers, etc.). The use of Oracle in configuring and managing HP-UX, Solaris, Linux and AIX servers to support large databases and applications was also discussed.

Other Unix systems discussed included Solaris, Linux, and AIX, and material was presented on how to perform alternate Information Assurance Officer duties for HP-UX, Solaris, Linux and AIX midtier systems. This chapter also showed entry-level security professionals how to provide support for Unix security error diagnosis, testing strategies, and resolution of problems, which, is normally found in the SMC Ogden server HP-UX, AIX, Solaris, and Linux environments. In addition, the chapter showed security professionals how to provide implementation of DISA security requirements (STIG) and Unix SRR.

This chapter also helped security professionals gain experience in the installation and management of applications in Unix/Sun/Linux/AIX environments. In addition, it showed security professionals how to apply Defense Information Systems Agency (DISA) Security Technical Information Guidelines (STIG) with regard to installing and configuring/setting up Unix/Linux environments under mandatory security requirements.

The chapter showed security professionals how to work with full life-cycle information technology projects; as well as, provides proficiency in the environments of J2EE, EJB, Sun Solaris, IBM WebSphere, Oracle, DB/2, Hibernate, JMS/MQ Series, Web Service, SOAP, and XML. It also helped Unix/Solaris administrators on a large scale, with reference to multiuser enterprise systems.

With regard to certification exams, this chapter is designed to help students gain general experience (which includes operations experience) on large-scale computer systems or multiserver local area networks; broad knowledge and experience with system technologies (including networking concepts, hardware, and software); and the capability to determine system and network and application performance capabilities. It can also help students gain specialized experience in administrating Unix-based systems and Oracle configuration knowledge, with security administration skills.

Finally, let's move on to the real interactive part of this chapter: review questions/exercises, hands-on projects, case projects and optional team case project. The answers and/or solutions by chapter can be found in the Online Instructor's Solutions Manual.

CHAPTER REVIEW QUESTIONS/EXERCISES

True/False

1. True or False? Unix was originally created as a single-user system.
2. True or False? Unix security has a long tradition, and though many concepts of the earliest Unix systems still apply, a large number of changes have taken place that fundamentally altered the way the operating system implements these security principles.
3. True or False? Achieving a high level of system security for the Unix system is a complex process that involves technical, operational, and managerial aspects of system operation.
4. True or False? For any interactive session, Linux systems require the user to log into the system.

5. True or False? The superuser has almost unlimited power on a Unix system, which can be a significant problem.

Multiple Choice

1. When a user is granted access to resources on a computing system, it is of vital importance to establish and verify the identity of the requesting entity. This process is commonly referred to as:
   A. authorization.
   B. availability.
   C. integrity.
   D. authentication.
   E. confidentiality.
2. What allows for the loading of additional drivers for file systems?
   A. File access
   B. Identity-based access control
   C. Filesystems in user space
   D. Access control list
   E. Meta data
3. The login process is a system daemon that is responsible for coordinating authentication and process setup for interactive users. To do this, the login process does the following, except which one?
   A. Draw or display the login screen.
   B. Collect the credential.
   C. Present the user credential to only one of the configured user databases (typically, these can be files, NIS, Kerberos servers, or LDAP directories) for authentication.
   D. Create a process with the user's default command-line shell, with the home directory as working directory.
   E. Execute systemwide, user, and shell-specific start-up scripts.
4. What was introduced to simplify the administration of small groups of computers?
   A. Systemauth PAM
   B. Network Information System
   C. Noninteractive access
   D. Trusted hosts
   E. Trusted networks
5. The most sensible alternative to the traditional interactive session protocols such as Telnet is the:
   A. open-source package OpenSSH.
   B. SSH daemon.
   C. Secure Shell (SSH) system.
   D. SSH protocol.
   E. SSH-enabled file transfer program.

EXERCISE

Problem

On a Tuesday morning, a company support team was alerted by a customer who was trying to download a drive update. The customer reported that the FTP server was not responding to connection attempts. Upon failing to log in to the FTP server remotely via the secure shell, the support team member walked to a server room only to discover that the machine crashed and was not able to boot. The reason was simple: No operating system was found. The company gathered the standard set of network servers (all running some version of Unix or Linux): Web, email, DNS servers, and also a dedicated FTP server, used to distribute hardware drivers for the company inventory. In this case project, how would the company go about implementing an incident response plan?

Hands-On Projects

Project

Despite the risks of viruses and malicious attacks, most Linux Web servers are inadequately protected against intrusion. How would a company go about protecting their Linux Web servers against intrusion?

Case Projects

Problem

Rlogin is a software utility for Unix-like computer operating systems that allows users to log in on another host via a network, communicating via TCP port 513. Rlogin is most commonly deployed on corporate or academic networks, where user account information is shared between all the Unix machines on the network (often using NIS). But rlogin does have serious security problems. Please list rlogin's possible security problems.

Optional Team Case Project

Problem

Brute-force attacks against remote services such as SSH, FTP, and telnet are still the most common form of attack to compromise servers facing the Internet. So, how would security administrators go about thwarting these types of attack?

## Chapter 10

Eliminating the Security Weakness of Linux and Unix Operating Systems

Mario Santana

Terremark

1. INTRODUCTION TO LINUX AND UNIX

A simple Google search for define:unix yields many definitions. This definition comes from Microsoft: "A powerful multitasking operating system developed in 1969 for use in a minicomputer environment; still a widely used network operating system."[1]

What is Unix?

Unix is many things. Officially, it is a brand and an operating system specification. In common usage, the word *Unix* is often used to refer to one or more of many operating systems that derive from or are similar to the operating system designed and implemented about 41 years ago at AT & T Bell Laboratories. Throughout this chapter, we'll use the term *Unix* to include official Unix-branded operating systems as well as Unix-like operating systems such as BSD, Linux, and even Macintosh OS X.

History

Years after AT & T's original implementation, there followed decades of aggressive market wars among many operating system vendors, each claiming that its operating system was Unix. The ever-increasing incompatibilities between these different versions of Unix were seen as a major deterrent to the marketing and sales of Unix. As personal computers grew more powerful and flexible, running inexpensive operating systems like Microsoft Windows and IBM OS/2, they threatened Unix as the server platform of choice. In response to these and other marketplace pressures, most major Unix vendors eventually backed efforts to standardize the Unix operating system.

Unix Is a Brand

Since the early 1990s, the Unix brand has been owned by The Open Group. This organization manages a set of specifications with which vendors must comply to use the Unix brand in referring to their operating system products. In this way, The Open Group provides a guarantee to the marketplace that any system labeled as Unix conforms to a strict set of standards.

Unix Is a Specification

The Open Group's standard is called the Single Unix Specification. It is created in collaboration with the Institute of Electrical and Electronics Engineers (IEEE), the International Standards Organization (ISO), and others. The specification is developed, refined, and updated in an open, transparent process.

The Single Unix Specification comprises several components, covering core system interfaces such as system calls as well as commands, utilities, and a development environment based on the C programming language. Together, these describe a "functional superset of consensus-based specifications and historical practice."[2]

Lineage

The phrase *historical practice* in the description of the Single Unix Specification refers to the many operating systems historically referring to themselves as Unix. These include everything from AT & T's original releases to the versions released by the University of California at Berkeley and major commercial offerings by the likes of IBM, Sun, Digital Equipment Corporation (DEC), Hewlett-Packard (HP), the Santa Cruz Operation (SCO),

---

1. Microsoft, n.d., "Glossary of Networking Terms for Visio IT Professionals," retrieved September 22, 2008, from Microsoft TechNet: http://technet.microsoft.com/en-us/library/cc751329. aspx#XSLTsection142121120120.

2. The Open Group, n.d., "The Single Unix Specification," retrieved September 22, 2008, from What Is Unix: www.unix.org/what_is_unix/single_unix_specification.html.

Novell, and even Microsoft. But any list of Unix operating systems would be incomplete if it didn't mention Linux (see Figure 10.1).

What is Linux?

Linux is a bit of an oddball in the Unix operating system lineup. That's because, unlike the Unix versions released by the major vendors, Linux did not reuse any existing source code. Instead, Linux was developed from scratch by a Finnish university student named Linus Torvalds.

Most Popular Unix-like OS

Linux was written from the start to function very similarly to existing Unix products. And because Torvalds worked on Linux as a hobby, with no intention of making money, it was distributed for free. These factors and others contributed to making Linux the most popular Unix operating system today.

Linux Is a Kernel

Strictly speaking, Torvalds's pet project has provided only one part of a fully functional Unix operating system: the kernel. The other parts of the operating system, including the commands, utilities, development environment, desktop environment, and other aspects of a full Unix operating system, are provided by other parties, including GNU, XOrg, and others.

Linux is a Community

Perhaps the most fundamentally different thing about Linux is the process by which it is developed and improved. As the hobby project that it was, Linux was released by Torvalds on the Internet in the hopes that someone out there might find it interesting. A few programmers saw Torvalds's hobby kernel and began working on it for fun, adding features and fleshing out functionality in a sort of unofficial partnership with Torvalds. At this point, everyone was just having fun, tinkering with interesting concepts. As more and more people joined the unofficial club, Torvalds's pet project ballooned into a worldwide phenomenon.

Today, Linux is developed and maintained by hundreds of thousands of contributors all over the world. In 1996, Eric S. Raymond[3] famously described the distributed development methodology used by Linux as a bazaar—a wild, uproarious collection of people, each developing whatever feature they most wanted in an operating system, or improving whatever shortcoming most impacted them. Yet somehow, this quick-moving community resulted in a development process that was stable as a whole and that produced an amazing amount of progress in a very short time.

This is radically different from the way in which Unix systems have typically been developed. If the Linux community is like a bazaar, then other Unix systems can be described as a cathedral—carefully preplanned and painstakingly assembled over a long period of time, according to specifications handed down by master architects from previous generations. Recently, however, some of the traditional Unix vendors have started moving toward a more decentralized, bazaar-like development model similar in many ways to the Linux methodology.

Linux Is Distributions

The open-source movement in general is very important to the success of Linux. Thanks to GNU, XOrg, and other open-source contributors, there was an almost complete Unix already available when the Linux kernel was released. Linux only filled in the final missing component of a no-cost, open-source Unix. Because the majority of the other parts of the operating system came from the GNU project, Linux is also known as GNU/Linux.

To actually install and run Linux, it is necessary to collect all the other operating system components. Because of the interdependency of the operating system components—each component must be compatible with the others—it is important to gather the right versions of all these components. In the early days of Linux, this was quite a challenge!

Soon, however, someone gathered up a self-consistent set of components and made them all available from a central download location. The first such efforts include H. J. Lu's "boot/root" floppies and MCC Interim Linux. These folks did not necessarily develop any of these components; they only redistributed them in a more convenient package. Other people did the same, releasing new bundles called *distributions* whenever a major upgrade was available.

Some distributions touted the latest in hardware support; others specialized in mathematics or graphics or another type of computing; still others built a distribution that would provide the simplest or most attractive user experience. Over time, distributions have become more robust, offering important features such as package management, which allows a user to safely upgrade parts of the system without reinstalling everything else.

Linux Standard Base

Today there are dozens of Linux distributions. Different flavors of distributions have evolved over the years. A primary distinguishing feature is the package management

---

3. E. S. Raymond, September 11, 2000, "The Cathedral and the Bazaar," retrieved September 22, 2008, from Eric S. Raymond's homepage: www.catb.org/esr/writings/cathedral-bazaar/cathedral-bazaar/index.html.

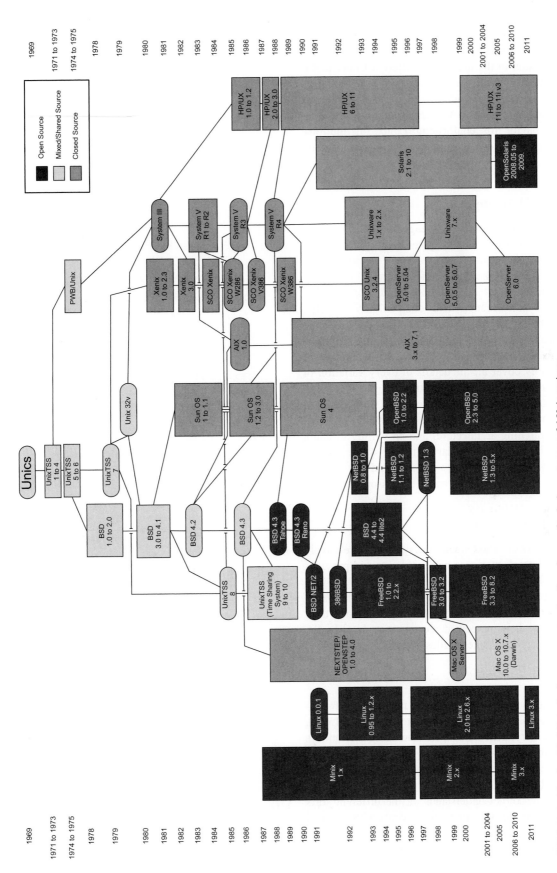

FIGURE 10.1 The simplified Unix family tree presents a timeline of some of today's most successful Unix variants.

system. Some distributions are primarily volunteer community efforts; others are commercial offerings. See Figure 10.2 for a timeline of Linux development.

The explosion in the number of different Linux distributions created a situation reminiscent of the Unix wars of previous decades. To address this issue, the Linux Standard Base was created to specify certain key standards of behavior for conforming Linux distributions. Most major distributions comply with the Linux Standard Base specifications.

A Word of Warning

Understanding the history and lineage of Unix is important for several reasons. First, it gives us insight into why some things work the way they do—often it's for historical reasons. Second, the wide variety of versions allows us to choose one that best fits our needs for security, functionality, performance, and compatibility. Finally, and most importantly, this understanding shows us that the rich history and many flavors of Unix make it impossible to treat security as a recipe. Similarly, this chapter cannot possibly cover all the details of every variation of the Unix commands that we will introduce.

Instead of memorizing some steps that will harden a Unix system, we must understand the underlying concepts and the overarching architecture, and be willing to adapt our knowledge to the particular details of whatever version we're working with. Keep this in mind as you read this chapter, especially as you apply the lessons in it.

System Architecture

The architecture of Unix operating systems is relatively simple. The kernel interfaces with hardware and provides core functionality for the system. File systems provide permanent storage and access to many other kinds of functionality. Processes embody programs as their instructions are being executed. Permissions describe the actions that users may take on files and other resources.

Kernel

The operating system kernel manages many of the fundamental details that an operating system needs to deal with, including memory, disk storage, and low-level networking. In general, the kernel is the part of the operating system that talks directly to hardware; it presents an abstracted interface to the rest of the operating system components.

Because the kernel understands all the different sorts of hardware that the operating system deals with, the rest of the operating system is freed from needing to understand all those underlying details. The abstracted interface presented by the kernel allows other parts of the operating

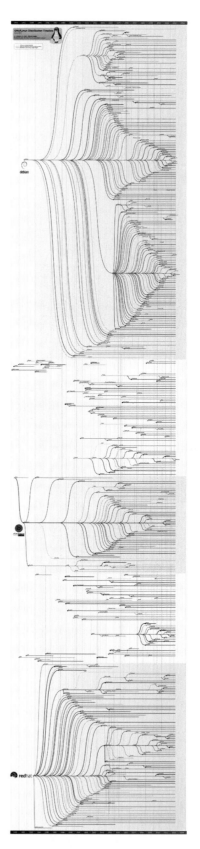

FIGURE 10.2   History of Linux distributions.

system to read and write files or communicate on the network without knowing or caring about what kinds of disks or network adapter are installed.

File System

A fundamental aspect of Unix is its file system. Unix pioneered the hierarchical model of directories that contain files and/or other directories to allow the organization of data into a tree structure. Multiple file systems could be accessed by connecting them to empty directories in the root file system. In essence, this is very much like grafting one hierarchy onto an unused branch of another. There is no limit to the number of file systems that can be mounted in this way.

The file system hierarchy is also used to provide more than just access to and organization of local files. Network data shares can also be mounted, just like file systems on local disks. And special files such as device files, first in/first out (FIFO) or pipe files, and others give direct access to hardware or other system features.

Users and Groups

Unix was designed to be a time-sharing system and as such has been a multiuser since its inception. Users are identified in Unix by their usernames, but internally each is represented as a unique identifying integer called a *user ID*, or *UID*. Each user can also belong to one or more groups. Like users, groups are identified by their names, but they are represented internally as a unique integer called a *group ID*, or *GID*. Each file or directory in a Unix file system is associated with a user and a group.

Permissions

Unix has traditionally had a simple permissions architecture, based on the user and group associated with files in the file system. This scheme makes it possible to specify read, write, and/or execute permissions, along with a special permission setting whose effect is context-dependent. Furthermore, it's possible to set these permissions independently for the file's owner; the file's group, in which case the permission applies to all users, other than the owner, who are members of that group, and to all other users. The chmod command is used to set the permissions by adding up the values of all desired permission types, as shown in Table 10.1.

The Unix permission architecture has historically been the target of criticism for its simplicity and inflexibility. It is not possible, for example, to specify a different permission setting for more than one user or more than one group. These limitations have been addressed in more recent file system implementations using extended file attributes and access control lists.

TABLE 10.1 Unix Permissions and Chmod.

Chmod Usage	Read	Write	Execute	Special
User	u + r or 0004	u + w or 0002	u + x or 0001	u + s or 4000
Group	u + r or 0040	u + w or 0020	u + x or 0010	u + s or 2000
Other	u + r or 0400	u + w or 0200	u + x or 0100	u + s or 1000

Processes

When a program is executed, it is represented in a Unix system as a process. The kernel keeps track of many pieces of information about each process. This information is required for basic housekeeping and advanced tasks such as tracing and debugging. This information represents the user, group, and other data used for making security decisions about a process's access rights to files and other resources.

2. HARDENING LINUX AND UNIX

With a basic understanding of the fundamental concepts of the Unix architecture, let's take a look at the practical work of securing a Unix deployment. First, we'll review considerations for securing Unix machines from network-borne attacks. Then we'll look at security from a host-based perspective. Finally, we'll talk about systems management and how different ways of administering a Unix system can impact security.

Network Hardening

Defending from network-borne attacks is arguably the most important aspect of Unix security. Unix machines are used heavily to provide network-based services, running Web sites, domain name server (DNS), firewalls, and many more. To provide these services, Unix systems must be connected to hostile networks, such as the Internet, where legitimate users can easily access and make use of these services.

Unfortunately, providing easy access to legitimate users makes the system readily accessible to bad actors who would subvert access controls and other security measures to steal sensitive information, change reference data, or simply make services unavailable to legitimate users. Attackers can probe systems for security weaknesses, identify and exploit vulnerabilities, and generally wreak digital havoc with relative impunity from anywhere around the globe.

Minimizing Attack Surface

Every way in which an attacker can interact with the system poses a security risk. Any system that makes available a large number of network services, especially complex services such as the custom Web applications of today, suffers a higher likelihood that inadequate permissions or a software bug or some other error will present attackers with an opportunity to compromise security. In contrast, even a very insecure service cannot be compromised if it is not running.

A pillar of any security architecture is the concept of minimizing the attack surface. By reducing the number of enabled network services and the available functionality of those services that are enabled, a system presents a smaller set of functions that can be subverted by an attacker. Other ways to reduce attackable surface areas are to deny network access from unknown hosts when possible and to limit the privileges of running services in order to minimize the damage they might be subverted to cause.

Eliminate Unnecessary Services

The first step in reducing an attack surface is to disable unnecessary services provided by a server. In Unix, services are enabled in one of several ways. The "Internet daemon," or *inetd*, is a historically popular mechanism for managing network services. Like many Unix programs, inetd is configured by editing a text file. In the case of inetd, this text file is /etc/inetd.conf; unnecessary services should be commented out of this file. Today a more modular replacement for inetd, called *xinetd*, is gaining popularity. The configuration for xinetd is not contained in any single file but in many files located in the /etc/xinetd.d/ directory. Each file in this directory configures a single service, and a service may be disabled by removing the file or by making the appropriate changes to the file.

Many Unix services are not managed by inetd or xinetd, however. Network services are often started by the system's initialization scripts during the boot sequence. Derivatives of the BSD Unix family historically used a simple initialization script located in /etc/rc. To control the services that are started during the boot sequence, it is necessary to edit this script.

Recent Unices (the plural of Unix), even BSD derivatives, use something similar to the initialization scheme of the System V or higher family. In this scheme, a "run level" is chosen at boot time. The default run level is defined in /etc/inittab; typically, it is 3 or 5. The initialization scripts for each run level are located in /etc/rc *X*.d, where *X* represents the run-level number. The services that are started during the boot process are controlled by adding or removing scripts in the appropriate run-level directory. Some Unices provide tools to help manage these scripts, such as the rcconf command in Debian and derivatives or the chkconfig command in Red Hat Linux and derivatives. Other methods of managing services in Unix include the Service Management Facility of Solaris 10 or higher. No matter how a network service is started or managed, however, it must necessarily listen for network connections to make itself available to users. This fact makes it possible to positively identify all running network services by looking for processes that are listening for network connections. Almost all versions of Unix provide a command that makes this a trivial task. The netstat command can be used to list various kinds of information about the network environment of a Unix host. Running this command with the appropriate flags (usually −lut) will produce a listing of all open network ports, including those that are listening for incoming connections (see Figure 10.3).

Finally, let's take a brief look at how services that are necessary can be configured securely. The following checklist (see checklist: An Agenda for Action When Securing Web Server Activities) presents several points to consider when securing a Web server.

Securely Configure Necessary Services

Every such listening port should correspond to a necessary service that is well understood and securely configured. Although we cannot cover every service that might be run on a Unix system, we'll explore a few of the more common services.

```
travis ~ # netstat -lut
Active Internet connections (only servers)
Proto Recv-Q Send-Q Local Address        Foreign Address      State
tcp       0      0 *:sunrpc             *:*                  LISTEN
tcp       0      0 *:41182              *:*                  LISTEN
tcp6      0      0 [::]:sunrpc          [::]:*               LISTEN
tcp6      0      0 [::]:37434           [::]:*               LISTEN
udp       0      0 *:sunrpc             *:*
udp       0      0 *:725                *:*
udp       0      0 *:743                *:*
udp       0      0 *:45308              *:*
udp6      0      0 [::]:sunrpc          [::]:*
udp6      0      0 [::]:725             [::]:*
udp6      0      0 [::]:58154           [::]:*
```

FIGURE 10.3   Output of netstat −lut.

An Agenda for Action when Securing Web Server Activities

The following items are possible actions that organizations should consider; some of the items may not apply to all organizations. Some important points to consider when securing Apache or any other Web server include[4] (check all tasks completed):

_____**1.** Keep up to date with server software updates.

_____**2.** Mitigate denial-of-service attacks by maximizing performance and limiting the resources consumed.

_____**3.** Minimize permissions on Web content directories and files.

_____**4.** Minimize capabilities for dynamic content.

_____**5.** When dynamic content (Web applications) is necessary, carefully check the security of the dynamic content scripts.

_____**6.** Monitor server logs for malicious or anomalous activity.

One of the most popular services to run on a Unix system is a Web server. The Apache Web server is one of the most popular because it is free, powerful, and flexible, with many third-party add-ons to make it even more powerful and flexible. All this power and flexibility can also make secure Apache configuration a nontrivial exercise.

Another popular service on Unix servers is the Secure Shell service, or SSH. This service enables secure remote access to the Unix console. To configure it for maximum security, disable the use of passwords and require private key authentication. SSH also allows an administrator to strictly limit which commands can be executed by a given account—a feature that can minimize the risk of SSH accounts used for automated or centralized management functions.

Unix systems are often used to run database software. These databases can contain sensitive information, in which case they must be carefully configured to secure that data; however, even when the data is of little value, the database server itself can be used as a stepping stone in a larger compromise. That's one reason why it's important to secure any Unix system and the services it runs. There are many different kinds of database software, and each one must be hardened according to its own unique capabilities. From the Unix point of view, however, the security of any database can be greatly enhanced by using one of the firewall technologies described below to limit which remote hosts can access the database software.

Host-based

Obviously, it is impossible to disable all the services provided by a server. However, it is possible to limit the hosts that have access to a given service. Often it is possible to identify a well-defined list of hosts or subnets that should be granted access to a network service. There are several ways in which this restriction can be configured.

A classical way of configuring these limitations is through the *tcpwrappers* interface. The tcpwrappers functionality is to limit the network hosts that are allowed to access services provided by the server. These controls are configured in two text files, /etc/hosts. allow and /etc/hosts.deny. This interface was originally designed to be used by inetd and xinetd on behalf of the services they manage. Today most service-providing software directly supports this functionality.

Another, more robust method of controlling network access is through firewall configurations. Most modern Unices include some form of firewall capability: IPFilter, used by many commercial Unices; IPFW, used by most of the BSD variants; and IPTables, used by Linux. In all cases, the best way to arrive at a secure configuration is to create a default rule to deny all traffic and then to create the fewest, most specific exceptions possible.

Modern firewall implementations are able to analyze every aspect of the network traffic they filter as well as aggregate traffic into logical connections and track the state of those connections. The ability to accept or deny connections based on more than just the originating network address and to end a conversation when certain conditions are met makes modern firewalls a much more powerful control for limiting attack surface than tcpwrappers.

Chroot and Other Jails

Eventually, some network hosts must be allowed to access a service if it is to be useful at all. In fact, it is often necessary to allow anyone on the Internet to access a service, such as a public Web site. Once a malicious user can access a service, there is a risk that the service will be subverted into executing unauthorized instructions on behalf of the attacker. The potential for damage is limited only by the permissions that the service process has to access resources and to make changes on the system. For this reason, an important security measure is to limit the power of a service to the bare minimum necessary to allow it to perform its duties.

A primary method of achieving this goal is to associate the service process with a user who has limited permissions. In many cases, it's possible to configure a user with very few permissions on the system and to associate that user with a service process. In these cases, the service

---

4. Apache.org, "Security Tips," retrieved August 22, 2012 from http://httpd.apache.org/docs/2.4/misc/security_tips.html.

can only perform a limited amount of damage, even if it is subverted by attackers.

Unfortunately, this is not always very effective or even possible. A service must often access sensitive server resources to perform its work. Configuring a set of permissions to allow access to only the sensitive information required for a service to operate can be complex or impossible.

In answer to this challenge, Unix has long supported the chroot and ulimit interfaces as ways to limit the access that a powerful process has on a system. The chroot interface limits a process's access on the file system. Regardless of actual permissions, a process run under a chroot jail can only access a certain part of the file system. Common practice is to run sensitive or powerful services in a chroot jail and make a copy of only those file system resources that the service needs in order to operate. This allows a service to run with a high level of system access, yet be unable to damage the contents of the file system outside the portion it is allocated.[5]

The ulimit interface is somewhat different in that it can configure limits on the amount of system resources a process or user may consume. A limited amount of disk space, memory, CPU utilization, and other resources can be set for a service process. This can curtail the possibility of a denial-of-service attack because the service cannot exhaust all system resources, even if it has been subverted by an attacker.[6]

Access Control

Reducing the attack surface area of a system limits the ways in which an attacker can interact and therefore subvert a server. Access control can be seen as another way to reduce the attack surface area. By requiring all users to prove their identity before making any use of a service, access control reduces the number of ways in which an anonymous attacker can interact with the system.

In general, access control involves three phases. The first phase is identification, where a user asserts his identity. The second phase is authentication, where the user proves his identity. The third phase is authorization, where the server allows or disallows particular actions based on permissions assigned to the authenticated user.

Strong Authentication

It is critical, therefore, that a secure mechanism is used to prove the user's identity. If this mechanism were to be subverted, an attacker would be able to impersonate a user to access resources or issue commands with

whatever authorization level has been granted to that user. For decades, the primary form of authentication has been through the use of passwords. However, passwords suffer from several weaknesses as a form of authentication, presenting attackers with opportunities to impersonate legitimate users for illegitimate ends. Bruce Schneier has argued for years that "passwords have outlived their usefulness as a serious security device."[7] More secure authentication mechanisms include two-factor authentication and PKI certificates.

Two-Factor Authentication

Two-factor authentication involves the presentation of two of the following types of information by users to prove their identity: something they know, something they have, or something they are. The first factor, something they know, is typified by a password or a PIN— some shared secret that only the legitimate user should know. The second factor, something they have, is usually fulfilled by a unique physical token (see Figure 10.4). RSA makes a popular line of such tokens, but cell phones, matrix cards, and other alternatives are becoming more common. The third factor, something they are, usually refers to biometrics.

Unix supports various ways to implement two-factor authentication into the system. Pluggable Authentication Modules, or PAMs, allow a program to use arbitrary authentication mechanisms without needing to manage any of the details. PAMs are used by Solaris, Linux, and other Unices. BSD authentication serves a similar purpose and is used by several major BSD derivatives.

With PAM or BSD authentication, it is possible to configure any combination of authentication mechanisms, including simple passwords, biometrics, RSA tokens, Kerberos, and more. It's also possible to configure a different combination for different services. This kind of flexibility allows a Unix security administrator to implement a very strong authentication requirement as a prerequisite for access to sensitive services.

PKI

Strong authentication can also be implemented using a Private Key Infrastructure (PKI). Secure Socket Layer (SSL), is a simplified PKI designed for secure communications, familiar from its use in securing traffic on the Web. Through use of a similar foundation of technologies, it's possible to issue and manage certificates to authenticate users rather than Web sites. Additional technologies, such as a trusted platform module or a smart

---

5. W. Richard Stevens, *Advanced Programming in the UNIX Environment* Addison-Wesley, Reading, 1992.
6. Ibid.

7. B. Schneier, December 14, 2006, *Real-World Passwords*, retrieved October 9, 2008, from Schneier on Security: www.schneier.com/blog/archives/2006/12/realworld_passw.html.

FIGURE 10.4 Physical tokens used for two-factor authentication.

card, simplify the use of these certificates in support of two-factor authentication.

Dedicated Service Accounts

After strong authentication, limiting the complexity of the authorization phase is the most important part of access control. User accounts should not be authorized to perform sensitive tasks. Services should be associated with dedicated user accounts, which should then be authorized to perform only those tasks required for providing that service.

Additional Controls

In addition to minimizing the attack surface area and implementing strong access controls, there are several important aspects of securing a Unix network server.

Encrypted Communications

One of the ways an attacker can steal sensitive information is to eavesdrop on network traffic. Information is vulnerable as it flows across the network, unless it is encrypted. Sensitive information, including passwords and intellectual property, are routinely transmitted over the network. Even information that is seemingly useless to an attacker can contain important clues to help a bad actor compromise security.

File Transfer Protocol (FTP), World Wide Web (WWW), and many other services that transmit information over the network support the Secure Sockets Layer (SSL) standard for encrypted communications. For server software that doesn't support SSL natively, wrappers like *stunnel* provide transparent SSL functionality.

No discussion of Unix network encryption can be complete without mention of Secure Shell, or SSH. SSH is a replacement for Telnet and RSH, providing remote command-line access to Unix systems as well as other functionality. SSH encrypts all network communications using SSL, mitigating many of the risks of Telnet and RSH.

Log Analysis

In addition to encrypting network communications, it is important to keep a detailed activity log to provide an audit trail in case of anomalous behavior. At a minimum, the logs should capture system activity such as logon and logoff events as well as service program activity, such as FTP, WWW, or Structured Query Language (SQL) logs.

Since the 1980s, the *syslog* service has been used to manage log entries in Unix. Over the years, the original implementation has been replaced by more feature-rich implementations, such as *syslog-ng* and *rsyslog*. These systems can be configured to send log messages to local files as well as remote destinations, based on independently defined verbosity levels and message sources.

The syslog system can independently route messages based on the facility, or message source, and the level, or message importance. The facility can identify the message as pertaining to the kernel, the email system, user activity, an authentication event, or any of various other services. The level denotes the criticality of the message and can typically be one of *emergency, alert, critical, error, warning, notice, informational*, and *debug*. Under Linux, the *klog* process is responsible for handling log messages generated by the kernel; typically, klog is configured to route these messages through syslog, just like any other process.

Some services, such as the Apache Web server, have limited or no support for syslog. These services typically include the ability to log activity to a file independently. In these cases, simple scripts can redirect the contents of these files to syslog for further distribution and/or processing.

Relevant logs should be copied to a remote, secure server to ensure that they cannot be tampered with. Additionally, file hashes should be used to identify any attempt to tamper with the logs. In this way, the audit trail provided by the log files can be depended on as a source of uncompromised information about the security status of the system.

IDS/IPS

Intrusion detection systems (IDSs) and intrusion prevention systems (IPSs) have become commonplace security items on today's networks. Unix has a rich heritage of such software, including Snort, Prelude, and OSSEC. Correctly deployed, an IDS can provide an early warning of probes and other precursors to attack.

Host Hardening

Unfortunately, not all attacks originate from the network. Malicious users often gain access to a system through legitimate means, bypassing network-based defenses. Various steps can be taken to harden a Unix system from a host-based attack such as this.

Permissions

The most obvious step is to limit the permissions of user accounts on the Unix host. Recall that every file and directory in a Unix file system is associated with a single user and a single group. User accounts should each have permissions that allow full control of their respective home directories. Together with permissions to read and execute system programs, this allows most of the typical functionality required of a Unix user account. Additional permissions that might be required include mail spool files and directories as well as crontab files for scheduling tasks.

Administrative Accounts

Setting permissions for administrative users is a more complicated question. These accounts must access very powerful system-level commands and resources in the routine discharge of their administrative functions. For this reason, it's difficult to limit the tasks these users may perform. It's possible, however, to create specialized administrative user accounts, then authorize these accounts to access a well-defined subset of administrative resources. Printer management, Web site administration, email management, database administration, storage management, backup administration, software upgrades, and other specific administrative functions common to Unix systems lend themselves to this approach.

Groups

Often it is convenient to apply permissions to a set of users rather than a single user or all users. The Unix group mechanism allows for a single user to belong to one or more groups and for file system permissions and other access controls to be applied to a group.

File System Attributes and ACLs

It can become unfeasibly complex to implement and manage anything more than a simple permissions scheme using the classical Unix file system permission capabilities. To overcome this issue, modern Unix file systems support access control lists, or ACLs. Most Unix file systems support ACLs using extended attributes that could be used to store arbitrary information about any given file or directory. By recognizing authorization information in these extended attributes, the file system implements a comprehensive mechanism to specify arbitrarily complex permissions for any file system resource.

ACLs contain a list of *access control entries*, or ACEs, which specify the permissions that a user or group has on the file system resource in question. On most Unices, the chacl command is used to view and set the ACEs of a given file or directory. The ACL support in modern Unix file systems provides a fine-grained mechanism for managing complex permissions requirements. ACLs do not make the setting of minimum permissions a trivial matter, but complex scenarios can now be addressed effectively.

Intrusion Detection

Even after hardening a Unix system with restrictive user permissions and ACLs, it's important to maintain logs of system activity. As with activity logs of network services, host-centric activity logs track security-relevant events that could show symptoms of compromise or evidence of attacks in the reconnaissance or planning stages.

Audit Trails

Again, as with network activity logs, Unix has leaned heavily on syslog to collect, organize, distribute, and store log messages about system activity. Configuring syslog for system messages is the same as for network service messages. The kernel's messages, including those messages generated on behalf of the kernel by klogd under Linux, are especially relevant from a hostcentric point of view.

An additional source of audit trail data about system activity is the history logs kept by a login shell such as *bash*. These logs record every command the user issued at the command line. The bash shell and others can be configured to keep these logs in a secure location and to attach timestamps to each log entry. This information is invaluable in identifying malicious activity, both as it is happening and after the fact.

File Changes

Besides tracking activity logs, monitoring file changes can be a valuable indicator of suspicious system activity. Attackers often modify system files to elevate privileges, capture passwords or other credentials, establish backdoors to ensure future access to the system, and support other illegitimate uses. Identifying these changes early can often foil an attack in progress before the attacker is able to cause significant damage or loss.

Programs such as Tripwire and Aide have been around for decades; their function is to monitor the file system for unauthorized changes and raise an alert when one is found. Historically, they functioned by scanning the file system and generating a unique *hash*, or fingerprint, of each file. On future runs, the tool would recalculate the hashes and identify changed files by the difference in the hash. Limitations of this approach include the need to regularly scan the entire file system, which can be a slow operation, as well as the need to secure the database of file hashes from tampering.

Today many Unix systems support file change monitoring: Linux has dnotify and inotify; Mac OS X has FSEvents, and other Unices have File Alteration Monitor. All these present an alternative method of identifying file changes and reviewing them for security implications.

Specialized Hardening

Many Unices have specialized hardening features that make it more difficult to exploit software vulnerabilities or to do so without leaving traces on the system and/or to show that the system is so hardened. Linux has been a popular platform for research in this area; even the National Security Agency (NSA) has released code to implement its strict security requirements under Linux. Here we outline two of the most popular Linux hardening packages. Other such packages exist for Linux and other Unices, some of which use innovative techniques such as virtualization to isolate sensitive data, but they are not covered here.

GRSec/PAX

The grsecurity package provides several major security enhancements for Linux. Perhaps the primary benefit is the flexible policies that define fine-grained permissions it can control. This role-based access control capability is especially powerful when coupled with grsecurity's ability to monitor system activity over a period of time and generate a minimum set of privileges for all users. Additionally, through the PAX subsystem, grsecurity manipulates program memory to make it very difficult to exploit many kinds of security vulnerabilities. Other benefits include a very robust auditing capability and other features that strengthen existing security features, such as chroot jails.

SELinux

Security Enhanced Linux, or SELinux, is a package developed by the NSA. It adds mandatory access control, or MAC, and related concepts to Linux. MAC involves assigning security attributes as well as system resources such as files and memory to users. When a user attempts to read, write, execute, or perform any other action on a system resource, the security attributes of the user and the resource are both used to determine whether the action is allowed, according to the security policies configured for the system. (See Figure 10.5.[8])

Systems Management Security

After hardening,a Unix host from network-borne attacks and hardening it from attacks performed by an authorized user of the machine, we will take a look at a few systems management issues. These topics arguably fall outside the purview of security as such; however, by taking certain considerations into account, systems management can both improve and simplify the work of securing a Unix system.

Account Management

User accounts can be thought of as keys to the "castle" of a system. As users require access to the system, they must be issued keys, or accounts, so they can use it. When a user no longer requires access to the system, her key should be taken away or at least disabled.

This sounds simple in theory, but account management in practice is anything but trivial. In all but the smallest environments, it is infeasible to manage user accounts without a centralized account directory where necessary changes can be made and propagated to every

---

8. Copyright RedHat, Inc, "Introduction to SELinux," retrieved May 14, 2012 from http://www.centos.org/docs/5/html/Deployment_Guide-en-US/ch-selinux.html.

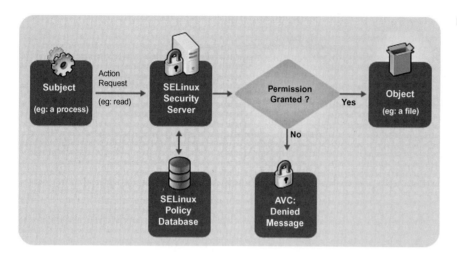

FIGURE 10.5   SELinux decision process.

server on the network. Through PAM, BSD authentication, and other mechanisms, modern Unices support LDAP, SQL databases, Windows NT and Active Directory, Kerberos, and myriad other centralized account directory technologies.

Patching

Outdated software is perhaps the number-one cause of easily preventable security incidents. Choosing a modern Unix with a robust upgrade mechanism and history of timely updates, at least for security fixes, makes it easier to keep software up to date and secure from well-known exploits. One of the main differentiating factors between the different Unix and Linux families is the software management and upgrade system. There are over 50 different package and upgrade management tools in use on the various Unix flavors.

Backups

When all else fails—especially when attackers have successfully modified or deleted data in ways that are difficult or impossible to positively identify—good backups will save the day. When backups are robust, reliable, and accessible, they put a ceiling on the amount of damage an attacker can do. Unfortunately, good backups don't help if the greatest damage comes from disclosure of sensitive information; in fact, backups could exacerbate the problem if they are not taken and stored in a secure way.

3. PROACTIVE DEFENSE FOR LINUX AND UNIX

As security professionals, we devote ourselves to defending systems from attack. However, it is important to understand the common tools, mind-sets, and motivations that drive attackers. This knowledge can prove invaluable

in mounting an effective defense against attack. It's also important to prepare for the possibility of a successful attack and to consider organizational issues so that a secure environment can be developed.

Vulnerability Assessment

A vulnerability assessment looks for security weaknesses in a system. Assessments have become an established best practice, incorporated into many standards and regulations. They can be network-centric or host-based.

Network-based Assessment

Network-centric vulnerability assessment looks for security weaknesses a system presents to the network. Unix has a rich heritage of tools for performing network vulnerability assessments. Most of these tools are available on most Unix flavors.

Nmap is a free, open-source tool for identifying hosts on a network and the services running on those hosts. It's a powerful tool for mapping out the true services being provided on a network. It's also easy to get started with nmap.

Nessus is another free network security tool, though its source code isn't available. It's designed to check for and optionally verify the existence of known security vulnerabilities. It works by looking at various pieces of information about a host on the network, such as detailed version information about the operating system and any software providing services on the network. This information is compared to a database that lists vulnerabilities known to exist in certain software configurations. In many cases, Nessus is also capable of confirming a match in the vulnerability database by attempting an exploit; however, this is likely to crash the service or even the entire system. Many other tools are available for performing network vulnerability assessments. Insecure.Org, the folks behind the nmap tool, also maintain a great list of security tools.[9]

Host-based Assessment

Several tools can examine the security settings of a system from a host-based perspective. These tools are designed to be run on the system that's being checked; no network connections are necessarily initiated. They check things such as file permissions and other insecure configuration settings on Unix systems.

One such tool, *lynis*, is available for various Linux distributions as well as some BSD variants. Another tool is the Linux Security Auditing Tool, or *lsat*. Ironically, lsat supports more versions of Unix than lynis does, including Solaris and AIX.

No discussion of host-based Unix security would be complete without mentioning *Bastille*. Although lynis and lsat are pure auditing tools that report on the status of various security-sensitive host configuration settings, Bastille was designed to help remediate these issues. Recent versions have a reporting-only mode that makes Bastille work like a pure auditing tool.

Incident Response Preparation

Regardless of how hardened a Unix system is, there is always a possibility that an attacker—whether it's a worm, a virus, or a sophisticated custom attack—will successfully compromise the security of the system. For this reason, it is important to think about how to respond to a wide variety of security incidents.

Predefined Roles and Contact List

A fundamental part of incident response preparation is to identify the roles that various personnel will play in the response scenario. The manual, hands-on gestalt of Unix systems administration has historically forced Unix systems administrators to be familiar with all aspects of the Unix systems they manage. These should clearly be on the incident response team. Database, application, backup, and other administrators should be on the team as well, at least as secondary personnel that can be called on as necessary.

Simple Message for End Users

Incident response is a complicated process that must deal with conflicting requirements to bring the systems back online while ensuring that any damage caused by the attack—as well as whatever security flaws were exploited to gain initial access—is corrected. Often, end users

without incident response training are the first to handle a system after a security incident has been identified. It is important that these users have clear, simple instructions in this case, to avoid causing additional damage or loss of evidence. In most situations, it is appropriate to simply unplug a Unix system from the network as soon as a compromise of its security is confirmed. It should not be used, logged onto, logged off from, turned off, disconnected from electrical power, or otherwise tampered with in any way. This simple action has the best chance, in most cases, to preserve the status of the incident for further investigation while minimizing the damage that could ensue.

Blue Team/Red Team Exercises

Any incident response plan, no matter how well designed, must be practiced to be effective. Regularly exercising these plans and reviewing the results are important parts of incident response preparation. A common way of organizing such exercises is to assign some personnel (the Red Team) to simulate a successful attack, while other personnel (the Blue Team) are assigned to respond to that attack according to the established incident response plan. These exercises, referred to as Red Team/Blue Team exercises, are invaluable for testing incident response plans. They are also useful in discovering security weaknesses and in fostering a sense of *esprit des corps* among the personnel involved.

Organizational Considerations

Various organizational and personnel management issues can also impact the security of Unix systems. Unix is a complex operating system. Many different duties must be performed in the day-to-day administration of Unix systems. Security suffers when a single individual is responsible for many of these duties; however, that is commonly the skill set of Unix system administration personnel.

Separation of Duties

One way to counter the insecurity of this situation is to force different individuals to perform different duties. Often, simply identifying independent functions, such as backups and log monitoring, and assigning appropriate permissions to independent individuals is enough. Log management, application management, user management, system monitoring, and backup operations are just some of the roles that can be separated.

Forced Vacations

Especially when duties are appropriately separated, unannounced forced vacations are a powerful way to bring fresh perspectives to security tasks. It's also an effective deterrent to internal fraud or mismanagement of security

---

9. Insecure.Org, 2008, "Top 100 Network Security Tools," retrieved October 9, 2008, from http://sectools.org.

responsibilities. A more robust set of requirements for organizational security comes from the Information Security Management Maturity Model, including its concepts of transparency, partitioning, separation, rotation, and supervision of responsibilities.[10]

4. SUMMARY

This chapter provides the technical security policies, requirements, and implementation details for eliminating the security weaknesses of Linux and Unix operating systems. The chapter also contains general requirements for Linux and Unix operating systems, as well as specific requirements. This chapter may also be used as a guide for enhancing the security configuration of any Linux or Unix-like system. The chapter also contains all requirements, check, and fix procedures that are expected to be applicable to most Linux and Unix-like operating systems.

Finally, let's move on to the real interactive part of this chapter: review questions/exercises, hands-on projects, case projects and optional team case project. The answers and/or solutions by chapter can be found in the Online Instructor's Solutions Manual.

CHAPTER REVIEW QUESTIONS/EXERCISES

True/False

1. True or False? Unix is a brand and an operating system specification.
2. True or False? The architecture of Unix operating systems is relatively difficult.
3. True or False? Defending from network-borne attacks is arguably the least important aspect of Unix security.
4. True or False? The first step in reducing an attack surface is to disable unnecessary services provided by a server.
5. True or False? Every listening port should not correspond to a necessary service that is well understood and securely configured.

Multiple Choice

1. What can be seen as another way to reduce the attack surface area?
   A. Dedicated service accounts
   B. PKI
   C. Two-factor authentication
   D. Strong authentication
   E. Access control

2. Information is vulnerable as it flows across the network, unless it is:
   A. log analyzed.
   B. clear texted.
   C. basically authenticated.
   D. encrypted.
   E. All of the above.

3. The Unix group mechanism allows for a single user to belong to one or more:
   A. attributes.
   B. ACLs.
   C. permissions.
   D. groups.
   E. focus groups.

4. Even after hardening a Unix system with restrictive user permissions and ACLs, it's important to maintain logs of:
   A. audit trails.
   B. system messages.
   C. system activity.
   D. bash.
   E. All of the above.

5. An additional source of audit trail data about system activity is the history logs kept by a login shell such as:
   A. log.
   B. file.
   C. password.
   D. bash.
   E. All of the above.

EXERCISE

Problem

Is Linux a secure operating system?

Hands-On Projects

Project

Is it more secure to compile driver support directly into the kernel, instead of making it a module?

Case Projects

Problem

Why does logging in as root from a remote machine always fail?

Optional Team Case Project

Problem

How do you enable shadow passwords on your Red Hat 4.2 or higher, or 5.x or higher Linux box?

---

10. ISECOM 2008, "Security Operations Maturity Architecture," retrieved October 9, 2008, from ISECOM: www.isecom.org/soma.

## Chapter 11

Internet Security

Jesse Walker
Intel Corporation

The Internet, with all its accompanying complications, is integral to our lives. The security problems besetting the Internet are legendary and have become daily annoyances—and worse—to many users. Given the Net's broad impact on our lives and the widespread security issues associated with it, it is worthwhile understanding what can be done to improve the immunity of our communications from attack.

The Internet can serve as a laboratory for studying network security issues; indeed, we can use it to study nearly every kind of security issue. We will pursue only a modest set of questions related to this theme. The goal of this chapter is to understand how cryptography can be used to address some of the security issues affecting communications protocols. To do so, it will be helpful to first understand the Internet architecture. After that we will survey the types of attacks that are possible against communications. With this background we will be able to understand how cryptography can be used to preserve the confidentiality and integrity of messages.

Our goal is modest: It is only to describe the network architecture and its cryptographic-based security mechanisms sufficiently to understand some of the major issues confronting security systems designers and to appreciate some of the major design decisions they have to make to address these issues.

1. INTERNET PROTOCOL ARCHITECTURE

The Internet was designed to create standardized communication between computers. Computers communicate by exchanging messages. The Internet supports message exchange through a mechanism called *protocols*. Protocols are very detailed and stereotyped rules explaining exactly how to exchange a particular set of messages. Each protocol is defined as a set of automata and a set of message formats. Each protocol specification defines one automaton for sending a message and another for receiving a message. The automata specify the timing of symbols that represent the messages; the automata implicitly define a grammar for the messages, indicating whether any particular message is meaningful or is interpreted by the receiver as gibberish. The protocol formats restrict the information that the protocol can express.

Security has little utility as an abstract, disembodied concept. What the word *security* should mean depends very much on the context in which it is applied. The architecture, design, and implementation of a system each determine the kind of vulnerabilities and opportunities that exist and which features are easy or hard to attack or defend.

It is fairly easy to understand why this is true. An attack on a system is an attempt to make the system act outside its specification. An attack is different from "normal" bugs that afflict computers and that occur through random interactions between the system's environment and undetected flaws in the system architecture, design, or implementation. An attack, on the other hand, is an explicit and systematic attempt by a party to search for flaws that make the computer act in a way its designers did not intend.

Computing systems consist of a large number of blocks or modules assembled together, each of which provides an intended set of functions. The system architecture hooks the modules together through *interfaces*, through which the various modules exchange information to activate the functions provided by each module in a coordinated way. These interfaces may be explicit, such as a formal grammar that the automata are supposed to conform, or they may be implicit, as when a parser accepts a larger grammar than is in the specification. An attacker exploits the architecture to compromise the computing system by interjecting inputs into these interfaces that do not conform to the intended specification of inputs into one of the automata. If the targeted module has not been carefully crafted, unexpected inputs can cause it to behave in unintended ways. This implies that the security of a system is determined by its decomposition into modules, which an adversary exploits by injecting messages into the interfaces the architecture exposes. Accordingly, no satisfying discussion of any system is feasible without an understanding of the system architecture. Our first goal, therefore, is to review the architecture of the

Internet communication protocols in an effort to gain a deeper understanding of its vulnerabilities.

Communications Architecture Basics

Since communication is an extremely complex activity, it should come as no surprise that the system components providing communication decompose into modules. One standard way to describe each communication module is as a black box with a well-defined service interface. A minimal communications service interface requires four primitives:

- *A send primitive, which an application using the communications module uses to send a message via the module to a peer application executing on another networked device.* The *send* primitive specifies a message payload and a destination, as well as a format for how messages are encoded from this information. The communication module responding to the *send* transmits the message to the specified destination, reporting its requestor as the message source.
- *A confirm primitive, to report that the module has sent a message to the designated destination in response to a send request or to report when the message transmission failed, along with any failure details that might be known.* It is possible to combine the *send* and *confirm* primitives, but network architectures rarely take this approach at their lowest layer. The *send* primitive is normally defined to allow the application to pass a message to the communications module for transmission by transferring control of a buffer containing the message. The *confirm* primitive then releases the buffer back to the calling application when the message has indeed been sent. This scheme affects "a conservation of buffers" and enables the communications module and the application using it to operate in parallel, thus enhancing the overall communication performance.
- *A listen primitive, which the receiving application uses to provide the communications module with buffers into which it should put messages arriving from the network.* Each buffer the application posts must be large enough to receive a message of the maximum expected size. The receiving automata must be carefully designed to respond correctly to arriving messages that are too large for the receive buffer.
- *A receive primitive, to deliver a received message from another party to the receiving application.* This releases a posted buffer back to the application and usually generates a signal to notify the application of message arrival. The released buffer contains the received message and the (alleged) message source.

Sometimes the *listen* primitive is replaced with a *release* primitive. In this model, the receive buffer is owned by the receiving communications module instead of the application, and the application must recycle buffers containing received messages back to the communication module upon completion. In this case the buffer size selected by the receiving module determines the maximum message size. In a moment we will explain how network protocols work around this restriction.

It is customary to include a fifth service interface primitive for communications modules:

- *A status primitive, to report diagnostic and performance information about the underlying communications.* This might report statistics, the state of active associations with other network devices, and the like.

Communications is affected by providing a communications module black box on systems, connected by a signaling medium. The medium connecting the two devices constitutes the network communications path. The media can consist of a direct link between the devices or, more commonly, several intermediate relay systems between the two communicating endpoints. Each relay system is itself a communicating device with its own communications module, which receives and then forward messages from the initiating system to the destination system.

Under this architecture, a message is transferred from an application on one networked system to an application on a second networked system as follows:

First, the application sourcing the message invokes the *send* primitive exported by its communications module. This causes the communications module to (attempt) to transmit the message to a destination provided by the application in the *send* primitive.

The communications module encodes the message onto the network's physical medium representing a link to another system. If the communications module implements a *best-effort* message service, it generates the *confirm* primitive as soon as the message has been encoded onto the medium. If the communication module implements a *reliable* message service, the communication delays generation of the *confirm* until it receives an acknowledgment from the message destination. If it has not received an acknowledgment from the receiver after some period of time, it generates a *confirm* indicating that the message delivery failed.

The encoded message traverses the network medium and is placed into a buffer by the receiving communications module of another system attached to the medium. This communications module examines the destination. The module then examines the destination specified by the message. If the module's local system is not the destination, the module reencodes the message onto the medium representing another link; otherwise the module uses the *deliver* primitive to pass the message to the receiving application.

Getting More Specific

This stereotyped description of networked communications is overly simplified. Actually, communications are torturously more difficult in real network modules. To overcome this complexity, communications modules are themselves partitioned further into layers, each providing a different networking function. The Internet decomposes communications into five layers of communications modules:

- The PHY layer
- The MAC layer
- The network layer
- The transport layer
- The sockets layer

These layers are augmented by a handful of cross-layer coordination modules. The Internet depends on the following cross-layer modules:

- ARP
- DHCP
- DNS
- ICMP
- Routing

An application using networking is also part of the overall system design, and the way it uses the network has to be taken into consideration to understand system security.

The PHY Layer

The PHY (pronounced *fie*) layer is technically not part of the Internet architecture per se, but Ethernet jacks and cables, modems, Wi-Fi adapters, and the like represent the most visible aspect of networking, and no security treatment of the Internet can ignore the PHY layer entirely.

The PHY layer module is medium dependent, with a different design for each type of medium: Ethernet, phone lines, Wi-Fi, cellular phone, OC-768, and the like are based on different PHY layer designs. It is the job of the PHY layer to translate between digital bits as represented on a computing device and the analog signals crossing the specific physical medium used by the PHY. This translation is a physics exercise.

To send a message, the PHY layer module encodes each bit of each message from the sending device as a media-specific signal or wave form, representing the bit value 1 or 0. Once encoded, the signal propagates along the medium from the sender to the receiver. The PHY layer module at the receiver decodes the medium-specific signal back into a bit. There are often special symbols representing such things as the frame start and frame end symbols, and training symbols to synchronize the receiver with the transmitter. These special symbols provide control only and are distinct from the symbols representing bits. Wave forms different from the defined symbols are undefined and discarded by the receiver.

It is possible for the encoding step at the transmitting PHY layer module to fail, for a signal to be lost or corrupted while it crosses the medium, and for the decoding step to fail at the receiving PHY layer module. It is the responsibility of higher layers to detect and recover from these potential failures.

The MAC Layer

Like the PHY layer, the MAC (pronounced *mack*) layer is not properly a part of the Internet architecture, but no satisfactory security discussion is possible without considering it. The MAC module is the "application" that uses and controls a particular PHY layer module. A MAC layer is always designed in tandem with a specific PHY (or vice versa), so a PHY–MAC pair together is often referred to as the *data link* layer.

MAC is an acronym for *media access control*. As its name suggests, the MAC layer module determines when to send and receive *frames*, which are messages encoded in a media-specific format. The job of the MAC is to pass frames over a link between the MAC layer modules on different systems.

Although not entirely accurate, it is useful to think of a MAC module as creating *links*, each of which is a communication channel between different MAC modules. It is further useful to distinguish physical links and virtual links. A *physical link* is a direct point-to-point channel between the MAC layers in two endpoint devices. A *virtual link* can be thought of as a shared medium to which more than two devices can connect at the same time. There are no physical endpoints per se; the medium acts as though it is multiplexing links between each pair of attached devices. Some media such as modern Ethernet are implemented as physical point-to-point links but act more like virtual links in that more than a single destination is reachable via the link. This is accomplished by MAC layer switching, which is also called *bridging*. Timing requirements for coordination among communicating MAC layer modules make it difficult to build worldwide networks based on MAC layer switching, however. Mobile devices such as smart phones, laptops, and notepads also make large-scale bridging difficult, since these devices can shift their attachment points to the network, thus invalidating the data structures used by switches to effect switching. Finally, some media such as Wi-Fi (IEEE 802.11) are *shared* or *broadcast media*. In a shared medium all devices can access the channel, and the MAC design must specify an access control policy that the MAC enforces; this behavior is what gives the MAC layer its name. Ethernet was originally a shared medium, but evolved into its present switched point-to-point structure in order to simplify medium access control. The access control function of a MAC is always a complex security concern.

A MAC frame consists of a header and a data payload. The frame header typically specifies information such as the source and destination for the link endpoints. Devices attached to the medium via their MAC + PHY modules are identified by *MAC addresses*. Each MAC module has its own MAC address assigned by its manufacturer and is supposed to be a globally unique identifier. The *destination address* in a frame allows a particular MAC module to identify frames intended for it, and the *source address* allows the receiver to identify the purported frame source. The frame header also usually includes a preamble, which is a set of special PHY timing signals used to synchronize the interpretation of the PHY layer data signals representing the frame bits.

The payload portion of a frame is the data to be transferred across the network. The maximum payload size is always fixed by the medium type. It is becoming customary for most MACs to support a maximum payload size of 1500 bytes = 12,000 bits, but this is not universal. The maximum fixed size allows the MAC to make efficient use of the underlying physical medium. Since messages can be of an arbitrary length exceeding this fixed size, a higher-layer function is needed to partition messages into segments of the appropriate length.

As we have seen, it is possible for bit errors to creep into communications as signals representing bits traverse the PHY medium. MAC layers differ a great deal in how they respond to errors. Some PHY layers, such as the Ethernet PHY, experience exceedingly low error rates, and for this reason, the MAC layers for these PHYs make no attempt to more than detect errors and discard the mangled frames. Indeed, with these MACs it is cheaper for the Internet to resend message segments at a higher layer than at the MAC layer. These are called *best-effort MACs*. Others, such as the Wi-Fi MAC, experience high error rates due to the shared nature of the channel and natural interference among radio sources; experience has shown that these MACs can deliver better performance by retransmitting damaged or lost frames. It is customary for most MAC layers to append a checksum computed over the entire frame, called *a frame check sequence* (FCS). The FCS allows the receiver to detect bit errors accumulated due to random noise and other physical phenomena during transmission and due to decoding errors. Most MACs discard frames with FCS errors. Some MAC layers also perform error correction on the received bits to remove random bit errors rather than relying on retransmissions.

The Network Layer

The purpose of the network layer module is to represent messages in a media-independent manner and to forward them between various MAC layer modules representing different links. The media-independent message format is called an *Internet Protocol*, or *IP, datagram*. The network layer implements the IP layer and is the lowest layer of the Internet architecture per se.

As well as providing media independence, the network layer provides a vital forwarding function that works even for a worldwide network like the Internet. It is impractical to form a link directly between each communicating system on the planet. Indeed, the cabling costs alone are prohibitive—no one wants billions, or even dozens, of cables connecting their computer to other computers—and too many MAC + PHY interfaces can quickly exhaust the power budget for a single computing system. Hence, each machine is attached by a small number of links to other devices, and some of the machines with multiple links comprise a *switching fabric*. The computing systems constituting the switching fabric are called *routers*.

The forwarding function supported by the network layer module is the key component of a router and works as follows: When a MAC module receives a frame, it passes the frame payload to the network layer module. The payload consists of an *IP datagram*, which is the media-independent representation of the message. The receiving network layer module examines the datagram to see whether to deliver it locally or to pass it on toward the datagram's ultimate destination. To accomplish the latter, the network layer module consults a *forwarding table* to identify some neighbor router closer to the ultimate destination than itself. The forwarding table also identifies the MAC module to use to communicate with the selected neighbor and passes the datagram to that MAC layer module. The MAC module in turn retransmits the datagram as a frame encoded for its medium across its link to the neighbor. This process happens recursively until the datagram is delivered to its ultimate destination.

The network layer forwarding function is based on *IP addresses*, a concept that is critical to understanding the Internet architecture. An IP address is a media-independent name for one of the MAC layer modules within a computing system. Each IP address is structured to represent the "location" of the MAC module within the entire Internet. This notion of location is relative to the graph comprising routers and their interconnecting links, called the *network topology*, not to actual geography. Since this name represents a location, the forwarding table within each IP module can use the IP address of the ultimate destination as a sort of signpost pointing at the MAC module with the greatest likelihood of leading to the ultimate destination of a particular datagram.

An IP address is different from the corresponding MAC address already described. A MAC address is a permanent, globally unique identifier, identifying a particular interface on a particular computing device, whereas an IP address can be dynamic due to device mobility. An IP address cannot be assigned by the equipment manufacturer, since a computing device can change locations frequently. Hence, IP addresses are administered and blocks allocated to different organizations with an Internet presence. It is common, for instance, for an Internet service provider (ISP) to acquire a large block of IP addresses for use by its customers.

An IP datagram has a structure similar to that of a frame: It consists of an IP header, which is "extra" overhead used to control the way a datagram passes through the Internet, and a data payload, which contains the message being transferred. The IP header indicates the ultimate source and destinations, represented as IP addresses.

The IP header format limits the size of an IP datagram payload to 64 K ($2^{16} = 65,536$) bytes. It is common to limit datagram sizes to the underlying media size, although datagrams larger than this do occur. This means that normally each MAC layer frame can carry a single IP datagram as its data payload. IP version 4 or higher, still the dominant version deployed on the Internet today, allows fragmentation of larger datagrams, to split large datagrams into chunks small enough to fit the limited frame size of the underlying MAC layer medium. IPv4 or higher reassembles any fragmented datagrams at the ultimate destination. IP version 6 or higher, which is becoming more widely deployed due to its widespread use in smart phone networks and Asia, does not support fragmentation and reassembly; this removes from IPv6 or higher one of the attack vectors enabled by IPv4 or higher.

Network layer forwarding of IP datagrams is best effort and is not reliable. Network layer modules along the path taken by any message can lose and reorder datagrams. It is common for the network layer in a router to recover from congestion—that is, when the router is overwhelmed by more receive frames than it can process—by discarding late-arriving frames until the router has caught up with its forwarding workload. The network layer can reorder datagrams when the Internet topology changes, because a new path between source and destination might be shorter or longer than an old path, so datagrams in flight before the change can arrive after frames sent following the change. The Internet architecture delegates recovery from these problems to high-layer modules.

Some applications, such as those utilizing voice and video, do not respond well to reordering because it imposes a severe performance penalty on the application. In order to better accommodate the needs of these types of message traffic, the Internet has begun to implement protocols such as MPLS, which mimics the switched circuit mechanisms

of phone networks. That is, these protocols create *flows* through the Internet that suppress datagram reordering. Circuit switching uses network resources differently than best-effort forwarding, and network links in the core of the network usually require greater bandwidth for the two technologies to successfully coexist.

The Transport Layer

The transport layer is implemented by TCP and similar protocols. Not all transport protocols provide the same level of service as TCP, but a description of TCP will suffice to help us understand the issues addressed by the transport layer. The transport layer provides a multitude of functions.

First, the transport layer creates and manages instances of two-way channels between communication endpoints. These channels are called *connections*. Each connection represents a virtual endpoint between a pair of communication endpoints. A connection is named by a pair of IP addresses and *port numbers*. Two devices can support simultaneous connections using different port numbers for each connection. It is common to differentiate applications on the same host through the use of port numbers.

A second function of the transport layer is to support delivery of messages of arbitrary length. The 64 K byte limit of the underlying IP module is too small to carry really large messages, and the transport layer module at the message source chops messages into pieces called *segments* that are more easily digestible by lower-layer communications modules. The segment size is negotiated between the two transport endpoints during connection setup. The segment size is chosen by discovering the smallest maximum frame size supported by any MAC + PHY link on the path through the Internet used by the connection setup messages. Once this is known, the transmitter typically partitions a large message into segments no larger than this size, plus room for an IP header. The transport layer module passes each segment to the network layer module, where it becomes the payload for a single IP datagram. The destination network layer module extracts the payload from the IP datagram and passes it to the transport layer module, which interprets the information as a message segment. The destination transport reassembles this into the original message once all the necessary segments arrive.

Of course, as noted, MAC frames and IP datagrams can be lost in transit, so some segments can be lost. It is the responsibility of the transport layer module to detect this loss and retransmit the missing segments. This is accomplished by a sophisticated acknowledgment algorithm defined by the transport layer. The destination sends a special acknowledgment message, often piggybacked with a data segment being sent in the opposite direction, for each segment that arrives. Acknowledgments can be lost as well, and if the message source does not receive the acknowledgment within a time window, the source retransmits the unacknowledged segment. This process is repeated a number of times, and if the failure continues, the network layer tears down the connection because it cannot fulfill its reliability commitment.

One reason for message loss is congestion at routers, something blind retransmission of unacknowledged segments will only exacerbate. The network layer is also responsible for implementing congestion control algorithms as part of its transmit function. TCP, for instance, lowers its transmit rate whenever it fails to receive an acknowledgment message in time, and it slowly increases its rate of transmission until another acknowledgment is lost. This allows TCP to adapt to congestion in the network, helping to minimize frame loss.

It can happen that segments arrive at the destination out of order, since some IP datagrams for the same connection could traverse the Internet through different paths due to dynamic changes in the underlying network topology. The transport layer is responsible for delivering the segments in the order sent, so the receiver caches any segments that arrive out of order prior to delivery. The TCP reordering algorithm is closed tied to the acknowledgment and congestion control scheme so that the receiver never has to buffer too many out-of-order received segments and the sender not too many sent but unacknowledged segments.

Segment data arriving at the receiver can be corrupted due to undetected bit errors on the data link and copy errors within routers and the sending and receiving computing systems. Accordingly, all transport layers use a checksum algorithm called a *cyclic redundancy check* (CRC) to detect such errors. The receiving transport layer module typically discards segments with errors detected by the CRC algorithm, and recovery occurs through retransmission by the sender when it fails to receive an acknowledgment from the receiver for a particular segment.

The Sockets Layer

The top layer of the Internet, the sockets layer, does not *per se* appear in the architecture at all. The sockets layer provides a set of interfaces, each of which represents a logical communications endpoint. An application can use the sockets layer to create, manage, and destroy connection instances using a socket as well as send and receive messages over the connection. The sockets layer has been designed to hide much of the complexity of the transport layer, thereby making TCP easier to use. The sockets layer has been highly optimized over the years to deliver as much performance as possible, but it does impose a performance penalty. Applications with very demanding performance requirements tend to utilize the transport

layer directly instead of through the sockets layer module, but this comes with a very high cost in terms of software maintenance.

In most implementations of these communications modules, each message is copied twice, at the sender and the receiver. Most operating systems are organized into user space, which is used to run applications, and kernel space, where the operating system itself runs. The sockets layer occupies the boundary between user space and kernel space. The sockets layer's *send* function copies a message from memory controlled by the sending application into a buffer controlled by the kernel for transmission. This copy prevents the application from changing a message it has posted to send, but it also permits the application and kernel to continue their activities in parallel, thus better utilizing the device's computing resources. The sockets layer invokes the transport layer, which partitions the message buffer into segments and passes the address of each segment to the network layer. The network layer adds its headers to form datagrams from the segments and invokes the right MAC layer module to transmit each datagram to its next hop. A second copy occurs at the boundary between the network layer and the MAC layer, since the data link must be able to asynchronously match transmit requests from the network layer to available transmit slots on the medium provided by its PHY. This process is reversed at the receiver, with a copy of datagrams across the MAC-network layer boundary and of messages between the socket layer and application.

Address Resolution Protocol

The network layer uses Address Resolution Protocol, or ARP, to translate IP addresses into MAC addresses, which it needs to give to the MAC layer in order to deliver frames to the appropriate destination.

The ARP module asks the question, "Who is using IP address *X*?" The requesting ARP module uses a request/response protocol, with the MAC layer broadcasting the ARP module's requests to all the other devices on the same physical medium segment. A receiving ARP module generates a response only if its network layer has assigned the IP address to one of its MAC modules. Responses are addressed to the requester's MAC address. The requesting ARP module inserts the response received in an address translation table used by the network layer to identify the next hop for all datagrams it forwards.

Dynamic Host Configuration Protocol

Remember that unlike MAC addresses, IP addresses cannot be assigned in the factory, because they are dynamic and must reflect a device's current location within the Internet. A MAC module uses Dynamic Host

Configuration Protocol, or DHCP, to acquire an IP address for itself to reflect the device's current location with respect to the Internet topology.

DHCP makes the request: "Please configure my MAC module with an IP address." When one of a device's MAC layer modules connects to a new medium, it invokes DHCP to make this request. The associated DHCP module generates such a request that conveys the MAC address of the MAC module, which the MAC layer module broadcasts to the other devices attached to the same physical medium segment. A DHCP server responds with a unicast DHCP response binding an IP address to the MAC address. When it receives the response, the requesting DHCP module passes the assigned IP address to the network layer to configure in its address translation table.

In addition to binding an IP address to the MAC module used by DHCP, the response also contains a number of network configuration parameters, including the address of one or more routers, to enable reaching arbitrary destinations, the maximum datagram size supported, and the addresses of other servers, such as DNS servers, that translate human-readable names into IP addresses.

Domain Naming Service

IP and MAC addresses are efficient means for identifying different network interfaces, but human beings are incapable of using these as reliably as computing devices can. Instead, human beings rely on names to identify the computing devices with which they want to communication. These names are centrally managed and called *domain names*. The Domain Naming Service, or DNS, is a mechanism for translating human-readable names into IP addresses.

The translation from human-readable names to IP addresses happens within the socket layer module. An application opens a socket with the name of the intended destination. As the first step of opening a connection to that destination, the socket sends a request to a DNS server, asking the server to translate the name into an IP address. When the server responds, the socket can open the connection to the right destination, using the IP address provided.

It is becoming common for devices to register their IP addresses under their names with DNS once DHCP has completed. This permits other devices to locate the registering device so that they can send messages to it.

Internet Control Message Protocol

Internet Control Message Protocol (ICMP) is an important diagnostic tool for troubleshooting the Internet. Though ICMP provides many specialized message services, three are particularly important:

- *Ping*. Ping is a request/response protocol designed to determine the reachability of another IP address. The

requestor sends a ping request message to a designated IP address. If the ping message is delivered, the interface using the destination IP address sends a ping response message to the IP address that sourced the request. The responding ICMP module copies the contents of the ping request into the ping response so that the requestor can match responses to requests. The requestor uses pings to measure the roundtrip time to a destination, among other things.

- *Traceroute*. Traceroute is another request/response protocol. An ICMP module generates a traceroute request to discover the path it is using to traverse the Internet to a destination IP address. The requesting ICMP module transmits a destination. Each router that handles the traceroute request adds a description of its own IP address that received the message and then forwards the updated traceroute request. The destination sends all this information back to the message source in a traceroute response message.

- *Destination unreachable*. When a router receives a datagram for which it has no next hop, it generates a "destination unreachable" message and sends it back to the datagram source. When the message is delivered, the ICMP module marks the forwarding table of the message source so that its network layer will reject further attempts to send messages to the destination IP address. An analogous process happens at the ultimate destination when a message is delivered to a network layer, but the application targeted to receive the message is no longer online. The purpose of "destination unreachable" messages is to suppress messages that will never be successfully delivered in order to reduce network congestion.

Routing

The last cross-layer module we'll discuss is *routing*. Routing is a middleware application to maintain the forwarding tables used by the network layer. Each router advertises itself by periodically broadcasting "hello" messages through each of its MAC interfaces. This allows routers to discover the presence or loss of all neighboring routers, letting them construct the one-hop topology of the part of the Internet directly visible through their directly attached media. The routing application in a router then uses a sophisticated gossiping mechanism to exchange this view of the local topology with their neighbors. Since some of a router's neighbors are not its own direct neighbors, this allows each router to learn the two-hop topology of the Internet. This process repeats recursively until each router knows the entire topology of the Internet. The cost of using each link is part of the information gossiped. A routing module receiving this information uses all of it to compute a lowest-cost route to each destination. Once this is accomplished, the routing module reconfigures the forwarding table maintained by its network layer module. The routine module updates the forwarding table whenever the Internet topology changes, so each network layer can make optimal forwarding decisions in most situations and at the very worst reach any other device that is also connected to the Internet.

There are many different routing protocols, each of which is based on different gossiping mechanisms. The most widely deployed routing protocol between different administrative domains within the Internet is the border gateway protocol (BGP). The most widely deployed routing protocols within wired networks controlled by a single administrative domain are OSPF and RIP. AODV, OLSR, and TBRPF are commonly used in Wi-Fi meshes. Different routing protocols are used in different environments because each one addresses different scaling and administrative issues.

Applications

Applications are the ultimate reason for networking, and the Internet architecture has been shaped by applications' needs. All communicating applications define their own language in which to express what they need to say. Applications generally use the sockets layer to establish communication channels, which they then use for their own purposes.

Since the network modules have been designed to be a generic communications vehicle, that is, designed to meet the needs of all (or at least most) applications, it is rarely meaningful for the network to attempt to make statements on behalf of the applications. There is widespread confusion on this point around authentication and key management, which are the source of many exploitable security flaws.

2. AN INTERNET THREAT MODEL

Now that we have reviewed the architecture of the Internet protocol suite, it is possible to constructively consider the security issues it raises. Before doing so, let's first set the scope of the discussion.

There are two general approaches to attacking a networked computer. The first is to compromise one of the communicating parties so that it responds to queries with lies or otherwise communicates in a manner not foreseen by the system designers of the receiver. For example, it has become common to receive email with virus-infected attachments, whereby opening the attachment infects the receiver with the virus. These messages typically are sent by a machine that has already been compromised, so the sender is no longer acting as intended by the manufacturer of the computing system. Problems of this type are

called *Byzantine failures*, named after the Byzantine Generals problem.

The Byzantine Generals problem imagines several armies surrounding Byzantium. The generals commanding these armies can communicate only by exchanging messages transported by couriers between them. Of course the couriers can be captured and the messages replaced by forgeries, but this is not really the issue, since it is possible to devise message schemes that detect lost messages or forgeries. All the armies combined are sufficient to overwhelm the defenses of Byzantium, but if even one army fails to participate in a coordinated attack, the armies of Byzantium have sufficient strength to repulse the attack. Each general must make a decision as to whether to participate in an attack on Byzantium at dawn or withdraw to fight another day. The question is how to determine the veracity of the messages received on which the decision to attack will be made—that is, whether it is possible to detect that one or more generals have become traitors and so will say their armies will join the attack when in fact they plan to hold back so that their allies will be slaughtered by the Byzantines.

Practical solutions addressing Byzantine failures fall largely within the purview of platform rather than network architecture, although the interconnectivity topology is an important consideration. For example, since viruses infect a platform by buffer overrun attacks, platform mechanisms to render buffer overrun attacks futile are needed. Secure logging, to make an accurate record of messages exchanged, is a second deterrent to these sorts of attacks; the way to accomplish secure logging is usually a question of platform design. Most self-propagating viruses and worms utilize the Internet to propagate, but they do not utilize any feature of the Internet architecture per se for their success. The success of these attacks instead depends on the architecture, design, implementation, and policies of the receiving system. Although these sorts of problems are important, we will rarely focus on security issues stemming from Byzantine failures.

What will instead be the focus of the discussion are attacks on the messages exchanged between computers themselves. As we will see, even with this more limited scope, there are plenty of opportunities for things to go wrong.

The Dolev–Yao Adversary Model

Security analyses of systems traditionally begin with a model of the attacker, and we follow this tradition. Daniel Dolev and Andrew Chi-Chih Yao formulated the standard attack model against messages exchanged over a network. The *Dolev-Yao model* makes the following assumptions about an attacker:

- *Eavesdrop.* An adversary can listen to any message exchanged through the network.

- *Forge*. An adversary can create and inject entirely new messages into the datastream or change messages in flight; these messages are called *forgeries*.
- *Replay*. A special type of forgery, called a *replay*, is distinguished. To replay a message, the adversary resends legitimate messages that were sent earlier.
- *Delay and rush*. An adversary can delay the delivery of some messages or accelerate the delivery of others.
- *Reorder*. An adversary can alter the order in which messages are delivered.
- *Delete*. An adversary can destroy in-transit messages, either selectively or all the messages in a datastream.

This model assumes a very powerful adversary, and many people who do not design network security solutions sometimes assert that the model grants adversaries an unrealistic amount of power to disrupt network communications. However, experience demonstrates that it is a reasonably realistic set of assumptions in practice; examples of each threat abound, as we will see. One of the reasons for this is that the environment in which the network operates is exposed and therefore open to attack by a suitably motivated adversary; unlike memory or microprocessors or other devices internal to a computer, there is almost no assurance that the network medium will be deployed in a "safe" way (Indeed, malware has progressed to the point where internal buses and memories can no longer be considered secure against knowledgeable attackers, which is forcing a migration of network security techniques into the platforms themselves). That is, it is comparatively easy for an attacker to anonymously access the physical network fabric, or at least the medium monitored to identify attacks against the medium and the networked traffic it carries. And since a network is intended as a generic communications vehicle, it becomes necessary to adopt a threat model that addresses the needs of all possible applications.

Layer Threats

With the Dolev−Yao model in hand, we can examine each of the architectural components of the Internet protocol suite for vulnerabilities. We next look at threats each component of the Internet architecture exposes through the prism of this model. The first Dolev−Yao assumption about adversaries is that they can eavesdrop on any communications.

Eavesdropping

An attacker can eavesdrop on a communications medium by connecting a receiver to the medium. Ultimately, such a connection has to be implemented at the PHY layer because an adversary has to access some physical media somewhere to be able to listen to anything at all. This connection to the PHY medium might be legitimate, such as when an authorized device is uncompromised, or illegitimate, such as an illegal wiretap; it can be intentional, as when an eavesdropper installs a rogue device, or unintentional, such as a laptop with wireless capabilities that will by default attempt to connect to any Wi-Fi network within range.

With a PHY layer connection, the eavesdropper can receive the analog signals on the medium and decode them into bits. Because of the limited scope of the PHY layer function—there are no messages, only analog signals representing bits and special control symbols—the damage an adversary can do with only PHY layer functionality is rather limited. In particular, to make sense of the bits, an adversary has to impose the higher-layer frame and datagram formats onto the received bits. That is, any eavesdropping attack has to take into account at least the MAC layer to learn anything meaningful about the communications. Real eavesdroppers are more sophisticated than this: They know how to interpret the bits as a medium-specific encoding with regard to the frames that are used by the MAC layer. They also know how to extract the media-independent representation of datagrams conveyed within the MAC frames, as well as how to extract the transport layer segments from the datagrams, which can be reassembled into application messages.

The defenses erected against any threat give some insight into the perceived danger of the threat. People are generally concerned about eavesdropping, and it is easy to illicitly attach listening devices to most PHY media, but detection and removal of wiretaps has not evolved into a comparatively large industry. An apparent explanation of why this is so is that it is easier and more cost effective for an attacker to compromise a legitimate device on the network and configure it to eavesdrop than it is to install an illegitimate device. The evidence for this view is that the antivirus/antibot industry is gigantic by comparison.

There is another reason that an antiwiretapping industry has never developed for the Internet. Almost every MAC module supports a special mode of operation called *promiscuous mode*. A MAC module in promiscuous mode receives every frame appearing on the medium, not just the frames addressed to itself. This allows one MAC module to snoop on frames that are intended for other parties. Promiscuous mode was intended as a troubleshooting mechanism to aid network administrators in diagnosing the source of problems. However, it is also a mechanism that can be easily abused by anyone motivated to enable promiscuous mode on their own networking devices.

Forgeries

A second Dolev−Yao assumption is that the adversary can forge messages. Eavesdropping is usually fairly innocuous compared to forgeries, because eavesdropping merely leaks information, whereas forgeries cause an unsuspecting receiver to take actions based on false information. Hence, the prevention or detection of forgeries is one of the central goals of network security mechanisms. Different kinds of forgeries are possible for each architectural component of the Internet. We will consider only a few for each layer of the Internet protocol suite, to give a taste of their variety and ingenuity.

Unlike the eavesdropping threat, where knowledge of higher layers is essential to any successful compromise, an attacker with only a PHY layer transmitter (and no higher-layer mechanisms) can disrupt communications by *jamming* the medium—that is, outputting noise onto the medium in an effort to disrupt communications. A jammer creates signals that do not necessarily correspond to any wave forms corresponding to bit or other control symbols. The goal of a pure PHY layer jammer is denial of service (DoS)—that is, to fill the medium sufficiently so that no communications can take place.

Sometimes it is feasible to create a jamming device that is sensitive to the MAC layer formats above it, to selectively jam only some frames. Selective jamming requires a means to interpret bits received from the medium as a higher-layer frame or datagram, and the targeted frames to jam are recognized by some criterion, such as being sent from or to a particular address. So that it can enable its own transmitter before the frame has been entirely received by its intended destination, the jammer's receiver must recognize the targeted frames before they are fully transmitted. When this is done correctly, the jammer's transmitter interferes with the legitimate signals, thereby introducing bit errors in the legitimate receiver's decoder. This results in the legitimate receiver's MAC layer detecting the bit errors while trying to verify the frame check sequence, causing it to discard the frame. Selective jamming is harder to implement than continuous jamming, but it is also much harder to detect, because the jammer's signal source transmits only when legitimate devices transmit as well, and only the targeted frames are disrupted. Successful selective jamming usually causes administrators to look for the source of the communications failure on one of the communicating devices instead of in the network for a jammer.

There is also a higher-layer analog to jamming, called *message flooding*. Denial of service (DoS) is also the goal of message flooding. The technique used by message flooding is to create and send messages at a rate high enough to exhaust some resource. It is popular today, for instance, for hackers to compromise thousands of unprotected machines, which they use to generate simultaneous messages to a targeted site. Examples of this kind of attack are to completely fill the physical medium

connecting the targeted site to the Internet with network layer datagrams—this is usually hard or impossible—or to generate transport layer connection requests at a rate faster than the targeted site can respond. Other variants—request operations that lead to disk I/O or require expensive cryptographic operations—are also common. Message flooding attacks have the property that they are legitimate messages from authorized parties but simply timed so that collectively their processing exceeds the maximum capacity of the targeted system.

Let's turn away from resource-clogging forgeries and examine forgeries designed to cause a receiver to take an unintended action. It is possible to construct this type of forgery at any higher layer: forged frames, datagrams, network segments, or application messages.

To better understand how forgeries work, we need to examine Internet "identities" more closely—MAC addresses, IP addresses, transport port numbers, and DNS names—as well as the modules that use or support their use. The threats are a bit different at each layer.

Recall that each MAC layer module is manufactured with its own "hardware" address, which is supposed to be a globally unique identifier for the MAC layer module instance. The hardware address is configured in the factory into nonvolatile memory. At boot time, the MAC address is transferred from nonvolatile memory into operational RAM maintained by the MAC module. A transmitting MAC layer module inserts the MAC address from RAM into each frame it sends, thereby advertising an "identity." The transmitter also inserts the MAC address of the intended receiver on each frame, and the receiving MAC layer matches the MAC address in its own RAM against the destination field in each frame sent over the medium. The receiver ignores the frame if the MAC addresses don't match and receives the frame otherwise.

In spite of this system, it is useful—even necessary sometimes—for a MAC module to change its MAC address. For example, sometimes a manufacturer accidentally recycles MAC addresses so that two different modules receive the same MAC address in the factory. If both devices are deployed on the same network, neither works correctly until one of the two changes its address. Because of this problem, all manufacturers provide a way for the MAC module to alter the address in RAM. This can always be specified by software via the MAC module's device driver, by replacing the address retrieved from hardware at boot time.

Since the MAC address can be changed, attacks will find it. A common attack in Wi-Fi networks, for instance, is for the adversary to put the MAC module of the attacking device into promiscuous mode, to receive frames from other nearby systems. It is usually easy to identify another client device from the received frames and extract its MAC address. The attacker then reprograms its own MAC module to transmit frames using the address of its victim. A goal of this attack is usually to "hijack" the session of a customer paying for Wi-Fi service; that is, the attacker wants free Internet access for which someone else has already paid. Another goal of such an attack is often to avoid attribution of the actions being taken by the attacker; any punishment for antisocial or criminal behavior will likely be attributed to the victim instead of the attacker because all the frames that were part of the behavior came from the victim's address.

A similar attack is common at the network layer. The adversary will snoop on the IP addresses appearing in the datagrams encoded in the frames and use these instead of their own IP addresses to source IP datagrams. This is a more powerful attack than that of utilizing only a MAC address, because IP addresses are global; an IP address is an Internet-wide locator, whereas a MAC address is only an identifier on the medium to which the device is physically connected.

Manipulation of MAC and IP addresses leads directly to a veritable menagerie of forgery attacks and enables still others. A very selective list of examples must suffice to illustrate the ingenuity of attackers:

- TCP uses sequence numbers as part of its reliability scheme. TCP is supposed to choose the first sequence number for a connection randomly. If an attacker can predict the first sequence number for a TCP connection, an attacker who spoofs the IP address of one of the parties to the connection can hijack the session by interjecting its own datagrams into the flow that use the correct sequence numbers. This desynchronizes the retry scheme for the device being spoofed, which then drops out from the conversation. This attack seems to have become relatively less common than other attacks over the past few years, since most TCP implementations have begun to utilize better random number generators to seed their sequence numbers.

- An attacker can generate an ARP response to any ARP request, thus claiming to use any requested IP address. This is a common method to hijack another machine's IP address; it is a very effective technique when the attacker has a fast machine and the victim machine has less processing power, and so responds more slowly.

- An attacker can generate DHCP response messages replying to DHCP requests. This technique is often used as part of a larger forgery, such as the evil twin attack, whereby an adversary masquerades as an access point for a Wi-Fi public hot spot. The receipt of DHCP response messages convinces the victim it is connecting to an access point operated by the legitimate hotspot.

- A variant is to generate a DHCP request with the hardware MAC address of another device. This method is useful when the attacker wants to ascribe action it takes over the Internet to another device.

- An attacker can impersonate the DNS server, responding to requests to resolve human-readable names into IP addresses. The IP address in the response messages points the victim to a site controlled by the attacker. This is becoming a common attack used by criminals attempting to commit financial fraud, such as stealing credit card numbers.

Replay

Replay is a special forgery attack. It occurs when an attacker records frames or datagrams and then retransmits them unchanged at a later time.

This might seem like an odd thing to do, but replay attacks are an especially useful way to attack stateful messaging protocols, such as a routing protocol. Since the goal of a routing protocol is to allow every router to know the current topology of the network, a replayed routing message can cause the routers receiving it to utilize out-of-date information.

An attacker might also respond to an ARP request sent to a sabotaged node or to a mobile device that has migrated to another part of the Internet by sending a replayed ARP response. This replay indicates the node is still present, thus masking the true network topology.

Replay is also often a valuable tool for attacking a message encryption scheme. By retransmitting a message, an attacker can sometimes learn valuable information from a message decrypted and then retransmitted without encryption on another link.

A primary use of replay, however, is to attack session start-up protocols. Protocol start-up procedures establish session state, which is used to operate the link or connection and determine when some classes of failures occur. Since this state is not yet established when the session begins, start-up messages replayed from prior instances of the protocol will fool the receiver into allocating a new session. This is a common DoS technique.

Delay and Rushing

Delay is a natural consequence of implementations of the Internet architecture. Datagrams from a single connection typically transit a path across the Internet in bursts. This happens because applications at the sender, when sending large messages, tend to send messages larger than a single datagram. The transport layer partitions these messages into segments to fit the maximum segment size along the path to the destination. The MAC tends to output all the frames together as a single blast after it has accessed the medium. Therefore, routers with many links can receive multiple datagram bursts at the same time. When this happens, a router has to temporarily buffer the burst, since it can output only one frame conveying a datagram per link at a time. Simultaneous arrival of bursts of datagrams is one source of congestion in routers. This condition usually manifests itself at the application by slow communications time over the Internet. Delay can also be intentionally introduced by routers, such as via traffic shaping.

Attackers can induce delays in several ways. We illustrate this idea by describing two different attacks. It is not uncommon for an attacker to take over a router, and when this happens, the attacker can introduce artificial delay, even when the router is uncongested. As a second example, attackers with bot armies can bombard a particular router with "filler" messages, the only purpose of which is to congest the targeted router.

Rushing is the opposite problem: a technique to make it appear that messages can be delivered sooner than can be reasonably expected. Attackers often employ rushing attacks by first hijacking routers that service parts of the Internet that are fairly far apart in terms of network topology. The attackers cause the compromised routers to form a *virtual link* between them. A virtual link emulates a MAC layer protocol but running over a transport layer connection between the two routers instead of a PHY layer. The virtual link, also called a *wormhole*, allows the routers to claim they are connected directly by a link and so are only one hop apart. The two compromised routers can therefore advertise the wormhole as a "low-cost" path between their respective regions of the Internet. The two regions then naturally exchange traffic through the compromised routers and the wormhole.

An adversary usually launches a rushing attack as a prelude to other attacks. By attracting traffic to the wormhole endpoints, the compromised routers can eavesdrop and modify the datagrams flowing through them. Compromised routers at the end of a wormhole are also an ideal vehicle for selective deletion of messages.

Reorder

A second natural event in the Internet is datagram *reordering*. The two most common reordering mechanisms are forwarding table updates and traffic-shaping algorithms. Reordering due to forwarding takes place at the network layer; traffic shaping can be applied at the MAC layer or higher.

The Internet reconfigures itself automatically as routers set up new links with neighboring routers and tear down links between routers. These changes cause the routing application on each affected router to send an update to its neighbors, describing the topology change. These changes are gossiped across the network until every router is aware of what happened. Each router receiving such an update modifies its forwarding table to reflect the new Internet topology.

Since the forwarding table updates take place asynchronously from datagram exchanges, a router can select a different forwarding path for each datagram between even the same two devices. This means that two datagrams sent in order at the message source can arrive in a different order at the destination, since a router can update its forwarding table between the selection of a next hop for different datagrams.

The second reordering mechanism is traffic shaping, which gets imposed on the message flow to make better use of the communication resources. One example is quality of service. Some traffic classes, such as voice or streaming video, might be given higher priority by routers than best-effort traffic, which constitutes file transfers. Higher priority means the router will send datagrams carrying voice or video first while buffering the traffic longer. Endpoint systems also apply traffic-shaping algorithms in an attempt to make real-time applications work better, without gravely affecting the performance of applications that can wait for their data. Any layer of the protocol stack can apply traffic shaping to the messages it generates or receives.

An attacker can emulate reordering any messages it intercepts, but since every device in the Internet must recover from message reordering anyway, reordering attacks are generally useful only in very specific contexts. We will not discuss them further.

Message Deletion

Like reordering, *message deletion* can happen through normal operation of the Internet modules. A MAC layer will drop any frame it receives with an invalid frame check sequence. A network layer module will discard any datagram it receives with an IP header error. A transport layer will drop any data segment received with a data checksum error. A router will drop perfectly good datagrams after receiving too many simultaneous bursts of traffic that lead to congestion and exhaustion of its buffers. For these reasons, TCP was designed to retransmit data segments in an effort to overcome errors.

The last class of attack possible with a Dolev−Yao adversary is message deletion. Two message deletion attacks occur frequently enough to be named: *black-hole attacks* and *gray-hole attacks*.

Black-hole attacks occur when a router deletes all messages it is supposed to forward. From time to time, a router is misconfigured to offer a zero-cost route to every destination in the Internet. This causes all traffic to be sent to this router. Since no device can sustain such a load, the router fails. The neighboring routers cannot detect the failure rapidly enough to configure alternate routes, and they fail as well. This continues until a significant portion of the routers in the Internet fail, resulting in a black hole: Messages flow into the collapsed portion of the Internet and never flow out. A black-hole attack intentionally misconfigures a router. Black-hole attacks also occur frequently in small-scale sensor, mesh, and peer-to-peer file networks.

A gray-hole attack is a selective deletion attack. Targeted jamming is one type of selective message deletion attack. More generally, an adversary can discard any message it intercepts in the Internet, thereby preventing its ultimate delivery. An adversary intercepting and selectively deleting messages can be difficult to detect and diagnose, and so is a powerful attack. It is normally accomplished via compromised routers.

A subtler, indirect form of message deletion is also possible through the introduction of *forwarding loops.* Each IP datagram header has a *time-to-live* (TTL) field, limiting the number of hops that a datagram can make. This field is set to 255 by the initiator and decremented by each router through which the datagram passes. If a router decrements the TTL field to zero, it discards the datagram.

The reason for the TTL field is that the routing protocols that update the forwarding tables can temporarily cause forwarding loops because updates are applied asynchronously as the routing updates are gossiped through the Internet. For instance, if router A gets updated prior to router B, A might believe that the best path to some destination C is via B, whereas B believes the best route to C is via A as the next hop. Messages for C will ping-pong between A and B until one or both are updated with new topology information.

An attacker who compromises a router or forges its routing traffic can intentionally introduce forwarding routes. This causes messages addressed to the destinations affected by the forgery to circulate until the TTL field gets decremented to zero. These attacks are also difficult to detect, because all the routers are behaving according to their specifications, but messages are being mysteriously lost.

Summary

The most striking point to observe about all of the enumerated attacks is that all take advantage of the natural features and structure of the Internet architecture: No one is making any of the protocols misbehave, just "misusing" the Internet's own features against "legitimate" use. Any I/O channel of any system—and communications over the Internet certainly falls into this bucket—is assumed under the control of an adversary under the Dolev–Yao model. The input parse for any such channel is therefore a programming environment to which we freely grant the adversary access via the language describing protocol messages on the channel. This means our communications architectures necessarily expose our systems to attack, unless we close all possible communications channels. Doing so is impractical because not all people and organizations with which they are affiliated necessarily trust one another for all possible communications, and openness is a necessary condition for our economic models. Vulnerability to attack is therefore a necessary consequence of communications and a judicious mix of security mechanisms with friends and open links with potential business partners is inevitable. Absolutely secure networks and systems have only limited utility.

3. DEFENDING AGAINST ATTACKS ON THE INTERNET

Now that we have a model for thinking about the threats against communication and we understand how the Internet works, we can examine how its communications can sometimes be protected. Here we will explain how cryptography is used to protect messages exchanged between various devices on the Internet and illustrate the techniques with examples.

As might be expected, the techniques vary according to scenario. Methods that are effective for an active session do not work for session establishment. Methods that are required for session establishment are too expensive for an established session. It is interesting that similar methods are used at each layer of the Internet architecture for protecting a session and for session establishment and that each layer defines its own security protocols. Many find the similarity of security solutions at different layers curious and wonder why security is not centralized in a single layer. We will explain why the same mechanisms solve different problems at different layers of the architecture, to give better insight into what each is for.

Layer Session Defenses

A *session* is a series of one or more related messages. The easiest and most straightforward defenses protect the exchange of messages that are organized into sessions, so we will start with session-oriented defenses.

Cryptography, when used properly, can provide reliable defenses against eavesdropping. It can also be used to detect forgery and replay attacks, and the methods used also have some relevance to detecting reordering and message deletion attacks. We will discuss how this is accomplished and illustrate the techniques with TLS, IPsec, and 802.11i.

Defending against Eavesdropping

The primary method used to defend against eavesdropping is encryption. Encryption was invented with the goal of making it infeasible for any computationally limited adversary to be able to learn anything useful about a message that cannot already be deduced by some other means, such as its length. Encryption schemes that appear to meet this goal have been invented and are in widespread use on the Internet. Here we will describe how they are used.

There are two forms of encryption: symmetric encryption, in which the same key is used to both encrypt and decrypt, and asymmetric encryption, in which encryption and decryption use distinct but related keys. The properties of each are different. Asymmetric encryption tends to be used only for applications related to session initiation and assertions about policy (although this is not universally true). The reason for this is that a single asymmetric key operation is generally too expensive across a number of dimensions—computation time, size of encrypted payloads, power consumption—to be applied to a message stream of arbitrary length. We therefore focus on symmetric encryption and how it is used by network security protocols.

A symmetric encryption scheme consists of three operations: *key generate*, *encrypt*, and *decrypt*. The key generate operation creates a *key*, which is a secret. The key generate procedure is usually application specific; we describe some examples of key generate operations in our discussion of session start-up. Once generated, the key is used by the encrypt operation to transform *plaintext* messages—that is, messages that can be read by anyone—into *ciphertext*, which is messages that cannot be read by any computationally limited party who does not possess the key. The key is also used by the decrypt primitive to translate ciphertext messages back into plaintext messages.

There are two kinds of symmetric encryption algorithms. The first type is called a *block cipher*, and the second a *stream cipher*. Block and stream ciphers make different assumptions about the environment in which they operate, making each more effective than the other at different protocol layers.

A block cipher divides a message into chunks of a fixed size called *blocks* and encrypts each block separately. Block ciphers have the random access property, meaning that a block cipher can efficiently encrypt or decrypt any block utilizing an *initialization vector* in conjunction with the key. This property makes block ciphers a good choice for encrypting the content of MAC layer frames and network layer datagrams, for two reasons.

First, the chunking behavior of a block cipher corresponds nicely to the packetization process used to form datagrams from segments and frames from datagrams. Second, and perhaps more important, the Internet architecture models the lower layers as "best-effort" services, meaning that it assumes that datagrams and frames are sent and then forgotten. If a transmitted datagram is lost due to congestion or bit error (or attack), it is up to the transport layer or application to recover. The random access property makes it easy to restart a block cipher anywhere it's needed in the datastream. Popular examples of block ciphers include AES, DES, and 3DES, used by Internet security protocols.

Block ciphers are used by the MAC and network layers to encrypt as follows: First, a block cipher mode of operation is selected. A block cipher itself encrypts and decrypts only single blocks. A mode of operation is a set of rules extending the encryption scheme from a single block to messages of arbitrary length. The most popular modes of operation used in the Internet are counter (CTR) mode and cipher-block chaining (CBC) mode. Both require an initialization vector, which is a counter value for counter mode and a randomly generated bit vector for the cipher-block chaining mode. To encrypt a message, the mode of operation first partitions the message into a sequence of blocks whose size equals that of the cipher, padding if needed to bring the message length up to a multiple of the block size. The mode of operation then encrypts each block under the key while combining initialization vectors with the block in a mode-specific fashion.

For example, counter mode uses a counter as its initialization vector, which it increments, encrypts, and then exclusive-ORs the result with the block:

$$\text{counter} \rightarrow \text{counter} + 1; \quad E \leftarrow \text{Encrypt}_{Key}(\text{counter});$$

$$\text{CipherTextBlock} \leftarrow E \oplus \text{PlainTextBlock}$$

where $\oplus$ denotes exclusive OR. The algorithm outputs the new (unencrypted) counter value, which is used to encrypt the next block and CipherTextBlock.

The process of assembling a message from a message encrypted under a mode of operation is very simple: Prepend the original initialization vector to the sequence of ciphertext blocks, which together replace the plaintext payload for the message. The right way to think of this is that the initialization vector becomes a new message header layer. Also prepended is a *key identifier*, which indicates to the receiver which key it should utilize to decrypt the payload. This is important because in many cases it is useful to employ multiple connections between the same pair of endpoints, and so the receiver can have multiple decryption keys to choose from for each message received from a particular source.

A receiver reverses this process: First, it extracts the initialization vector from the data payload, then it uses this and the ciphertext blocks to recover the original plaintext message by reversing the steps in the mode of operation.

This paradigm is widely used in MAC and network layer security protocols, including 802.11i, 802.16e, 802.1ae, and IPsec, each of which utilizes AES in modes related to counter and cipher-block chaining modes.

A stream cipher treats the data as a continuous stream and can be thought of as encrypting and decrypting data one bit at a time. Stream ciphers are usually designed so that each encrypted bit depends on all previously encrypted ones, so decryption becomes possible only if all the bits arrive in order; most true stream ciphers lack the random access property. This means that in principle stream ciphers only work in network protocols when they're used on top of a reliable data delivery service such as TCP. Therefore, they work correctly below the transport layer only when used in conjunction with reliable data links. Stream ciphers are attractive from an implementation perspective because they can often achieve much higher throughputs than block ciphers. RC4 is an example of a popular stream cipher.

Stream ciphers typically do not use a mode of operation or an initialization vector at all, or at least not in the same sense as a block cipher. Instead, they are built as pseudorandom number generators, the output of which is based on a key. The random number generator is used to create a sequence of bits that appear random, called a *key stream*, and the result is exclusive OR'd with the plaintext data to create ciphertext. Since XOR is an idempotent operation, decryption with a stream cipher is just the same operation: Generate the same key stream and exclusive OR it with the ciphertext to recover the plaintext. Since stream ciphers do not utilize initialization vectors, Internet protocols employing stream ciphers do not need the extra overhead of a header to convey the initialization vector needed by the decryptor in the block cipher case. Instead, these protocols rely on the ability of the sender and receiver to keep their respective key stream generators synchronized for each bit transferred. This implies that stream ciphers can only be used over a reliable medium such as TCP—that is, a transport that guarantees delivery of all bits in the proper order and without duplication.

Transport layer security (TLS) is an example of an Internet security protocol that uses the stream cipher RC4. TLS runs on top of TCP, which is a reliable transport and therefore meets one of the preconditions for use of RC4.

Assuming that a symmetric encryption scheme is well designed, its efficacy against eavesdropping depends on four factors. Failing to consider *any* of these factors can cause the encryption scheme to fail catastrophically.

Independence of Keys

This is perhaps the most important consideration for the use of encryption. All symmetric encryption schemes assume that the encryption key for each and every session is generated independently of the encryption keys used for every other session. Let's parse this thought:

- *Independent* means selected or generated by a process that is indistinguishable by *any* polynomial time statistical test from the uniform distribution applied to the key space. One common failure is to utilize a key generation algorithm that is not random, such as using the MAC or IP address of a device or time of session creation as the basis for a key, or even basing the key on a password. Schemes that use such public values instead of randomness for keys are easily broken using brute-force search techniques such as dictionary attacks. A second common failure is to pick an initial key randomly but create successive keys by some simple transformation, such as incrementing the initial key, exclusive OR 'ing the MAC address of the device with the key, and so on. Encryption using key generation schemes of this sort are easily broken using differential cryptanalysis and related key attacks.

- *Each and every* mean each and every. For a block cipher, reusing the same key twice with the same initialization vector can allow an adversary to recover information about the plaintext data from the ciphertext *without* using the key. Similarly, each key always causes the pseudorandom number generator at the heart of a stream cipher to generate the same key stream, and reuse of the same key stream again will leak the plaintext data from the ciphertext without using the key.

- Methods effective for the coordinated generation of random keys at the beginning of each session constitute a complicated topic. We address it in our discussion of session start-up later in the chapter.

Limited Output

Perhaps the second most important consideration is to limit the amount of information encrypted under a single key. The modern definition of security for an encryption scheme revolves around the idea of indistinguishability of the scheme's output from random. This goes back to a notion of ideal security proposed by Claude E. Shannon (a research mathematician working for Bell Labs). This has a dramatic effect on how long an encryption key may be safely used before an adversary has sufficient information to begin to learn something about the encrypted data.

Every encryption scheme is ultimately a deterministic algorithm using a finite state space, and no deterministic algorithm using a finite state space can generate an infinite amount of output that is indistinguishable from random. This means that encryption keys must be replaced on a regular basis. The amount of data that can be safely encrypted under a single key depends very much on the encryption scheme. As usual, the limitations for block ciphers and stream ciphers are a bit different.

Let the block size for a block cipher be some integer $n > 0$. Then, for any key K, for every string S_1 there is another string S_2 so that:

$$\text{Encrypt}_K(S_2) = S_1 \text{ and } \text{Decrypt}_K(S_1) = S_2$$

This says that a block cipher's encrypt and decrypt operations are *permutations* of the set of all bit strings whose length equals the block size. In particular, this property says that every pair of distinct n bit strings results in distinct n bit ciphertexts for any block cipher. However, by an elementary theorem from probability called the birthday paradox, random selection of n bit strings should result in a 50 percent probability that some string is chosen at least twice after about $2^{n/2}$ selections. This has a sobering consequence for block ciphers. It says that an algorithm as simple as naïve guessing can distinguish the output of the block cipher from random after about $2^{n/2}$ blocks have been encrypted. This means that an encryption key should never be used to encrypt even close to $2^{n/2}$ blocks before a new, independent key is generated.

To make this specific, DES and 3DES have a block size of 64 bits; AES has a 128-bit block size. Therefore a DES or 3DES key should be used much less than to encrypt $2^{64/2} = 2^{32}$ blocks, whereas an AES key should never be used to encrypt as many as 2^{64} blocks; doing so begins to leak information about the encrypted data without use of the encryption key. As an example, 802.11i has been crafted to limit each key to encrypting 2^{48} before forcing generation of a new key.

This kind of arithmetic does not work for a stream cipher, since its block size is 1 bit. Instead, the length of time a key can be safely used is governed by the periodicity of the pseudorandom number generator at the heart of the stream cipher. RC4, for instance, becomes distinguishable from random after generating about 2^{31} bytes. Note that $31 \approx 32 = \sqrt{256}$, and 256 bytes is the size of the RC4 internal state. This illustrates the rule of thumb that there is a birthday paradox relation between the maximum number of encrypted bits of a stream cipher key and its internal state.

Key Size

The one "fact" about encryption that everyone knows is that larger keys result in stronger encryption. This is indeed true, provided that the generate keys operation is designed according to the independence condition. One common mistake is to properly generate a short key—say, 32 bits long—that is then concatenated to get a key of the length needed by the selected encryption scheme—say, 128 bits. Another similar error is to generate a short key and manufacture the remainder of the key with known public data, such as an IP address. These methods result in a key that is only as strong as the short key that was generated randomly.

Mode of Operation

The final parameter is the mode of operation—that is, the rules for using a block cipher to encrypt messages whose length is different from the block cipher width. The most common problem is failure to respect the documented terms and conditions defined for using the mode of operation.

As an illustration of what can go wrong—even by people who know what they are doing—the cipher-block chaining mode requires that the initialization vector be chosen randomly. The earliest version of the IPsec standard used the cipher-block chaining mode exclusively for encryption. This standard recommended choosing initialization vectors as the final block of any prior message sent. The reasoning behind this recommendation was that, because an encrypted block cannot be distinguished from random if the number of blocks encrypted is limited, a block of a previously encrypted message ought to suffice. However, the advice given by the standard was erroneous because the initialization vector selection algorithm failed to have one property that a real random selection property has: The initialization vector is not unpredictable. A better way to meet the randomness requirement is to increment a counter, prepend it to the message to encrypt, and then encrypt the counter value, which becomes the initialization vector. This preserves the unpredictability property at a cost of encrypting one extra block.

A second common mistake is to design protocols using a mode of operation that was not designed to encrypt multiple blocks. For example, failing to use a mode of operation at all—using the naked encrypt and decrypt operations, with no initialization vector—is itself a mode of operation called *electronic code book* mode. Electronic code book mode was designed to encrypt messages that never span more than a single block—for example, encrypting keys to distribute for other operations. Using electronic code book mode on a message longer than a single block leaks a bit per block, however, because this mode allows an attacker to disguise when two plaintext blocks are the same or different. A classical example of this problem is to encrypt a photograph using electronic code book mode. The main outline of the photograph shows through plainly. This is not a failure of the encryption scheme; it is, rather, using encryption in a way that was never intended.

Now that we understand how encryption works and how it is used in Internet protocols, we should ask why it is needed at different layers. What does encryption at each layer of the Internet architecture accomplish? The best way to answer this question is to watch what it does.

Encryption applied at the MAC layer encrypts a single link. Data is encrypted prior to being put on a link and is decrypted again at the other end of a link. This leaves the IP datagrams conveyed by the MAC layer frames exposed inside each router as they wend their way across the Internet. Encryption at the MAC layer is a good way to transparently prevent data from leaking, since many devices never use encryption. For example, many organizations are distributed geographically and use direct point-to-point links to connect sites; encrypting the links connecting sites prevents an outsider from learning the organization's confidential information merely by eavesdropping. Legal wiretaps also depend on this arrangement because they monitor data inside routers. The case of legal wiretaps also illustrates the problem with link layer encryption only: If an unauthorized party assumes control of a router, he or she is free to read all the datagrams that traverse the router.

IPsec operates essentially at the network layer. Applying encryption via IPsec prevents exposure of the datagrams' payload end to end, so the data is still protected within routers. Since the payload of a datagram includes both the transport layer header and its data segments, applying encryption at the IPsec layer hides the applications being used as well as the data. This provides a big boost in confidentiality but also leads to more inefficient use of the Internet, since traffic-shaping algorithms in routers critically depend on having complete access to the transport headers. Using encryption at the IPsec layer also means the endpoints do not have to know whether each link a datagram traverses through the Internet applies encryption; using encryption at this layer simplifies the security analysis over encryption applied at the MAC layer alone. Finally, like MAC layer encryption, IPsec is a convenient tool for introducing encryption transparently to protect legacy applications, which by and large ignored confidentiality issues. A downside of IPsec is that it still leaves data unprotected within the network protocol implementation, and malware can sometimes hook itself between the network and sockets layer to inspect traffic.

The transport layer encryption function can be illustrated by TLS. Like IPsec, TLS operates end to end, but TLS encrypts only the application data carried in the transport data segments, leaving the transport header exposed. Thus, with TLS, routers can still perform their traffic-shaping function, and we still have the simplified security analysis that comes with end-to-end encryption. A second advantage is that TLS protects data essentially from application to application, making malware attacks against the communication channel per se more difficult. There are of course downsides. The first disadvantage of this method is that the exposure of the transport headers gives the attacker greater knowledge about what might be encrypted in the payload. The second disadvantage is that it is somewhat more awkward to introduce encryption transparently at the transport layer; encryption at the transport layer requires cooperation by the application to perform properly. This analysis says that it is reasonable to employ encryption at any one of the network protocol layers because each solves a slightly different problem.

Before leaving the topic of encryption, it is worthwhile to emphasize what encryption does and does not do. Encryption, when properly used, is a *read access control*. If used correctly, no one who lacks access to the encryption key can read the encrypted data. Encryption, however, is *not a write access control*; that is, it does not guarantee the integrity of the encrypted data. Counter mode and stream ciphers are subject to bit-flipping attacks, for instance. An attacker launches a bit-flipping attack by capturing a frame or datagram, changing one or more bits from 0 to 1 (or vice versa) and retransmitting the altered frame. The resulting frame decrypts to some result—the altered message decrypts to something—and if bits are flipped judiciously, the result can be intelligible. As a second example, cipher-block chaining mode is susceptible to cut-and-paste attacks, whereby the attack cuts the final few blocks from one message in a stream and uses them to overwrite the final blocks of a later stream. At most, one block decrypts to gibberish; if the attacker chooses the paste point judiciously, for example, so that it falls where the application ought to have random data anyway, this can be a powerful attack. The upshot is that even encrypted data needs an integrity mechanism to be effective, which leads us to the subject of defenses against forgeries.

Defending against Forgeries and Replays

Forgery and replay detection are usually treated together because replays are a special kind of forgery. We follow this tradition in our own discussion. Forgery detection, not eavesdropping protection, is the central concern for designs to secure network protocol. This is because every accepted forgery of an encrypted frame or datagram is a question whose answer can tell the adversary something about the encryption key or plaintext data. Just as one learns any subject in school, an attacker can learn about the encrypted stream or encryption key faster by asking questions rather than sitting back and passively listening.

Since eavesdropping is a passive attack, whereas creating forgeries is active, turning from the subject of eavesdropping to that of forgeries changes the security goals subtly. Encryption has a security goal of prevention—to prevent the adversary from learning anything useful about the data that cannot be derived in other ways. The comparable security goal for forgeries would be to prevent the adversary from creating forgeries, which is not feasible. This is because any device with a transmitter appropriate for the medium can send forgeries by creating frames and datagrams using addresses employed by other parties. What is feasible is a form of asking forgiveness instead of permission: Prevent the adversary from creating *undetected* forgeries.

The cryptographic tool underlying forgery detection is called a *message authentication code*. Like an encryption scheme, a message authentication code consists of three operations: a *key generation* operation, a *tagging* operation, and a *verification* operation. Also like encryption, the key generation operation, which generates a symmetric key shared between the sender and receiver, is usually application specific. The tagging and verification operations, however, are much different from encrypt and decrypt.

The tagging operation takes the symmetric key, called an *authentication key*, and a message as input parameters and outputs a *tag*, which is a cryptographic checksum depending on the key and message to produce its output.

The verification operation takes three input parameters: the symmetric key, the message, and its tag. The verification algorithm recomputes the tag from the key and message and compares the result against the tag with the received message. If the two fail to match, the verify algorithm outputs a signal that the message is a forgery. If the input and locally computed tag match, the verify algorithm declares that the message is authenticated.

The conclusion drawn by the verify algorithm of a message authentication code is not entirely logically correct. Indeed, if the tag is n bits in length, an attacker could generate a random n bit string as its tag and it would have one chance in 2^n of being valid. A message authentication scheme is considered good if there are no polynomial time algorithms that are significantly better than random guessing at producing correct tags.

Message authentication codes are incorporated into network protocols in a manner similar to encryption. First, a sequence number is prepended to the data that is being forgery protected; the sequence number, we will see, is used to detect replays. Next, a message authentication code tagging operation is applied to the sequence number and message body to produce a tag. The tag is appended to the message, and a key identifier for the authentication key is prepended to the message. The message can then be sent. The receiver determines whether the message was a forgery by first finding the authentication key identified by the key identifier, then by checking the correctness of the tag using the message

authentication code's verify operation. If these checks succeed, the receiver finally uses the sequence number to verify that the message is not a replay.

How does replay detection work? When the authentication key is established, the sender initializes to zero the counter that is used in the authenticated message. The receiver meanwhile establishes a replay window, which is a list of all recently received sequence numbers. The replay window is initially empty. To send a replay protected frame, the sender increments his counter by one and prepends this at the front of the data to be authenticated prior to tagging. The receiver extracts the counter value from the received message and compares this to the replay window. If the counter falls before the replay window, which means it is too old to be considered valid, the receiver flags the message as a replay. The receiver does the same thing if the counter is already represented in the replay window data structure. If the counter is greater than the bottom of the replay window and is a counter value that has not yet been received, the frame or datagram is considered "fresh" instead of a replay.

The process is simplest to illustrate for the MAC layer. Over a single MAC link it is ordinarily impossible for frames to be reordered, because only a single device can access the medium at a time; because of the speed of electrons or photons comprising the signals representing bits, at least some of the bits at the start of a frame are received prior to the final bits being transmitted (satellite links are an exception). If frames cannot be reordered by a correctly operating MAC layer, the replay window data structure records the counter for the last received frame, and the replay detection algorithm merely has to decide whether the replay counter value in a received frame is larger than that recorded in its replay window. If the counter is less than or equal to the replay window value, the frame is a forgery; otherwise it is considered genuine. 802.11i, 802.16, and 802.1ae all employ this approach to replay detection. This same approach can be used by a message authentication scheme operating above the transport layer, by protocols such as TLS and SSH (Secure Shell), since the transport eliminates duplicates and delivers bits in the order sent. The replay window is more complicated at the network layer, however, because some reordering is natural, given that the network reorders datagrams. Hence, for the network layer the replay window is usually sized to account for the maximum reordering expected in the "normal" Internet. IPsec uses this more complex replay window.

This works for the following reason: Every message is given a unique, incrementing sequence number in the form of its counter value. The transmitter computes the message authentication code tag over the sequence number and the message data. Since it is not feasible for a computationally bounded adversary to create a valid tag for the data with probability significantly greater than $1/2^n$, a tag validated by the receiver implies that the message, including its sequence number, was created by the transmitter. The worst thing that could have happened, therefore, is that the adversary has delayed the message. However, if the sequence number falls within the replay window, the message could not have been delayed longer than reordering due to the normal operation of forwarding and traffic shaping within the Internet.

A replay detection scheme limits an adversary's opportunities to delete and to reorder messages. If a message does not arrive at its destination, its sequence number is never set in the receive window, so it can be declared a lost message. It is easy to track the percentage of lost messages, and if this exceeds some threshold, then communications become unreliable, but more important, the cause of the unreliability can be investigated. Similarly, messages received outside the replay window can also be tracked, and if the percentage becomes too high, messages are arriving out of order more frequently than might be expected from normal operation of the Internet, pointing to a configuration problem, an equipment failure, or an attack. Again, the cause of the anomaly can be investigated. Mechanisms like these are often how attacks are discovered in the first place. The important lesson is that attacks and even faulty equipment or misconfigurations are often difficult to detect without collecting reliability statistics, and the forgery detection mechanisms can provide some of the best reliability statistics available.

Just like encryption, the correctness of this analysis depends critically on the design enforcing some fundamental assumptions, regardless of the quality of the message authentication code on which it might be based. If any of the following assumptions are violated, the forgery detection scheme can fail catastrophically to accomplish its mission.

Independence of Authentication Keys

This is absolutely paramount for forgery detection. If the message authentication keys are not independent, an attacker can easily create forged message authentication tags based on authentication keys learned in other ways. This assumption is so important that it is useful to examine in greater detail.

The first point is that a message authentication key utterly fails to accomplish its mission if it is shared among even three parties; only two parties must know any particular authentication key. This is very easy to illustrate. Suppose A, B, and C were to share a message authentication key, and suppose A creates a forgery-protected message it sends to C. What can C conclude when it receives this message? C cannot conclude that the message actually originated from A, even though its addressing indicates it did, because B could have

produced the same message and used A's address. C cannot even conclude that B did not change some of the message in transit. Therefore, the algorithm loses all its efficacy for detecting forgeries if message authentication keys are known by more than two parties. They must be known by at least two parties or the receiver cannot verify that the message and its bits originated with the sender.

This is much different than encryption. An encryption/decryption key can be distributed to every member of a group, and as long as the key is not leaked from the group to a third party, the encryption scheme remains an effective read access control against parties that are not members of the group. Message authentication utterly fails if the key is shared beyond two parties. This is due to the active nature of forgery attacks and the fact that forgery handling, being a detection rather than a prevention scheme, already affords the adversary more latitude than encryption toward fooling the good guys.

So for forgery detection schemes to be effective, message authentication keys must be shared between exactly two communicating devices. As with encryption keys, a message authentication key must be generated randomly because brute-force searches and related key attacks can recover the key by observing messages transiting the medium.

No Reuse of Replay Counter Values with a Key

Reusing a counter with a message authentication key is analogous to reusing an initialization vector with an encryption key. Instead of leaking data, however, replay counter value reuse leads automatically to trivial forgeries based on replayed messages. The attacker's algorithm is trivial: Using a packet sniffer, record each of the messages protected by the same key and file them in a database. If the attacker ever receives a key identifier and sequence number pair already in the database, the transmitter has begun to reuse replay counter values with a key. The attacker can then replay any message with a higher sequence number and the same key identifier. The receiver will be fooled into accepting the replayed message.

This approach implies that known forgery detection schemes cannot be based on static keys. To the contrary, we could attempt to design such a scheme. One could try to checkpoint in nonvolatile memory the replay counter at the transmitter and the replay window at the receiver. This approach does not work, however, in the presence of a Dolev–Yao adversary. The adversary can capture a forgery-protected frame in flight and then delete all successive messages. At its convenience later, the adversary resends the captured message. The receiver, using its static message authentication key, will verify the tag and, based on its replay window retrieved from nonvolatile storage, verify that the message is indeed in sequence and so accept the message as valid. This experiment demonstrates that forgery detection is not entirely satisfactory because sequence numbers do not take timeliness into account. Secure clock synchronization, however, is a difficult problem with solutions that enjoy only partial success. The construction of better schemes that account for timing remains an open research problem.

Key Size

If message authentication keys must be randomly generated, they must also be of sufficient size to discourage brute-force attack. The key space has to be large enough to make exhaustive search for the message authentication key cost prohibitive. Key sizes for message authentication comparable with those for encryption are sufficient for this task.

Message Authentication Code Tag Size

We have seen many aspects that make message authentication codes somewhat more fragile encryption schemes. Message authentication code size is one in which forgery detection can on the contrary effectively utilize a smaller block size than an encryption scheme. Whereas an encryption scheme based on a 128-bit block size has to replace keys every 2^{48} or so blocks to avoid leaking data, an encryption scheme can maintain the same level of security with about a 48-bit message authentication code tag. The difference is that the block cipher-based encryption scheme leaks information about the encrypted data due to the birthday paradox, whereas an attacker has to create a valid forgery based on an exhaustive search due to the active nature of a forgery attack. In general, to determine the size of a tag needed by a message authentication code, we have only to determine the maximum number of messages sent in the lifetime of the key. As a rule of thumb, if this number of messages is bounded by 2^n, the tag need only be $n + 1$ bits long. This is only a rule of thumb because some MACs cannot be safely truncated to this minimal number of bits.

As with encryption, for many it is confusing that forgery detection schemes are offered at nearly every layer of the Internet architecture. To understand the preceding concept, it is again useful to ask what message forgery detection accomplishes at each layer.

If a MAC module requires forgery detection for every frame received, physical access to the medium being used by the module's PHY layer affords an attacker no opportunity to create forgeries. This is a very strong property. It means that the only MAC layer messages attacking the receiver are either generated by other devices authorized to attach to the medium or else are forwarded by the network layer modules of authorized devices, because all frames received directly off the medium generated by

unauthorized devices will be discarded by the forgery detection scheme. A MAC layer forgery detection scheme therefore essentially provides a write access control of the physical medium, closing it to unauthorized parties. Installing a forgery detection scheme at any other layer will not provide this kind of protection. Requiring forgery detection at the MAC layer is therefore desirable whenever feasible.

Forgery detection at the network layer provides a different kind of assurance. IPsec is the protocol designed to accomplish this function. If a network layer module requires IPsec for every datagram received, this essentially cuts off attacks against the device hosting the module to other authorized machines in the entire Internet; datagrams generated by unauthorized devices will be dropped. With this forgery detection scheme it is still possible for an attacker on the same medium to generate frames attacking the device's MAC layer module, but attacks against higher layers become computationally infeasible. Installing a forgery detection scheme at any other layer will not provide this kind of protection. Requiring forgery detection at the network layer is therefore desirable whenever feasible as well.

Applying forgery detection at the transport layer offers different assurances entirely. Forgery detection at this level assures the receiving application that the arriving messages were generated by the peer application, not by some virus or Trojan-horse program that has linked itself between modules between protocol layers on the same or different machine. This kind of assurance cannot be provided by any other layer. Such a scheme at the network or MAC layers only defends against message injection by unauthorized devices on the Internet generally or directly attached to the medium, not against messages generated by unauthorized processes running on an authorized machine. Requiring forgery detection at the transport layer therefore is desirable whenever it is feasible.

The conclusion is that forgery detection schemes accomplish different desirable functions at each protocol layer. The security goals that are achievable are always architecturally dependent, and this comes through clearly with forgery detection schemes.

We began the discussion of forgery detection by noting that encryption by itself is subject to attack. One final issue is how to use encryption and forgery protection together to protect the same message. Three solutions could be formulated to this problem. One approach might be to add forgery detection to a message first—add the authentication key identifier, the replay sequence number, and the message authentication code tag—followed by encryption of the message data and forgery detection headers. TLS is an example Internet protocol that takes this approach. The second approach is to reverse the order of encryption and forgery detection: First encrypt, then compute the tag over the encrypted data and the encryption headers. IPsec is an example Internet protocol defined to use this approach. The last approach is to apply both simultaneously to the plaintext data. SSH is an Internet protocol constructed in this manner.

Session Start-up Defenses

If encryption and forgery detection techniques are such powerful security mechanisms, why aren't they used universally for all network communications? The problem is that not everyone is your friend; everyone has enemies, and in every human endeavor there are those with criminal mind-sets who want to prey on others. Most people do not go out of their way to articulate and maintain relationships with their enemies unless there is some compelling reason to do so, and technology is powerless to change this.

More than anything else, the keys used by encryption and forgery detection are relationship signifiers. Possession of keys is useful not only because they enable encryption and forgery detection but because their use assures the remote party that messages you receive will remain confidential and that messages the peer receives from you actually originated from you. They enable the accountable maintenance of a preexisting relationship. If you receive a message that is protected by a key that only you and I know, and you didn't generate the message yourself, it is reasonable for you to conclude that I sent the message to you and did so intentionally.

If keys are signifiers of preexisting relationships, much of our networked communications cannot be defended by cryptography, because we do not have preexisting relationships with everyone. We send and receive email to and from people we have never met. We buy products online from merchants we have never met. None of these relationships would be possible if we required all messages to be encrypted or authenticated. What is always required is an open, unauthenticated, risky channel to establish new relationships; cryptography can only assure us that communication from parties with whom we already have relationships is indeed occurring with the person with whom we think we are communicating.

A salient and central assumption for both encryption and forgery detection is that the keys these mechanisms use are fresh and independent across sessions. A session is an instance of exercising a relationship to effect communication. This means that secure communications require a state change, transitioning from a state in which two communicating parties are not engaged in an instance of communication to one in which they are. This state change is *session establishment*.

Session establishment is like a greeting between human beings. It is designed to synchronize two entities communicating over the Internet and establish and synchronize their keys, key identifiers, sequence numbers and replay windows, and, indeed, all the states to provide mutual assurance that the communication is genuine and confidential.

The techniques and data structures used to establish a secure session are different from those used to carry on a conversation. Our next goal is to look at some representative mechanisms in this area. The field is vast, and it is impossible to do more than skim the surface briefly to give the reader a glimpse of the beauty and richness of the subject. Secure session establishment techniques typically have three goals, as described in the following sections of this chapter.

Mutual Authentication

First, session establishment techniques seek to mutually authenticate the communicating parties to each other. *Mutually authenticate* means that both parties learn the "identity" of the other. It is not possible to know what is proper to discuss with another party without also knowing the identity of the other party. If only one party learns the identity of the other, it is always possible for an imposter to masquerade as the unknown party.

There are a couple of points to make about this issue. The first is what "learn" means. The kind of learning needed for session establishment is the creation of common knowledge: You know both identities, the peer knows both identities, and the peer knows you know both identities (and vice versa). A lower level of knowledge always enables opportunities for subverting the session establishment protocol.

The second point is what an identity is. Identities in session establishment protocols work differently than they do in real life. In session establishment, an identity is a commitment to a key that identifies you or your computing system. That is, an identity commits its sender to utilizing a particular key during session establishment, and the receiver to reject protocol messages generated using other keys.

Key Secrecy

Second, session establishment techniques seek to establish a session key that can be maintained as a secret between the two parties and is known to no one else. The session key must be independent from all other keys for all other session instances and indeed from all other keys. This implies that no adversary with limited computational resources can distinguish the key from one selected uniformly at random. Generating such an independent session key is both harder and easier than it sounds; it is always possible to do so if a preexisting relationship already exists between the two communicating parties, and it is impossible to do so reliably if a preexisting relationship does not exist. Relationships begat other relationships, and nonrelationships are sterile with respect to the technology.

Session State Consistency

Finally, the parties need to establish a consistent view of the session state. This means that they both agree on the identities of both parties; they agree on the session key instance; they agree on the encryption and forgery detection schemes used, along with any associated state such as sequence counters and replay windows; and they agree on which instance of communication this session represents. If they fail to agree on a single shared parameter, it is always possible for an imposter to convince one of the parties that it is engaged in a conversation that is different from its peer's conversation. As with identities, agree means the two establish common knowledge of all of these parameters, and a session establishment protocol can be considered secure in the Dolev–Yao model only if the protocol proves that both parties share common knowledge of all of the parameters.

Mutual Authentication

There are an enormous number of ways to accomplish the mutual authentication function needed to initiate a new session. Here we examine two approaches that are used in various protocols within the Internet.

A Symmetric Key Mutual Authentication Method

Our old friend the message authentication code can be used with a static, long-lived key to create a simple and robust mutual authentication scheme. Earlier we stressed that the properties of message authentication are incompatible with the use of a static key to provide forgery detection of session-oriented messages. The incompatibility is due to the use of sequence numbers for replay detection. We will replace sequence numbers with unpredictable quantities in order to resocialize static keys. The cost of this resocialization effort will be a requirement to exchange extra messages.

Suppose parties A and B want to mutually authenticate. We will assume that ID_A is B's name for the key it shares with A, whereas ID_B is A's name for the same key B. We will also assume that A and B share a long-lived message authentication key K and that K is known only to A and B. We will assume that A initiates the authentication. A and B can mutually authenticate using a three-message exchange, as follows: For message 1, A generates a random number R_A and sends a message containing its identity ID_A and random number to B:

$$A \rightarrow B: ID_A, R_A \qquad (1)$$

The notation $A \rightarrow B: m$ means that A sends message m to B. Here the message being passed is specified as ID_A, R_A, meaning it conveys A's identity ID_A (or, more precisely, the name of the key K) and A's random number R_A. This message asserts B's name for A, to tell B which is the right long-lived key it should use in this instance of the authentication protocol. The random number R_A plays the role of the sequence number in the session-oriented case. It is random in order to provide an unpredictable challenge. If B responds correctly, then this proves that the response is live and was not pre-recorded. R_A also acts as a transaction identifier for the response to A's message 1 (it allows A to recognize which response goes with which message 1). This is important in itself, because without the ability to interleave different instances of the protocol A would have to wait forever for any lost message in order to obtain a correct theory.

If B is willing to have a conversation with A at this time, it fetches the correct message authentication key K, generates its own random number R_B, and computes a message authentication code tag T over the message ID_B, ID_A, R_A, R_B, that is, over the message consisting of both names and both random numbers. B appends the tag to the message, which it then sends to A in response to message 1:

$$B \rightarrow A: ID_B, ID_A, R_A, R_B, T \qquad (2)$$

B includes A's name in the message to tell A which key to use to authenticate the message. It includes A's random number R_A in the message to signal the protocol instance to which this message responds.

The magic begins when A validates the message authentication code tag T. Since independently generated random numbers are unpredictable, A knows that the second message could not have been produced before A sent the first, because it returns R_A to A. Since the authentication code tag T was computed over the two identities ID_B and ID_A and the two random numbers R_A and R_B using the key K known only to A and B, and since A did not create the second message itself, A knows that B must have created message 2. Hence, message 2 is a response from B to A's message 1 for this instance of the protocol. If the message were to contain some other random number than R_A, A would know the message is not a response to its message 1.

If A verifies message 2, it responds by computing a message authentication code tag T' computed over ID_A and B's random number RB, which it includes in message 3:

$$A \rightarrow B: ID_A, R_B, T' \qquad (3)$$

Reasoning as before, B knows A produced message 3 in response to its message 2, because message 3 could not have been produced prior to message 2 and only A could have produced the correct tag T'. Thus, after message 3 is delivered, A and B both have been assured of each other's identity, and they also agree on the session instance, which is identified by the pair of random numbers R_A and R_B.

A deeper analysis of the protocol reveals that message 2 must convey both identities and both random numbers protected from forgery by the tag T. This construction binds A's view of the session with B's, and this is providing A with B's view of what they know in common. This binding prevents interleaving or man-in-the-middle attacks. As an example, without this binding, a third party, C, could masquerade as B to A and as A to B. Similarly, message 3 confirms the common knowledge: A knows that B knows that A knows ID_A, ID_B, R_A, and R_B if B verifies the third message; similarly, if B verifies message 3, B knows that A knows that B knows the same parameters.

It is worth noting that message 1 is not protected from either forgery or replay. This lack of any protection is an intrinsic part of the problem statement. During the protocol, A and B must transition from a state where they are unsure about the other's identity and have no communication instance instantiating the long-term relationship signified by the encryption key K to a state where they fully agree on each other's identities and a common instance of communication expressing their long-lived relationship. A makes the transition upon verifying message 2, and there are no known ways to reassure it about B until this point of the protocol. B makes the state transition once it has completed verification of message 3. The point of the protocol is to transition from a mutually suspicious state to a mutually trusted state.

An Asymmetric Key Mutual Authentication Method

Authentication based on asymmetric keys is also possible. In addition to asymmetric encryption, there is also an asymmetric key analog of a message authentication code called a *signature scheme*. Just like a message authentication code, a signature scheme consists of three operations: *key generate*, *sign*, and *verify*. The key generate operation outputs two parameters, a signing key S and a related verification key V. S's key holder is never supposed to reveal S to another party, whereas V is meant to be a public value. Under these assumptions, the sign operation takes the signing key S and a message M as input parameters and outputs a signature s of M. The verify operation takes the verification key V, message M, and signature s as inputs, and returns whether it verifies that s was created from S and M. If the signing key S is indeed known by only one party, the signature s must have been produced by that party. This is because it is infeasible for a computationally limited party to compute the signature s without S. Asymmetric signature schemes are often called *public/private key schemes* because S is maintained as a secret,

never shared with another party, whereas the verification key is published to everyone.

Signature schemes were invented to facilitate authentication. To accomplish this goal, the verification key must be public, and it is usually published in a certificate, which we will denote as $cert(ID_A, V)$, where ID_A is the identity of the key holder of S and V is the verification key corresponding to A. The certificate is issued by a well-known party called a *certificate authority*. The sole job of the certificate authority is to introduce one party to another. A certificate $cert(ID_A, V)$ issued by a certificate authority is an assertion that entity A has a public verification key V that is used to prove A's identity.

As with symmetric authentication, hundreds of different authentication protocols can be based on signature schemes. The following is one example among legions of examples:

$$A \rightarrow B: cert(ID_A, V), R_A \qquad (4)$$

Here $cert(ID_A, V)$ is A's certificate, conveying its identity ID_A and verification key V; R_A is a random number generated by A. If B is willing to begin a new session with A, it responds with the message:

$$B \rightarrow A: cert(ID_B, V'), R_B, R_A, sig_B(ID_A, R_B, R_A) \qquad (5)$$

R_B is a random number generated by B, and $sig_B(ID_A, R_B, R_A)$ is B's signature over the message with fields ID_A, R_B, and R_A. Including IDA under B's signature is essential because it is B's way of asserting that A is the target of message 2. Including RB and RA in the information signed is also necessary to defeat man-in-the-middle attacks. A responds with a third message:

$$A \rightarrow B: cert(ID_A, V), R_b, sig_B(ID_B, R_B) \qquad (6)$$

A Caveat

Mutual authentication is necessary to establish identities. Identities are needed to decide on the access control policies to apply to a particular conversation, that is, to answer the question, Which information that the party knows is suitable for sharing in the context of this communications instance? Authentication—mutual or otherwise—has very limited utility if the communications channel is not protected against eavesdropping and forgeries.

One of the most common mistakes made by Wi-Fi hotspot operators, for instance, is to require authentication but disable eavesdropping and forgery protection for the subsequent Internet access via the hotspot. This is because anyone with a Wi-Fi radio transmitter can access the medium and hijack the session from a paying customer. Another way of saying this is that authentication is useful only when it's used in conjunction with a secure channel. This leads to the topic of session key establishment. The most common use of mutual authentication is to establish ephemeral session keys using the long-lived authentication keys. We will discuss session key establishment next.

Key Establishment

Since it is generally infeasible for authentication to be meaningful without a subsequent secure channel, and since we know how to establish a secure channel across the Internet if we have a key, the next goal is to add key establishment to mutual authentication protocols. In this model, a mutual authentication protocol establishes an ephemeral session key as a side effect of its successful operation; this session key can then be used to construct all the encryption and authentication keys needed to establish a secure channel. All the session states, such as sequence number, replay windows, and key identifiers, can be initialized in conjunction with the completion of the mutual authentication protocol.

It is usually feasible to add key establishment to an authentication protocol. Let's illustrate this with the symmetric key authentication protocol, based on a message authentication code, discussed previously. To extend the protocol to establish a key, we suppose instead that A and B share two long-lived keys K and K'. The first key K is a message authentication key as before. The second key K' is a derivation key, the only function of which is to construct other keys within the context of the authentication protocol. This is accomplished as follows: After verifying message 2 (from line 2 previously), A computes a session key SK as:

$$SK \leftarrow prf(K', R_A, R_B, ID_A, ID_B, length) \qquad (7)$$

Here prf is another cryptographic primitive called a *pseudorandom function*. A pseudorandom function is characterized by the properties that (a) its output is indistinguishable from random by any computationally limited adversary and (b) it is hard to invert; that is, given a fixed output O, it is infeasible for any computationally limited adversary to find an input I so that $O \leftarrow prf(I)$. The output SK of (7) is *length* bits long and can be split into two pieces to become encryption and message authentication keys. B generates the same SK when it receives message 3. An example of a pseudorandom function is any block cipher, such as AES, in cipher-block chaining MAC mode. Cipher-block chaining MAC mode is just like cipher-block chaining mode, except all but the last block of encrypted data is discarded.

This construction meets the goal of creating an independent, ephemeral set of encryptions of message authentication keys for each session. The construction creates independent keys because any two outputs of a *prf* appear

to be independently selected at random to any adversary that is computationally limited. A knows that all the outputs are statistically distinct, because A picks the parameter to the prf R_A randomly for each instance of the protocol; similarly for B. And using the communications instances identifiers RA, RB along with A and B's identities ID_A and ID_B are interpreted as a "contract" to use SK only for this session instance and only between A and B.

Public key versions of key establishment based on signatures and asymmetric encryption also exist, but we will close with one last public key variant based on a completely different asymmetric key principle called the *Diffie−Hellman algorithm*.

The Diffie−Hellman algorithm is based on the discrete logarithm problem in finite groups. A group G is a mathematical object that is closed under an associative multiplication and has inverses for each element in G. The prototypical example of a finite group is the integers under addition modulo a prime number p.

The idea is to begin with an element g of a finite group G that has a long period. This means $g^1 = g$, $g^2 = g$ X g, $g^3 = g^2$ X g, …. Since G is finite, this sequence must eventually repeat. It turns out that $g = g^{n+1}$ for some integer $n > 1$, and $g^n = e$ is the group's neutral element. The element e has the property that h X $e = e$ X $h = h$ *for* every element h in G, and n is called the *period* of g. With such an element it is easy to compute powers of g, but it is hard to compute the logarithm of g^k. If g is chosen carefully, no polynomial time algorithm is known that can compute k from g^k. This property leads to a very elegant key agreement scheme:

$$A \rightarrow B: cert(ID_A, V), g^a$$
$$B \rightarrow A: g^b, cert(ID_B, V'), sig_B(g^a, g^b, ID_A)$$
$$A \rightarrow B: sig_A(g^b, g^a, ID_B)$$

The session key is then computed as SK $\leftarrow$ prf(K, $g^a g^b$, ID_A, ID_B), where K $\leftarrow$ prf(0, g^{ab}). In this protocol, a is a random number chosen by A, b is a random number chosen by B, and 0 denotes the all zeros key. Note that A sends g^a unprotected across the channel to B.

The quantity g^{ab} is called the *Diffie−Hellman key*. Since B knows the random secret b, it can compute $g^{ab} = (g^a)^b$ from A's public value g^a, and similarly A can compute g^{ab} from B's public value g^b. This construction poses no risk, because the discrete logarithm problem is intractable, so it is computationally infeasible for an attacker to determine a from g^a. Similarly, B may send g^b across the channel in the clear, because a third party cannot extract b from g^b. B's signature on message 2 prevents forgeries and assures that the response is from B. Since no method is known to compute g^{ab} from g^a and g^b, only A and B will know the Diffie−Hellman key at the end of the protocol. The step K$\leftarrow$ prf(0, g^{ab}) extracts all

---

An Agenda for Action in Selecting Internet Security Process Activities

The following high-level checklist should be addressed in order to find the following Internet security practices helpful (check all tasks completed):

_____**1.** Login pages should be encrypted.
_____**2.** Data validation should be done server-side.
_____**3.** Manage your Web site via encrypted connections.
_____**4.** Use strong, cross-platform compatible encryption.
_____**5.** Connect from a secured network.
_____**6.** Don't share login credentials.
_____**7.** Prefer key-based authentication over password authentication.
_____**8.** Maintain a secure workstation.
_____**9.** Use redundancy to protect the Web site.
_____**10.** Make sure you implement strong security measures that apply to all systems — not just those specific to Web security.
_____**11.** Validate logins trough SSL encryption.
_____**12.** Do not use clear text protocols to manage your server.
_____**13.** Implement security policies that apply to all systems.

---

the computational entropy from the Diffie–Hellman key. The construction $SK \leftarrow prf(K, g^a g^b, ID_A, ID_B)$ computes a session key, which can be split into encryption and message authentication keys as before.

The major drawback of Diffie–Hellman is that it is subject to man-in-the-middle attacks. The preceding protocol uses signatures to remove this threat. B's signature authenticates B to a and also binds g^a and g^b together, preventing man-in-the-middle attacks. Similarly, A's signature on message 3 assures B that the session is with A.

These examples illustrate that it is practical to construct session keys that meet the requirements for cryptography, if a long-lived relationship already exists.

State Consistency

We have already observed that the protocol specified in (1) through (3) achieves state consistency when the protocol succeeds. Both parties agree on the identities and on the session instance. When a session key SK is derived, as in (7), both parties also agree on the key. Determining which parties know which pieces of information after each protocol message is the essential tool for a security analysis of this kind of protocol. The analysis of this protocol is typical for authentication and key establishment protocols.

Finally, allowing Internet access in the workplace can create two challenges: ensuring employee efficiency and mitigating security risks. Since you can't simply take away Internet privileges, you must find a way to boost employee productivity while maintaining Internet security. So, with the preceding in mind, because of the frequency of poor security practices or far-too-common security failures on the Internet, let's briefly look at the importance of the process that is used to gather all of these faults into an Internet security checklist and give them a suitable solution.

4. INTERNET SECURITY CHECKLIST

Internet security is a fast-moving challenge and an ever-present threat. There is no one right way to secure a Web site, and all security methods are subject to instant obsolescence, incremental improvement, and constant revision. All public facing Web sites are open to constant attack. So, are you willing and able to invest the time it takes to administer a dynamic, 24×7, world-accessible, database-driven, interactive, user-authenticated Web site? Do you have the time and resources to respond to the constant flow of new Internet security issues? The following high-level checklist helps to answer the preceding questions and addresses a number of far-too-common security failures on the Internet (see checklist: An Agenda for Action in Selecting Internet Security Process Activities).

5. SUMMARY

This chapter examined how cryptography is used on the Internet to secure protocols. It reviewed the architecture of the Internet protocol suite, for even the meaning of what security means is a function of the underlying system architecture. Next it reviewed the Dolev–Yao model, which describes the threats to which network communications are exposed. In particular, all levels of network protocols are completely exposed to eavesdropping and manipulation by an attacker, so using cryptography properly is a first-class requirement to derive any benefit from its use. We learned that effective security mechanisms to protect session-oriented and session establishment protocols are different, although they can share many cryptographic primitives. Cryptography can be very successful in protecting messages on the Internet, but doing so requires preexisting, long-lived relationships. How to build secure open communities is still an open problem; it is probably an intractable question because a solution would imply the elimination of conflict between human beings who do not know each other.

Finally, let's move on to the real interactive part of this chapter: review questions/exercises, hands-on projects, case projects, and optional team case project. The answers and/or solutions by chapter can be found in the online Instructor's Solutions Manual.

CHAPTER REVIEW QUESTIONS/EXERCISES

True/False

1. True or False? The Internet was designed to create standardized communication between computers.
2. True or False? Since communication is an extremely complex activity, it should come as no surprise that the system components providing communication decompose into modules.
3. True or False? Practical solutions addressing Byzantine failures fall largely within the purview of platform rather than network architecture, although the interconnectivity topology is an important consideration.
4. True or False? Security analyses of systems traditionally begin with a model of the user.
5. True or False? A user can eavesdrop on a communications medium by connecting a receiver to the medium.

Multiple Choice

1. The Internet supports message exchange through a mechanism called:
   A. interfaces.
   B. send primitive.
   C. protocols.
   D. confirm primitive.
   E. listen primitive.
2. A minimal communications service interface requires the following four primitives, except which one?
   A. Send
   B. Clear
   C. Confirm
   D. Listen
   E. Receive
3. A report of diagnostic and performance information about underlying communications is known as a:
   A. send primitive.
   B. confirm primitive.
   C. shift cipher.

D. status primitive.
   E. deliver primitive.
4. What is technically not part of the Internet architecture per se?
   A. PHY Layer
   B. Chi-square statistic
   C. Polyalphabetic cipher
   D. Kerckhoff's principle
   E. Unicity distance
5. What is a request/response protocol designed to determine the reachability of another IP address?
   A. Traceroute
   B. Chisquare test
   C. Statistical test
   D. Ping
   E. Destination unreachable

EXERCISE

Problem

How would an organization go about deciding an authentication strategy?

Hands-On Projects

Project

How would an organization go about deciding an authorization strategy?

Case Projects

Problem

When should an organization use message security versus transport security?

Optional Team Case Project

Problem

With regard to a Microsoft-based Internet security system, how would an organization go about using its existing Active Directory infrastructure?

## Chapter 12

The Botnet Problem

Daniel Ramsbrock
George Mason University

Xinyuan Wang
George Mason University

A *botnet* is a collection of compromised Internet computers being controlled remotely by attackers for malicious and illegal purposes. The term comes from programs that are called *robots*, or *bots* for short, because of their automated behavior.

Bot software is highly evolved Internet malware, incorporating components of viruses, worms, spyware, and other malicious software. The person controlling a botnet is known as the *botmaster* or *bot-herder*; and he or she seeks to preserve that person's anonymity at all costs. Unlike previous malware such as viruses and worms, the motivation for operating a botnet is financial. Botnets are extremely profitable, earning their operators hundreds of dollars per day. Botmasters can either rent botnet processing time to others or make direct profits by sending spam, distributing spyware to aid in identity theft, and even extorting money from companies via the threat of a distributed denial-of-service (DDoS) attack.[1] It is no surprise that many network security researchers believe that botnets are one of the most pressing security threats on the Internet today.

Bots are at the center of the undernet economy. Almost every major crime problem on the Net can be traced to them.
　　　　　　　　　—Jeremy Linden, formerly of Arbor Networks[2]

1. INTRODUCTION

You sit down at your computer in the morning, still squinting from sleep. Your computer seems a little slower than usual, but you don't think much of it. After checking the news, you try to sign into eBay to check on your auctions. Oddly enough, your password doesn't seem to work. You try a few more times, thinking maybe you changed it recently—but without success.

Figuring you'll look into it later, you sign into online banking to pay some of those bills that have been piling up. Luckily, your favorite password still works there—so it must be a temporary problem with eBay. Unfortunately, you are in for more bad news: The $0.00 balance on your checking and savings accounts isn't just a "temporary problem." Frantically clicking through the pages, you see that your accounts have been completely cleaned out with wire transfers to several foreign countries.

You check your email, hoping to find some explanation of what is happening. Instead of answers, you have dozens of messages from "network operations centers" around the world, informing you in no uncertain terms that your computer has been scanning, spamming, and sending out massive amounts of traffic over the past 12 hours or so. Shortly afterward, your Internet connection stops working altogether, and you receive a phone call from your service provider. They are very sorry, they explain, but due to something called "botnet activity" on your computer, they have temporarily disabled your account. Near panic now, you demand an explanation from the network technician on the other end. "What exactly is a botnet? How could it cause so much damage overnight? "

Although this scenario might sound far-fetched, it is entirely possible; similar things have happened to thousands of people over the last few years. Once a single bot program is installed on a victim computer, the possibilities are nearly endless. For example, the attacker can get your online passwords, drain your bank accounts, and use your computer as a remote-controlled "zombie" to scan for other victims, send out spam emails, and even launch DDoS attacks.

---

1. T. Holz, "A Short Visit to the Bot Zoo," *IEEE Security and Privacy*, 3(3), 2005, pp. 76—79.
2. S. Berinato, "Attack of the Bots," *WIRED*, 14(11), November 2006, www.wired.com/wired/archive/14.11/botnet.html.

This chapter describes the botnet threat and the countermeasures available to network security professionals. First, it provides an overview of botnets, including their origins, structure, and underlying motivation. Next, the chapter describes existing methods for defending computers and networks against botnets. Finally, it addresses the most important aspect of the botnet problem: how to identify and track the botmaster in order to eliminate the root cause of the botnet problem.

2. BOTNET OVERVIEW

Bots and botnets are the latest trend in the evolution of Internet malware. Their black-hat developers have built on the experience gathered from decades of viruses, worms, Trojan horses, and other malware to create highly sophisticated software that is difficult to detect and remove. Typical botnets have several hundred to several thousand members, though some botnets have been detected with over 5.9 million members.[3] As of January 2011, industry analysts estimated that up to 590 million computers (about 36 percent of all Internet hosts) were infected with bot software.[4]

Origins of Botnets

Before botnets, the main motivation for Internet attacks was fame and notoriety. By design, these attacks were noisy and easily detected. High-profile examples are the Melissa email worm (1999), ILOVEYOU (2000), Code Red (2001), Slammer (2003), and Sasser (2004).[5] Although the impact of these viruses and worms was severe, the damage was relatively short-lived and consisted mainly of the cost of the outage plus man-hours required for cleanup. Once the infected files had been removed from the victim computers and the vulnerability patched, the attackers no longer had any control.

By contrast, botnets are built on the very premise of extending the attacker's control over his victims. To achieve long-term control, a bot must be stealthy during every part of its life cycle, unlike its predecessors.[2] As a result, most bots have a relatively small network footprint and do not create much traffic during typical operation. Once a bot is in place, the only required traffic consists of incoming commands and outgoing responses, constituting the botnet's command and control (C&C) channel. Therefore, the scenario at the beginning of the chapter is not typical of all botnets. Such an obvious attack points to either a brazen or an inexperienced botmaster, and there are plenty of them.

The concept of a remote-controlled computer bot originates from Internet Relay Chat (IRC), where benevolent bots were first introduced to help with repetitive administrative tasks such as channel and nickname management.[1,2] One of the first implementations of such an IRC bot was Eggdrop, originally developed in 1993 and still one of the most popular IRC bots.[6] Over time, attackers realized that IRC was in many ways a perfect medium for large-scale botnet C&C. It provides an instantaneous one-to-many communications channel and can support very large numbers of concurrent users.[6]

Botnet Topologies and Protocols

In addition to the traditional IRC-based botnets, several other protocols and topologies have emerged recently. The two main botnet topologies are centralized and peer-to-peer (P2P). Among centralized botnets, IRC is still the predominant protocol,[7,8,9] but this trend is decreasing and several recent bots have used HTTP for their C&C channels.[7,9] Among P2P botnets, many different protocols exist, but the general idea is to use a decentralized collection of peers and thus eliminate the single point of failure found in centralized botnets. P2P is becoming the most popular botnet topology because it has many advantages over centralized botnets.[10]

Centralized

Centralized botnets use a single entity (a host or a small collection of hosts) to manage all bot members. The advantage of a centralized topology is that it is fairly easy to implement and produces little overhead. A major disadvantage is that the entire botnet becomes useless if the central entity is removed, since bots will attempt to

3. Joris Evers, "'Bot Herders' May Have Controlled 1.5 Million PCs," http://news.cnet.com/Bot-herders-may-have-controlled-1.5-million-PCs/2100-7350_3-5906896.html.

4. A. Greenberg, "Spam Crackdown 'A Drop in the Bucket,'" *Forbes*, June 14, 2007, www.forbes.com/security/2007/06/14/spam-arrest-fbi-tech-security-cx_ag_0614spam.html.

5. P. Barford and V. Yegneswaran, "An Inside Look at Botnets," Special Workshop on Malware Detection, Advances in Information Security, Springer Verlag, 2006.

6. E. Cooke, F. Jahanian, and D. McPherson, "The Zombie Roundup: Understanding, Detecting, and Disturbing Botnets," in Proc. 1st Workshop on Steps to Reducing Unwanted Traffic on the Internet (SRUTI), Cambridge, July 7, 2005, pp. 39–44.

7. N. Ianelli and A. Hackworth, "Botnets as a Vehicle for Online Crime," in Proc. 18th Annual Forum of Incident Response and Security Teams (FIRST), Baltimore, MD, June 25–30, 2006.

8. M. Rajab, J. Zarfoss, F. Monrose, and A. Terzis, "A Multifaceted Approach to Understanding the Botnet Phenomenon," in Proc. of the 6th ACM SIGCOM Internet Measurement Conference, Rio de Janeiro, Brazil, October 2006.

9. Trend Micro, "Taxonomy of Botnet Threats," Trend Micro Enterprise Security Library, November 2006.

10. Symantec, "Symantec Internet Security Threat Report, Trends for July–December 2007," Volume 13, April 2008.

connect to nonexistent servers. To provide redundancy against this problem, many modern botnets rely on dynamic DNS services and/or fast-flux DNS techniques. In a fast-flux configuration, hundreds or thousands of compromised hosts are used as proxies to hide the identities of the true C&C servers. These hosts constantly alternate in a round-robin DNS configuration to resolve one hostname to many different IP addresses (none of which are the true IPs of C&C servers). Only the proxies know the true C&C servers, forwarding all traffic from the bots to these servers.[11]

As we've described, the IRC protocol is an ideal candidate for centralized botnet control, and it remains the most popular among in-the-wild botmasters,[7,8,9] although it appears that will not be true much longer. Popular examples of IRC bots are Agobot, Spybot, and Sdbot.[11] Variants of these three families make up most active botnets today. By its nature, IRC is centralized and allows nearly instant communication among large botnets. One of the major disadvantages is that IRC traffic is not very common on the Internet, especially in an enterprise setting. As a result, standard IRC traffic can be easily detected, filtered, or blocked. For this reason, some botmasters run their IRC servers on non-standard ports. Some even use customized IRC implementations, replacing easily recognized commands such as JOIN and PRIVMSG with other text. Despite these countermeasures, IRC still tends to stick out from the regular Web and email traffic due to uncommon port numbers.

Recently, botmasters have started using HTTP to manage their centralized botnets. The advantage of using regular Web traffic for C&C is that it must be allowed to pass through virtually all firewalls, since HTTP comprises a majority of Internet traffic. Even closed firewalls that only provide Web access (via a proxy service, for example) will allow HTTP traffic to pass. It is possible to inspect the content and attempt to filter out malicious C&C traffic, but this is not feasible due to the large number of existing bots and variants. If botmasters use HTTPS (HTTP encrypted using SSL/TLS), then even content inspection becomes useless and all traffic must be allowed to pass through the firewall. However, a disadvantage of HTTP is that it does not provide the instant communication and built-in, scale-up properties of IRC: Bots must manually poll the central server at specific intervals. With large botnets, these intervals must be large enough and distributed well to avoid overloading the server with simultaneous requests. Examples of HTTP

bots are Bobax[12] and Rustock, with Rustock using a custom encryption scheme on top of HTTP to conceal its C&C traffic.[13]

Peer-To-Peer

As defenses against centralized botnets have become more effective, more and more botmasters are exploring ways to avoid the pitfalls of relying on a centralized architecture and therefore a single point of failure. Symantec reports a "steady decrease" in centralized IRC botnets and predicts that botmasters are now "accelerating their shift ... to newer, stealthier control methods, using protocols such as ... peer-to-peer."[10] In the P2P model, no centralized server exists, and all member nodes are equally responsible for passing on traffic. "If done properly, [P2P] makes it near impossible to shut down the botnet as a whole. It also provides anonymity to the [botmaster], because they can appear as just another node in the network," says security researcher Joe Stewart of Lurhq.[14] There are many protocols available for P2P networks, each differing in the way nodes first join the network and the role they later play in passing traffic along. Some popular protocols are BitTorrent, WASTE, and Kademlia.[11] Many of these protocols were first developed for benign uses, such as P2P file sharing.

One of the first malicious P2P bots was Sinit, released in September 2003. It uses random scanning to find peers, rather than relying on one of the established P2P bootstrap protocols.[11] As a result, Sinit often has trouble finding peers, which results in overall poor connectivity.[15] Due to the large amount of scanning traffic, this bot is easily detected by intrusion detection systems (IDSs).[16]

Another advanced bot using the P2P approach is Nugache, released in April 2006.[11] It initially connects to a list of 22 predefined peers to join the P2P network, then downloads a list of active peer nodes from there. This implies that if the 22 "seed" hosts can be shut down, no new bots will be able to join the network, but existing nodes can still function.[17] Nugache encrypts all

11. J. Grizzard, V. Sharma, C. Nunnery, B. Kang, and D. Dagon, "Peer-to-Peer Botnets: Overview and Case Study," in Proc. First Workshop on Hot Topics in Understanding Botnets (HotBots), Cambridge, April 2007.

12. J. Stewart, "Bobax Trojan Analysis," SecureWorks, May 17, 2004, http://secureworks.com/research/threats/bobax.

13. K. Chiang and L. Lloyd, "A Case Study of the Rustock Rootkit and Spam Bot," in Proc. First Workshop on Hot Topics in Understanding Botnets (HotBots), Cambridge, April 10, 2007.

14. R. Lemos, "Bot Software Looks to Improve Peerage," SecurityFocus, May 2, 2006, www.securityfocus.com/news/11390.

15. P. Wang, S. Sparks, and C. Zou, "An Advanced Hybrid Peer-to-Peer Botnet," in Proc. First Workshop on Hot Topics in Understanding Botnets (HotBots), Cambridge, April 10, 2007.

16. J. Stewart, "Sinit P2P Trojan Analysis," SecureWorks, December 8, 2004, www.secureworks.com/research/threats/sinit.

17. R. Schoof and Ralph Koning, "Detecting Peer-to-Peer Botnets," unpublished paper, University of Amsterdam, February 4, 2007, http://staff.science.uva.nl/~delaat/sne-2006-2007/p17/report.pdf.

communications, making it harder for IDSs to detect and increasing the difficulty of manual analysis by researchers.[14] Nugache is seen as one of the first of the more sophisticated P2P bots, paving the way for future enhancements by botnet designers.

The most famous P2P bot so far is Peacomm, more commonly known as the Storm Worm. It started spreading in January 2007 and continues to have a strong presence. To communicate with peers, it uses the Overnet protocol, based on the Kademlia P2P protocol. For bootstrapping, it uses a fixed list of peers (146 in one observed instance) distributed along with the bot. Once the bot has joined Overnet, the botmaster can easily update the binary and add components to extend its functionality. Often the bot is configured to automatically retrieve updates and additional components, such as an Simple Mail Transfer Protocol (SMTP) server for spamming, an email address harvesting tool, and a DoS module. Like Nugache, all of Peacomm's communications are encrypted, making it extremely hard to observe C&C traffic or inject commands appearing to come from the botmaster. Unlike centralized botnets relying on a dynamic DNS provider, Peacomm uses its own P2P network as a distributed DNS system that has no single point of failure. The fixed list of peers is a potential weakness, although it would be challenging to take all these nodes offline. Additionally, the attackers can always set up new nodes and include an updated peer list with the bot, resulting in an "arms race" to shut down malicious nodes.[11]

3. TYPICAL BOT LIFE CYCLE

Regardless of the topology being used, the typical life cycle of a bot is similar:

1. *Creation.* First, the botmaster develops his bot software, often reusing existing code and adding custom features. He might use a test network to perform dry runs before deploying the bot in the wild.
2. *Infection.* There are many possibilities for infecting victim computers, including the following four. Once a victim machine becomes infected with a bot, it is known as a *zombie.*
    - Software vulnerabilities. The attacker exploits a vulnerability in a running service to automatically gain access and install his/her software without any user interaction. This was the method used by most worms, including the infamous Code Red and Sasser worms.[5]
    - *Drive-by download.* The attacker hosts his file on a Web server and entices people to visit the site. When the user loads a certain page, the software is automatically installed without user interaction,

usually by exploiting browser bugs, misconfigurations, or unsecured ActiveX controls.
    - *Trojan horse.* The attacker bundles his malicious software with seemingly benign and useful software, such as screen savers, antivirus scanners, or games. The user is fully aware of the installation process, but he does not know about the hidden bot functionality.
    - *Email attachment*: Although this method has become less popular lately due to rising user awareness, it is still around. The attacker sends an attachment that will automatically install the bot software when the user opens it, usually without any interaction. This was the primary infection vector of the ILOVEYOU email worm from 2000.[5] The recent Storm Worm successfully used enticing email messages with executable attachments to lure its victims.[18]

3. *Rallying.* After infection, the bot starts up for the first time and attempts to contact its C&C server(s) in a process known as *rallying*. In a centralized botnet, this could be an IRC or HTTP server, for example. In a P2P botnet, the bots perform the bootstrapping protocol required to locate other peers and join the network. Most bots are very fault-tolerant, having multiple lists of backup servers to attempt if the primary ones become unavailable. Some C&C servers are configured to immediately send some initial commands to the bot (without botmaster intervention). In an IRC botnet, this is typically done by including the commands in the C&C channel's topic.
4. *Waiting.* Having joined the C&C network, the bot waits for commands from the botmaster. During this time, very little (if any) traffic passes between the victim and the C&C servers. In an IRC botnet, this traffic would mainly consist of periodic keep-alive messages from the server.
5. *Executing.* Once the bot receives a command from the botmaster, it executes it and returns any results to the botmaster via the C&C network. The supported commands are only limited by the botmaster's imagination and technical skills. Common commands are in line with the major uses of botnets: scanning for new victims, sending spam, sending DoS floods, setting up traffic redirection, and many more.

Following the execution of a command, the bot returns to the waiting state to await further instructions. If the victim computer is rebooted or loses its connection to the C&C network, the bot resumes in the rallying state. Assuming it can reach its C&C network, it will then continue in the waiting state until further commands arrive.

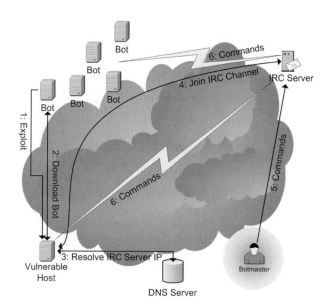

FIGURE 12.1   Infection sequence of a typical centralized IRC-based botnet.

Figure 12.1 shows the detailed infection sequence in a typical IRC-based botnet:

1. An existing botnet member computer launches a scan, then discovers and exploits a vulnerable host.
2. Following the exploit, the vulnerable host is made to download and install a copy of the bot software, constituting an infection.
3. When the bot starts up on the vulnerable host, it enters the rallying state: It performs a DNS lookup to determine the current IP of its C&C server.
4. The new bot joins the botnet's IRC channel on the C&C server for the first time, now in the waiting state.
5. The botmaster sends his commands to the C&C server on the botnet's IRC channel.
6. The C&C server forwards the commands to all bots, which now enter the executing state.

4. THE BOTNET BUSINESS MODEL

Unlike the viruses and worms of the past, botnets are motivated by financial profit. Organized crime groups often use them as a source of income, either by hiring "freelance" botmasters or by having their own members create botnets. As a result, network security professionals are up against motivated, well-financed organizations that can often hire some of the best minds in computers and network security. This is especially true in countries such as Russia, Romania, and other eastern European nations where there is an abundance of IT talent at the high school and university level but legitimate IT job prospects are very limited. In such an environment, criminal organizations easily

recruit recent graduates by offering far better opportunities than the legitimate job market.[18-21] One infamous example of such a crime organization is the Russian Business Network (RBN), a Russian Internet service provider (ISP) that openly supports criminal activity.[19] They are responsible for the Storm Worm (Peacomm), the March 2007 DDoS attacks on Estonia, and a high-profile attack on the Bank of India in August 2007,[22] along with many other attacks.

It might not be immediately obvious how a collection of computers can be used to cause havoc and produce large profits. The main point is that botnets provide *anonymous* and *distributed* access to the Internet. The anonymity makes the attackers untraceable, and a botnet's distributed nature makes it extremely hard to shut down. As a result, botnets are perfect vehicles for criminal activities on the Internet. Some of the main profit-producing methods are explained here,[23] but criminals are always devising new and creative ways to profit from botnets:

- *Spam.* Spammers send millions of emails advertising phony or overpriced products, phishing for financial data and login information, or running advance-fee schemes such as the Nigerian 419 scam. Even if only a small percentage of recipients respond to this spam, the payoff is considerable for the spammer. It is estimated that up to 90 percent of all spam originates from botnets.[2]

- *DDoS and extortion.* Having amassed a large number of bots, the attacker contacts an organization and threatens to launch a massive DDoS attack, shutting down its Web site for several hours or even days. Another variation on this method is to find vulnerabilities, use them to steal financial or confidential data, and then demand money for the "safe return" of the data and to keep it from being circulated in the underground economy.[21] Often, companies would rather pay off the attacker to avoid costly downtime, lost sales, and the lasting damage to its reputation that would result from a DDoS attack or data breach.

18. D. Bizeul, "Russian Business Network Study," unpublished paper, November 20, 2007, www.bizeul.org/files/RBN_study.pdf.
19. A. E. Cha, "Internet Dreams Turn to Crime," *The Washington Post*, May 18, 2003, www.washingtonpost.com/ac2/wp-dyn/A2619-2003May17.
20. B. I. Koerner, "From Russia with Løpht," *Legal Affairs*, May–June 2002, http://legalaffairs.org/issues/May-June-2002/feature_koerner_may-jun2002.msp.
21. M. Delio, "Inside Russia's Hacking Culture," *WIRED*, March 12, 2001, www.wired.com/culture/lifestyle/news/2001/03/42346.
22. L. Tung, "Infamous Russian ISP Behind Bank of India Hack" *ZDNet*, September 4, 2007, http://news.zdnet.co.uk/security/0,1000000189, 39289057,00.htm?r = 2.
23. P. Bächer, T. Holz, M. Kötter, and G. Wicherski, "Know Your Enemy: Tracking Botnets," March 13, 2005; see www.honeynet.org/papers/bots.

- *Identity theft.* Once a bot has a foothold on a victim's machine, it usually has complete control. For example, the attacker can install keyloggers to record login and password information, search the hard drive for valuable data, or alter the DNS configuration to redirect victims to look-alike Web sites and collect personal information, known as *pharming*. Using the harvested personal information, the attacker can make fraudulent credit-card charges, clean out the victim's bank account, and apply for credit in the victim's name, among many other things.

- *Click fraud.* In this scenario, bots are used to repeatedly click Web advertising links, generating per-click revenue for the attacker.[2] This represents fraud because only the clicks of human users with a legitimate interest are valuable to advertisers. The bots will not buy the product or service as a result of clicking the advertisement.

These illegal activities are extremely profitable. For example, a 2006 study by the Germany Honeynet Project estimated that a botmaster can make about $430 per day just from per-install advertising software.[24] A 20-year-old California botmaster indicted in February 2006 earned $100,000 in advertising revenue from his botnet operations.[25] However, both of these cases pale in comparison to the estimated $20 million worth of damage caused by an international ring of computer criminals known as the A-Team.[26]

Due to these very profitable uses of botnets, many botmasters make money simply by creating botnets and then renting out processing power and bandwidth to spammers, extortionists, and identity thieves. Despite a recent string of high-profile botnet arrests, these are merely a drop in the bucket.[4] Overall, botmasters still have a fairly low chance of getting caught due to a lack of effective traceback techniques. The relatively low risk combined with high yield makes the botnet business very appealing as a fundraising method for criminal enterprises, especially in countries with weak computer crime enforcement.

5. BOTNET DEFENSE

When botnets emerged, the response was similar to previous Internet malware: Antivirus vendors created signatures and removal techniques for each new instance of the

bot. This approach initially worked well at the host level, but researchers soon started exploring more advanced methods for eliminating more than one bot at a time. After all, a botnet with tens of thousands of members would be very tedious to combat one bot at a time.

This part of the chapter describes the current defenses against centralized botnets, moving from the host level to the network level, then to the C&C server, and finally to the botmaster himself.

Detecting and Removing Individual Bots

Removing individual bots does not usually have a noticeable impact on the overall botnet, but it is a crucial first step in botnet defense. The basic antivirus approach using signature-based detection is still effective with many bots, but some are starting to use polymorphism, which creates unique instances of the bot code and evades signature-based detection. For example, Agobot is known to have thousands of variants, and it includes built-in support for polymorphism to change its signature at will.

To deal with these more sophisticated bots and all other polymorphic malware, detection must be done using behavioral analysis and heuristics. Researchers Stinson and Mitchell have developed a taint-based approach called BotSwat that marks all data originating from the network. If this data is used as input for a system call, there is a high probability that it is bot-related behavior, since user input typically comes from the keyboard or mouse on most end-user systems.[27]

Detecting C&C Traffic

To mitigate the botnet problem on a larger scale, researchers turned their attention to network-based detection of the botnet's C&C traffic. This method allows organizations or even ISPs to detect the presence of bots on their entire network, rather than having to check each machine individually.

One approach is to examine network traffic for certain known patterns that occur in botnet C&C traffic. This is, in effect, a network-deployed version of signature-based detection, where signatures have to be collected for each bot before detection is possible. Researchers Goebel and Holz implemented this method in their Rishi tool, which evaluates IRC nicknames for likely botnet membership based on a list of known botnet naming schemes. As with all signature-based approaches, it often leads to an "arms race" where the

24. R. Naraine, "Money Bots: Hackers Cash in on Hijacked PCs," *eWeek*, September 8, 2006, www.eweek.com/article2/0,1759,2013924,00.asp.

25. P. F. Roberts, "DOJ Indicts Hacker for Hospital Botnet Attack," *eWeek*, February 10, 2006, www.eweek.com/article2/0,1759,1925456,00.asp.

26. T. Claburn, "New Zealander 'AKILL' Pleads Guilty to Botnet Charges," *Information Week*, April 3, 2008, www.informationweek.com/news/security/cybercrime/showArticle.jhtml?articleID = 207001573.

27. E. Stinson and J. Mitchell, "Characterizing Bots' Remote Control Behavior," in Proc. 4th International Conference on Detection of Intrusions & Malware and Vulnerability Assessment (DIMVA), Lucerne, Switzerland, July 12–13, 2007.

attackers frequently change their malware and the network security community tries to keep up by creating signatures for each new instance.[28]

Rather than relying on a limited set of signatures, it is also possible to use the IDS technique of anomaly detection to identify unencrypted IRC botnet traffic. This method was successfully implemented by researchers Binkley and Singh at Portland State University, and as a result they reported a significant increase in bot detection on the university network.[29]

Another IDS-based detection technique called BotHunter was proposed by Gu et al. in 2007. Their approach is based on IDS dialog correlation techniques: It deploys three separate network monitors at the network perimeter, each detecting a specific stage of bot infection. By correlating these events, BotHunter can reconstruct the traffic dialog between the infected machine and the outside Internet. From this dialog, the engine determines whether a bot infection has taken place with a high accuracy rate.[30]

Moving beyond the scope of a single network/organization, traffic from centralized botnets can be detected at the ISP level based only on transport layer flow statistics. This approach was developed by Karasaridis et al., and it solves many of the problems of packet-level inspection. It is passive, highly scalable, and only uses flow summary data (limiting privacy issues). Additionally, it can determine the size of a botnet without joining and can even detect botnets using encrypted C & C. The approach exploits the underlying principle of centralized botnets: Each bot has to contact the C&C server, producing detectable patterns in network traffic flows.[31]

Beyond the ISP level, a heuristic method for Internet-wide bot detection was proposed by Ramachandran et al. in 2006. In this scheme, query patterns of DNS blackhole lists (DNSBLs) are used to create a list of possible bot-infected IP addresses. It relies on the fact that botmasters need to periodically check whether their spam-sending bots have been added to a DNSBL and have therefore become useless. The query patterns of botmasters to a DNSBL are very different from those of

legitimate mail servers, allowing detection.[32] One major limitation is that this approach focuses mainly on the sending of spam. It would most likely not detect bots engaged in other illegal activities, such as DDoS attacks or click fraud, since these do not require DNSBL lookups.

Detecting and Neutralizing the C&C Servers

Though detecting C&C traffic and eliminating all bots on a given local network is a step in the right direction, it still doesn't allow the takedown of an entire botnet at once. To achieve this goal in a centralized botnet, access to the C&C servers must be removed. This approach assumes that the C&C servers consist of only a few hosts that are accessed directly. If hundreds or thousands of hosts are used in a fast-flux proxy configuration, it becomes extremely challenging to locate and neutralize the true C&C servers.

In work similar to BotHunter, researchers Gu et al. developed BotSniffer in 2008. This approach represents several improvements, notably that BotSniffer can handle encrypted traffic, since it no longer relies only on content inspection to correlate messages. A major advantage of this approach is that it requires no advance knowledge of the bot's signature or the identity of C&C servers. By analyzing network traces, BotSniffer detects the spatial-temporal correlation among C&C traffic belonging to the same botnet. It can therefore detect both the bot members and the C&C server(s) with a low false positive rate.[33]

Most of the approaches mentioned under "Detecting C&C Traffic" can also be used to detect the C&C servers, with the exception of the DNSBL approach.[33] However, their focus is mainly on detection and removal of individual bots. None of these approaches mentions targeting the C&C servers to eliminate an entire botnet.

One of the few projects that has explored the feasibility of C&C server takedown is the work of Freiling et al. in 2005.[34] Although their focus is on DDoS prevention, they describe the method that is generally used in the wild to remove C&C servers when they are detected. First, the bot binary is either reverse-engineered or run in

28. J. Goebel and T. Holz, "Rishi: Identify Bot Contaminated Hosts by IRC Nickname Evaluation," in Proc. First Workshop on Hot Topics in Understanding Botnets (HotBots), Cambridge, April 10, 2007.

29. J. Binkley and S. Singh, "An Algorithm for Anomaly-based Botnet Detection," in Proc. 2nd Workshop on Steps to Reducing Unwanted Traffic on the Internet (SRUTI), San Jose, July 7, 2006, pp. 43–48.

30. G. Gu, P. Porras, V. Yegneswaran, M. Fong, and W. Lee, "BotHunter: Detecting Malware Infection through IDS-driven Dialog Correlation," in Proc. 16th USENIX Security Symposium, Boston, August 2007.

31. A. Karasaridis, B. Rexroad, and D. Hoeflin, "Wide-scale Botnet Detection and Characterization," in Proc. First Workshop on Hot Topics in Understanding Botnets (HotBots), Cambridge, MA, April 10, 2007.

32. A. Ramachandran, N. Feamster, and D. Dagon, "Revealing Botnet Membership Using DNSBL Counter-intelligence," in Proc. 2nd Workshop on Steps to Reducing Unwanted Traffic on the Internet (SRUTI), San Jose, CA, July 7, 2006, pp. 49–54.

33. G. Gu, J. Zhang, and W. Lee, "BotSniffer: Detecting Botnet Command and Control Channels in Network Traffic," in Proc. 15th Network and Distributed System Security Symposium (NDSS), San Diego, February 2008.

34. F. Freiling, T. Holz, and G. Wicherski, "Botnet Tracking: Exploring a Root-Cause Methodology to Prevent Denial-of-Service Attacks," in Proc. 10th European Symposium on Research in Computer Security (ESORICS), Milan, Italy, September 12–14, 2005.

a sandbox to observe its behavior, specifically the hostnames of the C&C servers. Using this information, the proper dynamic DNS providers can be notified to remove the DNS entries for the C&C servers, preventing any bots from contacting them and thus severing contact between the botmaster and his botnet. Dagon et al. used a similar approach in 2006 to obtain experiment data for modeling botnet propagation, redirecting the victim's connections from the true C&C server to their sinkhole host.[35] Even though effective, the manual analysis and contact with the DNS operator is a slow process. It can take up to several days until all C&C servers are located and neutralized. However, this process is essentially the best available approach for shutting down entire botnets in the wild. As we mentioned, this technique becomes much harder when fast-flux proxies are used to conceal the real C&C servers or a P2P topology is in place.

Attacking Encrypted C&C Channels

Although some of the approaches can detect encrypted C&C traffic, the presence of encryption makes botnet research and analysis much harder. The first step in dealing with these advanced botnets is to penetrate the encryption that protects the C&C channels.

A popular approach for adding encryption to an existing protocol is to run it on top of SSL/TLS; to secure HTTP traffic, ecommerce Web sites run HTTP over SSL/TLS, known as HTTPS. Many encryption schemes that support key exchange (including SSL/TLS) are susceptible to man-in-the-middle (MITM) attacks, whereby a third party can impersonate the other two parties to each other. Such an attack is possible only when no authentication takes place prior to the key exchange, but this is a surprisingly common occurrence due to poor configuration.

The premise of an MITM attack is that the client does not verify that it's talking to the real server, and vice versa. When the MITM receives a connection from the client, it immediately creates a separate connection to the server (under a different encryption key) and passes on the client's request. When the server responds, the MITM decrypts the response, logs and possibly alters the content, then passes it on to the client reencrypted with the proper key. Neither the client nor the server notices that anything is wrong because they are communicating with each other over an encrypted connection, as expected. The important difference is that unknown to either party, the traffic is being decrypted and reencrypted by the MITM in transit, allowing him to observe and alter the traffic.

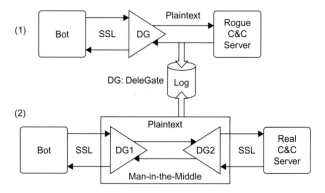

FIGURE 12.2 Setups for man-in-the-middle attacks on encrypted C&C channels.

In the context of bots, two main attacks on encrypted C&C channels are possible: (1) "gray-box" analysis, whereby the bot communicates with a local machine impersonating the C&C server, and (2) a full MITM attack, in which the bot communicates with the true C&C server. Figure 12.2 shows a possible setup for both attacks, using the DeleGate proxy[36] for the conversion to and from SSL/TLS.

The first attack is valuable to determine the authentication information required to join the live botnet: the address of the C&C server, the IRC channel name (if applicable), plus any required passwords. However, it does not allow the observer to see the interaction with the larger botnet, specifically the botmaster. The second attack reveals the full interaction with the botnet, including all botmaster commands, the botmaster password used to control the bots, and possibly the IP addresses of other bot members (depending on the configuration of the C&C server). Figures 12.3–12.5 show the screenshots of the full MITM attack on a copy of Agobot configured to connect to its C&C server via SSL/TLS. Specifically, Figure 12.3 shows the botmaster's IRC window, with his commands and the bot's responses. Figure 12.4 shows the encrypted SSL/TLS trace, and Figure 12.5 shows the decrypted plaintext that was observed at the DeleGate proxy. The botmaster password *botmasterPASS* is clearly visible, along with the required username, *botmaster*.

Armed with the botmaster username and password, the observer could literally take over the botnet. He could log in as the botmaster, then issue a command such as Agobot's .bot.remove, causing all bots to disconnect from the botnet and permanently remove themselves from the infected computers. Unfortunately, there are legal issues with this approach because it constitutes unauthorized access to all the botnet computers, despite the fact that it is in fact a benign command to remove the bot software.

35. D. Dagon, C. Zou, and W. Lee, "Modeling Botnet Propagation Using Time Zones," in Proc. 13th Network and Distributed System Security Symposium (NDSS), February 2006.

36. "DeleGate Multi-purpose Application Gateway," www.delegate.org/delegate (accessed May 4, 2008).

FIGURE 12.3 Screenshot showing the botmaster's IRC window.

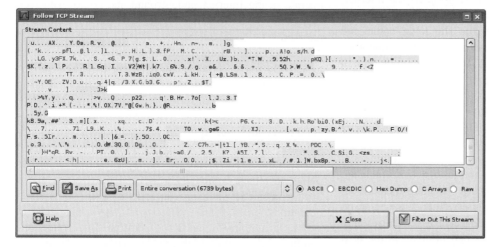

FIGURE 12.4 Screenshot showing the SSL/TLS-encrypted network traffic.

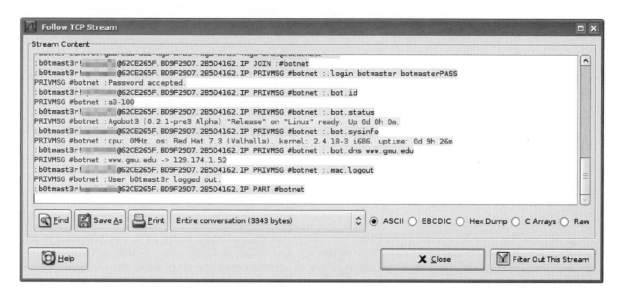

FIGURE 12.5 Screenshot showing decrypted plaintext from the DeleGate proxy.

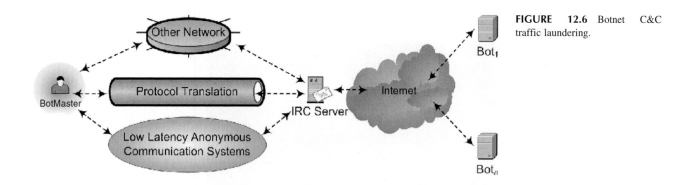

FIGURE 12.6 Botnet C&C traffic laundering.

Locating and Identifying the Botmaster

Shutting down an entire botnet at once is a significant achievement, especially when the botnet numbers in the tens of thousands of members. However, there is nothing stopping the botmaster from simply deploying new bots to infect the millions of vulnerable hosts on the Internet, creating a new botnet in a matter of hours. In fact, most of the machines belonging to the shutdown botnet are likely to become infected again because the vulnerabilities and any attacker-installed backdoors often remain active, despite the elimination of the C&C servers. Botnet-hunting expert Gadi Evron agrees: "When we disable a command-and-control server, the botnet is immediately recreated on another host. We're not hurting them anymore," he said in a 2006 interview.[37]

The only permanent solution of the botnet problem is to go after the root cause: the botmasters. Unfortunately, most botmasters are very good at concealing their identities and locations, since their livelihood depends on it. Tracking the botmaster to her true physical location is a complex problem that is described in detail in the next part of the chapter. So far, there is no published work that would allow automated botmaster traceback on the Internet, and it remains an open problem.

6. BOTMASTER TRACEBACK

The botnet field is full of challenging problems: obfuscated binaries, encrypted C&C channels, fast-flux proxies protecting central C&C servers, customized communication protocols, and many more (see Figure 12.6). Arguably the most challenging task is locating the botmaster. Most botmasters take precautions on multiple levels to ensure that their connections cannot be traced to their true locations.

The reason for the botmaster's extreme caution is that a successful trace would have disastrous consequences.

He could be arrested, his computer equipment could be seized and scrutinized in detail, and he could be sentenced to an extended prison term. Additionally, authorities would likely learn the identities of his associates, either from questioning him or by searching his computers. As a result, he would never again be able to operate in the Internet underground and could even face violent revenge from his former associates when he is released.

In the United States, authorities have recently started to actively pursue botmasters, resulting in several arrests and convictions. In November 2005, 20-year-old Jeanson James Ancheta of California was charged with botnet-related computer offenses.[38] He pleaded guilty in January 2006 and could face up to 25 years in prison.[39] In a similar case, 20-year-old Christopher Maxwell was indicted on federal computer charges. He is accused of using his botnet to attack computers at several universities and a Seattle hospital, where bot infections severely disrupted operations.[26]

In particular, the FBI's Operation Bot Roast has resulted in several high-profile arrests, both in the United States and abroad.[40] The biggest success was the arrest of 18-year-old New Zealand native Owen Thor Walker, who was a member of a large international computer crime ring known as the A-Team. This group is reported to have infected up to 1.3 million computers with bot software and caused about $20 million in economic damage. Despite this success, Walker was only a minor player, and the criminals in control of the A-Team are still at large.[27]

37. R. Naraine, "Is the Botnet Battle Already Lost?" *eWeek*, October 16, 2006, www.eweek.com/article2/0,1895,2029720,00.asp.

38. P. F. Roberts, "California Man Charged with Botnet Offenses," *eWeek*, November 3, 2005, www.eweek.com/article2/0,1759,1881621,00.asp.

39. P. F. Roberts, "Botnet Operator Pleads Guilty," *eWeek*, January 24, 2006, www.eweek.com/article2/0,1759,1914833,00.asp.

40. S. Nichols, "FBI 'Bot Roast' Scores String of Arrests," *vnunet.com*, December 3, 2007, www.vnunet.com/vnunet/news/2204829/bot-roast-scores-string-arrests.

Unfortunately, botmaster arrests are not very common. The cases described here represent only several individuals; thousands of botmasters around the world are still operating with impunity. They use sophisticated techniques to hide their true identities and locations, and they often operate in countries with weak computer crime enforcement. The lack of international coordination, both on the Internet and in law enforcement, makes it hard to trace botmasters and even harder to hold them accountable to the law.[20]

Traceback Challenges

One defining characteristic of the botmaster is that he originates the botnet C&C traffic. Therefore, one way to find the botmaster is to track the botnet C&C traffic. To hide himself, the botmaster wants to disguise his link to the C&C traffic via various traffic-laundering techniques that make tracking C&C traffic more difficult. For example, a botmaster can route his C&C traffic through a number of intermediate hosts, various protocols, and low-latency anonymous networks to make it extremely difficult to trace. To further conceal his activities, a botmaster can also encrypt his traffic to and from the C&C servers. Finally, a botmaster only needs to be online briefly and send small amounts of traffic to interact with his botnet, reducing the chances of live traceback. Figure 12.6 illustrates some of the C&C traffic-laundering techniques a botmaster can use.

Stepping Stones

The intermediate hosts used for traffic laundering are known as *stepping stones*. The attacker sets them up in a chain, leading from the botmaster's true location to the C&C server. Stepping stones can be SSH servers, proxies (such as SOCKS), IRC bouncers (BNCs), virtual private network (VPN) servers, or any number of network redirection services. They usually run on compromised hosts, which are under the attacker's control and lack audit/logging mechanisms to trace traffic. As a result, manual traceback is tedious and time consuming, requiring the cooperation of dozens of organizations whose networks might be involved in the trace.

The major challenge posed by stepping stones is that all routing information from the previous hop (IP headers, TCP headers, and the like) is stripped from the data before it is sent out on a new, separate connection. Only the content of the packet (the application layer data) is preserved, which renders many existing tracing schemes useless. An example of a technique that relies on routing header information is *probabilistic packet marking* (PPM). This approach was introduced by Savage et al. in 2000, embedding tracing information in an unused

IP header field.[41] Two years later, Goodrich expanded this approach, introducing "randomize-and-link" for better scalability.[42] Another technique for IP-level traceback is the log/hash-based scheme introduced by Snoeren et al.[43] and enhanced by Li et al.[44] These techniques were very useful in combating the fast-spreading worms of the early 2000s, which did not use stepping stones. However, these approaches do not work when stepping stones are present, since IP header information is lost.

Multiple Protocols

Another effective and efficient method to disguise the botmaster is to launder the botnet C&C traffic across other protocols. Such protocol laundering can be achieved by either *protocol tunneling* or *protocol translation*. For example, a sophisticated botmaster could route its command and control traffic through SSH (or even HTTP) tunnels to reach the command and control center. The botmaster could also use some intermediate host X as a stepping stone, use some real-time communication protocols other than IRC between the botmaster host and host X, and use IRC between the host X and the IRC server. In this case, host X performs the protocol translation at the application layer and serves as a conduit of the botnet C&C channel. One protocol that is particularly suitable for laundering the botnet command and control is instant messaging (IM), which supports real-time text-based communication between two or more people.

Low-Latency Anonymous Network

Besides laundering the botnet C&C across stepping stones and different protocols, a sophisticated botmaster could anonymize its C&C traffic by routing it through some low-latency anonymous communication systems. For example, Tor—the second generation of onion routing—uses an overlay network of onion routers to provide anonymous outgoing connections and anonymous hidden services. The botmaster could use Tor as a virtual tunnel to anonymize his TCP-based C&C traffic to the IRC server of the botnet. At the same time, the IRC server of the botnet could utilize Tor's hidden services to anonymize the

41. S. Savage, D. Wetherall, A. Karlin, and T. Anderson, "Practical Network Support for IP Traceback," in Proc. ACM SIGCOMM 2000, September 2000, pp. 295–306.

42. M. T. Goodrich, "Efficient Packet Marking for Large-scale IP Traceback," in Proc. 9th ACM Conference on Computer and Communications Security (CCS 2002), October 2002, pp. 117–126.

43. A. Snoeren, C. Patridge, L. A. Sanchez, C. E. Jones, F. Tchakountio, S. T. Kent, and W. T. Strayer, "Hash-based IP Traceback," in Proc. ACM SIGCOMM 2001, September 2001, pp. 3–14.

44. J. Li, M. Sung, J. Xu, and L. Li, "Large-scale IP Traceback in Highspeed Internet: Practical Techniques and Theoretical Foundation," in Proc. 2004 IEEE Symposium on Security and Privacy, IEEE, 2004.

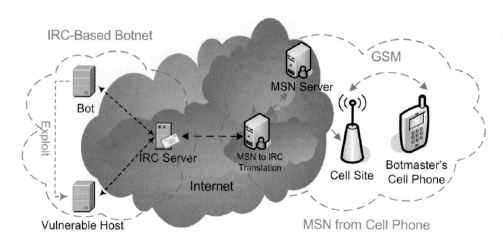

FIGURE 12.7 Using a cell phone to evade Internet-based traceback.

IRC server of the botnet in such a way that its network location is unknown to the bots, and yet it could communicate with all the bots.

Encryption

All or part of the stepping stone chain can be encrypted to protect it against content inspection, which could reveal information about the botnet and botmaster. This can be done using a number of methods, including SSH tunneling, SSL/TLS-enabled BNCs, and IPsec tunneling. Using encryption defeats all content-based tracing approaches, so the tracer must rely on other network flow characteristics, such as packet size or timing, to correlate flows to each other.

Low-Traffic Volume

Since the botmaster only has to connect briefly to issue commands and retrieve results from his botnet, a low volume of traffic flows from any given bot to the botmaster. During a typical session, only a few dozen packets from each bot can be sent to the botmaster. Tracing approaches that rely on analysis of packet size or timing will most likely be ineffective because they typically require a large amount of traffic (several hundred packets) to correlate flows with high statistical confidence. Examples of such tracing approaches[45,46,47] all use timing information to embed a traceable watermark. These approaches can handle stepping stones, encryption, and even low-latency

anonymizing network, but they cannot be directly used for botmaster traceback due to the low traffic volume.

Traceback Beyond the Internet

Even if all three technical challenges can be solved and even if all Internet-connected organizations worldwide cooperate to monitor traffic, there are additional traceback challenges beyond the reach of the Internet (see Figure 12.7). Any IP-based traceback method assumes that the true source IP belongs to the computer the attacker is using and that this machine can be physically located. However, in many scenario this is not true—for example, (1) Internet-connected mobile phone networks, (2) open wireless (Wi-Fi) networks, and (3) public computers, such as those at libraries and Internet cafés.

Most modern cell phones support text-messaging services such as Short Message Service (SMS) and many smart phones also have full-featured IM software. As a result, the botmaster can use a mobile device to control her botnet from any location with cell phone reception. To enable her cell phone to communicate with the C&C server, a botmaster needs to use a protocol translation service or a special IRC client for mobile phones. She can run the translation service on a compromised host, an additional stepping stone. For an IRC botnet, such a service would receive the incoming SMS or IM message, then repackage it as an IRC message and send it on to the C&C server (possibly via more stepping stones), as shown in Figure 12.7. To eliminate the need for protocol translation, the botmaster can run a native IRC client on a smart phone with Internet access. Examples of such clients are the Java-based WLIrc[48] and jmIrc[49] open-source projects. In Figure 12.8, a Nokia smartphone is shown

45. X. Wang, S. Chen, and S. Jajodia, "Network Flow Watermarking Attack on Low-latency Anonymous Communication Systems," in Proc. 2007 IEEE Symposium on Security and Privacy, May 2007.

46. X. Wang, S. Chen, and S. Jajodia, "Tracking Anonymous, Peer-to-Peer VoIP Calls on the Internet," in Proc. 12th ACM Conference on Computer and Communications Security (CCS 2005), October 2005.

47. X. Wang and D. Reeves, "Robust Correlation of Encrypted Attack Traffic through Stepping Stones by Manipulation of Interpacket Delays," in Proc. 10th ACM Conference on Computer and Communications Security (CCS 2003), October 2003, pp. 20–29.

48. "WLIrc Wireless IRC Client for Mobile Phones," http://wirelessirc.sourceforge.net (accessed May 3, 2008).

49. "jmIrc: Java mobile IRC-client (J2ME)," http://jmirc.sourceforge.net (accessed May 3, 2008).

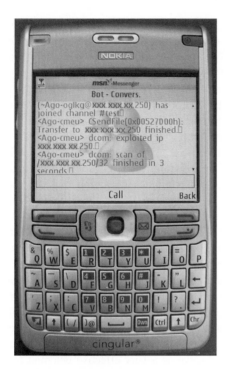

FIGURE 12.8   Using a Nokia smartphone to control an Agobot-based botnet. *(Photo courtesy of Ruishan Zhang.)*

downtown area, such a radius can contain thousands of people and just as many computers. Again, short of searching everyone in the vicinity, the police will be unable to find the botmaster.

Finally, many places provide public Internet access without any logging of the users' identities. Prime examples are public libraries, Internet cafés, and even the business centers at most hotels. In this scenario, a real-time trace would actually find the botmaster, since he would be sitting at the machine in question. However, even if the police are late by only several minutes, there might no longer be any record of who last used the computer. Physical evidence such as fingerprints, hair, and skin cells would be of little use, since many people use these computers each day. Unless a camera system is in place and it captured a clear picture of the suspect on his way to/from the computer, the police again will have no leads.

This part of the chapter illustrated a few common scenarios where even a perfect IP traceback solution would fail to locate the botmaster. Clearly, much work remains on developing automated, integrated traceback solutions that work across various types of networks and protocols.

Finally, let's briefly look at how to prevent botnets. The most important thing to remember is that prevention is an ongoing process. An organization can't just set everything up and expect to be protected forever. Also, it's important to remember that unless an organization employs common sense and prudent Internet communication habits, they're courting disaster.

running MSN Messenger, controlling an Agobot zombie via MSN-IRC protocol translation. On the screen, a new bot has just been infected and has joined the IRC channel following the botmaster's .scan.dcom command.

When a botnet is being controlled from a mobile device, even a perfect IP traceback solution would only reach as far as the gateway host that bridges the Internet and the carrier's mobile network. From there, the tracer can ask the carrier to complete the trace and disclose the name and even the current location of the cell phone's owner. However, there are several problems with this approach. First, this part of the trace again requires lots of manual work and the cooperation of yet another organization, introducing further delays and making a real-time trace unlikely. Second, the carrier won't be able to determine the name of the subscriber if he is using a prepaid cell phone. Third, the tracer could obtain an approximate physical location based on cell site triangulation. Even if he can do this in real time, it might not be very useful if the botmaster is in a crowded public place. Short of detaining all people in the area and checking their cell phones, police won't be able to pinpoint the botmaster.

A similar situation arises when the botmaster uses an unsecured Wi-Fi connection. This could either be a public access point or a poorly configured one that is intended to be private. With a strong antenna, the botmaster can be located up to several thousand feet away. In a typical

7. PREVENTING BOTNETS

One of the most common problems during botnet incident handling (preventing botnets), particularly in widespread incidents, is poor communication and coordination. Anyone involved in an incident, including users, can inadvertently cause additional problems because of a limited view or understanding of the situation. To improve communication and coordination, an organization should designate in advance a few individuals or a small team to be responsible for coordinating the organization's responses to botnet incidents. The coordinator's primary goal is to maintain situational awareness by gathering all pertinent information, making decisions that are in the best interests of the organization, and communicating pertinent information and decisions to all relevant parties within the organization in a timely manner. For botnet incidents, the relevant parties often include end users, who might be given instructions on how to avoid infecting their systems, how to recognize the signs of an infection, and what to do if a system appears to be infected. The coordinator also needs to provide technical guidance and instructions to all staff assisting with containment, eradication, and recovery efforts, as well as giving management regular updates on the status of the response and the current and likely future impact of the incident.

Because widespread botnet incidents often disrupt email services, internal Web sites, Voice over IP, and other forms of communication, organizations should have several communication mechanisms established, so that good communication and coordination among incident handlers, technical staff, management, and users can be sustained during adverse events. Possible communication methods include the organization's phone system, cell phones, pagers, email, fax, and paper. Even under good conditions, it is often effective to use different communication methods for different audiences (for example, communicating to users through email, but using a standard conference call phone number for discussions among key technical personnel). Management updates could occur in person, through conference calls, or through a voice mailbox greeting that is updated regularly with the incident status and other helpful information.

Organizations should also establish a point of contact for answering questions about the legitimacy of botnet alerts. Many organizations use the IT help desk as the initial point of contact and give help desk agents access to sources of information on real botnet threats and virus hoaxes, so that they can quickly determine the legitimacy of an alert and provide users with guidance on what to do. Organizations should caution users not to forward botnet alerts to others without first confirming that the alerts are legitimate.

Organizations should also ensure that they have the necessary tools (hardware and software) and resources to assist in handling botnet incidents. Examples of tools include packet sniffers and protocol analyzers. Additional tools include antivirus software, spyware detection and removal utilities, and host-based IPS software that incident handlers should be able to use. Incident handling teams may choose to build hash sets of known good operating system and application files, so that they are better prepared to determine how the botnet has altered a system. Examples of resources include lists of contact and on-call information, commonly used port numbers, and known critical assets.

So, if an organization practices careful Internet communication habits and follows the key tools and resources for botnet incident handlers tips described in the checklist that follows, the chances of the computer remaining secure are very good (see checklist: An Agenda for Action for Preventing Botnet Activities).

8. SUMMARY

Botnets are one of the biggest threats to the Internet today, and they are linked to most forms of Internet crime. Most spam, DDoS attacks, spyware, click fraud, and other attacks originate from botnets and the shadowy organizations behind them. Running a botnet is immensely profitable, as several recent high-profile arrests have shown. Currently, many botnets still rely on a centralized IRC C&C structure, but more and more botmasters are using P2P protocols to provide resilience and avoid a single point of failure. A recent large-scale example of a P2P botnet is the Storm Worm, widely covered in the media.

A number of botnet countermeasures exist, but most are focused on bot detection and removal at the host and network level. Some approaches exist for Internet-wide detection and disruption of entire botnets, but we still lack effective techniques for combating the root of the problem: the botmasters who conceal their identities and locations behind chains of stepping-stone proxies.

The three biggest challenges in botmaster traceback are stepping stones, encryption, and the low traffic volume. Even if these problems can be solved with a technical solution, the trace must be able to continue beyond the reach of the Internet. Mobile phone networks, open wireless access points, and public computers all provide an additional layer of anonymity for the botmasters.

Short of a perfect solution, even a partial traceback technique could serve as a very effective deterrent for botmasters. With each botmaster that is located and arrested, many botnets will be eliminated at once. Additionally, other botmasters could decide that the risks outweigh the benefits when they see more and more of their colleagues getting caught. Currently, the economic equation is very simple: Botnets can generate large profits with relatively low risk of getting caught. A botmaster traceback solution, even if imperfect, would drastically change this equation and convince more botmasters that it simply is not worth the risk of spending the next 10–20 years in prison.

Finally, let's move on to the real interactive part of this chapter: review questions/exercises, hands-on projects, case projects, and optional team case project. The answers and/or solutions by chapter can be found in the Online Instructor's Solutions Manual.

CHAPTER REVIEW QUESTIONS/EXERCISES

True/False

1. True or False? A botnet is a collection of compromised Internet computers being controlled remotely by attackers for malicious and legal purposes.
2. True or False? The person controlling a botnet is known as the botmaster or bot-herder.
3. True or False? Centralized botnets use a double entity (a host or a small collection of hosts) to manage all bot members.
4. True or False? The attacker exploits a vulnerability in a running service to automatically gain access and install his software without any user interaction.
5. True or False? After infection, the bot starts up for the first time and attempts to contact its C&C server(s) in a process known as waiting.

An Agenda for Action for Preventing Botnet Activities

In order to provide a timely, comprehensive, relevant, and accurate Internet communication security strategy, the following set of preventative botnet activities must be adhered to (check all tasks completed):

Botnet Incident Handler Communications and Facilities

_____ 1. **Contact information: This includes** phone numbers and email addresses for team members and others within and outside the organization (primary and backup contacts), who may have helpful information, such as antivirus vendors and other incident response teams.

_____ 2. **On-call information is used** for other teams within the organization, including escalation information.

_____ 3. **Pagers or cell phones that are** to be carried by team members for off-hour support, onsite communications.

_____ 4. **Alternate Internet access method which is used** for finding information about new threats, downloading patches and updates, and reaching other Internet-based resources when Internet access is lost during a severe botnet incident.

_____ 5. **War room is used** for central communication and coordination; if a permanent war room is not necessary, the team should create a procedure for procuring a temporary war room when needed.

Botnet Incident Analysis Hardware and Software

_____ 6. **Laptops**, which provide easily portable workstations for activities such as analyzing data and sniffing packets.

_____ 7. **Spare workstations, servers, and networking equipment**, which may be used for trying out botnets in an isolated environment. If the team cannot justify the expense of additional equipment, perhaps equipment in an existing test lab could be used, or a virtual lab could be established using OS emulation software.

_____ 8. **Blank media**, such as CDs and flash drives, for storing and transporting botnet samples and other files as needed

_____ 9. **Packet sniffers and protocol analyzers that are used** to capture and analyze network traffic that may contain botnet activity.

_____ 10. **Up-to-date, trusted versions of OS executables and analysis utilities, which are** stored on flash drives or CDs, to be used to examine systems for signs of botnet infection (antivirus software, spyware detection and removal utilities, system administration tools, forensics utilities).

Botnet Incident Analysis Resources

_____ 11. **Port lists, that include** commonly used ports and known Trojan horse and backdoor ports.

_____ 12. **Documentation** for OSs, applications, protocols, and antivirus and intrusion detection signatures.

_____ 13. **Network diagrams and lists of critical assets**, such as Web, email, and File Transfer Protocol (FTP) servers.

_____ 14. **Baselines** of expected network, system and application activity.

Botnet Incident Mitigation Software

_____ 15. **Media**, which includes OS boot disks and CDs, flash drives, OS media, storage media. and application media.

_____ 16. **Security patches** from OS and application vendors.

_____ 17. **Disk imaging software and backup images** of OS, applications, and data stored on secondary media.

Multiple Choice

1. A collection of compromised Internet computers being controlled remotely by attackers for malicious and illegal purposes is known as:
   A. malware.
   B. spyware.
   C. botmaster.
   D. botnet.
   E. bot-herder.

2. The botmaster develops his or her bot software, often reusing existing code and adding custom features. This is known as:
   A. infection.
   B. rallying.
   C. creation.
   D. waiting.
   E. executing.

3. Once a victim machine becomes infected with a bot, it is known as a:
   A. vampire.
   B. werewolf.
   C. chost.
   D. succubus.
   E. zombie.

4. After infection, the bot starts up for the first time and attempts to contact its C&C server(s) in a process known as:
   A. infection.
   B. creation.
   C. rallying.
   D. waiting.
   E. executing.

5. Having joined the C&C network, the bot waits for commands from the botmaster. This is known as:
   A. infection.

B. creation.

C. rallying.

D. executing.

E. waiting.

EXERCISE

Problem

On a Wednesday morning, a new worm is released on the Internet. The worm exploits a Microsoft Windows vulnerability that was publicly announced three weeks before, at which time patches were released. The worm spreads itself through two methods: emailing itself to all addresses that it can locate on an infected host; and identifying and sending itself to hosts with open Windows shares. The worm is designed to generate a different attachment name for each copy that it mails; each attachment has a randomly generated file name that uses one of over a dozen file extensions. The worm also chooses from more than 200 email subjects and a similar number of email bodies. When the worm infects a host, it gains administrative rights and attempts to download a distributed denial-of-service (DDoS) agent from different Internet Protocol (IP) addresses using File Transfer Protocol (FTP). The number of IP addresses providing the agent is unknown. Although the antivirus vendors quickly post warnings about the worm, it spreads very rapidly, before any of the vendors have released signatures. The organization has already incurred widespread infections before antivirus signatures become available four hours after the worm started to spread. What questions should the botnet incident response team be asking?

Hands-On Projects

Project

On a Monday night, one of the organization's network intrusion detection sensors alerts on a suspected outbound DDoS activity involving a high volume of Internet Control Message Protocol (ICMP) pings. The intrusion analyst reviews the alerts; although the analyst cannot confirm that the alerts are accurate, they do not match any known false positives. The analyst contacts the botnet incident response team so that it can investigate the activity further. Because the DDoS activity uses spoofed source IP addresses, it takes considerable time and effort to determine which host or hosts within the organization are producing it; meanwhile, the DDoS activity continues. The investigation shows that eight servers appear to be generating the DDoS traffic. Initial analysis of the servers shows that each contains signs of a DDoS rootkit. What questions should the botnet incident response team be asking?

Case Projects

Problem

On a Saturday afternoon, several users contact the help desk to report strange popup windows and toolbars in their Web browsers. The users' descriptions of the behavior are similar, so the help desk agents believe that the users' systems have been affected by the same thing and that the most likely cause is Web-based malicious mobile code. What questions should the botnet incident response team be asking?

Optional Team Case Project

Problem

Shortly after an organization adopts a new instant messaging platform, its users are hit with a widespread botnet attack that propagates itself through the use of instant messaging. Based on the initial reports from security administrators, the attack appears to be caused by a worm. However, subsequent reports indicate that the attacks also involve Web servers and Web clients. The instant messaging and Web-based attacks appear to be related to the worm because they display the same message to users. What questions should the botnet incident response team be asking?

## Chapter 13

Intranet Security

Bill Mansoor
Information Systems Audit and Control Association (ISACA)

Headline dramas like the ones shown in the accompanying sidebar (Intranet Security as News in the Media) (in the mainstream media) are embarrassing nightmares to top brass in any large corporation. These events have a lasting impact on a company's bottom line because the company's reputation and customer trust take a direct hit. Once events like these occur, customers and current and potential investors never look at the company in the same trusting light again, regardless of remediation measures. The smart thing, then, is to avoid the limelight. The onus of preventing such embarrassing security gaffes falls squarely on the shoulders of the IT security chiefs (Chief Information Security Officer and security officers), who are sometimes hobbled by unclear mandates from government regulators and lack of sufficient budgeting to tackle the mandates.

- Intranet Security as News in the Media
- "State Department Contract Employees Fired, Another Disciplined for Looking at Passport File"[1]
- "Laptop stolen with a million customer data records "[2]
- "eBayed VPN kit hands over access to council network "[3]
- "(Employee) caught selling personal and medical information about ... FBI agent to a confidential source ... for $500"[4]
- "Data thieves gain access to TJX through unsecured wireless access point"[5]

However, federal governments across the world are not taking breaches of personal data lightly (see sidebar, TJX: Data Breach with 45 Million Data Records Stolen). In view of a massive plague of publicized data thefts in the past decade, recent mandates such as the Health Insurance Portability and Accountability Act (HIPAA), Sarbanes-Oxley, and the Payment Card Industry-Data Security Standard (PCI-DSS) Act within the United States now have teeth. These laws even spell out stiff fines and personal jail sentences for CEOs who neglect data breach issues.

TJX: Data Breach with 45 Million Data Records Stolen

The largest-scale data breach in history occurred in early 2007 at TJX, the parent company for the TJ Maxx, Marshalls, and HomeGoods retail chains.

In the largest identity-theft case ever investigated by the U.S. Department of Justice, 11 people were convicted of wire fraud. The primary suspect was found to perpetrate the intrusion by wardriving and taking advantage of an unsecured Wi-Fi access point to get in and set up a "sniffer" software instance to capture credit-card information from a database.[12]

Although the intrusion was earlier believed to have taken place from May 2006 to January 2007, TJX later found that it took place as early as July 2005. The data compromised included portions of credit- and debit-card transactions for approximately 45 million customers.[6]

As seen in the TJX case, intranet data breaches can be a serious issue, impacting a company's goodwill in the open marketplace as well as spawning class-action lawsuits.[7] Gone are the days when intranet security was a superficial exercise; security inside the firewall was all

1. Jake Tapper, and Radia Kirit, "State Department Contract Employees Fired, Another Disciplined for Looking at Passport File," ABCnews. com, March 21, 2008, http://abcnews.go.com/Politics/story?id= 4492773&page=1.
2. Laptop security blog, Absolute Software, http://blog.absolute.com/ category/real-theft-reports.
3. John Leyden, "eBayed VPN Kit Hands over Access to Council Network," theregister.co.uk, September 29, 2008, www.theregister.co. uk/2008/09/29/second_hand_vpn_security_breach.
4. Bob Coffield, "Second Criminal Conviction under HIPAA," Health Care Law Blog, March 14, 2006, http://healthcarebloglaw.blogspot.com/ 2006/03/second-criminal-conviction-under-hipaa.html.
5. "TJX Identity Theft Saga Continues: 11 Charged with Pilfering Millions of Credit Cards," Networkworld.com magazine, August 5, 2008, www. networkworld.com/community/node/30741?nwwpkg=breaches? ap1=rcb.

6. "The TJX Companies, Inc. Updates Information on Computer Systems Intrusion," February 21, 2007, www.tjx.com/Intrusion_ Release_email.pdf.
7. "TJX Class Action Lawsuit Settlement Site," The TJX Companies, Inc., and Fifth Third Bancorp, Case No. 07-10162, www.tjxsettlement. com.

but nonexistent. There was a feeling of implicit trust in the internal user. After all, if you hired that person, training him for years, how could you not trust him?

In the new millennium, the Internet has come of age, and so have its users. The last largely computer-agnostic generation has exited the user scene; their occupational shoes have been filled with the X and Y generations. Many of these young people have grown up with the Internet, often familiar with it since elementary school. It is not uncommon today to find young college students who started their programming interests in the fifth or sixth grade.

With such a level of computer expertise in users, the game of intranet security has changed (see sidebar: Network Breach Readiness: Many Are Still Complacent). Resourceful as ever, these new users have gotten used to the idea of being hyperconnected to the Internet using mobile technology such as personal digital assistants (PDAs), smartphones, and firewalled barriers. For a corporate intranet that uses older ideas of using access control as the cornerstone of data security, such mobile access to the Internet at work needs careful analysis and control. The idea of building a virtual moat around your well-constructed castle (investing in a firewall and hoping to call it an intranet) is gone. Hyperconnected "knowledge workers" with laptops, PDAs, and USB keys that have whole operating systems built in have made sure of it.

Network Breach Readiness: Many are Still Complacent

The level of readiness for breaches among IT shops across the country is still far from optimal. The Ponemon Institute, a security think tank, surveyed some industry personnel and came up with some startling revelations. Hopefully, these statistics will change in the future:

- Eighty-five percent of industry respondents reported that they had experienced a data breach.
- Of those responding, 43 percent had no incident response plan in place, and 82 percent did not consult legal counsel before responding to the incident.
- Following a breach, 46 percent of respondents still had not implemented encryption on portable devices (laptops, PDAs) with company data stored on them.[8]

If we could reuse the familiar vehicle ad tagline of the 1980s, we would say that the new intranet is not "your father's intranet anymore." The intranet as just a simple place to share files and to list a few policies and procedures has ceased to be. The types of changes can be summed up in the following list of features, which shows

that the intranet has become a combined portal as well as a public dashboard. Some of the features can include:

- A searchable corporate personnel directory of phone numbers by department. Often the list is searchable only if the exact name is known.
- Expanded activity guides and a corporate calendar with links for various company divisions.
- Several Really Simple Syndication (RSS) feeds for news according to divisions such as IT, HR, Finance, Accounting, and Purchasing.
- Company blogs (weblogs) by top brass that talk about the current direction for the company in reaction to recent events, a sort of "mission statement of the month."
- A search engine for searching company information, often helped by a search appliance from Google. Microsoft also has its own search software on offer that targets corporate intranets.
- One or several "wiki" repositories for company intellectual property, some of it of a mission-critical nature. Usually granular permissions are applied for access here. One example could be court documents for a legal firm with rigorous security access applied.
- A section describing company financials and other mission-critical indicators. This is often a separate Web page linked to the main intranet page.
- A "live" section with IT alerts regarding specific downtimes, outages, and other critical time-sensitive company notifications. Often embedded within the portal, this is displayed in a "ticker-tape" fashion or like an RSS-type dynamic display.

Of course, this list is not exhaustive; some intranets have other unique features not listed here. In any case, intranets these days do a lot more than simply list corporate phone numbers.

Recently, knowledge management systems have presented another challenge to intranet security postures. Companies that count knowledge as a prime protected asset (virtually all companies these days) have started deploying "mashable" applications that combine social networking (such as Facebook and LinkedIn), texting, and microblogging (such as Twitter) features to encourage employees to "wikify" their knowledge and information within intranets. One of the bigger vendors in this space, Socialtext, has introduced a mashable wiki app that operates like a corporate dashboard for intranets.[9,10]

---

8. "Ponemon Institute Announces Result of Survey Assessing the Business Impact of a Data Security Breach," May 15, 2007, www.ponemon.org/press/Ponemon_Survey_Results_Scott_and_Scott_FINAL1.pdf.

9. James Mowery, "Socialtext Melds Media and Collaboration," cmswire.com, October 8, 2008, www.cmswire.com/cms/enterprise-20/socialtext-melds-media-and-collaboration-003270.php.

10. Rob Hof, "Socialtext 3.0: Will Wikis Finally Find Their Place in Business?" Businessweek.com magazine, September 30, 2008, www.business-week.com/the_thread/techbeat/archives/2008/09/socialtext_30_i.html.

Socialtext has individual widgets, one of which, "Socialtext signals," is a microblogging engine. In the corporate context, microblogging entails sending short SMS messages to apprise colleagues of recent developments in the daily routine. Examples could be short messages on progress on any major project milestone—for example, joining up major airplane assemblies or getting Food and Drug Administration (FDA) testing approval for a special experimental drug.

These emerging scenarios present special challenges to security personnel guarding the borders of an intranet. The border as it once existed has ceased to be. One cannot block stored knowledge from leaving the intranet when a majority of corporate mobile users are accessing intranet wikis from anywhere using inexpensive mini-notebooks that are given away with cell phone contracts.[11]

If we consider the impact of national and international privacy mandates on these situations, the situation is compounded further for C-level executives in multinational companies who have to come up with responses to privacy mandates in each country in which the company does business. The privacy mandates regarding private customer data have always been more stringent in Europe than in North America, which is a consideration for doing business in Europe.

It is hard enough to block entertainment-related Flash video traffic from time-wasting Internet abuse without blocking a video of last week's corporate meeting at headquarters. Only letting in traffic on an exception basis becomes untenable or impractical because of a high level of personnel involvement needed for every ongoing security change. Simply blocking YouTube.com or Vimeo.com is not sufficient. Video, which has myriad legitimate work uses nowadays, is hosted on all sorts of content-serving (caching and streaming) sites worldwide, which makes it well near impossible to block using Web filters. The evolution of the Internet Content Adaptation Protocol (ICAP), which standardizes Web site categories for content-filtering purposes, is under way. However, ICAP still does not solve the problem of the dissolving networking "periphery."[12]

Guarding movable and dynamic data—which may be moving in and out of the perimeter without notice, flouting every possible mandate—is a key feature of today's intranet. The dynamic nature of data has rendered the traditional confidentiality, integrity, and availability (CIA) architecture somewhat less relevant. The changing nature of data security necessitates some specialized security considerations:

- Intranet security policies and procedures (P&Ps) are the first step toward a legal regulatory framework. The P&Ps needed on any of the security controls listed below should be compliant with federal and state mandates (such as HIPAA, Sarbanes-Oxley, the European Directive 95/46/EC on the protection of personal data, and PCI-DSS, among others). These P&Ps have to be signed off by top management and placed on the intranet for review by employees. There should be sufficient teeth in all procedural sections to enforce the policy, explicitly spelling out sanctions and other consequences of noncompliance, leading up to discharge.

- To be factual, none of these government mandates spell out details on implementing any security controls. That is the vague nature of federal and international mandates. Interpretation of the security controls is better left after the fact to an entity such as the National Institute of Standards and Technology (NIST) in the United States or the Geneva-based International Organization for Standardization (ISO). These organizations have extensive research and publication guidance for any specific security initiative. Most of NIST's documents are offered as free downloads from its Web site.[13] ISO security standards such as 27002 ~ 27005 are also available for a nominal fee from the ISO site.

Policies and procedures, once finalized, need to be automated as much as possible (one example is mandatory password changes every three months). Automating policy compliance takes the error-prone human factor out of the equation (see sidebar: Access Control in the Era of Social Networking). Numerous software tools are available to help accomplish security policy automation.

Access Control in the Era of Social Networking

In an age in which younger users have grown up with social networking sites as part of their digital lives, corporate intranet sites are finding it increasingly difficult to block them from using these sites at work. Depending on the company, some are embracing social networking as part of their corporate culture; others, especially government entities, are actively blocking these sites. Detractors mention as concerns wasted bandwidth, lost productivity, and the possibility of infections with spyware and worms.

However, blocking these sites can be difficult because most social networking and video sites such as Vimeo and YouTube can use port 80 to vector Flash videos into an

---

11. Matt Hickey, "MSI's 3.5G Wind 120 Coming in November, Offer Subsidized by Taiwanese Telecom," Crave.com, October 20, 2008, http://news.cnet.com/8301-17938_105-10070911-1.html?tag=mncol;title.

12. Network Appliance, Inc., RFC Standards white paper for Internet Content Adaptation Protocol (ICAP), July 30, 2001, www.content-networking.com/references.html.

---

13. National Institute of Standards and Technology, Computer Security Resource Center, http://csrc.nist.gov/.

intranet—which is wide open for HTTP access. Flash videos have the potential to provide a convenient Trojan horse for malware to get into the intranet.

To block social networking sites, one needs to block either the Social Networking category or the specific URLs (such as YouTube.com) for these sites in the Web-filtering proxy appliance. Flash videos are rarely downloaded from YouTube itself. More often a redirected caching site is used to send in the video. The caching sites also need to be blocked; this is categorized under Content Servers.

1. SMARTPHONES AND TABLETS IN THE INTRANET

The proliferation of mobile devices for personal and business usage has gained an unprecedented momentum, which only reminds one of the proliferation of personal computers at the start of the 1980s. Back then the rapid proliferation of PCs was rooted in the wide availability of common PC software and productivity packages such as Excel or Borland. Helping with kids' homework and spreadsheets at home was part of the wide appeal.

A large part of the PC revolution was also rooted in the change in interactivity patterns. Interaction using GUIs and mice had made PCs widely popular compared to the DOS character screen. The consumer PC revolution did not really take off until Windows PCs and Mac Classics brought along mice starting in the early 1990s. It was a quantum leap for ordinary people unfamiliar with DOS commands.

Today, which some now call the post-PC era,[14] the interaction between people and computers has again evolved. The finger (touch) has again replaced keyboards and mice as an input device in smartphones and tablets—which invariably use a mobile-oriented OS like Android or iOS as opposed to MAC OS, Linux, or Windows. Android and iOS were built from the ground up with the "touch interface" in mind.

This marks a sea-change.[15] By the next couple of years, most smartphones will end up with the computing power of a full-size PC that is only five years older. These powerful smartphones and portable tablets (such as iPads and android devices) enabled with multimedia and gaming capabilities are starting to converge toward becoming one and the same device. The increasing speed and functionality for the price ("bang for the buck") will only gather a more rapid pace as user demand becomes more intense. The success of smartphones and tablet devices over traditional full-size laptops stems from two primary reasons:

1. **The functionality and ease of use of using "voice," "gesture," and "touch" interfaces.** As opposed to the use of mice and keyboards, voice-enabled, touch, and gesture-based interfaces used in mobile devices offer a degree of ease unseen in traditional laptops.

2. **The availability of customized apps (applications).** Given the number of specialized apps found in the Apple App Store (and Android's equivalent "market"), they offer increased versatility for these new mobile devices compared to traditional laptops. In Apple's case, the closed ecosystem of apps (securely allowed only after testing for security) decreases the possibility of hacking iPads using uncertified apps.

In the recent iPhone 4s, the use of "Siri" as a speech-aware app only portends the increasing ease of usage for this class of device.[16] Using Siri, the iPhone can be issued voice commands to set appointments, to read back messages, and to notify people if one is going to be late—among a myriad other things—all without touching any keypad. In the recently introduced android version 4.0 or higher, face recognition authentication using the on-board camera is also an ease-of-use feature. There are bugs in these applications of course, but they indisputably point toward a pattern of interactivity change compared to a traditional laptop. There are a few other trends to watch in the integration of mobile devices in the enterprise:

1. Mobile devices let today's employees stretch work far beyond traditional work hours. Because of rich interactivity and ease of use, these devices blur the boundary between work and play. Companies benefit from this employee availability at non-traditional work hours. The very concept of being at work has changed compared to even 10 years ago.

2. The iteration life cycles of mobile devices are now more rapid. Unlike laptops that had life cycles of almost three years, new version of the iPad comes out almost every year with evolutionary changes. This makes it less and less feasible for IT to set standardization for mobile devices or even pay for them. IT is left in most cases with supporting these devices. IT can, however, put in recommendations on which device it is able or unable to support for feasibility reasons.

3. Because of these cost reasons, it is no longer feasible for most IT departments to dictate the brand or platform of mobile device employees use to access the

14. Ina Fried, "Steve Jobs: Let the Post-PC Era Begin," CNET News, June 1, 2010, http://news.cnet.com/8301-13860_3-20006442-56.html?tag=content;siu-container.

15. Associated Press, "Apple Describes Post-PC Era, Surprise of Success," March 7, 2012, http://news.yahoo.com/apple-describes-post-pc-era-surprise-success-2126136,25.html.

16. "Siri—Your Wish Is Its Command," http://www.apple.com/iphone/features/siri.html.

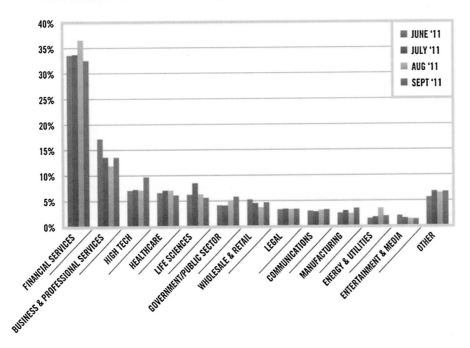

FIGURE 13.1 Net activation by industry. Source: *http://i.zdneMt.com/blogs/zdnet-good-technology-ios-survey-1.jpg?tag=content;siu-container.*

corporate network. It is often a BYOD (Bring Your Own Device) situation. As long as specialized software can be used to partition the personally owned mobile device for storing company data safely (which cannot be breached), this approach is feasible.

4. The mobile device that seems to be numerically most ready for the enterprise is the same one that has been the most successful commercially, the Apple iPad. Already in its third iteration in 2012 since the first one came out in 2010, the iPad 3 with its security and VPN features seems to be ready to be managed by most Mobile Device Management (MDM) packages. It has been adopted extensively by executives and sales staff at larger corporate entities.[17] It is also starting to be adopted by state and local government to expedite certain e-government initiatives.[18]

5. Compared to the Apple iPhone, however, the Android smartphones generally have had better adoption rates.

Blackberry adoption, however, is on the wane.[19] Smartphones will need to have more specially designed Web pages to cope with interactivity on a smaller screen.

6. According to a major vendor in the Mobile Device Management space ("Good Technology") the financial services sector saw the highest level of iPad (iOS) activation, accounting for 46 percent for the third quarter in 2011—which tripled the amount of activation in any other industry (see Figure 13.1).[20]

When it comes to mobile devices (see sidebar: The Commoditization of Mobile Devices and Impact upon Businesses and Society) and smartphones, one can reasonably surmise that the act of balancing security versus business considerations has clearly tilted toward the latter. The age of mobile devices is here, and IT has to adapt security measures to conform to it. The common IT security concept of protecting the host may have to convert to protecting the network from itinerant hosts.

17. Rachel King, "SAP CIO Bussman on Tablets and Mobile Strategy for Enterprise," September 19, 2011, http://www.zdnet.com/blog/btl/sap-cio-bussman-on-tablets-and-mobile-strategy-for-enterprise/58247.

18. "Better Health Channel—iPhone and iPad Mobile Application," Retrieved March 19, 2012, http://www.egov.vic.gov.au/victorian-government-resources/government-initiatives-victoria/health-and-community-victoria/health-victoria/better-health-channel-iphone-and-ipad-mobile-application.html.

19. Brad Reed, "iOS vs. Android vs. BlackBerry OS vs. Windows Phone," Retrieved November 2, 2011, http://www.networkworld.com/news/2011/102011-tech-arguments-android-ios-blackberry-windows-252223.html.

20. Rachel King, "iPad Driving Massive Growth for iOS in Enterprise (Survey)," October 20, 2011, http://www.zdnet.com/blog/btl/ipad-driving-massive-growth-for-ios-in-enterprise-survey/61229?tag=content;siu-container.

The Commoditization of Mobile Devices and Impact upon Businesses and Society

There are quite a few increasingly visible trends that portend the commoditization of mobile devices and their resulting impact on businesses.

1. The millennial generation is more familiar with mobile technology—Due to widespread usage of smartphones and iPhones as communication devices for computing usage (other than simply voice) in the last few years and now iPads which have taken their place, their familiarity with mobile hardware is far higher than previous generations. The technological sophistication of these devices has forced the majority of the current generation of young people to be far more tech savvy than previous generations as they have grown up around this mobile-communication-enabled environment.

2. Mobile devices are eating into the sales of PCs and laptops—The millennial generation is no longer simply content with traditional bulky PCs and laptops as computing devices. Lightweight devices with pared-down mobile OSs and battery-efficient mobile devices with 10-hour lives are quickly approaching the computing power of traditional computers and in addition are far more portable. The demand of lowered cost, immediacy, and ease of usage of mobile devices have caused traditional laptop sales to slow down in favor of tablet and iPad sales.

3. Social media usage by mobile devices—Sites like FaceBook, Twitter, and Flickr encourage collaboration and have given rise to usage of these sites using nothing other than mobile devices, whereas this was not possible previously. Most smartphones (even an increasingly common class of GPS-enabled point-and-shoot cameras) enable upload of images and videos to these sites directly from the device itself using Wi-Fi connections and Wi-Fi-enabled storage media (SD cards). This has engendered a mobile lifestyle for this generation that sites such as FaceBook, Twitter, and Flickr are only too happy to cater to. Employees using social media represent new challenges to businesses because protection of business data (enforced by privacy-related federal and state regulations and mandates) has become imperative. Business data has to be separated and protected from personal use of public social media, if they have to exist on the same mobile device. Several vendors already offer products that enable this separation. In industry parlance this area of IT is known as Mobile Device Management.

4. The mobile hardware industry has matured—Margins have been pared to the bone. Mobile devices have become a buyers' market. Because of wider appeal, it is no longer just the tech savvy (opinion leaders and early adopters) who determine the success of a mobile product. It will be the wider swath of nontechie users looking for attractive devices with a standardized set of often-used functions that will determine the success of a product. This will sooner than later force manufacturers to compete on price rather than product innovation. This downward pressure on price will also make it cost-effective for businesses to adopt these mobile devices within their corporate IT infrastructure. Amazon's Kindle and Barnes &Noble's Nook are both nimbly designed and priced at around a $200 price-point compared to the $500 iPad. They have begun to steal some market share from full-featured tablets like the iPad but of course enterprise adoption for the cheaper devices remains to be sorted out.

5. Users expect the "cloud" to be personal—Users in their personal lives have become used to customizing their Internet digital persona by being offered limitless choices in doing so. In their usage of the business cloud," they expect the same level of customization. This customization can be easily built into the backend using the likes of Active Directory and collaboration tools such as Microsoft's SharePoint once a user authenticates through the VPN. Customization can be built upon access permissions in a granular manner per user while tracking their access to company information assets. This accumulated data trend can be used later to refine ease of use for remote users using the company portal.

In 2011, Apple shipped 172 million portable computing devices including iPads, iPods, and iPhones. Among these were 55 million iPads. The sales of mostly android tablets by other manufacturers are also increasing at a rapid pace. By the end of the first decade of the new millennium, it has become clear that sales of iPads and tablets are making serious dents in the sale of traditional PCs—indicating a shift in consumer preference toward a rapid commoditization of computing. Figure 13.2 from the Forrester Research consumer PC and Tablet forecast helps illustrate this phenomenon.[21]

Several reasons can be attributed to this shift. The millennial generation was already reinventing the idea of how business is conducted and where. Because of increased demands on employee productivity, business had to be conducted in real time at the employee's location (home, hotel, airport) and not just at the traditional workplace. With gas prices hovering in the United States around $5.00 a gallon (essentially a doubling of prices over the first half-decade of the millennium), traditional 9-to-5 work hours with long commutes are no longer practical. iPads and tablets therefore had become *de rigueur* for not only field employees but also workers at headquarters. Instead of imposing rigid 9-to-5 attendance on employees, progressive companies had to let employees be flexible in meeting

---

21. Zack Whittaker, "One Billion Smartphones by 2016, Says Forrester," February 13, 2012, http://www.zdnet.com/blog/btl/one-billion-smartphones-by-2016-says-forrester/69279.

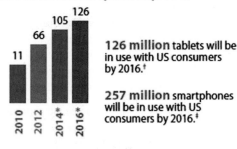

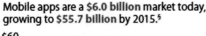

126 million tablets will be in use with US consumers by 2016.†

257 million smartphones will be in use with US consumers by 2016.‡

Mobile apps are a $6.0 billion market today, growing to $55.7 billion by 2015.§

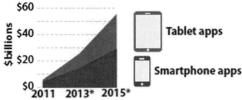

Sources: †Forrester Research Consumer PC And Tablet Forecast, 2011 to 2016 (US); ‡Forrester Research Mobile Adoption Forecast, 2012 to 2017 (US); §February 28, 2011, "Mobile App Internet Recasts The Software And Services Landscape" Forrester report
*Forecast

FIGURE 13.2 Mobile device adaptation. Source: *http://i.zdnet.com/blogs/screen-shot-2012-02-13-at-173416.png.*

sales or deliverables on their own deadlines, which improved employee morale and productivity.

Popular devices like the iPad, Samsung Galaxy Android tablet, and many types of smartphones are already capable of accessing company intranets using customized intranet apps. This assures that access to critical company data needed for a sale or demo does not stand in the way of closing an important deal. All this had already been enabled by laptops, but the touchpad-enabled tablet eases this process by using more functional media usage and richer interactivity features.

Ultimately, it will matter less about what device employees use to access the company portal or where they are because their identity will be the deciding factor in what information they will gain access to. Companies will do better in providing customized "private cloud environments" for workers accessible from anywhere. Employees may still use PCs while at the office (see sidebar: Being Secure in the Post-PC Era) and mobile devices while in the field conducting business, but they will increasingly demand the same degree of ease in accessing company data regardless of their location or the means used to access it. The challenge for IT will be in catering to these versatile demands without losing sight of security and protecting privacy.

Being Secure in the Post-PC Era

The post-PC era began with the advent of tablets such as iPads as enterprise mobile computing devices. Secure use of tablets in the enterprise presupposes a number of conditionalities:

1. **Backend enterprise network infrastructure support has to be ready** and has to be strong to handle mobile devices interacting with SSL VPNs. Specifically, enterprises need to consider each device platform and their unique issues and idiosyncrasies in trying to connect using an SSL VPN. SSL (or Web) VPNs are preferred because IPSec and L2TP VPNs were not known to be easy to implement on mobile devices (especially Android tablets) as SSL VPNs. PPTP VPNs are dated and not known to have sufficient encryption and security compared to SSL VPNs.

2. **Testing of remote access scenarios such as VPNs is key.** Client Apps for each supported platform (iOS, Android, Windows Phone) against the existing or proposed VPN appliance will need to be thoroughly tested.

3. **This is fundamentally a new paradigm for delivering applications** (email, dashboards, databases) to users. Starting with a practical and functional client App from ground zero will be a better philosophy than sticking to existing GUI ideas or concepts. Instead of pretty but nonfunctional interfaces, spare but well-tested and robust mobile interfaces will afford users time-savings and efficiency to get their job done quicker. Once they are reliably working, additional functions can be slowly added to the app in successive versions.

2. SECURITY CONSIDERATIONS

Quite a few risks need to be resolved when approaching intranet security with regard to mobile devices:

1. **Risk of size and portability**—Mobile devices are prone to loss. An Apple staffer's "loss" of a fourth-generation iPhone to a Gizmodo staffer during a personal outing to a bar is well known. There is no denying that smartphones because of their size are easy theft targets in the wrong place at the wrong time. Loss of a few hundred dollars of hardware, however, is nothing when an invaluable client-list is lost and falls into a competitor's hands. These are nightmare scenarios that keep CIOs up at night.

2. **Risk of access via multiple paradigms**—Mobile devices can access unsafe sites using cellular networks and download malware into storage. The malware in turn can bypass the company firewall to enter the company network to wreak havoc. Old paradigms of security by controlling security using perimeter network access are no longer feasible.

3. **Social media risks**—By definition, mobile devices are designed in such a way that they can easily access

social media sites, which are the new target for malware propagating exploits. Being personal devices, mobile media devices are much more at risk of getting exploits sent to them and being "pw" (so to speak).

These issues can be approached and dealt with by using a solid set of technical as well as administrative controls:

1. **Establish a customized corporate usage policy for mobile devices**—This policy/procedure must be signed by new hires at orientation and by all employees who ask for access to the corporate VPN using mobile devices (even personal ones). This should ideally be in the form of a contract and should be signed by the employee before a portion of the employee's device storage is partitioned for access and storage of corporate data. Normally, there should be yearly training highlighting the do's and dont's of using mobile devices in accessing a corporate VPN. The first thing emphasized in this training should be how to secure company data using passwords and if cost-effective, two-factor authentication using hardware tokens.

2. **Establish a policy for reporting theft or misplacement**—This policy should identify at the very least how quickly one should report thefts of mobile devices containing company data and how quickly remote wipe should be implemented. The policy can optionally detail how the mobile devices feature (app) enabling location of the misplaced stolen device will proceed.

3. **Establish a well-tested SSL VPN for remote access**—Reputed vendors having experience with mobile device VPN clients should be chosen. The quality, functionality, adaptability of usage (and proven reputation) of the VPN clients should be key in determining the choice of the vendor. The advantage of an SSL VPN compared to IPsec or L2TP for mobile usage is well known. The SSL VPNs should be capable of supporting two-factor authentication using hardware tokens. For example, Cisco's "Cisco AnyConnect Secure Mobility Client" and Juniper's "Junos Pulse App" are free app downloads available within the Apple iTunes App store. Other VPN vendors will also have these apps available, and they can be tested to see how smooth and functional the access process is.

4. **Establish inbound and outbound malware scanning**—Inbound scanning should occur for obvious reasons, but outbound scanning should also be scanned in case the company's email servers become SPAM relays and get blacklisted on sites such as Lashback or get blocked to external sites by force.

5. **Establish WPA2 encryption for Wi-Fi traffic access**—WPA2 for now is the best encryption available compared to WEP encryption, which is dated and not recommended.

6. **Establish logging metrics and granular controls**—Keeping regular tabs on information asset access by users and configuring alerting on unusual activity (such as large-scale access or exceeded failed-logon thresholds) is a good way to prevent data leakage.

Mobile devices accessing enterprise intranets using VPNs are subject to the same factors as any other device remotely accessing VPNs, namely (see Figure 13.3):

1. Protection of data while in transmission
2. Protection of data while at rest
3. Protection of the mobile device itself (in case it fell into the wrong hands)
4. App security

At a minimum, the following standards are recommended for managing tablets and smartphones with Mobile Device Management (MDM) appliances:

1. **Protection of data while in transmission:** Transmission security for mobile devices is concerned primarily with VPN security as well as Wi-Fi security. With regard to VPNs, the primary preference for most mobile devices should be for Web-based or SSL VPNs. The reason is that IPsec and L2TP VPN implementations are still buggy as of this writing on all but iOS devices (iPhones and iPads). SSL VPNs can also be implemented as clientless. Regarding Wi-F,i the choice is to simply configure WPA2 Enterprise using 128-bit AES encryption for mobile devices connecting via Wi-Fi. Again, MDM appliances can be used to push out these policies to the mobile devices.

2. **Protection of data while at rest:** The basis of protecting stored data on a mobile device is the password. The stronger the password, the harder to break the encryption. Some devices (including the iPad) support 256-bit AES encryption. Most recent mobile devices also support remote wipe and progressive wipe. The latter feature will progressively increase the time of the lockout duration until finally initiating an automatic remote wipe of all data on the device. These wipe features are designed to protect company data from falling into the wrong hands. All these features can be queried and are configurable for mobile devices via either Exchange ActiveSync policies or configuration policies from MDM appliances.

3. **Protection of the mobile device:** Passwords for mobile devices have to conform to the same corporate "strong password" policy as for other wired network devices. This means the password length, content (minimum of eight characters, alphanumeric, special characters etc.), password rotation and expiry (remember: last three and every two to three months), and

Deployment Scenario

The example depicts a typical deployment with a VPN server/concentrator as well as an authentication server controlling access to enterprise network services.

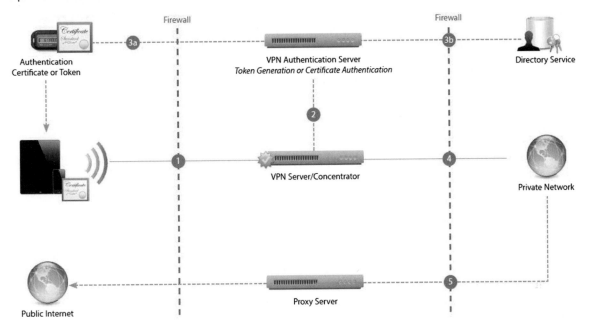

FIGURE 13.3   Mobile device VPN access to company network using token authentication *Courtesy: Apple Inc.*

password lockout (three to five attempts) have to be enforced. Complete sets of configuration profiles can be pushed to tablets, smartphones, and iPads using MDM appliances specifying app installation privileges, YouTube, and iTunes content ratings permissions, among many others.

4. **App security:** In recent versions of both Android and iOS, significant changes have been made so that app security has become more bolstered. For example, in both OSs, apps run in their own silos and can't access other app or system data. While iPhone apps are theoretically capable of accessing the users' contact information and also their locations in some cases, Apple's signing process for every app that appears in the iTunes app store takes care of this. It is possible on the iOS devices to encrypt data using either software methods such as AES, RC4, 3DES, or hardware accelerated encryption activated when a lockout occurs. In iOS, designating an app as managed can prevent its content from being uploaded to iCloud or iTunes. In this manner, MDM appliances or Exchange ActiveSync can prevent leakage of sensitive company data.

While there are quite a few risks in deploying mobile devices within the Intranet, with careful configuration these risks can be minimized to the point where the myriad benefits outweigh the risks. One thing is certain:

These mobile devices and the efficiency they promise are for real, and they are not going away.

Empowering employees is the primary idea in the popularity of these devices. And corporate IT will only serve its own interest by designing enabling security around these devices and letting employees be more productive.

3. PLUGGING THE GAPS: NAC AND ACCESS CONTROL

The first priority of an information security officer in most organizations is to ensure that there is a relevant corporate policy on access controls. Simple on the surface, the subject of access control is often complicated by the variety of ways the intranet is connected to the external world.

Remote users coming in through traditional or SSL (browser-based) virtual private networks (VPNs), control over use of USB keys, printouts, and CD-ROMs all require that a comprehensive endpoint security solution be implemented.

The past couple of years have seen large-scale adoption of network access control (NAC) products in the midlevel and larger IT shops to manage endpoint security. Endpoint security ensures that whoever is plugging into or accessing any hardware anywhere within the intranet has to comply with the minimum baseline corporate security policy standards. This can include add-on access credentials but goes far beyond access. Often these solutions ensure that traveling corporate laptops are compliant with a minimum patching level, scans, and antivirus definition levels before being allowed to connect to the intranet.

The NAC appliances that enforce these policies often require that a NAC fat client is installed on every PC and laptop. This rule can be enforced during logon using a logon script. The client can also be part of the standard OS image for deploying new PCs and laptops.

Microsoft has built an NAC-type framework into some versions of its client OSs (Vista and XP SP3) to ease compliance with its NAC server product called MS Network Policy Server, which closely works with its Windows 2008 Server product (see sidebar: The Cost of a Data Breach). The company has been able to convince quite a few industry networking heavyweights (notably Cisco and Juniper) to adopt its NAP standard.[22]

The Cost of a Data Breach

As of July 2007, the average breach cost per incident was $4.8 million.

- This works out to $182 per exposed record.
- It represents an increase of more than 30 percent from 2005.
- Thirty-five percent of these breaches involved the loss or theft of a laptop or other portable device.
- Seventy percent were due to a mistake or malicious intent by an organization's own staff.
- Since 2005, almost 150 million individuals' identifiable information has been compromised due to a data security breach.
- Nineteen percent of consumers notified of a data breach discontinued their relationship with the business, and a further 40 percent considered doing so.[23]

Essentially, the technology has three parts: a policy-enforceable client, a decision point, and an enforcement point. The client could be an XP SP3 or Vista client (either a roaming user or guest user) trying to connect to the company intranet. The decision point in this case would be the Network Policy Server product, checking to see whether the client requesting access meets the minimum baseline to allow it to connect. If it does not, the decision point product would pass this data on to the enforcement point, a network access product such as a router or switch, which would then be able to cut off access.

The scenario would repeat itself at every connection attempt, allowing the network's health to be maintained on an ongoing basis. Microsoft's NAP page has more details and animation to explain this process.[24]

Access control in general terms is a relationship triad among internal users, intranet resources, and the actions internal users can take on those resources. The idea is to give users only the least amount of access they require to perform their job. The tools used to ensure this in Windows shops utilize Active Directory for Windows logon scripting and Windows user profiles. Granular classification is needed for users, actions, and resources to form a logical and comprehensive access control policy that addresses who gets to connect to what, yet keeping the intranet safe from unauthorized access or data-security breaches. Quite a few off-the-shelf solutions geared toward this market often combine inventory control and access control under a "desktop life-cycle" planning umbrella.

Typically, security administrators start with a "Deny-All" policy as a baseline before slowly building in the access permissions. As users migrate from one department to another, are promoted, or leave the company, in large organizations this job can involve one person by herself. This person often has a very close working relationship with Purchasing, Helpdesk, and HR, getting coordination and information from these departments on users who have separated from the organization and computers that have been surplused, deleting and modifying user accounts and assignments of PCs and laptops.

Helpdesk software usually has an inventory control component that is readily available to Helpdesk personnel to update and/or pull up to access details on computer assignments and user status. Optimal use of form automation can ensure that these details occur (such as deleting a user on the day of separation) to avoid any possibility of an unwelcome data breach.

4. MEASURING RISK: AUDITS

Audits are another cornerstone of a comprehensive intranet security policy. To start an audit, an administrator should know and list what he is protecting as well as know the relevant threats and vulnerabilities to those resources.

Assets that need protection can be classified as either tangible or intangible. *Tangible assets* are, of course, removable media (USB keys), PCs, laptops, PDAs, Web

22. "Juniper and Microsoft Hook Up for NAC work," May 22, 2007, PHYSORG.com, www.physorg.com/news99063542.html.
23. Kevin Bocek, "What Does a Data Breach Cost?" SCmagazine.com, July 2, 2007, www.scmagazineus.com/What-does-a-data-breach-cost/article/35131.
24. NAP Program details, Microsoft.com, www.microsoft.com/windows server2008/en/us/nap-features.aspx.

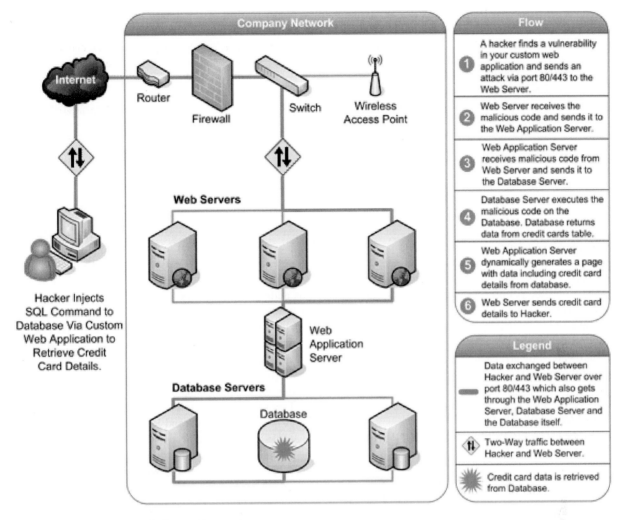

FIGURE 13.4   SQL injection attack. Source: © *acunetix.com.*

servers, networking equipment, DVR security cameras, and employees' physical access cards. *Intangible assets* can include company intellectual property such as corporate email and wikis, user passwords, and, especially for HIPAA and Sarbanes-Oxley mandates, personally identifiable health and financial information, which the company could be legally liable to protect.

Threats can include the theft of USB keys, laptops, PDAs, and PCs from company premises. This results in a data breach (for tangible assets), weak passwords, and unhardened operating systems in servers (for *intangible assets*).

Once a correlated listing of assets and associated threats and vulnerabilities has been made, we have to measure the impact of a breach, which is known as *risk*. The common rule of thumb to measure risk is:

$$\text{Risk} = \text{Value of asset} \times \text{Threat} \times \text{Vulnerability}$$

It is obvious that an Internet-facing Web server faces greater risk and requires priority patching and virus

scanning because the vulnerability and threat components are high in that case (these servers routinely get sniffed and scanned over the Internet by hackers looking to find holes in their armor). However, this formula can standardize the priority list so that the actual audit procedure (typically carried out weekly or monthly by a vulnerability-scanning device) is standardized by risk level. Vulnerability-scanning appliances usually scan server farms and networking appliances only because these are high-value targets within the network for hackers who are looking for either unhardened server configurations or network switches with default factory passwords left on by mistake. To illustrate the situation, look at Figure 13.4, which illustrates an SQL injection attack on a corporate database.[25]

25. "Web Application Security—Check Your Site for Web Application Vulnerabilities," www.acunetix.com/websitesecurity/webapp-security.htm.

Questions for a Nontechnical Audit of Intranet Security

1. Is all access (especially to high-value assets) logged?
2. In case of laptop theft, is encryption enabled so that the records will be useless to the thief?
3. Are passwords verifiably strong enough to comply with the security policy? Are they changed frequently and held to strong encryption standards?
4. Are all tangible assets (PCs, laptops, PDAs, Web servers, networking equipment) tagged with asset tags?

5. Is the process for surplusing obsolete IT assets secure (that is, are disks wiped for personally identifiable data before surplusing happens)?
6. Are email and Web usage logged?
7. Are peer-to-peer (P2P) and instant messaging (IM) usage controlled?

Based on the answers you get (or don't get), you can start the security audit procedure by finding answers to these questions.

The value of an asset is subjective and can be assessed only by the IT personnel in that organization (see sidebar, Questions for a Nontechnical Audit of Intranet Security). If the IT staff has an ITIL (Information Technology Infrastructure Library) process under way, the value of an asset will often already have been classified and can be used. Otherwise, a small spreadsheet can be created with classes of various tangible and intangible assets (as part of a hardware/software cataloguing exercise) and values assigned that way.

5. GUARDIAN AT THE GATE: AUTHENTICATION AND ENCRYPTION

To most lay users, authentication in its most basic form is two-factor authentication—meaning a username and a password. Although adding further factors (such as additional autogenerated personal identification numbers [PINs] and/or biometrics) makes authentication stronger by magnitudes, one can do a lot with just the password within a two-factor situation. Password strength is determined by how hard the password is to crack using a password-cracker application that uses repetitive tries using common words (sometimes from a stored dictionary) to match the password. Some factors will prevent the password from being cracked easily and make it a stronger password:

- Password length (more than eight characters)
- Use of mixed case (both uppercase and lowercase)
- Use of alphanumeric characters (letters as well as numbers)
- Use of special characters (such as !, ?, %, and #)

The ACL in a Windows AD environment can be customized to demand up to all four factors in the setting or renewal of a password, which will render the password strong. Prior to a few years ago, the complexity of a password (the last three items in the preceding list) was favored as a measure of strength in passwords. However, the latest preference as of this writing is to use

uncommon passwords—joined-together sentences to form passphrases that are quite long but don't have much in the way of complexity. Password authentication ("what you know") as two-factor authentication is not as secure as adding a third factor to the equation (a dynamic token password). Common types of third-factor authentication include biometrics (fingerprint scan, palm scan, or retina scan—in other words, "what you are") and token-type authentication (software or hardware PIN—generating tokens—that is, "what you have"). Proximity or magnetic swipe cards and tokens have seen common use for physical premises-access authentication in high-security buildings (such as financial and R & D companies), but not for network or hardware access within IT.

When remote or teleworker employees connect to the intranet via VPN tunnels or Web-based SSL VPNs (the outward extension of the intranet once called an *extranet*), the connection needs to be encrypted with strong 3DES or AES type encryption to comply with patient data and financial data privacy mandates. The standard authentication setup is usually a username and a password, with an additional hardware token-generated random PIN entered into a third box. Until lately, RSA as a company was one of the bigger players in the hardware-token field; incidentally, it also invented the RSA algorithm for public-key encryption.

As of this writing, hardware tokens cost under $30 per user in quantities of greater than a couple hundred pieces, compared to about a $100 only a decade ago. Most vendors offer free lifetime replacements for hardware tokens. Instead of a separate hardware token, some inexpensive software token generators can be installed within PC clients, smartphones, and BlackBerry devices. Tokens are probably the most cost-effective enhancement to security today.

6. WIRELESS NETWORK SECURITY

Employees using the convenience of wireless to log into the corporate network (usually via laptop) need to have their laptops configured with strong encryption to prevent data breaches. The first-generation encryption type known as Wireless Equivalent Privacy (WEP) was easily deciphered (cracked) using common hacking tools and is no longer widely used. The latest standard in wireless authentication is WPA or WPA2 (802.11i), which offers stronger encryption compared to WEP. Although wireless cards in laptops can offer all the previously noted choices, they should be configured with WPA or WPA2 if possible.

There are quite a few hobbyists roaming corporate areas looking for open wireless access points (transmitters) equipped with powerful Wi-Fi antennas and wardriving software, a common package being Netstumbler. Wardriving was originally meant to log the presence of open Wi-Fi access points on Web sites (see sidebar: Basic Ways to Prevent Wi-Fi Intrusions in Corporate Intranets), but there is no guarantee that actual access and use (*piggybacking*, in hacker terms) won't occur, curiosity being human nature. If there is a profit motive, as in the TJX example, access to corporate networks will take place, although the risk of getting caught and the resulting risk of criminal prosecution will be high. Furthermore, installing a RADIUS server is a must to check access authentication for roaming laptops.

7. SHIELDING THE WIRE: NETWORK PROTECTION

Firewalls are, of course, the primary barrier to a network. Typically rule based, firewalls prevent unwarranted traffic from getting into the intranet from the Internet. These days firewalls also do some stateful inspections within packets to peer a little into the header contents of an incoming packet, to check validity—that is, to check whether a streaming video packet is really what it says it is, and not malware masquerading as streaming video.

Intrusion prevention systems (IPSs) are a newer type of inline network appliance that uses heuristic analysis (based on a weekly updated signature engine) to find patterns of malware identity and behavior and to block malware from entering the periphery of the intranet. The IPS and the intrusion detection system (IDS), however, operate differently.

IDSs are typically *not* sitting inline; they sniff traffic occurring anywhere in the network, cache extensively, and can correlate events to find malware. The downside

Basic Ways to Prevent Wi-Fi Intrusions in Corporate Intranets

1. Reset and customize the default Service Set Identifier (SSID) or Extended Service Set Identifier (ESSID) for the access point device before installation.
2. Change the default admin password.
3. Install a RADIUS server, which checks for laptop user credentials from an Active Directory database (ACL) from the same network before giving access to the wireless laptop. See Figures 13.5 and 13.6 for illustrated explanations of the process.
4. Enable WPA or WPA2 encryption, not WEP, which is easily cracked.
5. Periodically try to wardrive around your campus and try to sniff (and disable) nonsecured network-connected rogue access points set up by naïve users.
6. Document the wireless network by using one of the leading wireless network management software packages made for that purpose.

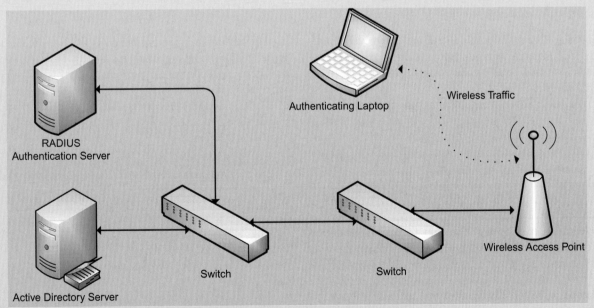

FIGURE 13.5 Wireless EAP authentication using Active Directory and authentication servers.

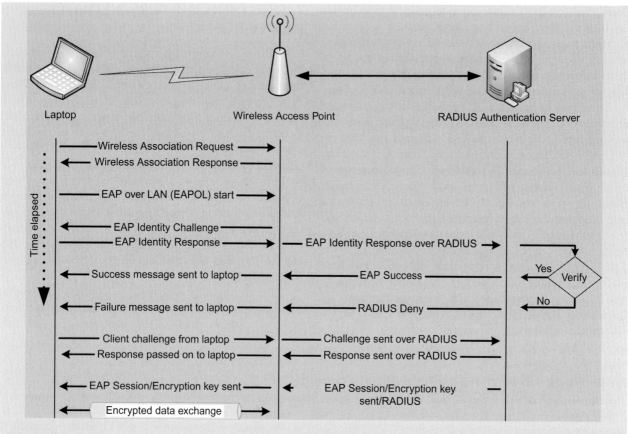

FIGURE 13.6 High-level wireless Extensible Authentication Protocol (EAP) workflow.

Note: Contrary to common belief, turning off the SSID broadcast won't help unless you're talking about a home access point situation. Hackers have an extensive suite of tools with which to sniff SSIDs for lucrative corporate targets, which will be broadcast anyway when connecting in clear text (unlike the real traffic, which will be encrypted).

of IDSs is that unless their filters are extensively modified, they generate copious amounts of false positives—so much so that "real" threats become impossible to sift out of all the noise.

IPSs, in contrast, work *inline* and inspect packets rapidly to match packet signatures. The packets pass through many hundreds of parallel filters, each containing matching rules for a different type of malware threat. Most vendors publish new sets of malware signatures for their appliances every week. However, signatures for common worms and injection exploits such as SQL-slammer, Code-red, and NIMDA are sometimes hardcoded into the application-specific integrated chip (ASIC) that controls the processing for the filters. Hardware-enhancing a filter helps avert massive-scale attacks more efficiently because it is performed in hardware, which is more rapid and efficient compared to software signature matching. Incredible numbers of malicious packets can be dropped from the wire using the former method.

The buffers in an enterprise-class IPS are smaller than those in IDSs and are quite fast—akin to a high-speed switch to preclude latency (often as low as 200 microseconds during the highest load). A top-of-the-line midsize IPS box's total processing threshold for all input and output segments can exceed 5 gigabits per second using parallel processing.[26]

However, to avoid overtaxing CPUs and for efficiency's sake, IPSs usually block only a very limited number of important threats out of the thousands of malware signatures listed. Tuning IPSs can be tricky—just enough blocking to silence the false-positive noise but making sure all critical filters are activated to block important threats.

---

26. IPS specification datasheet. "TippingPoint® intrusion prevention system (IPS) technical specifications," www.tippingpoint.com/pdf/resources/datasheets/400918-007_IPStechspecs.pdf.

Types of Redundancy for Inline Security Appliances

1. Security appliances usually have dual power supplies (often hot-swappable) and are designed to be connected to two separate UPS devices, thereby minimizing the chances of a failure within the appliance itself. The hot-swap capability minimizes replacement time for power supplies.

2. We can configure most of these appliances to either shut down the connection or fall back to a level-two switch (in case of hardware failure). If reverting to a fallback state, most IPSs become basically a bump in the wire and, depending on the type of traffic, can be configured to fail open so that traffic remains uninterrupted. Also, inexpensive, small third-party switchboxes are available to enable this failsafe high-availability option for a single IPS box. The idea is to keep traffic flow active regardless of attacks.

3. IPS or firewall devices can be placed in dual-redundant failover mode, either in active-active (load-sharing) or active-passive (primary-secondary) mode. The devices commonly use a protocol called Virtual Router Redundancy Protocol (VRRP) where the secondary pings the primary every second to check live status and assumes leadership to start processing traffic in case pings are not returned from the primary. The switchover is instantaneous and transparent to most network users. Prior to the switchover, all data and connection settings are fully synchronized at identical states between both boxes to ensure failsafe switchover.

4. Inline IPS appliances are relatively immune to attacks because they have highly hardened Linus/Unix operating systems and are designed from the ground up to be robust and low-maintenance appliances (logs usually clear themselves by default).

The most important factors in designing a critical data infrastructure are resiliency, robustness, and redundancy regarding the operation of inline appliances. Whether one is talking about firewalls or inline IPSs, redundancy is paramount (see sidebar: Types of Redundancy for Inline Security Appliances). Intranet robustness is a primary concern where data has to available on a 24/7 basis.

Most security appliances come with syslog reporting (event and alert logs sent usually via port 514 UDP) and email notification (set to alert beyond a customizable threshold) as standard. The syslog reporting can be forwarded to a security event management (SEM) appliance, which consolidates syslogs into a central threat console for benefit of event correlation and forwards warning emails to administrators based on preset threshold criteria. Moreover, most firewalls and IPSs can be configured to forward their own notification email to administrators in case of an impending threat scenario.

For those special circumstances where a wireless-type LAN connection is the primary one (whether microwave beam, laser beam, or satellite-type connection), redundancy can be ensured by a secondary connection of equal or smaller capacity. For example, in certain northern Alaska towns where digging trenches into the hardened icy permafrost is expensive and rigging wire across the tundra is impractical due to the extreme cold, the primary network connections between towns are always via microwave link, often operating in dual redundant mode.

8. WEAKEST LINK IN SECURITY: USER TRAINING

Intranet security awareness is best communicated to users in two primary ways—during new employee orientation and by ongoing targeted training for users in various departments with specific user audiences in mind. A formal security training policy should be drafted and signed off by management, with well-defined scopes, roles, and responsibilities of various individuals, such as the CIO and the information security officer, and posted on the intranet. New recruits should be given a copy of all security policies to sign off on before they are granted user access. The training policy should also spell out the roles of the HR, Compliance, and PR departments in the training program.

Training can be given using the PowerPoint Seminar method in large gatherings before monthly "all-hands" departmental meetings and also via an emailed Web link to a Flash video format presentation. The latter can also be configured to have an interactive quiz at the end, which should pique audience interest in the subject and help them remember relevant issues.

With regard to topics to be included in the training, any applicable federal or industry mandate such as HIPAA, SOX, PCI-DSS, or ISO 27002 should be discussed extensively first, followed by discussions on tackling social engineering, spyware, viruses, and so on.

The topics of data theft and corporate data breaches are frequently in the news. These topics can be extensively discussed, with emphasis on how to protect personally identifiable information in a corporate setting. Password policy and access control topics are always good things to discuss; users at a minimum need to be reminded to sign off their workstations before going on break.

9. DOCUMENTING THE NETWORK: CHANGE MANAGEMENT

Controlling the IT infrastructure configuration of a large organization is more about change control than other

---

Change Management Spreadsheet Details to Submit to a CM Meeting

- Name and organizational details of the change-requestor
- Actual change details, such as the time and duration of the change
- Any possible impacts (high, low, medium) to significant user groups or critical functions
- The amount of advance notice needed for impacted users via email (typically two working days)
- Evidence that the change has been tested in advance
- Signature and approval of the supervisor and her supervisor (manager)

- Whether and how rollback is possible
- Post-change, a "postmortem tab" has to confirm whether the change process was successful and any revealing comments or notes for the conclusion.
- One of the tabs can be an "attachment tab" containing embedded Visio diagrams or word documentation embedded within the Excel sheet to aid discussion.

---

things. Often the change control guidance comes from documents such as the ITIL series of guidebooks.

After a baseline configuration is documented, change control—a deliberate and methodical process that ensures that any changes are made to the baseline IT configuration of the organization (such as changes to network design, AD design, and so on)—is extensively documented and authorized only after prior approval. This is done to ensure that unannounced or unplanned changes are not allowed to hamper the day-to-day efficiency and business functions of the overall intranet infrastructure.

In most government entities, even very small changes are made to go through change management (CM); however, management can give managers leeway to approve a certain minimal level of ad hoc change that has no potential to disrupt operations. In most organizations where mandates are a day-to-day affair, no ad hoc change is allowed unless it goes through supervisory-level change management meetings.

The goal of change management is largely to comply with mandates—but for some organizations, waiting for a weekly meeting can slow things significantly. If justified, an emergency CM meeting can be called to approve a time-sensitive change.

Practically speaking, the change management process works as follows: A formal change management document is filled out (usually a multitab online Excel spreadsheet) and forwarded to the change management ombudsman (maybe a project management person). For some CM form details, see the sidebar: Change Management Spreadsheet Details to Submit to a CM Meeting.

The document must have supervisory approval from the requestor's supervisor before proceeding to the ombudsman. The ombudsman posts this change document on a section of the intranet for all other supervisors and managers within the CM committee to review in advance. Done this way, the change management committee, meeting in its weekly or biweekly change approval meetings, can voice reservations or ask clarification questions of the change-initiating person, who is usually present to explain

the change. At the end of the deliberations the decision is then voted on to either approve, deny, modify, or delay the change (sometimes with preconditions).

If approved, the configuration change is then made (usually within the following week). The postmortem section of the change can then be updated to note any issues that occurred during the change (such as a rollback after change reversal and the causes).

In recent years, some organizations have started to operate the change management collaborative process using social networking tools at work. This allows disparate flows of information, such as emails, departmental wikis, and file-share documents, to belong to a unified thread for future reference.

10. REHEARSE THE INEVITABLE: DISASTER RECOVERY

Possible disaster scenarios can range from the mundane to the biblical in proportion. In intranet or general IT terms, successfully recovering from a disaster can mean resuming critical IT support functions for mission-critical business functions. Whether such recovery is smooth and hassle-free depends on how prior disaster-recovery planning occurs and how this plan is tested to address all relevant shortcomings adequately.

The first task when planning for disaster recovery (DR) is to assess the business impact of a certain type of disaster on the functioning of an intranet using business impact analysis (BIA). BIA involves certain metrics; again, off-the shelf software tools are available to assist with this effort. The scenario could be a natural hurricane-induced power outage or a human-induced critical application crash. In any one of these scenarios, one needs to assess the type of impact in time, productivity, and financial terms.

BIAs can take into consideration the breadth of impact. For example, if the power outage is caused by a hurricane or an earthquake, support from generator vendors or the electricity utility could be hard to get, because of the large demands for their services. BIAs also need to take into account historical and local weather priorities. Though there could be possibilities of hurricanes occurring in California or earthquakes occurring along the Gulf Coast of Florida, for most practical purposes the chances of those disasters taking place in those locales are pretty remote. Historical data can be helpful for prioritizing contingencies.

Once the business impacts are assessed to categorize critical systems, a disaster recovery (DR) plan can be organized and tested. The criteria for recovery have two types of metrics: a recovery point objective (RPO) and a recovery time objective (RTO).

In the DR plan, the RPO refers to how far back or "back to what point in time" that backup data has to be recovered. This timeframe generally dictates how often tape backups are taken, which can again depend on the criticality of the data. The most common scenario for medium-sized IT shops is daily incremental backups and a weekly full backup on tape. Tapes are sometimes changed automatically by the tape backup appliances.

One important thing to remember is to rotate tapes (that is, put them on a life-cycle plan by marking them for expiry) to make sure that tapes have complete data integrity during a restore. Most tape manufacturers have marking schemes for this task. Although tapes are still relatively expensive, the extra amount spent on always having fresh tapes ensures that there are no nasty surprises at the time of a crucial data recovery.

RTO refers to how long it takes to restore backed up or recovered data to its original state for resuming normal business processes. The critical factor here is cost. It will cost much more to restore data within an hour using an online backup process or to resume operations using a hotsite rather than a five-hour restore using stored tape backups. If business process resumption is critical, cost becomes a less important factor.

DR also has to take into account resumption of communication channels. If network and telephone links aren't up, having a timely tape restore does little good to resume business functions. Extended campus network links are often dependent on leased lines from major vendors such as Verizon and AT & T, so having a trusted vendor relationship with agreed-on SLA standards is a requirement.

Depending on budgets, one can configure DR to happen almost instantly, if so desired, but that is a far more costly option. Most shops with "normal" data flows are okay with business being resumed within the span of about three to fours hours or even a full working day after a major disaster. Balancing costs with business expectations is the primary factor in the DR game. Spending inordinately for a rare disaster that might never happen is a waste of resources. It is fiscally imprudent (not to mention futile) to try to prepare for every contingency possible.

Once the DR plan is more or less finalized, a DR committee can be set up under an experienced DR professional to orchestrate the routine training of users and managers to simulate disasters on a frequent basis. In most shops this means management meeting every two months to simulate a DR "war room" (command center) situation and employees going through a mandatory interactive six-month disaster recovery training, listing the DR personnel to contact.

Within the command center, roles are preassigned, and each member of the team carries out his or her role as though it were a real emergency or disaster. DR coordination is frequently modeled after the U.S. Federal Emergency Management Agency (FEMA) guidelines, an active entity that has training and certification tracks for DR management professionals.

Simulated "generator shutdowns" in most shops are scheduled on a biweekly or monthly basis to see how the systems actually function. The systems can include uninterrupible power supplies (UPSs), emergency lighting, email and cell phone notification methods, and alarm enunciators and sirens. Since electronics items in a server room are sensitive to moisture damage, gas-based Halon fire-extinguishing systems are used. These Halon systems also have a provision to test them (often twice a year) to determine their readiness. The vendor will be happy to be on retainer for these tests, which can be made part of the purchasing agreement as a service level agreement (SLA). If equipment is tested on a regular basis, shortcomings and major hardware maintenance issues with major DR systems can be easily identified, documented, and redressed.

In a severe disaster situation, priorities need to be exercised on what to salvage first. Clearly, trying to recover employee records, payroll records, and critical business mission data such as customer databases will take precedence. Anything irreplaceable or not easily replaceable needs priority attention.

We can divide the levels of redundancies and backups to a few progressive segments. The level of backup sophistication would of course be dependent on (1) criticality and (2) time-to-recovery criteria of the data involved.

At the very basic level, we can opt not to back up any data or not even have procedures to recover data, which means that data recovery would be a failure. Understandably, this is not a common scenario.

More typical is contracting with an archival company of a local warehouse within a 20-mile periphery. Tapes are backed up onsite and stored offsite, with the archival company picking up the tapes from your facility on a daily basis. The time to recover is dependent on retrieving the tapes from archival storage, getting them onsite, and starting a restore. The advantages here are lower cost.

However, the time needed to transport tapes and recover them might not be acceptable, depending on the type of data and the recovery scenario.

Often a "coldsite" or "hotsite" is added to the intranet backup scenario. A coldsite is a smaller and scaled-down copy of the existing intranet data center that has only the most essential pared-down equipment supplied and tested for recovery but not in a perpetually ready state (powered down as in "cold," with no live connection). These cold-sites can house the basics, such as a Web server, domain name servers, and SQL databases, to get an informational site started up in very short order.

A hotsite is the same thing as a coldsite except that in this case the servers are always running and the Internet and intranet connections are "live" and ready to be switched over much more quickly than on a coldsite. These are just two examples of how the business resumption and recovery times can be shortened.

Recovery can be made very rapidly if the hotsite is linked to the regular data center using fast leased-line links (such as a DS3 connection). Backups synched in real time with identical RAID disks at the hotsite over redundant high-speed data links afford the shortest recovery time.

In larger intranet shops based in defense-contractor companies, there are sometimes requirements for even faster data recovery with far more rigid standards for data integrity. To-the-second real-time data synchronization in addition to hardware synchronization ensures that duplicate sites thousands of miles away can be up and running within a matter of seconds—even faster than a hotsite. Such extreme redundancy is typically needed for critical national databases (that is, air traffic control or customs databases that are accessed 24/7, for example).

At the highest level of recovery performance, most large database vendors offer "zero data loss" solutions, with a variety of cloned databases synchronized across the country that automatically failover and recover in an instantaneous fashion to preserve a consistent status—often free from human intervention. Oracle's version is called Data Guard; most mainframe vendors offer a similar product, varying in their offerings of tiers and features.

The philosophy here is simple: The more dollars you spend, the more readiness you can buy. However, the expense has to be justified by the level of criticality for the availability of the data.

11. CONTROLLING HAZARDS: PHYSICAL AND ENVIRONMENTAL PROTECTION

Physical access and environmental hazards are very relevant to security within the intranet. People are the primary weak link in security (as previously discussed), and controlling the activity and movement of authorized personnel and preventing access to unauthorized personnel fall within the purview of these security controls. This important area of intranet security must first be formalized within a management-sanctioned and published P&P.

Physical access to data center facilities (as well as IT working facilities) is typically controlled using card readers. These were scanning types in the last two decades but are increasingly being converted to near-field or proximity-type access card systems. Some high-security facilities (such as bank data centers) use smartcards, which use encryption keys stored within the cards for matching keys.

Some important and common-sense topics should be discussed within the subject of physical access. First, disbursal of cards needs to be a deliberate and high-security affair requiring the signatures of at least two supervisory-level people who can be responsible for the authenticity and actual need for access credentials for a person to specific areas.

Access-card permissions need to be highly granular. An administrative person will probably never need to be in the server room, so that person's access to the server room should be blocked. Areas should be categorized and catalogued by sensitivity and access permissions granted accordingly.

Physical data transmission access points to the intranet have to be monitored via digital video recording (DVR) and closed-circuit cameras if possible. Physical electronic eavesdropping can occur to unmonitored network access points in both wireline and wireless ways. There have been known instances of thieves intercepting LAN communication from unshielded Ethernet cable (usually hidden above the plenum or false ceiling for longer runs). All a data thief needs is to place a TAP box and a miniature (Wi-Fi) wireless transmitter at entry or exit points to the intranet to copy and transmit all communications. At the time of this writing, these transmitters are the size of a USB key. The miniaturization of electronics has made data theft possible for part-time thieves. Spy-store sites give determined data thieves plenty of workable options at relatively little cost.

Using a DVR solution to monitor and store access logs to sensitive areas and correlating them to the time-stamps on the physical access logs can help forensic investigations in case of a physical data breach, malfeasance, or theft. It is important to remember that DVR records typically rotate and are erased every week. One person has to be in charge of the DVR so records are saved to optical disks weekly before they are erased. DVR tools need some tending to because their sophistication level often does not come up to par with other network tools.

Written or PC-based sign-in logs must be kept at the front reception desk, with timestamps. Visitor cards should have limited access to private and/or secured areas. Visitors must provide official identification, log times coming in and going out, and names of persons to be visited and the reason for their visit. If possible, visitors should be escorted to and from the specific person to be visited, to minimize the chances of subversion or sabotage.

Entries to courthouses and other special facilities have metal detectors, but these may not be needed for every facility. The same goes for bollards and concrete entry barriers to prevent car bombings. In most government facilities where security is paramount, even physical entry points to parking garages have special personnel (usually deputed from the local sheriff's department) to check under cars for hidden explosive devices.

Contractor laptops must be registered and physically checked in by field support personnel. And if these laptops are going to be plugged into the local network, the laptops need to be virus-scanned by data-security personnel and checked for unauthorized utilities or suspicious software (such as hacking utilities, Napster, or other P2P threats).

Supply of emergency power to the data center and the servers has to be robust to protect the intranet from corruption due to power failures. Redundancy has to be exercised all the way from the utility connection to the servers themselves. This means there has to be more than one power connection to the data center (from more than one substation/transformer, if it is a larger data center). There has to be provision of alternate power supply (a ready generator to supply some, if not all, power requirements) in case of power failure.

Power supplied to the servers has to come from more than one single UPS because most servers have two removable power inputs. Data center racks typically have two UPSs on the bottom supplying power to two separate power strips on both sides of the rack for this redundancy purpose (for seamless switchover). In case of a power failure, the UPSs instantly take over the supply of power and start beeping, alerting personnel to gracefully shut down servers. UPSs usually have reserve power for brief periods (less than 10 minutes) until the generator kicks in, relieving the UPS of the large burden of the server power loads. Generators come on trailers or are skid-mounted and are designed to run as long as fuel is available in the tank, which can be about three to five days, depending on the model and capacity to generate (in thousands of kilowatts).

Increasingly, expensive polluting batteries have made UPSs in larger data centers fall out of favor compared to flywheel power supplies, which are a cleaner, battery-less technology to supply interim power. Maintenance of this technology is half as costly as UPS, and it offers the same functionality. Provision has to be made for rechargeable emergency luminaires within the server room, as well as all areas occupied by administrators, so entry and exit are not hampered during a power failure.

Provision for fire detection and firefighting must also be made. As mentioned previously, Halon gas fire-suppression systems are appropriate for server rooms because sprinklers will inevitably damage expensive servers if the servers are still turned on during sprinkler activation.

Sensors have to be placed close to the ground to detect moisture from plumbing disasters and resultant flooding. Master shutoff valve locations for water have to be marked and identified and personnel trained on performing shutoffs periodically. Complete environmental control packages with cameras geared toward detecting any type of temperature, moisture, and sound abnormality are offered by many vendors. These sensors are connected to monitoring workstations using Ethernet LAN cabling. Reporting can occur through emails if customizable thresholds are met or exceeded.

12. KNOW YOUR USERS: PERSONNEL SECURITY

Users working within intranet-related infrastructures have to be known and trusted. Often data contained within the intranet is highly sensitive, such as new product designs and financial or market-intelligence data gathered after much research and at great expense.

Assigning personnel to sensitive areas in IT entails attaching security categories and parameters to the positions, especially within IT. Attaching security parameters to a position is akin to attaching tags to a photograph or blog. Some parameters will be more important than others, but all describe the item to some extent. The categories and parameters listed on the personnel access form should correlate to access permissions to sensitive installations such as server rooms. Access permissions should be compliant to the organizational security policy in force at the time. Personnel, especially those who will be handling sensitive customer data or individually identifiable health records, should be screened before hiring to ensure that they do not have felonies or misdemeanors on their records.

During transfers and terminations, all sensitive access tools should be reassessed and reassigned (or de-assigned, in case termination happens) for logical and physical access. Access tools can include such items as encryption tokens, company cell phones, laptops or PDAs, card keys, metal keys, entry passes, and any other company identification provided for employment. For people who are leaving the organization, an exit interview should be taken. System access should be terminated on the hour after former personnel have ceased to be employees of the company.

13. PROTECTING DATA FLOW: INFORMATION AND SYSTEM INTEGRITY

Information integrity protects information and data flows while they are in movement to and from the users' desktops to the intranet. System integrity measures protect the systems that process the information (usually servers such as email or file servers). The processes to protect information can include antivirus tools, IPS and IDS tools, Web-filtering tools, and email encryption tools.

Antivirus tools are the most common security tools available to protect servers and users' desktops. Typically, enterprise-level antivirus software from larger vendors such as Symantec or McAfee will contain a console listing all machines on the network and will enable the administrators to see graphically (color or icon differentiation) which machines need virus remediation or updates. All machines will have a software client installed that does some scanning and reporting of the individual machines to the console. To save bandwidth, the management server that contains the console will be updated with the latest virus (and spyware) definition from the vendor. Then it is the management console's job to slowly update the software client in each computer with the latest definitions. Sometimes the client itself will need an update, and the console allows this to be done remotely.

IDS detects malware within the network from the traffic and communication malware used. There are certain patterns of behavior attached to each type of malware, and those signatures are what IDSs are used to match. IDSs are mostly defunct nowadays. The major problems with IDSs were that (1) IDSs used to produce too many false positives, which made sifting out actual threats a huge, frustrating exercise, and (2) IDSs had no teeth; that is, their functionality was limited to reporting and raising alarms. IDS devices could not stop malware from spreading because they could not block it.

Compared to IDSs, IPSs have seen much wider adoption across corporate intranets because IPS devices sit inline processing traffic at the periphery and they can block traffic or malware, depending on a much more sophisticated heuristic algorithm than IDS devices. Although IPSs are all mostly signature based, there are already experimental IPS devices that can stop threats, not on signature, but based only on suspicious or anomalous behavior. This is good news because the numbers of "zero-day" threats are on the increase, and their signatures are mostly unknown to the security vendors at the time of infection.

Web-filtering tools have gotten more sophisticated as well. Ten years ago Web filters could only block traffic to specific sites if the URL matched. Today most Web filter vendors have large research arms that try to categorize specific Web sites under certain categories. Some vendors have realized the enormity of this task and have allowed the general public to contribute to this effort. The Web site www.trustedsource.org is an example; a person can go in and submit a single or multiple URLs for categorization. If they're examined and approved, the site category will then be added to the vendor's next signature update for their Web filter solution.

Web filters not only match URLs, but they also do a fair bit of packet-examining these days—just to make sure that a JPEG frame is indeed a JPEG frame and not a worm in disguise. The categories of Web sites blocked by a typical midsized intranet vary, but some surefire blocked categories would be pornography, erotic sites, discrimination/hate, weapons/illegal activities, and dating/relationships.

Web filters are not just there to enforce the moral values of management. These categories—if not blocked at work—openly enable an employee to offend another employee (especially pornography or discriminatory sites) and are fertile grounds for a liability lawsuit against the employer.

Finally, email encryption has been in the news because of the various mandates such as Sarbanes-Oxley and HIPAA. Both mandates specifically mention email or communication encryption to encrypt personally identifiable financial or patient medical data while in transit. Lately, the state of California (among other states) has adopted a resolution to discontinue fund disbursements to any California health organization that does not use email encryption as a matter of practice. This has caught quite a few California companies and local government entities unaware because email encryption software is relatively hard to implement. The toughest challenge yet is to train users to get used to the tool. Email encryption works by entering a set of credentials to access the email rather than just getting email pushed to the user, as within the email client Outlook.

14. SECURITY ASSESSMENTS

A security assessment (usually done on a yearly basis for most midsized shops) not only uncovers various misconfigured items on the network and server-side sections of IT operations; it also serves as a convenient blueprint for IT to activate necessary changes and get credibility for budgetary assistance from the accounting folks.

Typically, most consultants take two to four weeks to conduct a security assessment (depending on the size of the intranet), and they primarily use open-source vulnerability scanners such as Nessus. GFI LANguard, Retina, and Core Impact are other examples of commercial vulnerability-testing tools. Sometimes testers also use other proprietary suites of tools (special open-source tools

Types of Scans Conducted on Servers and Network Appliances during a Security Assessment

- Firewalls and IPS devices configuration
- Regular and SSL VPN configuration
- Web server hardening (most critical; available as guides from vendors such as Microsoft)
- DMZ configuration
- Email vulnerabilities
- DNS server anomalies
- Database servers (hardening levels)
- Network design and access control vulnerabilities
- Internal PC health such as patching levels and incidence of spyware, malware, and so on

like the Metasploit Framework or Fragrouter) to conduct "payload-bearing attack exploits," thereby evading the firewall and the IPS to gain entry. In the case of intranet Web servers, cross-site scripting attacks can occur (see sidebar: Types of Scans Conducted on Servers and Network Appliances during a Security Assessment).

The results of these penetration tests are usually compiled as two separate items: (1) as a full-fledged technical report for IT and (2) as a high-level executive summary meant for and delivered to top management to discuss strategy with IT after the engagement.

15. RISK ASSESSMENTS

Risk is defined as the probability of loss. In IT terms we're talking about compromising data CIA (confidentiality, integrity, or availability). Risk management is a way to manage the probability of threats causing an impact. Measuring risks using a risk assessment exercise is the first step toward managing or mitigating a risk. Risk assessments can identify network threats, their probabilities, and their impacts. The reduction of risk can be achieved by reducing any of these three factors.

Regarding intranet risks and threats, we're talking about anything from threats such as unpatched PCs getting viruses and spyware (with hidden keylogging software) to network-borne denial-of-service attacks and even

large, publicly embarrassing Web vandalism threats, such as someone being able to deface the main page of the company Web site. The last is a very high-impact threat but mostly perceived to be a remote probability—unless, of course, the company has experienced this before. The awareness among vendors as well as users regarding security is at an all-time high due to security being a high-profile news item.

Any security threat assessment needs to explore and list exploitable vulnerabilities and gaps. Many midsized IT shops run specific vulnerability assessment (VA) tools in-house on a monthly basis. eEye's Retina Network Security Scanner and Foundstone's scanning tools appliance are two examples of VA tools that can be found in use at larger IT shops. These tools are consolidated on ready-to-run appliances that are usually managed through remote browser-based consoles. Once the gaps are identified and quantified, steps can be taken to gradually mitigate these vulnerabilities, minimizing the impact of threats.

In intranet risk assessments, we identify primarily Web server and database threats residing within the intranet, but we should also be mindful about the periphery to guard against breaches through the firewall or IPS.

Finally, making intranet infrastructure and applications can be a complex task. This gets even more complex and even confusing when information is obtained

An Agenda for Action for Intranet Security Implementation Process Activities

The following high-level checklist should be addressed in order to find the following intranet security implemnetation process questions helpful (check all tasks completed):

_____ 1. How to validate the intranet?
_____ 2. How to validate web applications?
_____ 3. How to ensure and verify accuracy of file transfer through the e-mails?
_____ 4. Does one need third-party certificates for digital signatures?
_____ 5. How to ensure limited and authorized access to closed and open systems?
_____ 6. How can one safely access the company intranet while traveling?
_____ 7. How to best protect the intranet from Internet attacks?
_____ 8. How to handle security patches?
_____ 9. Does the stakeholder expect to be able to find a procedure using a simple search interface?
_____ 10. How many documents will be hosted?
_____ 11. What design will be used (centralized, hub and spoke, etc.)?
_____ 12. Who will be involved in evaluating projects?
_____ 13. What is the budget?
_____ 14. Who will be responsible for maintaining the site after it goes "live"?

from the different sources that are normally found at security conferences around the world. Frequently, these conference sources give a high-level overview, talking about generic compliance; but none gives a full picture and details that are required for quick implementation. So, with the preceding in mind, and because of the frequency of poor security practices or far-too-common security failures on the intranet, let's briefly look at an intranet security implementation process checklist.

16. INTRANET SECURITY IMPLEMENTATION PROCESS CHECKLIST

With this checklist, you get all of your questions in one place. This not only saves time, it's also cost effective. The following high-level checklist lists all of the questions that are typically raised during the implementation process (see checklist: An Agenda for Action for Intranet Security Implementation Process Activities).

17. SUMMARY

It is true that the level of Internet hyperconnectivity among generation X and Y users has mushroomed lately, and the network periphery that we used to take for granted as a security shield has been diminished largely because of the explosive growth of social networking and the resulting connectivity boom. However, with the various new types of incoming application traffic (VoIP, SIP, and XML traffic) to their networks, security administrators need to stay on their toes and deal with these new protocols by implementing newer tools and technology. One recent example of new technology is the application-level firewall for connecting outside vendors to intranets (also known as an XML firewall, placed within a DMZ) that protects the intranet from malformed XML and SOAP message exploits coming from outside sourced applications.[27]

In conclusion, we can say that with the myriad security issues facing intranets today, most IT shops are still well equipped to defend themselves if they assess risks and, most important, train their employees regarding data security practices on an ongoing basis. The problems with threat mitigation remain largely a matter of meeting gaps in procedural controls rather than technical measures. Trained and security-aware employees are the biggest deterrent to data thefts and security breaches.

Finally, let's move on to the real interactive part of this chapter: review questions/exercises, hands-on projects, case projects and optional team case project. The

answers and/or solutions by chapter can be found in the Online Instructor's Solutions Manual.

CHAPTER REVIEW QUESTIONS/EXERCISES

True/False

1. True or False? In the corporate context, microblogging entails sending short SMS messages to apprise colleagues of recent developments in the daily routine.
2. True or False? Popular devices like the iPad, Samsung Galaxy Android tablet, and many types of smartphones are already capable of accessing company intranets using customized intranet apps.
3. True or False? Quite a few risks need to be resolved when approaching intranet security concerning mobile devices.
4. True or False? Mobile devices accessing enterprise intranets using VPNs have to be subject to the same factors as any other device remotely accessing VPNs.
5. True or False? While there are few risks in deploying mobile devices within the Intranet, with careful configuration these risks can be increased to the point where the myriad benefits outweigh the risks.

Multiple Choice

1. The intranet, as just a simple place to share files and to list a few policies and procedures, has ceased to be. The types of changes can be summed up in the following list of features, which shows that the intranet has become a combined portal as well as a public dashboard. Some of the features include the following, except which one?
   A. A corporate personnel directory of phone numbers by department.
   B. Several RSS feeds for news according to divisions such as IT, HR, Finance, Accounting, and Purchasing.
   C. A search engine for searching company information, often helped by a search appliance from Google.
   D. A section describing company financials and other mission-critical indicators.
   E. A "live" section with IT alerts regarding specific downtimes, outages, and other critical time-sensitive company notifications.
2. Intranet security policies and procedures (P&Ps) are:
   A. The functionality and ease of use of using voice, gesture, and touch interfaces
   B. The first step toward a legal regulatory framework
   C. The availability of customized apps (applications)
   D. The change in the very concept of "being at work" compared to even 10 years ago
   E. The more rapid iteration life cycles of mobile devices

---

27. Latest standard (version 1.1) for SOAP message security standard from OASIS, a consortium for Web Services Security, www.oasisopen.org/committees/download.php/16790/wss-v1.1-spec-os-SOAPMessage Security.pdf.

3. The millennial generation is more familiar with:
   A. PCs and laptops.
   B. social media.
   C. mobile technology.
   D. mobile hardware industry.
   E. cloud.
4. Backend enterprise network infrastructure support has to be ready and has to be strong to handle mobile devices interacting with:
   A. iPads.
   B. IPSec.
   C. L2TP VPNs.
   D. SSL VPNs.
   E. PPTP VPNs.
5. What policy/procedure must be signed by new hires at orientation and by all employees who ask for access to the corporate VPN using mobile devices (even personal ones)?
   A. WPA2 encryption for Wi-Fi traffic access
   B. Inbound and outbound malware scanning
   C. A well-tested SSL VPN for remote access
   D. A policy for reporting theft or misplacement
   E. A customized corporate usage policy for mobile devices

EXERCISE

Problem

How can an organization prevent security breaches to their intranet?

Hands-On Projects

Project

How would an organization handle an intranet attack?

Case Projects

Problem

How would an organization go about handling an unauthorized access of an intranet?

Optional Team Case Project

Problem

How would an organization go about handling the misuse of user privileges on an intranet?

## Chapter 14

Local Area Network Security

Dr. Pramod Pandya
California State University

Securing available resources on any corporate or academic data network is of paramount importance because most of these networks connect to the Internet for commercial or research activities. Therefore, the network is under attack from hackers on a continual basis, so network security technologies are ever evolving and playing catch-up with hackers. Around 29 years ago the number of potential users was small and the scope of any activity on the network was limited to local networks only. As the Internet expanded in its reach across national boundaries and as the number of users increased, potential risk to the network grew exponentially. Over the past 18 years ecommerce-related activities such as online shopping, banking, stock trading, and social networking have permeated extensively, creating a dilemma for both service providers and their potential clients, as to who is a trusted service provider and a trusted client on the network. Of course, this being a daunting task for security professionals, they have needed to design security policies appropriate for both the servers and their clients. The security policy must be a factor in clients' level of access to the resources. So, in whom do we place trust, and how much trust? Current network designs implement three levels of trust: most trusted, less trusted, and least trusted. Figure 14.1 reflects these levels of trust, as described here:

- The most trusted users belong to the *intranet*. These users have to authenticate to a centralize administrator to access the resources on the network.
- The less trusted users may originate from the intranet as well as the external users who are authenticated to access resources such as email and Web services.
- The least trusted users are the unauthenticated users; most of them are simply browsing the resources on the Internet with no malice intended. Of course, some are scanning the resources with the intent to break in and steal data.

These are the objectives of network security:

- *Confidentiality.* Only authorized users have access to the network.

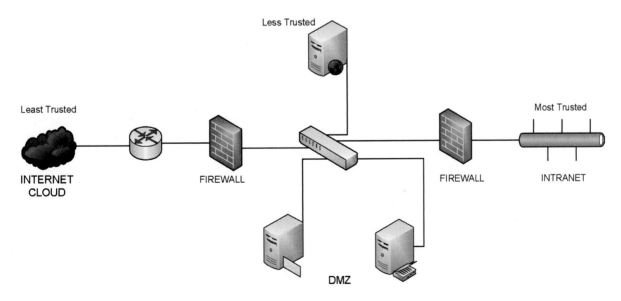

FIGURE 14.1 The DMZ.

- *Integrity.* Data cannot be modified by unauthorized users.
- *Access.* Security must be designed so that authorized users have uninterrupted access to data.

Finally, the responsibility for the design and implementation of network security, is headed by the chief information officer (CIO) of the enterprise network. The CIO has a pool of network administrators and legal advisers to help with this task. The network administrators define the placing of the network access controls, and the legal advisors underline the consequences and liabilities in the event of network security breaches. We have seen cases of customer records such as credit-card numbers, Social Security numbers, and personal information being stolen. The frequency of these reports have been on the increase in the past years, and consequently this has led to a discussion on the merits of encryption of stored data. One of the most quoted legal requirements on the part of any business, whether small or big, is the protection of consumer data under the Health Insurance Portability and Accountability Act (HIPAA), which restricts disclosure of health-related data and personal information.

1. IDENTIFY NETWORK THREATS

Network security threats can be in one of two categories: (1) disruptive type or (2) unauthorized access type.

Disruptive

Most LANs are designed as collapsed backbone networks using a layer-2 or layer-3 switch. If a switch or a router were to fail due to power failure, a segment or the entire network may cease to function until the power is restored. In some case, the network failure may be due to a virus attack on the secondary storage, thus leading to loss of data.

Unauthorized Access

This access type can be internal (employee) or external (intruder), a person who would attempt to break into resources such as database, file, and email or web servers that they have no permission to access. Banks, financial institutions, major corporations, and major retail businesses employ data networks to process customer transactions and store customer information and any other relevant data. Before the birth of the Internet Age, interin-stitutional transactions were secured because the networks were not accessible to intruders or the general public. In the past 14 years, access to the Internet is almost universal; hence institutional data networks have

become the target of frequent intruder attacks to steal customer records. One frequently reads in the news about data network security being compromised by hackers, leading to loss of credit card and debit card numbers, Social Security numbers, drivers' license numbers, and other sensitive information such as purchasing profiles. Over the years, although network security has increased, the frequency of attacks on the networks has also increased because the tools to breach the network security have become freely available on the Internet. In 1988 the U.S. Department of Defense established the Computer Emergency Response Team (CERT), whose mission is to work with the Internet community to prevent and respond to computer and network security breaches. Since the Internet is widely used for commercial activities by all kinds of businesses, the federal government has enacted stiffer penalties for hackers.

2. ESTABLISH NETWORK ACCESS CONTROLS

In this part of the chapter, we outline steps necessary to secure networks through network controls. These network controls are either software or hardware based and are implemented in a hierarchical structure to reflect the network organization. This hierarchy is superimposed on the network from the network's perimeter to the access level per user of the network resources. The functions of the network control are to detect an unauthorized access, to prevent network security from being breached, and finally, to respond to a breach—thus the three categories of detect, prevent, and respond.

The role of prevention control is to stop unauthorized access to any resource available on the network. This could be implemented as simply as a password required to authenticate the user to access the resource on the network. For an authorized user this password can grant login to the network to access the services of a database, file, Web, print, or email server. The network administrator would need a password to access the switch or a router. The prevention control in this case is software based. An analog of hardware-based control would be, for example, if the resources such as server computers, switches, and routers are locked in a network access control room.

The role of the detection control is to monitor the activities on the network and identify an event or a set of events that could breach network security. Such an event may be a virus, spyware, or adware attack. The detection control software must, besides registering the attack, generate or trigger an alarm to notify of an unusual event so that a corrective action can be taken immediately, without compromising security.

TABLE 14.1 Mission-Critical Components of any Enterprise Network.

Resources	Threats					
	Fire, Flood, Earthquake	Power Failure	Spam	Virus	Spyware, Adware	Hijacking
Perimeter Router						
DNS Server						
WEB Server						
Email Server						
Core Switches						
Databases						

The role of the response control is to take corrective action whenever network security is breached so that the same kind of breach is detected and any further damage is prevented.

3. RISK ASSESSMENT

During the initial design phase of a network, the network architects assess the types of risks to the network as well as the costs of recovering from attacks for all the resources that have been compromised. These cost factors can be realized using well-established accounting procedures such as cost/benefit analysis, return on investment (ROI), and total cost of ownership (TCO). These risks could range from natural disaster to an attack by a hacker. Therefore, you need to develop levels of risks to various threats to the network. You need to design some sort of spreadsheet that lists risks versus threats as well as responses to those identified threats. Of course, the spreadsheet would also mark the placing of the network access controls to secure the network.

4. LISTING NETWORK RESOURCES

We need to identify the assets (resources) that are available on the corporate network. Of course, this list could be long, and it would make no sense to protect all the resources, except for those that are mission-critical to the business functions. Table 14.1 identifies mission-critical components of any enterprise network. You will observe that these mission-critical components need to be prioritized, since they do not all provide the same functions. Some resources provide controlled access to a network; other resources carry sensitive corporate data. Hence the threats posed to these resources do not carry the same degree of vulnerabilities to the network. Therefore, the network access control has to be articulated and applied to each of the components listed, in varying degrees. For

example, threats to DNS server pose a different set of problems from threats to the database servers. Next, we itemize the threats to these resources and specific network access controls.

5. THREATS

We need to identify the threats posed to the network from internal users as opposed to those from external users. The reason for such a distinction is that the internal users are easily traceable, compared to the external users. If a threat to the data network is successful, and it could lead to loss or theft of data or denial of access to the services offered by the network, it would lead to monetary loss for the corporation. Once we have identified these threats, we can rank them from most probable to least probable and design network security policy to reflect that ranking.

From Table 14.2, we observe that most frequent threats to the network are from viruses, and we have seen a rapid explosion in antivirus, antispamware, and spyware and adware software. Hijacking of resources such as domain name services, Web services, and perimeter routers would lead to what's most famously known as denial of service (DoS) or distributed denial of service (DDoS). Power failures can always be complemented by standby power supplies that could keep the essential resources from crashing. Natural disasters such as fire, floods, or earthquakes can be most difficult to plan for; therefore we see a tremendous growth in data protection and backup service provider businesses.

6. SECURITY POLICIES

The fundamental goals of security policy are to allow uninterrupted access to the network resources for authenticated users and to deny access to unauthenticated users. Of course, this is always a balancing act between the users' demands on network resources and the

TABLE 14.2 The Most Frequent Threats to the Network Are from Viruses.

Rank	Threat
1	Virus
2	Spam
3	Spyware, Adware
4	Hijacking
5	Power Failure
6	Fire, Flood, Earthquake

evolutionary nature of information technology. The user community would prefer open access, whereas the network administrator insists on restricted and monitored access to the network.

The hacker is, in the final analysis, the arbitrator of the network security policy, since it is always the unauthorized user who discovers the potential flaw in the software. Hence, any network is as secure as the last attack that breached its security. It would be totally unrealistic to expect a secured network at all times, once it is built and secured. Therefore, network security design and its implementation represent the ultimate battle of the minds between the chief information security officer (CISO) and the devil, the hacker. We can summarize that the network security policy can be as simple as to allow access to resources, or it can be several hundred pages long, detailing the levels of access and punishment if a breach is discovered. Most corporate network users now have to sign onto the usage policy of the network and are reminded that security breaches are a punishable offence. The critical functions of a good security policy are:

- Appoint a security administrator who is conversant with users' demands and on a continual basis is prepared to accommodate the user community's needs.
- Set up a hierarchical security policy to reflect the corporate structure.
- Define ethical Internet access capabilities.
- Evolve the remote access policy.
- Provide a set of incident-handling procedures.

7. THE INCIDENT-HANDLING PROCESS

The incident-handling process is the most important task of a security policy for the reason that you would not want to shut down the network in case of a network security breach. The purpose of the network is to share the resources; therefore an efficient procedure must be

developed to respond to a breach. If news of the network security breach becomes public, the corporation's business practices could become compromised, thus resulting in compromise of its business operations. Therefore set procedures must be developed jointly with the business operations manager and the chief information officer. This calls for a modular design of the enterprise network so that its segments can be shut down in an orderly way, without causing panic.

Toward this end, we need a set of tools to monitor activities on the network—we need an intrusion detection and prevention system. These pieces of software will monitor network activities and log and report an activity that does not conform to usual or acceptable standards as defined by the software. Once an activity is detected and logged, response is activated. It is not merely sufficient to respond to an incident; the network administrator also has to activate tools to trace back to the source of this breach. This is critical so that the network administrator can update the security procedures to make sure that this particular incident does not take place.

8. SECURE DESIGN THROUGH NETWORK ACCESS CONTROLS

A network is as secure as its weakest link in the overall design. To secure it, we need to identify the entry and exit points into the network. Since most data networks have computational nodes to process data and storage nodes to store data, stored data may need to be encrypted so that if network security is breached, stolen data may still remain confidential unless the encryption is broken. As we hear of cases of stolen data from either hacked networks or stolen nodes, encrypting data while it's being stored appears to be necessary to secure data.

The entry point to any network is a perimeter router, which sits between the external firewall and the Internet; this model is applicable to most enterprise networks that engage in some sort of ecommerce activities. Hence our first network access control is to define security policy on the perimeter router by configuring the appropriate parameters on the router. The perimeter router will filter traffic based on the range of IP addresses.

Next in the line of defense is the external firewall that filters traffic based on the state of the network connection. Additionally, the firewall could also check the contents of the traffic packet against the nature of the Transmission Control Protocol (TCP) connection requested. Following the firewall we have the so-called demilitarized zone, or DMZ, where we would place the following servers: Web, DNS, and email. We could harden these servers so that potential threatening traffic can be identified and appropriate incident response generated.

The DMZ is placed between two firewalls, so our last line of defense is the next firewall that would inspect the traffic and possibly filter out the potential threat. The nodes that are placed on the intranet can be protected by commercially available antivirus software. Last but not least, we could install on the network an intrusion detection and prevention system that will generate real-time response to a threat.

Next we address each of the network control access points. The traditional network design includes an access layer, a distribution layer, and the core layer. In the case of a local area network (LAN) we will use the access and distribution layers; the core layer would simply be our perimeter router that we discussed earlier. Thus the LAN will consist of a number of segments reflecting the organizational structure. The segments could sit behind their firewall to protect one another as well, in case of network breach; segments under attack can be isolated, thus preventing a cascade-style attack on the network.

9. IDS DEFINED

An intrusion detection system, or IDS, can be both software and hardware based. IDSs listen to all the activities taking place on both the computer (node on a network) and the network itself. One could think of an IDS as like traffic police, whose function is to monitor the data packet traffic and detect and identify those data packets that match predefined unusual pattern of activities. An IDS can also be programmed to teach itself from its past activities to refine the rules for unusual activities. This should not come as a surprise, since the hackers also get smarter over time.

As we stated, the IDS collects information from a variety of system and network resources, but in actuality it captures packets of data as defined by the TCP/IP protocol stack. In this sense IDS is both a sniffer and analyzer software. IDS in its sniffer role would either capture all the data packets or select ones as specified by the configuration script. This configuration script is a set of rules that tell the analyzer what to look for in a captured data packet, then make an educated guess per rules and generate an alert. Of course, this could lead to four possible outcomes with regard to intrusion detection: false positive, false negative, true positive, or true negative. We address this topic in more detail later in the chapter. IDSs performs a variety of functions:

- Monitor and analyze user and system activities
- Verify the integrity of data files
- Audit system configuration files
- Recognize activity of patterns, reflecting known attacks
- Statistical analysis of any undefined activity pattern

An IDS is capable of distinguishing different types of network traffic, such as an HTTP request over port 80

from some other application such as SMTP being run over port 80. We see here that an IDS understands which TCP/IP applications run over which preassigned port numbers, and therefore falsifying port numbers would be trivially detectable. This is a very easy illustration, but there are more complex attacks that are not that easy to identify, and we shall cover them later in this chapter.

The objective of intrusion detection software packages is to make possible the complex and sometimes virtually impossible task of managing system security. With this in mind, it might be worthwhile to bring to our attention two industrial-grade IDS software packages: Snort (NIDS), which runs on both Linux and Windows, and GFI LANguard S.E.L.M., a host intrusion detection system (HIDS), which runs on Windows only. Commercial-grade IDS software is designed with user-friendly interfaces that make it easy to configure scripts, which lay down the rules for intrusion detection. Next let's examine some critical functions of an IDS:

- Can impose a greater degree of flexibility to the security infrastructure of the network
- Monitors the functionality of routers, including firewalls, key servers, and critical switches
- Can help resolve audit trails, thus often exposing problems before they lead to loss of data
- Can trace user activity from the network point of entry to the point of exit
- Can report on file integrity checks
- Can detect whether a system has been reconfigured by an attack
- Can recognize a potential attack and generate an alert
- Can make possible security management of a network by nonexpert staff

10. NIDS: SCOPE AND LIMITATIONS

Network-based IDS (NIDS) sensors scan network packets at the router or host level, auditing data packets and logging any suspicious packets to a log file. Figure 14.2 is an example of a NIDS. The data packets are captured by a sniffer program, which is a part of the IDS software package. The node on which the IDS software is enabled runs in promiscuous mode. In promiscuous mode, the NIDS node captures all the data packets on the network as defined by the configuration script. NIDSs have become a critical component of network security management as the number of nodes on the Internet has grown exponentially over last few years. Some of the common malicious attacks on networks are:

- IP address spoofing
- MAC address spoofing
- ARP cache poisoning
- DNS name corruption

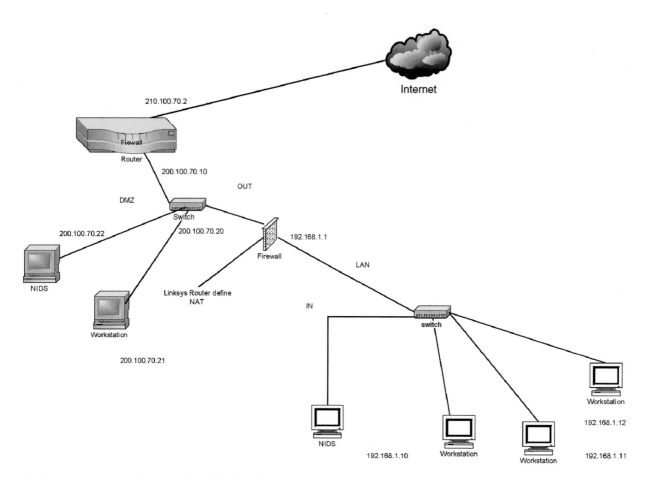

FIGURE 14.2   An example of a network-based intrusion detection system.

11. A PRACTICAL ILLUSTRATION OF NIDS

In this part of the chapter, we illustrate the use of Snort as an example of a NIDS. The signature files are kept in the directory signatures under the directory .doc. Signature files are used to match defined signature against a pattern of bytes in the data packets, to identify a potential attack. Files marked as rules in the rules directory are used to trigger an alarm and write to the file alert.ids. Snort is installed on a node with IP address 192.168.1.22. The security auditing software Nmap is installed on a node with IP address 192.168.1.20. Nmap software is capable of generating ping sweeps, TCP SYN (half-open) scanning, TCP connect() scanning, and much more. Figure 14.2 has a node labeled *NIDS* (behind the Linksys router) on which Snort would be installed. One of the workstations would run Nmap software.

UDP Attacks

A UDP attack is generated from a node with IP address 192.168.1.20 to a node with IP address 192.168.1.22. Snort is used to detect a possible attack.

Snort's detect engine uses one of the files in DOS under directory rules to generate the alert file alert.ids. We display a partial listing (see Listing 14.1) of the alert.ids file.

Listing 14.2 shows a partial listing of DOS rules file. The rules stated in the DOS rules file are used to generate the alert.ids file.

TCP SYN (Half-Open) Scanning

This technique is often referred to as *half-open* scanning because you don't open a full TCP connection. You send a SYN packet, as though you were going to open a real connection, and wait for a response. A SYN|ACK indicates that the port is listening. An RST is indicative of a nonlistener. If a SYN|ACK is received, you immediately send an RST to tear down the connection (actually, the kernel does this for you). The primary advantage of this scanning technique is that fewer sites will log it! SYN scanning is the -*s* option of Nmap.

A SYN attack is generated using Nmap software from a node with IP address 192.168.1.20 to a node with IP address 192.168.1.22. Snort is used to detect for a

```
[**] [1:0:0] DOS Teardrop attack [**]              LISTING 14.1   An alert.ids file.

[Priority: 0]

01/26-11:37:10.667833 192.168.1.20:1631 -> 192.168.1.22:21

UDP TTL:128 TOS:0x0 ID:60940 IpLen:20 DgmLen:69

Len: 41

[**] [1:0:0] DOS Teardrop attack [**]

[Priority: 0]

01/26-11:37:10.668460 192.168.1.20:1631 -> 192.168.1.22:21

UDP TTL:128 TOS:0x0 ID:60940 IpLen:20 DgmLen:69

Len: 41

[**] [1:0:0] DOS Teardrop attack [**]

[Priority: 0]

01/26-11:37:11.667926 192.168.1.20:1631 -> 192.168.1.22:21

UDP TTL:128 TOS:0x0 ID:60941 IpLen:20 DgmLen:69

Len: 41

[**] [1:0:0] DOS Teardrop attack [**]

[Priority: 0]

01/26-11:37:11.669424 192.168.1.20:1631 -> 192.168.1.22:21

UDP TTL:128 TOS:0x0 ID:60941 IpLen:20 DgmLen:69

Len: 41

[**] [1:0:0] DOS Teardrop attack [**]

[Priority: 0]

01/26-11:37:12.669316 192.168.1.20:1631 -> 192.168.1.22:21

UDP TTL:128 TOS:0x0 ID:60942 IpLen:20 DgmLen:69

Len: 41
```

possible attack. Snort's detect engine uses scan and ICMP rules files under directory rules to generate the alert file alert.ids. A partial listing of alert.ids file is shown in Listing 14.3.

A partial listing of the scan rules appears in Listing 14.4. Listing 14.5 contains a partial listing of the ICMP rules. The following points must be noted about NIDS:

- One NIDS is installed per LAN (Ethernet) segment.
- Place NIDS on the auxiliary port on the switch and then link all the ports on the switch to that auxiliary port.
- When the network is saturated with traffic, the NIDS might drop packets and thus create a potential "hole."
- If the data packets are encrypted, the usefulness of an IDS is questionable.

Some Not-So-Robust Features of NIDS

Network security is a complex issue with myriad possibilities and difficulties. In networks, security is also a weakest link phenomenon, since it takes vulnerability on one node to allow a hacker to gain access to a network and thus create chaos on the network. Therefore IDS products are vulnerable.

An IDS cannot compensate for weak identification and authentication. Hence you must rely on other means of identification and authentication of users. This is best implemented by token-based or biometric schemes and one-time passwords.

An IDS cannot conduct investigations of attacks without human intervention. Therefore when an incident does occur, steps must be defined to handle the incident. The incident must be followed up to determine the responsible party, then the vulnerability that allowed the problem to occur should be diagnosed and corrected. You will observe that an IDS is not capable of identifying the attacker, only the IP address of the node that served as the hacker's point of entry.

An IDS cannot compensate for weaknesses in network protocols. IP and MAC address spoofing is a very common form of attack in which the source IP or MAC address does not correspond to the real source IP or MAC

```
# (C) Copyright 2001, Martin Roesch, Brian Caswell, et al. All rights reserved.
# $Id: dos.rules,v 1.30.2.1 2004/01/20 21:31:38 jh8 Exp $
# -----------
# DOS RULES
# -----------
alert ip $EXTERNAL_NET any -> $HOME_NET any (msg:"DOS Jolt attack"; fragbits: M;
dsize:408; reference:cve,CAN-1999-0345; classtype:attempted-dos; sid:268; rev:2;)
alert udp $EXTERNAL_NET any -> $HOME_NET any (msg:"DOS Teardrop attack"; id:242;
fragbits:M; reference:cve,CAN-1999-0015; reference:url,www.cert.org/advisories/CA-1997-
28.html; reference:bugtraq,124; classtype:attempted-dos; sid:270; rev:2;) alert udp any 19 <>
any 7 (msg:"DOS UDP echo+chargen bomb"; reference:cve,CAN-1999-0635;
reference:cve,CVE-1999-0103; classtype:attempted-dos; sid:271; rev:3;)
alert ip $EXTERNAL_NET any -> $HOME_NET any (msg:"DOS IGMP dos attack";
content:"|02 00|"; depth: 2; ip_proto: 2; fragbits: M+; reference:cve,CVE-1999-0918;
classtype:attempted-dos; sid:272; rev:2;)
alert ip $EXTERNAL_NET any -> $HOME_NET any (msg:"DOS IGMP dos attack";
content:"|00 00|"; depth:2; ip_proto:2; fragbits:M+; reference:cve,CVE-1999-0918;
classtype:attempted-dos; sid:273; rev:2;)
alert icmp $EXTERNAL_NET any -> $HOME_NET any (msg:"DOS ath"; content:"+++ath";
nocase; itype: 8; reference:cve,CAN-1999-1228; reference:arachnids,264; classtype:attempted-
dos; sid:274; rev:2;)
```

LISTING 14.2　The DOS rules file.

address of the hacker. Spoofed addresses can be mimicked to generate DDoS attacks.

An IDS cannot compensate for problems in the integrity of information the system provides. Many hacker tools target system logs, selectively erasing records corresponding to the time of the attack and thus covering the hacker's tracks. This calls for redundant information sources.

An IDS cannot analyze all the traffic on a busy network. A network-based IDS in promiscuous mode, can capture all of the data packets; and, as the traffic level raises, NIDS can reach a saturation point and begin to lose data packets.

An IDS cannot always deal with problems involving packet-level attacks. The vulnerabilities lie in the difference between IDS interpretation of the outcome of a network transaction and the destination node for that network session's actual handling of the transaction. Therefore, a hacker can send a series of fragmented network transactions.

Packets that elude detection and can also launch attacks on the destination node. Even worse, the hacker can lead to DoS on the IDS itself.

An IDS has problems dealing with fragmented data packets. Hackers would normally use fragmentation to confuse the IDS and thus launch an attack.

12. FIREWALLS

A firewall is either a single node or a set of nodes that enforce an access policy between two networks. Firewall technology evolved to protect the intranet from unauthorized users on the Internet. This was the case in the earlier years of corporate networks. Since then, the network administrators have realized that networks can also be attacked from trusted users as well as, for example, the employee of a company. The corporate network consists of hundreds of nodes per department and thus aggregates to over a thousand or more, and now there is a need to protect data in each department from other departments. Hence, a need for internal firewalls arose to protect data from unauthorized access, even if they are employees of the corporation. This need has, over the years, led to design of segmented IP networks, such that internal firewalls would form barriers within barriers, to restrict a potential break-in to an IP segment rather than expose the entire corporate network to a hacker. For this reason, network security has grown into a multibillion-dollar business.

Almost every intranet, whether of one node or many nodes, is always connected to the Internet, and thus a potential number of hackers wait to attack it. Thus every intranet is an IP network, with TCP- and UDP-based

```
[**] [1:469:1] ICMP PING NMAP [**]
[Classification: Attempted Information Leak] [Priority: 2]
01/24-19:28:24.774381 192.168.1.20 -> 192.168.1.22
ICMP TTL:44 TOS:0x0 ID:29746 IpLen:20 DgmLen:28
Type:8 Code:0 ID:35844 Seq:45940 ECHO
[Xref => http://www.whitehats.com/info/IDS162]
[**] [1:469:1] ICMP PING NMAP [**]
[Classification: Attempted Information Leak] [Priority: 2]
01/24-19:28:24.775879 192.168.1.20 -> 192.168.1.22
ICMP TTL:44 TOS:0x0 ID:29746 IpLen:20 DgmLen:28
Type:8 Code:0 ID:35844 Seq:45940 ECHO
[Xref => http://www.whitehats.com/info/IDS162]
[**] [1:620:6] SCAN Proxy Port 8080 attempt [**]
[Classification: Attempted Information Leak] [Priority: 2]
01/24-19:28:42.023770 192.168.1.20:51530 -> 192.168.1.22:8080
TCP TTL:50 TOS:0x0 ID:53819 IpLen:20 DgmLen:40
******S* Seq: 0x94D68C2 Ack: 0x0 Win: 0xC00 TcpLen: 20
[**] [1:620:6] SCAN Proxy Port 8080 attempt [**]
[Classification: Attempted Information Leak] [Priority: 2]
01/24-19:28:42.083817 192.168.1.20:51530 -> 192.168.1.22:8080
TCP TTL:50 TOS:0x0 ID:53819 IpLen:20 DgmLen:40
******S* Seq: 0x94D68C2 Ack: 0x0 Win: 0xC00 TcpLen: 20
[**] [1:615:5] SCAN SOCKS Proxy attempt [**]
[Classification: Attempted Information Leak] [Priority: 2]
01/24-19:28:43.414083 192.168.1.20:51530 -> 192.168.1.22:1080
TCP TTL:59 TOS:0x0 ID:62752 IpLen:20 DgmLen:40
******S* Seq: 0x94D68C2 Ack: 0x0 Win: 0x1000 TcpLen: 20
[Xref => http://help.undernet.org/proxyscan/]
```

LISTING 14.3   Alert.ids file.

applications running over it. The design of TCP and UDP protocols require that every client/server application interacts with other client/server applications through TCP and UDP port numbers. As we stated earlier, these TCP and UDP port numbers are well known and hence give rise to a necessary weakness in the network. TCP and UDP port numbers open up "holes" in the networks by their very design. Every Internet and intranet point of entry has to be guarded, and you must monitor the traffic (data packets) that enter and leave the network.

A firewall is a combination of hardware and software technology, namely a sort of sentry, waiting at the points of entry and exit to look out for an unauthorized data packet trying to gain access to the network. The network administrator, with the help of other IT staff, must first identify the resources and the sensitive data that need to be protected from the hackers. Once this task has been accomplished, the next task is to identify who would have access to these identified resources and the data. We should pointed out that most of the networks in any

corporation are never designed and built from scratch but are added to an existing network as the demand for networking grows with the growth of the business. So, the design of the network security policy has multilayered facets as well.

Once the network security policy is defined and understood, we can identify the proper placement of the firewalls in relation to the resources on the network. Hence, the next step would be to actually place the firewalls in the network as nodes. The network security policy now defines access to the network, as implemented in the firewall. These access rights to the network resources are based on the characteristics of TCP/IP protocols and the TCP/UDP port numbers.

Firewall Security Policy

The firewall enables the network administrator to centralize access control to the campuswide network. A firewall logs every packet that enters and leaves the

```
# (C) Copyright 2001,2002, Martin Roesch, Brian Caswell, et al.
# All rights reserved.
# $Id: scan.rules,v 1.21.2.1 2004/01/20 21:31:38 jh8 Exp $
# ------------
# SCAN RULES
# ------------
# These signatures are representitive of network scanners. These include
# port scanning, ip mapping, and various application scanners. #
# NOTE: This does NOT include web scanners such as whisker. Those are
# in web* #
alert tcp $EXTERNAL_NET 10101 -> $HOME_NET any (msg:"SCAN myscan"; stateless; ttl:
>220; ack: 0; flags: S;reference:arachnids,439; classtype:attempted-recon; sid:613; rev:2;)
alert tcp $EXTERNAL_NET any -> $HOME_NET 113 (msg:"SCAN ident version request";
flow:to_server,established; content: "VERSION|0A|"; depth: 16;reference:arachnids,303;
classtype:attempted-recon; sid:616; rev:3;)
alert tcp $EXTERNAL_NET any -> $HOME_NET 80 (msg:"SCAN cybercop os probe";
stateless; flags: SF12; dsize: 0; reference:arachnids,146; classtype:attempted-recon; sid:619;
rev:2;)
alert tcp $EXTERNAL_NET any -> $HOME_NET 3128 (msg:"SCAN Squid Proxy attempt";
stateless; flags:S,12; classtype:attempted-recon; sid:618; rev:5;)
alert tcp $EXTERNAL_NET any -> $HOME_NET 1080 (msg:"SCAN SOCKS Proxy attempt";
stateless; flags: S,12; reference:url,help.undernet.org/proxyscan/; classtype:attempted-recon;
sid:615; rev:5;)
alert tcp $EXTERNAL_NET any -> $HOME_NET 8080 (msg:"SCAN Proxy Port 8080
attempt"; stateless; flags:S,12; classtype:attempted-recon; sid:620; rev:6;)
alert tcp $EXTERNAL_NET any -> $HOME_NET any (msg:"SCAN FIN"; stateless; flags:F,12;
reference:arachnids,27; classtype:attempted-recon; sid:621; rev:3;)
alert tcp $EXTERNAL_NET any -> $HOME_NET any (msg:"SCAN ipEye SYN scan"; flags:S;
stateless; seq:1958810375; reference:arachnids,236; classtype:attempted-recon; sid:622; rev:3;)
alert tcp $EXTERNAL_NET any -> $HOME_NET any (msg:"SCAN NULL"; stateless; flags:0;
seq:0; ack:0; reference:arachnids,4; classtype:attempted-recon; sid:623; rev:2;)
```

LISTING 14.4   Scan rules.

network. The network security policy implemented in the firewall provides several types of protection, including the following:

- Block unwanted traffic
- Direct incoming traffic to more trustworthy internal nodes
- Hide vulnerable nodes that cannot easily be secured from external threats
- Log traffic to and from the network

A firewall is transparent to authorized users (both internal and external), whereas it is not transparent to unauthorized users. However, if the authorized user attempts to access a service that is not permitted to that

user, a denial of that service will be echoed, and that attempt will be logged.

Firewalls can be configured in a number of architectures, providing various levels of security at different costs of installation and operations. Figure 14.2 is an example of a design termed a *screened Subnet*. In this design, the internal network is a private IP network, so the resources on that network are completely hidden from the users who are external to that network, such as users from the Internet. In an earlier chapter we talked about public versus private IP addresses. It is agreed to by the IP community that nodes with private IP addresses will not be accessible from outside that network. Any number of corporations may use the same private IP network

```
# (C) Copyright 2001,2002, Martin Roesch, Brian Caswell, et al.
# All rights reserved.
# $Id: icmp.rules,v 1.19 2003/10/20 15:03:09 chrisgreen Exp $
# ------------
# ICMP RULES
# ------------
#
# Description:
# These rules are potentially bad ICMP traffic. They include most of the
# ICMP scanning tools and other "BAD" ICMP traffic (Such as redirect host)
#
# Other ICMP rules are included in icmp-info.rules
alert icmp $EXTERNAL_NET any -> $HOME_NET any (msg:"ICMP ISS Pinger";
content:"|495353504e475251|";itype:8;depth:32; reference:arachnids,158; classtype:attempted-
recon; sid:465; rev:1;)
alert icmp $EXTERNAL_NET any -> $HOME_NET any (msg:"ICMP L3retriever Ping";
content: "ABCDEFGHIJKLMNOPQRSTUVWABCDEFGHI"; itype: 8; icode: 0; depth: 32;
reference:arachnids,311; classtype:attempted-recon; sid:466; rev:1;)
alert icmp $EXTERNAL_NET any -> $HOME_NET any (msg:"ICMP Nemesis v1.1 Echo";
dsize: 20; itype: 8; icmp_id: 0; icmp_seq: 0; content:
"|0000000000000000000000000000000000000000|";                reference:arachnids,449;
classtype:attempted-recon; sid:467; rev:1;)
alert icmp $EXTERNAL_NET any -> $HOME_NET any (msg:"ICMP PING NMAP"; dsize: 0;
itype: 8; reference:arachnids,162; classtype:attempted-recon; sid:469; rev:1;)
alert icmp $EXTERNAL_NET any -> $HOME_NET any (msg:"ICMP icmpenum v1.1.1"; id:
666; dsize: 0; itype: 8; icmp_id: 666; icmp_seq: 0; reference:arachnids,450; classtype:attempted-
recon; sid:471; rev:1;) alert icmp $EXTERNAL_NET any -> $HOME_NET any (msg:"ICMP
redirect host";itype:5;icode:1; reference:arachnids,135; reference:cve,CVE-1999-0265;
classtype:bad-unknown; sid:472; rev:1;)
alert icmp $EXTERNAL_NET any -> $HOME_NET any (msg:"ICMP redirect
net";itype:5;icode:0; reference:arachnids,199; reference:cve,CVE-1999-0265; classtype:bad-
unknown; sid:473; rev:1;)
alert icmp $EXTERNAL_NET any -> $HOME_NET any (msg:"ICMP superscan echo";
content:"|0000000000000000|"; itype: 8; dsize:8; classtype:attempted-recon; sid:474; rev:1;)
alert icmp $EXTERNAL_NET any -> $HOME_NET any (msg:"ICMP traceroute ipopts";
ipopts: rr; itype: 0; reference:arachnids,238; classtype
```

LISTING 14.5 ICMP rules.

address without creating packets with duplicated IP addresses. This feature of IP networks, namely private IP networks, adds to network security. In Figure 14.2, we used a Linksys router to support a private IP network (192.168.1.0) implementation. For the nodes on the 192.168.1.0 network to access the resources on the Internet, the Linksys router has to translate the private IP address of the data packet to a public IP address. In our scenario, the Linksys router would map the address of the node on the 192.168.1.0 network, to an address on the public network, 200.100.70.0. This feature is known as Network Address Translation (NAT), which is enabled on the Linksys router. You can see in Figure 14.2 that the Linksys router demarks the internal (IN) network from the external (OUT) network.

We illustrate an example of network address translation, as shown in Listing 14.6. The script configures a Cisco router that translates an internal private IP address

```
ip nat pool net-sf 200.100.70.50 200.100.70.60 netmask 255.255.255.0
ip nat inside source list 1 pool net-sf
!
interface Ethernet0
ip address 192.168.1.1 255.255.255.0
ip nat inside
!
interface Ethernet1
ip address 200.100.70.20 255.255.255.0
ip nat outside
access-list 1 deny 192.168.1.0 0.0.0.255
```

LISTING 14.6 Network Address Translation (NAT).

to a public IP address. Of course, configuring a Linksys router is much simpler using a Web client. An explanation of the commands and their details follow the script.

Configuration Script for sf Router

The access-list command creates an entry in a standard traffic filter list:

- Access-list "access-list-number" permit|deny source [source-mask]
- Access-list number: identifies the list to which the entry belongs; a number from 1 to 99
- Permit|deny: this entry allows or blocks traffic from the specified address
- Source: identifies source IP address
- Source-mask: identifies the bits in the address field that are matched; it has a 1 in position indicating "don't care" bits, and a 0 in any position that is to be strictly followed

The IP access-group command links an existing access list to an outbound interface. Only one access list per port, per protocol, and per direction is allowed.

- Access-list-number: indicates the number of the access list to be linked to this interface
- In|out: selects whether the access list is applied to the incoming or outgoing interface; out is the default

NAT is a feature that operates on a border router between an inside private addressing scheme and an outside public addressing scheme. The inside private address is 192.168.1.0 and the outside public address is chosen to be 200.100.70.0. Equivalently, we have an intranet on the inside and the Internet on the outside.

13. DYNAMIC NAT CONFIGURATION

First a NAT pool is configured from which outside addresses are allocated to the requesting inside hosts: IP NAT pool "pool name" "start outside IP address" "finish

outside IP address." Next the access-list is defined to determine which inside networks are translated by the NAT router: access-list "unique access-list number" permit|deny "inside IP network address." Finally the NAT pool and the access list are correlated:

- IP NAT inside source list "unique access list number" pool "pool name"
- Enable the NAT on each interface of the NAT router
- IP NAT inside+++++++++++++++++++ IP NAT outside

You will note that only one interface may be configured as outside, yet multiple interfaces may be configured as inside, with regard to Static NAT configuration:

- IP NAT inside source static "inside IP address" "outside IP address"
- IP NAT inside source static 192.168.1.100 200.100.70.99

14. THE PERIMETER

In Figure 14.3, you will see yet another IP network labeled *demilitarized zone* (DMZ). You may ask, why yet another network? The rationale behind this design is as follows.

The users that belong to IN might want to access the resources on the Internet, such as read their email and send email to the users on the Internet. The corporation needs to advertise its products on the Internet.

The DMZ is the perimeter network, where resources have public IP addresses, so they are seen and heard on the Internet. The resources such as the Web (HTTP), email (SMTP), and domain name server (DNS) are placed in the DMZ, whereas the rest of the resources that belong to this corporation are completely hidden behind the Linksys router. The resources in the DMZ can be attacked by the hacker because they are open to users on the Internet. The relevant TCP and UDP port numbers on the servers in the DMZ have to be left open to the incoming

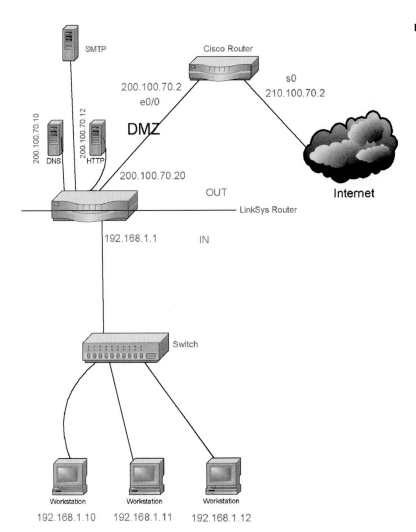

FIGURE 14.3   An illustrative firewall design.

and outgoing traffic. Does this create a potential "hole" in the corporate network? The answer to this is both yes and no. Someone can compromise the resources in the DMZ without the entire network being exposed to a potential attack.

The first firewall is the Cisco router, and it is the first line of defense, were network security policy implemented. On the Cisco router it is known as the Access Control List (ACL). This firewall will allow external traffic to inbound TCP port 80 on the Web server, TCP port 25 on the email server, and TCP and UDP port 53 on the DNS server. The external traffic to the rest of the ports will be denied and logged.

The second line of defense is the Linksys router that will have well-known ports closed to external traffic. It too will monitor and log the traffic. It is acceptable to place email and the Web server behind the Linksys router on the private IP network address. Then you will have to open up the TCP ports 80 and 25 on the Linksys router so

that the external traffic can be mapped to ports 80 and 25, respectively. This would slow down the traffic because the Linksys router (or any commercial-grade router) would have to constantly map the port numbers back and forth. Finally, the DNS server would always need to be placed in the DMZ with a public IP address, since it will be used to resolve domain names by both internal and external users. This decision has to be left to the corporate IT staff.

15. ACCESS LIST DETAILS

The Cisco router in Figure 14.3 can be configured with the following access list to define network security policy. Building an access list in the configuration script of the router does not activate the list unless it is applied to an interface. "ip access-group 101 in" applies the access-list 101 to the serial interface of the router. Some of the access-list commands are explained here. For more information on Cisco access-list commands, visit the Cisco Web site (www.cisco.com):

- ip access-group group no. {in|out}: default is out
- What is the group number?
- The group number is the number that appears in the access-list command line
- What is {in|out}?
- In implies that the packet enters the router's interface from the network
- Out implies that the packet leaves the router's interface to the network

All TCP packets are IP packets, but all IP packets are not TCP packets. Therefore, entries matching on IP packets are more generic than matching on TCP, UDP, or ICMP packets. Each entry in the access list is interpreted (see Listing 14.7) from top to bottom for each packet on the specified interface. Once a match is reached, the remaining access-list entries are ignored. Hence, the order of entries in an access list is very critical, and therefore more specific entries should appear earlier on.

This permits TCP from any host to any host if the ACK or RST bit is set, which indicates that it is part of an established connection. You will note that in a TCP Full Connect, the first packet from the source node does not have the ACK bit set. The keyword *established* is meant to prevent an untrusted user from initiating a connection while allowing packets that are part of already established TCP connections to go through:

- Access-list 101 permit udp any gt 1023 host 200.100.70.10 eq 53
- Permit UDP protocol from any host with port greater than 1023 to the DNS server at port 53
- Access-list 101 permit ip any host 200.100.70.12
- Permit IP from any host to 200.100.70.12

  or

- Access-list 101 permit TCP any 200.100.70.12 eq 80
- Permit any host to engage with our HTTP server on port 80 only
- Access-list 101 permit icmp any echo-reply
- Permit ICMP from any host to any host if the packet is in response to a ping request
- Access-list 101 deny ip any any

```
interface serial0

ip address 210.100.70.2

ip access-group 101 in

!

access-list 101 permit tcp any any established
```

LISTING 14.7 Access-list configuration script.

The last access-list command is implicit (that is, not explicitly stated). The action of this last access-list is to deny all other packets.

16. TYPES OF FIREWALLS

Conceptually, there are three types of firewalls:

- *Packet filtering.* Permit packets to enter or leave the network through the interface on the router on the basis of protocol, IP address, and port numbers.
- *Application-layer firewall.* A proxy server that acts as an intermediate host between the source and the destination nodes.
- *Stateful-inspection layer.* Validates the packet on the basis of its content.

17. PACKET FILTERING: IP FILTERING ROUTERS

An IP packet-filtering router permits or denies the packet to either enter or leave the network through the interface (incoming and outgoing) on the basis of the protocol, IP address, and the port number. The protocol may be TCP, UDP, HTTP, SMTP, or FTP. The IP address under consideration would be both the source and the destination addresses of the nodes. The port numbers would correspond to the well-known port numbers. The packet-filtering firewall has to examine every packet and make a decision on the basis of defined ACL; additionally it will log the following guarded attacks on the network:

- A hacker will attempt to send IP spoofed packets using raw sockets (we will discuss more about usage of raw sockets in the next chapters)
- Log attempted network scanning for open TCP and UDP ports—NIDS will carry out this detective work in more detail
- SYN attacks using TCP connect(), and TCP half open
- Fragment attacks

18. APPLICATION-LAYER FIREWALLS: PROXY SERVERS

These are proxy servers that act as an intermediary host between the source and the destination nodes. Each of the sources would have to set up a session with the proxy server, then the proxy server would set up a session with the destination node. The packets would have to flow through the proxy server. There are examples of Web and FTP proxy servers on the Internet. The proxy servers would also have to be used by the internal users, that is, the traffic from the internal users will have to run through the proxy server to the outside network. Of course, this slows the flow of packets, but you must pay the price for added network security.

19. STATEFUL INSPECTION FIREWALLS

In here the firewall will examine the contents of the packets before permitting them to either enter or leave the network. The contents of the packets must conform with the protocol declared with the packet. For example, if the protocol declared is HTTP, the contents of the packet must be consistent with the HTTP packet definition.

20. NIDS COMPLEMENTS FIREWALLS

A firewall acts as a barrier, if so designed, among various IP network segments. Firewalls may be defined among IP intranet segments to protect resources. In any corporate network, there will always be more than one firewall because an intruder could be one of the authorized network users. Hence the following points should be noted:

- Not all threats originate outside the firewall.
- The most trusted users are also the potential intruders.
- Firewalls themselves may be subject to attack.

Since the firewall sits at the boundary of the IP network segments, it can only monitor the traffic entering and leaving the interface on the firewall that connects to the network. If the intruder is internal to the firewall, the firewall will not be able to detect the security breach. Once an intruder has managed to transit through the interface of the firewall, the intruder would go undetected, which could possibly lead to stealing sensitive information, destroying information, leaving behind viruses, staging attacks on other networks, and most important, leaving spyware software to monitor the activities on the network for future attacks. Hence, a NIDS would play a critical role in monitoring activities on the network and continually looking for possible anomalous patterns of activities.

Firewall technology has been around for the past 25 years, so much has been documented about its weaknesses and strengths. Information about firewalls is freely available on the Internet. Hence a new breed of hackers have utilized *tunneling* as a means of bypassing firewall security policy. NIDS enhances security infrastructure by monitoring system activities for signs of attack and then, based on the system settings, responds to the attack as well as generates an alarm. Response to a potential attack is known as the *incident response* or *incident handling*, which combines investigation and diagnosis phases. Incident response has been an emerging technology in the

past 7 years and is now an integral part of intrusion detection and prevention technology.

Finally, but not least, securing network systems is an ongoing process in which new threats arise all the time. Consequently, firewalls, NIDS, and intrusion prevention systems are continuously evolving technologies. In this chapter and subsequent chapters our focus has been and will be wired networks. However, as wireless data networks proliferate and seamlessly connect to the cellular voice networks, the risk of attacks on the wired networks is growing exponentially.

21. MONITOR AND ANALYZE SYSTEM ACTIVITIES

Figure 14.1 shows the placement of a NIDS, one in the DMZ and the other in the private network. This suggests at least two points on the network from which we capture data packets. The next question is the timing of the information collection, although this depends on the degree of threat perceived to the network.

If the level of perceived threat to the network is low, an immediate response to the attack is not very critical. In such a case, interval-oriented data capturing and analysis is most economical in terms of load placed on a NIDS and other resources on the network. Additionally, there might not be full-time network security personnel to respond to an alarm triggered by the NIDS.

If the level of perceived threat is imminent and the time and the data are mission-critical to the organization, real-time data gathering and analysis are of extreme importance. Of course, the real-time data gathering would impact the CPU cycles on the NIDS and would lead to a massive amount of data storage. With real-time data capturing and analysis, real-time response to an attack can be automated with notification. In such a case, network activities can be interrupted, the incident could be isolated, and system and network recovery could be set in motion.

Analysis Levels

Capturing and storing data packets are among the manageable functions of any IDS. How do we analyze the data packets that represent potential or imminent threats to the network?

We need to examine the data packets and look for evidence that could point to a threat. Let's examine the makeup of data packets. Of course, any packet is almost encapsulated by successive protocols from the Internet model, with the data as its kernel. Potential attacks could be generated by IP or MAC spoofing, fragmented IP packets leading to some sort of DoS, saturating the resource with flooding, and much more. We should remind readers that since humans are not going to examine the data packets, this process of examination is relegated to an algorithm. This algorithm must compare the packets with a known format of the packet (signature) that suggests an attack is in progress, or it could be that there is some sort of unusual activity on the network. How does one distinguish abnormal from normal sets of activities? There must be some baseline (statistical) that indicates normal, and deviation from it would be an indicator of abnormal. We explore these concepts in the following paragraphs.

We can identify two levels of analysis: signature and statistical.

22. SIGNATURE ANALYSIS

Signature analysis includes some sort of pattern matching of the contents of the data packets. There are patterns corresponding to known attacks. These known attacks are stored in a database, and a pattern is examined against the known pattern, which defines signature analysis. Most commercial NIDS products perform signature analysis against a database of known attacks, which is part of the NIDS software. Even though the databases of known attacks may be proprietary to the vendor, the client of this software should be able to increase the scope of the NIDS software by adding signatures to the database. Snort is open-source NIDS software, and the database of known attacks is maintained and updated by the user community. This database is an ASCII (human-readable) file.

23. STATISTICAL ANALYSIS

First we have to define what constitutes a normal traffic pattern on the network. Then we must identify deviations away from normal patterns as potential threats. These deviations must be arrived at by statistical analysis of the traffic patterns. A good example would be how many times records are written to a database over a given time interval, and deviations from normally accepted numbers would be an indication of an impending attack. Of course, a clever hacker could mislead the detector into accepting attack activity as normal by gradually varying behavior over time. This would be an example of a false negative.

24. SIGNATURE ALGORITHMS

Signature analysis is based on the following algorithms:

- Pattern matching
- Stateful pattern matching
- Protocol decode-based analysis
- Heuristic-based analysis
- Anomaly-based analysis

Pattern Matching

Pattern matching is based on searching for a fixed sequence of bytes in a single packet. In most cases the pattern is matched against only if the suspect packet is associated with a particular service or, more precisely, destined to and from a particular port. This helps to reduce the number of packets that must get examined and thus speed up the process of detection. However, it tends to make it more difficult for systems to deal with protocols that do not live on well-defined ports.

The structure of a signature based on the simple pattern-matching approach might be as follows: First, the packet is IPv4 or higher and TCP, the destination port is 3333, and the payload contains the fictitious string *psuw*, trigger an alarm. In this example, the pattern *psuw* is what we were searching for, and one of the IDS rules implies to trigger an alarm. One could do a variation on this example to set up more convoluted data packets. The advantage of this simple algorithm is:

- This method allows for direct correlation of an exploit with the pattern; it is highly specific.
- This method is applicable across all protocols.
- This method reliably alerts on the pattern matched.

The disadvantages of this pattern-matching approach are as follows:

- Any modification to the attack can lead to missed events (false negatives).
- This method can lead to high false-positive rates if the pattern is not as unique as the signature writer assumed.
- This method is usually limited to inspection of a single packet and, therefore, does not apply well to the stream-based nature of network traffic such as HTTP traffic. This scenario leads to easily implemented evasion techniques.

Stateful Pattern Matching

This method of signature development adds to the pattern-matching concept because a network stream comprises more than a single atomic packet. Matches should be made in context within the state of the stream. This means that systems that perform this type of signature analysis must consider arrival order of packets in a TCP stream and should handle matching patterns across packet boundaries. This is somewhat similar to a stateful firewall.

Now, instead of looking for the pattern in every packet, the system has to begin to maintain state information on the TCP stream being monitored. To understand the difference, consider the following scenario. Suppose that the attack you are looking for is launched from a client connecting to a server and you have the pattern-match method deployed on the IDS. If the attack is launched so that in any given single TCP packet bound for the target on port 3333 the string is present, this event triggers the alarm. If, however, the attacker causes the offending string to be sent such that the fictitious *gp* is in the first packet sent to the server and *o* is in the second, the alarm does not get triggered. If the stateful pattern-matching algorithm is deployed instead, the sensor has stored the *gp* portion of the string and is able to complete the match when the client forwards the fictitious *p*. The advantages of this technique are as follows:

- This method allows for direct correlation of an exploit with the pattern.
- This method is applicable across all protocols.
- This method makes evasion slightly more difficult.
- This method reliably alerts on the pattern specified.

The disadvantages of the stateful pattern matching-based analysis are as follows:

- Any modification to the attack can lead to missed events (false negatives).
- This method can lead to high false-positive rates if the pattern is not as unique as the signature writer assumed.

Protocol Decode-based Analysis

In many ways, intelligent extensions to stateful pattern matches are protocol decode-based signatures. This class of signature is implemented by decoding the various elements in the same manner as the client or server in the conversation would. When the elements of the protocol are identified, the IDS applies rules defined by the request for comments (RFCs) to look for violations. In some instances, these violations are found with pattern matches within a specific protocol field, and some require more advanced techniques that account for such variables as the length of a field or the number of arguments.

Consider the fictitious example of the *gwb* attack for illustration purposes. Suppose that the base protocol that the attack is being run over is the fictitious OBL protocol, and more specifically, assume that the attack requires that the illegal fictitious argument *gpp* must be passed in the OBL Type field. To further complicate the situation, assume that the Type field is preceded by a field of variable length called OBL Options. The valid list of fictitious options are *gppi, nppi, upsnfs,* and *cvjmep*. Using the simple or the stateful pattern-matching algorithm in this case leads to false positives because the option *gppi*

contains the pattern that is being searched for. In addition, because the field lengths are variable, it would be impossible to limit such false positives by specifying search start and stop locations. The only way to be certain that *gpp* is being passed in as the OBL type argument is to fully decode the protocol.

If the protocol allows for behavior that the pattern-matching algorithms have difficulty dealing with, not doing full protocol decodes can also lead to false negatives. For example, if the OBL protocol allows every other byte to be a NULL if a value is set in the OBL header, the pattern matchers would fail to see fx00ox00ox00. The protocol decode-enabled analysis engine would strip the NULLS and fire the alarm as expected, assuming that *gpp* was in the Type field. Thus, with the preceding in mind, the advantages of the protocol decode-based analysis are as follows:

- This method can allow for direct correlation of an exploit.
- This method can be more broad and general to allow catching variations on a theme.
- This method minimizes the chance for false positives if the protocol is well defined and enforced.
- This method reliably alerts on the violation of the protocol rules as defined in the rules script.

The disadvantages of this technique are as follows:

- This method can lead to high false-positive rates if the RFC is ambiguous and allows developers the discretion to interpret and implement as they see fit. These gray area protocol violations are very common.
- This method requires longer development times to properly implement the protocol parser.

Heuristic-based Analysis

A good example of this type of signature is a signature that would be used to detect a port sweep. This signature looks for the presence of a threshold number of unique ports being touched on a particular machine. The signature may further restrict itself through the specification of the types of packets that it is interested in (that is, SYN packets). Additionally, there may be a requirement that all the probes must originate from a single source. Signatures of this type require some threshold manipulations to make them conform to the utilization patterns on the network they are monitoring. This type of signature may be used to look for very complex relationships as well as the simple statistical example given.

The advantages for heuristic-based signature analysis are that some types of suspicious and/or malicious activity cannot be detected through any other means. The disadvantages are that algorithms may require tuning or modification to better conform to network traffic and limit false positives.

Anomaly-based Analysis

From what is seen normally, anomaly-based signatures are typically geared to look for network traffic that deviates. The biggest problem with this methodology is to first define what normal is. Some systems have hardcoded definitions of normal, and in this case they could be considered heuristic-based systems. Some systems are built to learn normal, but the challenge with these systems is in eliminating the possibility of improperly classifying abnormal behavior as normal. Also, if the traffic pattern being learned is assumed to be normal, the system must contend with how to differentiate between allowable deviations and those not allowed or representing attack-based traffic. The work in this area has been mostly limited to academia, although there are a few commercial products that claim to use anomaly-based detection methods. A subcategory of this type of detection is the profile-based detection methods. These systems base their alerts on changes in the way that users or systems interact on the network. They incur many of the same limitations and problems that the overarching category has in inferring the intent of the change in behavior.

Statistical anomalies may also be identified on the network either through learning or teaching of the statistical norms for certain types of traffic, for example, systems that detect traffic floods, such as UDP, TCP, or ICMP floods. These algorithms compare the current rate of arrival of traffic with a historical reference; based on this, the algorithms will alert to statistically significant deviations from the historical mean. Often, a user can provide the statistical threshold for the alerts. The advantages for anomaly-based detection are as follows:

- If this method is implemented properly, it can detect unknown attacks.
- This method offers low overhead because new signatures do not have to be developed.
- In general, these systems are not able to give you intrusion data with any granularity. It looks like something terrible may have happened, but the systems cannot say definitively.
- This method is highly dependent on the environment in which the systems learn what normal is.

The following are Freeware tools to monitor and analyze network activities:

- Network Scanner, Nmap, is available from www.insecure.org. Nmap is a free open-source utility to monitor open ports on a network. The MS-Windows version is a zip file by the name nmap-3.75-win32. zip. You also need to download a packet capture library, WinPcap, under Windows. It is available from http://winpcap.polito.it. In addition to these programs, you need a utility to unzip the zipped file, which you can download from various Internet sites.
- PortPeeker is a freeware utility for capturing network traffic for TCP, UDP, or ICMP protocols. With PortPeeker you can easily and quickly see what traffic is being sent to a given port. This utility is available from www.Linklogger.com.
- Port-scanning tools such as Fport 2.0 or higher and SuperScan 4.0 or higher are easy to use and freely available from www.Foundstone.com.
- Network sniffer Ethereal is available from www.ethereal.com. Ethereal is a packet sniffer and analyzer for a variety of protocols.
- EtherSnoop light is a free network sniffer designed for capturing and analyzing the packets going through the network. It captures the data passing through your network Ethernet card, analyzes the data, and represents it in a readable form. EtherSnoop light is a fully configurable network analyzer program for Win32 environments. It is available from www.arechisoft.com.
- A fairly advanced tool, Snort, an open-source NIDS, is available from www.snort.org.
- UDPFlood is a stress testing tool that could be identified as a DoS agent; it is available from www.Foundstone.com.
- An application that allows you to generate a SYN attack with a spoofed address so that the remote host's CPU cycle's get tied up is Attacker, and is available from www.komodia.com.

Finally, organizations employing legacy LANs should be aware of the limited and weak security controls available to protect communications. Legacy LANs are particularly susceptible to loss of confidentiality, integrity, and availability. Unauthorized users have access to well-documented security flaws and exploits that can easily compromise an organization's systems and information, corrupt the organization's data, consume network bandwidth, degrade network performance, launch attacks that prevent authorized users from accessing the network, or use the organization's resources to launch attacks on other networks. Organizations should mitigate risks to their LANs by applying countermeasures to address specific threats and vulnerabilities. So, with the preceding in mind, let's briefly look at a local area network security countermeasures checklist, which describes management, operational, and technical countermeasures that can be effective in reducing the risks commonly associated with legacy LANs.

An Agenda for Action for Local Area Network Security Countermeasures Implementation Activities

Policy considerations for legacy LANs should include the following (check all tasks completed):

Roles and Responsibilities:

_____1. Which users or groups of users are and are not authorized to use organization LANs?

_____2. Which parties are authorized and responsible for installing and configuring access points (APs) and other LAN equipment?

LAN Infrastructure Security:

_____3. Physical security requirements for LANs and LAN devices, including limitations on the service areas of LANs.

_____4. Types of information that may and may not be sent over LANs, including acceptable use guidelines.

_____5. How LAN transmissions should be protected, including requirements for the use of encryption and for cryptographic key management.

LAN Client Device Security:

_____6. The conditions under which LAN client devices are and are not allowed to be used and operated.

_____7. Standard hardware and software configurations that must be implemented on LAN client devices to ensure the appropriate level of security.

_____8. Limitations on how and when LAN clients device may be used, such as specific locations.

_____9. Guidelines on reporting losses of LAN client devices and reporting LAN security incidents.

_____10. Guidelines for the protection of LAN client devices to reduce theft.

LAN Security Assessments:

_____11. The frequency and scope of LAN security assessments.

_____12. The actions to be taken to address rogue or misconfigured devices that are identified.

Other Recommendations for Management Countermeasures are as Follows:

_____13. Consider designating an individual to track the progress of security standards, features, threats, and vulnerabilities. This helps to ensure the continued secure implementation of LAN technology.

_____14. Maintain an inventory of legacy access points (APs) and connecting devices. This inventory is useful when conducting audits of technologies, particularly in identifying rogue devices.

---

25. LOCAL AREA NETWORK SECURITY COUNTERMEASURES IMPLEMENTATION CHECKLIST

With this checklist, these countermeasures do not guarantee a secure LAN environment and cannot prevent all adversary penetrations. Also, security comes at a cost—financial expenses related to security equipment, inconvenience, maintenance, and operation. Each organization needs to evaluate the acceptable level of risk based on numerous factors, which will affect the level of security implemented by that organization. To be effective, LAN security should be incorporated throughout the entire life cycle of LAN solutions. Organizations should create a networking security policy that addresses legacy LAN security. Such a policy and an organization's ability to enforce compliance with it are the foundations for all other countermeasures (see checklist: "An Agenda For Action For Local Area Network Security Countermeasures Implementation Activities"):

26. SUMMARY

Local area networks (LANs) are significantly impacting the way organizations do business. As more and more critical work migrates from mainframes to LANs, the need for better controls becomes apparent. This chapter discussed the security and control issues involved with LANs; the types of critical and sensitive data now residing on LANs; the impact of loss, change or disclosure; and, realistic remedies for identified vulnerabilities. Also covered, were how transition technologies, topologies, and architectures create complex security, recovery, and integrity problems. In addition, the security features of popular LAN systems software and add-on packages were also identified. Next, the need for policies, procedures, and administrative controls were covered.

In conclusion, this chapter discussed the basics of how and where to implement effective controls in a local area network (LAN). Security pitfalls existing in both the hardware and software components that make up a LAN were identified. The significant challenges presented by the fast growth of LANs in the workplace was met head on with guidelines for reducing security exposures. Although this chapter di not address the specific implementations of any single network operating system, the topics discussed apply to all of these systems.

Finally, let's move on to the real interactive part of this Chapter: review questions/exercises, hands-on projects, case projects and optional team case project. The answers and/or solutions by chapter can be found in the Online Instructor's Solutions Manual.

CHAPTER REVIEW QUESTIONS/EXERCISES

True/False

1. True or False? Most LANs are designed as collapsed backbone networks using a layer-1 or layer-4 switch.
2. True or False? The LAN consists of a number of segments reflecting the network structure.
3. True or False? The most trusted users belong to the Internet.
4. True or False? During the final design phase of a network, the network architects assess the types of risks to the network; as well as, the costs of recovering from attacks for all the resources that have been compromised.
5. True or False? The fundamental goals of security policy are to allow uninterrupted access to the network resources for authenticated users and to deny access to unauthenticated users.

Multiple Choice

1. The critical functions of a good security policy include the following, except which one?
   A. Appoint a security administrator who is conversant with users' demands and on a continual basis is prepared to accommodate the user community's needs.
   B. Monitor and analyze user and system activities.
   C. Set up a hierarchical security policy to reflect the corporate structure.
   D. Define ethical Internet access capabilities.
   E. Provide a set of incident-handling procedures.
2. IDSs perform the following functions, except which one?
   A. Monitor and analyze user and system activities.
   B. Verify the integrity of data files.
   C. Customize the availability of 'apps' (applications).
   D. Audit system configuration files.
   E. Recognize activity of patterns, reflecting known attacks.
3. IDSs perform the following critical functions, except which one?
   A. Can impose a greater degree of flexibility to the security infrastructure of the network.
   B. Monitors the functionality of routers, including firewalls, key servers, and critical switches.
   C. Can help resolve audit trails, thus often exposing problems before they lead to loss of data.
   D. Can trace the mobile hardware industry.
   E. Can make possible security management of a network by nonexpert staff.

4. Some of the common malicious attacks on networks include the following, except which one?
   A. IP address spoofing
   B. MAC address spoofing
   C. ARP cache poisoning
   D. DNS name corruption
   E. PPTP VPNs address hacking
5. The following points should be noted about network intrusion detection system (NIDS), except which one?
   A. Inbound and outbound NIDS malware scanning.
   B. One NIDS is installed per LAN (Ethernet) segment.
   C. Place NIDS on the auxiliary port on the switch and then link all the ports on the switch to that auxiliary port.
   D. When the network is saturated with traffic, the NIDS might drop packets and thus create a potential "hole."
   E. If the data packets are encrypted, the usefulness of an IDS is questionable.

EXERCISE

Problem

What minimum requirements does a computer need to meet to be able to connect to a local area network?

Hands-On Projects

Project

A medium size company needs to know what components they will need to establish a Local Area Network. They plan to have 1,200 users with e-mail, file and print, and Internet services. They also plan to have 20 servers used as LAN, proxy, and database servers. Four departments will need sufficient bandwidth and access applications from a database server. They are also going to expand to eight branch offices located in different states, two with only 10 users needing just a single Internet. What hardware components does the company need to build the LAN for all areas?

Case Projects

Problem

How can an organization correctly route traffic? A small organization has an application server with two network interface cards (NICs): LAN (A) equals a corporate network (in which clients connect to a server for application use); and, LAN (B) equals a digital subscriber line (DSL) Internet and remote connection. The application on this application server is designed to send alerts to the clients (connected via LAN (A)) and it also has email functionality (configured using POP3) that needs to be outbound via LAN (B), due to LAN (A) blocking this traffic. Right now, LAN (A) does not have a default gateway defined, which is allowing the email functionality to work just fine; clients can connect to the servers application via LAN (A) as well; but, the alerts that the application is supposed to send to the client does not work. When LAN (B) is disabled completely, the clients connect to the server application; and, the application successfully sends alerts to the clients as it is designed to do; but, the email functionality no longer works because of the blocked outbound traffic. So, what is the proper way to set this up? Is it something that can be corrected by using static routes? Routing and Remote Access Service (RRAS) perhaps?

Optional Team Case Project

Problem

How would a small company go about connecting a LAN to WAN server? In other words, how would the company connect their default LAN IP (193.279.2. ...) through a Cisco router to a WAN IP (213.81. ...)?

## Chapter 15

Wireless Network Security

Chunming Rong
University of Stavanger, Norway

Gansen Zhao
Sun Yat-sen University, China

Liang Yan
University of Stavanger, Norway

Erdal Cayirci
University of Stavanger, Norway

Hongbing Cheng
University of Stavanger, Norway

With the rapid development of technology in wireless communication and microchips, wireless technology has been widely used in various application areas. The proliferation of wireless devices and wireless networks in the past decade shows the widespread use of wireless technology.

Wireless networks are a general term to refer to various types of networks that communicate without the need of wire lines. Wireless networks can be broadly categorized into two classes based on the structures of the networks: wireless ad hoc networks and cellular networks. The main difference between these two is whether a fixed infrastructure is present.

Three of the well-known cellular networks are the GSM network, the CDMA network, and the 802.11 wireless LAN. The GSM network and the CDMA network are the main network technologies that support modern mobile communication, with most of the mobile phones and mobile networks that are built based on these two wireless networking technologies and their variants. As cellular networks require fixed infrastructures to support the communication between mobile nodes, deployment of the fixed infrastructures is essential. Further, cellular networks require serious and careful topology design of the fixed infrastructures before deployment, because the network topologies of the fixed infrastructures are mostly static and will have a great impact on network performance and network coverage.

Wireless ad hoc networks do not require a fixed infrastructure; thus it is relatively easy to set up and deploy a wireless ad hoc network (see Figure 15.1). Without the

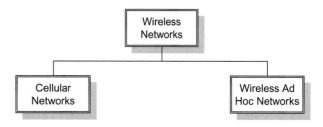

FIGURE 15.1 Classification of wireless networks.

fixed infrastructure, the topology of a wireless ad hoc network is dynamic and changes frequently. It is not realistic to assume a static or a specific topology for a wireless ad hoc network. On the other hand, wireless ad hoc networks need to be self-organizing; thus mobile nodes in a wireless ad hoc network can adapt to the change of topology and establish cooperation with other nodes at runtime.

Besides the conventional wireless ad hoc networks, there are two special types that should be mentioned: wireless sensor networks and wireless mesh networks. Wireless sensor networks are wireless ad hoc networks, most of the network nodes of which are sensors that monitor a target scene. The wireless sensors are mostly deprived devices in terms of computation power, power supply, bandwidth, and other computation resources. Wireless mesh networks are wireless networks with either a full mesh topology or a partial mesh topology in which some or all nodes are directly connected to all other nodes. The redundancy in

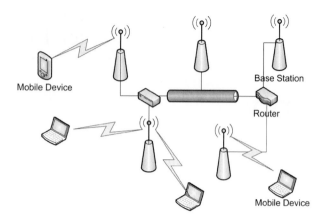

FIGURE 15.2   Cellular networking.

connectivity of wireless networks provides great reliability and excellent flexibility in network packet delivery.

1. CELLULAR NETWORKS

Cellular networks require fixed infrastructures to work (see Figure 15.2). A cellular network comprises a fixed infrastructure and a number of mobile nodes. Mobile nodes connect to the fixed infrastructure through wireless links. They may move around from within the range of one base station to outside the range of the base station, and they can move into the ranges of other base stations. The fixed infrastructure is stationary, or mostly stationary, including base stations, links between base stations, and possibly other conventional network devices such as routers. The links between base stations can be either wired or wireless. The links should be more substantial than those links between base stations and mobile nodes in terms of reliability, transmission range, bandwidth, and so on.

The fixed infrastructure serves as the backbone of a cellular network, providing high speed and stable connection for the whole network, compared to the connectivity between a base station and a mobile node. In most cases, mobile nodes do not communicate with each other directly without going through a base station. A packet from a source mobile node to a destination mobile node is likely to be first transmitted to the base station to which the source mobile node is connected. The packet is then relayed within the fixed infrastructures until reaching the destination base station to which the destination mobile node is connected. The destination base station can then deliver the packet to the destination mobile node to complete the packet delivery.

Cellular Telephone Networks

Cellular telephone networks offer mobile communication for most of us. With a cellular telephone network, base stations are distributed over a region, with each base station covering a small area. Each part of the small area is called a *cell*. Cell phones within a cell connect to the base station of the cell for communication. When a cell phone moves from one cell to another, its connection will also be migrated from one base station to a new base station. The new base station is the base station of the cell into which the cell phone just moved.

Two of the technologies are the mainstream for cellular telephone networks: the global system for mobile communication (GSM) and code division multiple access (CDMA).

GSM is a wireless cellular network technology for mobile communication that has been widely deployed in most parts of the world. Each GSM mobile phone uses a pair of frequency channels, with one channel for sending data and another for receiving data. Time division multiplexing (TDM) is used to share frequency pairs by multiple mobiles.

CDMA is a technology developed by a company named Qualcomm and has been accepted as an international standard. CDMA assumes that multiple signals add linearly, instead of assuming that colliding frames are completely garbled and of no value. With coding theory and the new assumption, CDMA allows each mobile to transmit over the entire frequency spectrum at all times. The core algorithm of CDMA is how to extract data of interest from the mixed data.

802.11 Wireless LANs

Wireless LANs are specified by the IEEE 802.11 series standard [1], which describes various technologies and protocols for wireless LANs to achieve different targets, allowing the maximum bit rate from 2 Mbits per second to 248 Mbits per second. Wireless LANs can work in either access point (AP) mode or ad hoc mode, as shown in Figure 15.3. When a wireless LAN is working in AP mode, all communication passes through a base station, called an *access point*. The access point then passes the communication data to the destination node, if it is connected to the access point, or forwards the communication data to a router for further routing and relaying. When working in ad hoc mode, wireless LANs work in the absence of base stations. Nodes directly communicate with other nodes within their transmission range, without depending on a base station.

One of the complications that 802.11 wireless LANs incur is medium access control in the data link layer. Medium access control in 802.11 wireless LANs can be either distributed or centralized control by a base station. The distributed medium access control relies on the Carrier Sense Multiple Access (CSMA) with Collision Avoidance (CSMA/CA) protocol. CSMA/CA allows network nodes to compete to transmit data when a channel is idle and uses the Ethernet binary exponential backoff algorithm to decide a waiting time before retransmission when a

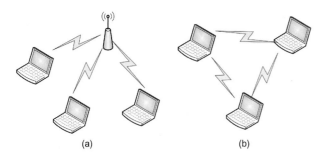

FIGURE 15.3   (a) A wireless network in AP mode; (b) a wireless network in ad hoc mode.

collision occurs. CSMA/CA can also operate based on MACAW (Multiple Access with Collision Avoidance for Wireless) using virtual channel sensing. Request packets and clear-to-send (CTS) packets, are broadcast before data transmission by the sender and the receiver, respectively. All stations within the range of the sender or the receiver will keep silent in the course of data transmission to avoid interference on the transmission.

The centralized medium access control is implemented by having the base station broadcast a beacon frame periodically and poll nodes to check whether they have data to send. The base station serves as a central control over the allocation of the bandwidth. It allocates bandwidth according to the polling results. All nodes connected to the base station must behave in accordance with the allocation decision made by the base station. With the centralized medium access control, it is possible to provide quality-of-service guarantees because the base station can control on the allocation of bandwidth to a specific node to meet the quality requirements.

2. WIRELESS AD HOC NETWORKS

Wireless ad hoc networks are distributed networks that work without fixed infrastructures and in which each network node is willing to forward network packets for other network nodes. The main characteristics of wireless ad hoc networks are as follows:

- Wireless ad hoc networks are distributed networks that do not require fixed infrastructures to work. Network nodes in a wireless ad hoc network can be randomly deployed to form the wireless ad hoc network.
- Network nodes will forward network packets for other network nodes. Network nodes in a wireless ad hoc network directly communicate with other nodes within their ranges. When these networks communicate with network nodes outside of their ranges, network packets will be forwarded by the nearby network nodes; and, other nodes that are on the path from the source nodes to the destination nodes.
- Wireless ad hoc networks are self-organizing. Without fixed infrastructures and central administration,

wireless ad hoc networks must be capable of establishing cooperation between nodes on their own. Network nodes must also be able to adapt to changes in the network, such as the network topology.

- Wireless ad hoc networks have dynamic network topologies. Network nodes of a wireless ad hoc network connect to other network nodes through wireless links. The network nodes are mostly mobile. The topology of a wireless ad hoc network can change from time to time, since network nodes move around from within the range to the outside, and new network nodes may join the network, just as existing network nodes may leave the network.

Wireless Sensor Networks

A wireless sensor network is an ad hoc network mainly comprising sensor nodes, which are normally used to monitor and observe a phenomenon or a scene. The sensor nodes are physically deployed within or close to the phenomenon or the scene. The collected data will be sent back to a base station from time to time through routes dynamically discovered and formed by sensor nodes.

Sensors in wireless sensor networks are normally small network nodes with very limited computation power, limited communication capacity, and limited power supply. Thus a sensor may perform only simple computation and can communicate with sensors and other nodes within a short range. The life spans of sensors are also limited by the power supply.

Wireless sensor networks can be self-organizing, since sensors can be randomly deployed in some inaccessible areas. The randomly deployed sensors can cooperate with other sensors within their range to implement the task of monitoring or observing the target scene or the target phenomenon and to communicate with the base station that collects data from all sensor nodes. The cooperation might involve finding a route to transmit data to a specific destination, relaying data from one neighbor to another neighbor when the two neighbors are not within reach of each other, and so on.

Wireless Multimedia Sensor Networks

Wireless multimedia sensor networks (WMSNs), developed based on wireless sensor networks, are the networks of wireless, interconnected smart devices that enable processing video and audio streams, still images, and scalar sensor data. WMSNs will enable the retrieval of multimedia streams and will store, process in real-time, correlate, and fuse multimedia content captured by heterogeneous sources. The characteristics of a WMSN diverge consistently from traditional network paradigms, such as the Internet and even from scalar sensor networks. Most potential applications of a WMSN require the sensor network paradigm to be rethought to provide mechanisms to deliver multimedia content with a predetermined level of quality of service (QoS). Whereas minimizing energy consumption has been the main objective in sensor network research, mechanisms to efficiently deliver application-level QoS and to map these requirements to network-layer metrics, such as latency and jitter, have not been primary concerns. Delivery of multimedia content in sensor networks presents new, specific system design challenges, which are the object of this article. potential to enable many new applications, includeing Multimedia Surveillance Sensor Networks, Traffic Avoidance, Enforcement, and Control SystemsAdvanced Health Care Delivery. Environmental and Structural Monitoring and Industrial Process Control.

Internet of Things

The Internet of Things (IoT) is an emerging global Internetbased information architecture facilitating the exchange of goods and services in global supply chain networks, the connection of physical things to the Internet makes it possible to access remote sensor data and to control the physical world from a distance. The applications of Internet of Things are based on real physical objectives. For example, the lack of certain goods would automatically be reported to the provider which in turn immediately causes electronic or physical delivery. From a technical point of view, the IoT architecture is based on data communication tools, primarily RFID-tagged items (Radio-Frequency Identification). The IoT has the purpose of providing an IT-infrastructure facilitating the exchanges of "things" in a secure and reliable manner. The most popular industry proposal for the new IT-infrastructure of the IoT is based on an Electronic Product Code (EPC), introduced by EPCglobal and GS1. The "things" are physical objects carrying RFID tags with a unique EPC; the infra-structure can offer and query EPC Information Services (EPCIS) both locally and remotely to clients. Since some important business processes are concerned, a high degree of reliability about IoT is needed. Generally, the following security and privacy requirements are necessary for IoT:

1. Resilience to attacks: IoT system has to avoid single points of failure and should adjust itself to node failures.
2. Data authentication: Retrieved address and object information must be authenticated is a principle for efficient applications.
3. Access control: Information providers of IoT must be able to implement access control scheme on their confidential data.

4. Client privacy: there should be suitable measures to prevent others retrieving clients' private information and data.

Mesh Networks

One of the emerging technologies of wireless network are wireless mesh networks (WMNs). Nodes in a WMN include mesh routers and mesh clients. Each node in a WMN works as a router as well as a host. When it's a router, each node needs to perform routing and to forward packets for other nodes when necessary, such as when two nodes are not within direct reach of each other and when a route to a specific destination for packet delivery is required to be discovered.

Mesh routers may be equipped with multiple wireless interfaces, built on either the same or different wireless technologies, and are capable of bridging different networks. Mesh routers can also be classified as access mesh routers, backbone mesh routers, or gateway mesh routers. Access mesh routers provide mesh clients with access to mesh networks; backbone mesh routers form the backbone of a mesh network; and a gateway mesh router connects the backbone to an external network.

Each mesh client normally has only one network interface that provides network connectivity with other nodes. Mesh clients are not usually capable of bridging different networks, which is different from mesh routers.

Similar to other ad hoc networks, a wireless mesh network can be self-organizing. Thus nodes can establish and maintain connectivity with other nodes automatically, without human intervention. Wireless mesh networks can divided into backbone mesh networks and access mesh networks.

3. SECURITY PROTOCOLS

Wired Equivalent Privacy (WEP) was defined by the IEEE 802.11 standard [1]. WEP is designed to protect linkage-level data for wireless transmission by providing confidentiality, access control, and data integrity, to provide secure communication between a mobile device and an access point in a 802.11 wireless LAN.

4. WEP

Implemented based on shared key secrets and the RC4 stream cipher [2], WEP's encryption of a frame includes two operations (see Figure 15.4). It first produces a checksum of the data, and then it encrypts the plaintext and the checksum using RC4:

- *Checksumming*. Let c be an integrity checksum function. For a given message M, a checksum $c(M)$ is

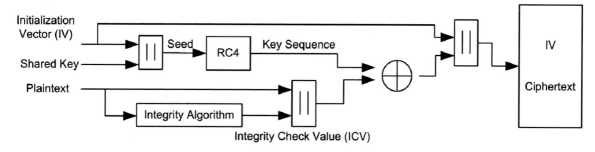

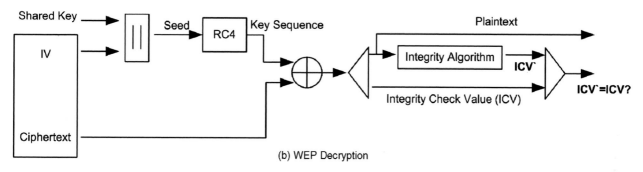

(a) WEP Encryption

(b) WEP Decryption

FIGURE 15.4   WEP encryption and decryption.

calculated and then concatenated to the end of M, obtaining a plaintext $P = \,<M, c(M)>$. Note that the checksum $c(M)$ does not depend on the shared key.

- *Encryption.* The shared key k is concatenated to the end of the initialization vector (IV) v, forming $<v,k>$. $<v,k>$ is then used as the input to the RC4 algorithm to generate a keystream $RC4(v,k)$. The plaintext P is exclusive-or' ed (XOR, denoted by $\oplus$) with the keystream to obtain the ciphertext: $C = P \oplus RC4(v,k)$.

Using the shared key k and the IV v, WEP can greatly simplify the complexity of key distribution because it needs only to distribute k and v but can achieve a relatively very long key sequence. IV changes from time to time, which will force the *RC 4* algorithm to produce a new key sequence, avoiding the situation where the same key sequence is used to encrypt a large amount of data, which potentially leads to several types of attacks [3,4].

WEP combines the shared key k and the IV v as inputs to seed the *RC 4* function. 802.11B [1] specifies that the seed shall be 64 bits long, with 24 bits from the IV v and 40 bits from the shared key k. Bits 0 through 23 of the seed contain bits 0 through 23 of the IV v, and bits 24 through 63 of the seed contain bits 0 through 39 of the shared key k. When a receiver receives the ciphertext C, it will XOR the ciphertext C with the corresponding keystream to produce the plaintext M' as follows:

$$M' = C \oplus RC4(k, v) = (P \oplus RC4(k, v)) \oplus RC4(k, v) = M$$

WPA and WPA2

Wi-Fi Protected Access (WPA) is specified by the IEEE 802.11i standard. The standard is aimed at providing a stronger security compared to WEP and is expected to tackle most of the weakness found in WEP [5−7].

WPA

WPA has been designed to target both enterprise and consumers. Enterprise deployment of WPA is required to be used with IEEE 802.1x authentication, which is responsible for distributing different keys to each user. Personal deployment of WPA adopts a simpler mechanism, which allows all stations to use the same key. This mechanism is called the *Pre-Shared Key* (PSK) mode.

The WPA protocol works in a similar way to WEP. WPA mandates the use of the *RC 4* stream cipher with a 128 − bit key and a 48 − bit initialization vector (IV), compared with the 40 − bit key and the 24 − bit IV in WEP.

WPA also has a few other improvements over WEP, including the Temporal Key Integrity Protocol (TKIP) and the Message Integrity Code (MIC). With TKIP, WPA will dynamically change keys used by the system periodically. With the much larger IV and the dynamically changing key, the stream cipher *RC4* is able to produce a much longer keystream. The longer keystream improved WPA's protection against the well-known key recovery attacks on WEP, since finding two packets encrypted using the same key sequences is literally impossible due to the extremely long keystream.

With MIC, WPA uses an algorithm named Michael to produce an authentication code for each message, which is termed the *message integrity code*. The message integrity code also contains a frame counter to provide protection over replay attacks.

WPA uses the Extensible Authentication Protocol (EAP) framework [8] to conduct authentication. When a user (supplicant) tries to connect to a network, an authenticator will send a request to the user asking the user to authenticate herself using a specific type of authentication mechanism. The user will respond with corresponding authentication information. The authenticator relies on an authentication server to make the decision regarding the user's authentication.

WPA2

WPA2 is not much different from WPA. Though TKIP is required in WPA, Advanced Encryption Standard (AES) is optional. This is aimed to provide backward compatibility for WPA over hardware designed for WEP, as TKIP can be implemented on the same hardware as those for WEP, but AES cannot be implemented on this hardware. TKIP and AES are both mandatory in WPA2 to provide a higher level of protection over wireless connections. AES is a block cipher, which can only be applied to a fixed length of data block. AES accepts key sizes of 128 bits, 196 bits, and 256 bits.

Besides the mandatory requirement of supporting AES, WPA2 also introduces supports for fast roaming of wireless clients migrating between wireless access points. First, WPA2 allows the caching of a Pair-wise Master Key (PMK), which is the key used for a session between an access point and a wireless client; thus a wireless client can reconnect a recently connected access point without having to reauthenticate. Second, WPA2 enables a wireless client to authenticate itself to a wireless access point that it is moving to while the wireless client maintains its connection to the existing access point. This reduces the time needed for roaming clients to move from one access point to another, and it is especially useful for timing-sensitive applications.

SPINS: Security Protocols for Sensor Networks

Sensor nodes in sensor networks are normally low-end devices with very limited resources, such as memory, computation power, battery, and network bandwidth.

Perrig et al. [9] proposed a family of security protocols named SPINS, which were specially designed for low-end devices with severely limited resources, such as

sensor nodes in sensor networks. SPINS consists of two building blocks: Secure Network Encryption Protocol (SNEP) and the "micro" version of the Timed, Efficient, Streaming, Loss-tolerant Authentication Protocol (μTESLA). SNEP uses symmetry encryption to provide data confidentiality, two-party data authentication, and data freshness. μTESLA provides authentication over broadcast streams. SPINS assumes that each sensor node shares a master key with the base station. The master key serves as the base of trust and is used to derive all other keys.

SNEP

As illustrated in Figure 15.5, SNEP uses a block cipher to provide data confidentiality and message authentication code (MAC) to provide authentication. SNEP assumes a shared counter C between the sender and the receiver and two keys, the encryption key K_{encr} and the authentication key K_{mac}. For an outgoing message D, SNEP processes it as follows:

- The message D is first encrypted using a block cipher in counter mode with the key K_{encr} and the counter C, forming the encrypted text $E = \{D\} <Kencr, C>$.
- A message authentication code is produced for the encrypted text E with the key K_{mac} and the counter C, forming the MAC $M = MAC(K_{mac}, C|E)$ where $MAC()$ is a one-way function and $C|E$ stands for the concatenation of C and E.
- SNEP increments the counter C.

To send the message D to the recipient, SNEP actually sends out E and M. In other words, SNEP encrypts D to E using the shared key K_{encr} between the sender and the receiver to prevent unauthorized disclosure of the data, and it uses the shared key K_{mac}, known only to the sender and the receiver, to provide message authentication. Thus data confidentiality and message authentication can both be implemented.

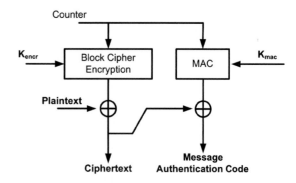

FIGURE 15.5   Sensor Network Encryption Protocol (SNEP).

The message D is encrypted with the counter C, which will be different in each message. The same message D will be encrypted differently even it is sent multiple times. Thus semantic security is implemented in SNEP. The MAC is also produced using the counter C; thus it enables SNEP to prevent replying to old messages.

μTESLA

TESLA [10−12] was proposed to provide message authentication for multicast. TESLA does not use any asymmetry cryptography, which makes it lightweight in terms of computation and overhead of bandwidth.

μTESLA is a modified version of TESLA, aiming to provide message authentication for multicasting in sensor networks. The general idea of μTESLA is that the sender splits the sending time into intervals. Packets sent out in different intervals are authenticated with different keys. Keys to authenticate packets will be disclosed after a short delay, when the keys are no longer used to send out messages. Thus packets can be authenticated when the authentication keys have been disclosed. Packets will not be tampered with while they are in transit since the keys have not been disclosed yet. The disclosed authentication keys can be verified using previous known keys to prevent malicious nodes from forging authentication keys.

μTESLA has four phases: sender setup, sending authenticated packets, bootstrapping new receivers, and authenticating packets. In the sender setup phase, a sender generates a chain of keys, K_i ($0 \le i \le n$). The keychain is a one-way chain such that K_i can be derived from K_j if $i \le j$, such as a keychain K_i ($i = 0, \ldots, n$), $K_i = F(K_{i+1})$, where F is a one-way function. The sender also decides on the starting time T_0, the interval duration T_{int}, and the disclosure delay d (unit is interval), as shown in Figure 15.6.

To send out authenticated packets, the sender attaches a MAC with each packet, where the MAC is produced using a key from the keychain and the data in the network packet. μTESLA has specific requirements on the use of keys for producing MACs. Keys are used in the same order as the key sequence of the keychain. Each of the

keys is used in one interval only. For the interval $T_i = T_0 + i \times T_{int}$, the key K_i is used to produce the MACs for the messages sent out in the interval T_i. Keys are disclosed with a fixed delay d such that the key K_i used in interval T_i will be disclosed in the interval T_{i+d}. The sequence of key usage and the sequence of key disclosure are demonstrated in Figure 15.6.

To bootstrap a new receiver, the sender needs to synchronize the time with the receiver and needs to inform the new receiver of a key K_j that is used in a past interval T_j, the interval duration T_{int}, and the disclosure delay d. With a previous key K_j, the receiver will be able to verify any key K_p where $j \le p$ using the one-way keychain's property. After this, the new receiver will be able to receive and verify data in the same way as other receivers that join the communication prior to the new receiver.

To receive and authenticate messages, a receiver will check all incoming messages if they have been delayed for more than d. Messages with a delay greater than d will be discarded, since they are suspect as fake messages constructed after the key has been disclosed. The receiver will buffer the remaining messages for at least d intervals until the corresponding keys are disclosed. When a key K_i is disclosed at the moment $T_i + d$, the receiver will verify K_i using K_{i-1} by checking if $K_{i-1} = F(K_i)$. Once the key K_i is verified, K_i will be used to authenticate those messages sent in the interval T_i.

5. SECURE ROUTING

Secure Efficient Ad hoc Distance (SEAD) [13] vector routing is adesign based on Destination-Sequenced Distance Vector (DSDV) routing [14]. SEAD augments DSDV with authentication to provide security in the construction and exchange of routing information.

SEAD

Distance vector routing works as follows. Each router maintains a routing table. Each entry of the table contains a specific destination, a metric (the shortest distance to the destination), and the next hop on the shortest path from the current router to the destination. For a packet that needs to be sent to a certain destination, the router will look up the destination from the routing table to get the matching entry. Then the packet is sent to the next hop specified in the entry.

To allow routers to automatically discover new routes and maintain their routing tables, routers exchange routing information periodically. Each router advises its neighbors of its own routing information by broadcasting its routing table to all its neighbors. Each router will update its routing table according to the information it hears from its neighbors. If a new destination is found

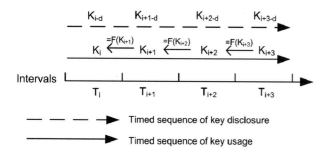

FIGURE 15.6 Sequences of intervals, key usages, and key disclosure.

from the information advertised by a neighbor, a new entry is added to the routing table with the metric recalculated based on the advertised metric and the linking between the router and the neighbor. If an existing destination is found, the corresponding entry is updated only when a new path that is shorter than the original one has been found. In this case, the metric and the next hop for the specified destination are modified based on the advertised information.

Though distance vector routing is simple and effective, it suffers from possible routing loops, also known as the counting to infinity problem. DSDV [14] is one of the extensions to distance vector routing to tackle this issue. DSDV augments each routing update with a sequence number, which can be used to identify the sequence of routing updates, preventing routing updates being applied in an out-of-order manner. Newer routing updates are advised with sequence numbers greater than those of the previous routing updates. In each routing update, the sequence number will be incremented to the next even number. Only when a broken link has been detected will the router use the next odd sequence number as the sequence number for the new routing update that is to be advertised to all its neighbors. Each router maintains an even sequence number to identify the sequence of every routing update. Neighbors will only accept newer routing updates by discarding routing updates with sequence numbers less than the last sequence number heard from the router.

SEAD provides authentication on metrics' lower bounds and senders' identities by using the one-way hash chain. Let H be a hash function and x be a given value. A list of values is computed as follows:

$$h_0, h_1, h_2, \ldots, h_n$$

where $h_0 = x$ and $h_{i+1} = H(h_i)$ for $0 \leq i \leq n$. Given any value h_k that has been confirmed to be in the list, to authenticate if a given value d is on the list or not one can compute if d can be derived from h_k by applying H a certain number of times, or if h_k can be derived from d by applying H to d a certain number of times. If either d can be derived from h_k or h_k can be derived from d within a certain number of steps, it is said that d can be authenticated by h_k.

SEAD assumes an upper bound $m - 1$ on the diameter of the ad hoc network, which means that the metric of a routing entry will be less than m. Let $h_0, h_1, h_2, \ldots, h_n$ be a hash chain where $n = m \times k$ and $k \in Z^+$. For an update with the sequence number i and the metric value of j, the value $h_{(k-i)m+j}$ is used to authenticate the routing update entry. By using $h_{(k-i)m+j}$ to authenticate the routing update entry, a node is actually disclosing the value $h_{(k-i)m+j}$ and subsequently all h_p where $p \geq (k-i)m+j$, but not any value h_q where $q \leq (k-i)m+j$.

Using a hash value corresponding to the sequence number and metric in a routing update entry allows the authentication of the update and prevents any node from advertising a route to some destination, forging a greater sequence number or a smaller metric. To authenticate the update, a node can use any given earlier authentic hash value h_p from the same hash chain to authenticate the current update with sequence number i and metric j. The current update uses the hash value $h_{(k-i)m+j}$ and $(k-i)m + J \leq P$, thus h_p can be computed from $h_{(k-i)\ m+j}$ by applying H for $(k-i)m + j - p$ times.

The disclosure of $h_{(k-i)m+j}$ does not disclose any value h_q where $q \leq (k-i)m+j$. Let a fake update be advised with a sequence number p and metric q, where $p \geq i$ and $q \leq j$, or $q \leq j$. The fake update will need to use the hash value $h_{(k-P)\ m+q}$. If the sequence number p is greater than i or the metric q is less than j, $(k-p)m + q < (k-i)m + j$. This means that a hash value $h_{(k-p)m+q}$ that has not been disclosed is needed to authenticate the update. Since the value $h_{(k-p)m+q}$ has not been disclosed, the malicious node will not be able to have it to fake a routing update.

Ariadne

Ariadne [15] is a secure on-demand routing protocol for ad hoc networks. Ariadne is built on the Dynamic Source Routing protocol (DSR) [16].

Routing in Ariadne is divided into two stages: the route discovery stage and the route maintenance stage. In the route discovery stage, a source node in the ad hoc network tries to find a path to a specific destination node. The discovered path will be used by the source node as the path for all communication from the source node to the destination node until the discovered path becomes invalid. In the route maintenance stage, network nodes identify broken paths that have been found. A node sends a packet along a specified route to some destination. Each node on the route forwards the packet to the next node on the specified route and tries to confirm the delivery of the packet to the next node. If a node fails to receive an acknowledgment from the next node, it will signal the source node using a ROUTE ERROR packet that a broken link has been found. The source node and other nodes on the path can then be advised of the broken link.

The key security features Ariadne adds onto the route discovery and route maintenance are node authentication and data verification for the routing relation packets. Node authentication is the process of verifying the identifiers of nodes that are involved in Ariadne's route discovery and route maintenance, to prevent forging routing packets. In route discovery, a node sends out a ROUTE REQUEST packet to perform a route discovery. When the ROUTE REQUEST packet reaches the destination node, the destination node verifies the originator identity before responding. Similarly, when the source node receives a ROUTE REPLY packet, which is a response to the ROUTE REQUEST packet, the source node will also authenticate the identity of the sender. The authentication of node identities can be of one of the three methods: TELSA, digital signatures, and Message Authentication Code (MAC).

Data verification is the process of verifying the integrity of the node list in route discovery for the prevention of adding and removing nodes from the node list in a ROUTE RQUEST. To build a full list of nodes for a route to a destination, each node will need to add itself into the node list in the ROUTE REQUEST when it forwards the ROUTE REQUEST to its neighbor. Data verification protects the node list by preventing unauthorized adding of nodes and unauthorized removal of nodes.

6. ARAN

Authenticated Routing for Ad hoc Networks (ARAN) [17] is a routing protocol for ad hoc networks with authentication enabled. It allows routing messages to be authenticated at each node between the source nodes and the destination nodes. The authentication that ARAN has implemented is based on cryptographic certificates.

ARAN requires a trusted certificate server, the public key of which is known to all valid nodes. Keys are assumed to have been established between the trusted certificate server and nodes. For each node to enter into a wireless ad hoc network, it needs to have a certificate issued by the trusted server. The certificate contains the IP address of the node, the public key of the node, a time stamp indicating the issue time of the certification, and the expiration time of the certificate. Because all nodes have the public key of the trusted server, a certificate can be verified by all nodes to check whether it is authentic. With an authentic certificate and the corresponding private key, the node that owns the certificate can authenticate itself using its private key.

To discover a route from a source node to the destination node, the source node sends out a route discovery packet (RDP) to all its neighbors. The RDP is signed by the source node's private key and contains a nonce, a time stamp, and the source node's certificate. The time stamp and the nonce work to prevent replay attacks and flooding of the RDP.

The RDP is then rebroadcast in the network until it reaches the destination. The RDP is rebroadcast with the signature and the certificate of the rebroadcaster. On receiving an RDP, each node will first verify the source's signature and the previous node's signature on the RDP.

On receiving an RDP, the destination sends back a reply packet (REP) along the reverse path to the source after validating the RDP. The REP contains the nonce specified in the RDP and the signature from the destination node.

The REP is unicast along the reverse path. Each node on the path will put its own certificate and its own signature on the RDP before forwarding it to the next node. Each node will also verify the signatures on the RDP. An REP is discarded if one or more invalid signatures are found on the REP.

When the source receives the REP, it will first verify the signatures and then the nonce in the REP. A valid REP indicates that a route has been discovered. The node list on a valid REP suggests an operational path from the source node to the destination node that is found.

As an on-demand protocol, nodes keep track of route status. If there has been no traffic for a route's lifetime or a broken link has been detected, the route will be deactivated. Receiving data on an inactive route will force a node to signal an error state by using an error (ERR) message. The ERR message is signed by the node that produces it and will be forwarded to the source without modification. The ERR message contains a nonce and a time stamp to ensure that the ERR message is fresh.

7. SLSP

Secure Link State Routing Protocol (SLSP) [18] is a secure routing protocol for an ad hoc network building based on link state protocols. SLSP assumes that each node has a public/private key pair and has the capability of signing and verifying digital signatures. Keys are bound with the Medium Access Code and the IP address, allowing neighbors within transmission range to uniquely verify nodes if public keys have been known prior to communication.

In SLSP, each node broadcasts its IP address and the MAC to its neighbor with its signature. Neighbors verify the signature and keep a record of the pairing IP address and the MAC. The Neighbor Lookup Protocol (NLP) of SLSP extracts and retains the MAC and IP address of each network frame received by a node. The extracted information is used to maintain the mapping of MACs and IP addresses.

Nodes using SLSP periodically send out link state updates (LSUs) to advise the state of their network links. LSU packets are limited to propagating within a zone of their origin node, which is specified by the maximum number of hops. To restrict the propagation of LSU packets, each LSU packet contains the *zone radius* and the *hops traversed* fields. Let the maximum hop be R; X, a random number; and H be a hash function. *Zone-radius* will be initialized to $H^R(X)$ and *hops−traversed* be initialized to $H(X)$. Each LSU packet also contains a *TTL* field initialized as $R - 1$. If $TTL < 0$ or $H(hops−traversed) = zone-radius$, a node will not rebroadcast the LSU packet. Otherwise, the node will replace the *hops–traversed* field with *H(hops–traversed)* and decrease *TTL* by one. In this way, the hop count is authenticated. SLSP also uses signatures to protect LSU packets. Receiving nodes can verify the authenticity and the integrity of the received LSU packets, thus preventing forging or tampering with LSU packets.

8. KEY ESTABLISHMENT

Because wireless communication is open and the signals are accessible by anyone within the vicinity, it is important for wireless networks to establish trust to guard the access to the networks. Key establishment builds relations between nodes using keys; thus security services, such as authentication, confidentiality, and integrity can be achieved for the communication between these nodes with the help of the established keys.

The dynamically changing topology of wireless networks, the lack of fixed infrastructure of wireless ad hoc and sensor networks, and the limited computation and energy resources of sensor networks, have all added complication to the key establishment process in wireless networks.

Bootstrapping

Bootstrapping is the process by which nodes in a wireless network are made aware of the presence of others in the network. On bootstrapping, a node gets its identifying credentials that can be used in the network the node is trying to join. Upon completion of the bootstrapping, the wireless network should be ready to accept the node as a valid node to join the network.

To enter a network, a node needs to present its identifying credential to show its eligibility to access the network. This process is called *preauthentication*. Once the credentials are accepted, network security associations are established with other nodes.

These network security associations will serve as further proof of authorization in the network. Security associations can be of various forms, including symmetric keys, public key pairs, hash key chains, and so on. The security associations can be used to authenticate nodes. Security associations may expire after a certain period of time and can be revoked if necessary. For example, if a node is suspected of being compromised, its security association will be revoked to prevent the node accessing the network. The actual way of revocation depends on the form of the security associations.

Bootstrapping in Wireless Ad Hoc Networks

Wireless ad hoc networks bring new challenges to the bootstrapping process by their lack of a centralized security infrastructure. It is necessary to build a security infrastructure in the bootstrapping phase. The trust infrastructure should be able to accept nodes with valid credentials to enter the network but stop those nodes without valid credentials from joining the network and establish security association between nodes within the network.

To build such a trust infrastructure, we can use any one of the following three supports: prior knowledge, trusted third parties, or self-organizing capability. Prior knowledge is information that has been set on valid nodes in advance, such as predistributed secrets or preset shared keys. This information can be used to distinguish legitimate nodes from malicious ones. Only nodes with prior knowledge will be accepted to enter the network. For example, the predistributed secrets can be used to authenticate legitimate nodes, so the network can simply reject those nodes without the predistributed secrets so that they can't enter the network.

Trusted third parties can also be used to support the establishment of the trust infrastructure. The trusted third party can be a Certificate Authority (CA), a base station of the wireless network, or any nodes that are designated to be trusted. If trusted third parties are used, all nodes must mutually agree to trust them and derive their trust on others from the trusted third parties. One of the issues with this method is that trusted third parties are required to be available for access by all nodes across the whole network, which is a very strong assumption for wireless networks as well as an impractical requirement.

It is desirable to have a self-organizing capability for building the trust infrastructure for wireless networks, taking into account the dynamically changing topology of wireless ad hoc networks. Implementing a self-organizing capability for building the trust infrastructure often requires an out-of-band authenticated communication channel or special hardware support, such as tamper-proof hardware tokens.

Bootstrapping in Wireless Sensor Networks

Bootstrapping nodes in wireless sensor networks is also challenging for the following reasons:

- *Node capture.* Sensor nodes are normally deployed in an area that is geographically close or inside the monitoring environment, which might not be a closed and confined area under guard. Thus sensor nodes are vulnerable to physical capture because it might be difficult to prevent physical access to the area.
- *Node replication.* Once a sensor node is compromised, it is possible for adversaries to replicate sensor nodes by using the secret acquired from the compromised node. In this case, adversaries can produce fake legitimate node that cannot be distinguished by the network.

- *Scalability.* A single-sensor network may comprise a large number of sensor nodes. The more nodes in a wireless sensor network, the more complicated it is for bootstrapping.
- *Resource limitation.* Sensor nodes normally have extremely limited computation power and memory as well as limited power supply and weak communication capability. This makes some of the deliberate algorithms and methods not applicable to wireless sensor networks. Only those algorithms that require a moderate amount of resources can be implemented in wireless sensor networks.

Bootstrapping a sensor node is achieved using an incremental communication output power level to discover neighbors nearby. The output power level is increased step by step from the minimum level to the maximum level, to send out a HELLO message. This will enable the sensor node to discover neighbors in the order of their distance from the sensor node, from the closest to the farthest away.

Key Management

Key management schemes can be classified according to the way keys are set up (see Figure 15.7). Either keys are managed based on the contribution from all participating nodes in the network or they are managed based on a central node in the network. Thus key management schemes can be divided into contributory key management schemes, in which all nodes work equally together to manage the keys, and distributed key management schemes, in which only one central node is responsible for key management [19].

Classification

The distributed key management scheme can be further divided into symmetric schemes and public key schemes. Symmetric key schemes are based on private key cryptography, whereby shared secrets are used to authenticate legitimate nodes and to provide secure communication between them. The underlying assumption is that the shared secrets are known only to legitimate nodes involved in the interaction. Thus proving the

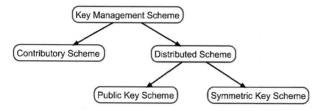

FIGURE 15.7   Key management schemes.

knowledge of the shared secrets is enough to authenticate legitimate nodes. Shared secrets are distributed via secure channels or out-of-band measures. Trust on a node is established if the node has knowledge of a shared secret.

Public key schemes are built on public key cryptography. Keys are constructed in pairs, with a private key and a public key in each pair. Private keys are kept secret by the owners. Public keys are distributed and used to authenticate nodes and to verify credentials. Keys are normally conveyed in certificates for distribution. Certificates are signed by trusted nodes for which the public keys have been known and validated. Trust on the certificates will be derived from the public keys that sign the certificates. Note that given $g^i(mod\ p)$ and $g^j(mod\ p)$, it is hard to compute $g^{i*j}(mod\ p)$ without the knowledge of i and j.

Contributory Schemes

Diffie-Hellman (D-H) [20] is a well-known algorithm for establishing shared secrets. The D-H algorithm's strength depends on the discrete log problem: It is hard to calculate s if given the value g^s (mod p), where p is a large prime number.

Diffie-hellman Key Exchange

D-H was designed for establishing a shared secret between two parties, namely node A and node B. Each party agrees on a large prime number p and a generator g. A and B each choose a random value i and j, respectively. A and B are then exchanged with the public values g^i (mod p) and g^j (mod p). On the reception of g^j (mod p) from B, A is then able to calculate the value $g^{j \times i}$ (mod p). Similarly, B computes $g^{i \times j}$ (mod p). Thus a shared secret, $g^{i \times j}$ (mod p), has been set up between A and B.

9. ING

Ingemarsson, Tang, and Wong (ING) [21] extends the D-F key exchange to a group of n members, $d_1, \ldots, d_n$. All group members are organized in a ring, where each member has a left neighbor and a right neighbor. Node d_i has a right neighbor d_{i-1} and a left neighbor d_{i+1}. Note that for node d_i, its right neighbor is d_{i+1}; for node d_{i+1}, its left neighbor is d_i.

Same as the D-F algorithm, all members in an ING group assume a large prime number p and a generator g. Initially, node d_i will choose a random number r_i. At the first round of key exchange, node d_i will compute g^{r_i} (mod p) and send it to its left neighbor d_{i+1}. At the same time, node d_i also receives the public value $g^{r_{i-1}}$ (mod p) from its right neighbor d_{i-1}. From the second round on, let q be the value that node d_i received in the previous round, node d_i will compute a new public value q^{d_i} (mod p). After $n-1$ rounds, the node d_i would have received a public value, g^k (mod p) where $k = \Pi_{m=1}^{i-1} r_m \times \Pi_{s=i+1}^{n} r_s$, from its right neighbors. With the public value received at the $n-1$th round, the node d_i can raise it to the power of r_i to compute the value g^l (mod p) where $l = \Pi_{m=1}^{n} r_m$.

Hypercube and Octopus (H & O)

The Hypercube protocol [22] assumes that there are 2^d nodes joining to establish a shared secret and all nodes are organized as a d-dimensional vector space $GF(2)^d$ Let $b_1, \ldots, b_d$ be the basic of $GF(2)^d$. The hypercube protocol takes d rounds to complete:

- In the first round, every participant $v \in GF(2)^d$ chooses a random number r_v and conducts a D-H key exchange with another participant $v + b_1$, with the random values r_v and r_{v+b1}, respectively.
- In the ith round, every participant $v \in GF(2)^d$ performances a D-H key exchange with the participant $v + b_i$, where both v and $v + b_i$ use the value generated in the previous round as the random number for D-H key exchange.

This algorithm can be explained using a complete binary tree to make it more comprehensible. All the nodes are put in a complete binary tree as leaves, with leaves at the 0−level and the root at the d-level. D-H key exchanges are performed from the leaves up to the root. The key exchange takes d rounds:

- In the first round, each leaf chooses a random number k and performs a D-H key exchange with its sibling leaf, which has a random number j, and the resulting value $g^{k \times j}$ (mod p) is saved as the random value for the parent node of the above two leaves.
- In the ith round, each node at the $i-1$ level performs a D-H key exchange with its sibling node using the random numbers m and n, respectively, that they received in the previous round. The resulting value $g^{m \times n}$ (mod p) is saved as the random value for the parent node of the above two nodes.

After d rounds, the root of the complete binary tree contains the established shared secret. The hypercube protocol assumes that there are 2^d network nodes. The octopus protocol removes the assumption and extends the hypercube protocol to work with an arbitrary number of nodes. Thus the octopus protocol can be used to establish a shared key for a node set containing an arbitrary number of nodes.

Distributed Schemes

A partially distributed threshold CA scheme [23] works with a normal PKI system where a CA exists. The private key of the CA is split and distributed over a set of n server nodes using a (k,n) secret-sharing scheme [24]. The (k,n) secretsharing scheme allows any k or more server nodes within the n server nodes to work together to reveal the CA's private key. Any set of nodes with fewer than k nodes will not be able to reveal the CA's private key. With the threshold signature scheme [25], any k of the n nodes can cooperate to sign a certificate. Each of the k nodes produces a piece of the signature on the request of signing a given certificate. With all the k pieces of the signature, a valid signature, which is the same as the one produced using the CA's private key, can be produced by combining the k pieces of the signature.

Partially Distributed Threshold CA Scheme

In this way, the partial distributed threshold CA scheme can avoid the bottleneck of the centralized CA of conventional PKI infrastructures. As long as there are at least k of the n nodes available, the network can always issue and sign new certificates. Attacks to any single node will not bring the whole CA down. Only when an attack manages to paralyze $n - k$ or more nodes will the CA's signing service not be available.

To further improve the security of the private key that is distributed over the n nodes, proactive security [26] can be imposed. Proactive security forces the private key shares to be refreshed periodically. Each refreshment will invalidate the previous share held by a node. Attacks on multiple nodes must complete within a refresh period to succeed. To be specific, only when an attack can compromise k or more nodes within a refresh period can the attack succeed.

While conventional PKI systems depend on directories to publish public key certificates, it is suggested that certificates should be disseminated to communication peers when establishing a communication channel with the partial distributed threshold CA scheme. This is due to the fact that the availability of centralized directories cannot be guaranteed in wireless networks. Therefore it is not realistic to assume the availability of a centralized directory.

Self-organized Key Management (PGP-A)

A self-organized key management scheme (PGP-A) [27] has its basis in the Pretty Good Privacy (PGP) [28] scheme. PGP is built based on the "web of trust" model, in which all nodes have equal roles in playing a CA.

Each node generates its own public/private key pair and signs other nodes' public keys if it trusts the nodes. The signed certificates are kept by nodes in their own certificate repositories instead of being published by centralized directories in the X.509 PKI systems [29].

PGP-A treats trust as transitive. So, trust can be derived from a trusted node's trust on another node, that is, if node A trusts node B, and node B trusts node C, then A should also trust C if A knows the fact that node B trusts node C.

To verify a key of a node u, a node j will merge its certificate repository with those of j's trusted nodes, and those of the nodes trusted by j's trusted nodes, and so forth. In this way, node j can build up a web of trust in which node j is at the center of the web and j's directly trusted nodes as node j's neighbors. Node l is linked with node k if node k trusts node l. Node j can search the web of trust built as above to find a path from j to u. If such as path exists, let it be a sequence of nodes S: $node_i$ where i = 1, ..., n, n be the length of the path, and $node_1 = j$ and $node_n = u$. This means that $node_i$ trust $node_{i+1}$ for all i = 1, ..., n−1. Therefore u can be trusted by j. The path S represents a verifiable chain of certificates. PGP-A does not guarantee that a node u that should be trusted by node j will always be trusted by node j, since there are chances that the node j fails to find a path from node j to node u in the web of trust. This might be due to the reason that node j has not acquired enough certificates from its trusted nodes to cover the path from node j to node u.

Self-Healing Session Key Distribution

The preceding two key management schemes are public key management schemes. The one discussed here, a self-healing session key distribution [30], is a symmetric key management scheme. In such a scheme, keys can be distributed either by an online key distribution server or by key predistribution. A key predistribution scheme normally comprises the key predistribution phase, the shared-key discovery phase, and the path key establishment phase.

In the key predistribution phase, a key pool of a large number of keys is created. Every key can be identified by a unique key identifier. Each network node is given a set of keys from the key pool. The shared-key discovery phase begins when a node tries to communicate with the others. All nodes exchange their key identifiers to find out whether there are any keys shared with others. The shared keys can then be used to establish a secure channel for communication. If no shared key exists, a key path will need to be discovered. The key path is a sequence of nodes with which all adjacent nodes share a key. With

the key path, a message can travel from the first node to the last node securely, by which a secure channel can be established between the first node and the last node.

The self-healing session key distribution (S-HEAL) [30] assumes the existence of a group manager and pre-shared secrets. Keys are distributed from the group manager to group members. Let h be a polynomial, where for a node i, node i knows about h(i). Let K be the group key to be distributed, K is covered by h in the distribution: f(x) = h(x) + K. The polynomial f(x) is the information that the group manager sends out to all its group members. For node j, node j will calculate K = f(j) − h(j) to reveal the group key. Without the knowledge of h(j), node j will not be able to recover K.

To enable revocation in S-HEAL, the polynomial h(x) is replaced by a bivariate polynomial s(x,y). The group key is covered by the bivariate polynomial s(x,y) when it is distributed to group members, in the way that f(N,x) = s(N,x) + K. Node i must calculate s(N,i) to recover K. The revocation enabled S-HEAL tries to stop revoked nodes to calculate s(N,i), thus preventing them to recover K.

Let s of degree t; then t + 1 values are needed to compute s(x,i). Assuming that s(i,i) is predistributed to node i, node i will need another t values to recover s(N,i), namely $s(r_1,x)$, ..., $s(r_t,x)$. These values will be disseminating to group members together with the key update. If the group manager wants to revoke node i, the group manager can set one of the values $s(r_1,x)$, ..., $s(r_t,x)$ to s(i,x). In this case, node i obtains only t values instead of t + 1 values. Therefore, node i will not be able to compute s(x,i), thus it will not be able to recover K. This scheme can only revoke maximum t nodes at the same time.

Now, let's take a very brief look at wireless network security management countermeasures. Security comes at a cost: either in dollars spent on security equipment, in inconvenience and maintenance, or in operating expenses. Some organizations may be willing to accept risk because applying various management countermeasures may exceed financial or other constraints.

10. MANAGEMENT COUNTERMEASURES

Management countermeasures ensure that all critical personnel are properly trained on the use of wireless technology. Network administrators need to be fully aware of the security risks that wireless networks and devices pose. They must work to ensure security policy compliance and to know what steps to take in the event of an attack (see checklist: "An Agenda For Action When Implementing Wireless Network Security Policies").

Management countermeasures for securing wireless networks begin with a comprehensive security policy. A security policy, and compliance therewith, is the foundation on which other countermeasures (the operational and technical) are rationalized and implemented. Finally, the most important countermeasures are trained and aware users.

11. SUMMARY

Organizations should understand that maintaining a secure wireless network is an ongoing process that requires greater effort than for other networks and systems. Moreover, it is important that organizations more frequently assess risks and test and evaluate system security controls when wireless technologies are deployed. Maintaining a secure wireless network (and associated devices) requires significant effort, resources and vigilance and involves the following steps:

- Maintaining a full understanding of the topology of the wireless network.
- Labeling and keeping inventories of the fielded wireless and handheld devices.
- Creating frequent backups of data.
- Performing periodic security testing and assessment of the wireless network.
- Performing ongoing, randomly timed security audits to monitor and track wireless and handheld devices.
- Applying patches and security enhancements.
- Monitoring the wireless industry for changes to standards to enhance to security features and for the release of new products.
- Vigilantly monitoring wireless technology for new threats and vulnerabilities.

Organizations should not undertake wireless deployment for essential operations until they understand and can acceptably manage and mitigate the risks to their information, system operations, and risk to the continuity of essential operations. As described in this chapter, the risks provided by wireless technologies are considerable. Many current communications protocols and commercial products provide inadequate protection and thus present unacceptable risks to organizational operations. Agencies must proactively address such risks to protect their ability to support essential operations, before deployment. Furthermore, many organizations poorly administer their wireless technologies. Some examples include deploying equipment with factory default settings; failing to control or inventory their access points; not implementing the security capabilities provided; and, not developing or employing a security architecture suitable to the wireless environment (firewalls between wired and wireless systems, blocking unneeded services/ports, using strong cryptography, etc.). To a large extent, most of the risks can be mitigated. However, mitigating these risks requires considerable tradeoffs between technical solutions and costs. Today, the vendor and standards community is aggressively working towards more robust, open, and secure solutions for the near future.

Finally, let's move on to the real interactive part of this Chapter: review questions/exercises, hands-on projects, case projects and optional team case project. The answers and/or solutions by chapter can be found in the Online Instructor's Solutions Manual.

CHAPTER REVIEW QUESTIONS/EXERCISES

True/False

1. True or False? Wireless networks are a general term to refer to various types of networks that communicate without the need of wire lines.
2. True or False? Cellular networks require fixed infrastructures to work.

An Agenda for Action when Implementing Wireless Network Security Policies

The items below are possible actions that organizations should consider; some of the items may not apply to all organizations. A wireless network security policy should be able to do the following (check all tasks completed):

_____1. Identify who may use WLAN technology in an organization.

_____2. Identify whether Internet access is required.

_____3. Describe who can install access points and other wireless equipment.

_____4. Provide limitations on the location of and physical security for access points.

_____5. Describe the type of information that may be sent over wireless links.

_____6. Describe conditions under which wireless devices are allowed.

_____7. Define standard security settings for access points.

_____8. Describe limitations on how the wireless device may be used, such as location.

_____9. Describe the hardware and software configuration of any access device.

_____10. Provide guidelines on reporting losses of wireless devices and security incidents.

_____11. Provide guidelines on the use of encryption and other security software.

_____12. Define the frequency and scope of security assessments.

3. True or False? Wireless ad hoc networks are distributed networks that work without fixed infrastructures and in which each network node is willing to forward network packets for other network nodes.

4. True or False? WEP is designed to protect linkage-level data for wireless transmission by providing confidentiality, access control, and data integrity, to provide secure communication between a mobile device and an access point in a 802.11 wireless LAN.

5. True or False? The WPA standard is aimed at providing a stronger security compared to WEP and is expected to tackle most of the weakness found in WEP.

Multiple Choice

1. Personal deployment of WPA adopts a simpler mechanism, which allows all stations to use the same key. This mechanism is called the:
   A. RC 4 stream cipher
   B. Temporal Key Integrity Protocol (TKIP)
   C. Pre-Shared Key (PSK) mode
   D. Message Integrity Code (MIC)
   E. Extensible Authentication Protocol (EAP) framework

2. What are low-end devices with very limited resources, such as memory, computation power, battery, and network bandwidth:
   A. SPINS
   B. Sequences of intervals
   C. Key usages
   D. Sensor nodes
   E. All of the above

3. Secure Efficient Ad hoc Distance (SEAD) vector routing is a design based on a:
   A. Secure on-demand routing protocol
   B. ROUTE RQUEST
   C. Message Authentication Code (MAC)
   D. Authenticated Routing for Ad hoc Networks (ARAN)
   E. Destination-Sequenced Distance Vector (DSDV) routing

4. What requires a trusted certificate server, where the public key is known to all valid nodes?
   A. ARAN.
   B. RDP.
   C. REP.
   D. ERR.
   E. All of the above.

5. What is a secure routing protocol for an ad hoc network building based on link state protocols?
   A. Neighbor Lookup Protocol (NLP).
   B. Secure Link State Routing Protocol (SLSP).
   C. Bootstrapping protocol.

   D. Preauthentication protocol.
   E. All of the above.

EXERCISE

Problem

What is WEP?

Hands-On Projects

Project

What is a WEP key?

Case Projects

Problem

Organization A is considering implementing a WLAN so that employees may use their laptop computers anywhere within the boundaries of their office building. Before deciding, however, Organization A has its computer security department perform a risk assessment. The security department first identifies WLAN vulnerabilities and threats. The department, assuming that threat-sources will try to exploit WLAN vulnerabilities, determines the overall risk of operating a WLAN and the impact a successful attack would have on Organization A. The manager reads the risk assessment and decides that the residual risk exceeds the benefit the WLAN provides. The manager directs the computer security department to identify additional countermeasures to mitigate residual risk before the system can be implemented. What are those additional countermeasures?

Optional Team Case Project

Problem

Organization C is considering purchasing mobiles devices for its sales force of 300 employees. Before making a decision to purchase the mobiles devices, the computer security department performs a risk assessment. What did the computer security department find out from the risk assessment?

REFERENCES

[1] L. M. S. C. of the IEEE Computer Society. Wireless LAN medium access control (MAC) and physical layer (PHY) specifications, technical report, IEEE Standard 802.11, 1999 ed., 1999.

[2] R.L. Rivest, The RC4 encryption algorithm, RSA Data Security, Inc., March 1992 technical report.

[3] E. Dawson, L. Nielsen, Automated cryptanalysis of XOR plaintext strings, Cryptologia 20 (2) (April 1996).

[4] S. Singh, The Code Book: The Evolution of Secrecy from Mary, Queen of Scots, to Quantum Cryptography, Doubleday, 1999.

[5] W.A. Arbaugh, An inductive chosen plaintext attack against WEP/WEP2, IEEE Document 802.11-01/230, May 2001.

[6] J.R. Walker, Unsafe at any key size; an analysis of the WEP encapsulation, IEEE Document 802.11-00/362, October 2000.

[7] N. Borisov, I. Goldberg, D. Wagner, Intercepting Mobile Communications: The Insecurity of 802.11, MobiCom 2001.

[8] B. Aboba, L. Blunk, J. Vollbrecht, J. Carlson, E.H. Levkowetz, Extensible Authentication Protocol (EAP), request for comment, Network Working Group, 2004.

[9] A. Perrig, R. Szewczyk, V. Wen, D. Culler, J.D. Tygar, SPINS: Security protocols for sensor networks, MobiCom '01: Proceedings of the 7th annual international conference on Mobile computing and networking, 2001.

[10] A. Perrig, R. Canetti, D. Xiaodong Song, J.D. Tygar, Efficient and secure source authentication for multicast, NDSS 01: Network and Distributed System Security Symposium, 2001.

[11] A. Perrig, J.D. Tygar, D. Song, R. Canetti, Efficient authentication and signing of multicast streams over lossy channels, SP '00: Proceedings of the 2000 IEEE Symposium on Security and Privacy, 2000.

[12] A. Perrig, R. Canetti, J.D. Tygar, D. Song, RSA CryptoBytes 5 (2002).

[13] Y.-C. Hu, D.B. Johnson, A. Perrig, SEAD: secure efficient distance vector routing for mobile wireless ad hoc networks, WMCSA '02: Proceedings of the Fourth IEEE Workshop on Mobile Computing Systems and Applications, IEEE Computer Society, Washington, DC, 2002. p. 3.

[14] C.E. Perkins, P. Bhagwat, Highly dynamic destination-sequenced distance-vector routing (DSDV) for mobile computers, SIGCOMM Comput. Commun. Rev. 24 (4) (1994) 234–244.

[15] Y.-C. Hu, A. Perrig, D. Johnson, Ariadne: a secure on-demand routing protocol for ad hoc networks, Wire. Netw. J. 11 (1), (2005).

[16] D.B. Johnson, D.A. Maltz, Dynamic source routing in ad hoc wireless networks, Mobile Computing, Kluwer Academic Publishers, 1996, pp. 153–181.

[17] K. Sanzgiri, B. Dahill, B.N. Levine, C. Shields, E.M. Belding-Royer, A secure routing protocol for ad hoc networks, 10th IEEE International Conference on Network Protocols (ICNP'02), 2002.

[18] P. Papadimitratos, Z.J. Haas, Secure link state routing for mobile ad hoc networks, saint-w, 00, 2003.

[19] E. Cayirci, C. Rong, Security in Wireless Ad hoc, Sensor, and Mesh Networks, John Wiley & Sons, 2008.

[20] W. Diffie, M.E. Hellman, New directions in cryptography, IEEE Trans. Inf. Theory IT-22 (6) (1976) 644–654.

[21] I. Ingemarsson, D. Tang, C. Wong, A conference key distribution system, IEEE Trans. Inf. Theory 28 (5) (September 1982) 714–720.

[22] K. Becker, U. Wille, Communication complexity of group key distribution, ACM conference on computer and communications security, 1998.

[23] L. Zhou, Z.J. Haas, Securing ad hoc networks, IEEE Netw. 13 (1999) 24–30.

[24] A. Shamir, How to share a secret, Comm. ACM 22 (11) (1979).

[25] Y. Desmedt, Some recent research aspects of threshold cryptography, ISW (1997) 158–173.

[26] R. Canetti, A. Gennaro, D. Herzberg, Naor, proactive security: long-term protection against break-ins, CryptoBytes 3 (1) (Spring 1997).

[27] S. Capkun, L. Buttyán, J.-P. Hubaux, Self-organized public-key management for mobile ad hoc networks, IEEE Trans. Mob. Comput. 2 (1) (2003) 52–64.

[28] P. Zimmermann, The Official PGP User's Guide, The MIT Press, 1995.

[29] ITU-T. Recommendation X.509, ISO/IEC 9594-8, Information Technology: Open Systems Interconnection – The Directory: Public-key and Attribute Certificate Frameworks, fourth ed., 2000, ITU.

[30] J. Staddon, S.K. Miner, M.K. Franklin, D. Balfanz, M. Malkin, D. Dean, Self-healing key distribution with revocation, IEEE Symposium on Security and Privacy, 2002.

## Chapter 16

Wireless Sensor Network Security

Harsh Kupwade Patil
Southern Methodist University

Thomas M. Chen
Swansea University

1. INTRODUCTION TO THE WIRELESS SENSOR NETWORK (WSN)

In recent times, advances in microelectronic mechanical systems (MEMS) and wireless communication technologies have led to the proliferation of wireless sensor networks (WSNs). A WSN can be broadly described as a network of nodes that makes a collaborative effort in sensing certain specified data around its periphery and thereby controls the surrounding environment. A typical sensor network consists of a large number of low-cost, low-powered sensor nodes that are deployable in harsh operating environments. Because of their varied applications in civilian and military sectors, WSNs have gained a lot of popularity in the past decade. For instance, applications can include habitat monitoring, air and water quality management, hazard and disaster monitoring, health care, remote sensing, smart homes, and so on. Figure 16.1 depicts a usual wireless sensor network in which sensor nodes are distributed in an ad-hoc, decentralized fashion. Usually, WSNs are connected to a legacy network (IP network or 3 G network) using one or more sink nodes or base stations. Furthermore, routing in WSN is typically carried in a hop-by-hop fashion.

In general, WSN protocols should be designed to minimize energy consumption and preserve the life of the network. Information gathering in WSN is done by asking for information regarding a specific attribute of the phenomena or by asking for statistics about a specific area of the sensor field. This requires a protocol that can handle requests for a specific type of information, which includes datacentric routing and data aggregation. The last important characteristic of wireless sensor networks is that the position of the nodes may not be engineered or predetermined, and therefore, must provide data routes that are self-organizing.

Although WSNs have gained a lot of popularity, they present some serious limitations when one is implementing security. WSNs present extreme resource limitations in available storage (memory) space, computing, battery life, and bandwidth. Hence, sensor networks present major challenges for integrating traditional security techniques in such resource-constraint networks. In addition, the ad-hoc, decentralized nature of WSNs would pose even greater challenges in applying conventional security mechanisms. Hence, researchers face the challenge of taking all these constraints in consideration while providing adequate security to such sensor networks.

WSN Architecture and Protocol Stack

Most of the traditional networks (for example, IP networks) are built on the Open System Interconnection (OSI) model. However, WSNs operate in a resource-constrained environment and therefore deviate from the traditional OSI model. A WSN stack usually consists of six layers: an application layer, middleware, transport, network, data link, and physical layer. In addition to these six layers that are mapped to each sensor node, there are three more planes that span across the entire sensor network and have more visibility to address issues such as mobility, power, and task management (see Figure 16.2).

Application Layer

The application layer aims to create an abstraction of the main functions of the sensing application, thereby making the lower software and hardware levels transparent to the end user. The application layer involves several processes running simultaneously and handles user requests relating to data aggregation, location finding, sleep/awake cycle control, time synchronization, authentication, encryption, key distribution, and other security measures. It also defines the order and format of message exchange between the two communication parties.

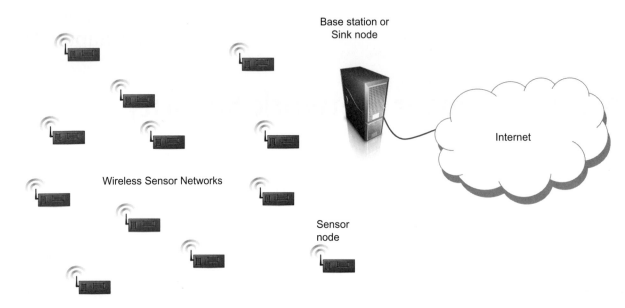

FIGURE 16.1   Wireless sensor network.

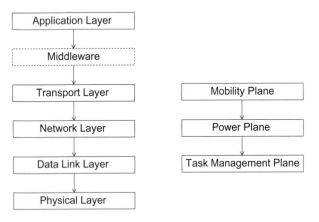

FIGURE 16.2   WSN protocol stack.

Middleware

The middle layer provides an application programming interface (API) for applications existing in the upper layers. It also may involve complex functionalities such as resource sharing and task management.

Transport Layer

The transport layer is responsible for flow and congestion control. It also performs error control to detect corrupted frames that arrive from lower layers. Due to the severe operating environment and reduced transmission power, it is difficult to achieve high end-to-end link reliability compared to traditional wireless networks. In addition, the transport layer performs fragmentation of sender data and reassembly of received data frames.

Network Layer

The network layer's primary goals are to perform routing operations and self-configuration. It is responsible for link failures and provides regular updates to neighboring nodes. However, assuring network connectivity at all times is a major challenge due to dynamically changing network topology. The routing protocols in WSN are very different from traditional routing protocols because of the need to optimize network life by performing intelligent routing.

Data Link Layer

The data link layer is an interface between the network and physical layer. It is further subdivided into two modules: Medium Access Control (MAC) and Logical Link Control (LLC). The MAC module plays a critical role in conserving network life by efficiently allocating medium access to the contending nodes. The LLC is on top of the MAC layer and is responsible for cyclic redundancy check (CRC), sequencing information, and addition of appropriate source and destination information. The data link layer is also responsible for the multiplexing of data streams and data frame detection. So, with the preceding in mind: first create a network infrastructure, which includes establishing communication links between possibly thousands of nodes, and provides the network self-organizing capabilities. Second, the data link layer can fairly and efficiently share communication resources between all the nodes.

Physical Layer

The physical layer is responsible for converting digital bits into analog symbols and vice versa. It involves modulation and demodulation, frequency selection, power control, and symbol synchronization. WSNs usually operate in frequencies ranging from 915 MHz to 2.4 GHz. It is recommended using a lower-frequency band, as there is higher attenuation when operating in higher-frequency bands. However, with the limited availability of the bandwidth in the lower frequencies, the WSN is forced to operate at higher frequencies. The environment in which sensors are operating plays a major role in signal attenuation. Thus, sensors placed on the ground or floating on water experience greater attenuation and consequently require higher transmit power. The choice of modulation scheme is one of the prime factors in deciding the transmit power. The modulation scheme decides the bit error rate (BER), spectrum efficiency, and number of bits per symbol. For example, an M-ary modulation scheme is able to transmit more bits per symbol than other binary modulation schemes such as Phase Shift Keying (PSK). However, M-ary schemes result in higher BERs and require more transmit power than the binary modulation schemes. Hence binary modulation schemes are more applicable to WSN.

Mobility Plane

Sensor nodes can be fixed on moving objects such as animals, vehicles, and people, which will lead to a dynamic topology. In the event of some mobility by sensor nodes, the mobility in collaboration with the network layer is responsible for maintaining the list of active neighboring nodes. It is also responsible for interacting periodically with the mobility planes of other neighboring nodes, so that it can create and maintain a table of active, power-efficient routes.

Power Plane

The power plane focuses on the awareness of power at each horizontal and vertical layer. It is responsible for shutting off the sensors if they are not participating in any routing decisions or simply if the sensing activity is complete. The power planes of each node work collectively on deciding efficient routes to sink nodes and maintain the sleep/awake cycles of sensor nodes.

Task Management Plane

The task management plane is responsible for achieving a common goal. The goal is met by taking the properties of each layer and across each layer in a power-aware manner.

Vulnerabilities and Attacks on WSN

A taxonomy allows organizations to reason about attacks at a level higher than a simple list of vulnerabilities (see Figure 16.3). It provides a classification system that ideally suggests ways to mitigate attacks by prevention, detection, and recovery.

In general, attacks can be divided into active and passive attacks:

Passive Attack

In this type of attack, the attacker is able to intercept and monitor data between communicating nodes, but does not tamper or modify packets for fear of raising suspicion of malicious activity among the nodes. For example, in traffic analysis, the attacker may not be able to decode encrypted data, but can find useful information by analyzing headers of packets, their sizes, and the frequency of transmission. In WSN, reconnaissance can also be performed to understand information exchange between communicating nodes, particularly at data aggregation points. Furthermore, routing information can be exploited using traffic analysis.

Active Attack

In this type of attack, the attacker actively participates in all forms of communication (control and data) and may modify, delete, reorder, and replay messages or even send spoofed illicit messages to nodes in the network. Some other active attacks include node capturing, tampering with routing information, and resource exhaustion attacks. Peculiar to WSN, the attacker can modify the

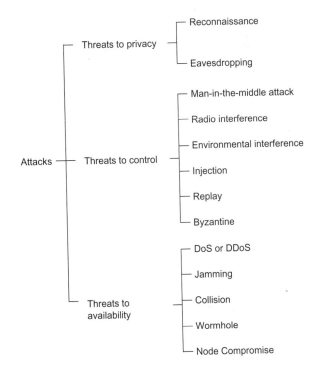

FIGURE 16.3 Taxonomy of attacks for WSN.

environment surrounding sensors, which could affect the sensed phenomena.

2. THREATS TO PRIVACY

In WSN, threats to privacy can be further classified into reconnaissance and eavesdropping.

Reconnaissance

Reconnaissance refers to intelligence gathering or probing to access the vulnerabilities in a network in order to launch a full-scale attack later. Reconnaissance attacks can be further classified into active and passive. Passive reconnaissance attacks include the collection of network information through indirect or direct methods, but without probing the target; active reconnaissance attacks involve the process of gathering traffic with the intention of eliciting responses from the target.

Eavesdropping

Eavesdropping is the act of listening secretly to a private conversation. However, in the paradigm of WSN, eavesdropping is an operation to learn the "aggregate data" that is being collected by the entire network. Hence, eavesdropping between two specific sensor nodes may not help the attacker in thoroughly understanding the entire network. It can be further classified into *active* and *passive* eavesdropping:

- *Active eavesdropping:* In this case, the adversary actively sends queries to other nodes in an attempt to goad them to respond to his queries, and in exchange will be able to comprehend the precise task assigned to the nodes in the network. Usually, the attacker launches a "man-in-the-middle attack" (discussed below) to infiltrate the network and enforce himself on the active path.
- *Passive eavesdropping:* The attacker inserts him- or herself into the active path, unbeknownst to other nodes in the network. He or she then passively listens to all traffic sent over the broadcast medium. It may be difficult to detect a passive eavesdropping attack, as the attacker may be operating in a stealth mode.

Threats to Control

The nodes in the network are unaware that the entire flow control is being handled by the attacker.

Man-in-the-Middle Attack

The man-in-the-middle attack is one of the classical attacks that can be executed in a WSN environment. In this type of attack, the attacker intrudes into the network and attempts to establish an independent connection between a set of nodes and the sink node. He can be in either a passive or an active state. In a passive state, he simply relays every message among the nodes with the intention of performing an eavesdropping attack. In an active state, he can tamper with the intercepted data in an effort to break authentication. In addition, the attack can be executed at the physical, data link, network, and application layers [1].

Radio Interference

With the increase in the number of wireless technologies using the same open spectrum band (2.4 GHz, 5 GHz, or 900 MHz), there is bound to be radio interference. For example, in a dense urban environment, where cordless phones share the same spectrum, radio interference can cause a sharp degradation of individual node performance. Similar problems can be projected for sensor networks with the increase in sensor nodes per network. The result of such interference could lead to change in the information bits transmitted over the wireless medium, thereby making the bits unintelligible and ultimately being dropped by the receiver [2]. Hence, radio interference could lead to a denial-of-service attack. The worst-case scenario in radio interference is jamming.

Injection Attack

After the attacker has clandestinely intruded into the WSN network, he may impersonate a few of the sensor nodes (or even sink nodes) and may inject malicious data into the network. The malicious data might be false advertisement of neighbor-node information to other nodes, leading to impersonation of sink nodes and aggregation of all data.

Replay Attack

A replay attack is a common attack in WSN, whereby an attacker is able to intercept user data and retransmit user data at a later time. This attack is particularly useful in breaking weak authentication schemes, which do not consider the time stamp when authenticating nodes. This attack is also useful during shared key-distribution processes.

Byzantine Attack

In a Byzantine attack, the outside adversary is able to take full control of a subset of authenticated nodes that can be further used to attack the network from inside. Such attacks by malicious behavior are known as Byzantine attacks. Some examples of Byzantine attacks are black holes, flood rushing, wormholes, and overlay network wormholes:

- *Black-hole attack*: In this type of attack, the attacker drops packets selectively, or all control and data packets that are routed through him. Therefore, any packet routed through this intermediate malicious node will suffer from partial or total data loss.
- *Flood rushing attack*: This type of attack is common to wireless networks and exploits the flood duplicate suppression technique. In this attack, the attacker attempts to overthrow the existing routing path by sending a flood of packets through an alternate route, which will result in discarding the legitimate route and adopting the adversarial route. Usual authentication schemes cannot prevent this attack, as the adversaries are authenticated nodes.
- *Wormhole attack:* In this type of attack, two conniving sensor nodes, or laptops, tunnel control and data packets between each other, with the intention of creating a shortcut in the WSN. Such a low-latency tunnel between the two conniving nodes will likely increase the probability of it being selected as an active path. This type of attack is very closely related to the sinkhole attack, because one of the conniving nodes could falsely advertise to be the sink node and thereby attract more traffic than usual. One of the main differences between a Byzantine wormhole and a traditional wormhole is that in a Byzantine wormhole, the tunnel exists between two compromised nodes, while in a traditional wormhole, two legitimate nodes are tricked into believing that a secure tunnel exists between them.
- *Byzantine overlay network wormhole attack:* This type of attack is a variant of the wormhole attack and occurs when the wormhole attack is extended to multiple sensor nodes; resulting in an overlay of compromised nodes. It provides a false illusion, to honest nodes, that they are surrounded by legitimate nodes, resulting in frequent reuse of the adversarial path.

Sybil Attack

The Sybil attack was first introduced by John R. Douceur while studying security in peer-to-peer networks [3], and later Karlof and Wagner showed that this type of attack poses a serious threat to routing mechanisms in WSN [4]. Sybil is an impersonation attack in which a malicious node masquerades as a set of nodes by claiming false identities, or generating new identities in the worst case [5]. Such attacks can be easily executed in a WSN environment because the nodes are invariably deployed in an unstructured and distributed environment, and communicate via radio transmission. They are especially detrimental in applications such as data aggregation, voting systems, reputation evaluation, and geographic routing. By using a Sybil attack in location-aware routing, it is possible to be in multiple locations at the same time.

Sinkhole Attack

In a sinkhole attack, the adversary impersonates a sink node and attracts the whole of traffic to a node or a set of nodes. Similar to a black-hole attack, the attacker takes control of a few compromised nodes and advertises false routing information to its neighbors, thereby luring all traffic to him.

Threats to Availability

Due to threats to the WSN, some portion of the network or some of the functionalities or services provided by the network could be damaged and unavailable to the participants of the network. For instance, some sensors could die earlier than their expected lifetimes. Thus, availability service ensures that the necessary functionalities or the services provided by the WSN are always carried out, even in the case of attacks.

Denial of Service (DoS) or DDoS

A denial-of-service attack occurs when an attacker floods the victim with bogus or spoofed packets with the intent of lowering the victim's response rate. In the worst-case scenario, it makes the victim totally unresponsive. For instance, in a WSN environment where nodes have limited computational capacity, a DoS attack from a resource-abundant adversary can overwhelm the nodes by flooding packets, which will exhaust communication bandwidth, memory, and processing power. From an attacker's point of view, this attack is also useful in wireless networks where nodes are required to deliver time-critical data. Jamming the wireless links can also lead to a DoS attack. An extension of a DoS attack is a distributed DoS attack, where an attacker takes control of a few nodes in the network, leading to a distributed flood attack against the victim.

HELLO Flood Attack

One of the common techniques for discovering neighbors is to send HELLO packets. If a node receives a HELLO packet, it indicates that it is within the range of communication. However, a laptop-class adversary could easily send HELLO packets with sufficient power to convince the sensor nodes that it is in proximity of communication and may be a potential neighbor. The adversary could also impersonate a sink node or a cluster node.

Jamming

Jamming is one of the most lethal types of attacks in WSN and is a direct way to compromise the entire wireless network. In this type of attack, the attacker jams a spectrum band with a powerful transmitter and prevents any member of the network in the affected area from transmitting or receiving any packet. Jamming attacks can be divided into constant jamming and sporadic jamming. Sporadic jamming can be very effective at times when a change in one bit of a data frame will force the receiver to drop it. In this kind of attack, it is difficult for the victim to identify whether his band is being jammed intentionally or due to channel interference; his immediate reaction is usually to increase his transmitting power, thereby depleting resources at a faster rate. Jamming attacks target the physical and MAC layers. Four types of jamming attacks (random, reactive, deceptive, and constant) would result in DoS attacks [6]. Xu et al. conclude that intrusion detection schemes can be very complex with reference to differentiating malicious attacks from link impairment.

Collision

Collision attacks target the MAC layer to create costly exponential backoff. Whenever collision occurs, the nodes should retransmit packets affected by collision, thus leading to multiple retransmissions. The amount of energy expended by the attacker is much less than the energy expended (battery exhaustion) by the sensor nodes. Collision attacks can be categorized under resource exhaustion attacks.

Node Compromise

Node compromise is one of the most common and detrimental attacks in WSN. As sensors can be deployed in harsh environments such as a battlefield, ocean bed, or the edge of an active volcano, they are easily susceptible to capture by a foreign agent. In the case of a battlefield scenario, the enemy could make an effort to dig into nodes with the intention of extracting useful data (extracting private keys in sensor nodes). Furthermore, it could be reprogrammed and launched into a battlefield to operate on behalf of the enemy.

Attacks Specific to WSN

Wireless sensor networks are vulnerable to eavesdropping problems as the data transmission highly depends on the assumption that the receiving node faithfully receives and forwards the same transmitted packet containing specified parameters. But during peer-to-peer communication the parameters may be spoofed, replaced, altered, repeated, or even diminished by the single frequency or intentional intruders who can easily analyze the traffic flow and fabricate new parameters containing wrong information and transmit them to the sink nodes.

Attacks on Beaconing Protocol

A beaconing protocol uses a breadth-first spanning tree algorithm to broadcast routing updates. The sink node periodically broadcasts updated routing information to its immediate neighboring nodes. These neighboring nodes then rebroadcast this information to their immediate neighbors, and the process continues recursively. During this process, each intermediate node makes a note of its parent node (the parent node is the first node that was able to make contact with its subordinate node and relay the routing information). When all the active nodes are operational, they should send all the sensed data to their parent node. However, this protocol is vulnerable to many attacks. For example, a simple impersonation attack, leading to a sinkhole attack, can totally compromise the entire network [4,7].

Authentication can be used to prevent such impersonation attacks, but it does not prevent a laptop-class adversary from launching a selective forwarding attack, an eavesdropping attack, or a black-hole attack. The attacker creates a wormhole between two conniving laptop-class adversaries. The two laptops are placed near the sink node and the targeted area, respectively. The laptop near the sink node attracts its entire neighbor's traffic and simply tunnels these authenticated messages to its colluder. The laptop attacker, close to the sink node, plays a passive role in forwarding these messages. Due to his furtive nature, it is difficult for his neighbors to detect whether he is malicious. Once the authenticated messages reach the remote laptop adversary, he could launch a black-hole attack or a selective forwarding attack.

Let us consider a situation in which digital signatures are being used for authentication and, while the routing updates are in progress, the sink node's private key is leaked. As soon as the sink node realizes that its private key is being compromised, it immediately broadcasts a new public key. All the nodes in close proximity to the sink node will update their local copy of the sink node's public key. The laptop close to the sink node will perform the same operation and convey this information to its colluding laptop. The remote laptop can now easily impersonate the sink node and launch a sinkhole attack. In addition, she can further create routing loops, which is a resource-exhaustion attack.

Attacks on Geographic- and Energy-Aware Routing (GEAR)

GEAR proposes a location- and energy-aware, recursive routing algorithm to address the problem of uneven energy consumption in routing in WSN. In GEAR, every node gauges the energy levels of its neighbors along with the distance from the target before making a routing decision. In such situations, a laptop-class attacker can advertise that he has larger energy levels than his neighboring node and attract all traffic to him. Thenceforth, he can execute a Sybil, black-hole, or selective forwarding attack.

As attacks on WSN become more sophisticated, the demand for new security solutions is continually increasing. Hence, an array of new security schemes have been designed and implemented in the past decade [8,9]. Most of these schemes have been designed to provide solutions on a layer-by-layer basis rather than on a per-attack basis; in doing so, they have left a gap between layers that may lead to cross-layer attacks.

In general, any security suite should ensure authentication, integrity, confidentiality, availability, access control, and nonrepudiation (see checklist: An Agenda for Action When Implementing a Security Suite). In addition, physical safety is absolutely necessary to avoid tampering or destruction of nodes.

Security in WSN Using a Layered Approach

Most researchers have come up with a security solution to WSN based on a layered approach. However, a layered approach has noticeable flaws such as redundant security or inflexible security solutions.

Security Measures in the Physical Layer

To prevent radio interference or jamming, the two common techniques used are frequency-hopping spread spectrum (FHSS) and direct-sequence spread spectrum (DSSS). In FHSS, the signal is modulated at frequencies such that it hops from one frequency to another in a random fashion at a fixed time interval. The transmitter and the corresponding receiver hop between frequencies using the same pseudorandom code for modulation and demodulation. If an eavesdropper intercepts a FHSS signal, unless she has prior knowledge of the spreading signal code, she will not be able to demodulate the signal. Furthermore, spreading the signal across multiple frequencies will considerably reduce interference.

In DSSS, a spreading code is used to map each data bit in the original signal to multiple bits in the transmitted signal. The pseudorandom code (spreading code) spreads the input data across a wider frequency range compared

---

An Agenda for Action when Implementing a Security Suite

A construction of tamper-resistant sensor nodes is absolutely necessary. However, such tamper-resistant schemes come at a higher manufacturing cost and are restricted to applications that are not only critical, but use fewer nodes; they should be able to do the following when implementing a security suite (check all tasks completed):

_____ 1. *Authentication:* The main objective of authentication is to prevent impersonation attacks. Hence, authentication can be defined as the process of assuring that the identity of the communicating entity is what it claims to be.

_____ 2. *Integrity:* The goal of integrity is to affirm that the data received is not altered by an interceptor during communication (by insertion, deletion, or replay of data) and is exactly as it was sent by the authorized sender. Usually, cryptographic methods such as digital signatures and hash values are used to provide data integrity.

_____ 3. *Confidentiality:* The goal of confidentiality is to protect the data from unauthorized disclosure. A common approach to achieving confidentiality is to encrypt user data.

_____ 4. *Availability:* The goal of availability is to ensure that the system (network) resources are available and usable by an authorized entity, upon its request. It tries to achieve survivability of the network at all times.

_____ 5. *Access control:* The goal of access control is to enforce access rights to all resources in its system. It tries to prevent unauthorized use of system and network resources. Access control is closely related to authentication attributes. It plays a major role in preventing leakage of information during a node-compromise attack. One of the conventional approaches to access control is to use threshold cryptography. This approach hides data by splitting it into a number of shares. To retrieve the final data, each share should be received through an authenticated process.

_____ 6. *Nonrepudiation:* Nonrepudiation can be best explained with an example. Let Alice and Bob be two nodes, who wish to communicate with each other. Let Alice send a message (M) to Bob. Later, Alice claims that she did not send any message to Bob. Hence, the question that arises is how Bob should be protected if Alice denies any involvement in any form of communication with Bob. Nonrepudiation aims to achieve protection against communicating entities that deny that they ever participated in any sort of communication with the victim.

to the input frequency. In the frequency domain, the output signals appear as noise. Since the pseudorandom code provides a wide bandwidth to the input data, it allows the signal power to drop down below the noise threshold without losing any information. Therefore, this technique is hard for an eavesdropper to detect, due to lower energy levels per frequency and more tolerance to interference. The above-mentioned schemes can provide security only as long as the hopping pattern or the spreading code is not disclosed to any adversary.

Security Measures in the Data Link Layer

Link-layer security plays an important role in providing hop-by-hop security. Its protocols are useful in handling fair channel access, neighbor-node discovery, and frame error control. Legacy security protocols such as Secure Socket Layer (SSL) or Internet Protocol Security (IPSec) cannot be applied directly to WSN because they do not provide data aggregation or allow in-network processing, which are prime requirements in designing security protocols.

To prevent denial-of-service (DoS) attacks on WSN, it is proposed that each intermediate node in the active routing path perform an authentication and integrity check. However, if a few intermediate nodes in the active path have very low energy levels, and if they are forced to perform authentication checks, they will expend all their energy and disrupt the active path. On the other hand, if we look at end-to-end authentication in WSN, it is more energy-efficient, since the sink node (resource-abundant) is the only node that performs authentication and integrity checks. Nevertheless, this scheme is vulnerable to many types of security attacks (black hole, selective forwarding, and eavesdropping). Hence there is a need for adaptive schemes that consider the energy levels of each node when deciding on the authentication schemes.

Early security approaches focused on symmetric keying techniques, and authentication was achieved using Message Authentication Code (MAC). One of the common MAC schemes is a cipher-block chaining message authentication code. However, this scheme is not secure for variable-length input messages. Hence the end user (sensor nodes) has to pad the input messages to be equal to a multiple of the block cipher. Therefore, each node has to waste energy, padding input data. To overcome this issue, other block cipher models such as CTR and OCB have been proposed. With reference to confidentiality, symmetric encryption schemes used to protect WSN are DES, AES, RC5, and Skipjack (block ciphers) and RC4 (a stream cipher). Usually, block ciphers are preferred to stream ciphers because they allow authentication and encryption.

A few proposed link-layer security frameworks include TinySec, Sensec, SNEP, MiniSec, SecureSense

[9,10], and ZigBee Alliance [11]. However, these schemes have limitations. For example, in TinySec a single key is manually programmed into all the sensor nodes in the network. A simple node-capture attack on any one of these nodes may result in the leakage of the secret key and the compromising of the entire network. A stronger keying mechanism is needed to secure TinySec. In addition, TinySec requires padding for input messages that are less than 8 bytes. It uses block cipher to encrypt messages, and for messages that are less than 8 bytes, the node will have to use extra energy to pad the message before encrypting.

3. SECURITY MEASURES FOR WSN

In all WSN applications, authentication and further encryption are fundamental security requirements and are useful in mitigating impersonation attacks. They are also useful in preventing the ever-increasing DoS and DDoS attacks on limited resource-constraint environments such as WSN.

Authentication

Three scenarios exist in WSN that require authenticated communication:

- Sink node to sensor nodes and vice versa
- Sensor node with other sensor nodes
- Outside user and sensor nodes

Most of the time critical applications in WSN require a message to be sent as promptly as possible. The intermediate nodes between the sender and receiver are responsible for relaying the message to the receiver. If one of the nodes is compromised, the malicious node can inject falsified packets into the network while routing messages. Such an act could lead to falsified distribution of such messages and, in turn, deplete the energy levels of other honest nodes. Hence, there is a need to filter messages as early as possible by authenticating every message, consequently conserving relaying energy.

In most WSN applications, the sensor nodes are expected to aggregate, process, store, and supply sensed data upon the end user's query. For example, in a military application, soldiers would require constant interaction with motion sensors that detect any movement along the border. In such situations, a large number of mobile or static end users could query the sensor nodes for sensed data. Usually, such interactions are realized through broadcast/multicast operations. Therefore, in such situations, a broadcast authentication mechanism is required before the query is sent. Furthermore, access control is also required, which would only allow the authorized user to access data to which he is entitled. Broadcast authentication was first addressed in μTESLA [9]. In this scheme, users are assumed to be a few trustworthy sink nodes. This scheme uses one-way hash functions, and the hash pre-images are used as keys to the Message Authentication Code (MAC) algorithm.

However, the messages are transmitted through a wireless medium, which consumes a considerable amount of time. In addition, the hop-by-hop routing nature of WSN further creates a delay in transmission. Hence, there is an increased need for rapid generation and verification of signature schemes.

The existing symmetric schemes such as μTESLA and its variants use Message Authentication Code (MAC) to gain efficiency in terms of processing and energy consumption. However, these symmetric schemes suffer from delayed authentication and sluggish performance for large-scale networks, and they are susceptible to DoS attacks due to late authentication. Furthermore, multiple senders cannot send authenticated broadcast messages simultaneously. For example, if a single node is interested in broadcasting a message, it would have to send a Unicast message to its respective sink node, which would then broadcast the message to all the other nodes on its behalf. Because of resource constraint, asymmetric schemes—for example, digital signatures that would require public key certificates—were pronounced inefficient. Hence, to address this problem, new avenues are being explored to introduce authentication in public-key cryptography in WSN [12].

Lightweight Private Key Infrastructure (PKI) for WSN

Although the applicability of PKI-based approaches has been deemed inappropriate for a resource-constraint environment such as WSN, security researchers have been proposing new lightweight PKI-based approaches for WSN. For instance, a simplified version of Secure Socket Layer (SSL) has been proposed in WSN [13]. Although this SSL version has a smaller overhead when compared to the usual SSL/TLS protocol, it is still not directly applicable to mobile sensor nodes because it would lead to increased communication and computational overhead. For instance, in an ad-hoc mobile sensor network, the nodes keep changing their location, and any change in their position would compel them to initiate the SSL protocol before informing their neighbors of their new location. In addition, schemes such as TinyPK have been designed that are in conjunction with TinySec and facilitate authentication and key agreement between sensor nodes [14]. However, TinyPK implements the Diffie-Hellman key-exchange protocol, which is susceptible to an active man-in-the-middle attack. Huang et al. [15]

proposed a hybrid architecture for authenticated key establishment of a session key between a leaf node and a sink node or an end user. This protocol leverages on the difference in the computational and communication capabilities between the leaf node and the resource-abundant device (sink node or end user). During the inception of the protocol, both parties exchange certificates issued by a certificate authority (CA) to extract each other's public keys. However, the corresponding private keys are discovered after both parties run the protocol. This step in this protocol can easily be exploited by an adversary by replaying a valid certificate that would result in a DoS attack. As a result, the nodes are forced to perform expensive computations and waste their resources and bandwidth. In addition, [16] showed a serious vulnerability in Huang et al.'s scheme wherein an end user can easily discover the long-term private key of a leaf node after having one normal run of the protocol.

To expunge the transmission of public key certificates, Ren, Lou, and Zhang [17] propose a Hybrid Authentication Scheme (HAS) for a multiuser broadcast authentication scheme in WSN. In this scheme, each sensor node is preloaded with the required public key information of the end user using the Bloom filter and Merkle hash tree [18,19]. However, HAS with the Merkle hash tree does not facilitate user scalability (a new user can only be added into the network after revocation of the old user).

Key Management in WSN

Recent advances in Integrated Circuit (IC) fabrication have led to the proliferation of wireless sensor networks, which comprise low-cost sensors with limited storage and processing power. WSNs have applicability in diverse fields, such as military, ocean, and wildlife monitoring; earthquake monitoring; safety monitoring in buildings; and in new smart home technology proposed by 4 G technologies. However, such networks deviate from the legacy-embedded wireless networks in terms of scalability, dynamic nature with regard to the addition or deletion of nodes, and deployment areas. Hence, there is a greater challenge in providing security by taking such harsh operational requirements into consideration. One such challenge is in the area of key distribution and its management. In addition, the lack of a-priori information about the topology of WSN makes key management fairly complex. Key distribution provides communication secrecy (confidentiality) and authentication among sensor nodes, and key revocation refers to the task of removing compromised keys from the network. Key distribution can be further divided into symmetric and asymmetric key-distribution protocols.

In recent years, considerable work has been done in proposing new symmetric key-distribution protocols in WSN, but less effort has been invested in the area of asymmetric key-distribution algorithms in WSN, which have low computational and storage requirements. Of late, significant work has been done to show the applicability of implementing binary-field algorithms on sensor nodes [20]. Consequently, such implementations have resulted in considerable reductions in computational time and memory access.

In general, key-distribution schemes in WSN can be broadly classified into four classes: symmetric key algorithms, trusted server mechanisms, random key-predistribution schemes, and public key algorithms. Later in this chapter, we review a few existing key-distribution schemes in WSN.

Symmetric Key Algorithms

In this class, a single shared key is used to perform the encryption and decryption operations in a communication network.

Fully Pairwise-Shared Keys

In this scheme, every node in the network shares a unique, preshared, symmetric key with every other node in the network. The keys are preloaded into the sensor nodes before deployment. Hence, in a network of n nodes, there would be a total of $n(n-1)/2$ unique keys. Subsequently, every node stores $n-1$ keys, one for each of the other nodes in the network. In this class of protocols, the compromise of a few sensor nodes will not result in the complete collapse of the entire network. However, the applicability of this approach in large sensor networks is not pragmatic, as each node would need to store $n-1$ keys, thus resulting in the rapid exhaustion of its limited memory space. In addition, nodes usually communicate with their immediate one-hop neighbors, thereby eliminating the need to establish unique keys with every node in the network. Although symmetric key algorithms are limited in terms of key distribution, they provide basic cryptographic primitives, which can be used in combination with asymmetric key cryptographic algorithms.

Trusted Server Mechanisms

In this category, key distribution is done via centralized trusted servers, which are usually static in nature. In WSN, the sink node or the base station can act as a key-distribution center (KDC). Usually, unique symmetric keys are shared between the sink node and the ordinary nodes. If two nodes were to communicate with each other, they would first authenticate with the base station,

after which the base station generates a link key and sends it securely to both parties.

An example of a base-station-mediated key-agreement protocol is the Security Protocol for Sensor Networks: SPINS [9]. Using this protocol, one can preload only one unique single key in every node of the network. Hence, a node capture will not result in the total compromise of the network. In addition, centralized revocation is possible through authenticated unicasts from the trusted base station. The main drawback of this scheme is that the trusted base station represents a single point of compromise for security information, and may also induce a focused communication load centered on the base station, which may lead to early battery exhaustion for the nodes closest to the base station. Another concern is that certain networks do not have a suitable, highly functional, and tamper-proof device that can be used as a secure KDC.

λ-Secure n × n Key-Establishment Schemes

Now let's address the problem of key distribution and key establishment [21,22] between all pairs of n principals. Although these schemes were originally intended for group keying in traditional networks, and not for sensor networks, they are included here because of their relevance to the development of subsequent key-distribution schemes for sensor networks. The schemes of both Blom and Blundo et al. have an important resiliency property— the λ-secure property: The coalition of no more than λ-compromised sensor nodes reveals nothing about the pairwise key between any two noncompromised nodes.

The main advantage of this class of schemes is that they allow a parameterizable trade-off between security and memory overhead. Whereas the full pairwise scheme involves the storage of $O(n)$ keys at each node and is n-secure, this class of schemes allows the storage of $O(\lambda)$ keys in return for a λ-secure property, and it is perfectly resilient to node compromise until $\lambda + 1$ nodes have been compromised, at which point the entire network's communications are compromised.

Random Key-Predistribution Schemes

In this method, keys are predistributed by preloading random keying material on sensor nodes with the intention of establishing a common secret key between the communicating entities. Upon deployment, these nodes carry out a lookup process to see if a shared key exists between them. As keys are preloaded in a random manner, a certain set of nodes may not share a common key with each other. In such cases, nodes could make use of their immediate neighbors who share keys as bridges between the nodes that do not share a common key. One of the early key-sharing algorithms using random graph theory was proposed by Eschenauer and Gligor [23].

Basic Random Key-Predistribution Scheme

In this scheme, let m denote the number of distinct cryptographic keys that can be stored on the key ring of a sensor node. This scheme is divided into three phases as follows.

Phase I: Key Predistribution

In this initialization phase, a random pool (set) of keys Q are picked from the total possible key space. In addition, for each node, m keys are randomly selected from the key pool Q and stored into the node's memory. Each of the m keys has identifiers that will be used to map the keys by the receiving nodes during the discovery phase of this scheme (discussed next). This set of m keys is called the node's key ring. The number of keys in the key pool $|Q|$ (key pool size) is chosen such that any two random subsets of size m in Q will share at least one key, with some probability p.

Phase II: Shared-Key Discovery

On deployment, neighboring sensor nodes begin the discovery process to find out if they share a common key with each other; if they do, then they establish a secure link. There could be many modes for the discovery phase, such as broadcasting the list of identifiers existing in their key ring in clear text or through a challenge-response mechanism. If the probability p were chosen correctly for the network's neighbor density, then the resultant graph of secure links would be connected with some high probability. The remaining links in the graph are then filled in by routing key-establishment messages, along this connected network of initial secure links. From a security perspective, although this approach does not reveal any important information to the adversary, it is still susceptible to a passive traffic analysis attack.

Phase III: Path-Key Establishment

Upon completing the discovery phase, if two nodes in the network discover that they do not share a key between them, they send an encrypted message to neighbors with whom they share a key, with a request to secure connection with the unshared node. This model assumes that after the completion of *Phase II*, there exist many keys in each key ring that can be used for third-party path-key establishment. Hence, the neighboring nodes generate pairwise keys for nodes that do not directly share a key.

Let us now find this probability p that any two nodes with key ring sizes m in the network share at least one common key from the pool Q. Let p' be the probability

that two nodes do not share a key between them. Then, p is defined as

$$p = 1 - p' \qquad (16.1)$$

In this case, keys from the key ring are drawn from Q without replacement. The total number of possible key rings t_1 is as follows:

$$t_1 = \frac{Q!}{m!(Q-m)!} \qquad (16.2)$$

Now, the total number of possible key rings that do not share a key with a particular key ring t_2 is the number of key rings drawn from the remaining Q-m unused keys in the pool:

$$t_2 = \frac{(Q-m)!}{m!(Q-2m)!} \qquad (16.3)$$

Then, the probability that no key is shared between any two rings is t_2/t_1. Hence, the probability p is

$$p = 1 - \frac{t_2}{t_1} = 1 - \frac{((Q-m)!)^2}{Q!(Q-2m)!} \qquad (16.4)$$

Usually, the value of p is very large in comparison to m, and using the Sterling's approximation for $n!$, the value of p is

$$p = 1 - \frac{\left(1 - \dfrac{m}{Q}\right)^{2(Q-m+0.5)}}{\left(1 - \dfrac{2m}{Q}\right)^{(Q-2m+0.5)}} \qquad (16.5)$$

Figure 16.4 shows the value of p for different values of Q and m. We observe that with the increase in Q, there is a negligible increase in the key ring size m for the same value of p. For example, for $p = 0.5$ and $Q = 6000$, the value of $m = 68$. Subsequently, if the pool size is increased to 10,000, for the same value of $p = 0.5$, m is only increased to 95.

In this scheme, all nodes use the same key pool Q. This implies that the security of the network is gradually eroded as keys from Q are compromised by an adversary that captures more and more nodes. In this scheme, the number of exposed keys is roughly linear to the number of nodes compromised. This characteristic of the basic scheme motivated development of key-predistribution schemes that have better resiliency to node capture. The basic scheme was extended by the q-composite scheme proposed by [24].

q-Composite Scheme

In a q-composite key scheme, instead of designing for a given probability p of sharing a single key, the parameters are altered such that any two nodes have a given probability p of sharing at least q different keys from the key

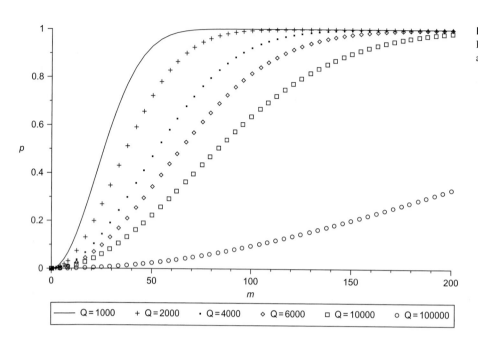

FIGURE 16.4 Probability of sharing at least one shared key using Eschenauer and Gligor's scheme.

pool. All q keys are used in the generation of the key, which encrypts communications between sensor nodes; hence, to eavesdrop on the secured link, the adversary now has to compromise all q keys, instead of just one. As q increases, it is exponentially harder for the attacker to break a link by taking possession of a given set. However, increasing the probability of overlap in this fashion naturally involves reducing the size of the key pool Q. Thus, the smaller key-pool size makes the scheme more vulnerable to an adversary that is capable of compromising larger numbers of sensor nodes.

The key-predistribution phase of this model is similar to *Phase I*, which is discussed later in the chapter, with the only exception being the key-pool size Q. In the shared key-discovery phase, each node must find nodes that share all common keys with each other. The discovery mechanism is similar to that of *Phase II*. Although a broadcast-based approach is susceptible to an eavesdropping attack, alternative methods that are slower but more secure are suggested where the nodes use the Merkle puzzle for key discovery [18]. After the discovery phase, each node would be able to recognize its immediate neighboring nodes with which it would share at least q keys. Subsequently, each node could establish a link between nodes that share at least q keys by hashing the keys in some canonical order. For example, $K = \text{hash}(k_1 \,||\, k_2 \,||\, k_3 \,||\, \ldots \,||\, k_q)$.

In this scheme, the key pool size $|Q|$ plays a critical role because with a larger Q, the probability of any two nodes sharing at least q keys would be much less. Consequently, after bootstrapping, the network may not be connected. On the contrary, if $|Q|$ is small, the security of the network is compromised. Hence, $|Q|$ should be such that the probability of sharing at least q key should be greater than or equal to the probability of successfully achieving a key setup with any of its neighbors. The approach used to calculate the probability of any two nodes sharing exactly i keys $p'(i)$ is similar to calculating p, as shown in Eq. (16.4), and is given as

$$p'(i) = \frac{\dbinom{|Q|}{i}\dbinom{|Q|-i}{2(m-i)}\dbinom{2(m-i)}{m-i}}{\dbinom{|Q|}{m}^2} \qquad (16.6)$$

For example, in Figure 16.5, we find the value of $|Q|$ for a given m and i. In this case, for $m = 200$ and $i = 10$, we achieve a maximum $p'(i)$ for $|Q| = 3900$.

In general, random key predistribution presents a desirable trade-off between the insecurity of using a single network-wide key and the impractical high memory overhead of using unique pairwise keys. Its main advantage is that it provides much lower memory overhead than the full pairwise key scheme, while being more resilient to node compromise than the single-network-wide key scheme. Furthermore, it is fully distributed and does not require a trusted base station. The main disadvantages of this approach are the probabilistic nature of the scheme, which makes it difficult to provide the guarantee of the initial graph of secure links being connected under nonuniform conditions or sparse deployments. Furthermore, since keys can be shared between a large number of nodes, this class of schemes does not provide very high resilience against node compromise and subsequent exposure of node keys.

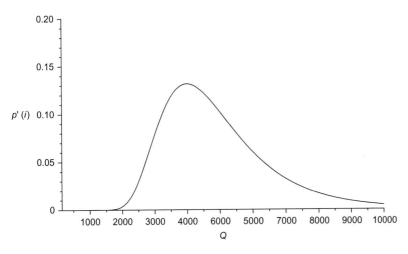

FIGURE 16.5   Key-pool set $|Q|$ selection based on $p'(i)$ for $m = 200$ and $i = 10$.

Random Pairwise Key Scheme

The random pairwise key scheme proposed by [24], is a hybrid of the random key-predistribution scheme and the full pairwise key scheme. In the analysis of random key predistribution, it was deduced that as long as any two nodes can form a secure link with at least a probability p, the entire network will be connected with secure links with high probability. Based on this observation, Chan noted that it is not necessary to perform full pairwise key distribution to achieve a network where any two nodes can find a secure pathway to each other. Instead of preloading $n - 1$ unique pairwise keys in each node, the random pairwise key scheme preloads $m \ll n$ unique pairwise keys from each node. The m keys of a key ring are a small, random subset of the $n - 1$ possible unique keys that this node could share with the other n nodes in the network. By using the same reasoning as the random key-predistribution scheme, as long as these m keys provide sufficient probability p of enabling any two neighboring nodes to establish a secure link, the resultant graph of initial secure links will have a high probability of being connected. The remaining links are then established using this initial graph exactly as in the random key-predistribution scheme.

Chan et al. (2003) present a preliminary initial distributed-node-revocation scheme that makes use of the fact that possessing unique pairwise keys allows nodes to perform node-to-node identity authentication. In their scheme, each of the m nodes that shares a unique pairwise key with the target node (the node's participants) carries a preloaded vote that it can use to signify a message that the target is compromised. These m votes form a Merkle hash tree with m leaves [18]. To vote against the target node, a node performs a network-wide broadcast of its vote (its leaf in the Merkle hash tree) along with the log m internal hash values, which will allow the other participants of the target to verify that this leaf value is part of

the Merkle hash tree. Once the t participants of a given target have voted, and the votes have been verified by the other m participants using the Merkle hash tree, all m nodes will erase any pairwise keys shared with the target, thus revoking it from the network.

The random pairwise key scheme inherits both strengths and weaknesses from the full pairwise key scheme and the random key-distribution scheme. Under the random pairwise key scheme, the nodes captured do not reveal information to the rest of the network, and central revocation can be accomplished by just unicasting to each of the nodes that share keys with the revoked node. It also involves a much lower memory overhead than the full pairwise keys scheme. Unfortunately, like the random key-predistribution schemes, it is probabilistic and cannot be guaranteed to work in nonuniform or sparse deployments.

Multispace Key Schemes

This class of schemes is a hybrid between random key predistribution and the λ-secure $n \times n$ key-establishment schemes. (These schemes were first proposed by [25].) Recall that in random key predistribution, a key pool is first selected from the universe of possible keys. Each sensor node is then preloaded with a set of keys from the key pool such that any two nodes possess some chosen probability p of sharing enough keys to form a secure link. Multispace key schemes use the same basic notion of random key predistribution but use key spaces, where individual keys are used in random key predistribution. Hence, the key pool is replaced by a pool of key spaces, and each node randomly selects a subset of key spaces from the pool of key spaces, such that any two nodes will have some common key space with probability p. Each key space represents a unique instance of a different λ-secure $n \times n$ key-establishment scheme [21]. If two nodes possess the same key space, they can then perform the relevant λ-secure $n \times n$ key-establishment scheme to generate a secure session key.

The main advantage of multispace schemes is that node compromise under these schemes reveals much less information to the adversary than occurs with the random key-predistribution schemes. However, they retain the disadvantage of being probabilistic in nature (no guarantee of success in nonuniform or sparse deployments). Furthermore, they experience the threshold-based sudden security failure mode that is a characteristic of the λ-secure schemes. Other schemes have combined λ-secure schemes with constructions other than random key-space selection. Liu and Ning [26], in particular, describe a deterministic grid-based construction in which key spaces are used to perform intermediary-based key establishment between nodes.

Deterministic Key-Predistribution Schemes

One drawback of the random key-distribution approach is that it does not guarantee success. [27], as well as [28], propose the use of combinatorial design techniques to allocate keys to nodes in such a way as to always ensure key sharing between any two nodes. The amount of memory required per node is typically some fractional power of the overall supported network size ($O(\sqrt{n})$). The main drawback of these schemes is that the same keys are shared between many nodes, leading to weaker resistance to node compromise. [24] have proposed a deterministic scheme using peer nodes as intermediaries in key establishments with similar memory overheads; compared with the combinatorial design approach, this scheme trades off increased communication cost for greater resistance against node compromise.

Public Key Algorithms

Although these algorithms are based on asymmetric key cryptography and are more resource intensive than symmetric key algorithms, they offer better security services, which are much needed and highly advantageous in WSN. As a result, there is motivation to pursue research in developing secure and efficient key-distribution mechanisms suitable in a resource-constraint environment such as WSN. Most of the implementations use Rivest, Shamir, Adleman (RSA) or elliptic curve cryptography (ECC) [12,20].

For example, TinyPK uses the Diffie-Hellman key-exchange technique for key agreement between nodes and is based on the legacy RSA cryptosystem. The main motive of this protocol is to facilitate secure communication between external users and the sensor networks. The external user's identity is established by a CA, where his or her public key is signed by the CA's private key.

Considering the state of the art in large-number factorization, key-size values are usually set to 1024 bits in RSA as lower values are considerably vulnerable to security attacks. In addition, the public key exponent e is set to 3, and all the resource-intensive operations are carried out on external servers. In this model, resource-abundant devices bear the burden of RSA private key operations, and, hence, the sensor nodes maintain higher energy levels during operations.

4. SECURE ROUTING IN WSN

Routing is one of the most fundamental operations in any network that attempts to ensure the delivery of messages from a source to a selected destination. It is a two-step method that involves the process of discovering a suitable route between the concerned source and its destination, and the forwarding of messages using this discovered route. In traditional networks (IP or 3 G networks), routing operations are dedicated to special nodes, such as routers. However, WSNs consist of resource-constraint devices operating in an ad-hoc decentralized manner that requires all the network operations to be done by these ordinary sensor nodes. Some real-time applications (remote-sensing operations) require the routing protocols to facilitate the timely delivery of messages. However, such applications are too resource intensive in WSN and require routing protocols that can balance the energy consumption of the entire network. Furthermore, the number of nodes operating in a WSN scenario is much larger than conventional networks. Consequently, there is a need for the mass production of low-cost nodes. However, with the increase in the number of sensor nodes to meet the current demand for sensor applications, construction of each node to be tamper resistant would be very expensive. As a result, nodes could be susceptible to a node-capture attack. Hence, routing protocols used in traditional networks cannot be applied directly to a resource-constraint environment such as WSN. As a result, new arrays of routing protocols have been designed for WSN [29].

5. ROUTING CLASSIFICATIONS IN WSN

Routing protocols in WSN can be classified by several criteria. Such criteria would be data centricity, location information, network layering and in-network processing, path redundancy, a Quality of Service (QoS) requirement, and network heterogeneity.

Datacentric Communication

Conventional networks such as IP networks use a node-centric routing model in which information is exchanged using a unique addressing scheme (IP version 4 or 6 or higher). Based on the route the query took to reach the destined node, each source node independently sends data via the shortest path to the concerned sink node. In contrast, a datacentric model is more focused on the aggregated data rather than on identifying the exact node's identifiers. Although the request/response scheme is similar in both of the models, the sink node or cluster head initiates a request for interested data and the responsible nodes respond with the requested data; they vary in the manner in which the nodes send data back to the sink node or cluster heads. The intermediate routing nodes inspect the data that is being sent to the sink node and perform some form of consolidation operation, such that the sink node receives aggregated data from different sources. Figures 16.6 and 16.7 illustrate the distinction between address-centric and datacentric models in WSN. Figure 16.6 shows the address-centric model in which two sources (nodes C and E) send information to the sink node via the shortest path. Node C sends via node A, and node E sends via nodes D and B.

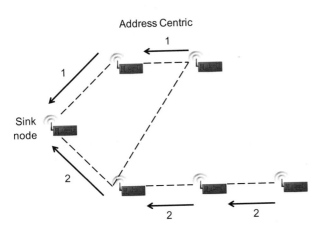

FIGURE 16.6   Address-Centric communication in WSN.

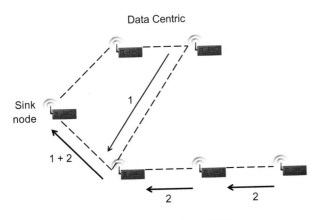

FIGURE 16.7   Datacentric communication in WSN.

In contrast, Figure 16.7 shows the datacentric model in which data from node C is directly sent to node B for consolidation, and, subsequently, the aggregated data is sent to the sink node. In cases where node C cannot directly contact node B, an intermediate node closer to node B is responsible for forwarding the data to node B. On comparing both models, the datacentric model is more energy efficient because only four messages are utilized in sending information from two different sources to the sink node, as opposed to five messages in the address-centric model (Figure 16.6).

Location Information

The physical location of a node in a network is an essential metric for designing routing protocols in a WSN. For example, the protocols could be designed for short- or long-range communication, depending on the position of the nodes. In addition, the positions of the nodes influence the design of the forwarding mechanism, which, in turn, affects the overall energy consumption of the system. In situations in which routing tables or global knowledge of the network is not required, location-based routing could be useful from a scalability point of view. However, one of the major challenges with such networks is that each node should be aware of its position with reference to the sink node. Additionally, the use of Global Positioning System (GPS)-based chips could weigh heavily on the limited resources available in a sensor-network environment, leading to an increase in the price and energy consumption of the system.

Network Layering and In-Network Processing

The architecture of a network could be flat, in the sense that all sensors have the same role. In other words, all sensors forward their sensed data to the sink without necessarily passing through a particular node. A network is said to be *nonlayered* if all sensors form only one group in which the sensors collaborate to accomplish a common monitoring task. On the other hand, the sensors in a network can be grouped into *clusters*, each of which is managed by a specific sensor called a *cluster head*. These types of networks are considered to be *layered*, and, any sensed data should pass through one or more cluster heads before reaching the sink. These cluster heads are supposed to be powerful enough to process the data they receive before sending it to the sink.

All other sensors only need to sense the environment and send their data to the cluster heads for further processing. In some sensing applications, redundancy and correlation exist in the gathered data. Hence, it would be desirable to only transmit more representative data. For example, in monitoring the temperature of a room, the variation in the data within a given region is expected to be small. Thus, the sink is not interested in receiving all the temperature measures, but rather only some of them. This can significantly reduce the communication overhead introduced by data forwarding and improve network performance. In addition, the concept of layering makes a network more scalable and leads to more efficient usage of the energy of sensors, thus extending the network's lifetime.

Extending the network's lifetime is an ultimate goal in the design of a WSN. Given that most of the energy of a sensor is mainly consumed in processing, sensing, and communication, an efficient design approach should take into account these three components of energy consumption. A question that network designers are mostly concerned about is, *How can the lifetime of a network be extended?* To address this problem, several energy-efficient routing and data-dissemination protocols have been proposed that focus on how to forward the data until they reach the sink, regardless of the type of data being transmitted from the source sensors to the sink. Among those protocols, one class does not update the data at the intermediate sensors. That is, each intermediate sensor only acts as a pure data relay without altering any of the data it has received. Another class of protocols introduces the concept of *in-network processing* to handle unnecessary redundancy and correlation contained in the sensed data.

In many applications, the data sensed by the sensors has a certain amount of redundancy and correlation. It would be desirable if the sink could only receive relevant data, for faster and better decision making. For this purpose, the sensed data should be processed at intermediate sensors before reaching the sink. The benefit of this in-network processing, such as data fusion, can be seen when vector data rather than scalar data are being transmitted. For example, in an application monitoring the temperature of a room, the sensed data is scalar (integer or real values). Hence, the cost of data communication is not very high, and the data fusion or aggregation is not as costly. But continuously sending unnecessary and redundant data will consume a huge amount of energy. If a sensing application has to send a large amount of data, for example, images, to the sink for further analysis and processing, it would consume a huge amount of energy. In this case, it would be more beneficial if those images, sensed by different sensors, could be aggregated and only a few of them sent. However, it is also true that processing those images for data fusion requires a considerable amount of energy. Moreover, there will be a delay due to the processing of those images. Therefore, there is a trade-off between data communication and fusion, in these types of information-intensive networks, where the sensed data is not scalar but rather vector.

Path Redundancy

The design of WSN not only should consider scalability and energy efficiency but should also be robust in nature, which means that a network remains operational despite the occurrence of sensor-node and link failures. The reasons for the failure could be intentional (security attack) or unintentional (defective node or natural calamity). One of the approaches to make the system more robust is to incorporate multipath routing. In short, multipath routing implies the existence of multiple paths (disjoint or partially disjoint) between source node and destination sensors (cluster heads or sink node) [30].

Although maintaining alternate paths in a routing table introduces some overhead and consumes more energy, multipath routing is an effective technique to improve robustness when link failures occur. Link failures could occur for many different reasons, such as frequent topological changes due to unreliable wireless communication links. Moreover, multipath routing enables recovery from sensor and link failures and provides the necessary resilience to the network at the cost of excessive redundancy.

Quality of Service (QoS)

WSN applications have varied requirements that are usually expressed in terms of some metrics, such as delay, fault tolerance, and reliability. For example, real-time applications (video surveillance) are dependent on delay bounds.

Hence, for such applications, the sensed data must reach the sink within a certain time. In addition, a desired property of WSN applications is fault tolerance, which means that a network should remain functional in the event of sensor or link failures. Another desired property is reliability, wherein the aggregated data should be received by the sink, as correctly as possible. This would ensure accurate decision making by the sink node. However, metrics such as fault tolerance and reliability necessitate the deployment of additional sensors, yielding additional energy consumption, so that the network can recover swiftly and deliver accurate sensed data to the sink, despite some sensor or link failures. Hence, routing and data-dissemination protocols should consider the trade-offs between fault tolerance, reliability, energy, and delay. Recall that energy is a constraint that should be considered by any routing and data-dissemination protocol to guarantee efficient usage of the amount of energy available at each sensor.

Network Dynamics

Requirements such as limited-energy use (discussed previously) and goals such as mobility have had direct impact on the design decisions of WSN network topology. In theory, a deterministic sensor deployment approach would provide even coverage of the area that has to be sensed. In addition, this approach would require fewer sensor nodes for accomplishing the required sensing task. However, in a real environment with an uneven terrain, it can be extremely challenging to apply a deterministic sensor deployment strategy. As a result, we are only left with the option of distributing the nodes in a random fashion. Consequently, not all areas of the sensing region are evenly covered by the sensors, thus leading to a coverage hole. In addition, there is a possibility of not all sensor nodes in the network being connected with each other or even with the sink node. In such situations, mobility plays an important role and becomes the main source of network dynamics that can be used to solve problems. In any sensor network, the aggregated data will be transmitted over some established paths between the source sensors and the cluster heads or sink node. And the establishment of optimal paths depends on whether the sensors are static or mobile. Hence, routing and data-dissemination protocols can be classified based on whether a network is static or dynamic.

In a static network, every node in the network is static—that is, both the sensors and the sink node remain in their fixed positions during their collaborative operation of monitoring a physical environment. Therefore, there is not much overhead required to maintain routes between the sensors and the sink and between the sensors themselves. In particular, the positions of the sensors and the sink can be learned before data exchange by exchanging some control messages. In certain cases, if the terrain is familiar, node positions can be preconfigured in nodes before deployment. Furthermore, neighbors of a given sensor do not change unless a new sensor has joined the network or an existing sensor has left the network, either by its own will or because of exhaustion of its battery life.

In a mobile network, either the sensors or the sinks or cluster heads are moving. As a result, the routes between the sensors and the sink are changing frequently in such a dynamic environment. Hence, a currently active route could at any time become inactive. This route instability would result in additional overhead and delay in discovering valid routes for data transmission and forwarding. To overcome this drawback, routing algorithms have been proposed in which the ordinary sensors and sinks are designed to be static, whereas certain relay nodes such as cluster heads could be mobile. One such example is the mobile ubiquitous LAN extensions (MULES)-based architecture [31].

In conclusion, the need for mobility in WSN is application dependent. For example, in applications that measure temperature, humidity, sound, or light in an enclosed area, there is no need to have mobile sensors or a mobile sink. However, in monitoring a moving object in a battle-field environment, or in monitoring endangered species, there is a need for mobile sensors in the network to efficiently track the object. In such scenarios, it has been observed that the use of mobile relays helps increase the lifetime of a WSN.

Network Heterogeneity

Early research on sensor networks focused on homogeneous network architecture. However, recently heterogeneous sensor networks have experienced increasing popularity because they significantly increase the lifetime and reliability of the system. A heterogeneous sensor network usually consists of a large number of low-cost nodes for the sensing operation and a few resource-abundant nodes that primarily perform data filtering, aggregation, and transport operations. Although heterogeneous networks have gained precedence over homogeneous networks, the efficient realization of heterogeneity in a sensor network requires prior systematic planning for placing these heterogeneous resources in a resource-aware manner [32].

Routing Protocols in WSN

Routing in ad-hoc networks has been very challenging owing to node mobility. Hence, a routing path established in the beginning between the source and the destination may not exist at a later time interval. Furthermore, in a resource-constraint environment such as WSN, the energy levels of the intermediate nodes must be considered in making routing decisions.

Routing protocols in WSN can be broadly classified into proactive, reactive, hybrid, and location-aware routing protocols [33]. In a proactive routing scheme, each node maintains an up-to-date routing table by frequently querying its immediate neighbors for routing information. An example of such a scheme is the Destination Sequenced Distance Vector (DSDV) routing protocol [34]. However, one of the major drawbacks of such schemes is the additional overhead due to frequent routing updates. In contrast, reactive routing involves on-the-fly route establishment and is demand driven. It is based on a request−response model. The initial discovery phase, to find the destined node, could involve flooding, and the response phase establishes the transient active routing path. Examples include Ad-hoc On-Demand Distance Vector (AODV) routing and Dynamic Source Routing (DSR) [35,36].

Various hybrid protocols use the node-discovery method of the proactive routing protocol, along with the on-the-fly routing-path establishment method to produce a hybrid version of the protocol. The Zone Routing Protocol (ZRP) is an example of such a hybrid scheme [37]. In position-aware routing protocols, the nodes select the geographically closest neighboring node when making routing decisions. An example of such a protocol is the Geographic- and Energy-Aware Routing (GEAR) protocol [38]. However, GEAR does not take security into consideration. Most of the security schemes in WSN have focused on symmetric-key cryptography, due to the notion that asymmetric-key cryptography (RSA-based algorithms) was computationally intensive. However, symmetric-key cryptography has major drawbacks with regard to key management, and the security is based on preshared secret keys. With the successful implementation of pairing-based cryptographic algorithms in WSN, a new platform is provided to implement asymmetric-key cryptographic schemes in WSN [20].

Selective-Forwarding Attack in WSN

Many routing protocols in WSN use a breadth-first spanning-tree algorithm to broadcast routing updates [5,39]. The sink node periodically broadcasts updated routing information to its immediate cluster heads. Then, these cluster heads re-broadcast this information to their immediate neighbors, and the process continues recursively. During this process, each intermediate node makes a note of its parent node, where the parent node is the first node that was able to make contact with its subordinate node and relay the routing information. When all the active nodes are operational, they should send all the sensed data to their parent node. However, this protocol is vulnerable to many attacks.

Cross-Layer Design Approach in WSN

Recently, a flurry of cross-layer design schemes have been proposed in WSN. As the fusion of secure networking and wireless communication occupies center stage in sensor networks, the traditional layered protocol architecture on which most of the networks form their basis has come under scrutiny. Although the layered approach has been repeatedly used in wired networks, it has been argued that the same approach cannot be directly applied in resource-constraint, wireless ad-hoc networks such as WSN. To combat this approach, security researchers have proposed several cross-layer design schemes in an ad-hoc environment [40]. Unlike the layering approach, where protocols at each layer are designed independently, cross-layer designs aim at exploiting the dependence between different protocol layers to achieve maximum performance gains. In the current state of the art in the paradigm of cross-layer design schemes in ad-hoc wireless networks, several diverse interpretations exist. One of the main reasons for such varied explanations is that the design effort is largely dominated by researchers who have made independent efforts in designing different layers of the stack. Many of the cross-layer designs depend on other cross-layer designs and hence raise the fundamental question of the coexistence of different cross-layer design proposals. In addition, the question of time synchronization between various cross-layer schemes and the roles each layer of the stack plays is an active area of research. The wireless medium allows richer modalities of communication than wired networks. For example, nodes can make use of the inherent broadcast nature of the wireless medium and cooperate with each other.

Employing modalities such as node cooperation in protocol design also calls for cross-layer design. The goal of designing security solutions with a cross-layer design approach takes us to a new paradigm of security research. The main objective of security solutions in a network is to provide security services such as authentication, integrity, confidentiality, and availability to the users. In wireless ad-hoc networks, due to the unreliable nature of the shared radio medium, attackers can launch varying attacks, ranging from passive reconnaissance attacks to active man-in-the-middle attacks. Routing in WSN is hop by hop and assumes a trusted, cooperative environment as intermediate nodes act as relays. However, compromised intermediate nodes can launch varying routing attacks, such as black-hole, wormhole, flood rushing, and selective-forwarding attacks. In this part of the chapter, we review the existing state of the art in the cross-layer design from a security perspective. In addition, as an example, we look at a cross-layer key-distribution mechanism.

In recent times, several cross-layer design schemes have been proposed. Cross-layer feedback optimization could be implemented on the sink or the sensor nodes. The cross-layer interactions among the layers can be categorized in different ways. For example, lower to upper (violation in the flow control from bottom to top), upper to lower (violation in the flow control from top to bottom), and lower and upper. In all these cases, new interfaces will be created between layers. In addition, cross-layer designs can be categorized by the integration of adjacent layers, design coupling without interfaces, and horizontal calibrations.

Lower to Upper

The requirement of information from the lower layer to the upper layer at runtime results in the creation of a new interface between these two layers. In this case, the lower layers update necessary information to the appropriate upper layers via the interface. For example, the data link layer is made aware of the transmit power, and the bit error rate information by the physical layer so that it can adjust its error-correction mechanism. Subsequently, the transport layer can inform the application layer about the TCP packet loss, as it would help the upper layer in the stack (application layer) to adjust its transmitting rate. In addition, it should be noted that self-adaptation loops should not be part of a cross-layer design approach, as they do not require new interfaces to be created between the necessary lower and upper layers. For example, in an auto-rate fallback mechanism for rate selection in a wireless networking environment with multirate physical layers, the Medium Authentication Code (MAC) layer rate selection is dependent on the received acknowledgment that is observable at the MAC layer. Hence, this mechanism would not qualify as a cross-layer design approach as there is no need to create new interfaces for rate adoption.

Upper to Lower

The upper layers provide updated information to the necessary lower layers via an interface. For example, if the application layer senses a delay or loss of data, a direct notification to the data link layer by the application layer would help adapt its error correction mechanism. In addition, delay sensitive packets could be treated with priority. As proposed by Larzon, Bodin, and Schelen [41], lower-to-upper information flow is treated as notifications (the lower layer notifies the upper layer about the underlying network condition), whereas the upper-to-lower information flow is treated as hints (upper layers provide hints to the lower layers on the means to process application data).

Lower and Upper

In this case, both the upper and lower layers are at liberty to transmit notifications about their current state and send queries to the other layers. During runtime, layers executing different tasks can collaborate with each other on an iterative loop basis, resulting in a back and forth communication between them. For example, a back and forth information flow between layers is seen in a proposal to solve the multiple access problem for contention-based wireless ad-hoc networks using joint scheduling and suggesting a distributed power-control algorithm for such networks [42]. In addition, direct communication between layers at runtime could indicate the advantage of making the variables at each layer visible to the other layers of the stack. However, one disadvantage of this approach

would be in managing the shared memory spaces between the layers when variables and internal states are shared between different layers.

Integration of Adjacent Layers

The formation of a super-layer by combining two or more adjacent layers would result in a new cross-layer design scheme. The resulting layer would simply provide the union of the services that were provided by the individual layers. For example, a collaborative design of the data-link and physical layer would suffice to produce a super-layer. From a network security perspective, a super-layer that combines network and data link layer would help prevent advanced Address Resolution Protocol (ARP) poisoning attacks.

Design Coupling without Interfaces

Coupling two or more layers during the design phase would avoid creating extra interfaces at runtime that could result in a new cross-layer design approach. However, in deployed networks, one of the architectural challenges would be to integrate the coupled layer with already-existing fixed layers.

Vertical and Horizontal Calibration across Layers

Vertical calibration: Vertical calibration refers to the efficient utilization of parameters across different layers of the vertical stack. The parameters set at the application level could dictate terms to the lower layers and vice versa. For example, the transport protocol (TCP or UDP) chosen at the transport layer would assert reliable or unreliable communication and would directly affect the layers below it. Consequently, the joint adjustment at different layers of the vertical stack would result in a more holistic performance of the system than the adjustment of individual parameters.

Horizontal Calibration

Horizontal calibration could be very useful in a resource-constraint environment such WSN. In this case, not only individual parameters pertaining to that layer are taken into consideration, but parameters pertaining to other compatriot layers are also considered. For example, while routing packets, if the network level state of intermediate nodes is taken into consideration, it would be easy to detect nonactive nodes and could subsequently result in an energy-efficient routing protocol. However, challenges do exist in case the participating nodes do not adhere to the same cross-layer approach as the initiating node.

6. WSN SECURITY FRAMEWORK AND STANDARDS

The standardization of wireless sensor networks proceeds along two main directives: the IEEE 802.15.4 standard [43] and ZigBee [11]. The IEEE 802.15.4 standard defines the physical and Medium access control (MAC) layers, and ZigBee defines the network and application layers. In WSN implementations, the two protocol stacks can be combined to provide low data rate and long-lasting applications on battery-powered wireless devices.

IEEE 802.15.4

The IEEE 802.15.4 MAC layer provides marginal support for security, and the advanced security features (key management and authentication) are the responsibility of the upper layers in the WSN protocol stack. In addition, the MAC layer security services assume that the keys are generated, transmitted, and stored by the upper layers in a secure manner.

The security services provided by the MAC layer include access control, data encryption, frame integrity, and sequential freshness. It should be noted that the security features of the MAC layer are optional and that the use of this feature is at the discretion of the applications existing on the application layer.

ZigBee

The ZigBee Alliance is an association of companies working together to develop standards (and products) for reliable, cost-effective, low-power wireless networking [2]. ZigBee is an emerging technology and is being used in a wide range of products and applications across consumer, commercial, industrial, and government markets worldwide. It builds upon the IEEE 802.15.4 standard described previously. The ZigBee specifications provide authentication, data freshness, message integrity, and encryption:

- *Authentication:* Network-level authentication is achieved by using a common network key. This prevents outsider attacks while adding very little in memory cost. Device level authentication is achieved by using unique link keys between pairs of devices. This prevents insider and outsider attacks but has higher memory cost.
- *Freshness:* ZigBee devices use incoming and outgoing freshness counters to maintain data freshness. These counters are reset every time a new key is created. Devices that communicate once per second will not overflow their freshness counters for 136 years.
- *Message Integrity:* ZigBee specifications provide the options of providing 0-, 32-, 64- or 128-bit data integrity for the transmitted messages. The default is 64-bit integrity.
- *Encryption:* ZigBee uses 128-bit Advanced Encryption Standard (AES) encryption. Encryption protection is possible at the network or device level. Network-level encryption is achieved by using a common network key. Device-level encryption is achieved by using unique link keys between pairs of devices. Encryption can be turned off without impacting freshness, integrity, or authentication, as some applications may not need any encryption.

The closest competitor to ZigBee in personal area network technology is Bluetooth. Although Bluetooth claims a much faster data rate (1 Mbps vs. 250 kbps), ZigBee specifies a longer transmission range and is specifically designed for low-power consumption. If Bluetooth is used in modular robotics applications, it requires a central coordinator and is limited to small networks. However, ZigBee does not have this limitation.

7. SUMMARY

Organizations and individuals benefit when wireless sensor networks and devices are protected. After assessing the risks associated with wireless sensor network technologies, organizations can reduce the risks by applying countermeasures to address specific threats and vulnerabilities. These countermeasures include management, operational, and technical controls. While these countermeasures will not prevent all penetrations and adverse events, they can be effective in reducing many of the common risks associated with wireless sensor networks technology.

Finally, let's move on to the real interactive part of this chapter: review questions/exercises, hands-on projects, case projects, and optional team case project. The answers and/or solutions by chapter can be found in the Online Instructor's Solutions Manual.

CHAPTER REVIEW QUESTIONS/EXERCISES
True/False

1. True or False? Although WSNs have gained a little popularity, there are some serious limitations when implementing security.
2. True or False? WSNs operate in a resource-constrained environment and therefore deviate from the traditional Open System Interconnection (OSI) model.
3. True or False? In WSN, threats to privacy can be further classified into reconnaissance.

4. True or False? The man-in-the-middle attack is not one of the classical attacks that can be executed in a WSN environment.
5. True or False? Due to threats to the WSN, some portion of the network or some of the functionalities or services provided by the network could be damaged and available to the participants of the network.

Multiple Choice

1. The middle layer provides one of the following for applications existing in the upper layers:
   A. RC 4 stream cipher
   B. Temporal Key Integrity Protocol (TKIP)
   C. Application programming interface
   D. Message Integrity Code (MIC)
   E. Extensible Authentication Protocol (EAP) framework
2. Which of the following is responsible for flow and congestion control?
   A. Middle layer
   B. Network layer
   C. Transport layer
   D. Data link layer
   E. All of the above
3. What allows organizations to reason about attacks at a level higher than a simple list of vulnerabilities?
   A. Secure on-demand routing protocol
   B. Taxonomy
   C. Message Authentication Code (MAC)
   D. Authenticated Routing for Ad hoc Networks (ARAN)
   E. Destination-Sequenced Distance Vector (DSDV) routing
4. In what type of attack is the attacker able to intercept and monitor data between communicating nodes, but does not tamper or modify packets for fear of raising suspicion of malicious activity among the nodes?
   A. Active attack
   B. Privacy attack
   C. Eavesdropping attack
   D. Man-in-the-middle attack
   E. Passive attack
5. What occurs when an attacker floods the victim with bogus or spoofed packets with the intent of lowering the response rate of the victim?
   A. HELLO flood attack
   B. Denial-of-service attack
   C. Sinkhole attack
   D. Sybil attack
   E. All of the above

EXERCISE

Problem

What is wireless sensor networking data acquisition?

Hands-On Projects

Project

What is the difference between the Wi-Fi NI CompactDAQ chassis and a wireless sensor node?

Case Projects

Problem

How do you add wireless sensors to your hard-wired security system?

Optional Team Case Project

Problem

How do you install window sensors for a wireless burglar alarm?

REFERENCES

[1] M. Anand, G. Ives, I. Lee. Quantifying Eavesdropping Vulnerability in Sensor Networks. Departmental papers, Department of Computer and Information Science, University of Pennsylvania, 2005.
[2] W. Xu, W. Trappe, Y. Zhang, T. Wood, in: Proceedings of the Sixth ACM International Symposium on Mobile Ad Hoc Networking and Computing (MobiHoc '05). ACM, 2005, pp. 48–57.
[3] J.R. Douceur, The sybil attack. in: First International Workshop on Peer-to-Peer Systems (IPTPS '02), 2002.
[4] C. Karlof, D. Wagner, Secure Routing in Wireless Sensor Networks: Attacks and Countermeasures. First International Workshop on Sensor Network Protocols and Applications. IEEE, 2003, pp. 113–127.
[5] J. Newsome, E. Shi, D. Song, A. Perrig. The sybil attack in sensor networks: analysis & defenses. Third International Symposium on Information Processing in Sensor Networks, IPSN. IEEE, 2004, pp. 259–268.
[6] W. Xu, W. Trappe, Y. Zhang, Defending wireless sensor networks from radio interference through channel adaptation, ACM Trans. Sensor Network 4(4), 18–34.
[7] Sun Zheng, Xiao-guang Zhang, Hui Li, Anqi Li. The application of TinyOS beaconing WSN routing protocol in mine safety monitoring. International Conference on Mechtronic and Embedded Systems and Applications, MESA. IEEE, 2008, pp. 415–419.
[8] M. Healy, T. Newe, E. Lewis Security for wireless sensor networks: a review. SAS 2009 – IEEE Sensors Applications Symposium. IEEE, 2009, pp. 80–85.

[9] A. Perrig, R. Szewczyk, J. Tygar, V. Wen, D. Culler, SPINS: Security protocols for sensor, Wireless Networks 8 (5) (2002) 521–534.

[10] C. Karlof, N. Sastry, D. Wagner. TinySec: A Lnk Layer Security Architecture for Wireless Sensor Networks. Second ACM Conference on Embedded Networked Sensor Systems. ACM, 2004, pp. 162–175.

[11] Z. Alliance, Zigbee Specification, 2013. <http://www.zigbee.org/Specifications.aspx>.

[12] H. Kupwade Patil, S.A. Szygneda, Security for Wireless Sensor Networks Using Identity-Based Cryptography, CRC Press, 2012.

[13] A.S. Wander, N. Gura, H. Eberle, V. Gupta, S.C. Shantz. Energy analysis of public-key cryptography for wireless sensor networks. Third IEEE International Conference on Pervasive Computing and Communications. IEEE, 2005, pp. 324–328.

[14] R. Watro, D. Kong, S. Cuti, C. Gardiner, C. Lynn, P. Kruus. TinyPK: securing sensor networks with public key technology. 2nd ACM Workshop on Security of ad hoc and Sensor Networks. ACM, 2004, pp. 59–64.

[15] Q. Huang, J. Cukier, H. Kobayashi, B. Liu, J. Zhang. Fast Authenticated Key Establishment Protocols for Organizing Sensor Networks. Workshop on Sensor Networks and Applications (WSNA). ACM, 2003, pp. 141–150.

[16] X. Tian, D. Wong, R. Zhu., Analysis and improvement of an authenticated key exchange protocol for sensor networks, *Commun. Lett.* (IEEE) 9 (11) (2005) 970–972.

[17] K. Ren, W. Lou, Y. Zhang, Multi-user broadcast authentication in wireless sensor networks. Proceedings of Sensor, Mesh and Ad Hoc Communications and Networks. IEEE, 2012, pp. 223–232.

[18] R.C. Merkle, Protocols for public key cryptosystems. Symposium on Security and Privacy. IEEE, 1980, pp. 122–134.

[19] M. Mitzenmacher, Compressed bloom filters. Edited by ACM. Transactions on Networking 10 (5) (2002) 604–612.

[20] D. Aranha, R. Dahab, J. López, L. Oliveira, Efficient implementation of elliptic curve cryptography in wireless sensors, Adv. Math. Commun. 4 (2) (2010) 169–187.

[21] R. Blom, An optimal class of symmetric key generation systems. Advances in Cryptology: Proceedings of Eurocrypt '84, 1984, pp. 335–338.

[22] C. Blundo, A.D. Santis, A. Herzberg, S. Kutten, Perfectly-secure key distribution for dynamic conferences, Advances in Cryptology—Crypto '92, Springer-Verlag, Berlin, 1992471–486.

[23] L. Eschenauer, V.D. Gligor. A key management scheme for distributed sensor networks. Proceedings of the 9th ACM Conference on Computer and Communication Security. ACM, 2002.

[24] C. Perrig, D. Song. Random key pre-distribution schemes for sensor networks. Proceedings of the 2003 IEEE Symposium on Security and Privacy. IEEE, 2003, pp. 197–213.

[25] W. Du, J. Deng, Y. Han, P. Varshney. A pairwise key pre-distribution scheme for wireless sensor networks. Proceedings of the Tenth ACM Conference on Computer and Communications Security (CCS 2003). ACM, 2003, pp. 42–51.

[26] D. Liu, P. Ning. Establishing pairwise keys in distributed sensor networks, Proceedings of the 10th ACM Conference on Computer and Communications Security (CCS 2003). ACM, 2003, pp. 52–61.

[27] J. Lee, D. Stinson, Deterministic key predistribution schemes for distributed sensor networks, Lecture Notes in Computer Science, 3357, Springer-Verlag, 2005294–307.

[28] S. Camtepe, B. Yener, Combinatorial design of key distribution mechanisms for wireless sensor networks, *IEEE Trans. Networking* (IEEE) 15 (2) (2007) 346–358.

[29] J.N. Al-Karaki, A.E. Kamal, Routing techniques in wireless sensor networks: a survey, *Wireless Commun.* (IEEE) 11 (2004) 6–28.

[30] D. Ganesan, R. Govindan, S. Shenker, D. Estrin, Highly-resilient, energy-efficient multipath routing in wireless sensor networks, *Mobile Comput. Commun. Rev.* (ACM SIGMOBILE) 5 (4) (2001) 10–24.

[31] R.C. Shah, S. Roy, S. Jain, W. Brunette, Data MULEs: modeling a three-tier architecture for sparse sensor networks, *Sensor Network Protocols Appl.* IEEE (2003) 30–41.

[32] M. Yarvis, N. Kushalnagar, H. Singh, A. Rangarajan, Y. Liu, S. Singh. Exploiting heterogeneity in sensor networks. 24th Annual Joint Conference of the IEEE Computer and Communications Societies. IEEE, 2005, pp. 878–890.

[33] Y. Xiao, X. Shen, D. Du, Wireless Network Security, Springer, 2007.

[34] C. Perkins, P. Bhagwat, Highly dynamic destination sequenced distance-vector routing for mobile computers, *ACM's Comput. Commun. Rev.* (ACM) (1994) 234–244.

[35] C. Perkins, E. Royer. Ad-hoc on-demand distance vector routing. Proc. of the 2nd IEEE Workshop on Mobile Computing Systems and Applications, 1999, pp. 90–100.

[36] D. Johnson, D. Maltz, Dynamic sourcerrouting, Mobile Computing, Kulwer Academic Press, 1996153–181

[37] Z. Haas, M. Pearlman, The performance of query control scheme for the zone routing protocol, *Trans. Networking* (IEEE) (2001) 427–438.

[38] Y. Yu, R. Govindan, D. Estrin. Geographical and energy aware routing: a recursive data dissemination protocol for wireless sensor networks. Tech Report, UCLA, 2001.

[39] Kuo-Feng Ssu, Wang Wei-Tong, Chang Wen-Chung, Detecting sybil attacks in wireless sensor networks using neighboring information, Comput. Networks (Elsevier) 53 (18) (December 2009) 3042–3056.

[40] S. Shakkottai, T.S. Rappaport, P.C. Karlsson., Cross-layer design for wireless networks, *Commun. Mag.* IEEE (2003) 74–80.

[41] L.-A. Larzon, U. Bodin, O. Schelen. Hints and notifications. Wireless Communications and Networking Conference. IEEE, 2002, pp. 635–641.

[42] T. ElBatt, A. Ephremides, Joint scheduling and power control for wireless ad hoc networks, IEEE Trans. Wireless Commun. 3 (1) (2004) 74–85.

[43] Std.802.15.4, IEEE. Wireless Medium Access Control (MAC) and Physical Layer (PHY) Specifications for Low Rate Wireless Personal Area Networks (LR-WPANs). IEEE Press, 2003.

## Chapter 17

Cellular Network Security

Peng Liu
Pennsylvania State University

Thomas F. LaPorta
Pennsylvania State University

Kameswari Kotapati
Pennsylvania State University

1. INTRODUCTION

Cellular networks are high-speed, high-capacity voice and data communication networks with enhanced multimedia and seamless roaming capabilities for supporting cellular devices. With the increase in popularity of cellular devices, these networks are used for more than just entertainment and phone calls. They have become the primary means of communication for finance-sensitive business transactions, lifesaving emergencies, and life-/ mission-critical services such as E-911. Today these networks have become the lifeline of communications.

A breakdown in a cellular network has many adverse effects, ranging from huge economic losses due to financial transaction disruptions; loss of life due to loss of phone calls made to emergency workers; and communication outages during emergencies such as the September 11, 2001, attacks. Therefore, it is a high priority for cellular networks to function accurately.

It must be noted that it is not difficult for unscrupulous elements to break into a cellular network and cause outages. The major reason for this is that cellular networks were not designed with security in mind. They evolved from the old-fashioned telephone networks that were built for performance. To this day, cellular networks have numerous well-known and unsecured vulnerabilities providing access to adversaries. Another feature of cellular networks is network relationships (also called *dependencies*) that cause certain types of errors to propagate to other network locations as a result of regular network activity. Such propagation can be very disruptive to a network, and in turn it can affect subscribers. Finally, Internet connectivity to cellular networks is another major contributor to cellular networks' vulnerability because it gives Internet users direct access to cellular network vulnerabilities from their homes.

To ensure that adversaries do not access cellular networks and cause breakdowns, a high level of security must be maintained in cellular networks. However, though great efforts have been made to improve cellular networks in terms of support for new and innovative services, greater number of subscribers, higher speed, and larger bandwidth, very little has been done to update the security of cellular networks. Accordingly, these networks have become highly attractive targets to adversaries, not only because of their lack of security but also due to the ease with which these networks can be exploited to affect millions of subscribers.

In this chapter we analyze the security of cellular networks. Toward understanding the security issues in cellular networks, the rest of the chapter is organized as follows. We present a comprehensive overview of cellular networks with a goal of providing a fundamental understanding of their functioning. Next we present the current state of cellular network security through an in-depth discussion on cellular network vulnerabilities and possible attacks. In addition, we present a cellular network specific attack taxonomy. Finally, we present a review of current cellular network vulnerability assessment techniques and conclude with a discussion.

2. OVERVIEW OF CELLULAR NETWORKS

The current cellular network is an evolution of the early-generation cellular networks that were built for optimal performance. These early-generation cellular networks were proprietary and owned by reputable organizations. They were considered secure due to their proprietary ownership and their *closed nature*, that is, their control infrastructure was unconnected to any public network (such as the Internet) to which end subscribers had direct access. Security was a nonissue in the design of these networks.

Recently, connecting the Internet to cellular networks has not only imported the Internet vulnerabilities to cellular networks, it has also given end subscribers direct access to the control infrastructure of a cellular network, thereby opening the network. Also, with the increasing demand for these networks, a large number of new network operators have come into the picture. Thus, the current cellular environment is no longer a safe, closed network but rather an insecure, open network with many unknown network operators having nonproprietary access to it. Here we present a brief overview of the cellular network architecture.

Overall Cellular Network Architecture

Subscribers gain access to a cellular network via radio signals enabled by a radio access network, as shown in Figure 17.1. The radio access network is connected to the wireline portion of the network, also called the *core network*. Core network functions include servicing subscriber requests and routing traffic. The core network is also connected to the Public Switched Telephone Network (PSTN) and the Internet, as illustrated in Figure 17.1[1].

The PSTN is the circuit-switched public voice telephone network that is used to deliver voice telephone calls on the *fixed landline telephone network*. The PSTN uses Signaling System No. 7 (SS7), a set of telephony signaling protocols defined by the International Telecommunication Union (ITU) for performing telephony functions such as call delivery, call routing, and billing. The SS7 protocols provide a universal structure for telephony network signaling, messaging, interfacing, and network maintenance. PSTN connectivity to the core network enables mobile subscribers to call fixed network subscribers, and vice versa. In the past, PSTN networks

were also closed networks because they were unconnected to other public networks.

The core network is also connected to the Internet. Internet connectivity allows the cellular network to provide innovative multimedia services such as weather reports, stock reports, sports information, chat, and electronic mail. Interworking with the Internet is possible using protocol gateways, federated databases, and multiprotocol mobility managers [2]. Interworking with the Internet has created a new generation of services called *cross-network services*. These are multivendor, multidomain services that use a combination of Internet-based data and data from the cellular network to provide a variety of services to the cellular subscriber. A sample cross-network service is the *Email Based Call Forwarding Service* (CFS), which uses Internet-based email data (in a mail server) to decide on the call-forward number (in a call-forward server) and delivers the call via the cellular network.

From a functional viewpoint, the core network may also be further divided into the circuit-switched (CS) domain, the packet-switched (PS) domain, and the IP Multimedia Subsystem (IMS). In the following, we further discuss the core network organization.

Core Network Organization

Cellular networks are organized as collections of interconnected *network areas*, where each network area covers a fixed geographical region (as shown in Figure 17.2). At a particular time, every subscriber is affiliated with two networks: the *home network* and the *visiting network*.

Every subscriber is permanently assigned to the home network (of his device), from which they can roam onto other visiting networks. The home network maintains the subscriber profile and his current location. The visiting network is the network where the subscriber is currently roaming. It provides radio resources, mobility management, routing, and services for roaming subscribers. The visiting network provides service capabilities to the subscribers on behalf of the home environment [3].

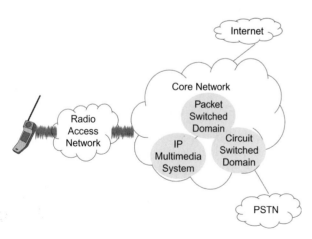

FIGURE 17.1   Cellular network architecture.

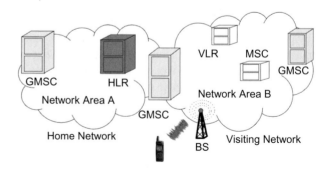

FIGURE 17.2   Core network organization.

The core network is facilitated by network servers (also called *service nodes*). Service nodes are composed of (1) a variety of *data sources* (such as cached read-only, updateable, and shared data sources) to store data such as subscriber profile and (2) *service logic* to perform functions such as computing data items, retrieving data items from data sources, and so on.

Service nodes can be of different types, with each type assigned specific functions. The major service node types in the circuit-switched domain include the Home Location Register (HLR), the Visitor Location Register (VLR), the Mobile Switching Center (MSC), and the Gateway Mobile Switching Center (GMSC) [4].

All subscribers are permanently assigned to a fixed HLR located in the home network. The HLR stores permanent subscriber profile data and relevant temporary data such as current subscriber location (pointer to VLR) of all subscribers assigned to it. Each network area is assigned a VLR. The VLR stores temporary data of subscribers currently roaming in its assigned area; this subscriber data is received from the HLR of the subscriber. Every VLR is always associated with an MSC. The MSC acts as an interface between the radio access network and the core network. It also handles circuit-switched services for subscribers currently roaming in its area. The GMSC is in charge of routing the call to the actual location of the mobile station. Specifically, the GMSC acts as interface between the fixed PSTN network and the cellular network. The radio access network comprises a transmitter, receiver, and speech transcoder called the base station (BS) [5].

Service nodes are geographically distributed and serve the subscriber through collaborative functioning of various network components. Such collaborative functioning is possible due to the inter-component network relationships (called dependencies). A *dependency* means that a network component must rely on other network components to perform a function. For example, there is a *dependency* between service nodes to service subscribers. Such a dependency is made possible through signaling messages containing data items. Service nodes typically request other service nodes to perform specific operations by sending them signaling messages containing data items with predetermined values. On receiving signaling messages, service nodes realize the operations to perform based on values of data items received in signaling messages. Further, dependencies may exist between data items so that received data items may be used to derive other data items. Several application layer protocols are used for signaling messages. Examples of signaling message protocols include Mobile Application Part (MAP), ISDN User Part (ISUP), and Transaction Capabilities Application Part (TCAP) protocols.

Typically in a cellular network, to provide a specific service a preset group of signaling messages is exchanged between a preset group of service node types. The preset group of signaling messages indicates the operations to be performed at the various service nodes and is called a *signal flow*. In the following, we use the *call delivery service* [6] to illustrate a signal flow and show how the various geographically distributed service nodes function together.

Call Delivery Service

The *call delivery service* is a basic service in the circuit-switched domain. It is used to deliver incoming calls to any subscriber with a mobile device regardless of their location. The signal flow of the call delivery service is illustrated in Figure 17.3. The call delivery service signal

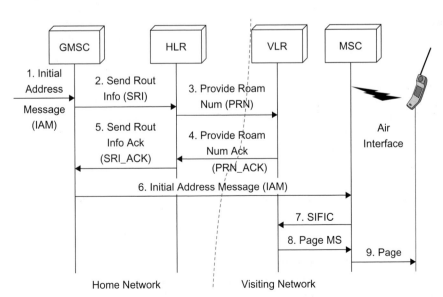

FIGURE 17.3 Signal flow in the call delivery service.

flow comprises MAP messages SRI, SRI_ACK, PRN, and PRN_ACK; ISUP message IAM; and TCAP messages SIFIC, Page MS, and Page.

Figure 17.3 illustrates the exchange of signal messages between different network areas. It shows that when a subscriber makes a call using his mobile device, the call is sent in the form of a signaling message IAM to the nearest GMSC, which is in charge of routing calls and passing voice traffic between different networks. This signaling message IAM contains data items such as *called number* that denotes the mobile phone number of the subscriber receiving this call. The *called number* is used by the GMSC to locate the address of the HLR (home network) of the called party. The GMSC uses this address to send the signaling message SRI.

The SRI message is an intimation to the HLR of the arrival of an incoming call to a subscriber with *called number* as mobile phone number. It contains data items such as the *called number* and *alerting pattern*. The *alerting pattern* denotes the pattern (*packet-switched data, short message service,* or *circuit-switched call*) used to alert the subscriber receiving the call. The HLR uses the *called number* to retrieve from its database the current location (pointer to VLR) of the subscriber receiving the call. The HLR uses this subscriber location to send the VLR the message PRN. The PRN message is a request for call routing information (also called *roaming number*) from the VLR where the subscriber is currently roaming. The PRN message contains the *called number*, *alerting pattern*, and other *subscriber call profile* data items.

The VLR uses the *called number* to store the *alerting pattern* and *subscriber call profile* data items and assign the *roaming number* for routing the call. This *roaming number* data item is passed on to the HLR (in message PRN_ACK), which forwards it to the GMSC (in message SRI_ACK). The GMSC uses this *roaming number* to route the call (message IAM) to the MSC where the subscriber is currently roaming. On receipt of the message IAM, the MSC assigns the *called number* resources for the call and also requests the *subscriber call profile* data items, and *alerting pattern* for the *called number* (using message SIFIC) from the VLR, and receives the same in the Page MS message. The MSC uses the *alerting pattern* in the incoming call profile to *derive* the *page type* data item. The *page type* data item denotes the manner in which to alert the mobile station. It is used to page the mobile subscriber (using message Page). Thus subscribers receive incoming calls irrespective of their locations.

If data item values are inaccurate, a network can misoperate and subscribers will be affected. Hence, accurate functioning of the network is greatly dependent on the integrity of data item values. Thus signal flows allow the various service nodes to function together, ensuring that the network services its subscribers effectively.

3. THE STATE OF THE ART OF CELLULAR NETWORK SECURITY

This part of the chapter presents the current state of the art of cellular network security. Because the security of a cellular network is the security of each aspect of the network, that is, radio access network, core network, Internet connection, and PSTN connection, we detail the security of each in detail.

Security in the Radio Access Network

In a cellular network, the radio access network uses radio signals to connect the subscriber's cellular device with the core network. Hence it would seem that attacks on the radio access network could easily happen because anyone with a transmitter/receiver could capture these signals. This was very true in the case of early-generation cellular networks (first and second generations), where there were no guards against eavesdropping on conversations between the cellular device and BS; cloning of cellular devices to utilize the network resources without paying; and cloning BSs to entice users to camp at the cloned BS in an attack is called a *false base station attack*, so that the target user provides secret information to the adversary.

In the current generation (third-generation) of cellular networks, all these attacks can be prevented because the networks provide adequate security measures. Eavesdropping on signals between the cellular device and BS is not possible, because cipher keys are used to encrypt these signals. Likewise, replay attacks on radio signals are voided by the use of non-repeating random values. Use of integrity keys on radio conversations voids the possibility of deletion and modification of conversations between cellular devices and BSs. By allowing the subscriber to authenticate a network, and vice versa, this generation voids the attacks due to cloned cellular devices and BSs. Finally, as the subscriber's identity is kept confidential by only using a temporary subscriber identifier on the radio network, it is also possible to maintain subscriber location privacy [7].

However, the current generation still cannot prevent a denial-of-service attack from occurring if a large number of registration requests are sent via the radio access network (BS) to the visiting network (MSC). Such a DoS attack is possible because the MSC cannot realize that the registration requests are fake until it attempts to authenticate each request and the request fails. To authenticate each registration request, the MSC must fetch the authentication challenge material from the corresponding HLR. Because the MSC is busy fetching the authentication challenge material, it is kept busy and the genuine registration requests are lost [7]. Overall there is a great improvement in the radio network security in the current third-generation cellular network.

Security in Core Network

Though the current generation of a cellular network has seen many security improvements in the radio access network, the security of the core network is not as improved. Core network security is the security at the service nodes and security on links (or wireline signaling message) between service nodes.

With respect to wireline signaling message security, of the many wireline signaling message protocols, protection is only provided for the Mobile Application Part (MAP) protocol. The MAP protocol is the cleartext application layer protocol that typically runs on the security-free SS7 protocol or the IP protocol. MAP is an essential protocol and it is primarily used for message exchange involving subscriber location management, authentication, and call handling. The reason that protection is provided for only the MAP protocol is that it carries authentication material and other subscriber-specific confidential data; therefore, its security was considered top priority and was standardized [8–10]. Though protection for other signaling message protocols was also considered important, it was left as an improvement for the next-generation networks [11].

Security for the MAP protocol is provided in the form of the newly proposed protocol called Mobile Application Part Security (MAPSec), when MAP runs on the SS7 protocol stack, or Internet Protocol Security (IPSec) when MAP runs on the IP protocol. Both MAPSec and IPSec, protect MAP messages on the link between service nodes by negotiating security associations. Security associations comprise keys, algorithms, protection profiles, and key lifetimes used to protect the MAP message. Both MAPSec and IPSec protect MAP messages by providing source service node authentication and message encryption to prevent eavesdropping, MAP corruption, and fabrication attacks.

It must be noted that though MAPSec and IPSec are deployed to protect individual MAP messages on the link between service nodes, signaling messages typically occur as a group in a signal flow, and hence signaling messages must be protected not only on the link but also in the intermediate service nodes. Also, the deployment of MAPSec and IPSec is optional; hence if any service provider chooses to omit MAPSec/IPSec's deployment, the efforts of all other providers are wasted. Therefore, to completely protect MAP messages, MAPSec/IPSec must be used by every service provider.

With respect to wireline service nodes, while MAPSec/IPSec protects links between service nodes, there is no standardized method for protecting service

nodes [7]. Remote and physical access to service nodes may be subject to operator's security policy and hence could be exploited (insider or outsider) if the network operator is lax with security. Accordingly, the core network suffers from the possibility of node impersonation, corruption of data sources, and service logic attacks. For example, unauthorized access to HLR could deactivate customers or activate customers not seen by the building system. Similarly, unauthorized access to MSC could cause outages for a large number of users in a given network area.

Corrupt data sources or service logic in service nodes have the added disadvantage of propagating this corruption to other service nodes in a cellular network [12–14] via signaling messages. This fact was recently confirmed by a security evaluation of cellular networks [13] that showed the damage potential of a compromised service node to be much greater than the damage potential of compromised signaling messages. Therefore, it is of utmost importance to standardize a scheme for protecting service nodes in the interest of not only preventing node impersonation attacks but also preventing the corruption from propagating to other service nodes.

In brief, the current generation core networks are lacking in security for all types of signaling messages, security for MAP signaling messages in service nodes, and a standardized method for protecting service nodes. To protect all types of signaling message protocols and ensure that messages are secured not only on the links between service nodes but also on the intermediate service nodes (that is, secured end to end), and prevent service logic corruption from propagating to other service nodes, the End-to-End Security (EndSec) protocol was proposed [13].

Because signaling message security essentially depends on security of data item values contained in these messages, EndSec focuses on securing data items. EndSec requires every data item to be signed by its source service nodes using public key encryption. By requiring signatures, if data items are corrupt by compromised intermediate service nodes en route, the compromised status of the service node is revealed to the service nodes receiving the corrupt data items. Revealing the compromised status of service nodes prevents corruption from propagating to other service nodes, because service nodes are unlikely to accept corrupt data items from compromised service nodes.

EndSec also prevents misrouting and node impersonation attacks by requiring every service node in a signal flow to embed the PATH taken by the signal flow in every EndSec message. Finally, EndSec introduces several control messages to handle and correct the detected corruption. Note that EndSec is not a standardized protocol.

Security Implications of Internet Connectivity

Internet connectivity introduces the biggest threat to the security of cellular networks. This is because cheap PC-based equipment with Internet connectivity can now access gateways connecting to the core network (of a cellular network). Therefore, any attack possible in the Internet can now filter into the core network via these gateways. For example, Internet connectivity was the reason for the slammer worm to filter into the E-911 service in Bellevue, Washington, making it completely unresponsive [15]. Other attacks that can filter into the core network from the Internet include spamming and phishing of short messages [16].

We expect low-bandwidth DoS attacks to be the most damaging attacks brought on by Internet connectivity [16,17,18]. These attacks demonstrate that by sending just 240 short messages per second, it is possible to saturate a cellular network and cause the MSC in charge of the region to be flooded and lose legitimate short messages per second. Likewise, it shows that it is possible to cause a specific user to lose short messages by flooding that user with a large number of messages, causing a buffer overflow. Such DoS attacks are possible because the short message delivery time in a cellular network is much greater than the short message submission time using Internet sites [17].

Also, short messages and voices services use the same radio channel, so contention for these limited resources may still occur and cause a loss of voice service. To avoid loss of voice services due to contention, separation of voice and data services on the radio network (of a cellular network) has been suggested [14]. However, such separation requires major standardization and overhaul of the cellular network and is therefore unlikely be implemented very soon. Other minor techniques such as queue management and resource provisioning have been suggested [17].

Though such solutions could reduce the impact of short message flooding, they cannot eliminate other types of low-bandwidth, DoS attacks such as attacks on connection setup and teardown of data services. The root cause for such DoS attacks from the Internet to the core network of a cellular network was identified as the difference in the design principles of these networks. Though the Internet makes no assumptions on the content of traffic and simply passes it on to the next node, the cellular network identifies the traffic content and provides a highly tailored service involving multiple service nodes for each type of traffic [18].

Until this gap is bridged, such attacks will continue, but bridging the gap itself is a major process because either the design of a cellular network must be changed to match the Internet design, or vice versa, which is unlikely to happen soon. Hence a temporary fix would be to secure the gateways connecting the Internet and core network. As a last note, Internet connectivity filters attacks not only into the core network, but also into the PSTN network. Hence PSTN gateways must also be guarded.

Security Implications of PSTN Connectivity

PSTN connectivity to cellular networks allows calls between the fixed and cellular networks. Though the PSTN was a closed network, the security-free SS7 protocol stack on which it is based was of no consequence. However, by connecting the PSTN to the core network that is in turn connected to the Internet, the largest open public network, the SS7-based PSTN network has "no security left" [19].

Because SS7 protocols are plaintext and have no authentication features, it is possible to introduce fake messages, eavesdrop, cause DoS by traffic overload, and incorrectly route signaling messages. Such introduction of SS7 messages into the PSTN network is very easily done using cheap PC-based equipment. Attacks in which calls for 800 and 900 numbers were rerouted to 911 servers so that legitimate calls were lost are documented [20]. Such attacks are more so possible due to the IP interface of the PSTN service nodes and Web-based control of these networks.

Because PSTN networks are to be outdated soon, there is no interest in updating these networks. So, they will remain "security free" until their usage is stopped [19].

So far, we have addressed the security and attacks on each aspect of a cellular network. But an attack that is common to all the aspects of a cellular network is the *cascading attack*. Next we detail the cascading attack and present the corresponding vulnerability assessment techniques.

4. CELLULAR NETWORK ATTACK TAXONOMY

In this part of the chapter, we present a cellular network specific attack taxonomy. This attack taxonomy is called the *three-dimensional taxonomy* because attacks are classified based on the following three dimensions: (1) adversary's physical access to the network when the attack is launched; (2) type of attack launched; and (3) vulnerability exploited to launch the attack.

The three-dimensional attack taxonomy was motivated by a *cellular network specific abstract model*, which is an atomic model of cellular network service nodes. It enables better study of interactions within a cellular network and aids in derivation of several insightful characteristics of attacks on the cellular network.

The abstract model not only led to the development of the three-dimensional attack taxonomy that has been instrumental in uncovering (1) *cascading attacks*, a type of attack in which the adversary targets a specific network location but attacks another location, which in turn propagates the attack to the target location, and (2) *cross-infrastructure cyber-attack*, a new breed of attack in which a cellular network may be attacked from the Internet [21]. In this part of the chapter we further detail the three-dimensional attack taxonomy and cellular network abstract model.

Abstract Model

The abstract model dissects functionality of a cellular network to the basic atomic level, allowing it to systematically isolate and identify vulnerabilities. Such identification of vulnerabilities allows attack classification based on vulnerabilities, and isolation of network functionality aids in extraction of interactions between network components, thereby revealing new vulnerabilities and attack characteristics.

Because service nodes in a cellular network comprise sophisticated *service logic* that performs numerous network functions, the abstract model logically divides the service logic into basic atomic units, called *agents* (represented by the elliptical shape in Figure 17.4). Each agent performs a single function. Service nodes also manage data, so the abstract model also logically divides data sources into data units specific to the agents they support. The abstract model also divides the data sources into *permanent* (represented by the rectangular shape in Figure 17.4) or *cached* (represented by the triangular shape in Figure 17.4) from other service nodes.

The abstract model developed for the CS domain is illustrated in Figure 17.4. It shows agents, permanent and cached data sources for the CS service nodes. For example, the *subscriber locator agent* in the HLR is the agent that tracks the subscriber location information. It receives and responds to location requests during an incoming call and stores a subscriber's location every time they move. This location information is stored in the *location data source*. Readers interested in further details may refer to [21,22].

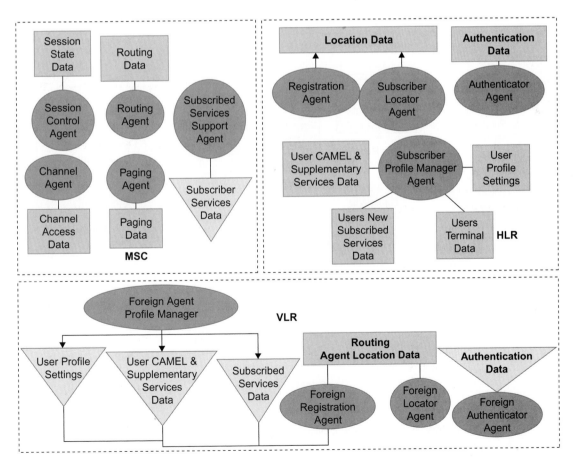

FIGURE 17.4 Abstract model of circuit-switched service nodes.

Abstract Model Findings

The abstract model led to many interesting findings. We outline them as follows:

Interactions

To study the network interactions, service nodes in signal flows (call delivery service) were replaced by their corresponding abstract model agents and data sources. Such an abstract-model – based signal flow based on the call delivery service is shown in Figure 17.5.

In studying the abstract model signal flow, it was observed that interactions happen (1) between agents typically using procedure calls containing data items; (2) between agents and data sources using queries containing data items; and (3) between agents belonging to different service nodes using signaling messages containing data items.

The common behavior in all these interactions is that they typically involve *data items* whose values are set or modified in agents or data source, or it involves data items passed between agents, data sources, or agents and data sources. Hence, the value of a data item not only can be corrupt in an agent or data source, it can also be easily passed on to other agents, resulting in propagation of

corruption. This propagation of corruption is called the *cascading effect*, and attacks that exhibit this effect are called *cascading attacks*. In the following, we present a sample of the cascading attack.

Sample Cascading Attack

In this sample cascading attack, cascading due to corrupt data items and ultimately their service disruption are illustrated in Figure 17.6. Consider the call delivery service explained previously. Here the adversary may corrupt the *roaming number* data item (used to route the call) in the VLR. This corrupt *roaming number* is passed on in message PRN_ACK to the HLR, which in turn passes this information to the GMSC. The GMSC uses the incorrect *roaming number* to route the call to the incorrect MSC$_B$, instead of the correct MSC$_A$. This results in the caller losing the call or receiving a wrong-number call. Thus corruption cascades and results in service disruption.

The type of corruption that can cascade is *system-acceptable incorrect value corruption*, a type of corruption in which corrupt values taken on system-acceptable values, albeit incorrect values. Such a corruption can cause the roaming number to be incorrect but a system-acceptable value.

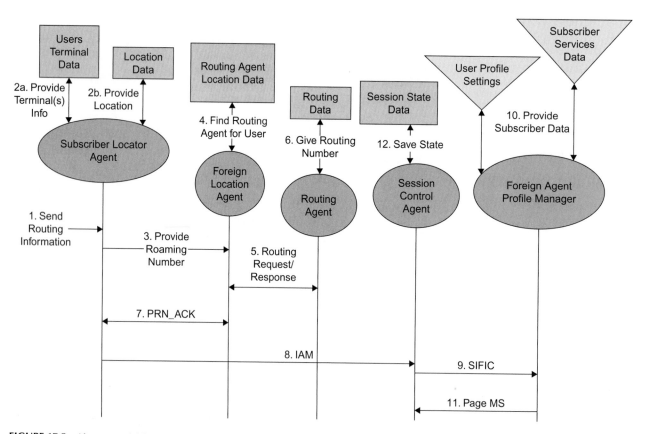

FIGURE 17.5   Abstract model-based signal flow for the call delivery service.

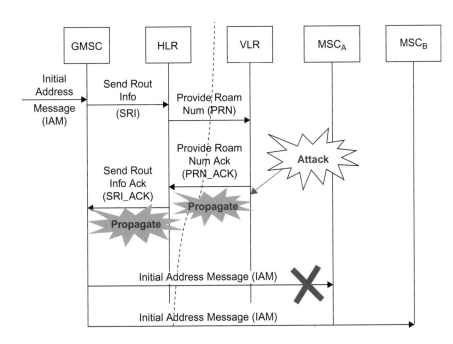

FIGURE 17.6 Sample cascading attacks in the call delivery service.

Note that it is easy to cause such system-acceptable incorrect value corruption due to the availability of Web sites that refer to proprietary working manuals of service nodes such as the VLR [23,24]. Such command insertion attacks have become highly commonplace, the most infamous being the telephone tapping of the Greek government and top-ranking civil servants [25].

Cross-Infrastructure Cyber Cascading Attacks

When cascading attacks cross into cellular networks from the Internet through *cross-network services*, they're called *cross-infrastructure cyber cascading attacks*. This attack is illustrated on the CFS in Figure 17.7.

As the CFS forwards calls based on the emails received, corruption is shown to propagate from the mail server to a call-forward (CF) server and finally to the MSC. In the attack, using any standard mail server vulnerabilities, the adversary may compromise the mail server and corrupt the email data source by deleting emails from people the victim is expecting to call. The CF server receives and caches incorrect email from the mail server.

When calls arrive for the subscriber, the call-forwarding service is triggered, and the MSC queries the CF server on how to forward the call. The CF server checks its incorrect email cache, and because there are no emails from the caller, it responds to the MSC to forward the call to the victim's voicemail when in reality the call should have been forwarded to the cellular device. Thus

the effect of the attack on the mail server propagates to the CF service nodes. This is a classic example of a cross-infrastructure cyber cascading attack, whereby the adversary gains access to the cross-network server, and attacks by modifying data in the data source of the cross-network server. Note that it has become highly simplified to launch such attacks due to easy accessibility to the Internet and subscriber preference for Internet-based cross-network services.

Isolating Vulnerabilities

From the abstract model, the major vulnerable-to-attacks network components are: (1) data sources; (2) agents (more generally called service logic); and (3) signaling messages. By exploiting each of these vulnerabilities, data items that are crucial to the correct working of a cellular network can be corrupted, leading to ultimate service disruption through cascading effects.

In addition, the effect of corrupt signaling messages is different from the effect of corrupt data sources. By corrupting data items in a data source of a service node, all the subscribers attached to this service node may be affected. However, by corrupting a signaling message, only the subscribers (such as the caller and called party in case of call delivery service) associated with the message are affected. Likewise, corrupting the agent in the service node can affect all subscribers using the agent in the service node. Hence, in the three-dimensional taxonomy, a vulnerability exploited is considered as an attack dimension, since the effect on each vulnerability is different.

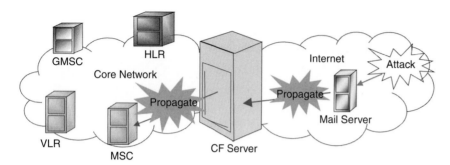

FIGURE 17.7   Cross-infrastructure cyber cascading attacks on call-forward service.

Likewise, the adversary's physical access to a cellular network also affects how the vulnerability is exploited and how the attack cascades. For example, consider the case when a subscriber has access to the air interface. The adversary can only affect messages on the air interface. Similarly, if the adversary has access to a service node, the data sources and service logic may be corrupted. Hence, in the three-dimensional taxonomy, the physical access is considered a category as it affects how the vulnerability is exploited and its ultimate effect on the subscriber.

Finally, the way the adversary chooses to launch an attack ultimately affects the service in a different way. Consider a passive attack such as *interception*. Here the service is not affected, but it can have a later effect on the subscriber, such as identity theft or loss of privacy. An active attack such as *interruption* can cause complete service disruption. Hence, in the three-dimensional taxonomy, the attack means are considered a category due the ultimate effect on service. In the next part of the chapter, we detail the cellular network specific three-dimensional taxonomy and the way the previously mentioned dimensions are incorporated (see checklist: "An Agenda For Action When Incorporating The Cellular Network Specific Three-Dimensional Attack Taxonomy").

Table 17.1 shows a sample tabulation of Level I attacks grouped in Case 1. For example, with Level I

An Agenda for Action when Incorporating the Cellular Network Specific Three-Dimensional Attack Taxonomy

The three dimensions in the taxonomy include Dimension I: Physical Access to the Network, Dimension II: Attack Categories and Dimension III: Vulnerability Exploited. In the following, we outline each dimension (check all tasks completed):

_____**1.** Dimension I—Physical Access to the Network: In this dimension, attacks are classified based on the adversary's level of physical access to a cellular network. Dimension I may be further classified into *single infrastructure attacks* (Level I–III) and *cross-infrastructure cyber-attacks* (Level IV–V):

_____**a.** *Level I: Access to air interface with physical device.* Here the adversary launches attacks via access to the radio access network using standard inexpensive "off-the-shelf" equipment [26]. Attacks include false base station attacks, eavesdropping, and man-in-the-middle attacks and correspond to attacks previously mentioned.

_____**b.** *Level II: Access to links connecting core service nodes.* Here the adversary has access to links connecting to core service nodes. Attacks include disrupting normal transmission of signaling messages and correspond to message corruption attacks previously mentioned.

_____**c.** *Level III: Access core service nodes.* In this case, the adversary could be an insider who managed to gain physical access to core service nodes. Attacks include editing the service logic or modifying data sources, such as subscriber data (profile, security and services) stored in the service node and corresponding to corrupt service logic, data source, and node impersonation attacks previously mentioned.

_____**d.** *Level IV: Access to links connecting the Internet and the core network service nodes.* This is a cross-infrastructure cyber-attack. Here the adversary has access to links connecting the core network and Internet service nodes. Attacks include editing and deleting signaling messages between the two networks. This level of attack is easier to achieve than Level II.

_____**e.** *Level V: Access to Internet servers or cross-network servers:* This is a cross-infrastructure cyber-attack. Here the adversary can cause damage by editing the service logic or modifying subscriber data (profile, security and services) stored in the cross-network servers. Such an attack was previously outlined earlier in the chapter. This level of attack is easier to achieve than Level III.

____ 2. Dimension II—Attack Type: In this dimension, attacks are classified based on the type of attack. The attack categories are based on Stallings [27] work in this area:

____ a. *Interception.* The adversary intercepts signaling messages on a cable (Level II access) but does not modify or delete them. This is a passive attack. This affects the privacy of the subscriber and the network operator. The adversary may use the data obtained from interception to analyze traffic and eliminate the competition provided by the network operator.

____ b. *Fabrication or replay.* In this case, the adversary inserts spurious messages, data, or service logic into the system, depending on the level of physical access. For example, via a Level II access, the adversary inserts fake signaling messages; and via a Level III access, the adversary inserts fake service logic or fake subscriber data into this system.

____ c. *Modification of resources.* Here the adversary modifies data, messages, or service logic. For example, via a Level II access, the adversary modifies signaling messages on the link; and via a Level III access, the adversary modifies service logic or data.

____ d. *Modification of resources.* Here the adversary modifies data, messages, or service logic. For example, via a Level II access, the adversary modifies signaling messages on the link; and via a Level III access, the adversary modifies service logic or data.

____ e. *Denial of service.* In this case, the adversary takes actions to overload a network results in legitimate subscribers not receiving service.

____ f. *Interruption.* Here the adversary causes an interruption by destroying data, messages, or service logic.

____ 3. Dimension III—Vulnerability Exploited: In this dimension, attacks are classified based on the vulnerability exploited to cause the attack. Vulnerabilities exploited are explained as follows:

____ a. *Data.* The adversary attacks the data stored in the system. Damage is inflicted by modifying, inserting, and deleting the data stored in the system.

____ b. *Messages.* The adversary adds, modifies, deletes, or replays signaling messages.

____ c. *Service logic.* Here the adversary inflicts damage by attacking the service logic running in the various cellular core network service nodes.

____ d. *Attack classification.* In classifying attacks, we can group them according to *Case 1: Dimension I versus Dimension II*, and *Case 2: Dimension II versus Dimension III*. Note that the Dimension I versus Dimension III case can be transitively inferred from Case 1 and Case 2.

TABLE 17.1 Sample Case 1 Classification.

	Interception	Fabrication/Insertion	Modification of Resources	Denial of Service	Interruption
Level I	• Observe time, rate, length, source, and destination of victim's locations.	• Using modified cellular devices, the adversary can send spurious registration messages to the target network.	• With a modified base station and cellular devices, the adversary modifies conversations between subscribers and their base stations.	• The adversary can cause DoS by sending a large number of fake registration messages.	• Jam victims' traffic channels so that victims cannot access the channels.
	• With modified cellular devices, eavesdrop on victim.	• Likewise, using modified base stations, the adversary can signal victims to camp at their locations.			• Broadcast at a higher intensity than allowed, thereby hogging the bandwidth.

access an adversary causes interception attacks by observing traffic and eavesdropping. Likewise, fabrication attacks due to Level I access include sending spurious registration messages. Modification of resources due to Level I access includes modifying conversations in the radio access network. DoS due to Level I access occurs when a large number of fake registration messages are sent to keep the network busy so as to not provide service to legitimate subscribers. Finally, interruption attacks due to Level I access occur when adversaries jam the radio access channel so that legitimate subscribers cannot access the network. For further details on attack categories, refer to [22].

5. CELLULAR NETWORK VULNERABILITY ANALYSIS

Regardless of how attacks are launched, if attack actions cause a system-acceptable incorrect value corruption, the corruption propagates, leading to many unexpected cascading effects. To detect remote cascading effects and identify the origin of cascading attacks, cellular network vulnerability assessment tools were developed.

These tools, including the *Cellular Network Vulnerability Assessment Toolkit* (CAT) and the *advanced Cellular Network Vulnerability Assessment Toolkit* (aCAT) [12,28], receive the input from users regarding which data item(s) might be corrupted and output an attack graph. The CAT attack graph not only shows the network location and service where the corruption might originate, it also shows the various messages and service nodes through which the corruption propagates.

An attack graph is a diagrammatic representation of an attack on a real system. It shows various ways an adversary can break into a system or cause corruption and the various ways in which the corruption may propagate within the system. Attack graphs are typically produced manually by red teams and used by systems administrators for protection. CAT and aCAT attack graphs allow users to trace the effect of an attack through a network and determine its side effects, thereby making them the ultimate service disruption.

Cellular networks are at the nascent stage of development with respect to security, so it is necessary to evaluate security protocols before deploying them. Hence, aCAT can be extended with security protocol evaluation capabilities into a tool [13] called *Cellular Network Vulnerability Assessment Toolkit for evaluation* (eCAT). eCAT allows users to quantify the benefits of security solutions by removing attack effects from attack graphs based on the defenses provided. One major advantage of this approach is that solutions may be evaluated before expensive development and deployment.

It must be noted that developing such tools — CAT, aCAT, and eCAT — presented many challenges: (1) cellular networks are extremely complex systems; they comprise several types of service nodes and control protocols, contain hundreds of data elements, and support hundreds of services; hence developing such toolkits requires in-depth working knowledge of these systems; and (2) every cellular network deployment comprises a different physical configuration; toolkits must be immune to the diversity in physical configuration; and finally (3) attacks cascade in a network due to regular network activity as a result of dependencies; toolkits must be able to track the way that corruption cascades due to network dependencies.

The challenge of in-depth cellular network knowledge was overcome by incorporating the toolkits with cellular network specifications defined by the Third Generation Partnership Project (3GPP) and is available at no charge [29]. The 3GPP is a telecommunications standards body formed to produce, maintain, and develop globally applicable "technical specifications and technical reports" for a third-generation mobile system based on evolved GSM core networks and the radio access technologies that they support [24].

Usage of specifications allows handling of the diversity of physical configuration, as specifications detail the functional behavior and not the implementation structure of a cellular network. Specifications are written using simple flow-like diagrams called the Specification and Description Language (SDL) [30], and are referred to as *SDL specifications*. Equipment and service providers use these SDL specifications as the basis for their service implementations.

Corruption propagation is tracked by incorporating the toolkits with novel dependency and propagation models to trace the propagation of corruption. Finally, Boolean properties are superimposed on the propagation model to capture the impact of security solutions.

CAT is the first version of the toolkit developed for cellular network vulnerability assessment. CAT works by taking user input of *seeds* (data items directly corrupted by the adversary and the cascading effect of which leads to a goal) and *goals* (data parameters that are derived incorrectly due to the direct corruption of seeds by the adversary) and uses SDL specification to identify cascading attacks. However, SDL is limited in its expression of relationships and inexplicit in its assumptions and hence cannot capture all the dependencies; therefore CAT misses several cascading attacks.

To detect a complete set of cascading effects, CAT was enhanced with new features, to aCAT. The new features added to aCAT include (1) a network dependency model that explicitly specifies the exact dependencies in a cellular network; (2) infection propagation rules that identify the reasons that cause corruption to cascade; and (3) a small amount of expert knowledge. The network dependency model and infection propagation rules may be applied to SDL specifications and help alleviate their limited expression capability. The expert knowledge helps capture the inexplicit assumptions made by SDL.

In applying these features, aCAT captures all those dependencies that were previously unknown to CAT, and thereby aCAT was able to detect a complete set of cascading effects. Through extensive testing of aCAT, several interesting attacks were found and the areas where SDL is lacking was identified.

To enable evaluation of new security protocols, aCAT was extended to eCAT. eCAT uses Boolean probabilities in attack graphs to detect whether a given security protocol can eliminate a certain cascading effect. Given a security protocol, eCAT can measure effective coverage, identify the types of required security mechanisms to protect the network, and identify the most vulnerable network areas. eCAT was also used to evaluate MAPSec, the new standardized cellular network security protocol. Results from MAPSec's evaluation gave insights into MAPSec's performance and the network's vulnerabilities. In the following, we detail each toolkit.

Cellular Network Vulnerability Assessment Toolkit (CAT)

In this part of the chapter, we present an overview of CAT and its many features. CAT is implemented using the Java programming language. It is made up of a number of subsystems (as shown in Figure 17.8). The *knowledge base* contains the cellular network knowledge obtained from SDL specifications. SDL specifications contain simple flowchart-like diagrams. The flowcharts are converted into data in the *knowledge base*. The *integrated data structure* is similar to that of the knowledge base; it holds intermediate attack graph results.

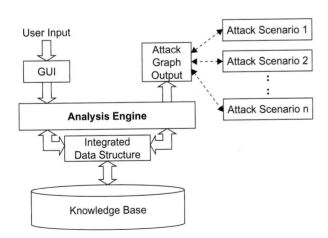

FIGURE 17.8   Architecture of CAT.

The GUI subsystem takes user input in the form of seeds and goals. The analysis engine contains algorithms (forward and midpoint) incorporated with cascading effect detection rules. It explores the possibility of the user input *seed* leading to the cascading effect of the user input *goal*, using the knowledge base, and outputs the cascading attack in the form of attack graphs.

Using these attack graphs, realistic attack scenarios may be derived. Attack scenarios explain the effect of the attack on the subscriber in a realistic setting. Each attack graph may have multiple interpretations and give rise to multiple scenarios. Each scenario gives a different perspective on how the attack may affect the subscriber.

Cascading Effect Detection Rules

The Cascading Effect Detection Rules were defined to extract cascading effects from the SDL specifications contained in the knowledge base. They are incorporated into the algorithms in the analysis engine. These rules define what constitutes propagation of corruption from a signaling message to a block, and vice versa, and propagation of corruption within a service node. For example, when a service node receives a signaling message with a corrupt data item and stores the data item, it constitutes propagation of corruption from a signaling message to a block. Note that these rules are high level.

Attack Graph

The CAT attack graph may be defined as a state transition showing the paths through a system, starting with the conditions of the attack, followed by attack action, and ending with its cascading effects. In Figure 17.9, we present the CAT attack graph output, which was built using user input of *ISDN Bearer Capability* as a seed and *Bearer Service* as goal. The attack graph constitutes nodes and edges. Nodes represent states in the network with respect to the attack, and *edges* represent network state transitions. For description purposes, each node has been given a node label followed by an alphabet, and the attack graph has been divided into layers.

Nodes may be broadly classified as *conditions, actions*, and *goals*, with the conditions of the attack occurring at the lowest layer and the final cascading effect at the highest layer. In the following, we detail each node type.

Condition Nodes

Nodes at the lowest layer typically correspond to the conditions that must exist for the attack to occur. These condition nodes directly follow from the taxonomy. They are an adversary's physical access, target service node, and vulnerability exploited. For example, the adversary

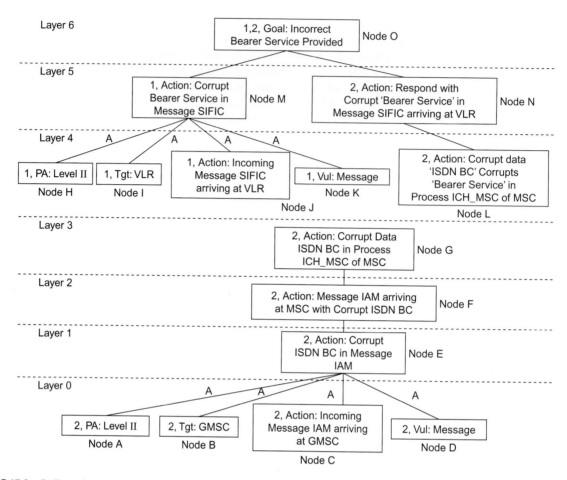

FIGURE 17.9 CAT attack graph output.

has access to links connecting to the GMSC service node, that is, Level II physical access; this is represented as Node A in the attack graph. Likewise, the adversary corrupts data item ISDN Bearer Capability in the IAM message arriving at the GMSC. Hence the target of the attack is the GMSC and is represented by Node B. Similarly, the adversary exploits vulnerabilities in a message (IAM); and, this is represented by Node D in the attack graph.

The CAT attack graphs show all the possible conditions for an attack to happen. In other words, we see not only the corruption due to the seed ISDN Bearer Capability in the signaling message, but also IAM arriving at the GMSC. But, there are also other possibilities, such as the corruption of the goal Bearer Service in the signaling message SIFIC, represented by Node M.

Action Nodes

Nodes at higher layers are actions that typically correspond to effects of the attack propagating through the network. Effects typically include propagation of corruption between service nodes, such as from MSC to VLR (Node N), propagation of corruption within service nodes such

as ISDN Bearer Capability corrupting Bearer Service (Node L), and so on. Actions may further be classified as adversary actions, normal network operations, or normal subscriber activities. Adversary actions include insertion, corruption, or deletion of data, signaling messages, or service logic represented by Node E. Normal network operations include sending (Node N) and receiving signaling messages (Node E). Subscriber activity may include updating personal data or initiating service.

Goal Nodes

Goal nodes typically occur at the highest layer of the attack graph. They indicate corruption of the goal items due to the direct corruption of seeds by the adversary (Node A).

Edges

In our graph, edges represent network transitions due to both normal network actions and adversary actions. Edges help show the global network view of adversary action. This is the uniqueness of our attack graph.

Transitions due to adversary action are indicated by an edge marked by the letter A (edges connecting Layer 0 and Layer 1). By inclusion of normal network transitions in addition to the transitions caused by the adversary, our attack graph shows not only the adversary's activity but also the *global network view of the adversary's action*. This is a unique feature of the attack graph.

Trees

In the graph, trees are distinguished by the tree numbers assigned to its nodes. For example, all the nodes marked with number 2 belong to Tree 2 of the graph. Some nodes in the graph belong to multiple trees. Tree numbers are used to distinguish between AND and OR nodes in the graph. Nodes at a particular layer with the same tree number(s) are AND nodes. For example, at Layer 4, Nodes H, I, J, and K are AND nodes; they all must occur for Node M at Layer 5 to occur. Multiple tree numbers on a node are called OR nodes. The OR node may be arrived at using alternate ways. For example, Node O at Layer 6 is an OR node, the network state indicated by Node O may be arrived at from Node M or Node N.

Each attack tree shows the attack effects due to corruption of a seed at a specific network location (such as signaling message or process in a block). For example, Tree 1 shows the attack due to the corruption of the seed Bearer Service at the VLR. Tree 2 shows the propagation of the seed ISDN Bearer Capability in the signaling message IAM. These trees show that the vulnerability of a cellular network is not limited to one place but can be realized due to the corruption of data in many network locations.

In constructing the attack graph, CAT assumes that an adversary has all the necessary conditions for launching the attack. The CAT attack graph format is well suited to cellular networks because data propagates through the network in various forms during the normal operation of a network; thus an attack that corrupts a data item manifests itself as the corruption of a different data item in a different part of the network after some network operations take place.

Attack Scenario Derivation

The CAT attack graph is in cellular network semantics, and realistic attack scenarios may be derived to understand the implications of the attack graph. Here we detail the principles involved in the derivation of realistic attack scenarios:

End-User effect

Goal node(s) are used to infer the end effect of the attack on the subscriber. According to the goal node in Figure 17.9, the SIFIC message to the VLR has incorrect goal item Bearer Service. The SIFIC message is used to inform the VLR the calling party's preferences such as voice channel requirements and request the VLR to set up the call based on the calling party and receiving party preferences.

If the calling party's preferences (such as Bearer Service) are incorrect, the call setup by the VLR is incompatible with the calling party, and the communication is ineffective (garbled speech). From the goal node, it can be inferred that Alice, the receiver of the call, is unable to communicate effectively with Bob, the caller, because Alice can only hear garbled speech from Bob's side.

Origin of Attack

Nodes at Layer 0 indicate the origin of the attack, and hence the location of the attack may be inferred. The speech attack may originate at the signaling messages IAM, or the VLR service node.

Attack Propagation and Side Effects

Nodes At All Other Layers Show The Propagation Of Corruption Across The Various Service Nodes In The Network. From Other Layers In Figure 17.9, It Can Be Inferred That The Seed Is The ISDN Bearer Capability And The Attack Spreads From The MSC To The VLR.

Example Attack Scenario

Using these guidelines, an attack scenario may be derived as follows. Trudy, the adversary, corrupts the ISDN Bearer Capability of Bob, the victim, at the IAM message arriving at the GMSC. The GMSC propagates this corruption to the MSC, which computes, and hence corrupts, the Bearer Service. The corrupt Bearer Service is passed on to the VLR, which sets up the call between Bob, the caller, and Alice, the receiver. Bob and Alice cannot communicate effectively because Alice is unable to understand Bob.

Though CAT has detected several cascading attacks, its output to a great extent depends on SDL's ability to capture data dependencies. SDL is limited in its expression capability in the sense that it does not always accurately capture the relationship between data items, and in many cases, SDL does even specify the relationship. Without these details CAT may miss some cascading effects due to loss of data relationships. CAT's output to a minor extent also depends on user input in the sense that to accurately capture all the cascading effect of a seed, the user's input must comprise all the seeds that can occur in the cascading effect; otherwise the exact cascading effect is not captured. To alleviate CAT's inadequacies, aCAT was developed.

Advanced Cellular Network Vulnerability Assessment Toolkit (aCAT)

In this section, we present aCAT, an extension of CAT with enhanced features. These enhanced features include (1) incorporating expert knowledge to compensate for the lacking caused by SDL's inexplicit assumptions; expert knowledge added to the knowledge base with the SDL specifications; (2) defining a network dependency model that accurately captures the dependencies in a cellular network; the network dependency model is used to format the data in knowledge base, thereby clarifying the nature of the network dependency; and (3) defining infection propagation rules that define fine-grained rules to detect cascading attacks; these infection propagation rules are incorporated into the analysis engine, which comprises the forward, reverse, and combinatory algorithms. aCAT is also improved in terms of its user input requirements. It requires as input either seeds or goals, whereas CAT required both seeds and goals.

In principle, cascading attacks are the result of propagation of corruption between network components (such as signaling messages, caches, local variables, and service logic) due to dependencies that exist between these network components. Hence, to uncover these attacks, the network dependency model and infection propagation (IP) rules were defined. In the following, we detail the network dependency model and infection propagation model using Figure 17.10.

Network Dependency Model

The network dependency model accurately defines fine-grained dependencies between the various network components. Given that service nodes comprise agents and data sources (from the abstract model), the dependencies are defined as follows. In interagent dependency, agents communicate with each other using agent invocations (as shown by 6 in Figure 17.10) containing data items. Thus, agents are related to each other through data items. Likewise, in agent to data source dependency, agents communicate with data sources using Read and Write operations containing data items. Therefore, agents and data items are related to each other through data items. Within agents, derivative dependencies define relationships between data items. Here data items are used as input to derive data items using derivation operations such as AND, OR operations. Therefore, data items are related to each other through derivation operation. For further detail on the network dependency model, refer to [12].

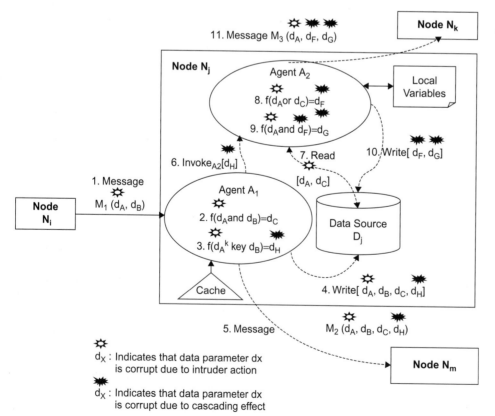

FIGURE 17.10 Network dependency model.

d_X : Indicates that data parameter dx is corrupt due to intruder action

d_X : Indicates that data parameter dx is corrupt due to cascading effect

Infection Propagation (IP) Rules

These are finegrained rules to detect cascading effects. They are incorporated into the algorithms in the analysis engine. An example of the IP rule is that an output data item in the AND dependency is corrupt only if both the input data items are corrupt (as shown by 9 in Figure 17.10). Likewise, an output data item in the OR dependency is corrupt if a single input data item is corrupt (as shown by 8 in Figure 17.10). Similarly, corruption propagates between agents when the data item used to invoke the agent is corrupt, and the same data item is used as an input in the derivative dependency whose output may be corrupt (as shown by 6, 8 in Figure 17.10). Accordingly, corruption propagates from an agent to a data source if the data item written to the data source is corrupt (as shown by 4 in Figure 17.10). Finally, corruption propagates between service nodes if a data item used in the signaling message between the service nodes is corrupt, and the corrupt data item is used to derive corrupt output items or the corrupt data item is stored in the data source (as shown by 1, 3 or 1, 4 in Figure 17.10) [12].

With such a fine-grained dependency model and infection propagation rules, aCAT was very successful in identifying cascading attacks in several key services offered by a cellular network, and it was found that aCAT can indeed identify a better set of cascading effects in comparison to CAT. aCAT has also detected several interesting and unforeseen cascading attacks that are subtle and difficult to identify by other means. These newly identified cascading attacks include the alerting attack, power-off/power-on attack, mixed identity attack, call redirection attack, and missed calls attack.

Alerting Attack

In the following we detail aCAT's output, a cascading attack called the *alerting attack*, shown in Figure 17.11. From goal nodes (Node A at Level 5, and Node C at Level 4) in the alerting attack, it can be inferred that the Page message has incorrect data item *page type*. The Page message is used to inform subscribers of the arrival of incoming calls, and "page type" indicates the type of call. "Page type" must be compatible with the subscriber's mobile station or else the subscriber is not alerted. From the goal node it may be inferred that Alice, a subscriber of the system, is not alerted on the arrival of an incoming call and hence does not receive incoming calls. This attack is subtle to detect because network administrators find that the network processes the incoming call correctly and that the subscriber is alerted correctly. They might not find that this alerting pattern is incompatible with the mobile station itself.

Also, nodes at Level 0 indicate the origin of the attack as signaling messages SRI, PRN, the service nodes VLR,

or the HLR. From the other levels it may be inferred that the seed is the *alerting pattern* that the adversary corrupts in the SRI message and the attack spreads from the HLR to the VLR and from the VLR to the MSC. For more details on these attacks, refer to [12].

Cellular Network Vulnerability Assessment Toolkit for Evaluation (eCAT)

In this part of the chapter, we present eCAT an extension to aCAT. eCAT was developed to evaluate new security protocols before their deployment. Though the design goals and threat model of these security protocols are common knowledge, eCAT was designed to find (1) the effective protection coverage of these security protocols in terms of percentage of attacks prevented; (2) the other kinds of security schemes required to tackle the attacks that can evade the security protocol under observation; and (3) the most vulnerable network areas (also called *hotspots*) [13].

eCAT computes security protocol coverage using attack graphs generated by aCAT and Boolean probabilities in a process called *attack graph marking* and quantifies the coverage using *coverage measurement formulas* (CMF). Attack graph marking also identifies network hotspots and exposes if the security protocol being evaluated protects these hotspots. eCAT was also used to evaluate MAPSec, as it is a relatively new protocol, and evaluation results would aid network operators.

Boolean Probabilities

Boolean probabilities are used in attack graphs to distinguish between nodes eliminated (denoted by 0, or shaded node in attack graph) and nodes existing (denoted by 1, or unshaded node in attack graph) due to the security protocol under evaluation. By computing Boolean probabilities for each node in the attack graph, eCAT can extract the attack effects that may be eliminated by the security protocol under evaluation.

Attack Graph Marking

To mark attack graphs, user input of Boolean probabilities must be provided for Layer 0 nodes. For example, if the security protocol under evaluation is MAPSec, then because MAPSec provides security on links between nodes, it eliminates Level 2 physical access. For example, consider the attack graph generated by eCAT shown in Figure 17.12. Here, Node 5 is set to 0, while all other nodes are set to 1.

eCAT uses the input from Layer 0 nodes to compute the Boolean probabilities for the rest of the nodes starting from Layer 1 and moving upward. For example, the

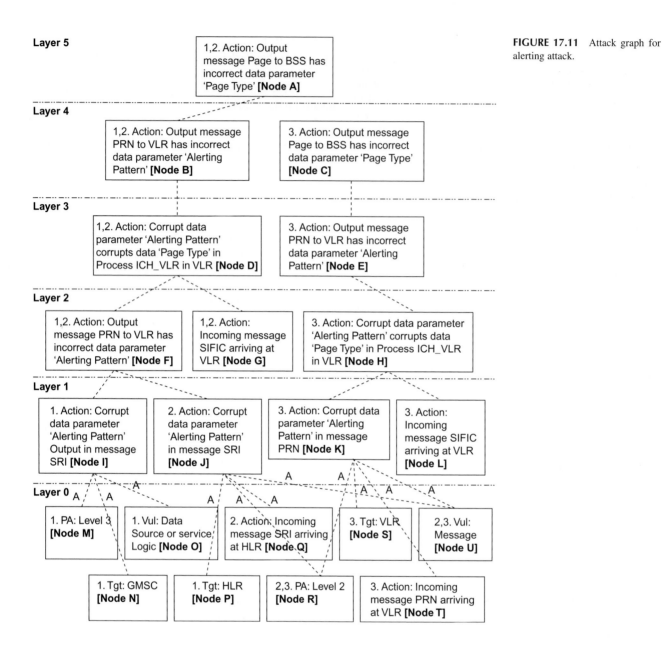

FIGURE 17.11 Attack graph for alerting attack.

Boolean probability of the AND node (Node 18) is the product of all the nodes in the previous layer with the same tree number. Because Node 5 has the same tree number as Node 18, and Node 5's Boolean probability is 0, Node 18's Boolean probability is also 0. This process of marking attack graphs is continued until Boolean probability of all the nodes is computed till the topmost layer.

Hotspots

Graph marking also marks the network hotspots in the attack graph. With respect to the attack graph, hotspots are the Layer 0 nodes with the highest tree number count. For example in Figure 17.12, Node 3 and Node 4 are the hotspots. A high tree number count indicates an increased

attractiveness of the network location to adversaries. This is because by breaking into the network location indicated by the hotspot node, the adversary has a higher likelihood of success and can cause the greatest amount of damage.

Extensive testing of eCAT on several of the network services using MAPSec has revealed hotspots to be "Data Sources and Service Logic." This is because a corrupt data source or service logic may be used by many different services and hence cause many varied cascading effects, spawning a large number of attacks (indicated by multiple trees in attack graphs). Thus attacks that occur due to exploiting service logic and data source vulnerabilities constitute a major portion of the networkwide vulnerabilities and so a major problem. In other words, by exploiting service logic and data sources, the likelihood

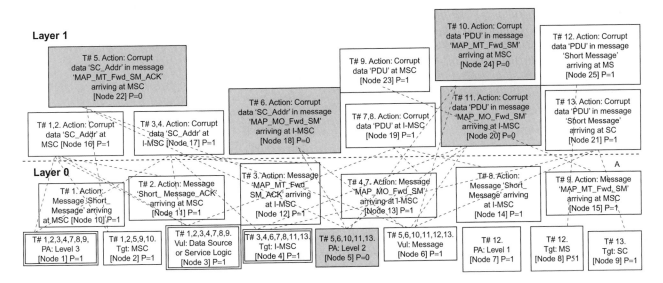

FIGURE 17.12   Fragment of a marked attack graph generated by eCAT.

of attack success is very high. Therefore data source and service logic protection mechanisms must be deployed. It must be noted that MAPSec protects neither service logic nor data sources; rather, it protects MAP messages.

Coverage Measurement Formulas

The CMF comprises the following set of three formulas to capture the coverage of security protocols: (1) *effective coverage*, to capture the average effective number of attacks eliminated by the security protocol; the higher the value of Effective Coverage the greater the protection the security protocol; (2) *deployment coverage*, to capture the coverage of protocol deployments; and (3) *attack coverage*, to capture the attack coverage provided by the security protocol; the higher this value, the greater is the security solution's efficacy in eliminating a large number of attacks on the network.

Extensive use of CMF on several of the network services has revealed that MAPSec has an average network-wide attack coverage of 33%. This may be attributed to the fact that message corruption has a low spawning effect. Typically a single message corruption causes a single attack, since messages are typically used by a single service. Hence MAPSec is a solution to a small portion of the total network vulnerabilities.

Finally, in evaluating MAPSec using eCAT, it was observed that though MAPSec is 100% effective in preventing MAP message attacks, it cannot prevent a successfully launched attack from cascading. For MAPSec to be truly successful, every leg of the MAP message transport must be secured using MAPSec. However, the overhead for deploying MAPSec can be high, in terms of both

processing load and monetary investment. Also, as MAP messages travel through third-party networks en route to their destinations, the risk level of attacks without MAPSec is very high. Hence, MAPSec is vital to protect MAP messages.

In conclusion, because MAPSec can protect against only 33% of attacks, it alone is insufficient to protect the network. A complete protection scheme for the network must include data source and service logic protection.

6. SUMMARY

Next to the Internet, cellular networks are the most highly used communication network. It is also the most vulnerable, with inadequate security measures making it a most attractive target to adversaries that want to cause communication outages during emergencies. As cellular networks are moving in the direction of the Internet, becoming an amalgamation of several types of diverse networks, more attention must be paid to securing these networks. A push from government agencies requiring mandatory security standards for operating cellular networks would be just the momentum needed to securing these networks.

Of all the attacks discussed in this chapter, cascading attacks have the most potential to stealthily cause major network misoperation. At present there is no standardized scheme to protect from such attacks. EndSec is a good solution for protecting from cascading attacks, since it requires every data item to be signed by the source service node. Because service nodes are unlikely to corrupt data items and they are to be accounted for by their signatures, the possibility of cascading attacks is greatly reduced. EndSec has the added advantage of providing end-to-end security for all types of signaling messages. Hence, standardizing EndSec and mandating its deployment would be a good step toward securing the network.

Both Internet and PSTN connectivity are the open gateways that adversaries can use to gain access and attack the network. Because the PSTN's security is not going to be improved, at least its gateway to the core network must be adequately secured. Likewise, since neither the Internet's design nor security will be changed to suit a cellular network, at least its gateways to the core network must be adequately secured.

Finally, because a cellular network is an amalgamation of many diverse networks, it has too many vulnerable points. Hence, the future design of the network must be planned to reduce the number of vulnerable network points and reduce the number of service nodes that participate in servicing the subscriber, thereby reducing the number of points from which an adversary may attack.

Finally, let's move on to the real interactive part of this Chapter: review questions/exercises, hands-on projects, case projects and optional team case project. The answers and/or solutions by chapter can be found in the Online Instructor's Solutions Manual.

CHAPTER REVIEW QUESTIONS/EXERCISES

True/False

1. True or False? Cellular networks are high-speed, high-capacity voice and data communication networks with enhanced multimedia and seamless roaming capabilities for supporting cellular devices.
2. True or False? The current cellular network is an evolution of the early-generation cellular networks that were built for optimal performance.
3. True or False? It would seem that attacks on the radio access network could not easily happen, because anyone with a transmitter/receiver could capture these signals.
4. True or False? Though the current generation of a cellular network has seen many security improvements in the radio access network, the security of the core network is not as improved.
5. True or False? Internet connectivity introduces the biggest threat to the security of cellular networks.

Multiple Choice

1. Cellular networks are organized as collections of interconnected:
   A. Message Integrity Codes (MIC)
   B. Temporal Key Integrity Protocols (TKIP)
   C. Application Program Interfaces
   D. Network Areas
   E. Extensible Authentication Protocol (EAP) framework
2. The core network is facilitated by network servers, which are also called?
   A. Middle Layers
   B. Network Layers
   C. Transport Layers
   D. Service Nodes
   E. All of the above
3. What is a basic service in the circuit-switched domain?
   A. Secure on-demand routing protocol service
   B. Taxonomy service
   C. Caller delivery service
   D. Authenticated Routing for Ad hoc Networks (ARAN) service
   E. Destination-Sequenced Distance Vector (DSDV) routing service
4. The cloning of cellular devices to utilize the network resources without paying; and cloning BSs to entice users to camp at the cloned BS in an attack, is called a:
   A. False base station attack.
   B. Privacy attack.
   C. Eavesdropping attack
   D. Man-in-the-Middle Attack.
   E. Passive attack.
5. What introduces the biggest threat to the security of cellular networks?
   A. HELLO Flood connectivity.
   B. Denial-of-service attack connectivity.
   C. Internet connectivity.
   D. Sybil connectivity.
   E. All of the above.

EXERCISE

Problem

What are the limitations of cellular network security?

Hands-On Projects

Project

What are the security issues in cellular networks?

Case Projects

Problem

What types of attacks are cellular networks open to?

Optional Team Case Project

Problem

What additional security mechanisms are available to cellular networks?

REFERENCES

[1] 3GPP, architectural requirements, Technical Standard 3G TS 23.221 V6.3.0, 3G Partnership Project, May 2004.

[2] K. Murakami, O. Haase, J. Shin, T.F. LaPorta, Mobility management alternatives for migration to mobile internet session-based services, IEEE J. Sel. Areas Commun. (J-SAC) 22 (June 2004) 834–848. special issue on Mobile Internet.

[3] 3GPP, 3G security, Security threats and requirements, Technical Standard 3G TS 21.133 V3.1.0, 3G Partnership Project, December 1999.

[4] 3GPP, network architecture, Technical Standard 3G TS 23.002 V3.3.0, 3G Partnership Project, May 2000.

[5] V. Eberspacher, GSM Switching, Services and Protocols, John Wiley & Sons, 1999.

[6] 3GPP, Basic call handling - technical realization, Technical Standard 3GPP TS 23.018 V3.4.0, 3G Partnership Project, April 1999.

[7] 3GPP, A guide to 3rd generation security, Technical Standard 3GPP TR 33.900 V1.2.0, 3G Partnership Project, January 2001.

[8] B. Chatras, C. Vernhes, Mobile application part design principles, in: Proceedings of XIII International Switching Symposium, vol. 1, June 1990, pp. 35–42.

[9] J.A. Audestad, The mobile application part (map) of GSM, technical report, Telektronikk 3.2004, Telektronikk, March 2004.

[10] 3GPP, Mobile Application part (MAP) specification, Technical Standard 3GPP TS 29.002 V3.4.0, 3G Partnership Project, April 1999.

[11] K. Boman, G. Horn, P. Howard, V. Niemi, Umts security, Electron. Commun. Eng. J. 14 (5) (October 2002) 191–204. Special issue security for mobility.

[12] K. Kotapati, P. Liu, T.F. LaPorta, Dependency relation-based vulnerability analysis of 3G networks: can it identify unforeseen cascading attacks? Special Issue of Springer Telecommunications Systems on Security, Privacy and Trust for Beyond 3G Networks, March 2007.

[13] K. Kotapati, P. Liu, T.F. LaPorta, Evaluating MAPSec by marking attack graphs, ACM/Kluwer J. Wire. Netw. J. (WINET) 12 (March 2008).

[14] K. Kotapati, P. Liu, T.F. LaPorta, EndSec: an end-to-end message security protocol for cellular networks, IEEE workshop on security, privacy and authentication in wireless networks (SPAWN

[15] D. Moore, V. Paxson, S. Savage, C. Shannon, S. Staniford, N. Weaver, Inside the slammer worm, IEEE Secur. Privacy 1 (4) (2003) 33–39.

[16] W. Enck, P. Traynor, P. McDaniel, T.F. LaPorta, Exploiting open functionality in sms-capable cellular networks, CCS '05: Proceedings of the 12th ACM Conference on Computer and Communications Security, ACM Press, 2005.

[17] P. Traynor, W. Enck, P. McDaniel, T.F. LaPorta, Mitigating attacks on open functionality in SMS-capable cellular networks, MobiCom '06: Proceedings of the 12th Annual International Conference on Mobile Computing and Networking, ACM Press, 2006, pp. 182–193

[18] P. Traynor, P. McDaniel, T.F. LaPorta, On attack causality in internet-connected cellular networks, USENIX Security Symposium (SECURITY), August 2007.

[19] T. Moore, T. Kosloff, J. Keller, G. Manes, S. Shenoi. Signaling system 7 (SS7) network security, in: Proceedings of the IEEE 45th Midwest Symposium on Circuits and Systems, August 2002.

[20] G. Lorenz, T. Moore, G. Manes, J. Hale, S. Shenoi, Securing SS7 telecommunications networks, in: Proceedings of the 2001 IEEE Workshop on Information Assurance and Security, June 2001.

[21] K. Kotapati, P. Liu, Y. Sun, T.F. LaPorta, A taxonomy of cyber attacks on 3G networksISI, Lecture Notes in Computer Science Proceedings IEEE International Conference on Intelligence and Security Informatics, Springer-Verlag, May 2005, pp. 631–633

[22] K. Kotapati, Assessing Security of Mobile Telecommunication Networks, Ph. D dissertation, Penn State University, August 2008.

[23] Switch, 5ESS Switch, www.alleged.com/telephone/5ESS/.

[24] Telcoman, Central Offices, www.thecentraloffice.com/.

[25] V. Prevelakis, D. Spinellis, The Athens affair, IEEE Spectrum (July 2007).

[26] H. Hannu, Signaling Compression (SigComp) Requirements & Assumptions, RFC 3322 (Informational), January 2003.

[27] W. Stallings, Cryptography and Network Security: Principles and Practice, Prentice Hall, 2000.

[28] K. Kotapati, P. Liu, T. F. LaPorta, CAT - a practical graph & SDL based toolkit for vulnerability assessment of 3G networks, in: Proceedings of the 21st IFIP TC-11 International Information Security Conference, Security and Privacy in Dynamic Environments, SEC 2006, May 2006.

[29] 3GPP2 3GPP, Third Generation Partnership Project, www.3gpp.org/, 2006.

[30] J. Ellsberger, D. Hogrefe, A. Sarma, SDL, Formal Object-oriented Language for Communicating Systems, Prentice Hall, 1997.

## Chapter 18

RFID Security

Chunming Rong
University of Stavanger, Norway

Gansen Zhao
Sun Yat-sen University, China

Liang Yan
University of Stavanger, Norway

Erdal Cayirci
University of Stavanger, Norway

Hongbing Cheng
University of Stavanger, Norway

1. RFID INTRODUCTION

Generally, an RFID system consists of three basic components: RFID tags, RFID readers, and a back-end database:

- *RFID tags or RFID transponders.* These are the data carriers attached to objects. A typical RFID tag contains information about the attached object, such as an identifier (ID) of the object and other related properties of the object that may help to identify and describe it.
- *The RFID reader or the RFID transceiver.* These devices can read information from tags and may write information into tags if the tags are rewritable.
- *Back-end database.* This is the data repository responsible for the management of data related to the tags and business transactions, such as ID, object properties, reading locations, reading time, and so on.

RFID System Architecture

RFID systems' architecture is illustrated in Figure 18.1. Tags are attached to or embedded in objects to identify or annotate them. An RFID reader send out signals to a tag for requesting information stored on the tag. The tag responses to the request by sending back the appropriate information. With the data from the back-end database, applications can then use the information from the tag to proceed with the business transaction related to the object.

Tags

In RFID systems, objects are identified or described by information on RFID tags attached to the objects. An RFID tag basically consists of a microchip that is used for data storage and computation and a coupling element for communicating with the RFID reader via radio frequency communication, such as an antenna. Some tags may also have an on-board battery to supply a limited amount of power.

RFID tags can respond to radio frequencies sent out by RFID readers. On receiving the radio signals from a RFID reader, an RFID tag either send back the requested data stored on the tag or write the data into the tag, if the tag is rewritable. Because radio signals are used, RFID tags do not require line of sight to connect with the reader and precise positioning, as barcodes do. Tags may also generate a certain amount of electronic power from the radio signals they receive, to power the computation and transmission of data.

RFID tags can be classified based on four main criteria: power source, type of memory, computational power, and functionality.

A basic and important classification criterion of RFID tags is to classify tags based on power source. Tags can be categorized into three classes: active, semi-active, and passive RFID tags.

Active RFID tags have on-board power sources, such as batteries. Active RFID tags can proactively send radio signals to an RFID reader and possibly to other tags [1]

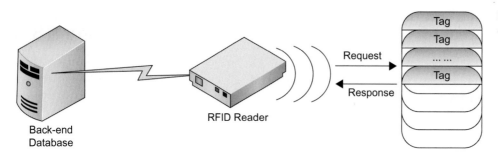

FIGURE 18.1 RFID system architecture.

as well. Compared with tags without on-board power, active tags have longer transmission range and are more reliable. Active tags can work in the absence of an RFID reader. On the other hand, the on-board power supply also increases the costs of active tags.

Semi-active RFID tags also have on-board power sources for powering their microchips, but they use RFID readers' energy field for actually transmitting their data [2] when responding to the incoming transmissions. Semi-active tags have the middle transmission range and cost.

Passive RFID tags do not have internal power sources and cannot initiate any communications. Passive RFID tags generate power from radio signals sent out by an RFID reader in the course of communication. Thus passive RFID tags can only work in the presence of an RFID reader. Passive tags have the shortest transmission range and the cheapest cost. The differences of active, semi-active and passive tags are shown in Table 18.1.

RFID tags can be classified into three categories according to the type of memory that a tag uses: read-only tags, write-once/read-many tags, and fully rewritable tags. The information on read-only tags cannot be changed in the life-cycle of the tags. Write-once/read-many tags can be initialized with application-specific information. The information on fully rewritable tags can be rewritten many times by an RFID reader.

According to the computational power, RFID tags can be classified into three categories: basic tags, symmetric-key tags, and public-key tags. Basic tags do not have the ability to perform cryptography computation. Symmetric-key tags and public-key tags have the ability to perform symmetric-key and public−key cryptography computation, respectively.

RFID tags can also be classified according to their functionality. The MIT Auto-ID Center defined five classes of tags according to their functionality in 2003 [3]: Class 0, Class 1, Class 2, Class 3, and Class 4 tags. Every class has different functions and different requirements for tag memory and power resource. Class 0 tags are passive and do not contain any memory. They only announce their presence and offer electronic article surveillance

TABLE 18.1 Tags Classified by Power Source.

Power Source	Active Tags	Semiactive Tags	Passive Tags
On-board power supply	Yes	Yes	No
Transmission range	Long	Medium	Short
Communication pattern	Proactive	Passive	Passive
Cost	Expensive	Medium	Cheap

(EAS) functionality. Class 1 tags are typically passive. They have read-only or write-once/read-many memory and can only offer identification functionality. Class 2 tags are mostly semi-active and active. They have fully rewritable memory and can offer data-logging functionality. Class 3 tags are semi-active and active tags. They contain on-board environmental sensors that can record temperature, acceleration, motion, or radiation and require fully rewritable memory. Class 4 tags are active tags and have fully rewritable memory. They can establish ad hoc wireless networks with other tags because they are equipped with wireless networking components.

RFID Readers

An RFID reader (transceiver) is a device used to read information from and possibly also write information into RFID tags. An RFID reader is normally connected to a back-end database for sending information to that database for further processing.

An RFID reader consists of two key functional modules: a high-frequency (HF) interface and a control unit. The HF interface can perform three functions: generating the transmission power to activate the tags, modulating the signals for sending requests to RFID tags, and receiving and demodulating signals received from tags. The control unit of an RFID reader has also three basic functions: controlling the communication between the RFID reader and RFID tags, encoding and decoding signals, and communicating with the back-end server for sending information to the back-end database or executing the commands from the back-end server. The control unit can perform more functions in the case of complex RFID systems, such as executing anticollision algorithms in the cause of communicating with multitags, encrypting requests sent by the RFID reader and decrypting responses received from tags, and performing the authentication between RFID readers and RFID tags [4].

RFID readers can provide high-speed tag scanning. Hundreds of objects can be dealt with by a single reader within a second; thus it is scalable enough for applications such as supply chain management, where a large number of objects need to be dealt with frequently. RFID readers need only to be placed at every entrance and exit. When products enter or leave the designated area by passing through an entrance or exit, the RFID readers can instantly identify the products and send the necessary information to the back-end database for further processing.

Back-End Database

The back-end database is in the back-end server that manages the information related to the tags in an RFID system. Every object's information can be stored as a record in the database, and the information on the tag attached to the object can serve as a pointer to the record.

The connection between an RFID reader and a back-end database can be assumed as secure, no matter via wireless link or not, because constraints for readers are not very tight and security solutions such as SSL/TLS can be implemented for them [5].

RFID Standards

Currently, as different frequencies are used for RFID systems in various countries and many standards are adopted for different kinds of application, there is no agreement on a universal standard that's accepted by all parties. Several kinds of RFID standards [6] are being used today. These standards include contactless smart cards, item management tags, RFID systems for animal identification, and electronic product code (EPC) tags. These standards specify the physical layer and the link layer characteristics of RFID systems but do not cover the upper layers.

Contactless smart cards can be classified into three types according to the communication ranges. The ISO standards for them are ISO 10536, ISO 14443, and ISO 15693. ISO 10536 sets the standard for close-coupling smart cards, for which the communication range is about 0–1 cm. ISO 14443 sets the standard for proximity-coupling smart cards, which have a communication range

of about 0–10 cm. ISO 15693 specifies vicinity-coupling smart cards, which have a communication range of about 0–1 m. The proximity-coupling and vicinity-coupling smart cards have already been implemented with some cryptography algorithms such as 128-bit AES, triple DES, and SHA-1 and challenge-response authentication mechanisms to improve system security [7].

Item management tag standards include ISO 15961, ISO 15962, ISO 15963, and ISO 18000 series [8]. ISO 15961 defines the host interrogator, tag functional commands, and other syntax features of item management. ISO 15962 defines the data syntax of item management, and ISO 15963 is "Unique Identification of RF tag and Registration Authority to manage the uniqueness." For the ISO 18000 standards series, part 1 describes the reference architecture and parameters definition; parts 2, 3, 4, 5, 6, and 7 define the parameters for air interface communications below 135 kHz, at 13.56 MHz, at 2.45 GHz, at 860 MHz, at 960 MHz, and at 433 MHz, respectively.

Standards for RFID systems for animal identification include ISO 11784, ISO 11785, and ISO 14223 [5]. ISO 11784 and ISO 11784 define the code structure and technical concepts for radiofrequency identification of animals. ISO 14223 includes three parts: air interface, code and command structure, and applications. These kinds of tags use low frequency for communication and have limited protection for animal tracking [7].

The EPC standard was created by the MIT Auto-ID, which is an association of more than 100 companies and university labs. The EPC system is currently operated by EPCglobal [8]. A typical EPC network has four parts [5]: the electronic product code, the identification system that includes RFID tags and RFID readers, the Savant middleware, and the object naming service (ONS). The first- and second-generation EPC tags cannot support strong cryptography to protect the security of the RFID systems due to the limitation of computational resources, but both of them can provide a kill command to protect the privacy of the consumer [7].

EPC tag encoding includes a Header field followed by one or more Value fields. The Header field defines the overall length and format of the Value fields. There are two kinds of EPC format: EPC 64-bit format and EPC 96-bit format. In the most recent version [9], the 64-bit format was removed from the standard. As shown in Table 18.2, both the formats include four fields: a header (8 bits), an EPC manager number (28 bits), an object class (24 bits), and a serial number (36 bits). The header and the EPC manager number are assigned by EPCglobal [8], and the object class and the serial number are assigned by EPC manager owner. The EPC header identifies the length, type, structure version, and generation of the EPC. The EPC manager number is the entity responsible for maintaining the subsequent partitions of the EPC.

TABLE 18.2 EPC Basic Format.

Header	EPC	Object Class	Serial
	Manager		Number
	Number		

TABLE 18.3 RFID Application Purpose.

Application Type	Identification Purpose
Asset management	Determine item presence
Tracking	Determine item location
Authenticity verification	Determine item source
Matching	Ensure affiliated items are not separated
Process control	Correlate item information for decision making
Access control	Person authentication
Automated payment	Conduct financial transaction

The object class identifies a class of objects. Serial number identifies the instance.

RFID Applications

Recently more and more companies and organizations have begun to use RFID tags rather than traditional barcode because RFID systems have many advantages over traditional barcode systems. First, the information stored in the RFID tags can be read by RFID readers without a line of sight; whereas, barcodes can only be scanned within the line of sight. Second, the distance between a tag and a reader is longer compared with the barcode system. For example, an RFID reader can read information from a tag at a distance as long as 300 feet, whereas the read range for a barcode is typically no more than 15 feet. Third, RFID readers can scan hundreds of tags in seconds. Fourth, since today most RFID tags are produced using silicon technology, more functions can be added to them, such as large memory for more information storage and calculation ability to support various kinds of encryption and decryption algorithms, so privacy can be better protected and the tags cannot be easily cloned by attackers. In addition, the information stored in the barcode cannot be changed after being imprinted on the barcode, whereas for the RFID tags with rewritable memory the information can be updated when needed.

With these characteristics and advantages, RFID has been widely adopted and deployed in various areas. Currently, RFID can be used in passports, transportation payments, product tracking, lap scoring, animal identification, inventory systems, RFID mandates, promotion tracking, human implants, libraries, schools and universities, museums, and social retailing. These myriad applications of RFID can be classified into seven classes according to the purpose of identifying items [10]. These classes are asset management, tracking, authenticity verification, matching, process control, access control, and automated payment. Table 18.3 lists the identification purposes of various application types.

Asset management involves determining the presence of tagged items and helping manage item inventory. One possible application of asset management is electronic article surveillance (EAS). For example, every good in a supermarket is attached to an EAS tag, which will be deactivated if it is properly checked out. Then RFID readers at the supermarket exits can detect unpaid goods automatically when they pass through.

Tracking is used to identify the location of tagged items. If the readers are fixed, a single reader can cover only one area. To effectively track the items, a group of readers is needed, together with a central system to deal with the information from different readers.

Authenticity verification methods are used to verify the source of tagged items. For example, by adding a cryptography-based digital signature in the tag, the system can prevent tag replication to make sure that a good is labeled with the source information.

Matching is used to ensure that affiliated items are not separated. Samples for matching applications include mothers and their newborn babies to match each other in the hospital and for airline passengers to match their checked luggage and so prevent theft.

Access control is used for person authentication. Buildings may use contactless RFID card systems to identify authorized people. Only those authorized people with the correct RFID card can authenticate themselves to the reader to open a door and enter a building. Using a car key with RFID tags, a car owner can open his own car automatically, another example of RFID's application to access control.

Process control involves decision making by correlating tagged item information. For example, RFID readers in different parts of an assembly line can read the information on the products, which can be used to help production managers make suitable decisions.

Automated payment is used to conduct financial transactions. The applications include payment for toll expressways and at gas stations. These applications can improve the speed of payment to hasten the processing of these transactions.

2. RFID CHALLENGES

RFID systems have been widely deployed in some areas. Perhaps this happened beyond the expectations of RFID researchers and RFID service providers. There are many limitations of the RFID technology that restrain the deployment of RFID applications, such as the lack of universal standardization of RFID in the industry and the concerns about security and privacy problems that may affect the privacy and security of individuals and organizations. The security and privacy issues pose a huge challenge for RFID applications. Here we briefly summarize some of the challenges facing RFID systems.

Counterfeiting

As described earlier in the chapter, RFID tags can be classified into three categories based on the equipped computation power: basic tags, symmetric-key tags, and public-key tags. Symmetric-key and public-key tags can implement cryptography protocols for authentication with private key, and public keys, respectively. Basic tags are not capable of performing cryptography computation. Although they lack the capability to perform cryptography computation, they are most widely used for applications such as supply chain management and travel systems. With the widespread application of fully writable or even reprogrammable basic tags, counterfeiters can easily forge basic tags in real-world applications, and these counterfeit tags can be used in multiple places at the same time, which can cause confusion.

The counterfeiting of tags can be categorized into two areas based on the technique used for tampering with tag data: modifying tag data and adding data to a blank tag. In real-world applications, we face counterfeit threats such as the following [7]:

- The attacker can modify valid tags to make them invalid or modify invalid tags to make them valid.
- The attacker can modify a high-priced object's tag as a low-priced object or modify a low-priced object's tag as a high-priced object.
- The attacker can modify an object's tag to be the same as the tags attached to other objects.
- The attacker can create an additional tag for personal reasons by reading the data from an authorized tag and adding this data to a blank tag in real-world applications, such as in a passport or a shipment of goods.

Sniffing

Another main issue of concern in deploying RFID systems is the sniffing problem. It occurs when third parties use a malicious and unauthorized RFID reader to read the information on RFID tags within their transmission range.

Unfortunately, most RFID tags are indiscriminate in their responses to reading requests transmitted by RFID readers and do not have access control functions to provide any protection against an unauthorized reader. Once an RFID tag enters a sufficiently powered reader's field, it receives the reader's requests via radio frequency. As long as the request is well formed, the tag will reply to the request with the corresponding information on the tag. Then the holder of the unauthenticated reader may use this information for other purposes.

Tracking

With multiple RFID readers integrated into one system, the movements of objects can be tracked by fixed RFID readers [11]. For example, once a specific tag can be associated with a particular person or object, when the tag enters a reader's field the reader can obtain the specific identifier of the tag, and the presence of the tag within the range of a specific reader implies specific location information related to the attached person or object. With location information coming from multiple RFID readers, an attacker can follow movements of people or objects. Tracking can also be performed without decrypting the encrypted messages coming from RFID readers [5]. Generally, the more messages the attacker describes, the more location or privacy information can be obtained from the messages.

One way to track is to generate maps of RFID tags with mobile robots [12]. A sensor model is introduced to compute the likelihood of tag detections, given the relative pose of the tag with respect to the robot. In this model a highly accurate FastSLAM algorithm is used to learn the geometrical structure of the environment around the robots, which are equipped with a laser range scanner; then it uses the recursive Bayesian filtering scheme to estimate the posterior locations of the RFID tags, which can be used to localize robots and people in the environment with the geometrical structure of the environment learned by the FastSLAM algorithm.

There is another method to detect the motion of passive RFID tags that are within a detecting antenna's field. Response rate at the reader is used to study the impact of four cases of tag movements that can provide prompt and accurate detection and the influence of the environment. The idea of multiple tags/readers is introduced to improve performance. The movement-detection algorithms can be improved and integrated into the RFID monitoring system to localize the position of the tags. The method does not require any modification of communication protocols nor the addition of hardware. In real-world applications, there exists the following tracking threat: The attacker can track the potential victim by monitoring the movement of the person and performing some illegal actions against the potential victim [13].

Now, let's take a very brief look at denial of service threats. Availability enables a Web services application to detect a Denial of Service (DoS) attack, to continue operation as long as possible, and then to gracefully recover and resume operations after a DoS attack. There is a need for techniques to replicate data and services to ensure continuity of operations in the event of a fault or threat (see checklist: "An Agenda For Action When Thwarting DoS Threats"). There is also a need for management and monitoring solutions to provide service performance and availability monitoring to meet certain service level objectives.

Other Issues

Besides the four basic types of attack (counterfeiting, sniffing, tracking, and denial of service) in real-world applications, there also exists some other threats to RFID systems.

Spoofing

Spoofing attacks take place when an attacker successfully poses as an authorized user of a system [13]. Spoofing attacks are different from counterfeiting and sniffing attacks, though they are all falsification types of attack. Counterfeiting takes place when an attacker forges the RFID tags that can be scanned by authorized readers. Sniffing takes place when an attacker forges authorized readers that can scan the authorized tags to obtain useful information. But the forging object of spoofing is an authorized user of a system. There exist the following spoofing threats in real-world applications [13]:

- *The attacker can pose as an authorized EPC global Information Service Object Naming Service (ONS) user.* If the attacker successfully poses as an authorized ONS user, he can send queries to the ONS to gather EPC numbers. Then, from the EPC numbers, the attacker may easily obtain the location, identification, or other privacy information.
- *The attacker can pose as an authorized database user in an RFID system.* The database stores the complete

---

An Agenda for Action when Thwarting DoS Threats

Denial of service (DoS) takes place when RFID readers or back-end servers cannot provide excepted services. DoS attacks are easy to accomplish and difficult to guard against [13]. The following are nine DoS threats (check all tasks completed):

____1. *Killing tags to make them disabled to disrupt readers' normal operations.* EPCglobal had proposed that a tag have a "kill" command to destroy it and protect consumer privacy. If an attacker knows the password of a tag, it can "kill" the tag easily in real-world applications. Now Class-0, Class-1 Generation-1, and Class-1 Generation-2 tags are all equipped with the kill command.

____2. Carry a blocker tag that can disrupt the communication between an RFID reader and RFID tags. *A blocker tag is a cheap, passive RFID device that can simulate many basic RFID tags at one time and render specific zones private or public. An RFID reader can only communicate with a single RFID tag at any specific time. If more than one tag responds to a request coming from the reader at the same time, "collision" happens. In this case, the reader cannot receive the information sent by the tags, which makes the system unavailable to authorized uses.*

____3. Carry a special absorbent tag that can be tuned to the same radio frequencies used by legitimate tags. *The absorbent tag can absorb the energy or power generated by radiofrequency signals sent by the reader, and the resulting reduction in the reader's*

energy may make the reader unavailable to communicate with other tags.

____4. *Remove, physically destroy, or erase the information on tags attached to or embedded in objects.* The reader will not communicate with the dilapidated tags in a normal way.

____5. *Shield the RFID tags from scrutiny using a Faraday cage. A Faraday cage is a container made of a metal enclosure that can prevent reading radio signals from the readers* [14].

____6. *Carry a device that can actively broadcast more powerful return radio signals or noises than the signals responded to by the tags so as to block or disrupt the communication of any nearby RFID readers and make the system unavailable to authorized users.* The power of the broadcast is so high that it could cause severe blockage or disruption of all nearby RFID systems, even those in legitimate applications where privacy is not a concern [14].

____7. *Perform a traditional Internet DoS attack and prevent the back-end servers from gathering EPC numbers from the readers.* The servers do not receive enough information from the readers and cannot provide the additional services from the server.

____8. *Perform a traditional Internet DoS attack against the object-naming service (ONS). This can deny the service.*

____9. *Send URL queries to a database and make the database busy with these queries. The database may then deny access to authorized users.*

information from the objects, such as manufacturer, product name, read time, read location, and other privacy information. If the attacker successfully poses as an authorized database user and an authorized user of ONS, he can send queries to the ONS for obtaining the EPC number of one object, then get the complete information on the object by mapping the EPC number to the information stored in the database.

- *The attacker can also pose as an ONS server.* If the attacker's pose is successful, he can easily use the ONS server to gather EPC numbers, respond to invalid requests, deny normal service, and even change the data or write malicious data to the system.

Repudiation

Repudiation takes place when a user denies doing an action or no proof exists to prove that the action has been implemented [13]. There are two kinds of repudiation threats:

- The sender or the receiver denies performing the send and receive actions. A non-repudiation protocol can be used to resolve this problem.
- The owner of the EPC number or the back-end server denies that it has the information from the objects to which the tags are attached.

Insert Attacks

Insert attacks take place when an attacker inserts some system commands to the RFID system where data is normally expected [15]. In real-world applications, there exists the following attack: A system command rather than valid data is carried by a tag in its data storage memory.

Replay Attacks

Replay attacks take place when an attacker intercepts the communication signals between an RFID reader and an RFID tag and records the tag's response. Then the RFID tag's response can be reused if the attacker detects that the reader sends requests to the other tags for querying [16]. There exist the following two threats:

- The attacker can record the communications between proximity cards and a building access reader and play it back to access the building.
- The attacker can record the response that an RFID card in a car gives to an automated highway toll collection system, and the response can be used when the car of the attacker wants to pass the automated toll station.

Physical Attacks

Physical attacks are very strong attacks that physically obtain tags and have unauthorized physical operations on the tags. But it is fortunate that physical attacks cannot be implemented in public or on a widespread scale, except for Transient Electromagnetic Pulse Emanation Standard (TEMPEST) attacks. There exist the following physical attacks [1,17]:

- *Probe attacks.* The attacker can use a probe directly attached to the circuit to obtain or change the information on tags.
- *Material removal.* The attacker can use a knife or other tools to remove the tags attached to objects.
- *Energy attacks.* The attacks can be either of the contact or contactless variety. It is required that contactless energy attacks be close enough to the system.
- *Radiation imprinting.* The attacker can use an X-ray band or other radial bands to destroy the data unit of a tag.
- *Circuit disruption.* The attacker can use strong electromagnetic interference to disrupt tag circuits.
- *Clock glitch.* The attacker can lengthen or shorten the clock pulses to a clocked circuit and destroy normal operations.

Viruses

Viruses are old attacks that threaten the security of all information systems, including RFID systems. RFID viruses always target the back-end database in the server, perhaps destroying and revealing the data or information stored in the database. There exist the following virus threats:

- An RFID virus destroys and reveals the data or information stored in the database.
- An RFID virus disturbs or even stops the normal services provided by the server.
- An RFID virus threatens the security of the communications between RFID readers and RFID tags or between back-end database and RFID readers.

Social Issues

Due to the security challenges in RFID, many people do not trust RFID technologies and fear that they could allow attackers to purloin their privacy information.

Weis [16] presents two main arguments. These arguments make some people choose not to rely on RFID technology and regard RFID tags as the "mark of the beast." However, security issues cannot prevent the success of RFID technology.

The first argument is that RFID tags are regarded as the best replacement for current credit cards and all other ways of paying for goods and services. But RFID tags can also serve as identification. The replacement of current ways of paying by RFID tag requires that people accept RFID tags instead of credit cards, and they cannot sell or buy anything without RFID tags.

There is a second argument [16]: "Since RFID tags are also used as identification, they should be implanted to avoid losing the ID or switching it with someone. Current research has shown that the ideal location for the implant is indeed the forehead or the hand, since they are easy to access and unlike most other body parts they do not contain much fluid, which interferes with the reading of the chip."

Comparison of All Challenges

Previously in this chapter we introduced some of the challenges that RFID systems are facing. Every challenge or attack can have a different method or attack goal, and the consequences of the RFID system after an attack may also be different. In this part of the chapter, we briefly analyze the challenges according to attack methods, attack goals, and the consequences of RFID systems after attacks (see Table 18.4).

The first four challenges are the four basic challenges in RFID systems that correspond to the four basic use cases. *Counterfeiting* happens when counterfeiters forge RFID tags by copying the information from a valid tag or adding some well-formed format information to a new tag in the RFID system. *Sniffing* happens when an unauthorized reader reads the information from a tag, and the information may be utilized by attackers. *Tracking* happens when an attacker who holds some readers unlawfully monitors the movements of objects attached by an RFID tag that can be read by those readers. *Denial of service* happens when the components of RFID systems deny the RFID service.

The last seven challenges or attacks can always happen in RFID systems (see Table 18.4). *Spoofing* happens when an attacker poses as an authorized user of an RFID system on which the attacker can perform invalid operations. *Repudiation* happens when a user or component of an RFID system denies the action it performed and there is no proof that the user did perform the action. *Insert attacks* happen when an attacker inserts some invalid system commands into the tags and some operations may be implemented by the invalid command. *Replay attacks* happen when an attacker intercepts the response of the tag and reuses the response for another communication. *Physical attacks* happen when an attacker does some physical operations on RFID tags and these attacks disrupt communications between the RFID readers and tags. A *virus* is the security challenge of all information systems; it can disrupt the operations of RFID systems or reveal the information in those systems. *Social issues* involve users' psychological attitudes that can influence the users' adoption of RFID technologies for real-world applications.

TABLE 18.4 Comparison of all Challenges or Attacks in RFID Systems.

Challenge or Attack	Attack Method	Attack Goal	Direct Consequence
Counterfeiting	Forge tags	Tag	Invalid tags
Sniffing	Forge readers	Reader	Reveals information
Tracking	Monitor the movement of objects	Objects of an RFID system	Tracks the movement of object
Denial of service	RF jamming, kill normal command, physical destroy, and so on	Reader, back-end database or server	Denies normal services
Spoofing	Pose as an authorized user	User	Invalid operations by invalid user
Repudiation	Deny action or no proof that the action was implemented	Tag, reader, back-end database or server	Deniable actions
Insert attacks	Insert invalid command	Tag	Invalid operations by invalid commands
Replay attacks	Reuse the response of tags	Communication between RFID tags and readers	Invalid identification
Physical attacks	Physical operations on tag	Tag	Disrupts or destroys communication between RFID tags and readers
Virus	Insert invalid data	Back-end database or server	Destroys the data or service of system
Social issues	Social attitude	Psychology of potential user	Restricts the widespread application

3. RFID PROTECTIONS

According to their computational power, RFID tags can be classified into three categories: basic tags, symmetric-key tags, and public-key tags. In the next part of the chapter, we introduce some protection approaches for these three kinds of RFID tags.

Basic RFID System

Prices have been one of the biggest factors to be considered when we're making decisions on RFID deployments. Basic tags are available for the cheapest price, compared with symmetric-key tags and public-key tags. Due to the limited computation resources built into a basic tag, basic tags are not capable of performing cryptography computations. This imposes a huge challenge to implement protections on basic tags; cryptography has been one of the most important and effective methods to implement protection mechanisms. Recently several approaches have been proposed to tackle this issue.

Most of the approaches to security protection for basic tags focus on protecting consumer privacy. A usual method is by tag killing, proposed by EPCglobal. In this approach, when the reader wants to kill a tag, it sends a kill message to the tag to permanently deactivate it. Together with the kill message, a 32-bit tag-specific PIN code is also sent to the object tag, to avoid killing other tags. On receiving this kill message, a tag will deactivate itself, after which the tag will become inoperative. Generally, tags are killed when the tagged items are checked out in shops or supermarkets. This is very similar to removing the tags from the tagged items when they are purchased. It is an efficient method of protecting the privacy of consumers, since a killed tag can no longer send out information.

The disadvantage of this approach is that it will reduce the post-purchase benefits of RFID tags. In some cases, RFID tags need to be operative only temporarily. For example, RFID tags used in libraries and museums for tagging books and other items need to work at all times and should not be killed or be removed from the tagged items. In these cases, instead of being killed or removed, tags can be made temporarily inactive. When a tag needs to be reawoken, an RFID reader can send a wake message to the tag with a 32-bit tag-specific PIN code, which is sent to avoid waking up other tags. This also results in the management of PIN codes for tags, which brings some inconvenience.

Another approach to protecting privacy is tag relabeling, which was first proposed by Sarma et al [18]. In this scheme, to protect consumers' privacy, identifiers of RFID tags are effaced when tagged items are checked out, but the information on the tags will be kept for later

use. Inoue and Yasuuran [19] proposed that consumers can store the identifiers of the tags and give each tag a new identifier. When needed, people can reactivate the tags with the new identifiers. This approach allows users to manage tagged items throughout the items' life cycle. A third approach is to allocate each tag a new random number at each checkout; thus attackers cannot rely on the identifiers to collect information about customers [20]. This method does not solve the problem of tracking [20]. To prevent tracking, random numbers need to be refreshed frequently, which will increase the burden on consumers. Juels proposed a system called the *minimalist system* [21], in which every tag has a list of pseudonyms, and for every reader query, the tag will respond with a different pseudonym from the list and return to the beginning of the list when this list is exhausted. It is assumed that only authorized readers know all these tag pseudonyms. Unauthorized readers that do not know these pseudonyms cannot identify the tags correctly. To prevent unauthorized readers getting the pseudonyms list by frequent query, the tags will response to an RFID reader's request with a relatively low rate, which is called *pseudonym throttling*. Pseudonym throttling is useful, but it cannot provide a high level of privacy for consumers, because with the tag's small memory, the number of pseudonyms in the list is limited. To tackle this problem, the protocol allows an authorized RFID reader to refresh a tag's pseudonyms list.

Juels and Pappu [22] proposed to protect consumers' privacy by using tagged banknotes. The proposed scheme used public-key cryptography to protect the serial numbers of tagged banknotes. The serial number of a tagged banknote is encrypted using a public key to generate a ciphertext, which is saved in the memory of the tag. On receiving a request of the serial number, the tag will respond with this ciphertext. Only law enforcement agencies know the related private key and can decrypt this ciphertext to recover the banknote's serial number. To prevent tracking of banknotes, the ciphertext will be reencrypted periodically. To avoid the ciphertext of a banknote being reencrypted by an attacker, the tagged banknote can use an optical write — access key. A reader that wants to reencrypt this ciphertext needs to scan the write — access key first. In this system only one key pair, a public key and a private key, is used. But this is not enough for the general RFID system. Using multiple key pairs will impair the privacy of RFID systems, since if the reader wants to reencrypt the ciphertext, it needs to know the corresponding public key of this tag.

So, a universal reencryption algorithm has been introduced [23]. In this approach, an RFID reader can reencrypt the ciphertext without knowing the corresponding public key of a tag. The disadvantage of this approach is that attackers can substitute the ciphertext with a new ciphertext, so the integrity of the ciphertext cannot be protected. By signing the ciphertext with a digital signature, this problem can be solved [24], since only the authenticated reader can access the ciphertext.

Floerkemeier (et al.) [25] introduced another approach to protect consumer privacy by using a specially designed protocol. In their approach, they first designed the communication protocol between RFID tags and RFID readers. This protocol requires an RFID reader to provide information about the purpose and the collection type for the query. In addition, a privacy-enforcing device called a *watchdog tag* is used in the system. This watchdog tag is a kind of sophisticated RFID tag that is equipped with a battery, a small screen, and a long-range communication channel. A watchdog tag can be integrated into a PDA or a cell phone and can decode the messages from an RFID reader and display them on the screen for the user to read. With a watchdog tag, a user can know not only the information from the RFID readers in the vicinity of the tag but also the ID, the query purpose, and the collection type of the requests sent by the RFID readers. With this information, the user is able to identify the unwanted communications between tags and an RFID reader, making this method useful for users to avoid the reader ID spoofing attack.

Rieback, Crispo, and Tanebaum [26] proposed another privacy-enforcing device called RFID Guardian, which is also a battery-powered RFID tag that can be integrated into a PDA or a cell phone to protect user privacy. RFID Guardian is actually a user privacy protection platform in RFID systems. It can also work as an RFID reader to request information from RFID tags, or it can work like a tag to communicate with a reader. RFID Guardian has four different security properties: auditing, key management, access control, and authentication. It can audit RFID readers in its vicinity and record information about the RFID readers, such as commands, related parameters, and data, and provide these kinds of information to the user. Using this information, the user can sufficiently identify illegal scanning. In some cases, a user might not know or could forget the tags in his vicinity. With the help of RFID Guardian, the user can detect all the tags within radio range. Then the user can deactivate the tags according to his choice.

For RFID tags that use cryptography methods to provide security, one important issue is key management. RFID Guardian can perform two-way RFID communications and can generate random values. These features are very useful for key exchange and key refresh. Using the features of coordination of security primitives, context awareness, and tag-reader mediation, RFID Guardian can provide access control for RFID systems [26]. Also, using two-way RFID communication and standard challenge-response algorithms, RFID Guardian can provide off-tag authentication for RFID readers.

Another approach for privacy protecting is proposed by Juels, Rivest, and Szydlo [14]. In this approach, a cheap, passive RFID tag is used as the blocker tag. Since this blocker tag can simulate many RFID tags at the same time, it is very difficult for an RFID reader to identify the real tag carried by the user. The blocker tag can both simulate all the possible RFID tags and simulate only a select set of the tags, making it convenient for the user to manage the RFID tags. For example, the user can tell the blocker tag to block only the tags that belong to a certain company. Another advantage of this approach is that if the user wants to reuse these RFID tags, unlike the "killed" tags that need to be activated by the user, the user need only remove the blocker tag. Since the blocker tag can shield the serial numbers of the tags from being read by RFID readers, it can also be used by attackers to disrupt proper operation of an RFID system. A thief can also use the blocker tag to shield the tags attached to the commodities in shops and take them out without being detected.

RFID System Using Symmetric-Key Cryptography

Symmetric-key cryptography, also called *secret-key cryptography* or *single-key cryptography*, uses a single key to perform both encryption and decryption. Due to the limited amount of resources available on an RFID chip, most available symmetric-key cryptographs are too costly to be implemented on an RFID chip. For example, a typical implementation of Advanced Encryption Standard (AES) needs about 2000–3000 gates. This is not appropriate for low-cost RFID tags. It is only possible to implement AES in high-end RFID tags. A successful case of implementing a 128-bit AES on high-end RFID tags has been reported [27].

Using the Symmetric Key to Provide Authentication and Privacy

Symmetric-key cryptography can be applied to prevent tag cloning in RFID systems using a challenge and response protocol. For example, if a tag shares a secret key K with a reader and the tag wants to authenticate itself to the reader, it will first send its identity to the reader. The reader will then generate a nonce N and send it to the tag. The tag will use this nonce and the secret K to generate a hash code $H = h(K,N)$ and send this hash code to the reader. The reader can also generate a hash code $H' = h(K,N)$ and compare these two codes to verify this tag. Using this scheme, it is difficult for an attacker to clone the tags without knowing the secret keys.

Different kinds of symmetric-key cryptography protocol-based RFID tags have been used recently in daily life. For example, an RFID device that uses this symmetric-key challenge-response protocol, called a digital signature transponder, has been introduced by Texas Instruments. This transponder can be built into cars to prevent car theft and can be implemented into wireless payment devices used in filling stations.

One issue of RFID systems that use symmetric-key cryptography is key management. To authenticate itself to an RFID reader, each tag in the system should share a different secret key with the reader, and the reader needs to keep all the keys of these tags. When a tag wants to authenticate itself to an RFID reader, the reader needs to know the secret key shared between them. If the reader does not know the identification of the tag in advance, it cannot determine which key can be used to authenticate this tag. If the tag sends its identification to the reader before the authentication for the reader to search the secret key, the privacy of the tag cannot be protected, since other readers can also obtain the identification of this tag.

To tackle this problem, one simple method is *key searching*. The reader will search all the secret keys in its memory to find the right key for the tag before authentication. There are some protocols proposed for the key search for RFID tags. One general kind of key search scheme [11] has been proposed. In this approach, the tag first generates a random nonce N and hashes this N using its secret key K to generate the hash code. Then it sends both this hash code and N to the reader. Using this nonce N, the reader will generate the hash code with all the secret keys and compare them with the received hash code from the tag. If there is a match, it means it found the right key. In this scheme, since the nonce N is generated randomly every time, the privacy of the tag can be protected.

The problem with this approach is that if there are a large number of tags, the key searching will be very costly. To reduce the cost of the key searching, a modification of this scheme was proposed [28]; in [12], in this approach, a scheme called *tree of secret* is used. Every tag is assigned to a leaf in the tree, and every node in the tree has its secret key. This way the key search cost for each tag can be reduced, but it will add some overlap to the sets of keys for each tag.

Another approach to reduce the cost of key searching is for the RFID tags and RFID reader to keep synchronization with each other. In this kind of approach, every tag will maintain a counter for the reader query times. For each reader's query, the tag should respond with a different value. The reader will also maintain counters for all the tags' responses and maintain a table of all the possible response values. Then, if the reader and tags can keep synchronization, the reader can know the approximate current counter number of the tags. When the reader

receives a response from a tag, it can search the table and quickly identify this tag.

Other Symmetric-Key Cryptography-based Approaches

In addition to the basic symmetric-key challenge-response protocol, some symmetric-key cryptography-based approaches have been proposed recently to protect the security and privacy of RFID systems.

One approach is called YA-TRAP: Yet Another Trivial RFID Authentication Protocol, proposed by Tsudik [29]. In this approach, a technique for the inexpensive untraceable identification of RFID tags is introduced. Here *untraceable* means it is computationally difficult to gather the information about the identity of RFID tags from the interaction with them. In YA-TRAP, for the purpose of authentication, only minimal communication between the reader and tags is needed, and the computational burden on the back-end server is very small.

The back-end server in the system is assumed to be secure and maintains all tag information. Each tag should be initialized with three values: K_i, T_0, and T_{max}. K_i is both the identifier and the cryptographic key for this tag. The size of K_i depends on the number of tags and the secure authentication requirement; in practice, 160 bits is enough. T_0 is the initial timestamp of this tag. The value of T_0 of each tag does not need to vary. This means that a group of tags can have the same T_0. T_{max} is the maximum value of T_0, and a group of tags can also have the same T_{max} value. In addition, each tag has a seeded pseudorandom number generator.

YA-TRAP works as follows: First, each tag should store a timestamp T_t in its memory. When an RFID reader wants to interrogate a RFID tag, it will send the current timestamp T_r to this tag. Receiving T_r, the tag will compare T_r with the timestamp value it stores and with T_{max}. If $T_r < T_t$ or $T_r > T_{max}$, this tag will respond to the reader with a random value generated by the seeded pseudo random number generator. Otherwise, the tag will replace T_t with T_r and calculate $H_r = HMAC_{K_i}(T_t)$, and then send H_r to the reader. Then the reader will send T_r and H_r to the back-end server. The server will look up its database to find whether this tag is a valid tag. If it's not, the server will send a tag-error message to the reader. If this is a valid tag, the server will send the meta-ID of this tag or the valid message to the reader, according to different application requirements. Since the purpose of this protocol is to minimize the interaction between the reader and tags and minimize the computation burden of the back-end server, it has some vulnerability. One of them is that the adversary can launch a DoS attack to the tag. For example, the attack can send a timestamp $t < T_{max}$, but this t is wildly inaccurate with the current time. In this case, the tag will update its timestamp with the wrong time and the legal reader cannot get access to this tag.

In Ref. [16], another approach called *deterministic hash locks* [11] was proposed. In this scheme, the security of RFID systems is based on the one-way hash function. During initialization, every tag in the system will be given a meta-ID, which is the hash code of a random key. This meta-ID will be stored in the tag's memory. Both the meta-ID and the random key are also stored in the back-end server. After initialization, all the tags will enter the locked state. When they stay in the locked state, tags will respond only with the meta-ID when interrogated by an RFID reader. When a legitimate reader wants to unlock a tag, as shown in Figure 18.2, it will first send a request to the tag. After receiving the meta-ID from the tag, the reader will send this meta-ID to the back-end server. The back-end server will search in its database using this meta-ID to get the random key. Then it will send this key to the reader, and the reader will send it to the tag. Using this random key, the tag will hash this key and compare the hash code with its meta-ID. The tag will unlock itself and send its actual identification to the reader if these two values match. Then the tag will return to the locked state to prevent hijacking of illegal readers. Since the illegal reader cannot contact the back-end server to get the random key, it cannot get the actual identification of the tag.

One problem with deterministic hash locks is that when the tag is queried, it will respond with its meta-ID. Since the meta-ID of the tag is a static one and cannot change, the tag can be tracked easily. To solve this problem, Weis, Sarma, Rivest, and Engels proposed the Randomized Hash Locks protocol to prevent tracking of the tag. In this protocol, each tag is equipped with not only the one-way hash function but also a random number generator. When the tag is requested by a reader, it will use the random number generator to generate a random number and will hash this random number together with its identification. The tag will respond with this hash code and the random number to the reader. After receiving this response from the tag, the reader will get all identifications of the tags from the back-end server. Using these identifications, the reader will perform brute-force search by hashing the identification of each tag together with the random number and compare the hash code. If there is a

match, the reader can know the identification of the tag. In this approach, the tag response to the reader is not dependent on the request of the reader, which means that the tag is vulnerable to replay attack. To avoid this, Juels and Weis proposed a protocol called Improved Randomized Hash-Locks [30].

RFID System using Public-Key Cryptography

Symmetric-key cryptography can provide security for RFID systems, but it is more suitable to be implemented in a closed environment. If the shared secret keys between them are leaked, it will impose a big problem for the security of RFID systems. Public-key cryptography is more suitable for open systems, since both RFID readers and tags can use their public keys to protect the security of RFID systems. In addition, using public-key cryptography can not only prevent leakage of any information to the eavesdropper attack during communication between reader and tags, it also can provide digital signatures for both the readers and tags for authentication. In the public-key cryptography system, an RFID reader does not need to keep all the secret keys for each tag and does not need to search the appropriate key for each tag as it does in a symmetric-key cryptography system. This will reduce the system burden for key management. Although public-key cryptography has some advantages over symmetric-key cryptography, it is commonly accepted that public-key cryptography is computationally more expensive than symmetric-key cryptography. Because of the limitations of memory and computational power of the ordinary RFID tags, it is difficult for the public-key cryptography to be implemented in RFID systems. In recent years, some research shows that some kinds of public key-based cryptographies such as elliptic curve cryptography and hyperelliptic curve cryptography are feasible to be implemented in high-end RFID tags [31].

Authentication with Public-Key Cryptography

Basically, there are two different kinds of RFID tag authentication methods that use public-key cryptography: one is online authentication and the other is offline authentication [32].

For the authentication of RFID tags in an online situation, the reader is connected with a database server. The database server stores a large number of challenge-response pairs for each tag, making it difficult for the attacker to test all the challenge-response pairs during a limited time period. During the challenge-response pairs enrollment phase, the physical uncloneable function part of RFID systems will be challenged by a Certification Authority with a variety of challenges, and accordingly it will generate responses for these challenges. The physical

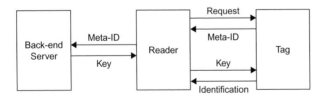

FIGURE 18.2   Tag unlock.

uncloneable function is embodied in a physical object and can give responses to the given challenges [31]. Then these generated challenge-response pairs will be stored in the database server.

In the authentication phase, when a reader wants to authenticate a tag, first the reader will send a request to the tag for its identification. After getting the ID of the tag, the reader will search the database server to get a challenge-response pair for this ID and send the challenge to the tag. After receiving the challenge from the reader, the tag will challenge its physical uncloneable function to get a response for this challenge and then send this response to the reader. The reader will compare this received response with the response stored in the database server. If the difference between these two responses is less than a certain predetermined threshold, the tag can pass the authentication. Then the database server will remove this challenge-response pair for this ID.

One paper [31] details how the authentication of RFID tags works in an offline situation using public key cryptography. To provide offline authentication for the tags, a PUF-Certificate-Identify-based identification scheme is proposed. In this method, a standard identification scheme and a standard signature scheme are used. Then the security of RFID systems depends on the security of the PUF, the standard identification scheme, and the standard signature scheme. For the standard identification scheme, an elliptic curve discrete log based on Okamoto's Identification protocol [33] is used. This elliptic curve discrete log protocol is feasible to be implemented in the RFID tags.

Identity-Based Cryptography Used in the RFID Networks

An identity-based cryptographic scheme is a kind of public-key-based approach that was first proposed by Shamir [34] in 1984. To use identity-based cryptography in RFID systems, since both the RFID tags and the reader have their identities, it is convenient for them to use their own identities to generate their public keys.

An RFID system based on identity-based cryptography should be set up with the help of a PKG. When the reader and tags enter the system, each of them is allocated a unique identity stored in their memory. The process of key generation and distribution in the RFID system that uses identity-based cryptography is shown in Figure 18.3 and is outlined here:

1. PKG generates a "master" public key PU_{pkg} and a related "master" private key PR_{pkg} and saves them in its memory.
2. The RFID reader authenticates itself to the PKG with its identity ID_{re}.

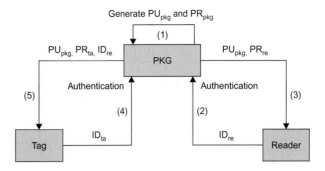

FIGURE 18.3   Key generation and distribution.

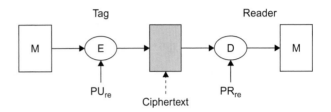

FIGURE 18.4   Message encryption.

3. If the reader can pass the authentication, PKG generates a unique private key PR_{re} for the reader and sends this private key together with PU_{pkg} to reader.
4. When an RFID tag enters the system, it authenticates itself to the PKG with its identity ID_{ta}.
5. If the tag can pass the authentication, PKG generates a unique private key PR_{ta} for the tag and sends PR_{ta} together with PU_{pkg} and the identity of the reader ID_{re} to the tag.

After this process, the reader can know its private key PR_{re} and can use PU_{pkg} and its identity to generate its public key. Every tag entered into the system can know its own private key and can generate a public key of its own and a public key of the reader.

If an RFID tag is required to transmit messages to the reader in security, since the tag can generate the reader's public key PU_{re}, it can use this key PU_{re} to encrypt the message and transmit this encrypted message to the reader. As shown in Figure 18.4, after receiving the message from the tag, the reader can use its private key PR_{re} to decrypt the message. Since only the reader can know its private key PR_{re}, the security of the message can be protected.

Figure 18.5 illustrates the scheme for the reader to create its digital signature and verify it. First, the reader will use the message and the hash function to generate a hash code, and then it uses its private key PR_{re} to encrypt this hash code to generate the digital signature and attach it to the original message and send both the digital signature and message to the tag. After receiving them, the

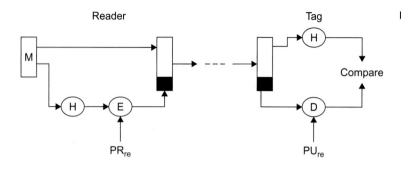

FIGURE 18.5   A digital signature from a reader.

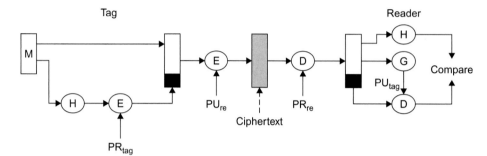

FIGURE 18.6   A digital signature from a tag.

RFID tag can use the public key of the reader PU_{re} to decrypt the digital signature to recover the hash code. By comparing this hash code with the hash code generated from the message, the RFID tag can verify the digital signature.

Figure 18.6 illustrates the scheme for the RFID tag to create its digital signature and verify it. In RFID systems, the reader cannot know the identity of the tag before reading it from the tag. The reader cannot generate the public key of the tag, so the general protocol used in identity-based networks cannot be used here. In our approach, first, the tag will use its identity and its private key PR_{ta} to generate a digital signature. When the tag needs to authenticate itself to the reader, it will add this digital signature to its identity, encrypt it with the public key of the reader PU_{re}, and send to the reader; only the reader can decrypt this ciphertext and get the identity of the tag and the digital signature. Using the tag identity, the reader can generate the tag's public key PU_{ta}. Then the reader can use this public key to verify the digital signature.

As mentioned, the most important problem for the symmetric-key approach in RFID systems is the key management. The RFID tags need a great deal of memory to store all the secret keys related with each tag in the system for message decryption. Also, if the RFID reader receives a message from a tag, it cannot know which tag this message is from and therefore cannot know which key it can use to decrypt the message. The reader needs to search all the keys until it finds the right one. In RFID systems using identity-based cryptography, every tag can use the public key of the reader to generate the ciphertext that can be decrypted using the reader's private key, so the reader does not need to know the key of the tags; all it needs to keep is its own private key.

In some RFID applications such as epassports and visas, tag authentication is required. However, the symmetric-key approach cannot provide digital signatures for RFID tags to authenticate them to RFID readers. By using an identity-based scheme, the tags can generate digital signatures using their private keys and store them in the tags. When they need to authenticate themselves to RFID readers, they can transmit these digital signatures to the reader, and the reader can verify them using the tags' public keys.

In identity-based cryptography RFID systems, since the identity of the tags and reader can be used to generate public keys, the PKG does not need to keep the key directory, so it can reduce the resource requirements. Another advantage of using identity-based cryptography in RFID systems is that the reader does not need to know the public keys of the tags in advance. If the reader wants to verify the digital signature of an RFID tag, it can read the identity of the tag and use the public key generated from the identity to verify the digital signature.

An inherent weakness of identity-based cryptography is the key escrow problem. But in RFID systems that use identity-based cryptography, because all the devices can be within one company or organization, the PKG can be highly trusted and protected, and the chance of key escrow can be reduced.

Another problem of identity-based cryptography is revocation. For example, people always use their public information such as their names or home addresses to generate their public key. If a person's private keys are compromised by an attacker, since public information cannot be changed easily, this will make it difficult to regenerate new public keys. In contrast, in RFID systems the identity of the tag is used to generate the public key. If the private key of one tag has been compromised, the system can allocate a new identity to the tag and use this new identity to effortlessly create a new private key to the tag.

4. SUMMARY

Like any information technology (IT), radio frequency identification (RFID) presents security and privacy risks that must be carefully mitigated through management, operational, and technical controls in order to realize the numerous benefits the technology has to offer. When practitioners adhere to sound security engineering principles, RFID technology can help a wide range of organizations and individuals realize substantial productivity gains and efficiencies. These organizations and individuals include hospitals and patients, retailers and customers, and manufacturers and distributors throughout the supply chain. This chapter provided detailed coverage of RFID technology, the associated security and privacy risks, and recommended practices that will enable organizations to realize productivity improvements while safeguarding sensitive information and protecting the privacy of individuals. While RFID security is a rapidly evolving field with a number of promising innovations expected in the coming years, these guidelines focus on controls that are commercially available today.

Finally, let's move on to the real interactive part of this Chapter: review questions/exercises, hands-on projects, case projects and optional team case project. The answers and/or solutions by chapter can be found in the Online Instructor's Solutions Manual.

CHAPTER REVIEW QUESTIONS/EXERCISES

True/False

1. True or False? Data carriers attached to objects are called RFID tags.
2. True or False? Currently, as different frequencies are used for RFID systems in various countries and many standards are adopted for different kinds of application, there is an agreement on a universal standard that's accepted by all parties.
3. True or False? Recently more and more companies and organizations have begun to use RFID tags rather than traditional barcode because RFID systems have many advantages over traditional barcode systems.
4. True or False? RFID tags can be classified into three categories based on the equipped computation power: basic tags, symmetric-key tags, and public-key tags.
5. True or False? Another main issue of concern in deploying RFID systems is the sniffing problem.

Multiple Choice

1. Besides the four basic types of attack (counterfeiting, sniffing, tracking, and denial of service) in real-world applications, there also exists some other threats to RFID systems, like:
   A. Spoofing
   B. Temporal Key Integrity Protocols (TKIP)
   C. Application Program Interfaces
   D. Network Areas
   E. Extensible Authentication Protocol (EAP) framework
2. What happens when counterfeiters forge RFID tags by copying the information from a valid tag or adding some well-formed format information to a new tag in the RFID system?
   A. Middle Layers
   B. DOS
   C. Tracking
   D. Sniffing
   E. Counterfeiting
3. What tags are available for the cheapest price, compared with symmetric-key tags and public-key tags?
   A. Symmetric-key tags
   B. Public-key tags
   C. Basic tags
   D. Authenticated Routing tags
   E. All of the Above
4. What uses a single key to perform both encryption and decryption?
   A. False base cryptography.
   B. Symmetric-key cryptography.
   C. Eavesdropping cryptography.
   D. Man-in-the-Middle cryptography.
   E. Passive cryptography.
5. What can provide security for RFID systems, but it is more suitable to be implemented in a closed environment?
   A. HELLO Flood connectivity.
   B. Denial-of-service attack connectivity.
   C. Internet connectivity.
   D. Symmetric-key cryptography.
   E. All of the above.

EXERCISE

Problem

What provisions are made for code security?

Hands-On Projects

Project

How can you ensure the security of electronic product code (EPC) data?

Case Projects

Problem

Personnel and asset tracking in a health care environment, is a hypothetical case study to illustrate how RFID security might be implemented in practice. Although the case study is fictional, it is intended to resemble real-world activities, including how decision makers address common and expected RFID security problems and their solutions. The case study does not cover *all* of the aspects of RFID system engineering or operations that an organization may encounter in its RFID implementation, but rather a representative sample of salient issues. The case study follows.

The Fringe Science Research Center (FSRC) is a health care facility dedicated to the study of highly contagious diseases—those transmitted through casual human contact. The Center has 80 beds for patient care, a radiology unit with four rooms of sophisticated imaging equipment, and eight laboratories with various diagnostic and research capabilities. The Center confronts the same management issues as many hospitals, including locating portable diagnostic equipment when needed and accounting for missing assets. Another important concern is the ability to quickly locate patients and staff as they move about the facility. Poor asset management results in higher costs, reduced efficiency, and lower quality of care.

The mission of the FSRC also leads to specialized requirements. To prevent unnecessary outbreaks of disease and to understand how transmission occurs, FSRC needs to track the interactions among its staff, patients, and visitors. These tracked interactions provide useful information to researchers about who came into contact with whom and at what time. Additionally, the FSRC must alert caregivers of disease-specific protocols when they are in close proximity to particular patients, including prohibiting staff contact in some cases. It must track blood, urine, and stool samples from patient to laboratory. Finally, the FSRC would like to track the history of in-house diagnostic equipment and trace how the equipment is used to support patients throughout each day. Currently, paper processes are used to achieve these objectives, but they are very labor-intensive and error-prone, sometimes with fatal consequences.

FSRC executives tasked the FSRC's Chief Information Officer (CIO) to use RFID technology to improve the FSRC's traditional asset management function; as well as, meet its specialized requirements. Working with the FSRC executives, how did the CIO go about commissioning a project to reengineer FSRC business practices by using RFID technology as a primary tool to improve organizational performance?

Optional Team Case Project

Problem

Supply chain management of hazardous materials, is also a hypothetical case study to illustrate how RFID security might be implemented in practice. Although the case study is fictional, it is intended to resemble real-world activities, including how decision makers address common and expected RFID security problems and their solutions. The case study does not cover *all* of the aspects of RFID system engineering or operations that an organization may encounter in its RFID implementation, but rather a representative sample of salient issues. The case study follows.

The RAD corporation oversees the movement of radioactive research materials between production facilities, national laboratories, military installations, and other relevant locations. The RAD oversight of the supply chain for these materials involves many of the same issues as in most any other supply chain. RAD wants to know who is in possession of what quantity of materials at any given time. It also wants to locate materials at a site quickly, without having to search through numerous containers to find them. Bar code technology does not provide that capability.

Some of RAD's requirements are more unique. For instance, much of the transported radionuclide material must be closely monitored because extreme temperatures or excessive vibration can make it useless for its intended applications. Consequently, RAD wants temperature and vibration sensors to continuously measure environmental conditions and record readings on the tag. Additionally, the handling of RAD-regulated materials is a homeland and national security issue. If the materials were to fall into unauthorized hands, they could endanger the public welfare. So, with the preceding in mind, how would RAD's project team go about conducting a risk assessment?

REFERENCES

[1] S.A. Weis, Security and Privacy in Radio-Frequency Identification Devices.
[2] M. Langheinrich, RFID and Privacy.
[3] Auto-ID Center, Draft Protocol Specification for a Class 0 Radio Frequency Identification Tag, February 2003.
[4] K. Finkenzeller, RFID Handbook: Fundamentals and Applications in Contactless Smart Cards and Identification.

[5]   P. Peris-Lopez, J.C. Hernandez-Castro, J. Estevez-Tapiador, A. Ribagorda, RFID systems: a survey on security threats and proposed solutions, 11th IFIP International Conference on Personal Wireless Communications − PWC06, Volume 4217 of Lecture Notes in Computer Science, Springer-Verlag, September 2006, pp. 159−170.

[6]   RFID Handbook, second ed., J. Wiley & Sons.

[7]   T. Phillips, T. Karygiannis, R. Huhn, Security standards for the RFID market, IEEE Secur. & Privacy (November/December 2005) 85−89.

[8]   EPCglobal, www.epcglobalinc.org/, June 2005.

[9]   EPCglobal Tag Data Standards, Version 1.3.

[10]   Guidelines for Securing Radio Frequency Identification (RFID) Systems, Recommendations of the National Institute of Standards and Technology, NIST Special Publication 800−98.

[11]   S. Weis, S. Sarma, R. Rivest, D. Engels, Security and privacy aspects of low-cost radio frequency identification systems, in: W. Stephan, D. Hutter, G. Muller, M. Ullmann (Eds.), International Conference on Security in Pervasive computing-SPC 2003, vol. 2802, Springer-Verlag, 2003, pp. 454−469.

[12]   D. Haehnel, W. Burgard, D. Fox, K. Fishkin, M. Philipose, Mapping and localization with WID technology, International Conference on Robotics & Automation, 2004.

[13]   D.R. Thompson, N. Chaudhry, C.W. Thompson, RFID Security Threat Model.

[14]   A. Juels, R.L. Rivest, M. Syzdlo, The blocker tag: selective blocking of RFID tags for consumer privacy, in: V. Atluri (Ed.), 8th ACM Conference on Computer and Communications Security, 2003, pp. 103−111.

[15]   F. Thornton, B. Haines, A.M. Das, H. Bhargava, A. Campbell, J. Kleinschmidt, RFID Security.

[16]   C. Jechlitschek, A Survey Paper on Radio Frequency Identification (RFID) Trends.

[17]   S.H. Weingart, Physical Security Devices for Computer Subsystems: A Survey of Attacks and Defenses.

[18]   S.E. Sarma, S.A. Weis, D.W. Engels, RFID systems security and privacy implications, Technical Report, MITAUTOID-WH-014, AutoID Center, MIT, 2002.

[19]   S. Inoue, H. Yasuura, RFID privacy using user-controllable uniqueness, in: RFID Privacy Workshop, MIT, November 2003.

[20]   N. Good, J. Han, E. Miles, D. Molnar, D. Mulligan, L. Quilter, J. Urban, D. Wagner, Radio frequency ID and privacy with information goods, in: Workshop on Privacy in the Electronic Society (WPES), 2004.

[21]   A. Juels, Minimalist cryptography for low-cost RFID tags, in: C. Blundo, S. Cimato (Eds.), The Fourth International Conference on Security in Communication Networks − SCN 2004, Vol. 3352 of Lecture Notes in Computer Science, Springer-Verlag, 2004, pp. 149−164.

[22]   A. Juels, R. Pappu, Squealing euros: privacy protection in RFID-enabled banknotes, in: R. Wright (Ed.), Financial Cryptography '03, vol. 2742, Springer-Verlag, 2003, pp. 103−121.

[23]   P. Golle, M. Jakobsson, A. Juels, P. Syverson, Universal re-encryption for mixnets, in: T. Okamoto (Ed.), RSA Conference-Cryptographers' Track (CT-RSA), vol. 2964, 2004, pp. 163−178.

[24]   G. Ateniese, J. Camenisch, B. de Madeiros, Untraceable RFID tags via insubvertible encryption, in: 12th ACM Conference on Computer and Communication Security, 2005.

[25]   C. Floerkemeier, R. Schneider, M. Langheinrich, Scanning with a Purpose Supporting the Fair Information Principles in RFID Protocols, 2004.

[26]   M.R. Rieback, B. Crispo, A. Tanenbaum, RFID Guardian: a battery-powered mobile device for RFID privacy management, in: C. Boyd, J.M. González Nieto (Eds.), Australasian Conference on Information Security and Privacy − ACISP 2005, Vol. 3574 of Lecture Notes in Computer Science, Springer-Verlag, 2005, pp. 184−194.

[27]   M. Feldhofer, S. Dominikus, J. Wolkerstorfer, Strong authentication for RFID systems using the AES algorithm, in: M. Joye, J.-J. Quisquater (Eds.), Workshop on Cryptographic Hardware and Embedded Systems CHES 04, Vol. 3156 of Lecture Notes in Computer Science, Springer-Verlag, 2004, pp. 357−370.

[28]   D. Molnar, D. Wagner, Privacy and security in library RFID: issues, practices, and architectures, in: B. Pfitzmann, P. McDaniel (Eds.), ACM Conference on Communications and Computer Security, ACM Press, 2004, pp. 210−219.

[29]   G. Tsudik, YA-TRAP: Yet another trivial RFID authentication protocol, in: Fourth Annual IEEE International Conference on Pervasive Computing and Communications Workshops (PERCOMW'06), 2006, pp. 640−643.

[30]   A. Juels, S. Weis, Defining strong privacy for RFID, in: Pervasive Computing and Communications Workshops, 2007.

[31]   P. Tuyls, L. Batina, RFID tags for anticounterfeiting, in: D. Pointcheval (Ed.), Topics in Cryptology-CT-RSA 2006, Springer-Verlag, 2006.

[32]   L. Batina, J. Guajardo, T. Kerins, N. Mentens, P. Tuyls, I. Verbauwhede, Public-key cryptography for RFID-tags. in: Printed handout of Workshop on RFID Security, RFIDSec06, 2006, pp. 61−76.

[33]   T. Okamoto, Provably secure and practical identification schemes and corresponding signature schemes, in: E.F. Brickell (Ed.), Advances in Cryptology | CRYPTO'92, Vol. 740 of LNCS, Springer-Verlag, 1992, pp. 31−53.

[34]   A. Shamir, Identity-based cryptosystems and signature scheme, Advances in Cryptology: Proceedings of CRYPTO 84, LNCS, 1984, pp. 47−53.

## Chapter 19

Optical Network Security

Lauren Collins

kCura Corporation

1. OPTICAL NETWORKS

The movement of data is not just about buying the best equipment out there. It is having the knowledge and logic to manipulate the hardware, create the configurations, shape the data, and possibly most important: secure that data. Having a vast amount of experience in getting data delivered quickly, a professional such as an architect for Electronic Trading embraces a strategy to capture the opportunities for the trader. This challenges the engineer to present opportunities for the trader, as well as to secure that formula to achieve long-standing success. However, when that data is compromised, a new obstacle presents itself. If everyone in the market has common knowledge on the trades and they have the fastest network, what sets them apart to capitalize on those markets?

Different types of businesses are confronted with different classes of security breaches. Cell phone providers may have an eavesdropping device attached to their network, which may leak news and confidential governmental matters if the proper tap is set. Mutual fund firms could have someone trying to access their quarterly statement prior to the release of information, which could be worth millions. Scanner taps may be present in International Interpol networks in order to gain knowledge of the location of government officials. Pharmaceutical players could also have a sniffer in their network to leak breaking news of a controversial drug recall.

Optical networks are potentially vulnerable to attacks based on the people who have access to the equipment and whether or not their curiosity to "tap" into the data supersedes their job function. Depending on the service provider architecture, equipment at each end may have multiple individuals representing several companies who access the equipment. This supplements the statement: "Assumptions should never be made that your data is safe." Both modern encryption methods and highly sophisticated methods to implement security procedures should be considered. This encryption protection derives from quantum mechanics, and military intelligence has monitored communications throughout the years, including tapping into undersea cabling. This chapter endeavors to familiarize readers with the various types of optical networks, how each type may be secured, how to identify vulnerabilities, and how to take corrective action.

Fiber

An optical fiber is a flexible, transparent fiber made of glass or plastic and is of comparable thickness to fishing wire. Engineers design networks utilizing optical fibers that permit transmissions over longer distances and at higher data rates than other forms of media communication. Fiber cabling is composed of two layers, the core and the cladding. Shown in Figure 19.1, the core is surrounded by the cladding layer, and the cladding layer has a higher index of refraction than the core.

Refraction of Light

As a light ray passes from one transparent medium to another, it changes direction; this phenomenon is called refraction of light. How much that light ray changes its direction depends on the refractive index of the mediums. In Figure 19.2, a ray's direction is altered when that ray enters the water.

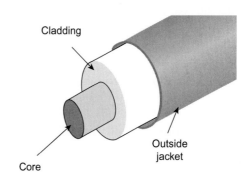

FIGURE 19.1 Fiber layers: cladding and core.

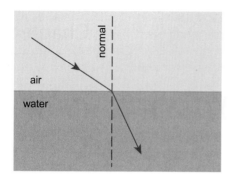

FIGURE 19.2   Refraction: Medium change from air to water alters the ray direction.

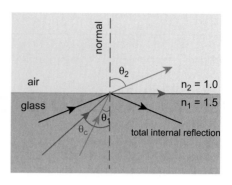

FIGURE 19.4   Total internal reflection: Angle of light affects transition to medium.

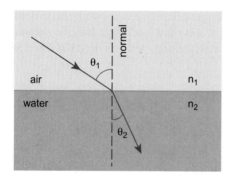

FIGURE 19.3   Snell's law portrays refractive indexes and angles.

Refractive Index

The refractive index is the speed of light in a vacuum (abbreviated c, $c = 299{,}792.458$ km/second) divided by the speed of light in a material (abbreviated v). The refractive index measures how much a material refracts light. The refractive index of a material, abbreviated as n, is defined as

$$n = c/v$$

When light tries to pass from a lower to a higher index of refraction at the proper angle, the light will refract back instead. This series of refractions allows light to continuously travel through to the other end of the fiber. In 1621, the Dutch physicist Willebrord Snell derived the relationship between the different angles of light as it passes from one transparent medium to another. Figure 19.3 illustrates light passing from one transparent material to another; that light bends according to Snell's law, which is defined as [1]:

$$n_1 \sin(\theta_1) = n_2 \sin(\theta_2)$$

where:

    n_1 is the refractive index of the medium the light is leaving
    θ_1 is the incident angle between the light beam and the normal (normal is 90° to the interface between two materials)

n_2 is the refractive index of the material the light is entering
θ_2 is the refractive angle between the light ray and the normal

Note:

For the case of $\theta_1 = 0°$ (a ray perpendicular to the interface), the solution is $\theta_2 = 0°$ regardless of the values of n_1 and n_2. That means a ray entering a medium perpendicular to the surface is never bent.

The preceding is also valid for light going from a dense (higher n) to a less dense (lower n) material. The symmetry of Snell's law shows that the same ray paths are applicable in the opposite direction.

Total Internal Reflection

When a light ray crosses an interface into a medium with a higher refractive index, it bends toward the normal. Conversely, light traveling across an interface from a higher refractive index medium to a lower refractive index medium will bend away from the normal. This has an interesting implication: At some angle, known as the **critical angle θ_c**, light traveling from a higher refractive index medium to a lower refractive index medium will be refracted at 90°; in other words, it will be refracted along the interface.

If the light hits the interface at any angle larger than this critical angle, it will not pass through to the second medium at all. Instead, all of it will be reflected back into the first medium, a process known as total internal reflection, as shown in Figure 19.4.

The critical angle can be calculated from Snell's law, putting in an angle of 90° for the angle of the refracted ray θ_2. This gives θ_1:

$$\theta_1 = \arcsin[(n_2/n_1) * \sin(\theta_2)]$$

Since

$$\theta_2 = 90°$$

So

$$\sin(\theta_2) = 1$$

Then

$$\theta_c = \theta_1 = \arcsin(n_2/n_1)$$

For example, with light trying to emerge from glass with $n_1 = 1.5$ into air ($n_2 = 1$), the critical angle θ_c is arcsin(1/1.5), or 41.8. For any angle of incidence larger than the critical angle, Snell's law will not be able to be solved for the angle of refraction because it will show that the refracted angle has a sine larger than 1, which is not possible. In that case all the light is totally reflected off the interface, obeying the law of reflection.

Single Mode Versus Multimode

There are two types of fiber: single-mode fiber (SMF) and multimode fiber (MMF). Single-mode fiber has a narrow core, allowing only a single mode of light to propagate within the core. Inversely, multimode has a wide core and allows multiple modes of light to propagate. Both fibers are 125 microns in outside diameter. Single mode has a core size between 8 and 10 microns (μm). SMF will support distances up to several thousand kilometers, taking into consideration appropriate amplification, dispersion compensation, and tuning of the heat and light signal where the hardware and software are concerned. This mode requires more expensive, articulate light sources, typically operating at a wavelength of 1310 nanometers or 1550 nanometers (nm). Multimode has a core size between 62.5 μm OM1 and 50 μm OM2. The wider core allows for use of incoherent light sources utilizing many rays, or modes. MMF is conventionally more cost effective than SMF, and operates at a wavelength of 850 nm or 1310 nm. There is also an OM3 MMF with a core size of 50 μm. This cable is aqua in color, rather than the traditional orange, and is designed to achieve 10 Gbps at 300 m. Be advised that you cannot use single-mode fiber and connect to multimode hardware and vice versa. At a minimum, this could lead to a 20-dB loss, or 99 percent of the power and worst case could burn your equipment out and render it useless.

Layers Within Sites

When networking distant locations together, certain considerations need to be made so that data may flow and procedures can be put in place to ensure that access to equipment is done carefully. When considering that there are numerous physical locations in any organization, there are also multiple layers of communications that may take place at each of those locations. For example, Central Offices (COs) are organized into metropolitan areas and are usually interconnected by fiber. Equipment is placed in these buildings, and access may only derive from a customer accessing this or her first service CO, not diving further into the network layers or involving any access to other locations. Networks can further structure layers consisting of nodes, integrating switching components and/or the cross-connection of such equipment, linking those logical adjacencies to provide a streamlined solution.

The circuits that link layer 1 traffic may be presented as point-to-point (PTP), IP/Multiprotocol Label Switching (MPLS), or IP services (Internet). IP services are typically provided by MPLS, composed of routers. PTP services are provided through three different layers: (1) Wideband cross-connect (1.5 Mbps), (2) broadband cross-connect (45 Mbps–1 Gbps), composed of Optical Switching and SONET, and (3) Optical Multiplexing ROADM (2.5 Gbps and up). Figure 19.5 depicts a model in which two core services, IP and PTP, are introduced and the relationship among these services is delineated, as are their links and the circuits respective to associated layers.

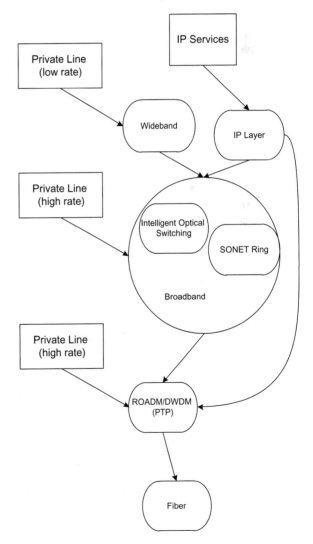

FIGURE 19.5 Geographical site: circuit layers.

2. SECURING OPTICAL NETWORKS

Information can be hidden in several dimensions of an optic: its phase, spatial frequency, wavelength, or the divergence of light. Since optical networks operate at such instantaneous transmission speeds, processing can offer advantages in matters of security.

Techniques

Tucking away an optically based message in one small section of a two-dimensional array, forces unauthorized users to find the messages' position before they can even start to decode it. Take this a bit further, and if you have an 8-bit optical system, one can decode as many as 256 gray shades, rather than dealing with those lovely one's and zero's that binary folks encode in hopes of securing information. Before that conspicuous user can begin the time-consuming, labor-intensive process to decode, he or she will need to gain access to the optic device in order to process the information. Altogether, these properties exponentially increase the mathematical possibilities for code-breakers to consider when they are confronted with optics and the techniques for encryption.

A typical optical system has components such as a light source, data, detectors, display devices, and sometimes, spatial light modulators. One can arrange these components in one of multiple configurations so that they can simulate the desired data.

Fourier Analysis

Jean Baptiste Joseph Fourier was a French mathematician and physicist known for introducing the Fourier series and corresponding applications to issues relevant to heat transfer and vibrations [2]. In 1822 Fourier presented his work on the flow of heat, which was based on two adjacent molecules proportional to one another, having a diminutive variance of their temperatures. This theory was amended several times by other contributors until 1888, when three works were published. One of the publications was purely mathematical, whereas the other two were, in essence, physics. Fourier had claimed that any function of a variable, whether continuous or discontinuous, could be expanded in a series of sines of multiples of the variable. Fourier's study, later found to be erroneous, showed that discontiguous functions are the sum of infinite series, such a breakthrough. This study of convergence was the fundamental one accepted for centuries, and the proposal of partial difference equation for conductive diffusion of heat is now taught to every student engaged in the study of mathematical physics.

Statement of the Equation

For functions $u(x,y,z,t)$ of three spatial variables (x,y,z) and the time variable t, the heat equation is:

$$\frac{\partial u}{\partial t} - \alpha \left(\frac{\partial^2 u}{\partial x^2} + \frac{\partial^2 u}{\partial y^2} + \frac{\partial^2 u}{\partial z^2} \right) = 0$$

In any coordinate system:

$$\frac{\partial u}{\partial t} - \alpha \nabla^2 u = 0$$

where α is a positive constant and Δ or ∇^2 denotes the Laplace operator. In the physical problem of temperature variation, $u(x,y,z,t)$ is the temperature and α is the thermal diffusivity. Per mathematical treatment, it is sufficient to consider the case $\alpha = 1$.

These equations are relative to this security discussion where such formulas are found to lead into the answer without even introducing decoding or breaking encryption. This equation, where the study of heat is concerned, finds a use in the Black-Scholes model. In financial mathematics, Black-Scholes is a mathematical model of a financial market that will contain assured derivative investment instruments. From this model, one can construe the formula that paved the way for derivatives to become commodities that could be traded in their own class. The economic housing explosion around 2006 encouraged options trading globally and ended in a subprime eruption, which cost banks hundreds of billions of dollars.

Conceptually, any system with a binary signal consists of bits that signify voltage or waves. This signal generally takes the form of a square wave that oscillates between two different states and those states representing two different voltage levels shown in Figure 19.6.

Square waves inherit their own set of difficulties when they are being sent at high frequencies, such as they would be when transmitted over fiber. Any waveform is comprised of an infinite integer of sine waves and/or cosine waves too, whether those waves are measured in the frequency of a square or harmonic wave. Consider 100 Mbit of a digital

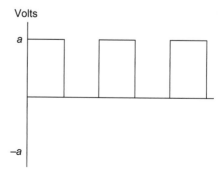

FIGURE 19.6   Square waves represent two states of voltage.

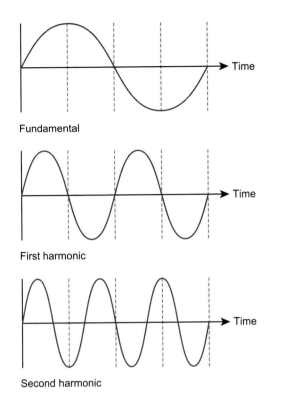

Fundamental

First harmonic

Second harmonic

FIGURE 19.7 Frequency and waves cycle from positive to negative in both data and sound.

signal, which is similarly composed of a 100-MHz sine wave at 300 MHz, 500 MHz, 700 MHz, respectively, and so on. Relate this data whether you are streaming real-time stock quotes or recording music from an acoustic guitar, represented in Figure 19.7. The frequency is measured in cycles per second, or hertz (Hz). Frequencies unforeseeable to the human eye and inaudible to the human ear exist and can be portrayed dynamically and simultaneously through optics.

In order to analyze forms such as a digital square wave, mathematics conceptualizes in the process of Fourier analysis. We can use Fourier analysis in an equation that defines waves translated in time:

$$f(X) = a_0 + \sum_{n=1}^{\infty} \left[a_n \cos\left(\frac{n\pi X}{L}\right) + b_n \sin\left(\frac{n\pi X}{L}\right) \right]$$

$$a_0 = \frac{1}{2L} \int_{-L}^{L} f(X) dX$$

$$a_n = \frac{1}{L} \int_{-L}^{L} f(X) \cos\left(\frac{n\pi X}{L}\right) dX$$

$$b_n = \frac{1}{L} \int_{-L}^{L} f(X) \sin\left(\frac{n\pi X}{L}\right) dX$$

where the values of a_n and b_n are effortlessly calculated. The summation sign Σ_n represents the sum over all the variables with an index n. For example, $\Sigma_n n^2 = 1^2 + 2^2 + 3^2 + \ldots$ The integral sign $\int_{-L}^{L}$ represents the sum over a continuous variable x from $x = -L$ to $x = +L$. A trivial example is $\int_{-L}^{L} dx = 2L$.

3. IDENTIFYING VULNERABILITIES

Optical fiber can be tapped more inexpensively and easily than ever, so a comprehensive, modular security strategy is necessary to ensure protection of a company's valuable information assets (see checklist: An Agenda for Action When Conducting an Optical Network Security Vulnerability Assessment). Some Wavelength Division Multiplexing (WDM) systems offer a cost-efficient capability to fully encrypt certain channels of traffic and monitor for intrusions at the physical layer. The result is a sophisticated security solution—without threatening degradation of the superior, low-latency performance for an organization's most demanding local and storage area network local area network (LAN) and storage area network (SAN) applications.

Signal Intelligence

Where data is ready and available, usually near where the cable terminates, it is easy to introduce a tap. Since taps are a cost-effective measure of hacking, and are not difficult to set up, this piece of hardware is more frequently used to access data. Based on knowledge, you can first gain access to the cabling and then extract light from the glass fibers. Most cabling is difficult to access since it may be underground, at the ocean floor, covered in concrete, or running through a conduit in elevator shafts. However, an adequate amount of cabling is accessible for those willing to look. Many companies boast about their fiber networks and list their fiber paths online, making them easy for hackers to locate. Hone in on the location of the cable, gain access to it, and pull data from the cable. The hack is now a success.

Bending is a process through which you insert a clip-on coupler. There is no interruption to the light signal, and only a small amount of light is leaked through the polymer cabling. Once the light has been retrieved, data can be captured by a photo detector. The next piece of equipment needed sniffs data off of the glass fibers. This device facilitates the connection to a network interface card (NIC), which will capture packets and filter data for information corresponding to IP, MAC addresses, DNS information, and any keywords in the data passed without encryption. This method would cost less than $2000 for the equipment to be acquired and positioned. Any firm that does not rely on data down to the nanosecond would

An Agenda for Action when Conducting an Optical Network Security Vulnerability Assessment

A security vulnerability assessment evaluates an optical network system's security performance; measures security trends and exceptions related to security policy, procedures, and user access; performs an audit of intrusion-detection data; and provides recommendations for improvement by conducting the following activities (check all tasks completed):

_____**1.** Conduct a planning meeting to set expectations and milestones and to define deliverables.

_____**2.** Define criteria for network security optimization, including utilization, fault conditions, error thresholds, and throughput.

_____**3.** Collect and analyze data for trends and exceptions that may impact network security.

_____**4.** Monitor and inspect security logs to trend usage of systems and suspicious activity.

_____**5.** Review network security component placement and configuration for optimal load distribution and traffic management.

_____**6.** Assess security performance against established criteria.

_____**7.** Provide impact analysis of new software versions, features, and configurations.

_____**8.** Provide hardware and software recommendations to optimize system and network performance.

_____**9.** Provide recommendations for network and security component tuning,,including system optimization, filtering, route redistribution, trunk and port configuration, and protocol, policy, and feature configuration.

_____**10.** Identify and measure the optical network security system for trends and exceptions related to security policy, procedures, and user access.

_____**11.** Assess the (advanced technology) security system performance against the established baseline and analyze for areas of improvement.

_____**12.** Analyze access-control policies and make recommendations for improvement.

_____**13.** Develop a Security Assessment Report highlighting recommendations for improving security.

_____**14.** Present and review the Security Assessment Report.

---

not notice any change in accessing their data when this procedure of tapping data has taken place.

Splicing is another method that is not as functional and, though seldom used, can result in detection due to the transient interruption of the light. Consider a cable that is capable of transporting 100 million concurrent connections; those connections require instantaneous signal rerouting to maintain network integrity. Splicing would interrupt that fiber integrity, even for a millisecond, and the connection would noticeably drop and potentially converge depending on the network routing.

Access to Equipment

Many firms collocate their infrastructure at a secured data center. These facilities utilize access lists to allow individuals access to the site and additionally into secured areas. Some of these areas are located in shared space, where a firm may have *n* number of cabinets in a large area among other firms. The cabinets may have locks on them to secure the equipment from others in that shared space, or an escort may be mandated for particular areas.

Regarding Metro facilities that are only open to Telecom companies, there are certainly areas of access that may be open to others. Technicians may be on-site to repair or to maintain equipment. While many organizations are putting protocols in place to secure equipment

and data, these facilities are open for both ease of access and for cross-functional work to be completed. One method to troubleshoot line latency or recurring line outages may be to tap that circuit, granting permission for the placement of the equipment that could cross the line, obscuring justice.

4. CORRECTIVE ACTIONS

All fiber runs should be enclosed and protected from anyone who might try to gain access to the cabling. The room where the cable terminates, known as the demarcation point, is a point where some may find data readily accessible.

Securing Equipment

Chapter 60 delves much deeper into the concept of securing the infrastructure. Wiring closets, public areas, and junction boxes should be secured and monitored.

Encryption

Sensitive data should always be encrypted to protect that data in the event an attacker gains access to the data. There are particular vendors who develop instruments to protect optical networks; such instruments offer protection at the physical layer as well as intrusion detection. These vendors identify possible threats and alert administrators of possible events, including excessive packet-receiving overloads, signal loss, transitory loss of power, and malicious infringement. One solution offered, though cost sensitive, is a real-time protocol agnostic monitoring system for optical networks. When an intrusion is detected, the path is shut down and traffic is rerouted to an alternate path. These independent solutions offer protection against corporate eavesdropping, government and financial espionage, network disturbances, and terrorism.

At this point, detection solutions notwithstanding, encryption of transmitted data is the only measure to prevent information from being pilfered from optical networks. The trend is leaning toward encryption at the data layer, which reduces latency and overhead associated with transporting large amounts of data at high speeds. Some make the mistake of encrypting data at the data layer and also at the physical layer, in the transmission of the data. While both may seem to cover all bases, only encryption is needed since the hindrance put forth will deter eavesdroppers. This will also save money where one will not have to add to latency and the overhead to support and manage additional equipment.

5. SUMMARY

An optical signal undergoes many transmission impairments throughout its entire path in an optical network. The peculiar behavior of the transmission medium and active/passive elements in the network makes an optical network vulnerable to unscrupulous attacks, thereby jeopardizing the security of information. In optical networks, data travel optically from source to destination without any optical-electrical conversions, thereby making the networks transparent to modulation format, bitrate, and protocol. This transparency poses many survivability vulnerabilities to attacks. This chapter discussed in detail the possible attack scenarios at the physical layer and also presented a conceptual modeling of attack problems and possible protection schemes in optical networks. However, attacks exploiting device characteristics necessitate comparatively more involved diagnostic expertise, complex remedial measures, and even more systematic detection schemes and control protocols. Future research will deal with the issue of practically feasible attack detection and restoration approaches.

Finally, let's move on to the real interactive part of this chapter: review questions/exercises, hands-on projects, case projects, and optional team case project. The answers and/or solutions by chapter can be found in the Online Instructor's Solutions Manual.

CHAPTER REVIEW QUESTIONS/EXERCISES

True/False

1. True or False? Optical networks are not vulnerable to attacks based on the people who have access to the equipment and whether their curiosity to "tap" into the data supersedes their job function.
2. True or False? An optical fiber is a flexible, transparent fiber made of glass or plastic and is of comparable thickness to fishing wire.
3. True or False? As a light ray passes from one transparent medium to another, it does not change direction; this phenomenon is called refraction of dark.
4. True or False? The refractive index is less than the speed of light in a vacuum (abbreviated c, $c = 299,792.458$ km/second) divided by the speed of light in a material (abbreviated v).
5. True or False? There are two types of fiber: single-mode fiber (SMF) and multimode fiber (MMF).

Multiple Choice

1. The circuits that link layer 1 traffic may be presented as:
   A. spoofing.
   B. point-to-point (PTP).
   C. application programming interfaces.
   D. network areas.
   E. Extensible Authentication Protocol (EAP) framework.
2. What type of waves inherit their own set of difficulties when being sent at high frequencies (such as they would be when transmitted over fiber)?
   A. Square
   B. Rectangle
   C. Triangle
   D. Octagon
   E. Trapizoid
3. In order to analyze forms such as a digital square wave, mathematics conceptualizes in the process of:
   A. Security Vulnerability Analysis.
   B. Wavelength Division Multiplexing.
   C. Signal Intelligence.
   D. Fourier analysis.
   E. All of the above.
4. What is the process of inserting a clip-on coupler?
   A. Splicing
   B. Accessing
   C. Bending
   D. Correcting
   E. Cabling
5. Sensitive data should always be _____ to protect that data in the event an attacker gains access to the data.
   A. encrypted
   B. protected

C. corrected
D. monitored
E. all of the above

EXERCISE

Problem

Is it possible to secure the files stored on a network attached storage (NAS) optical storage server?

Hands-On Projects

Project

How does optical network security work across the multiple protocols?

Case Projects

Problem

Can optical network security be controlled down to the directory level?

Optional Team Case Project

Problem

Can optical network security be set on a virtual volume?

REFERENCES

[1] Wolfram Research [Snell's law], 100 Trade Center, Drive, Champaign, IL 61820–7237, USA.

[2] Joseph Fourier, The Analytical Theory of Heat, The University of Adelaide Library, University of Adelaide, South Australia 5005, 1878.

## Chapter 20

Optical Wireless Security

Scott R. Ellis, EnCE, RCA

kCura Corporation

1. OPTICAL WIRELESS SYSTEMS OVERVIEW

In this section, we examine the origins of using light as a means of communication, and we discuss how, over time, it developed into free space optic (FSO) technology. This section will also cover the use of the technology.

History

The use of light and optics is long standing. The ancient Greeks used their polished shields to send reflected light signals while in battle. In 1880, Alexander Graham Bell and his assistant, Charles Sumner Tainger, jointly created a device they called a photophone, or radiophone. Using it, they could transmit sound on a beam of light. The device was based on the photovoltaic properties of crystalline selenium and worked very similarly to the telephone. Bell did not, however, predict the laser or fiber optics, which needed to predicate any potential success of such a device. World War II saw the use of the invention for secure communication. Early on, its users recognized that clear, targeted, line-of-sight communication, invisible to everyone else, allowed for a high degree of security. FSO technology is inherently secure primarily because of this. It wouldn't be until the 1960s and the invention of lasers that this form of communication would mature into Bell's 1880s vision.

Today

FSO uses optical pulse-modulated signals—light—to transmit data from point to point. The technology is similar to fiber optics, with the exception that instead of being contained in glass fiber, the signal is transmitted through varying degrees of atmospheric conditions. Each FSO unit consists of an optical transmitter and receiver with full duplex capability. This means it is bidirectional.

Typically, these devices are mounted on buildings. Part of the security of these devices is, of course, ensuring that no harm or damage can come to the device, due to its perceived attractiveness by natural aviary populations (make sure you can keep pigeons off of it). The devices contain an array of optics that is used to signal between the device pair at distances of up to several kilometers.

Because these systems are mounted on buildings and because (conceivably) something could happen that could cause a unit to point or be directed into human (or even pigeon) eyes, there are some safety considerations. FSO systems operate in the infrared range. When discussing these devices, and the range in which they operate, the term *wavelength* is used.

Theory of Operation

It is common knowledge that radio frequency (rf) transmissions are easily intercepted and that the technology of securing the transmissions can, if it is secured at all, usually be circumvented, given enough time and effort. It takes little effort to simply drive around and find an "open" wireless connection, even though Light is both a wave and a particle, but most often is discussed in terms of wavelength. Generally, FSO uses infrared (IR), optical light-emitting diode (LED) laser technology at between 780 and 1550 nm. The higher ranges are thought to be less damaging to the cornea as the beam is absorbed by the cornea and never strikes the retina.

The greatest challenge that faces widespread acceptance of FSO is atmospheric conditions. Factors such as fog, smog, heavy rain, or even clouds of dust raised by construction or in areas near desert locales are detrimental to the optical signal. The greater the distance that the beam attempts to traverse, the greater the likelihood that it will fail. Additionally, scintillation—viewed by human eyes as "heat mirages"—is a perturbation in the homogeneous atmospheric density that can significantly distort the photonic transmission. Units with adaptive power will reduce the power to the laser in clear weather and increase it in inclement conditions. Adaptive power features will also increase the life span of the units. Many units are built with features that will increase the physical security. Features such as the following all contribute to increase the security by significantly reducing overshoot signals:

- Adaptive power—prevents overpowering during clear weather
- High frequency—prevents the use of commercially available optics to detect the signal
- Narrow beamwidth—reduces overshoot footprint
- Higher quality optics—prevents a narrower overshoot footprint

Placement on buildings can determine the amount of security as well as signal degradation due to atmospheric conditions. Higher elevations on buildings may increase the amount of disruption to fog; lower elevations may increase the amount of disruption to construction activities like severe dust. Placement should also ensure that the unit has some sort of backstop that can prevent overshoot footprint.

Finally, as it relates to physical security, the diffraction grating effect of shining a light through a small hole must be considered. As any sophomore physics student knows, the equation of light diffraction through an aperture is:

$$I = I_0 \left(\frac{\sin \beta}{\beta} \right)^2$$

where

$$\beta = \frac{\pi W \sin \theta}{\lambda}$$

W = the size of the aperture.

As can be seen, as the aperture gets larger and the wavelength gets smaller, the central disk of illumination varies inversely with the size of the aperture. An FSO manufacturer that simply assembles parts from various manufacturers without consideration of diffraction grating will be more vulnerable to overspread than a conscientious manufacture that has thoroughly engineered its product.

2. DEPLOYMENT ARCHITECTURES

Deployment of the technology varies. The commonly used variations are mesh, ring, point to multipoint (PMP), and point to point (P2P). Some concern over building movement may be appropriate—there are devices capable of autocorrecting up to a few degrees of range. Most devices are designed with movement-handling capabilities. Building architects may have more information; it would be very disappointing to install a system in July, only to find out, nearly nine months later, that March through May winds cause unacceptable disruptions in service, caused by building sway.

Mesh

In a mesh architecture, every node is connected to every other node in a mesh-like lattice work of connections (see Figure 20.1). An increase in the number of nodes increases the quality of the mesh. Mesh networks offer a high degree of reliability. Mesh and ring architectures are larger scale, metropolitan-style deployments that may be used by large carriers and service providers.

Ring

Large cities, such as Hong Kong, may use ring architecture to deliver quality, high-bandwidth Internet services to the entire city. Ring architecture is a blend of mesh and Point to Point/point-to-point (PTP) (see Figure 20.2). With a broad geographical deployment, the ring itself resides at the center, near or at a large communications trunk, or several. It may or may not link multiple trunk sites for redundancy, which also increases the diameter of the ring to extend the range over the area. Communication points are then established as links that radiate outward from the ring, like the spokes of a wheel.

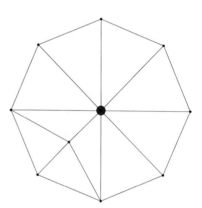

FIGURE 20.1 In a mesh schema, all points are interconnected. This provides a high degree of redundancy.

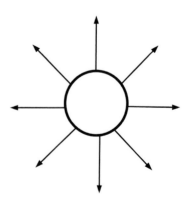

FIGURE 20.2 In a ring schema, a heavy-duty, high-bandwidth ring exists at the center. This provides a high degree of redundancy, as well as pushing the threshold for distance and strength of signal.

Point to Point

Point-to-point architecture comes in two flavors: PTP and PMP. As the names imply, the only difference lay in the one-to-one relationship versus a one-to-many relationship. This architecture primarily suits smaller deployments, such as an organization that may have multiple office locations or an office that has set up space across the street.

In a PTP network, multiple single connections are chained together, linearly, to increase the range of the network. Perhaps the only connection to be made is across town, or perhaps multiple locations are served along the way. It effectively increases the range of the product or defeats the shortened range that may occur during inclement conditions.

In a PMP schema, all connections to various locations radiate outward from a central location. A single node acts as the source, with a central communications closet in the building serving to link the devices at the central location. For example, by placing the optical wireless devices at all four sides of a single, hub building, you can extend the network to surrounding buildings. Such a deployment would be most suitable for organizations with campus-styled building layouts. Figure 20.3 illustrates the connection points of such an arrangement.

3. HIGH BANDWIDTH

FSO devices boast speeds of up to 10 Gbps in an unhindered atmosphere. Bandwidth decreases in the presence of smog and fog down to complete loss of signal. For this reason, when selecting FSO, it is important to consider the local weather and the distances involved.

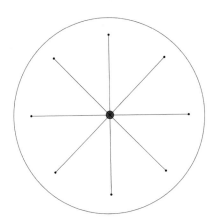

FIGURE 20.3 In a PMP schema, a single, central trunk provides high-bandwidth service to multiple, closely linked optical wireless transmitters. This provides a low-cost solution to providing high-bandwidth network services in a small geographical area, where cost savings is more important than redundancy or high availability.

4. LOW COST

Security is expensive. The larger the physicality of the surface area, the greater is the area that needs protection from attack. Assuming that line of sight and lease rights are forthcoming and easily procured, setting up a land-based metropolitan network in a city such as Chicago could be very expensive. The price difference of using fiber versus FSO in an installation to connect two offices that are 400 m apart is not just a small percentage. It is several orders of magnitude more expensive to install fiber.

5. IMPLEMENTATION

In theory, FSO has great potential to become far more commonplace and enjoy much greater acceptance in the information technology community than it currently enjoys. At the time of this writing, FSO installations can be found in places such as corporate and educational campuses.

Future use could see the removal of wired communications across long distances in open country, with tall poles housing FSO equipment. It is common knowledge that the technology has already been successfully used in space communications and that Artemis, the European Space Agency Advanced Relay and Technology Mission Satellite, successfully linked with an aircraft at a distance of over 40,000 km. The use of optical boosting equipment could introduce even greater adoption in long-distance (many millions of miles) communications with deep space missions.

High data rates, lightweight equipment, low-energy requirements, little interference, and nearly guaranteed clear and unobstructed paths between space platforms makes space the ideal environment for FSO networks. They would also be somewhat tap proof, though it is conceivable that an enemy satellite could interpose and successfully relay the signal, undetected, the whole while recording and transmitting it back to Wreaking Havoc headquarters (HQ).

6. SURFACE AREA

Microwave and radio frequency (RF) antennas that are typically used to interconnect remote stations have a radial dispersion of 5 to 25 degrees. The actual wavelength of light for optical wireless is in the near-infrared range of 800−1500 nm.

Narrow beams are usually less than 0.5 degrees. By using the diagram and formula given in Figure 20.4, the approximate spread of the beam can be calculated providing the distance is known.

Generally speaking, optical wireless devices operate at the same wavelength as fiber-optic networks. Thus, a

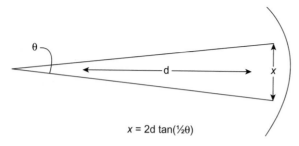

$$x = 2d\tan(\tfrac{1}{2}\theta)$$

FIGURE 20.4 The width of the broadcast at x distance can be calculated using simple trigonometry. Different manufacturers boast different theta and use this formula to calculate the spread based on equipment specifications.

small wavelength creates frequencies in the several hundred terahertz (THz) range. This is much higher than commercial microwave communications. The lower power and tighter beam of the wireless optics prevent wide angles of reflection, which can be intercepted in an attack (see checklist: An Agenda for Action When Implementing the Security of FSO). Government organizations were among the first to recognize that the greater ability to control the wireless beam inherently meant a higher degree of freedom. The 128 and 256 advanced encryption standard is frequently used in microwave transmissions; while this is all well and good, many are concerned that it can be broken.

To intercept an optical wireless system, the hacker must know the location of either the origin or the target. The intruder must also have unhindered access to a location where he can set up his electronic equipment without being caught or disturbed. Since this location is usually a commercial location, at an elevation well above ground, the ability to insert becomes tremendously more challenging. FSO devices also employ multiplex, bidirectional signals. If the insertion is occlusive, then the units *know* when the signal has been disrupted. They will not continue to broadcast without the reverse bias feedback that

indicates a successful connection. The interloper will only intercept connections establishing signals.

Additionally, the very high installations that are typical of optical wireless present additional challenges. But what about light scattered from rain, fog, dust, aerosol, or the like? Optical wireless transmissions use extremely low power levels, but the main reason for discounting this possible attack is the scattering of light in many different directions from the transmitted path.

The amount of radiation that can be collected with a detector capable of processing the signal is well beneath the range of what most detectors would consider noise. Because the beam is a laser, once the beam is scattered, the scattered photons still maintain their cohesion. However, being lasers, they tend to move in a very straight line with little incoherence. Capturing enough of the scattered light would require a collector that encapsulates the entire beam, and even then, it may not be enough. Ultimately, though, if the fog is such that one can see the actual beam (imagine a laser pen shining through fog), then it is conceivable that a collector could be designed that would be able to read the signal and translate its longitudinal section. The most likely scenario is that such an intercept device would only capture useless noise and would be so large as to make it extremely noticeable and unwieldy.

Lastly, a hacker could conceivably parachute onto the roof of a building and set his or her intercept device down on top of or next to the network FSO he or she wished to crack. For this reason, take the following precautions:

- FSOs should have backstops to prevent overshoot to neighboring office windows or rooftops.
- They should be mounted in difficult to reach places.
- They should have physical security such as keycard and/or biometric access.
- They should be protected by motion detection systems and motion-activated video surveillance.

An Agenda for Action when Implementing the Security of FSO

The five items in this checklist are, in the author's experience; the most important and critical things to address (and they are listed in order of priority) in any project that aspires to achieve true security of the physical infrastructure. The easiest way to gain access to classified access is always the first way that will be attempted by those who wish to gain unauthorized access. So, assuming that data access prevention through traditional hacking attacks is in place, the key to security of FSO lies in the following (check all tasks completed):

_____**1.** *Intrusion alerts*: When a signal is lost or disrupted, make sure your management software is capable of pinpointing when and where the interruption occurred.

_____**2.** *Entrusted access:* Make sure that, either real or verified, the people working with the data are not selling it out the back door—that they are incorruptible.

_____**3.** *Physical security of hardware:* Prevent actual physical access by unauthorized personnel.

_____**4.** *Eavesdropping on transmissions*: Make sure that any mechanism that collects the data in transit is thwarted.

_____**5.** *Data security*: Make sure that the data is encrypted, so that should it be intercepted it cannot be understood.

7. SUMMARY

The advantages of FSO technology are easily summarized. Its security is achieved primarily through the difficulty in interception of the signal. Additional security can easily be introduced in the form of traffic encryption, though this will subtract from the overall, available bandwidth. Deployment of the technology is easy because large areas can be quickly spanned with the installation of just two devices. Additionally, the technology is unaffected by electromagnetic interference, and it has low rates of error in the transmission, which means higher overall bandwidth. It also has no licensing fees, unlike microwave transmissions, and with a range of 2 KM, this is a very attractive feature.

While it does face its challenges, such as fog and very dense weather, in such areas where this is common, it could serve to offer a layer of Disaster Recovery (DR) protection. If land links are compromised due to earthquake, flood, or hurricane, FSO can offer a way of bringing signal in to an area quickly from an unaffected area.

Regardless of the configuration used, and its strengths and weaknesses, FSO is a technology that should be examined and considered as a potentially essential element in any large-area communications architecture. In the end, it is important to realize that security is never a *one-step* task. It has multiple dimensions, and every product has its security weaknesses and strengths. The most important aspect is to choose a technology that, in the existing enterprise, meshes well with existing security features, or is capable of being adapted easily and quickly to them.

The most attractive feature of FSO systems is the tremendous transmission security provided by the very narrow width of the beam used. Lasers can be aimed with a great deal of precision, and considering that the aperture of a laser beam that is very much larger than the actual wavelength of the laser, diffraction interference is minimal. This prevents even further scattering that could potentially be used to even detect that laser transmissions are occurring. The combination of keeping the location of the transceivers secret, the lack of distortion scattering, and the narrow beamwidth offers a high level of security in that the beam is virtually undetectable.

Finally, let's move on to the real interactive part of this chapter: review questions/exercises, hands-on projects, case projects, and optional team case project. The answers and/or solutions by chapter can be found in the Online Instructor's Solution Manual.

CHAPTER REVIEW QUESTIONS/EXERCISES

True/False

1. True or False? FSO uses optical pulse-modulated signals—light—to transmit data from point to point.

2. True or False? It is not common knowledge that radio frequency transmissions are easily intercepted and that the technology of securing the transmissions can, if it is secured at all, usually be circumvented, given enough time and effort.

3. True or False? Most devices are not designed with movement-handling capabilities.

4. True or False? In a mesh architecture, every other node is connected to every other node in a mesh-like lattice work of connections.

5. True or False? Ring architecture is a blend of mesh and PTP.

Multiple Choice

1. What architecture comes in two flavors: PTP and PMP?
   A. Spoofing
   B. Point-to-point
   C. Application programming interfaces
   D. Network areas
   E. Extensible Authentication Protocol (EAP) framework

2. What devices boast speeds of up to 10 Gbps in an unhindered atmosphere?
   A. SSO
   B. RSO
   C. FSO
   D. OSO
   E. TSO

3. The larger the physicality of the surface area, the greater is the area that needs protection from:
   A. attack.
   B. high expenses.
   C. price differences.
   D. lease rights.
   E. All of the above.

4. In theory, what has great potential to become far more commonplace and enjoy much greater acceptance in the information technology community than is currently the case?
   A. Splicing
   B. Accessing
   C. Bending
   D. FSO
   E. Cabling

5. Microwave and RF antennas that are typically used to interconnect remote stations have a radial dispersion of:
   A. 5−20 degrees.
   B. 5−30 degrees.
   C. 5−35 degrees.
   D. 5−40 degrees.
   E. 5−25 degrees.

EXERCISE

Problem

Are wireless fiber-optic networks more secure than standard wiring or airwaves?

Hands-On Projects

Project

How would you set up a fiber tap?

Case Projects

Problem

After homing in on the target and gaining access to the fiber-optic cable itself, what is the next step to extract light and, ultimately, data from the fiber-optic cable?

Optional Team Case Project

Problem

Can a light shield actually be created?

Managing Information Security

Information Security Essentials for IT Managers: Protecting Mission-Critical Systems

Albert Caballero

Terremark Worldwide, Inc.

1. INFORMATION SECURITY ESSENTIALS FOR IT MANAGERS, OVERVIEW

Information security management as a field is ever increasing in demand and responsibility because most organizations spend increasingly larger percentages of their IT budgets in attempting to manage risk and mitigate intrusions, not to mention the trend in many enterprises of moving all IT operations to an Internet-connected infrastructure, known as enterprise cloud computing.[1] For information security managers, it is crucial to maintain a clear perspective of all the areas of business that require protection. Through collaboration with all business units, security managers must work security into the processes of all aspects of the organization, from employee training to research and development. Security is not an IT problem, it is a business problem.

Information security means protecting information and information systems from unauthorized access, use, disclosure, disruption, modification, or destruction[2]

Scope of Information Security Management

Information security is a business problem in the sense that the entire organization must frame and solve security problems based on its own strategic drivers, not solely on technical controls aimed to mitigate one type of attack. The evolution of a risk-based paradigm, as opposed to a technical solution paradigm for security, has made it clear that a secure organization does not result from securing technical infrastructure alone. Furthermore, securing the organization's technical infrastructure cannot provide the appropriate protection for these assets, nor will it protect many other information assets that are in no way dependent on technology for their existence or protection. Thus, the organization would be lulled into a false sense of security if it relied on protecting its technical infrastructure alone.[3]

CISSP Ten Domains of Information Security

In the information security industry there have been several initiatives to attempt to define security management and how and when to apply it. The leader in certifying information security professionals is the Internet Security Consortium, with its CISSP (see sidebar, "CISSP Ten Domains: Common Body of Knowledge") certification.[4]

In defining required skills for information security managers, the ISC has arrived at an agreement on ten domains of information security that is known as the *Common Body of Knowledge* (CBK). Every security manager must understand and be well versed in all areas of the CBK.[5]

In addition to individual certification there must be guidelines to turn these skills into actionable items that can be measured and verified according to some international standard or framework. The most widely used standard for maintaining and improving information security

---

1. "Cloud computing, the enterprise cloud," Terremark Worldwide Inc. Website, http://www.theenterprisecloud.com/

2. "Definition of information security," Wikipedia, http://en.wikipedia.org/wiki/Information_security

3. Richard A. Caralli, William R. Wilson, "The challenges of security management," Survivable Enterprise Management Team, Networked Systems Survivability Program, Software Engineering Institute, http://www.cert.org/archive/pdf/ESMchallenges.pdf

4. "CISSP Ten domains" ISC2 Web site https://www.isc2.org/cissp/default.aspx

5. Micki, Krause, Harold F. Tipton, *Information Security Management Handbook sixth edition*, Auerbach Publications, CRC Press LLC

CISSP Ten Domains: Common Body of Knowledge

- *Access control.* Methods used to enable administrators and managers to define what objects a subject can access through authentication and authorization, providing each subject a list of capabilities it can perform on each object. Important areas include access control security models, identification and authentication technologies, access control administration, and single sign-on technologies.

- *Telecommunications and network security.* Examination of internal, external, public, and private network communication systems, including devices, protocols, and remote access.

- *Information security and risk management.* Including physical, technical, and administrative controls surrounding organizational assets to determine the level of protection and budget warranted by highest to lowest risk. The goal is to reduce potential threats and money loss.

- *Application security.* Application security involves the controls placed within the application programs and operating systems to support the security policy of the organization and measure its effectiveness. Topics include threats, applications development, availability issues, security design and vulnerabilities, and application/data access control.

- *Cryptography.* The use of various methods and techniques such as symmetric and asymmetric encryption to achieve desired levels of confidentiality and integrity. Important areas include encryption protocols and applications and Public Key Infrastructures.

- *Security architecture and design.* This area covers the concepts, principles, and standards used to design and implement secure applications, operating systems, and all platforms based on international evaluation criteria such as Trusted Computer Security Evaluation Criteria (TCSEC) and Common Criteria.

- *Operations security.* Controls over personnel, hardware systems, and auditing and monitoring techniques such as maintenance of AV, training, auditing, and resource protection; preventive, detective, corrective, and recovery controls; and security and fault-tolerance technologies.

- *Business continuity and disaster recovery planning.* The main purpose of this area is to preserve business operations when faced with disruptions or disasters. Important aspects are to identify resource values, perform a business impact analysis, and produce business unit priorities, contingency plans, and crisis management.

- *Legal, regulatory, compliance, and investigations.* Computer crime, government laws and regulations, and geographic locations will determine the types of actions that constitute wrongdoing, what is suitable evidence, and what type of licensing and privacy laws your organization must abide by.

- *Physical (environmental) security.* Concerns itself with threats, risks, and countermeasures to protect facilities, hardware, data, media, and personnel. Main topics include restricted areas, authorization models, intrusion detection, fire detection, and security guards.

---

is ISO/IEC 17799:2005. ISO 17799 (see Figure 21.1) establishes guidelines and principles for initiating, implementing, maintaining, and improving information security management in an organization.[6]

A new and popular framework to use in conjunction with the CISSP CBK and the ISO 17799 guidelines is ISMM. ISMM is a framework (see Figure 21.2) that describes a five-level evolutionary path of increasingly organized and systematically more mature security layers. It is proposed for the maturity assessment of information security management and the evaluation of the level of security awareness and practice at any organization, whether public or private. Furthermore, it helps us better understand where, and to what extent, the three main processes of security (prevention, detection, and recovery) are implemented and integrated.

ISMM helps us better understand the application of information security controls outlined in ISO 17799.

Figure 21.3 shows a content matrix that defines the scope of applicability between various security controls mentioned in ISO 17799's ten domains and the corresponding scope of applicability on the ISMM Framework.[7]

What is a Threat?

Threats to information systems come in many flavors, some with malicious intent, others with supernatural powers or unexpected surprises. Threats can be deliberate acts of espionage, information extortion, or sabotage, as in many targeted attacks between foreign nations; however, more often than not it happens that the biggest threats can be forces of nature (hurricane, flood) or acts of human error or failure. It is easy to become consumed in attempting to anticipate and mitigate every threat, but this is simply not possible. Threat agents are threats only when they are provided the opportunity to take advantage of a vulnerability, and ultimately there is no guarantee

---

6. "ISO 17799 security standards," ISO Web site, http://www.iso.org/iso/support/faqs/faqs_widely_used_standards/widely_used_standards_other/information_security.htm

7. Saad Saleh AlAboodi, *A New Approach for Assessing the Maturity of Information Security*, CISSP.

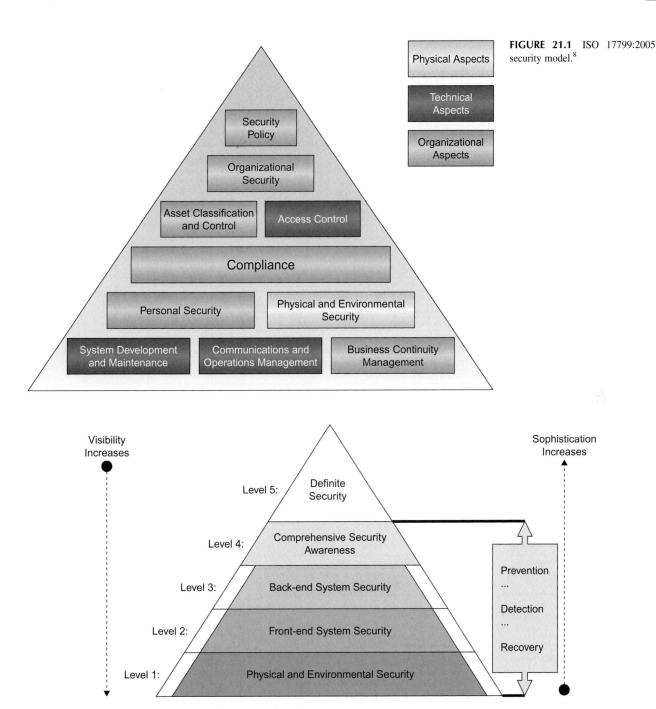

FIGURE 21.1   ISO 17799:2005 security model.[8]

FIGURE 21.2   ISMM framework.[9]

that the vulnerability will be exploited. Therefore, determining which threats are important can only be done in the context of your organization. The process by which a threat can actually cause damage to your information assets is as follows: A threat agent *gives rise to* a threat that *exploits* a vulnerability and can *lead to* a security risk that *can damage* your assets and *cause* an exposure. This can be *counter-measured by* a safeguard that *directly affects* the threat agent. Figure 21.4 shows the building blocks of the threat process.

8. "ISO 17799 security standards," ISO Web site, http://www.iso.org/iso/support/faqs/faqs_widely_used_standards/widely_used_standards_other/information_security.htm

9. Saad Saleh AlAboodi, *A New Approach for Assessing the Maturity of Information Security*, CISSP.

ISO 17799			ISMM (Scope of Applicability)				
Domain Number	Domain Name	Domain Subname	Layer 1	Layer 2	Layer 3	Layer 4	Layer 5
1	Security policy	N/A	✓	✓	✓	✓	
2	Organizational security	Information security infrastructure	✓	✓	✓		
		Security of third-party access	✓	✓	✓	✓	
		Outsourcing	✓	✓	✓	✓	
3	Asset classification and control	Accountability for assets	✓	✓	✓		
		Information classification	✓	✓	✓		
4	Personnel security	Security in job definition and resourcing	✓				
		User training	✓	✓	✓	✓	
		Responding to security incidents/malfunctions	✓	✓	✓	✓	
5	Physical and environmental security	Secure areas	✓				
		Equipment security	✓				
		General controls	✓				
6	Communications and operations management	Operational procedures and responsibilities		✓	✓		
		System planning and acceptance		✓	✓		
		Protection against malicious software		✓			
		Housekeeping		✓	✓		
		Network management			✓		
		Media handling and security	✓				
		Exchange of information and software		✓			
7	Access control	Business requirement for access control	✓	✓	✓		
		User access management		✓			
		User responsibilities		✓			
		Network access control			✓		
		Operating system access control			✓		
		Application access control		✓			
		Monitoring system access and use		✓	✓		
		Mobile computing and teleworking		✓	✓		
8	System development and maintenance	Security requirement of systems		✓	✓		
		Security in application systems		✓			
		Cryptographic controls			✓		
		Security of system files		✓	✓		
		Security in development and support processes		✓	✓		
9	Business continuity management	N/A				✓	✓
10	Compliance	Compliance with legal requirements				✓	
		Review of security policy and compliance				✓	
		System audit considerations				✓	

FIGURE 21.3 A content matrix for ISO 17799 and its scope of applicability.

Common Attacks

Threats are exploited with a variety of attacks, some technical, others not so much. Organizations that focus on the technical attacks and neglect items such as policies and procedures or employee training and awareness are setting up information security for failure. The mantra that the IT department or even the security department, by themselves, can secure an organization is as antiquated as black-and-white television. Most threats today are a mixed blend of automated information gathering, social engineering, and combined exploits, giving the perpetrator endless vectors through which to gain access. Examples of attacks vary from a highly technical remote exploit over the Internet, social-engineering an administrative assistant to reset his password, or simply walking right through an unprotected door in the back of your building. All scenarios have the potential to be equally devastating to the integrity of the organization. Some of the most common attacks are briefly described in the sidebar, "Common Attacks."[10]

Impact of Security Breaches

The impact of security breaches on most organizations can be devastating; however, it's not just dollars and cents that are at stake. Aside from the financial burden of

10. Symantec Global Internet, Security Threat Report, Trends for July–December 07, Volume XII, Published April 2008 http://eval. symantec.com/mktginfo/enterprise/white_papers/b-whitepaper_internet_security_threat_report_xiii_04-2008.en-us.pdf

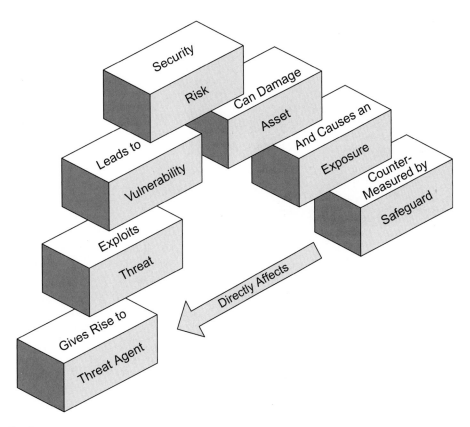

FIGURE 21.4   The threat process.

Common Attacks

- *Malicious code (malware).* Malware is a broad category; however, it is typically software designed to infiltrate or damage a computer system without the owner's informed consent. As shown in Figure 21.5, the most commonly identifiable types of malware are viruses, worms, backdoors, and Trojans. Particularly difficult to identify are root kits, which alter the kernel of the operating system.
- *Social engineering.* The art of manipulating people into performing actions or divulging confidential information. Similar to a confidence trick or simple fraud, the term typically applies to trickery to gain information or computer system access; in most cases, the attacker never comes face to face with the victim.
- *Industrial espionage.* Industrial espionage describes activities such as theft of trade secrets, bribery, blackmail, and technological surveillance as well as spying on commercial organizations and sometimes governments.
- *Spam, phishing, and hoaxes.* Spamming and phishing (see Figure 21.6), although different, often go hand in hand. Spamming is the abuse of electronic messaging systems to indiscriminately send unsolicited bulk messages, many of which contain hoaxes or other undesirable contents such

as links to phishing sites. Phishing is the criminally fraudulent process of attempting to acquire sensitive information such as usernames, passwords, and credit card details by masquerading as a trustworthy entity in an electronic communication.
- *Denial-of-service (DoS) and distributed denial-of-service (DDoS).* These are attempts to make a computer resource unavailable to its intended users. Although the means to carry out, motives for, and targets of a DoS attack may vary, it generally consists of the concerted, malevolent efforts of a person or persons to prevent an Internet site or service from functioning efficiently or at all, temporarily or indefinitely.
- *Botnets.* The term *botnet* (see Figure 21.7) can be used to refer to any group of bots, or software robots, such as IRC bots, but this word is generally used to refer to a collection of compromised computers (called zombies) running software, usually installed via worms, Trojan horses, or backdoors, under a common command-and-control infrastructure. The majority of these computers are running Microsoft Windows operating systems, but other operating systems can be affected.

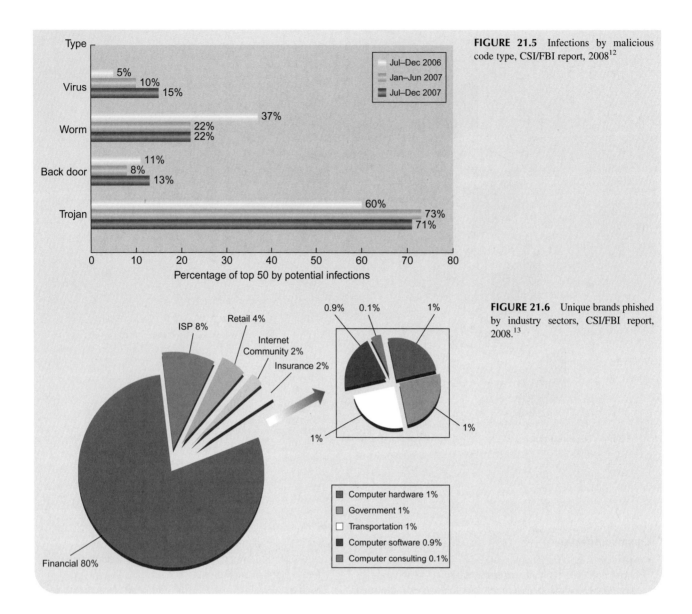

FIGURE 21.5 Infections by malicious code type, CSI/FBI report, 2008[12]

FIGURE 21.6 Unique brands phished by industry sectors, CSI/FBI report, 2008.[13]

having to deal with a security incident, especially if it leads to litigation, other factors could severely damage an organization's ability to operate, or damage the reputation of an organization beyond recovery. Some of the preliminary key findings from the 2008 CSI/FBI Security Report[11] (see Figure 21.8) include:

- Financial fraud cost organizations the most, with an average reported loss of close to $500,000.

- The second most expensive activity was dealing with bots within the network, reported to cost organizations an average of nearly $350,000.
- Virus incidents occurred most frequently, respondents said — at almost half (49%) of respondent organizations.

  Some things to consider:
- How much would it cost your organization if your ecommerce Web server farm went down for 12 hours?
- What if your mainframe database that houses your reservation system was not accessible for an entire afternoon?

11. Robert Richardson, "2008 CSI Computer Crime & Security Survey," (The latest results from the longest-running project of its kind) http://i.cmpnet.com/v2.gocsi.com/pdf/CSIsurvey2008.pdf

12. Robert Richardson, "2008 CSI Computer Crime & Security Survey," (The latest results from the longest-running project of its kind) http://i.cmpnet.com/v2.gocsi.com/pdf/CSIsurvey2008.pdf

13. Robert Richardson, "2008 CSI Computer Crime & Security Survey," (The latest results from the longest-running project of its kind) http://i.cmpnet.com/v2.gocsi.com/pdf/CSIsurvey2008.pdf

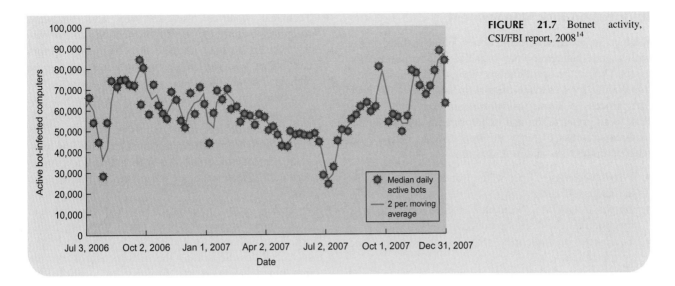

FIGURE 21.7 Botnet activity, CSI/FBI report, 2008[14]

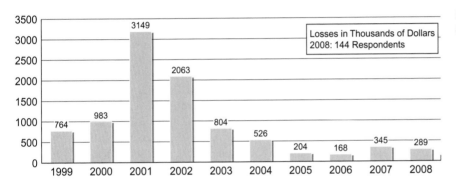

FIGURE 21.8 2008 CSI/FBI Security Survey results.[15]

- What if your Web site was defaced and rerouted all your customers to a site infected with malicious Java scripts?
- Would any of these scenarios significantly impact your organization's bottom line?

2. PROTECTING MISSION-CRITICAL SYSTEMS

The IT core of any organization is its mission-critical systems. These are systems without which the mission of the organization, whether building aircraft carriers for the U.S. military or packaging Twinkies to deliver to food markets, could not operate. The major components to protecting these systems are detailed throughout this chapter; however, with special emphasis on the big picture an information security manager must keep in mind, there are some key components that are crucial for the success and continuity of any organization. These are information assurance, information risk management, defense in depth, and contingency planning.

Information Assurance

Information assurance is achieved when information and information systems are protected against attacks through the application of security services such as availability, integrity, authentication, confidentiality, and nonrepudiation. The application of these services should be based on the protect, detect, and react paradigm. This means that in addition to incorporating protection mechanisms, organizations need to expect attacks and include attack detection tools and procedures that allow them to react to and recover from these unexpected attacks.[16]

14. Robert Richardson, "2008 CSI Computer Crime & Security Survey," (The latest results from the longest-running project of its kind) http://i.cmpnet.com/v2.gocsi.com/pdf/CSIsurvey2008.pdf

15. Robert Richardson, "2008 CSI Computer Crime & Security Survey," (The latest results from the longest-running project of its kind) http://i.cmpnet.com/v2.gocsi.com/pdf/CSIsurvey2008.pdf

16. "Defense in Depth: A practical strategy for achieving Information Assurance in today's highly networked environments," National Security Agency, Information Assurance Solutions Group - STE 6737.

Information Risk Management

Risk is, in essence, the likelihood of something going wrong and damaging your organization or information assets. Due to the ramifications of such risk, an organization should try to reduce the risk to an acceptable level. This process is known as *information risk management*. Risk to an organization and its information assets, similar to threats, comes in many different forms. Some of the most common risks and/or threats are:

- *Physical damage.* Fire, water, vandalism, power loss and natural disasters.
- *Human interaction.* Accidental or intentional action or inaction that can disrupt productivity.
- *Equipment malfunctions.* Failure of systems and peripheral devices.
- *Internal or external attacks.* Hacking, cracking, and attacking.
- *Misuse of data.* Sharing trade secrets; fraud, espionage, and theft.
- *Loss of data.* Intentional or unintentional loss of information through destructive means.
- *Application error.* Computation errors, input errors, and buffer overflows.

The idea of risk management is that threats of any kind must be identified, classified, and evaluated to calculate their damage potential.[17] This is easier said than done.

Administrative, Technical, and Physical Controls

For example, administrative, technical, and physical controls, are as follows:

- Administrative controls consist of organizational policies and guidelines that help minimize the exposure of an organization. They provide a framework by which a business can manage and inform its people how they should conduct themselves while at the workplace and provide clear steps employees can take when they're confronted with a potentially risky situation. Some examples of administrative controls include the corporate security policy, password policy, hiring policies, and disciplinary policies that form the basis for the selection and implementation of logical and physical controls. Administrative controls are of paramount importance because technical and physical controls are manifestations of the administrative control policies that are in place.

- Technical controls use software and hardware resources to control access to information and computing systems, to help mitigate the potential for errors and blatant security policy violations. Examples of technical controls include passwords, network- and host-based firewalls, network intrusion detection systems, and access control lists and data encryption. Associated with technical controls is the *Principle of Least Privilege*, which requires that an individual, program, or system process is not granted any more access privileges than are necessary to perform the task.

- Physical controls monitor and protect the physical environment of the workplace and computing facilities. They also monitor and control access to and from such facilities. Separating the network and workplace into functional areas are also physical controls. An important physical control is also separation of duties, which ensures that an individual cannot complete a critical task by herself.

Risk Analysis

During risk analysis there are several units that can help measure risk. Before risk can be measured, though, the organization must identify the vulnerabilities and threats against its mission-critical systems in terms of business continuity. During risk analysis, an organization tries to evaluate the cost for each security control that helps mitigate the risk. If the control is cost effective relative to the exposure of the organization, then the control is put in place. The measure of risk can be determined as a product of threat, vulnerability, and asset values—in other words:

$$\text{Risk} = \text{Asset} \times \text{Threat} \times \text{Vulnerability}$$

There are two primary types of risk analysis: quantitative and qualitative. *Quantitative risk analysis* attempts to assign meaningful numbers to all elements of the risk analysis process. It is recommended for large, costly projects that require exact calculations. It is typically performed to examine the viability of a project's cost or time objectives. Quantitative risk analysis provides answers to three questions that cannot be addressed with deterministic risk and project management methodologies such as traditional cost estimating or project scheduling[18]:

- What's the probability of meeting the project objective, given all known risks?

---

17. Shon Harris, *All in One CISSP Certification Exam Guide 4th Edition*, McGraw Hill Companies

18. Lionel Galway, *Quantitative Risk Analysis for Project Management, A Critical Review*, WR-112-RC, February 2004, Rand.org Web site, http://www.rand.org/pubs/working_papers/2004/RAND_WR112.pdf

- How much could the overrun or delay be, and therefore how much contingency do we need for the organization's desired level of certainty?
- Where in the project is the most risk, given the model of the project and the totality of all identified and quantified risks?

Qualitative risk analysis does not assign numerical values but instead opts for general categorization by severity levels. Where little or no numerical data is available for a risk assessment, the qualitative approach is the most appropriate. The qualitative approach does not require heavy mathematics; instead, it thrives more on the people participating and their backgrounds. Qualitative analysis enables classification of risk that is determined by people's wide experience and knowledge captured within the process. Ultimately it is not an exact science, so the process will count on expert opinions for its base assumptions. The assessment process uses a structured and documented approach and agreed likelihood and consequence evaluation tables. It is also quite common to calculate risk as a single loss expectancy (SLE) or annual loss expectancy (ALE) by project or business function.

Defense in Depth

The principle of *defense in depth* is that layered security mechanisms increase security of a system as a whole. If an attack causes one security mechanism to fail, other mechanisms may still provide the necessary security to protect the system.[19] This is a process that involves people, technology, and operations as key components to its success; however, those are only part of the picture. These organizational layers are difficult to translate into specific technological layers of defenses, and they leave out areas such as security monitoring and metrics. Figure 21.9 shows a mind map that organizes the major categories from both the organizational and technical aspects of defense in depth and takes into account people, policies, monitoring, and security metrics.

Contingency Planning

Contingency planning is necessary in several ways for an organization to be sure it can withstand some sort of security breach or disaster. Among the important steps required to make sure an organization is protected and able to respond to a security breach or disaster are business impact analysis, incident response planning, disaster recovery planning, and business continuity planning. These contingency plans are interrelated in several ways

and need to stay that way so that a response team can change from one to the other seamlessly if there is a need. Figure 21.10 shows the relationship between the four types of contingency plans with the major categories defined in each.

Business impact analysis must be performed in every organization to determine exactly which business process is deemed mission-critical and which processes would not seriously hamper business operations should they be unavailable for some time. An important part of a business impact analysis is the recovery strategy that is usually defined at the end of the process. If a thorough business impact analysis is performed, there should be a clear picture of the priority of each organization's highest-impact, therefore risky, business processes and assets as well as a clear strategy to recover from an interruption in one of these areas.[20]

An Incident Response (IR) Plan

It is a detailed set of processes and procedures that anticipate, detect, and mitigate the impact of an unexpected event that might compromise information resources and assets. Incident response plans are composed of six major phases:

1. *Preparation.* Planning and readying in the event of a security incident.
2. *Identification.* To identify a set of events that have some negative impact on the business and can be considered a security incident.
3. *Containment.* During this phase the security incident has been identified and action is required to mitigate its potential damage.
4. *Eradication.* After it's contained, the incident must be eradicated and studied to make sure it has been thoroughly removed from the system.
5. *Recovery.* Bringing the business and assets involved in the security incident back to normal operations.
6. *Lessons learned.* A thorough review of how the incident occurred and the actions taken to respond to it where the lessons learned get applied to future incidents.

When a threat becomes a valid attack, it is classified as an information security incident if[21] :

- It is directed against information assets
- It has a realistic chance of success
- It threatens the confidentiality, integrity, or availability of information assets

---

19. OWASP Definition of Defense in Depth http://www.owasp.org/index.php/Defense_in_depth

20. M. E. Whitman, H. J. Mattord, *Management of Information Security*, Course Technology, 2nd Edition, March 27, 2007.

21. M. E. Whitman, H. J. Mattord, *Management of Information Security*, Course Technology, 2nd Edition, March 27, 2007.

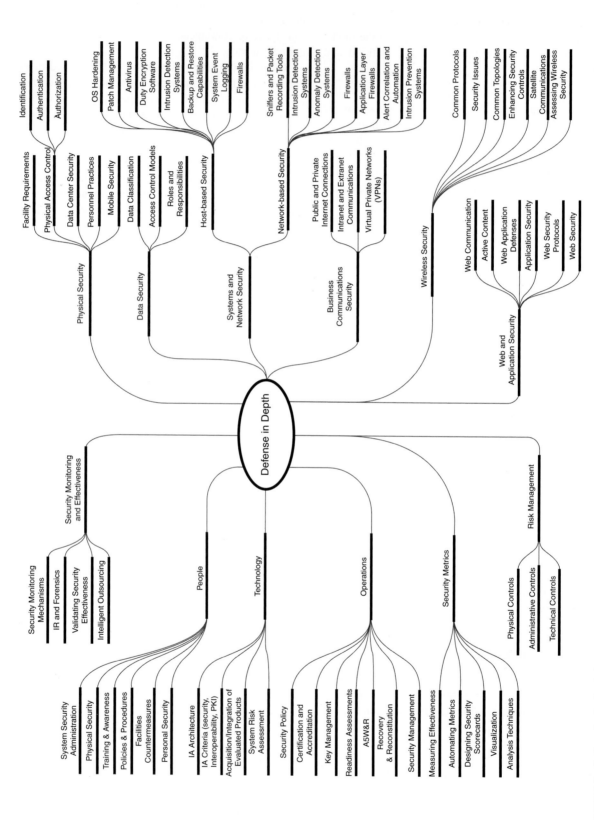

FIGURE 21.9 Defense-in-depth mind map.

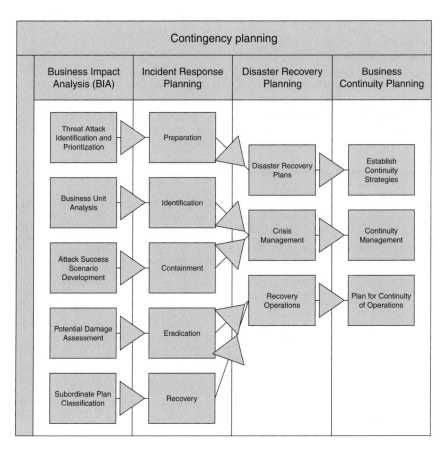

FIGURE 21.10   The relationship between the four types of contingency plans.

Business Continuity Planning (BCP)

It ensures that critical business functions can continue during a disaster and is most properly managed by the CEO of the organization. The BCP is usually activated and executed concurrently with *disaster recovery planning* (DRP) when needed and reestablishes critical functions at alternate sites (DRP focuses on reestablishment at the primary site). BCP relies on identification of critical business functions and the resources to support them using several continuity strategies, such as exclusive-use options like hot, warm, and cold sites or shared-use options like time-share, service bureaus, or mutual agreements.[22]

Disaster recovery planning is the preparation for and recovery from a disaster. Whether natural or manmade, it is an incident that has become a disaster because the organization is unable to contain or control its impact, or the level of damage or destruction from the incident is so severe that the organization is unable to recover quickly. The key role of DRP is defining how to reestablish

operations at the site where the organization is usually located.[23] Key points in a properly designed DRP:

- Clear delegation of roles and responsibilities
- Execution of alert roster and notification of key personnel
- Clear establishment of priorities
- Documentation of the disaster
- Action steps to mitigate the impact
- Alternative implementations for various systems components
- DRP must be tested regularly

3. INFORMATION SECURITY FROM THE GROUND UP

The core concepts of information security management and protecting mission-critical systems have been explained. Now, how do you actually apply these concepts to your organization from the ground up? You literally start at the ground (physical) level and work yourself up to the top (application) level. This model can be applied to many IT frameworks, ranging from networking models such as OSI or TCP/IP stacks to operating systems or other problems such as organizational information security and protecting mission-critical systems.

22. M. E. Whitman, H. J. Mattord, *Management of Information Security*, Course Technology, 2nd Edition, March 27, 2007.
23. M. E. Whitman, H. J. Mattord, *Management of Information Security*, Course Technology, 2nd Edition, March 27, 2007.

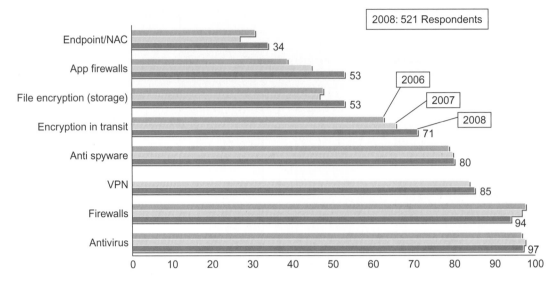

FIGURE 21.11   Security technologies used by organizations, CSI/FBI report, 2008.

There are many areas of security, all of which are inter-related. You can have an extremely hardened system running your ecommerce Web site and database; however, if physical access to the system is obtained by the wrong person, a simple yanking of the right power plug can be game over. In other words, to think that any of the following components is not important to the overall security of your organization is to provide malicious attackers the only thing they need to be successful — that is, the path of least resistance. The next parts of this chapter each contain an overview of the technologies (see Figure 21.11) and processes of which information security managers must be aware to successfully secure the assets of any organization:

- Physical security
- Data security
- Systems and network security
- Business communications security
- Wireless security
- Web and application security
- Security policies and procedures
- Security employee training and awareness

Physical Security

Physical security as defined earlier concerns itself with threats, risks, and countermeasures to protect facilities, hardware, data, media and personnel. Main topics include restricted areas, authorization models, intrusion detection, fire detection, and security guards. Therefore physical safeguards must be put in place to protect the organization from damaging consequences. The security rule defines physical safeguards as "physical measures, policies, and procedures to protect a covered entity's electronic information systems and related buildings and equipment, from natural and environmental hazards, and unauthorized intrusion."[24] A brief description of the baseline requirements to implement these safeguards at your facility follow.

Facility Requirements

Entering and accessing information systems to any degree within any organization must be controlled. What's more, it is necessary to understand what is allowed and what's not; if those parameters are clearly defied, the battle is half won. Not every building is a high-security facility, so it's understandable that some of the following items might not apply to your organization; however, there should be a good, clear reason as to why they don't. Sample questions and comments to consider:[25]

- Are policies and procedures developed and implemented that address allowing authorized and limiting unauthorized physical access to electronic information systems and the facility or facilities in which they are housed?
- Do the policies and procedures identify individuals (workforce members, business associates, contractors, etc.) with authorized access by title and/or job function?
- Do the policies and procedures specify the methods used to control physical access, such as door locks, electronic access control systems, security officers, or video monitoring?

24. 45 C.F.R. § 164.310 Physical safeguards, http://law.justia.com/us/cfr/title45/45-1.0.1.3.70.3.33.5.html
25. 45 C.F.R. § 164.310 Physical safeguards, http://law.justia.com/us/cfr/title45/45-1.0.1.3.70.3.33.5.html

The facility access controls standard has four implementation specifications[26] :

- *Contingency operations.* Establish (and implement as needed) procedures that allow facility access in support of restoration of lost data under the disaster recovery plan and emergency mode operations plan in the event of an emergency.
- *Facility security plan.* Implement policies and procedures to safeguard the facility and the equipment therein from unauthorized physical access, tampering, and theft.
- *Access control and validation procedures.* Implement procedures to control and validate a person's access to facilities based on her role or function, including visitor control and control of access to software programs for testing and revision.
- *Maintenance records.* Implement policies and procedures to document repairs and modifications to the physical components of a facility that are related to security (for example, hardware, walls, doors, and locks).

Administrative, Technical, and Physical Controls

Understanding what it takes to secure a facility is the first step in the process of identifying exactly what type of administrative, technical, and physical controls will be necessary for your particular organization. Translating the needs for security into tangible examples, here are some of the controls that can be put in place to enhance security:

- *Administrative controls.* These include human resources exercises for simulated emergencies such as fire drills or power outages as well as security awareness training and security policies.
- *Technical controls.* These include physical intrusion detection systems and access control equipment such as biometrics.
- *Physical controls.* These include video cameras, guarded gates, man traps, and car traps.

Data Security

Data security is at the core of what needs to be protected in terms of information security and mission-critical systems. Ultimately it is the data that the organization needs to protect in many cases, and usually data is exactly what perpetrators are after, whether trade secrets, customer information, or a database of Social Security numbers — the data is where it's at!

---

26. 45 C.F.R. § 164.310 Physical safeguards, http://law.justia.com/us/cfr/title45/45-1.0.1.3.70.3.33.5.html

To be able to properly classify and restrict data, the first thing to understand is how data is accessed. Data is accessed by a *subject*, whether that is a person, process, or another application, and what is accessed to retrieve the data is called an *object*. Think of an object as a cookie jar with valuable information in it, and only select subjects have the permissions necessary to dip their hands into the cookie jar and retrieve the data or information that they are looking for. Both subjects and objects can be a number of things acting in a network, depending on what action they are taking at any given moment, as shown in Figure 21.12.

Data Classification

Various *data classification* models are available for different environments. Some security models focus on the confidentiality of the data (such as Bell-La Padula) and use different classifications. For example, the U.S. military uses a model that goes from most confidential (Top Secret) to least confidential (Unclassified) to classify the data on any given system. On the other hand, most corporate entities prefer a model whereby they classify data by business unit (HR, Marketing, R & D ...) or use terms such as Company Confidential to define items that should not be shared with the public. Other security models focus on the integrity of the data (for example, Bipa); yet others are expressed by mapping security policies to data classification (for example, Clark-Wilson). In every case there are areas that require special attention and clarification.

Access Control Models

Three main *access control models* are in use today: RBAC, DAC, and MAC. In Role-Based Access Control (RBAC), the job function of the individual determines the group he is assigned to and determines the level of access he can attain on certain data and systems. The level of access is usually defined by IT personnel in accordance with policies and procedures. In Discretionary Access Control (DAC), the end user or creator of the data object is allowed to define who can and who cannot access the data; this has become less popular in recent history. Mandatory Access Control (MAC) is more of a militant style of applying permissions, where permissions are the same across the board to all members of a certain level or class within the organization. The following are data security "need to knows":

- *Authentication versus authorization.* It's crucial to understand that simply because someone becomes authenticated does not mean that they are authorized to view certain data. There needs to be a means by which a person, after gaining access through authentication, is limited in the actions they are authorized to

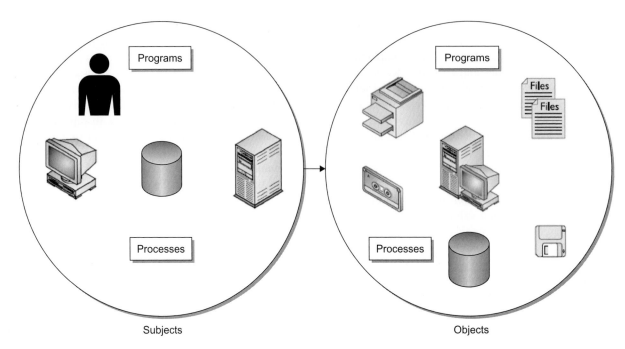

FIGURE 21.12 Subjects access objects.

perform on certain data (such as read-only permissions).

- *Protecting data with cryptography* is important for the security of both the organization and its customers. Usually the most important item that an organization needs to protect, aside from trade secrets, is its customers' personal data. If there is a security breach and the data that is stolen or compromised was previously encrypted, the organization can feel more secure in that the collateral damage to their reputation and customer base will be minimized.
- *Data leakage prevention and content management* is an up-and-coming area of data security that has proven extremely useful in preventing sensitive information from leaving an organization. With this relatively new technology, a security administrator can define the types of documents, and further define the content within those documents, that cannot leave the organization and quarantine them for inspection before they hit the public Internet.
- *Securing email systems* is one of the most important and overlooked areas of data security. With access to the mail server, an attacker can snoop through anyone's email, even the company CEO's! Password files, company confidential documents, and contacts for all address books are only some of the things that a compromised mail server can reveal about an organization, not to mention root/administrator access to a system in the internal network.

Systems and Network Security

Systems and network security[27] is at the core of information security. Though physical security is extremely important and a breach could render all your systems and network security safeguards useless, without hardened systems and networks, anyone from the comfort of her own living room can take over your network, access your confidential information, and disrupt your operations at will. Data classification and security are also quite important, if for nothing else to be sure that only those who need to access certain data can and those who do not need access cannot; however, that usually works well for people who play by the rules. In many cases when an attacker gains access to a system, the first order of business is escalation of privileges. This means that the attacker gets in as a regular user and attempts to find ways to gain administrator or root privileges. The following are brief descriptions of each of the components that make for a complete security infrastructure for all host systems and network connected assets.

Host-Based Security

The host system is the core of where data sits and is accessed, so it is therefore also the main target of many

27. "GSEC, GIAC Security Essentials Outline," SANS Institute, https://www.sans.org/training/description.php?tid = 672

intruders. Regardless of the operating system platform that is selected to run certain applications and databases, the principles of hardening systems are the same and apply to host systems as well as network devices, as we will see in the upcoming sections. Steps required to maintain host systems in as secure a state as possible are as follows:

1. *OS hardening.* Guidelines by which a base operating system goes through a series of checks to make sure no unnecessary exposures remain open and that security features are enabled where possible. There is a series of organizations that publish OS hardening Guides for various platforms of operating systems.

2. *Removing unnecessary services.* In any operating system there are usually services that are enabled but have no real business need. It is necessary to go through all the services of your main corporate image, on both the server side and client side, to determine which services are required and which would create a potential vulnerability if left enabled.

3. *Patch management.* All vendors release updates for known vulnerabilities on some kind of schedule. Part of host-based security is making sure that all required vendor patches, at both the operating system and the application level, are applied as quickly as business operations allow on some kind of regular schedule. There should also be an emergency patch procedure in case there is an outbreak and updates need to be pushed out of sequence.

4. *Antivirus.* Possibly more important than patches are antivirus definitions, specifically on desktop and mobile systems. Corporate antivirus software should be installed and updated frequently on all systems in the organization.

5. *Intrusion detection systems (IDSs).* Although many seem to think IDSs are a network security function, there are many good host-based IDS applications, both commercial and open source, that can significantly increase security and act as an early warning system for possibly malicious traffic and/or files for which the AV does not have a definition.

6. *Firewalls.* Host-based firewalls are not as popular as they once were because many big vendors such as Symantec, McAfee, and Checkpoint have moved to a host-based client application that houses all security functions in one. There is also another trend in the industry to move toward application-specific host-based firewalls like those specifically designed to run on a Web or database server, for example.

7. *Data encryption software.* One item often overlooked is encryption of data while it is at rest. Many solutions have recently come onto the market that offer the ability to encrypt sensitive data such as credit card and Social Security numbers that sit on your file server or inside the database server. This is a huge protection in the case of information theft or data leakage.

8. *Backup and restore capabilities.* Without the ability to back up and restore both servers and clients in a timely fashion, an issue that could be resolved in short order can quickly turn into a disaster. Backup procedures should be in place and restored on a regular basis to verify their integrity.

9. *System event logging.* Event logs are significant when you're attempting to investigate the root cause of an issue or incident. In many cases, logging is not turned on by default and needs to be enabled after the core installation of the host operating system. The OS hardening guidelines for your organization should require that logging be enabled.

Network-Based Security

The network is the communication highway for everything that happens between all the host systems. All data at one point or another passes over the wire and is potentially vulnerable to snooping or spying by the wrong person. The controls implemented on the network are similar in nature to those that can be applied to host systems; however, network-based security can be more easily classified into two main categories: detection and prevention. We will discuss security monitoring tools in another section; for now the main functions of network-based security are to either detect a potential incident based on a set of events or prevent a known attack.

Most network-based security devices can perform detect or protect functions in one of two ways: signature-based or anomaly-based. Signature-based detection or prevention is similar to AV signatures that look for known traits of a particular attack or malware. Anomaly-based systems can make decisions based on what is expected to be "normal" on the network or per a certain set of standards (for example, RFC), usually after a period of being installed in what is called "learning" or "monitor" mode.

Intrusion Detection

Intrusion detection is the process of monitoring the events occurring in a computer system or network and analyzing them for signs of possible incidents that are violations or imminent threats of violation of computer security policies, acceptable-use policies, or standard security practices. Incidents have many causes, such as malware (worms, spyware), attackers gaining unauthorized access to systems from the Internet, and authorized system users who misuse their privileges or attempt to gain additional privileges for which they are not authorized.[28] The most common detection technologies and their security functions on the network are as follows:

- *Packet sniffing and recording tools.* These tools are used quite often by networking teams to troubleshoot connectivity issues; however, they can be a security professional's best friend during investigations and root-cause analysis. When properly deployed and maintained, a packet capture device on the network allows security professionals to reconstruct data and reverseengineer malware in a way that is simply not possible without a full packet capture of the communications.
- *Intrusion detection systems.* In these systems, appliances or servers monitor network traffic and run it through a rules engine to determine whether it is malicious according to its signature set. If the traffic is deemed malicious, an alert will fire and notify the monitoring system.
- *Anomaly detection systems.* Aside from the actual packet data traveling on the wire, there are also traffic trends that can be monitored on the switches and routers to determine whether unauthorized or anomalous activity is occurring. With Net-flow and S-flow data that can be sent to an appliance or server, aggregated traffic on the network can be analyzed and can alert a monitoring system if there is a problem. Anomaly detection systems are extremely useful when there is an attack for which the IDS does not have a signature or if there is some activity occurring that is suspicious.

Intrusion Prevention

Intrusion prevention is a system that allows for the active blocking of attacks while they are inline on the network, before they even get to the target host. There are many ways to prevent attacks or unwanted traffic from coming into your network, the most common of which is known as a firewall. Although a firewall is mentioned quite commonly and a lot of people know what a firewall is, there are several different types of controls that can be put in place in addition to a firewall that can seriously help protect the network. Here are the most common prevention technologies:

- *Firewalls.* The purpose of a firewall is to enforce an organization's security policy at the border of two

networks. Typically most firewalls are deployed at the edge between the internal network and the Internet (if there is such a thing) and are configured to block (prevent) any traffic from going in or out that is not allowed by the corporate security policy. There are quite a few different levels of protection a firewall can provide, depending on the type of firewall that is deployed, such as these:

- *Packet filtering.* The most basic type of firewalls perform what is called *stateful packet filtering*, which means that they can remember which side initiated the connection, and rules (called access control lists, or ACLs) can be created based not only on IPs and ports but also depending on the state of the connection (meaning whether the traffic is going into or out of the network).
- *Proxies.* The main difference between proxies and stateful packet-filtering firewalls is that proxies have the ability to terminate and reestablish connections between two end hosts, acting as a proxy for all communications and adding a layer of security and functionality to the regular firewalls.
- *Application layer firewalls.* The app firewalls have become increasingly popular; they are designed to protect certain types of applications (Web or database) and can be configured to perform a level of blocking that is much more intuitive and granular, based not only on network information but also application-specific variables so that administrators can be much more precise in what they are blocking. In addition, app firewalls can typically be loaded with server-side SSL certificates, allowing the appliance to decrypt encrypted traffic, a huge benefit to a typical proxy or stateful firewall.
- *Intrusion prevention systems.* An intrusion prevention system (IPS) is software that has all the capabilities of an intrusion detection system and can also attempt to stop possible incidents using a set of conditions based on signatures or anomalies.

Business Communications Security

Businesses today tend to communicate with many other business entities, not only over the Internet but also through private networks or guest access connections directly to the organization's network, whether wired or wireless. Business partners and contractors conducting business communications obviously tend to need a higher level of access than public users but not as extensive as permanent employees, so how does an organization handle this phenomenon? External parties working on internal projects are also classed as business partners. Some general rules for users to maintain security control of external entities are shown in Figure 21.13.

---

28. Karen Scarfone and Peter Mell, NIST Special Publication 800–94: "Guide to Intrusion Detection and Prevention Systems (IDPS)," Recommendations of the National Institute of Standards and Technology, http://csrc.nist.gov/publications/nistpubs/800-94/SP800-94.pdf

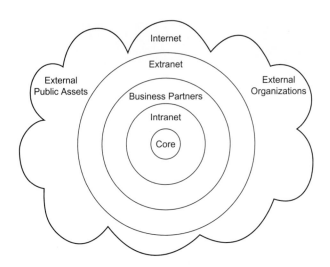

FIGURE 21.13   The business communications cloud.

General Rules for Self-Protection

The general rules for self-protection are as follows:

- Access to a user's own IT system must be protected in such a way that system settings (in the BIOS) can only be changed subject to authentication.
- System start must always be protected by requiring appropriate authentication (requesting the boot password). Exceptions to this rule can apply if:
- Automatic update procedures require this, and the system start can only take place from the built-in hard disk.
- The system is equipped for use by a number of persons with their individual user profiles, and system start can only take place from the built-in hard disk.
- Unauthorized access to in-house resources including data areas (shares, folders, mailboxes, calendar, etc.) must be prevented in line with their need for protection. In addition, the necessary authorizations for approved data access must be defined.
- Users are not permitted to operate resources without first defining any authorizations (such as no global sharing). This rule must be observed particularly by those users who are system managers of their own resources.
- Users of an IT system must lock the access links they have opened (for example, by enabling a screensaver or removing the chip card from the card reader), even during short periods of absence from their workstations.
- When work is over, all open access links must be properly closed or protected against system/data access (such as if extensive compilation runs need to take place during the night).

- Deputizing rules for access to the user's own system or data resources must be made in agreement with the manager and the acting employee.

Handling Protection Resources

The handling of protection resources are as follows:

- Employees must ensure that their protection resources cannot be subject to snooping while data required for authentication is being entered (e.g., password entry during login).
- Employees must store all protection resources and records in such a way that they cannot be subjected to snooping or stolen.
- Personal protection resources must never be made available to third parties.
- In the case of chip cards, SecurID tokens, or other protection resources requiring a PIN, the associated PIN (PIN letter) must be stored separately.
- Loss, theft, or disclosure of protection resources is to be reported immediately.
- Protection resources subject to loss, theft, or snooping must be disabled immediately.

Rules for Mobile IT Systems

In addition to the general rules for users, the following rules may also apply for mobile IT systems:

- Extended self-protection.
- A mobile IT system must be safeguarded against theft (that is, secured with a cable lock, locked away in a cupboard).
- The data from a mobile IT system using corporate proprietary information must be safeguarded as appropriate (e.g., encryption). In this connection, CERT rules in particular are to be observed.
- The software provided by the organization for system access control may only be used on the organization's own mobile IT systems.

Operation on Open Networks

Rules for operation on open networks are as follows:

- The mobile IT system must be operated in open network environments using a personal firewall.
- The configuration of the personal firewall must be in accordance with the corporate policy or, in the case of other personal firewall systems, must be subject to restrictive settings.
- A mobile IT system must be operated in an unprotected open network only for the duration of a secure access link to the organization's own network. The connection establishment for the secure access link

IEEE Standard or Amendment	Maximum Data Rate	Typical Range	Frequency Band	Comments
802.11	2 Mbps	50–100 meters	2.4 GHz	
802.11a	54 Mbps	50–100 meters	5 GHz	Not compatible with 802.11b
802.11b	11 Mbps	50–100 meters	2.4 GHz	Equipment based on 802.11b has been the dominant WLAN technology
802.11g	54 Mbps	50–100 meters	2.4 GHz	Backward compatible with 802.11b

FIGURE 21.14 IEEE Common Wireless Standards: NIST SP800−97.[30]

must be performed as soon as possible, at least within five minutes.

- Simultaneous operation on open networks (protected or unprotected) and the organization's own networks is forbidden at all times.
- Remote access to company internal resources must always be protected by means of strong authentication.
- For the protection of data being transferred via a remote access link, strong encryption must always be used.

Additional Business Communications Guidelines

Additional business communications guidelines should be defined for the following:

- External IT systems may not be connected directly to the intranet. Transmission of corporate proprietary data to external systems should be avoided wherever possible, and copies of confidential or strictly confidential data must never be created on external IT systems.
- Unauthorized access to public data areas (shares, folders, mailboxes, calendars, etc.) is to be prevented. The appropriate authentication checks and authorization requirements must be defined and the operation of resources without such requirements is not permitted (no global sharing).
- Remote data access operations must be effected using strong authentication and encryption, and managers must obtain permission from the owner of the resources to access.
- For secure remote maintenance by business partners, initialization of the remote maintenance must take place from an internal system, such as via an Internet connection protected by strong encryption. An employee must be present at the system concerned during the entire remote maintenance session to monitor the remote maintenance in accordance with the policy, and the date, nature, and extent of the remote maintenance must be logged at a minimum.

Wireless Security

Wireless networking enables devices with wireless capabilities to use information resources without being physically connected to a network. A wireless local area network (WLAN) is a group of wireless networking nodes within a limited geographic area that is capable of radio communications. WLANs are typically used by devices within a fairly limited range, such as an office building or building campus, and are usually implemented as extensions to existing wired local area networks to provide enhanced user mobility. Since the beginning of wireless networking, many standards and technologies have been developed for WLANs. One of the most active standards organizations that address wireless networking is the Institute of Electrical and Electronics Engineers (IEEE), as outlined in Figure 21.14.[29] Like other wireless technologies, WLANs typically need to support several security objectives. This is intended to be accomplished through a combination of security features built into the wireless networking standard. The most common security objectives for WLANs are as follows:

- *Access control.* Restrict the rights of devices or individuals to access a network or resources within a network.
- *Confidentiality.* Ensure that communication cannot be read by unauthorized parties.
- *Integrity.* Detect any intentional or unintentional changes to data that occur in transit.
- *Availability.* Ensure that devices and individuals can access a network and its resources whenever needed.

29. Sheila Frankel, Bernard Eydt, Les Owens, Karen Scarfone, NIST Special Publication 800−97: "Establishing Wireless Robust Security Networks: A Guide to IEEE 802.11i," Recommendations of the National Institute of Standards and Technology, http://csrc.nist.gov/publications/nistpubs/800-97/SP800-97.pdf
30. Sheila Frankel, Bernard Eydt, Les Owens, Karen Scarfone, NIST Special Publication 800−97: "Establishing Wireless Robust Security Networks: A Guide to IEEE 802.11i," Recommendations of the National Institute of Standards and Technology, http://csrc.nist.gov/publications/nistpubs/800-97/SP800-97.pdf

Access Control

Typically there are two means by which to validate the identities of wireless devices attempting to connect to a WLAN: open-system authentication and shared-key authentication. Neither of these alternatives is secure. The security provided by the default connection means is unacceptable; all it takes for a host to connect to your system is a Service Set Identifier (SSID) for the AP (which is a name that is broadcast in the clear) and, optionally, a MAC Address. The SSID was never intended to be used as an access control feature.

A MAC address is a unique 48-bit value that is permanently assigned to a particular wireless network interface. Many implementations of IEEE 802.11 allow administrators to specify a list of authorized MAC addresses; the AP will permit devices with those MAC addresses only to use the WLAN. This is known as *MAC address filtering.* However, since the MAC address is not encrypted, it is simple to intercept traffic and identify MAC addresses that are allowed past the MAC filter. Unfortunately, almost all WLAN adapters allow applications to set the MAC address, so it is relatively trivial to spoof a MAC address, meaning that attackers can easily gain unauthorized access. Additionally, the AP is not authenticated to the host by open-system authentication. Therefore, the host has to trust that it is communicating to the real AP and not an impostor AP that is using the same SSID. Therefore, open system authentication does not provide reasonable assurance of any identities and can easily be misused to gain unauthorized access to a WLAN or to trick users into connecting to a malicious WLAN.[31]

Confidentiality

The WEP protocol attempts some form of confidentiality by using the RC4 stream cipher algorithm to encrypt wireless communications. The standard for WEP specifies support for a 40-bit WEP key only; however, many vendors offer nonstandard extensions to WEP that support key lengths of up to 128 or even 256 bits. WEP also uses a 24-bit value known as an *initialization vector* (IV) as a seed value for initializing the cryptographic keystream. Ideally, larger key sizes translate to stronger protection, but the cryptographic technique used by WEP has known flaws that are not mitigated by longer keys. WEP is not the secure alternative you're looking for.

A possible threat against confidentiality is network traffic analysis. Eavesdroppers might be able to gain information by monitoring and noting which parties communicate at particular times. Also, analyzing traffic patterns can aid in determining the content of communications; for example, short bursts of activity might be caused by terminal emulation or instant messaging, whereas steady streams of activity might be generated by videoconferencing. More sophisticated analysis might be able to determine the operating systems in use based on the length of certain frames. Other than encrypting communications, IEEE 802.11, like most other network protocols, does not offer any features that might thwart network traffic analysis, such as adding random lengths of padding to messages or sending additional messages with randomly generated data.[32]

Integrity

Data integrity checking for messages transmitted between hosts and APs exists and is designed to reject any messages that have been changed in transit, such as by a manin-the-middle attack. WEP data integrity is based on a simple encrypted checksum — a 32-bit cyclic redundancy check (CRC-32) computed on each payload prior to transmission. The payload and checksum are encrypted using the RC4 keystream, and then transmitted. The receiver decrypts them, recomputes the checksum on the received payload, and compares it with the transmitted checksum. If the checksums are not the same, the transmitted data frame has been altered in transit, and the frame is discarded. Unfortunately, CRC-32 is subject to bit-flipping attacks, which means that an attacker knows which CRC-32 bits will change when message bits are altered. WEP attempts to counter this problem by encrypting the CRC-32 to produce an integrity check value (ICV). WEP's creators believed that an enciphered CRC-32 would be less subject to tampering. However, they did not realize that a property of stream ciphers such as WEP's RC4 is that bit flipping survives the encryption process — the same bits flip whether or not encryption is used. Therefore, the WEP ICV offers no additional protection against bit flipping.[33]

31. Sheila Frankel, Bernard Eydt, Les Owens, Karen Scarfone, NIST Special Publication 800–97: "Establishing Wireless Robust Security Networks: A Guide to IEEE 802.11i," Recommendations of the National Institute of Standards and Technology, http://csrc.nist.gov/publications/nistpubs/800-97/SP800-97.pdf

32. Sheila Frankel, Bernard Eydt, Les Owens, Karen Scarfone, NIST Special Publication 800–97: "Establishing Wireless Robust Security Networks: A Guide to IEEE 802.11i," Recommendations of the National Institute of Standards and Technology, http://csrc.nist.gov/publications/nistpubs/800-97/SP800-97.pdf

33. Sheila Frankel, Bernard Eydt, Les Owens Karen, Scarfone, NIST Special Publication 800–97: "Establishing Wireless Robust Security Networks: A Guide to IEEE 802.11i," Recommendations of the National Institute of Standards and Technology, http://csrc.nist.gov/publications/nistpubs/800-97/SP800-97.pdf

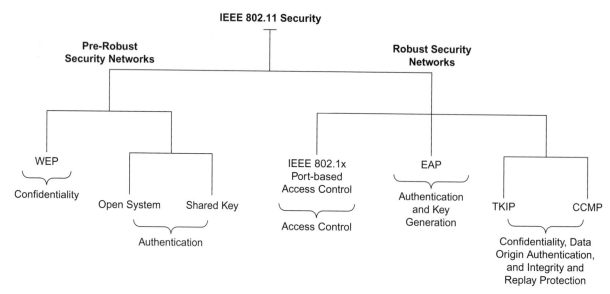

FIGURE 21.15   High-level taxonomy of the major pre-RSN and RSN security mechanisms.[35]

Availability

Individuals who do not have physical access to the WLAN infrastructure can cause a denial of service for the WLAN. One threat is known as jamming, which involves a device that emits electromagnetic energy on the WLAN's frequencies. The energy makes the frequencies unusable by the WLAN, causing a denial of service. Jamming can be performed intentionally by an attacker or unintentionally by a non-WLAN device transmitting on the same frequency. Another threat against availability is flooding, which involves an attacker sending large numbers of messages to an AP at such a high rate that the AP cannot process them, or other STAs cannot access the channel, causing a partial or total denial of service. These threats are difficult to counter in any radio-based communications; thus, the IEEE 802.11 standard does not provide any defense against jamming or flooding. Also, as described in Section 3.2.1, attackers can establish rogue APs; if STAs mistakenly attach to a rogue AP instead of a legitimate one, this could make the legitimate WLAN effectively unavailable to users. Although 802.11i protects data frames, it does not offer protection to control or management frames. An attacker can exploit the fact that management frames are not authenticated to deauthenticate a client or to disassociate a client from the network.[34]

Enhancing Security Controls

The IEEE 802.11i amendment allows for enhanced security features beyond WEP and the simple IEEE 802.11 shared-key challenge-response authentication. The amendment introduces the concepts of Robust Security Networks (RSNs) (see Figure 21.15) and Robust Security Network Associations (RSNAs). There are two RSN data confidentiality and integrity protocols defined in IEEE 802.11i—Temporal Key Integrity Protocol (TKIP) and Counter Mode with Cipher-Block Chaining Message Authentication Code Protocol (CCMP).

At a high level, RSN includes IEEE 802.1x port-based access control, key management techniques, and the TKIP and CCMP data confidentiality and integrity protocols. These protocols allow for the creation of several diverse types of security networks because of the numerous configuration options. RSN security is at the link level only, providing protection for traffic between a wireless host and its associated AP or between one wireless host and another. It does not provide end-to-end application-level security, such as between a host and an email or Web server, because communication between these entities requires more than just one link. For infrastructure mode, additional measures need to be taken to provide end-to-end security.

34. Sheila Frankel, Bernard Eydt, Les Owens Karen, Scarfone, NIST Special Publication 800–97: "Establishing Wireless Robust Security Networks: A Guide to IEEE 802.11i," Recommendations of the National Institute of Standards and Technology, http://csrc.nist.gov/publications/nistpubs/800-97/SP800-97.pdf

35. Sheila Frankel, Bernard Eydt, Les Owens Karen, Scarfone, NIST Special Publication 800–97: "Establishing Wireless Robust Security Networks: A Guide to IEEE 802.11i," Recommendations of the National Institute of Standards and Technology, http://csrc.nist.gov/publications/nistpubs/800-97/SP800-97.pdf

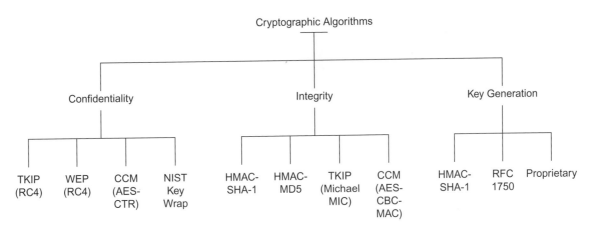

FIGURE 21.16 Taxonomy of the cryptographic algorithms included in the IEEE 802.11 standard.[36]

The IEEE 802.11i amendment defines an RSN as a wireless network that allows the creation of RSN Associations (RSNAs) only. An RSNA is a security relationship established by the IEEE 802.11i 4-Way Handshake. The 4-Way Handshake validates that the parties to the protocol instance possess a pairwise master key (PMK), synchronize the installation of temporal keys, and confirm the selection of cipher suites. The PMK is the cornerstone of a number of security features absent from WEP. Complete robust security is considered possible only when all devices in the network use RSNAs. In practice, some networks have a mix of RSNAs and non-RSNA connections. A network that allows the creation of both pre-RSN associations (pre-RSNA) and RSNAs is referred to as a Transition Security Network (TSN). A TSN is intended to be an interim means to provide connectivity while an organization migrates to networks based exclusively on RSNAs. RSNAs enable the following security features for IEEE 802.11 WLANs:

- Enhanced user authentication mechanisms
- Cryptographic key management
- Data confidentiality
- Data origin authentication and integrity
- Replay protection

An RSNA relies on IEEE 802.1x to provide an authentication framework. To achieve the robust security of RSNAs, the designers of the IEEE 802.11i amendment used numerous mature cryptographic algorithms and techniques. These algorithms can be categorized as being used for confidentiality, integrity (and data origin authentication), or key generation. All the algorithms specifically referenced in the IEEE 802.11 standard (see

Figure 21.16) are symmetric algorithms, which use the same key for two different steps of the algorithm, such as encryption and decryption.

TKIP is a cipher suite for enhancing WEP on pre-RSN hardware without causing significant performance degradation. TKIP works within the processing constraints of first-generation hosts and APs and therefore enables increased security without requiring hardware replacement. TKIP provides the following fundamental security features for IEEE 802.11 WLANs:

- Confidentiality protection using the RC4 algorithm[38]
- Integrity protection against several types of attacks[39] using the Michael message digest algorithm (through generation of a message integrity code [MIC])[40]
- Replay prevention through a frame-sequencing technique
- Use of a new encryption key for each frame to prevent attacks, such as the Fluhrer-Mantin-Shamir (FMS) attack, which can compromise WEP-based WLANs[41]
- Implementation of countermeasures whenever the STA or AP encounters a frame with a MIC error, which is a strong indication of an active attack

Web and Application Security

Web and application security has come to center stage recently because Web sites and other public-facing applications have had so many vulnerabilities reported that it is often trivial to find some part of the application that is vulnerable to one of the many exploits out there. When an attacker compromises a system at the application level, often it is too trivial to take advantage of all the capabilities said application has to offer, including querying the back-end database or accessing proprietary information. In the past it was not necessary to implement security during the development phase of an application, and since most security professionals are not programmers, that

---

36. Sheila Frankel, Bernard Eydt, Les Owens, Karen Scarfone, NIST Special Publication 800–97: "Establishing Wireless Robust Security Networks: A Guide to IEEE 802.11i," Recommendations of the National Institute of Standards and Technology, http://csrc.nist.gov/publications/nistpubs/800-97/SP800-97.pdf

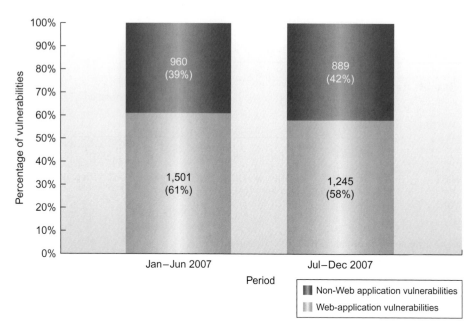

FIGURE 21.17   Symantec Web application vulnerabilities by share.

worked out just fine; however, due to factors such as rushing software releases and a certain level of complacency where end users expect buggy software and apply patches, the trend of inserting security earlier in the development process is catching steam.

Web Security

Web security is unique to every environment; any application and service that the organization wants to deliver to the customer will have its own way of performing transactions. Static Web sites with little content or searchable areas of course pose the least risk, but they also offer the least functionality. Who wants a Web site they can't sell anything from? Implementing something like a shopping cart or content delivery on your site opens up new, unexpected aspects of Web security. Among the things that need to be considered are whether it is worth developing the application in-house or buying one off the shelf and rely on someone else for the maintenance ad patching. With some of these thoughts in mind, here are some of the biggest threats associated with having a public-facing Web site:

- Vandalism
- Financial fraud
- Privileged access
- Theft of transaction information
- Theft of intellectual property
- Denial-of-service (DoS) attacks
- Input validation errors
- Path or directory traversal
- Unicode encoding
- URL encoding

Some Web application defenses that can be implemented have already been discussed; they include:

- Web application firewalls
- Intrusion prevention systems
- SYN proxies on the firewall

Application Security

An integrated approach to application security (see Figure 21.17) in the organization is required for successful deployment and secure maintenance of all applications. A corporate initiative to define, promote, assure, and measure the security of critical business applications would greatly enhance an organization's overall security. Some of the biggest obstacles, as mentioned in the previous section, are that security professionals are not typically developers, so this means that often application security is left to IT or R & D personnel, which can lead to gaping holes. Components of an application security program consist of[37]:

- *People.* Security architects, managers, technical leads, developers and testers.
- *Policy.* Integrate security steps into your SDLC and ADLC; have security baked in, not bolted on. Find security issues early so that they are easier and cheaper to fix. Measure compliance; are the processes working? Inventory and categorize your applications.

37. "AppSec2005DC-Anthony Canike-Enterprise AppSec Program PowerPoint Presentation," OWASP, http://www.owasp.org/index.php/Image:AppSec2005DC-Anthony_Canike-Enterprise_AppSec_Program.ppt

- *Standards.* Which controls are necessary, and when and why? Use standard methods to implement each control. Provide references on how to implement and define requirements.
- *Assessments.* Security architecture/design reviews, security code reviews, application vulnerability tests, risk acceptance review, external penetration test of production applications, white-box philosophy. Look inside the application, and use all the advantages you have such as past reviews, design documents, code, logs, interviews, and so on. Attackers have advantages over you; don't tie your hands.
- *Training.* Take awareness and training seriously. All developers should be performing their own input validation in their code and need to be made aware of the security risks involved in sending unsecure code into production.

Security Policies and Procedures

A quality information security program begins and ends with the correct information security policy (see Figure 21.18). Policies are the least expensive means of control and often the most difficult to implement. An information security policy is a plan that influences and determines the actions taken by employees who are presented with a policy decision regarding information systems. Other components related to a security policy are practices, procedures, and guidelines, which attempt to explain in more detail the actions that are to be taken by employees in any given situation. For policies to be effective, they must be properly disseminated, read, understood, and agreed to by all employees as well as backed by upper management. Without upper management support, a security policy is bound to fail. Most information security policies should contain at least:

- An overview of the corporate philosophy on security

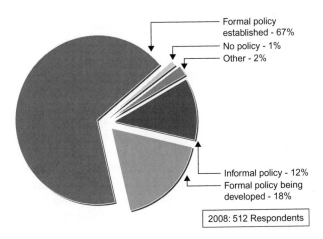

2008: 512 Respondents

Formal policy established - 67%
No policy - 1%
Other - 2%

Informal policy - 12%
Formal policy being developed - 18%

FIGURE 21.18 Information security policy within your organization, CSI/FBI report, 2008.

- Information about roles and responsibilities for security shared by all members of the organization
- Statement of purpose
- Information technology elements needed to define certain controls or decisions
- The organization's security responsibilities defining the security organization structure
- References to IT standards and guidelines, such as Government Policies and Guidelines, FISMA, http://iase.disa.mil/policy-guidance/index.html#FISMA and NIST Special Publications (800 Series), and http://csrc.nist.gov/publications/PubsSPs.html.

Some basic rules must be followed when you're shaping a policy:

- Never conflict with the local or federal law.
- Your policy should be able to stand up in court.
- It must be properly supported and administered by management.
- It should contribute to the success of the organization.
- It should involve end users of information systems from the beginning.

Security Employee Training and Awareness

The Security Employee Training and Awareness (SETA) program is a critical component of the information security program. It is the vehicle for disseminating security information that the workforce, including managers, need to do their jobs. In terms of the total security solution, the importance of the workforce in achieving information security goals and the importance of training as a countermeasure cannot be overstated. Establishing and maintaining a robust and relevant information security awareness and training program as part of the overall information security program is the primary conduit for providing employees with the information and tools needed to protect an agency's vital information resources. These programs will ensure that personnel at all levels of the organization understand their information security responsibilities to properly use and protect the information and resources entrusted to them. Agencies that continually train their workforces in organizational security policy and role-based security responsibilities will have a higher rate of success in protecting information.[38]

As cited in audit reports, periodicals, and conference presentations, people are arguably the weakest element in the security formula that is used to secure systems and networks. The people factor, not technology, is a critical one

---

38. Pauline Bowen, Joan Hash and Mark Wilson, NIST Special Publication 800–100: Information Security Handbook: A Guide for Managers. Recommendations of the National Institute of Standards and Technology, http://csrc.nist.gov/publications/nistpubs/800-100/SP800-100-Mar07-2007.pdf

	Awareness	Training	Education
Attribute	"What"	"How"	"Why"
Level	Information	Knowledge	Insight
Objective	Recognition	Skill	Understanding
Teaching Method	<u>Media</u> Videos Newsletters Posters, etc.	<u>Practical Instruction</u> Lecture Case study workshop Hands-on practice	<u>Theoretical Instruction</u> Discussion Seminar Background reading
Test Measure	True/False Multiple Choice (identify learning)	Problem Solving (apply learning)	Essay (interpret learning)
Impact Timeframe	Short-term	Intermediate	Long-term

FIGURE 21.19 Matrix of security teaching methods and measures that can be implemented.

that is often overlooked in the security equation. It is for this reason that the Federal Information Security Management Act (FISMA) and the Office of Personnel Management (OPM) have mandated that more and better attention must be devoted to awareness activities and role-based training, since they are the only security controls that can minimize the inherent risk that results from the people who use, manage, operate, and maintain information systems and networks. Robust and enterprisewide awareness and training programs are needed to address this growing concern.[39]

The Ten Commandments of SETA

The Ten Commandments of SETA consist of the following:

1. Information security is a people, rather than a technical, issue.
2. If you want them to understand, speak their language.
3. If they cannot see it, they will not learn it.
4. Make your point so that you can identify it and so can they.
5. Never lose your sense of humor.
6. Make your point, support it, and conclude it.
7. Always let the recipients know how the behavior that you request will affect them.
8. Ride the tame horses.
9. Formalize your training methodology.
10. Always be timely, even if it means slipping schedules to include urgent information.

---

39. Pauline Bowen, Joan Hash and Mark Wilson, NIST Special Publication 800–100: Information Security Handbook: A Guide for Managers. Recommendations of the National Institute of Standards and Technology, http://csrc.nist.gov/publications/nistpubs/800-100/SP800-100-Mar07-2007.pdf

Depending on the level of targeted groups within the organization, the goal is first awareness, then training, and eventually the education of all users as to what is acceptable security. Figure 21.19 shows a matrix of teaching methods and measures that can be implemented at each level.

Targeting the right people and providing the right information are crucial when you're developing a security awareness program. Therefore, some of the items that must be kept in mind are focusing on people, not so much on technologies; refraining from using technical jargon; and using every available venue, such as newsletters or memos, online demonstrations, and in-person classroom sessions. By not overloading users and helping them understand their roles in information security, you can establish a program that is effective, identifies target audiences, and defines program scope, goals, and objectives. Figure 21.20 presents a snapshot according to the 2008 CSI/FBI Report, showing where the SETA program stands in 460 different U.S. organizations.

4. SECURITY MONITORING AND EFFECTIVENESS

Security monitoring and effectiveness are the next evolutions to a constant presence of security-aware personnel who actively monitor and research events in real time. A substantial number of suspicious events occur within most enterprise networks and computer systems every day and go completely undetected. Only with an effective security monitoring strategy, an incident response plan, and security validation and metrics in place will an optimal level of security be attained. The idea is to automate and correlate as much as possible between both events and vulnerabilities

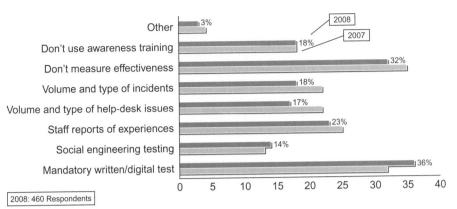

FIGURE 21.20 Awareness training metrics.

and to build intelligence into security tools so that they alert you if a known bad set of events has occurred or a known vulnerability is actually being attacked.

To come full circle; You need to define a security monitoring and log management strategy, an integrated incident response plan, validation, and penetration exercises against security controls and security metrics to help measure whether there has been improvement in your organization's handling of these issues.

Security Monitoring Mechanisms

Security monitoring involves real-time or near-real-time monitoring of events and activities happening on all your organization's important systems at all times. To properly monitor an organization for technical events that can lead to an incident or an investigation, usually an organization uses a security information and event management (SIEM) and/or log management tool. These tools are used by security analysts and managers to filter through tons of event data and to identify and focus on only the most interesting events.

Understanding the regulatory and forensic impact of event and alert data in any given enterprise takes planning and a thorough understanding of the quantity of data the system will be required to handle (see checklist: "An Agenda For Action When Implementing A Critical Security Mechanism"). The better logs can be stored,

---

An Agenda for Action when Implementing a Critical Security Mechanism

Without a solid log management strategy, it becomes nearly impossible to have the necessary data to perform a forensic investigation; and, without monitoring tools identifying threats and responding to attacks against confidentiality, integrity, or availability, it becomes much more difficult. For a network to be compliant and an incident response or forensics investigation to be successful, it is critical that a mechanism be in place to do the following (check all tasks completed):

_____1. Securely acquire and store raw log data for as long as possible from as many disparate devices as possible while providing search and restore capabilities of these logs for analysis.

_____2. Monitor interesting events coming from all important devices, systems, and applications in as near real time as possible.

_____3. Run regular vulnerability scans on your hosts and devices; and, correlate these vulnerabilities to intrusion detection alerts or other interesting events, identifying high-priority attacks as they happen, and minimizing false positives. SIEM and log management solutions in general can assist in security information monitoring (see Figure 21.21); as well as, regulatory compliance and incident response.

_____4. Aggregate and normalize event data from unrelated network devices, security devices, and application servers into usable information.

_____5. Analyze and correlate information from various sources such as vulnerability scanners, IDS/IPS, firewalls, servers, and so on, to identify attacks as soon as possible and help respond to intrusions more quickly.

_____6. Conduct network forensic analysis on historical or real-time events through visualization and replay of events.

_____7. Create customized reports for better visualization of your organizational security posture.

_____8. Increase the value and performance of existing security devices by providing a consolidated event management and analysis platform.

_____9. Improve the effectiveness and help focus IT risk management personnel on the events that are important.

_____10. Meet regulatory compliance and forensics requirements by securely storing all event data on a network for long-term retention and enabling instant accessibility to archived data.

FIGURE 21.21 Security monitoring.

understood, and correlated, the better the possibility of detecting an incident in time for mitigation. In this case, what you don't know *will* hurt you. Responding to incidents, identifying anomalous or unauthorized behavior, and securing intellectual property has never been more important.

Incidence Response and Forensic Investigations

Network forensic investigation is the investigation and analysis of all the packets and events generated on any given network in hope of identifying the proverbial needle in a haystack. Tightly related is incident response, which entails acting in a timely manner to an identified anomaly or attack across the system. To be successful, both network investigations and incident response rely heavily on proper event and log management techniques. Before an incident can be responded to there is the challenge of determining whether an event is a routine system event or an actual incident. This requires that there be some framework for incident classification (the process of examining a possible incident and determining whether or not it requires a reaction). Initial reports from end users, intrusion detection systems, host- and network-based malware detection software, and systems administrators are all ways to track and detect incident candidates.[40]

As mentioned in earlier sections, the phases of an incident usually unfold in the following order: preparation, identification (detection), containment, eradication, recovery and lessons learned. The preparation phase requires detailed understanding of information systems and the

threats they face; so to perform proper planning an organization must develop predefined responses that guide users through the steps needed to properly respond to an incident. Predefining incident responses enables rapid reaction without confusion or wasted time and effort, which can be crucial for the success of an incident response. Identification occurs once an actual incident has been confirmed and properly classified as an incident that requires action. At that point the IR team moves from identification to containment. In the containment phase, a number of action steps are taken by the IR team and others. These steps to respond to an incident must occur quickly and may occur concurrently, including notification of key personnel, the assignment of tasks, and documentation of the incident. Containment strategies focus on two tasks: first, stopping the incident from getting any worse, and second, recovering control of the system if it has been hijacked.

Once the incident has been contained and system control regained, eradication can begin, and the IR team must assess the full extent of damage to determine what must be done to restore the system. Immediate determination of the scope of the breach of confidentiality, integrity, and availability of information and information assets is called *incident damage assessment*. Those who document the damage must be trained to collect and preserve evidence in case the incident is part of a crime investigation or results in legal action.

At the moment that the extent of the damage has been determined, the recovery process begins to identify and resolve vulnerabilities that allowed the incident to occur in the first place. The IR team must address the issues found and determine whether they need to install and/or replace/upgrade the safeguards that failed to stop or limit the incident or were missing from system in the first place. Finally, a discussion of lessons learned should always be conducted to prevent future similar incidents from occurring and review what could have been done differently.[41]

Validating Security Effectiveness

The process of validating security effectiveness comprises making sure that the security controls that you have put in place are working as expected and that they are truly mitigating the risks they claim to be mitigating. There is no way to be sure that your network is not vulnerable to something if you haven't validated it yourself. Ensuring that the information security policy addresses your organizational needs and assessing compliance with your security policy across

40. M. E. Whitman, H. J. Mattord, *Management of Information Security*, Course Technology, 2nd Edition, March 27, 2007.

41. M. E. Whitman, H. J. Mattord, *Management of Information Security*, Course Technology, 2nd Edition, March 27, 2007.

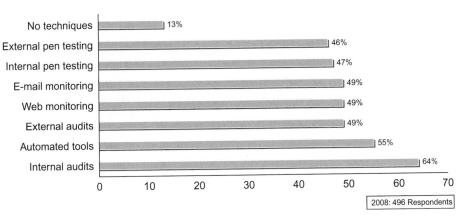

FIGURE 21.22 Security validation techniques, CSI/FBI survey, 2008.

all systems, assets, applications, and people is the only way to have a concrete means of validation.

Here are some areas where actual validation should be performed — in other words, these are areas where assigned IT personnel should go with policy in hand, log in, and verify the settings and reports before the auditors do:

- Verifying operating system settings
- Reviewing security device configuration and management
- Establishing ongoing security tasks
- Maintaining physical security
- Auditing security logs
- Creating an approved product list
- Reviewing encryption strength
- Providing documentation and change control

Vulnerability Assessments and Penetration Tests

Validating security (see Figure 21.22) with internal as well as external vulnerability assessments and penetration tests is a good way to measure an increase or decrease in overall security, especially if similar assessments are conducted on a regular basis. There are several ways to test security of applications, hosts, and network devices. With a vulnerability assessment, usually limited scanning tools or just one scanning tool is used to determine vulnerabilities that exist in the target system. Then a report is created and the manager reviews a holistic picture of security. With authorized penetration tests it's a little different. In that case the data owner is allowing someone to use just about any means within reason (in other words, many different tools and techniques) to gain access to the system or information. A successful penetration test does not provide the remediation avenues that a vulnerability assessment does; rather, it is a good test of how difficult it would be for someone to truly gain access if he were trying.

5. SUMMARY

This chapter emphasized how IT managers are expected to develop, document, and implement an organization-wide program to provide information security essentials for protecting mission-critical systems that support the operations and assets of the organization. An effective information security program should include:

- Periodic assessments of risk, including the magnitude of harm that could result from the unauthorized access, use, disclosure, disruption, modification, or destruction of information and information systems that support the operations and assets of the organization.
- Policies and procedures that are based on risk assessments, cost-effectively reduce information security risks to an acceptable level, and ensure that information security is addressed throughout the life cycle of each organizational information system.
- Subordinate plans for providing adequate information security for networks, facilities, information systems, or groups of information systems, as appropriate.
- Security awareness training to inform personnel (including users of information systems that support the operations and assets of the organization) of the information security risks associated with their activities and their responsibilities in complying with organizational policies and procedures designed to reduce these risks.
- Periodic testing and evaluation of the effectiveness of information security policies, procedures, practices, and security controls to be performed with a frequency depending on risk, but no less than annually.
- A process for planning, implementing, evaluating, and documenting remedial actions to address any deficiencies in the information security policies, procedures, and practices of the organization.
- Procedures for detecting, reporting, and responding to security incidents.

- Plans and procedures to ensure continuity of operations for information systems that support the operations and assets of the organization.

  In other words, IT managers must be prepared to:

- Plan for security.
- Ensure that appropriate officials are assigned security responsibility.
- Periodically review the security controls in their information systems.
- Authorize system processing prior to operations and, periodically, thereafter.

The preceding management responsibilities presume that responsible IT managers understand the risks and other factors that could adversely affect their missions. Moreover, these managers must understand the current status of their security programs and the security controls planned or in place to protect their information and information systems in order to make informed judgments and investments that appropriately mitigate risk to an acceptable level. The ultimate objective is to conduct the day-to-day operations of the organization and to accomplish the organization's mission critical systems with adequate security, or security commensurate with risk, including the magnitude of harm resulting from the unauthorized access, use, disclosure, disruption, modification, or destruction of information.

Finally, let's move on to the real interactive part of this Chapter: review questions/exercises, hands-on projects, case projects and optional team case project. The answers and/or solutions by chapter can be found in the Online Instructor's Solutions Manual.

CHAPTER REVIEW QUESTIONS/EXERCISES

True/False

1. True or False? Information security management as a field is ever decreasing in demand and responsibility because most organizations spend increasingly larger percentages of their IT budgets in attempting to manage risk and mitigate intrusions, not to mention the trend in many enterprises of moving all IT operations to an Internet-connected infrastructure, known as enterprise cloud computing.
2. True or False? Information security is a business problem in the sense that the entire organization must frame and solve security problems based on its own strategic drivers, not solely on technical controls aimed to mitigate one type of attack.
3. True or False? In defining required skills for information security managers, the ISC has arrived at an agreement on ten domains of information security

that is known as the *Common Body of Knowledge* (CBK).

4. True or False? Threats to information systems come in many flavors, some with malicious intent, others with supernatural powers or expected surprises.
5. True or False? Threats are exploited with a variety of attacks, some technical, others not so much.

Multiple Choice

1. The art of manipulating people into performing actions or divulging confidential information, is known as:
   A. Malware
   B. Industrial espionage
   C. Social engineering
   D. Spam
   E. Phishing
2. What describes activities such as theft of trade secrets, bribery, blackmail, and technological surveillance as well as spying on commercial organizations and sometimes governments?
   A. Spam
   B. Phishing
   C. Hoaxes
   D. Industrial espionage
   E. Denial-of-service
3. What is the abuse of electronic messaging systems to indiscriminately send unsolicited bulk messages, many of which contain hoaxes or other undesirable contents such as links to phishing sites?
   A. Spamming
   B. Phishing
   C. Hoaxes
   D. Distributed denial-of-service
   E. All of the Above
4. What is the criminally fraudulent process of attempting to acquire sensitive information such as usernames, passwords, and credit-card details by masquerading as a trustworthy entity in an electronic communication?
   A. Splicing
   B. Phishing
   C. Bending
   D. FSO
   E. Cabling
5. What requires that an individual, program, or system process is not granted any more access privileges than are necessary to perform the task?
   A. Administrative controls
   B. Principle of Least Privilege
   C. Technical controls
   D. Physical controls
   E. Risk analysis

EXERCISE

Problem

What is continuous monitoring?

Hands-On Projects

Project

If your information system is subject to continuous monitoring, does that mean it does not have to undergo security authorization?

Case Projects

Problem

Why is continuous monitoring not replacing the traditional security authorization process?

Optional Team Case Project

Problem

What is front-end security and how does it differ from back-end security?

## Chapter 22

Security Management Systems

James T. Harmening

Computer Bits, Inc.

1. SECURITY MANAGEMENT SYSTEM STANDARDS

To give organizations a starting point to develop their own security management systems, the International Organization for Standardization (ISO) and the International Electrotechnical Commission (IEC) have developed a family of standards known as the Information Security Management System 27000 Family of Standards. This group of standards, starting with ISO/IEC 27001, gives organizations the ability to certify their security management systems. For more details see WWW.ISO.ORG. As an alternative some organizations are following the SANS 20 Critical Security Controls (http://www.sans.org/critical-security-controls/) set of twenty critical security controls that lead you through a twenty step audit process for your organization.

The ISO/IEC-27001 certification process takes place in several stages. The first stage is an audit of all documentation and policies that currently exist for a system. The documentation is usually based directly on the requirements of the standard, but it does not have to be. Organizations can come up with their own sets of standards, as long as all aspects of the standard are covered. The second stage actually tests the effectiveness of the existing policies. The third stage is a reassessment of the organization to make sure it still meets the requirements. This third stage keeps organizations up to date over time as standards for security management systems change. This certification process is based on a Plan-Do-Check-Act iterative process:

- *Plan* the security management system and create the policies that define it.
- *Do* implement the policies in your organization.
- *Check* to ensure the security management system's policies are protecting the resources they were meant to protect.
- *Act* to respond to incidents that breach the implemented policies.

Certifying your security management system helps ensure that you keep the controls and policies constantly up to date to meet certification requirements. Getting certified also demonstrates to your partners and customers that your security management systems will help keep your business running smoothly if network security events were to occur.

Though the ISO/IEC 27000 Family of Standards allows for businesses to optionally get certified, the Federal Information Security Management Act (FISMA) requires all government agencies to develop security management systems. The process of complying with FISMA is very similar to the process of implementing the ISO 27000 family of standards.

The first step of FISMA compliance is determining what constitutes the system you're trying to protect. Next, you need to perform risk assessment to determine what controls you'll need to put in place to protect your system's assets. The last step is actually implementing the planned controls. FISMA then requires mandatory yearly inspections to make sure an organization stays in compliance.

One of the advantages of the Sans 20 Critical Security Controls is the 20 individual touchstones that can be acted upon by the organization. It starts with some basic audit information. In step one you inventory all authorized and unauthorized devices. This may mean accessing each workstation and reviewing the system logs to identify if USB, Music, or phones have been plugged into the computer. The second step is to audit the software in the same way. Many times a user will download software and not know they have violated their organizations I.T. policies. These two basic checks need to be done annually for some organizations and more frequently for others. For more details access the SANS.ORG website.

2. TRAINING REQUIREMENTS

Many security management system training courses for personnel are available over the Internet. These courses provide information for employees setting up security management systems and for those using the computer and network resources of the company that are referenced in the policies of the security management system.

Training should also include creating company security policies and creating user roles that are specific to the organization. Planning policies and roles, ahead of time, will help prevent confusion in the event of a problem, since everyone will know their responsibilities. Documenting these roles is also very important.

3. PRINCIPLES OF INFORMATION SECURITY

The act of securing information has been around for as long as the idea of storing information. Over time, three main objectives of information security have been defined:

- *Confidentiality*. Information is only available to the people or systems that need access to it. This is done by encrypting information that only certain people are able to decrypt or denying access to those who don't need it. This might seem simple at first, but confidentiality must be applied to all aspects of a system. This means preventing access to all backup locations and even log files if those files can contain sensitive information.
- *Integrity*. Information can only be added or updated by those who need to update that data. Unauthorized changes to data cause it to lose its integrity, and access to the information must be cut off to everyone until the information's integrity is restored. Allowing access to compromised data will cause those unauthorized changes to propagate to other areas of the system.
- *Availability*. The information needs to be available in a timely manner when requested. Access to no data is just as bad as access to compromised data. No process can be performed if the data on which the process is based is unavailable.

4. ROLES AND RESPONSIBILITIES OF PERSONNEL

All personnel who come into contact with information systems need to be aware of the risks from improper use of those systems. Network administrators need to know the effects of each change they make to their systems and how that affects the overall security of that system. They also need to be able to efficiently control access to those systems in cases of emergency, when quick action is needed.

Users of those systems need to understand what risks can be caused by their actions and how to comply with

company policy. Several roles should be defined within your organization:

- *Chief information officer/director of information technology*. This person is responsible for creating and maintaining the security policies for your organization.
- *Network engineer*. This person is responsible for the physical connection of your network and the connection of your network to the Internet. He or she is also responsible for the routers, firewalls, and switches that connect your organization.
- *Network administrator*. This person handles all other network devices within the organization, such as servers, workstations, printers, copiers, tablets, video conference, smart phones, and wireless access devices. Server and workstation software is also the responsibility of the network administrator.
- *End users*. These people are allowed to operate the computer in accordance with company policies, to perform their daily tasks. They should not have administrator access to their PCs or, especially, servers.

There are also many other specific administrators some companies might require. These are Microsoft Exchange Administrators, Database Administrators, and Active Directory Administrators, to name a few. These administrators should have specific tasks to perform and a specific scope in which to perform them that is stated in the company policy.

5. SECURITY POLICIES

Each organization should develop a company policy detailing the preferred use of company data or company software. An example of a policy is: No person shall transfer any data to any device that was not purchased by the company. This policy can help prevent unauthorized access to company data. Some companies ban all removable media within the organization.

Security policies should govern how the computer is to be used on a day-to-day basis. Very often, computer users are required to have Internet access to do research pertaining to their jobs. This isn't hard to restrict in a specialized setting such as a law firm where only a handful of sites contain pertinent information. In other cases it can be nearly impossible to restrict all Web sites except the ones that contain information that applies to your organization or your research. In those cases it is imperative that you have company policies that dictate what Web sites users are able to visit and for what purposes. When unrestricted Internet access is allowed, it is a good practice to use software that will track the Web sites a user visits, to make sure they are not breaking company policy. For many companies they create a white list of allowable sites, for others they use a black list to prevent certain sites from being accessed. Some of the more advanced firewalls give a list of categories that are allowed or blocked.

6. SECURITY CONTROLS

There are three types of security controls that need to be implemented for a successful security policy to be put into action. They are physical controls, technical controls, and administrative controls.

Physical controls consist of things such as magnetic swipe cards, RFID, or biometric security to prevent access to stored information or network resources. Physical controls also consist of environmental controls such as HVAC units, power generators, and fire suppression systems. One of the most common failures is people leaving their computers on and another person using their computer to gain access to information/data that they should not be allowed to access. Many companies utilize password screen savers or require a computer to be "locked" before they leave their workstation. Another common security measure is to encrypt the drives on a computer. One free whole disk encryption utility commonly deployed is True Crypt. (www.truecrypt.org). This prevents the data from being accessed from a stolen laptop or computer.

Technical controls can also be called software or system controls which are used to limit access to network resources and devices that are used in the organization. They can be individual usernames and passwords used to access individual devices or access control lists that are part of a network operating system. Many organizations are putting in password expiration dates of 30−60 days and even account deletion for accounts not accessed for more than 90 days. In addition, passwords that contain, numbers, upper and lowercase letters, special characters and have a length that exceeds 8 characters are required by some organizations in order to ensure stronger passwords.

Administrative controls consist of policies created by an organization that determine how they will work. These controls guide employees by describing how their jobs are to be done and what resources they are supposed to use to do them. This is probably the weakest section of each companies policies. The lack of written policies makes the implementation of security very difficult. More organizations should spend time setting up their policies and keep their employees up to date on what expectations they have for each employee.

7. NETWORK ACCESS

The first step in developing a security management system is documenting the network resources and which group of users may access those resources. Users should only have access to the resources that they need to complete their jobs efficiently. An example of when this will come in handy is when the president of the company wants access to every network resource and then his computer becomes infected with a virus that starts infecting all network files. Access Control Lists (ACLs) should be planned ahead of time and then implemented on the network to avoid complications with the network ACL hierarchy.

An ACL dictates which users have access to certain network resources. Network administrators usually have access to all files and folders on a server. Department administrators will have access to all files used by their departments. End users will have access to a subset of the department files that they need to perform their jobs. ACLs are developed by the head of IT for an organization and the network administrator and implemented by the network administrator.

Implementing ACLs prevents end users from being able to access sensitive company information and helps them perform their jobs better by not giving them access to information that can act as a distraction.

Access control can also apply to physical access as well as electronic access. Access to certain networking devices could cause an entire organization to stop functioning for a period of time, so access to those devices should be carefully controlled.

Through the use of Remote Authentication Dial In User Service (RADIUS) is an added layer of security to your network. Many of these systems employ a random number generator key fob's that displays a random number and changes it every 30−60 seconds. With this extra step of user authentication a person can combine a private key along with the random number to access the network. For example, an RSA SecureID token generates an 8 digit number, combine that with the users own 4 digit private password, an administrator can help to stop unauthorized access to their system.

8. RISK ASSESSMENT

Before security threats can be blocked, all risks must first be identified and assessed (see checklist: "An Agenda For Action When Identifying And Assessing Risks"). Risk assessment forms the foundation of a good security management system. Network administrators must document all aspects of their network setup. This documentation should provide information on the network firewall, servers, clients, and any other devices physically connected or wirelessly connected to the network.

9. INCIDENT RESPONSE

Knowing what to do in case of a security incident is crucial to being able to track down what happened and how

An Agenda for Action when Identifying and Assessing Risks

The most time should be spent documenting how the private computer network will be connected to the Internet for Web browsing and email. Some common security risks that should be identified and assessed are (check all tasks completed):

_____ 1. USB storage devices: Devices that can be used to copy proprietary company data off the internal network. Many organizations use software solutions to disable unused USB ports on a system; others physically block the connections.

_____ 2. Remote control software: Services such as GoToMyPc or Log Me In do not require any special router or firewall configuration to enable remote access.

_____ 3. Email: Filters should be put in place that prevent sensitive company information from simply being emailed outside the organization.

_____ 4. General Internet use: There is always a possibility of downloading a malicious virus from the Internet unless all but trusted and necessary Web sites are restricted to internal users. This can be accomplished by a content-filtering firewall or Web proxy server.

_____ 5. Laptops: Lost laptops pose a very large security risk, depending on the type on data stored on

them. Policies need to be put in place to determine what types of information can be stored on these devices and what actions should be taken if a laptop is lost.

_____ 6. Peer-to-peer applications: P2P applications that are used to download illegal music and software cause a risk because the files that are downloaded are not coming from known sources. People who download an illegal version of an application could be downloading a worm that can affect the entire network.

_____ 7. Television/DVR/Blu-Ray Devices: With the expansion of technology, even televisions have internet access and storage.

_____ 8. VOIP telephones: The proliferation of Voice over IP telephones brings another device into our network environment. Some companies prefer to have their phones on a separate physical network, preventing slow response times and bad phone quality, while others have routers and switches that will prioritize the traffic of the phone calls in order to maintain good phone quality.

---

to make sure it never happens again. When a security incident is identified, it is imperative that steps are taken so that forensic evidence is not destroyed in the investigation process. Forensic evidence includes the content of all storage devices attached to the system at the time of the incident and even the contents stored in memory of a running computer.

Using an external hard drive enclosure to browse the content of the hard drive of a compromised system will destroy date and timestamps that a forensic technician can use to tie together various system events.

When a system breach or security issue has been detected, it is recommended to consult someone familiar with forensically sound investigation methods. If forensic methods are not used, it can lead to evidence not being admissible in court if the incident results in a court case.

There are specific steps to take with a computer system, depending on the type of incident that occurred. Unless a system is causing damage to itself by deleting files or folders that can be potential evidence, it is best to leave the system running for the forensic investigator. The forensic investigator will:

- Document what is on the screen by photographing it. He/She will also photograph the actual computer system and all cable connections.

- Capture the contents of the system's memory. This is done using a small utility installed from a removable drive that will create a forensic image of what is in the system's physical memory. This can be used to document Trojan activity. If memory is not imaged and the computer was used to commit a crime, the computer's user can claim that a malicious virus, which was only running in memory, was responsible.

- Turn off the computer. If the system is running a Windows workstation operating system such as Windows Vista Workstation or Windows Azure, the forensic technician will pull the plug on the system. If the system is running a server operating system such as Windows Server 2008, Windows 7 Server, Windows Server 2012, Windows 8 or a Linux- or Unix-based operating system such as Red Hat, Fedora, or Ubuntu, the investigator will properly shut down the system.

- Create a forensic image of the system's hard drive. This is done using imaging software and usually a hardware write-blocker to connect the system's hard drive to the imaging computer. A hardware write-blocker is used to prevent the imaging computer from writing anything at all to the hard drive. Windows, by default, will create a recycle bin on a new volume that it is able to mount, which would cause the evidence to lose forensic value. Investigators are then able to search through the system without making any changes to the original media.

10. SUMMARY

Organizations interested in implementing a comprehensive security management system should start by documenting all business processes that are critical to an organization and then analyzing the risks associated with them, then implement the controls that can protect those processes from external and internal threats. Internet threats are not usually the cause of someone with malicious intent but someone who accidentally downloads a Trojan or accidentally moves or deletes a directory or critical files. The final step is performing recursive checking of the policies your organization has put in place to adjust for new technologies that need to be protected or new ways that external threats can damage your network. The easiest way to implement security management systems is to use the Plan-Do-Act-Check (PDAC) process to step though the necessary procedures. A locked door, a good password, and good supervision of employees is key to good security management.

Finally, let's move on to the real interactive part of this Chapter: review questions/exercises, hands-on projects, case projects and optional team case project. The answers and/or solutions by chapter can be found in the Online Instructor's Solutions Manual.

CHAPTER REVIEW QUESTIONS/EXERCISES

True/False

1. True or False? To give organizations a starting point to develop their own security management systems, the International Organization for Standardization (ISO) and the International Electrotechnical Commission (IEC) have developed a family of standards known as the Information Security Management System 27000 Family of Standards.
2. True or False? Training should also include creating company security policies and creating user roles that are specific to the organization.
3. True or False? The act of securing information has not been around for as long as the idea of storing information.
4. True or False? All personnel who come into contact with information systems need to be aware of the risks from improper use of those systems.

5. True or False? Each organization should not develop a company policy detailing the preferred use of company data or company software.

Multiple Choice

1. _____ what is on the screen by photographing it?
   A. Capture
   B. Turn off
   C. Document
   D. Create
   E. All of the above
2. _____the contents of the system's memory?
   A. Turn off
   B. Document
   C. Create
   D. Capture
   E. All of the above
3. _____the computer?
   A. Capture
   B. Create
   C. Document
   D. Distribute
   E. Turn off
4. _____a forensic image of the system's hard drive?
   A. Create
   B. Turn off
   C. Capture
   D. Document
   E. All of the above
5. Devices that can be used to copy proprietary company data off the internal network are known as:
   A. Remote control software
   B. Email
   C. USB storage
   D. General Internet use
   E. Risk analysis

EXERCISE

Problem

Why should an organization certify their security management system?

Hands-On Projects

Project

How does ISO/IEC 27001 (BS 7799) relate to other security management system standards (ISO 9001 and 14001)?

Case Projects

Problem

Why should an organization invest in implementing an SMS and certifying it using ISO/IEC 27001 (BS 7799-2)?

Optional Team Case Project

Problem

How is risk assessment related to ISO/IEC 27001 (BS 7799)?

## Chapter 23

Policy-driven System Management

Henrik Plate
SAP Research Sophia-Antipolis, 805 Avenue Dr M. Donat, 06250 Mougins, France

Cataldo Basile
Politecnico di Torino, Corso Duca degli Abruzzi 24, 10129 Torino, Italy

Stefano Paraboschi
Universitá degli studi di Bergamo, via Salvecchio 19, 24129 Bergamo, Italy

1. INTRODUCTION

This chapter begins with a high-level view of security management and the development of security concepts, followed by an introduction of core concepts and terms relevant for PBM in particular, the layering of policies with different abstraction levels in a so-called policy hierarchy. Sections 3 and 4 explain high-level security objectives and principles, policies, and technologies relevant for the various policy abstraction levels and architecture layers in more detail, thereby putting particular focus on access control policies, related enforcement technologies, and selection criteria when touching lower abstraction levels. Section 5 summarizes the policy-related functionality of a small selection of existing products and technologies. As there does not yet exist a large-scale deployment of a policy-based computing system, all of the examples provide focus on selected aspects of PBM. Section 6 explains the approach of two research projects on the subject matter: Ponder, a project conducted in the early 1990s and considered a forerunner in this research domain, and PoSecCo, an ongoing EU research project that relates PBM to organizational structures and processes, seek to optimize and semiautomate the policy refinement process, and support policy-based configuration audits. The products and projects introduced in Sections 5 and 6 will be positioned with regard to the security life-cycle phases covered, policy types and abstraction levels supported, and architecture layers concerned. Note that we put special emphasis on access control (AC), thereby leaving other security-related topics and technologies aside (privacy or Digital Rights Management).

2. SECURITY AND POLICY-BASED MANAGEMENT

This section briefly summarizes today's practice with regard to security management, followed by a description of its deficiencies and an explanation of how PBM can help overcome them. Thereafter, we explain basic concepts of PBM and conclude with a short summary of autonomic computing, which aims at policy-based self-management of future information systems.

System Architecture and Security Management

IT systems are traditionally structured according to several architecture layers, each layer thereby offering a number of security capabilities that can support organizations in reaching desired security objectives. Architectures that exemplify the layered structure of IT systems are the three-tier architecture of Web applications, or, more recently, the cloud computing reference architecture [1]. Typical architecture layers comprise, for instance, user frontends, software services, and applications that implement the business logic, platform services that provide a runtime environment, or infrastructure services that offer connectivity or computing resources.

Ideally, capabilities offered on different layers are combined in a complementary manner as to implement *Defense in Depth*, a security principle recommending the setup of multiple, complementary lines of defense against malicious attacks or other threats to security. Since many of the

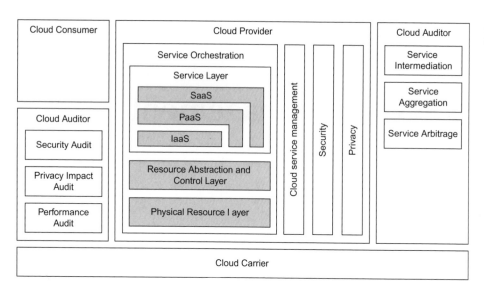

FIGURE 23.1 NIST cloud computing reference architecture [1].

security mechanisms[1] employed on different layers do not work in isolation but impact each other, security is typically seen to be orthogonal to the various technology layers in order to have a holistic view of security (cf. Figure 23.1). This view is also supported by the IT Infrastructure Library[2] (ITIL), a widely adapted methodology for the management of IT services, which aims at overcoming IT silos— specialized people, expertise, and tools that focus on the management of system slices (databases or networks).

High-level security objectives, common controls, as well as processes regarding the design, implementation, and operation of an information security management system and a security concept are described in various standards and guidelines (the ISO 27000 series of standards as well as national adaptations[3]). These processes structure the design of secure systems in several phases that generally follow the idea of the Plan-Do-Check-Act (PDCA) cycle introduced by [3].

The *Plan* phase starts with the specification of security objectives and the definition of protection requirements by C-level executives, data protection officers, or business stakeholders. Larger organizations and those known to have special requirements can do this on the basis of a comprehensive risk analysis, while others follow a best-practice approach. Other sources of high-level objectives comprise general laws and regulations (SOX or privacy laws) or industry-specific standards such as those from the U.S. Food and Drug Administration (FDA), or the Data Security Standard (DSS) authored by the Payment Card Industry (PCI), which is relevant for every organization that stores or processes cardholder information [4].

Once those high-level objectives are defined, suitable security controls need to be identified and assessed by means of a cost-benefit analysis; as a result, some of the controls will be selected for implementation. This activity is complicated by the fact that the security capabilities of controls residing on different architecture layers can overlap and even conflict. Application servers, for instance, also support IP address filtering.[4] Firewalls, as another example, emerged to analyze application-level communication protocols.

The *Do* phase sees the implementation of security controls, which includes, among other activities, the transformation of high-level policies to a representation that can be interpreted by the security mechanisms selected. Here, system and security administrators knowledgeable in the various technologies enter the scene. The *Check* phase concerns the performance review and monitoring of security mechanisms as to understanding whether they are still suitable to meet the initial objectives (design effectiveness) and whether they work as designed (operation effectiveness). Finally, the *Act* phase covers continuous improvements of the security mechanisms in reaction to (small) requirement and system changes.

The Promise of Policy-based Management

Security management as performed today involves a variety of stakeholders with different job functions, expertise,

---

1. Note that we use the terms *security mechanism* and *security control* interchangeably in order to denote a technical security capability provided by software or hardware components. In other contexts, the term *security control* typically has a broader meaning, and denotes technical and nontechnical measures to reach a given security objective.
2. http://www.itil-officialsite.com
3. The Federal Office for Information Security (BSI) in Germany, for example, maintains the standard BSI 100-1 to describe general requirements for an Information Security Management System (ISMS) in greater detail and following a more didactic approach [2].

---

4. The Apache HTTP Server, for example, supports AC rules with conditions over source IP addresses or domain names.

and objectives, and the use of different tools and terminology. Human-centric processes, however, are the main contributor to the significant increase of costs related to system management. On average, 70 percent of IT budgets are spent to maintain and manage current IT infrastructures [5]. And despite significant spending, many organizations "cannot prove enforcement [of security policies] or it is prohibitively expensive to do so" [6]. At the same time, human intervention is prone to errors, in particular when it comes to repetitive tasks involving low-level technology aspects. A series of studies show that inaccurate configuration settings are among the most common reasons for insecure and incompliant systems, many times leading to actual data breaches [7,8]. A UK security report, for instance, found that, "whilst many of the organizations investigated actually had firewalls installed, poor configuration of these devices rendered most of them useless" [9]. Moreover, "in over 96% of cases, … PCI DSS was not adequately adhered to." Inaccurate configurations are typically introduced during the implementation and operations phase of a security concept, for instance, when configurations are altered to reflect system or business process changes.

In light of the above, the promise of PBM with regard to system management is twofold. On the one hand, it aims at reducing management costs by the automation of activities that today require human intervention. On the other hand, it aims at improving service quality (in part through the avoidance of human failure). Both goals shall be achieved by sparing humans from low-level and repetitive tasks that relate to technical implementation details of IT systems.

One property of policy-based systems that contributes to these goals is the fact that security decision rules of system elements are not represented by hard-coded algorithms, which would result in modifications or replacements of system elements whenever security rules change. Policy-based systems instead rely on declarative statements made available to and interpreted by the respective system element. This separation of policy specification and enforcement is cost-beneficial and increases the flexibility to adapt a system to changing security requirements.

PBM aligns very well with the security life cycle, since both of them follow a top-down approach that starts with the specification of high-level objectives and ends with the enforcement of low-level policies by security mechanisms. In PBM, high-level security objectives that control overall system behavior are still given by humans, but subsequent steps related to the selection, implementation, and operation of appropriate mechanisms become more and more automated.

In order to reach its goals, PBM must address the following problems: the identification, assessment, and selection of appropriate security mechanisms, the refinement of higher-level policies to lower-level representations until a point where selected enforcement mechanisms can interpret them, the analysis and resolution of policy conflicts occurring on several abstraction levels, within and across policy enforcement mechanisms, and, finally, the organization of policies and their distribution to enforcement devices.

Policy Basics

Generally speaking, a *policy* is a "definite goal, course or method of action to guide and determine present and future decisions" [10]. The term policy is broadly used in the domain of computer science and information security, and denotes many different things (firewall policies, access control policies, acceptable use policies, or security policies). Sometimes, the term refers to a single policy rule, and in other contexts to a collection of such rules.

For our purposes, a policy constrains the behavior of computing systems. More formally, following [11], a policy is defined over a target system, which is associated with a number of attributes that have a certain type, and all of which together determine the system state. The behavior of a system is then defined as a continuous ordered set of states, where the order is imposed by time. Considering the set of all possible behaviors, a policy represents a set of constraints on the possible behaviors (it defines a subset of acceptable behaviors). Based on this generic definition, in [11] policies are classified into different types, in particular *configuration constraint policies* that constrain the values of configurable system attributes, *metric constraint policies* that constrain observable but not directly influenceable attributes, *action policies* that, upon the observation of a given state, trigger operations in order to reach a desired target state, and *alert policies* that notify users as soon as the system state satisfies certain conditions.

A password policy, for instance, that demands a certain password length and complexity can be considered as a configuration constraint policy over attributes belonging to an authentication mechanism. An access control policy, for instance, can be considered as an action policy, where the condition is defined over attributes of the subject, resource, or other entities, and the action is either deny or allow.

While the generality of the above definition covers a broad range of policies, many more specific definitions were created for single policy application domains. In that context, *policy information models* are often used to visualize the constituting policy elements and their structural relationships. Condition-Action (CA) and Event-Condition-Action (ECA) hereby represent very basic policy models, where a single action or set of actions are to

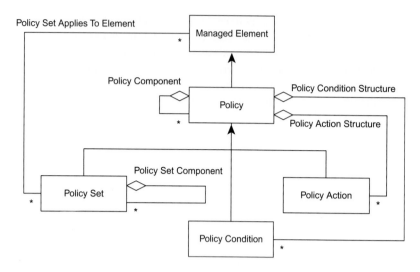

FIGURE 23.2   CIM policy model [12].

be executed upon certain conditions.[5] The CIM Policy Model, for instance, uses UML to model the structure of CA policies that can be associated with CIM managed elements (see Figure 23.2).[6]

Security-related information models such as for AC typically specify conditions under which a subject can be granted to perform an operation defined over a target (or resource). On first sight, typical AC policy models seem to differ from the CA/ECA models mentioned before. However, this is only because event and action are not made explicit but exist implicitly in the form of the access request issued by the subject, and the deny or allow action that determines whether access can be granted.

Information models are useful for illustrating the conceptual structure of policies, but *policy languages* are required to represent concrete policies. A plethora of such languages exist, ranging from natural language for the expression of high-level policies on the one hand to precise mathematical models to support computer-based reasoning on the other hand. In many cases, the syntax and vocabulary of a policy language are tailored to a specific application domain, and some languages were designed without explicitly denoting the underlying information model. XACML, for instance, is a widely used XML-based language for expressing access control policies. CIM-SPL (Simple Policy Language), for instance, can be used to represent CIM policies according to the CIM Policy Model.

Policy Hierarchy and Refinement

The PBM approach naturally leads to a so-called policy continuum [13], a hierarchy of policies that are subject to different abstraction levels. Such policies undergo an

iterative refinement process that transforms high-level and abstract policies into lower-level representations that can be eventually interpreted by enforcement mechanisms situated in a given IT system.

The highest policy abstraction level is typically referred to as business view [14], goal policies [15,16],[7] corporate policies [17], or high-level user-specified policies [11]. Such policies use business terms and relate to, for instance, corporate goals, business-critical risks, or regulatory and legal requirements. They abstract from the IT system in question and often specify goals without detailing how to attain them. They are typically authored by management and business users that indeed neither need nor want to depend on technology when specifying business goals. Being independent from the IT system, business policies typically remain more stable than lower-level representations that are more exposed to system changes. Since business policies are often written in an informal and possibly ambiguous way (with the support of spreadsheets and policy documents, they are seldom subject to automated reasoning that supports the detection of policy conflicts).

The PCI DSS requirement, which demands the use of "strong cryptography and security protocols to safeguard cardholder data during transmission over public networks," is a typical example for a high-level business policy [4]. It merely states an objective without prescribing a specific enforcement technology, and it remains agnostic of a given IT system. "Response time must not exceed 2 sec" is another example for a high-level goal policy [16], since it does not specify suitable actions to improve the response time once the threshold is reached.

The number of intermediate abstraction levels following business policies varies between the various

---

5. The ECA model also specifies the event that triggers the evaluation.
6. The Common Information Model (CIM) is a DMTF standard that uses an object-oriented approach to model computing systems and today is widely used in IT management systems.

7. Though in [16] utility function policies are considered as the highest policy level, we consider them here as meta-policies that define the relative importance of goal policies.

classification schemes. In [16], for instance, action policies are presented that specify how a goal policy can be reached, and in [11] a distinction is made between abstract, technology-independent and concrete, technology-specific policies as intermediate levels. Common to the transformation of higher to lower abstraction levels is that policies are step-by-step enriched with additional details, thereby keeping the policy structure intact. Policy goals become substituted by actions and mechanisms that support reaching the goal. In order to enforce the PCI DSS requirement, for instance, one has to specify the security technology to be used (SSL/TLS or IPsec). As another example, the action policy "Increase CPU share by 5% if response time exceeds 2 sec" refines the above goal policy, thereby using the form Condition-Action. Moreover, policy components such as subjects, targets, conditions, or actions become refined and enriched until they correspond to identifiable elements in a given IT system. Logical roles, for instance, are substituted by technical roles used in the respective system components, or logical names for computers or groups of computers become substituted by IP addresses or address ranges. The kind of lower-level information to be enriched depends on the enforcement mechanism chosen (IP addresses for network-level firewalls vs. protocols or URLs for application-level firewalls), while the actual information is determined by the system in question.

The lowest policy abstraction level is typically referred to as executable or deployment policies [11], or policy mechanism information [15]. These policies can be deployed into and interpreted by a given system component, which then acts as a policy enforcement point. The format or language to express executable policies depends on technologies and vendors. Typical examples for executable policies are, for instance, configuration parameters that establish the use of Transport Layer Security (TLS) for Internet-facing Web applications that process cardholder data, or a configuration rule that increases or decreases the priority of operating system processes depending on response time changes. It is noteworthy that system management tools available today typically focus on a subset of policy representations instead of taking a holistic view on the entire policy hierarchy. Microsoft Group Policy, for instance, concentrates only on the executable policy layer but does not support policy analysis or translation of upper-layer policy representations. SAP Access Control, as another example, supports concrete policies for role-based access control systems and their translation to vendor-specific representations on the executable policy layer.

Policy Organization and Conflicts

Larger systems make it impractical to specify policies for individual system elements. Accordingly, PBM must support the grouping of both policies and system elements to facilitate the scoping of policies (the specification of system elements to which a given set of policies shall apply). Today, system management is typically structured by administrative domains that govern a subset of the entire system, which is organized in a hierarchical fashion. This hierarchy is then used to group system elements and policies.

Microsoft Group Policy, for instance, supports the linking of policies to a hierarchy of domains, sites, and organizational units. In [15] the term *managed domain* was introduced to denote a collection of managed objects that are grouped for management purposes. In [11] the use of roles is presented as a means to group policies. Policies for (Web servers can be created, distributed, and evaluated as a group).

Once a set of policies is somehow structured and assigned to managed elements, the system has to determine which policy or policies shall be evaluated in the course of a given event. This selection is supported by different strategies, sometimes considering the entire set of policies, sometimes terminating the search as soon as an applicable policy is found. Policies assigned to tree structures allow, for instance, preference of more specific over more general policies or vice versa. A strategy implemented by most firewalls is to order policy rules, evaluate the first one with matching conditions, and ignore the rest. Other means are to prioritize policies and evaluate the one with the highest priority in case several policies have matching conditions, or to specify meta-policies.

Moreover, a group of policies can be subject to anomalies and conflicts. A (modal) policy conflict between, for instance, firewall policy rules arises if two rules have overlapping conditions (on the source IP address), but conflicting actions (allow and deny). As another example, a modal conflict between obligation and access control policies exist if a subject is obliged to perform a given action but does not have the required authorization [18]. Such conflicts are relatively easy to spot in case they concern just one enforcement point (a firewall), but are more complex if several enforcement points are concerned. Accordingly, continuing the firewall example, a classification is presented in [19] of intra- and inter-firewall policy conflicts (conflicts that arise from the interpretation of policy rules by a single firewall and those that result from a sequence of policy evaluations performed by several firewalls). Furthermore, conflicts can also occur between policies targeting different architecture layers, which are again more difficult to identify and require a holistic view on policies. More details on policy conflicts can be found in Chapter 45, Detection of Conflicts in Security Policies.

Policy Distribution

Once refined to low-level representations (executable policies according to the terminology used by) [11], policies need to be distributed to those system elements that need to evaluate and enforce them at system runtime. To overcome problems inherent to manual deployment, a variety of tools support administrators in the automated deployment of policies in large-scale distributed systems.

Today, such tools include, on the one hand, tailor-made configuration scripts that copy configuration files by, for instance, means of Secure Shell (SSH) connections. This category of tools also comprises, on the other hand, configuration management systems such as SAP Solution Manager or HP OpenView, which maintain central configuration repositories, support versioning, and implement ITIL-defined workflows in order to prevent unauthorized and erroneous configuration changes. Other examples comprise Local Configuration (LCFG), a large scale UNIX configuration system that facilitates configuration management in UNIX environments, and Microsoft Group Policy, which supports Windows environments. Configuration management systems increase the correctness and consistency of configuration information, speed up deployment processes, and support a variety of other security-related activities such as IT audits. However, they do not yet free humans from the burden of dealing with low-level details of system management, since the initial specification of low-level configuration parameters is still left to administrators. In other words, they cover neither high-level policy representations nor the translation from abstract policies to concrete configuration parameters.

Generic Policy Architecture

Policy-based systems require a set of common functionalities related to the creation, storage, distribution, and enforcement of policies. The standardization bodies Internet Engineering Task Force (IETF) and Distributed Management Task Force, Inc. (DMTF) started defining a generic architecture for policy-based systems [20], which was subsequently refined and now represents a common basis for policy-related work, thereby abstracting from specific technologies, vendors, or types of policies.

In this generic architecture, the policy administration point (PAP) provides a user interface to allow end users to create, translate, validate, and manage policies that will be stored in a policy repository. At system runtime, a policy decision point (PDP) identifies and evaluates applicable policies provided by the repository in order to decide whether appropriate actions need to be taken. In the course of policy evaluation, a policy information point (PIP) supplies complementary information required for taking a policy decision. Last, the so-called policy enforcement point (PEP) is responsible for ensuring that the outcome of policy decisions is enforced in the system.

The runtime interaction of these components can be illustrated as the example of an access request to a protected resource (cf. Figure 23.3). Here, the PEP mediates any access request of a user to a protected resource. The PEP sends a corresponding request to the PDP, thereby providing identifiers of the authenticated user and the protected resource. The PDP searches for applicable policies and seeks complementary information from the PIP, for instance, user-role assignments stored in an LDAP directory. The Policy Decision Point (PDP) terminates the policy evaluation by deciding whether access to this resource shall be denied or granted to the user in question, which in turn will be enforced by the PEP. The preceding could be implemented with the help of, for instance, XACML, which not only specifies a language for the definition of access control policies, but also defines a protocol for the interaction of PEP and PDP.

Note that most of today's security mechanisms, including some of those presented later in this chapter, implement several of these policy-related functions in an integrated manner, rather than supporting a clean, protocol-based separation as outlined by the generic architecture. Firewalls, for instance, typically integrate the functionalities of PEP, PDP,

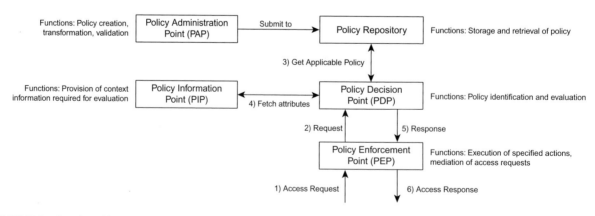

FIGURE 23.3 Generic architecture of policy-based systems.

and repository, which is motivated by significant performance advantages compared to a communication of possibly distributed components.

Autonomic Computing

The term *autonomic computing* has been coined by IBM to denote computing systems that manage themselves [21]. Inspired by biological and social systems, autonomic (computing) systems are composed of autonomic elements (aka agents) that autonomously enforce high-level policies they were provided with by humans or other system elements, and thereby discover, interact, and negotiate with other autonomic elements. Two out of the four self-management properties stipulated by IBM are *self-protection* and *self-healing*. Self-protection refers to the capability of autonomic systems to detect and correlate distributed events that result from attacks, cascading failures, or problematic changes inadvertently introduced by users, and to react appropriately in order to defend the system against security compromise. Self-healing concerns the detection, diagnosis, and correction of localized problems that result from software bugs or hardware failures. The correction of a software bug could result, for instance, in the search, application, and test of software patches. The contribution of IBM's autonomic computing manifesto [22] does not primarily concern technology; the foundation was already laid, but in giving perspective to the future and long-term development of IT, as a means to tie several research domains to a bigger context, and to address nontechnical questions that emerge when IT components behave in an autonomous fashion.

As illustrated by Figure 23.4, an autonomic element comprises an autonomic manager, which seeks enforcing the policy by observing and manipulating one or several managed elements under its control. Managed elements essentially correspond to software as it exists today, and all of the security mechanisms presented in Section 5 can be managed elements. The autonomic manager monitors managed elements through the use of sensors, analyzes such information, and, where necessary, plans appropriate actions that are executed through effectors. In the course of

policy distribution, and in contrast to existing distribution technologies, the autonomic manager receives a high-level policy that must be refined to lower-level representations understood by its managed elements. Policy translation as well as the analysis and planning phases of the MAPE-K (Monitor, Analyze, Plan, Execute, Knowledge) control loop are guided by a knowledge base populated by the agent developer. In case managed elements do not provide a required security capability by themselves, a software agent may also act as a policy enforcement point. Ponder, for instance, relies on agents to enforce authorization policies specified over the target managed element.

Accreditation

The following checklist addresses accreditation criteria for security and policy-based management (see checklist: An Agenda for Action When Addressing Accreditation Criteria for Security and Policy-Based Management) systems. The numbering of this checklist generally follows the numbering of other checklists found in the rest of the book, as well as, other tasks that must be completed:

- All items on this checklist shall be addressed.
- Place an "X" beside each item that represents a nonconformity (formerly called deficiency).
- Place a "C" beside each item on which you are making a comment.
- Place an "OK" beside each item that you observed or verified at the laboratory.

3. CLASSIFICATION AND LANGUAGES

The availability of tools for policy-based security management will support the realization of all the classical security objectives, such as confidentiality, integrity, availability. Indeed, the design of a secure system, in most cases, separately considers each of the objectives, whereas a holistic view is needed in order to capture the interdependencies that exist among separate security services. For instance, the specification of authorizations requires the availability of adequate authentication

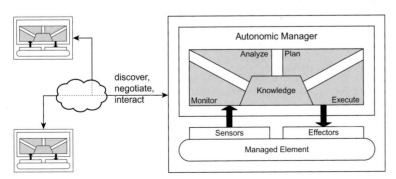

FIGURE 23.4 MAPE-K reference model for autonomic elements

An Agenda for Action When Addressing Accreditation Criteria for Security and Policy-Based Management

All organizations must adhere to the following accreditation process (check all tasks completed):

_____ **1.** The management system documentation was most recently reviewed on _____. Changes and additions required by the reviewers were made by the laboratory.

_____ **2.** The management system documentation was found adequate for _continuation of the assessment process._

_____ **3.** Changes and additions to the management system documentation, which were required by the reviewers, were made by the laboratory.

_____ **4.** The initial on-site was conducted on _____.

_____ **5.** Resolutions of findings from the initial on-site visit will be reviewed during the assessment visit.

_____ **6.** The results of the initial evaluations have been read and will be reviewed during the assessment visit.

_____ **7.** The laboratory shall establish and maintain policies and procedures for maintaining laboratory impartiality and integrity in the conduct of information technology security evaluations.

_____ **8.** When conducting evaluations under the NIAP Common Criteria Scheme, the laboratory policies and procedures shall ensure that:

    _____ **a.** Laboratory staff members cannot both develop and evaluate the same Protection Profile, Security Target, or IT product.

    _____ **b.** Laboratory staff members cannot provide consulting services for and then participate in the evaluation of the same Protection Profile, Security Target, or IT product.

_____ **9.** The laboratory shall have physical and electronic controls augmented with an explicit policy and set of procedures for maintaining separation, both physical and electronic, between the laboratory evaluators and laboratory consultants, product developers, system integrators, and others who may have an interest in and/or may unduly influence the evaluation outcome.

_____ **10.** The management system shall include policies and procedures to ensure the protection of proprietary information.

_____ **11.** The protection of proprietary information protection shall specify how proprietary information will be protected from persons outside the laboratory, from visitors to the laboratory, from laboratory personnel without a need to know, and from other unauthorized persons.

_____ **12.** The management system requirements are designed to promote laboratory practices that ensure the technical accuracy and integrity of the security evaluation and adherence to quality assurance practices appropriate to common criteria testing.

_____ **13.** The laboratory shall maintain a management system that fully documents the laboratory's policies, practices, and the specific steps taken to ensure the quality of the IT security evaluations.

_____ **14.** The reference documents, standards, and publications, shall be available for use by laboratory staff developing and maintaining the management system and conducting evaluations.

_____ **15.** Each applicant and accredited laboratory shall have written and implemented procedures.

_____ **16.** Records shall be kept of all management system activities.

_____ **17.** The procedures for review of contracts shall include procedures to ensure that the laboratory has adequate staff and resources to meet its evaluation schedule and complete evaluations in a timely manner.

_____ **18.** The laboratory shall maintain a functional recordkeeping system that is used to track each security evaluation.

_____ **19.** Records shall be easily accessible and contain complete information for each evaluation.

_____ **20.** Required records of evaluation activities shall be traceable to common criteria evaluator actions and common evaluation methodology work units.

_____ **21.** Computer-based records shall contain entries indicating the date created and the individual(s) who performed the work, along with any other information required by the management system.

_____ **22.** Entries in laboratory notebooks shall be dated and signed or initialed.

_____ **23.** All records shall be maintained in accordance with laboratory policies and procedures and in a manner that ensures record integrity.

_____ **24.** There shall be appropriate back-ups and archives.

_____ **25.** There must be enough evaluation evidence in the records so an independent body can determine what evaluation work was actually performed for each work unit and can concur with the verdict.

_____ **26.** Records should include evaluator notebooks, records relating to the product, work-unit level records, and client-site records.

_____ **27.** Laboratory records shall be maintained, released, or destroyed in accordance with the laboratory's proprietary information policy and contractual agreements with customers.

_____ **28.** Records covering the following are required:

    _____ **a.** All quality system activities.

    _____ **b.** Staff training dates and competency reviews.

    _____ **c.** All audits and management reviews.

_____**d.** Creation of and changes to evaluation procedures and methodology.

_____**e.** Acceptance/rejection of products submitted for evaluation.

_____**f.** Complete tracking of multiple versions of evaluation evidence and evaluation technical reports.

_____**g.** Complete tracking of evaluation activities to the work-unit level including initial analysis, verdicts, and any subsequent changes to those verdicts (based on modifications of evidence or additional analysis).

_____**h.** Source code, binary executables, data and configuration information sufficient to reproduce any testing performed during the evaluation must be retained; this includes source code and binary executables for any test tools (when available) along with test data and configuration information/files.

_____**i.** Calibration records for any equipment where reported results include an estimate of error.

_____**j.** The calibration records should include: the range of calibration, the resolution of the instrument and its allowable error, calibration date and schedule, date and result of last calibration, identity of the laboratory individual or external service responsible for calibration; and source of reference standard and traceability.

_____**k.** The configuration of all test equipment used during an evaluation along with analysis of that equipment to confirm the suitability of test equipment to perform the desired testing.

_____**29.** The internal audit shall cover the laboratory management system and the application of the management system to all laboratory activities.

_____**30.** The audit shall cover compliance with contractual and laboratory management system requirements.

_____**31.** Audits shall cover all aspects of the evaluation activities, including the evaluation work performed.

_____**32.** In the case where only one member of the laboratory staff is competent to conduct a specific aspect of a test method, and performing an audit of work in this area would result in that person auditing his or her own work, then audits may be conducted by another staff member.

_____**33.** The audit shall cover the evaluation methodology for that test method and shall include a review of documented procedures and instructions, adherence to procedures and instructions, and review of previous audit reports.

_____**34.** External experts may also be used in these situations.

_____**35.** The most recent internal audit report shall be available for review during on-site assessments.

_____**36.** The laboratory shall perform at least one complete internal audit prior to the first full on-site assessment.

_____**37.** A partial internal audit should be performed prior to the initial on-site assessment.

_____**38.** The records will be reviewed before or during the on-site assessment visit.

_____**39.** The most recent management review report shall be available for review during on-site assessments.

_____**40.** The laboratory shall perform at least one management review prior to the first full on-site assessment.

_____**41.** A management review should be performed prior to the initial on-site assessment.

_____**42.** The records should be reviewed before or during the on-site assessment visit.

_____**43.** The quality manual shall contain, or refer to, documentation that describes and details the laboratory's implementation of procedures covering all of the technical requirements.

_____**44.** The laboratory shall maintain a competent administrative and technical staff appropriate for common criteria-based IT security evaluations.

_____**45.** The laboratory shall maintain position descriptions, training records, and resumes for responsible supervisory personnel and laboratory staff members who have an effect on the outcome of security evaluations.

_____**46.** The laboratory shall maintain a list of personnel designated to fulfill requirements, including: laboratory director, Authorized Representative, Approved Signatories, evaluation team leaders, and senior evaluators.

_____**47.** The laboratory shall also identify a staff member as quality manager who has overall responsibility for the management system, the quality system, and maintenance of the management system documents.

_____**48.** An individual may be assigned or appointed to serve in more than one position; however, to the extent possible, the laboratory director and the quality manager positions should be independently staffed.

_____**49.** When key laboratory staff are added, the notification of changes shall include a current resume for each new staff member.

_____**50.** Laboratories shall document the required qualifications for each staff position.

_____**51.** The staff information may be kept in the official personnel folders or in separate, official folders that contain only the information that the assessors need to review.

_____**52.** Laboratory staff members who conduct IT security evaluation activities shall have a Bachelor of Science in Computer Science, Computer Engineering, or related technical discipline or equivalent experience.

____53. Laboratory staff collectively shall have knowledge or experience in the following areas: operating systems, data structures, design/analysis of algorithms, database systems, programming languages, computer systems architectures, and networking.

____54. In addition, the laboratory staff shall have knowledge or experience for any specific technologies upon which an evaluation is conducted.

____55. The laboratory shall have documented a detailed description of its training program for new and current staff members.

____56. Each new staff member shall be trained for assigned duties.

____57. The training program shall be updated and current staff members shall be retrained when the common criteria, common evaluation methodology, or scope of accreditation changes, or when the individuals are assigned new responsibilities.

____58. Each staff member may receive training for assigned duties either through on-the-job training, formal classroom study, attendance at conferences, or another appropriate mechanism.

____59. Training materials that are maintained within the laboratory shall be kept up to date.

____60. Staff members shall be trained in the following areas:

____a. general knowledge of the test methods including generation of evaluation reports

____b. computer science concepts

____c. computer security concepts

____d. working knowledge of the common criteria

____e. working knowledge of the common cethodology

____61. The laboratory shall review annually the competence of each staff member for each test method the staff member is authorized to conduct.

____62. The staff member's immediate supervisor, or a designee appointed by the laboratory director, shall conduct annually an assessment and an observation of performance for each staff member.

____63. A record of the annual review of each staff member shall be dated and signed by the supervisor and the employee.

____64. A description of competency review programs shall be maintained in the management system.

____65. Individuals hired to perform common criteria testing activities are sometimes referred to as "subcontractors."

____66. To that end, all individuals performing evaluation activities must satisfy all requirements, irrespective of the means by which individuals are compensated.

____67. The records for each staff member having an effect on the outcome of evaluations shall include: position description, resume/CV/bio (matching person to job), duties assigned, annual competence review, and training records and training plans.

____68. In order to maintain confidentiality and impartiality, the laboratory shall maintain proper separation between personnel conducting evaluations and other personnel inside the laboratory or outside the laboratory, but inside the parent organization.

____69. The laboratory shall have adequate facilities to conduct IT security evaluations.

____70. This (checklist number 69) includes laboratory facilities for security evaluation, staff training, recordkeeping, document storage, and software storage.

____71. A protection system shall be in place to safeguard customer proprietary hardware, software, test data, electronic and paper records, and other materials.

____72. The protection system shall protect the proprietary materials and information from personnel outside the laboratory, visitors to the laboratory, laboratory personnel without a need to know, and other unauthorized persons.

____73. Laboratories shall have systems (firewall, intrusion detection) in place to protect internal systems from untrusted external entities.

____74. If evaluation activities are conducted at more than one location, all locations shall meet the requirements and mechanisms shall be in place to ensure secure communication between all locations.

____75. The laboratory shall have regularly updated protection for all systems against viruses and other malware.

____76. The laboratory shall have an effective backup system to ensure that data and records can be restored in the event of their loss.

____77. If the laboratory is conducting multiple simultaneous evaluations, it shall maintain a system of separation between the products of different customers and evaluations.

____78. This (checklist number 77) includes the product under evaluation, the test platform, peripherals, documentation, electronic media, manuals, and records.

____79. PKI enabled electronic mail capability is required for communications.

____80. Internet access also is required for obtaining revisions to the common criteria, common evaluation methodology, guidance, and interpretations.

____81. Evaluation activities will be conducted outside of the laboratory, and the management system shall include appropriate procedures for conducting security evaluation activities at customer sites or other offsite locations.

____82. The customer site procedures should explain how to secure the site, where to store records and documentation, and how to control access to the test facility.

_____83. If the laboratory is conducting its evaluation at the customer site or other location outside the laboratory facility, the environment shall conform, as appropriate, to the requirements for the laboratory environment.

_____84. If a customer's system on which an evaluation is conducted is potentially open to access by unauthorized entities during evaluation, the evaluation laboratory shall control the evaluation environment.

_____85. This (checklist number 84) is to ensure that the systems are in a defined state compliant with the requirements for the evaluation before starting to perform evaluation work and that the systems ensure that unauthorized entities do not gain access to the system during evaluation.

_____86. The test methods of ISO/IEC 17025 are analogous to evaluation methodology using the common criteria (CC), the common evaluation methodology (CEM), and additional laboratory-developed methodology.

_____87. The version of the CC and CEM to be used in each evaluation shall be established in consultation with NIAP and the sponsor.

_____88. For the purposes of achieving product validation through the common criteria scheme, laboratories may be required to comply with both international interpretations and NIAP-specified guidance.

_____89. The common criteria, common evaluation methodology, guidance and interpretations, and the laboratory's procedures for conducting security evaluations shall be maintained up to date and be readily available to the staff.

_____90. The laboratory shall have documented procedures for conducting security evaluations using the common criteria and common evaluation methodology, and for complying with guidance or interpretations

_____91. The laboratory shall ensure that documented procedures are followed.

_____92. Security evaluations may be conducted at the customer site, the laboratory, or another location that is mutually agreed to.

_____93. When evaluation activities are conducted outside the laboratory, the laboratory shall have additional procedures to ensure the integrity of all tests and recorded results.

_____94. The additional procedures shall also ensure that the same requirements that apply to the laboratory and its facility are maintained at the nonlaboratory site.

_____95. When exceptions to the evaluation methodology are deemed necessary for technical reasons; and to ensure that the new methodology continues to meet all requirements and policies, the customer shall be informed, and details of these exceptions shall be described in the evaluation report.

_____96. The laboratory shall maintain on-site systems adequate to support IT security evaluations in keeping with the tests for which it is seeking accreditation.

_____97. The laboratory shall have an electronic report generation capability.

_____98. The laboratory shall document and maintain records on all test equipment or test suites used during common criteria testing.

_____99. The laboratory is responsible for configuration and operation of all equipment within its control.

_____100. Computer systems and other platforms used during the conduct of testing shall be under configuration control.

_____101. The laboratory shall have procedures to ensure that any equipment (hardware and software) used for testing is in a known state prior to use for testing.

_____102. Measurement traceability is required when applicable.

_____103. The equipment used for conducting security evaluations shall be maintained in accordance with the manufacturer's recommendations, or in accordance with internally documented laboratory procedures, as applicable.

_____104. Test equipment refers to software and hardware products or other assessment mechanisms used by the laboratory to support the evaluation of the security of an IT product.

_____105. Laboratories shall calibrate their test equipment.

_____106. In common criteria testing, calibration means verification of correctness and suitability.

_____107. Any test tools used to conduct security evaluations that are not part of the unit under evaluation shall be studied in isolation to make sure they correctly represent and assess the test assertions they make.

_____108. Test tools should also be examined to ensure they do not interfere with the conduct of the test and do not modify or impact the integrity of the product under test in any way.

_____109. Laboratories shall have procedures that ensure appropriate configuration of all test equipment.

_____110. Laboratories shall maintain records of the configuration of test equipment and all analysis to ensure the suitability of test equipment to perform the desired testing.

_____111. For common criteria testing, "traceability" is interpreted to mean that security evaluation activities are traceable to the underlying common criteria requirements and work units in the common evaluation methodology.

_____112. Test tools and evaluation methodology demonstrate that the tests they conduct and the test assertions they make are traceable to specific criteria and methodology.

_____113. The laboratory shall use documented procedures for sampling.

_____**114.** Whenever sampling is used during an evaluation, the laboratory shall document its sampling strategy, the decision-making process, and the nature of the sample.

_____**115.** Sampling shall be part of the evaluation record.

_____**116.** The laboratory shall protect products under evaluation and calibrated tools from modification, unauthorized access, and use.

_____**117.** The laboratory shall maintain separation between and control over the items from different evaluations, to include the product under evaluation, its platform, peripherals, and documentation.

_____**118.** When the product under evaluation includes software components, the laboratory shall ensure that configuration management mechanisms are in place to prevent inadvertent modifications to the software components during the evaluation process.

_____**119.** The laboratory shall have procedures to ensure proper retention, disposal, or return of software and hardware after the completion of the evaluation.

_____**120.** The laboratory shall have procedures for conducting final review of evaluation results and the laboratory records of the evaluation prior to their submission to the customer.

_____**121.** The laboratory shall issue evaluation reports of its work that accurately, clearly, and unambiguously present the evaluator analysis, test conditions, test setup, test and evaluation results, and all other required information.

_____**122.** Evaluation reports shall provide all necessary information to permit the same or another laboratory to reproduce the evaluation and obtain comparable results.

_____**123.** There may be two types of evaluation reports: (a) reports that are to be submitted, and(b) reports that are produced under contract and intended for use by the customer.

_____**124.** The evaluation report shall contain sufficient information for the exact test conditions and results to be reproduced at a later time if a reexamination or retest is necessary.

_____**125.** Reports intended for use only by the customer shall meet customer laboratory contract obligations and be complete.

_____**126.** The electronic version shall have the same content as the hardcopy version and use an application format (Adobe PDF or Microsoft Word).

_____**127.** Evaluation reports that are delivered in electronic form via electronic mail shall be digitally signed or have a message authentication code applied to ensure integrity of the report and the identity of the laboratory that produced the report.

_____**128.** The laboratory shall provide a secure means of conveying the necessary information for the verification of the signature or the message authentication code.

_____**129.** Confidentiality mechanisms shall be employed to ensure that the evaluation report cannot be disclosed to anyone other than the intended recipient(s).

_____**130.** Each applicant and accredited laboratory shall have written and implemented procedures.

_____**131.** Implementation is used here to mean that the appropriate management system and technical documents have been written, experts and expertise obtained, training conducted, activity conducted, activity audited, and a management review conducted.

_____**132.** Procedures are an integral part of the laboratory management system and shall be included in all aspects of the laboratory operation.

_____**133.** A laboratory shall implement all of the procedures that are required to meet the accreditation requirements.

_____**134.** Failure to have implemented procedures may lead to suspension of accreditation.

_____**135.** General procedures for the following activities are required and shall be implemented before accreditation can be granted:

_____**a.** Internal audits and management review.

_____**b.** Writing and implementing procedures.

_____**c.** Writing and implementing instructions.

_____**d.** Staff training and individual development plans.

_____**e.** Contract review.

_____**f.** Staff members who work at home and at alternate work sites outside the laboratory (telecommuting).

_____**g.** referencing NVLAP accreditation and use of the NVLAP logo.

_____**136.** The following program-specific procedures shall be implemented before the activity is undertaken; as well as, procedures for writing common methodology work-unit level instructions before an evaluation is conducted:

_____**a.** Writing a work plan for an evaluation.

_____**b.** Selecting the members of an evaluation team.

_____**c.** Writing an Evaluation Technical Report (ETR).

_____**d.** Writing an Observation Report (OR).

_____**e.** Conducting an evaluation at a customer's site (if the laboratory offers such services).

_____**f.** Conducting evaluations: for specific technologies (firewalls, operating systems, biometric devices).

_____**g.** Vulnerability analysis.

_____**h.** Conducting independent testing.

_____**i.** Requesting and incorporating interpretations.

_____**j.** Working with NIAP or other validators during an evaluation.

_____**k.** Records and recordkeeping for evaluations.

services and, in the construction of a secure information system, it is the direct responsibility of the security designer to manage the integration between authentication and authorization. This dependency can be automatically implemented by PBM, with strong guarantees about its correct realization.

An important aspect of the design and implementation of a secure information system is the correct consideration of the security principles. They represent fundamental guidelines derived from experience. One of the most well-known security principles is the "least privilege" principle, which claims that elements of a system should only be authorized to execute the minimum set of actions that are required in order to fulfill the specified tasks. A crucial obstacle to realization of this principle is the difficulty in managing security policies. For instance, today most Web applications and Web services use a single account to access the data stored in the database supporting the application, and the presence of a single vulnerability in the Web application may jeopardize the protection of the complete database content. Finer granularity controls and the application of "defense in depth" are services made available by tools for policy-based security management that permit better compliance with the "least privilege" principle.

The realization of policy-based security management has to consider the collection of approaches and solutions offered by current technology. Access control is one of the critical components in the realization of a secure system, and many different models have been proposed to organize and support access control policies. The level of support of the high-level security requirements strongly depends on the features of the access control model that the underlying technological system is able to support. For instance, the high-level requirements can use the concept of "role," in a way consistent with the features of the role-based-access control (RBAC) model, but the underlying system may not offer native support to it; the tool will then be responsible for introducimg a mapping from the high-level RBAC policies to the specific model supported by the system.

Next, the main security objectives are presented. Then, well-known security principles are presented, and for each of them we describe how the realization of a policy-based security management can help achieve them in the realization of a secure information system. Finally, the major access control models are described, and it will be shown how a modern approach for policy-based security management can flexibly support them.

Security Objectives

In computer security, the acronym CIA describes the basic security objectives of *Confidentiality*, *Integrity*, and *Availability*, which a secure system is typically designed to support. These three basic objectives are the basis for realizing a large variety of security functions and satisfying the security requirements of most applications. In some applications there is the need to support only part of them, but a secure system is applicable to concrete scenarios only if all three of them are offered by the system and can be immediately adopted when the need arises.

Confidentiality is the property that is typically associated with the use of encryption. Indeed, when the concern about security derives from the transmission on a channel of sensitive information, encryption represents the crucial technology able to protect the information content of the transferred information from being readable by adversaries who have access to the communication channel. In information systems, the confidentiality of information stored within the system is mostly realized using the access control services, which are responsible for monitoring every access to a protected resource. Only read accesses that are consistent with the policy will be allowed by the system. In some cases, encryption can support the realization of an access control policy for read operations, but this is reserved for information systems with outsourced resources or for representation of data at the low level (hard disks support the encryption of the information contained in them).

Integrity is arguably the most important security service in the design of business applications. Integrity guarantees that all information stored and sent along communication channels is not manipulated by unauthorized users without detection. Integrity in network traffic commonly relies on the use of hash functions, message authentication codes, encryption functions, and digital signatures. Integrity for services requires that the function of the service is not manipulated (supported by code signing) and that only authenticated users that have been authorized to invoke a given service are actually able to have their service requests processed by the system. The critical aspect for achieving integrity protection is that the access policy is configured in a way consistent with the security requirements.

Availability focuses on the resistance against attacks that aim at disrupting the offer of services. This aspect, as a security service, is particularly important for military applications. In the business environment, this is typically considered together with safety and reliability aspects and represents the property that the system is able to continuously provide the services, independently from the variety of threats, due to adversaries or random events that may make the system inoperable. There may be specific business scenarios where the security aspect is extremely relevant (Web application providers that are victims of flooding attacks by adversaries who want to blackmail the service owners), but in most cases the scope is the complete collection of all the possible malfunctions that can block the system.

Beyond confidentiality, integrity, and availability, other services are often added in this classification as basic security services, but they can typically be considered as variants or combinations of the main services. *Authenticity* can be considered a variant of integrity, where resources and services have to prove their origin and users have to prove the control of a specified identity. *Accountability* is also a variant of integrity, where the goal is to guarantee that actions on the system are always recorded without loss and associated with the verified identity of the user. In this way, *nonrepudiability* can also be guaranteed, since users cannot deny that they were responsible for the actions they executed on the system.

Security Principles

Security principles denote the basic guidelines that should be used when designing a secure system. Experience shows that a crucial success factor in the design of a secure system is the correct consideration of the security principles. Vulnerabilities and attacks in most cases can be ascribed to the inadequate application of some principle.

Several classifications of these principles exist. A classical and seminal analysis is the one by Saltzer and Schroeder [23], which lists the following principles: least privilege, economy of mechanism, separation of privilege, psychological acceptability, fail-safe defaults, complete mediation, open design, and least common mechanism.

The *least privilege* principle requires that the set of authorizations that each user gets in the system has to be the minimum set that permits the user to execute his or her role. The same principle can be adopted for the configuration of the privileges of programs and services. The idea is that the *need-to-know* approach has to be used when giving access to resources or services. A critical requirement to correctly apply the principle is to have available an expressive authorization language, which permits a fine-grained definition of the boundaries of the access domain of each user and process. The critical obstacle to the application of this principle, when a flexible access control language is available, is the difficulty to precisely forecast the domain of resources that the user will need to access in the execution of his tasks. The application of PBM offers great support to the realization of this principle, as the policy is specified in a more abstract and structured way and the limitations to the accesses of users can be better delineated. The application of the defense-in-depth approach is a variant of this principle that receives significant support from the advanced support of PBM.

The *economy of mechanism* principle establishes that the protection has to be obtained with a mechanism that is as simple as possible; otherwise it becomes harder to guarantee that the system is able to protect the resource. This principle becomes harder to respect in modern information systems, where resources are typically stored in a layered system. For example, a sensitive credit-card number can be used by an application, which stores it into a database, which stores it into a table stored on a disk managed by an operating system, which may be executed in a virtual machine running in parallel with a multitude of other processes; each layer may offer to the adversary its own opportunities to bypass the protection offered by the application. The protection then depends on the robust implementation at every layer. The use of encryption can mitigate the problem, but its adoption is far from trivial in most circumstances. PBM helps to have a consistent representation of an access policy across the multiple layers, increasing the strength at each layer.

The *separation of privilege* principle clarifies that greater protection can be obtained by requiring distinct actors for the execution of an action. In this way the system is more robust against breaches of trust in the principles legitimately receiving access privileges. An access control model supporting separation of duty constraints supports this principle. PBM can support separation of duty constraints even when the underlying access model does not offer native support to this construct.

The *psychological acceptability* principle states that the security solution has to be understandable by the users, both in its design and during its use. PBM offers clear support to this principle in the design phase, as it offers a way to understand the variety of security configurations that characterize a modern information system.

The *fail-safe defaults* principle suggests the use of a secure default configuration, where in the absence of further information, an access has to be denied. The use of abstract policies can support the system-level specification of default protective actions that will be enforced by all the elements in the system.

The *complete mediation* principle requires that every access to a protected resource must be monitored and verified for consistency with the access policy. The complete coverage of accesses offered by PBM can provide more robust guarantees that each access path is captured by the system.

The *open design* principle establishes that the security of the system must not depend on the obscurity of its design; rather it has to depend on knowledge of a few well-managed secrets. In PBM, the availability of a high-level description of the policy limits the reliance on the assumption that the system can be protected by keeping hidden the protection measures. Instead, modern security practices are promoted.

The *least common mechanism* principle concerns the design of solutions where a single resource or piece of software is used to mediate accesses for different users. Any vulnerability in such an element can then lead to a compromise of the system. PBM helps the realization of this privilege, as it simplifies the configuration in a consistent way of multiple devices.

Access Control Models

The term *access control* commonly denotes the combination of the authentication, authorization, and auditing services. Each of the three services is organized in two parts: a policy, directing how the system resources should be accessed; and a mechanism, responsible for implementation of the policy. Of the six components, the one that mostly characterizes the access control system is the *authorization policy*.

The authorization policy, given an access request produced by a user with the intention to execute a specific action on a resource, has the goal of specifyin whether or not the request has to be authorized. Many proposals have emerged for representation of the authorization policy. The design of the authorization policy has to carefully balance the requirements of expressivity with the strict efficiency constraints that limit the amount of computational resources that can be dedicated to processing each access request. There are a few long-term trends, clearly visible in the evolution of IT technology, that have a specific impact: The evolution of computer systems is significantly increasing the amount of computational resources available to process an access request; the application of access control increasingly occurs in distributed systems where the delay due to network access can support a more complex evaluation; and application requirements are becoming more complex and require the evaluation of sophisticated conditions. These trends lead to a progressive increase of the amount of resources available to process each access request and to a corresponding enrichment of the access control models used for representation of the authorization policies. We summarize the evolution of these models, describing their main features. Each model typically extends previous proposals and offers specific new functionalities.

The classical access control model, which today is still the basis of most operating systems and databases, is the discretionary access control (DAC) model, which starts from the assumption that users have the ability to manage the information they access without restrictions and users are able to specify the access policy for the resources they create. The access policy can be represented by (Subject, Resource, Action) triples that describe each permitted action. The elements of the policy can be organized by resource (offering access control lists) or by subject (offering capabilities). This access control model presents a number of variants; for instance, a user can transfer the privileges he received; also, programs can be configured to give to users invoking the program the privileges of the owner of the program.

A first evolution of the DAC model was represented by the mandatory access control (MAC) models, which establish policies that restrict the set of operations that users can apply over the resources they are authorized to access. The most famous of these models is the Bell-LaPadula model [24], which has been designed taking inspiration from the approaches used for protecting information in military and intelligence environments, classifying resources according to their secrecy level, and giving users clearances to access resources up to a certain level; restrictions are then imposed on the flow of information. The restrictions guarantee that information will not flow from a high level to a low level, independently of the actions of the users. Alternative MAC models have been defined supporting integrity (the Biba model [25]) and protection of conflict-of-interest requirements (the Chinese Wall model [26]). All these models, when applied on real systems, showed significant shortcomings, mostly due to their rigidity; the presence of covert channels in real systems limited the robustness of the approach. The idea of establishing restrictions on the operations of a resource that depend on properties of resources and users is an advanced aspect that characterizes recent access control solutions.

The role-based access control (RBAC) model [27] assumes that the assignment of privileges to users is mediated by the specification of roles. Roles represent functions in an organization, which require a collection of privileges to execute their tasks. Users are assigned to a role depending on the organizational function that is given to them. The model is particularly interesting for large enterprises, where this structure of the access policy greatly facilitates the management of the security requirements. The evolution of the access policy can be better controlled, with a clear strategy to support the evolution of the required resource privileges and of the organization. The use of roles in general requires two kinds of authorizations: system authorization specifying the privileges a role should acquire and role authorization specifying the subjects that can enact the defined roles. This increase in structural complexity is in most cases mitigated by a significant reduction in the size of the policy and by an easier management. The RBAC model has been successful and has been adopted in many environments, with dedicated support in the SQL3 standard and modern operating systems.

A modern family of solutions is represented by attribute-based access control (ABAC) models. These models assume that authorizations can express conditions on properties of the resource and the subject. For instance, assuming that each resource has an attribute that denotes the identifier of the subject that created the resource, a single authorization can specify the ownership privilege for all the creators of every resource; this would either require an ad-hoc mechanism in the access control module or the creation of a distinct authorization for every resource. The advantages in terms of flexibility and expressive power of the ABAC model are evident. The main obstacle to its adoption in real systems has always been the worry about the performance impact of such a solution. In the scenario of access control for cooperating Web services, this worry is mitigated by the high cost of each access that makes acceptable the cost required for evaluating predicates on resource ad user properties. The XACML proposal is a notable example of a language that supports an ABAC model. The evolution of access control solutions is expected to lead to a wider adoption of ABAC models.

Another family of authorization models focuses on the specification of the constraint that different users have to be involved in executing a task. This is consistent with the "separation of privilege" principle presented earlier, which urges the design of secure systems to be robust against breaches of trust, by making critical actions only executable with the cooperation of a defined number of distinct users. The classical example is the withdrawal at a bank of an amount larger than a given threshold, which requires the cooperation of a bank teller and the supervision of the branch director. The damage that can be done by a corrupt or blackmailed bank employee is then limited.

Several models have been proposed for representation of these access control restrictions, commonly called Separation of Duty (SoD) constraints. Today the design of such a model typically occurs extending a role-based model, specifying different privileges for roles that are required in the execution of a given process, then imposing that the same subject cannot enact two roles. There are two variants of SoD conflicts: Static SoD and Dynamic SoD. Static SoD assumes that the roles are rigidly assigned to users, who will always enact the same role in every action. Dynamic SoD assumes that the conflict has to be evaluated within the domain of a specific action instance, where distinct users have to enact conflicting roles. The same user may enact conflicting roles, as long as they are enacted in different action instances. Static SoD is the model receiving greater support, typically at the level of policy definition, with the availability of techniques that permit the identification of assignments of privileges to users that may violate the constraint. SAP Access Control, for instance, supports the detection of static SoD conflicts during role design and provisioning. Dynamic SoD requires robust support from the execution system, and this remains a critical requirement. Dynamic SoD requires some robust way to keep track of the history of accesses within an action. An extensive analysis of these issues appears in Chapter 45.

We note again that PBM can offer the opportunity to use a sophisticated high-level policy model for the design of the policy, taking the responsibility for mapping the high-level representation to the concrete access control model that the system responsible for the implementation of the system can offer. This is one advantage of using such an approach. The PoSecCo project, described later in the chapter, offers an abstract flexible policy language, with support for RBAC and ABAC models. This policy can be translated into a collection of policies for the low-level systems that are used in the IT infrastructure, each with its own restrictions. This represents an interesting approach for applying modern access control models in a scenario where common network protocols, operating systems, DBMSs, Web servers, and application servers are used.

To conclude this analysis, we want to quickly present the concept of *obligation*, which presents specific features that clearly distinguish it from the concept of authorization presented above. Obligations are Embedded and Communications Alliance (ECA) policies that serve to determine future actions a subject has to perform (on a target) as a reaction to specific events. As noted by Sloman [28], obligation policies are enforced at the subject, while access control policies are enforced at the resource side. They also differ from the provisional access control model, proposed by Jajodia [29], that extends the traditional yes/no access control answers by saying that subjects must cause a set of conditions to be evaluated to true "prior" to authorize a request. Obligations are used in many management fields such as Quality of Service (increase resources if a SLA is not satisfied), privacy management (delete user information after 6 months), auditing (raise an alarm if some events occur), dynamic network reconfiguration based on security or network events (activate backup links in case of DDoS), and activity scheduling (periodic backups). Complex events can be specified from basic events using event expressions managed also using external monitoring or event services and reused in many policies. Due to their operative and temporal nature, obligations are not only used in security-relevant policies but also for workflow management. Unlike access control, obligations policies are often unenforceable; that is, the system cannot ensure that each obligation will be actually fulfilled by the subject [30]. There is a lack of security controls able to enforce obligations. Even if ad hoc agents have been sometimes proposed [31] and some tool is available, to be practically used, obligation policies are often mapped to other enforceable authorization mechanisms [32].

4. CONTROLS FOR ENFORCING SECURITY POLICIES IN DISTRIBUTED SYSTEMS

The fulfillment of high-level security objectives in distributed systems goes beyond the specification of AC policies and their enforcement, which is typically done at the endpoint (close to the resource that requires protection). Complications that arise in distributed systems result from the topological arrangement and interaction of system elements over trustworthy and untrustworthy networks. The satisfaction of CIA properties in distributed systems can primarily count on two different categories of security controls. Firewalls that separate network portions with different security levels, provide security checks before allowing incoming and outgoing network traffic, and communication protection mechanisms, like VPNs, that allow two endpoints to securely communicate over untrustworthy networks. Next, the difficulty in choosing the "best" security control in a given context, as well as an alternative firewall and communication protection technologies, is explained in much more detail.

Criteria for Control Selection

As previously described, the plan phase of the security life cycle requires the identification and selection of appropriate security controls. Evaluating the alternatives is, however, not an easy task because different control technologies have different features, performance, management costs, and security implications. First of all, there is a large availability of security controls. They may be available at the endpoints (personal firewalls, channel protection mechanisms), or in the infrastructure (VPN gateways, border firewalls).

Firewalls are displaced in many points of the corporate networks to separate the internal network in portions at different security levels (the administrator's from the guests' subnet). Firewalls have different functionalities, as explained in the next section, which can be used to enforce different policies, but they have different performance. Performance critical elements often run on dedicated appliances, as it often happens for the border firewalls, the main elements of defense as they separate the internal network from the remainder of the (unsecure) Internet. Filtering capabilities are also available at the OS level (iptables in Linux), or they can be freely installed both to be used for host protection (personal firewall) or to implement a filtering mechanism (forwarding firewall). Best-practices suggest discarding unallowed traffic as soon as possible, that is, as close as possible to the source. But other factors need to be carefully considered; for instance, the performance, or the trustworthiness of the control to configure, based on the vendor/product reputation and on an analysis of historical data of vulnerabilities (number, seriousness, exposure time) [33]. As previously anticipated, firewall configurations are an ordered list of rules; the action enforced is the one taken from the first matching rule. Software-based implementations of the resolution algorithm have linear processing time; this means that the higher the number of rules, the higher the overhead and the lower the performance. Therefore, optimizing the rule set is mandatory to have reasonable performance.

Hardware-based implementations use expensive hardware and sophisticated algorithms [34] (the Content-Addressable Memories, to improve the performance to a constant time; that is, the firewall takes (more or less) the same time regardless of the rule set size). However, when the hardware resources are saturated, no other rules can be added. For instance, Netscreen 100 products allow the specification of no more than 733 rules. More expensive appliances need to be bought if more rules are needed; thus, in this case, the optimization of the rule set may also reduce the expenses.

The enforcement of a communication protection policy shares the same decisional problems, but it is even worse due to the availability of different technologies working at different levels of the ISO/OSI stack. The most well-known solutions are IPsec, which works at the network layer, the TLS protocol, which works up to the transport layer, and WS-Security, which prescribes how to protect SOAP messages using XML Signature and XML Encryption. In most cases, these protections are available directly in the kernel (IPsec), in the server software (TLS), and in the application containers (WS-Security). Therefore, the decision of the most appropriate one does not depend on the availability but on other considerations, such as the efficiency of the solution, the configuration and management costs, the ease of use for the clients, and the overall security. These technologies can be divided into channel protection, when the protection is applied to data during the transmission and is valid up to the other communication party, and message protection, when the protection is applied to data prior to be transmitted (WS-Security and S/MIME) so that the communication medium becomes irrelevant. The decision between channel and message protection is also very sensitive and requires a careful analysis of the systems to be configured. This difficulty can be exemplified with the help of, for instance, WS-Security. This technology can be used to encrypt sensitive information exchanged by Web services and is considered very secure, as application data remains encrypted along the entire communication channel, whereas application data protected by TLS is often subject to TLS offloading, which results in unencrypted data exchange within a service providers' network. The choice of using WS-Security, however, must consider the potential impact on other security mechanisms in place. It can, for instance, inhibit the work of application-level or content-inspection firewalls. It can also prevent data leakage prevention systems to detect the leakage of sensitive information in outbound calls. Moreover, message protection technologies have worse performance compared to channel protection ones. Figure 23.5 presents the logical view of the techniques available at the different layers together and illustrates the possibility of nesting them. Note that, practically, the implementation of the WS-

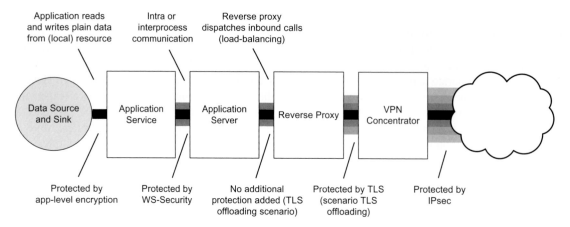

FIGURE 23.5 Logical view of data protection offered by different technologies in Web service environments (scenario SSL offloading).

Security is typically offered by plug-ins or modules of the Application Services (Rampart is the security module of Axis2).

In addition to the above considerations, distributed systems are intrinsically redundant for availability purposes. Together with duplicated functionalities, many backup solutions are available to connect different endpoints, even if they may be disabled. Redundant controls are often used in combinations (configured with the same policy) to mitigate the risk of attacks in case one of the controls has some vulnerability. In other words, one needs not only to decide on (and subsequently configure) the main security controls, but also to have backup solutions that cope with failures or attacks.

Another aspect that complicates the selection of security controls is that they cannot be considered in isolation. In general, every time a security control blocks or alters the information transmitted (changing the addresses), as for NATting and packet enveloping, or the content, like the encrypted communications, there is a risk that another control is hampered; thus, another high-level policy is not enforced.

Other parameters that need to be considered when selecting and configuring security controls are management costs (including the configuration costs), deployment costs, efforts related to the creation of the initial configuration (controls provided with a GUI are often preferred to a script-based approach), or efforts related to implement configuration changes (automatic remote deployment systems are preferred to manual ones). Moreover, the expressiveness of the policy is important. Depending on the layer where each solution works, security controls can decide based on MAC or IP addresses and ports, up to application layer information as users, and roles, or other semantically rich information.

In summary, automatic or semiautomatic tool support would significantly facilitate the selection and evaluation of appropriate security controls and their configuration.

The PoSecCo project, for instance, proposes an optimized control selection and configuration generation starting from end-to-end requirements.

Firewall Technologies

An overview of firewall types is given by the NIST in [35]. The simplest firewall feature is *packet filtering*, which makes decisions on each received packet based on information in IP and transport headers. Rules for packet filters are sometimes referred to as five-tuples, as they include conditions on IP source and destination addresses, source and destination ports, and the IP protocol field. Packet filters are very efficient and very often work at wire speed even without dedicated hardware. However, they cannot be used to express complex filtering policies (to allow FTP in passive mode), and in general, compared to more sophisticated firewalls, more rules are needed to specify the same policy. However, many studies proved that their performance is seriously affected by the quality of the rule set. Reducing overlapping rules (that match the same packets) and eliminating redundant ones (never activated rules) [36][37], together with a careful rule reordering based on traffic profile [38], strongly increase the overall performance.

Stateful inspection improves packet filters by tracking connection states at the transport layer by examining certain values of TCP headers and maintaining a *state table*. State values are used to take decisions (allowing all the TCP packets from an "established" (the responses)) or "related" connection (the FTP data connections), or blocking packets that do not comply with the TCP protocol specification. Some controls that implement the stateful inspection are also able to track other protocols (permit DNS response only after DNS query), and ICMP echo-reply only after an echo-request. Stateful inspection may enforce bandwidth control (to limit the number of connections allowed to a given destination, or the packet

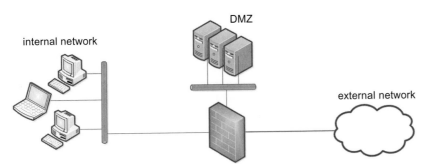

FIGURE 23.6 A screened subnet with a DMZ created using a three-legged firewall.

rate per destination address or port base). Presently, stateful firewalls are the most frequently used technology as they allow sufficiently expressive policies, but they are also appropriate where performance is critical (for border protection) as they are often sold with dedicated hardware appliances. As stated previously, analyzing the rule set and optimizing it allow organizations to save money as less expensive hardware can be bought.

Another capability is the *stateful protocol analysis*, also known as *deep packet inspection*; that is, the ability to read the data and reconstruct the state of application layer protocols. Elements able to perform deep packet inspection are often referred to as *application firewalls*. Due to the large variety of application protocols, these security controls can be "customized" to a specific protocol to perform a more focused analysis; therefore they are named specialized application firewalls, the most widespread being the Web Application Firewall (WAF). The WAF can block traffic depending on the values of HTTP properties and fields (e.g., they can filter email messages that contain attachments of a given type), or block possibly harmful protocol operations, as it is often the case for the FTP "put" command or HTTP unsafe methods (TRACK, TRACE, DELETE). Additionally, application firewalls are able to check traffic compliance to protocol standards or to a set of nonharmful implementations ("RFC compliance") and to identify unexpected sequences of commands. Application firewalls enable fine-grained decisions (to allow or deny access to web pages), not only considering their URLs but also checking whether Java or ActiveX are used, or filter TLS connections from/to endpoints whose certificates have been issued by an untrustworthy certification authority. At the application level, information is often represented in the form of strings (MIME objects, URLs, filenames). For this reason, conditions are often formulated using regular expressions.

An improved type of application firewall is the *application-proxy gateway*, which enforces an access control policy using a proxy agent. It accepts the incoming connections and uses circuit relay services to forward the allowed ones. It hides the details about an internal network, as its address is the only visible one. Additionally, it keeps track of authenticated users, thus permitting the

specification of rules that prescribe the maximum number of users allowed, or the maximum number of connections on a per user base. More precisely, the proxy is named "tunneling proxy" if it does not modify requests and responses after a successful authentication, "forward proxy" if it retrieves the resource on behalf of the client (and it belongs to the client's network), and "reverse proxy" if they answer to client requests on behalf of a server or a set of servers (and it belongs to the servers' network). Finally, some firewalls support "content inspection," that is, the ability to analyze and take decisions based on the payload of application protocols.

These components are the bricks needed to create more complex firewall architectures that achieve a better level of protection. For instance, the screened subnet, presented in [39], creates an intermediate level of protection between internal and external networks by creating a demilitarized zone (DMZ), with limited access to the internal network, where the services to be provided to the external network are usually put (see Figure 23.6).

As the firewalls separate network portions at different security levels, they often implement the network address translation (NAT) functionality. NAT is the functionality that changes IP addresses and ports into the received packets. When source IP addresses are modified, the mapping can be one-to-one, if every IP address is statically changed, or many-to-one, when an entire network is mapped on one or a few (public) IP addresses. In the latter case also TCP/UDP port numbers are modified to perform the required multiplexing; for this reason, this technique is named network address and port translation (NAPT). Unlike circuit relay, the NAT does not break the IP stack as the change is made transparently. First proposed to avoid IPv4 address exhaustion, now it is commonly used to hide private networks, but it introduces drawbacks on the connectivity quality and requires careful configuration. On the other end, it can be useful to masquerade the actual IP address of publicly available services or when load balancing systems are used, that forward requests on a pool of services. In that case, the destination NAT is used. For Web servers and Web services, another technique is used that permits associating the resources with URLs in a dynamic way, both to expose "fancy URLs" usable by the search engines and to redirect content.

Although the importance of a correct configuration of filtering devices is easily understood for the security of the internal network, a "polite" configuration of firewalls can produce a significant impact on the security of the entire Internet. To this purpose, two best-practices have been proposed: *ingress filtering* and *egress filtering*. Ingress filtering is a technique that consists in accepting packets from the outside only if they actually come from the networks that they claim to be from. According to RFC 2827 [40], a systematic ingress filtering starting at the periphery of the Internet would reduce or permit mapping DDoS attacks. Packet filtering at source IP level is usually enough to enforce it. Egress filtering consists in configuring the filtering infrastructure to block the unauthorized or malicious traffic from the internal network. It can be implemented using a packet filter that verifies that the source IP address in all packets is within the allocated IP block used by the company, or in more advanced ways using proxies that authenticate users before allowing them to access the Internet.

Channel and Message Protection Technologies

This part of the chapter presents two channel protection technologies: IPsec, which works at layer 3, and the TLS protocol, which works at layer 4, and two message protection technologies, WS-security, which protects SOAP objects (used by Web services), and S/MIME, which protects MIME email messages. IPsec is a suite of protocols that offers various security services for traffic at the IP layer, for both the IPv4 and IPv6 protocols. The protection is guaranteed by means of two security protocols, the Authentication Header (AH) and the Encapsulating Security Payload (ESP). AH guarantees the integrity and symmetric authentication of IP packets; both the payload and the nonvariable fields of the header. ESP may provide the integrity, authentication, and confidentiality of IP packets payload (but not of the header). Both optionally provide an anti-replay service by maintaining a window with the last 32 or 64 packets. These protocols can be used in two modes: *transport mode* and *tunnel mode*. The transport mode is between two network nodes to provide security services to upper layers and therefore protects only the payload. This type of configuration is named end-to-end security (see Figure 23.7(a). In tunnel mode, a secure channel is established between two endpoints, the gateways, each one associated with the IP addresses of the subnet they control. When packets arrive at one gateway from a subnet and are directed to the other one, they are first encapsulated in a new packet exchanged between the gateways (by means of IP in IP); then its payload (that is, the entire original packet) is protected. This type of configuration is named basic VPN (see Figure 23.7c). Additionally, IPsec in tunnel mode can be used to secure the remote access (to allow a user to connect to a gateway without knowing his IP address a priori via user-level authentication), as shown in Figure 23.7(b). The connections to protect are specified by means of a Security Policy, stored in the Security Policy Database (SPDB). The details to protect a connection are summarized by means of a Security Association (SA). An SA is a univocally identified set of parameters that characterize a unidirectional connection, including symmetric cryptographic

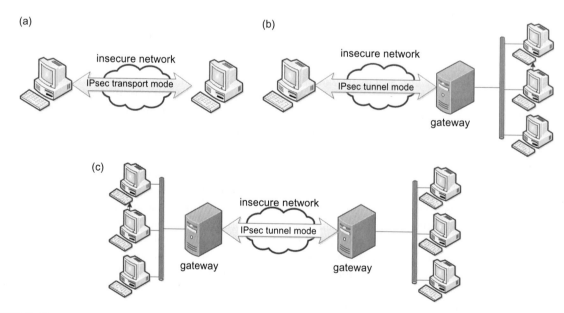

FIGURE 23.7   IPsec.

algorithms, keys, the selected protocol (AH or ESP), and a lifetime. The SA can be manually written by administrators or negotiated using an ad-hoc key management solution, the Internet Key Exchange (IKE) protocol [41], and are stored in a Security Association Database (SADB). A prior offline agreement is needed to write or negotiate the SA and configure IPsec accordingly. In some cases, vendors provide software for simplified remote client configuration (CISCO VPN client). In general IPsec has good performance but it has high management costs. IKE supports certificate-based user authentication; a very granular policy can be enforced.

Transport Layer Security (TLS) is a suite of protocols that allow a client and a server to authenticate each other, to negotiate the security services to enforce, and the cryptographic keys before starting to exchange data at the application layer in a client-server scenario. It was first issued by Netscape as Secure Socket Layer (SSL), then absorbed with minor (but security relevant) revisions by the IETF as Transport Layer Security [42]. TLS works at the transport layer; that is, it is encapsulated in a reliable transport protocol, like TCP. Additionally, there exists the Datagram TLS (DTLS) that guarantees the same security properties with datagram protocols, like UDP [43] and DCCP [44]. The protection is summarized using a cipher suite, a string that indicates the peer authentication and key exchange algorithm, the hash algorithm used to calculate the message authentication code (HMAC for TLS, keyed digest for SSL), and the encryption algorithm (TLS RSA WITH AES 128 CBC SHA). The cipher suites are negotiated using the TLS Handshake Protocol, which also supports server authentication using X.509 certificates. It optionally supports server-requested client authentication. As the TLS Handshake Protocol is very expensive both computationally and in terms of exchanged data, there exists a resume functionality based on a session identification mechanism. The protection is applied to application data by the TLS Record Protocol, which divides in blocks the application data to protect, optionally compresses it, calculates the message authentication code, ciphers, and adds the TLS record header before transmitting each block. The main advantage of TLS over IPsec is that it requires less configuration effort at the client side, as the TLS client is available in every browser together with a list of trusted certification authorities. Nevertheless, its performance is a little worse [45]. For remote access, TLS VPN permits two types of usage: the clientless approach, when an authenticated user can select a set of predefined resources from a Web page, or the thin client, when by means of an ActiveX- or Java-based plug-in an authenticated user can run other applications across the VPN. However, TLS VPNs are subject to other security issues; for instance, as they allow a Web-based approach, they are more vulnerable to password cracking

attacks, they may be the vector for malware to the internal network, and, if split tunneling is used, they may allow a compromised remote machine to become a router for the internal network. Additionally, they may increase the risk exposure due to keystroke loggers, open sessions, or cached data on shared machines, as they easily allow anywhere connections also from public machines.

As anticipated previously, when there is the risk of offloading— for instance, in the case of email systems where relaying servers temporarily store the emails before forwarding them to the user's inbox—channel protection solutions working at network and transport layer are not enough. In fact, the assumption that all the intermediaries and the endpoint are trusted does not hold any more. In this case, the protection needs to be applied directly to the exchanged messages. The emails, represented with the MIME format, are protected with the Secure/MIME (S/MIME) [46]. S/MIME applies sender's authentication, message integrity, nonrepudiation of origin, privacy, and data security using X.509 certificates. S/MIME protected messages are conveyed using an ad-hoc MIME type, the application/pkcs7-mime. There are two types of protected messages for security purposes: the "enveloped-data," when data are ciphered with a session key that is then encrypted with the public keys taken from the certificates of all the recipients, and the "signed-data," when data are signed with the private key of the sender's certificate. Message protections can be nested in any order; however, the available implementations include the enveloped-only, signed-only, or signed-then-enveloped messages. S/MIME messages are represented using the Cryptographic Message Syntax format [47], an extension of PKCS#7.

Analogously, in the case of Web services, a SOAP-level security mechanism has been made available, the Web Service Security (WS-Security or WSS). It has been defined as a SOAP extension protocol that specifies how to sign or encrypt messages using XML Signature and XML Encryption. Additionally, it can be used to transport credentials (like X.509 certificates) and security tokens (like SAML assertions or Kerberos tokens) that can also be associated with messages. WS-Security can be used to enforce an end-to-end security at the application layer when Web services are used. Using WS-Security is computationally expensive due to the use of cryptographic algorithms, and it increases the size of the messages. Compared to TLS or IPsec, it is significantly less performing, but it allows for more granular application of the protection, as it can be applied to single XML fields and for the enforcement of more sophisticated authentication and authorization policies. Due to the granularity of the enforcement, configuring and managing changes with WS-Security may require significantly more effort than channel protection techniques, thus posing a major burden to administrators.

5. PRODUCTS AND TECHNOLOGIES

This section introduces a small and diverse selection of mature technologies and products related to PBM, which can now be used to improve system security and compliance. Note that none of them takes a holistic view of PBM. Instead, each example looks at different facets of system security and works with different abstraction levels of security policy. The solutions from SAP, Microsoft, and CISCO exemplify the state of the art in managing authorizations for enterprise applications, endpoint security, and network security devices, respectively. XACML has been selected as an example for policy specification languages, herewith acknowledging its increasing adoption by industry. Moreover, it has been specifically created for dealing with access control, while other languages such as Ponder or CIM-SPL are general-purpose languages. Finally, SELinux is a prominent open-source example for the policy-based configuration of operating systems.

SAP Access Control

SAP access control is an enterprise software application that enables organizations to control access and prevent fraud across enterprise applications, while minimizing the time and cost of compliance. The solution is centered on a repository of access and authorization-based risks related to single or multiple functions executed in the course of business processes. Each business function is linked to one or several actions that implement the respective functionality in a given enterprise application. Users can specify their own risk rules or rely on a standard rule set for business processes implemented by standard ERP applications from SAP, Oracle, and others. A typical SoD risk related to the business process Procure-to-Pay is, for instance, that single users within the same organizational unit have permission to both maintain vendor master data and initiate payment runs, which could be misused to perform fraud (cf. Figure 23.8).

The rule set is the basis for the analysis and reporting of risks caused by the assignment of authorizations to roles and users, performed at the design and, respectively, runtime of an enterprisewide authorization concept. At design time, SAP access control supports the management of roles from multiple SAP or non-SAP systems with a single unified role repository; any new or changed role is subject to risk analysis in order to prevent SoD violations within a single role. Role design is further supported by approval workflows, role refinement according to organizational hierarchies, and eventually results in the automated generation and deployment of technical roles in the respective target application. At runtime, risk analysis is performed during (de)provisioning workflows in order to detect SoD violations that could result from the assignment of multiple roles to a given user. Such workflows are triggered by HR events (as a result of a new hire) or self-services, include approval steps, and eventually result in the automated provisioning of roles (and identities) to all systems concerned.

SAP access control focuses on the design and operation of authorization concepts for the application layer. The definition of risks and, subsequently, roles is rather subject to the design phase of a security concept, while the mapping of generic business functions to the respective applications and authorizations as well as the support of change and provisioning workflows belongs to the implementation and operations phases. With regard to policy abstraction levels, one can distinguish abstract and application-independent business functions and roles on the one hand, and the concrete and application-specific counterparts on the other hand.

Microsoft Group Policy

Microsoft Group Policy is a technology that facilitates the management of configuration settings in Windows

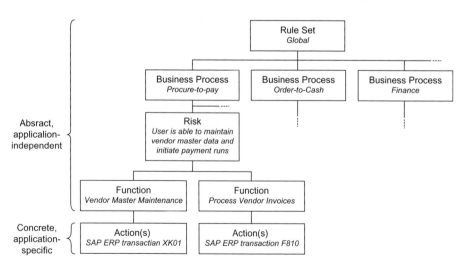

FIGURE 23.8 Example risk specified in SAP access control.

environments. More specifically, domain-based Group Policy supports centralized configuration management and scales up to IT networks that span across multiple sites and domains, thereby relying on Active Directory Domain Services (AD DS).

Although it can be used for configuring all kinds of features, Group Policy is particularly useful for the enforcement of security policies concerning password policies or the setup of endpoint firewalls. Settings governed by Group Policy cannot be modified by standard users, which ensures that security-relevant settings remain as specified and cannot be changed advertently or inadvertently. Technically, a so-called Group Policy Object (GPO) comprises policy settings, each of these prescribing a desired value for a given software configuration parameter. GPOs are linked to a hierarchy of domains, sites, and organizational units in order to determine to which systems and users a GPO shall apply (cf. Figure 23.9). The settings are deployed in regular intervals and manifest primarily in the Windows registry. Group Policy supports inheritance, whereby more specific GPOs prevail over GPOs that are linked to upper-level hierarchy nodes. Policy settings that concern systems are applied after startup, while user-related settings apply after logon.

Figure 23.9 displays the Group Policy Management Console, which administrators use to associate GPOs with hierarchy elements. The Default Domain Policy, for instance, is a GPO associated with the entire company domain, which renders the contained policy settings applicable to all users and systems in the entire domain. On the right-hand side, it becomes visible that this GPO comprises mainly security-related settings (the minimum password length as specified in the registry). While settings can be maintained with the help of the Group Policy Management Editor, further tools extend Group Policy with regard to approval workflows, delegation, or role-based administration.

With regard to the notion of policy abstraction levels, it shall be noted that Group Policy does not support the specification of high-level policies, but works on the level of concrete and software-specific configuration parameters that determine the behavior of a given software feature.

CISCO

CISCO, a leading provider of computer network hardware, offers products to enforce, manage, and monitor the security of network infrastructures for clouds, data centers, and in general for medium to large enterprise networks. It sells a set of modular appliances for network security, including the ASA series (Adaptive Security Appliances), the Catalyst series, and the IOS series, that can be expanded with firewalls (stateful, application layer and content inspection), IPsec- and TLS-based VPN components, and intrusion prevention systems, to scale and reach the company needs. These tools also permit the dynamic definition of zones to partition the network according to security levels (to create the DMZs) and the definition of NAT rules. It also freely provides VPN clients to allow remote access to IPsec VPNs.

All the CISCO devices can be configured using a command-line script-based approach, which they themselves declared as "cumbersome" [48]. For this reason, they

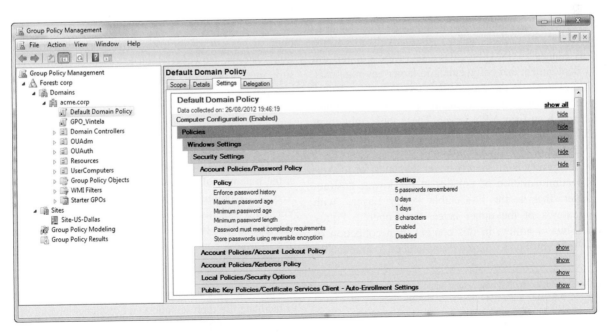

FIGURE 23.9 Microsoft Group Policy Management Console.

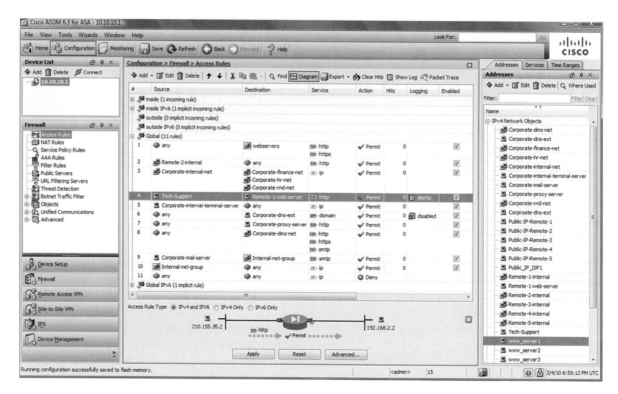

FIGURE 23.10   The CISCO ASDM GUI-based firewall appliance management.

also provide Web-based or stand-alone user-friendly applications that allow administrators to simplify the configuration, troubleshooting, and central management of appliances. For instance, the Adaptive Security Device Manager (ASDM), with a representative interface presented in Figure 23.10, provides setup wizards and administration tools, together with dashboards that provide an at-a-glance view of appliance status, and debugging tools such as packet trace and packet capture. Alternatively, the Cisco Security Manager (CSM) provides a set of tools to perform policy deployment and enforcement in larger environments. Another example is the Easy VPN that allows the central management (and pushing) of channel protection configurations through an Easy VPN server. These tools only cover CISCO appliances and cannot be used with products of other vendors or open-source products.[8]

CISCO products efficiently cover demands for the traditional administration of policies at the lowest abstraction layer, that is, the Executable Policy Layer,[9] with some features of the upper layer, the Concrete Policy Layer. Thus, a policy, in this context, is a collection of rules to configure Cisco appliances, graphically represented in a GUI or represented as a collection of command-line instructions. Human errors and inconsistencies, the leading factor to move toward a PBM approach, may be reduced because of a more efficient data representation and management (the reuse of low-level security rules and objects (IP addresses, ports, and URLs)), because of the availability of simple integrated debugging tools, such as packet capture, ping, and traceroute, or because of the integration with intrusion prevention systems. However, high-level specifications are not supported. Today this status is common to all the companies producing security appliances.

XACML

The eXtensible Access Control Model Language (XACML) is the outcome of the work of an OASIS committee. The XACML Committee released version 1.0 in 2003 [50]. Version 3.0 or higher is expected to be approved in 2013. The goal of the language is to define an XML representation of access control policies, focusing on the description of authorizations.

The main goal of XACML is to offer a platform-independent representation of access control policies in order to facilitate the representation and exchange among systems of the access control restrictions that systems have to apply. XACML is a member of a large family of specifications that

---

8. A step toward the multiproduct multivendor management of security controls is Firewall Builder [49], which permits support of CISCO devices as well as other open-source firewalls such as iptables and pf with a single GUI and a set of translation and deployment scripts.

9. *Source:* http://www.cisco.com/en/US/products/ps6121/index.html.

offer an XML schema for the portable representation of information to be shared in a distributed system.

The model behind the language assumes that the basic building block is a rule, which is associated with a resource, a subject, and an action. Rules are structured in policies, and policies build policy sets. The specification of the elements of the rules and policies can use the XPath language, supporting the representation of flexible predicates on resource and subject properties. Based on this, XACML can be considered an example of an ABAC model, with the possibility of defining compact policies. This choice is consistent with the general architecture of a policy management system described in Figure 23.3, with the roles of PEP, PDP, PIP, and PAP.

XACML can be considered a successful initiative, with a lot of interest dedicated to it in the research and industrial community. Systems exist that are able to evaluate XACML policies and implement the components of the XACML architecture; many prototypes have been built that use a variant of XACML to manage advanced policies (for obligations, delegations, privacy profiles [51]). The most significant industrial use of XACML today is to offer a representation of the internal policies of a system in a format that can be understood by other components. A very interesting opportunity is the realization of a family of adapters able to create, starting from an XACML policy, the access control configuration of a real system. The XACML Committee has worked on the definition of a variety of profiles that define restrictions and introduce terms for the definition of polices that make them processable by automatic tools. Currently, however, there is only support for a limited number of systems. An interesting profile is the one for the representation of RBAC policies [52].

The XACML language has an interesting role in the design of a PBM system, as it can be used to represent policies in a portable way, using the services of ad-hoc translators to map the XACML policy to the concrete implementation. Also, the ability of some profiles to map a high-level view of the policy to the concrete setting is consistent with the goals of the approach advocated in this chapter. It is not clear whether XACML will emerge as the central component for the realization of such architectures, but certainly it deserves careful consideration in this area.

SELinux

Security Enhanced Linux (SELinux) is the outcome of a project initially sponsored by the National Security Agency aiming at improving the protection of the Linux operating system, with a first implementation made available in 2000. The module was initially offered as a default option in a few distributions, and, since version 2.6 or higher of the Linux kernel, SELinux is a stable part of the operating system.

SELinux enriches the native discretionary model that characterizes Unix-like operating systems. Limitations of this model have been known for a long time and SELinux introduced an additional layer of protection. The approach took inspiration from classical mandatory models and looked at the experience in the use of these models. This led to an offer of higher expressivity and the possibility of flexibly controlling the behavior of the system. Initial experience in the use of SELinux demonstrated the difficulty of putting an additional layer of access control in an existing system: Users encountered frequent situations where the new access control services were blocking the execution of legitimate applications. Progressively, the technology has evolved, and the policies have been greatly refined. Today the presence of SELinux in a system that only uses standard applications and modules does not exhibit anomalies, at the same time offering increased protection against misuse.

The approach used by SELinux relies on the idea of associating a context with three components (role, user name, and domain) to users and processes of the system. Labels with the same structure are assigned to resources in the system. Processes typically inherit the context of the user that invoked the process, except when an explicit policy rule permits change of the running context. A policy defines the compatibility rules among contexts and labels. Typically, processes are only authorized to access resources characterized by a label compatible with the process context (in the same domain). Specific resources that may need to be accessed by a variety of processes will be associated with less restrictive rules. In general, the SELinux policy permits building a rigid compartmentalization among the resources of a system, greatly limiting the possibility that a vulnerability in some process or protocol would lead to the manipulation of a critical resource and the consequent compromise of the system.

An interesting feature of SELinux is the way the policy is defined and applied. A policy language is used to express the policy that a system must follow. Tools are also offered that assist the administrator in the design of the policy. The policy is then compiled, a low-level configuration is produced, and each element is then associated with the resources that will be protected. The compilation phase is introduced to improve the performance and to distribute the policy to all the elements of the system responsible for the protection. This approach is consistent with the idea of using a high-level representation of the policy valid for the whole system, which is then mapped to a low-level configuration to realize its objectives. This can be considered a realization at the level of a single system of the PBM approach, which has as its goal the security management of distributed systems. The success of SELinux can be considered a valid demonstration of the advantages of such an approach. Recently, the SEAndroid initiative has started, which aims at improving the security of the Android environment with the adaptation of the SELinux approach to it.

6. RESEARCH PROJECTS

Policies and policy-based management has been a research topic for several decades, and, due to its ambition as well as technological advancements, will remain so for a number of years. This section introduces the approach of two public-funded projects to PBM. First, we will introduce Ponder, a project conducted in the early 1990s that is considered a forerunner in the use of policies for system management. Second, we will describe PoSecCo, a project started in 2010, which looks at optimization problems related to policy refinement, the embedding of PBM into organizational processes, as well as policy-based audits. One important difference between the two is that Ponder relies on agents to enforce (AC) policies, while PoSecCo discovers and uses standard security capabilities available in virtually every given system.

Ponder

Ponder is a generic policy framework that was developed by the Policy Research Group of Imperial College in London. It features a policy specification language [28] and a toolkit with a management console tool for dynamically managing policies using policy enforcement agents. Its goal is to support security and management policy specification in large-scale distributed systems.

The Ponder language is *declarative* and *object-oriented*. Everything is represented by an object interface, and policies are written in terms of interface methods. It includes grouping constructs and policy inheritance useful for scalability purposes in large systems. The basic policy types in Ponder are (positive and negative) authorization, refrain, obligation, and delegation policies. Meta-policies are also supported to constrain the acceptable types of policies in the system. Policies can be specified directly as instances or as reusable parameterized template-like policy types from which multiple instances can be created by passing the actual parameters.

In Ponder, administrators create and edit policies using an administration tool. The administration tool includes a policy compiler that transforms the policies to policy classes that are stored in a policy server that acts as a central point of management. Policies can be loaded, unloaded, enabled, and disabled. The description of the system to manage is made using *domains*. A domain is a filesystem-like hierarchy that is used to group objects such as users, resources, services, and devices into categories for management purposes with parent–children policy propagation methods. A *domain service* keeps track of objects in the domain hierarchy and is responsible for evaluating policy subject and target sets at runtime. As domains change dynamically, the domain server maintains the references to all the installed policies that apply to each subdomain. When the domain hierarchy changes, the relevant policy objects are notified of the change.

The enforcement is left to a set of enforcement agents. When policies are loaded, policy objects distribute enforcement classes to the enforcement agents, which are destroyed when policies are unloaded. On the other hand, the enforcement classes react to enable and disable events. In case of authorization policies, the enforcement agent is the access controller of the target object, and for obligation and refrain policies, it is the subject policy management agent. Policy management agents of obligation policies register themselves to receive certain events from the *event server* that collects system events and notifies the registered event subscribers so that obligation policies can be triggered. The Ponder architecture is sketched in Figure 23.11.

Ponder presented some limitation on flexibility due to the centralized management of the enforcement. For this reason, Ponder2 has been developed. Ponder2 provides a new framework for an event-based enforcement wherein management services implement self-management cells that interact with each other through asynchronous events. It comprises an API, a shell that can be used to perform various maintenance actions, and a compiler/interpreter for PonderTalk, the Ponder2 management and policy specification language based on SmallTalk. Ponder2 inherits from its ancestor the authorization and obligation policy models, but it acts differently by giving more emphasis to

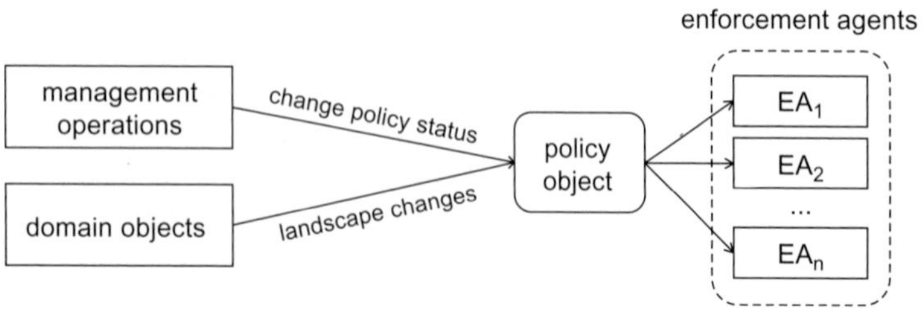

FIGURE 23.11   Ponder reference architecture.

enforcement agents

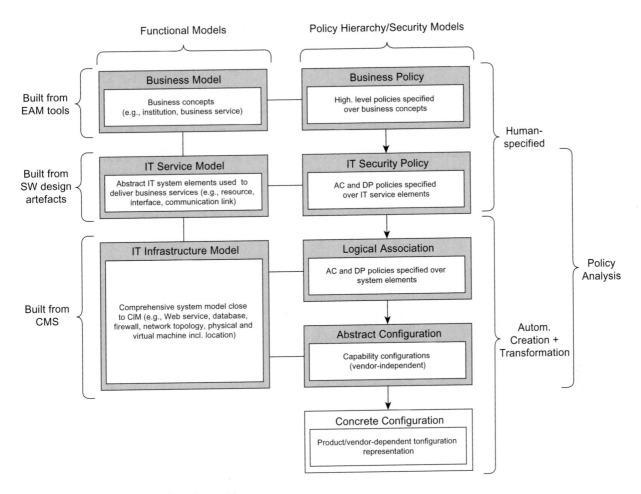

Functional Models | Policy Hierarchy/Security Models

FIGURE 23.12 PoSecCo system and security models.

the dynamic aspects of a system. For example, it supports changes, activation, and deactivation of policies while the system is running, without requiring the system to stop.

PoSecCo

The research project PoSecCo[10] focuses on securing shared IT systems that are used by service providers to deliver to end-users business (application) services, which consist of elements that are in parts operated internally and in other parts provided by outsourcing or cloud providers. Since the project relies on off-the-shelf security capabilities (for enforcing security policies), rather than developing new kinds of policy enforcement points, it bridges the gap between policy-related research and purist policy systems on the one hand, and today's IT systems and management practice on the other hand. This approach aims at rendering research results more applicable to real-world systems and is accompanied by the

consideration of economic and organizational considerations around the design and runtime of a security concept.

System and Security Model

The policy hierarchy of PoSecCo consists of five layers, four of which correspond to different abstraction levels linked to a functional counterpart, while the fifth represents concrete configuration information for security mechanisms. Figure 23.12 visualizes the relationships between functional and security models belonging to the different abstraction levels and also mentions how each of the models is built.

A *Business policy* represents a high-level requirement provided by management or stemming from laws, regulations, or customers. Business policies are associated with risks that express the probability of a threat to negatively impact assets or asset classes [53]. The latter are generic concepts that can be linked to arbitrary elements of the *Business Model*, which in turn comprises general business concepts relevant for organizations (institution, business service, customer, organizational role, business information).

10. Policy and Security Configuration Management (http://www. posecco.eu).

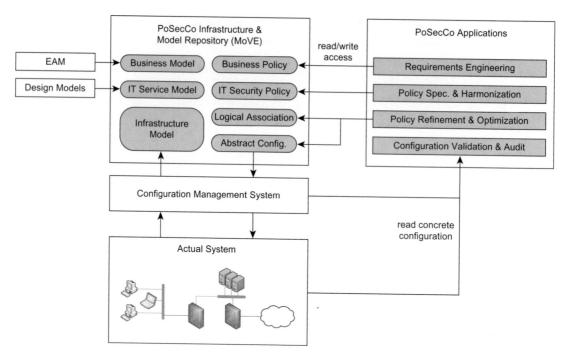

FIGURE 23.13   PoSecCo architecture.

Business policies have a defined structure and can be organized in a hierarchy, but its core is represented in natural language. Business policies are typically created by business and legal stakeholders (management or data protection officers). There exists no dedicated policy language for representing business policies, and the semiformal nature of business policies hampers automated reasoning.

An *IT security policy* represents an Access Control or Data Protection (DP) policy that contributes to the fulfillment of one or several business policies. They are specified over concepts of the *IT Service Model*, which describes the interaction of logical IT resources in order to realize a given business service. Logical IT resources abstract software components present in an actual system, which allows the specification of security policies without considering implementation details. IT security policies are again specified by humans, in particular by security architects, who have the required knowledge to specify appropriate AC or DP policies. IT security policies (as well as lower-level policy representations) are represented by means of an ontology (OWL-DL), which allows the automation of reasoning tasks (conflict or enforceability analysis).

A *Logical association* specifies a security property over two system elements that represent endpoints of a communication link. As such, they refine an IT security policy to the level of the real system, which is described by the *Infrastructure Model*. This topology-aware representation of an IT Security Policy represents the basis for the search and selection of security capabilities that are suitable for enforcing a given policy. A policy demanding

a "secure channel" between two communication endpoints, for instance, can be enforced by several capabilities offered "along the way" (the capability of VPN concentrators to establish a VPN connection), or the capability of an application server to support SSL/TLS. The refinement to logical associations and the discovery of suitable enforcement mechanisms is again done with the help of an ontology. Every security mechanism found is then assessed by performance, cost, and security functions that aim at choosing the "best" alternative.

Once a human chooses one (or several) of the security mechanisms proposed for implementation, a so-called abstract configuration is created, which configures a capability in a vendor and product-independent manner. The abstract configuration again gets transformed into a concrete configuration that is understood by the device offering the respective capability. Its representation or format is hence determined by the respective system element.

The policy hierarchy is constructed during the *Plan* and *Do* phases of the classical security life cycle and terminates with the deployment of concrete configurations. The hierarchy will then be used to deal with ongoing requirement and system changes at operations time.

System architecture. The PoSecCo architecture (cf. Figure 23.13) is centered on a model repository called MoVE,[11] which has been chosen to manage all functional and security models. Each of them is stored and versioned independently of each other, but related concepts can be

---

11. Model Versioning and Evolution (http://move.q-e.at/).

associated by cross-model links. The model repository offers a coarse-grained XMI interface for reading and writing entire models, as well as fine-grained create, read, update and delete (CRUD) operations for the manipulation of single-model elements. Moreover, it supports the definition of state-machines for single classes, whereby state changes result in corresponding events that can be used to trigger other actions. Finally, MoVE offers an OCL interface to query the models.

The business and IT service models of PoSecCo are created by interfacing Enterprise Architecture Management (EAM) systems and by reading software design artifacts (UML component diagrams). The infrastructure model is built by using the WBEM standards from DMTF to read information from Configuration Management Systems (CMS). Such tools represent an important building block of ITIL and commonly support CIM, which is in large part equivalent to the PoSecCo infrastructure model. CMS are also expected to transform and deploy the abstract configuration as soon as it has been completed at the end of the policy refinement process.

The policy hierarchy will then be constructed by so-called *PoSecCo applications* in a top-down manner, each of them using the MoVE API to read and manipulate model elements of its respective abstraction layer. The orchestration of these applications in the course of the plan and implementation phases of the security life cycle is realized by means of an event bus.[12] The change of policies on each abstraction layer results in state transitions that on the one hand persist in MoVE, and on the other hand are published to topics to which other PoSecCo applications can subscribe. The successful harmonization of IT policies by the application of *Policy Specification and Harmonization*, for instance, leads to a state transition from *UNVERIFIED* to *VERIFIED*, which is notified to the application *Policy Refinement and Optimization* for the continuation of the policy refinement.

Requirements Engineering

This PoSecCo application offers a Web-based environment for the specification, management, and monitoring of hierarchically organized security requirements (business policies in terms of PoSecCo). Requirements can be linked to various stakeholders within an organization as to express responsibility, accountability, or interest, which allows tying the hierarchy of requirements to the organizational structure. Different fulfillment models allow

---

12. An event bus is a middleware component supporting the publish/ subscribe communication model, where software components do not directly interact with each other, but communicate through events or messages mediated by the event bus. Events are produced (published) by a source component and consumed by one or multiple target components.

specifying under which conditions a requirement is considered fulfilled, partially fulfilled or not fulfilled, and whether such state changes can happen in an automated fashion or require human confirmation (which is limited in time as to force the continuous revalidation of requirements). Furthermore, different reporting views allow users to monitor requirements as to see the compliance rate of organizational units with given laws or regulations.

Policy Specification and Harmonization

This application offers the administrator access to the set of requirements specified in the previous phase and supports him or her in constructing a collection of instances of the IT Security Policy model able to represent the requirements. The IT Security Policy model focuses on the representation of access control and data protection requirements. The access control part supports the high-level formal description of the authentication and authorization profiles of applications.

For the authentication profile, the model considers the description of a variety of authentication techniques. The most common solution is the use of usernames and passwords, but richer solutions based on certificates, hardware tokens, and cryptographic credentials are supported. The model distinguishes between "direct" authentication solutions, where the system managing the authentication phase and verifying the correctness of the claimed identity of the user is the same that will offer the services, and "indirect" authentication solutions, where some support is received by external systems, responsible for the secure retrieval of the protected credential for the complete execution of the authentication phase.

For the authorization profile, the IT Security Policy model permits the representation of modern access control models. The central concepts of this part are the system authorization and the role authorization. These two constructs are integrated, and the possibility is offered to express declarative restrictions on the subject and the resource of an authorization. Authorizations have a sign, positive or negative, and, in general, DAC, MAC, RBAC, and ABAC models can be represented. The expressivity of the authorization model is loosely comparable to what can be achieved with XACML, even if the different assumptions about the structure of subjects and resources do not permit establishing a formal containment relationship between the models.

Once the IT policy has been defined, reasoning services are offered to verify whether the policy satisfies a number of consistency constraints. The checks that are supported focus on identification of modality conflicts, redundant authorizations, and violations of Separation-of-Duty (SoD) constraints. Modality conflicts arise when rules with conflicting signs apply to the same access request and a specified conflict resolution policy is not able to establish which of the rules has to be applied. The detection requires expanding all the subject and resource hierarchies that are used in the design of the IT Policy. Redundant authorizations are detected by looking for authorization rules that are dominated by other rules. These redundant rules can be omitted from the IT policy without changing system behavior. SoD constraints are specified using negative role authorizations, and violations are detected by identifying subjects that are able to acquire two roles denoted as conflicting. All the checks are implemented thanks to the use of Semantic Web tools, translating the IT policy into an OWL representation and then invoking adequate reasoning services. The outcome of this phase is a harmonized IT policy that is passed to the next phase.

Policy Refinement and Optimization

The harmonized IT Security Policy is the input, together with the landscape to configure, to the refinement phase that produces abstract configurations for the security controls available in the landscape. The Policy Refinement and Optimization application is a modular framework that drives the administrator in all the refinement phases and allows him or her to make informed decisions and to provide missing information. In fact, the Policy Refinement and Optimization application allows the selection of different refinement strategies (prefer the enforcement of security at the application layer, or message protection over channel protection, use infrastructure rather than the endpoint controls), or a manual selection of the devices to configure for each IT Security Policy.

The refinement is performed in two phases: the ontology-based refinement and the landscape configuration. During the ontology refinement, the IT Security Policy is enriched according to the landscape information using specialized ontologies that characterize the meaning of security concepts for each policy type (AC vs. DP) and for each device type (databases vs. operating systems). Moreover, the generated configurations are further adapted for the control that will actually enforce it (Windows vs. Linux AC policies) in order to simplify the transformation from abstract to concrete configurations. Additionally, the ontology also permits the automatic reasoning on the target landscape (to classify element according to the security level), to capture the complex dependencies among all the entities involved in policy enforcement and identify possible issues. Depending on the IT Security Policy to refine and the chosen strategy, the available controls are proposed for configuration according to their policy expressiveness and enforcement granularity, management costs, and the like, but the selection of the controls to actually configure is manually done by the administrators who have full control of AC policy enforcement. At the end of the

ontology refinement, the configurations for access control endpoint security controls are generated (operating systems, databases, Web service containers). Additionally, for the IT Security Policies that require a further refinement (to configure the firewalls to allow users to reach the services they are authorized to use), for the ones that administrators decided to enforce using infrastructure elements (using VPN gateways to protect the communications between two networks), or for the ones that are not enforceable with endpoint security, the ontology refinement outputs the Logical Associations that are the input for the landscape configuration phase.

The landscape configuration takes into account all the information about the target landscape, including all the infrastructure controls and the entire network topology. Since at this level many different alternatives are usually available (different available controls, different configuration modes, different paths, etc.), the selection of the controls to configure and the rules to configure them are decided through an optimization process that decides not only based on single-control configuration, but also at the global landscape level. Many target functions can be selected by the administrator to maximize the overall performance, to minimize the risk exposure, and other balanced combinations. Additionally, the entire process can be customized with additional constraints; for instance, it is possible to implement the defense in depth, to configure at least two redundant controls. For example, the best-practice for firewall configuration imposed to block prohibited traffic as soon as possible may force the use of the border firewall to implement most of the IT policy. According to security and performance considerations, the Policy Refinement and Optimization application can move some of the rules from the border firewall to the periphery to avoid performance degradation. Another example concerns channel protection controls, where it is possible to avoid redundant channels or to aggregate end-to-end connections into basic VPNs according to the trustworthiness of the involved networks to improve performance. At the end of these phases, all the missing abstract configurations are generated. The set of abstract configurations is provided to Configuration Management Systems, which are expected first to transform them into the representation required by the respective system element and then to deploy this concrete configuration as to enforce the policy.

Configuration Validation and Audit

The deployment of concrete configuration marks the end of the implementation phase of the security life cycle. The PoSecCo application *Configuration Validation and Audit* then checks the presence of a concrete configuration in order to validate the *operation effectiveness* of implemented security controls. This is achieved by using and extending the Security Content Automation Protocol (SCAP), a collection of standards developed by the NIST in order to foster the standardized representation, exchange, and automated processing of security knowledge. OVAL (Open Vulnerability Assessment Language), in particular, is used to check whether or not the PoSecCo-generated configuration is in place. Configuration discrepancies will be reflected by policy state changes on upper abstraction levels. The PCI DSS requirement to protect cardholder data, for instance, linked to the concrete configuration of a server's SSL feature, will enter the state *UNDER ANALYSIS* during the assessment of a configuration discrepancy, and *NOT FULFILLED* in case the assessment concludes that the discrepancy impacts security up to a point that the originating requirement is not fulfilled any longer (in case MD5 instead of SHA1 is used as a hash algorithm). In that context, OVAL has been extended to support the checking of application-level configurations in distributed environments, and to abstract check specifications from the way configuration is actually collected [54].

Operation effectiveness is one element of common IT audits, but alone is not sufficient to check whether a control framework put in place by an organization does address all security objectives and requirements. It is complemented by a check of the framework's *design effectiveness* in order to see whether planned controls are, in principle, suitable to reach the desired objectives (independent from the question of whether they have been implemented and properly configured). PoSecCo will support auditors and other stakeholders in this activity by allowing them to explore a subset of the models stored in MoVE and to formulate (OCL) queries. The subset defined depends on the actual audit scope, for example, a given business service and all connected elements. As an example, an auditor could query the model to check whether cardholder data is transmitted over communication links without a corresponding data protection policy. Finally, the model will also be used to generate draft audit programs that refer to OVAL checks for concrete configuration; these programs can be further enriched by auditors prior to the automated execution in the auditee's system. Here, the aim is to overcome today's audit practice of taking samples, but to enable complete and automated validation of all relevant configurations.

7. SUMMARY

This chapter briefly sketched different aspects of policy-based system management. It outlines achievements made since the late 1980s, when policies were first considered for system management purposes concerningareas such as policy information models, specification languages, or policy refinement and conflict detection. Some of this work

culminated in international standards that foster a broader adoption of PBM. IBM succeeded in establishing the vision of autonomic computing, which forecasts the long-term development of future IT systems founded on mature and broadly applied policy technologies and techniques. This vision drives technology researchers from academia and industry, but it also serves as a vehicle to discuss nontechnical matters related to autonomous and self-managing IT systems (ethical and socioeconomic questions).

Today, we observe that policy concepts are increasingly adopted by commercial products used in real-life systems. It comes without surprise that this application started by looking into single domains (network management), specification of access control policies, or system management. This restricted focus facilitates the implementation, and already suffices to realize economic benefits and service quality improvements. As yet, however, there exists no implementation of a PBM system that takes a holistic view of the many different kinds of policies at their various abstraction levels, and that considers the interdependencies of security mechanisms at various architecture layers. Moreover, today's application of PBM targets primarily the management of administrative domains belonging to one organizational entity, while new technologies and business models, such as virtualization and cloud services, result in the collaboration of many organizations across all layers of the application stack.

As such, at least two major technical challenges need to be addressed in order to move toward autonomous systems: (1) the detection of policy conflicts across architectural layers (cf. Chapter 45) and (2) the policy-based negotiation and collaboration of system elements that belong to different organizational entities (business partners). Efforts in the latter direction comprise, for instance, work on the high-level description of nonfunctional service properties and requirements, including security, which represents the basis for discovery and negotiation capabilities. This topic also stretches across compositional security, which investigates the preservation of security properties when systems are constructed from smaller components (with given properties).

We believe that the further development and increased adoption of policy technology by the IT industry strongly depends on the use of common specification languages, protocols, and architectures. While typical problems related to standardization also apply to the area of PBM (the fact that long-running standardization processes are sometimes outpaced by technological developments or undermined by strong market participants who seek to establish proprietary technology), we observe that past standardization efforts related to policies prove to be very successful. The DMTF standards CIM and WBEM are broadly supported by state-of-the-art tools for system management.

Finally, let's move on to the real interactive part of this chapter: review questions/exercises, hands-on projects, case projects, and optional team case project. The answers and/or solutions by chapter can be found in the Online Instructor's Solutions Manual.

CHAPTER REVIEW QUESTIONS/EXERCISES

True/False

1. True or False? Policy-driven system management or policy-based management (PBM) is a research domain that aims at automatizing the management of small-scale computing systems.
2. True or False? IT systems are untraditionally structured according to several architecture layers, each layer offering a number of security capabilities that can support organizations in reaching desired security objectives.
3. True or False? Security management as performed today involves a variety of stakeholders with different job functions, expertise, and objectives, and using different tools and terminology.
4. True or False? Generally speaking, a policy is a definite goal, course or method of action to guide and determine present and future decisions.
5. True or False? The approach of PBM naturally leads to a so-called policy continuum, a hierarchy of policies that are subject to the same abstraction levels.

Multiple Choice

1. What makes it impractical to specify policies for individual system elements?
   A. Smaller systems
   B. Larger systems
   C. Management systems
   D. Network systems
   E. All of the above
2. What increases the correctness and consistency of configuration information, speeds up deployment processes, and supporst a variety of other security-related activities such as IT audits?
   A. Smaller systems
   B. Larger systems
   C. Configuration management systems
   D. Network systems
   E. All of the above
3. What requires a set of common functionalities related to the creation, storage, distribution, and enforcement of policies?
   A. Smaller systems
   B. Larger systems
   C. Policy-based systems

D. Configuration management systems
E. Network systems
4. What term has been coined by IBM to denote computing systems that manage themselves?
   A. Autonomic computin
   B. Self-protection
   C. Self-healing
   D. Autonomic elements
   E. All of the above
5. An important aspect in the design and implementation of a secure information system is the correct consideration of:
   A. remote control software
   B. email
   C. USB storage
   D. security principles
   E. risk analysis

EXERCISE

Problem

How long does ISO certification/accreditation take?

Hands-On Projects

Project

What happens after ISO certification/accreditation?

Case Projects

Problem

What if an organization has an accident, incident, or complaint?

Optional Team Case Project

Problem

What is the difference between major and minor nonconformance?

ACKNOWLEDGMENTS

This work was partially funded by the European Community in the scope of the research project PoSecCo (project no. 257129), under the Information and Communication Technologies (ICT) theme of the 7th Framework Programme for R&D (FP7). The PoSecCo general approach, methodology, and architecture stem from the joint efforts of all consortium partners. The work by Stefano Paraboschi was partially supported by the PRIN 2008 project PEPPER (2008SY2PH4).

REFERENCES

[1] F. Liu, J. Tong, J. Mao, R. Bohn, J. Messina, L. Badger, et al., NIST Cloud Computing Reference Architecture, National Institute of Standards and Technology (NIST), 2011.

[2] BSI: Standard 100-1: Information Security Management Systems (ISMS). URL: <https://www.bsi.bund.de/SharedDocs/Downloads/EN/BSI/Publications/BSIStandards/standard_100-1_e_pdf.pdf>, 2008.

[3] W.E. Deming, Out of the Crisis, MIT Center for Advanced Engineering Study, 1986.

[4] PCI Security Standards Council LLC: PCI DSS requirements and security assessment procedures. (2010).

[5] IBM: IBM Corporate Strategy Analysis of IDC Data. (2007).

[6] K. Kark, L.M. Orlov, S. Bright, How to manage your information security policy framework (2006).

[7] W.H. Baker, A. Hutton, C.D. Hylender, C. Novak, C. Porter, B. Sartin, et al., 2009 data breach investigations report. URL <http://www.verizonbusiness.com/resources/security/reports/2009_databreach_rp.pdf> 2009.

[8] J. Williams, D. Wichers, Top 10 most critical web application security risks. URL <https://www.owasp.org/index.php/Top_10_2010-A6> 2010.

[9] C. Maple, A. Philips, UK security breach investigations report 2010. URL <http://www.7safe.com/breach_report/Breach_report_2010.pdf> 2010.

[10] E.A. Westerinen, RFC 3198—Terminology for policy-based management. URL <http://www.ietf.org/rfc/rfc3198> 2001.

[11] D. Agrawal, S. Calo, K.W. Lee, J. Lobo, D. Verma, Policy Technology for Self-Managing Systems, IBM Press, 2009.

[12] Moore: RFC 3460—Policy Core Information Model (PCIM) extensions. URL <http://www.ietf.org/rfc/rfc3460> 2003.

[13] J. Strassner, How policy empowers business-driven device management, Proceedings of the 3rd International Workshop on Policies for Distributed Systems and Networks (POLICY'02). POLICY '02, IEEE Computer Society, Washington, DC, USA, 2002214ff.

[14] R. Boutaba, I. Aib, Policy-based management: a historical perspective, J. Netw. Syst. Manage. 15 (4) (2007) 447–480.

[15] M. Sloman, Policy driven management for distributed systems, J. Netw. Sys.Manage. 2 (1994) 333–360.

[16] S.R. White, J.E. Hanson, I. Whalley, D.M. Chess, J.O. Kephart, An architectural approach to autonomic computing, Auton. Comput., Int. Conf. on 0 (2004) 2–9.

[17] R. Wies, Policy definition and classification: Aspects, criteria, and examples. In: IEEE/IFIP Workshop on Distributed Systems Operations and Management. (1994) 10–12.

[18] E. Lupu, M. Sloman, Conflicts in policy-based distributed systems management. Software engineering, IEEE Transactions on 25 (6) (1999) 852–869.

[19] E. Al-Shaer, H. Hamed, R. Boutaba, M. Hasan, Conflict classification and analysis of distributed firewall policies. Selected areas in communications, IEEE J. 23 (10) (2005) 2069–2084.

[20] G. Waters, J. Wheeler, A. Westerinen, L. Rafalow, R. Moore, Policy framework architecture (IETF Internet-Draft <draft-ietf-policy-arch-00.txt>) (1999).

[21] M.C. Huebscher, J.A. McCann, A survey of autonomic computing—degrees, models, and applications, ACM Comput. Surv. 40 (3) (2008) 7:1–7.28.

[22] P. Horn, Autonomic computing: IBMs perspective on the state of information technology. URL <http://researchweb.watson.ibm.com/autonomic/manifesto/autonomic_computing.pdf> 2001.

[23] J.H. Saltzer, M.D. Schroeder, The protection of information in computer systems, Proc. of the IEEE 63 (9) (1975) 1278–1308.

[24] D.E. Bell, L.J. LaPadula, Secure Computer Systems: Mathematical Foundations, Technical Report MTR-2547, Vol. 1, MITRE Corp, Bedford, MA, 1973.

[25] K.J. Biba, Integrity considerations for secure computer systems. Technical Report ESD-TR-76-372, USAF Electronic systems division, Bedford, MA (1977). (Also available through National Technical Information Service, Springfield, VA, NTIS AD-A039324.)

[26] D.F.C. Brewer, M.J. Nash, The Chinese wall security policy, IEEE Symp. Secur. Priv. (1989) 206–214.

[27] D. Ferraiolo, R. Kuhn, Role-based access control. In: 15th NIST-NCSC National Computer Security Conference (1992) 554–563.

[28] N. Damianou, N. Dulay, E. Lupu, M. Sloman, The ponder policy specification language, Proceedings of the International Workshop on Policies for Distributed Systems and Networks. POLICY '01, Springer-Verlag, London, UK, 200118–38

[29] S. Jajodia, M. Kudo, V.S. Subrahmanian, Provisional authorizations, E-Commerce Security and Privacy, Springer, 2001133–159

[30] K. Irwin, T. Yu, W.H. Winsborough, Assigning responsibilities for failed obligations. In: Proceedings of the IFIPTM Joined iTrust and PST Conference on Privacy, Trust Management and Security (iTrust). (June 2008) 327–342.

[31] P. Gama, P. Ferreira, Obligation policies: an enforcement platform, Proceedings of the Sixth IEEE International Workshop on Policies for Distributed Systems and Networks. POLICY '05, IEEE Computer Society, Washington, DC, USA, 2005203–212

[32] N. Li, H. Chen, E. Bertino, On practical specification and enforcement of obligations, Proceedings of the second ACM conference on Data and Application Security and Privacy. CODASPY '12, New York, NY, USA, ACM, 201271–82

[33] S. Bugiel, L.V. Davi, S. Schulz, Scalable trust establishment with software reputation, Proceedings of the sixth ACM workshop on Scalable trusted computing. STC '11, New York, NY, USA, ACM, 201115–24

[34] D. Taylor, J. Turner, Scalable packet classification using distributed crossproducting of field labels. Dept. of Computer Science and Engineering, George Washington University, Washington, DC, Tech. Rep. WUCSE-2004-38 (2004).

[35] K. Scarfone, P. Hoffman, NIST Special Publication 800-41: Guidelines on Firewalls and Firewall Policy, National Institute of Standards and Technology (NIST), 2009.

[36] E. Al-Shaer, H. Hamed, Modeling and management of firewall policies, IEEE Trans. Net. Serv. Manage. 1 (1) (2004) 2–10.

[37] C. Basile, A. Cappadonia, A. Lioy, Network-level access control policy analysis and transformation, IEEE/ACM Trans. Net. 20 (4) (2012) 985–998.

[38] A. El-Atawy, T. Samak, E. Al-Shaer, H. Li, Using Online Traffic Statistical Matching for Optimizing Packet Filtering Performance, INFOCOM, 2007866–874

[39] W.R. Cheswick, S.M. Bellovin, A.D. Rubin, Firewalls and Internet Security; Repelling the Wily Hacker, second ed., Addison-Wesley, Reading, MA, 2003.

[40] P. Ferguson, D. Senie, Network ingress filtering: defeating denial of service attacks which employ IP source address spoofing. RFC 2827 (Best Current Practice), Updated by RFC 3704 (2000).

[41] D. Harkins, D. Carrel, The internet key exchange (IKE). RFC 2409 (Proposed Standard), Obsoleted by RFC 4306, updated by RFC 4109 (1998).

[42] T. Dierks, E. Rescorla, The transport layer security (TLS) protocol version 1.2. RFC 5246 (Proposed Standard), Updated by RFCs 5746, 5878, 6176 (2008).

[43] E. Rescorla, N. Modadugu, Datagram Transport Layer Security Version 1.2. RFC 6347 (Proposed Standard) (2012).

[44] T. Phelan, Datagram Transport Layer Security (DTLS) over the Datagram Congestion Control Protocol (DCCP). RFC 5238 (Proposed Standard) (2008).

[45] A. Alshamsi, T. Saito, A technical comparison of IPsec and SSL, Proceedings of the 19th International Conference on Advanced Information Networking and Applications - Volume 2. AINA '05, IEEE Computer Society, Washington, DC, USA, 2005 395−398.

[46] B. Ramsdell, S. Turner, Secure/Multipurpose Internet Mail Extensions (S/MIME) Version 3.2 Message Specification. RFC 5751 (Proposed Standard) (2010).

[47] R. Housley, Cryptographic Message Syntax (CMS). RFC 5652 (Standard) (2009).

[48] Cisco Systems, Inc.: (Cisco adaptive security device manager — <http://www.cisco.com/en/US/products/ps6121/index.html>).

[49] NetCitadel LLC: (Firewall builder 5 user's guide - <http://www.fwbuilder.org/>.

[50] S. Godik, T. Moses (Eds.), eXtensible Access Control Markup Language (XACML) Version 1.0, 2003.

[51] C.A. Ardagna, S.D.C. di Vimercati, S. Paraboschi, E. Pedrini, P. Samarati, M. Verdicchio, Expressive and deployable access control in open web service applications, IEEE T. Serv. Comput. 4 (2) (2011) 96−109.

[52] A. Anderson (Ed.), XACML Profile for Role Based Access Control (RBAC) (2004).

[53] F. Innerhofer-Oberperer, R. Breu, M. Hafner, Living security—collaborative security management in a changing world. parallel and distributed computing and networks/720, Softw. Eng. (2011).

[54] M. Casalino, M. Mangili, H. Plate, S. Ponta, Detection of configuration vulnerabilities in distributed (web) environments (2012).

## Chapter 24

Information Technology Security Management

Rahul Bhaskar
California State University

Bhushan Kapoor
California State University

1. INFORMATION SECURITY MANAGEMENT STANDARDS

A range of standards are specified by various industry bodies. Although specific to an industry, these standards can be used by any organization and adapted to its goals. Here we discuss the main organizations that set standards related to information security management.

Federal Information Security Management Act

At the U.S. federal level, the National Institute of Standards and Technology (NIST) has specified guidelines for implementing the Federal Information Security Management Act (FISMA). This act aims to provide the following standards shown in Figure 24.1.

The "Federal Information Security Management Framework Recommended by NIST"[2] sidebar describes the risk management framework as specified in FISMA. The activities specified in this framework are paramount in implementing an IT security management plan. Although specified for the federal government, this framework can be used as a guideline by any organization.

International Standards Organization

Another influential international body, the International Standards Organization and the International Electro Technical Commission, published ISO/IEC 17799:2005.[3]

• Standards for categorizing information and information systems by mission impact
• Standards for minimum security requirements for information and information systems
• Guidance for selecting appropriate security controls for information systems
• Guidance for assessing security controls in information systems and determining security control effectiveness
• Guidance for certifying and accrediting information systems

FIGURE 24.1 Specifications in the Federal Information Security Management Act.[1]

---

1. "Federal Information Security Management Act," National Institute of Standards and Technology, http://csrc.nist.gov/groups/SMA/fisma/index.html, 2008 (downloaded 10/20/2008).

2. "Federal Information Security Management Act," National Institute of Standards and Technology, http://csrc.nist.gov/groups/SMA/fisma/index.html, 2008 (downloaded 10/20/2008).

3. "Information technology | Security techniques | Code of practice for information security management, ISO/IEC 17799," The International Standards Organization and The International Electro Technical Commission, www.iso.org/iso/iso_catalogue/catalogue_tc/catalogue_detail.htm?csnumber = 39612, 2005 (downloaded 10/20/2008).

Federal Information Security Management Framework Recommended by NIST

Step 1: Categorize
In this step, information systems and internal information should be categorized based on impact.

Step 2: Select
Use the categorization in the first step to select an initial set of security controls for the information system and apply tailoring guidance as appropriate, to obtain a starting point for required controls.

Step 3: Supplement
Assess the risk and local conditions, including the security requirements, specific threat information, and cost/benefit analyses or special circumstances. Supplement the initial set of security controls with the supplement analyses.

Step 4: Document
The original set of security controls and the supplements should be documented.

Step 5: Implement
The security controls you identified and supplemented should be implemented in the organization's information systems.

Step 6: Assess
The security controls should be assessed to determine whether the controls are implemented correctly, are operating as intended, and are producing the desired outcome with respect to meeting the security requirements for the system.

Step 7: Authorize
Upon a determination of the risk to organizational operations, organizational assets, or individuals resulting from their operation, authorize the information systems.

Step 8: Monitor
Monitor and assess selected security controls in the information system on a continuous basis, including documenting changes to the system.

These standards establish guidelines and general principles for initiating, implementing, maintaining, and improving information security management in an organization. The objectives outlined provide general guidance on the commonly accepted goals of information security management. The standards consist of best practices of control objectives and controls in the areas of information security management shown in Figure 24.2.

These objectives and controls are intended to be implemented to meet the requirements identified by a risk assessment.

2. OTHER ORGANIZATIONS INVOLVED IN STANDARDS

Other organizations that are involved in information security management include The Internet Society[4] and the Information Security Forum.[5] These are professional societies with members in the thousands. The Internet Society is the organization home for the groups responsible for Internet infrastructure standards, including the Internet Engineering Task Force (IETF) and the Internet Architecture Board (IAB). The Information Security Forum is a global nonprofit organization of several hundred leading organizations in financial services, manufacturing, telecommunications, consumer goods, government, and other areas. It provides research into best practices and advice, summarized in its biannual Standard of Good Practice, which incorporates detailed specifications across many areas.

3. INFORMATION TECHNOLOGY SECURITY ASPECTS

The various aspects to IT security in an organization that must be considered include:

- Security policies and procedures
- Security organization structure
- IT security processes
  - Processes for a business continuity strategy
  - Processes for IT security governance planning
- Rules and regulations

Security Policies and Procedures

Security policies and procedures constitute the main part of any organization's security. These steps are essential for implementing IT security management: authorizing security roles and responsibilities to various security personnel; setting rules for expected behavior from users and security role players; setting rules for business continuity plans; and more. The security policy should be generally agreed to by most personnel in the organization and should have the support of the highest-level management. This helps in prioritization at the overall organization level.

The following list, illustrated in Figure 24.3, is a sample of some of the issues an organization is expected to

---

4. "ISOC's Standards and Technology Activities," Internet Society, www.isoc.org/standards, 2008 (downloaded 10/20/2008).
5. "The Standard of Good Practice," Information Security Forum, https://www.securityforum.org/html/frameset.htm, 2008 (downloaded 10/20/2008).

| Security Policy |
| Organization of Information Security |
| Asset Management |
| Human Resources Security |
| Physical and Environmental Security |
| Communication and Operations Management |
| Access Control |
| Information Systems Acquisition, Development and Maintenance |
| Information Security Incident Management |
| Business Continuity Management |
| Compliance |

FIGURE 24.2   International Standards Organization best-practice areas.[7]

| Access Control Standards |
| Accountability |
| Audit Trails |
| Backups |
| Disposal of Media |
| Disposal of Printed Matter |
| Information Ownership |
| Managers Responsibility |
| Equipment |
| Communication |
| Procedures and Processes at Work |

FIGURE 24.3   Security aspects an organization is expected to address in its policies.

address in its policies.[6] Note, however, that the universal list is virtually endless, and each organization's list will consist of issues based on several factors, including its size and the value and sensitivity of the information it owns or deals with. Some important issues included in most security policies are:

- *Access control standards.* These are standards on controlling the access to various systems. These include password change standards.

- *Accountability.* Every user should be responsible for her own accounts. This implies that any activity under a particular user ID should be the responsibility of the user whose ID it is.

- *Audit trails.* There should be an audit trail recorded of all the activities under a user ID. For example, all the login, log-out activities for 30 days should be recorded. Additionally, all unauthorized attempts to access, read, write, and delete data and execute programs should be logged.

---

6. "Information technology | Security techniques | Code of practice for information security management, ISO/IEC 17799," The International Standards Organization and The International Electro Technical Commission, www.iso.org/iso (downloaded 10/20/2008).

7. "Information technology | Security techniques | Code of practice for information security management, ISO/IEC 17799," The International Standards Organization and The International Electro Technical Commission, www.iso.org/iso (downloaded 10/20/2008).

- *Backups.* There should be a clearly defined backup policy. Any backups should be kept in a secure area. A clear policy on the frequency of the backups and their recovery should be communicated to the appropriate personnel.
- *Disposal of media.* A clear policy should be defined regarding the disposal of media. This includes a policy on which hardware and storage media, such as disk drives, diskettes, and CD-ROMs, are to be destroyed. The level and method of destruction of business-critical information that is no longer needed should be well defined and documented. Personnel should be trained regularly on the principles to follow.
- *Disposal of printed matter.* Guidelines as to the disposal of printed matter should be specified and implemented throughout the organization. In particular, business-critical materials should be disposed properly and securely.
- *Information ownership.* All the data and information available in the organization should have an assigned owner. The owner should be responsible for deciding on access rights to the information for various personnel.
- *Managers' responsibility.* Managers at all levels should ensure that their staff understands the security policy and adheres to it continuously. They should be held responsible for recording any deviations from the core policy.
- *Equipment.* An organization should have specific guidelines about modems, portable storage, and other devices. These devices should be kept in a secured physical environment.
- *Communication.* Well-defined policy guidelines are needed for communication using corporate information systems. These include communications via emails, instant messaging, and so on.
- *Work procedures and processes.* Employees of an organization should be trained to secure their workstations when not in use. The policy can impose a procedure of logging off before leaving a workstation. It can also include quarantining any device (such as a laptop) brought from outside the organization before plugging it into the network.

Security Organization Structure

Various security-related roles need to be maintained and well defined. These roles and their brief descriptions are described here.[8]

End User

End users have a responsibility to protect information assets on a daily basis through adherence to the security policies that have been set and communicated. End-user compliance with security policies is key to maintaining information security in an organization because this group represents the most consistent users of the organization's information.

Executive Management

Top management plays an important role in protecting the information assets in an organization. Executive management can support the goal of IT security by conveying the extent to which management supports security goals and priorities. Members of the management team should be aware of the risks that they are accepting for the organization through their decisions or failure to make decisions. There are various specific areas on which senior management should focus, but some that are specifically appropriate are user training, inculcating and encouraging a security culture, and identifying the correct policies for IT security governance.

Security Officer

The security officer "directs, coordinates, plans, and organizes information security activities throughout the organization."[9]

Data/Information Owners

Every organization should have clearly identified data and information owners. These executives or managers should review the classification and access security policies and procedures. They should also be responsible for periodic audit of the information and data and its continuous security. They may appoint a data custodian in case the work required to secure the information and data is extensive and needs more than one person to complete.

Information System Auditor

Information system auditors are responsible for ensuring that the information security policies and procedures have been adhered to. They are also responsible for establishing the baseline, architecture, management direction, and compliance on a continuous basis. They are an essential part of unbiased information about the state of information security in the organization.

Information Technology Personnel

IT personnel are responsible for building IT security controls into the design and implementations of the systems. They are also responsible for testing these controls

8. Tipton and Krause, "Information Security Governance," *Information Security Management Handbook*, Auerbach Publications, 2008.

9. Tipton and Krause, "Information Security Governance," *Information Security Management Handbook*, Auerbach Publications, 2008.

periodically or whenever there is a change. They work with the executives and other managers to ensure compliance in all the systems under their responsibility.

Systems Administrator

A systems administrator is responsible for configuring the hardware and the operating system to ensure that the information systems and their contents are available for business as and when needed. These adminstrators are placed ideally in an organization to ensure security of these assets. They play a key role because they own access to the most vulnerable information assets of an organization.

IT Security Processes

To achieve effective IT security requires processes related to security management. These processes include business continuity strategy, processes related to IT security governance planning, and IT security management implementation.

Processes for a Business Continuity Strategy

As is the case with any strategy, the business continuity strategy depends on a commitment from senior management. This can include some of the analysis that is obtained by business impact assessment/risk analysis focused on business value drivers (see checklist: "An Agenda For Action For The Contingency Planning Process"). These business value drivers are determined by the main stakeholders from the organizations. Examples of these value drivers are customer service and intellectual property protection.[11]

Processes for IT Security Governance Planning

IT security governance planning includes prioritization as its major function. This helps in utilizing the limited sources of the organization. Determining priorities among the potential conflicting interests is the main focus of these processes. This includes budget setting, resource allocation, and, most important, the political process needed to prioritize in an organization.

Rules and Regulations

An organization is influenced by rules and regulations that influence its business. In a business environment marked by globalization, organizations have to be aware of both national and international rules and regulations. From an information security management perspective, various rules and regulations must be considered. These are listed in Figure 24.4. We give more details on some rules and regulations here:

- The Health Insurance Portability and Accountability Act (HIPAA) requires the adoption of national standards for electronic healthcare transactions and national identifiers for providers, health insurance plans, and employers. Healthcare providers have to protect the personal medical information of the customer to comply with this law. Similarly, the Gramm-Leach-Bliley Act of 1999 (GLBA), also known as the Financial Services Modernization Act of 1999, requires financial companies to protect the information about individuals that it collects during transactions.

- The Sarbanes-Oxley Act of 2002 (SOX). This law requires companies to protect and audit their financial data. The chief information officer and other senior executives are held responsible for reporting and

10. "Contingency Planning Process," DRII — The Institute for Continuity Management, https://www.drii.org/professional_prac/profprac_appen-dix.html#BUSINESS_CONTINUITY_PLANNING_INFORMATION, 2008 (downloaded 10/24/2008).

11. C. R. Jackson, "Developing Realistic Continuity Planning Process Metrics," *Information Security Management Handbook*, Auerbach Publications, 2008.

Health Insurance Portability and Accountability Act (HIPAA)
Gramm-Leach-Bliley Act
Sarbanes-Oxley Act of 2002
Security Breach Notification Laws
Personal Information Protection and Electronic Document Act (PIPEDA)
Computer Fraud and Abuse Act
USA PATRIOT Act

FIGURE 24.4 Rules and regulations related to information security management.

auditing an organization's financial information to regulatory and other agencies.

- State Security Breach Notification Laws (California and many others) require businesses, nonprofits, and state institutions to notify consumers when unencrypted "personal information" might have been compromised, lost, or stolen.
- The Personal Information Protection and Electronics Document Act (PIPEDA) supports and promotes electronic commerce by protecting personal information that is collected, used, or disclosed in certain circumstances, by providing for the use of electronic means to communicate or record information or transactions, and by amending the Canada Evidence Act, the Statutory Instruments Act, and the Statute Revision Act that is in fact the case.
- The Computer Fraud and Abuse Act, or CFAA (also known as Fraud and Related Activity in Connection with Computers), is a U.S. law passed in 1986 and intended to reduce computer crimes. It was amended in 1994, 1996, and 2001 by the U.S.A. PATRIOT Act.[12]

The following sidebar, "Computer Fraud and Abuse Act Criminal Offences," lists criminal offences covered under this law.[13]

The U.S.A. PATRIOT Act of 2001 increased the scope and penalties of this act by:

- Raising the maximum penalty for violations to ten years (from five) for a first offense and 20 years (from ten) for a second offense
- Ensuring that violators only need to intend to cause damage generally, not intend to cause damage or other

specified harm over the $5000 statutory damage threshold

- Allowing aggregation of damages to different computers over a year to reach the $5000 threshold
- Enhancing punishment for violations involving any (not just $5000 in) damage to a government computer involved in criminal justice or the military
- Including damage to foreign computers involved in U.S. interstate commerce
- Including state law offenses as priors for sentencing;
- Expanding the definition of loss to expressly include time spent investigating
- Responding (this is why it is important for damage assessment and restoration)

These details are summarized in Figure 24.5.

The PATRIOT Act of 2001 came under criticism for a number of reasons. There are fears that the Act is an invasion of privacy and infringement on freedom of speech. Critics also feel that the Act unfairly expands the powers of the executive branch and strips away many crucial checks and balances.

The original act has a sunset clause that would have caused many of the law's provisions to expire in 2005. The Act was reauthorized in early 2006 with some new safeguards and with expiration dates for its two most controversial powers, which authorize roving wiretaps and secret searches of records.

4. SUMMARY

Information technology security management consists of processes to enable organizational structure and technology to protect an organization's IT operations and assets against internal and external threats, intentional or otherwise. These processes are developed to ensure confidentiality, integrity, and availability of IT systems. There are various aspects to the IT security in an organization that need to be considered. These include security policies and procedures, security organization structure, IT security processes, and rules and regulations.

---

12. "Fraud and Related Activities in Relation to the Computers," U.S. Code Collection, Cornell University Law School, www4.law.cornell.edu/uscode/18/1030.html, 2008 (downloaded 10/24/2008).
13. "Fraud and Related Activities in Relation to the Computers," U.S. Code Collection, Cornell University Law School, www4.law.cornell.edu/uscode/18/1030.html, 2008 (downloaded 10/24/2008).

Maximum Penalty
Extent of Damage
Aggregation of Damage
Enhancement of Punishment
Damage to Foreign Computers
State Law Offenses
Expanding the Definition of Loss
Response

FIGURE 24.5 U.S.A. PATRIOT Act increase in scope and penalties.

Computer Fraud and Abuse Act Criminal Offences

(a) Whoever —

(1) having knowingly accessed a computer without authorization or exceeding authorized access, and by means of such conduct having obtained information that has been determined by the United States Government pursuant to an Executive order or statute to require protection against unauthorized disclosure for reasons of national defense or foreign relations, or any restricted data, as defined in paragraph y. of section 11 of the Atomic Energy Act of 1954, with reason to believe that such information so obtained could be used to the injury of the United States, or to the advantage of any foreign nation willfully communicates, delivers, transmits, or causes to be communicated, delivered, or transmitted, or attempts to communicate, deliver, transmit or cause to be communicated, delivered, or transmitted the same to any person not entitled to receive it, or willfully retains the same and fails to deliver it to the officer or employee of the United States entitled to receive it;

(2) intentionally accesses a computer without authorization or exceeds authorized access, and thereby obtains —

(A) information contained in a financial record of a financial institution, or of a card issuer as defined in section 1602 (n) of title 15, or contained in a file of a consumer reporting agency on a consumer, as such terms are defined in the Fair Credit Reporting Act (15 U.S.C. 1681 et seq.);

(B) information from any department or agency of the United States; or

(C) information from any protected computer if the conduct involved an interstate or foreign communication;

(3) intentionally, without authorization to access any non-public computer of a department or agency of the United States, accesses such a computer of that department or agency that is exclusively for the use of the Government of the United States or, in the case of a computer not exclusively for such use, is used by or for the Government of the United States and such conduct affects that use by or for the Government of the United States;

(4) knowingly and with intent to defraud, accesses a protected computer without authorization, or exceeds authorized access, and by means of such conduct furthers the intended fraud and obtains anything of value, unless the object of the fraud and the thing obtained consists only of the use of the computer and the value of such use is not more than $5,000 in any 1-year period;

(5)

(A)

(i) knowingly causes the transmission of a program, information, code, or command, and as a result of such conduct, intentionally causes damage without authorization, to a protected computer;

(ii) intentionally accesses a protected computer without authorization, and as a result of such conduct, recklessly causes damage; or

(iii) intentionally accesses a protected computer without authorization, and as a result of such conduct, causes damage; and

(B) by conduct described in clause (i), (ii), or (iii) of subparagraph (A), caused (or, in the case of an attempted offense, would, if completed, have caused) —

(i) loss to 1 or more persons during any 1-year period (and, for purposes of an investigation, prosecution, or other proceeding brought by the United States only, loss resulting from a related course of conduct affecting 1 or more other protected computers) aggregating at least $5,000 in value;

(ii) the modification or impairment, or potential modification or impairment, of the medical examination, diagnosis, treatment, or care of 1 or more individuals;

(iii) physical injury to any person;

(iv) a threat to public health or safety; or

(v) damage affecting a computer system used by or for a government entity in furtherance of the administration of justice, national defense, or national security;

(6) knowingly and with intent to defraud traffics (as defined in section 1029) in any password or similar information through which a computer may be accessed without authorization, if —

(A) such trafficking affects interstate or foreign commerce; or

(B) such computer is used by or for the Government of the United States;

(7) with intent to extort from any person any money or other thing of value, transmits in interstate or foreign commerce any communication containing any threat to cause damage to a protected computer; shall be punished as provided in subsection (c) of this section.

(b) Whoever attempts to commit an offense under subsection (a) of this section shall be punished as provided in subsection (c) of this section.

(c) The punishment for an offense under subsection (a) or (b) of this section is —

(1)

(A) a fine under this title or imprisonment for not more than ten years, or both, in the case of an offense under subsection (a)(1) of this section which does not occur after a conviction for another offense under this section, or an attempt to commit an offense punishable under this subparagraph; and

(B) a fine under this title or imprisonment for not more than twenty years, or both, in the case of an offense under subsection (a)(1) of this section which occurs after a conviction for another offense under this section, or an attempt to commit an offense punishable under this subparagraph;

(2)

(A) except as provided in subparagraph (B), a fine under this title or imprisonment for not more than one year, or both, in the case of an offense under subsection (a)(2), (a)(3), (a)(5)(A)(iii), or (a)(6) of this section which does not occur after a conviction for another offense under this section, or an attempt to commit an offense punishable under this subparagraph;

(B) a fine under this title or imprisonment for not more than 5 years, or both, in the case of an offense under subsection (a)(2), or an attempt to commit an offense punishable under this subparagraph, if —

(i) the offense was committed for purposes of commercial advantage or private financial gain;

(ii) the offense was committed in furtherance of any criminal or tortious act in violation of the Constitution or laws of the United States or of any State; or

(iii) the value of the information obtained exceeds $5,000; and

(C) a fine under this title or imprisonment for not more than ten years, or both, in the case of an offense under subsection (a)(2), (a)(3) or (a)(6) of this section which occurs after a conviction for another offense under this section, or an attempt to commit an offense punishable under this subparagraph;

(3)

(A) a fine under this title or imprisonment for not more than five years, or both, in the case of an offense under subsection (a)(4) or (a)(7) of this section which does not occur after a conviction for another offense under this section, or an attempt to commit an offense punishable under this subparagraph; and

(B) a fine under this title or imprisonment for not more than ten years, or both, in the case of an offense under subsection (a)(4), (a)(5)(A)(iii), or (a)(7) of this section which occurs after a conviction for another offense under this section, or an attempt to commit an offense punishable under this subparagraph;

(4)

(A) except as provided in paragraph (5), a fine under this title, imprisonment for not more than 10 years, or both, in the case of an offense under subsection (a)(5)(A)(i), or an attempt to commit an offense punishable under that subsection;

(B) a fine under this title, imprisonment for not more than 5 years, or both, in the case of an offense under subsection (a)(5)(A)(ii), or an attempt to commit an offense punishable under that subsection;

(C) except as provided in paragraph (5), a fine under this title, imprisonment for not more than 20 years, or both, in the case of an offense under subsection (a)(5)(A)(i) or (a)(5)(A)(ii), or an attempt to commit an offense punishable under either subsection, that occurs after a conviction for another offense under this section; and

(5)

(A) if the offender knowingly or recklessly causes or attempts to cause serious bodily injury from conduct in violation of subsection (a)(5)(A)(i), a fine under this title or imprisonment for not more than 20 years, or both; and

(B) if the offender knowingly or recklessly causes or attempts to cause death from conduct in violation of subsection (a)(5)(A)(i), a fine under this title or imprisonment for any term of years or for life, or both.

(d)

(1) The United States Secret Service shall, in addition to any other agency having such authority, have the authority to investigate offenses under this section.

(2) The Federal Bureau of Investigation shall have primary authority to investigate offenses under subsection (a)(1) for any cases involving espionage, foreign counterintelligence, information protected against unauthorized disclosure for reasons of national defense or foreign relations, or Restricted Data (as that term is defined in section 11y of the Atomic Energy Act of 1954 (42 U.S.C. 2014 (y)), except for offenses affecting the duties of the United States Secret Service pursuant to section 3056 (a) of this title.

(3) Such authority shall be exercised in accordance with an agreement which shall be entered into by the Secretary of the Treasury and the Attorney General.

(e) As used in this section —

(1) the term "computer" means an electronic, magnetic, optical, electrochemical, or other high speed data processing device performing logical, arithmetic, or storage functions, and includes any data storage facility or communications facility directly related to or operating in conjunction with such device, but such term does not include an automated typewriter or typesetter, a portable hand held calculator, or other similar device;

(2) the term "protected computer" means a computer —

(A) exclusively for the use of a financial institution or the United States Government, or, in the case of a computer not exclusively for such use, used by or for a financial institution or the United States Government and the conduct constituting the offense affects that use by or for the financial institution or the Government; or

(B) which is used in interstate or foreign commerce or communication, including a computer located outside the United States that is used in a manner that affects interstate or foreign commerce or communication of the United States;

(3) the term "State" includes the District of Columbia, the Commonwealth of Puerto Rico, and any other commonwealth, possession or territory of the United States;

(4) the term "financial institution" means —

(A) an institution, with deposits insured by the Federal Deposit Insurance Corporation;

(B) the Federal Reserve or a member of the Federal Reserve including any Federal Reserve Bank;

(C) a credit union with accounts insured by the National Credit Union Administration;

(D) a member of the Federal home loan bank system and any home loan bank;

(E) any institution of the Farm Credit System under the Farm Credit Act of 1971;

(F) a broker-dealer registered with the Securities and Exchange Commission pursuant to section 15 of the Securities Exchange Act of 1934;

(G) the Securities Investor Protection Corporation;

(H) a branch or agency of a foreign bank (as such terms are defined in paragraphs (1) and (3) of section 1(b) of the International Banking Act of 1978); and

(I) an organization operating under section 25 or section 25(a) [2] of the Federal Reserve Act;

(5) the term "financial record" means information derived from any record held by a financial institution pertaining to a customer's relationship with the financial institution;

(6) the term "exceeds authorized access" means to access a computer with authorization and to use such access to obtain or alter information in the computer that the accesser is not entitled so to obtain or alter;

(7) the term "department of the United States" means the legislative or judicial branch of the Government or one of the executive departments enumerated in section 101 of title 5;

(8) the term "damage" means any impairment to the integrity or availability of data, a program, a system, or information;

(9) the term "government entity" includes the Government of the United States, any State or political subdivision of the United States, any foreign country, and any state, province, municipality, or other political subdivision of a foreign country;

(10) the term "conviction" shall include a conviction under the law of any State for a crime punishable by imprisonment for more than 1 year, an element of which is unauthorized access, or exceeding authorized access, to a computer;

(11) the term "loss" means any reasonable cost to any victim, including the cost of responding to an offense, conducting a damage assessment, and restoring the data, program, system, or information to its condition prior to the offense, and any revenue lost, cost incurred, or other consequential damages incurred because of interruption of service; and

(12) the term "person" means any individual, firm, corporation, educational institution, financial institution, governmental entity, or legal or other entity.

(f) This section does not prohibit any lawfully authorized investigative, protective, or intelligence activity of a law enforcement agency of the United States, a State, or a political subdivision of a State, or of an intelligence agency of the United States.

(g) Any person who suffers damage or loss by reason of a violation of this section may maintain a civil action against the violator to obtain compensatory damages and injunctive relief or other equitable relief. A civil action for a violation of this section may be brought only if the conduct involves 1 of the factors set forth in clause (i), (ii), (iii), (iv), or (v) of subsection (a)(5)(B). Damages for a violation involving only conduct described in subsection (a)(5)(B)(i) are limited to economic damages. No action may be brought under this subsection unless such action is begun within 2 years of the date of the act complained of or the date of the discovery of the damage. No action may be brought under this subsection for the negligent design or manufacture of computer hardware, computer software, or firmware.

(h) The Attorney General and the Secretary of the Treasury shall report to the Congress annually, during the first 3 years following the date of the enactment of this subsection, concerning investigations and prosecutions under subsection (a)(5).

Security policies and procedures are essential for implementing IT security management: authorizing security roles and responsibilities to various security personnel; setting rules for expected behavior from users and security role players; setting rules for business continuity plans; and more. The security policy should be generally agreed to by most personnel in the organization and have support from high-level management. This helps in prioritization at the overall organization level. The IT security processes are essentially part of an organization's risk management processes and business continuity strategies. In a business environment marked by globalization, organizations have to be aware of both national and international rules and regulations. Their information security and privacy policies must conform to these rules and regulations.

Finally, let's move on to the real interactive part of this Chapter: review questions/exercises, hands-on projects, case projects and optional team case project. The answers and/or solutions by chapter can be found in the Online Instructor's Solutions Manual.

CHAPTER REVIEW QUESTIONS/EXERCISES

True/False

1. True or False? Security policies and procedures do not constitute the main part of any organization's security.
2. True or False? Various security-related roles do not need to be maintained and well defined.
3. True or False? End users have a responsibility to protect information assets on a daily basis through adherence to the security policies that have been set and communicated.
4. True or False? Top management does not play an important role in protecting the information assets in an organization.
5. True or False? The security officer "directs, coordinates, plans, and organizes information security activities throughout the organization.

Multiple Choice

1. Who are responsible for ensuring that the information security policies and procedures have been adhered to?
   A. Information owners
   B. Information system auditors
   C. Security officers
   D. Executive management
   E. All of the above
2. Who is responsible for building IT security controls into the design and implementations of the systems?
   A. Information owners
   B. Information system auditors

C. IT personnel
   D. Systems Administrator
   E. All of the above
3. Who is responsible for configuring the hardware and the operating system to ensure that the information systems and their contents are available for business as and when needed?
   A. Information System Auditor
   B. Information Owners
   C. Systems Administrator
   D. Security Officer
   E. Executive Management
4. What analyzes the impact of outage on critical business function operations?
   A. Risk assessment
   B. Recovery strategy identification
   C. Recovery strategy selection
   D. Business impact analysis
   E. All of the above
5. What documents the processes, equipment, and facilities required to restore the IT assets?
   A. Contingency plan development
   B. User training
   C. Plan verification
   D. Plan maintenance
   E. Recovery strategy selection

EXERCISE

Problem

Why does an organization need a Business Continuity Plan (BCP)?

Hands-On Projects

Project

How often should the BCP / DR (Disaster Recovery) plans be reviewed?

Case Projects

Problem

What are some guidelines for identifying mission critical functions?

Optional Team Case Project

Problem

Why should an organization certify their IT security management system?

## Chapter 25

Online Identity and User Management Services

Tewfiq El Maliki

University of Applied Sciences of Geneva, tewfiq.elmaliki@hesge.ch

Jean-Marc Seigneur

University of Geneva, jean-marc.seigneur@reputaction.com

1. INTRODUCTION

Anytime, anywhere mobile computing is becoming easier, more attractive and even cost-effective: the mobile devices carried by the roaming users offer more and more computing power and functionalities including sensing and providing location-awareness [1]. A lot of computing devices are also deployed in the environments where the users evolve; for example, intelligent home appliances or RFID-enabled fabrics. In this ambient intelligent world, the choices of identity mechanisms will have a large impact on social, cultural, business and political aspects. Moreover, Internet of things will generate more complicated privacy problems [2]. Identity has become a burden on the online world. When it is stolen it engenders a massive fraud, principally in online services which generate a lack of confidence in doing business for providers and frustration for users.

Therefore, the whole of society would suffer from the demise of privacy which is a real human need. As people have hectic live and cannot spend their time administering their digital identities, we need consistent identity management platforms and technologies enabling usability and scalability among others [3]. In this paper, we survey how the requirements have evolved for mobile user-centric identity management and their associated technologies.

The chapter is organized as follows. First, we present the evolution of identity management requirements. Section 4 surveys how the different most advanced identity management technologies fulfill present day requirements. Section 5 covers "social login" that is the major identity management technical solution that has emerged after writing the first version of this book chapter and that has nowadays gained a stronger user adoption than the other solutions surveyed in Section 4 although a few of them are used underneath "social login". Section 6 discusses how mobility can be achieved in the field of identity management in an ambient intelligent/ubiquitous computing world.

2. EVOLUTION OF IDENTITY MANAGEMENT REQUIREMENTS

In this section, we first define what we mean by a digital identity. Later in the chapter, we summarize all the different requirements and detail the most important ones in the following subsections, namely, privacy, usability and mobility.

Digital Identity Definition

A digital identity is a representation of an entity in a specific context [4]. For a long time, a digital identity was considered as the equivalent of our real life identity which indicates some of our attributes:

- Who we are, Name, Citizenship, Birthday;
- What we like, our favorite Reading, Food, Clothes, etc;
- What our reputation is, whether we are honest, without any problems, etc.

A digital identity was seen as an extended identity card or passport containing almost the same information. However, recent work [5] has argued that the link between the real-world identity and a digital identity is not always mandatory. For example, on e-Bay what matters is to know whether the seller's digital identity reputation has been remarkable and that the seller can prove that she controls that digital identity. It is less important to know that her real-world national identity is from the Bermuda Islands, where suing anybody is rather unlikely to succeed. It should be underlined that in a major identity management initiative [6], a digital identity is defined as "the distinguishing character or personality of an individual. An identity consists of traits, attributes, and preferences upon which one may receive personalized services. Such services could exist online, on mobile devices at work, or in many other places", that is, without mentioning a mandatory link to the real-world identity behind the digital identity.

The combination of virtual world with ubiquitous connectivity has changed the physical constraints to entirely new set of requirements as the associated security issues such phishing, spam, and identity theft has emerged. They are aggravated by the mobility of the user, the temporary and anonymity of cyber relationships. We are going toward new truly virtual world with always the implication of human. Therefore, we are facing the problem of determining the identity of our interlocutor and the accuracy of his/her claims. Simply using strong authentication will not resolve all these security issues. Digital identity management is a key issue that will ensure not only the service and functionality expectations but also security and privacy.

Identity Management Overview

A model of identity can been as follows [7]:

- User who wants to access to a service
- Identity Provider (IdP): is the issuer of user identity
- Service Provider (SP): is the relay party imposing identity check
- Identity (Id): is a set user's attributes
- Personal Authentication Device (PDA): Device holding various identifiers and credentials and could be used for mobility

Figure 25.1 lists the main components of identity management. The relationship between entities, identities and identifiers are shown in Figure 25.2, which illustrates that an entity, such as a user, may have multiple identities, and each identity may consist of multiple attributes that can be unique or non-unique identifiers.

Identity management refers to "the process of representing, using, maintaining, deprovisioning and authenticating entities as digital identities in computer networks".

Authentication is the process of verifying claims about holding specific identities. A failure at this stage will threaten the validity in the entire system. The technology is constantly finding stronger authentication using claims based on:

- Something you know: password, PIN
- Something you have: one-time-password
- Something you are: your voice, face, fingerprint (Biometrics)
- Your position
- Some combination of the four.

The BT report [3] has highlighted some interesting points to meet the challenges of identity theft and fraud:

- Developing risk calculation and assessment methods
- Monitoring user behavior to calculate risk
- Building trust and value with the user or consumer
- Engaging the cooperation of the user or consumer with transparency and without complexity or shifting the liability to consumer
- Taking a staged approach to authentication deployment and process challenges, using more advanced technologies

Digital identity should mange three connected vertexes: usability, cost and risk as illustrated in Figure 25.3.

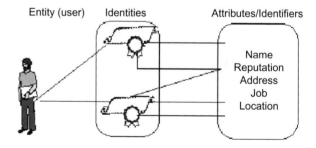

FIGURE 25.2   Relationship between identities, identifiers and entity.

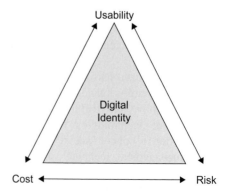

FIGURE 25.3   Digital identity environment to manage.

FIGURE 25.1   Identity management main components.

The user should be aware of the risk he/she facing if his/her device/software's security is compromised. The usability is the second aspect that should be guaranty to the user unless he/she will find the system difficult which could be a source of security problem. Indeed, a lot of users when they are flooded by passwords write them down and hide them in a secrete place under their keyboard. Furthermore, the difficulty to deploy and manage a large number of identities discourages the use of identity management system. The cost of a system should be well studied and balanced related to risk and usability. Many systems such as one-Time-Password token are not widely used because they are too costly for a widespread deployment for large institutions. Traditionally identity management was seen as service provider centric as it was designed to fulfill the requirements of service provider, such as cost effectiveness and scalability. The users were neglected in many aspects because they were forced to memorize difficult or too many passwords. Identity management systems are elaborated to deal with the following core facets [8]:

- Reducing identity theft: The problem of identity theft is becoming a major one, mainly in the online environment. The providers need more efficient system to tackle this problem.
- Management: The amount of digital identities per person will increase, so the users need convenient support to manage these identities and the corresponding authentication.
- Reachability: The management of reachability allows user to handle their contacts to prevent misuse of their address (spam) or unsolicited phone calls.
- Authenticity: Ensuring authenticity with authentication, integrity and non-repudiation mechanisms can prevent from identity theft.
- Anonymity and pseudonymity: providing anonymity prevent from tracking or identifying the users of a service.
- Organization personal data management: A quick method to create, modify a delete work accounts is needed, especially in big organizations.

Without improved usability of identity management [8], for example, weak passwords used by users on many Web sites, the number of successful attacks will remain high. To facilitate interacting with unknown entities, simple recognition rather than authentication of a real-world identity has been proposed, which usually involves manual enrollment steps in the real-world [5]. Usability is indeed enhanced, if there is no manual task needed. There might be a weaker level of security but that level may be sufficient for some actions, such as, logging to a mobile game platform. Single Sign-On (SSO) is the name given to the requirements of eliminating multiple password issues and dangerous password. When we use multiple user Id's and passwords just to use the emails systems and file servers at work, we feel the inconvenience that comes from having multiple identities. The second problem is the scattering of identity data which causes problems for the integration of IT systems. Moreover, it simplifies the end-user experience and enhances security via identity-based access technology.

Microsoft first largest identity management system was Passport Network. It was a very large and widespread Microsoft Internet service to be an identity provider for the MSN and Microsoft properties, and to be an identity provider for the Internet. However, with Passport, Microsoft was suspected by many persons of intending to have an absolute control over the identity information of Internet users and thus exploiting them for its own interests. Passport failed to become the Internet identity management tool. Since then, Microsoft has clearly understood that an identity management solution cannot succeed unless some basic rules are respected [9]. That's why Microsoft's Identity Architect, Kim Cameron, has stated the seven laws of identity. His motivation was purely practical in determining the prerequisites of successful identity management system. He formulated the essential principles to maintain privacy and security.

1. User control and consent over the handling of their data.
2. Minimal disclosure of data, and for specified purpose.
3. Information should only be disclosed to people who have a justifiable need for it.
4. The system must provide identifiers for both bilateral relationships between parties, and for incoming unsolicited communications.
5. It must support diverse operators and technologies.
6. It must be perceived as highly reliable and predictable.
7. There must be a consistent user experience across multiple identity systems and using multiple technologies.

Most systems do not fulfill several of these tests particularly they are deficient in fine-tuning the access control over identity to minimize disclosure of data. The formulated Cameron's principles are very clear but they are not enough explicit to compare finely identity management systems. That's why we will define explicitly the identity requirements.

Privacy Requirement

Privacy is a central issue, due to the fact that the official authorities of almost all countries have legal strict policies related to identity. It is often treated in the case of identity management because the management deals with personal information and data. Therefore, it is important to give a definition. Alan F. Westin defines privacy as "*the claim of individuals, groups and institutions to determine for themselves, when, how and to what extent information about them is communicated to others*" [2]. However, we will use Cooley's broader definition of privacy [10]: "the right to be let alone", because it also emphasizes the problems related to disturbing the user's attention, for example, by email spam.

User Centricity

The evolution of the identity management system is toward the simplification of user experience and reinforcing authentication. It is well known that a poor usability implies the weakness of authentication. Mainly federated management has responded to some of these requirements by facilitating the use and the managing of identifiers and credentials in the boundary of a federated domain. Nevertheless, it is improbable that only one federated domain will subsist. Moreover, different levels of sensitivity and risks of different services will need different kinds of credentials. It is obvious that we should give users support and atomization of the identity management on the user's side.

A new paradigm must be introduced to solve the problems of usability, scalability and universal SSO. Therefore, a user-oriented paradigm has emerged which is called user-centric identity management. The word user controlled management [11] is the first used to explain user-centric management model. Recent federated identity management systems keep strong end-user controls over how identity information is disseminated amongst members of the federation. This new paradigm gives the user full control over his/her identity by notifying him the information collected and by guarantying his/her consent for any type of manipulation over collected information. A user control and consent is also defined as the first law in Cameron's Laws of Identity [9]. A user-centric identity

management system supports the user's control and considers user-centric architecture and usability aspects. There is no uniform definition but "user-centric identity management is understood to mean digital identity infrastructure where an individual end-user has substantially independent control over the dissemination and use of their identifier(s) and personally-identifiable information (PII)."[12] See Figure 25.4. We can also give this definition of user centricity.

In user-centric identity management the user has the full control over hi/hers identity and consistent user experience during all transaction when accessing his/her services.

In other terms it means that it allows the user to keep at least some or total control over his/her personal data. One of the principles of user-centric identity is the idea that the user of a Web service should have full control over his/her identity information (see checklist: "An Agenda For Action For The User-Centric Identity Paradigm").

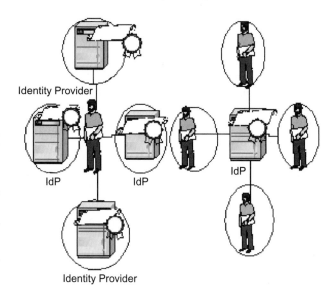

Identity Provider

IdP　　IdP　　IdP

Identity Provider

FIGURE 25.4　IdP centric and User-centric models.

An Agenda for Action for the User-Centric Identity Paradigm

A lot of technology discussion and solution has been focusing on service provider and rarely on user's perspectives. User-centric identity paradigm is a real evolution because it moves information technology architecture forward for the users with the following advantages. These are as follows (check all tasks completed):

____**1** Empower the total control of users over their privacy.

____**2** Usability, as users are using the same identity for each identity transaction.

____**3** Give a consistent user's experience thanks to uniformity of identity interface.

____**4** Limit identity attacks (Phishing).

____**5** Limit reachability/disturbances, such as spam.

____**6** Review policies on both sides when necessary, identity providers and service providers (Web sites).

____**7** Huge scalability advantages as the Identity Provider does not have to get any prior knowledge about the Service Provider.

____**8** Assure secure conditions when exchanging data.

____**9** Decouple digital identity from applications.

____**10** Pluralism of Operators and Technologies.

User-centricity approach allows the user to gain access anonymously as she detains the full control on his/her identity. Of course, full anonymity [26] and unlinkability may lead to increased misuse by anonymous users. Then, Pseudonymity is alternative which is more suitable to the e-commerce environment. In this regard, anonymity must be guaranty at the application and at network levels. Some frameworks have been proposed to ensure user-centric anonymity using the concepts of One-task Authorization key and Binding Signature [26].

Usability Requirement

The security is also compromised with the proliferation of the user's password and even by it's weakness. Indeed, some users note their passwords on scratch pads, because their memorization poses problem. The recent FFIEC guidance on authentication in online banking reports that "Account fraud and identity theft are frequently the result of single factor (Id/password) authentication exploitation" [14]. From then on, the security must be user oriented as he/her is the effective person concerned with it and a lot of recent attacks take advantage from the lack of awareness of users attacks (i.e. spoofing, pharming and phishing) [15]. Without strong control and improved usability [16] of identity management some attacks will be always possible. To facilitate interacting with unknown entities, simple recognition rather than authentication of a real-world identity, which usually involves manual enrollment steps in the real-world, has been proposed [5]. Usability is indeed enhanced if there is no manual task needed. There might be a weaker level of security reached but that level may be sufficient for some actions, such as, logging to a mobile game platform.

Single Sign-On (SSO) is the name given to the requirements of eliminating multiple password issues and dangerous password. When we use multiple user Id's and passwords just to use the emails systems and file servers at work, we feel the pain that comes from having multiple identities. The second problem is the scattering of identity data which causes problem for the integration of IT systems. Moreover, it simplifies the end-user experience and enhances security via identity-based access technology. Therefore, we offer these features:

- Flexible authentication
- Directory independence
- Session and password management
- Seamless

3. THE REQUIREMENTS FULFILLED BY IDENTITY MANAGEMENT TECHNOLOGIES

This section provides an overview of identity management solutions from identity 1.0 to identity 2.0 and how they address the requirements introduced in Section 2. We will focus on related standards XRI and LID issued from Yadis project and platforms mainly ID-WSF, OpenID, Higgins, InfoCard and Sxip. At the end, we treat the identity management in the field of mobility.

Evolution of Identity Management

This section provides an overview of almost all identity management 1.0 (See Figure 25.5). First of all, we describe the silo model, then different kind of centralized model and the federated identity management.

4. IDENTITY MANAGEMENT 1.0

In the real world I use my identity card to prove who I am. How about the online world?

The first digital identity appeared when the user was associated with the pair (username, password) or any other shared secret. This method is used for authentication when connecting to an account or a directory. It proves your identity if you follow the guidelines strictly otherwise there is no proof. In fact, it is a single authority using opaque trust decision without any credentials (cryptographic proofs) choice or portability.

In the context of Web access, the user must enroll for every non-related service, generally with different user interfaces and follows diverse policies and protocols. Thus, the user has a non-consistent experience and deals with different identity copies. In addition, some problems related to privacy have also emerged. Indeed, our privacy was potentially invaded by sites. It is clear that sites have a privacy policy, but there is no control from the user on his/her identity. What are the conditions for using these

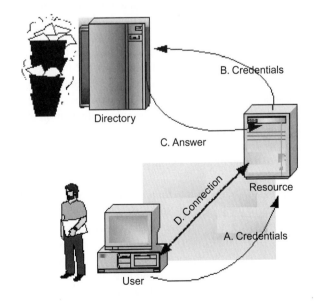

FIGURE 25.5   Identity 1.0 principle.

data? How can we improve our privacy? And to what granularity we allow them to use it?

The same problem is revealed when having access to resources. The more resources, the more management we have. It is an asymmetric trust. And, the policy decision maybe opaque.

It allows access with an opaque trust decision and a single centralized authority without a credentials choice. It is a silo model [17] because it is neither portable nor scalable. This is Identity 1.0.

The identity management appeared with these problems in the 1980s. The fist identity management system was the Rec. X.500, developed by ITU [1], covering directory services like Directory Access Protocol (DAP). ISO was also associated to the development of the standard. Like a lot of ITU standards, this one was very heavy and complex. A light version appeared in the 1990s for DAP. It was LDAP which was standardized by the IETF and widespread and adopted by Netscape. Microsoft has invented an equivalent Active Directory, and for users, they introduced Passport. It is also the ITU which standardized X.509 for identities related to certificates. It is the format currently recognized. It is a small file, generated by an authority of certification.

If there is a loss or a usurpation of the certificate, it can always be revoked by the authority of certification. This is for single user and what about business corporations who have automated their procedures and have a proliferation of applications with de-provisioning but still been in a domain-centric model. What about resources shared between domains?

Silo Model

The main identity management system deployed currently in the world of the Internet is known as the silo model, as shown in Figure 25.6. Indeed, the identity provider and service provider are mixed up and they share the same space. The identity management environment is put in place and operated by a single entity for a fixed users' community.

Users of different services must have different accounts and therefore reenter the same information about their identity which increases the difficulty of management. Moreover, the users are overloaded by identity and password to memorize which produces a significant barrier to usage.

A real problem is the forgetfulness of passwords due to the infrequent use of some of these data. This can obviously lead to a higher cost of service provisions. This is for single users, what about Enterprises that have automated their procedures and have a proliferation of applications with de-provisioning but are still in a domain-centric model? What about resources shared between domains?

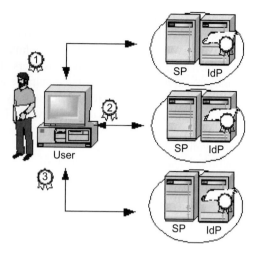

FIGURE 25.6 Identity silo model.

Silo model is not interoperable and is deficient in many aspects. That's why the federated identity management model is now emerging and it is very appreciated by enterprises. A federated identity management system consists of software components and protocols that handle in a decentralized manner the identity of individuals throughout their identity life cycle [19].

Solution by Aggregation

Aggregating identity information and finding the relationship between identity records is important to aggregate identity. There are some alternatives:

- The first approach consolidates authentication and attributes in only one site and is called a centralized management solution like Microsoft Passport. This solution avoids the redundancies and inconsistencies in the silo model and gives the user a seamless experience [7]. The evolution was as follows [17,19]:
  - Building a single central identity data store which is feasible only for small organizations.
  - Creating a meta-directory that synchronizes data from other identity data stored elsewhere.
  - Creating a virtual directory that provides a single integrated view of the identity data stored.
  - A Single Sign On Identity model which allows users to be authenticated by one service provider.
- The second approach decentralizes the responsibility of IdP to multiple such IdPs which can be selected by the end users. This is a federate system where some attributes of identity are stored in distributed IdPs. A federated directories model, by linking identity data stored together, has emerged. Protocols are defined in several standards such as in Shibboleth [20], Web services federation language 2003.

Centralized vs. Federation Identity Management

Microsoft Passport is a centralized system, entirely controlled by Microsoft and closely tied to other Microsoft products. Individuals and companies have proven to be reluctant adopters of a system so tightly controlled by one dominant company.

Centrally managed repositories in centralized identity infrastructures can't solve the problem of cross-organizational authentication and authorization. This approach has several drawbacks as the IdP does not only become a single point of failure but may also not be trusted. That's why Microsoft Passport was not successful. In contrast, the federation identity will leave the identity resources in their various distributed locations but produce a federation that links them to solve identity duplication, provision and management.

A Simple Centralized Model

A relatively simple centralized identity management model is to build a platform that centralizes identities. A separate entity acts as an exclusive user credentials provider for all service providers. This approach merges both authentication and attributes in only one site. This architecture, which could be called Common user identity management model, is illustrated in Figure 25.7. All identities for each SP are gathered to a unique identity management site (IdP). SPs have to provide each identity to IdP.

In this environment, users can have access to all service providers using the same set of identifiers and credentials. A centralized certificated CAs could be implemented with a PKI or SPKI [21]. This architecture is very efficient in a close domain where users could be identified by a controlled email address. Although such architecture seems to be scalable, the concentration of privacy related information has a lot of difficulties in social acceptance in terms of privacy [22].

Meta-Directories

SPs can share certain identity-related data on a meta-level. This can be implemented by consolidating all service providers' specific identities to a meta-identifier linked to credentials.

There are collections of directories information from various directory sources. We aggregated them to provide a single view of data. Therefore, we can show these advantages:

- A single point of reference provides an abstraction boundary between application and the actual implementation.
- A single point of administration avoids the multiple directories, too.
- Redundant directory information can be eliminated, reducing the administration tasks.

This approach can be seeing from the user's point of view to his/her password as synchronization across multiple service providers. Thus, the password is automatically changed with all the others.

This architecture can be used in large enterprises where all services are linked to a meta-directory, as shown in Figure 25.8. In this case, the ease-of-use is clear as the administration is done by a single authority.

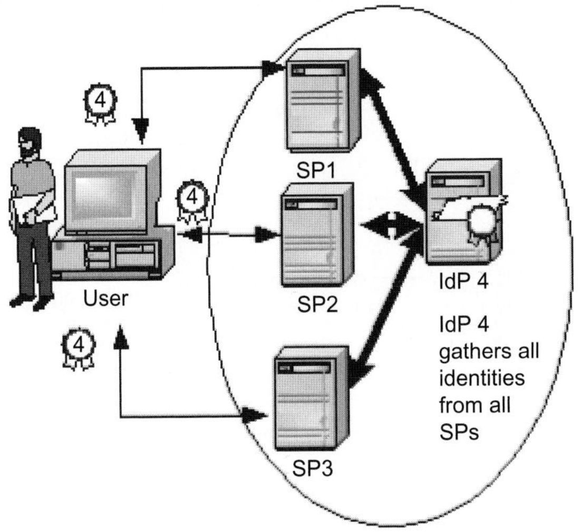

![Figure 25.7 and 25.8 diagrams]

FIGURE 25.7   Simple centralized identity management.

FIGURE 25.8   Meta-directory model.

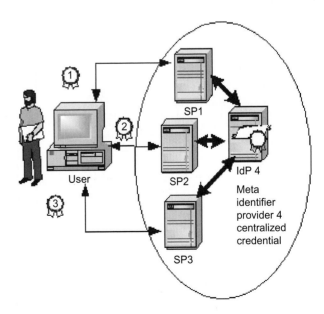

Virtual Directories

Virtual directories are directories that are not located in the same physical structure as the Web home directory, but look as if they were to Web clients. The actual directories may be at a completely different location in the physical directory structure; for example, on another hard disk or on a remote computer. They are similar in concept to meta-directories in that they provide a single directory view from multiple independent directories. They differ in the means used to accomplish this goal. MD software agents replicate and synchronize data from various directories in what might be batch processes. In contrast, VD provide a single view of multiple directories using real-time queries based on mapping from fields in the virtual scheme to fields in the physical schemes of the real directories.

Single-Sign-On (SSO)

We use multiple user's Ids and passwords just to use the emails systems and file servers at work and we feel pain from managing multiple identities. The second problem is the scattering of identity data which causes problem for the integration of IT systems.

Single Sign-On (see Figure 25.9) is a solution proposed to eliminate multiple password issues and dangerous password. Moreover, it simplifies the end-user experience and enhances security via identity-based access technology. Therefore, it offers these features:

- Flexible authentication,
- Seamless

- Directory independence and
- Session and password management.

Federated Identity Management

We have seen different approaches to manage user's identity; they are not clearly interoperable and are deficient in unifying standard-based frameworks. On one hand, maintenance of privacy and identity control are fundamental when offering identity to users, on the other hand the same users ask for more easy to use and rapid access. The balance of the two sides leads to federated network identity. That's why these environments are now emerging. A federated identity management system (See Figure 25.10) consists of software components and protocols that handle the identity of individuals throughout their identity life cycle.

This architecture gives the user the illusion that there is a single identifier authority. Even though the user has many identifiers, he doesn't need to know exactly all of them. Only one identifier is enough to have access to all services in the federated domain.

Each SP is responsible for the name space of his users and all SPs are federated by linking the identity domains. Thus, the Federated identity model is based on a set of SPs called a circle of trust by the Liberty Alliance. This set of SPs follows an agreement on mutual security and authentication in order to allow SSO. Indeed, the federated identity management combines SSO and authorization tools using a number of mutual SPs' technologies and standards. This practice makes the recognition and entitlement of user identities by other SPs easy. The Figure 22-10 shows the set of federated domains and the possibility for other SPs to have access to the same user with different identifiers.

The essential difference between federated identity systems and centralized identity management is that there

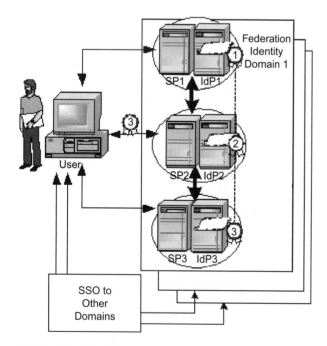

FIGURE 25.9 Single-Sign-On model.

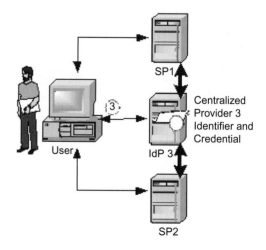

FIGURE 25.10 Federated identity management model.

is no single entity that operates the identity management system. Federated systems support multiple identity providers and a distributed and partitioned store for identity information. Therefore, a federated identity network allows a simplified sign-on to users by giving rapid access to resources, but it doesn't require the user's personal information to be stored centrally. With this identity network approach, users authenticate themselves once and can control how their personal information and preferences are used by the service providers.

Federated identity standards, like those produced by the Liberty Alliance [23], provide Single-Sign-On over all offered services and enable users to manage the sharing of their personal information through identity and service providers as well as the use of personalized services in order to give access to convergent services. The interoperability between disparate security systems is assumed by an encapsulation layer through a trust domain which links a set of trusted service providers.

However there are some disadvantages with federated identity management. The first one is the lack of privacy of the user as his/her personal attributes and information can be mapped using correlation between identifiers. Anonymity could be violated. The second one is the scalability of users as they have access to the network from different domains by authentication to their relative IdPs. Therefore, the problem of passwords will continue across multiple federated domains.

A major challenge is to integrate all these components into a distributed network and to deal with these drawbacks. This challenge cannot be taken up without new paradigms and supported standards.

The evolution of identity management system is toward also simplification of user experience and reinforcing authentication. It is very known that a poor usability implies the weakness of authentication. A new paradigm should be introduced to solve those problems while still being compatible at least with federated identity management.

That is why user-centric identity management, has emerged [7,17]. This paradigm is embraced by multiple industry products and initiative such as Microsoft Cardspace [24], Sxip [25] and Higgins Trust Framework [26]. This is Identity 2.0.

Identity 2.0

The user of Internet services is overwhelmed with identities. he/she is seldom able to transfer his/her identity from one site to another. The reputation that he/she gains in one network is useful to transfer to other networks. Nevertheless, he/she cannot profit from his/her constructed reputation and he/she should rebuild his/her identity and reputation another time, and so on. The actual systems

don't allow users to decide about the sharing of their attributes related to their identity with other users. This causes a lack of privacy control. Some solutions propose an advanced social system that would model the social interaction like the real world.

The solutions must be easy to use and enable users to share the credentials among many services and must be transparent from the end-user perspective. The principle of modern identity is to separate the acquisition process from the presentation process. It is the same for the identification process and authorization process. Moreover, it provides scalability and privacy. Doing so, we can have more control on my identity.

The scale, security and usability advantages of user-centric identity are what make it the underpinning for Identity 2.0. The main objective of Identity 2.0 protocol is to provide users with full control over their virtual identities. An important aspect of Identity 2.0 is protection against increasingly Web attacks like Phishing attacks as well as the inadvertent disclosure of confidential information while enabling convenient management.

Identity 2.0 would allow users to use one identity respecting transparency and flexibility. It is focused around the user and not around directory or identity provider. It requires identified transactions between users and relaying party using credentials, thus providing more traceable transactions. To maximize the privacy of users, some credentials could be given to the users in advance. Doing so, the IdP could not easily know when the user is utilizing the credentials.

The Identity 2.0 (See Figure 25.11) endorses completely the paradigms of user-centric identity management enabling the full control of user on his/her identity. Service Provider will therefore be required to change their approaches by including request and authentication

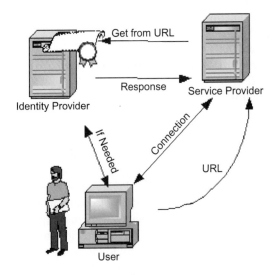

FIGURE 25.11   URL-based Id 2.0.

of users' identity. Identity 2.0 systems are interested in using the concept of a user's identity as credentials about the user, from their attributes like their name, address, to less traditional things like their desires, customer service history, and other attributes that are usually not so much associated with a user identity.

Identity 2.0 Initiatives

When a Website collects data from users he cannot confirm whether or not the collected data is pertinent and reliable as the users often enter nonsense information into online forms. This is due to the lack of Website to control and verify the users' data. Furthermore, due to the law limitation on the requested data, the Website cannot provide true customized services even though users require them. In the other side, users have not direct control on what the Website will do with their data. In addition, the users enter many times the same data when accessing the first time different Websites. Doing so, they have a huge difficulty to manage their large number of identities.

To mitigate these problems, different models of identity management have been considered. One such model, Identity 2.0, proposes an Internet-scalable and user-centric identity architecture that mimics real world interactions.

Many research labs have collaborated to develop the Identity 2.0 Internet based Identity Management services. It is based on the concept of user-centric identity management, supporting enhanced identity verification and privacy, and user consent and control over any access to personal information for Internet-based transactions. There are various Identity 2.0 initiatives:

1. **LID**
2. **XRI**
3. **SAML**
4. **Shibboleth**
5. **ID-WSF**
6. **OpenID**
7. **Microsoft's CardSpace (formerly InfoCard)**
8. **SXIP**
9. **Higgins**

LID

Like LDAP, LID is under the principle of simplicity because many existing identity schemes are too complicated to be largely adoptable. It simplifies more complex protocol; but instead of being less capable due to fewer features, it has run success that their more complex predecessors lacked. This was because their simplification reduced the required complexity to the point where many people could easily support them, and that was one of the goals of LID.

Light-Weight Identity (LID) is a set of protocols capable of representing and using digital identities on the Internet in a simple manner, without relying on any central authority. LID is the original URL-based identity protocol, and part of the OpenID movement.

LID supports digital identities for humans, human organizations and non-humans (software agents, things, Websites, etc.) It implements Yadis, a meta-data discovery service and is pluggable on all levels.

XRI/XDI

We have XRI EXtensible Resource Identifier (see Figure 25.12) and XDI which fractional solution without Web services integrated. They are open standards as they are royalty-free open standards. XRI is about Addressing. XDI is about Data Sharing protocol and uses basically XRI. Both XRI and XDI are being developed under the support of OASIS. I-name and I-number registry services for privacy-protected digital addressing use XRI. It can be used as an identifier for persons, machines and agents.

XRIs offer a human-friendly form of persistent identifier. That's why it is convenient identifier for SSO system. They Supports both persistent and reassignable identifiers in the same syntax and establish a global context symbols. Moreover, they enable identification of the same logical resource across multiple contexts and multiple versions of the same logical resource.

XDI (XRI Data Exchange) is a Secure Distributed Data Sharing Protocol. It is also an architecture and specification for privacy-controlled data exchange where all data is identified using XRIs. The XDI platform includes explicit specification for caching with both push and pull synchronization. XDI universal schema can represent any complex data and have the ability of cross context addressing and linking.

SAML

The Security Assertion Markup Language (SAML) is an OASIS specification [27] that provides a set of rules for the structure of identity assertions, protocols to move assertions, bindings of protocols for typical message transport mechanisms, and profiles. Indeed, SAML (see Figure 25.13) is a set of XML and SOAP-based services

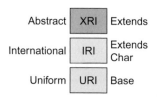

FIGURE 25.12 XRI layers.

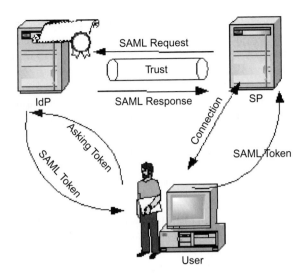

FIGURE 25.13   SAML token exchange.

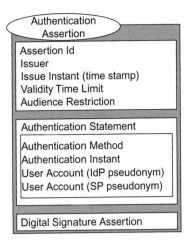

FIGURE 25.14   SAML assertion.

and formats for the exchange of authentication and authorization information between security systems.

The initial versions of SAML v1.0 and v1.1 define protocols for SSO, delegated administration, and policy management. The most recent version is SAML 2.0. It is now a common language to the majority platform to change secure unified assertion. He is very useful and simple as it is based on XML. An assertion is a datum produced by a SAML authority referring to authentication, attribute information, or authorizations applying to the user with respect to a specified resource.

This protocol (see Figure 25.14) enables interoperability between security systems (Browser Single Sign On, Web Services Security, etc.). Other aspects of federated identity management as permission-based attribute sharing are also supported.

An SAML is sometimes criticized for its complexity of the specifications and the relative constraint of its security rules. Recently, the SAML community has shown significant interest in extending SAML to reach less stringent requirements for low-sensitivity use cases. The advantages of SAML are robustness of its security and privacy model, and the guarantee of its interoperability between multiple vendor implementations through the Liberty Alliance's Conformance Program.

Shibboleth

Shibboleth [20] is a project which goal is to allow universities to share the Web resources subject to control access. Thereafter, it allows inter-operation between institutions using it. It develops architectures, policy structure, practical technologies, and an open source implementation. It is building components for both the identity providers and the reliant parties. The key concept

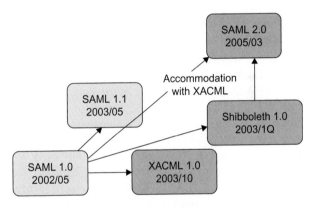

FIGURE 25.15   Convergence between SAML & Shibboleth.

includes "federated" management identity whose meaning is almost the same as the Liberty term's [28]. Access control is fundamentally based on user attributes, validated by SAML Assertions. In Figure 25.15, we can see the evolution of SAML, Shibboleth and XACML [29].

ID-WSF

In 2001, a business alliance was formed to serve as open standards organization for federated identity management and it was named Liberty alliance [23,30]. Its goals are to guaranty interoperability, support privacy, and promote adoption of its specifications, guidelines and best practices. The key objectives of the Liberty Alliance (see Figure 25.16) are to:

- Enable users to protect their privacy and identity
- Enable SPs' to manage their clients
- Provide an open federated SSO
- Provide a network identity infrastructure that supports all current emerging network access devices

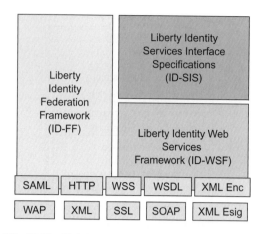

FIGURE 25.16 High-Level Overview of the Liberty Alliance Architecture.

Roadmap to Interoperable Federated Identity Services

The Liberty Alliance's work in the first phase is to enable federated network identity management. It offers among others SSO and linking accounts in the set of SPs' in the boundary of the circle of trust. This work of this phase is referred to as Identity Federation Framework (ID-FF).

In the second phase, the specifications offer enhancing identity federation and interoperable identity-based Web services. This body is referred to as Identity Web Services Framework (ID-WSF). This framework involves support of the new open standard such as WS-Security developed in OASIS. ID-WSF is a platform for the discovery and invocation of identity services — Web services associated with a given identity-. In the typical ID-WSF use case, after a user authenticates to an IdP this fact is asserted to a SP through SAML-based SSO. Embedded within the assertion is information that the SP can optionally use to discover and invoke potentially numerous and distributed identity services for that user. For some scenarios which present an unacceptable privacy risk as it suggests the possibility of a user's identity being exchanged without their consent or even knowledge. ID-WSF has a number of policy mechanisms to guard against this risk but ultimately, it is worth noting that many identity transactions (automated bill payments) already occur without the user's active real-time consent — and users appreciate this efficiency and convenience.

To build additional interoperable identity services such as registration services, contacts, calendar, geolocation services, alert services, it's envisaged to use ID-WSF. This specification is referred to as the Identity Services Interfaces Specifications (ID-SIS).

The Liberty Alliance specifications define the protocol messages, profiles, and processing rules for identity federation and management. They rely heavily on other standards such as SAML and WS-Security which is another OASIS specification that defines mechanisms implemented in SOAP headers.

These mechanisms are designed to enhance SOAP messaging by providing a quality of protection through message integrity, message confidentiality, and single message authentication. Additionally, Liberty has contributed portions of its specification back into the technical committee working on SAML. Other identity management enabling standards include:

- Service Provisioning Markup Language (SPML)
- XML Access Control Markup Language (XACML)
- XML Key Management Specification (XKMS)
- XML Signature
- XML Encryption

The WS-* (the Web Services protocol specifications) are a set of specifications that is currently under development by Microsoft and IBM. It is a part of larger effort to define a security framework for Web services, the resultant of proposals are often referred to as WS-*. It includes specifications as WS-Policy, WS-Security Conversation, WS-Trust, and WS-Federation. This last one has functionality for enabling pseudonyms and attribute-based interactions. Therefore, WS-Trust's has the ability to ensure security tokens as a means of brokering identity and trust across domain boundaries [22].

The Liberty Alliance is developing and delivering specification that enables federate network identity management. Figure 25.16 shows an Overview of the Liberty Alliance architecture as describe in the introduction to the Liberty Alliance identity architecture.

OpenID 2.0

Brad Fitzpatrick is at the origin of the development of the OpenID 1.0. The intent of the OpenID framework is to specify layers that are independent and small enough to be acceptable and adopted by market [12]. OpenID is basically providing simple attribute sharing for low-value transactions. It does not depend on any preconfigured trust model. The version 1.0 has deal with http based URL authentication protocol. OpenID authentication 2.0 is becoming an open platform that supports both URL and XRI user identifiers. In addition, it would like to be modular, lightweight and user oriented. Indeed, OpenID auth. 2.0 allows user to choose/control/manage his/her identity address. Moreover, the user choose his/her Identity Provider and have a large interoperability of his/her identity and can dynamically uses new services that stand out attribute verification and reputation without any loose of features. No software is required on user's side as the user interacts directly with the identity provider's site. This approach jeopardize the user identity because it could be hacked or theft. Moreover the user has no ability to examine tokens before they are sent.

At the beginning of identity management each technology came with its own futures without any interest for others. Later, the OpenID 1.0 community has realized the importance of integrating other technologies as OASIS XRDS which is useful for his simplicity and extensibility.

OpenID Stack

The first layer is for supporting users' identification. Using URL or XRI form, we can identify an user. URL use IP or DNS resolution and is unique and ubiquitously supported. It can be as a personal digital address as used by blogers even though it is not yet largely used.

XRI (EXtensible Resource Identifier) is being developed under the support of OASIS and is about Addressing. I-names are a generic term for XRI authority names that provide abstract identifiers for the entity to which they are assigned. They can be used as the entry point to access data under the control of that authority. Like a domain name, the physical location of the information is transparent to the requester.

OpenID 2.O provides a private digital address to allow a user to be only identified in specific conditions. This is guaranty the user privacy in a public domain.

Discovery Yadis is used for identity service discovery for URLs and XRI resolution protocol for XRIs. The both use OASIS format called XRDS (Extensible Resource Description Sequence). The protocol is simple and describes any type of service.

Authentication This service lets a user to prove his/her URL or I-name using credentials (cryptographic proof). This protocol is explained in Figure 25.17. The OpenID doesn't need a centralized authority for enrollment and it is therefore a federated identity management. With the OpenID 2.0 the IdP offers the user the option of selecting a digital address to send to the SP. To ensure anonymity,

IdP can randomly generate a digital address used specially for this SP.

Data Transport This layer ensures the data exchange between the IdP and SP. It supports push and pulls methods and it is independent from authentication procedures. Therefore, the synchronization of data and secure messaging and other service will be enabled. The data formats are those defined by SAML, SDI (XRI Data interchange) or any other data formats. This approach will enable evolution of the OpenID platform.

The four layers construct the foundation of the OpenID ensuring user centricity (see Figure 25.18). There are three points to guaranty this paradigm:

1. User choose his/her digital identity
2. User choose IdP
3. User choose SP

OpenID is decentralized and well founded and at the same time simple, easy to use and to deploy. It provides open development process and single sign-on for the Web and ease of integration into scripted Web platforms (Drupal, WordPress, etc).

So, it is a greater future for him. You can learn about OpenID at openidenabled.com also the community of OpenId can be joined at opened.net.

InfoCard

Rather than invent another technology for creating and representing digital identities, Microsoft has adopted the federated user-centric identity meta-system. This is a serious solution that provides a consistent way to work with multiple digital identities. Using standard protocols that anyone can implement on any platform, the identity

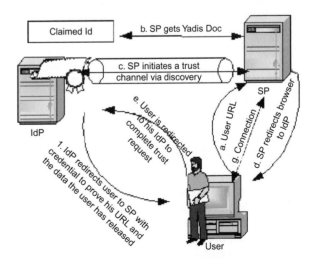

FIGURE 25.18   OpenID 1.1 protocol flow.

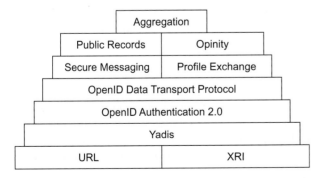

FIGURE 25.17   OpenID protocol stack.

meta-system allows the acquisition and use of any kind of security tokens to convey identity.

The "Infocard" is the Microsoft's codename for this new technology that tackles the problem of managing and disclosing identity information. The "InfoCard" implements the core of the Identity Metasystem, using open standard protocols to negotiate, request and broker identity information between trusted IdPs and SPs. "InfoCard" is a technology that helps developers to integrate a consistent identity infrastructure into applications, Web sites and Web services.

By providing a way for users to select identities and more, Windows CardSpace [24] plays an important part in the identity meta-system.

It provides the consistent user experience required by the identity meta-system. It is specifically hardened against tampering and spoofing to protect the end user's digital identities and maintain end-user control. Windows CardSpace enables users to provide their digital identities in a familiar, secure and easy way.

In the terminology of Microsoft, relying party is in our model service provider (SP). To prove an identity over a network, the user emitted credentials which are some proofs about his/her identity. For example in the simplest digital identity the user name is the identity while the password is said to be the authentication credential. In the terminology of Microsoft and others, there are called security token and contain one or more claims. Each claim contains information about the users, like the user name or home address, etc. In addition, security token encloses prove that the claims are correctly emitted by the real user and are belonging to him. This is could be done cryptographically using different forms such as X.509 certificates and Kerberos tickets but unfortunately there are not practical to convoy different kind of claim. The standard SAML as seen before is the indicated one for this purpose as it can be used to define security tokens. Indeed, SAML token could enclose any desired information and thus become as largely useful in the network to show and control digital identity. CardSpace runs on Windows Vista, XP, Server 2003 and Server 2008, based on .NET3, and also uses Web service protocols:

- WS-Trust
- WS-Policy
- WS-SecurityPolicy
- WS-MetaDataExchange

CardSpace runs in a self virtual desktop on the PC. Thereby, it locks out other processes and reduces the possibility of intercepting information by a spyware.

Figure 25.19 shows that the architecture is fitting exactly to the principle of Identity 2.0. The user access one of any of his/her relying parties (SPs) using an application that supports CardSpace.

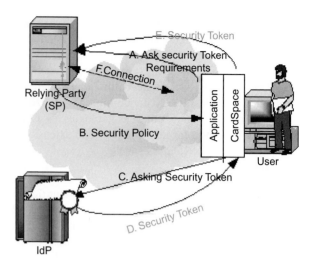

FIGURE 25.19 Interactions among the users, identity providers and relying party.

When the choice is made, the application asks for the requirement of security token of this specific SP that will answer with SP policy. It really contains information about the claims and the accepted token formats. Once this is done, the application passes these requirements to CardSpace which asks the security token from an appropriate identity provider.

Once this security token has been received, CardSpace transmits via application to the relying party. The relying party can then use this token to authenticate the user.

Please note that each identity is emitted by an identity provider and is stored at the user side. It contains the emitter, the kind of security token he/she can issue and the details about the claims' enclose. All difficulties are hidden to the user as he/she has only to choose one of InfoCard when the process of authentication is launched. Indeed, once the requirements information are returned and passed to CardSpace, the system displays the card selection matching the requirements on screen. In this regard, the user has a consistent experience as all applications based on CardSpace will have the same interface, and the user do not have to worry about the protocol used to express identity's security token. The PIN number is entered by user and the choice of his/her card is done in a private Windows desktop to prevent locally-running process.

SXIP 2.0

In 2004, The SXIP 1.0 grows from efforts to build a balanced online identity solution that met the requirements of the entire online community. Indeed, SXIP 2.0 is the new generation of the SXIP 1.0 protocol that was a platform that gives users control over their online identities and enables online communities to have a richer relationship with their membership. SXIP 2.0 defines entities' terminology as:

- Homesite: URL-based identity given by IdP.
- Membersite: SP that uses SXIP 2.0.
- User: equivalent to the user in our model.

The Simple eXtensible Identity Protocol (SXIP) [25] was designed to address the principles defined by the Identity 2.0 model (see Figure 25.20), which proposes an Internet-scalable and user-centric identity architecture that mimics real-world interactions.

If a SP has integrated a SXIP to his Website, which is easy done by using SDKs, he is a Membersite. When a subscriber of SXIP would like to access this Membersite:

1. Types his/her URL address and clicks on [Sxip in]
2. Types his/her URL identity issued by IdP (called Homesite)
3. Browser is redirected to the Homesite
4. Enters his/her username and password, being informed that the Membersite has requested data, selects the related data and verify it and can select to automatically release data for other visit to this Membersite and confirms
5. Browser is redirected to the Membersite
6. Have access to the content of the site.

SXIP 2.0 is a platform based on a fully decentralized architecture providing an open and simple set of process for exchanging identity information. SXIP 2.0 has significantly reduced the problems resulting from moving identity data form one site to another. It is URL-based protocol that allows a seamless user experience and fits exactly to user-centric paradigm. In that sense, the user has full control on his/her identity and has an active role in the exchange of his/her identity data. Therefore, he/she can profit from portable authentication to connect many Websites. Doing so, user has more choice and convenience when exchanging his/her identity data and enables indirectly Websites to offer enhanced services to their subscribers.

SXIP 2.0 provides the following features:

- Decentralized architecture: SXIP 2.0 is completely decentralized and is a federated identity management. The online identity is URL-based and the user identity is separated from the authority that issues the identifiers for this identity. In this regard, we can easily move the location of the identity data without losing the associated identifier.
- Dynamic discovery: A simple and dynamic discovery mechanism ensures that users are always informed online about his/her home site that is exporting identity data.
- Simple implementation: SXIP 2.0 is open source using different high level development languages such as Perl, Python, PHP, and Java. Therefore, the integration of SXIP 2.0 into a Website is effortless. It does not require PKI as it uses a URL-based protocol that do not need it.
- Support for existing technologies: SXIP 2.0 uses simple Web browsers, the primary client and means of data exchange, providing users with choice in the release of their identity data.
- Interoperability: SXIP 2.0 can coexist with other URL-based protocols.
- Richer data at an Internet scale: SXIP 2.0 messages consist of lists of simple name value pairs. It can exchanged simple text, claims using SAML and third-party claims in one exchange and present them in many separate exchange. In addition, the Identity provider is not bothersome every time identity is requested.

Finally by using SXIP 2.0, Websites can also be authoritative about users for data, such as third-party claims. Those are keys to build online reputation, further enriching the online exchange of identity data.

Higgins

Higgins [31] is a project supported principally by IBM and it is a part of IBM's Eclipse open source foundation. It will also offer libraries for Java, C and C++, and plug-ins for popular browsers. It is really an open source trust framework which goals are to support existing and new applications that give users more convenience, privacy and control over their identity information. The aim objective is to develop an extensible,

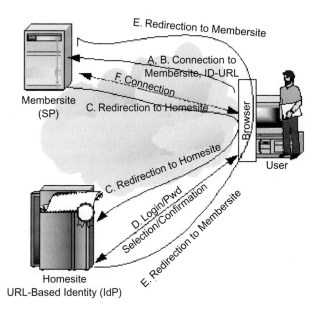

FIGURE 25.20 SXIP entities interactions.

platform-independent, identity protocol-independent, software framework that provides a foundation for user-centric identity management. Indeed, it enables applications to integrate identity, profiles and relationship across heterogeneous systems.

The main goal of Higgins as an identity management systems are interoperability, security and privacy that are a decoupled architecture. This system is a real user-centric based on a federated identity management. The user has the ability to use a pseudonym or simply reply anonymously in case you would not give your name.

We use the term context to cover a range of underlying implementations. A context can be thought of as a distributed container-like object that contains digital identities of multiple people or processes. The platform intends to address four challenges:

- The need to manage multiple contexts,
- The need for interoperability,
- The need to respond to regulatory, public or customer pressure to implement solutions based on trusted infrastructure that offers security and privacy, and
- The lack of common interfaces to identity/networking systems.

Higgins matches exactly the user-centric paradigms because it offers consistent user experience based on card icons for the management and release of identity data. Thereby, there is less vulnerability to Phishing and other attacks. Moreover, user privacy is enabled by sharing only what is needed. Thus, the user has a full control on his/her personal data. Identity Attribute Service enables aggregation and federation of identity systems and even silos. For enterprises, it integrates all data related to identity, profile, reputation, and relationship information across and among complex systems.

Higgins is a trust framework that enables users and enterprises to adopt, share across multiple systems and integrate to new or existing application, digital identity, profiles, and cross-relationship information. In fact, it facilitates as well the integration of different identity management systems as the management of identity, profile, reputation and relationship data across repositories. Using context providers, directories and communications technologies (Microsoft/IBM WS-*, LDAP, email, etc.) can be plugged into the Higgins framework. Higgins has become an Eclipse plug-in, and is a project of the Eclipse Foundation. Any application developed with Higgins will enable users to share identity with other users under a strict control.

Higgins is benefic for developers, users and enterprise. Higgins relieves the developers from knowing all the details of multiple identity systems, thanks to one API that support many protocols and technologies: CardSpace, OpenID, XRI, LDAP, etc. An Application written to the Higgins API can integrate the identity, profile, and relationship information across these heterogeneous systems. The goal of the framework is to be useful in the development of applications accessed through browsers, rich clients, and Web services. Thus, the Higgins Project is supported by IBM and Novell and thwart InfoCard Microsoft's project.

The Higgins framework intents to define in terms of service descriptions, messages and port types consistent with an SOA model and to develop a Java binding and implementation as an initial reference. Applications can use Higgins to create a unified, virtual view of identity, profile and relationship information. A key focus of Higgins is providing a foundation for new "user-centric identity" and personal information management applications.

Finally, Higgins provides virtual integration; user-centric federated management model and trust brokering that are applied to identity, profile and relationship information. Furthermore, Higgins provides common interfaces to identity and thanks to data context it encloses enhanced automation process. Those features are also offered across multiple contexts, disparate systems and implementations. In this regard, Higgins is a full interoperable framework.

The Higgins service acts together with a set of so-called context providers which can represent a department, association, informal network and so on. A context is the environment of Higgins and digital identities, the policies and protocols that govern their interactions. Context providers adjust existing legacy systems to the framework, or implement new ones Context providers may also contain the identities of a machine or human. A context encloses a group of digital identities and their related claims and links. A Context maintains a set of Claims about properties and values (name, address, etc.). It is like security token for Cardspace. The set of profile properties, the set of roles, and the access rights for each role are defined by and controlled by the Context Provider.

Context providers act as adapters to existing systems. Adapter providers can connect for example to LDAP servers, identity management systems like CardSpace, mailing list and social networking systems. A Higgins context provider (see Figure 25.21) has the ability to implement the Context interface and thus empower the applications layered on top of Higgins.

Summarizing Table

The 10 requirements at the top of Table 25.1, are those discussed earlier in the chapter. In this table, white means that the requirement is not covered, grey partially and black fully fulfilled.

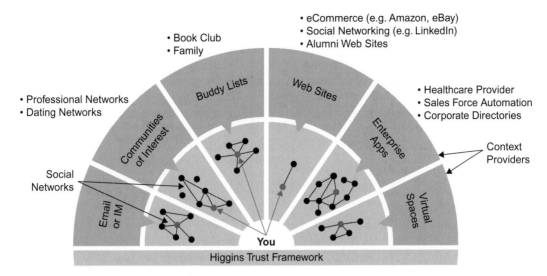

FIGURE 25.21   Higgins Trust Framework and context [26].

At the moment, service providers have to choose between so many authentications and identity management systems and users are left to face the non-convenience of a variety of digital identities. The main initiatives have different priorities and some unique advantages, while overlapping in many areas. The most pressing requirements for users are interoperability, usability and centricity. Thanks to Higgins the majority of identity requirements are guaranty. Therefore, using it, the user is free to visit all Web sites without being worried about the identity management system used by the provider.

5. SOCIAL LOGIN AND USER MANAGEMENT

At the time of the writing of the second version of this book chapter (end of 2012), none of the identity management technologies surveyed earlier in the chapter, have reached major user adoption. A few of them have been discontinued. For example, Sxip went bankrupt [32]. Others have moved very slowly. Higgins has only released a partial implementation of its vision and seems on hold. Liberty Alliance moved to a new initiative called the Kantara initiative [23]. However, a new type of solutions, which was not really expected at time of writing the first version of the book chapter, has emerged and gained quite large users adoption. This type of solutions is provided by major online social networks that have reached mass market very fast and where users have spent time configuring their profile. Then, those major online networks have built on top of previously surveyed standard identity management technological building blocks tools to facilitate logging to other Web sites and online

services with the identities managed on their services. The good news is that most of them have based their work on OpenID. Therefore although OpenID is less known by the greater public, it still exists underneath. They are also extensively relying on OAuth [33] that was built when OpenID was investigated for Twitter [34]. It is also possible to authenticate through OAuth but OAuth goes beyond OpenID regarding authorizations (in addition to authentication). The major online social networks providers that have created tools to allow their users to easy log in into other Web sites and services are: Facebook [35], Twitter, LinkedIn [36] and Google [37].

The Web sites and services that use the "social login" tools of one of these providers provide an easier access to their service to users who already have an account on this external provider. With a few confirming clicks, the user has joined the new service without having to spend time filling out her personal information again. Although this solution has gained large adoption because it fulfilled the user-friendliness requirement, there are still a few flaws remaining.

First, there is concern about the privacy protection requirement. For example, based on Facebook privacy bugs and issues due to privacy protection laws in different countries, one cannot claim that a Facebook user is really under control of her personal data disclosed to Facebook. It does not correspond to a user-centric approach. Thus, the Web site or service that reuses Facebook identity management service does not really fulfill the privacy requirement discussed above. The same privacy issues apply to the other "social login" providers.

Second issue concerns allowing users who may not have an account in one of the chosen "social login" provider to still login. Although the "social login" providers have created tools to connect their identity management

TABLE 25.1 Evaluation of Identity 2.0 Technologies.

Requirement	Empowering the total control of users over their privacy rivacy	Usability, as users are using the same identity for each identity transaction	Giving a consistent user's experience thanks to uniformity of identity interface	Limiting identity attacks i.e. phishing	Limiting reachability/ disturbances, such as spam	Reviewing policies on both sides when necessary, identity providers and service providers	Huge scalability advantages as the identity provider does not have to get any prior knowledge about the service provider	Assuring secure conditions when exchanging data	Decoupling digital identity from applications	Pluralism of operators and technologies
XRI/XDI										
ID/WSF										
Shibboleth										
CardSpace										
OpenID										
SXIP										
Higgins										

system to another Web site or service, adding multiple login forms to a Web site or service takes times and may confuse the user as many forms may be possible for registering. In addition, most "social login" providers often change their Application Programming Interface (API) without backward compatibility. Thus, the Web site or service may lose its registration functionality for some time before it can apply the required changes.

It is why a new type of providers has emerged on top of these "social login" providers. Those providers do the hard work to maintain a tool that allows a user to create an account with all the "social login" providers as well as store and manage users information on behalf of the service or Web site that uses this tool. The owners of Web sites and services install this tool on their Web site or service without having to worry when one of the "social login" providers change their API. The price of allowing a user to create an account with any of the main online social networks providers without having to maintain each "social login" module has to be weighed against the subscription price to one of these user management providers such as Janrain [38], OneAll [39], LoginRadius [40] or Gigya [41].

6. IDENTITY 2.0 FOR MOBILE USERS

In this section, we discuss identity management in the realm of mobile computing devices. These devices are used more and more, and have different constraints than fixed desktop computers.

Introduction

The number of devices such as mobile phones, smart cards and RFIDs [42], is increasing daily and becoming huge. Mobile phones have attracted particular interest because of their large penetration and pervasiveness that exceeds that of personal computers. Furthermore, the emergence of both IP-TV and wireless technology has facilitated the proliferation of intelligent devices, mobile phones, RFIDs, and other forms of information technology that are developing at a rapid speed. These devices include a fixed identifier that could be linked to the user's identity. This identifier provides a mobile identity which takes into account information about the location and the mobile user's personal data [43].

Mobile Web 2.0

Mobile Web 2.0 as a content-based service is an up-to-date offering of services within the mobile network. As the number of people having access to mobile devices exceeds those using a desktop computer, *mobile Web* will be a key factor for the next generation network. At the

moment, mobile Web suffers from lack of interoperability and usability due to the small screen size and lower computational capability. Fortunately, these limitations are only temporary and within 5 years they will be easily overcome. There will be convergence in the next generation public networks towards the mobile network which will bring mobility to the forefront. Thus, mobile identity management will play a central role in addressing issues such as usability, privacy and security which are key challenges for researcher in the mobile network. Since the initial launch of mobile Web services, customers have increasingly turned to their wireless phones to connect with family and friends and also to obtain the latest news and information or even to produce content with their mobile and then publish them. Mobile Web 2.0 [27] is the enforcement of evolution and will enhance the experience of users by providing connections in an easier and more efficient way. For this reason, it will be welcome by the key actors as a well-established core service identity management for the next generation mobile network. This mobile identity management will be used not only to identify, acquire, access and pay for services but also to offer context-aware services as well as location based services.

Mobility

The mobile identity may not be stored at the same location but could be distributed among many locations, authorities and devices. Indeed, identity is mobile in many respects [1]:

1. There is a device mobility where a person is using the same identity while using different devices;
2. There is a location mobility where a person is using the same devices while changing the location; and
3. There is context mobility where a person is receiving services based on different societal roles: as a parent, as a professional and so on.

The three kind of mobility are not isolated but they interacted more often and became concurrently modified creating much more complex situations that what implied from single mode. Mobile identity management addresses three main challenges: a. usability via context awareness b. trust based on the perception of secure operation and c. the protection of privacy [1].

Evolution of Mobile Identity

Mobile identity management is in its infancy. GSM networks, for example, provide management of SIM identities as a kind of mobile identity management, but they do not meet all the requirements for a complete Mobile identity management. Unlike static identity, already implemented in

Web 2.0 identity, dynamic aspects, such as the user's position or the temporal context, gain increasingly importance for new kinds of mobile applications [44].

Mobile identity (MId) infrastructure solutions have evolved over time and can be classified into three solutions. The first proposed solution is just an extension of wired identity management to mobile Internet. This is the widespread solution, which is limited to the users of mobile devices running the same operating system as wired solution. This limitation is expected to evolve over time mainly with the large deployment of Web services. Some specifications, such as Liberty Alliance specifications, have been developed for identity management including mobility. However, several limitations are observed when the MId system is derived from fixed context. These limitations are principally due to the assumptions during their design and they do not match well with extra requirement of mobility [1].

Many improvements such as interoperability, privacy and security are to be operated. Also, older centralized PKI must be replaced by a modern trust management system or at least a decentralized PKI.

The second solution is capable of providing an alternative to the prevalent Internet derived MId infrastructure. This consists of either connected (Cellular phones) or unconnected (Smartcards) mobiles devices.

The third one consists of using implantable radio frequency identity (RFID) devices. This approach is expected to increase rapidly even if the market penetration is smaller than cellular phones.

In addition, the sensitivity risk of data related to different applications and services are seldom at the same level and the number of identifiers used by a person is in constant increasing. Thus, there is a real need of different kind of credentials associated with different kind of applications. Indeed, a tool at the user side capable of managing the credentials and identifies is inevitable. With the increasing capacity of CPU power and the spreading number of mobile phone with a SIM card, mobile phones can be considered as a Personal Authentication Device (PDA). They can hold securely the users' credentials, password and even identities. Thereby, we introduced a new efficient Identity management device at the user side able to facilitate the memorization in one hand, and strengthen the security by limiting the number of passwords and their weakness in other hand. All wired identity management can be deployed using PDA. In addition, many different authentication architectures become possible and easy to implement such as dual channel authentication.

PDA as Solution to Strong Authentication

PDA is a tamper-resistant hardware device which could include smart card and sensors or not. As it is used for authentication it is called a personal authentication device (PDA) [45]. This term has been early used in the context of security by Wong and al. [46]. The approach is the same and the only thing change so far is the performance of the mobile device has radically changed. This is the opportunity to emphasis the user centricity as the PDA could strengthen the user experience and to facilitate the automation and system support of the identity management at the user side. The Figure 25.22 illustrated the combination of PDA and silo model. The user stores his/her identity in the PDA. Whenever he/she would like to connect to a Service provider.

1. He/she authenticates her/himself with a PIN code to use the PDA.
2. The user choose the Password to be used for his/her connection to the specific service provider.
3. The user launch and log to the specific service provider by entering his/her Username and the Password.

The PDA is a good device to tackle the weakness and non-convenience of password authentication. Thereby, we have a user friendly and user centric application and even introducing stronger authentication. The fundamental advantage of PDA comparing with common PC using common operating systems such as windows or linux is that PDA has a robust isolation of processes. Therefore, compromising one application does not compromise all the applications. This advantage is becoming less important for mobile phone as flexibility is introduced by manufacturers a lot of vulnerabilities is also introduced. We have seen many viruses for mobile phones and even nowadays we have viruses for RFID. This vulnerability can compromise authentication and even biometrics authentication. That's why we should be very vigilant in implementing security in

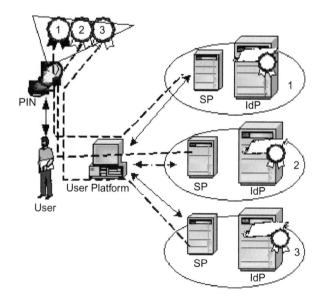

FIGURE 25.22 Integration of PDA in silo model.

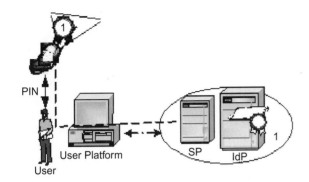

FIGURE 25.23 Single channel authentication.

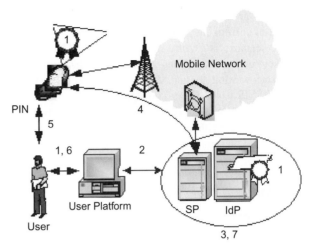

FIGURE 25.25 Scenario of SMS double channel authentication.

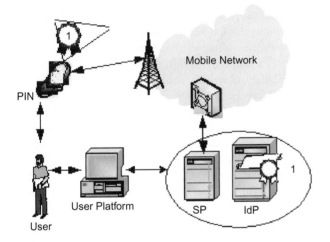

FIGURE 25.24 Dual channel authentication.

PDA devices. An ideal device is the USB stick running a standalone OS, and integrating a biometric reader and mobile network access. A can find some of them with fingerprint reader for a reasonable price.

Two main categories can group many authentication architectures that could be implemented in a PDA. There are single and dual channel authentications. Thereby, the cost, the risk and the non-convenience could be tackled at the same time.

Figure 25.23 illustrates the principle of single channel authentication, which is the first application of the PDA. Figure 25.24 illustrates the second principle of dual-channel authentication, which is more secure.

Different Kinds of Strong Authentication Through a Mobile PDA

The mobile network mainly GSM can help to overcome a lot of security vulnerabilities such as phishing or man-in-the-middle. It attracts all business that would like to deploy double channel authentication but are worry about cost and usability. The near-ubiquity of the mobile network has made feasible the utilization of this approach and even being adopted by some banks.

SMS Based One-Time Password (OTP)

The main advantages in mobile network are the facility and usability to send and receive SMSs. Moreover, they could be used to setup and download easily Java program to the mobile device. In addition, mobile devices are using smart card that can securely calculate and store claims.

The cost is minimized by adopting a mobile device using SMS to receive OTP instead of a special hardware that can generate OTP. The scenario implemented by some banks is illustrated in Figure 25.25. First of all, the user switches his/her mobile phone and enters his PIN code then:

1. The user log into his online account by entering his/her Username and Password (U/P)
2. The Web site received the couple U/P
3. The server verifies the couple
4. Send a SMS message with OTP
5. The user reads the message
6. The user enters the OPT into online account
7. The server verify the OPT and give access

The problem of this approach is the fact that the cost is assumed by the service provider. In addition, some drawbacks are very common mainly in some developing countries such as lack of coverage and SMS latency. Of course, the attack of the man-in-the-middle is not overcome by this approach.

Soft Token Application

In this case, the PDA is used as a token emitter. The application is previously downloaded. SMS could be sent to the user in order to set up the application that will play the role of soft token.

The scenario is exactly identical to the SMS but only the user generates his/her OTP using the soft token instead of waiting for a SMS message. The cost is less than the SMS based OTP. This approach is a single channel authentication that is not dependent on mobile network coverage neither on his latency. Furthermore, the attack of the man-in-the-middle is not tackle.

Full Option Mobile Solution

We have seen in the two previously scenarios that the attacks of the man-in-the-middle is not addressed. It exist a counterattack to this security issue consisting of using the second channel to completely control all the transactions over the online connection. Of course, the security of this approach is based on the assumption that it is difficult for an attacker to steal the user's personal mobile phone or to attack the mobile network. Anyway, we have developed an application to crypt the SMS message which minimizes the risk of attacks. The scenario is illustrated in the Figure 25.26 and it is as follows:

1. The user login on online account using token
2. The server receives the token
3. The server verifies the token
4. the access is given to the service
5. the user request a transaction
6. SMS message is send with the requested transaction and a confirmation code
7. The user verifies the transaction
8. He enters the confirmation code
9. The server verifies and execute the transaction
10. The server sends a transaction confirmation

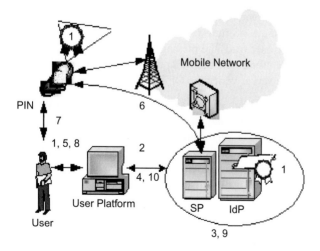

FIGURE 25.26 Secure transaction via SMS.

Future of Mobile User-Centric Identity Management in an Ambient Intelligence (AmI) World

AmI manifests itself through a collection of everyday devices incorporating computing and networking capabilities that enable them to interact with each other, make intelligent decisions and interact with users through user friendly multimodal interfaces. Ambient intelligence is driven by users' needs and the design of its capabilities should be driven by users' requirements.

Ambient Intelligence technologies are expected to combine concepts of ubiquitous computing and intelligent systems putting humans in the center of technological developments. Indeed, the Internet extension to home and mobile networks, the multiplication of modes of connection will make the individual the central point. Therefore, the identity is a challenge in this environment and will guarantee the infatuation with Ambient Intelligence. Moreover, AmI will be the future environment where we shall be surrounded by mobile devices which will be more and more used for mobile interactions with things, places and people.

The low-cost and the shrinking size of sensors as well as the ease of deployment will aid ambient intelligence research efforts for rapid prototyping. Evidently, a sensor combined with unique biometric identifiers is becoming more frequently utilized in access a system, and supposedly provide proof of a person's identity and thus accountability for subsequent actions. To explore these new AmI technologies, it is easier to investigate a scenario related to ubiquitous computing in an ambient intelligence environment.

AmI Scenario

A person having a mobile device, GPS (or equivalent) and an ad-hoc communication network connected to sensors, visits an intelligent environment supermarket and would like to acquire some merchandise. We illustrate below how this person can benefit from mobile identity.

When this person enters the supermarket, he/she is identified by means of his/her mobile device or implemented RFID tag and a special menu is displayed to him/her. His/her profile, related to his/her context identity, announces a discount if there is one.

The members of his/her social network could propose him/her a connection if they are present and even guide him to their location. Merchandise on display could communicate with his/her device to show prices and details. Location-based services could be offered to quickly find his/her specific articles.

His device could help him to find diabetic foods or any restrictions associated with specific articles. A secure Web connection could be initiated to give more information about purchases and the user account.

An adaptive screen could be used by the supermarket to show him/her information that is too extensive for his/her device screen. Payment could be carried out using payment identity stored in his/her device and even a biometric identity to prevent identity theft.

Identity information and profiling should be portable and seamless for interoperability. The identity must be managed to ensure user control. Power and performance management in this environment is a must. The concept of authentication between electronic devices is also highlighted.

In order to use identity management, the user needs an appropriate tool to facilitate the management for the disclosure of personal data. A usable and secure tool should be proposed to help even inexperienced users manage their general security needs when using the network.

We need mobile identity management, which is a concept that allows the user to keep his or her privacy, depending on the situation. By using identity management, the user's device acts in a similar way to the user. In different contexts, the user presents a different appearance. Devices controlled by identity management change their behavior similar to the way in which a user would.

Requirements for Mobile User-centric Identity Management in an AmI world

As the network evolution is toward mobility with the proliferation of ubiquitous and pervasive computing systems, the importance of identity management to build trust relationships in the context of electronic and mobile (e/m) government and business is evident [47,48]. Thereby, all these systems require advanced, automated identity management systems in order to be cost effective and easy to use.

Several mobile devices such as mobile phones, smart cards of RFID are used for mobility. As mobile devices have fixed identifiers, they are essentially providing a mobile identity that can be liked to a user. Mobile identity takes into account location data of mobile users in addition to their personal data. A recent court decision in the UK has established as proof of location of the accused the location trace of his mobile phone which implies a de facto recognition of the identity of a citizen as the identity of her mobile telephones [1].

That is why Mobile identity management (MIdm) is necessary to empower mobile users to manage their mobile identities to enforce their security and privacy interests. Mobile identity management is a special kind of identity management. For this purpose, mobile users must be able to control the disclosure of their mobile identity dependent on the respective service provider and also their location via mobile identity management systems.

Ambient Intelligence emphasizes the principles of secure communication anywhere, anytime, with anything.

The evolution of AmI will directly influence identity management with this requirement to ensure mutual interaction between users and things. *Being Anywhere* will imply more and more mobility, interoperability and profiling. *At Anytime* will imply online as well as offline connection as the network does not have a 100% coverage and will imply power as well as performance management in order to optimize use battery. *With anything* will imply sensor use, biometrics and RFID interaction; and *Securely* implies more and more integration of privacy, authentication, anonymity and prevention of identity theft.

From multilateral security [49,50], Jendricke [31] has derived privacy principles for MIdm and we have completed them below with a few other important principles. Management systems are as follows:

1. Context-detection
   a. Sensors
   b. Biometrics
   c. RFID
2. Anonymity
3. Security
   a. Confidentiality
   b. Integrity
   c. Non-repudiation
   d. Availability
4. Privacy
   a. Protection of location information
5. Trustworthiness
   a. Segregation of power, separating knowledge, integrating independent parties
   b. Using Open Source
   c. Trusted seals of approval seal
6. Law Enforcement / Liability
   a. Digital evidence
   b. Digital signatures
   c. Data retention
7. Usability
   a. Comfortable and informative user interfaces
   b. Training and education
   c. Reduction of system' complexity
   d. Raising awareness
8. Affordability
   a. Power of market :Produce MIMS that are competitive and are able to reach a remarkable penetration of market
   b. Using open source building blocks
   c. Subsidies for development, use, operation, etc.
9. Power management: the energy provided by the batteries of mobile devices is limited and that energy must be used with care on energy-friendly applications and services
10. Online and offline identity proof
11. Small screen size and lower computational capability

12. Interoperability

    a. Identity needs to be portable to be understood by any device.

7. SUMMARY

The Internet is being used more and more; but, the fact that the Internet has not been developed with an adequate identity layer is a major security risk. Password fatigue and online fraud are a growing problem and are damaging user confidence. However it is a difficult problem to solve both from a technical point of view and a business model point of view. Users are not prepared to pay themselves for identity management and expect the service provider should provide it to them. It is the reason that a number of major initiatives trying to provide a more adequate identity layer for the Internet surveyed above and already present in the first version of this chapter have been discontinued due to a failing business model, for example, Sxip. If the user experience is too long or require retyping personal information, many users may not take the time to join the new service. "Social login" provided by online social networks has emerged as the main identity management solution adopted by the users to log in to new Web sites and services because they did not have to type their personal information again. It has been to the detriment to the privacy of the users but it is clear that it does not worry the users because they are not able to take into account the effect of this privacy leak in the long term. They prefer accessing the service they want to use, such as Facebook, even if it may impact their privacy in the long term. Thus, although "social login" do not fulfill all identity management requirements that have been presented in this chapter since its first version, "social login" has won over many other identity management initiatives, even if a few of them are still used underneath, e.g., OpenId. User management providers listed in Section 4 and aggregating several "social login" solutions for Web sites and services are promising. Another development concerns mobile identity management and those new user management providers may also play an importation role in this respect.

Finally, let's move on to the real interactive part of this Chapter: review questions/exercises, hands-on projects, case projects and optional team case project. The answers and/or solutions by chapter can be found in the Online Instructor's Solutions Manual.

CHAPTER REVIEW QUESTIONS/EXERCISES

True/False

1. True or False? A digital identity is a representation of an entity in a general context.

2. True or False? Identity management refers to "the process of representing, using, maintaining, deprovisioning and authenticating entities as digital identities in computer networks."

3. True or False? Privacy is a central issue, due to the fact that the official authorities of almost all countries have legal strict policies related to identity.

4. True or False? The evolution of the identity management system is away from the simplification of user experience and reinforcing authentication.

5. True or False? The security is also compromised with the proliferation of the user's password and even by it's strength.

Multiple Choice

1. The main identity management system deployed currently in the world of the Internet is known as the?

    A. Federated identity management model

    B. Identity life cycle

    C. Aggregate identity

    D. Executive management model

    E. Silo model

2. _____ in centralized identity infrastructures, can't solve the problem of cross-organizational authentication and authorization?

    A. Centrally managed repositories

    B. Information system auditors

    C. IT personnel

    D. Systems Administrators

    E. All of the above

3. A relatively simple _____ model is to build a platform that centralizes identities?

    A. Common user identity management

    B. Simple centralized identity management

    C. Unique identity management

    D. Meta directory

    E. Executive Management

4. What provides an abstraction boundary between application and the actual implementation?

    A. Single point of administration

    B. Redundant directory information

    C. Single point of reference

    D. Business impact analysis

    E. All of the above

5. What directories are not located in the same physical structure as the Web home directory, but look as if they were to Web clients?

    A. Single Sign-On

    B. Seamless

    C. Session

    D. Virtual

    E. Flexible

EXERCISE

Problem

What is a digital identity?

Hands-On Projects

Project

Why would a bank issue digital identities?

Case Projects

Problem

Does the digital identity capture the physical signature of the person?

Optional Team Case Project

Problem

What if I am already using digital certificates or credentials?

REFERENCES

[1] G. Roussos, U. Patel, Mobile Identity Management: An Enacted View, Birkbeck College, University of London, City University, London, 2003.

[2] A. Westin, Privacy and Freedom, Athenaeum, New York, NY, 1967.

[3] J. Madelin, et al., BT report on: comprehensive identity management Balancing cost, risk and convenience in identity management, 2007.

[4] T. Miyata, et al., A survey on identity management protocols and standards, IEICE Trans. Inf. Syst. (2006).

[5] J.-M. Seigneur, Trust, Security and Privacy in Global Computing, PhD Thesis, Trinity College Dublin, 2005.

[6] Introduction to the Liberty Alliance Identity Architecture. Rev. 1.0, March 2003.

[7] A.B. Spantzel, et al., User Centricity: A taxonomy and open issues, IBM Zurich Research Laboratory, 2006.

[8] Independent Center for Privacy Protection (ICPP) and Studio Notarile Genghini(SNG), Identity Management Systems (IMS): Identification and Comparison Study, 2003.

[9] K. Cameron, Laws of Identity, 5/12/2005.

[10] T.M. Cooley, A Treatise on the Law of Torts, Callaghan, Chicago, 1888.

[11] Identity Management Systems (IMS): Identification and Comparison Study, Independent Center for Privacy Protection (ICPP) and Studio Notarile Genghini(SNG), 2003.

[12] David Recordon VeriSign Inc, Drummond Reed, OpenID 2.0: A Platform for User-Centric Identity Management, 2006.

[13] A user centric anonymous authorisation framework in ecommerce environment Richard Au, Harikrishna Vasanta, KimKwang Raymond Choo, Mark Looi Information Security Research Centre Queensland University of Technology, Brisbane, Australia.

[14] Federal financial institutions examination council. Authentication in an internetbanking environment. <http://www.ffiec.gov/press/pr101205.htm>, October 2005.

[15] A. Erzberg, A. Gbara, TrustBar: protecting even Naïve) Web Users from Spoofing and Phishing Attacks. <http://wwwcs.biu.ac.il/~erzbea/papaers/ecommerce/spoofing.htm>, 2004.

[16] Introduction to Usability. <http://www.usabilityfirst.com/intro/index.tx1>, 2005.

[17] A. Jøsang, S. Pope, User Centric Identity Management, AusCERT Conference, 2005.

[18] ITU (International Telecommunication Union), Geneva. <http://www.itu.org/>.

[19] A. Jøsang, et al., Usability and Privacy in identity management architectures, (AISW2007) Ballarat, Australia, 2007.

[20] Internet2, Shibboleth project. <http://shibboleth.Internet2.edu>.

[21] C. Esslison et al., RFC 2693- SPKI Certification Theory. IETF. <http://www.ietf.org/rfc/rfc2693.txt>, Sep. 1999.

[22] T. Miyata, et al., A survey on identity management protocols and standards, IEICE Trans. Inf. Syst. (2006).

[23] Kantara Initiative. <http://kantarainitiative.org/>.

[24] Microsoft, a technical ref. for InfoCard in windows. <http://msdn.microsoft.com/winfx/reference/infocard/,2005>.

[25] J. Merrels, SXIP Identity. DIX: Digital Identity Exchange Protocol. Internet Draft, March 2006.

[26] Higgings trust framework project. <http://www.eclipse.org/higgins/>, 2006.

[27] A. Jaokar, T. Fish. Mobile Web 2.0, a book 2007.

[28] Liberty developer tutorial. <http://www.projectliberty.org/resources/LAP_DIDW_Oct-15_2003_jp.pdf>.

[29] XACML. <http://www.oasis-open.org/committees/tc_home.php?wg_abbrev=xacml>.

[30] Liberty alliance, liberty ID-FF architecture overview. Liberty alliance project, 2005.

[31] U. Jendricke et al., Mobile identity management, UBICOMP, 2002.

[32] Sxip bankruptcy. <http://techcrunch.com/2008/05/22/identity-20-startup-sxips-into-the-deadpool/>.

[33] IETF OAuth. <https://www.ietf.org/mailman/listinfo/oauth>.

[34] Twitter. <http://www.twitter.com>.

[35] Facebook. <http://www.facebook.com>.

[36] LinkedIn. <http://www.linkedin.com>.

[37] Google. <http://www.google.com>.

[38] Janrain. <http://www.janrain.com>.

[39] OneAll. <http://www.oneall.com>.

[40] LoginRadius. <http://www.loginradius.com>.

[41] Gigya. <http://www.gigya.com>.

[42] S. Garfinkel, B. Rosenberg, RFID, Applications, Security and Privacy, Addison Wesley, Boston, 2006.

[43] S.A. Weis, al., Security and privacy aspects of low-Cost radio frequency identification systems, *Proc. of the First International Conference on Security in Pervasive Computing*, March 2003.

[44] User-centric identity management in open mobile environments Mario Hoffmann Fraunhofer-Institute for secure telecooperation (SIT).

[45] A. Jøsang, et al., Trust Requirements in Identity Management, AISW, 2005.

[46] Wong, et al., Polonius: an identity authentication system, Proceedings of the 1985 IEEE Symposium on security and Privacy.

[47] MyGrocer Consortium, Mygrocer whitepaper, 2002.

[48] M. Wieser, The Computer for the twenty-first century, *Scientific American*, 1991.

[49] K. Rannenberg, Multilateral security? a concept and examples for balanced security, *Proc. of the Ninth ACM new security Paradigms Workshop* 2000.

[50] K. Reichenbach, al., individual management of personal reachability in mobile communications, Proc. of the IFIP TC11 (Sec'97).

## Chapter 26

Intrusion Prevention and Detection Systems

Christopher Day
Terremark Worldwide, Inc.

1. WHAT IS AN 'INTRUSION' ANYWAY?

Information security concerns itself with the confidentiality, integrity and availability of information systems and the information or data they contain and process. An 'intrusion' then is any action taken by an adversary that has a negative impact on the confidentiality, integrity, or availability of that information. Given such a broad definition of 'intrusion' it is instructive to examine a number of commonly occurring classes of information system (IS) intrusions.

2. PHYSICAL THEFT

Having physical access to a computer system allows an adversary to bypass most security protections put in place to prevent unauthorized access. By stealing a computer system, the adversary has all the physical access he or she could want and unless the sensitive data on the system is strongly encrypted (see sidebar, "Definition of Encryption"), the data is very likely to be compromised. This issue is most prevalent with laptop loss and theft. Given the processing and storage capacity of even low-cost laptops today, a great deal of sensitive information can be put at risk if a laptop containing this data is stolen. In May of 2006, it was revealed that over 26 million military veterans' personal information including names, social security numbers, addresses, and some disability data was on a Veteran Affairs staffer's laptop that was stolen from his home [2a]. The stolen data was of the type that is often used to commit identity theft and due to the large number of impacted veterans, there was a great deal of concern about this theft and the lack of security around such a sensitive collection of data. In another example, in May of 2012 it was revealed that an unencrypted laptop containing medical records for 2,159 patients was stolen Boston Children's Hospital staffer while travelling overseas for a conference [2b].

Definition of Encryption

Encryption is the process of protecting the content or meaning of a message or other kinds of data [3]. Modern encryption algorithms are based on complex mathematical functions that scramble the original, clear-text message or data in such a way that makes it difficult or impossible for an adversary to read or access the data without the proper key to reverse the scrambling. The encryption key is typically a large number of values that when fed into the encryption algorithm scrambles and unscrambles the data being protected and without which it is extremely difficult or impossible to decrypt encrypted data. The science of encryption is called cryptography and is a broad and technical subject.

3. ABUSE OF PRIVILEGES (THE INSIDER THREAT)

An insider is an individual who, due to their role in the organization, has some level of authorized access to the IS environment and systems. The level of access can range from that of a regular user to a system administrator with nearly unlimited privileges. When an insider abuses their privileges the impact can be devastating. Even a relatively limited-privilege user is already starting with an advantage over an outsider due to their knowledge of the IS environment, critical business processes, and potential knowledge of security weaknesses or 'soft spots'. An insider may use their access to steal sensitive data such as customer databases, trade secrets, national security secrets, or personally identifiable information (PII) (see sidebar, "Definition of Personally Identifiable Information"). Because they are a trusted user and given that many intrusion detection systems are designed to monitor for attacks from outsiders, an insider's privileged abuse can go on for a long time unnoticed thus compounding the damage. In 2010, US soldier Bradley Manning allegedly utilized his legitimate access to the

Secret Internet Protocol Router Network (SIPRNet) to pass classified information to the whistleblower website WikiLeaks in what has been described as the largest known theft of classified information in US history [4]. An appropriately privileged user may also use their access to make unauthorized modifications to systems that can undermine the security of the environment. These changes can range from creating "backdoor" accounts used to preserve access in the event of termination to installing so-called "logic bombs" which are programs designed to cause damage to systems or data at some predetermined point in time, often as a form of retribution for some real or perceived sleight.

Definition of Personally Identifiable Information

Personally Identifiable Information (PII) is a set of information such as name, address, social security number, financial account number, credit card number, and driver's license number. This class of information is considered particularly sensitive due to its value to identify thieves and others who commit financial crimes such as credit card fraud. Most states in the United States have some form of data breach disclosure law which imposes a burden of notification on any organization which suffers unauthorized access, loss, or theft of unencrypted PII. It is worth noting that all of the current laws provide a level of 'Safe Harbor' for organizations that suffer a PII loss if the PII was encrypted. California's SB1386 was the first and arguably most well known of the disclosure laws.

---

4. UNAUTHORIZED ACCESS BY OUTSIDER

An outsider is considered anyone who does not have authorized access privileges to an information system or environment. To gain access the outsider may try to gain possession of valid system credentials via social engineering or even by guessing username and password pairs in a brute force attack. Alternatively, the outsider may attempt to exploit a vulnerability in the target system to gain access. Often the result of successfully exploiting a system vulnerability leads to some form of high-privileged access to the target, such as an "Administrator" or Administrator-equivalent account on a Microsoft Windows system or "root" or root-equivalent account on a UNIX or Linux-based system. Once an outsider has this level of access on a system he or she effectively "owns" that system and can steal data or use the system as a launching point to attack other systems.

5. MALWARE INFECTION

Malware can be generally defined as "a set of instructions that run on your computer and make your system do something that allow an attacker to make it do what he

wants it to do" [5]. Historically, malware (see sidebar, "Classifying Malware") in the form of viruses and worms was more of a disruptive nuisance than a real threat but it has been evolving as the weapon of choice for many attackers due to the increased sophistication, stealthiness, and scalability of intrusion-focused malware. Today, we see malware being used by intruders to gain access to systems, search for valuable data such as PII and passwords, monitor real-time communications, provide remote access/control, and automatically attack other systems just to name a few capabilities. Using malware as an attack method also provides the attacker with a "stand-off" capability that reduces the risk of identification, pursuit, and prosecution. By "stand-off" we mean the ability to launch the malware via a number of anonymous methods such as an insecure, open public wireless access point and once the malware has gained access to the intended target or targets, manage the malware via a distributed command and control system such as Internet Relay Chat (IRC), web site pages, dynamic DNS, as well as completely novel mechanisms. Not only does the command and control network help mask the location and identity of the attacker but it also provides a scalable way to manage many compromised systems at once, maximizing the results for the attacker. In some cases the number of controlled machines can be astronomical, such as with the Storm worm infection which, depending on the estimate, ranged somewhere between one and ten million compromised systems [6]. These large collections of compromised systems are often referred to as "bot-nets".

Classifying Malware

Malware takes many forms but can be roughly classified by function and replication method.

- *Virus*: Self-replicating code that attaches itself to another program. It typically relies on human interaction to start the host program and activate the virus. A virus usually has a limited function set and its creator has no further interaction with it once released. Examples are Melissa, Michelangelo, and Sobig.
- *Worm*: Self-replicating code that propagates over a network, usually without human interaction. Most worms take advantage of a known vulnerability in systems and compromise those that aren't properly patched. Worm creators have begun experimenting with updateable code and payloads, such as seen with the Storm worm [5]. Examples are Code Red, SQL Slammer, and Blaster.
- *Backdoor*: A program that bypasses standard security controls to provide an attacker access, often in a stealthy way. Backdoors rarely have self-replicating capability and are either installed manually by an attacker after compromising a system to facilitate future access or by other self-propagating malware as payload. Examples are Back Orifice, Tini, and netcat (netcat has legitimate uses as well).

- *Trojan Horse*: A program that masquerades as a legitimate, useful program while also performing malicious functions in the background. Trojans are often used to steal data or monitor user actions and can provide a backdoor function as well. Examples of two well-known programs that have had Trojaned versions circulated on the Internet are tcpdump and Kazaa.
- *User-level Rootkit*: Trojan/ backdoor code that modifies operating system software so the attacker can maintain privileged access on a machine but remain hidden. For example, the rootkit will remove malicious processes from user-requested process lists. This form of rootkit is called user-level because it manipulates operating system components utilized by users. This form of rootkit can often be uncovered by the use of trusted tools and software since the core of the operating system is still unaffected. Examples of user-level rootkits are the Linux Rootkit (LRK) family and FakeGINA.
- *Kernel-level Rootkit*: Trojan/ backdoor code that modifies the core or kernel of the operating system to provide the intruder the highest level of access and stealth. A kernel-level rootkit inserts itself into the core of the operating system, the kernel, and intercepts system calls and thus can remain hidden even from trusted tools brought onto the system from the outside by an investigator. Effectively, nothing the compromised system tells a user can be trusted and detecting and removing kernel-level rootkits is very difficult and often requires advanced technologies and techniques. Examples are Adore and Hacker Defender.
- *Blended Malware*: More recent forms of malware combine features and capabilities discussed above into one program. For example, one might see a Trojan Horse that once activated by the user inserts a backdoor utilizing user-level rootkit capabilities to stay hidden and provide a remote handler with access. Examples of blended malware are Lion and Bugbear.

6. THE ROLE OF THE '0-DAY'

The Holy Grail for vulnerability researchers and exploit writers is to discover a previously unknown and exploitable vulnerability, often referred to as a 0-day exploit (pronounced 'zero day' or 'oh day'). Given that others have not discovered the vulnerability, all systems running the vulnerable code will be unpatched and possible targets for attack and compromise. The danger of a given 0-day is a function of how widespread the vulnerable software is and what level of access it gives the attacker. For example, a reliable 0-day for something as widespread as the ubiquitous Apache Web server that somehow yields root or Administrator-level access to the attacker is far more dangerous and valuable than an exploit that works against an obscure point-of-sale system used by only a few hundred users (unless the attacker's target is that very set of users).

In addition to potentially having a large, vulnerable target set to exploit, the owner of a 0-day also has the advantage that most intrusion detection and prevention systems will not trigger on the exploit for the very fact that it has never been seen before and the various IDS/IPS technologies will not have signature patterns for the exploit yet. We will discuss this issue in more detail later.

It is this combination of many unpatched targets and the ability to potentially evade many forms of intrusion detection and prevention systems that make 0-days such a powerful weapon in the hands of an attacker. Many legitimate security and vulnerability researchers explore software systems to uncover 0-days and report them to the appropriate software vendor in the hopes of preventing malicious individuals from finding and using them first. Those who intend to use 0-days for illicit purposes guard the knowledge of a 0-day very carefully lest it become widely and publically known and effective countermeasures, including vendor software patches, can be deployed.

One of the more disturbing issues regarding 0-days is their lifetimes. The lifetime of a 0-day is the amount of time between the discovery of the vulnerability and public disclosure through vendor or researcher announcement, mailing lists, and so on. By the very nature of 0-day discovery and disclosure it is difficult to get reliable statistics on lifetimes but one vulnerability research organization claims their studies indicate an average 0-day lifetime of 348 days [7]. Hence, if malicious attackers have a high-value 0-day in hand, they may have almost a year to put it to most effective use. If used in a stealthy manner so as not to tip off system defenders, vendors, and researchers this sort of 0-day can yield many high-value compromised systems for the attackers. While there has been no official substantiation, there has been a great deal of speculation that the "Titan Rain" series of attacks against sensitive United States government networks between 2003 and 2005 utilized a set of 0-days against Microsoft software [8,9].

7. THE ROGUE'S GALLERY: ATTACKERS AND MOTIVES

Now that we have examined some of the more common forms computer system intrusions take, it is worthwhile to discuss those who are behind these attacks and attempt to understand their motivations. The appropriate selection of intrusion detection and prevention technologies is dependent on the threat being defended against, the class of adversary and the value of the asset being protected.

While it is always risky to generalize, those who attack computer systems for illicit purposes can be placed into a number of broad categories. At minimum this gives us a "capability spectrum" of attackers to begin to understand motivations and, therefore, threats.

Script Kiddy

The pejorative term "script kiddy" is used to describe those who have little or no skill at writing or understanding how vulnerabilities are discovered and exploits written but download and utilize other's exploits available on the Internet to attack vulnerable systems. Typically, script kiddies are not a threat to a well managed, patched environment as they are usually relegated to using publically known and available exploits for which patches and detection signatures already exist.

Joy Rider

This type of attacker is often represented by those with potentially significant skills in discovering vulnerabilities and writing exploits but who rarely have any real malicious intent when they access systems they are not authorized on. In a sense they are "exploring" for the pleasure of it. However, while their intentions are not directly malicious, their actions can represent a major source of distraction and cost to system administrators who must respond to the intrusion especially if the compromised system contained sensitive data such as PII where a public disclosure may be required.

Mercenary

Since the late nineties there has been a growing market for those who possess the skills to compromise computer systems and are willing to sell them and those willing to purchase these skills [10]. Organized crime is a large consumer of these services and computer crime has seen a significant increase in both frequency and severity over the last decade, primarily driven by direct, illicit financial gain and identity theft [11]. In fact, so successful have these groups become that a full-blown market has emerged including support organizations offering technical support for rented bot-nets and online trading environments for the exchange of stolen credit card data and PII. Stolen data has a tangible financial value as can be seen by Table 26.1, which indicates the dollar value ranges for various types of PII.

Nation-State Backed

Nations performing espionage against other nations do not ignore the potential for intelligence gathering via information technology systems. Sometimes this espionage takes the form of malware injection and system compromises such as the previously mentioned Titan Rain attack while other times it may take the form of electronic data interception of unencrypted e-mail and other messaging protocols. A number of nations have developed or are

TABLE 26.1 PII Values.

Goods and Services	Percentage	Range of Prices
Financial Accounts	22%	$10–$1,000
Credit Card Information	13%	$.40-$20
Identity Information	9%	$1–$15
eBay Accounts	7%	$1–$8
Scams	7%	$2.5–$50/week for hosting $25 for design
Mailers	6%	$1–$10
Email Addresses	5%	$.83-$10/MB
Email Passwords	5%	$4–$30
Drop (request or offer)	5%	10%–50% of drop amount
Proxies	5%	$1.50–$30

(Complied from Miami Electronic Crimes Task Force and Symantec Global Internet Security Threat Report (2008)).

developing an information warfare capability designed to impair or incapacitate an enemy's Internet-connected systems, command-and-control systems, and other information technology capability [12]. These sorts of capabilities were demonstrated in 2007 against Estonia, allegedly by Russian sympathizers, utilizing a sustained series of denial-of-service attacks designed to make certain Websites unreachable as well as interfere with online activities such as e-mail and mission-critical systems such as telephone exchanges [13].

8. A BRIEF INTRODUCTION TO TCP/IP

Throughout the history of computing, there have been numerous networking protocols, the structured rules computers use to communicate with each other, but none have been as successful and become as ubiquitous as the Transmission Control Protocol/Internet Protocol (TCP/IP) suite of protocols. TCP/IP is the protocol suite used on the Internet and the vast majority of enterprise and government networks have now implemented TCP/IP on their networks. Due to this ubiquity almost all attacks against computer systems seen today are designed to be launched over a TCPI/IP network and thus the majority of intrusion detection and prevention systems are designed to operate with and monitor TCP/IP-based networks. Therefore, to better understand the nature of these technologies it is important to have a working knowledge of TCP/IP. While a complete description of TCP/IP is beyond the scope of this chapter, there are numerous excellent references and tutorials for those interested in learning more [14,15]. Three features that have made TCP/IP so popular and widespread are [16]:

1. Open protocol standards that are freely available. This and independence from any particular operating system or computing hardware means TCP/IP can be deployed on nearly any computing device imaginable.
2. Hardware, transmission media and device independence. TCP/IP can operate over numerous physical devices and network types such as Ethernet, Token Ring, optical, radio, and satellite.
3. A consistent and globally scalable addressing scheme. This ensures that any two uniquely addressed network nodes can communicate (notwithstanding any traffic restrictions implemented for security or policy reasons) with each other even if those nodes are on different sides of the planet.

9. THE TCP/IP DATA ARCHITECTURE AND DATA ENCAPSULATION

The best way to describe and visualize the TCP/IP protocol suite is to think of it as a layered stack of functions, as shown in Figure 26.1.

Each layer is responsible for a set of services and capabilities provided to the layers above and below it. This layered model allows developers and engineers to modularize the functionality in a given layer and minimize the impacts of changes on other layers. Each layer performs a series of functions on data as it is prepared for network transport or received from the network. How those functions are performed internal to a given layer is hidden from the other layers and as long as the agreed upon rules and standards are adhered to with regards to

how data is passed from layer to layer, the inner workings of a given layer are isolated from any other.

The Application Layer is concerned with applications and processes, including those that users interact with such as browsers, e-mail, instant messaging and other network-aware programs. There may also be numerous applications in the Application Layer running on a computer system that interact with the network but users have little interaction with such as routing protocols.

The Transport Layer is responsible for handling data flow between applications on different hosts on the network. There are two Transport protocols in the TCP/IP suite: the Transport Control Protocol (TCP) and the User Datagram Protocol (UDP). TCP is a connection or session oriented protocol which provides a number of services to the above application such as reliable delivery via Positive Acknowledgement with Retransmission (PAR), packet sequencing to account for out-of-sequence receipt of packets, receive buffer management, and error detection. In contrast, UDP is a low-overhead, connectionless protocol that provides no delivery acknowledgement or other session services. Any necessary application reliability must be built into the application whereas with TCP, the application need not worry about the details of packet delivery. Each protocol serves a specific purpose and allows maximum flexibility to application developers and engineers. There may be numerous network services running on a computer system each built on either TCP or UDP (or, in some cases, both) so both protocols utilize the concept of *ports* to identify a specific network service and direct data appropriately. For example, a computer may be running a Web server and standard Web services are offered on TCP port 80. That same computer could also be running an e-mail system utilizing the Simple Mail Transport Protocol (SMTP) which is by standard offered on TCP port 25. Finally, this server may also be running a Domain Name Server (DNS) server on both TCP and UDP port 53. As can be seen, the concept of ports allows multiple TCP and UDP services to be run on the same computer system without interfering with each other.

The Network Layer is primarily responsible for packet addressing and routing through the network. The Internet Protocol (IP) manages this process within the TCP/IP protocol suite. One very important construct found in IP is the concept of an IP address. Each system running on a TCP/IP network must have at least one unique address for other computer systems to direct traffic to it. An IP address is represented by a 32-bit number which is usually represented as four integers ranging from 0 to 255 separated by decimals such as 192.168.1.254. This representation is often referred to as a *dotted quad*. The IP address actually contains two pieces of information in it: the network address and the node address. To know where the network address ends and the node address

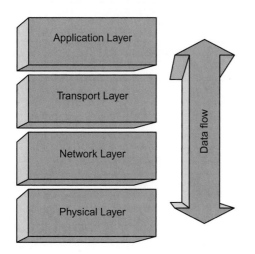

FIGURE 26.1 TCP/IP data architecture stack.

begins a *subnet mask* is used to indicate the number of bits in the IP address assigned to the network address and is usually designated as a slash and a number such as '/24'. If the example address of 192.168.1.254 has a subnet mask of /24, then we know that the network address is 24 bits or 192.168.1 and the node address is 254. If we were presented with a subnet mask of /16 then we would know the network address is 192.168 while the node address is 1.254. Subnet masking allows network designers to construct subnets of various sizes ranging from two nodes (a subnet mask of /30) to literally millions of nodes (a subnet of /8) or anything in between. The topic of subnetting and its impact on addressing and routing is a complex one and the interested reader is referred to [14] for more detail.

The Physical Layer is responsible for interaction with the physical network medium. Depending on the specifics of the medium this may include functions such as collision avoidance, the transmission and reception of packets or datagrams, basic error checking, and so on. The Physical Layer handles all of the details of interfacing with the network medium and isolates the upper layers from the physical details.

Another important concept in TCP/IP is that of data encapsulation. Data is passed up and down the stack as it travels from a network-aware program or application in the Application Layer, is packaged for transport across the network by the Transport and Network Layer and eventually placed on the transmission medium (copper or fiber optic cable, radio, satellite, and so on) by the Physical Layer. As data is handed down the stack, each layer adds its own header (a structured collection of fields of data) to the data passed to it by the above layer. Figure 26.2 illustrates three important headers: the IP header, the TCP header, and the UDP header. The reader will note the various headers are where layer-specific

IP, Version 4 Header

4-bit version	4-bit header length	8-bit type of service	16-bit total packet length (value in bytes)	
16-bit IP/fragment identification			3-bit flags	13-bit fragment offset
8-bit time to live (TTL)		8-bit protcol ID	16-bit header checksum	
32-bit source IP address				
32-bit destination IP address				
options (if present)				
data (inlcuding upper layer headers)				

TCP Header

16-bit source port number			16-bit destination port number	
32-bit sequence number				
32-bit acknowledgement number				
4-bit TCP header length	6-bit reserved	6-bit flags	16-bit window size	
16-bit TCP checksum			16-bit urgent pointer	
options (if present)				
data (if any)				

UDP Header

16-bit source port number	16-bit destination port number
16-bit UDP length (header plus data)	16-bit UDP checksum
data (if any)	

(sourced from Request for Comment (RFC) 791, 793, 768)

FIGURE 26.2 IP, TCP, and UDP headers.

constructs such as IP address and TCP or UDP port numbers are placed so the appropriate layer can access this information and act on the accordingly.

The receiving layer is not concerned with the content of the data passed to it, only that the data is given to it in a way compliant with the protocol rules. The Physical Layer places the completed packet (the full collection of headers and application data) onto the transmission medium for handling by the physical network. When a packet is received, the reverse process occurs. As the packet travels up the stack, each layer removes its respective header, inspects the header content for instructions on which upper layer in the protocol stack to hand the remaining data to, and passes the data to the appropriate layer. This process is repeated until all TCP/IP headers have been removed and the appropriate application is handed the data. The encapsulation process is illustrated in Figure 26.3.

To best illustrate these concepts, let us explore a somewhat simplified example. Figure 26.4 illustrates the various steps in this example. Assume a user, Alice, wishes to send an e-mail to her colleague Bob at Cool Company.com:

1. Alice launches her e-mail program and types in Bob's e-mail address, *bob@coolcompany.com*, as well as her message to Bob. Alice's e-mail program constructs a properly formatted SMTP-compliant message, resolves Cool Company's e-mail server address utilizing a DNS query, and passes the message to the TCP component of the Transport Layer for processing.

2. The TCP process adds a TCP header in front of the SMTP message fields including such pertinent information as the source TCP port (randomly chosen as a port number greater than 1024, in this case 1354), the destination port (port 25 for SMTP e-mail), and other TCP-specific information such as sequence numbers and receive buffer sizes.

3. This new data package (SMTP message plus TCP header) is then handed to the Network Layer and an IP header is added with such important information as the source IP address of Alice's computer, the destination IP address of Cool Company's e-mail server, and other IP specific information such as packet lengths, error-detection checksums, and so on.

4. This complete IP packet is then handed to the Physical Layer for transmission onto the physical network medium, which will add network layer headers as appropriate. Numerous packets may be needed to fully transmit the entire e-mail message depending on the various network media and protocols that must be traversed by the packets as they leave Alice's network and travel the Internet to Cool Company's e-mail server. The details will be handled by the intermediate systems and any required updates or changes to the packet headers will be made by those systems.

5. When Cool Company's e-mail server receives the packets from its local network medium via the Physical Layer, it removes the network frame and hands the remaining data to the Network Layer.

6. The Network Layer strips off the IP header and hands the remaining data to the TCP component of the Transport Layer.

7. The TCP process removes and examines the TCP header to, among other tasks, examine the destination port (again, 25 for e-mail), and finally hand the SMTP message to the SMTP server process.

8. The SMTP application performs further application specific processing as well delivery to Bob's e-mail application by starting the encapsulation process all over again to transit the internal network between Bob's PC and the server.

It is important to understand that network-based computer system attacks can occur at every layer of the TCP/IP stack and thus an effective intrusion detection and prevention program must be able to inspect at each layer and act accordingly. Intruders may manipulate any number of fields within a TCP/IP packet to attempt to bypass security processes or systems including the application-specific data, all in an attempt to gain access and control of the target system.

10. SURVEY OF INTRUSION DETECTION AND PREVENTION TECHNOLOGIES

Now that we have discussed the threats and those who pose them to information systems as well as examined

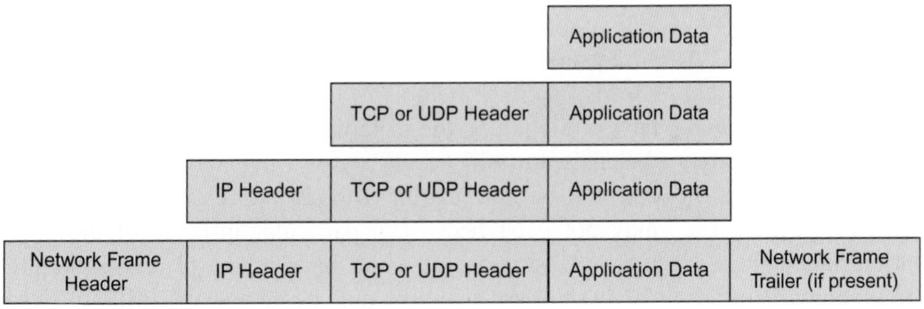

FIGURE 26.3   TCP/IP encapsulation.

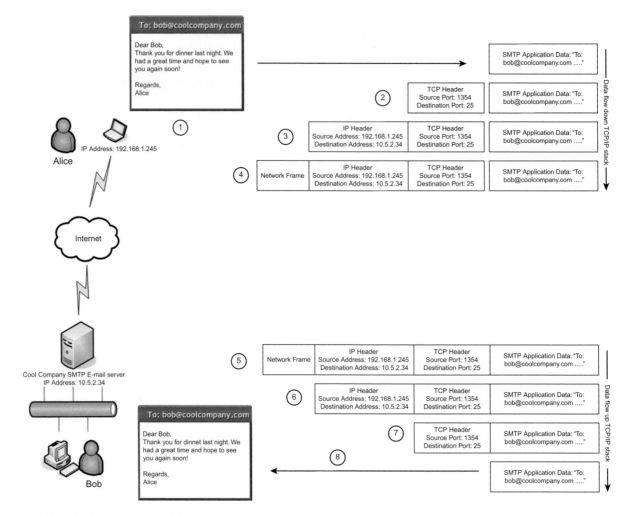

FIGURE 26.4   Application and network interaction example.

the underlying protocol suite in use on the Internet and enterprise networks today we are prepared to explore the various technologies available to detect and prevent intrusions. It is important to note that while technologies such as firewalls, a robust patching program and disk and file encryption can be part of a powerful intrusion prevention program these are considered static preventative defenses and will not be discussed here. In this section, we will discuss various dynamic systems and technologies that can assist in the detection and prevention of attacks on information systems.

11. ANTI-MALWARE SOFTWARE

We have discussed malware and its various forms previously. Anti-malware software, in the past typically referred to as anti-virus software, is designed to analyze files and programs for known signatures, or patterns, in the data that make up the file or program and indicates malicious code is present. This signature scanning is often accomplished in a multi-tiered approach where the entire hard drive of the computer is scanned sequentially during idle periods and any file accessed is scanned immediately to help prevent dormant code in a file that has not been scanned from becoming active. When an infected file or malicious program is found, it is prevented from running and either quarantined (moved to a location for further inspection by a system administrator) or simply deleted from the system. There are also appliance-based solutions that can be placed on the network to examine certain classes of traffic such as e-mail before being delivered to the end systems.

In any case, the primary weakness of the signature-based scanning method is that if the software does not have a signature for a particular piece of malware then the malware will be effectively invisible to the software and will be able to run without interference. A signature may not exist because a particular instance of the anti-malware software may not have an up to date signature database or the malware may be new or modified so as to avoid detection. To overcome this increasingly common issue, more sophisticated anti-malware software will monitor for known-malicious behavioral patterns instead of, or in addition to, signature based scanning. Behavioral pattern monitoring can take many forms such as observing the system calls all programs make and identifying patterns of calls that are anomalous or known-malicious. Another common method is to create a white list of allowed known-normal activity and prevent all other activity or at least prompt the user when a non-while listed activity is attempted. While these methods overcome some of the limitations of the signature-based model and can help detect previously never seen malware, they come with the price of higher false positive rates and/or additional administrative burdens.

While anti-malware software can be evaded by new or modified malware, it still serves a useful purpose as a component in a defense-in-depth strategy, as illustrated in Figure 26.5. A well maintained anti-malware

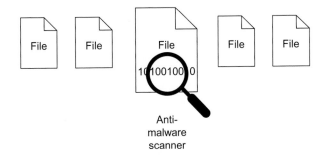

FIGURE 26.5 Anti-malware file scanning

infrastructure will detect and prevent known forms, thus freeing up resources to focus on other threats, but it can also be used to help speed and simplify containment and eradication of a malware infection once an identifying signature can be developed and deployed.

12. NETWORK-BASED INTRUSION DETECTION SYSTEMS

For many years, network-based intrusion detection systems (NIDS) have been the workhorse of information security technology and in many ways have become synonymous with intrusion detection [17]. NIDS function in one of three modes: signature detection, anomaly detection, and hybrid. A signature-based NIDS operates by passively examining all the network traffic flowing past its sensor interface or interfaces and examines the TCP/IP packets for signatures of known attacks as illustrated in Figure 26.6.

TCP/IP packet headers are also often inspected to search for nonsensical header field values sometimes used by attackers in an attempt to circumvent filters and monitors. In much the same way that signature-based anti-malware software can be defeated by never before seen malware or malware sufficiently modified to no longer possess the signature used for detection, signature-based NIDS will be blind to any attack it does not have a signature for. While this can be a very serious limitation, signature-based NIDS are still useful due to most system's ability for the operator

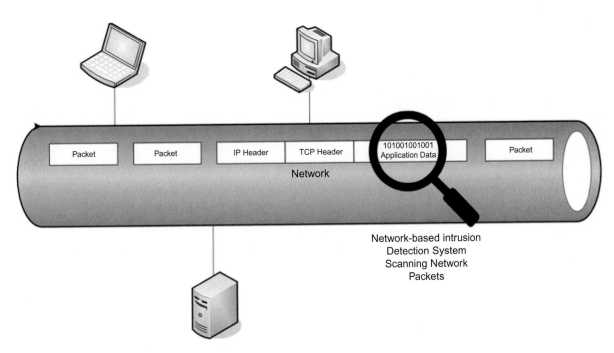

FIGURE 26.6 NIDS device scanning packets flowing past sensor interface.

to add custom signatures to sensors. This allows security and network engineers to rapidly deploy monitoring and alarming capability on their networks in the event they discover an incident or are suspicious about certain activity. Signature-based NIDS are also useful to monitor for known-attacks and ensure none of those are successful at breaching systems, freeing up resources to investigate or monitor other more serious threats.

NIDS designed to detect anomalies in network traffic build statistical or baseline models for the traffic they monitor and raise an alarm on any traffic that deviates significantly from those models. There are numerous methods for detecting network traffic anomalies but one of the most common involves checking traffic for compliance with various protocols standards such as TCP/IP for the underlying traffic and application layer protocols such as HTTP for Web traffic, SMTP for e-mail and so on. Many attacks against applications or the underlying network attempt to cause system malfunctions by violating the protocol standard in ways unanticipated by the system developers and which the targeted protocol handling layer does not deal with properly. Unfortunately, there are entire classes of attacks that do not violate any protocol standard and thus will not be detected by this model of anomaly detection. Another model commonly used is to build a model for user behavior and to generate an alarm when a user deviates from the 'normal' patterns. For example, if Alice never logs into the network after 9 pm and suddenly a logon attempt is seen from Alice's account at 3 am, this would constitute a significant deviation from normal usage patterns and generate an alarm. Some of the main drawbacks of anomaly detection systems are defining the models of what is normal and what is malicious, defining what is a significant enough deviation from the norm to warrant an alarm, and defining a sufficiently comprehensive model or models to cover the immense range of behavioral and traffic patterns that are likely to be seen on any given network. Due to this complexity and the relative immaturity of adaptable, learning anomaly detection technology, there are very few production-quality systems available today. However, due to not relying on static signatures and the potential of a successful implementation of an anomaly detection NIDS for detecting 0-day attacks and new or custom malware is so tantalizing that much research continues in this space.

A hybrid system takes the best qualities of both signature-based and anomaly detection NIDS and integrates them into a single system to attempt to overcome the weaknesses of both models. Many commercial NIDS now implement a hybrid model by utilizing signature matching due to its speed and flexibility while incorporating some level of anomaly detection to, at minimum, flag suspicious traffic for closer examination by those responsible for monitoring the NIDS alerts.

Aside from the primary criticism of signature-based NIDS their depending on static signatures, common additional criticisms of NIDS are they tend to produce a lot of false alerts either due to imprecise signature construction or poor tuning of the sensor to better match the environment, poor event correlation resulting in many alerts for a related incident, the inability to monitor encrypted network traffic, difficulty dealing with very high speed networks such as those operating at 10 gigabits per second, and no ability to intervene during a detected attack. This last criticism is one of the driving reasons behind the development of intrusion prevention systems.

13. NETWORK-BASED INTRUSION PREVENTION SYSTEMS

While NIDS are designed to passively monitor traffic and raise alarms when suspicious traffic is detected, network-based intrusion prevention systems (NIPS) are designed to go one step further and actually try to prevent the attack from succeeding. This is typically achieved by inserting the NIPS device inline with the traffic it is monitoring. Each network packet is inspected and only passed if it does not trigger some sort of alert based on a signature match or anomaly threshold. Suspicious packets are discarded and an alert is generated.

The ability to intervene and stop known attacks, in contrast to the passive monitoring of NIDS, is the greatest benefit of NIPS. However, NIPS suffers from the same drawbacks and limitations as discussed for NIDS such as heavy reliance on static signatures, inability to examine encrypted traffic, and difficulties with very high network speeds. In addition, false alarms are much more significant due to the fact that the NIPS may discard that traffic even though it is not really malicious. If the destination system is business or mission critical, this action could have significant negative impact on the functioning of the system. Thus, great care must be taken to tune the NIPS during a training period where there is no packet discard before allowing it to begin blocking of any detected, malicious traffic.

14. HOST-BASED INTRUSION PREVENTION SYSTEMS

A complementary approach to network-based intrusion prevention is to place the detection and prevention system on the system requiring protection as an installed software package. Host-based intrusion prevention systems (HIPS), while often utilizing some of the same signature-based technology found in NIDS and NIPS, also take advantage of being installed on the protected system to protect by monitoring and analyzing what other processes on the system are doing at a very detailed level. This process monitoring is very similar to that which we discussed in the anti-malware software section and involves observing system calls, interprocess communication, network traffic, and other behavioral patterns for suspicious activity. Another benefit of HIPS is that encrypted network traffic can be analyzed after the decryption process has occurred on the protected system thus providing an opportunity to detect an attack that would have been hidden from a NIPS or NIDS device monitoring network traffic.

Again, as with NIPS and NIDS, HIPS is only as effective as its signature database, anomaly detection model, or behavioral analysis routines. Also, the presence of HIPS on a protected system does incur processing and system resource utilization overhead and on a very busy system, this overhead may be unacceptable. However, given the unique advantages of HIPS, such as being able to inspect encrypted network traffic, it is often used as a complement to NIPS and NIDS in a targeted fashion and this combination can be very effective.

15. SECURITY INFORMATION MANAGEMENT SYSTEMS

Modern network environment generate a tremendous amount of security event and log data via firewalls, network routers and switches, NIDS/NIPS, servers, anti-malware systems and so on. Envisioned as a solution to help manage and analyze all of this information, security information management (SIM) systems have since evolved to provide data reduction, to reduce the sheer quantity of information that must analyzed, and event correlation capabilities that assist a security analyst to make sense of it all [18]. A SIM system not only acts as a centralized repository for such data, it helps organize it and provides an analyst the ability to do complex queries across this entire database. One of the primary benefits of a SIM system is that data from disparate systems is normalized into a uniform database structure thus allowing an analyst to investigate suspicious activity or a known incident across different aspects and elements of the IT environment. Often an intrusion will leave various types of 'footprints' in the logs (see checklist: "An Agenda For Action For Logging Capabilities") of different systems involved in the incident and bringing these all together and providing the complete picture for the analyst or investigator is the job of the SIM.

Even with modern and powerful event correlation engines and data reduction routines, however, a SIM system is only as effective as the analyst examining the output. Fundamentally, SIM systems are a reactive technology, like NIDS, and because extracting useful and actionable information from them often requires a strong understanding of the various systems sending data to the SIM, the analysts skill set and experience become very critical to the effectiveness of the SIM as an intrusion detection system [19]. SIM systems also play a significant role during incident response as often times, evidence of an intrusion can be found in the various logs stored on the SIM.

16. NETWORK SESSION ANALYSIS

Network session data represents a high-level summary of 'conversations' occurring between computer systems [20]. No specifics about the content of the conversation such as packet payloads is maintained but various elements about the conversation are kept and can be very useful when investigated an incident or as an indicator of

---

An Agenda for Action for Logging Capabilities

Network-based intrusion detection and prevention systems (IDPSs) typically perform extensive logging of data related to detected events. This data can be used to confirm the validity of alerts, to investigate incidents, and to correlate events between the IDPS and other logging sources. Data fields commonly logged by network-based IDPSs include the following (check all tasks completed):

_____ 1. Timestamp (usually date and time).

_____ 2. Connection or session ID (typically a consecutive or unique number assigned to each TCP connection or to like groups of packets for connectionless protocols).

_____ 3. Event or alert type.

_____ 4. Rating (priority, severity, impact, confidence).

_____ 5. Network, transport, and application layer protocols.

_____ 6. Source and destination IP addresses.

_____ 7. Source and destination TCP or UDP ports, or ICMP types and codes.

_____ 8. Number of bytes transmitted over the connection.

_____ 9. Decoded payload data, such as application requests and responses.

_____ 10. State-related information (authenticated username).

_____ 11. Prevention action performed (if any).

_____ 12. Most network-based IDPSs can also perform packet captures. Typically this is done once an alert has occurred, either to record subsequent activity in the connection or to record the entire connection if the IDPS has been temporarily storing the previous packets.

suspicious activity. There are a number of ways to generate and process network session data ranging from vendor specific implementations such as Cisco's NetFlow [21] to session data reconstruction from full traffic analysis using tools such as Argus [22]. However the session data is generated, there are a number of common elements constituting the session such as source IP address, source port, destination IP address, destination port, timestamp information, and an array of metrics about the session such as bytes transferred and packet distribution.

Using the collected session information, an analyst can examine traffic patterns on a network to identify which systems are communicating with each other and identify suspicious sessions that warrant further investigation. For example, a server configured for internal use by users and having no legitimate reason to communicate with addresses on the Internet will cause an alarm to be generated if suddenly a session or sessions appear between the internal server and external addresses. At that point the analyst may suspect a malware infection or other system compromise and investigate further. Numerous other queries can be generated to identify sessions that are abnormal in some way or another such as excessive byte counts, excessive session lifetime, or unexpected ports being utilized. When run over a sufficient timeframe, a baseline for traffic sessions can be established and the analyst can query for sessions that don't fit the baseline. This sort of investigation is a form of anomaly detection based on high-level network data versus the more granular types discussed for NIDS and NIPS.

Another common usage of network session analysis is to combine it with the use of a honeypot or honeynet (see sidebar, "Honeypots and Honeynets"). Any network activity, other than known-good maintenance traffic such as patch downloads, seen on these systems is, by definition, suspicious as there are no production business functions or users assigned to these systems. Their sole purpose is to act as a lure for an intruder. By monitoring network sessions to and from these systems, an early warning can be raised without even necessarily needing to perform any complex analysis.

Honeypots and Honeynets

A honeypot is a computer system designed to act as a lure or trap for intruders. This is most often achieved by configuring the honeypot to look like a production system possibly containing valuable or sensitive information and providing legitimate services but in actuality neither the data or the services are real. A honeypot is carefully monitored and, since there is no legitimate reason for a user to be interacting with it, any activity seen targeting it is immediately considered suspicious. A honeynet is a collection of honeypots designed to mimic a more complex environment than one system can support [23].

---

17. DIGITAL FORENSICS

Digital forensics is the "application of computer science and investigative procedures for a legal purpose involving the analysis of digital evidence" [24]. Less formally digital forensics is the use of specialized tools and techniques to investigate various forms of computer-oriented crime including fraud, illicit use such as child pornography, and many forms of computer intrusions.

Digital forensics as a field can be divided into two subfields: network forensics and host-based forensics. Network forensics focuses on the use of captured network traffic and session information to investigate computer crime. Host-based forensics focuses on the collection and analysis of digital evidence collected from individual computer systems to investigate computer crime. Digital forensics is a vast topic and a comprehensive discussion is beyond the scope of this chapter and interested readers are referred to [25] for more detail.

In the context of intrusion detection, digital forensic techniques can be utilized to analyze a suspected compromised system in a methodical manner. Forensic investigations are most commonly used when the nature of the intrusion is unclear, such as those perpetrated via a 0-day exploit, but wherein the root cause must be fully understood either to ensure the exploited vulnerability is properly remediated or to support legal proceedings. Due to the increasing use of sophisticated attack tools and stealthy and customized malware designed to evade detection, forensic investigations are becoming increasingly common and sometimes only a detailed and methodical investigation will uncover the nature of an intrusion. The specifics of the intrusion may also require a forensic investigation such as those involving the theft of Personally Identifiable Information (PII) in regions covered by one or more data breach disclosure laws.

18. SYSTEM INTEGRITY VALIDATION

The emergence of powerful and stealthy malware, kernel-level rootkits, and so-called clean-state attack frameworks that leave no trace of an intrusion on a computer's hard drive have given rise to the need for technology that can analyze a running system and its memory and provide a series of metrics regarding the integrity of the system. System integrity validation (SIV) technology is still in its infancy and a very active area of research but primarily focuses on live system memory analysis and the notion of deriving trust from known-good system elements [26]. This is achieved by comparing the system's running state including the processes, threads, data structures, and modules loaded into memory to the static elements on disk that the running state was supposedly loaded from. Through a number of cross-validation processes, discrepancies between what is running in memory and what should be running can be identified. When properly implemented, SIV can be a powerful tool for detecting intrusions, even those utilizing advanced techniques.

19. SUMMARY

It should now be clear that intrusion detection and prevention is not a single tool or product but a series of layered technologies coupled with the appropriate methodologies and skill sets. Each of the technologies surveyed in this chapter have their own specific strengths and weaknesses and a truly effective intrusion detection and prevention program must be designed to play to those strengths and minimize the weaknesses. Combining NIDS and NIPS with network session analysis and a comprehensive SIM, for example, helps to offset the inherent weakness of each technology as well as provides the information security team greater flexibility to bring the right tools to bear for an ever-shifting threat environment.

An essential element in a properly designed intrusion detection and prevention program is an assessment of the threats faced by the organization and a valuation of the assets to be protected. There must be an alignment of the value of the information assets to be protected and the costs of the systems put in place to defend them. The program for an environment processing military secrets and needing to defend against a hostile nation state must be far more exhaustive than that for a single server containing no data of any real value that must simply keep out assorted script kiddies.

For many organizations, however, their information systems are business and mission critical enough to warrant considerable thought and planning with regards to the appropriate choices of technologies, how they will be implemented, and how they will be monitored. Only through flexible, layered, and comprehensive intrusion detection and prevention programs can organizations hope to defend their environment against current and future threats to their information security.

Finally, let's move on to the real interactive part of this Chapter: review questions/exercises, hands-on projects, case projects and optional team case project. The answers and/or solutions by chapter can be found in the Online Instructor's Solutions Manual.

CHAPTER REVIEW QUESTIONS/EXERCISES

True/False

1. True or False? Information security concerns itself with the integrity and availability of information systems and the information or data they contain and process.

2. True or False? Having physical access to a computer system allows an adversary to bypass most security protections put in place to prevent unauthorized access.

3. True or False? An insider is an individual who, due to their role in the organization, has some level of authorized access to the IS environment and systems.

4. True or False? An outsider is considered anyone who does not have authorized access privileges to an information system or environment.

5. True or False? Malware can be generally defined as "a set of instructions that run on your computer and make your system do something that allow an attacker to make it do what he wants it to do."

Multiple Choice

1. What is a self-replicating code that attaches itself to another program?
   A. Worm
   B. Virus
   C. Backdoor
   D. Trojan Horse
   E. User-level Rootkit

2. What is a self-replicating code that propagates over a network, usually without human interaction?
   A. Backdoor
   B. Virus
   C. Worm
   D. Trojan Horse
   E. User-level Rootkit

3. What is a program that bypasses standard security controls to provide an attacker access, often in a stealthy way?
   A. Trojan Horse
   B. Virus
   C. Worm
   D. Backdoor
   E. User-level Rootkit

4. What is a program that masquerades as a legitimate, useful program while also performing malicious functions in the background?
   A. Trojan Horse
   B. Virus
   C. Worm
   D. Backdoor
   E. User-level Rootkit

5. What is the Trojan/ backdoor code that modifies operating system software so the attacker can maintain privileged access on a machine but remain hidden?
   A. Trojan Horse
   B. Virus
   C. Worm
   D. Backdoor
   E. User-level Rootkit

EXERCISE

Problem

How do intrusion detection systems (IDSs) work?

Hands-On Projects

Project

Why should an organization use an IDS, especially when they already have firewalls, anti virus tools, and other security protections on their system?

Case Projects

Problem

What are the different types of IDSs?

Optional Team Case Project

Problem

How do does one go about selecting the best IDS for their organization?

REFERENCES

[1]   NIST Special Publication on Intrusion Detection Systems, NIST, 100 Bureau Drive, Stop 1070, Gaithersburg, MD 20899-1070, [US Department of Commerce, 1401 Constitution Avenue, NW, Washington, DC 20230], 2006.

[2a] M. Bosworth, VA Loses Data on 26 Million Veterans, consumer-affairs.com. <http://www.consumeraffairs.com/news04/2006/05/va_laptop.html>, 2006.

[2b] B. Prince, Stolen Laptop Exposes Boston Hospital Patient Data, darkreading.com.   <http://www.darkreading.com/compliance/167901112/security/attacks-breaches/240001031/stolen-laptop-exposes-boston-hospital-patient-data.html>, 2012.

[3]   B. Schneier, *Applied Cryptograhpy*, Wiley, 1996.

[4]   S. Fishman, Bradley Manning's Army of One, New York Magazine, July 3, 2011.

[5]   E. Skoudis, Malware: *Fighting Malicious Code*, Prentice Hall, 2003.

[6]   P. Gutman, World's Most Powerful Supercomputer Goes Online, *Full Disclosure*.   <http://seclists.org/fulldisclosure/2007/Aug/0520.html>, 2007.

[7]   J. Aitel, The IPO of the 0-day. <http://www.immunityinc.com/downloads/0day_IPO.pdf>, 2007.

[8]   M.H. Sachs, Cyber-Threat Analytics. <www.cyber-ta.org/downloads/files/Sachs_Cyber-TA_ThreatOps.ppt>, 2006.

[9]   J. Leyden, Chinese Crackers Attack US.Gov, The Register. <http://www.theregister.co.uk/2006/10/09/chinese_crackers_attack_us/>, 2006.

[10] P. Williams, Organized Crime and Cyber-Crime: Implications for Business. <http://www.cert.org/archive/pdf/cybercrime-business.pdf>, 2002.

[11] C. Wilson, Botnets, Cybercrime, and Cyberterrorism: Vulnerabilities and Policy Issues for Congress. <http://fas.org/sgp/crs/terror/RL32114.pdf>, 2008.

[12] M. Graham, Welcome to Cyberwar Country, USA, WIRED. <http://www.wired.com/politics/security/news/2008/02/cyber_command>, 2008.

[13] M. Landler, J. Markoff, <http://www.nytimes.com/2007/05/29/technology/29estonia.html> Digital Fears Emerge After Data Siege in Estonia, New York Times, 2007.

[14] R. Stevens, TCP/IP *Illustrated, Volume 1*: The Protocols, Addison-Wesley Professional, 1994.

[15] D.E. Comer, Internetworking with TCP/IP Vol. 1: Principles, Protocols, and Architecture, fourth ed., Prentice Hall, 2000.

[16] C. Hunt, TCP/IP Network Administration, third ed., O'Reilly Media, Inc., 2002.

[17] S. Northcutt, *Network Intrusion Detection*, third ed., Sams, 2002.

[18] J.L. Bayuk, Stepping Through the InfoSec Program, ISACA, 2007.

[19] B. Schneier, Security Information Management Systems (SIMS), Schneier on Security. <http://www.schneier.com/blog/archives/2004/10/security_inform.html>, October 20, 2004.

[20] R. Bejtlich, *The Tao of Network Security Monitoring: Beyond Intrusion Detection*, Addison-Wesley Professional, 2004.

[21] Cisco Website, Cisco IOS NetFlow. <http://www.cisco.com/web/go/netflow>.

[22] Argus Website, Argus — Auditing Network Activity. <http://qosient.com/argus/>, August 13, 2012.

[23] Honeynet Project Website, The Honeynet Project. <www.honeynet.org>, 2012.

[24] K. Zatyko, Commentary: Defining Digital Forensics, *Forensics Magazine*. <http://www.forensicmag.com/articles.asp?pid=130>, 2007.

[25] K. Jones, Real Digital Forensics: *Computer Security and Incident Response*, Addison-Wesley Professional, 2005.

[26] Volatile Systems Website, Volatile Systems. <www.volatilesystems.com>, 2012.

## Chapter 27

TCP/IP Packet Analysis

Pramod Pandya

CSU Fullerton

1. THE INTERNET MODEL

This chapter will provide an overview of communication protocols that are necessary for transfer of data between or among communicating nodes (computers) connected through networks. An application program generates a continuous stream of data, which cannot be sent over a network as a continuous stream, but must be packetized per defined protocol and then sent over the network. Therefore, communicating nodes exchange packets of data over the network. Each of the packets is delineated with a header, contents, and a trailer. The header, the trailer, and the length of the packet are defined by the protocol that identifies the characteristic of the packet. A set of protocols are necessary for data communications between or among nodes. Hence a layered approach to data communication protocols is defined. This layered approach is known as the Internet model, which consists of five layers from top to bottom as illustrated in Figure 27.1. The Internet model is a submodel of the well-known Open System Interconnection (OSI) model with seven peer-to-peer layers. Communicating nodes on a network operate on a peer-to-peer basis using the protocols appropriate to a given layer.

Next, we will briefly review the logical functions of each of the layers from the Internet model before we provide a detailed discussion of each layer (see checklist: An Agenda for Action for the TCP/IP Layered Model). Let us examine the layers from bottom to top.

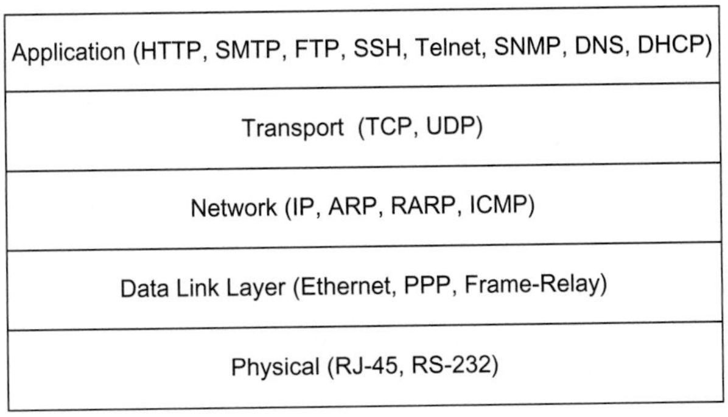

The Physical Layer

The physical layer defines a commonly agreed standard for the mechanical, electrical, and functional specifications of the interface and the transmission media. The mechanical standard defines the kind of the connector, its size, and number of pins that are used to connect the computer to the bound medium (copper, or fiber), thus creating a network of computers. The electrical standard defines the allowable electrical voltage. The functional characteristic defines the binary logic that is used to represent the actual data bits. The reader should be aware that the data transmitted by the node attached to the network is transmitted serially in a synchronous manner to the other nodes on the network. This synchronous transmission requires that the data bits are organized to belong to packets. Thus even though data bits are placed on the medium one bit at a time, a bit on its own represents known information. Bits simply represent a predefined level of voltage. The physical layer is concerned with the following:

- Physical characteristics of interfaces and media
- Representation of bits
- Data rate
- Synchronization of bits
- Line configuration
- Physical topology
- Transmission mode

The Data Link Layer

The data link layer has two sublayers: the logical link control (LLC) and the media access control (MAC). The LLC is responsible for flow and error control. The MAC specifies how the node accesses the media, and the most commonly MAC for a Local Area Network (LAN) is carrier sense multiple access with collision detection

| Application (HTTP, SMTP, FTP, SSH, Telnet, SNMP, DNS, DHCP) |
| Transport (TCP, UDP) |
| Network (IP, ARP, RARP, ICMP) |
| Data Link Layer (Ethernet, PPP, Frame-Relay) |
| Physical (RJ-45, RS-232) |

FIGURE 27.1 The Internet model.

An Agenda for Action for the TCP/IP Layered Model

Knowing the fundamentals and how to diagnose/troubleshoot the network, with a focus on how to do an analysis of the TCP/IP packet, is vital to anyone who is in the networking field today, whether it be at the service provider level or enterprise level. This checklist focuses on the layered model approach to analyze the world of TCP/IP networking (check all tasks completed):

Layer 1: The Physical Layer:
_____**1.** Function of Layer 1
_____**2.** Transmission Type: Simplex/Half Duplex/Full Duplex
_____**3.** T1, DS1 Super Frame, DS1 Extended Super Frame
_____**4.** Wireless Physical Layer
_____**5.** Wired Ethernet Physical Layer
_____**6.** Wireless PHY Analysis
_____**7.** Wireless Wi-Fi Layers
_____**8.** 802.11 Fundamentals, BSS, ESS, Standards
_____**9.** Wireless Operations, Beacons, Management Frames
_____**10.** Wireless Data Capture

Layer 2: The Datalink Layer (Ethernet):
_____**11.** Ethernet Defined, Mechanisms and the OSI Model
_____**12.** Sublayers and Logical Link Control
_____**13.** Topologies
_____**14.** CSMA/CD and Full Duplex
_____**15.** Hubs and Switches

_____**16.** Ethernet Frame Formats
_____**17.** The MAC Address
_____**18.** ARP Protocol, Inverse, and Reverse ARP
_____**19.** Spanning Tree, RSTP Protocols
_____**20.** Ethernet Spanning Tree Analysis
_____**21.** VLANs and VLAN Trunking Protocol
_____**22.** Ethernet VLAN and VTP Analysis

Layer 3: The Network Layer —Internet Protocol (IP):
_____**23.** IP Protocol Functions, Format
_____**24.** IP Addressing, Reserved and Broadcast Addresses
_____**25.** IP Routing
_____**26.** Fragmenting Packets
_____**27.** IP Fragmentation
_____**28.** ICMP Protocol, Format, and Troubleshooting
_____**29.** ICMP Troubleshooting

Layer 4: The Transport Layer —TCP and UDP Protocols:
_____**30.** TCP Protocol Characteristics, Format
_____**31.** TCP Connection States
_____**32.** Three-Way-Handshake
_____**33.** TCP Sockets
_____**34.** TCP Segmentation
_____**35.** TCP Three-Way Handshake
_____**36.** Flow Control, Sliding Windows
_____**37.** Packet Loss, Re-transmission, and TCP Slow Start
_____**38.** Nagle Algorithm

(CSMA/CD, IEEE 802.3). The CSMA/CD is also known as Ethernet. All the nodes on a LAN share the medium for data transmission; thus two nodes on a LAN can create collision if they transmit bits at the same time. Ethernet is therefore a broadcast protocol, and the nodes are required to listen for signal level on the medium before transmitting data, thus avoiding collision. The wired Ethernet data transmission runs at 10, 100, and 1000 megabits per second (MBPS). The Ethernet protocol organizes the data bits in a packet known as the FRAME. The Ethernet frame is a data structure with a specific number of fields as illustrated in Figure 27.2. The data link layer has the following responsibilities:

- Framing
- Physical addressing
- Flow control

Preamble	SFD	Destination address	Source address	Length PDU	Data and padding	CRC

FIGURE 27.2　Ethernet frame.

- Error control
- Access control

Each field of the Ethernet Frame has the following characteristics.

- *Preamble.* The preamble contains seven bytes (56 bits) of alternating 0s and 1s that alert the receiving node to the coming frame and enable it to synchronize its input timing. The preamble is not part of the frame.
- *Start frame delimiter (SFD).* The SFD field is 1 byte long (10101011) and signals the beginning of the frame. The last two one bits signal that the next field is the destination address.
- *Destination address (DA).* The DA field is 6 bytes long and specifies the physical address of the destination node on the network.
- *Source address (SA).* The SA field is 6 bytes long and specifies the physical address of the sending node on the network.
- *Length/type.* The length/type field is less than 1518; it is a length field and defines the length of the data field that follows. If the value of the field is greater than 1536, it defines the upper layer protocol that uses the services of the Internet.

- *Data.* The data field carries encapsulated data from the upper protocols. Its minimum length is 46 and a maximum 1500 bytes.
- *CRC.* This field is used to detect for a damaged Ethernet frame, using an algorithm known as Cyclic Redundancy Check.

Addressing in a LAN Select and Type an H3 Here

In a LAN, each node is assigned a physical address, also known as a MAC/Ethernet address. This address is unique to each of the nodes on the LAN and is 6 bytes (48 bits) long, which is burnt on the Ethernet card (also known as the network interface card, NIC). Ethernet is a byte-count protocol. A node on a LAN broadcasts a frame that is heard by all other nodes, and only the node whose Ethernet address matches with the DA in the Ethernet frame copies the frame into its buffer. If the DA address is a broadcast address (all 1's), then all the nodes on that LAN would copy the frame. Hackers can disguise the MAC address of their data packets to protect their identity by spoofing their MAC address. The utility that allows spoofing the MAC address is known as SMAC, which is available from Internet sites.

Benefits and Applications of Spoofing the MAC Address

Perform Security Vulnerability Testing, Penetration Testing on MAC Address-based Authentication and Authorization Systems (Wireless Access Points); as well as the following:

- Troubleshoot network problems.
- Troubleshoot ARP tables, routers, switching.
- Troubleshoot system problems.
- Test network management tools.
- Test incident response procedures on simulated network problems.
- Test Intrusion Detection Systems (IDS), whether they are Host-and Network-Based IDS.

(Disclaimer: Authorization to perform these tests must be obtained from the system owner(s).)

The Network Layer

The network layer consists of four protocols: the Internet Protocol (IP), Address Resolution Protocol (ARP), Reverse Address Resolution Protocol (RARP), and Internet Control Message Protocol (ICMP). The IP protocol is a connectionless protocol; hence it is not responsible for guaranteed delivery of data packets known as datagrams. The datagram encapsulates the data from the transport layer. The IP is responsible for addressing the datagram with the source and destination addresses of the nodes. It is also responsible for routing the datagram from the source node to the destination node, as well as making sure that the length of the datagram is compatible with the allowable packet length if the datagram is to travel through a Wide Area Network (WAN). In such a case, the router that connects a LAN to a WAN uses the Maximum Transfer Unit (MTU) packet length for the appropriate protocol such as X.25 or ATM running on the WAN. This function of the IP protocol is known as fragmentation, which is used by hackers to exploit any vulnerability in networks.

IP Packet Format

We will now consider the internals of the protocol and discuss its packet format and fields. IP uses 14 separate fields in the packet format. The fields fall into two basic categories. *Header management fields* handle the packet structure, version, data length, and protection of IP header. *Packet flow fields*, such as Type of Service, Fragmentation, and Time to Live, handle end-to-end delivery of packets. A detailed description of the fields of the IP Packet shown in Figure 27.3 is as follows:

- Version: 4 bits. The version of IP used.
- Header Length: This 4-bit field defines the total length of the datagram header in 4-byte words. The length of the header is from 20 to 60 bytes. With no Options, the header length is 20 bytes long.
- Differentiated Service (DS): 8 bits. This field was previously known as service type. Specifies how the upper layer protocol wants the current datagram to be handled.
- Total Length: 16 bits. The IP datagram length in bytes, including the IP header. Length of data = total length − header length.

Version	Header Len		DS	Total Length
Identification			Flags	Fragment Offset
TTL		Protocol		Header Checksum
Source IP address				
Destination IP address				
Options				
Data				

FIGURE 27.3   IP datagram.

- Identification: 16 bits. Contains an integer that identifies the current datagram.
- Flags: 3 bits. Consists of a 3-bit field of which the first bit is reserved. The second bit set to 1 means that the datagram must not be fragmented, and if it cannot pass through any network, then an ICMP error message is generated and the datagram is discarded. If the second bit is set to 0, then the datagram may be fragmented. The third bit set to 1 means that there are more fragments to follow. If the value of the third bit is set to 0, it means that this is the last or only fragment.
- Fragment Offset: 13 bits. Indicates the position of the fragment's data relative to the beginning of the data in the original datagram. It is the offset of the data in the original datagram measured in units of 8 bytes. Figure 27.4, Fragmentation Example, shows a datagram with data size of 4000 bytes fragmented into three fragments. The bytes in the original datagram are numbered 0 to 3999. The first fragment carries bytes 0 to 1399. The offset for this datagram is $0/8 = 0$. The second fragment carries bytes 1400 to 2799; the offset value for this fragment is $1400/8 = 175$. The third fragment carries bytes 2800 to 3999. The offset value for this fragment is $2800/8 = 350$.
- Protocol: 8 bits. The upper-layer protocol that is the source or destination of the data.
- Header Checksum: 16 bits. Calculated over the IP header to verify header's correctness. It does not calculate the checksum over any of the data because that is covered by the Layer 2 CRC.
- Source IP address: 32 bits. The IP address of the sending host.

- Destination IP address: 32 bits. The IP address of the receiving host.
- Options.
- Data. IP datagrams can be sent with several options enabled. They are rarely used because most routers and firewalls do not allow them.

Figure 27.5, IPv4 Captured Packet, displays the contents of an IP packet. The fields we discussed are all displayed in the lower-left pane under the IPv4 Header. The Header length is 20 bytes; thus there are no IP Options. The data field is therefore $48 - 20 = 20$ bytes long. The Flags indicate not to fragment the datagram.

Internet Protocol Addressing: Classful Addressing

The Internet Protocol (IP) provides an interface to an IP network, which is a logical, not physical, as provided by the data link layer protocol. The reader will note that the physical address is hard-coded on the network interface card, whereas the logical address is assigned to a node through the TCP/IP stack with programmable parameters. This feature permits designing an IP network with security parameters and makes it scaleable.

IP address ranges are categorized by a class of address. The first 3 bits of the 32-bit address determine the class of the address. Tables 27.1 and 27.2 show the bit settings and how IP addresses are classified. At the network (IP) layer, each device connected to the network must be assigned a unique IP address. We will restrict the overview to IPv4 (a 32-bit number).

Some IP network addresses per Table 27.3 are reserved (private-use), and hence can be used by anyone

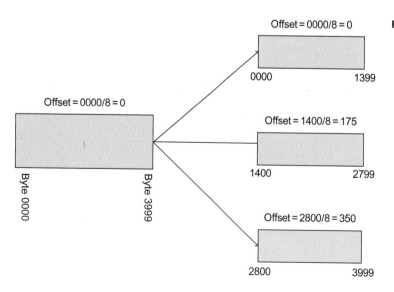

Offset = 0000/8 = 0

0000   1399

Offset = 0000/8 = 0

Byte 0000   Byte 3999

Offset = 1400/8 = 175

1400   2799

Offset = 2800/8 = 350

2800   3999

FIGURE 27.4 Fragmentation example.

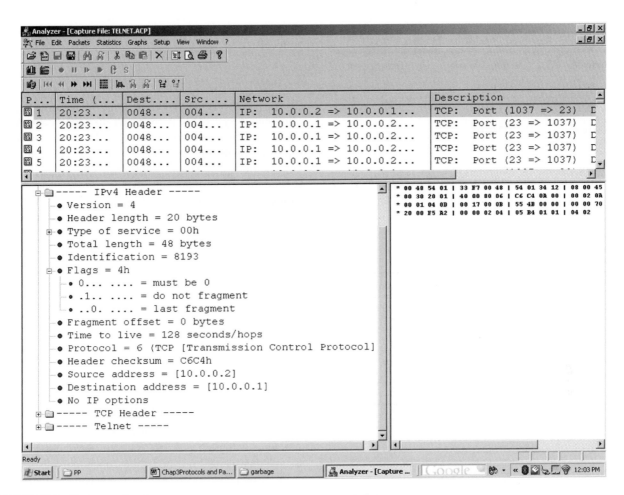

FIGURE 27.5   IPv4 captured packet.

TABLE 27.1 The Class in Binary Notation.

	First Byte	Second Byte	Third Byte	Fourth Byte
Class A	0			
Class B	10			
Class C	110			
Class D	1110			
Class E	11110			

TABLE 27.2 The Class in Decimal Notation.

	First Byte	Second Byte	Third Byte	Fourth Byte
Class A	1 TO 126			
Class B	128 TO 191			
Class C	192 TO 223			
Class D	224 TO 239			
Class E	240 TO 255			

without having to pay any fees. The rest of IP network addresses (public-use) have to be leased from an organization that keeps track of them.

In classful addressing (Table 27.4), an IP address is divided into Netid and Hostid. For each of the class, Table 27.4 represents the breakdown of bytes that represent the network id and the bytes that represent the host id.

Subnet Mask and Subnetting

Each class of a network address has an associated subnet mask as represented in Table 27.5. The IP protocol uses the subnet mask associated with the class of network address to extract the destination network address from the IP address of the destination node from the IP

TABLE 27.3 Reserved IP Address Ranges.

Address	Subnet Mask	Description
0.0.0.0	255.0.0.0	"This" Network
10.0.0.0	255.0.0.0	Private Network
127.0.0.0	255.0.0.0	Loopback
172.16.0.0	255.255.0.0	Private Network
192.168.1.0	255.255.255.0	Private Network

TABLE 27.4 Netid and Hostid.

	First Byte	Second Byte	Third Byte	Fourth Byte
Class A	Netid	Hostid	Hostid	Hostid
Class B	Netid	Netid	Hostid	Hostid
Class C	Netid	Netid	Netid	Hostid
Class D	Multi	Class	add	Ress
Class E	Reserved	For	FUTURE	USE

TABLE 27.5 Subnet Mask.

	First Byte	Second Byte	Third Byte	Fourth Byte
Class A	255	0	0	0
Class B	255	255	0	0
Class C	255	255	255	0
Class D	1110			
Class E	11110			

datagram, and thus make a routing decision. IP is a routable protocol; hence IP datagrams can be routed. In classful routing, each interface on the network must be assigned a subnet mask corresponding to its class of network address. This scheme enables the interface in making the routing decision for the IP datagram.

Subnetting is a mechanism by which a given network address is divided into several logical groups of networks. The subnetting allows managing, supervising, and securing a large number of hosts, such that each of the subnets can be assigned a security policy independent of other subnets. Routing of IP datagram from one subnet to another subnet requires the subnets to be interconnected using a set of routers. These routers run a set of routing protocols.

Routing Internet Protocol (RIP)

RIP is an intradomain routing protocol used inside an autonomous system. It is based on distance vector routing. The number of networks that the datagram can travel before it reaches its destination is defined as the metric. This metric is also known as the hop count. Any route in an autonomous system using RIP cannot have more than 15 hops. This protocol is used by the routers to build the route table dynamically. RIP is implemented with all the MS-Windows Network Operating System, so that you can build a router using multiple network cards in a PC.

Open Shortest Path First (OSPF)

OSPF is an intradomain routing protocol based on link state routing. Its domain is autonomous. In link state routing, each node in the domain has the entire topology of the domain—the list of nodes and links, how they are connected.

Border Gateway Protocol (BGP)

BGP is based on a path vector routing algorithm. It is an interdomain routing protocol. In path vector routing, we assume that there is one node in each autonomous system that acts on behalf of the entire autonomous system. This node builds the routing table and advertises it to another such node in other autonomous systems. The idea is the same as the distance vector protocol except that only one node in each of the autonomous systems can communicate with other such nodes. RIP, OSPF, and BGP are implemented in Linux, so that you can build a router using a multiple network cards in a PC.

Address Resolution Protocol (ARP)

The IP protocol is capable of routing an IP datagram within the same IP segment (network address), or else it would need a router to route the datagram to a different IP segment (network address). The IP protocol uses the IP address specified in the destination IP field and the subnet mask to extract the destination IP network address to which the datagram must be routed. The IP protocol looks up in its routing table to determine if the destination network is directly accessible by the node or whether it needs the router to route the datagram to the destination network. The reader needs to be reminded that the Ethernet protocol on the host node needs the MAC address of the destination node to prepare the Ethernet frame. The host node has a routing table with IP addresses mapped to Ethernet addresses, known as ARP

(Address Resolution Protocol) cache. If the ARP cache does not have the MAC address mapped to its corresponding IP address entry, then an ARP request is generated by the host node to discover the MAC address corresponding to its IP address. If the destination node is on the same network, then this is resolved by the destination node upon its ARP reply and the destination MAC address corresponding to destination IP address is resolved. If the datagram needs to be routed out of the network address, then the IP protocol on the host node generates an ARP request to resolve the IP address to the MAC address of the Ethernet interface on the router to which the network segment connects. In such a case, the MAC address of the router interface is used as an intermediate MAC address. Once the IP address to the MAC address is resolved, the Ethernet protocol can next build the Ethernet frame and encapsulate the IP datagram. An ARP packet is directly encapsulated (bypassing IP datagram) into an Ethernet frame, as shown Figure 27.6.

The destination address in the Ethernet frame is all 1's, indicating that it is a broadcast address. Figure 27.7 illustrates the ARP packet format. Each field is described as follows:

- *Hardware type*. 16-bit field that defines the type of the network on which ARP is running. Ethernet is given the type 1.

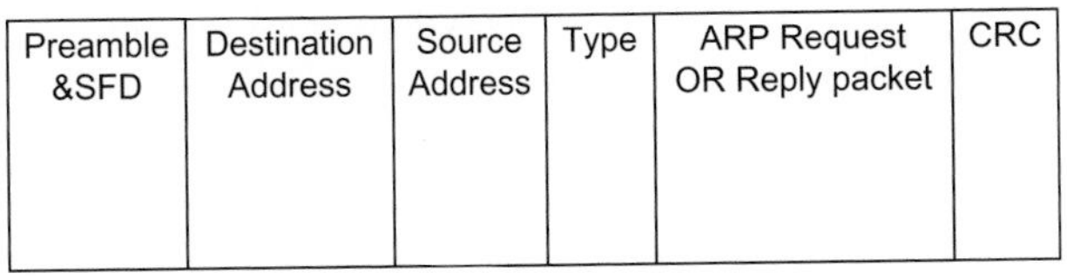

FIGURE 27.6 Encapsulation of an ARP packet in an Ethernet frame.

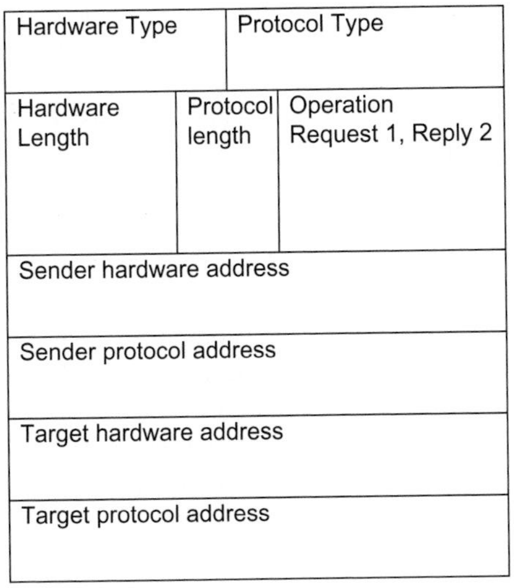

FIGURE 27.7 ARP packet.

- *Protocol type*. 16-bit field defines the protocol. For IPv4, the value of this field is 0×800.
- *Hardware length*. An 8-bit field that defines the length of the physical address, which is 6 bytes for the Ethernet address.
- *Protocol length*. An 8-bit field that defines the length of the logical address, which is 4 bytes for the IPv4 protocol.
- *Operation*. A 16-bit field defining the type of packet. Two packet types are ARP request (1) and ARP reply (2).
- *Sender hardware address*. The physical address of the sender node.
- *Sender protocol address*. The logical address of the sender node.
- *Target hardware address*. A field set to all 0s for an ARP request.
- *Target protocol address*. A field set to the IP address of the target node.

Figure 27.8 is a screen capture of an Ethernet frame using a sniffer program. Ping is executed from a node with an IP address 192.168.1.3 to a node with an IP address 192.168.1.4. The screen capture is divided into three panes. The upper pane displays six columns of information. You will observe that a packet number 6 is highlighted in the upper pane; it shows that an ARP request was generated with a source address 00045AA29675, destination address FFFFFFFFFFFF, which is a broadcast address. Under the description column in the upper pane, the node with an IP address 192.168.1.3 is broadcasting on the network to find the MAC address corresponding to the IP address 192.1681.4. The Ethernet frame in the lower-right pane shows a destination address of FFFFFFFFFFFF, which is a broadcast address.

Figure 27.9 represents the contents of the Ethernet frame and the ARP packet it encapsulates. The contents of the ARP packet displays the IP and MAC address of the sender's node. You will observe that the Target hardware address is 16 zeros, and the Target IP address is 192.168.1.4.

Reverse Address Resolution Protocol (RARP)

This protocol was designed so that a diskless node on a network can obtain an IP address given its physical address. This protocol has been replaced in terms of its usage by BOOTP and DHCP.

Internet Control Message Protocol (ICMP)

ICMP messages are encapsulated inside IP datagrams. ICMP is used for controlling the flow of data in the network, for reporting errors, and for performing diagnostics.

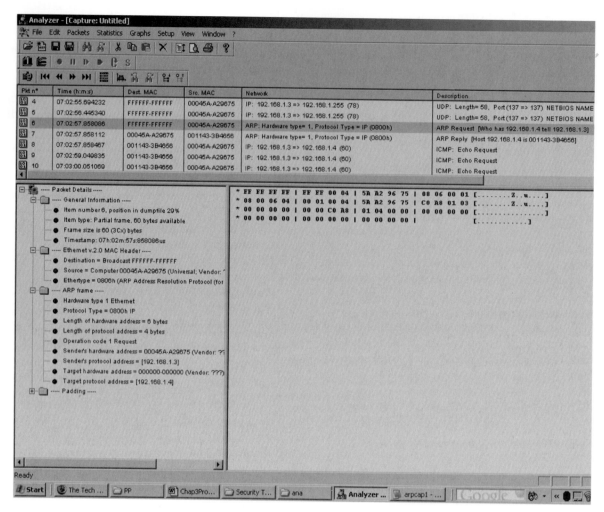

FIGURE 27.8   Captured Ethernet frame.

ICMP messages are divided in two categories: error-reporting messages (Figure 27.10) and query messages (Figure 27.11).

A very important troubleshooting tool within the ICMP protocol is ping, the packet Internet Groper. The ping command is used to verify connectivity with another host on a network. The ping command uses a series of echo requests and echo reply messages to query the status of a node on a network. The ping command can be exploited by a would-be hacker to check and monitor the status of nodes on a network before launching any attack. The current practice is to turn off a response to an echo request, thus effectively hiding the node from external users of the network.

The Transport Layer

The Transmission Control Protocol (TCP) is a transport layer protocol that provides for a connection-oriented, reliable service to applications. A connection-oriented protocol establishes a connection, manages the data transfer, and terminates the connection. Thus TCP provides end-to-end connectivity using a virtual connection between the endpoints; therefore all the data segments are sent over this same virtual path. In addition, TCP uses flow, error, and congestion control to manage transfer of data between the two endpoints. TCP offers full-duplex and multiplex service to applications. TCP uses IP address and port number (16-bit number) to identify the sending and receiving processes, respectively. The combination of IP address and port number is called a socket, and a TCP connection is uniquely identified by the two end sockets. The data generated by an application are encapsulated in TCP segments. Some of the most common applications and their port numbers are illustrated in Figure 27.12. Figure 27.13 shows the layout of the TCP header.

What follows is a description of a TCP header per Figure 27.13. This is extremely useful for decoding TCP

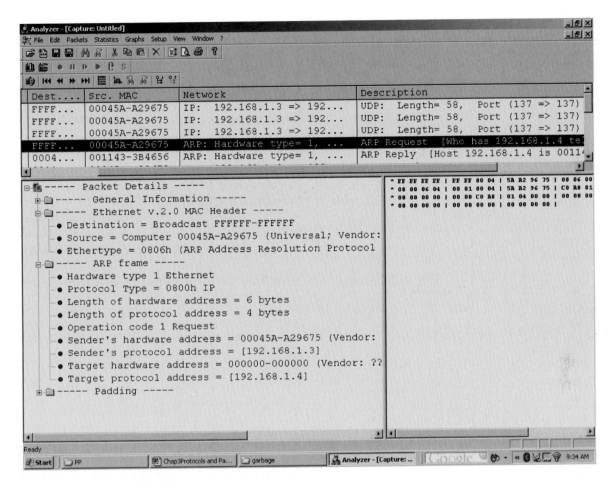

FIGURE 27.9   Contents of an ARP packet.

Type	Message
3	Destination unreachable
4	Source quench
11	Time exceede
12	Parameter problem
5	Redirection

FIGURE 27.10   Error-reporting messages.

Type	Message
8 or 0	Echo request or reply
13 or 14	Timestamp request or reply
17 or 18	Address mask request reply
10 or 9	Router solicitation or advertisement

FIGURE 27.11   Query messages.

segments, if you are to become an expert in the field of network intrusion, detection, and prevention:

- *Source Port Number.* 16-bit port number on the source host.
- *Destination Port Number.* 16-bit port number on the destination host.

- *Sequence Number.* This 32-bit field identifies the byte in the stream of data from the sending TCP to the receiving TCP. It is the sequence number of the first byte of data in this segment represents.
- *Acknowledgment Number.* This 32-bit field contains the next sequence number that the destination node wants to receive.
- *Header Length.* 4 bits. The length of the header is 32-bit words.

- *Reserved.* 6 bits.
- *Flags:* There are 6 bits for flags.
- *URG:* If the first bit is set, an urgent message is being carried.
- *ACK:* If the second bit is set, the acknowledgment number is valid.

7	Echo
23	Telnet
20,21	FTP
25	SMTP
53	DNS
67,68	DHCP
80	HTTP
110	POP3
445	SMB
1701	L2TP
1720	VoIP

FIGURE 27.12   Common applications and their port numbers.

- *PSH:* If the third bit is set, it is notification from the sender to the receiver that the receiver should pass all the data to the application quickly.
- *RST:* If the fourth bit is set, it signals a request to reset the TCP connection.
- *SYN:* The fifth bit of the flag field of the packet is set when initiating a connection.
- *FIN:* The sixth bit is set to terminate a connection.
- *Window Size.* This field defines the size of the window, in bytes that a receiver can accept. The length of this field is 16 bits; hence the maximum size of the window is 65,535 bytes.
- *Checksum.* This 16-bit field contains the checksum.
- *Urgent Pointer.* This 16-bit field, which is valid only if the URG flag is set, is used when the segment contains urgent data.
- *Options.* Up to 40 bytes of optional information in the TCP header.

Figure 27.14 displays a screenshot of a captured TCP segment. This segment has a SYN set to 1, indicating that the node with an IP address of 10.0.0.2, port number 1037, is attempting to establish an active TCP connection, with IP address 10.0.0.1 at a port number 23. The Acknowledgment field has a value of zero.

A TCP Connection—Three-way Handshaking

A unique sequence of three data packets are exchanged at the beginning of an active TCP connection as illustrated in Figure 27.15:

- The client initiates a connection by sending a synchronizing (SYN) packet.
- The server responds with a SYN + ACK packet.

Source Port Number				Destination Port Number				
Sequence Number								
Acknowledgement Number								
Hdr Len	Reserved	URG	ACK	PSH	RST	SYN	FIN	Window size
TCP Checksum				Urgent Pointer				
Options								
Data								

FIGURE 27.13   TCP header.

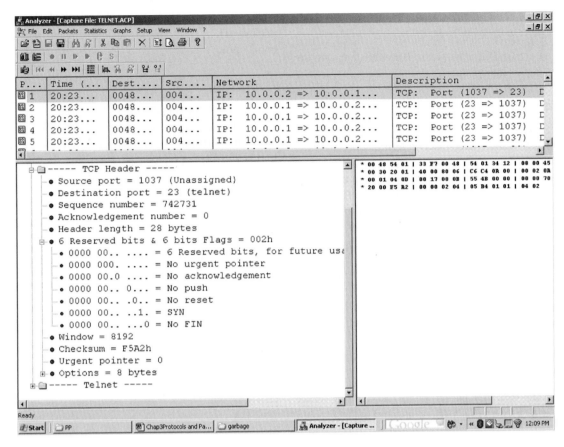

FIGURE 27.14   A captured screenshot of a TCP segment.

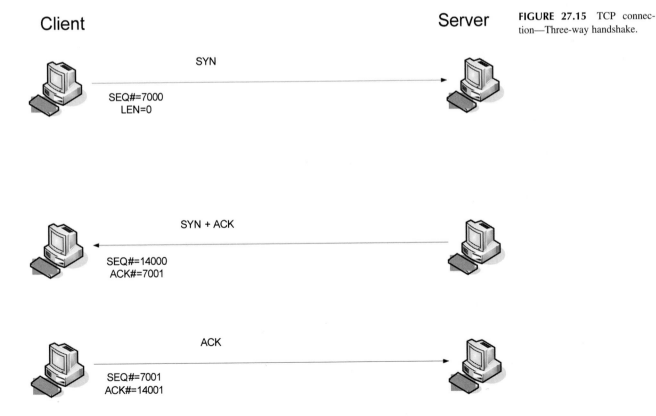

FIGURE 27.15 TCP connection—Three-way handshake.

- Finally the client acknowledges the SYN + ACK packet with its own ACK packet.

Thus an active TCP connection is established, and the two nodes can exchange data.

State Transition Diagram

To keep track of all the different events happening during connection establishment, connection termination, and data transfer, the TCP software is implemented as a finite state machine. At any one moment, the machine is in one of the states. It remains in that state until an event takes place. The event can change the state, and perform predefined action. Transition states for TCP protocol are given in Figure 27.16. Using netstat utility, you can discover the state of a TCP connection between two nodes. This information could be of help in network intrusion detection.

Maximum segment lifetime (MSL) is the maximum time a segment can exist in the Internet before it is dropped. The common value for MSL is between 30 and 60 seconds.

Connection Termination—In a three-way handshake

The client sends a FIN packet to the server; the server responds with FIN + ACK packet; and the client sends a

ACK packet to confirm the receipt of the FIN + ACK packet. This would lead to the closing of the TCP connection.

Half-Close

An example of a Half-Close TCP session is when a client sends all the data to a server. At this point, the client closes its port on an outbound direction, but the inbound port is still kept open to receive the data.

Connection Reset

An RST segment can be sent by a receiving node to a sending node to the following:

- Deny a connection.
- Abort an existing connection.
- Terminate an idle connection.

SYN Flooding Attack

The full TCP connection establishment procedure is susceptible to a serious security flaw. A node can continuously send SYN segments to a server. This server in turn responds with SYN + ACK segments. During this process, the resources on the server get overloaded, leading

State	Description
CLOSED	No connection
LISTEN	Waiting for SYN
SYN-SENT	SYN sent; waiting for ACK
SYN-RECVD	SYN+ACK sent; waiting for ACK
ESTABLISHED	Connection established; data transfer in progress
FIN-WAIT-1	First FIN sent; waiting for ACK
FIN-WAIT-2	ACK to first FIN received; waiting for second FIN
CLOSE-WAIT	First FIN received, ACK sent; waiting for application to close
TIME-WAIT	Second FIN received, ACK sent; waiting for 2MSL time-out
LAST-ACK	Second FIN sent; waiting for ACK
CLOSING	Both sides have decided to close simultaneously

FIGURE 27.16 State Transitions for TCP.

to the server crash. This results in denial-of-service (DOS) attack.

User Datagram Protocol (UDP)

UDP is a transport layer protocol that provides a connectionless, unreliable service to applications. Each application that makes a call to a UDP service uses UDP port numbers to open a socket for service from a server node.

The Application Layer

Some of the Internet-based applications are vulnerable to attack by hackers. The reason for this is that the TCP/UDP port numbers where services are available are attacked to penetrate the network. To secure the networks from unauthorized users, firewalls are built around networks, and a minimum number of ports are kept open. Additionally, intrusion detection systems (IDS) are placed on the networks to monitor for anomalous traffic pattern.

Dynamic Host Configuration Protocol (DHCP)

The DHCP application has two components: a client, and a server. In an IP network, a DHCP server is configured to assign IP addresses to clients upon a request. In such a case, a DHCP client uses the UDP protocol to broadcast a request for an IP address. A DHCP server then might respond with an IP address. This IP address is leased for a fixed duration of time to the client.

Domain Name Server (DNS)

Nodes on an Internet when accessing Web service need to resolve the domain name to an IP address. This process is known as name resolution, whereby the client node uses the UDP protocol to broadcast for name resolution. If a DNS server is attacked, then the organization that relied on the DNS for name resolution is prevented from providing services to its client. If the top-level DNS servers are attacked, then most of the Internet becomes inaccessible, resulting in millions of dollars of loss of revenue. This is a result of a DNS server overloaded with name resolution queries. The most serious attack could be when a DNS session is hijacked, resulting in directing clients to unauthorized Web sites, leading to loss of confidence in E-commerce- based activities.

Traceroute

The traceroute in UNIX or tracert in Windows can be used to trace the route of a packet from source to destination node. The traceroute program uses two ICMP messages, time exceeded and destination unreachable, to find the route of a packet.

IpConfig

IpConfig is a Windows-based utility that displays the configured TCP/IP stack parameters such as the node's IP address, subnet mask, the Default Gateway's IP address, and the DNS's IP address. In addition, it also displays whether the IP address is static or a leased IP address.

Ping

Ping is a utility that allows you query the status of a remote node on a network. If the node is accessible, then the node responds to the query, which uses ICMP protocol.

Netstat

Netstat is a utility that displays protocol statistics with TCP/IP connections and port numbers. The utility will display the dynamic status of TCP/UDP ports.

2. SUMMARY

This chapter reviewed the significance of the TCP/IP stack in data networking. You should be able to examine the TCP/IP packet, analyze it, and explain the applications that are using the TCP/IP stack. The material in this chapter forms a building block for network intrusion detection. The exercises at the end of the chapter allow you to practice with the utilities on a network to reinforce the TCP/IP protocol concepts.

So, let's move on to the real interactive part of this chapter: review questions/exercises, hands-on projects, case projects, and optional team case project. The answers and/or solutions by chapter can be found in the Online Instructor's Solutions Manual.

CHAPTER REVIEW QUESTIONS/EXERCISES

True/False

1. True or False? The physical layer defines a commonly agreed standard for the mechanical, electrical, and the functional specifications of the interface and the transmission media.
2. True or False? The data link layer has two layers: the logical link control (LLC), and the media access control (MAC).
3. True or False? In a LAN, each node is assigned a physical address, also known as a MAC/Ethernet address.
4. True or False? The network layer consists of three protocols: The Internet Protocol (IP), the Address Resolution Protocol (ARP), and the Internet Control Message Protocol (ICMP).

5. True or False? The Internet Protocol (IP) provides an interface to an IP network, which is logical, not physical, as provided by the data link layer protocol.

Multiple Choice

1. What are categorized by a class of address?
   A. Worms
   B. Viruses
   C. IP address ranges
   D. Trojan horses
   E. User-level rootkits
2. Each class of a network address has an associated _____?
   A. backdoor
   B. virus
   C. subnet mask
   D. Trojan horse
   E. user-level rootkit
3. What is an intradomain routing protocol used inside an autonomous system?
   A. Trojan horse
   B. Virus
   C. RIP
   D. Backdoor
   E. User-level rootkit
4. What is an intradomain routing protocol based on link state routing?
   A. Trojan horse
   B. Virus
   C. OSPF
   D. RIP
   E. User-level rootkit

5. What is based on a path vector routing algorithm?
   A. OSPF
   B. RIP
   C. Worm
   D. Backdoor
   E. BGP

EXERCISE

Problem

Explain how an organization can detect that the other end of a TCP/IP connection has crashed? Can the organization use keepalives for this?

Hands-On Projects

Project

Explain what is the full form of the OSI and TCP/IP model.

Case Projects

Problem

Explain how applications coexist over TCP and UDP.

Optional Team Case Project

Problem

Explain the role of TCP/IP in data transmission from source to destination?

## Chapter 28

The Enemy (The Intruder's Genesis)

Dr. Pramod Pandya
CSU Fullerton

1. INTRODUCTION

In last few years, we have read and experienced the nature of such threats, resulting in loss of credit-card numbers, Social Security numbers, passwords, and other sensitive information. Security for the network has grown from a simpleminded approach to a multilevel approach, depending on the complexity of the network. As the number of Intranets connected to the Internet has grown, threat to network security has progressed from simple need for network security engineers to need for information security engineers. The primary function of network security engineers was to design network architecture to secure and protect network resources from unauthorized users, namely, hackers. The goal of information security engineers was to define and design the information architectural infrastructure to secure and protect information resources from being stolen by unauthorized users, namely hackers. Why then the need for a cybersecurity engineer? We have now seen that the Internet has more than a couple of billion users connecting to it from all over the world. Since all these users are not from one nation, it does pose a much greater security as the network traffic enters and leaves at the nation boundaries. Hence the Internet has morphed into a cyberspace and thus a need for a cybersecurity engineer. The reader can appreciate that the "Enemy" is not a just a hacker bounded by the nation-state boundary, but can be just from anywhere in cyberspace!

The latest incident-response report from the Industrial Control Systems Cyber Emergency Response Team (ICS-CERT)—part of the Department of Homeland Security (DHS)—warns of ongoing cyberattacks against the computer networks of U.S. natural gas pipeline companies. Cybersecurity experts believe that attacks on the critical commercial and public infrastructure will increase more rapidly in the future economic wars as the nation-states compete for natural resources and intelligence.

At the other extreme in the cyberspace is social media networking, which has dominated the conversation. The young and the mature alike all have accounts on Facebook to connect with each other. Facebook has a vital interest in making sure that its clientele feel confident about sharing their experiences and personal moments with their friends. Sharing becomes a lot less appealing when there is a risk of contagion. A growing number of companies have created their presence on Facebook and would want to make sure that the users on the Facebook would feel safe and confident to click on links that would direct them to a company's e-commerce site for marketing, customer support, and product reach. Presently, more information about individuals and companies has been made publicly available on Facebook, LinkedIn, Twitter, and other social media Web sites (cyberspace) than ever before. Social media sites can be used by companies to gather information about their competitors, and by hackers to exploit the information, the passwords, and much more.

A host of software-based hacking tools or toolkits are available freely from the various Web sites on the Internet. Hacker would initially take a survey of a network, scan for network devices, then look for open ports on those network devices, take an audit of available sensitive information on the vulnerable network devices, and finally design an attack plan to secure the sensitive information. Of course, this approach to compromise the network is designed so that the trace back to the hacker is lost in the maze of the Internet. It is not possible to completely secure the network (see Figure 28.1) against hackers, as most networks have at least one open port that permits communications with the rest of the Internet. This is the dilemma facing all network security professionals: how to safeguard the network from unauthorized access. The following steps are undertaken by those intending to hack a network:

- Gather information about nodes on the target network.
- Look for vulnerabilities in the target network— "holes."

Methodology

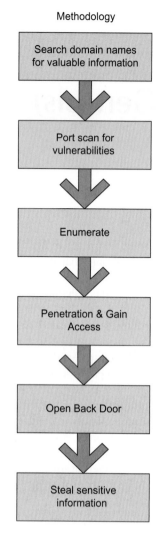

FIGURE 28.1 The six-step process necessary to gain control of a network.

- Exploit the "holes" to access the nodes in the target network.
- Secure access to the target network, without leaving the traces behind, for launching future attacks on the target network, or third-party networks.

Figure 28.1 shows the six-step process necessary to gain control of a network.

2. ACTIVE RECONNAISSANCE

The first step involves searching for Internet domain names, to help to identify those entities that would hold valuable information worth gaining access to. The next step is to map the domain names to network addresses, and finally map out the detail infrastructure of that network. Now we can begin to discover IP addresses of the network nodes and attempt to identify DNS servers,

database servers, email servers, and Web servers. These various servers would hold the sensitive information of value. The next phase would be to place the DNS servers, email, and Web servers and database servers on the network and reproduce a complete network, including its functional specification. Once the target network is mapped out, we will use network-based tools to get all the information about that server, and then make a preparation to design a scheme to attack the network.

The domain name registered by the target corporate network can be found by entering the organization's domain name in a search at www.internic.net/whois.html. Thus, we can learn addresses for the target networks' DNS servers, Web servers, and email servers. The GFI Languard NSS software has a utility "whois" that easily allows discovering all the information regarding a domain name registered to a corporate network. DNS Zone transfers refer to learning about the servers and their IP addresses from zone files. Information collected is used to determine what TCP and or UDP services such as HTTP, SMTP, or FTP are in either "listening," "wait," or "closed" state, including the types of operating system and applications currently in use.

The examples of port scanning, and enumeration illustrated in this chapter were obtained using the network in Figure 28.2. The network consists of the following computers:

- kailash a Windows 2000 server—Domain PANDYA
- kalidas a Windows XP workstation
- nanjun a Linux server

Network Mapping

Network mapping (see Figure 28.3) is the process of discovering information about the topology of the target network, thus finding the IP addresses of gateways, routers, email, Web, FTP servers, and database servers. The next step is to sweep the target network to find live nodes by sending ping packets and waiting for response from the target nodes. ICMP messages can be blocked, so an alternative is to send a TCP or UDP packet to a port such as 80 (http) that is frequently open, and live machines will send a SYN-ACK packet in response. Once the live nodes are mapped, standard utility such as traceroute can provide additional information about the network topology by discovering the paths taken by packets to each host, which provides information about the routers and gateways in the network and the general network layout.

The screenshot in Figure 28.3 is obtained using a network security scanner from GFI Languard (http://www.gfi.com). This software is a commercial product, but a trial version 6.0 can be downloaded for 14 days.

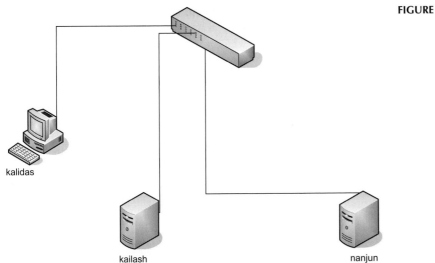

FIGURE 28.2   Switched Ethernet network.

kalidas

kailash   nanjun

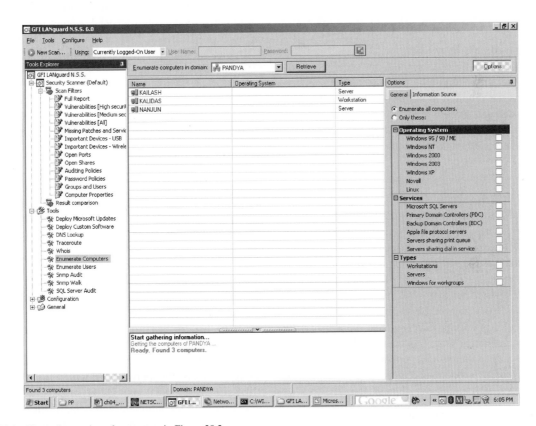

FIGURE 28.3   Network mapping of computers in Figure 28.2.

Nmap

The Nmap main page is described as a security/network exploration tool and port-scanner. The basic command line syntax to invoke Nmap is as follows:

- nmap [scan type(s)] [options] {target specification}
- Nmap has a huge list of command-line options, generally categorized into target specification, host listing, port specifications, service identification, scan technique, scripted scans, and output options. Some of the Nmap switches only work when run as the root (superuser).

- nmap -sL 192.168.1.0/24—Lists all the hosts scanned (all responding IPs in the subnet from 192.168.1.1 to 192.168.1.254).
- nmap -p80,443 192.168.1.10-20—Scans the IP address range looking for open ports 80 and 443.

- nmap -p T:80,8080,6588,800 172.16.0.1/22 — Scans all hosts between 172.16.0.1 and 172.16.3.254, looking for open TCP ports 80, 8080, 6588, and 800 (the default listening ports for various proxy servers).
- nmap -sP 192.168.1.10,20 — Ping scans two hosts in a fast scan.
- nmap -PN 192.168.1.0/29 — Scans all the hosts in the 192.168.1.1 to 192.168.1.6 range. Sometimes host-based firewalls deny ping requests, and it is difficult to scan such hosts. The -PN scan is useful in such cases; it scans the hosts assuming them to be online.
- nmap -A -F 192.168.1.1 — Detects target OS and services running on it, in fast-scan mode.

Idlescan

This scan will probe 192.168.1.95 while pretending that the scan packets come from another host; the target's logs will show that the scan originated from 192.168.1.10. This is called a zombie host.

Zombie hosts are those controlled by other hosts on the network. Not all hosts can be used as zombies, as certain conditions are required to be met before this is possible. (Using packages such as hping may enable you to find a zombie host on the network.) The -v switch increases the verbosity of the output.

Decoy Host

This command is especially useful while testing IDS/IPS. The -sS option will perform a SYN scan on the target host. While doing so, it will spoof the packet contents to make the target host see them as coming from the specified (-D) decoy hosts. The -sI and -D switches can't be combined, for obvious reasons.

Now, a word of caution: Be careful not to cause an unintended denial-of-service (DoS) attack while using the -D option. To understand how this could happen, we need to know how a TCP handshake operates. TCP, being a connection-oriented protocol that guarantees delivery of packets, operates with a three-way handshake:

- The client initiates the communication by a SYN.
- The server acknowledges with a SYN-ACK.
- The client again sends an ACK, and now they can communicate.

If the -D switch is used, and there is a live host at the decoy IP address, then the SYN-ACK reaches the actual host at the decoy IP address, and not the host running the Nmap scan. Since the real host at the decoy address did not initiate the connection, it closes the connection by sending a TCP Reset (RST). There's no problem with this.

However, a problem occurs if the decoy IP address is not active on the network — there is no RST sent to the scan target, which keeps the connection open. As Nmap continues to generate more and more requests to the target with the decoy IP as the source, the scan target has a growing list of open connections for which it maintains the "connection-initiated" state. This ends up consuming more and more resources on the target and may cause a DoS to other, legitimate hosts and communications.

FIN Scan

The Nmap FIN scan comes in handy in such circumstances. The standard use of a FIN packet is to terminate the TCP connection — typically after the data transfer is complete. Instead of a SYN packet, Nmap initiates a FIN scan by using a FIN packet. Since there is no earlier communication between the scanning host and the target host, the target responds with an RST packet to reset the connection. However, by doing so, it reveals its presence. A FIN scan is initiated using a command like nmap -sF 192.168.1.1.

Port Scanning

The second step in reconnaissance is known as port scanning. All networks are secured by one firewall on the perimeter of the network, and this firewall is configured to permit HTTP and SMTP traffic to pass through. Other application traffic is forced to use a secured tunnel to pass through the network. Of course, the perimeter firewall is configured to monitor the traffic, and a log is kept for analysis. Internal network is built using Ethernet segments to reflect the infrastructure of the organization. IP network segments are then superimposed on the Ethernet segments. Each IP network segment is secured from each other by a firewall. Each of the IP segments is connected to the layer-3 switch, thus further protecting each IP segment from an external attack. The IP traffics from the layer-3 switch are directed to pass through a Demilitarized ZONE (DMZ) before it enters the perimeter router. The nodes in the DMZ are DNS, SMTP, and HTTP servers, which are permitted for both inbound and outbound traffic. The attacker would scan the ports on the perimeter firewall and look for open ports on the firewall. The firewall would have the ports such as 80 and 25 (well-known) open for Web and email services. The goal of the attacker is to find which ports in "listen," "wait," or "closed" state.

TCP Full Connect. Full TCP connection is a three-way handshake between a source host and a target host to establish a normal connection. This is used to determine the open TCP ports on the target network, even though the packets have to pass through the firewall. If an intrusion detection system (IDS) is installed on the target network and configured to trigger an alarm to indicate an anomalous behavior on the network, then this activity will be recorded by IDS.

Ping

This mode sends a short UDP packet to the target's UDP ports and looks for an ICMP "Port Unreachable" message in response. The absence of that message indicates either that the port is in use or the target does not return the ICMP message, which can lead to false positives (A *false positive* occurs when an IDS reports as an intrusion an event that is in fact legitimate network activity). This mode, too, is easily recognized by IDS.

TCP SYN Half Open

In Chapter 27, we talked about the mode of the TCP session. This mode normally sends out a SYN packet to the target port and listens for the appropriate response. Open ports respond with SYN + ACK, and closed ports respond with ACK + RST or RST. This mode is less likely to be recorded by IDS, since the TCP connection is not fully complete, and consequently the attacker might get away with this mode of intrusion.

Fragmentation Scanning

In this method of scanning, you break up IP packets into a number of fragments. Consequently, you are splitting up the TCP header over several packets to make it harder for packet filters and so forth to detect what you are doing. IP fragmentation can also lead to a DoS.

Port Numbers

Public IP addresses are controlled by the Internet Assigned Numbers Authority (IANA) www.iana.org, and are unique globally. Port numbers are unique only within a computer system, and they are 16-bit unsigned numbers. The port numbers are divided into three ranges: the Well Known Ports (0..1023), the Registered Ports (1024..49151), and the Dynamic and/or Private Ports (49152..65535).

Well-Known Ports

Port numbers 0 to 1023 are well-known ports. These well-known ports (also called standard ports) are assigned to services by the IANA. On Unix, the text file named /etc/services (on Windows 2000 the file named %windir%\ system32\ drivers\ etc\ services) lists these service names and the ports they use. Here are a few lines extracted from this file:

- echo   7/tcp   Echo
- ftp-data   20/udp   File Transfer [Default Data]
- ftp   21/tcp   File Transfer [Control]
- ssh   22/tcp   SSH Remote Login Protocol
- telnet   23/tcp   Telnet
- domain   53/udp   Domain Name Server
- www-http   80/tcp   World Wide Web HTTP

Nonstandard Ports

By a nonstandard port, we simply mean a port whose number is higher than 1023. In this range also, several services are "standard." For example:

- wins   1512/tcp # Microsoft Windows Internet Name Service
- yahoo   5010 # Yahoo! Messenger
- x11   6000-6063/tcp # X Window System

Once the IP address of a target system is known, an attacker can then begin the process of port scanning, looking for holes in the system through which the attacker can gain access to the network nodes. We have already discussed the significance of TCP and UDP port numbers, and the well-known and not so well-known services that run at these ports. Each of these ports is a potential entryway or "hole" into the network. If a port is open, there is a service listening on it; well-known services have assigned port numbers, such as http on TCP port 80 or telnet on TCP port 23. Port scanning is the process of sending packets (TCP or UDP) to each port on a system to find out which ones are open.

A port scanner such as Nmap is capable of a wider variety of TCP scans that are harder to detect. Nmap allows an option for a TCP SYN stealth scan in which the third message is not an ACK but a FIN that forces the TCP connection to be closed before fully opening. This half-open connection is not logged at the target, but may be noticed by routers or firewalls that record the original SYN packet.

Nmap also allows options that give the attacker more control over the packets sent. The attacker can set the rate at which packets are sent, since changing the timing to space out the packets can help avoid raising the target's suspicions that it is being scanned. If the rate is set too fast, packets can be lost, and incorrect results will be returned. The attacker can also fragment the packets to avoid intrusion detection systems, many of which only look for the whole suspicious packet to be sent at once. Nmap even allows the attacker to set the source port, for example, to 80 to appear as Web traffic to a packet filter, as well as to set a decoy source address to obscure the real address by sending an extra packet per decoy address.

Bounce Scans

In the bounce scan, the attacker would attempt to fool or mislead the victim into believing that the attack originated from a different source IP address, often known as the distributed denial-of-service attacks (DDoS). Such an attack would make it difficult to trace the attacker's IP address. Most commercial Internet sites such as Yahoo, Google, Microsoft, and others support proxy services so that all Web traffic can be directed to a single server for filtering as well as caching to improve performance. We have seen cases of DDOS in spite of the proxy servers' setup to protect the networks.

Vulnerability Scanning

One essential type of tool for any attacker or defender is the vulnerability scanner. These tools allow the attacker to connect to a target system and check for such vulnerabilities as configuration errors, default configuration settings that allow attackers access, and the most recently reported system vulnerabilities. Most commercial Network Security Services (NSS) are expensive and do not come with the source code, while the open-source NSSs are free and the source code is readily available. The open-source tool Nessus is an extremely powerful network scanner and can be configured to run a variety of attacks. Nessus includes a variety of plug-ins that can be enabled, depending on the type of security checks the user wishes to perform. Nessus includes its own scripting language, called Nessus Attack Scripting Language (NASL), which can be used to create individualized attacks and incorporate them with the other plug-ins. Although attacks could be written in C, Perl, Python, or a variety of other languages, NASL was designed to be an attack language. The screenshot in Figure 28.4 was obtained using a network security scanner from GFI Languard.

3. ENUMERATION

Now we should be ready to generate a laundry list of resources that we identified to be vulnerable using the scanning devices; this is known as Enumeration. Our list would have at a minimum the following resources that we discovered to be vulnerable; DNS, Web, and email servers in the DMZ. If we had managed to penetrate through the firewall, then of course, most of the resources on the Intranet would now be vulnerable to our attacks. We have now completed the Active Reconnaissance, phase one of Figure 28.1.

4. PENETRATION AND GAIN ACCESS

Vulnerable resources on the network have been itemized, so we are ready now to devise an attack scheme and to

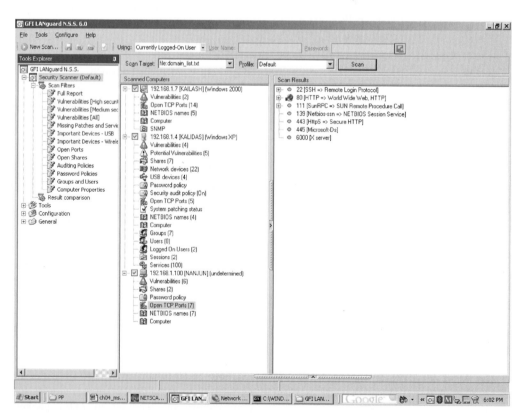

FIGURE 28.4 Vulnerable open ports on the computers in Figure 28.2.

proceed with penetration techniques. Database and HTTP servers are now ready to be compromised.

Stack-Based Buffer Overflow Attacks

Stack-based buffer overflow attacks take advantage of poorly written applications and operating systems architecture. A computer program is a process that is executed by the central processing unit (CPU). Each process manages its memory and input/output. Typically, a process is broken into functions and one main function. This main function is the entry point to the program. Once the program enters the execution mode, the functions in the program get executed as they are called by other functions in a given order. When a called function has completed execution, the control must be returned to the calling function. Herein lay\\ies the problem: When a function is in the execution mode, it needs to store data it is manipulating; this data is stored in a region of memory called a stack. If this region of memory gets overwritten, this will lead to crashing the program—buffer overflow results.

A special-purpose register keeps track of the currently executing instruction, and points to the address of this instruction —Instruction Pointer (IP). This IP is stored on the stack during the function call. Now as you can see, if buffer overflow takes place, then the return addresses get smashed, and the CPU will return to whatever address is available in the IP. The attacker will take advantage of this flow in the architecture by placing the address in the IP.

Once a stack overflow is successful, the returned address gets altered. This altered address is where the attacker will place the payload which could be a virus, a malware, or a Trojan horse. The playload is injected thus, and the attacker will have control of the target network node.

Password Attacks

Every node on a network is secured by assigning a password to access the resources available on the network or on that node. The current policy set by the network administrators is to force the users to change the password over a defined time interval. A new password cannot be a previous password, and it must be alphanumeric and of a certain minimum length to make it difficult for someone to break it. Users' passwords are normally encrypted and stored in a file. If a user forgets the password, then the password will need to be reset as there is no way of recovering the password. An attacker would attempt to get hold of the file that has encrypted passwords. Using password cracking tools as listed below, hacker might be able to recover the plaintext passwords.

Password Cracking Tool: John the Ripper is a password cracker available under Linux and Windows. DoS attacks have become more complicated, concealing malicious client requests as legitimate ones. Also, a distributed approach, the DDoS (distributed denial of service) is now being adopted, which involves generating multiple requests to create a flood scenario. One type of DDoS flood attack is the TCP SYN queue flood.

A SYN queue flood attack takes advantage of the TCP protocol's "three-way handshake." A client sends a TCP SYN (S flag) packet to begin a connection to the server. The target server replies with a TCP SYN-ACK (SA flag) packet, but the client does not respond to the SYN-ACK, leaving the TCP connection "half-open." In normal operations, the client should send an ACK (a flag) packet followed by the data to be transferred, or an RST reply to reset the connection. On the target server, the connection is kept open, in a "SYN_RECV" state, as the ACK packet may have been lost due to network problems.

In a DDoS, multiple attackers make many such half-connections to the target server, in a storm of requests. When the server's SYN buffer is full with half-open TCP connections, it stops accepting SYN connections, thus resulting in denial of service to legitimate clients.

Such DDoS attacks are generally carried out using "botnets" of other compromised systems across the Internet, which through backdoors and Trojans are directed to send artificial SYN flood traffic to targeted servers. To defend against such attacks, a strong monitoring system is required, as there is a very fine line between legitimate and fake clients. SYN queue flood attacks can be mitigated by tuning the kernel's TCP/IP parameters.

Sniffing

The most popular packet sniffer—Wireshark—is a computer program that can monitor the traffic passing over a network or part of a network. Wireshark is normally placed on a network node and configured to run in a promiscuous mode to capture every packet traversing on that network. Sniffer can be configured to capture traffic at any one of the Internet's models, such as layer 2 (Ethernet), layer 3 (IP), layer 3 (TCP or UDP), layer 4 (SMTP, HTTP, DNS, DHCP), or layer 5 (Applications).

Once the data traffic is captured, the hacker would have analyzed the contents of the packets and be able to draw inferences about what is being captured. Hackers would thus have access to port numbers, IP addresses, and application details.

Sniffing Tools

One popular sniffing tool is called Wireshark (http://www.wireshark.com/). The other popular sniffing tool is TCPDump, which can provide very detailed information on the captured data traffic (http://www.tcpdump.org/).

IP Address Spoofing

IP address spoofing normally involves what is known as IP packet crafting. Once again it is a computer program that allows the attacker to target a perimeter router into accepting the IP packet with a disguised IP source address. The real IP source address is spoofed. The purpose of IP spoofing is to make it difficult to trace back to the attacker's node. IP packet crafting is possible by overriding the function of the kernel of the operating system.

MAC Address Modifying Utility: SMAC

Similar to IP address spoofing is a utility that will allow the Ethernet address (MAC) to be spoofed (http://www.klcconsulting.net/smac). The attacker could use nmap to generate packets with the fake IP address in their headers. In this scenario, the target will send any response packets to the spoofed address, so its usefulness is limited to situations where the attacker needs to obscure the source of packets, such as in a denial-of-service attack.

DNS Spoofing

In this case, the domain name system server is spoofed to alter entries of domain names to reflect the attackers' IP address. This results in sending Web or email traffic to the attackers' machine. This attack is achieved by creating multiple forged packets wherein the IP, port, and service type entries are modified to serve the purpose.

Session Hijacking

Session hijacking is an act of taking over an ongoing active connection between two nodes on a network. Hijackers would have been monitoring an active session over a network, using a combination of sniffing and spoofing tools for a while. There is a TCP and UDP session hijacking. The hacker would have to continue to monitor the type of application layer protocol being used between two nodes, since the application layer protocol would decide the type of application being hijacked. We give examples of application layer protocols such as HTTP, SMTP, and DNS used to exchange data between any two active nodes on the network. We remind the reader that all three application layer protocols just stated use the TCP protocol at the layer 3 of the Internet model. Hence the hijacker would have to monitor the TCP port number 80 (HTTP), 25 (SMTP), and 57 (DNS) in order to hijack an active session.

TCP Session Hijacking

Let us recall that a TCP session starts out with a three-way handshake between the two nodes (one node is a client, and the other node is a server) that would like to establish a session between them. The nodes would exchange a sequence of TCP segments with well-defined sequence numbers to establish an active session. This active session is normally terminated by an exchange of FIN (finish) packet or abruptly with RST (reset) packets.

If a would-be hijacker were to correctly guess the sequence number of TCP segments between the two nodes, then it is quite possible that the hijacker could hijack the session before that session gets established between the original TCP client and the server. The original client would still send an ACK segment to the server, but the server would assume that it has received a duplicate segment with a matching sequence number, and thus ignore, as this happens quite a lot of times on the network. This scenario is not a complete description of session hijacking, but just an overview.

Route Table Modification

In this scenario, the attacker would block the packets by modifying the routing tables so that the packets flow through the network that the attacker has the control over. This is known as redirection of traffic and is normally achieved using ICMP (Internet Control Message Protocols) packets.

UDP Hijacking

The DNS protocol would need to be hijacked, if the attacker would want to pretend to be a Web server. The attacker would grab a copy of the HTTP request packet originating from a client to a Web server. Then the attacker would extract the request for a HTTP session from the packet and insert the attacker's IP address, and forward the packet to the client. The client would then establish the HTTP session with the attacker's node, unless the client verified the IP address to confirm that the session has not been hijacked.

Session-Hijacking Tool: Hunt

Hunt (http://packetstormsecurity.org/sniffers/hunt) has sniffing and session hijacking modes. Hunt uses ARP spoofing to establish the attacker's machine as a relay between, say Alice and Bob. When a system prepares to send a packet over a LAN, it first sends out an Address Resolution (ARP) query to all the other systems on the LAN, asking which of them has the Medium Access Control (MAC) address that corresponds to the IP address in the packet's header. The destination system replies with its MAC address, which the source system stores in its ARP cache for a certain period of time. For that period, the source system uses the data from its ARP cache to send transmissions to that destination. The attacker subverts this process by sending an unsolicited ARP response to Alice that maps Bob's IP address to a fake MAC address, and by sending an unsolicited ARP response to Bob that maps Alice's IP address to a fake MAC address. Both Bob's and Alice's systems overwrite these fake MAC addresses into their ARP caches, so that the packets they send to each other will go to fake addresses. They now cannot send packets to each other for the lifetime of the ARP cache.

Web Hijacking

Hackers may cause serious damage by either defacing the site or using the Web server to spread a virus. Unlike most other attacks, the techniques used in Web attacks range from layer 2 to layer 7 attacks, thus making the Web server susceptible to a wider variety of possible hacking attempts. Since the firewall port must be opened for the Web service (by default, port 80), it cannot help in preventing layer 7 attacks, which makes the detection of Web attacks difficult.

SQL Injection

As we saw earlier, Web portals use database servers in the backend, whereby the Web page connects to the database, queries for data, and presents the fetched data in a Web format to the browser. SQL injection attacks can occur if the input on the client side is not filtered appropriately before it is sent to the database in a query form. This can result in the possibility of manipulating SQL statements in order to perform invalid operations on the database.

A common example for this attack would be that of an SQL server, which is accessed by a Web application, wherein the SQL statements are not filtered by middleware or validation code components. This can lead to the attacker being able to craft and execute his own SQL statements on the backend database server, which could be simple SELECT statements to fetch and steal data, or could be as serious as dropping an entire data table.

5. MAINTAIN ACCESS

All types of service providers on the Internet that hold their clients' sensitive information, are required to notify their clients if a network breach has occurred. This has been mandated by every state in the country. Attackers must remove any evidence of intrusion associated with establishing access, modifying privileges, installing rootkits, and injecting backdoors.

Covering Tracks

Once a network has been compromised, the attacker must make sure that the attacker did not leave footprints behind. Every network runs some sort of security software such as the network intrusion detection system (NDIS), and the intrusion prevention system (IPS). The NDIS detects an intrusion and then reports it so that an appropriate response can be directed to the intrusion.

Backdoors and Trojan Horses

Trojan horses are code disguised as a benign program, but behave in an unexpected manner, usually a malicious manner. Trojan horses are normally injected into a foreign host while that host is browsing the Internet or downloading free utilities from the Internet. The host is normally quite unaware that a malicious program has been injected. This malicious program could hijack future HTTP sessions, monitor the activities on that host, and then relay that information back to the attacker's host and much more. Some noteworthy Trojans are ZeuS, ZeroAccess, TDSS Downloader, Alureon, Gbot, Butterfly bot, and BO2K.

Backdoors and Trojan horses have several things in common. They both come with two pieces of software, the client and the server. The server is the piece that the "remote administrator" will use to infect the victim's computer. The client is the piece that the attacker will use to monitor the victim's computer. Both programs allow for complete access to the victim's files. The hacker can copy, move, rename, delete, and even change any file or folder in the victim's computer.

Backdoor Tool: Netcat

Netcat (http://netcat.sourceforge.net) is a multipurpose networking tool capable of a variety of functions ranging from port scanning and opening connections to remote ports to creating backdoor shells for root access. It runs in either client mode or listening (server) mode.

Rootkits

One way an intruder can maintain access to a compromised system is by installing a rootkit as a Loadable Kernel Module in Linux or as a driver in MS-Windows. Furthermore, rootkits may be injected as user mode, in which case it might be detectable by a virus checker. Kernel-mode rootkits would run with the system privileges by adding a code or replacing portions of the core operating system. Kernel-mode rootkits are difficult to detect and remove, as they have the same level of security as the operating system. A rootkit contains a set of tools and replacement executables for many of the operating system's critical components, used to hide evidence of the attacker's presence and to give the attacker backdoor access to the system. Rootkits require root access to install, but once they are set up, the attacker can get root access back at any time. A rootkit may also consist of spyware and other programs that monitor traffic and keystrokes and can create a "backdoor" into the system for the hacker to gain access to the hacked node. Third-party software to detect and remove rootkits, Trojans, and Malware can be found at the following URLs:

- http://www.gmer.net
- http://usa.kaspersky.com
- http://www.spamfighter.com

6. DEFEND NETWORK AGAINST UNAUTHORIZED ACCESS

Now that we have completed the discussion on how the hacker might gain control of the target network, we will briefly discuss network perimeter defense (see checklist: An Agenda for Action for Network Security Self-Assessment), known as a firewall, as illustrated in Figure 28.5. Most firewalls are both a hardware and software integrated into one device. The firewall sits on the perimeter that defines the inside of the network from the un-trusted outside. A firewall should provide protection against intruders while allowing trusted users to connect to the network and use the resources therein. To set this scenario, first an access policy has to be defined. This policy is then turned into a set of security rules and is implemented as scripts on the firewall. Hence, firewall rules are defined. Thus, firewalls will examine the packets on the basis of the security policy and will either permit or deny the traffic. The security policy would be made up of a range of IP addresses, port numbers, network protocols (TCP, UDP, IP), and application protocols (HTTP, SMTP, FTP, Telnet). A firewall would have some of the ports open for both authorized inbound and outbound traffic, but the rest of the ports would be closed. Open ports remain a necessary vulnerability; they allow connections to applications, but they may also turn into open doors for attack. In the end, as long as ports remain open, network applications are susceptible to attack. Use of intrusion detection systems (IDS) may certainly help in detecting would-be attackers and thus provide some sense of security.

7. SUMMARY

In this chapter we presented a series of steps undertaken by the intruder to gain unlawful access to networks. The intruder first has to scan the network, thus obtaining the

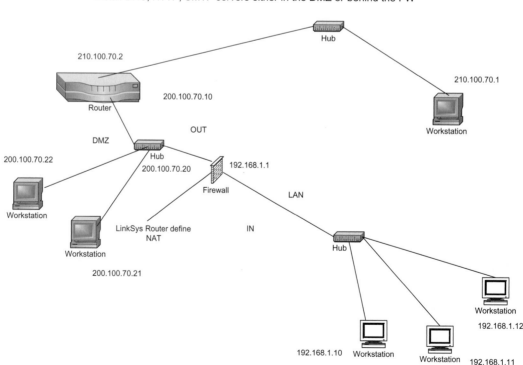

FIGURE 28.5   Network perimeter defense, known as a firewall.

An Agenda for Action for Network Security Self-Assessment

The first step to a self-defending network includes a careful and complete assessment of your network. The Network Security Self-Assessment Checklist shown here can help you quickly assess whether you have network security that is proactive, reactive, or open. The network security practices on this checklist will help ensure that your network is as secure as it can be. It will help you develop proactive, rather than reactive, security and will significantly limit your exposure to threats and the associated liabilities (check all tasks completed).

_____1. Conducting network and endpoint security assessments.

_____2. Classifying all network and information assets.

_____3. Deploying integrated security solutions with intelligent self-defending capabilities.

_____4. Identifying areas of regulatory similarities to minimize overhead and avoid duplicate investments in network security. For example, GLBA, the USA Patriot Act, and SOX all require consideration of capabilities for:

    _____a. Firewalls

    _____b. Encryption

    _____c. Access Controls

    _____d. Virtual Private Networks

    _____e. Intrusion Detection and Prevention

    _____f. Anti-virus Software

    _____g. Monitoring, Auditing, and Reporting

_____5. Aligning your people, processes, and technology to protect your institution.

_____6. Educating each employee on his or her security duties and responsibilities.

_____7. Managing security as an essential, dynamic, and ongoing project.

_____8. Regularly testing your network and endpoint security to identify weaknesses.

_____9. Responding immediately and appropriately to known and unknown or emerging security threats.

_____10. Updating your security practices to comply with new laws, rules, and guidelines and protect against new threats.

_____11. Identifying and reporting security-related events to executive management and the board of directors.

---

information regarding the resources available on the network. Once the intruder has completed the profile of the network and identified the "holes" in the network, he or she is ready to launch the attack. Next, the intruder would attempt to gain access to the network with the tools that are freely accessible on the Internet. If the intruder is successful in hacking into the network, then he or she could establish a backdoor entrance to the network. In later chapters we will introduce the topic of how network penetration can be achieved, with the tools that are freely available on the Internet. The reader should be warned that network intrusion is a punishable offense.

Now, let's move on to the real interactive part of this chapter: review questions/exercises, hands-on projects, case projects, and optional team case project. The answers and/or solutions by chapter can be found in the Online Instructor's Solutions Manual.

CHAPTER REVIEW QUESTIONS/EXERCISES

True/False

1. True or False? Network mapping is the process of discovering information about the topology of the target network, thus finding the IP addresses of gateways, routers, email, Web, FTP servers, and database servers.

2. True or False? The Nmap main page is described as an exploration tool and port-scanner.

3. True or False? Zombie hosts are those controlled by others on the network.

4. True or False? The decoy host command is not especially useful while testing IDS/IPS.

5. True or False? The standard use of a FIN packet is to not terminate the TCP connection — typically after the data transfer is complete.

Multiple Choice

1. Discover network interconnection and configuration, and look for network vulnerabilities:
   A. DOS
   B. Sniffing
   C. SYN flooding
   D. Reconnaissance
   E. All of the above

2. Removal and/or alteration of data, installing "backdoors," and hiding the tracks of attack activities is known as
   A. enumeration
   B. scanning
   C. DoS
   D. operational attacks
   E. all of the above

3. The port scanning technique is used to discover open _____ ports.
   A. TCP
   B. NetBIOS

C. PDP

D. HTTP

E. All of the above

4. The three-way TCP handshake is established during which of the TCP scanning sessions?

A. TCP connect()

B. TCP SYN

C. TCP FIN

D. TCP Open

E. All of the above

5. TCP SYN scanning is also known as

A. full open

B. half open

C. full close

D. half close

E. All of the above

EXERCISE

Problem

Download IP-tools and install the software:

1. Visit the Web site, http://www.ks-soft.net.
2. Download the software "IP-Tools."
3. Install IP-tools on your computer.

Hands-On Projects

Project

Download LANguard N.S.S. (Commercial grade Network Security Scanner, N.S.S.):

1. Visit the Web site, http://www.gfi.com.
2. Download LANguard N.S.S., a trial version.
3. Install the software on your computer.
4. Under Tools Explorer, select Whois.
5. Enter the Internet domain such as cox.net to discover the name servers and the IP addresses of the cox.net domain.

Case Projects

Problem

Using LANguard software to rnumerate the computers in your Windows domain:

1. Open LANguard application.
2. Under Tools Explorer, select Tools, and then Enumerate Computers.
3. Enter the domain in which you wish to enumerate.
4. Click the Retrieve TAB.
5. Copy the list of the computers thus displayed.

Optional Team Case Project

Problem

In this case study, you are to learn about RAW Sockets and to compare them with standard TCP/IP or Winsocks. This should prepare you to understand how TCP/IP packets are normally generated by the kernel, and to learn how a hacker bypassed the kernel to inject custom packets to attack a network.

## Chapter 29

Firewalls

Dr. Errin W. Fulp
Wake Forest University

Note: This chapter is available in its entirety online at store.elsevier.com/product.jsp?isbn=9780123943972 (click the Resources tab at the bottom of the page). It is also available in print in *Managing Information Security*.

1. ABSTRACT

The purpose of the firewall and its location is to have network connections traverse the firewall, which can then stop any unauthorized packets. A simple firewall will filter packets based on IP addresses and ports. A useful analogy is filtering your postal mail based only on the information on the envelope. You typically accept any letter addressed to you and return any letter addressed to someone else. This act of filtering is essentially the same for firewalls. This chapter refers to the secure network as the internal network; the insecure network is the external network. The remainder of this chapter provides an overview of firewall policies, designs, features, and configurations. Of course, technology is always changing, and network firewalls are no exception. However, the intent of this chapter is to describe aspects of network firewalls that tend to endure over time.

2. CONTENTS

## Chapter 30

Penetration Testing

Sanjay Bavisi
EC-Council

1. INTRODUCTION

Last year I walked into a restaurant in Rochester, New York, with a business partner; I was wearing an EC-Council official polo shirt. The back of the shirt was embroidered with the words "Licensed Penetration Tester." On reading those words on my shirt, a group of young executives seated behind me started an intense dialogue among themselves.

They were obviously not amused at my "behavior," since that was a restaurant for decent people! On my way out, I walked up to them and asked if they were amazed at what that statement meant. They replied "Absolutely!" When I explained to them the meaning of a Licensed Penetration Tester, they gave a loud laugh and apologized to me. They admitted that they had thought I was a pervert.

Each time I am at an airport, I get some stares when I put on that shirt. So the question is, what is penetration testing?

2. WHAT IS PENETRATION TESTING?

Penetration testing is the exploitation of vulnerabilities present in an organization's network. It helps determine which vulnerabilities are exploitable and the degree of information exposure or network control that the organization could expect an attacker to achieve after successfully exploiting a vulnerability. No penetration test is or ever can be "just like a hacker would do it," due to necessary limitations placed on penetration tests conducted by "white hats." Hackers don't have to follow the same rules as the "good guys" and they could care less whether your systems crash during one of their "tests." We'll talk more about this later. Right now, before we can talk any more about penetration testing, we need to talk about various types of vulnerabilities and how they might be discovered.

Before we can exploit a vulnerability in a penetration test, we have to discover what vulnerabilities exist within (and outside of) the organization. A vulnerability is a potential weakness in an organization's security. I use the term "potential" because not all vulnerabilities are exploitable or worth exploiting. A flaw may exist and may even be documented, but perhaps no one has figured out (yet) how to exploit it. Some vulnerabilities, although exploitable, might not yield enough information in return for the time or resources necessary to exploit them. Why break into a bank and steal only a dollar? That doesn't make much sense, does it?

Vulnerabilities can be thought of in two broad categories: logical and physical. We normally think of logical vulnerabilities as those associated with the organization's computers, infrastructure devices, software, or applications. Physical vulnerabilities, on the other hand, are normally thought of as those having to do with either the actual physical security of the organization (such as a door that doesn't always lock properly), the sensitive information that "accidentally" ends up in the dumpster, or the vulnerability of the organization's employees to social engineering (a vendor asking to use a computer to send a "quick email" to the boss).

Logical vulnerabilities can be discovered using any number of manual or automated tools and even by browsing the Internet. For those of you who are familiar with Johnny Long's *Google Hacking* books: *"Passwords*, for the *love of God!!!* Google found *passwords!"* The discovery of logical vulnerabilities is usually called *security scanning*, *vulnerability scanning*, or just *scanning*. Unfortunately, there are a number of "security consultants" who run a scan, put a fancy report cover on the output of the tool, and pass off these scans as a penetration test.

Physical vulnerabilities can be discovered as part of a physical security inspection, a "midnight raid" on the organization's dumpsters, getting information from employees, or via unaccompanied access to a usually nonpublic area (I really need to use the bathroom!).

Vulnerabilities might also exist due to a lack of company policies or procedures or an employee's failure to follow the policy or procedure. Regardless of the cause of the vulnerability, it might have the potential to compromise the organization's security. So, of all the vulnerabilities that have been discovered, how do we know which ones pose the greatest danger to the organization's network? We test them! We test them to see which ones we can exploit and exactly what could happen if a "real" attacker exploited that vulnerability.

Because few organizations that I know of have enough money, time, or resources to eliminate every vulnerability discovered, they have to prioritize their efforts; this is one of the best reasons for an organization to conduct a penetration test. At the conclusion of the penetration test, they will know which vulnerabilities can be exploited and what can happen if they are exploited. They can then plan to correct the vulnerabilities based on the amount of critical information exposed or network control gained by exploiting the vulnerability. In other words, a penetration test helps organizations strike a balance between security and business functionality. Sounds like a perfect solution, right? If only it were so!

There are organizations that do not care about the "true risks" that their organizations face. Instead, they are more interested in being able to tell their shareholders or their regulating agencies that they've conducted a penetration test and "passed" it. If the penetration test is structured so that only certain systems are tested, or if the test is conducted during a known timeframe, the test results will be favorable to the organization, but the test isn't a true reflection of its network security posture. This kind of "boutique testing" can lead to a false sense of security for the organization, its employees, and its stakeholders.

3. HOW DOES PENETRATION TESTING DIFFER FROM AN ACTUAL "HACK?"

Earlier, I mentioned that penetration testing isn't and never can be "just like a hacker would do it." How come? Except in the case of "directed" sabotage or espionage, it's not personal between your organization and attackers. They don't care who you are, where you are, or what your organization does to earn its living. They just want to hack something. The easier it is to attack your network, the more likely it is that you'll be a target. Ask your network administrator to look at the network intrusion detection logs (or look at them yourself if you're a network admin). See how many times in a 24-hour period your organization's network gets scanned for potential vulnerabilities.

Once an attacker has decided that you're his or her (yes, there *are* female hackers—good ones, too!) next target, they may take weeks or months to perform the first step of an attack: reconnaissance. As a penetration tester or company providing penetration testing services, I doubt that you're going to get hired to spend six months doing reconnaissance and another couple of months conducting an attack. So, the first difference between a penetration test and a real attack is the length of time taken to conduct all the activities needed to produce a successful outcome. As "good guys," we don't have the luxury of time

that the "bad guys" do. So we're handicapped to begin with. The two things I tell clients are:

1. I cannot spend the months planning to attack you like a real hacker can
2. I cannot break the law, I am limited by a code of ethics, and have to maintain "ethical" boundaries.

In some (not all) cases, once attackers find a suitable vulnerability to attack, they will. They don't care that the vulnerability resides on a mission-critical system, if the vulnerability will crash the system, or that the system might become unusable in the middle of the busiest time of day. If that vulnerability doesn't "pan out," they find another and try again. They keep it up until they run out of vulnerabilities that they can exploit, or they're discovered, or they manage to successfully breach the network or crash the system. Penetration test teams normally don't have this luxury, either. Usually the test team has X amount of time to find a vulnerability and get in or the test is over and the network is declared "safe and secure." If the test team didn't have enough time to test all the vulnerabilities—oh, well. The test is still over, they still didn't get in, and so our network *must* be safe! Few seem to think about the fact that a "real" attacker may, just by blind luck, choose one of the unable-to-be-tested-because-of-time-limitations vulnerabilities and be able to waltz right into the network without being detected. One of the most important things for a tester and/or clients to grasp is the fact that no test will find everything, there are always things that can be missed, be it due to time constraints, or the team did not have the right conditions to find the weakness. It is best to proceed with the understanding that there will always be things we might miss, our job as a tester is to find what we can within the scope of the assessment and time constraints. At the end of the day, the goal of the test is to provide the client a report that will assist them in improving their security posture, there is no such thing as perfect security and there will never be.

Some systems are declared "off limits" to testing because they're "too important to have crash" during a test. An organization may specify that testing can only occur during certain hours or on certain days because of a real or perceived impact on business operations. This is the second difference between a penetration test and a real attack: Hackers don't play by any rules. They attack what they want when they want and how they want. Just to be clear: I'm not advocating denial-of-service testing during the busiest time of an organization's day, or unrestricted testing at any time. I'm just trying to make a point that *no* system is too critical to test. From a hacker's perspective, there are no "off-limits" systems, just opportunities for attack. We'll talk more about differences between real attacks and penetration tests when we talk about the various types of testing in the next section. For example, in a bank or financial company you never get to test their financial databases, there is just too much risk, and when that is the revenue that the company uses to survive they are not going to let you test it, and real hackers would not have this limitation.

4. TYPES OF PENETRATION TESTING

Some sources classify penetration testing into two types—internal and external—and then talk about the "variations" of these types of tests based on the amount of information the test team has been given about the organization prior to starting the test. Other sources use a reverse-classification system, typing the penetration test based on the amount of information available to the test team and then the location from which the test is conducted. I much prefer the latter method, since it removes any chance of misunderstanding about what testing is going to be conducted where. *Warning:* If you're planning to take the CISSP or some of the other network security certification examinations, stick with the "old skool" "classification by location, then type" definitions for penetration testing types and variations.

When a penetration test is conducted against Internet-facing hosts, it is known as *external testing*. When conducted against hosts inside the organization's internal network, it is known as *internal testing*. Obviously, a complete penetration test will encompass testing of both external and internal hosts. The "variations" of penetration tests are normally classified based on how much information the test team has been given about the organization. The three most commonly used terms for penetration types are *white-box*, *gray-box*, and *black-box testing*. Before we talk about these penetration testing variations, you need to understand that we can conduct any of them (white, gray, or black) either externally or internally. If we want a complete test, we need to test both externally *and* internally. Got it? Good! Now we can talk about what is involved with each type of testing.

We'll start with white-box testing. The "official" definition of white-box testing usually includes verbiage about providing information so as to be able to assess the security of a specific target or assess security against a specific attack. There are several problems with this definition in real life. The first is that it sounds as though you would only conduct a white-box test if you were looking to verify the security of one specific host or looking to verify the security of your network against one specific attack. But it would be foolhardy to test for only one vulnerability. Since the "variations" we're talking about are supposed to be centered on the amount of information available to the test team, let's look at a white-box test from an information availability perspective.

Who in your organization knows the most about your network? Probably the network administrator. Any organization that has recently terminated employment of a network administrator or member of the IT Department under less than favorable circumstances has a big problem. There is the potential that the organization's network could be attacked by this former employee who has extreme knowledge about the network. In a white-box test, therefore, the test team should be given about the same amount of information that a network administrator would have. Probably the team won't be given passwords, but they'll be given network ranges, topologies, and so on.

Gray-box testing, by "official" definition, provides "some" knowledge to the test team, about the sort of thing a normal, unprivileged user might have: hostnames, maybe a few IP addresses, the fact that the organization allows senior management to "remote" into the network, and so on. Common, though not necessarily public, knowledge about the "inner workings" of the organization's network is the level of information provided to the test team. Some sources claim that this testing type (as well as the information disclosed in a white-box test) "puts the tester at an advantage" over an attacker because the test team possesses information that an attacker wouldn't have. But that's not necessarily the case. Any organization that has terminated a "normal user" has the potential for an attack based on that user's inside knowledge of the network.

Now let's talk about everyone's favorite: black-box penetration testing. Again, we'll start with the common definition, which usually says something like "provides the test team with little or no information except for possibly the company name." The test team is required to obtain all their attack information from public sources such as the Internet. There's usually some sentence somewhere in the description that says how a black-box test is always much better than any other type of test because it most closely mimics the way an attacker would conduct an attack. The definition might be right (and I might even be inclined to agree with it) if the organization has never terminated a network admin or any other employee with network access. I might also be more in agreement with this train of thought if the majority of attacks were conducted by unknown persons from the far reaches of the globe instead of former employees or currently employed "insiders"!

Depending on what article or book you happen to be reading at the time, you might also see references to application penetration testing, Web penetration testing, shrink-wrap penetration testing, wireless penetration testing, telephony penetration testing, Bluetooth penetration testing ... and the list goes on. I've seen every possible device in a network listed as a separate penetration test. The bottom line is that if it's present in the network, an organization needs to discover what vulnerabilities exist on it and then test those vulnerabilities to discover what could happen if they're successfully exploited.

I guess since Morgan Kaufmann asked me to write this chapter, I can give you my opinion: I don't like black-box penetration testing. I don't want any network of mine tested "just like a hacker would do it." I want my network tested *better* than any hacker ever could, because I don't want to end up on the front page of *The New York Times* as the subject of a "latest breach" article. My client's data are much too important to take that chance.

The success of every penetration test rests on the experience of the test team. If some hacker has more experience than the test team I hire, I'm in trouble! So how do I even the odds? Instead of hiring a team to do a black box, in which they're going to spend hours searching for information and poking around, I give them the necessary information to test the network thoroughly, right up front. By doing so, their time is actually spent testing the network, not carrying out a high-tech scavenger hunt. Any good penetration test team is still going to do reconnaissance and tell me what information is available about my organization from public sources anyway. No, I'm not going to give up the administrative password to my network. But I am going to tell them what my IP ranges are, whether or not I have wireless, and whether I allow remote access into the network, among other things.

In addition to the types and variations of penetration testing, we also need to talk about announced and unannounced testing. Which of these two methods will be used depends on whether your intent is to test the network itself or the network's security staff. In an announced test, the penetration testing team works in "full cooperation" with the IT staff and the IT staff has "full knowledge" about the test, such as what will be tested and when. In an unannounced test, only specific members of the tested organization (usually the higher levels of management) are aware that the testing will take place. Even they may only know a "window" of time for testing, not the exact times or dates.

If you follow the published guidelines, an unannounced test is used when testing an organization's incident response capability is called for. Announced tests are used when the organization simply wants to test network devices. Is this really how it happens in the real world? Sometimes it isn't.

Most organizations that conduct annual testing do so at about the same time every year, especially if it's a government organization. So there's really no such thing as an "unannounced" test. Everyone knows that sometime between *X* and *Y* dates, they're going to be tested. In some organizations this means that during that timeframe there suddenly appears to be an increased awareness of network security. Machines get patched quicker. Logs are reviewed daily. Abnormal activities are reported immediately. After the testing window is over, however, it's back to the same old routine until the next testing window, next year.

What about announced testing, you ask? Think about it: If you're a network administrator and you know a test is coming, you're going to make sure that everything is as good as you can make it. Once again, there's that increased emphasis on security—until the testing window is over, that is.

Let's take a minute to recap what we've talked about so far. We've learned that a penetration test is used to exploit discovered vulnerabilities and to help determine what an attacker could do if they successfully exploited a vulnerability. We learned that not all vulnerabilities are actually a concern, because there might not be a way to exploit them or what we'd get by exploiting them wouldn't justify the time or effort we spent in doing so. We learned that there are different types and variations of penetration tests, that they can be announced or unannounced, and that none of them are actually "just like a hacker would do it." Probably the most important thing we've learned so far is that if we really and truly want to protect our network from a real-life attack, we have to offset the biggest advantage that a hacker has: time. We discovered that we can do this by giving the testing team sufficient information to thoroughly test the network instead of surfing the Internet on our dime. In today's penetration testing world , when we get hired to do a general penetration test, we inform the client that the level of skill we are going to emulate, shall be the skill set of an average hacker within the parameters set by the client. This means we will use a combination of tools and manual techniques and proven methodologies . Given the general scope of the assignment, this will not enable us to reverse engineer all of the applications and run debugging tools to find vulnerabilities, and write our own exploits, as it is too time consuming and obviously outside of the scope of the engagement.

5. PHASES OF PENETRATION TESTING

There are three phases in a penetration test, and they mimic the phases that an attacker would use to conduct a real attack. These phases are the pre-attack phase, the attack phase, and the post-attack phase, as shown in Figure 30.1.

The activities that take place in each phase (as far as the penetration testing team is concerned) depend on how the rules of engagement have specified that the penetration test be conducted. To give you a more complete picture, we talk about these phases from the perspective of a hacker and from that of a penetration team conducting the test under "black-box" conditions.

The Pre-Attack Phase

The pre-attack phase (see Figure 30.2) consists of the penetration team's or hacker's attempts to investigate or explore the potential target. This reconnaissance effort is

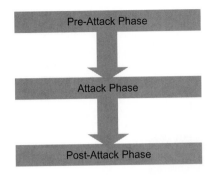

FIGURE 30.1   The three phases in a penetration test.

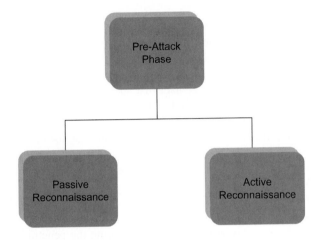

FIGURE 30.2   The pre-attack phase.

normally categorized into two types: active reconnaissance and passive reconnaissance.

Beginning with passive reconnaissance, which does not "touch" the network and is therefore undetectable by the target organization, the hacker or penetration tester will gather as much information as possible about the target company. Once all available sources for passive reconnaissance have been exhausted, the test team or attacker may move into active reconnaissance.

During active reconnaissance, the attacker may actually "touch" the network, thereby increasing the chance that they will be detected or alert the target that someone is "rattling the doorknobs." Some of the information gathered during reconnaissance can be used to produce a provisional map of the network infrastructure for planning a more coordinated attack strategy later. Ultimately it boils down to information gathering in all its many forms. Hackers will often spend more time on pre-attack or reconnaissance activities than on the actual attack itself.

The Attack Phase

This stage involves the actual compromise of the target. The hacker or test team may exploit a logical or physical vulnerability discovered during the pre-attack phase or use other methods such as a weak security policy to gain access to a system. The important point here is to understand that although there could be several possible vulnerabilities, the hacker needs only one to be successful to compromise the network.

By comparison, a penetration test team will be interested in finding and exploiting as many vulnerabilities as possible because neither the organization nor the test team will know which vulnerability a hacker will choose to exploit first (see Figure 30.3). Once inside, the attacker may attempt to escalate his or her privileges, install one or more applications to sustain their access, further exploit the compromised system, and/or attempt to extend their control to other systems within the network. When they've finished having their way with the system or network, they will attempt to eliminate all evidence of their presence in a process some call "covering their tracks."

The Post-Attack Phase

The post-attack phase is unique to the penetration test team. It revolves around returning any modified system(s) to the pretest state. With the exception of covering their tracks, a real attacker couldn't care less about returning a compromised system to its original state. The longer the system remains compromised, the longer they can legitimately claim credit for "pwning" (owning) the system.

Obviously, in a real penetration test, the following list would include reversal of each and every change made to the network to restore it to its pre-attack state. Some of the activities that the test team may have to accomplish are shown here:

- Removal of any files, tools, exploits, or other test-created objects uploaded to the system during testing
- Removal or reversal of any changes to the registry made during system testing
- Reversal of any access control list (ACL) changes to file(s) or folder(s) or other system or user object(s)
- Restoration of the system, network devices, and network infrastructure to the state the network was in prior to the beginning of the test

The key element for the penetration test team to be able to restore the network or system to its pre-attack state is documentation. The penetration testing team documents every step of every action taken during the test, for two reasons. The obvious one is so that they can reverse their steps to "cleanse" the system or network. The second reason is to ensure repeatability of the test. Why is repeatability an issue?

An important part of the penetration test team's job is not only to find and exploit vulnerabilities but also to recommend appropriate mitigation strategies for discovered

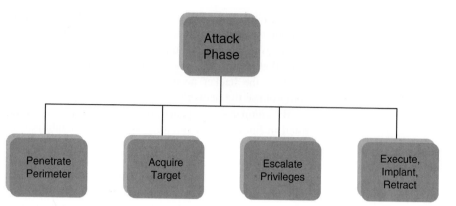

FIGURE 30.3 The attack phase.

vulnerabilities. This is especially true for those vulnerabilities that were successfully exploited. After the tested organization implements the recommended corrections, it should repeat the penetration test team's actions to ensure that the vulnerability has indeed been eliminated and that the applied mitigation has not had "unintended consequences" by creating a new vulnerability. The only way to do that is to recreate the original test that found the vulnerability in the first place, make sure it's gone, and then make sure there are no new vulnerabilities as a result of fixing the original problem.

As you might imagine, there are lots of possible ways for Murphy to stick his nose into the process we just talked about. How do penetration test teams and tested organizations try to keep Murphy at bay? Rules!

6. DEFINING WHAT'S EXPECTED

Someone once said: "You can't win the game if you don't know the rules!" That statement makes good sense for a penetration test team as well. Every penetration test must have a clearly defined set of rules by which the penetration test "game" is played. These rules are put into place to help protect both the tested organization and the penetration test team from errors of omission and commission (under normal circumstances). According to the National Institute of Standards and Technology (NIST), the "rule book" for penetration tests is often called the "Rules of Engagement." Rules of Engagement define things like which IP addresses or hosts are and are not allowed to be tested, which techniques are and are not allowed to be used, when testing is permitted or prohibited, points of contact for both the test team and the tested organization, IP addresses of machines from which testing is conducted, and measures to prevent escalation of an incident response to law enforcement, just to name a few.

There isn't a standard format for the Rules of Engagement, so it is not the only document that can be used to control a penetration test. Based on the complexity of the tested organization and the scope of the penetration test, the penetration test team may also use detailed test plan(s) for either or both logical and physical testing. In addition to these documents, both the client and the penetration test company conducting the operation will require some type of formal contact that spells out either explicitly, or incorporates by reference, such items as how discovered sensitive material will be handled, an indemnification statement, nondisclosure statement, fees, project schedule, reporting, and responsibilities. These are but a few of the many items that penetration testing control documents cover, but they should be sufficient for you to understand that all aspects of the penetration test need to be described somewhere in a document.

We now know what's expected during the penetration test. Armed with this information, how does the penetration test team plan to deliver the goods? It starts with a methodology.

7. THE NEED FOR A METHODOLOGY

When you leave for vacation and you've never been to your destination before, you're likely make a list of things you need or want to do before, during, or after the trip. You might also take a map along so you know how to get there and not get lost or sidetracked along the way. Penetration test teams also use a map of sorts. It's called their *methodology.*

A methodology is simply a way to ensure that a particular activity is conducted in a standard manner, with documented and repeatable results. It's a planning tool to help ensure that all mandatory aspects of an activity are performed.

Just as a map will show you various ways to get to your destination, a good penetration testing methodology does not restrict the test team to a single way of compromising the network. While on the road to your dream vacation, you might find your planned route closed or under construction and you might have to make a detour. You might want to do some sightseeing, or maybe visit long-lost relatives along the way.

Similarly, in a penetration test, your primary attack strategy might not work, forcing you to find a way around a particular network device, firewall, or intrusion prevention system. While exploiting one vulnerability, you may discover another one that leads you to a different host or a different subnet. A well-written methodology allows the test team the leeway necessary to explore these "targets of opportunity" while still ultimately guiding them to the stated goals of the test.

Most penetration test companies will have developed a standard methodology that covers all aspects of a penetration test. This baseline methodology document is the starting point for planning a particular test. Once the control documentation has been finalized, the penetration test team will know exactly what they can and cannot test. They will then modify that baseline methodology based on the scope statement in the Rules of Engagement for the penetration test that they are going to conduct.

Different clients are subject to different regulatory requirements such as HIPAA, Sarbanes-Oxley, Gramm-Leach-Bliley, or others, so the penetration test team's methodology must also be flexible enough to cover these and other government or private industry regulations.

In a minute, we'll talk about the sources of penetration testing methodologies, but for now, just understand that a methodology is not a "nice to have," it's a "must have." Without a methodology to be used as the basis to plan and execute a penetration test, there is no reliability. The team will be lost in the network, never knowing if they've fulfilled the requirements of the test or not until they're writing the report. By then, it's too late—for them and for the organization.

8. PENETRATION TESTING METHODOLOGIES

Back to our map example for a minute. Unless you're a cartographer, you're probably not going to make your own map to get to your dream vacation destination. You'll rely on a map that someone else has drawn, tested, and published. The same holds true for penetration testing methodologies. Before we talk about how a methodology, any methodology, is used in a penetration test, let's discuss penetration testing methodologies in general. There are probably as many different methodologies as there are companies conducting penetration tests, but all of them fit into one of two broad categories: open source or proprietary.

Open-source methodologies are just that: available for use by anyone. Probably the best-known open-source methodology, and de facto standard, is the Open Source Security Testing Methodology Manual (OSSTMM), the brainchild of Pete Herzog. You can get the latest copy of this document at www.isecom.org. Another valuable

open-source methodology is the Open Web Application Security Project (OWASP), geared to securing Web applications, available at www.owasp.org.

Proprietary methodologies have been developed by particular entities offering network security services or certifications. The specific details of the processes that produce the output of the methodology are usually kept private. Companies wanting to use these proprietary methodologies must usually undergo specific training in their use and abide by quality standards set by the methodology proponent. Some examples of proprietary methodologies include IBM, ISS, Foundstone, and our own EC Council Licensed Penetrator Tester methodology.

9. METHODOLOGY IN ACTION

A comprehensive penetration test is a systematic analysis of all security controls in place at the tested organization. The penetration test team will look at not only the logical and physical vulnerabilities that are present but also at the tested organization's policies and procedures to assess whether or not the controls in place adequately protect the organization's information infrastructure.

Let's examine the use of a penetration testing methodology in more detail to demonstrate how it's used to conduct a penetration test. Of course, as the President of the EC-Council, I'm going to take the liberty of using our LPT methodology as the example.

EC-Council LPT Methodology

Figure 30.4 is a block representation of some of the major areas of the LPT methodology as taught in the EC-Council's Licensed Penetration Tester certification course. The first two rows of the diagram (except for the Wireless Network Penetration Testing block) represent a fairly normal sequence of events in the conduct of a penetration test. The test team will normally start by gathering information, then proceed with vulnerability discovery and analysis, followed by penetration testing from the network perimeter, and graduating to the internal network.

After that, beginning with wireless testing, what the test team actually does will depend on what applications or services are present in the network and what is allowed to be tested under the Rules of Engagement. I've chosen not to show every specific step in the process as part of the diagram. After all, if I told you everything, there wouldn't be any reason for you to get certified as a Licensed Penetration Tester, would there?

The methodology (and course) assumes that the penetration test team has been given authorization to conduct a complete test of the target network, including using denial-of-service tactics so that we can acquaint our LPT

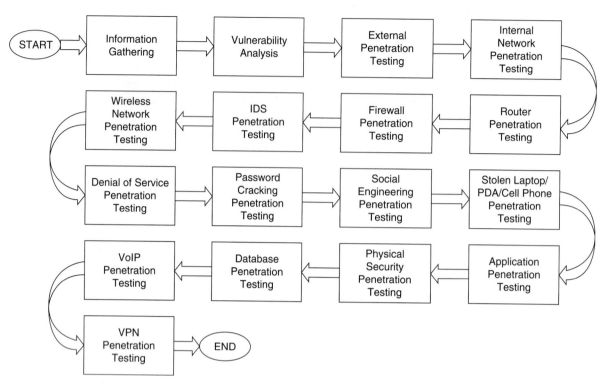

FIGURE 30.4   Block representation of some of the major areas of the LPT methodology.

candidates with the breadth of testing they may be called on to perform. In real life, a test team may seldom actually perform DoS testing, but members of the penetration test team must still be proficient in conducting this type of test, to make recommendations in their reports as to the possible consequences of an attacker conducting a DoS attack on the company's network infrastructure. Here I give you a quick overview of each of the components.

Information Gathering

The main purpose of information gathering is to understand more about the target company. As we've already talked about, there are a number of ways to gather information about the company from public domain sources such as the Internet, newspapers, and third-party information sources.

Vulnerability Analysis

Before you can attack, you have to find the weak points. A vulnerability analysis is the process of identifying logical weaknesses in computers and networks as well as physical weaknesses and weaknesses in policies, procedures, and practices relating to the network and the organization.

External Penetration Testing

External testing is normally conducted before internal testing. It exploits discovered vulnerabilities that are accessible from the Internet to help determine the degree of information exposure or network control that could be achieved by the successful exploitation of a particular vulnerability from outside the network.

Internal Network Penetration Testing

Internal testing is normally conducted after external testing. It exploits discovered vulnerabilities that are accessible from inside the organization to help determine the degree of information exposure or network control that could be achieved by the successful exploitation of a particular vulnerability from inside the network.

Router Penetration Testing

Depending on where they are located in the network infrastructure, routers may forward data to points inside or outside the target organization's network. Take down a router; take down all hosts connected to that router. Because of their importance, routers that connect the target organization to the Internet may be tested twice: once from the Internet and again from inside the network.

Firewall Penetration Testing

Firewall(s) are another critical network infrastructure component that may be tested multiple times, depending on where they reside in the infrastructure. Firewalls that are exposed to the Internet are a primary line of defense for the tested organization and so will usually be tested from the Internet and from within the DMZ for both ingress and egress vulnerabilities and proper rule sets. Internal firewalls are often used to segregate portions of the internal network from each other. Those firewalls are also tested from both sides and for ingress and egress filtering to ensure that only applicable traffic can be passed.

IDS Penetration Testing

As networks have grown more complex and the methods to attack them have multiplied, more and more organizations have come to rely on intrusion detection (and prevention) systems (IDS/IPS) to give them warning or prevent an intrusion from occurring. The test team will be extremely interested in testing these devices for any vulnerabilities that will allow an attacker to circumvent setting of the IPS/IDS alarms.

Wireless Network Penetration Testing

If the target company uses wireless (and who doesn't these days), the test team will focus on the availability of "outside" wireless networks that can be accessed by employees of the target company (effectively circumventing the company's firewalls), the "reach" of the company's own wireless signal outside the physical confines of the company's buildings, and the type and strength of encryption employed by the wireless network. With the explosion of smart phones this has expanded significantly, and requires much time and consideration in the testing methodology if an organization is syncing their smart phones, or more importantly using a Blackberry Enterprise Server (BES), one of our Master Trainers while doing a penetration test for a large financial organization was able to compromise the BES and this machine holds all of the files from the Blackberry device, over the years the Blackberry has made improvements in their security, but when an organization deploys a BES then they have accepted the risk that if that gets a vulnerability and is compromised then all of the data that is stored on ALL of the organizations Blackberry devices is compromised, think about that, what do you have on your Blackberry today? It is not only Blackberry, but all of the smart phones carry with them similar risks, not to mention each and every application on the device is susceptible to the same vulnerabilities as our systems have been for years. There is a saying " Hack the iPhone, there is an app for that."

Denial-of-Service Penetration Testing

If the test team is lucky enough to land a penetration test that includes DoS testing, they will focus on crashing the company's Web sites and flooding the sites or the internal network with enough traffic to bring normal business processes to a standstill or a crawl. They may also attempt to cause a DoS by locking out user accounts instead of trying to crack the passwords.

Password-Cracking Penetration Testing

Need we say more?

Social Engineering Penetration Testing

The test team may use both computer- and human-based techniques to try to obtain not only sensitive and/or nonpublic information directly from employees but also to gain unescorted access to areas of the company that are normally off-limits to the public. Once alone in an off-limits area, the social engineer may then try to obtain additional sensitive or nonpublic information about the company, its data, or its customers. This has taken on a whole new level, whereas before the most common method was by phone, we now have all the email attacks, and the variants that have proven largely successful, and now with the advent of social networking by the vast majority of the online population the attack surface for this has no boundaries, and it is not just Facebook and Twitter, it is the combination of these different profiles that can be used to social engineer information from perspective victims.

Stolen Laptop, PDA, and Cell Phone Penetration Testing

Some organizations take great pains to secure the equipment that is located within the physical confines of their buildings but fail to have adequate policies and procedures in place to maintain that security when mobile equipment leaves the premises. The test team attempts to temporarily "liberate" mobile equipment and then conducts testing to gain access to the data stored on those devices. They will most often attempt to target either or both members of the IT Department and the senior members of an organization in the hopes that their mobile devices will contain the most useful data.

Application Penetration Testing

The test team will perform meticulous testing of an application to check for code-related or "back-end" vulnerabilities that might allow access to the application itself, the underlying operating system, or the data that the application can access.

Physical Security Penetration Testing

The test team may attempt to gain access to the organizational facilities before, during, or after business hours using techniques meant to defeat physical access control systems or alarms. They may also conduct an overt "walk-thorough" accompanied by a member of the tested organization to provide the tested company with an "objective perspective" of the physical security controls in place. Either as a part of physical security testing or as a part of social engineering, the team may rifle through the organization's refuse to discover what discarded information could be used by an attacker to compromise the organization and to observe employee reaction to an unknown individual going through the trash.

Database Penetration Testing

The test team may attempt to directly access data contained in the database using account password-cracking techniques or indirectly access data by manipulating triggers and stored procedures that are executed by the database engine.

Voice-Over-IP Penetration Testing

The test team may attempt to gain access to the VoIP network for the purpose of recording conversations or to perform a DoS to the company's voice communications network. In some cases, if the organization has not followed the established "best practices" for VoIP, the team may attempt to use the VoIP network as a jumping-off point to conduct further compromise of the organization's network backbone.

VPN Penetration Testing

A number of companies allow at least some of their employees to work remotely, either from home or while they are "on the road." In either case, a VPN represents a trusted connection to the internal network. The test team will attempt to gain access to the VPN by either compromising the remote endpoint or gaining access to the VPN tunnel so that they have a "blessed" connection to the internal company network.

In addition to testing the applicable items in the blocks on the previous diagram, the penetration test team must also be familiar with and able to test for compliance with the regulatory requirements to which the tested organization is subject. Each standard has specific areas that must be tested, the process and procedures of which may not be part of a standard penetration test.

I'm sure that as you read the previous paragraphs, there was a nagging thought in the back of your mind: What are the risks involved? Let's talk about the risks.

10. PENETRATION TESTING RISKS

The difference between a real attack and a penetration test is the penetration tester's intent, authority to conduct the test, and lack of malice. Because penetration testers may use the same tools and procedures as a real attacker, it should be obvious that penetration testing can have serious repercussions if it's not performed correctly.

Even if your target company ceased all operations for the time the penetration test was being conducted, there is still a danger of data loss, corruption, or system crashes that might require a reinstall from "bare metal." Few, if any, companies can afford to stop functioning while a penetration test is being performed. Therefore it is incumbent on both the target organization and the penetration test team to do everything in their power to prevent an interruption of normal business processes during penetration testing operations.

Target companies should be urged to back up all their critical data before testing begins. They should always have IT personnel present to immediately begin restoration in the unfortunate event that a system crashes or otherwise becomes unavailable. The test team must be prepared to lend all possible assistance to the target company in helping to restore any system that is affected by penetration testing activities.

11. LIABILITY ISSUES

Although we just discussed some of the risks involved with conducting a penetration test, the issue of liability deserves its own special section. A botched penetration test can mean serious liability for the penetration test company that conducted the testing. The penetration test company should ensure that the documentation for the penetration test includes a liability waiver.

The waiver must be signed by an authorized representative of the target company and state that the penetration testing firm cannot be held responsible for the consequences of items such as:

- Damage to systems
- Unintentional denial-of-service conditions
- Data corruption
- System crashes or unavailability
- Loss of business income

12. LEGAL CONSEQUENCES

The legal consequences of a penetration test gone wrong can be devastating to both the target company and the penetration testers performing the test. The company may become the target of lawsuits by customers. The penetration testers may become the target of lawsuits by the target company. The only winners in this situation are the lawyers. It is imperative that proper written permission is obtained from the target company before *any* testing is conducted.

Legal remedies are normally contained in a penetration testing contract that is drawn up in addition to the testing control documentation. Both the penetration test company and the target company should seek legal counsel to review the agreement and to protect their interests. The authorization to perform testing must come from a senior member of the test company, and that senior member must be someone who has the authority to authorize such testing, not just the network administrator or LAN manager.

Authorized representatives of both the penetration test company and the target company must sign the penetration testing contract to indicate that they agree with its contents and the contents of all documentation that may be included or included by reference, such as the Rules of Engagement, the test plan, and other test control documentation.

13. "GET OUT OF JAIL FREE" CARD

We just talked about how the target company and the penetration test company protect themselves. What about that individual team member crawling around in the dumpster at 2:00 A.M., or the unfortunate team member who's managed to get into the company president's office and log onto his or her computer? What protection do those individuals have when that 600-pound gorilla of a security guard clamps his hand on their shoulder and asks what they're doing?

A "Get Out of Jail Free" card might just work wonders in these and other cases. Though not really a card, it's usually requested by the penetration test team as "extra insurance" during testing. It is presented if they're detained or apprehended while in the performance of their duties, as proof that their actions are sanctioned by the officers of the company. The card may actually be a letter on the tested company's letterhead and signed by the senior officer authorizing the test. It states the specific tasks that can be performed under the protection of the letter and specifically names the bearer.

It contains language that the bearer is conducting activities and testing under the auspices of a contract and that no violation of policy or crime is or has been committed. It includes a 24-hour contact number to verify the validity of the letter. As you can imagine, these "Get Out of Jail Free" cards are *very* sensitive and are usually distributed to team members immediately before testing begins, collected, and returned to the target company immediately after the end of any testing requiring their use.

There is a tremendous amount of work involved in conducting a thorough and comprehensive penetration test. What we've just discussed is but a 40,000-foot fly-over of what actually happens during the process. But we're not done yet! The one area that we haven't discussed is the personnel performing these tests.

14. PENETRATION TESTING CONSULTANTS

The quality of the penetration test performed for a client is directly dependent on the quality of the consultants performing the work, singularly and in the aggregate. There are hundreds if not thousands of self-proclaimed "security services providers" out there, both companies and individuals. If I'm in need of a penetration test, how can I possibly know whether the firm or individual I'm going to select is really and truly qualified to test my network comprehensively, accurately, and safely? What if I end up hiring a consultancy that employs hackers? What if the consultant(s) aren't hackers, but they just don't know what they're doing?

In these, the last pages of this chapter, I want to talk about the people who perform penetration testing services. First, you get another dose of my personal opinion. Then we'll talk about security services providers, those who provide penetration testing services. We'll talk about some of the questions that you might want to ask about their operations and their employees. Here's a hint for you: If the company is evasive in answering the questions or outright refuses to answer them—run!

What determines whether or not a penetration tester is "experienced"? There are few benchmarks to test the knowledge of a penetration tester. You can't ask her for a score: "Yes, I've performed 27 penetration tests, been successful in compromising 23 of those networks, and the overall degree of difficulty of each one of those tests was 7 on a scale of 1 to 10."

There really isn't a Better Business Bureau for penetration testers. You can't go to a Web site and see that XSecurity has had three complaints filed against them for crashing networks they've been testing or that "John Smith" has tested nine networks that were hacked within the following 24 hours. (Whoa! What an idea … ! Nah, wouldn't work.) Few companies would want to admit that they chose the wrong person or company to test their networks, and that kind of information would surely be used by attackers in the "intelligence-gathering phase" as a source of information for future attacks on any company that chose to report. Well, if we can't do that, what can we do?

We pretty much have to rely on "word of mouth" that such-and-such a company does a good job. We have to pretty much rely on the fact that the tester has been

---

An Agenda for Action for the Experiences of the Test Team

The checklist that follows should give you some indication of questions you can ask to determine the "experiences" of your test team (check all tasks completed):

_____ 1. Have they conducted research and development in the security arena?

_____ 2. Have they published research papers or articles in technical journals?

_____ 3. Have they presented at seminars, either locally or internationally?

_____ 4. What certifications do they hold?

_____ 5. Where are those certifications from?

_____ 6. Do they maintain membership/affiliation/ accreditation in organizations such as the EC-Council, ISC2, ISACA, and others?

_____ 7. Have they written or contributed to security-related books and articles?

_____ 8. How about some simple questions to ask of the company that will perform your test?

---

certified to a basic standard of knowledge by a reputable certification body. We pretty much have to rely on the skill set of the individual penetration tester and that "the whole is more than the sum of its parts" thing called synergy, which is created when a group of penetration testers works together as a team.

I'm not going to insult you by telling you how to go ask for recommendations. I will tell you that there are security certification providers who are better than others and who hold their candidates to a higher standard of knowledge and professionalism than others. Since it's hard to measure the "synergy" angle, let's take a closer look at what skill sets should be present on the penetration team that you hire.

15. REQUIRED SKILL SETS

Your penetration test "dream team" should be well versed in areas such as these:

- Networking concepts
- Hardware devices such as routers, firewalls, and IDS/IPS
- Hacking techniques (ethical hacking, of course!)
- Databases
- Open-source technologies
- Operating systems
- Wireless protocols
- Applications
- Protocols
- Many others

That's a rather long list to demonstrate a simple concept: Your penetration team should be able to show proof that they have knowledge about all the hardware, software, services, and protocols in use within your network.

Okay. They have technical skills. Is that enough?

16. ACCOMPLISHMENTS

Are the members of the test team "bookworms" or have they had practical experience in their areas of expertise?

Have they contributed to the security community (see checklist: "An Agenda For Action For The Experiences Of The Test Team")?

17. HIRING A PENETRATION TESTER

Here are some of the questions you might consider asking prospective security service providers or things to think about when hiring a test team:

- Is providing security services the primary mission of the security service provider, or is this just an "additional revenue source" for another company?
- Does the company offer a comprehensive suite of services tailored to your specific requirements, or do they just offer service packages?
- Does the supplier have a methodology? Does their methodology follow a recognized authority in security such as OSSTMM, OWASP, or LPT?
- Does the supplier hire former hackers? Do they perform background checks on their employees?
- Can they distinguish (and articulate) between infrastructure and application testing?
- How many consultants does the supplier have who perform penetration testing? How long have those consultants been practicing?
- What will the final report look like? Does it meet your needs? Is the supplier willing to modify the format to suit your needs (within reason)?
- Is the report just a list of what's wrong, or does it contain mitigation strategies that will be tailored to your particular situation?
- Is the supplier a recognized contributor to the security community?
- Do they have references available to attest to the quality of work already performed?
- That ought to get a company started down the road to hiring a good penetration test team. Now let's talk about why a company should hire you, either as an individual or as a member of a penetration testing team.

18. WHY SHOULD A COMPANY HIRE YOU?

When a prospective client needs a penetration test, they may publish a request for proposal (RFP) or just make an announcement that they are accepting solicitations for security services. When all the bids come in, they will only consider the most qualified candidates. How to you make sure that your or your company's bid doesn't end up in the "circular file?"

Qualifications

Highlight your or your company's qualifications to perform the desired services. Don't rely on "alphabet soup" after your name or your team's names to highlight qualifications. Take the time to explain the meaning of CISSP, LPT, or MCSE.

Work Experience

The company will provide some information about itself. Align your response by highlighting work (without naming specific clients!) in the same or related fields and of related size.

Cutting-Edge Technical Skills

It doesn't bode well when you list one of your primary skills as "MCSE in Windows NT 3.51 and NT 4.0 or higher." Maintain your technical proficiency and showcase your most recent and most highly regarded certification accomplishments, such as CCNA, CEH, CHFI, CCNP, MCSE, LPT, CISA, and CISM.

Communication Skills

Whether your communicate with the prospective client through written or verbal methods, made sure you are well written or well spoken. Spell-check your written documents, and then look them over again. There are some errors that spell checkers just won't find. "Dude, I'm gonna hack yer network!" isn't going to cut it in a second-round presentation.

Attitude

Let's face it: Most of us in the security arena have a bit of an ego and sometimes come off as a bit arrogant. Though that may hold some sway with your peers, it won't help your case with a prospective client. Polite and professional at all times is the rule.

Team Skills

There is no synergy if there is no team. You must be a good team player who can deal with subordinates, superiors, and clients professionally, even in the most critical moments of an engagement.

Okay. You've done all this. What else do you need to know to get hired? What about the concerns of the company that will hire you?

Company Concerns

You can have a sterling record and the best qualifications around and still not get hired. Here are some of the "influencing factors" companies may consider when looking to hire a penetration testing team:

- Companies usually want to work in collaboration with reputable and well-established firms such as Foundstone, ISS, EC-Council, and others.
- Companies may want to verify the tools that will be run during a test and the equipment on which the tools run.
- Companies will want references for the individuals on the team as well as recommendations about the company itself.
- Companies demand security-related certifications such as CISSP, CEH, and TICSA to confirm the authenticity of the testing company.
- Companies usually have an aversion to hiring those who are known or suspected hackers.
- Companies may require security clearances.
- Companies may inquire about how and where their data will be stored while in the testing company's possession.

Okay, you get the idea, right?

19. SUMMARY

Anybody got an aspirin? I'm sure you probably need one after reading all the information I've tried to throw at you in this chapter. I've only barely scratched the surface of what a penetration test is, what it's meant to accomplish, how it's done, and how you report the findings to the client, but I'm out of space to tell you more.

Let me take these last couple of inches on the page to summarize. If you've got a network, the question is not "if you'll be attacked, but "when." If you're going to make your network as safe as possible, you need to find the weaknesses and then test them to see which ones are really, truly the things that need to be fixed "yesterday." If you only conduct a penetration test once a year, a real hacker has 364 "unbirthdays" in which to attack and compromise your network. Don't give them the opportunity.

Get someone on your staff certified as an ethical hacker and a Licensed Penetration Tester so that they can perform ethical hacks and penetrations on a regular basis to help protect your network.

Finally, let's move on to the real interactive part of this Chapter: review questions/exercises, hands-on projects, case projects and optional team case project. The answers and/or solutions by chapter can be found in the Online Instructor's Solutions Manual.

CHAPTER REVIEW QUESTIONS/EXERCISES

True/False

1. True or False? Penetration testing is the exploitation of vulnerabilities absent in an organization's network.
2. True or False? Some sources classify penetration testing into two types—internal and external—and then talk about the "variations" of these types of tests based on the amount of information the test team has been given about the organization prior to starting the test.
3. True or False? When a penetration test is conducted against Internet-facing hosts, it is known as *external testing*.
4. True or False? There are three phases in a penetration test, and they mimic the phases that an attacker would use to conduct a real attack.
5. True or False? The pre-attack phase consists of the penetration team's or hacker's attempts to investigate or explore the potential target.

Multiple Choice

1. What stage involves the actual compromise of the target?
   A. Worm Phase
   B. Virus Phase
   C. Backdoor Phase
   D. More popular Phase
   E. Attack Phase
2. What is unique to the penetration test team?
   A. Backdoor Phase
   B. Virus Phase
   C. Post-Attack Phase
   D. Packet filter Phase
   E. User-level Rootkit Phase
3. What is simply a way to ensure that a particular activity is conducted in a standard manner, with documented and repeatable results?
   A. Stateful firewalls
   B. Virus
   C. Methodology
   D. Backdoor
   E. User-level Rootkit
4. What have been developed by particular entities offering network security services or certifications?
   A. Application layer firewalls
   B. Proprietary methodologies
   C. Worms
   D. Backdoors
   E. User-level Rootkit
5. What test is a systematic analysis of all security controls in place at the tested organization?
   A. Trojan Horse
   B. Firewalls
   C. Worm
   D. Comprehensive penetration
   E. User-level Rootkit

EXERCISE

Problem

Penetration testing can also be useful for determining?

Hands-On Projects

Project

The discovery phase of penetration testing includes two parts. The first part is the start of actual testing, and covers information gathering and scanning. Network port and service identification is conducted to identify potential targets. In addition to port and service identification, what other techniques are used to gather information on the targeted network?

Case Projects

Problem

While vulnerability scanners check only for the possible existence of a vulnerability, the attack phase of a penetration test exploits the vulnerability to confirm its existence. Most vulnerabilities exploited by penetration testing fall into which of the following categories?

Optional Team Case Project

Problem

Identify some penetration testing logistics.

## Chapter 31

What is Vulnerability Assessment?

Almantas Kakareka
Demyo, Inc.

1. INTRODUCTION

In computer security, the term *vulnerability* is applied to a weakness in a system that allows an attacker to violate the integrity of that system. Vulnerabilities may result from weak passwords, software bugs, a computer virus or other malware (malicious software), a script code injection, or from unchecked user input, just to name a few.

A security risk is classified as vulnerability if it is recognized as a possible means of attack. A security risk with one or more known instances of a working or fully implemented attack is classified as an *exploit*. Constructs in programming languages that are difficult to use properly can be large sources of vulnerabilities.

Vulnerabilities always existed, but when the Internet was in its early stage they were not as often used and exploited. The media did not report news of hackers who were getting put in jail for hacking into servers and stealing vital information.

Vulnerability assessment may be performed on many objects, not only computer systems/networks. For example, a physical building can be assessed so it will be clear what parts of the building have what kind of flaw. If the attacker can bypass the security guard at the front door and get into the building via a back door, it is definitely vulnerability. Actually, going through the back door and using that vulnerability is called an *exploit*. The physical security is one of the most important aspects to be taken into account. If the attackers have physical access to the server, the server is not yours anymore! Just stating, "Your system or network is vulnerable" doesn't provide any useful information. Vulnerability assessment without a comprehensive report is pretty much useless. A vulnerability assessment report should include:

- Identification of vulnerabilities
- Risk rating of each vulnerability (Critical, High, Medium, Low)
- Quantity of vulnerabilities

It is enough to find one critical vulnerability, which means the whole network is at risk, as shown in Figure 31.1.

FIGURE 31.1 One critical vulnerability affects the entire network.

Vulnerabilities should be sorted by severity and then by servers/services. Critical vulnerabilities should be at the top of the report and should be listed in descending order, that is, critical, then high, medium, and low.

2. REPORTING

Reporting capability is of growing importance to administrators in a documentation-oriented business climate where you must not only be able to do your job, you must also provide written proof of how you've done it. In fact, respondents to Sunbelt's survey[1] indicate that flexible and prioritizing reporting is their number-one favorite feature.

A scan might return hundreds or thousands of results, but the data is useless unless it is organized in a way that can be understood. That means that ideally you will be able to sort and cross-reference the data, export it to other programs and formats (such as CSV, HTML, XML, MHT, MDB, Excel, Word, and/or various databases), view it in different ways, and easily compare it to the results of earlier scans.

Comprehensive, flexible, and customizable reporting is used within your department to provide a guideline of technical steps you need to take, but that's not all. Good reports also give you the ammunition you need to justify to management the costs of implementing security measures.

1. "Vulnerability Assessment Scanning:Why Sunbelt Network Security Inspector (SNSI)?" Sunbelt Software, [http://img2.insight.com/graphics/uk/content/microsite/sunbelt/sunbelt_network_security_inspector_white-paper.pdf], February 2004.

3. THE "IT WON'T HAPPEN TO US" FACTOR

Practical matters aside, CEOs, CIOs, and administrators are all human beings and thus subject to normal human tendencies—including the tendency to assume that bad things happen to "other people," not to us. Organizational decision makers assume that their companies aren't likely targets for hackers ("Why would an attacker want to break into the network of Widgets, Inc., when they could go after the Department of Defense or Microsoft or someone else who's much more interesting?").[1]

4. WHY VULNERABILITY ASSESSMENT?

Organizations have a tremendous opportunity to use information technologies to increase their productivity. Securing information and communications systems will be a necessary factor in taking advantage of all this increased connectivity, speed, and information. However, no security measure will guarantee a risk-free environment in which to operate. In fact, many organizations need to provide easier user access to portions of their information systems, thereby increasing potential exposure. Administrative error, for example, is a primary cause of vulnerabilities that can be exploited by a novice hacker, whether an outsider or insider in the organization. Routine use of vulnerability assessment tools along with immediate response to identified problems will alleviate this risk. It follows, therefore, that routine vulnerability assessment should be a standard element of every organization's security policy. Vulnerability assessment is used to find unknown problems in the systems. The main purpose of vulnerability assessment is to find out what systems have flaws and take action to mitigate the risk. Some industry standards such as DSS PCI require organizations to perform vulnerability assessments on their networks. The sidebar "DSS PCI Compliance" gives a brief look.

DSS PCI Compliance

PCI DSS stands for Payment Card Industry Data Security Standard. This standard was developed by leading credit-card companies to help merchants be secure and follow common security criteria to protect sensitive customers' credit-card data. Before that every credit card company had a similar standard to protect customer data on the merchant side. Any company that does transactions via credit cards needs to be PCI compliant. One of the requirements to be PCI compliant is to regularly test security systems and processes. This can be achieved via vulnerability assessment. Small companies that don't process a lot of transactions are allowed to do self-assessment via

questionnaire. Big companies that process a lot of transactions are required to be audited by third parties.[2]

5. PENETRATION TESTING VERSUS VULNERABILITY ASSESSMENT

There seems to be a certain amount of confusion within the security industry about the difference between penetration testing and vulnerability assessment. They are often classified as the same thing but in fact they are not. Penetration testing sounds a lot more exciting, but most people actually want a vulnerability assessment and not a penetration test, so many projects are labeled as penetration tests when in fact they are 100% vulnerability assessments.

A penetration test mainly consists of a vulnerability assessment, but it goes one step further. A penetration test is a method for evaluating the security of a computer system or network by simulating an attack by a malicious hacker. The process involves an active analysis of the system for any weaknesses, technical flaws, or vulnerabilities. This analysis is carried out from the position of a potential attacker and will involve active exploitation of security vulnerabilities. Any security issues that are found will be presented to the system owner, together with an assessment of their impact and often with a proposal for mitigation or a technical solution.

A vulnerability assessment is what most companies generally do, since the systems they are testing are live production systems and can't afford to be disrupted by active exploits that might crash the system. Vulnerability assessment is the process of identifying and quantifying vulnerabilities in a system. The system being studied could be a physical facility such as a nuclear power plant, a computer system, or a larger system (for example, the communications infrastructure or water infrastructure of a region). Vulnerability assessment has many things in common with risk assessment. Assessments are typically performed according to the following steps:

1. Cataloging assets and capabilities (resources) in a system
2. Assigning quantifiable value and importance to the resources
3. Identifying the vulnerabilities or potential threats to each resource
4. Mitigating or eliminating the most serious vulnerabilities for the most valuable resources

This is generally what a security company is contracted to do, from a technical perspective—not to actually penetrate the systems but to assess and document the

2. PCI Security Standards Council, Copyright© 2006–2013 PCI Security Standards Council, LLC. All rights reserved. [www.pcisecurity standards.org], 2013.

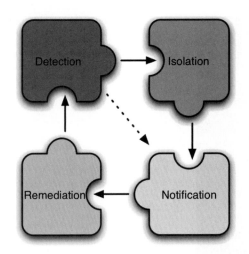

FIGURE 31.2 Vulnerability mitigation cycle.

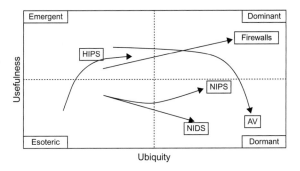

FIGURE 31.3 Usefulness/ubiquity relationship.

possible vulnerabilities and to recommend mitigation measures and improvements. Vulnerability detection, mitigation, notification, and remediation are linked, as shown in Figure 31.2.[3]

6. VULNERABILITY ASSESSMENT GOAL

The theoretical goal of network scanning is elevated security on all systems or establishing a network-wide minimal operation standard. Figure 31.3 shows how usefulness is related to ubiquity:

- HIPS: Host-Based Intrusion Prevention System
- NIDS: Network-Based Intrusion Detection System
- AV: Antivirus
- NIPS: Network-Based Intrusion Prevention System

7. MAPPING THE NETWORK

Before we start scanning the network we have to find out what machines are alive on it. Most of the scanners

have a built-in network mapping tool, usually the Nmap network mapping tool running behind the scenes. The Nmap Security Scanner is a free and open-source utility used by millions of people for network discovery, administration, inventory, and security auditing. Nmap uses raw IP packets in novel ways to determine what hosts are available on a network, what services (application name and version) those hosts are offering, what operating systems they are running, what type of packet filters or firewalls are in use, and more. Nmap was named "Information Security Product of the Year" by *Linux Journal* and *Info World*. It was also used by hackers in the movies *Matrix Reloaded, Die Hard* 4, and *Bourne Ultimatum*. Nmap runs on all major computer operating systems, plus the Amiga. Nmap has a traditional command-line interface, as shown in Figure 31.4; and, zenmap is the official nmap security scanner GUI (see Figure 31.5).

It is a multiplatform (Linux, Windows, Mac OS X, BSD, etc.), free and open-source application that aims to make Nmap easy for beginners to use while providing advanced features for experienced Nmap users. Frequently used scans can be saved as profiles to make them easy to run repeatedly. A command creator allows interactive creation of Nmap command lines. Scan results can be saved and viewed later. Saved scan results can be compared with one another to see how they differ. The results of recent scans are stored in a searchable database.

Gordon Lyon (better known by his nickname, Fyodor) released Nmap in 1997 and continues to coordinate its development. He also maintains the Insecure.Org, Nmap.Org, SecLists.Org, and SecTools.Org security resource sites and has written seminal papers on OS detection and stealth port scanning. He is a founding member of the Honeynet project and coauthored the books *Know Your Enemy: Honeynets* and *Stealing the Network: How to Own a Continent*. Gordon is President of Computer Professionals for Social Responsibility (CPSR), which has promoted free speech, security, and privacy since 1981.[4]

Some systems might be disconnected from the network. Obviously, if the system is not connected to any network at all it will have a lower priority for scanning. However, it shouldn't be left in the dark and not be scanned at all, because there might be other nonnetwork related flaws, for example, a Firewire exploit that can be used to unlock the Windows XP SP2 system. Exploits work like this: An attacker approaches a locked Windows XP SP2 station, plugs a Firewire cable into it, and uses special commands to unlock the locked machine. This technique is possible because Firewire has direct access

---

3. Darknet, © Darknet—The Darkside 2000—2013. [www.darknet.org.uk/2006/04/penetration-testing-vs-vulnerability-assessment/], 2013.

4. insecure.org, http://insecure.org/fyodor/

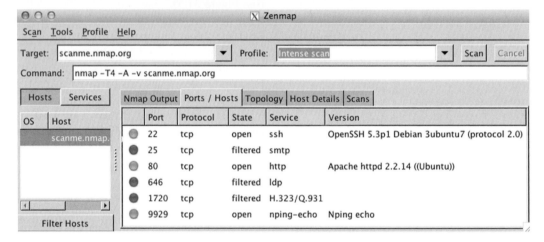

```
sh-3.2# nmap -sV scanme.nmap.org

Starting Nmap 5.61TEST4 ( http://nmap.org ) at 2012-02-25 15:08 EST
Nmap scan report for scanme.nmap.org (74.207.244.221)
Host is up (0.17s latency).
Not shown: 994 closed ports
PORT       STATE     SERVICE     VERSION
22/tcp     open      ssh         OpenSSH 5.3p1 Debian 3ubuntu7 (protocol 2.0)
25/tcp     filtered  smtp
80/tcp     open      http        Apache httpd 2.2.14 ((Ubuntu))
646/tcp    filtered  ldp
1720/tcp   filtered  H.323/Q.931
9929/tcp   open      nping-echo  Nping echo
Service Info: OS: Linux; CPE: cpe:/o:linux:kernel

Service detection performed. Please report any incorrect results at http://(
Nmap done: 1 IP address (1 host up) scanned in 11.31 seconds
sh-3.2#
```

FIGURE 31.4   Nmap command-line interface.

FIGURE 31.5   Zenmap graphical user interface.

to RAM. The system will accept any password and unlock the computer.[5]

8. SELECTING THE RIGHT SCANNERS

Scanners alone don't solve the problem; using scanners well helps solve *part* of the problem. Start with one scanner but consider more than one. It is a good practice to use more than one scanner. This way you can compare results from a couple of them. Some scanners are more focused on particular services. Typical scanner architecture is shown in Figure 31.6.

For example, Nessus is an outstanding general-purpose scanner, but Web application-oriented scanners such as HP Web Inspect or Hailstorm will do a much

better job of scanning a web application. In an ideal situation, scanners would not be needed because everyone would maintain patches and tested hosts, routers, gateways, workstations, and servers. However, the real world is different; we are humans and we tend to forget to install updates, patch systems, and/or configure systems properly. Malicious code will always find a way into your network! If a system is connected to the network, that means there is a possibility that this system will be infected at some time in the future. The chances might be higher or lower depending on the system's maintenance level. The system will never be secure 100%. There is no such thing as 100% security; if well maintained, it might be 99.9999999999% secure, but never 100%. There is a joke that says, if you want to make a computer secure, you have to disconnect it from the network and power outlet and then put it into a safe and lock it. This system will be *almost* 100% secure (although not useful), because social engineering cons may call your employees and ask

5. Nilay Patel, "Windows passwords easily bypassed over Firewire," © 2013 AOL Inc. All rights reserved. [http://www.engadget.com/2008/03/04/windows-passwords-easily-bypassed-over-firewire/], Mar 4th, 2008.

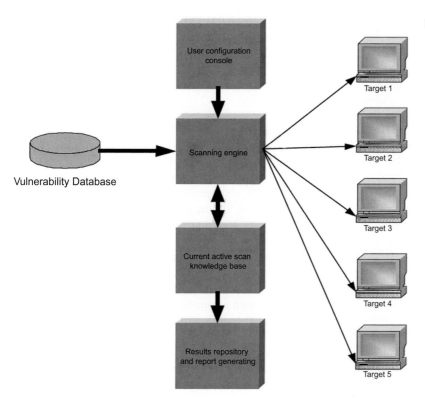

FIGURE 31.6   Typical scanner architecture.

them to remove that system from the safe and plug it back into the network.[6,7]

9. CENTRAL SCANS VERSUS LOCAL SCANS

The question arises: Should we scan locally or centrally? Should we scan the whole network at once, or should we scan the network based on subdomains and virtual LANs? Table 31.1 shows pros and cons of each method.

With localized scanning and central scanning verification, central scanning becomes a verification audit. The question again arises, should we scan locally or centrally? The answer is both. Central scans give overall visibility into the network. Local scans may have higher visibility into the local network. Centrally driven scans serve as the baseline. Locally driven scans are key to vulnerability reduction. Scanning tools should support both methodologies. Scan managers should be empowered to police their own area and enforce policy. So what will hackers target? Script kiddies will target any easily exploitable system; dedicated hackers will target some particular network/organization (see sidebar, "Who Is the Target?").

6. Hewlett-Packard Development Company, L.P. © 2013 Hewlett-Packard Development Company, L.P. [http://www.hpenterprisesecurity.com/], 2013.
7. "Cenzic Desktop: Application Security for Cloud and Web," © 2012 Cenzic, Inc. All rights reserved. Cenzic, Inc., 655 Campbell Technology Parkway, Suite #100Campbell, CA 95008 [http://www.cenzic.com/products/desktop/index.html], 2013.

TABLE 31.1 Pros and Cons of Central Scans and Local Scans.

	Centrally Controlled and Accessed Scanning	Decentralized Scanning
Pros	Easy to maintain	Scan managers can scan at will
Cons	Slow; most scans must be queued	Patching of the scanner is often overlooked

Who is the Target?

"We are not a target." How many times have you heard this statement? Many people think that they don't have anything to hide, they don't have secrets, and thus nobody will hack them. Hackers are not only after secrets but after resources as well. They may want to use your machine for hosting files, use it as a source to attack other systems, or just try some new exploits against it.

If you don't have any juicy information, you might not be a target for a skilled hacker, but you will always be a target for script kiddies. In hacker culture terms, *script kiddie* describes an inexperienced hacker who is using available tools, usually with a GUI, to do any malicious activity. Script kiddies lack technical expertise to write or create any tools by themselves. They try to infect or deface as many systems as they can with the least possible effort. If they can't hack your system/site in a couple of minutes, usually they move to an easier target. It's rather different with skilled hackers, who seek financial or other benefits from hacking the system. They spend a lot of time just exploring the system and collecting as much information as possible before trying to hack it. The proper way of hacking is data mining and writing scripts that will automate the whole process, thus making it fast and hard to respond to.

10. DEFENSE IN DEPTH STRATEGY

Defense in depth is an information assurance (IA) strategy in which multiple layers of defense are placed throughout an IT system. Defense in depth addresses security vulnerabilities in personnel, technology, and operations for the duration of the system's life cycle. The idea behind this approach is to defend a system against any particular attack using several varying methods. It is a layering tactic, conceived by the National Security Agency (NSA) as a comprehensive approach to information and electronic security. Defense in depth was originally a military strategy that seeks to delay, rather than prevent, the advance of an attacker by yielding space in order to buy time. The placement of protection mechanisms, procedures, and policies is intended to increase the dependability of an IT system where multiple layers of defense prevent espionage and direct attacks against critical systems. In terms of computer network defense, defense-in-depth measures should not only prevent security breaches, they should give an organization time to detect and respond to an attack, thereby reducing and mitigating the impact of a breach. Using more than one of the following layers constitutes defense in depth:

- Physical security (deadbolt locks)
- Authentication and password security
- Antivirus software (host based and network based)
- Firewalls (hardware or software)
- Demilitarized zones (DMZs)
- Intrusion detection systems (IDSs)
- Intrusion prevention systems (IPSs)
- Packet filters (deep packet inspection appliances and stateful firewalls)
- Routers and switches
- Proxy servers
- Virtual private networks (VPNs)
- Logging and auditing
- Biometrics
- Timed access control
- Proprietary software/hardware not available to the public

11. VULNERABILITY ASSESSMENT TOOLS

There are many vulnerability assessment tools. Popular scanning tools according to www.sectools.org are listed here.

Nessus

Nessus is one of the most popular and capable vulnerability scanners, particularly for UNIX systems. It was initially free and open source, but they closed the source code in 2005 and removed the free "Registered Feed" version in 2008. It now costs $1,200 per year, which still beats many of its competitors. A free "Home Feed" is also available, though it is limited and only licensed for home network use. Nessus is constantly updated, with more than 46,000 plugins. Key features include remote and local (authenticated) security checks, a client/server architecture with a web-based interface, and an embedded scripting language for writing your own plugins or understanding the existing ones. The open-source version of Nessus was forked by a group of users who still develop it under the OpenVAS name.

GFI LANguard

This is a network security and vulnerability scanner designed to help with patch management, network and software audits, and vulnerability assessments. The price is based on the number of IP addresses you wish to scan. A free trial version of up to 5 IP addresses is available.

Retina

Commercial vulnerability assessment scanner by eEye. Like Nessus, Retina's function is to scan all the hosts on a network and report on any vulnerabilities found. It was written by eEye, well known for security research.

Core Impact

Core Impact isn't cheap (be prepared to spend at least $30,000), but it is widely considered to be the most powerful exploitation tool available. It sports a large, regularly updated database of professional exploits, and can do neat tricks like exploiting one machine and then establishing an encrypted tunnel through that machine to reach and exploit other boxes. Other good options include Metasploit and Canvas.

ISS Internet Scanner

Application-level vulnerability assessment Internet Scanner started off in 1992 as a tiny open-source scanner by Christopher Klaus. Now he has grown ISS into a billion-dollar company with myriad security products.

X-Scan

A general scanner for scanning network vulnerabilities, X-Scan is a multithreaded, plug-in-supported vulnerability scanner. X-Scan includes many features, including full NASL support, detecting service types, remote OS type/version detection, weak user/password pairs, and more. You may be able to find newer versions available at the X-Scan site if you can deal with most of the page being written in Chinese.

12. SARA

Security Auditor's Research Assistant SARA is a vulnerability assessment tool that was derived from the infamous SATAN scanner. Updates are released twice a month and the company tries to leverage other software created by the open-source community (such as Nmap and Samba).

QualysGuard

A Web-based vulnerability scanner delivered as a service over the Web, QualysGuard eliminates the burden of deploying, maintaining, and updating vulnerability management software or implementing ad hoc security applications. Clients securely access QualysGuard through an easy-to-use Web interface. QualysGuard features 5000+ unique vulnerability checks, an inference-based scanning engine, and automated daily updates to the QualysGuard vulnerability knowledge base.

13. SAINT

Security Administrator's Integrated Network Tool (SAINT) is another commercial vulnerability assessment tool (like Nessus, ISS Internet Scanner, or Retina). It runs on Unix and used to be free and open source but is now a commercial product.

14. MBSA

Microsoft Baseline Security Analyzer (MBSA) is an easy-to-use tool designed for the IT professional that helps small and medium-sized businesses determine their security state in accordance with Microsoft security recommendations, and offers specific remediation guidance. Built on the Windows Update Agent and Microsoft Update infrastructure, MBSA ensures consistency with other Microsoft management products, including Microsoft Update (MU), Windows Server Update Services (WSUS), Systems Management Server (SMS),

and Microsoft Operations Manager (MOM). Apparently MBSA, on average, scans over three million computers each week.[8]

15. SCANNER PERFORMANCE

A vulnerability scanner can use a lot of network bandwidth, so you want the scanning process to complete as quickly as possible. Of course, the more vulnerabilities in the database and the more comprehensive the scan, the longer it will take, so this can be a tradeoff. One way to increase performance is through the use of multiple scanners on the enterprise network, which can report back to one system that aggregates the results.

16. SCAN VERIFICATION

The best practice is to use few scanners during your vulnerability assessment, then use more than one scanning tool to find more vulnerabilities. Scan your networks with different scanners from different vendors and compare the results. Also consider penetration testing, that is, hire white/gray-hat hackers to hack your own systems.

17. SCANNING CORNERSTONES

All orphaned systems should be treated as hostile. Something in your organization that is not maintained or touched poses the largest threat. For example, say that you have a Web server and you inspect every byte of DHTML and make sure it has no flaws, but you totally forget to maintain the SMTP service with open relay that it is also running. Attackers might not be able to deface or harm your Web page, but they will be using the SMTP server to send out spam emails via your server. As a result, your company's IP ranges will be put into spammer lists such as spamhaus and spamcop.[9,10]

18. NETWORK SCANNING COUNTERMEASURES

A company wants to scan its own networks, but at the same time the company should take countermeasures to protect itself from being scanned by hackers. Here is a checklist of countermeasures (see checklist: "An Agenda For Action For The Use Of Network Scanning Countermeasures") to use when you're considering technical modifications to networks and filtering devices to

8. "SecTools.Org: Top 125 Network Security Tools," SecTools.Org [www.sectools.org], 2013.
9. The Spamhaus Project Ltd., © 1998–2013 The Spamhaus Project Ltd. All rights reserved. [www.spamhaus.org], 2013.
10. Cisco Systems, Inc., ©1992–2010 Cisco Systems, Inc. All rights reserved. [www.spamcop.net], 2010.

An Agenda for Action for the Use of Network Scanning Countermeasures

Here is a checklist of network scanning countermeasures; and, if a commercial firewall is in use (check all tasks completed):

_____**1.** Filter inbound Internet Control Message Protocol (ICMP) message types at border routers and firewalls. This forces attackers to use full-blown TCP port scans against all your IP addresses to map your network correctly.

_____**2.** Filter all outbound ICMP type 3 unreachable messages at border routers and firewalls to prevent UDP port scanning and firewalking from being effective.

_____**3.** Consider configuring Internet firewalls so that they can identify port scans and throttle the connections accordingly. You can configure commercial firewall appliances (such as those from Check Point, NetScreen, and WatchGuard) to prevent fast port scans and SYN floods being launched against your networks. On the open-source side, many tools such as port sentry can identify port scans and drop all packets from the source IP address for a given period of time.

_____**4.** Assess the way that your network firewall and IDS devices handle fragmented IP packets by using fragtest and fragroute when performing scanning and probing exercises. Some devices crash or fail under conditions in which high volumes of fragmented packets are being processed.

_____**5.** Ensure that your routing and filtering mechanisms (both firewalls and routers) can't be bypassed using specific source ports or source-routing techniques.

_____**6.** If you house publicly accessible FTP services, ensure that your firewalls aren't vulnerable to stateful circumvention attacks relating to malformed PORT and PASV commands.

If a commercial firewall is in use, ensure the following:

_____**7.** The latest firmware and latest service pack is installed.

_____**8.** Antispoofing rules have been correctly defined so that the device doesn't accept packets with private spoofed source addresses on its external interfaces.

_____**9.** Investigate using inbound proxy servers in your environment if you require a high level of security. A proxy server will not forward fragmented or malformed packets, so it isn't possible to launch FIN scanning or other stealth methods.

_____**10.** Be aware of your own network configuration and its publicly accessible ports by launching TCP and UDP port scans along with ICMP probes against your own IP address space. It is surprising how many large companies still don't properly undertake even simple port-scanning exercises.[11]

---

reduce the effectiveness of network scanning and probing undertaken by attackers.

19. VULNERABILITY DISCLOSURE DATE

The time of disclosure of vulnerability is defined differently in the security community and industry. It is most commonly referred to as "a kind of public disclosure of security information by a certain party." Usually vulnerability information is discussed on a mailing list or published on a security Web site and results in a security advisory afterward. Mailing list named "Full Disclosure Mailing List" is a perfect example how vulnerabilities are disclosed to public. It is a must read for any person interested in IT security. This mailing list is free of charge and is available at http://seclists.org/fulldisclosure/.

The *time of disclosure* is the first date that security vulnerability is described on a channel where the disclosed information on the vulnerability has to fulfill the following requirements:

• The information is freely available to the public.
• The vulnerability information is published by a trusted and independent channel/source.

• The vulnerability has undergone analysis by experts such that risk rating information is included upon disclosure.

The method of disclosing vulnerabilities is a topic of debate in the computer security community. Some advocate immediate full disclosure of information about vulnerabilities once they are discovered. Others argue for limiting disclosure to the users placed at greatest risk and only releasing full details after a delay, if ever. Such delays may allow those notified to fix the problem by developing and applying patches, but they can also increase the risk to those not privy to full details. This debate has a long history in security; see full disclosure and security through obscurity. More recently a new form of commercial vulnerability disclosure has taken shape, as some commercial security companies offer money for exclusive disclosures of zero-day vulnerabilities. Those offers provide a legitimate market for the purchase and sale of vulnerability information from the security community.

---

11. Chris McNab, Network Security Assessment, O'Rielly, Chapter 4: IP Network Scanning [www.trustmatta.com/downloads/pdf/Matta_IP_Network_Scanning.pdf], pp. 36–72, 2013.

From the security perspective, a free and public disclosure is successful only if the affected parties get the relevant information prior to potential hackers; if they did not, the hackers could take immediate advantage of the revealed exploit. With security through obscurity, the same rule applies but this time rests on the hackers finding the vulnerability themselves, as opposed to being given the information from another source. The disadvantage here is that fewer people have full knowledge of the vulnerability and can aid in finding similar or related scenarios.

It should be unbiased to enable a fair dissemination of security-critical information. Most often a channel is considered trusted when it is a widely accepted source of security information in the industry (such as CERT, SecurityFocus, Secunia, www.exploit-db.com). Analysis and risk rating ensure the quality of the disclosed information. The analysis must include enough details to allow a concerned user of the software to assess his individual risk or take immediate action to protect his assets.

Find Security Holes before they Become Problems

Vulnerabilities can be classified into two major categories:

- Those related to errors made by programmers in writing the code for the software
- Those related to misconfigurations of the software's settings that leave systems less secure than they could be (improperly secured accounts, running of unneeded services, etc.)

Vulnerability scanners can identify both types. Vulnerability assessment tools have been around for many years. They've been used by network administrators and misused by hackers to discover exploitable vulnerabilities in systems and networks of all kinds. One of the early well-known Unix scanners, System Administrator Tool for Analyzing Networks (SATAN), later morphed into SAINT (Security Administrator's Integrated Network Tool). These names illustrate the disparate dual nature of the purposes to which such tools can be put.

In the hands of a would-be intruder, vulnerability scanners become a means of finding victims and determining those victims' weak points, like an undercover intelligence operative who infiltrates the opposition's supposedly secure location and gathers information that can be used to launch a full-scale attack. However, in the hands of those who are charged with protecting their networks, these scanners are a vital proactive defense mechanism that allows you to see your systems through the eyes of the enemy and take steps to lock the doors, board up the windows, and plug up seldom used passageways through which the "bad guys" could enter, before they get a chance.

In fact, the first scanners were designed as hacking tools, but this is a case in which the bad guys' weapons have been appropriated and used to defend against them. By "fighting fire with fire," administrators gain a much-needed advantage. For the first time, they are able to battle intruders proactively.[8] Once the vulnerabilities are found, we have to remove them (see sidebar, "Identifying and Removing Vulnerabilities").

Identifying and Removing Vulnerabilities

Many software tools can aid in the discovery (and sometimes removal) of vulnerabilities in a computer system. Though these tools can provide an auditor with a good overview of possible vulnerabilities present, they cannot replace human judgment. Relying solely on scanners will yield false positives and a limited-scope view of the problems present in the system.

Vulnerabilities have been found in every major operating system including Windows, Mac OS, various forms of Unix and Linux, OpenVMS, and others. The only way to reduce the chance of a vulnerability being used against a system is through constant vigilance, including careful system maintenance (e.g., applying software patches), best practices in deployment (e.g., the use of firewalls and access controls), and auditing during development and throughout the deployment life cycle.

20. PROACTIVE SECURITY VERSUS REACTIVE SECURITY

There are two basic methods of dealing with security breaches:

- The *reactive method* is passive; when a breach occurs, you respond to it, doing damage control at the same time you track down how the intruder or attacker got in and cut off that means of access so it won't happen again.
- The *proactive method* is active; instead of waiting for the hackers to show you where you're vulnerable, you put on your own hacker hat in relation to your own network and set out to find the vulnerabilities yourself, before anyone else discovers and exploits them.

The best security strategy employs both reactive and proactive mechanisms. Intrusion detection systems (IDS), for example, are reactive in that they detect suspicious network activity so that you can respond to it appropriately.

Vulnerability assessment scanning is a proactive tool that gives you the power to anticipate vulnerabilities and keep out attackers instead of spending much more time and money responding to attack after attack. The goal of proactive security is to prevent attacks before they happen, thus decreasing the load on reactive mechanisms. Being proactive is more cost effective and usually easier; the difference can be illustrated by contrasting the time and cost required to clean up after vandals break into your home or office with the effort and money required to simply install better locks that will keep them out.

Despite the initial outlay for vulnerability assessment scanners and the time spent administering them, potential return on investment is very high in the form of time and money saved when attacks are prevented. *Threat Intelligence* is another example of proactive security methods. The goal of threat intelligence is to monitor dark corners of Internet for hacks, exploits, malicious code being sent to your networks. For example company XYZ, Inc. receives threat intelligence information that one of their web servers administrator level access is for sale in Russian underground forums. For this company it will be so much cheaper to shut down the server as soon as possible, so there will be the least amount of damage done.[12]

21. VULNERABILITY CAUSES

The following are examples of vulnerability causes:

- Password management flaws
- Fundamental operating system design flaws
- Software bugs
- Unchecked user input

Password Management Flaws

The computer user uses weak passwords that could be discovered by brute force. The computer user stores the password on the computer where a program can access it. User has so many accounts on different web sites, that it is impossible to have a different password and still remember it. The result: user uses the same password on many web sites (déjà vu anyone?).

Fundamental Operating System Design Flaws

The operating system designer chooses to enforce suboptimal policies on user/program management. For example, operating systems with policies such as *default permit* grant every program and every user full access to the

entire computer. This operating system flaw allows viruses and malware to execute commands on behalf of the administrator.

Software Bugs

The programmer leaves an exploitable bug in a software program. The software bug may allow an attacker to misuse an application through (for example) bypassing access control checks or executing commands on the system hosting the application. Also the programmer's failure to check the size of data buffers, which can then be overflowed, can cause corruption of the stack or heap areas of memory (including causing the computer to execute code provided by the attacker).

Unchecked User Input

The program assumes that all user input is safe. Programs that do not check user input can allow unintended direct execution of commands or SQL statements (known as Buffer overflows, SQL injection, or other non-validated inputs). For example a form on the web page is asking how old are you? A regular user would enter 32, a hacker would try -3.2, which is somewhat legit input. The goal for entering bogus data is to find out how application reacts and monitor for input validation flaws. The biggest impact on the organization would be if vulnerabilities were found in core devices on the network (routers, firewalls, etc.), as shown in Figure 31.7.

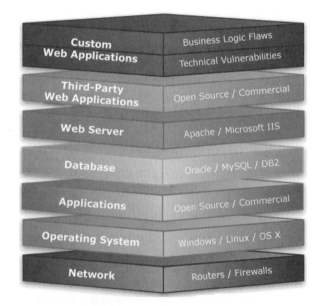

FIGURE 31.7   Vulnerabilities with the biggest impact.

12. "Threat Intelligence," © 2013 Demyo, Inc., Demyo, Inc. [http://demyo.com/services/threat-intelligence/], 2013.

22. DIY VULNERABILITY ASSESSMENT

If you perform credit-card transactions online, you're most likely PCI DSS compliant or working on getting there. In either case, it is much better to resolve compliancy issues on an ongoing basis rather than stare at a truck-load of problems as the auditor walks into your office. Though writing and reviewing policies and procedures is a big part of reaching your goal, being aware of the vulnerabilities in your environment and understanding how to remediate them are just as important. For most small businesses, vulnerability assessments sound like a lot of work and time that you just don't have. What if you could have a complete understanding of all vulnerabilities in your network and a fairly basic resolution for each, outlined in a single report within a couple of hours? Sound good? What if I also told you the tool that can make this happen is currently free and doesn't require an IT genius to run it? Sounding better?

It isn't very pretty and it's not always right, but it can give you some valuable insight into your environment. Tenable's Nessus vulnerability scanner is one of the most widely used tools in professional vulnerability assessments today. In its default configuration, all you need to do is provide the tool with a range of IP addresses and click Go. It will then compare its database of known vulnerabilities against the responses it receives from your network devices, gathering as much information as possible without killing your network or servers, usually. It does have some very dangerous plug-ins that are disabled by default, and you can throttle down the amount of bandwidth it uses to keep the network noise levels to a minimum. The best part about Nessus is that it's, very well documented, and used by over 75,000 organizations worldwide, so you know you're dealing with trustworthy product. I urge you to take a look Tenable's enterprise offerings as well. You might just be surprised at how easy it is to perform a basic do-it-yourself vulnerability assessment! Related links:

- Tenable's Nessus: www.nessus.org
- Tenable Network Security: www.tenablesecurity.com

23. SUMMARY

Network and host-based vulnerability assessment tools are extremely useful in determining what vulnerabilities might exist on a particular network. However, these tools are not useful if the vulnerability knowledge base is not kept current. Also, these tools can only take a snapshot of the systems at a particular point in time. Systems administrators will continually update code on the target systems and will continuously add/delete services and configure the system. All found vulnerabilities should be promptly patched (especially critical ones).

Finally, let's move on to the real interactive part of this Chapter: review questions/exercises, hands-on projects, case projects and optional team case project. The answers and/or solutions by chapter can be found in the Online Instructor's Solutions Manual.

CHAPTER REVIEW QUESTIONS/EXERCISES

True/False

1. True or False? Reporting capability is of growing importance to administrators in a documentation-oriented business climate where you must not only be able to do your job, you must also provide written proof of how you've done it.
2. True or False? Organizations have a tremendous opportunity to use information technologies to increase their productivity.
3. True or False? PCI DSS stands for Payment Card Information Data Security Standard.
4. True or False? There seems to be a certain amount of confusion within the security industry about the similarities between penetration testing and vulnerability assessment.
5. True or False? The theoretical goal of network scanning is elevated security on all systems or establishing a network-wide minimal operation standard.

Multiple Choice

1. What runs on all major computer operating systems, plus the Amiga.?
   A. Nmap
   B. Zenmap
   C. Security scanner GUI
   D. More popular Phase
   E. Attack Phase
2. What is an outstanding general-purpose scanner, but Web application-oriented scanners such as HP Web Inspect or Hailstorm will do a much better job of scanning a web application?
   A. Nessus
   B. SATAN
   C. Central
   D. Local
   E. User-level Rootkit scan
3. With localized scanning and central scanning verification, central scanning becomes a:
   A. Stateful firewall
   B. Virus
   C. Methodology
   D. Verification audit
   E. User-level Rootkit

4. What is an information assurance (IA) strategy in which multiple layers of defense are placed throughout an IT system?
   A. Physical security
   B. Authentication and password security
   C. Defense in depth
   D. Antivirus software
   E. Firewalls Rootkit
5. What is one of the most popular and capable vulnerability scanners, particularly for UNIX systems?
   A. Nessus
   B. GFI LANguard
   C. Retina
   D. Core Impact
   E. ISS Internet Scanner

EXERCISE

Problem

What will happen if a Vulnerability is exploited and who exploits vulnerabilities?

Hands-On Projects

Project

Will scanning interrupt or affect the servers?

Case Projects

Problem

What is Open Vulnerability and Assessment Language (OVAL®)?

Optional Team Case Project

Problem

How is OVAL different from commercial vulnerability scanners?

## Chapter 32

Security Metrics: An Introduction and Literature Review

George O.M. Yee

Department of Systems and Computer Engineering, Carleton University, Ottawa, Canada K1S 5B6, gmyee@sce.carleton.ca

1. INTRODUCTION

We live in a world where attacks against computer systems are a fact of life. Barely a day goes by without headlines appearing about the latest systems compromised, in terms of Web sites being brought down by DDoS (distributed denial of service) attacks, or the loss of privacy due to malware-infected computers. In response, systems owners have invested more and more funds into various forms of protection mechanisms (firewalls, biometrics, data encryption) as well as improved design of systems and work flows to provide more resistance against these attacks. However, the return on these investments or the subsequent increase in the level of security has been largely unknown, leading to the following dilemmas:

- How much more do I need to spend to be "safe" from attack?
- Will the changes made to my software to improve security be effective?
- Are my company's work flows or processes sufficiently secure?
- How will adding the third-party software component impact security?
- How can legislation requiring certain levels of security be enforced if the level of security is unknown?

These questions can be answered if there is some way to measure the cyber system's level of security. Properly defined, effective *security metrics* appear to be the solution. An analogy can be made with performance engineering, where there is a need to know if the performance of a computer system is sufficient to satisfy users when they are under a certain processing load. A performance analysis to obtain *performance metrics* such as throughput and service time is an effective approach to knowing if the performance is sufficient, and if not, identifying the location of performance bottlenecks. Similarly, in the security domain, it should be possible to perform a security analysis of a computer system to obtain security metrics that would indicate whether the system is secure from various forms of attack, and if not, where and what are the vulnerabilities.

Security metrics do exist and are being used. However, most of them are far from giving the results described above. They can be ineffective and not meaningful. For example, a traditional metric is the number of viruses detected and eliminated, say at a firewall. This metric is not meaningful since (a) it says nothing about the number of viruses that were not detected and that got through, and (b) it does not explain why so many viruses are trying to get through in the first place [1]. Rather, a security metric should:

- Measure quantities that are meaningful for establishing the security posture of a computer system or of an organization.
- Be reproducible.
- Be objective and unbiased.
- Be able to measure a progression toward a goal over time.

More details on what makes a good (or a bad) security metric are given in Section 3. The above qualities of a good security metric also describe certain metrics that have a basis in science, such as the throughput metric in performance engineering. Throughput measures the number of jobs completed per second by a computing system. It is a quantitative measure of a computing system based on the laws of physics. It is also meaningful, reproducible, objective, and unbiased, and it can measure the improving performance of a system over time toward a throughput goal. This leads to the question of what sort of scientific framework could give rise to such science-based metrics. This topic will be discussed further in Section 3.

An interesting practical application of security metrics is in determining the security posture of a computer system in real time. One envisages a security dashboard that displays security metrics associated with vulnerability points. The dashboard would display security alerts corresponding to strategic subsets and groupings of the metrics that exceed critical thresholds. Security officers monitoring the dashboard would then be able to take remedial action, upon which the security alerts would be replaced by "system back to normal" messages. One can further envisage the dashboard as having intelligence sufficient to recommend courses of remedial action appropriate to particular security alerts. The possibility of achieving this vision based on commercial systems now available will be assessed in Section 5. The objectives of this chapter are:

1. To introduce the reader with little or no background in security metrics to the topic
2. To discuss the nature of security metrics
3. To explain how one can get started in using security metrics
4. To show the reader where to find further information by presenting the results of a literature search (including research papers) on security metrics.

The rest of this chapter is organized as follows. Section 2 further elaborates on the need for security metrics. Section 3 discusses the nature of security metrics, including the need to put security metrics on a scientific basis and what that means; Section 4 gives an overview on how one could get started using security metrics; Section 5 provides an assessment of the feasibility of achieving a security dashboard that is driven by security metrics; Section 6 presents the results of a literature search on security metrics; and Section 7 gives conclusions.

2. WHY SECURITY METRICS?

Over 100 years ago, Lord Kelvin, the distinguished British mathematical physicist and engineer, observed that measurement is vital to knowledge and to continued progress in physical science. Lord Kelvin stated that "to measure is to know," and "if you can not measure it, you can not improve it."

These observations are evident in many activities in our modern world. One has only to recall school exams, and at the time of this writing, the 2012 London Olympics. Indeed, the Olympics is fraught with measurement, and an athlete depends on measuring his or her progress in order to improve in his or her chosen sport. Returning to the topic of computer systems performance that was mentioned in the Introduction, we note that measuring the performance of a computer system prior to its deployment in a highly demanding environment is the only way to know in advance if it will perform adequately once deployed. In addition, in order to improve the

performance, one has to know where the performance bottlenecks lie, something that can only be found by measuring it. Thus, it appears that Lord Kelvin's words are applicable to many modern activities, as they were during his own time.

These observations on measurements are also relevant to the information technology (IT) world. Organizations and consumers rely on information technology to deliver goods and services. Information technology heads are challenged to use computer systems effectively and to protect them from security threats and risks. Many efforts have been made to develop security measurements to help organizations make informed decisions about the design of systems, the selection of controls, and the efficiency of security operations. But the development of standardized metrics for computer system security has been a difficult challenge, and past efforts have only met with partial success (see Section 3). Security metrics are needed to:

- Provide a quantitative and objective basis for security operations.
- Support decision making (is investment in more security controls needed)?
- Support software quality since software security is part of software quality,
- Support the reliable maintenance of security operations (how often do users need to change their passwords)?
- Support the incremental improvement of software's resistance to attacks.

This list is by no means exhaustive, but it does serve to illustrate the usefulness of good security metrics. In addition, the following are the main uses of security metrics [2]:

- "Strategic support—Assessments of security properties can be used to aid different kinds of decision making, such as program planning, resource allocation, and product and service selection.
- Quality assurance—Security metrics can be used during the software development life cycle to eliminate vulnerabilities, particularly during code production, by performing functions such as measuring adherence to secure coding standards, identifying likely vulnerabilities that may exist, and tracking and analyzing security flaws that are eventually discovered.
- Tactical oversight—Monitoring and reporting of the security status or posture of an IT system can be carried out to determine compliance with security requirements (policy, procedures, and regulations), gauge the effectiveness of security controls and manage risk, provide a basis for trend analysis, and identify specific areas for improvement."

It should be clear from the above that security metrics play very important roles in today's computing systems.

3. THE NATURE OF SECURITY METRICS

Security metrics as quantifiers of the effectiveness of the organization's security practices over time have always been difficult to define and evaluate. How can an organization determine whether it is secure? This can only be truly determined by the organization undergoing a real crisis. Yet, such a crisis is exactly what the security controls were designed to prevent.

Traditional Security Metrics

Traditional security metrics have not been developed in a rigorous, systematic manner [1]. It may in fact, have given rise to false impressions of security, leading to unsafe or ineffective implementations of security controls.

The Organization Perspective

A security metric is therefore given the task of measuring the security of the organization, which is discernible only when the organization is in a security crisis, thereby defeating the whole point of having the metric in the first place. An important requirement of a security metric then is that it is capable of measuring the organization's security level at any time and not only when the organization is in a crisis. The bottom line is that management needs some way to measure the organization's security level. Organizations need to ask:

- How many *security controls* does it take to be "safe"?
- *When* does the organization know it is "safe"?
- How can the cost of new security controls be *justified*?
- Is the organization getting *good value* for its money?
- How can the organization *compare* its security posture with that of other similar organizations and with best practices?

Traditionally, these questions are answered using risk assessment. In particular, the answers relate to how much residual risk the organization is willing to accept, depending on business needs and budget limits. However, risk management may be a red herring and may not necessarily lead to stronger security.

Consider, for example, a risk assessment that lists a number of threats, along with the cost to mitigate each threat or risk. Some items on the list would be very low cost, while other items would be very expensive (see Figure 32.1). Often, management may choose to purchase the most security controls for the least amount of money,

FIGURE 32.1 Is buying more inexpensive security controls better than buying fewer but more expensive ones?.

possibly ignoring the most expensive controls. Management assumes that buying more inexpensive controls is better value than buying fewer expensive ones. Thus, there is a tendency to buy large numbers of less expensive security tools and avoid the more expensive, less glamorous controls. The latter tends to be organizational, requiring cultural change (disaster recovery plan) rather than specific self-contained solutions (such as firewalls and intrusion detection systems—IDSs). In carrying out such a purchase policy, management believes it is buying more security for less money.

However, how can it be said that more security is purchased? What increased security does each additional purchase achieve, and how can the organization determine this? How do we even know that the purchases have been made in the correct order? Perhaps the organization is being exposed to *more* risk because of the haphazard way in which the security controls were obtained?

Security metrics programs need to be built from the ground up to allow for new approaches to these traditional security metrics problems. A more systematic and even scientifically based approach (see below) to security metrics can:

- Come up with reproducible and justifiable measurements
- Objectively measure something of value to the organization
- Determine real progress in security posture
- Apply to a broad range of organizations while producing consistent results
- Fix the order in which security controls should be applied
- Help determine the resources needed to apply to a security program

Issues Associated with Definition and Application

To be called a metric, a measurement has to be combined with time. Furthermore, a metric by itself is not going to save an organization that is in trouble with its security posture. It is necessary to think through and analyze the true meaning of the metric. The art is to develop security metrics that are simple and that provide useful management information corresponding to security-related objectives. The metrics have to inform the organization by demonstrating progress.

Clearly, a security metric needs to count or measure *something*. But count or measure what? How can security be measured? Consider the following security metrics (in italics) [1] that are common but problematic in that they ignore the attendant core issues:

- *Number of computer viruses or malware detected.* The intended use of this metric is to measure the effectiveness of the anti-malware controls. However, it fails to consider why so much malware is getting through in the first place, and what about the malware that got through but were undetected!

- *Number of security incidents and investigations.* This metric presumably measures the effectiveness of security events monitoring. However, it does not consider the thresholds at which the incident or investigation is triggered. Nor does it consider their causes; for example, are incidents triggered due to flaws in work processes?

- *Cost of security breaches.* This metric is intended to measure the true business loss due to security failures. However, it ignores the residual risks that the organization chose to live with. Furthermore, it does not differentiate between costs incurred for normal operations, despite safeguards that were in place, or costs that result from abnormal conditions such as crises or disasters.

- *Resources assigned to security functions.* The intended use of this metric is to measure the true business cost of running a security program. However, it fails to consider the causes of high cost such as the possibility that people may be less productive due to inefficient tools or procedures.

- *Compliance with security policy.* This metric is intended to measure the level of compliance or adhesion to security goals. However, it can be misleading since it fails to consider how compliance is related to effectiveness, the order of compliance that may be relevant, and what happens once compliance is achieved—will the security program be complete then?

A security metric for an organization should measure the quality of the organization's security program and be capable of showing progress. The latter is important so that one can know if new investments in improving security are making any difference. None of the above metrics really possess these capabilities. The following illustration shows why incident totals are unreliable:

Imagine a small town with one police officer. He does no other police work other than patrolling the highway with a radar gun, pulling over hundreds of speeders. Now imagine a large town with many police officers. They do not use radar guns and have caught very few speeders but have a large defensive driving program and an active anti-drunk-driving program. Is the small town safer than the large town? The count of speeders is only as good as the sensing mechanism, but that number has no depth to it. What about the small town with nonspeeders who are drunk—are they not potentially more dangerous? [1]

Consider the anti-malware tool in light of this illustration. The fact that the tool detected a large amount of malware probably makes the security team feel good that the tool works and that so much malware has been caught. However, this says very little about the organization's security level. Why is so much malware present in the first place? How much malware remains undetected? What does it say about the quality of the security program? In fact, just the opposite may be what we want: The tool doesn't detect any malware because malware is unable to penetrate the security controls that are in place!

Time spent on a security-related task (software patching, security incident investigation) is often used as a security metric. This may be useful from a project management point of view in order to ensure that there is sufficient time to complete a project, but it is next to useless as a measure of security. This is because more time spent does not necessarily translate into better security. For example, the additional time may have been due to inefficient procedures or work processes. Moreover, such procedures may have been responsible for triggering the incidents that called for the investigation (security-related task) in the first place!

The business cost of a security incident is another unreliable security metric. This metric comes with the built-in assumption that something bad has happened, but what if that something has already been considered as acceptable to the organization in terms of the residual risk it is willing to live with? On the other hand, the security incident may in fact have been caused by poor security practices. Or perhaps one of these two possibilities happened, but the incident management was so good that the costs were kept to a minimum. How can these three possibilities be separated? This metric may measure the effectiveness of incident response in terms of minimizing the business cost, but it may not be a good rating of the quality of the organization's security practices since it cannot distinguish whether or not the costs were due to poor security practices.

Security metrics should have the following **ideal characteristics**. They should

- *Measure quantities that are meaningful for establishing the security posture of a computer system or of an organization.* As discussed above, some traditional security metrics fail to measure the security level, which should be their first objective.

- *Have results that are reproducible*. This means that the value of the security metric should be the same as the original value if reevaluated by another party, given that the factors on which the metric is evaluated remain the same. It will be seen below that this is a key requirement of being "scientifically-based."
- *Be objective and unbiased*. This requirement is self explanatory.
- *Be able to measure a progression toward a goal over time*. As already mentioned, it is important to be able to measure over time whether or not investments in improving security have in fact improved security [1].

Unfortunately, traditional security metrics found in practice lack one or more of the above characteristics. Such metrics were haphazard and opportunistic in the sense that whatever measures were readily available were taken up and reported. Moving even beyond the ideal characteristics of a security metric above, security metrics should be "scientifically based." The meaning of this will be discussed in the next section.

Scientifically Based Security Metrics

It would be very useful to have computer security based on science, similar to computer systems performance being based on the science of physics. For then security could be analyzed, just as performance is analyzed, and security metrics could be systematically derived and predicted, just as performance metrics are derived and predicted. Unfortunately, it is not known at the time of this writing that security can be based on science, due to at least two fundamental problems [3] as follows:

Problem 1: "The first is the difference between mathematical abstractions [for security metrics] and real implementations. The gap between theoretical cryptography results and practical cryptanalysis illustrates this: although no one has found a fast factoring algorithm, RSA implementations are regularly broken because of side channels (such as timing and power consumption), poor random-number generation, insecure key storage, message formats and padding, and programming bugs.[1] For system security, the gap between models simple enough to use for metrics and actual implementations is even larger. To make progress, we need metrics that work on more concrete models of actual systems, or ways to build systems that refine models without introducing security vulnerabilities." In other words, security metrics must be simple enough to understand, but by so being, they

cannot capture enough of what is going on in a computer system to accurately reflect security levels.

Problem 2: "The second problem is that it seems unlikely that we can reason well about adversary creativity. This argues for metrics that assume that adversaries can efficiently search the entire space of possible actions. Perhaps we can develop complexity metrics that analyze that space and the maximum effectiveness of different search strategies." In other words, to understand the security of a computer system, it is necessary to understand attacker creativity in creating new attacks. However, at the present time, we are not very good at capturing and predicting this behavior. This then calls for metrics that assume that the attacker is capable of launching every possible attack, which are difficult to design since we would need to know every possible attack.

However, the preceding assumes basing security on a "weak sense of science" [3] and the "strong sense of science" (explained below). It is possible to base security on the "methodological sense of science." Let us examine these senses of science more closely. Three interpretations of science can be considered for security metrics [3], as follows:

- *Weak sense*: science as the generalization and systematization of knowledge—for example, consider the body of knowledge within physics, where laws and descriptions of behavior have been systematized and interwoven into an integral whole.
- *Strong sense*: science used to develop laws with which predictions can be made—for example, in physics, laws of motion have been developed and used to predict the future position of planets.
- *Methodological sense*: science used for research by forming hypotheses and proving or disproving the hypotheses with experiments. The results of the experiments must be confirmable by independent experimenters. Hence the experiments must be repeatable and yield the same results. This is the embodiment of the scientific method, and established sciences have in fact been built up in this fashion.

Basing security metrics on the weak sense of science is currently at best unknown as there has not been sufficient research to show that it is even possible outside of perhaps a highly specialized subarea of security. Basing the metrics on the strong sense is likewise untenable since it is more likely that laws can be developed only after systematization of the knowledge (the strong sense is more likely after the weak sense has been established). This leaves the methodological sense, which appears to be a possible basis on which a framework for computer security metrics can

---

1. J.P. Degabriele, K.G. Paterson, G.J. Watson, Provable security in the real world, *IEEE Security & Privacy* 9 (3) (2011) 33–41.

be developed. Such a development, however, is currently undergoing research and is beyond the scope of this chapter. However, the reader is invited to consult this author's papers on this subject in the near future.

Assuming that scientifically based security metrics are available, the following question now arises: What type of security metrics should be used—those based on science or those having the ideal characteristics? It is recommended that both types can be used. The choice can be made based on practicality and system requirements. Scientifically based metrics would be more rigorous and therefore require more work to define and evaluate. Perhaps scientifically based metrics can be reserved for critical systems such as those involving public utilities, public safety, hospital systems, and defense applications, which have more stringent requirements for security.

4. GETTING STARTED WITH SECURITY METRICS

As a security professional in your organization, you would like to start a security metrics program and begin using security metrics. But how do you start such a program (see checklist: An Agenda for Action for Getting Started with Security Metrics")?

An Agenda for Action for Getting Started with Security Metrics

This checklist consists of some essential items that must first be in place, after which suggestions are given (in no particular order) to guide you in starting a security metrics program in your organization [4] (check all tasks completed): Essentials: The following items are essential for any successful security metrics program:

_____1. **Design your security metrics based on ideal characteristics.**

_____2. **Make sure you collect and store all the data needed for the metrics as specified in your design of the metrics.** This task may sometimes be automated by programming the system to automatically output the data needed to a repository.

_____3. **Obtain a picture of how metrics-minded your organization is through discussion with management and co-workers.** Ensure that everyone understands and buys in to processes that include metrics, which will be critical when you collect the data needed for the metrics.

Suggestions for Security Metrics Design: The following Suggestions are Essential for any Successful Security Metrics Design:

_____4. **Base your security metrics on the ideal characteristics.** Strive to base your security metrics on the ideal characteristics as described in Section 3.

_____5. **Use your service-level agreement to guide your metrics design.** Your organization's security policies or service-level agreements will point to areas for which security metrics may be needed. Use them to refine your measurement targets. By so doing, you will be relating what you measure to what is expected of you, and your organization (especially upper management) will more immediately recognize the value of your results.

_____6. **Start with basic measurements, understand them, then expand.** Start with a basic metric that is easy to understand and then work to make that metric more useful or replace it with a better one that you've discovered along the way. Be well organized and prioritize your efforts so that you can build up and maintain a portfolio of metrics that have maximal value.

Suggestions for Organization and Management:

_____7. **Form a team of stakeholders as early as possible.** As soon as possible, contact and put together a cross-functional team of metrics-minded people to build the plan around collecting, analyzing, reporting, interpreting, and responding to security metrics. Work with the experts who understand the data, and the management who will need to champion changes throughout the organization.

_____8. **Define your metrics data repository.** A central agreed location for storing trusted data required for metrics evaluation will help to create confidence and trust in the data. Also, it may save you much time defending the data later on, should questions arise over its reliability.

_____9. **Be consistent in using your metrics.** Don't spend a month on observing and analyzing and then move on if nothing is found. Consistent, steady vigilance is the key to identifying trends or variances; erratic monitoring and analysis will mislead you into a false sense of security and reduce your ability to continuously reflect and refine based on known patterns.

_____10. **Be ready to change based on your findings.** A common behavioral pattern is to take a finding, create a countermeasure around it, and then never look back. Be intellectually and ethically honest when you make new discoveries, particularly if they show a need to change an established rule, position, or policy. Learn to be comfortable with the idea that you may learn something new that will require a policy or process change.

_____11. **Be open to incorporating expertise and data from others.** Since attacks are often not limited to one area, you may need to integrate data from other system components into your analysis. In this case, ask for input from teams who know these other components better. They may shed light on interdependencies or relationships that are critical to better metric design. Leverage the findings established together with these teams to extract any support that may be needed from managers.

_____ 12. **Test your analytics.** Carry out a Metrics Penetration Test (MPT), which is a test to determine if your analytic procedures will zero in on the behaviors you are trying to isolate. For example, have a colleague attempt to crack a login password at an odd hour of the day to see if your "Unusual Login Attempts" metric triggers the flags you expect to see. Incorporate the results from these MPTs in operational reviews to continue evolving and maturing your analytic methodologies.

Additional advice for establishing a security metrics program can be found in books such as Jaquith [5] and Hayden [6]. In addition, NIST [7] provides guidelines for establishing measures for assessing security controls and other security-related activities.

5. METRICS IN ACTION—TOWARDS AN INTELLIGENT SECURITY DASHBOARD

SIEM (Security Information and Event Management) describes security dashboard-like commercial applications or services that are widely available from security vendors. According to Wikipedia[2], SIEM technology "provides real-time analysis of security alerts generated by network hardware and applications. SIEM solutions come as software, appliances or managed services, and are also used to log security data and generate reports for compliance purposes". The same Wikipedia page also gives the following list f SIEM capabilities:

- **Data Aggregation:** SIEM/LM (log management) solutions aggregate data from many sources, including network, security, servers, databases, applications, providing the ability to consolidate monitored data to help avoid missing crucial events.
- **Correlation:** looks for common attributes, and links events together into meaningful bundles. This technology provides the ability to perform a variety of correlation techniques to integrate different sources, in order to turn data into useful information.
- **Alerting:** the automated analysis of correlated events and production of alerts, to notify recipients of immediate issues.
- **Dashboards:** SIEM/LM tools take event data and turn it into informational charts to assist in seeing patterns, or identifying activity that is not forming a standard pattern.
- **Compliance:** SIEM applications can be employed to automate the gathering of compliance data, producing reports that adapt to existing security, governance and auditing processes.

- **Retention:** SIEM/SIM [Security Information Management] solutions employ long-term storage of historical data to facilitate correlation of data over time, and to provide the retention necessary for compliance requirements.

The question at hand is: Is it possible to use SIEM technology as a base up on which to build an intelligent security dashboard that displays security alerts and responds to the alerts by either suggesting corrective action or automatically taking corrective action (depending on the action), or both? The above list of SIEM capabilities suggests that the "alerting" and "dashboard" capabilities map directly to the security dashboard's display of security alerts, and that the "data aggregation" and "correlation" capabilities map directly to the security dashboard's suggesting or taking of corrective action. Thus it does seem viable to use SIEM technology as the base on which to build the security dashboard. Additional research is required to determine what security metrics should be used to trigger the security alerts. In addition, research is needed to know how to construct the security dashboard's corrective action engine, which may be built using artificial intelligence techniques. The construction of an intelligent security dashboard based on SIEM technology does indeed appear feasible.

6. SECURITY METRICS IN THE LITERATURE

This section presents the results of a literature search using the following sources: the Internet, the IEEE Xplore and ACM Digital Library databases, and the homepages of university researchers. The publications found can be categorized as concerning:

- The nature of security metrics
- Measuring the security of a computer system
- Managing IT security risks
- Measuring the effectiveness of a security process

Measuring the security of a computer system differs from the other categories in that (i) it considers the component makeup of the computer system, (ii) it is about the use of scientific tools (modeling) to measure the security, and (iii) it only measures the security of the computer

---

2. "Security information and event management", accessed Mar. 27, 2012 at: http://en.wikipedia.org/wiki/Security_information_and_event_management.

system and not other aspects such as operational security or security process. Note that a publication may appear in more than one category.

It should also be noted that a publication may not fit neatly within a particular category. This is natural since security metrics may have a different meaning for different people, and different authors approach the subject from their own varied backgrounds and environments. The above categories do, however, help to group the papers in a broad sense. Of course, the security metrics coverage within these publications is limited by the data sources searched, since not all research is published or published in these sources. Nevertheless, one can say that given the dominance of IEEE and ACM publication repositories over other sources, this coverage is reasonably high.

The following sections divide up the publications into tables according to each of the categories mentioned above. References to the publications in each table are of the form "Table n [$i, j, k, \ldots$]", for publications $i, j, k, \ldots$ in Table n.

The Nature of Security Metrics

Table 32.1 lists the publications in this category, which treats questions such as "how is a security metric defined?" (Table 32.1 [3,4,7]), "what makes a good

security metric?" (Table 32.1 [4,6,7]), "what is a security metrics taxonomy?" (Table 32.1 [3]), "are security metrics scientifically based?" (Table 32.1 [2,5]), "what are good areas for security metrics research?" (Table 32.1 [5]), and "who are the U.S. industrial and government players in security metrics, and what security metrics initiatives have they undertaken?" (Table 32.1 [1]). Publications Table 32.1 [2,4−6] elaborate the ideas of Section 3 by discussing what makes a good security metric and a scientific basis for security metrics.

Measuring the Security of a Computer System

Table 32.2 lists the publications in this category, which contains the largest number of publications of all the categories. These papers propose a range of techniques that use metrics to evaluate the security of a computer system and mostly apply to the software. The techniques involve the computer system's components and generally do not treat supporting areas such as software development practice, security operations, or security process. The papers here are based on various frameworks and serve to illustrate the earlier discussion of a scientific framework for computer system security metrics.

TABLE 32.1 The Nature of Security Metrics.

No.	Publication	Summary
1	"Measuring Cyber Security and Information Assurance," IATAC SOAR, May 8, 2009.	Provides broad coverage of United States, including laws, standards, best practices, government programs, industry initiatives, measurable data, tools, and technologies.
2	S. Stolfo, S. Bellovin, D. Evans, "Measuring Security," *IEEE Security & Privacy*, May/June 2011.	Discusses a scientific basis for security and security metrics with examples and ideas for research; focuses on security of a computer system.
3	R. Savoia, "Towards a Taxonomy for Information Security Metrics" QoP'07, 2007.	Proposes a high-level security metrics taxonomy for Information Communications Technology (ICT) product companies; gives an example of a security metrics taxonomy.
4	D. Chapin, S. Akridge, "How Can Security Be Measured?" *Information Systems Control Journal*, Vol. 2, 2005.	Discusses what is wrong with traditional security metrics, giving characteristics of good metrics; discusses security maturity models with examples.
5	Wayne Jansen, "Directions in Security Metrics Research," NIST, April 2009.	Overviews security measurement and proposes possible research areas such as formal models of security measurement and artificial intelligence techniques.
6	O. Saydjari, "Is Risk a Good Security Metric?" Panel, Proceedings of QoP'06, 2006.	Succinct descriptions of risk as a security metric, alternative security metrics, and what makes a good metric.
7	Andrew Jaquith, *Security Metrics: Replacing Fear, Uncertainty, and Doubt*, Addison-Wesley, 2007.	Discusses security metrics for enterprise application; security metrics applied broadly, not only to computing systems but also to all sorts of enterprise processes.
8	Lance Hayden, IT Security Metrics: *A Practical Framework for Measuring Security & Protecting Data*, McGraw-Hill Osborne Media, June 2010.	Similar to the Jaquith book in its focus on the enterprise; covers security metrics in terms of effectiveness, implementation, operations, compliance, costs, people, organizations; includes four case studies.

TABLE 32.2 Measuring the Security of a Computer System.

No.	Publication	Summary
1	S. Stolfo, S. Bellovin, D. Evans, "Measuring Security," *IEEE Security & Privacy*, May/June 2011.	Discusses scientific basis for security and security metrics with examples and ideas for research; focuses on security of a computer system.
2	Wayne Jansen, "Directions in Security Metrics Research," NIST, April 2009.	Overviews security measurement and proposes possible research areas such as formal models of security measurement and artificial intelligence techniques.
3	M. Howard, J. Pincus, J. Wing, "Measuring Relative Attack Surfaces," in *Computer Security in the 21st Century*, Springer, pp. 109–137, 2005.	Proposes "attack surfaces" as a measure of one system's security relative to another; an attack surface is described along three dimensions: targets and enablers, channels and protocols, and access rights.
4	M. Howard, "Attack Surface: Mitigate Security Risks by Minimizing the Code You Expose to Untrusted Users," 2004.	Offers ractical advice to developers on how to reduce the attack surface of their code; based on actual Microsoft products such as Windows XP and Windows Server 2003.
5	L. Wang, A. Singhal, S. Jajodia, "Toward Measuring Network Security Using Attack Graphs," Proceedings of QoP'07, 2007.	Proposes a framework for assessing the security of a network based on attack graphs or access paths for attack; for example, given two networks, if one has more paths of attack than the other, it is the less secure of the two; references Table 32.2 for attack resistance.
6	S. Noel, L. Wang, A. Singhal, S. Jajodia, "Measuring Security Risks of Networks Using Attack Graphs," *International Journal of Next-Generation Computing*, Vol. 1, No. 1, pp 113–123, 2010.	Gives an expanded version of Table 32.2[5]; provides a method for quantitatively analyzing the security of a network using attack graphs; the attack graphs are first populated with known vulnerabilities and likelihoods of exploitation and then "exercised" to obtain a metric of the overall security and risks of the network.
7	L. Wang, S. Jajodia, A. Singhal, S. Noel, "k-Zero Day Safety: Measuring the Security Risk of Networks against Unknown Attacks," Proceedings of 15th European Symposium on Research in Computer Security (ESORICS 2010), Springer-Verlag Lecture Notes in Computer Science (LNCS), Vol. 6345, 20–22 September, pages 573–587, 2010.	Proposes "k-zero day safety" as a security metric that counts the number of unknown zero day vulnerabilities that would be required to compromise a network asset, regardless of what those vulnerabilities might be. The metric is defined in terms of an abstract model of networks and attacks. Algorithms for computing the metric are included.
8	L. Wang, A. Singhal, S. Jajodia, "Measuring the Overall Security of Network Configurations Using Attack Graphs," Proc. 21st Annual IFIP WG 11.3 Working Conference on Data and Applications Security (DBSec 2007), Springer Lecture Notes in Computer Science, Vol. 4602, Steve Barker and Gail-Joon Ahn, eds., Redondo Beach, CA, pages 98–112, 2007.	Proposes an attack graph-based attack resistance metric for measuring the relative security of network configurations; incorporates two composition operators for computing the cumulative attack resistance from given individual resistances and accounts for the dependency between individual attack resistances; referenced by Table 32.2[5] for attack resistance.
9	L. Wang, T. Islam, T. Long, A. Singhal, S. Jajodia, "An Attack Graph-Based Probabilistic Security Metric," Proceedings of 22nd Annual IFIP WG 11.3 Working Conference on Data and Applications Security (DBSEC 2008) , Springer-Verlag Lecture Notes in Computer Science (LNCS), Vol. 5094, pages 283–296, 2008.	Proposes an attack graph-based metric for the security of a network that incorporates the likelihood of potential multistep attacks combining multiple vulnerabilities in order to reach the attack goal; the definition of the metric is claimed to have an intuitive and meaningful interpretation that is useful in real-world decision making.
10	A. Singhal, X. Ou, "Techniques for Enterprise Network Security Metrics," Fifth Cyber Security and Information Intelligence Research Workshop (CSIIRW '09), Knoxville, TN, USA, 2009.	Presents an attack graph-based method for evaluating the security of a network based on likelihood of attack (similar to Table 32.2); stresses the derivation of the metric based on composition of component vulnerabilities whose security levels are already known. This is a short paper with accompanying slides.
11	M. Frigault, L. Wang, A. Singhal, S. Jajodia, "Measuring Network Security Using Dynamic Bayesian Network," Proceedings of QoP'08, 2008.	A Dynamic Bayesian Network (DBN) model is used to capture the dynamic nature of vulnerabilities that change over time. An attack graph is converted to a DBN by applying conditional probabilities to the nodes, calculated from the Common Vulnerabilities Scoring System (CVSS). The security of the network is calculated from the probabilities of the attacks being successful.

(Continued)

TABLE 32.2 (Continued)

No.	Publication	Summary
12	M. Frigault, L. Wang, "Measuring Network Security Using Bayesian Network-Based Attack Graphs," Annual IEEE International Computer Software and Applications Conference, 2008.	Proposes measuring network security using Bayesian network-based attack graphs so that relationships such as exploiting one vulnerability makes another vulnerability easier to exploit may be captured; differs from Table 32.2 in that Table 32.2 uses Dynamic Bayesian Networks, whereas this paper uses regular Bayesian networks.
13	L. Krautsevich, F. Martinelli, A. Yautsiukhin, "Formal Approach to Security Metrics. What Does 'More Secure' Mean for You?" Proceedings of ECSA 2010, 2010.	Initial proposal and analysis of a number of mathematically based definitions of security metrics such as "number of attacks", "minimal cost of attack", "maximal probability of attack", and even "attack surface" from Table 32.2[3].
14	C. Wang, W. Wulf, "Towards a Framework for Security Measurement," Proceedings of 20th National Information Systems Security Conference, 1997.	Proposes an initial framework for estimating the security strength of a system by decomposing the system into its security sensitive components and assigning security scores to each component; aggregate the component scores to get an estimate for the security strength of the system.
15	P. Halonen, K. Hätönen, "Towards Holistic Security Management through Coherent Measuring," Proceedings of ECSA 2010, 2010.	Discusses the problems of applying security metrics to telecommunication systems; compares security metric taxonomies, and discusses the need for security impact metrics; presents a broad view of security metrics.
16	D. Mellado, E. Fernández-Medina, M. Piattini, "A Comparison of Software Design Security Metrics," Proceedings of ECSA 2010, 2010.	Surveys various security metrics and standards that may be applicable to software design; compares the relevance of the various approaches to security properties such as authenticity and confidentiality.
17	J. Wang, H. Wang, M. Guo, M. Xia, "Security Metrics for Software Systems," Proceedings of ACMSE '09, 2009.	Presents a security metrics formulation in terms of weaknesses and vulnerabilities, rated by CVSS scores for CVE (Common Vulnerabilities and Exposures) names; does not show how one would determine such scores for a brand-new piece of software; not clear how the final security metric can be used to improve security.
18	R. Scandariato, B. De Win, W. Joosen, "Towards a Measuring Framework for Security Properties of Software," Proceedings of QoP '06, 2006.	Claims that software has security properties that can be measured, much like it has maintainability properties such as complexity; proposes a number of software security properties along with corresponding metrics.
19	O. Saydjari, "Is Risk a Good Security Metric?" Panel, Proceedings of QoP'06, 2006.	Presents succinct descriptions of risk as a security metric, alternative security metrics, and what makes a good metric.
20	Z. Dwaikat, F. Parisi-Presicce, "Risky Trust: Risk-Based Analysis of Software Systems," Proceedings of SESS'05, 2005.	Proposes an approach to evaluate the security of a software system in development; security requirements are derived, and a method is given for evaluating the likelihood of requirements violation based on the individual risks of system components.
21	Y. Liu, I. Traore, A. M. Hoole, "A Service-oriented Framework for Quantitative Security Analysis of Software Architectures," Proceedings of 2008 IEEE Asia-Pacific Services Computing Conference, 2008.	Proposes a User System Interaction Effect (USIE) model for systematically deriving and analyzing security concerns in service-oriented architectures. The model is claimed to provide a foundation for software services security metrics, and one such metric is defined and illustrated.
22	Y. Liu, I. Traore, "Properties for Security Measures of Software Products," *Applied Mathematics & Information Sciences*, I(2), pp. 129–156, 2007.	Describes and formalizes properties that characterize security-related internal software attributes; these properties form a framework that can be used to rigorously identify and evaluate new security metrics; this framework is claimed to be sound but not complete; the properties are claimed to be necessary but not sufficient conditions for good security metrics.

(Continued)

TABLE 32.2 (Continued)

No.	Publication	Summary
23	Y. Liu, I. Traore, "UML-based Security Measures of Software Products," Proceedings of International Workshop on Methodologies for Pervasive and Embedded Software (MOMPES'04), 2004.	Proposes the USIE model mentioned above for Table 32.2 (probably first publication of the model) and derives it from UML (Unified Modeling Language) sequence diagrams; this model can be used as a basis for architectural-level security metrics, and as an example, confidentiality metrics are defined based on the model.
24	E. Chew, M. Swanson, K. Stine, N. Bartol, A. Brown, W. Robinson, "Performance Measurement Guide for Information Security," NIST SP 800-55, Revision 1, 2008.	Provides guidelines for developing, selecting, and implementing information system-level and security program-level measures for assessing the implementation, performance, and impact of security controls and other security related activities.
25	"Recommended Security Controls for Federal Information Systems and Organizations," NIST SP 800-53, 2009.	Describes recommended security controls; includes risk assessment as a control; this publication is used by the "Performance Measurement Guide for Information Security" (Table 32.2) as a basis for developing security measures.
26	T. E. Hart, M. Chechik, D. Lie, "Security Benchmarking Using Partial Verification," Proceedings of HotSec 08, 2008.	Proposes quantifying insecurity using the partial results of verification attempts—instrumented code (assertions) is property checked until a failure is found. The aggregate of such failures determines the level of insecurity of the software.
27	T. Maibaum, "Challenges in Software Certification," SQRL Report 59, McMaster University, May 2010.	Considers the requirements of software certification, proposing that certification should be product based, not development process based; considers the Common Criteria (CC) as a possible product-based model for certification; although this paper is on software certification, it is relevant to security metrics in that it describes the elements of the CC that are pertinent to evaluating the security of a software product.

TABLE 32.3 Managing IT Security Risks.

No.	Publication	Summary
1	Andrew Jaquith, *Security Metrics: Replacing Fear, Uncertainty, and Doubt*, Addison-Wesley, 2007.	Discusses security metrics for enterprise application; security metrics applied broadly, not only to computing systems but also to all sorts of enterprise processes.
2	Lance Hayden, *IT Security Metrics: A Practical Framework for Measuring Security & Protecting Data*, McGraw-Hill Osborne Media, June 2010.	Similar to the Jaquith book in its focus on the enterprise; covers security metrics in terms of effectiveness, implementation, operations, compliance, costs, people, organizations; includes four case studies.
3	J. Talbot, M. Jakeman, *Security Risk Management Body of Knowledge*, book, Wiley, 2009.	Describes the security risk management process; discusses the pros and cons of various risk measures, including risks of threats and attacks.
4	G. Stoneburner, A. Goguen, A. Feringa, "Risk Management Guide for Information Technology Systems," NIST SP 800-30, 2002.	Provides a foundation for developing a risk management program; contains definitions and guidelines for assessing and mitigating risks within IT systems.

Managing IT Security Risks

Table 32.3 lists the publications in this category, which treats the management of risks for IT vulnerabilities taking into account the probability and impact of occurrence.

Managing risks is a process, made up of (a) identifying the risks, (b) assessing the risks, and (c) reducing the risks to acceptable levels using established procedures. In addition, some of the papers (Table 32.3 [4]) provide guidance

TABLE 32.4 Measuring the Effectiveness of a Security Process.

No.	Publication	Summary
1	Andrew Jaquith, *Security Metrics: Replacing Fear, Uncertainty, and Doubt*, Addison-Wesley, 2007.	Discusses security metrics for enterprise application; security metrics applied broadly, not only to computing systems but also to all sorts of enterprise processes.
2	Lance Hayden, *IT Security Metrics: A Practical Framework for Measuring Security & Protecting Data*, McGraw-Hill Osborne Media, June 2010.	Similar to the Jaquith book in its focus on the enterprise; covers security metrics in terms of effectiveness, implementation, operations, compliance, costs, people, organizations; includes four case studies.
3	D. Chapin, S. Akridge, "How Can Security Be Measured?" *Information Systems Control Journal*, Vol. 2, 2005.	Discusses what is wrong with traditional security metrics, giving characteristics of good metrics; discusses security maturity models with examples.
4	S.S. Alaboodi, "Towards Evaluating Security implementations Using the Information Security Maturity Model (ISMM)," MASc thesis, University of Waterloo, 2007.	Extensions and abstractions of the ISMM are proposed with the goals of using the extended model to identify the security level of implementations as well as promote the optimization of IT and security expenditures.
5	Carnegie-Mellon University, "The Systems Security Engineering Capability Maturity Model (SSE-CMM)—Model Description Document," Version 3, June 15, 2003. Accessed Mar. 16, 2012, at: http://www.sse-cmm.org/model/model.asp	Describes essential characteristics of a sound security engineering process; addresses security engineering activities that span the entire security engineering life cycle, including process metrics; applies to all types and sizes of security engineering organizations, including commercial, government, and academic organizations.
6	R. F. Lentz, "Advanced Persistent Threats & Zero Day Attacks," slide presentation, 2010.	Describes the stages of the Cyber Security Maturity Model, which can be measures of where an organization stands in terms of its security posture.
7	R. F. Lentz, "Cyber Security Maturity Model," slide presentation, 2011.	Describes advanced persistent threats and the stages of the Cyber Security Maturity Model; appears to be an updated version of Table 32.4 [6].

on selecting security controls for mitigating the identified risks. Security risk management metrics serve to:

- quantify the risks,
- calculate the risks using formulas, and
- quantify the effectiveness of the risk management process.

Here, the difference between the first and second points is that "quantify the risks" is not limited to producing numbers (stating that "plan B" is riskier than "plan A"). Note that, currently, the quantifications of risks and the risk management process are applicable to all of IT, including, for example, operations and software development. They do not focus on evaluating the security of a computer system with sufficient detail. Therefore, the papers in this category, in a broad sense, extend beyond the evaluation of the security of a computer system. Papers that use risks in conjunction with system components and metrics to evaluate security (not risk management) have been placed in Table 32.2.

Measuring the Effectiveness of a Security Process

Table 32.4 lists the publications in this category, which cover metrics that evaluate the effectiveness of security processes or show where an organization is at in terms of a security maturity model. Note that security processes usually describe security within an enterprise. On the other hand, a security maturity model can apply to an enterprise, a geographical region, and even a country.

7. SUMMARY

Security metrics provide a quantitative basis for security operations and security-related decision making. They can be used to measure security improvements over time and can therefore show if a series of new investments in security controls is giving better security. Traditional security metrics have been selected haphazardly and have been problematic in that they often targeted aspects of a computer system that were irrelevant to the question at hand. Security metrics should be based on the ideal characteristics given in Section 3. Security metrics for application in critical areas such as public safety and health care should be scientifically based once scientifically based security metrics are available and mature. Key aspects of starting a security metrics program for an organization include designing the security metrics based on the ideal characteristics and forming a security metrics cross-functional team. An intelligent security dashboard that not only displays alerts but also automatically handles them is an exciting application of security metrics. It appears that current SIEM technology can be a basis for such a dashboard, but more research work is needed. Security metrics publications cover the nature of security metrics, measuring the security of a computer system, managing risk, and measuring the effectiveness of a security process.

Finally, let's move on to the real interactive part of this chapter: review questions/exercises, hands-on projects, case projects, and optional team case project. The answers and/or solutions by chapter can be found in the Online Instructor's Solutions Manual.

CHAPTER REVIEW QUESTIONS/EXERCISES

True/False

1. True or False? Assessments of security properties cannot used to aid different kinds of decision making, such as program planning, resource allocation, and product and service selection.
2. True or False? Security metrics cannot be used during the software development life cycle to eliminate vulnerabilities, particularly during code production, by performing functions such as measuring adherence to secure coding standards, identifying likely vulnerabilities that may exist, and tracking and analyzing security flaws that are eventually discovered.
3. True or False? Monitoring and reporting of the security status or posture of an IT system can be carried out to determine compliance with security requirements (policy, procedures, and regulations), gauge the effectiveness of security controls and manage risk, provide a basis for trend analysis, and identify specific areas for improvement.
4. True or False? A security metric is given the task of measuring the security of the organization, which is undiscernible only when the organization is in a security crisis, thereby defeating the whole point of having the metric in the first place.
5. True or False? A risk assessment lists a number of threats along with the cost to mitigate each threat or risk.

Multiple Choice

1. The intended use of this metric _____ is to measure the effectiveness of the anti-malware controls.
   A. Number of security incidents and investigations
   B. Cost of security breaches
   C. Number of computer viruses or malware detected
   D. Resources assigned to security functions
   E. Compliance with security policy
2. What presumably measures the effectiveness of security events monitoring?
   A. Resources assigned to security functions
   B. Cost of security breaches
   C. Number of computer viruses or malware detected
   D. Number of security incidents and investigations
   E. Compliance with security policy
3. What metric is intended to measure the true business loss due to security failures?
   A. Cost of security breaches
   B. Resources assigned to security functions
   C. Number of computer viruses or malware detected
   D. Number of security incidents and investigations
   E. Compliance with security policy
4. The intended use of this metric _____ is to measure the true business cost of running a security program?
   A. Cost of security breaches
   B. Number of security incidents and investigations
   C. Number of computer viruses or malware detected
   D. Resources assigned to security functions
   E. Compliance with security policy
5. What metric is intended to measure the level of compliance or adhesion to security goals?
   A. Cost of security breaches
   B. Number of security incidents and investigations
   C. Number of computer viruses or malware detected
   D. Resources assigned to security functions
   E. Compliance with security policy

EXERCISE

Problem

How do organizations identify suitable security metrics?

Hands-On Projects

Project

How should security metrics be reported?

Case Projects

Problem

What if the metrics are bad?

Optional Team Case Project

Problem

How do metrics support decision making?

REFERENCES

[1] D. Chapin, S. Akridge, How can security be measured? Inf. Syst. Control J. 2 (2005).

[2] W. Jansen, Directions in security metrics research NIST NISTIR 7564, April 2009.

[3] S. Stolfo, S. Bellovin, D. Evans, Measuring security, IEEE Security Privacy (May/June 2011).

[4] J. Gottlieb, 10 tips for getting started with security metric. Available as of September 5, 2012 from: <http://threatpost.com/en_us/blogs/10-tips-getting-started-security-metrics-081712>.

[5] A. Jaquith, Security Metrics: Replacing Fear, Uncertainty, and Doubt, Addison-Wesley, 2007.

[6] Lance Hayden, IT Security Metrics: A Practical Framework for Measuring Security & Protecting Data, McGraw-Hill Osborne Media, June 2010.

[7] E. Chew, M. Swanson, K. Stine, N. Bartol, A. Brown, W. Robinson, Performance measurement guide for information security NIST SP 800-55, Revision 1, 2008.

## Part III

Cyber, Network, and Systems Forensics Security and Assurance

## Chapter 33

Cyber Forensics

Scott R. Ellis
kCura Corporation

1. WHAT IS CYBER FORENSICS?

Definition: Cyber forensics is the acquisition, preservation, and analysis of electronically stored information (ESI) in such a way that ensures its admissibility for use as either evidence, exhibits, or demonstratives in a court of law.

Rather than discussing at great length what cyber forensics is (the rest of the chapter will take care of that), let's, for the sake of clarity, define what cyber forensics is *not*. It is not an arcane ability to tap into a vast, secret repository of information about every single thing that ever happened on, or to, a computer. Often, it involves handling hardware in unique circumstances and doing things with both hardware and software that are not, typically, things that the makers or manufacturers ever intended (see sidebar: "Angular Momentum").

Not every single thing a user ever did on a computer is 100% knowable beyond a shadow of a doubt or even beyond reasonable doubt. Some things are certainly *knowable* with varying degrees of certainty. and there is nothing that can happen on a computer through the use of a keyboard and a mouse that cannot be replicated with a software program or macro of some sort. It is fitting, then, that many of the arguments of cyber forensics become philosophical, and that *degrees of certainty* exist and beg definition. Such as: How heavy is the burden of proof? Right away, lest arrogant thoughtlessness prevail, anyone undertaking a study of cyber forensics must understand the core principles of what it means to be in a position of authority and to what varying degrees of certainty an examiner may attest to without finding he has overstepped his mandate (see sidebar, "Angular Momentum"). The sections "Testifying in Court" and "Beginning to End in Court" in this chapter, and the article "Cyber forensics and Ethics, Green Home Plate Gallery View," address these concerns as they relate to ethics and testimonial work.

Angular Momentum

Hard drive platters spin very fast. The 5¼-inch floppy disk of the 1980s has evolved into heavy, metallic platters that spin at ridiculous speeds. If your car wheels turned at 10,000 RPM, you would zip along at 1000 mph. Some hard drives spin at 15,000 RPM. That's really fast. But though HD platters will not disintegrate (as CD-ROMs have been known to do), anecdotal evidence suggests that in larger, heavier drives, the bearings can become so hot that they liquefy, effectively stopping the drive in its tracks. Basic knowledge of surface coating magnetic properties tells us that if the surface of a hard drive becomes overly hot, the basic magnetic properties, the "zeroes and ones" stored by the particulate magnetic domains, will become unstable. The stability of these zeroes and ones maintains the consistency of the logical data stored by the medium. The high speeds of large, heavy hard drives generate heat and ultimately result in drive failure.

Forensic technicians are often required to handle hard drives, sometimes while they have power attached to them. For example, a computer may need to be moved while it still has power attached to it. Here is where a note about angular momentum becomes necessary: A spinning object translates pressure applied to its axis of rotation 90 degrees from the direction of the force applied to it. Most hard drives are designed to park the heads at even the slightest amount of detected g-shock. They claim to be able to withstand thousands of "g's," but this simply means that if the hard drive was parked on a neutron star it would still be able to park its heads. This is a relatively meaningless, static attribute. Most people should understand that if you drop your computer, you may damage the internal mechanics of a hard drive and, if the platters are spinning, the drive may be scored. Older drives, those that are more than three years old, are especially susceptible to damage. Precautions should be taken to keep older drives vibration free and cool.

With very slight, gentle pressures, a spinning hard drive can be handled much as you would handle a gyro and

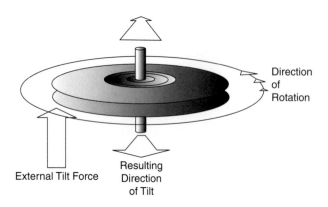

FIGURE 33.1 A spinning object distributes applied force differently than a stationary object. Handle operating hard drives with extreme care.

with little potential for damage. It can be handled in a way that won't cause the heads to park.

Note: Older drives are the exception, and any slight motion at all can cause them to stop functioning.

Most hard drives have piezoelectric shock detectors that will cause the heads to park the instant a certain g-shock value is reached. Piezoelectrics work under the principle that when a force is exerted along a particular axis, certain types of crystals will emit an electrical charge. Just like their pocket-lighter counterparts, they don't always work and eventually become either desensitized or over-sensitized; if the internal mechanism of the hard drive is out of tolerance, the shock detector may either work or it won't park the heads correctly and the heads will shred the surface of the platters. Or, if it does work, it may thrash the surface anyway as the heads park and unpark during multiple, repeated shocks. A large, heavy drive (such as a 1 TB drive) will behave exactly as would any heavy disk spinning about an axis—just like a gyro (see Figure 33.1). So, when a vector of force is applied to a drive and it is forced to turn in the same direction as the vector, instead of its natural 90 degree offset, the potential for damage to the drive increases dramatically.

Such is the case of a computer mounted in brackets inside a PC in transit. The internal, spinning platters of the drive try to shift in opposition to the direction the external drive turned; it is an internal tug of war. As the platters attempt to lean forward, the drive leans to the left instead. If there is any play in the bearings at all, the cushion of air that floats the drive heads can be disrupted and the surface of the platters can scratch. If you must move a spinning drive (and sometimes you must), be very careful, go very slowly, and let the drive do all the work. If you must transport a running hard drive, ensure that the internal drive is rotating about the x axis, that it is horizontally mounted inside the computer, and that there is an external shock pad. Some PCs have vertically mounted drives.

Foam padding beneath the computer is essential. If you are in the business of transporting running computers that have been seized, a floating platform of some sort wouldn't be a bad idea. A lot of vibrations, bumps, and jars can shred less durably manufactured HDs. This author once shredded

his own laptop hard drive by leaving it turned on, carrying it 15 city blocks, and then for an hour-long ride on the train. You can transport and move computers your entire life and not have an issue. But the one time you do, it could be an unacceptable and unrecoverable loss.

Never move an older computer. If the computer cannot be shut down, then the acquisition of the computer must be completed on site. Any time a computer is to be moved while it's running, everyone involved in the decision-making process should sign off on the procedure and be aware of the risk.

Lesson learned: Always make sure that a laptop put into standby mode has actually gone into standby mode before closing the lid. Windows can be tricky like that sometimes.

2. ANALYSIS OF DATA

Never underestimate the power of a maze. There are two types of mazes that maze experts generally agree on: unicursive and multicursive. In the unicursive maze, the maze has only one answer; you wind along a path and with a little patience you end up at the end. Multicursory mazes, according to the experts, are full of wrong turns and dead ends.

The fact of the matter is, however, when one sets foot into a multicursive maze, one need only recognize that it is, in fact, two unicursory mazes put together, with the path through the maze being the seam. If you take the unicursory tack and simply *always stay to the right (or the left*, as long as you are consistent), you will traverse the entire maze and have no choice but to traverse and complete it successfully.

This is not a section about mazes, but they are analogous in that there are two approaches to cyber forensics: one that churns through every last bit of data and one that takes shortcuts. This is called *analysis*. Quite often as a forensic analyst, the sheer amount of data that needs to be sifted will seem enormous and unrelenting. But there is a path that, if you know it, you can follow it through to success. Here are a few guidelines on how to go about conducting an investigation. For starters, we talk about a feature that is built into most forensic toolsets. It allows the examiner to "reveal all" in a fashion that can place hundreds of thousands of files at the fingertips for examination. It can also create a bad situation, legally and ethically.

Cyber Forensics and Ethics, Green Home Plate Gallery View[1]

A simplified version of this article was published on the Chicago Bar Association blog in late 2007. This is the original version, unaltered.

---

1. "Cyber forensics and ethics," Green Home Plate Gallery View, Chicago Bar Association Blog, September 2007.

EnCase is a commonly used forensic software program that allows a cyber forensic technologist to conduct an investigation of a forensic hard disk copy. One of the functions of the software is something known as "green-home-plate-gallery-view." This function allows the forensic technologist to create, in *plain view*, a gallery of every single image on the computer.

In EnCase, the entire folder view structure of a computer is laid out just as in Windows Explorer with the exception that to the left of every folder entry are two boxes. One is shaped like a square, and the other like a little "home plate" that turns green when you click on it; hence the "green-home-plate." The technical name for the home plate box is "Set Included Folders." With a single click, every single file *entry* in that folder and its subfolders becomes visible in a table view. An additional option allows the examiner to switch from a table view of entries to a gallery view of *thumbnails*. Both operations together create the "green-home-plate-gallery-view" action.

With two clicks of the mouse, the licensed EnCase user can gather up every single image that exists on the computer and place it into a single, scrollable, thumbnail gallery. In a court-ordered investigation where the search may be for text-based documents such as correspondence, green-home-plate-gallery-view has the potential of being *misused* to visually search the computer for imaged/scanned documents. I emphasize *misused* because, ultimately, this action puts every single image on the computer in *plain view*. It is akin to policemen showing up for a domestic abuse response with an x-ray machine in tow and x-raying the contents of the whole house.

Because this action enables one to view every single image on a computer, including those that may not have anything to do with the forensic search at hand, it raises a question of ethics, and possibly even legality. Can a forensic examiner green-home-plate-gallery-view without reasonable cause?

In terms of a search where the search or motion specifically authorized searching for text-based "documents," green-home-plate-gallery-view is not the correct approach, nor is it the most efficient. The action exceeds the scope of the search and it may raise questions regarding the violation of rights and/or privacy. To some inexperienced examiners, it may seem to be the quickest and easiest route to locating all the documents on a computer. More experienced examiners may use it as a quick litmus test to "peek under the hood" to see if there are documents on the computer.

Many documents that are responsive to the search may be in the form of image scans or PDFs. Green-home-plate-gallery-view renders them visible and available, just for the scrolling. Therein lies the problem: If anything incriminating turns up, it also has the ring of truth in a court of law when the examiner suggests that he was innocently searching for financial documents when he inadvertently discovered, in *plain view*, offensive materials that were outside the scope of his original mandate. But just because something has the ring of truth does not mean that the bell's been rung.

For inexperienced investigators, green-home-plate-gallery-view (see Figure 33.2) may truly seem to be the only recourse and it may also be the one that has yielded the most convictions. However, because there is a more efficient method to capture and detect text, one that can protect privacy and follows the constraints of the search mandate, it should be used.

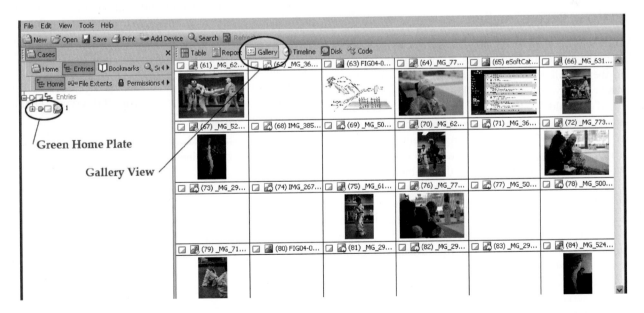

FIGURE 33.2   Green-home-plate-gallery-view.

Current forensic technology allows us, through electronic file signature analysis, sizing, and typing of images, to capture and export every image from the subject file system. Next, through optical character recognition (OCR), the experienced professional can detect every image that has text and discard those that do not. In this manner, images are protected from being viewed, the subject's privacy is protected, and all images with text are located efficiently. The resultant set can then be hashed and reintroduced into EnCase as single files, hashed, and indexed so that the notable files can be bookmarked and a report generated.

Technically, this is a more difficult process because it requires extensive knowledge of imaging, electronic file signature analysis, automated OCR discovery techniques, and hash libraries. But to a trained technician, this is actually faster than green-home-plate-gallery-view, which may yield thousands of images and may take hundreds of hours to accurately review.

In practice, the easiest way is seldom the most ethical way to solve a problem; neither is it always the most efficient method of getting a job done. Currently, there are many such similar scenarios that exist within the discipline of cyber forensics. As the forensic technology industry grows and evolves, professional organizations may eventually emerge that will provide codes of ethics and some syncretism in regard to these issues. For now, however, it falls on attorneys to retain experienced cyber forensic technologists who place importance on developing appropriate ethical protocols. Only when these protocols are in place can we successfully understand the breadth and scope of searches and prevent possible violations of privacy.

Database Reconstruction

A disk that hosts an active database is a very busy place. Again and again throughout this chapter, a single recurring theme will emerge: Data that has been overwritten cannot, by any conventionally known means, be recovered. If it could be, then Kroll Ontrack and every other giant in the forensics business would be shouting this service from the rooftops and charging a premium price for it. Experimentally, accurate statistics on the amount of data that will be overwritten by the seemingly random action of a write head may be available, but most likely it functions by rules that are different for every system based on the amount of usage, the size of the files, and the size of the unallocated clusters. Anecdotally, the formula goes something like this; the rules change under any given circumstances, but this story goes a long way toward telling how much data will be available:

On a server purposed with storing surveillance video, there are three physical hard drives. Drive C serves as the operating system (OS) disk and program files disk; Drives E and F, 350 gigabytes (GB) each, serve as storage disks. When the remote DVR units synchronize each evening, every other file writes to every other disk of the two storage drives. Thirty-day-old files automatically get deleted by the synchronization tool.

After eight months of use, the entire unallocated clusters of each drive, 115 GB on one drive and 123 GB on the other, are completely filled with MPG data. An additional 45 GB of archived deleted files are available to be recovered from each drive.

In this case, the database data were MPG movie files. In many databases, the data, the records (as the database indexes and grows and shrinks and is compacted and optimized), will grow to populate the unallocated clusters. Database records found in the unallocated clusters are not an indicator of deleted records. Database records that exist in the unallocated clusters that don't exist in the live database *are* a sign of deleted records.

Lesson learned: Don't believe everything you see. Check it out and be sure. Get second, third, and fourth opinions when you're uncertain.

3. CYBER FORENSICS IN THE COURT SYSTEM

Cyber forensics is one of the few cyber-related fields in which the practitioner will be found in the courtroom on a given number of days of the year. With that in mind, the following sections are derived from the author's experiences in the courtroom, the lessons learned there, and the preparation leading up to giving testimony. To most lawyers and judges, cyber forensics is a mysterious black art. It is as much a discipline of the art to demystify and explain results in plain English as it is to conduct an examination. It was with special consideration of the growing prevalence of the use of electronically stored information (ESI) in the courtroom, and the general unfamiliarity with how it must be handled as evidence, that spawned the idea for the sidebar "Preserving Digital Evidence in the Age of eDiscovery."

Preserving Digital Evidence in the Age of eDiscovery[2]

Society has awoken in these past few years to the realities of being immersed in the digital world. With that, the harsh realities of how we conduct ourselves in this age of binary processing are beginning to take form in terms of both new laws and new ways of doing business. In many actions, both civil and criminal, digital documents are the new "smoking gun." And with the new Federal laws that

---

2. Scott R. Ellis, "Preserving digital evidence in the age of ediscovery," *Daily Southtown*, 2007.

open the floodgates of accessibility to your digital media, the sanctions for mishandling such evidence become a fact of law and a major concern.

At some point, most of us (any of us) could become involved in litigation. Divorce, damage suits, patent infringement, intellectual property theft, and employee misconduct are just some examples of cases we see. When it comes to digital evidence, most people simply aren't sure of their responsibilities. They don't know how to handle the requests for and subsequent handling of the massive amounts of data that can be crucial to every case. Like the proverbial smoking gun, "digital evidence" must be handled properly.

Recently, a friend forwarded us an article about a case ruling in which a routine email exhibit was found inadmissible due to authenticity and hearsay issues. What we should take away from that ruling is that electronically stored information (ESI), just like any other evidence, must clear standard evidentiary hurdles. Whenever ESI is offered as evidence, the following evidence rules must be considered.

In most courts, there are four types of evidence. Cyber files that are extracted from a subject machine and presented in court typically fall into one or more of these types:

- *Documentary evidence* is paper or digital evidence that contains human language. It must meet the authenticity requirements outlined below. It is also unique in that it may be disallowed if it contains hearsay. Emails fall into the category of documentary evidence.
- *Real evidence* must be competent (authenticated), relevant, and material. For example, a computer that was involved in a court matter would be considered real evidence provided that it hasn't been changed, altered, or accessed in a way that destroyed the evidence. The ability to use these items as evidence may be contingent on this fact, and that's is why preservation of a cyber or digital media must be done.
- *Witness testimony*. With ESI, the technician should be able to verify how he retrieved the evidence and that the evidence is what it purports to be, and he should be able to speak to all aspects of computer use. The witness must both remember what he saw and be able to communicate it.
- *Demonstrative evidence* uses things like PowerPoint, photographs, or cyber-aided design (CAD) drawings of crime scenes to demonstrate or reconstruct an event. For example, a flowchart that details how a person goes to a Web site, enters her credit-card number, and makes a purchase would be considered demonstrative.

For any of these items to be submitted in court, they each must, to varying degrees, pass the admissibility requirements of relevance, materiality, and competence. For evidence to be *relevant*, it must make the event it is trying to prove either more or less probable. A forensic analyst may discover a certain Web page on the subject

hard drive that shows the subject visited a Web site where flowers are sold and that he made a purchase. In addition to perhaps a credit-card statement, this shows that it is more probable that the subject of an investigation visited the site on his computer at a certain time and location.

Materiality means that something not only proves the fact (it is relevant to the fact that it is trying to prove) but is also *material* to the issues in the case. The fact that the subject of the investigation purchased flowers on a Web site may not be material to the matter at hand.

Finally, *competency* is the area where the forensic side of things becomes most important. Assuming that the purchase of flowers from a Web site is material (perhaps it is a stalking case), how the evidence was obtained and what happened to it after that will be put under a microscope by both the judge and the party objecting to the evidence. The best evidence collection experts are trained professionals with extensive experience in their field. The best attorneys will understand this and will use experts when and where needed. Spoliation results from mishandled ESI, and spoiled data is generally inadmissible. It rests upon everyone involved in a case—IT directors, business owners, and attorneys—to get it right. Cyber forensics experts cannot undo damage that has been done, but if involved in the *beginning*, they can prevent it from happening.

4. UNDERSTANDING INTERNET HISTORY

Of the many aspects of user activity, the Internet history is usually of the greatest interest. In most investigations, people such as HR, employers, and law enforcement seek to understand the subject's use of the Internet. What Web sites did he visit? When did he visit them? Did he visit them more than once? The article "What Have You Been Clicking On" (see sidebar) seeks to demystify the concept of temporary Internet files (TIF).

What Have You Been Clicking On?

You've probably heard the rumor that whenever you click on something on a Web page, you leave a deeply rooted trail behind you for anyone (with the right technology) to see. In cyber forensics, just like in archeology, these pieces that a user leaves behind are called *artifacts*. An artifact is a thing made by a human. It tells the story of a behavior that happened in the past.

On your computer, that story is told by metadata stored in databases as well as by files stored on your local machine. They reside in numerous places, but this article will address just three: Internet history, Web cache, and temporary Internet files (TIF). Because Internet Explorer (IE) was developed in a time when bandwidth was precious, storing data locally prevents a browser from having to retrieve the same data every time the same Web page is visited. Also, at the time, no established technology existed that, through a Web browser, could show data on a local machine without first putting the file on the local machine. A Web browser, essentially, was a piece of software that combined FTP and document-viewing technology into one application platform, complete with its own protocol, HTTP.

In IE, press **Ctrl + H** to view your history. This will show a list of links to all the sites that were viewed over a period of four weeks. The history database only stores the name and date the site was visited. It holds no information about files that may be cached locally. That's the job of the Web cache.

To go back further in history, an Internet history viewer is needed. A Google search for "history.dat viewer" will turn up a few free tools.

The Web cache database, index.dat, is located in the TIF folder; it tracks the date, the time the Web page downloaded, the original Web page filename, and its local name and location in the TIF. Information stays in the index.dat for a long time, much longer than four weeks. You will notice that if you set your computer date back a few weeks and then press **Ctrl + H**, you can always pull the last four weeks of data for as long as you have had your computer (and not cleared your cache). Using a third-party viewer to view the Web cache shows you with certainty the date and origination of a Web page. The Web cache is a detailed inventory of everything in the TIF. Some history viewers will show Web cache information, too.

The TIF is a set of local folders where IE stores Web pages your computer has downloaded. Typically, the size varies depending on user settings. But Web sites are usually small, so 500 MB can hold thousands of Web pages and images! Viewing these files may be necessary. Web mail, financial, and browsing interests are all stored in the TIF. However, malicious software activity, such as pop-ups, exploits, viruses, and Trojans, can cause many strange files to appear in the TIF. For this reason, files that are in the TIF should be compared to their entry in the Web cache. Time stamps on files in the TIF may or may not accurately show when a file was written to disk. System scans periodically alter Last Accessed and Date Modified time stamps! Because of hard-disk caching and delayed writing, the Date Created time stamp may not be the actual time the file arrived. Cyber forensics uses special tools to analyze the TIF, but much is still left to individual interpretations.

Inspection of all the user's Internet artifacts, when intact, can reveal what a user was doing and whether or not a click trail exists. Looking just at time stamps or IE history isn't enough. Users can easily delete IE history, and time stamps aren't always accurate. Missing history can disrupt the trail. Missing Web cache entries or time stamp—altering system scans can destroy the trail. Any conclusions are best not preceded by a suspended leap through the air (you may land badly and trip and hurt yourself). Rather, check for viruses and bad patching, and get the artifacts straight. If there is a click trail, it will be revealed by the Web cache, the files in the TIF, and the history. Bear in mind that when pieces are missing, the reliability of the click trail erodes, and professional examination may be warranted.

5. TEMPORARY RESTRAINING ORDERS AND LABOR DISPUTES

A temporary restraining order (TRO) will often be issued in intellectual property or employment contract disputes. The role of the forensic examiner in a TRO may be multifold, or it may be limited to a simple, one-time acquisition of a hard drive. Often when an employee leaves an organization under less than amicable terms, accusations will be fired in both directions and the resulting lawsuit will be a many-headed beast. Attorneys on both sides may file motions that result in forensic analysis of emails, user activity, and possible contract violations as well as extraction of information from financial and customer relationship management (CRM) databases.

Divorce

Typically the forensic work done in a divorce case will involve collecting information about one of the parties to be used to show that trust has been violated. Dating sites, pornography, financial sites, expatriate sites, and email should be collected and reviewed.

Patent Infringement

When one company begins selling a part that is patented by another company, a lawsuit will likely be filed in federal court. Subsequently, the offending company will be required to produce all the invoices relating to sales of that product. This is where a forensic examiner may be required. The infringed-on party may find through their own research that a company has purchased the part from the infringer and that the sale has not been reported. A thorough examination of the financial system will reveal all the sales. It is wise when doing this sort of work to contact the financial system vendor to get a data dictionary that defines all the fields and the purpose of the tables.

Invoice data is easy to collect. It will typically reside in just two tables: a header and a detail table. These tables will contain customer codes that will need to be joined to the customer table, so knowing some SQL will be a great help. Using the database server for the specific database technology of the software is the gold standard for this sort of work. Getting the collection to launch into VMware is the platinum standard, but sometimes an image won't want to boot. Software utilities such as Live View do a great job of preparing the image for deployment in a virtualized environment.

When to Acquire, When to Capture Acquisition

When a forensics practitioner needs to capture the data on a hard disk, he/she does so in a way that is forensically sound. This means that, through any actions on the part of the examiner, no data on the hard drive is altered and a complete and total copy of the surface of the hard drive platters is captured. Here are some common terms used to describe this process:

- Collection
- Mirror
- Ghost
- Copy
- Acquisition

Any of these terms is sufficient to describe the process. The one that attorneys typically use is *mirror* because they seem to understand it best. A "forensic" acquisition simply means that the drive was write-protected by either a software or hardware write blocker while the acquisition was performed.

Acquisition of an entire hard drive is the standard approach in any case that will require a deep analysis of the behaviors and activities of the user. It is not always the standard procedure. However, most people will agree that a forensic procedure must be used whenever information is copied from a PC. Forensic, enterprise, and ediscovery cases all vary in their requirements for the amount of data that must be captured. In discovery, much of what is located on a computer may be deemed "inaccessible," which is really just fancy lawyer talk for "it costs too much to get it." Undeleting data from hundreds of computers in a single discovery action in a civil case would be a very rare thing to happen and would only take place if massive malfeasance was suspected. In these cases, forensic creation of logical evidence files allows the examiner to capture and copy relevant information without altering the data.

Creating Forensic Images Using Software and Hardware Write Blockers

Both software and hardware write blockers are available. Software write blockers are versatile and come in two flavors. One is a module that "plugs" into the forensic software and can generally be used to write block any port on the computer. The other method of software write blocking is to use a forensic boot disk. This will boot the computer from the hard drive. Developing checklists that can be repeatable procedures is an ideal way to ensure solid results in any investigation.

Software write blockers are limited by the port speed of the port they are blocking, plus some overhead for the write-blocking process. But then, all write blockers are limited in this manner.

Hardware write blockers are normally optimized for speed. Forensic copying tools such as Logicube and Tableau are two examples of hardware write blockers, though there are many companies now that make them. LogiCube will both hash and image a drive at a rate of about 3 GB a minute. They are small and portable and can replace the need for bulky PCs on a job site. There are also appliances and large enterprise software packages that are designed to automate and alleviate the labor requirements of large discovery/disclosure acquisitions that may span thousands of computers.

Live Capture of Relevant Files

Before conducting any sort of a capture, all steps should be documented and reviewed with counsel before proceeding. Preferably, attorneys from both sides on a matter and the judge agree to the procedure before it is enacted. Whenever a new procedure or technique is introduced late on the job site, if there are auditors or observers present, the attorneys will argue, which can delay the work by several hours. Most forensic software can be loaded to a USB drive and launched on a live system with negligible forensic impact to the operating environment. Random Access Memory (RAM) captures are becoming more popular; currently this is the only way to capture an image of physical RAM. Certain companies are rumored to be creating physical RAM write blockers. Launching a forensic application on a running system will destroy a substantial amount of physical RAM as well as the paging file. If either RAM or the paging file is needed, the capture must be done with a write blocker.

Once the forensic tool is launched, either with a write blocker or on a live system, the local drive may be previewed. The examiner may only be interested in Word documents, for example. Signature analysis is a lengthy process in preview mode, as are most searches. A better method, if subterfuge is not expected: Filtering the table pane by extension produces a list of all the docs. "Exporting" them will damage the forensic information, so instead you need to create a logical evidence file (LEF). Using EnCase, a user can create a condition to view all the .DOC files and then dump the files into a logical evidence file in about 30 seconds. Once the logical evidence file is created, it can later be used to create a CD-ROM. There are special modules available that will allow an exact extraction of native files to CD to allow further processing for a review tool.

Redundant Array of Independent (or Inexpensive) Disks (RAID)

Acquiring an entire RAID set disk by disk and then reassembling them in EnCase is probably the easiest way of dealing with a RAID and may be the only way to capture a software RAID. Hardware RAIDs can be most efficiently captured using a boot disk. This allows the capture of a single volume that contains all the unique data in an array. It can be trickier to configure and as with everything, practice makes perfect. Be sure you understand how it works. The worst thing that can happen is that the wrong disk or an unreadable disk gets imaged and the job has to be redone at your expense.

File System Analyses

FAT12, FAT16, and FAT32 are all types of file systems. Special circumstances aside, most forensic examiners will find themselves regularly dealing with either FAT or NTFS file systems. FAT differs from NTFS primarily in the way that it stores information about how it stores information. Largely, from the average forensic examiner's standpoint, very little about the internal workings of these file systems is relevant. Most modern forensic software will do the work of reconstructing and extracting information from these systems, at the system level, for you. Nonetheless, an understanding of these systems is critical because, at any given time, an examiner *just might* need to know it. The following are some examples showing where you might need to know about the file system:

- Rebuilding RAID arrays
- Locating lost or moved partitions
- Discussions of more advanced information that can be gleaned from entries in the MFT or FAT

The difference between FAT12, 16, and 32 is in the size of each item in the File Allocation Table (FAT). Each has a correspondingly sized entry in the FAT. For example, FAT12 has a 12-bit entry in the FAT. Each 12-bit sequence represents a cluster. This places a limitation on the file system regarding the number of file extents available to a file. The FAT stores the following information:

- Fragmentation
- Used or unused clusters
- A list of entries that correspond to each cluster on the partition
- Marks a cluster as used, reserved, unused, or bad
- The cluster number of the next cluster in the chain

Sector information is stored in the directory. In the FAT file system, directories are actually files that contain as many 32-byte slots as there are entries in the folder. This is also where deleted entries from a folder can be discovered. Figure 33.3 shows how the sector view is represented by a common forensic analysis tool.

NTFS

NTFS is a significant advancement in terms of data storage. It allows for long filenames, almost unlimited storage, and a more efficient method of accessing information. It also provides for much greater latency in deleted files, that is, deleted files stick around a lot longer in NTFS than they do in FAT. The following items are unique to NTFS. Instead of keeping the filenames in folder files, the entire file structure of NTFS is retained in a flat file database called the Master File Table (MFT):

- Improved support for metadata
- Advanced data structuring improves performance and reliability
- Improved disk space utilization with a maximum disk size of 7.8 TB, or 2^{64} sectors; sector sizes can vary in NTFS and are most easily controlled using a third-party partitioning tool such as Partition Magic.
- Greater security

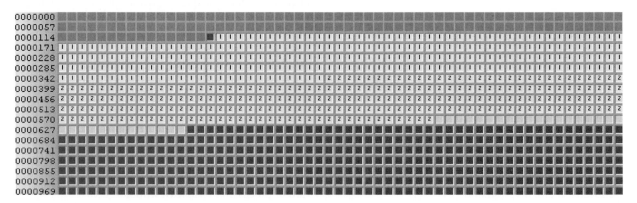

FIGURE 33.3   The sector view.

The Role of the Forensic Examiner in Investigations and File Recovery

The forensic examiner is at his best when he is searching for deleted files and attempting to reconstruct a pattern of user behavior. The sidebar "Oops! Did I Delete That?" first appeared in the Chicago *Daily Southtown* column "Bits You Can Use." In addition, this section also includes a discussion of data recovery and an insurance investigation article (see sidebar, "Don't Touch That Computer! Data Recovery Following Fire, Flood, or Storm").

Oops! Did I Delete That?

The file is gone. It's not in the recycle bin. You've done a complete search of your files for it, and now the panic sets in. It's vanished. You may have even asked people to look through their email because maybe you sent it to them (you didn't). Oops. Now what?

Hours, days, maybe even years of hard work seem to be lost. Wait! Don't touch that PC! Every action you take on your PC at this point may be destroying what is left of your file. It's not too late yet. You've possibly heard that things that are deleted are never really deleted, but you may also think that it will cost you thousands of dollars to recover deleted files once you've emptied the recycle bin. Suffice it to say, unless you are embroiled in complicated ediscovery or forensic legal proceedings where preservation is a requirement, recovering some deleted files for you may cost no more than a tune-up for your car.

Now the part where I told you: "Don't touch that PC!" I meant it. Seriously: Don't touch that PC. The second you realize you've lost a file, stop doing anything. Don't visit any Web sites. Don't install software. Don't reformat your hard drive, do a Windows repair, or install undelete software. In fact, if it's not a server or running a shared database application, pull the plug from the back of the PC. Every time you "write" to your hard drive, you run the risk that you are destroying your lost file. In the case of one author we helped, ten years of a book were "deleted." With immediate professional help, her files were recovered.

Whether you accidentally pulled your USB drive from the slot without stopping it first (corrupting your MFT), intentionally deleted it, or have discovered an "OS not found" message when you booted your PC, you need your files back and you need them now. However, if you made the mistake of actually overwriting a file with a file that has the same name and thereby replaced it, "Abandon hope all ye who enter here." Your file is trashed, and all that may be left are some scraps of the old file, parts that didn't get overwritten but can be extracted from file slack. If your hard drive is physically damaged, you may also be looking at an expensive recovery.

Here's the quick version of how deleted files become "obliterated" and unrecoverable:

Step 1: The MFT that contains a reference to your file marks the deleted file space as available.

Step 2: The actual sectors where the deleted file resides *might* be either completely or partially overwritten.

Step 3: The MFT record for the deleted file is overwritten and destroyed. Any ability to *easily* recover your deleted file at this point is lost.

Step 4: The sectors on the PC that contain your deleted file *are* overwritten and eventually only slight traces of your lost file remain. Sometimes the MFT record may be destroyed before the actual sectors are overwritten. This happens a lot, and these files are recoverable with a little extra work.

It's tremendously amazing how fast this process can occur. It's equally amazing how slowly this process can occur. Recently I retrieved hundreds of files from a system that had periodically been deleting files, and new files were written to the disk on a daily basis. Yet recovery software successfully recovered hundreds of complete files from nearly six months ago! A lot of free space on the disk contributed to this success. A disk that is in use and is nearly full will be proportionally less likely to contain old, deleted files.

The equipment and training investment to perform these operations is high, so expect that labor costs will be higher, but you can also expect some degree of success when attempting to recover files that have been accidentally deleted. Let me leave you with two dire warnings: Disks that have experienced surface damage (scored platters) are unrecoverable with current technology. And never, ever, ever disrupt power to your PC when it's performing a defrag. The results are disastrous.

Don't Touch That Computer! Data Recovery Following Fire, Flood, or Storm

Fire, flood, earthquakes, landslides, and other catastrophes often result in damaged cyber equipment—and loss of electronic data. For claims managers and adjusters, this data loss can manifest itself in an overwhelming number of insurance claims, costing insurers millions of dollars each year.

The improper handling of computers immediately following a catastrophic event is possibly one of the leading causes of data loss—and once a drive has been improperly handled, the chances of data retrieval plummet. Adjusters often assume a complete loss when, in fact, there are methods that can save or salvage data on even the most damaged computers.

Methods to Save or Salvage Data

One of the first steps toward salvaging cyber data is to focus on the preservation of the hard drive. Hard drives are highly precise instruments, and warping of drive components by even fractions of a millimeter will cause damage to occur in the very first moments of booting up. During these moments the drive head can shred the surface of the platters, rendering the data unrecoverable.

Hard drives are preserved in different ways, depending on the damaging event. If the drive is submerged in a flood, the drive should be removed and resubmerged in clean, distilled water and shipped to an expert. It is important that this is done immediately. Hard drive platters that are allowed to corrode after being exposed to water, especially if the drive experienced seepage, will oxidize and data will be destroyed. A professional can completely disassemble the drive to ensure that all of its parts are dry, determine what level of damage has already occurred, and then decide how to proceed with the recovery. Care must always be taken during removal from the site to prevent the drive from breaking open and being exposed to dust.

Fire or Smoke Damage

After a fire or a flood, the hard drive should not be moved and in no circumstances should it be powered up. A certified cyber forensic expert with experience in handling damaged drives should be immediately contacted. Typically, these experts will be able to dismantle the drive and move it without causing further damage. They are able to assess the external damage and arrive at a decision that will safely triage the drive for further recovery steps. Fire-damaged drives should never be moved or handled by laymen.

Shock Damage

Shock damage can occur when someone drops a computer or it is damaged via an automobile accident; in more catastrophic scenarios, shock damage can result when servers fall through floors during a fire or are even damaged by bulldozers that are removing debris. This type of crushing damage often results in bending of the platters and can be extensive. As in fire and flood circumstances, the drive should be isolated and power should not be applied.

A drive that has been damaged by shock presents a unique challenge: from the outside, the computer may look fine. This is typical of many claims involving laptop computers damaged during an automobile collision. If the computer consultant can verify that the drive was powered down at the time the accident occurred, most will be comfortable attempting to power up a drive that has been in a collision, to begin the data capture process. At the first sign of a change in the dynamics of the drive, a head clicking or a drive spinning down, power will be cut from the drive and the restoration will continue in a clean room where the drive will be opened up and protected from harmful dust.

The Importance of Off-Site Cyber Backup

One of the best ways to maximize cyber data recovery efforts is to have off-site cyber backup. For adjusters arriving at the scene, this should be one of the first questions asked. An offsite backup can take many forms. Some involve the use of special data centers that synchronize data constantly. There are companies that provide this service. Other backups, for smaller companies, may be as mundane (but effective) as removing a tape backup of critical data from the site on a daily basis. With proper rotation and several tapes, a complete backup of data is always offsite. Prices for these services vary widely depending on how much data needs to be backed up and how often.

Case Studies

Scenario 1

John ran a home-based IT business. After his home burned down, John posted an insurance claim for a $500,000 loss for lost income, damaged cyber equipment, and lost wages. He also charged the insurance company $60,000 for the three months he spent recovering data from the drives. Because he was only able to recover 25% of the data, he posted an additional claim for the cost of reconstructing the Web sites that he hosted from his home.

For the cyber forensic consultant, this case raised several questions. As an IT professional, John should have known better than to touch the hard drive and attempt to recover any of the data himself. Also, when a claimant intentionally or unintentionally inflicts damage on his or her own property after an event, who is responsible? Through a thorough evaluation of the circumstances and intense questioning of the claimant, the claim was eventually reduced to a substantially smaller amount.

Scenario 2

Sammie's Flowers has 113 retail outlets and one central headquarters where they keep photography, custom software, catalog masters, and the like. There is no offsite backup. Everything is on CD-ROMs or on the hard drive of the company's server.

One night lightning struck the headquarters building and it burned down. An IT appraiser lacking the appropriate cyber forensic skills evaluated the cyber equipment after the fire. No attempts were made to recover data from the hard drives or to start the computers; because of their damaged physical condition, they were simply thrown into a dumpster.

One year later, the insured filed a claim for $37 million. Under the terms of the insured's policy, coverage for valuable papers and business personal property was most pertinent to the case. The policy limit for valuable papers is small and easily reached. The coverage limit for business personal property, on the other hand, *will* cover the $37 million claim—if the court decides that the cyber data that was lost qualifies as "business valuable papers." Though this case is still pending, the cost of resolving this claim could be astronomic, and had a cyber data recovery expert been consulted, the claim amount could have been reduced by millions.

Scenario 3

Alisa, a professional photographer, was in a car accident that damaged her laptop computer. She had been using the PC at a rest stop prior to the accident and later reported to the adjuster that when she booted it up after the accident she heard "a strange clicking and clacking sound." Unfortunately for Alisa, that was the sound of data being destroyed. She posted a $500,000 claim to her insurance company under her business policy—including the cost of 2000 lost images and the cost of equipment, site, model, and agency fees for a one-day photography shoot. Had the PC, which had a noticeable crack in it caused by the accident, been professionally handled, the chances are good the data could have been recovered and the claim would have been significantly reduced.

Cyber equipment is always at risk of being damaged—whether by flood, fire, lightning, or other catastrophic means. However, damage does not always equal data loss. Indeed, companies and their adjusters can be quick to write off damaged storage media when, in fact, recovery may be possible. By taking the immediate measures of protecting the computers from touch and power and by calling in professional cyber forensic experts to assess the damage, insurers can reap the benefits in reduced claim amounts.

Password Recovery

The following is a short list of the ways and types of passwords that can be recovered. Many useful tools that can be downloaded from the Internet for free will crack open system files that store passwords. Software programs, such as Peachtree (a financial database), Windows 8, certain FTP programs, and the like all store passwords in a way that allows their easy retrieval.

Recovering license keys for software is often an important step in reconstructing or virtualizing a disk image. Like passwords, without a valid license key the software won't work. There are a number of useful programs that can recover software license keys from the registry of a computer that can be found with a quick Google search. Understanding the mind of the user can also be helpful in locating things such as password storage tools or simply thinking to search a computer for the word *password*. Many, many Web sites will pass the password down to a client machine through the Password field in HTML documents. Some developers have wised up to this "feature" and they strip it out before it comes down, but most of them do it on the client side. This means that with the proper intercepting tool, the password can be captured midstream on its way down to the client, before it gets stripped out.

Password cracking can be achieved with a minimal amount of skill and a great deal of patience. Having some idea of what the password is before cracking it will be helpful. You can also purchase both online services as well as software tools that will strip the password right out of a file, removing it completely. Word documents are particularly vulnerable, and zip files are particularly invulnerable. However, there is a method (and a free download) that can figure out the password of a zip file if a sample of a file that is known to be in the zip can be provided.

File Carving

In most investigations, the very first place a file system examination begins is with live files. Live files are those files that still have MFT entries. Link file, trash bin,

Outlook Temporary (OLK) folders, recent items, ISO lists, Internet history, TIF, and thumb databases all constitute a discernible, unique pattern of user activity. As such, they hold particular interest. By exploring these files an examiner can make determinations about file origins, the usage of files, the distribution of files, and of course the current location of the files. But sometimes the subject has been very clever and removed all traces of activity. Or the suspect item may be a server, used merely as a repository for the files. Or maybe someone just wants to recover a file that they deleted a long, long time ago (see sidebar, "Oops, Did I Delete That?").

When such need arises, the vast graveyard called the *unallocated clusters* could hold the last hope that the file can be recovered. By searching the unallocated clusters using a search tool designed for such things, and by using a known keyword in the file, one may locate the portion within the unallocated clusters where a file used to reside. Typically, search hits will be stored under a tab or in a particular area of the forensic toolset, and they may be browsed, one by one, along with a small excerpt from the surrounding bits. By clicking on the search hit, another pane of the software window may show a more expanded view of the hit location. If it is a document, with text, then that is great and you may see other words that were also known to have been in the target file. Now, in TV shows like *CSI*, of course the document is always there, and by running some reverse 128-bit decryption sequencer to an inverted 12-bit decryption sequencer that reloops the hashing algorithm through a 256-bit decompiler by rethreading it into a multiplexing file marker, they can just right click and say "export this" and the file will print out, even if it's not even on the computer that is being examined and never was. (Yes, I made all that up.)

In the real world, more often than not we find that our examinations are spurred and motivated and wholly created by someone's abject paranoia. In these cases, no amount of digging will ever create the evidence that they want to see. That leaves only creative use of time stamps on documents to attempt to create an aroma of guilt about the subject piece. Sometimes we find that even after rooting through 300 GB of unallocated clusters, leaving no stone unturned, the *file just isn't there*. But sometimes, all pessimism aside, we find little bits and pieces of interesting things all salted around throughout the unallocated clusters.

The first place to turn is the automated carvers. By familiarizing ourselves with the hexadecimal patterns of file signatures (and I've provided a nice table for you here), we may view the hex of the unallocated clusters in a hex editor or in the hex pane of the examination tool. Or possibly we already know the type of file. Let's say that we know the type of file because our client told us that they only use Word as their document editor. We scroll to the beginning of the section of text, which might look like this:

Figure sample file signature
From the text pane view of EnCase:
Ð Ï · â¡ ± á ·············· > ··· þ ÿ ·········
From the Hex view:
00 00 00 00 00 00 00 00 00 00 00 00 00 00 00 4F 6F 70 73
21 20 20 44 69 64
20 49 20 64 65 6C 65 74 65 20 74 68 61 74 3F 0D 42 79
20 53 63 6F 74 74 20
52 2E 20 45 6C 6C 69 73 0D 73 65 6C 6C 69 73 40 75 73
2E 72 67 6C 2E 63 6F
6D 0D 0D 54 68 65 20 66 69 6C 65 20 69 73 20 67 6F 6E
65 2E 20 20 49 74 92
73 20 6E 6F 74 20 69 6E 20 74 68 65 20 72 65 63 79 63
6C 65 20 62 69 6E 2E
20 59 6F 75 92 76 65 20 64 6F 6E 65 20 61 20 63 6F 6D
70 6C 65 74 65 20 73

Scrolling down in the text pane, we then find the following:

·············· *Oops! Did I delete that? By Scott R. Ellis The file is gone. It's not in the recycle bin. You've* ·······.

By simply visually scanning the unallocated clusters, we can pick up where the file begins and, if the file signature isn't in the provided list of signatures or if for some reason the carving scripts in the forensic software are incorrectly pulling files, they may need to be manually set up. Truly, for Word files, that is all you need to know. You need to be able to determine the end and the beginning of a file. Some software will ignore data in the file before and after the beginning and end of file signatures. This is true for many, many file types; I can't tell you which ones because I haven't tried them all. There are some file types that need a valid end-of-file (EOF) marker, but most don't. However, if you *don't* capture the true EOF (sensible marker or no), the file may look like garbage or all the original formatting will be scrambled or it won't open. Some JPEG viewers (such as Adobe Photoshop) will throw an error if the EOF is not found. Others, such as Internet Explorer, won't even notice. Here's the trick—and it is a trick, and don't let anyone tell you differently; they might not teach this in your average university cyber forensics class: Starting with the file signature, highlight as many of the unallocated clusters *after* the file signature that you think would possibly be big enough to hold the entire file size. Now double that, and export it as raw data. Give it a .DOC extension and open it in Word. *Voilá!* The file has been reconstructed. Word will know where the document ends and it will show you that document. If you happen to catch a few extra documents at the end, or a JPG or whatever, Word will ignore them and show only the first document.

Unless some sort of drastic "wiping action" has taken place, as in the use of a third-party utility to delete data, I have almost always found that a great deal of deleted data is *immediately* available in EnCase (forensic software) within 20–25 minutes after a hard disk image is mounted, simply by running "recover folders" and sitting back and waiting while it runs. This is especially true when the drive has not been used at all since the time the data was deleted. Preferably, counsel will have taken steps to ensure that this is the case when a computer is the prime subject of an investigation. Often this is not the case, however. Many attorneys, IT, and HR directors "poke around" for information all on their own.

It is conceivable that up to 80% of deleted data on a computer may be readily available, without the necessity of carving, for up to two or three years, as long as the computer hasn't seen extreme use (large amounts of files, or large amounts of copying and moving of very large files) that could conceivably overwrite the data.

Even so, searching unallocated clusters for file types typically does not require the creation of an index. Depending on the size of the drive, it may take four or five hours for the carving process to complete, and it may or may not be entirely successful, depending on the type of files that are being carved. For example, MPEG videos do not carve well at all, but there are ways around that. DOC and XLS files usually carve out quite nicely.

Indexing is something that is done strictly for the purpose of searching massive amounts of files for large numbers of keywords. We rarely use EnCase to search for keywords; we have found it better to use Relativity, our review environment, to allow the people who are interested in the keywords to do the keyword searching themselves as they perform their review. Relativity is built on an SQL platform on which indexing is a known and stable technology.

In other words (as in the bottom line), spending 15 to 25 minutes with a drive, an experienced examiner can provide a very succinct answer as to how long it would take to provide the files that they want. And, very likely, the answer could be, "Another 30 minutes and it will be yours." Including time to set up, extract, and copy to disk, if everything is in perfect order, two hours is the upper limit. This is based on the foundation that the deleted data they are looking for was deleted in the last couple of weeks of the use of the computer. If they need to go back more than a couple of months, an examiner may end up carving into the unallocated clusters to find "lost" files—these are files for which part of or all of the master file table entry has been obliterated and portions of the files themselves may be overwritten.

Carving is considered one of the consummate forensic skills. Regardless of the few shortcuts that exist, carving requires a deep, disk-level knowledge of how files are stored, and it requires a certain intuition that cannot be "book taught." Examiners gain this talent from years of looking at raw disk data. Regardless, even the most efficient and skilled of carvers will turn to their automated carving tools. Two things that the carving tools excel at is carving out images and print spool files (EMFs). What are they really bad at? The tools I use don't even begin to work properly to carve out email files. General regular program (GREP) searching doesn't provide for branching logic, so you can't locate a qualified email header, every single time, and capture the end of it. The best you can do is create your own script to carve out the emails. GREP does not allow for any sort of true logic that would be useful or even efficient at capturing something as complex as the many variations of email headers that exist, but it does allow for many alterations of a single search term to be formulated with a single expression. For example, the words *house*, *housing*, *houses*, and *housed* could all be searched for with a single statement such as "hous [(e)|(es)|(ing)|(ed)]". GREP can be useful, but it is not really a shortcut. Each option added to a GREP statement doubles the length of time the search will take to run. Searching for *house(s)* has the same run time as two separate keywords for *house* and *houses*. It also allows for efficient pattern matching. For example, if you wanted to find all the phone numbers on a computer for three particular area codes, you could formulate a GREP expression like this. Using a test file and running the search each time, an expression can be built that finds phone numbers in any of three area codes:

(708)|(312)|(847) Checks for the three area codes
[\(]?(708)|(312)|(847)[\-\)\.]? Checks for parentheses and other formatting
[\(]?(708)|(312)|(847)[\-\)\.]?###[\-\.]?#### Checks for the rest of the number

This statement will find any 10-digit string that is formatted like a phone number, as well as any 10-digit string that contains one of the three area codes. This last option, to check for any 10-digit number string, if run against an entire OS, will likely return numerous results that aren't phone numbers. The question marks render the search for phone number formatting optional.

The following are the characters that are used to formulate a GREP expression. Typically, the best use of GREP is its ability to formulate pattern-matching searches. In GREP, the following symbols are used to formulate an expression:

.   The period is a wildcard and means a space must be occupied by any character.

*   The asterisk is a wildcard that means any character or no character. It will match multiple repetitions of the character as well.

?   The character preceding the question mark must repeat 0 or 1 times. It provides instructions as to how to search for the character or grouping that precedes it.

+   This is like the question mark, only it *must* exist at least one or more times.

Matches a number.

[·]   Matches a list of characters. *[hH]i* matches *hi* and *Hi* (but not *hHi!*).

∧   This is a "not" and will exclude a part from a string.

[-]   A range of characters such as (a-z) will find any single letter, a through z.

\   This will escape the standard GREP search symbols so that it may be included as part of the search. For example, a search string that has the (symbol in it (such as a phone number) needs to have the parentheses escaped so that the string can be included as part of the search.

| This is an "or." See previous sample search for area codes.

\x   Searches for the indicated hex string.

By preceding a hex character with \x marks the next two characters as hexadecimal characters. Using this to locate a known hex string is more efficient than relying on it to be interpreted from Unicode or UTF.

Most forensic applications have stock scripts included that can carve for you. Many of the popular cyber forensics applications can carve for you. They have scripted modules that will run, and all you have to do is select the signature you want and *voilá*, it carves it right out of the unallocated clusters for you. Sounds pretty slick, and it is slick—when it works. The problem is that some files, such as MPEG video, don't have a set signature at the beginning and end of each file. So how can we carve them? Running an MPEG carver will make a mess. It's a far better thing to do a "carve" by locating MPEG data, highlighting it, exporting it to a file, and giving it an MPEG extension.

Things to Know: How Time Stamps Work

Let's take an example: Bob in accounting has been discovered to be pilfering from the cash box. A forensics examiner is called in to examine his cyber system to see if he has been engaging in any activities that would be against company policy and to see if he has been accessing areas of the network that he shouldn't be. They want to know what he has been working on. A quick examination of his PC turns up a very large cache of pornography. A casual glance at the Entry Modified time stamp shows that the images were created nearly one year before Bob's employment, so automatically the investigator disregards the images and moves onto his search for evidence of copying and deleting sensitive files to his local machine. The investigator begins to look at the deleted files. His view is filtered, so he is not looking at anything but deleted files. He leaves the view in "gallery" view so that he can see telltale images that may give clues as to any Web sites used during the timeframe of the suspected breaches. To his surprise, the investigator begins seeing images from that porn cache. He notices now that when a deleted file is overwritten, in the gallery view of the software the image that overwrote the deleted file is displayed. He makes the logical conclusion that the Entry Modified time stamp is somehow wrong.

On a Windows XP machine, an archive file is extracted. Entry Modified time stamps are xx:xx:xx, even though the archive was extracted to the file system on yy:yy:yy. Normally when a file is created on a system, it takes on the system date as its Date Created time stamp. Such is not the case with zip files.

Entry Modified, in the world of cyber forensics, is that illustrious time stamp that has cinched many a case. It is a hidden time stamp that users never see, and few of them actually know about it. As such, they cannot change it. A very little-known fact about the Entry Modified time stamp is that it is constrained. It can be no later than the Date Created time stamp. (This is not true in Vista.) When a zip file is created, the Date Created and Date Modified time stamps become the same.

Experimental Evidence

Examining and understanding how time stamps behave on individual PCs and operating systems provide some of the greatest challenges facing forensic examiners. This is not due to any great difficulty, but rather because of the difficulty in clearly explaining it to others. This examiner once read a quote from a prosecutor in a local newspaper that said, "We will clearly show that he viewed the image on three separate occasions." In court the defense's expert disabused her of the notion she held that Last Written, Last Accessed, Entry Modified, and Date Created time stamps were convenient little recordings of user activity. Rather, they are references mostly used by the operating system for its own arcane purposes. Table 33.1 compares the three known Windows time stamps with the four time stamps in EnCase.

XP

A zip file was created using a file with a Date Created time stamp of 12/23/07 10:40:53AM (see ID 1 in Table 19.2). It was then extracted and the time stamps were examined.

Using Windows XP compressed folders, the file was then extracted to a separate file on a different system (ID 2 in Table 33.2). Date Created and Entry Modified time stamps, upon extraction, inherited the original Date Created time stamp of 12/23/12 10:40:53AM and Last Accessed of 04/28/13 01:56:07PM.

TABLE 33.1 Comparison of Three Known Windows Time stamps with the Four EnCase Time Stamps.

Windows	EnCase	Purpose
Date Created	Date Created	Typically this is the first time a file appeared on a system. It is not always accurate.
Date Modified	Last Written	Usually this is the time when a system last finished writing or changing information in a file.
Last Accessed	Last Accessed	This time stamp can be altered by any number of user and system actions. It should not be interpreted as the file having been opened and viewed.
N/A	Entry Modified	This is a system pointer that is inaccessible to users through the Explorer interface. It changes when the file changes size.

TABLE 33.2 Date Created Time Stamp.

ID	Name	Last Accessed	File Created	Entry Modified
1	IMG_3521.CR2	04/28/08 01:56:07PM	12/23/07 10:40:53AM	03/15/08 09:11:15AM
2	IMG_3521.CR2	04/28/08 01:56:07PM	12/23/07 10:40:53AM	04/28/08 01:57:12PM

TABLE 33.3 Altering the Entry Modified Time Stamp.

ID	Name	Last Accessed	File Created	Entry Modified
1	*IMG_3521.CR2*	*04/28/08 01:56:07PM*	*12/23/07 10:40:53AM*	*03/15/08 09:11:15AM*
2	IMG_3521.CR2	05/21/08 03:32:01PM	12/23/07 10:40:53AM	05/21/08 03:32:01PM

The system Entry Modified (not to be confused with Date Modified) became 04/28/13 01:57:12PM.

Various operating systems can perform various operations that will, *en masse*, alter the Entry Modified time stamp (see Table 33.3). For example, a tape restoration of a series of directories will create a time stamp adjustment in Entry Modified that corresponds to the date of the restoration. The original file is on another system somewhere and is inaccessible to the investigator (because he doesn't know about it).

In Table 33.3, Entry Modified becomes a part of a larger pattern of time stamps after an OS event. On a computer on which most of the time stamps have an Entry Modified time stamp that is sequential to a specific timeframe, it is now more difficult to determine when the file actually arrived on the system. As long as the date stamps are not inherited from the overwriting file by the overwritten file, examining the files that were overwritten by ID2 (Table 19.3), can reveal a No Later Than time. In other words, the file could not have appeared on the system prior to the file that it overwrote.

Vista

A zip file was created using a file with a Date Created time stamp of dd:mm:yyyy(a) and a date modified of dd:mm:yy(a). Using Windows Vista compressed folders, the file was then extracted to a separate file on the same system. Date Modified time stamps, on extraction, inherited the original time stamp of dd:mm:yyyy(a), but the Date Created time stamp reflected the true date. This is a significant change from XP. There are also tools available that will allow a user to mass-edit time stamps. Forensic examiners must always bear in mind that there are some very savvy users who research and understand antiforensics.

Email Headers and Time Stamps, Email Receipts, and Bounced Messages

There is much confusion in the ediscovery industry and in cyber forensics in general about how best to interpret email time stamps. Though it might not offer the perfect "every case" solution, this section reveals the intricacies of dealing with time stamps and how to interpret them correctly.

Regarding sources of email, SMTP has to relay email to its own domain. HELO/EHLO allows a user to connect to the SMTP port and send email.

As most of us are aware, in 2007 the U.S. Congress enacted the Energy Policy Act of 2005 (http://www.epa.gov/oust/fedlaws/publ_109-058.pdf, Section 110. Daylight Savings). This act was passed into law by President George W. Bush on August 8, 2005. Among other provisions, such as subsidies for wind energy, reducing air pollution, and providing tax breaks to homeowners for making energy-conserving changes to their homes, it amended the Uniform Time Act of 1966 by changing the start and end dates for Daylight Savings Time (DST) beginning in 2007. Previously, clocks would be set ahead by an hour on the first Sunday of April and set back on the last Sunday of October. The new law changed this as follows: Starting in 2007 clocks were set ahead one hour on the first Sunday of March and then set back on the first Sunday in November. Aside from the additional confusion now facing everyone when we review email and attempt to translate Greenwich Mean Time (GMT) to a sensible local time, probably the only true noteworthy aspect of this new law is the extra daylight time afforded to children trick-or-treating on Halloween. Many observers have questioned whether or not the act actually resulted in a net energy savings.

In a world of remote Web-based email servers, it has been observed that some email sent through a Web mail interface will bear the time stamp of the time zone wherein the server resides. Either your server is in the Central Time zone or the clock on the server is set to the wrong time/time zone. Servers that send email mark the header of the email with the GMT stamp numerical value (noted in bold in the example that follows) as opposed to the actual time zone stamp. For example, instead of saying 08:00 CST, the header will say 08:00 (-0600). The GMT differential is used so that every email client interprets that stamp based on the time zone and time setting of itself and is able to account for things like Daylight Savings Time offsets. This is a dynamic interpretation; if I change the time zone of my computer, it will change the way Outlook *shows* me the time of each email, but it doesn't actually physically change the email itself. For example, if an email server is located in Colorado, every email I send appears to have been sent from the Mountain Time zone. My email client interprets the Time Received of an email based on when my server received the mail, *not* when my email client downloads the email from my server.

If a server is in the Central Time zone and the client is in Mountain Time, the normal Web mail interface will not be cognizant of the client's time zone. Hence those are the times you'll see. I checked a Webmail account on a server in California that I use and it does the same thing. Here I've broken up the header to show step by step how it moved. Here is, first, the entire header in its original context, followed by a breakdown of how I interpret each transaction in the header:

****

Received: from p01c11m096.mxlogic.net (208.65.144.247) by mail.us.rgl.com

(192.168.0.12) with Microsoft SMTP Server id 8.0.751.0; Fri, 30 Nov 200721:03:15-0700

Received: from unknown [65.54.246.112] (EHLO bay0-omc1-s40.bay0.hotmail.com)

by p01c11m096.mxlogic.net (mxl_mta-5.2.0-1) with ESMTP id 23cd0574.3307895728.120458.00-105.p01c11m096. mxlogic.net (envelope-from

<timezone32@hotmail.com>); Fri, 30 Nov 2007 20:59:46-0700 (MST)

Received: from BAY108-W37 ([65.54.162.137]) by bay0-omc1-s40.bay0.hotmail.com

with Microsoft SMTPSVC(6.0.3790.3959); Fri, 30 Nov 2007 19:59:46-0800

Message-ID: <BAY108-W374BF59F8292A9D2C95F08BA7 20@phx.gbl>

Return-Path: timezone32@hotmail.com

Content-Type: multipart/alternative; boundary = " = _reb-r538638D0-t4750DC32"

X-Originating-IP: [71.212.198.249]

From: Test Account <timezone3@hotmail.com>

To: Bill Nelson <attorney@attorney12345.com>, Scott Ellis <sellis@us.rgl.com>

Subject: FW: Norton Anti Virus

Date: Fri, 30 Nov 2007 21:59:46 -0600

Importance: Normal

In-Reply-To: <BAY108-W26EE80CDDA1C4C632124ABA7 20@phx.gbl>

References: <BAY108-W26EE80CDDA1C4C632124ABA7 20@phx.gbl>

MIME-Version: 1.0

X-OriginalArrivalTime: 01 Dec 2007 03:59:46.0488

(UTC) FILETIME = [9CAC5B80:01C833CE]

X-Processed-By: Rebuild v2.0-0

X-Spam: [F = 0.0038471784; B = 0.500(0);

spf = 0.500; CM = 0.500; S = 0.010(2007110801);

MH = 0.500(2007113048); R = 0.276(1071030201529);

SC = none; SS = 0.500]

X-MAIL-FROM: <timezone3@hotmail.com>

X-SOURCE-IP: [65.54.246.112]

X-AnalysisOut: [v = 1.0 c = 0 a = Db0T9Pbbji75CibVO CAA:9

a = rYVTvsE0vOPdh0IEP8MA:]

X-AnalysisOut: [7 a = TaS_S6-EMopkTzdPlCr4MVJL5D QA:4 a = NCG-xuS670wA:10 a = T-0]

X-AnalysisOut:[QtiWyBeMA:10a = r9zUxlSq4yJzxRie7pAA:7 a = EWQMng83CrhB0XWP0h]

X-AnalysisOut: [vbCEdheDsA:4 a = EfJqPEOeqlMA:10 a = 37WNUvjkh6kA:10]

****

Looks like a bunch of garbage, right? Here it is, step by step, transaction by transaction, in reverse chronological order:

1. My server in Colorado receives the email (GMT differential is in bold):

Received: from p01c11m096.mxlogic.net (208.65.144.247) by mail.us.rgl.com

(192.168.0.12) with Microsoft SMTP Server id 8.0.751.0; Fri, 30 Nov 2007 21:03:15 -0700

2. Prior to that, my mail-filtering service in Colorado receives the email:

Received: from unknown [65.54.246.112] (EHLO bay0-omc1-s40.bay0.hotmail.com)

by p01c11m096.mxlogic.net (mxl_mta-5.2.0-1) with ESMTP id 23cd0574.3307895728.120458.00-105.p01c11m096. mxlogic.net (envelope-from

<timezone3@hotmail.com>); Fri, 30 Nov 2007 20:59:46 -0700 (MST)

— The email server receives the sender's email in this next section. On most networks, the mail server is rarely the same machine on which a user created the email. This next item in the header of the email shows that the email server is located in the Pacific Time zone. 65.54.246.112, the x-origin stamp, is the actual IP address of the computer that sent the email:

Received: from BAY108-W37 ([65.54.162.137]) by bay0-omc1-s40.bay0.hotmail.com

with Microsoft SMTPSVC(6.0.3790.3959); Fri, 30 Nov 2007 19:59:46 -0800

Message-ID: <BAY108-W374BF59F8292A9D2C95F08 BA720@phx.gbl>

Return-Path: timezone310@hotmail.com

— This content was produced on the server where the Webmail application resides. Technically, the email was created on the Web client application with only one degree of separation between the originating IP and the sender IP. By examining the order and type of IP addresses logged in the header, a trail can be created that shows the path of mail servers that the email traversed before arriving at its destination. This machine is the one that is likely in the Central Time zone, since it can be verified by the -0600 in the following. The X-originating IP address is the IP address of the sender's external Internet connection IP address in her house and the X-Source IP address is the IP address of the Webmail server she logged into on this day. This IP address is also subject to change because they have many Webmail servers as well. In fact, comparisons to older emails sent on different dates show that it is different. Originating IP address is also subject to change since a DSL or cable Internet is very likely a dynamic account, but it (likely) won't change as frequently as the X-source:

Content-Type: multipart/alternative; boundary = "=_reb-r538638D0-t4750DC32"
X-Originating-IP: [71.212.198.249]
From: Test Account <@hotmail.com>
To: Bill Nelson <attorney@attorney12345.com>, Scott Ellis <sellis@us.rgl.com>
Subject: FW: Norton Anti Virus
Date: Fri, 30 Nov 2007 21:59:46 **-0600**
Importance: Normal
In-Reply-To: <BAY108-W26EE80CDDA1C4C632124 ABA 720@phx.gbl>
References: <BAY108-W26EE80CDDA1C4C632124 ABA7 20@phx.gbl>
MIME-Version: 1.0
X-OriginalArrivalTime: 01 Dec 2007 03:59:46.0488 (UTC) FILETIME = [9CAC5B80:01C833CE]
X-Processed-By: Rebuild v2.0-0
X-Spam: [F = 0.0038471784; B = 0.500(0); spf = 0.500; CM = 0.500; 5 = 0.010(2007110801); MH = 0.500 (2007113 048); R = 0.276(1071030201529); SC = none; SS = 0.500]
X-MAIL-FROM: <timezone310@hotmail.com>
X-SOURCE-IP: [65.54.246.112]
X-AnalysisOut:
[v = 10c = 0a = Db0T9Pbbji75CibVOCAA:9 a = rYVTvsE0vOPdh0IEP8MA:]
X-AnalysisOut:[7a = TaS_S6-EMopkTzdPlCr4MVJL5DQA:4 a = NCG-xuS670wA:10a = T-0]

X-AnalysisOut: [QtiWyBeMA:10 a = r9zUxlSq4yJzxRie 7p AA:7 a = EWQMng83CrhB0XWP0h]
X-AnalysisOut: [vbCEdheDsA:4 a = EfJqPEOeqlMA:10 a = 37WNUvjkh6kA:10]
From: *Test Account [mailto:timezone310@hotmail.com*
Sent: *Friday, November 30, 2007 10:00 PM*
To: *Bill Nelson; Scott Ellis*
Subject: *FW: Norton Anti Virus*
Bill and Scott,
By the way, it was 8:57 my time when I sent the last email, however, my hotmail shows that it was 9:57 pm. Not sure if their server is on Central time or not. Scott, can you help with that question? Thanks.
Anonymous
From:*timezone3@hotmail.com*
To:*attorney@attorney12345.com; sellis@us.rgl.com*
CC:*timezone310@hotmail.com*
Subject: Norton Anti Virus
Date: Fri, 30 Nov 2007 21:57:16 -0600
Bill and Scott,
I am on the computer now and have a question for you. Can you please call me?
Anonymous

Steganography "Covered Writing"

Steganography tools provide a method that allows a user to hide a file in plain sight. For example, there are a number of stego software tools that allow the user to hide one image inside another. Some of these do it by simply appending the "hidden" file at the tail end of a JPEG file and then add a pointer to the beginning of the file. The most common way that steganography is discovered on a machine is through the detection of the steganography software on the machine. Then comes the arduous task of locating 11 of the files that may possibly contain hidden data. Other, more manual stego techniques may be as simple as hiding text behind other text. In Microsoft Word, text boxes can be placed right over the top of other text, formatted in such a way as to render the text undetectable to a casual observer. Forensic tools will allow the analyst to locate this text, but on opening the file the text won't be readily visible. Another method is to hide images behind other images using the layers feature of some photo enhancement tools, such as Photoshop.

StegAlyzerAS is a tool created by Backbone Security to detect steganography on a system. It works by both searching for known stego artifacts as well as by searching for the program files associated with over 650 steganography toolsets. Steganography hash sets are also available within the NIST database of hash sets. Hash sets are databases of MD5 hashes of known unique files associated with a particular application.

6. FIRST PRINCIPLES

In science, *first principles* refer to going back to the most basic nature of a thing. For example, in physics, an experiment is *ab initio* (from first principles) if it only subsumes a parameterization of known irrefutable laws of physics. The experiment of calculation does not make assumptions through modeling or assumptive logic.

First principles, or *ab initio*, may or may not be something that a court will understand, depending on the court and the types of cases it tries. Ultimately the very best evidence is that which can be easily duplicated. In observation of a compromised system in its live state, even if the observation photographed or videoed may be admitted as evidence but the events viewed cannot be duplicated, the veracity of the events will easily be questioned by the opposition.

During an investigation of a defendant's PC, an examiner found that a piece of software on the computer behaved erratically. This behavior had occurred after the computer had been booted from a restored image of the PC. The behavior was photographed and introduced in court as evidence. The behavior was mentioned during a cross-examination and had not, originally, been intended as use for evidence; it was simply something that the examiner recalled seeing during his investigation, that the list of files a piece of software would display would change. The prosecution was outraged because this statement harmed his case to a great deal. The instability and erratic behavior of the software was one of the underpinnings of the defense. The examiner, in response to the prosecutor's accusations of ineptitude, replied that he had a series of photographs that demonstrated the behavior. The prosecutor requested the photos, but the examiner didn't have them in court. He brought them the next day, at which time, when the jury was not in the room, the prosecutor requested the photos, reviewed them, and promptly let the matter drop.

It would have been a far more powerful thing to have produced the photographs at the time of the statement; but it may have also led the prosecution to an *ab initio* effort—one that may have shown that the defense expert's findings were irreproducible. In an expert testimony, the more powerful and remarkable a piece of evidence, the more likely it is to be challenged by the opposition. It is an intricate game because such a challenge may ultimately destroy the opposition's case, since a corroborative result would only serve to increase the veracity and reliability of the expert's testimony. Whether you are defense, prosecution, or plaintiff, the strongest evidence is that which is irrefutable and relies on first

principles. Aristotle defined it as those circumstances where "for the same (characteristic) simultaneously to belong and not belong to the same (object) in the same (way) is impossible." In less obfuscating, 21st-century terms, the following interpretation is applicable: One thing can't be two different things at the same time in the same circumstance; there is only one truth, and it is self-evidentiary and not open to interpretation. For example, when a computer hard drive is imaged, the opposition may also image the same hard drive. If proper procedures are followed, there is no possible way that different MD5 hashes could result. Black cannot be white.

The lesson learned? Never build your foundation on irreproducible evidence. To do so is tantamount to building the case on "circumstantial" evidence.

7. HACKING A WINDOWS XP PASSWORD

There are many, many methods to decrypt or "hack" a Windows password. This section lists some of them. One of the more interesting methods of cracking passwords through the use of forensic methods is hacking the Active Directory. It is not covered here, but suffice it to say that there is an awesome amount of information stored in the Active Directory file of a domain server. With the correct tools and settings in place, Bitlocker locked PCs can be accessed and passwords can be viewed in plaintext with just a few simple, readily available scripts.

Net User Password Hack

If you have access to a machine, this is an easy thing, and the instructions to do it can easily be found on YouTube. Type **net users** at the Windows command line. Pick a user. Type **net user***username*****. (You have to type the asterisk or it won't work.) You will then, regardless of your privileges, be allowed to change any password, including the local machine administrator password.

Lanman Hashes and Rainbow Tables*

- The following procedure can be used to "reverse-engineer" the password from where it is stored in Windows. Lan Manager (or Lanman, or LM) has been used by Windows, in versions prior to Windows Vista, to store passwords that are shorter than 15 characters. The vast majority of passwords are stored in this format. LM hashes are computed via a short series of actions. The following items contribute to the weakness of the hash.
- Password is converted to all uppercase.
- Passwords longer than seven characters are divided into two halves. By visual inspection of the hash, this allows us to determine whether the second half is

padding. We can do this by viewing all the LM hashes on a system and observing whether the second halves of any of the hashes are the same. This will speed up the process of decrypting the hash.

- There is no salt. In cryptography, *salt* is random bits that are thrown in to prevent large lookup tables of values from being developed.

Windows will store passwords using the Lanman hash. Windows Vista has changed this. For all versions of Windows except Vista, about 70 GB of what are called *rainbow tables* can be downloaded from the Internet. Using a tool such as the many that are found on Backtrack will capture the actual hashes that are stored for the password on the physical disk. Analysis of the hashes will show whether or not the hashes are in use as passwords. Rainbow tables, which can be downloaded from the Web in a single 70 GB table, are simply lookup tables of every possible iteration of the hashes. By entering the hash value, the password can be easily and quickly reverse-engineered and access to files can be gained. A favorite method of hackers is to install command-line software on remote machines that will allow access to the Lanman hashes and will send them via FTP to the hacker. Once the hacker has admin rights, he owns the machine.

Password Reset Disk

Emergency Boot CD (EBCD) is a Linux-based tool that allows you to boot a computer that has an unknown password. Using this command-line tool, you can reset the administrator password very easily. It will not tell you the plaintext of the password, but it will clear it so that the machine can be accessed through something like VMware with a blank password.

Memory Analysis and the Trojan Defense

One method of retrieving passwords and encryption keys is through memory analysis—physical RAM. RAM can be acquired using a variety of relatively nonintrusive methods. HBGary.com offers a free tool that will capture RAM with very minimal impact. In addition to extracting encryption keys, RAM analysis can be used to either defeat or corroborate the Trojan defense. The Responder tool from HBGary (single-user license) provides in-depth analysis and reporting on the many malware activities that can be detected in a RAM environment. The Trojan defense is commonly used by innocent and guilty parties to explain unlawful actions that have occurred on their computers. The following items represent a brief overview of the types of things that can be accomplished through RAM analysis:

- A hidden driver is a 100% indicator of a bad guy. Hidden drivers can be located through analysis of the physical memory.
- Using tools such as FileMon, TCPView, and RegMon, you can usually readily identify malware infections. There is a small number of advanced malwares that are capable of doing things such as rolling up completely (poof, it's gone!) when they detect the presence of investigative tools or that are capable of escaping a virtualized host. All the same, when conducting a malware forensic analysis, be sure to isolate the system from the network.
- RAM analysis using a tool such as HBGary's Responder can allow reverse-engineering of the processes that are running and can uncover potential malware behavioral capabilities. As this science progresses, a much greater ability to easily and quickly detect malware can be expected.

User Artifact Analysis

There is nothing worse than facing off against an opposing expert who has not done his artifact analysis on a case. Due to an increasing workload in this field, experts are often taking shortcuts that, in the long run, really make more work for everyone. In life and on computers, the actions people take leave behind artifacts. The following is a short list of artifacts that are readily viewed using any method of analysis:

- Recent files
- OLK files
- Shortcuts
- Temporary Internet Files (TIF)
- My Documents
- Desktop
- Recycle Bin
- Email
- EXIF data

Users create all these artifacts, either knowingly or unknowingly, and aspects of them can be reviewed and understood to indicate that certain actions on the computer took place—for example, a folder in My Documents called "fast trains" that contains pictures of Europe's TGV and surrounding countryside, TIF sites that show the user booking travel to Europe, installed software for a Casio Exilim digital camera, EXIF data that shows the photos were taken with a Casio Exilim, and email confirmations and discussions about the planned trip all work together to show that the user of that account on that PC did very likely take a trip to Europe and did take the photos. Not that there is anything wrong with taking pictures of trains, but if the subject of the investigation is a suspected terrorist and he has ties with a group that was discovered to be planning an attack on a train, this evidence would be very valuable.

It is the sum of the parts that matters the most. A single image of a train found in the user's TIF would be virtually meaningless. Multiple pictures of trains in his TIF could also be meaningless; maybe he likes trains or maybe someone sent him a link that he clicked to take him to a Web site about trains. *It's likely he won't even remember having visited the site*. It is the forensic examiner's first priority to ensure that all the user artifacts are considered when making a determination about any behavior.

Recovering Lost and Deleted Files

Unless some sort of drastic "wiping action" has taken place, as in the use of a third-party utility to delete data or if the disk is part of a RAIDed set, I have almost always found that deleted data is *immediately* available in EnCase (forensic software I use) within 20 to 25 minutes after a hard disk image is mounted. This is especially true when the drive has not been used at all since the time the data was deleted.

Software Installation

Nearly every software installation will offer to drop one on your desktop, in your Start menu, and on your quick launch tool bar at the time of program installation. Whenever a user double-clicks on a file, a link file is created in the Recent folder located at the root of Documents and Settings. This is a hidden file.

Recent Files

In Windows XP (and similar locations exist in other versions), link files are stored in the Recent folder under Documents and Settings. Whenever a user double-clicks on a file, a link file is created. Clicking the Start button in Windows and navigating to the My Recent Documents link will show a list of the last 15 documents that a user has clicked on. What most users don't realize is that the C:\Documents and Settings\\$user name\$\Recent folder will potentially reveal *hundreds* of documents that have been viewed by the user. This list is indisputably a list of documents that the user has viewed. Interestingly, in Windows 2000, if the Preserve History feature of the Windows Media Player is turned off, no link files will be created. The only way to make any legitimate determination about the use of a file is to view the Last Accessed time, which has been shown in several cases to be inconsistent and unreliable in certain circumstances. Be very careful when using this time stamp as part of your defense or prosecution. It is a loaded weapon, ready to go off.

Start Menu

The Start menu is built on shortcuts. Every item in the Start file has a corresponding .LNK file. Examining Last Accessed or Date Created time stamps may shed light on when software was installed and last used.

Email

Extracting email is an invaluable tool for researching and finding out thoughts and motives of a suspect in any investigation. Email can be extracted from traditional client-based applications such as Outlook Express, Lotus Notes, Outlook, Eudora, and Netscape Mail as well as from common Webmail apps such as Gmail, Hotmail, Yahoo Mail, and Excite. Reviewing log files from server-based applications such as Outlook Webmail can show a user, for example, accessing and using his Webmail after employment termination. It is important that companies realize that they should terminate access to such accounts the day a user's employment is terminated.

Internet History

Forensic analysis of a user's Internet history can reveal much useful information. It can also show the exact code that may have downloaded on a client machine and resulted in an infection of the system with a virus. Forensic examiners should actively familiarize themselves with the most recent, known exploits.

Typed URLs is a registry key. It will store the last 10 addresses that a user has typed into a Web browser address field. I once had a fed try to say that everything that appeared in the drop-down window was a "typed" URL. This is not the case. The only definitive source of showing the actual typed URLs is the registry key. Just one look at the screen shown in Figure 33.4 should clearly demonstrate that the user never would have "typed" all these entries. Yet that is exactly what a Department of Homeland Security Agent sat on the witness stand and swore, under oath, was true. In Figure 33.4, simply typing in **fil** spawns a list of URLs that were never typed but rather are the result of either the user having opened a file or a program having opened one. The highlighted file entered the history shown as a result of installing the software, not as a result of the user "typing" the filename. Many items in the history wind their way into it through regular software use, with files being accessed as an indirect result of user activity.

8. NETWORK ANALYSIS

Many investigations require a very hands-off approach in which the only forensics that can be collected is network

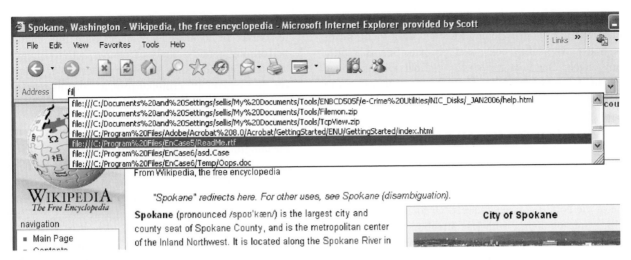

FIGURE 33.4 Spawning a list of URLs that were never typed (the Google one is deleted).

traffic. Every machine is assigned an IP address and a MAC address. It is like an IP address on layer 3, but the MAC address sits on Layer 2. It is quite like a phone number in that it is unique. Software that is used to examine network traffic is categorized as a *sniffer*. Tools such as Wireshark and Colasoft are two examples of sniffers. They can be used to view, analyze, and capture all the IP traffic that comes across a port.

Switches are not promiscuous, however. To view the traffic coming across a switch you can either put a hub in line with the traffic (between the target and the switch) and plug the sniffer into the hub with it, or ports can be spanned. Spanning, or mirroring, allows one port on a switch to copy and distribute network traffic in a way such that the sniffer can see everything. The argument could be made in court that the wrong port was accidentally spanned, but this argument quickly falls apart because all network packets contain both the machine and IP address of a machine. ARP poisoning is the practice of spoofing another user's IP address, however. This would be the smartest defense, but if a hub is used on a switched port, with the hub wired directly to the port, a greater degree of forensic certainty can be achieved. The only two computers that should be connected to the hub are the examiner and target machines.

Protocols

In the world of IP, the various languages of network traffic that are used to perform various tasks and operations are called *protocols*. Each protocol has its own special way of organizing and forming its packets. Unauthorized protocols viewed on a port are a good example of a type of action that might be expected from a rogue machine or employee. Network sniffing for email (SMTP and POP)

traffic and capturing it can, depending on the sniffer used, allow the examiner to view live email traffic coming off the target machine. Viewing the Web (HTTP) protocol allows the examiner to capture images and text from Web sites that the target is navigating, in real time.

Analysis

Once the capture of traffic has been completed, analysis must take place. Colasoft offers a packet analyzer that can carve out and filter out the various types of traffic. A good deal of traffic can be eliminated as just "noise" on the line. Filters can be created that will capture the specific protocols, such as VoIP. Examination of the protocols for protocol obfuscation can (if it is not found) eliminate the possibility that a user has a malware infection, and it can identify a user that is using open ports on the firewall to transmit illicit traffic. They sneak legitimate traffic over open ports, masking their nefarious activities over legitimate ports, knowing that the ports are open. This can be done with whitespace inside of an existing protocol, with HTTP, VoIP, and many others. The thing to look for, which will usually be clearly shown, is something like:

VOIP > SMTP

This basically means that VOIP is talking to a mail server. This is not normal.[3]

Another thing to look for is protocols coming off a box that isn't purposed for that task. It's all context: who should be doing what with whom. Why is the workstation suddenly popping a DNS server? A real-world example is when a van comes screaming into your neighborhood.

---

3. M. J. Staggs, FireEye, Network Analysis talk at CEIC 2008.

Two guys jump out and break down the door of your house and grab your wife and kids and drag them out of the house. Then they come and get you. Seems a little fishy, right? But it is a perfectly normal thing to have happen if the two guys are firemen, the van was a fire truck, and your house is on fire.

9. CYBER FORENSICS APPLIED

This section details the various ways in which cyber forensics is applied professionally. By no means does this cover the extent to which cyber forensics is becoming one of the hottest computer careers. It focuses on the consulting side of things, with less attention to corporate or law enforcement applications. Generally speaking, the average forensic consultant handles a broader variety of cases than corporate or law enforcement disciplines, with a broader applicability.

10. TRACKING, INVENTORY, LOCATION OF FILES, PAPERWORK, BACKUPS, AND SO ON

These items are all useful areas of knowledge in providing consultative advisement to corporate, legal, and law-enforcement clients. During the process of discovery and warrant creation, knowledge of how users store and access data at a very deep level is critical to success.

Testimonial

Even if the work does not involve the court system directly—for example, a technician that provides forensic backups of computers and is certified—you may someday be called to provide discovery in a litigation matter. Subsequently, you may be required to testify.

Experience Needed

In cyber forensics, the key to a successful technologist is experience. Nothing can substitute for experience, but a good system of learned knowledge that represents at least the last 10 years is welcome.

Job Description, Technologist

Practitioners must possess extreme abilities in adapting to new situations. The environment is always changing.

Job description:
Senior Forensic Examiner and eDiscovery Specialist Prepared by Scott R. Ellis, 11/01/2007.

- Forensics investigative work which includes imaging hard drives, extracting data and files for ediscovery production, development of custom scripts as required to extract or locate data. On occasion this includes performing detailed analyses of user activity, images, and language that may be of an undesirable, distasteful, and potentially criminal format. For this reason, a manager must be notified immediately upon the discovery of any such materials.
- Creation of detailed reports that lay out findings in a meaningful and understandable format. All reports will be reviewed and OK'd by manager before delivery to clients.
- Use of software tools such as FTK, EnCase, VMware, Recovery for Exchange, IDEA, LAW, and Relativity.
- Processing ediscovery and some paper discovery.
- Be responsive to opportunities for publication such as papers, articles, blog, or book chapter requests. All publications should be reviewed by manager and marketing before being submitted to requestor.
- Use technology such as servers, email, time reporting, and scheduling systems to perform job duties and archive work in client folders.
- Managing lab assets (installation of software, Windows updates, antivirus, maintaining backup strategy, hardware installation, tracking hardware and software inventory).
- Some marketing work
- Work week will be 40 hours per week, with occasional weekends as needed to meet customer deadlines.
- Deposition or testimony as needed.
- Occasional evenings and out of town to accommodate client schedules for forensic investigative work.
- Occasional evenings and out of town to attend seminars, CPE or technology classes as suggested by self or by manager, and marketing events.
- Other technology related duties as may be assigned by manager in the support of the company mission as it relates to technology or forensic technology matters.

Job Description Management

A manager in cyber forensics is usually a working manager. He is responsible for guiding and developing staff as well as communicating requirements to the executive level. His work duties will typically encompass everything mentioned in the previous description.

Commercial Uses

Archival, ghosting images, dd, recover lost partitions, etc. are all applications of cyber forensics at a commercial level. Data recovery embraces a great many of the practices typically attributed to cyber forensics. Archival and retrieval of information for any number of purposes, not just litigation, is required as is a forensic level of system knowledge.

Solid Background

To become a professional practitioner of cyber forensics, there are three requirements to a successful career. Certainly there are people, such as many who attain certification through law-enforcement agencies, that have skipped or bypassed completely the professional experience or scientific training necessary to be a true cyber forensic scientist. That is not to degrade the law-enforcement forensic examiner. His mission is traditionally quite different from that of a civilian, and these pros are frighteningly adept and proficient at accomplishing their objective, which is to locate evidence of criminal conduct and prosecute in court. Their lack of education in the traditional sense should never lead one to a desultory conclusion. No amount of parchment will ever broaden a mind; the forensic examiner must have a broad mind that eschews constraints and boxed-in thinking.

The background needed for a successful career in cyber forensics is much like that of any other except that, as a testifying expert, publication will give greater credence to a testimony than even the most advanced pedigree. The exception would be the cyber forensic scientist who holds a Ph. D. and happened to write her doctoral thesis on just the thing that is being called into question on the case. Interestingly, at this time, this author has yet to meet anyone with a Ph. D. (or any university degree for that matter), in cyber forensics. We can then narrow down the requirements to these three items. Coincidentally, these are also the items required to qualify as an expert witness in most courts:

- Education
- Programming and Experience
- Publications

The weight of each of these items can vary. To what degree depends on who is asking, but suffice it to say that a deficiency in any area may be overcome by strengths in the other two. The following sections provide a more in-depth view of each requirement.

Education/Certification

A strong foundation at the university level in mathematics and science provides the best mental training that can be obtained in cyber forensics. Of course, anyone with an extremely strong understanding of computers can surpass and exceed any expectations in this area. Of special consideration are the following topics. The best

forensic examiner has a strong foundation in these areas and can qualify not just as a forensic expert with limited ability to testify as to the functions and specific mechanical abilities of software, but as a cyber expert who can testify to the many aspects of both hardware and software.

Understand how database technologies, including MS SQL, Oracle, Access, My SQL, and others, interact with applications and how thin and fat clients interact and transfer data. Where do they store temporary files? What happens during a maintenance procedure? How are indexes built, and is the database software disk aware?

Programming and Experience

Background in cyber programming is an essential piece. The following software languages must be understood by any well-rounded forensic examiner:

- Java
- JavaScript
- ASP/.NET
- HTML
- XML
- Visual Basic
- SQL

Develop a familiarity with the purpose and operation of technologies that have not become mainstream but have a devoted cult following. At one time such things as virtualization, Linux, and even Windows lived on the bleeding edge, but from being very much on the "fringe" have steadily become more mainstream.

- If it runs on a computer and has an installed base of greater than 10,000 users, it is worth reviewing.
- Internet technologies should be well understood. JavaScript, Java, HTML, ASP, ASPRX, cold fusion, databases, etc. are all Internet technologies that may end up at the heart of a forensic examiner's investigation.
- Experience. Critical to either establishing oneself in a career as a corporate cyber forensic examiner or as a consultant, experience working in the field provides the confidence and knowledge-base needed to successfully complete a forensic examination. From cradle to grave, from the initial interviews with the client to forensic collection, examination, reporting, and testifying, experience will guide every step. No suitable substitute exists. Most forensic examiners come into the career later in life after serving as a network or software consultant. Some arrive in this field after years in law enforcement where almost anyone who can turn on a computer winds up taking some cyber forensic training.

Communications

- Cyber forensics is entirely about the ability to look at a cyber system and subsequently explain, in plain English, the analysis. A typical report may consist of the following sections:
  - Summary
  - Methodology
  - Narrative
  - Healthcare information data on system
  - User access to credit-card numbers
  - Date range of possible breach and order handlers
  - Distinct list of operators
  - Russell and Crist Handlers
  - All other users logged in during Crist/Russel Logins
- Login failures activity coinciding with account activity
- All Users:
  - User access levels possible ingress/egress
  - Audit trail
  - Login failures
  - Conclusion
  - Contacts/examiners

Each section either represents actual tables, images, and calculated findings, or it represents judgments, impressions, and interpretations of those findings. Finally, the report should contain references to contacts involved in the investigation. A good report conveys the big picture, and translates findings into substantial knowledge without leaving any trailing questions asked and unanswered. Sometimes findings are arrived at through a complex procedure such as a series of SQL queries. Conclusions that depend on such findings should be as detailed as necessary so that opposing experts can reconstruct the findings without difficulty.

Almost any large company requires some measure of forensic certified staff. Furthermore, the forensic collection and ediscovery field continues to grow. Virtually every branch of law enforcement—FBI, CIA, Homeland Security, and state and local agencies—all use cyber forensics to some degree. Accounting firms and law firms of almost any size greater than 20 need certified forensic and ediscovery specialists that can both support their forensic practice areas as well as grow business.

Publications

Publishing articles in well-known trade journals goes a long way toward establishing credibility. The following things are nearly always true:

- A long list of publications not only creates in a jury the perception that the expert possess special knowledge that warrants publication; it also shows the expert's ability to communicate. Articles published on the Internet typically do not count unless they are for well-known publications that have a printed publication as well as an online magazine.
- Publishing in and of itself creates a certain amount of risk. Anything that an expert writes or says or posts online may come back to haunt him in court. Be sure to remember to check, double check, and triple check anything that could be of questionable interpretation.
- When you write, you get smarter. Writing forces an author to conduct research and refreshes the memory on long unused skills.

Getting published in the first place is perhaps the most difficult task. Make contact with publishers and editors at trade shows. Ask around, and seek to make contact and establish relationships with published authors and bloggers. Most important, always seek to gain knowledge and deeper understanding of the work.

11. TESTIFYING AS AN EXPERT

Testifying in court is difficult work. As with any type of performance, the expert testifying must know her material, inside and out. She must be calm and collected and have confidence in her assertions. Often, degrees of uncertainty may exist within a testimony. It is the expert's duty to convey those "gray" areas with clarity and alacrity. She must be able to confidently speak of things in terms of degrees of certainty and clear probabilities, using language that is accessible and readily understood by the jury.

In terms of degrees of certainty, often we find ourselves discussing the "degree of difficulty" of performing an operation. This is usually when judges ask whether or not an operation has occurred through direct user interaction or through an automated, programmatic, or normal maintenance procedure. For example, it is well within the normal operation of complex database software to reindex or compact its tables and reorganize the way the data is arranged on the surface of the disk. It is not, however, within the normal operation of the database program to completely obliterate itself and all its program, help, and system files 13 times over a period of three weeks, all in the time leading up to requests for discovery from the opposition. Such information, when forensically available, will then be followed by the question of "Can we know *who* did it?" And that question, if the files exist on a server where security is relaxed, can be nearly impossible to answer.

Degrees of Certainty

Most cyber forensic practitioners ply their trade in civil court. A typical case may involve monetary damages or loss. From a cyber forensics point of view, evidence that you have extracted from a computer may be used by the attorneys to establish liability, that the plaintiff was damaged by the actions of the defendant. Your work may be the lynchpin of the entire case. You cannot be wrong. The burden to prove the amount of damages is less stringent once you've established that damage was inflicted, and since a single email may be the foundation for that proof, its provenance should prevail under even the most expert scrutiny. Whether or not the damage was inflicted may become a point of contention that the defense uses to pry and crack open your testimony.

The following sections may prove useful in your answers. The burden of proof will fall on the defense to show that the alleged damages are not accurate. There are three general categories of "truth" that can be used to clarify for a judge, jury, or attorney the weight of evidence. See the section on "Rules of Evidence" for more on things such as relevance and materiality.

Generally True

Generally speaking, something is generally true if under normal and general use the same thing always occurs. For example, if a user deletes a file, generally speaking it will go into the recycle bin. This is not true if:

- The user holds down a Shift key when deleting
- The recycle bin option "Do not move files to the recycle bin. Remove files immediately when deleted," is selected

- An item is deleted from a server share or from another computer that is accessing a local user share

Reasonable Degree of Certainty

If it smells like a fish and looks like a fish, generally speaking, it is a fish. However, without dissection and DNA analysis, there is the possibility that it is a fake, especially if someone is jumping up and down and screaming that it is a fake. Short of expensive testing, one may consider other factors. Where was the fish found? Who was in possession of the fish when it was found? We begin to rely on more than just looking at the fish to see if it is a fish.

Cyber forensic evidence is much the same (see checklist: "An Agenda For Action For Retrieval And Identification Of Evidence"). For example, in an employment dispute, an employee may be accused of sending sensitive and proprietary documents to her personal Webmail account. The employer introduces forensic evidence that the files were sent from her work email account during her period of employment on days when she was in the office.

Pretty straightforward, right? Not really. Let's go back in time to two months before the employee was fired. Let's go back to the day after she got a very bad performance review and left for the day because she was so upset. Everyone knew what was going on, and they knew that her time is limited. Two weeks later she filed an EEOC complaint. The IT manager in this organization, a seemingly mild-mannered, helpful savant, was getting

---

An Agenda for Action for Retrieval and Identification of Evidence

The computer forensics specialist should ensure that the following provisional list of actions for retrieval and identification of evidence are adhered to (Check All Tasks Completed):

_____1. Protect the subject computer system during the forensic examination from any possible alteration, damage, data corruption, or virus introduction.

_____2. Discover all files on the subject system. This includes existing normal files, deleted yet remaining files, hidden files, password-protected files, and encrypted files.

_____3. Recover all (or as much as possible) of discovered deleted files.

_____4. Reveal (to the greatest extent possible) the contents of hidden files as well as temporary or swap files used by both the application programs and the operating system.

_____5. Access (if possible and legally appropriate) the contents of protected or encrypted files.

_____6. Analyze all possibly relevant data found in special (and typically inaccessible) areas of a disk. This includes but is not limited to what is called unallocated space on a disk (currently unused, but possibly the repository of previous data that is relevant evidence), as well as slack space in a file (the remnant area at the end of a file in the last assigned disk cluster, that is unused by current file data, but once again, may be a possible site for previously created and relevant evidence).

_____7. Print out an overall analysis of the subject computer system, as well as a listing of all possibly relevant files and discovered file data.

_____8. Provide an opinion of the system layout; the file structures discovered; any discovered data and authorship information; any attempts to hide, delete, protect, and encrypt information; and anything else that has been discovered and appears to be relevant to the overall computer system examination.

_____9. Provide expert consultation and/or testimony, as required.

ready to start his own company as a silent partner in competition with his employer. He wanted information. His partners want information in exchange for a 20% stake. As an IT manager, he had administrative rights and could access the troubled employee's email account and began to send files to her Webmail account. As an IT administrator, he had system and network access that would easily allow him to crack her Webmail account and determine the password. All he had to do was spoof her login page and store it on a site where he could pick it up from somewhere else. If he was particularly interested in keeping his own home and work systems free of the files, he could wardrive her house, hack her home wireless (lucky him, it is unsecured), and then use terminal services to access her home cyber, log into her Webmail account (while she is home), and view the files to ensure that they appear as "read." This scenario may seem farfetched but it is not; this is not hard to do.

For anyone with the IT manager's level of knowledge, lack of ethics, and opportunity, this is likely the *only* way that he would go about stealing information. There is no other way that leaves him so completely out of the possible running of suspects.

There is no magic wand in cyber forensics. The data is either there or it isn't, despite what Hollywood says about the subject. If an IT director makes the brash decision to reinstall the OS on a system that has been compromised and later realizes he might want to use a forensic investigator to find out what files were viewed, stolen, or modified, he can't just dial up his local forensics tech and have him pop in over tea, wave his magic wand, and recover all the data that was overwritten. Here is the raw, unadulterated truth: If you have 30 GB of unallocated clusters and you copy the DVD *Finding Nemo* onto the drive until the disk is full, nobody (and I really mean this), *nobody* will be able to extract a complete file from the unallocated clusters. Sure, they might find a couple of keyword hits in file slack and maybe, just maybe, if the stars align and Jupiter is in retrograde and Venus is rising, maybe they can pull a tiny little complete file out of the slack or out of the MFT. Small files, less than 128 bytes, are stored directly in the MFT and won't ever make it out to allocated space. This can be observed by viewing the $MFT file.

When making the determination "reasonable degree of forensic certainty," *all* things must be considered. Every possible scenario that could occur must flash before the forensic practitioner's eyes until only the most reasonable answer exists, an answer that is supported by all the evidence, not just part of it. This is called *interpretation*, and it is a weigh of whether or not a preponderance of evidence actually exists. The forensic expert's job is not to decide whether a preponderance of evidence exists. His job is to fairly, and truthfully, present the facts and his

interpretation of the individual facts. Questions an attorney might ask a cyber forensics practitioner on the stand:

- Did the user delete the file?
- Could someone else have done it?
- Could an outside process have downloaded the file to the computer?
- Do you know for certain how this happened?
- Did you see Mr. Smith delete the files?
- How do you know he did?
- Isn't it true, Mr. Expert, that you are being paid to be here today?

These are not "Yes or no" questions. Here might be the answers:

- I'm reasonably certain he did.
- Due to the security of this machine, it's very unlikely that someone else did it.
- There is evidence to strongly indicate that the photos were loaded to the computer from a digital camera, not the Internet.
- I am certain, without doubt, that the camera in Exhibit 7a is the same camera that was used to take these photos and that these photos were loaded to the computer while username CSMITH was logged in.
- I have viewed forensic evidence that strongly suggests that someone with Mr. Smith's level of access and permissions to this system did, in fact, delete these files on 12/12/2009.
- I'm not sure I didn't just answer that.
- I am an employee of The Company. I am receiving my regular compensation and today is a normal workday for me.

Be careful, though. Reticence to answer in a yes-or no fashion may be interpreted by the jury as uncertainty. If certainty exists, say so. But it is always better to be honest and admit uncertainty than to attempt to inflate one's own ego by expressing certainty where none exists. Never worry about the outcome of the case. You can't care about the outcome of the trial. Guilt or innocence cannot be a factor in your opinion. You must focus on simply answering the questions in front of you that demand to be answered.

Certainty without Doubt

Some things on a computer can happen only in one fashion. For example, if a deleted item is found in the recycle bin, there are steps that must be taken to ensure that "it is what it is":

- Was the user logged in at the time of deletion?
- Are there link files that support the use or viewing of the file?

TABLE 33.4 Example of a Forensic View of Files Showing Some Alteration or Masking of Dates.

Filename	Date Created	File Properties	Original Path
Kitty.jpg	5/12/2007	File, Archive	
summaryReport.doc	7/12/2007	File, Deleted, Overwritten	Kitty.jpg
Marketing_flyer.pdf	2/12/2008	File, Deleted, Overwritten	Kitty.jpg

- Was the user with access to the user account at work that day?
- What are the permissions on the folder?
- Is the deleted file in question a system file or a user-created file located in the user folders?
- Is the systems administrator beyond reproach or outside the family of suspects?

If all of these conditions are met, you may have arrived at certainty without doubt. Short of reliable witnesses paired with physical evidence, it is possible that there will always be other explanations, that uncertainty to some degree can exist. It is the burden of the defense and the plaintiff to understand and resolve these issues and determine if, for example, hacker activity is a plausible defense. I have added the stipulation of reliable witnesses because, in the hands of a morally corrupt forensic expert with access to the drive and a hex editor, a computer can be undetectably altered. Files can be copied onto a hard drive in a sterile manner that, to most trained forensic examiners, could appear to be original. Even advanced users are capable of framing the evidence in such a way as to render the appearance of best evidence, but a forensic examination may lift the veil of uncertainty and show that data has been altered, or that something *isn't quite right*. For example, there are certain conditions that can be examined that can show with certainty that the time stamps on a file have been somehow manipulated or are simply incorrect, and it is likely that the average person seeking to plant evidence will not know these tricks (see Table 33.4). The dates on files that were overwritten may show that "old" files overwrote newer files. This is impossible.

As shown here, the file kitty.jpg overwrites files that appear to have been created on the system after it. Such an event may occur when items are copied from a CDROM or unzipped from a zip file.

12. BEGINNING TO END IN COURT

In most courts in the world, the accuser goes first and then the defense presents its case. This is for the very logical reason that if the defense goes first, nobody would

know what they are talking about. The Boulder Bar has a Bar manual located at www.boulder-bar.org[4] that provides a more in-depth review of the trial process than can be presented here. Most states and federal rules are quite similar, but nothing here should be taken as legal advice; review the rules for yourself for the courts where you will be testifying. The knowledge isn't necessary, but the less that you seem to be a fish out of water, the better. This section *does not* replace true legal advice, it is strictly intended for the purpose of education. The manual located at the Boulder Bar Web site was created for a similar reason that is clearly explained on the site. The manual there was specifically developed without any "legalese," which makes it very easy to understand.

Defendants, Plaintiffs, and Prosecutors

When someone, an individual or an organization, decides it has a claim of money or damages against another individual or entity, they file a claim in court. The group filing the claim is the plaintiff, the other parties are the defendants. Experts may find themselves working for strictly defendants, strictly plaintiffs, or a little bit of both. In criminal court, charges are "brought" by an indictment, complaint, information, or a summons and complaint.

Pretrial Motions

Prior to the actual trial, there may be many, many pretrial motions and hearings. When a motion is filed, such as when the defense in a criminal case is trying to prevent certain evidence from being seen or heard by the jury, a hearing is called and the judge decides whether the motion has any merit. In civil court, it may be a hearing to decide whether the defense has been deleting, withholding, or committing other acts of discovery abuse. Cyber forensic practitioners will find that they may be called to testify at any number of hearings prior to the trial, and then they may not be needed at the trial at all,

---

4. Boulder Bar, www.boulder-bar.org/bar_media/index.html.

or the defense and plaintiff may reach a settlement and there will be no trial at all.

Trial: Direct and Cross-Examination

Assuming that there is no settlement or plea agreement, a case will go to trial. The judge will first ask the prosecutor or plaintiff whether they want to make an opening statement. Then the defense will be asked. Witnesses will be called, and if it is the first time appearing in the particular trial as an expert, the witness will be qualified, as discussed in a moment. The party putting on the witness will conduct a direct examination and the other side will very likely cross-examine the witness afterward. Frequently the two sides will have reviewed the expert report and will ask many questions relating directly to it. "Tricks" may be pulled by either attorney at this point. Certain prosecutors have styles and techniques that are used in an attempt to either rattle the expert's cage or simply intimidate him into a state of nervousness so that he will appear uncertain and unprepared. These prosecutors are not interested in justice. They are interested in winning because their career rotates around their record of wins/losses.

Rebuttal

After a witness has testified and undergone direct examination and cross-examination, the other side may decide to bring in an expert to discuss or refute. The defendant may then respond to the prosecution's witness in *rebuttal*. In criminal court, when the state or the government (sometimes affectionately referred to by defense attorneys as "The G") brings a case against an individual or organization, the attorneys that prosecute the case are called the state's attorney, district attorney, assistant U.S. attorney (AUSA), or simply prosecutor.

Surrebuttal

This is the plaintiff (or prosecutor's!) response to rebuttal. Typically the topics of surrebuttal will be limited to those topics that are broached in rebuttal, but the rules for this are probably best left to attorneys to decipher; this author has occasionally been asked questions that should have been deemed outside the bounds of the rebuttal. This could most likely be attributed to a lack of technical knowledge on the part of the attorneys involved in the case.

Testifying: Rule 702. Testimony by Experts

Rule 702 is a federal rule of civil procedure that governs expert testimony. The judge is considered the "gatekeeper," and she alone makes the decision as to whether or not the following rule is satisfied:

If scientific, technical, or other specialized knowledge will assist the trier of fact to understand the evidence or to determine a fact in issue, a witness qualified as an expert by knowledge, skill, experience, training, or education, may testify thereto in the form of an opinion or otherwise, if (1) the testimony is based upon sufficient facts or data, (2) the testimony is the product of reliable principles and methods, and (3) the witness has applied the principles and methods reliably to the facts of the case (U.S. Courts, Federal Rules of Evidence, Rule 702).

There are certain rules for qualifying as an expert. In court, when an expert is presented, both attorneys may question the expert on matters of background and expertise. This process is referred to as *qualification* and, if an "expert" does not meet the legal definition of expert, he may not be allowed to testify. This is a short bullet list of items that will be asked in qualifying as an expert witness:

- How long have you worked in the field?
- What certifications do you hold in this field?
- Where did you go to college?
- Did you graduate? What degrees do you have?
- What are your publications?

You may also be asked if you have testified in other proceedings. It is important to always be honest when on the stand. Perjury is a very serious crime and can result in jail time. All forensics experts should familiarize themselves with Federal Rules 701–706 as well as understand the purpose, intent, and results of a successful *Daubert* challenge, wherein an expert's opinion or the expert himself may be challenged and, if certain criteria are met, may have his testimony thrown out. It is accepted and understood that experts may have reasonably different conclusions given the same evidence.

When testifying, stay calm (easier said than done). If you've never done it, approaching the bench and taking the witness stand may seem like a lot of fun. In a case where a lot is on the line and it all depends on the expert's testimony, nerves will shake and cages will be rattled. The best advice is to stay calm. Drink a lot of water. Drinking copious amounts of water will, according to ex-Navy Seal Mike Lukas, dilute the affect of adrenalin in the bloodstream.

Testifying in a stately and austere court of law may seem like it is the domain of professors and other ivory tower enthusiasts. However, it is something that pretty much anyone can do that has a valuable skill to offer, regardless of educational background. Hollywood often paints a picture of the expert witness as a consummate professorial archetype bent on delivering "just the facts." It is true that expert witnesses demand top dollar in the consulting world. Much of this is for the reason that a great deal is at stake once the expert takes the stand. There is also a very high inconvenience factor. When on the stand for days at a time, one can't simply take phone calls, respond to emails, or perform other work for other clients. There is a certain amount of business interruption that the fees must make up for somehow.

Testifying is interesting. Distilling weeks of intense, technical investigation into a few statements that can be understood by everyone in the courtroom is no small task. It is a bit nerve wracking, and one can expect to have high blood pressure and overactive adrenalin glands for the day. Drinking lots of water will ease the nerves better than anything (nonpharmaceutical). It can have other side effects, however, but it is better to be calm and ask the judge for a short recess as needed than to have shaky hands and a trembling voice from nerves. Caffeine is a bad idea.

Correcting Mistakes: Putting Your Head in the Sand

The interplay of examiner and expert in the case of cyber forensics can be difficult. Often the forensic examiner can lapse into speech and explanations that are so common-place to her that she doesn't realize she is speaking fluent geek-speak. The ability to understand how she sounds to someone who doesn't understand technology must be cultivated. Practice by explaining to any six-year-old what it is you do.

Direct Testimony

Under direct questioning, your attorney will ask questions to which you will know the answer. A good expert will, in fact, have prepared a list of questions and reviewed the answers with the attorney and explained the context and justification for each question thoroughly. If it is a defense job, you will likely go first and testify as to what your investigation has revealed. Avoid using big words and do make some eye contact with the jury if you feel you need to explain something to them, but generally speaking, you should follow the attorney's lead. If she wants you to clarify something for the jury, you should do so, and at that time you should look at the jury. Generally, the rule of thumb is to look at the attorney who asked you the question. If the judge says, "Please explain to the jury . . ." then by all means, look at the jury.

Cross-Examination

The purpose of a cross-examination is to get the testifying expert to make a mistake or to discredit him. Sometimes (rarely) it is actually used to further understand and clarify things that were discussed in direct. In most cases, the attorney will do this by asking you questions about your experience or about the testimony the expert gave under direct. But there is another tactic that attorneys use. They ask a question that is completely unrelated to the topic you talked about. They know that the vast majority of time you spend is on the issues in your direct. For example, you may give a testimony about Last Accessed time stamps. Your entire testimony may be about Last Accessed time stamps. It may be the only issue in the case you are aware of. Then, on cross, the attorney asks a question about the behavior of the mail icon that appears on each line next to the subject line in an email. "Great," the expert thinks. "They recognize my expertise and are asking questions."

Stop. They are about to ask you an arcane question about a behavior in a piece of software in the hopes that you are overconfident and will answer from the hip and get the answer wrong. Because if you get this wrong, then everything else you said must be wrong, too. *Whenever* you are asked a question that does not relate to your previous testimony, pause. Pause for a long time. Give your attorney time to object. He might not know that he should object, but the fact is that you might get the answer wrong and even if there is no doubt in your mind that you know the answer, you should respond that you had not prepared to answer that question and would like to know more details. For example, what is the version of the software? What is the operating system? What service pack? If it is Office, what Office service pack? You need to make it clear that you need more information before you answer the question because, frankly, if the opposition goes down this road, they will try to turn *whatever* you say into the wrong answer.

As a forensic examiner, you may find yourself thinking that the reason they are asking these questions in such a friendly manner is because they forgot to ask their own expert and are trying to take advantage of your time because possibly this came up in a later conversation. This could very well be the case. Maybe the counselor is not trying to trip up the expert. Maybe the Brooklyn Bridge *can* be purchased for a dollar, too.

What is the best response to a question like this? If you give it a 10 count and your attorney hasn't objected, and the asking attorney has not abandoned the question, you may have to answer. There are many schools of thought on this. It is best to understand that a number of responses can facilitate an answer to difficult questions. One such response might be, "That is not really a forensics question" (if it's not), or "I'm not sure how that question relates back to the testimony I just gave." Or, if it is a software question, you can say, "Different software behaves differently, and I don't think I can answer that question without more details. I don't typically memorize the behavior of every piece of software, and I'm afraid that if I answer from memory I may not be certain." At the end of the day, the expert should only speak to what he knows *with certainty*. There is very little room for error. Attorneys can back-pedal a certain amount to "fix" a mistake, but a serious mistake can follow you for a very long time and can hamper future testimony. For example, if you make statements about time stamps in one trial, and then in the next trial you make statements that interpret them differently, there is a good chance that the opposition will use this against you.

Fortunately, when cyber forensic experts testify in a defense trial, the testimony can last a number of hours. Great care is usually taken by the judge to ensure that understanding of all the evidence is achieved. This can create a very long transcript that is difficult to read, understand, and recall with accuracy. For this reason, rarely will bits and pieces of testimony be used against a testifying expert in a future trial. This is not, of course, to say that it can't or won't happen.

It is important, in terms of both setting expectations and understanding legal strategy, for an expert witness to possess passable knowledge of the trial process. Strong familiarity with the trial process can benefit both the expert and the attorneys as well as the judge and the court reporter.

13. SUMMARY

Computers have appeared in the course of litigation for over 36 years. In 1977, there were 291 U.S. federal cases and 246 state cases in which the word *computer* appeared and which were sufficiently important to be noted in the Lexis database. In 2012, according to industry analysts, those figures in the U.S. have risen dramatically, to 3,250,514 U.S. federal cases and 2,750,177 state cases in which the word *cyber* appeared. In the UK, there were only 20 in 1977, with a rise to 220,372 in 2012. However, as early as 1968, the computer's existence was considered sufficiently important for special provisions to be made in the English Civil Evidence Act.

The following description is designed to summarize the issues rather than attempt to give a complete guide. As far as one can tell, noncontentious cases tend not to be reported, and the arrival of computers in commercial disputes and in criminal cases did not create immediate difficulties. Judges sought to allow cyber-based evidence on the basis that it was no different from forms of evidence with which they were already familiar: documents, business books, weighing machines, calculating machines, films, and audio tapes. This is not to say that such cases were without difficulty; however, no completely new principles were required. Quite soon, though, it became

apparent that many new situations were arising and that analogies with more traditional evidential material were beginning to break down. Some of these were tackled in legislation, as with the English 1968 Act and the U.S. Federal Rules of Evidence in 1976. But many were addressed in a series of court cases. Not all of the key cases deal directly with computers. But they do have a bearing on them as they relate to matters that are characteristic of cyber-originated evidence. For example, cyber-originated evidence or information that is not immediately readable by a human being is usually gathered by a mechanical counting or weighing instrument. The calculation could also be performed by a mechanical or electronic device.

The focus of most of this legislation and judicial activity was determining the admissibility of the evidence. The common law and legislative rules are those that have arisen as a result of judicial decisions and specific law. They extend beyond mere guidance. They are rules that a court must follow; the thought behind these rules may have been to impose standards and uniformity in helping a court test authenticity, reliability, and completeness. Nevertheless, they have acquired a status of their own and in some cases prevent a court from making ad hoc common sense decisions about the quality of evidence. The usual effect is that once a judge has declared evidence inadmissible (that is, failing to conform to the rules), it is never put to a jury; for a variety of reasons that will become apparent shortly. It is not wholly possible for someone interested in the practical aspects of computer forensics (that is, the issues of demonstrating authenticity, reliability, completeness, or lack thereof) to separate out the legal tests.

Finally, let's move on to the real interactive part of this Chapter: review questions/exercises, hands-on projects, case projects and optional team case project. The answers and/or solutions by chapter can be found in the Online Instructor's Solutions Manual.

CHAPTER REVIEW QUESTIONS/EXERCISES

True/False

1. True or False? Cyber forensics is the acquisition, preservation, and analysis of electronically stored information (ESI) in such a way that ensures its admissibility for use as either evidence, exhibits, or demonstratives in a court of law.

2. True or False? EnCase is a commonly used forensic software program that does not allow a cyber forensic technologist to conduct an investigation of a forensic hard disk copy.

3. True or False? On a server purposed with storing surveillance video, there are three physical hard drives.

4. True or False? Cyber forensics is one of the many cyber-related fields in which the practitioner will be found in the courtroom on a given number of days of the year.

5. True or False? A temporary restraining order (TRO) will often be issued in intellectual property or employment contract disputes.

Multiple Choice

1. Typically the forensic work done in a _____ will involve collecting information about one of the parties to be used to show that trust has been violated.
   A. Security incident
   B. Security breach
   C. Computer virus
   D. Divorce case
   E. Security policy

2. When one company begins selling a part that is _____ by another company, a lawsuit will likely be filed in federal court.
   A. Assigned
   B. Breached
   C. Detected
   D. Patented
   E. Measured

3. When a forensics practitioner needs to capture the data on a hard disk, he/she does so in a way that is:
   A. Forensically acquired
   B. Forensically mirrored
   C. Forensically sound
   D. Forensically imaged
   E. Forensically booted

4. Before conducting any sort of a capture, all steps should be documented and reviewed with a _____ before proceeding

   A. Observer
   B. Investigator
   C. Counsel
   D. Forensic Expert
   E. Judge

5. FAT12, FAT16, and FAT32 are all types of file systems?
   A. FAT12
   B. FAT16
   C. FAT32
   D. FAT64
   E. All of the above

EXERCISE

Problem

Why Cyber Forensics?

Hands-On Projects

Project

How long does data recovery take?

Case Projects

Problem

Are there instances where data cannot be recovered?

Optional Team Case Project

Problem

What can an organization do to protect their data and minimize their chances of losing data?

## Chapter 34

Cyber Forensics and Incident Response

Cem Gurkok

Verizon Terremark

1. INTRODUCTION TO CYBER FORENSICS

Cyber forensics and incident response go hand in hand. Cyber forensics reduces the occurrence of security incidents by analyzing the incident to understand, mitigate, and provide feedback to the actors involved. To perform incident response and related activities, organizations should establish an incident plan, a computer security incident response team (CSIRT), or a computer emergency response team (CERT) to execute the plan and associated protocols.

Responding to Incidents

In an organization, there is a daily occurrence of events within the IT infrastructure, but not all of these events qualify as incidents. It is important for the incident response team to be able to distinguish the difference between events and incidents. Generally, incidents are events that violate an organization's security policies, end-user agreements, or terms of use. SANS (sans.org) defines an incident as an adverse event in an information system or network, or the threat of an occurrence of such an event. Denial-of-service attacks, unauthorized probing, unauthorized entry, destruction or theft of data, and changes to firmware or operating systems can be considered incidents.

Generally, incident response handling comprises incident reporting, incident analysis, and incident response. Incident reporting takes place when a report or indications of an event are sent to the incident response team. The team then performs an incident analysis by examining the report, available information, and evidence or artifacts related to the event to qualify the event as an incident, correlate the data, and assess the extent of damage, source, and plan potential solutions. Once the analysis is over, then the team responds to mitigate the incident by containing and eradicating the incident. This is followed by the creation of a detailed report about the incident.

Applying Forensic Analysis Skills

Forensic analysis is usually applied to determine who, what, when, where, how, and why an incident took place. The analysis may include investigating crimes and inappropriate behavior, reconstructing computer security incidents, troubleshooting operational problems, supporting due diligence for audit record maintenance, and recovering from accidental system damage. The incident response team should be trained and prepared to be able to collect and analyze the related evidence to answer these questions. Data collection is a very important aspect of incident response since evidence needs to be collected in a forensically sound manner to protect its integrity and confidentiality. The incident responder needs to have the necessary skills and experience to be able to meet the collection requirements.

Forensic analysis is the process whereby the collected data is reviewed and scrutinized for the lowest level of evidence (deleted data in slack space) it can offer. The analysis may involve extracting email attachments, building timelines based on file times, reviewing browser history and in-memory artifacts, decrypting encrypted data, and malware reverse engineering. Once the analysis is complete, the incident responder will produce a report describing all the steps taken starting from the initial incident report till the end of the analysis. One of the most important skills a forensic analyst can have is note taking and logging, which becomes very important during the reporting phase and, if it ever comes to it, in court. These considerations related to forensics should be addressed in organizational policies. The forensic policy should clearly define the responsibilities and roles of the actors involved. The policies should also address the types of activities that should be undertaken under certain circumstances and the handling of sensitive information.

Distinguishing between Unpermitted Corporate and Criminal Activity

We previously defined incidents as events that are not permitted by a certain organization's policies. The incident response team should also be aware of several federal laws that can help them to identify criminal activity to ensure that the team does not commit a crime while responding to the incident. Some of these federal laws are:

- The Foreign Intelligence Surveillance Act of 1978
- The Privacy Protection Act of 1980
- The Computer Fraud and Abuse Act of 1984
- The Electronic Communications Privacy Act of 1986
- The Health Insurance Portability and Accountability Act of 1996 (HIPAA)
- The Identity Theft and Assumption Deterrence Act of 1998
- The USA Patriot Act of 2001

When an incident response team comes across incidents relevant to these laws, they should consult with their legal team. They should also contact appropriate law enforcement agencies.

2. HANDLING PRELIMINARY INVESTIGATIONS

An organization should be prepared beforehand to properly respond to incidents and mitigate them in the shortest time possible. An incident response plan should be developed by the organization and tested on a regular basis. The plan should be written in an easily understood and implemented fashion. The incident response team and related staff should also be trained on an ongoing basis to keep them up to date with the incident response plan, latest threats, and defense techniques.

Planning for Incident Response

Organizations should be prepared for incidents by identifying corporate risks, preparing hosts and network for containment and eradication of threats, establishing policies and procedures that facilitate the accomplishment of incident response goals, creating an incident response team, and preparing an incident response toolkit to be used by the incident response team.

Communicating with Site Personnel

All departments and staff that have a part in an incident response should be aware of the incident response plan and should be regularly trained as to its content and implementation. The plan should include the mode of communication with the site personnel. The site personnel should clearly log all activity and communication, including the date and time in a central repository that is backed up regularly. This information should be reviewed by all of the incident response team members to assure all

players are on the same page. Continuity and the distribution of information within the team is critical in the swift mitigation of an incident. An incident response team leader should be assigned to an incident and should make sure all team members are well informed and acting in a coordinated fashion.

Knowing Your Organization's Policies

An organization's policies will have an impact on how incidents are handled. These policies are usually very comprehensive and effective computer forensics policies that include considerations, such as contacting law enforcement, performing monitoring, and conducting regular reviews of forensic policies, guidelines, and procedures. Banks, insurance companies, law firms, governments, and health care institutions have such policies. Generally, policies should allow the incident response team to monitor systems and networks and perform investigations for reasons described in the policies. Policies may be updated frequently to keep up with the changes to laws and regulations, court rulings, and jurisdictions.

Forensics policies define the roles and responsibilities of the staff involved, including users, incident handlers, and IT staff. The policy indicates when to contact internal teams or reach out to external organizations. It should also discuss how to handle issues arising from jurisdictional conflicts. Policies also discuss the valid use of anti-forensics tools and techniques (sanitation and privacy versus malicious use, such as hiding evidence). How to maintain the confidentiality of data and the retention time of the data is also governed by organizational policies.

Minimizing the Impact on Your Organization

The goals of incident response include minimizing disruption to the computer and network operations, and limiting the exposure and compromise of sensitive data. To be able to meet these goals, incident response preparedness, planning, and proper execution following related policies are crucial. Incident response teams should minimize the downtimes of business critical systems once the evidence has been gathered and the systems have been cleared of the effects of the incident. Incident response teams should also identify an organization's risks and work with appropriate teams to continuously test and eliminate any vulnerability. Red team/blue team-type exercises whereby one team plays the role of malicious people and the other team the role of incident responders can provide good training for the staff and expose previously unknown risks and vulnerabilities. To minimize the impact of incidents, organizations should also establish and enforce security policies and procedures, gain management support for security policies and incident response, keep systems updated and patched, train IT staff and end users, implement a strong credential policy, monitor network traffic and system logs, and implement and routinely test a backup policy.

Identifying the Incident Life Cycle

SANS (sans.org) defines the phases of the incident life cycle (see Figure 34.1).

Preparation

It's a matter of when rather than if an incident will happen. Therefore, it has become a top priority for an organization to be prepared for an incident. To be prepared, an organization must establish security plans and controls, make sure these plans and controls are continuously reviewed and updated to keep up with the evolving threats, and see that they are enforced in case of an incident. Organizations should be prepared to act swiftly to minimize the impact of any incident to maintain business continuity. Incident response teams should continuously train; test, and update the incident response plan to keep their skills honed.

Detection, Collection, and Analysis

The detection of an incident involves the observance and reporting of irregularities or suspicious activities to security or IT department staff members. Once an event has been reported and escalated to the incident response team, the event is evaluated to determine whether it warrants classification as an incident. If the event has been classified as an incident, the incident response team should move in to perform data collection on the affected systems that will later be used for analysis. During collection, it is important to work in accordance with the organization's policies and procedures and preserve a valid chain-of-custody. The person involved in collecting the data should make sure that the integrity of the data is maintained on both the original and working copies of the

evidence. Once the relevant information has been captured, the incident response team should analyze the data to determine who, what, when, where, how, and why an incident took place.

Containment, Eradication, and Recovery

Once the involved systems and offending vectors have been analyzed, the incident response team should move in to contain the problem and eradicate it. It is crucial to contain an incident as fast as possible to minimize its impact on the business. This action can be as easy as disconnecting the system from the network or as hard as isolating a whole server farm from the production environment. Containment and eradication should strive to protect service integrity, sensitive data, hardware, and software. The recovery phase depends on the extent of the incidence. For example, it is easier to recover from an intrusion that was detected while it was affecting a single user than from an intrusion in which the lateral movement of the intruder is extensive. Most of the time, recovery involves backing up the unaffected data to use on the new systems. Operating systems and applications are usually installed fresh to avoid any type of contamination.

Post-Incident Activity

The post-incident phase involves documenting, reporting, and reviewing the incident. Documentation actually starts as soon as an event has been classified as an incident. The report should include all of the documentation compiled during the incident, the analysis methods and techniques, and all other findings. The person writing the report should keep in mind that the report might someday be used by law enforcement or in court. Finally, the incident response team should go over the report with the IT department and other involved parties to discuss how to improve the infrastructure to prevent similar incidents.

Capturing Volatile Information

Computer systems contain volatile data that is temporarily available either until a process exits or a system is shut down. Therefore, it is important to capture this data before making any physical or logical changes to the system to avoid tampering with evidence. Many incident responders have unwittingly destroyed memory-only resident artifacts by shutting down a system in the name of containment.

Volatile data is available as system memory (including slack and free space), network configuration, network connections and sockets, running processes, open files, login sessions, and operating system time. System memory can be captured by using sampling tools (MoonSols Windows Memory Toolkit, GMG Systems' KnTDD) as a

FIGURE 34.1   Incident response life cycle.

file and analyzed with the Volatility Framework to obtain the volatile data previously mentioned. The volatile data can also be captured individually with tools that are specific for each data type. The Microsoft Windows Sysinternals suite provides an extensive set of tools that can capture volatile data, such as login sessions, registry, process information, service information, shares, and loaded DLLs.

3. CONTROLLING AN INVESTIGATION

To control an investigation, the incident response team should have a forensics investigation plan, a forensics toolkit, and documented methods to secure the affected environment. An investigator should always keep in mind that the evidence collected and the analysis performed might be presented in court or used by law enforcement. Related documentation should be detailed and contain dates and times for each activity performed. To avoid challenges to the authenticity of evidence, investigators should be able to secure the suspect infrastructure, log all activity, and maintain a chain of custody.

Collecting Digital Evidence

It is important to an investigator to preserve data related to an incident as soon as possible to avoid the rapid degradation or loss of data in digital environments. Once the affected systems have been determined, volatile data should be captured immediately, followed by nonvolatile data, such as system users and groups, configuration files, password files and caches, scheduled jobs, system logs, application logs, command history, recently accessed files, executable files, data files, swap files, dump files, security software logs, hibernation files, temporary files, and complete file listings with times.

Chain of Custody and Process Integrity

The incident response team should be committed to collect and preserve evidence using methods that can support future legal or organizational proceedings. A clearly defined chain of custody is necessary to avoid allegations of tampering evidence. To accomplish this task, the team should keep a log of every entity who had physical custody of the evidence, document all of the actions performed on the evidence with the related date and time, make a working copy of the evidence for analysis, verify the integrity of the original and working copy, and store the evidence in secured location when not in use [1]. Also, before touching a physical system, the investigator should take a photograph of it. To ensure the integrity of the process, a detailed log should be kept of all the

collection steps, and information about every tool used in the incident response process should be included.

Advantages of Having a Forensic Analysis Team

Forensic analysis is usually associated with crime investigations. Nowadays, due to the increase in computer-related malicious activity and growing digital infrastructure, forensic analysis is involved in incident response, operational troubleshooting, log monitoring, data recovery, data acquisition, audits, and regulatory compliance. Therefore, organizations can no longer rely on law enforcement due to resource and jurisdictional limitations. A violation of organizational policies and procedures might not concern law enforcement, leaving the organization to its own devices. It has become evident to organizations that maintaining capabilities to perform forensic analysis has become a business requirement to satisfy organizational and customer needs. While it may make sense for some organizations to maintain an internal team of forensic analysts, some might find it more beneficial to hire outside parties to carry out this function. Organizations should take cost, response time, and data sensitivity into consideration before making this decision [1]. Keeping an internal forensic analysis team might reduce cost depending on the scale of the incident, provide faster response due to familiarity with the infrastructure, and prevent sensitive data from being viewed by third parties.

Legal Aspects of Acquiring Evidence: Securing and Documenting the Scene

Securing the physical scene and documenting it should be one of the first steps an incident responder should take. This activity involves photographing the system setup, cabling, and general area, collecting and documenting all cables and attached devices, write-protecting all media, using anti-static packaging for transportation, maintaining proper temperature for stored devices, avoiding exposure to excessive electromagnetic fields, and logging all access to the area. The incident response team should keep an inventory of evidence handling supplies (chain of custody forms, notebooks, evidence storage bags, evidence tape), blank media, backup devices, and forensics workstations.

Processing and Logging Evidence

The goal of an investigation is to collect and preserve evidence that can be used for internal proceedings or courts of law. Investigators should be able to prove that the evidence has not been tampered with. To be able to get this evidence, the incident response team members should receive training specifically addressing these issues and should practice these skills on an ongoing basis to stay sharp.

To properly process and log evidence, investigators should keep the evidence within a secured and controlled environment where all access is logged, and should document the collected evidence and its circulation among investigative entities. We cannot stress how important it is to associate each activity with a date and time.

4. CONDUCTING DISK-BASED ANALYSIS

To be able to process evidence in a manner that is admissible in a court of law, a lab and accompanying procedures should be established. This will ensure that the data integrity is not breached and that the data remains confidential—in other words, that the evidence remains forensically sound.

Forensics Lab Operations

To ensure forensic soundness, an investigator's process needs to be reliable, repeatable, and documented. To have a controlled and secure environment for the investigator to follow these steps, a forensic lab becomes a necessity.

The lab should be established in a physically secure building that is monitored 24/7; have a dedicated staff; have regularly upgraded and updated workstations dedicated to forensic analysis with related software installed; and have a disaster recovery plan in place.

Acquiring a Bit-Stream Image

Acquiring a bit-stream image involves producing a bit-by-bit copy of a hard drive on a separate storage device. By creating an exact copy of a hard drive, an investigator preserves all data on a disk, including currently unused and partially overwritten sectors. The imaging process should not alter the original hard drive to preserve the copy's admissibility as evidence. Selecting a proper imaging tool is crucial to produce a forensically sound copy. The National Institute of Standards and Technology (NIST) lists the requirements for a drive imaging tool as follows [1]:

- The tool shall make a bit-stream duplicate or an image of an original disk or a disk partition on fixed or removable media.
- The tool shall not alter the original disk.
- The tool shall be able to access both IDE and SCSI disks.
- The tool shall be able to verify the integrity of a disk image file.
- The tool shall log input/output (I/O) errors.
- The tool's documentation shall be correct.

The imaging of a hard drive can be performed using specialized hardware tools or by using a combination of computers and software.

Specialized Hardware

The Image MASSter Solo series hard drive duplicators generally support SATA, IDE, USB, eSATA, uSATA, SAS hard drives, and flash memory devices. They can hash the disk images, besides providing write-blocking, to ensure the integrity of the copies. The imaging process can be either disk-to-disk or disk-to-file.

The Digital Intelligence Forensic Duplicator units have the same properties as the Image MASSter Solo series. But they provide access to different hard drive formats through their protocol modules.

Software: Linux

The dd or dcfldd has been fully tested and vetted by NIST as a forensic imaging tool. It is a freeware utility for any Linux-based system and can copy every sector of hard drives. dcfldd is a dd-based software that enhances dd's output by providing status and time-to-completion output as the disk gets imaged and can split the output to smaller chunks. It can also hash the output to ensure data integrity. The following command as seen in Table 34.1 will read block sizes of 512 bytes, produce 2 GB chunks of a disk device defined as /dev/sdb, and calculate the MD5 hashes every 2 GB to ensure integrity. The hash values will be written to a file named md5.og. In the event of a read error, dcfldd will write zeroes in the copy.

Windows The AccessData FTK (Forensic Toolkit) Imager tool is a commercial disk-imaging tool distributed by AccessData. FTK supports storage of disk images in EnCase's file format, as well as in bit-by-bit (dd) format.

On the other hand, the Guidance EnCase tool is a commercial disk-imaging tool distributed by Guidance Software. Disk images are stored in the proprietary EnCase Evidence File Format, which contains compressed data prefixed with case metadata and contains hashes of the image data.

Enabling a Write Blocker

Write blockers are hardware- or software-based tools that allow the acquisition of hard drive images while

---

TABLE 34.1 Creating an Image of a Drive.

$ dcfldd if = /dev/sdb hash = md5 hashwindow = 2G md5log = md5.log hashconv = after bs = 512 conv = noerror, sync split = 2G splitformat = aa of = driveimage.dd preventing any data from being written to the source hard drive. Therefore ensuring the integrity of the data involved. Write blockers can do this by only allowing read commands to pass through by blocking write commands or by letting only specific commands through. While copying data with a hardware write blocker, both the source and destination drives should be connected to the write blocking device, and in case of a software blocker, the blocking software should be activated first before copying [2]. After imaging is performed with a write blocker, calculating the hashes of both the source and destination images is essential to ensure data integrity. Some hardware write blockers that are used in the industry are as follows:

- Tableau Forensic Bridges
- WiebeTech WriteBlocker

Establishing a Baseline

It is important to maintain the integrity of the data being analyzed throughout the investigation. When dealing with disk drives, to maintain integrity, calculating the hashes of the analyzed images becomes crucial. Before copying or performing any analysis, the investigator should take a baseline hash of the original drives involved. The hash could be either just MD5 or a combination of MD5, SHA-1, and SHA-512. The baseline hash can be compared with hashes of any copies that are made thereafter for analysis or backup to ensure that the integrity of the evidence is maintained.

Physically Protecting the Media

After making copies of the original evidence hard drives, they should be stored in a physically secure location, such as a safe in a secured storage facility. These drives could be used as evidence in the event of prosecution. The chain of custody should also be maintained by labeling the evidence and keeping logs of date, time, and persons with whom the evidence has come into contact. During transportation, the hard drives should be placed in anti-static bags and should not be exposed to harsh environmental conditions. If possible, photographs of the evidence should be taken whenever they are processed, starting from the original location until the image acquisition stages.

Disk Structure and Recovery Techniques

Once a forensically sound copy of the evidence has been made, we can proceed to analyze its contents. There are different kinds of storage media: hard disk drives (HDD), solid state drives (SSD), digital video disks (DVD), compact disks (CD), flash memory, and other kinds. An investigator needs to be mindful about how each media stores data differently. For example, while data in the unused space on an HDD is stored as long as new data is not written, the data in the unused space of a SSD is destroyed within minutes of switching it on. This difference in retaining data makes it difficult to obtain a forensically sound image and recovering data (see checklist: An Agenda for Action for Data Recovery).

An Agenda for Action for Data Recovery

The cyber forensic specialist should ensure that the following provisional list of actions for data recovery are adhered to (check all tasks completed):

_____ 1. Make sure you are ready and have procedures in place for disasters like floods, tornadoes, earthquakes, and terrorism when they strike.

_____ 2. Make sure you are ready and have a plan in place to take periodic image copies and send them off-site.

_____ 3. Perform change accumulation to reduce the number of logs required as input to the recovery, which saves time at the recovery site. However, performing this step consumes resources at the home site.

_____ 4. Evaluate your environment to decide how to handle the change accumulation question/problem in action/task 3.

_____ 5. Make sure you have procedures in place to implement your plan.

_____ 6. Check your assets to make sure they're ready as part of your plan.

_____ 7. Make sure you build your recovery Job Control Language (JCL) correctly. JCL is tricky, and you need to get it exactly right. Data integrity and your business rely on this task.

_____ 8. Make sure you clean your RECON data sets. It can take hours if done manually, and it's an error-prone process. When your system is down, can you afford to make mistakes with this key resource?

_____ 9. Make sure you test your plan. There's a lot to think about. In the real world, there's much more.

_____ 10. Make sure your plan works before you are required to use it!

_____ 11. Make sure you have procedures in place to deal with issues of increased availability, shrinking expertise, and growing complexity, failures of many types, and the costs of data management and downtime.

Disk Geometry Components

With regard to HDD geometry, the surface of each HDD platter is arranged in concentric magnetic tracks on each side. To make accessing data more efficient, each track is divided into addressable sectors or blocks as seen in Figure 34.2. This organization is known as formatting. Sectors typically contain 512 bytes or 2048 bytes of data in addition to the address information. Newer HDDs use 4096 byte sectors. The HDD controller uses the format and address information to locate the specific data processed by the operating system.

Now, with regard to SSD geometry: Compared to HDDs, SSDs store data in 512-kilobyte sectors or blocks, which are in turn divided into 4096-byte long pages. These structures are located in arrays of NAND (Negated AND or NOT AND) transistors.

Inspecting Windows File System Architectures

File systems, including Windows, can be defined in six layers: Physical (absolute sectors), data classification (partitions), allocation units (clusters), storage space management (FAT or MFT), and information classification (folders), and application level storage (files). Knowing these layers will guide the investigator as to what tool is needed to extract information from the file system. Windows file systems have gone through an evolution starting from FAT and continuing to NTFS.

FAT (File Allocation Table)

FAT has been available widely on Windows systems starting with the MS-DOS operating system. This file system's incarnations include FAT12, FAT16, FAT32, and exFAT. The volume is organized into specific-sized chunks based on the version numbering of the file system. FAT12 has a cluster size of 512 bytes to 8 kilobytes, whereas FAT16 has cluster sizes ranging from 512 bytes to 64 kilobytes. FAT32 file systems can support disk sizes up to 2 terabytes using cluster sizes ranging from 512 bytes to 32 kilobytes. FAT file systems begin with the boot sector and proceed with FAT areas 1 and 2, the root directory, files and other directories. FAT provides a table to the operating system as to which cluster in the volume is used for a file or folder. In a FAT file system, file deletion is accomplished by overwriting the first character of the object's name with 0xE5 or 0×00 and by setting the table entry of the related clusters to zero. FAT file times are stored by using the local system's time information.

New Technology File System (NTFS)

As the name suggests, NTFS was developed to overcome the limitations inherent in the FAT file system. These limitations were the lack of access control lists (ACLs) on file system objects, journaling, and compression, encryption, named streams, rich metadata, and many other features. The journaling features of NTFS make it capable of recovering itself by automatically restoring the consistency of the file system when an error takes place [1]. It also should be noted that NTFS file times are stored in the Universal Coordinated Time (UTC) compared to FAT where the operating system's local time is used. There are mainly two artifacts in NTFS that interests a forensics investigator: MFT (master file table) and ADS (alternate data streams).

Master File Table (MFT) MFT or $MFT can be considered one of the most important files in the NTFS file system. It keeps records of all files in a volume, the files' location in the directory, the physical location of the files on the drive, and file metadata. The metadata includes file and folder create dates, entry modified dates, access dates, last written dates, physical and logical file size, and ACLs of the files. The file and directory metadata is stored as an MFT entry that is 1024 bytes in size. The first 16 entries in the MFT belong to system files, such as the MFT itself. From a forensics investigator's perspective, entries are very interesting because when a file is deleted an entry gets marked as unallocated while the file content on the drive remains intact. The file name in the MFT entry can be overwritten due to MFT tree structure reorganization, so most of the time file names are not maintained. File data eventually is overwritten as the unallocated drive space gets used.

Alternate Data Streams (ADS) NTFS supports multiple data streams for files and folders. Files are composed of unnamed streams that contain the actual file data besides additional named streams (mainfile.txt:one-stream). All streams within a file share the file's metadata, including file size. Since the file size does not change with the addition of ADSs, it becomes difficult to detect their

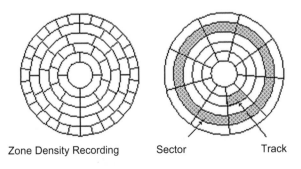

Zone Density Recording   Sector   Track

FIGURE 34.2 Physical structure of a drive.

existence. Open source forensics tools, such as The Sleuth Kit (TSK), can be used to parse MFT entries and reveal the existence of ADSs. Specifically, the TSK command fls can be used to list the files and the associated ADSs.

Locating and Restoring Deleted Content

Depending on the method of deletion, time elapsed since the deletion, and drive fragmentation; files can be fully or partially recovered. A deleted or unlinked file is a file whose MFT entry has been marked as unallocated and is no longer present in the user's view. The file can be recovered based on the metadata still present in the MFT entry, given that too much time has not passed since the deletion. The Sleuth Kit (TSK) can be used to parse the MFT to locate and recover these files. The investigator would need to execute the command fls to get a listing of the deleted file's inode and use that inode to extract the file data with the command icat.

Orphaned files' MFT entries on the one hand are no longer fully intact, and therefore the related metadata, such as file name might not be available. On the other hand, the file's data may still be recovered using the same method employed for deleted files.

Unallocated files' MFT entries have been reused and/or unlinked. In this scenario, the only way to recover the file would be to "carve" the data out of the unallocated drive space. Carving involves using tools (foremost, scalpel) that recognize specific file formats, such as headers and footers to find the beginning and end of the file and extract the data.

Overwritten files' MFT entries and content have been reallocated or reused. Complete recovery would not be possible. Fragments of the file can be recovered by searching through the unallocated spaces on the drive with tools, such as grep.

5. INVESTIGATING INFORMATION-HIDING TECHNIQUES

Hidden data can exist due to regular operating system activities or deliberate user activities. This type of data includes alternate data streams, information obscured by malicious software, data encoded in media (steganography), hidden system files, and many others.

Uncovering Hidden Information

Collection of hidden data can be a challenge for an investigator. The investigator needs to be aware of the different data-hiding techniques to employ the proper tools.

Scanning and Evaluating Alternate Data Streams

Open-source forensics tools, such as The Sleuth Kit (TSK), can be used to parse MFT entries and reveal the existence of ADSs. Specifically, the TSK command fls can be used to list the files and the associated ADSs as seen in Table 34.2.

In the example above, we can see that the file ads-file.txt contains two streams named suspicious.exe and another-stream. The numbers seen in the beginning of each listing is the inode. This value identifies each file and folder in the file system. We should note that 63 bytes were skipped starting from the beginning of the drive since that data belongs to the master boot record (MBR). To extract the file data from the file system, the TSK command icat can be used in combination with the inode values, as seen in Table 34.3.

Executing Code from a Stream

Malicious software can attempt to hide its components in ADSs to obscure themselves from investigators. Such components could be executable files. Executable ADSs can be launched with the Windows start command or by other scripting languages, such as VBScript or Perl by referring to the ADS file directly: start ads-file.jpg:suspicious.exe. Executable hidden in ADSs can be automatically launched on system start-up by defining it to do so in the Windows registry key "HKEY_LOCAL_MACHINE\Software\Microsoft\Windows\CurrentVersion\Run" by creating a string value containing the full path of the ADS file.

Steganography Tools and Concepts

Steganography is the science of hiding secret messages in nonsecret messages or media in a manner that only the

---

TABLE 34.2 Listing Files from a Raw Disk Image.

```
$fls—o 63-rp evidence-diskimage.dd
r/r 11315-158-1: ads-folder/ads-file.txt
r/r 11315-158-4: ads-folder/ads-file.txt:suspicious.exe
r/r 11315-158-3: ads-folder/host.txt:another-stream
```

TABLE 34.3 Extracting a File from a Raw Image with its Inode.

```
$ icat —o 63 evidence-diskimage.dd 11315-158-4 >
suspicious.exe
```

person who is aware of the mechanism can successfully find and decode it. Messages can be hidden in images, audio files, videos, or other computer files without altering the actual presentation or functionality. While steganography is about hiding the message and its transmission, cryptography only aims to obscure the message content itself through various algorithms. Steganography can be performed by using the least significant bits in image files, placing comments in the source code, altering the file header, spreading data over a sound file's frequency spectrum, or hiding encrypted data in pseudorandom locations in a file. Several tools perform steganography:

- S-Tools is a freeware steganography tool that hides files in BMP, GIF, and WAV files. The message can be encrypted with algorithms, such as IDEA, DES, 3DES, and MDC before being hidden in the images.
- Spam Mimic is a freeware steganography tool that embeds messages in spam email content. This tool would be useful when real spam messages are numerous and the fake spam message would not wake any suspicion.
- Snow is a freeware steganography tool that encodes message text by appending white space characters to the end of lines. The tool's name stands for and exploits the steganographic nature of whitespace. It also can employ ICE encryption to hide the content of the message in case of the detection of steganography. While most of the time it's visually undetectable, it can be discovered by a careful investigator or a script looking for this tool's artifacts.
- OutGuess is an open-source tool that hides messages in the redundant bits of data sources. OutGuess can use any data format as a medium as long as a handler is provided.

Detecting Steganography

During an incident, an investigator might suspect that steganography has been used by the suspect due to an admission, a discovery of specific tools, or other indicators. Traces of the use of steganography tools can be found in the recently used files (MRU) key, the USERASSIST key, and the MUICache key in the Windows registry; prefetch files, Web browser history, deleted file information in the file system; and in the Windows Search Assistant utility. File artifacts generated by these tools can also be a good indicator of the tools' use.

The presence of files (JPEG, MP3) that present similar properties, but different hash values, might also generate

suspicion. The investigator might be able to discover such pairs of carrier and processed files to apply discovery algorithms to recover the hidden messages. Steganalysis tools can also be used to detect the presence of steganography:

- Stegdetect is an open-source steganalysis tool that is capable of detecting steganographic content in images that have been generated by JSteg, JPHide, Invisible Secrets, OutGuess, F5, Camouflage, and appendX.
- StegSpy is a freeware steganalysis tool that can currently identify steganography generated by the Hiderman, JPHideandSeek, Masker, JPegX, and Invisible Secrets tools.
- Stegbreak is used to launch dictionary attacks against JSteg-Shell, JPHide, and OutGuess 0.13b-generated messages.

Scavenging Slack Space

File slack or slack space refers to the bytes between the logical end of a file and the end of the cluster in which the file resides. Slack space is a source of information leak, which can result in password, email, registry, event log, database entries, and word processing document disclosures. File slack has the potential of containing data from the system memory. This can happen if a file can't fill the last sector in a cluster and the Windows operating system uses randomly selected data from the system memory (RAM slack) to fill the gap. RAM slack can contain any information loaded into memory since the system was turned on. The information can include file content resident in memory, usernames and passwords, and cryptographic keys. File slack space can also be used to hide information by malicious users or software, which can become challenging if the investigator is not specifically looking for such behavior. Volume slack is the space that remains on a drive when it's not used by any partition. This space can contain data if it was created as a result of deleting a partition. While the partition metadata no longer exists, its contents still remain on the drive. Partition slack is the area between the ending of a logical partition and the ending of a physical block in which the partition is located. It is created when the number of sectors in a partition is not a multiple of the physical block size. Registry slack is formed when a registry key is deleted and the size value is changed to a positive value. Normally, key sizes are negative values when read as signed integers. The registry key data still remains on the drive. Jolanta Thomassen created a Perl script called "regslack" to parse registry hives and extract deleted keys by exploiting the negative to positive conversion information.

Inspecting Header Signatures and File Mangling

Users or malware with malicious intent can alter or mangle file names or the files themselves to hide files that are used to compromise systems or contain data that has been gathered as a result of their malicious actions. These techniques include but are not limited to renaming files, embedding malicious files in regular files (Pdf, Doc, Flash), binding multiple executable in a single executable, and changing file times to avoid event time-based analysis. For example, a malicious Windows executable "bad.exe" can be renamed "interesting.pdf" and be served by a Web page to an unsuspecting user. Depending on the Web browser, the user would get prompted with a dialog asking whether the user would like to run the program; and most of the time the user will dismiss the dialog by clicking the OK button. To analyze a file disguised in different file extensions, a header-based file-type checker, such as the Linux "file" command or the tool TrID (also available in Windows), can be used. Table 34.4 presents a sample of the malware Trojan.Spyeye hidden in a file with an Acrobat Pdf document extension being detected by the tool file.

Combining Files

Combining files is a very popular method among malware creators. Common file formats, such as Microsoft Office files and Adobe Pdf and Flash files, can be used as containers to hide malicious executables. One example is a technique where a Windows executable is embedded in a PDF file as an object stream and marked with a compression filter. The stream is usually obfuscated with XOR. The Metasploit Framework provides several plug-ins to generate such files for security professionals to conduct social engineering in the form of phishing attacks. The example in Table 34.5 uses Metasploit to generate a Pdf file with an embedded executable file.

To discover such embedding, an investigator can use Didier Stevens's tool Pdf-parser to view the objects in a Pdf file.

Binding Multiple Executable Files

Binding multiple executable files provides the means to pack all dependencies and resource files a program might need while running into a single file. This is advantageous since it permits a malicious user to leave a smaller footprint on a target system and makes it harder for an investigator to locate the malicious file. Certain tools, such as the WinZip Self-Extractor, nBinder or File Joiner can create one executable file by archiving all related files whose execution will be controlled by a stub executable. When executed, the files will be extracted, and the contained program will be launched automatically. Some of these file binders can produce files that can't be detected by some anti-viruses, and if downloaded and run by an unsuspecting user, it can result in a system compromise.

File Time Analysis

File time analysis is one of the most frequently used techniques by investigators. File times are used to build a storyline that could potentially reveal how and when an event on a system caused a compromise. The file time of a malicious executable could be linked to a user's browser history to find out which sites were visited before the compromise occurred.

The problem with this type of analysis is that sometimes the file times can be tampered with and can't be relied upon as evidence. The tool Timestomp, created by James Foster and Vincent Liu, allows for the deletion or modification of file MACE times (modified, accessed, created, entry modified in MFT times) in the MFT's $STANDARD_INFORMATION attribute. Timestomp

---

TABLE 34.4 Inspecting File Headers.

```
$ file hidden.pdf
hidden.pdf: PE32 executable for MS Windows (GUI)
Intel 80386 32-bit

Example of a PDF Header:
0000000: 2550 4446 2d31 2e36 0a25 e4e3 cfd2 0a31 %
PDF-1.6.%.....1

Example of a Windows Executable Header:
0000000: 4d5a 9000 0300 0000 0400 0000 ffff 0000
MZ.............
```

TABLE 34.5 Creating a Malicious PDF file with the Metasploit Framework.

```
$ ./msfcli exploit/windows/fileformat/
adobe_pdf_embedded_exe INFILENAME = /samples/base.pdf
payload = windows/meterpreter/bind_tcp E
[*] Please wait while we load the module tree...
....
INFILENAME = > ./base.pdf
payload = > windows/meterpreter/bind_tcp
[*] Reading in './base.pdf'...
[*] Parsing './base.pdf'...
[*] Parsing Successful.
[*] Using 'windows/meterpreter/bind_tcp' as payload...
[*] Creating 'evil.pdf' file...
[+] evil.pdf stored at .../local/evil.pdf
```

```
timestomp.exe c:\test.txt -z "Saturday 10/08/2005 2:02:02 PM"
timestomp.exe c:\test.txt -a "Saturday 10/08/2005 2:02:02 PM"
```

Standard Information		File Name Info.	
Creation	10/8/2005 : 14:2:2	Creation	10/15/2008 : 0:37:35
Modifica.	10/8/2005 : 14:2:2	Modifica.	10/15/2008 : 0:37:35
MFT	10/8/2005 : 14:2:2	MFT	10/15/2008 : 0:38:49
Last Acc.	10/8/2005 : 14:2:2	Last Acc.	10/15/2008 : 0:37:35

FIGURE 34.3 Changing timestamps as a result of time stomping.

can't change the file MACE times in the MFT's $FILE_NAME attribute because this attribute is meant to be modified by Windows system internals only. This time-tampering method can be defeated by using Mark McKinnon's MFT Parser tool to view all eight file times to detect discrepancies, as seen in Figure 34.3.

Executable compile times can also be used as a data point during timeline analysis. The open-source Python module pefile can be used to extract this information from the executable header. For example, if malicious software changes MACE times to a future date, but keeps its original compile time, this can be flagged as suspicious by an investigator as seen in Table 34.6.

6. SCRUTINIZING EMAIL

Although many noncommercial users are favoring Webmail nowadays, most corporate users are still using local email clients, such as Microsoft Outlook or Mozilla Thunderbird. Therefore, we should still look at extracting and analyzing email content from local email stores. Email message analysis might reveal information about the sender and recipient, such as email addresses, IP addresses, data and time, attachments, and content.

Investigating the Mail Client

An email user will generally utilize a local client to compose and send his or her message. Depending on the user's configuration, the sent and received messages will exist in the local email database. Deleted emails can also be stored locally for some time depending on the user's preferences. Most corporate environments utilize Microsoft Outlook. Outlook will store the mail in a PST (portable storage table) or OST (offline storage table) format. Multiple PST files can exist in various locations on the user's file system and can provide valuable information to an investigator about the user's email specific activity.

Interpreting Email Headers

Generally speaking, email messages are composed of three sections: header, body, and attachments. The header

TABLE 34.6 Compilation Time of an Executable Extracted with Pefile.

Compilation timedatestamp: 2010-03-23 23:42:40
Target machine: 0 × 14C (Intel 386 or later processors and compatible processors)
Entry point address: 0 × 000030B1

TABLE 34.7 An Email Header.

Return-Path: <example_from@acme.edu>
X-SpamCatcher-Score: 1 [X]
Received: from [**1.1.1.1**] (HELO acme.edu)
    by fe3.acme.edu (CommuniGate Pro SMTP 4.1.8)
    with ESMTP-TLS id 61258719 for example_to@mail.acme.edu; Mon, 23 Aug 2004 11:40:10 -0400
Message-ID: <4129F3CA.2020509@acme.edu>
Date: Mon, 23 Aug 2005 11:40:36 -0400
From: Jim Doe <example_from@acme.edu>
User-Agent: Mozilla/5.0 (Windows; U; Windows NT 5.1; en-US; rv:1.0.1) Gecko/20020823 Netscape/7.0
X-Accept-Language: en-us, en
MIME-Version: 1.0
To: John Doe <example_to@mail.acme.edu>
Subject: Sales Development Meeting
Content-Type: text/plain; charset=us-ascii; format=flowed
Content-Transfer-Encoding: 7bit

contains source and destination information (email and IP addresses), date and time, email subject, and the route the email takes during its transmission. Information stored in a header can either be viewed through the email client or through an email forensics tool, such as libpff (an open-source library to access email databases), FTK, or EnCase.

The "Received" line in Table 34.7 shows that the email was sent from IP address 1.1.1.1. An investigator should not rely on this information as concrete evidence because it can be easily changed by a malicious sender (email spoofing). The time information in the header might also be incorrect due to different time zones, user system inaccuracies, and tampering.

Recovering Deleted Emails

While most users treat emails as transient, the companies they work for have strict data retention policies that can enforce the storage of email, sometimes indefinitely. User emails usually are stored in backup archives or electronic-discovery systems to provide means for analysis in case there is an investigation. The email servers also can keep messages in store, although the users remove them from their local systems. Therefore, nowadays it has become somewhat difficult for a corporate user to delete an email permanently. Recovery is usually possible from various backup systems. In cases where there is no backup source and users delete an email from their local system, we need to perform several steps on the user's storage drive, depending on the level of deletion:

- If the user deletes the message, but does not empty the deleted messages folder, the user can move the messages from the deleted folder to the original folder quite easily.
- If the user deletes the email message and removes it from the deleted messages folder, then the investigator needs to apply disk forensics techniques to recover the email. In case of a Microsoft Outlook PST file, when a message is deleted it is marked as deleted by Outlook and the data remains on the disk unless the location on the drive is overwritten by new data. Commercial tools, such as AccessData's FTK or Guidance's EnCase, can be used to recover deleted messages. Another approach would be to use Microsoft's "Scanpst.exe" tool. To apply this technique, the investigator should first back up the PST and then deliberately corrupt the PST file with the command "DEBUG <FILE.pst> -f 107 113 20 −q." If the file is too large and there is insufficient system memory, then the investigator should use a hex editor to make the changes marked in red in the PST file as shown in Figure 34.4.

Once the PST file has been corrupted, then the "Scanpst.exe" tool should be located on the drive. And it should also be executed to repair the file, as seen in Figure 34.5.

7. VALIDATING EMAIL HEADER INFORMATION

Email header information can be tampered with by users who do not wish to disclose their source information or by malicious users who would like to fake the origin of the message to avoid detection and being blocked by spam filters. Email header information can be altered by spoofing, by using an anonymizer (removes identifying information), and using a mail relay server.

Detecting Spoofed Email

A spoofed email message is a message that appears to be from an entity other than the actual sender entity. This can be accomplished by altering the sender's name, email address, email client type, and/or the source IP address in the email header. Spoofing can be detected by looking at the "Received:" and "Message-ID:" lines of the header. The "Received:" field will have each email server hop the message has taken before it has been received by the email client. An investigator can use the email server IP addresses in the header to get their hostnames from their DNS records and verify them by comparing to the actual outgoing and incoming email servers' information. The "Message-ID:" field uniquely identifies a message and is used to prevent multiple deliveries. The domain information in the "Message-ID:" field should match the domain information of the sender's email address. If this is not the case, the email is most probably spoofed. An investigator should also look out for different "From:" and "Reply-To:" email addresses and unusual email clients displayed in the "X-Mailer:" field.

Verifying Email Routing

Email routing can be verified by tracing the hops an email message has taken. This can be accomplished by verifying the "Received" field information through DNS records and if possible obtaining email transaction logs from the email servers involved. The "Message-ID" information can be searched for in the logs to make sure that

```
Offset   0  1  2  3  4  5  6  7  8  9  A  B  C  D  E  F
00000000 21 42 44 4E 4B E7 0A 20 20 20 20 20 20 20 20 20   !BDNKç.
00000010 20 20 20 20 00 00 00 00 04 00 00 00 01 00 00 00    ..........
00000020 B3 93 07 00 00 00 00 00 F8 7E 27 00 D2 D8 00 00   ³".....ø~'.ÒØ..
00000030 09 35 01 00 09 2A 01 00 00 36 01 00 28 6E 04 00   .5...*...6..(n..
00000040 84 37 01 00 00 36 01 00 00 36 01 00 E0 DA 00 00   „7...6...6..àÚ..
```

FIGURE 34.4 Manipulating a PST file for recovery.

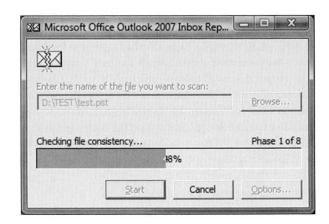

FIGURE 34.5 Use of the Scanpst.exe tool.

the message has actually traveled the route declared in the "Received" field.

8. TRACING INTERNET ACCESS

Knowing the path a perpetrator has taken becomes very valuable when an investigator is building a case to present in court. It adds credibility to the claim and solidifies the storyline by connecting the events. For example, knowing the path an attacker has taken to steal a company's source code can reveal the extent of the compromise (loss of domain credentials, customer information leakage, and intellectual property loss), show intent, and prevent the same attack from happening. Tracing Internet access can also be valuable in the case of employees viewing content that is not compliant with workplace rules.

Inspecting Browser Cache and History Files

An investigator can use various data points to trace a perpetrator's activity by analyzing the browser cache and Web history files in the gathered evidence. Every action of a user on the Internet can generate artifacts. The browser cache contains files that are saved locally as a result of a user's Web browsing activity. The history files contain a list of visited URLs, Web searches, cookies, and bookmarked Web sites. These files can be located in different folders, depending on the operating system (OS), OS version, and browser type.

Exploring Temporary Internet Files

A browser cache stores multimedia content (images, videos), and Web pages (HTML, JavaScript, CSS) to increase the load speed of a page when viewed the next time. For the Internet Explorer Web browser on Windows XP and 2003, the cache files can be located in the folder "Documents and Settings\%username%\Local Settings \Temporary Internet Files"; in Windows Vista/7/2008, they are located in the folder "Users\%username%\AppData\ Local\Microsoft\Windows\Temporary Internet Files":

- On Windows XP/2003 Firefox stores the cached files in the folder "C:\Documents and Settings\%username\Local Settings\ Application Data\Mozilla\Firefox\Profiles", and for Windows Vista/7/2008 in "C:\Users\%username% \AppData\Roaming\Mozilla\Firefox\ Profiles."
- On Windows XP/2003 Google chrome Web browser stores the cached files in the folder "C:\Documents and Settings\%username\Application Data\ Google \Chrome\Default\Cache", and for Windows Vista/7/ 2008 in "C:\Users\%username%\AppData\Local \Google\Chrome\ Default\Cache".
- The MAC times of these cached files can be used during a timeline analysis to find when certain artifacts,

such as malware, get dropped by malicious or compromised Web sites. Malicious executable, Pdf files, or Java files can be located in the cache unless the cache is cleared by the user or malware.

Visited URLs, Search Queries, Recently Opened Files

The Internet Explorer Web browser stores the visited URL, search query, and opened file information in the file "index.dat," accompanied by last modified and last accessed, and expiration times. This file on Windows XP/ 2003 systems can be located in the folder "Documents and Settings\%username%\Local Settings\Temporary Internet Files\Content.IE5," and in Windows Vista/7/2008 systems, it is located in the folder "Users\%username% \AppData\ Local\Microsoft\Windows\Temporary Internet Files\Content.IE5," The "index.dat" file contains a LEAK record, which is a record that remains when it's marked as deleted, but can't be deleted due a related temporary Internet file (TIF) still being used.

Mozilla Firefox stores the URL, search, and open files-related history in a SQLite 3 database file Places. sqlite. These files on Windows XP/2003 systems can be located in the folder "C:\Documents and Settings\%username\Local Settings\ Application Data\Mozilla\Firefox \Profiles," and in Windows Vista/7/2008 systems, it is located in the folder "C:\Users\%username%\AppData \Roaming\Mozilla\Firefox\Profiles."

Google Chrome also stores its user activity data in SQLite 3 database files. These files on Windows XP/ 2003 systems can be located in the folder "C:\Documents and Settings\%username\Application Data\ Google \Chrome\default," and in Windows Vista/7/2008 systems, it is located in the folder "C:\Users\%username% \AppData\Local\Google\Chrome\ default."

All three browsers' history files, cookies, and cache files can be parsed and interpreted by log2timeline, a tool created by Kristinn Gudjonsson. log2timeline is capable of parsing multiple data sources and producing a timeline with, including but not limited to, file MAC times, registry write times, and Windows event logs. The tool can be pointed to a raw drive image (dd image), and as a result it can produce a "super" timeline in CSV format for all pursuable time-based data sources, as seen Figure 34.6 and Table 34.8.

Researching Cookie Storage

Internet Explorer cookies can be found in the folder "Documents and Settings\%username%\ Cookies" in Windows XP/2003 systems, and in Windows Vista/7/2008 systems, in "Users\%username%\AppData\Roaming\ Microsoft\Windows\Cookies." The cookies are stored in plaintext format.

FIGURE 34.6   log2timeline GUI.

TABLE 34.8 Using log2timeline from the Command Line.

log2timeline -p -r -f win7 -z EST5EDT /storage/disk-image001.dd -w supertimeline001.csv

Mozilla Firefox stores its cookies in a SQLite 3 database Cookies.sqlite located in the folder "C:\Documents and Settings\%username\Local Settings\ Application Data \Mozilla\Firefox\Profiles," and, in Windows Vista/7/2008 systems, it is located in the folder "C:\Users\%username %\AppData\Roaming\Mozilla\Firefox\Profiles".

Google Chrome stores its cookies in a SQLite 3 database file "C:\Documents and Settings\%username \Application Data\ Google\Chrome\default\Cookies" in Windows XP/2003 systems and in the file "C:\Users\%username%\AppData\Local\Google\Chrome\default\Cookies" in Windows Vista/7/2008 systems. The cookies files of all three browser types can be parsed and viewed by the tool log2timeline, as previously mentioned.

Reconstructing Cleared Browser History

It is possible to come across cleared browser histories during an investigation. The user could have deliberately deleted the files to hide their Web browsing activity, or a malware could have removed its traces to avoid detection and analysis. Nevertheless, an investigator will look into various locations on the suspect system to locate the deleted browser history files. The possible locations are unallocated clusters, cluster slack, page files, system files, hibernation files, and systems restore points. Using AccessData's FTK Imager on the suspect drive or drive image, an investigator can promptly locate the orphaned files and see if the browser files are present there. The next step would be to use the FTK Imager to look at the unallocated spaces, which should end up being a time-consuming analysis as seen in Figure 34.7. If the drive has not been used too much, an investigator has a high chance of locating the files in the unallocated space.

Auditing Internet Surfing

Knowing what employees are browsing on the Web while they are at work has become necessary to prevent employees from visiting sites that host malicious content (sites with exploits and malware), content that is not compliant with workplace rules, and content that is illegal. Employees can use the Web to upload confidential corporate information, which can cause serious problems for the employer.

Tracking User Activity

User activity can be tracked by using tools that monitor network activity, DNS (Domain Name Server) requests, local user system activity, and proxy logs. Network activity, on the other hand, can be monitored by looking at netflows. Netflow is a network protocol developed by Cisco Systems for monitoring IP traffic. It captures source and destination IP addresses, IP protocol, source and destination ports, and IP types of service.

Local user system activity can be monitored by installing specific agents on the users' systems that can report their activity back to a centralized server. SpectorSoft offers a product called Spector 360 that can be installed on a user system and a central server. The agents on the user systems can track user browser activity by hooking into system APIs and enforce rules set by the employer.

DNS requests can be monitored at the corporate DNS server level or by looking at network traffic. When a user requests a Web page with its domain name, the name gets translated to an IP address via DNS. User activity can be tracked by monitoring for domains that are not approved by the employer or domains hosting illegal content in the DNS server's logs.

Most corporate environments utilize a proxy server to funnel Web traffic through. A proxy server acts as the middle-man for requests from users seeking resources from external servers. This position of the proxy server permits tracking user browsing activity and can be used to filter or block certain behavior. Content protected by SSL (Secure Socket Layer protocol) can also be tracked by proxies, by setting the proxy up as an intercept proxy.

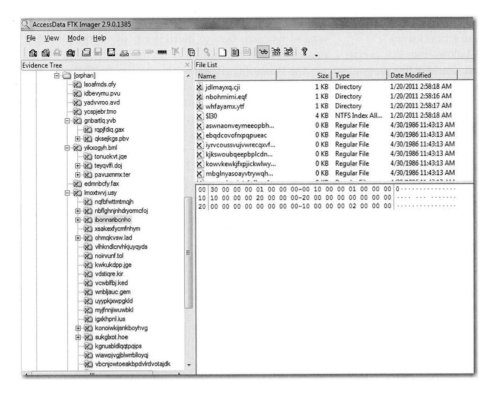

FIGURE 34.7 Use of AccessData FTK Imager.

Squid is one of the most popular open-source proxies available and can carry out the necessary functions to track and block user activity.

Uncovering Unauthorized Usage

Unauthorized Web usage can take multiple forms, such as downloading or viewing noncompliant or illegal content, uploading confidential information, launching attacks on other systems, and more. Once the unauthorized usage has been detected by the previously mentioned means, an investigator can focus on the user's system to corroborate the unauthorized activity. This can be done by analyzing browser history files and related file system activities. Building a "super" timeline with the tool log2timeline can become very useful to find the created cache and cookie files and the browser history entries around the same time the unauthorized activity was detected.

9. SEARCHING MEMORY IN REAL TIME

Analyzing memory in real time can provide very crucial information about the activities of malware or a hacker that would be otherwise unavailable if one were only looking at a system's drives. This information can be network connections and sockets, system configuration settings, collected private information (usernames, passwords, credit-card numbers), memory-only resident executables, and much more. Real-time analysis involves analyzing volatile content and therefore requires swift action by the investigator. The investigator has to quickly act to capture an image of the memory using tools, such as MoonSols Windows Memory Toolkit, GMG Systems' KnTDD, or F-response. F-response is different from the other memory-imaging tools since it provides real-time access to the target systems memory. Real-time access can reduce the time to analyze by permitting the investigator to analyze the memory right away without waiting for the whole memory to be downloaded into a file. You can read more about F-response at www.f-reponse.com.

Comparing the Architecture of Processes

Generally speaking, Windows architecture uses two access modes; user and kernel modes. The user mode includes application processes, such as programs and protected subsystems. The protected subsystems are so named because each of these is a separate process with its own protected virtual address space in memory. The kernel mode is a privileged mode of functioning in which the application has direct access to the virtual memory. This includes the address spaces of all user mode processes and applications and the associated hardware. The kernel mode is also called the protected mode, or Ring 0:

- Windows processes are generally composed of an executable program, consisting of initial code and data, a private virtual address space, system resources that are accessible to all threads in the process, a unique identifier, called a process id, at least one thread of execution, and a security context (an access token).

- A Windows thread is what Windows uses for execution within a process. Without threads, the program used by the process cannot run. Threads consist of contents of the registers representing the state of the processor, two stacks (one for the thread for executing kernel-mode instructions, and one for user-mode), private storage area used by the subsystems, run-time libraries and DLLs (dynamic-link libraries), and a unique identifier named a thread ID.

- DLLs are a set of callable subroutines linked together as a binary file that can be dynamically loaded by applications that use the subroutines. Windows user-mode entities utilize DLLs extensively. Using DLLs is advantageous for an application since applications can share DLLs. Windows ensures that there is only one copy of a DLL in memory. Each DLL has its own import address table (IAT) in its compiled form.

Identifying User and Kernel Memory

Windows refers to Intel's linear memory address space as a virtual address space (VAS) since Windows uses the disk space structure to manage physical memory. In other words 2 GB of VAS is not a one-to-one match to physical memory. 32-bit Windows divides VAS into user space (linear addresses 0x00000000 − 0x7FFFFFFF, 2 GB) and kernel space (linear addresses 0x80000000—0xFFFFFFFF, 2 GB), where user space gets the lower end of the address range and kernel space gets the upper end. To get an idea of how user space is arranged, we can use the !peb command in the Windows debugger. A list of loaded kernel modules can be obtained by running the command 'lm n' in the Windows debugger.

Inspecting Threads

While it is assumed that user and kernel codes are restricted to their own address spaces, a thread can jump from user space to kernel space by the instruction SYSENTER and jump back with the instruction SYSEXIT. Malicious threads can also exist within valid kernel or other user processes. Such hidden or orphan kernel threads can be detected using the Volatility Framework with the plug-in threads, which are shown in Table 34.9.

Discovering Rogue DLLs and Drivers

DLLs can be used for malicious purposes by injecting them through AppInit_DLLs registry value, SetWindowsHookEx() API call, and using remote threads via the CreateRemoteThread() Windows API call. Injected DLLs can be detected using the Volatility Framework's apihooks plug-in. The plug-in provides detailed information regarding

the DLLs loaded, such as IAT, process, hooked module, hooked function, from-to instructions, and hooking module, as seen in Table 34.10.

The Volatility Framework plug-in malfind can find hidden or injected DLLs in user memory based on VAD (Virtual Address Descriptor) tags and page. Use of the malfind plug-in to discover injected code is shown in Table 34.11.

The plug-in dlllist in the Volatility Framework can also be used to list all DLLs for a given process in memory and find DLLs injected with the CreateRemoteThread and LoadLibrary technique. This technique does not hide the DLL and, therefore, will not be detected by the plug-in malfind, as seen in Table 34.12.

Employing Advanced Process Analysis Methods

Processes can be analyzed using tools, such as the Windows Management Instrumentation (WMI) and walking dependency trees.

TABLE 34.9 Use of the Plug-In Threads.

$ python vol.py threads −f /memory_samples/tigger.vmem -F OrphanThread
Volatile Systems Volatility Framework 2.2_alpha
[x86] Gathering all referenced SSDTs from KTHREADs...
Finding appropriate address space for tables...
————
ETHREAD: 0xff1f92b0 Pid: 4 Tid: 1648
Tags: OrphanThread,SystemThread
Created: 2010-08-15 19:26:13
Exited: 1970-01-01 00:00:00
Owning Process: System
Attached Process: System
State: Waiting:DelayExecution
BasePriority: 0x8
Priority: 0x8
TEB: 0x00000000
StartAddress: 0xf2edd150 UNKNOWN
ServiceTable: 0x80552180
 [0] 0x80501030
 [1] 0x00000000
 [2] 0x00000000
 [3] 0x00000000
Win32Thread: 0x00000000
CrossThreadFlags: PS_CROSS_THREAD_FLAGS_SYSTEM
0xf2edd150 803d782aeff200   CMP BYTE [0xf2ef2a78], 0x0
0xf2edd157 7437   JZ 0xf2edd190
0xf2edd159 56   PUSH ESI
0xf2edd15a bef0d0edf2   MOV ESI, 0xf2edd0f0
0xf2edd15f ff35702aeff2   PUSH DWORD [0xf2ef2a70]
0xf2edd165 ff   DB 0xff
0xf2edd166 15   DB 0x15
0xf2edd167 0c   DB 0xc

TABLE 34.10 Use of the Apihooks Plug-in to Detect Hooking.

```
$ python vol.py -f coreflood.vmem -p 2015 apihooks
Volatile Systems Volatility Framework 2.1_alpha
*************************************************************
Hook mode: Usermode
Hook type: Import Address Table (IAT)
Process: 2015 (IEXPLORE.EXE)
Victim module: iexplore.exe (0x400000 - 0x419000)
Function: kernel32.dll!GetProcAddress at 0x7ff82360
Hook address: 0x7ff82360
Hooking module: <unknown>
Disassembly(0):
0x7ff82360 e8fbf5ffff   CALL 0x7ff81960
0x7ff82365 84c0   TEST AL, AL
0x7ff82367 740b   JZ 0x7ff82374
0x7ff82369 8b150054fa7f   MOV EDX, [0x7ffa5400]
0x7ff8236f 8b4250   MOV EAX, [EDX + 0x50]
0x7ff82372 ffe0   JMP EAX
0x7ff82374 8b4c2408   MOV ECX, [ESP + 0x8]
```

TABLE 34.11 Use of the Malfind Plug-In to Discover Injected Code.

```
$ python vol.py -f zeus.vmem malfind -p 1645
Volatile Systems Volatility Framework 2.1_alpha
Process: explorer.exe Pid: 1645 Address: 0x1600000
Vad Tag: VadS Protection: PAGE_EXECUTE_READWRITE
Flags: CommitCharge: 1, MemCommit: 1, PrivateMemory: 1,
Protection: 6
0x01600000 b8 35 00 00 00 e9 cd d7 30 7b b8 91 00 00 00
e9   .5......0{......
0x01600010 4 f df 30 7b 8b ff 55 8b ec e9 ef 17 c1 75 8b
ff   O.0{..U.....u..
0x01600020 55 8b ec e9 95 76 bc 75 8b ff 55 8b ec e9 be
53   U....v.u..U....S
0x01600030 bd 75 8b ff 55 8b ec e9 d6 18 c1 75 8b ff 55
8b   .u..U......u..U.
0x1600000 b835000000   MOV EAX, 0x35
0x1600005 e9cdd7307b   JMP 0x7c90d7d7
0x160000a b891000000   MOV EAX, 0x91
0x160000 f e94fdf307b   JMP 0x7c90df63
0x1600014 8bff   MOV EDI, EDI
0x1600016 55   PUSH EBP
```

TABLE 34.12 Use of the Dlllist Plug-In to Detect DLL Iijection.

```
$ python vol.py dllist -f sample.vmem -p 468
Volatile Systems Volatility Framework 2.2_alpha
*************************************************************
wuauclt.exe pid: 468
Command line : "C:\WINDOWS\system32\wuauclt.exe"
Service Pack 2
Base   Size Path
_____   ____   ___
0x00400000   0x1e000 C:\WINDOWS\system32\
wuauclt.exe
0x7c900000   0xb0000 C:\WINDOWS\system32\ntdll.dll
0x7c800000   0xf4000 C:\WINDOWS\system32\kernel32.dll
0x77c10000   0x58000 C:\WINDOWS\system32\msvcrt.dll
0x76b20000   0x11000 C:\WINDOWS\system32\ATL.DLL
0x77d40000   0x90000 C:\WINDOWS\system32\
USER32.dll
0x77f10000   0x46000 C:\WINDOWS\system32\GDI32.dll
0x77dd0000   0x9b000 C:\WINDOWS\system32\ADVAPI32.
dll
0x77e70000   0x91000 C:\WINDOWS\system32\
RPCRT4.dll
```

line interfaces and through batch scripts without having to rely on any other programming language. The command wmic uses class aliases to query related information. It can be executed remotely as well as locally by specifying target node or hostname and credentials. Various commands that can be used to extract various process-related information through wmic are shown in Table 34.13.

WMI output can be used to get a clean baseline of a system to periodically run comparisons. The comparisons can show any new process that has appeared on the system and can help to update the baseline if the new process is a known one.

Evaluating Processes with Windows Management Instrumentation (WMI)

WMI is a set of extensions to the Windows Driver Model that provides an operating system interface where components can provide information and notifications. The WMI classes Win32_Process can help collect useful information about processes. The Windows command wmic extends WMI for operation from several command-

Walking Dependency Trees

Viewing the dependencies of a process can provide valuable information about the functionality of a process. A process's dependencies may be composed of various Windows modules, such as executables, DLLs, OCX (object linking and embedding control extension) files, and SYS files (mostly real-mode device drivers). Walking a dependency tree means to explore a process's dependencies in a hierarchical view, such as a tree. The free tool Dependency Walker provides an interface that presents such a view, which is shown in Figure 34.8.

Figure 34.8 lists all of the functions that are exported by a given Windows module and the functions that are actually being called by other modules. Another view

TABLE 34.13 List of WMI Commands to Get Process Information.

wmic /node: /user: process where get ExecutablePath,parentprocessid	Find the path to a specific running executable and its parent process (for all, leave off 'where name = ').
wmic /node: /user: process where get name, processid,commandline,creationdate	Find command-line invocation of a specific executable, as well as the creation time for the process (for all, leave off "where name = ").
wmic startup list full	Find all files loaded at start-up and the registry keys associated with autostart.
wmic process list brief | find "cmd.exe"	Search for a specific process name, such as cmd.exe.

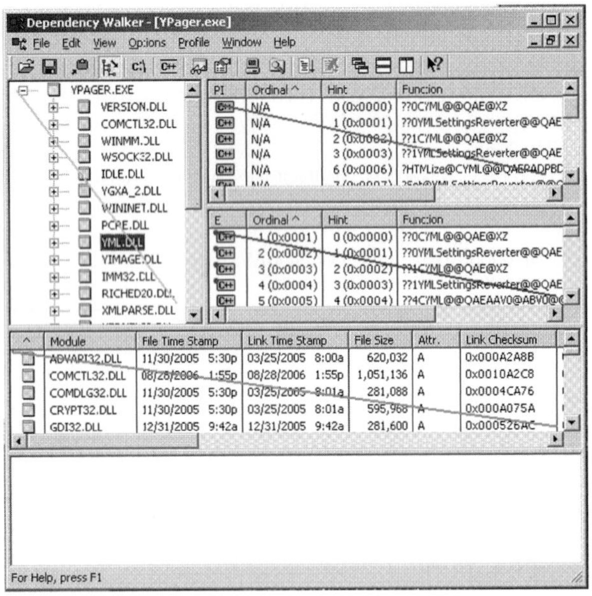

FIGURE 34.8   Using the dependency walker.

displays the minimum set of required files, along with detailed information about each file, including a full path to the file, base address, version numbers, machine type, and debug information. Dependency Walker can be used in conjunction with the tool Process Explorer (a free Microsoft tool) to detect malicious DLLs. This can be achieved by comparing the DLL list in Process Explorer to the imports displayed by the Dependency Walker.

Auditing Processes and Services

Auditing changes in process and service properties, as well as their counts on a system, can provide valuable information to an investigator about potentially malicious activity. Rootkits, viruses, trojans, and other malicious software can be detected by the auditing process and service creation or deletion across a period of time. This technique is frequently used in malware behavioral analysis in sandboxes. We can audit Windows processes and

services by using tools that utilize system APIs or system memory for live analysis. To view information through the system APIs, we can use the tool Process Hacker. The Process Hacker provides a live view of processes and services that are currently being executed or are present on the system. It provides an interface to view and search process information in detail, such as process privileges, related users and groups, DLLs loaded, handles opened, and thread information, which is shown in Figure 34.9. Service information can also be viewed in the services tab. Process and service information can be saved periodically and compared across time to detect any suspicious variations.

System memory can also be analyzed with the Volatility Framework for audit purposes. Periodic memory samples can be obtained using tools, such as F-response, MoonSols Windows Memory Toolkit, or GMG Systems' KnTDD. The Volatility Framework plug-in pslist can be used to audit processes, while the plug-in svcscan can be used to audit services.

Investigating the Process Table

The process table (PT) is a data structure kept by the operating system to help context switching, scheduling, and other activities. Each entry in the process table, called process context blocks (PCBs), contains information about a process, such as process name and state, priority, and process id. The exact content of a context block depends on the operating system. For example, if the operating system supports paging, then the context block contains a reference to the page table. While to a user a process is identified by the process id (PID), in the operating system the process is represented by entries in the process table. The process control block is a large data structure that contains information about a specific process. In Linux this data structure is called task_struct, whereas in Windows it is called an EPROCESS structure. Each EPROCESS structure contains a LIST_ENTRY structure called ActiveProcessLinks, which contains a link to the previous (Blink) EPROCESS structure and the next (Flink) EPROCESS structure.

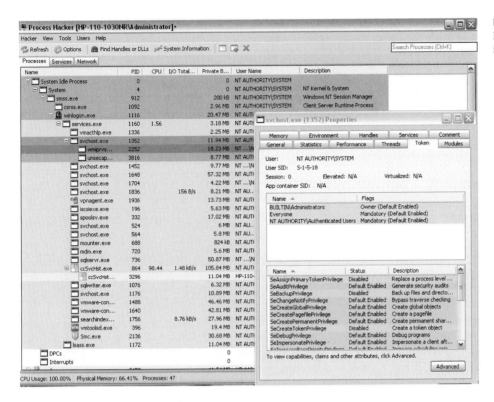

FIGURE 34.9 Using Process Hacker to view process and service information.

A listing of processes represented in the PT can be obtained by using the plug-in pslist in the Volatility Framework. This plug-in generates its output by walking the doubly-linked list. Certain malware or malicious users can hide processes by unlinking them from this linked list by performing direct kernel object manipulation (DKOM). To detect this kind of behavior, the Volatility Framework plug-in psscan can be used since it relies on scanning the memory to detect pools similar to that of an EPROCESS structure instead of walking the linked list.

Discovering Evidence in the Registry

We have already covered one method to inject code into a process. Another method is to add a value in the AppInit_DLLs registry key (HKEY_LOCAL_MACHINE \Software\Microsoft\Windows NT\CurrentVersion\Windows \AppInit_DLLs) that makes a new process to load a DLL of malicious origin.

AppInit_DLLs is a mechanism that allows an arbitrary list of DLLs to be loaded into each user mode process on the system. Although a code-signing requirement was added in Windows 7 and Windows Server 2008 R2, it is still being utilized by various malicious software to hide and persist on a system.

The Volatility Framework can also be used to analyze the registry that has been loaded to memory. The plug-ins that are available from the Volatility Framework for registry analysis are shown in Table 34.14.

TABLE 34.14 List of Volatility Framework Plug-Ins to extract Registry Information from Memory.

hivescan	finds the physical address of CMHIVE structures, which represent a registry hives in memory.
hivelist	takes a physical address of one CMHIVE, returns the virtual address of all hives, and their names
printkey	takes a virtual address of a hive and a key name (e.g., "ControlSet001\Control"), and display the key's timestamp, values, and subkeys.
hashdump	dump the LanMan and NT hashes from the registry.
lsadump	dump the LSA secrets (decrypted) from the registry.
cachedump	dump any cached domain password hashes from the registry.

A listing of services can be obtained from the registry in memory from the registry key "HKEY_LOCAL_MACHINE\SYSTEM\CurrentControlSet\Services." This key contains the database of services and device drivers that get read into the Windows service control manager's (SCM) internal database. SCM is a remote procedure call (RPC) server that interacts with the Windows service processes.

TABLE 34.15 List of Volatility Framework plug-ins to detect rootkit hooking.

Rootkit Technique	The Volatility Framework Plug-In
IAT (import address table) Hooks	Apihooks—detect overwritten IAT entry for a PE file
EAT (export address table) Hooks	apihooks
Inline API Hooks	apihooks
IDT (interrupt descriptor table) Hools	Idt—detects overwritten IDT entries that point to malicious interrupts or processor exceptions
Driver IRP (I/O request packets) Hooks	Driverirp—detects overwritten IRP function table entries (modified to monitor buffer data)
SSDT (system service descriptor table) Hooks	Ssdt—detects hooking of pointers to kernel mode functions in the SSDT that occurs per thread
Hiding with Orphan Threads in Kernel	Threads—detects orphan threads that can unlink or unload its driver

Other registry keys that might be of interest are the keys located in the registry key "HKEY_LOCAL_ MACHINE\ SOFTWARE\ Microsoft\ Windows\CurrentVersion." The keys that are part of the auto start registries are "Run," "RunOnce," "RunOnce\Setup," "RunOnceEx," "RunServices," and "RunServicesOnce." Malware can set values in these keys to persist across system restarts and get loaded during system start-up.

Deploying and Detecting a Rootkit

Rootkits are composed of several tools (scripts, binaries, configuration files) that permit malicious users to hide their actions on a system so they can control and monitor the system for an indefinite time. Rootkits can be installed either through an exploit payload or after system access has been achieved. Rootkits are usually used to provide concealment, command and control (C2), and surveillance. A rootkit will usually try to hide system resources, such as processes, Registry information, files, and network ports. API hooking is a popular rootkit technique that intercepts system calls to make the operating system report inaccurate results that conceal the presence of the rootkit. To skip all of the system-level subversion, we can look into the memory directly to detect rootkits. The Volatility Framework provides various plug-ins to detect rootkit concealment techniques, as seen in Table 34.15.

10. SUMMARY

In this chapter we have seen the importance of having a well-documented incident response plan and process, and having an incident response team that is experienced in cyber forensics analysis. Besides having these important components, an organization needs to have strong policies and procedures that back them. Incident response is not only about countering the incident, but also about learning from it and improving on the weaknesses exposed. We should always keep in mind that preparedness is paramount since it is a matter of when rather than if an incident will strike.

With regard to the near future, the amount of data that needs to be gathered and analyzed is increasing rapidly, and as a result we are seeing the emergence of big-data analytic tools that can process disparate data sources to deal with large cases. Tomorrow's incident response teams will need to be skilled in statistical analysis as well as forensics to be able to navigate in this increasingly hostile and expanding cyberspace. As you can see, incident response and cyber forensics needs to be a step ahead of the potential causes of threats, risks, and exploits.

Finally, let's move on to the real interactive part of this chapter: review questions/exercises, hands-on projects, case projects, and optional team case project. The answers and/or solutions by chapter can be found in the Online Instructor's Solutions Manual.

CHAPTER REVIEW QUESTIONS/EXERCISES

True/False

1. True or False? Cyber forensics and incident response go hand in hand.
2. True or False? In an organization there is a daily occurrence of events within the IT infrastructure, but not all of these events qualify as incidents.
3. True or False? Forensic analysis is not usually applied to determine who, what, when, where, how, and why an incident took place.

4. True or False? When an incident response team comes across incidents relevant to these laws, they should consult with their legal team.
5. True or False? An organization should be prepared beforehand to properly respond to incidents and mitigate them in the longest time possible.

Multiple Choice

1. How do incident response and cyber forensics fit together?
   A. They don't
   B. Incident response helps cyber forensics in analyzing evidence
   C. Cyber forensics provides answers to questions that need to be answered for proper incident response
   D. None of the above
   E. All of the above
2. Which option below might be classified as an incident?
   A. Phishing attack
   B. Unauthorized access
   C. Intellectual property theft
   D. Denial-of-service attack
   E. All of the above
3. Which of these options should be considered volatile data and be captured immediately?
   A. Configuration files
   B. Database files
   C. Documents
   D. System Memory
   E. All of the above
4. Which considerations would be involved in monitoring employee email?
   A. Technical factors
   B. Legal factors
   C. Organizational factors
   D. All of the above
   E. None of the above
5. Which tool below can be used to extract the MFT of a Windows system from a drive?
   A. The Sleuthkit
   B. The Volatility Framework
   C. The KntDD
   D. Truecrypt
   E. All of the above

EXERCISE

Problem

How does an organization ship its hard drives?

Hands-On Projects

Project

How does an organization get its data back?

Case Projects

Problem

As an exercise to practice what you have learned in this chapter, you will analyze your own Windows workstation:

1. Create an image of your disk drive and save it to an external drive using AccessData FTK Imager.
2. Create a memory sample from your system using MoonSols Windows Memory Toolkit and save it to an external drive.
3. Create a super timeline of the disk image using log2timeline and list the files created within 24 hours.
4. Using the Volatility Framework, get a list of the following objects from the memory sample: processes, DLLs, modules, services, connections, sockets, API hooks.

Optional Team Case Project

Problem

When should an organization consider using a computer forensic examiner?

REFERENCES

[1] Guide to Integrating Forensic Techniques into Incident Response, NIST, 2006.
[2] Disk Imaging Tool Specification, NIST, 2001.

## Chapter 35

Securing e-Discovery

Scott R. Ellis, EnCE, RCA, RCIA
kCura Corporation

Few, if any, corporations are exempt from litigation. For some, the risk of litigation far outweighs the cost associated with managing and structuring their internal information systems in such a way as to facilitate discovery actions. In other words, the cost of doing "business as usual" in the event of large-scale litigation can actually bankrupt a company. Preparedness to respond swiftly and accurately to discovery requests can prevent costly processing and overly inclusive review. In the legal industry, any request for information typically arrives in the form of a court-ordered "discovery request." Essentially, when one organization sues another organization, they each are allowed to request the disclosure of any relevant documents relating to the litigated matter. For some corporations, these actions occur daily. For them, adhering to some sort of framework of security that allows them to quickly engage and respond to such requests becomes extremely important. There exist many models that outline and assist to define the entire process of electronic discovery, such as the Electronic Discovery Reference Model (EDRM).[1] This chapter does not aspire to redefine, reorganize, or even correct or suggest a need for correction in any such model.

The field of e-discovery relates to litigation as a whole (see checklist: An Agenda for Action for Discovery of Electronic Evidence). Most aspects of civil lawsuits will, at some point, brush up against the EDRM, whether they be civil or criminal. Recent years have seen deeper adoption and application of the Federal Rules of Civil Procedure (FRCP) by criminal courts as well. Cultivating an understanding of the FRCP therefore becomes a necessity for any attorney who wishes to practice law in the federal court system.

It follows then that corporations should also develop a similar, if not deeper, awareness of the EDRM life cycle. While this chapter acknowledges and makes reference to regulatory and legal compliance requirements, it does not seek to explain them or detail them. Such legal, risk, and compliance issues are going to be industry dependent. First on any e-discovery manager's list should be the need to discover whether or not data (and what data!) should be preserved beyond the scope of immediate purposefulness. Figure 35.1 presents the basic diagram of the EDRM life cycle.

When one organization sues another, they may become subject to a court requirement that they preserve any information pertaining to the matter. Even a letter from an opposing attorney requesting that the defendant secure and "hold" any documents that may pertain to the matter (and even in the case of a threatening letter that does not specifically request a hold when the circumstances indicate a reasonable likelihood of litigation) may trigger a need to preserve information, as litigation may be imminent. In the United States, the process of collecting, processing, reviewing, and producing this body, this collective corpus of "documents" that may contain email, images, executables, databases, text files, documents, spreadsheets, structured systems, and so on that may be relevant to the litigation is commonly called "discovery." Essentially, *anything*, any potentially relevant information that exists in electronic form, is fair game. Furthermore, in some industries, there may be regulatory compliance laws that dictate the length of time that data must be preserved. One such example is Sarbanes-Oxley, or SOX,[2] which states:

Whoever knowingly alters, destroys, mutilates, conceals, covers up, falsifies, or makes a false entry in any record, document, or tangible object with the intent to impede, obstruct, or influence the investigation or proper administration of any matter within the jurisdiction of any department or agency of the United States or any case filed under title 11, or in relation to or contemplation of any such matter or case, shall be fined under this title, imprisoned not more than 20 years, or both.

There are, in fact, *criminal* penalties for getting this wrong, in addition to civil monetary sanctions.

---

1. EDRM (edrm.net).

2. Section 802(a) of the SOX, 18 USC 1519.

An Agenda for Action for Discovery of Electronic Evidence

The cyber forensics specialist should ensure the following are adhered to (check all tasks completed):

_____**1.** Do not alter discovered information.

_____**2.** Always back up discovered information.

_____**3.** Document all investigative activities.

_____**4.** Accumulate the computer hardware and storage media necessary for the search circumstances.

_____**5.** Prepare the electronic means needed to document the search.

_____**6.** Ensure that specialists are aware of the overall forms of information evidence that are expected to be encountered as well as the proper handling of this information.

_____**7.** Evaluate the current legal ramifications of information discovery searches.

_____**8.** Back up the information discovery file or files.

_____**9.** Start the lab evidence log.

_____**10.** Mathematically authenticate the information discovery file or files.

_____**11.** Proceed with the forensic examination.

_____**12.** Find the MD5 message digest for the original information discovery file or files.

_____**13.** Log all message digest values in the lab evidence log.

_____**14.** When forensic work is complete, regenerate the message digest values using the backups on which work was performed; log these new values alongside the hashes that were originally generated. If the new values match the originals, it's reasonable to conclude that no evidence tampering took place during the forensic examination of the information file(s).

_____**15.** Briefly compare the physical search and seizure with its logical (data-oriented) counterpart, information discovery.

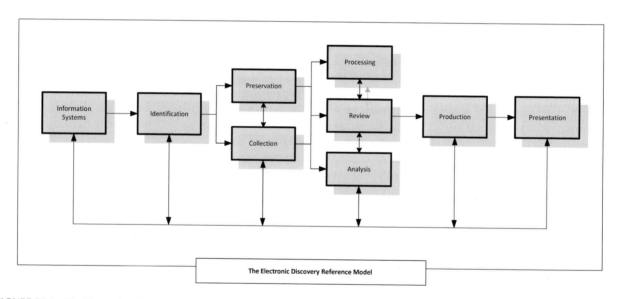

FIGURE 35.1 The Electronic Discovery Reference Model provides a loose framework for how to manage electronic discovery and what to expect from a process viewpoint.

Technologists should be aware that the regulations exist, and they should ensure that their organizations are compliant by working with a qualified law firm or legal department. There exist mountains of this sort of regulatory legalese. Whether or not it applies to your organization is important to the work and the level of security detailed in this chapter and to its implementation. Understanding all of the challenges of regulatory compliance in your organization will likely be a departmental or cross-departmental responsibility—that is, an entire department or team will provide oversight of this increasingly important aspect of conducting business.

The EDRM model, and its accompanying diagram, represent just *one* way of how data may flow from an information system to a discovery information system to a courtroom. The large box in Figure 35.2 represents the confines of a discovery information system. Shaded boxes represent zone boundaries where information may move

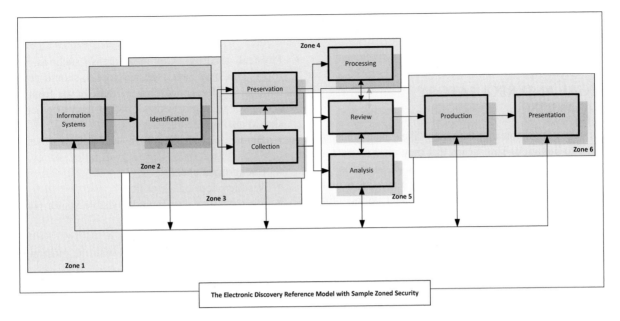

FIGURE 35.2   Underpinning the EDRM with zone security throughout the e-discovery life cycle.

from one vendor to another. Dotted line boxes are used to refer to areas of interest or to break out details or suggest technologies. In this example, overlapping zones identify areas of functionality where data is passed from one vendor to the next. Some vendors do service zones 1–6, but in this example, each zone represents a different vendor handling data. A similar, real diagram of a corporate EDRM would attach a similar diagram, complete with vendor names and data transfer protocols, to an EDRM procedure document for each and every case where data may be processed using different vendors. For security purposes, it is wisest to keep the number of vendors to a minimum, with set and established data conduits.

There are disparate, often overlapping, zones in this diagram because it is very common for multiple vendors to be involved in processing data in a lawsuit. This is done because very few vendors perform the work required in all zones. From start to finish, from standard information management strategies through to presenting data in the courtroom, few, if any, can do everything and do it well. Even fewer corporations manage any of this work internally. Later, this chapter will refer back to the numbers on the boxes and will describe the various security measures taken at each zone interface, as well as the benefits of shifting certain work to fewer vendors or moving certain tasks to internal, corporate IT. Some of this fragmentation can also be attributed to the defibrillating effect of the change in the Federal Rules on the entire paper discovery industry in 2006. Many of these small, e-discovery shops already existed, but were amped up by the sudden demand for their services. So, rather than

using the EDRM as one (and perhaps the most accurate) example, this chapter:

1. Explains it from an industry insider perspective
2. Collates issues of performance, urgency, accuracy, risk, and security to a zoned model that underpins the EDRM
3. Explains the very real need for organizations to secure certain operations internally
4. Provides examples through real-world experiences of flawed discovery and what should have been done differently
5. Discusses how security *from* the information, as well as security *of* it, plays a critical role throughout much of the EDRM

1. INFORMATION MANAGEMENT

The framework of the EDRM begins with information management. Much in the same way that there exists a model for electronic discovery, there also exists an information governance reference model (IGRM) that pays particular attention to the needs of an IT management organization that concerns itself, and prepares itself, for possible future litigation. To be successful, information management must consider all the stakeholders in an environment; it must apply successful collaboration across all groups in an enterprise; it must consider the security of the data and protection of systems; and it must engage information technology to implement the procedures and guidelines created. It must also be secure. There is no worse feeling than the sinking sensation you will feel than when @nonymous hacks your systems and posts your entire discovery database online, along with your CEO's email box.

2. LEGAL AND REGULATORY OBLIGATION

Certain types of organizations are more likely than others to be prone to litigation. This means that they must operate at a heightened sense of awareness as it pertains to e-discovery processes. In particular, law firms have both ethical and legal obligations to protect client confidential data. Guidelines pertaining to the security requirements and the specific safeguards required by law are all outlined in the Federal Rules of Civil Procedure. This chapter is not meant to replace that. Rather, this chapter seeks to familiarize its readers with the basic flow of information throughout a lawsuit so that proper security can be executed. Without knowledge and deep understanding of the inner workings of a lawsuit and the functions that are required for the successful management of it, security will surely fail.

Securing the Field of Play

This chapter is titled "Securing e-Discovery," but it has much broader reaching implications. Just about any organization may be subject to litigation. What, then, is a security model, if it is one that doesn't anticipate litigation? A security model that does not anticipate the possible need to collect large amounts of data, port it into other systems, and ensure that the data is relevant risks being unresponsive to a request from the court and possible noncompliance with an order from a judge. Much in the same way that not knowing the speed limit will not get you out of a ticket, not knowing how or where your data is stored will not prevent a judge from sending someone else to your offices to show you how your systems interoperate. This person will be an expert, probably chosen by the opposition, interviewed by the judge, and you will be paying his bill, which may be as much as $400/hr. or higher. What follows are several steps to:

- Assess, evaluate, and remediate the current state of security and discovery preparedness
- Get things in order
- Set the stage for data collection and effective response to a discovery request

Step 1: Examine the Information Management Environment

Are you secure? Your internal systems may be a mess of disparate data and IT fiefdoms, but first, let's close the doors and staunch the flow. Areas where sensitive data,

or easily obtained access to sensitive data stores, should be secured are as follows:

- Physical security—Common areas, such as lunchrooms that may have external access, should never be unmanned. Reception areas that have front door access, or may have corridors that lead to other areas should also be secured with:
  - Biometric security for physical access to sensitive data areas
  - Background checks
  - Visible photo badge policy
  - Visitor policy that includes visible visitor photo ID badges
- Data center ISO 9001 security.
- Firewalls should be configured with the most minimal access possible.
- Antivirus should be nonintrusive and should be pointing at points of ingress. File repositories should run scheduled scans—virus signature databases are frequently updated, a file that is clean today may trip an alert after a signature update. Entire system scans should be scheduled jobs that run during nightly or weekly maintenance.
- Acceptable use policy—Users are the number one incursion vector. Ensure that your acceptable use policy is well formed and *understood.*
- Response plans (what do we do when someone we don't know tries to tailgate us into the office? What do we do when tables are suddenly missing in our database?)

Step 2: Measure: How Secure is the System?

Penetration testing should be performed against the enterprise systems. Any organization that wishes to conduct collections must understand that sensitive data will be copied and corraled into a new area. This area should be secured. If any one of the above steps is not followed, as an IT director you will almost certainly come into work and find that the penetration team has placed a chocolate cake on your desk and changed your desktop image. The organization that will conduct the penetration testing should be testing the following things:

1. Internal, physical penetration. Can they put someone at a desktop and access the system? Can they insert "malicious" code into your system? This may be as simple as accessing the BIOS of a machine, changing the boot order, and booting a new machine on your network.
2. Penetration testing of any and all external facing software, especially web sites.
3. Internal penetration testing—Can internal systems be breached by someone sitting at a desktop, with varying levels of access?
4. Penetration testing of any critical software as a service (SAAS) system. For example, if the testers can trick

the HR director into logging in to a spoofed or cross-site scripted payroll site that contains sensitive employee data, a flaw in your security system exists.

5. Penetration testing of known services that protect essential data. Ensure that they can't be hacked easily. Many of the methods for hacking services such as Amazon Cloud or ADP are easy to spot. All software as a service (SAAS) providers should have implemented or be in the process of implementing two-factor authentication. If they are not, then your data shouldn't be there and should be moved.

6. Examine the VLAN architecture, in both virtual and physical topologies. Virtual switches offer a whole host of challenges of which many IT administrators are unaware.

7. Socially engineered attacks—Most attacks have a social component. The attacker knows what he wants, he knows who works at the company, and he knows their name, too. Or it may be completely impersonal, and the hacker simply saw an email address he liked and wants to play with it.

8. Stolen and lost access badges—The easiest way to access a building is if you have an RFID pass. Criminals know that the badges that workers wear can get them unquestioned access to a building. And, as a bonus, the badges are easy to steal (people wear them dangling from their clothing and often even drop them on the street—this author has found at least three, potentially all-access badges on the streets of Chicago.) Badges can certainly contain a photo; but name, workplace, address, and so on, should be encoded in the chip. There should be a mail-to address on the card that *is not* the same as the location to which the card grants access.

Step 3: Remediate Issues

Number 4 is perhaps the most important item in the above list. Most penetrations that result in loss of data are socially engineered and will, at some stage, include some social element. Someone will receive an email with a link that will take the user to a spoofed Web page where the users will log in, thinking they are logging into their own systems.

Example

Mattie, an internal HR director, uses a custom-built payroll system that is built on top of a known technology. The password reset notifications sent out by the system *always look the same*. The hacker is aware of the system used. Perhaps he used to be an employee or a contractor. Perhaps he saw it on the software vendor's Web site and thought that Mattie's company was a client. He then culled Mattie's name from a published employee directory. Or maybe he worked out her email address by calling and asking questions about employment. It doesn't matter. He gets in by sending Mattie an email that appears to be from an internal email address. Its header has been forged. The email claims that multiple attempts have been made to log in using employee x's log-in, and she will need to reset their password. The email provides a link to the "system." Mattie follows the link, sees her internal log-in screen, and enters HER log-in information and is immediately redirected to her internal log-in screen. She blinks, and says to herself "That's odd, didn't I just log in?"

Mattie is pretty savvy; her company has a security training program. She immediately logs in and changes her password, and then reports the incident. The hacker had her log-in credentials momentarily, and if not for her quick thinking, he would have used it to successfully export the entire payroll, which he then would have held hostage or simply posted on the Internet.

How do you stop this sort of thing from happening? Spam filters may be able to trap these emails, but what if it comes in on a personal account? Most people would just raise their eyebrows and say, "That's interesting," and chances are good they wouldn't follow it, but you can't count on it. One step would be to not give the outside world access to internal, sensitive systems. Then the redirect would fail, and even if the hacker traps the sign on, he has to breach the physical location. Another way to prevent it would be to ensure two-factor authentication.

There are loopholes in any external facing system. Wherever a human being interfaces with an electronic system, this is an avenue of ingress that can be exploited. A seemingly secure operation such as entering a password and checking a fob on a keychain or a text message on a cell phone to access a system has a weakness. There is a password that remains constant, which means it can be observed or logged, and there is a keychain or cell phone that can be stolen, cloned, or replaced. Additionally, many different types of accounts can be *linked* together now, and hackers can daisy chain enough information together from the different password hints provided by these accounts that they can successfully leapfrog right into secure areas.

Gaining access to one employee's twitter account could conceivably be the single breach a hacker needs to be able to gain access to all of corporate systems—especially if the victim has access to everything and passwords set to automatic on his laptop, has linked password recovery of corporate accounts to both personal and work email addresses, and is someone who plays an active part in the online community and has a high level of visibility.

Here are some security items that should be ensured in each zone. Later, this chapter will explain the specific vulnerabilities of each zone while describing how to collapse the zones to more manageable, securable corridors:

1. Examine the security policy *as it exists today*. Don't just document how it should be and tell everyone how

it should be. Rather, show them how it is and tell them what to stop doing. Better yet, *stop them.* Don't allow employees to use their work email addresses in any nonwork-related capacity. Don't let them use their personal email addresses on corporate systems.

2. Don't allow employees to use their personal email addresses as password recovery points for any work-related systems.

3. Office systems should never be accessed from personal laptops, which may be unsecured or may have lapsed antivirus. If circumstances necessitate this allowance, then provide licenses to antivirus and firewall technologies to employees for free. After all, they are accessing work systems and ostensibly performing work while at home from personal systems. If the corporation can't see the wisdom in providing security, then disallow it and take the productivity hit.

4. Enforce work-personal email uniqueness. Somebody1@website1.com should not be under the same user as somebody1@website2.com. For example, your work email and personal email address prefixes must be different.

5. Do use encrypted tunnels, AES 256 entire drive encryption, and secure messenger services for moving sensitive data.

Securing e-discovery data will be challenging, and there will be many hurdles to overcome. Human behavior—changing it—presents the greatest challenge. Infallible controls must be put into place to protect this data, as it will likely represent the most sensitive data in the organization. Successful information management will facilitate the identification and securing of relevant data. Relevancy will play a key part in this process. Take the approach that there is an existing compromise—that there is already someone in your network. Minimize risk of exposure as much as possible—they can't get what isn't there.

Identification

The EDRM model breaks identification into a separate phase of e-Discovery than information management. This was perhaps for ease and beautification of the EDRM diagram. It is important to note that, from a fountainhead perspective, information management most certainly belongs in this position on the EDRM diagram. However, from a physical management perspective, information management encompasses the entire spectrum of the EDRM life cycle, with each segment, along the way, underscored by an information management system. Securing e-discovery then becomes a matter of interfacing and connecting to disparate information management systems that are designed to perform different tasks, or it becomes a matter of absorbing those systems into the collective corporate information system.

For very large or highly litigated corporations faced with a new lawsuit every day, it is not a matter of whether or not they will save money by bringing e-discovery internally, it is a matter of *how much.* By doing this, by bringing the identification systems in-house, corporations can then create a security cordon that contains the team infrastructure, the software used to identify relevant data, and the access and permission controls to the identification system, which should tie directly to its users. Typically, this would be the internal legal department. This cordoned system can then act as a launch pad for secure transmission corridors to vendors for further data processing.

For many corporations, and many IT experts, however, the term *legal hold* means very little. From a high level, very few corporations will be faced with litigation on a daily basis. There are several reasons for this:

1. They aren't big enough to make it worthwhile.
2. They are very transparent in what they do already.
3. They don't think that anything they are doing could ever cause a lawsuit to be filed.
4. They never thought they would ever need to sue another company.
5. The corporation is able to quickly settle any matters that do arise.
6. It's a shell corporation, and the owners are untraceable.
7. Economically, the corporation would collapse after just one discovery motion, so they declare bankruptcy and fold.
8. They haven't made anyone angry yet.

Generally, companies such as these don't concern themselves with e-discovery. However, some of them should. Item 3 above, in particular, causes many companies to be caught unawares. Some people simply don't realize that copying someone else's product is illegal, and they will even brag about it to complete strangers. These people are heading the wrong way down a one-way track. Any organization with revenues in the millions of dollars is very likely doing something on a scale that someone will notice, take offense to it, and file a suit.

NOTE: The Sedona Conference is an organization comprised of leading judges and attorneys who provide guidelines and frameworks for the proper conduct of legal hold, as well as other e-discovery activities.

When faced with a litigation hold requirement, business stakeholders should inform their technologists of as many details of the lawsuit as possible. Key stakeholders in a legal action are:

• Officers of the corporation
• In-House Counsel or other representation
• IT directors
• Managers of custodians

Each of these people should understand what makes a potential lawsuit. This will better enable both the attorneys and the information technologist to work together to produce the relevant documents.[3] What makes a potential lawsuit? Let's take a look[4]:

1. Something happens that causes loss of income, life, or injuries.
2. The corporation or person knew the potentially dangerous condition existed and had a legal duty to safeguard the damaged party.
3. The corporation did nothing, and was not in the process of remedying it, and prevention would have been the normal practice of a "reasonably prudent party."

Many types of lawsuits fit this scenario. One example[5] would be of a school that runs its own bus service and, every year, offers safety training to its Kindergarten children on the third day of school. Because it occurs at the end of the day on the third day of school, it means the children have *already* ridden the bus five times, with no safety training. At the same time, prevailing practices among similar schools require safety training before using the bus.

NOTE: Optionally, what can make a lawsuit even stronger is if the corporation tried to hide what happened. Best case scenario (for the plaintiff, not the defendant!) would be a case where the plaintiff is awarded punitive damages due to intentional misconduct. The author includes this information in part because it is interesting, and in part as a warning. Punitive damages may involve multiplying monetary damages, such as a tripling of the award.

One year, an incident occurs on the first day of school where an older child convinces one of the Kindergarteners that he needs to exit the bus at the next stop through the rear exit door, while the bus is moving. He attempts to do it but is stopped by the bus driver. The parent of the child writes an angry letter to the school and advises them that they should be providing safety training *before* the Kindergarteners are ever allowed on the bus. The school fears a lawsuit (even though no loss occurred), and the parent is put on an internal watch-list as "litigious."

The school then thanks the parent for the letter but does nothing. The school fails to actually respond to the threat. This is because the school administrators didn't understand the above rules. Now, this incident is inactionable because there was no loss to society. However, a year passes by and on the first day of school the incident recurs, with the same older child, and this time it leads to the injury of a Kindergarten child and a lawsuit is filed. The parent of the child in the first incident informs the parent of the child in the second incident, and even provides him with a copy of the email he had sent. The email letter becomes the centerpiece in the lawsuit, but the school denies that the email was ever sent.

The plaintiffs are granted access to the school, and over a single weekend they create exact duplicate copies of every PC and server in the district. The judge in the case is convinced that the school network, in its entirety, was instrumental in the incident—and FRCP 37 covers this. Whether or not criminal charges will be filed remains on the table.

Unbeknownst to the defendants, the judge e issues a civil search warrant, one that allows civilian experts—employed by the plaintiffs—to access the site and make forensic copies of all digital media located on the premises. This *includes* any thumb drives that employees may happen to be carrying on their person! To ensure that this civil search warrant was carried out, arrival on site was heralded by 20 black SUVs—a squad of fully armored and m16 carrying federal U.S. marshals—that pulled up into the school parking lot at 3 PM on a Friday afternoon when school was being let out. The school computer system administrator is located and ordered by federal marshals to relinquish complete and total access, passwords, tokens, and so on. Now enter the e-discovery and forensic experts who will take the school's information systems apart, piece by piece, and make forensic copies of every hard drive. They will render the entire school's information system as subject to discovery.[6] Upon inspection of the systems, the experts located a deleted copy of the email and dozens of other complaints about the school safety system

---

3. This is not to be interpreted as legal advice, but is based on the courtroom and work life experiences of the author, working and testifying within the federal and state judiciaries of the United States and with litigating attorneys for over a dozen years.

4. It follows, then, that a deeper understanding of the entire motivation and rationale behind these lawsuits will enable a system security architect to better anticipate and understand the nature of what is happening, and what is about to happen, to him. Or rather, what is about to happen to his security model. The following examples very closely parallel several of the lawsuits within which this author has served as an expert witness. For exemplification and clarity, certain aspects of the cases, including the overall nature of each, have been changed. Where applicable, references to actual cases have been included for further study.

5. This and any other stories, unless referencing actual cases, are completely fictionalized accounts. Names, situations, and places have been changed

6. *Covad v. Revonet*—Mag. Judge Facciola, in a landmark decision, reduced Revonet's arguments to dust when he ordered that the entire network was relevant to the action and ordered them to allow a team of COVAD forensic experts to enter the Revonet Sioux Falls location and create exact, forensic copies of all PCs, laptops, and servers. Over 125 forensic images were created at a cost of many thousands of dollars. Ultimately, Revonet declared bankruptcy. Revonet failed to provide a believable and reliable basis for determining that only particular subsidiary databases contained relevant documents, thereby rendering the entire networked database, and this included all PCs, subject to the other party's expert forensic handling and searching for relevant documents. United States District Court for the District of Columbia, Civil Action 06-1892-CKK-JMF, Document 95, Filed 05/27/2009.

in general, all of which created sensational drama in front of the jury, and resulted in a judgment against the district of many millions of dollars.[7]

This situation plays out in courtrooms around the world on a daily basis. Companies are simply aggregations of humans trying to make money. Sometimes they engage in activities that are unsafe or illegal in an effort to save money (or make money). Sometimes these activities are activities that put others at risk.

A less distressing, and also fictional, example would be the case of *HappyFlyers v. MadFlyers.* MadFlyers is a small company that manufactures model, remote control helicopters. Unfortunately, their engineer retired (he wasn't very good anyway), sales are slipping, and everyone is buying the competition's (Happy Flyers) helicopters, even though they are more expensive. MadFlyers CEO Gerardo Gutierrez purchases one of the Happy Flyers choppers and says, "What the heck!" and sends it off to his chop shop in China where they reverse engineer it and make a near exact replica. MadFlyers then sells thousands of the helicopters for half the price. Unbeknownst to Gerardo, the CEO of Happy Flyers heard about this, visited one of his shops, and purchased one of the knock-off choppers. Additionally, Gerardo isn't the only one who copied the helicopter. Six other manufacturers also felt the heat and similarly copied patented sections of Happy Flyers copter. Also unbeknownst to Gerardo is the fact that he has crossed paths with a patent house. Basically, Happy Flyers is a shell company, owned by a holding corporation that owns and protects many patents. The only actual work it does is to search the marketplace for potential violations of the patents it owns, new patents to purchase, and file lawsuits when violations are found.

Gerardo finds himself subpoenaed, and he is asked to settle for an undisclosed amount. Of the seven companies that were targeted in this patent infringement suit, MadFlyers refuses to admit what they did. They claim they sold "only five or six" of the helicopters. They also claim that they are working to pull and find all the invoices from their system, but they are having trouble accessing it. Again and again, Gerardo claims the system is difficult to access and that reports can't be run, that he has to go to the warehouse and do them one at a time, and so on. Ultimately, the judge allows an independent and neutral forensic examiner, escorted by federal marshalls, to enter the Mad Flyers warehouse facility in California, where several servers and PCs are imaged.

Subsequently, in court, the expert testimony reveals that he uncovered nearly a million dollars worth of sales of the phony copter, and that the sales were recovered

from the database as orphan line item records, meaning that the original order had been deleted, but because someone had gone into the backend of the sales/order system to do it, and had done it incorrectly, the detail of each order remained behind while, from the front end, it would most likely appear that the sales never existed. The judge orders both parties to retire to a conference room and settle this matter, and he warns the defendant that *he will not like* the judgment that will be handed out should be fail to come back into the courtroom without a settlement. They settle for an undisclosed amount.

Identification, then, becomes a matter of asking a number of questions. First, one must understand what is happening to him or her in a lawsuit, and the degree to which uncooperativeness will aggravate the situation, and make the judge angry. Angry federal judges are not fun people. Don't make them angry. To facilitate the litigation hold process, many companies use legal hold software to manage the custodians and administer legal holds. A typical legal hold product will allow the legal hold administrator to perform the following identifications, and then inform the owners of the data, the *custodians*, to *hold* any and all relevant data to the matter. One piece of software, titled "Method," offers the following capabilities, which guide the hold administrator to input the correct information:

1. It will initiate the process of identifying *who are the custodians*—the people who have the data that is material or relevant[8] to the lawsuit.
2. Where is the data?
3. Are there backups, are there thumb drives floating around, etc.
4. It will provide instructions for next actions.

The role of a security architect, a system administrator, a CIO, a CTO, a technology director, and the like, goes beyond simple security and encompasses a holistic security model and a level of awareness that demands attention to the facts at hand. This means that, in the

---

7. Remember, this entire account is a fictionalized amalgamation of many cases and experiences of the author.

8. Two words that are often confused with one another are *material* and *relevant*. Here is an example of this confusion: Elaine alleges that she remembers witnessing a certain event at a certain time and what she was wearing because it rained on Tuesday. Elaine, while walking outside on Tuesday, got soaking wet. She preserved her dress in order to prove that it rained on Tuesday. The dress is material in that it will be offered to prove a specific issue in the case. Elaine's testimony would then be relevant, as she will testify that she wore the dress on Tuesday, and it became wet because it rained. Relevancy tends to tie together one or more material facts. For example, testimony to prove that the dress is a dress, or that the dress is wet, would not be relevant. However, any information pertaining to the purchase of the dress, the type of dress, documentation about how wet it was, and so on might be deemed as being *responsive* to the matter, which means the documents are eligible for evaluation in the process of admitting evidence, and means they are "discoverable."

model laid out in Figure 35.1, the interfaces of each zone must be identified and assessed. Mechanisms must be in place to deal with the movement of data, and the administrator must be equipped with a responsible, responsive plan that he or she can engage when litigation becomes apparently imminent. The EDRM model may take different shapes and forms in differing types of litigation, and reflect that no two IT infrastructures are built in the same way. In fact, we expect to see vast variations just within one information management system.

This chapter seeks to impart an understanding of the EDRM as it relates to information security. To do this, it underpins the structure of a lawsuit with the structure of a zoned security model, which will also vary substantially from one organization to the next and even from one lawsuit to the next. The point of this chapter is to provide an acceptable, sufficiently adaptable model whereby the flows of information between zones, and the type of information in motion, may be fully understood and modeled. By also demonstrating how risk can be mitigated by adjusting the activities, the reader of this chapter should begin to understand how malleable this model is and how the various decisions made to hire vendors, purchase licenses for internal use, and hire internal or external counsel can have a deep impact on the overall security model.

Identification Integration

From a security standpoint, then, how do we plan? By securing information identified as relevant internally, and by developing policies and procedures that govern how

information is retained, we can then respond quickly and accurately to any demand for disclosure. In addition, we can do it while minimizing the risk of exposing the data in a vulnerable environment, or unintentionally releasing data. A corporation can then prevent unauthorized delivery of sensitive personal and corporate information into the hands of strangers. This section is titled Identification Integration because it will discuss how to integrate an identification system into the information management segment of the EDRM. Ultimately, it is most secure for all zones to be collapsed into this segment, because this is where the corporation can maintain the most complete control over the security of its information.

When the identification process is executed internally, as in Figure 35.3, observe how the entirety of Zone 2 becomes encapsulated by Zone 1. Zone 3 then collapses into a simple, manageable form, leaving us with a fathomable disconnect between Zone 2 and Zone 4. Zone 3 can then be treated as a secured conduit. Often, however, companies have no internal resources to which to turn when faced with electronic discovery requests. E-discovery is a relatively new field that experienced a surge of growth and acceptance in December 2006 with the new Federal Rules of Civil Procedure, which finally formalized the consideration of electronic evidence and codified it into law. Since 2006, hundreds of companies that specialize in electronic discovery (e-discovery) management have sprung into existence. Many of these companies possess vast experience in the field, but some of them are simply companies that once specialized in paper discovery and have now scrambled to hire anyone who has even a modicum of knowledge of the process so that

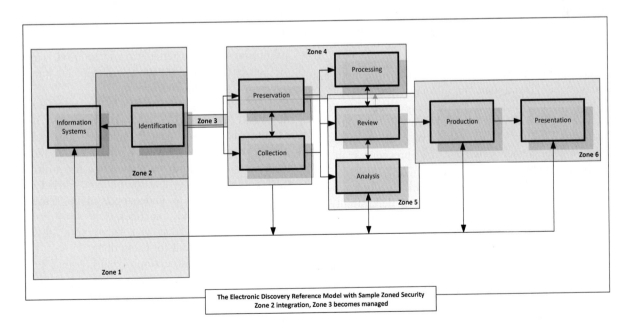

The Electronic Discovery Reference Model with Sample Zoned Security
Zone 2 integration, Zone 3 becomes managed

FIGURE 35.3 Collapsing Zone 2.

they don't collapse along with the paper industry. They have populated their staff with "experts" who have insufficient skills in searching and culling techniques, and lack significant expertise in deploying infrastructure to support the big data lawsuits of this decade.

Such companies are not easily identified—they possess all the tools and all of the staff, and they may even host very large cases for big-name clients. However, software vendors that publish effective software solutions do exist, and they may have some sort of "Best of Breed" programs. In these programs, clients are tested by the vendor to ensure that they possess the capability to successfully manage the program. Vendors will list these best of breed companies on their Web sites in special areas. The best software vendors will participate in programs such as Gartner's Magic Quadrant study. Every year, Gartner publishes a study of the competing players in almost all the major technology markets. A firm grasp of the principles put forth in this chapter will provide the background needed to build out a successful, and defensible, corporate EDRM implementation.

Securing Zone 1

Zone 2 in this model is now subsumed by Zone 1. This is not to say that the information in Zone 2 inherits the permissions of Zone 1. It still maintains its own rules, but now it can do so using the same framework of information security that secures Zone 1. Security managers of Zone 1 may now also manage items in Zone 2 because they have internalized the function of identification. Perhaps they have hired internal counsel and installed an appliance that allows them to capture and cull information that is deemed relevant. Perhaps the identification process was as simple as walking over to Joe's desk, pulling the plug on his PC, taking it to a secure area, and bagging and tagging it. Always, when securing a computer that may be a pivotal item in a court case, standard, forensically sound procedures should be used to secure it. Any further reads and writes to the drive will be deemed as suspicious. Chapter 33 in this book, on cyber forensics, provides much greater detail on the procedures that should be used here.

Zone 2 notwithstanding, Zone 1 must then adopt some new standards of data security. In terms of defensibility, data must be preserved in such a way that is customary and necessary for continued business operation. It makes no sense for some companies to retain seven years worth of email. For some companies, however, this may be necessary. Zone 1, the information management phase, encompasses all that a business must do to simply operate, securely, day to day. When developing a model of security that incorporates electronic discovery, consider

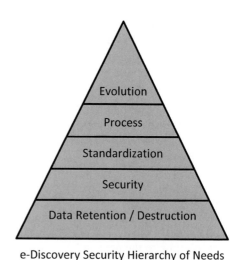

e-Discovery Security Hierarchy of Needs

FIGURE 35.4 Getting it right. Not unlike Maslow's (see Figure 35.4) hierarchy of needs, enterprises need to focus on the most important tasks first—start at the bottom of the triangle and work toward the top. It makes no sense to be worrying about the nuances of converting .eml files to XML for more efficient storage if you don't even know where all of your backup tapes are going, or if your backups are even completing successfully.

that there is a new model of need. Consider that businesses have a similar hierarchy of needs as Maslow's.

Each layer of the triangle describes the phase of development. The items at the bottom of the triangle *must* be executed effectively before implementing process. Process that you implement on top of a fragmented or an incomplete backup and retention strategy will be forced to change or adapt later on, and change is costly. Failure in this may also have deadly business consequences. Losing all of your responsive data in a lawsuit could be a business-ending event:

- **Evolution**—finding better ways to improve what you are doing. Be faster, better, stronger. Do more in-house, and do it more efficiently.
- **Process**—defining and understanding your information flow.
- **Standardization**—things like making sure everyone uses the same software, stores information in the same places, and uses approved technology for information transmittals. Ensuring that the policies carried out on the bottom rung are understood, make sense, and adhere to business best practices.
- **Security**—ensuring that you know your data isn't walking out your front (or back) door.
- **Data Retention/destruction**—ensuring that you are keeping what you want to keep, destroying what you don't want, and backing up data at risk.

Starting at the bottom and working up the pyramid provide architects with a scalable model of data security.

Alternatively, starting at the top and working to the bottom is similar to folding one's clothes before washing them. It makes little sense.

Securing Zone 2

Securing Zone 2, once it has been collapsed into Zone 1, then becomes a matter of definition. The breadth and scope of the discovery, the manner in which potentially relevant information will be identified, all scream for a comprehensive plan. This plan should detail the steps needed to identify the following items of information:

1. Custodians.
2. Keywords or time periods of relevancy. Discerning this may be a matter of conducting interviews and documenting the location of data.
3. Do backups exist? What format?
4. Is all information accessible? Inaccessible information, or data that has been destroyed *after it became apparent that litigation was likely* will present special challenges. It is important that all IT personnel understand that tampering with evidence may have very dire consequences.

This phase is about identification. As it relates to security, the following items should be of interest and should be secured from distribution:

1. Strategy plan—All items should be marked with the words "Confidential" and "Attorneys' Eyes Only."
2. Create an Identification Team roster.
3. Plans and spreadsheets that detail source lists should be stored securely. Applications that can track media should be created.
4. Access to software used to initiate a legal hold should be password protected, and only team members, trained in its use, should access it.

All information pertaining to litigation should be treated with the same amount of security with which one would handle sensitive financial data, if not more so. In the end, emails collected may contain data relating to *all* aspects of the enterprise—from logistical data to personal messages sent by the CEO to his administrative assistant—there could truly be very sensitive data released to the opposition. And, in the event of a "no-holds-barred" judgment? All data could go to the opposition—all of it. When it comes to the deeply probative nature of a lawsuit, there can be no doubt that, at some point, information from many sources may be culled. Here are some helpful tips.

- Build a solid identification system from the start. This will allow system administrators to respond rapidly and securely, with only responsive data.

- Create a solid, but not overly restrictive, communication system that raises corporate awareness. Inform corporate system users that the corporate system should not be used for personal communication.
- See to it that employees shred and destroy any personal emails they have sent.
- 'For employees' personal communication, make sure they use their own personal devices. In today's highly equipped society, there is no reason to use the corporate system for anything personal.
- Make it Group Policy at the corporatewide level to delete temporary Internet files upon exiting the application.
- Consider that some inter-relay chat messaging systems can be configured to save and send missed chats as emails, and create a policy that covers how these chat logs should be treated.
- Be aware of "cloud" data—data that a corporation may have created and is potentially relevant, but could be stored in a third-party SAAS system. Is this data easily exported? Can it be accessed and exported with custom queries?

Keeping personal communication off the enterprise system has several benefits. Aside from the inherent security benefit (users may launch harmful attachments from personal emails that are not scanned by the corporate email system), consider that with a Security Awareness Program:

- The amount of potentially discoverable data will be reduced.
- The potential exposure to harmful and misleading personal conversations diminishes or disappears.
- The program itself raises awareness that users should not write any emails that they wouldn't want to be made publicly available.

A strong security policy will allow the legal hold team to perform their work within a predefined and secure framework. An "anything goes" policy, while seemingly very employee friendly, can have disastrous results: When the professional, corporate system commingles with employees' personal lives, the amount of data increases, and the opportunities for email from disgruntled employees who have their own interpretations that they may willingly be sharing with those outside the organization, on the corporate system, increase. Keeping to the hierarchy and defining this stage of the EDRM within the corporation is key to securing this zone. Creating a responsive and secure information identification program *within* the information management system is essential to maintaining the utmost security of corporate data. When Zone 2 is subsumed by Zone 1, a secure conduit can be opened for the movement of data and for the subsequent integration of all zones into a secure work flow. The alternative to assimilation of Zone 2 by Zone 1 is that outside consultants be granted unfettered access to entire systems, and that it be secure.

Many possible vendor arrangements can be made when dealing with the identification of data. Ultimately, whichever configuration is arrived at must meet several rules of e-discovery security[9]:

1. Information must always be encrypted when transmitted over the Internet.
2. Data cannot be lost: Create multiple backups and have a DR site as well. In the end, there is no such thing as a real "backup" of electronic data. There are only redundant points of failure.
3. Data can only be accessed by authorized personnel.
4. Data has not been changed or altered maliciously, which can be verified independently. This verification can be accomplished rather easily using methods that are well known in the e-discovery industry. An e-discovery vendor's sales team may not be up to speed on this, but their technical staff should know all about it.
5. Stored or archived data is encrypted. Data stored outside your system should reside on encrypted systems. A bankruptcy of the firm or vendor hosting your e-discovery data could mean that your data resides on systems that will be sold at auction.
6. Data can easily be located and destroyed when no longer needed.

Once these rules are understood, we are ready to delve deeper into the EDRM life cycle, and discuss the transition of data from Zone 2 to Zone 3 in Preservation, Collection, and Processing. Zone 3, then, becomes a securable conduit with easily established secure data transfer protocols, and security experts can shift their focus to battening down Zone 4.

Securing Zone 4: Preservation, Collection, and Processing

In the EDRM, preservation refers primarily to the act of requesting that all custodians cease and desist any and all deletion activities and any automatic deletion procedures respecting potentially responsive data. Effectively, though, the end result of the act of preservation, collection and processing, is that data is preserved. Until data has actually been collected, logged, and securely stored, it has not been preserved in the traditional sense of the word.

9. These items are derived from the Health Insurance Portability and Accountability Act (HIPAA; Pub.L. 104-191, 110 Stat. 1936, enacted August 21, 1996), which is not specific to e-discovery. In the end, it is up to organizations to make certain that they have complied with whatever standards are applicable in their industry.

Preservation

Typically, at the outset of litigation, or when litigation is reasonably likely, a requirement called a "legal hold" or "litigation hold" will apply. In a sense, this is the order that triggers identification. Some organizations should have the ability to immediately pull the requested data; for others, however, the criticality of collection matters very little. Once data has been identified, it then must be preserved in a forensic manner. This necessitates a discussion on metadata. You can't preserve and secure data if you don't know what the data is, where it is, or what data is necessary to be captured. Often, at the heart of this debate lies a conversation about *metadata* and about data *forensics*.

What is Metadata?

Metadata is data about data. For example, this chapter includes the following metadata, which can be derived using programs such as EnCase or FTK, which are forensic analysis tools:

As can be seen in Table 35.1, this metadata includes operating system (OS) information such as file created, modified, accessed, and last written. These timestamps may be very important because they will provide timeline

TABLE 35.1 A Listing of some of the OS Metadata that can be Derived from EnCase.

Metadata	Item
Filename	**Chapter 64.docx**
File Ext	docx
File Category	Document
Description	File, Archive
Last Accessed	09/27/2012 04:34:03PM
File Created	09/27/2012 04:34:03PM
Last Written	09/25/2012 08:32:27AM
Entry Modified	09/27/2012 04:34:03PM
Logical Size	418,950
Physical Size	421,888
Starting Extent	0D-C10609788
File Extents	1
Physical Location	44,717,031,424
Physical Sector	87,337,952
Full Path	C:\User\Chapter 64 - Securing eDiscover\Chapter 64.docx

data when investigating some sort of breech. One such example would be an employee accessing documents during her tenure as an employee versus her accessing the file systems post-termination. Chapter 33 includes a description of these timestamps and what they mean. This metadata must be preserved. Other items that may fall into the category of "metadata" to be preserved include drafts, outlines, and all their subsequent markup, hidden text, track changes, and so on. As can be seen in Table 35.2, a much more extensive list can be produced using a software tool to extract and compile the data into a structure format.

TABLE 35.2 This Table Lists all of the Metadata that can be Extracted from a Document. This Extraction was Performed using a Tool called Relativity Processing.[10]

Metadata Field	Data
Time Zone Field	1038662
Processing Custodian	1038663
Originating Processing Set	2352
Control Number	REL000000020
Virtual path	
Level	1
Container ID	
Container name	
Container extension	
File Path	\\server\FileShare\dan\INV\0\5.DOCX
Processing duplicate hash	05D5DD668238B1DF9D18B57DF5469DCCB343-D6859556FEB2CF21ACBD2452A272
Processing Errors	
Extracted Text	\\server\FileShare\dan\INV\INTERMEDIATE\0\5.TXT
OutsideInFileId	1336
OutsideInFileType	Microsoft Word 2010
Folder Path	
ChildControlNumbers	REL000000021;REL000000022;REL000000023;REL000000024;REL000000025;REL000000026
Author	Ellis
Comments	
EmailConversation	
ConversationFamily	
EmailConversationIndex	
CreatedOn	9/28/2012 14:30
LastModified	9/28/2012 16:43
LastPrinted	
EmailReceivedOn	
EmailSentOn	

(Continued)

10. The data used in this example is from the word document for this chapter.

TABLE 35.2 (Continued)

Metadata Field	Data
FileExtension	DOCX
DocumentSubject	
EmailBCCSmtp	
EmailKeywords	
EmailCCSmtp	
EmailSenderSmtp	
EmailSubject	
EmailToSmtp	
Email/DomainParsedFrom	
Email/DomainParsedTo	
Email/DomainParsedCC	
Email/DomainParsedBCC	
HiddenText	TRUE
FileName	Chapter 64 Securing eDiscovery Final.docx
FileSize	588272
FileType	Microsoft Office Word Open XML Format
RelativityGroupId	REL000000020
EmailImportance	
MD5Hash	9AC20F60696D0ECC861D3893F9AFC5A0
AttachmentCount	6
OtherProps	Office/LastAuthor = Ellis;Office/Revision = ;
	InternalCreatedOn = 9/28/2012 2:30:00 PM ;
	LastSaved = 9/28/2012 4:43:00 PM; Office/EmbeddedItems = True;
	TrackChanges = True
ParentDate	
ParentControlNumber	
SHA1Hash	B2E8BA743F154EE1687B9011572907A3C5636A57
SHA256Hash	BF6B62AE6B5CFB4F274640C6123949063FBEA-9C233A26FB443FCE4AE6483E11D

Ultimately, these tables demonstrate that a lot of data can be considered *metadata.* Whether or not they are, actually metadata is a philosophical argument. Regardless, a comprehensive policy can prevent the accumulation of this sort of data.

NOTE: Some companies set up all of their documents so that, upon sending through email, all sensitive track changes data are removed.

What is Data Forensics?

The word "forensic" means that the data meets or exceeds the standards required in a court of law for the information to be presented as evidence. Information, when properly preserved, must comply with several rules in order to be admissible. Not least among the rules is the need for proof that the information was not altered. There are two ways that this can be accomplished. For civilian organizations, the preferred method is to hash the data and preserve the resulting hash. A hash is an algorithm that reads ALL the data on disk and creates a unique identifier. Nothing but a perfect copy of the data would result in the same hash. In other areas, the witness is enough. Ideally, the following scenario will provide sufficient proof of preservation to allow admissibility to court. Bear in mind, though, that exceptions abound. Just because one of these rules is broken doesn't mean that the evidence won't be admitted. Certain judges in any court, where the judge has the ultimate authority to decide law, may even allow a hard drive to be admitted that had neither chain of custody nor a hash that matched the original drive's hash.[11] Ultimately, it boils down to the judge's interpretation of the Rules of Evidence and how they may be applicable to electronic data:

1. The hard drive or files are acquired using a forensically proven method and hashed.
2. Paperwork that describes where the files were found and how the files were captured must be created and stored in a secure location with the images.
3. A witness must be available who can say that she personally collected the files and stored them.

These rules protect the electronically stored information from tampering or even accidental destruction. These rules must be followed during a collection activity. Collection is the actual practice of data forensics in motion. Remember, though, that data can become corrupt just sitting on a disk.

Collection

Collection is the logical successor to identification; in the EDRM diagram, preservation shows a double-sided arrow pointing between collection and preservation. Preservation applies first in the sense that the litigation hold requires that responsive data be preserved rather than deleted. Collection is an activity, and collected records are the result of that activity, and the collected records themselves must be preserved. Whether or not true preservation occurs is wholly dependent on whether or not the rules mentioned in the previous section were followed and whether or not the collection is properly conducted. Securing the data is entirely key to both. This creates a zone that cannot and should not be integrated with other zones. It should stand alone as an entity unto itself. A collection activity may manifest in several scenarios; each has unique security requirements:

- The electronically stored information (ESI) collected is stored internally.

---

11. *US v. Gore.*

- The ESI was collected by your staff from a remote location.
- The ESI is being collected from your location by opposing counsel's vendors.

Each of these scenarios requires special treatment. Security approaches will vary within each circumstance. There are many products that are used to do this work; they fall into several categories:

1. Boot device only
2. Network boot only
3. Network collection (this includes use of a crossover)
4. Direct or drive-to-drive acquisition.

Each of the above options will allow for two types of collections. Which one is needed depends on the case and on the type of litigation. If there is any possibility that locating a deleted file can alter the outcome of the case, then choose option 2, below, unilaterally:

1. Logical files
2. Physical disk image

Physical disk images present a very unique concern in the world of security. To a certain extent, a hard drive acts as a recording device. However, if there is a lot of churn on the PC, if many files are created and deleted, the files have the potential to multiply like rabbits. Imagine that the hard drive is like an onion slice, only with millions of concentric rings. If the hard drive is frequently defragmented, the layers of the onion build up over time. Often, what happens in the world of IT is that a user will "fill up" her hard drive. When this happens, the IT support technician, or perhaps the user, will clean up the computer by deleting files. Perhaps she will delete 50 gigabytes (GB) of data from accumulated logs, windows temp files, and email. That night, defragmentation runs, and all of the files that were on the outer ring of the drive are moved inward, filling the space where the deleted files previously existed, and leaving copies out on the outer edges. Windows delete *does not* overwrite the file. It only marks the space as free. The deleted file is easily recovered using a tool that can examine the master file table. To even the most incompetent of forensic examiners, there are now copies of her files that can very easily be located. And because she deleted so much data (perhaps a Windows log file had grown out of control at some point), it will be some time before the data reaches that outer ring and overwrites it. Defragmentation is good but must be followed by a secure wipe of the unallocated clusters.

Data Retention Policies

This leads us directly into data retention policies, which require that the security administrator understand the nature and location of any sensitive data, and ensure that a sound and responsible policy be formulated around it. It dovetails into collection because, ultimately, the data that exists may be data that gets collected. A rigorous data retention policy will prevent the exposure of outdated and irrelevant files.

Deleted files are a security concern because they may still be extant. The following items present deleted data security challenges:

1. Email databases.
2. SQL log files. Often, SQL log files are not properly maintained. See the sidebar: "Managing SQL Server Log Files" for directions on how to keep the logs in such a way that they will remain efficient and continually overwrite themselves. It is not uncommon to find an unmaintained log that contains 150 GB of past transactions. Left to its own devices, SQL will allow a log file to grow interminably, or until disk space runs out.
3. Decommissioned servers.
4. Old backup tapes.
5. Forgotten share locations. The author of this chapter once located one year of database versions. The database was central to the case.
6. Internet Explorer cache files. This is the backstage pass to a full-blown, no-holds-barred collection order by the judge. Internet cache files, unless regularly cleaned, will grow to be quite large and will contain a recorded history of user activity. Many companies use online tools for contact management. The Internet history, then, may contain a record going back several years of every contact created in the system.
7. Local drives. Users like to save files where they know they can find them. Most users have been bitten by IT enough times to want to make certain that they keep their most important files on a local drive.
8. Shadow copies, versioning.
9. Partial files in file slack. When a file writes to a windows cluster, it takes the whole cluster. You can't store two files in one extant. However, if one file takes up an entire sector and then just one byte of the next sector, if another file (deleted) lived in that next sector, it would be recoverable. It is difficult to recover these files, but in the normal course of an examination of a PC, a forensic investigator will stumble across many items of interest. Due to deletion activity and defragmentation, there may exist many, many copies of a single file. When that file gets deleted, and partially overwritten, it may still exist in dozens, if not hundreds, of other places.
10. Decommissioned laptops and PCs.
11. Hard drive upgrades. Stacks of hard drives, regardless of being slated for destruction, become discoverable when a legal hold is issued.
12. PDAs, tablets.
13. Digital cameras.
14. Smart media cards.
15. CDs, DVDs, USB thumb drives, digital audio and video tapes, voice mail, and surveillance servers.

There are many enterprise software packages available that handle secure deletion. Secure deletion means at least one complete overwriting of the data. Some organizations operate at a heightened level of anxiety and may require as many as 35 overwrites of the data. Gutmann theorized that 35 overwrites of data are required to fully obliterate the data from the surface of the drive. In terms of meeting modern security requirements, this is probably excessive. The Gutmann algorithm, devised by Peter Gutmann and Colin Plumb, was targeting certain types of drives, of a certain track density, and so they suggested that near perfect obliteration of any residual magnetic data could be accomplished by writing a series of 35 patterns over the disk regions being deleted. The patterns are designed specifically for three different types of drive data encoding techniques that were prevalent in the 1980s.[12]

Sidebar: Managing SQL Log Files

- Ensure that log file backups are set to run at least once every hour. Consider running them more often in the following scenarios:
- You want to recover with less than one hour of data loss.
- More data can be written to the log file in one hour than is desirable.
- The amount of data written to the log file in one hour causes the log file to fill up the drive. SQL marks the log file as reusable once it is backed up, so it shouldn't grow too large.

Note: Some single transactions in processing software are quite large and may result in log file growth through multiple transaction log backups. This can prevent successful log backups.

- Ensure that the growth of the log files is set to at least 512 MB.
- In certain situations, many gigabytes of data may pour into a log file before the next scheduled log backup marks space as available. Unanticipated growth can also occur when extremely large transactions run. Should this occur, use some sort of log file size monitoring tool to control the size.
- When necessary, grow the log file size in anticipation of any large influx of new data.

---

12. Secure Deletion of Data from Magnetic and Solid-State Memory, Peter Gutmann, July 22–25, 1996, Sixth USENIX Security Symposium Proceedings, San Jose, CA. http://www.cs.auckland.ac.nz/~pgut001/pubs/secure_del.html.

To this date, no software or hardware product exists that can read the outer edges of a disk track and recompile overwritten data on a modern hard drive—unless, of course, one believes in a secret government facility that nobody knows exists that hosts an array of scanning probe microscopes (SPM), as well as scientists and analysts. Secure deletion, then, means at least one complete overwriting of the data and includes file slack (regions of sectors that are not being used by the file) and unallocated clusters. Doing it twice would be advisable; if there are two station points in the workflow, it will ensure at least some protection from human error.

Some organizations operate at a higher level of anxiety and may require as many as 35 overwrites of the data, using the Gutmann algorithm. The reason for this level of deletion was due perhaps to misunderstanding of the theory and a paper published by Peter Gutmann. In his paper, he described the potential to recover data from the outer edges of tracks using scanning probe microscopy, and the potential to recover overwritten data through a form of error-canceling read in which the calculated signal from the current data is subtracted from the signal that's actually read, with the difference being due to the influence of previously-written data.[13]

The procedure itself—the use of a robot-controlled drive mechanism and an oscilloscope to collect data from an 80-MB disk pack—has, in fact, been accomplished, and it was verified that the data did have the appearance of a true bit-stream that could then be further analyzed for comparative data.[14] This would be a very challenging operation, but it is conceivable that, if portions of the files are known, it could be extended to "decrypt" three or four passes at different locations in the same track. However, modern drives are far denser, and due to the use of advanced recording techniques, the potential for this sort of attack to be successful is extremely unlikely.[15]

Ultimately, there are software products that can perform truly secure deletion on modern drives with just one pass. Additionally, secure deletion should take place as part of the defragmentation routine. In any security-conscious enterprise, the secure wiping of the unallocated clusters should always happen *after* a defrag.

There are only two ways to destroy electronically stored data. You can overwrite the media, using software, or you can physically destroy the hard drive. SSDs present unique challenges as well.[16] For the physical-destruction option, any severe deformation, perforation,

or incineration of the platters will suffice. Commercially available products such as diskstroyer have received good reviews as well.

The security of collection, then, is not just about the security of how the collected data is stored—this will be discussed in the next few sections. Rather, it begins with the security of the data itself that is being collected: You most know where data lives, and you must work to ensure that you know what data is being taken. It also means that the data must be stored in such a way as to take all possible and reasonable precautions to prevent data loss. Data loss, whenever it occurs, must be fully documented and explained, and it must not have occurred due to human error or willful neglect. This also means the data must be securable and identifiable.

The practice of collection can be divided into two categories: internal and external. Internal collection occurs when an organization looks inward and investigates itself using staff or consultant data forensic examiners. The motivation to perform the work stems from internal concerns, such as incidents involving earlier misconduct by a terminated employee, and there are internal stakeholders. An external collection occurs in litigation, where many parties may be involved.

Internal Collection

Many large corporations have their own internal forensic groups. However, even large corporations may turn to specialized forensic experts when unique circumstances arise. An internally conducted collection, though, will be one where staff employees, who are members of the enterprise domain, perform the work of securing, copying, and storing the discoverable information. A number of methods are employed:

1. Appliances are installed throughout the network.
2. Enterprise software allows administrators to capture everything from individual files to entire disk images, remotely, with two options:
   a. Systems are monitored for breaches in security policy and, when a breach is detected, the user system is locked down and the evidence is collected.
   b. Systems are not monitored, and collections are conducted only when suspicious behavior is observed or upon employee termination.
3. Physical collection—The drive is harvested, imaged, and stored, and then a standard disk image is redeployed to the machine.

In each of these methods, the end result is that a large amount of redundant data must be secured and preserved for, possibly, a very, very long time. Lawsuits can last many years, or regulatory compliance may require retention of up to a decade. It follows, then, that the location,

13. Email from Peter Gutmann to author, dated 10/5/2012.
14. Digital Archeology with Drive-Independent Data Recovery, Christopher Fenton, ELEN E9002 Research Project Final Report, Summer 2011. http://tinyurl.com/3jhe2os.
15. Email from Peter Gutmann to author, dated 10/5/2012.
16. http://www.cs.auckland.ac.nz/~pgut001/pubs/secure_del.html#recommendations.

nature (matter), and status of all data be tracked carefully. This data should be secured at a much higher level than other data in the enterprise as it is, most likely, a corporate espionage goldmine of all of the business's most sensitive data:

- Two-factor authentication
- Physical access with surveillance and biometric access controls
- AES 256-bit encryption where possible
- Hardware and data destruction policies
- Group-based access by matter

Often, internal forensic examiners provide advice and expertise in externally related matters, but often, depending on the matter at hand, these examiners will work tangentially with external consultants on projects that involve externally driven litigation.

External Collection

Often, when external adversarial forces are at play, enterprises choose to involve external collection experts. Ostensibly, this shift stabilizes liability and planning from internal sources, already taxed with managing internal risk, to an outside firm. These external firms should be experienced and should be able to easily integrate their tools to your systems for a speedy and accurate collection of data. They are often managed by in-house counsel in tandem with external counsel. In the rather small world of e-discovery vendors, the vendors selected by both sides will likely have worked together in the past. Interview any potential vendor carefully.

Occasionally, a court will allow, even at the protest of the opposing defense's argument, plaintiff's staff ESI specialists to conduct an on-site collection. It does happen—but it is not the normal course of events. A corporation that responds and complies with discovery requests in a timely fashion, demonstrating cooperation, will not face sanctions. Typically, by the time it comes to the "other side," being allowed to put their experts in the living room of an ex-employee or the data center of the opposition, things have become fairly combative in the courtroom. The reason for this is usually the utter failure of one side or the other to adhere to the bottom layer of the e-Discovery Security Hierarchy of Needs. This short list details some of the reasons why a judge may allow the opposition's experts full access to the other side's data center:

1. Failure to produce relevant documents on the agreed to timeline
2. Failure to produce relevant documents in the agreed upon format
3. Denial that any relevant documents exist
4. Failure to appear

5. Refusal to pay costs associated with discovery, or claims of financial destitution
6. Failure to provide a believable and reliable basis for determining whether something is or isn't relevant.

All of this exemplifies the need for a robust backup and data retention policy. Acceptable use policies are also a key part of this. Zone 3, as shown in Figure 35.3, becomes a matter of physical or encrypted tunnel transport of data. Often, the amount of data involved in a collection can approach many terabytes or petabytes in size. Movement of such large volumes of data, when it requires processing, becomes infeasible. Fortunately, with proper encryption, moving the data via hard drives, using accepted shipping methods, provides adequate security. Backups of data should be retained, and pass-phrases that allow access to the data should be transmitted securely. Should the need to transport dozens of drives via courier arise, ensure that the courier has a copy of the order on his person and in the hardened transport case, with the drives.

Collection "Don'ts"

Enterprises faced with litigation for the first time often make severe mistakes. A good example of a first-time litigation is where an employee storms out of the investors' Office of Alice Rabbit and Hole, and the next week begins working for a rival investment firm, Tweedle Dee and Dum. Suddenly, clients that were long-time, loyal customers are dropping their accounts with Alice and moving to...yes, the Tweedle, where the ex-employee now works. Later, the CEO of Alice receives a brochure, passed along from a client. It outlines a new pricing structure for the opposing firm's services that mirror the work being done at Alice, work that the ex-employee participated in developing. The brochure appears to be the exact same layout with only a few slight differences.

The CEO calls his IT director and demands an explanation. The IT director panics and saying "I'll get to the bottom of this!" immediately goes to access the ex-employee's laptop. She finds it on the workbench of an IT associate, halfway through a reload of the OS. She halts the work. Next, she browses the network to the ex-employee's share and begins to browse the directory contents, searching for content that the user shouldn't have had in her drive area—files that were thought to be restricted to marketing. She finds interesting files, and then she connects a hard drive to her network and copies all of Alice's files to the hard drive. Then, thinking to herself, "Gee, I could really use all that space she was hogging," she deletes all of the ex-employee's files from the network share.

Ultimately, Alice may still have a case—until, of course, a private investigator discovers that the ex-employee and the IT director had had an affair. Ultimately, the case would have been far simpler and easier to execute had an intact laptop been available, a laptop that may have shown evidence of the ex-employee using Webmail to airlift files from the corporate network. Furthermore, a protocol in place to handle disgruntled employee departures would have been prudent. The CEO should have instructed his IT director to engage the protocol, which would have resulted in forensic quality images of everything the ex-employee had ever touched. Now, there will be a long-drawn-out legal battle that will be very costly, because Alice Rabbit and Hole have, essentially, a weakened position.

Processing

One might think that, once the data has been identified, properly collected, and shipped, the heavy lifting is completed. It is, in fact, only just beginning. The following searches may now need to be executed against a data set that is largely unstructured. Processing takes unstructured data and structures it so that future searches may be efficiently executed. Processing software provides, at a minimum, the following functionality:

- File types.
- While a collection may have targeted spreadsheets and documents, to be thorough the effort may have swept up files that are not the correct file type. Or the collection technologies used targeted areas such as unallocated clusters, compressed files, or entire file systems, and the types of files that were of interest didn't become apparent until later in the EDRM life cycle. The processing tool will recognize these files and will not process them.
- Date range culling.
- Database conversion.
- Files stored in databases, or information stored in databases, present unique challenges. A customer database that uses a Web interface to access the data may require a design team to re-create pages that display the information, which can then be reviewed, or they may simply be required to search the database. This requires that the database server be hosted by the processing agent.
- Keyword searches.
- Custodian organization.
- De-encrypting of encrypted files—the ability to enter in passwords or to "try" lists of passwords.
- It will remove National Institute of Science and Technology (NIST) items (De-NIST). Earlier, file hash values were discussed as being unique identifiers for a file that possesses a certain content. As passwords are broken, unusual compression algorithms

unlocked, and hidden files uncovered, standard system and program files may be uncovered (this may be conducted multiple times, any step of the way).

- Deduplication Customized lists of hash values are created, and duplicates are removed. There are three ways to do this: globally, by custodian, and by family or child. When the context of the item does not matter, then global deduplication is best. If the context, such as the location of the file, who sent it, and its location, matters, then dedupe families only. Often, users will have local archives of files, which will contain large volumes of copies. A 5–6 TB corpus can easily be reduced through deNIST'ing and deduplication.

Ultimately, some combination of all of the above may be necessary as well. For example, after identifying that any email sent by an employee during a certain date range may be relevant, further analysis may be needed.

Securing the Processing Architecture—Zone 4

In Figure 35.3, Zone 4 encapsulates preservation, collection, and processing. Each of these items requires special treatment. In reality, preservation is a process that begins with identification, issuing a legal hold, and collecting the data; and data must be "processed" each step of the way. Data is not truly preserved until it has been securely copied, logged, and moved to a staging area where it can be accessed and reviewed at a high level for relevancy. In Figure 35.5, the upside-down triangle represents a funnel.

The EDRM is actually a drawn-out preservation and display process, and as we move through it, the amount of data being manipulated should shrink. However, sometimes things happen. For example, perhaps many compressed archives will be discovered, or deleted partitions recovered. There may be momentary bursts of data. Recall also that the entire process is cyclical. There may be many separate requests for disclosure in a single case. Storage and sizing become major challenges of

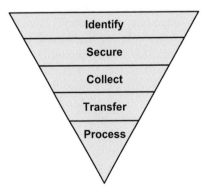

FIGURE 35.5 The preservation effort doesn't end with a simple backup and archive of the data. Throughout the EDRM cycle, the act of preserving metadata and file integrity remains important.

e-discovery architects, and securing the storage becomes a great challenge for security architects.

As storage bursts, emergency measures may need to be executed to meet deadlines. If emergency protocols do not exist, they cannot be executed. An example of an emergency protocol would be to have agreements with companies that sell storage and servers to execute on pre-authorized purchase orders within 24 hours. This is normal, and hardware vendors are prepared for such requests as they also tie into DR strategies.

In both planned and unplanned situations, servers will get moved, disk arrays transferred, and SAN fabrics re-architected. An adept security plan considers this contingency, is adaptable, and provides for extremely rapid scaling of the environment. This is not a "let's budget it for Q3" item. This is a "We need it, and we need it now, or we could get fined a million dollars" situation or, from the law firm or vendor perspective. "We need it, and we need it now, or we are going to lose an $85 m a year client." This sort of work occurs not only at small businesses across the world, but in the very largest enterprises that exist.

British Petroleum (BP) and the *Deepwater Horizon* case will, when all is said and done, very likely involve thousands of people and many terabytes of data, and will involve many millions, if not over a billion, in legal costs alone. Duplicative work can double and triple costs. Deficiencies in process can create even greater inefficiencies.

In 2007, this author was involved in managing the electronic data for a large class action suit that involved a consumer loss. Thousands of consumers had a home remodeling component that had failed due to manufacturing defects. The electronic discovery included thousands of joint photographic expert group (JPG) digital photographs. Nearly all of the photos were far larger than needed; a short experiment proved that the images could be reduced in size with no discernible loss of quality. Simply observing that 80 GB of images could be reduced in size to 10 GB can reduce storage costs by 8 times! Why is this important to security? Properly securing e-discovery includes ensuring manageability of the data. Data that booms in size rapidly begins to break down the barriers of security. Escalating costs cause corners to be cut and will leach funds away from the security budget. In the e-discovery industry, all-hands-on-deck emergencies are common, if not daily, events at many firms. Maintaining security should be the first priority. New servers introduced should be sanitized of any data, disjoined from other security groups, and should not have outbound Internet access.

The processing arena should be cordoned through DMZ technologies as described in Figure 35.6. Differing technologies have differing methods of access. At every

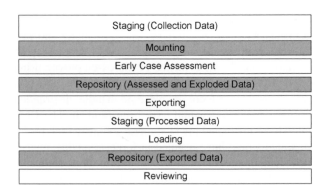

FIGURE 35.6 Each of the shaded areas represents either a static location or the process that creates the data that resides in that repository. Shaded areas indicate key areas where virus scanning activities may take place.

step of the way, intrusion detection systems, intrusion prevention, and virus and malware detection systems should be dovetailed with each processing step. Figure 35.6 provides a sample configuration of how different servers may be tied to security cordons that are designed to minimize the risk of infected files being inadvertently viewed, which in turn can inadvertently execute malicious code. Staging areas, which are large disk repositories where data is stored as it is being accessed and manipulated, allow, tangentially, for other processes to be used to scan and monitor these areas.

Staging (Collection Data)

Figure 35.6 introduced the concept of staging and the issue of having a secure staging area. In large litigation cases, collected files can arrive in many formats. Also, depending on the vendor, the work that remains to be done may differ. For the sake of simplicity, in this diagram, the assumption is that many forensic images of disks have arrived and have been stored on a high-capacity storage array.

Mounting

Subsequently, for processing, the forensic images are mounted as drive letters. At this time, performing a virus scan is not necessary. The files are read-only—if a virus was found, nothing could be done except to make note of it and exclude it, or mark it for manual review if it is a relevant file. In fact, depending on the method and software used to process the data, this is one of the options. However, at this stage, forensic tools are used to cull the data, and viruses that exist in system files may be ignored if they are in uninteresting locations. As part of culling, other processes may simply export all data from the mounted layer to a secondary staging area, and then may scan the entire area and quarantine infected files. Infected files may, of course, include files that are relevant.

A virus scanning utility that allows for cleansing of the infected files should be used.

Early Case Assessment (ECM)

During the assessment process, the risk of a user coming into contact with a virus increases. Decommissioned hard drives, unflushed quarantine directories, USB drives, thumb drives, spam email, and so on, can all rise to the surface. Especially, as the processing tool fails, one may come into direct contact with the file that failed, and the reason for the failure may be that the file is infected. As the ECA software service searches files, relevant files may be loaded into RAM by an unsuspecting user wishing to review a file. The file may be infected and may not appear in the viewer properly, so the user may choose to access the file and open it. When this happens, the virus is triggered, and a malicious hacker receives a notification on his bootleg cell phone that one of his viruses has been activated. Imagine his delight when, upon accessing the servers, he discovers that he has complete control over all of the electronic data of a highly sensitive litigation. Perhaps it is a merger. Perhaps it is a high-profile divorce, or bankruptcy, or product liability.

Additionally, technicians working with the files may erroneously believe that the processing software *failed* to process the file. They won't realize that the file is infected, and they may actually spread the virus by sending it to the software vendor. All files that are identified as suspect during processing should be quarantined and scanned before further evaluation.

Security around these areas cannot be tight enough. These systems should not have Internet access, and there should be double-layered, interwoven defenses of firewalls, intrusion detection, and intrusion prevention, even in disconnected systems. Some viruses are merely designed to infect other files and/or inflict damage. Once activated, nothing is to stop the virus from wreaking havoc on the servers. Ultimately, the infected files may have to be produced to the opposition in the lawsuit. Imagine how unhappy they will be if they discover that their entire network became infected by files in the production they received from opposing counsel. Referring back to Figure 35.2, outside of Zone 1, Zone 4 presents the greatest security challenges.

Processing

In this step of the EDRM, by now potentially relevant data has been identified. It may be a handful of files, or it may be millions of files. The current atmosphere of electronic discovery is one of "more is less" and so the discipline finds itself faced with issue of "Big Data." The end result of processing is that a "package" is created, or a series of them, that contain all of the natives and all of the metadata information, extracted from the natives. This includes something called "extracted text." Extracted text is nothing more than the body of language encapsulated in a file. For example, in this chapter, the extracted text would include all of the alphanumeric characters, with no formatting. It would also include any hidden comments, track changes, and any markup notes. This will all be stored as Unicode, so that special characters may be preserved and later searched. This package of data, which may actually be many terabytes, will then be transmitted to a new location. This new location may be internal to the corporation, to a law firm, or to a vendor data center. Review and analysis represents a major shift, or interface, where large amounts of data are likely to shift into a different area. That is, a copy of everything processed is now ready to be looked at and loaded into a hosted review tool.

Securing Zone 5: Hosting/Review

For some organizations, the hosted review may be integrated within the processing cordon. However, for many it is not, so this chapter treats it as though the data will be moving to a separate entity, either internal or external to the organization. Once the package has been received in the hosting review center, it must be loaded to the review software. Some software processing platforms may integrate directly with the review tool. For example, the software product Relativity includes a processing package—data may be pumped directly, SQL server to SQL server, from the processing center to the hosted review platform. Antivirus scans should continue, for two reasons. First, this system will very likely be connected to the Internet. Large-scale litigation requires many reviewers, and these many review shops are located all over the world. The enterprise data is about to go global. Second, virus definitions are frequently updated. A file that scanned "virus free" yesterday may not actually be virus free and may just be a time bomb, waiting to be set off.

More is Less

This returns us to the "more is less" philosophy prevalent in e-discovery culture in 2012. This philosophy is being countered by recent developments in automated review. In the sidebar "Relativity-Assisted Review," Constantine Pappas discusses assisted review, which is a way of programmatically eliminating documents from the potentially relevant population of documents. This sort of technology may often reduce the cost of analysis as well as the amount of data that needs to be reviewed by humans. If exposure is measured by surface area, then an increase in the volume of documents in e-discovery effectively increases that surface area. Primarily, this is because additional computer systems will need to be set up (more Web servers for a hosted review) and because of an increase in human eyes that are performing the review. By leveraging predictive coding tools *before* releasing all of the data, exposure may be significantly reduced. The exposure here is the exposure of sensitive corporate data to hundreds of reviewers. Fewer reviewers means more security and less potential that someone will steal corporate data. It also means that, if the system is hacked, fewer files will escape. Exposure is not curtailed, but it is certainly reduced.

Software products that provide review services should be secure. They will have received "A" ratings from security auditing service companies. In response to security concerns, security consulting firms work diligently to ensure that proper security precautions are integrated into the platform for things such as:

- JavaScript injection
- Structured Query Language (SQL) injection
- Cross-site scripting
- At least AES 256 encryption of Web site and installers
- FIPS
- Signed
- Secure Session Cookies

Additionally, any security manager or software provider should be cognizant of new threats. Frequently, clients and peers, along with blogs and journals, are great sources of information. Keeping an eye out and seriously considering all threats or descriptions of potential threats, regardless of the source of information, can mean the difference between correcting a potential SQL injection vulnerability and having it remain to be discovered by a hacker.

Sidebar: Relativity-Assisted Review

Relativity-Assisted Review is a workflow process designed to save time and money during the electronic discovery phase of a lawsuit or investigation. The process captures human decisions on sample sets of documents and in turn applies those decisions to other documents in the same database that meets a predetermined conceptual similarity threshold. It is an iterative workflow, divided into phases called rounds. The number of rounds necessary to complete the project varies, depending on validation criteria and other case-specific variables.

The tool employs text analytics categorization, specifically an engine called Latent Semantic Indexing (LSI). First, the documents to be categorized are indexed; these analytics indexes typically filter out email header information and other repeated content that could otherwise serve to confound effective machine learning.

Once the index has been created, a sample set of documents is generated. A random statistical sample is very often employed, although it is also quite common to choose known documents that are believed to be excellent candidates for machine learning. Sampling by this latter method is called judgmental sampling.

Human reviewers will then apply values to a designation field (typically as either Responsive or Non-Responsive) for each sample document. Once all documents in the sample set have been reviewed, they are submitted for Categorization by the system. When Categorization is complete, the categorized documents are then sampled into new validation rounds, which human reviewers check for accuracy. Each instance in which a reviewer corrects the system is called an overturn, and the process of sampled validation review and Categorization is repeated until the overturn rate reaches an acceptable level or no longer changes. This effect is called stabilization and indicates completion of the Assisted Review phase of the discovery project.

Ultimately, the 'More is Less' process can greatly reduce the costs and time required to review a large number of records. This is accomplished by being able to isolate and either de-prioritize or disregard the Non-Responsive population, which is typically an overwhelming majority of most data sets. In addition, the tool amplifies human expertise, taking each coding decision and multiplying it many times over. This process greatly augments both consistency and decision-making transparency when compared with traditional linear review. Review tools, even Web-based ones, are most often secured in one of the following methods:

1. Simple forms security over HTTPS to a Web server.
2. Two-factor authentication with an integration of the application with something like RSA.
3. Portal-based access. One organization, Juniper, uses Uniform Resource Locator (URL)-rewriting to control access to Web-based applications, adding an additional layer of token-based authentication security to an already secure application.
4. Thin-client remote access. Remote desktop access uses something like Citrix to allow users server-next-door speeds when using the Web-based tool. It also prevents any information from being downloaded to the users' machines. This may assist with the compliance to some safe harbor rules and for overseas access and review of data. Some countries, such as UK, have very stringent policies on disclosure of motherland data to overseas entities.
5. Site-based security—Vendors own and control the review arenas, and the machines are locked down so that data cannot be loaded to a thumb drive. Users view documents in a basic dumb-terminal setup.

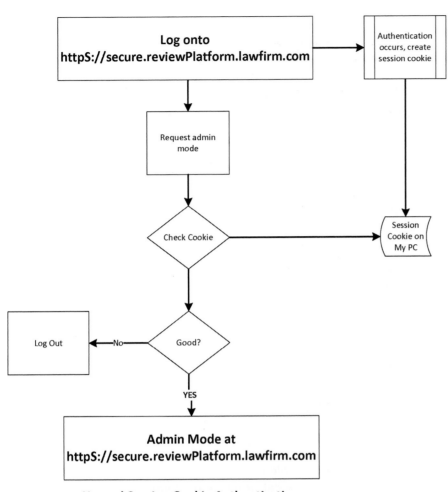

FIGURE 35.7 In a normal authentication, the cookie is generated by the browser and shared with the server. Subsequently, the browser is authenticated using the same cookie.

Normal Session Cookie Authentication

Consider the flowchart in Figures 35.7 and 35.8. In this flowchart, the ease with which an infiltrator can secure admin access is described. These electronic discovery systems contain, at times, extremely sensitive data.

Review and analysis are in the same vertical in the EDRM. Essentially, they are one and the same—analysis often takes place exclusively in the review platform. However, while there are many things that many review platforms can do, there are many things that they cannot. Not all review platforms can perform:

- Entity Relationship Mapping
- Voice recognition
- Threading
- Benford's Law
- Gap Analysis
- Deduplication
- Manage projects
- Bypass painful load file management
- Audio and visual search

Often, once documents have been coded by reviewers, data must be exported from the review platform and into some sort of analysis tool or another. This data may still be considered to be proprietary to the corporate entity and should remain under the same controls as any other data. A good review application will have permission-based security on various functions, such as the ability to download natives or to export data to Excel spreadsheets. Security will consider that many different software products will have special requirements and require varying levels of security permissions on the network.

Review platforms also must have storage capacity, and the same storage capacity issues can occur here that come up in processing. Additionally, there are, in fact, virus threats even at this stage, where one would think that everything had already been scanned three or four times.

Consider the zeroth day threat, where a threat is considered to be occurring on the "zeroth" day when, as of yet, it has not been discovered. It is true that files that are in the repository of a review platform have most likely

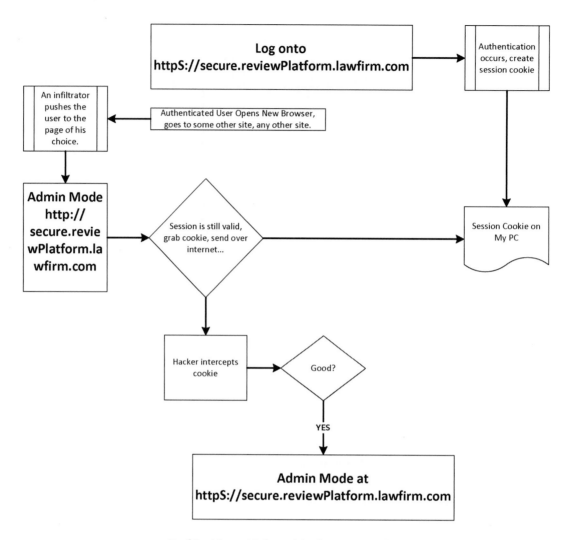

Surf Jacking a Vulnerable Session Cookie

FIGURE 35.8 In a poorly secured application, the cookie becomes vulnerable to "surf-jacking," whereby a malicious user can seize control of a session.

already been scanned, so continual scanning of a file repository would be overkill if you have other intrusion countermeasures in place. Use something like a network intrusion prevention system (NIPs) for the Web and two-factor authentication on any other types of access. The reason for the scanning shown on the review repository in Figure 35.6 is to address zeroth day threats that could be lurking.

The term *zeroth* day is, in reality, somewhat misleading. This author once had a desktop that scanned clean by antivirus tool A (I KNEW it was infected). Scanning the machine again using Antivirus tool B (and then C, D, E, and F) also revealed nothing. The only thing to do was to shut the machine down and preserve it. A month later a scan, using the exact same scanning tools but with updated definition, located the virus.

Sometimes the scanners we are using just don't have the definitions yet. DO require scanning of an adequately protected file repository when virus definitions are updated. In particular, be cognizant of virus definitions that cover loose files. Scanning the file repository in a targeted way can reduce the load on the system. For example, when an antivirus company releases a signature update that specifically addresses infected Excel spreadsheets, scan all spreadsheets with that particular signature.

Scanning activities should also occur in a staging area whenever new loads of files arrive, regardless of the source, but especially ones that have been processed without regard to any sort of an EDRM security zone model. This chapter puts forth a zoned security model that underpins the entire EDRM: Any processing vendor that operates as though it is an island should be cause for concern.

Securing Zone 6: Production and Presentation

These two areas of the EDRM are zoned together in this model. In this model, there are two types of production. The first kind is called a "disclosure" in some countries. In the United States, it is just "discovery." Effectively, the first kind of production is the release of information in the format agreed to in the pre-discovery "meet and confer" conference to the opposing counsel. Production data that is to be delivered to opposing counsel should be delivered in a compressed and encrypted format. 7Zip is one such tool that is both free and effective. It allows for compressing in several different formats, and it offers all of the flexibility needed to compress large amounts of data. Alternatively, whole drive encryption may be more efficient, at least from a workflow perspective, and the drives can be locked in TSA-approved containers and shipped overnight.

Other kinds of production include privilege log, attorneys' eyes only logs, and other same-side productions, which may be delivered to other counsels, expert witnesses, or other vendors for further processing. Use a media tracking application in conjunction with a labeling system (RFID or bar code) to control media. The location and who has handled or come into contact with electronic discovery will help to determine the source of a security weakness; it will also help with the continued, ongoing assessment of risk.

In the EDRM, the presentation vertical simply refers to courtroom technologies and the presentation of documents and other information. Several software products will allow things like video, document, and transcript presentation via a projector. In the past, law firms would spend thousands of dollars on large, printed, foam-board charts and graphs to make their points to juries and judges. This trend has declined in the past decade, with more and more attorneys bringing laptops into the courtroom. There are few courts that are not media ready, wired for sound, with microphone and video, and with strategically placed monitors and projectors.

The quality of monitors, however, should be checked, as should all systems. Some courtrooms are slow to upgrade and will either not have monitors available or will make available monitors that are of such poor quality that they can hardly be viewed. This may swing the decision as to whether or not a mobile network should be set up in the courtroom. There will rarely be hard-wired network access available, though there may be a public wireless point that will likely be shared. Secure any wireless access by ensuring that a software firewall exists on any laptops that will be entering the court room.

Security

Zone 6 security, then, involves a thorough tracking of media and securing any deliveries of data or findings to a separate vendor entity for processing into a more presentable format. At this stage, the e-discovery process is complete. It is show time. If the documents are in the production, they will soon be out of the control of the enterprise. Questioning and ensuring the security of these documents should not be overlooked: The attorneys may not know, or even think, to worry about this. It is up to the director of electronic discovery at the originating corporate level to follow the progress, to ensure security at every touch point, and to ensure that a program is in place that educates any attorneys as to the importance of data security and what they can do to help. Insist on encryption and on secure storage of delivered productions. This is not an unreasonable thing to do. Requesting "attorney's eyes only" is also not abnormal. Confidentiality and nondisclosure agreements should be signed and understood by anyone who will come into contact with sensitive, proprietary, and confidential corporate data.

3. SUMMARY

This chapter has endeavored to condense the experiences of over a decade of forensic, litigation, security, discovery, and software design and use-cases into some 40 pages. It has attempted to do this in such a way as to lay a foundation of understanding. Through learning the business and understanding the ins-and-outs of it, a proper security framework for individually unique enterprises and unique legal cases can be established.

The industry is rapidly changing. New technologies are emerging, and companies, such as kCura, Recommind, and AccessData, which were once micro-shops, are growing and absorbing more of the EDRM's functions into their offerings. As these platforms grow, they will inevitably become more robust and will offer the full life cycle in one product, or suite. Ultimately, the organizations that are suing each other will experience the greatest security when the data can be kept and processed in as few disparate locations as possible.

The preceding will only be achieved by consolidating and collapsing the security zones to the point where there only exist the corporate information system and a legal system whereby attorneys are able to securely present their work in a court of law. If the EDRM can be run in such a way that *only* responsive data leaves the building, then the surface area of exposure shrinks and security increases.

Finally, let's move on to the real interactive part of this chapter: review questions/exercises, hands-on projects, case projects, and an optional team case project. The answers and/or solutions by chapter can be found in the Online Instructor's Solutions Manual.

CHAPTER REVIEW QUESTIONS/EXERCISES

True/False

1. True or False? The field of e-discovery does not relate to litigation as a whole.
2. True or False? The framework of the EDRM begins with information security.
3. True or False? Certain types of organizations are more likely than others to be prone to litigation.
4. True or False? There are loopholes in any external facing system.
5. True or False? The EDRM model breaks identification into the same phase of e-Discovery as information management.

Multiple Choice

1. Finding better ways to improve what you are doing is known as:
   A. process.
   B. standardization.
   C. data retention.
   D. evolution.
   E. security.
2. Defining and understanding your information flow is known as:
   A. evolution.
   B. standardization.
   C. data retention.
   D. process.
   E. security.
3. Making sure everyone uses the same software, stores information in the same places, and uses approved technology for information transmittals is known as:
   A. evolution.
   B. data retention.
   C. standardization.
   D. process.
   E. security.
4. Ensuring that you know your data isn't walking out your front (or back) door, is known as:
   A. security.
   B. data retention.
   C. standardization.s
   D. process.
   E. evolution.
5. Ensuring that you are keeping what you want to keep, destroying what you don't want, and backing up data at risk is known as:
   A. security.
   B. data retention.
   C. standardization.
   D. data destruction.
   E. all of the above.

EXERCISE

Problem

Can an organization's internal IT staff conduct an investigation and extract electronic evidence?

Hands-On Projects

Project

What happens to electronic information after it is deleted?

Case Projects

Problem

What can an organization do immediately to safeguard the integrity and admissibility of electronic evidence?

Optional Team Case Project

Problem

What is spoliation, and how can an organization protect against it?

## Chapter 36

Network Forensics

Yong Guan

Iowa State University

1. SCIENTIFIC OVERVIEW

With the phenomenal growth of the Internet, more and more people enjoy and depend on the convenience of its provided services. The Internet has spread rapidly almost all over the world. Up to December 2006, the Internet had been distributed to over 233 countries and world regions and had more than 1.09 billion users.[1] Unfortunately, the wide use of computers and the Internet also opens doors to cyber attackers. There are different kinds of attacks that an end user of a computer or Internet can meet. For instance, there may be various viruses on a hard disk, several backdoors open in an operating system, or a lot of phishing emails in an emailbox. According to the annual *Computer Crime Report* of the Computer Security Institute (CSI) and the U.S. Federal Bureau of Investigation (FBI), released in 2006, cyber attacks cause massive money losses each year.

However, the FBI/CSI survey results also showed that a low percentage of cyber crime cases have been reported to law enforcement (in 1996, only 16%; in 2006, 25%), which means that in reality, the vast majority of cyber criminals are never caught or prosecuted. Readers may ask why this continues to happen. Several factors contribute to this fact:

- In many cases, businesses are often reluctant to report and publicly discuss cyber crimes related to them. The concern of negative publicity becomes the number-one reason because it may attract other cyber attackers, undermine the confidence of customers, suppliers, and investors, and invite the ridicule of competitors.
- Generally, it is much harder to detect cyber crimes than crimes in the physical world. There are various antiforensics techniques that can help cyber criminals evade detection, such as information-hiding techniques (steganography, covert channels), anonymity proxies, stepping stones, and botnets. Even more challenging,

cyber criminals are often insiders or employees of the organizations themselves.
- Attackers may walk across the boundaries of multiple organizations and even countries. To date, the lack of effective solutions has significantly hindered efforts to investigate and stop the rapidly growing cyber criminal activities. It is therefore crucial to develop a forensically sound and efficient solution to track and capture these criminals.

Here we discuss the basic principles and some specific forensic techniques in attributing real cyber criminals.

2. THE PRINCIPLES OF NETWORK FORENSICS

Network forensics can be generally defined as a science of discovering and retrieving evidential information in a networked environment about a crime in such a way as to make it admissible in court. Different from intrusion detection, all the techniques used for the purpose of network forensics should satisfy both legal and technical requirements. For example, it is important to guarantee whether the developed network forensic solutions are practical and fast enough to be used in high-speed networks with heterogeneous network architecture and devices. More important, they need to satisfy general forensics principles such as the rules of evidence and the criteria for admissibility of novel scientific evidence (such as the *Daubert* criteria).[2,3,4] The five rules are that evidence must be:

- *Admissible.* Must be able to be used in court or elsewhere.

1. Internet World Stats, www.internetworldstats.com.

2. G. Palmer, "A road map for digital forensic research," Digital Forensic Research Workshop (DFRWS), Final Report, Aug. 2001.
3. C. M. Whitcomb, "An historical perspective of digital evidence: A forensic scientist's view," IJDE, 2002.
4. S. Mocas, "Building theoretical underpinnings for digital forensics research," Digital Investigation, Vol. 1, pp. 61−68, 2004.

- *Authentic*. Evidence relates to incident in relevant way.
- *Complete*. No tunnel vision, exculpatory evidence for alternative suspects.
- *Reliable*. No question about authenticity and veracity.
- *Believable*. Clear, easy to understand, and believable by a jury.

The evidence and the investigative network forensics techniques should satisfy the criteria for admissibility of novel scientific evidence (*Daubert v. Merrell*):

- Whether the theory or technique has been reliably tested
- Whether the theory or technique has been subject to peer review and publication
- What is the known or potential rate of error of the method used?
- Whether the theory or method has been generally accepted by the scientific community

The investigation of a cyber crime often involves cases related to homeland security, corporate espionage, child pornography, traditional crime assisted by computer and network technology, employee monitoring, or medical records, where privacy plays an important role.

There are at least three distinct communities within digital forensics: law enforcement, military, and business and industry, each of which has its own objectives and priorities. For example, prosecution is the primary objective of the law enforcement agencies and their practitioners and is often done after the fact. Military operations' primary objective is to guarantee the continuity of services, which often have strict real-time requirements. Business and industry's primary objectives vary significantly, many of which want to guarantee the availability of services and put prosecution as a secondary objective.

Usually there are three types of people who use digital evidence from network forensic investigations: police investigators, public investigators, and private investigators. The following are some examples:

- Criminal prosecutors. Incriminating documents related to homicide, financial fraud, drug-related records.
- Insurance companies. Records of bill, cost, services to prove fraud in medical bills and accidents.
- Law enforcement officials. Require assistance in search warrant preparation and in handling seized computer equipment.
- Individuals. To support a possible claim of wrongful termination, sexual harassment, or age discrimination.

The primary activities of network forensics are investigative in nature. The investigative process encompasses the following:

- Identification
- Preservation
- Collection
- Examination
- Analysis
- Presentation
- Decision

In the following discussion, we focus on several important network forensic areas (see checklist: "An Agenda For Action For Network Forensics").

An Agenda for Action for Network Forensics

The cyber forensics specialist should ensure the following are adhered to (Check All Tasks Completed):

_____**1.** Provide expert data visualization techniques to the problem of network data pattern analysis.

_____**2.** Apply standard research and analysis techniques to datasets provided by a company or organization.

_____**3.** Apply the lessons learned from company-provided datasets to open datasets as the research advances.

_____**4.** Provide initial datasets, project initiation, and training in network traffic datasets and analysis techniques.

_____**5.** Provide expert network forensical rule-based algorithms for incorporation by researchers.

_____**6.** Repeatedly test and verify new visualization techniques and procedures to ensure that new patterns are, in fact, accurate representations of designated activities.

_____**7.** Develop a test database.

_____**8.** Develop a design methodology for visualizing test data.

_____**9.** Develop a query interface to the database.

_____**10.** Map data structures to a visualization model.

_____**11.** Build a prototype.

_____**12.** Refine a prototype.

_____**13.** Incorporate live Internet data.

_____**14.** Test live Internet data.

_____**15.** Deliver a final build.

_____**16.** Produce new visualization techniques to streamline and enhance analysis of network forensic data.

_____**17.** Produce a Web browser compatible prototype that demonstrates these techniques to visualize and query vast amounts of data. The resulting interactive visualization interface will advance the usability of the system, solve the volumetric problem with analyzing these datasets, and advance the adaptation of the solution in the INFOSEC market.

_____**18.** Routinely archive all e-mail as it is received on your server for a certain period of time (say, 30–60 days).

_____**19.** Clear the archives after an additional specified time.

_____**20.** Physically segregate the back-up copies of the e-mail system from back-ups of the rest of the computer system.

_____**21.** Automatically erase e-mail from the computer system, including back-ups, after a short period (15–30 days).

_____**22.** Apply uniform retention and deletion standards and features outside the server to workstations and laptops.

_____**23.** Formulate and distribute a statement that the automatic deletion of electronic records will be suspended and steps taken to preserve records in the event of investigation or litigation.

_____**24.** Maintain an appropriate SOP document. All agencies that seize and/or examine digital evidence must do this.

_____**25.** Clearly set forth in this SOP document all elements of an agency's policies and procedures concerning digital evidence, which must be issued under the agency's management authority.

_____**26.** Review the SOPs on an annual basis to ensure their continued suitability and effectiveness.

_____**27.** Make sure that the procedures that you use are generally accepted in the field or supported by data gathered and recorded in a scientific manner.

_____**28.** Maintain written copies of appropriate technical procedures.

_____**29.** Use hardware and software that is appropriate and effective for the seizure or examination procedure.

_____**30.** Record all activity relating to the seizure, storage, examination, or transfer of digital evidence in writing.

_____**31.** Make sure that all digital evidence is available for review and testimony.

_____**32.** Make sure that any action that has the potential to alter, damage, or destroy any aspect of original evidence is performed by qualified persons in a forensically sound manner.

_____**33.** Be alert. One of the best ways to ensure that your network is secure is to keep abreast of developing threats. Security experts agree that ignorance is the most detrimental security problem. Most hacks occur because someone wasn't paying attention.

Web sites such as the CERT home page (http://www.cert.org) are excellent places to get current information.

_____**34.** Apply all service patches. Many companies will sit on patches rather than put them to use. Others are not diligent enough about searching for and downloading the latest virus definitions. Smart hackers bank on the negligence of others.

_____**35.** Limit port access. Although just about any application that uses TCP requires a port, you can minimize exposure by limiting the number of ports accessible through a firewall. NNTP (Network News Transport Protocol) is an excellent example: Unless your shop requires newsgroup access, port 119 should be shut down.

_____**36.** Eliminate unused user IDs and change existing passwords. Poor maintenance is almost as dangerous as ignorance.

_____**37.** Make sure that system administrators routinely audit and delete any idle user IDs.

_____**38.** Make sure that in order to limit the likelihood of successful random guessing, that all user and system passwords be system-generated or system-enforced.

_____**39.** Avoid the use of SNMP across the firewall.

_____**40.** Check routers to make sure they do not respond to SNMP commands originating outside the network.

_____**41.** Secure remote access. Try to break into your own network. You can learn a lot by hacking into your own system.

_____**42.** Test your packet-filtering scheme. If you can gain access to your systems from a workstation outside your network, you can easily test your packet-filtering scheme without any outside exposure. If you do spot a weakness, you'll be one step ahead of the hackers.

_____**43.** Ask a consultant when in doubt. If you don't have the technical wherewithal in-house or if your staff is too busy working on other projects, don't hesitate to call in a consultant. Many companies offer security assessment and training services.

_____**44.** Assess your company's networking needs and shut down any ports that aren't necessary for day-to-day operations, such as port 53 for DNS access and port 119 for NNTP (Network News Transfer Protocol) services.

_____**45.** Be sure to eliminate unused user IDs and to avoid provisioning SNMP services through the firewall.

3. ATTACK TRACEBACK AND ATTRIBUTION

When we face the cyber attacks, we can detect them and take countermeasures. For instance, an intrusion detection system (IDS) can help detect attacks; we can update operating systems to close potential backdoors; we can install antivirus software to defend against many known viruses. Although in many cases we can detect attacks and mitigate their damage, it is hard to find the real attackers/criminals. However, if we don't trace back to the attackers, they can always conceal themselves and launch new attacks. If we have the ability to find and punish the attackers, we believe this will help significantly reduce the attacks we face every day.

Why is traceback difficult in computer networks? One reason is that today's Internet is stateless. There is too much data in the Internet to record it all. For example, a typical router only forwards the passed packets and does not care where they are from; a typical mail transfer agent (MTA) simply relays emails to the next agent and never minds who is the sender. Another reason is that today's Internet is almost an unauthorized environment. Alice can make a VoIP call to Bob and pretend to be Carol; an attacker can send millions of emails using your email address and your mailbox will be bombed by millions of replies. Two kinds of attacks are widely used by attackers and also interesting to researchers all over the world. One is IP spoofing; the other is the stepping-stone attack. Each IP packet header contains the source IP address. Using IP spoofing, an attacker can change the source IP address in the header to that of a different machine and thus avoid traceback.

In a stepping-stone attack, the attack flow may travel through a chain of stepping stones (intermediate hosts) before it reaches the victim. Therefore, it is difficult for the victim to know where the attack came from except that she can see the attack traffic from the last hop of the stepping-stone chain. Figure 36.1 shows an example of IP stepping-stone attack.

Next we introduce the existing schemes to trace back IP spoofing attacks, then we discuss current work on stepping-stone attack attribution.

IP Traceback

Here we review major existing IP traceback schemes that have been designed to trace back to the origin of IP packets through the Internet. We roughly categorize them into four primary classes:

- Active probing[5,6]
- ICMP traceback[7,8,9]
- Packet marking[10,11,12,13,14]
- Log-based traceback[15,16,17,18]

Active Probing

Stone[19] proposed a traceback scheme called *CenterTrack*, which selectively reroutes the packets in question directly from edge routers to some special tracking routers. The tracking routers determine the ingress edge router by observing from which tunnel the packet arrives. This approach requires the cooperation of network administrators, and the management overhead is considerably large.

Burch and Cheswick[20] outlined a technique for tracing spoofed packets back to their actual source without relying on the cooperation of intervening ISPs. The victim actively changes the traffic in particular links and observes the influence on attack packets, and thus can determine where the attack comes from. This technique cannot work well on distributed attacks and requires that the attacks remain active during the time period of traceback.

---

5. H. Burch and B. Cheswick, "Tracing anonymous packets to their approximate source," in *Proceedings of USENIX LISA* 2000, Dec. 2000, pp. 319–327.

6. R. Stone, "Centertrack: An IP overlay network for tracking DoS floods," in *Proceedings of the 9th USENIX Security Symposium*, Aug. 2000, pp. 199–212.

7. S. M. Bellovin, "ICMP traceback messages," Internet draft, 2000.

8. A. Mankin, D. Massey, C.-L. Wu, S. F. Wu, and L. Zhang, "On design and evaluation of 'Intention-Driven' ICMP traceback," in *Proceedings of 10th IEEE International Conference on Computer Communications and Networks*, Oct. 2001.

9. S. F. Wu, L. Zhang, D. Massey, and A. Mankin, "Intention-driven ICMP trace-back," Internet draft, 2001.

10. A. Belenky and N. Ansari, "IP traceback with deterministic packet marking," *IEEE Communications Letters*, Vol. 7, No. 4, pp. 162–164, April 2003.

11. D. Dean, M. Franklin, and A. Stubblefield, "An algebraic approach to IP traceback," *Information and System Security*, Vol. 5, No. 2, pp. 119–137, 2002.

12. K. Park and H. Lee, "On the effectiveness of probabilistic packet marking for IP traceback under denial of service attack," in *Proceedings of IEEE INFOCOM* 2001, Apr. 2001, pp. 338–347.

13. S. Savage, D. Wetherall, A. Karlin, and T. Anderson, "Network support for IP traceback," *IEEE/ACM Transactions on Networking*, Vol. 9, No. 3, pp. 226–237, June 2001.

14. D. Song and A. Perrig, "Advanced and authenticated marking schemes for IP traceback," in *Proceedings of IEEE INFOCOM* 2001, Apr. 2001.

15. J. Li, M. Sung, J. Xu, and L. Li, "Large-scale IP traceback in high-speed Internet: Practical techniques and theoretical foundation," in *Proceedings of* 2004 *IEEE Symposium on Security and Privacy*, May 2004.

16. S. Matsuda, T. Baba, A. Hayakawa, and T. Nakamura, "Design and implementation of unauthorized access tracing system," in *Proceedings of the* 2002 *Symposium on Applications and the Internet* (*SAINT* 2002), Jan. 2002.

17. K. Shanmugasundaram, H. Brönnimann, and N. Memon, "Payload attribution via hierarchical Bloom filters," in *Proceedings of the* 11*th ACM Conference on Computer and Communications Security*, Oct. 2004.

18. A. C. Snoeren, C. Partridge, L. A. Sanchez, C. E. Jones, F. Tchakountio, B. Schwartz, S. T. Kent, and W. T. Strayer, "Single-packet IP traceback," *IEEE/ACM Transactions on Networking*, Vol. 10, No. 6, pp. 721–734, Dec. 2002.

19. R. Stone, "Centertrack: An IP overlay network for tracking DoS floods," in *Proceedings of the 9th USENIX Security Symposium*, Aug. 2000, pp. 199–212.

20. H. Burch and B. Cheswick, "Tracing anonymous packets to their approximate source," in *Proceedings of USENIX LISA* 2000, Dec. 2000, pp. 319–327.

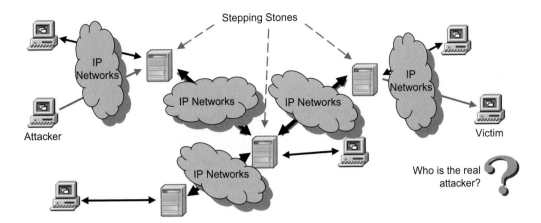

FIGURE 36.1   Stepping-stone attack attribution.

ICMP Traceback (iTrace)

Bellovin[21] proposed a scheme named *iTrace* to trace back using ICMP messages for authenticated IP marking. In this scheme, each router samples (with low probability) the forwarding packets, copies the contents into a special ICMP traceback message, adds its own IP address as well as the IP of the previous and next-hop routers, and forwards the packet to either the source or destination address. By combining the information obtained from several of these ICMP messages from different routers, the victim can then reconstruct the path back to the origin of the attacker.

A drawback of this scheme is that it is much more likely that the victim will get ICMP messages from routers nearby than from routers farther away. This implies that most of the network resources spent on generating and utilizing iTrace messages will be wasted. An enhancement of iTrace, called *Intention-Driven iTrace*, has been proposed.[22,23] By introducing an extra "intention-bit," it is possible for the victim to increase the probability of receiving iTrace messages from remote routers.

Packet Marking

Savage et al.[24] proposed a *Probabilistic Packet Marking* (PPM) scheme. Since then several other PPM-based

schemes have been developed.[25,26,27] The baseline idea of PPM is that routers probabilistically write partial path information into the packets during forwarding. If the attacks are made up of a sufficiently large number of packets, eventually the victim may get enough information by combining a modest number of marked packets to reconstruct the entire attack path. This allows victims to locate the approximate source of attack traffic without requiring outside assistance.

The *Deterministic Packet Marking* (DPM) scheme proposed by Belenky and Ansari[28] involves marking each individual packet when it enters the network. The packet is marked by the interface closest to the source of the packet on the edge ingress router. The mark remains unchanged as long as the packet traverses the network. However, there is no way to get the whole paths of the attacks.

Dean et al.[29] proposed an *Algebraic Packet Marking* (APM) scheme that reframes the traceback problem as a polynomial reconstruction problem and uses techniques from algebraic coding theory to provide robust methods of transmission and reconstruction. The advantage of this

21. S. M. Bellovin, "ICMP traceback messages," Internet draft, 2000.

22. A. Mankin, D. Massey, C.-L. Wu, S. F. Wu, and L. Zhang, "On design and evaluation of 'Intention-Driven' ICMP traceback," in *Proceedings of 10th IEEE International Conference on Computer Communications and Networks*, Oct. 2001.

23. S. F. Wu, L. Zhang, D. Massey, and A. Mankin, "Intention-driven ICMP trace back," Internet draft, 2001.

24. S. Savage, D. Wetherall, A. Karlin, and T. Anderson, "Network support for IP traceback," IEEE/*ACM Transactions on Networking*, Vol. 9, No. 3, pp. 226–237, June 2001.

25. D. Song and A. Perrig, "Advanced and authenticated marking schemes for IP traceback," in *Proceedings of IEEE INFOCOM* 2001, Apr. 2001.

26. K. Park and H. Lee, "On the effectiveness of probabilistic packet marking for IP traceback under denial of service attack," in *Proceedings of IEEE INFOCOM* 2001, Apr. 2001, pp. 338–347.

27. D. Dean, M. Franklin, and A. Stubblefield, "An algebraic approach to IP traceback," *Information and System Security*, Vol. 5, No. 2, pp. 119–137, 2002.

28. A. Belenky and N. Ansari, "IP traceback with deterministic packet marking," *IEEE Communications Letters*, Vol. 7, No. 4, pp. 162–164, April 2003.

29. D. Dean, M. Franklin, and A. Stubblefield, "An algebraic approach to IP traceback," *Information and System Security*, Vol. 5, No. 2, pp. 119–137, 2002.

scheme is that it offers more flexibility in design and more powerful techniques that can be used to filter out attacker-generated noise and separate multiple paths. But it shares similarity with PPM in that it requires a sufficiently large number of attack packets.

Log-Based Traceback

The basic idea of log-based traceback is that each router stores the information (digests, signature, or even the packet itself) of network traffic through it. Once an attack is detected, the victim queries the upstream routers by checking whether they have logged the attack packet in question. If the attack packet's information is found in a given router's memory, that router is deemed to be part of the attack path. Obviously, the major challenge in log-based traceback schemes is the storage space requirement at the intermediate routers.

Matsuda et al.[30] proposed a hop-by-hop log-based IP traceback method. Its main features are a logging *packet feature* that is composed of a portion of the packet for identification purposes and an algorithm using a data-link identifier to identify the routing of a packet. However, for each received packet, about 60 bytes of data should be recorded. The resulting large memory space requirement prevents this method from being applied to high-speed networks with heavy traffic.

Although today's high-speed IP networks suggest that classical log-based traceback schemes would be too prohibitive because of the huge memory requirement, logbased traceback became attractive after Bloom filter-based (i.e., hash-based) traceback schemes were proposed. *Bloom filters* were presented by Burton H. Bloom[31] in 1970 and have been widely used in many areas such as database and networking.[32] A Bloom filter is a spaceefficient data structure for representing a set of elements to respond to membership queries. It is a vector of bits that are all initialized to the value 0. Then each element is inserted into the Bloom filter by hashing it using several independent uniform hash functions and setting the corresponding bits in the vector to value 1. Given a query as to whether an element is present in the Bloom filter, we hash this element using the same hash functions and check whether all the corresponding bits are set to 1.

If any one of them is 0, then undoubtedly this element is not stored in the filter. Otherwise, we would say that it is present in the filter, although there is a certain probability that the element is determined to be in the filter though it is actually not. Such false cases are called *false positives*.

The space-efficiency of Bloom filters is achieved at the cost of a small, acceptable false-positive rate. Bloom filters were introduced into the IP traceback area by Snoeren et al.[33] They built a system named the *Source Path Isolation Engine* (SPIE), which can trace the origin of a single IP packet delivered by the network in the recent past. They demonstrated that the system is effective, space-efficient, and implementable in current or next-generation routing hardware. Bloom filters are used in each SPIE-equipped router to record the digests of all packets received in the recent past. The digest of a packet is exactly several hash values of its nonmutable IP header fields and the prefix of the payload. Strayer et al.[34] extended this traceback architecture to IP-v6. However, the inherent false positives of Bloom filters caused by unavoidable collisions restrain the effectiveness of these systems. To reduce the impact of unavoidable collisions in Bloom filters, Zhang and Guan[35] propose a topologyaware single-packet IP traceback system, namely TOPO. The router's local topology information, that is, its immediate predecessor information, is utilized. The performance analysis shows that TOPO can reduce the number and scope of unnecessary queries and significantly decrease false attributions. When Bloom filters are used, it is difficult to decide their optimal control parameters *a priori*. They designed a *k*-adaptive mechanism that can dynamically adjust the parameters of Bloom filters to reduce the false-positive rate.

Shanmugasundaram et al.[36] proposed a *payload attribution system* (PAS) based on a *hierarchical Bloom filter* (HBF). HBF is a Bloom filter in which an element is inserted several times using different parts of the same element. Compared with SPIE, which is a packet-digesting scheme, PAS only uses the payload excerpt of a packet. It is useful when the packet header is unavailable.

30. S. Matsuda, T. Baba, A. Hayakawa, and T. Nakamura, "Design and implementation of unauthorized access tracing system," in *Proceedings of the* 2002 *Symposium on Applications and the Internet* (*SAINT* 2002), Jan. 2002.

31. B. H. Bloom, "Space/time trade-offs in hash coding with allowable errors," *Communications of the ACM*, Vol. 13, No. 7, pp. 422–426, July 1970.

32. A. Broder and M. Mitzenmacher, "Network applications of Bloom filters: A survey," *Proceedings of the 40th Annual Allerton Conference on Communication, Control, and Computing*, Oct. 2002, pp. 636–646.

33. A. C. Snoeren, C. Partridge, L. A. Sanchez, C. E. Jones, F. Tchakountio, B. Schwartz, S. T. Kent, and W. T. Strayer, "Single-packet IP traceback," *IEEE/ACM Transactions on Networking*, Vol. 10, No. 6, pp. 721–734, Dec. 2002.

34. W. T. Strayer, C. E. Jones, F. Tchakountio, and R. R. Hain, "SPIE-IPv6: Single IPv6 packet traceback," in *Proceedings of the 29th IEEE Local Computer Networks Conference* (*LCN* 2004), Nov. 2004.

35. L. Zhang and Y. Guan, "TOPO: A topology-aware single packet attack traceback scheme," in *Proceedings of the 2nd IEEE Communications Society/CreateNet International Conference on Security and Privacy in Communication Networks* (*SecureComm* 2006), Aug. 2006.

36. S. Savage, D. Wetherall, A. Karlin, and T. Anderson, "Network support for IP traceback," *IEEE/ACM Transactions on Networking*, Vol. 9, No. 3, pp. 226–237, June 2001.

Li et al.[37] proposed a Bloom filter-based IP trace-back scheme that requires an order of magnitude smaller processing and storage cost than SPIE, thereby being able to scale to much higher link speed. The baseline idea of their approach is to sample and log a small percentage of packets, and 1 bit packet marking is used in their sampling scheme. Therefore, their traceback scheme combines packet marking and packet logging together. Their simulation results showed that the traceback scheme can achieve high accuracy and scale well to a large number of attackers. However, as the authors also pointed out, because of the low sampling rate, their scheme is no longer capable of tracing one attacker with only one packet.

Stepping-Stone Attack Attribution

Ever since the problem of detecting stepping stones was first proposed by Staniford-Chen and Heberlein,[38] several approaches have been proposed to detect encrypted stepping-stone attacks.

The ON/OFF based approach proposed by Zhang and Paxson[39] is the first timing-based method that can trace stepping stones, even if the traffic were to be encrypted. In their approach, they calculated the correlation of different flows by using each flow's OFF periods. A flow is considered to be in an OFF period when there is no data traffic on it for more than a time period threshold. Their approach comes from the observation that two flows are in the same connection chain if their OFF periods coincide.

Yoda and Etoh[40] presented a deviation-based approach for detecting stepping-stone connections. The deviation is defined as the difference between the average propagation delay and the minimum propagation delay of two connections. This scheme comes from the observation that the deviation for two unrelated connections is large enough to be distinguished from the deviation of connections in the same connection chain.

Wang et al.[41] proposed a correlation scheme using interpacket delay (IPD) characteristics to detect stepping stones. They defined their correlation metric over the IPDs in a sliding window of packets of the connections to be correlated. They showed that the IPD characteristics may be preserved across many stepping stones.

Wang and Reeves[42] presented an active watermark scheme that is designed to be robust against certain delay perturbations. The watermark is introduced into a connection by slightly adjusting the interpacket delays of selected packets in the flow. If the delay perturbation is not quite large, the watermark information will remain along the connection chain. This is the only active stepping-stone attribution approach.

Strayer et al.[43] presented a State-Space algorithm that is derived from their work on wireless topology discovery. When a new packet is received, each node is given a weight that decreases as the elapsed time from the last packet from that node increases. Then the connections on the same connection chain will have higher weights than other connections.

However, none of these previous approaches can effectively detect stepping stones when delay and chaff perturbations exist simultaneously. Although no experimental data is available, Donoho et al.[44] indicated that there are theoretical limits on the ability of attackers to disguise their traffic using evasions for sufficiently long connections. They assumed that the intruder has a maximum delay tolerance, and they used wavelets and similar multiscale methods to separate the short-term behavior of the flows (delay or chaff) from the long-term behavior of the flows (the remaining correlation). However, this method requires the intrusion connections to remain for long periods, and the authors never experimented to show the effectiveness against chaff perturbation. These evasions consist of local jittering of packet arrival times and the addition of superfluous packets.

Blum et al.[45] proposed and analyzed algorithms for stepping-stone detection using ideas from computational learning theory and the analysis of random walks. They achieved provable (polynomial) upper bounds on the

37. J. Li, M. Sung, J. Xu, and L. Li, "Large-scale IP traceback in high-speed Internet: Practical techniques and theoretical foundation," in *Proceedings of* 2004 *IEEE Symposium on Security and Privacy*, May 2004.
38. S. Staniford-Chen and L. T. Heberlein, "Holding intruders accountable on the Internet," in *Proceedings of the 1995 IEEE Symposium on Security and Privacy*, May 1995.
39. Y. Zhang and V. Paxson, "Detecting stepping stones," in *Proceedings of the 9th USENIX Security Symposium*, Aug. 2000, pp. 171–184.
40. K. Yoda and H. Etoh, "Finding a connection chain for tracing intruders," in *Proceedings of the 6th European Symposium on Research in Computer Security* (*ESORICS* 2000), Oct. 2000.
41. X. Wang, D. S. Reeves, and S. F. Wu, "Inter-packet delay based correlation for tracing encrypted connections through stepping stones," in *Proceedings of the 7th European Symposium on Research in Computer Security* (*ESORICS* 2002), Oct. 2002.

42. X. Wang and D. S. Reeves, "Robust correlation of encrypted attack traffic through stepping stones by manipulation of interpacket delays," in *Proceedings of the 10th ACM Conference on Computer and Communications Security* (*CCS* 2003), Oct. 2003.
43. W. T. Strayer, C. E. Jones, I. Castineyra, J. B. Levin, and R. R. Hain, "An integrated architecture for attack attribution," BBN Technologies, Tech. Rep. BBN REPORT-8384, Dec. 2003.
44. D. L. Donoho, A. G. Flesia, U. Shankar, V. Paxson, J. Coit, and S. Staniford, "Multiscale stepping-stone detection: Detecting pairs of jittered interactive streams by exploiting maximum tolerable delay," in *Proceedings of the 5th International Symposium on Recent Advances in Intrusion Detection* (*RAID* 2002), Oct. 2002.
45. A. Blum, D. Song, and S. Venkataraman, "Detection of interactive stepping stones: Algorithms and confidence bounds," in *Proceedings of the 7th International Symposium on Recent Advances in Intrusion Detection* (RAID 2004), Sept. 2004.

number of packets needed to confidently detect and identify stepping-stone flows with proven guarantees on the false positives and provided lower bounds on the amount of chaff that an attacker would have to send to evade detection. However, their upper bounds on the number of packets required is large, while the lower bounds on the amount of chaff needed for attackers to evade detection is very small. They did not discuss how to detect stepping stones without enough packets or with large amounts of chaff and did not show experimental results.

Zhang et al.[46] proposed and analyzed algorithms that represent that attackers cannot always evade detection only by adding limited delay and independent chaff perturbations. They provided the upper bounds on the number of packets needed to confidently detect stepping-stone connections from nonstepping stone connections with any given probability of false attribution.

Although there have been many stepping-stone attack attribution schemes, there is a lack of comprehensive experimental evaluation of these schemes. Therefore, there are no objective, comparable evaluation results on the effectiveness and limitations of these schemes. Xin et al.[47] designed and built a scalable testbed environment that can evaluate all existing stepping-stone attack attribution schemes reproducibly, provide a stable platform for further research in this area, and be easily reconfigured, expanded, and operated with a user-friendly interface. This testbed environment has been established in a dedicated stepping-stone attack attribution research laboratory. An evaluation of proposed stepping-stone techniques is currently under way.

A group from Iowa State University proposed the first effective detection scheme to detect attack flows with both delay and chaff perturbations. A scheme named "datatick" is proposed that can handle significant packet merging/splitting and can attribute multiple application layer protocols (e.g., X-Windows over SSH, Windows Remote Desktop, VNC, and SSH). A scalable testbed environment is also established that can evaluate all existing stepping-stone attack attribution schemes reproducibly. A group of researchers from North Carolina State University and George Mason University utilizes timing-based watermarking to trace back stepping-stone attacks. They have proposed schemes to handle repacketization of the attack flow and a "centroid-based" watermarking scheme to detect attack flows with chaff. A group from

Johns Hopkins University demonstrates the feasibility of a "post-mortem" technique for traceback through indirect attacks. A group from Telcordia Technologies proposed a scheme that reroutes the attack traffic from uncooperative networks to cooperative networks such that the attacks can be attributed. The BBN Technologies' group integrates single-packet traceback and stepping-stone correlation. A distributed traceback system called FlyTrap is developed for uncooperative and hostile networks. A group from Sparta integrates multiple complementary traceback approaches and tests them in a TOR anonymous system.

A research project entitled Tracing VoIP Calls through the Internet, led by Xinyuan Wang from George Mason University, aims to investigate how VoIP calls can be effectively traced. Wang et al. proposed to use the watermarking technology in stepping-stone attack attribution into VoIP attribution and showed that VoIP calls can still be attributed.[48]

Strayer et al. has been supported by the U.S. Army Research Office to research how to attribute attackers using botnets. Their approach for detecting botnets is to examine flow characteristics such as bandwidth, duration, and packet timing, looking for evidence of botnet command and control activity.[49]

4. CRITICAL NEEDS ANALYSIS

Although large-scale cyber terrorism seldom happens, some cyber attacks have already shown their power in damaging homeland security. For instance, on October 21, 2002, all 13 Domain Name Server (DNS) root name servers sustained a DoS attack.[50] Some root name servers were unreachable from many parts of the global Internet due to congestion from the attack traffic. Even now, we do not know the real attacker and what his intention was.

Besides the Internet itself, many sensitive institutions, such as the U.S. power grid, nuclear power plants, and airports, may also be attacked by terrorists if they are connected to the Internet, although these sites have been carefully protected physically. If the terrorists want to launch large-scale attacks targeting these sensitive institutions through the Internet, they will probably have to try several times to be successful. If we only sit here and do not fight back, they will finally find our vulnerabilities

46. L. Zhang, A. G. Persaud, A. Johnson, and Y. Guan, "Detection of Stepping Stone Attack under Delay and Chaff Perturbations," in 25th IEEE International Performance Computing and Communications Conference (IPCCC 2006), Apr. 2006.

47. J. Xin, L. Zhang, B. Aswegan, J. Dickerson, J. Dickerson, T. Daniels, and Y. Guan, "A testbed for evaluation and analysis of stepping stone attack attribution techniques," in Proceedings of TridentCom 2006, Mar. 2006.

48. X. Wang, S. Chen, and S. Jajodia "Tracking anonymous peer-to-peer VoIP calls on the Internet," In Proceedings of the 12th ACM Conference on Computer Communications Security (CCS 2005), November 2005.

49. W. T. Strayer, R. Walsh, C. Livadas, and D. Lapsley, "Detecting botnets with tight command and control," Proceedings of the 31st IEEE Conference on Local Computer Networks (LCN), November 15–16, 2006.

50. P. Vixie, G. Sneeringer, and M. Schleifer, "Events of Oct. 21, 2002", November 24, 2002, www.isc.org/ops/f-root/october21.txt.

and reach their evil purpose. However, if we can attribute them to the source of attacks, we can detect and arrest them before they succeed.

Although there have been a lot of traceback and attribution schemes on IP spoofing and stepping-stone attacks, we still have a lot of open issues in this area. The biggest issue is the deployment of these schemes. Many schemes (such as packet marking and log-based traceback) need the change of Internet protocol on each intermediate router. Many schemes need many network monitors placed all over the world. These are very difficult to implement in the current Internet without support from government, manufacturers, and academics. It is necessary to consider traceback demands when designing and deploying next-generation networks.

5. RESEARCH DIRECTIONS

There are still some open problems in attack traceback and attribution.

VoIP Attribution

Like the Internet, the Voice over Internet Protocol (VoIP) also provides unauthorized services. Therefore, some security issues existing in the Internet may also appear in VoIP systems. For instance, a phone user may receive a call with a qualified caller ID from her credit-card company, so she answers the critical questions about Social Security number, data of birth, and so on. However, this call actually comes from an attacker who fakes the caller ID using a computer. Compared with a Public Switched Telephone Network (PSTN) phone or mobile phone, IP phones lack monitoring. Therefore, it is desirable to provide schemes that can attribute or trace back to the VoIP callers.

Tracking Botnets

A botnet is a network of compromised computers, or bots, commandeered by an adversarial botmaster. Botnets usually spread through viruses and communicate through the IRC channel. With an army of bots, bot controllers can launch many attacks, such as spam, phishing, key logging, and denial of service. Today more and more scientists are interested in how to detect, mitigate, and trace back botnet attacks.

Traceback in Anonymous Systems

Another issue is that there exist a lot of anonymous systems available all over the world, such as Tor.[51] Tor is a toolset for anonymizing Web browsing and publishing, instant messaging, IRC, SSH, and other applications that use TCP. It provides anonymity and privacy for legal users, and at the same time, it is a good platform via which to launch stepping-stone attacks. Communications over Tor are relayed through several distributed servers called *onion routers*. So far there are more than 800 onion routers all over the world. Since Tor may be seen as a special stepping-stone attack platform, it is interesting to consider how to trace back attacks over Tor.

Online Fraudster Detection and Attribution

One example is the auction frauds on eBay-like auction systems. In the past few years, Internet auctions have become a thriving and very important online business. Compared with traditional auctions, Internet auctions virtually allow everyone to sell and buy anything at anytime from anywhere, at low transaction fees. However, the increasing number of cases of fraud in Internet auctions has harmed this billion-dollar worldwide market. Due to the inherent limitation of information asymmetry in Internet auction systems, it is very hard, if not impossible, to discover all potential (committed and soon to be committed) frauds. Auction frauds are reported as ascending in recent years and have become serious problems. The Internet Crime Complaint Center (IC3) and Internet FraudWatch have both reported Internet auction frauds as the most prevalent type of Internet fraud.[52,53] Internet FraudWatch reported that auction fraud represented 34% (the highest percentage) of total Internet frauds in 2006, resulting in an average loss of $1,331. Internet auction houses had tried to prevent frauds by using certain types of reputation systems, but it has been shown that fraudulent users are able to manipulate these reputation systems. It is important that we develop the capability to detect and attribute auction fraudsters.

Tracing Phishers

Another serious problem is the fraud and identity theft that result from phishing, pharming, and email spoofing of all types. Online users are lured to a faked web site and tricked to disclose sensitive credentials such as passwords, Social Security numbers, and credit-card numbers. The phishers collect these credentials in order to illegitimately gain access to the user's account and cause financial loss or other damages to the user. In the past, phishing attacks often involve various actors as a part of

51. Tor system, http://tor.eff.org.

52. Internet Crime Complaint Center, Internet crime report, 2006 ic3 annual report, 2006.
53. Internet National Fraud Information Center, 2006 top 10 Internet scam trends from NCL's fraud center, 2006.

a secret criminal network and take approaches similar to those of money laundering and drug trafficking. Tracing phishers is a challenging forensic problem and the solutions thereof would greatly help law enforcement practitioners and financial fraud auditors in their investigation and deterrence efforts.

Tracing Illegal Content Distributor in P2P Systems

Peer-to-peer (P2P) file sharing has gained popularity and achieved a great success in the past 15 years. Though the well-known and popular P2P file sharing applications such as BitTorrent (BT), eDonkey, and Foxy may vary from region to region, the trend of using P2P networks can be seen almost everywhere. In North America, a recent report stated that around 41%−44% of all bandwidth was used up by P2P file transfer traffic. With the increasing amount of sensitive documents and files accidentally shared through P2P systems, it is important to develop forensic solutions for locating initial illegal content uploaders in P2P systems. However, one technique would not be applicable to all P2P systems due to their architectural and algorithmic differences among different P2P systems. There are many legal and technical challenges for tracing illegal content distributors in P2P systems.

6. SUMMARY

Organizations should have a capability to perform computer and network forensics. Forensics is needed for various tasks within an organization, including investigating crimes and inappropriate behavior, reconstructing computer security incidents, troubleshooting operational problems, supporting due diligence for audit record maintenance, and recovering from accidental system damage. Without such a capability, an organization will have difficulty determining what events have occurred within its systems and networks, such as exposures of protected, sensitive data. Also, handling evidence in a forensically sound manner puts decision makers in a position where they can confidently take the necessary actions.

One of the most challenging aspects of network forensics is that the available data is typically not comprehensive. In many cases, if not most, some network traffic data has not been recorded and consequently has been lost. Generally, analysts should think of the analysis process as a methodical approach that develops conclusions based on the data that is available and assumptions regarding the missing data (which should be based on technical knowledge and expertise). Although analysts should strive to locate and examine all available data regarding an event, this is not practical in some cases,

particularly when there are many redundant data sources. The analyst should eventually locate, validate, and analyze enough data to be able to reconstruct the event, understand its significance, and determine its impact. In many cases, additional data is available from sources other than network traffic related sources (data files or host OSs).

Organizations typically have many different sources of network traffic data. Because the information collected by these sources varies, the sources may have different value to the analyst, both in general and for specific cases. The following items describe the typical value of the most common data sources in network forensics.

IDS Software

IDS data is often the starting point for examining suspicious activity. Not only do IDSs typically attempt to identify malicious network traffic at all TCP/IP layers, but also they log many data fields (and sometimes raw packets) that can be useful in validating events and correlating them with other data sources. Nevertheless, as noted previously, IDS software does produce false positives, so IDS alerts should be validated. The extent to which this can be done depends on the amount of data recorded related to the alert and the information available to the analyst about the signature characteristics or anomaly detection method that triggered the alert.

Security Event Management Software

Ideally, SEM can be extremely useful for forensics because it can automatically correlate events among several data sources, then extract the relevant information and present it to the user. However, because SEM software functions by bringing in data from many other sources, the value of SEM depends on which data sources are fed into it, how reliable each data source is, and how well the software can normalize the data and correlate events.

NFAT Software

NFAT software is designed specifically to aid in network traffic analysis, so it is valuable if it has monitored an event of interest. NFAT software usually offers features that support analysis, such as traffic reconstruction and visualization; Firewalls, Routers, Proxy Servers, and Remote Access Servers. By itself, data from these sources is usually of little value. Analyzing the data over time can indicate overall trends, such as an increase in blocked connection attempts. However, because these sources typically record little information about each event, the data provides little insight into the nature of the events. Also, many events might be logged each day, so the sheer volume of data can be overwhelming. The primary value of the data is to correlate events recorded by other sources. For example, if a host is compromised and a network IDS sensor detected the attack, querying the firewall logs for events involving the apparent attacking IP address might confirm where the attack entered the network and might indicate other hosts that the attacker attempted to compromise. In addition, address mapping (NAT) performed by these devices is important for network forensics because the apparent IP address of an attacker or a victim might actually have been used by hundreds or thousands of hosts. Fortunately, analysts usually can review the logs to determine which internal address was in use.

DHCP Servers

DHCP servers typically can be configured to log each IP address assignment and the associated MAC address, along with a timestamp. This information can be helpful to analysts in identifying which host performed an activity using a particular IP address. However, analysts should be mindful of the possibility that attackers on an organization's internal networks falsified their MAC addresses or IP addresses, a practice known as spoofing.

Packet Sniffers

Of all the network traffic data sources, packet sniffers can collect the most information on network activity. However, sniffers might capture huge volumes of benign data as well.millions or billions of packets.and typically provide no indication as to which packets might contain malicious activity. In most cases, packet sniffers are best used to provide more data on events that other devices or software has identified as possibly malicious. Some organizations record most or all packets for some period of time so that when an incident occurs, the raw network data is available for examination and analysis. Packet sniffer data is best reviewed with a protocol analyzer, which interprets the data for the analyst based on knowledge of protocol standards and common implementations.

Network Monitoring

Network monitoring software is helpful in identifying significant deviations from normal traffic flows, such as those caused by DDoS attacks, during which, hundreds or thousands of systems launch simultaneous attacks against particular hosts or networks. Network monitoring software can document the impact of these attacks on network bandwidth and availability, as well as providing information about the apparent targets. Traffic flow data can also be helpful in investigating suspicious activity

identified by other sources. For example, it might indicate whether a particular communications pattern has occurred in the preceding days or weeks.

ISP Records

Information from an ISP is primarily of value in tracing an attack back to its source. This is particularly true when the attack uses spoofed IP addresses.

Send Network Traffic to the IP Address

Organizations should not send network traffic to an apparent attacking IP address to validate its identity. Any response that is generated cannot conclusively confirm the identity of the attacking host. Moreover, if the IP address is for the attacker.s system, the attacker might see the traffic and react by destroying evidence or attacking the host sending the traffic. If the IP address is spoofed, sending unsolicited network traffic to the system could be interpreted as unauthorized use or an attack. Under no circumstances should individuals attempt to gain access to others. systems without permission.

Because network forensics can be performed for many purposes with dozens of data source types, analysts may use several different tools on a regular basis, each well-suited to certain situations. Analysts should be aware of the possible approaches to examining and analyzing network traffic data and should select the best tools for each case, rather than applying the same tool to every situation. Analysts should also be mindful of the shortcomings of tools; for example, a particular protocol analyzer might not be able to translate a certain protocol or handle unexpected protocol data (illegal data field value). It can be helpful to have an alternate tool available that might not have the same deficiency.

Network forensic analysis tools (NFAT) typically provide the same functionality as packet sniffers, protocol analyzers, and SEM software in a single product. Whereas SEM software concentrates on correlating events among existing data sources (which typically include multiple network traffic.related sources), NFAT software focuses primarily on collecting, examining, and analyzing network traffic. NFAT software also offers additional features that further facilitate network forensics, such as the following:

- Reconstructing events by replaying network traffic within the tool, ranging from an individual session (instant messaging [IM] between two users) to all sessions during a particular time period. The speed of the replaying can typically be adjusted as needed.
- Visualizing the traffic flows and the relationships among hosts. Some tools can even tie IP addresses,

domain names, or other data to physical locations and produce a geographic map of the activity.

- Building profiles of typical activity and identifying significant deviations.
- Searching application content for keywords (confidential., proprietary).

Finally, let's move on to the real interactive part of this Chapter: review questions/exercises, hands-on projects, case projects and optional team case project. The answers and/or solutions by chapter can be found in the Online Instructor's Solutions Manual.

CHAPTER REVIEW QUESTIONS/EXERCISES

True/False

1. True or False? In many cases, businesses are often eager to report and publicly discuss cyber crimes related to them.
2. True or False? Network forensics can be generally defined as a science of discovering and retrieving evidential information in a networked environment about a crime in such a way as to make it nonadmissible in court.
3. True or False? When we face the cyber attacks, we can detect them and take countermeasures.
4. True or False? The *Deterministic Packet Marking* (DPM) scheme proposed by Belenky and Ansari[28] involves marking each general packet when it enters the network.
5. True or False? The basic idea of log-based traceback is that each router stores the information (digests, signature, or even the packet itself) of network traffic through it.

Multiple Choice

1. Like the Internet, the _____ also provides unauthorized services.
   A. Voice over Internet Protocol (VoIP)
   B. Botnets
   C. Data retention
   D. Evolution
   E. Security
2. What is a network of compromised computers, or bots, commandeered by an adversarial botmaster.
   A. Botnet
   B. Traceback
   C. Data retention
   D. Process
   E. Security

3. _____ file sharing has gained popularity and achieved a great success in the past 15 years.:
   A. Evolution
   B. Data retention
   C. Peer-to-peer (P2P)
   D. Process
   E. Security
4. In many cases, businesses are often reluctant to report and publicly discuss _____ related to them:
   A. Security
   B. Data retention
   C. Standardization
   D. Cyber crimes
   E. Evolution
5. Generally, it is much harder to detect cyber crimes than crimes in the:
   A. Physical world
   B. Data retention
   C. Standardization
   D. Data destruction
   E. All of the above

EXERCISE

Problem

How does network forensics help an organization pinpoint the source of intermittent performance issues and conduct investigations to identify the source of data leaks, HR violations, or security breaches?

Hands-On Projects

Project

24 × 7 access to all network data and network forensics mining tools, allows an organization to do what?

Case Projects

Problem

How would network forensics go about addressing a pesky intermittent network issue, benchmark application performance for SLAs, or investigate a data breach?

Optional Team Case Project

Problem

When network forensics solutions are in place, what types of forensic investigations can an organization conduct?

Encryption Technology

## Chapter 37

Data Encryption

Dr. Bhushan Kapoor
California State University

Dr. Pramod Pandya
California State University

Data security is not limited to wired networks but is equally critical for wireless communications such as in Wi-Fi and cellular. A very recent case was highlighted when the Indian government requested to Research In Motion (RIM) to share the encryption algorithm used in the BlackBerry cellular device. Of course, RIM refused to share the encryption algorithm. This should demonstrate that encryption is an important technology in all forms of communication. It is hard to accept that secured systems could ever remain secured, since they are designed by us and therefore must be breakable by one of us, given enough time. Every human-engineered system must have a flaw, and it is only a matter of time before someone finds it, thus demanding new innovations by exploring applications from algebraic structures such as groups and rings, elliptic curves, and quantum physics.

Over the past 20 years we have seen classical cryptography evolve to quantum cryptography, a branch of quantum information theory. Quantum cryptography is based on the framework of quantum physics, and it is meant to solve the problem of key distribution, which is an essential component of cryptography that enables us to secure data. The key allows the data to be coded so that to decode it, one would need to know the key that was used to code it. This coding of the given data using a key is known as *encryption*, and decoding of the encrypted data, the reverse step-by-step process, is known as *decryption*. At this stage we point out that the encryption algorithm comes in two flavors: symmetric and asymmetric, of which we will get into the details later on. Securing data requires a three-pronged approach: detection, prevention, and response. Data normally resides on storage media that are accessible over a network. This network is designed with a perimeter around it, such that a single access point provides a route for inbound and outbound traffic through a router supplemented with a firewall.

Data encryption prevents data from being exposed to unauthorized access and makes it unusable. Detection enables us to monitor the activities of network users and provides a means to differentiate levels of activities and offers a possible clue to network violations. Response is equally important, since a network violation must not be allowed to be repeated. Thus the three-pronged approach is evolutionary, and therefore systems analysis and design principles must be taken into account when we design a secured data network.

1. NEED FOR CRYPTOGRAPHY

Data communication normally takes place over an unsecured channel, as is the case when the Internet provides the pathways for the flow of data. In such a case the cryptographic protocols would enable secured communications by addressing the following.

Authentication

Alice sends a message to Bob. How can Bob verify that the message originated from Alice and not from Eve pretending to be Alice? Authentication is critical if Bob is to believe the message—for example, if the bank is trying to verify your Social Security or account number.

Confidentiality

Alice sends a message to Bob. How can Bob be sure that the message was not read by Eve? For example, personal communications need to be maintained as confidential.

Integrity

Alice sends a message to Bob. How does Bob verify that Eve did not intercept the message and change its contents?

Nonrepudiation

Alice could send a message to Bob and later deny that she ever sent a message to Bob. In such a case, how could Bob ever determine who actually sent him the message?

2. MATHEMATICAL PRELUDE TO CRYPTOGRAPHY

We will continue to describe Alice and Bob as two parties exchanging messages and Eve as the eavesdropper. Alice sends either a character string or a binary string that constitutes her message to Bob. In mathematical terms we have the *domain* of the message. The message in question needs to be secured from the eavesdropper Eve—hence it needs to be encrypted.

Mapping or Function

The encryption of the message can be defined as *mapping* the message from the domain to its range such that the inverse mapping should recover the original message. This mapping is a mathematical construct known as the *function*.

So we have a domain, and the range of the function is defined such that the elements of the domain will always map to the range of the function, never outside it. If f represents the function, and the message $m \in$ the domain, then:

$$f(m) = M \in \text{the range}$$

This function can represent, for example, swapping (shifting by k places) the characters positions in the message as defined by the function:

$$f(m,k) = M \in \text{the range}$$

The inverse of this function f must recover the original message, in which case the function is invertible and one-to-one defined. If we were to apply two functions such as f followed by g, the composite function $(g \circ f)$ must be defined and furthermore invertible and one-to-one to recover the original message:

$$(g \circ f)(m) = g(f(m))$$

We will later see that this function is an algorithm that tells the user in a finite number of ways to disguise (encrypt) the given message. The inverse function, if it does exist, would enable us to recover the original message, which is known as the decryption.

Probability

Information security is the goal of the secured data encryption; hence if the encrypted data is truly randomly distributed in the message space (range), to the hacker the encrypted message is equally likely to be in any one of the states (encrypted). This would amount to maximum entropy, so one could reasonably ask as to the likelihood of a hacker breaking the encrypted message, that is, what is the probability of an insecure event taking place? This is conceptually similar to a system being in statistical equilibrium, when it could be equally likely to be in any one of the states. This could lay the foundations of cryptoanalysis in terms of how secure the encryption algorithm is, and can it be broken in polynomial time?

Complexity

Computational complexity deals with problems that could be solved in polynomial time, for a given input. If a given encryption algorithm is known to be difficult to solve and may have a number of solutions, the hacker would have a surmountable task to solve it. Therefore, secured encryption can be examined within the scope of computational complexity to determine whether a solution exists in polynomial time. There is a class of problems that have solutions in polynomial time for a given input, designated as P. By contrast, NP is the set of all problems that have solutions in polynomial time but the correctness of the problem cannot be ascertained. Therefore, NP is a larger set containing the set P. This is useful, for it leads us to NP-completeness, which reduces the solvability of problems in class P to class NP.

Consider a simple example—a set $S = \{4, 7, 12, 1, 10\}$ of five numbers. We want any three numbers to add to 23. Each of the numbers is either selected once only or not selected. The target is 23. Is there an algorithm for the target 23? If there is one, do we have more than one solution? Let's explore whether we can add three numbers to reach a target of 25. Is there a solution for a target of 25? Does a solution exist, and can we investigate in polynomial time? We could extend this concept of computational complexity to crack encryption algorithm that is public, but the key used to encrypt and decrypt the message is kept private. So, in essence the cryptoanalysis deals with discovering the key.

3. CLASSICAL CRYPTOGRAPHY

The conceptual foundation of cryptography was laid out around 3,000 years ago in India and China. The earlier work in cryptology was centered on messages that were expressed using alphanumeric symbols; hence encryption involved simple algorithms such as shifting characters within the string of the message in a defined manner, which is now known as shift cipher. We will also introduce the necessary mathematics of cryptography: integer and modular arithmetic, linear congruence, Euclidean and

Extended Euclidean algorithms, Fermat's theorem, and elliptic curves. We will specify useful notations in context.

Take the set of integers:

$$Z = \{\ldots\ldots\ldots, -3, -2, -1, 0, 1, 2, 3, \ldots\ldots\ldots\ldots\}$$

For any integers a and n, we say that n divides a if the remainder is zero after the division, or else we write:

$$a = q \cdot n + r \quad q: \text{quotient}, \, r: \text{remainder}$$

The Euclidean Algorithm

Given two positive integers, a and b, find the greatest common divisors of a and b. Let d be the greatest common divisors (gcd) of a and b, then,

$$d = \gcd(a, b)$$

Use the following example:

$$\gcd(36, 10) = \gcd(10, 6) = \gcd(6, 4) = \gcd(4, 2)$$
$$= \gcd(2, 0) = 2$$

Hence:

$$\gcd(36, 10) = 2$$

The Extended Euclidean Algorithm

Let a and b be two positive integers, then

$$d = \gcd(a, b) = ax + by$$

Use the following example:

$$\gcd(540, 168) = \gcd(168, 36) = \gcd(36, 24)$$
$$= \gcd(24, 12) = \gcd(12, 0) = 12$$

$$540 = 3(168) + 36 \qquad 36 = 540 - 3(168)$$
$$168 = 4(36) + 24 \qquad 24 = 168 - 4(36)$$
$$36 = 1(24) + 12 \qquad 12 = 36 - 1(24)$$
$$12 = 540 - 3(168) - 168 + 4(36)$$
$$= 540 - 4(168) + 4(36)$$
$$= 540 - 4(168) + 4(540) - 12(168)$$
$$= 5(540) - 16(168)$$

Therefore:

$$x = 5 \quad \text{and} \quad y = -16$$

Hence:

$$12 = (5)540 - (16)168$$

Modular Arithmetic

For a given integer a, positive integer m, and the remainder r,

$$r = a \, (\text{mod } m)$$

Consider examples:

$$2 = 27 \bmod 5$$
$$10 = -18 \bmod 14$$

{divide -18 by 14 leaves -4 as a remainder, then add 14 to -4 so that $(-4 + 14) = 10$ so the remainder is nonnegative}

A set of *residues* is a set consisting of remainders obtained by dividing positive integers by a chosen positive number m (modulus).

$$Z_m = a \, (\text{mod } m) = \{0, 1, 2, 3, \ldots\ldots, m - 1\}$$

Take $m = 7$, then

$$Z_7 = \{0, 1, 2, 3, 4, 5, 6\}$$

Congruence

In arithmetic we normally use the relational operator, equal ($=$), to express that the pair of numbers are equal to each other, which is a binary operation. In cryptography we use *congruence* to express that the residue is the same for a set of integers divided by a positive integer. This essentially groups the positive integers into equivalence classes. Let's look at some examples:

$$2 \equiv 2 \bmod 10; \, 2 \equiv 12 \bmod 10; 2 \equiv 22 \bmod 10$$

Hence we say that the set $\{2, 12, 22\}$ are congruent mod 10.

Residue Class

A residue class is a set of integers congruent mod m, where m is a positive integer.

Take $m = 7$:

$$[0] = \{\ldots\ldots, -21, -14, -7, 0, 7, 14, 21, \ldots\ldots\}$$
$$[1] = \{\ldots\ldots, -20, -3, -6, 1, 8, 15, 22, \ldots\ldots\}$$
$$[2] = \{\ldots\ldots, -19, -12, -5, 2, 9, 16, 23, \ldots\ldots\}$$
$$[3] = \{\ldots\ldots, -18, -11, -4, 3, 10, 17, 24, \ldots\}$$
$$[4] = \{\ldots\ldots, -17, -10, -3, 4, 11, 18, 25, \ldots\}$$
$$[5] = \{\ldots\ldots, -16, -9, -2, 5, 12, 19, 26, \ldots\}$$
$$[6] = \{\ldots\ldots, -15, -8, -1, 6, 13, 20, 27, \ldots\}$$

Some more useful operations defined in Z_m:

$$(a + b) \bmod m = \{(a \bmod m) + (b \bmod m)\} \bmod m$$
$$(a - b) \bmod m = \{(a \bmod m) - (b \bmod m)\} \bmod m$$
$$(a * b) \bmod m = \{(a \bmod m) * (b \bmod m)\} \bmod m$$

$$10^n (\bmod x) = \langle 10 \bmod x \rangle^n \bmod m$$

Inverses

In everyday arithmetic, it is quite simple to find the inverse of a given integer if the binary operation is either additive or multiplicative, but such is not the case with modular arithmetic.

We will begin with the additive inverse of two numbers $a, b \in Z_m$

$$(a + b) \equiv 0 \ (\bmod \ m)$$

That is, the additive inverse of a is $b = (m - a)$.
Given

$$a = 4, \quad \text{and} \quad m = 10$$

then:

$$b = m - a = 10 - 4 = 6$$

Verify:

$$4 + 6 \equiv 0 \ (\bmod \ 10)$$

Similarly, the multiplicative inverse of two integers $a, b \in Z_m$ if

$$a * b \equiv 1 \ (\bmod \ m)$$

a has a multiplicative inverse $b \in Z_m$ if and only if

$$\gcd(m, a) = 1$$

in which case (m, a) are relative prime.

We remind the reader that a prime number is any number greater than 1 that is divisible (with a remainder 0) only by itself and 1. For example, $\{2, 3, 5, 7, 11, 13, \ldots\}$ are prime numbers, and we quote the following theorem for the reader.

Fundamental Theorem of Arithmetic

Each positive number is either a prime number or a composite number, in which case it can be expressed as a product of prime numbers.

Let's consider a set of integers mod 10 to find the multiplicative inverse of the numbers in the set:

$$Z_{10} = \{0, 1, 2, 3, 4, 5, 6, 7, 8, 9\}$$
$$(1 * 1) \bmod 10 = 1$$
$$(3 * 7) \bmod 10 = 1$$
$$(9 * 9) \bmod 10 = 1$$

then there are only three pairs (1,1); (3,7); and (9,9):

$$Z_{10*} = \{1, 3, 7, 9\}$$

The numbers $\{0, 2, 4, 5, 6, 8\}$ have no multiplicative inverse.

Consider a set:

$$Z_6 = \{0, 1, 2, 3, 4, 5\}$$

Then,

$$Z_{6*} = \{1, 5\}$$

You will note that Z_{n*} is a subset of Z_n with unique multiplicative inverse.

Each member of Z_n has a unique additive inverse, whereas each member of Z_{n*} has a unique multiplicative inverse.

Congruence Relation Defined

The a is congruent to b (mod m) if m divides $(a - b)$, that is, the remainder is zero.

$$a \equiv b \bmod m$$

Examples: $87 \equiv 27 \bmod 4$, $67 \equiv 1 \bmod 6$.
Next we quote three theorems:

Theorem 1: Suppose that $a \equiv c \bmod m$ and $b \equiv = d$ mod m, then

$$a + b \equiv c + d (\bmod \ m)$$
$$a * b \equiv c * d (\bmod \ m)$$

Theorem 2: Suppose $a*b \equiv a*c \ (\bmod \ m)$

$$\text{and } \gcd(a, m) = 1$$
$$\text{then } b \equiv c \ (\bmod \ m)$$

Theorem 3: Suppose $a*b \equiv a*c \ (\bmod \ m)$

$$\text{and } d = \gcd(a, m)$$
$$\text{then } b \equiv c \ (\bmod \ m/d)$$

Example to illustrate the use of the theorems just stated:

$$6 \equiv 36 \ (\bmod \ 10)$$

then

$$3 \times 2 \equiv 3 \times 12 \ (\bmod \ 10)$$

since

$$\gcd(3, 10) = 1$$

therefore,

$$2 \equiv 12 \ (\bmod \ 10)$$

also

$$2 = \gcd(6, 10)$$

therefore,

$$1 \equiv 6 \ (\text{mod } 5)$$

Given,

$$14x \equiv 12 \ (\text{mod } 18)$$

find x.

Since

$$\gcd(14, \ 18) = 2$$

therefore,

$$7x \equiv 6 \ (\text{mod } 9)$$

you will observe that,

$$\gcd(7, \ 9) = 1$$

therefore,

$$x \equiv 6(7^{-1}) \ \text{mod } 9$$

and the multiplicative inverse of 7^{-1} is 4, therefore,

$$x \equiv (6 * 4) \ (\text{mod } 9) = 6$$

Substitution Cipher

Shift ciphers, also known as *additive ciphers*, are an example of a monoalphabetic character cipher in which each character is mapped to another character, and a repeated character maps to the same character irrespective of its position in the string. We give a simple example of an additive cipher, where the key is 3, and the algorithm is "add." We restrict the mapping to {0, 1, ..., 7} (see Table 37.1)—that is, we use mod 8. This is an example of finite domain and the range for mapping, so the inverse of the function can be determined easily from the ciphertext.

Observations:

- The domain of the function is $x = \{0,1,2,3,4,5,6,7\}$.
- The range of the function is $y = \{0,1,2,3,4,5,6,7\}$.
- The function is 1 to 1.
- The function is invertible.
- The inverse function is $x = (y - 3) \ \text{mod } 8$.

The affine cipher has two operations, addition and multiplication, with two keys. Once again the arithmetic is mod m, where m is a chosen positive integer.

$$y = (kx + b) \ \text{mod } m$$

where k and b are chosen from integers {0, 1, 2, 3,.........., $(m - 1)$}, and x is the symbol to be encrypted.

The decryption is given as:

$$x = [(y - b) * k^{-1}] \text{mod } m$$

where

$$k^{-1}$$

is the multiplicative inverse of k in Z_{n*}
$(—b)$ is the additive inverse in Z_n
Consider,

$$y = (5 * x + 3) \text{mod } 8$$

Then,

$$x = (y - 3)5 \text{mod } 8$$

In this case, the multiplicative inverse of 5 happens to be 5.

Monoalphabetic substitution ciphers are easily broken, since the key size is small (see Table 37.2).

$$Z_8 = \{0, 1, 2, \ 3, 4, 5, 6, 7, \}$$
$$Z_{8*} = \{1, 3, 5\}$$

Transposition Cipher

A transposition cipher changes the location of the character by a given set of rules known as *permutation*. A cyclic group defines the permutation with a single key to encrypt, and the same key is used to decrypt the ciphered message. Table 37.3 provides an illustration.

4. MODERN SYMMETRIC CIPHERS

Computers internally represent printable data in binary format as strings of zeros and ones. Therefore any data is

TABLE 37.2 Monoalphabetic Substitution Cipher.

X	0	1	2	3	4	5	6	7
y	3	0	5	2	7	4	1	6

TABLE 37.1 Table of values for $y = (x + 3)$ mod 8, given values of $x = \{0,1,... 7\}$.

X	0	1	2	3	4	5	6	7
y	3	4	5	6	7	0	1	2

TABLE 37.3 Transposition Cipher.

1	2	3	4	5
3	1	4	5	2

represented as a large block of zeros and ones. The processing speed of a computer is used to encrypt the block of zeros and ones. Securing all the data in one go would not be practical, nor would it secure the data; hence the scheme to treat data in chunks of blocks, leading to the concept of block ciphers.

The most common value of a block is 64, 128, 256, or 512 bits. You will observe that these values are powers of 2, since computers process data in binary representation using modular arithmetic with modulus 2. We need an algorithm and a key to encrypt the blocks of binary data such that the ciphered data is confusing and diffusing to the hacker. The algorithm is made public, whereas the key is kept secret from unauthorized users so that hackers could establish the robustness of the cipher by attempting to break the encrypted message. The logic of the block cipher is as follows:

- Each bit of ciphertext should depend on all bits of the key and all bits of the plaintext.
- There should be no evidence of statistical relationship between the plaintext and the ciphertext.

In essence, this is the goal of an encryption algorithm: Confuse the message so that there is no apparent relationship between the ciphertext and the plaintext. This is achieved by the substitution rule (S-boxes) and the key.

If changing one bit in the plaintext has a minimal effect on the encrypted text, it might be possible for the hacker to work backward from the encrypted text to the plaintext by changing the bits. Therefore a minimal change in the plaintext should lead to a maximum change in the ciphertext, resulting in spreading, which is known as *diffusion*. Permutation or P-boxes implement the diffusion.

The symmetric cipher consists of an algorithm and a key. The algorithm is made public, whereas the key is kept secret and is known only to the parties that are exchanging messages. Of course, this does create a huge problem, since every pair that is going to exchange messages will need a secret key, growing indefinitely in number as the number of pairs increases. We also would need a mechanism by which to manage the secret keys. We will address these issues later on.

The symmetric algorithm would consist of finite rounds of S-boxes and P-boxes. Once the plaintext is encrypted using the algorithm and the key, it would need to be decrypted using the same algorithm and key. The decryption algorithm and the key would need to work backward in some sense to revert the encrypted message to its original message.

So you begin to see that the algorithm must consist of a finite number of combinations of S-boxes and P-boxes; encryption is mapping from message space (domain) to another message space (range), that is, mapping should be a closed operation, a "necessary" condition on the encryption algorithm. This implies that message strings get mapped to message strings, and of course these message strings belong to a set of messages. We are not concerned with the semantics of the message; we leave this to the message sender and receiver. The S-boxes and P-boxes would define a set of operations on the messages or bits that represent the string of messages. Therefore we require that this set of operations should also be able to undo the encryption, that is, mapping must be invertible in the mathematical sense. Hence the set of operations must have definite relationships among them, resulting in some structural and logical connection. In mathematics an example of this is an algebraic structure such as group, ring, and field, which we explore in the next section.

S-Box

The reader should note that an S-box can have a 3-bit input binary string, and its output may be a 2-bit. The S-box may use a key or be keyless. Let $S(x)$ be the linear function computed by the following function [1]:

$$S(x_1x_2x_3) = [(1 + x_1 + x_2 + x_3 + x_1 \bullet x_2) \bmod 2]$$
$$[(1 + x_3 + x_1 \bullet x_3 + x_1 \bullet x_2) \bmod 2]$$

Such a function is referred to as an *S-box*. For a given 4-bit block of plaintext $x_1x_2x_3x_4$ and the 3-bit key, $k_1k_2k_3$, let

$$E(x_1x_2x_3x_4, \ k_1k_2k_3) = x_1x_2(x_3x_4 \oplus S(x_2x_1x_2 \oplus k_1k_2k_3))$$

where $\oplus$ represents exclusive OR

Given ciphertext, $y_1y_2y_3y_4$ computed with E and the key, $k_1k_2k_3$, compute

$$D(y_1y_2y_3y_4, \ k_1k_2k_3) = (y_1y_2 \oplus S(y_4y_3y_4 \oplus k_1k_2k_3))y_3y_4$$

S-boxes are classified as linear if the number of output bits is the same as the number of input bits, and they're nonlinear if the number of output bits is different from the number of input bits. Furthermore, S-boxes can be invertible or noninvertible.

P-Boxes

A *P-box* (permutation box) will permute the bits per specification. There are three different types of P-boxes, as shown in Tables 37.4, 37.5, and 37.6.

In the compression P-box, inputs 2 and 4 are blocked.

The expansion P-box maps elements 1, 2, and 3 only.

Let's consider a permutation group with the mapping defined, as shown in Table 37.7.

This group is a cyclic group with elements:

$$G = (e, \ a, \ a^2, \ a^3, \ a^4, \ a^5, \ a^6)$$

The identity mapping is given by $a^7 = e$. The inverse element is a^{-1}.

Table 37.7 shows a permutation of an 8-bit string (11110010).

TABLE 37.4 Straight P-Box.

1	2	3	4	5
4	1	5	3	2

TABLE 37.5 Compression P-Box.

1	2	3	4	5
1		2		3

TABLE 37.6 Expansion P-Box.

1	3	3	1	2
1	2	3	4	5

TABLE 37.7 The Permutation Group.

	1	2	3	4	5	6	7	8
a	2	6	3	1	4	8	5	7
	1	1	1	1	0	0	1	0
	1	0	1	1	1	0	0	1
a^2	6	8	3	2	1	7	4	5
	0	0	1	1	1	1	1	0
a^3	8	7	3	6	2	5	1	4
	0	1	1	0	1	0	1	1
a^4	7	5	3	8	6	4	2	1
	1	0	1	0	0	1	1	1
a^5	5	4	3	7	8	1	6	2
	0	1	1	1	0	1	0	1
a^6	4	1	3	5	7	2	8	6
	1	1	1	0	1	1	0	0
$a^7 = e$	1	2	3	4	5	6	7	8
	1	1	1	1	0	0	1	0

Product Ciphers

Modern block ciphers are divided into two categories. The first category of the cipher uses both invertible and noninvertible components. A Feistel cipher belongs to the first category, and DES is a good example of a Feistel cipher. This cipher uses the combination of S-boxes and P-boxes with compression and expansion (noninvertible).

The second category of cipher only uses invertible components, and Advanced Encryption Standard (AES) is an example of a non-Feistel cipher. AES uses S-boxes with an equal number of inputs and outputs and a straight P-box that is invertible.

Alternation of substitutions and transpositions of appropriate forms when applied to a block of plaintext can have the effect of obscuring statistical relationships between the plaintext and the ciphertext and between the key and the ciphertext (diffusion and confusion).

5. ALGEBRAIC STRUCTURE

Modern encryption algorithms such as DES, AES, RSA, and ElGamal, to name a few, are based on algebraic structures such as group theory and field theory as well as number theory. We will begin with a set S, with a finite number of elements and a binary operation (*) defined between any two elements of the set:

$$* : S \times S \to S$$

that is, if a and $b \in S$, then $a * b \in S$. This is important because it implies that the set is closed under the binary operation. We have seen that the message space is finite, and we want to make sure that any algebraic operation on the message space satisfies the closure property. Hence, we want to treat the message space as a finite set of elements. We remind the reader that messages that get encrypted must be finally decrypted by the received party, so the encryption algorithm must run in polynomial time; furthermore, the algorithm must have the property that it be reversible, to recover the original message. The goal of encryption is to confuse and diffuse the hacker to make it almost impossible for the hacker to break the encrypted message. Therefore, encryption must consist of finite number substitutions and transpositions. The algebraic structure *classical group* facilitates the coding of encryption algorithms.

Next we give some relevant definitions and examples before we proceed to introduce the essential concept of a Galois field, which is central to formulation of a Rijndael algorithm used in the Advanced Encryption Standard.

Definition Group

A definition group $(G, \bullet)$ is a finite set G together with an operation $\bullet$ satisfying the following conditions [2]:

- Closure: $\forall a, b \in G$, then $(a \bullet b) \in G$
- Associativity: $\forall a, b, c \in G$, then $a \bullet (b \bullet c) = (a \bullet b) \bullet c$
- Existence of identity: $\exists a$ unique element $e \in G$ such that $\forall a \in G: a \bullet e = e \bullet a$
- $\forall a \in G: \forall a^{-1} G: a^{-1} a = a^{-1} \bullet a = e$

Definitions of Finite and Infinite Groups (Order of a Group)

A group G is said to be finite if the number of elements in the set G is finite; otherwise the group is infinite.

Definition Abelian Group

A group G is abelian if for all $a, b \in G$, $a \bullet b = b \bullet a$

The reader should note that in a group, the elements in the set do not have to be numbers or objects; they can be mappings, functions, or rules.

Examples of a Group

The set of integers Z is a group under addition $(+)$, that is, $(Z, +)$ is a group with identity $e = 0$, and inverse of an element a is $(-a)$. This is an additive abelian group, but infinite.

Nonzero elements of Q (rationale), R (reals), and C (complex) form a group under multiplication, with the identity element $e = 1$, and a^{-1} being the multiplicative inverse.

For any $n \geq 1$, the set of integers modulo n forms a finite additive group of n elements.

$G = <Z_n, +>$ is an abelian group.

The set of Z_{n*} with multiplication operator, $G = <Z_{n*}, x>$ is also an abelian group.

The set Z_{n*}, is a subset of Z_n and includes only integers in Z_n that have a unique multiplicative inverse.

$$Z_{13} = \{0, 1, 2, 3, 4, 5, 6, 7, 8, 9, 10, 11, 12\}$$
$$Z_{13*} = \{1, 2, 3, 4, 5, 6, 7, 8, 9, 10, 11, 12\}$$

Definition: Subgroup

A subgroup of a group G is a non empty subset H of G, which itself is a group under the same operations as that of G. We denote that H is a subgroup of G as $H \subseteq G$, and $H \subset G$ is a proper subgroup of G if the set $H \neq G$ [2]:

Examples of subgroups:

Under addition, $Z \subseteq Q \subseteq R \subseteq C$.

$H = <Z_{10}, +>$ is a proper subgroup of $G = <Z_{12}, +>$

Definition: Cyclic Group

A group G is said to be cyclic if there exists an element $a \in G$ such that for any $b \in G$, and $i \geq 0$, $b = a^i$. Element a is called a generator of G.

The group $G = <Z_{10*}, x>$ is a cyclic group with generators $g = 3$ and $g = 7$.

$$Z_{10*} = \{1, 3, 7, 9\}$$

The group $G = <Z_6, +>$ is a cyclic group with generators $g = 1$ and $g = 5$.

$$Z_6 = \{0, 1, 2, 3, 4, 5\}$$

Rings

Let R be a non-empty set with two binary operations addition $(+)$ and multiplication $(*)$. Then R is called a *ring* if the following axioms are met:

- Under addition, R is an abelian group with zero as the additive identity.
- Under multiplication, R satisfies the closure, the associativity, and the identity axiom; 1 is the multiplicative identity, and that $1 \neq 0$.
- For every a and b that belongs to R, $a \bullet b = b \bullet a$.
- For every a, b, and c that belongs to R, then $a \bullet (b + c) = a \bullet b + a \bullet c$.

Examples

Z, Q, R, and C are all rings under addition and multiplication. For any $n > 0$, Z_n is a ring under addition and multiplication modulo n with 0 as identity under addition, 1 under multiplication.

Definition: Field

If the nonzero elements of a ring form a group under multiplication, the ring is called a *field*.

Examples

Q, R, and C are all fields under addition and multiplication, with 0 and 1 as identity under addition and multiplication.

Note: Z under integer addition and multiplication is not a field because any nonzero element does not have a multiplicative inverse in Z.

Finite Fields $GF(2^n)$

Construction of finite fields and computations in finite fields are based on polynomial computations. Finite fields play a significant role in cryptography and cryptographic protocols such as the Diffie and Hellman key exchange protocol, ElGamal cryptosystems, and AES.

For a prime number p, the quotient Z/p (or F_p) is a finite field with p number of elements. For any positive integer q, $GF(q) = F_q$. We define A to be algebraic structure such as a ring, group, or field.

Definition: A polynomial over A is an expression of the form

$$f(x) = \sum_{i=0}^{n} a_i x^n$$

where n is a nonnegative integer, the coefficient $a_i \in A$, $0 \le i \le n$, and $x \notin A$ [2].

Definition: A polynomial $f \in A[x]$ is said to be irreducible in $A[x]$ if f has a positive degree and $f = gh$ for some $g, h \in A[x]$ implies that either g or h is a constant polynomial [2].

The reader should be aware that a given polynomial can be reducible over one structure but irreducible over another.

Definition: Let f, g, q, and $r \in A[x]$ with $g \ne 0$. Then we say that r is a *remainder* of f divided by g:

$$r \equiv f(\bmod g)$$

The set of remainders of all the polynomials in $A[x]$ (mod g) denoted as $A[x]_g$.

Theorem: Let F be a field and f be a nonzero polynomial in $F[x]$. Then $F[x]_f$ is a ring and is a field if f is irreducible over F.

Theorem: Let F be a field of p elements, and f be an irreducible polynomial over F. Then the number of elements in the field $F[x]f$ is p^n [2].

For every prime p and every positive integer n there exists a finite field of p^n number of elements.

For any prime number p, Z_p is a finite field under addition and multiplication modulo p with 0 and 1 as the identity under addition and multiplication.

Z_p is an additive ring and the nonzero elements of Z_p, denoted by Z_{p*}, forms a multiplicative group.

Galois field, $GF(p^n)$ is a finite field with number of elements p^n, where p is a prime number and n is a positive integer.

Example: Integer representation of a finite field (Rijndael) element.

Polynomial $f(x) = x^8 + x^4 + x^3 + x + 1$ is irreducible over F_2.

The set of all polynomials(mod f) over F_2 forms a field of 2^8 elements; they are all polynomials over F_2 of degree less than 8. So any element in the field $F_2[x]_f$

$$b_7 x^7 + b_6 x^6 + b_5 x^5 + b_4 x^4 + b_3 x^3 + b_2 x^2 + b_1 x^1 + b_0$$

where $b_7, b_6, b_5, b_4, b_3, b_2, b_1, b_0 \in F_2$ thus any element in this field can represent an 8-bit binary number.

We often use F_{2^8} field with 256 elements because there exists an isomorphism between Rijndael and F_{2^8}.

Data inside a computer is organized in bytes (8 bits) and is processed using Boolean logic, that is, bits are manipulated using binary operations addition and multiplication. These binary operations are implemented using the logical operator XOR, or in the language of finite fields, $GF(2)$. Since the extended ASCII defines 8 bits per byte, an 8-bit byte has a natural representation using a polynomial of degree 8. Polynomial addition would be mod 2, and multiplication would be mod polynomial degree 8. Of course this polynomial degree 8 would have to be irreducible. Hence the Galois field $GF(2^8)$ would be the most natural tool to implement the encryption algorithm. Furthermore, this would provide a close algebraic formulation.

Consider polynomials over $GF(2)$ with $p = 2$ and $n = 1$.

$$1,\ x,\ x + 1,\ x^2 + x + 1,\ x^2 + 1,\ x^3 + 1$$

For polynomials with negative coefficients, -1 is the same as $+1$ in $GF(2)$. Obviously, the number of such polynomials is infinite. Algebraic operations of addition and multiplication in which the coefficients are added and multiplied according to the rules that apply to $GF(2)$ are sets of polynomials that form a ring.

Modular Polynomial Arithmetic Over GF(2)

The Galois field $GF(2^3)$: Construct this field with eight elements that can be represented by polynomials of the form

$$ax^2 + bx + c \text{ where } a, b, c \in GF(2) = \{0,\ 1\}$$

Two choices for a, b, c give $2 \times 2 \times 2 = 8$ polynomials of the form

$$ax^2 + bx + c \in GF_2[x]$$

What is our choice of the irreducible polynomials for this field?

$$(x^3 + x^2 + x + 1),\ (x^3 + x^2 + 1),\ (x^3 + x^2 + x),$$
$$(x^3 + x + 1),\ (x^3 + x^2)$$

These two polynomials have no factors: $(x^3 + x^2 + 1)$, $(x^3 + x + 1)$

So we choose polynomial $(x^3 + x + 1)$. Hence all polynomial arithmetic multiplication and division is carried out with respect to $(x^3 + x + 1)$.

The eight polynomials that belong to $GF(2^3)$:

$$\{0,\ 1,\ x,\ x^2,\ 1 + x,\ 1 + x^2,\ x + x^2,\ 1 + x + x^2\}$$

You will observe that GF(8) = $\{0,1,2,3,4,5,6,7\}$ is not a field, since every element (excluding zero) does not have a multiplicative inverse such as $\{2, 4, 6\}$ (mod 8) [2].

Using a Generator to Represent the Elements of $GF(2^n)$

It is particularly convenient to represent the elements of a Galois field with the help of a generator element. If α, is a generator element, then every element of $GF(2^n)$, except for the 0 element, can be written as some power of α. A generator is obtained from the irreducible polynomial that was used to construct the finite field. If $f(\alpha)$ is the irreducible polynomial used, then α, is that element that satisfies the equation $f(\alpha) = 0$. You do not actually solve this equation for its roots, since an irreducible polynomial cannot have actual roots in the field GF(2).

Consider the case of $GF(2^3)$, defined with the irreducible polynomial $x^3 + x + 1$. The generator α, is that element that satisfies $\alpha^3 + \alpha + 1 = 0$. Suppose α is a root in $GF(2^3)$ of the polynomial $p(x) = 1 + x + x^3$, that is, $p(\alpha) = 0$, then

$$\alpha^3 = -\alpha - 1 \ (\text{mod } 2) = \alpha + 1$$
$$\alpha^4 = \alpha(\alpha + 1) = \alpha^2 + \alpha$$
$$\alpha^5 = \alpha^4 \cdot \alpha = (\alpha^2 + \alpha)\alpha = \alpha^3 + \alpha^2 = (\alpha^2 + \alpha + 1)$$
$$\alpha^6 = \alpha^5 \cdot \alpha = \alpha \cdot (\alpha^2 + \alpha + 1) = (\alpha^2 + 1)$$
$$\alpha^7 = (\alpha^2 + 1) \cdot \alpha = (2\alpha + 1)$$

All powers of α generate nonzero elements of GF_8. The polynomials of $GF(2^3)$ represent bit strings, as shown in Table 37.8.

We now consider all polynomials defined over $GF(2)$, modulo the irreducible polynomial $x^3 + x + 1$. When an algebraic operation (polynomial multiplication) results in a polynomial whose degree equals or exceeds that of the irreducible polynomial, we will take for our result the remainder modulo the irreducible polynomial. For example,

$$(x^2 + x + 1) * (x^2 + 1) \bmod (x^3 + x + 1)$$
$$= (x^4 + x^3 + x^2) + (x^2 + x + 1) \bmod (x^3 + x + 1)$$
$$= (x^4 + x^3 + x + 1) \bmod (x^3 + x + 1)$$
$$= -x^2 + x$$
$$= x^2 + x$$

Recall that $1 + 1 = 0$ in GF(2). With multiplications modulo $(x^3 + x + 1)$, we have only the following eight polynomials in the set of polynomials over GF(2):

$$\{0, 1, x, x + 1, x^2, x^2 + 1, x^2 + x, x^2 + x + 1\}$$

We refer to this set as $GF(2^3)$, where the power of 2 is the degree of the modulus polynomial. The eight elements of Z_8 are to be integers modulo 8. Similarly, $GF(2^3)$ maps all the polynomials over GF(2) to the eight polynomials shown. But you will note the crucial difference between $GF(2^3)$ and 2^3: $GF(2^3)$ is a field, whereas Z_8 is *not* [2].

$GF(2^3)$ is a Finite Field

We know that $GF(2^3)$ is an abelian group because the operation of polynomial addition satisfies all the requirements of a group operator and because polynomial addition is commutative. $GF(2^3)$ is also a commutative ring because polynomial multiplication is a distributive over polynomial addition. $GF(2^3)$ is a finite field because it is a finite set and because it contains a unique multiplicative inverse for every nonzero element.

$GF(2^n)$ is a finite field for every n. To find all the polynomials in $GF(2^n)$, we need an irreducible polynomial of degree n. AES arithmetic is based on $GF(2^8)$. It uses the following irreducible polynomial:

$$f(x) = x^8 + x^4 + x^3 + x + 1$$

The finite field $GF(2^8)$ used by AES obviously contains 256 distinct polynomials over GF(2). In general, GF(p^n) is a finite field for any prime p. The elements of GF(p^n) are polynomials over GF(p) (which is the same as the set of residues Z_p).

Next we show how the multiplicative inverse of a polynomial is calculated using the Extended Euclidean algorithm:

$$\text{Multiplicative inverse of } (x^2 + x + 1)$$
$$\text{in } F_2[x]/(x^4 + x + 1) \text{ is } (x^2 + x)$$
$$(x^2 + x)(x^2 + x + 1) = 1 \bmod (x^4 + x + 1)$$

$$\text{Multiplicative inverse of } (x^6 + x + 1)$$
$$\text{in } F_2[x]/(x^8 + x^4 + x^3 + x + 1)$$
$$\text{is } (x^6 + x^5 + x^2 + x + 1)$$

$$(x^6 + x + 1)(x^6 + x^5 + x^2 + x + 1) = 1$$
$$\bmod (x^8 + x^4 + x^3x + 1)[2, 3]$$

6. THE INTERNAL FUNCTIONS OF RIJNDAEL IN AES IMPLEMENTATION

Rijndael is a block cipher. The messages are broken into blocks of a predetermined length, and each block is encrypted independently of the others. Rijndael operates on blocks that are 128-bits in length. There are actually three variants of the Rijndael cipher, each of which uses a different key length. The permissible key lengths are 128, 192, and 256 bits. The details of Rijndael may be found in Bennett and Gilles (1984), but we give an overview here [2,3].

TABLE 37.8 The Polynomials of CF(2^3).

Polynomial	Bit String
0	000
1	001
x	010
$x + 1$	011
x^2	100
$x^2 + 1$	101
$x^2 + x$	110
$x^2 + x + 1$	111

Mathematical Preliminaries

Within a block, the fundamental unit operated on is a byte, that is, 8 bits. Bytes can be interpreted in two different ways. A byte is given in terms of its bits as $b_7b_6b_5b_4b_3b_2b_1b_0$. We may think of each bit as an element in GF(2), the finite field of two elements (mod 2). First, we may think of a byte as a vector, $b_7b_6b_5b_4b_3b_2b_1b_0$ in $GF(2^8)$. Second, we may think of a byte as an element of $GF(2^8)$, in the following way: Consider the polynomial ring GF(2)[X]. We may mod out by any polynomial to produce a factor ring. If this polynomial is irreducible and of degree n, the resulting factor ring is isomorphic to $GF(2^n)$. In Rijndael, we mod out by the irreducible polynomial $X8 + X4 + X3 + X + 1$ and so obtain a representation for $GF(2^8)$. The Rijndael algorithm deals with five units of data in the encryption scheme:

- Bit: A binary digit with a value of 0 or 1
- Byte: A group of 8 bits
- Word: A group of 32 bits
- Block: A block in AES is defined to be 128, 192 or 256 bits
- State: The data block is known as a *state*, and it is made up of a 4×4 matrix of 16 bytes (128 bits)

State

For our discussion purposes, we will consider a data block of 128 bits with a *ky* size of 128 bits. The state is 128 bits long. We think of the state as divided into 16 bytes, a_{ij} where $0 \le i, j \le 3$. We think of these 16 bytes as an array, or matrix, with 4 rows and 4 columns, such that a_{00} is the first byte, b_0 and so on (see Figure 37.1).

AES uses several rounds (10, 12, or 14) of transformations, beginning with a 128-bit block. A round is made up of four parts: S-box, permutation, mixing, and subkey addition. We discuss each part here [2,3].

The S-Box (SubByte)

S-boxes, or substitution boxes, are common in block ciphers. These are 1-to-1 and onto functions, and therefore an inverse exists. Furthermore, these maps are nonlinear to make them immune to linear and differential cryptoanalysis. The S-box is the same in every round, and it acts

$$\begin{bmatrix} a_{00}=b_0 a_{01}=b_4 a_{02}=b_8 a_{03}=b_{12} \\ a_{10}=b_1 a_{11}=b_5 a_{12}=b_9 a_{13}=b_{13} \\ a_{20}=b_2 a_{21}=b_6 a_{22}=b_{10} a_{23}=b_{14} \\ a_{30}=b_3 a_{31}=b_7 a_{32}=b_{11} a_{33}=b_{15} \end{bmatrix}$$

FIGURE 37.1   State.

independently on each byte. Each byte belongs to $GF(2^8)$ domain with 256 elements. For a given byte we compute the inverse of that byte in the $GF(2^8)$ field. This sends a byte x to x^{-1} if x is nonzero and sends it to 0 if it is zero. This defines a nonlinear transformation, as shown in Table 37.9.

Next we apply an affine (over GF(2)) transformation. Think of the byte x as a vector in $GF(2^8)$. Consider the invertible matrix A, as shown in Figure 37.2.

The structure of matrix A is relatively simple, successively shifting the prior row by 1. If we define the vector $v \in GF(2^8)$ to be (1, 1, 0, 0, 0, 1, 1, 0), then the second half of the S-box sends byte x to byte y through the affine transformation defined as:

$$y = A \cdot x^{-1} \oplus 1$$

Since the matrix A has an inverse, it is possible to recover x using the following procedure known as the InvSubByte:

$$x = [A^{-1}(y \oplus b)]^{-1}$$

We will demonstrate the action of an S-box by choosing an uppercase letter S, for which the hexadecimal representation is 53_{16} and binary representation is shown in Tables 37.10 and 37.11.

The letter S has a polynomial representation:

$$(x^6 + x^4 + x + 1)$$

The multiplicative inverse of $(x^6 + x^4 + x + 1)$ is $(x^7 + x^6 + x^3 + x)$, which is derived using the Extended Euclidean algorithm.

Next we multiply the multiplicative inverse x^{-1} with an invertible matrix A (see Figure 37.3) and add a column vector (b) and get the resulting column vector y (see Table 37.12). This corresponds to SubByte transformation and it is nonlinear [2].

$$y = A * x^{-1} + b$$

The column vector y represents a character ED_{16} in hexadecimal representation.

The reader should note that this transformation using the $GF(2^8)$ field is a pretty tedious computation, so instead we use an AES S-box lookup table (a 17×17 matrix expressed in hexadecimal) to replace the character with a replacement character. This corresponds to the SubByte transformation, and corresponding to the SubByte table there is an InvSubByte table that is the inverse of the SubByte table. The InvSubByte can be found in the references or is readily available on the Internet.

We will work with the following string: QUANTUMCRYPTOGOD, which is 16 bytes long, to illustrate AES (see Table 37.13). The state represents

TABLE 37.9 SubByte Transformation.

	0	1	2	3	4	5	6	7	8	9	A	B	C	D	E	F
0	63	7C	77	7B	F2	6B	6F	C5	30	01	67	2B	FE	D7	AB	76
1	CA	82	C9	7D	FA	59	47	F0	AD	D4	A2	AF	9C	A4	72	C0
2	B7	FD	93	26	36	3F	F7	CC	34	A5	E5	F1	71	D8	31	15
3	04	C7	23	C3	18	96	05	9A	07	12	80	E2	EB	27	B2	75
4	09	83	2C	1A	1B	6E	5A	A0	52	3B	D6	B3	29	E3	2F	84
5	53	D1	00	ED	20	FC	B1	5B	6A	CB	BE	39	4A	4C	58	CF
6	D0	EF	AA	FB	43	4D	33	85	45	F9	02	7F	50	3C	9F	A8
7	51	A3	40	8F	92	9D	38	F5	BC	B6	DA	21	10	FF	F3	D2
8	CD	0C	13	EC	5F	97	44	17	C4	A7	7E	3D	64	5D	19	73
9	60	81	4F	DC	22	2A	90	88	46	EE	B8	14	DE	5E	0B	DB
A	E0	32	3A	0A	49	06	24	5C	C2	D3	AC	62	91	95	E4	79
B	E7	CB	37	6D	8D	D5	4E	A9	6C	56	F4	EA	65	7k	AE	08
C	BA	78	25	2E	1C	A6	B4	C6	E8	DD	74	1F	4B	BD	8B	8A
D	70	3E	B5	66	48	03	F6	0E	61	35	57	B9	86	C1	1D	9E
E	E'I	F8	98	11	69	D9	8E	94	9B	1E	87	E9	CE	55	28	DF
F	8C	A1	89	0D	BF	E6	42	68	41	99	2D	0F	B0	54	BB	16

$$A = \begin{bmatrix} 10001111 \\ 11000111 \\ 11110001 \\ 11110001 \\ 01111100 \\ 00111110 \\ 00011111 \end{bmatrix} \qquad b = \begin{pmatrix} 1 \\ 1 \\ 0 \\ 0 \\ 0 \\ 1 \\ 1 \\ 0 \end{pmatrix}$$

FIGURE 37.2 The invertible matrix.

TABLE 37.10 Hexadecimal and Binary Representation.

a_7	a_6	a_5	a_4	a_3	a_2	a_1	a_0
0	1	0	1	0	0	1	1

TABLE 37.11 Hexadecimal and Binary Representation.

a_7	a_6	a_5	a_4	a_3	a_2	a_1	a_0
1	1	0	0	1	0	1	0

our string as a 4×4 matrix in the given arrangement using a hexadecimal representation of each byte (see Figure 37.4).

We apply SubByte transformation (see Figure 37.5) using the lookup table, which replaces each byte as defined in Table 37.13.

The next two rounds of ShiftRows and Mixing in the encryption lead to a diffusion process. The ShiftRow is a permutation.

ShiftRows

In the first step, we take the state and apply the following logic. The first row is kept as is. The second row is shifted left by one byte. The third row is shifted left by two bytes, and the last row is shifted left by three bytes. The resulting state is shown in Figure 37.6.

InvShiftRows in decryption shift bytes toward the right, similar to ShiftRows.

Mixing

The second step, the MixColumns transformation, mixes the columns. We interpret the bytes of each column as the coefficients of a polynomial in $GF(2^8)[x]/(x^4 + 1)$. Then we multiply each column by the polynomial '03'

$$\begin{bmatrix} 10001111 \\ 11000111 \\ 11100011 \\ 11110001 \\ 11111000 \\ 01111100 \\ 00111110 \\ 00011111 \end{bmatrix} \begin{pmatrix} 0 \\ 1 \\ 0 \\ 1 \\ 0 \\ 0 \\ 1 \\ 1 \end{pmatrix} + \begin{pmatrix} 1 \\ 1 \\ 0 \\ 0 \\ 0 \\ 1 \\ 1 \\ 0 \end{pmatrix} \textbf{(mod 2)} = \begin{pmatrix} 1 \\ 0 \\ 1 \\ 1 \\ 0 \\ 1 \\ 1 \\ 1 \end{pmatrix}$$

FIGURE 37.3 Multiplying the multiplicative inverse with an invertibile matrix.

TABLE 37.12 Vectory.

Y_7	Y_6	Y_5	Y_4	Y_3	Y_2	Y_1	Y_0
1	1	1	0	1	1	0	1

$x^3 + {}'02'\ x^2 + {}'01'x + {}'02'$. Multiplication of the bytes is done in $GF(2^8)$ with mod $(x^4 + 1)$.

The mixing transformation remaps the four bytes to a new four bytes by changing the contents of the individual bytes (see Figure 37.7). The MixColumns transformation is applied to each column of the state, hence each column is multiplied by a constant matrix to obtain a new state, S'_{0i}.

$$S'_{0i} = 2 \circ S_{0i} \oplus 3 \circ S_{1i} \oplus S_{2i} \oplus S_{3i}$$

$$S'_{00} = 2 \circ S_{00} \oplus 3 \circ S_{10} \oplus S_{20} \oplus S_{30}$$

$$S_{20} \oplus S_{30} = 53 \oplus 1B$$

$$= (01010011) \oplus (00011011)$$

$$= (01001000)$$

$$2 \circ S_{00} = (00000010) \circ (D1)$$

$$= (x) \circ (11010001)$$

$$= (x)(x^7 + x^6 + x^4 + 1)$$

$$= (x^8 + x^7 + x^5 + x) \bmod (x^8 + x^4 + x^3 + x + 1)$$

$$= (x^7 + x^5 + x^4 + x^3 + 1)$$

$$= (10111001)$$

$$3 \circ S_{10} = (00000011)\ (FC)$$

$$= (00000011)(11111100)$$

$$= \{(x + 1)\ (x^7 + x^6 + x^5 + x^4 + x^3 + x^2)\}$$

$$\bmod(x^8 + x^4 + x^3 + x + 1)$$

$$= (00011111)$$

$$S'_{00} = (10111001) \oplus (00011111) \oplus (01001000)$$

$$= (11101110) = 0 \times EE$$

Subkey Addition

From the original key, we produce a succession of 128-bit keys by means of a key schedule. Let's recap that a word is a group of 32 bits. A 128-bit key is labeled as shown in Table 37.14.

word $W_0 = (k_0k_1k_2k_3)$ word $W_1 = (k_4k_5k_6k_7)$
word $W_2 = (k_8k_9k_{10}k_{11})$ word $W_3 = (k_{12}k_{13}k_{14}k_{15})$

which is then written as a 4×4 matrix (see Figure 37.8), where W_0 is the first column, W_1 is the second column, W_2 is the third column, and W_3 is the fourth column.

AES uses a process called *key expansion* that creates $(10 + 1)$ round keys from the given cipher key. We start with four words and end with 44 words—four word per round key. Thus

$$(W_0,\text{.....................}W_{42}, W_{43})$$

The algorithm to generate 10 round keys is as follows:
The initial cipher key consists of words: $W_0W_1W_2W_3$
The other 10 round keys are made using the following logic:
If $(j \bmod 4) \neq 0$

$$W_j = W_{j-1} \oplus W_{j-4}$$

else

$$W_j = Z \oplus W_{j-4}$$

where $Z = \text{SubWord}(\text{RotWord}(W_{j-1})) \oplus \text{RCon}_{j/4}$.

RotWord (rotate word) takes a word as an array of four bytes and shifts each byte to the left with wrapping. SubWord (substitute word) uses the SubByte lookup table to substitute the byte in the word [2,3]. RCon (round constants) is a four-byte value in which the rightmost three bytes are set to zero [2,3].

Let's work through an example, as shown in Figure 37.9.

Key: 2B 7E 15 16 28 AE D2 A6 AB F7 15 88 09 CF 4F 3C

$W_0 = $ 2B 7E 15 16 $W_1 = $ 28 AE D2 A6 $W_2 = $ AB F7 15 88 $W_3 = $ 09 CF 4F 3C

Compute W_4:

$$W_4 = Z \oplus W_0$$

$$\text{RotWord}(W_3) = \text{RotWord}(09\ CF\ 4F\ 3C)$$

$$= (CF4F3C09)$$

$$\text{SubWord}(CF\ 4F\ 3C\ 09) = (8A\ 84\ EB\ 01)$$

$$Z = (8A\ 84\ EB\ 01) \oplus (01\ 00\ 00\ 00)_{16} = 8B\ 84\ EB\ 01$$

Hence,

$$W_4 = (8B\ 84\ EB\ 01) \oplus (2B\ 7E1516) = A0\ FA\ FE\ 17$$

TABLE 37.13 Illustrating AES.

b_0	b_1	b_2	b_3	b_4	b_5	b_6	b_7	b_8	b_9	b_{10}	b_{11}	b_{12}	b_{13}	b_{14}	b_{15}
Q	U	A	N	T	U	M	C	R	Y	P	T	O	C	O	D
51	55	41	4E	54	55	4D	43	52	59	50	54	4F	47	4F	44

$$\text{State} = \begin{bmatrix} 5154524F \\ 55555947 \\ 414D504F \\ 4E435444 \end{bmatrix}$$

FIGURE 37.4 The state represents a string as a 4×4 matrix in the given arrangement using hexadecimal representation of each byte.

$$\text{State} = \begin{bmatrix} D1200084 \\ FCFCCBA0 \\ 83E35384 \\ 2F1A201B \end{bmatrix}$$

FIGURE 37.5 Applying the SubByte transformation.

$$\text{State} = \begin{bmatrix} D1200084 \\ FCCBA0FC \\ 538483E3 \\ 1B2F1A20 \end{bmatrix}$$

FIGURE 37.6 ShiftRows.

$$\begin{bmatrix} S'_{0i} \\ S'_{1i} \\ S'_{2i} \\ S'_{3i} \end{bmatrix} = \begin{bmatrix} 2311 \\ 1231 \\ 1123 \\ 3112 \end{bmatrix} \begin{bmatrix} S_{0i} \\ S_{1i} \\ S_{2i} \\ S_{3i} \end{bmatrix}$$

FIGURE 37.7 Mixing transformation.

Putting it Together

Put the input into the state: XOR is the state with the 0-th round key. We start with this because any actions before the first (or after the last) use of the key are pointless, since they are publicly known and so can be undone by an attacker. Then apply 10 of the preceding rounds, skipping the column mixing on the last round (but proceeding to a final key XOR in that round). The resulting state is the ciphertext. We use the following labels to describe the encryption procedure (see Table 37.15):

Key 1 : K1 : $W_0 W_1 W_2 W_3$
Key 2 : K2 : $W_4 W_5 W_6 W_7$

Key 11: K11 : $W_{40} W_{41} W_{42} W_{43}$
The Initial State (IS) is the plaintext
The Output State (OSI)
SubByte (SB), ShiftRows (SR), MixColumns (MC)
Round
Pre-round PlainText $\oplus$ K1 = = = = $\rightarrow$ OSI

Next we cycle through the decryption procedure: InvSubByte (ISB), InvShiftRows (ISR), InvMix Columns (IMC)

Round

AES is a non-Feistel cipher, hence each set of transformations such as SubByte, ShiftRows, and MixColumns are invertible so that the decryption must consist of steps to recover the plaintext. You will observe that the round keys are used in the reverse order (see Table 37.16).

7. USE OF MODERN BLOCK CIPHERS

DES and AES are designed to encrypt and decrypt data blocks of fixed size. Most practical examples have data blocks of fewer than 64 bits or greater than 128 bits, and to address this issue currently, five different modes of operation have been set up. These five modes of operation are known as Electronic Code Book (ECB), Cipher-Block Chaining (CBC), Output Feedback (OFB), Cipher Feedback (CFB), and Counter (CTR) modes.

The Electronic Code Book (ECB)

In this mode, the message is split into blocks, and the blocks are sequentially encrypted. This mode is vulnerable to attack using the frequency analysis, the same sort used in simple substitution. Identical blocks would get encrypted to the same blocks, thus exposing the key [1].

Cipher-Block Chaining (CBC)

A logical operation is performed on the first block with what is known as an *initial vector* using the secret key so as to randomize the first block. The output of this step is logically combined with the second block and the key to

TABLE 37.14 Subkey Addition.

k_0	k_1	k_2	k_3	k_4	k_5	k_6	k_7	k_8	k_9	k_{10}	k_{11}	k_{12}	k_{13}	k_{14}	k_{15}

$$\begin{bmatrix} k_{00}k_{01}k_{02}k_{03} \\ k_{10}k_{11}k_{12}k_{13} \\ k_{20}k_{21}k_{22}k_{23} \\ k_{30}k_{31}k_{32}k_{33} \end{bmatrix}$$

FIGURE 37.8   A 4×4 matrix.

$$\begin{bmatrix} 2B28AB09 \\ 7EAEF7CF \\ 15D2154F \\ 16A6883C \end{bmatrix}$$

FIGURE 37.9   RotWord and SubWord.

generate encrypted text, which is then used with the third block and so on [1].

8. PUBLIC-KEY CRYPTOGRAPHY

In this section we cover what is known as *asymmetric encryption*, which uses a pair of keys rather than one key, as used in symmetric encryption. This single-key encryption between the two parties requires that each party has its secret key, so that as the number of parties increases so does the number of keys. In addition, the distribution of the secret key becomes unmanageable as the number of keys increases. Of course, a longtime use of the same secret key between any pair would make it more vulnerable to cryptoanalysis attack. So, to deal with these inextricable problems, a key distribution facility was born. Symmetric encryption is considered more practical in dealing with vast amounts of data consisting of strings of zeros and ones. Yet another scheme was invented to secure data while in transition, using tools from a branch of mathematics known as number theory. To begin, let's review the necessary number theory concepts [2,3].

Review: Number Theory

Asymmetric-key encryption uses prime numbers, which are a subset of positive integers. Positive integers are all odd and even numbers, including the number 1, such that some of the numbers are composite, that is, products of numbers therein. This critical fact plays a significant role in generating keys. Next we will go through some statements of fact for the sake of completeness.

Coprimes

Two positive integers are said to be coprime or relatively prime if gcd(a, b) = 1.

Cardinality of Primes

The number of primes is infinite. Given a number *n*, how many prime numbers are smaller than or equal to *n*? The answer to this question was discovered by Gauss and Lagrange as:

$$\{n/\ln(n) < \Pi (n) < \{n/\ln(n) - 1.08366\}$$

where $\Pi(n)$ is the number of primes smaller than or equal to *n*.

Check whether a given number 107 is a prime number. We take the square root of 107 to the nearest whole number, which is 10. Then count the number of primes less than 10, which are 2, 3, 5, 7. Next we check whether any one of these numbers will divide 107. In our example none of these numbers can divide 107, so 107 is a prime number.

Euler's Phi-Function $\phi(n)$: Euler's totient function finds the number of integers that are both smaller than *n* and coprime to *n*.

- $\phi(1) = 0$
- $\phi(p) = p - 1$ if p is a prime
- $\phi(m \times n) = \phi(n) \times \phi(m)$ if m and n are coprime
- $\phi(p^e) = p^e - p^{e-1}$ if p is a prime

Examples:

$\phi(2) = 1$; $\phi(3) = 2$; $\phi(4) = 2$; $\phi(5) = 4$; $\phi(6) = 2$; $\phi(7) = 6$; $\phi(8) = 4$

Factoring

The fundamental theorem of arithmetic states that every positive integer can be written as a product of prime numbers. There are a number of algorithms to factor large composite numbers.

Fermat's Little Theorem

In the 1970s, the creators of digital signatures and public-key cryptography realized that the framework for their research was already laid out in the body of work by Fermat and Euler. Generation of a key in public-key cryptography involves exponentiation modulo of a given modulus.

TABLE 37.15 The Encryption Procedure.

1.	OS1 →	SB →	SR →	MC ⊕	K2 →	OS2
2.	OS2 →	SB →	SR →	MC ⊕	K3 →	OS3
3.	OS3 →	SB →	SR →	MC ⊕	K4 →	OS4
4.	OS4 →	SB →	SR →	MC ⊕	K5 →	OS5
5.	OS5 →	SB →	SR →	MC ⊕	K6 →	OS6
6.	OS6 →	SB →	SR →	MC ⊕	K7 →	OS7
7.	OS7 →	SB →	SR →	MC ⊕	K8 →	OS8
8.	OS8 →	SB →	SR →	MC ⊕	K9 →	OS9
9.	OS9 →	SB →	SR →	MC ⊕	K10 →	OS10
10.	OS10 →	SB →	SR →	⊕	K11 →	Cipher Text (C)

TABLE 37.16 Round.

	C ⊕	K11 →				OS10
1	OS10 →	ISR →	ISB ⊕	K10 →	IMC →	OS9
2	OS9 →	ISR →	ISB ⊕	K9 →	IMC →	OS8
10	SI →		ISR →	ISB ⊕	K1 →	PlainText

$a \equiv b \pmod{m}$ then $a^e \equiv b^e \pmod{m}$ for any positive integer e

$$a^{e+d} \equiv a^e \cdot a^d \pmod{m}$$

$$(ab)^e \equiv a^e \cdot b^e \pmod{m}$$

$$(a^d)^e \equiv a^{de} \pmod{m}$$

Examples:

$$2^{13} \pmod{33} \equiv 2^{8+4+1} \equiv 25.16.2 \equiv 25.32 \equiv 8 \pmod{33}$$

$$6^{43} \pmod{13}$$

$$2^2 \equiv 4 \quad 3^2 \equiv 9$$

$$2^4 \equiv 4^2 \equiv 16 \equiv 33^4 \equiv 3$$

$$2^8 \equiv 3^2 \equiv 93^8 \equiv 9$$

$$2^{16} \equiv 9^2 \equiv 81 \equiv 33^{16} \equiv 3$$

$$2^{32} \equiv 3^2 \equiv 9 \pmod{13} \quad 3^{32} \equiv 9 \pmod{13}$$

Theorem. Let *p* be a prime number.

1. If a is coprime to p, then $a^{p-1} \equiv 1 \pmod{p}$
2. $a^p \equiv a \pmod{p}$ for any integer a

Examples:

$$43^{58} \equiv 1 \pmod{59}$$
$$86^{97} \equiv 86 \pmod{97}$$

Theorem: Let p and q be distinct primes.

1. If a is coprime to pq, then

$$a^{k(p-1)(q-1)} \equiv 1 \pmod{pq}, \text{k is any integer}$$

2. For any integer a,

$$a^{k(p-1)(q-1)+1} \equiv a \pmod{pq}, \text{k is any positive integer}$$

Example:

$$62^{60} \equiv 62^{(7-1) \cdot (11-1)} \equiv 1 \pmod{77}$$

Discrete Logarithm

Here we will deal with multiplicative group $G = <Z_{n*}x>$. The order of a finite group is the number of elements in the group G. Let's take an example of a group,

$$G = <Z_{21*}, \ x>$$

$$\phi(21) = \phi(3) \times \phi(7) = 2 \times 6 = 12$$

that is, 12 elements in the group, and each is coprime to 21.

$$\{1, 2, 4, 5, 8, 9, 10, 11, 13, 16, 17, 19, 20\}$$

The order of an element, ord(a) is the smallest integer i such that

$$a^i \equiv e \pmod{}$$

where $e = 1$.

Find the order of all elements in $G = <Z_{10*}x>$
$$\phi(10) = \phi(2) \times \phi(5) = 1 \times 4 = 4$$
$$\{1, 3, 7, 9\}$$

Lagrange's theorem states that the order of an element divides the order of the group. In our example $\{1, 2, 4\}$ each of them divide 4, therefore we need to check only these powers to find the order of the element.

$$1^1 \equiv 1 \ (\text{mod } 10) \rightarrow \text{ord}(1) = 1$$
$$3^1 \equiv 3 \ (\text{mod } 10); 3^2 \equiv 9(\text{mod } 10); 3^4 \equiv 1 \ (\text{mod } 10)$$
$$\rightarrow \text{ord}(3) = 4$$
$$7^1 \equiv 7 \ (\text{mod } 10); 7^2 \equiv 9 \ (\text{mod } 10); 7^4 \equiv 1(\text{mod } 10)$$
$$\rightarrow \text{ord}(7) = 4$$
$$9^1 \equiv 9 \ (\text{mod } 10); 9^2 \equiv 1 \ (\text{mod } 10) \rightarrow \text{ord}(9) = 2$$

If $a \in G = <Z_{n*}, x>$, then $a^{\phi(n)} = 1 \ \text{mod n}$

Euler's theorem shows that the relationship $a^i \equiv 1 \ (\text{mod n})$ holds whenever the order (i) of an element equals $\phi(\text{n})$.

Primitive Roots

In the multiplicative group, if $G = <Z_{n*}, x>$ when the order of an element is the same as $\phi(n)$, then that element is called the primitive root of the group. This property of primitive root is used in ElGamal cryptosystem.

$G = <Z_{8*}, x>$ has no primitive roots. The order of this group is $\phi(8) = 4$.

$$Z_{8*} = \{1, 3, 5, 7\}$$

1, 2, 4 each divide the order of the group, which is 4.

$$1^1 \equiv 1 \ (\text{mod } 8) \rightarrow \text{ord}(1) = 1$$
$$3^1 \equiv 3 \ (\text{mod } 8); 3^2 \equiv 1 \ (\text{mod } 8) \quad \rightarrow \text{ord}(3) = 2$$
$$5^1 \equiv 5 \ (\text{mod } 8); 5^2 \equiv 1 \ (\text{mod } 8) \quad \rightarrow \text{ord}(5) = 2$$
$$7^1 \equiv 7 \ (\text{mod } 8); 7^2 \equiv 1 \ (\text{mod } 8) \quad \rightarrow \text{ord}(7) = 2$$

In this example none of the elements has an order of 4, hence this group has no primitive roots. We will rearrange our data as shown in Table 37.17 [2, 3].

Let's take another example: $G = <Z_{7*}, x>$, then $\phi(7) = 6$, hence the order of the group is 6 with these members $\{1, 2, 3, 4, 5, 6\}$, which are all coprime to 7. We note that the order of each of these elements $\{1, 2, 3, 4, 5, 6\}$ is the smallest integer i such that $a^i \equiv 1 \ (\text{mod } 7)$. We note that the order of an element divides the order of the group. Thus the only numbers that divide 6 are $\{1, 2, 3, 6\}$:

A. $1^1 \equiv 1 \ (\text{mod } 7); 1^2 \equiv 1 \ (\text{mod } 7); 1^3$
$$\equiv 1 \ (\text{mod } 7); 1^2 \equiv 1 \ (\text{mod } 7);$$
$$1^5 \equiv 1 \ (\text{mod } 7); 1^6 \equiv 1 \ (\text{mod } 7); \rightarrow \text{ord}(1) = 1$$

B. $2^1 \equiv 2 \ (\text{mod } 7); 2^2 \equiv 4 \ (\text{mod } 7); 2^3$
$$\equiv 1 \ (\text{mod } 7); 2^4 \equiv 2 \ (\text{mod } 7);$$
$$2^5 \equiv 4 \ (\text{mod } 7); 2^6 \equiv 1 \ (\text{mod } 7); \rightarrow \text{ord}(2) = 3$$

C. $3^1 \equiv 3 \ (\text{mod } 7); 3^2 \equiv 2 \ (\text{mod } 7); 3^3$
$$\equiv 6 \ (\text{mod } 7); 3^4 \equiv 4 \ (\text{mod } 7);$$
$$3^5 \equiv 5 \ (\text{mod } 7); 3^6 \equiv 1 \ (\text{mod } 7); \rightarrow \text{ord}(3) = 6$$

D. $4^1 \equiv 4 \ (\text{mod } 7); 4^2 \equiv 2 \ (\text{mod } 7); 4^3$
$$\equiv 1 \ (\text{mod } 7); 4^4 \equiv 4 \ (\text{mod } 7);$$
$$4^5 \equiv 2 \ (\text{mod } 7); 4^6 \equiv 1 \ (\text{mod } 7); \rightarrow \text{ord}(4) = 3$$

E. $5^1 \equiv 5 \ (\text{mod } 7); 5^2 \equiv 4 \ (\text{mod } 7); 5^3$
$$\equiv 6 \ (\text{mod } 7); 5^4 \equiv 2 \ (\text{mod } 7);$$
$$5^5 \equiv 3 \ (\text{mod } 7); 5^6 \equiv 1 \ (\text{mod } 7); \rightarrow \text{ord}(5) = 6$$

F. $6^1 \equiv 6 \ (\text{mod } 7); 6^2 \equiv 1 \ (\text{mod } 7); 6^3$
$$\equiv 6 \ (\text{mod } 7); 6^4 \equiv 1 \ (\text{mod } 7)$$
$$6^5 \equiv 6 \ (\text{mod } 7); 6^6 \equiv 1 \ (\text{mod } 7) \rightarrow \text{ord}(6) = 2$$

Since the order of the elements $\{3, 5\}$ is 6, which is the order of the group, therefore the primitive roots of the group are $\{3, 5\}$. In here the smallest integer i = 6, $\phi(7) = 6$.

Solve for x in each of the following:

$$5^x \equiv 6 \ (\text{mod } 7)$$

We can rewrite the above as:

$$x = \log_5 6 \ (\text{mod } 7)$$

Using the third term in E). we see that x must be equal to 3.

The group $G = <Z_{n*}, x>$ has primitive roots only if n is 2, 4, p^t, or $2p^t$, where p is an odd prime not including 2, and t is an integer.

If the group $G = <Z_{n*}, x>$ has any primitive roots, the number of primitive roots is $\phi(\phi(n))$.

Group $G = <Z_{n*}, x>$ has primitive roots, then it is cyclic, and each of its primitive roots is a generator of the whole group.

Group $G = <Z_{10*}, x>$ has two primitive roots because $\phi(10) = 4$, and $\phi(\phi(10)) = 2$. These two primitive roots are $\{3, 7\}$.

$$3^1 \bmod 10 = 3 \ 3^2 \bmod 10 = 9 \ 3^3 \bmod 10 = 7 \ 3^4 \bmod 10 = 1$$
$$7^1 \bmod 10 = 7 \ 7^2 \bmod 10 = 9 \ 7^3 \bmod 10 = 3 \ 7^4 \bmod 10 = 1$$

Group $G = <Z_{p*}, x>$ is always cyclic.

The group $G = <Z_{p*}, x>$ has the following properties:

- Its elements are from 1 to $(p - 1)$ inclusive.
- It always has primitive roots.
- It is cyclic, and its elements can be generated using g where x is an integer from 1 to $\phi(n) = p - 1$.

TABLE 37.17 No Primitive Group.

	i = 1	i = 2	i = 3	i = 4	i = 5	i = 6	i = 7
a = 1	x:1	x:1	x:1	x:1	x:1	x:1	x:1
a = 3	x:3	x:1	x:3	x:1	x:3	x:1	x:3
a = 5	x:5	x:1	x:5	x:1	x:5	x:1	x:5
a = 7	x:7	x:1	x:7	x:1	x:7	x:1	x:7

- The primitive roots can be used as the base of a discrete logarithm.

Now that we have reviewed the necessary mathematical preliminaries, we will focus on the subject matter of asymmetric cryptography, which uses a public and a private key to encrypt and decrypt the plaintext. If Alice wants to send plaintext to Bob, she uses Bob's public key, which is advertised by Bob, to encrypt the plaintext and then send it to Bob via an unsecured channel. Bob decrypts the data using his private key, which is known to him only. Of course this would appear to be an ideal replacement for the asymmetric-key cipher, but it is much slower, since it has to encrypt each byte; hence it is useful in message authentication and communicating the secret key (see sidebar, "The RSA Cryptosystem").

9. CRYPTANALYSIS OF RSA

RSA algorithm relies that p and q, the distinct prime numbers, are kept secret, even though $m = p \times q$ is made public. So if n is an extremely large number, the problem reduces to find the factors that make up the number n, which is known as *the factorization attack*.

Factorization Attack

If the middleman, Eve, can factor n correctly, then she correctly guesses p, q, and $\phi(m)$. Reminding ourselves that the public key e is public, then Eve has to compute the multiplicative inverse of e:

$$d \equiv e^{-1} \pmod{m}$$

So if the modulus m is chosen to be 1024 bits long, it would take considerable time to break the RSA system unless an efficient factorization algorithm could be found [2,3] (see sidebars "Chosen-Ciphertext Attack" and "The eth Roots Problem").

Discrete Logarithm Problem

Discrete logarithms are perhaps simplest to understand in the group Z_{p*}, where p is the prime number. Let g be the generator of Z_{p*}, then the discrete logarithm problem

---

The RSA Cryptosystem

Key generation algorithm:
1. Select two prime numbers p and q such that p≠q.
2. Construct m = p × q.
3. Set up a commutative ring $R = <Z_\phi, +, x>$ which is public since m is made public.
4. Set up a multiplicative group $G = <Z_{r(m)*}, x>$ which is used to generate public and private keys. This group is hidden from the public since $\phi(m)$ is kept hidden.
   $\phi(m) = (p - 1)(q - 1)$
5. Choose an integer e such that, $1 < e < \phi(m)$ and e is coprime to $\phi(m)$.
6. Compute the secret exponent d such that, $1 < d < \phi(m)$ and that ed≡1 (mod $\phi(m)$).
7. The public key is "e" and the private key is "d." The value of p, q, and $\phi(m)$ are kept private.

Encryption:
1. Alice obtains Bob's public key (m, e).
2. The plaintext x is treated as a number to lie in the range $1 < x < m - 1$.
3. The ciphertext corresponding to x is $y = x^e \pmod{m}$.
4. Send the ciphertext y to Bob.

Decryption: Example:
1. Bob uses his private key (m, d).
2. Compute the $x = y^d \pmod{m}$. Why RSA works:

1. Choose $p = 7$ and $q = 11$, then $m = p \times q = 7 \times 11 = 77$ $R = <Z_{77}, +, x>$ and $\phi(77) = \phi(7)\phi(11) = 6 \times 10 = 60$
2. The corresponding multiplicative group $G = <Z_{60}^*, x>$.
3. Choose $e = 13$ and $d = 37$ from Z_{60}^* such that $e \times d \equiv 1 \pmod{60}$.

Plaintext = 5 $y = x^e \pmod{m} = 5^{13} \pmod{77} = 26 \times x = y^d \pmod{m} = 26^{37} \pmod{77} = 5$

Note: 384-bit primes or larger are deemed sufficient to use RSA securely. The prime number $e = 2^{16} + 1$ is often used in modern RSA implementations[2,3].

Chosen-Ciphertext Attack

Z_n is a set of all positive integers from 0 to $(n-1)$. Z_{n*} is a set all integers such that $\gcd(n,a) = 1$, where $a \in Z_{n*}$

$$Z_n^* \subset Z_n$$

$\Phi(n)$ calculates the number of elements in Z_{n*} that are smaller than n and coprime to n.

$$\Phi(21) = \Phi(3) \times \Phi(7) = 2 \times 6 = 12$$

Therefore, the number of integers in $\in Z_{21*}$ is 12.

$$Z_{21}^* = \{1, 2, 4, 5, 8, 10, 11, 13, 16, 17, 19, 20\}$$

Each of which is coprime to 21.

$$Z_{14}^* = \{1, 3, 5, 9, 11, 13\}$$

Each of which is coprime to 14.

$\Phi(14) = \Phi(2) \times \Phi(7) = 1 \times 6 = 6$ number of integers in Z_{14}^*

Example: Choose $p = 3$ and $q = 7$, then $m = 3 \times 7 = 21$. Encryption and decryption take place in the ring, $R = \langle Z_{21}, +, x \rangle$

$$\Phi(21) = \Phi(2) \Phi(6) = 12$$

Key-Generation Group, $G = \langle Z_{12}^*, x \rangle$

$$\Phi(12) = \Phi(4)\Phi(3) = 2 \times 2 = 4 \text{ number in}$$

$$Z_{12}^* = \{1, 5, 7, 11\}$$

Alice encrypts the message P using the public key e of Bob and sends the encrypted message C to Bob.

$$C = P^e \bmod m$$

Eve, the middleman, intercepts the message and manipulates the message before forwarding to Bob.

1. Eve chooses a random integer $X \in Z_m^*$ (since m is public).
2. Eve calculates $Y = C \times X^e \pmod{m}$.
3. Bob receives Y from Eve, and he decrypts Y using his private key d.
4. $Z = Y^d \pmod{m}$.
5. Eve can easily discover the plaintext P as follows:

$$Z = Y^d \pmod{m} = [C \times X^e]^d \pmod{m}$$

$$= [C^d \times X^{ed}] \pmod{m} = [C^d \times X] \pmod{m}$$

Hence $Z = [P \times X] \pmod{m}$.

Using the Extended Euclidean algorithm, Eve can then compute the multiplicative inverse of X, and thus obtain P:

$$P = Z \times X^{-1} \pmod{m} \ [2,3]$$

reduces to computing a, given $(g, p, g^a \bmod p)$ for a randomly chosen $a < (p - 1)$.

If we want to find the kth power of one of the numbers in this group, we can do so by finding its kth power as an integer and then finding the remainder after division by p. This process is called *discrete exponentiation*. For example, consider Z_{23*}. To compute 3^4 in this group, we first compute $3^4 = 81$, then we divide 81 by 23, obtaining a remainder of 12. Thus $3^4 = 12$ in the group Z_{23*}

A *discrete logarithm* is just the inverse operation. For example, take the equation $3^k \equiv 12 \pmod{23}$ for k. As shown above $k = 4$ is a solution, but it is not the only solution. Since $3^{22} \equiv 1 \pmod{23}$, it also follows that if n is an integer, then $3^{4+22n} \equiv 12 \times 1^n \equiv 12 \pmod{23}$. Hence the equation has infinitely many solutions of the form $4 + 22n$. Moreover, since 22 is the smallest positive integer m satisfying $3^m \equiv 1 \pmod{23}$, that is, 22 is the order

The eth Roots Problem

Given:
  A composite number n, product of two prime numbers
    p and q
  An integer $e \geq 3$
  $\gcd(e, \Phi(n)) = 1$
  An integer $c \in Z_{12}^*$
  Find an integer m such that $m^e \equiv c \bmod n$ [2,3].

of 3 in Z_{23*} these are all solutions. Equivalently, the solution can be expressed as $k \equiv 4 \pmod{22}$ [2,3].

10. DIFFIE-HELLMAN ALGORITHM

The purpose of this protocol is to allow two parties to set up a shared secret key over an insecure communication channel so that they may exchange messages. Alice and Bob agree on a finite cyclic group G and a generating element g in G. We will write the group G multiplicatively [2,3].

1. Alice picks a prime number p, with the base g, exponent a to generate a public key A
2. $A = g^a \bmod p$
3. (g, p, A) are made public, and a is kept private.
4. Bob picks a prime number p, base b, and an exponent b to generate a public key B.
5. $B = g^b \bmod p$
6. (g, p, B) are made public, and b is kept private,
7. Bob using A generates the shared secret key S.
8. $S = A^b \bmod p$
9. Alice using B generates the shared secret key S.
10. $S = B^a \bmod p$

Thus the shared secret key S is established between Bob and Alice.

Example:

Alice: $p = 53$, $g = 18$, $a = 10$
$\quad A = 18^{10} \bmod 53 = 24$
Bob: $p = 53$, $g = 18$, $b = 11$
$\quad B = 18^{11} \bmod 53 = 48$
$\quad S = 24^{11} \bmod 53 = 48^{10} \bmod 53 = 15$

Diffie-Hellman Problem

The middleman Eve would know (g, p, A, B) since these are public. So for Eve to discover the secret key S, she would have to tackle the following two congruences:

$$g^a \equiv A \bmod p \quad \text{and} \quad g^b \equiv B \bmod p$$

If Eve had some way of solving the discrete logarithm problem (DLP) in a time-efficient manner, she could discover the shared secret key S; no probabilistic polynomial-time algorithm exists that solves this problem. The set of values:

$$(g^a \bmod p, \; g^b \bmod p, \; g^a b \bmod p)$$

is called the *Diffie-Hellman problem*.

If the DLP problem can be efficiently solved, then so can the Diffie-Hellman problem.

11. ELLIPTIC CURVE CRYPTOSYSTEMS

For simplicity, we shall restrict our attention to elliptic curves over Zp, where p is a prime greater than 3. We mention, however, that elliptic curves can more generally be defined over any finite field [4]. An *elliptic curve E* over Z_p is defined by an equation of the form

$$y^2 = x^3 + ax + b \qquad ((37.1))$$

where a, $b \in Z_p$, and $4a^3 + 27b^2 \neq 0 \pmod{p}$, together with a special point O called the *point at infinity*. The set E (Z_p) consists of all points (x, y), $x \in Z_p$, $y \in Z_p$, which satisfy the defining equation (1), together with O.

An Example

Let $p = 23$ and consider the elliptic curve $E: y^2 = x^3 + x + 1$, defined over Z_{23}. (In the notation of Equation 24.1, we have $a = 1$ and $b = 1$.) Note that $4a^3 + 27b^2 = 4 + 4 = 8 \neq 0$, so E is indeed an elliptic curve. The points in $E(Z_{23})$ are O and the following are shown in Table 37.18.

Addition Formula

There is a rule for adding two points on an elliptic curve $E(Zp)$ to give a third elliptic curve point. Together with this addition operation, the set of points $E(Zp)$ forms a group with O serving as its identity. It is this group that is used in the construction of elliptic curve cryptosystems.

TABLE 37.18 Elliptic Curve Cryptosystems.

(0, 1)	(6, 4)	(12, 19)
(0, 22)	(6, 19)	(13, 7)
(1, 7)	(7, 11)	(13, 16)
(1, 16)	(7, 12)	(17, 3)
(3, 10)	(9, 7)	(17, 20)
(3, 13)	(9, 1 6)	(18, 3)
(4, 0)	(11, 3)	(18, 20)
(5, 4)	(11, 20)	(19, 5)
(5, 19)	(12, 4)	(19, 18)

The addition rule, which can be explained geometrically, is presented here as a sequence of algebraic formula [4].

1. $P + O = O + P = P$ for all $P \in E(Z_p)$
2. If $P = (x, y) \in E(Zp)$ then $(x, y) + (x, -y) = O$ (The point $(x, -y)$ is denoted by $-P$, and is called the *negative* of P; observe that $-P$ is indeed a point on the curve.)
3. Let $P = (x1, y1) \in E(Zp)$ and $Q = (x2, y2) \in E(Zp)$, where $P \neq -Q$. Then $P + Q = (x3, y3)$,

where:

$$x_3 = (\lambda^2 - x_1 - x_2) \bmod p$$
$$y_3 = (\lambda(x_1 - x_3) - y_1) \bmod p$$
$$\lambda = \frac{y_2 - y_1}{x_2 - x_1} \bmod p \text{ if } P \neq Q \text{ or}$$
$$\lambda = \frac{3x_1^2 + \alpha}{2y_1} \bmod p \text{ if } P = Q$$

We will digress to modular division: 4/3 mod 11. We are looking for a number, say t, such that $3 * t \bmod 11 = 4$. We need to multiply the left and right sides by 3^{-1}

$$3^{-1} * 3 * t \bmod 11 = 3^{-1} * 4$$
$$t \bmod 11 = 3^{-1} * 4$$

Next we use the Extended Euclidean algorithm and get (inverse) 3^{-1} is 4 ($3 * 4 = 12 \bmod 11 = 1$).

$$4 * 4 \bmod 11 = 5$$

Hence,

$$4/3 \bmod 11 = 5$$

Example of Elliptic Curve Addition

Consider the elliptic curve defined in the previous example. (Also see sidebar, "EC Diffie-Hellman Algorithm.") [4].

EC Diffie-Hellman Algorithm

1. Alice has her elliptic curve, and she chooses a secret random number d and computes a number on the curve $Q_A = d_A * P[4]$.

   Alice's public key: (p, a, b, Q_A)

   Alice's private key: d_A

2. Bob has his elliptic curve, and he chooses a secret random number d and computes a number on the curve $Q_B = d_B * P$:

   Bob's public key: (p, a, b, Q_B)

   Bob's private key: d_B

3. Alice computes the shared secret key as

$$S = d_A * Q_B$$

4. Similarly, Bob computes the shared secret key as

$$S = d_B * Q_A$$

5. The shared secret key computed by Alice and Bob are the same for:

$$S = d_B * Q_A = d_B * d_A * P$$

1. Let $P = (3, 10)$ and $Q = (9, 7)$. Then $P + Q = (x3, y3)$ is computed as follows:

$$\lambda = \frac{7 - 10}{9 - 3} = \frac{-3}{6} = \frac{-1}{2} = 11 \in Z_{23}$$

$x_3 = 11^2 - 3 - 9 = 6 - 3 - 9 = -6 \equiv 17 \pmod{23}$, and $y_3 = 11(3 - (-6))\ -10 = 11(9)\ -10 = 89 \equiv 20 \pmod{23}$.

Hence $P + Q = (17, 20)$.

2. Let $P = (3,10)$. Then $2P = P + P = (x_3, y_3)$ is computed as follows:

$$\lambda = \frac{3(3^2) + 1}{20} = \frac{5}{20} = \frac{1}{4} = 6 \in Z_{23}$$

$x_3 = 6^2 - 6 = 30 \equiv 7 \pmod{23}$, and $y_3 = 6(3 - 7) - 10 = -24 - 10 = -11 \in 12 \pmod{23}$. Hence $2P = (7, 12)$.

Consider the following elliptic curve with Z_p^*

$$y^2 \bmod p = (x^3 + ax + b) \bmod p$$

Set $p = 11$ and $a = 1$ and $b = 2$. Take a point $P\ (4, 2)$ and multiply it by 3; the resulting point will be on the curve with $(4, 9)$.

EC Security

Suppose Eve the middleman captures (p, a, b, Q_A, Q_B). Can Eve figure out the shared secret key without knowing either (d_B, d_A)? Eve could use

$$Q_A = P * d_A$$

to compute the unknown d_A, which is known as the Elliptic Curve Discrete Logarithm problem [4].

12. MESSAGE INTEGRITY AND AUTHENTICATION

We live in the Internet age, and a fair number of commercial transactions take place on the Internet. It has often been reported that transactions on the Internet between two parties have been hijacked by a third party, hence data integrity and authentication are critical if ecommerce is to survive and grow.

This section deals with message integrity and authentication. So far we have discussed and shown how to keep a message confidential. But on many occasions we need to make sure that the content of a message has not been changed by a third party, and we need some way of ascertaining whether the message has been tampered with. Since the message is transmitted electronically as a string of ones and zeros, we need a mechanism to make sure that the count of the number of ones and zeros does not become altered, and furthermore, that zeros and ones are not changed in their position within the string.

We create a pair and label it as message and its corresponding message digest. A given block of messages is run through an algorithm hash function, which has its input the message and the output is the compressed message, the message digest, which is a fixed-size block but smaller in length. The receiver, say, Bob, can verify the integrity of the message by running the message through the hash function (the same hash function as used by Alice) and comparing the message digest with the message digest that was sent along with the message by, say, Alice. If the two message digests agree on their block size, the integrity of the message was maintained in the transmission.

Cryptographic Hash Functions

A cryptographic hash function must satisfy three criteria:

- Preimage resistance
- Second preimage resistance (weak collision resistance)
- Strong collision resistance

Preimage Resistance

Given a message m and the hash function hash, if the hash value h = hash(m) is given, it should be hard to find any m such that h = hash(m).

Second Preimage Resistance (Weak Collision Resistance)

Given input m_1, it should be hard to find another message m_2 such that hashing) = hash(m_2) and that $m_1 \neq m_2$

Strong Collision Resistance

It ought to be hard to find two messages $m_1 \neq m_2$ such that hash(m_1) = hash(m_2). A hash function takes a fixed size input n-bit string and produces a fixed size output m-bit string such that m less than n in length. The original hash function was defined by Merkle-Damgard, which is an iterated hash function. This hash function first breaks up the original message into fixed-size blocks of size n. Next an initial vector H_0 (digest) is set up and combined with the message block M_1 to produce message digest H_1, which is then combined with M_2 to produce message digest H_1, and so on until the last message block produces the final message digest.

$$H_i = f(H_{i-1}, M_i) \quad i \geq 1$$

Message digest MD2, MD4, and MD5 were designed by Ron Rivest. MD5 as input block size of 512 bits and produces a message digest of 128 bits [1].

Secure Hash Algorithm (SHA) was developed by the National Institute of Standards and Technology (NIST). SHA-1, SHA-224, SHA-256, SHA-384, and SHA-512 are examples of the secure hash algorithm. SHA-512 produces a message digest of 512 bits.

Message Authentication

Alice sends a message to Bob. How can Bob be sure that the message originated from Alice and not someone else pretending to be Alice? If you are engaged in a transaction on the Internet using a Web client, you need to make sure that you are not engaged with a dummy Web site or else you could submit your sensitive information to an unauthorized party. Alice in this case needs to demonstrate that she is communicating and not an imposter.

Alice creates a message digest using the message (M), then using the shared secret key (known to Bob only) she combines the key with a message digest and creates a message authentication code (MAC). She then sends the MAC and the message (M) to Bob over an insecure channel. Bob uses the message (M) to create a hash value and then recreates a MAC using the secret shared key and the hash value. Next he compares the received MAC from Alice with his MAC. If the two match, Bob is assured that Alice was indeed the originator of the message [1].

Digital Signature

Message authentication is implemented using the sender's private key and verified by the receiver using the sender's public key. Hence if Alice uses her private key, Bob can verify that the message was sent by Alice, since Bob would have to use Alice's public key to verify. Alice's public key cannot verify the signature signed by Eve's private key [1].

Message Integrity Uses a Hash Function in Signing the Message

Nonrepudiation is implemented using a third party that can be trusted by parties that want to exchange messages with one another. For example, Alice creates a signature from her message and sends the message, her identity, Bob's identity, and the signature to the third party, who then verifies the message using Alice's public key that the message came from Alice. Next the third party saves a copy of the message with the sender's and the recipient's identity and the time stamp of the message.

The third party then creates another signature using its private key from the message that Alice left behind. The third party then sends the message, the new signature, and Alice's and Bob's identity to Bob, who then uses the third party's public key to ascertain that the message came from the third party [1].

RSA Digital Signature Scheme

Alice and Bob are the two parties that are going to exchange the messages. So, we begin with Alice, who will generate her public and private key using two distinct prime numbers—say, p and q. Next she calculates $n = p \times q$. Using $\Phi(n) = (p-1)(q-1)$, picks e and computes d such that $e \times d = 1 \mod (\Phi(n))$. Alice declares (e, n) public, keeping her private key d secret.

Signing: Alice takes the message and computes the signature as:

$$S = M^d (\mod n)$$

She then sends the message M and the signature S to Bob.

Bob receives the message M and the signature S, and then, using Alice's public key e and the signature S, recreates the message $M' = S^e \pmod{n}$. Next Bob compares M' with M, and if the two values are congruent, Bob accepts the message [1].

RSA Digital Signature and the Message Digest

Alice and Bob agree on a hash function. Alice applies the hash function to the message M and generates the message digest, D = hash(M). She then signs the message digest using her private key,

$$S = D^d(mod\ n)$$

Alice sends the signature S and the message M to Bob. He then uses Alice's public key, and the signature S recreates the message digest $D' = S^e\ (mod\ n)$ as well as computes the message digest D = hash(M) from the received message M. Bob then compares D with D', and if they are congruent modulo n, he accepts the message [1].

Next, let's take a very very brief look at the Triple Data Encryption Algorithm (TDEA), including its primary component cryptographic engine, the Data Encryption Algorithm (DEA). When implemented, TDEA may be used by organizations to protect sensitive unclassified data. Protection of data during transmission or while in storage may be necessary to maintain the confidentiality and integrity of the information represented by the data.

13. TRIPLE DATA ENCRYPTION ALGORITHM (TDEA) BLOCK CIPHER

TDEA is made available for use by organizations and Federal agencies within the context of a total security program consisting of physical security procedures, good information management practices, and computer system/ network access controls. The TDEA block cipher includes a Data Encryption Algorithm (DEA) cryptographic engine that is implemented as a component of TDEA. TDEA functions incorporating the DEA cryptographic engine are designed in such a way that they may be used in a computer system, storage facility, or network to provide cryptographic protection to binary coded data. The method of implementation will depend on the application and environment. TDEA implementations are subject to being tested and validated as accurately performing the transformations specified in the TDEA algorithm.

Applications

Cryptography is utilized in various applications and environments. The specific utilization of encryption and the implementation of TDEA is based on many factors particular to the computer system and its associated components. In general, cryptography is used to protect data while it is being communicated between two points or while it is stored in a medium vulnerable to physical theft or technical intrusion (hacker attacks). In the first case, the key must be available by the sender and receiver simultaneously during communication. In the second case, the key must be maintained and accessible for the duration of the storage period. The following checklist (see checklist: "An Agenda For Action Of Conformance Requirements For The Installation, Configuration And Use Of TDEA") lays out an agenda for action for conformance to many of the requirements that are the responsibility of entities installing, configuring or using

---

An Agenda for Action of Conformance Requirements for the Installation, Configuration and Use of TDEA

These requirements include the following (Check All Tasks Completed):

_____**1.** TDEA functions incorporating the DEA cryptographic engine shall be designed in such a way that they may be used in a computer system, storage facility, or network to provide cryptographic protection to binary coded data.

_____**2.** Each 64-bit key shall contain 56 bits that are randomly generated and used directly by the algorithm as key bits.

_____**3.** A key bundle shall not consist of three identical keys.

_____**4.** The TDEA block cipher shall be used to provide cryptographic security only when used in an approved mode of operation.

_____**5.** The following specifications for keys shall be met in implementing the TDEA modes of operation. The bundle and the individual keys shall:

    _____**a.** Be kept secret.

    _____**b.** Be generated using an approved method12 that is based on the output of an approved random bit generator.

    _____**c.** Be independent of other key bundles.

    _____**d.** Have integrity whereby each key in the bundle has not been altered in an unauthorized manner since the time it was generated, transmitted, or stored by an authorized source.

    _____**e.** Be used in the appropriate order as specified by the particular mode.

    _____**f.** Be considered a fixed quantity in which an individual key cannot be manipulated while leaving the other two keys unchanged; and cannot be unbundled except for its designated purpose.

_____**6.** One key bundle shall not be used to process more than 232 64-bit data blocks when the keys conform to Keying Option 1.

_____**7.** When Keying Option 2 is used, the keys shall not be used to process more than 220 blocks.

applications or protocols that incorporate the recommended use of TDEA.

14. SUMMARY

In this chapter we have attempted to cover cryptography from its very simple structure such as substitution ciphers to the complex AES and elliptic curve crypto-systems. There is a subject known as *cryptoanalysis* that attempts to crack the encryption to expose the key, partially or fully. We briefly discussed this in the section on the discrete logarithm problem. Over the past 10 years, we have seen the application of quantum theory to encryption in what is termed *quantum cryptology*, which is used to transmit the secret key securely over a public channel. The reader will observe that we did not cover the Public Key Infrastructure (PKI) due to lack of space in the chapter.

Finally, let's move on to the real interactive part of this Chapter: review questions/exercises, hands-on projects, case projects and optional team case project. The answers and/or solutions by chapter can be found in the Online Instructor's Solutions Manual.

CHAPTER REVIEW QUESTIONS/EXERCISES

True/False

1. True or False? Data security is limited to wired networks but is equally critical for wireless communications such as in Wi-Fi and cellular.
2. True or False? Data communication normally takes place over a secured channel, as is the case when the Internet provides the pathways for the flow of data.
3. True or False? The encryption of the message can be defined as *mapping* the message from the domain to its range such that the inverse mapping should recover the original message.
4. True or False? Information security is the goal of the secured data encryption; hence if the encrypted data is truly randomly distributed in the message space (range), to the hacker the encrypted message is equally unlikely to be in any one of the states (encrypted).
5. True or False? Computational complexity deals with problems that could be solved in polynomial time, for a given input.

Multiple Choice

1. The conceptual foundation of _____ was laid out around 3,000 years ago in India and China.
   A. Cryptography
   B. Botnets
   C. Data retention
   D. Evolution
   E. Security
2. In cryptography we use _____ to express that the residue is the same for a set of integers divided by a positive integer.
   A. Congruence
   B. Traceback
   C. Data retention
   D. Process
   E. Security
3. What is a set of integers congruent mod *m*, where *m* is a positive integer?
   A. Evolution
   B. Residue class
   C. Peer-to-peer (P2P)
   D. Process
   E. Security
4. _____ also known as *additive ciphers*, are an example of a monoalphabetic character cipher in which each character is mapped to another character, and a repeated character maps to the same character irrespective of its position in the string:
   A. Security
   B. Data retention
   C. Shift ciphers
   D. Cyber crimes
   E. Evolution
5. A transposition cipher changes the location of the character by a given set of rules known as:
   A. Physical world
   B. Data retention
   C. Standardization
   D. Permutation
   E. All of the above

EXERCISE

Problem

How is the DEA cryptographic engine used by TDEA to cryptographically protect (encrypt) blocks of data consisting of 64 bits under the control of a 64-bit key?

Hands-On Projects

Project

Please expand on a discussion of how each TDEA forward and inverse cipher operation is a compound operation of the DEA forward and inverse transformations.

Case Projects

Problem

For all TDEA modes of operation, three cryptographic keys (*Key*1, *Key*2, *Key*3) define a TDEA key bundle. The bundle and the individual keys should do what?

Optional Team Case Project

Problem

There are a few keys that are considered weak for the DEA cryptographic engine. The use of weak keys can reduce the effective security afforded by TDEA and should be avoided. Give an example of Keys that are considered to be weak (in hexadecimal format).

REFERENCES

[1] T.H. Barr, Invitation to Cryptology, Prentice Hall, 2002.

[2] W. Mao, Modern Cryptography, Theory & Practice, Prentice Hall, New York, 2004.

[3] B.A. Forouzan, Cryptography and Network Security, McGraw-Hill, 2008.

[4] A. Jurisic, A.J. Menezes, Elliptic curves and cryptograph, Dr. Dobb's Journals (April 01, 1997)http://www.ddj.com/architect/184410167.

## Chapter 38

Satellite Encryption

Daniel S. Soper

Information Systems and Decision Sciences Department, Mihaylo College of Business and Economics, California State University, Fullerton, dsoper@fullerton.edu

1. INTRODUCTION

For virtually all of human history, the communication of information was relegated to the surface of the Earth. Whether written or spoken, transmitted by land, by sea, or by air, all messages had one thing in common – they were, like those who created them, inescapably bound to the terrestrial surface. In February 1945, however, the landscape of human communication was forever altered when an article by the highly influential science fiction writer Arthur C. Clarke proposed the extraordinary possibility that artificial satellites placed into orbit above the Earth could be used to facilitate mass communication on a global scale. A year later, a Project RAND report concluded that "A satellite vehicle with appropriate instrumentation [could] be expected to be one of the most potent scientific tools of the 20th century", and that "The achievement of a satellite craft would produce repercussions comparable to the explosion of the atomic bomb." It was only 12 short years after Clarke's historic prediction that mankind's first artificial satellite, *Sputnik 1*, was transmitting information from orbit back to Earth. In the decades that followed, satellite technology evolved rapidly from its humble beginnings to become an essential tool for such diverse activities as astronomy, commerce, communications, scientific research, defense, navigation, and the monitoring of global climate conditions. In the 21st century, satellites are helping to fuel globalization, and societies everywhere are relying heavily on the power of satellite technology to enable the modern lifestyle. It is for these reasons that satellite communications must be protected. Before examining satellite encryption in particular, however, a brief review of satellite communication in general may be useful.

For communications purposes, modern satellites can be classified into two categories: those that communicate exclusively with the surface of the Earth (which will be referred to here as "Type 1" satellites), and those that communicate not only with the surface of the Earth, but also with other satellites or spacecraft (which will be referred to here as "Type 2" satellites). The distinction between these two types of satellite communication is depicted in Figure 38.1 below.

As shown in Figure 38.1, there are several different varieties of communications links that a particular

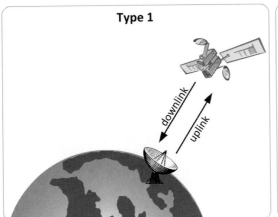
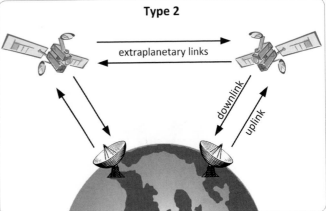

FIGURE 38.1   Comparison of Type 1 and Type 2 satellite communication capabilities.

satellite may support. Classifying satellites as Type 1 or Type 2 provides us with a useful framework for understanding and discussing basic satellite communications capabilities, and allows us to gain insight into the sort of communications links that may need to be protected. In the case of Type 1 satellites, the spacecraft may support *uplink* capabilities, *downlink* capabilities, or both. An uplink channel is a communications channel through which information is transmitted from the surface of the Earth to an orbiting satellite or other spacecraft. By contrast, a downlink channel is a communications channel through which information is transmitted from an orbiting satellite or other spacecraft to the terrestrial surface. While Type 2 satellites may possess the uplink and downlink capabilities of a Type 1 satellite, they are also capable of establishing links with spacecraft or other Type 2 satellites for purposes of extraplanetary communication. Type 2 satellites that can act as an intermediary between other spacecraft and the terrestrial surface can be classified as relay satellites. Note that whether a particular link is used for sending or receiving information depends upon the perspective of the viewer. From the ground, for example, an uplink channel is used to send information, but from the perspective of the satellite, the uplink channel is used to receive information.

2. THE NEED FOR SATELLITE ENCRYPTION

Depending on the type of satellite communications link that needs to be established, substantially different technologies, frequencies, and data encryption techniques may be required in order to secure a satellite-based communications channel. The reasons for this lie as much in the realm of human behavior as they do in the realm of physics. Broadly speaking, it is not unreasonable to conclude that satellite encryption would be entirely unnecessary if every human being were perfectly

trustworthy. That is to say, the desire to protect our messages from the possibility of extraterrestrial interception and decipherment notwithstanding, there would be no need to encrypt satellite communications if only those individuals entitled to send or receive a particular satellite transmission actually attempted to do so. In reality, however, human beings, organizations, and governments commonly possess competing or contradictory agendas, thus implying the need to protect the confidentiality, integrity, and availability of information transmitted via satellite.

Keeping such human behavioral concerns in mind, we can also understand the need for satellite encryption from a physical perspective. Consider, for example, a Type 1 communications satellite that has been placed into orbit above the equator of the Earth. Transmissions from the satellite to the terrestrial surface (the downlink channel) would commonly be made by way of a parabolic antenna. Although such an antenna facilitates focusing the signal, the signal nevertheless disperses in a conical fashion as it departs the spacecraft and approaches the surface of the planet. The result is that the signal may be made available over a wider geographic area than would be optimally desirable for security purposes. As with terrestrial radio, in the absence of encryption, anyone within range of the signal who possesses the requisite equipment could receive the message. In this particular example, the geographic area over which the signal would be dispersed would depend both on the focal precision of the parabolic antenna, and the altitude of the satellite above the Earth. These concepts are illustrated in Figure 38.2 below.

Because the sender of a satellite message may have little or no control over to whom the transmission is theoretically available, protecting the message requires that its contents be encrypted. For similar reasons, extraplanetary transmissions sent between Type 2 satellites must also be protected. After all, with thousands of satellites orbiting

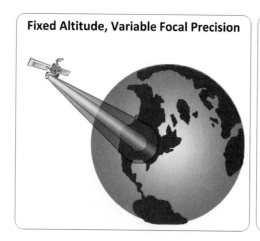

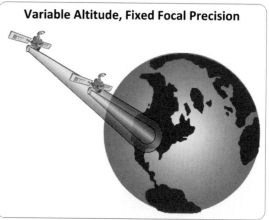

FIGURE 38.2   Effect of altitude and focal precision on satellite signal dispersion.

the planet, the chances of an inter-satellite communication being intercepted are quite good!

Aside from these considerations, the sensitivity of the information being transmitted must also be taken into account. Different entities possess different motivations for wanting to ensure the security of messages transmitted via satellite. An individual, for example, may want her private telephone calls or bank transaction details to be protected. An organization may likewise want to prevent its proprietary data from falling into the hands of its competition, while a government may want to protect its military communications and national security secrets from being intercepted or compromised by an enemy. As is the case with terrestrial communications, the sensitivity of the data being transmitted via satellite must dictate the extent to which those data are protected. If the emerging global Information Society is to fully capitalize on the benefits of satellite-based communication, its citizens, organizations, and governments must be assured that their sensitive data are not being exposed to unacceptable risk. In light of these considerations, satellite encryption will almost certainly play a key role in the future advancement of mankind.

3. IMPLEMENTING SATELLITE ENCRYPTION

It was noted earlier in this chapter that information can be transmitted to or from satellites using three general types of communication links: surface-to-satellite links (uplinks), satellite-to-surface links (downlinks), and inter-satellite or inter-spacecraft links (extraplanetary links). Technological considerations notwithstanding, the specific encryption mechanism used to secure a transmission depends not only on which of these three types of links is being utilized, but also on the nature and purpose of the message being transmitted. For purposes of simplicity, the value of transmitted information can be classified along two dimensions: high-value, and low-value. The decision as to what constitutes high-value and low value information largely depends on the perspective of the beholder — after all, one man's trash is another man's treasure. Nevertheless, establishing this broad distinction allows satellite encryption to be considered in the context of the conceptual model shown in Figure 38.3 below.

Type of Satellite Communications Link

Data Value		Uplink	Downlink	Extraplanetary Link
	High-Value	Category 01	Category 03	Category 05
	Low-Value	Category 02	Category 04	Category 06

FIGURE 38.3 Satellite communications categories as a function of data value and type of link.

As shown in Figure 38.3, any satellite-based communication can be classified into one of six possible categories. Each of these categories will be addressed later in the chapter by considering the encryption of both high-value and low-value data in the context of the three types of satellite communication links. Before considering the specific facets of encryption pertaining to satellite uplink, extraplanetary, and downlink transmissions, however, an examination of several of the more general issues associated with satellite encryption may be useful.

General Satellite Encryption Issues

One of the problems common to all forms of satellite encryption relates to signal degradation. Satellite signals are typically sent over long distances using comparatively low-power transmissions, and must frequently contend with many forms of interference, including terrestrial weather, solar and cosmic radiation, and many other forms of electromagnetic noise. Such disturbances can cause errors or gaps to emerge in the signal that carries a satellite transmission from its source to its destination. Depending on the encryption algorithm chosen, this situation can be particularly problematic for encrypted satellite transmissions, since the entire encrypted message may be irretrievably lost if even a single bit of data is out of place. To resolve this problem, a checksum or cryptographic hash function may be applied to the encrypted message to allow errors to be identified and reconciled upon receipt. This approach comes at a cost however — appending checksums or error-correcting code to an encrypted message increases the length of the message, and by extension increases the time required for the message to be transmitted. The result, of course, is that a satellite's actual overall communications capacity is commonly lower than its theoretical capacity, due to the extra burden that is placed on its limited resources by this communications overhead.

Another common problem associated with two-way encrypted satellite communications relates to establishing the identity of the sender of a message. Most modern satellites, for example, are designed to receive and respond to signals that control their onboard functions. Such satellites need to be certain that the control signals they receive from the ground originate from an authorized source. In addition to control signals, senders of other types of satellite transmissions commonly need to be authenticated as well. An intelligence agency receiving a satellite transmission from one of its operatives, for example, needs to establish that the transmission is genuine. To establish the identity of the sender, the message needs to be encrypted in such a way that from the recipient's perspective, only a legitimate sender could have encoded the message. The sender, of course, also wants to ensure that the message is protected while in transit, and thus desires that only an authorized recipient would be able to decode the message upon receipt. Both parties to the communication must therefore agree to use an encryption algorithm that serves to identify the authenticity of the sender while affording a sufficient level of protection to the message while it is in transit to its destination. Although keyless encryption algorithms may satisfy these two criteria, such algorithms are usually avoided in satellite communications, since the satellite may become useless if the keyless encryption algorithm were to be compromised, and satellites are expensive to replace. This problem also extends to the terrestrial equipment used to encrypt satellite signals prior to transmission and decrypt those signals after receipt. Keyed encryption algorithms are therefore typically used to protect information transmitted via satellite. Even keyed methods of encryption can be problematic when it comes to satellite communications, however.

To gain insight into the problems associated with keyed encryption, one might first consider the case of a symmetrically keyed encryption algorithm, wherein the same key is used to both encode and decode a message. If party A wants to communicate with party B via satellite using this method, then both A and B must agree on a secret key in advance of the communication. As long as the key remains secret, it also serves to authenticate both parties. If party A also wants to communicate with party C, however, then A and C must agree on their own unique secret key, otherwise party B could masquerade as

A or C, and vice-versa. A keyed encryption approach to two-way satellite communication thus requires that each party establish a unique secret key with every other party with whom they would like to communicate. To further compound this problem, each party must obtain all of its secret keys in advance, because possession of an appropriate key is a necessary prerequisite to establishing a secure communications channel with another party.

To resolve these issues, an asymmetrically keyed encryption algorithm may be adopted, wherein the key used to encrypt a message is different from the key used to decrypt the message. Such an approach requires each party to maintain only two keys, one of which is kept private, and the other of which is made publicly-available. If party A wants to send party B a secure transmission, A first asks B for her public key, which can be transmitted over an unsecured connection. Party A then encodes a secret message using B's public key. The message is secure because only B's private key can decode the message. To authenticate herself to B, party A needs only to re-encode the entire message using her own private key before transmitting the message to B. Upon receiving the message, B can establish whether it was sent by A, because only A's private key could have encoded a message that can be decoded with A's public key. This process is depicted in Figure 38.4 below.

Unfortunately, even this approach to secure two-way satellite communication is not entirely foolproof. To understand why, consider how a malicious party M might interject himself between A and B in order to intercept

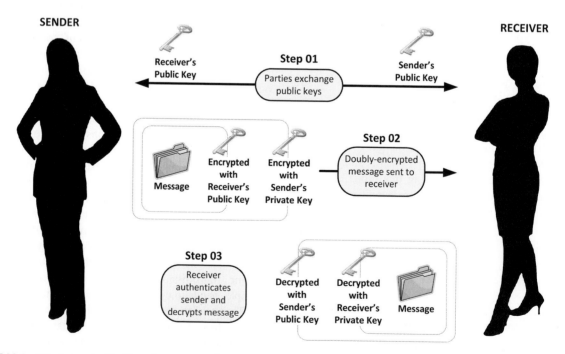

FIGURE 38.4　Ensuring sender identity and message security with asynchronously keyed encryption.

the secure communication. To initiate the secure transmission, A must request B's public key over an unsecure channel. If this request is intercepted by M, then M can supply A with his own (that is, M's) public key. A will then encrypt the message with M's public key, after which she will re-encrypt the result of the first encryption operation with her own private key. A will then transmit the encrypted message to B, which will once again be intercepted by M. Using A's public key in conjunction with his own private key, M will be able to decrypt and read the message. A will not know that the message has been intercepted, and B will not know that a message was even sent. Note that intercepting a secure communication is particularly easy for M if he owns or controls the satellite through which the message is being routed. In addition to the risk of interception, asynchronously keyed encryption algorithms are typically at least 10,000 times slower than synchronously keyed encryption algorithms — a situation that may place an enormously large burden on a satellite's limited computational resources. Until a means is developed of dynamically and securely distributing synchronous keys, satellite-based encryption will always require trade-offs among security, computational complexity, and ease of implementation.

Uplink Encryption

Protecting a transmission that is being sent to a satellite from at or near the surface of the Earth requires much more than just cryptographic techniques; to wit, encrypting the message itself is a necessary but insufficient condition for protecting the transmission. The reason for this is that the actual transmission of the encrypted message to the satellite is but the final step in a long chain of custody that begins when the message is created and ends when the message is successfully received by the satellite. Along the way, the message may pass through many people, systems, or networks, the control of which may or may not reside entirely in the hands of the sender. If one assumes that the confidentiality and integrity of the message have not been compromised as the message has passed through all of these intermediaries, then but two primary security concerns remain: the directional accuracy of the transmitting antenna, and the method used to encrypt the message. In the case of the former, the transmitting antenna must be sufficiently well-focused to allow the signal to be received by — and ideally *only* by — the target satellite. With thousands of satellites in orbit, a strong potential exists for a poorly focused transmission to be intercepted by another satellite, in which case the only remaining line of defense for a message is the strength of the encryption algorithm with which it was encoded. For this reason, a prudent sender should always assume that their message could be intercepted while in transit to and from the satellite, and should implement message encryption accordingly.

When deciding upon which encryption method to use, the sender must simultaneously consider the value of the data being transmitted, the purpose of the transmission, and the technological and computational limitations of the target satellite. A satellite's computational and technological capabilities are a function of its design specifications, its current workload, and any degradation that has occurred since the satellite was placed into orbit. These properties of the satellite can therefore be considered constraints — any encrypted uplink communications must work within the boundaries of these limitations. That having been said, the purpose of the transmission also features prominently in the choice of which encryption method to use. Here we must distinguish between two types of transmissions: commands, which instruct the satellite to perform one or more specific tasks, and transmissions-in-transit, which are intended to be retransmitted to the surface or to another satellite or spacecraft. Not only are command instructions of high value, but they are also not typically burdened with the same low-latency requirements of transmissions-in-transit. Command instructions should therefore always be highly encrypted, because control of the satellite could be lost if they were to be intercepted and compromised. What remains, then, are transmissions-in-transit, which may be of either high value, or of low value. One of the basic tenants of cryptography states that the value of the data should dictate the extent to which the data are protected. As such, minimal encryption may be acceptable for low-value transmissions-in-transit. For such transmissions, adding an unnecessarily complex layer of encryption may increase the computational burden on the satellite, which in turn may delay message delivery and limit the satellite's ability to perform other tasks simultaneously. High-value transmissions-in-transit should be protected with a robust encryption scheme that reflects the value of the data being transmitted. The extent to which a highly encrypted transmission-in-transit will negatively impact a satellite's available resources depends upon whether or not the message needs to be processed before being retransmitted. If the message is simply being relayed through the satellite without any additional processing, then the burden on the satellite's resources may be comparatively small. If, however, a highly encrypted message needs to be processed by the satellite prior to retransmission (if the message needs to be decrypted, processed, and then re-encrypted), the burden on the satellite's resources may be substantial. Processing high-value, highly encrypted transmissions-in-transit may therefore vastly reduce a satellite's throughput capabilities when considered in conjunction with its technological and computational limitations.

Extraplanetary Link Encryption

Before a signal is sent to the terrestrial surface, it may need to be transmitted across an extraplanetary link. Telemetry from a remote spacecraft orbiting Mars, for example, may need to be relayed to scientists by way of an Earth-orbiting satellite. Alternatively, a television signal originating in China may need to be relayed around the Earth by several intermediary satellites in order to reach its final destination in the United States. In such circumstances, several unique encryption-related issues may arise, each of which is associated with the routing of an extraplanetary transmission through one or more satellite nodes. Perhaps the most obvious of these issues is the scenario that arises when the signal transmitted from the source satellite or spacecraft is not compatible with the receiving capabilities of the target. For example, the very low power signals transmitted from a remote exploratory spacecraft may not be detectable by a particular listening station on the planet's surface, or the data rate or signal modulation with which an extraplanetary transmission is sent may not be supported by the final recipient. In this scenario, the intermediary satellite through which the signal is being routed must act as an interpreter or translator of sorts, a situation which is illustrated in Figure 38.5 below.

From an encryption perspective, the situation illustrated above implies that the intermediary satellite may need to decrypt the extraplanetary message, and re-encrypt it using a different encryption scheme prior to retransmission. A similar issue may arise for legal or political reasons. Consider, for example, a message that is being transmitted from one country to another by way of several intermediary satellites. The first country may have no standing policies regarding the encryption of messages sent via satellite, while the second country may have policies that strictly regulate the encryption standards of messages received via satellite. In this case, one or more of

the orbiting satellites may need to alter the encryption of a message in transit in order to satisfy the legal and regulatory guidelines of both countries.

Downlink Encryption

Several different issues impact the way in which information is protected as it is transmitted from orbiting satellites to the surface of the Earth. As with uplink encryption, the technological and computational capabilities of the spacecraft may constrain the extent to which a particular message can be protected. If, for example, an older communications satellite does not possess the requisite hardware or software capabilities to support a newly developed downlink encryption scheme, then that scheme simply cannot be used with the satellite. Similarly, if the utilization of a particular encryption scheme would reduce the efficiency or message-handling capacity of a satellite to a level that is deemed unacceptable, then the satellite's operators may choose to prioritize capacity over downlink security. The precision with which a satellite is able to focus a downlink transmission may also impact the choice of encryption scheme — as noted earlier in this chapter, a widely dispersed downlink signal can be more readily intercepted than can a signal transmitted with a narrow focus. While each of these computational and technological limitations must be considered when selecting a downlink encryption scheme, they are by no means the only factors requiring consideration.

Unlike uplink signals, which can only originate from the surface of the planet, messages to be transmitted over a downlink channel can come from one of three different sources: the terrestrial surface, from another spacecraft, or from the satellite itself. The source of the message to be broadcast to the planet's surface plays a critical role in determining the method of protection for that message. Consider, for example, a message that originates from the surface or from another spacecraft. In

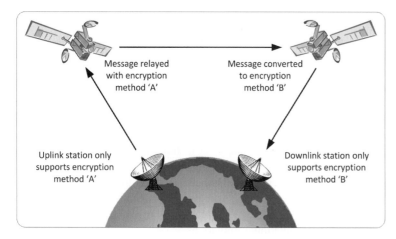

FIGURE 38.5 In-transit translation of encrypted messages in satellite communication.

Message relayed with encryption method 'A'

Message converted to encryption method 'B'

Uplink station only supports encryption method 'A'

Downlink station only supports encryption method 'B'

this case, one of two possible scenarios may exist. First, the satellite transmitting the message to Earth may be serving only as a simple signal repeater or amplifying transmitter; that is to say, the message is already encrypted upon receipt, and the satellite is simply relaying the previously encrypted message to the surface. In this case, the satellite transmitting the downlink signal has very little to do with the encryption of the message, and only the integrity of the message and the retransmission capabilities of the satellite at the time the message is received need be considered. In the second scenario, a satellite may need to filter a message or alter its encryption method prior to downlink transmission. For example, a satellite may receive signals that have been optimized for extraplanetary communication from a robotic exploration spacecraft in the far reaches of the solar system. Prior to retransmission, the satellite may need to decrypt the data, process it, and then re-encrypt the data using a different encryption scheme more suited to a downlink transmission. In this case, the technological capabilities of the satellite, the timeliness with which the data need to be delivered, and the value of the data themselves dictate the means through which those data are protected prior to downlink transmission.

Finally, one might consider the scenario in which the data being transmitted to the terrestrial surface originate from the satellite itself, rather than from the surface or from another spacecraft. Such data can be classified as either telemetry relating to the status of the satellite, or as information that the satellite has acquired or produced while performing an assigned task. In the case of the former, telemetry relating to the status of the satellite should always be highly protected, as it may reveal details about the satellite's capabilities, inner workings, or control systems if it were to be intercepted and compromised. In the case of the latter, however, the value of the data that the satellite has acquired or produced should dictate the extent to which those data are protected. Critical military intelligence, for example, should be subjected to a much higher standard of encryption than data that are comparatively less valuable. In the end, a satellite operator must weigh many factors when deciding upon the extent to which a particular downlink transmission should be protected. It is tempting to conclude that the maximum level of encryption should be applied to every downlink transmission. Doing so, however, would unnecessarily burden satellites' limited resources, and would vastly reduce the communications capacity of the global satellite network. Instead, a harmonious balance needs to be sought between a satellite's technological and computational capabilities, and the source, volume, and value of the data that it is asked to handle. Only by achieving such a balance can the maximum utility of a satellite be realized.

4. PIRATE DECRYPTION OF SATELLITE TRANSMISSIONS

As a general rule, it is reasonable to assume that encrypted satellite messages contain content that is important or valuable in some way. After all, why would a sender go to the trouble of encrypting a message if its contents were not of value? Unfortunately, the fact that encrypted satellite transmissions contain valuable information is sufficient motivation for some individuals, organizations, and governments to attempt to decrypt and benefit from such information, even if they are not its intended recipients. In the world of encrypted satellite communications, this problem of pirate signal decryption is compounded by two additional factors. First, the dispersive nature of satellite-to-ground transmissions – as illustrated in Figure 38.2 – creates an environment in which many people other than the intended recipient have access to the encrypted signal. This is, of course, also one of the great benefits of satellite communication, since it allows providers of commercial services such as satellite-based television and radio to ensure that their signals are available to as many potential customers as possible. Second, equipment designed to receive satellite signals is, at least in the developed world, both abundant and relatively inexpensive.

As opposed to satellite *transmitters* or *transceivers* – both of which can send messages to satellites – the vast majority of the satellite communications devices in use today are classified simply as *receivers*, which can receive satellite transmissions but cannot send them. These differences are illustrated in Figure 38.6 below.

There are literally hundreds of millions of GPS devices, commercial satellite television receivers, and satellite radio devices in use in the world today, and while all are designed to receive satellite signals, only a tiny fraction can actually send them. When viewed through the eyes of a signal pirate, the combination of these

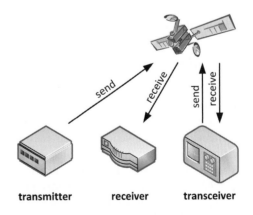

FIGURE 38.6 Communications capabilities of satellite transmitters, receivers, and transceivers.

factors makes encrypted satellite transmissions a very tempting target. There are three reasons for this: First, since the encrypted signal is already available, no additional effort (such as physical wiretapping) is required in order to gain access to the signal itself. Second, since compatible receiving equipment is relatively inexpensive and widely available, acquiring the equipment necessary to receive an encrypted satellite signal is not at all difficult for most would-be pirates. Finally, although pirating encrypted satellite transmissions is illegal in many countries, the fact that most satellite communications devices are simple receivers that cannot transmit any information back to the sender means that the probability of a signal pirate being detected and subsequently punished is quite low.

Since signal piracy has become a rampant phenomenon in the realm of commercial satellite communications, a survey of the history of satellite signal piracy should prove useful. As described earlier in this chapter, modern digital satellite communication relies on keyed encryption algorithms for message security. In this model, the sender first encodes a message by running the digital data through an encryption algorithm with a chosen key. The resulting encrypted data are then relayed to the receiver by way of a satellite transmission, after which the receiver can decrypt the message using the appropriate key. Anyone wishing to access the encrypted satellite transmission must therefore satisfy three conditions if he or she is to be successful. First, the receiver must have access to the encrypted signal. This typically means that the receiver must possess compatible receiving equipment, and must be geographically located within the satellite's signal dispersion zone. Next, the receiver must know which encryption algorithm was used to encode the message. This is usually not a significant problem, since the encryption algorithm is typically embedded within the hardware or software of the receiving device. Finally, presuming that the first two conditions have been met, the receiver must apply the proper key in order to unlock the encrypted digital message. It is toward this final condition that efforts aimed at signal piracy are most often directed.

Circuit-based Security

Since most satellite receivers are not capable of two-way communication, they are also generally not capable of negotiating a new key with the sender of the encrypted message in real-time. The sender of the message must therefore find some other way of supplying its authorized receivers with the proper key, and many different approaches have been developed with this problem in mind. In early secure satellite communications, the means of decoding encrypted transmissions were often built directly into the receiving devices themselves in the form of fixed solid-state circuitry. The "key" in these cases would be the one unique circuit design that would allow a given message to be decrypted. Anyone who owned such a receiver could therefore decode the encrypted transmission, and the sender maintained security by regulating who was given access to compatible receiving devices.

From a security perspective, this early approach was plagued by several obvious flaws. First, anyone able to clone the circuitry of the receiving device would have immediate access to the encrypted message. Circuit components and circuit design knowledge were quite rare in the early days of satellite communication, but it was not long until a would-be signal pirate with a little knowledge could walk into his or her local electronics supply store and buy everything needed to build a simple satellite receiver. Since the security of this approach depended on maintaining the secrecy of the circuit design, the entire system would be compromised as soon as knowledge of that design was made available outside of the circle of authorized recipients. The security of the system could thence only be restored by replacing all of the legitimate receivers with new receivers that contained a different unique circuitry key. If only a few people were authorized to receive the encrypted messages, then replacing the compromised devices might not be terribly problematical. If thousands or even millions of people were authorized to receive the encrypted messages, however, then replacing all of the compromised receivers could be a financially and logistically daunting prospect. Clearly, a better approach was needed.

Removable Security Cards

The next major evolutionary step in secure satellite communications arrived with the introduction of removable security cards. In this model, the receiving devices themselves were of a generalist design inasmuch as they could receive satellite messages encrypted with any number of algorithms or keys. Decoding the encrypted message, however, required that a proprietary security card be inserted into the receiver. It was thus the security card and not the receiver itself which contained the proper circuitry for decrypting the signal. This approach had three major advantages. First, service offerings could be readily stratified into multiple layers. A satellite television customer who wanted to purchase a premium movie channel, for example, could be sent a security card capable of decrypting that channel. Second, the security cards could be rotated according to some predefined schedule. Secret military communications, for example, might use a different security card every day or every week in order to enhance the overall security of the system. Third, if the security of the decryption circuitry were ever compromised, the sender would only need to replace the security cards themselves. This would, of course, be much less expensive than replacing all of the receivers completely.

Unfortunately, this security card-based approach suffered from many of the same fundamental flaws as earlier approaches. Namely, an aspiring signal pirate could gain access to the encrypted signal simply by cloning the circuitry of the security card. Once successful, the pirate could rest comfortably knowing that the probability he or she would be detected was virtually zero. This problem came to a head when the first several generations of security cards developed by direct broadcast satellite television companies were cracked almost immediately after being released. Not only did this create a great deal of embarrassment and bad press for these companies, but it also spawned a lively and flourishing black market for pirated satellite security cards. Eventually, a new generation of security cards that incorporated what are known as application-specific integrated circuits (ASICs) was released in order to combat this problem. As the name implies, an ASIC is an integrated circuit that is designed for a very specific purpose — in this case, to decode encrypted satellite signals. Since integrated circuits are much smaller than standard circuitry and can contain thousands if not millions of logic gates, reverse-engineering an ASIC's circuit pathways is an extremely difficult task that requires highly specialized equipment such as a circuit probe or an electron microscope. While the introduction of ASICs all but eliminated the black market for cloned satellite security cards, signal piracy is still prevalent today as pirates have found ways of tinkering with or reprogramming existing cards to allow them to illicitly receive premium or restricted content. There is little reason to believe that this long-lived battle between signal pirates and satellite content providers will end anytime soon.

5. SATELLITE ENCRYPTION POLICY

Given the rapid adoption of satellite communications — and the potential security implications associated therewith — many governments and multinational coalitions are increasingly establishing policy instruments with a view toward controlling and regulating the availability and use of satellite encryption in both the public and private sectors. Such policy instruments have wide-reaching economic, political, and cultural implications that commonly extend well beyond national boundaries. One might, for example, consider the export controls placed on satellite encryption technology by the United States government, which many consider to be the most stringent in the world. Broadly, these export controls were established in support of two primary objectives. First, the maintenance of a restrictive export policy allows the government to review and assess the merits of any newly developed satellite encryption technologies that have been proposed for export. If the export of those technologies is ultimately approved, the government will possess a detailed understanding of how the technologies operate, potentially allowing for their encryption schemes to be defeated if deemed necessary. Second, such controls allow the government to prevent satellite encryption technologies of particularly high merit from leaving the country, especially if the utilization of those technologies by foreign entities would interfere with U.S. intelligence-gathering activities. Although these stringent controls may appear to be a legacy of the xenophobic policies of the Cold War, they are nevertheless still seen as prudent measures in a world where information and communication technologies can be readily leveraged to advance extreme agendas. Unfortunately, such controls have potentially negative economic implications, insofar as U.S. firms may be barred from competing in the increasingly lucrative global market for satellite communication technologies.

The establishment and maintenance of satellite encryption policy also needs to be considered in the context of satellite systems of global import. Consider, for example, the NAVSTAR Global Positioning System (GPS), whose constellation of satellites enables anyone with a GPS receiver to accurately determine their current location, time, elevation, velocity, and direction of travel anywhere on or near the surface of the Earth. In recent years, GPS capabilities have been incorporated into the navigational systems of automobiles, ocean-going vessels, trains, commercial aircraft, military vehicles, and many other forms of transit all over the world. Despite its worldwide use, the NAVSTAR GPS satellites are currently operated by the 2nd Space Operations Squadron of the United States Air Force, implying that satellite encryption policy decisions related to the GPS system are controlled by the U.S. Department of Defense. One of the options available to the United States government through this arrangement is the ability to selectively or entirely block the transmission of civilian GPS signals, while retaining access to GPS signals for military purposes. Additionally, the United States government reserves the right to introduce errors into civilian GPS signals, thus making them less accurate. Since the U.S. government exercises exclusive control over the GPS system, users all over the world are forced to place a great deal of trust in the goodwill of its operators, and in the integrity of the encryption scheme for the NAVSTAR uplink channel. Given the widespread use of GPS navigation, a global catastrophe could ensue if the encryption scheme used to control the NAVSTAR GPS satellites were to be compromised. Because the GPS system is controlled by the U.S. military, the resiliency and security of this encryption scheme cannot be independently evaluated.

In the reality of a rapidly globalizing and interconnected world, the effectiveness of national satellite encryption policy efforts may not be sustainable in the long run. Satellite encryption policies face the same legal difficulties as so many other intrinsically international issues; to wit, outside of international agreements, the ability of a specific country to enforce its laws extends only so far as its geographic boundaries. This problem is particularly relevant in the context of satellite communications, since the satellites themselves orbit the Earth, and hence do not lie within the geographic boundaries of any one nation. Considered in conjunction with the growing need of governments to share intelligence resources and information with their allies, future efforts targeted toward satellite encryption policy-making may increasingly fall under the auspices of international organizations and multinational coalitions.

Finally, let's briefly look at Satellite Encryption Service (SES). SES provides dedicated and reliable satellite encryption based transmission for specific data networks and mission critical applications, where landline access may not be available; as well as, wideband video broadcast transmission. The connection from the satellite earth station to the Service Delivery Platform (SDP) is included in this service.

6. SATELLITE ENCRYPTION SERVICE

Satellite Encryption Service can be used as dedicated transmission service for voice, data, and video traffic transmission and wideband broadcast applications, such as broadband distance learning and broadcast of data/multimedia files. The service provides full-duplex, half-duplex, and simplex (broadcast) encrypted transmissions using C-band, Ku-band, and Ka-band satellites.

SES provides dedicated and ad-hoc (reservation-based) encrypted satellite transmission. This transmission can be used by any application services at a customer specified bandwidth between two or more distance learning, broadcast quality National Television System Committee (NTSC) video and associated audio, digital compressed video and associated audio, including encrypted communications specified end points. The connection between the locations receiving this encryption service is permanently established unless a service request for modification, move, or disconnect is received.

This encryption service can be used for applications such as voice, data, video, and multimedia; and, may include Government end-to-end encrypted communications. As previously stated, SES also provides reservation based wideband encrypted satellite broadcast transmission that can be used for numerous applications.

SES connects to and interoperates with specified permanent or temporary locations (SDPs, such as PBX, Multiplexer, router, video codec, earth station, and VSAT (fixed and transportable/deployable)). This results in a satellite encryption strategy being guided by a set of pre-cutover activities (see checklist: "An Agenda For Action For SES Pre-cutover Activities").

An Agenda for Action for SES Pre-Cutover Activities

In order to provide timely, comprehensive, relevant, and accurate satellite encryption strategy, the following set of pre-cutover activities must be adhered to (check all tasks completed):

Administrative

_____1. Has a Hierarchy Code (HC) been provided to the vendor?

_____2. Have Local Contacts (recommend at least two per location) been identified and contact information provided?

_____3. Has a Project Specific Transition Plan Identifier been assigned?

_____4. Note (P_OPS) in the Service Request Number (SRN) if this is parallel encryption service.

Pre-Ordering/Design Decisions

_____5. Has the vendor developed the functional and performance specifications for Satellite Encryption Service (SES) systems and Sensor Evolutionary Developments (SEDs) in accordance with requirements? This task will include the development of

the operational concept for SES within the overall network architecture.

_____6. Has the vendor identified all necessary interfaces between the wireline and wireless systems and SES?

_____7. Has the vendor defined the contours of the SES coverage to make and receive calls?

_____8. Has the vendor presented a plan to continue to provide any changes to satellite footprints for each satellite system providing the coverage?

_____9. Determine the Parallel Operations Period – all orders for parallel service will have to be so noted in the Service Request Number (SRN).

_____10. Fall-Back plan: Has the vendor provided a detailed fall-back/back-out plan to all stakeholders?

Site Preparation

_____11. Has the vendor conducted site surveys at all locations if required and provided site survey reports?

_____12. Has the vendor delivered an acceptable, detailed, system design? This design plan, at a minimum, will address network topology, configuration, addressing (fleet mapping), coverage, availability, reliability, scalability, security, Service Enabling Devices (SEDs), and disaster recovery requirements.

User Training

_____**13.** Has the vendor provided any required training and documentation for users?

Installation

_____**14.** Has the vendor managed the SEDs required for the installation and operation of the SES to include ensuring that SEDs are transported to the appropriate site of deployment and/or stored until installation is complete?

Network Management

_____**15.** Has the vendor submitted a detailed, overall management plan for the SES to include operational support?

Documentation

_____**16.** Has the vendor provided all required documentation (Systems Specifications Document, System Design Document, and Test Documentation when completed)?

Execute Tests

_____**17.** Have the Network Management Organization and vendor reviewed the results of this testing to insure all is ready for the actual cutover?

_____**18.** Conduct pre-cutover testing

7. THE FUTURE OF SATELLITE ENCRYPTION

Despite the many challenges faced by satellite encryption, the potential advantages afforded by satellites to mankind are so tantalizing and alluring that the utilization of satellite-based communication can only be expected to grow for the foreseeable future. As globalization continues its indefatigable march across the terrestrial surface, access to secure, high-speed communications will be needed from even the most remote and sparsely populated corners of the globe. Satellites by their very nature are well-positioned to meet this demand, and will therefore play a pivotal role in interconnecting humanity and enabling the forthcoming global Information Society. Furthermore, recent developments in the area of quantum cryptography promise to further improve the security of satellite-based encryption. This rapidly advancing technology allows the quantum state of photons to be manipulated in such a way that the photons themselves can carry a synchronous cryptographic key. The parties involved in a secure communication can be certain that the cryptographic key has not been intercepted, because eavesdropping upon the key would introduce detectable quantum anomalies into the photonic transmission. By using a constellation of satellites in low earth orbit, synchronous cryptographic keys could be securely distributed via photons to parties wishing to communicate, thus resolving the key exchange problem. The parties could then establish secure communications using more traditional satellite channels. The further development and adoption of technologies such as quantum cryptography ensures that satellite-based communication has a bright — and secure — future.

There are, of course, risks to relying heavily on satellite-based communication. Specifically, if the ability to access critical satellite systems fails due to interference or damage to the satellite, disastrous consequences may ensue. What might happen, for example, if interference from a solar flare were to disrupt the constellation of global positioning satellites? What might happen if a micrometeoroid storm were to damage all of the weather satellites monitoring the progress of a major hurricane? What might happen to a nation's ability to make war if anti-satellite weapons were deployed to destroy its military communications and intelligence-gathering satellites? Questions such as these highlight the risks of relying too heavily on artificial satellites. Nevertheless, as the costs associated with building, launching, and operating satellites continue to decline, the utilization of satellite technology will, for the foreseeable future, become an increasingly common part of the human experience.

8. SUMMARY

This chapter focused on encrypted satellite data transmissions (uplink and downlink) in the critical national infrastructure and private industry. Over the last 16 years, the Federal Government and corporations, have become increasingly reliant on the commercial satellite communications industry. Today, the satellite industry is providing encrypted voice, data, and video services in support of Government and commercial operations, including national security and emergency preparedness (NS/EP) missions. The commercial industry is also supplying the majority of the encrypted satellite communications used for military and surveillance operations along and outside the border of Iran and within Afghanistan. As part of the critical national infrastructure, encrypted satellite networks provide unparalleled coverage of remote geographical areas and difficult terrain. They complement terrestrial networks also used to provide NS/EP communications support.

The terrestrial components of encrypted satellite networks contain many of the same subsystems found in other communications networks. As a result, encrypted satellite and terrestrial networks share similar cyber vulnerabilities and mitigation measures. However, because satellites must be controlled remotely from Earth, satellite operators take special care to mitigate two risks: (1) remote introduction of a false spacecraft command; and (2) a malicious third party preventing the spacecraft from executing authorized commands or interfering with satellite telemetry reception.

Satellite operators use redundant and geographically diverse facilities to protect terrestrial infrastructure from man-made and natural threats and to ensure continuity of encrypted critical satellite network functions. Ground stations are connected by redundant, path-diverse, cryptographically secured communications links and employ preventative measures such as buffer zones and robust security systems to protect from attack. Further, operators maintain personnel security procedures, including background checks, employee badges, logged entry and exit, and on-site security guards, as part of their best practice security efforts.

Consistent with Government policy, most satellite companies use the National Security Agency-approved satellite command uplink encryption for satellites supporting U.S. Government services. As operators replace their older, legacy satellites that are technically incapable of encrypting commands, newer satellites are likely to be fully compliant with the Government's policy direction.

Finally, let's move on to the real interactive part of this Chapter: review questions/exercises, hands-on projects, case projects and optional team case project. The answers and/or solutions by chapter can be found in the Online Instructor's Solutions Manual.

CHAPTER REVIEW QUESTIONS/EXERCISES

True/False

1. True or False? Depending on the type of satellite communications link that needs to be established, substantially different technologies, frequencies, and data encryption techniques may be required in order to secure a satellite-based communications channel.

2. True or False? For purposes of simplicity, the value of transmitted information can be classified along three dimensions: high-value, medium value and low-value.

3. True or False? One of the problems common to all forms of satellite encryption relates to signal degradation.

4. True or False? Protecting a transmission that is being sent to a satellite from at or near the surface of the Earth requires much more than just cryptographic techniques; to wit, encrypting the message itself is a necessary but insufficient condition for protecting the transmission.

5. True or False? Before a signal is sent to the terrestrial surface, it may need to be transmitted across an extra-planetary link.

Multiple Choice

1. For communications purposes, modern satellites can be classified into two categories:
   A. Type 1
   B. Type 2
   C. Type 3
   D. Type 4
   E. Type 5

2. Any satellite-based communication can be classified into one of:
   A. Two possible categories
   B. Six possible categories
   C. Four possible categories
   D. Eight possible categories
   E. Seven possible categories

3. In addition to the risk of interception, asynchronously keyed encryption algorithms are typically at least:
   A. 10,000 times slower than synchronously keyed encryption algorithms
   B. 20,000 times slower than synchronously keyed encryption algorithms
   C. 30,000 times slower than synchronously keyed encryption algorithms
   D. 40,000 times slower than synchronously keyed encryption algorithms
   E. 50,000 times slower than synchronously keyed encryption algorithms

4. As opposed to satellite *transmitters* or *transceivers* — both of which can send messages to satellites — the vast majority of the satellite communications devices in use today are classified simply as:
   A. Devices
   B. Signals
   C. Transmissions
   D. Receivers
   E. Messages

5. What is an integrated circuit that is designed for a very specific purpose:
   A. ASIC
   B. NAVSTAR
   C. GPS
   D. SES
   E. SDP

EXERCISE

Problem

How would you go about breaking the encryption algorithms known as A5-GMR-1 and A5-GMR-2 that are used to secure civilian communications between mobile phones and satellites based on the GMR-1 and GMR-2 satphone standards?

Hands-On Projects

Project

Finding the right satellite encryption solution is critical for financial services providers in order to meet compliance requirements. A bank needed a cost-effective, secure and reliable way to back up its data files, and faced a decision between choosing a hardware solution or finding the right software that would work on their system. What motivated the bank's search for a satellite encryption solution and what approach did it take to find that solution?

Case Projects

Problem

This case study illustrates a need for a new satellite receiver platform with a unique encryption system. Please identify what type of platform should be developed.

Optional Team Case Project

Problem

A commercial satellite encryption communications solutions and hardware company had run into major impediments on both cost and delivery. Please identify how the company redesigned their commercial grade satellite receiver to achieve an increase in delivery at a reduced cost.

Public Key Infrastructure

Terence Spies

Voltage Security

Note: This chapter is available in its entirety online at store.elsevier.com/product.jsp?isbn=9780123943972 (click the Resources tab at the bottom of the page).

1. ABSTRACT

This chapter will explain the cryptographic background that forms the foundation of PKI systems, the mechanics of the X.509 PKI system (as elaborated by the Internet Engineering Task Force), the practical issues surrounding the implementation of PKI systems, a number of alternative PKI standards, and alternative cryptographic strategies for solving the problem of secure public key distribution. PKI systems are complex objects that have proven to be difficult to implement properly. This chapter aims to survey the basic architecture of PKI systems, and some of the mechanisms used to implement them. It does not aim to be a comprehensive guide to all PKI standards or to contain sufficient technical detail to allow implementation of a PKI system. These systems are continually evolving, and the reader interested in building or operating a PKI is advised to consult the current work of standards bodies referenced in this chapter.

2. CONTENTS

Chapter 39

Public Key Infrastructure

## Chapter 40

Password-based Authenticated Key Establishment Protocols

Jean Lancrenon
Interdisciplinary Centre for Security Reliability and Trust (SnT)

Dalia Khader
Interdisciplinary Centre for Security Reliability and Trust (SnT)

Peter Y.A. Ryan
Interdisciplinary Centre for Security Reliability and Trust (SnT); University of Luxembourg,CSC

Feng Hao
Newcastle University

1. INTRODUCTION TO KEY EXCHANGE

What Are Key Exchange Protocols?

One of the main goals of cryptography is to provide secure communication channels between different parties. Security here means various flavors of data secrecy, message integrity, and communicant authenticity. One way to construct secure channels between parties is for them to share suitable *keys* that they keep secret and use as input to encryption and message authentication algorithms. Roughly, keys deemed suitable for such cryptographic applications are required to be *long* (e.g. from one hundred to several hundreds of bits, depending on the application and desired level of security) and *random*. This basically guarantees that they cannot be predicted or exhaustively searched for in a reasonable amount of time. We are now faced with the question of establishing keys over an insecure network. Key exchange protocols are meant to provide an answer. More formally, a key exchange protocol is a cryptographic procedure in which two or more entities exchange messages to jointly determine a strong cryptographic key that cannot be computed by outsiders [1].

One may wonder whether there is a vicious circle here, since the problem of exchanging keys over an insecure network can be viewed as a particular case of secure message transmission. The point is that the successful exchange of a single key can lead to efficiently securing much larger amounts of data. Typically, a fresh key is established for each new conversation in which the parties may want to engage; such conversations are called sessions, and the keys used to secure them are called session keys.

The Historic Example: The Diffie-Hellman Key Exchange

In 1976, Whitfield Diffie and Martin Hellman proposed a method for creating session keys over an insecure channel [2]. Suppose Alice $\mathcal{A}$ and Bob $\mathcal{B}$ wish to share a key. We assume that they share the following public information: the description of a large integer n, a cyclic group G of order n, and a generator g for G. (See part IV, *Encryption Technology*, Chapter 37, *Data Encryption*, in the sequel, for basic definitions of groups, generators, etc.) We will briefly address the security of the public data later; what is important to note for now is that potential adversaries know it as well.

The *Diffie-Hellman Key Exchange* runs as follows:

- $\mathcal{A}$ chooses $x \in \mathbb{Z}_n$ randomly, computes $X := g^x$, and sends X to $\mathcal{B}$. x is kept secret;
- Upon receiving X, $\mathcal{B}$ chooses $y \in \mathbb{Z}_n$ randomly, computes $Y := g^y$, and sends Y back to $\mathcal{A}$. He computes $K_{\mathcal{B}} := X^y$, and keeps y secret;
- Finally, upon receiving Y, $\mathcal{A}$ computes $K_{\mathcal{A}} := Y^x$.

The properties of cyclic groups (see Chapter 37) ensure that $K_{\mathcal{A}} = K_{\mathcal{B}} = g^{xy}$. Thus, $\mathcal{A}$ and $\mathcal{B}$ end up sharing

FIGURE 40.1 Diffie-Hellman key exchange.

the same group value, from which a session key can be derived. We now turn to explaining why this is (the starting point to) an appropriate solution.

The **secrecy** of the key is based on the observation that for well-chosen n, computing g^{xy} knowing only the tuple (n, G, g, g^x, g^y) appears to be infeasible in a reasonable amount of time, provided x and y are chosen sufficiently randomly.[1] This is known as the *Computational Diffie-Hellman Assumption* (CDH). It is widely believed that, for many concrete groups, the assumption indeed holds. (Examples of such groups will appear in section 3 of this chapter.) Note that CDH is related to the difficulty of the *Discrete Logarithm Problem* (DLP) where for randomly chosen x, computing x knowing only g and g^x is difficult.

In fact, in some groups it is widely believed that the *Decisional Diffie-Hellman Assumption* (DDH) holds: If x, y, and z are chosen sufficiently randomly, there is no efficient statistical test that can tell apart $(n, G, g, g^x, g^y, g^{xy})$ and (n, G, g, g^x, g^y, g^z). This basically means that g^{xy} appears truly random even given g^x and g^y. This implies that the protocol in Figure 40.1 will achieve the required **randomness** property of the key g^{xy}. However, in practice it is more common to compute the key as a *function of* g^{xy}; often, a *cryptographic hash function* is used. (See Chapter 37 for basic properties of cryptographic hash functions.) One reason to do this is to obtain a key of correct length for higher-level applications. This function needs to have special properties to guarantee that the key ultimately computed remains random.[2] Finally, n being a large number, g^{xy} is a large value, making it relatively easy to derive **long** keys from it.

We point out that a huge amount of key exchange protocols still use the Diffie-Hellman construct as a basis for computing secret keys. (In fact, all three protocols described at the end of this chapter use it in one way or another.) The main issue at hand now is authenticating the exchange.

Authentication

Using the classic protocol in the preceding, we illustrate the main problem that arises when one does not pay attention to the authenticity of the key exchange itself. That would be the protocol's vulnerability to *active* attacks.

Man in the Middle

In addition to $\mathcal{A}$ and $\mathcal{B}$, let $\mathcal{M}$ be a malicious adversary intercepting communications between $\mathcal{A}$ and $\mathcal{B}$. By impersonating $\mathcal{A}$ to $\mathcal{B}$ and vice versa, and injecting her own messages in the protocol flow, $\mathcal{M}$ can fool $\mathcal{A}$ and $\mathcal{B}$ into thinking they are communicating with each other, while in fact they are both communicating with $\mathcal{M}$. The attack runs as follows (see Figure 40.2):

- $\mathcal{M}$ intercepts $\mathcal{A}$'s first message to $\mathcal{B}$, that is $X = g^x$. She chooses some value u and sends instead $U := g^u$ to $\mathcal{B}$, claiming it is from $\mathcal{A}$.
- $\mathcal{B}$ selects y, computes $Y = g^y$, and sends Y back to $\mathcal{A}$. $\mathcal{B}$ also computes what it thinks is the correct Diffie-Hellman value, $U^y = g^{uy}$.
- $\mathcal{M}$ intercepts Y, and instead computes $V := g^v$ for some value v, which it returns to $\mathcal{A}$. $\mathcal{A}$ thus computes $V^x = g^{vx}$.
- $\mathcal{M}$ now computes $X^v = g^{vx}$ and $Y^u = g^{uy}$. It shares the former value with $\mathcal{A}$, the latter value with $\mathcal{B}$, and can now begin a falsified session with both parties, impersonating each to the other.

This is called a *man-in-the-middle* attack; its success is due to the absence of any mechanism authenticating the message flow between $\mathcal{A}$ and $\mathcal{B}$. In other words, in the basic Diffie-Hellman protocol described above, neither party really knows whether or not the message it received is indeed from whom it claims to be.

Implicit and Explicit Authentication

Essentially two flavors of authentication can be provided by a key exchange protocol. We say that *implicit authentication* is reached if after completing its role in a protocol run, a party is guaranteed that if it has not conversed with the intended partner, whomever it really has communicated with will fail at computing the same session key. *Explicit authentication* is reached if, after completing its role in a protocol run, a party obtains the guarantee that it was speaking to its intended partner, and that this partner has computed the correct session key.

The latter of these two notions is more desirable than the former because the honest party can start using the computed session key in a higher application knowing that its intended partner can actually participate, whereas if the exchange is implicitly authenticated, it may very well be that the honest party will open a session alone.

---

1. Strictly speaking, these values need to be chosen *uniformly at random*. In practice, they are computed by *pseudo-random number generators*. Also, n is often required to be of special form.
2. In case only the CDH assumption holds, this additional step is vital for security.

Often, implicitly authenticated protocols are converted into explicitly authenticated ones with a mechanism known as *key confirmation*, in which an honest party is guaranteed that its intended partner indeed did compute the correct session key. These considerations will appear again in section 2 of this chapter.

Examples of how to construct authenticated key exchange schemes are described below. For *any* such scheme to work, *some form of secret, long-term keying information must be in place for both parties.*

Classical Key Exchange

In what is considered classical key exchange, the long-term keying material that a user is required to possess is usually one of two kinds: (i) a cryptographically secure key for a symmetric cryptographic algorithm (e.g. a 128-bit AES encryption key, see Chapter 37) or (ii) a cryptographically secure public key/secret key pair for an asymmetric cryptographic algorithm (e.g., a 1024-bit RSA modulus, and appropriate encryption and decryption exponents e and d; see Chapter 37). In the former case, the long-term key needs to be also known to the other party; for key management purposes, it is actually more convenient to have the users share their respective keys with a trusted server, which will then aid those users and their target desired partners in the network to establish session keys between themselves. In the latter case, the public key is what the other party will use, and a trusted *Certificate Authority* (CA) will ensure that this key is indeed bound to the user it is purportedly associated with via a *Certificate* in a *Public Key Infrastructure* (PKI). (See Chapter 37 for a general introduction to PKI.)

In the paragraphs that follow, we give an overview of the symmetric-key Needham-Schroeder key exchange protocol and the PKI-based Station-to-Station key exchange protocol (see Figures 40.3 and 40.4).

Long-term Symmetric Keys

The symmetric-key Needham-Schroeder key establishment protocol, which is the main building block of the popular Kerberos system, was first proposed in 1978 [4] and slightly modified in 1987 [5]. In addition to the two parties $\mathcal{A}$ and $\mathcal{B}$, there is a trusted server $\mathcal{T}$. $\mathcal{A}$ (resp., $\mathcal{B}$) shares a secret long symmetric key K_{AT} (resp., K_{BT}) with $\mathcal{T}$. The protocol we shall describe now is the original version from [4] (see Figure 40.3).

Let E denote a symmetric-key encryption algorithm; for any key K, E_K is the encryption function obtained from E under key K. Also, M and N will be used to designate *nonces*. (A *NONCE* is a *N*umber used *ONCE*. Here, they are strings of some agreed upon length picked randomly.) The protocol runs as follows:

- $\mathcal{A}$ sends $ID_\mathcal{A}$, $ID_\mathcal{B}$, $N_\mathcal{A}$, to $\mathcal{T}$, where $N_\mathcal{A}$ is a nonce she picked randomly;

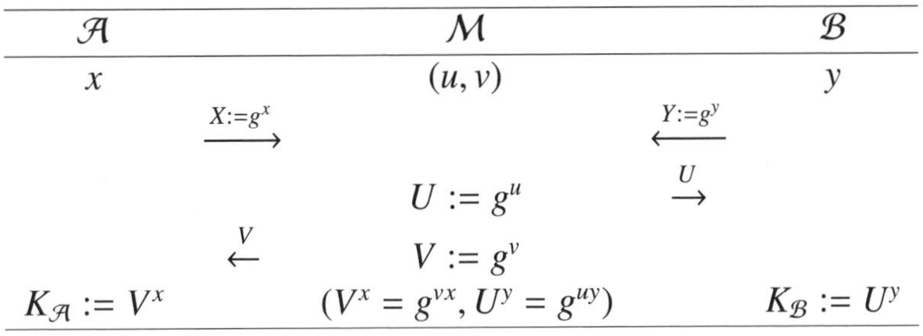

FIGURE 40.2 Man-in-the-middle attack.

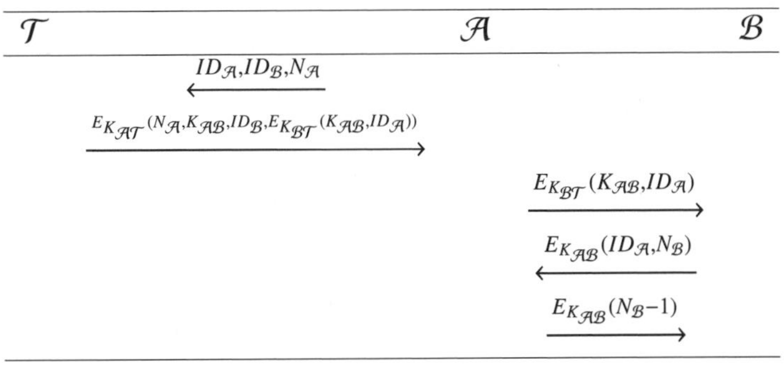

FIGURE 40.3 Needham-Schroeder [4].

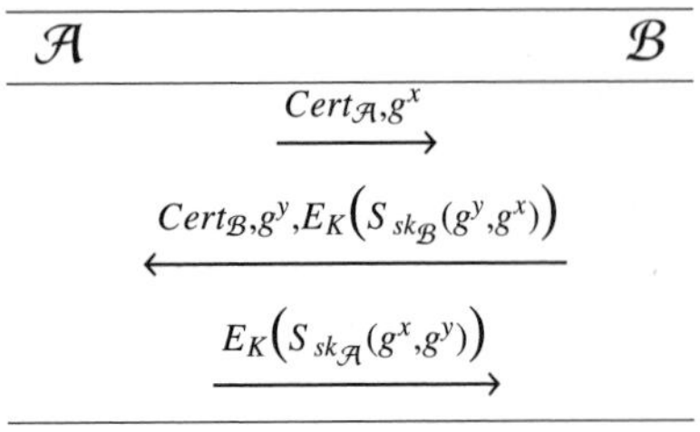

FIGURE 40.4   Station-To-Station [3].

- $\mathcal{T}$ computes $E_{K_{AT}}(N_A, K_{AB}, ID_B, E_{K_{BT}}(K_{AB}, ID_A))$ and sends it back to $\mathcal{A}$, where K_{AB} is a key $\mathcal{T}$ chooses randomly for $\mathcal{A}$ and $\mathcal{B}$. K_{AB} will be the session key;
- $\mathcal{A}$ decrypts the message received and checks that the identity of her intended partner is correct and that the nonce N_A is the one picked previously. If any checks fail, the protocol is aborted. Otherwise, she sends $E_{K_{BT}}(K_{AB}, ID_A)$ to $\mathcal{B}$;
- $\mathcal{B}$ decrypts the received message and discovers the identity of his intended partner ID_A. $\mathcal{B}$ computes $E_{K_{AB}}(ID_A, N_B)$ and sends it to $\mathcal{A}$, where N_B is a nonce generated randomly;
- $\mathcal{A}$ decrypts the message received using key K_{AB}, and checks to see if the identity is correct. If it is, she computes $E_{K_{AB}}(N_B - 1)$, and sends it to $\mathcal{B}$;
- Finally, $\mathcal{B}$ decrypts the last message received using key K_{AB}, and checks to see if the decrypted value is indeed equal to $N_B - 1$.

The protocol seems complex, but the underlying authentication mechanism that is exploited throughout is essentially this: When one entity, say $\mathcal{A}$, encrypts a string (m, N), where m is some message and N is a nonce that $\mathcal{A}$ chose randomly, and that nonce is returned to $\mathcal{A}$ subsequently, then $\mathcal{A}$ has the proof that the nonce N and message m were indeed decrypted by the correct entity. Thus, $\mathcal{A}$ can safely continue participating in the protocol. In contrast, if the returned value of the nonce is not what is expected, the protocol is abandoned. Using randomly chosen nonces from one exchange to the next associates unique numbers to each exchange. This keeps a man in the middle from replaying stale data from previous unrelated exchanges. Also, incorporating identities in the clear (and in the encryptions) prevents the adversary from trying to transmit messages to unintended recipients. Finally, notice that the last two flows are composed of encryptions under the session key K_{AB}. This is used to prove to each party that the other actually possesses the right key. We shall return to this important property later.

Relying on Public-Key Infrastructure

Another type of preestablished long-term keying material that can be used is *certified public key/secret key pairs*.

This requires a trusted CA to *digitally sign* messages binding parties' identities to their public keying material. These signed messages are known as *certificates*. Let pk_{CA} and sk_{CA} be the CA's public verification and private signature keys respectively. (See Chapter 37 for information on digital signatures.) The certificate of a given party will also contain descriptions of the instantiated mathematical objects used in the public-key algorithms. Let $Cert_A$ (resp., $Cert_B$) denote $\mathcal{A}$'s (resp., $\mathcal{B}$'s) certificate. Below we describe the main flows of the well-known Station-To-Station protocol (STS; see [3]). Let G be a cyclic group of order denote n in which DDH is believed to hold, g be a generator for G, E be a symmetric encryption algorithm, and S be the signature algorithm of a digital signature scheme. (See Chapter 37.) The protocol runs as follows:

- $\mathcal{A}$ sends to $\mathcal{B}$ the data $Cert_A$ and g^x, where x is chosen at random, and $Cert_A$ contains the group parameters and a description of E. It also contains $\mathcal{A}$'s public signature verification key, pk_A;
- $\mathcal{B}$ first verifies the CA's signature on $Cert_A$ using CA's public key pk_{CA}. If this check fails, $\mathcal{B}$ aborts the protocol. Otherwise, he replies to $\mathcal{A}$ with $Cert_B$, g^y, $c_B := E_K(S_{sk_B}(g^y, g^x))$, where y is chosen at random, $\mathcal{B}$ computes $K = g^{xy}$, $S_{sk_B}(g^y, g^x)$ is a digital signature under key sk_B of (g^y, g^x), and finally c_B is an encryption of the signature under K;
- $\mathcal{A}$ checks the CA's signature on $Cert_B$ using pk_A. If this check fails, the protocol is aborted. Otherwise, she computes $K := g^{xy}$ and decrypts c_B using K to obtain $S_{sk_B}(g^y, g^x)$. She verifies this signature on message (g^y, g^x) using pk_B. If this check fails, the protocol is aborted. Otherwise, she computes a signature $S_{sk_A}(g^x, g^y)$ on (g^x, g^y) using her private signing key sk_A, and then computes an encryption $c_A := E_K(S_{sk_A}(g^x, g^y))$ that she sends back to $\mathcal{B}$;
- Finally, $\mathcal{B}$ decrypts c_A using K and verifies the obtained signature using $\mathcal{A}$'s public verification key pk_A. The session key is set to being $K = g^{xy}$.

In this scheme, the authentication is basically provided by the digital signatures. A party is certain that a message was indeed signed by another entity if the signature verification equation under that entity's public key holds. The CA's role is to make sure that an adversary cannot simply replace an honest party's public key with her own in a certificate, since this would require forging a signature under the CA's key. Also, similarly to the Needham-Schroeder protocol, the values g^x and g^y can be viewed as numbers that, in addition to computing a joint session key, serve as unique identifiers for the key exchange, in order to prevent replay attacks. Notice also that the session key K is actually used in the protocol to encrypt the signatures, allowing the parties to demonstrate to one another that they have computed the correct session key.

2. PASSWORD-AUTHENTICATED KEY EXCHANGE

The Need for User-Friendly, Password-Based Solutions

All of the methods described so far have a common property: Whether the long-term keying material is symmetric and shared by both users, or asymmetric and certified using a PKI, keys are long and difficult to use in common applications. One could argue that this information could be embedded in security tokens that users could carry such as smartcards, USB security tokens, and so on. However, this requires additional hardware that will certainly have a cost. It may also introduce compatibility issues in cases when the tokens need to be plugged into another device. Finally, such tokens can always be compromised through loss or theft.

Another method that has been considered to authenticate users involves using human *biometrics*. While such data is indeed unique to the user and—in a certain sense—unforgettable, its use raises many other issues, such as privacy considerations or variability of readings. A further drawback is that biometrics cannot be replaced in case of compromise. The necessary hardware to put in place is also quite expensive.

Nowadays, the most common form of authentication in use is via knowledge of passwords. Passwords are cheap and convenient. They are easy to choose, use, and change when needed, and they are typically human-memorable. The pervasiveness of this method of authentication is the main motivation behind research in *Password-Authenticated Key Exchange* (PAKE).

The objective of a PAKE protocol is to perform an authenticated key exchange like those described above, but assuming that the long-term keying material is **just a password that both parties involved share**.[3] Such a scheme combines the effectiveness of key exchange in producing cryptographically strong session keys with the convenience of authenticating oneself by demonstrating knowledge of a simple password.

However, convenience is often accompanied by security degradation in cryptography; using passwords instead of strong cryptographic keys is no exception and brings forth some important issues that we try to explain in the following sections.

New Security Threats

Using passwords rather than long, cryptographically strong keys to authenticate key exchange protocol flows

---

3. There are also variations of this: For instance, one party may hold the password and the other a function of this password. Typically, the function will be a hash function.

is not straightforward. For instance, a password cannot just replace a strong symmetric key as input to a classical key exchange protocol. There are mainly two reasons for this.

First for all, passwords are low-entropy data. This makes them vulnerable to *dictionary attacks*, which are essentially brute-force guessing attacks. Second, passwords are quite often mismanaged (e.g., written down or used across several applications). This frequently leads to password compromise, which must be taken into account in PAKE design.

Dictionary Attacks

In classical key exchange, exhaustively searching for the correct long-term key can simply not be done feasibly by construction: It is completely random and very long. A password on the other hand is likely to be short and produced with less-than-ideal randomness from a small set of values, making exhaustive search possible. We illustrate the effects of this phenomenon with a "dummy" protocol.

Assume that A and B share a password pw and the description of some group G and generator g for G. Further assume that they share the description of some cryptographic hash function H. A and B can attempt to engage in the following variant of the Diffie-Hellman key exchange introduced earlier:

- A first chooses $x \in \mathbb{Z}_n$ randomly and computes g^x and $h := H(pw, g^x, ID_A, ID_B)$. By the properties of the function H, the value h binds A's identity ID_A, her target recipient's identity ID_B, and her password to her chosen value. It also effectively hides the password. A sends (g^x, h, ID_A) to B;
- Upon receiving h and g^x, B computes $H(pw, g^x, ID_A, ID_B)$ and checks that it equals h. He thus gains assurance that he indeed received the data from A. He now chooses $y \in \mathbb{Z}_n$ randomly, computes $h' := H(pw, g^y, g^x, ID_A, ID_B)$, and sends back (g^y, h', ID_B). He computes the key g^{xy};
- Finally, A checks to see if h' is equal to $H(pw, g^y, g^x, ID_A, ID_B)$, and if so computes the key g^{xy}.

This protocol is vulnerable to a dictionary attack: An eavesdropper can simply record the first message, (g^x, h, ID_A), and test candidate passwords pw' against h. If for some value pw' the adversary obtains $h = H(pw', g^x, ID_A, ID_B)$, it is very likely that she has found the password. Note that the password is *never directly revealed in the protocol*.

This kind of attack is arguably the most important one to prevent in PAKE design because an attacker need not be online to perform it. Offline attackers have more time and computational power for the simple reason that they may be impossible to interrupt. Indeed, in the above example it was only necessary for the adversary to record an exchange. From then on, there is no way to interfere with the adversary's behavior. We call such attacks *offline dictionary attacks*. To prevent them, it is necessary that protocol runs leak not a single bit of information on the underlying password, even if the attacker is engaging in the protocol, and injecting her own data by trying to impersonate a party. This has an important consequence for authentication; we will return to this point later.

Online dictionary attacks are active attacks in which the adversary tries to guess the password through successive login attempts: The adversary engages over and over in the protocol, trying out different passwords, and when the opposing party stops aborting, the adversary knows it guessed the right password. It is clear that protocol design cannot prevent this attack from occurring; however, a well-constructed PAKE should only allow one password to be tested per login attempt. From that point on, it is up to the application supporting the protocol to specify how many failed attempts can be tolerated before, for instance, locking the targeted account.

Forward Secrecy and Known Session Keys

A user's password in a PAKE protocol is viewed as a long-term key (i.e., it is expected to be used many times to create random, independent session keys). It obviously plays a role in the computations of session keys' exchange transcripts and may even appear as an argument to the formula producing the session keys themselves. These relationships cannot be ignored.

On the one hand, passwords are notoriously mismanaged data: They are routinely lost, shared (with unintended parties), and used across several applications. This very often leads to the password getting compromised. Once this occurs, there clearly is no way of stopping an adversary with knowledge of the password from impersonating its rightful owner, at least until the breach is discovered. However, the scheme should ensure that despite this breach, past established session keys remain secure. This property is known as *forward secrecy*.

On the other hand, we have the session keys: There are potentially many of them, and there are no restrictions whatsoever concerning their use. This includes of course running them as input to possibly insecure algorithms. Also, session keys are ephemeral data by nature, but disposing of them after they have served their purpose may not be such an easy task in practice. Given all of this, it is wise to assume that whole session keys may actually be compromised during or after their use. Hence, a PAKE should guarantee that such a disclosure does not breach its security. In particular, this must not leak any password information either. This is referred to as the *known-session key security*.

Other Security Properties

Dictionary attacks are specific to PAKE protocols. However, the forward secrecy and known-session key security were actually first considered in classical key exchange and subsequently carried over to the password-based case. It may be tempting to do this with all security properties that can be defined for key exchange in general, but this is not always possible. For instance, resistance to *key compromise impersonation*—in which an adversary who compromised a user's long-term key can then impersonate other parties to that user—is not satisfied by a PAKE: The other holder of the password can always be impersonated to the attacked user.

Another notion of security that is specific to the password-based case is that of *server compromise resistance* (see [6] or [7]). It arises in the following case: when one of the two parties is a server holding a function of the user's password rather than the password itself. Any ordinary PAKE can be easily converted into one that fits this situation by simply hashing the password for instance. (Ordinary PAKEs are sometimes referred to as *balanced* protocols while the server compromise-resistant ones are known as *augmented* PAKEs.) This captures a realistic scenario: One server may hold functions of many different users which open sessions with it to access various resources. Resistance to server compromise then basically states that the server cannot impersonate a user unless it first performs a dictionary attack on the data it holds. Let us mention that this notion has been disputed, essentially because if server data is indeed compromised, it makes no sense to consider the related passwords safe since they are trivially vulnerable to offline searches. In the remainder of this chapter, we concentrate on balanced PAKEs.

Key Confirmation and Authentication in PAKE

We mentioned earlier that resistance to offline dictionary attacks has an effect on authentication; we return to this issue now. As explained earlier, a PAKE protocol transcript cannot be allowed to leak a single bit of information on the password. This implies that no mechanism can be in place to directly ensure at either end of the protocol that the correct password is being used by the other party. For instance, the password cannot satisfy any kind of efficiently verifiable equation, which happens to be the flaw of the dummy protocol in Figure 40.5. In contrast, this is exactly how a digital signature scheme functions, the key

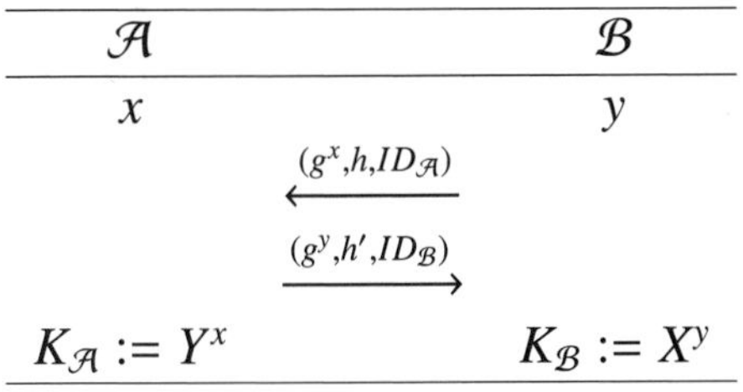

FIGURE 40.5   Dummy password authentication protocol.

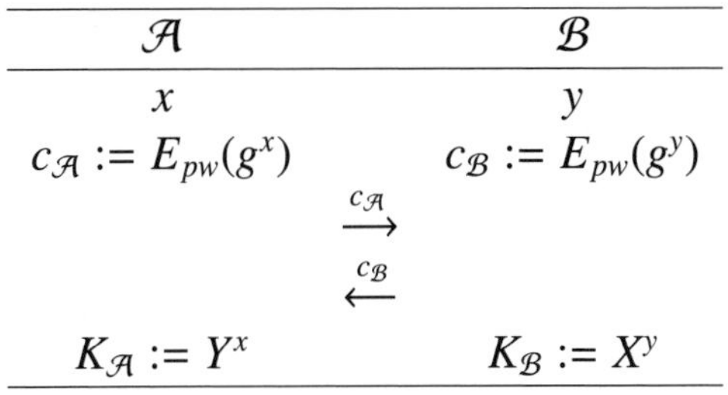

FIGURE 40.6   Encrypted key exchange.

difference again being that the long-term secret is cryptographically strong. This is the method behind STS.

This makes key confirmation the only way to obtain explicit authentication: Both parties are sure that they have been talking to their intended partner if and only if they can determine that they have computed the same session key. This is especially important in the password-based setting because a server cannot tell a failed login attempt from a successful one without explicit authentication. Yet, this obviously needs to be determined before granting or denying the right to opening a session, and in the latter case, incrementing a rejection counter.

3. CONCRETE PROTOCOLS

In this section we describe three concrete PAKEs. We give an overview of their properties, security guarantees, and known flaws. All three protocols require the parties—A and B—to share the description of a cyclic group G of large order n. Such information can be directly hard-coded into the program specification running the protocol. Of course, A and B also share a password pw.

PAKE research mainly began in the early 1990s [8]. Since then, the research community has produced many different protocols. We chose to present the three algorithms below mainly because they are simple to describe, quite efficient, and have been proposed for standardization. Information relative to their industrial and commercial deployment is described later in this chapter.

For each protocol, we begin by describing the heart of the mechanism itself: the protocol flows that contain the information for computing the shared key. We then go on to discuss the security properties and weaknesses. Finally, we give full descriptions of the protocols, or variants thereof, that have been proposed for standardization. In particular, these descriptions also contain various examples of key confirmation procedures.

Encrypted Key Exchange

The first PAKE ever designed was proposed in 1992 by Bellovin and Merrit [8] and is known as Encrypted Key Exchange, or EKE (see Figure 40.6). The authors were the first to tackle the problem of preventing offline dictionary attacks. To describe the main protocol flow, we first need some notation. E will denote a symmetric encryption algorithm, with D the associated decryption algorithm. (See Chapter 37.) We will designate encryption under key k with E_k and the corresponding decryption with D_k. Similarly to the description of the group G, algorithms E and D are hard-coded into the program specification. Concretely, the group G used will be the multiplicative group $\mathbb{Z}_p^*$ of invertible integers modulo some large prime p of the form $p = 2q + 1$ for some prime q. Thus, G is of order $p - 1$. (See Chapter 37.) Let g be a generator of G. It is conjectured that the CDH assumption holds in this case.

The protocol works as follows:

- A first chooses $x \in \mathbb{Z}_{p-1}$ randomly and computes g^x and $c_A := E_{pw}(g^x)$. She sends c_A to B;
- Upon receiving c_A, B recovers g^x by computing $D_{pw}(c_A)$. He now chooses $y \in \mathbb{Z}_{p-1}$ randomly, computes $c_B := E_{pw}(g^y)$, and sends back c_B. He computes the key g^{xy};
- Finally, A recovers g^y by computing $D_{pw}(c_B)$, and computes the key g^{xy}.

Security and Efficiency

Security and Efficiency by Design

The main idea behind the dictionary attack resistance of this protocol is that if the data encrypted using algorithm E under key pw is random enough, then verification of the password becomes infeasible. More concretely, if pw' is some other password, the string $D_{pw'}(c_A)$ cannot be told apart from g^x because x, and therefore g^x, is random. In theory, this is a very elegant observation, but we shall see below that it is highly nontrivial to implement in practice, an issue we address in the next sections. Online dictionary attacks are essentially prevented by the fact that if the algorithm E is indeed suitable, it should yield different encryption functions for different passwords.

Forward secrecy is argued to hold for a very simple reason: The shared value g^{xy} is completely independent of the password. Indeed, assuming the password has been discovered, the only information an attacker can get consists of the two values g^x and g^y from which g^{xy} cannot be computed. Similarly, since random numbers are independently generated from one session key to the next, compromise of previous keys does not affect the security of new ones.

In terms of efficiency, the protocol performs quite well. Since it only requires adding (symmetric) encryption and decryption operations at each user's end, it is only slightly more costly than the original Diffie-Hellman protocol. (Of course, the ultimate efficiency of the protocol depends also on how the encryption function is instantiated, but in general symmetric encryption mechanisms are quite efficient.) Since it requires the CDH assumption to hold in the underlying group, it is necessary to have p be at least 1024 bits long. Therefore, the random numbers that should be chosen by each party need to be 1024 bits long as well.

Security in Theory

It should also be mentioned that the security of EKE's main protocol flows has been studied from a purely theoretical point of view [9]. In this work, the protocol and several of its variants have been *proven secure*; that is, a very precise mathematical proof of security was given (we refer to [9] for exact definitions) assuming that the encryption function satisfies some idealized properties. This is methodologically important and theoretically interesting; however, such proofs do not necessarily immediately translate into real-world security guarantees, as demonstrated in the following section.

Flaws

The protocol, as it is defined, can be made vulnerable to dictionary attacks. The main issue is that even if it is a strictly random element of G, g^x is not randomly distributed in E's plaintext space. Concretely, this means that we cannot expect that for every possible candidate password pw', the decryption $D_{pw'}(c_A)$ will fall into $\mathbb{Z}_p^*$; therefore, every time such a test fails, a password can be ruled out. It has been shown (see, e.g., [10]) that the password in use can be very quickly determined by observing just a few protocol runs. Such attacks are known as *partition attacks* because from one protocol run to the next, the list of potentially valid passwords is roughly halved.

Bellovin and Merrit had already noticed this in their work introducing EKE [8]. They proposed some countermeasures such as choosing p as close as possible to the next power of 2, or encrypting $g^x + jp$ rather than g^x where jp is added using a nonmodular operation, and j is constructed in a particular way (see [8] for details). Unfortunately, these ad-hoc fixes are not completely

satisfactory. As of yet, they have not been adequately modeled so as to systematically measure their contribution to the protocol's security, and it is not clear that they can be. This makes them difficult to analyze precisely. Furthermore, they do not solve the problem completely anyway: The number of strings obtained by decryption that an adversary can gain meaningful information from may be reduced, but it does not drop to zero.

These instantiation issues illustrate the subtlety of defending against dictionary attacks in practice; another example comes from examining the choice of the underlying group itself. Here we have $G = \mathbb{Z}_p^*$ for a prime p. The idea behind this choice is that any bitstring that corresponds to an integer between 1 and $p - 1$ is necessarily an element of the group. Hence, if a trial decryption of c_A with some candidate password yields such a bitstring, there is no way to tell if that password was correct or not. On the other hand, other groups commonly used in cryptography are built in such a way that their elements verify special properties; these cannot be used here again because from trial decryptions may result strings that do not verify these properties, indicating that the tested password was not the right one.

These flaws are not captured in the theoretical security studies we mentioned above precisely because the modeling of encryption by an idealized process completely hides problems that may arise with concrete instantiations.

Proposed Standardization

In 2000, Bellare and Rogaway proposed a PAKE protocol based essentially on EKE for IEEE standardization: AuthA [11]. One of the main concerns the authors raise in their work involves instantiating the encryption function. The security flaws discussed above clearly show that this needs to be done very carefully. In particular, there is no straightforward way to directly replace the ideal cipher with a concrete symmetric encryption algorithm. The authors propose to replace the encrypting operation with multiplying the group element by a hash of the password, allowing them to rely on idealizing a hash function rather than an encryption function. This seems less dangerous because hoping that one concrete fixed function looks random enough is viewed as more reasonable than hoping the same of an entire family of functions parameterized by poorly chosen secrets. Also, it is easier to hash into a group than to force a decryption function to map into a group for all possible decryption keys, so using groups other than $\mathbb{Z}_p^*$ is conceivable in this case. For simplicity, we will assume that $G = \mathbb{Z}_p^*$, with p a prime of the form $p = 2q + 1$, where q is a prime as well. As usual, let g be a generator of G, E be the encryption algorithm, and D be the corresponding decryption algorithm. Finally, let H be a hash function. We assume that $\mathcal{A}$ and $\mathcal{B}$ know this data.

AuthA runs as follows:

- $\mathcal{A}$ first chooses $x \in \mathbb{Z}_{p-1}$ randomly and computes g^x and $c_\mathcal{A} := E_{pw}(g^x)$. She sends $c_\mathcal{A}$ to $\mathcal{B}$;
- Upon receiving $c_\mathcal{A}$, $\mathcal{B}$ recovers g^x by computing $D_{pw}(c_\mathcal{A})$. He now chooses $y \in \mathbb{Z}_{p-1}$ randomly, computes $c_\mathcal{B} := E_{pw}(g^y)$, g^{xy}, $MK := H(g^x, g^y, g^{xy})$ (MK for "Master Key"), $h := H(MK, 1)$, and sends $c_\mathcal{B}$ and h to $\mathcal{B}$;
- Upon receiving $c_\mathcal{B}$ and h, $\mathcal{A}$ recovers g^y by computing $D_{pw}(c_\mathcal{B})$, and computes g^{xy} and $MK := H(g^x, g^y, g^{xy})$. She then checks to see if the value h received is equal to $H(MK, 1)$. If not, the protocol is aborted. Otherwise, she computes $K := H(MK, 0)$, $h' := H(MK, 2)$, accepts the session key to be K, and sends h' back to $\mathcal{B}$;
- Finally, upon receiving h', $\mathcal{B}$ checks to see if this value is equal to $H(MK, 2)$. If not, the protocol is aborted. Otherwise, $\mathcal{B}$ computes $K := H(MK, 0)$, which he accepts as the session key.

AuthA as described above is one of four different possibilities considered by the authors in [11]. We have chosen to describe the one in which there is mutual authentication through an additional key confirmation process. This process is depicted in Figure 40.7. Ignoring the flaws of the encrypted flows for now, we concentrate first on explaining how the key is confirmed using the hash function. (Another example is given in the full version of SPEKE below.) We return afterwards to considerations on the encryption.

Key Confirmation and Mutual Authentication

In the second step, once $\mathcal{B}$ has computed g^{xy}, he also computes a so-called master key MK from g^{xy}. This data, and the properties of the hash function H, will allow him to prove to $\mathcal{A}$ that he has computed the correct key and will also let him verify that $\mathcal{A}$ has done so as well. In the third step of the protocol, $\mathcal{A}$ computes the master key as well. If h_1 is indeed equal to $H(MK, 1)$, $\mathcal{A}$ is assured that both she and the entity that computed h_1 hold the same master key, therefore also the same value g^{xy}, and

therefore the same password. Since by assumption only $\mathcal{B}$ should know this password, $\mathcal{A}$ concludes that she is indeed speaking with $\mathcal{B}$, and that $\mathcal{B}$ can compute the same session key. A similar argument can be made on $\mathcal{B}$'s end, with h_2.

On the Security of Hash-and-Multiply Instantiations of the Encryption Process

Since at the heart of AuthA lie the main flows of EKE, it suffers from the same flaws. We return now to examining how E can be instantiated using a hash function rather than a block cipher. Two methods for accomplishing this have been suggested by the authors in [11]. Let H' be a hash function different from H and that maps strings into the group G. For a group element z and a password pw, the encryption of z under key pw can be:

i. $E_{pw}(z) := z.H'(pw)$, or
ii. $E_{pw}(z) := (r, z.H'(pw, r))$ for some randomly chosen string r.

In both formulas, $z.H'$ is the group multiplication of z by H'.

Using this method, we no longer need to rely on idealizing a block cipher to mathematically prove security. However, we still need to rely on idealizing a hash function. While this is viewed as more "realizable" in practice, it still does not guarantee security, and it can be vulnerable to attacks. A thorough theoretical study in idealized models of the security of various variants of AuthA, including ones in which the encryption is instantiated through hash-and-multiply methods, can be found in [12] and [13]. In these works, once again the protocols are proven secure under idealized assumptions. Yet, real-world attacks on these same variants of AuthA, including those in which hashing replaces encrypting, can be found in [14]. They all involve essentially attacking the procedure used for encryption. The authors also propose a possible instantiation of their own for the hash-and-multiply method, but still warn that it may be subject to attack.

$\mathcal{A}$		$\mathcal{B}$
		$MK := H(g^x, g^y, g^{xy})$
	$\overset{h}{\leftarrow}$	$h := H(MK, 1)$
$MK := H(g^x, g^y, g^{xy})$		
Verify $h = H(MK, 1)$		
$h' := H(MK, 2)$	$\overset{h'}{\rightarrow}$	
		Verify $h' = H(MK, 2)$

FIGURE 40.7   Key confirmation with a master key.

Simple Password Exponential Key Exchange

Another popular protocol that was first proposed in 1996 by Jablon [15] is Simple Password Exponential Key Exchange (see Figure 40.8), or SPEKE. It was initially designed to avoid having to encrypt data using the password as the key, so as to avoid the problems that EKE suffers from. Instead, the password is used to derive the group's generator. The group G considered for SPEKE is the unique prime order subgroup of order q of the multiplicative group $\mathbb{Z}_p^*$, where again p is chosen to be a prime of the form $p = 2q + 1$. We assume that passwords can easily be viewed as elements in $\mathbb{Z}_p^*$. The protocol runs as follows:

- $\mathcal{A}$ first chooses $x \in \mathbb{Z}_q$ randomly and computes $X := pw^{2x}$. She sends X to $\mathcal{B}$;
- Upon receiving X, $\mathcal{B}$ chooses $y \in \mathbb{Z}_q$ randomly, computes $Y := pw^{2y}$, and sends back Y. He computes the key $X^{2y} = pw^{4xy}$;
- Finally, $\mathcal{A}$ computes the key $Y^{2x} = pw^{4xy}$.

In each of the flows and in the final key computation, the squaring operation is necessary to make sure the resulting element of $\mathbb{Z}_p^*$ is actually in G. (This prevents so-called *subgroup confinement attacks*; see [15].)

Security and Efficiency

Security and Efficiency by Design

Offline dictionary attack resistance in SPEKE is basically due to the fact that pw^2 generates G. This implies that pw^{2x} and pw^{2y} are random, independent elements in G, so they leak no information on pw. In case the key pw^{4xy} is leaked to the adversary as well, there does not seem to be any way to compute the password other than by first computing the discrete logarithm of the key to the base, say pw^{2x}, and then computing pw from pw^{2y}. Since DLP is presumed hard in G, this is infeasible. Finally, forward secrecy is basically ensured through the DDH assumption, which holds in G. (We mention here that it does not hold in the whole of $\mathbb{Z}_p^*$, however.)

$\mathcal{A}$	$\mathcal{B}$
x	y
$X := pw^{2x}$	$Y := pw^{2y}$
	$\xrightarrow{\quad X \quad}$
	$\xleftarrow{\quad Y \quad}$
$K_{\mathcal{A}} := Y^{2x}$	$K_{\mathcal{B}} := X^{2y}$

FIGURE 40.8 Simple password exponential key exchange.

The protocol is clearly very efficient, as it essentially consists of a Diffie-Hellman Key Exchange. As with EKE, the prime p has to be at least 1024 bits in length, so as to be sure the computing discrete logarithms will be difficult. Thus, also as in EKE, the random numbers chosen by the parties are quite large: at least 1023 bits in this case.

Security in Theory

Similarly to EKE, SPEKE's security has been theoretically studied. Namely, a proof of security for it can be found in [16]. However, without getting into the specific details, the result only guarantees that a *constant* number of passwords may be tested per online impersonation attempt, rather than at most one. Also, the model assumes idealized hash functions, similarly to the use of idealized encryption to analyze SPEKE. Finally, it is interesting to note that the formal proof of security rests on a rather rarely seen computational hardness assumption: the *decision additive-inverted Diffie-Hellman problem*. We refer to [16] for details.

Flaws

It has been shown in [17] that is possible to test many more than one password per impersonation attempt. For this to occur, the adversary first needs to find sets of passwords that are *exponentially equivalent*.

A set of passwords $\{pw_i\}$ is said to form an *exponential equivalence class* if there exists some integer a and a set of integers $\{j_i\}$ such that for all i we have $pw_i = a^{j_i}$. Since the password space is a small subset of $\mathbb{Z}_p^*$, an adversary can potentially find many such classes efficiently simply by computing successive sets of integers of the form a^j for various values of a and j. The point is, by impersonating one party and sending the single value a^r for any integer r, one protocol execution allows the adversary to test all of the passwords in the set $\{pw_i\}$. The details on this attack can be found in [17].

Now, testing implies that the adversary is able to verify its guess against the values it receives from the honest party. This is not strictly possible in the protocol described above; however, we already explained that PAKE protocols need key confirmation to achieve mutual authentication. Adding the key confirmation mechanism is what lets the adversary verify its guess, completing the attack.

We emphasize that this is not an argument against key confirmation, which is important for PAKE, but rather a reminder that in assessing a protocol's security correctly, all flows and the interactions between them should be considered simultaneously.

Proposed Standardization

A fully constrained SPEKE requires the parties to share knowledge of a large prime p of the form $p = 2q + 1$

where q is also prime. They also share the description of two distinct cryptographic hash function H_1 and H_2. The protocol runs as follows:

- $\mathcal{A}$ chooses $x \in \mathbb{Z}_q$ randomly and computes $X := H_1(pw)^{2x}$. She sends X to $\mathcal{B}$;
- Upon receiving X, $\mathcal{B}$ chooses $y \in \mathbb{Z}_q$ randomly, computes $Y := H_1(pw)^{2y}$ and X^{2y}. If this last value is 1 or $p - 1$, he aborts the protocol. Otherwise, he computes $K := H_2(X^{2y})$ and $h := H_2(H_2(K))$. He sends Y and h to $\mathcal{A}$, and the session key will be K;
- Upon receiving Y and h, $\mathcal{A}$ computes Y^{2x}. If this value is 1 or $p - 1$, she aborts the protocol. Otherwise, she computes $K = H_2(Y^{2x})$, and checks to see if h is equal to $H_2(H_2(K))$. If not, she aborts the protocol. Otherwise, she computes $h' = H_2(K)$, and sends h' back to $\mathcal{B}$. She sets the session key to being K;
- Finally, upon receiving h', $\mathcal{B}$ checks to see if h' equals $H_2(K)$. If not, he aborts; otherwise, he sets the session key to K.

A slight variant of SPEKE has been proposed for IEEE 1363.2 standardization by its inventor [15]. It differs from the protocol presented earlier in two ways. First, a key confirmation mechanism has been added, using the hash function H_2. Second, rather than squaring the password in $\mathbb{Z}_p^*$, it is first hashed using H_1. The efficiency of the protocol remains essentially the same, as hashing is a cheap operation. The key confirmation mechanism used here is portrayed in Figure 40.9. We now discuss the use of the additional operations that are performed.

Checking that X^{2y} and Y^{2x} are different from 1 and $p - 1$ ensures that the initial jointly computed value is not the group's neutral element. This is necessary to prevent *subgroup confinement attacks*, see [15] for details. It is interesting to observe what is accomplished by the hashing operations.

Key Confirmation and Mutual Authentication

In the second protocol step, $\mathcal{B}$ computes h as $H_2(H_2(K))$ and sends this data to $\mathcal{A}$. The properties of the hash function guarantee that only the holder of the correct key K could have computed this string. Thus, in verifying that the value h she receives equals $H_2(H_2(K))$ where K here

is the value of the session key she computes at her end, $\mathcal{A}$ gains confirmation that all along she has been communicating to an entity that must have had the correct password, since it was able to compute the right key. Since by assumption only $\mathcal{B}$ should know the password, $\mathcal{A}$ can safely conclude that she is indeed talking to $\mathcal{B}$, and furthermore that he has computed the session key. By a similar reasoning with h', $\mathcal{B}$ receives confirmation that he is indeed talking to $\mathcal{A}$, and that $\mathcal{A}$ holds the key.

Note that the reason $H_2(H_2(K))$ is sent *before* $H_2(K)$ is that when sent in this order, neither value can be computed by an adversary in time to attempt any damage. If $H_2(K)$ were sent first, an adversary could compute $H_2(H_2(K))$ on her own and fool $\mathcal{B}$ into thinking $\mathcal{A}$ has the key, while she may actually have nothing.

Defending against Exponential Equivalence

The role of the function H_1 is to prevent the attack described earlier. Hashing the password before squaring it makes it more difficult for an adversary to exploit exponential equivalence. However, known hash functions are not designed to guarantee that applying them to different values leads to integers that are not exponentially equivalent. See [17] for more details on this.

Password-Authenticated Key Exchange by Juggling

The last protocol we discuss is the J-PAKE [18] protocol of Hao and Ryan, first proposed in 2008. This protocol can be instantiated with any prime order cyclic group G in which the DDH assumption holds. Let G be such a group, g be a generator of G, and denote the order of G by q. J-PAKE also requires a *Zero Knowledge Proof* (ZKP) protocol for proving knowledge of discrete logarithms. Before describing J-PAKE, we briefly explain the role of the ZKP.

Interlude: Proving Knowledge of Discrete Logarithms

A ZKP protocol is run between two entities, the *prover* $\mathcal{P}$ and the *verifier* $\mathcal{V}$. The purpose of the protocol is for $\mathcal{P}$ to convince $\mathcal{V}$ that a certain statement is true without revealing any more information on that statement. For this to be

$\mathcal{A}$		$\mathcal{B}$
	$\overset{h}{\longleftarrow}$	$h := H_2(H_2(K))$
Verify $h := H_2(H_2(K))$		
$h' := H_2(K)$	$\overset{h'}{\longrightarrow}$	
		Verify $h' := H_2(K)$

FIGURE 40.9 Key confirmation with double hashing.

of any use to $\mathcal{V}$, it should be infeasible for a cheating $\mathcal{P}$ to trick $\mathcal{V}$ into believing a false statement.

Concretely, in our case $\mathcal{P}$ and $\mathcal{V}$ each know the description of group G and generator g, $\mathcal{P}$ holds a secret value $x \in \mathbb{Z}_q$, and $\mathcal{V}$ holds the public value g^x. The ZKP should allow $\mathcal{P}$ to convince $\mathcal{V}$ that $\mathcal{P}$ truly knows x, without revealing any information about x to $\mathcal{V}$ beyond that already revealed by g^x. Also, if $\mathcal{P}$ does not know x, it should be unable to produce a statement that would convince $\mathcal{V}$ that it does.

We denote $ZKP(x, g)$ the output of the algorithm that computes a proof of knowledge of x to the base g. We will give an example of how to instantiate ZKP with Schnorr signatures further below. More on ZKPs can be found for instance in [19].

J-PAKE

Let pw be the password that $\mathcal{A}$ and $\mathcal{B}$ share. We assume that it can be viewed as an element of $\mathbb{Z}_q$ and that $pw \neq 0$ [18]. The key exchange protocol runs as follows (see Figure 40.10):

- $\mathcal{A}$ chooses x_1 and x_2 randomly in $\mathbb{Z}_q$, with $x_2 \neq 0$, and computes $X_1 := g^{x_1}$, $X_2 := g^{x_2}$, and proofs of knowledge $ZKP(x_1, g)$ and $ZKP(x_2, g)$. She sends $(X_1, X_2, ZKP(x_1, g), ZKP(x_2, g))$ to $\mathcal{B}$;
- Upon receiving the first message, $\mathcal{B}$ verifies the knowledge proofs. He then chooses x_3 and x_4 randomly in $\mathbb{Z}_q$, with $x_4 \neq 0$, and computes X_3, X_4, $ZKP(x_3, g)$, and $ZKP(x_4, g)$. The tuple $(X_3, X_4, ZKP(x_3, g), ZKP(x_4, g))$ is sent back to $\mathcal{A}$;
- $\mathcal{A}$ verifies the knowledge proofs. She then computes $X_{\mathcal{A}} := (X_1 X_3 X_4)^{x_2 pw}$, a proof of knowledge $ZKP(x_2 pw, X_1 X_3 X_4)$, and sends $(X_{\mathcal{A}}, ZKP(x_2 pw, X_1 X_3 X_4))$ to $\mathcal{B}$;
- $\mathcal{B}$ once again verifies the new knowledge proof. He then similarly computes $X_{\mathcal{B}} := (X_3 X_1 X_2)^{x_4 pw}$, $ZKP(x_4 pw, X_3 X_1 X_2)$, and returns $(X_{\mathcal{B}}, ZKP(x_4 pw, X_3 X_1 X_2))$ to $\mathcal{A}$. He finally computes key $K_{\mathcal{B}} := (X_{\mathcal{A}}(X_2)^{-x_4})^{x_4 pw}$;

- Upon receiving $(X_{\mathcal{B}}, ZKP(x_4 pw, X_3 X_1 X_2))$, $\mathcal{A}$ verifies the knowledge proof, and computes the key $K_{\mathcal{A}} := (X_{\mathcal{B}}(X_4)^{-x_2})^{x_2 pw}$.

A careful examination of the group elements sent shows that $K_{\mathcal{A}} = K_{\mathcal{B}} = g^{(x_1 + x_3) x_2 x_4 pw}$.

A Concrete ZKP Protocol

The authors of [18] suggest using Schnorr signatures [20] to prove knowledge of exponents to a given base. We review how this is done here. We keep the earlier notation that was shown; let H be a hash function. Suppose prover $\mathcal{P}$ wishes to prove knowledge of x such that $X = g^x$ to verifier $\mathcal{V}$. The prover does the following:

i. $\mathcal{P}$ selects v randomly from $\mathbb{Z}_q$;
ii. $\mathcal{P}$ sets $V := g^v$ and $h := H(\mathcal{P}, g, V, X)$;
iii. $\mathcal{P}$ sets $r := v - xh$;
iv. $\mathcal{P}$'s proof is (V, r).

To verify the proof, $\mathcal{V}$ first checks that V is a valid group element, that is, is of order q, and then checks that $V = g^r X^h$, where he recomputes h using H, his input (g, X, V), and $\mathcal{P}$'s identity.

The security of Schnorr signatures used as ZKPs is well known. Details on how this can be proven can be found in [1]. (See Schnorr's identification scheme.)

J-PAKE's Security

The offline dictionary attack resistance is essentially due to the fact that the DDH assumption holds in G. The transmitted group elements that depend on the password are $(X_1 X_3 X_4)^{x_2 pw}$ and $(X_3 X_1 X_2)^{x_4 pw}$, and even given the first four group elements sent, these values still look like random values; hence, the password is completely protected from eavesdropping adversaries. If the adversary is active, that is, posing for instance as $\mathcal{B}$, then the value $(X_1 X_3 X_4)^{x_2 pw}$ it receives from $\mathcal{A}$ still looks like a random element again

$\mathcal{A}$		$\mathcal{B}$	**FIGURE 40.10** J-PAKE protocol.
(x_1, x_2)		(x_3, x_4)	
	$\xrightarrow{\left(X_1, X_2, ZKP(x_1, g), ZKP(x_2, g) \right)}$		
	$\xleftarrow{\left(X_3, X_4, ZKP(x_3, g), ZKP(x_4, g) \right)}$		
$X_{\mathcal{A}} := (X_1 X_3 X_4)^{x_2 pw}$		$X_{\mathcal{B}} := (X_3 X_1 X_2)^{x_4 pw}$	
	$\xrightarrow{\left(X_{\mathcal{A}}, ZKP(x_2 pw, X_1 X_3 X_4) \right)}$		
	$\xleftarrow{\left(X_{\mathcal{B}}, ZKP(x_4 pw, X_3 X_1 X_2) \right)}$		
$K_{\mathcal{A}} := (X_{\mathcal{B}}(X_4)^{-x_2})^{x_2 pw}$		$K_{\mathcal{B}} := (X_{\mathcal{A}}(X_2)^{-x_4})^{x_4 pw}$	

under the DDH assumption. This is because it contains a factor of the form $g^{x_1 x_2}$, where x_1 and x_2 are chosen randomly by the honest party $\mathcal{A}$. Now, one may think that the malicious $\mathcal{B}$ could try to cancel out or otherwise manipulate x_1 in this formula by computing X_3 as some function of X_1; but this is not possible by virtue of the fact that X_3 needs to be accompanied by a proof of knowledge of x_3.

One must also pay attention to the accompanying zero-knowledge proofs, since the last two proofs that are transmitted prove knowledge of exponents that are computed using the password. However, by design these proofs leak no more information about these exponents than what is already known.

Forward secrecy is also guaranteed by the DDH assumption essentially because even given the tuple

$$(q, G, g, g^{x_1}, g^{x_2}, g^{x_3}, g^{x_4}, g^{(x_1 + x_3 + x_4)x_2}, g^{(x_3 + x_1 + x_2)x_4})$$

the adversary cannot tell apart the value $g^{(x_1 + x_3)x_2 x_4}$ from a random group element, much less compute it. Finally, known-session key security follows from the fact that fresh random values are chosen in each protocol run. Thus, session keys are all independent.

Flaws

As of yet, no flaws have been found in J-PAKE's security. On the other hand, the security rests in part on that of the ZKP protocol used. To be able to efficiently integrate such a tool into the protocol, it is necessary to make it noninteractive, and current state-of-the-art techniques can only provably achieve this in models that use idealized hash functions (this is known as the *random oracle* model). In particular, Schnorr's signature scheme is proven secure using an idealized hash function. This observation has not yet led to any practical attacks on J-PAKE, but one must remain cautious.

It can be argued that the protocol may not be very practical given the number of sent messages and exponentiations needed, especially taking into account the additional computations that are necessary to prove knowledge of discrete logarithms. However, in comparing J-PAKE with EKE and SPEKE, one must also bear in mind the underlying groups that are involved. J-PAKE can work in groups with special structure provided the DDH assumption holds. For instance, G can be the multiplicative subgroup of order q of the group $\mathbb{Z}_p^*$ where p is a prime of the form $p = rq + 1$ for r coprime to q and q prime, and $r > 2$. The length of q can thus be around 160 bits rather than 1024. This makes selecting random elements in $\mathbb{Z}_q$ much more efficient. Other groups that can be used to increase efficiency are elliptic curve groups. The reader can find a good presentation of the DDH assumption and

examples of families of groups that are believed to verify it in [21].

Proposed Standardization

J-PAKE has also been submitted as a potential candidate for IEEE standardization. In [18], the inventors of the protocol suggest either of the methods employed for EKE and SPEKE to achieve key confirmation. Taking into account this added exchange, the protocol remains secure.

Patents and Deployment

Both EKE and an augmented version of EKE have been patented by Lucent Technologies, now Alcatel-Lucent (U. S. patent 5,241,599 [22] and U.S. patent 5,440,635 [23], respectively). The former expired in 2011, and the latter will expire in 2013. SPEKE is also covered by U.S Patent 6,226,383 [24], which is owned by Phoenix technologies. It is due to expire in 2017 [24].

The patent issue has been a brake to deployment of PAKEs. For instance, at the beginning of 2012 there were no publicly known implementations of EKE according to the Gèant project (see the DJ3.1.2,1 document on roaming developments in the Gèant deliverables link on **www. geant.net**). There have been, however, IETF information notes on integrating EKE to the EAP (see checklist; An Agenda for Action for Implementing Procedures for Extensible Authentication Protocol (EAR) Methods) authentication framework. (RFC 6124, which can be found at **http://tools.ietf.org/html/rfc6124**, seems to be the latest.)

SPEKE on the other hand seems easier to locate. It is used in BlackBerry devices (produced by Research in Motion), for instance, in the Enterprise Server or Playbook Tablet. (The reader can search for SPEKE in the general knowledge base of BlackBerry's Website: **http://btsc.webapps.blackberry.com/btsc/microsites/ microsite.do**.) It is also used in Entrust's TruePass end-to-end Web security product. (See the Entrust TruePass Technical Portfolio Overview document in the list of white papers of Entrust's Website: **http://www.entrust. com/resources/whitepapers.cfm**.) Funk Software— now Juniper Networks—and Interlink Networks have also used SPEKE for RADIUS systems in the past, although Interlink has discontinued SPEKE in its RAD-series product line starting version 7.1 or higher. (See the release notes in the documentation provided on their Website: **http://www.interlinknetworks.com/ aaa_documentation.htm#notes**), and SPEKE no longer appears in Juniper's online glossary, suggesting that it may have stopped using the algorithm as well. (See **http://www.juniper.net/techpubs/en_US/release-**

An Agenda for Action for Implementing Procedures for Extensible Authentication Protocol (EAP) Methods

Every EAP method consists of several procedures that are necessary to ensure the security goals, enable crypto-agility and backward compatibility, and prevent attacks. These procedures can be executed sequentially, in parallel or in an interleaved fashion. For example, authentication and key establishment could be combined into an authenticated key establishment process. If the authentication or key establishment algorithm is not negotiated as part of the ciphersuite negotiation, both the ciphersuite negotiation and the algorithm can be started at the same time. The EAP methods under consideration may include the following procedures (check all tasks completed):

_____1. Ciphersuite negotiation to enable crypto-agility and backward compatibility.

_____2. Mutual authentication of a peer and the EAP server to ensure that federal peers and federal EAP servers provide assurance of their acclaimed identities to each other.

_____3. Key establishment between a peer and the EAP server to provide keying material to protect the remainder of the EAP execution and the wireless link.

_____4. Service information exchange to ensure the detection of malicious information sent by rogue authenticators or other rogue intermediary entities.

_____5. Message protection to utilize the established keying material to protect the remainder of the EAP execution.

independent/glossary/index.html, last checked August 30, 2012.)

As for J-PAKE, it is in the public domain and is used by Mozilla in Firefox Sync. (See the "How Firefox does it" paragraph in the Mozilla Services Sync Client documentation at: **http://docs.services.mozilla.com/sync/life-ofasync.html**.)

4. SUMMARY

In this chapter, we have given a short overview on a specific variant of authenticated key exchange protocols: that in which authentication between parties is established through knowledge of a simple, human-memorable password. Since passwords are overwhelmingly present in today's digital world, the study and development of these methods is important.

The most notable aspect of security introduced by this concept is defending against dictionary attacks, in which online or offline attackers attempt to test password guesses against transcripts of protocol executions. Recall that passwords are vulnerable to this precisely because of the low entropy they suffer from in order to achieve user-friendliness.

We have also presented three such protocols—namely, EKE, SPEKE, and J-PAKE—and discussed their security properties. Research in this area is still quite active; many other protocols besides those described here have been proposed and analyzed from both practical and theoretical standpoints. We refer to [12], [13], and [18] for more extensive bibliographies.

Finally, let's move on to the real interactive part of this chapter: review questions/exercises, hands-on projects, case projects, and optional team case project. The answers and/or solutions by chapter can be found in the Online Instructor's Solutions Manual.

CHAPTER REVIEW QUESTIONS/EXERCISES

True/False

1. True or False? A fresh key is established for each new conversation in which the parties may want to engage; such conversations are called sessions, and the keys used to secure them are called session keys.

2. True or False? A huge amount of key exchange protocols still use the Diffie-Hellman construct as a basis for computing secret keys.

3. True or False? There are essentially two flavors of authentication that can be used within a key exchange protocol.

4. True or False? In what is considered classical key exchange, the long-term keying material that a user is required to possess is usually one of two kinds: (i) a cryptographically secure key for a symmetric cryptographic algorithm (a 128-bit AES encryption key; see Chapter 37) or (ii) a cryptographically secure public key/secret key pair for an asymmetric cryptographic algorithm.

5. True or False? Another type of established long-term keying material that can be used is certified public key/secret key pairs.

Multiple Choice

1. Another method that has been considered to authenticate users involves using human
   A. passwords
   B. PAKE
   C. cryptography
   D. biometrics
   E. key exchange

2. Passwords are low-entropy data. This makes them vulnerable to _____, which are essentially brute-force guessing attacks
   A. security attacks
   B. key exchanges
   C. dictionary attacks
   D. protocol attacks
   E. PAKE attacks

3. What are active attacks in which the adversary tries to guess the password through successive login attempts: The adversary engages over and over in the protocol, trying out different passwords, and when the opposing party stops aborting, the adversary knows it guessed the right password?
   A. Evolution attacks
   B. Residue class attacks
   C. Online dictionary attacks
   D. Certification authority attacks
   E. Security attacks

4. A user's password in a _____ is viewed as a long-term key (it is expected to be used many times to create random, independent session keys).
   A. session key
   B. PAKE protocol
   C. known-session key security
   D. forward secrecy
   E. security protocol

5. Resistance to _____ (in which an adversary who compromised a user's long term key can then impersonate other parties to that user), is not satisfied by a PAKE: the other holder of the password can always be impersonated to the attacked user.
   A. physical world
   B. data retention
   C. standardization
   D. key compromise impersonation
   E. signature

EXERCISE

Problem

A PAKE protocol transcript cannot be allowed to leak a single bit of information on the password. Please explain further.

Hands-On Projects

Project

The security of EKE's main protocol flows has been studied from a purely theoretical point of view. Please explain and expand on this topic further.

Case Projects

Problem

The protocol is clearly very efficient, as it essentially consists of a Diffie-Hellman Key Exchange. Please explain and expand on this topic further.

Optional Team Case Project

Problem

A ZKP protocol is run between two entities, the prover P and the verifier V. Please explain further.

REFERENCES

[1] D. Stinson, Cryptography: Theory and Practice, Third Edition, Discrete Mathematics and its Applications, Chapman and Hall/CRC, 2006.

[2] W. Diffie, M. Hellman, New directions in cryptography, IEEE. Trans. Inf. Theory IT-11 (November 1976) 644−654.

[3] W. Diffie, P. van Oorschot, M. Wiener, Authentication and Authenticated Key Exchanges, Designs, Codes and Cryptography, Vol. 2, Kluwer Academic Publishers, 1992 (2), pp. 107−125.

[4] R. Needham, M. Schroeder, Using encryption for authentication in large networks of computers, Commun. ACM, 21 (12), pp. 993−999.

[5] R. Needham, M. Schroeder, Authentication revisited, SIGOPS Oper. Syst. Rev. 21 (1) (January 1987).

[6] S. Bellovin, M. Merrit, Augmented Encrypted Key Exchange: A Password-Based Protocol Secure Against Dictionary Attacks and Password File Compromise, AT&T Bell Laboratories, 1993.

[7] D. Jablon, Extended password protocols immune to dictionary attack, Proceedings of WETICE 97 Enterprise Security Workshop, (June 1997), pp. 248−255.

[8] S. Bellovin, M. Merrit, Encrypted key exchange: password-based protocols secure against dictionary attacks, Proc. IEEE. Symp. Res. Secur. Priv. (May 1992).

[9] M. Bellare, D. Pointcheval, P. Rogaway, Authenticated key exchange secure against dictionary attacks, Adv. in Cryptology, Eurocrypt 2000, LNCS 1807 (2000) 139−155Springer

[10] S. Patel, Number-theoretic attacks on secure password schemes, Proceedings of the 1997 IEEE Symposium on Security and Privacy, (1997), pp. 236−247.

[11] M. Bellare, P. Rogaway, The AuthA protocol for password-based authenticated key exchange, Contributions to IEEE P1363.2, (March 2000). Available from: <http://grouper.ieee.org/groups/1363/passwdPK/submissions.html>.

[12] E. Bresson, O. Chevassut, D. Pointcheval, Proc. of the 10th CCS Security Proofs for an Efficient Password-Based Key Exchange, ACM Press, New York, 2003.

[13] E. Bresson, O. Chevassut, D. Pointcheval, PKC 2004, LNCS New Security Results on Encrypted Key Exchange, Springer-Verlag, Berlin, 2004.

[14] Z. Zhao, Z. Dong, Y. Wang, Security analysis of a password-based authentication protocol proposed to IEEE 1363, Theor. Comput. Sci. 352 (1) (2006) 280−287.

[15] D. Jablon, Strong password-only authenticated key exchange, ACM Comput. Commun. Rev. 26 (5) (October 1996) 5−26.

[16] P. MacKenzie, On the security of the SPEKE password-authenticated key exchange protocol, IACR e-print archive, <http://eprint.iacr.org/2001/057>.

[17] M. Zhang, Analysis of the SPEKE password-authenticated key exchange protocol, IEEE Commun. Lett. 8 (1) (January 2004) 63−65.

[18] F. Hao, P.Y.A. Ryan, Password authenticated key exchange by juggling, Secur. Protoc. Workshop (2008) 159−171.

[19] W. Mao, Modern Cryptography: Theory and Practice, HP Professional Series, Pearson Education, Prentice Hall PTR, 2004.

[20] C. Schnorr, Efficient signature generation by smart cards, J. Cryptology 4 (3) (1991) 161−174.

[21] D. Boneh, The decision diffie-hellman problem, Proceedings of the Third International Symposium on Algorithmic Number Theory, LNCS 1423, (1998), pp. 48−63.

[22] AT&T Bell Laboratories, Cryptographic Protocol for Secure Communications, US Patent 5,241,599, filed October 1991.

[23] AT&T Bell Laboratories, Cryptographic Protocol for Remote Authentication, US Patent 5,440,635, filed August 1993.

[24] Integrity Sciences Inc. Cryptographic methods for remote authentication, US Patent 6,226,383, filed March 1997.

## Chapter 41

Instant-Messaging Security

Samuel J.J. Curry
RSA

Instant messaging (IM) has been through several phases in the technology roller-coaster from exciting, cutting edge technology used by the socially avant-garde to a solid tool in the productivity toolkit of the most conservative organization. You would have to practically live under a rock (or at least not own a computer, personal digital assistant [PDA], or cell phone) to not have used it, much less to not know what it is. Luddites[1] notwithstanding, most people who use IM and even many people in information technology (IT) do not know how it works, why it is here, and what it means. In many deployments, IM can be a valuable contributor to business infrastructure, but it shouldn't be adopted without due consideration of business value (that is, is this worth doing?), business risk (that is, what is at stake?), and the people, processes, and technologies that will make it valuable and secure. This chapter should help you make a plan, keep it current, and make sure that it makes a difference.

1. WHY SHOULD I CARE ABOUT INSTANT MESSAGING?

When considering IM, it is important to realize that it is first and foremost a technology; it is not a goal in and of itself. Like an ERP[2] system, an email system, a database, a directory, or a provisioning system, IM must ultimately serve the business: it is a means to an end. The end should be measured in terms of *quantifiable* returns and should be put in context. Before engaging in an IM project, you should be clear about why you are doing it. The basic reasons you should consider IM are:

- Employee satisfaction
- Improving efficiency

- Performing transactions (some business transactions have been built, as you'll see later, to use IM infrastructures; those who do this are aware of it and those who have not seen it before are frequently horrified)
- Improving communications
- Improving response times and timelines

Business decisions revolve around the principle of acceptable risk for acceptable return, and as a result, your *security* decisions with respect to IM are effectively *business* decisions. To those of you reading this with a security hat on, you've probably experienced the continued rapprochement of security and business in your place of work (and in some cases the splitting of security into both a technical and a business discipline): IM is no exception to that. So let's look at IM, trends, the business around it, and then the security implications.

2. WHAT IS INSTANT MESSAGING?

IM is a technology in a continuum of advances (q.v.) that have arisen for communicating and collaborating over the Internet. The most important characteristic of IM is that it has the appearance of being in "real time," and for all intents and purposes it is in real time.[3] Of course, some IM systems allow for synchronization with folks who are offline and come online later through buffering and batching delivery, although these aren't really "instant" messaging (ironically, this is coming back with the advent of some features in social networking applications and environments like Facebook).

IM technologies predate the Internet, with many early mainframe systems and bulletin board systems (BBS) having early chat-like functionality, where two or more

---

1. Luddites were a British social movement in the textile industry who protested against the technological changes of the Industrial Revolution in the 19th century (http://en.wikipedia.org/wiki/Luddites).
2. Enterprise resource planning is a category of software that ties together operations, finance, staffing, and accounting. Common examples include SAP and Oracle software.

3. The debate over what constitutes real time is a favorite in many technical circles and is materially important when dealing with events and their observation in systems in which volumes are high and distances and timing are significant. When dealing with human beings and the relatively simple instances of whom we interact with and our perceptions of communications, it is far simpler to call this "real time" than "near real time."

people could have a continuous dialogue. In the post-mainframe world, when systems became more distributed and autonomous, chatting and early IM technologies came along, too. In the world of the Internet, two basic technologies have evolved: communications via a central server and communications directly between two peers. Many IM solutions involve a hybrid of these two basic technologies, maintaining a directory or registry of users that then enable a peer-to-peer (P2P) connection.

Some salient features that are relevant for the purposes of technology and will be important later in our approaches to securing instant messaging are as follows:

- *Simultaneity.* IM is a real time or "synchronous" form of communication—real-time opportunity and real-time risk.
- *Recording.* IM transactions are a form of written communication, which means that there are logs and sessions can be captured. This is directly analogous to email, although it can be hard to instrument in a P2P connection.
- *Nonrepudiation.* Instant messaging usually involves a dialogue and the appearance of nonrepudiation by virtue of an exchange, but there is no inherent nonrepudiation in most IM infrastructures. For example, talking to "Bobby" via IM does not in any way prove that it is registered to "Bobby" or is actually "Bobby" at the time you are talking to the other user.
- *Lack of confidentiality and integrity.* There is no guarantee that sessions are private or unaltered in most IM infrastructures without the implementation of effective encryption solutions.
- *Availability.* Most companies do not have guaranteed service-level agreements around availability and yet they depend on IM, either consciously or unknowingly and suffer the costs of supporting the service when it fails.

Most users of an IM infrastructure also treat IM as an informal form of communication. It's also not subject to the normal rules of behavior, formatting, and formality of other forms of business communication, such as letters, memoranda, and email.

3. THE EVOLUTION OF NETWORKING TECHNOLOGIES

Over time, technology changes and, usually, advances. Advancements in this context generally refer to being able to do more transactions with more people for more profit. Of course, generalizations of this sort tend to be true on the macroscopic level only since at the microscopic level the tiny deltas in capabilities, offerings, and the vagaries of markets drive many small changes, some

of which are detrimental. However, over the long term and at the macroscopic level, advances in technology enable us to do more things with more people more easily and in closer to real time.

There are more than a few laws that track the evolution of some distinct technology trends and the positive effects that are expected. A good example of this is Moore's Law, which has yet to be disproven and has proven true since the 1960s. Moore's Law, put simply, postulates that the number of transistors that can be effectively integrated doubles roughly every two years, and the resultant computing power or efficiency increases along with that. Most of us in technology know Moore's Law, and it is arguable that we as a society depend on it for economic growth and stimulus: There is always more demand for more computing power (or has been to date and for the foreseeable future). A less known further example is Gilder's Law[4] (which has since been disproven) that asserts that a similar, related growth in available bandwidth occurs over time.

Perhaps the most important "law" with respect to networks and for instant messaging is Metcalfe's Law, which states that the value of a telecommunications network increases exponentially with a linear increase in the number of users. (Actually, it states that it is proportional to the square of the users on the network.)

Let's also assume that over time the value of a network will increase; the people who use it will find new ways to get more value out of it. The number of connections or transactions will increase, and the value and importance of that network will go up. In a sense, it takes time once a network has increased in size for the complexity and number of transactions promised by Metcalfe's Law to be realized. What does all this have to do with IM? Let's tie it together:

- Following from Moore's Law (and to a lesser extent Gilder), computers (and their networks) will get faster and therefore more valuable—and so connecting them in near real time (of which IM is an example of real-time communications) is a *natural occurrence* and will *increase value.*
- Following from Metcalfe, over time networks will become increasingly valuable to users of those networks.

In other words, IM as a phenomenon is really a tool for increasing connections among systems and networks and for getting more value. For those of us in the business world, this is good news: using IM, we should be able to realize more value from that large IT investment and should be able to do more business with more people more efficiently. That is the "carrot," but there is a stick,

---

4. www.netlingo.com/lookup.cfm?term=Gilder's%20Law.

too: It is not all good news, because where there is value and opportunity, there is also threat and risk.

4. GAME THEORY AND INSTANT MESSAGING

Whenever gains or losses can be quantified for a given population, game theory applies. Game theory is used in many fields to predict what is basically the *social* behavior or organisms in a system: people in economics and political science, animals in biology and ecology, and so on. When you can tell *how much* someone stands to gain or lose, you can build reasonably accurate predictive models for how they will behave; and this is in fact the foundation for many of our modern economic theories. The fact of the matter is that now that the Internet is used for business, we can apply game theory to human behavior with Internet technologies, too, and this includes IM.

On the positive side, if you are seeing more of your colleagues, employees, and friends adopt a technology, especially in a business context, you can be reasonably sure that there is some gain and loss equation that points to an increase in value behind the technology. Generally, people should not go out of their way to adopt technologies simply for the sake of adopting them on a wide scale (though actually, many people do just this and then suffer for it; technology adoption on a wide scale and over a long period of time generally means that something is showing a return on value). Unfortunately, in a business context, this may not translate into more business or more value for the business. Human beings not only do things for quantifiable, money-driven reasons; they also do things for moral and social reasons.

Let's explore the benefits of adopting IM technology within a company, and then we can explore the risks a little more deeply.

Your Workforce

Whether you work in an IT department or run a small company, your employees have things they need to do: process orders, work with peers, manage teams, talk to customers and to partners. IM is a tool they can and will use to do these things. Look at your workforce and their high-level roles: Do they need IM to do their jobs? IM is an entitlement within a company, not a right. The management of entitlements is a difficult undertaking, but it isn't without precedent. For older companies, you probably had to make a decision similar to the IM decision with respect to email or Internet access. The first response from a company is usually binary: Allow everyone or disallow everyone. This reactionary response is natural, and in many cases some roles are denied entitlements such as email or Internet access on a regular basis. Keep in mind

that in some industries, employees make the difference between a successful, aggressively growing business and one that is effectively in a "maintenance mode" or, worse, is actively shrinking. In the remainder of this chapter, we outline factors in your decision making, as follows with the first factor.

Factor #1

Do your employees need IM? If so, which employees need IM and what do they need it for?

Examples of privileged IM entitlement include allowing developers, brokers, sales teams, executives, operations, and/or customer support to have access. *Warning:* If you provide IM for some parts of your company and not for others, you will be in a situation in which some employees have a privilege that others do not. This will have two, perhaps unintended, consequences:

- Employees without IM will seek to get it by abusing backdoors or processes to get this entitlement.
- Some employees will naturally be separated from other employees and may become the object of envy or of resentment. This could cause problems.

We have also touched on employee satisfaction, and it is important to understand the demographics of your workplace and its social norms. It is important to also consider physical location of employees and general demographic considerations with respect to IM because there could be cultural barriers, linguistic barriers, and, as we will see later, generational ones, too.

Factor #2

Is IM important as a job satisfaction component?

Economists generally hold that employees work for financial, moral, and social reasons. Financial reasons are the most obvious and, as we've seen, are the ones most easily quantified and therefore subject to game theory; companies have money, and they can use it to incent the behaviors they want. However, we as human beings also work on things for moral reasons, as is the case with people working in nonprofit organizations or in the open-source movement. These people work on things that matter to them for moral reasons.

However, the social incentives are perhaps the most important for job satisfaction. In speaking recently with the CIO of a large company that banned the use of external IM, the CIO was shocked that a large number of talented operations and development people refused lucrative offers on the grounds that IM was disallowed with people outside the company. This led to a discussion of the motivators for an important asset for this company: attracting and keeping the right talent. The lesson is that if you want to attract the best, you may have to allow them to use technologies such as IM.

After you have determined whether or not IM is needed for the job (Factor #1), interview employees on the uses of IM in a social context: with whom do they IM and for what purposes? Social incentives include a large number of social factors, including keeping in touch with parents, siblings, spouses, and friends but also with colleagues overseas, with mentors, and for team collaboration, especially over long distances.

Generational Gaps

An interesting phenomenon is observable in the generation now in schools and training for the future: They multitask frequently. Generational gaps and their attendant conflicts are nothing new; older generations are in power and are seen to bear larger burdens, and younger generations are often perceived in a negative light. Today IM may be at the forefront of yet another generational conflict.

If you've observed children recently, they do more all at once than adults have done in the past 20 years. This is a generation that grows up in a home with multiple televisions, multiple computers, cell phones from a young age, PowerPoint in the classroom, text messaging, email,[5] and IM.

The typical older-generation values in a generational conflict that we must watch out for are assuming that the younger generation is inherently more lazy, is looking for unreasonable entitlement, wants instant gratification, or is lacking in intelligence and seasoning. If you catch yourself doing this, stop yourself and try to empathize with the younger folks. Likewise, the younger generation has its pitfalls and assumptions; but let's focus on the younger, emerging generation, because they will soon be entering the workforce. If you find yourself assuming that multitasking and responding to multiple concurrent stimuli is distracting and likely to produce a lack of efficiency, stop and run through a basic question: Is what's true for you immediately true for the people you are interacting with? This leads to Factors 3 and 4.

Factor #3

Does IM improve or lessen efficiency?

With respect to IM, does IM (and the interruptions it creates) have to mean that someone is less efficient, or could they be more efficient because of it? As we've

seen, it is possible that many younger employees can have multiple IM conversations and can potentially get a lot more done in less time compared to either sending out multiple emails or waiting for responses. In many respects, this question is similar to the questions that the BlackBerry raised when it was introduced to the workforce, and there are three ways that it can be answered:

- In some cases, jobs require isolation and focus, and a culture of IM can create conditions that are less effective.
- In some cases, it doesn't matter.
- In some cases, some employees may be much more effective when they receive maximum stimulus and input.

Factor #4

Will this efficiency change over time, or is it in fact different for different demographics of my workforce?

Consider generational differences and the evolution of your workforce. This may all be moot, or there may be a *de facto* acceptance of IM over time, much as there was with email and other, older technologies in companies. It is interesting to note that younger, newer companies never consider the important factors with respect to IM because *they culturally assume it is a right*. This assumption may form the basis of some real conflicts in the years to come. Imagine companies that shut off new technologies being sued over "cruel and unusual" work conditions because they are removing what employees assume to be a right. Of course, this conflict is small now, but it is important to have a process for dealing with new technologies within the corporation rather than being blindsided by them as they emerge or, worse, as a new generation of users find themselves cut off from stimuli and tools that they consider necessary for their job or for their quality of life. In the end, the first four factors should help you define the following three items:

- Do you need IM as a company?
- Why do employees need it?
  - To do their jobs?
  - To improve efficiency?
  - To do more business?
  - To work with peers?
  - To improve employee satisfaction?
- Who needs it?

Without answers to these questions, which are all about the workforce as a whole, the role of IM will not be easily understood nor established within the company.

---

5. To my amusement, my goddaughter, who is 11, recently told me that "email was old fashioned" and she couldn't believe that I used it so heavily for work!

Transactions

Some companies have taken a bold step and use IM infrastructure for actual business processes. These are typically younger, fast-growing companies that are looking for more real-time transactions or processes. They typically accept a higher level of risk in general in exchange for greater potential returns. The unfortunate companies are the ones that have built product systems and processes on an IM infrastructure *unknowingly* and now have to deal with potentially unintended consequences of that infrastructure.

How does this happen? The infrastructures for IM on the Internet are large, ubiquitous, and fairly reliable, and it is natural that such infrastructures will get used. As we saw in the section on the evolution of Internet technologies, users will find ways to increase complexity and the value of networks over time, in essence fulfilling Metcalfe's Law. This is why some companies find that a small team using IM (where a built in business process on an IM application has grown fast, with real-time response times for some processes) has now reached the point where sizeable business and transactions are conducted over IM.

Factor #5

Does your company have a need or dependency on IM to do business?

If this is the case, you need to understand immediately which applications and infrastructures you rely on. You should begin a process for examining the infrastructure and mapping out the business processes:

- Where are the single points of failure?
- Where does liability lie?
- What is availability like?
- What is the impact of downtime on the business?
- What is the business risk?
- What are your disaster recovery and business continuity options?

The answers to these questions will lead to natural action plans. They will also follow the basic rule of acceptable risk for acceptable return, unless you find you have a regulatory implication (in which case, build action plans immediately).

Factor #6

Are you considering deploying a technology or process on an IM infrastructure?

If this is the case, you need to understand immediately which applications and infrastructures you will rely on. You should begin a process for understanding the

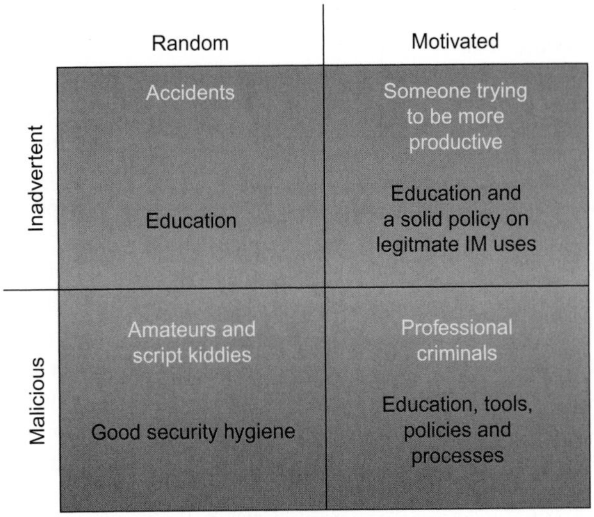

FIGURE 41.1 Populations that present a corporate risk and the correct responses to each.

infrastructure and quantifying and managing the business risk. Again, make sure, as with the workforce, that you in fact need the IM infrastructure in the first place.

5. THE NATURE OF THE THREAT

There are some clear threats, internal and external, and both inadvertent and malicious. These different threats call for the implementation of different countermeasures. Figure 41.1 shows a simple grid of the populations that a security professional will have to consider in the context of their security postures for IM.

Malicious Threat

We've looked at the good guys, who are basically looking within the company or are perhaps partners looking to use a powerful, real-time technology for positive reasons: more business with more people more efficiently. Now it is time to look at the bad guys: black hats.[6]

In the "old days," black hats were seen to be young kids in their parents' basements, or perhaps a disgruntled techie with an axe to grind. These were people who would invest a disproportionate amount of time in an activity, spending hundreds of hours to gain fame or notoriety or to enact revenge. This behavior led to the "worm of the week" and macro-viruses. They were, in effect, not a systematic threat but were rather background noise. We

---

6. This term was a difficult one to choose. I opted not to go with *crackers* or *hackers* but rather with *black hats* because that is the most neutral term to refer to malicious computer exploiters.

will calls these folks "amateurs" for reasons that will become clear.

There have also always been dedicated black hats, or "professionals," who plied their trade for gain or as mercenaries. These folks were at first in the minority and generally hid well among the amateurs. In fact, they had a vested interest in seeing the proliferation of "script kiddies" who could "hack" easily: This activity created background noise against which their actions would go unnoticed. Think of the flow of information and activity, of security incidents as a CSI scene where a smart criminal has visited barber shops, collected discarded hair from the floors, and then liberally spread them around the crime scene to throw off the DNA collection of forensic investigators. This is what the old-world professionals did and why they rejoiced at the "worms of the week" that provided a constant background noise for them to hide their serious thefts.

Now we come to the modern age, and the professionals are in the majority. The amateurs have grown up and found that they can leave their parents' basements and go out and make money working for real organizations and companies, plying their skills to abuse the Internet and systems for real gain. This is what led to the proliferation of Spyware; and because it is an *economic* activity, we can quantify losses and gains for this population and can begin to apply game theory to predicting their behaviors and *the technologies that they will abuse for gain.*

There is a new category as well around the *Advanced Persistent Threat* or APT.[7] These attackers are likewise professionals and highly motivated by a mission. They are also well funded and include both nation states and hacktivists looking for key intelligence and access: economic, military or political access, information and control.

On the one hand, the bad guys are now a vested interest, as has been well documented[8] and analyzed; they are a sustained, real, commercial interest and present a clear and present risk to most IT infrastructures. On the other hand, there are well-funded APTs that are specifically determined to break in and achieve their mission, which you are empowered and responsible for stopping. Keep in mind the following general rules about these online miscreants:

- It is not about ego or a particular trick; they are not above using or abusing any technology.
- They do what they do to make money or to achieve their mission. This is your money, your IP and your

trust they are threatening. They are a risk to you and to your company.

- They are sophisticated; they have supply and distribution agreements and partners, they have SLAs[9] and business relationships, they have allies and enemies, and they even have quality labs, alliances and conferences. They are not merely immature adults or precocious adolescents.

In general, online criminals will seek to exploit IM if they can realize value in the target and if they can efficiently go after it. IM represents a technology against which it is easy for black hats to develop exploits, and even relatively small returns (such as a 1% click rate on SPIM, which stands for *spam instant messaging*) would have enormous potential value.

Factor #7

Does the value to the company of information and processes carried over IM represent something that is a valuable target (because it can either affect your business or realize a gain)? Do you have have information or processes that are valuable to your customers or partners? This should include the ability to blackmail employees and partners: Can someone learn things about key employees that they could use to threaten or abuse employees and partners?

The answer to this question will help put in perspective the potential for IM technology to be abused.

Factor #8

If the IM technology were abused or compromised, what would be the risk to the business or to a customer or partner?

SPIM, worms, viruses, spyware, Trojans, rootkits, backdoors and other threats can spread over IM as readily as email, file shares, and other transmission vectors—in fact, it is arguable that it can spread more readily via IM. Will an incident over IM cause an unacceptable risk to the business? This should be answered in the same way as "Will an incident over email cause an unacceptable risk to the business?" For most organizations the answer should always be yes.

Vulnerabilities

Like any form of software (or hardware), IM applications and infrastructure are subject to vulnerabilities and weaknesses from poor configuration and implementation. Most of these applications do not have the same degree of rigor

---

7. I prefer Josh Corman's term of *Advanced Persistent Adversary* since this most accurately reflects the Human nature of this class of threat. However, I will use APT as the more common term of the day.

8. www.rsa.com/blog/blog. aspx#Security-Blog.

9. Service-level agreement.

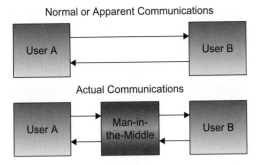

Normal or Apparent Communications

Actual Communications

FIGURE 41.2 Normal versus man-in-the-middle communications.

around maintenance, support, and patching as other enterprise software applications. As a result, it is important to have processes for penetration testing and security audits and to establish a relationship, if possible, with manufacturers and distributors for enterprise caliber support. In many cases, the total cost of ownership of an IM infrastructure and applications may rise considerably to make up for this lack. For this reason, using the freeware services may be a temptation, but the risks may quickly outweigh the savings.

Man-in-the-Middle Attacks

A man-in-the-middle attack is a class of attack in which a third party acts as a legitimate or even invisible broker. As shown in Figure 41.2, an attacker is posing to each user in an IM transaction as a legitimate part of the process while in fact recording or relaying information. This is a common attack philosophy, and without basic mutual authentication or encryption tools, it is inexpensive for black hats to carry out in a wide-scale manner.

As a security professional, it is possible to monitor IM protocols and the IP addresses with which they communicate, allowing IM to and from only certain recognized hubs. Even this is not perfect, because "X-in-the-middle" attacks in their most generic form can include everything from Trojans and keyloggers to line taps. It is also possible to monitor communications among peers, although effectively looking for man-in-the-middle attacks in this way is difficult.

Phishing and Social Engineering

Social engineering is the practice of fooling someone into giving up something they wouldn't otherwise surrender through the use of psychological tricks. Social engineers rely on the normal behavior of people presented with data or a social situation to respond in a predictable, human way. An attack of this sort will rely on presenting trusted logos and a context that seems normal but is in fact designed to create a vulnerability that the social engineer

can exploit. This is relevant to IM because people can choose IM identities *similar to ones with whom the user normally communicates.* The simplest attack of all is to get an identity that is similar to a boss, sibling, friend, or spouse and then provide information to get information. Employees should be educated to always directly check with end users to ensure that they are in fact communicating with whom they believe they are communicating.

Knowledge is the Commodity

It goes without saying that knowledge of business transactions is itself something that can be turned to profit. The contents of a formula, the nature of an experiment, the value and type of a financial transaction are all important to competitors and to speculators. Stock values rise and fall on rumors of activity, and material knowledge of what is happening can be directly translated into profit.

There are companies, organizations, and individuals that launder money and reap huge profits on the basis of insider information and intellectual property, and the bad guys are looking for exactly this information. Know what is being communicated and educate your employees about the open, real-time, and exposed nature of IM. Make sure that you have solid policies on what is acceptable to communicate over IM.

Factor #9

What intellectual property, material information, corporate documents, and transaction data are at risk over IM?

Make sure that you know what people use IM for and, if you do not have the means to control it, consider denying access to IM or implementing content-filtering technologies. With false positives and technology failing to track context of communications, do not rely heavily on a technological answer; make sure you have educational options and that you document use of IM in your environment.

Data and Traffic Analysis

The mere presence of communications is enough, in some circumstances, to indicate material facts about a business or initiative. This is particularly well understood by national governments and interests with "signals intelligence." You do not have to know what someone is saying to have an edge. This has been seen throughout history, with the most obvious and numerous examples during World War II: If you know that someone is communicating, that is in effect intelligence.

Communicating with a lawyer, making a trade, and the synchronizing in real time of that information with public data may construe a material breach if it's intercepted. Wherever possible, artificial traffic levels and data content flags to the outside world should be used to disguise the nature and times of communication for transactions that indicate insider information or transactions that you otherwise wouldn't want the world to know about.

Factor #10

What do transaction types and times tell people about your business? Is it acceptable for people to have access to this information?

Some of the most important events in history have occurred because of intelligence not of what was said but rather how, and most important why, a communication occurred.

Unintentional Threats

Perhaps the most insidious threat isn't the malicious one; it is the inadvertent one. Employees are generally seeking to do more work more efficiently. This is what leads to them using their public, Web-based emails for working at home rather than only working in the office. Very often people who are working diligently do something to try to work faster, better, or in more places and they inadvertently cause a business risk. These are, in effect, human behaviors that put the company at risk, and the answer is both an educational one and one that can benefit from the use of certain tools.

Intellectual Property Leakage

Just as employees shouldn't leave laptops in cars or work on sensitive documents in public places such as an airport or coffee shop, they also should not use public IM for sensitive material. Intellectual property leakage of source code, insider information, trade secrets, and so on are major risks with IM when used incorrectly, although it should be noted that when deployed correctly, such transactions can be done safely over IM (when encrypted and appropriate, with the right mutual authentication).

Inappropriate Use

As with Web browsing and email, inappropriate use of IM can lead to risks and threats to a business. In particular, IM is an informal medium. People have their own lingo in IM, with acronyms[10] peculiar to the medium (B4N = bye for now, HAND = have a nice day, IRL = in real life, and so on). The very informal nature of the medium means that it is generally not conducted in a businesslike manner; it is more like our personal

---

10. A good source on these is found at AOL (www.aim.com/acronyms.adp).

interactions and notes. When the social glue of an office becomes less business-oriented, it can lead to inappropriate advances, commentary, and exposure. Outlining inappropriate use of IM, as with any technology, should be part of the general HR policy of a company, and correct business use should be part of a regular regimen of business conduct training.

Factor #11

What unintended exposure could the company face via IM? Which populations have this information and require special training, monitoring, or protection?

Make sure that your company has a strategy for categorization and management of sensitive information, in particular personally identifiable information, trade secrets, and material insider information.

Regulatory Concerns

Last, but far from least, are the things that simply must be protected for legal reasons. In an age where customer information is a responsibility, not a privilege, where credit-card numbers and Social Security numbers are bartered and traded and insider trading can occur in real time (sometimes over IM), it is imperative that regulatory concerns be addressed in an IM policy. If you can't implement governance policies over IM technology, you might have to ban IM use until such time as you can govern it effectively—and you very well may have to take steps to actively root out and remove IM applications, with drastic consequences for those who break the company's IM policy. Examples of these are common in financial institutions, HR organizations, and healthcare organizations.

Factor #12

Do you have regulatory requirements that require a certain IM posture and policy?

No matter how attractive the technology, you may not be able to adopt IM if the regulatory concerns aren't addressed. If you absolutely need it, the project to adopt compliant IM will be driven higher in the priority queue; but the basic regulatory requirement and penalties could be prohibitive if this isn't done with utmost care and attention.

Remember also that some countries have explicit regulations about monitoring employees. In some jurisdictions in Europe and Asia in particular, it is *illegal to monitor employee behavior and actions*. This may seem alien to some in the United States, but multinationals and companies in other regions must conform to employee rights requirements.

6. COMMON IM APPLICATIONS

IM is a fact of life. Now it is time to decide which applications and infrastructures your company can and will be exposed to. You most likely will want to create a policy and to track various uses of IM and develop a posture and educational program about which ones are used in which contexts. You will want to review common IM applications in the consumer or home user domain because they will find their ways into your environment and onto your assets. For example, many people install IM applications for personal use on laptops that they then take out of the company environment; they aren't using them at work, but those applications are on systems that have company intellectual property and material on them and they are used on insecure networks once they leave the building.

Consumer Instant Messaging

Numbers of subscribers are hard to come by in a consistent manner, although some analyst firms and public sites present disparate numbers. Wikipedia has a current view and commentary on relative sizes of IM networks and concentrations that are worth examining and verifying in a more detailed fashion. The major IM programs are AIM at 100 million, Yahoo! Messenger at 248 million, Windows Live Messenger/MSN at 330 million users, Skype at 882 million, and Tencent at a staggering 900 million (which is up enormously from the first edition of this book). There is also a good comparison of the technologies and infrastructure in use with various tools as well. Others include a host of smaller applications such as ICQ (at 50 million) continue to proliferate.

It is important to keep in mind who owns the infrastructures for private IM applications. In effect, the IM backbone passes information in the clear (unless an encryption program is used, and the owners of the infrastructure can see and collect data on who is communicating with whom, how, and what they are saying.

It could, for instance, with respect to quarterly earnings or an investigation or lawsuit, be materially important to know with whom the CFO is communicating and at what times. As a result, companies are well advised to educate employees on the risks of IM in general and the acceptable uses for certain applications. It may be acceptable to talk to your husband or wife on Yahoo! or QQ, but is it acceptable to talk to your lawyer that way?

Enterprise Instant Messaging

Some companies, such as IBM and Microsoft, offer IM solutions for internal use only. These are readily deployed and allow for good, real-time communications within the company. They of course do not address the issues of bridging communications with the outside world and the general public, but they are good for meeting some needs for improved productivity and efficiency that are clearly business related. The risk that these pose is in complacency—assuming that the IM application is exclusively used within the organization. Very often, they are used from public places or from private homes and even in some cases from employee-owned assets. As such, the ecosystem for remote access should be carefully considered.

Instant-Messaging Aggregators

There are some programs, such as Trillian,[11] for pulling together multiple IM applications. The danger here is similar to many applications that aggregate passwords or information: They should be legitimate companies, such as Cerulean Studios, with real privacy and security policies. Many illegitimate applications pose as IM aggregators, especially "free" ones, and are really in the business of establishing a spyware presence on PCs, especially corporate-owned PCs. To be clear, there are real, legitimate IM aggregators with real value, and you should look to do business with them, read their end-user license agreements (EULAs), and deploy and manage them correctly. There are also *illegitimate* companies and organizations that manufacture spyware but that pose as IM aggregators; these will come into your environment via well-meaning end users.

Most *illegitimate* applications should be caught with antispyware applications (note that some antivirus applications have antispyware capabilities; verify that this is the case with your vendor) that are resident on PCs, but there are some basic steps you should make sure that your security policies and procedures take into account:

- Make sure that you have antivirus and antispyware software, that it is up to date and that it is active.
- Make sure that end users know the risks of these applications, especially on non-corporate systems (home or user-owned systems).
- Make sure that you survey communications into and out of the network for "phone home," especially encrypted communications and that you have a standard policy and procedure on what course of action to take should suspicious communications be discovered.

Backdoors: Instant Messaging Via Other Means (HTML)

Some IM applications have moved to HTML-based integrations with their network. The reason is obvious: This

---

11. Manufactured by Cerulean Studios: http://www.ceruleanstudios.com.

is a way around the explicit IM protocols being blocked on corporate networks. Employees want to keep using their IM tools for personal or professional reasons, and they are finding workarounds. The obvious counter to this is HTML content filtering, especially at the gateways to networks. If your policy disallows IM, make sure the content-filtering blacklists are sensitive to IM IP addresses and communications. Many IM applications will actively scan for ports that are available on which they can piggyback communications, meaning that if you have any permissive rules for communications, the IM application will find it.

Mobile Dimension

Computing platforms and systems keep getting smaller and converging with their larger cousins; PDAs and phones are everywhere, and most major IM networks have an IM client for BlackBerry, cell phones, and the like. On corporate-owned assets with the latest generation of mobile technologies, it is fairly simple to lock down these applications to conform to the corporate IM policy. In some instances, however, it is more complex, especially in situations where PDAs are employee-owned or managed. In these cases, you actually have a larger potential problem and need a PDA and phone policy; the IM policy is secondary to that.

7. DEFENSIVE STRATEGIES

There are four basic postures that you can take within your company with respect to IM (actually this applies to all end-user applications more generally, although it needs to be rationalized for IM in particular):

- *Ban all IM.* This is the least permissive and most likely to fail over time. It is normally only advisable in cases of extremely high risk and in businesses that are very resistant to technology. This will be the hardest to enforce socially if not technically.
- *Allow internal IM.* This is the most common first step, but it demands a careful understanding and policies and procedures to enforce the ban on *external* or consumer IM.
- *Allow all IM.* Outright allowing all IM is not a common first policy, though some companies on due consideration may consider it.
- *Create a sophisticated IM policy.* This is the most difficult to do, but a sophisticated and granular IM policy, integrated with classic security measures, asset management, and a rigorous information policy, is the hallmark of a mature security organization. Incidentally, many of these exist already. It is not necessary to reinvent all of them if these sorts of policies

have already been worked through and are a Web search away.

8. INSTANT-MESSAGING SECURITY MATURITY AND SOLUTIONS

Companies will likely go through an evolution of the security policy with respect to IM. Many (particularly older companies) begin with a ban and wind up over time settling on a sophisticated IM policy that takes into account asset policies, information policies, human behavior, risk, and corporate goals around employee satisfaction, efficiency, and productivity.

Asset Management

Many asset management solutions such as CA Unicenter, IBM Tivoli, and Microsoft SMS manage systems and the software they have. They are most effective for managing corporate-owned assets; make sure that employees have the right tools, correctly licensed and correctly provisioned. They also make sure that rogue, unlicensed software is minimized and can help enforce IM applications bans as in the case of a "ban of all IM" policy or a ban on external or consumer IM.

Built-In Security

Enterprise IM applications are generally the most readily adopted of solutions within a company or organization. Many of these IM platforms and "inside the firewall" IM applications provide some built-in security measures, such as the ability to auto-block inbound requests from unknown parties. Many of these features are good for hardening obvious deficiencies in the systems, but by themselves they do not typically do enough to protect the IM infrastructure.

Keep in mind also that "inside the firewall" is often misleading; people can readily sign on to these applications via virtual private network from outside the firewall or even from home computers, with a little work. Make sure the access policies and security features built into internal applications are understood and engaged correctly.

It is also generally good to ensure that strong authentication (multifactor authentication) is used in cases where people will be gaining remote access to the internal IM application. You want to make sure that the employee in question is in fact the employee and not a family member, friend, or someone who has broken into the employee's home or hotel room.

Content Filtering

A class of relatively new security products has arisen over the past few years specifically designed to do content filtering on IM. These are still not widely adopted and, when adopted, apply to only a limited set of users. Most companies that use these tools are those with strong regulatory requirements and then only to a limited set of users who expose the company most. The most common examples are insiders in financial firms or employees who can access customer data. Real-time leaks in a regulated or privileged environment are generally the most serious drivers here.

Classic Security

The perimeter is dead—long live the Internet. It is almost hackneyed these days to say that perimeter-centric security is dead; firewalls and IDSs aren't the solution. In many ways, modern security is about proving a negative—it can't be done. Human beings seeking to do better at their jobs, to communicate with friends and family, or to actively invade and bypass security will find new ways and new vectors around existing security controls. Having said that, it is important to realize that our job as security professionals is to first remove the inexpensive and easy ways to do get around security controls and then to efficiently *raise the security bar* for getting at what matters: the information. It is important to do a real, quantitative analysis of your cost threshold for the controls you are going to put in place and the amount by which it raises the bar and compare these to the risk and likelihood of loss.

In this regard, the traditional software for perimeter security *still serves a purpose;* in fact, many of these vendors are quite innovative at adding new features and new value over time. The classic products of proxies, corporate firewalls, virtual private networks, intrusion detection, and anti-malware continue to raise the bar for the most simple and inexpensive attack vectors and for stopping inadvertent leakage. This is true of adding layered protection to IM, and the classic security products should be leveraged to raise the security bar (that is, to lower basic business risk). They won't solve the problem, but it is important to use them in a layered approach to reducing business risk.

Compliance

Some industries have strict regulations that require that information be handled in certain ways. These industries have no choice but to comply or face punitive and legal damages and increased risk to their business. It is vital to consult with auditors and compliance departments regarding the implications of IM on corporate compliance.

Also, explicitly keep in mind employee rights legislation that may prohibit monitoring employees' IM communications. There are jurisdictions in which this kind of monitoring is illegal.

Data Loss Prevention

There is a new class of data loss prevention (DLP) product that can discover, classify, categorize, monitor, and enforce information-centric policies (at endpoint, network, datacenter, and "gateway" touchpoints) for a user population—either the whole company or a subset of the workforce population. There are tradeoffs to be made among applications of this type, in particular when it comes to false positives (wrongly identifying information as sensitive) and efficiency at particular times (filtering HR information during benefits enrollment periods or filtering financial-related information at the close of a quarter). This class of product can be massively powerful for enforcing the policy as a useful tool, but its efficiency and impact on *employee* efficiency need to be carefully applied. Further, the vital discovery, classification, and categorization features should be well understood, as should monitoring and enforcement applications.

Logging

Security information and event management (SIEM) systems are only as effective as what they instrument. In combination with content-filtering and DLP, this technology can be extremely effective. The best "real-world" analogy is perhaps insider trading. It is not impossible to commit insider trading, but it isn't as widespread as it could be because the Securities and Exchange Commission (and other regulatory bodies outside the United States) has effective logging and anomaly detection and reporting functions to catch transgressors. Logging in the form of SIEM on the right controls is both a good measure for active protection and a deterrent; just be sure to mention in your education processes that this is happening, to realize the deterrence benefit.

Anomaly Detection

Going beyond even correlation in a SIEM context, it's possible to look for patterns and trends in data – neural networks, Bayesian engines and other correlation engines can be used to determine baselines, deviation from baselines and to spot anomalies. The most effective of these will also tie into a risk analysis engine and should inform authentication and authorization engines in your company. The general direction of authentication technologies is towards establishing context, "continuous" authentication and a constant estimation of the likely risk inherent in someone whenever they do a transaction of any sort.

Archival

In conjunction with regulatory requirements, you may have either a process or audit requirement to keep logs for a certain period of time. Archival, storage, and retrieval systems are likely to form an important part of your post-event analysis and investigation and forensics policies and may actually be legally required for regulatory purposes.

9. PROCESSES

The lifeblood of any policy is the process and the people who enforce that policy. You will need a body of processes and owners that is documented and well maintained. Some of the processes you may need include, but aren't limited to, the following.

Instant-Messaging Activation and Provisioning

When someone is legitimately entitled to IM, how specifically do they get access to the application? How are they managed and supported? If you have IM, you will have issues and will have to keep the application and service current and functioning.

Application Review

Make sure that you know the state of the art in IM. Which applications have centralized structures, and what nations and private interests host these? Which applications are poorly written, contain weaknesses or, worse, have remote control vulnerabilities and are potentially Spyware?

People

Make sure your IT staff and employees know the policies and why they matter. Business relevance is the best incentive for conformity. Work on adding IM to the corporate ethics, conduct, information, and general training policies.

Revise

Keep the policy up to date and relevant. Policies can easily fall into disuse or irrelevance, and given the nature of advances in Internet technologies, it is vital that you regularly revisit this policy on a quarterly or semiannual basis.

Also ensure that your policy is enforceable; a policy that is not enforceable or is counterintuitive is useless.

Audit

Be sure to audit your environment. This is not auditing in the sense of a corporate audit, although that may also be a requirement, but do periodic examinations of network traffic for sessions and traffic that are out of policy. IM will leave proprietary protocol trails and even HTML trails in the network. Look in particular for rogue gateways and rogue proxies that have been set up by employees to work around the corporate policy.

10. SUMMARY

Remember game theory with respect to your workforce and business; people will find ways to do more with the tools, networks, and systems at their disposal. They will find ways to use ungoverned technology, such as IM, to do more things with more people more efficiently. The

---

The 12 Factors

Factor #1: Do your employees need IM? If so, which employees need IM and *what do they need it for?*

Factor #2: Is IM important as a job satisfaction component?

Factor #3: Does IM improve or lessen efficiency?

Factor #4: Will this efficiency change over time, or is it in fact different for different demographics of my workforce?

Factor #5: Does your company have a need or dependency on IM to do business?

Factor #6: Are you considering deploying a technology or process on an IM infrastructure?

Factor #7: Does the value to the company of information and processes carried over IM represent something that is a valuable target (because it can either affect your business or realize a gain)? This should include the ability to blackmail employees and partners; can someone learn things about key employees that they could use to threaten or abuse employees and partners?

Factor #8: If the IM technology were abused or compromised, what would be the risk to the business?

Factor #9: What intellectual property, material information, corporate documents, and transaction information is at risk over IM?

Factor #10: What do transaction types and times tell people about your business? Is it okay for people to have access to this information?

Factor #11: What unintended exposure could the company face via IM? Which populations have this information and require special training, monitoring, or protection?

Factor #12: Do you have regulatory requirements that require a certain IM posture and policy?

An Agenda for Action for Regulatory Requirements and the Basic Business Assets that must be Protected

This will mean having a posture on the following items, at a minimum (Check All Tasks Completed):

_____**1.** You must have formal, written policies for each of the following:

_____**a.** Intellectual property identification, monitoring, and protection

_____**b.** Sensitive information identification, monitoring, and protection

_____**c.** Entitlements by role for IM specifically

_____**d.** Legitimate, accepted uses for IM and specifically prohibited ones (if any)

_____**e.** Monitoring of IM traffic

_____**f.** Enforcement of IM policies

_____**g.** Logging of IM traffic

_____**h.** Archival of IM logs

_____**i.** Regulatory requirements and needs and the processes to satisfy them around IM

_____**2.** Education

_____**a.** With respect to IM

_____**b.** With respect to regulations

_____**c.** With respect to intellectual property

_____**d.** With respect to social engineering

_____**e.** About enforcement, monitoring, and archival requirements (remember that these can have a deterrence benefit)

_____**3.** Applications

_____**a.** Dealing with consumer IM and the applications employees will try to use

_____**b.** Internal, enterprise IM applications

_____**c.** Asset management

_____**4.** Processes

_____**a.** Provisioning IM and accounts

_____**b.** Deprovisioning (via asset management processes) illegal IM clients

_____**c.** Revoking IM entitlements and accounts

_____**5.** Do you have basic security hygiene configured correctly for an environment that includes IM?

_____**a.** Asset management software

_____**b.** Firewalls and proxies

_____**c.** Intrusion detection systems

_____**d.** Anti-malware

_____**e.** Virtual private networks and remote access

_____**f.** Strong authentication

_____**g.** Authorization

_____**6.** Advanced security

_____**a.** Monitoring and enforcement with DLP

_____**b.** Monitoring and SIEM

_____**c.** Anomaly and pattern detection

---

siren call of real-time communications is too much to resist for a motivated IT department and a motivated workforce who want to do more with the tools that are readily available to them.

Let's review a few lists and what you must consider in formulating an IM security policy—and remember that this must always be *in service* to the business. In the following sidebar, "The 12 Factors," consider the factors and the posture in which these put you and your company.

Now consider your responses to these factors in the context of your employees, your partners, your competitors, and the active threats your company will face. Next, consider the basic risks and returns and the infrastructure that you deploy:

• Where are the single points of failure?
• Where does liability lie?
• What is availability like?
• What is the impact of downtime on the business?
• What is the business risk?
• What are your disaster recovery and business continuity options?

Last, consider regulatory requirements and the basic business assets you must protect. You will most likely have to create or update your security policy to consider IM. (see checklist, "An Agenda For Action For Regulatory Requirements And The Basic Business Assets That Must Be Protected").

IM, like any other technology, can serve the business or be a risk to it. The best situation of all is where it is quantified like any other technology and helps promote

---

Acme Inc.'s Answers to the 12 Factors

Factor #1: Do your employees need IM? If so, which employees need IM and *what do they need it for?*

Yes! All nonline working employees should have IM to allow for increased internal communications.

Factor #2: Is IM important as a job satisfaction component? Yes!

Factor #3: Does IM improve or lessen efficiency? IM should improve efficiency by allowing employees to get immediate answers/results and to be able to pull groups together quickly, compared to emails.

Factor #4: Will this efficiency change over time, or is it in fact different for different demographics of my workforce? Efficiency should grow as adoption and comfort levels with IM technologies grow.

Factor #5: Does your company have a need for or dependency on IM to do business?

IM cannot be used for external business transactions or discussions.

Factor #6: Are you considering deploying a technology or process on an IM infrastructure?

Yes. We would need to implement an internal tool to perform IM services.

Factor #7: Does the value to the company of information and processes carried over IM represent something that is a valuable target (because it can either affect your business or realize a gain)? This should include the ability to blackmail employees and partners; can someone learn things about key employees that they could use to threaten or abuse employees and partners?

Yes. All IM communications must remain internal.

Factor #8: If the IM technology were abused or compromised, what would be the risk to the business? Data loss: intellectual property.

Business plan loss: Sensitive information that we can't afford to let the competition see.

Customer data theft: Some Personally Identifiable Information (PII), but all customer-related information is treated as PII.

Factor #9: What intellectual property, material information, corporate documents, and transaction information is at risk over IM?

All internal data would be at risk.

Factor #10: What do transaction types and times tell people about your business? Is it okay for people to have access to this information?

Data will always remain on a need-to-know basis and the IM implementation must not result in the loss of data.

Factor #11: What unintended exposure could the company face via IM? Which populations have this information and require special training, monitoring, or protection? Unintentional internal transfer of restricted data to internal staff without the required internal clearances.

Factor #12: Do you have regulatory requirements that require a certain IM posture and policy? We are under PCI, HIPAA, ISO 27001, and SAS70 Type II guidelines.

the ability to attract talent and keep it while serving the business—driving more business with more people more efficiently and while minimizing risk for business return.

Example Answers to Key Factors

Let's take the example of Acme Inc., as shown in the sidebar, "Acme Inc.'s Answers to the 12 Factors." Acme is a publicly traded company that has international offices and groups that span geographies.

Giving answers to these simple questions mean that the scope of risk and the business relevance is known. These answers can now be used to formulate a security policy and begin the IT projects that are needed for enforcement and monitoring.

Finally, let's move on to the real interactive part of this Chapter: review questions/exercises, hands-on projects, case projects and optional team case project. The answers and/or solutions by chapter can be found in the Online Instructor's Solutions Manual.

CHAPTER REVIEW QUESTIONS/EXERCISES

True/False

1. True or False? When considering IM, it is important to realize that it is first and foremost a technology; it is not a goal in and of itself.
2. True or False? IM is a technology in a continuum of advances (q.v.) that have arisen for communicating and collaborating over a local area network.
3. True or False? Perhaps the most important "law" with respect to networks and for instant messaging is Metcalfe's Law, which states that the value of a telecommunications network increases exponentially with a linear increase in the number of users. (Actually, it states that it is proportional to the square of the users on the network.)
4. True or False? Whenever gains or losses can be quantified for a given population, game theory does not apply.
5. True or False? Whether you work in an IT department or run a small company, your employees have things they need to do: process orders, work with peers, manage teams, talk to customers and to partners. IM is a tool they can and will use to do these things.

Multiple Choice

1. Employees without _____ will seek to get it by abusing backdoors or processes to get this entitlement.
   A. XM
   B. IMS
   C. IM
   D. EM
   E. EXO
2. Some companies have taken a bold step and use _____ for actual business processes?
   A. Metcalfe's Law
   B. Malicious threat
   C. Spyware
   D. IM infrastructure
   E. APT
3. Like any form of software (or hardware), IM applications and infrastructure are subject to _____ and weaknesses from poor configuration and implementation.
   A. Evolution
   B. Residue class

C. Vulnerabilities
D. Certification Authority
E. Security

4. A _____ attack is a class of attack in which a third party acts as a legitimate or even invisible broker.
   A. Trojan horse
   B. X-in-the-middle
   C. Man-in-the-middle
   D. keylogger
   E. tap

5. What is the practice of fooling someone into giving up something they wouldn't otherwise surrender through the use of psychological tricks?
   A. Phishing
   B. IM identity
   C. Knowledge
   D. Intellectual property
   E. Social engineering

EXERCISE

Problem

How does IM differ from email?

Hands-On Projects

Project

How does one manage their IM content?

Case Projects

Problem

What are the current best practices for capturing IM?

Optional Team Case Project

Problem

How can one schedule IM content?

Privacy and Access Management

## Chapter 42

Privacy on the Internet

Marco Cremonini
Università degli Studi di Milano

Chiara Braghin
Università degli Studi di Milano

Claudio Agostino Ardagna
Università degli Studi di Milano

1. PRIVACY IN THE DIGITAL SOCIETY

Privacy in today's digital society is one of the most debated and controversial topics. Many different opinions about what privacy actually is and how it could be preserved have been expressed, but still we can set no clearcut border that cannot be trespassed if privacy is to be safeguarded.

The Origins, the Debate

As it often happens when a debate heats up, the extremes speak louder and, about privacy, the extremes are those that advocate the ban of the disclosure of whatever personal information and those that say that all personal information is already out there, therefore privacy is dead. Supporters of the wide deployment and use of anonymizing technologies are perhaps the best representatives of one extreme. However, these are just the extremes; in reality privacy in the digital society is a fluid concept that such radical positions cannot fully contain. It is a fact that even those supporting full anonymity recognize that there are several limitations to its adoption, either technical or functional. On the other side, even the most skeptical cannot avoid dealing with privacy issues, either because of laws and norms or because of common sense. Sun Microsystems, for example, is actually supporting privacy protection and is a member of the Online Privacy Alliance, an industry coalition that fosters the protection of individuals' privacy online.

Looking at the origins of the concept of privacy, Aristotle's distinction between the public sphere of politics and the private sphere of the family is often considered the root. Much later, the philosophical and anthropological debate around these two spheres of an individual's life evolved. John Stuart Mill, in his essay, *On Liberty*, introduced the distinction between the realm of governmental authority as opposed to the realm of self-regulation. Anthropologists such as Margaret Mead have demonstrated how the need for privacy is innate in different cultures that protect it through concealment or seclusion or by restricting access to secret ceremonies.

More pragmatically, back in 1898, the concept of privacy was expressed by U.S. Supreme Court Justice Brandeis, who defined privacy as "The right to be let alone."[1] This straightforward definition represented for decades the reference of any normative and operational privacy consideration and derivate issues and, before the advent of the digital society, a realistically enforceable ultimate goal. Internet has changed the landscape because the very concept of being let alone while interconnected becomes fuzzy and fluid.

In 1948, privacy gained the status of fundamental right of any individual, being explicitly mentioned in the United Nations Universal Declaration of Human Rights (Article 12): "No one shall be subjected to arbitrary interference with his privacy, family, home or correspondence, nor to attacks upon his honor and reputation. Everyone has the right to the protection of the law against such interference or attacks."[2] However, although privacy has been recognized as a fundamental right of each individual, the Universal Declaration of Human Rights does not explicitly define what privacy is, except for relating it to possible interference or attacks.

About the digital society, less rigorously but otherwise effectively in practical terms, in July 1993, *The New Yorker* published a brilliant cartoon by Peter Steiner that since then has been cited and reproduced dozen of times to refer to the supposed intrinsic level of privacy—here in the sense of anonymity or hiding personal traits—that can be achieved by carrying out social relations over the Internet. That famous cartoon shows one dog that types on a computer keyboard and says to the other one: "On the Internet, no one knows you're a dog."[3] The Internet, at least at the very beginning of its history, was not perceived as threatening to individuals' privacy; rather, it was seen as increasing it, sometimes too much, since it could easily let people disguise themselves in the course of personal relationships. Today that belief may look naïve with the rise of threats to individual privacy that have accompanied the diffusion of the digital society. Nevertheless, there is still truth in that cartoon because, whereas privacy is much weaker on the Internet than in real space, concealing a person's identity and personal traits is technically even easier. Both aspects concur and should be considered.

A commonly used definition of privacy is by Alan Westin: "Privacy is the claim of individuals, groups and institutions to determine for themselves, when, how and to what extent information about them is communicated to others."[4] The definition is rather generic since it does not specify what kind of personal information is to be considered. In the digital society, in particular in the context of network communication, the information can be the identity of the sender, the identity of the receiver, the identity of both, the fact that there is a communication is ongoing, the host/cell/location of the participants taking part to the communication, etc. In order to address these different aspects of privacy, some terms are often used in place of privacy. In [5,6] the differences among *anonymity, unobservability*, and *unlinkability* are pointed out. In the digital society scenario, anonymity is defined as the state of not being identifiable, unobservability as the state of being indistinguishable, and unlinkability as the impossibility of correlating two or more actions/items/pieces of information.

Privacy, however defined and valued, is a tangible state of life that must be attainable in both the physical and the digital society. The reason that in the two realms—the physical and the digital—privacy behaves differently has been widely debated, too, and many of the critical factors that make a difference in the two realms, the impact of technology and the Internet, have been spelled out clearly. However, given the threats and safeguards that technologies make possible, it often remains unclear what the goal of preserving privacy over the Internet should be—being that extreme positions are deemed unacceptable.

Lessig, in his book *Free Culture*,[7] provided an excellent explanation of the difference between privacy in the physical and in the digital world: "The highly inefficient architecture of real space means we all enjoy a fairly robust amount of privacy. That privacy is guaranteed to us by friction. Not by law [...] and in many places, not by norms [...] but instead, by the costs that friction imposes on anyone who would want to spy. [...] Enter the Internet, where the cost of tracking browsing in particular has become quite tiny. [...] The friction has disappeared, and hence any 'privacy' protected by the friction disappears, too."

Thus, privacy can be seen as the friction that reduces the spread of personal information, that makes it more difficult and economically inconvenient to gain access to it. The merit of this definition is to put privacy into a relative perspective, which excludes the extremes that advocate no friction at all or so much friction to stop the flow of information. It also reconciles privacy with security, being both aimed at setting an acceptable level of protection while allowing the development of the digital society and economy rather than focusing on an ideal state of perfect security and privacy.

Privacy Threats

Threats to individual privacy have become publicly appalling since July 2003, when the California Security Breach Notification Law [8] went into effect. This law was the first one to force state government agencies, companies, and nonprofit organizations that conduct business in California to notify California customers if personally identifiable information (PII) stored unencrypted in digital archives was, or is reasonably believed to have been, acquired by an unauthorized person.

The premise for this law was the rise of *identity theft*, which is the conventional expression that has been used to refer to the illicit impersonification carried out by fraudsters who use PII of other people to complete electronic transactions and purchases. The California Security Breach Notification Law lists as PII: Social Security number, driver's license number, California Identification Card number, bank account number, credit- or debit-card number, security codes, access codes, or passwords that would permit access to an individual's financial account (see checklist, "An Agenda For Action For Protecting One's Identity"). By requiring by law the immediate notification to the PII owners, the aim is to avoid direct consequences such as financial losses and derivate consequences such as the burden to restore an individual's own credit history. Starting on January 1, 2008, the data security breach notification law in California also applies to medical information and health insurance data.

Besides the benefits to consumers, this law has been the trigger for similar laws in the United States—today, the majority of U.S. states have one—and has permitted the flourishing of regular statistics about privacy breaches, once almost absent. Privacy threats and analyses are now widely debated, and research focused on privacy problems has become one of the most important.

An Agenda for Action for Protecting One's Identity

You'll want to protect the privacy of your personal information while you're online. Here's a checklist of some of the most important things you can do to protect your identity and prevent others from easily getting your personal information: (Check All Tasks Completed):

_____1. Check a site's privacy policy before you enter any personal information and know how it will be used.

_____2. Make sure you have a secure internet connection, by checking for the unbroken key or closed lock icon in your browser, before you enter any personal information onto a webpage.

_____3. Only give a credit card number when buying something.

_____4. Register your credit cards with your card provider's online security services, such as Verified by Visa and MasterCard SecureCode.

_____5. Use just one credit card for online purchases; if possible, use an account with a low spending limit or small available balance.

_____6. Don't use a debit card for your online purchases. Credit cards are better because bank-provided security guarantees apply to credit cards, so an unauthorized charge is limited to $50.

_____7. Don't select the "remember my password" option when registering online.

_____8. Change your passwords every 60 to 90 days and don't use personal information as your password, instead use a string of at least five letters, numbers and punctuation marks.

_____9. Don't store your passwords near your computer or in your purse or wallet.

_____10. Don't give more information than a site requires.

_____11. Keep your anti-virus software up-to-date to reduce the risk of malicious code running on your PC.

_____12. Don't go online unless you have a personal firewall enabled to add a layer of protection to your PC by stopping unknown connections to your PC.

_____13. Don't reply directly to e-mail messages asking for personal information.

_____14. Type web addresses directly into your web browser instead of clicking on e-mail links.

_____15. Get anti-virus and anti-spam filtering software and keep it up to date by using its automatic update feature, if your service provider or employer doesn't provide it for you.

_____16. Check out online retailers' ratings at BizRate and the Better Business Bureau and the before buying.

The DataLossDB, maintained by the Open Security Foundation, [9] publishes one of the most complete references for privacy breaches and data losses, recording incidents involving data losses back from 2003 to date.

Looking at the largest incidents, the magnitude of some breaches is astonishing: In 2009, about 130 million records were lost by Heartland Payment Systems, USA; in 2007, about 94 million records were hacked at TJX stores in the United States; in 2011, the target was Sony Corp. and its 77 million customer's records. Many other incidents in the dozen of million size are recorded and have gained the headlines on the press, involving all sort of confidential information managed by very different kind of organizations. Most of the incidents have been consequence of hacking from outside the corporate network, but with notable exceptions. In 2004, an employee of America Online Inc. stole 92 million email addresses and sold them to spammers; in 2006 a computer containing about 26 million personal records of the U.S. Department of Veterans Affairs was stolen, in 2007 two CDs were lost containing the entire HM Revenue and Customs (GB) child benefit database (about 25 million records) and 7 million banking details. Similarly, lost tape backups or other storage media containing million of personal records were the reason for severe data loss incidents in 2008 at T-Mobile, at Deutsch Telekom company, at LaSalle Bank, USA, and at GS Caltex in South Korea.

It is interesting to note that the existence of criminals looking after huge archives of personal data is not a phenomenon that appeared with the advent of the Internet and modern interconnected digital networks. In 1984, hackers accessed a credit-reporting database, likely managed on mainframe systems, at TRW Inc. containing 90 million records, and in 1986, document about 16 million vital records of Canadian taxpayers was stolen from Toronto's District Taxation Center.

Whereas these incidents are the most notable, the phenomenon is distributed over the whole spectrum of breach sizes. Hundreds of privacy breaches are reported in the order of a few thousand records lost and all categories of organizations are affected, from public agencies, universities, banks and financial institutions, manufacturing and retail companies, and so on. To this end, it is interesting to quote the authors of the 2011 Data Breach Investigations Report by the Verizon RISK team [10]: "2010 exhibited a much more even distribution. The main factor in this shift is the lack of "mega-breaches" in our combined caseload. Many incidents involving the compromise of multi-millions of records (or more) in the last few years occurred in financial institutions. Without one or two of these skewing the results, things naturally balance out a bit more. Another factor to consider is that criminals seemed to gain interest in stealing data other than payment cards. Account takeovers, theft of IP and other sensitive data, stolen authentication credentials, botnet activity, etc. (which are typically less mega-breachable) affected firms at increased rates in 2010". This is a precious warning not to focus excessively on that "mega-breaches" that get the headlines as the sole indicator of the status of privacy on the Internet. Even in 2010, when huge breaches did not happened (2011 is different, as we illustrated), privacy threats and incidents soared in numbers, while not in the amount of records stolen. Therefore, the threats are real and still well alive even for small-to-medium firms and organizations.

Again from the DataLossDB, we have an overview about the incidence of data breaches by breach type, business type and vector. With respect to breach type, the main ones are: 19% due to hacking; 15% due to stolen laptops; 11% due to malicious Web services; and 11% due to frauds.

A plethora of other reasons for breach, from disposal documents, media and computers to lost or missing storage media, malwares and emails are responsible for almost 40% of all breaches.

With respect to business type, incidents are distributed as follows: 49% affect business; 19% governments; 16% medical institutions; and 16% education.

Finally, the vectors mainly exploited to conduct privacy and data breaches are: 55% of incidents originate from outside an organization; 39% from inside; and 6% unknown.

It is interesting to note how, for incidents originated from inside an organization, the majority is accidental, rather than intentional. This fact points out the relevant role of mistakes, disorganization, mismanagement and all other accidental reasons that may pose severe threats to data privacy.

2. THE ECONOMICS OF PRIVACY

The existence of strong economic factors that influence the way privacy is managed, breached, or even traded off has long been recognized [11,12]. However, it was with the expansion of the online economy, in the 1990s and 2000s, that privacy and economy become more and more entangled. Many studies have been produced to investigate, from different perspectives and approaches, the relation between the two. A comprehensive survey of works that analyzed the economic aspects of privacy can be found in [13].

Two issues among the many have gained most of the attention: assessing the value of privacy and examining to what extent privacy and business can coexist or are inevitably conflicting one with the other. For both issues the debate is still open and no ultimate conclusion has been reached yet.

Privacy and Business

The relationship between privacy and business has been examined from several angles by considering which incentives could be effective for integrating privacy with business processes and, instead, which disincentives make business motivations to prevail over privacy.

Froomkin [14] analyzed what he called "privacy-destroying technologies" developed by governments and businesses. Examples of such technologies are collections of transactional data, automated surveillance in public places, biometric technologies, and tracking mobile devices and positioning systems. To further aggravate the impact on privacy of each one of these technologies, their combination and integration result in a cumulative and reinforcing effect. On this premise, Froomkin introduces the role that legal responses may play to limit this apparently unavoidable "death of privacy."

Odlyzko [15,16] is a leading author that holds a pessimistic view of the future of privacy, calling "unsolvable" the problem of granting privacy because of price discrimination pressures on the market. His argument is based on the observation that the markets as a whole, especially Internet-based markets, have strong incentives to price discriminate, that is, to charge varying prices when there are no cost justifications for the differences. This practice, which has its roots long before the advent of the Internet and the modern economy—one of the most illustrative examples is 19th-century railroad pricing practices—provides relevant economic benefits to the vendors and, from a mere economic viewpoint, to the efficiency of the economy. In general, charging different prices to different segments of the customer base permits vendors to complete transactions that would not take place otherwise. On the other hand, the public has often contrasted plain price discrimination practices since they perceive them as unfair. For this reason, many less evident price discrimination practices are in place today, among which bundling is one of the most recurrent. Privacy of actual and prospective customers is threatened by such economic pressures toward price discrimination because the more the customer base can be segmented—and thus known with greatest detail—the better efficiency is achieved for vendors. The Internet-based market has provided a new boost to such practices and to the acquisition of personal information and knowledge of customer habits.

More pragmatically, some analyses have pointed out that given the current privacy concerns, an explicitly fair management of customers' privacy may become a positive competitive factor [17]. Similarly, Hui et al. [18] have identified seven types of benefits that Internet businesses can provide to consumers in exchange for their personal information.

Privacy and the Web

With respect to the often difficult relation between business goals and privacy requirements, a special attention should be given to Web-based business and the many tools and mechanisms that have been developed to improve the knowledge about customers, their habits and preferences in order to offer to them purchase suggestions and personalized services. The drawback of such business goals is the spread of profiling and the inevitable erosion of customers and users privacy.

Despite the hype that from time to time involves popular search engines like Google or digital social networks like Facebook for their practices of collecting huge amount of information about users accessing their services, detailed and comprehensive analyses of the data collection and management activity on the Internet are still a few and often focused on one specific, while relevant, company.

One of the most informative analysis was published by Krishnamurthy and Wills at the World Wide Web Conference of 2009 [19]. In their work, they reported the results of a study spanning over several years and focused on the technical ways by which third-party aggregators acquire data and the depth of user-related information acquired. The choice of third-party aggregators is useful, because if web sites and services collecting user data are countless, third-party aggregators are a few.

The common technique adopted to track users is to use a cookie, which, in short, is a text file containing information about the user's access to a web service, often encoded in opaque formats, that a web server sends to a client, the client stores locally through its web browser and he exchanges with the server in case of further connections to the same server. Javascript, is the other main technique for tracking users: being code executed at client's side, they have access to information stored by the browser. The two mechanisms provide first- (in case of web-based services like ecommerce sites) and third-party aggregators recording many behavioral information, which, together with physical information like IP addresses, permit to identify users when surfing through the catalogue of an ecommerce site, correlate accesses to different sites and, in general, provide web analytics information about traffic measurements, user profiling and geolocation identification.

From the mentioned study, one notable result is that the top-10 third-party aggregators serve up to 80% of first-party servers analyzed. Interestingly, the authors observe that due to the raising concerns about privacy, modern web browsers now provide means to block third-party Javascript and cookies, but, as expected, the arms race between users profiling and privacy never settle down and tracking techniques are evolving to bypass those new limitations. In particular, being first-party scripts and cookies still usually allowed, being them the key to an improved user experience and variety of functionality, third-party aggregators are more and more "hiding" their content in first-party servers. Data examined by the study confirm this, exhibiting a striking growth of first-party cookies, Javascript and hidden third-party objects in the timeframe considered. Therefore, it is safe to conclude that, despite new tools and features aimed at privacy protection, blocking third-party content used for tracking users is extremely difficult, without severely impair the user experience.

Considering the limitations that affect technical means in protecting privacy, it is natural to turn the attention to regulations and guidelines too. One example of guidelines is the "Guide to Protecting the Confidentiality of Personally Identifiable Information (PII)" published by the National Institute for Standard and Technology (NIST) in 2010 [20]. The aim is "to assist Federal agencies in protecting the confidentiality of personally identifiable information (PII) in information systems". It is inspired by the Fair Information Practices, which are the principles underlying most privacy laws and privacy best practices. This publication by NIST consists of a comprehensive set of guidelines, merging consideration about information security and privacy, mostly focused on preventing frauds or massive data breaches. With regard to profiling and tracking, however, the NIST guidelines seem ineffective.

The case of the new proposed regulation by the European Union [21] is different. Being still a proposal, it may be subject to changes, amendments and its adoption delayed; therefore only preliminary considerations are possible. However, the overall rational seems clear. First, the regulation is aimed at establishing a uniform legislation among all European member states, resolving the current heterogeneity of approaches that leads to different practices and privacy protection levels. Then, it mandates a notification procedure in case of data breach, similar, in the spirit, to the many US states legislations. Finally, and most pertinent to the issues discussed in the present section, it remarkably reinforces the *opt-in* approach (i.e., this means that by default, personal information could not be acquired and managed by first- and third-parties unless the user explicitly express his/her consent, and it is opposed to the *opt-out* approach generally adopted in the USA) and imposes strong management requirements to first- and third-parties. More in particular, the proposed regulation is driven by the assumption that personal data belong and still fully belong to data owners even when collected by first- and third-parties. As a consequence, the regulation has several prescriptions about the extent of knowledge that data owners should be provided with from organizations collecting their data, the full right to inspect, modify and delete personal data stored and even transmitted to others by those organizations, and even prescriptions about the provisioning of an European-based support service by data collectors. Therefore, the new EU regulation, if approved in the current form, could sensibly interfere with the practices adopted by data aggregators and first-parties for tracking and profiling users. However, given its status, it is still early to draw firm conclusions about its effectiveness and real impact in the arms race between business and privacy requirements.

3. PRIVACY-ENHANCING TECHNOLOGIES

Technical improvements of Web and location technologies have fostered the development of online applications that use the private information of users (including physical position of individuals) to offer enhanced services. The increasing amount of available personal data and the decreasing cost of data storage and processing makes it technically possible and economically justifiable to gather and analyze large amounts of data. In this context, users are much more concerned about their privacy, which has been recognized as one of the main reasons that prevents users from using the Internet for accessing online services. A number of useful privacy-enhancing technologies (PETs) have been developed for dealing with privacy issues, and previous works on privacy protection have focused on a wide variety of topics [22–26]. In this section, we discuss the privacy protection problem in three different contexts. We start by giving an overview of languages and approaches for the specification of access control policies in distributed networks; we then discuss languages and solutions for the definition of privacy-aware access control policies and privacy preferences in distributed networks; we finally describe the problem of protecting privacy in mobile and pervasive environments, and we give an overview of solutions for preserving the location privacy of the users from different perspectives [27].

Access Control Models and Languages

Access control systems have been introduced for regulating and protecting access to resources and data owned by parties. Originally, access control models and languages have been defined for centralized and closed environments: users were assumed to be known by the system, and to be identified and authenticated before any authorization process could start. The advent of distributed environments has changed the overall scenario making the above assumptions not possible and traditional access control inapplicable. In an open scenario, in fact, the users are usually not known to the server a-priori and, therefore, identification and authentication are not always possible/wanted. Suitable access control models and languages need to depart from identification and authentication, and to provide a solution that fits the requirements of an open scenario.

Recent works have focused on the definition of attribute-based and credential-based access control, where authorization policies specify the set of attributes and credentials that a user must possess, or conditions over credentials and attributes that a user needs to satisfy to access a resource. In this context, credential-based languages refer to those solutions that use properties of the users, included in credentials signed by third parties, to evaluate access control policies. In general, credentials are characterized by a type (Identity Card), a unique identifier, and an issuer (US government), and certify a set of properties for the user (*FirstName* = John, *LastName* = Doe). Similarly, attribute-based languages refer to those solutions that evaluate policies using attributes that are self-certified by the owner, without a signature made by a third party. Several different models and languages have been defined, prescribing access decisions on the basis of some properties that the requesting party may have. First, logic-based languages ([28–31]) have been proposed with the main goal of providing high-expressive solutions allowing the definition of policies that well adapt to the dynamics and complexity of distributed environments. However, although highly expressive and powerful, logic languages are difficult to adopt in practice especially in a distributed scenario where simplicity, interoperability, and easiness of use are fundamental requirements. [32–34] In addition to frameworks and solutions supporting logic-based access control policies, different automated trust negotiation approaches [35–37] have been developed to establish trust between unknown parties. A trust negotiation is a bidirectional exchange of requests and responses between two parties to the aim of establishing trust by incremental data disclosure. Trust negotiation research has investigated algorithms and protocols that *i)* allow a party to select credentials that have to be released to the counterpart and *ii)* protect sensitive information in credentials and/or policies during the negotiation process. In general, trust negotiation protocols provide low performance, with high overhead, and are therefore not suitable for many distributed use cases. The research community has then focused on the definition of access control models and languages that support the requirements of distributed environments, and address the issues of logic-based languages and trust negotiation approaches.

The *eXtensible Access Control Markup Language (XACML)*[38], which is the result of a standardization effort by OASIS, provides an attribute-based access control solution that balances between expressivity and simplicity, is flexibile and extensible, and integrates well with open environments. XACML proposes an XML-based language to express and interchange access control policies, defines an architecture for the evaluation of policies, and specifies a communication protocol for messages interchange.

Main features of XACML are: *(1) policy combination*, a method for combining policies on the same resource independently specified by different entities; *(2) combining algorithms*, different algorithms representing ways of combining multiple decisions into a single decision; *(3) attribute-based restrictions*, the definition of policies based on properties associated with subjects and resources rather than on their identities; *(4) multiple subjects*, the definition of more than one subject relevant to a decision request; *(5) policy distribution*, policies can be defined by different parties and enforced at different enforcement points; *(6) implementation independence*, an abstraction layer that isolates the policy-writer from the implementation details; and *(7) obligations*, a method for specifying the actions that must be fulfilled in conjunction with the policy enforcement.

Focusing on the language, XACML is based on a model providing a formal representation of policies. Each XACML policy has an element *Policy* or *PolicySet* as root, which in turn may contain other *Policy* or *PolicySet* elements. Each *Policy* element is composed by a *Target* that evaluates policy applicability to a request, a set of *Rule* that corresponds to positive authorizations (i.e., with attribute *effect* = permit) or negative authorizations (i.e., with attribute *effect* = deny), a set of *Obligation* specifying actions to be done during the enforcement of an access decision, and a rule combing algorithm (attribute *RuleCombiningAlgId*) that establishes how conflicting decisions taken by different rules can be reconciled in a single decision (i.e., deny overrides, permit overrides, first applicable, only one applicable).

Today, XACML is considered as the de-facto standard for attribute-based access control in distributed environments and is adopted in many different scenarios. In addition, although the XACML language is not specifically designed for managing privacy, it has represented a relevant innovation in the field of access control policies and has set the basis for the definition of many authorization languages with enhanced functionalities, including support for anonymity, trust negotiation, credentials, complex conditions (recursion, delegation, chain of trust), dialog management [39−41].

Languages for Privacy-Aware Access Control and Privacy Preferences

The importance gained by privacy requirements has brought with it the definition of access control models that are enriched with the ability of supporting privacy requirements. These enhanced access control models encompass two privacy aspects: to guarantee the desired level of privacy of information exchanged between different parties by controlling the access to services/resources, and to control all secondary uses of information disclosed for the purpose of access control enforcement. Users requiring access to a server application need then to protect access to their personal data by specifying and evaluating privacy policies.

The most important proposal in this field is the *Platform for Privacy Preferences Project* (P3P), a World Wide Web Consortium (W3C) project aimed at protecting the privacy of users by addressing their need to assess that the privacy practices adopted by a server provider comply with users' privacy requirements. The goal of P3P is twofold: *i)* to allow Web sites to state their data-collection practices in a standardized, machine-readable way, and *ii)* to provide users with a solution to understand which data will be collected and how those data will be used. To this aim, P3P allows Web sites to declare their privacy practices in a standard and machine-readable XML format known as *P3P policy*. A P3P policy contains the specification of the data it protects, the data recipients allowed to access the private data, consequences of data release, purposes of data collection, data retention policy, and dispute resolution mechanisms. Supporting privacy preferences and policies in Web-based transactions allows users to automatically understand and match server practices against their privacy preferences. Thus, users do not need to read the privacy policies at every site they interact with, but they are always aware of the server practices in data handling. The corresponding language that would allow users to specify their preferences as a set of preference rules is called a *P3P Preference Exchange Language* (APPEL)[42]. APPEL can be used by users' agents to reach automated or semi-automated decisions regarding the acceptability of privacy policies from P3P-enabled Web sites. Unfortunately, interactions between P3P and APPEL have shown that users can explicitly specify just what is unacceptable in a policy, whereas the APPEL syntax is cumbersome and error prone for users.

Other approaches have focused on the definition of access control frameworks that integrate both policy evaluation and privacy functionalities. A solution that introduced a privacy-aware access control system has been defined by Ardagna et al. [43]. This framework allows the integration, evaluation, and enforcement of policies regulating access to service/data and release of personal identifiable information, and provides a mechanism to define constraints on the secondary use of personal data for the protection of users' privacy. In particular, the following types of privacy policies have been specified:

- *Access control policies.* They govern access/release of services/data managed by the party (as in traditional access control).

- *Release policies.* They govern release of properties/credentials/personal identifiable information (PII) of the party and specify under which conditions this information can be disclosed.
- *Data handling policies.* They define how personal information will be (or should be) dealt with at the receiving parties.

An important feature of this framework is to support requests for certified data, issued and signed by trusted authorities, and uncertified data, signed by the owner itself. It also allows to define conditions that can be satisfied by means of zero-knowledge proof [44] and based on the physical position of the users [45].

Most of the research on security and privacy has focused on the server-side of the problem, while symmetric approaches have been used and implemented at the client-side to protect the privacy of the users (privacy preference definition based on policies). In the last few years, however, some solutions for privacy protection that strictly focus on clients' needs have been defined.

Privacy in Mobile Environments

The concept of *location privacy* can be defined as the right of individuals to decide how, when, and for which purposes their location information could be released to other parties. The lack of location privacy protection could be exploited by adversaries to perform various attacks [46]:

- *Unsolicited advertising,* when the location of a user could be exploited, without her consent, to provide advertisements of products and services available nearby the user position.
- *Physical attacks or harassment,* when the location of a user could allow criminals to carry out physical assaults on specific individuals.
- *User profiling and tracking,* when the location of a user could be used to infer other sensitive information, such as state of health, personal habits, or professional duties, by correlating visited places or paths.
- *Political, religious, sexual persecution and discrimination,* when the location of a user could be used to reduce the freedom of individuals, and mobile technologies are used to identify and persecute opponents.
- *Denial of service,* when the location of a user could motivate an access denial to services under some circumstances.

A further complicating factor is that location privacy can assume several meanings and introduce different requirements, depending on the scenario in which the users are moving and on the services the users are interacting with. The following categories of location privacy can then be identified:

- *Identity privacy* protects the identity of the users associated with or inferable from location information. To this purpose, protection techniques aim at minimizing the disclosure of data that can let attackers infer a user identity. Identity privacy is suitable in application contexts that do not require the identification of the users for providing a service.
- *Position privacy* protects the position of individual users by perturbing corresponding information and decreasing the accuracy of location information. Position privacy is suitable for environments where users' identities are required for a successful service provisioning. A technique that most solutions exploit, either explicitly or implicitly, consists of reducing the accuracy by scaling a location to a coarser granularity (from meters to hundreds of meters, from a city block to the whole town, and so on).
- *Path privacy* protects the privacy of information associated with users movements, such as the path followed while travelling or walking in an urban area. Several location-based services (personal navigation systems) could be exploited to subvert path privacy or to illicitly track users.

Since location privacy definition and requirements differ depending on the scenario, no single technique is able to address the requirements of all location privacy categories. Therefore, in the past, the research community, focusing on providing solutions for the protection of location privacy of users, has defined techniques that can be divided into three main classes: *anonymity-based, obfuscation-based,* and *policy-based* techniques. These classes of techniques are partially overlapped in scope and could be potentially suitable to cover requirements coming from one or more of the categories of location privacy. It is easy to see that anonymity-based and obfuscation-based techniques can be considered dual categories. Anonymity-based techniques have been primarily defined to protect identity privacy and are not suitable for protecting position privacy, whereas obfuscation-based techniques are well suited for position protection and not appropriate for identity protection. Anonymity-based and obfuscation-based techniques could also be both exploited for protecting path privacy. Policy-based techniques are in general suitable for all location privacy categories, although they are often difficult to understand and manage for end users.

Among the classes of techniques just introduced, current research on location privacy has mainly focused on supporting anonymity and partial identities. Beresford and Stajano [47] propose a method, called *mix zones,* which uses an anonymity service based on an infrastructure that delays and reorders messages from sub-scribers. Within a mix zone (an area where a user cannot be tracked), a user is anonymous, meaning that the identi-ties of all users coexisting in the same zone are mixed and become indiscernible. Other works are based on the concept of k-anonymity [48] applied to location privacy. Bettini et al. [49] design a framework able to evaluate the risk of sensitive location-based information dissemina-tion. Their proposal puts forward the idea that the geo-localized history of the requests submitted by a user can be considered as a quasi-identifier that can be used to dis-cover sensitive information about the user. Gruteser and Grunwald [50] develop a middleware architecture and an adaptive algorithm to adjust location information resolu-tion, in spatial or temporal dimensions, to comply with users' anonymity requirements. To this purpose, the authors introduced the concepts of *spatial cloaking*. Spatial cloaking guarantees k-anonymity by enlarging the area where a user is located to an area containing k indis-tinguishable users. Cornelius et al. [51] describe *AnonySense*, a privacy-aware architecture that implements complex applications using collaborative and opportunis-tic sensing by mobile devices. The proposed solution pro-tects the privacy of the involved users by submitting sensing tasks to mobile devices in an anonymous way, and by collecting anonymized (but verified) sensed data. Chow et al. [52] provide a spatial cloaking solution for P2P environments and protocols, based on information sharing, historical location, and cloaked area adjustment schemes.

Anonymity has also been exploited to protect the path privacy of the users. Chow and Mokbel [53] provide a survey of the most advanced techniques for privacy pro-tection in continuous LBS and trajectory data publication.

Alternatively, when the user identity is required for location-based service provision, obfuscation-based tech-niques have been deployed. Obfuscation is the process of degrading the quality of location information for privacy reasons. An important issue is to manage the trade-off between individual needs for high-quality information services and for location privacy. Ardagna et al. [54] define an approach based on obfuscation for protecting the location privacy of the users against malicious adver-saries. The proposed solution is based on a metric called *relevance*, which models the level of location privacy, and balances location privacy with the accuracy needed for the provision of reliable location-based services. The authors introduce different obfuscation-based techniques aimed at preserving location privacy by artificially per-turbing location information (modeled as planar and cir-cular areas). These techniques, which can be used alone or in combination, degrade the location information accu-racy by (1) enlarging the radius, (2) reducing the radius, and (3) shifting the center of the measured location. The

robustness of the obfuscation techniques is tested against attackers with different knowledge and capabilities, to verify their suitability in a real environment. Hashem and Kulik [55] present a decentralized approach to privacy in wireless ad-hoc networks that mixes both k-anonymity and obfuscation concepts. First of all, the users obfuscate their precise location; then, they anonymize the request by transforming the obfuscated area in a k-anonymous area that contains the obfuscated area of other k-1 users. After creating the anonymous area, an algorithm selects a query requester with a near-uniform randomness, thus ensuring sender anonymity.

Finally, policy-based techniques are based on the notion of privacy policies and are suitable for all the cate-gories of location privacy. In particular, privacy policies define restrictions that must be enforced when location of users is used by or released to external parties. As an example, the IETF Geopriv working group [56] addresses privacy and security issues related to the disclosure of location information over the Internet. The main goal is to define an environment supporting both location infor-mation and policy data.

4. NETWORK ANONYMITY

In recent years, Internet has become an essential aspect of our daily activities, thus the interest in security and pri-vacy issues on the Internet has grown exponentially. In particular, in such a distributed environment, privacy should also imply anonymity: a person shopping online may not want her visits to be tracked, the sending of email should keep the identities of the sender and the recipient hidden from observers, and so on. That is, when surfing the Web, users want to keep secret not only the information they exchange but also the fact that they are exchanging information and with whom. Such a problem has to do with traffic analysis, and it requires ad hoc solu-tions. Traffic analysis is the process of intercepting and examining messages to deduce information from patterns in communication. It can be performed even when mes-sages are encrypted and cannot be decrypted. In general, the greater the number of messages observed or even intercepted and stored, the more can be inferred from the traffic. It cannot be solved just by encrypting the header of a packet or the payload: in the first case, the packet could still be tracked as it moves through the network; the second case is ineffective as well since it would still be possible to identify who is talking to whom.

In this section, we first describe the onion routing pro-tocol [57−59], one of the better-known approaches that is not application-oriented. Then, we provide an overview of other techniques for assuring anonymity and privacy over networks and we discuss the problem of mail anonymity.

Onion Routing and TOR

Onion routing is intended to provide real-time bidirectional *anonymous connections* that are resistant to both eavesdropping and traffic analysis in a way that is transparent to applications. That is, if Alice and Bob communicate over a public network by means of onion routing, they are guaranteed that the content of the message remains confidential and no external observer or internal node is able to infer that they are communicating.

Onion routing works beneath the application layer, replacing socket connections with anonymous connections and without requiring any change to proxy-aware Internet services or applications. It was originally implemented on Sun Solaris 2.4 in 1997, including proxies for Web browsing (HTTP), remote logins (rlogin), email (SMTP), and file transfer (FTP) and now runs on most common operating systems. It consists of a fixed infrastructure of onion routers, where each router has a long-standing socket connection to a set of neighboring ones. Only a few routers, called *onion router proxies*, know the whole infrastructure topology. In onion routing, instead of making socket connections directly to a responding machine, initiating applications make a socket connection to an onion routing proxy that builds an anonymous connection through several other onion routers to the destination. In this way, the onion routing network allows the connection between the initiator and responder to remain anonymous. Although the protocol is called onion routing, the routing that occurs during the anonymous connection is at the application layer of the protocol stack, not at the IP layer. However, the underlying IP network determines the route that data actually travels between individual onion routers. Given the onion router infrastructure, the onion routing protocol works in three phases:

- Anonymous connection *setup*
- *Communication* through the anonymous connection
- Anonymous connection *destruction*

During the first phase, the initiator application, instead of connecting directly with the destination machine, opens a socket connection with an onion routing proxy (which may reside in the same machine, in a remote machine, or in a firewall machine). The proxy first establishes a path to the destination in the onion router infrastructure, then sends an *onion* to the first router of the path. The onion is a layered data structure in which each layer of the onion (public-key encrypted) is intended for a particular onion router and contains (1) the identity of the next onion router in the path to be followed by the anonymous connection; (2) the expiration time of the onion; and (3) a key seed to be used to generate the keys to encode the data sent through the anonymous connection in both directions. The onion is sent through the path established by the proxy: an onion router that receives an onion peels off its layer, identifies the next hop, records on a table the key seed, the expiration time and the identifiers of incoming and outgoing connections and the keys that are to be applied, pads the onion and sends it to the next onion router. Since the most internal layer contains the name of the destination machine, the last router of the path will act as the destination proxy and open a socket connection with the destination machine. Note that only the intended onion router is able to peel off the layer intended to it. In this way, each intermediate onion router knows (and can communicate with) only the previous and the next-hop router. Moreover, it is not capable of understanding the content of the following layers of the onion. The router, and any external observer, cannot know *a priori* the length of the path since the onion size is kept constant by the fact that each intermediate router is obliged to add padding to the onion corresponding to the fixed-size layer that it removed.

Once the anonymous connection is established, data can be sent in both directions. The onion proxy receives data from the initiator application, breaks it into fixed-size packets, and adds a layer of encryption for each onion router in the path using the keys specified in the onion. As data packets travel through the anonymous connection, each intermediate onion router removes one layer of encryption. The last router in the path sends the plaintext to the destination through the socket connection that was opened during the setup phase. This encryption layering occurs in the reverse order when data is sent backward from the destination machine to the initiator application. In this case, the initiator proxy, which knows both the keys and the path, will decrypt each layer and send the plaintext to the application using its socket connection with the application. As for the onion, data passed along the anonymous connection appears different to each intermediate router and external observer, so it cannot be tracked. Moreover, compromised onion routers cannot cooperate to correlate the data stream they see.

When the initiator application decides to close the socket connection with the proxy, the proxy sends a destroy message along the anonymous connection and each router removes the entry of the table relative to that connection.

There are several advantages in the onion routing protocol. First, the most trusted element of the onion routing infrastructure is the initiator proxy, which knows the network topology and decides the path used by the anonymous connection. If the proxy is moved in the initiator machine, the trusted part is under the full control of the initiator. Second, the total cryptographic overhead is the same as for link encryption but, whereas in link encryption one corrupted router is enough to disclose all the data, in onion routing routers cannot cooperate to correlate the little they know and disclose the information. Third, since an onion has an expiration time, replay attacks are not possible. Finally, if anonymity is also desired, then all identifying information must be additionally removed from the data stream before being sent over the anonymous connection. However, onion routing is not completely invulnerable to traffic analysis attacks: if a huge number of messages between routers is recorded and usage patterns analyzed, it would be possible to make a close guess about the routing, that is, also about the initiator and the responder. Moreover, the topology of the onion router infrastructure must be static and known *a priori* by at least one onion router proxy, which make the protocol little adaptive to node/router failures.

Tor [60] is the second generation onion routing. It addresses some of the limitations highlighted earlier, providing a reasonable tradeoff among anonymity, usability, and efficiency. In particular, it provides perfect forward secrecy and it does not require a proxy for each supported application protocol. Tor is also an effective *circumvention tool* (a tool to bypass Internet filtering in order to access content blocked by governments, workplaces or schools). All circumvention tools use the same core method to bypass network filtering: they proxy connections through third party sites that are not filtered themselves. [61] is a report on the usage of these tools. One of the most interesting result is the small usage of circumvention tools with respect to the number of filtering countries, explained by the authors by the fact that users are probably not aware of the existence of this kind of tools or are not able to find them.

Network Anonymity Services

Some other approaches offer some possibilities for providing anonymity and privacy, but they are still vulnerable to some types of attacks. For instance, many of these approaches are designed for World Wide Web access only; being protocol-specific, these approaches may require further development to be used with other applications or Internet services, depending on the communication protocols used in those systems.

David Chaum [62] introduced the idea of *mix networks* in 1981 (further extended subsequently, like in [63]) to enable unobservable communication between users of the Internet: it provides of sender and receiver and sender anonymity. Mixes are intermediate nodes that may reorder, delay, and pad incoming messages to complicate traffic analysis. A mix node stores a certain number of incoming messages that it receives and sends them to the next mix node in a random order. Thus, messages are modified and reordered in such a way that it is nearly impossible to correlate an incoming message with an outgoing message. Messages are sent through a series of mix nodes and encrypted with mix keys. If participants exclusively use mixes for sending messages to each other, their communication relations will be unobservable, even if the attacker records all network connections. Also, without additional information, the receiver does not have any clue about the identity of the message's sender. As in onion routing, each mix node knows only the previous and next node in a received message's route. Hence, unless the route only goes through a single node, compromising a mix node does not enable an attacker to violate either the sender nor the recipient privacy. Mix networks are not really efficient, since a mix needs to receive a large group of messages before forwarding them, thus delaying network traffic. However, onion routing has many analogies with this approach and an onion router can be seen as a real-time Chaum mix.

Reiter and Rubin [64] proposed an alternative to mixes, called *crowds*, a system to make only browsing anonymous: it aims at hiding from Web servers and third-parties information about either the user or the information she retrieves. This is obtained by preventing a Web server from learning any information linked to the user, such as the IP address or domain name, the page that referred the user to its site, or the user's computing platform. The approach is based on the idea of "blending into a crowd," that is, hiding one's actions within the actions of many others. Before making any request, a user joins a crowd of other users. Then, when the user submits a request, it is forwarded to the final destination with probability *p* and to some other member of the crowd with probability *1-p*. When the request is eventually submitted, the end server cannot identify its true initiator. Even crowd members cannot identify the initiator of the request, since the initiator is indistinguishable from a member of the crowd that simply passed on a request from another.

Anonymous Remailers

An anonymous remailer is a system that provides sender anonymity for electronic mail. The basic idea is that a mail server receives messages and then forwards them without revealing where they originally came from. There are different types of anonymous remailer servers. A *type-0* remailer (or *Pseudonymous* remailer) removes the server address, sets a random pseudonym to the sender and sends the message to the intended recipient. In this way, the recipient may send a message back to the sender. The server keeps a list containing the matching of the pseudonyms to sender real email addresses. The remailer is vulnerable to traffic analysis, moreover if the server is compromised and an attacker is able to obtain the matching list all the senders are revealed.

Type-I remailers (or *Cypherpunk* remailers) were developed to deal with the problems highlighted above. The basic idea is the same: the remailer receive the message, removes the sender address and then send it to the recipient, but there are some changes: (i) the message may be encrypted with the remailer public key; (ii) the remailer does not keep any log that could be used to identify senders; and (iii) the message is not sent directly to the recipient but to a *chain* of remailers. In this way, a single remailer does not know both the sender and the recipient. The drawback is that it is not possible to reply to the message and that they are still vulnerable to some kinds of attack. For this reason, Type-II (or Mixmaster) and type-III (or Mixminion) remailers have been proposed, but they are not really used in practice since they require specially customized software in order to send mails.

5. SUMMARY

In this Chapter we have discussed privacy from different viewpoints, from historical to technological. The very nature of the concept of privacy requires such an enlarged perspective because it often appears indefinite, being constrained into the tradeoff between the undeniable need of protecting personal information and the evident utility, in many contexts, of the availability of the same information. The digital society and the global interconnected infrastructure eased accessing and spreading of personal information; therefore, developing technical means and defining norms and fair usage procedures for privacy protection are now more demanding than in the past.

Economic aspects have been introduced since they are likely to strongly influence the way privacy is actually managed and protected. In this area, research has provided useful insights about the incentive and disincentives toward better privacy.

We presented some of the more advanced solutions that research has developed to date, either for anonymizing stored data, hiding sensitive information in artificially inaccurate clusters, or introducing third parties and middleware in charge of managing online transactions and services in a privacy-aware fashion. Location privacy is a topic that has gained importance in recent years with the advent of mobile devices and that is worth a specific consideration.

Furthermore, the important issue of anonymity on the internet has been investigated. To let individuals surf the Web, access online services, and interact with remote parties in an anonymous way has been the goal of many efforts for years. Some important technologies and tools are available and are gaining popularity.

To conclude, whereas privacy on the internet and in the digital society does not look to be in good shape, the augmented sensibility of individuals to its erosion, the many scientific and technological efforts to introduce novel solutions, and a better knowledge of the problem with the help of fresh data contribute to stimulating the need for better protection and fairer use of personal information. For this reason, it is likely that internet privacy will remain an important topic in the years to come and more innovations toward better management of privacy issues will emerge.

Finally, let's move on to the real interactive part of this Chapter: review questions/exercises, hands-on projects, case projects and optional team case project. The answers and/or solutions by chapter can be found in the Online Instructor's Solutions Manual.

CHAPTER REVIEW QUESTIONS/EXERCISES

True/False

1. True or False? Privacy in today's digital society is one of the most debated and controversial topics.
2. True or False? As it often happens when a debate heats up, the extremes speak louder and, about privacy, the extremes are those that advocate the ban of the disclosure of whatever personal information and those that say that all personal information is already out there, therefore privacy is alive.
3. True or False? Threats to individual privacy have become publicly appalling since July 2012, when the California Security Breach Notification Law [8] went into effect.
4. True or False? The existence of strong economic factors that influence the way privacy is managed, breached, or even traded off has not been recognized.
5. True or False? The relationship between privacy and business has been examined from several angles by considering which incentives could be ineffective for integrating privacy with business processes and, instead, which disincentives make business motivations to prevail over privacy.

Multiple Choice

1. With respect to the often difficult relation between business goals and privacy requirements, a special attention should be given to _____ business and the many tools and mechanisms that have been developed to improve the knowledge about customers, their habits and preferences in order to offer to them purchase suggestions and personalized services.
   A. Privacy-enhancing technology
   B. Location technology
   C. Web-based
   D. Technical improvement

E. Web Technology

2. Technical improvements of _____ and location technologies have fostered the development of online applications that use the private information of users (including physical position of individuals) to offer enhanced services?
   A. Privacy-enhancing technology
   B. Location technology
   C. Web-based
   D. Web
   E. Web Technology

3. What systems have been introduced for regulating and protecting access to resources and data owned by parties?
   A. Access control
   B. *XACML*
   C. XML-based language
   D. Certification Authority
   E. Security

4. The importance gained by privacy requirements has brought with it the definition of _____ that are enriched with the ability of supporting privacy requirements.
   A. Access control models
   B. Languages
   C. Privacy-Aware Access Control
   D. Privacy preferences
   E. Taps

5. What govern access/release of services/data managed by the party (as in traditional access control)?
   A. Release policies
   B. Access control policies
   C. Data handling policies
   D. Intellectual property
   E. Social engineering

EXERCISE

Problem

What should I know about privacy policies?

Hands-On Projects

Project

How can I protect my privacy when shopping online?

Case Projects

Problem

How can I prevent web sites from sharing my web browsing habits?

Optional Team Case Project

Problem

How can I prevent my computer from keeping a history of where I browse?

REFERENCES

[1] S.D. Warren, L.D. Brandeis, The right to privacy, Harv. Law Rev. IV (5) (1890).

[2] United Nations, Universal Declaration of Human Rights. <www.un.org/Overview/rights.html>, 1948.

[3] P. Steiner, On the internet, nobody knows you're a dog, Cartoonbank, The New Yorker. <www.cartoonbank.com/item/22230>, 1993.

[4] A. Westin, Privacy and Freedom, New York, 1987.

[5] A. Pfitzmann, M. Waidner, Networks without user observability – design options, Proceedings of Workshop on the Theory and Application of Cryptographic Techniques on Advances in Cryptology (EuroCrypt'85), vol. 219, LNCS Springer, Linz, Austria, 1986.

[6] A. Pfitzmann, M. Köhntopp, Anonymity, unobservability, and pseudonymity—a proposal for terminology, Designing Privacy Enhancing Technologies, Springer, Berlin, 2001.

[7] L. Lessig, Free Culture, Penguin Group, 2003 <www.free-culture.cc/>.

[8] California Security Breach Notification Law, Bill Number: SB 1386. <http://info.sen.ca.gov/pub/01-02/bill/sen/sb_1351-1400/sb_1386_bill_20020926_chaptered.html>, February 2002.

[9] DataLossDB. <http://datalossdb.org/>, 2012.

[10] Data Breach Investigations Report, the Verizon RISK team. <http://www.verizonbusiness.com/Products/security/dbir/>, 2011.

[11] J. Hirshleifer, The private and social value of information and the reward to inventive activity, Am. Econ. Rev. 61 (1971) 561−574.

[12] R.A. Posner, The economics of privacy, Am. Econ. Rev. 71 (2) (1981) 405−409.

[13] K.L. Hui, I.P.L. Png, Economics of privacy, in: T. Hendershott (Ed.), Handbooks in Information Systems, vol. 1, Elsevier, 2006.

[14] A.M. Froomkin, The death of privacy? 52 *Stanford Law Rev.* (2000) 1461−1469.

[15] A.M. Odlyzko, Privacy, economics, and price discrimination on the internet, in: N. Sadeh (Ed.), Proceedings of the Fifth International Conference on Electronic Commerce (ICEC2003), ACM, 2003, pp. 355−366.

[16] A.M. Odlyzko, Privacy and the clandestine evolution of ecommerce, Proceedings of the Ninth International Conference on Electronic Commerce (ICEC2007), ACM, 2007.

[17] M. Brown, R. Muchira, Investigating the relationship between internet privacy concerns and online purchase behavior, J. Electron. Comm. Res. 5 (1) (2004) 62−70.

[18] K.L. Hui, B.C.Y. Tan, C.Y. Goh, Online information disclosure: motivators and measurements, ACM Trans. Internet Technol. 6 (4) (2006) 415−441.

[19] B. Krishnamurthy, C.E. Wills, Privacy Diffusion on the Web: A Longitudinal Perspective, WWW 2009, Madrid, Spain, April 20−24, 2009.

[20] E. McCallister, T. Grance, K.A. Scarfone, NIST Special Publication 800−122 Guide to Protecting the Confidentiality of

Personally Identifiable Information (PII). <http://www.nist.gov/manuscript-publication-search.cfm?pub_id = 904990>, April 2010.

[21] European Commission, Protection of personal data. <http://ec.europa.eu/justice/newsroom/data-protection/news/120125_en.htm>, 2012.

[22] R. Chandramouli, Privacy protection of enterprise information through inference analysis, Proceedings of IEEE Sixth International Workshop on Policies for Distributed Systems and Networks (POLICY 2005), Stockholm, Sweden, 2005, pp. 47−56.

[23] L.F. Cranor, Web Privacy with P3P, O'Reilly & Associates, 2002.

[24] G. Karjoth, M. Schunter, Privacy policy model for enterprises, Proceedings of the Fifteenth IEEE Computer Security Foundations Workshop, Cape Breton, Nova Scotia, 2002.

[25] B. Thuraisingham, Privacy constraint processing in a privacy-enhanced database management system, Data Knowl. Eng. 55 (2) (2005) 159−188.

[26] M. Youssef, V. Atluri, N.R. Adam, Preserving mobile customer privacy: an access control system for moving objects and customer profiles, Proceedings of the Sixth International Conference on Mobile Data Management (MDM 2005), Ayia Napa, Cyprus, 2005, pp. 67−76.

[27] P. Samarati, Protecting respondents' identities in microdata release, in: IEEE Transactions on Knowledge and Data Engineering (TKDE), November−December, 2001, vol. 13, 6.

[28] P. Bonatti, P. Samarati, A unified framework for regulating access and information release on the Web, J. Comput. Secur. 10 (3) (2002) 241−272.

[29] K. Irwin, T. Yu, Preventing attribute information leakage in automated trust negotiation, Proceedings of the Twelfth ACM Conference on Computer and Communications Security (CCS 2005), Alexandria, VA, USA, November 2005.

[30] S. Jajodia, P. Samarati, M. Sapino, V. Subrahmanian, Flexible support for multiple access control policies, ACM Trans. Database Syst. 26 (2) (June 2001) 214−260.

[31] M. Winslett, N. Ching, V. Jones, I. Slepchin, Assuring security and privacy for digital library transactions on the web: client and server security policies, Proceedings of the Fourth International Forum on Research and Technology Advances in Digital Librarie.

[32] World Wide Web Consortium (W3C), Platform for privacy preferences (P3P) project. <www.w3.org/TR/P3P/>, 2002.

[33] P. Ashley, S. Hada, G. Karjoth, M. Schunter, E-P3P privacy policies and privacy authorization, Proceedings of the ACM Workshop on Privacy in the Electronic Society (WPES 2002), Washington, 2002, pp. 103−109.

[34] P. Ashley, S. Hada, G. Karjoth, C. Powers, M. Schunter, Enterprise privacy authorization language (epal 1.1). <www.zurich.ibm.com/security/enterprise-privacy/epal>, 2003.

[35] K. Seamons, M. Winslett, T. Yu, Limiting the disclosure of access control policies during automated trust negotiation, Proceedings of the Network and Distributed System Security Symposium (NDSS 2001), San Diego, CA, USA, April 2001.

[36] T. Yu, M. Winslett, K. Seamons, Supporting structured credentials and sensitive policies trough interoperable strategies for automated trust, ACM Trans. Inf. Syst. Secur. (TISSEC) 6 (1) (February 2003) 1−42.

[37] P. Bonatti, D. Olmedilla, Driving and monitoring provisional trust negotiation with metapolicies, Proceedings of the IEEE Sixth International Workshop on Policies for Distributed Systems and Networks (POLICY 2005), Stockholm, Sweden, June 2005.

[38] eXtensible Access Control Markup Language (XACML) Version 2.0. <http://docs.oasis-open.org/xacml/2.0/access_control-xacml-2.0-core-spec-os.pdf>, February 2005.

[39] V. Cheng, P. Hung, D. Chiu, Enabling web services policy negotiation with privacy preserved using XACML, Proceedings of the Fortieth Hawaii International International Conference on Systems Science (HICSS 2007), Hawaii, USA, January 2007.

[40] D. Haidar, N. Cuppens, F. Cuppens, H. Debar, XeNA: an access negotiation framework using XACML, Ann. Telecomm. 64 (1−2) (January 2009).

[41] D. Chadwick, S. Otenko, T. Nguyen, Adding support to XACML for dynamic delegation of authority in multiple domains, Proceedings of the Tenth Conference in Communications and Multimedia Security (CMS 2006), Heraklion, Crete, Greece, October 2006.

[42] C. Ardagna, S. De Capitani di Vimercati, S. Paraboschi, E. Pedrini, P. Samarati, M. Verdicchio, Expressive and Deployable Access Control in Open Web Service Applications, IEEE Trans. Serv. Comput. (TSC) 4 (2) (April−June, 2011) 86−109.

[43] World Wide Web Consortium (W3C). A P3P Preference Exchange Language 1.0 (APPEL1.0). <www.w3.org/TR/P3P-preferences/>, 2002.

[44] C.A. Ardagna, M. Cremonini, S. De Capitani di Vimercati, P. Samarati, A privacy-aware access control system, J. Comput. Secur. 16 (4) (2008) 369−392.

[45] J. Camenisch, E. Van Herreweghen, Design and implementation of the idemix anonymous credential system, Proceedings of the Ninth ACM Conference on Computer and Communications Security (CCS 2002), Washington, 2002, pp. 21−30.

[46] C.A. Ardagna, M. Cremonini, E. Damiani, S. De Capitani di Vimercati, P. Samarati, Supporting location-based conditions in access control policies, Proceedings of the ACM Symposium on Information, Computer and Communications Security (ASIACCS '06), Taipei, 2006, pp. 212−222.

[47] A.R. Beresford, F. Stajano, Mix zones: user privacy in location-aware services, Proceedings of the Second IEEE Annual Conference on Pervasive Computing and Communications Workshops (PERCOMW04), Orlando, 2004, pp. 127−131.

[48] P. Samarati, L. Sweeney, Generalizing data to provide anonymity when disclosing information (abstract), *Proceedings of the Seventeenth ACM SIGACT-SIGMOD-SIGART Symposium on Principles of Database Systems* (PODS '98), ACM, New York, NY, USA, 1998.

[49] C. Bettini, X.S. Wang, S. Jajodia, Protecting privacy against location-based personal identification, Proceedings of the Second VLDB Workshop on Secure Data Management (SDM'05), Trondheim, Norway, 2005, pp. 185−199.

[50] M. Gruteser, D. Grunwald, Anonymous usage of location-based services through spatial and temporal cloaking, Proceedings of the First International Conference on Mobile Systems, Applications, and Services (MobiSys), San Francisco, 2003, pp. 31−42.

[51] C. Cornelius, A. Kapadia, D. Kotz, D. Peebles, M. Shin, N. Triandopoulos, Anonysense: privacy-aware people-centric sensing, Proceedings of the Sixth International Conference on Mobile Systems, Applications, and Services (MobiSys 2008), Breckenridge, CO, USA, June 2008.

[52] C.-Y. Chow, M.F. Mokbel, X. Liu, Spatial cloaking for anony-mous location-based services in mobile peer-to-peer environ-ments, Geoinformatica 15 (2011) 351—380.

[53] C.-Y. Chow, M.F. Mokbel, Trajectory privacy in location based services and data publication, ACM SIGKDD Explorations Newslett. 13 (1) (June 2011) 19—29.

[54] C.A. Ardagna, M. Cremonini, S. De Capitani di Vimercati, P. Samarati, An obfuscation-based approach for protecting location privacy, in: IEEE Transactions on Dependable and Secure Computing (TDSC), January-February, 2011, vol. 8, 1, pp. 13—27.

[55] T. Hashem L. Kulik, Safeguarding location privacy in wireless ad-hoc networks, Proceedings of the Nineth International Conference on Ubiquitous Computing (UbiComp 2007), Innsbruck, Austria, September 2007.

[56] Geographic Location/Privacy (geopriv). <www.ietf.org/html.char-ters/geopriv-charter.html>, September 2006.

[57] D. Goldschlag, M. Reed, P. Syverson, Hiding routing information (Volume 1174 of Lecture Notes in Computer Science) in: R. Anderson (Ed.), Information Hiding: First International Workshop, Springer-Verlag, 1999, pp. 137—150.

[58] D. Goldschlag, M. Reed, P. Syverson, Onion routing for anony-mous and private internet connections, Commun. ACM 42 (2) (1999) 39—41.

[59] M. Reed, P. Syverson, D. Goldschlag, Anonymous connections and onion routing, IEEE J. Sel. Areas Commun. 16 (4) (1998) 482—494.

[60] R. Dingledine, N. Mathewson, P. Syverson, Tor: the second-generation onion router, Proceedings of the Thirteenth USENIX Security Symposium, San Diego, 2004.

[61] H. Roberts, E. Zuckerman, J. York, R. Faris, J. Palfrey, Circumvention Tool Usage Report, Berkman Center Internet Soc. (October 2010).

[62] D. Chaum, Untraceable electronic mail, return address, and digital pseudonyms, Commun. ACM 24 (2) (1981) 84—88.

[63] O. Berthold, H. Federrath, S. Kopsell, Web MIXes: a system for anonymous and unobservable Internet access (Vol. 2009 of Lecture Notes in Computer Science) in: H. Federrath (Ed.), Anonymity 2000, Springer-Verlag, 2000, pp. 115—119.

[64] M. Reiter, A. Rubin, Anonymous web transactions with crowds, Commun. ACM 42 (2) (1999) 32—48.

## Chapter 43

Privacy-Enhancing Technologies[1]

Simone Fischer-Hbner
Professor, Karlstad University, Karlstad/Sweden

Stefan Berthold
Karlstad University

Privacy is considered a core value and is recognized either explicitly or implicitly as a fundamental human right by most constitutions of democratic societies. In Europe, the foundations for the right to privacy of individuals were embedded in the European Convention on Human Rights and Fundamental Freedoms of 1950 (Art. 8) and the Charter of Fundamental Rights of the European Union in 2009 (Art. 7 & 8). In 1980, the OECD recognized the importance of privacy protection with the publication of the OECD Privacy Guidelines [1], which served as the foundation for many national privacy laws.

1. THE CONCEPT OF PRIVACY

Privacy as a social and legal issue has long been a concern of social scientists, philosophers, and lawyers. The first definition of privacy by legal researchers was given by the two American lawyers Samuel D. Warren and Louis D. Brandeis in their famous *Harvard Law Review* chapter "The Right to Privacy" [2], in which they defined privacy as "the right to be let alone." At that time, the risks of modern technology in the form of photography used by the yellow press to infringe privacy rights was the motivation for Warren and Brandeis's discussion of the individual's right to privacy.

In the age of modern computing, an early and often referred to definition of privacy was given by Alan Westin: "Privacy is the claim of individuals, groups and institutions to determine for themselves, when, how and to what extent information about them is communicated to others" [3]. Even though, according to Westin's definition, natural persons (humans) as well as legal persons (groups and institutions) have a right to privacy, in most legal systems, privacy is defined as a basic human right that only applies to natural persons.

In general, the concept of personal privacy has several dimensions. This chapter mainly addresses the dimension of informational privacy, which can be defined, similarly as by Westin and by the German Constitutional Court in its Census decision,[2] as the right to informational self-determination (the right of individuals to determine for themselves when, how, and to what extent information about them is communicated to others). Furthermore, so-called spatial privacy can be defined as another dimension of the concept of privacy, which also covers the "right to be let alone," where spatial privacy is defined as the right of individuals to control what is presented to their senses [4]. Further dimensions of privacy, which will, however, not be the subject of this chapter, are territorial privacy, which concerns the setting of limits on intrusion into the domestic, workplace, and other environments (public spaces), and bodily privacy, which concerns protecting a person against undue interference, such as physical searches, drug testing, or information violating his or her moral sense (see [5,6]).

Data protection concerns protecting personal data in order to guarantee privacy and is only part of the concept of privacy. Privacy, however, is not an unlimited or absolute right, because it can be in conflict with other rights or legal values and because individuals cannot participate fully in society without revealing personal data. Nevertheless, even in cases where privacy needs to be restricted, the very core of privacy still needs to be protected. For this reason, the objective of privacy and data protection laws is to define fundamental privacy principles that need to be enforced if personal data is collected, stored, or processed.

1. Parts of this work were conducted within the scope of the PetWeb II project funded by the Norwegian Research Council (NFR) and the U-PrIM project funded by the Swedish Knowledge (KK) Foundation.

2. German Constitutional Court, Census decision, 1983 (BVerfGE 65,1).

An Agenda for Action for Privacy-Enhancing Technologies

The Privacy-Enhancing Technology (PET) Concept: (Check All Tasks Completed)

_____ 1. Enforces making sparing use of data.
_____ 2. Makes privacy the default.
_____ 3. Transfers control to individuals.
_____ 4. Sends tags to a secure mode automatically.
_____ 5. Can prove that automatic activation of the secure mode always works.
_____ 6. Prevents eavesdropping of tag-reader communication.
_____ 7. Protects individuals from producer.
_____ 8. Protects individuals from retailer.
_____ 9. Protection includes in-store problem.
_____ 10. Protects tag in secure mode against presence-spotting.
_____ 11. Does not require individuals to take active protection measures.
_____ 12. Does not interfere with active protection measures.
_____ 13. Avoids creation and use of central database(s).
_____ 14. Avoids creation and use of databases at all.
_____ 15. Enables functionality after point-of-sale in a secure way.
_____ 16. Can be achieved without changing Radio Frequency Identification (RFID) physical technology.
_____ 17. Does not make tags much more expensive.
_____ 18. Does not introduce additional threats to privacy.
_____ 19. Introduces additional benefits for privacy.
_____ 20. Provides benefits for the retailer.

---

2. LEGAL PRIVACY PRINCIPLES

In this section, we present an overview to internationally well-accepted, basic legal privacy principles, for which PETs implementing these principles have been developed. These principles are also part of the general EU Data Protection Directive 95/46/EC [7], which is an important legal instrument for protection of privacy in Europe, as it codifies general privacy principles that have been implemented in the national privacy laws of all EU member states and of many other states. The principles also correspond to principles of the OECD Privacy Guidelines to which we will also refer.

Legitimacy

Personal data processing has to be legitimate, which according to Art. 7 EU Directive 95/46/EC is usually the case if the data subject[3] has given his unambiguous (and informed) consent, if there is a legal obligation, or if there is contractual agreement (cf. the Collection Limitation Principle of the OECD Guidelines). The requirement of informed consent poses special challenges for the design of user interfaces (UIs) for PETs.

Purpose Specification and Purpose Binding (Also Called Purpose Limitation)

Personal data must be collected for specified, explicit, and legitimate purposes and may not be further processed in a way that is incompatible with these purposes (Art. 6 I (b) EU Directive 95/46/EC). The purpose limitation principle

is of key importance for privacy protection, as the sensitivity of personal data does not only depend on how "intimate" the details are, which the personal data are describing, but is also mainly influenced by the purposes of data processing and context of use. For this reason, the data processing purposes need to be specified in advance by the lawmaker or by the data processor before obtaining the individual's consent, and personal data may later not be (mis)used for any other purposes (cf. Purpose Specification and Use Limitation Principles of the OECD Guidelines). The objective of privacy policy languages and tools is to enforce this principle.

Data Minimization

The processing of personal data must be limited to data that are adequate, relevant, and not excessive (Art. 6 I (c) EU Directive 95/46/EC). Besides, data should not be kept in a personally identifiable form any longer than necessary (Art. 6 I (e) EU Directive 95/46/EC—cf. Data Quality Principle of the OECD Guidelines, which requires that data should be relevant to the purposes for which they are to be used). In other words, the collection of personal data and the extent to which personal data are used should be minimized because obviously privacy is best protected if no personal data at all (or at least as little data as possible) are collected or processed. The data minimization principle derived from the Directive also serves as a legal foundation for PETs (see checklist: An Agenda for Action for Privacy-Enhancing Technologies). that aim at protecting "traditional" privacy goals, such as anonymity, pseudonymity, or unlinkability for users and/ or other data subjects.

---

3. A data subject is a person about whom personal data is processed.

Transparency and Rights of the Data Subjects

Transparency of data processing means informing a data subject about the purposes and circumstances of data processing, identifying who is requesting personal data, how the personal data flow, where and how long the data are stored, and what type of rights and controls the data subject has in regard to his personal data. The Directive 95/46/EC provides data subjects with respective information rights according to its Art. 10. Transparency is a prerequisite for informational self-determination, as "a society, in which citizens can no longer know who does, when, and in which situations know what about them, would be contradictory to the right of informational self-determination."[4] Further rights of the data subjects include the right of access to data (Art. 12 (a) EU Directive 95/46/EC), the right to object to the processing of personal data (Art. 14 EU Directive 95/46/EC), and the right to correction, erasure, or blocking of incorrect or illegally stored data (Art. 12 (b) EU Directive 95/46/EC, cf. Openness and Individual Participation Principle of the OECD Guidelines).

Security

The data controller needs to install appropriate technical and organizational security mechanisms to guarantee the confidentiality, integrity, and availability of personal data (Art. 17 EU Directive 95/46/EC) (cf. Security Safeguards Principle of the OECD Guidelines). Classical security mechanisms, such as authentication, cryptography, access control, or security logging, which need to be implemented for technical data protection, will, however, not be discussed in this chapter.

In January 2012, the EU Commission published a proposal for a new EU Regulation [8], which defines a single set of modernized privacy rules and which (once the regulation is in force) will be directly valid across the EU. In particular, it includes the principle of data protection/privacy by design and by default (Art. 23), requiring building PETs already into the initial system design. Besides, the requirements of transparency for data handling and easily accessible policies (Art. 11) are explicitly included. Furthermore, the right to be forgotten (Art. 17) and a right to data portability (Art. 18) are newly included, which require technical support by appropriate PETs.

3. CLASSIFICATION OF PETS

Privacy-enhancing technologies (PETs) can be defined as technologies that enforce legal privacy principles in order to protect and enhance the privacy of users of information technology (IT) and/or data subjects (see [9]). While many fundamental PET concepts for achieving data minimization were already introduced, mostly by David Chaum, in the 1980s (see [10–12]), the term *privacy-enhancing technologies* was first introduced in 1995 in a report on "privacy-enhancing technologies, which was jointly published by the Dutch Registratiekamer and the Information and Privacy Commissioner in Ontario/Canada [13]. PETs can basically be divided into three different classes.

The first class comprises PETs for enforcing the legal privacy principle of data minimization by minimizing or avoiding the collection and use of personal data of users or data subjects. These types of PETs provide the "traditional" privacy goals of *anonymity*, *unlinkability*, *unobservability*, and *pseudonymity*, which will be elaborated on in the next section. This class of PETs can be further divided, dependent on whether data minimization is achieved on the communication or application level. Examples for some of the most prominent data minimization technologies will be presented in Section 6.

While data minimization is the best strategy for protecting privacy, there are many occasions in daily life when individuals simply have to reveal personal data, or when users want to present themselves by disseminating personal information (especially on social network sites). In these cases, the privacy of the individuals concerned still needs to be protected by adhering to other relevant legal privacy requirements). The second class of PETs therefore comprises technologies that enforce legal privacy requirements, such as informed consent, transparency, right to data subject access, purpose specification, and purpose binding and security, in order to safeguard the lawful processing of personal data. In this chapter, so-called transparency-enhancing technologies will be discussed, which are PETs that enforce or promote informed consent and transparency. Besides, we will refer to privacy models and privacy authorization languages for enforcing the principle of purpose binding.

The third class of PETs comprises technologies that combine PETs of the first and second class. An example is provided by privacy-enhancing identity management technologies such as the ones that have been developed within the EU FP6 project PRIME (Privacy and Identity Management for Europe) [14]. The PRIME architecture supports strong privacy by default by anonymizing the underlying communication and achieving data minimization on the application level by the use of anonymous credential protocols. Besides privacy presentation and

---

4. German Constitutional Court, Census decision, 1983 (BVerfGE 65,1).

negotiation tools, privacy authorization language for enforcing negotiated policies and tools allowing users to "track" and access their data that they released to remote services sides ensure the technical enforcement of all privacy requirements mentioned in the section above.

4. TRADITIONAL PRIVACY GOALS OF PETS

In this section, privacy goals for achieving data minimization are defined, which we call traditional privacy goals because early PETs that were developed already in the 1980s followed these goals. Data minimization as an abstract strategy describes the avoidance of unnecessary or unwanted data disclosures. The most fundamental information that can be disclosed about an individual is who he is, that is, an identifier, or which observable events he is related to. If this information can be kept secret, the individual remains anonymous. Pfitzmann and Hansen, who pioneered the technical privacy research terminology, define anonymity as follows: Anonymity of a subject means that the subject is not identifiable within a set of subjects, the anonymity set [14].

By choosing the term *subject*, Pfitzmann and Hansen aim to define the term *anonymity* as generally as possible. The subject can be any entity defined by facts (names or identifiers, or causing observable events, such as by sending messages). If an adversary cannot narrow down the sender of a specific message to less than two possible senders, the actual sender of the message remains anonymous. The two or more possible senders in question form the anonymity set. The anonymity set, and particularly its size, will be the first privacy metrics discussed in Section 5, Privacy Metrics.

An adversary that discovers the relation between a fact or an event and a subject identifies the subject. Relations cannot only exist between facts or events and subjects, but may exist between facts, actions, and subjects. An adversary may, for instance, discover that two messages have been sent by the same subject, without knowing this subject. The two messages would be part of the equivalence relation [15] that is formed by all messages that have been sent by the same subject. Knowing this equivalence relation (and maybe even others) helps the adversary to identify the subject. Pfitzmann and Hansen define the inability of the adversary to discover these equivalence relations as unlinkability.

Unlinkability of two or more items of interest (IOIs (subjects, messages, actions, . . .)) from an attacker's perspective means that within the system (comprising these and possibly other items), the attacker cannot sufficiently distinguish whether these IOIs are related or not [14].

A special type of unlinkability is the unlinkability of a sender and recipient of a message (or so-called

relationship anonymity), which means that the relation of who is communicating with whom is kept secret. Data minimization can also be implemented through obfuscating the presence of facts and events. The idea is that adversaries who are unable to detect the presence of facts or events cannot link them to subjects. Pfitzmann and Hansen define this privacy goal as undetectability.

Undetectability of an item of interest (IOI) from an attacker's perspective means that the attacker cannot sufficiently distinguish whether it exists or not [14].

The strongest privacy goal in data minimization is unobservability, which combines undetectability and anonymity: Unobservability of an item of interest (IOI) means:

- undetectability of the IOI against all subjects uninvolved in it and
- anonymity of the subject(s) involved in the IOI even against the other subject(s) involved in that IOI [14].

The third and last way to implement data minimization, apart from obfuscating the facts, the events (undetectability, unobservability), or the relation between them and the subjects (unlinkability), is the use of pseudonyms in the place of subjects. Pseudonyms may be random numbers, email addresses, or (cryptographic) certificates. In order to minimize the disclosed information, pseudonyms must not be linkable to the subject. The corresponding privacy goal is pseudonymity: Pseudonymity is the use of pseudonyms as identifiers [14].

Pseudonymity is related to anonymity, as both concepts aim at protecting the real identity of a subject. The use of pseudonyms, however, allows maintaining a reference to the subject's real identity (for accountability purposes [16]). A trusted third party could, for instance, reveal the real identities of misbehaving pseudonymous users. Pseudonymity also enables a user to link certain actions under one pseudonym. For example, a user could reuse the same pseudonym in an online auction system (such as eBay) for building up a reputation.

The degree of anonymity protection provided by pseudonyms depends on the amount of personal data of the pseudonym holder that can be linked to the pseudonym, and on how often the pseudonym is used in various contexts/for various transactions. The best privacy protection can be achieved if for each transaction a new so-called transaction pseudonym is used that is unlinkable to any other transaction pseudonyms and at least initially unlinkable to any other personal data items of its holder (see also [14]).

5. PRIVACY METRICS

Privacy metrics aim to quantify the effectiveness of schemes or technologies with regard to the privacy goals defined in the previous section. A simple metrics for measuring anonymity is the anonymity set [14]. The anonymity set comprises all subjects that may have caused an event that is observed by the adversary. The subjects in the set cover up for each other against the adversary. The adversary can thus not hold a single subject responsible for the observed event as long as the set size of the anonymity set is greater than one. Greater set sizes are useful for protecting against (stronger) adversaries that would accept false positives up to a certain threshold among the subjects that are held responsible. In this case, the set size has to exceed such a threshold.

The anonymity set size is also related to the metrics in k-anonymity [17]. K-anonymity is defined as a property or a requirement for databases that must not leak sensitive private information. This concept was also applied as an anonymity metrics in location-based services [18] and in VoIP [19,20]. The underlying assumption is that database tables store two kinds of attributes. The first kind is identifying information, and the second is identifying sensitive information. The claim is that the database table is anonymous if every search for identifying information results in a group of at least k candidate records. The k in k-anonymity is thus the privacy parameter that determines the minimum group size. Groups of candidate records form anonymity sets of identifiers in the database table.

The k-anonymity as a privacy property and k as a metrics are not undisputed. In particular, the fact that k-anonymity only depends on the identifying information in the database table—that is, it is independent of the sensitive information—leads to remaining privacy risks [21]. A simple attack building on the k-anonymity's blindness for sensitive information is described in [22]. The trick is to search for candidate groups where the sensitive attribute has a constant value for all candidates. The sensitive attribute value is immediately disclosed for all records in the candidate group; thus, privacy is breached. A solution to these risks is a new privacy property, l-diversity, with the privacy parameter l. The claim of l-diversity is that a database table is anonymous if the diversity of sensitive attribute values is at least l ($>$ 1) in every candidate group. In some cases, l-diversification would not sufficiently protect from attribute disclosure or would be too difficult to establish. A third property, t-closeness [23], is solving this problem. T-closeness restricts the distribution of sensitive information within a candidate group. The claim is that a database table is anonymous if the distribution of sensitive information within each candidate group differs from the table's distribution at most up to a threshold t.

All these privacy metrics with the exception of the anonymity set are tailored to static database tables. Changes in the data set are possible, but the privacy

properties have to be reestablished afterward. T-closeness as one of the latest developed properties in this category is a close relative to information-theoretic privacy metrics. Information-theoretic metrics measure the information that an adversary learns by observing an event or a system, for example, all observable events in a communication system. The information always depends on the knowledge the adversary had before his observation, the a-priori knowledge. Knowledge is expressed as a probability distribution over the events. For a discrete set of events $X = \{x_1, x_2, \ldots, x_n\}$ and the probability mass function $\Pr: X \rightarrow [0, 1]$, Shannon [24] defines the self-information of x_i, $1 \leq i \leq n$, as

$$I(x_i) = -\log_2 \Pr(x_i)$$

The self-information $I(x_i)$ is what an adversary learns when he observes the event x_i with his a-priori knowledge about all possible events encoded in the probability mass function Pr. The self-information takes the minimal value zero for $\Pr(x_i) = 1$; that is, the adversary will learn minimal information from observing x_i, if he is a-priori certain that x_i will be observed. The self-information approaches infinity for $\Pr(x_i) \rightarrow 0$; that is, the more information the adversary learns, the less likely the observed events are. The expected self-information of a system with the events X is the entropy of the system. Shannon defines the entropy as

$$H(X) = \sum_{x_i \in X} \Pr(x_i) \cdot I(x_i)$$

The entropy is maximal when the distribution of all events is uniform; that is, $\Pr(x_i) = \frac{1}{n}$ for all $1 \leq i \leq n$. The maximal entropy is thus

$$H_{\max} = -\log_2 \frac{1}{n} = \log_2 n$$

The entropy is minimal when one event x_i is perfectly certain; that is, $\Pr(x_i) = 1$ and $\Pr(x_j) = 0$ for all $x_j \in X$ and $x_j \neq x_i$.

The "degree of anonymity" is the entropy of the communication system in question [25,26]. This degree of anonymity measures the anonymity of the message's sender within the communication system. When the adversary learns the actual sender of the message, he will learn the self-information $I(x_i)$ where each $x_i \in X$ encodes the fact that one specific subject is the sender of the message. The probability distribution Pr encodes the a-priori knowledge of the adversary about the sender. A uniform distribution (maximal entropy) indicates minimal a-priori knowledge (maximal sender anonymity). Absolute certainty, on the other hand (minimal entropy), indicates perfect a-priori knowledge (minimal sender anonymity). The degree of anonymity can be used to compare communication systems with different features (numbers of subjects) when normalized [25] with max entropy H_{max} and otherwise without normalization [26].

The same entropy-based metrics can be applied to measure the anonymity provided by facts about a subject [27]. The adversary's a-priori knowledge, encoded in the probability mass function Pr, comprises how well a feature vector with facts about a subject fits to each subject $x_i \in X$. The adversary learns the self-information $I(x_i)$ when learning that the feature vector applies to the subject x_i. The entropy $H(X)$ can be seen as the confusion of the adversary before he learns the subject that the feature vector is applying to.

The entropy can be used to calculate the expected anonymity set size, which is $2^{H(X)}$. The expected anonymity set size is equal to the anonymity set size, if Pr corresponds to the uniform distribution (if the message [25,26] or feature vector [27] is not more or less linkable to one subject than to any other subject in X). The anonymity set size can be seen as an overestimation of the expected anonymity set size, if Pr does not correspond to the uniform distribution; that is, some subjects are more linkable than others in the anonymity set. In this case, the expected anonymity set size or the degree of anonymity is the more accurate metrics.

Metrics that are based on entropy have the disadvantage that the a-priori knowledge Pr of the adversary has to be known when evaluating the metrics. When this a-priori knowledge can be derived from publicly available observations (message routing data in a network [25,26]), the metrics are easy to apply. If the Pr depends on personal information which is not available to nonadversaries [27], the metrics are hard to evaluate without additional tools being effective (legal transparency tools).

6. DATA MINIMIZATION TECHNOLOGIES

In this section, we will present the most relevant PETs for minimizing data on both communication and application levels. It is important to note that applications (such as eCommerce applications) can only be designed and used anonymously if their users cannot be identified on a communication level (via their IP addresses). Hence anonymous communication is a prerequisite for achieving anonymity, more generally or data minimization, on the application level.

Anonymous Communication

Already in 1981, David Chaum presented the Mix net protocol for anonymous communication, which has become the fundamental concept for many practical anonymous communication technologies that have been broadly used for many years. In this section, we will provide an overview to anonymous communication

technologies that we think are most relevant from a practical and scientific point of view.

DC Network

David Chaum's DC (Dining Cryptographer) network protocol [28] is an anonymous communication protocol, which, even though it cannot be easily used in practice, is still very interesting from a scientific perspective. It provides unconditional sender anonymity, recipient anonymity, and unobservability, even if we assume a global adversary who can observe all communication in the network. Hence, it can guarantee the strongest anonymity properties of all known anonymous communication protocols. DC nets are based on binary superposed sending. Before any message can be sent, each participant in the network (user station) has to exchange via a secure channel a random bit stream with at least one other user station. These random bit streams serve as secret keys and are at least as long as the messages to be sent. For each single sending step (round), every user station adds modulo 2 (superposes), all the key bits it shares and its message bit, if there is one. Stations that do not wish to transmit messages send zeros by outputting the sums of their key bits (without any inversions). The sums are sent over the net and added up modulo 2. The result, which is broadcast to all user stations, is the sum of all sent message bits because every key bit was added twice (see Figure 43.1). If exactly one participant transmits a

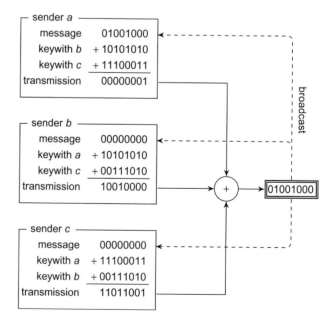

FIGURE 43.1 A DC network with three users. Sender a sends a message, but from observing the communication in the network alone, the adversary cannot tell whether it was sent by a, b, or c (and not even if a meaningful message was sent at all).

message, the message is successfully broadcast as the result of the global sum to each participant. Collisions are easily detected (as the message sent by a user and the one that is broadcast back to him will be different) and have to be resolved, for example, by retransmitting the message after a random number of rounds.

In theory, superposed sending provides, in the information-theoretic sense, perfect (unconditional) sender anonymity and unobservability, as the fact that someone is sending a meaningful message (and not only zeros) is hidden by a one-time pad encryption. From a metrics perspective, all senders in the DC network form the anonymity set. No user is more likely to be the sender of the message than any other user for an outside adversary. Perfect recipient anonymity can be achieved by reliable broadcasting. However, the DC network and the one-time pad share the same practical shortcomings which have prevented them from being broadly used: the security of DC networks depends on the perfect randomness of keys and the secure distribution of keys. Moreover, each key is to be used only once, and the keys need to be perfectly unavailable to the adversary (the adversary may not get hold of the keys before or after the message has been sent).

Mix Nets

Mix nets [12] are more practical than DC networks, but do not provide security against adversaries with unlimited resources. Nevertheless, most anonymity networks (Mixmaster, Tor, Onion Routing, and AN.ON) build on the mix net concept. A mix is a relay or proxy server that performs four steps to hide the relation between incoming and outgoing messages (see Figure 43.2):

1. Duplicates (replayed messages) are discarded. Without this functionality, an adversary could launch a replay attack by sending two identical messages to be forwarded as two identical output messages by the mix. The adversary could thus link these messages and therefore "bridge over" the mix.
2. All messages are (randomly) delayed (by temporarily storing them in a buffer). Without this functionality (if messages were immediately forwarded), the anonymity set for one message would be reduced to one sender (no anonymity at all).

3. All messages are recoded. This is usually done by cryptography. Without this functionality, the adversary could link the input with the output messages by comparing the contents of the messages.
4. The sending sequence of delayed messages is determined independently of the receiving sequence. Without the delay and reordering of messages, an adversary could link the input to the output messages by a time correlation attack (he could be sure that the first message is the first message out).
5. Mixes can be used to achieve unlinkability of sender and recipient, sender anonymity as well as recipient anonymity. For achieving the latter two properties, different recoding functions are used. For providing sender anonymity, asymmetric cryptography is used. The mix user (or more precisely his machine) encrypts the message m with the public key e_R of the recipient and achieves $enc_{e_R}(m)$. He then encrypts $enc_{e_R}(m)$ together with the address of the recipient and a nonce with public key e_1 of the mix and sends the resulting message $enc_{e_1}(r_1, A_R, enc_{e_R}(m))$ to the mix. Adding the nonce is necessary to achieve nondeterministic encryption, which prevents an adversary from monitoring the output message $enc_{e_R}(m)$ and address A_R of the recipient, and then simply encrypt both values with the public key of the mix and compare it with the messages sent to the mix. Moreover, it prevents the mix from discarding one of two messages when identical contents are intended to be sent. The mix decrypts the message with its private key, discards the nonce, and sends $enc_{e_R}(m)$ to the address A_R of the recipient.
6. Using a single mix can only provide anonymity if it is fully trustworthy and cannot be compromised. For improving security, several mixes can be used in a chain or a "cascade." Let us assume that the sender (or more precisely his machine) chooses a chain of n mixes with addresses A_i and public keys e_i, $i = 1 \ldots n$. The sender will first add layers of encryptions using the public keys of the mixes in the path in reverse order. Each layer includes the message to be forwarded by the mix, the address to which the message should be sent (next mix in the chain or the final recipient), plus a nonce to be discarded. The resulting message $enc_{e_1}(r_1, A_2, enc_{e_2}(\ldots enc_{e_n}(r_n, A_R, enc_{e_R}(m))\ldots))$ is sent to the first mix (with the address A_1). Each mix on the path decrypts the message with its privacy key and thereby gets a nonce that is discarded as well as an encrypted message and address to which it sends this message. The last mix in the path finally sends $enc_{e_R}(m)$ to the recipient. Unlinkability of sender and recipient can in principle also be provided in the presence of an adversary who monitors all communication lines, as long as the crypto operations cannot be broken and one mix in the path is trustworthy, that is, one

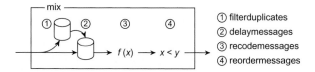

FIGURE 43.2 Processing steps within a mix.

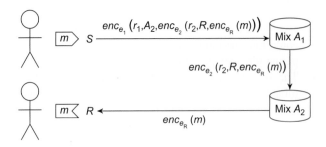

FIGURE 43.3   Sender anonymity with two mixes.

mix that is not controlled by the adversary. Figure 43.3 illustrates how sender anonymity can be achieved with a path consisting of two mixes.

For achieving recipient anonymity, symmetric cryptography is used as arecoding function.[5] The recipient first chooses a sequence of n mixes with addresses A_i and public keys e_i, $i = 1 \ldots n$, a sequence of m symmetric encryption keys $j = 0 \ldots n$, and a label L_R and creates an anonymous return address $R_S = (k_0, A_1, R_1)$, which contains a symmetric key k_0, the address of the first mix A_1 in the chain, and another anonymous return address R_1, which is calculated according to the following scheme:

$R_j = enc_{e_i}(k_j, A_{j+1}, R_{j+1})$ for $j = 1 \ldots n$, where A_{n+1} is the address of the recipient and $R_{n+1} = L_R$.

The recipient makes the anonymous return address available to the sender, who uses key k_0 to encrypt his message m. The encrypted message $ENC_{k_0}\{m\}$ is then sent along with the return address R_1 to the first mix A_1. The first mix decrypts $R_1 = enc_{e_1}(k_1, A_2, R_2)$, encrypts $ENC_{k_0}\{m\}$ with the symmetric key k_1, and sends the encrypted message $ENC_{k_1}\{ENC_{k_0}\{m\}\}$ along with R_2 to the next mix with the address A_2. This is repeated for all mixes along the path. The last mix in the path finally forwards $ENC_{k_n}\{\ldots ENC_{k_1}\{ENC_{k_0}\{m\}\} \ldots\}$ and L_R to the recipient. The label L_R of the return address indicates to the recipient which sequence of symmetric keys he has to use to decrypt the message.

The two schemes above provide either sender or recipient anonymity. By combining both schemes, it is possible for two communication partners to communicate anonymously in both directions. Suppose that Alice anonymously sends a message including an anonymous return address to a discussion forum. Bob can then anonymously send his reply via a self-chosen sequence of mixes to the first mix used in the anonymous return address. If Bob's message also contains an anonymous return address,

Alice can reply as well in the same manner. Thus, Alice and Bob can communicate without knowing each other's identities.

The mix net protocol was invented by Chaum in 1981 for high-latency communication, such as email communication. In the mid-1990s, when interactive Internet services became broadly used, low-latency anonymous communication protocols were developed. The most broadly used low-latency protocols AN.ON and Onion Routing/Tor, which are based on the mix net concept, will be briefly presented in the next sections.

AN.ON

AN.ON [29] is an anonymity service that was developed and operated since the late 1990s at the Technical University of Dresden. Because it aims at providing a network of mixes for low-latency traffic routing, symmetric cryptography is replacing asymmetric cryptography where possible (asymmetric cryptography is only used to exchange symmetric session keys between mixes and users). Moreover, low latency requires that message delays are reduced, and in fact, AN.ON mixes implement practically no message delay. The downside of reducing delays is that the size of the message buffer in the mixes and thus the anonymity set decrease. In order to increase the size of anonymity sets, AN.ON provides standard routes through the mix network, the so-called mix cascades. A mix cascade typically contains a sequence of two or three mixes, and every message sent to the cascade runs through the mixes in the same order as any other message sent to the same cascade. Predefined and stable mix cascades have a number of advantages over dynamic routing:

1. Mixes can be audited and certified with regard to their performance, their geographical position, the legislation in which they operate, and the operator (the company or the governmental institution operating the mix infrastructure).
2. Cascades can be designed to cross different nations, different legislations, and different operators in order to enjoy the protection of the most liberal regulation; they can also be designed to provide a certain performance.
3. Security measures focus on a small number of mixes while the costs can be distributed to a large number of users.

Disadvantages of implementing mix cascades include:

1. Each mix is a possible bottleneck and thus needs to provide a stable and high-bandwidth installation, as one mix going offline stops all cascades in which it was involved.

---

5. In the following, we will use capital letters and curly brackets for the symmetric encryption function ENC.

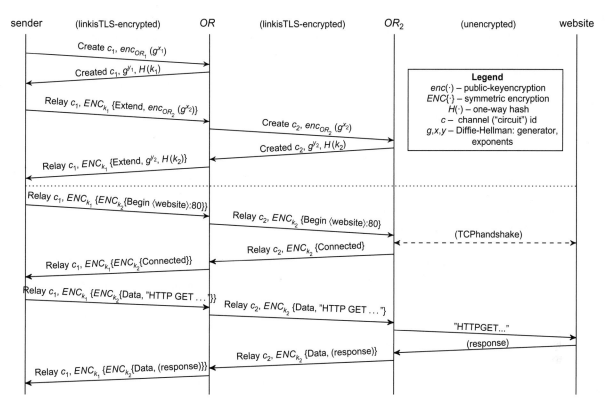

FIGURE 43.4   The Tor key negotiation and a simple Web site request [31].

2. Setting up and operating mixes is expensive due to the considerable organizational overhead for establishing mix cascades and due to the high performance requirements.

Onion Routing/Tor

Onion Routing [30] is a low-latency, mix-based routing protocol developed in the 1990s at the Naval Research Laboratory. It provides anonymous socket connections by means of proxy servers. Onion Routing uses the mix net concept of layers of public key encryption (the so-called onion) to build up an anonymous bidirectional virtual circuit between communication partners. The initiator's proxy (for the service being requested) constructs a "forward onion," which encapsulates a series of routing nodes ("mixes") forming a path to the responder, and sends it with a create command to the first node. Each layer of the onion is encrypted with the public key of each node on the path and contains symmetric crypto function/key pairs as a payload. After sending the onion, the anonymous path is established and the initiator's proxy sends data through this anonymous connection. The symmetric function/key pairs are applied by each node on the path to crypt data that will be sent along the virtual circuit. All information (onions, data, and network control) are sent through the Onion Routing network in uniform-sized cells. All cells arriving at an onion router within a fixed time interval are mixed together to reduce correlation by network insiders. Reply onions, which correspond to untraceable return addresses, allow for a responder to send back anonymously a reply after its original circuit is broken.

Since individual routing nodes in each circuit only know the identities of adjacent nodes, and since the nodes further encrypt multiplexed virtual circuits, traffic analysis is made difficult. However, if the first node behind the initiator's proxy and the last node of the circuit cooperate, they will be able to determine the source and recipient of communication through the number of cells sent over this circuit or through the duration for which the virtual circuit was used.

Tor [31], the second generation of Onion Routing, has added several improvements. In particular, it provides forward secrecy. Once the session keys are deleted they cannot be obtained any longer. Even if all communication has been wiretapped, the long-term secret keys of the onion routers ("mixes") become compromised. Therefore, instead of using hybrid encryption for distributing symmetric session keys, the Diffie-Hellman key negotiation protocol is used, which provides forward secrecy. The key negotiation and a simple communication via two onion routers are outlined in Figure 43.4. The symmetric session key shared by the user with the first onion router

OR_1 is negotiated by means of a Diffie-Hellman handshake. The first half of the handshake g^{x_1} is encrypted with the public key of OR_1 (to prevent man-in-the-middle attacks), and $enc_{OR_1}(g^{x_1})$ is then sent to OR_1. The onion router replies with the second half of the handshake; that is, g^{y_1} and a hash over the negotiated session key $k_1 = g^{x_1 y_1}$. Any further communication between the sender and OR_1 will be crypted with this negotiated symmetric session key. In order to extend the path from the sender over OR_1 to a second onion router OR_2, the sender transmits $ENC_{k_1}\{OR_2, enc_{OR_2}(g^{x_2})\}$ to OR_1. The first onion router decrypts the symmetric encryption and forwards the encrypted first half of a new Diffie-Hellman handshake $enc_{OR_2}(g^{x_2})$ to OR_2. The second onion router replies with the second half of the handshake g^{y_2} and the hash over the session key $k_2 = g^{x_2 y_2}$. The reply $ENC_{k_1}\{g^{y_2}, hash(k_2)\}$ is forwarded by OR_1 back to the sender. Only the sender and OR_1 are now in possession of k_1 and only the sender and OR_2 are now in possession of k_2. The communication between sender and OR_2 can now be crypted with k_2. Once a circuit has been established, the symmetric encryption with the negotiated session keys is applied by each node on the path to crypt data that will be sent along the circuit. Advantages of Tor over AN.ON are as follows:

1. Tor provides forward secrecy.
2. It is easy to set up new onion routers ("mixes"), which are run by many volunteers all over the world.
3. There are lower performance requirements for each "mix."
4. Each mix is a possible bottleneck, however, in Tor, "mixes" that do not perform can be excluded from the dynamic routing.

Disadvantages include:

1. Anyone can set up "mixes" independent of their performance, that is, bandwidth, latency, security.
2. There is no audit or certification, thus a lack of reliable data about legislation and operator.
3. Bridging the "mixes" and thus breaching anonymity by controlling the entry node and the exit node is easier for adversaries, since they can easily set up their own new nodes. In particular, an adversary can easily try to attract user traffic by establishing a few well-performing exit nodes and a lot of stable intermediate mix nodes that eventually become entry nodes [32].

Data Minimization at Application Level

Even if the communication channel is anonymized, users can still reveal personal and identifying data on the application level; often users have to reveal more personal data than needed. Hence, data minimization techniques are also needed on the application level. Many such data minimization techniques are based on cryptographic protocols (see also [33] for an overview). The classical types of privacy-protecting cryptography that have already been applied for decades are of course encryption schemes themselves. However, there are a number of more recent crypto schemes for protecting data and authenticating information, which are variations or extensions of basic crypto schemes they have "surprising properties" that in many cases can offer better data minimization properties [33]. In this chapter, some of the most relevant examples of mainly cryptographic mechanisms for protecting privacy at application level will be given.

Blind Signatures and Anonymous eCash

Blind signatures are an extension of digital signatures and provide privacy by allowing someone to obtain a signature from a signer on a document without the signer seeing the actual content of the "blinded" document he is signing. Hence, if the signer is later presented with the signed "unblinded" document, he cannot relate it with the signing session and with the person on behalf of whom he has signed the document. Blind signatures were invented by David Chaum as a basic building block for anonymous eCash (see below). They can also be used to achieve anonymity of other applications, such as eVoting, and also serve as a basic building block for other privacy crypto protocols, such as anonymous credentials (see below).

David Chaum et al. have invented protocols based on blind signatures [10,34,35], which allow electronic money to flow perfectly tracelessly from the bank through consumer and merchant before returning to the bank. Chaum's cryptographic "online" payment protocol based on blind signatures can be summarized as follows (see also Figure 43.5).

Let (e, n) be the bank's private key indicating a certain value of a signature under this key (in this example: one dollar) and (d, n) the bank's public key.[6] f is a suitable one-way function. Electronic money has the form $(x, f(x)^d \pmod n)$, where the one-way function is needed to prevent forgery of electronic money (see also [36] for more explanations).

1. The customer Alice (his computer) first generates a bank note number x (of at least 100 digits) at random and (in essence) multiplies it with a blinding factor r, which he has also chosen at random: $B = r^e \cdot f(x) \pmod n$. He then signs the blinded bank note number with his private key and sends it to the bank.
2. The bank verifies and removes Alice's signature. Then, it signs the blinded note (and thereby creates

---

6. Using the RSA encryption scheme.

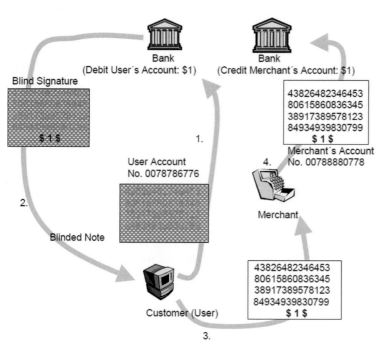

FIGURE 43.5 The flow of eCash's untraceable electronic money [35].

the blinded signature) with its "worth one dollar" signature:

$$B^d \ (\mathrm{mod}\ n) = (r^e \cdot f(x))^a \ (\mathrm{mod}\ n) = r \cdot f(x)^d \ (\mathrm{mod}\ n).$$

The bank then withdraws one dollar from his account and returns the note with the blind signature.

3. Alice divides out the blinding factor and thereby extracts: $C = \frac{B^d}{r}(\mathrm{mod}\ n) = f(x)^d \ (\mathrm{mod}\ n)$ from B. For paying the online merchant Bob one dollar, Alice sends him the pair $(x, f(x)^d \ (\mathrm{mod} n))$.

4. Bob verifies the bank's signature and immediately contacts the bank to verify that the note has not already been spent.

5. The bank verifies its signature, checks the note against a list of those notes already spent, and credits Bob's account by one dollar.

The blind signature scheme provides (unconditional) anonymity of the electronic money: Even if the bank and the merchant cooperate, they cannot determine who spent the notes. Since the bank does not know the blinding factors, it cannot correlate the note it was signing blindly for Alice with the note that was spent. (However, Alice's identity is only protected if he also uses an anonymized communication channel and if he does not personally reveal identifying information, such as a personal delivery address).

In addition to the online eCash protocol version, where the bank needs to be constantly online for checking whether notes have already been spent, in [28] a protocol for offline electronic money is presented by Chaum et al. With the offline protocol, a user remains unconditionally anonymous as long as he spends each bank note only once. If, however, a note is spent twice, the bank will get enough information to identify the spender's account. Disappointingly, there has been a lack of adoption of anonymous eCash (attempts of commercial deployment of Chaum's schemes failed in the late 1990s), and today, there are still no widely deployed anonymous electronic payment services.

Zero-Knowledge Proofs

A zero-knowledge proof is defined as an interactive proof in which a prover can prove to a verifier that a statement is true without revealing anything else than the veracity of the statement. Zero-knowledge proofs were first presented in 1985 by Goldwasser et al. [37]. A zero-knowledge proof must fulfill the following three properties:

- *Completeness:* If the statement is true, the honest verifier will be convinced of this fact by an honest prover.
- *Soundness:* If the statement is false, no cheating prover can convince the honest verifier that it is true, except with some very small probability.
- *Zero-knowledge:* If the statement is true, no cheating verifier learns anything other than this fact.

Zero-knowledge proofs are building blocks for data-minimizing technologies, such as anonymous credential systems. The anonymous credential protocol IdeMix is, for example, based on proofs of knowledge, in which a prover proves that he knows a secret value or that he is able to solve some number theoretic problem, which would contradict the assumption that the problem cannot be solved by a polynomially bounded Turing machine.

Anonymous Credentials

A traditional credential (often also called certificate or attribute certificate) is a set of personal attributes, such as birth date, name or personal number, signed (and thereby certified) by the certifying party (the so-called issuer), and bound to its owner by cryptographic means (by requiring the user's secret key to use the credential). In terms of privacy, the use of (traditional or anonymous) credentials is better than the direct request to the certifying party, as this prevents the certifying party from profiling the user. Traditional credentials require, however, that all attributes are disclosed together if the user wants to prove certain properties, so that the verifier can check the issuer's signature. This makes different uses of the same credential linkable to each other. Moreover, the verifier and issuer can link the different uses of the user's credential to the issuing of the credential.

Anonymous credentials (also called private certificates) were first introduced by Chaum [10] and later enhanced by Brands [38] and by Camenisch and Lysyanskaya [39] and have stronger privacy properties than traditional credentials. Microsoft's U-Prove technology based on Brands's protocols and IBM's IdeMix technology based on the credential protocols by Camenisch et al. are currently the practically most relevant anonymous credential technologies.

Anonymous credentials allow the user to essentially "transform" the certificate into a new one that contains only a subset of attributes of the original certificate (it allows proving only a subset of its attributes to a verifier (*selective disclosure property*)). Instead of revealing the exact value of an attribute, anonymous credential systems also enable the user in the transformation to apply any mathematical function to the (original) attribute value, allowing him to prove only attribute properties without revealing the attribute itself. Besides, with the IdeMix protocol by Camenisch et al., the issuer's signature is also transformed in such a way that the signature in the new certificate cannot be linked to the original signature of the issuer [33]. Hence, different credential uses cannot be linked by the verifier and/or issuer (*unlinkability property*). Cryptographically speaking, with IdeMix, the user is basically using a zero-knowledge proof to convince the verifier of possessing a signature generated by the issuer on a statement containing the subset of attributes.

Figure 43.6 provides a scenario illustrating how data minimization can be achieved in an identity management online transaction: First, user Alice obtains an anonymous driving license credential issued by the Swedish Road authority (the so-called identity provider), with personal attributes typically stored in the license, including her birth date. Later, she would like to purchase a video from an online shop (the so-called relying party, which is also the verifier in this scenario), which is only permitted for adults. After sending a service request, the online shop will answer her with a data request for a proof that she is older than 18. Alice can now take advantage of the selective disclosure feature of the anonymous credential protocol to prove with her credential just the fact that she is older than 18 without revealing her birth date or any other attributes of her credential. If Alice later wants to purchase another video that is only permitted for adults at the same video online shop, she can use the same anonymous credential for a proof that she is over 18. If the IdeMix protocol is used, the video shop is unable to recognize that the two proofs are based on the same credential. Hence, the two rental transactions cannot be linked to the same person.

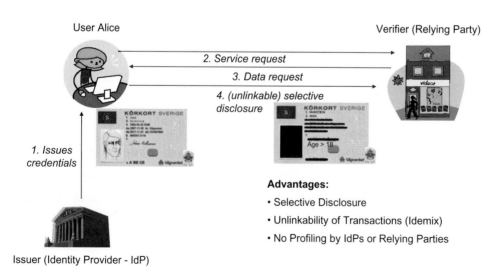

FIGURE 43.6 Example for achieving data minimization for an online transaction by the use of anonymous credentials.

User Alice

Verifier (Relying Party)

2. *Service request*

3. *Data request*

4. *(unlinkable) selective disclosure*

1. Issues credentials

Issuer (Identity Provider - IdP)

Advantages:

- Selective Disclosure
- Unlinkability of Transactions (Idemix)
- No Profiling by IdPs or Relying Parties

Private Information Retrieval

Private Information Retrieval (PIR) allows a user to retrieve an item (record) from a database server without revealing which item he is interested in; that is, the privacy of the item of interest is provided. A typical application example is a patent database from which inventors would like to retrieve information without revealing their interests. A trivial approach would be to simply download the entire database and to make a local selection, which would, however, be too costly bandwidth-wise. In [40], one of the first PIR solutions was introduced, which requires the existence of $t + 1$ noncooperating identical database servers (with n records each). To each server, one n-bit query vector (out of a set of $t + 1$ query vectors) is sent via an encrypted channel, where each bit represents one record of the queried database: If the bit is one, then the record is selected; otherwise not. The user creates t of the query vectors randomly. The remaining $t + 1$st vector is calculated by XOR-ing (superposing) all random vectors and flipping the bit representing the record of interest. One of the query vectors is sent to each database. All selected records are superposed (XOR-ed). The result is exactly the requested database item. If each of the bits in the t random query vectors is set to 1 with a probability of 0.5, then an adversary who has access to at most t of the requests or responses associated with the query vectors will gain no information about the database item that the user is retrieving.

A disadvantage of a multi-database solution is, however, that several identical databases must be obtained. Especially updates are complex, as changes should take place simultaneously. Besides information-theoretic PIR schemes with database replication, several single-database (computational) PIR schemes have been subsequently developed and advanced (see, for instance, [41,42] for surveys and references). Oblivious transfer [42] is private information retrieval, where additionally the user may not learn any item other than the one that he requested.

7. TRANSPARENCY-ENHANCING TOOLS

As we elaborated above, transparency is a basic legal principle. It is also an important social trust factor, as trust in an application can be enhanced if procedures are clear, transparen,t and reversible, so that users feel they are in control [43]. Transparency-enhancing technologies provide tools to the end users or their proxies acting on behalf of the user's interests (such as data protection commissioners), for making personal data processing more transparent to them.

Classification

Transparency-enhancing tools (TETs) for privacy purposes can be classified into the following categories (see also [44]):

1. TETs that provide information about the intended data collection and processing to the data subject, in order to enhance the data subject's privacy;
2. TETs that provide the data subject with an overview of what personal data have been disclosed to which data controller under which policies;
3. TETs that provide the data subject, or his proxy, online access to his personal data, to information on how his data have been processed and whether this was in line with privacy laws and/or negotiated policies, and/or to the logic of data processing in order to enhance the data subject's privacy;
4. TETs that provide "counter-profiling" capabilities to the data subject, helping him to "guess" how his data match relevant group profiles, which may affect his future opportunities or risks;

TETs of the first and last categories are also called *ex-ante* TETs, as they provide transparency of any intended data processing to the data subjects before they are releasing any personal data. TETs of the second and third categories provide transparency in regard to the processing of personal data, which the user has already disclosed, and are therefore called *ex-post* TETs.

Ex-ante Transparency-Enhancing Tools

Examples of ex-ante TETs are privacy policy languages tools and Human Computer Interaction (HCI) components that make privacy policies of services sides more transparent, such as the Platform for Privacy Preferences (P3P) language [45] and P3P user agents, such as the privacy bird.[7] P3P enables Web sites to express their privacy policy (basically stating what data are requested by whom, for what purposes, and how long the data will be retained) in a standard (machine-readable XML) format that can be retrieved automatically and interpreted easily by user agents and matched with the user's privacy preferences. Thus, P3P user agents enable users to be better informed of a Web site's data-handling practices (in both machine- and human-readable formats).

Recently developed visualization techniques for displaying P3P-based privacy policies are based on the metaphor of a "Nutrition Label," assuming that people already understand other nutrition, warning, and energy labeling, which consequently can also allow users to find and digest policy-related information with a proposed privacy

---

7. http://www.privacybird.org.

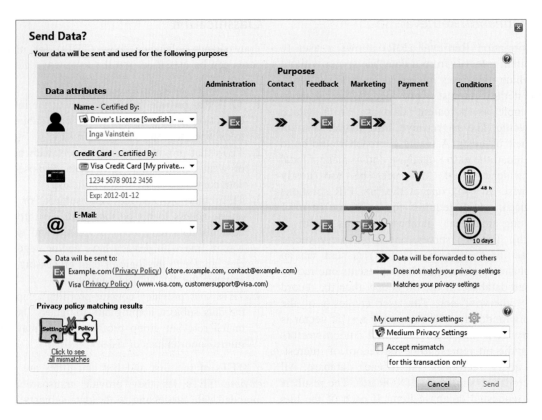

FIGURE 43.7   "Send Data?" PPL user interface [48].

label design more accurately and quickly (see [46]). A more advanced policy language, the PrimeLife Policy Language (PPL), was developed in the EU FP7 project PrimeLife [47]. PPL is a language used to specify not only the privacy policies of data controllers but also those of third parties (so-called downstream controllers) to whom data are further forwarded as well as privacy preferences of users. It is based on two widespread industry standards, XACML (eXtensible Access Control Markup Language) and SAML (Security Assertion Markup Language). The data controller and downstream data controller have policies basically specifying which data are requested from the user and for which purposes and obligations (e.g., under the obligation that the data will be deleted after a certain time period). PPL allows specifying both uncertified data requests and certified data requests based on proofs of the possession of (anonymous IdeMix or traditional X.509) credentials that fulfill certain properties. The user's preferences allow expressing for each data item to which data controllers and downstream data controllers the data can be released and how the user expects his data to be treated. The PPL engine conducts an automated matching of the data controller's policy and the user's preferences. The result can be a mutual agreement concerning the usage of data in the form of a so-called sticky policy, which should be enforced by the access control systems at the backend

sides and which will "travel" with the data transferred to downstream controllers.

As PPL has many features that P3P does not provide (downstream data controllers, credential selection for certified data, and obligations), the design of usable PPL user interfaces provides many challenges. The "Send Data?" user interfaces for letting the PPL engine interact with the user for displaying the result of policy matches, identity/credential selection and for obtaining informed consent to disclose selected certified and uncertified data items were developed and presented [48]. Figure 43.7 depicts an example PPL "Send Data?" dialogue.

The PPL user interfaces follow the Art. 29 Data Protection Working Party recommendation of providing policy information in a multilayered format [49] for making policies more understandable and usable. According to this recommendation, a short privacy notice on the top layer offers individuals the core information required under Art. 10 EU Directive 95/46/EC, including at least the identity of the service provider and the purpose of data processing. In addition, a clear indication (in the form of URLs—in our example the "privacy policy" URLs of the two data controllers) must be given as to how the individuals can access the other layers presenting the additional information required by Art. 10 and national privacy laws.

Ex-Post Transparency-Enhancing Tools[8]

An important transparency-enhancing tool that falls into categories 2 and 3 of our classification is the data track that has been developed in the PRIME[9] and PrimeLife[10] projects [51]. The data track is a user side transparency tool, which includes both a history function and online access functions. The history function keeps for each transaction, in which a user discloses personal data to a communication partner, a record for the user on which personal data are disclosed to whom (the identity of the controller), for which purposes, which credentials and/or pseudonyms have been used in this context, as well as the details of the negotiated or given privacy policy. These transaction records are either stored at the user side or centrally (in the Cloud—see [52]) in a secure and privacy-friendly manner. User-friendly search functionalities, which allow the user to easily get an overview about who has received what data about him or her, are also included. The Online access functions allow end users to exercise their rights to access their data at the remote services sides online. In this way, they can compare what data they have disclosed to a services side with what data are still stored by the services side. This allows them to check whether data have been changed, processed, or deleted (in accordance with data retention periods of the negotiated or given privacy policy). Online access is granted to a user if he can provide a unique transaction ID (currently implemented as a 16-byte random number), which is shared between the user (stored in his data track) and the services side for each transaction of personal data disclosure. This in principle also allows anonymous or pseudonymous users to access their data.

While the data track is still in the research prototype stage, the Google Dashboard is already available in practice and grants its users access to a summary of the data stored with a Google account, including account data and the users' search query history, which are, however, only a part of the personal data that Google processes. It does not provide any insight into how these data provided by the users (the users' search queries) have subsequently been processed by Google. Besides, access is provided only to authenticated Google users.

Further examples of transparency tools that allow users to view and control how their personal data have been processed and to check whether this is in compliance with a negotiated or given privacy policy are based on secure logging systems that usually extend the Kelsey-Schneier log [53] and protect the integrity and the confidentiality of the log data. Such a secure logging system and an automated privacy audit facility are key components of a privacy evidence approach proposed by [54]. This privacy evidence system allows a user to inspect all log entries that are recording actions of that user with a special view tool and permits sending the log view created by that tool to the automated privacy audit component, which compares the log view with the privacy policy and to construct privacy evidence. This privacy evidence indicates to the user whether the privacy policy has been violated.

The unlinkability of log entries, which means that they should not be stored in the sequence of their creation, is needed to prevent an adversary from correlating the log with other information sources, such as other external logs, which could allow him to identify data subjects to whom the entries refer (cf. [55]). Also, anonymous access is needed to prevent an adversary from observing who views which log entries and in this way conclude to whom the log entries refer. Wouters et al. [56] have presented such a secure and privacy-friendly Logging for eGovernment Services. However, it addresses the unlinkability of logs between logging systems in eGovernment rather than the unlinkability of log entries within a log. Moreover, it does not address insider attacks, nor does it allow anonymous access to log entries.

Within the PrimeLife project, a secure logging system has been developed, which addresses these aspects of the unlinkability of log entries and anonymous user access. In particular, it fulfills the following requirements (see [55]):

- Only the data subject can decrypt log entries after they have been committed to the log.
- A user can check the integrity of his log entries. A service provider can check the integrity of the whole log file.
- It is not possible for an attacker to secretly modify log entries, which have been committed to the log before the attacker took over the system (forward integrity).
- It is practically impossible to link log entries, which refer to the same user.
- For efficiency reasons, it should be possible for a data subject to read his log entries without the need to download and/or fully traverse the whole log database.

The need and requirements of tools that can anticipate profiles (category 4 of our definition above) have been analyzed within studies of the FIDIS project (see, for instance, [57]). To the best of our knowledge, no practical transparency-enhancing tools fulfill the requirements. In academia, promising approaches [58,59] have been formulated and are the subject of research.

---

8. This section corresponds to most parts of Section 2.4.2 that the leading author has contributed to ENISA's study on "Privacy, Accountability and Trust—Challenges and Opportunities," published in 2011 [50].

9. EU FP6 project PRIME (Privacy and Identity Management for Europe), www.prime-project.eu.

10. EU FP7 project PrimeLife (Privacy and Identity Management for Life), www.primelife.eu.

8. SUMMARY

This chapter has provided an introduction to the area of privacy-enhancing technologies. We presented the legal foundation of PETs and provided a classification of PETs, as well as a selection of some of the most relevant PETs. Following the Privacy by Design paradigm for effectively protecting privacy, privacy protection should be incorporated into the overall system design (it should be embedded throughout the entire system life cycle).

While technical PET solutions to many practical privacy issues have existed for many years, these solutions have not been widely adopted by either industry or users. The main factors contributing to this problem are low demand by industry, which, rather, is under competitive business pressure to exploit and monetize user data, and low user awareness in combination with a lack of easily usable, efficient PET implementations (see also [60]). While this chapter is part of a technical computer security handbook and has therefore focused on the technical (and partly legal) aspects of PETs, clearly the economic, social, and usability aspects of PETs also need further attention in the future.

Finally, let's move on to the real interactive part of this chapter: review questions/exercises, hands-on projects, case projects, and optional team case project. The answers and/or solutions by chapter can be found in the Online Instructor's Solutions Manual.

CHAPTER REVIEW QUESTIONS/EXERCISES

True/False

1. True or False? Data protection concerns the protection of personal data in order to guarantee privacy and is only a part of the concept of privacy.
2. True or False? Personal data processing has to be legitimate, which according to Art. 7 EU Directive 95/46/EC is usually the case if the data subject[11] has given his ambiguous (and informed) consent, if there is a legal obligation, or if there is contractual agreement (cf. the Collection Limitation Principle of the OECD Guidelines).
3. True or False? Personal data must be collected for specified, explicit, and legitimate purposes and may be further processed in a way incompatible with these purposes (Art. 6 I b EU Directive 95/46/EC).
4. True or False? The processing of personal data must not be limited to data that are adequate, relevant

and not excessive (Art. 6 I (c) EU Directive 95/46/EC).
5. True or False? Transparency of data processing means informing a data subject about the purposes and circumstances of data processing, identifying who is requesting personal data, how the personal data flow, where and how long the data are stored, and what type of rights and controls the data subject has in regard to his personal data.

Multiple Choice

1. What needs to install appropriate technical and organizational security mechanisms to guarantee the confidentiality, integrity, and availability of personal data (Art. 17 EU Directive 95/46/EC)?
   A. Privacy-enhancing technology
   B. Location technology
   C. Web-based
   D. Technical improvement
   E. Data controller
2. What can be defined as technologies that are enforcing legal privacy principles in order to protect and enhance the privacy of users of information technology (IT) and/or data subjects?
   A. Information technology
   B. Location technology
   C. Web-based
   D. Privacy-enhancing technologies
   E. Web technology
3. What as an abstract strategy describes the avoidance of unnecessary or unwanted data disclosures?
   A. Data minimization
   B. *XACML*
   C. XML-based language
   D. Certification authority
   E. Security
4. What aim quantifies the effectiveness of schemes or technologies with regard to the privacy goals defined in the previous section?
   A. Privacy metrics
   B. Languages
   C. Privacy-Aware Access Control
   D. Privacy preferences
   E. Taps
5. What is a prerequisite for achieving anonymity, more generally, or data minimization, on an application level?
   A. Release policies
   B. Anonymous communication
   C. Data-handling policies
   D. Intellectual property
   E. Social engineering

---

11. A data subject is a person about whom personal data is processed.

EXERCISE

Problem

Why now? Why is the National Strategy for Trusted IDs in Cyberspace needed?

Hands-On Projects

Project

Won't having a single password and credential be less secure and private than having many usernames and passwords?

Case Projects

Problem

Who will make sure that companies follow the rules?

Optional Team Case Project

Problem

Will new laws be needed to create the Identity Ecosystem?

REFERENCES

[1] OECD, Guidelines on the Protection of Privacy and Transborder Flows of Personal Data, September 1980.

[2] S.D. Brandeis, L.D. Warren, The right to privacy, Harv. Law Rev. 5 (1890) 193–220.

[3] A. Westin, Privacy and Freedom, Atheneum, New York, 1967.

[4] G. Hogben, Annex A, i PRIME project deliverable D14.0a– PRIME Framework V0, June 2004.

[5] Global Internet Liberty Campaign, PRIVACY AND HUMAN RIGHTS—An International Survey of Privacy Laws and Practice, [Online]. Available: <http://gilc.org/privacy/survey>.

[6] R. Rosenberg, The Social Impact of Computers, Academic Press, 1992.

[7] European union, directive 95/46/EC of the European Parliament and of the Council of 24 October 1995 on the protection of individuals with regard to the processing of personal data and on the free movement of such data, Off. J. L 281 (1995).

[8] Proposal for a REGULATION OF THE EUROPEAN PARLIAMENT AND OF THE COUNCIL on the protection of individuals with regard to the processing of personal data and on the free movement of such data (General Data Protection Regulation), COM(2012) 11 final, 2012/00, January 25, 2012. [Online]. Available: <http://ec.europa.eu/justice/data-protection/document/review2012/com_2012_11_en.pdf>.

[9] S. Fischer-Hübner, Anonymity, Encyclopedia of Database Systems, Springer, Heidelberg, 2009, pp. 90–91.

[10] D. Chaum, Security without identification: card computers to make big brother obsolete, Informatik Spektrum 10 (1987) 262–277.

[11] D. Chaum, The dining cryptographers problem: unconditional sender and recipient untraceability, J. Cryptol. 1 (1) (January 1988) 65–75.

[12] D. Chaum, Untraceable electronic mail, return addresses, and digital pseudonyms, Commun. ACM 24 (2) (February 1981) 84–88.

[13] Registratiekamer & Information and Privacy Commissioner of Ontairo, Privacy-Enhancing Technologies: The Path to Anonymity, Achtergrondstudies en Verkenningen 5B, vol. I & II, Rijswijk, August 1995.

[14] A. Pfitzmann och M. Hansen, Anonymity, Unlinkability, Undetectability, Unobservability, Pseudonymity, and Identity Management—A Consolidated Proposal for Terminology (2010). [Online]. Available: <http://dud.inf.tu-dresden.de/Anon_Terminology.shtml>.

[15] S. Steinbrecher, S. Köpsell, Modelling unlinkability, in: Workshop on Privacy Enhancing Technologies, 2003.

[16] Common Criteria for Information Technology Security Evaluation, Version 3.1, Part 2: Security Functional Requirements, Common Criteria Project (September 2006). [Online]. Available: <www.commoncriteriaportal.org>.

[17] L. Sweeney, k-Anonymity: a model for protecting privacy, Int. J. Uncertain. Fuzz. Knowl. Based Syst. 10 (5) (2002) 571–588.

[18] M. Gruteser, D. Grunwald, Anonymous usage of location-based services through spatial and temporal cloaking, Proceedings of the 1st International Conference on Mobile Systems, Applications and Services (MobiSys), 2003.

[19] W. Wang, M. Motani, V. Srinivasan, Dependent link padding algorithms for low latency anonymity systems, Proceedings of the 15th ACM Conference on Computer and Communications Security (CCS), 2008.

[20] M. Srivatsa, A. Iyengar, L. Liu, Privacy in VoIP networks: a k-anonymity approach, Proceedings of the IEEE INFOCOM 2009, 2009.

[21] A. Narayanan, V. Shmatikov, Robust de-anonymization of large sparse datasets, Proceedings of the IEEE 29th Symposium on Security and Privacy, Oakland, CA, USA, 2008.

[22] A. Machanavajjhala, D. Kifer, J. Gehrke, M. Ventikasubramaniam, l-Diversity: privacy beyond k-anonymity, ACM Trans. Knowl. Discov. Data 1 (2007).

[23] N. Li, T. Li, S. Venkatasubramanian, t-Closeness: privacy beyond k-Anonymity and l-Diversity, Proceedings of the IEEE 23rd International Conference on Data Engineering, 2007.

[24] C.E. Shannon, A mathematical theory of communications, Bell Syst. Tech. J. 27 (1948) 379–423623–656

[25] C. Diaz, S. Seys, J. Claessens, B. Preneel, Towards measuring anonymity, Workshop on Privacy Enhancing Technologies, 2002.

[26] A. Serjantov, G. Danezis, Towards an information theoretic metric for anonymity, Workshop on Privacy Enhancing Technologies, 2002.

[27] S. Clauss, A framework for quantification of linkability within a privacy-enhancing identity management system, Emerg. Trends Inf. Commun. Secur. (ETRICS) (2006).

[28] D. Chaum, The dining cryptographers problem: unconditional sender and recipient untraceabilit, J. Cryptol. 1 (1) (January 1988) 65–75.

[29] [Online]. <http://anon.inf.tu-dresden.de>, [Använd August 29, 2012].

[30] D.M. Goldschlag, M.G. Reed, P.F. Syverson, Hiding routing information, Inf. Hiding (1996).

[31] R. Dingledine, N. Mathewson, P. Syverson, Tor: The Second-Generation Onion Router, Naval Research Lab, Washington, DC, 2004.

[32] R. Böhme, G. Danezis, C. Díaz, S. Köpsell, A. Pfitzmann, On the PET Workshop Panel "Mix Cascades Versus Peer-to-Peer: Is One Concept Superior?", Workshop on Privacy-Enhancing Technologies (PET) 2004, 2005.

[33] Jan Camenish, Maria Dubovitskaya, Markulf Kohlweiss, Jorn Lapon, Gregory Neven, Cryptographic mechanisms for privacy, Privacy and Identity Management for Life, Springer, Heidelberg, 2011, pp. 117–134.

[34] D. Chaum, A. Fiat, M. Naor, Untraceable Electronic Cash, Adv. Cryptol. Crypto'88 (1988).

[35] D. Chaum, Achieving electronic privacy, Sci. Am. (1992) 76–81.

[36] S. Fischer-Hübner, LNCS IT-Security and Privacy—Design and Use of Privacy-Enhancing Security Mechanisms, Springer, Heidelberg, 2001.

[37] S. Goldwasser, S. Micali, C. Rackoff, The knowledge complexity of interactive proof systems, Proceedings of the 17th ACM Symposium on Theory of Computing, 1985, pp. 291–304.

[38] S. Brands, Rethinking Public Key Infrastructure and Digital Certificates—Building in Privacy, PhD thesis. Eindhoven. Institute of Technology, 1999.

[39] J. Camenisch, A. Lysyanskaya, Efficient non-transferable anonymous multi-show credential system with optional anonymity revocation, Adv. Cryptol. Eurocrypt 2045 (2001) 93–118.

[40] D. Cooper, K. Birman, Preserving privacy in a network of mobile computers, Proceedings of the 1995 IEEE Symposium on Security and Privacy, Oakland, May 1995.

[41] R. Ostrovsky, W. Skeith, A Survey of Single-Database Private Information Retrieval: Techniques and Applications, Public Key Cryptography−PKC 2007, Springer, 2007.

[42] H. Lipmaa, Oblivious Transfer or Private Information Retrieval, [Online]. Available: <http://www.cs.ut.ee/∼lipmaa/crypto/link/protocols/oblivious.php>.

[43] R. Leenes, M. Lips, R. Poels, M. Hoogwout, User aspects of Privacy and Identity Management in Online Environments: Towards a theoretical model of social factors, PRIME Framework V1 (Chapter 9) project Deliverable, 2005.

[44] H. Hedbom, A survey on transparency tools for privacy purposes, Proceedings of the 4th FIDIS/IFIP Summer School, published by Springer, 2009, Brno, September 2008.

[45] W3C, P3P—The Platform for Privacy Preferences 1.1 (P3P1.1) Specification, 2006. [Online]. Available: <http://www.w3.org/P3P/>.

[46] P. Kelley, L. Cesca, J. Bresee, L. Cranor, Standardizing privacy notices: an online study of the nutrition label approach, Proceedings of the 28th International Conference on Human Factors in Computing Systems ACM, 2010, p. 1573.

[47] PrimeLife, Privacy and Identity Management in Europe for Life-Policy Languages, [Online]. Available: <http://primelife.ercim.eu/results/primer/133-policy-languages>.

[48] J. Angulo, S. Fischer-Hübner, E. Wästlund, T. Pulls, Towards usable privacy policy display & management for primelife, Inf. Manag. Comput. Secur. (Emerald) 20 (1) (2012) 4−17.

[49] Opinion on More Harmonised Information provisions. 11987/04/EN WP 100, Chapter 29 Data Protection Working Party, November 25, 2004. [Online]. Available: <http://ec.europa.eu/justice_home/fsj/privacy/docs/wpdocs/2004/wp100_en.pdf>.

[50] ENISA, Privacy, Accountability and Trust—Challenges and Opportunities, 2011. [Online]. Available: <http://www.enisa.europa.eu/activities/identity-and-trust/privacy-and-trust/library/deliverables/pat-study>.

[51] E. Wästlund, S. Fischer-Hübner, End User Transparency Tools: UI Prototypes, PrimeLife Deliverable D4.2.2. <www.primelife.eu>, June 2010.

[52] T. Pulls, Privacy-Friendly Cloud Storage for the Data Track: An Educational Transparency Tool, NordSec—17th Nordic Conference on Secure IT Systems will be held at Blekinge Institute of Technology, Karlskrona, October 2012.

[53] B. Schneier, J. Kelsey, Cryptographic Support for Secure Logs on Untrusted Machines, The Seventh USENIX Security Symposium Proceedings, USENIX Press, 1998, pp. 53−62.

[54] S. Sackmann, J.A.R. Strüker, Personalization in privacy-aware highly dynamic systems, Commun. ACM 49 (9) (September 2006).

[55] H. Hedbom, T. Pulls, P. Hjärtquist, A. Lavén, Adding Secure Transparency Logging to the PRIME Core, i 5th IFIP WG 9.2,9.6/11.7,11.4,11.6 / PrimeLife International Summer School, revised selected papers, published by Springer in 2010, Nice, France, 2009.

[56] K. Wouters, K. Simoens, D. Lathouwers, B. Preneel, Secure and Privacy-Friendly Logging for eGovernment Services, 3rd International Conference on Availability, Reliability and Security (ARES 2008), IEEE, 2008, pp. 1091−1096.

[57] M. Hildebrandt, Biometric Behavioral Profiling and Transparency Enhancing Tools, FIDIS Deliverable D 7.12, <www.fidis.net>, 2009.

[58] S. Berthold, R. Böhme, Valuating privacy with option pricing theory, in: T. Moore, D.J. Pym, C. Ioannidis (Eds.), Economics of Information Security and Privacy, Red. Springer, 2010, pp. 187−209.

[59] S. Berthold, Towards a Formal Language for Privacy Options, Privacy and Identity Management for Life, 6th IFIP WG 9.2,9.6/11.7, 11.4, 11.6/PrimeLife International Summer School 2010, Revised Selected Papers, 2011.

[60] S. Fischer-Hübner, C.J. Hoofnagle, I. Krontiris, K. Rannenberg, M. Waidner, Online privacy: towards informational self-determination on the internet (Dagstuhl Perspectives Workshop 11061), Dagstuhl Manifestos 1 (1) (2011) 1−20.

## Chapter 44

Personal Privacy Policies[1]

George O.M. Yee
Carleton University

Larry Korba
National Research Council of Canada, Ottawa

1. INTRODUCTION

The rapid growth of the Internet has been accompanied by a similar rapid growth in Internet based e-services targeting consumers. E-services are available for banking, shopping, stock investing, and healthcare, to name a few areas. However, each of these services requires a consumer's personal information in one form or another. This leads to concerns over privacy.

For e-services to be successful, privacy must be protected. In a recent U.S. study by MasterCard International, 60% of respondents were concerned with the privacy of transmitted data.[2] An effective and flexible way of protecting privacy is to manage it using privacy policies. In this approach, each provider of an e-service has a privacy policy specifying the private information required for that e-service. Similarly, each consumer of an e-service has a privacy policy specifying the private information she is willing to share for the e-service. Prior to the activation of an e-service, the consumer and provider of the e-service exchange privacy policies. The service is only activated if the policies are compatible (we define what "compatible" means in a moment). Where the personal privacy policy of an e-service consumer conflicts with the privacy policy of an e-service provider, we have advocated a negotiations approach to resolve the conflict.[3,4]

In our approach, the provider requires private information from the consumer for use in its e-service and so reduces the consumer's privacy by requesting such information. This reduction in consumer privacy is represented by the requirements for consumer private information in the provider's privacy policy. The consumer, on the other hand, would rather keep her private information to herself, so she tries to resist the provider's attempt to reduce her privacy. This means that the consumer would only be willing to have her privacy reduced by a certain amount, as represented by the privacy provisions in her privacy policy. There is a *match* between a provider's privacy policy and the corresponding consumer's policy where the amount of privacy reduction allowed by the consumer's policy is at least as great as the amount of privacy reduction required by the provider's policy (more details on policy matching follow). Otherwise, there is a *mismatch*. Where time is involved, a private item held for less time is considered less private. A privacy policy is considered *upgraded* if the new version represents more privacy than the prior version. Similarly, a privacy policy is considered *downgraded* if the new version represents less privacy than the prior version.

So far so good, but what should go into a personal privacy policy? How are these policies constructed? Moreover, what can be done to construct policies that do not lead to negative unexpected outcomes (an outcome that is harmful to the user in some manner)? Consumers need help in formulating personal privacy policies. The creation of such policies needs to be as easy as possible or consumers would simply avoid using them. Existing privacy specification languages such as P3P and APPE[5,6]

1. NRC Paper number: NRC 50334
2. T. Greer, and M. Murtaza, "E-commerce security and privacy: Managerial vs. technical perspectives," Proceedings, *15th IRMA International Conference (IRMA 2004)*, New Orleans, May 2004.
3. G. Yee, and L. Korba, "Bilateral e-services negotiation under uncertainty," Proceedings, *The 2003 International Symposium on Applications and the Internet (SAINT 2003)*, Orlando, Jan 2003.
4. G. Yee, and L. Korba, "The negotiation of privacy policies in distance education," Proceedings, *14th IRMA International Conference*, Philadelphia, May 2003.
5. W3C Platform, "The platform for privacy preferences," retrieved Sept. 2, 2002, from www.w3.org/P3P/.
6. W3C APPEL, "A P3P preference exchange language 1.0 (APPEL1.0)," W3C Working Draft 15, April 2002, retrieved Sept. 2, 2002, from: http://www.w3.org/TR/P3P-preferences/.

that are XML-based are far too complicated for the average Internet user to understand. Understanding or changing a privacy policy expressed in these languages effectively requires knowing how to program. What is needed is an easy, semiautomated way of deriving a personal privacy policy.

In this chapter, we present two semiautomated approaches for obtaining personal privacy policies for consumers. We also show how these policies should be specified to avoid negative unexpected outcomes. Finally, we describe our Privacy Management Model that explains how personal privacy policies are used to protect consumer privacy, including how policies may be negotiated between e-service consumer and e-service provider.

The "Content of Personal Privacy Policies" section examines the content of personal privacy policies by identifying some attributes of private information collection. The "Semiautomated Derivation of Personal Privacy Policies" section shows how personal privacy policies can be semiautomatically generated. The "Specifying Well-Formed Personal Privacy Policies" section explains how to ensure that personal privacy policies do not lead to negative unexpected outcomes. "The Privacy Management Model" section presents our Privacy Management Model, which explains how personal privacy policies can be used to protect consumer privacy, including how they may be negotiated between e-service consumer and e-service provider. The "Discussion and Related Work" section discusses our approaches and presents related work. The chapter ends with conclusions and a description of possible future work in these areas.

2. CONTENT OF PERSONAL PRIVACY POLICIES

In Canada, privacy legislation is enacted in the *Personal Information Protection and Electronic Documents Act* (PIPEDA)[7] and is based on the Canadian Standards Association's Model Code for the Protection of Personal Information,[8] recognized as a national standard in 1996. This code consists of ten Privacy Principles that for convenience, we label CSAPP.

Privacy Legislation and Directives

Data privacy in the European Union is governed by a very comprehensive set of regulations called the Data Protection Directive.[9] In the United States, privacy protection is achieved through a patchwork of legislation at the federal and state levels. Privacy legislation is largely sector-based.[10]

Requirements from Privacy Principles

In this section, we identify some attributes of private information collection or personally identifiable information (PII) collection using CSAPP as a guide (see checklist, "An Agenda For Action For Developing Privacy Policies To Guide Customer /Client Relations"). We then apply the attributes to the specification of privacy policy contents. Note that we use the terms *private information* and *PII* interchangeably. We use CSAPP because it is representative of privacy legislation in other countries (European Union, Australia) and has withstood the test of time, originating from 1996. In addition, CSAPP is representative of the Fair Information Practices, a set of standards balancing the information needs of the business with the privacy needs of the individual.[11] Table 44.1 shows CSAPP.

In Table 44.1, we interpret *organization* as "provider" and *individual* as "consumer." In the following, we use CSAPP.n to denote Principle n of CSAPP. Principle CSAPP.2 implies that there could be different providers requesting the information, thus implying a *collector* attribute. Principle CSAPP.4 implies that there is a *what* attribute, that is, what private information is being collected? Principles CSAPP.2, CSAPP.4, and CSAPP.5 state that there are *purposes* for which the private information is being collected. Principles CSAPP.3, CSAPP.5, and CSAPP.9 imply that the private information can be disclosed to other parties, giving a *disclose-to* attribute. Principle CSAPP.5 implies a *retention time* attribute for the retention of private information. Thus, from the CSAPP we derive five attributes of private information collection: *collector, what, purposes, retention time*, and *disclose-to*.

The Privacy Principles also prescribe certain operational requirements that must be satisfied between provider and consumer, such as identifying purpose and consent. Our service model and the exchange of privacy

---

7. Canadian Standards Association, "Model code for the protection of personal information," retrieved Sept. 5, 2007, from www.csa.ca/standards/privacy/code/Default.asp?articleID=5286&language=English.

8. Office of the Privacy Commissioner of Canada, "The personal information protection and electronic documents act," retrieved May 1, 2008, from www.privcom.gc.ca/legislation/02_06_01_e.asp.

9. European Union, "Directive 95/46/EC of the European Parliament and of the Council of 24 October 1995 on the protection of individuals with regard to the processing of personal data and on the free movement of such data," unofficial text retrieved Sept. 5, 2003, from http://aspe.hhs.gov/datacncl/eudirect.htm.

10. Banisar, D., "Privacy and data protection around the world," Proceedings, *21st International Conference on Privacy and Personal Data Protection*, September 13, 1999.

11. K. S. Schwaig, G. C. Kane, and V. C. Storey, "Privacy, fair information practices and the fortune 500: the virtual reality of compliance," *The DATA BASE for Advances in Information Systems*, 36(1), pp. 49–63, 2005.

An Agenda for Action for Developing Privacy Policies to Guide Customer /Client Relations

The checklist suggests issues to consider when drafting privacy principles to safeguard the personal information of your clients and customers: (Check All Tasks Completed):

A. Organizational Policies:

_____1. Does your organization have policies that outline its privacy practices and expectations for handling the personal information of its clients, customers, users, members and/or listees?

_____2. Are your organization's privacy policies communicated regularly? Opportunities include in employees' initial training sessions, in regular organization-wide training programs, in employee handbooks, on posters and posted signs, on company intranet and Internet Web sites, in brochures available to clients.

_____3. Are all employees who handle personal information included in the training programs, including temporary employees, back-up personnel, and contract staff?

_____4. Is your organization familiar with and has it adopted International Standards Organization (ISO) security standards, known as ISO 27001?

B. Privacy Principles:

_____5. **Openness.** A general practice of openness about practices and policies should exist. Means should be available to establish the existence and nature of personal information and the main purposes of its use.

_____6. **Purpose specification.** The purpose for collecting personal information should be specified at the time of collection. Further uses should be limited to those purposes.

_____7. **Collection limitation.** Personal information should be collected by lawful and fair means and with the knowledge and consent of the subject. To the greatest extent possible, companies should employ principles of data minimization, that is, collecting only data that is actually necessary to conduct their business, and collecting such information only for the stated purpose.

_____8. **Use limitation.** Personal information should not be disclosed for secondary purposes without the consent of the subject or by authority of law.

_____9. **Individual participation.** Individuals should be allowed to inspect and correct their personal information. Whenever possible, personal information should be collected directly from the individual.

_____10. **Quality.** Personal information should be accurate, complete and timely, and be relevant to the purposes for which it is to be used.

_____11. **Security safeguards.** Personal information should be protected by reasonable security safeguards against such risks as loss, unauthorized access, destruction, use, modification or disclosure. Access to personal information should be limited to only those within the organization with a specific need to see it.

_____12. **Accountability.** Someone within the organization, such as the chief privacy officer or an information manager, should be held accountable for complying with its privacy policy. Privacy audits to monitor organizational compliance should be conducted on a regular basis, as should employee training programs.

C. Data and Network Security:

_____13. Do you have staff specifically assigned to data security?

_____14. Do staff members participate in regular training programs to keep abreast of technical and legal issues?

_____15. Have you developed a security breach response plan in the event that your company or organization experiences a data breach?

_____16. Have you developed security guidelines for laptops and other portable computing devices when transported off-site?

_____17. Is physical access restricted to computer operations and paper/micrographic files that contain personally identifiable information?

_____18. Do you have procedures to prevent former employees from gaining access to computers and paper files?

_____19. Are sensitive files segregated in secure areas/computer systems and available only to qualified persons?

_____20. Are filing cabinets containing sensitive information locked? Are computers, laptops, and networks password protected?

_____21. Do you have audit procedures and strict penalties in place to prevent telephone fraud and theft of equipment and information?

_____22. Do all employees follow strict password and virus protection procedures?

_____23. Are employees required to change passwords often, using "foolproof" methods?

_____24. Is encryption used to protect sensitive information (a particularly important measure when transmitting personally-identifiable information over the Internet)?

_____25. Do you regularly conduct systems-penetration tests to determine if your systems are hacker proof?

_____26. If your organization is potentially susceptible to industrial espionage, have you taken extra precautions to guard against leakage of information?

TABLE 44.1 CSAPP: The Ten Privacy Principles from the Canadian Standards Association.

Principle	Description
1. Accountability	An organization is responsible for personal information under its control and shall designate an individual or individuals accountable for the organization's compliance with the privacy principles.
2. Identifying Purposes	The purposes for which personal information is collected shall be identified by the organization at or before the time the information is collected.
3. Consent	The knowledge and consent of the individual are required for the collection, use, or disclosure of personal information, except when inappropriate.
4. Limiting Collection	The collection of personal information shall be limited to that which is necessary for the purposes identified by the organization. Information shall be collected by fair and lawful means.
5. Limiting Use, Disclosure, and Retention	Personal information shall not be used or disclosed for purposes other than those for which it was collected, except with the consent of the individual or as required by the law. In addition, personal information shall be retained only as long as necessary for fulfillment of those purposes.
6. Accuracy	Personal information shall be as accurate, complete, and up to date as is necessary for the purposes for which it is to be used.
7. Safeguards	Security safeguards appropriate to the sensitivity of the information shall be used to protect personal information.
8. Openness	An organization shall make readily available to individuals specific information about its policies and practices relating to the management of personal information.
9. Individual Access	Upon request, an individual shall be informed of the existence, use and disclosure of his or her personal information and shall be given access to that information. An individual shall be able to challenge the accuracy and completeness of the information and have it amended as appropriate.
10. Challenging Compliance	An individual shall be able to address a challenge concerning compliance with the above principles to the designated individual or individuals accountable for the organization's compliance.

policies automatically satisfy some of these requirements, namely Principles CSAPP.2, CSAPP.3, and CSAPP.8. The satisfaction of the remaining operational requirements depends on compliance mechanisms (Principles CSAPP. 1, CSAPP.4, CSAPP.5, CSAPP.6, CSAPP.9, and CSAPP. 10) and security mechanisms (Principle CSAPP.7).

Privacy Policy Specification

Based on these explorations, the contents of a privacy policy should, for each item of PII, identify (1) the *collector*—the person who wants to collect the information, (2) *what*—the nature of the information, (3) *purposes*—the purposes for which the information is being collected, (4) *retention time*—the amount of time for the provider to keep the information, and (5) *disclose-to*—the parties to whom the information will be disclosed. Figure 44.1 gives three examples of consumer personal privacy policies for use with an e-learning provider, an online bookseller, and an online medical help clinic. The *policy use* field indicates the type of online service for which the

policy will be used. Since a privacy policy may change over time, we have a *valid* field to hold the time period during which the policy is valid. Figure 44.2 gives examples of provider privacy policies corresponding to the personal privacy policies of Figure 44.1.

A privacy policy thus consists of "header" information (*policy use, owner, valid*) together with one or more 5-tuples, or privacy rules:

$$< collector, what, purposes, retention\ time, disclose-to >$$

where each 5-tuple or rule represents an item of private information and the conditions under which the information may be shared. For example, in Figure 44.1, the personal policy for e-learning has a header (top portion) plus two rules (bottom portion); the personal policy for a bookseller has only one rule.

3. SEMIAUTOMATED DERIVATION OF PERSONAL PRIVACY POLICIES

A semiautomated derivation of a personal privacy policy is the use of mechanisms (described in a moment) that may

Policy Use: E-learning Owner: Alice Consumer Valid: unlimited	Policy Use: Bookseller Owner: Alice Consumer Valid: June 2009	Policy Use: Medical Help Owner: Alice Consumer Valid: July 2009
Collector: any What: name, address, tel Purposes: identification Retention Time: unlimited Disclose-To: none Collector: any What: course marks Purposes: records Retention Time: 2 years Disclose-To: none	Collector: any What: name, address, tel Purposes: identification Retention Time: unlimited Disclose-To: none	Collector: any What: name, address, tel Purposes: contact Retention Time: unlimited Disclose-To: pharmacy Collector: Dr. A. Smith What: medical condition Purposes: treatment Retention Time: unlimited Disclose-To: pharmacy

FIGURE 44.1 Example of consumer personal privacy policies.

Policy Use: E-learning Owner: E-learning Unlimited Valid: unlimited	Policy Use: Bookseller Owner: All Books Online Valid: unlimited	Policy Use: Medical Help Owner: Medics Online Valid: unlimited
Collector: E-learning Unlimited What: name, address, tel Purposes: identification Retention Time: unlimited Disclose-To: none Collector: E-learning Unlimited What: course marks Purposes: records Retention Time: 1 years Disclose-To: none	Collector: All Books Online What: name, address, tel Purposes: identification Retention Time: unlimited Disclose-To: none Collector: All Books Online What: credit card Purposes: payment Retention Time: until paid Disclose-To: none	Collector: Medics Online What: name, address, tel Purposes: contact Retention Time: unlimited Disclose-To: pharmacy Collector: Medics Online What: medical condition Purposes: treatment Retention Time: 1 year Disclose-To: pharmacy

FIGURE 44.2 Example of corresponding provider privacy policies.

be semiautomated to obtain a set of privacy rules for a particular policy use. We present two approaches for such derivations. The first approach relies on third-party surveys (see sidebar, "Derivation Through Third Party Surveys") of user perceptions of data privacy (Figure 44.3). The second approach is based on retrieval from a community of peers.

Consumers may interactively adapt their existing privacy policies for new service provider policies based on the PSLs of the WPRs and the new provider policies, as illustrated in Figure 44.4. In Figure 44.4, the Policy Interpreter interactively allows the user to establish (using a privacy slider) the privacy levels of required rules based on the new provider policy and the PSLs from a policy provider. Policy Search then retrieves the user policy that most closely matches the user's privacy-established rules. This policy may then be further amended interactively via the Policy Interpreter to obtain the required personal privacy policy. This assumes the availability of an easy-to-understand interface for the user interaction as well as software to automatically take care of any needed conversions of rules back into the policy language (APPEL).

An Example

Suppose a consumer wants to generate a personal privacy policy for a company called E-learning Unlimited. For simplicity, suppose the privacy policy of E-learning Unlimited has only one WPR, namely $<$ *course marks, records, 12 months* $>$. The steps are implemented as follows:

1. The third-party survey generates the following results for the WPR (the lowest privacy sensitivity level is $M = 1$, the highest is $N = 5$).

   WPR (p_i) PSL ($S_{k,i}$)
   $<$ *course marks, records, 6 months* > 3
   $<$ *course marks, records, 6 months* > 4
   $<$ *course marks, records, 6 months* > 4
   $<$ *course marks, records, 6 months* > 5
   $<$ *course marks, records, 12 months* > 1
   $<$ *course marks, records, 12 months* > 1
   $<$ *course marks, records, 12 months* > 2
   $<$ *course marks, records, 12 months* > 3

   Note that the higher the number of months the marks are retained, the lower the PSL (the lower

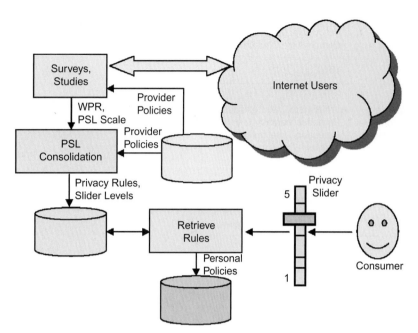

FIGURE 44.3 Derivation of personal privacy policies from surveys.

Derivation Through Third-Party Surveys

(a) A policy provider makes use of third-party surveys performed on a regular basis, as well as those published in research literature, to obtain user privacy sensitivity levels (PSLs) or perceptions of the level of privacy for various combinations of *<what, purposes, retention time>* in provider policy rules. We call *<what, purposes, retention time>* WPR, for short. This gives a range of PSLs for different WPRs in different provider policies. Formally:

Let p_i represent a WPR from a provider policy, I represent the set of p_i over all provider policies, $f_{k,i}$ represent the privacy sensitivity function of person k to sharing p_i with a service provider. We restrict $f_{k,i}$ to an integer value in a standard interval *[M,N]*, that is, $M \leq f_{k,i} \leq N$ for integers M, N (e.g., M = 1, N = 5). Then the PSLs $s_{k,i}$ are obtained as

$$s_{k,i} = f_{k,i}(p_i) \forall k \in K, i \in I$$

where K is the set of consumers interested in the providers' services. This equation models a person making a choice of what PSL to assign a particular p_i.

(b) Corresponding to a service provider's privacy policy (which specifies the privacy rules required), a policy provider (or a software application used by the policy provider) consolidates the PSLs from (a) such that the WPRs are selectable by a single value privacy level from a "privacy slider" for each service provider policy. There are different ways to do this consolidation. One way is to assign a WPR the median of its PSL range as its privacy level (illustrated in a moment). The outcome of this process is a set of consumer privacy rules (expressed using a

policy language such as APPEL) ranked by privacy level for different providers, and with the *collector* and *disclose-to* fields as "any" and "none," respectively. (The consumer can change these fields later if desired.) Formally, using the notation introduced in (a):

Let P represent a provider's privacy policy. Then for each WPR $p_i \in P$, we have from (a) a set of PSLs: $S_i(P) = \{s_{k,i} \mid p_i \in P, \forall k \in K\}$. Our goal is to map $S_i(P)$ to a single privacy level from a privacy slider. Let g be such a mapping. Then this step performs the mapping $g(S_i(P)) = n$, where n is the privacy slider value. For example, the mapping g can be "take the median of" (illustrated below) or "take the average of." We have assumed that the range of slider values is the same as *[M,N]* in (a). If this is not the case, g would need to incorporate normalization to the range of slider values.

(c) Consumers obtain online from the policy provider the privacy rules that make up whole policies. They do this by first specifying the provider for which a consumer privacy policy is required. The consumer is then prompted to enter the privacy level using the privacy slider for each WPR from the service provider's policy. The selected rules would then automatically populate the consumer's policy. The consumer then completes his privacy policy by adding the header information (i.e., *policy use, owner, valid*) and, if desired, add specific names to *collector* and *disclose-to* for all rules. This can be done through a human-computer interface that shelters the user from the complexity of the policy language. In this way, large populations of consumers may quickly obtain privacy policies for many service providers that reflect the privacy sensitivities of the communities surveyed.

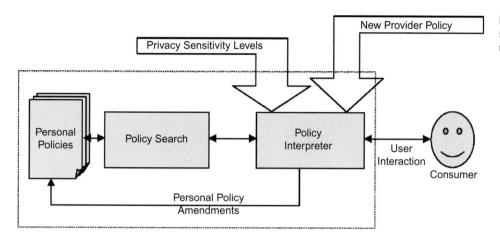

FIGURE 44.4 Adapting an existing personal privacy policy to a new provider.

the privacy perceived by the consumer). The different PSLs obtained constitute one part of the privacy sensitivity scale.

2. In this step, the policy provider consolidates the PSL in Step 1 using the median value from the corresponding PSL range. Thus for the four course-mark retention times of 6 months, the lowest value is 3, the highest value is 5, and the median is 4. Therefore the rule < *any, course marks, records, 6 months, none-* > is ranked with privacy level 4. Similarly, the rule < *any, course marks, records, 12 months, none* > is ranked with privacy level 2.

3. To obtain her privacy rules, the consumer specifies the service provider as E-learning Unlimited and a privacy slider value of 4 (for example) when prompted. She then obtains the rule:

< *any, course marks, records, 6 months, none* >

and proceeds to complete the policy by adding the header values and if desired, specific names for *collector* and *disclose-to*.

Retrieval from a Community of Peers

This approach assumes an existing community of peers already possessing specific use privacy policies with rules according to desired levels of privacy. A new consumer joining the community searches for personal privacy rules. The existing personal privacy policies may have been derived using the third-party surveys, as previously. Each privacy policy rule is stored along with its privacy level so that it may be selected according to this level and *purpose*. Where a rule has been adapted or modified by the owner, it is the owner's responsibility to ensure that the slider privacy value of the modified rule is consistent with the privacy sensitivity scale from surveys.

- All online users are peers and everyone has a privacy slider. The new consumer broadcasts a request for

privacy rules to the community (see Figure 44.5a), specifying *purpose* and slider value. This is essentially a peer-to-peer search over all peers.

- The community responds by forwarding matching (in terms of *purpose* and slider value) rules to the consumer (see Figure 44.5b). This matching may also be fuzzy.

- The consumer compares the rules and selects them according to *what*, possibly popularity (those that are from the greater number of peers), and best fit in terms of privacy. After obtaining the rules, the consumer completes the privacy policies by completing the headers and possibly changing the *collector* and *disclose-to* as in the preceding derivation from surveys approach.

- The consumer adapts a privacy policy to the service provider's policy, as in the derivation by surveys approach (Figure 44.4), to try to fulfill provider requirements.

4. SPECIFYING WELL-FORMED PERSONAL PRIVACY POLICIES

This section explains how unexpected outcomes may arise from badly specified personal privacy policies. It then gives guidelines for specifying "well-formed" policies that avoid unexpected outcomes.

Unexpected Outcomes

We are interested in unexpected outcomes that result from the matching of consumer and provider policies. Unexpected outcomes result from (1) the way the matching policy was obtained, and (2) the content of the matching policy itself. We examine each of these sources in turn.

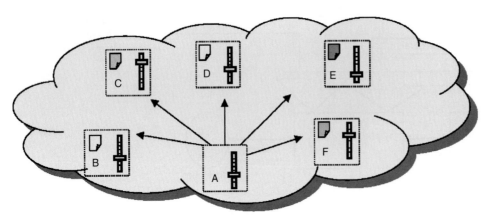

FIGURE 44.5 Retrieval of private policy rules from a community of peers.

(a) New consumer "A" broadcasts request for privacy rules to the community

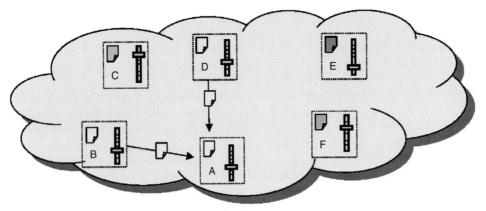

(b) Consumers B and D answer A's request

Outcomes from the Way the Matching Policy was Obtained

The matching policy can be obtained through policy upgrades or downgrades. These policy changes can occur while the policy is being formulated for the first time or after a mismatch occurs, in an attempt to obtain a match (during policy negotiation[12,13]). Recall from the "Introduction" section that an upgraded policy reflects a higher level of privacy. On the other hand, a downgraded policy reflects a lower level of privacy.

Policy Upgrades

Given that a provider always tries to reduce a consumer's privacy, it is possible that the policy nonmatch was due to the provider's policy requiring too much privacy

reduction. Suppose then that the match occurred after the provider upgraded its privacy policy to represent more privacy, that is, require less privacy reduction. This could mean that the provider is requiring less information that is private. In this case, the provider or consumer may not realize the extra costs that may result from not having access to the private information item or items that were eliminated through upgrading. For example, leaving out the social security number may lead to more costly means of consumer identification for the provider. As another example, consider the provider and consumer policies of Figure 44.6. In this figure, suppose All Books Online upgraded its privacy policy by eliminating the credit-card requirement. This would lead to a match with Alice's privacy policy, but it could cost Alice longer waiting time to get her order, since she may be forced into an alternate and slower means of making payment (e.g., mailing a check) if payment is required prior to shipping.

Policy Downgrades

Since the consumer resists the provider's privacy reduction, it is possible that the policy nonmatch was due to

12. G. Yee, and L. Korba, "Bilateral e-services negotiation under uncertainty," Proceedings, *The 2003 International Symposium on Applications and the Internet (SAINT 2003)*, Orlando, Jan 2003.

13. G. Yee, and L. Korba, "The negotiation of privacy policies in distance education," Proceedings, *14th IRMA International Conference*, Philadelphia, May 2003.

Policy Use: Book Seller Owner: All Books Online Valid: unlimited	Policy Use: Book Seller Owner: Alice Consumer Valid: December 2009
Collector: All Books Online What: name, address, tel Purposes: identification Retention Time: unlimited Disclose-To: none Collector: All Books Online What: credit card Purposes: payment Retention Time: until payment complete Disclose-To: none	Collector: any What: name, address, tel Purposes: identification Retention Time: unlimited Disclose-To: none

FIGURE 44.6 Example online bookseller provider (left) and consumer privacy policies (right).

Policy Use: Medical Help Owner: Nursing Online Valid: unlimited	Policy Use: Medical Help Owner: Alice Consumer Valid: December 2009
Collector: Nursing Online What: name, address, tel Purposes: contact Retention Time: unlimited Disclose-To: pharmacy Collector: Nursing Online What: medical condition Purposes: treatment Retention Time: 1 year Disclose-To: pharmacy	Collector: any What: name, address, tel Purposes: contact Retention Time: unlimited Disclose-To: pharmacy Collector: Dr. A. Smith What: medical condition Purposes: treatment Retention Time: unlimited Disclose-To: pharmacy

FIGURE 44.7 Example of medical help provider (left) and consumer privacy policies (right).

the consumer's policy allowing too little privacy reduction. Suppose then that the match occurred after the consumer downgraded her privacy policy to represent less privacy, that is, to allow for more privacy reduction. This could mean that the consumer is willing to provide more information that is private. Then the provider or consumer may not realize the extra costs that result from having to safeguard the additional private information item or items that were added through downgrading. For example, the additional information might be a critical health condition that the consumer does not want anyone else to know, especially her employer, which could result in loss of her employment. The provider had better add sufficient (costly) safeguards to make sure that the condition is kept confidential. The provider may not have fully realized the sensitivity of the extra information.

Outcomes from the Content of the Matching Policy

We give here some example unexpected outcomes due to the content of the matching policy. We examine the content of the header and privacy rules in turn, as follows.

Valid Field

If the *valid* field of the consumer's policy is not carefully specified, the provider may become confused upon expiry if there is not another consumer policy that becomes the new policy. In this state of confusion the provider could inadvertently disclose the consumer's private information to a party that the consumer does not want to receive the information.

Collector Field

Specification of who is to collect the consumer's private information needs to consider what happens if the collector is unavailable to receive the information. For example, consider the privacy policies of Figure 44.7. The policies are not compatible, since Alice will reveal her medical condition only to Dr. Smith, whereas the provider would like any doctor or nurse on staff to take the information. Suppose the provider upgrades its policy to satisfy Alice by allowing only Dr. Smith to receive information on Alice's condition. Then an unexpected outcome is that Alice cannot receive help from Nursing Online because Dr. Smith is not available (he might have been seriously injured in an accident), even though the policies would match and the service could theoretically proceed. There are various ways to solve this particular situation (one way is simply to have an overriding condition that in an emergency, Alice *must* give her condition to any doctor or nurse on staff), but our point still holds: An improperly specified *collector* attribute can lead to unexpected serious consequences.

Retention Time

Care must also be taken to specify the appropriate retention time for a particular information item. The responsibility for setting an appropriate retention time lies with both the provider and the consumer. For example, consider once again the policies of Figure 44.7. Suppose Alice changes her privacy rule for medical condition from *Dr. A. Smith* to *any* and from *unlimited* to *2 years*. Then the policies match and the service can proceed. At the end of two years, the provider complies with the consumer's privacy policy and discards the information it has on Alice's medical condition. But suppose that after the two years, medical research discovers that Alice's condition is terminal unless treated with a certain new drug. Then Nursing Online cannot contact Alice to warn her, since it no longer knows that Alice has that condition. Poor Alice! Clearly, both the provider and the consumer are responsible for setting the appropriate retention time. One could conclude that in the case of a medical condition, the retention time should be *unlimited*. However, *unlimited* can also have its risks, such as retaining information beyond the point at which it no longer applies. For example, Alice could one day be cured of her condition. Then retention of Alice's condition could unjustly penalize Alice if it somehow leaked out when it is no longer true.

Disclose-to Field

If the *disclose-to* attribute of the consumer's privacy policy is not specified or improperly specified, providers can share the consumer's private information with other providers or consumers with resulting loss of privacy. Consider the following examples.

Suppose Alice has a critical health condition and she does not want her employer to know for fear of losing her job (the employer might dismiss her to save on sick leave or other benefits—this really happened![14]). Suppose that she is able to subscribe to Nursing Online as in the preceding examples. Then through the execution of the service, Nursing Online shares her condition with a pharmacy to fill her prescription. Suppose the company that Alice works for is a pharmaceutical supplier and needs to know contact information of patients in the area where Alice lives so that the company can directly advertise to them about new drugs effective for Alice's condition. Suppose further that the pharmacy with which Nursing Online shared Alice's condition is a consumer of the pharmaceutical supplier and the pharmacy's privacy policy does not restrict the sharing of patient information that it receives secondhand. Then the pharmaceutical supplier, Alice's employer, can learn of her health condition from the pharmacy, and Alice could lose her job—an unexpected outcome with serious consequences. A possible solution to this situation is for Alice to specify *pharmacy, no further* for *disclose-to*. Then to comply with Alice's policy, Nursing Online, as a consumer of the pharmacy, in its privacy policy with the pharmacy would specify *none* for the *disclose-to* corresponding to Alice's condition, thus preventing Alice's employer from learning of her condition and so preserving her privacy.

As another example, suppose Alice, as a consumer, uses graphics services from company A and company B.

Her privacy policy with these companies stipulates that the rates she pays them is private and not to be disclosed to any other party. Suppose she pays company A a higher rate than company B. Now suppose companies A and B are both consumers of company C, which provides data on rates paid for graphics services. To use company C's services, companies A and B must provide company C with deidentified information regarding rates they are paid. This does not violate the privacy policies of consumers of companies A and B, because the information is deidentified. However, company B now learns of the higher rate paid company A and seeks a higher rate from Alice. There does not appear to be any solution to this situation, since Alice has already specified *disclose-to* as *none*. This example shows that there can be unexpected outcomes that may not be preventable.

We have presented a number of unexpected outcomes arising from the way the policy match was obtained and how the content of the policy was specified. Our outcomes are all negative ones because they are the ones we need to be concerned about. There are also, of course, positive unexpected outcomes, but they are outside the scope of this chapter.

5. PREVENTING UNEXPECTED NEGATIVE OUTCOMES

The problem at hand is how to detect and prevent the unexpected outcomes that are negative or dangerous. Since all unexpected outcomes derive from the personal privacy policy (at least in this work), it is necessary to ensure "well-formed" policies that can avoid unexpected negative outcomes. Further, if a non-well-formed policy matches the first time and leads to negative outcomes, it is too late to do anything about it. Based on the discussion of the preceding section, let's define our terms.

Definition 1

An *unexpected negative outcome* is an outcome of the use of privacy policies such that (1) the outcome is unexpected by both the provider and the consumer, and (2) the outcome leads to either the provider or the consumer or both experiencing some loss, which could be private information, money, time, convenience, job, and so on, even losses that are safety and health related.

Definition 2

A *well-formed (WF)* privacy policy (for either consumer or provider) is one that does not lead to unexpected negative outcomes. A *near well-formed (NWF)* privacy policy is one in which the attributes *valid, collector, retention time*, and *disclose-to* have each been considered against

---

14. J. K. Kumekawa, "Health information privacy protection: crisis or common sense?", retrieved Sept. 7, 2003, from www.nursingworld.org/ojin/topic16/tpc16_2.htm.

all *known* misspecifications that can lead to unexpected negative outcomes.

In Definition 2, the misspecifications can be accumulated as a result of experience (trial and error) or by scenario exploration (as earlier). We have already presented a number of them in the preceding section. An NWF privacy policy is the best that we can achieve at this time. Clearly, such a policy does not guarantee that unexpected negative outcomes will not occur; it just reduces the probability of an unexpected negative outcome.

Rules for Specifying near Well-Formed Privacy Policies

Let's consider once more the content of a personal privacy policy by looking at the header and the privacy rules. The header (Figure 44.1) consists of *policy use, owner,* and *valid. Policy use* and *owner* serve only to identify the policy and, assuming they are accurately specified, they are unlikely to lead to unexpected negative outcomes. That leaves *valid.* As discussed, *valid* must be specified so that it is never the case that the provider is in possession of the consumer's private information without a corresponding valid consumer policy (i.e., with the policy expired). Another way to look at this is that it must be true that the provider is no longer in possession of the consumer's information at the point of policy expiration. Hence we can construct a rule for specifying *valid.*

Rule for Specifying Valid

The time period specified for valid *must be at least as long as the longest retention time in the privacy policy.* This rule ensures that if the provider is in possession of the consumer's private information, there is always a corresponding consumer privacy policy that governs the information, which is what is needed to avoid the unexpected outcomes from an improperly specified *valid.*

Let's now consider the content of a privacy rule. The privacy rule consists of the attributes *collector, what, purposes, retention time,* and *disclose-to* (Figure 44.1). *What* and *purposes* serve only to identify the information and the purposes for which the information will be put to use. Assuming they are accurately specified, they are unlikely to lead to unexpected negative outcomes. That leaves *collector, retention-time,* and *disclose-to,* which we discussed. Based on this discussion, we can formulate specification rules for these attributes.

Rule for Specifying Collector

When specifying an individual for collector, *the consequences of the unavailability of the individual to receive the information must be considered. If the consequences do not lead to unexpected negative outcomes (as far as can be determined), proceed to specify the individual. Otherwise, or if there is doubt, specify the name of the provider (meaning anyone in the provider's organization).*

Rule for Specifying Retention Time

When specifying retention time, *the consequences of the expiration of the retention time (provider destroys corresponding information) must be considered. If the consequences do not lead to unexpected negative outcomes (as far as can be determined), proceed to specify the desired time. Otherwise, or if there is doubt, specify the length of time the service will be used.*

Rule for Specifying Disclose-To

When specifying disclose-to, *the consequences of successive propagation of your information starting with the first party mentioned in the* disclose-to *must be considered. If the consequences do not lead to unexpected negative outcomes (as far as can be determined), proceed with the specification of the* disclose-to *party or parties. Otherwise, or if there is doubt, specify* none *or name of receiving party, no further.*

These rules address the problems discussed in the section "Outcomes from the Content of the Matching Policy" that lead to unexpected negative outcomes. Except for *valid,* in each case we require the consumer or provider to consider the consequences of the intended specification, and propose specification alternatives, where the consequences lead to unexpected negative outcomes or there is doubt. By definition, application of these rules to the specification of a privacy policy will result in a near well-formed policy. Undoubtedly, mathematical modeling of the processes at play together with state exploration tools can help to determine whether or not a particular specification will lead to unexpected negative outcomes. Such modeling and use of tools is part of future research.

Approach for Obtaining Near Well-Formed Privacy Policies

We propose that these rules for obtaining near well-formed policies be incorporated during initial policy specification. This is best achieved using an automatic or semiautomatic method for specifying privacy policies, such as the methods in the section "Semiautomated Derivation of Personal Privacy Policies." The rule for *valid* is easy to implement. Implementation of the remaining rules may employ a combination of artificial intelligence and human-computer interface techniques to assist the human specifier to reason out the consequences. Alternatively, the rules may be applied during manual policy specification in conjunction with a tool for determining possible consequences of a particular specification.

6. THE PRIVACY MANAGEMENT MODEL

In this part of the chapter, we explain how our Privacy Management Model works to protect a consumer's privacy through the use of personal privacy policies.

How Privacy Policies are Used

An e-service provider has a privacy policy stating what PII it requires from a consumer and how the information will be used. A consumer has a privacy policy stating what PII the consumer is willing to share, with whom it may be shared, and under what circumstances it may be shared. An entity that is both a provider and a consumer has separate privacy policies for these two roles. A privacy policy is attached to a software agent, one that acts for the consumer and another that acts for the provider. Prior to the activation of a particular service, the agent for the consumer and the agent for the provider undergo a privacy policy exchange, in which the policies are examined for compatibility (see Figure 44.8). The service is only activated if the policies are compatible, in which case we say that there is a "match" between the two policies.

The Matching of Privacy Policies

We define here the meaning of a match between a consumer personal privacy policy and a service provider privacy policy. Such matching is the comparison of corresponding rules that have the same *purposes* and similar *what*. Let I represent the set of rules in a consumer privacy policy and let J represent the set of rules in a service provider privacy policy. Let $p_{i,c}$, $i \in I$ and $p_{j,p}$, $j \in J$ represent corresponding WPRs of the consumer policy and the provider policy, respectively, that have the same *purposes* and similar *what*. We want to ascribe a function pr that returns a numerical level of privacy from the consumer's point of view when applied to $p_{i,c}$ and $p_{j,p}$. A high pr means a high degree of privacy; a low pr means a low degree of privacy—from the consumer's point of view. It is difficult to define pr universally because

privacy is a subjective notion, and one consumer's view of degree of privacy may be different from another consumer's view. However, the privacy rules from the policy provider have corresponding privacy slider values and they are just what we need. We simply look up $p_{i,c}$ and $p_{j,p}$ in the policy provider database and assign the corresponding privacy slider values to them. This look-up and assignment can be done automatically.

Definition 3 (Matching Collector and Disclose-to)

The *collector* parameter from a consumer policy matches the *collector* parameter from a provider policy if and only if they are textually the same or the *collector* parameter from the consumer policy has the value *any*. The matching of *disclose-to* parameters is defined in the same way.

Definition 4 (Matching Rules)

There is a *match* between a rule in a consumer privacy policy and the corresponding (same *purposes* and similar *what*) rule in the provider policy if and only if:

$$pr(p_{i,c}) \leq (p_{j,p}), i \in I, j \in J$$

and the corresponding *collector* and *disclose-to* parameters match. If there is no corresponding rule in the provider policy, we say that the consumer rule corresponds to the *null* rule in the provider policy (called *consumer n-correspondence*), in which case the rules automatically match. If there is no corresponding rule in the consumer policy, we say that the provider rule corresponds to the *null* rule in the consumer policy (called *provider n-correspondence*), in which case the rules automatically mismatch.

In Definition 4, a match means that the level of privacy in the provider's rule is greater than the level of privacy in the consumer's rule (the provider is demanding less information than the consumer is willing to offer). Similarly, a consumer rule automatically matches a provider null rule because it means that the provider is not even asking for the information represented by the consumer's rule (ultimate rule privacy). A provider rule automatically mismatches a consumer null rule because it means the provider is asking for information the consumer is not willing to share, whatever the conditions (ultimate rule lack of privacy).

FIGURE 44.8 Exchange of privacy policies (PP) between consumer agent (CA) and provider agent (PA).

TABLE 44.2 Example Negotiation Dialogue Showing Offers and Counteroffers.

Provider	Employee
Okay for your exam results to be seen by your management?	Yes, but only David and Suzanne can see them.
Okay if only David and Bob see them?	No, only David and Suzanne can see them.
Can management from Divisions B and C also see your exam results?	Okay for management from Division C but not Division B.
How about letting Divisions C and D see your results?	That is acceptable.

Definition 5 (Matching Privacy Policies)

A consumer privacy policy matches a service provider privacy policy if and only if all corresponding (same *purposes* and similar *what*) rules match. And, there are no cases of provider *n*-correspondence, although there may be cases of consumer *n*-correspondence.

Definition 6 (Upgrade and Downgrade of Rules and Policies)

A privacy rule or policy is considered *upgraded* if the new version represents more privacy than the prior version. A privacy rule or policy is considered *downgraded* if the new version represents less privacy than the prior version.

In comparing policies, it is not always necessary to carry out the comparison of each and every privacy rule as required by Definitions 4 and 5. We mention three shortcuts here.

Shortcut 1

Both policies are the same except one policy has fewer rules than the other policy. According to Definitions 4 and 5, there is a match if the policy with fewer rules belongs to the provider. There is a mismatch if this policy belongs to the consumer.

Shortcut 2

Both policies are the same except one policy has one or more rules with less retention time than the other policy. According to Definitions 4 and 5, there is a match if the policy with one or more rules with less retention time belongs to the provider. There is a mismatch if this policy belongs to the consumer.

Shortcut 3

Both policies are the same except one policy has one or more rules that clearly represent higher levels of privacy than the corresponding rules in the other policy. According to Definitions 4 and 5, there is a match if the policy with rules representing higher levels of privacy belongs to the provider. There is a mismatch if this policy belongs to the consumer.

Thus, in our example policies (Figures 44.1 and 44.2), there is a match for e-learning according to Shortcut 2, since the policy with lower retention time belongs to the provider. There is a mismatch for bookseller according to Shortcut 1, since the policy with fewer rules belongs to the consumer. There is a mismatch for medical help according to Shortcut 3, since the policy with the rule representing a higher level of privacy is the one specifying a particular collector (Dr. Smith), and this policy belongs to the consumer.

Personal Privacy Policy Negotiation

Where there is no match between a consumer's personal privacy policy and the privacy policy of the service provider, the consumer and provider may negotiate with each other to try to achieve a match.[15,16] Consider the following negotiation to produce a privacy policy for an employee taking a course from an e-learning provider. Suppose the item for negotiation is the privacy of examination results. The employer would like to know how well the employee performed on a course in order to assign him appropriate tasks at work. Moreover, management (Bob, David and Suzanne) would like to share the results with management of other divisions, in case they could use the person's newly acquired skills. The negotiation dialogue can be expressed in terms of offers, counter-offers, and choices, as follows in Table 44.2 (read from left to right and down).

As shown in this example, negotiation is a process between two parties, wherein each party presents the other with offers and counter-offers until either an agreement is reached or no agreement is possible. Each party

15. G. Yee, and L. Korba, "Bilateral e-services negotiation under uncertainty," Proceedings, *The 2003 International Symposium on Applications and the Internet (SAINT 2003)*, Orlando, Jan 2003.

16. G. Yee, and L. Korba, "The negotiation of privacy policies in distance education," Proceedings, *14th IRMA International Conference*, Philadelphia, May 2003.

chooses to make a particular offer based on the value that the choice represents to that party. Each party chooses a particular offer because that offer represents the maximum value among the alternatives.

Each party in a negotiation shares a list of items to be negotiated. For each party and each item to be negotiated, there is a set of alternative positions with corresponding values. This set of alternatives is explored as new alternatives are considered at each step of the negotiation. Similarly, the values can change (or become apparent), based on these new alternatives and the other party's last offer.

Let R be the set of items r_i to be negotiated, $R = \{r_1, r_2, ..., r_n\}$. Let $A_{1,r,k}$ be the set of alternatives for party 1 and negotiation item r at step k, $k = 0,1,2,...,$ in the negotiation. $A_{1,r,0}$ is party 1's possible opening positions. Let $O_{1,r,k}$ be the alternative $a \in A_{1,r,k}$ that party 1 chooses to offer party 2 at step k. $O_{1,r,0}$ is party 1's chosen opening position. For example, for the first negotiation, the provider's opening position is *exam results can be seen by management*. Then for each alternative $a \in A_{1,r,k}, V_k(a)$ is the value function of alternative a for party 1 at step k, $k > 0$, and

$$V_k(a) = f(I, O_{1,r,k-1}, O_{2,r,k-1}, \cdots)$$

where I is the common interest or purpose of the negotiation (e.g. negotiating privacy policy for "Psychology 101"), $O_{1,r,k-1}$ is the offer of party 1 at step $k \geq 1$, $O_{2,r,k-1}$ is the offer of party 2 at step $k \geq 1$, plus other factors which could include available alternatives, culture, sex, age, income level, and so on. These other factors are not required here, but their existence is without doubt since how an individual derives value can be very complex. Let $a_m \in A_{1,r,k}$ such that $V_k(a_m) = max \{V_k(a), a \in A_{1,r,k}\}$.

Then at step k, $k > 0$ in the negotiation process, party 1 makes party 2 an offer $O_{1,r,k}$ where

$$O_{1,r,k} = a_m \quad if \quad V_k(a_m) > V_k(O_{2,r,k-1}), \qquad (1)$$
$$= O_{2,r,k-1} \quad if \quad V_k(a_m) \leq V_k(O_{2,r,k-1}). \qquad (2)$$

Equation 1 represents the case where party 1 makes a counter-offer to party 2's offer. Equation 2 represents the case where party 1 accepts party 2's offer and agreement is reached! A similar development can be done for party 2. Thus, there is a negotiation tree $\vec{r}$ corresponding to each item r to be negotiated, with two main branches extending from r at the root (see Figure 44.9). The two main branches correspond to the two negotiating parties. Each main branch has leaves representing the alternatives at each step. At each step, including the opening positions at step 0, each party's offer is visible to the other for comparison. As negotiation proceeds, each party does a traversal of its corresponding main branch. If the negotiation is successful, the traversals converge at the successful alternative (one of the parties adopts the other's offer as his own, Equation 2) and the negotiation tree is said to be complete. Each party may choose to terminate the negotiation if the party feels no progress is being made; the negotiation tree is then said to be *incomplete*.

In Figure 44.9, the influences arrows show that a particular alternative offered by the other party at step k will influence the alternatives of the first party at step $k + 1$. Figure 44.10 illustrates the negotiation tree using the above privacy of examination results negotiation.

Personal privacy policy negotiation may be used to avoid negative unexpected outcomes, even if the privacy policies involved are near well formed, since near well-formed policies may still not match. At a policies

FIGURE 44.9 Negotiation tree $\vec{r}$ for a policy negotiation.

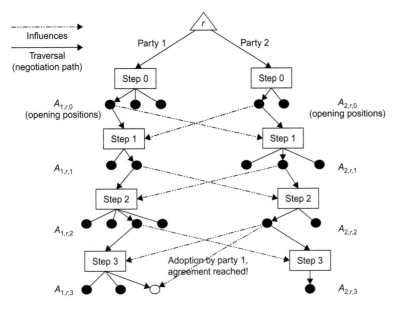

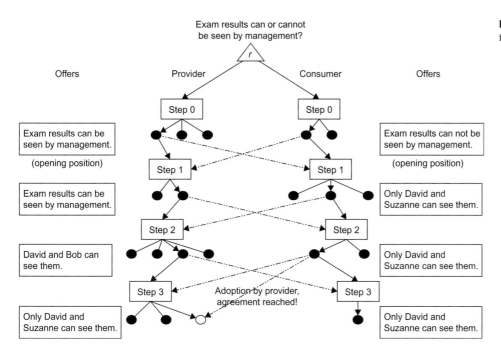

FIGURE 44.10 Negotiation tree for the first part of our negotiation.

mismatch, the consumer or the provider upgrades or downgrades the individual policy to try to get a match. In so doing, each could inadvertently introduce new values into the policy or remove values from the policy that result in negative unexpected outcomes or loss of NWF-ness. We propose the use of privacy policy negotiation between consumer and provider agents to guide the policy upgrading or downgrading to avoid undoing the values already put in place for NWF-ness in the initial specification. Alternatively, negotiation may expose a needed application of the above rules for a policy to be near well formed. This is also a consequences exploration, but here both provider and consumer do the exploration while negotiating in real time.

For example, in the All Books Online example of the "Outcomes From How the Matching Policy Was Obtained" section, where Alice does not need to provide her credit card, negotiation between Alice and All Books Online could have identified the consequence that Alice would need to wait longer for her order and direct her to another, more viable alternative, such as agreeing to provide her credit card. Similarly, in the example (same section) where the provider has to introduce more costly safeguards to protect the consumer's added highly sensitive information, negotiation could have uncovered the high sensitivity of the new information and possibly result in a different less costly alternative chosen (e.g., the new information may not be needed after all).

Table 44.3 illustrates how negotiation can detect and prevent the unexpected negative outcome of Alice having no access to medical service when it is needed (read from left to right and down). The result of this negotiation is

that Nursing Online will be able to provide Alice with nursing service whenever Alice requires it, once she makes the change in her privacy policy reflecting the results of negotiation. If this negotiation had failed (Alice did not agree), Alice will at least be alerted to the possibility of a bad outcome, and may take other measures to avoid it. This example shows how negotiation may persuade the consumer to resolve a mismatch by applying the above rule for specifying *collector*.

Table 44.4 gives another example of negotiation at work using Alice's bookseller policy from Figure 44.1. This policy mismatched because Alice did not want to provide her credit-card information. At the end of the negotiation, Alice modifies her privacy policy and receives service from All Books Online.

Personal Privacy Policy Compliance

As we have seen, the above Privacy Principles require a provider to be accountable for complying with the Privacy Principles (CSAPP.1) and the privacy wishes of the consumer. In practice, a provider is required to appoint someone in its organization to be accountable for its compliance to Privacy Principles (CSAPP.1). This person is usually called the chief privacy officer (CPO). An important responsibility of the CPO is to put in place a procedure for receiving and responding to complaints or inquiries about the privacy policy and the practice of handling personal information. This procedure should be easily accessible and simple to use. The procedure should also refer to the dispute resolution process that the organization has adopted. Other responsibilities of the CPO

TABLE 44.3 Preventing Unexpected Negative Outcomes: Nursing Online.

Nursing Online (Provider)	Alice (Consumer)
Okay if a nurse on our staff is told your medical condition?	No, only Dr. Alexander Smith can be told my medical condition.
We cannot provide you with any nursing service unless we know your medical condition.	Okay, I'll see Dr. Smith instead.
You are putting yourself at risk. What if you need emergency medical help for your condition and Dr. Smith is not available?	You are right. Do you have any doctors on staff?
Yes, we always have doctors on call. Okay to allow them to know your medical condition?	That is acceptable. I will modify my privacy policy to share my medical condition with your doctors on call.

TABLE 44.4 Preventing Unexpected Negative Outcomes: All Books Online.

All Books Online (Provider)	Alice (Consumer)
Okay if you provide your credit-card information?	No, I do not want to risk my credit-card number getting stolen.
If you do not provide your credit-card information, you will need to send us a certified check before we can ship your order. This will delay your order for up to three weeks.	I still don't want to risk my credit-card number getting stolen.
Your credit-card information will be encrypted during transmission and we keep your information in secure storage once we receive it. You need not worry.	Okay, I will modify my privacy policy to share my credit-card information.

include auditing the current privacy practices of the organization, formulating the organization's privacy policy, and implementing and maintaining this policy. *We propose that the CPO's duties be extended to include auditing the provider's compliance to the consumer's personal privacy policy.*

Further discussion of personal privacy policy compliance is beyond the scope of this chapter. We mention in passing that an alternative method of ensuring compliance is the use of a Privacy Policy Compliance System (PPCS) as presented in.[17]

7. DISCUSSION AND RELATED WORK

We have presented methods for the semiautomatic derivation of personal privacy policies. Given our Privacy Management Model, there needs to be a way for consumers to derive their personal privacy policies easily or consumers will simply not use the approach. The only "alternative" that we can see to semiautomated derivation is for the consumer to create his/her personal privacy

policy manually. This can be done by a knowledgeable and technically inclined consumer, but would require a substantially larger effort (and correspondingly less likely to be used) than the semiautomated approaches. In addition to ease of use, our approaches ensure consistency of privacy rules by community consensus. This has the added benefit of facilitating provider compliance, since it is undoubtedly easier for a provider to comply to privacy rules that reflect the community consensus than rules that only reflect the feelings of a few.

We believe our approaches for the semiautomatic derivation of personal privacy policies are quite feasible, even taking account of the possible weaknesses described in this chapter. In the surveys approach, the consumer has merely to select the privacy level when prompted for the rules from the provider's policy. In fact, the user is already familiar with the use of a privacy slider to set the privacy level for Internet browsers (e.g., Microsoft Internet Explorer, under Internet Options). We have implemented the surveys approach in a prototype that we created for negotiating privacy policies. We plan to conduct experiments with this implementation, using volunteers to confirm the usability of the surveys approach. In the retrieval approach, the consumer is asked to do a little bit more—compare and select the rules received—but

17. G. Yee, and L. Korba, "Privacy policy compliance for web services," Proceedings, *2004 IEEE International Conference on Web Services (ICWS 2004)*, San Diego, July 2004.

this should be no more complex than today's ecommerce transactions or the use of a word-processing program. Likewise, adapting a personal policy to a provider policy should be of the same level of complexity. Like anything else, the widespread use of these methods will take a little time to achieve, but people will come around to using them, just as they are using ecommerce; it is merely a matter of education and experience. Further, consumers are becoming more and more aware of their privacy rights as diverse jurisdictions enact privacy legislation to protect consumer privacy. In Canada, the Personal Information Protection and Electronic Documents Act has been in effect across all retail outlets since January 1, 2004, and consumers are reminded of their privacy rights every time they visit their optician, dentist, or other business requiring their private information.

We now discuss some possible weaknesses in our approaches. The surveys approach requires trust in the policy provider. Effectively, the policy provider becomes a trusted third party. Clearly, the notion of a trusted third party as a personal policy provider may be controversial to some. Any error made by the policy provider could affect PII for many hundreds or thousands of people. A certification process for the policy provider is probably required. For instance, in Canada, the offices for the provincial and federal privacy commissioners could be this certification body. They could also be policy providers themselves. Having privacy commissioners' offices take on the role of policy providers seems to be a natural fit, given their mandate as privacy watchdogs for the consumer. However, the process would have a cost. Costs could be recovered via micro-charges to the consumer, or the service provider for the policies provided. Aggregated information from the PII surveys could be sold to service providers who could use them to formulate privacy policies that are more acceptable to consumers.

There is a challenge in the retrieval approach regarding how to carry it out in a timely fashion. Efficient peer-to-peer search techniques will collect the rules in a timely manner, but the amount of information collected by the requester may be quite large. Furthermore, since the various rules collected will probably differ from one another, the requestor will have to compare them to determine which ones to select. Quick comparisons to reduce the amount of data collected could be done through a peer-to-peer rules search that employs a rules hash array containing hashed values for different portions of the rule.

In the section on policy compliance, a weakness of having the CPO be responsible for protecting consumer privacy is that the CPO belongs to the provider's organization. Will he be truly diligent about his task to protect the consumer's privacy? To get around this question, the CPO can use secure logs to answer any challenges doubting his organization's compliance. Secure logs

automatically record all the organization's use of the consumer's private information, both during and after the data collection. Cryptographic techniques[18] provide assurance that any modification of the secure log is detectable. In addition, database technology such as Oracle9i can tag the data with its privacy policy to evaluate the policy every time data is accessed.[19] The system can be set up so that any policy violation can trigger a warning to the CPO.

An objection could be raised that our approaches are not general, having been based on privacy policy content that was derived from Canadian privacy legislation. We have several answers for this objection. First, as we pointed out, Canadian privacy legislation is representative of privacy legislation in many countries. Therefore the content of privacy policies derived from Canadian privacy legislation is applicable in many countries. Second, as we also pointed out, Canadian privacy legislation is also representative of the Fair Information Practices standards, which have universal applicability. Third, all privacy policies regardless of their content will have to converge on the content that we presented, since such content is required by legislation. Finally, our approaches can be customized to any form of privacy policy, regardless of the content. We next discuss related work.

The use of privacy policies as a means of safeguarding privacy for ebusiness is relatively new. There is relatively little research on the use of personal privacy policies. For these reasons, we have not been able to find many authors who have written on the derivation of personal privacy policies. Dreyer and Olivier[20] worked on generating and analyzing privacy policies for computer systems, to regulate private information flows within the system, rather than generating personal privacy policies. Brodie et al.[21] describe a privacy management workbench for use by organizations. Within this workbench are tools to allow organizational users tasked with the responsibility to author organizational privacy policies. The tools allow these users to use natural language for policy creation and to visualize the results to ensure that they accomplished their intended goals. These authors do not address the

18. B. Schneier, and J. Kelsey, "Secure audit logs to support computer forensics," *ACM Transactions on Information and System Security*, 2(2), pp. 159–176, ACM, May 1999.

19. G. Yee, K. El-Khatib, L. Korba, A. Patrick, R. Song, and Y. Xu, "Privacy and trust in e-government," chapter in *Electronic Government Strategies and Implementation*, Idea Group Inc., 2004.

20. L. C. J. Dreyer, and M. S. Olivier, "A workbench for privacy policies," Proceedings, *The Twenty-Second Annual International Computer Software and Applications Conference (COMPSAC '98)*, pp. 350–355, August 19–21, 1998.

21. C. Brodie, C.-M. Karat, J. Karat, and J. Feng, "Usable security and privacy: a case study of developing privacy management tools," *Symposium On Usable Privacy and Security (SOUPS) 2005*, July 6–8, Pittsburgh, 2005.

creation of personal privacy policies. Irwin and Yu[22] present an approach for dynamically asking the user suitable questions to elicit the user's privacy preferences. They present a framework for determining which questions are suitable. However, there is no use of community consensus which means the resulting policies could be highly subjective. This means that providers would find it more difficult to use such policies to help them formulate provider privacy policies that would be acceptable to the majority of consumers.

Other work that uses privacy policies is primarily represented by the W3C Platform for Privacy Preferences.[23] This provides a Web site operator with a way of expressing the site's privacy policy using a P3P standard format and to have that policy automatically retrieved and interpreted by user agents (e.g., browser plug-in). The user can express rudimentary privacy preferences and have those preferences automatically checked against the web site's policy before proceeding. However, P3P cannot be used to fulfill the requirements of privacy legislation, has no compliance mechanism, and represents a "take it or leave it" view to privacy—if you don't like the privacy policy of the Web site, you leave it. There is no provision for negotiation. In addition, Jensen and Potts[24] evaluated the usability of 64 online privacy policies and the practice of posting them and determined that significant changes needed to be made to the practice in order to meet usability and regulatory requirements. Finally, Stufflebeam et al.[25] presented a case study in which they used P3P and Enterprise Privacy Authorization Language (EPAL) to formulate two healthcare Web site privacy policies and described the shortcomings they found with using these languages.

Negative outcomes arising from privacy policies may be regarded as a feature interaction problem, where policies "interact" and produce unexpected outcomes.[26] Traditionally, feature interactions have been considered mainly in the telephony or communication services domains.[27] More recent papers, however, have focused on other domains such as the Internet, multimedia systems, mobile systems,[28] and Internet personal appliances.[29] In this work, we have chosen not to frame negative outcomes from privacy policies as a feature interaction problem. In so doing, we have obtained new insights and results. Apart from feature interactions, other possible related work has to do with resolving conflicts in access control and mobile computing (e.g.[30,31]). However, it is believed that these methods and similar methods in other domains will not work for privacy due to the subjective nature of privacy, that is, personal involvement to consider each privacy rule is necessary.

Most negotiation research is on negotiation via autonomous software agents, focusing on methods or models for agent negotiation[32] and can incorporate techniques from other scientific areas such as game theory (e.g.[33]), fuzzy logic (e.g.[34]) and genetic algorithms (e.g.[35]). The research also extends to autonomous agent negotiation for specific application areas, such as ecommerce[36] and service-level agreements for the Internet.[37] Apart from

22. K. Irwin, and T. Yu, "Determining user privacy preferences by asking the right questions: an automated approach," Proceedings of the 2005 ACM Workshop on Privacy in the Electronic Society (WPES 2005), November 7, Alexandria, 2005.

23. W3C Platform, "The platform for privacy preferences," retrieved Sept. 2, 2002, from www.w3.org/P3P/.

24. Jensen, C., and Potts, C., "Privacy policies as decision-making tools: an evaluation of online privacy notices," Proceedings of the 2004 Conference on Human Factors in Computing Systems (CHI 2004), April 24–29, Vienna, 2004.

25. W. Stufflebeam, A. Anton, Q. He, and N. Jain, "Specifying privacy policies with P3P and EPAL: lessons learned," Proceedings of the 2004 ACM Workshop on Privacy in the Electronic Society (WPES 2004), October 28, Washington, D.C., 2004.

26. G. Yee, and L. Korba, "Feature interactions in policy driven privacy management", Proceedings, Seventh International Workshop on Feature Interactions in Telecommunications and Software Systems, Ottawa, Ontario, Canada, June 2003.

27. D. Keck, and P. Kuehn, "The feature and service interaction problem in telecommunications systems: a survey," in IEEE Transactions on Software Engineering, Vol. 24, No. 10, October 1998.

28. L. Blair, and J. Pang, "Feature interactions: life beyond traditional telephony," Distributed Multimedia Research Group, Computing Dept., Lancaster University, UK.

29. M. Kolberg, E. Magill, D. Marples, and S. Tsang, "Feature interactions in services for internet personal appliances," Proceedings, IEEE International Conference on Communications (ICC 2002), Vol. 4, pp. 2613–2618, 2002.

30. T. Jaeger, R. Sailer, and X. Zhang, "Resolving constraint conflicts", Proceedings of the Ninth ACM Symposium on Access Control Models and Technologies, June 2004.

31. L. Capra, W. Emmerich, and C. Mascolo, "A micro-economic approach to conflict resolution in mobile computing," Proceedings of the 10th ACM SIGSOFT Symposium on Foundations of Software Engineering, November 2002.

32. P. Huang, and K. Sycara, "A Computational model for online agent negotiation", Proceedings of the 35th Annual Hawaii International Conference on System Sciences, 2002.

33. Y. Murakami, H. Sato, and A. Namatame, "Co-evolution in negotiation games," Proceedings, Fourth International Conference on Computational Intelligence and Multimedia Applications, 2001.

34. R. Lai, and M. Lin, "Agent negotiation as fuzzy constraint processing," Proceedings of the 2002 IEEE International Conference on Fuzzy Systems (FUZZ-IEEE'02), Vol. 2, 2002.

35. M. Tu, E. Wolff, and W. Lamersdorf, "Genetic algorithms for automated negotiations: a FSM application approach," Proceedings, 11th International Workshop on Database and Expert Systems Applications, 2000.

36. M. Chung, and V. Honavar, "A Negotiation Model in Agent-mediated Electronic Commerce," Proceedings, International Symposium on Multimedia Software Engineering, 2000.

37. T. Nguyen, N. Boukhatem, Y. Doudane, and G. Pujolle, "COPSSLS: A service level negotiation protocol for the internet," IEEE Communications Magazine, Vol. 40, Issue 5, May 2002.

negotiation by autonomous software agents, research has also been carried out on support tools for negotiation (e.g.[38]), which typically provide support in position communication, voting, documentation communication, and big picture negotiation visualization and navigation.

8. SUMMARY

The protection of personal privacy is paramount if e-services are to be successful. A personal privacy policy approach to privacy protection seems best. However, for this approach to work, consumers must be able to derive their personal privacy policies easily. To describe semiautomated approaches to derive personal privacy policies, we first defined the content of a personal privacy policy using the Canadian Privacy Principles. We then presented two semiautomated approaches for obtaining the policies: one based on third-party surveys of consumer perceptions of privacy, the other based on retrieval from a peer community. Both approaches reflect the privacy sensitivities of the community, giving the consumer confidence that his/her privacy preferences are interpreted with the best information available. We then explained how personal privacy policies can lead to negative unexpected outcomes if not properly specified. We proposed specification rules that can be applied in conjunction with semiautomated policy derivation to result in near well-formed policies that can avoid the negative unexpected outcomes. We closed with our Privacy Management Model, which explains how privacy policies are used and the meaning of privacy policy matching. We described policy negotiation, not only for resolving policies that do not match, but also as an effective means for avoiding negative unexpected outcomes. Finally, we suggested how consumers could be assured that providers will comply with personal privacy policies.

We have based our work on our particular formulation of a privacy policy. An obvious question is whether our approaches apply to other formulations of privacy policies. We believe the answer is yes, for the following reasons: (1) privacy policy formulations (i.e., contents) cannot differ too much from one another since they must all conform to privacy legislation and our policy is a minimal policy that so conforms, and (2) if necessary, we can fit our approaches to any formulation by applying the same logic we used in this work.

Possible topics for future work include (1) looking at other methods for easily deriving personal privacy policies, (2) conducting experiments with volunteers, using the implementation of the surveys approach in our privacy policy negotiation prototype to confirm usability and resolve any scalability/performance issues, (3) investigating other possible unexpected outcomes from the interaction of privacy policies, (4) designing tools for outcomes exploration to identify the seriousness of each consequence, (5) exploring other methods for avoiding or mitigating negative unexpected outcomes from the interaction of privacy policies, and (6) investigating ways to facilitate personal privacy policy negotiation, such as improving trust, usability and response times.

Finally, let's move on to the real interactive part of this Chapter: review questions/exercises, hands-on projects, case projects and optional team case project. The answers and/or solutions by chapter can be found in the Online Instructor's Solutions Manual.

CHAPTER REVIEW QUESTIONS/EXERCISES

True/False

1. True or False? The provider requires private information from the consumer for use in its e-service and so increases the consumer's privacy by requesting such information.
2. True or False? The Privacy Principles also prescribe certain operational requirements that must be satisfied between provider and consumer, such as identifying purpose and consent.
3. True or False? A semiautomated derivation of a personal privacy policy is the use of mechanisms (described in a moment) that may be semiautomated to obtain a set of privacy rules for a particular policy use.
4. True or False? The matching policy can be obtained through policy upgrades or downgrades.
5. True or False? Given that a provider always tries to reduce a consumer's privacy, it is possible that the policy nonmatch was due to the provider's policy requiring too much privacy reduction.

Multiple Choice

1. Since the consumer resists the provider's privacy reduction, it is possible that the _____ was due to the consumer's policy allowing too little privacy reduction.
   A. Privacy-enhancing technology
   B. Location technology
   C. Web-based
   D. Policy nonmatch
   E. Data controller
2. If the _____ field of the consumer's policy is not carefully specified, the provider may become

---

38. D. Druckman, R. Harris, and B. Ramberg, "Artificial computer-assisted international negotiation: a tool for research and practice," Proceedings of the 35th Annual Hawaii International Conference on System Sciences, 2002.

confused upon expiry if there is not another consumer policy that becomes the new policy.
A. Information technology
B. Location technology
C. Valid
D. Privacy-enhancing Technologies
E. Web Technology

3. Specification of who is to collect the consumer's _____ needs to consider what happens if the collector is unavailable to receive the information.
A. Data minimization
B. *XACML*
C. Private information
D. Certification Authority
E. Security

4. Care must also be taken to specify the appropriate _____ for a particular information item.
A. Privacy metrics
B. Retention time
C. Privacy-Aware Access Control
D. Privacy preferences
E. Taps

5. If the _____ attribute of the consumer's privacy policy is not specified or improperly specified, providers can share the consumer's private information with other providers or consumers with resulting loss of privacy.
A. Release policies
B. Anonymous communication
C. Data handling policies
D. Disclose-to
E. Social engineering

EXERCISE

Problem

A medical office photocopied more of a car accident victim's record than necessary and released extremely sensitive but irrelevant information to the insurance company.

Information about the woman's child, given up for adoption 40 years ago, eventually became part of the court record, a public document. What type of questions should you be asking with regards to this case?

Hands-on Projects

Project

An automobile dealer did not shred loan applications before tossing them into the garbage. A "dumpster diver" retrieved one and used the financial information to commit thousands of dollars of fraud against someone who had applied for a car loan. What type of questions should you be asking with regards to this case?

Case Projects

Problem

A medical doctor, who was filing for bankruptcy, faxed a financial document to his attorney. He entered the wrong telephone number, and the document was instead transmitted to the local newspaper. What type of questions should you be asking with regards to this case?

Optional Team Case Project

Problem

Five used copiers purchased from an office supply warehouse for about $400 each contained a gold mine of personal data. Using a forensic software program available free on the Internet, tens of thousands of documents were downloaded. Some of the data available included 106 pages of pay stubs with names, addresses and Social Security numbers; 400 pages of individual medical records; detailed domestic violence complaints and a list of wanted sex offenders; and a list of targets in a major drug raid. What type of questions should you be asking and comments made with regards to this case?

## Chapter 45

Detection of Conflicts in Security Policies

Cataldo Basile

Politecnico di Torino, Corso Duca degli Abruzzi 24, 10129 Torino, Italy

Matteo Maria Casalino

SAP Research Sophia-Antipolis, 805 Avenue Dr M. Donat, 06250 Mougins, France

Simone Mutti

Università degli Studi di Bergamo, via Marconi 5, 24044 Dalmine, Italy

Stefano Paraboschi

Università degli Studi di Bergamo, via Marconi 5, 24044 Dalmine, Italy

1. INTRODUCTION

The evolution of information systems is continuously increasing the capabilities and range of offered services, leading to infrastructures that see the participation of a larger number of users, a greater level of integration among separate systems, and a correspondingly larger impact of possible misbehaviors. Security solutions are available to protect the correct delivery of services, but these solutions have to adapt to the increasing complexity of system architectures. In this scenario, the management of security becomes a critical task. The goal is not only part of natural business practices, but it is also required to show compliance with respect to the many regulations promulgated by governments.

In modern information systems, a particular area of security requirement is access control management, with security policies that describe how resources and services should be protected. These policies offer a classification of the actions on the system that distinguishes them into authorized and forbidden, depending on a variety of parameters. Given the critical role of security and their large size and complexity, concerns arise about the policy's correctness. It is no longer possible to rely on the security designer to guarantee that the policy correctly represents how the system should protect access to resources.

Examples will be used to support the explanation and try to make the description self-contained. We want to provide an understanding of what we perceive as the main applications of these techniques.

The chapter is organized as follows. Section 2 introduces the concept of conflict in a security policy; then, the resolution of conflicts is discussed, and the relationship with separation of duty constraints is illustrated. Section 3 presents conflicts that arise in the execution of a security policy; the example of security policies for Java EE is used as an example. Section 4 offers an extensive analysis of conflict detection for network policies; significant attention is dedicated to this area, as it represents the domain where there is large experience in the use of conflict detection. Section 5 illustrates how Semantic Web technology can support the detection of conflicts in generic policies. Section 6 draws a few concluding remarks.

2. CONFLICTS IN SECURITY POLICIES

A typical top-down representation of the protection of an information system might consist of the five layers shown in Figure 45.1.

Security Requirements

Security requirements are a high-level, declarative representation of the rules according to which access control must be regulated. Security requirements largely ignore details of the system used to deliver the service, but focus on business concepts. This layer uses terminology and level of detail typical of the managers and are commonly expressed using natural language. For this reason, formal consistency verification cannot be automatically applied to the security requirements, and so human intervention will be required to complete the task.

Policies

Policies represent how business requirements are mapped to the systems used for service provisioning. Policies can

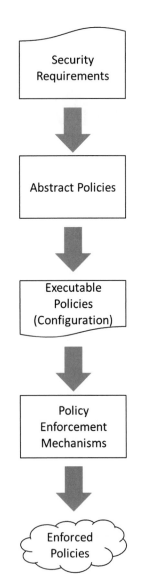

FIGURE 45.1 Top-down representation of the protection of an information system.

be defined at different levels, and the use of a higher level specification requires adopting an approach, possibly associated with a software tool, that supports the generation of lower level representations.

Abstract Policies

Abstract policies provide a formal representation of access control and its behavior. A policy may state, for instance, that an internal database storing credit-card information must not be accessible from the Internet. It is declarative because it does not detail the actual mechanism used for enforcing this policy. First, the policy is intended to define the desired behavior of the services. Since the policy will apply to abstract service definitions (services that are not yet instantiated), the specification cannot use full topological details.

Executable Policies

Executable policies describe the access control policy in a way that can immediately be processed by an access control component. Executable policies can be considered the security configuration of a system and are expressed in the specific language that a system recognizes. For instance, a policy for a relational Data Base Management System (DBMS) will typically be expressed by a sequence of Structured Query Language (SQL) statements.

Policy Enforcement Mechanisms

Policy enforcement mechanisms correspond to the low-level functions that implement the executable policies. It is convenient in the design and analysis of the system to separate the consideration of the policies (abstract and executable) from the mechanisms responsible for enforcing them, as each has its own weaknesses and threats.

Research has proposed multiple approaches for policy specification. Recent proposals have often been characterized by a direct integration with the languages and models of the modern Web scenario. These models include industry standards such as XACML [1], which is interesting because it can mostly be characterized as an abstract policy language, but it is also associated with tools that are able to directly process it, making it an executable policy. There are other abstract policy languages that a computer can directly process, such as rule-based policy notation using an if-then-else format, or proposals based on the representation of policies using Deontic logic for obligation and permissibility rules. Academic efforts produced solutions ranging from theoretical languages like the one proposed by Jajodia et al. in [2] to executable policy languages such as Ponder [3]. In the Semantic Web area have emerged proposals such as Rei [4] and KAoS [5]. Policy languages based on Semantic Web technologies allow policies to be described over heterogeneous domain data and promote a common understanding among participants, who might not use the same information model.

A crucial advantage of using a formal policy representation, particularly at the abstract level, is the possibility of an early identification of anomalies. Security policies in real systems often exhibit contradictions (inconsistencies in the policy that can lead to an incorrect realization of the security requirements) and redundancies (elements of the policy that are dominated by other elements, increasing the cost of security management without providing benefits to the users or applications). The availability of a high-level and complete representation of the security policies supports the construction of services for the analysis of the policies able to identify these anomalies and possibly suggest corrections. A classical taxonomy of conflicts is shown in Figure 45.2.

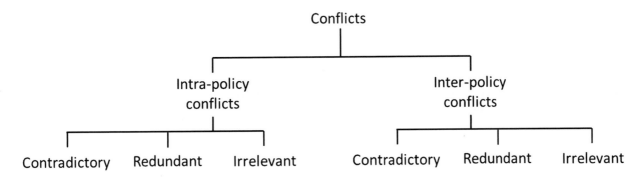

FIGURE 45.2   Taxonomy of conflicts.

#	Sign	User	Action	Resource
1	+	Alice	read	file1
2	+	Bob	write	file2
3	-	Alice	read	file1
4	+	Bob	write	folder (contains file1 and file2)

FIGURE 45.3   Examples of contradictory and redundant conflicts.

As depicted in Figure 45.2, conflicts can be divided into two categories: (a) *intra-policy* conflicts that may exist within a single policy and (b) *inter-policy* conflicts that may exist between at least two policies. For each category we have the following subcategories: (a) contradictory, (b) redundant, and (c) irrelevant.

Contradictory

Contradictory conflicts arise when principals are authorized to do an action *a* on a resource *r* by *a* positive authorization, and are forbidden to do the same action *a* on the resource *r* by a negative authorization. In this case, the two authorizations are said to be incompatible. For example, in Figure 45.3 authorization 1 is in conflict with authorization 3. In fact, authorization 1 states that Alice can read file1, and authorization 3 states that Alice cannot read file1.

Contradictory authorizations make the policy inconsistent. The security administrator has to be alerted, to correct this error by editing or removing the conflict. In network policies, a classification is introduced that further refines this type of conflict.

Redundant

Redundant conflicts arise when an authorization is dominated by other authorizations and does not contribute to the policy (its removal would not modify the behavior of

the system). Given two authorizations a_1 and a_2 with the same action and sign, let us call p_i (respectively, r_i) the principals (respectively, resources) associated, directly or indirectly, with a_i. If $p_2 \subseteq p_1$ and $r_2 \subseteq r_1$ and a_2 is not involved in any conflict with other authorizations, then a_2 is redundant with respect to a_1, and can be safely removed from the policy without modifying the behavior of the system. For example, in Figure 45.3 authorization 2 is redundant with respect to authorization 4 because authorization 4 dominates (it is expressed on the folder) authorization 2 (it is expressed on file1, but it is contained in the folder).

Irrelevant

Irrelevant conflicts occur when the conflict can never manifest itself in a system. This may happen when the specification of the elements of the authorizations cannot lead to activation of all the authorizations involved in the conflict. Recognizing that a conflict is irrelevant may be hard, depending on the expressive power of the language used for representation of authorizations. Examples are presented in Section 4 when discussing conflicts in network policies.

This classification is a starting point for evaluation of the conflicts. In the next section we present some examples of conflicts and discuss the introduction of techniques for resolution of conflicts, able to solve contradictions in the policy.

Conflict Resolution

Security policies in real systems often exhibit conflicts and redundancies. The availability of a high-level and complete representation of the security policies supports the construction of services for the analysis of the policies able to identify these anomalies and possibly suggest corrections. Contradictions in the policy are also called *modality conflicts*. They arise when principals are authorized to do an action *a* on a resource *r* by a positive authorization, and forbidden to do the same action *a* on resource *r* by a negative authorization.

In this case, the two authorizations are said to be *incompatible*. An example has been presented before, with authorization 1 and authorization 3 in Figure 45.3.

In the literature and in systems, several criteria have been proposed and implemented to manage at policy execution time this kind of conflict [6], aiming at removing the ambiguity in the policy and solving the conflict. Consider, in that regard, the case of a generic network firewall device, whereby packet filtering rules are evaluated in a given order and, as such, any conflict among them (more than one rule matching to the same packet) is deterministically solved by evaluating the result dictated by the first matching rule. The rules that handle the composition of authorizations in order to solve the conflicts do not necessarily have to be fixed. More sophisticated languages are in fact equipped with specific constructs to instruct the policy evaluator to apply one out of several possible composition strategies. The XACML language [1], for instance, defines so-called combining algorithms to compose the results of different access control rules. Examples of the available options are the "*deny-overrides*" algorithm, where rules prescribing access denial take precedence. This means that in case of conflict, the negative authorization always wins, so a forbidden action will never be permitted. For the example presented in Figure 45.3, this means that authorization 3, being negative for subject Alice, has priority over authorization 1, so Alice is not allowed to read file1. Another strategy that sees extensive adoption in operating systems is the "*first-applicable*" one, where rules are evaluated in order, such as in the aforementioned case of a network firewall. In a similar fashion, the Apache Web server access control configuration language permits specification of the order of priority of rule evaluation: For example, the "Order allow, deny" directive determines the priority of permissions over denials.

Other important criteria are those based on identification of a dominance relationship among rules. This is represented by the criterion "*most specific wins*," which states that, when one authorization dominates the other, the more specific wins. In most cases this represents an adequate and flexible solution. A critical problem of this approach is that specificity may not always be defined for conflicting authorizations, for a variety of reasons.

A first case is represented by the authorizations supporting a hierarchy for any element of the (<*subject, action, resource*>) triple, with the possibility to be contained in more than one ancestor. For example, for a given action and resource, authorization *A3* has a positive sign and is applied to group *G1*, and authorization *A4* has a negative sign and is applied to group *G2*, with *G1* and *G2* not contained one into the other and with a user *u*

belonging to both groups. In this situation, the "*most specific wins*" does not solve the conflict. A second case occurs when containment hierarchies are possible on more than one element. For example, authorization A5 has a positive sign and applies to user *u* when accessing elements in the resource group RG; authorization *A6* has a negative sign and applies to user group *UG* when accessing element *r*; if *u* is a member of *UG* and *r* is included in *RG*, the "*most specific wins*" criterion is not able to manage the conflict. Other solutions have been proposed that rely on the explicit specification of a priority for each authorization. If a partial order is specified, using the same priority for sets of authorizations, the possibility of unresolved conflicts remains. If priorities build a total order on authorizations, conflicts would be solved, but it appears quite difficult to assign in an efficient way priorities that are consistent with the application semantics.

An option that can solve all the conflicts is to combine multiple resolution criteria, applying each one only after the previous ones were not able to solve the conflict. For instance, the "*most specific wins*" can be applied first, and the "*deny overrides*" can be used to solve the remaining conflicts. This is in most cases a solution preferable to identification of some fixed ordering of the authorization that is not consistent with the semantics of the policy. Another option that has a significant potential, particularly when dealing with abstract policies that will be mapped to executable policies, is to use the "*most specific wins*" criterion as a first step, and let the conflict detection solutions notify the security administrator of the remaining conflicts, in order to either modify the policy or introduce an ad-hoc solution. Support for this approach can be offered by use of Semantic Web tools, as discussed in Section 5.

Separation of Duty

The conflicts presented until now derive from the presence of positive and negative authorizations in the same policy that can be applied to the same access request. A different kind of conflict derives from the definition in the security policy of constraints that the authorizations have to satisfy. An important class of constraints is *Separation of Duty (SoD)*. These constraints follow the common best practice for which sensitive combinations of permissions should not be held by the same individual, in order to avoid the violation of business rules. The purpose of this constraint is to discourage fraud by spreading the responsibility and authority for an action or task, thereby raising the risk involved in committing a fraudulent act, by requiring the involvement of more than one individual. The idea of Separation of Duty long existed before the information age and is extensively used in some areas, like the bank industry and the military.

Role-Based Access Control can be adapted to express this kind of constraint because the role hierarchy allows an easy mapping of real-world business rules to the access control model.

A well-known example is the process of creating and approving purchase orders. If a single person creates and approves purchase orders, it is easy and tempting for them to create and approve a phony order and pocket the money. If different people must create and approve orders, then committing fraud requires a conspiracy of at least two people, which significantly lowers the risk.

The two main categories of Separation of Duty are (a) Static Separation of Duty (*SSoD*) and (b) Dynamic Separation of Duty (*DSoD*) (see Figure 45.4). The former category (also known as strong exclusion) is the simplest way to implement SoD. Given two roles *role*$_1$ and *role*$_2$, the Static SoD between these two roles means that a user *u* must not exist who can activate both *role*$_1$ and *role*$_2$. For instance, if *Order Creator* and *Order Approver* are strongly exclusive roles, then no one who may assume the Order Creator role would be allowed to assume the Order Approver role, and vice versa no one who may assume the *Order Approver* role would be allowed to assume the *Order Creator* role.

The latter category (also known as weak exclusion) states that "A principal may be a member of any two exclusive roles, but he must not activate both at the same time." This definition implies that the system will keep precise track of each task. Before doing any task, the system will check that the separation of duty is not violated. Dynamic separation of duty allows the users to perform the roles that would be strongly exclusive in static systems.

Violations of the Separation of Duty constraints policy are another kind of conflict. Support for this conflict can be adequately provided by the implementation of conflict detection services, which are able to notify the security designer of inconsistencies in the policy. Resolution of such a conflict will typically require either revising the policy, restricting the user's ability to enact conflicting roles, or modifying the specification of the constraint. The efficient identification of these violations can use ad-hoc solutions. An interesting option is represented by the use of Semantic Web tools, as discussed in Section 5.

3. CONFLICTS IN EXECUTABLE SECURITY POLICIES

We have so far focused on how conflicts have been studied in the context of abstract security policies, where the specific details on the implementation of the policy enforcement mechanisms are not part of the model. Therefore they are not assumed to possibly introduce any issue in the policy evaluation.

In this section we instead consider the case of concrete policy evaluation frameworks, where an *evaluation algorithm* determines the effect of a given policy according to:

- An executable representation of the policy
- Context-dependent information

The executable policy can be seen as the configuration of the security enforcement mechanism, and it can be referred to as its *security configuration*. A security configuration is typically expressed according to a respective *configuration language*. The semantics of this language is ultimately given by the evaluation algorithm that computes the result of a configuration at operations time. As a consequence, configuration authors need to have a thorough understanding of the semantics evaluation, such that they can configure the behavior of the enforcing mechanism exactly according to the policy they want the system to implement.

Security configuration languages and corresponding evaluation semantics typically incorporate mechanisms to cope with conflicts that may arise at the evaluation stage. This can be achieved, on the one hand, by constraining the expressiveness of the configuration language so that

FIGURE 45.4 NIST RBAC model.

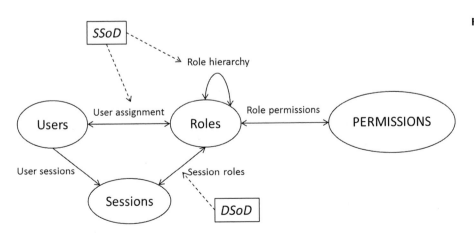

some inconsistencies are syntactically ruled out; for instance, contradictions in the policy (cf. Section 2) cannot occur in the case of an access control configuration language that only allows specifying collections of positive (respectively, negative) authorization rules. On the other hand, solutions to resolve the conflicting situations can be included in the evaluation semantics. For example, the rules that determine the semantics of the composition of different constructs of the language can be designed to handle conflicts by applying a predetermined strategy, as discussed earlier.

Although policy conflicts are sorted out in the evaluation semantics of security configuration languages, errors can still be introduced by inexperienced configuration authors. As a matter of fact, the gap of abstraction that lies between a security configuration and the corresponding enforced abstract policy is not dissimilar to the difference between a program's source code and the behavior realized by an interpreter while executing the program (cf. Figure 45.5). As such, policies that enforce unintended security properties can stem from misconfigured security enforcement devices, like bugs in the program's source code produce an incorrect runtime behavior.

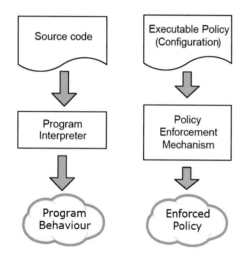

FIGURE 45.5 Analogy between program interpretation and the low portion of Figure 45.1.

To solve this issue, researchers have been studying the characteristics of security policy languages and their semantics in order to:

- Identify in particular counterintuitive corner-cases or anomalous situations that likely stem from misconfigurations.
- Propose models to automatically detect and possibly solve such misconfigurations.

In the following we discuss these issues in the scenario of Java Enterprise Edition. The treatment will also use some concrete examples of the security configuration language.

Java EE Access Control

The Java Enterprise Edition (Java EE) platform consists in a set of API and a runtime environment that allow development and execution of distributed Web-based applications. The basic execution model of a Java EE Web application is depicted in Figure 45.6. HTTP requests coming over the network are processed by the Java EE application server and abstracted to *HttpServlet Request* Java objects, which constitute the input of the Web application. Web applications are composed of *Web Components*, dealing with the client's requests and computing responses, and *JavaBeans Components* which can be optionally involved to encapsulate the business logic of large-scale Web applications.

The interface between the Web Components and the application server, providing their execution environment, is standardized in the Java EE Servlet Specification [7]. This document establishes a contract between application server implementations on one side and Web applications on the other, prescribing, among others, a number of mechanisms to deal with security in Java EE Web applications.

Such mechanisms belong to two categories: programmatic security and declarative security. Programmatic security describes functionalities that developers can use through an API to implement security within their application's code. Declarative security refers instead to the enforcement of security properties (such as HTTP-based

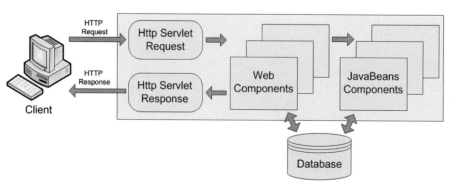

FIGURE 45.6 Execution model of a Java EE Web application [7].

access control) achieved not through dedicated source code in the application, but rather through the declarative specification of security configurations. In the latter case, the enforcement of security at runtime is completely transparent to the Web application's developer. When the Web application is deployed within the application server, it comes together with a configuration file, the so-called deployment descriptor, where security and several other aspects of the Web application's runtime environment are configured. Analogous mechanisms are likewise available for JavaBeans Components, as described in a dedicated specification [8].

As we are interested in discussing examples of security configuration languages, in this section we focus on declarative security. We first provide an overview about its evaluation semantics and then examine different approaches to the analysis of Java EE security configurations.

The deployment descriptor of Web Components is a XML document that conforms to a grammar (XML schema) defined as part of the Servlet Specification. The security-related fragment of this grammar is the subtree rooted at the *security constraint* XML tag.

Every security constraint associates a set of resources (i.e., URLs of the Web application) with the required security properties. Two categories of security properties can be configured: *authorization constraints*, which are access control on URLs, and *user data constraints*, which stand for confidentiality or integrity requirements on data exchanged between the client and the Web application. Access control is configured by associating URL patterns and a (possibly empty) set of HTTP methods to at most one authorization constraint, that is, the set of roles allowed to access the mentioned resources. Wildcards are allowed in the definition of both URL patterns and granted roles: in particular (i) the special role name '*' is shorthand for all the roles defined inside the deployment descriptor, and (ii) entire URL hierarchies can be specified with URL patterns ending with the '/*' wildcard.

Similarly, requirements on data confidentiality or integrity are specified by associating URL patterns and HTTP methods with one or more transport guarantee XML nodes, containing either the CONFIDENTIAL or INTEGRAL keywords.

According to the informal semantics from [9], in order to have access granted, a user must be a member of *at least one of the roles* named in the security constraint (or implied by '*') that matches her/his HTTP request. An empty authorization constraint means that *nobody* can access the resources, whereas access is granted to *any* (possibly unauthenticated) user in case the authorization constraint is omitted. Unauthenticated access is also allowed by default to any unconstrained resources. It's worth noting that an intuitively insignificant syntactic difference, such as omitting the authorization constraint

instead of specifying an empty one, corresponds to a major gap in semantics, respectively, *allow all* or *deny all* behaviors are obtained.

In case the same URL pattern and HTTP method occur in different security constraints, they have to be conceptually composed, as they apply to overlapping sets of resources. For what concerns access control, if two nonempty authorization constraints are composed, the result is the *union* of the two sets of allowed roles. If one of the two allows unauthenticated access, the composition also does. In contrast, if one of the sets of roles is empty, their composition is empty; that is, the *intersection* of the two sets is performed in this case. Constraints on more specific URL patterns (/a/b) always override more general ones (/a/*). The composition of user data constraints, instead, is always the union of the single requirements.

The following snippet is an example of two overlapping security constraints. As a result of their composition, no access is granted to the URL hierarchies '*' and '/acme/wholesale/*' via the *DELETE* and *PUT HTTP* methods. Access to '/acme/wholesale/*' via *GET* is restricted to users having the role *SALESCLERK*. HTTP requests with any method other than the aforementioned are instead granted to anyone:

```
<security-constraint>
<web-resource-collection>
<url-pattern>/*</url-pattern>
<url-pattern>/acme/wholesale/*</url-pattern>
<http-method>DELETE</http-method>
<http-method>PUT</http-method>
</web-resource-collection>
<auth-constraint/>
</security-constraint>
<security-constraint>
<web-resource-collection>
<url-pattern>/acme/wholesale/*</url-pattern>
<http-method>GET</http-method>
<http-method>PUT</http-method>
</web-resource-collection>
<auth-constraint>SALESCLERK</auth-constraint>
</security-constraint>
```

It is suggested [10] that the evaluation semantics of security constraints for Java EE Web Components is partly counterintuitive, specifically in its fragments concerning composition, which is where, as argued earlier, the rules to deal with conflicts are encoded. The peculiar handling of unconstrained HTTP methods and the fact that more specific URL patterns shall override less specific ones, for instance, may lead to unexpected behaviors, as illustrated in the following example.

Let us consider again a couple of security constraints introduced above. According to the aforementioned interpretation, the *HTTP DELETE* requests to the URL */acme* are denied, as the first constraint applies. In contrast, requests to the same URL but through any unconstrained method, such as *GET*, are allowed to anyone.

We now assume that a system administrator, wanting to deny *GET* requests to the URL */acme*, added the following constraint:

```
<security-contraint>
<web-resource-collection>
<url-pattern>/acme</url-pattern>
<http-method>GET</http-method>
</web-resource-collection>
<auth-constraint/>
</security-contraint>
```

Since this new constraint is the most specific for the URL */acme*, and it does not specify any behavior for methods other that *GET*, it introduces a side effect by allowing requests that were previously denied. For example, the *DELETE* requests to */acme* become *allowed to anyone*, after introducing this constraint. This behavior is particularly counterintuitive because the new constraint does not include any reference to the *DELETE* method, which is nevertheless affected. Also, although apparently it specifies *access denial* (empty authorization constraint), it implicitly carries *access permission* semantics for every unconstrained method.

The authors of [10] argue for the need of a formal characterization of the semantics of security constraints, which can be used as a reference to check the correctness of the behavior of both application server implementations and Web application configurations. Hence, they propose a set-theoretic model that captures the expressiveness of Java EE Web Components' authorization constraints, where resources form a set ordered according to the URL tree hierarchy and sets of roles, ordered by inclusion, form a lattice of permissions.

4. CONFLICTS IN NETWORK SECURITY POLICIES

The identification of conflicts in security policies has been particularly investigated in the scenario of the configuration of computer networks. This area of security sees a significant industrial interest, is today one of the most critical components in the protection of an information system from external threats, and relies on a protection model that is well understood and adequate to the realization of a number of ad-hoc solutions. We consider it interesting then to analyze the solutions that have been devised for detection of policy conflicts in this scenario.

The analysis will give a more precise understanding of the problems that can be faced when managing conflicts in a real system, and the results of the work in this area provide important guidelines that can drive the design of this functionality in the different scenarios where security policies are defined. First, we will consider the configuration of firewalls. Then, we will analyze how the configuration of channel protection solutions can identify other kinds of conflicts in the policy.

Filtering Intra-policy Conflicts

Firewalls are devices used to separate parts of networks parts that have different security levels; in fact, they are able to enforce an authorization policy that selects the traffic to be allowed according to a security policy expressed as a set rules, often named the access control list (ACL). The rules are composed by a *condition* clause, formed by a series of predicates over some packet header fields, and an action clause, determining the action to be enforced, typically allowing or denying the traffic.

When a new packet arrives at one of the firewall network interfaces, the values from its headers are used to evaluate the condition clause predicates [10,11]. A packet matches a rule if all the predicates of the rule are true. If a packet matches only one rule, the action enforced is taken of its action clause. However, in an ACL, a packet can match more than one rule; therefore rules are prioritized and the action from the matching rule at the highest priority is enforced. This approach is often named the "*first applicable*" resolution strategy, based on ordering rules by priority and starting from the highest priority one; the action enforced is the one from the first matching rule. However, hardware-based approaches use ad-hoc algorithms and fast memories that speed up the matching process considerably. In practice, the ACL is not scanned linearly, as the action is selected by fast look-up algorithms [12]. It also may happen that a packet does not match any of the ACL rules.In that case, a default action is enforced; typically, the traffic is denied and the packet is dropped.

Firewalls are categorized according to their capabilities or the layer at which they work (that is, the headers they can consider). The simplest firewall capability is the *packet filter*, working at the network and transport ISO/OSI layer, that takes decisions based on five fields: IP address and ports of the source and destination, and the IP protocol type. Packet filters do not maintain state information (distinguishing packets that belong to an established TCP connection), and they are also referred to as *stateless firewalls*.

A firewall that performs the stateful packet inspection is named a *stateful firewall*, and it usually maintains information about the TCP state, but also about other stateless protocols (ICMP echo-request echo-reply sequences) or stateful application-layer protocols (understanding the opening of FTP data ports in active or passive mode). At the highest level of the ISO/OSI stack, there are the *application firewalls*. Because application protocols are very heterogeneous, application firewalls are usually tailored to one or more specific protocols to perform a more focused analysis. The most widespread one is the Web Application Firewall (WAF), which observes HTTP properties and fields, including MIME objects, and, if integrated with the Web service it protects, can also circumvent common attacks and vulnerability exploits. Additionally, application firewalls are able to check the "RFC compliance" that verifies whether the protocol traffic is consistent with the standards or with a set of nonharmful implementations. Therefore, the condition clause of stateful and application firewalls also contains predicates over state information and application protocol fields.

Condition clauses are not just modeled as logical predicates; in fact, many works represent them as using geometrical models that are proven equivalent. According to the geometric view, every packet is a point in a decision space, composed by many dimensions, one for each field for which it is possible to state a condition. A rule thus becomes a hyper-rectangle. For instance, the decision space of packet filters is often named five-tuple space. A packet matches a rule if it is in the rule hyperrectangular area. For instance, a simple bidimensional case is represented in Figure 45.7.

As firewalls are a major security shield against attacks and intrusions, their correct configuration has always worried administrators. However, most firewalls are very poorly configured, as Wool highlighted in a study in 2004 whose trend was recently confirmed [13,14]. Historically, three approaches are used to verify the correctness of intra-firewall policies: manual testing, query-based approaches, and use of conflict and anomaly analysis tools. Recently, companies have been using complex distributed systems with many firewalls and redundant controls; therefore, all these approaches have been designed or extended to the inter-firewall policies analysis.

In the inter-firewall policy analysis, verification of the correctness of the action enforced by a firewall is extended to a more general case, evaluating the actual reachability by analyzing the actions enforced by all the firewalls encountered in a communication path.

Manual Testing

Manual testing is the first and the simplest case. It can be performed by actually trying a set of connections to verify if they succeed and comparing them with the authorization policy, or using software able to probe hosts, servers, and other devices for open ports and available features, that is, the vulnerability scanner. Many scanners are available to this purpose, mostly as open-source software, like nmap [15], Amap [16], and Nessus [17]. They are sophisticated and can be used to detect more complex cases (to recognize OS and software fingerprints, or to distinguish filtered ports from closed ones) or to identify known vulnerabilities. This approach is very time consuming and requires an effort that, especially in large networks, is beyond the administrator's possibilities. Additionally, it requires actual deployment of the policy and physical access to the network, which may also be flooded by probe packets that may interfere with normal network functioning. Although scanners' output is very detailed, they need a further step to be compared with the firewall policy and to actually know if it has been correctly implemented.

5. QUERY-BASED CONFLICT DETECTION

The first attempts to overcome the limitations of the manual approach consisted in representing a firewall policy using an abstract format in order to perform queries and figure out the actual firewall behavior, by evaluating the action it would enforce instead of actually trying the connections. Firewall queries can be considered as questions concerning firewall behavior [16]. Examples of questions of interest to administrators are: "Which clients can access the server s1?", or "Which server is reachable from the Internet?" This query-based approach easily extends to the analysis of firewalls in distributed systems. In fact, the firewall questions can be easily extended to more general reachability problems.

Querying a firewall requires an abstract representation of the policy it implements and an abstract representation of the issued question. One major theoretical problem is the query aggregation. In fact, the number of cases to be considered, for instance, to answer the previous questions, is too large: For a five-tuple IPv4 packet filter there are 2^{104} different packets, potentially corresponding to cases to consider.[1] It is critical to use IP address ranges instead of single addresses and port intervals, merging adjacent

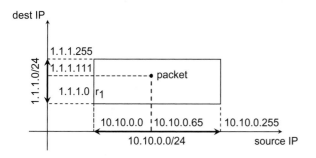

FIGURE 45.7 Geometric representation of a rule and a packet.

1. 32 bits for source and destination IPv4 addresses, 16 bits for ports, and 8 for the protocol type.

intervals. The aggregation of the results is also complex and computationally expensive, as the union of rectangles is not always a rectangle.

The first tool produced was Fang [18], a simulation-based engine that performs simple query aggregation. Its successor, Firewall Analyzer (formerly known as Lumeta) [19,20], also provided standard queries and import functionalities to automate the analysis and to facilitate the job of the administrators. Another early work from Hazelhurst [21] concentrated on a simple query-based analysis.

Recently, Liu proposed the Structured Firewall Query Language (SFQL) and an associated intra-firewall query engine [22], which he extended to analysis of corporate networks composed of packet filters also having network address and port translation capabilities (NAT and NAPT) [11]. SFQL is a SQL-like language that permits specifying queries in a compact and familiar syntax. Assuming that D is the field name for the destination address, S for source address, N for the destination port, and P for the protocol type, the following query answers the following question: "Which are the IP (source) addresses of computers that can reach the web service s_1 available at 10.0.0.1:80/TCP?" Please see the following lines of code:

```
Select S
from firewall
where {S ∈ all} ∧
{D ∈ 10.0.0.1} ∧
{N ∈ {80}} ∧
{P ∈ {TCP}} ∧
{decision = accept}
```

The main limitation of the firewall querying approach is that the questions to issue are selected by administrators who have to identify the meaningful queries, write them correctly, aggregating if needed the results of more queries (similarly to the SQL union clause), and analyze the results which may be very large. However, they "often do not know what to query" [18]. In literature, only the Firewall Analyzer addressed this problem, proposing a set of standard queries.

Conflict Detection by Anomaly Classification

A different method to identify whether the firewall policy is correct consists in performing an exhaustive analysis of the access control list (ACL), to detect all the situations that may be evidence of a misconfiguration. Even though the terms *conflict* and *anomaly* are often used synonymously, in this field they have different meanings: a *conflict* is an occurrence that may stop the correct working (having two matching rules in a router that only allows for one matching rule at the time); an *anomaly* is a

particular relation between one or more ACL rules that administrators have to consider, as it may be the evidence of specification mistakes, but that is perfectly allowed by the examined control.

Sloman [23–25] initially introduced the concept of conflicting policy, but the methods he presents are not directly applicable to firewall policies and in general to all the low-level configurations. Many seminal papers present solutions for analysis of packet filtering. First works concentrated on efficient representations of the ACL, as conflicting rules decrease performance or were not allowed in devices, due to the limited computation capabilities.

The approaches are mainly equivalent, even if they use different rule representations. Hazelhurst presented solutions based on binary decision diagrams (BDDs) [21], Hari [26] proposed the use of tries, Baboescu [27] the use of bit vectors, and Srinivasan [28] the Tuple Space Search classification algorithm.

The first formalization of the anomaly concept has been proposed by Al- Shaer who focused on the intra-policy analysis of packet filters [10]. He introduced the concept of anomaly, defined as "the existence of two or more filtering rules that may match the same packet, or the existence of a rule that can never match any packet" and identified five rule-pair anomaly types: *shadowing, correlation, generalization*, and *irrelevance* and presented an algorithm to discover and manage anomalies in ordered rule lists. Given two rules r_1 and r_2 where r_1 is the highest priority rule, the rule-pair anomalies are:

1. *Shadowing anomaly*: r_2 is shadowed when r_1 matches all the packets that r_2 matches, so that r_2 will never be activated (see Figure 45.9b);
2. *Correlation anomaly*: r_1 and r_2 are correlated if (1) they enforce different ac- tions and (2) there exists some packet matching both r_1 and r_2 and (3) there exists some packet matching r_1 but not r_2 and vice versa (see Figure 45.8b);
3. *Generalization anomaly*[2] : r_2 is a generalization of r_1 if (1) they enforce dif- ferent actions and (2) all the packets matching r_1 also match r_2, but not the contrary (see Figure 45.8c);
4. *Redundancy anomaly*: r_2 is redundant if r_1 matches the same packets and enforces the same action as r_2, so the removal of r_2 will not change the policy behavior (see Figure 45.9a);
5. *Irrelevance anomaly*: A rule is irrelevant if does not match any packet that could pass through the firewall. It does not concern relations between rules, but rather between a rule and the enforcing device.

---

2. In [29] this is named exception.

For instance, with reference to Table 45.1, r_1 is a generalization of r_2, r_2 shadows r_3, makes r_4 redundant, and is correlated to r_5. Finally, r_6 is irrelevant if the traffic from IP address 5.5.5.5 cannot reach the firewall interfaces.

Al-Shaer's classification has a limitation because it detects only anomalies in rule pairs; anomalies that arise when more rules are considered are not discussed. Basile [29,30] generalized Al-Shaer's classification to multi-rule anomalies, that is, anomalies that involve more than two rules. The firewall policies are categorized

as *conflicting* when at least two rules contradict each other (that includes the correlation, generalization and shadowing anomalies), and suboptimal when the removal of one or more rules does not affect the behavior of the firewall (that includes shadowing and redundancy). Suboptimality is caused by *hidden rules* (rules that are never activated, regardless of the number of rules that hide them). Hidden rules are further classified as *general redundant* if all the rules hiding them enforce the same action (as presented in Figure 45.9a), and *general shadowed*, if at least one enforces a different action (as presented in Figure 45.9b).

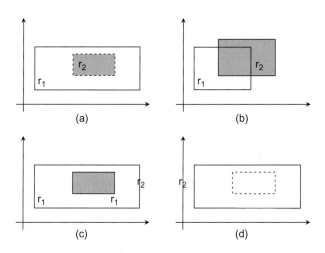

FIGURE 45.8 Al-Shaer's rule-pair anomaly classification for packet filters.

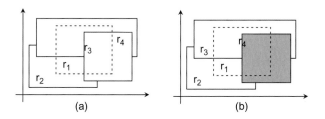

FIGURE 45.9 Multi-rule anomaly classification.

A More in-Depth View of Packet Filter Conflict Analysis

Al-Shaer's classification is the starting point for several works that tried to improve the identification of the anomalies using different techniques. Bouhoula [31] used rule field logical relations, so permitting the analysis of different firewall rule formats, not only the five-tuples. Thanasegaran [32] used bit vectors that support the detection of rule-pair anomalies more efficiently and the definition of new fields, but they fail to effectively express conditions on ordered fields (ranges of port numbers). Ferraresi [33] presented a slightly alternative conflict classification and a proven correct algorithm that produces a conflict-free rule list. Other works propose ruleset optimization by redundancy removal, Gouda [34] provided algorithms to verify the consistency, completeness, and compactness of packet filters, and Liu [35] introduced techniques for detection of redundancy based on Firewall Decision Diagrams. Alfaro [36] proposed a set of algorithms to remove anomalies between packet filters and NIDS in distributed systems, recently implemented in the MIRAGE tool [37]. Hu [38] also introduced an ontology-based anomaly management framework that delegates set operations to binary decision diagrams (BDDs). A completely different approach is presented by Bandara [39], who uses argumentation logic and achieves excellent performance. A

TABLE 45.1 A Sample Filtering Policy with Anomalies.

	priority	source IP	source port	dest IP	dest port	protocol	action
r_1	1	10.0.0.64/28	any	1.1.1.64/28	80	TCP	DENY
r_2	2	10.0.0.0/24	any	1.1.1.0/24	80	TCP	ALLOW
r_3	3	10.0.0.2	any	1.1.1.1	80	TCP	DENY
r_4	4	10.0.0.250	any	1.1.1.1	80	TCP	ALLOW
r_5	5	10.0.0.16/24	any	1.1.1.16/24	80	TCP	DENY
r_6	6	5.5.5.5	any	6.6.6.6	any	any	ALLOW

complementary approach is represented by Liu's Firewall Compressor [40], which minimizes the ACL size by manipulating the specified rules to obtain an equivalent ACL with a minimal number of rules. Redundant and shadowed rules disappear, but correlated rules are not examined. The compressed ACL only serves deployment purposes, as it is no longer manageable by the administrators.

Stateful Firewall Analysis

Anomaly analysis of stateful firewalls is a less explored field. It is difficult to share the optimism of Buttyàn [41], who stated that "stateful is not harder than stateless." Their scenario is oversimplified, as they added one single field to the five-tuple decision space to describe all the possible states. The stateful case is harder at least for two reasons: There are new anomalies that do not appear in the stateless case, and it is computationally more complex as many fields need to be considered. Gouda and Liu presented in [42] a model of stateful firewalls that maps the stateful filtering functionalities to the packet filter case, in order to use the available detection algorithms. For this reason, they model stateful firewalls using two components: the stateful section and the stateless section. The stateful section inspects the transport headers and maintains a *state table* that associates each of the connections observed with a set of Boolean variables, for example, the established state for the TCP connections. A set of (hard-coded) *stateful rules* regulates how the state table is updated, according to previous states and received packets. The stateless section is simply a packet filter that also includes predicates over the boolean variables in the state table, and the anomalies found are Al-Shaer's. Cuppens [43] extended Al-Shaer's classification adding stateful conflicts, situations connected to the specific protocol state machines, for example, rules that deny TCP setup and termination for allowed connections, or rules that block allowed related FTP connections.

Finally, there is currently no extensive work to detect anomalies in application firewalls, if we exclude the effort to validate the factory-provided regular expressions used to avoid attacks in Web application firewalls. An example representative of the complexity of the analysis in this case is described by the following rules (the first rule is used to avoid DoS attacks):

1. Deny packets with the SYN and ACK set to true from the external nodes;
2. Allow TCP connections from the internal node having IP 1.1.1.1 to the external server 2.2.2.2 (in the Internet).

These rules are apparently disjoint, as one poses a condition on different values of the IP addresses and TCP

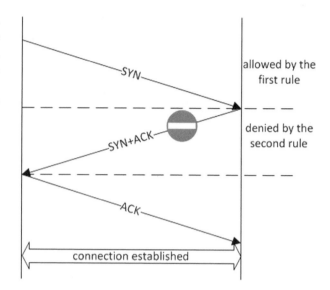

FIGURE 45.10   Blocked three-way handshake.

flags. However, according to the TCP specification, the three-way handshake cannot be terminated; the result then is that the connection from 1.1.1.1 and 2.2.2.2 is forbidden (see Figure 45.10).

Inter-Firewall Analysis

Al-Shaer [44] has also provided the first classification of anomalies in distributed systems. He considers the case of two serially connected stateless firewalls, named, respectively, upstream and downstream firewalls. Assuming fw_u is the upstream firewall and fw_d is the downstream firewall, four anomaly types are identified:

- *Shadowing anomaly*—occurs if fw_u blocks traffic accepted by fw_d (see Figure 45.11a);
- *Spuriousness anomaly*—occurs if fw_u permits traffic denied by fw_d (see Figure 45.11b);
- *Redundancy anomaly*—occurs if fw_u denies traffic already blocked by fw_u (see Figure 45.11c);
- *Correlation anomaly* occurs when a rule ru in fw_u and a rule rd in fw_d are correlated (see Figure 45.11d).

Another work that addresses conflict analysis in distributed systems is presented in [42]. This work defines for every pair of nodes in the network two separate end-to-end policies: the allowed packets, named accept property, and the denied packets, named discard property. Based on an abstract representation of the firewall ACL, the Firewall Decision Diagram [32], they calculate the effects on the communication between two nodes n_1 and n_2 by superposing the actions taken by all the cascading firewalls encountered in the path between n_1 and n_2. Then, they compare the results with the accept and discard properties; a conflict arises when an accept or

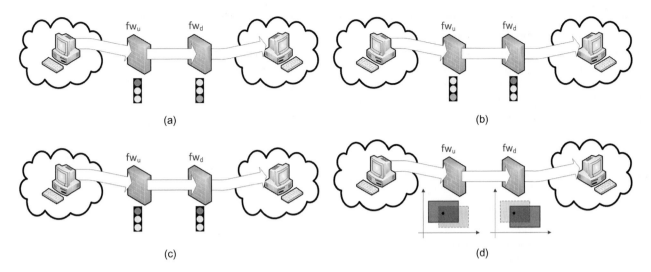

FIGURE 45.11   Al-Shaer's rule-pair anomaly classification for distributed packet filters.

discard property is not satisfied. Finally, a tool able to detect Al-Shaer's anomalies in distributed systems is FIREMAN, which also checks if a distributed policy complies with an end-to-end policy [43].

Channel Protection Conflicts

The configuration of secure channels is also an error-prone activity; thus administrators need assistance and conflict detection mechanisms. A few differences can be highlighted with respect to the filtering case: The number of rules is usually orders of magnitude less than in the firewall case. However, they enforce more complex actions, they may enforce more than one action in case of multiple matches, and they have more complex dependencies on the actual distributed system topology.

Different technologies are available to protect channels, and these technologies work at different levels of the ISO/OSI stack. The most well-known solutions are: IPsec, which works at the network layer; and the TLS protocol, which works up to the transport layer. IPsec allows the creation of secure communication channels between two endpoints. IPsec can enforce authentication and integrity of IP payload and header using the Authentication Header (AH) protocol, and confidentiality, authenticity, and integrity of the IP payload using the Encapsulating Security Payload (ESP). These endpoints can be the communicating peers (client and server or two peers) or two gateways used to allow securely connecting two subnets or two offices connected over a public/insecure network (the Internet) and to establish a virtual private network (VPN). Also, TLS is used as the base protocol to create VPNs; when this technology is employed, the terms *OpenVPN* or *clientless VPN* are used. These techniques have many similarities from

the configuration point of view; therefore they share the same anomalous situations. However, only IPsec VPNs have received attention from researchers, nevertheless, the results on IPsec VPNs are easily extendable to the OpenVPN scenario.

IPsec Intra-Policy Conflict Detection

The IPsec configuration rules (the Security Policy) are stored in the local Security Policy Database (SPDB). These rules select the traffic to be protected by means of (condition clause) predicates on the source and destination IP addresses, IP protocol type fields, and traffic direction (in/out). Three types of anomalies can be found in this scenario: (intra-policy) local anomalies, (intra-policy) topology-dependent local anomalies, and inter-policy anomalies.

Local anomalies are analogous to the packet filter scenario (see checklist:"An Agenda for Action for Developing Security Policies for Packet Filtering), and they can be identified using the same techniques (only a simple adaptation is needed). It is not surprising that Al-Shaer proposed the application of its classification for packet filters presented in [10] to intra-IPsec policy analysis [45], extending an early work from Fu et al. [46].

The anomaly types are exactly the same: shadowed, redundant, correlated, and generalized rule pairs can be found in an IPsec SPDB. However, the effort required for the analysis is greater. The main difference is that the actions that can be enforced using IPsec are more complex, as confidentiality, authenticity, and integrity (of the IP payload only using ESP, or IP payload and header using AH) can be selected. Moreover, cryptographic algorithms need to be evaluated and compared. For instance, is it better to protect a channel using "ESP with HAMC-SHA1

An Agenda for Action for Developing Security Policies for Packet Filtering

IPSec can perform host-based packet filtering to provide limited firewall capabilities for end systems. You can configure IPSec to permit or block specific types of unicast IP traffic based on source and destination address combinations and specific protocols and specific ports. For example, nearly all the systems illustrated in the following checklist can benefit from packet filtering to restrict communication to only specific addresses and ports. You can strengthen security by using IPSec packet filtering to control exactly the type of communication that is allowed between systems (check all tasks completed):

_____1. The internal network domain administrator can assign an Active Directory-based IPSec policy (a collection of security settings that determines IPSec behavior) to block all traffic from the perimeter network (also known as a demilitarized zone [DMZ], demilitarized zone, or screened subnet).

_____2. The perimeter network domain administrator can assign an Active Directory-based IPSec policy to block all traffic to the internal network.

_____3. The administrator of the computer running Microsoft SQL Server on the internal network can create an exception in the Active Directory-based IPSec policy to permit Structured Query Language (SQL) protocol traffic to the Web application server on the perimeter network.

_____4. The administrator of the Web application server on the perimeter network can create an exception in the Active Directory-based policy to permit SQL traffic to the computer running SQL server on the internal network.

_____5. The administrator of the Web application server on the perimeter network can also block all traffic from the Internet, except requests to TCP port 80 for the HyperText Transfer Protocol (HTTP) and TCP port 443 for HTTPS (HTTP over Secure Sockets Layer/Transport Layer Protocol [SSL/TLS]), which are used by Web services. This provides additional security for traffic allowed from the Internet in case the firewall was misconfigured or compromised by an attacker.

_____6. The domain administrator can block all traffic to the management computer, but allow traffic to the perimeter network.

and AES256" or a channel using "ESP with RC2128 encapsulated in AH with HMAC-MD5"? The answer is not easy and depends on the requirements specified at the business level.

Together with the previous anomalies, other types of anomaly appear from the analysis of a local SPDB: the intra-policy channel overlapping and the multitransform anomalies. These anomalies depend on the possibility of applying in the same SPDB more than one transformation; choosing the correct order, modes, and algorithms becomes crucial.

The overlapping occurs when a SPDB contains more than one rule having the same source s and destination d that use different tunneling devices, g_1 and g_2 (see Figure 45.12). For instance, if the SPDB contains the following rules:

- (short tunnel) tunnel to g_1 with protection p_1
- (long tunnel) tunnel to g_2 with protection p_2

and are applied in this order, the following communications are performed:

1. $s \rightarrow g_2$ protected with p_1 and p_2

2. $g_2 \rightarrow g_1$ protected with p_1 (p_2 is removed at g_2)
3. $g_1 \rightarrow d$ with no protection

Therefore, the rule order matters. In fact, if the rules are applied in the opposite order, the communications are, as expected:

1. $s \rightarrow g_1$ protected with p_1 and p_2
2. $g_1 \rightarrow g_2$ protected with p_2 (p_1 is removed at g_1)
3. $g_2 \rightarrow d$ with no protection

This anomaly can also occur with a transport transform (instead of the long tunnel) followed by a tunnel (short tunnel). Applying more than one transformation increases the risk of reducing the protection level. In fact, it is not always true that the combination of more transformations results in a stronger protection. Moreover, since the application of each transformation requires computational resources, using more than one transformation must be justified from the security point of view. The multitransform anomaly occurs when a weaker protection is applied after a stronger one. For instance, applying ESP after AH reduces the overall security because ESP transport does not provide IP header protection. On the other hand,

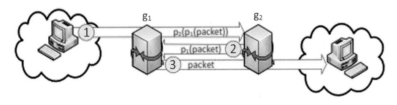

FIGURE 45.12   IPsec intra-policy overlapping conflict.

applying AH after ESP is often justified to preserve the header integrity. Additionally, a multitransform anomaly may also occur when the increase of cost/benefit in terms of security is not justified, as when one is applying ESP with AES256 after having applied ESP with AES128. Resolving these anomalies is very delicate. Every case needs to be considered individually, as the "protection strength" needs to be measured and compared to the performance loss, but an official measure does not exist and every organization may have its own evaluation criteria.

IPsec Inter-Policy Conflict Detection

Together with the explicit deny action, communications can also be blocked in case of misconfigurations or if the peer authentication fails, if the *security association* defining the algorithms and keys to use to protect the channel is not available and not negotiable, or if there is more than one security association when a unique security association is expected. Therefore, the types of anomaly are analogous to the ones presented in distributed systems. In fact, IPsec communications can be shadowed (block traffic already blocked by the upstream device) and spurious (allow traffic already blocked by the upstream device).

Additionally, it is possible to highlight the *inter-policy channel overlapping*, presenting the same mechanism as the intra-policy case but involving more than two elements. To protect communication between source s and destination d, there are three gateways, g_1, g_2, and g_3, which are encountered in this order by packets from s to d (see Figure 45.13). The following policy is enforced:

- s creates a secure channel (transport mode) to g_2 with protection p_1.
- g_1 creates a tunnel to g_3 with protection p_2.

Therefore, the resulting communications are:

1. $s \rightarrow g_1$ protected with p_1
2. $g_1 \rightarrow g_3$ protected with p_1 and p_2
3. $g_3 \rightarrow g_2$ protected with p_1 (p_2 is removed at g_3)
4. $g_2 \rightarrow d$ with no protection

IPsec devices are managed by different people often working in different units; therefore the inter-policy conflicts are relatively frequent. Sun et al. [47] proposed a new architecture that stores all the IPsec policy centrally and offers access via a manager which also enforces an access control policy. Additionally, the proposed work aims at automatically manipulating the SPDB to avoid or recover some of the anomalies presented before.

6. SEMANTIC WEB TECHNOLOGY FOR CONFLICT DETECTION

The term *Semantic Web* refers to both a vision and a set of technologies. The vision is articulated, in particular by the World Wide Web Consortium (W3C), as an extension to the current idea of the Web in which knowledge and data could be published in a form easy for computers to understand and reason with. Doing so would support more sophisticated software systems that share knowledge, information and data on the Web just as people do by publishing text and multimedia. Under the stewardship of the W3C, a set of languages, protocols, and technologies have been developed to partially realize this vision, to enable exploration and experimentation, and to support the evolution of the concepts and technology. The current set of W3C standards is based on RDF [48], a language that provides a basic capability of specifying graphs with a simple interpretation as a *semantic network* and serializing them in XML and several other popular Web systems (e.g., JSON). Since it is a graph-based representation, RDF data are often reduced to a set of triples where each represents an edge in the graph or, alternatively, a binary predicate. The Web Ontology Language (OWL) [49] is a family of knowledge representation languages based on Description Logic (DL) [50] with a representation in RDF. OWL supports the specification and use of ontologies that consist of terms representing individuals, classes of individuals, properties, and axioms that assert constraints over them.

The use of OWL to describe and verify the properties of policies offers several important advantages, which are particularly critical in distributed environments possibly involving coordination across multiple organizations. First, most policy languages define constraints over classes of targets, objects, actions, and other kinds of information (location). A substantial part of the development of a policy is often devoted to the precise specification of these classes. This is especially important if the policy is shared between multiple organizations that must adhere to or enforce the policy, even though they have their own native schemas or data models for the domain in question. The

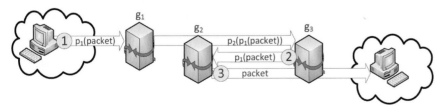

FIGURE 45.13 To protect communication between sources and destination d, there are three gateways: g_1, g_2, and g_3.

second advantage is that OWL's grounding in logic facilitates the translation of policies expressed in OWL to other formalisms, either for further analysis or for execution.

Semantic Web technology offers an extensive collection of tools that can be used to model and represent policy conflicts. Several approaches can be adopted, with different profiles in terms of abstractness and efficiency. There are three main approaches to discover conflicts: standard reasoners, ad-hoc reasoning methods, and rule-based inferencing. In the next subsections we characterize these three alternatives.

Use of Standard Reasoners

The standard reasoner is one of the core elements of an ontology-based system. Starting from the information contained in the ontology described in OWL, it is able to perform several tasks (it is able to check the consistency and validity of the ontology, classify its information, answer queries, and generate inferences) using a variety of techniques deriving from the work of the artificial intelligence community.

In particular, standard *Description Logic* (DL) reasoning performed w.r.t. a formal ontology can check complex consistency constraints in the model. Such constraints are different from the usual ones from database and *UML*-like systems. In OWL-DL, which is the portion of OWL restricted to the expressivity of DL, we can express:

- Constraints on properties, domains, and ranges
- Definitions of concepts (classes) in terms of relationships with other elements
- Boolean operations on classes

One of the main differences between DL-based schema definitions and UML or ER definitions concerns the constraints on property domains and ranges. Properties can be defined in a general way, and their behavior in terms of range type can be precisely described while refining the ontology concepts. This promotes the definition and reuse of high-level properties, without losing the ability to force precise typing. In this way, the resolution of some conflicts can be explicitly expressed in the policy, without the need to rely on an external conflict resolution option or implicit priorities. For instance, authorizations associated with a subject administrator can be denoted as having higher priority, dominating in possible conflicts with other authorizations.

Ad-Hoc Reasoning Methods

Standard *Description Logic* reasoners can answer complex questions and verify structural and nonstructural constraints. Furthermore, DL-based language expressiveness often exceeds classical solutions (like UML for design

and SQL for data storage models). This supports the description and verification of more complex structural constraints. For example, if we consider the approach used in [51], where the roles are represented as individuals of the class Role, the *roleHierarchy : Role → Role* property[3] is used to connect each role to its direct subroles and the *canHaveRole + : Identity → Role* property is used to represent the roles that each identity (user) can activate, directly or indirectly, thanks to the presence of positive role authorizations. Thus, *roleHierarchy* (r_1, r_2) means that role r_1 is a super-role of r_2. Its transitive closure *canBe + : Role → Role* can be used to identify all the direct or indirect subroles. The subrole (as well as its inverse super-role) relationship is not a containment and does not define a taxonomy on identities (a super-role of role R is intended to be more privileged than R and is available to a more restricted set of identities).

With these tools it is possible, for instance, to offer an immediate management of Separation of Duty constraints. The user role assignment relation is represented using role authorizations, which specialize authorizations with the specification of the role that the principal is allowed or forbidden to assume. A Separation of Duty constraint between role r_1 and r_2 can then be expressed using a negative role authorization r_{auth} that forbids role r_1 to enact role r_2. Separation of Duty constraints are enforced both at the role hierarchy level (in this way we directly prevent a role r_1 from being declared super-role of another role r_2, such that r_1 and r_2 are in a SoD constraint) and at the user hierarchy level (to prevent two roles r_1 and r_2 from being assigned to a user, directly or indirectly, that are involved in a SoD constraint).

To show a more concrete example, we assume that class *RoleAuthorization* ⊆ Authorization represents the role authorizations, and properties *grantedTo: RoleAuthorization → Principal* and *enabledRole: Role Authorization → Role* are used to represent, respectively, the role enabled by the role authorization and the principal to which the role is assigned. In order to keep track of all SoD conflicts on roles, we can define a class *SoDOnRole* ⊆ *Role*. Separation of Duty constraints on the role hierarchy can be expressed adding to the ontology the following set of axioms:

$$\forall auth \in RoleAuthorization:sign(auth, -),$$
$$grantedTo(auth, r_1), enabledRole(auth, r_2)$$

$$SoDOnRole \equiv \exists canBe + .\{r_1\} \cap \exists canBe + .\{r_2\}$$

The interpretation of these axioms is that, for each negative role authorization, there is an instance in class

---

SoDOnRole only if there exists a single role that belongs to r1 and to r2. We can thus enforce the SoD at the role hierarchy level by simply adding the axiom $SoDOnRole \sqsubseteq \bot$ to the ontology, which declares as consistent the ontology only if the class is empty.

In a similar way to what we have done for the identification of SoD conflicts at the role hierarchy level, we can define a class $SoDOnUser \sqsubseteq Identity$ that keeps track of the conflicts on the user hierarchy. We then express SoD constraints using the following axioms:

$$\forall auth \in RoleAuthorization{:}sign(auth, -),$$
$$grantedTo(auth, r_1), \ enabledRole(auth, r_2)$$

$$SoDOnUser \equiv \exists canHaveRole + .\{r_1\} \cap \exists canHaveRole + .\{r_2\}$$

and to enforce the SoD constraints we simply have to add to the ontology the axiom $SoDOnUser \sqsubseteq \bot$.

This approach can be easily extended to handle other kinds of SoD constraints, such as *Permission-based SoD* (which requires that no user be allowed to do both actions a_1 and a_2) or *Object-based SoD* (which requires that no user can access both resources res_1 and res_2). However, DL systems, as well as *Semantic Web* tools in general, are designed and implemented with a focus on knowledge management services, such as knowledge integration, schema matching, and instance retrieval. Such a specialization raises some limitations on the use of pure DL reasoning in real scenarios, in which reasoning must be carried out on a well-defined and complete description of a closed system.

Closed World Assumption (CWA)

Closed World Assumption (CWA) reasoning is a generally accepted requirement in model-driven systems. Conversely, DL reasoners usually work under the Open World Assumption (OWA). This means that the facts asserted in the model (about the layout topology or the authorization policies) are not assumed to be complete. Obviously, this can become a problem if model characteristics are described in terms of the existence of some properties or some relationships between model elements.

Reasoning on Complex Property Paths

Reasoning on complex property paths (commutatively of nontrivial graphs) rapidly brings to the undecidability of the formal logics the language is based on. Checking the closure of complex paths is beyond the expressive power of classical database systems, but unfortunately it is sometimes necessary in order to check structural constraints. This is the case, for example, for the consistency loop in Figure 45.14, stating that:

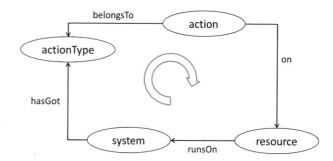

FIGURE 45.14   A simple consistency constraint.

an authorization of executing an action must be assigned to a resource (Database) that runs on a system (DBMS) compatible with the action type (Select, Create, Delete).

Unique Name Assumption (UNA)

Unique Name Assumption (UNA) is a commonly accepted assumption in most model-driven tools. It consists in assuming that different names will always denote different elements in the model. This is usually not true in DL reasoners because of the essential nature of knowledge integration problems. In fact, in the Semantic Web scenario, different authors may describe the same entities (both shared conceptualizations and physical objects), assigning a new name, generally in the form of an URI, defined independently from other users.

These properties must be carefully considered when applying DL and Semantic Web tools to the detection of policy conflicts. The obstacles introduced can be solved as long as attention is paid to them. Misbehaviors of the system can otherwise be observed.

Rule-Based Inferencing

Rule inference reasoning is widely used in knowledge management systems. Recently, some combinations of theorem proving systems (like DL ones) and rule inference systems have been proposed, to address some limitations of decidable theorem proving systems.

Semantic Web Rule Language (SWRL) is the W3C standard proposal for integrating rule-based inferencing into systems that represent knowledge as a set of RDF triples and introducing some limitations to the use of the rules, in order to preserve joint system decidability. In a real scenario, the main advantage of combining rules and classical theorem-proving systems is the support for complex property chains. In fact, even if some *OWL* profiles introduce the support for the chaining of properties (a.k.a roles in DL terminology), this may not be sufficient to express some complex topological properties. For example, the simple consistency loop shown in Figure 45.14 is not enforceable at the schema level using only DL axioms. In order to perform a consistency check on Figure 45.14, a simple SWRL rule like this one is needed:

$on\ (\ ?\ a_1\ ,\ ?\ r_1\ )\ ,\ belongsTo\ (\ ?\ a_1\ ,\ ?\ act_1\ )\ ,\ runsOn\ (\ ?\ r_1\ ,\ ?\ s_1\ )\ ,\ hasGot\ (\ ?\ s_1\ ,\ ?\ act_2\ )\ ,\ differentFrom\ (\ ?\ act_1\ ,\ ?\ act_2\ )\ ->\ Error\ (\ ?\ a_1\ ,\ Error\ )$

The above SWRL rule verifies whether there is an action a1 belonging to action type act1 that is applied to resource r1, which runs on service s1, which has an action type act2; if act1 and act2 are verified to be incompatible (using the *differentFrom* predicate), an instance of class Error is created, recording a1. Essentially, using this rule we can verify that all the *system* instances on which the action is granted are compatible with the *actionType*. Violations are recorded into Error.

As a technical note, we observe that as a general outcome of the adoption of the *Open World Assumption*, even if we could enforce the existence of the loops, we would not be able to require that such loops be explicitly stated into the assertional part of the semantic model (*A-box*). At the opposite end, due to decidability issues (DL safe rules), the rule-based component of the language operates in a kind of *Closed World Assumption* (CWA) limited to the nodes. This means that a forward chaining rule can be triggered by any property derived by the reasoning, but involving only nodes that are explicitly named in the A-box. Then, we can operate only on nodes and properties explicitly stated in the semantic model. Furthermore, rules can freely combine as antecedent triple patterns to capture complex topological structures, and this solves the lack of complex property chains of *Description Logics*. This means that we can check for loops, or for the absence of loops, by adding custom rules to the ontology. However, SWRL safe rules can consume only positive knowledge, so they can be used to directly detect errors that consist in the existence of some structure in the ontology, that is, the existence of a loop.

To summarize, Semantic Web technology offers an interesting potential for detecting conflicts in a variety of settings. The integration with a rich environment of tools, open source and commercial, together with the increasing familiarity that users are acquiring on them, makes this option particularly interesting for the realization of sophisticated conflict-detection solutions. These approaches support the flexible definition and identification of conflicts, going beyond the classifications introduced in this chapter and adapting the model to the specific requirements of every application scenario.

7. SUMMARY

The detection and management of conflicts in security policies is an important topic for both the research and industrial community. The chapter was not exhaustive in its treatment of the topic, though it is quite extensive. The goal was to focus on the detection of conflicts, considering abstract and executable policies, and illustrating in greater detail the detection of policy conflicts in computer networks, which is the area that today sees the greater industrial support. Support in industrial products can be expected to appear in the near future for security policies in other scenarios and at a variety of abstraction levels. The discussion of Semantic Web technology has shown how this family of tools can be applied to this task, offering a strategy that can be of particular interest for deployment in real systems.

We expect that conflict detection techniques will become common components of tools for the design and configuration of security. The *PoSecCo* project, which is described in Chapter 23, aims at realizing a policy-based security management, and it represents an interesting example of such a system.

Finally, let's move on to the real interactive part of this chapter: review questions/exercises, hands-on projects, case projects, and optional team case project. The answers and/or solutions by chapter can be found in the Online Instructor's Solutions Manual.

CHAPTER REVIEW QUESTIONS/EXERCISES

True/False

1. True or False? The evolution of information systems is continuously increasing the capabilities and range of offered services, leading to infrastructures that see the participation of a larger number of users, a greater level of integration among separate systems, and a correspondingly larger impact of possible misbehaviors.
2. True or False? A typical top-down representation of the protection of an information system might consist of five layers.
3. True or False? Security requirements are a low-level, declarative representation of the rules according to which access control must be regulated.
4. True or False? Policies represent how security requirements are mapped to the systems used for service provisioning.
5. True or False? Abstract policies provide a formal representation of access control and its behavior.

Multiple Choice

1. What describes the access control policy in a way that can be immediately processed by an access control component?
   A. Privacy-enhancing technology
   B. Location technology
   C. Web-based

D. Executable policies

E. Data controller

2. What mechanisms correspond to the low-level functions that implement the executable policies?

A. Policy enforcement

B. Location technology

C. Valid

D. Privacy-enhancing technologies

E. Web technology

3. What conflicts arise when principals are authorized to do an action *a* on a resource *r* by *a* positive authorization, and forbidden to do the same action *a* on the resource *r* by a negative authorization?

A. Data minimization

B. *XACML*

C. Private information

D. Contradictory

E. Security

4. What conflicts arise when an authorization is dominated by other authorizations and does not contribute to the policy (its removal would not modify the behavior of the system)?

A. Privacy metrics

B. Retention time

C. Redundant

D. Privacy preferences

E. Taps

5. What conflicts occur when the conflict can never manifest itself in a system?

A. Irrelevant

B. Anonymous communication

C. Data-handling policies

D. Disclose-to

E. Social engineering

EXERCISE

Problem

What is meant by the phrase "where technically feasible?"

Hands-On Projects

Project

What is meant by the phrase "reasonable business judgment?"

Case Projects

Problem

What is meant by *data, documents, documentation*, "*logs*, and *records*? What are the differences between these terms?

Optional Team Case Project

Problem

What are some sample security policy test procedures?

ACKNOWLEDGMENTS

This work was partially funded by the European Community in the scope of the research project PoSecCo (project no. 257129), under the Information and Communication Technologies (ICT) theme of the 7th Framework Programme for R&D (FP7). The work by Stefano Paraboschi was partially supported by the PRIN 2008 project PEPPER (2008SY2PH4) and the PRIN 2010-11 project GenData-2020.

REFERENCES

[1] A. Anderson, eXtensible access control markup language (XACML), Identity. <http://www.oasis-open.org/committees/xacml/>, 2006.

[2] S. Jajodia, P. Samarati, V.S. Subrahmanian, A logical language for expressing authorizations, Proceedings of the 1997 IEEE Symposium on Security and Privacy. SP '97, IEEE Computer Society, Washington, DC, USA, 199731−41.

[3] N. Damianou, N. Dulay, E. Lupu, M. Sloman, The ponder policy specification language, Proceedings of the International Workshop on Policies for Distributed Systems and Networks. POLICY '01, Springer-Verlag, London, UK, 200118−38.

[4] L. Kagal, T. Finin, A. Joshi, A policy language for a pervasive computing environment, Proceedings of the 4th IEEE International Workshop on Policies for Distributed Systems and Networks. POLICY '03, IEEE Computer Society, Washington, DC, USA, 200363−74.

[5] G. Tonti, J.M. Bradshaw, R. Jeffers, R. Montanari, N. Suri, A. Uszok, Se- mantic web languages for policy representation and reasoning: a comparison of KAoS, in: D. Fensel, K.P. Sycara, J. Mylopoulos (Eds.), International Semantic Web Conference, Springer, 2003, pp. 419−437.

[6] E. Lupu, M. Sloman, Conflicts in policy-based distributed systems management, IEEE TSE 25 (6) (1999).

[7] N. Coward, Y. Yoshida, Java Servlet Specification Version 2.4. Technical report, 2003.

[8] M. Casalino, R. Thion, M.S. Hacid, Access control configuration for j2ee web applications: a formal perspective, in: S. Fischer-Hbner, S. Katsikas, G. Quirchmayr (Eds.), *Trust, Privacy and Security in Digital Business*. Volume 7449 of Lecture Notes in Computer Science, Springer, Berlin Heidelberg, 2012, pp. 30−35.

[9] A. Rubinger, B. Burke, R. Monson-Haefel, Enterprise JavaBeans 3.1. Java Series. O'Reilly Media, Incorporated, 2010.

[10] E. Al-Shaer, H. Hamed, Modeling and management of firewall policies, IEEE Trans. Net. Serv. Manage 1 (1) (2004) 2−10.

[11] A.R. Khakpour, A.X. Liu, Quantifying and querying network reachability. In: Proc. of the 2010 IEEE 30th Int. Conf. on Distributed Computing Systems, Washington, DC, USA, 2010, pp. 817−826.

[12] D. Taylor, Survey and taxonomy of packet classification techniques, ACM Comput. Surv. 37 (3) (2005) 238−275.

[13] A. Wool, A quantitative study of firewall configuration errors, Computer 37 (2004) 62−67.

[14] A. Wool, Trends in firewall configuration errors: measuring the holes in swiss cheese, IEEE Internet Comput. 14 (2010) 58−65.

[15] Insecure.Com LLC: Network mapper <http://nmap.org/>.

[16] T. Hachers Choice, Amap <http://thc.org/thc-amap/>.

[17] T.N. Security, Nessus vulnerability scanner. <http://www.tenable.com/products/nessus/nessus-product-overview>.

[18] A. Mayer, A. Wool, E. Ziskind, Fang: a firewall analysis engine, in: Proc. of the 2000 IEEE Symposium on Security and Privacy, Washington, DC, USA, 2000, pp. 177−187.

[19] A. Wool, Architecting the lumeta firewall analyzer, in: Proc. of the 10th Conference on USENIX Security Symposium, Vol. 10, Berkeley, CA, USA, 2001, 7−7.

[20] A. Mayer, A. Wool, E. Ziskind, Offline firewall analysis, Int. J. Inf. Secur. 5 (3) (2006) 125−144.

[21] S. Hazelhurst, A. Attar, R. Sinnappan, Algorithms for improving the dependability of firewall and filter rule lists, in: Proc. of the 2000 Int. Conf. on Dependable Systems and Networks, Washington, DC, USA, 2000, pp. 576−585.

[22] A.X. Liu, M.G. Gouda, Firewall policy queries, IEEE Trans. Parallel Distrib. Syst. 20 (2009) 766−777.

[23] J.D. Moffett, M.S. Sloman, Policy conflict analysis in distributed system management, J. Organ. Comput. 4 (1) (1993) 1−22.

[24] E. Lupu, M. Sloman, Conflicts in policy-based distributed system management, IEEE Trans. Software Eng. 25 (6) (1999) 852−869.

[25] M. Sloman, Policy driven management for distributed systems, J. Net. Syst. Manage 2 (4) (1994) 333−360.

[26] H. Adiseshu, S. Suri, G.M. Parulkar, Detecting and resolving packet filter conflicts, INFOCOM (2000) 1203−1212.

[27] F. Baboescu, G. Varghese, Fast and scalable conflict detection for packet classi- fiers, Comput. Netw. 42 (6) (2003) 717−735.

[28] V. Srinivasan, S. Suri, G. Varghese, Packet classification using tuple space search, in: Proc. of the conference on Applications, technologies, architectures, and protocols for computer communication, New York, NY, USA, 1999, pp. 135−146.

[29] C. Basile, A. Cappadonia, A. Lioy, Geometric interpretation of policy specification, in: IEEE Policy 2008, New York, NY, 2008, pp. 78−81.

[30] C. Basile, A. Cappadonia, A. Lioy, Network-level access control policy analysis and transformation, IEEE/ACM Trans. Networking (2012).

[31] M. Benelbahri, A. Bouhoula, Tuple based approach for anomalies detection within firewall filtering rules, in: ISCC 2007, Aveiro, Portugal, 2007, pp. 63−70.

[32] S. Thanasegaran, Y. Yin, Y. Tateiwa, Y. Katayama, N. Takahashi, A topological approach to detect conflicts in firewall policies, in: IPDPS 2009, Rome, Italy, 2009, pp. 1−7.

[33] S. Ferraresi, S. Pesic, L. Trazza, A. Baiocchi, Automatic conflict analysis and resolution of traffic filtering policy for firewall and security gateway, in: ICC'07, Glasgow, Scotland, 2007, pp. 1304−1310.

[34] M.G. Gouda, X.Y.A. Liu, Firewall design: consistency, completeness, and com- pactness, in: Proc. of the 24th Int. Conf. on Distributed Computing Systems (ICDCS'04), Washington, DC, USA, 2004, pp. 320−327.

[35] A.X. Liu, M.G. Gouda, Complete redundancy detection in firewalls, in: Proc. of the 19th annual IFIP WG 11.3 working conference on Data and Applications Security, 2005, pp. 193−206.

[36] J.G. Alfaro, N. Boulahia-Cuppens, F. Cuppens, Complete analysis of configuration rules to guarantee reliable network security policies, Int. J. Inf. Secur. 7 (2) (2008) 103−122.

[37] J. Garcia-Alfaro, F. Cuppens, N. Cuppens-Boulahia, S. Preda, Mirage: a management tool for the analysis and deployment of network security policies, in: Proc. of the 5th Int. Workshop on data privacy management, 2011, pp. 203−215.

[38] H. Hu, G.J. Ahn, K. Kulkarni, Ontology-based policy anomaly management for autonomic computing, in: D. Georgakopoulos, J.B.D. Joshi (Eds.), CollaborateCom, 2011, pp. 487−494.

[39] A.K. Bandara, A.C. Kakas, E.C. Lupu, A. Russo, Using argumentation logic for firewall configuration management, Integr. Network Manage. (2009) 180−187.

[40] A.X. Liu, E. Torng, C.R. Meiners, Firewall compressor: an algorithm for mini- mizing firewall policies, INFOCOM (2008) 176−180.

[41] L. Buttyan, G. Pek, T.V. Thong, Consistency verification of stateful firewalls is not harder than the stateless case, Infocommun. J. 54 (2009/2-3) (2009) 1−8.

[42] M.G. Gouda, A.X. Liu, A model of stateful firewalls and its properties, in: Proc. of the IEEE Int. Conf. on Dependable Systems and Networks (DSN-05), Yokohama, Japan, 2005.

[43] F. Cuppens, N. Cuppens-Boulahia, J. Garca-Alfaro, T. Moataz, X. Rimasson, Handling stateful firewall anomalies, in: Information Security and Privacy Research—27th IFIP TC 11 Information Security and Privacy Conference, SEC 2012, Heraklion, Crete, Greece, June 4−6, 2012. Proceedings. vol. 376, 2012, pp. 174−186.

[44] E. Al-Shaer, H. Hamed, R. Boutaba, M. Hasan, Conflict classification and analysis of distributed firewall policies, IEEE JSAC 23 (10) (2005) 2069−2084.

[45] H. Hamed, E. Al-Shaer, W. Marrero, Modeling and verification of ipsec and vpn security policies, Proceedings of the 13TH IEEE International Conference on Network Protocols. ICNP '05, IEEE Computer Society, Washington, DC, USA, 2005259−278.

[46] Z. Fu, S.F. Wu, H. Huang, K. Loh, F. Gong, I. Baldine, et al. Ipsec/vpn security policy: correctness, conflict detection, and resolution, in: POLICY, 2001, pp. 39−56.

[47] H.M. Sun, S.Y. Chang, Y.H. Chen, B.Z. He, C.K. Chen, The design and im- plementation of IPsec conflict avoiding and recovering system. TENCON 2007 -2007 IEEE Region 10 Conference, 2007, pp. 1−4.

[48] O. Lassila, R.R. Swick, Resource description framework (RDF), Model and Syntax Specification, 1999.

[49] S. Bechhofer, F. van Harmelen, J. Hendler, I. Horrocks, D.L. McGuinness, P.F. Patel- Schneider, et al., OWL Web Ontology Language Reference. Technical report, W3C. <http://www.w3.org/TR/owl-ref/>, 2004.

[50] F. Baader, D. Calvanese, D.L. McGuinness, D. Nardi, P.F. Patel-Schneider (Eds.), Description Logic Handbook, Cambridge University Press, 2003.

[51] T. Finin, A. Joshi, L. Kagal, J. Niu, R. Sandhu, W. Winsborough, et al., R owl bac: representing role based access control in OWLl, in: Proc. of SACMAT 2008, (ACM).

## Chapter 46

Supporting User Privacy Preferences in Digital Interactions

Sara Foresti

Dipartimento di Informatica Università degli Studi di Milano via Bramante 65, 26013 Crema (CR), Italy

Pierangela Samarati

Dipartimento di Informatica Università degli Studi di Milano via Bramante 65, 26013 Crema (CR), Italy

1. INTRODUCTION

The advancements in Information and Communications Technology (ICT) allow users to take more and more advantage of the availability of online services (and resources) that can be accessed anywhere anytime. In such a scenario, the server providing the service and the requesting user may be unknown to each other. As a consequence, traditional access control systems [1] based on the preliminary identification and authentication of users requesting access to a service cannot be adopted and are usually not suited to open scenarios [2–4]. The solutions proposed to allow servers to regulate access to the services they offer, while not requiring users to manage a huge number of accounts, rely on *attribute-based access control* mechanisms [5–13]. Policies regulating access to services define conditions that the requesting client must satisfy to gain access to the service of interest. Upon receiving a request to access a service, the server will not return a yes/no reply, but it will send the client the conditions that she must satisfy to be authorized to access the service. To prove to the server the possession of the attributes required to gain the access, the client releases *digital certificates* (*credentials*) signed by a trusted third party, the *certification authority*, who declares under its responsibility that the certificate holder possesses the attributes stated in the certificate. Practically, credentials are the digital representation of paper certificates (id card, passport, credit card). The adoption of credentials in access control has several advantages. First, credential-based access control enables clients to conveniently access Web services, without the need to remember a different <*username, password*> pair for each system with which she wants to interact. Second, it offers better protection against adversaries interested in improperly acquiring users' access privileges.

The use of credentials to enforce access control restrictions in open environments has been widely studied in the last 15 years. Most attention has, however, been devoted to the server side of the problem, proposing a number of novel *policy languages*, for specifying access control rules [5,6,11–13]; *policy engines*, for the evaluation of access requests and the enforcement of policy restrictions [10,11,13,14]; and strategies for *communicating* access conditions to the requesting clients, possibly engaging a negotiation protocol [10,11,13–18]. Since the interacting parties are assumed to be unknown to each other, the client may not know which attributes/credentials to release to gain access to the service of interest. As a consequence, the server should send the client its policy, which may, however, be considered sensitive and therefore needs to be adequately protected before being disclosed. Most of the current approaches implicitly assume that clients adopt an approach symmetrical to the one used by servers for regulating access to the sensitive information certified by their credentials. Although these solutions are expressive and powerful, they do not fully support the specific protection requirements of the clients. In fact, clients are interested in a solution that is expressive and flexible enough to support an intuitive and user-friendly definition of the sensitivity/privacy levels that they perceive as characterizing their data. These preferences are used to choose which credentials to release when more than one subset of credentials satisfy the access control policy defined by the server (to buy a medicine, a patient needs to prove her identity by releasing either her identity card or her passport).

This chapter provides an overview of the privacy issues arising in open environments, both from the client and from the server points of view, and illustrates some solutions proposed to overcome these problems. The remainder of this chapter is organized as follows. Section 2 introduces basic concepts and describes the desiderata of privacy-aware access control systems operating in open environments. Sections 3, 4, 5, and 6 illustrate some recent proposals that permit clients to specify privacy preferences that are then used to determine which credentials to disclose to gain access to a service of interest. Section 7 focuses on the server side of the problem, describing approaches that permit regulating the disclosure of sensitive access control policies. Section 8 presents some open issues that still need to be addressed. Finally, Section 9 presents our summary and concluding remarks.

2. BASIC CONCEPTS AND DESIDERATA

In this section, we describe the concepts that are the basis of the proposals we will describein the chapter, and we discuss the desiderata that an attribute-based access control system should satisfy to effectively support both client and server privacy preferences.

Client Portfolio

The information that a client can provide to a server to gain access to a service is organized in a *portfolio* including both *credentials* signed by third parties and certifying client properties, and *declarations* stating uncertified properties uttered by the client [6]. Each credential c in the client portfolio is characterized by: a unique identifier $id(c)$, an issuer $issuer(c)$, a set of attributes $attributes(c)$, and a credential type $type(c)$. The type of credential determines the set of attributes it certifies. Credential types are traditionally organized in a rooted *hierarchy*, where intermediate nodes represent abstractions defined over specific credential types that correspond to the leaves of the hierarchy [19]. Formally, a hierarchy H of credential types is a pair $(T, \leq_{isa})$, where T is the set of all credential types and abstractions defined over them, and $\leq_{isa}$ is a partial-order relationship on T. Given two credential types t_i and

t_j, $t_i \leq_{isa} t_j$ if t_j is an abstraction of t_i. For instance, *photo_id* is an abstraction of credential types *id_card* and *passport* (i.e., $id\_card \leq_{isa} photo\_id$ and $passport \leq_{isa} photo\_id$). The root of the hierarchy is node *, representing any credential type. We note that declarations are usually modeled as a type of credential, signed by the client herself. Figure 46.1 illustrates a hierarchy of credential types.

The hierarchy of credential types is a knowledge shared between the client and the server. In fact, while a client knows exactly the different instances of credential types composing her portfolio, the server formulates its requests over credential types since it cannot be aware of the instances composing the client portfolio. We note that a client may possess different credentials of the same type (she can have more than one credit card).

Depending on the cryptographic protocol used for their generation, credentials can be classified as *atomic* or *nonatomic*. Atomic credentials are the most common kind of credentials used today in distributed systems (X.509 certificates) and can only be released as a whole. As a consequence, even if an atomic credential certifies attributes that are not required to gain access to a service, if the client decides to release it, these attributes will be disclosed to the server. Nonatomic credentials have recently been proposed as a successful approach to limit data disclosure (U-Prove and Idemix [20,21]). Credentials generated adopting these technologies permit the client to selectively release a subset of the attributes certified by the credential (as well as the existence of the credential itself). Note that the release of an attribute (or a set thereof) certified by a nonatomic credential entails the disclosure of the existence in the client portfolio of the credential itself. Clearly, declarations are nonatomic credentials.

Attributes within credentials are characterized by a *type*, a *name*, and a *value* (attribute *Name* of type *Name* with value *Bob*), which can either depend only on the client or on the specific credential certifying the attribute. In the first case, the attribute is *credential-independent* since

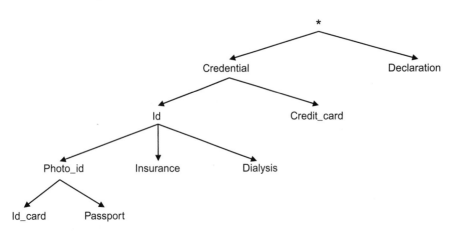

FIGURE 46.1 An example of hierarchy of credential types.

TABLE 46.1 An Example of a Client Portfolio.

id(c)	Atomic	Type(c)	Attributes(c)
MyIdCard	✓	id_card	Name, DoB, City
MyPassport		passport	Name, DoB, Country
MyVISA	✓	credit_card	Name, *VISANum*, *VISALimit*
MyAmEx	✓	credit_card	Name, *AmExNum*, *AmExLimit*
MyDialysis		dialysis	Name, City
MyInsurance	✓	insurance	Name, *Company*, *Coverage*
MyDecl		declaration	Name, DoB, City, Country, *VISANum*, *VISALimit*, *AmExNum*, *AmExLimit*, *Company*, *Coverage*, e-mail

its value is the same, independently from the credential certifying it (*Name* and *DoB* are credential-independent attributes). In the second case, the attribute is *credential-dependent* since its value depends not only on the credential holder, but also on the specific instance of the credential certifying it (attribute type *CCNum*, representing the credit-card number, is a credential-dependent attribute since each credit card has a different number).

For instance, Table 46.1 illustrates a client portfolio composed of four atomic and three nonatomic credentials. In the table, credential-independent attributes are in roman, while credential-dependent attributes are in *italic*.

Disclosure Policies

Attribute-based access control restricts access to server service, depending on the attributes and credentials that the requesting client discloses to the server. The policy regulating access to services is therefore defined over attributes and credentials provided by clients. Since the server may not know the requesting client and therefore will ignore the credential instances in her portfolio, the access control policy is defined considering only the hierarchy of credential types, which represents a common knowledge to the interacting parties. An access control policy is defined as a Boolean formula composed of basic conditions *cond* of the form ($term_1$ o $term_2$), where o is a predicate operator ($>$, $<$, $=$), and $term_1$ and $term_2$ are its operands. The operands of a basic condition can be either constant values or (certified or declared) attributes represented by terms of the form *c.a*, where *c* is a variable representing a credential and *a* is the name of the attribute. For instance, basic condition *Coverage* > 10,000 USD requires that the coverage offered by insurance is higher than 10,000 USD to access the service. The server may also define restrictions on the type of credentials that should certify the requested attributes and/or require that a set of attributes in the policy are certified by the same

credential. As an example, policy (*type(c)* = *insurance*) ∧ (*c.Company* ≠ 'A') ∧ (*c.Coverage* > 10,000 USD) requires that attributes *Company* and *Coverage* are certified by the same credential *c*, of type *insurance*.

Trust Negotiation

Since clients and servers operating in open environments are assumed to be unknown to each other, they interact with the aim of building a trust relationship that will permit the client to gain access to a service offered by the server. This trust relationship is built step by step through the exchange of credentials. Since credentials may certify sensitive information, their release is often regulated, as for services, by access control policies. Usually, these conditions require the counterpart's release of another credential (or set thereof). As an example, a user agrees to release the certificate stating her dialysis condition to a server only if the server proves (through a certificate) to be a medical institution or a pharmacy recognized by the Health Ministry.

To gain access to a service, the client and the server must then find a sequence of certificate exchange, called *strategy*, satisfying the access control policies of both parties. For instance, with reference to the above example, a successful strategy that permits the user to buy the medicine of interest consists of the following steps: (1) the patient sends her request to the pharmacy; (2) the pharmacy answers with a request for a certificate proving that the user has a nephrological disease; (3) the client, in turn, asks the pharmacy for the certificate proving that it is recognized by the Health Ministry; (4) the pharmacy releases to the client the requested certificate; (5) the client then discloses to the pharmacy her dialysis certificate; and (6) finally, the server grants access to the service. Different approaches have been proposed in the literature with the aim of identifying a successful trust negotiation strategy [10,11,13–18] that depends not only on the policies defined by the parties and on the credentials at their disposal, but also on their choice of disclosure/non-disclosure of their data. As an example, an eager strategy would disclose a credential as soon as the policy regulating its release is satisfied, while a more parsimonious strategy permits the release of a credential only if there exists a *successful strategy* that will finally grant the client access to the service. Given the policies and credentials of the interacting client and server, more than one successful strategy may exist. For instance, with reference to the portfolio in Table 46.1, policy $(type(c) = id) \land (c. DoB < 01/01/1994)$ can be satisfied by the client releasing either credential *MyIdCard* or credential *MyPassport*. Although all the successful strategies may seem equivalent, this is generally not true. Both the client and the server may prefer to release a credential over another one because they perceive a different sensitivity level associated with the information that credentials certify. For instance, the client may prefer to release her *id_card* over her *passport*.

Client Privacy Preferences

Given the server request, the client needs to determine which credentials and/or attributes to disclose to satisfy it. This task becomes more difficult if different subsets of credentials and/or attributes in the client portfolio can be used to fulfill the server policy, since the client needs to choose among them. Ideally, the choice should be driven by the sensitivity level that the client perceives for her credentials and attributes, as she will be more willing to disclose less sensitive portfolio components. It is therefore necessary to provide clients with a flexible and effective system that automatically determines the release strategy that better satisfies her privacy preferences. To this purpose, a flexible and expressive model for representing privacy preferences needs to be defined. The following checklist illustrates the main desiderata that a privacy-aware access control system should satisfy (see checklist: An Agenda for Action for a Privacy-Aware Access Control System) [22].

An Agenda for Action for a Privacy-Aware Access Control System

The main desiderata that a privacy-aware access control system should satisfy are as follows (check all tasks completed):

_____1. *Fine-grained preference specification.* The privacy preferences associated with attributes and credentials in the client portfolio reflect the sensitivity perceived by the credential owner for the personal information represented by the attribute/credential. The model should support the definition of privacy preferences for each instance of attribute and credential in the client portfolio, meaning that different instances of the same credential type (and credential-dependent attribute) might be associated with different privacy preferences. For instance, with reference to the portfolio in Table 46.1, the client may prefer to release his VISA credit card instead of his AmEx.

_____2. *Inheritance of privacy preferences.* To provide flexibility in the definition of privacy preferences and a user-friendly mechanism for their specification, the model should take advantage of the hierarchy of credential types characterizing the client portfolio. When the client portfolio is composed of a huge number of attributes and credentials, it might be difficult for the client to specify a different preference value for each credential and attribute. Privacy preferences associated with abstractions of credential types could, however, be inherited by all its specifications, if not overwritten by a more specific preference value, thus reducing the client overhead. For instance, with reference to the hierarchy of credential types in Figure 46.1 and the portfolio in

Table 46.1, the client may specify a single privacy preference associated with credential type *photo_-id*, which is automatically inherited by credentials *MyIdCard* and *MyPassport*.

_____3. *Partial-order relationship and composition operator.* The domain of privacy preferences should be characterized by a (partial) order relationship $\succeq$ that permits precisely determining whether a given piece of personal information is more or less sensitive than another. The domain should also be characterized by a composition operator $\oplus$, which permits computing the privacy preference value characterizing the release of a set of attributes and/or credentials. As an example, if the domain of privacy preferences is the set of positive integer numbers, the partial-order relationship could be the "greater than" relationship ($\geq$), while the composition operator could be the sum operator ($+$).

_____4. *Sensitive associations.* In different scenarios, the combined release of a set of attributes and/or credentials is considered more (or less) sensitive than the release of each portfolio component singularly taken. For instance, with reference to the portfolio in Table 46.1, the client may consider the combined release of attributes *DoB* and *City* more sensitive than the release of each of the two attributes, since their combination could be exploited to infer the identity of the client [23]. On the other hand, she may value the release of *City* and *Country* less sensitively than the release of the two attributes singularly taken, due to the dependency between the values of the two attributes. As a consequence, the model should support the definition of a privacy preference value for the combined release of a set of attributes and/or credentials that is different from the result of the combination of the privacy preferences of the items in the set.

_____5. *Disclosure constraints.* There are situations where the client needs to specify restrictions on the combined release of portfolio components, since she wants to keep the association among a subset of attributes and/or credentials confidential, or limit their combined release. For instance, with reference to the portfolio in Table 46.1, the client may not be willing to release credential *MyDialysis* together with attribute *DoB*, to prevent the server from exploiting this information for data-mining purposes (to analyze the age of people with nephrologic diseases).

_____6. *Context-based preferences.* The privacy preferences associated with attributes and credentials may vary depending on the context in which their release is requested (and also depending on the requested service and/or on the server providing it). For instance, the client may be more willing to release her dialysis certificate to a pharmacy for buying a medicine than to a hotel for booking a room.

_____7. *History-based preferences.* The preference of the client toward disclosing one credential (attribute, respectively) over another one may depend on the

history of past interactions with the server offering the service. As a matter of fact, if the server already knows the attributes and credentials released by the client during a previous interaction, the client may be more willing to release the same (or a different) set of portfolio components. For instance, with reference to the portfolio in Table 46.1, assume that the client released credential *MyVISA* to a server to buy a service. When interacting again with the same server to buy another service, the client may prefer to use the same credit card, instead of also releasing credential *MyAmEx.*

_____8. *Proof of possession.* Thanks to novel technologies, clients can release proofs of possession of certificates and proofs of the satisfaction of conditions [20,21]. As a consequence, the model should also permit the client to specify privacy preferences associated with proofs (besides attributes and credentials on which proofs are defined). For instance, with reference to the portfolio in Table 46.1, the client may consider more sensitive the release of her *DoB* than the release of a proof that she is at least 18.

_____9. *User-friendly preference specification.* The definition of privacy preferences should be easy for the client, who may not be familiar with access control systems. As a consequence, it is necessary to provide clients with interfaces that permit easily defining preferences without introducing inconsistencies.

Server Privacy Preferences

With attribute-based access control, servers regulate access to their services based on the attributes and certificates presented by the requesting client. Upon receiving an access request, the server needs to communicate to the client the policy that she should satisfy to possibly gain access to the service. The access control policy could, however, be sensitive, and the server may not be willing to disclose it completely to the client: While the communication of the complete policy favors the privacy of the client (since she can avoid disclosing her attributes and credentials if they would not satisfy the conditions in the policy), the communication of the attributes involved in the policy only favors the privacy of the server (since the specific conditions are not disclosed). Also, different portions of the same policy may be subject to different confidentiality requirements. For instance, assume that a pharmacy grants clients access to the online medicine purchase service only if the clients' insurance coverage is higher than 10,000 USD and the insurance company is not on the pharmacy black list. The pharmacy might not

mind disclosing the fact that only clients with insurance coverage greater than 10,000 USD can access its services, but it does not want to reveal its black list. The system managing the disclosure of server policies should satisfy the following desiderata.

- *Disclosure policy.* The server should be able to define, at a fine-granularity level, how policy release should be regulated.
- *Policy communication.* The communication of the access control policy regulating access to the requested service to the client should guarantee that privacy requirements are satisfied and that the client has enough information to determine the set of attributes and/or credentials she needs to disclose to possibly gain access to the service. It is therefore necessary to define a mechanism that adequately transforms the access control policy before communicating it to the client.
- *Integration with client mechanisms.* The approach designed to regulate policy release should be integrated with the one designed to manage the release of portfolio components at the client side.

Note that in a negotiation process, both the client requesting access to a service and the server providing it possess a portfolio that regulates the disclosure of credentials and attributes composing it, according to their access control policy.

3. COST-SENSITIVE TRUST NEGOTIATION

This section discusses a solution that takes disclosure preferences into consideration in attribute-based access control [24]. The authors propose to associate a *sensitivity cost* $w(c)$ with each credential c in the client (and server) portfolio, and with each access control policy p regulating credentials disclosure and access to services. A policy p is defined as a Boolean formula over the credentials in the counterparty's portfolio. A Boolean variable representing credential c in policy p is *true* if c has already been disclosed; it is *false* otherwise. The sensitivity cost associated with credential c (policy p, respectively) models how much the credential's owner (party who defined the policy, respectively) values the release of the credential (policy, respectively) and the disclosure of the sensitive information that the credential certifies. Intuitively, a client (server, respectively) is more willing to disclose credentials (policies, respectively) with lower sensitivity cost, and, vice versa, she prefers to keep credentials (policies, respectively) with high sensitivity cost confidential. For instance, Tables 46.2 and 46.3, respectively, illustrate a client portfolio (server portfolio, respectively). For each credential, the table reports the policy regulating its

disclosure, the sensitivity cost of the credential, and the sensitivity cost of its policy. Constant value TRUE is used in policy definition to model the case when the release of a credential is free; that is, it is not regulated by a policy. (The portfolio in Table 46.2 is a simplified version of the portfolio in Table 46.1.)

The goal of the client and the server engaging in a negotiation protocol is to *minimize* the sensitivity cost of the credentials and policies exchanged during a successful negotiation strategy. This optimization problem can be formulated as follows [24].

Problem 1: Minimum Sensitivity Cost problem

Let C_s be the set of server credentials and services; P_s the set of policies regulating the disclosure of server credentials and access to services; C_c the set of client credentials; P_c the set of policies regulating the disclosure of client credentials; $w:C_s \cup P_s \cup C_c \cup P_c \rightarrow \mathbb{R}$ the sensitivity cost function; and $s \in C_s$ the service requested by the client. Find an exchange sequence of credentials and policies such that:

1. s is released to the client;
2. the policy regulating the disclosure of each credential released to the counterpart is satisfied before credential release;
3. the sum of the sensitivity costs of released credentials and policies is minimum.

The problem of computing a Minimum Sensitivity Cost strategy is NP-hard [24], and therefore any algorithm that solves it at optimum has exponential cost in the size of its input (the number of credentials and policies in $C_s \cup P_s \cup C_c \cup P_c$). In [24] the authors propose two different heuristic approaches for computing a good (although nonoptimal) solution to the problem. These heuristics have polynomial computational complexity and can be adopted when policies can be freely disclosed and when they are associated with a sensitivity cost, respectively.

Nonsensitive Policies

The solution proposed for the simplified scenario where policies are not associated with a sensitivity cost (they can be freely released) is based on the definition of a *policy graph* modeling the policies regulating credential disclosure at both the client and server side. A policy graph $G(V,A,w)$ is defined as a weighted graph with:

- a vertex v_c for each credential c in $C_s \cup C_c$;
- a vertex v_s for each service s in C_s;
- a vertex v_T for constant value TRUE;

TABLE 46.2 An Example of Client Portfolio and Policies Regulating its Disclosure.

id(c)	w(c)	Policy p Regulating c	w(p)
MyIdCard	2	TRUE	0
MyPassport	4	TRUE	0
MyCreditCard	10	POS_register	5
MyDialysis	20	pharmacy_register	10
MyInsurance	15	pharmacy_register	10

TABLE 46.3 An Example of Server Portfolio and Policies Regulating its Disclosure.

id(c)	w(c)	Policy p regulating c	w(p)
MyPOSRegister	2	TRUE	0
MyPharmacyRegister	5	passport ∨ id_card	4

- a vertex v for each disjunction in the policies regulating credential release;
- an edge (v_i, v_j), with v_i and v_j vertexes representing credentials, if the release of the credential represented by v_i is a necessary condition to gain access to the credential represented by v_j;
- an edge (v_i, v_j), with v_i a vertex representing a credential and v_j a vertex representing a disjunction, if v_i is one of the clauses of the disjunction represented by v_j.

The weight of a vertex representing a credential corresponds to the sensitivity cost of the credential it represents, while other vertexes do not have weight. For instance, consider the access control policies in Tables 46.2 and 46.3 and service *MedicineBooking*, regulated by policy $p = dialysis \vee (id\_card \wedge (credit\_card \vee insurance))$. Figure 46.2(a) illustrates the policy graph modeling the access control policies in the system.

The first step of the negotiation process consists in disclosing the policies regulating credential release and access to services at the client and at the server side. This information permits one to correctly build the policy graph. Note that this disclosure is permitted thanks to the assumption that policies are not sensitive in this simplified scenario. The minimum sensitivity cost problem then translates into the equivalent problem of determining a *Minimum Directed Acyclic Graph* for the policy graph, starting at vertex v_T (representing value TRUE) and

ending at vertex v_s representing the requested service s. Formally, a Minimum Directed Acyclic Graph is defined as follows.

Definition 1: Minimum Directed Acyclic Graph

Let $G(V, A, w)$ be a policy graph, v_T be the vertex representing value TRUE, and v_s be the vertex representing service s. A directed acyclic graph starting at v_T and ending at v_s is a subgraph $G'(V', A', w)$ of G such that:

1. G' is acyclic;
2. $v_T, v_s, \in V'$;
3. $\nexists(v_i, v_T) \in A', v_i \in V'$;
4. $\nexists(v_s, v_i) \in A', v_i \in V'$;
5. $\forall v_i \in V', \exists v_T | v_i$, where $v_T | v_i$ is a path starting at v_T and ending at v_i;
6. $\forall v_i \in V', \forall(v_i, v_j) \in A$, where v_i represents a credential, $(v_i, v_j) \in A', v_j \in V'$;
7. $\nexists G''(V'', A'', w)$ that satisfies all the previous conditions and such that $\sum_{v \in V''} w(v) < \sum_{v \in V'} w(v)$.

It is easy to see that a directed acyclic graph starting at v_T and ending at v_s represents a successful negotiation strategy for service s. Therefore, the minimum sensitivity cost problem and the problem of computing a minimum directed acyclic graph from vertex v_T to vertex v_s are

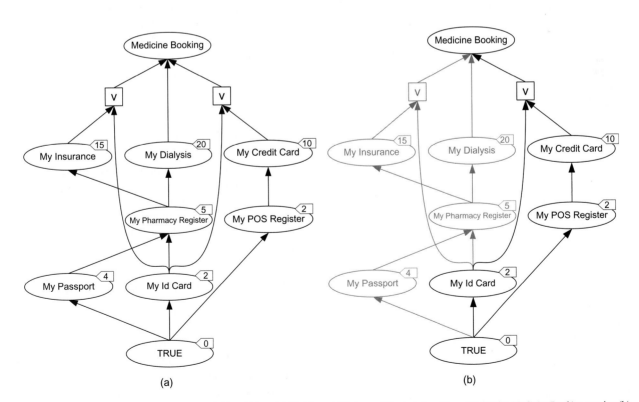

(a)   (b)

FIGURE 46.2 Policy graph for the policies in Tables 46.2 and 46.3 (a), and Minimum Directed Acyclic graph for the *MedicineBooking* service (b).

equivalent. The heuristic algorithm proposed in [24] is based on a variation of the well-known Dijkstra algorithm [25]. In [24] the authors experimentally prove that the proposed algorithm computes an optimal solution in most cases. For instance, consider the policy graph in Figure 46.2(a) and assume that the client is interested in the *MedicineBooking* service. Figure 46.2(b) illustrates a Minimum Directed Acyclic Graph for the *MedicineBooking* service with cost 14, where the vertexes and edges in the policy graph that also belong to the Minimum Directed Acyclic Graph are in black, while the other vertexes and edge are in gray.

Sensitive Policies

The solution [24] for the more complex scenario where both credentials and policies regulating their release are associated with a sensitivity cost is based on a *greedy strategy* that consists of two steps. During the first step, the interacting parties adopt an eager strategy (each party discloses to the counterpart the name of a credential as soon as the policy for its release is satisfied) to mutually exchange the name and sensitivity cost associated with credentials that could be useful for identifying a successful negotiation strategy with minimum cost. If this first step finds such a strategy, the client and the server start the second step of the protocol, which consists in enforcing the strategy discovered during the first step. For instance, with reference to the policy graph in Figure 46.2 (a), the first step consists of the sequence of releases illustrated in Figure 46.3. First, the client and the server reveal to each other the name and sensitivity cost of credentials whose release is not regulated by a policy, that is, *MyIdCard* and *MyPassport* for the client and *MyPOSRegister* for the server. These releases satisfy the

policy regulating the release of *MyCreditCard* at the client side and *MyPharmacyRegister* at the server side, whose names and sensitivity costs are disclosed. These releases, in turn, satisfy the policies regulating the disclosure of credentials *MyInsurance* and *MyDialysis* at the client side and service *MedicineBooking* at the server side. The exchange then represents a successful negotiation strategy. Note that the edges in Figure 46.3 are labeled with the cumulative sensitivity cost of the negotiation process (*MyCreditCard* is associated with cost $12 = w(MyCreditCard) + w(MyPOSRegister)$). The successful negotiation strategy computed by the first step is enforced during the second step of the protocol. Therefore, the server first discloses credential *MyPOSRegister*, and the client releases *MyIdCard*. When the client receives the credential from the server, she discloses *MyCreditCard*, thus gaining access to the *MedicineBooking* service. The overall sensitivity cost of the strategy is 14.

Open Issues

Although effective, the model and algorithms [24] suffer from some limitations. A first drawback is that the proposed approach assumes that the disclosure of access control policies does not need to be regulated, while policy release may be subject to restrictions. Also, this solution assumes that the objective of a privacy-aware negotiation protocol is to minimize the overall sensitivity cost of credentials and policies disclosed during the negotiation process. However, the goal of the two parties may be different. For instance, with reference to our example, the pharmacy offering the *MedicineBooking* service may not be interested in minimizing the sensitivity cost of the policies and credentials it needs to disclose to offer the service. On the contrary, the patient wants to minimize the sensitivity cost of the credentials she must disclose to the pharmacy. We also note that the model [24] does not satisfy all the desiderata to support privacy preferences in attribute-based access control scenarios. In fact, it only supports the definition of privacy preferences as sensitivity costs, which have a numerical domain characterized by a total order relationship ($\geq$) and by a composition operator ($+$).

4. POINT-BASED TRUST MANAGEMENT

The problem of minimizing the amount of sensitive information disclosed by a trust negotiation protocol [26] is addressed in this section, where the authors propose a *point-based trust management model*. This model assumes that policies regulating access to services and release of credentials are based on the definition of quantitative measures. More precisely, the server associates a

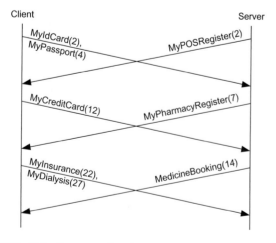

FIGURE 46.3 Sequence of exchanges between the client and the server to determine a successful negotiation strategy.

TABLE 46.4 An Example of Points *pt* and Privacy Scores *ps* Associated by the Server and the Client, Respectively, with the Credential in the Client Portfolio.

	id_card	Passport	Credit_card	Dialysis	Insurance
pt	1	1	2	3	2
ps	2	4	10	20	15

number *pt* of *points* with each credential type *t*. This value represents the trustworthiness perceived by the server for the credential issuer (credentials issued by a more reliable party will be associated with a higher number of points and vice versa). To restrict the access to its services, the server then associates a *thresholdthr* with each service. To gain access to a service *s*, the client must disclose a subset of credentials in her portfolio such that the sum of the points of the released credentials is higher than or equal to the threshold fixed by the server for *s*. Analogously, the client associates a *privacy scoreps* with each credential in her portfolio, which represents how much she values the release of the credential to an external server. The higher the privacy value of a credential, the lower the client willingness in its release. As a consequence, a client who is interested in accessing a service *s* must determine a subset of credentials in her portfolio that satisfies the threshold fixed by the server for *s*, while minimizing the privacy score of released credentials. Table 46.4 presents an example of points and privacy scores associated by the server and the client, respectively, to the credentials composing the client's portfolio.

Since the server policy might be considered sensitive, the server does not reveal the threshold associated with its services to the client. Analogously, the client does not reveal to the counterpart the privacy scores she associates with the credentials in her portfolio. As a consequence, when a client requests access to a service, she needs to identify a subset of the credentials in her portfolio that satisfies the server threshold (the access control policy regulating the release of the service) without knowing it and without revealing to the server credentials' privacy scores. More formally, the *Credential Selection* problem is an optimization problem that can be formulated, as discussed in Problem 2 below.

Problem 2: Credential Selection Problem

Let $C = \{c_1, \ldots, c_n\}$ be the set of credentials in the client portfolio; $pt(type(c_i))$ be the points associated by the server with credential type $type(c_i)$, $i = 1, \ldots, n$; $ps(c_i)$ be the privacy score associated by the client with credential c_i, $i = 1, \ldots, n$; s be the service requested by the client; and *thr* be the release threshold associated with *s*. Find a subset $D \subseteq C$ of credentials such that:

1. $\sum_{c \in D} pt(type(c)) \geq thr$;
2. $\nexists D' \subseteq C$ s.t. $\sum_{c \in D'} pt(type(c)) \geq thr$ and $\sum_{c \in D'} ps(c) < \sum_{c \in D} ps(c)$.

The first condition states that the subset of credentials in the client portfolio must satisfy the server policy, while the second condition states that the sensitive information disclosed is minimum. For instance, with reference to the points and privacy scores in Table 46.4, let us assume that the server offering service *s* (*MedicineBooking* in our example) defines a threshold $thr = 3$. The release of her *id_card* and of her *credit_card* permits the client to gain access to the service of interest ($pt(id\_card) + pt(credit\_card) = 3 \geq thr$), while minimizing the overall privacy score of released information ($ps(id\_card) + ps(credit\_card) = 12$).

Dynamic Programming Algorithm

The Credential Selection problem is NP-hard and can be rewritten into a knapsack problem, where each credential *c* can be inserted into the knapsack with weight $pt(type(c))$ and value $ps(c)$ [26]. Since the knapsack algorithm maximized the value of the items inserted in the knapsack to satisfy its capacity, while the goal of the client is that of minimizing the sensitivity of the credentials necessary to reach the threshold of interest, the solution to the credential selection problem is computed by inserting in the knapsack those credentials that will not be released. Intuitively, the knapsack problem is complementary to our problem and therefore the approach in [26] finds the complementary solution to the Credential Selection problem by exploiting a known dynamic programming algorithm for the knapsack problem [25]. The knapsack capacity *KC* is computed as the complementary of the threshold fixed by the server with respect to the clients portfolio, that is, $KC = \sum_{c \in C} pt(type(c)) - thr$, which is the difference between the sum of points associated with credential types in the client's portfolio and the threshold fixed by the server to gain access to the service. With reference to the example above, $KC = (1 + 1 + 2 + 3 + 2) - 3 = 6$.

The dynamic programming solution to the knapsack problem is based on the definition of a matrix *M* with $n + 1$ rows, where *n* is the number of items that can be inserted into the knapsack (credentials in our scenario), and $KC + 1$ columns. All the cells in the first row and in the first column of the matrix are set to zero ($M[i, 0] = 0$, $i = 0, \ldots, n$, and $M[0, j] = 0$, $j = 0, \ldots, KC$). The value of the other cells in the matrix is computed according to the following formula:

$$M[i,j] = \begin{cases} M[i-1,j], & j < pt(type(c_i)) \\ \max(M[i-1,j], \\ \quad M[i-1,i-pt(c_i)] + ps(c_i)), & j \geq pt(type(c_i)) \end{cases}$$

The values of the cells in the matrix are computed, in the order, starting from top to bottom and from left to right (by increasing value of i and j, respectively). Each cell in the matrix represents the total value of the knapsack, obtained inserting (a subset) of the items preceding the current element in the matrix without exceeding the knapsack capacity. It is obtained as the current value of the knapsack either including or not including the current element.

Table 46.5 illustrates the matrix computed considering points and privacy scores in Table 46.4. The first row in the matrix represents an empty knapsack. Cells $M[id\_card,1],\ldots,M[id\_card,6]$ in the first row model the insertion of credential *id_card* in the empty knapsack. As a consequence, the knapsack has weight 2. Cell $M[passport,2]$ is obtained by comparing the solution represented by cell $M[id\_card,2]$ (which models a knapsack including only *id_card*) with the solution $M[id\_card,1 \cup]\{passport\}$ obtained by also inserting credential *passport* into the knapsack. The weight of the two alternative solutions is, respectively, 2 and $2 + 4 = 6$. Since $6 > 2$, $M[passport,2]$ is set to 6 and it represents a knapsack including credentials *id_card* and *passport*. The other cells in the matrix are computed in the same way.

The optimal solution to the knapsack problem is represented by the value in cell $M[n,KC]$, which represents the value of the knapsack obtained trying to insert all the candidate elements in the knapsack without exceeding its capacity. To determine the elements that belong to the optimal solution, it is necessary to keep track of which item has been inserted at each step. For instance, consider the matrix in Table 46.5, cell $M[insurance,6] = 39$ is the sum of the cells in gray in the table; that is, it represent a solution including the credentials *passport*, *dialysis*, and *insurance*. Since the credentials included in the knapsack are not disclosed, the credentials disclosed by the client to gain the access are *id_card* and *credit_card*, which, as already noted, satisfy the threshold fixed by the server for the *MedicineBooking* service while minimizing privacy scores.

The traditional dynamic programming algorithm described above for the knapsack problem assumes that the client knows the points assigned by the server to credential types (or that the server knows the privacy scores that the client associates with the credentials in her portfolio). Since this assumption does not hold in the considered scenario, in [26] the authors propose to enhance the basic algorithm to permit the client and the server to interact with each other for computing a solution to the knapsack problem without the need for the client and the server to reveal to each other their secret parameters. The proposed solution consists of a secure two-party dynamic-programming protocol, which relies on homomorphic encryption to provide privacy guarantees to sensitive information [27,28].

Open Issues

The model and algorithm introduced in [26] suffer from different shortcomings. First, the client and the server must share, as common knowledge, the set of possible credentials on which the negotiation process should be based. Such knowledge may, however, put the privacy of the server policy at risk. The proposed model also assumes that the access control policy defined by the server consists of a threshold value, but in many real-world scenarios the server needs to define more expressive policies. Furthermore, the focus of the proposal, as well as the model in [24], is more on the negotiation process than on the management of the privacy preferences of the interacting parties. The solution in [26], however, represents an important step toward defining a privacy-aware access control model, even if it does not satisfy all the desiderata. In fact, this approach only supports the definition of privacy preferences as privacy scores, which have a numerical domain characterized by a total order relationship ($\geq$) and by a composition operator ($+$).

5. LOGICAL-BASED MINIMAL CREDENTIAL DISCLOSURE

The solutions in [24,26] are based on the assumption that privacy preferences can be expressed as numerical values, defined over a domain characterized by a total order relationship and an additive operator. While this assumption permits one to easily integrate privacy preferences with

TABLE 46.5 An Example of a Dynamic Programming Matrix for the Portfolio in Table 46.4.

	0	1	2	3	4	5	6
0	0	0	0	0	0	0	0
id_card	0	2	2	2	2	2	2
passport	0	4	6	6	6	6	6
credit_card	0	4	10	14	16	16	16
dialysis	0	4	14	20	24	30	34
insurance	0	4	15	20	29	35	39

traditional negotiation processes, the usability of the resulting system may be limited. In fact, it might not be easy for the final user to express her privacy preferences through numeric values, also because the adoption of numeric preference values may cause unintended side effects (dominance relationships are not explicitly defined but are implied by the values assigned to the portfolio components). To overcome these limitations, in [29], the authors propose adopting *qualitative* (instead of quantitative) preference values. The proposed solution is based on the assumption that credentials are singleton (certify one attribute only) and that the policy defined by the server is publicly available. The goal of the approach is to determine, among the successful negotiation strategies, the one that better suits the client preferences (i.e., the set of credentials that minimizes the amount of sensitive information disclosed to the server to gain access to the requested service). When the number of successful strategies is limited, the client can explicitly choose the one she prefers. However, when the number of credentials in the client portfolio increases and the server policy becomes complex, the number of successful trust negotiation strategies may grow quickly. For instance, assume that the client portfolio is composed of credentials {*Name, DoB, City, VISANum, VISALimit, AmExNum, AmExLimit, Insurance, InsCoverage, Dialysis*}, and that the policy regulating access to the *MedicineBooking* service is ((*Name* ∧ (*DoB* ∨ *City*) ∨ *Dialysis* ∨ *Insurance*) ∧ ((*VISANum* ∧ *VISALimit*) ∨ (*AmExNum* ∧ *AmExLimit*) ∨ (*InsCoverage* ∧ *DoB*)). There are 12 strategies that satisfy the access control policy. It is therefore necessary to define a mechanism that permits exploiting qualitative

disclosure preferences defined by the client to limit the number of strategies among which she is explicitly asked to choose.

Qualitative Preferences

Given the set $C = \{c_1, \ldots, c_n\}$ of credentials in the client portfolio, the release of a subset of credentials is modeled as a binary n-dimension vector D, where $D[i] = 1$ if c_i is released and $D[i] = 0$; otherwise, $i = 1, \ldots n$. For instance, with reference to the previous example, Table 46.6 summarizes the subsets of portfolio credentials satisfying the policy regulating service *MedicineBooking*. Disclosure D_1 represents the release of {*Name, DoB, VISANum, VISALimit*}.

The model [29] proposed permits one to specify privacy preferences at different granularity levels. Dominance relationship $\succ_i$ defines disclosure preferences for credential c_i. Usually, credential-level preferences state that $0 \succ_i 1$, $i = 1, \ldots n$, meaning that the client prefers not to disclose credential c_i. To compare the disclosure of different subsets of credentials in the client portfolio, credential-level preferences are composed according to the *Pareto composition* operator $\succ_P$. A disclosure set D_i dominates, according to the Pareto composition, a disclosure set D_j if, for each credential c_l in the portfolio, either $D_i[l] \succ_l D_j[l]$ or $D_i[l] =_l D_j[l]$, meaning that D_i releases a proper subset of the credentials in D_j. For instance, consider the disclosure sets in Table 46.6, $D_3 \succ_P D_6$ since $D_3[DoB] \succ_{DoB} D_6[DoB]$, that is, $D_6 = D_3 \cup \{DoB\}$.

TABLE 46.6 Disclosure Strategies that Satisfy the Access Control Policy of Service *MedicineBooking*.

	Name	DoB	City	VISANum	VISALimit	AmExNum	AmExLimit	Insurance	InsCoverage	Dialysis
D_1	1	1	0	1	1	0	0	0	0	0
D_2	1	1	0	0	0	1	1	0	0	0
D_3	1	1	0	0	0	0	0	0	1	0
D_4	1	0	1	1	1	0	0	0	0	0
D_5	1	0	1	0	0	1	1	0	0	0
D_6	1	1	1	0	0	0	0	0	1	0
D_7	0	0	0	1	1	0	0	0	0	1
D_8	0	0	0	0	0	1	1	0	0	1
D_9	0	1	0	0	0	0	0	0	1	1
D_{10}	0	0	0	1	1	0	0	1	0	0
D_{11}	0	0	0	0	0	1	1	1	0	0
D_{12}	0	1	0	0	0	0	0	1	1	0

The most interesting kind of preferences modeled by the solution [29] is represented by *amalgamated preferences*, which compare the release of sets of credentials that are not related by a subset–containment relationship. Amalgamated preferences are of the form $c_i \to c_j$, meaning that the client prefers to release credential c_i over credential c_j. This preference defines a dominance relationship, denoted $\succ_{\{i,j\}}^{(1,0)(0,1)}$, among disclosure sets. More formally, disclosure set D_k dominates, according to amalgamated preference $c_i \to c_j$, disclosure set D_l if $D_k[i] = 1$, $D_k[j] = 0$, $D_l[i] = 0$, $D_l[j] = 1$, and $D_k[x] = D_l[x]$, for all $x \neq i$, $x \neq j$. For instance, consider the disclosure sets in Table 46.6 and amalgamated preference *Insurance $\to$ Dialysis*, then $D_{10} \succ_{\{Insurance,Dialysis\}}^{(1,0)(0,1)} D_7$ since they both disclose credentials *VISANum* and *VISALimit*, but D_{10} releases *Insurance* while D_7 releases *Dialysis*. Analogously, $D_{11} \succ_{\{Insurance,Dialysis\}}^{(1,0)(0,1)} D_8$ and $D_{12} \succ_{\{Insurance,Dialysis\}}^{(1,0)(0,1)} D_9$. Note that the binary subvectors on the top of the dominance operator can be any pair of binary subvectors of the same length. Amalgamated preferences can be conveniently represented through a graph, whose vertexes model credentials and whose edges represent disclosure preferences among them. Note that, to avoid inconsistencies in the definition of privacy preferences, the disclosure graph must be acyclic. The model [29] also permits specifying conditions associated with preferences, meaning that a dominance relationship holds only if the associated condition is satisfied (e.g., only if a given credential has already been disclosed). For instance, the client may prefer to release credential *Insurance* over her *Name* if credential *InsCoverage* has already been released (since the server is aware of the fact that the client has subscribed an insurance). These conditions are graphically represented by labels associated with the edges of the preference graph. Figure 46.4 illustrates an example of a graph representing amalgamated preferences for the portfolio in our example. Consider the disclosure sets in Table 46.6, according to the preferences in the graph, $D_1 \succ_{\{DoB,City\}}^{(1,0)(0,1)} D_4$ and $D_2 \succ_{\{DoB,City\}}^{(1,0)(0,1)} D_5$ since the disclosure of *DoB* is preferred to the disclosure of *City*. Also, $D_{12} \succ_{\{Insurance,Name\}}^{(1,0)(0,1)} D_3$ since credential *InsCoverage* has already been released, and

therefore the client prefers to release *Insurance* instead of *Name*.

Both the dominance relationship defined by the Pareto composition and the dominance relationships induced by amalgamated preferences permit a comparison of disclosure sets that differ only for the release of the subset of credentials on which the dominance relationship has been defined. However, it may happen that two disclosure sets cannot be compared considering one dominance relationship only, but they can be compared combining two or more disclosure preferences. For instance, consider the graph in Figure 46.4 and the disclosure sets in Table 46.6. Disclosure sets D_1 and D_2 cannot be directly compared, but it is immediate to see that D_1 dominates D_2 by combining amalgamated preferences *VISANum $\to$ AmExNum* and *VISALimit $\to$ AmExLimit*. In fact, D_1 discloses the attributes of the VISA credit card, while D_2 discloses the attributes of the AmEx credit card. In [29] the authors propose incrementally composing certificate-level and amalgamated preferences. The transitive closure of all the preferences in the system permits defining a *complete preference relationship*, denoted $\succ\succ$, which summarizes all the preference relationships expressed by the client. As a consequence, given the access control policy p regulating the release of the service requested by the client, the approach in [29] permits one to limit the set of successful disclosure strategies among which the client needs to choose. In fact, the choice can be restricted to the *optimal disclosure sets*—that is, to the sets of credentials in the client portfolio that satisfy p and that are not dominated by another disclosure set that satisfies p. More formally, the set of optimal disclosure sets is defined as follows [29].

Definition 2: Optimal Disclosure Sets

Let $C = \{c_1, \ldots, c_n\}$ be the set of credentials in the client portfolio; s the service requested by the client; p the access control policy regulating the release of s; $\mathcal{D} = \{D_1, \ldots, D_m\}$ the set of disclosure sets that satisfy p, with $D_i \subseteq C$, $i = 1, \ldots, n$; and $\succ\succ$ a complete preference relationship over C. An optimal disclosure set $\mathcal{D}_{\succ\succ}$

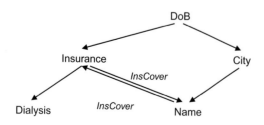

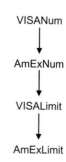

FIGURE 46.4 An example of a set of amalgamated preferences.

of $\mathscr{D}$ wrt $\succ\succ$ is defined as: $\mathscr{D}_{\succ\succ} = \{D \in \mathscr{D} | \nexists D' \in \mathscr{D}, D' \succ \succ D\}$.

The disclosure sets in $\mathscr{D}_{\succ\succ}$ are optimal and cannot be compared with respect to the disclosure preferences defined by the client (i.e., they are equivalent according to client preferences). To finally decide which set of credentials to disclose to the server, the client needs to choose, among the negotiation strategies in $\mathscr{D}_{\succ\succ}$, the one she prefers to disclose. For instance, with reference to the disclosure sets in Table 46.6 and the preferences in Figure 46.4, $\mathscr{D}_{\succ\succ} = \{D_1, D_{10}, D_{12}\}$.

Open Issues

The solution proposed in [29] has the great advantage over the approaches of modeling and managing qualitative preferences. In fact, it permits specifying privacy preferences at the attribute granularity, and it defines a partial-order relationship and different composition operators over the domain of privacy preferences, therefore making it easy for the client to use. However, it still needs to be enhanced to comply with all the desiderata that a privacy-aware access control system should satisfy. The main shortcoming from which the proposal in [29] suffers is that it requires client intervention in the choice of the set of credentials to disclose among the successful strategies in the optimal set. Also, the proposed model assumes that each credential in the client portfolio certifies one attribute only, while often credentials include a set of attributes that cannot be singularly released (atomic credentials).

6. PRIVACY PREFERENCES IN CREDENTIAL-BASED INTERACTIONS

The first solution that formally models the client portfolio to permit the client to specify fine-grained privacy preferences, as well as constraints on the disclosure of portfolio components, has been proposed in [19]. One of the main advantages of the portfolio modeling in [19] is that it permits one to represent both atomic and nonatomic credentials, declarations, and the attributes composing them, clearly distinguishing between credential-dependent and credential-independent attributes. As a consequence, this modeling permits one to easily associate privacy preferences with each credential and attribute in the client portfolio. More precisely, the client portfolio is modeled as a bipartite graph $G(V_C \cup V_A, E_{CA})$, with a vertex for each credential and each attribute in the portfolio and an edge connecting each credential to the attributes it certifies. It is important to note that each credential-independent attribute is represented by a vertex in G, while each credential-dependent attribute is represented by several vertexes (one for each credential certifying it). For

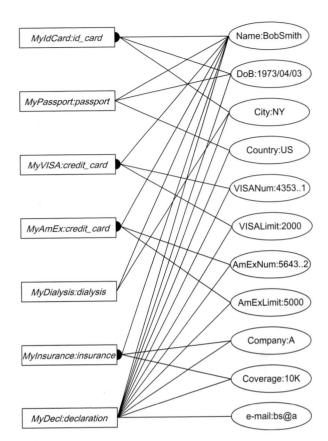

FIGURE 46.5   Portfolio graph of the portfolio in Table 46.1.

instance, Figure 46.5 illustrates the graph representing the portfolio in Table 46.1, where we distinguish atomic credentials by attaching all the edges incident to the vertex representing the credential to a black semicircle. The label of vertexes representing credentials is of the form *id*:type, where *id* is the identifier of the credential and *type* is its type. The label of vertexes representing attributes is of the form name:value.

Sensitivity Labels

The client can define her privacy preferences at a fine-granularity level by associating a *sensitivity label* with each credential and attribute (or combinations thereof) in her portfolio. These labels represent how much the client values the disclosure of the portfolio components. The domain Λ of sensitivity labels can be any set of values characterized by a partial-order relationship $\succcurlyeq$, and a composition operator $\oplus$. This generic definition of sensitivity labels captures different methods for expressing preferences. For instance, sensitivity labels could be positive integer values, where the order relationship $\succcurlyeq$ is the traditional $\geq$ relationship and the composition operator can either be the sum ($+$) or the maximum. In the example, for simplicity, we will consider numerical sensitivity labels. Labeling function λ associates a sensitivity label in Λ with each credential c, with each attribute a in the client portfolio, and possibly with subsets thereof. Figure 46.5 illustrates the portfolio graph in Figure 46.5, extended by associating each vertex with its sensitivity label and by including new vertexes that represent associations and disclosure constraints. The semantics of the sensitivity labels associated with portfolio components can be summarized as follows.

- $\lambda(a)$: defines the sensitivity of attribute a singularly taken and reflects how much the client values its disclosure. For instance, with reference to the portfolio graph in Figure 46.5, $\lambda(VISANum) \geq \lambda(DoB)$ since the client considers the number of her VISA more sensitive than her date of birth.
- $\lambda(c)$: defines the sensitivity of the *existence* of credential c. This label reflects how much the client values the additional information carried by the credential itself, independently from the attributes it certifies. For instance, with reference to the portfolio graph in Figure 46.5, $\lambda(MyDialysis)$ reflects the sensitivity associated by the client with the credential certifying her nephrological disease, independently from the fact that this credential also certifies attributes *Name* and *City*. Clearly, the existence of the credential itself has a sensitivity that goes beyond the demographical information it certifies.

The sensitivity label associated with the combined release of a set of credentials and attributes generally corresponds to the composition through operator $\oplus$ of the sensitivity labels of each portfolio component in the released set. For instance, the release of atomic credential *MyIdCard* has sensitivity label $\lambda(MyIdCard) \oplus \lambda(Name) \oplus \lambda(DoB) \oplus \lambda(City)$. There are, however, cases where the combined release of some portfolio components may cause a higher or lower information disclosure than the sensitivity label obtained composing the labels of the released credentials and attributes. To capture these situations, the model in [19] permits the client to specify sensitivity labels for subsets of portfolio components, representing how much the client values the release of the *association* of their values. The sensitivity labels of associations must then be considered when composing the sensitivity labels of the attributes and/or credentials in the association. Graphically, associations are represented by additional vertexes in the portfolio graph, connected to the attributes and/or credentials composing the associations. In particular, the following two kinds of associations are modeled.

- *Sensitive views* model situations where the combined release of a set of portfolio components carries *more* information than the composition of the sensitive

labels of its components. For instance, with reference to the portfolio graph in Figure 46.5, $\lambda(\{DoB, City\}) = 4$ models the additional sensitivity carried by the combined release of the two attributes.

- *Dependencies* model situations where the combined release of a set of portfolio components carries *less* information than the composition of the sensitive labels (see Figure 46.6) of its components. For instance, with reference to the portfolio graph in Figure 46.5, $\lambda(\{City, Country\}) = -2$ represents the sensitivity to be removed when the two attributes are released together, since the knowledge of the *City* where a user leaves permits one to easily infer her *Country*. The sensitivity label associated with a dependency $\mathscr{A} = \{c_i, \ldots, c_j, a_k, \ldots, a_l\}$ can assume any value, provided the sensitivity label of the combined release of all the credentials and attributes in $\mathscr{A}$ dominates the sensitivity label of the most sensitive element in $\mathscr{A}$ ($\lambda(c_i) \oplus \ldots \oplus \lambda(c_j) \oplus \lambda(a_k) \oplus \ldots \oplus \lambda(a_l) \oplus \lambda(\mathscr{A}) \succcurlyeq \max(\lambda(x), x \in \mathscr{A}))$.

In addition to sensitivity labels associated with credentials, attributes, and subsets thereof, the client may need to specify disclosure constraints that cannot be expressed through sensitivity labels. To this purpose, in [30] the authors extend the original model introduced in [19] with the following two kinds of constraints.

- *Forbidden views* represent subsets of portfolio components whose combined release is prohibited. For instance, with reference to the portfolio graph in Figure 46.5, forbidden view $\{DoB, MyDialysis\}$ prevents the combined release of attribute *DoB* and credential *MyDialysis* and is graphically represented by a cross-shaped vertex connected with the attribute and credential in the constraint.
- *Disclosure limitations* represent subsets of portfolio components characterized by restrictions of the form *at most n* elements in the set can be jointly disclosed. For instance, with reference to the portfolio graph in Figure 46.5, disclosure limitation $\{Name, City, Country, e-mail\}_2$ permits release at most of two attributes in the set and is graphically represented by a cross-shaped vertex with label 2 and connected with all the attributes in the set.

Disclosure

Given the client portfolio, it is important to note that not all the subsets of portfolio components represent a valid disclosure; that is, not all the sets of credentials and attributes can be communicated to the server to gain access to the requested service. First, a subset QUOTE of portfolio components represents a *disclosure* only if it satisfies the following three conditions.

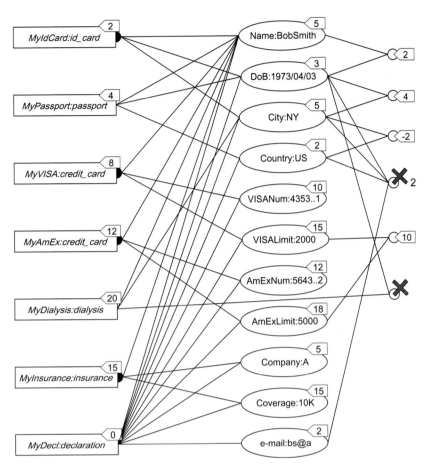

FIGURE 46.6 Portfolio graph extended with sensitivity labels, associations, and constraints.

1. *Certifiability*: Each disclosed attribute is certified by at least a credential, whose existence is disclosed as well ($\forall a \in D, \exists c \in D s.t.\ a \in attributes(c)$).

2. *Atomicity*: If an attribute certified by an atomic credential is disclosed, all the attributes in the credential are disclosed ($\exists c \in D s.t. c$ is atomic, $\forall a \in attributes(c), a \in D$).

3. *Association exposure*: If all the attributes and/or credentials composing an association are disclosed, then the association itself is disclosed ($\forall x \in \mathscr{A}, x \in D$ then $\mathscr{A} \in D$).

These conditions permit one to easily take into account both atomic and nonatomic credentials, as well as associations, in the computation of the sensitivity label characterizing the disclosure of a set of credentials and attributes. For instance, consider the portfolio graph in Figure 46.5. An example of disclosure D is represented in Figure 46.7 (a), where released elements are reported in black while nonreleased elements are reported in gray. Figure 46.7(b) represents instead a subset of the portfolio components that does not represent a disclosure, since it violates the above properties. The *sensitivity* of a disclosure D is computed by composing the sensitivity label of all the credentials, attributes, and associations composing it. For instance, the sensitivity of the disclosure in Figure 46.7(a) is $\lambda(D) = \lambda(MyPassport) + \lambda(MyVISA) + \lambda(MyDecl) + \lambda(Name) + \lambda(DoB) + \lambda(VISANum) + \lambda(VISALimit) + \lambda(e\text{-}mail) + \lambda(\{Name, DoB\}) = 4 + 8 + 0 + 5 + 3 + 10 + 15 + 2 + 2 = 49$. A disclosure is said to be *valid* if it does not violate disclosure constraints. Only valid disclosures can be released. For instance, the disclosure in Figure 46.7(a) is valid, while the one in Figure 46.7(c) is not valid since it violates forbidden view $\{DoB, MyDialysis\}$.

Given the server policy p regulating the disclosure of the service of interest, it is necessary to determine a *minimum disclosure* (a valid disclosure with minimum sensitivity label) satisfying p. The authors [19] assume that server policies are formulated as Boolean formulas composed of terms of the form $t.\{a_i, \ldots, a_j\}$ in disjunctive normal form. A clause $t.\{a_i, \ldots, a_j\}$ in the server policy requires the disclosure of a credential c of type t that certifies attributes $\{a_i, \ldots, a_j\}$. A valid disclosure D satisfies a term $t.\{a_i, \ldots, a_j\}$ if $\exists c \in D s.t.\ type(c) \leq_{isa} t$ and $\{a_i, \ldots, a_j\} \subseteq attributes(c)$. For instance, assume that the policy regulating access to the *MedicineBooking* service is $id.\{Name\} \wedge credit\_card.\{Name, Number, Limit\} \wedge *$.

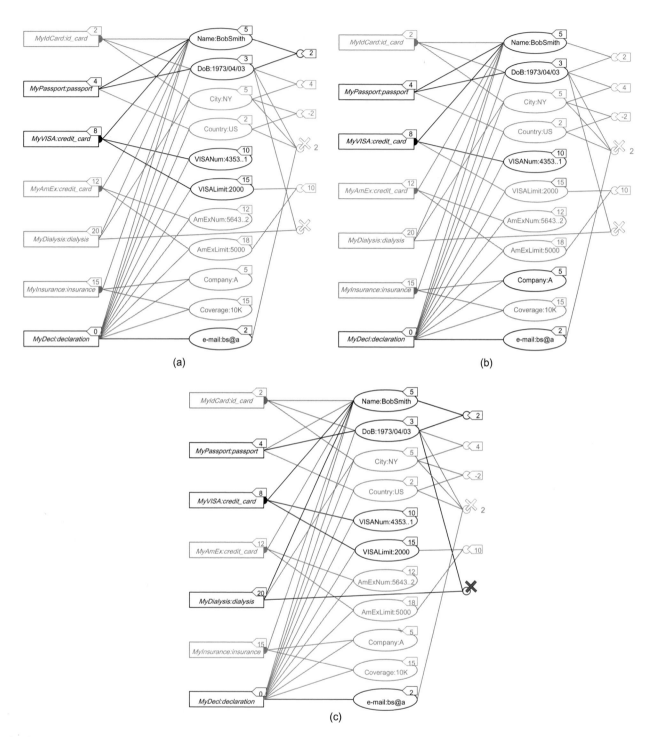

FIGURE 46.7   An example of valid disclosure (a), arbitrary subset of portfolio elements (b), and nonvalid disclosure (c).

{*DoB,e-mail*}. The disclosure in Figure 46.7(a) satisfies the policy and grants the client access to the requested service: Term *id*.{*Name*} is satisfied by the release of attribute *Name* from credential *MyIdCard*; term *credit_-card*.{*Name,Number,Limit*} is satisfied by the release of

atomic credential *MyVISA*; and term *.{*DoB,e-mail*} is satisfied by the release of attribute *DoB* from credential *MyIdCard* and by the declaration of attribute *e-mail*. Formally, the minimum disclosure problem can then be formulated, as discussed in Problem 3 below.

Problem 3: Minimum Disclosure Problem

Let $C = \{c_1, \ldots, c_n\}$ be the set of credentials in the client portfolio; $A = \{a_1, \ldots, a_m\}$ the set of attributes in the client portfolio; $(T, \leq_{isa})$ the hierarchy of credential types; A the set of sensitive associations; F the set of forbidden views; L the set of disclosure limitations; λ the labeling function; and p the server policy. Find a subset $D \subseteq C \cup A$ such that:

1. $\forall a \in D, \exists c \in D s.t. \ a \in attributes(c)$ (certifiability);
2. $\exists c \in D s.t. c$ is atomic, $\forall a \in attributes(c), a \in D$ (atomicity);
3. $\forall x \in \mathscr{A}, x \in D$ then $\mathscr{A} \in D$ (association exposure);
4. (forbidden views satisfaction);
5. $\forall l_i \in L, \nexists l' \subseteq D s.t. |l'| \geq i$, with i the threshold fixed by constraint l_i (disclosure limitation satisfaction);
6. $\exists$ a clause $t_1.\{a_{i1}, \ldots, a_{j1}\} \wedge \ldots \wedge t_l.\{a_{il}, \ldots, a_{jl}\}$ in p such that for each term $t.\{a_i, \ldots, a_j\}$ in the clause, $\exists c \in D s.t. type(c) \leq_{isa} t$ and $\{a_i, \ldots, a_j\} \subseteq attributes(c)$ (policy satisfaction);
7. $\nexists D'$ satisfying all the conditions above and such that $\lambda(D) \succ \lambda(D')$.

For instance, the disclosure in Figure 46.7(a) represents a minimal disclosure for our example. The problem of computing a minimal disclosure is NP-hard [19]. In [19] the authors propose a graph-based heuristic algorithm to compute a minimal disclosure (a disclosure that, though not minimal, has a low sensitivity label). In [30] the authors define a modeling of the problem as an instance of the Max-SAT problem, and use Max-SAT solvers to compute an optimum solution in a limited computational time.

The model in [19] has been extended in [31] to permit the client to complement her privacy preferences with *context-based restrictions* that limit the disclosure of credentials on the basis of the context of her request. In the same paper, the authors also propose to take the *history*

of past interactions into account in the choice of the set of credentials and attributes to disclose for gaining access to the requested service.

Open Issues

The modeling of the client portfolio proposed in [19] permits the client to specify sensitivity labels at the attribute granularity level and to take advantage of new constructs for taking sensitive associations and disclosure constraints into consideration in the choice of the set of portfolio components to disclose. This approach, however, leaves space for further improvements. Sensitivity labels modeling privacy preferences may not be easy to define for final users. In fact, as already noted in [29], it is hard to associate a quantitative value with each portfolio component (and possible subset thereof), while it would be easier to define a partial-order relationship between subsets of portfolio components.

7. FINE-GRAINED DISCLOSURE OF SENSITIVE ACCESS POLICIES

In [32], the authors address the problem of regulating the disclosure of access control policies by proposing a model that permits the server to specify a *disclosure policy* regulating if and how an access control policy should be communicated to the client. To this purpose, the approach in [32] models access control policies as *policy trees*. Policy tree $T(N)$ representing policy p has a node for each operator, attribute, and constant value in p. The internal nodes of the tree represent operators, whose operands are represented by the subtrees rooted at its children. For instance, Figure 46.8 represents the policy tree of $p = (type(c_1) = credit\_card \wedge c_1.Limit > 1{,}000) \vee (type(c_2) = insurance \wedge c_2.Company \neq `A' \wedge c_2.Company \neq `B')$.

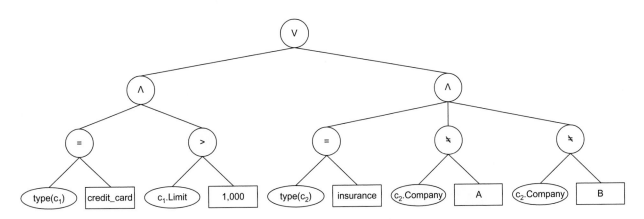

FIGURE 46.8   An example of policy tree.

Disclosure Policy

The disclosure policy regulating the release of a policy p to a client regulates the visibility of each node in the policy tree $T(N)$. The disclosure policy is formally defined as a coloring function $\gamma:N \to \{green, yellow, red\}$ that associates with each node n in the policy tree a color in the set $\{green, yellow, red\}$, thus obtaining a *colored policy tree* $T(N, \gamma)$. The semantics of the colors, with respect to the client visibility of a node, can be summarized as follows:

- *green*: The node is released.
- *yellow*: The label of the node is removed (the operator, attribute, or constant value it represents) before its release, while its presence in the tree and its children are preserved.
- *red*: The label of the node is removed and possibly also its presence in the tree.

As an example, Figure 46.9 illustrates a possible coloring regulating the disclosure of the policy tree in the figure. In the figure, QUOTE nodes are white, QUOTE nodes are gray, and QUOTE nodes are black.

Although the server can decide to associate an arbitrary color with each node in the tree, a disclosure policy is *well defined* if it is meaningful. More precisely, a disclosure policy is well defined if it satisfies the following conditions.

1. If a leaf node representing a constant value is *green*, then its sibling (which represents an attribute) is *green* and its parent (which represents an operator) is not *red*.
2. If a node representing an operator is *green*, at least one of its children must be either *green* or *yellow*.
3. The nodes in a subtree representing a condition on credential type must be either all *green* or all *red*.

Figure 46.10 presents an example of non−well-defined coloring for the policy tree in Figure 46.9. In fact, since only node 'A' is *green* in the subtree representing condition $c_2.Company \neq$ 'A', the server would disclose value 'A' instead of the condition. Analogously,

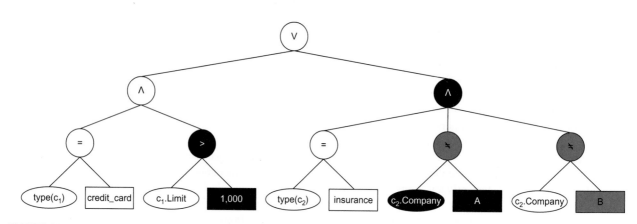

FIGURE 46.9   An example of coloring for the policy tree.

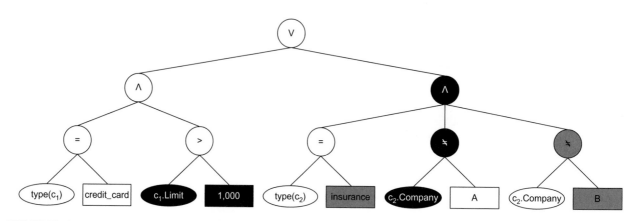

FIGURE 46.10   An example of non−well-defined colored policy tree.

only node $>$ is *green* in the subtree of condition c_1. *Limit* $> 1,000$, and the server would disclose the operator $>$ only to the client. Finally, node *insurance* is *yellow* in the sub-tree of condition *type*(c_2) $=$ *insurance*, while the other nodes are *green*. The disclosed condition would then only release operand *type*(c_2) and operator $=$, which does not give the client any information to possibly gain access to the service.

Policy Communication

When the client sends a request for accessing a service to the server, the server transforms its access control policy into a client policy view according to the disclosure policy. The colored policy tree $T(N, \gamma)$ regulating policy disclosure is therefore transformed into an equivalent *client policy tree view* by: (1) removing the label of *yellow* and *red* nodes; (2) removing unnecessary *red* leaves; and (3) collapsing internal *red* nodes in a parent–child relationship in a single *red* node. To this purpose, the server visits the tree following a post-order strategy and applies, in the order, the following three classes of transformation rules.

- *Prune rules.* These rules remove unnecessary leaf nodes. Two kinds of prune rules can be applied on an internal node *n* whose children are leaf nodes.
  - *Red predicate rule.* If *n* is *red*, all its *red* children are removed. For instance, consider the colored policy tree in Figure 46.10; according to this rule, the node representing constant value 1,000 is removed.
  - *Red children rule.* If all the children of *n* are *red*, they are removed and the color of node *n* is set to *red*. For instance, consider the colored policy tree in Figure 46.10; according to this rule, the nodes representing attribute *Company* and constant value 'A' in condition (c_2.*Company* $\neq$ 'A') are removed.

Also, the color of the node representing operator $\neq$ is set to red.

- *Collapse rule.* This rule operates on internal *red* nodes and removes their non-leaf *red* children. For instance, consider the colored policy tree in Figure 46.9; the node representing operator $\neq$ in condition (c_2.*Company* $\neq$ 'A') is removed since its parent (i.e., the second child of the root node) is *red*.
- *Hide label rule.* This rule removes the labels of *yellow* and *red* nodes.

Figure 46.11 illustrates the client policy tree view obtained by applying the transformation rules described above to the colored policy tree in Figure 46.10.

The disclosure of a client policy tree view may be meaningless for the client, since it may not represent in a "fair way" the server access control policy [32]. Intuitively, a client policy tree view fairly represents the server policy if it includes at least a subset of attributes that permit the access control policy evaluation. In fact, in this case, the client can decide whether to release the requested attributes to possibly gain access to the service of interest. Clearly, the server should disclose only fair policies. For instance, the policy view represented by the tree in Figure 46.7 is fair, since all the attributes and credential types in the original policy are preserved in the client view. The client can decide whether to release either one of her credit cards or her insurance to possibly gain access to the *MedicineBooking* service.

Open Issues

The solution proposed in [32] to protect the confidentiality of access control policies, while permitting the client-server interaction in open environments, is effective and permits the definition of disclosure restrictions at a fine granularity level. However, this proposal represents only a first step in the definition of an effective system

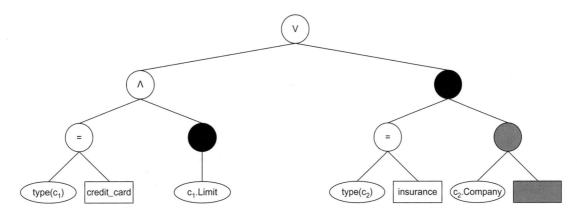

FIGURE 46.11 Policy tree view of the colored policy tree.

regulating policy disclosure. In fact, the proposed model permits one to check whether a disclosure policy generates a fair client policy tree view, but it does not propose an approach for possibly revising the disclosure policy when the client policy tree view is not fair (and therefore prevents the definition of a successful negotiation strategy). Also, the model could be extended to consider the disclosure of proofs of possession and/or proofs of satisfaction of condition.

8. OPEN ISSUES

The enforcement of access privileges in open environments, taking into account both client privacy preferences and policy confidentiality requirements still presents different open issues that need to be addressed.

- *Inheritance of privacy preferences.* Most of the solutions proposed in the literature assume that the client associates a preference with each credential and/or attribute in her portfolio. Although the solution in [19] uses the hierarchy of credential types for checking whether the disclosure of a subset of the portfolio components satisfies a given server request, it does not consider this hierarchy in the definition of privacy preferences. An interesting open issue consists in exploiting the hierarchy of credential types to make the definition of privacy preferences more user-friendly.
- *Proof of possession.* The values modeling privacy preferences are traditionally associated with credentials and/or attributes and express how much their owner values their release. Recent technologies, however, permit release of proofs of possession of credentials and proofs of satisfaction of conditions defined on attributes. The release of a proof is usually considered less sensitive than the release of the credential/attribute on which the proof is based. This different disclosure risk should therefore be adequately modeled.
- *Shared knowledge.* Attribute-based access control solutions traditionally assume that the hierarchy of credential types and attribute names represent a common knowledge for the server and the client. However, this assumption does not always hold in real-life scenarios, where there may be mismatches due also to the fact that servers refer to credential and attribute types while clients refer to their instances. Access control models should be extended to handle this problem.
- *Integration.* Both the solutions developed to support client privacy preferences and the solutions proposed to protect the confidentiality of server policies do not consider the privacy requirements of the counterpart. It is therefore important to study new models that consider both client and server privacy needs.

The approaches proposed in the literature for the support of client privacy preferences present advantages and disadvantages complementary to each other. For instance, the solution in [29] has the advantage of usability, while the approach in [19] supports sensitive associations and disclosure constraints. An interesting open issue is therefore the definition of a model that combines the advantages of all the proposed approaches.

9. SUMMARY

We have analyzed the privacy issues that may arise in open scenarios, where the client accessing a service and the server offering it may be unknown to each other and need to exchange information to build a trust relationship. We have illustrated both the problem of taking client privacy preferences into account in credential disclosure and the problem of maintaining the confidentiality of server access control policies. For each of these problems, we have described some recent approaches for their solution and illustrated some open issues that still need to be addressed.

Finally, let's move on to the real interactive part of this chapter: review questions/exercises, hands-on projects, case projects, and optional team case project. The answers and/or solutions by chapter can be found in the Online Instructor's Solutions Manual.

CHAPTER REVIEW QUESTIONS/EXERCISES

True/False

1. True or False? The advancements in Information and Communications Technology (ICT) allow users to take more and more advantage of the availability of online services (and resources) that can be accessed anywhere anytime.
2. True or False? The information that a client can provide to a server to gain access to a service is organized in a *portfolio* including both *credentials* signed by third parties and certifying client properties, and *declarations* stating certified properties uttered by the client.
3. True or False? Attribute-based access control restricts access to server service depending on the attributes and credentials that the requesting client discloses to the server.
4. True or False? Since clients and servers operating in open environments are assumed to be unknown to each other, they interact with the aim of building a trust relationship that will permit the client to gain access to a service offered by the server.
5. True or False? Given the server request, the client needs to determine which credentials and/or attributes to disclose to satisfy it.

Multiple Choice

1. With _____, servers regulate access to their services based on the attributes and certificates presented by the requesting client?
   A. privacy-enhancing technology
   B. location technology
   C. attribute-based access control
   D. executable policies
   E. data controller

2. The goal of the client and the server engaging in a negotiation protocol is that of _____ the sensitivity cost of the credentials and policies exchanged during a successful negotiation strategy.
   A. policy enforcement
   B. location technology
   C. valid
   D. minimizing
   E. Web Technology

3. The solution proposed for the simplified scenario where policies are not associated with a sensitivity cost (they can be freely released) is based on the definition of a _____ modeling the policies regulating credential disclosure at both the client and server side.
   A. data minimization
   B. *XACML*
   C. policy graph
   D. contradictory
   E. security

4. The solution for the more complex scenario where both credentials and policies regulating their release are associated with a sensitivity cost is based on a _____that consists of two steps.
   A. privacy metrics
   B. greedy strategy
   C. redundant
   D. privacy preferences
   E. taps

5. Since the _____ might be considered sensitive, the server does not reveal the threshold associated with its services to the client.
   A. irrelevant
   B. anonymous communication
   C. datahandling policies
   D. disclose-to
   E. server policy

EXERCISE

Problem

If an organization uses a distributed access control system, does it have to give up other access control methods or security measures?

Hands-On Projects

Project

Who does an organization have to trust with regard to a distributed access control system?

Case Projects

Problem

Exactly how is a user authenticated?

Optional Team Case Project

Problem

Do all distributed access control system users have to have client certificates issued by the same certificate authority?

ACKNOWLEDGMENTS

We would like to thank Sabrina De Capitani di Vimercati for suggestions and comments on the chapter organization and presentation. This work was partially supported by the Italian Ministry of Research within the PRIN 2008 project "PEPPER" (2008SY2PH4).

REFERENCES

[1] P. Samarati, S. De Capitani di Vimercati, Access control: policies, models, and mechanisms, in: R. Focardi, R. Gorrieri (Eds.), Foundations of Security Analysis and Design, Vol. 2171 of LNCS, Springer-Verlag, 2001.

[2] S. Cimato, M. Gamassi, V. Piuri, R. Sassi, F. Scotti, Privacy-aware biometrics: design and implementation of a multimodal verification system, in: Proc. of ACSAC 2008, Anaheim, CA, USA, December 2008.

[3] M. Gamassi, V. Piuri, D. Sana, F. Scotti, Robust fingerprint detection for access control, in: Proc. of RoboCare 2005, Rome, Italy, May 2005.

[4] R. Sandhu, P. Samarati, Authentication, access control and intrusion detection, in: A. Tucker (Ed.), CRC Handbook of Computer Science and Engineering, CRC Press, 1997.

[5] C.A. Ardagna, S. De Capitani di Vimercati, S. Paraboschi, E. Pedrini, P. Samarati, M. Verdicchio, Expressive and deployable access control in open web service applications, IEEE TSC 4 (2) (April–June 2011) 6–109.

[6] P. Bonatti, P. Samarati, A uniform framework for regulating service access and information release on the web, JCS 10 (3) (2002) 241–272.

[7] S. De Capitani di Vimercati, S. Foresti, S. Jajodia, S. Paraboschi, G. Psaila, P. Samarati, Integrating trust management and access control in data-intensive web applications, ACM TWEB 6 (2) (May 2012) 6:1–6:43.

[8] S. De Capitani di Vimercati, S. Foresti, S. Jajodia, P. Samarati, Access control policies and languages in open environments, in: T.

Yu, S. Jajodia (Eds.), Secure Data Management in Decentralized Systems, Springer-Verlag, 2007.

[9] S. De Capitani di Vimercati, S. Jajodia, S. Paraboschi, P. Samarati, Trust management services in relational databases, in: Proc. of ASIACCS 2007, Singapore, March 2007.

[10] K. Irwin, T. Yu, Preventing attribute information leakage in automated trust negotiation, in: Proc. of ACM CCS 2005, Alexandria, VA, USA, November 2005.

[11] A.J. Lee, M. Winslett, J. Basney, V. Welch, The Traust authorization service, ACM TISSEC 11 (1) (February 2008) 1−33.

[12] T. Ryutov, L. Zhou, C. Neuman, T. Leithead, K.E. Seamons, Adaptive trust negotiation and access control, in: Proc. of SACMAT 2005, Stockholm, Sweden, June 2005.

[13] T. Yu, M. Winslett, K.E. Seamons, Supporting structured credentials and sensitive policies trough interoperable strategies for automated trust, ACM TISSEC 6 (1) (February 2003) 1−42.

[14] J. Li, N. Li, W.H. Winsborough, Automated trust negotiation using cryptographic credentials, in: Proc. of ACM CCS 2005, Alexandria, VA, USA, November 2005.

[15] C.A. Ardagna, E. Damiani, S. De Capitani di Vimercati, S. Foresti, P. Samarati, Trust management, in: M. Petkovic, W. Jonker (Eds.), Security, Privacy and Trust in Modern Data Management, Springer-Verlag, 2007.

[16] K.E. Seamons, M. Winslett, T. Yu, Limiting the disclosure of access control policies during automated trust negotiation, in: Proc. of NDSS 2001, San Diego, CA, USA, April 2001.

[17] W. Winsborough, K.E. Seamons, V. Jones, Automated trust negotiation, Proc. of DISCEX 2000, Hilton Head Island, SC, USA, January 2000.

[18] T. Yu, M. Winslett, A unified scheme for resource protection in automated trust negotiation, in: Proc. of the IEEE Symposium on Security and Privacy 2003, Berkeley, CA, USA, May 2003.

[19] C.A. Ardagna, S. De Capitani di Vimercati, S. Foresti, S. Paraboschi, P. Samarati, Minimizing disclosure of private information in credential-based interactions: a graph-based approach, in: Proc. of PASSAT 2010, Minneapolis, MN, USA, August 2010.

[20] S. Brands, Rethinking Public Key Infrastructure and Digital Certificates - Building in Privacy, MIT Press, 2000.

[21] J. Camenisch, A. Lysyanskaya, An efficient system for non-transferable anonymous credentials with optional anonymity revocation, in: Proc. of EUROCRYPT 2001, Innsbruck, Austria, May 2001.

[22] C.A. Ardagna, S. De Capitani di Vimercati, S. Foresti, S. Paraboschi, P. Samarati, Supporting user privacy preferences on information release in open scenarios, in: Proc. of the W3C Workshop on Privacy and Data Usage Control, Cambridge, MA, USA, October 2010.

[23] P. Samarati, Protecting respondents' identities in microdata release, IEEE TKDE 13 (6) (November/December 2001) 1010−1027.

[24] W. Chen, L. Clarke, J. Kurose, D. Towsley, Optimizing cost-sensitive trust-negotiation protocols, in: Proc. of INFOCOM 2005, Miami, FL, USA, March 2005.

[25] T.H. Cormen, C.E. Leiserson, R.L. Rivest, C. Stein, Introduction to Algorithms, Second ed., MIT Press, 2001.

[26] D. Yao, K.B. Frikken, M.J. Atallah, R. Tamasia, Private information: to reveal or not to reveal, ACM TISSEC 12 (1) (October 2008) 1−27.

[27] I. Damgrad, M. Jurik, A generalisation, a simplification and some applications of Paillier's probabilistic public-key system, in: Proc. of PKC 2001, Cheju Island, Korea, February 2001.

[28] P. Paillier, Public-key cryptosystems based on composite degree residuosity classes, in: Proc. of EUROCRYPT 1999, Prague, Czech Republic, May 1999.

[29] P. Kärger, D. Olmedilla, W.-T. Balke, Exploiting preferences for minimal credential disclosure in policy-driven trust negotiations, in: Proc. of SDM 2008, Atlanta, GA, USA, August 2008.

[30] C.A. Ardagna, S. De Capitani di Vimercati, S. Foresti, S. Paraboschi, P. Samarati, Supporting privacy preferences in credential-based interactions, in: Proc. of WPES 2010, Chicago, IL, USA, October 2010.

[31] C.A. Ardagna, S. De Capitani di Vimercati, S. Foresti, S. Paraboschi, P. Samarati, Minimising disclosure of client information in credential-based interactions, IJIPSI 1 (2/3) (2012) 205−233.

[32] C.A. Ardagna, S. De Capitani di Vimercati, S. Foresti, G. Neven, S. Paraboschi, F.-S. Preiss, et al., Fine-grained disclosure of access policies, in: Proc. of ICICS 2010, Barcelona, Spain, December 2010.

## Chapter 47

Privacy and Security in Environmental Monitoring Systems: Issues and Solutions

Sabrina De Capitani di Vimercati
Dipartimento di Informatica, Università degli Studi di Milano, Crema, Italy

Angelo Genovese
Dipartimento di Informatica, Università degli Studi di Milano, Crema, Italy

Giovanni Livraga
Dipartimento di Informatica, Università degli Studi di Milano, Crema, Italy

Vincenzo Piuri
Dipartimento di Informatica, Università degli Studi di Milano, Crema, Italy

Fabio Scotti
Dipartimento di Informatica, Università degli Studi di Milano, Crema, Italy

1. INTRODUCTION

Environmental monitoring systems allow the study of physical phenomena and the design of prediction and reaction mechanisms to dangerous situations. In its general form, a monitoring system consists of a certain number of sensors designed to measure different physical quantities, one or more processing nodes, and a communication network. The sensors provide output analogical signals, which are conditioned and converted into the digital domain. The digital signals are then transmitted to the computing devices, which perform the aggregation of the obtained data to understand the measured phenomenon.

In our modern society, these systems are becoming increasingly important for keeping the state of the environment under control. In fact, they have a fundamental role in detecting new environmental issues and in providing evidence that can help prioritize environmental policies. Such systems are also useful to better understand the relationship between the environment, economical activities, and daily life and health of people. For instance, weather affects agricultural prosperity and forest well-being, while environmental pollution affects human health and reduces the quality of water, land, cultivation, and forest. There is then great interest in monitoring the environment to associate possible effects with observed phenomena and predict critical or dangerous situations.

For instance, today we know that there is a direct link between exposure to PM10 and PM2,5 and different pathologies of vascular systems. Moreover, natural resource management and preservation can also greatly benefit from using monitoring systems to observe the status and its evolution so as to initiate conservation actions when needed. Similarly, natural disaster detection, observation, and, eventually, prediction can be based on monitoring the geographical areas of interest. Another sector in which these systems are becoming highly significant is the monitoring of critical infrastructure, in particular encompassing railways, highways, gas pipelines, and electric energy distribution networks.

In the last several years, the environmental monitoring systems have been subject to fundamental changes due to rapid advancements in technology as well as the development of a global information infrastructure such as the Internet that allows an easy and rapid diffusion of information worldwide. As an example, advances in spectral and spatial resolutions, new satellite technologies, and progress in communication technologies have improved the level of detail of satellite Earth observations, thus making available high-resolution spatial and spectral data. Although such technological developments have the positive effect of expanding the application fields where environmental data can be successfully used, there is also a negative effect related to increased misuse of environmental data and systems. As a matter of fact, seemingly innocuous environmental information can lead to privacy concerns. For instance, ambient environmental monitoring data could be used to identify small geographic areas. Property owners identified in the vicinity of a hazardous waste site or other pollution sources could experience decreased property values or increased insurance costs.

In this chapter, we aim at providing a comprehensive analysis of the main security and privacy issues that can arise when collecting, processing, and sharing environmental data. The main contribution of this chapter is the analysis of these security and privacy issues, which involve both the infrastructure of the environmental monitoring systems and the data collected and disseminated, along with possible countermeasures for mitigating them. The remainder of the chapter is organized as follows. Section 2 discusses the different kinds of systems and architectures used for environmental monitoring. Section 3 resents what kinds of environmental data are typically collected and analyzed. Section 4 illustrates the main security and privacy issues related to the collection, processing, and sharing of environmental data. Section 5 discusses how such security and privacy risks can be counteracted by adopting suitable protection techniques. Finally, Section 6 concludes the chapter.

2. SYSTEM ARCHITECTURES

Environmental monitoring systems have evolved from a simple computer with sensors to composite structures that include specialized subcomponents addressing particular data collection issues. These systems are typically classified by considering the system architecture, the geographical extension of the monitored phenomenon, or the number of functions performed by the system.

Based on the system architecture, environmental monitoring systems can be classified as *centralized*, *distributed*, and *remote sensing systems* [1]. Centralized systems comprise a single processor or controller, a limited number of sensors, and a simple output presentation interface (a single value on a display). Data are collected by sensors and transmitted to the processing unit that performs data analysis and feature extraction required by the application, and stores all relevant information as specified by the application itself. They may have small dimensions and be easily transported. Examples of centralized environmental monitoring systems are radiation detectors, gas detectors, and laboratory equipment. Centralized systems also include monitoring systems based on a single observation point or systems that use robotic architectures to monitor hostile or remote environments [2].

Distributed systems are composed of a high number of sensing nodes and can exploit distributed computing and

storing abilities. A sensing node contains a limited number of sensors, a processing unit, and a network communication channel. Sensing nodes collect data may perform some local processing, and route data and information toward some processing nodes in the distributed structure. Some nodes have interfaces to deliver the results of their elaborations and storage devices to save acquired sensor data and processed information. Sensing nodes are deployed in a fixed position or may be mobile on boards of robots to explore the environment [3]. Some intelligence may be distributed in sensing and processing nodes to provide local abilities for data processing to extract knowledge as near to the sensors as possible, reducing the transmitted data or taking earlier local actions [4]. Sensing nodes can have self-configuration capabilities to adapt their operation to the environment and allow for easier deployment, especially when the environmental conditions are harsh or humans cannot reach the monitored place. Mechanisms are also introduced for effecting automatic network configuration if nodes are added or removed [4], for determining if node measurements are not necessary and thus save energy, or for allowing the nodes to move when a more suitable position is found [5]. Self-calibration techniques are used to set the operating parameters [6]. The distributed structures may help in limiting costs and may impact the environment (small and inexpensive sensors, shorter and cheaper sensor connections, small low-cost processing units for real-time operation, and possibly wireless transmission for limited interconnection costs).

In the simplest network topology, a central node processes data (Figure 47.1); even though continuous data transmission from sensing nodes leads to higher energy consumption, adjacent nodes may measure redundant or highly correlated data, and scalability may be limited due to computational and bandwidth issues.

To overcome these problems, hierarchical sensor networks have been used. These networks are usually

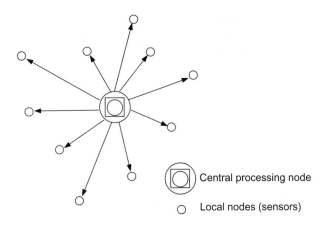

FIGURE 47.1 Sensor network with a central processing node.

composed of three-levels: *local nodes* (sensors), *intermediate nodes* (local aggregation centers, gateways, or base stations), and a *central processing* node. Some nodes may coordinate some sensors (cluster) by performing synchronization and data fusion [4] (Figure 47.2). Computation is distributed in the hierarchical structure to create abstract views of the environment at different abstraction levels and compact the information by extracting the relevant knowledge as locally as possible. Local processing should be performed carefully to avoid possible erroneous interpretation of the corresponding data at higher levels. Appropriate data aggregation techniques must be adopted to achieve a global understanding of the measured phenomena, while avoiding data loss and redundant transmissions [7].

Communications are a critical aspect of sensor networks. They can be wired as in the conventional architectures or wireless (wireless sensor networks [WSN]). Use of cables to power sensors and transmit the data can create difficulties. Low-power communication protocols and wireless interconnections are often used [8]. In these architectures, the geographical position of nodes may not be known a-priori: GPS or GIS systems are used to trace the positions of the data collected from sensors.

Sensing can be performed by using sensors for the specific quantities to be measured and placed locally at the point in which the measure has to be taken. In some environments, direct local sensing may be difficult or even impossible due to costs or environmental/operating conditions. To overcome this problem, for some

quantities indirect measures can be taken by observing the point of interest from some distance. Visual sensor networks (VSNs) are an example of this approach: Their nodes are equipped with image-capturing devices and use image-based monitoring techniques. However, they require more complex devices, greater memory usage, higher bandwidth, and nodes with more power consumption. Hierarchical sensor network architectures, consisting of heterogeneous nodes, can be used to reduce the costs and computational load [9].

Remote sensing systems are based on signals and images acquired by sensors installed on artificial satellites or aircraft and are used for vast geographical phenomena. These systems can capture several types of quantities at a significant distance, for example, by aircraft or artificial satellites. Such systems can be passive or active. In the first case, the sensors only detect quantities naturally produced by the object (the radiations of the reflected sunlight emitted by the objects). Many passive sensors can be used according to the chosen wavelength and signal dimension (radiometers, multispectral, and hyperspectral imaging). Instead, active systems send a signal to the object to be monitored and measure the reflected pulse (RADAR, LIDAR, laser altimeters). Remote sensing techniques can be merged with terrestrial sensor networks to integrate local data with large-scale observations to enhance the observation quality [10].

Environmental monitoring systems can also be classified, according to their geographical extension, as *large-scale*, *regional*, or *localized* monitoring systems [11]. Large-scale environmental monitoring systems are deployed when there is the need to cover a vast geographical area, such as several countries, or even the whole earth globe. They are typically based on distributed networks or remote sensing, and they are used, for example, for monitoring seismic activity [12–14], geophysical monitoring [15], earth pollution [16,17], global water quality [18], wildfire [19], meteorological data [20–23], arctic ice and snow [20,24], desert sand storms [25], or their combinations (see checklist: An Agenda for Action for Privacy and Security of Environmental Compliance Monitoring Systems) [26–29].

Regional monitoring systems typically cover areas such as cities, forests, or region. They are used, for example, for monitoring water quality [30], air quality [31,32], meteorological information [33–36], regional oceanographic processes [33,36], or wildfires [37–41].

Localized systems are used for monitoring very localized points, for example, lakes, volcanoes, indoor environments, or buildings. Several practical cases are available, for example, for the quality of the water in lakes, rivers, or small bays [42–44], the state of glaciers [45], underwater currents [46], air quality in small environments [47–49], and urban pollution (noise [50],

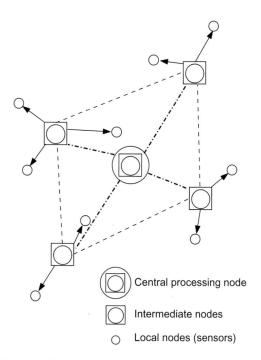

Central processing node

Intermediate nodes

Local nodes (sensors)

FIGURE 47.2 Hierarchical sensor network.

An Agenda for Action for Privacy and Security of Environmental Compliance Monitoring Systems

The EPA's national compliance monitoring program is responsible for maximizing compliance with federal environmental statutes dealing with prevention and control of air pollution, water pollution, hazardous waste, toxic substances, and pesticides. Under these statutes, the EPA and its regulatory partners monitor activities under 44 separate statutory programs. The statutory and regulatory requirements of these programs apply to approximately 41 million regulated entities, such as sewage treatment plants, gas stations, and hospitals. The EPA regulates chemicals and monitors compliance with environmental laws and regulations designed to reduce pollution to protect public health and the environment. Without compliance with the environmental requirements, the promulgation of laws and regulations has little impact. Compliance monitoring consists of a variety of activities including (check all tasks completed):

_____ **1.** Conduct of compliance inspections, civil investigations, and evaluations under the air program.
_____ **2.** Determination of facility/site compliance status.
_____ **3.** Entry of results of activities into national data systems.
_____ **4.** Response to citizen complaints.
_____ **5.** Participation in development of rules to ensure they are enforceable.
_____ **6.** Development of compliance monitoring tools such as inspection checklists/guides.
_____ **7.** Procurement and dissemination of new compliance monitoring technologies such as remote sensing and hand-held computers.
_____ **8.** Development and delivery of training for compliance monitoring personnel.
_____ **9.** Support in the development of enforcement cases.
_____ **10.** Development of state, tribal, local, and international compliance monitoring capacity.
_____ **11.** Funding and oversight of regional, state, and tribal compliance monitoring programs.

radiation [51]). Localized systems are also used for disaster prevention (for active volcanoes [52], landslides [53], and critical infrastructures [54,55]).

More complex measurement systems, called *heterogeneous sensor networks*[11], have been created by integrating combinations of subsystems of the above types, with different scales and functions, especially when applications use systems already deployed in the environment of interest or when quantities must be measured in a heterogeneous setting. Some examples of this kind of system are the UK Climate Change Network [21,23] for land and aquatic places in the UK, the Global Earth Observation System (GEOSS) [28] for different environmental processes all over the world, and the ORION project [56] for oceans. Heterogeneous systems may combine information from local sensor networks with satellite information, for example, linking local sensor networks on a planetary scale [10] or aggregating local imaging data with satellite imaging techniques [57].

Environmental monitoring systems are also characterized by the type of functionalities performed [11]. In *monofunction systems*, the measured quantities are directed to provide knowledge for a single application, as in monitoring volcanoes [52] or buildings [55]. In *multiple-function systems*, data are collected (possibly in subsets of different types from different locations) and used by different applications and even for different global purposes, thus integrating various monitoring systems into a single infrastructure ([58]. Multiple-function systems also support environmental monitoring, border control, and surveillance applications, while [26,27] dealing with climate and resource monitoring, topography, and disaster prevention).

3. ENVIRONMENTAL DATA

Before describing the security and privacy issues that characterize an environmental monitoring system, it is fundamental to clarify what kinds of environmental data can be typically collected and possibly released to the public. Different data types are used in environmental monitoring systems, depending on the context. The used sensors can, in fact, measure data related to different physical quantities: movement, speed, acceleration, force, pressure, humidity, radiation, luminosity, chemical concentration, audio, video, and so on. Usually, the acquired data consist in monodimensional or multidimensional signals (images/frame sequences). The data used by large-scale environmental monitoring systems are inherent to the physical quantities chosen to measure a single phenomenon, and the data are captured and aggregated at a high frequency to perform a continuous monitoring of the phenomenon.

In most cases, the geographical positions of the measuring nodes are fixed, known a priori, and released publicly. For instance, the system described in [34] was composed of 192 measurement stations with fixed and known positions, and performed a continuous monitoring of air temperature, humidity, precipitation, solar radiation, wind speed and direction, and atmospheric pressure. The system described in [12,14] was composed by more than 150 measurement stations with fixed and known positions, and measured data from seismographs. The system proposed in [16,17] used different UV radiation detectors to perform a continuous monitoring of radiation. In the case of regional or localized environmental monitoring networks with multiple functions, nodes may not have fixed or known a-priori positions, are equipped with GPS devices, use wireless transmission techniques, and are powered using batteries. For this reason, the data transmission frequency is often smaller than the one used in large-scale environmental monitoring systems. For instance, the system described in [33,36] performed the continuous monitoring of the waves along the coasts of Louisiana and the Mexican gulf, measuring the wave height, their period, the direction of propagation, the water level, and the direction and speed of the currents. Different kinds of nodes with wireless transmission capabilities can be used. For instance, a volcano monitoring system is described in [52] and uses nodes with infrasound sensors and GPS devices. An experimental visual sensor network for fire monitoring is proposed in [37,40].

At a high level, the life cycle of environmental data can be divided in three macro-steps: *collection*, *storage*, and *publication*. Data are collected from the environment and stored at the sensor and/or processing nodes. The format of the stored data depends on the specific purpose for which such data have been collected. Authorized parties can access the environmental data for analysis or other purposes. The environmental data (or a subset of them) can then be made publicly or semipublicly available. The data are typically published in the form of *macrodata* (tables reporting aggregated information about an environmental phenomenon) or *microdata* (records reporting data related to specific physical measurements) [59].

In the remainder of this chapter, we illustrate some security and privacy risks that may arise in the data life cycle. To fix ideas and to clarify the following discussion, we refer our examples to a scenario characterized by a localized network in the city of San Francisco, which is under the control of the local municipality. The system is distributed and the sensor nodes are organized according to a centralized configuration. The collected data are stored at processing node PN. *Alice* is an adversary that tries to violate the monitoring system and to discover sensitive information. We also consider a fictitious factory A, which improperly releases pollutants and production rejects into the environment.

4. SECURITY AND PRIVACY ISSUES IN ENVIRONMENTAL MONITORING

Environmental monitoring systems and the data they collect can be vulnerable to security and privacy risks [60]. In particular, security risks are related to the threats that can undermine the *confidentiality*, *integrity*, and *availability* of both the data and the monitoring systems in their entirety (e.g., system architecture and communication infrastructure). Conversely, privacy risks are related

to those threats that can allow an adversary to use the environmental data for *inferring sensitive information*, which is not intended for disclosure and should be kept private. Security and privacy risks are not independent: They are often correlated, and an adversary can exploit a security violation for breaching data privacy. As an example, suppose that *Alice* successfully violates the physical security of processing node PN, causing a security violation that can allow her to access private information related to the pollutant levels in the air of San Francisco. This security violation can allow *Alice* to infer pathologies of the citizens of a given area of the city, therefore violating their privacy.

In this section, we present and illustrate through examples the main security and privacy risks that can arise in the context of environmental monitoring. Note that, in the following discussion, we consider neither the classical security problems related to failures of systems and applications due to errors, nor the reliability and dependability aspects characterizing the system, as our goal is to focus on the less well-known security and privacy issues.

Security Risks

Broadly speaking, in our environmental monitoring scenario, security risks are related to all threats that can: (1) damage the infrastructure of the monitoring system; (2) violate communication channels connecting different components of the monitoring system; or (3) allow unauthorized parties to intrude into the monitoring system for malicious purposes. We now describe these threats in detail.

Damages to the System Infrastructure

Any attack performed with the aim of physically damaging the monitoring system can put at risk the confidentiality, integrity, and availability of the collected environmental data. For instance, suppose that the local municipality of San Francisco wants to build a new playground for children and, to determine the safest location, it analyzes the collected environmental data to discard polluted areas of the city. Suppose also that *Alice* maliciously damages the sensor nodes close to factory A, to hide evidence of the pollutants and production rejects release. Clearly, this compromises the collection of the environmental data, since these sensor nodes become unavailable (data availability violation). An analysis of the partial environmental data available to the local municipality can erroneously identify an area close to factory A as the safest area for building the new playground. If this were to happen, children would be exposed to pollutants and production rejects. The same risks apply when all sensor nodes are working properly but the processing node gets attacked and becomes unavailable: In this case, the analysis of the environmental data would not be based on the latest measurements of the sensor nodes, and the results might be compromised. Note that these attacks can impact any of the three steps of the environmental data life cycle, as similar problems arise when an adversary succeeds in compromising the nodes collecting data (collection step), the database where environmental data are stored (storage step), or the systems where they are published (publication step).

Violation of the Communication Channels

All communication channels connecting the different components of a sensor network can represent a possible target for an adversary. In particular, the adversary might be a *passive adversary*; that is, she could be interested only in monitoring the communication channels to observe information that she would not be able to access, or an *active adversary*; that is, she could attempt to delete or modify data transmitted on such channels. These two scenarios configure two "classical" security attacks, which can intuitively violate the confidentiality and integrity of the data. Besides such attacks, an adversary can also be interested in monitoring the *accesses* performed on the data by the authorized parties, to discover some sensitive information about them. For instance, the fact that an authorized party accesses data related to the concentration of particulates reveals that the party is interested in discovering the polluted areas. If the party is a building constructor, this may imply that the party is interested in building a new apartment complex, and therefore the adversary can speculate on the costs of the lands. Effective protection of data access also requires the protection of *access patterns*: An adversary should not be able to see whether two accesses performed by two different parties aimed at the same data. For instance, *Alice* should not be able to see if two competitors are interested in performing similar analysis on the environmental data. If so, *Alice* would be able to sell this knowledge to one of the two competitors. Note how the latter two attack scenarios configure two examples of a security violation causing a privacy breach.

Unauthorized Access

Environmental data should be available only to users and parties authorized by the data owner. Clearly, restrictions on accesses to environmental data only apply when such data are not publicly released. Unauthorized accesses can possibly involve the database where environmental data are stored after their collection and analysis, or the sensor nodes. The storage server can be a local server, under the control of the data owner, or an external, third-party storage server. In the first case, the server can be considered trusted (data can be safely stored), and access control should only be enforced against users requesting access to the stored data. In the second case, the external storage server is not considered trusted, and therefore access restrictions should also take into account the fact that the server itself should not be able to access the stored data. An adversary intruding into sensor nodes can be interested in accessing raw data to update them, or to inject false data so that tampered data are sent to the processing node. For instance, *Alice* can be interested in manipulating the measurements performed by the sensor nodes close to factory A to reduce the concentration of a specific harmful substance. An adversary intruding into the storage servers is clearly interested in accessing environmental data after their collection, normalization, and analysis. Note that collected data can also be stored together with other datasets and, as a consequence, the adversary can discover correlations and dependencies among these different data sets. In all these cases, both data confidentiality and integrity are at risk.

Privacy Risks

Privacy risks are related to all threats that can allow an adversary to infer sensitive information from the collected environmental data. Such inferences can be *direct*, that is, caused by observations in the data collection (an adversary observing production rejects can discover confidential details of the productive processes of a company), or *indirect* (studies on the presence of polluting substances in geographical areas or workplaces can be correlated with studies on the relationship between correlating pollutants and diseases, revealing possible illnesses of individuals living in those areas). Inferred sensitive information can involve individuals, the environmental area on which data have been collected, and also areas close to or correlated with it. As an example, the knowledge that some geographical areas are polluted with harmful substances can also affect individuals who live in other areas if they own properties in the polluted areas. In fact, due to such knowledge, the value of their properties could decrease. Privacy risks can occur when environmental data are made publicly available (publication step) or when they are (properly or improperly) accessed; they can be a consequence of data correlations and associations, observations of data evolutions, unusual data, or knowledge of users' locations.

Data Correlation and Association

A possible means through which sensitive information can be inferred is represented by the natural correlations existing among different phenomena. To illustrate, consider a life and sickness insurance company in San Francisco. Suppose that a third-party organization releases a study illustrating the relationship existing between pollutants and rare diseases. Suppose also that the insurance company accesses this study. By analyzing environmental data collected by the local municipality and comparing them with the study, the insurance company can decide to increase the risk associated with citizens living in polluted areas of San Francisco and re-compute their insurance policies. In addition to correlation, also the association of environmental data with other information coming from different sources can be exploited for inferring sensitive information. For instance, suppose that *Alice* can access a collection of data recording the medical histories of a community of patients. *Alice* might then link such data with airborne pollution studies (by exploiting city and county zones that are used to identify population exposed to specific airborne pollutants) and thereby violate patients' privacy.

Data Evolutions

To obtain more meaningful data, sensor nodes can perform several measurements of quantities of interest over time. For instance, a measuring station can continuously record the noise level in a given area of a city. While a high number of samples allows for better analysis of a given phenomenon, such repeated measurements can open the door to possible inference channels leaking sensitive information. For instance, suppose that *Alice* wants to discover the timetable of the freight trains traversing the railroad in San Francisco, which is kept secret by the local train company. Suppose also that the environmental monitoring of the local municipality includes measurements of the noise pollution in the city. Having access to the measurements collected close to the railway, *Alice* can notice peaks in the noise levels and correlate this information with the public timetables of passenger trains, thus reconstructing the freight trains' timetable.

Unusual Data

Intuitively, if the measurements obtained from an environmental monitoring system deviate from what is expected or considered as usual, a high risk of sensitive information inference can arise. To illustrate, suppose that the results of the environmental monitoring of the San Francisco city area show a high level of radioactivity. If the neighbor cities do not show such a high level of radioactivity, then these values can be considered surprising, and may witness the existence of a neighbor location storing radioactive material (nuclear weapons, or rejects of nuclear power plants). Otherwise, if the same level of

radioactivity is observed also in other cities, the radioactivity in San Francisco can be due to some peculiarities of the soil.

Users' Locations

Mobile phones and smartphones are portable computers that more and more users have and carry with them all times. In the near future, we can imagine that our phones will be equipped with sensors and applications specifically targeted to the environmental monitoring, leading to a *pervasive* environmental monitoring where the sensing will be directly performed by users who will collect data related to the locations they visit. Since users move around the space, measurements have to be tagged with the location in which they have been captured. An adversary able to track the movements of a given user can violate her privacy discovering her frequent addresses (home and workplace), usual movements (from home to work), and habits, and, accordingly, can infer sensitive information about her. For instance, suppose that *Alice* gains access to the set of location-tagged environmental measurements performed by her colleague *Bob* with his smartphone. *Alice* can notice that *Bob* visits a clinic for cardiovascular diseases every day, discovering that *Bob*, or one of his relatives or close friends, suffers form a heart problem.

5. COUNTERMEASURES

We now describe possible countermeasures that can be adopted to avoid or mitigate the security and privacy risks described in the previous section. In the remainder of this chapter, we will refer our examples to the environmental data in Table 47.1, reporting a possible example of a collection of noise and PM10 values measured in the San Francisco area. Each row reports the GPS coordinates of the node that performed the measurement, personal information (name, date of birth, and ZIP code) of the owner of the area in which the sensor node is placed, and the noise and PM10 values measured by the node, expressed in dB and $\mu g/m^3$, respectively.

Counteracting Security Risks

The security risks related to the system architecture can be prevented by hardening the physical security of the whole system architecture and by adopting intrusion detection systems [61]. Fault-tolerance solutions can also be helpful when an adversary turns out to be successful and some parts of the system report damages. For instance, a simple solution for ensuring the availability of the data stored in the processing node consists in replicating the data on several machines, possibly located in

TABLE 47.1 An Example of a Collection of Environmental Data.

Sensor Position	Owner Personal Data				
	Name	DoB	ZIP	PM10	Noise
37.739404, − 122.483128	Arnold	21/06/1980	94210	60	40
37.748313, − 122.583017	Bob	12/06/1980	94211	60	42
37.737222, − 122.451906	Carol	07/06/1980	94152	42	60
37.746131, − 122.442895	David	26/06/1980	94112	30	51
37.735048, − 122.533784	Emma	01/07/1970	95113	50	38
37.744957, − 122.534673	Fred	10/07/1970	95141	20	40
37.733864, − 122.625562	George	05/07/1970	95217	35	43
37.742772, − 122.416451	Hillary	12/07/1970	95235	38	61

different sites. The classical attacks on the communication channels can be prevented by encrypting the traffic, though lightweight solutions appear to be suitable for an environmental monitoring scenario, where data measurements are typically performed by sensor nodes with limited computational capabilities [62]. More challenging are the problems of ensuring appropriate protection against nonclassical attacks that analyze data access and access patterns, and of enforcing access restrictions under the assumption that the set of authorized users can dynamically change and might not be known a priori. In the remainder of this section, we illustrate possible strategies that can be adopted for addressing these two issues.

Protecting Environmental Data Access Patterns

The problem of protecting data access and access patterns from external observers and the storage server itself has been mainly studied in the database field [63]. A possible solution to the problem of ensuring that an adversary cannot infer any sensitive information from the observations of accesses to data is to change the physical location (blocks of the hard disk) where data are stored at each access. The technique in [63] goes in this direction, enabling authorized parties to access the stored data while guaranteeing: (1) *content* confidentiality (data privacy is maintained); (2) *access* confidentiality (the fact that an access aims at a specific data item is protected); and (3) *pattern* confidentiality (the fact that two different accesses aim at the same data items is protected) from any observer, including the storage server itself. The technique is originally proposed in scenarios of data outsourcing, but it nicely fits a scenario in which a collection of environmental data needs to be stored and maintained

private, and each access to certain information is performed by a request issued by a *trusted client*, directly interacting with the storage server.

Adopting this proposal, content, access, and pattern confidentiality are guaranteed by organizing data in an ad-hoc data structure, called a *shuffle index*. Such a shuffle index assumes data to be organized in an unchained $B + -$tree, and encrypts data at the node level, so that real (plaintext) values are protected from the (possibly untrusted) storage server. In the $B + -$tree, data are indexed over a candidate key defined for the data collection, and actual data items are stored in the leaves of the tree according to their index values. Accesses to the data items stored in the tree are based on the value of the associated indexes. Note that, to avoid improper leakage of information to the storage server, the $B + -$tree does not include any link from a leaf to the next one. The rationale behind this is that such links would expose the order relationship among index values in different nodes.

Data encryption ensures content confidentiality, while access and pattern confidentiality are safeguarded by the client by means of: (1) hiding the real (target) request within cover (fake) requests; (2) caching target searches recently performed by users; and (3) shuffling, at each request, the content among blocks stored at the server. These three strategies work as follows:

- Cover searches hide a request in a set of fake ones, thus introducing confusion on the requested target. Cover searches are executed in parallel to the target search, and the number of cover searches can be customized to tune the offered protection level.
- Cache avoids the client to search in the $B + -$tree for the same target in two close queries. The client maintains a local copy of the nodes forming a path in the

B + −tree reaching a target value. The size of the cache determines the number of last target searches that are maintained in the cache itself.

- Shuffling implies modifying the data structure at every access and shuffling content among its blocks. The shuffling operation destroys the one-to-one correspondence otherwise existing between a block and the node of the B + −tree stored in it. In this way, repeated accesses to the same node might actually refer to searches for different data items, while different accesses to different nodes might refer to searches for the same data item.

Enforcing Access Restrictions on Environmental Data

To prevent unauthorized access to the system, an access control mechanism is needed. A peculiarity of the environmental monitoring scenario is that the set of users authorized to access collected environmental data is typically very dynamic and may not be known a priori. For instance, consider the monitoring of air pollutants in the area of San Francisco. The collected and analyzed data could be accessed for analysis by the local municipality, but also by young researchers of local universities, which may have collaborations with other universities and therefore be part of a dynamic research group. According to this observation, the identity of the users accessing the data may not always be known in advance, and traditional identity-based access control techniques [64] might not be applicable. To overcome this problem, attribute-based access control might represent a viable solution [65]. In this case, rather than considering users' identities, the authorizations stating who can access what data are defined by taking into consideration properties (age, nationality, occupation) of the authorized parties. For instance, suppose that the local municipality of San Francisco aims at giving access to the collected environmental data only to U.S. citizens. To this aim, the access control policy might grant access to users showing that they hold a U.S. passport, regardless of their identity. Attribute-based access control has been introduced as a means of enforcing this kind of access restrictions in open environments. It is based on the assumption that typically each interacting party (e.g., a client and a server) has a portfolio of *credentials* and *declarations*, either issued and certified by trusted authorities or self-declared by the party herself [65]. More precisely, a credential includes a list (possibly empty) of certified attributes of the form ⟨attribute name, attribute value⟩ representing the subject's attributes (e.g., name and surname contained in an electronic passport), the issuer's public key, the subject's public key, a validity period, and a digital signature. Declarations are pairs of the form ⟨attribute name,

attribute value⟩ specifying the party's attributes (the professional status communicated by a user during a registration process) and are produced by the party itself, without any certification from a legal authority. A common assumption underlying attribute-based access control systems is that the set of credentials and declarations that can be released by a party is stored in a profile associated with the party itself.

Attribute-based authorizations involve a *subject*, an *object*, and a set of *actions* to which the authorization refers. A *subject* can be defined as a Boolean formula over declarations and/or credentials. Analogously, an *object* can be defined as a Boolean formula of *predicates* specifying given conditions on the metadata associated with objects. An authorization therefore states that all subjects with a profile that satisfies the conditions in the *subject* field can perform *actions* on the objects whose metadata satisfy the conditions in the *object* field [65]. An authorization might also contain other elements imposing further conditions on the authorization, such as the purpose of access or generic conditions that must be satisfied by the access request. For instance, consider the environmental data in Table 47.1. To read (action) a specific set of PM10 measurements in the San Francisco area (object) collected from a certain set of ZIP codes (condition to be satisfied by the object profile), an authorization can require the proof of majority age and a U.S. nationality (conditions to be satisfied by the subject's profile).

When an access request is submitted to the storage server (service provider), it is evaluated with respect to the authorizations applicable to it. An access request is allowed if the conditions for the required access are satisfied; it is denied if none of the specified conditions that might grant the requested access can be fulfilled. However, it may happen that the currently available information is insufficient to determine whether the access request should be granted or denied: In such cases, additional information is needed, and the requester receives an undefined response with a list of requests that she must fulfill to gain the access.

Counteracting Privacy Risks

To protect environmental data from inferences, it is necessary to adopt techniques limiting the analysis that an adversary can perform on them, and obfuscating correlations, associations, and dependencies among them. As previously mentioned, these kinds of inferences can arise whenever environmental data are properly or improperly accessed (when they are stored or outsourced), or when they are made publicly available. In the first case, the privacy of environmental data can be protected by adopting privacy-enhancing solutions devised for data storage and outsourcing (e.g., encryption and fragmentation). In the latter case, solutions investigated in the context of privacy-preserving data publishing can be adopted. In the remainder of this section, we discuss some of these possible solutions and briefly overview how location privacy can be ensured in the context of environmental monitoring.

Encrypting Stored and Outsourced Environmental Data

Properly storing and maintaining a collection of environmental data that can include, for example, raw data, analysis results, and evidence of correlations among environmental factors is not a trivial problem due to the possible inferences that can arise when accessing such data. Ensuring an appropriate degree of data privacy is of paramount importance, especially when the storage server is not trusted for accessing the data. Clearly, storing environmental data in *encrypted form* can represent an intuitive solution to guarantee protection against inferences. In fact, an encrypted data collection will be accessible for analysis only to authorized users—that is, those who are provided by the data owner with a decryption key.

Ensuring proper access to encrypted data is, however, a challenging problem, since different users are typically authorized to access different portions of the stored data. To ensure that all authorized parties can access *all and only* the data for which they have the appropriate authorization, data encryption can be combined with access control, leading to a peculiar kind of encryption usually referred to as *selective encryption* [66,67]. By adopting selective encryption, the keys with which data items are encrypted are regulated by the authorizations holding on the data, and different data items are encrypted with different keys, mapping an *authorization policy* into an equivalent *encryption policy*. As a consequence, an authorization to access a data item translates into knowledge of the key with which the data item is encrypted (for efficiency reasons, selective encryption is typically assumed to use symmetric encryption). An intuitive solution for enforcing selective encryption consists in encrypting each data item with a different key and providing each user with a set of keys, including all those used to encrypt the data items she can access. Such a naïve solution is, however, not viable in practice due to the unacceptable key management burden left to users: Each user would be required to manage as many keys as the number of data items she is authorized to access. This issue can be conveniently overcome by adopting *key derivation* methods. Basically, a key derivation method allows the computation of an encryption key starting from another key and some public information [66]. Adopting a key derivation technique, each user in the system is provided with a unique key. The set of keys in the system is then built in such a way that, starting from her own key and according to a *key derivation structure*, each user can compute all and only the keys needed for decrypting the resources she can access.

Among the possible key derivation strategies, *token-based* key derivation [66] results are particularly appealing for storing or outsourcing (environmental) data. In fact, this solution minimizes the amount of re-encrypting and re-keying required to enforce changes and updates to the authorization policy. Broadly speaking, token-based key derivation works as follows. Given a key k_i in the set of keys of the system, identified by public label l_i, a different key k_j can be derived from k_i and l_j through a so-called *token* $d_{i,j}$, computed as $k_j \oplus h(k_i, l_j)$, where $\oplus$ is the bitwise xor operator and h is a cryptographic function (e.g., a secure hash function). Note that the key derivation can be iteratively applied via a chain of tokens, and, since tokens are public pieces of information, all tokens defined in the system are stored in a public catalog. For instance, given three different keys k_i, k_j, and k_h, and two tokens $d_{i,j}$ and $d_{j,h}$, a user who knows (or can derive) key k_i can first use $d_{i,j}$ to derive k_j and, from k_j and $d_{j,h}$, she can then derive k_h. The effect of providing a user with a set $K = \{k_1, \ldots, k_n\}$ of keys is therefore conveniently obtained by providing the user with a single key $k_i \in K$ and publishing a set of tokens allowing the (direct or indirect) derivation of all keys $k_j \in K$, $i \neq j$. In this way, the user can derive all the n encryption keys, while having to worry about a single one.

To implement updates in the authorization policy regulating access to the stored data (insertion/deletion of a user or data item and grant/revoke of a permission), a subset of the keys and of the tokens defined in the system must be updated, and some data items must accordingly be re-encrypted. To limit computational burden, the solution in [66] proposes a two-layer encryption strategy called *over-encryption*. By adopting over-encryption, policy updates can be performed on encrypted resources themselves, without the need of decrypting them: In this way, the storage server itself can directly manage policy updates.

Fragmenting Stored or Outsourced Environmental Data

When encryption results are too heavy or when encrypting the whole data is an overdue, alternative solutions can be adopted. In fact, if what is sensitive is the data association instead of specific data values, solutions based on the vertical fragmentation of the data can be adopted. The intuition is very simple: When the joint visibility of some pieces of information is sensitive, such pieces of information are split in different portions that are not joinable. Fragmentation can be adopted by itself or coupled with encryption. For instance, suppose that the collected environmental data include information about the concentration of a pollutant in an area, the area, and the owner of the properties within the area. Suppose also that the data holder wants to protect the identities of the owners of polluted properties. Such a collection of environmental data can be easily split in two fragments: One fragment includes the concentration of the pollutant and the corresponding area (with the information about the properties's owner possibly encrypted), and the other fragment includes the information about the owners.

Data fragmentation has been deeply studied in the context of data outsourcing and publication in order to vertically fragment the set of attributes composing the schema of a relation to be outsourced or published in such a way to satisfy all confidentiality constraints defined by the data holder. Confidentiality constraints are subsets of attributes composing the original schema. Depending on the number of attributes involved, confidentiality constraints can be classified as: (1) *singleton constraints*, stating that the values of the attribute involved in the constraint are sensitive and cannot be released (the SSNs of patients hospitalized for a given respiratory disease due to PM10 exposure are sensitive per se and should be kept private); and (2) *association constraints*, stating that the association among the values of the attributes in the constraint is sensitive and cannot be released (the association between the name and the respiratory illness of a patient can be considered sensitive and should be protected from disclosure). Several fragmentation techniques have been proposed in the literature, and these techniques can be classified based on how they fragment the original relation schema and whether they adopt encryption.

The first strategy [68] couples fragmentation with encryption and is based on the assumption that fragments can be stored on two noncommunicating servers. When some confidentiality constraints cannot be solved by fragmentation, at least one attribute appearing in such constraints is encrypted. This technique strictly relies on the absence of communications between the servers storing the fragments. However, since collusions among servers can restore the original relation schema compromising the protection of sensitive data, alternative techniques have been proposed for enforcing confidentiality constraints.

The technique in [69] enforces confidentiality constraints coupling fragmentation with encryption, while removing the assumption of absence of communication among the storage servers. This technique satisfies singleton constraints by encrypting the values of the involved attributes. Association constraints are satisfied by adopting either fragmentation (storing the involved attributes in different fragments) or encryption (encrypting at least one of the involved attributes). However, this technique favors

fragmentation over encryption: If a confidentiality constraint can be satisfied via encryption or fragmentation, such a constraint will be enforced with fragmentation. To ensure that no sensitive association can be reconstructed, each attribute must appear in the clear in at most one fragment. This makes the different fragments not joinable, and, therefore, all fragments might also be stored on a single storage server. Also, to guarantee the possibility for authorized users to run queries against the data collection, at the physical level each fragment stores all attributes of the original relation schema, either in the clear or encrypted, so that no confidentiality constraint is violated. For instance, consider the environmental data reported in Table 47.1, and suppose that there are seven confidentiality constraints ($c_0, \ldots, c_6$) as reported in Figure 47.3.

Intuitively, these confidentiality constraints state that: (1) the list of the sensor GPS positions is considered sensitive (c_0); (2) the association of the landowners' names with any other information in the relation is considered sensitive ($c_1, \ldots, c_4$); and (3) attributes DoB and ZIP can be exploited to infer the identity of the landowners and, therefore, their associations with the collected noise and PM10 values are considered sensitive (c_5 and c_6). Table 47.2 represents a possible fragmentation of Table 47.1 satisfying all the defined confidentiality constraints.

Attribute Enc_T contains the encrypted version of all attributes appearing in the original relation but not in the clear in the fragment. Note that attribute SensorPosition is the only attribute not appearing in the clear in any fragment since it is the only attribute involved in a singleton. Therefore, attribute Enc_T of the first fragment on the left-hand side in Table 47.2 includes in encrypted form the set {SensorPosition, DoB, ZIP, PM10, Noise} of attributes. Similarly, attribute Enc_T of the second and third fragment in Table 47.2 includes the sets {SensorPosition, Name } and {SensorPosition, Name, DoB, ZIP} of attributes, respectively.

Favoring fragmentation over encryption, the technique in [69] aims at limiting the overhead conveyed by encryption. There are, however, situations calling for a complete departure from encryption. The technique in [70] avoids the use of encryption and relies solely on fragmentation for satisfying confidentiality constraints. The assumption is that the data owner is willing to store a limited portion

- $c_0 = \{\text{SensorPosition}\}$
- $c_1 = \{\text{Name, DoB}\}$
- $c_2 = \{\text{Name, ZIP}\}$
- $c_3 = \{\text{Name, PM10}\}$
- $c_4 = \{\text{Name, Noise}\}$
- $c_5 = \{\text{DoB, ZIP, PM10}\}$
- $c_6 = \{\text{DoB, ZIP, Noise}\}$

FIGURE 47.3 An example of confidentiality constraints.

TABLE 47.2 An Example of Fragmentation (Multiple Fragments).

Name	Enc_T	DoB	ZIP	Enc_T	PM10	Noise	Enc_T
Arnold	Gfg5656d!	21/06/1980	94210	Jhfdshjew	60	40	Jr8kds32j-
Bob	Dfgh45rer	12/06/1980	94211	Hde832a8	60	42	Jhu2982nd
Carol	Fg9324gd	07/06/1980	94152	Jw92[oq\	42	60	Njef9832m
David	Hd72pjc"L	26/06/1980	94112	He82n1-x	30	51	Ne983mvs
Emma	543rfet4[f	01/07/1970	95113	Nhw92d3	50	38	][NJ9,PDH
Fred	2q34rxa1q	10/07/1970	95141	9832ie9f	20	40	Jd0wKL34
George	Jkr8478'q	05/07/1970	95217	Hj282nf2	35	43	/.USHSD8
Hillary	0932hjdfk	12/07/1970	95235	83jdpvjw	38	61	[/'jdipw8m

TABLE 47.3 An Example of Fragmentation (No Encryption, Two Fragments).

T_Id	Sensor Position	Name	ZIP	T_Id	DoB	PM10	Noise
1	37.739404, − 122.483128	Arnold	94210	1	21/06/1980	60	40
2	37.748313, − 122.583017	Bob	94211	2	12/06/1980	60	42
3	37.737222, − 122.451906	Carol	94152	3	07/06/1980	42	60
4	37.746131, − 122.442895	David	94112	4	26/06/1980	30	51
5	37.735048, − 122.533784	Emma	95113	5	01/07/1970	50	38
6	37.744957, − 122.534673	Fred	95141	6	10/07/1970	20	40
7	37.733864, − 122.625562	George	95217	7	05/07/1970	35	43
8	37.742772, − 122.416451	Hillary	95235	8	12/07/1970	38	61

of the data, whenever needed for enforcing confidentiality constraints. In this context, confidentiality constraints are satisfied by storing (at least) one attribute for each constraint at the data owner side. This fragmentation technique builds a pair of fragments, one stored on the data owner and the other one at the external storage server. Assuming that the storage capacity of the data owner is limited, each attribute of the original schema should appear in only one fragment in order to avoid replication of attributes that are already stored at the server side. To illustrate, consider the environmental data set in Table 47.1 and the set of confidentiality constraints in Figure 47.3, in which there is a possible fragmentation where attributes SensorPosition, Name and ZIP are stored at the data owner side, while attributes DoB, PM10 and Noise are stored externally. Note that, unlike the fragmentation in Table 47.2, no attribute is encrypted (all attributes belonging to the original schema appear in the clear in exactly one fragment).

By adopting this technique, we see that the execution of queries involving attributes stored in the two fragments requires that the two fragments must have a common key attribute, so as to guarantee a lossless join property (attribute T_Id in the fragments in Table 47.3). To increase the utility of fragmented data, the fragmentation process can also take into consideration *visibility constraints*, expressing views of data that the fragmentation should satisfy. Visibility constraints permit the expression of different needs of visibility, such as visibility over the *values* of a single attribute, visibility over the *association* among the values of the attributes, or *alternative* visibility over different attributes [71]. Furthermore, fragments can be complemented with a sanitized release of the sensitive associations broken by fragmentation. Such a release takes the form of *loose associations*, defined in a way to guarantee a specified degree of privacy. A loose association reveals some information on the association broken by fragmentation by hiding tuples participating in the associations in groups, and providing information on the associations only at the group level (in contrast to the tuple level) [71,72].

Protecting Published Environmental Data

When environmental data are publicly released, the possible countermeasures for their protection depend on the format of the data themselves (see Section 3). In the following, we illustrate how it is possible to publish environmental data while ensuring appropriate privacy protection, in the cases of both macrodata and microdata.

Publishing Environmental Macrodata

If environmental data are published through macrodata tables, they are released as aggregate values and do not contain information specifically related to single individuals or single environmental measurements. However, sensitive information can still be leaked. For instance, consider a macrodata table reporting the concentration of a pollutant during the day and night for each county of a given region. The cells of the macrodata table that contain a high value can be considered sensitive since they indicate that the persons living in the high-polluted counties may have a high probability of suffering from specific illnesses. The content of these cells therefore needs to be somehow protected.

A macrodata table can be protected before or after tabulation. In the first case, the objective is to apply some protection techniques to the collected data (data swapping, sampling, noise addition), so that the computed aggregate values can be considered safe. In the latter case, the protection techniques typically operate in two steps since they first discover sensitive cells, that is, cells that can be easily associated with a specific respondent, and then protect them [59]. We now describe how sensitive cells can be discovered and protected.

Detecting Sensitive Cells Sensitive cells can be identified according to different strategies [72]. An intuitive strategy is the so-called *threshold rule*, according to which a cell is sensitive if the number of respondents who contribute to the value stored in the cell is less than a given threshold. The *(n,k)-rule* states that a cell is sensitive if less than n respondents contribute to more than $k\%$ of the total cell value. Other examples of techniques are the *p-percent rule* and the *pq-rule*. According to the *p-percent rule*, a cell is sensitive if the total value of the cell minus the largest reported value v_1 minus the second largest reported value v_2 is less than $(p/100) \cdot v_1$ (the reported value of some respondents can be estimated too accurately). The *pq-rule* is similar to the *p-percent rule* but takes into consideration the value q representing how

accurately a respondent can estimate another respondent's sensitive value ($p < q < 100$).

Protecting Sensitive Cells Once detected, sensitive cells can be protected by applying several techniques: *Cell suppression*, *rounding*, *roll-up categories*, *sampling*, *controlled tabular adjustment (CTA) function*, and *confidential edit* are possible examples of protection techniques. In particular, cell suppression consists in protecting a cell by removing its value (*primary suppression*). However, if some partial (marginal) totals of the table are revealed or publicly known, it might still be possible to re-determine the value of a suppressed cell or restrict the uncertainty about it. To counteract this risk, additional cells can be suppressed (*secondary suppression*). The rounding technique modifies the original value of a sensitive cell by rounding it up or down to a near multiple of a chosen base number. The roll-up categories technique modifies the original macrodata table so that a less detailed (of smaller size) table is released. Sampling implies that, rather than through a census, the macrodata table is obtained through a sample survey. The CTA technique consists in replacing the value of a sensitive cell with a different value that is not considered sensitive with respect to the rule chosen to detect sensitive cells. In a subsequent step, linear programming techniques are used to selectively adjust the values of the nonsensitive cells. The rationale behind confidential edit is to compute the macrodata table on a data set that is being slightly modified with respect to the original collection. In particular, a sample of the original records is selected and matched (i.e., a set of records with the same values on a specific set of attributes) in other geographical regions, and the attributes of the matching records are then swapped.

Publishing Environmental Microdata

Microdata tables contain specific information related to single entities (called respondents). To illustrate, consider the environmental data reported in Table 47.1, and suppose that the local municipality of San Francisco decides to publicly release the PM10 values in the area. Table 47.4 illustrates a microdata table that the municipality can prepare from the collected data and can then publicly release. Intuitively, the publication of a microdata table increases the privacy risks, and extreme attention has to be devoted to ensuring that no sensitive information is improperly leaked due to the release of such a table. In particular, in our example, the municipality must protect the fact that a given individual lives in an area with a high concentration of PM10 since an adversary may infer that the individuals living in such areas have a high probability of suffering from respiratory diseases.

TABLE 47.4 An Example of an Environmental Microdata Table.

| Sensor Position | Owner Personal Data | | | |
	Name	DoB	ZIP	PM10
37.739404, − 122.483128	Arnold	21/06/1980	94210	60
37.748313, − 122.583017	Bob	12/06/1980	94211	60
37.737222, − 122.451906	Carol	07/06/1980	94152	42
37.746131, − 122.442895	David	26/06/1980	94112	30
37.735048, − 122.533784	Emma	01/07/1970	95113	50
37.744957, − 122.534673	Fred	10/07/1970	95141	20
37.733864, − 122.625562	George	05/07/1970	95217	35
37.742772, − 122.416451	Hillary	12/07/1970	95235	38

TABLE 47.5 An Example of a De-Identified Environmental Microdata Table.

| Sensor Position | Owner Personal Data | | | |
	Name	DoB	ZIP	PM10
***	***	21/06/1980	94210	60
***	***	12/06/1980	94211	60
***	***	07/06/1980	94152	42
***	***	26/06/1980	94112	30
***	***	01/07/1970	95113	50
***	***	10/07/1970	95141	20
***	***	05/07/1970	95217	35
***	***	12/07/1970	95235	38

Before publishing an environmental microdata table, all explicit identifiers have to be removed (or encrypted). For instance, Table 47.5 is a de-identified version of Table 47.4. In Table 47.5, the name of the landowners and the GPS position of the sensing devices (which would univocally identify the associated owner) have been removed by replacing them with value ***.

A de-identified table does not provide any guarantee of anonymity: In fact, besides identifiers, other attributes such as race, ZIP code, or gender (usually referred to as *quasi-identifiers*) can exist that might be linked to publicly available information to re-identify respondents. For instance, consider the public voter list reported in Table 47.1 and the de-identified microdata in Table 47.5

where there is only one landowner born on 21/06/1980 and living in the 94210 area. If this combination is unique in the external world as well, it identifies the first tuple of the microdata in Table 47.5 as pertaining to Adam Doe, 1201 Main Street, San Francisco 94210, thus revealing that Adam is the owner of an area where the level of PM10 is 60 $\mu g/m^3$.

Effective protection of data privacy can be achieved by adopting techniques that, for example, generalize the data while preserving data truthfulness: *k*-anonymity is the pioneering technique in this direction [73]. *k*-Anonymity enforces the well-known protection requirement, typically applied by statistical agencies, demanding that any released information should be indistinguishably related to no less than a certain number of respondents. This general requirement is reformulated in the context of *k*-anonymity as follows: *Each release of data must be such that every combination of values of quasi-identifiers can be indistinctly matched to at least k respondents.* Since, typically, each respondent is assumed to be represented by at most one tuple in the released table and vice-versa (each tuple includes information related to one respondent only), a microdata table satisfies the *k*-anonymity requirement if and only if: (1) each tuple in the released table cannot be related to less than *k* individuals in the population; and (2) each individual in the population cannot be related to less than *k* tuples in the table. Taking a safe approach, a microdata table is said to be *k*-anonymous if each combination of values of the quasi-identifier in the table appears with at least *k* occurrences. In this way, each respondent cannot be associated with less than *k* tuples in the table, and each tuple cannot be related to less than *k* respondents in the population, guaranteeing the satisfaction of the *k*-anonymity requirement.

To guarantee data truthfulness, *k*-anonymity is typically achieved by applying *generalization* and *suppression* over quasi-identifying attributes. Generalization substitutes the original values with more general values. For instance, the date of birth can be generalized by removing the day, or the day and the month of birth. Suppression consists in removing information from the microdata table. As an example, suppose that the quasi-identifier for Table 47.5 is composed by attributes DoB and ZIP. Table 47.7 represents a possible 2-anonymous version of the environmental data in Table 47.5. The 2-anonymous version has been produced by generalizing the date of birth of the landowners (releasing only the month and year) and the ZIP code (releasing only the first three digits of the code). It is easy to see that comparing the 2-anonymous table with the voter list in Table 47.6 and adversary cannot determine which one between the first two tuples is related to Adam Doe, since both of them share the same combination of attributes DoB and

TABLE 47.6 An Example of a Public Voter List.

Name	DoB	Address	ZIP	City	Job
…	…	…	…	…	…
Arnold Doe	21/06/1980	1201, Main Street	94210	San Francisco	Dentist
…	…	…	…	…	…

TABLE 47.7 An Example of a 2-Anonymous Microdata Table.

	Owner Personal Data			
Sensor Position	Name	DoB	ZIP	PM10
***	***	**/06/1980	942**	60
***	***	**/06/1980	942**	60
***	***	**/06/1980	941**	42
***	***	**/06/1980	941**	30
***	***	**/07/1970	951**	50
***	***	**/07/1970	951**	20
***	***	**/07/1970	952**	35
***	***	**/07/1970	952**	38

TABLE 47.8 An Example of a 3-Diverse Microdata Table.

	Owner Personal Data			
Sensor Position	Name	DoB	ZIP	PM10
***	***	**/**/1980	94***	60
***	***	**/**/1980	94***	60
***	***	**/**/1980	94***	42
***	***	**/**/1980	94***	30
***	***	**/**/1970	95***	50
***	***	**/**/1970	95***	20
***	***	**/**/1970	95***	35
***	***	**/**/1970	95***	38

ZIP. More precisely, each combination of values for attributes DoB and ZIP appear in the table with (at least) two different.

The k-Anonymity has been designed for counteracting *identity disclosure*; that is, it represents an effective solution for protecting the identities of the respondents of a microdata table. The original definition of k-anonymity has been extended to counteract the risk that sensitive information is leaked when releasing a microdata table (*attribute disclosure*). As an example, ℓ-diversity [74] and t-closeness [75] are two well-known extensions of k-anonymity, which slightly modify the k-anonymity requirement to ensure that neither identities nor sensitive information related to a respondent can be leaked when releasing a microdata table. The basic idea behind these approaches is to extend the k-anonymity requirement considering not only quasi-identifiers, but also sensitive attribute values when computing a privacy-preserving microdata table. To illustrate, consider the 2-anonymous microdata in Table 47.7. Although an adversary cannot precisely identify the tuple of Adam Doe between the first two in the table, they both share the same value for the PM10 measurement. As a consequence, the adversary is still able to discover that Adam Doe is the owner of a high polluted area. Table 47.8 illustrates a 3-diverse version of the microdata in Table 47.5, obtained by generalizing the date of birth to the year of birth, and the ZIP code by releasing only the first two digits. In this case, the tuple of Adam Doe can be one of the first four tuples of the table, but since these tuples assume three (hence the 3-diversity) different values for the PM10 concentration, the adversary cannot determine which is the concentration associated with Adam Doe's area.

The k-Anonymity, ℓ-diversity, and t-closeness have recently been modified and/or extended to suit particular releasing scenarios, characterized by particular assumptions, constraints, and privacy requirements, such as multiple table releases [76,77], data republication [78], nonpredefined or dynamic quasi-identifiers [79], customizable privacy protection [80].

Protecting the Privacy of Location Information in Environmental Data

The problem of protecting users' positions and movements has recently gained an increasing interest due to the proliferation of both mobile devices equipped with location capabilities and location-based services [81]. This has lad to the definition of different techniques for protecting location information, which can be nicely adapted to the scenario of pervasive environmental monitoring. In the remainder of this section, we survey three different classes of works that can be adopted in this scenario for protecting users' privacy.

The first class of works aims at protecting the privacy of anonymous users communicating with a location-based service provider whenever their real identities are not relevant for the service provision [81]. The goal of these techniques is to avoid the possibility to *re-identify* users observing their position. Since in traditional location-based services users communicate with the service provider posing queries associated with their position, the intuition is that of ensuring that a same location be shared by at least a certain number of different users. These techniques guarantee indistinguishability of users by typically enforcing the requirement of *k*-anonymity [72], specifically tailored to fit the location-based scenario. In our environmental context, instead of issuing queries to a service provider, users communicate some environmental measurements: This translates to the requirement that a same sensed location should be shared by at least a certain number of different sensing users.

The second class of works aims at obfuscating the real position of the users in scenarios in which users are not anonymized and must provide their real identity to the service provider. The idea is that of *degrading the accuracy* of the location measurement. An intuitive strategy might consist in hiding the real position of a user with a set of other *n* fake positions, characterized by the same probability [82]. A different strategy is based on the adoption of some *obfuscation operators*, with the goal of balancing the accuracy of the position and the privacy requirements of the users. For instance, the technique in [83] quantifies privacy with respect to the accuracy of the location measurement, since the more accurate the measurement, the less the privacy. The defined obfuscation operators change the radius, or the center, of the original location measurement and are used to degrade the accuracy of the location measurement in such a way that, for each user, her privacy preferences are satisfied.

The third class of works focuses on *path privacy*, and aims at releasing a path shared by multiple users so to make them indistinguishable [84]. For instance, these solutions are based on a dynamic grouping of users [85], and protect path privacy enforcing a modified version of *k*-anonymity that requires that all *k* users associated with a specific location remain grouped together as time passes. A different solution is instead based on the release of fake (simulated) locations [86]. This technique adopts probabilistic models of driving behaviors, applied for creating realistic driving trips, and GPS noise to decrease the precision of the starting point of a trip, and is therefore more suitable for scenarios in which environmental sensing devices are placed on vehicles.

6. SUMMARY

In this chapter, we provided an overview of the systems and architectures used for environmental monitoring. We also presented an overview of the main security and privacy issues in environmental monitoring systems and discussed possible countermeasures for mitigating such

issues. Our work can help in better understanding the security and privacy issues that characterized the environmental monitoring systems, and in designing novel environmental systems and applications that guarantee a privacy-aware collection, management, and dissemination of environmental data.

Finally, let's move on to the real interactive part of this chapter: review questions/exercises, hands-on projects, case projects, and optional team case project. The answers and/or solutions by chapter can be found in the Online Instructor's Solutions Manual.

CHAPTER REVIEW QUESTIONS/EXERCISES

True/False

1. True or False? Environmental monitoring systems allow the study of physical phenomena and the design of prediction and reaction mechanisms to dangerous situations.
2. True or False? Environmental monitoring systems have evolved from a simple computer with sensors to composite structures that include specialized components addressing particular data collection issues.
3. True or False? Before describing the security and privacy issues that characterize an environmental monitoring system, it is fundamental to clarify what kinds of environmental data can be typically collected and possibly released to the public.
4. True or False? Environmental monitoring systems and the data they collect cannot be vulnerable to security and privacy risks.
5. True or False? Any attack performed with the aim of physically damaging the monitoring system can put at risk the confidentiality, integrity, and availability of the collected environmental data.

Multiple Choice

1. All _____ connecting the different components of a sensor network can represent a possible target for an adversary.
   A. privacy-enhancing technology
   B. location technology
   C. communication channels
   D. executable policies
   E. data controller
2. What should be available only to users and parties authorized by the data owner.
   A. Policy enforcement
   B. Location technology
   C. Valid
   D. Environmental data
   E. Web technology

3. Which of the following are related to all threats that can allow an adversary to infer sensitive information from the collected environmental data?
   A. Data minimization
   B. XACML
   C. Privacy risks
   D. Contradictory
   E. Security

4. A possible means through which _____ can be inferred is represented by the natural correlations existing among different phenomena.
   A. privacy metrics
   B. greedy strategy
   C. sensitive information
   D. privacy preferences
   E. taps

5. To obtain more meaningful data, _____ can perform several measurements of quantities of interest over time.
   A. irrelevant
   B. sensor nodes
   C. data-handling policies
   D. disclose-to
   E. server policy

EXERCISE

Problem

What is the difference between the data gathered by the stationary and deployable monitors?

Hands-On Projects

Project

What are EPA's radiation air monitoring capabilities?

Case Projects

Problem

Are near-real-time radiation air monitors able to cover the whole United States?

Optional Team Case Project

Problem

What are deployable monitors? What do they measure?

ACKNOWLEDGMENTS

This work was supported in part by the Italian Ministry of Research within the PRIN 2008 project "PEPPER" (2008SY2PH4), and by the Università degli Studi di Milano within the "UNIMI per il Futuro −5 per Mille" project "PREVIOUS."

REFERENCES

[1] F. Amigoni, A. Brandolini, V. Caglioti, V.D. Lecce, A. Guerriero, M. Lazzaroni, et al., Agencies for perception in environmental monitoring, IEEE Trans. Instrum. Meas. 55 (4) (2006) 1038−1050.

[2] M. Dunbabin, L. Marques, Robots for environmental monitoring: significant advancements and applications, IEEE Robotics Autom. Mag. 19 (1) (March 2012) 24−39.

[3] A. Rodic, D. Katie, G. Mester, Ambient intelligent robot-sensor networks for environmental surveillance and remote sensing, 2009.

[4] M. Tubaishat, S. Madria, Sensor networks: an overview, IEEE Potentials 22 (2) (2003) 20−33.

[5] T. Wong, T. Tsuchiya, T. Kikuno, A self-organizing technique for sensor placement in wireless micro-sensor networks, 2004.

[6] H. Leung, S. Chandana, S. Wei, Distributed sensing based on intelligent sensor networks, IEEE Circuits Syst. Mag. 8 (2) (2008) 38−52.

[7] C.Y. Chong, S.P. Kumar, Sensor networks: evolution, opportunities and challenges, IEEE Proc. 91 (8) (2003).

[8] ZigBee Allianz, [Online]. Available: <http://www.zigbee.org>.

[9] P. Kulkarni, D. Ganesan, P. Shenoy, Q. Lu, SensEye: a multitier camera sensor network. in: Proc. of Multimedia 2005, Singapore, 2005.

[10] D. Aksoy, A. Aksoy, Satellite-linked sensor networks for planetary scale monitoring, in: Proc. of VTC 2004, Los Angeles, CA, USA, 2004.

[11] J.K. Hart, K. Martinez, Environmental sensor networks: a revolution in the earth system science? Earth Sci. Rev. 78 (3−4) (2006) 177−191.

[12] R. Butler, T. Lay, K. Creager, P. Earl, K. Fischer, J. Gaherty, et al., The global seismographic network surpasses its design goal, EOS 85 (23) (2004) 225−229.

[13] NOAA Center for Tsunami Research, DART (Deep-ocean Assessment and Reporting of Tsunamis), [Online]. Available: <http://nctr.pmel.noaa.gov/Dart>.

[14] Global Seismographic Network, [Online]. Available: <http://www.iris.edu/hq/programs/gsn>.

[15] Hawaii Institute of Geophysics and Planetology, [Online]. Available: <http://www.higp.hawaii.edu/>.

[16] G. Bernhard, C. Booth, J. Ehramjian, Real-time UV and column ozone from multi-channel UV radiometers deployed in the national science foundation's UV monitoring network, Ultraviolet Ground- and Space-Based Measurements, Models, and Effects III: Proceedings of SPIE, vol. 5156, 2003, pp. 167−178.

[17] NSF Polar Programs UV Monitoring Network, [Online]. Available: <http://uv.biospherical.com/>.

[18] GEMSTAT global environment monitoring system, [Online]. Available: <http://www.gemstat.org/>.

[19] J. Vogelmann, J. Kost, B. Tolk, S. Howard, K. Short, X. Chen, et al., Monitoring landscape change for LANDFIRE using multi-temporal satellite imagery and ancillary data, IEEE J. Sel. Topics Appl. Earth Observations Remote Sens. 4 (2) (June 2011) 252−264.

[20] G. Schaefer, R. Paetzold, SNOTEL (SNOwpack TELemetry) and SCAN (Soil Climate Analysis Network), Automated Weather Stations for Applications in Agriculture and Water Resources Management: Current Use and Future Perspectives, March 2000.

[21] UK climate change network, [Online]. Available: <http://www.ecn.ac.uk>.

[22] J. Kimball, L. Jones, K. Zhang, F. Heinsch, K. McDonald, W. Oechel, A satellite approach to estimate land CO2 atmosphere exchange for boreal and arctic biomes using MODIS and AMSR-E, IEEE Trans. Geosci. Remote Sens. 47 (2) (February 2009) 569–587.

[23] A. Lane, The UK environmental change network database: an integrated information resource for long-term monitoring and research, J. Environ. Manage. 51 (1) (1997) 87–105.

[24] S. Ngheim, P. Clemete-Colon, Arctic sea ice mapping with satellite radars, IEEE Aerosp. Electron. Syst. Mag. 24 (11) (November 2009) 41–44.

[25] J. Qu, X. Hao, M. Kafatos, L. Wang, Asian dust storm monitoring combining terra and aqua MODIS SRB measurements, IEEE Geosci. Remote Sens. Lett. 3 (4) (October 2006) 484–486.

[26] M. Shimada, T. Tadono, A. Rosenqvist, Advanced land observing satellite (ALOS) and monitoring global environmental change, IEEE Proc. 98 (5) (May 2010) 780–799.

[27] A. Rosenqvist, M. Shimada, N. Ito, M. Watanabe, ALOS PALSAR: a pathfinder mission for global-scale monitoring of the environment, IEEE Trans. Geosci. Remote Sens. 45 (11) (November 2007) 3307–3316.

[28] National Oceanic and Atmospheric Administration NOA, United States Department of Commerce, Global Earth Observation System, [Online]. Available: <http://www.noaa.gov/eos.html>.

[29] United States environmental protection agency, national environmental monitoring initiative, [Online]. Available: <http://www.epa.gov/cludygxb/html/choices.htm>.

[30] King county natural resources and parks, [Online]. Available: <http://www.kingcounty.gov/environment/dnrp.aspx>.

[31] M. Carotta, G. Martinelli, L. Crema, C. Malagu, M. Merli, G. Ghiotti, et al., Nanostructured thick-film gas sensors for atmospheric pollutant monitoring: quantitative analysis on field tests, Sens. Actuators B 76 (2001) 336–342.

[32] G. Andria, G. Cavone, V.D. Lecce, A. Lanzolla, Model characterization in measurements of environmental pollutants via data correlation of sensor outputs, IEEE Trans. Instrum. Meas. 54 (3) (June 2005) 1061–1066.

[33] WAVCIS Wave-Current-Surge Information System for Coastal Louisiana, [Online]. Available: <http://www.wavcis.lsu.edu>.

[34] G. Hoogenboom, The Georgia automated environmental monitoring network, Southeastern Climate Rev. 4 (0) (1993) 12–18.

[35] Chesapeake Bay Observatory System, [Online]. Available: <http://www.cbos.org>.

[36] G. Stone, X. Zhang, J. Li, A. Sheremet, Coastal observing systems: key to the future of coastal dynamics investigations, GCAGS/GCSSEPM Trans. 53 (2003) 783–799.

[37] A. Genovese, R. Donida Labati, V. Piuri, F. Scotti, Wildfire smoke detection using computational intelligence techniques, in: IEEE International Conference on Computational Intelligence for Measurement Systems and Applications (CIMSA 2011), Ottawa, Canada, 2011.

[38] A. Genovese, R. Donida Labati, V. Piuri, F. Scotti, Virtual environment for synthetic smoke clouds generation, in: IEEE International Conference on Virtual Environments, Human-Computer Interfaces and Measure ment Systems (VECIMS 2011), Ottawa, Canada.

[39] Z. Liu, A. Kim, Review of recent developments in fire detection technologies, J. Fire Prot. Eng. 13 (2) (May 2003) 129–149.

[40] Q. Li, Q. Hao, K. Zhang, Smart wireless video sensor network for fire alarm, in: Proc. of WiCOM 2010, Chengdu, China, 2010.

[41] B. Son, Y.-s. Her, J.-G. Kim, A design and implementation of forest-fires surveillance system based on wireless sensor networks for South Korea mountains, IJCSNS Int. J. Comput. Sci. Network Secur. 6 (9B) (September 2006).

[42] J. Tschmelak, G. Proll, J. Riedt, J. Kaiser, P. Kraemmer, L. Bárzaga, et al., Automated water analyser computer supported system (AWACSS) part I: project objectives, basic technology immunoassay development, software design and networking, Biosens. Bioelectron. 20 (8) (2005) 1499–1508.

[43] T. Bendikov, J. Kim, T. Harmon, Development and environmental applications of a nitrate selective microsensor based on doped polypyrrole films, in: 204th Meeting of the Electrochemical Society, 2003.

[44] C. Alippi, R. Camplani, C. Galperti, M. Roveri, A robust, adaptive solar-powered WSN framework for aquatic environmental monitoring, IEEE Sens. J. 11 (1) (January 2011) 45–55.

[45] K. Martinez, J. Hart, R. Ong, Environmental sensor networks, Computer 37 (8) (2004) 50–56.

[46] G. Acar, A. Adams, ACMENet: an underwater acoustic sensor network protocol for real-time environmental monitoring in coastal areas, Radar, Sonar and Navigation, IEE Proc. 153 (4) (August 2006) 365–380.

[47] K. Persaud, Smart gas sensor for monitoring environmental changes in closed systems: results from the MIR space station, Sens. Actuators B 2–3 (55) (1999) 118–126.

[48] A. Kumar, I. Singh, S. Sud, Energy efficient and low-cost indoor environment monitoring system based on the IEEE 1451 standard, IEEE Sens. J. 11 (10) (October 2011) 2598–2610.

[49] J. Guevara, F. Barrero, E. Vargas, J. Becerra, S. Toral, Environmental wireless sensor network for road traffic applications, Intell. Transport Syst. IET 6 (2) (June 2012) 177–186.

[50] S. Santini, A. Vitaletti, Wireless sensor networks for environmental noise monitoring, GI/ITG KuVS Fachgespraech Drahtlose Sensornetze, July 2007, pp. 98–101.

[51] L. Ioriatti, M. Martinelli, F. Viani, M. Benedetti, A. Massa, Realtime distributed monitoring of electromagnetic pollution in urban environments in: Geoscience and Remote Sensing Symposium, 2009 IEEE International, IGARSS 2009, 2009.

[52] G. Werner-Allen, J. Johnson, M. Ruiz, J. Lees, M. Welsh, Monitoring volcanic eruptions with a wireless sensor network, in: Proc. of EWSN 2005, Istanbul, Turkey, 2005.

[53] M.V. Ramesh, Real-time wireless sensor network for landslide detection, in: Proceedings of the 2009 Third International Conference on Sensor Technologies and Applications, Washington, DC, USA, 2009.

[54] L. Buttyan, D. Gessner, A. Hessler, P. Langendoerfer, Application of wireless sensor networks in critical infrastructure protection: challenges and design options, IEEE Wireless Commun. 17 (5) (October 2010) 44–49.

[55] T. Harms, S. Sedigh, F. Bastianini, Structural health monitoring of bridges using wireless sensor networks, IEEE Instrum. Meas. Mag. 13 (6) (December 2010) 14–18.

[56] ORION Project, [Online]. Available: <http://orion.lookingtosea.ucsd.edu>.

[57] E. Bradley, M. Toomey, C. Still, D. Roberts, Multi-scale sensor fusion with an online application: Integrating GOES, MODIS, and webcam imagery for environmental monitoring, IEEE J. Sel. Topics Appl. Earth Observations Remote Sens. 3 (4) (December 2010) 497–506.

[58] P. Ferraro, M. Bauersachs, J. Burns, G. Bataller, A system for the measurement of the Amazon, IEEE Aerosp. Electron. Syst. Mag. 22 (8) (August 2007) 9–19.

[59] V. Ciriani, S. De Capitani di Vimercati, S. Foresti, P. Samarati, Microdata protection, in: T. Jajodia, S. Yu (Eds.), Secure Data Management in Decentralized Systems, Springer-Verlag, 2007.

[60] S. De Capitani di Vimercati, G. Livraga, V. Piuri, F. Scotti, Privacy and security in environmental monitoring systems, in: Proc. of ESTEL 2012, Rome, Italy, 2012.

[61] W. Stallings, Network Security Essentials: Applications and Standards, fourth ed., Prentice Hall Press, Upper Saddle River, NJ, 2010.

[62] C. Castelluccia, A.C.-F. Chan, E. Mykletun, G. Tsudik, Efficient and provably secure aggregation of encrypted data in wireless sensor networks, ACM TOSN 5 (3) (2009) 1–36.

[63] S. De Capitani di Vimercati, S. Foresti, S. Paraboschi, G. Pelosi, P. Samarati, Efficient and private access to outsourced data, in: Proc. of ICDCS 2011, Minneapolis, MN, USA, 2011.

[64] S. De Capitani di Vimercati, P. Samarati, Access control in federated systems in: Proc. of NSPW, Lake Arrowhead, CA, USA, 1996.

[65] C. Ardagna, M. Cremonini, S. De Capitani di Vimercati, P. Samarati, A privacy-aware access control system, JCS 16 (4) (2008).

[66] S. De Capitani di Vimercati, S. Foresti, S. Jajodia, S. Paraboschi, P. Samarati, Encryption policies for regulating access to outsourced data, ACM TODS 35 (2) (2010) 1–46.

[67] S. De Capitani di Vimercati, S. Foresti, S. Jajodia, S. Paraboschi, P. Samarati, A data outsourcing architecture combining cryptography and access control, in: Proc. of CSAW 2007, Fairfax, VA, USA, 2007.

[68] G. Aggarwal, M. Bawa, P. Ganesan, H. Garcia-Molina, K. Kenthapadi, R. Motwani, et al., Two can keep a secret: a distributed architecture for secure database services, in: Proc. of CIDR 2005, Asilomar, CA, USA, 2005.

[69] V. Ciriani, S. De Capitani di Vimercati, S. Foresti, S. Jajodia, S. Paraboschi, P. Samarati, Combining fragmentation and encryption to protect privacy in data storage, ACM TISSEC 13 (9) (2010).

[70] V. Ciriani, S. De Capitani di Vimercati, S. Foresti, S. Jajodia, S. Paraboschi, P. Samarat, Keep a few: outsourcing data while maintaining confidentiality, in: Proc. of ESORICS 2009, Saint-Malo, France, 2009.

[71] S. De Capitani di Vimercati, S. Foresti, S. Jajodia, S. Paraboschi, P. Samarati, Fragments and loose associations: respecting privacy in data publishing, PVLDB 3 (1) (2010) 1370–1381.

[72] Federal Committee on Statistical Methodology, Statistical Policy Working Paper 22, second ed., Washington, DC, 2005.

[73] P. Samarati, Protecting respondents' identities in microdata release, IEEE TKDE 13 (6) (2001) 1010–1027.

[74] A. Machanavajjhala, D. Kifer, J. Gehrke, M. Venkitasubramaniam, l-diversity: privacy beyond k-anonymity, ACM TKDD 1 (1) (2007) 3–52.

[75] N. Li, T. Li, S. Venkatasubramanian, t-Closeness: privacy beyond k-anonymity and l-diversity, in: Proc. of ICDE 2007, Istanbul, Turkey, 2007.

[76] K. Wang, B. Fung, Anonymizing sequential releases, in: Proc. of KDD 2006, Philadelphia, PA, USA, 2006.

[77] M. Nergiz, C. Clifton, A. Nergiz, Multirelational k-anonymity, in: Proc. of ICDE 2007, Istanbul, Turkey, 2007.

[78] X. Xiao, Y. Tao, m-invariance: towards privacy preserving re-publication of dynamic datasets, in: Proc. of SIGMOD 2007, Beijing, China, 2007.

[79] M. Terrovitis, N. Mamoulis, P. Kalnis, Privacy-preserving anonymization of set-valued data, PVLDB 1 (1) (2008) 115–125.

[80] Frikken, Y. Zhang, Yet another privacy metric for publishing micro-data, in: Proc. of WPES 2008, Alexandria, VA, USA, 2008.

[81] C. Bettini, S. Jajodia, P. Samarati, X.S. Wang (Eds.), vol. LNCS 5599, Springer, 2009.

[82] M. Duckham, L. Kulik, A formal model of obfuscation and negotiation for location privacy, Munich, Germany, 2005.

[83] C. Ardagna, M. Cremonini, S. De Capitani di Vimercati, P. Samarati, An obfuscation-based approach for protecting location privacy, IEEE TDSC 8 (1) (2011) 13–27.

[84] C.-Y. Chow, M.F. Mokbel, Trajectory privacy in location-based services and data publication, SIGKDD Explorations Newsletter 13 (11) (2011) 19–29.

[85] C.-Y. a. M. M. Chow, Enabling private continuous queries for revealed user locations, in: Proc. of SSTD 2007, Boston, MA, USA, 2007.

[86] J. Krumm, Realistic driving trips for location privacy, in: Proc. of Pervasive 2009, Nara, Japan, 2009.

## Chapter 48

Virtual Private Networks

James T. Harmening

Computer Bits, Inc.

With the incredible advance of the Internet, it has become more and more popular to set up virtual private networks (VPNs) within organizations. Two types of VPNs are typically employed. The first will connect two separate local area networks (LANs), in different locations, to each other; while the second is a single remote computer connecting through the Internet, back to the home network. VPNs have been around for many years and have branched out into more and more varieties. (See Figure 48.1 for a high-level view of a VPN.) Once only the largest of organizations would utilize VPN technology to connect multiple networks over the Internet "public networks," but now VPNs are being used by many small businesses as a way to allow remote users access to their business networks from home or while traveling.

Consultants have changed their recommendations from dial-in systems and leased lines to VPNs for several reasons. Security concerns were once insurmountable, forcing the consultants to set up direct dial-in lines. Not that the public telephone system was much more secure, but it gave the feeling of security and with the right setup, dial-in systems approach secure settings. Sometimes they utilized automatic callback options and had their own encryption. Now, with advanced security, including random-number generator logins, a network administrator is far more likely to allow access to his network via a VPN. High-speed Internet access is now the rule instead of the exception. Costs have plummeted for the hardware and software to make the VPN connection as well. The proliferation of vendors, standardization of Internet Protocol (IP) networks, and ease of setup all played a role in the increasingly wide use and acceptance of VPN.

The key to this technology is the ability to route communications over a public network to allow access to office servers, printers, or data warehouses in an inexpensive manner. As high-speed Internet has grown and become prevalent throughout the world, VPNs over the public Internet have become common. Even inexpensive hotels are offering free Internet access to their customers. This is usually done through Wi-Fi connections, thus causing some concern for privacy, but the connections are out there. Moreover, the iPhone, Android, Windows, Blackberry, and other multifunction Web-enabled phones are giving mobile users access to the Internet via their phones. Finally, some of the best ways to access the Internet is via a wireless USB or PCMCIA card or wireless Hotspot from the major phone companies. These dedicated modem cards allow users to surf the Internet as

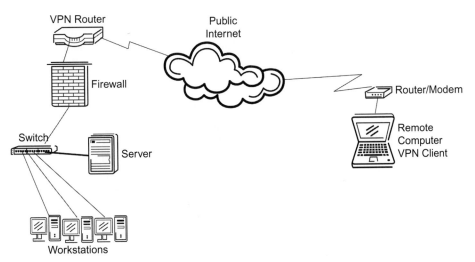

FIGURE 48.1 A high-level view of a VPN.

long as they are in contact with the cell towers of their subscribing company.

One of the sources of our information on the overview of VPNs is James Yonan's talk at Linux Fest Northwest in 2004. You can read the entire presentation online at openvpn.net.

"Fundamentally, a VPN is a set of tools which allow networks at different locations to be securely connected, using a public network as the transport layer."[1] This quote from Yonan's talk states the basic premise incredibly well. Getting two computers to work together over the Internet is a difficult feat, but making two different computer networks be securely connected together via the public Internet is pure genius. By connecting different locations over the Internet, many companies cut out the cost of dedicated circuits from the phone companies. Some companies have saved thousands of dollars by getting rid of their Integrated Services Digital Network (ISDN) lines, too. Once thought of as the high-speed (128,000 bits per second, or 128 kbs) Holy Grail, it is now utilized mainly by videoconferencing systems that require a direct sustained connection, but the two endpoints aren't usually known too much prior to the connection requirement. The ISDN lines are often referred to as glorified fast dial-up connections. Some companies utilize multiple ISDN connections to get higher-quality voice or video.

Not all VPNs had security in the early days. Packets of information were transmitted as cleartext and could be easily seen. To keep the network systems secure, the information must be encrypted. Throughout the past 25 years, different encryption schemes have gained and lost favor. Some are too easy to break with the advanced speed of current computers; others require too much processing power at the router level, thus making their implementation expensive. This is one of those areas where an early technology seemed too expensive, but through time and technological advancements, the hardware processing power has caught up with requirements of the software. Encryption that seems secure in our current environments is often insecure as time passes. With supercomputers doing trillions of computations a second, we are required to make sure that the technology employed in our networks is up to the task. There are many different types of encryption, as discussed later in the chapter.

Early in the VPN life-cycle, the goal for organizations was to connect different places or offices to remote computer systems. This was usually done with a dedicated piece of hardware at each site. This "point-to-point" setup allowed for a secure transmission between two sites, allowing users access to computer resources, data, and communications systems. Many of these sites were too expensive to access, so the advent of the point-to-point systems allowed access where none existed. Now multinational companies set up VPNs to access their manufacturing plants all over the world.

Accounting, order entry, and personnel databases were the big driving forces for disparate locations to be connected. Our desire to have more and more information and faster and faster access to information has driven this trend. Now individuals at home are connecting their computers into the corporate network either through VPN connections or SSL-VPN Web connections. This proliferation is pushing vendors to make better security, especially in unsecure or minimally secure environments. Giving remote access to some, unfortunately, makes for a target to hackers and crackers.

1. HISTORY

Like many innovations in the network arena, the telephone companies first created VPNs. ATT, with it's familiar "Bell logo" (see Figure 48.2), was one of the leading providers of Centrex systems. The goal was to take advantage of different telephone enhancements for conferencing and dialing extensions within a company to connect to employees. Many people are familiar with the Centrex systems that the phone companies offered for many years.

With Centrex the phone company did not require you to have a costly private branch exchange (PBX) switching system onsite. These PBXs were big, needed power, and cost a bundle of money. By eliminating the PBX and using the Centrex system, an organization could keep costs down yet have enhanced service and flexibility of the advanced phone services through the telephone company PBX.

The primary business of the phone companies was to provide voice service, but they also wanted to provide data services. Lines from the phone company from one company location to another (called *leased lines*) offered

FIGURE 48.2　ATT logo; the company was often referred to as Ma Bell.

---

1. James Yonan. "The User-Space VPN and OpenVPN " Copyright ©2003 James Yonan. All Rights Reserved. 5980 Stoneridge Drive, Suite 103, Pleasanton, CA 94588 United States, 2003.

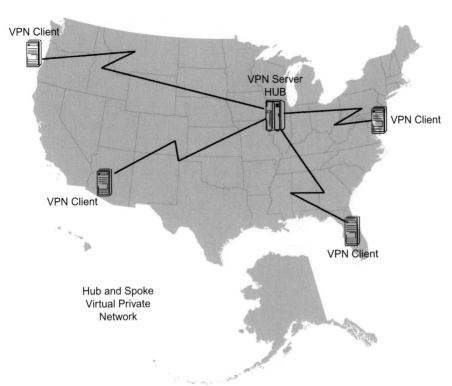

FIGURE 48.3   The hub in the early days.

VPN Client

VPN Server
HUB

VPN Client

VPN Client

VPN Client

Hub and Spoke
Virtual Private
Network

remote data access from one part of a company to another.

Many companies started utilizing different types of software to better utilize their leased lines. In the early days, the main equipment was located centrally, and all the offices connected to the "hub" (see Figure 48.3). This was a good system and many companies still prefer this network topography, but times are changing. Instead of having a hub-and-spoke design, some companies opted to daisy-chain their organization together, thus trying to limit the distance they would have to pay for their leased lines. So a company would have a leased line from New York to Washington, D.C., another from D.C. to Atlanta, and a third from Atlanta to Miami. This would cut costs over the typical hub-and-spoke system of having all the lines go through one central location (see Figure 48.4).

With the proliferation of the Internet and additional costs for Internet connections and leased-line connections, the companies pushed the software vendors to make cheap connections via the Internet. VPNs solved their problems and had a great return on investment (ROI). Within a year, the cost of the VPN equipment paid for itself through eliminating the leased lines. Though this technology has been around for years, some organizations still rely on leased lines due to a lack of high-speed Internet in remote areas.

In 1995, IPsec was one of the first attempts at bringing encryption to the VPN arena. One of the early downfalls of this technology was its complexity and requirement for fast processors on the routers to keep up with the high bandwidths. In 1995, according to ietf.org, "at least one hardware implementation can encrypt or decrypt at about 1 Gbps."[2] Yes, one installation that cost thousands of dollars.

Fortunately, Moore's Law has been at work, and today our processing speeds are high enough to get IPsec working on even small routers. Moore's Law is named after Intel cofounder Gordon Moore, who wrote in 1965: "the number of transistors on a chip will double about every two years."[3] This doubling of chip capacity allows for more and more computing to be done.

Another issue with early IPsec is that it is fairly inflexible, with differing IP addresses. Many home and home office computers utilize dynamic IP addresses. You may get a different IP address each time you turn on your computer and connect to the Internet. The IPsec connection will have to be reestablished and may cause a hiccup in your transmissions or the requirement that a password be reentered. This seems unreasonable to most users.

Another difficulty is the use of Network Address Translation (NAT) for some networks. Each computer on the network has the same IP address as far as the greater

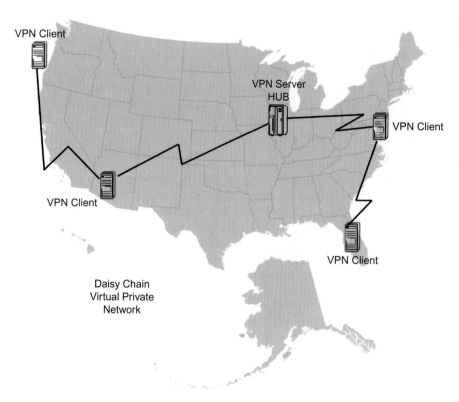

FIGURE 48.4 One central location for the hub-and-spoke system.

Internet is concerned. This is in part because of the shortage of legal IP addresses available in the IPv4 or higher address space. As we move closer and closer to the IPv6 or higher address space model, some of these issues will be moot, for a while. Soon, every device we own, including our refrigerators, radios, and heating systems, will have a static IP address. Maybe even our kitchen sinks will. Big Brother is coming, but won't it be cool to see what your refrigerator is up to? Want that ice cold beer a bit cooler, get on your Smartphone and tell the refrigerator you are on your way!

In the late 1990s Linux began to take shape as a great test environment for networking. A technology called *tun,* short for *tunnel,* allows data to be siphoned through the data stream to create virtual hardware. From the operating system perspective it looks like point-to-point network hardware, even though it is virtual hardware. Another technology, called *tap,* looks like Ethernet traffic but also uses virtual hardware to fool the operating system into thinking it is real hardware.

These technologies utilize a program running in the user area of the operating system software in order to look like a file. They can read and write IP packets directly to and from this virtual hardware, even though the systems are connected via the public Internet and could be on the other side of the world. Security is an issue with the tun/tap method. One way to build in security is to utilize the Secure Shell protocol (SSH) and

transport the data via a User Datagram Protocol (UDP) or Transmission Control Protocol (TCP) packet sent over the network.

It is important to remember that IP is an unreliable protocol. There are collisions on all IP networks; high traffic times give high collisions and lost packets, but the protocol is good at resending the packets so that eventually all the data will get to its destination. On the other hand, TCP is a reliable protocol. So, like military and intelligence, we have the added problem of a reliable transportation protocol (TCP) using an unreliable transportation (IP) method.

So, how does it work if it is unreliable? Well, eventually all the packets get there; TCP makes sure of that, and they are put in order and delivered to the other side. Some may have to be retransmitted, but most won't and the system should work relatively quickly.

One way that we can gain some throughput and added security is by utilizing encapsulation protocols. Encapsulation allows you to stuff one kind of protocol inside another type of protocol. The idea is to encapsulate a TCP packet inside a UDP packet. This forces the application to worry about dropped packets and reliability instead of the TCP network layer, since UDP packets are not a reliable packet protocol. This really increases speed, especially during peak network usage times.

So, follow this logic: The IP packets are encrypted, then encapsulated and stored for transport via UDP over the Internet. On the receiving end the host system receives, decrypts, and authenticates the packets and then sends them to the tap or tun virtual adapter at the other end, thus giving a secure connection between the two sides, with the operating system not really knowing or caring about the encryption or transport methods. From the OS point of view, it is like a data file being transmitted; the OS doesn't have to know that the hardware is virtual. It is just as happy thinking that the virtual data file is real—and it processes it just like it processes a physical file locally stored on a hard drive.

OpenVPN is just one of many Open Source VPNs in use today. Google it and you will see a great example of a VPN system that employs IPsec.

IPsec is another way to ensure security on your VPN connection. IPsec took the approach that it needed to replace the IP stack and do it securely. IPsec looks to do its work in the background, without utilizing operating system CPU cycles. This is wonderful for its non-impact on servers, but it then relies heavily on the hardware.

A faster-growing encryption scheme involves Secure Socket Layer (SSL) VPN, as we talk about it later in this chapter. This scheme gives the user access to resources like a VPN but through a Web browser. The end user only needs to install the browser plug-ins to get this VPN up and working, for remote access on the fly. One example of this SSL type of VPN is LogMeIn Rescue.[4] It sets up a remote control session within the SSL layer of the browser. It can also extend resources out to the remote user without initiating a remote-control session.

Finally, the future for standardizing (Transport Layer Security) TLS-based, user-space VPNs is growing quickly. With the ability to prevent eavesdropping before the transmissions begin, future VPN session will be even more secure. In 2011, the Internet Engineering Task Force (IETF) published the latest on TLS http://tools.ietf.org/html/rfc6176. With all these schemes and more, we should take a look at who is in charge of helping to standardize the hardware and software requirements of the VPN world.

2. WHO IS IN CHARGE?

For all this interconnectivity to actually work, there are several organizations that publish standards and work for cooperation among vendors in the sea of computer networking change. In addition to these public groups, there are also private companies that are working toward new protocols to improve speed and efficiency in the VPN arena.

FIGURE 48.5   Logo for IETF

FIGURE 48.6   Logo for IEEE.

The two biggest public groups are the Internet Engineering Task Force (www.ietf.org; see Figure 48.5) and the Institute of Electrical and Electronic Engineers (www.IEEE.org; see Figure 48.6). Each group has its own way of doing business and publishes its recommendations and standards.

As the IEEE Web site proclaims, the group's "core purpose is to foster technological innovation and excellence for the benefit of humanity." This is a wonderful and noble purpose. Sometimes they get it right and sometimes input and interference from vendors get in the way of moving technology forward—or worse yet, vendors go out and put up systems that come out before the specifications get published, leaving humanity with different standards. This has happened several times on the wireless networking standards group. Companies release their implementation of a standard prior to final agreement by the standards boards.

The group's vision is stated thus: "IEEE will be essential to the global technical community and to technical professionals everywhere, and be universally recognized for the contributions of technology and of technical professionals in improving global conditions."[5]

The Internet Engineering Task Force (IETF) is a large, open international community of network designers, operators, vendors, and researchers concerned with the evolution of the Internet architecture and the smooth operation of the Internet. It is open to any interested

4. H. Alvestrand "A Mission Statement for the IETF" Network Working Group RFC3935, October 2004.

5. A. Valencia, M. Littlewood, and T. Kolar 'Cisco Layer Two Forwarding (Protocol) "L2F"' Network Working Group RFC2341 May 1998.

FIGURE 48.7 The ANSI logo.

individual. The IETF Mission Statement is documented in RFC 3935. According to the group's mission statement, "The goal of the IETF is to make the Internet work better."[6]

Finally, we can't get away from acronyms unless we include the United States Government. An organization called the American National Standards Institute (ANSI; www.ansi.org) an over 90-year-old organization with responsibilities that include writing voluntary standards for the marketplace to have somewhere to turn for standardizing efforts to improve efficiencies and interoperability (see Figure 48.7).

There are many standards for many physical things, such as the size of a light bulb socket or the size of an outlet on your wall. These groups help set standards for networking. Two international groups that are represented by ANSI are the International Organization for Standardization (ISO) and International Electrotechnical Commission (IEC).

These organizations have ongoing workgroups and projects that are tackling the various standards that will be in use in the future releases of the VPN standard. They also have the standards written for current interoperability. However, this does not require a vendor to follow the standards. Each vendor can and will implement parts and pieces of standards, but unless they meet all the requirements of a specification, they will not get to call their system compatible.

There are several IEEE projects relating to networking and the advancement of interconnectivity. If you are interested in networking, the 802 family of workgroups is your best bet. Check out www.ieee802.org.

3. VPN TYPES

As we talked about earlier, this encryption standard for VPN access is heavy on the hardware for processing the encryption and decrypting the packets. This protocol operates at the Layer 3 level of the Open Systems Interconnection (OSI) model. The OSI model dates to 1982 by the International Organization for

Standardization.[7] IPsec is still used by many vendors for their VPN hardware.

IPsec

One of the weaknesses of VPNs we mentioned earlier is also a strength. Because the majority of the processing work is done by the interconnecting hardware, the application doesn't have to worry about knowing anything about IPsec at all.

There are two modes for IPsec. First, the transport mode secures the information all the way to each device trying to make the connection. The second mode is the transport mode, which is used for network-to-network communications. The latest standard for IPsec came out in 2005.

One of the downsides to IPsec is it's complexity at the Kernal level. With one buffer overflow, you can wreak havoc on the transmitted data.

L2TP

Layer Tunneling Protocol was released in 1999; then to improve the reliability and security of Point-to-Point Tunneling Protocol (PPTP), L2TP was created. It really is a layer 5 protocol because it uses the session layer in the OSI model.

This was more cumbersome than PPTP and forced the users at each end to have authentication with one another. It also has weak security, thus most implementations of the L2TP protocol utilize IPsec to enhance security.

There is a 32-bit header for each packet that includes flags, versions, Tunnel ID, and Session IDs. There is also a space for the packet size.

Because this is a very weak protocol, some vendors combined it with IPsec to form L2TP/IPsec. In this implementation you take the strong, secure nature of IPsec as the secure channel, and the L2TP will act as the tunnel.

This protocol is a server/user setup. One part of the software acts as the server and waits for the user side of the software to make contact. Because this protocol can handle many users or clients at a time, some Asymmetric Digital Subscriber Line (ADSL) providers use this L2TP protocol and share the resources at the telephone central office. Their modem/routers utilize L2TP to phone home to the central office and share a higher capacity line out to the Internet.

For more information, see the IETF.org publication RFC 2661. You can delve deeper into the failover mode of L2TP or get far more detail on the standard.

6. E. Rosen A. Viswanathan, R. Callon "Multiprotocol Label Switching Architecture" Network Working Group RFC 3031 January 2001.

7. Callan, Tim "MD5 Hack Interesting, But Not Threatening", Security Focus January 5, 2009.

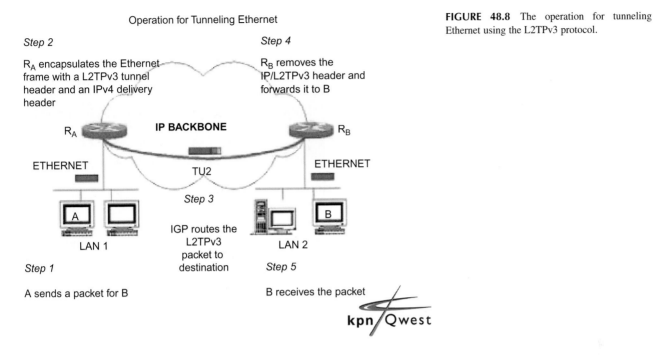

Operation for Tunneling Ethernet

Step 2

R_A encapsulates the Ethernet frame with a L2TPv3 tunnel header and an IPv4 delivery header

Step 4

R_B removes the IP/L2TPv3 header and forwards it to B

IP BACKBONE

R_A R_B

ETHERNET   TU2   ETHERNET

Step 3

IGP routes the L2TPv3 packet to destination

LAN 1   LAN 2

Step 1

A sends a packet for B

Step 5

B receives the packet

kpn/Qwest

FIGURE 48.8 The operation for tunneling Ethernet using the L2TPv3 protocol.

L2TPv3 or Higher

This is the draft advancement of the L2TP for large carrier-level information transmissions. In 2005, the draft protocol was released; it provides additional security features, improved encapsulation, and the ability to carry data links other than simply PPP over an IP network (Frame Relay, Ethernet, ATM). Figure 48.8 shows the operation for tunneling Ethernet using the L2TPv3 or higher protocol and was taken from *Psuedo-wire Services and L2TPv3 or higher* from KPN/Quest.[8]

L2F

Cisco's Layer 2 Forwarding protocol is used for tunneling the link layer (layer 2 in the OSI model). This protocol allows for virtual dial-up that allows for the sharing of modems, ISDN routers, servers, and other hardware.

This protocol was popular in the mid- to late-1990s and was utilized by Shiva's products to share a bank of modems to a network of personal computers. This was a fantastic cost savings for network administrators wanting to share a small number of modems and modem lines to a large user group. Instead of having 50 modems hooked up to individual PCs, you could have a bank of eight modems that could be used during the day to dial out and connect to external resources, becoming available at night for workers to dial back into the computer system for remote access to corporate data resources.

For those long-distance calls to remote computer systems, an employee could dial into the office network. For security and billing reasons, the office computer system would dial back to the home user. The home user would access a second modem line to dial out to a long distance computer system. This would eliminate all charges for the home user except for the initial call to get connected. RFC 2341 on IETF.org gives you the detailed standard.[9]

PPTP VPN

Point-to-Point Tunneling Protocol was created in the 1990s by Microsoft, Ascend, 3COM and a few other vendors, in order to try and serve the user community. This VPN protocol allowed for easy implementation with Windows machines because it was included in Windows. It made for fairly secure transmissions, though not as secure as IPsec. Although Microsoft has a great deal of influence in the computing arena, the IPsec and L2TP protocols are the standards-based protocols that most vendors use for VPNs.

Under PPTP, Microsoft has implemented MPPE—Microsoft Point-to-Point Encryption Protocol, which allows encryption keys of 40 to 128 bits. The latest updates were done in 2003 to strengthen the security of this protocol. A great excerpt from Microsoft Technet for Windows NT 4.0 or higher Server explains the process of

8. ibid

9. Duane Dunston "In this article, Duane Dunston gives a brief introduction to OpenVPN and interviews its founder James Yonan" October 2006 Linux Security www.linuxsecurity.com/content/view/117363/49"

PPTP extremely well; check out http://technet.microsoft.com/en-us/library/cc768084.aspx for more information.

MPLS

MPLS is another system for large telephone companies or huge enterprises to get great response times for VPN with huge amounts of data. MPLS stands for MultiProtocol Label Switching. This protocol operates between layer 2 and layer 3 of the OSI model we have mentioned before. The Internet Engineering Task Force Web page with the specifications for the label switching architecture can be found at www.ietf.org/rfc/rfc3031.txt.

This protocol has big advantages over Asynchronous Transfer Mode (ATM) and Frame Relay. The overhead is lower and with the ability to have variable length data packets, audio and video will be transmitted much more efficiently. Another big advantage over ATM is the ATM requirement that the two endpoints have to handshake and make a connection before any data is ever transmitted.

The name MultiProtocol Label Switching came from the underlying way in which the endpoints find each other. The switches using this technology find their destination through the lookup of a label instead of the lookup of an IP address. Label Edge Routers are the beginning and ending points of an MPLS network. The big competitor for future network expansion is L2TPv3 or higher.

MPVPN™

Ragula Systems Development Company created Multi Path Virtual Private Network (MPVPN) to enhance the quality of service of VPNs. The basic concept is to allow multiple connections to the Internet at both endpoints and use the combination of connections to create a faster connection. So if you have a T1 line and a DS3 at your office, you can aggregate both lines through the MPVPN device to increase your response times. The data traffic will be load balanced and will increase your throughput.

SSH

This protocol lets network traffic run over a secured channel between devices. SSH uses public-key cryptography. Tatu Ylönen from Finland created the first version of SSH in 1995 to thwart password thieves at his university network. The company he created is called SSH Communications Security and can be reached at www.ssh.com (see Figure 48.9).

Utilizing public-key cryptography is a double-edged sword. If an inside user authenticates an attacker's public key, you have just let them into the system, where they can deploy man-in-the-middle hacks. Also, the intent for

FIGURE 48.9   SSH Communications Security logo.

this security system was to keep out the bad guys at the gate. Once a person is authenticated, she is in and a regular user and can deploy software that would allow a remote VPN to be set up through the SSH protocol. Future versions of SSH may prevent these abuses.

SSL-VPN

Secure Socket Layer (SSL) VPN isn't really VPN at all. It's more of an interface that gives users the services that look like VPN through their Web browsers. There are many remote-control applications that take advantage of this layer in the Web browser to gain access to users' resources.

TLS

Transport Layer Security, the successor to SSL, is used to prevent eavesdropping on information being sent between computers. When using strong encryption algorithms, the security of your transmission is almost guaranteed.

Both SSL and TLS work very much the same way. First, the sessions at each endpoint contact each other for information about what encryption method is going to be employed. Second, the keys are exchanged. These could be RSA, Diffie-Hellman, ECDH, SRP, or PSK.

Finally, the messages are encrypted and authenticated, sometimes using Certificate of Authorities Public Key list. When you utilize SSL and TLS you may run into a situation where the server certificate does not match the information held in the Certificate of Authorities Public Key list. If this is the case, the user may override the error message or may choose not to trust the site and end the connection.

The whole public key/private key encryption is able to take place behind the scenes for a few reasons. During the beginning phase of the connection, the server and requesting computer generate a random number. Random numbers are combined and encrypted using the private keys. Only the owner of the public key can unencrypt the random number that is sent using their private key.

TLS is growing every year. One of the limiting factors is the size of the hash value in the final message is truncated to 96bits. So even though it could be using a 256 bit hash, the transmission cuts it to 96bits. In the future we may see something that addresses this.

4. AUTHENTICATION METHODS

Currently, usernames and passwords are the most common authentication method employed in the VPN arena. We may transport the data through an SSL channel or via a secured and encrypted transport model, but when it comes to gaining access to the system resources, most often you will have to log into the VPN with a username and password.

As we talked about earlier, there are some edge-based systems that require a dongle, and a random number is generated on gaining access to the login screen. These tiered layers of security can be a great wall that will thwart a hacker's attempt to gain access to your network system in favor of going after easier networks.

Not all authentication methods are the same. We will talk about a few different types of protection schemes and point out weaknesses and strengths.

With each type of encryption we are concerned with its voracity along with concerns over the verification and authentication of the data being sent. Transmission speeds and overhead in encrypting and decrypting data are another consideration, but as mentioned earlier, Moore's Law has helped a great deal.

Hashing

Using a computer algorithm to mix up the characters in your encryption is fairly common. If you have a secret and want another person to know the answer, but you are fearful that it will be discovered, you can mix up the letters.

HMAC

HMAC (keyed Hash Message Authentication Code) is a type of encryption that uses an algorithm in conjunction with a key. The algorithm is only as strong as the complexity of the key and the size of the output. For HMAC either 128 or 160 bits are used.

This type of Message Authentication Code (MAC) can be defeated. One way is by using the birthday attack. To ensure that your data is not deciphered, choose a strong key; use upper- and lowercase letters, numbers, and special characters. Also use 160 bits when possible.

MD5

Message Digest 5 is one of the best file integrity checks available today. It is also used in some encryption schemes, though the veracity of its encryption strength is being challenged.

The method uses a 128-bit hash value. It is represented as a 32-digit hexadecimal number. A file can be "hashed" down to a single 32-digit hex number. The likelihood of two files with the same hash is 2^{128} but with the use of rainbow tables and collision theory, there have been a few successes in cracking this encryption. As Tim Callan points out in his January 5, 2009 blog post, "Considering that it took the original researchers four tries over at least a month to successfully accomplish their attack against the RapidSSL brand, we're fully confident that no malicious organization had the opportunity to use this information against RapidSSL, or any other certificate authority authorized by VeriSign."

SHA-1

Secure Hash Algorithm was designed by the U.S. National Security Agency (NSA). There is also SHA-224, SHA-256, SHA-384, and SHA-512. The number of bits in SHA-1 is 160. The others have the number of bits following the SHA.

SHA-1 is purported to have been compromised, but the voracity of the reports has been challenged. In any case, the NSA has created the SHA-224 to SHA-512 specification to make it even more difficult to crack. At the Rump Session of CRYPTO 2006, Christian Rechberger and Christophe De Cannière claimed to have discovered a collision attack on SHA-1 that would allow an attacker to select at least parts of the message.

The basic premise is the same as the MD5 hash: The data is encrypted utilizing a message digest. This method is the basis for several common applications including SSL, PGP, SSH, S/MIME, and IPsec.

NSA is working on the next-generation SHA-3 and is seeking vendors to compete in creating the next-generation hashing algorithms. Submissions were due October 31, 2008 and the final 5 were chosen December 10, 2010. They are BLAKE, Grøstl, JH, Keccak, and Skein. The interesting thread among these, the winner will be chosen in 2013. Check the NIST website at http://csrc.nist.gov/groups/ST/hash/sha-3/index.html for the most recent updates.

5. SYMMETRIC ENCRYPTION

Symmetric encryption requires that both the sender and receiver have the same key and each computes a common key that is subsequently used. Two of the most common symmetric encryption standards are known as DES (Data

Encryption Standard) and AES (Advanced Encryption Standard). Once AES was released, DES was withdrawn as a standard and replaced with 3-DES, often referred to as Triple DES and TDES.

3-DES takes DES and repeats it two more times. So it is hashed with the 56-bit algorithm and password, and then done twice more. This prevents more brute-force attacks, assuming a strong key is used. Some VPN software is based on these symmetric keys, as we have discussed before.

Finally, a system of shared secrets allows encryption and decryption of data. This can either be done as a pre-shared password, which is known by both ends prior to communication, or some kind of key agreement protocol where the key is calculated from each end using a common identifier or public key.

6. ASYMMETRIC CRYPTOGRAPHY

The biggest example of asymmetric cryptography for VPNs is in the RSA protocol. Three professors at MIT, Ron Rivest, Adi Shamir, and Leonard Adelman (thus RSA), came up with the RSA encryption algorithm, which is an implementation of public/private key cryptography.

This is one of the coolest and most secure means of transmitting data. Not only is it used for transmission of data, but a person can also digitally sign a document with the use of RSA secure systems. Some states are creating systems for giving people their own digital signatures and holding the public keys in a server that can be accessed by all.

Although these systems have been around for a while, they are becoming more and more prevalent. For example, some states will allow accountants who sign up with them to transmit income tax forms electronically as long as they digitally sign the returns.

This algorithm uses two large random prime numbers. Prime number searching has been a pastime for many mathematical scientists. As the prime number gets larger and larger, its use for privacy and security systems is increased. Thus, many search for larger prime numbers. Through the use of these numbers and a key, the data is secured from prying eyes.

When you are in a public system and don't have the luxury of knowing the keys in advance, there are ways to create a key that will work. This system is very interesting and is known as the *exponential key exchange* because it uses exponential numbers in the initial key exchange to come to an agreed-on cipher.

7. EDGE DEVICES

As with any system, having two locked doors is better than one. With the advent of many remote computing systems, a new type of external security has come into favor. For instance, the setting up an edge device, allows for a unique username and password, or better yet, a unique username and a random password that only the user and the computer system knows.

These edge systems often employ authentication schemes in conjunction with a key fob that displays a different random number every 30 to 60 seconds. The server knows what the random number should be based on the time and only authenticates the person into the edge of the network if the username and password match. Once into the edge network, the user is prompted for a more traditional username and password to gain access to data, email, or applications under his username.

8. PASSWORDS

Your system and data are often only as good as the strength of your password. The weakest of passwords entails a single word or name. An attacker using common dictionary attacks will often break a weak password. For example, using the *word password* is usually broken very quickly.

Using multiple words or mixing spelling and upper- and lowercase will make your weak password a bit stronger. PasswOrd would be better. Adding numbers increases your passwords voracity. P2ssw9rd decreases your chance of getting hacked. Add in a few special characters and your password gets even more secure, as with P2#$w9rd.

But to get even stronger you need to use a password over 12 characters made up of upper- and lowercase letters, numbers, and special characters: P2#$w9rd.34HHlz. Stay away from acronyms. There are even some systems that don't allow any word from the English language to be used in any part of the password. The first time I ran into this, I was very frustrated, it is tough to teach an old dog new tricks.

Another way to keep your VPNs secure is to only allow access from fixed IP addresses. If the IP address isn't on the allowable list, you don't allow the computer in, no matter what. The unique address for each network card that is in the hardware is called the Media Access Control (MAC) address. This is another fixed ID that can be used to allow or disallow computers onto your VPN. The problem with this method is that both IP and MACs can be spoofed. So, if a person gets his hands on a valid MAC ID, he can get around this bit of security.

Some VPN systems will allow you to log in with a username and password, and then it will connect to a predefined IP address. So even if your passwords are stolen, unless the person knows the predefined IP address of the callback, they can't get into your system. This idea is a throwback to the dial-in networks that would allow a person to dial in, connect with their username and password, and then promptly disconnect and call the person's computer system back. It was an extra two minutes on the front end, but a great added level of security.

Finally, biometrics are beginning to play a role in authentication systems. For example, instead of a password, your fingerprint is used. Some systems use voiceprint, hand geometry, retinal eye scan, or facial geometry. We can foresee the day when a DNA reader uses your DNA as your password. Like a bloodhound who is able to follow you by the scent of the dead skin falling off your body (www.mythbusters.com), a sniffer device may be employed to analyze the DNA falling off your body. Homeland Security is looking into testing this technology at major airports in the U.S. I guess it beats taking naked pictures or giving you the personal pat down.

9. HACKERS AND CRACKERS

One of the inherent problems with remote access is security, Duane Dunston asked James Lonan from www. LinuxSecurity.com is "One of my major gripes with IPSec is that it adds a lot of complexity to the kernel. Complexity is really the enemy of security. The problem with putting complex security software in the kernel is that you ignore an important security principle: never design secure systems so that the failure of one component results in a catastrophic security breach. A single buffer overflow exploit in kernel space results in total system compromise – why not move the complexity into user space where the code might run in an empty chroot jail as user "nobody"? At least with this approach, a code insertion exploit can be more readily contained" (http://www.linuxsecurity.com/content/view/117363/49/).

Some good ways to prevent hackers and crackers from getting into your system is to enable the best security levels that your hardware has to offer. If you can utilize 512 or 256-bit encryption methods, then use them. If you can afford a random-number−generated edge security system, then use it.

Have your users change their VPN passwords frequently, especially if they are utilizing public Internet portals. Don't expect your local library to have the security that your own internal company has. If you access your VPN from an insecure public Internet hotspot, then make sure you change your VPN password.

Don't give out your VPN password for other people to use. This can cause you great difficulties if something sinister happens to the network and the connection is traced back to your username and password.

Another way to secure your network is to deactivate accounts that have not been used for 30 days. Yes, this can be a pain, but if a person is not regularly accessing the system, then maybe they don't need access in the first place.

Finally, remove stale VPN accounts from the system. One of the biggest problems with unauthorized VPN access is the employee who has retired but her account never got disabled. Maybe her logon and email were removed, but IT didn't remove her VPN account. Put in checks and balances on accounts.

10. MOBILE VPN

We have become a mobile computing society. We have Smartphones, iPads, Android Tablets, Netbooks, laptops, and Cars just to name a few of the things we carry that can connect to the internet. With this connectivity comes challenges to the VPN world. Having a policeman or fireman connected back to the station's computers while on the road can cause sub-nets to change, cell towers to change, phone carrier's to change not only the speed, but also the protocol for data service. Imagine having to deal with this, all while keeping a secure data connection to the office. Some vehicles are even equipped with radios that can transmit data through their own private network. Or the health professional who does well-care or sick-care visit's throughout the community and needs to enter information about their visit as they go. How does the VPN keep the connection, let alone keep it secure?

Host Identity Protocol (HIP) is the technology now being employed to keep us connected on our mobile devices. At this point there is no final standard, but the IETF (http://tools.ietf.org/html/rfc4423) is studying the technology and working with vendors to come up with a public standard. Each vendor uses this technology a little bit differently. But the market has pushed them to do so.

The basic premise is to have the tunnel bound to an IP address that is static on the phone, that static IP is used even though the tunnels change and go through different sub-nets and even different carriers. The VPN software does all the security and handshaking when the changes occur, thus leaving the user free to think they have a steady connection — no matter where they are at.

Think of some of the security risks as well as the speed problems. This harkens back to the days where an application had to be written with transmission speeds in mind, think more text, less graphics. Think re-usable graphics on different form pages, so the browser doesn't have to download them each time a page is changed.

Finally, let's briefly look at VPN deployments. Organizations planning VPN deployments should identify and define requirements, and evaluate several products to determine their fit into the organization.

11. VPN DEPLOYMENTS

VPN products vary in functionality, including protocol and application support. They also vary in breadth, depth, and completeness of features and security services. Some recommendations and considerations are included the following checklist: "An Agenda For Action For VPN Deployments").

An Agenda for Action for VPN Deployments

Some of the cryptographic requirements, including allowable hash functions and certificate key lengths have changed. Therefore, organizations who want to provide VPN services must ensure that their systems are upgradeable to the cipher suites and key lengths, and that their SSL VPN vendors guarantee that such upgrades will be available early enough for testing and deployment in the field. Thus, the following set of VPN deployments activities must be adhered to (check all tasks completed):

_____1. VPN manageability features such as status reporting, logging, and auditing should provide adequate capabilities for the organization to effectively operate and manage the SSL VPN and to extract detailed usage information.

_____2. The SSL VPN high availability and scalability features should support the organization's requirements for failover, load balancing and throughput.

_____3. State and information sharing is recommended to keep the failover process transparent to the user.

_____4. VPN portal customization should allow the organization to control the look and feel of the portal and to customize the portal to support various devices such as personal digital assistants (PDA) and smart phones.

_____5. SSL VPN authentication should provide the necessary support for the organization's current and future authentication methods and leverage existing authentication databases.

_____6. VPN authentication should also be tested to ensure interoperability with existing authentication methods.

_____7. The strongest possible cryptographic algorithms and key lengths that are considered secure for current practice should be used for encryption and integrity protection unless they are incompatible with interoperability, performance and export constraints.

_____8. SSL VPNs should be evaluated to ensure they provide the level of granularity needed for access controls.

_____9. Access controls should be capable of applying permissions to users, groups, and resources, as well as integrating with endpoint security controls.

_____10. Implementation of endpoint security controls is often the most diverse service among VPN products.

_____11. Endpoint security should be evaluated to ensure it provides the necessary host integrity checking and security protection mechanisms required for the organization.

_____12. Not all SSL VPNs have integrated intrusion prevention capabilities. Those that do should be evaluated to ensure they do not introduce an unacceptable amount of latency into the network traffic.

12. SUMMARY

This chapter assisted organizations in understanding VPN technologies and in designing, implementing, configuring, securing, monitoring, and maintaining SSL VPN solutions. The chapter also provided a phased approach to VPN planning and implementation that can help in achieving successful SSL VPN deployments. It also provided a comparison with other similar technologies such as IPsec VPNs and other VPN solutions.

Finally, let's move on to the real interactive part of this Chapter: review questions/exercises, hands-on projects, case projects and optional team case project. The answers and/or solutions by chapter can be found in the Online Instructor's Solutions Manual.

CHAPTER REVIEW QUESTIONS/EXERCISES

True/False

1. True or False? All VPNs had security in the early days.
2. True or False? ATT, with it's familiar "Bell logo," was one of the leading providers of Centrex systems.
3. True or False? In the early days, the main equipment was located locally, and all the offices connected to the "hub."
4. True or False? The encryption standard for VPN access is heavy on the software for processing the encryption and decrypting the packets.
5. True or False? Secure Socket Layer (SSL) VPN is really VPN.

Multiple Choice

1. What is another system for large telephone companies or huge enterprises to get great response times for VPNs with huge amounts of data?
   A. PPTP VPN
   B. L2F
   C. MPLS
   D. L2TPv3
   E. L2TP
2. What allows multiple connections to the Internet at both endpoints and use the combination of connections to create a faster connection?
   A. MPLS

B. SSH

C. MPVPN

D. SSL-VPN

E. TLS

3. What is used to prevent eavesdropping on information being sent between computers?

   A. SSL

   B. TLS

   C. RSA

   D. ECDH

   E. SRP

4. What are two of the most common authentication methods employed in the VPN arena?

   A. Usernames

   B. Encryption

   C. Random numbers

   D. Decryption

   E. Passwords

5. What is a type of encryption that uses an algorithm in conjunction with a key?

   A. MAC

   B. HMAC

   C. MD5

   D. SHA-1

   E. DES

EXERCISE

Problem

The problem described in this exercise is how do you connect remote users to a single main office. A medium-sized organization has a large population of users that work from remote locations once to several days each week. The organization is research-oriented, and many of these users require access to a broad range of internal IT resources to conduct their research. These resources include email, calendar, file sharing services, and secure shell access on a variety of hosts. The organization already offers remote access services in the form of a host-to-gateway IPsec solution. This works successfully, but has required significant IT labor resources to install and support the client software on user hosts. The current solution also does not provide remote access for hosts based in public locations such as hotels and kiosks. So, how does the organization implement a complementary remote access architecture?

Hands-On Projects

Project

A health care company formed from the merger of two large health care companies, started to experience a

succession of network stability issues. This was a big concern for the company. Strong network availability is a crucial business requirement for the company, as it predominantly operates in a moderate client environment. If users cannot connect to the central server, they cannot access either the applications or the data that are essential for them to do their jobs. After a competitive evaluation of multiple telecommunications services, what did the company decide to do with regards to replacing its existing point-to-point connections with an Virtual Private Network (VPN)?

Case Projects

Problem

This case study illustrates how a leading building construction company needed a highly scalable and flexible telecommunications solution. So, how would the company go about meeting all of its telecommunications requirements and ensure business continuity in order to back up its vital systems in the event of an unforeseen disaster?

Optional Team Case Project

Problem

An engineering company developed a site-to-site virtual private network (VPN). How was the company's VPN solution able to cut networking costs dramatically by integrating security applications with other platform components to create a tightly-integrated, multi-layer security perimeter?

RESOURCES

1 www.openvpn.net/papers/BLUG-talk/2.html,   copyright   James Yonan 2003

2 http://tools.ietf.org/html/draft-ietf-ipsec-esp-des-cbc-03   The   ESP DES-CBC Transform

3 www.intel.com/technology/mooreslaw/Gordon Moore 1965.

4 www.logmein.com

5 www.ieee.org/web/aboutus/visionmission.html   Copyright   IEEE 2008

6 www.ietf.org/rfc/rfc3935.txt Copyright The Internet Society 2004

7 http://en.wikipedia.org/wiki/Open_Systems_Interconnection

8 www.ripe.net/ripe/meetings/ripe-42/presentations/ripe42-eofpseudo-wires2/index.htmlKPN/Quest*Pseudo-wire Services and L2TPv3* presentation 5/14/2002

9 www.ietf.org/rfc/rfc2341.txt

10 http://en.wikipedia.org/wiki/MD5#Vulnerability

11 http://en.wikipedia.org/wiki/SHA-1#Cryptanalysis_and_validation

## Chapter 49

Identity Theft

Markus Jakobsson
Palo Alto Research Center

Alex Tsow
The MITRE Corporation

Note: This chapter is available in its entirety online at store.elsevier.com/product.jsp?isbn=9780123943972 (click the Resources tab at the bottom of the page).

1. ABSTRACT

This chapter focuses on identity manipulation tactics in email and Web pages. It describes the effects of features ranging from URL plausibility to trust endorsement graphics on a population of 398 subjects. The experiment presents these trust indicators in a variety of stimuli, since reactions vary according to context. In addition to testing specific features, the test gauges the potential of a tactic that spoofs third-party contractors rather than a brand itself. The results show that indeed graphic design can change authenticity evaluations and that its impact varies with context. We expected that authenticity-inspiring design changes would have the opposite effect when paired with an unreasonable request, but our data suggest that narrative strength, rather than underlying legitimacy, limits the impact of graphic design on trust and that these authenticity-inspiring design features improve trust in both legitimate and illegitimate media. Thus, it is not what is said that matters but how it is said: An eloquently stated unreasonable request is more convincing than a poorly phrased but quite reasonable request.

2. CONTENTS

## Chapter 50

VoIP Security

Harsh Kupwade Patil
Southern Methodist University

Dan Wing
Cisco Systems

Thomas M. Chen
Swansea University

1. INTRODUCTION

H.323 and *Session Initiation Protocol* (SIP) are the two standardized protocols for the realization of VoIP.[1,2] The multimedia conference protocol H.323 of the International Telecommunication Union (ITU) consists of multiple separate protocols such as the H.245 for control signaling and H.225 for call signaling. H.323 is difficult to implement because of its complexity and the bulkiness that it introduces into the client application.[3] In contrast, SIP is simpler than H.323 and also leaner on the client-side application. SIP uses the human-readable protocol (ASCII) instead of H.323's binary signal coding.

VoIP Basics

SIP is the *Internet Engineering Task Force* (IETF) standard for multimedia communications in an IP network. It is an application layer control protocol used for creating, modifying, and terminating sessions between one or more SIP *user agents*. It was primarily designed to support user location discovery, user availability, user capabilities, and session setup and management.

In SIP, the end devices are called *user agents* (UAs), and they send SIP requests and SIP responses to establish media sessions, send and receive media, and send other SIP messages (to send short text messages to each other or subscribe to an event notification service). A UA can be a SIP phone or SIP client software running on a PC or PDA.

Typically, a collection of SIP user agents belongs to an administrative domain, which forms a SIP network. Each administrative domain has a SIP proxy, which is the point of contact for UAs within the domain and for UAs or SIP proxies outside the domain. All SIP signaling messages within a domain are routed through the domain's own SIP proxy. SIP routing is performed using *Uniform Resource Identifiers* (URIs) for addressing user agents. Two types of SIP URIs are supported: the SIP URI and the TEL URI. A SIP URI begins with the keyword *sip* or *sips*, where *sips* indicates that the SIP signaling must be sent over a secure channel, such as TLS.[4] The SIP URI is similar to an email address and contains a user's identifier and the domain at which the user can be found. For example, it could contain a username such as *sip:alice@example.com*, a global E.164 telephone number[5] such as *sip*:11-972-310-9882@*example.com;user* = *phone*, or an extension such as *sip*:1234@*example.com*. The TEL URI only contains an E.164 telephone number and does not contain a domain name, for example, *tel*: + 1.408.555.1234.

A SIP proxy server is an entity that receives SIP requests, performs various database lookups, and then forwards ("proxies") the request to the next-hop proxy server. In this way, SIP messages are routed to their ultimate destination. Each proxy may perform some specialized function, such as external database lookups, authorization checks, and so on. Because the media does

---

1. ITU-T Recommendation H.323, Packet-Based Multimedia Communications System, www.itu.int/rec/T-REC-H.323-200606-I/en. 1998.
2. J. Rosenberg, H. Schulzrinne, G. Camarillo, J. Peterson, R. Sparks, M. Handley, and E. Schooler, "SIP: Session Initiation Protocol," IETF RFC 3261, June 2002.
3. H. Schulzrinne and J. Rosenberg, "A Comparison of SIP and H.323 for Internet telephony," in *Proceedings of NOSSDAV*, Cambridge, U.K., July 1998.

4. S. Fries and D. Ignjatic, "On the applicability of various MIKEY modes and extensions," IETF draft, March 31, 2008.
5. F. Audet, "The use of the SIPS URI scheme in the Session Initiation Protocol (SIP)," IETF draft, February 23, 2008.

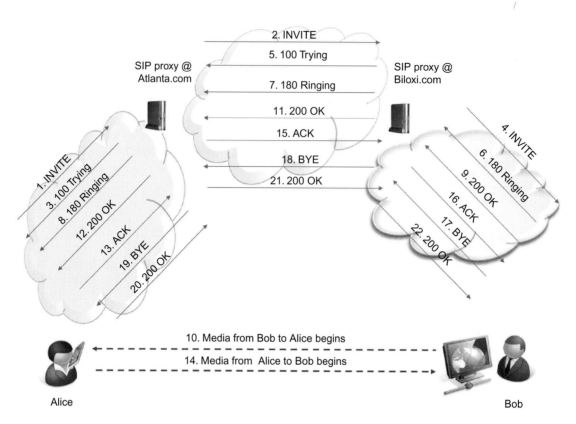

FIGURE 50.1   An example of a SIP session setup.

not flow through the SIP proxies—but rather only SIP signaling—SIP proxies are no longer needed after the call is established. In many SIP proxy designs, the proxies are stateless, which allows alternative intermediate proxies to resume processing for a failed (or overloaded) proxy. One type of SIP proxy called a *redirect server* receives a SIP request, performs a database query operation, and returns the lookup result to the requester (which is often another proxy). Another type of SIP proxy is a SIP *registrar server*, which receives and processes registration requests. Registration binds a SIP (or TEL) URI to the user's device, which is how SIP messages are routed to a user agent. Multiple UAs may register the same URI, which causes incoming SIP requests to be routed to all of those UAs, a process termed *forking*, which causes some interesting security concerns.

The typical SIP transactions can be broadly viewed by looking at the typical call flow mechanism in a SIP session setup, as shown in Figure 50.1. The term *SIP trapezoid* is often used to describe this message flow where the SIP signaling is sent to SIP proxies and the media is sent directly between the two UAs.

If Alice wants to initiate a session with Bob, she sends an initial SIP message *(INVITE)* to the local proxy for her domain (Atlanta.com). Her *INVITE* has Bob's URI (bob@biloxi.com) as the Request-URI, which is used to route the message. Upon receiving the initial message from Alice, her domain's proxy sends a provisional 100 *Trying* message to Alice, which indicates that the message was received without error from Alice. The Atlanta.com proxy looks at the *SIP Request-URI* in the message and decides to route the message to the Biloxi.com proxy. The Biloxi.com proxy receives the message and routes it to Bob. The Biloxi.com proxy delivers the *INVITE* message to Bob's SIP phone, to alert Bob of an incoming call. Bob's SIP phone initiates a provisional 180 *Ringing* message back to Alice, which is routed all the way back to Alice; this causes Alice's phone to generate a ringback tone, audible to Alice. When Bob answers his phone a 200 *OK* message is sent to his proxy, and Bob can start immediately sending media ("Hello?") to Alice. Meanwhile, Bob's 200 OK is routed from his proxy to Alice's proxy and finally to Alice's UA. Alice's UA responds with an *ACK* message to Bob and then Alice can begin sending media (audio and/or video) to Bob. Real-time media is almost exclusively sent using the Real-time Transport Protocol (RTP).[6] At this point the proxies are no longer involved in the call and hence the media will typically flow directly between Alice and Bob.

---

6. H. Schulzrinne, R. Frederick, and V. Jacobson, "RTP: A transport protocol for real-time applications," IETF RFC 1889, Jan. 1996.

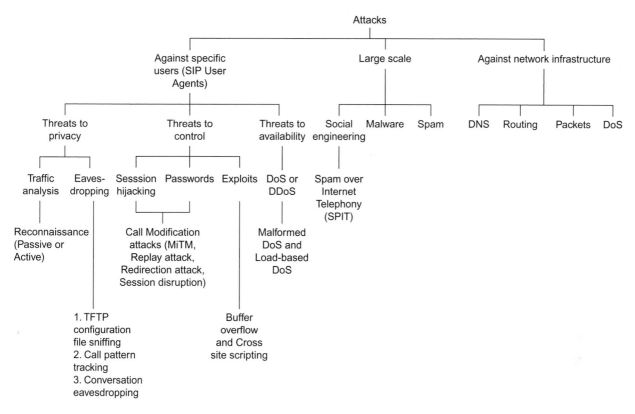

FIGURE 50.2 Taxonomy of threats.

That is, the media takes a different path through the network than the signaling. Finally, when either Alice or Bob want to end the session, they send a *BYE* message to their proxy, which is routed to the other party and is acknowledged.

One of the challenging tasks faced by the industry today is secure deployment of VoIP. During the initial design of SIP, the focus was more on providing new dynamic and powerful services along with simplicity rather than security. For this reason, a lot of effort is under way in the industry and among researchers to enhance SIP's security. The subsequent sections of this chapter deal with these issues.

2. OVERVIEW OF THREATS

Attacks can be broadly classified as attacks against specific users (SIP user agents), large scale (VoIP is part of the network) and against network infrastructure (SIP proxies or other network components and resources necessary for VoIP, such as routers, DNS servers, and bandwidth).[7] This chapter does not cover attacks against

infrastructure; the interested reader is referred to the literature.[8] The subsequent parts of this chapter deal with the attacks targeted toward the specific host and issues related to social engineering. The taxonomy of attacks is shown in Figure 50.2.

Reconnaissance of VoIP Networks

Reconnaissance refers to intelligent gathering or probing to assess the vulnerabilities of a network, to successfully launch a later attack; it includes *footprinting* the target (also known as *profiling* or *information gathering*). The two forms of reconnaissance techniques are passive and active. Passive reconnaissance attacks include the collection of network information through indirect or direct methods but without probing the target; active reconnaissance attacks involve generating traffic with the intention of eliciting responses from the target. Passive reconnaissance techniques would involve searching for publicly available SIP URIs in databases provided by VoIP service providers or on Web pages, looking for publicly accessible SIP proxies or SIP UAs. Examples include *dig* and

7. T. Chen and C. Davis, "An overview of electronic attacks," in *Information Security and Ethics: Concepts, Methodologies, Tools and Applications*, H. Nemati (ed.), Idea Group Publishing, to appear 2008.

8. A. Chakrabarti and G. Manimaran, "Internet infrastructure security: a taxonomy," IEEE Network, Vol. 16, pp. 13–21, Dec. 2002.

nslookup. Although passive reconnaissance techniques can be effective, they are time intensive.

If an attacker can watch SIP signaling, the attacker can perform number harvesting. Here, an attacker passively monitors all incoming and outgoing calls to build a database of legitimate phone numbers or extensions within an organization. This type of database can be used in more advanced VoIP attacks such as signaling manipulation or Spam over Internet Telephony (SPIT) attacks.

Active reconnaissance uses technical tools to discover information on the hosts that are active on the target network. The drawback to active reconnaissance, however, is that it can be detected. The two most common active reconnaissance attacks are call walking attacks and port-scanning attacks.

Call walking is a type of reconnaissance probe in which a malicious user initiates sequential calls to a block of telephone numbers to identify what assets are available for further exploitation. This is a modern version of *war-dialing*, common in the 1980s to find modems on the Public Switched Telephone Network (PSTN). Performed during non-business hours, call walking can provide information useful for social engineering, such as voice-mail announcements that disclose the called party's name.

SIP UAs and proxies listen on UDP/5060 and/or TCP/5060, so it can be effective to scan IP addresses looking for such listeners. Once the attacker has accumulated a list of active IP addresses, he can start to investigate each address further. The Nmap tool is a robust port scanner that is capable of performing a multitude of types of scans.[9]

In addition, honeypots and honeynets are becoming increasingly popular, as it would help detect, prevent or prepare to respond to attacks. A honeypot is a trap where vulnerabilities are deliberately introduced to lure attackers (hackers) and then analyze their activity (probing, security attack or compromise). While, a honeynet is a collection of honeypots. In the domain of VoIP, honeynets can be useful in preventing Spam over Internet Telephony (SPIT) and VoIP Phishing (Vishing).

Denial of Service

A denial-of-service (DoS) attack deprives a user or an organization of services or resources that are normally available. In SIP, DoS attacks can be classified as malformed request DoS and load-based DoS.

Malformed Request DoS

In this type of DoS attack, the attacker would craft a SIP request (or response) that exploits the vulnerability in a SIP proxy or SIP UA of the target, resulting in a partial or complete loss of function. For example, it has also been found that some user agents allow remote attackers to cause a denial of service ("486 Busy" responses or device reboot) via a sequence of SIP INVITE transactions in which the Request-URI lacks a username.[10] Attackers have also shown that the IP implementations of some hard phones are vulnerable to IP fragmentation attacks [CAN-2002-0880] and DHCP-based DoS attacks [CAN-2002-0835], demonstrating that normal infrastructure protection (such as firewalls) is valuable for VoIP equipment. DoS attacks can also be initiated against other network services such as DHCP and DNS, which serve VoIP devices.

Load-Based DoS

In this case, an attacker directs large volumes of traffic at a target (or set of targets) and attempts to exhaust resources such as the CPU processing time, network bandwidth, or memory. SIP proxies and session border controllers (SBCs) are primary targets for attackers because of their critical role of providing voice service and the complexity of the software running on them.

A common type of load-based attack is a flooding attack. In case of VoIP, we categorize flooding attacks into these types:

- Control packet floods
- Call data floods
- Distributed denial-of-service attack

Control Packet Floods

In this case, the attacker will flood SIP proxies with SIP packets, such as INVITE messages, bogus responses, or the like. The attacker might purposefully craft authenticated messages that fail authentication, to cause the victim to validate the message. The attacker might spoof the IP address of a legitimate sender so that rate limiting the attack also causes rate limiting of the legitimate user as well.

Call Data Floods

The attacker will flood the target with RTP packets, with or without first establishing a legitimate RTP session, in an attempt to exhaust the target's bandwidth or processing power, leading to degradation of VoIP quality for other users on the same network or just for the victim. Other common forms of load-based attacks that could affect the VoIP system are buffer overflow attacks, TCP SYN flood, UDP flood, fragmentation attacks, smurf attacks, and general overload attacks. Though VoIP equipment needs to

---

9. http://nmap.org/.

10. The common vulnerability and exposure list for SIP, http://cve.mitre.org/cgibin/cvekey.cgi?keyword = SIP.

protect itself from these attacks, these attacks are not specific to VoIP.

A SIP proxy can be overloaded with excessive legitimate traffic—the classic "Mother's Day" problem when the telephone system is most busy. Large-scale disasters (earthquakes) can also cause similar spikes, which are not attacks. Thus, even when not under attack, the system could be under high load. If the server or the end user is not fast enough to handle incoming loads, it will experience an outage or misbehave in such a way as to become ineffective at processing SIP messages. This type of attack is very difficult to detect because it would be difficult to sort the legitimate user from the illegitimate users who are performing the same type of attack.

Distributed Denial-of-Service Attack

Once an attacker has gained control of a large number of VoIP-capable hosts and formed a "zombies" network under the attacker's control, the attacker can launch interesting VoIP attacks, as illustrated in Figure 50.3. Each zombie can send up to thousands of messages to a single location, thereby resulting in a barrage of packets, which incapacitates the victim's computer due to resource exhaustion.

Loss of Privacy

The four major eavesdropping attacks are:

- Trivial File Transfer Protocol (TFTP) configuration file sniffing

- Traffic analysis
- Conversation eavesdropping

TFTP Configuration File Sniffing

Most IP phones rely on a TFTP server to download their configuration file after powering on. The configuration file can sometimes contain passwords that can be used to directly connect back to the phone and administer it or used to access other services (such as the company directory). An attacker who is sniffing the file when the phone downloads this configuration file can glean through these passwords and potentially reconfigure and control the IP phone. To thwart this attack vector, vendors variously encrypt the configuration file or use HTTPS and authentication.

Traffic Analysis

Traffic analysis involves determining who is talking to whom, which can be done even when the actual conversation is encrypted and can even be done (to a lesser degree) between organizations. Such information can be beneficial to law enforcement and for criminals committing corporate espionage and stock fraud.

Conversation Eavesdropping

An important threat for VoIP users is eavesdropping on a conversation. In addition to the obvious problem of confidential information being exchanged between people, eavesdropping is also useful for credit-card fraud and identity theft. This is because some phone calls—

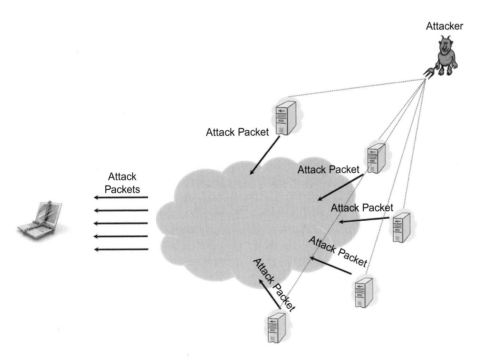

FIGURE 50.3 Distributed denial-of-service attack (DDoS).

especially to certain institutions—require users to enter credit-card numbers, PIN codes, or national identity numbers (Social Security numbers), which are sent as Dual-Tone Multi-frequency (DTMF) digits in RTP. An attacker can use tools like Wireshark, Cain & Abel, vomit (voice over misconfigured Internet telephones), VoIPong, and Oreka to capture RTP packets and extract the conversation or the DTMF digits.[11]

Man-in-the-Middle Attacks

The man-in-the-middle attack is a classic form of an attack where the attacker has managed to insert himself between the two hosts. It refers to an attacker who is able to read, and modify at will, messages between two parties without either party knowing that the link between them has been compromised. As such, the attacker has the ability to inspect or modify packets exchanged between two hosts or insert new packets or prevent packets from being sent to hosts. Any device that handles SIP messages as a normal course of its function could be a man in the middle: a compromised SIP proxy server or session border controller. If SIP messages are not authenticated, an attacker can also compromise a DNS server or use DNS poisoning techniques to cause SIP messages to be routed to a device under the attacker's control.

In a conventional enterprise network, VoIP phones are configured with different Virtual Local Area Network (VLAN) addresses as opposed to data devices. In such situations, the attacker would initially access the network by connecting his laptop to the existing data VLAN and then hop to the designated voice VLAN. This attack can be achieved in two ways: switch spoofing or double tagging. If a network switch is configured for autotrunking, the attacker converts it to a switch that needs to trunk. In the second method, the attacker sends data from one switch to another by sending frames with two 802.1Q headers (one for the victim's switch and the other for the attacking switch). The victim's switch accepts any incoming frames, while the target switch forwards the second frame (embedded with a false-tag) to the destination host based on the VLAN identifier present in the second 802.1q header. Once, inside the desired voice VLAN, the attacker could Address Resolution Protocol (ARP) poison the designated phones that would result in a Man-in-the-middle attack.

Replay Attacks

Replay attacks are often used to impersonate an authorized user. A replay attack is one in which an attacker captures a valid packet sent between the SIP UAs or

proxies and resends it at a later time (perhaps a second later, perhaps days later). As an example with classic unauthenticated telnet, an attacker that captures a telnet username and password can replay that same username and password. In SIP, an attacker would capture and replay valid SIP requests. (Capturing and replaying SIP responses is usually not valuable, as SIP responses are discarded if their Call-Id does not match a currently outstanding request, which is one way SIP protects itself from replay attacks.)

If Real-time Transport Protocol (RTP) is used without authenticating Real-time Transport Control Protocol (RTCP) packets and without sampling synchronization source (SSRC), an attacker can inject RTCP packets into a multicast group, each with a different SSRC, and force the group size to grow exponentially. A variant on a replay attack is the cut-and-paste attack. In this scenario, an attacker copies part of a captured packet with a generated packet. For example, a security credential can be copied from one request to another, resulting in a successful authorization without the attacker even discovering the user's password.

Impersonation

Impersonation is described as a user or host pretending to be another user or host, especially one that the intended victim trusts. In case of a phishing attack, the attacker continues the deception to make the victim disclose his banking information, employee credentials, and other sensitive information. In SIP, the From header is displayed to the called party, so authentication and authorization of the values used in the From header are important to prevent impersonation. Unfortunately, call forwarding in SIP (called *retargeting*) makes simple validation of the From header impossible. For example, imagine Bob has forwarded his phone to Carol and they are in different administrative domains (Bob is at work, Carol is his wife at home). Then Alice calls Bob. When Alice's INVITE is routed to Bob's proxy, her INVITE will be retargeted to Carol's UA by rewriting the Request-URI to point to Carol's URI. Alice's original INVITE is then routed to Carol's UA. When it arrives at Carol's UA, the INVITE needs to indicate that the call is from Alice. The difficulty is that if Carol's SIP proxy were to have performed simplistic validation of the From in the INVITE when it arrived from Bob's SIP proxy, Carol's SIP proxy would have rejected it—because it contained Alice's From. However, such retargeting is a legitimate function of SIP networks.

Redirection Attack

If compromised by an attacker or via a SIP man-in-the-middle attack, the intermediate SIP proxies responsible

---

11. D. Endler and M. Collier, *Hacking VoIP Exposed: Voice over IP Security Secrets and Solutions*, McGraw-Hill, 2007.

for SIP message routing can falsify any response. In this section we describe how the attacker could use this ability to launch a redirection attack. If an attacker can fabricate a reply to a SIP INVITE, the media session can be established with the attacker rather than the intended party. In SIP, a proxy or UA can respond to an INVITE request with a 301 Moved Permanently or 302 Moved Temporarily Response. The 302 Response will also include an Expires header line that communicates how long the redirection should last. The attacker can respond with a redirection response, effectively denying service to the called party and possibly tricking the caller into communicating with, or through, a rogue UA.

Session Disruption

Session disruption describes any attack that degrades or disrupts an existing signaling or media session. For example, in the case of a SIP scenario, if an attacker is able to send failure messages such as BYE and inject them into the signaling path, he can cause the sessions to fail when there is no legitimate reason why they should not continue. For this to be successful, the attacker has to include the Call-Id of an active call in the BYE message. Alternatively, if an attacker introduces bogus packets into the media stream, he can disrupt packet sequence, impede media processing, and disrupt a session. Delay attacks are those in which an attacker can capture and resend RTP SSRC packets out of sequence to a VoIP endpoint and force the endpoint to waste its processing cycles in re-sequencing packets and degrade call quality. An attacker could also disrupt a Voice over Wireless Local Area Network (WLAN) service by disrupting IEEE 802.11 WLAN service using radio spectrum jamming or a Wi-Fi Protected Access (WPA) Message Integrity Check (MIC) attack. A wireless access point will disassociate stations when it receives two invalid frames within 60 seconds, causing loss of network connectivity for 60 seconds. A one-minute loss of service is hardly tolerable in a voice application.

Exploits

Cross-Site Scripting (XSS) attacks are possible with VoIP systems because call logs contain header fields, and administrators (and other privileged users) view those call logs. In this attack, specially crafted From: (or other) fields are sent by an attacker in a normal SIP message (such as an INVITE). Then later, when someone such as the administrator looks at the call logs using a Web browser, the specially crafted From; causes a XSS attack against the administrator's Web browser, which can then do malicious things with the administrator's privileges. This can be a damaging attack if the administrator has already logged into other systems (HR databases, the SIP call controller, the firewall) and her Web browser has a valid cookie (or active session in another window) for those other systems.

Social Engineering

SPIT (Spam over Internet Telephony) is classified as a social threat because the callee can treat the call as unsolicited, and the term *unsolicited* is strictly bound to be a user-specific preference, which makes it hard for the system to identify this kind of transaction. SPIT can be telemarketing calls used for guiding callees to a service deployed to sell products. IM spam and presence spam could also be launched via SIP messages. IM spam is very similar to email spam; presence spam is defined as a set of unsolicited presence requests for the presence package. A subtle variation of SPIT called *Vishing* (VoIP phishing) is an attack that aims to collect personal data by redirecting users toward an interactive voice responder that could collect personal information such as the PIN for a credit card. From a signaling point of view, unsolicited communication is technically a correct transaction.

Unfortunately, many of the mechanisms that are effective for email spam are ineffective with VoIP, for many reasons. First, the email with its entire contents arrives at a server before it is seen by the user. Such a mail server can therefore apply many filtering strategies, such as Bayesian filters, URL filters, and so on. In contrast, in VoIP, human voices are transmitted rather than text. To recognize voices and to determine whether the message is spam or not is still a very difficult task for the end system. A recipient of a call only learns about the subject of the message when he is actually listening to it. Moreover, even if the content is stored on a voice mailbox, it is still difficult for today's speech recognition technologies to understand the context of the message enough to decide whether it is spam or not.

One mechanism to fight automated systems that deliver spam is to challenge such suspected incoming calls with a Turing test. These methods include:

- *Voice menu.* Before a call is put through, a computer asks the caller to press certain key combinations, for example "Press #55."
- *Challenge models.* Before a call is put through, a computer asks the caller to solve a simple equation and to type in the answer—for example, "Divide 10 by 2."
- *Alternative number.* Under the main number a computer announces an alternative number. This number may even be changed permanently by a call management server. All these methods can even be enforced by enriching the audio signal with noise or music. This prevents SPIT bots from using speech recognition.

Such Turing tests are attractive, since it is often hard for computers to decode audio questions. However, these puzzles cannot be made too difficult, because human beings must always be able to solve them.

One of the solutions to the SPIT problem is the whitelist. In a whitelist, a user explicitly states which persons are allowed to contact him. A similar technique is also used in Skype; where Alice wants to call Bob, she first has to add Bob to her contact list and send a contact request to Bob. Only when Bob has accepted this request can Alice make calls to Bob.

In general, whitelists have an introduction problem, since it is not possible to receive calls by someone who is not already on the whitelist. Blacklists are the opposite of whitelists but have limited effectiveness at blocking spam because new identities (which are not on the blacklist) can be easily created by anyone, including spammers.

Authentication mechanisms can be used to provide strong authentication, which is necessary for strong whitelists and reputation systems, which form the basis of SPIT prevention. Strong authentication is generally Public Key Infrastructure (PKI) dependent. Proactive publishing of incorrect information, namely SIP addresses, is a possible way to fill up spammers' databases with existing contacts. Consent-based communication is the other solution. Address obfuscation could be an alternative wherein spam bots are unable to identify the SIP URIs.

3. SECURITY IN VOIP

Much existing VoIP equipment is dedicated to VoIP, which allows placing such equipment on a separate network. This is typically accomplished with a separate VLAN. Depending on the vendor of the equipment, this can be automated using CDP (Cisco Discovery Protocol), LLDP (Link Layer Discovery Protocol), or 802.1x, all of which will place equipment into a separate "voice VLAN" to assist with this separation. This provides a reasonable level of protection, especially within an enterprise where employees lack much incentive to interfere with the telephone system.

Preventative Measures

However, the use of VLANs is not an ideal solution because it does not work well with softphones that are not dedicated to VoIP, because placing those softphones onto the "voice VLAN" destroys the security and management advantage of the separate network. A separate VLAN can also create a false sense of security that only benign voice devices are connected to the VLAN. However, even though 802.1x provides the best security, it is still possible for an attacker to gain access to the voice VLAN (with a suitable hub between the phone and

the switch). Mechanisms that provide less security, such as CDP or LLDP, can be circumvented by software on an infected computer. Some vendors' Ethernet switches can be configured to require clients to request inline Ethernet power before allowing clients to join certain VLANs (such as the voice VLAN), which provides protection from such infected computers. But, as mentioned previously, such protection of the voice VLAN prevents deployment of softphones, which is a significant reason that most companies are interested in deploying VoIP.

Eavesdropping

To counter the threat of eavesdropping, the media can be encrypted. The method to encrypt RTP traffic is Secure RTP (RFC3711), which does not encrypt the IP, UDP, or RTP headers but does encrypt the RTP payload (the "voice" itself). SRTP's advantage of leaving the RTP headers unencrypted is that header compression protocols (cRTP,[12] ROHC,[13]) and protocol analyzers (looking for RTP packet loss and (S)RTCP reports) can still function with SRTP-encrypted media.

The drawback of SRTP is that approximately 13 incompatible mechanisms exist to establish the SRTP keys. These mechanisms are at various stages of deployment, industry acceptance, and standardization. Thus, at this point in time it is unlikely that two SRTP-capable systems from different vendors will have a compatible SRTP keying mechanism. A brief overview of some of the more popular keying mechanisms is provided here.

One of the popular SRTP keying mechanisms, Security Descriptions, requires a secure SIP signaling channel (SIP over TLS) and discloses the SRTP key to each SIP proxy along the call setup path. This means that a passive attacker, able to observe the unencrypted SIP signaling and the encrypted SRTP, would be able to eavesdrop on a call. S/MIME is SIP's end-to-end security mechanism, which Security Descriptions could use to its benefit, but S/MIME has not been well deployed and, due to specific features of SIP (primarily forking and retargeting), it is unlikely that S/MIME will see deployment in the foreseeable future.

Multimedia Internet Keying (MIKEY) has approximately eight incompatible modes defined; these allow establishing SRTP keys.[14] Almost all these MIKEY modes are more secure than Security Descriptions

12. T. Koren, S. Casner, J. Geevarghese, B. Thompson, and P. Ruddy, "Enhanced compressed RTP (CRTP) for links with high delay," IETF RFC 3545, July 2003.

13. G. Pelletier and K. Sandlund, "Robust header compression version 2 (ROHCv2): Profiles for RTP, UDP, IP, ESP and UDP-Lite," IETF RFC 5225, April 2008.

14. S. Fries and D. Ignjatic, "On the applicability of various MIKEY modes and extensions," IETF draft, March 31, 2008.

because they do not carry the SRTP key directly in the SIP message but rather encrypt it with the remote party's private key or perform a Diffie-Hellman exchange. Thus, for most of the MIKEY modes, the attacker would need to actively participate in the MIKEY exchange and obtain the encrypted SRTP to listen to the media.

Zimmermann Real-time Transport Protocol (ZRTP)[15] is another SRTP key exchange mechanism, which uses a Diffie-Hellman exchange to establish the SRTP keys and detects an active attacker by having the users (or their computers) validate a short authentication string with each other. It affords useful security properties, including perfect forward secrecy and key continuity (which allows the users to verify authentication strings once, and never again), and the ability to work through session border controllers.

In 2006, the IETF decided to reduce the number of IETF standard key exchange mechanisms and chose DTLS-SRTP. DTLS-SRTP uses Datagram TLS (a mechanism to run TLS over a non-reliable protocol such as UDP) over the media path. To detect an active attacker, the TLS certificates exchanged over the media path must match the signed certificate fingerprints sent over the SIP signaling path. The certificate fingerprints are signed using SIP's identity mechanism.[16]

A drawback with SRTP is that it is imperative (for some keying mechanisms) or very helpful (with other keying mechanisms) for the SIP user agent to encrypt its SIP signaling traffic with its SIP proxy. The only standard for such encryption, today, is SIP-over-TLS which runs over TCP. To date, many vendors have avoided TCP on their SIP proxies because they have found SIP-over-TCP scales worse than SIP-over-UDP. It is anticipated that if this cannot be overcome we may see SIP-over-DTLS standardized. Another viable option, especially in some markets, is to use IPsec ESP to protect SIP.

Another drawback of SRTP is that diagnostic and troubleshooting equipment cannot listen to the media stream. This may seem obvious, but it can cause difficulties when technicians need to listen to and diagnose echo, gain, or other anomalies that cannot be diagnosed by examining SRTP headers (which are unencrypted) but can only be diagnosed by listening to the decrypted audio itself.

Identity

As described in the "Threats" section, it is important to have strong identity assurance. Today there are two mechanisms to provide for identity: P-Asserted-Identity,[17] which is used within a trust domain (within a company or between a service provider and its paying customers) and is simply a header inserted into a SIP request, and SIP Identity,[18] which is used between trust domains (between two companies) and creates a signature over some of the SIP headers and over the SIP body.

SIP Identity is useful when two organizations connect via SIP proxies, as was originally envisioned as the SIP architecture for intermediaries between two organizations—often a SIP service provider. Many of these service providers operate session border controllers (SBCs) rather than SIP proxies, for a variety of reasons. One of the drawbacks of SIP Identity is that an SBC, by its nature, will rewrite the SIP body (specifically the m = / c = lines), which destroys the original signature. Thus, an SBC would need to rewrite the From header and sign the new message with the SBC's own private key. This effectively creates hop-by-hop trust; each SBC that needs to rewrite the message in this way is also able to manipulate the SIP headers and SIP body in other ways that could be malicious or could allow the SBC to eavesdrop on a call. Alternative cryptographic identity mechanisms are being pursued, but it is not yet known whether this weakness can be resolved.

Traffic Analysis

The most useful protection from traffic analysis is to encrypt your SIP traffic. This would require the attacker to gain access to your SIP proxy (or its call logs) to determine who you called.

Additionally, your (S)RTP traffic itself could also provide useful traffic analysis information. For example, someone may learn valuable information just by noticing where (S)RTP traffic is being sent (the company's in-house lawyers are calling an acquisition target several times a day). Forcing traffic to be concentrated to a device can help prevent this sort of traffic analysis. In some network topologies this can be achieved using a NAT, and in all cases it can be achieved with an SBC.

Reactive

An intrusion prevention system (IPS) is a useful way to react to VoIP attacks against signaling or media. An IPS with generic rules and with VoIP-specific rules can detect an attack and block or rate-limit traffic from the offender.

15. P. Zimmermann, A. Johnston, and J. Callas, "ZRTP: Media path key agreement for secure RTP," IETF draft, July 9, 2007.

16. J. Peterson and C. Jennings, "Enhancements for authenticated identity management in the Session Initiation Protocol (SIP)," IETF RFC 4474, August 2006.

17. C. Jennings, J. Peterson and M. Watson, "Private extensions to the Session Initiation Protocol (SIP) for asserted identity within trusted networks," IETF RFC 3325, November 2002.

18. J. Peterson and C. Jennings, "Enhancements for authenticated identity management in the Session Initiation Protocol (SIP)," IETF RFC 4474, August 2006.

IPS

Because SIP is derived from, and related to, many well-deployed and well-understood protocols (HTTP), IDS/IPS vendors are able to create products to protect against SIP quite readily. Often an IDS/IPS function can be built into a SIP proxy, SBC, or firewall, reducing the need for a separate IDS/IPS appliance. An IDS/IPS is marginally effective for detecting media attacks, primarily to notice an excessive amount of bandwidth is being consumed and to throttle it or alarm the event.

A drawback of IPS is that it can cause false positives and deny service to a legitimate endpoint, thus causing a DoS in an attempt to prevent a DoS. An attacker, knowledgeable of the rules or behavior of an IPS, may also be able to spoof the identity of a victim (the victim's source IP address or SIP identity) and trigger the IPS/IDS into reacting to the attack. Thus, it is important to deny attackers that avenue by using standard best practices for IP address spoofing[19] and employing strong SIP identity. Using a separate network (VLAN) for VoIP traffic can help reduce the chance of false positives, as the IDS/IPS rules can be more finely tuned for that one application running on the voice VLAN.

Rate Limiting

When suffering from too many SIP requests due to an attack, the first thing to consider doing is simple rate limiting. This is often naïvely performed by simply rate limiting the traffic to the SIP proxy and allowing excess traffic to be dropped. Though this does effectively reduce the transactions per second the SIP proxy needs to perform, it interferes with processing of existing calls to a significant degree. For example, a normal call is established with an INVITE, which is reliably acknowledged when the call is established. If the simplistic rate limiting were to drop the acknowledgment message, the INVITE would be retransmitted, incurring additional processing while the system is under high load. A separate problem with rate limiting is that both attackers and legitimate users are subject to the rate limiting; it is more useful to discriminate the rate limiting to the users causing the high rate. This can be done by distributing the simple rate limiting toward the users rather than doing the simple rate limiting near the server.

On the server, a more intelligent rate limiting is useful. These are usually proprietary rate-limiting schemes, but they attempt to process existing calls before processing new calls. For example, such a scheme would allow

processing the acknowledgment message for a previously processed INVITE, as described above; process the BYE associated with an active call, to free up resources; or process high-priority users' calls (the vice president's office is allowed to make calls, but the janitorial staff is blocked from making calls).

By pushing rate limiting toward users, effective use can be made of simple packet-based rate limiting. For example, even a very active call center phone does not need to send 100 Mb of SIP signaling traffic to its SIP proxy; even 1 Mb would be an excessive amount of traffic. By deploying simplistic, reasonable rate limiting very near the users, ideally at the Ethernet switch itself, bugs in the call processing application or malicious attacks by unauthorized software can be mitigated.

A similar situation occurs with the RTP media itself. Even high-definition video does not need to send or receive 100 Mb of traffic to another endpoint and can be rate-limited based on the applications running on the dedicated device. This sort of policing can be effective at the Ethernet switch itself, or in an IDS/IPS (watching for excessive bandwidth), a firewall, or SBC.

Challenging

A more sophisticated rate-limiting technique is to provide additional challenges to a high-volume user. This could be done when it is suspected that the user is sending spam or when the user has initiated too many calls in a certain time period. A simple mechanism is to complete the call with an interactive voice response system that requests the user to enter some digits ("Please enter 5, 1, 8 to complete your call"). Though this technique suffers from some problems (it does not work well for hearing-impaired users or if the caller does not understand the IVR's language), it is effective at reducing the calls per second from both internal and external callers.

4. FUTURE TRENDS

Certain SIP proxies have the ability to forward SIP requests to multiple user agents. These SIP requests can be sent in parallel, in series, or a combination of both series and parallel. Such proxies are called *forking proxies*.

Forking Problem in SIP

The forking proxy expects a response from all the user agents who received the received the request; the proxy forwards only the "best" final response back to the caller. This behavior causes a situation known as the

---

19. P. Ferguson and D. Senie, "Network ingress filtering: Defeating denial of service attacks which employ IP source address spoofing," IETF 2827, May 2000.

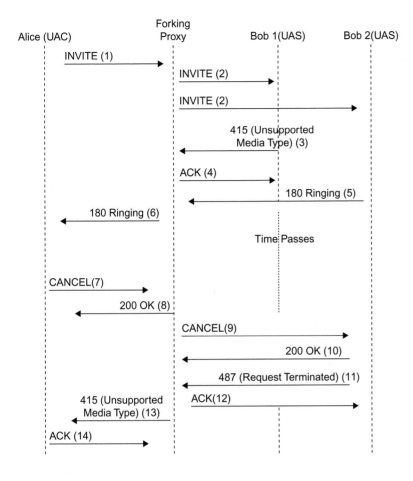

FIGURE 50.4   The heterogeneous error response forking problem.

heterogeneous error response forking problem [HERFP], which is illustrated in Figure 50.4.[20]

Alice initiates an INVITE request that includes a body format that is understood by UAS2 but not UAS1. For example, the UAC might have used a MIME type of multipart/mixed with a session description and an optional image or sound. As UAC1 does not support this MIME format, it returns a 415 (Unsupported Media Type) response. Unfortunately the proxy has to wait until all the branches generate the final response and then pick the "best" response, depending on the criteria mentioned in RFC 3261. In many cases the proxy has to wait a long enough time that the human operating the UAC abandons the call. The proxy informs the UAS2 that the call has been canceled, which is acknowledged by UAS2. It then returns the 415 (Unsupported Media Type) back to Alice, which could have been repaired by Alice by sending the appropriate session description.

Security in Peer-to-Peer SIP

Originally SIP was specified as a client/server protocol, but recent proposals suggest using SIP in a peer-to-peer setting.[21] One of the major reasons for using SIP in a peer-to-peer setting is its robustness, since there is no centralized control. As defined, "peer to peer (P2P) systems are distributed systems without any centralized control or hierarchical organization." This definition defines pure P2P systems. Even though many networks are considered P2P, they employ central authority or use supernodes. Early systems used flooding to route messages, which was found to be highly inefficient. To improve lookup time for a search request, structured overlay networks have been developed that provide load balancing and efficient routing of messages. They use distributed hash tables (DHTs) to provide efficient lookup.[22] Examples of

20. H. Schulzrinne, D. Oran, and G. Camarillo, "The reason header field for the Session Initiation Protocol (SIP)," IETF RFC 3326, December 2002.

21. K. Singh and H. Schulzrinne, "Peer-to-peer Internet telephony using SIP," in *15th International Workshop on Network and Operating Systems Support for Digital Audio and Video*, June 2005.

22. H. Balakrishnan, M. FransKaashoek, D. Karger, R. Morris, and I. Stoica, "Looking up data in P2P systems," *Communications of the ACM*, Vol. 46, No. 2, February 2003.

structured overlay networks are CAN, Chord, Pastry, and Tapestry.[23,24,25,26]

We focus on Chord Protocol because it is used as a prototype in most proposals for P2P-SIP. Chord has a ring-based topology in which each node stores at most $\log(N)$ entries in its finger table, which is like an application-level routing table, to point to other peers. Every node's IP address is mapped to an m bit chord identifier with a predefined hash function h. The same hash function h is also used to map any key of data onto a key ID that forms the distributed hash table. Every node maintains a finger table of $\log(N) = 6$ entries, pointing to the next-hop node location at distance 2^{i-1} (for $i = 1,2...m$) from this node identifier. Each node in the ring is responsible for storing the content of all key IDs that are equal to the identifier of the node's predecessor in the Chord ring. In a Chord ring each node n stores the IP address of m successor nodes plus its predecessor in the ring. The m successor entries in the routing table point to nodes at increasing distance from n. Routing is done by forwarding messages to the largest node-ID in the routing table that precedes the key-ID until the direct successor of a node has a longer ID than the key ID.

Singh and Schulzrinne envision a hierarchical architecture in which multiple P2P networks are represented by a DNS domain. A global DHT is used for interdomain routing of messages.

Join/Leave Attack

Security of structured overlay networks is based on the assumption that joining nodes are assigned node-IDs at random due to random assignment of IP addresses. This could lead to a join/leave attack in which the malicious attacker would want to control $O(\log N)$ nodes out of N nodes as search is done on $O(\log N)$ nodes to find the desired key ID. With the adoption of IPv6, the join/leave attack can be more massive because the attacker will

have more IP addresses. But even with IPv4, join/leave attacks are possible if the IP addresses are assigned dynamically. Node-ID assignment in Chord is inherently deterministic, thereby allowing the attacker to compute Node-IDs in advance where the attack could be launched by spoofing IP addresses. A probable solution would be to authenticate nodes before allowing them to join the overlay, which can involve authenticating the node before assigning the IP address.

Attacks on Overlay Routing

Any malicious node within the overlay can drop, alter, or wrongly forward a message it receives instead of routing it according to the overlay protocol. This can result in severe degradation of the overlay's availability. Therefore an adversary can perform one of the following:

Registration Attacks

One of the existing challenges to P2P-SIP registration is to provide confidentiality. This also includes message integrity to registration messages.

Man-in-the-middle Attacks

Let's consider the case where a node with ID 80 and a node with ID 109 conspire to form a man-in-the-middle attack, as shown in Figure 50.5. The honest node responsible for the key is node 180. Let's assume that a recursive approach is used for finding the desired key ID, wherein each routing node would send the request message to the appropriate node-ID until it reaches the node-ID responsible for the desired key-ID. The source node (node 30) will not have any control nor can it trace the request packet as it traverses through the Chord ring. Therefore node 32 will establish a dialog with node 119, and node 80 would impersonate node 32 and establish a dialog with node 108. This attack can be detected if an iterative routing mechanism is used wherein a source node checks whether the hash value is closer to the key-ID than the node-ID it received on the previous hop.[27] Therefore the source node (32) would get suspicious if node 80 redirected it directly to node 119, because it assumes that there exists a node with ID lower than Key ID 107.

Attacks on Bootstrapping Nodes

Any node wanting to join the overlay needs to be bootstrapped with a static node or cached node or discover the bootstrap node through broadcast mechanisms (SIP-

23. S. Ratnasamy, P. Francis, M. Handley, R. Karp, and S. Shenker, "A scalable content-addressable network," in *Proceedings of ACM SIGCOMM* 2001.

24. I. Stoica, R. Morris, D. Karger, M. F Kaashoek, and H. Balakrishnan, "Chord: A scalable peer-to-peer lookup service for internet applications," in *Proceedings of the 2001 Conference on Applications, Technologies, Architectures, and Protocols for Computer Communication*, pp. 149–160, 2001.

25. A. Rowstron and P. Druschel, "Pastry: Scalable, decentralized object location and routing for large-scale peer-to-peer systems," in *IFIP/ACM International Conference on Distributed Systems Platforms (Middleware)*, Heidelberg, Germany, pp. 329–350, 2001.

26. B. Y. Zhao, L. Huang, J. Stribling, S. C. Rhea, A. D. Joseph, and J. D. Kubiatowicz, "Tapestry: A resilient global-scale overlay for service deployment," *IEEE Journal on Selected Areas in Communications*, Vol. 22, No. 1, pp. 41–53, Jan. 2004.

27. M. Srivatsa and L. Liu, "Vulnerabilities and security threats in structured overlay networks: A quantitative analysis," in *Proceedings of 20th Annual Computer Science Application Conference*, Tucson, pp. 251–261, Dec. 6–10, 2004.

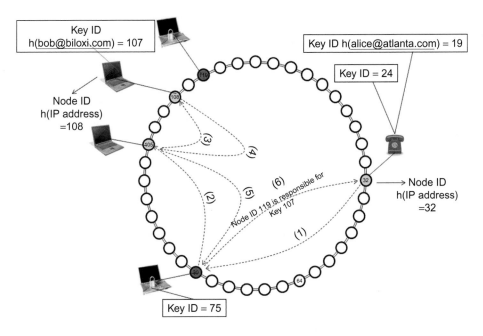

FIGURE   50.5 Man-in-the-middle attack.

multicast). In any case, if an adversary gains access to the bootstrap node, the joining node can easily be attacked. Securing the bootstrap node is still an open question.

Duplicate Identity Attacks

Preventing duplicate identities is one of the open problems whereby a hash of two IP addresses can lead to the same node-ID. The Singh and Schulzrinne approach reduces this problem somewhat by using a P2P network for each domain. Further, they suggest email-based authentication in which a joining node would receive a password via email and then use the password to authenticate itself to the network.

Free Riding

In a P2P system there is a risk of free riding in which nodes use services but fail to provide services to the network. Nodes use the overlay for registration and location service but drop other messages, which could eventually result in a reduction of the overlay's availability. The other major challenges that are presumably even harder to solve for P2P-SIP are as follows:

- Prioritizing signaling for emergency calls in an overlay network and ascertaining the physical location of users in real time may be very difficult.
- With the high dynamic nature of P2P systems, there is no predefined path for signaling traffic, and therefore it is impossible to implement a surveillance system for law enforcement agencies with P2P-SIP.

End-to-End Identity with SBCs

As discussed earlier,[28] End-to-End Identity with SBCs provides identity for SIP requests by signing certain SIP headers and the SIP body (which typically contains the Session Description Protocol (SDP)). This identity is destroyed if the SIP request travels through an SBC, because the SBC has to rewrite the SDP as part of the SBC's function (to force media to travel through the SBC). Today, nearly all companies that provide SIP trunking (Internet telephony service providers, ITSPs) utilize SBCs. In order to work with[29] those SBCs, one would have to validate incoming requests (which is new), modify the SDP and create a new identity (which they are doing today), and sign the new identity (which is new). As of this writing, it appears unlikely that ITSPs will have any reason to perform these new functions.

A related problem is that, even if we had end-to-end identity, it is impossible to determine whether a certain identity can rightfully claim a certain E.164 phone number in the From: header. Unlike domain names, which can have their ownership validated (the way email address validation is performed on myriad Web sites today), there is no de facto or written standard to determine whether an identity can rightfully claim to "own" a certain E.164.

28. J. Peterson and C. Jennings, "Enhancements for authenticated identity management in the Session Initiation Protocol (SIP)," IETF RFC 4474, August 2006.
29. J. Peterson and C. Jennings, "Enhancements for authenticated identity management in the Session Initiation Protocol (SIP)," IETF RFC 4474, August 2006.

An Agenda for Action for VoIP's Security Challenges

The following are some tips for ensuring a secure VoIP (Check All Tasks Completed):

_____**1.** Choose the VoIP protocols carefully.

_____**2.** Turn off unnecessary protocols.

_____**3.** Remember that each element in the VoIP infrastructure, accessible on the network like any computer, can be attacked.

_____**4.** Divide and conquer works well for VoIP networks.

_____**5.** Authenticate remote operations.

_____**6.** Separate VoIP servers and the internal network.

_____**7.** Make sure the VoIP security system can track the communications ports by reading inside the signaling packets to discover the ports selected and enable two endpoints to send media packets to each other.

_____**8.** Use Network Address Translation (NAT), even if in some cases, it poses a special problem for VoIP. NAT converts internal IP addresses into a single, globally unique IP address for routing across the Internet.

_____**9.** Use a security system that performs VoIP specific security checks.

It is anticipated that as SIP trunking becomes more commonplace, SIP spam will grow with it, and the growth of SIP spam will create the necessary impetus for the industry to solve these interrelated problems. Solving the end-to-end identity problem and the problem of attesting E.164 ownership would allow domains to immediately create meaningful whitelists. Over time these whitelists could be shared among SIP networks, end users, and others, eventually creating a reputation system. But as long as spammers are able to impersonate legitimate users, even creating a whitelist is fraught with the risk of a spammer guessing the contents of that whitelist (your bank, family member, or employer).

SIP Security Using Identity-Based Cryptography

Authentication in SIP has been a major concern and existing authentication schemes depend on PKI or shared secrets (passwords). Although PKI has existed for decades, the cost of maintaining the infrastructure has prevented enterprises from harnessing it to its fullest potential. In a PKI, the certificates contain a preset expiration date and if the validity date expires, or if the sender refreshes his keys, then the end user (callee) would have to obtain a new certificate from a public key repository. This retrieval process would involve the onerous task of certificate path construction and path validation processes. In such cases, Identity based cryptography can be extremely useful, as it eliminates the generation and maintenance of public key certificates. The basic idea behind an identity-based crypto-system is that end users can choose an arbitrary string (SIP URI) which represents their identity to compute their public key. As a result, it expunges the need for certificates from Certificate Authority (CA).[30] In addition, concatenation of user identity and Universally Unique Identifier (UUID) to generate a public key would greatly simplify the revocation process.

5. SUMMARY

With today's dedicated VoIP handsets, a separate voice VLAN provides a reasonable amount of security. Going forward, as non-dedicated devices become more commonplace, more rigorous security mechanisms will gain importance. This will begin with encrypted signaling and encrypted media and will evolve to include spam protection and enhancements to SIP to provide cryptographic assurance of SIP call and message routing.

As VoIP continues to grow, VoIP security solutions (see checklist, "An Agenda For Action For VoIP's Security Challenges") will have to consider consumer, enterprise and policy concerns. Some VoIP applications, commonly installed on PCs may be against corporate security policies (Skype). One of the biggest challenges with enabling encryption is with maintaining a public key infrastructure and the complexities involved in distributing public key certificates that would span to end users[31] and key synchronization between various devices belonging to the same end user agent.[32]

30. D. Berbecaru, A. Lioy, and M. Marian, "On the complexity of public key certificate validation," in *Proceedings of the 4th International Conference on Information Security, Lecture Notes in Computer Science*, Springer-Verlag, Vol. 2200, pp. 183−203, 2001.

31. C. Jennings and J. Fischl, "Certificate management service for the Session Initiation Protocol (SIP)," IETF draft April 5, 2008.

32. Z. Anwar, W. Yurcik, R. Johnson, M. Hafiz, and R. Campbell, "Multiple design patterns for voice over IP (VoIP) security," IPCCC 2006, pp. 485−492, April 10−12, 2006.

Using IPsec for VoIP tunneling across the Internet is another option; however, it is not without substantial overhead.[33] Therefore end-to-end mechanisms such as SRTP are specified for encrypting media and establishing session keys.

VoIP network designers should take extra care in designing intrusion detection systems that are able to identify never-before-seen activities and react according to the organization's policy. They should follow industry best practices for securing endpoint devices and servers. Current softphones and consumer-priced hardphones use the "haste-to-market" implementation approach and therefore become vulnerable to VoIP attacks. Therefore VoIP network administrators may evaluate VoIP endpoint technology, identify devices or software that will meet business needs and can be secured, and make these the corporate standards. With P2P-SIP, the lack of central authority makes authentication of users and nodes difficult. Providing central authority would dampen the spirit of P2P-SIP and would conflict the inherent features of distributed networks. A decentralized solution such as the reputation management system, where the trust values are assigned to nodes in the network based on prior behavior, would lead to a weak form of authentication because the credibility used to distribute trust values could vary in a decentralized system. Reputation management systems were more focused on file-sharing applications and have not yet been applied to P2P-SIP.

Finally, let's move on to the real interactive part of this Chapter: review questions/exercises, hands-on projects, case projects and optional team case project. The answers and/or solutions by chapter can be found in the Online Instructor's Solutions Manual.

CHAPTER REVIEW QUESTIONS/EXERCISES

True/False

1. True or False? H.323 and *Session Initiation Protocol* (SIP) are the two substandardized protocols for the realization of VoIP.
2. True or False? SIP is the *Internet Engineering Task Force* (IETF) substandard for multimedia communications in an IP network.
3. True or False? Attacks can be broadly classified as attacks against specific users (SIP user agents), large scale (VoIP is part of the network) and against network infrastructure (SIP proxies or other network components and resources necessary for VoIP, such as routers, DNS servers, and bandwidth).
4. True or False? *Reconnaissance* refers to intelligent gathering or probing to assess the vulnerabilities of a

network, to successfully launch a later attack; it includes *footprinting* the target (also known as *profiling* or *information gathering*).
5. True or False? A denial-of-service (DoS) attack deprives a user or an organization of services or resources that are not normally available.

Multiple Choice

1. In what type of DoS attack, would the attacker craft a SIP request (or response) that exploits the vulnerability in a SIP proxy or SIP UA of the target, resulting in a partial or complete loss of function?
A. Privacy-enhancing technology
B. Location technology
C. Promotional email
D. Malformed request DoS
E. Data controller
2. In what case, would an attacker direct large volumes of traffic at a target (or set of targets) and attempt to exhaust resources such as the CPU processing time, network bandwidth, or memory?
A. Policy enforcement
B. Location technology
C. Valid
D. Load-Based DoS
E. Bait
3. In what case, would the attacker flood SIP proxies with SIP packets, such as INVITE messages, bogus responses, or the like?
A. Data minimization
B. XACML
C. Control packet floods
D. Strong narrative
E. Security
4. What is it called when the attacker floods the target with RTP packets, with or without first establishing a legitimate RTP session, in an attempt to exhaust the target's bandwidth or processing power, leading to degradation of VoIP quality for other users on the same network or just for the victim?
A. Call data floods
B. Greedy strategy
C. Sensitive information
D. Phishing
E. Taps
5. Most IP phones rely on a TFTP server to download their _____ after powering on?
A. Irrelevant
B. Sensor nodes
C. Crimeware
D. Configuration file
E. Server policy

33. H. Kupwade Patil, Dean Willis, "Identity-based authentication in the Session Initiation Protocol", IETF draft, Feb 17, 2008.

EXERCISE

Problem

What are some of the disadvantages of VOIP?

Hands-On Projects

Project

Can one use their existing network equipment (routers, hubs, etc.) for a VOIP network?

Case Projects

Problem

What is a VOIP "softphone?"

Optional Team Case Project

Problem

Will a VOIP system continue to function during a power failure or cable outage?

Storage Security

## Chapter 51

SAN Security

John McGowan
EMC Corporation

Jeffrey Bardin
Independent consultant

John McDonald
EMC Corporation

Note: This chapter is available in its entirety online at store.elsevier.com/product.jsp?isbn=9780123943972 (click the Resources tab at the bottom of the page).

1. ABSTRACT

One thing to consider is that the most probable avenue of attack in a SAN is through the hosts connected to the SAN. There are potentially thousands of host, application, and operating system-specific security considerations that are beyond the scope of this chapter but should be followed as your systems and application administrators properly configure their owned devices. Information security, that aspect of security that seeks to protect data confidentiality, data integrity, and access to the data, is an established commercial sector with a wide variety of vendors marketing mature products and technologies, such as VPNs, firewalls, antivirus, and content management. Recently there has been a subtle development in security. Organizations are expanding their security perspectives to secure not only end-user data access and the perimeter of the organization but also the data within the datacenter. Several factors drive these recent developments. The continuing expansion of the network and the continued shrinking of the perimeter expose datacenter resources and the storage infrastructure to new vulnerabilities. Data aggregation increases the impact of a security breach. IP-based storage networking potentially exposes storage resources to traditional network vulnerabilities. Recently the delineation between a back-end datacenter and front-end network perimeter is less clear. Storage resources are potentially becoming exposed to unauthorized users inside and outside the enterprise. In addition, as the plethora of compliance regulations continues to expand and become more complicated, IT managers are faced with addressing the threat of security breaches from both within and outside the organization. Complex international regulations require a greater focus on protecting not only the network but the data itself. This chapter describes best practices for enhancing and applying security of SANs.

2. CONTENTS

## Chapter 52

Storage Area Networking Security Devices

Robert Rounsavall
Terremark Worldwide, Inc.

Storage area networking (SAN) devices have become a critical IT component of almost every business today. The upside and intended consequences of using a SAN are to consolidate corporate data as well as reduce cost, complexity, and risks. The tradeoff and downside to implementing SAN technology are that the risks of large-scale data loss are higher in terms of both cost and reputation. With the rapid adoption of virtualization, SANs now house more than just data; they house entire virtual servers and huge clusters of servers in "enterprise clouds."[1] In addition to all the technical, management, deployment, and protection challenges, a SAN comes with a full range of legal regulations such as PCI, HIPAA, SOX, GLBA, SB1386, and many others. Companies keep their informational "crown jewels" on their SANs but in most cases do not understand all the architecture issues and risks involved, which can cost an organization huge losses. This chapter covers all the issues and security concerns related to storage area network security.

1. WHAT IS A SAN?

The Storage Network Industry Association (SNIA)[2] defines a SAN as a data storage system consisting of various storage elements, storage devices, computer systems, and/or appliances, plus all the control software, all communicating in efficient harmony over a network. Put in simple terms, a SAN is a specialized, high-speed network attaching servers and storage devices and, for this reason, it is sometimes referred to as "the network behind the servers." A SAN allows "any-to-any" connections across the network, using interconnected elements such as routers, gateways, hubs, switches, and directors. It eliminates the traditional dedicated connection between a server and storage as well as the concept that the server effectively

"owns and manages" the storage devices. It also eliminates any restriction to the amount of data that a server can access, currently limited by the number of storage devices attached to the individual server. Instead, a SAN introduces the flexibility of networking to enable one server or many heterogeneous servers to share a common storage utility, which may comprise many storage devices, including disk, tape, and optical storage. Additionally, the storage utility may be located far from the servers that use it.

The SAN can be viewed as an extension to the storage bus concept, which enables storage devices and servers to be interconnected using similar elements to those used in local area networks (LANs) and wide area networks (WANs). SANs can be interconnected with routers, hubs, switches, directors, and gateways. A SAN can also be shared between servers and/or dedicated to one server. It can be local or extended over geographical distances.

2. SAN DEPLOYMENT JUSTIFICATIONS

Perhaps a main reason SANs have emerged as the leading advanced storage option is because they can often alleviate many if not all the data storage "pain points" of IT managers.[3] For quite some time IT managers have been in a predicament in which some servers, such as database servers, run out of hard disk space rather quickly, whereas other servers, such as application servers, tend to not need a whole lot of disk space and usually have storage to spare. When a SAN is implemented, the storage can be spread throughout servers on an as-needed basis. The following are further justifications and benefits for implementing a storage area network:

- They allow for more manageable, scalable, and efficient deployment of mission-critical data.

---

1. The Enterprise Cloud by Terremark, www.theenterprisecloud.com.
2. Storage Network Industry Association, www.snia.org/home.

3. SAN justifications: http://voicendata.ciol.com/content/enterprise_zone/ 105041303.asp.

- SAN designs can protect resource investments from unexpected turns in the economic environment and changes in market adoption of new technology.
- SANs help with the difficulty of managing large, disparate islands of storage from multiple physical and virtual locations.
- SANs reduce the complexity of maintaining scheduled backups for multiple systems and difficulty in preparing for unscheduled system outages.
- The inability to share storage resources and achieve efficient levels of subsystem utilization is avoided.
- SANs help address the issue of a shortage of qualified storage professionals to manage storage resources effectively.
- SANs help us understand how to implement the plethora of storage technology alternatives, including appropriate deployment of Fibre Channel as well as Internet small computer systems interface (iSCSI), Fibre Channel over IP (FCIP), and InfiniBand.
- SANs allow us to work with restricted budgets and increasing costs of deploying and maintaining them, despite decreasing prices for physical storage in terms of average street price per terabyte.

In addition to all these benefits, the true advantage of implementing a SAN is that it enables the management of huge quantities of email and other business-critical data such as that created by many enterprise applications, such as customer relationship management (CRM), enterprise resource planning (ERP), and others. The popularity of these enterprise applications, regulatory compliance, and other audit requirements have resulted in an explosion of information and data that have become the lifeblood of these organizations, greatly elevating the importance of a sound storage strategy. Selecting a unified architecture that integrates the appropriate technologies to meet user requirements across a range of applications is central to ensuring storage support for mission-critical applications. Then matching technologies to user demands allows for optimized storage architecture, providing the best use of capital and IT resources.

A large number of enterprises have already implemented production SANs, and many industry analysts have researched the actual benefits of these implementations. A Gartner[4] study of large enterprise data center managers shows that 64% of those surveyed were either running or deploying a SAN. Another study by the Aberdeen Group cites that nearly 60% of organizations that have SANs installed have two or more separate SANs. The study also states that 80% of those surveyed felt that they had satisfactorily achieved their main goals for implementing a SAN. Across the board, all vendor case studies and all industry analyst investigations have found the following core benefits of SAN implementation compared to a direct attached storage (DAS) environment:

- Ease of management
- Increased subsystem utilization
- Reduction in backup expense
- Lower Total Cost of Ownership (TCO)

3. THE CRITICAL REASONS FOR SAN SECURITY

SAN security is important because there is more concentrated, centralized, high-value data at risk than in normal distributed servers with built-in, smaller-scale storage solutions. On a SAN you have data from multiple devices and multiple parts of the network shared on one platform. This typically fast-growing data can be consolidated and centralized from locations all over the world. SANs also store more than just data; with the increasing acceptance of server virtualization, multiple OS images and the data they create are being retrieved from and enabled by SANs.

Why is SAN Security Important?

Some large-scale security losses have occurred by intercepting information incrementally over time, but the vast majority of breaches involve access or loss of data from the corporate SAN. (For deeper insight into the numbers, check out the Data Loss Web site. This website tracks incidents and is a clearinghouse of data loss each month.[5])

A wide range of adversaries can attack an organization simply to access its SAN, which is where all the company data rests. Common adversaries who will be looking to access the organization's main data store are:

- Financially motivated attackers and competitors
- Identity thieves
- Criminal gangs
- State-sponsored attackers
- Internal employees
- Curious business partners

If one or some of these perpetrators were to be successful in stealing or compromising the data in the SAN, and if news got around that your customer data had been compromised, it could directly impact your organization monetarily and cause significant losses in terms of:

- Reputation
- Time lost
- Forensics investigations

---

4. Gartner, www.gartner.com.

5. Data Loss Database, http://datalossdb.org/.

- Overtime for IT
- Business litigation
- Perhaps even a loss of competitive edge—for example, if the organization's proprietary manufacturing process is found in the wild

4. SAN ARCHITECTURE AND COMPONENTS

In its simplest form, a SAN is a number of servers attached to a storage array using a switch. Figure 52.1 is a diagram of all the components involved.

SAN Switches

Specialized switches called SAN switches are at the heart of a typical SAN. Switches provide capabilities to match the number of host SAN connections to the number of connections provided by the storage array. Switches also provide path redundancy in the event of a path failure from host server to switch or from storage array to switch. SAN switches can connect both servers and storage devices and thus provide the connection points for the fabric of the SAN. For smaller SANs, the standard SAN switches are called *modular switches* and can typically support eight or 16 ports (though some 32-port modular switches are beginning to emerge). Sometimes modular switches are interconnected to create a fault-tolerant fabric. For larger SAN fabrics, director-class switches provide a larger port capacity (64 to 128 ports per switch)

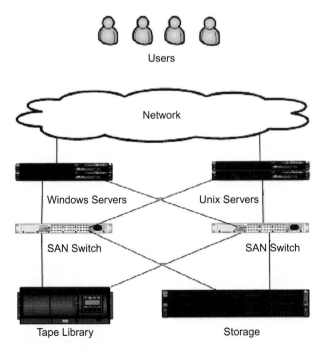

FIGURE 52.1   Simple SAN elements.

and built-in fault tolerance. The type of SAN switch, its design features, and its port capacity all contribute to its overall capacity, performance, and fault tolerance. The number of switches, types of switches, and manner in which the switches are interconnected define the topology of the fabric.

Network Attached Storage (NAS)

Network attached storage (NAS) is file-level data storage providing data access to many different network clients. The Business Continuity Planning (BCP) defined in this category address the security associated with file-level storage systems/ecosystems. They cover the Network File System (NFS), which is often used by Unix and Linux (and their derivatives') clients as well as SMB/CIFS, which is frequently used by Windows clients.

Fabric

When one or more SAN switches are connected, *a fabric* is created. The fabric is the actual network portion of the SAN. Special communications protocols such as Fibre Channel (FC), iSCSI, and Fibre Channel over Ethernet (FCoE) are used to communicate over the entire network. Multiple fabrics may be interconnected in a single SAN, and even for a simple SAN it is not unusual for it to be composed of two fabrics for redundancy.

HBA and Controllers

Host servers and storage systems are connected to the SAN fabric through ports in the fabric. A host connects to a fabric port through a Host Bus Adapter (HBA), and the storage devices connect to fabric ports through their controllers. Each server may host numerous applications that require dedicated storage for applications processing. Servers need not be homogeneous within the SAN environment.

Tape Library

A tape library is a storage device that is designed to hold, manage, label, and store data to tape. Its main benefit is related to cost/TB, but its slow random access relegates it to an archival device.

Protocols, Storage Formats and Communications

The following protocols and file systems are other important components of a SAN.

Block-Based IP Storage (IP)

Block-based IP storage is implemented using protocols such as iSCSI. This also includes Internet Fibre Channel Protocol (iFCP) and FCIP to transmit SCSI commands over IP networks.

Secure iSCSI

Internet SCSI or iSCSI, which is described in IETF RFC 3720, is a connection-oriented command/response protocol that runs over TCP. It is also used to access disk, tape, and other devices.

Secure FCIP

Fibre Channel over TCP/IP (FCIP), defined in IETF RFC 3821, is a pure Fibre Channel encapsulation protocol. It allows the interconnection of islands of Fibre Channel storage area networks through IP-based networks to form a unified storage area network.

Fibre Channel Storage (FCS)

Fibre Channel is a gigabit-speed network technology used for block-based storage. The Fibre Channel Protocol (FCP) is the interface protocol used to transmit SCSI on this network technology.

Secure FCP

Fibre Channel entities (host bus adapters or HBAs, switches, and storage) can contribute to the overall secure posture of a storage network. This is done by employing mechanisms such as filtering and authentication.

Secure Fibre Channel Storage Networks

A SAN is architected to attach remote computer storage devices (such as disk arrays, tape libraries, and optical jukeboxes) to servers in such a way that, to the operating system, the devices appear as though they're locally attached. These SANs are often based on a Fibre Channel fabric topology that utilizes the Fibre Channel Protocol (FCP).

SMB/CIFS

SMB/CIFS is a network protocol whose most common use is sharing files. This is especially true in Microsoft operating system environments.

Network File System (NFS)

NFS is a client/server application, communicating with a remote procedure call (RPC)-based protocol. It enables file systems physically residing on one computer system or NAS device to be used by other computers in the network, appearing to users on the remote host as just another local disk.

Online Fixed Content

An online fixed content system usually contains at least some data subject to retention policies and a retention-managed storage system/ecosystem is commonly used for such data.

5. SAN GENERAL THREATS AND ISSUES

A SAN is a prime target of all attackers due to the goldmine of information that can be attained by accessing it. Here we discuss the general threats and issues related to SANs.

SAN Cost: A Deterrent to Attackers

Unlike many network components such as servers, routers, and switches, SANs are quite expensive, which does raise the bar for attackers a little bit. There are not huge numbers of people with SAN protocol expertise, and not too many people have a SAN in their home lab, unless they are a foreign government that has dedicated resources to researching and exploiting these types of vulnerabilities. Why would anyone go to the trouble when it would be much easier to compromise the machines of the people who manage the SANs or the servers that are themselves connected to the SAN?

The barrier to entry to directly attack the SAN is high; however, the ability to attack the management tools and administrators who access the SAN is not. Most are administered via Web interfaces, software applications, or command-line interfaces. An attacker simply has to gain root or administrator access on those machines to be able to attack the SAN.

Physical Level Threats, Issues, and Risk Mitigation

There can be many physical risks involved in using a SAN. It is important to take them all into consideration when planning and investing in a storage area network:

- Locate the SAN in a secure datacenter
- Ensure that proper access controls are in place
- Cabinets, servers, and tape libraries come with locks; use them
- Periodically audit the access control list
- Verify whether former employees can access the location where the SAN is located
- Perform physical penetration and social engineering tests on a regular basis

Physical Environment

The SAN must be located in an area with proper ventilation and cooling. Ensure that your datacenter has proper cooling and verify any service-level agreements with a third-party provider with regard to power and cooling.

Hardware Failure Considerations

Ensure that the SAN is designed and constructed in such a way that when a piece of hardware fails, it does not cause an outage. Schedule failover testing on a regular basis during maintenance windows so that it will be completed on time.

Secure Sensitive Data on Removable Media to Protect "Externalized Data"

Many of the data breaches that fill the newspapers and create significant embarrassments for organizations are easily preventable and involve loss of *externalized data* such as backup media. To follow are some ideas to avoid unauthorized disclosure while data is in transit:

- Offsite backup tapes of sensitive or regulated data should be encrypted as a general practice and must be encrypted when leaving the direct control of the organization; encryption keys must be stored separately from data.
- Use only secure and bonded shippers if not encrypted. (Remember that duty-of-care contractual provisions often contain a limitation of liability limited to the bond value. The risk transfer value is often less than the data value.)
- Secure sensitive data transferred between datacenters.
- Sensitive/regulated data transferred to and from remote datacenters must be encrypted in flight.
- Secure sensitive data in third-party datacenters.
- Sensitive/regulated data stored in third-party datacenters must be encrypted prior to arrival (both in-flight and at-rest).
- Secure your data being used by ediscovery tools.

Know Thy Network (or Storage Network)

It is not only a best practice but critical that the SAN is well documented. All assets must be known. All physical and logical interfaces must be known. Create detailed physical and logical diagrams of the SAN. Identify *all* interfaces on the SAN gear. Many times people overlook the network interfaces for the out-of-band management. Some vendors put a sticker with login and password physically on the server for the out-of-band management ports. Ensure that these are changed. Know what networks can access the SAN and from where. Verify all entry points and exit points for data, especially sensitive data such as financial information or PII. If an auditor asks, it should be simple to point to exactly where that data rests and where it goes on the network.

Use Best Practices for Disaster Recovery and Backup

Guidelines such as the NIST Special Publication 800-34[6] outline best practices for disaster recovery and backup. The seven steps for contingency planning are outlined below:

1. *Develop the contingency planning policy statement.* A formal department or agency policy provides the authority and guidance necessary to develop an effective contingency plan.
2. *Conduct the business impact analysis (BIA).* The BIA helps identify and prioritize critical IT systems and components. A template for developing the BIA is also provided to assist the user.
3. *Identify preventive controls.* Measures taken to reduce the effects of system disruptions can increase system availability and reduce contingency life-cycle costs.
4. *Develop recovery strategies.* Thorough recovery strategies ensure that the system may be recovered quickly and effectively following a disruption.
5. *Develop an IT contingency plan.* The contingency plan should contain detailed guidance and procedures for restoring a damaged system.
6. *Plan testing, training, and exercises.* Testing the plan identifies planning gaps, whereas training prepares recovery personnel for plan activation; both activities improve plan effectiveness and overall agency preparedness.
7. *Plan maintenance.* The plan should be a living document that is updated regularly to remain current with system enhancements.

Logical Level Threats, Vulnerabilities, and Risk Mitigation

Aside from the physical risks and issues with SANs, there are also many logical threats. A threat is defined as any potential danger to information or systems. These are the same threats that exist in any network and they are also applicable to a storage network because Windows and Unix servers are used to access and manage the SAN. For this reason, it is important to take a defense-in-depth approach to securing the SAN. Some of the threats that face a SAN are as follows:

- *Internal threats (malicious).* A malicious employee could access the sensitive data in a SAN via management interface or poorly secured servers.
- *Internal threats (nonmalicious).* Not following proper procedure such as using change management could

---

6. NIST Special Publication 800-34, http://csrc.nist.gov/publications/nist-pubs/800-34/sp800-34.pdf.

bring down a SAN. A misconfiguration could bring down a SAN. Poor planning for growth could limit your SAN.

- *Outside threats.* An attacker could access your SAN data or management interface by compromising a management server, a workstation or laptop owned by an engineer, or other server that has access to the SAN.

The following parts of the chapter deal with protecting against these threats.

Begin with a Security Policy

Having a corporate information security policy is essential.[7] Companies should already have such policies, and they should be periodically reviewed and updated. If organizations process credit cards for payment and are subject to the Payment Card Industry (PCI)[8] standards, they are mandated to have a security policy. Federal agencies subject to certification and accreditation under guidelines such as DIACAP[9] must also have security policies.

Is storage covered in the corporate security policy? Some considerations for storage security policies include the following:

- Identification and classification of sensitive data such as PII, financial, trade secrets, and business-critical data
- Data retention, destruction, deduplication, and sanitization
- User access and authorization

Instrument the Network with Security Tools

Many of the network security instrumentation devices such as IDS/IPS have become a commodity, required for compliance and a minimum baseline for any IT network. The problem with many of those tools is that they are signature based and only provide alerts and packet captures on the offending packet alerts. Adding tools such as full packet capture and network anomaly detection systems can allow a corporation to see attacks that are not yet known. They can also find attacks that bypass the IDS/IPSs and help prove to customers and government regulators whether or not the valuable data was actually stolen from the network.

Intrusion Detection and Prevention Systems (IDS/IPS)

Intrusion detection and prevention systems can detect and block attacks on a network. Intrusion prevention systems are usually inline and can block attacks. A few warnings about IPS devices:

- Their number-one goal is to *not* bring down the network.
- Their number-two goal is to not block legitimate traffic.

Time after time attacks can slip by these systems. They will block the low-hanging fruit, but a sophisticated attacker can trivially bypass IDS/IPS devices. Commercial tools include TippingPoint, Sourcefire, ISS, and Fortinet. Open-source tools include Snort and Bro.

Network Traffic Pattern Behavior Analysis

Intrusion detection systems and vulnerability-scanning systems are only able to detect well-known vulnerabilities. A majority of enterprises have these systems as well as log aggregation systems but are unable to detect 0-day threats and other previously compromised machines. The answer to this problem is NetFlow data. NetFlow data shows all connections into and out of the network. There are commercial and open-source tools. Commercial tools are Arbor Networks and Mazu Networks. Open-source tools include nfdump and Argus.

Full Network Traffic Capture and Replay

Full packet capture tools allow security engineers to record and play back all the traffic on the network. This allows for validation of IDS/IPS alerts and validation of items that NetFlow or log data is showing. Commercial tools include Niksun, NetWitness, and NetScout. Open-source tools include Wireshark and tcpdump.

Secure Network and Management tools

It is important to secure the network and management tools. If physical separation is not possible, then at a very minimum logical separation must occur. For example:

- Separate the management network with a firewall.
- Ensure user space and management interfaces are on different subnets/VLANs.
- Use strong communication protocols such as SSH, SSL, and VPNs to connect to and communicate with the management interfaces.
- Avoid using out-of-band modems if possible. If absolutely necessary, use the callback feature on the modems.

---

7. Information Security Policy Made Easy, www.informationshield.
8. PCI Security Standards, https://www.pcisecuritystandards.org/.
9. DIACAP Certification and Accreditation standard, http://iase.disa.mil/ditscap/ditscap-to-diacap.html.

- Have a local technician or datacenter operators connect the line only when remote dial-in access is needed, and then disconnect when done.
- Log all external maintenance access.

Restrict Remote Support

Best practice is to not allow remote support; however, most SANs have a "call home" feature that allows them to call back to the manufacturer for support. Managed network and security services are commonplace. If remote access for vendors is mandatory, take extreme care. Here are some things that can help make access to the SAN safe:

- Disable the remote "call home" feature in the SAN until needed.
- Do not open a port in the firewall and give direct external access to the SAN management station.
- If outsourcing management of a device, ensure that there is a VPN set up and verify that the data is transmitted encrypted.
- On mission-critical systems, do not allow external connections. Have internal engineers connect to the systems and use a tool such as WebEx or GoToAssist to allow the vendor to view while the trusted engineer controls the mouse and keyboard.

Attempt to Minimize User Error

It is not uncommon for a misconfiguration to cause a major outage. Not following proper procedure can cause major problems. Not all compromises are due to malicious behaviors; some may be due to mistakes made by trusted personnel.

Establish Proper Patch Management Procedures

Corporations today are struggling to keep up with all the vulnerabilities and patches for all the platforms they manage. With all the different technologies and operating systems it can be a daunting task. Mission-critical storage management gear and network gear cannot be patched on a whim whenever the administrator feels like it. There are Web sites dedicated to patch management software. Microsoft Windows Software Update Services (WSUS) is a free tool that only works with Windows. Other commercial tools can assist with cross-platform patch management deployment and automation:

- Schedule updates.
- Live within the change window.
- Establish a rollback procedure.
- Test patches in a lab if at all possible. Use virtual servers if possible, to save cost.

- Purchase identical lab gear if possible. Many vendors will sell "nonproduction" lab gear at more than 50% discount. This allows for test scenarios and patching in a nonproduction environment without rolling into production.
- After applying patches or firmware, validate to make sure that the equipment was actually correctly updated.

Use Configuration Management Tools

Many large organizations have invested large amounts of money in network and software configuration management tools to manage hundreds or thousands of devices around the network. These tools store network device and software configurations in a database format and allow for robust configuration management capabilities. An example is HP's Network Automation System,[10] which can do the following:

- Reduce costs by automating time-consuming manual compliance checks and configuration tasks.
- Pass audit and compliance requirements easily with proactive policy enforcement and out-of-the-box audit and compliance reports (IT Infrastructure Library (ITIL), Cardholder Information Security Program (CISP), HIPAA, SOX, GLBA, and others).
- Improve network security by recognizing and fixing security vulnerabilities before they affect the network, using an integrated security alert service.
- Increase network stability and uptime by preventing the inconsistencies and misconfigurations that are at the root of most problems.
- Use process-powered automation to deliver application integrations, which deliver full IT life-cycle workflow automation without scripting.
- Support SNMPv3 and IPv6, including dual-stack IPv4 and IPv6 support. HP Network Automation supports both of these technologies to provide flexibility in your protocol strategy and implementation.
- Use automated software image management to deploy wide-scale image updates quickly with audit and rollback capabilities.

Set Baseline Configurations

If a commercial tool is not available, there are still steps that can be taken. Use templates such as the ones provided by the Center for Internet Security or the National Security Agency. They offer security templates for multiple operating systems, software packages, and network

---

10. HP Network Automation System, https://h10078.www1.hp.com/cda/hpms/display/main/hpms_content.jsp?zn = bto&cp = 1-11-271-273_4000_100_.

devices. They are free of charge and can be modified to fit the needs of the organization. In addition:

- Create a base configuration for all production devices.
- Check with the vendor to see if they have baseline security guides. Many of them do internally and will provide them on request.
- Audit the baseline configurations.
- Script and automate as much as possible.

Center for Internet Security[11]

The Center for Internet Security (CIS) is a not-for-profit organization that helps enterprises reduce the risk of business and ecommerce disruptions resulting from inadequate technical security controls and provides enterprises with resources for measuring information security status and making rational security investment decisions.

National Security Agency[12]

NSA initiatives in enhancing software security cover both proprietary and open-source software, and we have successfully used both proprietary and open-source models in our research activities. NSA's work to enhance the security of software is motivated by one simple consideration: Use our resources as efficiently as possible to give NSA's customers the best possible security options in the most widely employed products. The objective of the NSA research program is to develop technologic advances that can be shared with the software development community through a variety of transfer mechanisms. The NSA does not favor or promote any specific software product or business model. Rather, it promotes enhanced security.

Vulnerability Scanning

PCI requirements include both internal and external vulnerability scanning. An area that is commonly overlooked when performing vulnerability scans is the proprietary devices and appliances that manage the SAN and network. Many of these have Web interfaces and run Web applications on board. Vulnerability-scanning considerations are as follows:

- Use the Change Management/Change Control process to schedule the scans. Even trained security professionals who are good at not causing network problems sometimes cause network problems.
- Know exactly what will be scanned.
- Perform both internal and external vulnerability scans.

---

11. Center for Internet Security, www.cisecurity.org.
12. National Security Agency security templates, www.nsa.gov/snac/index.cfm.

- Scan the Web application and appliances that manage the SAN and the network.
- Use more than one tool to scan.
- Document results and define metrics to know whether vulnerabilities are increasing or decreasing.
- Set up a scanning routine and scan regularly with updated tools.

System Hardening

System hardening is an important part of SAN security. Hardening includes all the SAN devices and any machines that connect to it as well as management tools. There are multiple organizations that provide hardening guides for free that can be used as a baseline and modified to fit the needs of the organization:

- Do not use shared accounts. If all engineers use the same account, there is no way to determine who logged in and when.
- Remove manufacturers' default passwords.
- If supported, use central authentication such as RADIUS.
- Use the principle of least privilege. Do not give all users on the device administrative credentials unless they absolutely need them. A user just working on storage does not need the ability to reconfigure the SAN switch.

Management Tools

It is common for management applications to have vulnerabilities that the vendor will refuse to fix or deny that they are vulnerabilities. They usually surface after a vulnerability scan or penetration test. When vulnerabilities are found, there are steps that can be taken to mitigate the risk:

- Contact the vendor regardless. The vendor needs to know that there are vulnerabilities and they should correct them.
- Verify if they have a hardening guide or any steps that can be taken to mitigate the risk.
- Physically or logically segregate the tools and apply strict ACLs or firewall rules.
- Place it behind an intrusion prevention device.
- Place behind a Web application firewall, if a Web application.
- Audit and log access very closely.
- Set up alerts for logins that occur outside normal hours.
- Use strong authentication if available.
- Review the logs.

Separate Areas of the SAN

In the world of security, a defense-in-depth strategy is often employed with an objective of aligning the security measures with the risks involved. This means that there must be security controls implemented at each layer that may create an exposure to the SAN system. Most organizations are motivated to protect sensitive (and business/mission-critical) data, which typically represents a small fraction of the total data. This narrow focus on the most important data can be leveraged as the starting point for data classification and a way to prioritize protection activities. The best way to be sure that there is a layered approach to security is to address each aspect of a SAN one by one and determine the best strategy to implement physical, logical, virtual, and access controls.

Physical

Segregating the production of some systems from other system classes is crucial to proper data classification and security. For example, if it is possible to physically segregate the quality assurance data from the research and development data, there is a smaller likelihood of data leakage between departments and therefore out to the rest of the world.

Logical

When a SAN is implemented, segregating storage traffic from normal server traffic is quite important because there is no need for the data to travel on the same switches as your end users browsing the Internet, for example. Logical Unit Numbers (LUN) Masking, Fibre Channel Zoning, and IP VLANs can assist in separating data.

Virtual

One of the most prevalent uses recently for storage area networks is the storing of full-blown virtual machines that run from the SAN itself. With this newest of uses for SANs, the movement of virtual servers from one data store to another is something that is required in many scenarios and one that should be studied to identify potential risks.

Penetration Testing

Penetration testing like vulnerability scanning is becoming a regulatory requirement. Now people can go to jail for losing data and not complying with these regulations. Penetration-testing the SAN may be difficult due to the high cost of entry, as noted earlier. Most people don't have a SAN in their lab to practice pen testing.

Environments with custom applications and devices can be sensitive to heavy scans and attacks. Inexperienced people could inadvertently bring down critical systems. The security engineers who have experience working in these environments choose tools depending on the environment. They also tread lightly so that critical systems are not brought down. Boutique security firms might not have $100k to purchase a SAN so that their professional services personnel can do penetration tests on SANs. With the lack of skilled SAN technicians currently in the field, it is not likely that SAN engineers will be rapidly moving into the security arena. Depending on the size of the organization, there are things that can be done to facilitate successful penetration testing. An internal penetration testing team does the following:

- Have personnel cross-train and certify on the SAN platform in use.
- Provide the team access to the lab and establish a regular procedure to perform a pen test.
- Have a member of the SAN group as part of the pen-test team.
- Follow practices such as the OWASP guide for Web application testing and the OSSTMM for penetration-testing methodologies.

OWASP

The Open Web Application Security Project (OWASP; www.owasp.org) is a worldwide free and open community focused on improving the security of application software. Our mission is to make application security "visible" so that people and organizations can make informed decisions about application security risks.

OSSTMM

The Open Source Security Testing Methodology Manual (OSSTMM; www.isecom.org/osstmm/) is a peer-reviewed methodology for performing security tests and metrics. The OSSTMM test cases are divided into five channels (sections), which collectively test information and data controls, personnel security awareness levels, fraud and social engineering control levels, computer and telecommunications networks, wireless devices, mobile devices, physical security access controls, security processes, and physical locations such as buildings, perimeters, and military bases. The external penetration testing team does the following:

- Validates SAN testing experience through references and certification
- Avoids firms that do not have access to SAN storage gear
- Asks to see a sanitized report of a previous penetration test that included a SAN

Whether an internal or external penetration-testing group, it is a good idea to belong to one of the professional security associations in the area, such as the Information Systems Security Association (ISSA) or

Information Systems Audit and Control Association (ISACA).

ISSA

ISSA (www.issa.org) is a not-for-profit, international organization of information security professionals and practitioners. It provides educational forums, publications, and peer interaction opportunities that enhance the knowledge, skill, and professional growth of its members.

ISACA

ISACA (www.isaca.org) got its start in 1967 when a small group of individuals with similar jobs—auditing controls in the computer systems that were becoming increasingly critical to the operations of their organizations—sat down to discuss the need for a centralized source of information and guidance in the field. In 1969 the group formalized, incorporating as the EDP Auditors Association. In 1976 the association formed an education foundation to undertake large-scale research efforts to expand the knowledge and value of the IT governance and control field.

Encryption

Encryption is the conversion of data into a form called *ciphertext* that cannot be easily understood by unauthorized people. *Decryption* is the process of converting encrypted data back into its original form so that it can be understood.

Confidentiality

Confidentiality is the property whereby information is not disclosed to unauthorized parties. *Secrecy* is a term that is often used synonymously with confidentiality. Confidentiality is achieved using encryption to render the information unintelligible except by authorized entities.

The information may become intelligible again by using decryption. For encryption to provide confidentiality, the cryptographic algorithm and mode of operation must be designed and implemented so that an unauthorized party cannot determine the secret or private keys associated with the encryption or be able to derive the plaintext directly without deriving any keys.[13]

Data encryption can save a company time, money, and embarrassment. There are countless examples of lost and stolen media, especially hard drives and tape drives. A misplacement or theft can cause major headaches for

an organization. Take, for example, the University of Miami[14]:

A private off-site storage company used by the University of Miami has notified the University that a container carrying computer back-up tapes of patient information was stolen. The tapes were in a transport case that was stolen from a vehicle contracted by the storage company on March 17 in downtown Coral Gables, the company reported. Law enforcement is investigating the incident as one of a series of petty thefts in the area.

Shortly after learning of the incident, the University determined it would be unlikely that a thief would be able to access the back-up tapes because of the complex and proprietary format in which they were written. Even so, the University engaged leading computer security experts at Terremark Worldwide[15] to independently ascertain the feasibility of accessing and extracting data from a similar set of back-up tapes.

Anyone who has been a patient of a University of Miami physician or visited a UM facility since January 1, 1999, is likely included on the tapes. The data included names, addresses, Social Security numbers, or health information. The University will be notifying by mail the 47,000 patients whose data may have included credit card or other financial information regarding bill payment.

Even thought it was unlikely that the person who stole the tapes had access to the data or could read the data, the university still had to notify 47,000 people that their data may have been compromised. Had the tape drives been encrypted, they would not have been in the news at all and no one would have had to worry about personal data being compromised.

Deciding What to Encrypt

Deciding what type of data to encrypt (see checklist, "An Agenda For Action For The Encryption Of Data") and how best to do it can be a challenge. It depends on the type of data that is stored on the SAN. Encrypt backup tapes as well.

Many of the vendors implement encryption in different ways. NIST SP 800-57 contains best practices for key management and information about various cryptographic ciphers. The following are the recommended minimum symmetric security levels, defined as bits of strength (not key size):

- 80 bits of security until 2010 (128-bit AES and 1024-bit RSA)
- 112 bits of security through 2030 (3DES, 128-AES and 2048-bit RSA)
- 128 bits of security beyond 2030 (128-AES and 3072-bit RSA)

---

13. NIST Special Publication 800-57, Recommendation for Key Management Part 1, http://csrc.nist.gov/publications/nistpubs/800-57/SP800-57-Part1.pdf.

14. Data Loss Notification from the University of Miami, www6.miami.edu/dataincident/index.htm.

15. Terremark Worldwide, www.terremark.com

An Agenda for Action for the Encryption of Data

There are two main types of encryption to focus on: data in transit and data at rest. SNIA put out a white paper called *Encryption of Data At-Rest: Step-by-Step Checklist,* which outlines nine steps for encrypting data at rest[16] (Check All Tasks Completed):

_____**1.** Understand confidentiality drivers.
_____**2.** Classify the data assets.
_____**3.** Inventory data assets.
_____**4.** Perform data flow analysis.
_____**5.** Determine the appropriate points of encryption.
_____**6.** Design encryption solution.
_____**7.** Begin data realignment.
_____**8.** Implement solution.
_____**9.** Activate encryption.

```
4940 5f 72 65 6c 73 2f 74 68-65 6d 65 4d 61 6e 61 67   _rels/themeManag
4950 65 72 2e 78 6d 6c 2e 72-65 6c 73 50 4b 05 06 00   er.xml.relsPK···
4960 00 00 00 05 00 05 00 5d-01 00 00 9a 0a 00 00 00   ·······]········
4970 00 3c 3f 78 6d 6c 20 76-65 72 73 69 6f 6e 3d 22   ·<?xml version="
4980 31 2e 30 22 20 65 6e 63-6f 64 69 6e 67 3d 22 55   1.0" encoding="U
4990 54 46 2d 38 22 20 73 74-61 6e 64 61 6c 6f 6e 65   TF-8" standalone
49a0 3d 22 79 65 73 22 3f 3e-0d 0a 3c 61 3a 63 6c 72   ="yes"?>··<a:clr
49b0 4d 61 70 20 78 6d 6c 6e-73 3a 61 3d 22 68 74 74   Map xmlns:a="htt
49c0 70 3a 2f 2f 73 63 68 65-6d 61 73 2e 6f 70 65 6e   p://schemas.open
49d0 78 6d 6c 66 6f 72 6d 61-74 73 2e 6f 72 67 2f 64   xmlformats.org/d
49e0 72 61 77 69 6e 67 6d 6c-2f 32 30 30 36 2f 6d 61   rawingml/2006/ma
49f0 69 6e 22 20 62 67 31 3d-22 6c 74 31 22 20 74 78   in" bg1="lt1" tx
4a00 31 3d 22 64 6b 31 22 20-62 67 32 3d 22 6c 74 32   1="dk1" bg2="lt2
4a10 22 20 74 78 32 3d 22 64-6b 32 22 20 61 63 63 65   " tx2="dk2" acce
4a20 6e 74 31 3d 22 61 63 63-65 6e 74 31 22 20 61 63   nt1="accent1" ac
```

FIGURE 52.2 Notice the clear, legible text on the right.

Type of Encryption to Use

The type of encryption used should contain a strong algorithm and be publicly known. Algorithms such as ASE, RSA, SHA, and Twofish are known and tested. All the aforementioned encryption algorithms have been tested and proven to be strong if properly implemented. Organizations should be wary of vendors saying that they have their own "unknown" encryption algorithm. Many times it is just data compression or a weak algorithm that the vendor wrote by itself. Though it sounds good in theory, the thousands of mathematicians employed by the NSA spend years and loads of computer power trying to break well-known encryption algorithms.

Proving that Data is Encrypted

A well-architected encryption plan should be transparent to the end user of the data. The only way to know for sure that the data is encrypted is to verify the data. Data at rest can be verified using forensic tools such as dd for Unix or the free FTK[17] imager for Windows. Data in transit can be verified by network monitoring tools such as Wireshark.

Turn on event logging for any encryption hardware or software. Make sure it is logging when it turns on or off. Have a documented way to verify that the encryption was turned on while it had the sensitive data on the system (see Figure 52.2).

Encryption Challenges and Other Issues

No method of defense is perfect. Human error and computer vulnerabilities do pose encryption challenges (see Figure 52.3). A large financial firm had personal information on its network, including 34,000 credit cards with names and account numbers. The network administrator had left the decryption key on the server. After targeting the server for a year and a half, the attacker was able to get the decryption key and finally able to directly query the fully encrypted database and pull out 34,000 cards.

Logging

Logging is an important consideration when it comes to SAN security. There are all sorts of events that can be logged. When a security incident happens, having proper

16. www.snia.org/forums/ssif/knowledge_center/white_papers.
17. Access Data Forensic Toolkit Imager, www.accessdata.com/downloads.html.

```
d5fb0  ce 05 18 59 7c ce ea 49-37 70 23 ba 0f ca 50 ad  Ï··Y|ÎêI7p#°·ËP-
d5fc0  ac ee ce c0 db e4 9c 26-97 ec ed 77 cd 1e d2 44  ¬îÎÀÛä·&·iiwÍ·ÒD
d5fd0  c2 22 de e1 2a fe 58 1f-27 32 a0 b3 f5 04 a6 30  Â"Þá*þX·'2 ³õ·¦0
d5fe0  41 f3 f3 97 c1 2a 91 d3-82 73 a1 45 02 19 8c 1e  Aóó·Á*·Ó·s¡E····
d5ff0  cb 76 fc c2 8e b9 cf 94-b8 c3 4b ff ce 7f e4 5b  ËvüÂ·¹Ï·¸ÃKÿÎ·ä[
d6000  c0 fd 37 75 40 a9 d3 c5-9a 8c 0d 51 82 69 7b 64  Àý7u@©ÓÅ···Q·i{d
d6010  10 54 ea 66 43 8c a8 68-2b 5f 44 9a 72 e5 5f b5  ·TêfC·¨h+_D·rå_µ
d6020  aa 16 cb 09 f1 79 2e 7a-f7 a2 cf 8a 2f a3 ca df  ª·Ë·ñy.z÷¢Ï·/£Êß
d6030  3a af 68 ee 11 d1 d7 3b-6c 01 9b 6d 18 92 c7 4e  :¯hî·Ñ×;l·›m··ÇN
d6040  18 9c 6b ac 61 38 a1 e6-67 3e b0 b3 00 35 69 10  ··k¬a8¡æg>°³·5i·
d6050  de 74 dd c2 ff 2b 5f 61-04 6b c5 26 01 3d 85 4a  ÞtÝÂÿ+_a·kÅ&·=·J
d6060  c5 de 94 4c d9 ff 85 ba-ac 31 a3 5e 5f e2 45 0b  ÅÞ·LÙÿ·º¬1£^_âE·
d6070  6b 8d 77 1f 8b d2 15 e1-90 86 02 94 bf 1d 54 18  k·w··Ò·á····¿·T·
```

FIGURE 52.3 Notice Encrypted Data on the right-hand side.

log information can mean the difference between solving the problem and not knowing whether your data was compromised. NIST has an excellent guide to Security Log Management. The SANS Institute has a guide on the top five most essential log reports.

There are multiple commercial vendors as well as open-source products for log management. Log management has evolved from standalone syslog servers to complex architectures for Security Event/Information Management. Acronyms used for these blend together as SEM, SIM, and SEIM. In addition to log data, they can take in data from IDSs, vulnerability assessment products, and many other security tools to centralize and speed up the analysis and processing of huge amounts of logs. More of a difference is being made between Security Event Management and audit logging. The former is geared toward looking at events of interest on which to take action; the latter is geared to compliance. In today's legal and compliance environment an auditor will ask an enterprise to immediately provide logs for a particular device for a time period such as the previous 90 days. With a solid log management infrastructure, this request becomes trivial and a powerful tool to help solve problems. NIST Special Publication 800-92[18] makes the following recommendations:

- Organizations should establish policies and procedures for log management.
- Organizations should prioritize log management appropriately throughout the organization.
- Organizations should create and maintain a log management infrastructure.
- Organizations should provide proper support for all staff with log management responsibilities.
- Organizations should establish standard log management operational processes.

---

18. NIST SP 800-92 http://csrc.nist.gov/publications/nistpubs/800-92/SP800-92.pdf.

Policies and Procedures

To establish and maintain successful log management activities, an organization should develop standard processes for performing log management. As part of the planning process, an organization should define its logging requirements and goals.

Prioritize Log Management

After an organization defines its requirements and goals for the log management process, it should then prioritize the requirements and goals based on the organization's perceived reduction of risk and the expected time and resources needed to perform log management functions.

Create and Maintain a Log Management Infrastructure

A log management infrastructure consists of the hardware, software, networks, and media used to generate, transmit, store, analyze, and dispose of log data. Log management infrastructures typically perform several functions that support the analysis and security of log data.

Provide Support for Staff with Log Management Responsibilities

To ensure that log management for individual systems is performed effectively throughout the organization, the administrators of those systems should receive adequate support.

Establish a Log Management Operational Process

The major log management operational processes typically include configuring log sources, performing log analysis, initiating responses to identified events, and managing long-term storage.

What Events Should Be Logged for SANs?

For storage networks the same type of data should be collected as for other network devices, with focus on the storage management systems and any infrastructure that supports the SAN, such as the switches and servers. According to the SANS Institute, the top five most essential log reports[19] are as follows.

Attempts to Gain Access Through Existing Accounts Failed authentication attempts can be an indication of a malicious user or process attempting to gain network access by performing password guessing. It can also be an indication that a local user account is attempting to gain a higher level of permissions to a system.

Failed File or Resource Access Attempts Failed file or resource access attempts is a broad category that can impact many different job descriptions. In short, failed access attempts are an indication that someone is attempting to gain access to either a nonexistent resource or a resource to which they have not been granted the correct permissions.

Unauthorized Changes to Users, Groups and Services The modification of user and group accounts, as well as system services, can be an indication that a system has become compromised. Clearly, modifications to all three will occur legitimately in an evolving network, but they warrant special attention because they can be a final indication that all other defenses have been breached and an intrusion has occurred.

Systems Most Vulnerable to Attack As indicated in the original SANS Top 10 Critical Vulnerabilities list as well as the current Top 20, one of the most important steps you can take in securing your network is to stay up to date on patches. In an ideal world all systems would remain completely up to date on the latest patches; time management, legacy software, availability of resources, and so on can result in a less than ideal posture. A report that identifies the level of compliance of each network resource can be extremely helpful in setting priorities.

Suspicious or Unauthorized Network Traffic Patterns Suspect traffic patterns can be described as unusual or unexpected traffic patterns on the local network. This not only includes traffic entering the local network but traffic leaving the network as well. This report

option requires a certain level of familiarity with what is "normal" for the local network. With this in mind, administrators need to be knowledgeable of local traffic patterns to make the best use of these reports. With that said, there are some typical traffic patterns that can be considered to be highly suspect in nearly all environments.

6. SUMMARY

The financial and IT resource benefits of consolidating information into a storage area network are compelling, and our dependence on this technology will continue to grow as our data storage needs grow exponentially. With this concentration and consolidation of critical information come security challenges and risks that must be recognized and appropriately addressed. In this chapter we covered these risks as well as the controls and processes that should be employed to protect the information stored on a SAN. Finally, we have emphasized why encryption of data at rest and in flight is a critical protection method that must be employed by the professional SAN administrator. Our intention is for you to understand all these risks to your SAN and to use the methods and controls described here to prevent you or your company from becoming a data loss statistic.

Finally, let's move on to the real interactive part of this Chapter: review questions/exercises, hands-on projects, case projects and optional team case project. The answers and/or solutions by chapter can be found in the Online Instructor's Solutions Manual.

CHAPTER REVIEW QUESTIONS/EXERCISES

True/False

1. True or False? The Storage Network Industry Association (SNIA)[2] defines a SAN as a data storage system consisting of various storage elements, storage devices, computer systems, and/or appliances, plus some of the control software, all communicating in efficient harmony over a network.
2. True or False? Perhaps a main reason SANs have emerged as the leading storage option is because they can often alleviate many if not all the data storage "pain points" of IT managers.
3. True or False? SAN security is important because there is more concentrated, centralized, high-value data at risk than in normal distributed servers with built-in, smaller-scale storage solutions.
4. True or False? Some large-scale security gains have occurred by intercepting information incrementally over time, but the vast majority of breaches involve access or loss of data from the corporate SAN.

---

19. SANS Institute, www.sans.org/free_resources.php.

5. True or False? In its advanced form, a SAN is a number of servers attached to a storage array using a switch.

Multiple Choice

1. Specialized switches called _____ are at the heart of a typical SAN. Switches provide capabilities to match the number of host SAN connections to the number of connections provided by the storage array.
   A. SAN switches
   B. Location technology
   C. Promotional email
   D. Malformed request DoS
   E. Data controller
2. What is file-level data storage providing data access to many different network clients?
   A. Network attached storage (NAS)
   B. Location technology
   C. Valid
   D. Load-Based DoS
   E. Bait
3. When one or more SAN switches are connected, a _____ is created.
   A. Data minimization
   B. Fabric
   C. Target access
   D. Strong narrative
   E. Security
4. Host servers and storage systems are connected to the SAN fabric through _____ in the fabric.
   A. Call data floods
   B. Greedy strategy
   C. Ports

   D. SAN protocol
   E. Taps
5. What is a storage device that is designed to hold, manage, label, and store data to tape?
   A. Irrelevant
   B. Tape library
   C. IP storage access
   D. Configuration file
   E. Server policy

EXERCISE

Problem

What is block level access?

Hands-On Projects

Project

What is a Storage Array?

Case Projects

Problem

When should an organization use a SAN solution?

Optional Team Case Project

Problem

Does a SAN Connected server need to be located in a Data Center?

## Chapter 53

Risk Management

Sokratis K. Katsikas
University of Piraeus

Integrating security measures with the operational framework of an organization is neither a trivial nor an easy task. This explains to a large extent the low degree of security that information systems operating in contemporary businesses and organizations enjoy. Some of the most important difficulties that security professionals face when confronted with the task of introducing security measures in businesses and organizations are:

- The difficulty to justify the cost of the security measures
- The difficulty to establish communication between technical and administrative personnel
- The difficulty to assure active participation of users in the effort to secure the information system and to commit higher management to continuously supporting the effort
- The widely accepted erroneous perception of information systems security as a purely technical issue
- The difficulty to develop an integrated, efficient and effective information systems security plan
- The identification and assessment of the organizational impact that the implementation of a security plan entails

The difficulty in justifying the cost of the security measures, particularly those of a procedural and administrative nature, stems from the very nature of security itself. Indeed, the justification of the need for a security measure can only be proved "after the (unfortunate) event", whereas, at the same time, there is no way to prove that already implemented measures can adequately cope with a potential new threat. This cost does not only pertain to acquiring and installing mechanisms and tools for protection. It also includes the cost of human resources, the cost of educating and making users aware, and the cost for carrying out tasks and procedures relevant to security.

The difficulty in expressing the cost of the security measures in monetary terms is one of the fundamental factors that make the communication between technical and administrative personnel difficult. An immediate consequence of this is the difficulty in securing the continuous commitment of higher management to supporting the security enhancement effort. This becomes even more difficult when organizational and procedural security measures are proposed. Both management and users are concerned about the impact of these measures in their usual practice, particularly when the widely accepted concept that security is purely a technical issue is put into doubt.

Moreover, protecting an information system calls for an integrated, holistic study that will answer questions such as: Which elements of the information system do we want to protect? Which, among these, are the most important ones? What threats is the information system facing? What are its vulnerabilities? What security measures must be put in place? Answering these questions gives a good picture of the current state of the information system with regard to its security. As research[1] has shown, developing techniques and measures for security is not enough, since the most vulnerable point in any information system is the human user, operator, designer, or other human. Therefore, the development and operation of secure information systems must equally consider and take account of both technical and human factors. At the same time, the threats that an information system faces are characterized by variety, diversity, complexity, and continuous variation. As the technological and societal environment continuously evolves, threats change and evolve, too. Furthermore, both information systems and threats against them are dynamic; hence the need for continuous monitoring and managing of the information system security plan.

The most widely used methodology that aims at dealing with these issues is the information systems risk management methodology. This methodology adopts the

---

1. E. A. Kiountouzis and S. A. Kokolakis, "An analyst's view of information systems security", in *Information Systems Security: Facing the Information Society of the 21st Century*, Katsikas, S. K., and Gritzalis, D. (eds.), Chapman & Hall, 1996.

concept of risk that originates in financial management, and substitutes the unachievable and immeasurable goal of fully securing the information system with the achievable and measurable goal of reducing the risk that the information system faces to within acceptable limits.

1. THE CONCEPT OF RISK

The concept of risk originated in the 17th century with the mathematics associated with gambling. At that time, risk referred to a combination of probability and magnitude of potential gains and losses. During the 18th century, risk, seen as a neutral concept, still considered both gains and losses and was employed in the marine insurance business. In the 19th century, risk emerged in the study of economics. The concept of risk, then, seen more negatively, caused entrepreneurs to call for special incentives to take the risk involved in investment. By the 20th century a total negative connotation was made when referring to outcomes of risk in engineering and science, with particular reference to the hazards posed by modern technological developments.[2,3]

Within the field of IT security, the risk R is calculated as the product of P, the probability of an exposure occurring a given number of times per year times C, the cost or loss attributed to such an exposure, that is, $R = P \times C$.[4]

The most recent standardized definition of risk comes from the International Organization for Standardization (ISO),[5] where the risk is defined as "the effect of uncertainty on objectives". This definition, quite different from the definition in the past (2008) version of the same standard, is the result of the process of aligning definitions within the ISO 27000 series of standards with those within the ISO 31000 series. Notwithstanding the fact that this alignment facilitates the treatment of risk regardless of its kind (IT security, environmental, etc.) within an enterprise, it does not directly convey the true meaning of risk within the IT security context. Within this context, it makes much more sense to retain the older standardized definition of risk as "the potential that a given threat will exploit vulnerabilities of an asset or group of assets and thereby cause harm to the organization."

To complete this definition, definitions of the terms *threat, vulnerability*, and *asset* are in order. These are as follows: A threat is "a potential cause of an incident, that may result in harm to system or organization." A vulnerability is "a weakness of an asset or group of assets that can be exploited by one or more threats." An asset is "anything that has value to the organization, its business operations and their continuity, including information resources that support the organization's mission."[6] Additionally, harm results in impact, which is "an adverse change to the level of business objectives achieved."[7] The relationships among these basic concepts are pictorially depicted in Figure 53.1.

2. EXPRESSING AND MEASURING RISK

Information security risk "is measured in terms of a combination of the likelihood of an event and its consequence."[8] Because we are interested in events related to information security, we define an information security event as "an identified occurrence of a system, service or network state indicating a possible breach of information security policy or failure of safeguards, or a previously unknown situation that may be security relevant."[9] Additionally, an information security incident is "indicated by a single or a series of unwanted information security events that have a significant probability of compromising business operations and threatening information security."[10] These definitions actually invert the investment assessment model, where an investment is considered worth making when its cost is less than the product of the expected profit times the likelihood of the profit occurring. In our case, the risk R is defined as the product of the likelihood L of a security incident occurring times the impact I that will be incurred to the organization due to the incident, that is, $R = L \times I$.[11]

To measure risk, we adopt the fundamental principles and the scientific background of statistics and probability theory, particularly of the area known as Bayesian statistics, after the mathematician Thomas Bayes (1702–1761), who formalized the namesake theorem.

2. M. Gerber and R. von Solms, "Management of risk in the information age," *Computers & Security*, Vol. 24, pp. 16–30, 2005.

3. M. Douglas, "Risk as a forensic resource," *Daedalus*, Vol. 119, Issue 4, pp. 1–17, 1990.

4. R. Courtney, "Security risk assessment in electronic data processing," in the *AFIPS Conference Proceedings of the National Computer Conference 46*, AFIPS, Arlington, pp. 97–104, 1977.

5. ISO/IEC, "Information technology—Security techniques—information security risk management," ISO/IEC 27005:2011 (E).

6. British Standards Institute, "Information technology—Security techniques—Management of information and communications technology security—Part 1: Concepts and models for information and communications technology security management," BS ISO/IEC 13335-1:2004.

7. ISO/IEC, "Information technology—security techniques–information security risk management," ISO/IEC 27005:2008 (E).

8. ISO/IEC, "Information technology—security techniques–information security risk management," ISO/IEC 27005:2008 (E).

9. British Standards Institute, "Information technology—Security techniques—Information security incident management," BS ISO/IEC TR 18044:2004.

10. British Standards Institute, "Information technology—Security techniques—Information security incident management," BS ISO/IEC TR 18044:2004.

11. R. Baskerville, "Information systems security design methods: implications for information systems development," *ACM Computing Surveys*, Vol. 25, No. 4, pp. 375–414, 1993.

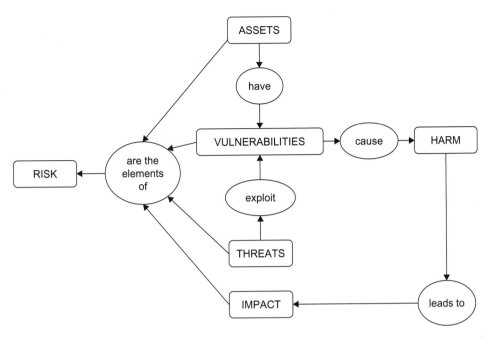

FIGURE 53.1 Risk and its related concepts.

Bayesian statistics is based on the view that the likelihood of an event happening in the future is measurable. This likelihood can be calculated if the factors affecting it are analyzed. For example, we are able to compute the probability of our data to be stolen as a function of the probability an intruder will attempt to intrude into our system and of the probability that he will succeed. In risk analysis terms, the former probability corresponds to the likelihood of the threat occurring and the latter corresponds to the likelihood of the vulnerability being successfully exploited. Thus, risk analysis assesses the likelihood that a security incident will happen by analyzing and assessing the factors that are related to its occurrence, namely the threats and the vulnerabilities. Subsequently, it combines this likelihood with the impact resulting from the incident occurring to calculate the system risk. Risk analysis is a necessary prerequisite for subsequently treating risk. Risk treatment pertains to controlling the risk so that it remains within acceptable levels. Risk can be reduced by applying security measures; it can be shared, by outsourcing or by insuring; it can be avoided; or it can be accepted, in the sense that the organization accepts the likely impact of a security incident.

The likelihood of a security incident occurring is a function of the likelihood that a threat appears and of the likelihood that the threat can successfully exploit the relevant system vulnerabilities. The consequences of the occurrence of a security incident are a function of the likely impact that the incident will have to the organization as a result of the harm that the organization assets will sustain. Harm, in turn, is a function of the value of the assets to the organization. Thus, the risk R is a function of four elements: (a) V, the value of the assets; (b) T, the severity and likelihood of appearance of the threats; (c) V, the nature and the extent of the vulnerabilities and the likelihood that a threat can successfully exploit them; and (d) I, the likely impact of the harm should the threat succeed, that is, $R = f(A, T, V, I)$.

If the impact is expressed in monetary terms, the likelihood being dimensionless, then risk can be also expressed in monetary terms. This approach has the advantage of making the risk directly comparable to the cost of acquiring and installing security measures. Since security is often one of several competing alternatives for capital investment, the existence of a cost/benefit analysis that would offer proof that security will produce benefits that equal or exceed its cost is of great interest to the management of the organization. Of even more interest to management is the analysis of the investment opportunity costs, that is, its comparison to other capital investment options.[12] However, expressing risk in monetary terms is not always possible or desirable, since harm to some kinds of assets (human life) cannot (and should not) be assessed in monetary terms. This is why risk is usually expressed in nonmonetary terms, on a simple dimensionless scale.

Assets in an organization are usually quite diverse. Because of this diversity, it is likely that some assets that have a known monetary value (hardware) can be valued in the local currency, whereas others of a more qualitative nature (data or information) may be assigned a numerical

12. R. Baskerville, "Risk analysis as a source of professional knowledge," *Computers & Security*, Vol. 10, pp. 749–764, 1991.

value based on the organization's perception of their value. This value is assessed in terms of the assets' importance to the organization or their potential value in different business opportunities. The legal and business requirements are also taken into account, as are the impacts to the asset itself and to the related business interests resulting from a loss of one or more of the information security attributes (confidentiality, integrity, availability). One way to express asset values is to use the business impacts that unwanted incidents, such as disclosure, modification, nonavailability, and/or destruction, would have to the asset and the related business interests that would be directly or indirectly damaged. An information security incident can impact more than one asset or only a part of an asset. Impact is related to the degree of success of the incident. Impact is considered as having either an immediate (operational) effect or a future (business) effect that includes financial and market consequences. Immediate (operational) impact is either direct or indirect.

Direct impact may result because of the financial replacement value of lost (part of) asset or the cost of acquisition, configuration and installation of the new asset or backup, or the cost of suspended operations due to the incident until the service provided by the asset(s) is restored. Indirect impact may result because financial resources needed to replace or repair an asset would have been used elsewhere (opportunity cost) or from the cost of interrupted operations or due to potential misuse of information obtained through a security breach or because of violation of statutory or regulatory obligations or of ethical codes of conduct.[13]

These considerations should be reflected in the asset values. This is why asset valuation (particularly of intangible assets) is usually done through impact assessment. Thus, impact valuation is not performed separately but is rather embedded within the asset valuation process.

The responsibility for identifying a suitable asset valuation scale lies with the organization. Usually, a three-value scale (low, medium, and high) or a five-value scale (negligible, low, medium, high, and very high) is used.[14]

Threats can be classified as deliberate or accidental. The likelihood of deliberate threats depends on the motivation, knowledge, capacity, and resources available to possible attackers and the attractiveness of assets to sophisticated attacks. On the other hand, the likelihood of accidental threats can be estimated using statistics and experience. The likelihood of these threats might also be related to the organization's proximity to sources of danger, such as major roads or rail routes, and factories dealing with dangerous material such as chemical materials or oil. Also the organization's geographical location will affect the possibility of extreme weather conditions. The likelihood of human errors (one of the most common accidental threats) and equipment malfunction should also be estimated.[15] As already noted, the responsibility for identifying a suitable threat valuation scale lies with the organization. What is important here is that the interpretation of the levels is consistent throughout the organization and clearly conveys the differences between the levels to those responsible for providing input to the threat valuation process. For example, if a three-value scale is used, the value *low* can be interpreted to mean that it is not likely that the threat will occur, there are no incidents, statistics, or motives that indicate that this is likely to happen. The value *medium* can be interpreted to mean that it is possible that the threat will occur, there have been incidents in the past or statistics or other information that indicate that this or similar threats have occurred sometime before, or there is an indication that there might be some reasons for an attacker to carry out such action. Finally, the value *high* can be interpreted to mean that the threat is expected to occur, there are incidents, statistics, or other information that indicate that the threat is likely to occur, or there might be strong reasons or motives for an attacker to carry out such action.[16]

Vulnerabilities can be related to the physical environment of the system, to the personnel, management, and administration procedures and security measures within the organization, to the business operations and service delivery or to the hardware, software, or communications equipment and facilities. Vulnerabilities are reduced by installed security measures. The nature and extent as well as the likelihood of a threat successfully exploiting the three former classes of vulnerabilities can be estimated based on information on past incidents, on new developments and trends, and on experience. The nature and extent as well as the likelihood of a threat successfully exploiting the latter class, often termed technical vulnerabilities, can be estimated using automated vulnerability-scanning tools, security testing and evaluation, penetration testing, or code review.[17] As in the case of threats, the responsibility for identifying a suitable vulnerability valuation scale lies with the organization. If a three-value scale is used, the value *low* can be interpreted to mean that the vulnerability is hard to exploit and the protection in place is good. The value *medium* can be interpreted to

13. ISO/IEC, "Information technology—security techniques—information security risk management," ISO/IEC 27005:2008 (E).

14. British Standards Institute, "ISMSs—Part 3: Guidelines for information security risk management," BS 7799-3:2006.

15. British Standards Institute, "ISMSs—Part 3: Guidelines for information security risk management," BS 7799-3:2006.

16. British Standards Institute, "ISMSs—Part 3: Guidelines for information security risk management," BS 7799-3:2006.

17. ISO/IEC, "Information technology—security techniques—information security risk management," ISO/IEC 27005:2008 (E).

An Agenda for Action for the Risk Management Framework

A risk-based approach to security control selection and speci-fication considers effectiveness, efficiency, and constraints due to applicable laws, directives, executive orders, policies, standards, or regulations. The following activities related to managing organizational risk (also known as the Risk Management Framework) are paramount to an effective infor-mation security program and can be applied to both new and legacy information systems within the context of the system development life cycle and the enterprise architecture (Check All Tasks Completed):

_____ **1.** Categorize the information system and the informa-tion processed, stored, and transmitted by that sys-tem based on an impact analysis.

_____ **2.** Select an initial set of baseline security controls for the information system based on the security cate-gorization; tailoring and supplementing the security control baseline as needed based on organization assessment of risk and local conditions.

_____ **3.** Implement the security controls and document how the controls are deployed within the information system and environment of operation.

_____ **4.** Assess the security controls using appropriate pro-cedures to determine the extent to which the con-trols are implemented correctly, operating as intended, and producing the desired outcome with respect to meeting the security requirements for the system.

_____ **5.** Authorize information system operation based upon a determination of the risk to organizational opera-tions and assets, individuals, other organizations and the Nation resulting from the operation of the information system and the decision that this risk is acceptable.

_____ **6.** Monitor and assess selected security controls in the information system on an ongoing basis including assessing security control effectiveness, document-ing changes to the system or environment of opera-tion, conducting security impact analyses of the associated changes, and reporting the security state of the system to appropriate organizational officials.

mean that the vulnerability might be exploited, but some protection is in place. The value *high* can be interpreted to mean that it is easy to exploit the vulnerability and there is little or no protection in place.[18]

3. THE RISK MANAGEMENT METHODOLOGY

The term *methodology* means an organized set of princi-ples and rules that drives action in a particular field of knowledge. A *method* is a systematic and orderly proce-dure or process for attaining some objective. A *tool* is any instrument or apparatus that is necessary to the perfor-mance of some task. Thus, methodology is the study or description of methods.[19] A methodology is instantiated and materializes by a set of methods, techniques, and tools. A methodology does not describe specific methods; nevertheless, it does specify several processes that need to be followed. These processes constitute a generic framework (see checklist, "An Agenda For Action For The Risk Management Framework"). They may be bro-ken down into sub-processes, they may be combined, or their sequence may change. However, every risk manage-ment exercise must carry out these processes in some form or another.

Risk management consists of six processes, namely context establishment, risk assessment, risk treatment, risk acceptance, risk communication and consultation, and risk monitoring and review.[20] This is more or less in line with the approach where four processes are identified as the constituents of risk management, namely, putting information security risks in the organizational context, risk assessment, risk treatment, and management decision-making and ongoing risk management activi-ties.[21] Alternatively, risk management is seen to comprise three processes, namely risk assessment, risk mitigation, and evaluation and assessment.[22] Table 53.1 depicts the relationships among these processes.[23,24]

Context Establishment

The context establishment process receives as input all relevant information about the organization. Establishing the context for information security risk management determines the purpose of the process. It involves setting

18. British Standards Institute, "ISMSs—Part 3: Guidelines for informa-tion security risk management," BS 7799-3:2006.

19. R. Baskerville, "Risk analysis as a source of professional knowl-edge," *Computers & Security*, Vol. 10, pp. 749-764, 1991.

20. ISO/IEC, "Information technology—security techniques−informa-tion security risk management," ISO/IEC 27005:2011 (E).

21. British Standards Institute, "ISMSs—Part 3: Guidelines for informa-tion security risk management," BS 7799-3:2006.

22. G. Stoneburner, A. Goguen and A. Feringa, *Risk Management guide for information technology systems*, National Institute of Standards and Technology, Special Publication SP 800-30, 2002.

23. ISO/IEC, "Information technology—security techniques−informa-tion security risk management," ISO/IEC 27005:2008 (E).

24. British Standards Institute, "ISMSs—Part 3: Guidelines for informa-tion security risk management," BS 7799-3:2006.

TABLE 53.1 Risk Management Constituent Processes.

ISO/IEC 27005:2011 (E)	BS 7799-3:2006	SP 800−30
Context establishment	Organizational context	
Risk assessment	Risk assessment	Risk assessment
Risk treatment	Risk treatment and management decision making	Risk mitigation
Risk acceptance		
Risk communication and consultation	Ongoing risk management activities	
Risk monitoring and review		Evaluation and assessment

the basic criteria to be used in the process, defining the scope and boundaries of the process, and establishing an appropriate organization operating the process. The output of context establishment process is the specification of these parameters.

The purpose may be to support an information security management system (ISMS); to comply with legal requirements and to provide evidence of due diligence; to prepare for a business continuity plan; to prepare for an incident reporting plan; or to describe the information security requirements for a product, a service, or a mechanism. Combinations of these purposes are also possible.

The basic criteria include risk evaluation criteria, impact criteria, and risk acceptance criteria. When setting risk evaluation criteria the organization should consider the strategic value of the business information process; the criticality of the information assets involved; legal and regulatory requirements and contractual obligations; operational and business importance of the attributes of information security; and stakeholders expectations and perceptions, and negative consequences for goodwill and reputation. The impact criteria specify the degree of damage or costs to the organization caused by an information security event. Developing impact criteria involves considering the level of classification of the impacted information asset; breaches of information security; impaired operations; loss of business and financial value; disruption of plans and deadlines; damage of reputation; and breaches of legal, regulatory or contractual requirements. The risk acceptance criteria depend on the organization's policies, goals, objectives and the interest of its stakeholders. When developing risk acceptance criteria the organization should consider business criteria; legal and regulatory aspects; operations; technology; finance; and social and humanitarian factors.[25]

The scope of the process needs to be defined to ensure that all relevant assets are taken into account in the subsequent risk assessment. Any exclusion from the scope needs to be justified. Additionally, the boundaries need to be identified to address those risks that might arise through these boundaries. When defining the scope and boundaries, the organization needs to consider its strategic business objectives, strategies, and policies; its business processes; its functions and structure; applicable legal, regulatory, and contractual requirements; its information security policy; its overall approach to risk management; its information assets; its locations and their geographical characteristics; constraints that affect it; expectations of its stakeholders; its socio-cultural environment; and its information exchange with its environment. This involves studying the organization (its main purpose, its business; its mission; its values; its structure; its organizational chart; and its strategy). It also involves identifying its constraints. These may be of a political, cultural, or strategic nature; they may be territorial, organizational, structural, functional, personnel, budgetary, technical, or environmental constraints; or they could be constraints arising from preexisting processes. Finally, it entails identifying legislation, regulations, and contracts.[26]

Setting up and maintaining the organization for information security risk management fulfills part of the requirement to determine and provide the resources needed to establish, implement, operate, monitor, review, maintain, and improve an ISMS.[27] The organization to be developed will bear responsibility for the development of the information security risk management process suitable for the organization; for the identification and analysis of the stakeholders; for the definition of roles and responsibilities of all parties, both external and internal to the organization; for the establishment of the required relationships between the organization and stakeholders, interfaces to the organization's high-level risk

---

25. ISO/IEC, "Information technology—security techniques—information security risk management," ISO/IEC 27005:2008 (E).

26. ISO/IEC, "Information technology—security techniques—information security risk management," ISO/IEC 27005:2008 (E).

27. ISO/IEC, "Information security management—specification with guidance for use," ISO 27001.

management functions, as well as interfaces to other relevant projects or activities; for the definition of decision escalation paths; and for the specification of records to be kept. Key roles in this organization are the senior management; the chief information officer (CIO); the system and information owners; the business and functional managers; the information systems security officers (ISSO); the IT security practitioners; and the security awareness trainers (security/subject matter professionals).[28] Additional roles that can be explicitly defined are those of the *risk assessor* and of the *security risk manager*.[29]

Risk Assessment

This process comprises three subprocesses, namely risk identification, risk analysis and risk evaluation. The process receives as input the output of the context establishment process. It identifies, quantifies or qualitatively describes risks and prioritizes them against the risk evaluation criteria established within the course of the context establishment process and according to objectives relevant to the organization. It is often conducted in more than one iterations, the first being a high-level assessment aiming at identifying potentially high risks that warrant further assessment, whereas the second and possibly subsequent iterations entail further in-depth examination of potentially high risks revealed in the first iteration. The output of the process is a list of assessed risks prioritized according to risk evaluation criteria.[30]

Risk identification seeks to determine what could happen to cause a potential loss and to gain insight into how, where, and why the loss might happen. It involves a number of steps, namely identification of assets; identification of threats; identification of existing security measures; identification of vulnerabilities; and identification of consequences. Input to the subprocess is the scope and boundaries for the risk assessment to be conducted, an asset inventory, information on possible threats, documentation of existing security measures, possibly preexisting risk treatment implementation plans, and the list of business processes. The output of the subprocess is a list of assets to be risk-managed together with a list of business processes related to these assets; a list of threats on these assets; a list of existing and planned security measures, their implementation and usage status; a list of vulnerabilities related to assets, threats and already installed security measures; a list of vulnerabilities that do not

relate to any identified threat; and a list of incident scenarios with their consequences, related to assets and business processes.[31]

Two kinds of assets can be distinguished, namely *primary assets*, which include business processes and activities and information, and *supporting assets*, which include hardware, software, network, personnel, site, and the organization's structure. Hardware assets comprise data-processing equipment (transportable and fixed), peripherals, and media. Software assets comprise the operating system; service, maintenance or administration software; and application software. Network assets comprise medium and supports, passive or active relays, and communication interfaces. Personnel assets comprise decision makers, users, operation/maintenance staff, and developers. The site assets comprise the location (and its external environment, premises, zone, essential services, communication and utilities characteristics) and the organization (and its authorities, structure, the project or system organization and its subcontractors, suppliers and manufacturers).[32]

Threats are classified according to their type and to their origin. Threat types are physical damage (fire, water, pollution); natural events (climatic phenomenon, seismic phenomenon, volcanic phenomenon); loss of essential services (failure of air-conditioning, loss of power supply, failure of telecommunication equipment); disturbance due to radiation (electromagnetic radiation, thermal radiation, electromagnetic pulses); compromise of information (eavesdropping, theft of media or documents, retrieval of discarded or recycled media); technical failures (equipment failure, software malfunction, saturation of the information system); unauthorized actions (fraudulent copying of software, corruption of data, unauthorized use of equipment); and compromise of functions (error in use, abuse of rights, denial of actions).[33] Threats are classified according to origin into deliberate, accidental or environmental. A deliberate threat is an action aiming at information assets (remote spying, illegal processing of data); an accidental threat is an action that can accidentally damage information assets (equipment failure, software malfunction); and an environmental threat is any threat that is not based on human action (a natural event, loss of power supply). Note that a threat type may have multiple origins.

Vulnerabilities are classified according to the asset class they relate to. Therefore, vulnerabilities are

28. G. Stoneburner, A. Goguen and A. Feringa, *Risk Management guide for information technology systems*, National Institute of Standards and Technology, Special Publication SP 800-30, 2002.

29. British Standards Institute, "ISMSs—Part 3: Guidelines for information security risk management," BS 7799-3:2006.

30. ISO/IEC, "Information technology—security techniques—information security risk management," ISO/IEC 27005:2011 (E).

31. ISO/IEC, "Information technology—security techniques—information security risk management," ISO/IEC 27005:2011 (E).

32. ISO/IEC, "Information technology—security techniques—information security risk management," ISO/IEC 27005:2011 (E).

33. ISO/IEC, "Information technology—security techniques—information security risk management," ISO/IEC 27005:2011 (E).

TABLE 53.2 Example Risk Calculation Matrix.

Asset Value	Level of Threat								
	Low			Medium			High		
	Level of Vulnerability								
	L	M	H	L	M	H	L	M	H
0	0	1	1	1	2	2	2	3	3
1	1	1	2	2	2	3	3	3	3
2	1	1	2	2	2	3	3	3	3
3	2	2	2	3	3	3	3	4	4
4	2	2	3	3	3	4	4	4	5
5	2	3	3	4	4	4	4	5	5
6	3	3	4	4	4	4	4	5	6
7	3	3	4	5	5	5	5	5	6
8	3	3	4	5	6	6	6	6	6
9	3	4	4	5	6	6	6	7	7
10	3	4	5	5	6	6	6	7	7

classified as hardware (susceptibility to humidity, dust, soiling; unprotected storage); software (no or insufficient software testing, lack of audit trail); network (unprotected communication lines, insecure network architecture); personnel (inadequate recruitment processes, lack of security awareness); site (location in an area susceptible to flood, unstable power grid); and organization (lack of regular audits, lack of continuity plans).[34]

Risk analysis is done either quantitatively or qualitatively. Qualitative analysis uses a scale of qualifying attributes to describe the magnitude of potential consequences (low, medium or high) and the likelihood that these consequences will occur. Quantitative analysis uses a scale with numerical values for both consequences and likelihood. In practice, qualitative analysis is used first, to obtain a general indication of the level of risk and to reveal the major risks. It is then followed by a quantitative analysis on the major risks identified.

Risk analysis involves a number of steps, namely assessment of consequences (through valuation of assets); assessment of incident likelihood (through threat and vulnerability valuation); and determination of the risk level. We discussed valuation of assets, threats, and vulnerabilities in an earlier section. Input to the subprocess is the output of the risk identification subprocess. Its output is a list of risks with value levels assigned.

Having valued assets, threats, and vulnerabilities, we should be able to calculate the resulting risk, if the function relating these to risk is known. Establishing an analytic function for this purpose is probably impossible and certainly ineffective. This is why, in practice, an empirical matrix is used for this purpose[35]. Such a matrix, an example of which is shown in Table 53.2, links asset values and threat and vulnerability levels to the resulting risk. In this example, asset values are expressed on a 0−10 scale, whereas threat and vulnerability levels are expressed on a Low-Medium-High scale. The risk values are expressed on a scale of 1 to 7. When linking the asset values and the threats and vulnerabilities, consideration needs to be given to whether the threat/vulnerability combination could cause problems to confidentiality, integrity, and/or availability. Depending on the results of these considerations, the appropriate asset value(s) should be chosen, that is, the one that has been selected to express the impact of a loss of confidentiality, or the one that has been selected to express the loss of integrity, or the one chosen to express the loss of availability. Using this method can lead to multiple risks for each of the assets, depending on the particular threat/vulnerability combination considered.[36]

34. ISO/IEC, "Information technology—security techniques—information security risk management," ISO/IEC 27005:2011 (E).

35. British Standards Institute, "ISMSs—Part 3: Guidelines for information security risk management," BS 7799-3:2006.

36. British Standards Institute, "ISMSs—Part 3: Guidelines for information security risk management," BS 7799-3:2006.

Finally, the risk evaluation process receives as input the output of the risk analysis process. It compares the levels of risk against the risk evaluation criteria and risk acceptance criteria that were established within the context establishment process. The process uses the understanding of risk obtained by the risk assessment process to make decisions about future actions. These decisions include whether an activity should be undertaken and setting priorities for risk treatment. The output of the process is a list of risks prioritized according to the risk evaluation criteria, in relation to the incident scenarios that lead to those risks.

Risk Treatment

When the risk is calculated, the risk assessment process finishes. However, our actual ultimate goal is treating the risk. The risk treatment process aims at selecting security measures to reduce, retain, avoid, or transfer the risks and at defining a risk treatment plan. The process receives as input the output of the risk assessment process and produces as output the risk treatment plan and the residual risks subject to the acceptance decision by the management of the organization.

The options available to treat risk are to modify it, to retain it, to avoid it, or to share it. Combinations of these options are also possible. The factors that might influence the decision are the cost each time the incident related to the risk happens; how frequently it is expected to happen; the organization's attitude toward risk; the ease of implementation of the security measures required to treat the risk; the resources available; the current business/technology priorities; and organizational and management politics.[37]

For all those risks where the option to modify the risk has been chosen, appropriate security measures should be implemented to reduce the risks to the level that has been identified as acceptable, or at least as much as is feasible toward that level. These questions then arise: How much can we reduce the risk? Is it possible to achieve zero risk?

Zero risk is possible when either the cost of an incident is zero or when the likelihood of the incident occurring is zero. The cost of an incident is zero when the value of the implicated asset is zero or when the impact to the organization is zero. Therefore, if one or more of these conditions are found to hold during the risk assessment process, it is meaningless to take security measures. On the other hand, the likelihood of an incident occurring being zero is not possible, because the threats faced by an open system operating in a dynamic, hence highly variable, environment, as contemporary information systems do, and the causes that generate them are extremely complex; human behavior, which is extremely difficult to predict and model, plays a very important role in securing information systems; and the resources that a business or organization has at its disposal are finite.

When faced with a nonzero risk, our interest focuses on reducing the risk to acceptable levels. Because risk is a non-decreasing function in all its constituents, security measures can reduce it by reducing these constituents. Since the asset value cannot be directly reduced,[38] it is possible to reduce risk by reducing the likelihood of the threat occurring or the likelihood of the vulnerability being successfully exploited or the impact should the threat succeed. Which of these ways (or a combination of them) an organization chooses to adopt to protect its assets is a business decision and depends on the business requirements, the environment, and the circumstances in which the organization needs to operate. There is no universal or common approach to the selection of security measures. A possibility is to assign numerical values to the efficiency of each security measure, on a scale that matches that in which risks are expressed, and select all security measures that are relevant to the particular risk and have an efficiency score of at least equal to the value of the risk. Several sources provide lists of potential security measures.[39,40] Documenting the selected security measures is important in supporting certification and enables the organization to track the implementation of the selected security measures.

When considering modifying (reducing) a risk, several constraints may appear. These may be related to the timeframe; to financial or technical issues; to the way the organization operates or to its culture; to the environment within which the organization operates; to the applicable legal framework or to ethics; to the ease of use of the appropriate security measures; to the availability and suitability of personnel; or to the difficulties of integrating new and existing security measures. Due to the existence of these constraints, it is likely that some risks will exist for which either the organization cannot install appropriate security measures or for which the cost of

---

37. ISO/IEC, "Information technology—security techniques—information security risk management," ISO/IEC 27005:2011 (E).

38. As we will see later, it is possible to indirectly reduce the value of an asset. For example, if sensitive personal data are stored and the cost of protecting them is high, it is possible to decide that such data are too costly to continue storing. This constitutes a form of risk avoidance. As another example, we may decide that the cost for protecting our equipment is too high and to resort to outsourcing. This is a form of risk sharing.

39. ISO/IEC, "Information security management—specification with guidance for use," ISO 27001.

40. British Standards Institute, "Information technology—Security techniques—Information security incident management," BS ISO/IEC 17799:2005.

implementing appropriate measures outweighs the potential loss through the incident related to the risk occurring. In these cases, a decision may be made to retain the risk and live with the consequences if the incident related to the risk occurs. These decisions must be documented so that management is aware of its risk position and can knowingly retain the risk. The importance of this documentation has led risk acceptance to be identified as a separate process.[41] A special case where particular attention must be paid is when an incident related to a risk is deemed to be highly unlikely to occur but, if it occurred, the organization would not survive. If such a risk is deemed to be unacceptable but too costly to reduce, the organization could decide to share it.

Risk sharing is an option whereby it is difficult for the organization to reduce the risk to an acceptable level or the risk can be more economically shared with a third party. Risks can be shared using insurance. In this case, the question of what is a fair premium arises.[42] Another possibility is to use third parties or outsourcing partners to handle critical business assets or processes if they are suitably qualified for doing so. Combining both options is also possible; in this case, the fair premium may be determined.[43]

Risk avoidance describes any action where the business activities or ways to conduct business are changed to avoid any risk occurring. For example, risk avoidance can be achieved by not conducting certain business activities, by moving assets away from an area of risk, or by deciding not to process particularly sensitive information. Risk avoidance entails that the organization consciously accepts the impact likely to occur if an incident occurs. However, the organization chooses not to install the required security measures to reduce the risk. There are several cases where this option is exercised, particularly when the required measures contradict the culture and/or the policy of the organization.

After the risk treatment decision(s) have been taken, there will always be risks remaining. These are called *residual risks*. Residual risks can be difficult to assess, but at least an estimate should be made to ensure that sufficient protection is achieved. If the residual risk is unacceptable, the risk treatment process should be repeated.

41. ISO/IEC, "Information technology—security techniques—information security risk management," ISO/IEC 27005:2011 (E).

42. C. Lambrinoudakis, S. Gritzalis, P. Hatzopoulos, A. N. Yannacopoulos, and S. K. Katsikas, "A formal model for pricing information systems insurance contracts," *Computer Standards and Interfaces*, Vol. 27, pp. 521–532, 2005.

43. S. Gritzalis, A. N. Yannacopoulos, C. Lambrinoudakis, P. Hatzopoulos, S. K. Katsikas, "A probabilistic model for optimal insurance contracts against security risks and privacy violation in IT outsourcing environments," *International Journal of Information Security*, Vol. 6, pp. 197–211, 2007.

Once the risk treatment decisions have been taken, the activities to implement these decisions need to be identified and planned. The risk treatment plan needs to identify limiting factors and dependencies, priorities, deadlines and milestones, resources, including any necessary approvals for their allocation, and the critical path of the implementation.

Risk Communication and Consultation

Risk communication is a horizontal process that interacts bi-directionally with all other processes of risk management. Its purpose is to establish a common understanding of all aspects of risk among all the organization's stakeholders. Common understanding does not come automatically, since it is likely that perceptions of risk vary widely due to differences in assumptions, needs, concepts, and concerns. Establishing a common understanding is important, since it influences decisions to be taken and the ways in which such decisions are implemented. Risk communication must be made according to a well-defined plan that should include provisions for risk communication under both normal and emergency conditions.

Risk Monitoring and Review

Risk management is an ongoing, never-ending process that is assigned to an individual, a team, or an outsourced third party, depending on the organization's size and operational characteristics. Within this process, implemented security measures are regularly monitored and reviewed to ensure that they function correctly and effectively and that changes in the environment have not rendered them ineffective. Because over time there is a tendency for the performance of any service or mechanism to deteriorate, monitoring is intended to detect this deterioration and initiate corrective action. Maintenance of security measures should be planned and performed on a regular, scheduled basis.

The results from an original security risk assessment exercise need to be regularly reviewed for change, since there are several factors that could change the originally assessed risks. Such factors may be the introduction of new business functions, a change in business objectives and/or processes, a review of the correctness and effectiveness of the implemented security measures, the appearance of new or changed threats and/or vulnerabilities, or changes external to the organization. After all these different changes have been taken into account, the risk should be recalculated and *necessary* changes to the risk treatment decisions and security measures identified and documented.

Regular internal audits should be scheduled and should be conducted by an independent party that does

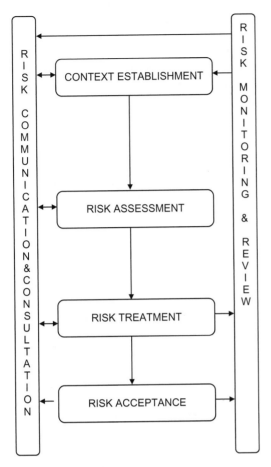

FIGURE 53.2   The risk management methodology.

not need to be from outside the organization. Internal auditors should not be under the supervision or control of those responsible for the implementation or daily management of the ISMS. Additionally, audits by an external body are not only useful, they are essential for certification.

Finally, complete, accessible, and correct documentation and a controlled process to manage documents are necessary to support the ISMS, although the scope and detail will vary from organization to organization. Aligning these documentation details with the documentation requirements of other management systems, such as ISO 9001, is certainly possible and constitutes good practice. Figure 53.2 pictorially summarizes the different processes within the risk management methodology, as we discussed earlier.

Integrating Risk Management into the System Development Life Cycle

Risk management must be totally integrated into the system development life cycle. This cycle consists of five

phases: initiation; development or acquisition; implementation; operation or maintenance; and disposal. Within the initiation phase, identified risks are used to support the development of the system requirements, including security requirements and a security concept of operations. In the development or acquisition phase, the risks identified can be used to support the security analyses of the system that may lead to architecture and design tradeoffs during system development. In the implementation phase, the risk management process supports the assessment of the system implementation against its requirements and within its modeled operational environment. In the operation or maintenance phase, risk management activities are whenever major changes are made to a system in its operational environment. Finally, in the disposal phase, risk management activities are performed for system components that will be disposed of or replaced to ensure that the hardware and software are properly disposed of, that residual data is appropriately handled, and that system migration is conducted in a secure and systematic manner.[44]

Critique of Risk Management as a Methodology

Risk management as a scientific methodology has been criticized as being shallow. The main reason for this rather strong and probably unfair criticism is that risk management does not provide for feedback of the results of the selected security measures or of the risk treatment decisions. In most cases, even though the trend has already changed, information systems security is a low-priority project for management, until some security incident happens. Then, and only then, does management seriously engage in an effort to improve security measures. However, after a while, the problem stops being at the center of interest, and what remains is a number of security measures, some specialized hardware and software, and an operationally more complex system. Unless an incident happens again, there is no way for management to know whether their efforts were really worthwhile. After all, in many cases the information system had operated for years in the past without problems, without the security improvements that the security professionals recommended.

The risk management methodology, as has already been stated, is based on the scientific foundations of statistical decision making. The Bayes Theorem, on which the theory is based, pertains to the statistical revision of *a priori* probabilities, providing *a posteriori*

44. G. Stoneburner, A. Goguen and A. Feringa, *Risk Management Guide for Information Technology Systems*, National Institute of Standards and Technology, Special Publication SP 800-30, 2002.

probabilities, and is applied when a decision is sought based on imperfect information. In risk management, the decision for quantifying an event may be a function of additional factors, other than the probability of the event itself occurring. For example, the probability for a riot to occur may be related to the stability of the political system. Thus, the calculation of this probability should involve quantified information relevant to the stability of the political system. The overall model accepts the possibility that any information ("The political system is stable") may be inaccurate. In comparison to this formal framework, risk management, as applied by the security professionals, is simplistic. Indeed, by avoiding the complexity that accompanies the formal probabilistic modeling of risks and uncertainty, risk management looks more like a process that attempts to guess rather than formally predict the future on the basis of statistical evidence.

Finally, the risk management methodology is highly subjective in assessing the value of assets, the likelihood of threats occurring, the likelihood of vulnerabilities being successfully exploited by threats, and the significance of the impact. This subjectivity is frequently obscured by the formality of the underlying mathematical-probabilistic models, the systematic way in which most risk analysis methods work, and the objectivity of the tools that support these methods.

If indeed the skepticism about the scientific soundness of the risk management methodology is justified, the question: Why, then, has risk management as a practice survived so long? becomes crucial. There are several answers to this question.

Risk management is a very important instrument in designing, implementing, and operating secure information systems, because it systematically classifies and drives the process of deciding how to treat risks. In doing so, it facilitates better understanding of the nature and the operation of the information system, thus constituting a means for documenting and analyzing the system. Therefore, it is necessary for supporting the efforts of the organization's management to design, implement, and operate secure information systems.

Traditionally, risk management has been seen by security professionals as a means to justify to management the cost of security measures. Nowadays, it does not only do that, but it also fulfills legislative and/or regulatory provisions that exist in several countries, which demand information systems to be protected in a manner commensurate with the threats they face.

Risk management constitutes an efficient means of communication between technical and administrative personnel, as well as management, because it allows us to express the security problem in a language comprensible by management, by viewing security as an investment that can be assessed in terms of cost/benefit analysis.[45]

Additionally, it is quite flexible, so it can fit in several scientific frameworks and be applied either by itself or in combination with other methodologies. It is the most widely used methodology for designing and managing information systems security and has been successfully applied in many cases.

Finally, an answer frequently offered by security professionals is that there simply is no other efficient way to carry out the tasks that risk management does. Indeed, it has been proved in practice that by simply using methods of management science, law, and accounting, it is not possible to reach conclusions that can adequately justify risk treatment decisions.

Risk Management Methods

Many methods for risk management are available today. Most of them are supported by software tools. Selecting the most suitable method for a specific business environment and the needs of a specific organization is very important, albeit quite difficult, for a number of reasons[46]:

- There is a lack of a complete inventory of all available methods, with all their individual characteristics.
- There exists no commonly accepted set of evaluation criteria for risk management methods.
- Some methods only cover parts of the whole risk management process. For example, some methods only calculate the risk, without covering the risk treatment process. Some others focus on a small part of the whole process (e.g., disaster recovery planning). Some focus on auditing the security measures, and so on.
- Risk management methods differ widely in the analysis level that they use. Some use high-level descriptions of the information system under study; others call for detailed descriptions.
- Some methods are not freely available to the market, a fact that makes their evaluation very difficult, if at all possible.

The National Institute of Standards and Technology (NIST) compiled, in 1991, a comprehensive report on risk management methods and tools.[47] The European Commission, recognizing the need for a homogenized and software-supported risk management methodology

45. R. Baskerville, "Information systems security design methods: implications for information systems development," *ACM Computing Surveys*, Vol. 25, No. 4, pp. 375–414, 1993.

46. R. Moses, "A European standard for risk analysis", in *Proceedings, 10th World Conference on Computer Security, Audit and Control*, Elsevier Advanced Technology, pp. 527–541, 1993.

47. NIST, *Description of automated risk management packages that NIST/NCSC risk management research laboratory have examined*, March 1991, available at http://w2.eff.org/Privacy/Newin/New_nist/risk-tool.txt, accessed August 07, 2012.

for use by European businesses and organizations, assigned, in 1993, a similar project to a group of companies. Part of this project's results was the creation of an inventory and the evaluation of all available risk management methods at the time.[48] In 2006 the European Network and Information Security Agency (ENISA) repeated the endeavor. Even though some results toward an inventory of risk management/risk assessment methods have been made available,[49] the process is still ongoing.[50] Some of the most widely used risk management methods[51] are briefly described in the sequel.

CRAMM (CCTA Risk Analysis and Management Methodology)[52] is a method developed by the British government organization CCTA (Central Communication and Telecommunication Agency), now renamed the Office of Government Commerce (OGC). CRAMM was first released in 1985. At present CRAMM is the U.K. government's preferred risk analysis method, but CRAMM is also used in many countries outside the U.K. CRAMM is especially appropriate for large organizations, such as government bodies and industry. CRAMM provides a staged and disciplined approach embracing both technical and non-technical aspects of security. To assess these components, CRAMM is divided into three stages: asset identification and valuation; threat and vulnerability assessment; and countermeasure selection and recommendation. CRAMM enables the reviewer to identify the physical, software, data, and location assets that make up the information system. Each of these assets can be valued. Physical assets are valued in terms of their replacement cost. Data and software assets are valued in terms of the impact that would result if the information were to be unavailable, destroyed, disclosed, or modified. CRAMM covers the full range of deliberate and accidental threats that may affect information systems. This stage concludes by calculating the level of risk. CRAMM contains a very large countermeasure library consisting of over 3000 detailed countermeasures organized into over 70 logical groupings. The CRAMM software uses the measures of risks determined during the previous stage and compares them against the security level (a threshold level associated with each countermeasure) to identify whether the risks are sufficiently large to justify the installation of a particular countermeasure. CRAMM provides a series of help facilities, including backtracking, what-if scenarios, prioritization functions, and reporting tools, to assist with the implementation of countermeasures and the active management of the identified risks. CRAMM is ISO/IEC 17799, ISO/IEC 27001, Gramm-Leach-Bliley Act (GLBA), and Health Insurance Portability and Accountability Act (HIPAA) compliant.

MAGERIT is an open methodology for Risk Analysis and Management, developed by the Spanish Ministry of Public Administration and offered as a framework and guide to the Public Administration. Given its open nature, it is also used outside the Administration. MAGERIT was first released in 1997. The current version v2 was published in 2005 and is structured into three books. Book I (Methodology) describes the core steps and basic tasks to carry out a project for risk analysis and management; the formal description of the project; the application to the development of information systems and it provides a large number of practical clues, as well as the theoretical foundations, together with some other complementary information. Book II (Catalogue of elements) provides standard elements and criteria for information systems and risk modeling: asset classes, valuation dimensions, valuation criteria, typical threats, and safeguards to be considered; it also describes the reports containing the findings and conclusions (value model, risk map, safeguard evaluation, risk status, deficiencies report and security plan), thus contributing to achieve uniformity. Book III (Practical techniques) describes techniques frequently used to carry out risk analysis and management projects such as: tabular and algorithmic analysis; threat trees, cost-benefit analysis, dataflow diagrams, process charts, graphical techniques, project planning, working sessions (interviews, meetings, presentations), and Delphi analysis.[53] The application of MAGERIT can be supported by the software PILAR / EAR, which exploits and increases its potentialities and effectiveness.[54]

48. INFOSEC 1992, Project S2014—Risk Analysis, *Risk Analysis Methods Database*, January 1993.

49. ENISA Technical department (Section Risk Management), *Risk Management: Implementation principles and Inventories for Risk Management/Risk Assessment methods and tools*, June 2006, available at http://www.enisa.europa.eu/activities/risk-management/current-risk/risk-management-inventory/files/deliverables/risk-management-principles-and-inventories-for-risk-management-risk-assessment-methods-and-tools/at_download/fullReport, accessed August 22, 2012.

50. "Risk Management," © 2005-2012 by the European Network and Information Security Agency (ENISA), ENISA - European Network and Information Security Agency, P.O. Box 1309, 71001 Heraklion, Crete, Greece [http://www.enisa.europa.eu/activities/risk-management], 2012.

51. ENISA Technical department (Section Risk Management), *Risk Management: Implementation principles and Inventories for Risk Management/Risk Assessment methods and tools*, June 2006, available at http://www.enisa.europa.eu/activities/risk-management/current-risk/risk-management-inventory/files/deliverables/risk-management-principles-and-inventories-for-risk-management-risk-assessment-methods-and-tools/at_download/fullReport, accessed August 22, 2012.

52. "CRAMM", © Siemens Enterprise 2011 [www.cramm.com], 2012.

53. Ministerio de Administraciones Publicas, *MAGERIT—version 2, Methodology for Information Systems Risk Analysis and Management, Book I — The Method*, available at http://administracionelectronica.gob.es/?_nfpb=true&_pageLabel=PAE_PG_CTT_Area_Descargas&langPae=es&iniciativa=184, accessed August 23, 2012.

54. "EAR/PILAR Environment for the Analysis of Risk," [http://www.pilar-tools.com/en/index.html], 2012.

The methodological approach offered by EBIOS (Expression des Besoins et Identification des Objectifs de Sécurité)[55] provides a global and consistent view of information systems security. It was first released in 1995. The method takes into account all technical entities and nontechnical entities. It allows all personnel using the information system to be involved in security issues and offers a dynamic approach that encourages interaction among the organization's various jobs and functions by examining the complete life cycle of the system. Promoted by the DCSSI (Direction Centrale de la Sécurité des Systèmes d' Information) of the French government and recognized by the French administrations, EBIOS is also a reference in the private sector and outside France. The EBIOS approach consists of five phases. Phase 1 deals with context analysis in terms of global business process dependency on the information system. Security needs analysis and threat analysis are conducted in Phases 2 and 3. Phases 4 and 5 yield an objective diagnostic on risks. The necessary and sufficient security objectives (and further security requirements) are then stated, proof of coverage is furnished, and residual risks made explicit. Local standard bases (German IT Grundschutz) are easily added on to its internal knowledge bases and catalogues of best practices. EBIOS is supported by a software tool developed by the Central Information Systems Security Division (France). The tool helps the user to produce all risk analysis and management steps according to the EBIOS method and allows all the study results to be recorded and the required summary documents to be produced. EBIOS is compliant with ISO/IEC 27001, ISO/IEC 13335 (GMITS), ISO/IEC 15408 (Common Criteria), ISO/IEC 17799, and ISO/IEC 21827 and consistent with the ISO/IEC 31000, ISO/IEC 27005 and ISO/IEC 27001 standards.

The Information Security Forum's (ISF) Standard of Good Practice[56] provides a set of high-level principles and objectives for information security together with associated statements of good practice. The Standard of Good Practice is split into five distinct aspects, each of which covers a particular type of environment. These are security management; critical business applications; computer installations; networks; and systems development. FIRM (Fundamental Information Risk Management) is a detailed method for monitoring and controlling information risk at the enterprise level. It has been developed as a practical approach to monitoring the effectiveness of information security. As such, it enables information risk to be managed systematically across enterprises of all sizes. It includes comprehensive implementation guidelines, which explain how to gain support for the approach and get it up and running. The Information Risk Scorecard is an integral part of FIRM. The Scorecard is a form used to collect a range of important details about a particular information resource such as the name of the owner, criticality, level of threat, business impact, and vulnerability. The ISF's Information Security Status Survey is a comprehensive risk management tool that evaluates a wide range of security measures used by organizations to control the business risks associated with their IT-based information systems. SARA (Simple to Apply Risk Analysis) is a detailed method for analyzing information risk in critical information systems. SPRINT (Simplified Process for Risk Identification) is a relatively quick and easy-to-use method for assessing business impact and for analyzing information risk in important but not critical information systems. The full SPRINT method is intended for application to important, but not critical, systems. It complements the SARA method, which is better suited to analyzing the risks associated with critical business systems. SPRINT first helps decide the level of risk associated with a system. After the risks are fully understood, SPRINT helps determine how to proceed and, if the SPRINT process continues, culminates in the production of an agreed plan of action for keeping risks within acceptable limits. SPRINT can help identify the vulnerabilities of existing systems and the safeguards needed to protect against them; and define the security requirements for systems under development and the security measures needed to satisfy them. The method is compliant to ISO/IEC 17799. The method was revised in 2011. The 2011 version is aligned with the requirements for an Information Security Management System (ISMS) set out in ISO 27001 and provides a wider and deeper coverage of ISO 27002 controls topics. It particularly covers many new topics, such as cloud computing, information leakage, consumer devices and security governance. Further, the 2011 Standard provides full coverage of COBIT v4 topics, and offers substantial alignment with other relevant standards and legislation such as PCI/DSS and the Sarbanes Oxley Act.

IT-Grundschutz (IT Baseline protection)[57] provides a method for an organization to establish an ISMS. It was first released in 1994. The full method, to which we will come back in Section 5, describes an ISMS comprising a governance structure and suite of information security

---

55. "EBIOS 2010 – Expression of Needs and Identification of Security Objectives", © French Network and Information Security Agency (FNISA) 2012, [http://www.ssi.gouv.fr/en/the-anssi/publications-109/methods-to-achieve-iss/ebios-2010-expression-of-needs-and-identification-of-security-objectives.html], 2012.

56. Information Security Forum, *The standard of good practice for information security*, 2007 and 2011 (available at https://www.securityforum.org/downloadresearch/downloadsogp/, accessed August 23, 2012).

57. "IT-Grundschutz", © Federal Office for Information Security (BSI). All rights reserved [https://www.bsi.bund.de/ContentBSI/EN/Topics/ITGrundschutz/itgrundschutz.html], 2012.

controls ranging from technological, organizational and sociological to infrastructural (physical) in nature. In its present form the IT Grundschutz comprises several parts, so the methods are separate from the catalog of threats. The part describing the risk analysis method is BSI Standard 100-3 "Risk Analysis Based on IT-Grundschutz" that uses the catalogs to specify security controls for 'normal' systems that are assumed to have 'normal' risks, using risk analysis only to identify additional risk and control requirements for 'high' or 'very high' systems. The IT security process suggested by IT-Grundschutz consists of the following steps: initialization of the process; definition of IT security goals and business environment; establishment of an organizational structure for IT security; provision of necessary resources; creation of the IT security concept; IT structure analysis; assessment of protection requirements; modeling; IT security check; supplementary security analysis; implementation planning and fulfillment; maintenance, monitoring, and improvement of the process; and IT-Grundschutz Certification (optional). IT-Grundschutz is supported by a software tool named *Gstool*[58] that has been developed by the Federal Office for Information Security (BSI). The method is compliant with ISO/IEC 17799 and ISO/IEC 27001.

MEHARI (Méthode Harmonisée d'Analyse de Risques Informatiques)[59] is a method designed by security experts of the CLUSIF (Club de la Sécurité Informatique Français) that replaced the earlier CLUSIF-sponsored MARION and MELISA methods. It was first released in 1996. It proposes an approach for defining risk reduction measures suited to the organization objectives. MEHARI provides a risk assessment model and modular components and processes. It enhances the ability to discover vulnerabilities through audit and to analyze risk situations. MEHARI includes formulas facilitating threat identification and threat characterization and optimal selection of corrective actions. MEHARI allows for providing accurate indications for building security plans, based on a complete list of vulnerability control points and an accurate monitoring process in a continual improvement cycle. It is compliant with ISO/IEC 17799 and ISO/IEC 13335.

The OCTAVE (Operationally Critical Threat, Asset, and Vulnerability Evaluation)[60] method, developed by the Software Engineering Institute of Carnegie-Mellon University, defines a risk-based strategic assessment and planning technique for security. It was first released in 1999. OCTAVE is self-directed in the sense that a small team of people from the operational (or business) units and the IT department work together to address the security needs of the organization. The team draws on the knowledge of many employees to define the current state of security, identify risks to critical assets, and set a security strategy. OCTAVE is different from typical technology-focused assessments in that it focuses on organizational risk and strategic, practice-related issues, balancing operational risk, security practices, and technology. The OCTAVE method is driven by operational risk and security practices. Technology is examined only in relation to security practices. OCTAVE-S is a variation of the method tailored to the limited means and unique constraints typically found in small organizations (less than 100 people). OCTAVE Allegro is tailored for organizations focused on information assets and a streamlined approach. The Octave Automated Tool has been implemented by the Advanced Technology Institute (ATI) to help users with the implementation of the OCTAVE method.

Callio Secura 17799[61] was first released in 2001. It is a multiuser Web application with database support that lets the user implement and certify an ISMS and guides the user through each of the steps leading to ISO 27001/17799 compliance and BS 7799-2 certification. Moreover, it provides document management functionality as well as customization of the tool's databases. It also allows carrying out audits for other standards, such as COBIT, HIPAA, and Sarbanes-Oxley, by importing the user's own questionnaires. Callio Secura is compliant with ISO/IEC 17799 and ISO/IEC 27001.

COBRA[62] is a standalone application for risk management from C&A Systems Security. It is a questionnaire-based Windows PC tool, using expert system principles and a set of extensive knowledge bases. It has also embraced the functionality to optionally deliver other security services, such as checking compliance with the ISO 17799 security standard or with an organization's own security policies. It can be used for identification of threats and vulnerabilities; it measures the degree of actual risk for each area or aspect of a system and directly links this to the potential business impact. It offers detailed solutions and recommendations to reduce the risks and provides business as well as technical reports. It is compliant with ISO/IEC 17799.

58. "IT-Grundschutz Tool – Performance features, © Federal Office for Information Security (BSI). All rights reserved, [https://www.bsi.bund.de/ContentBSI/EN/Topics/ITGrundschutz/ITGrundschutzGSTOOL/gstool.html], 2012.

59. "MEHARI: Information Risk Analysis and Management Methodology", Club de la securite de l' information francais, [https://www.clusif.asso.fr/en/production/mehari/], accessed August 24, 2012.

60. "OCTAVE", © 1995-2012 Carnegie Mellon University, [www.cert.org/octave/], 2012.

61. "Callio", © 2003-2009 ACinfotec Co. Ltd. All rights reserved. [http://www.acinfotec.com/callio.php], 2012.

62. "Security Risk Analysis & Assessment, and ISO 27000 Compliance, [www.riskworld.net/method.htm], 2012.

Alion's product CounterMeasures[63] performs web-based enterprise risk management based on the US-NIST 800 series and OMB Circular A-130 USA standards. The user standardizes the evaluation criteria and, using a "tailor-made" assessment checklist, the software provides objective evaluation criteria for determining security posture and/or compliance. CounterMeasures is available in both networked and desktop configurations. It is compliant with the NIST 800 series and OMB Circular A-130 USA standards.

Proteus[64] is a product suite from InfoGov. It was first released in 1999. Through its components the user can perform gap analysis against standards such as ISO 17799 or create and manage an ISMS according to ISO 27001 (BS 7799-2). Proteus Enterprise is a fully integrated Web-based Information Risk Management, Compliance and Security solution that is fully scalable. Using Proteus Enterprise, companies can perform any number of online compliance audits against any standard and compare between them. They can then assess how deficient compliance security measures affect the company both financially and operationally by mapping them onto its critical business processes. Proteus then identifies risks and mitigates those risks by formulating a work plan, maintains a current and demonstrable compliance status to the regulators and senior management alike. The system works with the company's existing infrastructure and uses RiskView to bridge the gap between the technical/regulatory community and senior management. Proteus is a comprehensive system that includes online compliance and gap analysis, business impact, risk assessment, business continuity, incident management, asset management, organization roles, policy repository, and action plans. Its compliance engine supports any standard (international, industry, and corporate specific) and is supplied with a choice of comprehensive template questionnaires. The system is fully scalable and can size from a single user up to the largest of multinational organizations. The product maintains a full audit trail. It can perform online audits for both internal departments and external suppliers. It is compliant with ISO/IEC 17799 and ISO/IEC 27001.

CORAS[65] is a method for conducting security risk analysis. CORAS provides a customized language for threat and risk modeling, and comes with detailed guidelines explaining how the language should be used to capture and model relevant information during the various stages of the security analysis. In this respect CORAS is model-based. The Unified Modelling Language (UML) is typically used to model the target of the analysis. For documenting intermediate results and for presenting the overall conclusions special CORAS diagrams are used, which are inspired by UML. The CORAS method provides a computerized tool designed to support documenting, maintaining and reporting analysis results through risk modeling. In the CORAS method a security risk analysis is conducted in eight steps: Preparations for the analysis; Customer presentation of the target; Refining the target description using asset diagrams; Approval of the target description; Risk identification using threat diagrams; Risk estimation using threat diagrams; Risk evaluation using risk diagrams; and risk treatment using treatment diagrams. The method is supported by a software tool.[66]

RiskWatch for Information Systems & ISO 17799[67] is the RiskWatch company's solution for information system risk management. Other relevant products in the same suite are RiskWatch for Financial Institutions, RiskWatch for HIPAA Security, RiskWatch for Physical & Homeland Security, RiskWatch for University and School Security, and RiskWatch for NERC (North American Electric Reliability Corporation) and C-TPAT-Supply Chain. The RiskWatch for Information Systems & ISO 17799 tool conducts automated risk analysis and vulnerability assessments of information systems. All RiskWatch software is fully customizable by the user. It can be tailored to reflect any corporate or government policy, including incorporation of unique standards, incident report data, penetration test data, observation, and country-specific threat data. Every product includes both information security as well as physical security. Project plans and a simple workflow make it easy to create accurate and supportable risk assessments. The tool includes security measures from the ISO 17799 and USNIST 800-26 standards, with which it is compliant.

The SBA (Security by Analysis) method[68] is a concept that has existed since the beginning of the 1980s. It is more of a way of looking at analysis and security work in computerized businesses than a fully developed method. It could be called the "human model" concerning risk and vulnerability analyses. The human model implies a very strong confidence in knowledge among staff and

63. "Countermeasures Risk Analysis Products and Services", © 2012 Alion Science and Technology Corporation, [www.countermeasures.com], 2012.

64. "Proteus Enterprise", © Information Governance Limited, Information Governance Limited PO Box 634, Farnham, Surrey, GU9 1HR, UK [www.infogov.co.uk], 2012.

65. "The CORAS Method", Sourceforge.net, [http://coras.sourceforge.net/index.html], 2012.

66. "The CORAS Tool", Sourceforge.net, [http://coras.sourceforge.net/coras_tool.html], 2012.

67. "RiskWatch International", Copyright © 2012 Risk Watch International, All Rights Reserved, Risk Watch International, 1237 N. Gulfstream Ave., Sarasota, FL 34236, USA, [www.riskwatch.com/index.php?option = com_content&task = view&id = 22&Itemid = 34], 2012.

68. "The SBA Method", Copyright © 2002 Norendal International All Rights Reserved, Norendal International PO Box 13 Cockermouth CA13 0GQ, UK, [www.thesbamethod.com], 2012.

individuals within the analyzed business or organizations. It is based on the idea that it is those who work with the everyday problems, regardless of position, who are better qualified to pinpoint the most important problems and to suggest the solutions. SBA is supported by three software tools. Every tool implements its own method, but they are all based on the same concept: gathering a group of people who represent the necessary breadth of knowledge. SBA Check is primarily a tool for anyone working with or responsible for information security issues. The role of analysis leader is central to the use of SBA Check. The analysis leader is in charge of ensuring that the analysis participants' knowledge of the operation is brought to bear during the analysis process in a way that is relevant, so that the description of the current situation and opportunities for improvement retain their consistent quality. SBA Scenario is a tool that helps evaluate business risks methodically through quantitative risk analysis. The tool also helps evaluate which actions are correct and financially motivated through risk management. SBA Project is an IT support tool and a method that helps identify conceivable problems in a project as well as providing suggestions for conceivable measures to deal with those problems. The analysis participants' views and knowledge are used as a basis for providing a good picture of the risk in the project.

4. RISK MANAGEMENT LAWS AND REGULATIONS

Many nations have adopted laws and regulations containing clauses that, directly or indirectly, pertain to aspects of information systems risk management. Similarly, a large number of international laws and regulations exist. In the following, a brief description of such documents with an international scope, directly relevant to information systems risk management,[69] is given.

The "Regulation (EC) No 45/2001 of the European Parliament and of the Council of 18 December 2000 on the protection of individuals with regard to the processing of personal data by the Community institutions and bodies and on the free movement of such data"[70] requires that any personal data processing activity by Community institutions undergoes a prior risk analysis to determine the privacy implications of the activity and to determine the appropriate legal, technical, and organizational measures to protect such activities. It also stipulates that such activity is effectively protected by measures, which must be state of the art, keeping into account the sensitivity and privacy implications of the activity. When a third party is charged with the processing task, its activities are governed by suitable and enforced agreements. Furthermore, the regulation requires the European Union's (EU) institutions and bodies to take similar precautions with regard to their telecommunications infrastructure, and to properly inform the users of any specific risks of security breaches.[71]

The European Commission's Directive on Data Protection went into effect in October 1998 and prohibits the transfer of personal data to non-EU nations that do not meet the European "adequacy" standard for privacy protection. The United States takes a different approach to privacy from that taken by the EU; it uses a sectoral approach that relies on a mix of legislation, regulation, and self-regulation. The EU, however, relies on comprehensive legislation that, for example, requires creation of government data protection agencies, registration of data bases with those agencies, and in some instances prior approval before personal data processing may begin. The Safe Harbor Privacy Principles[72] aim at bridging this gap by providing that an EU-based entity self-certifies its compliance with them.

The "Commission Decision of 15 June 2001 on standard contractual clauses for the transfer of personal data to third countries, under Directive 95/46/EC", the "Commission Decision of 27 December 2004 amending Decision 2001/497/EC as regards the introduction of an alternative set of standard contractual clauses for the transfer of personal data to third countries" and the : Commission Decision of 5 February 2010 on standard contractual clauses for the transfer of personal data to processors established in third countries under Directive 95/46/EC of the European Parliament and of the Council"[73] provide a set of voluntary model clauses that can be used to export personal data from a data controller who is subject to EU data protection rules to a data processor outside the EU who is not subject to these rules or to a similar set of adequate rules. Upon acceptance of the

69. J. Dumortier and H. Graux, "Risk management/risk assessment in European regulation, international guidelines and codes of practice," ENISA, June 2007 (available at http://www.enisa.europa.eu/activities/risk-management/current-risk/laws-regulation/downloads/risk-management-risk-assessment-in-european-regulation-international-guidelines-and-codes-of-practice, accessed August 24, 2012).

70. Official Journal of the European Communities, 12.1.2001, EN, L 8/1−8/22, 2001 (available at http://eur-lex.europa.eu/LexUriServ/LexUriServ.do?uri = OJ:L:2001:008:0001:0022:en:PDF, accessed December 23, 2012).

71. J. Dumortier and H. Graux, "Risk management/risk assessment in European regulation, international guidelines and codes of practice," ENISA, June 2007 (available at http://www.enisa.europa.eu/activities/risk-management/current-risk/laws-regulation/downloads/risk-management-risk-assessment-in-european-regulation-international-guidelines-and-codes-of-practice, accessed August 24, 2012).

72. "export.gov. Helping U.S. Companies export", [http://export.gov/safeharbor/eu/eg_main_018476.asp] 2012.

73. Official Journal of the European Union, 12.2.2010, EN, L 39/5−39/18, 2010.

model clauses, the data controller must warrant that the appropriate legal, technical, and organizational measures to ensure the protection of the personal data are taken. Furthermore, the data processor must agree to permit auditing of its security practices to ensure compliance with applicable European data protection rules.[74]

The Health Insurance Portability and Accountability Act of 1996[75] is a U.S. law with regard to health insurance coverage, electronic health, and requirements for the security and privacy of health data. Title II of HIPAA, known as the Administrative Simplification (AS) provisions, requires the establishment of national standards for electronic health care transactions and national identifiers for providers, health-insurance plans, and employers. Per the requirements of Title II, the Department of Health and Human Services has promulgated five rules regarding Administrative Simplification: the Privacy Rule, the Transactions and Code Sets Rule, the Security Rule, the Unique Identifiers Rule, and the Enforcement Rule. The standards are meant to improve the efficiency and effectiveness of the U.S. health care system by encouraging the widespread use of electronic data interchange.

The "Directive 2002/58/EC of the European Parliament and of the Council of 12 July 2002 concerning the processing of personal data and the protection of privacy in the electronic communications sector (Directive on privacy and electronic communications)"[76] requires that any provider of publicly available electronic communications services takes the appropriate legal, technical and organizational measures to ensure the security of its services; informs his subscribers of any particular risks of security breaches; and takes the necessary measures to prevent such breaches, and indicates the likely costs of security breaches to the subscribers.[77]

The "Directive 2006/24/EC of the European Parliament and of the Council of 15 March 2006 on the retention of data generated or processed in connection with the provision of publicly available electronic communications services or of public communications networks and amending Directive 2002/58/EC"[78] requires the affected providers of publicly accessible electronic telecommunications networks to retain certain communications data to be specified in their national regulations, for a specific amount of time, under secured circumstances in compliance with applicable privacy regulations; to provide access to this data to competent national authorities; to ensure data quality and security through appropriate technical and organizational measures, shielding it from access by unauthorized individuals; to ensure its destruction when it is no longer required; and to ensure that stored data can be promptly delivered on request from the competent authorities.[79]

The "Regulation (EC) No 1907/2006 of the European Parliament and of the Council of 18 December 2006 concerning the Registration, Evaluation, Authorisation and Restriction of Chemicals (REACH), establishing a European Chemicals Agency, amending Directive 1999/45/EC and repealing Council Regulation (EEC) No 793/93 and Commission Regulation (EC) No 1488/94 as well as Council Directive 76/769/EEC and Commission Directives 91/155/EEC, 93/67/EEC, 93/105/EC and 2000/21/EC"[80] implants risk management obligations by imposing a reporting obligation on producers and importers of articles covered by the regulation, with regard to the qualities of certain chemical substances, which includes a risk assessment and obligation to examine how such risks can be managed. This information is to be registered in a central database. It also stipulates that a Committee for Risk Assessment within the European Chemicals Agency established by the Regulation is established and requires that the information provided is kept up to date with regard to potential risks to human health or the environment, and that such risks are adequately managed.[81]

74. J. Dumortier and H. Graux, "Risk management/risk assessment in European regulation, international guidelines and codes of practice," ENISA, June 2007 (available at http://www.enisa.europa.eu/activities/risk-management/current-risk/laws-regulation/downloads/risk-management-risk-assessment-in-european-regulation-international-guidelines-and-codes-of-practice, accessed August 24, 2012).

75. "LegalArchiver.org", [www.legalarchiver.org/hipaa.htm], 2012.

76. Official Journal of the European Communities, 31.7.2002, EN, L 201/37-201/47, 2002 (available at http://eur-lex.europa.eu/LexUriServ/LexUriServ.do?uri = OJ:L:2002:201:0037:0037:EN:PDF, accessed August 24, 2012).

77. J. Dumortier and H. Graux, "Risk management/risk assessment in European regulation, international guidelines and codes of practice," ENISA, June 2007 (available at http://www.enisa.europa.eu/activities/risk-management/current-risk/laws-regulation/downloads/risk-management-risk-assessment-in-european-regulation-international-guidelines-and-codes-of-practice, accessed August 24, 2012).

78. Official Journal of the European Union, 13.4.2006, EN, L 105/54-105/63, 2006 (available at http://eur-lex.europa.eu/LexUriServ/LexUriServ.do?uri = OJ:L:2006:105:0054:0063:EN:PDF, accessed August 24, 2012).

79. J. Dumortier and H. Graux, "Risk management/risk assessment in European regulation, international guidelines and codes of practice," ENISA, June 2007 (available at http://www.enisa.europa.eu/activities/risk-management/current-risk/laws-regulation/downloads/risk-management-risk-assessment-in-european-regulation-international-guidelines-and-codes-of-practice, accessed August 24, 2012).

80. Official Journal of the European Union, 30.12.2006, EN, L 396/1-396/849 (available at http://eurlex.europa.eu/LexUriServ/LexUriServ.do?uri = OJ:L:2006:396:0001:0849:EN:PDF, accessed August 24, 2012).

81. J. Dumortier and H. Graux, "Risk management/risk assessment in European regulation, international guidelines and codes of practice," ENISA, June 2007 (available at http://www.enisa.europa.eu/activities/risk-management/current-risk/laws-regulation/downloads/risk-management-risk-assessment-in-european-regulation-international-guidelines-and-codes-of-practice, accessed August 24, 2012).

The "Council Framework Decision 2005/222/JHA of 24 February 2005 on attacks against information systems"[82] contains the conditions under which legal liability can be imposed on legal entities for conduct of certain natural persons of authority within the legal entity. Thus, the Framework decision requires that the conduct of such figures within an organization is adequately monitored, also because the decision states that a legal entity can be held liable for acts of omission in this regard. Additionally, the decision defines a series of criteria under which jurisdictional competence can be established. These include the competence of a jurisdiction when a criminal act is conducted against an information system within its borders.[83]

The "OECD Guidelines for the Security of Information Systems and Networks: Towards a Culture of Security" (25 July 2002)[84] aim to promote a culture of security; to raise awareness about the risk to information systems and networks (including the policies, practices, measures, and procedures available to address those risks and the need for their adoption and implementation); to foster greater confidence in information systems and networks and the way in which they are provided and used; to create a general frame of reference; to promote cooperation and information sharing; and to promote the consideration of security as an important objective. The guidelines state nine basic principles underpinning risk management and information security practices. No part of the text is legally binding, but noncompliance with any of the principles is indicative of a breach of risk management good practices that can potentially incur liability.[85]

The "Basel Committee on Banking Supervision—Risk Management Principles for Electronic Banking"[86] identifies 14 Risk Management Principles for Electronic Banking to help banking institutions expand their existing risk oversight policies and processes to cover their e-banking activities. The Risk Management Principles fall into three broad, and often overlapping, categories of issues that are grouped to provide clarity: board and management oversight; security controls; and legal and reputational risk management. The Risk Management Principles are not put forth as absolute requirements or even "best practice," nor do they attempt to set specific technical solutions or standards relating to e-banking. Consequently, the Risk Management Principles and sound practices are expected to be used as tools by national supervisors and to be implemented with adaptations to reflect specific national requirements and individual risk profiles where necessary.

The "Commission Recommendation 87/598/EEC of 8 December 1987, concerning a European code of conduct relating to electronic payments"[87] provides a number of general nonbinding recommendations. This includes an obligation to ensure that privacy is respected and that the system is transparent with regard to potential security or confidentiality risks, which must obviously be mitigated by all reasonable means.[88]

The "Public Company Accounting Reform and Investor Protection Act of 30 July 2002" (commonly referred to as *Sarbanes-Oxley* and often abbreviated to *SOX* or *Sarbox*)[89] even though indirectly relevant to risk management, is discussed here due to its importance. The Act is a U.S. federal law passed in response to a number of major corporate and accounting scandals including those affecting Enron, Tyco International, and WorldCom (now MCI). These scandals resulted in a decline of public trust in accounting and reporting practices. The legislation is wide ranging and establishes new or enhanced standards for all U.S. public company boards, management, and public accounting firms. Its provisions range from additional Corporate Board responsibilities to criminal penalties, and require the Securities and Exchange Commission (SEC) to implement rulings on requirements to comply with the new law. The first and most important part of the Act

82. Official Journal of the European Union, 16.3.2005, EN, L 69/67-69/71 (available at http://eurlex.europa.eu/LexUriServ/LexUriServ.do?uri = CELEX:32005F0222:EN:NOT, accessed August 24, 2012).

83. J. Dumortier and H. Graux, "Risk management/risk assessment in European regulation, international guidelines and codes of practice," ENISA, June 2007 (available at http://www.enisa.europa.eu/activities/risk-management/current-risk/laws-regulation/downloads/risk-management-risk-assessment-in-european-regulation-international-guidelines-and-codes-of-practice, accessed August 24, 2012).

84. Organisation for economic co-operation and development, "OECD Guidelines for the security of information systems and networks: Towards a culture of security", © OECD 2002 (available at http://www.oecd.org/sti/interneteconomy/15582260.pdf, accessed August 24, 2012).

85. J. Dumortier and H. Graux, "Risk management/risk assessment in European regulation, international guidelines and codes of practice," ENISA, June 2007 (available at http://www.enisa.europa.eu/activities/risk-management/current-risk/laws-regulation/downloads/risk-management-risk-assessment-in-european-regulation-international-guidelines-and-codes-of-practice, accessed August 24, 2012).

86. Basel Committee on Banking Supervision, "Risk management principles for electronic banking", July 2003, (available at www.bis.org/publ/bcbs98.pdf, accessed August 24, 2012).

87. Official Journal of the European Communities, 24.12.87, EN, No L 365/72-365/76 (available at http://eurlex.europa.eu/LexUriServ/LexUriServ.do?uri = CELEX:31987H0598:EN:pdf, accessed August 24, 2012).

88. J. Dumortier and H. Graux, "Risk management/risk assessment in European regulation, international guidelines and codes of practice," ENISA, June 2007 (available at http://www.enisa.europa.eu/activities/risk-management/current-risk/laws-regulation/downloads/risk-management-risk-assessment-in-european-regulation-international-guidelines-and-codes-of-practice, accessed August 24, 2012).

89. US Public Law 107-204-July 30, 2002, 116 STAT.745 (available at http://www.gpo.gov/fdsys/pkg/PLAW-107publ204/pdf/PLAW-107publ204.pdf, accessed August 24, 2012).

establishes a new quasi-public agency, the Public Company Accounting Oversight Board (www.pcaobus. org), which is charged with overseeing, regulating, inspecting, and disciplining accounting firms in their roles as auditors of public companies. The Act also covers issues such as auditor independence, corporate governance and enhanced financial disclosure.

The "Office of the Comptroller of the Currency (OCC) – Electronic Banking Guidance,"[90] is fairly high level. And, it should be indicative of the subject matter to be analyzed and assessed by banking institutions, rather than serving as a yardstick to identify actual problems.[91]

The "Payment Card Industry (PCI) Security Standards Council—Data Security Standard (DSS)"[92] provides central guidance allowing financial service providers relying on payment cards to implement the necessary policies, procedures, and infrastructure to adequately safeguard their customer account data. PCI DSS has no formal binding legal power. Nevertheless, considering its origins and the key participants, it holds significant moral authority, and noncompliance with the PCI DSS by a payment card service provider may be indicative of inadequate risk management practices.[93]

The "Directive 2002/65/EC of the European Parliament and of the Council of 23 September 2002 concerning the distance marketing of consumer financial services and amending Council Directive 90/619/EEC and Directives 97/7/EC and 98/27/EC (the 'Financial Distance Marketing Directive')"[94] requires that, as a part of the minimum information to be provided to a consumer prior to concluding a distance financial services contract, the consumer must be clearly and comprehensibly informed of any specific risks related to the service concerned.[95]

5. RISK MANAGEMENT STANDARDS

Various national and international, de jure, and de facto standards exist that are related, directly or indirectly, to information systems risk management. In the following, we briefly describe the most important international standards that are directly related to risk management.

The ISO/IEC 27000 series of standards has been reserved for a family of information security management standards derived from British Standard BS 7799. Several standards within the series have already been published; others are in various stages of development. A comprehensive presentation and discussion of these standards is provided by the ISO27001 security home[96]. Within this series, the "ISO/IEC 27001:2005—Information technology—Security techniques—Information security management systems—Requirements" standard[97] is designed to ensure the selection of adequate and proportionate security measures that protect information assets and give confidence to interested parties. The standard covers all types of organizations (commercial enterprises, government agencies, not-for-profit organizations) and specifies the requirements for establishing, implementing, operating, monitoring, reviewing, maintaining, and improving a documented ISMS within the context of the organization's overall business risks. Further, it specifies requirements for the implementation of security measures customized to the needs of individual organizations or parts thereof. Its application in practice is often combined with related standards, such as BS 7799-3:2006 which provides additional guidance to support the requirements given in ISO/IEC 27001:2005.

The "ISO/IEC 27005:2011 – Information technology – Security techniques – Information security risk management" standard[98] provides guidelines for information security risk management. It supports the general concepts specified in ISO/IEC 27001 and is designed to assist the satisfactory implementation of information security based on a risk management approach. ISO/IEC 27005:2011 is

90. "Office of the Comptroller of the Currency", US Department of the Treasury, [www.occ.treas.gov/netbank/ebguide.htm], 2012.

91. J. Dumortier and H. Graux, "Risk management/risk assessment in European regulation, international guidelines and codes of practice," ENISA, June 2007 (available at http://www.enisa.europa.eu/activities/risk-management/current-risk/laws-regulation/downloads/risk-management-risk-assessment-in-european-regulation-international-guidelines-and-codes-of-practice, accessed August 24, 2012).

92. "PCI Security standards council", Copyright © 2006-2012 PCI Security Standards Council, LLC, All rights reserved, PCI Security Standards Council, LLC401 Edgewater Place Suite 600, Wakefield, MA, USA 01880, [https://www.pcisecuritystandards.org/security_standards/documents.php], 2012.

93. J. Dumortier and H. Graux, "Risk management/risk assessment in European regulation, international guidelines and codes of practice," ENISA, June 2007 (available at http://www.enisa.europa.eu/activities/risk-management/current-risk/laws-regulation/downloads/risk-management-risk-assessment-in-european-regulation-international-guidelines-and-codes-of-practice, accessed August 24, 2012).

94. Official Journal of the European Communities, 9.10.2002, EN, L 271/16-271/271/24 (available at http://eurlex.europa.eu/LexUriServ/LexUriServ.do?uri = CELEX:32002L0065:EN:pdf, accessed August 24, 2012).

95. J. Dumortier and H. Graux, "Risk management/risk assessment in European regulation, international guidelines and codes of practice," ENISA, June 2007 (available at http://www.enisa.europa.eu/activities/risk-management/current-risk/laws-regulation/downloads/risk-management-risk-assessment-in-european-regulation-international-guidelines-and-codes-of-practice, accessed August 24, 2012).

96. "ISO 27001 security. Information security standards", Copyright © 2012 IsecT Ltd., Castle Peak, 1262 Taihape Road, RD9 Hastings 4179, New Zealand, [http://www.iso27001security.com/index.html], 2012.

97. ISO/IEC, "Information security management—specification with guidance for use," ISO 27001.

98. ISO/IEC, Information technology – Security techniques – Information security risk management, 2011.

applicable to all types of organizations (commercial enterprises, government agencies, non-profit organizations) which intend to manage risks that could compromise the organization's information security. ISO/IEC 27005 revised and superseded the Management of Information and Communications Technology Security (MICTS) standards ISO/IEC TR 13335-3:1998 plus ISO/IEC TR 13335-4:2000. The standard describes the risk management methodology, without specifying, recommending or even naming any specific method.

The "ISO 31000:2009 Risk management – principles and guidelines" standard provides principles and generic guidelines on risk management.[99] The standard is not sector or industry-specific, and it can be used by any public, private or community enterprise, association, group or individual. It can be applied to any type of risk, whatever its nature, whether having positive or negative consequences. This also means that the standard is not specific to information security or even to IT risks. It is intended that ISO 31000:2009 be utilized to harmonize risk management processes in existing and future standards. It provides a common approach in support of standards dealing with specific risks and/or sectors, and does not replace those standards.

The IEC 31010:2009 "Risk management – risk assessment techniques" is a supporting standard for ISO 31000 and provides guidance on selection and application of systematic techniques for risk assessment. The standard treats risk assessment as an integral part of risk management, helping managers understand risks that could affect the achievement of business objectives and assess the adequacy and effectiveness of various risk mitigation controls. It covers risk assessment concepts as well as processes and a range of techniques.[100]

The ISO Guide 73:2009 provides the definitions of generic terms related to risk management. It aims to encourage a mutual and consistent understanding of, and a coherent approach to, the description of activities relating to the management of risk, and the use of uniform risk management terminology in processes and frameworks dealing with the management of risk. For principles and guidelines on risk management, reference is made to ISO 31000:2009.[101]

The "BS 7799-3:2006—Information security management systems—Guidelines for information security risk management" standard[102] was the predecessor of ISO/IEC 27005. It gives guidance to support the requirements given in BS ISO/IEC 27001:2005 regarding all aspects of an ISMS risk management cycle and is therefore typically applied in conjunction with this standard in risk assessment practices. This includes assessing and evaluating the risks, implementing security measures to treat the risks, monitoring and reviewing the risks, and maintaining and improving the system of risk treatment. The focus of this standard is effective information security through an ongoing program of risk management activities. This focus is targeted at information security in the context of an organization's business risks. With the proliferation of ISO/IEC 27005, it is expected that BS 7799 -3 will eventually be withdrawn.

In Section 3 we discussed BSI Standard 100-3, i.e. the part of IT-Grundschutz (IT Baseline protection)[103] that describes the risk analysis method. BSI Standard 100-1 Information Security Management Systems (ISMS) is an overview of the IT-Grundshutz approach to developing and implementing an ISMS. BSI Standard 100-2 IT-Grundschutz Methodology is basically about governance of information security within the organization using an ISMS. BSI Standard 100-4 *Business Continuity Management* explains how to establish and maintain a BCM system. BSI IS audit guideline *Information Security Audit (IS Audit) - a guideline for IS audits based on IT-Grundschutz* is primarily aimed at IS auditors working for German federal agencies. IT-Grundschutz Catalogues contains detailed advice on information security threats, controls etc.

The "ISF Standard of Good Practice" standard[104] which we discussed as a risk management method in Section 3, is a commonly quoted source of good practices and serves as a resource for the implementation of information security policies and as a yardstick for auditing such systems and/or the surrounding practices.[105] The standard covers six distinct aspects of information security, each of which relates to a particular type of environment. The standard focuses on how information security supports an organization's key business processes.

The U.S. General Accounting Office "Information security risk assessment: practices of leading

99. ISO, Risk management – principles and guidelines, 2009
100. ISO/IEC, IEC 31010:2009 Risk management – Risk assessment techniques, 2009.
101. ISO, ISO Guide 73:2009 Risk management – Vocabulary, 2009
102. British Standards Institute, "ISMSs—Part 3: Guidelines for information security risk management," BS 7799-3:2006.

103. "IT-Grundschutz", Copyright © Federal Office for Information Security (BSI). All rights reserved, [https://www.bsi.bund.de/ContentBSI/EN/Topics/ITGrundschutz/itgrundschutz.html], 2012.
104. Information Security Forum, *The standard of good practice for information security*, 2007 and 2011 (available at https://www.security-forum.org/downloadresearch/downloadsogp/, accessed August 23, 2012).
105. J. Dumortier and H. Graux, "Risk management/risk assessment in European regulation, international guidelines and codes of practice," ENISA, June 2007 (available at http://www.enisa.europa.eu/activities/risk-management/current-risk/laws-regulation/downloads/risk-management-risk-assessment-in-european-regulation-international-guidelines-and-codes-of-practice, accessed August 24, 2012).

organizations" guide[106] is intended to help federal managers implement an ongoing information security risk assessment process by providing examples, or case studies, of practical risk assessment procedures that have been successfully adopted by four organizations known for their efforts to implement good risk assessment practices. More important, it identifies, based on the case studies, factors that are important to the success of any risk assessment program, regardless of the specific methodology employed.

The U.S. NIST SP 800-30 "Risk management guide for information technology systems"[107] developed by NIST in 2002, provides a common foundation for experienced and inexperienced, technical, and non-technical personnel who support or use the risk management process for their IT systems. Its guidelines are for use by federal organizations which process sensitive information and are consistent with the requirements of OMB Circular A-130, Appendix III. The guidelines may also be used by nongovernmental organizations on a voluntary basis, even though they are not mandatory and binding standards.

Finally, the U.S. NIST SP 800-39 "Managing Information Security Risk: Organization, Mission and Information System View" standard[108] provides guidelines for managing risk to organizational operations, organizational assets, individuals, other organizations, and the nation resulting from the operation and use of information systems. It provides a structured yet flexible approach for managing that portion of risk resulting from the incorporation of information systems into the mission and business processes of organizations.

6. SUMMARY

The information systems risk management methodology was developed with an eye to guiding the design and the management of security of an information system within the framework of an organization. It aims at analyzing and assessing the factors that affect risk, to subsequently treat the risk, and to continuously monitor and review the security plan. Central concepts of the methodology are those of the threat, the vulnerability, the asset, the impact, and the risk. The operational relationship of these

concepts materializes when a threat exploits one or more vulnerabilities to harm assets, an event that will impact the organization. Once the risks are identified and assessed, they must be treated, that is, modified, shared, avoided, or retained. Treating the risks is done on the basis of a carefully designed security plan, which must be continuously monitored, reviewed, and amended as necessary. Many methods implementing the whole or parts of the risk management methodology have been developed. Even though most of them follow closely the methodology as described in pertinent international standards, they differ considerably in both their underlying philosophy and in their specific steps. The risk management methodology has been and is being applied internationally with considerable success and enjoys universal acceptance. However, it does suffer several disadvantages that should be seriously considered in the process of applying it. Particular attention must be paid to the subjectivity of its estimates, which is often obscured by the formality of the underlying probabilistic models and by the systematic nature of most of the risk management methods. Subjectivity in applying the methodology is unavoidable and should be accepted and consciously managed. A number of international laws and regulations contain provisions for information system risk management, in addition to national provisions. The risk management methodology is standardized by international organizations.

Finally, let's move on to the real interactive part of this Chapter: review questions/exercises, hands-on projects, case projects and optional team case project. The answers and/or solutions by chapter can be found in the Online Instructor's Solutions Manual.

CHAPTER REVIEW QUESTIONS/EXERCISES

True/False

1. True or False? Information security risk "is measured in terms of a combination of the likelihood of an event and not its consequence."
2. True or False? The likelihood of a security incident occurring is a function of the likelihood that a threat appears and of the likelihood that the threat can successfully exploit the relevant system vulnerabilities.
3. True or False? The term *methodology* means an organized set of principles and rules that drives action in a particular field of knowledge.
4. True or False? The context establishment process receives as input all relevant information about the organization.
5. True or False? Risk identification seeks to determine what could happen to cause a potential loss and to gain insight into how, where, and why the loss might happen.

106. U.S. General Accounting Office, *Information security risk assessment: practices of leading organizations*, 1999.

107. G. Stoneburner, A. Goguen and A. Feringa, *Risk Management guide for information technology systems*, National Institute of Standards and Technology, Special Publication SP 800-30, 2002 (available at http://csrc.nist.gov/publications/nistpubs/800-30/sp800-30.pdf accessed August 29, 2012).

108. NIST, *Managing Information Security Risk: Organization, Mission and Information System View*, US NIST SP 800-39, 2011 (available at http://csrc.nist.gov/publications/nistpubs/800-39/SP800-39-final.pdf accessed August 29, 2012).

Multiple Choice

1. What are classified according to the asset class they relate to?
   A. Qualitative analysis
   B. Vulnerabilities
   C. Promotional email
   D. Malformed request DoS
   E. Data controller

2. When the risk is calculated, the _____ process finishes.
   A. Network attached storage (NAS)
   B. Risk assessment
   C. Valid
   D. Load-Based DoS
   E. Bait

3. What is a horizontal process that interacts bi-directionally with all other processes of risk management.
   A. Data minimization
   B. Fabric
   C. Target access
   D. Risk communication
   E. Security

4. What is an ongoing, never-ending process that is assigned to an individual, a team, or an outsourced third party, depending on the organization's size and operational characteristics?
   A. Risk management
   B. Greedy strategy
   C. Ports
   D. SAN protocol
   E. Taps

5. What must be totally integrated into the system development life cycle?
   A. Irrelevant
   B. Tape library
   C. IP storage access
   D. Configuration file
   E. Risk management

EXERCISE

Problem

What is continuous monitoring?

Hands-On Projects

Project

If an organization's information system is subject to continuous monitoring, does that mean it does not have to undergo security authorization?

Case Projects

Problem

Why is continuous monitoring not replacing the traditional security authorization process?

Optional Team Case Project

Problem

What is front-end security and how does it differ from back-end security?

Physical Security

Part VII

Physical Security

## Chapter 54

Physical Security Essentials

William Stallings

Independent consultant

Platt[1] distinguishes three elements of information system (IS) security:

- *Logical security.* Protects computer-based data from software-based and communication-based threats.
- *Physical security.* Also called *infrastructure security.* Protects the information systems that house data and the people who use, operate, and maintain the systems. Physical security must also prevent any type of physical access or intrusion that can compromise logical security.
- *Premises security.* Also known as *corporate or facilities security.* Protects the people and property within an entire area, facility, or building(s) and is usually required by laws, regulations, and fiduciary obligations. Premises security provides perimeter security, access control, smoke and fire detection, fire suppression, some environmental protection, and usually surveillance systems, alarms, and guards.

This chapter is concerned with physical security and with some overlapping areas of premises security. We begin by looking at physical security threats and then consider physical security prevention measures.

1. OVERVIEW

For information systems, the role of physical security is to protect the physical assets that support the storage and processing of information. Physical security involves two complementary requirements. First, physical security must prevent damage to the physical infrastructure that sustains the information system. In broad terms, that infrastructure includes the following:

- *Information system hardware.* Including data processing and storage equipment, transmission and

networking facilities, and offline storage media. We can include in this category supporting documentation.

- *Physical facility.* The buildings and other structures housing the system and network components.
- *Supporting facilities.* These facilities underpin the operation of the information system. This category includes electrical power, communication services, and environmental controls (heat, humidity, etc.).
- *Personnel.* Humans involved in the control, maintenance, and use of the information systems.

Second, physical security must prevent misuse of the physical infrastructure that leads to the misuse or damage of the protected information. The misuse of the physical infrastructure can be accidental or malicious. It includes vandalism, theft of equipment, theft by copying, theft of services, and unauthorized entry.

Figure 54.1, based on Bosworth and Kabay[2], suggests the overall context in which physical security concerns arise. The central concern is the information assets of an organization. These information assets provide value to the organization that possesses them, as indicated by the upper four items in Figure 54.1. In turn, the physical infrastructure is essential to providing for the storage and processing of these assets. The lower four items in Figure 54.1 are the concern of physical security. Not shown is the role of logical security, which consists of software- and protocol-based measures for ensuring data integrity, confidentiality, and so forth.

The role of physical security is affected by the operating location of the information system, which can be characterized as static, mobile, or portable. Our concern in this chapter is primarily with static systems, which are installed at fixed locations. A mobile system is installed in a vehicle, which serves the function of a structure for the system. Portable systems have no single installation point but may operate in a variety of locations, including buildings, vehicles, or in the open. The nature of the

1. F. Platt, "Physical threats to the information infrastructure," in S. Bosworth, and M. Kabay, (eds.), *Computer Security Handbook,* Wiley, 2002.

2. S. Bosworth and M. Kabay (eds.), *Computer Security Handbook,* Wiley, 2002.

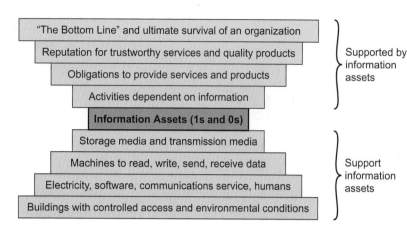

FIGURE 54.1 A context for information assets.

TABLE 54.1 Characteristics of Natural Disasters.

	Warning	Evacuation	Duration
Tornado	Advance warning of potential; not site specific	Remain at site	Brief but intense
Hurricane	Significant advance warning	May require evacuation	Hours to a few days
Earthquake	No warning	May be unable to evacuate	Brief duration; threat of continued aftershocks
Ice storm/blizzard	Several days warning generally expected	May be unable to evacuate	May last several days
Lightning	Sensors may provide minutes of warning	May require evacuation	Brief but may recur
Flood	Several days warning generally expected	May be unable to evacuate	Site may be isolated for extended period

Source: ComputerSite Engineering, Inc.

system's installation determines the nature and severity of the threats of various types, including fire, roof leaks, unauthorized access, and so forth.

2. PHYSICAL SECURITY THREATS

In this pat of the chapter, we first look at the types of physical situations and occurrences that can constitute a threat to information systems. There are a number of ways in which such threats can be categorized. It is important to understand the spectrum of threats to information systems so that responsible administrators can ensure that prevention measures are comprehensive. We organize the threats into the following categories:

- Environmental threats
- Technical threats
- Human-caused threats

We begin with a discussion of natural disasters, which are a prime, but not the only, source of environmental threats. Then we look specifically at environmental threats, followed by technical and human-caused threats.

Natural Disasters

Natural disasters are the source of a wide range of environmental threats to datacenters, other information processing facilities, and their personnel. It is possible to assess the risk of various types of natural disasters and take suitable precautions so that catastrophic loss from natural disaster is prevented.

Table 54.1 lists six categories of natural disasters, the typical warning time for each event, whether or not personnel evacuation is indicated or possible, and the typical duration of each event. We comment briefly on the potential consequences of each type of disaster.

A tornado can generate winds that exceed hurricane strength in a narrow band along the tornado's path. There is substantial potential for structural damage, roof damage, and loss of outside equipment. There may be damage from wind and flying debris. Off site, a tornado may cause a temporary loss of local utility and communications. Offsite damage is typically followed by quick restoration of services. Tornado damage severity is measured by the Fujita Tornado Scale (see Table 54.2).

Hurricanes, tropical storms, and typhoons, collectively know as tropical cyclones, are among the most devastating naturally occurring hazards. Depending on strength, cyclones may also cause significant structural damage and damage to outside equipment at a particular site. Off site, there is the potential for severe regionwide damage to public infrastructure, utilities, and communications. If on-site operation must continue, then emergency supplies for personnel as well as a backup generator are needed. Further, the responsible site manager may need to mobilize private poststorm security measures, such as armed guards.

Table 54.3 summarizes the widely used Saffir/Simpson Hurricane Scale. In general, damage rises by about a factor of four for every category increase.

A major earthquake has the potential for the greatest damage and occurs without warning. A facility near the epicenter may suffer catastrophic, even complete, destruction, with significant and long-lasting damage to

TABLE 54.2 Fujita Tornado Intensity Scale.

Category	Wind Speed Range	Description of Damage
F0	40–72 mph 64–116 km/hr	Light damage. Some damage to chimneys; tree branches broken off; shallow-rooted trees pushed over; sign boards damaged.
F1	73–112 mph 117–180 km/hr	Moderate damage. The lower limit is the beginning of hurricane wind speed; roof surfaces peeled off; mobile homes pushed off foundations or overturned; moving autos pushed off the roads.
F2	113–157 mph 181–252 km/hr	Considerable damage. roofs torn off houses; mobile homes demolished; boxcars pushed over; large trees snapped or uprooted; light-object missiles generated.
F3	158–206 mph 253–332 km/hr	Severe damage. Roofs and some walls torn off well-constructed houses; trains overturned; most trees in forest uprooted; heavy cars lifted off ground and thrown.
F4	207–260 mph 333–418 km/hr	Devastating damage. Well-constructed houses leveled; structure with weak foundation blown off some distance; cars thrown and large missiles generated.
F5	261–318 mph 419–512 km/hr	Incredible damage. Strong frame houses lifted off foundations and carried considerable distance to disintegrate; automobile-sized missiles fly through the air in excess of 100 yards; trees debarked.

TABLE 54.3 Saffir/Simpson Hurricane Scale.

Category	Wind Speed Range	Storm Surge	Potential Damage
1	74–95 mph 119–153 km/hr	4–5 ft 1–2 m	Minimal
2	96–110 mph 154–177 km/hr	6–8 ft 2–3 m	Moderate
3	111–130 mph 178–209 km/hr	9–12 ft 3–4 m	Extensive
4	131–155 mph 210–249 km/hr	13–18 ft 4–5 m	Extreme
5	155 mph >249 km/hr	>18 ft >5 m	Catastrophic

datacenters and other IS facilities. Examples of inside damage include the toppling of unbraced computer hardware and site infrastructure equipment, including the collapse of raised floors. Personnel are at risk from broken glass and other flying debris. Off site, near the epicenter of a major earthquake, the damage equals and often exceeds that of a major hurricane. Structures that can withstand a hurricane, such as roads and bridges, may be damaged or destroyed, preventing the movement of fuel and other supplies.

An ice storm or blizzard can cause some disruption of or damage to IS facilities if outside equipment and the building are not designed to survive severe ice and snow accumulation. Off site, there may be widespread disruption of utilities and communications and roads may be dangerous or impassable.

The consequences of lightning strikes can range from no impact to disaster. The effects depend on the proximity of the strike and the efficacy of grounding and surge protector measures in place. Off site, there can be disruption of electrical power and there is the potential for fires.

Flooding is a concern in areas that are subject to flooding and for facilities that are in severe flood areas at low elevation. Damage can be severe, with long-lasting effects and the need for a major cleanup operation.

Environmental Threats

This category encompasses conditions in the environment that can damage or interrupt the service of information systems and the data they house. Off site, there may be severe regionwide damage to the public infrastructure and, in the case of severe hurricanes, it may take days, weeks, or even years to recover from the event.

Inappropriate Temperature and Humidity

Computers and related equipment are designed to operate within a certain temperature range. Most computer systems should be kept between 10 and 32 degrees Celsius (50 and 90 degrees Fahrenheit). Outside this range, resources might continue to operate but produce undesirable results. If the ambient temperature around a computer gets too high, the computer cannot adequately cool itself, and internal components can be damaged. If the temperature gets too cold, the system can undergo thermal shock when it is turned on, causing circuit boards or integrated circuits to crack.

Another temperature-related concern is the internal temperature of equipment, which can be significantly higher than room temperature. Computer-related equipment comes with its own temperature dissipation and cooling mechanisms, but these may rely on, or be affected by, external conditions. Such conditions include excessive ambient temperature, interruption of supply of power or heating, ventilation, and air-conditioning (HVAC) services, and vent blockage.

High humidity also poses a threat to electrical and electronic equipment. Long-term exposure to high humidity can result in corrosion. Condensation can threaten magnetic and optical storage media. Condensation can also cause a short circuit, which in turn can damage circuit boards. High humidity can also cause a galvanic effect that results in electroplating, in which metal from one connector slowly migrates to the mating connector, bonding the two together.

Very low humidity can also be a concern. Under prolonged conditions of low humidity, some materials may change shape and performance may be affected. Static electricity also becomes a concern. A person or object that becomes statically charged can damage electronic equipment by an electric discharge. Static electricity discharges as low as 10 volts can damage particularly sensitive electronic circuits, and discharges in the hundreds of volts can create significant damage to a variety of electronic circuits. Discharges from humans can reach into the thousands of volts, so this is a nontrivial threat. In general, relative humidity should be maintained between 40% and 60% to avoid the threats from both low and high humidity.

Fire and Smoke

Perhaps the most frightening physical threat is fire. It is a threat to human life and property. The threat is not only from the direct flame but also from heat, release of toxic fumes, water damage from fire suppression, and smoke damage. Further, fire can disrupt utilities, especially electricity.

The temperature due to fire increases with time, and in a typical building, fire effects follow the curve shown in Figure 54.2. The scale on the right side of Figure 54.2 shows the temperature at which various items melt or are damaged and therefore indicates how long after the fire is started such damage occurs.

Smoke damage related to fires can also be extensive. Smoke is an abrasive. It collects on the heads of unsealed magnetic disks, optical disks, and tape drives. Electrical fires can produce an acrid smoke that may damage other equipment and may be poisonous or carcinogenic.

The most common fire threat is from fires that originate within a facility, and, as discussed subsequently, there are a number of preventive and mitigating measures that can be taken. A more uncontrollable threat is faced from wildfires, which are a plausible concern in the western United States, portions of Australia (where the term *bushfire* is used), and a number of other countries.

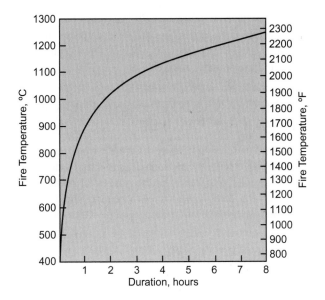

FIGURE 54.2 Fire effects.

Water Damage

Water and other stored liquids in proximity to computer equipment pose an obvious threat. The primary danger is an electrical short, which can happen if water bridges between a circuit board trace carrying voltage and a trace carrying ground. Moving water, such as in plumbing, and weather-created water from rain, snow, and ice also pose threats. A pipe may burst from a fault in the line or from freezing. Sprinkler systems, despite their security function, are a major threat to computer equipment and paper and electronic storage media. The system may be set off by a faulty temperature sensor, or a burst pipe may cause water to enter the computer room. For a large computer installation, an effort should be made to avoid any sources of water from one or two floors above. An example of a hazard from this direction is an overflowing toilet.

Less common but more catastrophic is floodwater. Much of the damage comes from the suspended material in the water. Floodwater leaves a muddy residue that is extraordinarily difficult to clean up.

Chemical, Radiological, and Biological Hazards

Chemical, radiological, and biological hazards pose a growing threat, both from intentional attack and from accidental discharge. None of these hazardous agents should be present in an information system environment, but either accidental or intentional intrusion is possible. Nearby discharges (from an overturned truck carrying hazardous materials) can be introduced through the ventilation system or open windows and, in the case of radiation, through perimeter walls. In addition, discharges in the vicinity can disrupt work by causing evacuations to be ordered. Flooding can also introduce biological or chemical contaminants.

In general, the primary risk of these hazards is to personnel. Radiation and chemical agents can also cause damage to electronic equipment.

Dust

Dust is a prevalent concern that is often overlooked. Even fibers from fabric and paper are abrasive and mildly conductive, although generally equipment is resistant to such contaminants. Larger influxes of dust can result from a number of incidents, such as a controlled explosion of a nearby building and a windstorm carrying debris from a wildfire. A more likely source of influx comes from dust surges that originate within the building due to construction or maintenance work.

Equipment with moving parts, such as rotating storage media and computer fans, are the most vulnerable to damage from dust. Dust can also block ventilation and reduce radiational cooling.

Infestation

One of the less pleasant physical threats is infestation, which covers a broad range of living organisms, including mold, insects, and rodents. High-humidity conditions can lead to the growth of mold and mildew, which can be harmful to both personnel and equipment. Insects, particularly those that attack wood and paper, are also a common threat.

Technical Threats

This category encompasses threats related to electrical power and electromagnetic emission.

Electrical Power

Electrical power is essential to the operation of an information system. All the electrical and electronic devices in the system require power, and most require uninterrupted utility power. Power utility problems can be broadly grouped into three categories: undervoltage, overvoltage, and noise.

An *undervoltage* occurs when the IS equipment receives less voltage than is required for normal operation. Undervoltage events range from temporary dips in the voltage supply to brownouts (prolonged undervoltage) and power outages. Most computers are designed to withstand prolonged voltage reductions of about 20% without shutting down and without operational error. Deeper dips or blackouts lasting more than a few milliseconds trigger a system shutdown. Generally, no damage is done, but service is interrupted.

Far more serious is an *overvoltage*. A surge of voltage can be caused by a utility company supply anomaly, by some internal (to the building) wiring fault, or by lightning. Damage is a function of intensity and duration and the effectiveness of any surge protectors between your equipment and the source of the surge. A sufficient surge can destroy silicon-based components, including processors and memories.

Power lines can also be a conduit for *noise*. In many cases, these spurious signals can endure through the filtering circuitry of the power supply and interfere with signals inside electronic devices, causing logical errors.

Electromagnetic Interference

Noise along a power supply line is only one source of electromagnetic interference (EMI). Motors, fans, heavy equipment, and even other computers generate electrical noise that can cause intermittent problems with the computer you are using. This noise can be transmitted through space as well as nearby power lines.

Another source of EMI is high-intensity emissions from nearby commercial radio stations and microwave relay antennas. Even low-intensity devices, such as cellular telephones, can interfere with sensitive electronic equipment.

Human-Caused Physical Threats

Human-caused threats are more difficult to deal with than the environmental and technical threats discussed so far. Human-caused threats are less predictable than other types of physical threats. Worse, human-caused threats are specifically designed to overcome prevention measures and/or seek the most vulnerable point of attack. We can group such threats into the following categories:

- *Unauthorized physical access.* Those who are not employees should not be in the building or building complex at all unless accompanied by an authorized individual. Not counting PCs and workstations, information system assets, such as servers, mainframe computers, network equipment, and storage networks, are generally housed in restricted areas. Access to such areas is usually restricted to only a certain number of employees. Unauthorized physical access can lead to other threats, such as theft, vandalism, or misuse.
- *Theft.* This threat includes theft of equipment and theft of data by copying. Eavesdropping and wiretapping also fall into this category. Theft can be at the hands of an outsider who has gained unauthorized access or by an insider.
- *Vandalism.* This threat includes destruction of equipment and destruction of data.

- *Misuse.* This category includes improper use of resources by those who are authorized to use them, as well as use of resources by individuals not authorized to use the resources at all.

3. PHYSICAL SECURITY PREVENTION AND MITIGATION MEASURES

In this part of the chapter, we look at a range of techniques for preventing, or in some cases simply deterring, physical attacks. We begin with a survey of some of the techniques for dealing with environmental and technical threats and then move on to human-caused threats.

Environmental Threats

We discuss these threats in the same order.

Inappropriate Temperature and Humidity

Dealing with this problem is primarily a matter of having environmental-control equipment of appropriate capacity and appropriate sensors to warn of thresholds being exceeded. Beyond that, the principal requirement is the maintenance of a power supply, discussed subsequently.

Fire and Smoke

Dealing with fire involves a combination of alarms, preventive measures, and fire mitigation. Martin provides the following list of necessary measures[3] :

- Choice of site to minimize likelihood of disaster. Few disastrous fires originate in a well-protected computer room or IS facility. The IS area should be chosen to minimize fire, water, and smoke hazards from adjoining areas. Common walls with other activities should have at least a one-hour fire-protection rating.
- Air conditioning and other ducts designed so as not to spread fire. There are standard guidelines and specifications for such designs.
- Positioning of equipment to minimize damage.
- Good housekeeping. Records and flammables must not be stored in the IS area. Tidy installation of IS equipment is crucial.
- Hand-operated fire extinguishers readily available, clearly marked, and regularly tested.
- Automatic fire extinguishers installed. Installation should be such that the extinguishers are unlikely to cause damage to equipment or danger to personnel.
- Fire detectors. The detectors sound alarms inside the IS room and with external authorities, and start

---

3. J. Martin, *Security, Accuracy, and Privacy in Computer Systems,* Prentice Hall, 1973.

automatic fire extinguishers after a delay to permit human intervention.

- Equipment power-off switch. This switch must be clearly marked and unobstructed. All personnel must be familiar with power-off procedures.
- Emergency procedures posted.
- Personnel safety. Safety must be considered in designing the building layout and emergency procedures.
- Important records stored in fireproof cabinets or vaults.
- Records needed for file reconstruction stored off the premises.
- Up-to-date duplicate of all programs stored off the premises.
- Contingency plan for use of equipment elsewhere should the computers be destroyed.
- Insurance company and local fire department should inspect the facility.

To deal with the threat of smoke, the responsible manager should install smoke detectors in every room that contains computer equipment as well as under raised floors and over suspended ceilings. Smoking should not be permitted in computer rooms.

For wildfires, the available countermeasures are limited. Fire-resistant building techniques are costly and difficult to justify.

Water Damage

Prevention and mitigation measures for water threats must encompass the range of such threats. For plumbing leaks, the cost of relocating threatening lines is generally difficult to justify. With knowledge of the exact layout of water supply lines, measures can be taken to locate equipment sensibly. The location of all shutoff valves should be clearly visible or at least clearly documented, and responsible personnel should know the procedures to follow in case of emergency.

To deal with both plumbing leaks and other sources of water, sensors are vital. Water sensors should be located on the floor of computer rooms as well as under raised floors and should cut off power automatically in the event of a flood.

Other Environmental Threats

For chemical, biological, and radiological threats, specific technical approaches are available, including infrastructure design, sensor design and placement, mitigation procedures, personnel training, and so forth. Standards and techniques in these areas continue to evolve.

As for dust hazards, the obvious prevention method is to limit dust through the use and proper filter maintenance and regular IS room maintenance. For infestations, regular pest control procedures may be needed, starting with maintaining a clean environment.

Technical Threats

To deal with brief power interruptions, an uninterruptible power supply (UPS) should be employed for each piece of critical equipment. The UPS is a battery backup unit that can maintain power to processors, monitors, and other equipment for a period of minutes. UPS units can also function as surge protectors, power noise filters, and automatic shutdown devices when the battery runs low.

For longer blackouts or brownouts, critical equipment should be connected to an emergency power source, such as a generator. For reliable service, a range of issues need to be addressed by management, including product selection, generator placement, personnel training, testing and maintenance schedules, and so forth.

To deal with electromagnetic interference, a combination of filters and shielding can be used. The specific technical details will depend on the infrastructure design and the anticipated sources and nature of the interference.

Human-Caused Physical Threats

The general approach to human-caused physical threats is physical access control. Based on Michael,[4] we can suggest a spectrum of approaches that can be used to restrict access to equipment. These methods can be used in combination:

- Physical contact with a resource is restricted by restricting access to the building in which the resource is housed. This approach is intended to deny access to outsiders but does not address the issue of unauthorized insiders or employees.
- Physical contact with a resource is restricted by putting the resource in a locked cabinet, safe, or room.
- A machine may be accessed, but it is secured (perhaps permanently bolted) to an object that is difficult to move. This will deter theft but not vandalism, unauthorized access, or misuse.
- A security device controls the power switch.
- A movable resource is equipped with a tracking device so that a sensing portal can alert security personnel or trigger an automated barrier to prevent the object from being moved out of its proper security area.
- A portable object is equipped with a tracking device so that its current position can be monitored continually.

4. M. Michael, "Physical security measures," In H. Bidgoli, (ed.), *Handbook of Information Security*, Wiley, 2006.

The first two of the preceding approaches isolate the equipment. Techniques that can be used for this type of access control include controlled areas patrolled or guarded by personnel, barriers that isolate each area, entry points in the barrier (doors), and locks or screening measures at each entry point. Physical access control should address not just computers and other IS equipment but also locations of wiring used to connect systems, the electrical power service, the HVAC equipment and distribution system, telephone and communications lines, backup media, and documents.

In addition to physical and procedural barriers, an effective physical access control regime includes a variety of sensors and alarms to detect intruders and unauthorized access or movement of equipment. Surveillance systems are frequently an integral part of building security, and special-purpose surveillance systems for the IS area are generally also warranted. Such systems should provide real-time remote viewing as well as recording.

4. RECOVERY FROM PHYSICAL SECURITY BREACHES

The most essential element of recovery from physical security breaches is redundancy. Redundancy does not undo any breaches of confidentiality, such as the theft of data or documents, but it does provide for recovery from loss of data. Ideally, all the important data in the system should be available off site and updated as near to real time as is warranted based on a cost/benefit tradeoff. With broadband connections now almost universally available, batch encrypted backups over private networks or the Internet are warranted and can be carried out on whatever schedule is deemed appropriate by management. At the extreme, a *hotsite* can be created off site that is ready to take over operation instantly and has available to it a near-real-time copy of operational data.

Recovery from physical damage to the equipment or the site depends on the nature of the damage and, importantly, the nature of the residue. Water, smoke, and fire damage may leave behind hazardous materials that must be meticulously removed from the site before normal operations and the normal equipment suite can be reconstituted. In many cases, this requires bringing in disaster recovery specialists from outside the organization to do the cleanup.

5. THREAT ASSESSMENT, PLANNING, AND PLAN IMPLEMENTATION

We have surveyed a number of threats to physical security and a number of approaches to prevention, mitigation, and recovery. To implement a physical security program, an organization must conduct a threat assessment to determine the amount of resources to devote to physical security and the allocation of those resources against the various threats. This process also applies to logical security.

Threat Assessment

In this part of the chapter, we follow Platt[5] in outlining a typical sequence of steps that an organization should take:

1. *Set up a steering committee.* The threat assessment should not be left only to a security officer or to IS management. All those who have a stake in the security of the IS assets, including all of the user communities, should be brought into the process.
2. *Obtain information and assistance.* Historical information concerning external threats, such as flood and fire is the best starting point. This information can often be obtained from government agencies and weather bureaus. In the United States, the Federal Emergency Management Agency (FEMA) can provide much useful information. FEMA has a number of publications available online that provide specific guidance in a wide variety of physical security areas (www.fema.gov/business/index.shtm). The committee should also seek expert advice from vendors, suppliers, neighboring businesses, service and maintenance personnel, consultants, and academics.
3. *Identify all possible threats.* List all possible threats, including those that are specific to IS operations as well as those that are more general, covering the building and the geographic area.
4. *Determine the likelihood of each threat.* This is clearly a difficult task. One approach is to use a scale of 1 (least likely) to 5 (most likely) so that threats can be grouped to suggest where attention should be directed. All the information from Step 2 can be applied to this task.
5. *Approximate the direct costs.* For each threat, the committee must estimate not only the threat's likelihood but also its severity in terms of consequences. Again a relative scale of 1 (low) to 5 (high) in terms of costs and losses is a reasonable approach. For both Steps 4 and 5, an attempt to use a finer-grained scale, or to assign specific probabilities and specific costs, is likely to produce the impression of greater precision and knowledge about future threats than is possible.
6. *Consider cascading costs.* Some threats can trigger consequential threats that add still more impact costs. For example, a fire can cause direct flame, heat, and

5. F. Platt, "Physical threats to the information infrastructure," in S. Bosworth, and M. Kabay, (eds.), *Computer Security Handbook,* Wiley, 2002.

smoke damage as well as disrupt utilities and result in water damage.

7. *Prioritize the threats.* The goal here is to determine the relative importance of the threats as a guide to focusing resources on prevention. A simple formula yields a prioritized list:

Importance = Likelihood × [Direct Cost + Secondary Cost]

where the scale values (1 through 5) are used in the formula.

8. *Complete the threat assessment report.* The committee can now prepare a report that includes the prioritized list, with commentary on how the results were achieved. This report serves as the reference source for the planning process that follows.

Planning and Implementation

Once a threat assessment has been done, the steering committee, or another committee, can develop a plan for threat prevention, mitigation, and recovery. The following is a typical sequence of steps an organization could take:

1. *Assess internal and external resources.* These include resources for prevention as well as response. A reasonable approach is again to use a relative scale from 1 (strong ability to prevent and respond) to 5 (weak ability to prevent and respond). This scale can be combined with the threat priority score to focus resource planning.

2. *Identify challenges and prioritize activities.* Determine specific goals and milestones. Make a list of tasks to be performed, by whom and when. Determine how you will address the problem areas and resource shortfalls that were identified in the vulnerability analysis.

3. *Develop a plan.* The plan should include prevention measures and equipment needed and emergency response procedures. The plan should include support documents, such as emergency call lists, building and site maps, and resource lists.

4. *Implement the plan.* Implementation includes acquiring new equipment, assigning responsibilities, conducting training, monitoring plan implementation, and updating the plan regularly.

6. EXAMPLE: A CORPORATE PHYSICAL SECURITY POLICY

To give the reader a feel for how organizations deal with physical security, we provide a real-world example of a physical security policy. The company is a European Union (EU)-based engineering consulting firm that specializes in the provision of planning, design, and management services for infrastructure development worldwide.

With interests in transportation, water, maritime, and property, the company is undertaking commissions in over 70 countries from a network of more than 70 offices.

Figure 54.3 is extracted from the company's security standards document. For our purposes, we have changed the name of the company to *Company* wherever it appears in the document. The company's physical security policy relies heavily on ISO 17799 *(Code of Practice for Information Security Management)*.

7. INTEGRATION OF PHYSICAL AND LOGICAL SECURITY

Physical security involves numerous detection devices, such as sensors and alarms, and numerous prevention devices and measures, such as locks and physical barriers. It should be clear that there is much scope for automation and for the integration of various computerized and electronic devices. Clearly, physical security can be made more effective if there is a central destination for all alerts and alarms and if there is central control of all automated access control mechanisms, such as smart card entry sites.

From the point of view of both effectiveness and cost, there is increasing interest not only in integrating automated physical security functions but in integrating, to the extent possible, automated physical security and logical security functions. The most promising area is that of access control. Examples of ways to integrate physical and logical access control include the following:

- Use of a single ID card for physical and logical access. This can be a simple magnetic-strip card or a smart card.
- Single-step user/card enrollment and termination across all identity and access control databases.
- A central ID-management system instead of multiple disparate user directories and databases.
- Unified event monitoring and correlation.

As an example of the utility of this integration, suppose that an alert indicates that Bob has logged on to the company's wireless network (an event generated by the logical access control system) but did not enter the building (an event generated from the physical access control system). Combined, these two events suggest that someone is hijacking Bob's wireless account.

For the integration of physical and logical access control to be practical, a wide range of vendors must conform to standards that cover smart card protocols, authentication and access control formats and protocols, database entries, message formats, and so on. An important step in this direction is FIPS 201-2 *(Personal Identity Verification (PIV) of Federal Employees and Contractors),* issued in 2011. The standard defines a reliable, governmentwide PIV system for use in applications

5. Physical and Environmental security

5.1. *Secure Areas*

5.1.1. ***Physical Security Perimeter*** - Company shall use security perimeters to protect all non-public areas, commensurate with the value of the assets therein. Business critical information processing facilities located in unattended buildings shall also be alarmed to a permanently manned remote alarm monitoring station.

5.1.2. ***Physical Entry Controls*** - Secure areas shall be segregated and protected by appropriate entry controls to ensure that only authorised personnel are allowed access. Similar controls are also required where the building is shared with, or accessed by, non-Company staff and organisations not acting on behalf of Company.

5.1.3. ***Securing Offices, Rooms and Facilities*** - Secure areas shall be created in order to protect office, rooms and facilities with special security requirements.

5.1.4. ***Working in Secure Areas*** - Additional controls and guidelines for working in secure areas shall be used to enhance the security provided by the physical control protecting the secure areas.

> *Employees of Company should be aware that additional controls and guidelines for working in secure areas to enhance the security provided by the physical control protecting the secure areas might be in force. For further clarification they should contact their Line Manager.*

5.1.5. ***Isolated Access Points*** - Isolated access points, additional to building main entrances (e.g. Delivery and Loading areas) shall be controlled and, if possible, isolated from secure areas to avoid unauthorised access.

5.1.6. ***Sign Posting Of Computer Installations*** - Business critical computer installations sited within a building must not be identified by the use of descriptive sign posts or other displays. Where such sign posts or other displays are used they must be worded in such a way so as not to highlight the business critical nature of the activity taking place within the building.

5.2. *Equipment Security*

5.2.1. ***Equipment Sitting and Protection*** - Equipment shall be sited or protected to reduce the risk from environmental threats and hazards, and opportunity for unauthorised access.

5.2.2. ***Power Supply*** - The equipment shall be protected from power failure and other electrical anomalies.

5.2.3. ***Cabling Security*** - Power and telecommunication cabling carrying data or supporting information services shall be protected from interception or damage commensurate with the business criticality of the operations they serve.

5.2.4. ***Equipment Maintenance*** - Equipment shall be maintained in accordance with manufacturer's instruction and/or documented procedures to ensure its continued availability and integrity.

5.2.5. ***Security of Equipment off-premises*** - Security procedures and controls shall be used to secure equipment used outside any Company's premises

> *Employees are to note that there should be security procedures and controls to secure equipment used outside any Company premises. Advice on these procedures can be sought from the Group Security Manager.*

5.2.6. ***Secure Disposal or Re-use of Equipment*** - Information shall be erased from equipment prior to disposal or reuse.

> *For further guidance contact the Group Security Manager.*

5.2.7. ***Security of the Access Network*** - Company shall implement access control measures, determined by a risk assessment, to ensure that only authorised people have access to the Access Network (including: cabinets, cabling, nodes etc.).

FIGURE 54.3 The Company's physical security policy.

5.2.8. **Security of PCs -** Every Company owned PC must have an owner who is responsible for its general management and control. Users of PCs are personally responsible for the physical and logical security of any PC they use. Users of Company PCs are personally responsible for the physical and logical security of any PC they use, as defined within the Staff Handbook.

5.2.9. **Removal of "Captured Data" -** Where any device (software or hardware based) has been introduced to the network that captures data for analytical purposes, all data must be wiped off of this device prior to removal from the Company Site. The removal of this data from site for analysis can only be approved by the MIS Technology Manager.

5.3. **General Controls**

5.3.1. **Security Controls -** Security Settings are to be utilised and configurations must be controlled

> *No security settings or software on Company systems are to be changed without authorisation from MIS Support*

5.3.2. **Clear Screen Policy -** Company shall have and implement clear-screen policy in order to reduce the risks of unauthorised access, loss of, and damage to information.

> *This will be implemented when all Users of the Company system have Windows XP operating system.*
>
> *When the User has the Windows XP system they are to carry out the following:*
>
> - *Select the Settings tab within the START area on the desktop screen.*
> - *Select Control Panel.*
> - *Select the icon called DISPLAY.*
> - *Select the Screensaver Tab.*
> - *Set a Screen saver.*
> - *Set the time for 15 Mins.*
> - *Tick the Password Protect box; remember this is the same password that you utilise to log on to the system.*
>
> *Staff are to lock their screens using the Ctrl-Alt-Del when they leave their desk*

5.3.3. **Clear Desk Policy –** Staff shall ensure that they operate a Clear Desk Policy

> *Each member of staff is asked to take personal and active responsibility for maintaining a "clear desk" policy whereby files and papers are filed or otherwise cleared away before leaving the office at the end of each day*

5.3.4. **Removal of Property -** Equipment, information or software belonging to the organisation shall not be removed without authorisation.

> *Equipment, information or software belonging to Company shall not be removed without authorisation from the Project Manager or Line Manager and the MIS Support.*

5.3.5. **People Identification -** All Company staff must have visible the appropriate identification whenever they are in Company premises.

5.3.6. **Visitors -** All Company premises will have a process for dealing with visitors. All Visitors must be sponsored and wear the appropriate identification whenever they are in Company premises.

5.3.7. **Legal Right of Entry -** Entry must be permitted to official bodies when entry is demanded on production of a court order or when the person has other legal rights. Advice must be sought from management or the Group Security Manager as a matter of urgency.

FIGURE 54.3   (Continued)

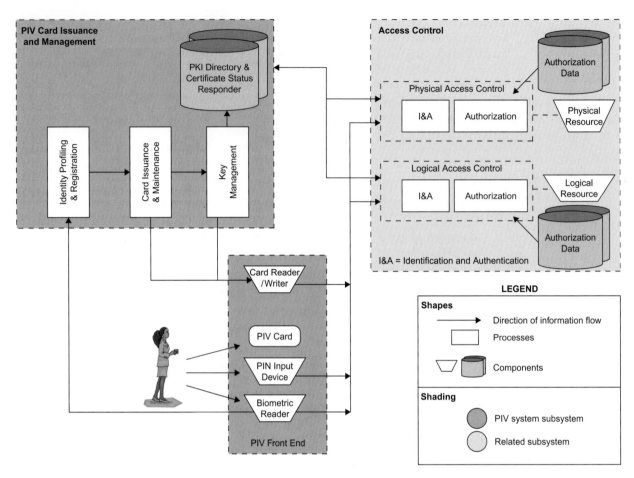

FIGURE 54.4 FIPS 201 PIV system model.

such as access to federally controlled facilities and information systems. The standard specifies a PIV system within which common identification credentials can be created and later used to verify a claimed identity. The standard also identifies federal governmentwide requirements for security levels that are dependent on risks to the facility or information being protected. The standard applies to private-sector contractors as well, and serves as a useful guideline for any organization.

Figure 54.4 illustrates the major components of FIPS 201-2 compliant systems. The PIV front end defines the physical interface to a user who is requesting access to a facility, which could be either physical access to a protected physical area or logical access to an information system. The PIV front-end subsystem supports up to three-factor authentication; the number of factors used depends on the level of security required. The front end makes use of a smart card, known as a *PIV card,* which is a dual-interface contact and contactless card. The card holds a cardholder photograph, X.509 certificates, cryptographic keys, biometric data, and the cardholder unique identifier (CHUID). Certain cardholder information may be read-protected and require a personal identification

number (PIN) for read access by the card reader. The biometric reader, in the current version of the standard, is a fingerprint reader.

The standard defines three assurance levels for verification of the card and the encoded data stored on the card, which in turn leads to verifying the authenticity of the person holding the credential. A level of *some confidence* corresponds to use of the card reader and PIN. A level of *high confidence* adds a biometric comparison of a fingerprint captured and encoded on the card during the card-issuing process and a fingerprint scanned at the physical access point. A *very high confidence* level requires that the process just described is completed at a control point attended by an official observer.

The other major component of the PIV system is the *PIV card issuance and management subsystem.* This subsystem includes the components responsible for identity proofing and registration, card and key issuance and management, and the various repositories and services (public key infrastructure [PKI] directory, certificate status servers) required as part of the verification infrastructure.

The PIV system interacts with an *access control subsystem,* which includes components responsible for

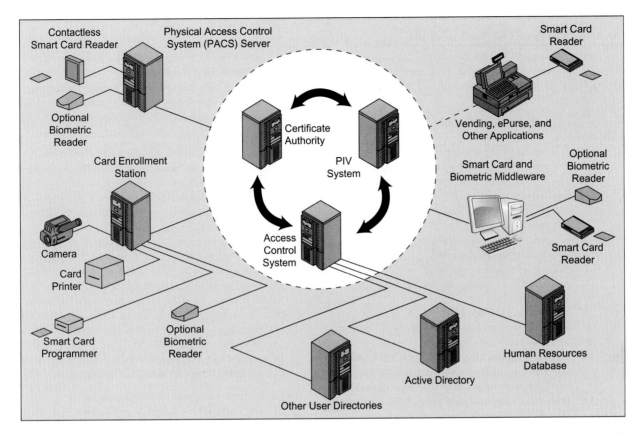

FIGURE 54.5 Convergence example (based on [FORR06]).

determining a particular PIV cardholder's access to a physical or logical resource. FIPS 201-1 standardizes data formats and protocols for interaction between the PIV system and the access control system.

Unlike the typical card number/facility code encoded on most access control cards, the FIPS 201 CHUID takes authentication to a new level, through the use of an expiration date (a required CHUID data field) and an optional CHUID digital signature. A digital signature can be checked to ensure that the CHUID recorded on the card was digitally signed by a trusted source and that the CHUID data have not been altered since the card was signed. The CHUID expiration date can be checked to verify that the card has not expired. This is independent of whatever expiration date is associated with cardholder privileges. Reading and verifying the CHUID alone provides only some assurance of identity because it authenticates the card data, not the cardholder. The PIN and biometric factors provide identity verification of the individual.

Figure 54.5, adapted from Forristal,[6] illustrates the convergence of physical and logical access control using FIPS 201-2. The core of the system includes the PIV and access control system as well as a certificate authority for

signing CHUIDs. The other elements of Figure 54.5 provide examples of the use of the system core for integrating physical and logical access control.

If the integration of physical and logical access control extends beyond a unified front end to an integration of system elements, a number of benefits accrue, including the following[7] :

- Employees gain a single, unified access control authentication device; this cuts down on misplaced tokens, reduces training and overhead, and allows seamless access.
- A single logical location for employee ID management reduces duplicate data entry operations and allows for immediate and real-time authorization revocation of all enterprise resources.
- Auditing and forensic groups have a central repository for access control investigations.
- Hardware unification can reduce the number of vendor purchase-and-support contracts.
- Certificate-based access control systems can leverage user ID certificates for other security applications, such as document esigning and data encryption.

---

6. J. Forristal, "Physical/logical convergence," *Network Computing,* November 23, 2006.

7. J. Forristal, "Physical/logical convergence," *Network Computing,* November 23, 2006.

An Agenda for Action for Physical Security

The brevity of a checklist can be helpful, but it in no way makes up for the detail of the text. Thus, the following set of Check Points for Physical Security must be adhered to (check all tasks completed):

Create a Secure Environment: Building and Room Construction:

_____1. Does each secure room or facility have low visibility (no unnecessary signs)?

_____2. Has the room or facility been constructed with full-height walls?

_____3. Has the room or facility been constructed with a fireproof ceiling?

_____4. Are there two or fewer doorways?

_____5. Are doors solid and fireproof?

_____6. Are doors equipped with locks?

_____7. Are window openings to secure areas kept as small as possible?

_____8. Are windows equipped with locks?

_____9. Are keys and combinations to door and window locks secured responsibly?

_____10. Have alternatives to traditional lock and key security measures (bars, anti-theft cabling, magnetic key cards, and motion detectors) been considered?

_____11. Have both automatic and manual fire equipment been properly installed?

_____12. Are personnel properly trained for fire emergencies?

_____13. Are acceptable room temperatures always maintained (between 50 and 80 degrees Fahrenheit)?

_____14. Are acceptable humidity ranges always maintained (between 20 and 80 percent)?

_____15. Are eating, drinking, and smoking regulations in place and enforced?

_____16. Has all non-essential, potentially flammable, material (curtains and stacks of computer paper) been removed from secure areas?

Guard Equipment:

_____17. Has equipment been identified as critical or general use, and segregated appropriately?

_____18. Is equipment housed out of sight and reach from doors and windows, and away from radiators, heating vents, air conditioners, and other duct work?

_____19. Are plugs, cabling, and other wires protected from foot traffic?

_____20. Are up-to-date records of all equipment brand names, model names, and serial numbers kept in a secure location?

_____21. Have qualified technicians (staff or vendors) been identified to repair critical equipment if and when it fails?

_____22. Has contact information for repair technicians (telephone numbers, customer numbers, maintenance contract numbers) been stored in a secure but accessible place?

_____23. Are repair workers and outside technicians required to adhere to the organization's security policies concerning sensitive information?

Rebuff Theft:

_____24. Has all equipment been labeled in an overt way that clearly and permanently identifies its owner (the school name)?

_____25. Has all equipment been labeled in a covert way that only authorized staff would know to look for (inside the cover)?

_____26. Have steps been taken to make it difficult for unauthorized people to tamper with equipment (by replacing case screws with Allen-type screws)?

_____27. Have security staff been provided up-to-date lists of personnel and their respective access authority?

_____28. Are security staff required to verify identification of unknown people before permitting access to facilities?

_____29. Are security staff required to maintain a log of all equipment taken in and out of secure areas?

Attend to Portable Equipment and Computers:

_____30. Do users know not to leave laptops and other portable equipment unattended outside of the office?

_____31. Do users know and follow proper transportation and storage procedures for laptops and other portable equipment?

Regulate Power Supplies:

_____32. Are surge protectors used with all equipment?

_____33. Are Uninterruptible Power Supplies (UPSs) in place for critical systems?

_____34. Have power supplies been "insulated" from environmental threats by a professional electrician?

_____35. Has consideration been given to the use of electrical outlets so as to avoid overloading?

_____36. Are the negative effects of static electricity minimized through the use of anti-static carpeting, pads, and sprays as necessary?

Protect Output:

_____37. Are photocopiers, fax machines, and scanners kept in open view?

_____38. Are printers assigned to users with similar security clearances?

_____39. Is every printed copy of confidential information labeled as "confidential"?

_____40. Are outside delivery services required to adhere to security practices when transporting sensitive information?

_____41. Are all paper copies of sensitive information shredded before being discarded?

Finally, let's briefly look at a physical security checklist. The effectiveness of the recommendations in the physical security checklist is most useful when initiated as part of a larger plan to develop and implement security policy throughout an organization.

8. PHYSICAL SECURITY CHECKLIST

While it may be tempting to simply refer to the following checklist as your security plan, to do so would limit the effectiveness of the recommendations. Some recommendations and considerations are included the following checklist: "An Agenda For Action For Physical Security").

9. SUMMARY

Physical security requires that building site(s) be safeguarded in a way that minimizes the risk of resource theft and destruction. To accomplish this, decision-makers must be concerned about building construction, room assignments, emergency procedures, regulations governing equipment placement and use, power supplies, product handling, and relationships with outside contractors and agencies.

The physical plant must be satisfactorily secured to prevent those people who are not authorized to enter the site and use equipment from doing so. A building does not need to feel like a fort to be safe. Well-conceived plans to secure a building can be initiated without adding undue burden on your staff. After all, if they require access, they will receive it—as long as they were aware of, and abide by, the organization's stated security policies and guidelines. The only way to ensure this is to demand that before any person is given access to your system, they have first signed and returned a valid Security Agreement. This necessary security policy is too important to permit exceptions.

Finally, let's move on to the real interactive part of this Chapter: review questions/exercises, hands-on projects, case projects and optional team case project. The answers and/or solutions by chapter can be found in the Online Instructor's Solutions Manual.

CHAPTER REVIEW QUESTIONS/EXERCISES

True/False

1. True or False? Information system hardware includes data processing and storage equipment, transmission and networking facilities, and online storage media.
2. True or False? Physical facility includes the buildings and other structures housing the system and network components.
3. True or False? Supporting facilities under scores the operation of the information system.
4. True or False? Personnel are humans involved in the control, maintenance, and use of the information systems.
5. True or False? It is possible to assess the risk of various types of natural disasters and take suitable precautions so that catastrophic loss from natural disaster is achieved.

Multiple Choice

1. What are the three elements of information system (IS) security?
   A. Logical security
   B. Physical security
   C. Maritime security
   D. Premises security
   E. Wireless security
2. In broad terms, which of the following is not included in the critical infrastructure?
   A. Environmental threats
   B. Information system hardware
   C. Physical facility
   D. Supporting facilities
   E. Personnel
3. Which of the following are threats?
   A. Environmental
   B. Natural
   C. Technical
   D. Access
   E. Human-caused
4. Which of the following is not a human-caused threat?
   A. Unauthorized physical access
   B. Theft
   C. Vandalism
   D. Decryption
   E. Misuse
5. Dealing with fire involves a combination of alarms, preventive measures, and fire mitigation. Which of the following is not a necessary measure?
   A. Choice of site to minimize likelihood of disaster
   B. Positioning of equipment to minimize damage
   C. Good housekeeping
   D. Fire detectors
   E. Physical contact

EXERCISE

Problem

A company's physical security team analyzed physical security threats and vulnerabilities for their systems. What type of vulnerabilities did the company focus on?

Hands-On Projects

Project

An engineering company operating within a highly regulated industry, in which privacy and compliance are of paramount importance, wanted to compare itself relative to its peers in physical security provision and establish a baseline from which to quantify improvement. Please identify the best practices; compare organizational and outsourcing models; compare security technologies utilized; and, calibrate investment in physical security against its peers.

Case Projects

Problem

This case study illustrates how a company uses intelligent video processing (a sub-system of its video surveillance system) to detect intrusions at land ports of entry. Virtual fences are integrated into each facility to compliment both the facility's perimeter physical security system (composed of a combination of fences, gates, and barriers) and the video surveillance system. What should happen if these virtual fences are breached?

Optional Team Case Project

Problem

A company wants to further develop its access control system (ACS) use of video, proximity-based ID cards, biometrics, RFID, VoIP, and remotely controlled gates for manned and unmanned access control. What does the company need to do to further develop its ACS?

## Chapter 55

Disaster Recovery

Scott R. Ellis and Lauren Collins
kCura Corporation

1. INTRODUCTION

In almost every organization, when a technology-oriented task is at hand, and where no one knows who would handle the request, it typically lands in the information technology department (IT). Whether the task consists of a special, faulty light bulb or a backup for a grease stop in the kitchen sink, organizations rely heavily on the IT department to know the unknown, and to fix anything that breaks.

Disaster recovery (DR), not unlike the plugged sink, is another task that many organizations fail to consider until after much of the technology groundwork has been laid, the corporation is profitable, and suddenly someone realizes that *not* having a DR site is a serious risk to the business. It is at this time that they begin to consider, and they begin to ponder, what a strategy might look like that enables the business to continue to run in the event of Force Majeure or some other disaster, such as if a hacker came in and tore their system down, or somehow seized control of it.

Hardware, physical or virtual, must be acquired and configured to capture the environment as it currently sits—and it must be able to continue with its synchronization. Whether this is by the minute, the hour, the day, or the week is a business decision. In fact, much of the DR strategy is driven by business continuity requirements. In the event of a disaster, there must be a plan in place that considers which individuals will act in the event of a disaster. Those individuals must know what constitutes a disaster, and the roles must be defined for those individuals.

2. MEASURING RISK AND AVOIDING DISASTER

A key component of a disaster recovery (DR) plan is for the committee to assess conceivable risks to the organization that could result in the disasters or emergency situations themselves. All events must be considered, and the impact must also be reflected upon so that the organization has the ability to continue and deliver business as usual. Quantitative and qualitative risks are considered separately in a DR plan; however, both come together when determining how an organizations reputation and earnings should be managed in the event of a disaster. Risk is assessed on an inherent and residual basis, allowing an entity to understand the extent to which potential events might impact objectives from two perspectives, likelihood and impact.

Assessing Risk in the Enterprise

Enterprise Risk Management (ERM) is not a template that can be given to every company to meet their needs and fit their business structure. Proper risk assessment identifies the risks throughout the organization and specifies the external and internal sources that the organization may face. The organization engages members from each organizational unit (Executives, HR, Finance, etc.), and asks questions such as "What do you perceive to be the largest risks to the company in terms of significance and likelihood?" and "What do you perceive to be the biggest risks within your control?" After a common understanding is met and all are aware of the risks, such risk assessments should be linked to strategic objectives as shown in Figure 55.1.

Once the company has an understanding of the top risks that can impact the organization, the executive team determines the company's risk appetite and risk tolerance. Risk appetite is the amount of risk, on a comprehensive level, that an entity is willing to accept in pursuit of value. Risk tolerance, on the other hand, is the range of acceptable variation around the company's objectives. The key is to determine the degree of maturity that meets the needs of your organization.

Steps in the Risk Process

There are five steps to consider for a company to come out ahead when a disaster hits to avoid risk and protect your data. The following checklist (see checklist: An

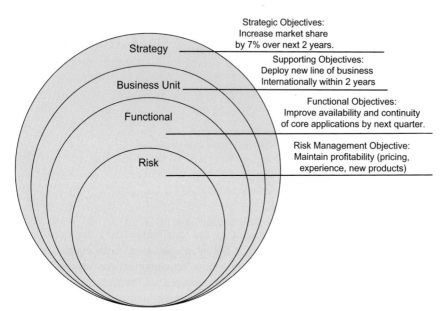

Strategic Objectives:
Increase market share
by 7% over next 2 years.

Supporting Objectives:
Deploy new line of business
Internationally within 2 years

Functional Objectives:
Improve availability and continuity
of core applications by next quarter.

Risk Management Objective:
Maintain profitability (pricing,
experience, new products)

FIGURE 55.1 Risk assessments are linked to strategic objectives in an organization as a whole to allow a company to understand the risks in the organization, the company's risk appetite, and risk tolerance.

Agenda for Action for Risk Assessment) is a list of these steps, from assessment to planning, architecting, specifying and implementing a full-bodied disaster recovery (DR) solution.

Downtime presents serious consequences for businesses, no matter what their function may be. It is difficult, if not impossible, to recoup lost revenue and rebuild a corporate reputation that is damaged by an outage. While professionals cannot expect to avoid every downtime event, the majority of system downtime is caused by preventable failures. Distinguishing between planned and unplanned system downtime allocates

---

An Agenda for Action for Risk Assessment

Steps in Risk Assessment (check all tasks completed):

_____ 1. Discover the potential threats:
     _____ **a.** Environmental (tornado, hurricane, flood, earthquake, fire, landslide, epidemic).
     _____ **b.** Organized or deliberate disruption (terrorism, war, arson).
     _____ **c.** Loss of utilities or services (electrical power failure, petroleum shortage, communications services breakdown).
     _____ **d.** Equipment or system failure (internal power failure, air conditioning failure, production line failure, equipment failure).
     _____ **e.** Security threat (leak of sensitive information, loss of records or data, cybercrime).
     _____ **f.** Supplementary emergency situations (workplace violence, public transportation disruption, health and safety hazard).

_____ 2. Determine requirements:
     _____ **a.** Prioritize processes
     _____ **b.** Determine recovery objectives
     _____ **c.** Plan for common incidents
     _____ **d.** Communicate the plan
     _____ **e.** Choose individuals who will test plan regularly and act in the event of a disaster

_____ 3. Understand DR options:
     _____ **a.** Determine how far to get the data out of the data center.
     _____ **b.** Will the data center be accessible at the same time as the disaster.
     _____ **c.** Determine the process to backup and/or replicate data off-site.
     _____ **d.** Determine the process to recreate an environment off-site.

_____ 4. Audit providers:
     _____ **a.** Compare list of providers with internal list of requirements.
     _____ **b.** Understand range of data protection solutions offered
     _____ **c.** Assess proximity (power grid/communications and contingencies).
     _____ **d.** Data center hardening features and their DR contingencies.

_____ 5. Record findings, implement/test, and revise if/as necessary:
     _____ **a.** Documentation is the heart of your plan.
     _____ **b.** Test and adjust plan as necessary, record findings.
     _____ **c.** As the environment changes and business needs change, revise the plan and test again.

different procedures as both present vastly diverse paths when bringing systems back up.

While both planned and unplanned downtime can be stressful, planned downtime must be finished on time. Unplanned is the worst. Unplanned can be good for teaching troubleshooting techniques to junior IT staff, but can be very frustrating to the workforce. The authors see fewer and fewer techs with troubleshooting experience, and more and more senior techs launching their own consultancies. The biggest cost is how it affects the customers and the impressions of the company that a severe outage can make on the organization's customers and clients. Planning, having people on staff with good troubleshooting skills, and documenting how the issue was found and fixed will help resolve the issue faster next time.

Matching the Response to the Threat

Separate each of your significant processes into one of three categories: Mission Critical, Business Critical or Organizationally Critical. By classifying processes into categories, you are able to define which parts of the organization would be recovered first in the event of an outage or disaster. How long can your organization or group live without access to a particular system? Should this system fail, how much data can the business realistically handle losing? Define, succinctly, what the organization considers a disastrously disruptive event and set the maximum amount of time you can go without access to your system. Then set the acceptable amount of data loss from the most recent backup, or replication. Repeat this step for each system and you will soon realize which systems have the highest priorities and highest impact. Look back in history and identify types of outages the firm has experienced and how those outages were dealt with. If one is more relevant than another, plan for that incident first.

3. THE BUSINESS IMPACT ASSESSMENT (BIA)

A business impact assessment is a solution that determines critical business processes based on their impact during a disruption. An organization must define resilience requirements, justify business continuity investments, and identify a robust risk mitigation strategy. Unplanned disruptions can be costly, resulting in major losses, customer dissatisfaction, and compliance issues. To counter such risks, developing an effective, end-to-end business resilience plan is a necessary component to business continuity and recovery solutions.

Identifying Business-Critical Activities

An organization must have a thorough understanding of the critical business processes and the tolerance of a business outage to define objectives to succeed in the event of an outage. A successful solution employs a vertical and horizontal, or top/down approach to understand, identify, and map critical business processes, functions, IT systems, resource dependencies, and delivery channels. The organization must analyze the cost of disruptions and place them into resilience tiers to assist in defining operational availability and disaster recovery requirements from a business perspective.

Additionally, Recovery Point Objectives (RPOs) and Recovery Time Objectives (RTOs) are perhaps the most important key metrics when architecting a disaster recovery solution. An RTO is the amount of time it takes to recover from a disaster event, and an RPO is the amount of data, measured in time, that your organization lost from that same event. The two business-driven metrics will set the stage for:

- Media chosen to recover (disk, tape, etc.)
- Location where data is being recovered
- Size of the recovery infrastructure and staff needed

Keep in mind that there are several intricacies to consider when assessing RTOs and RPOs. First, the objective in both stands for "objective" and should be defined as the target. If an RPO is five hours, then the architecture must ensure data loss of five hours or less. Therefore, when testing or recovering from a disaster, document and track actual thresholds achieved, including recovery point and recovery time. In many test cases, the time to recover does not meet the objective due to overhead time. Examples of overhead time are as follows:

- Selection of staff and determination in DR teams
- Declaration of the disaster and logistics to the recovery site
- Consideration of massive chaos is involved in initiating a recovery from a disaster event

When tracking and documenting actual versus objective, especially during testing, you will understand what is being accomplished in a given period of time. Figure 55.2 illustrates a flowchart of conflict resolution in the BIA and shows how time can be calculated when following the flow of the dependencies. Ultimately, this will allow a firm to defend future investment by honing your recovery methodologies and processes to better meet or exceed those objectives. Once the recovered data is made available and back to the application, the end users and owners of the applications only understand the RPO and RTO specific to usability of the application with an understood and acceptable amount of data loss in a specified amount of time.

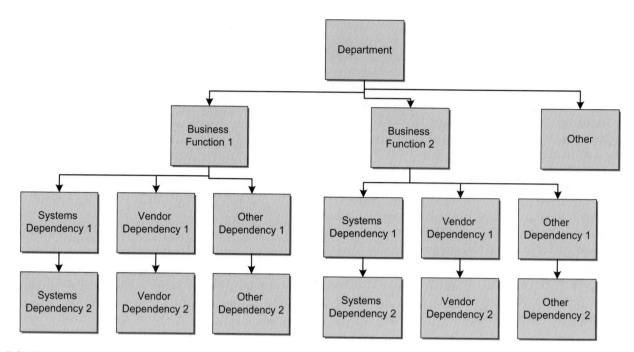

FIGURE 55.2 Flowchart illustrating the formula used to calculate the time a department receives items and performs actions prior to passing onto another department.

Specifying Required IT Support from Technical Staff

There are challenges associated with managing a high-density infrastructure coupled with the technology each department integrates into that infrastructure. To meet the continually increasing demand for faster, better, and more powerful technology, IT directors are deploying high-density equipment with great processing powers encompassing a small footprint in the data center.

Incongruent IT teams include storage, server, network, and application teams; all understand their specific roles in recovering from a disaster, which is why tests are so crucial. However, once the infrastructure is recovered with the associated application data, many more tasks are required to make the application usable and available to the end users. Consider, for example, what the DBAs need to do to the databases and what the application and software teams need to do in order to validate functionality. Thus, having these objects defined and metrics in place will help with the testing and checkpoints in the recovery process to ensure that the RTOs and RPOs are met successfully.

Designing Recovery Solutions

Many kinds of "disasters" can occur in business. Typically, one thinks mostly of natural disasters when one thinks of disasters. To do this when planning a disaster recovery solution is a fatal mistake. For example, consider a small company (or possibly even a large company!) where one or a small number of people control access to all data. Perhaps only one person has access to critical systems that, one day, may require reconfiguration or repair. What if that day comes sooner than expected, and what if that person was involved in a fatal car accident on the way to work? This sort of scenario and myriad others plague the information technology industry. The amount of risk tied up in IT director fiefdoms could, if exercised by a wide-scale disaster one day, bring about a nationwide business calamity. Think about the assorted systems that could be affected by the following "disasters:"

- Loss of bidirectional communication
- Loss of Internet connectivity
- Data loss
- Life lost

The final point, while not directly related to information technology and the preservation of business continuity through tragic, business-altering events is included because, at the heart of all the systems exist the human beings who operate and understand them. Recovery solutions should consider the human element. More importantly, a disaster recovery should be able to do just what the name implies—it should allow complete recovery, if not business continuity, through any disaster.

Consider, for example, a software company called Knowledge Inc. that provides critical software services to many of the Fortune 500 companies. On a Friday afternoon, a terrorist attack destroys their one, and only, location. The 400 + people who ran the company, except for those who were out sick or were on the road, are no more. Granted, the owner of the company has nothing to worry about anymore; he was in his office, but those 300 Fortune 500 companies, what about them? From their perspective, they are likely asking themselves why they never asked to see the DR plan for Knowledge Inc. They should have asked about the business recovery plan. Ostensibly, then, a DR plan contains two parts:

- Technology and data redundancy
- Business recovery

No business should ever *close down* due to a disaster. Yes, closing a business's books and winding down after a disaster could be the outcome of a disaster, but that should be a business decision, not a forced event. That is, the disaster itself, followed by a poorly executed or nonexistent DR plan, should not be a business-ending event. Closing the business or selling its assets may be the decision made by survivors and beneficiaries, but by preserving the business through proper DR planning, this should be just one of many options, not the only option after a disaster. As intimated earlier, disasters come in many forms, which can be loosely grouped into three categories:

1. Force Majeure
2. Conditional
3. Human

Force Majeure, or catastrophe, is obvious. Events such as hurricanes, earthquakes, fire, flood, war, volcanic eruptions, and terrorist acts all fall into this category.

Conditional is less obvious and revolves around the circumstances of an unexpected change in infrastructure conditions. For example, on a Monday afternoon, the Internet "goes down." Service doesn't' resume until Wednesday evening because it took that long for the service provider to find the problem. In another example, a construction crew saws through all three trunks that service the city of Chicago. As a result, 99% of the city loses its Internet. The other 1%? They had a recovery plan that included routing phones and Internet through a satellite dish on their roof.

The human category means loss of life and the business impact. For example, what if a strange new virus decimated more than half the organization's staff, and for some strange reason, it wiped out all but the most itinerant staff members, who have little knowledge of operations. A solid DR plan will consider that a disaster can occur, and all infrastructure may remain intact.

Establishing a Disaster Recovery Site

Once a disaster recovery plan has been created that includes both fail and no-fail infrastructure circumstances, a plan must be made that allows for varying degrees of infrastructure failure. For example, consider the conditions that must exist before someone says "Break out the black book!" and the organization *shifts* its mind-set into one of disaster recovery. For example, consider the following course of events:

1. The Internet goes down.
2. IT fails to back up Internet connections (there are three alternative paths to the Internet). Each path fails.
3. A DR link to the data center is powered up and established. This link is a point-to-point optical wireless linkup to the data center. There is no Internet at the data center either.
4. The DR link to the failover data center is powered up and established. This data center is also down.
5. Nobody knows what is happening yet, but one thing is certain: While the plan was okay, because there was even an alternative, nonphysical link to two data centers, one that was a failover site, it didn't help because the DR data center site was only a couple of miles from the primary.

In the event of a disaster, DR sites should be as logically separated from a catastrophe point of view as possible. To establish what makes a good DR site, let's explore disaster a little bit.

Site Choices: Configuration and Acquisition

Since this is a book about computer and information security, and not about business alternative planning, these next sections will focus primarily on force majeure and conditional disasters. The assumption it makes is that the business critical functions have been deemed complex and necessary enough that a geographically disparate location is desirable and necessary. For many, disaster recovery is about backup planning. A distinction between the two must be made. Backup and recovery addresses one thing, and only one thing: For example, a hacker accesses the system and deletes a small but critical table from a database. This is a backup and recovery option. You simply restore from backup, and you are up and running again. Disaster recovery is more severe, and it implies that the recovery of data after an incident that destroys equipment or data in tandem with an event of some sort has rendered equipment and communications at a particular site unusable. In this case the definition of unusable is one of a business nature:

- DR definition of *unusable*: Equipment or data or communications that are not functioning for such a length of time as to render irreparable damage to business revenues or relationships.

- *Unusable*, then, in the business sense, must be taken in the context of this sentence.
- Disaster recovery is a sequence of events that, regardless of extenuating circumstances, will restore the full functionality of data, communications, or equipment, located at some one site or many sites, that has been rendered unusable by some event.

Over time, some piece of equipment may become unserviceable, but in terms of disaster recovery, something is *unusable* only if its unserviceability inflicts damage on the business. Disaster recovery assumes one thing is true: that a major, business critical function has ceased operation due to one of the aforementioned reasons, and that it can no longer continue.

The following list details a number of disasters and chooses alternative locations. In the end, one may consider that the disaster is too unlikely to occur, and that if the disaster were to occur (such as an asteroid strike), there would likely be no point in continuing business anyway— simply surviving will be everyone's concern, and whether or not customers can purchase concert tickets will be moot if nobody is going to be going to concerts any time soon. Table 55.1 provides a sample listing of DR failover locations, the disaster that occurs, and the reason why it is a bad choice. This table seeks to provide a thought experiment framework whereby a planner may base a similar table for her location.

Choosing Suppliers: In-House Versus Third Party

As evidenced by Table 55.1, the complexity of choosing a DR location that is a perfect *ying* to your primary locations *yang* is not an easy task. If one assumes that the third-party provider has been in business for a while, has experience in the field, and is not just an investor who purchased an underground quarry in Kansas City and simply didn't know what to do with it, then the primary reason to contract a DR provider will be one of reliability.

Furthermore, the DR provider will host *other* companies, which means that they will likely be performing the sort of monthly and manual testing of their failover electrical and uplink capabilities that is required. This results in a savings due to the economy of scale. A company that has to test its systems understands that testing takes time, is expensive, and may result in unanticipated damage to equipment should a faulty failover mechanism result in a massive surge through the power grid.

Typically, businesses that aren't savvy or interested in the facts of disasters— that they do happen, and they can happen to them—may make a rather cursory attempt at DR. They may blend some non-DR site functions with the DR site. The mistake they make in doing this relates directly to redundancy—inherent to the DR strategy is that, essentially, both sites require each other to act as backup. If the DR site is being used, and it fails, it would need to failover to the primary site. Organizations that are greatly concerned about business

TABLE 55.1 The Portland Example Serves to Illustrate that While a Disaster Recovery Planned Site may Appear to be Perfectly Acceptable, even if Affected by Collateral After-Affects, the type of Infrastructure and the Routing of the Trunks, all May Play a Part. The ENTIRE Infrastructure of the Environment, and all the Unknown Interdependencies should be thoroughly Uncovered, Explored, and Understood.

Primary Site	Disaster	DR Location	Pass/Fail
Quad Cities	Flood	St. Louis	It flooded too.
Chicago	Military strike	New York	Communications in New York were also targeted.
Miami	Hurricane	Chicago	Pass.
San Francisco	Earthquake	San Jose	Fail. San Jose is under water.
Portland	Volcano	Seattle	Fail. The Seattle site depends on optical wireless, which are due to Portland's ash cloud and northerly winds.
New York	Tsunami	San Diego	Pass.
St. Louis	Tornado	Undisclosed location in Nevada	Pass. The use of a hardened, undisclosed location protects against additional threats, such as terrorist or military action, that may strike multiple communication centers simultaneously. With satellite uplinks, this location is ideal against myriad threats.

continuity will segregate business functions completely. When contracting a vendor to handle DR, the business will drive the requirements. Things like email, database applications, HR, and finance systems may not have the same impact of loss as, for example, a Web site that takes customer orders.

When building a DR plan, the planners must consider the scope of the disaster as well, how the vendor charges, and whether or not multiple vendors are required to fully comply with business needs. For example, for some companies, it is perfectly acceptable that employees could work for home in case the DR triggering event also closed the physical office. Other companies may have differing compliance issues and may require a secure facility. They may even require that employees travel to a distant location and work there. Now, arrangements have to be made for both PC access to network systems and food and lodging. This author recommends a nice resort that has conference center capabilities that could be set up to provide workstations. Do bear in mind that some employees will require family housing. Choosing to provision DR through in-house versus choosing an external vendor requires comparing and determining a number of factors:

- Skills—Decide whether or not the IT team has the skills and the time (or can hire someone.)

- Location—Determine whether or not the location is suitable. For example, a large law firm may already have multiple data centers. It begins to make sense to handle disaster recovery internally if the company is not segmented in such a way that use of its multiple data centers will cause internal turmoil (this speaks to the IT fiefdoms alluded to earlier.)

- Estimated downtime—The definition of a disaster has already been described as involving the length of the downtime. How much further past the qualifying outage window is tolerable? If the best that internal resources can do is 24 hours to get a remote DR site functional and the requirement is 2 hours, outside help should be sought.

Figure 55.3 diagrams a failover site. Data flows are unidirectional *to* the DR site. It is a common fallacy that the DR site can also provide some functionality to the enterprise and serve as more than just a graveyard for servers, waiting for the day they must spring to life and perform a critical duty.

Specifying Equipment

The challenge of a DR site is primarily cost, followed closely by configuration. Setting it up, planning redundancy, creating strategies for rerouting voice, messaging,

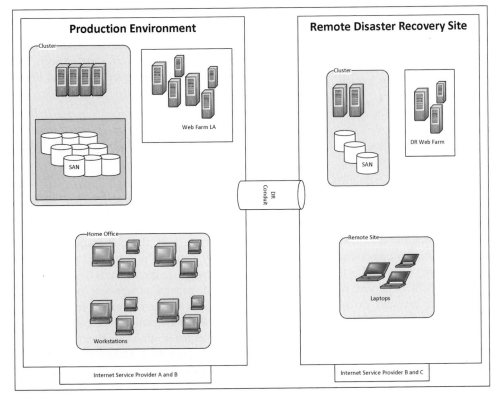

FIGURE 55.3 In a DR site, one can expect to see a slimming down of the amount of equipment needed. Configuring applications to work in such an environment will be a balance between labor costs and estimates of configuration time and the cost of additional servers. Rewriting application code to force a distributed application to work with a reduced server requirement may not be cost effective.

email, delivery of goods, and so on are things that can be written and kept within arm's reach of all employees. ALL employees should be aware of the DR plan. No single employee should be left wondering what his role is during a disaster.

Configuration and cost are closely related. In just one example (of many similar), consider a complex federated database where many applications and many databases commingle information and exist in harmony on a home-grown system across 30 or 40 SQL servers. Picking up something so complex, and moving it, is not a simple task. It may take many weeks of reconfiguration to get such as system to be functional at the DR site. The complexity of an application and the ease of setting it up in a DR site should always be considered *during the purchasing and application review phase*. Waiting until afterwards to think about the DR site can be a very costly mistake. A DR-ready application will be able to collapse down to just a couple of servers and will be able to provide core functionality, with additional functionality brought online with the addition of more servers as needed.

A DR site is a site that is to be used for a temporary period of time. Typically, the hope is that the DR failover will not be permanent. However, this should be a planned contingency—that it will be permanent and that you may need to rapidly scale the environment. This is not to say that a DR site should be a fully functional, duplicate site of the primary site that failed. Rather, it should be able to support essential business functions. Suppose, for example, an enterprise that hosts a document review platform. Many people would like to access the system, but in the contract with its clients, the business is only committed to support minimal, required activities, and they are listed. Contractually, activity should be restricted. Only known, business-critical activity should be conducted. Users should only be performing activities that are business critical for them or their customers.

From an equipment purchasing standpoint, then, only minimal hardware need be purchased. Some companies may even refer to their DR site as "the graveyard" and the DR plan as a "Dawn of the Dead" plan. However, from a strategic standpoint, rack space MUST be available for rapid growth. Should the disaster become lengthy, or should the outage be permanent, the enterprise must be able to scale rapidly. Many business computing sales companies will configure a "standing order." This is something that, for a price, can be held in a sort of "escrow" until needed. When an outage becomes extensive, or permanent, or is recognized as being permanent the moment it happened, then pulling the trigger on such an order could actually be automatic and scripted in the failover plan. After all, in the event of a Dawn of the Dead, the graveyard will need to be fed more brains.

4. SUMMARY

Creating an effective, risk-biased, deployable DR plan that carefully considers human and technology interests takes time and attention. The solution to just about all DR issues that crop up will be to *spend more money*. This is where the art of it, and the experience of the designers, will either make or break the plan. Inexperienced planners may make assumptions and will overlook critical aspects of how to deploy the plan. They may not take it seriously, but as has been seen in recent history, *expect the worst*. Maintaining a heightened state of awareness is the rule of the day. Experienced IT professionals will be able to design a plan that is effective.

These authors recommend that a disaster recovery team be made up of the most senior people in the company—people who have been with the company for a long time and know its every system inside and out. These are people who should have ten or more years of experience in IT, if not with the company itself. These are the people who can ensure that, should a disaster occur, business will continue—because they are the ones doing this work already— they are the ones who are called when something is broken and nobody else can get it right. They are the ones who can unclog a plugged firewall, who have the part number for that odd LED in the service rack memorized, and they are the ones who could, if needed, rebuild the entire infrastructure from scratch, preferably while they sleep. Essentially, that is what DR is. It is an essential-function rebuilding of the entire company. Asking it to be anything less is simply asking for failure.

Finally, let's move on to the real interactive part of this chapter: review questions/exercises, hands-on projects, case projects, and optional team case project. The answers and/or solutions by chapter can be found in the Online Instructor's Solutions Manual.

CHAPTER REVIEW QUESTIONS/EXERCISES

True/False

1. True or False? Disaster recovery (DR), not unlike the plugged sink, is another task that many organizations fail to consider until after much of the technology groundwork has been laid, the corporation is profitable, and suddenly someone realizes that *not* having a DR site is a serious risk to the business.
2. True or False? A general component of a disaster recovery (DR) plan is for the committee to assess conceivable risks to the organization that could result in the disasters or emergency situations themselves.
3. True or False? Enterprise Risk Management (ERM) is not a template that can be given to every company to meet their needs and fit their business structure.

4. True or False? Downtime presents moderate consequences for businesses, no matter what their function may be.

5. True or False? A business impact assessment is a solution that determines critical business processes based on their impact during a disruption.

Multiple Choice

1. An organization must have a thorough understanding of the _____ and the tolerance of a business outage to define objectives to succeed in the event of an outage.
   A. qualitative analysis
   B. vulnerabilities
   C. critical business processes
   D. malformed request DoS
   E. data controller

2. There are challenges associated with managing a _____, coupled with the technology each department integrates into that infrastructure.
   A. network attached storage (NAS)
   B. risk assessment
   C. valid
   D. high-density infrastructure
   E. bait

3. There are many types of _____ that can occur in business.
   A. data minimization
   B. fabric
   C. disasters
   D. risk communication
   E. security

4. Once a disaster recovery plan has been created that includes both fail and no-fail infrastructure circumstances, a plan must be made that allows for varying degrees of:
   A. risk management
   B. greedy strategy
   C. infrastructure failure
   D. SAN protocol
   E. taps

5. What are equipment or data or communications that are not functioning for such a length of time as to render irreparable damage to business revenues or relationships?
   A. Irrelevant
   B. Tape library
   C. IP storage access
   D. Configuration file
   E. Unusable

EXERCISE

Problem

What are the differences among a Continuity of Operations Plan (COOP), a Business Continuity Plan (BCP), a Critical Infrastructure Protection (CIP) Plan, a Disaster Recovery Plan (DRP), an Information System Contingency Plan (ISCP), a Cyber Incident Response Plan, and an Occupant Emergency Plan (OEP)?

Hands-On Projects

Project

What type of alternate site should an organization choose as a disaster recovery strategy?

Case Projects

Problem

When an event occurs, who should be notified?

Optional Team Case Project

Problem

With what other activities should the ISCP and the recovery solutions be coordinated?

## Chapter 56

Biometrics

Luther Martin
Voltage Security

Biometrics is the analysis of biological observations and phenomena. People routinely use biometrics to recognize other people, commonly using the shape of a face or the sound of a voice to do so. Biometrics can also be used to create automated ways of recognizing a person based on her physiological or behavioral characteristics. Using biometrics as the basis of technologies that can be used to recognize people is not a new idea; there is evidence that fingerprints were used to sign official contracts in China as early as AD 700 and may have been used by ancient Babylonian scribes to sign cuneiform tablets as early as 2000 BC.[1] In both of these cases, a fingerprint was pressed in clay to form a distinctive mark that could characterize a particular person. It is likely that the sophistication of the techniques used to analyze biometric data has increased over the past 4000 years, but the principles have remained essentially the same.

Using biometrics in security applications is certainly appealing. Determining a person's identity through the presence of a physical object such as a key or access card has the problem that the physical token can be lost or stolen. Shared secrets such as passwords can be forgotten. Determining a person's identity using biometrics seems an attractive alternative. It allows an identity to be determined directly from characteristics of the person. It is generally impossible for people to lose or forget their biometric data, so many of the problems that other means of verifying an identity are essentially eliminated if biometrics can be used in this role.

Not all biometric data is suitable for use in security applications, however. To be useful, such biometric data should be as unique as possible (uniqueness), should occur in as many people as possible (universality), should stay relatively constant over time (permanence), and should be able to be measured easily (measurability) and without causing undue inconvenience or distress to a user (acceptability). Examples of technologies that seem to meet these criteria to varying degrees are those that

recognize a person based on his DNA, geometry of his face, fingerprints, hand geometry, iris pattern, retina pattern, handwriting, or voice. Many others are also possible. Not all biometrics are equally suited for use in security applications. Table 56.1 compares the properties of selected biometric technologies, rating each property as high, medium, or low. This table shows that there is no "best" biometric for security applications. Though this is true, each biometric has a set of uses for which its particular properties make it more attractive than the alternatives.

Biometrics systems can be used as a means of authenticating a user. When they are used in this way, a user presents his biometric data along with his identity, and the biometric system decides whether or not the biometric data presented is correct for that identity. Biometrics used as a method of authentication can be very useful, but authentication systems based on biometrics also have very different properties from other authentication technologies, and these differences should be understood before biometrics are used as part of an information security system.

Systems based on biometrics can also be used as a means of identification. When they are used in this way, captured biometric data is compared to entries in a database, and the biometric system determines whether or not the biometric data presented matches any of these existing entries. When biometrics are used for identification, they have a property that many other identification systems do not have. In particular, biometrics do not always require the active participation of a subject. While a user always needs to enter her password when the password is used to authenticate her, it is possible to capture biometric data without the user's active involvement, perhaps even without her knowledge. This lets data be used in ways that other systems cannot. It is possible to automatically capture images of customers in a bank, for example, and to use the images to help identify people who are known to commit check fraud. Or it is possible to automatically capture images of airline passengers in an airport and use the images to help identify suspicious travelers.

---

1. R. Heindl, *System und Praxis der Daktyloskopie und der sonstigen technischen Methoden der Kriminalpolizei*, De Gruyter, 1922.

TABLE 56.1 Overview of Selected Biometric Technologies.

Biometric	Uniqueness	Universality	Permanence	Measurability	Acceptability
DNA	High	High	High	Low	Low
Face geometry	Low	High	Medium	High	High
Fingerprint	High	Medium	High	Medium	Medium
Hand geometry	Medium	Medium	Medium	High	Medium
Iris	High	High	High	Medium	Low
Retina	High	High	Medium	Low	Low
Signature dynamics	Low	Medium	Low	High	High
Voice	Low	Medium	Low	Medium	High

The use of biometrics for identification also has the potential to pose serious privacy issues. The interests of governments and individual citizens are often at odds. Law enforcement agencies might want to be able to track the movements of certain people, and the automated use of biometrics for identification can certainly support this goal. On the other hand, it is unlikely that most people would approve of law enforcement having a database that contains detailed information about their travels. Similarly, tax authorities might want to track all business dealings to ensure that they collect all the revenue they are due, but it seems unlikely that most people would approve of government agencies having a database that tracks all merchants they have had dealings with, even if no purchases were made. Using some biometrics may also inherently provide access to much more information that is needed to just identify a person. DNA, for example, can used to identify people, but it can also be used to determine information about genetic conditions that are irrelevant to the identification process. But if a user needs to provide a DNA sample as a means of identification, the same DNA sample could be used to determine genetic information that the user might rather have kept private.

Designing biometric systems has been dubbed a "grand challenge" by researchers,[2] indicating that a significant level of research will be required before it will be possible for real systems to approach the performance that is expected of the technology, but one that also has the possibility for broad scientific and economic impact when technology finally reaches that level. So, although biometric systems are useful today, we should expect to see them become even more useful in the future and for the technology to eventually become fairly commonly used.

2. A. Jain, et al., "Biometrics: A grand challenge," *Proceedings of the 17th International Conference on Pattern Recognition*, Cambridge, UK, August 2004, pp. 935–942.

1. RELEVANT STANDARDS

The American National Standard (ANS) X9.84, "Biometric Information Management and Security for the Financial Services Industry," is one of the leading standards that provide an overview of biometrics and their use in information security systems. It is a good high-level discussion of biometric systems, and the description of the technology in this chapter roughly follows the framework defined by this standard. This standard is particularly useful to system architects and others concerned with a high-level view of security systems. On the other hand, this standard does not provide many details of how to implement such systems.

There are also several international (ISO/IEC) standards that cover the details of biometric systems with more detail than ANS X9.84 does. These are listed in Table 56.2. These standards provide a good basis for implementing biometric systems and may be useful to both engineers and others who need to build a biometric system, and others who need the additional level of detail that ANS X9.84 does not provide. Many other ISO/IEC standards for biometric systems are currently under development that address other aspects of such systems, and in the next few years it is likely that the number of these standards that have been finalized will at least double from the number that are listed here. The JTC 1/SC 37 technical committee of the ISO is responsible for the development of these standards.

2. BIOMETRIC SYSTEM ARCHITECTURE

All biometric systems have a number of common subsystems. These are the following:

- A data capture subsystem
- A signal processing subsystem

TABLE 56.2 Current ISO/I EC Standards for Biometric Systems.

Standard	Title
ISO/IEC 19784-1:2006	Information technology – Biometric Application Programming Interface – Part 1: BioAPI Specification
ISO/IEC 19784-2:2007	Information technology – Biometric Application Programming Interface – Part 2: Biometric Archive Function Provider Interface
ISO/IEC 19785-1:2006	Information technology – Common Biometric Exchange Formats Framework (CBEFF) – Part 1: Data Element Specification
ISO/IEC 19785-2:2006	Information technology – Common Biometric Exchange Formats Framework (CBEFF) – Part 2: Procedures for the Operation of the Biometric Registration Authority
ISO/IEC 19794-1:2006	Information technology – Biometric data interchange format – Part 1: Framework
ISO/IEC 19794-2:2005	Information technology – Biometric data interchange format – Part 2: Finger minutiae data
ISO/IEC 19794-3:2006	Information technology – Biometric data interchange format – Part 3: Finger pattern spectral data
ISO/IEC 19794-4:2005	Information technology – Biometric data interchange format – Part 4: Finger image data
ISO/IEC 19794-5:2005	Information technology – Biometric data interchange format – Part 5: Face image data
ISO/IEC 19794-6:2005	Information technology – Biometric data interchange format – Part 6: Iris image data
ISO/IEC 19794-7:2006	Information technology – Biometric data interchange format – Part 7: Signature/sign time series data
ISO/IEC 19794-8:2006	Information technology – Biometric data interchange format – Part 8: Finger pattern skeletal data
ISO/IEC 19794-9:2007	Information technology – Biometric data interchange format – Part 9: Vascular image data
ISO/IEC 19795-1:2006	Information technology – Biometric performance testing and reporting – Part 1: Principles and framework
ISO/IEC 19795-2:2007	Information technology – Biometric performance testing and reporting – Part 2: testing methodologies for technology and scenario evaluation
ISO/IEC 24709.1: 2007	BioAPI Conformance Testing – Part 1: Methods and Procedures
ISO/IEC 24709.2: 2007	BioAPI Conformance Testing – Part 2: Test Assertions for Biometric Service Providers

- A matching subsystem
- A data storage subsystem
- A decision subsystem

An additional subsystem, the adaptation subsystem, may be present in some biometric systems but not others.

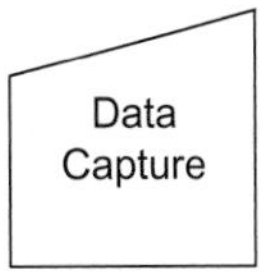

FIGURE 56.1   Symbol used to indicate a data capture subsystem.

Data Capture

A data capture subsystem collects captured biometric data from a user. To do this, it performs a measurement of some sort and creates machine-readable data from it. This could be an image of a fingerprint, a signal from a microphone, or readings from a special pen that takes measurements while it is being used. In each case, the captured biometric data usually needs to be processed in some way before it can be used in a decision algorithm. It is extremely rare for a biometric system to make a decision using an image of a fingerprint, for example. Instead, features that make fingerprints different from other fingerprints are extracted from such an image in the signal

processing subsystem, and these features are then used in the matching subsystem. The symbol that is used to indicate a data capture subsystem is shown in Figure 56.1.

The performance of a data capture subsystem is greatly affected by the characteristics of the sensor that it uses. A signal processing subsystem may work very well with one type of sensor, but much less well with another type. Even if identical sensors are used in each data capture subsystem, the calibration of the sensors may need to be consistent to ensure the collection of data that works well in other subsystems.

Environmental conditions can also significantly affect the operation of a data capture subsystem. Dirty sensors can result in images of fingerprints that are distorted or incomplete. Background noise can result in the collection of a data that makes it difficult for the signal processing subsystem to identify the features of a voice signal. Lighting can also affect any biometric data that is collected as an image so that an image collected against a gray background might not work as well as an image collected against a white background.

Because environmental conditions affect the quality and usefulness of captured biometric data, they also affect the performance of all the subsystems that rely on it. This means that it is essential to carry out all testing of biometric systems under conditions that duplicate the conditions under which the system will normally operate (see checklist, "An Agenda For Action For Biometrics Testing"). Just because a biometric system performs well in a testing laboratory when operated by well-trained users does not mean that it will perform well in real-world conditions. Because the data capture subsystem is typically the only one with which users directly interact, it is also the one that may require training of users to ensure that it provides useful data to the other subsystems.

Signal Processing

A signal processing subsystem takes the captured biometric data from a data capture subsystem and transforms the data into a form suitable for use in the matching subsystem. This transformed data is called a *reference*, or a *template* if it is stored in a data storage subsystem. A template is a type of reference, and it represents the average value that we expect to see for a particular user.

A signal processing subsystem may also analyze the quality of captured biometric data and reject data that is not of high enough quality. An image of a fingerprint that is not oriented correctly might be rejected, or a sample of speech that was collected with too much background noise might be rejected. The symbol that is used to indicate a signal processing subsystem is shown in Figure 56.2.

If the captured biometric data is not rejected, the signal processing subsystem then transforms the captured biometric data into a reference. In the case of fingerprints, for example, the signal processing subsystem may extract features such as the locations of branches and endpoints of the ridges that comprise a fingerprint. A biometric system that uses the speech of users to characterize them might convert the speech signal into frequency components using a Fourier transform and then look for patterns in the frequency components that uniquely characterize a particular speaker. A biometric that uses an image of a person's face might first look for large features such as the eyes, nose, and mouth and then look for distinctive features such as eyebrows or parts of the nose relative to the large ones, to uniquely identify a particular user. In

FIGURE 56.2   Symbol used to indicate a signal processing subsystem.

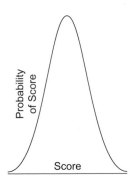

FIGURE 56.3   Distribution in comparison scores for a typical user.

any case, the output of the signal processing subsystem is the transformed data that comprises a reference. Although a reference contains information that has been extracted from captured biometric data, it may be possible to recover the captured biometric data, or a good approximation to it, from a template.[3]

Note that though several standards exist that define the format of biometric references for many technologies, these standards do not describe how references are obtained from captured biometric data. This means that there is still room for vendor innovation while remaining in compliance with existing standards.

Matching

A matching subsystem receives a reference from a signal processing subsystem and then compares the reference with a template from a data storage subsystem. The output of the matching subsystem is a numeric value called a *comparison score* that indicates how closely the two match.

Random variations occur in a data capture subsystem when it is used. This means that the reference created from the captured data is different each time, even for the same user. This makes the comparison score created for a particular user different each time they use the system, with random variations occurring around some average value. This concept is shown in Figure 56.3, in which the distribution of comparison scores that are calculated from

3. M. Martinez-Diaz, et al., "Hill-climbing and brute-force attacks on biometric systems: A case study in match-on-card fingerprint verification," *Proceedings of the 40th IEEE International Carahan Conference on Security Technology*, Lexington, October 2006, pp. 151–159.

An Agenda for Action for Biometrics Testing

Steps in technical requirements for biometrics testing accreditation (Check All Tasks Completed):

Personnel:

_____1. The laboratory shall maintain competent administrative and technical staff that are :

    _____**a.** Knowledgeable of all biometrics standards pertaining to the specific tests found on the laboratory's scope(s) of accreditation.

    _____**b.** Familiar with the biometrics terminology, biometrics modalities, biometrics systems and sub-systems.

    _____**c.** Familiar with the "acceptable use" (collection, storage, handling, etc.) of Personally Identifiable Information (PII) as described in federal and state laws.

    _____**d.** Familiar with the biometrics products testing protocols, procedures and tools, when applicable.

    _____**e.** Familiar with human-crew interaction and human-crew rights and responsibilities, when applicable.

_____2. The laboratory shall maintain a list of personnel designated to fulfill requirements including:

    _____**a.** Laboratory's director

    _____**b.** Authorized Representative

    _____**c.** Approved Signatories

    _____**d.** team leaders

    _____**e.** Key technical persons in the laboratory

_____3. The laboratory shall identify a staff member as quality manager with overall responsibility for quality assurance and for maintenance of the quality manual. An individual may be assigned or appointed to serve in more than one position; however, to the extent possible, the laboratory director and the quality manager positions should be independently staffed.

_____4. The laboratory key technical personnel who conduct biometrics products testing activities shall have at least a Bachelor of Science in Computer Science, Computer Engineering, Electrical Engineering, Human Factors or similar technical discipline or equivalent experience.

_____5. Laboratory staff collectively shall have knowledge of or experience in the following areas:

    _____**a.** Biometrics modalities available.

    _____**b.** Design/analysis of biometrics systems and sub-systems.

    _____**c.** Database systems.

    _____**d.** Biometrics products testing protocols and procedures.

    _____**e.** Biometrics data structures.

    _____**f.** Biometrics standards and special publications referenced in this handbook.

    _____**g.** Familiarity with operating systems under which the biometrics systems are operating.

    _____**h.** Any specific technology upon which testing is conducted.

_____6. The laboratory shall have documented a detailed description of its training program for new and current staff members. Each new staff member shall be trained for assigned duties.

_____7. The training program shall be updated and current staff members shall be retrained when relevant standards or scope of accreditation changes, or when the individuals are assigned new responsibilities. Each staff member may receive training for assigned duties either through on-the-job training, formal classroom study, attendance at conferences, or another appropriate mechanism.

_____8. Training materials that are maintained within the laboratory shall be kept up-to-date.

_____9. The laboratory shall have a competency review program and procedures for the evaluation and maintenance of the competency of each staff member for each test method the staff member is authorized to conduct.

_____10. An evaluation and an observation of performance shall be conducted annually for each staff member by the immediate supervisor or a designee appointed by the laboratory director.

_____11. A record of the annual evaluation of each staff member shall be dated and signed by the supervisor and the employee.

_____12. A description of competency review programs shall be maintained in the management system.

_____13. If the mechanism by which the laboratory employs staff members is through contracting, any key personnel who are contractors shall be identified and listed in the laboratory's application for accreditation.

_____14. If the mechanism by which the laboratory employs staff members is through contracting, any key personnel who are contractors shall be identified and listed in the laboratory's application for accreditation.

_____15. The laboratory personnel who handle PII documents shall obey all laboratory policies and procedures that implement the federal and state privacy laws that stress the "acceptable uses" of PII.

repeated captures of biometric data from a single user are random. Such random data tend to be close to an average value every time that they are calculated from captured biometric data but not exactly the average value.

This is much like the case we get in other situations where observed data has a random component. Suppose that we flip a fair coin 100 times and count how many times the result "heads" appears. We expect to see this result an average of 50 times, but this average value actually occurs fairly rarely; exactly 50 out of 100 flips coming up heads happen less than 8% of the time. On the other hand, the number of heads will usually be not too far from the average value of 50, with the number being between 40 and 60 more than 95% of the time. Similarly, with biometrics, captured data will probably be close, but not identical, to an average value, and it will also not be too different from the average value.

The comparison score calculated by a matching subsystem is passed to a decision subsystem, where it is used to make a decision about the identity of the person who was the source of the biometric data. The symbol that is used to indicate a matching subsystem is shown in Figure 56.4.

Data Storage

A data storage subsystem stores templates that are used by the matching subsystem. The symbol that is used to indicate a data storage subsystem is shown in Figure 56.5.

A database is one obvious candidate for a place to store templates, but it is possible to store a template on a portable data storage device such as a chip card or a smart card. The relative strengths and weaknesses of different ways of doing this are discussed in the section on security considerations.

Decision

A decision subsystem takes a comparison score that is the output of a matching subsystem and returns a binary

yes or no decision from it. This decision indicates whether or not the matching subsystem made a comparison which resulted in a match or not. The value yes is returned if the comparison was probably a match; the value no is returned is the comparison was probably not a match. The symbol that is used to indicate a decision subsystem is shown in Figure 56.6.

To make a yes or no decision, a decision subsystem compares a comparison score with a parameter called a threshold. The threshold value represents a measure of how good a comparison needs to be to be considered a match. If the comparison score is less than or equal to the threshold value then the decision subsystem returns the value yes. If the comparison score is greater than the threshold, it returns the value no. Comparison scores that will result in a yes or no response from a decision subsystem are shown in Figure 56.7. Comparison scores in the gray area of this illustration are close to the average value and result in a yes, whereas comparison scores that are outside the gray area are too far from the average value and result in a no. In Figure 56.7, the threshold value defines how far the gray area extends from the central average value. If the threshold is decreased, the size of the gray area will get narrower and decrease in size so that fewer comparison scores result in a yes answer. If the threshold is increased, the gray area will get wider and increase in size so that more comparison scores result in a yes answer.

Errors may occur in any decision subsystem. There are two general types of errors that can occur. In one

FIGURE 56.6   Symbol used to indicate a decision subsystem.

FIGURE 56.4   Symbol used to indicate a matching subsystem.

FIGURE 56.5   Symbol used to indicate a data storage subsystem.

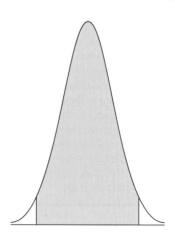

FIGURE 56.7   Comparison scores close to the average that result in a yes decision.

case, a decision subsystem makes the incorrect decision of *no* instead of *yes*. In this case, a user is indeed who she claims to be, but large random errors occur in the data capture subsystem and cause her to be incorrectly rejected. This type of error might result in the legitimate user Alice inaccurately failing to authenticate as herself.

This class of error is known as a *type*-1 error by statisticians,[4] a term that would almost certainly be a contender for an award for the least meaningful terminology ever invented if such an award existed. It was once called *false rejection* by biometrics researchers and vendors, a term that has more recently been replaced by the term *false nonmatch*. One way in which the accuracy of biometric systems is now typically quantified is by their false non-match rate (FNMR), a value that estimates the probability of the biometric system making a type-1 error in its decision subsystem.

In the second case, a decision subsystem incorrectly returns a *yes* instead of a no. In this case, random errors occur that let a user be erroneously recognized as a different user. This might happen if the user Alice tries to authenticate as the user Bob, for example. This class of error is known as a *type*-2 error by statisticians.[5] It was once called *false acceptance* by biometrics researchers and vendors, a term that has been more recently been replaced by the term *false match*. This leads to quantifying the accuracy of biometrics by their false match rate (FMR), a value that estimates the probability of the biometric system making a type-2 error.

For a particular biometric technology, it is impossible to simultaneously reduce both the FNMR and the FMR, although improving the technology does make it possible to do this. If the parameters used in a matching subsystem are changed so that the FNMR decreases, the FMR rate must increase; if the parameters used in a matching subsystem are changed so that the FMR decreases, the FNMR must increase. This relationship follows from the nature of the statistical tests that are performed by the decision subsystem and is not limited to just biometric systems. Any system that makes a decision based on statistical data will have the same property. The reason for this is shown in Figures 56.8 and 56.9.

Suppose that we have two users of a biometric system: Alice and Bob, whose comparison scores are distributed as shown in Figure 56.8. Note that the distributions of these values overlap so that in the area where they overlap, the comparison score could have come from either

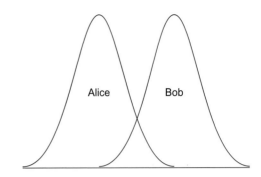

FIGURE 56.8   Overlap in possible comparison scores for Alice and Bob.

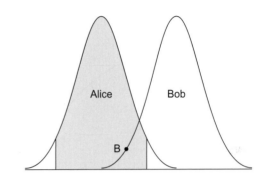

FIGURE 56.9   Type-2 error that causes a false match.

Alice or Bob, but we cannot tell which. If the average values that we expect for Alice and Bob are far enough apart, the chances of this happening may get extremely low, but even in such cases it is possible to have large enough errors creep into the data capture step to make even the rarest of errors possible.

Figure 56.9 shows how a false match can occur. Suppose that Bob uses our hypothetical biometric system but claims to be Alice when he does this, and the output of the matching subsystem is the point B that is shown in Figure 56.9. Because this point is close enough to the average that we expect from biometric data from Alice, the decision subsystem will erroneously decide that the biometric data that Bob presented is good enough to authenticate him as Alice. This is a false match, and it contributes to the FMR of the system.

Figure 56.10 shows how a false nonmatch can occur. Suppose that Alice uses our hypothetical biometric system and the output of the matching subsystem is the point A that is shown in Figure 56.10. Because this point is too far from the average that we expect when Alice uses the system, it is more likely to have come from someone else other than from Alice, and the decision subsystem will erroneously decide that the biometric data that Alice presented is probably not hers. This is a false nonmatch, and it contributes to the FNMR of the system.

Because the FNMR and FMR are related, the most meaningful way to represent the accuracy of a biometric

4. J. Neyman and E. Pearson, "On the use and interpretation of certain test criteria for purposes of statistical inference: Part I," *Biometrika*, Vol. 20 A, No. 1−2, pp. 175−240, July 1928.

5. S. King, H. Harrelson and G. Tran, "Testing iris and face recognition in a personnel identification application," 2002 Biometric Consortium Conference, February 2002.

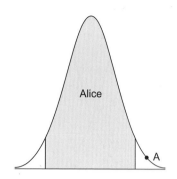

FIGURE 56.10 Type-1 error that causes a false nonmatch.

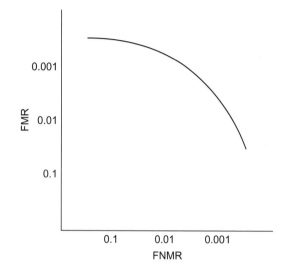

FIGURE 56.11 ROC for a hypothetical biometric system.

system is probably by showing the relationship between the two error rates. The relationship between the two is known by the term *receiver operating characteristic*, or ROC, a term that originated in the study of the sensitivity of radio receivers as their operating parameters change. Figure 56.11 shows an ROC curve for a hypothetical biometric. Such an ROC curve assumes that the only way in which the error rates are changed is by changing the threshold value that is used in the decision subsystem. Note that this ROC curve indicates that when the FMR increases the FNMR decreases, and vice versa.

By adjusting the threshold that a decision subsystem uses it is possible to make the FMR very low while allowing the FNMR to get very high or to allow the FMR to get very high while making the FNMR very low. Between these two extreme cases lies the case where the FMR and the FNMR are the same. This point is sometimes the equal error rate (EER) or crossover error rate (CER) and is often used to simplify the discussions of error rates for biometric systems.

Though using a single value does indeed make it easier to compare the performance of different biometric

systems, it can also be somewhat misleading. In high-security applications like those used by government or military organizations, keeping unauthorized users out may be much more important than the inconvenience caused by a high FNMR. In consumer applications, like ATMs, it may be more important to keep the FNMR low. This can help avoid the anger and accompanying support costs of dealing with customers who are incorrectly denied access to their accounts. In such situations, a low FNMR may be more important than the higher security that a higher FMR would provide. The error rates that are acceptable are strongly dependent on how the technology is being used, so be wary of trying to understand the performance of a biometric system by only considering the CER.

There is no theoretical way to accurately estimate the FMR and FNMR of biometric systems, so all estimates of these error rates need to be made from empirical data. Because testing can be expensive, the sample sizes used in such testing are often relatively small, so the results may not be representative of larger and more general populations. This is further complicated by the fact that some of the error rates that such testing attempts to estimate are fairly low. This means that human error from mislabeling data or other mistakes that occur during testing may make a bigger contribution to the measured error rates than the errors caused by a decision subsystem. It may be possible to create a biometric system that makes an error roughly only one time in 1 million operations, for example, but it is unrealistic to expect such high accuracy from the people who handle the data in an experiment that tries to estimate such an error rate. And because there are no standardized sample sizes and test conditions for estimating these error rates, there can be a wide range of reliability of error rate estimates. In one study,[5] a biometric system that performed well in a laboratory setting when used by trained users ended up correctly identifying enrolled users only 51% of the time when it was tested in a pilot project under real-world conditions, perhaps inviting an unenviable comparison with a system that recognizes a person by his ability to flip a coin and have it come up heads. Because of these effects, estimates of error rates should be viewed with a healthy amount of skepticism, particularly when extremely low rates are claimed.

Adaptation

Some biometric data changes over time. This may result in matches with a template becoming worse and worse over time, which will increase the FNMR of a biometric system. One way to avoid the potential difficulties associated with having users eventually becoming unrecognizable is to update their template after a successful authentication.

This process is called *adaptation*, and it is done by an optional part of a biometric system called an adaptation subsystem. If an adaptation subsystem is present, the symbol shown in Figure 56.12 is used to indicate it.

3. USING BIOMETRIC SYSTEMS

There are three main operations that a biometric system can perform. These are the following.

- *Enrollment.* During this operation, a biometric system creates a template that is used in later authentication and identification operations. This template, along with an associated identity, is stored in a data storage subsystem.
- *Authentication.* During this operation, a biometric system collects captured biometric data and a claimed identity and determines whether or not the captured biometric data matches the template stored for that identity. Although the term *authentication* is almost universally used in the information security industry for this operation, the term *verification* is often used by biometrics vendors and researchers to describe this.
- *Identification.* During this operation, a biometric system collects captured biometric data and attempts to find a match against any of the templates stored in a data storage subsystem.

Enrollment

Before a user can use a biometric system for either authentication or identification, a data storage subsystem needs to contain a template for the user. The process of initializing a biometric system with such a template is called *enrollment*, and it is the source of another error

Adaptation

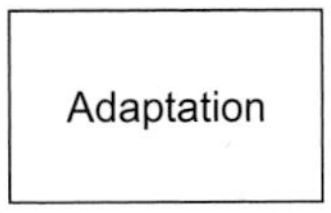

FIGURE 56.12 Symbol used to indicate an adaptation subsystem.

rate that can limit the usefulness of biometric systems. The interaction of the subsystems of a biometric system when enrolling a user is shown in Figure 56.13.

In the first step of enrollment, a user presents his biometric data to a data capture subsystem. The captured biometric data is then converted into a reference by a signal processing subsystem. This reference is then stored in a data storage subsystem, at which point it becomes a template. Such a template is typically calculated from several captures of biometric data to ensure that it reflects an accurate average value. An optional step includes using a matching subsystem to ensure that the user is not already enrolled.

The inherent nature of some captured biometric data as well as the randomness of captured biometric data can cause the enrollment process to fail. Some people have biometrics that are far enough outside the normal range of such data that they cause a signal processing subsystem to fail when it attempts to convert their captured data into a reference. The same types of random errors that contribute to the FMR and FNMR are also present in the enrollment process, and can be sometimes be enough to turn captured biometric data that would normally be within the range that the signal processing subsystem can handle into data that is outside this range. In some cases, it may even be impossible to collect some types of biometric data from some users, like the case where missing hands make it impossible to collect data on the geometry of the missing hands.

The probability of a user failing in the enrollment process is used to calculate the failure to enroll rate (FER). Almost any biometric can fail sometimes, either temporarily or permanently. Dry air or sticky fingers can cause fingerprints to temporarily change. A cold can cause a voice to temporarily become hoarse. A broken arm can temporarily change the way a person writes his signature. Cataracts can permanently make retina patterns impossible to capture. Some skin diseases can even permanently change fingerprints.

A useful biometric system should have a low FER, but because all such systems have a nonzero value for

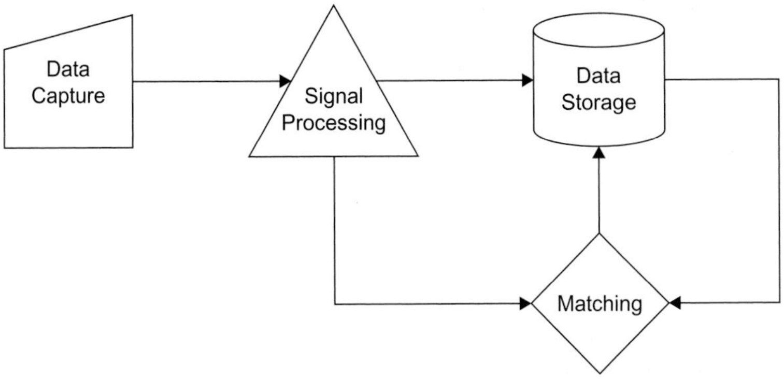

FIGURE 56.13 Enrollment in a biometric system.

this rate, it is likely that there will always be some users that cannot be enrolled in any particular biometric system, and a typical FER for a biometric system may be in the range of 1% to 5%. For this reason, biometric systems are often more useful as an additional means of authentication in multifactor authentication system instead of the single method used.

Authentication

After a user is enrolled in a biometric system, the system can be used to authenticate this user. The interaction of the subsystems of a biometric system when used to authenticate a user is shown in Figure 56.14.

To use a biometric system for authentication, a user first presents both a claimed identity and his biometric data to a data capture subsystem. The captured biometric data is then passed to a signal processing subsystem where features of the captured data are extracted and converted into a reference. A matching subsystem then compares this reference to a template from a data storage subsystem for the claimed identity and produces a comparison score. This comparison score is then passed to a decision subsystem, which produces a *yes* or *no* decision that reflects whether or not the biometric data agrees with the template stored for the claimed identity. The result of

the authentication operation is the value returned by the decision subsystem.

A false match that occurs during authentication will allow one user to successfully authenticate as another user. So if Bob claims to be Alice and a false match occurs, he will be authenticated as Alice. A false nonmatch during authentication will incorrectly deny a user access. So if Bob attempts to authenticate as himself, he will be incorrectly denied assess if a false nonmatch occurs.

Because biometric data may change over time, an adaptation subsystem may update the stored template for a user after they have authenticated to the biometric system. If this is done, it will reduce the number or times that users will need to go through the enrollment process again when their biometric data changes enough to increase their FNMR rate to an unacceptable level.

Identification

A biometric system can be used to identify a user that has already enrolled in the system. The interaction of the subsystems of a biometric system when used for identification is shown in Figure 56.15.

To use a biometric system for identification, a user presents his biometric data to a data capture subsystem.

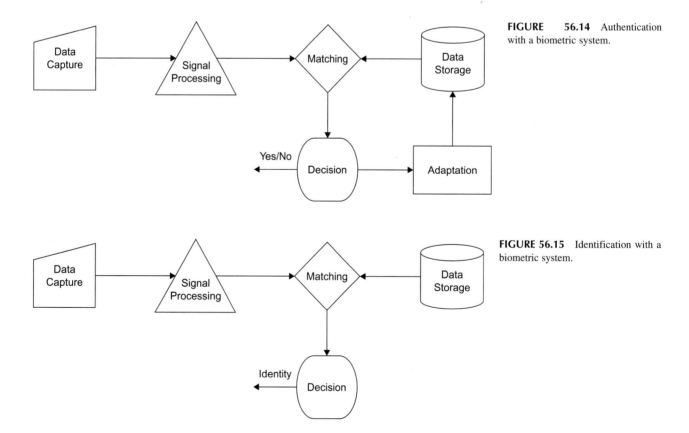

FIGURE   56.14 Authentication with a biometric system.

FIGURE 56.15 Identification with a biometric system.

The captured biometric data is then passed to a signal processing subsystem where features of the captured data are extracted and converted into a reference. A matching subsystem then compares this reference to each of the templates stored in a data storage subsystem and produces a comparison score. Each of these comparison scores are passed to a decision subsystem, which produces a *yes* or *no* decision that reflects whether or not the reference is a good match for each template. If a *yes* decision is reached, then the identity associated with the template is returned for the identification operation. It is possible for this process to return more that one identity. This may or may not be useful, depending on the application. If a *yes* decision is not reached for any of the templates in a data storage subsystem, then a response that indicates that no match was found is returned for the identification operation.

A false match that occurs during identification will incorrectly identify a user as another enrolled user. So if Bob uses a biometric system for identification, he might be incorrectly identified as Alice if a false match occurs. Because there are typically many comparisons done when a biometric system is used for identification, the FMR can increase dramatically because there is an opportunity for a false match with every comparison. Suppose that for a single comparison we have an FMR of ε_1 and that ε_n represents the FMR for n comparisons. These two error rates are related by $\varepsilon_n = 1 - (1 - \varepsilon_1)^n$. If $n \cdot \varepsilon_1 \ll 1$. then we have that $\varepsilon_n \approx n \cdot \varepsilon_1$. This means that for a small FMR, the FMR is increased by a factor equal to the number of enrolled users when a system is used for identification instead of authentication. So an FMR of 10^{-6} when a system is used for authentication will be increased to approximately 10^{-3} if the identification is done by comparing to 1000 templates. A false nonmatch during identification will fail to identify an enrolled user as one who is enrolled in the system. So Bob might be incorrectly rejected, even though he is actually an enrolled user.

4. SECURITY CONSIDERATIONS

Biometric systems differ from most other authentication or identification technologies in several ways, and these differences should be understood by anyone considering using such systems as part of an information security architecture. Biometric data is not secret, or at least it is not very secret. Fingerprints, for example, are not very secret because so-called latent fingerprints are left almost everywhere. On the other hand, reconstructing enough of a fingerprint from latent fingerprints to fool a biometric system is actually very difficult because latent fingerprints are typically of poor quality and incomplete. Because biometric data is not very secret, it may be useful to verify that captured biometric data is fresh instead

of being replayed. There are technologies available that make it more difficult for an adversary to present fake biometric data to a biometric system for this very purpose. The technology exists to distinguish between a living finger and a manufactured copy, for example. Such technologies are not foolproof and can themselves be circumvented by clever attackers. This means that they just make it more difficult for an adversary to defeat a biometric system, but not impossible.

It is relatively easy to require users to frequently change their passwords and to enforce the expiration of cryptographic keys after their lifetime has passed, but many types of biometric data last for a long time, and it is essentially impossible to force users to change their biometric data. So when biometric data is compromised in some way, it is not possible to reissue new biometric data to the affected users. For that reason, it may be useful to both plan for alternate forms of authentication or identification in addition to a biometric system and to not rely on a single biometric system being useful for long periods of time.

Biometrics used for authentication may have much lower levels of security than other authentication technologies. This, plus the fact there is usually a non-zero FER for any biometric system, means that biometric systems may be more useful as an additional means of authentication than as a technology that can work alone. Types of authentication technology can be divided into three general categories or "factors":

- Something that a user *knows*, such as a password or PIN
- Something that a user *has*, such as a key or access card
- Something that a user *is* or *does*, which is exactly the definition of a biometric

To be considered a *multifactor* authentication system, a system must use means from more than one of these categories to authenticate a user so that a system that uses two independent password-based systems for authentication does not qualify as a multifactor authentication system, whereas one that uses a password plus a biometric does. There is a commonly held perception that multifactor authentication is inherently more secure than authentication based on only a single factor, but this is not true. The concepts of *strong* authentication, in which an attacker has a small chance of bypassing the means of authentication, and multifactor authentication are totally independent. It is possible to have strong authentication based on only one factor. It is also possible to have weak authentication based on multiple authentication factors. So, including a biometric system as part of a multifactor authentication system should be done for reasons other than to simply use more than a single authentication factor. It may be more secure to use a password plus a PIN for authentication than to use a password plus a biometric, for example, even though both the password and PIN are the same type of authentication factor.

Error Rates

The usual understanding of biometric systems assumes that the FMR and FNMR of a biometric system are due to random errors that occur in a data capture subsystem. In particular, this assumes that the biometrics that are used in these systems are actually essentially unique. The existing market for celebrity lookalikes demonstrates that enough similarities exist in some physical features to justify the concern that similarities also exist in the more subtle characteristics that biometric systems use.

We assume, for example, that fingerprints are unique enough to identify a person without any ambiguity. This may indeed be true,[6] but there has been little careful research that demonstrates that this is actually the case. The largest empirical study of the uniqueness of fingerprints used only 50,000 fingerprints, a sample that could have come from as few as 5000 people, and has been criticized by experts for its careless use of statistics.[7] This is an area that deserves a closer look by researchers, but the expense of large-scale investigations probably means that they will probably never be carried out, leaving the uniqueness of biometrics an assumption that underlies the use of the technology for security applications. Note that other parts of information security also rely on assumptions that may never be proved. The security provided by all public-key cryptographic algorithms, for example, assumes that certain computational problems are intractable, but there are currently no proofs that this is actually the case.

The chances that the biometrics used in security systems will be found to be not unique enough for use in such systems is probably remote, but it certainly could happen. One easy way to prepare for this possibility is to use more than one biometric to characterize users. In such multi-modal systems, if one of the biometrics used is found to be weak, the others can still provide adequate strength. On the other hand, multi-modal systems have the additional drawback of being more expensive that a system that uses a single biometric.

Note that a given error rate can have many different sources. An error rate of 10% could be caused by an entire population having an error rate of 10%, or it could be caused by 90% of a population having an error rate of zero and 10% of the population having an error rate of 100%. The usability of the system is very different in each of these cases. In one case, all users are equally inconvenienced, but in the other case, some users are essentially unable to use the system at all. So understanding how errors are distributed can be important in understanding how biometric systems can be used. If a biometric system is used to control access to a sensitive facility, for example, it may not be very useful in this role if some of the people who need entry to the facility are unlucky enough to have a 100% FNMR. Studies have suggested that error rates are not uniformly distributed in some populations, but they are not quite as bad as the worst case. The nonuniform distribution of error rates that is observed in biometric systems is often called Doddington's Zoo and is named after the researcher who first noticed this phenomenon and the colorful names that he gave to the classes of users who made different contributions to the observed error rates.

Doddington's Zoo

Based on his experience testing biometric systems, George Doddington divided people into four categories: sheep, goats, lambs, and wolves.[8] Sheep are easily recognized by a biometric system and comprise most of the population. Goats are particularly unsuccessful at being recognized. They have chronically high FNMRs, usually because their biometric is outside the range that a particular system recognizes. Goats can be particularly troublesome if a biometric system is used for access control, where it is critical that all users be reliably accepted. Lambs are exceptionally vulnerable to impersonation, so they contribute to the FMR. Wolves are exceptionally good false matchers and they also make a significant contribution to the FMR.

Doddington's goats can also cause another problem. Because their biometric pattern is outside the range that a particular biometric system expects, they may be unable to enroll in such a system and thus be major contributors to the FER of the system.

Note that users that may be sheep for one biometric may turn out to be goats for another, and so on. Because of this it is probably impossible to know in advance how error rates are distributed for a particular biometric system, it is almost always necessary to test such systems thoroughly before deploying them on a wide scale.

6. S. Pankanti, S. Prabhakar and A. Jain, "On the individuality of fingerprints," *IEEE Transactions on Pattern Analysis and Machine Intelligence*, Vol. 24, No. 8, pp. 1010–1025, August 2002.

7. S. Cole, *Suspect Identities: A History of Fingerprinting and Criminal Identification*, Harvard University Press, 2002.

8. G. Doddington, et al., "Sheep, goats, lambs and wolves: A statistical analysis of speaker performance in the NIST 1998 speaker recognition evaluation," *Proceedings of the Fifth International Conference on Spoken Language Processing*, Sydney, Australia, November–December, 1998, pp. 1351–1354.

Birthday Attacks

Suppose that we have n users enrolled in a biometric system. This biometric system maps arbitrary inputs into $n + 1$ states that represent deciding on a match with one of the n users plus the additional "none of the above" user that represents the option of deciding on a match with none of the n enrolled users. From this point of view, this biometric system acts like a hash function so might try to use well-known facts about hash functions to understand the limits that this property puts on error rates. In particular, errors caused by the FMR of a biometric system look like a collision in this hash function, which happens when two different input values to a hash function result in the same output from the hash function. For this reason, we might think that the same "birthday attack" that can find collisions for a hash function can also increase the FMR of a biometric system. The reason for this is as follows.

For a hash function that maps inputs into m different message digests, the probability of finding at least one collision, a case where different inputs map to the same message digest, after calculating n message digests is approximately $1 - e^{-n^2/2m}$.[9] Considering birthdays as a hash function that maps people into one of 365 possible birthdays, this tells us that the probability of two or more people having the same birthday in a group of only 23 people is approximately $1 - e^{-23^2/2 \cdot 365} \approx 0.52$. This means that there is greater that a 50% chance of finding two people with the same birthday in a group of only 23 people, a result that is often counter to people's intuition. Using a biometric system is much like a hash function in that it maps biometric data into the templates in the data storage subsystem that it has a good match for, and collisions in this hash function cause a false match. Therefore, the FMR may increase as more users are added to the system, and if it does, we might expect the FMR rate to increase in the same way that the chances of a collision in a hash function do. This might cause false matches at a higher rate that we might expect, just like the chances of finding matching birthdays does.

In practice, however, this phenomenon is essentially not observed. This may be due to the nonuniform distribution in error rates of Doddingon's Zoo. If the threshold used in a decision subsystem is adjusted to create a particular FMR, it may be limited by the properties of Doddington's lambs. This may leave the sheep that comprise the majority of the user population with enough room to add additional users without getting too close to other sheep.

ANS X9.84 requires that the FMR for biometric systems provide at least the level of security provided by a

TABLE 56.3 Comparison of Security Provided by Biometrics and Other Common Mechanisms.

FMR	PIN Length	Password Length	Key Length
10^{-3}	3 digits	2 letters	10 bits
10^{-4}	4 digits	3 letters	13 bits
10^{-5}	5 digits	4 letters	17 bits
10^{-6}	6 digits	4 letters	20 bits
10^{-7}	7 digits	5 letters	23 bits
10^{-8}	8 digits	6 letters	27 bits

four-digit PIN, which equates to an FMR of no greater than 10^{-4} and recommends that they provide an FMR of no more than 10^{-5}. In addition, this standard requires that the corresponding FNMR be no greater than 10^{-2} at the FMR selected for use. These error rates may be too ambitious for some existing technologies, but it is certainly possible to attain these error rates with some technologies.

On the other hand, these error rates compare very unfavorably with other authentication technologies. For example, an FMR of 10^{-4} is roughly the same as the probability of randomly guessing a four-digit PIN, a three-character password, or a 13-bit cryptographic key. And although few people would find three-character passwords or 13-bit cryptographic keys acceptable, they might have to accept an FMR of 10^{-4} from a biometric system because of the limitations of affordable current technologies. Table 56.3 summarizes how the security provided by various FMRs compares to both the security provided by all-numeric PINs and passwords that use only case-independent letters.

Comparing Technologies

There are many different biometrics that are used in currently available biometric systems. Each of these competing technologies tries to be better than the alternatives in some way, perhaps being easier to use, more accurate, or cheaper to operate. Because there are so many technologies available, however, it should come as no surprise that there is no single "best" technology for use in biometric systems. Almost any biometric system that is available is probably the best solution for some problem, and it is impossible to list all of the cases where each technology is the best without a very careful analysis of each authentication or identification problem. So any attempt to make a simple comparison between the competing technologies will be inherently inaccurate. Despite this, Table 56.4 attempts to make such a high-level

---

9. D. Knuth, *The Art of Computer Programming, Volume 2: Sorting and Searching*, Addison-Wesley, 1973.

TABLE 56.4 Comparison of Selected Biometric Technologies.

Biometric	Ease of Use	Accuracy	Cost
DNA	Low	High	High
Face geometry	High	Medium	Medium
Fingerprint	High	High	Low
Hand geometry	Medium	Medium	Medium
Iris	High	High	High
Retina	Medium	High	High
Signature dynamics	Low	Medium	Medium
Voice	Medium	Low	Low
(Password)	(Medium)	(Low)	(Low)

comparison. In this table, the ease of use, accuracy and cost are rated as high, medium, or low.

Using DNA as a biometric provides an example of the difficulty involved in making such a rough classification. The accuracy of DNA testing is limited by the fairly large number of identical twins that are present in the overall population, but in cases other than distinguishing identical twins it is very accurate. So if identical twins need to be distinguished, it may not be the best solution. By slightly abusing the usual understanding of what a biometric is, it is even possible to think of passwords as a biometric that is based purely on behavioral characteristics, along with the FMR, FNMR, and FER rates that come with their use, but they are certainly outside the commonly understood meaning of the term. Even if they are not covered by the usual definition of a biometric, passwords are fairly well understood, so they provide a point of reference for comparing against the relative strengths of biometrics that are commonly used in security systems. The accuracy of passwords here is meant to be that of passwords that users select for their own use instead of being randomly generated. Such passwords are typically much weaker than their length indicates because of the structure that people need to make passwords easy to remember. This means that the chances of guessing a typical eight-character case-insensitive password is actually much greater than the 26^{-8} that we would expect for strong passwords. Studies of the randomness in English words have estimated that there is approximately one bit of randomness per letter.[10] If we conservatively double this to estimate that there are approximately two bits of randomness per

letter in a typical user-selected password, we get the estimate that an eight-character password probably provides only about 16 bits of randomness, which is close to the security provided by a biometric system with an FMR of 10^{-5}. This means that the security of passwords as used in practice is often probably comparable to that attainable by biometric systems, perhaps even less if weak passwords are used.

Storage of Templates

One obvious way to store the templates used in a biometric system is in a database. This can be a good solution, and the security provided by the database may be adequate to protect the templates that it stores. In other cases, it may be more useful for a user to carry his template with him on some sort of portable data storage device and to provide that template to a matching subsystem along with his biometric data. Portable, credit-card-sized data storage devices are often used for this purpose. There are three general types of such cards that are used in this way, and each has a different set of security considerations that are relevant to it.

In one case, a memory card with unencrypted data storage can be used to store a template. This is the least expensive option, but also the least secure. Such a memory card can be read by anyone who finds it and can easily be duplicated, although it may be impossible for anyone other that the authorized user to use it. Nonbiometric data stored on such a card may also be compromised when a card is lost.

In principle, a nonauthorized user can use such a card to make a card that lets them authenticate as an authorized user. This can be done as follows. Suppose that Eve, a nonauthorized user, gets the memory card that stores the template for the authorized user Alice. Eve may be able to use Alice's card to make a card that is identical in every way to Alice's card but that has Eve's template in place of Alice's. Then when Eve uses this card to authenticate, she uses her biometric data, which then gets compared to her template on the card and gets her authenticated as the user Alice. Note that doing this relies on a fairly unsecured implementation.

A case that is more secure and also more expensive is a memory card in which data storage is encrypted. The contents of such a card can still be read by anyone who finds it and can easily be duplicated, but it is infeasible for an unauthorized user to decrypt and use the data on the card, which may also include any nonbiometric data on the card. Encrypting the data storage also makes it impractical for an unauthorized user to make a card that will let them authenticate as an authorized user. Though it may be possible to simply replace one template with another if the template is stored unencrypted on a

---

10. C. Shannon, "Prediction and entropy of printed english," *Bell System Technical Journal*, Vol. 30, pp. 50–64, January 1951.

memory card, carrying out the same attack on a memory card that stores data encrypted requires being able to create a valid encrypted template, which is just as difficult as defeating the encryption.

The most secure as well as the most expensive case is where a smart card with cryptographic capabilities is used to store a template. The data stored on such a smart card can only be read and decrypted by trusted applications, so that it is infeasible for anyone who finds a lost smart card to read data from it or to copy it. This makes it infeasible for unauthorized users to use a smart card to create a way to authenticate as an authorized user. It also protects any nonbiometric data that might be stored on the card.

5. SUMMARY

Using biometric systems as the basis for security technologies for authentication or identification is currently feasible. Each biometric has properties that may make it useful in some situations but not others, and security systems based on biometrics have the same property. This means that there is no single "best" biometric for such use and that each biometric technology has an application where it is superior to the alternatives.

There is still a great deal of research that needs to be done in the field, but existing technologies have progressed to the point that security systems based on biometrics are now a viable way to perform authentication or identification of users, although the properties of biometrics also make them more attractive as part of a multifactor authentication system instead of the single means that is used.

Finally, let's move on to the real interactive part of this Chapter: review questions/exercises, hands-on projects, case projects and optional team case project. The answers and/or solutions by chapter can be found in the Online Instructor's Solutions Manual.

CHAPTER REVIEW QUESTIONS/EXERCISES

True/False

1. True or False? *Biometrics* is the analysis of biological observations and phenomena. People routinely use biometrics to recognize other people, commonly using the shape of a face or the sound of a voice to do so.
2. True or False? Not all biometric systems have a number of common subsystems.
3. True or False? A data subsystem collects captured biometric data from a user.
4. True or False? A signal processing subsystem takes the captured biometric data from a data subsystem and transforms the data into a form suitable for use in the matching subsystem.
5. True or False? A matching subsystem receives a reference from a signal processing subsystem and then compares a template from a data storage subsystem.

Multiple Choice

1. What subsystem stores templates that are used by the matching subsystem?
   A. Qualitative analysis
   B. Vulnerabilities
   C. Data storage
   D. Malformed request DoS
   E. Data controller
2. What subsystem takes a comparison score that is the output of a matching subsystem and returns a binary *yes* or *no* decision from it?
   A. Network attached storage (NAS)
   B. Risk assessment
   C. Valid
   D. Decision
   E. Bait
3. One way to avoid the potential difficulties associated with having users eventually becoming unrecognizable is to update their template after a successful authentication. This process is called:
   A. Adaptation
   B. Fabric
   C. Disasters
   D. Risk communication
   E. Security
4. During what operation, does a biometric system create a template that is used in later authentication and identification operations?
   A. Enrollment
   B. Greedy strategy
   C. Infrastructure failure
   D. SAN protocol
   E. Taps
5. During what operation, does a biometric system collect captured biometric data and a claimed identity and determines whether or not the captured biometric data matches the template stored for that identity?
   A. Irrelevant
   B. Authentication
   C. IP storage access
   D. Configuration file
   E. Unusable

EXERCISE

Problem

How are biometrics collected?

Hands-On Projects

Project

What are biometric templates?

Case Projects

Problem

Can one interact with a biometric device without touching
something?

Optional Team Case Project

Problem

Why are there so many different biometric modalilties?

## Chapter 57

Homeland Security

Rahul Bhaskar, Ph.D.
California State University

Bhushan Kapoor
California State University

Note: This chapter is available in its entirety online at store.elsevier.com/product.jsp?isbn=9780123943972 (click the Resources tab at the bottom of the page). It is also available in print in *Cyber Security and IT Infrastructure Protection*.

1. ABSTRACT

The September 11, 2001, terrorist attacks, permanently changed the way the United States and the world's other most developed countries perceived the threat from terrorism. Massive amounts of resources were mobilized in a very short time to counter the perceived and actual threats from terrorists and terrorist organizations. In the United States, this refocus was pushed as a necessity for what was called *homeland security*. The homeland security threats were anticipated for the IT infrastructure as well. It was expected that not only the IT at the federal level was vulnerable to disruptions due to terrorism-related attacks but, due to the ubiquity of the availability of IT, any organization was vulnerable. Soon after the terrorist attacks, the U.S. Congress passed various new laws and enhanced some existing ones that introduced sweeping changes to homeland security provisions and to the existing security organizations. The executive branch of the government also issued a series of Homeland Security Presidential Directives to maintain domestic security. These laws and directives are comprehensive and contain detailed provisions to make the U.S. secure from its vulnerabilities. Later in the chapter, we describe some principle provisions of these homeland security-related laws and presidential directives. Next, we discuss the organizational changes that were initiated to support homeland security in the United States. Then we highlight the 9-11 Commission that Congress charted to provide a full account of the circumstances surrounding the attacks and to develop recommendations for corrective measures that could be taken to prevent future acts of terrorism. We also detail the Intelligence Reform and Terrorism Prevention Act of 2004 and the Implementing the 9-11 Commission Recommendations Act of 2007. Finally, we summarize the chapter's discussion.

2. CONTENTS

## Chapter 58

Cyber Warfare

Anna Granova

Pretoria Society of Advocates

Marco Slaviero

SensePost Pty Ltd

The times we live in are called the Information Age for very good reasons: Today information is probably worth much more than any other commodity. Globalization, the other important phenomenon of the times we live in, has taken the value of information to new heights. On one hand, citizens of a country may now feel entitled to know exactly what is happening in other countries around the globe. On the other, the same people can use the Internet to mobilize forces to overthrow the government in their own country.[1] To this end, the capabilities of the Internet have been put to use and people have become accustomed to receiving information about everyone and everything as soon as it becomes available. The purpose of this chapter is to define the concept of cyber warfare (CW), discuss their most common tactics, weapons, and tools, compare CW terrorism with conventional warfare, and address the issues of liability and the available legal remedies under international law. To have this discussion, a proper model and definition of CW first needs to be established.

October 20, 1969, marked the first message sent on the Internet,[2] and more 40 years on we cannot imagine our lives without it. Internet banking, online gaming, and online shopping and social media have become just as important to some as food and sleep. As the world has become more dependent on automated environments, interconnectivity, networks, and the Internet, instances of abuse and misuse of information technology infrastructures have increased proportionately.[3] Such abuse has,

unfortunately, not been limited only to the abuse of business information systems and Web sites but over time has also penetrated the military domain of state security. Today this penetration of governmental IT infrastructures, including, among others, the military domain, is commonly referred to as *cyber warfare*. However, these concepts are not yet clearly defined and understood. Furthermore, this type of warfare is a multidisciplinary field requiring expertise from technical, legal, offensive, and defensive perspectives. Information security professionals are challenged to respond to this type of warfare issues in a professional and knowledgeable way.

1. CYBER WARFARE MODEL

The authors propose a model for CW by mapping important concepts regarding them on a single diagrammatic representation (see Figure 58.1). This aids in simplifying a complex concept as well as providing a holistic view on the phenomenon. To this end, this chapter addresses the

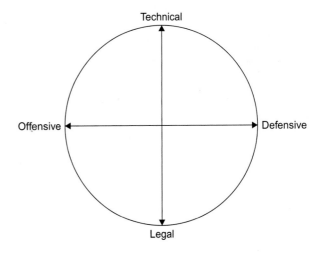

FIGURE 58.1 A perspective on CW.

1. *Egypt: AP Confirms Government has Disrupted Internet Service* (2011), http://pomed.org/blog/2011/01/egypt-ap-confirms-government-has-disrupted-internet-service.html/, accessed on 09 April 2012.

2. *An Internet History* (2008), www.services.ex.ac.uk/cmit/modules/the_internet/webct/ch-history.html, accessed on 19 February 2008.

3. *Symantec Global Internet Security Threat Report Trends for July−December 07* (2008) Vol. 13, published April 2008 available at http://eval.symantec.com/mktginfo/enterprise/white_papers/b-whitepaper_internet_security_threat_report_xiii_04-2008.en-us.pdf, accessed on 21 April 2008.

four axes of CW: technical, legal, offensive, and defensive, as depicted in Figure 58.1.

The technical side of CW deals with technical exploits on one side and defensive measures on the other. As is apparent from Figure 58.1, these range from the most destructive offensive strategies, such as a distributed denial-of-service (DDoS) attack or stuxnet, to various workstation emergency response teams, such as US-CERT.

Considered from a legal perspective, CW can range from criminal prosecutions in international courts to use of force in retaliation. Therefore, the four axes of CW continuously interact and influence each other, as will become clearer from the discussion that follows.

2. CYBER WARFARE DEFINED

The manner in which war is being conducted has evolved enormously,[4] and CW has not only been accepted as a new direction in military operations,[5] but also been incorporated into some of the top military forces in the world, with China implementing an CW policy as early as 1995,[6] with United States Cyber Command (USCYBERCOM) established in 2009,[7] followed by China in July 2010,[8] US Cyber Warfare Intelligence Center[9] unveiled in November 2010 and the Cyber Warfare Administration in Israel in breathed into life in 2012.[10] A number of definitions are relevant for the purposes of this chapter. Some authors[11] maintain that CW covers "the full range of competitive information operations from destroying IT equipment to subtle perception management, and from industrial espionage to marketing." If one regards the more "military" definition of CW, one could say that CW is "a subset of information operations"—in other words "actions taken to adversely affect information and information systems while defending one's own information and information systems."[12]

The UN Secretary-General's report on *Development in the Field on Information and Telecommunications in the context of International Security* describes CW as "actions aimed at achieving information superiority by executing measures to exploit, corrupt, destroy, destabilise, or damage the enemy's information and its functions."[13] This definition is very similar to one of the more recent and accepted definitions found in literature that states that CW is "actions taken in support of objectives that influence decision-makers by affecting the information and/or information systems of others while protecting your own information and/or information systems."[14] If one, however, looks at CW in purely a military light, the following technical definition seems to be the most appropriate: "The broad class of activities aimed at leveraging data, information and knowledge in support of military goals."[15]

In light of the preceding, it is clear that CW is all about information superiority because "the fundamental weapon and target of CW is information."[16] This being so, some authors[17] outline the basic strategies of CW as follows:

1. Deny access to information
2. Disrupt/destroy data
3. Steal data
4. Manipulate data to change its context or its perception

A slightly different perspective on the aims of CW is perhaps to see it as "an attack on information systems for military advantage using tactics of destruction, denial, exploitation or deception."[18] Since about 2008, however, the CW starting to cross over into the physical realm through one of its forms: cyber warfare, which can be defined as *politically motivated hacking to conduct sabotage and espionage*.

With these definitions in mind, it is now appropriate to consider whether CW is a concept that has been created by enthusiasts such as individual hackers to impress the rest of the world's population or is, in fact, part of daily military operations.

4. Schmitt, "Wired Warfare-Workstation Network Attack and *jus in bello*" 2002 *International Review of the Red Cross,* 365.

5. Rogers "Protecting America against Cyberterrorism" 2001 *United States Foreign Policy Agenda,* 15.

6. Ball "Security Challenges", Vol. 7, No. 2 (Winter 2011), pp. 81–103, http://www.securitychallenges.org.au/ArticlePDFs/vol7no2Ball.pdf, accessed on 09 April 2012.

7. *Cyber Command Achieves Full Operational Capability* (2010) http://www.defense.gov/releases/release.aspx?releaseid=14030 accessed on 09 April 2012.

8. Branigan "Chinese army to target cyber war threat" (2010), http://www.guardian.co.uk/world/2010/jul/22/chinese-army-cyber-war-department accessed on 09 April 2012.

9. *Construction begins on first cyber warfare intelligence center* (2010), http://www.af.mil/news/story.asp?id=123204543accessed on 09 April 2012.

10. *Israel to Establish Cyber Warfare Administration* (2012), http://www.israelnationalnews.com/News/News.aspx/151713 accessed on 09 April 2012.

11. Hutchinson and Warren, *CW — Corporate Attack and Defence in a Digital World (2001) and XVIIII.*

12. Schmitt, "Wired Warfare-Workstation Network Attack and *jus in bello*" 2002 *International Review of the Red Cross* 365. See also the definition by Goldberg available on line at http://psycom.net/CWar.2.html.

13. UNG.A.Res A/56/164 dated 3 July 2001.

14. Thornton, R, *Asymmetric Warfare — Threat and Response in the 20-First Century* 2007.

15. Vacca, J. R., *Computer Forensics: Computer Crime Scene Investigation (2nd Edition)* Charles River Media, 2005.

16. Hutchinson and Warren, *CW — Corporate Attack and Defence in a Digital World* (2001), p. xviiii.

17. Hutchinson and Warren, *CW — Corporate Attack and Defence in a Digital World* (2001) p. xviiii.

18. Vacca, J. R., *Computer Forensics: Computer Crime Scene Investigation (2nd Edition)* Charles River Media, 2005.

3. CW: MYTH OR REALITY?

Groves once said: "... nowhere it is safe ... no one knows of the scale of the threat, the silent deadly menace that stalks the network."[19] With the growing risk of terrorists and other hostile entities engaging in missions of sabotaging, either temporarily or permanently, important public infrastructures through cyber attacks, the number of articles[20] on the topic has grown significantly. To understand the gravity of CW and its consequences, the following real-life examples need to be considered. At the outset, however, it is important to mention that the reason there is so little regulation (see checklist, "An Agenda For Action For Regulating High Level Cyber Warfare Strategies") of computer-related activities with specific reference to CW both on national and international planes is that lawyers are very reluctant to venture into the unknown. The following examples, however, demonstrate that CW has consistently taken place since at least 1991. One of the first CW incidents was recorded in 1991 during the first Gulf War, where CW was used by the United States against Iraq.[21]

In 1998 an Israeli national hacked into the government workstations of the United States.[22] In 1999, a number of cyber attacks took place in Kosovo. During the attacks the Serbian and NATO Web sites were taken down with the aim of interfering with and indirectly influencing the public's perception and opinion of the conflict.[23]

These cyber attacks were executed for different reasons: Russians hacked U.S. and Canadian websites "in protest" against NATO deployment,[24] Chinese joined the online war because their embassy in Belgrade was bombed by NATO,[25] and U.S. nationals were paralyzing the White House[26] and NATO[27] Web sites "for fun." In 2000, classified information was distributed on the Internet,[28] and attacks were launched on NASA's laboratories,[29] the U.S. Postal Service, and the Canadian Defense Department.[30] As early as 2001, detected intrusions into the U.S. Defense Department's Web site numbered 23,662.[31] Furthermore, there were 1300 pending investigations into activities "ranging from criminal activity to national security intrusions."[32] Hackers also attempted to abuse the U.S. Federal Court's database[33] to compromise the peace process in the Middle East.[34]

In 2002, incidents of cyber terrorism in Morocco, Spain, Moldova, and Georgia[35] proved once again that a "hacker influenced by politics is a terrorist," illustrated by more than 140,000 attacks in less than 48 hours allegedly executed by the "G-Force" (Pakistan)[36]. During this period, a series of convictions on charges of conspiracy, the destruction of energy facilities,[37] the destruction of telecommunications facilities, and the disabling of air navigation facilities,[38] as well as cases of successful international luring and subsequent prosecutions, were recorded.[39]

In the second half of 2007, 499,811 new malicious code threats were detected, which represented a 571% increase from the same period in 2006.[40] With two thirds

---

19. Lloyd, I. J., *Information Technology Law* Oxford University Press 181 (5th Edition) 2008.

20. Groves, The War on Terrorism: Cyberterrorist be Ware, *Informational Management Journal,* Jan-Feb 2002.

21. Goodwin "Don't Techno for an Answer: The false promise of CW."

22. *Israeli citizen arrested in Israel for hacking United States and Israeli Government Workstations* (1998) http://www.usdoj.gov/criminal/cybercrime/ehudpr.hgm(accessed on 13 October 2002).

23. Hutchinson and Warren, *CW – Corporate Attack and Defence in a Digital World (2001).*

24. Skoric (1999), http://amsterdam.nettime.org/Lists-Archives/net-time-1-9906/msg00152.html, (accessed on 03 October 2002).

25. Messmer (1999) http://www.cnn.com/TECH/computing/9905/12/cyberwar.idg/, (accessed on 03 October 2002).

26. *"Web Bandit" Hacker Sentenced to 15 Months Imprisonment, 3 Years of Supervised Release, for Hacking USIA, NATO, Web Sites* (1999), www.usdoj.gov/criminal/cybercrime/burns.htm (accessed on 13 October 2002).

27. *Access to NATO's Web Site Disrupted* (1999), www.cnn.com/WORLD/europe/9903/31/nato.hack/ (accessed on 03 October 2002).

28. Lusher (2000), www.balkanpeace.org/hed/archive/april00/hed30.shtml (accessed on 03 October 2002).

29. *Hacker Pleads Guilty in New York City to Hacking into Two NASA Jet Propulsion Lab Workstations Located in Pasadena, California* (2000), www.usdoj.gov/criminal/cybercrime/rolex.htm (accessed on 13 October 2002).

30. (2000) www.usdoj.gov/criminal/cybercrime/VAhacker2.htm (accessed on 13 October 2002).

31. www.coe.int/T/E/Legal_affairs/Legal_co-operation/Combating_economic_crime/Cybercrime/International_conference/ConfCY(2001)5E-1.pdf (accessed on 9 October 2002).

32. Rogers, *Protecting America against Cyberterrorism* U.S. Foreign Policy Agenda (2001).

33. (2001) "Hacker Into United States Courts' Information System Pleads Guilty," www.usdoj.gov/criminal/cybercrime/MamichPlea.htm (accessed on 13 October 2002).

34. (2001) "Computer Hacker Intentionally Damages Protected Computer" www.usdoj.gov/criminal/cybercrime/khanindict.htm (accessed on 13 October 2002).

35. *Hacker Influenced by Politics is Also a Terrorist* (2002), www.utro.ru/articles/2002/07/24/91321.shtml (accessed on 24 July 2002).

36. www.echocct.org/main.html (accessed on 20 September 2002).

37. *Hackers Hit Power Companies* (2002) www.cbsnews.com/stories/2002/07/08/tech/main514426.shtml (accessed on 20 September 2002).

38. U.S. v. Konopka (E.D.Wis.), www.usdoj.gov/criminal/cybercrime/konopkaIndict.htm (accessed on 13 October 2002).

39. U.S. v. Gorshkov (W.D.Wash.), www.usdoj.gov/criminal/cybercrime/gorshkovSent.htm (accessed on 13 October 2002).

40. *Symantec Global Internet Security Threat Report Trends for July–December 07* (2008) Vol. 13, published April 2008 available at http://eval.symantec.com/mktginfo/enterprise/white_papers/b-whitepaper_internet_security_threat_report_xiii_04-2008.en-us.pdf accessed on 21 April 2008 at p.45.

An Agenda for Action for Regulating High Level Cyber Warfare Strategies

Please see the following recommendations for regulating high level cyber warfare strategies (Check All Tasks Completed):

_____**1.** The President of the United States should task the National Office for Cyberspace (NOC) to work with appropriate regulatory agencies to develop and issue standards and guidance for securing critical cyber infrastructure, which those agencies would then apply in their own regulations.

_____**2.** The NOC should work with the appropriate regulatory agencies and with the National Institute of Standards and Technology (NIST) to develop regulations for industrial control systems (ICS).

_____**3.** The government should reinforce regulations by making the development of secure control systems an element of any economic stimulus package.

_____**4.** The NOC should immediately determine the extent to which government-owned critical infrastructures are secure from cyber attack.

_____**5.** The president should direct the NOC and the federal Chief Information Officers Council, working with industry, to develop and implement security guidelines for the procurement of IT products (with software as the first priority).

_____**6.** The president should task the National Security Agency (NSA) and NIST, working with international partners, to reform the National Information Assurance Partnership (NIAP).

_____**7.** The president should take steps to increase the use of secure Internet protocols.

_____**8.** The president should direct the Office of Management OMB and the NOC to develop mandatory requirements for agencies to contract only with telecommunications carriers that use secure Internet protocols.

---

of more than 1 million identified viruses created in 2007,[41] the continued increase in malicious code threats has been linked to the sharp rise in the development of new Trojans and the apparent existence of institutions that employ "professionals" dedicated to creation of new threats.[42] In 2008 it has been reported in the media that "over the past year to 18 months, there has been 'a huge increase in focused attacks on our [United States] national infrastructure networks .... and they have been coming from outside the United States.'"[43]

It is common knowledge that over the past 15 years, the United States has tried to save both manpower and costs by establishing a system to remotely control and monitor the electric utilities, pipelines, railroads, and oil companies all across the United States.[44] The reality of the threat of CW has been officially confirmed by the

U.S. Federal Energy Regulatory Commission, which approved eight cyber-security standards for electric utilities, which include "identity controls, training, security 'parameters' physical security of critical cyber equipment, incident reporting and recovery."[45] In January 2008, a CIA analyst warned the public that cyber attackers have hacked into the workstation systems of utility companies outside the United States and made demands, which led to at least one instance where, as a direct result, a power outage that affected multiple cities took place.[46]

Furthermore, since 2007, there have been a number of high profile events, which can be categorized as cyber attacks. Estonia was first in line to suffer from this debilitating form of aggression: it unleashed a wave of DdoS attacks, where websites were swamped by tens of thousands of requests, which in turn disabled them by overcrowding the bandwidths for the servers running the websites of the Estonian government, political parties, half of media organizations and the top two banks.[47]

Russia was blamed for the Estonian cyber conflict which was caused by the removal of a statue of

41. *Symantec Global Internet Security Threat Report Trends for July−December 07* (2008) Vol. 13, published April 2008 available at http://eval.symantec.com/mktginfo/enterprise/white_papers/b-whitepaper_internet_security_threat_report_xiii_04-2008.en-us.pdf accessed on 21 April 2008 at p. 45.

42. *Symantec Global Internet Security Threat Report Trends for July−December 07* (2008) Vol. 13, published April 2008 available at http://eval.symantec.com/mktginfo/enterprise/white_papers/b-whitepaper_internet_security_threat_report_xiii_04-2008.en-us.pdf accessed on 21 April 2008 at p. 46.

43. Nakashima, E and Mufson, S, "Hackers have attacked foreign utilities, CIA Analysts says," 19 January 2008, available at www.washingtonpost.com/wp/dyn/conmttent/atricle/2008/01/18/AR2008011803277bf.html, accessed on 28 January 2008.

44. Nakashima, E and Mufson, S, "Hackers have attacked foreign utilities, CIA Analysts says," 19 January 2008, available at www.washingtonpost.com/wp/dyn/conmttent/atricle/2008/01/18/AR2008011803277bf.html, accessed on 28 January 2008.

45. Nakashima, E and Mufson, S, "Hackers have attacked foreign utilities, CIA Analysts says," 19 January 2008, available at www.washington-post.com/wp/dyn/conmttent/atricle/2008/01/18/AR2008011803277bf.html, accessed on 28 January 2008.

46. Nakashima, E and Mufson, S. (2008), "Hackers have attacked foreign utilities, CIA Analysts says," www.washingtonpost.com/wp/dyn/conmttent/atricle/2008/01/18/AR2008011803277bf.html, accessed on 28 January 2008.

47. Traynor "Russia accused of unleashing cyberwar to disable Estonia" (2007) http://www.guardian.co.uk/world/2007/may/17/topstories3.russia accessed on 19 April 2012.

significant importance to Russian people. The repeat of the showdown, but now with Georgia on the receiving end, was witnessed in 2008 when Georgia was literally blown offline during its military conflict with Russia.[48]

China also appears to be waging a persistent low-profile campaign against many foreign nations, such as Japan,[49] the United States[50] and the United Kingdom.[51] The United States themselves are not above suspicion: some experts hint that it might have been that country[52] that unleashed such a powerful "cyber weapon" as Stuxnet which impacted Iran's ability to conduct nuclear research.

With Duqu worm having been discovered on 01 September 2011, and showing similar capabilities as Stuxnet,[53] it is only a matter of time before one is able to find the country behind the worm by analyzing the motives behind the facility which will suffer its onslaught. The appropriate questions that then arise are: How can CW be brought about and how can one ward against it?

4. CYBER WARFARE: MAKING CW POSSIBLE

To conduct any form of warfare, one would require an arsenal of weapons combined with an array of defensive technologies as well as laboratories and factories for researching and producing both. As far as CW is concerned, three general strategies need to be considered: preparation, offensive strategies and defensive strategies.

Preparation

Without arms, wars cannot be fought. Weapons are not constructed overnight and so in order to be prepared to enter any war, a state must have stockpiles of weapons ready to be deployed; CW is no different. Preparation will play a major role in CW as hostile acts occur in seconds or minutes, but the acts themselves are the culmination of many man-years worth of work.

In addition to training personnel and producing cyber weapons, the preparation stage also consists of a wide range of information gathering activities. Effective warfare is premised on knowledge of the opponent's weaknesses, and having extensive knowledge of an adversary's technology and networks prior to any hostilities is important for planning.

Preparation thus broadly consists of research, reconnaissance and vulnerability enumeration. The preparation phase never reaches a conclusion; ongoing research produces new tools, vulnerabilities and exploits, reconnaissance must continually discover new targets while removing stale targets, and vulnerability enumeration must keep track of new and old targets, while testing for recent vulnerabilities.

Research

CW does not require the infrastructure investment that physical arms do,[54] however it requires highly trained personnel to develop cyber weapons and the process of training to the required skill levels occupies a significant portion of activities prior to hostilities breaking out. In addition, once personnel have the necessary skills they need time to uncover vulnerabilities and turn those into usable weapons. These are separate jobs; the notion of vulnerability research as a separate discipline to exploit writing is growing especially as the continued fragmentation of applications and hardware forces extreme specialization. In the commercial information security market, vulnerability research and exploit writing are often separate tasks handed to different individuals, especially where memory corruption bugs are concerned.

The bug finders' skills tend towards quickly understanding how an application or system is built, how they often fail using common usage patterns and the ability to reverse engineer protocols quickly. Good bug finders are adept at automating this process. Their task, for example,

48. Danchev "Coordinated Russia vs Georgia cyber attack in progress" (2008) http://www.zdnet.com/blog/security/coordinated-russia-vs-georgia-cyber-attack-in-progress/1670 accessed on 09 April 2012, Tikk "Cyber Attacks Against Georgia: Legal Lessons Identified" (2008) http://www.carlisle.army.mil/DIME/documents/Georgia%201%200.pdf accessed on 09 April 2012.

49. "Japan parliament hit by China-based cyber attack" (2011) http://www.telegraph.co.uk/news/worldnews/asia/japan/8848100/Japan-parliament-hit-by-China-based-cyber-attack.html accessed on 09 April 2012.

50. "Identified Massive Global Cyberattack Targeting U.S., U.N. Discovered; Experts Blame China" (2011) http://www.foxnews.com/scitech/2011/08/03/massive-global-cyberattack-targeting-us-un-discovered-experts-blame-china/ accessed on 09 April 2012, Finkle "Cyber attack from China targets chemical firms: Symantec" (2011) http://www.msnbc.msn.com/id/45105397/ns/technology_and_science-security/t/cyber-attack-china-targets-chemical-firms-symantec/ accessed on 09 April 2012, Gorman "U.S. Report to Warn on Cyberattack Threat From China" (2012) http://online.wsj.com/article/SB10001424052970203961204577267923890777392.html accessed on 09 April 2012.

51. Foster "China chief suspect in major cyber attack" (2012) http://www.telegraph.co.uk/technology/news/8679658/China-chief-suspect-in-major-cyber-attack.html accessed on 09 April 2012.

52. Langner "Cracking Stuxnet, a 21st-century cyber weapon" (2011) http://www.ted.com/talks/ralph_langner_cracking_stuxnet_a_21st_century_cyberweapon.html accessed on 09 April 2012, Waug "How the world's first cyber super weapon 'designed by the CIA' attacked Iran - and now threatens the world" (2011) http://www.dailymail.co.uk/sciencetech/article-2070690/How-worlds-cyber-super-weapon-attacked-Iran-threatens-world.html accessed on 09 April 2012.

53. Naraine "Duqu FAQ" http://www.securelist.com/en/blog/208193178/Duqu_FAQ#comments accessed on 09 April 2012.

54. Of the $707.5 billion requested for the U.S. Department of Defense 2012 budget, $159 million was earmarked for the Cyber Command.

is to find input that will cause a memory corruption to occur, after which the test case is handed to an exploit writer. Vulnerabilities are found at all layers and are introduced all stages of development, and vulnerability research strives to understand each component. Software bugs are not the only target; flaws in algorithms are highly valued and common misconfigurations often yield trivial exploits.

The exploit writer has extreme specialist knowledge of the inner working of the operating system on which the application runs, and is able to craft exploits that bypass operating system protections designed to thwart their exploits. With a working exploit in hand, the exploit writer then ensures it runs without crashing across a wide range of possible versions of the target software and operating system. The exploit will also often be obfuscated in some manner, to avoid detection. For the moment it serves to simplify cyber arms by thinking of them as exploits, but as we shall see, cyber weapons consist of further components.

The combined process of finding a bug and writing an exploit for it can take months. While not all vulnerabilities require that level of input, it is by no means extreme. Consider that cyber weapons are not simply just bugs and exploits; superficially, configuration and operational failures are prevalent but deeper issues in protocols and algorithms also exist.

Reconnaissance

This phase of preparation focuses on identifying government organs, industries, infrastructure, companies, organizations and individuals that are potential targets. This is fed by a country's intelligence services, and overlaps with targets for physical warfare. In producing targets, information is gathered on the purpose of the targets, likely data that they store, technologies in use, network presence (on public or private networks) and channels by which the target could be engaged.

A discovery exercise is conducted on targets to determine which network services, if any, are accessible. Access to targets over the Internet is certainly not a requirement for CW but, for those that are, prior knowledge of their presence saves time when hostilities break out.

Vulnerability Enumeration

With reconnaissance complete, the next preparation step is to discover vulnerable systems. Vulnerability scanning is a common activity in the commercial security industry, and numerous scanners exist. A scanner has a large database holding knowledge of tens of thousands of issues, as well as how to test for those issues. The kinds of tests vary; in some instances a test consists of simply checking

a software version number extracted from a service banner, but in other tests more complex methods are required such as harmless exploits that confirm the vulnerability but do not take further action. By unleashing the scanner on a wide range of targets, a database of vulnerable machines can be saved prior to an CW.

Vulnerable systems are not the only benefit of wide scale scanning. Even a database of version numbers or technology types will improve targeting, for example when vulnerabilities for a system are discovered in the future.

The problem with scanners is that they are not subtle. They often test for issues unrelated to the technology on which the service runs, and protection mechanisms such as IDS are tuned to detect vulnerability scans. One improvement is scanning for specific issues across the target's networks which reduces the likelihood of detection, as well as masking tests to evade signature-based detection methods.

Offensive Strategies

Scale is an important decision in deciding on an CW strategy. To extend the analogy of physical warfare, the strategic focus in CW could either be on small but highly experienced and trained tactical teams who are able to compromise targets at will, or to deploy an overwhelming number of moderately skilled operators. The analogy has flaws: whereas adding an extra operator in the physical realm increases the capabilities of that unit, adding extra CW operators past some point starts to see diminishing returns. The reason for this is that many CW operations can be automated and parallelized; additional *infrastructure* is often more valuable than additional personnel. Smaller teams decrease personnel and training costs, though they are more vulnerable to physical attacks against the teams.

A second consideration is the type of hostilities that CW covers. It will very likely be employed as a support to a kinetic war in the same way that ground troops value air cover. There is a second set of tactics that are *covert*, and these are akin to espionage. Regardless of whether the strategy is overt or covert, we refer to them a hostilities.

The arsenal of CW includes weapons of psychological and technical nature. Both are significant and a combination of the two can bring about astounding and highly disruptive results.

Psychological Weapons

Psychological weapons include social engineering techniques and psychological operations *(psyops)*. Psyops include deceptive strategies, which have been part of warfare in general for hundreds of years.

Sun Tzu, in his fundamental work on warfare, says that "All warfare is based on deception."[55] Deception has been described as "a contrast and rational effort ... to mislead an opponent."[56] In December 2005, it became known that the Pentagon was planning to launch a US $300 million operation to place pro-U.S. messages "in foreign media and on items such as T-shirts and bumper stickers without disclosing the U.S. government as the source."[57]

Trust is a central concept and a prerequisite for any psyops to succeed. Traditionally, trust was vested in institutions and roles; a stranger in uniform might be afforded recognition based on the trust (if any) one has in the organization they are representing, without knowing them personally. Computer networks have, for some time now, been attacked by so-called "Social Engineers" who excel in gaining and exploiting trust, and cybercrime activities such as phishing rely on victims associating mere graphics on a website with the trust they invest in their bank.

However, this does not represent an exhaustive list of psyops. Psyops can also target the general population by substituting the information on well-trusted news agencies' Web sites as well as public government sites with information favorable to the attackers. A good example is where the information on the Internet is misleading and does not reflect the actual situation on the ground.

Today, social networks are highly efficient tools for spreading information. The instantaneous broadcast nature of micro-blogging sites such as Twitter mean that consumers rely more on social tools for obtaining information about current events than traditional media. In the heat of the moment, fact-checking quality decreases and the probability of inserting false information into social platforms increases. Social networks are also useful in guiding public conversations; Russia's legislative elections of 2011 saw automated software posting thousands of messages on Twitter in order to drown out opposition.[58]

The problem with psyops is that they cannot be used in isolation because once the enemy stops trusting the information it receives and disregards the bogus messages posted for its attention, psyops become useless, at least for some time. Therefore, technical measures of CW should also be employed to achieve the desired effect, such as DoS and botnet attacks. That way, the enemy

might not only be deceived but the information the enemy holds can be destroyed, denied, or even exploited.

Technical Weapons

There are non-subtle differences between weapons that exist in the physical realm and those that exist within the cyber realm, and the differences are useful to highlight. Bluntly put, there is no patch for an Intercontinental Ballistic Missile. To refine this further, a significant challenge facing a cyber army is that, while their attacks can occur virtually instantly, the target is able to respond as rapidly. The response may be to rollout patches for known issues, develop new patches for new vulnerabilities, employ perimeter defenses to filter out the attack traffic or simply disconnect the targeted system or network (perhaps, in the worst case scenario, even disconnect a country.)

A further challenge is the carrying of CW traffic. In the physical world, air and water provide the channels by which weapons are deployed, but in the cyber realm the path between two points is governed by a very different geography. It is a truism that in order to attack a network, an access channel extending from the attacker to the target is required. It could be a disconnected channel using flashdrives, or a highly technical and difficult operation such as the conquest of military satellites with ground-based resources or breaking into submarine cables, but the attacker must have a viable means for delivering their attack. While these complex or unreliable channels are possible, a more likely carrier for CW traffic is commercial Internet infrastructure supplied and maintained by global Internet Service Providers (ISPs), as they provide publicly accessible network links between countries around the world. In relying on commercial ISPs, attackers have the benefit of plausible deniability on the one hand, and on the other the ability to extend their reach into the commercial space of the target country, before attacking government and military targets.

CW attacks have the advantage that their implementation can be deployed long before any declaration of war. Whereas it is difficult to deploy physical armaments in preparation for detonating them near a target prior to a declaration of war, cyber attacks do not have the same limitation. Preparing attack launch pads either by compromising systems or by renting data center space can be performed months if not years in advance of attacks. When CW commences, the attacker is already well placed to wreak damage. A particularly effective force will compromise their target's supply chain, infusing equipment with backdoors years before they are used.

Rules of engagement present a further challenge. Traditional weapons are deployed at predetermined points in a conflict: artillery is seldom deployed when friendly

55. Sun Tzu, *Art of War.*

56. Thornton, R., *Asymmetric Warfare – Threat and Response in the Twenty-First Century,* 2007.

57. www.infowar-monitor.net/modules.php?op=modload&name=News &sid=1302, accessed on 28 September 2006.

58. http://www.guardian.co.uk/world/2011/dec/09/russia-putin-twitter-facebook-battles accessed on 29 February 2012.

troops are in the vicinity of the target, nuclear weapons may be a disproportionate response to a minor border skirmish and attacking schools or hospital without authorization may lie outside of a force's rules of engagement. Each armament has known side effects and its impact can be predicted; a commander in a physical war will understand which weapons are appropriate in each circumstance and deploy those that achieve their objectives while remaining within the constraints that are their policies and procedures. However, these norms have not been established publicly for CW, where *appropriate response* has yet to be defined. The dynamic nature of CW also means that, regardless of tools and techniques developed in the preparation phase, tools will be rapidly written during hostilities in reaction to new information or circumstances, and these could be trialed in the field while a conflict is active. Without perfect knowledge of exactly what a system controls or influences, unexpected consequences will be common in CW as the effects of an attack cannot be completely predicted.

The final significant difference between CW weapons and physical armaments is that their deterrence value is markedly different. Physical weapons demonstrate capability, which a cautious enemy will note. Developing defenses and counter-attacks against new weapons takes time in the real world, and so publicly exposing weapons capabilities can serve to avoid conflict. In the digital realm however, revealing one's weapons to an opponent simply highlights the areas they need to monitor, patch or upgrade. If an opponent provides evidence of working exploits against SoftwareX then, as a first line of defense, all of the target's machines running SoftwareX are moved behind additional layers and a plan is formulated to migrate away from SoftwareX. The defense can also perform their own investigation into SoftwareX, to determine the possible bug. By the time a conflict occurs, the revealed weapons are no longer useful. It has been shown in the commercial software exploit market that merely publishing seemingly innocuous descriptions of bugs can lead to experienced bug finders rapidly repeating the discovery without additional help. Demonstrating cyber capabilities is a confidence game in which a little skin is shown, in order to imply the strength of weapons that remain hidden. This is very susceptible to bluffing and subterfuge. With all this in mind, what do cyber weapons look like?

Previous work defined them as individual tools such as viruses, Trojans and so on. However, CW is fought at a larger scale than individual attacks, exploits and vulnerabilities. A commander on an CW battlefield is concerned with achieving objects such as disabling powergrids to support a kinetic attack on a facility. The commander firstly requires a team and infrastructure that is able to communicate and act in a distributed fashion; channeling attacks across lone routes or network links exposes a single point of failure, and attacks should be launched from a platform that is close in network terms to the target. This platform may be some distance from the command post. The weapons should be capable of working across multiple locations, and the payloads too must run in parallel and from multiple points in the network. Secondly, the commander must remain in control of attacks. For example, a worm that is unleashed against a target cannot indiscriminately attack targets on the public Internet as this would not help achieve the goal, and possibly result in collateral damage of systems unrelated to the opponent. Attacks would either be directly controlled by the commander through a command channel, or the attack would be self-limiting in terms of time or through built-in target detection. Examples of target detection are hardcoded addresses (when the reconnaissance phase was effective,) or a set of heuristics for determining at run-time whether a potential target should be attacked. This was seen in the Stuxnet attack, where the malicious code contained numerous heuristics to determine when it had finally migrated to the target SCADA installation. Until those heuristics were triggered, the program did nothing except attempt to migrate further. Lastly, a feedback loop that keeps the commander updated on whether the attack has succeeded is important. If the attack has a physical effect (for example, knocking out a powergrid), then the feedback loop would include forces on the ground. However, where the impact is virtual, then detecting attack success is not so clear cut. Consider the objective of disabling an opponent's logistics capability by preventing access to their logistics application through a deluge of traffic. Should the application become unresponsive from an attacker's perspective then it is not immediately apparent if the cause of the outage was a successful attack or due to the attack being detected and all the attacker's traffic blocked. Telemetry is vitally important.

Remember that CW is an "attack on information systems for military advantage using tactics of destruction, denial, exploitation or deception." The tactics by which the advantage is gained are determined by the weaknesses in the opponents systems, not the weapons in one's arsenal. This is important as it suggests that CW is not defined simply in terms of a set of tools; rather, the purpose or intent behind the deployment of a tactic is what defines a tactic to be part of an CW action. We shall see that so-called cyber weapons, in many circumstances, are called viruses, Trojans and the like when deployed by criminals or fraudsters. In that sense, the actual malicious components are less interesting as they are seldom unique to the field of CW and have been covered in this book already. The broader set of CW tools includes vulnerability databases, deployment tools, payloads and control consoles.

Vulnerability Databases

The vulnerability database is the result of an effort to collect information about all known security flaws in software. From the outset, it is obvious this is a massive challenge as vulnerability information is generated by thousands of sources including software vendors, vulnerability researchers and users of the software. Public efforts exist to provide identifiers for security weaknesses in software applications, such as the MITRE Corporations' Common Vulnerabilities and Exposures (CVE) project, which defines itself as "dictionary of common names (CVE Identifiers) for publicly known information security vulnerabilities."[59] The CVE contains information about a particular vulnerability in a software product, but for CW this is only part of the required information. A truly useful CW vulnerability database will also include those opposing systems that have been discovered to exhibit a particular weakness. The weaknesses are not simply software vulnerabilities; in many cases misconfigurations lead to compromise, and these are not problems with the code but snags resulting from the manner in which the system was setup.

Deployment Tools

Commonly seen in commercial malware where they are known as "droppers", deployment techniques are a separate beast from the payload that executes after compromise. Deployment occurs by exploiting a vulnerability, attacking a misconfiguration, spreading misinformation, spoofing communications, collusion or coercion. Stuxnet, for example, was deployed via four previously unknown vulnerabilities in Microsoft Windows, as well as through known network-based attacks. What made Stuxnet particularly interesting is that one infection mechanism was via USB flashdisks, as the target was presumed to not have public Internet connectivity.

Development of deployment tools occupies a large portion of the preparation phase, as discovered vulnerabilities and their exploits written form the basis for deploying malicious code. A stockpile of these tools aids an CW action, especially where tools take advantage of unknown flaws in software (termed "zero day", "0day", "0-day" or "oh-day").

Payloads

Merely loading malicious code onto a target does not constitute a full attack. Seldom is compromise the sole CW tactic; rather, post-compromise is where the CW tactic is implemented. Payloads consist of the post-compromise logic, and can be swapped out depending on the intended tactic. In this way, deployment and payload are separate tools but combined to form a single attack. Potential actions by malicious code are covered elsewhere in the book, here we mention a sample of possible payloads that have been seen in examples of CW.

A DoS attack is an overt example of CW, in that its effects will be plainly visible to the target; an important system will no longer be accessible or usable. DoS attacks were amongst the first malicious tactics to be labeled as actual CW maneuvers in state-on-state disputes. In 2007, Estonia suffered a massive DoS attack that lasted three weeks, and interrupted financial and governmental functions, while in a dispute with Russia.[60] Whether the attack was conducted by organs of the Russian state has never been established; however, CW does not necessitate actions are conducted only by nation states. Standards for attribution are not clearly defined, as we shall see.

The adoption of Supervisory Control and Data Acquisition (SCADA) network-connected systems for the U.S. infrastructure, such as power, water, and utilities,[61] has made DoS attacks a lethal weapon of choice. Offline SCADA systems could have spectacular kinetic results. In 2010, a covert attack given the name Stuxnet was targeted at nuclear facilities in Iran. It succeeded in causing widespread damage by replacing control code on SCADA systems, and aimed to remain covert by feeding the operators false instrument information while the attack was underway.

Control Consoles

In the commercial information security business, attack consoles are a known quantity. Software such as CORE IMPACT,[62] CANVAS[63] and Metasploit[64] provide interfaces that help the operator find vulnerabilities in target systems and launch exploits against those targets. The consoles ship with knowledge of hundreds of vulnerabilities, and include exploits for each one. The consoles also contain a multitude of payloads that can be attached to any exploit, that perform tasks such as account creation, command shell access or attacks against machines further in the network. An CW control console would contain the same elements as a commercial attack console, but also include the previously prepared vulnerability database as well as sport advanced telemetry to determine attack success.

59. http://cve.mitre.org/about/index.html, accessed on 10 March 2012.

60. Geers, K. (2008), *Cyberspace and the Changing Nature of Warfare*, BlackHat Asia 2008.

61. McClure, S., Scambray, J., and Kurtz, G. (2003), *Hacking Exposed: Network Security Secrets & Solutions,* 4th ed., McGraw-Hill/Osborne, 505.

62. http://www.coresecurity.com/content/core-impact-overview, accessed on 10 March 2012.

63. http://immunityinc.com/products-canvas.shtml, accessed on 10 March 2012.

64. http://www.metasploit.com/, accessed on 10 March 2012.

Defensive Strategies

As far as prevention is concerned, experts agree that "there is no silver bullet against CW attacks."[65] In the US, defense against CW is split between two entities: the Department of Defense (DoD) is responsible for defending military resources, and the Department for Homeland Security (DHS) is responsible for protecting critical infrastructure. Purely in terms of military spending, the DoD requested $3.2 billion for cybersecurity in 2012, of which $159 million was intended for the U.S. Cyber Command (USCYBERCOM),[66] a military command who mission is to be the organization that "plans, coordinates, integrates, synchronizes, and conducts activities to: direct the operations and defense of specified Department of Defense information networks and; prepare to, and when directed, conduct full-spectrum military cyberspace operations in order to enable actions in all domains, ensure US/Allied freedom of action in cyberspace and deny the same to our adversaries."[67] From this mission statement, it is also clear that an offensive capability will be maintained. According to one military official, this was envisioned to be split approximately 85 percent defense and 15 percent offense.[68]

Without question, the defender's job is harder than the attackers in the environment that currently exists. This is not to say it is a truism; it is certainly possible to envision a world in which uniform security is applied throughout all connected networks, however that world does not exist today. The defender's dilemma from an CW perspective has multiple facets. Apart from the oft cited statement that a defender needs to cover all avenues of attack while the attackers needs only find a single vulnerability, CW also introduces the additional difficulty of defending networks that one potentially does not control. Would an CW defense command have full access to all critical infrastructure networks? This is unlikely; rather, individual actions would have to be delegated to administrators of those networks, who best know the ins and outs of their own networks.

For the most part, the attacks listed here are preventable and detectable. The problem facing a large target entity such as a sovereign nation is to coordinate its defense of many possible individual targets. Policies and procedures must be consistent and thoroughly followed. This is a mammoth task, given the heterogeneous nature of large computing systems. CW defense calls for rapid communication between all points worthy of defense and the central defense command.

Current solutions are of an organizational nature. Many developed countries have response teams such as the Computer Emergency Response Teams (CERT), but these deal only with technicalities of attacks. Higher-level involvement from government is required to act as a line of defense for CW. The U.S. DHS has forged a link with the private and public sector in the form of the US-CERT, with the blessing of a national strategy for cyber defense, and DHS coordinates with USCYBERCOM to ensure protection across military, government and critical infrastructure networks. In the U.K., a similar role is played by the National Infrastructure Security Co-ordination Centre.

South Africa, as an example country of the developing world, does not yet have a high-level commitment to digital defense; however, there are initiatives in the pipeline to address CW issues. A number of international efforts that aim at securing the Internet and preventing attacks such as the ones mentioned here have been implemented. One such initiative is the adoption of the European Convention of Cybercrime 2001, which deals with the commercial aspects of the Internet transactions. As far as the military aspects of CW are concerned, there have been calls from a number of countries, notably Russia, that the Internet be placed under control of the United Nations.[69]

One author suggests that, while completely excluding attackers is desirable, this may not be attainable, and so proposes that "the purpose of cyberdefense is to preserve [the ability to exert military power] in the face of attack,"[70] by concentrating on desirable qualities such robustness, system integrity and confidentiality. This is achieved by architecture decisions (air-gapped networks), policy positions (centralized planning including forensic abilities, decentralized execution), strategic analysis (determining the purpose of distributed attacks) and effective operations.

Key to any cyberdefense is attribution; without identifying the source of the attack one is unable to launch counterattacks. Attribution is rarely guaranteed except

65. Lonsdale, D. J., *The Nature of War and Information Age: Clausewitzian Future* at 140.

66. Miller, J.N., Statement to the House Committee on Armed Services, Subcommittee on Emerging Threats and Capabilities, *Hearing on the Department of Defense in Cyberspcae and U.S. Cyber Command*, March 16, 2011. Available at http://www.dod.mil/dodgc/olc/docs/testMiller03162011.pdf, accessed 11 March 2012.

67. U.S. Cyber Command Fact Sheet, http://www.defense.gov/home/features/2010/0410_cybersec/docs/CYberFactSheet%20UPDATED%20replaces%20May%2021%20Fact%20Sheet.pdf, accessed on 10 March 2012.

68. Holmes, E., "Donley Sets out Structure for Cyber Command", *Air Force Times*, February 26 2009.

69. (2003) *"Russia wants the UN to take control over the Internet,"* www.witrina.ru/witrina/internet/?file_body=20031118oon.htm, accessed on 10 May 2005.

70. Libicki, M.C., *Cyberdeterrence and Cyberwar*, Santa Monica, CA: RAND Corporation, 2009. http://www.rand.org/pubs/monographs/MG877 accessed on 29 February 2012.

when extremely simplistic markers are used. For example, using the source IP address of an attack does not imply that the owner of that addresses was aware of the attack. Botnets are typically built from thousands of vulnerable machines around the Internet and, while a machine may form part of an CW action, the owner cannot be punished militarily. Rather, the impact of the attack must be assessed in conjunction with information gleaned from other sources, in order to determine who the likely source was. Even then, the information may not be sufficient to point to state actors; industrial espionage or commercial attacks share many characteristics with CW, as we have already highlighted.

5. LEGAL ASPECTS OF CW

The fact that the Internet is, by definition, international implies that any criminal activity that occurs within its domain is almost always of an international nature.[71] The question that raises concern, however, is the degree of severity of the cyber attacks. This concern merits the following discussion.

Terrorism and Sovereignty

Today more than 110 different definitions of terrorism exist and are in use. There is consensus only on one part of the definition, and that is that the act of terrorism must "create a state of terror" in the minds of the people.[72]

The following definition of "workstation terrorism" as a variation of CW is quite suitable: "Computer terrorism is the act of destroying or of corrupting workstation systems with an aim of destabilizing a country or of applying pressure on a government,"[73] because the cyber attack's objective, *inter alia,* is to draw immediate attention by way of causing shock in the minds of a specific populace and thus diminishing that populace's faith in government.

Incidents such as hacking into energy plants, telecommunications facilities, and government Web sites cause a sense of instability in the minds of a nation's people, thereby applying pressure on the government of a particular country; therefore, these acts do qualify as terrorism and should be treated as such. Factual manifestations of war, that is, use of force and overpowering the enemy, ceased to be part of the classical definition of "war" after World War I,[74] and international writers began to pay

more attention to the factual circumstances of each case to determine the status of an armed conflict. This is very significant for current purposes because it means that, depending on the scale and consequences of a cyber attack, the latter may be seen as a fully fledged war,[75] and the same restrictions—for example, prohibition of an attack on hospitals and churches—will apply.[76]

CW may seem to be a stranger to the concepts of public international law. This, however, is not the case, for there are many similarities between CW and the notions of terrorism and war as embodied in international criminal law.

The impact of the aforesaid discussion on sovereignty is enormous. Admittedly a cornerstone of the international law, the idea of sovereignty, was officially entrenched in 1945 in article 2(1) of the United Nations (UN) Charter.[77] This being so, any CW attack, whatever form or shape it may take, will no doubt undermine the affected state's political independence, because without order there is no governance.

Furthermore, the prohibition of use of force[78] places an obligation on a state to ensure that all disputes are solved at a negotiation table and not by way of crashing of the other state's Web sites or paralyzing its telecommunications facilities, thereby obtaining a favorable outcome of a dispute under duress. Finally, these rights of nonuse of force and sovereignty are of international character and therefore "international responsibility"[79] for all cyber attacks may undermine regional or even international security.

Liability Under International Law

There are two possible routes that one could pursue to bring CW wrongdoers to justice: using the concept of "state responsibility," whereby the establishment of a material link between the state and the individual executing the attack is imperative, or acting directly against the person, who might incur individual criminal responsibility.

State Responsibility

Originally, states were the only possible actors on the international plane and therefore a substantial amount of jurisprudence has developed concerning state responsibility. There are two important aspects of state responsibility

71.   Corell   (2002),   www.un.org/law/counsel/english/remarks.pdf (accessed on 20 September 2002).

72. J. Dugard, International Law: A South African Perspective 149 (2nd ed. 2000).

73.   Galley   (1996),   http://homer.span.ch/~spaw1165/infosec/sts_en/ (accessed on 20 September 2002).

74. P. Macalister-Smith, Encyclopaedia of Public International Law 1135(2000).

75. Barkham, *Informational Warfare and International Law,* 34 Journal of International Law and Politics, Fall 2001, at 65.

76. P. Macalister-Smith, Encyclopaedia of Public International Law 1400 (2000).

77. www.unhchr.ch/pdf/UNcharter.pdf (accessed on 13 October 2002).

78. www.unhchr.ch/pdf/UNcharter.pdf (accessed on 13 October 2002).

79. *Spanish Zone of Morocco* claims 2 RIAA, 615 (1923) at 641.

that are important for our purposes: presence of a right on the part of the state claiming to have suffered from the cyber attack and imputation of the acts of individuals to a state.

Usually one would doubt that such acts as cyber attacks, which are so closely connected to an individual, could be attributable to a state, for no state is liable for acts of individuals unless the latter acts on its behalf.[80] The situation, however, would depend on the concrete facts of each case, as even an *ex post facto* approval of students' conduct by the head of the government[81] may give rise to state responsibility. Thus, this norm of international law has not become obsolete in the technology age and can still serve states and their protection on the international level.

Attribution in the context of CW, without somebody coming forward to claim responsibility for the attack, may prove to be a difficult, if not impossible, task because to hold a state liable one would have to show that the government had effective control over the attacker but, though its conduct, failed to curtail the latter's actions directed at another state and threatens international peace and security.[82]

As a result, even though many attacks emanate from China, for example, the Chinese government will only be responsible if it supported or at least was aware of the attacker and went along with that attacker's plans. Solid forensic investigation would therefore be required before there can be any hope in attributing responsibility.[83]

Individual Liability

With the advent of a human rights culture after the Second World War, there is no doubt that individuals have become participants in international law.[84] There are, however, two qualifications to the statement: First, such participation was considered indirect in that nationals of a state are only involved in international law if they act on the particular state's behalf. Second, individuals were regarded only as beneficiaries of the protection offered by the international law, specifically through international human rights instruments.[85]

Individual criminal responsibility, however, has been a much more debated issue, for introduction of such a concept would make natural persons equal players in international law. This, however, has been done in cases of Nuremberg, the former Yugoslavia, and the Rwanda tribunals, and therefore,[86] cyber attacks committed during the time of war, such as attacks on NATO web sites in the Kosovo war, should not be difficult to accommodate.

What made it easier is the fact that in 2010, the Review Conference for the International Criminal Court introduced article *8bis* to the Rome Statute of the International Criminal Court ("ICC") which finally defined the crime of "aggression" as "the planning, preparation, initiation or execution, by a person in a position effectively to exercise control over or to direct the political or military action of a State, of an act of aggression which, by its character, gravity and scale, constitutes a manifest violation of the Charter of the United Nations".[87]

There is no doubt that use of unilateral force which threatens universal peace is prohibited in international law.[88] The difficulty in holding an individual responsible is two-fold: confirming jurisdiction of the ICC over the accused and proving the intention to commit the crime covered by the Rome Statute the ICC administers.

First, only persons who are found within the territory of the state that is a signatory to the Rome Statute or such state's nationals may be tried before the ICC. Secondly, there may be difficulties with justification of use of the same terms and application of similar concepts to acts of CW, where the latter occurs independently from a conventional war. Conventionally, CW as an act of war sounds wrong, and to consider it as such requires a conventional classification. The definition of "international crimes" serves as a useful tool that saves the situation: arguably being part of *jus cogens*,[89] crimes described by terms such as "aggression," "torture," and "against humanity" provide us with ample space to fit all the possible variations of CW without disturbing the very foundation of international law. Thus, once again there is support for the notions of individual criminal responsibility for cyber attacks in general public international law, which stand as an alternative to state responsibility.

In conclusion, it is important to note that international criminal law offers two options to an agreed state, and it is up to the latter to decide which way to go. The fact that there are no clear pronouncements on the subject by an

---

80. M.N. Shaw, International Law 414 (2nd ed. 1986).

81. For example, in *Tehran Hostages Case (v.) I.C.J. Reports,* 1980 at 3, 34–35.

82. Huntley (2010) "Controlling the use of force in cyber space: the application of the law of armed conflict during a time of fundamental change in the nature of warfare" 60 Naval L. Rev. 1 2010.

83. Friesen (2009) "Resolving tomorrow's conflicts today: How new developments within the U.N. Security Council can be used to combat cyberwarfare" 58 Naval L. Rev. 89 2009.

84. J. Dugard, International Law: a South African Perspective (2nd ed. 2000), p. 1.

85. J. Dugard, International Law: a South African Perspective 1 (2nd ed. 2000), p. 234.

86. M.C. Bassiouni, International Criminal Law (2nd ed. 1999), p. 26.

87. Resolution RC/Res.6 http://www.icc-cpi.int/iccdocs/asp_docs/Resolutions/RC-Res.6-ENG.pdf accessed on 09 April 2012.

88. Green (2011) "Questioning the peremptory status of the prohibition of the use of force" 32 Mich. J. Int'l L. 215 2010–2011.

89. M.C. Bassiouni, International Criminal Law (2nd ed. 1999), p. 98.

international forum does not give a blank amnesty to actors on an international plane to abuse the apparent *lacuna,* ignore the general principles, and employ unlawful measures in retaliation.

Remedies Under International Law

In every discussion, the most interesting part is the one that answers the question: What are we going to do about it? In our case there are two main solutions or steps that a state can take in terms of international criminal law in the face of CW: employ self-defense or seek justice by bringing the responsible individual before an international forum. Both solutions, however, are premised on the assumption that the identity of the perpetrator is established.[90]

Self-Defense

States may only engage in self-defense in cases of an armed attack[91] which in itself has become a hotly debated issue.[92] This is due to recognition of obligation of nonuse of force in terms of Art.2(4) of the UN Charter as being not only customary international law but also *jus cogens.*[93]

Armed attack, however, can be explained away by reference to the time when the UN Charter was written, therefore accepting that other attacks may require the exercise of the right to self-defense.[94] What cannot be discarded is the requirement that this inherent right may be exercised only if it aims at extinguishing the armed attack to avoid the conclusion of it constituting a unilateral use of force.[95] Finally, a state may invoke "collective self-defense" in the cases of CW. Though possible, this type of self-defense requires, first, an unequivocal statement by a third state that it has been a victim of the attack, and second, such a state must make a request for action on its behalf.[96]

Therefore, invoking self-defense in cases of CW today, though possible,[97] might not be a plausible option, because it requires solid proof of an attack, obtained promptly and before the conclusion of such an attack,[98] which at this stage of technological advancement is quite difficult. The requirement that the attack should not be completed by the time the victim state retaliates hinges on the fact that once damage is done and the attack is finished, states are encouraged to turn to international courts and through legal debate resolve their grievances without causing more loss of life and damage to infrastructure. Since most states would deny any support of or acquiescence to the actions of its citizens in executing an attack, the more realistic court that one would turn to in pursuit of justice is the ICC.

International Criminal Court

The International Criminal Court (ICC) established by the Rome Statute of 1998 is not explicitly vested with a jurisdiction to try an individual who committed an act of terrorism. Therefore, in a narrow sense, cyber terrorism would also fall outside the competence of the ICC.

In the wide sense, however, terrorism, including cyber terrorism, could be and is seen by some authors as torture.[99] That being so, since torture is a crime against humanity, the ICC will, in fact, have a jurisdiction over cyber attacks, too.[100]

Cyber terrorism could also be seen as crime against peace, should it take a form of fully fledged "war on the Internet," for an "aggressive war" has been proclaimed an international crime on a number of occasions.[101] Though not clearly pronounced on by the Nuremberg Trials,[102] the term "crime of aggression" is contained in the ICC Statute and therefore falls under its jurisdiction.[103]

90. Murphy (2011) "Mission Impossible? International law and the changing character of war" 87 Int'l L. Stud. Ser. US Naval War Col. 13 2011, (2011) Lewis "Cyberwarfare and its impact on international security" http://www.un.org/disarmament/HomePage/ODAPublications/OccasionalPapers/PDF/OP19.pdf accessed on 09 April 2012.

91. U.N.Charter art. 51.

92. Cammack (2011) "The Stuxnet worm and potential prosecution by the international criminal court under the newly defined crime of aggression" 20 Tul. J. Int'l & Comp. L. 303 2011.

93. M.Dixon, Cases and Materials on International Law 570 (3rd ed., 2000).

94. P. Macalister-Smith, Encyclopaedia of Public International Law 362 (2000).

95. Military and Paramilitary Activities in and against Nicaragua *(Nic. v. U.S.A.),* www.icj-cij.org/icjwww/Icases/iNus/inus_ijudgment/inus_ijudgment_19860627.pdf (accessed on 11 October 2002).

96. M.Dixon, Cases and Materials on International Law 575 (3rd ed. 2000).

97. Barkham, *Informational Warfare and International Law,* Journal of International Law and Politics (2001), p. 80.

98. otherwise a reaction of a state would amount to reprisals, that are unlawful; see also *Nic.* v. *U.S.A.* case in this regard, www.icj-cij.org/icjwww/Icases/iNus/inus_ijudgment/inus_ijudgment_19860627.pdf (accessed on 11 October 2002).

99. J. Rehman, International Human Rights Law: A Practical Approach 464–465 (2002).

100. Rome Statute of the International Criminal Court of 1998 art.7, www.un.org/law/icc/statute/english/rome_statute(e).pdf (accessed on 13 October 2002).

101. League of Nations Draft Treaty of Mutual Assistance of 1923, www.mazal.org/archive/imt/03/IMT03-T096.htm (accessed on 13 October 2002); Geneva Protocol for the Pacific Settlement of International Disputes 1924, www.worldcourts.com/pcij/eng/laws/law07.htm (accessed on 13 October 2002).

102. P. Macalister-Smith, Encyclopaedia of Public International Law 873–874 (1992).

103. Art.5(1)(d) of the Rome Statute of the International Criminal Court 1998, www.un.org/law/icc/statute/english/rome_statute(e).pdf (accessed on 13 October 2002).

Cyber crimes can also fall under crimes against nations, since in terms of customary international law states are obliged to punish individuals committing crimes against third states.[104] Furthermore, workstation-related attacks evolved into crimes that are universally recognized to be criminal and therefore against nations. P. Macalister-Smith, Encyclopaedia of Public International Law 876 (1992). Therefore, thanks to the absence of *travaux préparatoires* of the Rome Statute, the ICC will be able to interpret provisions of the statute to the advantage of the international community, allow prosecutions of cyber terrorists, and ensure international peace and security.

In practical terms the above will mean that a cyber attack will most probably be interpreted as part of "any weapon"[105] within the scope of the definition of "aggression" of the Rome Statute and the attacker will face the full might of the law as long as he/she is the national of the member state or finds him/herself within the physical territorial boundaries of the state that is party to the Rome Statute even though the attacker's conduct may not be enough to make the country of its nationality liable for what he/she did.[106]

Other Remedies

Probably the most effective method of dealing with CW is by way of treaties. At the time of this writing, there has been only one such convention on a truly international level, the European Convention on Cybercrime 2001.

The effectiveness of the Convention can be easily seen from the list of states that have joined and ratified it. By involving such technologically advanced countries as the United States, Japan, the United Kingdom, Canada, and Germany, the Convention can be said to have gained the status of instant customary international law,[107] as it adds *opinio juris* links to already existing practice of the states.

Furthermore, the Convention also urges the member states to adopt uniform national legislation to deal with the ever-growing problem of this century[108] as well as provide a platform for solution of disputes on the international level.[109] Finally, taking the very nature of CW into

consideration, "hard" international law may be the solution to possible large-scale threats in future.

The fact that remedies bring legitimacy of a rule cannot be overemphasized, for it is the remedies available to parties at the time of a conflict that play a decisive role in the escalation of the conflict to possible loss of life. By discussing the most pertinent remedies under international criminal law, the authors have shown that its old principles are still workable solutions, even for such a new development as the Internet.

Developing Countries Response

The attractiveness of looking into developing countries' response to an CW attack lies in the fact that usually these are the countries that appeal to transnational criminals due to lack of any criminal sanctions for crimes they want to commit. For purposes of this chapter, the South African legal system will be used to answer the question of how a developing country would respond to such an instance of CW.

In a 1989 "end conscription" case, South African courts defined war as a "hostile contest between nations, states or different groups within a state, carried out by force of arms against the foreign power or against an armed and organised group within the state."[110] In the 1996 *Azapo* case, the Constitutional Court, the highest court of the land, held that it had to consider international law when dealing with matters like these.[111] In the 2005 *Basson* case, the Constitutional Court further held that South African courts have jurisdiction to hear cases involving international crimes, such as war crimes and crimes against humanity.[112]

A number of legislative provisions in South Africa prohibit South African citizens from engaging, directly or indirectly, in CW activities. These Acts include the Internal Security Intimidation Act 13 of 1991 and the Regulation of Foreign Military Assistance Act 15 of 1998. The main question here is whether the South African courts would have jurisdiction to hear matters in connection therewith. A number of factors will play a role. First, if the incident takes place within the air, water, or *terra firma* space of South Africa, the court would have jurisdiction over the matter.[113]

The implementation of the Rome Statute Act will further assist the South African courts to deal with the matter because it confers jurisdiction over the citizens who

104. P. Macalister-Smith, Encyclopaedia of Public International Law 876 (1992).
105. Article 8 *bis* 2(b) of the Rome Statute, http://www.icc-cpi.int/icc-docs/asp_docs/Resolutions/RC-Res.6-ENG.pdf acc3essed on 09 April 2012.
106. Schmitt (2011) "Cyber Operations and the *Jus in Bello*: Key Issues" 87 Int'l. L. Stud. Ser. US Naval War Col. 89 2011.
107. http://conventions.coe.int/Treaty/en/Treaties/Html/185.htm (accessed on 9 October 2002).
108. European Convention on Cybercrime of 2001 art. 23, http://conventions.coe.int/Treaty/en/Treaties/Html/185.htm (accessed on 9 October 2002).
109. European Convention on Cybercrime of 2001 art. 45, http://conventions.coe.int/Treaty/en/Treaties/Html/185.htm (accessed on 9 October 2002).

110. Transcription *Campaign and Another v. Minister of Defence and Another* 1989 (2) SA 180 (C).
111. *Azanian People's Organisation (AZAPO) v. Truth and Reconciliation Commission* 1996 (4) SA 671 (CC).
112. *State v. Basson* 2005, available at www.constitutionalcourt.org.za.
113. Supreme Court Act 59 of 1959 (South Africa).

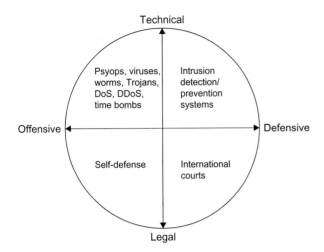

FIGURE 58.2 Holistic view of CW.

commit international crimes. It is well known that interference with the navigation of a civil aircraft, for example, is contrary to international law and is clearly prohibited in terms of the Montreal Convention.[114]

A further reason for jurisdiction is found in the 2004 Witwatersrand Local Division High Court decision of *Tsichlas v. Touch Line Media*,[115] where Acting Judge Kuny held that publication on a Web site takes place where it is accessed. In our case, should the sites in question be accessed in South Africa, the South African courts would have jurisdiction to hear the matter, provided that the courts can effectively enforce its judgment against the members of the group.

Finally, in terms of the new Electronic Communications and Transactions (ECT) Act,[116] any act or preparation taken toward the offense taking place in South Africa would confer jurisdiction over such a crime, including interference with the Internet. This means that South African courts can be approached if preparation for the crime takes place in South Africa. Needless to say, imprisonment of up to five years would be a competent sentence for each and every participant of CW, including coconspirators.[117]

6. HOLISTIC VIEW OF CYBER WARFARE

This chapter has addressed the four axes of the CW model[118] presented at the beginning of this discussion: technical, legal, offensive, and defensive. Furthermore, the specific subgroups of the axes have also been discussed. For the complete picture of CW as relevant to the

discussion at hand, however, Figure 58.2 places each subgroup into its own field.[119]

7. SUMMARY

This discussion clearly demonstrated that CW is not only possible, it has already taken place and is growing internationally as a preferred way of warfare. It is clearly demonstrated that successful strategies, offensive or defensive, are dependent on taking a holistic view of the matter. Information security professionals should refrain from focusing only on the technical aspects of this area, since it is shown that legal frameworks, national as well as international, also have to be considered. The prevailing challenge for countries around the globe is to foster collaboration among lawyers, information security professionals, and technical IT professionals. They should continue striving to at least keep the registry of CW arsenal and remedies updated, which may, in turn, incite adversaries to provide us with more material for research.

Finally, let's move on to the real interactive part of this Chapter: review questions/exercises, hands-on projects, case projects and optional team case project. The answers and/or solutions by chapter can be found in the Online Instructor's Solutions Manual.

CHAPTER REVIEW QUESTIONS/EXERCISES

True/False

1. True or False? The technical side of CW deals with technical exploits on one side and offensive measures on the other.
2. True or False? It is clear that CW is all about information superiority because "the fundamental weapon and target of CW is information.".
3. True or False? In addition to training personnel and producing cyber weapons, the preparation stage also consists of a wide range of information gathering activities.
4. True or False? CW does not require the infrastructure investment that physical arms do,[120] however it requires highly trained personnel to develop cyber weapons and the process of training to the required skill levels occupies a significant portion of activities prior to hostilities breaking out.
5. True or False? The reconnaissance phase of preparation focuses on identifying government organs, industries, infrastructure, companies, organizations and individuals that are not potential targets.

114. Montreal Convention of 1971.
115. *Tsichlas v. Touch Media* 2004 (2) SA 211 (W).
116. Electronic Communications and Transactions Act 25 of 2002.
117. Electronic Communication and Transaction Act 25 of 2002.
118. Supreme Court Act 59 of 1959 (South Africa).

119. Implementation of the Rome Statute of the International Criminal Court Act 27 of 2002 (South Africa).
120. Of the $707.5 billion requested for the U.S. Department of Defense 2012 budget, $159 million was earmarked for the Cyber Command.

Multiple Choice

1. What type of scanning is a common activity in the commercial security industry, where numerous scanners exist?
   A. Qualitative analysis
   B. Vulnerabilities
   C. Data storage
   D. Vulnerability
   E. DHS

2. What is an important decision in deciding on a CW strategy?
   A. Network attached storage (NAS)
   B. Risk assessment
   C. Scale
   D. Subcomponents
   E. Bait

3. What type of weapons include social engineering techniques and psychological operations *(psyops)*?
   A. Organizations
   B. Fabric
   C. Psychological
   D. Risk communication
   E. Security

4. There are _____ differences between weapons that exist in the physical realm and those that exist within the cyber realm, and the differences are useful to highlight.
   A. Cabinet-level state office
   B. Non-subtle
   C. Infrastructure failure
   D. SAN protocol
   E. Taps

5. What type of database is the result of an effort to collect information about all known security flaws in software?
   A. Irrelevant
   B. Consumer privacy protection
   C. IP storage access
   D. Vulnerability
   E. Unusable

EXERCISE

Problem

How can organizations address advanced persistent cyber threats?

Hands-On Projects

Project

How are cyber-attacks carried out?

Case Projects

Problem

What targets can be attacked?

Optional Team Case Project

Problem

What are the implications of a cyber-attack?

Practical Security

System Security

Lauren Collins

kCura Corporation

1. FOUNDATIONS OF SECURITY

Since the inception of technology, data security has revolved around cryptography. Since cryptography is only as good as the ability of a person or a program, new methods are constantly being implemented as technology becomes more sophisticated.

Differentiating Security Threats

Cipher text and secret keys are transported over the network and can be harvested for analysis, as well as impersonate a source or, worst case, cause a service denial. Thus, aiding encryption and complex distribution methods, a network needs to be secure and elegant. That is, the network should have applicable appliances that monitor and detect attacks, intelligence that discriminates between degradations/failures and attacks, and also a convention for vigorous countermeasure strategies to outmaneuver the attacker. Consequently, network security is a completely separate topic from data security.

Incident levels should be defined as low, medium, high, and catastrophic. Level 1 helpdesk professionals should be equipped to handle tasks such as these. Low-severity breach examples are:

- Malware or virus-infected system that is on the local area network (LAN)
- Account credentials compromised with general rights
- Spam e-mail incidents

Medium-severity incidents should be escalated to a system administrator or engineer. These would include:

- Website destruction
- Spam impacting an entire environment's performance
- Sensitive information leak
- Account credentials compromised with administrative rights

High-severity incidents would be handled by a senior engineer, architect, manager, or director. Examples include:

- Hacking of the environment
- International, federal, or state law violations:
    1. HIPAA (Health Insurance Portability and Accountability Act)—medical field
    2. FERPA (Family Education Rights and Privacy Act)—education field
    3. Pornography
    4. Illegal download and sharing of copyright material (music, movies, software)
- Disruption of business due to malicious acts
- Breach to systems where an act is in progress of leaking confidential information and hosts need to be disconnected altogether to halt the process

Modern enterprises and their security teams need to be prepared to work with an onslaught of new, rapidly evolving menaces. From novice script writers to sophisticated hackers working for criminal organizations, if an enterprise does not have policies in place to handle threats, they will pay the price in disconcerting, expensive data breaches. An effective threat management platform is one vibrant component for any security team who deals with evolving threats from the world outside of their control. Resources must be allocated to implement such a platform, and an agenda should be put in place while also testing the program. The following are five best practices to increase effectiveness when implementing a vulnerability management program:

1. **Control notifications and alerts.** The most important thing a company can do is get a handle on threat management and ensure an IT professional is available to review and respond to a notification or alert. In order to accomplish this, one or more individuals need to have responsibility assigned to them so that everyone is aware of which point person(s) will review logs and audits on a daily basis, or in the event of an attack. It is not uncommon to see organizations assign different

individuals to review different alerts consoles. Case in point: A firewall expert may review firewall changes and logs, while an applications engineer may review the logs and alerts from the Web application firewalls.

2. **Consider a holistic view.** In the domain of discovery avoidance, attackers are growing more and more cutting edge. A multichannel attack is the superficially innocuous spear where a user clicks on a link that leads to a rogue site that has been designed to look authentic. This user may then be deceived into entering sensitive data or clicking another link affecting the target machine with a bot. Once that user's sensitive information has been collected, the attacker can now attempt to log in to a system and dive deeper into the network for more valuable information. To catch multichannel attackers, alerts need to be organized in a meaningful way from all the systems into a single console where correlation rules filter activities and, when combined, creates a single, organized attack.

3. **Slash false positives.** Have you received so many email alerts that you ignore certain alerts and immediately delete them without further investigation? This author surely has. Excessive alerts and false positives intensify the noise ratio so greatly that it can be challenging (if not impossible) to scrutinize data to find truly malicious occurrences. If an organization's administrators cannot differentiate important alert signals through all the less significant events, the system becomes useless. To reduce the number of false positives fabricated, an enterprise should first analyze the alert output of its threat-warning console and then determine if the rules can be fine-tuned to reduce the false-positive noise. Also, filtering the alerts by level of confidence may be useful so that administrators can see which alerts are more likely to be relevant. One way to lower the alert levels without losing the critical alerts would be to set the threshold levels that match normal activity on the network. For example, if a company forces all users to change the password on the same 30-day cycle, they might find that failed logins increase significantly on the day after the end of the cycle. To account for this occurrence, a rule that normally signals an alert after two failed logins could be increased to four failed logins, only on days following the password change. Those logins could also be linked to other threat indicators, such as attempts to log in using the same username from multiple IP addresses, to increase accuracy.

4. **Integrate thresholds and procedures.** As mentioned in #3, aggregating threat information into a single console gives firms threat visibility across the entire infrastructure. You want more visibility? A firm can integrate that single console view with their new, refined thresholds and procedures. That's right: Always keep the mind-set that you want to be a moving target. By treating your monitoring system the same way as your infrastructure, as the infrastructure grows please ensure that your monitoring system accommodates that growth. Rules and log aggregation tools rightfully parse through information and flag legitimate attack activity for further investigation or response. Another key to integrating effectively is to make sure engineers and admins have access to proper escalation paths, communication protocols, and approved response activities.

5. **Corroborate remediation events.** In a heated situation, one can easily overlook validating events in logs upon review. Even when performing routine maintenance such as patch management, many firms fail to close the remediation loop by validating the entries. Did the patch get loaded properly? Did it close the intended vulnerability? Without testing, an organization cannot be certain the remediation was successful and the threat exposure gap was closed. There is a threat management cycle, and it must be completed utilizing steps for validation. This may include rescanning systems to validate patches and also, by performing application and network penetration, testing to confirm that fixes or controls are blocking vulnerabilities as expected.

Hardware and Peripheral Security

Network security deals with the secure transport of data. It requires more awareness and a thorough understanding of the different types of mechanisms and attack scenarios and how they can be differentiated. A topic these days for a controversial discussion is whether to allow employees to bring your own device (BYOD) to the office. Whether it is a mobile device, a desktop or laptop, or a tablet, companies must have policies in place to address security and who owns the data on the device. Several places institute a policy where an application like ActiveSync is used, and upon an employee's termination the device(s) can be wiped of all data. That usually sounds good to the employee upon signing the consent form, but imagine losing all your contacts, music and apps, and all the data on the device. Given the breadth of end users on mobile devices and the diversity of use cases, BYOD is driving not just the need for performance upgrades but also much more fine-grained network access controls.

There is also a method for detecting signatures and how that is used to classify attacks and enhance network security. Computing platforms used in the field are intricate and require interaction between multiple hardware components (processor, chipset, memory) for their normal operation. Maintaining the security of the platforms translates to verifying that no known security exploits are present in the runtime interaction between these hardware units which can be exploited by attackers. However, given the large number of state elements in the hardware units and many control signals influencing their mutual interaction, validating the security of a commercial computing platform thoroughly can be complicated and intractable. By exemplifying challenges to correctly implement security, it is necessary to provide examples of various classes of hardware-oriented security attacks. The following are logic and tools to use:

- For the enthusiastic newbies, there are pre-made, entry-level tool packages as shown in Figure 59.1. You can diagnose your hardware without writing even one line of code. Automatically generate your device driver, and run this nifty tool on any operating system.
- Digital oscilloscopes, logic analyzers, device programmers, and spectrum analyzers are all available on eBay and are no longer out of reach for hardware hackers. Utilizing this equipment, one can take advantage of essentially the same equipment used in production engineering facilities. In Figure 59.2, a logic analyzer displays signals and program variables as they change over time.
- Free tools are available that are open-source Printed Circuit Board (PCB) design tools, which include electronic design automation (EDA). These tools allow hackers to dive deep into the game without bringing a ton of years of electrical engineering to the table. Schematic captures are done interactively with an editor tool and allow one to gain insight on arrays and other miniscule passive components.

The magnificence of hardware hacking, similar to engineering design, is that rarely is there only one correct process or solution. The author's personal hardware hacking methodology consists of the following subsystems:

1. *Gather information:* Hardware hacking, much like any technology, is about gathering pertinent information from an assortment of resources. The answers include product specifications, design documents, marketing data, forums or blogs, and of course, social network sites. Social engineering techniques can be used to manipulate a human victim into divulging applicable information. Many will simply call a vendor's sales or technical engineer directly and invoke interest in a product, and will ask open-ended questions to obtain as much information as the respondent is willing to divulge.

2. *Hardware stripping:* This consists of obtaining the hardware and disassembling it to gather evidence regarding system functionality, design practices, and potential attack areas to target. The primary goal of tearing hardware down is to gain access to the circuit board, which will then allow a hacker to identify high-level subsystems, component types, and values, and in some cases, locate any antitampering mechanisms that would specifically impede physical attack or tampering. Clearly, having direct access to the circuitry allows an attacker to modify, remove, or add components.

3. *Assess external accessibility:* Any product interface that is made accessible to the outside world is an avenue of attack. Programming, debugging, or admin interfaces are of extreme interest, as it allows a hacker direct access to control the device with the same authority as a tech or engineer.

4. *Reverse engineering:* By extracting program code or data and disassembling the contents, a hacker will be able to obtain full insight into the product operation and functionality and potentially modify, recompile, and insert the code back into the product in order to bypass security mechanisms or inject malicious behavior.

The prolific adoption of embedded systems has led to a blurring between hardware and software. Software

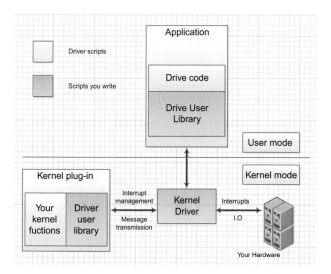

FIGURE 59.1 Architecture to access your hardware directly from the application level.

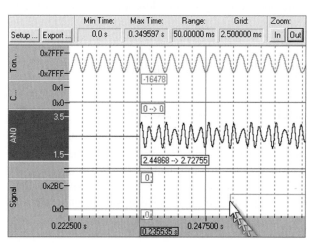

FIGURE 59.2 Signals recorded by the logic analyzer are easily configured to accurately measure signal changes and delta information, and will even allow you to zoom into the area at any point where a signal changed.

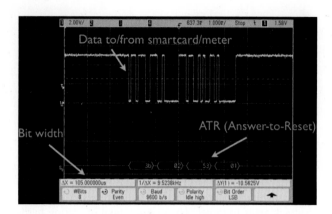

FIGURE 59.3 Oscillator output displaying the transmission between the smartcard and meter.

hackers can now use their skills, tools, and techniques in an embedded environment against firmware without having to grasp hardware-specific paradigms.

The best way to close the gap between hardware and software hacking is to allow them to work together in order to achieve the desired results. The leading example will enlighten the reader as to why electronic devices used in security or financial applications cannot and should not be fully trusted without thorough analysis and stress testing.

Example

Many large cities have installed digital parking meters throughout the streets, and claim they are secure and tamper proof. While a hacker has many opportunities to attack a metering device, this example focuses on the easily accessible, external smartcard interface. By placing an uninhabited shim between the smartcard and meter, the shim was used to gain the requisite signals and the communication was then captured using an oscilloscope. (It's good to have friends with cool toys). The serial decoding function of the oscilloscope, displayed in Figure 59.3, points out the actual data bytes that were transmitted from the meter, then to the card, and finally received by the meter from the card.

Patch Management and Policies

Does anyone receive auto-generated email alerts that are excessive, false positives? Not only can it be impossible to examine all of the information, but to assert whether or not the information is truly malicious is another tedious task. Many times this author has ignored countless emails when too many false positives have occurred, which could have been a warning of potential issues. Anytime an environment changes, individuals should be attentive to editing the notifications of the environment. An example would be when maintenance will be performed where five servers will be restarted multiple times for patches.

The alert should be paused for these five servers in an effort to not trigger false alerts where the rest of the team is not aware of the maintenance. If the team is aware of the maintenance, this is a prime example of a false alert that is overlooked, and think through this example happening 10 times a day. Hardly anyone will pay attention to the alerts if 99.99 percent of them are false positives.

Implementing consistent, updated patches may be cost prohibitive for a company, especially for a mission-critical environment. It is necessary to maintain the integrity of an environment and the data by applying both operating system and application security patches and updates. The security team or IT manager needs to ascertain a criterion for procedures as well as an established time frame to apply patches. Windows patches may alter program functionality and capability so severely that users are unable to effectively perform their job function. For instance, some Web applications were not compatible with Internet Explorer version 9, and if updates are set to automatic, troubleshooting this issue could be quite time consuming. Unless patches have been tested in a testing environment, and were successful, there should not be any patches released to the user community. There are patch management packages that offer automation, of course, after testing has proved to be successful. Figure 59.4 depicts an example of a patch management program. Patch names are shown in the left-hand column, the next column classifies the patch, then displays whether or not the patch was installed, and shows the release date along with the arrival date.

Package management systems are charged with the task of organizing all of the packages installed on a particular system. The characteristics of architectural tasks are shown in the following checklist: An Agenda for Action for Implementing Package Architectural Tasks.

IT admins may install and maintain software-utilizing instruments other than package management software. Dependencies will need to be managed, and additional

---

An Agenda for Action for Implementing Package Architectural Tasks

Please see the following package architectural characteristics tasks (check all tasks completed):

_____**1.** Manage dependencies to ensure a package is installed with all packages required.

_____**2.** Group packages related to utility.

_____**3.** Upgrade software to latest (tested) versions from a file repository.

_____**4.** Apply file records to manage encapsulated files.

_____**5.** Verify digital signatures upon substantiation of the source packages.

_____**6.** Corroborate file checksums to confirm authentic, comprehensive packages.

FIGURE 59.4   Patch management software is a helpful tool to track patches and whether or not the patch has been applied to a client.

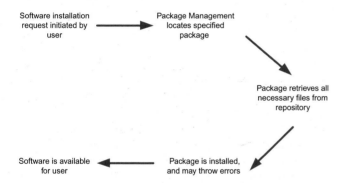

FIGURE 59.5   Cycle of a patch management software installation.

changes may have to be assimilated into the package manager. This does not seem like a very efficient way to some, although having control of source code and the ability to manipulate code may be an attractive advantage. In addition to the manual process of installing patches, license codes may need to be manually activated. When dealing with large environments, can you fathom typing in an activation code thousands of times? Not only is this counterproductive, but it is severely inefficient as noted in Figure 59.5.

Each hardware and software vendor may have differing frequencies for their approach to patch releases. Microsoft has "Patch Tuesday" which occurs the second Tuesday of a month. When Windows updates are set to Automatic, a computer will apply patches as they're released. These patches may not be tested in an environment, hence the importance of setting updates to manual and having a patch management system. A good practice is to release patches once a month, and to release them roughly a week after the vendor has published the patch. Network hardware patches may not need to be applied,

depending on the environment and whether or not the patch will compromise the function of the equipment. Additionally, patches may alter the command set or configuration, so be sure to back up your configuration prior to applying any patch or firmware update.

2. BASIC COUNTERMEASURES

With only 30 to 40 percent of firewall rules in use, security vulnerabilities arise due to misconfigurations. An organization may expose its network to access for which there is no business purpose.

Security Controls and Firewalls

At times, it is not an issue of data sneaking past network controls, but misconfiguration and reluctance to fix issues fearing that the business may be interrupted as changes are implemented. When a team identifies all users' network access, they are able to shape and control access based off rights and proper use. Risk is reduced by blocking unnecessary access paths prior to a security incident occurring. When a consultant is brought into a firm and shows the IT director all the paths, there are holes in the network that could be used for unauthorized access; heads roll, and a plan is soon in place to rectify the holes. Other firms are relatively weak when it comes to monitoring the data right in front of them. While many firms have the appropriate technologies, policies and awareness programs need to be in place for users and their resources. The level of awareness also needs to be known in unmanaged IP devices due to the number of vulnerabilities only increasing over time.

There are many options out there when considering a firewall for your environment. A great deal of firewalls also include other security features: unified threat management (UTM), data loss prevention (DLP), content filtering, intrusion detection and prevention services (IPS), and vulnerability management. A firewall is such a critical component of your infrastructure, and fault tolerance should not be considered optional. A network should be designed so that it is resilient enough to handle the failure of a single firewall. Most concerns with UTM are the amount of processors eaten up by the jobs being performed. With large organizations, you may find you're better off with specialty devices fulfilling each of the security functions covered by UTM. Conversely, UTMs are a great benefit for smaller companies with lower network traffic, especially where costs are concerned when selecting a bundled option.

There is a huge amount of virtual networks out there, both at company office sites and at data center facilities. Virtual firewalls are a way to maximize your security budget by consolidating multiple logical firewalls onto a single platform. Each virtual firewall has its own rules, interfaces, and configuration options that are completely independent from other virtual firewalls running in other infrastructure platforms, but in the same environment. Having this feature also adds the element that a configuration mistake will not only affect performance, but may block all traffic getting to and from the affected segment.

Whether the firewall is hardware or software based, the objective is to control whether or not traffic should be allowed in or out based on a predetermined set of rules. Imagine a security analyst parsing through hundreds pages of logs, where this would only account for 10 to 30 minutes of traffic and determining whether or not rule sets need to be altered.

Case in point: Also envision an issue arising where a complaint comes in from your company's Internet provider stating that your IP address raised a red flag and downloads of copyrighted material were performed. This Internet provider can even state the name of the movie that was downloaded. Other than the Internet provider expecting a response back describing the steps that will be taken to prevent subscriptions from downloading illegal content, internal management at this company expects actions to be taken as well. This is when a security admin will go in and parse through logs searching for the type of file that was downloaded, and if this was not already blocked it will need to be. Bit torrents may need to be blocked. However, depending on the type of work a company performs, there are many legal and necessary uses of bit torrents.

Application Security

An increasing number of organizations are questioning whether they should put a Web application firewall in front of an application, or if the code should just be fixed. Entire teams have committed to securing an application. Consultants travel all over to perform a deep dive of an application environment and suggest measures to correct loopholes. If the strategy shifted toward incorporating applications coupled with Web application firewalls, the company would be more productive integrating this plan as part of its broader application security architectures. Whether Structured Query Language (SQL) attacks or cross-site scripting was the vulnerability, a financial institution would still need about two years to patch 99 percent of the flaws in its applications. By this time, several revisions of the application will have been released, sending teams in downward spirals chasing their tails.

If you ask your customers or colleagues, there is not much collaboration between the security and development teams in an organization. The worst part is that developers are not usually motivated to address secure application development unless they are forced to in the midst of a security incident or to prove compliance initiatives. Developers are sometimes reviewed based on how much software they can build and release on time, and no one holds them accountable for the security portion. The application security challenge has become so difficult to address through development that an alternative plan relies on integrating defensive technologies like Web app firewalls, database audit and protection (DAP), and XML gateways into the infrastructure. Using Web app firewalls in conjunction with coding frameworks fits nicely into filling security functions.

Is it faster, cheaper, and more effective to use a device to shield an application from a security flaw? It may be, but meanwhile hacking strategies are also becoming more accessible, faster, free, and more attractive. Web application firewalls are an appliance, or server, that can monitor and block traffic both to and from the applications. They are common in companies such as credit-card payment firms, which have frequent code reviews. You cannot throw a piece of hardware in front of all applications and expect it to solve all your problems because it is a good idea to build your applications securely from the start.

Hardening and Minimization

The practice of safeguarding systems is to reduce the plane of exposure, also referred to as hardening. An environment where a multitude of cross-functional work is performed can increase the scale of the vulnerability surface since that plane grows larger based on the scope of work. A security engineer can reduce available trajectories of incidents by removing unnecessary software that is not related to business use, deleting usernames or logins for employees or contractors who are no longer at the firm, and also by disabling or removing unnecessary services.

Linux has so many powerful tools where a patch can be applied to the kernel and will close open network ports, integrate intrusion detection, and also assimilate intrusion prevention. While this may work for a smaller firm, the author does not recommend this solution for a robust, large environment. Exec Shield is an undertaking Red Hat began in 2002, with the goal of condensing the probability of worms or other automated remote breaches on Linux systems. After this was released, a patch was necessary that emulated a never execute (NX) bit for a CPU that lacks a native NX implementation in the hardware. This NX bit is a tool used in CPUs to isolate sections of memory that are used by either the storage of processor instructions, or code, or for storage of data. Intel and AMD now also use this architecture; however, Intel identifies this as execute disable (XD), and AMD appointed the name enhanced virus protection. An operating system with the capability to emulate and take advantage of a NX bit may prevent the heap memory and stack from being executable, and may also counteract executable memory from being writable. This facilitates the prevention of particular buffer overflow exploits from prospering, predominantly those that inject and execute code, for example, Sasser and Blaster worms. Such attacks are dependent on some portion of the memory, typically the stack, to be both executable and writable, and if it is not the stack fails.

In the realm of Wi-Fi, companies must implement tight network security controls. Device authentication is another layer of security that would not allow proximity hacking. For example, a car next door is parked in a parking lot and can easily hack onto a firm's network. Guest wireless is a common component to segregate guests off the company's network. With that being said, corporate users might be tempted to switch over to the public, guest network where there are fewer or no controls. This is where leakage may occur. Best practice would be to set up a guest network that issues only temporary credentials to allow connections. This will deter any employees from accessing and utilizing an unsecure connection, and also will not allow former guests or employees' access.

In an ideal world, all traffic would be monitored, but when a company does a cost/benefit analysis, it may seem excessive to do so. Directors make a judgment call based on the threat analysis to ascertain whether it is worth putting these controls into certain segments of the network. It is a terrible practice to have everyone on the same network, but unfortunately that is what most companies do. Whether money is not abundant enough to segment a network, or a security team is not in place to implement policies and maintain them, this is prevalent in most small and medium-sized businesses.

The best approach would be to have anomaly detection that baselines the network traffic and assesses patterns, identifying the anomalies. For the determined attacker, you need to be prepared on the host; so, you

need to have it tightly secured where users do not have admin rights. Having a good anti-virus and anti-malware software platform in place is mandatory, too. Depending on the business purpose, classifying data and ultimately segregating that data is also key. The only way to access that data would be through a secured connection through Citrix or some other key/fingerprint mechanism.

In programming, minimization is the method of eradicating all unnecessary character from source code, keeping its functionality. Unnecessary characters may include comments, white space characters, new line characters, comments, and occasionally block delimiters, which are used to enhance comprehension to the code but are not required for that code to execute. In computing machine learning, a generalized model must be selected from a finite data set, with the consequent challenge of overlifting. The model may become too strongly modified to the particularities of the training set and oversimplifying new data. By balancing complexity to institute security against success to seamlessly provide data to groups across the entire firm, one can master risk minimization.

3. SUMMARY

This chapter focused on how the objective of systems security is to improve protection of information system resources. All organizational systems have some level of sensitivity and require protection as part of good management practice. The protection of a system must be documented in a systems security plan.

The purpose of the systems security plan is to provide an overview of the security requirements of the system and describe the controls in place or planned for meeting those requirements. The systems security plan also delineates the responsibilities and expected behavior of all individuals who access the system. The systems security plan should be viewed as documentation of the structured process of planning adequate, cost-effective security protection for a system. It should reflect input from various managers with responsibilities concerning the system, including information owners and the system owner. Additional information may be included in the basic plan, and the structure and format should be organized according to organizational needs.

In order for the plans to adequately reflect the protection of the resources, a senior management official must authorize a system to operate. The authorization of a system to process information, granted by a management official, provides an important quality control. By authorizing processing in a system, the manager accepts its associated risk.

Management authorization should be based on an assessment of management, operational, and technical controls. Since the systems security plan establishes and documents the security controls, it should form the basis for the authorization, supplemented by the assessment report and the plan of actions and milestones. In addition, a periodic review of controls should also contribute to future authorizations. Re-authorization should occur whenever there is a significant change in processing, but at least every three years.

Finally, let's move on to the real interactive part of this chapter: review questions/exercises, hands-on projects, case projects, and optional team case project. The answers and/or solutions by chapter can be found in the Online Instructor's Solutions Manual.

CHAPTER REVIEW QUESTIONS/EXERCISES

True/False

1. True or False? Since the inception of technology, data security revolves around cryptography.
2. True or False? Cipher text and secret keys are transported over the network and can be harvested for analysis, and furthermore to impersonate a source or, worst case, cause a service denial.
3. True or False? Network security deals with the insecure transport of data.
4. True or False? Implementing inconsistent, updated patches may be cost prohibitive for a company, especially for a mission-critical environment.
5. True or False? With only 30 to 40% of firewall rules in use, security vulnerabilities arise due to misconfigurations.

Multiple Choice

1. At times, it is not an issue of data sneaking past network controls, but _____ and reluctance to fix issues fearing that the business may be interrupted as changes are implemented.
   A. qualitative analysis
   B. vulnerabilities
   C. data storage
   D. misconfiguration
   E. DHS
2. There are many options out there when considering a _____ for your environment.
   A. firewall
   B. risk assessment
   C. scale
   D. subcomponents
   E. bait
3. There are an increasing number of organizations questioning whether they should put a(n) _____ in front of an application, or if the code should just be fixed.
   A. organizations
   B. fabric
   C. psychological
   D. Web application firewall
   E. security
4. The practice of safeguarding systems is to reduce the plane of exposure, also referred to as:
   A. cabinet-level state office
   B. nonsubtle
   C. hardening
   D. SAN protocol
   E. taps
5. The purpose of the _____ is to provide an overview of the security requirements of the system and describe the controls in place or planned for meeting those requirements?
   A. systems security plan
   B. consumer privacy protection
   C. IP storage access
   D. vulnerability
   E. unusable

EXERCISE

Problem

If continuous monitoring does not replace security authorization, why is it important?

Hands-On Projects

Project

Who should be involved in continuous monitoring activities?

Case Projects

Problem

What role does automation play in continuous monitoring?

Optional Team Case Project

Problem

What security controls should be subject to continuous monitoring?

## Chapter 60

Securing the Infrastructure

Lauren Collins

kCura Corporation

1. COMMUNICATION SECURITY GOALS

Since the inception of technology, data security revolves around cryptography. Because cryptography is only as good as the ability of a person or a program, new methods are constantly implemented as technology becomes more sophisticated.

Network Design and Components

Cipher text and secret keys are transported over the network and can be harvested for analysis; furthermore they can impersonate a source or, worst case, cause a service denial. Thus, to aid encryption and complex distribution methods, a network needs to be secure and elegant. That is, the network should have applicable appliances that monitor and detect attacks, intelligence that discriminates between degradations/failures and attacks, and also a convention for vigorous countermeasure strategies to outmaneuver the attacker. Consequently, network security is a completely separate topic from data security; however, the devices chosen must complement your infrastructure.

The accumulation of advances in key technologies has enabled companies to envision the implementation of an infrastructure with no limitations. Among these advances are those in materials that underlie electronic components and optical technologies, including optical fibers. Improvements in electronic integrated circuits include both the speed at which these circuits can perform their functions and the achievable complexity that allows a single chip to perform complex tasks. Advances in signal processing techniques that use electronic circuits and software to convert information and information-carrying signals into forms suitable for transport over short or long distances arrange for data to be stored, processed, and transmitted lightning fast. Such advantages have even allowed engineers and scientists to work harder and think further out to develop new technologies to follow suit on hardware and software

transformations. Significant progress is required to realize and appreciate the vision of affordable media.

New algorithms and approaches complement the speed of transport networks, coupled with complex connection and session establishment and management. Total network approaches are required to resolve effective management of a cutting-edge infrastructure solution. Large costs are associated with installation and building out of fiber networks needed to provide an objective, robust network. Networks must be scalable and support multiple types of media, including coax, fiber, copper, and wireless, using both the shared media and switched approaches. Premise access must support the multiplexing of video, voice, and data sources requiring varied quality-of-service (QoS) levels and various bandwidths.

Several backbone options and avenues are available, due mostly to the era of electronic trading. These can be comprehensively separated into time division techniques and wavelength division techniques. Determining the potential of each technology would significantly contribute to a company's success, depending completely on the type of business involved. The time domain limits are determined by the speed of the electro-optic transducers, of the required buffer and memory, and of the switching and control logic required to manage the system. Additionally, high-speed regeneration technologies play a pivotal role in delivering benefits of time-division techniques to the system. Take long distances into consideration: Fiber properties such as loss and dispersion in the fiber limit the capabilities of the fiber span. Optical amplification, attenuators, and dispersion compensator devices can restore impairments induced by the fiber properties and allow the media to match the heat and light of the equipment chosen. Wavelength converters, wavelength filters, and wavelength division multipliers enable use of a greater capacity of the fiber. Optical regeneration techniques permit clock recovery and lead to full regeneration capabilities in the optical domain, avoiding unnecessary optical to electrical conversions.

Switching and Routing

Backbone networks require switches with tremendous capacity. Switches of this scale are not commercially available today, and much research, configuration, and testing must be done to make them perform a specific job. Total system throughputs of 15 terabits per second are possible with the latest and greatest equipment out there, and more is to come. A challenge for switching systems is to achieve systems that the access network can scale to either the amount of users or the amount of traffic being pumped through the network. Signaling systems for switch control must support a richer communication model than prior generations of switches. User channels can operate at any rate from a couple bits per second to a gig per second and beyond. Multipoint communication channels (one-to-many and many-to-many) are necessary for applications such as video and voice. This requires a signaling and control system that supports a multipoint call model, where a call may include multiple virtual circuits, each with its own individual characteristics. Certain applications place extreme demands on signaling systems.

Layer-specific functionality is now an important role of a switch. When ordering a switch, you now have to determine whether you only want layer 2 or whether layer 3 will be needed. Many switches have the capacity to install software to allow layer 3 capabilities; however, some layer 3 capabilities are tied to the hardware. The author's favorite layer 3 function is IP multicast through Internet Group Multicast Protocol (IGMP) snooping. IGMP snooping with proxy reporting actively sifts IGMP packets in an effort to reduce the amount of load the router is carrying that provides the multicast. When a join leaves and heads to the next routers, routes are filtered so that the smallest number of information is transported. A switch warrants that the router has one point to contend with, no matter how many listeners are out there in the network. The router is only aware of the most recent member who joined the group. Since a switch creates the layer 1 connection, both virtually and physically, it is no longer required to have systems interconnected to the same hardware or at the same physical location.

Several switches will meet an organization's needs, and several designs are available to fit in any data center or server room. Some switches, usually just in the home or small office setting, are not rackable and can be located on a desktop or server. Rack-mounted switches are intended to be used in racked environments and can range anywhere from 1 u to an entire cabinet of 42 u (u is the measurement relating to units). A chassis switch, as seen in Figure 60.1, is one that has either vertical or horizontal blades that allow for hot swapping and many different, custom options. There are many switch management features:

- Bandwidth and duplex settings for circuits
- Priority settings for ports

FIGURE 60.1   Chassis switch.

- Simple Network Management Protocol (SNMP) configuration to monitor devices and perform health checks
- Message authentication code (MAC) filtering and port security
- Link aggregation for versions < Elastic Sky X interface (ESXi) 5, trunking for versions of ESXi > 5
- Layer 2 and Layer 3 virtual local area network (VLAN)

Switching over to routers (no pun intended), we find that when choosing a router it is important to understand the job the router should perform. Just as there are many protocols, there are many types of routing platforms to accomplish services at the edge, at the distribution layer, or at the core. An edge router operates at the edge of a multiprotocol switching network. In a (MPLS) domain, IP datagrams are forwarded, and routing information is used to determine which labels should accompany the datagram. The packets are then labelled accordingly, and the labeled packets are forwarded into the MPLS domain.

Similarly, an edge router can strip the label and forward the resulting packet over utilizing standard IP forwarding logic. Distribution routers can aggregate traffic from multiple-access routers and are not dependent on site location or geographical region. Often, distribution routers are responsible for enforcing quality of service (QoS) across a (WAN), so they may have considerable amounts of memory installed, multiple wide area network (WAN) interfaces, and extensive on-board data processing routines. These types of routers are also capable of providing connectivity to large groups of servers, whether it be file servers or additional external networks. Core routers operate on the Internet backbone at an organization to transmit lightning fast speeds and to forward IP packets just as fast. Routing also needs to be done at the core level, in some instances, and differs since edge routers have different features and sit at the edge of a network. Conversely, core routers can sit at the edge of a network if the engineer desires to build the infrastructure this way.

Ports and Protocols

Between the protocols User Datagram Protocol (UDP) and Transmission Control Protocol (TCP), there are 65,535 ports available for communication between devices. Among this impressive number are three classes of ports:

1. Well-known ports: Range from 0–1,023
2. Registered ports: Range from 1,024–49,151
3. Dynamic/Private ports: Range from 49,152–65,535

Understandably, not all of the ports listed in those three categories are secure. As a result, reference Table 60.1, which enumerates the most commonly used ports and the service/protocol that utilizes the port.

Ideally, when architecting a system, one should plan out the intent for the environment and should only configure the services necessary for the network to pass traffic and servers to perform their intended functions.

Table 60.1 reflects protocols that may be open by default, as well as some that are necessary for the intended purpose of the environment. When installing equipment in Section I, it is imperative that the engineer be aware of the ports that need to be open for each device or piece of software and, if needed, can be referenced in the device white paper. It is also essential to recognize the variation between the numerous types of attacks and the respective ports on which such attacks would be executed. It is necessary to monitor the ports that are open in an effort to detect protocols that may leave the network vulnerable. Running netstat on a workstation will allow one to view the ports that are running and that are open. In addition, running a local port scan will also portray which ports are exposed.

Many protocols may still be used during an installation where system administrators and users are not aware, and those may leave the network vulnerable. Simple Network Management Protocol (SNMP) and Domain Naming Service (DNS) were deployed years ago, yet still present security risks. SNMP can be utilized for monitoring the health of network equipment, servers, and other peripheral

TABLE 60.1 Well-Known Port Numbers and Their Respective Service Description and Protocol.

Port	Service/Protocol
7	Echo/TCP & UDP
9	Systat/TCP & UDP
15	Netstat/TCP & UDP
20	FTP data transfer/TCP
21	FTP control/TCP
22	SSH/TCP
23	Telnet/TCP
24	Private mail/TCP & UDP
25	SMT{/TCP
39	RLP/TCP & UDP
42	ARPA/TCP & UDP
42	Windows Internet Name Service/TCP & UCP
43	WHOIS/TCP
49	TACACS/TCP & UDP
53	DNS/TCP & UDP
69	TFTP/UDP
80	HTTP/TCP
88	Kerbos/TCP & UDP
101	NIC hostname/TCP
110	POP3/TCP
115	SFTP/TCP
119	Network News Transfer Protocol/TCP
123	NTP/UDP
143	IMAP/TCP
152	Background File Transfer Protocol/TCP & UDP
156	SQL Service/TCP & UDP
161	SNMP/UDP
162	SNMPTRAP/TCP & UDP
175	VMNET/TCP
179	BGP/TCP
220	IMAP/TCP & UDP
264	Border Gateway Multicast Protocol/TCP & UDP
280	http-mgmt/TCP & UDP
389	LDAP/TCP & UDP
443	HTTPS/TCP
500	Internet Security Assoc and Key Mgmt (ISAKMP)/UDP

equipment. However, susceptibilities associated with the SNMP derive from use of SNMP v1. Although such vulnerabilities were raised years ago (about 10 years), exposures are still reported while utilizing the current version of SNMP. Liabilities allow for authentication evasion and execution of proprietary code when utilizing SNMP. The SNMP infrastructure has three components:

1. SNMP managed connections
2. SNMP instruments
3. SNMP network management servers

Where the devices are concerned, they load the agent, which in turn assembles information and forwards it to the management servers. Network management servers collect a substantial amount of significant network information and are possibly targets of attacks due to their use of SNMP v1, which is not secure. A community name is a point of security; however, it may be similar to a password. Usually, the community name is public and is not secure, nor is it changed, thus permitting information to leak out to invasions. Conversely, SNMP v2 uses Message Digest Version 5 (MD5) for authentication. The transmission can also be encrypted. SNMP v_3 is used across firms as the criteria; however, a number of devices are not compatible and are left to use SNMP v1 or SNMP v2.

SNMP assists spiteful users to learn too much about a system, making password speculations easier. SNMP is often disregarded when checking for vulnerabilities due to the User Datagram Protocol (UDP) ports 161 and 162. Ensure network management servers are physically secured and secured on the network layer. Consider utilizing a segregate management subnet, protecting it by using a router with an access list. Unless the service is required, it should be shut off by default. In order to defend a network infrastructure from incidents aimed at obsolete or unfamiliar ports and/or protocols, remove any unnecessary protocols while creating access-control lists to allow traffic on defined ports. This eliminates the possibility of any obscure protocols being utilized, while minimizing the danger of an incident.

Threats

Hijacking occurs when an intruder takes control of a session between a server and the client. The communication starts when a middle-man attack adds a request to the client, resulting in the client getting kicked off the session. Meanwhile, the rogue workstation talks with the server, and the attacker intercepts the source-side packets, replacing them with fresh packets that are sent over to the destination. This type of hijacking, referred to as TCP/IP hijacking, most commonly occurs during telnet and Web sessions when security is nonexistent, or lacking, and also when session timeouts are improperly configured.

During the course of a Web session, cookies are commonly used to authenticate and track users. While the authentic session is in session, an attacker may attempt to hijack a session by loading a modified cookie in the session page. Session hijacking may also ensue when a session timeout is set to be an extended period of time; this gives an attacker a chance to hijack a session. Telnet-type plaintext connections create the ideal situation for TCP hijacking. In an instance like this, when an attacker surveys the data passing in the TCP session, the attacker can take control of the user's session; this is yet another reason why it is called session hijacking. When a user is forced to authenticate prior to allowing transactions to occur, it helps to prevent hijacking attacks. Protection mechanisms include the use of unique sequence numbers (USNs) and Web session cookies. The more unique the cookies, the harder it is to crack and hijack. Additional preventative measures for this type of attack include the use of encrypted session keys and Secure Socket Layer (SSL) encryption.

Spoofing

Spoofing is a method of providing false identity information to gain unauthorized access. This can be achieved by modifying the source address of traffic or source of information. Spoofing seeks to bypass IP address filters by setting up a connection from a client and sourcing the packets with an IP address that is allowed through the filter. Blind spoofing occurs when the attacker only sends data and only makes assumptions of responses. Informed spoofing is when the attacker can participate in a session and can monitor the bidirectional communications. Services that can be spoofed are:

1. Email
2. Web
3. File transfers
4. Caller ID

Web spoofing occurs when an attacker creates a convincing, fabricated copy of an entire Web site. The fabricated Web site will appear just as a real Web site would, and it has all the pages and links. The attacker controls the fabricated Web site so that all network traffic between the user's browser and the site goes through the attacker. In the situation for email spoofing, a spammer or virus can forge the email packet information in an email so that it appears that the email is coming from a trusted host, a friend, or even your own email. When one leaves their email address at an Internet site, or exchange email with others, a spoofer may be able to use your email address as the sender address to blast spam. File transfer spoofing involves the FTP service, and FTP is sent in clear, plain text. The data can be intercepted by an attacker. The data can then be viewed and altered prior to sending it over to the receiver. These types of attacks are intended to pull information from a network of users to accomplish a more comprehensive attack. By setting up a filter to deny traffic originating from the Internet that shows an internal network address, using the signing capabilities of certificates on servers and clients will allow Web and email services to be more secure. Using an Internet Protocol Security (IPSEC) tunnel adds more security between critical servers and their clients by preventing these types of attacks from transpiring.

Intercepting Traffic

The man in the middle attack occurs when an attacker intercepts traffic and deceives the parties at both ends into believing they are communicating with one another. An attack like this is possible due to the nature of the three-way TCP handshake process using SYNchronize (SYN) and ACKnowledge (ACK) packets. Since TCP is a connection-oriented protocol, a three-way handshake takes place when establishing a connection and when closing the session. When a session is established, the client sends a SYN request; then the server sends an ACK (sometimes referred to as SYN-ACK-ACK), completing the connection. During this process, the attacker initiates the man-in-the-middle attack by using a program that appears to be a server to the client and appears to be a client to the server. In telnet and wireless communications, this attack is common. This is a difficult attack to perform due to physical routing matters, TCP sequencing number, and speed. Since the hacker must sniff both sides of the connection simultaneously, programs have been developed to aid the attacker in order to make man in the middle easier.

If an attack is performed on an internal network, physical access to that network is mandatory. By ensuring that access to wiring closets and switches are restricted, and that they're behind locked doors, physical access becomes difficult. Once the physical segment of the network has been secured, services and resources may allow a system to be inserted into a session, so those will need to be protected. DNS can be compromised and used to redirect the initial request for service, providing an opportunity to execute the man-in-the-middle attack. DNS access needs to be restricted, allowing read-only access for anyone but administrators. By using encryption and security controls and protocols, organizations can prevent these types of attacks on their infrastructure.

Packet Capturing

Packets are captured by sniffing devices in a replay attack. Once the relevant information is extracted, packets are put back on the network. An attack such as this can be used to replay a bank transaction or other comparable types of data transfers in the hopes of replicating or changing activities, such as transfers or deposits. Protecting oneself against a replay attack will involve some type of timestamp associated with the packets, or time-valued nonrepeating serial numbers. Additionally, integrating secure protocols, such as IPSEC, prevents replays of data traffic while providing authentication and data encryption.

Denial of Service

When resources have been disrupted or services that a user would expect to have access to are compromised, they have experienced a denial-of-service attack. These types of attacks are executed by manipulating protocols and can occur without the need to be validated by the network. An attack will usually involve flooding the listening port on a machine with packets. The purpose is to make that workstation so busy processing the new connections that it cannot process legitimate service requests. Several tools are available on the Internet that will produce a denial-of-service attack. IT administrators use them daily to test connectivity and troubleshoot issues on their networks, whereas malicious users will use the tool to cause connectivity issues. Some examples of DoS attacks are:

- SYN flood—This attack takes advantage of the TCP three-way handshake. A source system will send a flood of synchronization (SYN) requests and will never send the final acknowledgment (ACK), creating partially open TCP sessions. Since the TCP stack waits before resetting the port, the attack overflows the destination workstation connection buffer, making it impossible to service requests from valid users.
- Ping flood—This attack attempts to block service or reduce activity on a host by sending ping requests directly to the target. Variations of these attacks include the ping of death, where the packet size is too large and the system is unable to handle the number of packets.
- Ping/Smurfing—This attack is based on the Internet Control Message Protocol (ICMP) echo reply function. The common name is ping, the command line tool utilized to invoke the function. The attacker sends ping packets to the broadcast address of a network, replacing the original source address in the ping packets with the source address of the target, causing a flood of traffic to be sent to the unsuspecting network device.
- Fraggle—This attack is similar to smurfing. The difference is that fraggle uses UDP rather than ICMP. The attacker sends spoofed UDP packets to broadcast addresses, just as the smurf attack does. These UDP packets are directed to port 7, echo, or port 19, Chargen. When connected to port 19, a character generator attack can be run. Refer to Table 60.1 for the commonly exploited ports.
- Land—This attack exploits a behavior in the operating systems of several versions of Windows, Unix, Mac, and Cisco IOS with respect to their TCP/IP stacks. The

attacker spoofs a TCP/IP SYN packet to the victim system with the same source and destination IP address and the same source and destination ports. This confuses the system as it attempts to respond to the packet.

- Teardrop—This form of attack targets a known behavior of UDP in the TCP/IP stack of some operating systems. The Teardrop attack will send fragmented UDP packets to the target with odd offset values in subsequent packets. When the operating system attempts to rebuild the original packets from the fragments, the fragments overwrite each other, causing confusion. Since some operating systems cannot elegantly handle the error, the system will either crash or restart.

DoS attacks come in many flavors, shapes, and sizes. Take the first step to protect the firm from an attack: Understand the types of attacks and the nature in which they operate.

Distributed Denial of Service

A modest expansion of denial of service can be referred to as distributed DoS attacks. Masters are computers that run the client software, where zombies will run the software. The attacker will create a master, which in turn creates a large number of zombies, or recruits. The software that runs on the zombies can launch multiple types of attacks, such as UDP or SYN flooding on a particular target. Figure 60.2 depicts a distributed DoS attack.

Although distributed DoS attacks usually come from the outside of the network to deny services, the impact of the attacks displayed inside the network should also be cogitated. Internal distributed DoS attacks allow disgruntled employees or malicious users to disrupt services without any outside influence or interaction. To help protect your network, set up filters on external routers to drop packets involved in these types of attacks. Also, set up an additional filter that denies traffic originating from the Internet but showing an internal IP address. By doing this, ping and some services are lost to test network connectivity, but this is where administrators should be on a separated network segment than users and would be on a segment where the filtering did not occur. If the operating system supports it, one can reduce the amount of time before the reset of an unfinished TCP connection. Doing so makes it harder to keep resources unavailable for extended periods of time.

Tip: In the case of a distributed DoS attack, it is best to get in touch with your service provider so that they can divert traffic or block traffic at a higher level.

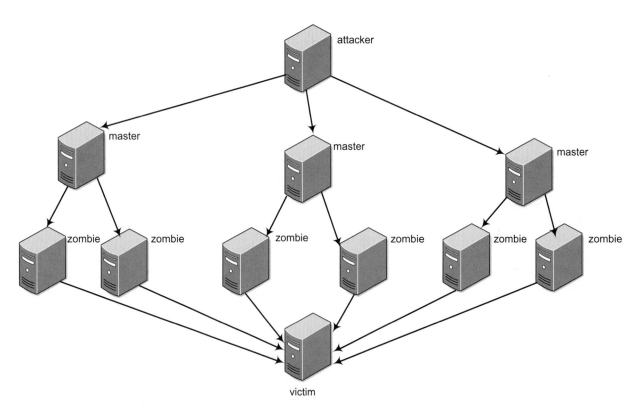

FIGURE 60.2   Distributed denial-of-service attack.

ARP Poisoning

Every network card has a 48-bit address that is unique and hard-coded into the card. For network communications to occur, this hardware address must be associated with an IP address. Address resolution protocol (ARP), which operates at layer 2 (data link layer) of the Open System Interconnection (OSI) model, associates MAC addresses to IP addresses. ARP is a lower-layer protocol that is straightforward and consists of requests and replies without validation. However, this simplicity leads to a lack of security.

When using a protocol analyzer to look at traffic, you will see an ARP request and an ARP reply, which are the two fundamental parts of ARP communication. There are also reverse ARP (RARP) requests and RARP replies. Devices maintain an ARP table that contains a cache of the IP addresses and MAC addresses that the device has already correlated. The host device searches its ARP table to see whether there is a MAC address corresponding to the destination host IP address. When there is no matching entry, it broadcasts an ARP request to the entire network. The broadcast is seen by all systems, but only the device that has the corresponding information replies. However, devices can accept ARP replies before even requesting them. This type of entry is known as an unsolicited entry because the information was not explicitly requested.

Because ARP does not require any type of validation, as ARP requests are sent, the requesting devices believe that the incoming ARP replies are from the correct devices. This can allow a perpetrator to trick a device into thinking any IP is related to any MAC address. In addition, they can broadcast fake or spoofed ARP replies to an entire network and attack all computers. This is known as ARP poisoning. Simply worded, the attacker deceives a device on your network, poisoning its table associations of other devices.

ARP poisoning can lead to attacks such as denial of service, man in the middle, and MAC flooding. Denial of service and man in the middle were discussed earlier in this chapter. MAC flooding is an attack directed at network switches. This type of attack is successful because of the nature of the way all switches and bridges work. The amount of space allocated to store source addresses of packets is limited. When the table becomes full, the device can no longer learn new information and becomes flooded. As a result, the switch can be forced into a hub-like state that will broadcast all network traffic to every device in the network. Macof is a tool that floods the network with random MAC addresses. Switches may get stuck in open repeating mode, leaving the network traffic susceptible to sniffing. Nonintelligent switches do not check the sender's identity, thereby allowing this condition to happen.

A lesser vulnerability of ARP is port stealing. Port stealing is a man-in-the-middle attack that exploits the binding between the port and the MAC address. The principle behind port stealing is that an attacker sends numerous packets with the source IP address of the victim and the destination MAC address of the attacker. This attack applies to broadcast networks built from switches. ARP traffic operates at layer 2, the data link layer of the OSI model, and is broadcast on local subnets. ARP poisoning is limited to attacks that are local, so an intruder needs either physical access to your network or control of a device on your network. To mitigate ARP poisoning on a small network, you can use static or script-based mapping for IP addresses and ARP tables. For larger networks, utilize equipment that offers port security. By doing so, one can only permit one MAC address for each physical port on the switch. In addition, you can deploy monitoring tools or an intrusion detection system (IDS) to signal when suspicious activity occurs.

DNS Poisoning

DNS poisoning enables a perpetrator to redirect traffic by changing the IP record for a specific domain, thus permitting the attacker to send legitimate traffic anywhere he chooses. This not only sends a requestor to a different Web site, but also caches this information for a short period and distributes the attack's effect to the servers users. DNS poisoning may also be referred to as DNS cache poisoning because it affects the information that is cached.

Because all Internet requests begin with a DNS query, if the IP address is not known locally then the request is sent to a DNS server. There are two types of DNS servers: authoritative and recursive. DNS servers share information, but recursive servers maintain information in their cache. This means caching or recursive servers can answer queries for resource records even if they cannot resolve the request directly. A flaw in the resolution algorithm allows the poisoning of DNS records on a server. All an attacker has to do is delegate a false name to the domain server along with providing a false address for the server. For example, an attacker creates a hostname hackattack.gov. Next, the attacker queries your DNS server to resolve the host hackattack.gov. The DNS server resolves the name and stores the information in its cache. Until the zone expiration, any further requests for hackattack.gov do not result in lookups but are answered by the server from its cache. It is now possible for the attacker to set your DNS server as the authoritative server for the zone with the domain registrar.

If the attacker conducts malicious activity, the attacker can make it appear that your DNS server is being used for those malicious activities.

DNS poisoning can result in many different implications. Domain name servers can be used for distributed DoS attacks. Malware can be downloaded to an unsuspecting user's computer from the rogue site, and all future requests by that computer will be redirected to the fake IP address. This could be used to build an effective botnet. This method of poisoning could also allow for cross-site scripting exploits, especially since Web 2.0 capabilities allow content to be pulled from multiple Web sites simultaneously.

To minimize the effects of DNS poisoning, check the DNS setup if you are hosting your own DNS. Be sure the DNS server is not open-recursive. An open-recursive DNS server responds to any lookup request, without checking where the request originated. Disable recursive access for other networks to resolve names that are not in your zone files. Also, use different servers for authoritative and recursive lookups and require that cached information is discarded except from the com servers and the root servers. As far as users are concerned, educate them. However, it is becoming increasingly difficult to spot an issue by watching the address bar on an Internet browser. Therefore, operating system vendors are adding more protection by notifying the user that a program is attempting to change the system's settings, thus preventing the DNS cache from being poisoned.

2. ATTACKS AND COUNTERMEASURES

To secure a network, a firewall can be successfully implemented and utilized whether it is software or hardware based. The purpose of a firewall is to control the incoming and outgoing traffic by analyzing packets and determining whether or not a rule set will allow the traffic in or not.

Network Firewall

In Figure 60.3, the firewall is protecting the network, rather than leaving it directly exposed to the Internet. The firewall will sit in conjunction with a network device and will serve as a gateway between two networks.

Firewalls inspect all traffic routed between two networks to determine whether or not that traffic meets predetermined criteria. If it does, the traffic is allowed through and routed to the appropriate destination. Otherwise, the traffic is blocked. Firewalls can also manage public access to private network resources, such as host applications. Hard drive space on firewalls is becoming increasingly important since log entries can grow to be terabytes of data, depending on the amount of traffic on your network. Consider your logging setup to log every attempt to enter into and exit the network. When half the company is surfing the Internet during their lunch time, one can fathom how large the log files can grow to be. Firewalls can also filter packets specific to network types and is known as protocol filtering. Since the decision to forward or reject traffic is dependent on the protocol used, a user attempting to access a server via HTTP, FTP, or telnet will either be allowed or denied based not only on their access to the server, but also on whether the firewall allows specific protocol access to that target server.

Firewalls use two approaches: Allow all traffic unless said traffic meets a certain criteria or deny all traffic unless it meets a certain criteria. Additionally, firewalls can fit into four categories: packet filters, circuit-level gateways, application-level gateways, and stateful multilayer inspection firewalls. Packet filtering firewalls sit at the Network Layer, or the IP layer of the TCP/IP Layer. Depending on the packet criteria, the firewall can drop the packet, forward it, or send a message to the initiator. Rules can include source and destination IP address, source and destination port number, and protocol used. The advantage of packet filtering firewalls is that they are affordable and have no impact on network performance. If a higher level firewall is used, packet filtering rules will not add any overhead to the network traffic. A lower level firewall will not support many other features that an organization may desire, such as network address translation (NAT). NAT is used in many different types of companies, whether it is a trading firm or a law firm. Understanding private and public IP addressing is the

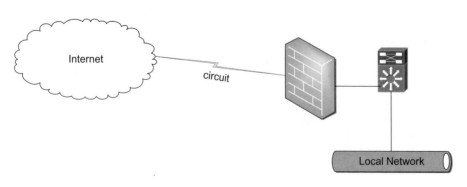

FIGURE 60.3 A firewall is placed between the outside world and the internal local network components.

first step in translating network addresses. Your internal network will communicate with internal IPs; however, if you have a client that needs to access a server on your network, giving them the internal IP on your network will not allow them access unless they're on your virtual private network (VPN). So, translating that IP to a public IP will allow the user to access that internal server, but the firewall is the tool that gives the user outside access by translating the IP. Additionally, the firewall needs to know that 66.55.44.123 is a public IP that belongs to internal IP 10.10.10.100. How will the user access the server? If a user wants to RDP to 10.10.10.100, the firewall must give RDP access to that server. Specific ports and protocols are allowed at the firewall level, too. When implementing a firewall, one must consider the following measures:

- Determine the access denial methodology: Most recommend denying all access by default right at the start. That would have a gateway that routes no traffic and is a brick wall with no doors in it. If you prefer a solid, secure environment, this is the first step, and then you can allow access from here.
- Determine inbound access: If all of your Internet traffic originates on the LAN, a NAT router will block all inbound traffic that is not in response to requests originating from within the LAN. As mentioned in the preceding example, only the external IP address is given to a client. The internal IP addresses of hosts behind the firewall are never revealed to the outside world, which makes intrusion difficult. Most hosts are nonpublic IPs, so it would make it difficult unless the attacker was on the internal network; however, it is the best practice. Packets coming in from the Internet in response to requests from local hosts are addressed to dynamically allocate port numbers on the public side of the NAT router. These numbers change rapidly, making it nearly impossible for an intruder to make assumptions of which port number they could use. You may also want to determine which criteria can be used when a packet originates from the Internet and whether or not to allow it into the LAN. The more rigorous the rules, the more secure your network will be. Ideally, you'll know which public IP addresses on the Internet originate inbound traffic, and by limiting inbound traffic to packets originating from specific hosts, you decrease the likelihood of hostile intrusion. Going further, earlier protocols were mentioned, and limiting communication-based off-protocol sets like HTTP or FTP adds greater security.
- Determine outbound access: When users only need access to the Internet, a proxy server may provide enough security, with access granted based off user rights. This type of firewall can be a great deal to manage since it requires manual configuration of each Web browser on every machine. Outbound protocol filtering can also be transparently achieved with packet filtering and no sacrifice on security. If you are using NAT without inbound mapping or traffic originating from the Internet, then it is possible to allow users access to all services on the Internet without compromising security. Consequently, there is a risk of employees acting irresponsibly through email or external hosts, but that is a management or HR issue and not IT.

Proxies

Proxy servers are capable of functioning on dedicated hardware or as software on a utility server. It acts as a transitional point of communication between two clients attempting to reach out to other servers. For example, if a client connects to a proxy server, requesting some file or connection, the proxy server will assess the request in an effort to simplify and regulate the intricacy of the communication, as shown in Figure 60.4.

Proxies can perform just as a firewall would by handling connection requests for packets coming into an application and by blocking any other packets. A proxy server can be thought of as a gateway from Network A to a certain network application, while acting as a proxy for the user on the network. When an administrator properly designs the function of a proxy, it is much more difficult for an outside attacker to access the internal network. However, an attacker may utilize a highly available system and use it as a proxy for their selfish means. This allows the proxy to deceive other machines, forcing them to think the proxy is safe and on their network, or their proxy. Utilizing internal, private IP addresses adds another layer for security; conversely, hackers could spoof the IP's attempt to gain access and transmit packets to a network.

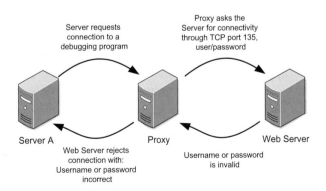

FIGURE 60.4 Communication between two servers connecting through a proxy, the third server.

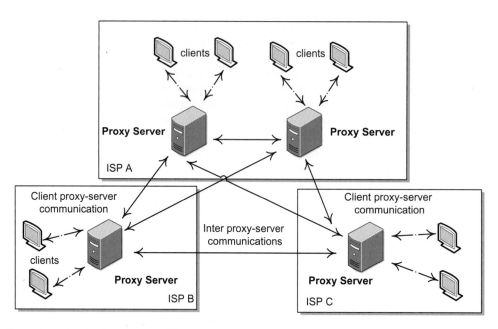

FIGURE 60.5 One session using the proxy server model.

Proxy servers have become prevalent in the gaming community since real-time, Internet gaming surfaced. Considering how many kids and adults are into gaming, the network for real-time streaming multiplayer gaming requires a low-latency proxy server-network topology. Client-server or peer-to-peer topologies provide a variety of positive aspects and can be applied intricately, leading to their high acquiescence for computer gaming. Both models also have many disadvantages, which results in weak QoS and constrains robust gaming architectures where there are a high amount of users. As soon as the player numbers increase, client-server and peer-to-peer topologies do not scale well. Additionally, the server in a client-server framework forms a single point of failure for the entire session. While the peer-to-peer method eradicates the problem of a single point of failure, a hacked client can cheat, since acquiesced game updates are not filtered by a server instance and concealed information becomes readily available to the player.

Architecting a proxy server setup, stemming from a peer-to-peer server-network, is shown in Figure 60.5. Utilizing several interconnected proxy servers for a one-user gaming session shows each proxy server having a full view of the comprehensive game architecture. Each client communicates with a single proxy, sending user selections and obtaining updates of the game status.

Proxy servers process user actions and forward them to other proxies, manipulating multicast at the IP or application level to synchronize the disseminated game state. With regard to low-latency Internet-centered sessions,

proxy servers need to be disbursed among different Internet service providers (ISPs), such that each client will connect to a proxy at its local ISP. Through testing, the author has set up the servers manually; however, testing proves that a dynamic setup of proxies falls in line with user demand and quick response times. Rather than replicating a gaming world, one could partition the approach across servers, compelling clients to exchange servers depending on their region. This approach may work well to accommodate slower flow of traffic, but it cannot be applied to the low-latency, graphic-intensive world. Pauses are annoying for users, as are noticeable server changes. Because the proxy has a wide spectrum to view the game state, best practices avoid a proxy server-network to attempt multiple reconnects during one session.

To manage replication utilizing proxy servers in a gaming infrastructure, ensure that the architecture is scalable, responsive, and consistent, simulating large amounts of data. Although trade-offs may be involved, implementing strong consistency patterns will increase the amount of inter-proxy communication. For example, proxies would order changes of the game state using timestamps or a physical clock mechanism. This would delay the transmission of acknowledgments of user actions to clients, thus reducing the responsiveness of the game. Talk about detrimental; especially when you've stood in line for 18 hours outside of the store, and now you're competing with 500,000 other users during the first hour of the game. A scalable, distributed model with real-time performance can only be achieved

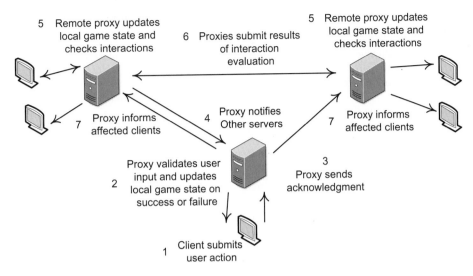

FIGURE 60.6 A user performing a single action—acknowledging and forwarding an action.

if all the servers do not talk to each other simultaneously; nonetheless, servers must be able to share the same data at all times. To implement this architecture, only allow one process to alter specific parts of replicated data (shown in Figure 60.6). Changes must be propagated to other processes, certifying the reliability of the replicated state immediately as the message arrives. The process in Figure 60.6 can be described by following these steps: (1) user actions are transferred from clients; (2) the server checks to see if the input is authorized to block cheating before changing the state; (3) consistency for the altered part of the game state is guaranteed, and the clients receive acknowledgments for movement commands in a short amount of time; (4) informs proxies about updating position values; (5) update local copies consequently; (6)in the case of interactions, notified proxies also check whether local clients are affected, and if local clients are affected, the proxy updates the game state of its local client and informs other servers; and (7) for all state updates received from other proxy servers, each proxy evaluates which local clients are affected and informs them. The architecture presented allows for management of a distributed state, with efficient synchronization of the game state in conjunction with fast acknowledgment of user actions.

3. SUMMARY

This chapter focused on how security is presented to protect the infrastructure. Smart grid cybersecurity must address not only deliberate attacks, such as from disgruntled employees, industrial espionage, and terrorists, but also inadvertent compromises of the information infrastructure due to user errors, equipment failures, and natural disasters.

Infrastructure Security Tasks Checklist

The primary intent of this chapter is to increase your awareness of specific technologies that secure the foundation of your infrastructure. Although this part of the chapter is called a checklist, each of the tasks in the checklist (An Agenda for Action for Implementing Infrastructure Security Tasks) requires so much elaboration that it is easy to lose the thread of organization. The guiding structure is to first summarize the major types of security vulnerabilities and mitigation techniques in general, and then traverse the OSI communication reference model layers (previously discussed) while discussing specific security considerations.

This chapter also addressed the critical cybersecurity needs in the areas of encryption key management, security requirements, testing criteria for remote upgrades, and privacy recommendations for third-party data usage. The chapter also provided foundational cybersecurity guidance, outreach, and foster collaborations in the cross-cutting issue of cybersecurity in the smart grid. Remember that a system is only as secure as its most vulnerable path, and it is difficult (if not impossible) to build a secure voice solution if the infrastructure foundation is insecure.

Finally, let's move on to the real interactive part of this chapter: review questions/exercises, hands-on projects, case projects, and optional team case project. The answers and/or solutions by chapter can be found in the Online Instructor's Solutions Manual.

An Agenda for Action for Implementing Infrastructure Security Tasks

Please see the following infrastructure security tasks (check all tasks completed):

Infrastructure security tasks are designed to thwart several types of threats:

_____1. Unauthorized traffic types going where they should not go (unauthorized access and denial of service).

_____2. Authorized traffic types using more bandwidth or other resources than they should (denial of service).

_____3. Unauthorized devices mimicking authorized devices (violating integrity).

_____4. Unauthorized devices intercepting communications intended for other devices (violating privacy).

At the infrastructure level, these threats are thwarted by:

_____5. Securing the routers and switches themselves so that they continue to perform their packet/frame forwarding and filtering functions.

_____6. Keeping unauthorized devices from being in the communication path by using filters and security mitigation features at different layers of the protocol stack and protecting against frame forgery and spoofing attempts to bypass the filters.

Filters that operate at most layers of the protocol stack under various feature names are appropriate at the following points in the network:

_____7. Ingress directly on hosts, servers, or endpoint devices (considered separately under host hardening, as opposed to infrastructure security features). (*Note:* This is distinct from filters that you can apply on Ethernet switches or other networking gear.)

_____8. Ingress Ethernet ports in wiring closet switches, where traffic first enters a network.

_____9. IP subnet boundaries where traffic crosses between VLANs.

_____10. Boundaries between network segments that are in different administrative domains

The following protocols that form the core of IP network functionality are critical components to consider as candidates for spoofing attacks:

_____11. Ethernet frame headers that contain source/destination link layer addresses.

_____12. IP packet headers that contain source/destination network layer addresses.

_____13. Address Resolution Protocol (ARP), which binds permanent Ethernet hardware addresses to configuration-specific IP logical addresses.

_____14. Dynamic Host Configuration Protocol (DHCP), which automatically assigns IP addresses to devices.

_____15. Domain Name Service (DNS), which maps human-readable names to IP addresses.

_____16. Hot Standby Router Protocol (HSRP), which provides a single virtual Ethernet hardware address and IP address for a group of routers that provide redundant default gateway services.

_____17. IEEE 802.1d Spanning Tree Protocol (STP), which controls the layer 2 Ethernet frame forwarding behavior in a switched Ethernet LAN or metropolitan area network (MAN).

_____18. IEEE 802.1q Ethernet trunk interfaces, which let a single physical Ethernet port share multiple VLANs.

_____19. Virtual Trunking Protocol (VTP) and other control protocols, which switch use to exchange VLAN configuration information.

_____20. Routing protocols that control the layer 3 packet forwarding behavior in a network.

CHAPTER REVIEW QUESTIONS/EXERCISES

True/False

1. True or False? Since the inception of technology, data security revolves around cryptography.

2. True or False? Cipher text and secret keys are transported over the network, and can be harvested for analysis, and furthermore to impersonate a source or, in a worst case, cause a service acceptance.

3. True or False? Backbone networks require switches with tremendous capacity.

4. True or False? Between the UDP and TCP protocols, there are 5,535 ports available for communication between devices.

5. True or False? Hijacking occurs when an intruder takes control of a session between a server and the port.

Multiple Choice

1. What is a method of providing false identity information to gain unauthorized access?
   A. Qualitative analysis
   B. Vulnerabilities
   C. Spoofing
   D. Misconfiguration
   E. DHS

2. What attack occurs when an attacker intercepts traffic and deceives the parties at both ends into believing they are communicating with one another?
   A. Firewall
   B. Risk assessment
   C. Scale
   D. Man in the middle
   E. Bait

3. What are captured by sniffing devices in a replay attack?
   A. Organizations
   B. Fabric
   C. Packets
   D. Web application firewall
   E. Security
4. When resources have been disrupted or services are compromised that a user would expect to have access to, they have experienced a:
   A. cabinet-level state office
   B. denial-of-service attack
   C. hardening
   D. SAN protocol
   E. taps
5. A modest expansion of denial of service can be referred to as:
   A. systems security plan
   B. consumer privacy protection
   C. IP storage access
   D. vulnerability
   E. distributed denial of service attacks

EXERCISE

Problem

Which Ethernet ports require 802.1x authentication?

Hands-On Projects

Project

What 802.1x authentication mechanism should one use?

Case Projects

Problem

Do all clients support 802.1x?

Optional Team Case Project

Problem

Does 802.1x have security vulnerabilities?

## Chapter 61

Access Controls

Lauren Collins

kCura Corporation

1. INFRASTRUCTURE WEAKNESSES: DAC, MAC, AND RBAC

The dichotomy between types of companies and implementing layers of security led to the use of three types of access control mechanisms: discretionary access control, mandatory access control, and role-based access control.

Discretionary Access Control

Discretionary access control (DAC), also known as file permissions, is the access control in Unix and Linux systems. Whenever you have seen the syntax drwxr-xs-x, it is the ugo abbreviation for owner, group, and other permissions in the directory listing. Ugo is the abbreviation for user access, group access, and other system user's access, respectively. These file permissions are set to allow or deny access to members of their own group, or any other groups. Modification of file, directory, and devices are achieved using the chmod command. Tables 61.1 and 61.2 illustrate the syntax to assign or remove permissions. Permissions can be assigned using the character format:

```
Chmod [ugoa] [+-=] [rwxXst] fileORdirectoryName
```

In DAC, usually the resource owner will control who access resources. Everyone has administered a system in which they decide to give full rights to everyone so that it is less to manage. The issue with this approach is that users are allowed not only to read, write, and execute files, but also to delete any files they have access to. This author has so often seen system files deleted in error by users, or simply by the user's lack of knowledge. This is an instance where DAC could be seen as a disadvantage, or less advantageous.

Mandatory Access Control

Mandatory access control (MAC) regulates user process access to resources based on an organizational security policy. This particular policy is a collection of rules that

TABLE 61.1 Notation to Add, Remove Access, and how to Explicitly Assign Access.

+	add access
−	remove access
=	access explicitly assigned

TABLE 61.2 Notation for File Permissions.

r	Permission to read file
	Permission to read a directory (also requires 'x')
w	Permission to delete or modify a file
	Permission to delete or modify files in a directory
x	Permission to execute a file/script
	Permission to read a directory (also requires 'r')
s	Set user or group ID on execution
u	Permissions granted to the user who owns the file
t	Set sticky bit. Execute file/script as a user root for regular user

specify what types of access are allowed on a system. System policy is associated with MAC comparably to how firewall rules are associated with firewalls. Security-enhanced Linux (SELinux) is a Linux kernel implementation of a supple MAC mechanism called type enforcement. These policies restrict users and processes to the minimal amount of privilege required to perform tasks. Type enforcement uses a type identifier and assigns it to every user and object; these authorizations are defined in a SELinux policy.

The SELinux implementation of MAC exercises a type of enforcement mechanism that necessitates every subject and object be assigned an identifier. We will use the terms *subject* and *object* for this example. Consider the subject as a user or a process, and the object as a file or a process. Characteristically, a subject cannot access an object unless the type identifier assigned to the subject is authorized to access the object. The default policy is to deny all access that is not specifically allowed. Authorization is determined by rules defined in the SELinux policy. The following is an example of rule-granting access:

```
allow httpd_t httpd_sys_content_t : file (ioctol
read getattr lock);
```

where the subject http daemon is assigned the type identifier of httpd_t and is granted permissions ioctol, read, gettattr, and lock for any file object assigned in the type identifier httpd_sys_content_t. Basically, the http daemon is allowed to read a rule that is assigned the type identifier httpsd_sys_content_t. This is a simpler rule; there are thousands of rules, varying in complexity. There are also many types of identifiers for use with subjects and objects. SELinux adds type enforcement to standard Linux distributions. To access an object, the user must have both the appropriate file permissions (DAC) and the correct SELinux access. ELinux security context covers three capacities:

1. The user
2. The role
3. The type identifier

By running the ls command with the -Z switch, conventional file information is displayed along with the security context for each element in the subdirectory. See the following example, where the security context for the index.html file encompasses user_u as the user, object_r as the role, and httpd_sys_content_t as the type identifier:

```
[web_admin@localhost html]$ ls -Z index.html
-rw-r-r-  web_admin  web_admin  user_u:object_r:
httpd_sys_content_t index.html
```

Role-Based Access Control

Role-based access control (RBAC) is a method whereby only authorized users can gain access to an environment and the sessions contained in the environment, as shown in Figure 61.1. Some refer to RBAC as role-based security due to the roles an organization creates to assign permissions to users, who perform specific functions, and such users acquire their roles and rights when their account is created. In Active Directory, either the users are in a department that assigns rights by department or the users have customized access based off their role to

perform a job function. Referring to the model in Figure 61.1, use the following conventions:

- Subject (S)—person or agent
- Role (R)—job function
- Permission (P)—authorization to access a resource or utility
- Session (SE)—mapping, including S, R, and/or P
- Subject Assignment (SA)
- Permission Agent (PA)
- Partial Instructional Role Hierarchy (RH)— $\geq$ (where $x \geq y$ requires x to inherit permissions of y)
  1. Subjects are allowed multiple roles.
  2. Roles are allowed to contain multiple subjects.
  3. Roles are allowed to assign multiple permissions.
  4. Permissions can be allocated to multiple roles.
  5. Operations can be allocated to multiple permissions.
  6. Permissions can be allocated many operations.

Whereas a constraint positions a provisional rule on the possibility of inherited permissions from contrasting rules; it can thus be utilized to attain applicable partitions of duties. As such, a user should not be permitted to both create a login or to empower such an account creation. RBAC is comprised of three principal guidelines:

1. Role assignment: A subject can implement permission once the subject has been designated or has allocated a role.
2. Role authorization: A subject's dynamic role requires permission for the subject. Refer to rule 1, above, which warrants users only inherit roles for which they are sanctioned.
3. Permission authorization: A subject can employ permission merely if the permission is approved for the subject's functional role. Refer to rules 1 and 2; rule 3 confirms users can only carry out permissions for which they are allowed.

Several additional controls can be applied on top of the former three rules, and roles can be combined in a hierarchy where higher level roles consider permissions retained by subroles. In larger organizations, typically those with over 500 users, administrators tend to combine MAC or DAC.

As previously mentioned, RBAC can be referred to as an adaptable secure access control. RBAC diverges from access control lists (ACLs) in that it appoints permissions to exclusive operations for users to perform their job functions, rather than to low-level data objects. Let's say an access control list could be utilized to allow or deny write access to a certain file system, but it is unable to dictate how that file could be changed.

As an example, in financial systems, an operation may seek to create a new trading account or to create a new database for a particular trading product. The assignment

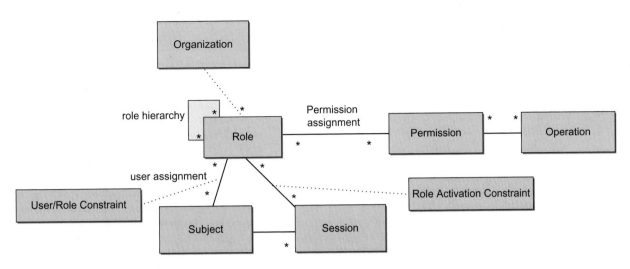

FIGURE 61.1   Role-based access control model that restricts environment access to authorized users.

of the permission to perform a particular operation is meaningful in this instance, since the operations are so granular with meaning to an application. You would not want college interns creating new trading accounts utilizing real money and would prefer that only an administrator of the risk department had those rights. Even concerning trading limits, imagine if traders could go into the application and raise their trading limits themselves. Risk controls are put into place to protect assets and rights.

RBAC is well suited to separate liabilities, ensuring that more than two people are involved in authorizing critical operations. Integrating RBAC benefits access control policies and aids the IT infrastructure where Active Directory, SQL Server, and any other proprietary applications are concerned.

Logical Access Controls

Logical access controls tools are used for credentials, validation, authorization, and accountability in an infrastructure and the systems within. These components enforce access control measures for systems, applications, processes, and information. This type of access control can also be embedded inside an application, operating system, database, or infrastructure administrative system. Physical access control is a mechanical form and can be thought of physical access to a room with a key. The line is often unclear whether or not an element can be considered physical or logical access control. Physical access is controlled by software, the chip on an access card and an electric lock grant access through software. Thus, physical access should be considered a logical access control. A benefit of having logical access controlled centrally in a system allows for a user's physical access permissions to be instantaneously revoked or amended. For example, when an employee is fired, his or her badge access can be

disabled, as can the employee's multiple system access accounts. Persons in possession of the proper access card, the appropriate security level, and in some cases a pin are granted entry to a room once the credentials are checked against a database.

Physical Access Controls

Physical access control is a mechanical form and can be thought of as physical access to a room with a key. The line is often unclear whether or not an element can be considered a physical or a logical access control. When physical access is controlled by software, the chip on an access card and an electric lock grants access through software (see checklist: An Agenda for Action for Evaluating Authentication and Access Control Software Products), which should be considered a logical access control. That being said, incorporating biometrics adds another layer to gain entry into a room. This is considered a physical access control. Identity authentication is based on a person's physical characteristics. The most common physical access controls are used at hospitals, police stations, government offices, data centers, and any area that contains sensitive equipment and/or data.

A significant element surrounding physical access controls as opposed to conventional security solutions is its capacity to capture multifaceted and detailed images of physical traits, encode such traits in files, and evaluate sets of data within seconds. Homeowners are now considering this layer of security since loved ones and belongings are sacred, and this layer of security is not possible to forge. Physical access controls not only enhance security but also allow for efficiency, only requiring one form of authentication, a physical trait (fingerprint, retina, palm of hand). This eliminates the risk of a card being stolen or a PIN being hacked.

An Agenda for Action for Evaluating Authentication and Access Control Software Products

Before one starts evaluating authentication and access control software products, they'll need to answer several questions about the technology; as well as the organization's specific needs (check all tasks completed):

_____1. **What needs to be protected?** The type and level of protection required depends on the assets you'll be safeguarding. After all, national security secrets need more extensive (and costly) protection than a public domain data collection. This is an important matter you will need to discuss with a security professional.

_____2. **Which type of authentication is best?** There are four basic ways of authenticating users: asking for something only the authorized user knows (such as a password), testing for the presence of something only the authorized user has (like a smart card), obtaining some nonforgeable biological or behavioral measurement of the user (like a fingerprint), or determining that the user is located at a place where only the authorized user can enter. The best (and most effective) solutions require a combination of two or more authentication methods.

_____3. **Is the software compatible with existing systems and devices?** The solution must be compatible with current operating systems and applications. Compatibility is a particularly big concern with biometric systems, since existing hardware and applications often must be adapted and/or reprogrammed to work with these tools.

_____4. **Does it offer an acceptable trade-off between security and convenience?** Organizations must balance the value of the information being protected with the authentication and access control software's ease of use. Solutions that are difficult to use may protect systems, but only at the expense of user convenience and productivity.

_____5. **How easy is it to upgrade and expand the software?** You'll want a product that you can use for many years. Over that time span, it will need to be upgraded to accommodate new security practices and technologies.

_____6. **Will the software work with other types of solutions, such as antifraud and user behavior-monitoring technologies?** These days, access control is often a part of a multifaceted enterprise security initiative. It's important to know if the software you're looking at plays well with others.

_____7. **What are the product's management features?** Authentication and access control software products are notoriously difficult to set up and maintain. Look for management features that are straightforward and easy to understand.

_____8. **Has the software ever been defeated? If so, how?** If the product has ever been hacked, you'll want to know what steps the vendor has taken to make its technology more secure.

_____9. How much does the software cost? Don't look at the license fee alone. The total product cost includes acquisition, customization, deployment, management, user training, extra hardware, productivity impact, and maintenance. Ask vendors for detailed statements, policies, and prices for each of these factors.

---

2. STRENGTHENING THE INFRASTRUCTURE: AUTHENTICATION SYSTEMS

Authentication might involve confirming the identity of a person or software program (see checklist: An Agenda for Action for Evaluating Authentication and Access Control Software Products). The introduction to this chapter mentioned three categories authentication may fall under. Whether it is knowledge specific to a user, a piece of information the user has, or the position the user is in, each of them aims to verify the user's identity. Each authentication factor covers a range of elements used to authenticate or verify a person's identity prior to being granted access. Examples include a computer approving a transaction request, electronically signing a document or other work product, administrators granting authority to users with management approval, and a chain of authority that must be established to keep the controls in place and consistent. Security investigations have determined that the standard for verification must include components from at least two factors, and preferably three. Three authentication factors are as follows:

1. *Ownership factors*: something tangible the user has (ID card, security token, software token, phone or cell phone)
2. *Knowledge factors*: a piece of information the user knows (password, pass phrase, PIN, or a challenge response, such as a security question only the user knows the answer to)
3. *Physical factors*: a physical trait of an individual (fingerprint, retinal pattern, signature, voice, or another biometrical identifier)

A common example of a two-factor authentication is when one uses his or her ATM card and has to enter a PIN. Some organizations not only require a username and password to authenticate to the VPN, but also give employees a token with a random set of numbers that change every 30 seconds. The author has visited multiple data center facilities, and while some differ in their choice of the second authentication factor, all data centers require two-factor authentication. While one data center may require use of a badge and your pointer finger fingerprint, others may use a PIN along with a biometric hand scan. Additionally, a handful of facilities include a third factor for authentication, a mantrap. The mantrap screens the person's height, weight, facial features, and retina. These facilities institute higher security standards and are generally financial or governmental collocation sites.

Kerberos and CHAP

Kerberos is a secure method for authenticating a request for a service in a network. Kerberos was developed in the Athena Project at the Massachusetts Institute of Technology (MIT). Based on the name of the Needham-Schroeder protocol, Kerberos is named after a three-headed dog who guarded the gates of Hades in Greek mythology. Kerberos lets a user request an encrypted "ticket" from an authentication process that can then be used to request a particular service from a server. The user's password does not have to pass through the network. MIT offers a download for both the client and server versions of Kerberos, or you can buy a copy.

One weakness is that Kerberos requires the continuous availability of a central server. Knock out the Kerberos server and no one can log in. This problem can be mitigated by using multiple Kerberos servers. The technology is also sensitive to clock settings and won't work properly unless the clocks of the involved hosts are synchronized. Default configuration requires that clock times be no more than 10 minutes apart. Additionally, the administration of the protocol is not standardized and differs between server implementations. And since the secret keys for all users are stored on the central server, a compromise of that server will jeapardize all users' secret keys.

Big data is a hot subject these days, and without question an increasing number of enterprise information security teams are going to be asked about the security-related ramifications of big data projects. There are many issues to look into, but here are a few ideas to make the big data environment more secure during architecture and implementation phases:

1. Create data controls as close to the data as possible, since much of this data isn't "owned" by the security team. The risk of having big data

traversing your network is that you have large amounts of confidential data—such as credit-card data, Social Security numbers, and personally identifiable information (PII)—residing in new places and being used in new ways. Also, you're usually not going to see terabytes of data siphoned from an organization, but you should be concerned about the search for patterns to find the content in these databases. Keep the security as close to the data as possible and don't rely on firewalls, IPS, DLP, or other systems to protect the data.

2. Verify that sensitive fields are indeed protected by using encryption so that when the data is analyzed, manipulated, or sent to other areas of the organization, you're limiting risk of exposure. All sensitive information needs to be encrypted once you have control over it.

3. After you've made the move to encrypt data, the next logical step is to concern yourself with key management. There are a few new ways to perform key management, including creating keys on an as-needed basis so you don't have to store them.

4. In Hadoop designs, review the Hadoop Distributed File System (HDFS) permissions of the cluster and verify that all access to HDFS is authenticated. When first implemented, Hadoop frameworks were notoriously bad at performing authentication of users and services. This allows users to impersonate as a user the cluster services themselves. You can be authenticated to the Hadoop framework using Kerberos, which can be used with HDFS access tokens to authenticate to the name node.

Challenge-Handshake Authentication Protocol (CHAP) is an authentication scheme used by Point-to-Point Protocol (PPP) hosts to authorize the identity of remote users and clients. CHAP occasionally validates the identity of the client by using a three-way handshake. This occurs simultaneously as the initial link is established, and can take place randomly at any time. Substantiation is based on a shared secret—for example, the user or client's password. Steps in the CHAP authentication scheme are as follows (reference Table 61.3):

1. Once the link has been established, the authenticator sends a "challenge" message to the peer.

2. The peer then responds with a determined value using a one-way hash function on the challenge and the secret combined.

3. The authenticator checks the response against the expected answer, or calculation of the expected hash value. If the values match, the authenticator acknowledges the authentication. If it does not match, the connection is terminated.

TABLE 61.3 Authentication Scheme used by CHAP Packets.

				CHAP Packets		
Description	1 Byte	1 Byte	2 Bytes	1 Byte	Variable	Variable
Challenge	Code = 1	ID	Length	Response length	Challenge value	Name
Response	Code = 2	ID	Length	Response length	Response value	Name
Success	Code = 3	ID	Length		Message	
Failure	Code = 4	ID	Length		Message	

Randomly, the Authenticator Sends Another Challenge to the Peer and Repeats the Steps Mentioned Above

The ID chosen for the random challenge is also used in the corresponding response, success, and failure packets. A new challenge with a new ID must be different from the last challenge with another ID. If the success or failure is lost, the same response can be sent again and will trigger the same success or failure indication. For MD5 as hash, the response value is MD5(ID||secret||challenge), the MD5 for the concatenation of ID, secret, and challenge.

Wireless Security Access Controls

The IT Department has just been notified that the company wishes to allow personnel to access the company network from personal devices. A common approach to achieve this is to create separately named networks, (SSIDs), and corresponding VLANs inside your wired network. Segregating VLANs will separate the traffic between the other network traffic. Public wireless can be placed on a separate VLAN rather than private wireless, and there could also be a Mobile Wireless VLAN added to separate laptop wireless traffic from mobile devices.

However, you still want network access protection and a secure and simple way for key personnel to register their own devices for secure access to a private wireless network. Ask your wireless vendor if it sells a visitor management feature or a registration portal capable of walking personal devices through authorization and Wi-Fi provisioning. Another method for network access protection and wireless access control could be using a Mobile Device Manager (MDM) to drive these tasks.

WPA2-Personal requires every device to supply a Pre-Shared Key (PSK) derived from a passphrase. For example, devices on your trading floor might be required to supply the same random string of 20 characters known only to your IT department and configured during

deployment. This method is often combined with MAC address filtering, so that only known devices with the right PSK are granted access. However, MAC address filters are easily bypassed, as are PSKs that are too short or too easy to guess. WPA2-Enterprise requires every device to complete an 802.1X log-on process that can support various authentication methods. For example, each device on your trading floor might be required to prove its identity with a unique digital certificate. Alternatively, each device might be required to supply a unique username and password configured during deployment and known only to your IT department. With this Wi-Fi access control method, you will be able to tell which individual machines are logged on. When used with certificates, WPA2-Enterprise is less vulnerable to password sharing and reuse, which are common problems when employees know a valid username/password or PSK and simply configure those into personal devices.

3. SUMMARY

Although only the most commonly used access mechanisms are discussed in this chapter, many extensions, combinations, and different mechanisms are possible. Trade-offs and limitations are involved with all mechanisms and access control designs, so it is the user's responsibility to determine the best-fit access control mechanisms that work for their business functions and requirements.

Also included in this chapter are the most commonly used access control policies. Since access control policies are targeted to specific access control requirements, unlike access control mechanisms, specific limitations cannot be inherently associated with them. And like access control mechanisms, it is up to the users to select the best policies for their needs. In addition to the limitations and issues, quality biometrics depends not only on the consideration of administration cost, but also on the flexibility of the mechanism helping the user in assessing or selecting among access control systems.

Finally, let's move on to the real interactive part of this chapter: review questions/exercises, hands-on projects, case projects, and optional team case project. The answers and/or solutions by chapter can be found in the Online Instructor's Solutions Manual.

CHAPTER REVIEW QUESTIONS/EXERCISES

True/False

1. True or False? The dichotomy between types of companies and implementing layers of security led to the use of three types of access control mechanisms: denial of access control, mandatory access control, and role-based access control.
2. True or False? Discretionary access control (DAC), also known as file permissions, is the access control in Unix and Windows systems.
3. True or False? Mandatory access control (MAC) regulates user process access to resources based on an organizational security policy.
4. True or False? Role-based access control (RBAC) is a method whereby only authorized users can lose access to an environment and the sessions contained in the environment.
5. True or False? Role-based access controls tools are used for credentials, validation, authorization, and accountability in an infrastructure and the systems within.

Multiple Choice

1. What is a mechanical form and can be thought of as physical access to a room with a key?
   A. Qualitative analysis
   B. Vulnerabilities
   C. Spoofing
   D. Physical access control
   E. DHS
2. What might involve confirming the identity of a person or software program?
   A. Firewall
   B. Risk assessment
   C. Scale
   D. Authentication
   E. Bait
3. What is a secure method for authenticating a request for a service in a network?

   A. Organizations
   B. Fabric
   C. Kerberos
   D. Web application firewall
   E. Security
4. What requires every device to supply a Pre-Shared Key (PSK) derived from a passphrase?
   A. Cabinet-level state office
   B. Denial-of-service attack
   C. WPA2-Personal
   D. SAN protocol
   E. Taps
5. What is an authentication scheme used by Point-to-Point Protocol (PPP) hosts to authorize the identity of remote users and clients?
   A. Systems security plan
   B. Consumer privacy protection
   C. IP storage access
   D. Vulnerability
   E. Challenge-Handshake Authentication Protocol (CHAP)

EXERCISE

Problem

Which type of authentication is best?

Hands-On Projects

Project

Is the access control and authentication software compatible with existing systems and devices?

Case Projects

Problem

Does access control and authentication software offer an acceptable trade-off between security and convenience?

Optional Team Case Project

Problem

How easy is it to upgrade and expand access control and authentication software?

## Chapter 62

Assessments and Audits

Lauren Collins

kCura Corporation

1. ASSESSING VULNERABILITIES AND RISK: PENETRATION TESTING AND VULNERABILITY ASSESSMENTS

Penetration testing usually occurs in the compliance sphere, both in the semantics we use to describe technical points like "regulating deployments" and in the language technology vendors employ to describe those implementations. Compliance, however, is intolerant when it comes to accuracy in writing, and elusive inconsistencies in words can mean the difference between compliance and noncompliance. Erratic interpretations of conditions can lead to incongruous control selection, vague or unsuitable management responses, misrepresentation of controls to auditors, and many other problems. These differences can result in the very violations we are striving to avoid by integrating assessments prior to audits occurring. Penetration tests are valuable for multiple reasons:

- To identify vulnerabilities that may be evasive or impractical to detect with automated network or application vulnerability scanning software
- To identify high-risk vulnerabilities resulting from an amalgamation of lower risk vulnerabilities exploited in a noteworthy sequence
- To regulate the viability of a particular set of attack vectors
- To assess the magnitude of potential business and operational impacts of successful incidents
- To test the ability of network defenders to successfully detect and counter incidents

Multiple techniques can be used to conduct a penetration test; the variance is the volume of knowledge of the implementation factors pertaining to the system undergoing testing. Black box testing assumes no prior familiarity with the testing environment. A tester lays out the scenario and gathers information about the infrastructure prior to formulating an analysis. Black box testing can become exponentially expensive as time goes on. Not only is it labor intensive, but it is also taxing on the network and could cause noticeable slowness due to scanning. White box testing specifies all the information necessary: source code, IP addressing schemes, network diagrams, and any other pertinent information that is available. Believe it or not, gray box testing is also out there. Gray box testing depends on the type of test one can administer; which is entirely based on the extent of the information available.

Vulnerability assessments and penetration tests are habitually exercised interchangeably among technical associates, auditors, and controllers. The misconception is that a penetration test and a vulnerability assessment are notably different exercises. As a result, it is necessary for compliance professionals to become educated on the differences of each in an effort to ensure they are appropriately satiating compliance intentions that the controls perform in an approach they would expect and that they are correctly demonstrating controlled deployments to peers. At a high level, a vulnerability assessment is any interest aimed at research and subsequently at detailed prospective attack points (the vulnerabilities) within a given set of data. In a corporate information technology context, it usually embraces an attentive study of information systems (applications, systems, network devices, etc.) in order to identify concerns that compromise the security of that environment. Potential concerns may include omission of patching, unprotected configurations, and weak passwords.

Vulnerability assessments can be conventional, or they can focus on a more meticulous level of the technology stack, such as an application-level vulnerability assessment. Best practice is to incorporate practical scanning manners, such as running an automated vulnerability scan to query the scope of systems and devices. The next step would be to run a report on the security issues that might be present. The point of the action is to specify as many potential issues as possible that may negatively impact the environment's security. A vulnerability assessment will contain an automated scan of the environment using a proprietary scanning tool. Furthermore, both types of activities can include vulnerability scoring and prioritization. In the case of a vulnerability assessment, the purpose is to provide information about the qualified severity level and remediation priority for the located issues. The penetration test, on the other hand, is designed to avoid providing attackers with information that gives them ideas on prolific attack opportunities.

From a regulatory compliance stance, the range of a vulnerability assessment or a penetration test will depend on the specific control objective you wish to meet. Since these conditions are sometimes used interchangeably, compliance specialists may find it necessary to ask some key questions rather than assume that a technical process or control implementation includes particular characteristics. Questions to ascertain if a vendor or partner is referring to vulnerability assessments or penetration testing include the following:

- Will the test include a vulnerability list, an activity report, or something else?
- What is the process output or report format?
- Will testers attempt to gain access to control sensitive resources?
- Is there a manual component, or is there just automated scanning?

By making invalid assumptions, you may not be receiving the controls and processes you hoped for. This could lead to more trouble than you had anticipated.

Make sure you understand what the partners or vendors mean when they are discussing vulnerability assessments and penetration testing. Ask questions.

Port Scanning and Password Cracking

Port scanning is one of the most popular techniques a hacker can use to discover services that can be compromised. For instance, a port scanner will send a TCP SYN request to the host (or range of hosts) set to scan. Ping sweeps are also an option when attempting to define which hosts are available before starting the TCP port scans. Most port scanners only scan TCP ports by default, and some will have UDP by default as well. Some software packages will perform the discovery and auditing of your systems and network, or if you're really good and know your way around the command line on a switch, you can navigate around a network quickly to locate and there are free open-source programs as well. Network Mapper (NMAP), an open-source license, will allow scanning of UDP packets and is shown in Figure 62.1. Other common programs that can be used, other than NMAP, are SuperScan and NetScan. A scan will probe the accessible hosts for up to 65,535 viable TCP and UDP ports. You can select specific ports you'd like to scan in order to return fewer results, and also filter to view the services

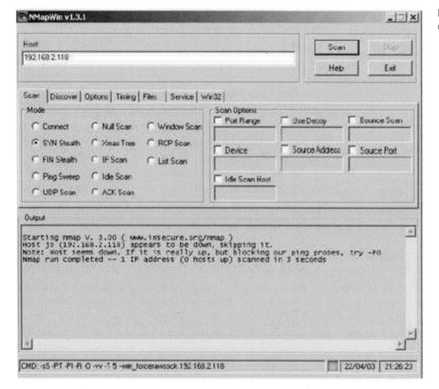

FIGURE 62.1 Network Mapper (NMAP), a utility used for scanning ports.

available. Port scans provide the following information from accessible hosts on the network:

- Network address of the hosts discovered
- Services and/or applications the hosts are running
- Hosts that are operational and reachable on the network

For your initial scan, it is recommended that you scan all ports from 1 to 65,535. There are many options to get as granular as you want. For instance, a scan can be performed on only well-known ports, or a scan may only involve a certain range of ports specific to your system. If the scanner is unable to find hosts that you are certain would show up, ICMP may be blocked. Once you have concluded what hosts are available and which ports are open, more sophisticate scans can be run to verify that the ports are open and that the tool is not reporting a false positive:

- *UDP Scan* is a basic UDP scan that looks for any open UDP ports on the host. This option is used to see what is running and determine whether or not Intrusion Detection Systems (IDS), firewalls, or other logging devices log the connection.
- *Connect* is a basic TCP scan that looks for any open TCP ports on the host. This scan is used to see what is running and determine whether or not IDS, firewalls, or other logging devices log the connection.
- *SYN Stealth* is a scan that initiates a half-open TCP connection, with the host potentially dodging IDS systems and logging. This option is a great scan for testing IDS systems, firewalls, and other logging devices.
- *FIN Stealth, Xmas Tree and Null* are scans that allow you to get creative by sending odd-shaped packets to the network hosts in order to see how the hosts respond. These scans basically alter the flags in the TCP headers of each packet, which allows you to test how each host handles them to point out weak TCP/IP implementations and patches that may need to be applied.

In Chapter 60, denial-of-service attack was one of the many attacks that were described. When running scans, it is possible to create your own denial-of-dervice attack and potentially crash applications or the entire network. Unfortunately, if there is a host on the network with a weak TCP/IP stack, there is no way to prevent your scan from becoming a DoS attack. To reduce the chance of this happening, use slow NMAP timing options when running scans. Refer to Figure 62.1 to see all the options available when running scans.

Password cracking is a process whereby a hacker or a system can retrieve passwords from records that have been stored or transmitted by a system. A popular tactic, and most common, is to try and guess the password. There is always the option to change the password and to

state you have forgotten it; that approach works more than most would assume and has destroyed many people's virtual lives. In an organization, it is always more secure to assign a user a new password rather than allow them to answer a set of questions to recover their forgotten password. Although only administrators can assign new passwords, the extra security layer is a must. When reflecting how all of us have answered a series of questions to regain a forgotten password, consider a program running through a file system, file by file, attempting to obtain the record where the answers to your challenge questions and password are makes complete sense. That is exactly how a password can be cracked.

Encryption is a common process that individuals and organizations practice, and although it may take longer to crack, an encrypted password is easily attainable. If MD5 or SHA1 hash is used to encrypt a string of characters, that encrypted password is then a string of characters that is stored in the database. Rainbow tables of encrypted hashes contain all possible uses of a password, and such tools are available for free downloads. When comparing the rainbow tables and the target hashes, newer computers have a powerful enough processor and graphics card to achieve quantifiable results quickly. Graphic processing units (GPUs) were designed to do supercomputing where high-end math calculations can be done quickly in electronic trading and password cracking. GPUs are much faster than CPUs at calculating predefined tasks and comprise faster memory and wider input/output (I/O) channels to facilitate rapid computations.

There are several ways to limit the effectiveness of the powerful tools available to hackers. Salted hashes are a randomly generated piece of information that is added to the data prior to running it through the hashing process. A salt is arbitrarily generated information that is added to the data before running through the hashing process. Now the encrypted value cannot be cracked using rainbow tables, and the salt will have to be stored in encrypted databases utilizing a different salt for each password. A hacker would have to decrypt the database as well as each password and its record. Two-factor authentication is another technique organizations can use to intensify security measures. This is a form of security that will add greater security, even in the event a hashed password has been breached.

OVAL and CVE

Open Vulnerability and Assessment Language (OVAL) is the standard for determining vulnerability and configuration issues on systems. OVAL is an open community that was created by MITRE, and it is where knowledge can be shared and the content stored may be accessible to the public in an effort to standardize security efforts and how

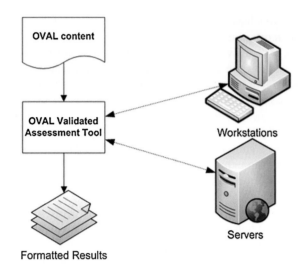

FIGURE 62.2 The assessment process of OVAL.

TABLE 62.1 Repositories Available Within OVAL.

Repository	Platform	Content
MITRE	Any platform	Open community based support for configuration and vulnerability information
Red Hat	Red Hat Enterprise Linux	Vulnerability content
NIST SCAP	Any platform	SCAP related

to assess and report systems and their states. OVAL utilizes a three-step system assessment:

1. Represent system information.
2. Articulate detailed machine states and report the results of the assessment.
3. Supply organizations with precise, stable, and actionable evidence to improve security.

Here is a case where OVAL could be useful: An organization designed their security procedures, protocols, and policies surrounding the Cisco products that were in their infrastructure. Three companies were acquired, and each of the three companies had hardware other than Cisco. Any vulnerability that was found prior to the acquisition and was corrected will no longer be valid once this other hardware is integrated into the infrastructure. Scanning your territory with three or four tools will now yield completely different results, making it more complex and prove that customized needs will have to be developed for the new assessment tool. Vendors, partners, and various other contributors will report the state of their systems, and this data should be referenced anytime your environment changes. The need for open standardization is clear in an example like this, and the process is represented in Figure 62.2.

Through public analysis, direct vendor support, and community contributions, OVAL provides vulnerability content that is reliable and verifiable. OVAL uses the robustness of XML to create a standard language for defining, assessing, and reporting vulnerabilities and configurations. Providing this vulnerability scanning content for the IT industry to collaborate and share technical details allows administrators and engineers to rapidly determine which systems are vulnerable and to rectify those vulnerabilities. And when there is a bug or a false positive, the community is astute to share fixes through use of publicly accessible repositories.

So, where do you go to get this content? There are tools that ship with vulnerability checks and receive regular content updates, or one of the OVAL repositories can assist. Table 62.1 represents the repository and its corresponding platform and content.

New repositories are added to OVAL's Web site after they have been created and verified. If you are assessing systems for use with the U.S. federal government, the NIST SCAP repository is your area of interest. Microsoft Security Guides, DISA Security Technical Implementation Guides, and Federal Desktop Core Configuration guides have been developed for assessing the systems established on current federal and vendor systems. Whether you are assessing the impact of the latest vulnerability or checking for federal compliance, the substantial public environment of OVAL developers and contributors will provide useful information to you and your infrastructure.

Common Vulnerabilities and Exposures (CVE) provides reference for information security vulnerability and exposures. MITRE assigns a CVE identifier to every vulnerability or exposure. A CVE is used to track vulnerability through different pieces of software, as a single CVE can affect multiple software packages and multiple vendors. The vulnerability is defined as a mistake in the software which may be directly oppressed by an attacker to compromise a system, and an exposure as a fault that could be used as an opportunity to launch an attack. CVE efforts include:

- Vulnerability Management
- Patch Management
- Vulnerability Alerting
- Intrusion Detection
- Security Content Automation Protocol (SCAP)
- National Vulnerability Database (NVD)
- US-CERT Bulletins
- CVE Numbering Authorities (CNAs)

When working with a common identifier, administrators and engineers find it less difficult to share data across separate databases, tools, and services. This data is not only easily accessible but can be integrated with ease. Unless a report comes up stating there is a bug, you're good to go. CVE is free and available for anyone who is interested in correlating data between diverse vulnerability or security tools, repositories, and services. Anyone could search or download CVE, copy it, redistribute it, reference it, and analyze it, provided you do not modify CVE itself. Companies are allowed to add links and pages to CVE's Web sites, products, publications, or other capacities. CVE Identifiers, or CVE names, are exclusive and collective identifiers for publicly known information. CVE-2001-0731 references a bug on how Google indexed a file without an external link. A CVE Identifier can be in the form of one of the following:

- Identifier number ("CVE-2001-0731")
- Description of the security vulnerability or exposure
- Any pertinent references (vulnerability reports and advisories or an OVAL-ID)

Using CVEs to identify vulnerabilities and exposures in your organization will allow for accurate and obtainable information from a vast selection of CVE information sources. CVE can help you make informed decisions and determine which of the capabilities are appropriate for your particular needs. Another plus is having the ability to create a suite of interoperable security tools and capabilities available as a translation mechanism.

2. RISK MANAGEMENT: QUANTITATIVE RISK MEASUREMENTS

By focusing on implementing best practices in your environment, you will be able to accomplish the following tasks:

- *Real-time alert configuration*: Data centers have become the core of a business, acting as an operations center. Managing logs is a significant step, and it is equally important to access and monitor alerts.
- *Proactive protection of the environment*: Log management tools and baseline analysis assist an organization to be proactive in their security methodology. Catching holes in security or issues existing, engineers can make a significant difference in time and money. Patching a server is an easy task, but when it is overlooked patch after patch, a vulnerability exists.
- *Incident containment*: When an unauthorized event occurs in an infrastructure, logs that are set up correctly can alert engineers and pinpoint the exact location quickly. If an engineer can see where the issue

resides in a timely manner, that network or server can be isolated to prevent further damage.

- *Creation of an audit trail for forensics analysis*: When an intrusion is suspected or data loss has occurred, a rockstar audit trail will allow forensic data engineers to retrace the steps taken by someone who has entered the environment and correlate that data into usable information.
- *Creation of online documentation as the environment evolves*: IT must keep an activity log, tracking all logs across all the environments. Understanding the various systems and how they're performing allows engineers to shape the infrastructure as the business needs change.

Establishing a Baseline

Two types of alerts should be logged: faults that are generated by the system and the applications running on it, and faults or errors reported by the system's users. Fault logging and analysis is often the only way of finding out what is unsuitable about a system or application. The analysis of fault logs can be used to identify trends that may indicate deeper issues, such as defective hardware or a lack of competence or training for system administrators or users. All operating systems and many applications, such as database software, provide event logging and basic alerting faculties. This logging functionality should be configured to log all faults and send alerts if the error threshold is above an acceptable, defined threshold. Fault logging and analysis is often the only way to find out what is wrong with a system or an application. Documentation is key when defining which faults to record or report, who is responsible to investigate the faults, and an expected resolution time.

Since data center environments continue to grow, it has become more evident that administrators need to properly manage logs. Checking in on servers, firewalls, appliances, and switching gear event logs will assist IT to do more than simply check for reactive issues. If the process is managed and kept accurate, engineers can create a proactive environment that is capable of spotting and controlling issues before they even arise. Logs can also help an environment plan for the future. Network logs can show engineers where they are lacking and how they can competently plan for growth.

Auditing and Logging

Many devices that provide protection to the infrastructure within networks allow the ability to log events and take actions based on those events. This application system and monitoring provide details both on what has happened to the device and on what is happening in real time. It provides security against lapses in perimeter and application defenses by alerting an administrator about issues, so that defensive measures can be enacted prior to any damage taking place. Without monitoring, an organization does not stand a chance of ascertaining whether a live application is under attack or if it has been compromised.

Business critical applications, processes handling valuable or sensitive information, previously compromised or abused systems, and those systems connected to third parties, all require active monitoring. Whenever suspicious behavior or critical events arise, an alert will be generated and must be acted on. Risk assessments must be done to determine logging levels and which actions are projected from a specified set of alerts. Logging and auditing work together, ensuring that users are only performing the activities they are authorized to perform. This data also plays a key role in preventing, spotting, tracking, and stopping unwanted or inappropriate activities. The levels of alerts, log reviews, and monitoring are an additional necessary component, and at least the following will need to be logged:

- Date, time, and other crucial events
- User ID or IP address
- Successful connections and failed attempts to access systems, data, or applications
- Files, servers, and networks accessed
- Changes to configurations
- Consumption of system utilities
- Exceptions and other security-related events, such as triggered alarms
- Activation of protection systems (intrusion detection systems and malware).

When these types of data are collected, that data will assist in access control monitoring and can provide audit trails when an incident is being investigated. Usually, logs are covered by some form of regulation of how many days it should be kept in case they are needed for an investigation. Employees need to be made aware of any firm monitoring policy activities on the network. Log files are a great source of information, but they serve absolutely no purpose if no one monitors them. When a firm purchases and deploys a solution, the product will not provide security unless the information is collected and analyzed on a regular basis. Some procedures require that the results be reviewed regularly to identify possible security threats and incidents. Each company differs in its processes based on the operations and content, and on how attractive that data may be.

Reviewing Policy Settings

Small networks can generate large amounts of information if the log settings are not optimal. Although log analyzers could automate the auditing and analysis of logs, storage for logs may be another challenge. This type of automated feedback frees up your resources, and your engineer can work to refine the log levels or parse through alerts of accurate threats. Recognizing true threats will help reduce the number of false positives. Eliminating false positives, while maintaining strict controls, is next to impossible. New threats and changes in the network infrastructure are ever changing and will likely affect the effectiveness of existing rule sets. Analyzing logs can provide a basis for focused security awareness training, reduced network misuse, and stronger policy enforcement.

Administrators have powerful access, and their activity should also be recorded and checked. A system restart may be prompted to correct serious errors, and those restarts may not be recorded if an administrator disables the alarm. Administrators' actions should be logged, notating start and finish times, who was involved and at what capacity, and what actions were taken. The name of the individual recording the information also should be recorded, along with the date and time. An organization with an internal audit team needs to maintain these records.

3. SUMMARY

An information security assessment and audit is the process of determining how effectively an entity being assessed (host, system, network, procedure, person—known as the assessment object) meets specific security objectives. Three types of assessment and audit methods can be used to accomplish this—testing, examination, and interviewing. *Testing* is the process of exercising one or more assessment and audit objects under specified conditions to compare actual and expected behaviors. *Examination* is the process of checking, inspecting, reviewing, observing, studying, or analyzing one or more assessment and audit objects to facilitate understanding, achieve clarification, or obtain evidence. *Interviewing* is the process of conducting discussions with individuals or groups within an organization to facilitate understanding, achieve clarification, or identify the location of evidence. Assessment and audit results are used to support the determination of security control effectiveness over time.

This chapter presents the basic technical aspects of conducting information security assessments and audits. It presents technical testing and examination methods and techniques that an organization might use as part of an assessment and audit, and it offers insights to assessors on their execution and the potential impact they may have on systems and networks. For an assessment and audit to be successful and have a positive impact on the security posture of a system (and ultimately the entire organization), elements beyond the execution of testing and

An Agenda for Action for Implementing Information Security Assessments and Audits

The processes and technical recommendations presented in this chapter enable organizations to (check all tasks completed):

_____ 1. Develop information security assessment and audit policy, methodology, and individual roles and responsibilities related to the technical aspects of assessment and audits.

_____ 2. Accurately plan for a technical information security assessment and audit by providing guidance on determining which systems to assess and the approach for assessment and audit, addressing logistical considerations, developing an assessment and audit plan, and ensuring legal and policy considerations are addressed.

_____ 3. Safely and effectively execute a technical information security assessment and audit using methods and techniques, and respond to any incidents that may occur during the assessment and audit.

_____ 4. Appropriately handle technical data (collection, storage, transmission, and destruction) throughout the assessment and audit process.

_____ 5. Conduct analysis and reporting to translate technical findings into risk mitigation actions that will improve the organization's security posture.

_____ 6. Establish an information security assessment and audit policy. This identifies the organization's requirements for executing assessments and audits, and provides accountability for the appropriate individuals to ensure assessments and audits are conducted in accordance with these requirements. Topics that an assessment and audit policy should address include the organizational requirements with which assessments and audits must comply; roles and responsibilities; adherence to an established assessment and audit methodology; assessment and audit frequency; and, documentation requirements.

_____ 7. Implement a repeatable and documented assessment and audit methodology. This provides consistency and structure to assessments and audits; expedites the transition of new assessment and

audit staff; and addresses resource constraints associated with assessments and audits. Using such a methodology enables organizations to maximize the value of assessments and audits while minimizing possible risks introduced by certain technical assessment and audit techniques. These risks can range from not gathering sufficient information on the organization's security posture for fear of impacting system functionality to affecting the system or network availability by executing techniques without the proper safeguards in place. Processes that minimize risk caused by certain assessment and audit techniques include using skilled assessors and auditors, developing comprehensive assessment plans, logging assessor and auditor activities, performing testing off-hours, and conducting tests on duplicates of production systems (development systems). Organizations need to determine the level of risk they are willing to accept for each assessment and audit, and tailor their approaches accordingly.

_____ 8. Determine the objectives of each security assessment and audit, and tailor the approach accordingly. Security assessments and audits have specific objectives, acceptable levels of risk, and available resources. Because no individual technique provides a comprehensive picture of an organization's security when executed alone, organizations should use a combination of techniques. This also helps organizations to limit risk and resource usage.

_____ 9. Analyze findings, and develop risk mitigation techniques to address weaknesses. To ensure that security assessments and audits provide their ultimate value, organizations should conduct root cause analysis upon completion of an assessment and audits to enable the translation of findings into actionable mitigation techniques. These results may indicate that organizations should address not only technical weaknesses, but weaknesses in organizational processes and procedures as well.

---

examination must support the technical process. Suggestions for these activities (including a robust planning process, root cause analysis, and tailored reporting) are also presented in this chapter (see checklist: An Agenda for Action for Implementing Information Security Assessments and Audits).

The information presented in this chapter is intended to be used for a variety of assessment and audit purposes. For example, some assessments and audits focus on verifying that a particular security control (or controls) meets requirements, while others are intended to identify,

validate, and assess a system's exploitable security weaknesses. Assessments and audits are also performed to increase an organization's ability to maintain a proactive computer network defense. Assessments and audits are not meant to take the place of implementing security controls and maintaining system security.

Finally, let's move on to the real interactive part of this chapter: review questions/exercises, hands-on projects, case projects, and optional team case project. The answers and/or solutions by chapter can be found in the Online Instructor's Solutions Manual.

CHAPTER REVIEW QUESTIONS/EXERCISES

True/False

1. True or False? Penetration testing usually occurs in the compliance sphere, both in the semantics we use to describe technical points like "regulating deployments" and in the language technology vendors use to describe those implementations.

2. True or False? Port scanning is one of the most popular techniques a hacker can use to discover services that can be compromised.

3. True or False? Open Vulnerability and Assessment Language (OVAL) is not the standard for determining vulnerability and configuration issues on systems.

4. True or False? Two types of alerts should be logged: faults that are generated by the system and the applications running on it, and faults or errors reported by the system's users.

5. True or False? Since data center environments continue to grow, it has become more evident that administrators need to properly manage logs.

Multiple Choice

1. Many devices that provide protection to the infrastructure within networks, allow the ability to _____ events, and take actions based on those events.
   - A. qualitative analysis
   - B. vulnerabilities
   - C. log
   - D. physical access control
   - E. DHS

2. Business critical applications, processes handling valuable or sensitive information, previously compromised or abused systems, and those systems connected to third parties, all require:
   - A. firewall
   - B. risk assessment
   - C. scale
   - D. authentication
   - E. active monitoring

3. What are usually covered by some form of regulation of how many days they should be kept in case they are needed for an investigation?
   - A. Organizations
   - B. Fabric
   - C. Kerberos
   - D. Logs
   - E. Security

4. What can generate large amounts of information if the log settings are not optimal?
   - A. Cabinet-level state office
   - B. Denial-of-service attack
   - C. WPA2-Personal
   - D. Small networks
   - E. Taps

5. Who has powerful access, where their activity should be recorded and checked?
   - A. Systems security plan
   - B. Consumer privacy protection
   - C. Administrators
   - D. Vulnerability
   - E. Challenge-Handshake Authentication Protocol (CHAP)

EXERCISE

Problem

Why are risk assessment and risk management relevant to information security?

Hands-On Projects

Project

How is risk assessment related to ISO/IEC 27001 (BS 7799)?

Case Projects

Problem

Does ISO/IEC 27001 (BS 7799) define the methodology for risk assessment?

Optional Team Case Project

Problem

After implementation, must the organization reassess risks?

## Chapter 63

Fundamentals of Cryptography

Scott R. Ellis, EnCE, RCA, RCIA

kCura Corporation

1. ASSURING PRIVACY WITH ENCRYPTION

Encryption provides a secure layer, at the storage byte level, under which information can be secured from prying eyes (see checklist: An Agenda for Action for Implementing Encryption and Other Information Security Functions). Data, or "plaintext" as it is called in cryptography, is rendered into cipher text through a ciphering process. Most importantly, encryption protects stored data. Files such as database data files, spreadsheets, documents, and reports can contain critical information—information which, if lost, could cause damage to:

- Sales generation
- Operations
- Reputation
- Competitive advantage
- Individuals
- Market capabilities
- Finances

Ultimately, the loss of enough data, especially were it due to incompetence, could be a business-ending event. Inadvertent disclosure of data, especially personally identifiable data, can mean financial liabilities and the need for restitution to injured parties.

Ensuring that files are encrypted in storage, everywhere, allows the files to be protected in the event of a breach of physical security. Should a hacker gain access to a system, database encryption will prevent her from accessing the database files. Whole-disk encryption will prevent her from accessing drive shares and pulling excel spreadsheets.

The past decade has seen additional liabilities and exposures of sensitive data in the form of lost backup tapes, lost laptops, and recycled computers that were not destroyed, encrypted, or wiped. After a third-party courier service lost a box of backup tapes, Bank of New York Mellon Corp. officials implemented a policy to encrypt data on all storage devices. Furthermore, they said they would limit the type and amount of confidential client data stored on tape backups. It took two losses of unencrypted data before the policy was launched.

Unfortunately, far too many companies wait for disaster to strike before they begin to think about all of the things they really need to do to ensure, or at least substantially mitigate, their risk of data loss. There are three primary reasons why industry executives are reticent to implement encryption:

1. The cost of doing it—the complexity of setting it up
2. Their feeling that it can't happen to them
3. The fear of data loss due to key loss—an inability to decrypt the data

The cost of implementing an encryption policy pales in comparison to the cost of a data loss due to a breach, or due to release of data simply because Joe Smith left his laptop on the train. In an interesting, real-life situation, the author of this chapter did, in fact, once find a small box of hard drives in a bag on a train. The drives were labeled backup01, backup02, and backup03. Fortunately, the box had a CDW Computer Centers, Inc. shipping label that identified a client number. After reaching out to a friend at the computer company on the label, who contacted the owner (a large university library), a reunion was arranged. The kindness and responsibility of strangers cannot serve, however, as a failsafe. If anything, the loss of ALL the backup data was narrowly averted. According to the library executive, the backup drives held *everything*. She also promised that the policy would be changing immediately.

Encryption also introduces an additional level of difficulty in the event of corruption. Certain segments of the drive, if they become corrupted, can make retrieval of the data more challenging. This necessitates

---

An Agenda for Action for Implementing Encryption and Other Information Security Functions

Encryption implementation recommendations presented in this chapter enable organizations to ask the following questions (check all tasks completed):

_____**1.** Does your product perform "cryptography," or otherwise contain any parts or components that are capable of performing any of the following "information security" functions?

_____**a.** encryption

_____**b.** decryption only (no encryption)

_____**c.** key management/public key infrastructure (PKI)

_____**d.** authentication (password protection, digital signatures)

_____**e.** copy protection

_____**f.** anti-virus protection

_____**g.** other (please explain): _____

_____**h.** NONE/NOT APPLICABLE

_____**2.** For items with encryption, decryption, and/or key management functions (1.a, 1.b, 1.c above):

_____**a.** What symmetric algorithms and key lengths (56-bit DES, 112 / 168-bit Triple-DES, 128 / 256-bit AES/Rijndael) are implemented or supported?

_____**b.** What asymmetric algorithms and key lengths (512-bit RSA / Diffie-Hellman, 1024 / 2048-bit RSA/Diffie-Hellman) are implemented or supported?

_____**c.** What encryption protocols (SSL, SSH, IPSEC, or PKCS standards) are implemented or supported?

_____**d.** What type of data is encrypted?

_____**3.** For products that contain an "encryption component," can this encryption component be easily used by another product, or else accessed/re-transferred by the end user for cryptographic use?

---

the storage, offsite, of secure, unencrypted backups. This may seem contrary to the purpose of this chapter, but consider that:

a. The data must be delivered to the unencrypted DR site *encrypted*.

b. Access to the unencrypted backup site should be manned access only with biometric access controls and no Internet or network connectivity.

c. As physical security and controls *increase*, the need for encryption *decreases*.

Such a high level of security allows the data to be under a much higher degree of control than the data in production data centers. A regular program of data movement, refreshing, and redundancy checks should be in place to ensure against data corruption. Placing data on a disk is no guarantee that two years later (if the disk has sat idle) the data will be coherent. Data can become corrupt just sitting on a disk.

Organizations should consider and design a program that understands and includes recipient and sender environments, and ensures that data encryption and decryption are as seamless and unintrusive as possible. In Figure 63.1, a clock-face approach to security balances the need for physical security against the need for encryption. Observe how, as the network segment approaches the 12th hour, everything is encrypted.

This model only inserts five categories of devices and activities. Each "hour" could conceivably have its own protocols. The analogy of "hour" is used by this author simply to explain and set forth this model as one plausible way of making it easier to think about security, and thus categorize applications based on the activity or on the type of encryption required.

Physical Versus Logical Security

In this clock-face model, the level of physical security decreases the need for encryption security. Physical and data security are applicable to each of the items shown in this diagram. For some items, such as digital cameras, security can get complicated. GPS locators and remote wiping are available for many personal devices, but digital cameras, for example, do not have any sort of a mechanism for encrypting their memory cards.

Consider ranking things in order of "Needs no encryption" to "Must be encrypted." As mentioned previously, the security requirement for encryption decreases as physical security increases. For example, a computer, sealed in cement and sunk to the bottom of the Mariana trench needs not be encrypted. Cell phones and laptops, on the other hand, should be. Create a panel of advisors to assist with the ranking. Depending on the workplace and the industry, the threat level of various areas could vary. *Moving items from one position on the clock face to a lower number effectively diminishes the immediate need for encryption. This can be accomplished by increasing physical security.* For example, whether a PC in an office is more deserving of encryption than a data center that is hooked into the Internet and has lots of virtual traffic through it may be dependent on other factors. Increasing the security in the office may effectively reduce the need for encryption to a level beneath that of the data center.

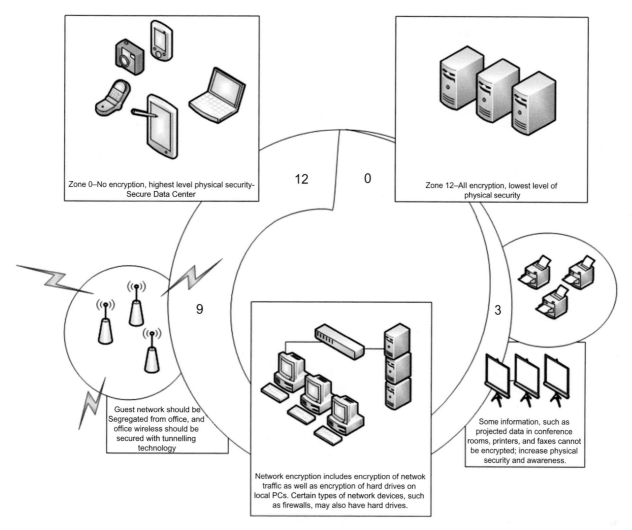

FIGURE 63.1 In a clock-face model, the most physically secure enterprise segments are at the zero hour, with the possibility of imminent attack or loss increasing up to the 12th hour. Note that the crescent line indicates increasing risk of loss, as well as a decrease in physical security.

Deciding which area is *more likely to be attacked first* requires some decision making—decisions that may, down the road, turn out to be wrong. Planning the implementation requires a *healthy* imagination, not a paranoid one. Too much paranoia can bog down the project, but a healthy dose of possible, real-life scenarios and a little imagination can make planning both enjoyable and effective. See the sidebar, Using Imagination to Effectively Plan, for an example scenario cooked up by the author with one of his coauthors.

As shown in Figure 63.1, devices can (generally) be ordered by Highest Concern for Encryption and least physical security to Least Concern for Encryption and highest physical security:

- Cell phones, PDAs, memory sticks, USB drives, tablets
- Data Center Web farm (financial data)
- Office PCs
- BackOffice Data Center

- Printers and Fax
- DR site (of course, in a failover, encryption protocols should be activated)
- Data Vault

Most organizations will need to take into account their own strategy. This allows for deployment of a planned implementation of encryption in an orderly and risk-biased way.

The Confidentiality, Integrity, and Availability (CIA) Model and Beyond

CIA, or confidentiality, integrity, and availability, is a model for establishing security and risk. It dovetails into the clock-face model presented herein in that CIA provides the litmus tests needed for assessing *into which* zone things must be placed.

Imagination Allows Accurate Ranking

One way of ranking is to imagine that a hacker is actually employed (unbeknownst to you) in your organization. One afternoon, after a particularly strange day of slowness in the network that you finally have been able to trace, you've narrowed it down to a group of three people: Justin Smirks, Nate Doomer, and Scotty Potomac.[1] You mention it to HR, who immediately panics, and later in the afternoon you learn (from an email) that Justin, Nate, and Scott were all fired, simultaneously, and they are really angry about it, and uttered some threats on their way out. "I'll get you, my pretty!" they hear Justin shouting as they drag Justin out kicking and screaming. Scott escapes security, grabs his backpack, crashes through the 23rd floor plate glass window with fist shaking in the air, and base jumps out to safety. Nate snarls, laughs, and vanishes in a puff of smoke, with an evil, lingering laugh, echoing through the corridors.

What are you going to do first (besides change your pants because you assume that Scott is "in" and did his damage on the way down, before his parachute finished opening)? In order of importance, would you say (very generally speaking) that it is more important to have disk encryption on the back-office systems or on the PCs? What is the highest priority?

It takes a special kind of mind to examine an organization and architect a solution that will decrease the vulnerable surface area of a system. Such a plan includes intrusion detection, prevention, firewall policy, and encryption, holistically. Unfortunately, the challenges of creating a comprehensive encryption strategy are daunting. To achieve affective encryption, it must be both seamless and the default action. There are three types of encryption that are well known:

1. Secret Key Cryptography (SKC): A single key decrypts and encrypts data.
2. Public Key Cryptography (PKC): A user's public key is used to encrypt data, and a private key is used to decrypt.
3. Hash Functions: A mathematical formula transforms the data to a set length of characters. For example, an MD5 hash reduces large blocks of information to a single, 128 bit, hexadecimal string.

Figure 63.2 demonstrates one example of how they are used and implemented in industry. Type 3 encryption is generally an augmentation of 1 and 2, used to send keys, to verify identity, and to ensure losslessness of information. By hashing a file before and after it is received, sender and recipient are then able to agree that they have the same file.

Users should be aware of the zones, what data lies within them, and the required encryption protocols. Auditors should check new processes, place them within the zones, and ensure compliance. If a new application happens to fail one of the tests, but passes another, move the application into a different zone until it can be made compliant. Zone 4 is "zone exceptions."

Step 1: Identify Areas of Risk:

1. The location of any personally identifiable information. This information takes priority.
2. Laptops, PDAs, any portable computers or systems, and remote workers that work with the data in item 1.
3. Email and other information transport communications.
4. Instant messages might be plaintext sent across the network and may be stored locally as well.
5. Vulnerable server drives and application communications.
6. Backups.

Step 2: Organize

Many organizations have very disparate legacy applications. Get organized—knowing the location, method of transport, and types of applications is critical. Understand where data is housed, how it gets transferred to other organizations, how employees generate and store data and where. Mapping out the ins and outs of how data gets generated and how it flows will both assist in understanding the overall security topology of the network and identify areas that should be encrypted. The end state may be that ALL information should be encrypted, and it may be that only some small amount of data should be encrypted. Ultimately, the following steps will assist in implementing and enterprise encryption strategy.

Step 3: Choose Cryptography Applications—Develop an Implementation Plan

All aspects of encryption that are planned for deployment should be fully understood. For example, using public key infrastructure (PKI) encryption gives users of the Internet the ability to exchange private data, securely, through the use of a public and private key pair that both recipient and sender share through a mutually agreed upon, trusted authority. Without this man-in-the middle trust factor, the process will not work. Essentially, the authority provides assignment and revocation of digital certificates that identify individuals and organizations. See the sidebar, How PKI Encryption Works, for more details on asymmetric key operations. The vendor selection team should have a great understanding.

Developing a strategy of encryption should be treated as a major project. From the outset, things like planning and compliance teams should be established. IT should be involved as well, and all access controls should be audited. Creating an encryption program makes sense, but only if the access controls system is tight. What good is an encrypted disk if the intruder can simply log in and see the unencrypted data right there? Additionally, the National Institute for Science and Technology (NIST) cryptographic toolkit provides standards and guidance over a wide range of the technology used in cryptography. Any vendors should be familiar with these standards and ensure compliance with them.

---

1. All persons listed in this sidebar are fictional. Any resemblance to any persons, living or dead, is purely noncoincidentally intentional.

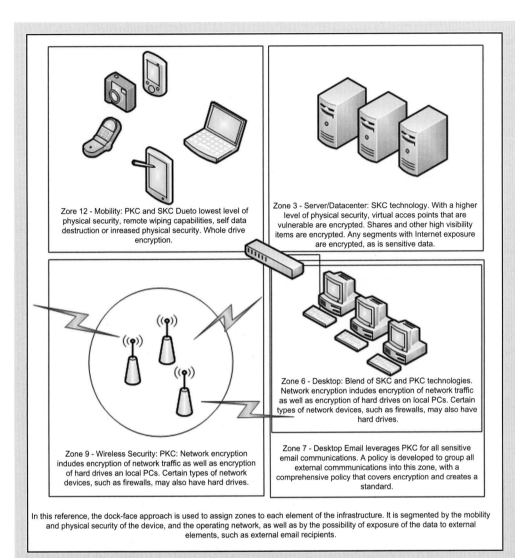

FIGURE 63.2 A sample of enterprise encryption. In this diagram, PKC and SKC forms of encryption are layered across the network in a zoned model of encryption.[2]

Zone 12 - Mobility: PKC and SKC Dueto lowest level of physical security, remote wiping capabilities, self data destruction or inreased physical security. Whole drive encryption.

Zone 3 - Server/Datacenter: SKC technology. With a higher level of physical security, virtual acces points that are vulnerable are encrypted. Shares and other high visibility items are encrypted. Any segments with Internet exposure are encrypted, as is sensitive data.

Zone 6 - Desktop: Blend of SKC and PKC technologies. Network encryption indudes encryption of network traffic as well as encryption of hard drives on local PCs. Certain types of network devices, such as firewalls, may also have hard drives.

Zone 9 - Wireless Security: PKC: Network encryption indudes encryption of network traffic as well as encryption of hard drives an local PCs. Certain types of network devices, such as firewalls, may also have hard drives.

Zone 7 - Desktop Email leverages PKC for all sensitive email communications. A policy is developed to group all external commmunications into this zone, with a comprehensive policy that covers encryption and creates a standard.

In this reference, the dock-face approach is used to assign zones to each element of the infrastructure. It is segmented by the mobility and physical security of the device, and the operating network, as well as by the possibility of exposure of the data to external elements, such as external email recipients.

The final plan should be endorsed by management, and should be communicated to staff. It should include consequences for noncompliance. This plan should also mesh well with data destruction and retention policies.

Step 4: Implement Encryption Protocols
Sadly, no single "enterprise encryption" solution exists. Many vendors offer products A–Z that can be deployed and integrated together in a piecemeal solution, but this sort of hodgepodge approach can also be defined and planned by an experienced project manager. Such a plan will consider possible regulatory compliance requirements as well.

Step 5: Periodic Audits
Periodic audits will help ensure compliance. Conduct them as needed or as things change in significant ways. Maintenance of zone plans and software security measures should be frequent. All documentation should be kept up to date.

Confidentiality

To the degree that some information must be made available only to a certain group of people, this determines the level of restriction needed. Unauthorized access to information must be prevented. In areas of the network where information transmissions are uncontrolled and breach the perimeter, encryption of confidential data must occur.

This is especially true of wireless networks. Frequently, wireless networks are set up with weak, flawed, or no security.

---

2. The diagram in Figure 63.2 represents the author's viewpoint of how encryption *might* be deployed across a network that he just imagined in his head. The purpose of this is to create a model, a framework of sorts, that can be copied and adjusted as needed. It is meant to start a conversation, not end one.

How PKI Encryption Works

In this scenario of message encryption, as shown in Figure 63.3, the infrastructure relies on the use of a public key to encrypt any message sent. This is called public key cryptography. Traditionally, cryptography relies on a secret key used for both encryption and decryption. The most serious flaw of this method is that the secret key can be uncovered, discovered, or stolen.

A public key cryptography approach has a higher level of trust because, on the Internet, the transmission of a private key could be intercepted. So, the public key infrastructure is the preferred approach on the Internet. (The private key system is sometimes known as symmetric cryptography and the public key system as asymmetric cryptography.)

A public key infrastructure requires the following components:

- The certificate authority (CA) that performs the following functions:
  - Issues and verifies digital certificate that includes the public key
- A registration authority (RA):
  - Provides verification for the certificate authority
  - Issues the digital certificate to a requestor

- Storage directories to house the certificates and public keys.
- A system of certificate management.

In public key cryptography, when someone uses the service, a public and private key are simultaneously created using the same algorithm, such as the Rivest-Shamir-Adleman (RSA) algorithm. The certificate authority creates the key.

Subsequently, the private key is sent only to the requesting party. Then, the public key is made available in a common storage location as defined above. The private key remains private.

The private key is then used to decrypt information that has been encrypted by someone else using your public key. People using the public key system can find another user's public key in a central repository and use it to encrypt information that they are sending to them. Users then decrypt the message using their private key. In fact, a message encrypted using a public key can only be decrypted in this fashion.

A number of services, such as RSA, Verisign, and PGP, are all examples of companies in this vertical. Each of them provides PKI services.

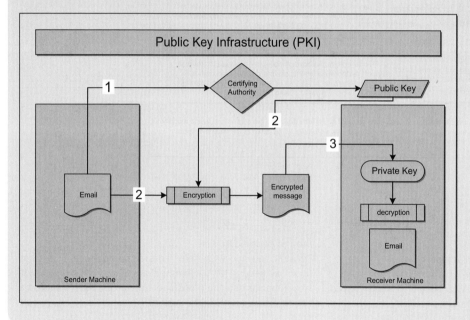

FIGURE 63.3 Step 1: The email requests the public key for the targeted recipient. Step 2: The email message is encrypted using the public key. Step 3: The email is unencrypted using the private key.

Integrity

Information should never be transmitted in ways that may disturb the integrity of the files or data. Unauthorized personnel should not be able to destroy or alter data. Hash values for files should be stored and transmitted with the file and accessed programmatically for validation.

Availability

Information that is so locked down that it is nearly inaccessible reduces the efficiency of operations. Information should be readily accessible to those who are authorized to view it.

Cryptographic Standards and Protocols: Block Ciphers—Approved Algorithms

Block ciphers utilize mathematical formulas that, when operated in cryptography, are called algorithms, and different flavors of algorithms are called ciphers. Block ciphers are a type of algorithm that converts plaintext into cypher text. They are called "block" ciphers because they work by enciphering a preset size of text at a time. Three well-known block ciphers are AES, Triple DES, and Skipjack.

AES

AES, published in FIPS 197 in February 2001, replaced DES. The government reviewed several different algorithms, but ultimately chose the Rijndael encryption algorithm to serve as a FIPS-approved symmetric encryption algorithm. The primary consideration here is that, by virtue of publishing under FIPS, the government created a standard whereby the U.S. government organizations (and others) may protect sensitive information.

Federal agencies also review the Office of Management and Budget (OMB) guidance, which suggests that AES is a standard that will be secure for 20 to 30 years. Furthermore, the OMB guidance warns agencies that the loss of cryptographic keys presents a risk to the availability of information needed to accomplish critical mission tasks and objectives.[3]

In today's world of extremely complex communication systems, the need for a full understanding of security, which includes a detailed understanding of the business itself first, has never been more apparent. The ability to protect and secure information depends entirely on the ability of those doing the protecting to understand the business. It cannot be solely dependent on the mathematical strengths of the encryption algorithm or the ability of someone to classify certain information. Likewise, you cannot count on the classification of the material to always be an accurate predictor of which encryption algorithm to use. Flexibility MUST be built into the system. There MUST be a way for the governing organization to stop, look, and listen. Many factors must be considered in choosing an algorithm and process for encryption, and these factors may, of course, change over time. An inflexible policy risks failure. The following factors are most relevant:

- How well the implementation of the algorithm will perform in specific software, firmware, or hardware configurations;

- The ability to develop a functional key management system, or of the algorithm to mesh with an existing solution;
- The fragility of the of the information to be protected; and/or
- Any requirements to interoperate, globally, where encryption algorithm restrictions may exist.

Considered in total, these requirements demand the implementation of a flexible implementation and policy that mixes the best of breed software with best practices derived from the individual business requirements.[4]

2. SUMMARY

Ultimately, the best encryption protocol would be completely seamless, effective, and transparent. A seamless encryption utility would provide, across the enterprise, a single-console approach to management. Phones, PDAs, hard drives, servers, network communications, and the like, all could be added to the encryption layer with the drag of a mouse. An effective algorithm is one that is not just unbreakable in the near foreseeable future, but rather, is simply unbreakable. A transparent system would provide encryption services without any observation by the user. They would not know, nor would they have reason to know, that their emails are encrypted using PKC technology. Unfortunately, modern information technology has not been able to provide any sort of all-encompassing program for managing secure communications. In the meantime, it is up to information technologists to cobble together a best of breed solution that protects and secures information simultaneously.

Finally, let's move on to the real interactive part of this chapter: review questions/exercises, hands-on projects, case projects, and optional team case project. The answers and/or solutions by chapter can be found in the Online Instructor's Solutions Manual.

CHAPTER REVIEW QUESTIONS/EXERCISES

True/False

1. True or False? Encryption provides an insecure layer, at the storage byte level, under which information can be secured from prying eyes.
2. True or False? Ultimately, the gain of enough data, especially were it due to incompetence, could be a business-ending event.

---

3. http://csrc.nist.gov/drivers/documents/ombencryption-guidance.pdf.

4. Additional information regarding the use of AES can be found in CNSS Policy No. 15, Fact Sheet No. 1 National Policy on the Use of the AES to Protect National Security Systems and National Security Information, June 2003.

3. True or False? Ensuring that files are encrypted in storage everywhere allows the files to be protected in the event of a breach of physical security.

4. True or False? The cost of implementing an encryption policy pales in comparison to the cost of a data loss due to a breach or to release of data simply because Joe Smith left his laptop on the train. In an interesting, real-life situation, the author of this chapter did, in fact, once find a small box of hard drives in a bag on a train.

5. True or False? Encryption also introduces additional levels of difficulty in the event of corruption.

Multiple Choice

1. The data must be delivered to the following unencrypted DR site:
   A. Qualitative analysis
   B. Vulnerabilities
   C. Log
   D. Encrypted
   E. DHS

2. Which unencrypted backup site should be manned accessed with only biometric access controls and no Internet or network connectivity?
   A. Firewall
   B. Risk assessment
   C. Scale
   D. Access
   E. Active monitoring

3. As physical security and controls *increase*, the need for encryption does which one of the following:
   A. Organizations
   B. Fabric
   C. Decreases
   D. Logs
   E. Security

4. Who or what should consider and design a program that understands and includes recipient and sender environments, and ensures that data encryption and decryption are as seamless and unintrusive as possible?
   A. Organizations
   B. Denial-of-service attack
   C. WPA2-Personal
   D. Small networks
   E. Taps

5. Deciding which area is *more likely to be attacked first* requires some _____ decisions that may, down the road, turn out to be wrong.
   A. Systems security plan
   B. Consumer privacy protection
   C. Administrators
   D. Decision making
   E. Challenge-Handshake Authentication Protocol (CHAP)

EXERCISE

Problem

What are the cryptographic module specification types?

Hands-On Projects

Project

What is cryptographic key management?

Case Projects

Problem

What types of self-tests must the cryptographic module perform?

Optional Team Case Project

Problem

What is the minimum information required in a cryptographic module security policy?

Advanced Security

## Chapter 64

Security Through Diversity

Kevin Noble

Verizon Terremark

The Internet and all the interconnected nodes reflect an aggregate of disparate technology, a new spectrum of human interaction, and the most competitive domain for nation states, industry and enterprise. The Internet is the mirror reflecting all things important or not. Revolutions are sparked, small grievances cascade into protest, aspects of wars are wages in the digital medium that is the Internet. Experimentally, the Internet is proving to be one of the most interesting medium to threaten with tangible and results beginning to be recognized as indistinguishable from any other threat. The interconnected scale assures threat can succeed with a high probability of success and yet avoiding attribution. Characteristics of success digital threats are creative with magnitude impact and requiring victims to adapt and pay attention. Most Internet related threats are opportunistic such as malware designed to steal access to bank accounts and computer virus infections primarily concerned with the theft of information. Yet none of these threat come close to the most successful attacks are excessive in magnitude of impact that cause economies to fail or governments to initiate a response other then to suppress social media.

Ubiquity and compatibility are driving forces of the computer revolution driving down cost while the application of 'security through diversity' is still emerging as a strategic decision. In most case geography and distribution of content achieve diversity. For the largest sites providing search capabilities, banking, social media, connective computing becomes critical and relevant as the scale and risk increases, protecting any single host with the application of diversity typically fails. Internet services provided through distribution and replication achieve geographical diversity and perhaps some security, intended or otherwise. Distribution and replication is resistant to denial of service and is an ideal response to cataclysmic events. Immense cataclysmic events require strategic contingency planning by nation states. In general, a decimated region such as the earthquake that hit Haiti in January 2010 required a rebuild of a telecommunications infrastructure. Mobile communication towers were deployed allowing mobile phones to communicate voice and SMS messages fairly quickly. As with many disasters, the distribution and volume of devices supported quickly provided a means to support the emergency needs and can be viewed as a principal of 'security through diversity' might be viewed as an aspect of ' resilience'. Emergency management can shorten the duration of recover and intercede in cascading events and coordinate efforts.

An example of an unnatural threat that probably caused permanent physical damage and destruction would be the stuxnet worm in June of 2010. The stuxnet worm may exemplify threats to come as it targeted programmable logic controllers for a specific set number of centrifuges. Generally, centrifuges operate at high speed at a steady pace. The stuxnet worm disrupted and delayed the uranium enrichment process by changing centrifuge speeds in such a way as to damage the equipment while falsely reporting nominal speeds through the programmable logic controllers. The stuxnet worm had a direct impact on an Iranian program that according to public information, delayed and disrupted the program successfully. The most successful targeted threats will achieve permanent physical damage and disruption.

To be successful, stuxnet had to contain enough exploits to vulnerabilities to ensure spreading and infecting enough host to achieve success. A defender that threat models may impose policies to forbid sharing of USB devices or an aggressive patch cycle. Direct Internet access was not a factor in the successful exploit of the device, many organization incorrectly consider devices and nodes safe based on "direct Internet access."

By volume, Internet related attacks that seek targets of opportunity for financial gain and financial loss can be insured to a point. Also significant in volume are 'targeted threats' where after an intrusion, sensitive data is targeted as part of a larger espionage effort. Information security practitioners focused on espionage related intrusions joke ponders "how many of the fortune 500 companies have been exploited?' the answer given is '500'".

Not a pervasive today but in 2001-2005 worms were effective and opportunistic. Aggressive targeted attacks are rare but tend to exceed in magnitude of other threats and usually have an effective duration to achieve specific goals such as denial of service (long duration) or the exfiltration of information (usually short). Exfiltration as an act itself usually only takes the time to find the location and compress and send the data out.

Specific DDoS attacks require enough magnitude and duration to achieve goals set by the attacker(s). In general DDoS must exceed the targets ability to resist for the intended duration or achieve short-term goals such as extortion. Response to DDoS threats generally require a balance of efforts to assure legitimate traffic remains while selectively banishing malicious traffic that can be dynamic, excessive, and requires logically adjusting content delivery, avoiding single point failures in location, services, and peering. The diversification in points of presence, scalable services, and working with service provides has proven successful.

Diversity as an aspect of resilience and part of a larger information security (see checklist: "An Agenda For Action For Implementing Information Technology Security") effort is costly and difficult. Decisions to hosting divergent technologies that provide the same service redundantly might keep you operational, but it comes with a necessary investment in effort and skill. Intentionally going against top trends appears to be happening naturally as technology refreshes and proliferates. Implementing diversity as doctrine may not be necessary, diversity of product selection has introduced risk to individuals while proliferation may protect all devices as a larger digital biosphere. For technology, mass manufacturing and commoditized hardware reduces cost, competition naturally introduces diversity. Software for the most part seeks to ensure uniformity across platforms and hardware, diversity in delivery comes at a price.

The most common diversity strategy is in use today by most large-scale businesses that choose to store data far enough away from the original site as to be unaffected by natural disasters and phenomena such as power outages. But is this enough? Natural disasters cover only one threat vector to sustainability and operational readiness. The information age must balance uniformity and ubiquity in the face of threats though adaptation and vigilances.

1. UBIQUITY

Most modern attacks take advantage of the fact that the majority of personal computers on the Internet are quite nearly in the same state. The way an attack works against a single host works identically on millions. At the global scale of interconnected systems, diversity is the best response to threats against ubiquity; it is the closest to a digital autoimmune system possible with the inclusion of patch remediation and defense in depth. Patch remediation only safeguards against known threats and assumes emerging threats pose little risk, the risk is worth absorbing or at least tolerated. Defense in depth as a strategy is requires threat modeling that includes methods to detect and suppress attacks. Business continuity planning rarely includes cyber threats or considers intrusions that can impact the core business.

At the smallest level of individual hosts, delayed patching of applications or with the operating system itself can be viewed as the single cell micro organism prone to automated compromise. Home users pay little attention to software updates unless prompted by self-updating software. Users rely on notification and antivirus software to protect and inoculation against common threats to the Internet as a whole more then providing individual protection. The modicum of protection from automatic updates and an antivirus solution is sufficient to individuals. Working with this knowledge, an attacker will seek to automate attacks by taking advantage of the ubiquity of systems, targets of opportunity. Consider the nation state threat, utilizing an exploit that works against a majority of home systems. The investment in

---

An Agenda for Action for Implementing Information Technology Security

The purpose of the checklist is a high level guide to assess the overall security and privacy status associated with a contracted IT service or outsourced business processing. The objective of checklist is to assist program managers, security officers, system owners and contracting officer representatives to identify areas of increased security risk and areas not in compliance with national and agency policy and standards. The key areas examined in this checklist include (Check All Tasks Completed):

_____**1.** IT, Physical and Personnel Security Policy

_____**2.** Organization/Contract General Provisions

_____**3.** System, Data and Device Inventory

_____**4.** System Certification and Accreditation

_____**5.** Contingency Planning

_____**6.** Continuous Monitoring/Risk Management

_____**7.** Weakness Management

_____**8.** Incident Handling and Response

_____**9.** Security Configuration Management

_____**10.** Security Training

developing an exploit provide a nation state with capability to disable and disrupt.

You don't have to be a nation state with an agenda to develop an offensive cyber capability. Imagine for a moment that you're an attacker or small collective of attackers. In general, the consideration is opportunistic and the effort is to develop exploits that within the collective skill set of the group, select popular operating systems with the most common software packages, and select the most ideal target within that subset. An economist might see the concept as a "probability density function," or what is simply referred to as "getting the most bang for the buck." Targets of opportunity are proportional to the ubiquity of the vulnerability itself. It is certain that as a given computer system moves away from the densest pool of common systems, an attacker needs to work harder to accommodate the difference, which thus can reduce the likelihood of compromise.

Ubiquity at scale introduces complexity in engineering updates, distribution considerations and that act as a safeguard. Large scale solutions leads to a natural diverse properties. Still, engineering to requirements with anticipated tolerances might still be the best approach for any design. "All security involves trade-offs."[1] To that end diversity is not a security strategy in itself but is an aspect of defense in depth, part of a holistic approach to security and possibly an insurance policy against unenforceable odds.

2. EXAMPLE ATTACKS AGAINST UNIFORMITY

Ubiquitous systems are good, cheap, replaceable, and reliable—until mass failure occurs. It certainly pays to know that ubiquity and uniformity are the absolute right choices in the absence of threats. That is not the world we occupy, even if not acknowledged. What would it take to survive an attack that had the potential to effectively disrupt a business or even destroy it?

If you operate in a service industry that is Internet based, this question is perhaps what keeps you up at night—an attack against all your systems and services, from which you might not recover. Denial of Service (DoS) is a simple and straightforward attack that involves an attacker making enough requests to saturate your network or service to the point at which legitimate business and communications fails. The distributed denial-of-service (DDoS) attack is the same type of attack against a uniform presence in the Internet space but with many attacking hosts operating in unison against a site or service.

Businesses with real bricks-and-mortar locations in addition to selling goods and services over the Internet can survive a sustainable DDoS attack against the Internet-based business because the bricks-and-mortar transactions can carry the company's survival. Inversely, businesses with the ubiquitous use of credit cards that require the merchant authorization process can suffer when the point-of-sale system can't process credit cards. That business will simply and routinely have to turn away customers who can only pay by credit card. Yet a business with both a strong Internet and a solid bricks-and-mortar presence can survive an outage through diversity.

For years DDoS was used as a form of extortion. Internet-based gambling businesses were frequent targets of this type of attack and frequently made payouts to criminal attackers. It is common for Internet-based businesses to utilize DDoS mitigation services to absorb or offload the undesired traffic. The various means that an attacker can use in combination to conduct DDoS have escalated into a shifting asymmetrical warfare, with each side adapting to new techniques deployed by the other side.

Companies have failed to counter the straightforward attack and have gone out of business or ceased operations. A company called Blue Security Inc. that specialized in combating unsolicited email messages (spam) by automating a reply message to the senders had its subscribers attacked. Blue Security's anti-spam model failed in 2006 when spammers attacked its very customers, causing the company to shut down the service in the interest of protecting the customers.[2]

Successfully mitigating and combating an attack is achieved by either having enough resources to absorb the attack or offloading the attack at some point prior to reaching a site or service. The DDoS attack is partially successful where the target is uniformly presented and responsive and does not react fast enough to the attacks. A common means to protect against DDoS or Internet-based outages is to have a diverse business model that does not rely only on the Internet as a means to conduct business. Diverse business models may hold considerable cost and bring in differential revenue, but they ensure that one model may in fact support the other through sustained attacks, disasters, or even tough times. Employing the concept of security through diversity gives decision makers more immediate options.

Though the DDoS attack represents the most simplistic and basic attack against an Internet-based institution, it does require an attacker to use enough resources against a given target to achieve bottlenecking or saturation. This represents the immediate and intentional attack, with one

1. Bruce Schneier, *Beyond Fear,* Springer-Verlag, 2003.

2. "Blue Security, spam victim or just a really bad idea," *InfoWorld/ Tech Watch* article, May 19, 2006.

or more attackers making a concentrated effort against a target.

3. ATTACKING UBIQUITY WITH ANTIVIRUS TOOLS

Attackers use obfuscation, encryption, and compression to install malicious code such as viruses, worms, and Trojans. These techniques are tactical responses to bypass common antivirus solutions deployed by just about everyone. The number of permutations possible on a single executable file while retaining functionality is on the order of tens of thousands, and these changes create just enough diversity in each iteration to achieve a successful infection. An attacker needs to mutate an executable only enough to bypass detection from signature-based antivirus tools, the most common antivirus solutions deployed.[3]

It is possible for anyone to test a given piece of malicious code against a litany of antivirus solutions. It is common practice for attackers and defenders both to submit code to sites such as www.virustotal.com for inspection and detection against 26 or more common antivirus solutions. Attackers use the information to verify whether a specific antivirus product will fail to detect code while defenders inspect suspected binaries.

At the root of the problem is the signature-based method used to inspect malicious code. Not all antivirus solutions use signature-based detection exclusively, but in essence, it is the fast, cheap, and, until recently, most effective method. If malware sample A looks like signature X, it is most likely X. A harder and less reliable way to detect malicious code is through a technique known as *heuristics*. Each antivirus will perform heuristics in a different manner, but it makes a guess or best-effort determination and will classify samples ranging from safe to highly suspect. Some antivirus solutions may declare a sample malicious, increasing the chances of finding a false positive.

Another factor in analysis is entropy, or how random the code looks upon inspection. Here again you can have false positives when following the trend to pack, distort, encrypt, and otherwise obfuscate malicious code. The measurement of entropy is a good key indicator that something has attempted to hide itself from inspection. Keep in mind that because commercial software uses these techniques as well, you have a chance of false positives.

At the 2008 annual DEFCON conference in Las Vegas, a new challenge was presented: Teams were provided with existing malicious code and modified the code without changing functionality, to bypass all the antivirus

solutions. The team that could best defeat detection won. The contest was called "race to zero." The organizers hoped to raise awareness about the decreased reliability on signature-based antivirus engines. It is very important to say again that the code is essentially the same except that it can avoid detection (or immediate detection).

Given that it is possible and relatively easy for attackers to modify existing malicious code enough to bypass all signature-based solutions yet retain functionality, it can be considered a threat against any enterprise that has a ubiquitous antivirus solution deployment. Infections are possible and likely and increasing; the risk is not a doomed enterprise, but usually information disclosure could lead to other things.

Those who choose Apple's OS X over PC operating systems enjoy what might be coined in some circles as immunity or resistance in the arena of malicious code. An attacker would have to invest time and effort into attack strategies against the Apple platform over and above the efforts of attacking Windows, for example. Without getting caught up in market share percentages, Apple is not as attractive for attackers (at the time of this writing) from the operating system perspective.

One might think the application of diversity can be applied simply by hosting differential operating systems. This is true but rarely works if derived from a strict security perspective. It could be beneficial to switch entirely to a less attacked platform or host a differential operating system in a single environment. On the sliding scales of diversity and complexity, you might have immune hosts to one attack type against a given operating system. This also means that internal information technology and support teams would have to maintain support skills that can support each different platform hosted. Usually business decisions make better drivers for using and supporting diverse operating systems than a strategy of diversity alone. In my observations, routine support will be applied where individuals have stronger skills and abilities while other platforms are neglected.

4. THE THREAT OF WORMS

In 2003 and 2004, the fast-spreading worm's probability represented the bigger threat for the Internet community at large because patching was not as commonplace and interconnectivity was largely ignored compared to today. A number of self-replicating viruses propagating to new hosts autonomously are known as *worms*. A worm-infected host would seek to send the worm to other hosts, using methods that would allow for extremely aggressive and rapid spread. Infected hosts did not experience much in the way of damage or intentional data loss but simply were not able to communicate with other hosts on heavily infected networks. Essentially, the worms became an

---

3. G. Ollmann, "X-morphic exploitation," IBM Global Technology Services, May 2007.

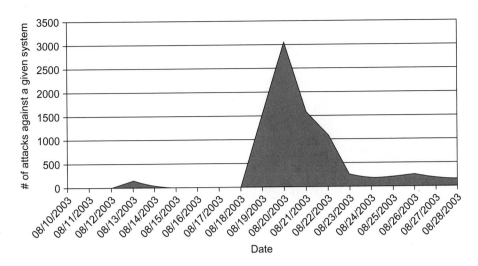

FIGURE 64.1   Tracking infected hosts as part of the Nachi outbreak.

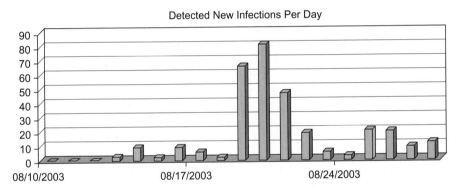

FIGURE 64.2   Nachi finding new hosts to infect.

uncontrolled DDoS tool, causing outages and performance issues in networks in which the worm gained enough hosts to saturate the networks by seeking yet more hosts.

While responding to the outbreaks of both the Nachi and MSBlas worms in 2003 for a large business, there was enough statistical information about both worms from the various logs, host-based protection, and packet captures to reconstruct the infection process (see Figure 64.1). The Nachi worm in particular appeared to have an optimized IP address-generating algorithm allowing nodes closer on the network to become infected faster. When you consider that the worm could only infect Windows-based systems against the total variety of hosts, you end up with a maximum threshold of targets. The network-accessible Windows hosts at the time of the worm attack were about 79.8% of the total network; other platforms and systems were based on Unix, printers, and routers. Certainly some of the hosts were patched against this particular vulnerability. Microsoft had released a patch prior to the outbreak. But at the time of the Nachi worm outbreak, patching was deployed at set intervals in excess of 60 days, and the particular vulnerability exploited by Nachi was not patched. The theoretical estimated number of systems that could succumb to infection was right at the total number of Windows systems on the network—just under 80%, as shown in Figure 64.2—meaning that the network was fairly uniform.[4]

Given this scenario, it would stand to reason that the infection would achieve 100% and only depend on each newly infected system coming up with the appropriate IP address to infect new hosts. Yet the data reveals that the total infection was only 36% of the total Windows systems and took 17 days to really become effective, as shown in Figure 64.3. It seemed that enough vulnerable Windows hosts had to be infected to seed the next wave of infected hosts.

The worm's pseudorandom IP address selection was a factor in the success of its spread; you had to have a vulnerable system online with a specific IP that was targeted at that time. Once enough seed systems became infected, even a poor pseudorandom IP generator would have been successful in allowing the worm to spread at speeds similar to a chemical chain reaction. Systems would become infected within seconds rather than minutes or hours of connecting to a network. Over the years the probability of

4. K. Noble, "Profile of an intrusion." research paper, Aug. 2003.

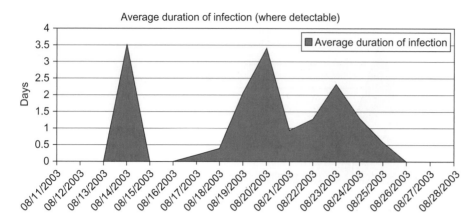

Average duration of infection (where detectable)

FIGURE 64.3 The Nachiworm requires continual infection to achieve network saturation.

a mass windows infection was reduced considerably by addressing vulnerabilities. Microsoft immunity response to reduce vulnerabilities is addressed by the 'Secure Development Lifecycle', a process that has proven effective to worm behavior of exploiting vulnerabilities automatically. It has been argues that massive worm outbreaks have declined because of the diverse number of systems has increased, the cost to develop an effective exploit has increased to a point where it would not be used carelessly, and DDoS can provide control while a worm may not.

Other factors for a successful defense against the worm included a deployment of host-based firewalls that blocked port traffic. The Nachi worm traffic was mostly from non-local untrusted networks making port filtering an easy block for the attack. Other factors that reduced the spread included the fact that a number of systems, such as mobile laptop computers, did not remain connected after business hours (users taking the laptops home, for example). Emergency patching and efforts to contain the spread by various groups was also a big factor in reducing the number of vulnerable systems. The Nachi worm itself also prevented infection to some systems by simply generating too much traffic, causing a DoS within the network. Network engineers immediately began blocking traffic as generated by the Nachi worm and blocking entire subnets altogether. The speed of the infection caused a dramatic increase in traffic on infected networks and induced a reaction by many network engineers looking for the root cause and attacking the problem by blocking specific traffic.

Additional resistance to infection from the Nachi worm in this case was achieved through unintended diversity in time, location, and events surrounding the vulnerable systems. Perhaps we can call this being lucky; vulnerable hosts were protected by not being connected or not needing to connect during the potential infection window. The last interesting thing about worms that achieved mass infection during 2003 is that those worms still generate traffic on the Internet today—perhaps an indication of a sustained infection, re-infection, or intentional attacks.

Though unintentional diversity and rapid response to the outbreak were success factors, an emerging response to automated attacks was intrusion detection systems (IDSs) being deployed in greater numbers. Though prevention is ideal, detection is the absolute first and necessary step in the process of defense. A natural transition to automating defense was the mass implementation of intrusion protection systems (IPSs), which detect and block based on predefined understandings of past attacks and in some cases block based on attack behavior.

Making a choice to be diverse as a means to improve security alone might not be beneficial. If you choose two different backup methodologies or split offices between two different operating systems just for the sake of security and not business as the driver, then cost in theory nearly doubles without gaining much. Ideally diversity is coupled with other concepts, such as security.

5. AUTOMATED NETWORK DEFENSE

Computer systems that transact information at great speed have similar properties to chemical reactions, once started, quite difficult or impossible to stop. The defense of the network can't happen at real time where humans alone provide security. Alternate, machines may not make the best decision about traffic and thresholds. A balanced approached that blends human decision with machine response is ideal. Network security defense from the perspective of the security provides is to leverage automation simply because it is cheap, trying to keep out most of the bad things while allowing everything else to traverse without interference, reflecting customer demand.

If a security service provider took time to inspect every anomaly to the point where overall traffic performance were degraded, it would be advantageous for an attacker to exploit the heavy inspection process to create a performance issue up to the point of denying service. This very consideration causes both the default policies on IPS and IPS customers to acquiesce and to allow a percentage of bad traffic as a trade for performance or connectivity in general.

At first you might be surprised at the position taken by IPS vendors and customers. Denying all anomalous and malicious traffic might be the sales pitch from IPS vendors, but the dichotomy of having a device designed for automated protection being used for automated DoS by an attacker against the very business it was suppose to protect would scare off anyone. IDS as an industry does nothing more than strike a balance between common attack prevention while allowing everything else—perhaps a worthy goal on some fronts.

6. DIVERSITY AND THE BROWSER

An evolutionary adaptation to security has driven attackers to exploit the Web browser. Because everyone has one, the Web browser represents the most promising avenue to information exploitation. Straightforward attacks involving simply spraying an attack across the Internet are not how one exploits browsers. Attacks usually take advantage of vulnerabilities only after a browser retrieves code from a malicious Web site. The remote attack is not a sustainable attack. Most popular browsers that host the means for automatic patching allow the browsers to be secured against known vulnerabilities. Still, not everyone takes advantage of new browser releases that include patches for remote exploits and serious issues. Attacking the user behind the browser along with attacking the browser seems to be a winning combination yielding a higher percentage of compromised hosts for attackers.

Conceptually, could the browser be the weapon of choice that collapses an entire enterprise? It is possible but highly unlikely. The two most common browsers are Microsoft's Internet Explorer and Mozilla's Firefox, making them the most targeted. Most browsers are not monolithic; adding code to view pages and perform animation are common practices. Browser extensibility allows anyone to integrate software components. Serious vulnerabilities and poor implementation in some of these extensions has led to exploitable code but usually demands a visit from a vulnerable browser. Since many of us don't use the same software package added to our browsers, this sort of threat, though risky to any enterprise from the standpoint of information disclosure, does not represent the sort of survivability issues security diversity seeks to remedy.

The application of diversity to browsers could be remedied by the selection of an uncommon browser or by choosing extensibility options offered by vendors other than the most common ones. The tradeoff is gaining a host of compatibility issues for the ability to thwart browser-specific attacks.

Operating systems (OSs) are the Holy Grail of attacked platforms simply because OS has all the control. Most attacks in some form or fashion seek to gain partial authority within the OS or to dominate and persist within the OS altogether. Rootkits seek to hide the behavior of code and allow code (usually malicious) to operate with impunity on a given system. Even when the browser or other services are attacked, it would probably be more advantageous for the attacker to seek a way into the OS without detection. Targeted threats are customized to evade detection and to leverage vulnerabilities discovered over time to infiltrate, these threats are difficult to detect and diversity at any layer is but an obstacle. Being a target means you have a specific value, either monetary or in information. Many fortune 500 companies have been targeted for trade secrets, industrial espionage, pending patents and were victimized and lost data, credibility and information but few went out of business as a result of an intrusion or series of intrusion. These types of threats do not appear to have a short term affect on the institutions except in the case where the company H.B. Gary was targeted and had nearly all the internal emails of the organization released publically. As a security firm, H.B. Gary lost considerable business unlike the institutions H.B. Gary sought to assist.

Opportunistic threats from generic malware and phishing affect individuals and the accounts and information they posses. Many individuals utilize a single account and password or a very short list of account and password pairs. Once accounts and passwords are exposed, attackers automate the use of those accounts against banking sites, social networking sites, and others. A unique and diverse set of accounts and password that are well protected offer the best defense against wholesale identity theft.

It is fairly safe to say that all systems host vulnerabilities, some are difficult to uncover and establishing a defense against future unknown vulnerabilities makes sense. Many well-developed operating systems can randomize memory layouts and as a means to reduce the predictability specific offsets for code execution. Attackers craft exploits to take advantage of vulnerabilities found in code and in some cases, well crafted exploits allow remote command execution. The Windows OS, with the lion's share of systems, is the ubiquitous platform of choice for attackers. Microsoft has made considerable efforts in the past few years to combat the threats and has introduced technologies such as stack cookies, safe handler and chain validation, heap protection, data execution prevention (DEP), and address space layout randomization (ASLR). Each is designed to thwart or deter automated attacks and protect code execution from exploitation through any vulnerability. ASLR can be defeated and many examples exist in the public, but ASLR affords protection at scale from generic automated attacks and the diversity of memory layouts from host with the same vulnerability are afforded protection.

Of each of these low-level defenses implemented in code today, ASLR seeks to increase security through diversity in the Vista OS. Theoretically, on a given system on which an attack is possible, it will not be possible again on another system or even the same system after a layout change that occurs after a reboot. Certainly altering the behavior between systems reduces risk.

The current implementation of ASLR on Vista requires complete randomized process address spacing to offer complete security from the next wave of attacks.[5] Certainly the balance of security falters and favors the attacker when promiscuous code meets any static state or even limited entropy of sorts.

7. SANDBOXING AND VIRTUALIZATION

The technique of *sandboxing* is sometimes used to contain code or fault isolation. Java, Flash, and other languages rely heavily on containing code as a security measure. Though sandboxing can be effective, it has the same issues as anything else that is ubiquitous—one flaw that can be exploited for a single sandbox can be exploited for all sandboxes.

Expanding the concept in a different way is the virtual hosting of many systems on a single system through the use of a *hypervisor*. Each instance of an OS connects to the physical host through the hypervisor, which acts as the hardware gateway and as a kernel of sorts. Frequently the concept of virtualization is coupled to security as the layer of abstraction and offers quite a bit of protection between environments in the absence of vulnerabilities.

The concept of virtualization has considerable long-term benefits by offering diversity within a single host but requires the same diligence as any physical system compounded by the number of virtual systems hosted. It is fair to say that each host that contains vulnerabilities may therefore put other hosts or the entire core of the hosting physical system at risk. The risk is no different than an entire room full of interconnected systems that have emergent properties. Frequently, security professionals and attackers alike use virtualization as a platform for testing code and the ability to suspend and record activity, similar to a VCR.

In many cases, the push to virtualized system or service is a business decision with operational cost being a key driver. Systems that share resources can leverage unused resources. However, with increased frequency, security is considered a benefit of virtualization. This is true only in the context of virtual environments achieving isolation between guests or host and guest. This is a clear goal of all the hypervisors on the market, from the VMware product line to Windows Virtualization products.

For quite some time it was possible for security researchers to work with malicious samples in a virtualized state. This allowed researchers to essentially use the context of a computer running on a computer with features similar to a digital video recorder, where time (for the malicious sample) can be recorded and played back at a speed of their choosing. That was true until the advent of malicious code with the ability to test whether it was hosted in a virtualized environment or not. Recent research has shown that it is possible for malicious code to escape the context of the virtual world and attack the host system or at least glean information from it.

Two competing factors nullify using virtualized environments as a means of archiving simple security through diversity. It will continue to be possible to detect hosting in a virtual environment, and it is possible to find the means to exploit virtual environments, even if the difficulty increases. However, this just means that you can't rely on the hypervisor alone. Vulnerabilities are at the heart of all software, and the evolutionary state of attacking the virtualized environments and the hypervisor will continue to progress.

The decline of virtualized environments as a security tool was natural as so many in the security field became dependent on hypervisors. In response, the security field will essentially adapt new features and functions to offset vulnerabilities and detect attacks. Examples include improved forensics and hosting virtualized environments in ways to avoid detection.

In nature, colorful insects represent a warning to others of toxicity or poison if eaten. Similarly, some in the security field have taken to setting virtualization flags on real, physical machines simply to foil malicious code. The more hostile malicious code will shut itself down and delete itself when it determines it is in a virtual host, thus preventing some infections.

8. DNS EXAMPLE OF DIVERSITY THROUGH SECURITY

It is fair to say that the Internet requires a means to resolve IP addresses to names and names back to IP addresses. The resolving capabilities are solved by

5. M. Dowd and A. Sotirov, 2008 Black Hat paper, "Bypassing browser memory protections," Black Hat USA 2008 Briefings and Training, Caesars Palace, Las Vegas August 2-7, 2008 [https://www.blackhat.com/presentations/bh-usa-08/Sotirov_Dowd/bh08-sotirov-dowd.pdf]

Domain Name Server with a well-defined explanation on how any DNS is supposed to function being published and publicly available. In most cases you may choose to use a provider's implementation of DNS as a resolver or deploy your own to manage internal names and perform a lookup from other domains.

If prior to 2008 you had selected the less popular DJBDNS[6] over the more popular BIND, you would have been inoculated (for the most part[7]) against the DNS cache-poisoning attack made famous by Dan Kaminski. Depending on your understanding of the attack against what you are trying to protect, theoretically all information transacted over the Internet was at the complete mercy of an attacker. Nothing could be trusted. This is actually not the limit of the capabilities, but it is the most fundamental. The threat to survivability was real and caused many to consider secure DNS alternatives after the attack was made public.

Rapid and automated response is the most common defense technique. Making the decision to act late is still beneficial but risky because the number of attackers capable of performing the attack increases with time. Reaction is both a good procedural defense and offers immunity and lessons learned. As part of the reaction, you could assume that the DNS is not trusted and continue to operate with the idea that some information not be from the intended sources. You could also make a decision to disconnect from the Internet until the threat is mitigated to a satisfactory level. Neither would seem reasonable, but it is important to know what threat would constitute such a reaction.

9. RECOVERY FROM DISASTER IS SURVIVAL

Disaster recovery is often thought of as being able to recover from partial data loss or complete data loss by restoring data from tape. With the considerably lower cost of dense media, it is now possible to continuously stream a copy of the data and recover at any point in time rather than the scheduled time associated with evening backup events. In many cases the backup procedure is tested frequently, whereas the recovery procedure is not.

Unfortunately, many assume that simply having backups means that recovery is inevitable or a foregone conclusion. For others, the risk associated with recovery has led to many organizations never testing the backups for fear of disruption or failure. Perhaps in the interest of diversity from the norm it is beneficial to frequently and procedurally test restore operations. Though security diversity is a survival technique, recovery is the paramount survival tool in everyone's arsenal.

When does diversity work against you? It might not be possible to quantify the advantage of selecting diversity over ubiquity other than the cost in procurement, training, and interoperability. It is quite possible that an investment in "bucking the system" and using uncommon systems and services won't just cause issues; it would drive your competitive advantage into oblivion. This is the single biggest reason to avoid security through diversity, and it will be pointed out repeatedly. Security through diversity starts early and is embraced as a matter of survival. Military and financial institutions abide by the diversity principals in investments and decision-making. Though a threat is not always understood, the institutionalizing lessons learned tend to live on, forcing change and adaptation that require diversity as a fundamental principal of survival.

10. SUMMARY

In the digital domain, Geo-dispersal or resources and disaster recovery concepts seems the ideal area in which to institute a separate and diverse architecture from that of a production environment. Segregation of resources and environments offers a tangible boundary that may increase resilience to threats. Software updates, early threat detection and suppression is but only part of a solution. As Dan Geer indicated in his essay on the evolution of security,[8] we already have an evolutionary approach to systems by centralizing enterprises into safe, climate-controlled environments. We protect systems with IDS all while making copies of critical data and systems, just in case. Making changes to systems as we acquire them is rarely undertaken to the level necessary to ensure survival; most systems have very few changes from the "out-of-box" state or factory default because we fear that the changes will make the system unstable or ineffective.

"Diversity ad absurdum" is cost prohibitive and not ill advised. Making a leap to complete diversity will inevitably fail for businesses and institutions. Competition in products and solutions is naturally coupled to diversity in much the same way as DNA differs in iterations of generations. At some point, security through diversity is an action to be considered through threat modeling, where it can be applied on as many fronts as possible and at the lowest levels as feasible. At the higher levels, consideration for a process to apply hygiene to processes, code snippets, and each protocol adds cost but acts to protect. A changed state might be more desirable then the original

---

6. D. J. Bernstein, author and developer of DJBDNS.

7. Though DNS queries might be verified where DJBDNS was deployed, the upstream DNS server could still be vulnerable, making it important to know from where you get your DNS names.

8. D. Geer, "The evolution of security," *ACM Queue,* April 2007.

state as an assurance against 'native attack code'. Forced change adds complexity and resilience at a cost yet might be required where untrusted computing takes place.

In selecting diversity and all the investment and issues that go along with it, an instant beneficial byproduct is a rich set of choices in many areas, not just security. Decision makers have options not available to monoculture networks and systems. For example, if you have deployed in production at least two different manufacturers, routers or firewalls, you will have people trained specifically for each or both. Instead of a competitive nature of driving out competition, you have the ability to match the appropriate models to various parts of a given network and not depend on the product catalog of a single vendor. In the immediate situation of threats to an entire product line, a diverse decision process such as exchanging routers is available. Someone with a single affected vendor has a limited choice bracket of solutions. Additionally, anyone trained or certified in more than one company's equipment portfolio can more easily adapt to any additional needs increasing choices and options.

Of all the security diversity solutions available, perhaps having a skilled and adaptable workforce trained in all the fundamental aspects of computer security offers the best solution. The simplistic statement of "the best defense is a good offense" in this case, means that security professionals should be able to defend from attacks, understand attacks, and be prepared to perform the forensic analysis and reverse-engineering needed to understand attacks. Adaptation and resiliency are key traits to diversity.

Security through diversity starts early and is embraced as a matter of survival. Military and financial institutions abide by the diversity principals in investments and decision-making. Though a threat is not always understood, the lessons learned during an attack tend to live on, forcing change and adaptation that require diversity as a fundamental principal of survival of a diverse skill set during a given threat to survival makes all the difference in the world.

Finally, let's move on to the real interactive part of this Chapter: review questions/exercises, hands-on projects, case projects and optional team case project. The answers and/or solutions by chapter can be found in the Online Instructor's Solutions Manual.

CHAPTER REVIEW QUESTIONS/EXERCISES

True/False

1. True or False? Ubiquity and compatibility are driving forces of the computer revolution driving down cost while the application of 'security through diversity' is not emerging as a strategic decision.

2. True or False? By volume, Internet related attacks that seek targets of opportunity for financial gain and financial loss, cannot be insured to a point.

3. True or False? Specific DDoS attacks require enough magnitude and duration to achieve goals set by the attacker(s).

4. True or False? The most common diversity strategy is in use today by most large-scale businesses that choose to store data far enough away from the original site as to be affected by natural disasters and phenomena such as power outages.

5. True or False? Most modern attacks take advantage of the fact that the majority of personal computers on the Internet are quite nearly in the same state.

Multiple Choice

1. What systems are good, cheap, replaceable, and reliable—until mass failure occurs?
   A. Ubiquitous
   B. Vulnerabilities
   C. Log
   D. Encrypted
   E. DHS

2. Who use obfuscation, encryption, and compression to install malicious code such as viruses, worms, and Trojans?
   A. Attackers
   B. Risk assessment
   C. Scale
   D. Access
   E. Active monitoring

3. A number of self-replicating viruses propagating to new hosts autonomously are known as:
   A. Organizations
   B. Fabric
   C. Worms
   D. Logs
   E. Security

4. Other factors for a successful defense against the worm included a deployment of host-based firewalls that blocked:
   A. Organizations
   B. Denial of service attack
   C. WPA2-Personal
   D. Port traffic
   E. Taps

5. If a security service provider took time to inspect every anomaly to the point where overall traffic performance were degraded, it would be advantageous for an attacker to exploit the heavy inspection process to create a performance issue up to the point of:
   A. Systems security plan
   B. Consumer privacy protection

C. Denying service

D. Decision making

E. Challenge-Handshake Authentication Protocol (CHAP)

EXERCISE

Problem

The most common diversity strategy is in use today by most large-scale businesses that choose to store data far enough away from the original site as to be unaffected by natural disasters and phenomena such as power outages. But is this enough?

Hands-On Projects

Project

Ubiquitous systems are good, cheap, replaceable, and reliable—until mass failure occurs. It certainly pays to know that ubiquity and uniformity are the absolute right choices in the absence of threats. That is not the world we occupy, even if not acknowledged. What would it take to survive an attack that had the potential to effectively disrupt a business or even destroy it?

Case Projects

Problem

Conceptually, could the browser be the weapon of choice that collapses an entire enterprise?

Optional Team Case Project

Problem

When does diversity work against you?

## Chapter 65

Online e-Reputation Management Services

Jean-Marc Seigneur
University of Geneva

1. INTRODUCTION

During the past three decades, the computing environment has changed from centralized stationary computers to distributed and mobile computing. This evolution has profound implications for the security models, policies and mechanisms needed to protect users' information and resources in an increasingly globally interconnected open computing infrastructure. In centralized stationary computer systems, security is typically based on the authenticated identity of other parties. Strong authentication mechanisms, such as Public Key Infrastructures (PKIs) [1,2], have allowed this model to be extended to distributed systems within a single administrative domain or within a few closely collaborating domains. However, small mobile devices are increasingly being equipped with wireless network capabilities that allow ubiquitous access to corporate resources and allow users with similar devices to collaborate while on the move. Traditional, identity-based security mechanism cannot authorize an operation without authenticating the claiming entity. This means that no interaction can take place unless both parties are known to each others' authentication framework. Spontaneous interactions would therefore require that a single, or a few trusted Certificate Authorities (CAs) emerge, which, based on the inability of a PKI to emerge over the past decade, seems highly unlikely in the foreseeable future. In the current environment, a user who wishes to partake in spontaneous collaboration with another party has the choice between enabling security and thereby disabling spontaneous collaboration or disabling security and thereby enabling spontaneous collaboration.

The state-of-the-art is clearly unsatisfactory, instead, mobile users and devices need the ability to autonomously authenticate and authorize other parties that they encounter on their way, without relying on a common authentication infrastructure. The user's mobility implies that resources left in the home environment must be accessed via interconnected third-parties. When the user moves to a foreign place for the first time, it is highly probable that the third-parties of this place are a priori unknown, strangers. However, to interact with these strangers is still necessary, for example, to access his/her remote home environment. It is a reality that users can move to potentially harmful places, for example, by lack of information or due to uncertainty, there is a probability that previously unknown computing third-parties used to provide mobile computing in foreign places are malicious. The assumption of a known and closed computing environment held for fixed, centralized and distributed computers until the advent of the Internet and more recently mobile computing. Legacy security models and mechanisms rely on the assumption of closed computing environments, where it is possible to identify and fortify a security perimeter, which protects against potentially malicious entities. However, in these models, there is no room for anytime anywhere mobility. Moreover, it is supposed that inside the security perimeter, there is a common security infrastructure, a common security policy or a common jurisdiction where the notion of identity is globally meaningful. It does not work in the absence of this assumption.

A fundamental requirement for Internet and mobile computing environments is to allow for potential interaction and collaboration with unknown entities. Due to the potentially large number of previously unknown entities and simple economic reasons, it makes no sense to assume the presence of a human administrator who configures and maintains the security framework for all users in the Internet, for example, in an online auction situation, or even in proximity, for example, when a user moves in a city from home to workplace. This means that either the individuals or their computing devices must decide about each of these potential interactions themselves. It applies to security decisions too, for example,

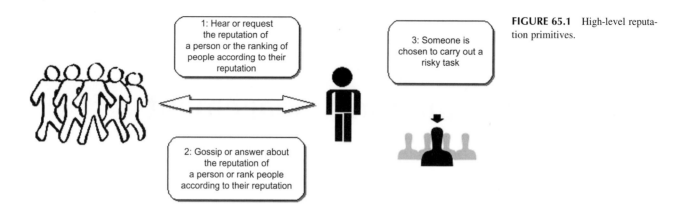

FIGURE 65.1 High-level reputation primitives.

concerning the enrollment of a large number of unknown entities. There is an inherent element of risk whenever a computing entity ventures into collaboration with a previously unknown party. One way to manage that risk is to develop models, policies and mechanisms that allow the local entity to assess the risk of the proposed collaboration and to explicitly reason about the trustworthiness of the other party in order to determine if the other party is trustworthy enough to mitigate the risk of collaboration. Formation of trust may be based on previous experience, recommendations from reachable peers or the perceived reputation of the other party. Reputation, for example, could be obtained through a reputation system such as the one used on eBay [3]. This chapter focuses on this new approach to computer security, namely, reputation management. Nowadays almost all communication and marketing agencies have online reputation monitoring and analysis as part of the services they propose to their customers. Although these services are the most well-known, this chapter covers all the types of services that compose a complete reputation management solution stack.

The next section of this chapter discusses the general understanding of the human notion of reputation. Section 3 explains how this concept of reputation fits into computer security. The fourth section presents the state of the art of attack-resistant reputation computation. Section 5 gives an overview of the current market of online reputation and e-reputation services. We conclude by underlining the need to standardize online reputation for increased adoption and robustness.

2. THE HUMAN NOTION OF REPUTATION

Reputation is an old human notion: the Romans named it "reputatio": "reputatio est vulgaris opinio ubi non est veritas." [4]. Reputation may be considered as a social control mechanism [5], where it is better to tell the truth than to have the reputation to be a liar. That social control mechanism may have been challenged in the past by the fact that people could change of region to clear their

reputation. However, as we move toward an information society world, changing of region should have less and less impact in this regard because reputation information is no more bound to a specific location, which is also a good news for reputable people who have to move to other regions for other reasons, such as a job relocation. For example, someone might want to know the reputation of a person that she or he does not know, especially when this person is considered to be chosen to carry out a risky task among a set of potential new collaborators. Another case may be that the reputation of a person is simply gossiped. The reputation information may be based on real, biased or faked facts, for example, faked by a malicious recommender who wants to harm the target person or biased by a recommender who is a close friend of the person to be recommended. The above Latin quote translates to "reputation is a vulgar opinion where there is no truth" [4]. The target of the reputation may also be an organization, a product, a brand, a location... The source of the reputation information may not be very clear, for example, it may come from gossips or rumors whose source is not exactly known or it may come from a known group of people. When the source is known, the term recommendation can be used. Reputation is different than a recommendation who is made by a known specific entity. The following Figure 65.1 gives an overview of the reputation primitives.

As La Rochefoucauld wrote[1] a long time ago, recommending is also a trusting behavior. It has not only an impact on the recommender's overall trustworthiness (meaning it goes beyond recommending trustworthiness) but also on the overall level of trust in the network of the involved parties. La Rochefoucauld highlighted that when

---

1. Original quotation in French: La confiance ne nous laisse pas tant de liberté, ses règles sont plus étroites, elle demande plus de prudence et de retenue, et nous ne sommes pas toujours libres d'en disposer: il ne s'agit pas de nous uniquement, et nos intérêts sont mêlés d'ordinaire avec les intérêts des autres. Elle a besoin d'une grande justesse pour ne livrer pas nos amis en nous livrant nous-mêmes, et pour ne faire pas des présents de leur bien dans la vue d'augmenter le prix de ce que nous donnons.

one recommends another, they should be aware that the outcome of their recommendation will reflect upon their trustworthiness and reputation since they are partly responsible for this outcome. Benjamin Franklin noted about recommendations that each time he made a recommendation, his recommending trustworthiness was impacted: "in consequence of my crediting such recommendations, my own are out of credit" [6]. However, his letter underlines that still he had to make recommendations about not very well-known parties because they made the request and not making recommendations could have upset them. This is in line with Covey's "Emotional Bank Account" [7,8], where any interaction modifies the amount of trust between the interacting parties and can be seen as favor or disfavor — deposit or withdrawal. As Romano underlined in her thesis, there are many definitions of trust in a wide range of domains [9], for example, psychology, economics, or sociology. In this chapter, we use Romano's definition of trust, which is supposed to integrate many aspects of previous work on trust research:

"Trust is a subjective assessment of another's influence in terms of the extent of one's perceptions about the quality and significance of another's impact over one's outcomes in a given situation, such that one's expectation of, openness to, and inclination toward such influence provide a sense of control over the potential outcomes of the situation." [9]

In social research, there are three main types of trust: interpersonal trust, based on the outcomes of past interactions with the trustee; dispositional trust, provided by the trustor's general disposition towards trust, independent of the trustee; and system trust, provided by external means such as insurance or laws [10]. Depending on the situation, a high level of trust in one of these types can become sufficient for the trustor to make the decision to trust. When there is insurance against a negative outcome, or when the legal system acts as a credible deterrent against undesirable behavior, it means that the level of system trust is high and the level of risk is negligible — therefore the levels of interpersonal and dispositional trust are less important. It is usually assumed that by knowing the link to the real-world identity, there is insurance against harm that may be done by this entity: in essence, this is security based on authenticated identity and legal recourse. In this case, the level of system trust seems to be high but one may argue that in practice the legal system does not provide a credible deterrent against undesirable behaviour (it makes no sense to sue someone for a single spam email, as the effort expended to gain redress outweighs the benefit).

The information on the outcomes of the past interactions with the trustee that are used for trust can come from different sources. First, the information on the outcomes may be based on direct observations: when the trustor has directly interacted with the requesting trustee and personally experienced the observation. Another type of observation is when a third-party observes itself an interaction between two parties and infers itself the type of outcome. Another source of information may be specific recommenders who report to the trustor the outcomes of interactions that have not been directly observed by the trustor but by themselves or other recommenders. In this case, care must be taken not to count twice or many more times the same outcomes reported by different recommenders. Finally, reputation is another source of trust information but more difficult to analyze because generally it is not exactly known who the recommenders are and the chance to count many times the same outcomes of interactions is higher. As said in the introduction, reputation may be biased by faked evidence or other controversial influencing means. Reputation evidence is the riskiest type of evidence to process. When the evidence recommender is known, it is possible to take into account the recommender trustworthiness. Since some recommenders are more or less likely to produce good recommendations, even malicious ones, the notion of recommending trustworthiness mitigates the risk of bad or malicious recommendations. Intuitively, recommendations must only be accepted from senders that the local entity trusts to make judgments close to those that it would have made about others. We call the trust in a given situation, the trust context. For example, recommending trustworthiness happens in the context of trusting the recommendation of a recommender. Intuitively, recommendations must only be accepted from senders that the local entity trusts to make judgments close to those that it would have made about others. In the remainder of this chapter, we define reputation as follows:

Reputation is the subjective aggregated value, as perceived by the requester, of the assessments by other people, who are not exactly identified, of some quality, character, characteristic or ability of a specific entity with whom the requester has never interacted with previously.

To be able to perceive the reputation of an entity is only one aspect of reputation management. The other aspects of reputation management for an entity consist of:

- Monitoring the entity reputation as broadly as possible in a proactive way;
- Analyzing the sources spreading the entity reputation;
- Influencing the number and content of these sources to spread an improved reputation.

Therefore, reputation management involves some marketing and public relations actions. Reputation management may be applied to different types of entities: personal reputation management, which is also called

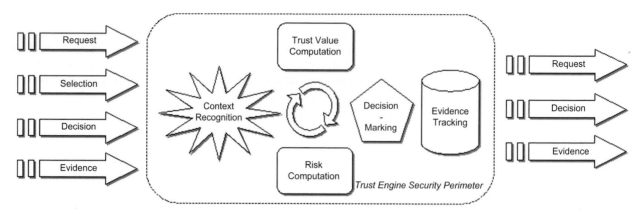

FIGURE 65.2 High-level components of a computational trust engine.

"personal branding" [11], business reputation management... It is now common for businesses to employ full time staff to influence the company's reputation via the traditional media channels. Politicians and stars also make use of public relations services. For mass people, in the past few media were available to easily retrieve people information, however as more and more people use the Web and leave digital traces, it now becomes possible to find information about any Web user via Google. For example, in a recent survey of hundred executive recruiters [12], 77% of these executive recruiters declared to use search engines to learn more about candidates.

3. REPUTATION APPLIED TO THE COMPUTING WORLD

Trust engines, based on computational models of the human notion of trust, have been proposed to make security decisions on behalf of their owner. For example, the EU-funded SECURE project [13] has built a generic and reusable trust engine that each computing entity would run. These trust engines allow the entities to compute levels of trust based on sources of trust evidence, that is, knowledge about the interacting entities: local observations of interaction outcomes or recommendations. Based on the computed trust value and given a trust policy, the trust engine can decide to grant or deny access to a requesting entity. Then, if access is given to an entity, the actions of the granted entity are monitored and the outcomes, positive or negative, are used to refine the trust value. The computed trust value represents the interpersonal trust part and is generally defined as follows:

- *A trust value is a non-enforceable estimate of the entity's future behavior in a given context based on past evidence.*

- *A trust metric consists of the different computations and communications that are carried out by the trustor (and his/her network) to compute a trust value in the trustee.*

Figure 65.2 depicts the high-level view of a computational trust engine called. This occurs when:

- A requested entity has to decide what action should be taken due to a request made by another entity, the requesting entity;
- The decision has been decided by the requested entity;
- Evidence about the actions and the outcomes is reported;
- The trustor has to select a trustee among several potential trustees.

A number of sub-components are used for the above cases:

- A component that is able to recognize the context, especially to recognize the involved entities. Depending on the confidence level in recognition of the involved entities, for example, the face has only been recognized with 82% of confidence, this may impact the overall trust decision. Context information may also consist of the time, the location and the activity of the user [14];
- Another component that can dynamically compute the trust value, that is, the trustworthiness of the requesting entity based on pieces of evidence (for example, direct observations, recommendations or reputation);
- A risk module that can dynamically evaluate the risk involved in the interaction based on the recognized context; risk evidence is also needed.

The chosen decision should maintain the appropriate cost/benefit ratio. In the background, another component is in charge of gathering and tracking evidence: recommendations, comparisons between expected outcomes of the chosen actions and real outcomes... This evidence is used to update risk and trust information. Thus, trust and risk follow a managed life-cycle.

Depending on dispositional trust and system trust, the weight of the trust value in the final decision may be small. The level of dispositional trust may be set due to two main facts. First, the user manually sets a general level of trust, which is used in the application to get the level of trust in entities, independently of the entities. Secondly, the current balance of gains and losses is very positive and the risk policy allows any new interactions as long as the balance is kept positive. Marsh uses the term "basic trust" [15] for dispositional trust; it may also be called self-trust.

Generally, as introduced by Rahman and Hailes [16], there are two main contexts for the trust values: "direct", which is about the properties of the trustee; and "recommend", which is the equivalent to recommending trustworthiness. In their case, recommending trustworthiness is based on consistency on the "semantic distance" between the real outcomes and the recommendations that have been made. The default metric for consistency is the standard deviation based on the frequency of specific semantic distance values: the higher the consistency, the smaller the standard deviation and the higher the trust value in recommending trustworthiness.

As said in the previous section, another source for trust in human networks consists of real-world recourse mechanisms, such as insurance or legal actions. Traditionally, it is assumed that if the actions made by a computing entity are bound to a real-world identity, the owner of the faulty computing entity can be brought to court and reparations are possible. In open environment with no unique authority, the feasibility of this approach is questionable. An example where prosecution is ineffective occurs when email spammers do not mind to move operations abroad where anti-spam laws are less developed to escape any risk of prosecution. It is a fact that worldwide there are multiple different jurisdictions. Therefore, security based on the authenticated identity may be superfluous. Furthermore, in the first place, there is the question of which authority is in charge of certifying the binding with the real-world identity, since there are no unique global authorities. "Who, after all, can authenticate US citizens abroad? The UN? Or thousands of pair wise national cross-certifications?" [17].

More importantly, is authentication of the real-world identity necessary to be able to use the human notion of trust? Indeed, a critical element for the use of trust is to retrieve trust evidence on the interacting entities but trust evidence does not necessarily consist of information about the real-world identity of the owner: trust evidence may simply be the count of positive interactions with a pseudonym as defended in [13]. As long as the interacting computing entities can be recognized, direct observations and recommendations can be exchanged in order to build trust, interaction after interaction. This level of trust can be used for trusting decisions. Thus, trust engines can provide dynamic protection without the assumption that real-world recourse mechanisms, such as legal recourse, are available in case of harm.

The terms trust/trusted/trustworthy, which appear in the traditional computer science literature, are not grounded on social science and often correspond to an implicit element of trust. For example, we have already mentioned above the use of trusted-third-parties, called CAs, which are common in PKI infrastructures. Another example is Trusted Computing [18], whose goal is to create enhanced hardware by using cost effective security hardware (more or less comparable to a smart card chip) that acts as the "root of trust". *They are trusted* means that they are assumed to make use of some (strong) security protection mechanisms. Therefore they can/must implicitly be blindly trusted and cannot fail. This cannot address security when it is not known who or whether or not to blindly trust. The term "trust management" has been introduced in computer security by Blaze et al. [19] but others have argued that their model still relies on an implicit notion of trust because it only describes "a way of exploiting established trust relationships for distributed security policy management without determining how these relationships are formed" [20]. There is a need for trust formation mechanisms from scratch between two strangers. Trust engines build trust explicitly based on evidence either personal, reported by known recommenders or through reputation mechanisms.

As said in the previous section, reputation is different than a recommendation who is made by a known specific entity. However, in the digital world, it is still less easy to exactly certify the identity of the recommender and in many cases the recommender can only be recognized up to some extent. The entity recognition occurs with the help of the context recognition module and the level of confidence in recognition may be taken into account in the final trust computation, for example, as done in advanced computational trust engines [13]. In the remainder of this chapter, for simplicity's sake since this chapter focuses on reputation rather than trust, we assume that each entity can be recognized with a perfect confidence level in recognition. Thus, we obtain the following two layers depicted in Figure 65.3, the identity management layer and the reputation management layer. In these layers, although we mention the world identity, we do not mean that the real-world identity behind each entity is supposed to be certified, we assume that it is sufficient to recognize the entity at a perfect level of confidence in recognition, for example, if a recommendation is received from an eBay account, it is sure that it comes from this

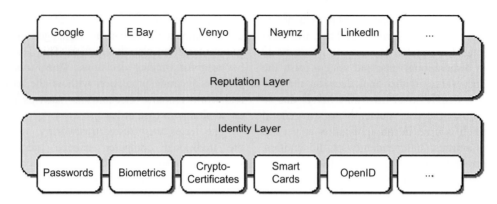

FIGURE 65.3   Identity management and reputation management layers.

account and that it is not spoofed. There are different rounded rectangles at the top of the reputation layer that represent a few of the different reputation services detailed in Section 5. There are also a number of rounded rectangles below the identity layer that represent the different types of authentication schemes that can be used to recognize an entity. Although password-based or OpenID[2]-based [21] authentication may be less secure than multi-modal authentication combining biometrics, smart cards and crypto-certificates [13], since we assume that the level of confidence in recognition is perfect as said above, the different identity management technologies are abstracted to a unique identity management layer for the remainder of the chapter.

As presented in the previous section, reputation management goes beyond mere reputation assessment and encompasses monitoring, analysis and influence of reputation sources. It is the reason that we introduce the following categories, depicted in Figure 65.4, for online reputation services:

- Reputation Calculation: Based on evidence gathered by the service, the service either computes a value representing the reputation of a specific entity or simply presents the reputation information without ranking.
- Reputation Monitoring, Analysis and Warnings: The service monitors Web-based media (Web sites, blogs, social networks, digitalized archived of paper-based press and trademarks...) to detect any information impacting the entity reputation and warns the user in case of important changes.
- Reputation Influencing, Promotion and Rewards: The service takes actions to influence the perceived reputation of the entity. The service actively promotes the

Reputation Calculation

Monitoring, Analysis and Warnings

Influencing, Promotion and Rewards

Interaction Facilitation and Follow-up

Reputation Certification and Assurance

Fraud Protection, Mediation, Cleaning and Recovery

FIGURE 65.4   Online reputation management services categories.

entity reputation, for example, by publishing Web pages carefully designed to reach a high rank in major search engines or paid online advertisements, such as, Google AdWords. Users reaching a higher reputation may gain other rewards than promotion, such as, discounts. Based on the monitoring services analysis, the service may be able to list the most important reputation sources and allow the users to influence these sources. For example, in a 2006 blog bribe case, it has been reported that free laptops preloaded with a new commercial operating system have been shipped for free to the most important bloggers in the field of consumer-oriented software in order to improve the reputation of the new operating software.

- Interaction Facilitation and Follow-up: The service provides an environment to facilitate the interaction and its outcome between the trustor and the trustee. For example, eBay provides the online auction system to sellers and buyers as well as monitors the follow-up

---

2. Please refer to Chapter 15 on Identity Management to learn more about OpenID.

of the commercial transaction between the buyer and the seller.

- Reputation Certification and Assurance: That type of service is closer to the notion of system trust than the human notion of reputation because it relies on externals means to avoid ending up in a harmful situation. For example, an insurance is paid as part of a commercial transaction. These services might need the certification of the link between the entity and its real-world identity in case of prosecutions. Our assumption does not hold for the services that require that kind of links but that category of services had to be covered because a few services surveyed below make use of them.

- Fraud Protection, Mediation, Cleaning and Recovery: The above promotion services aim at improving the ranking of reputation information provided by the user rather than external information provided by third-parties. However, even if external information is hidden behind more controlled information, it can still be found. It is the reason that some services try to force the owners of the external sites hosting the damaging reputation information to delete the damaging information. Depending on where the server is located, it is more or less difficult to achieve. It may be as simple as filling an online form on the site hosting the defaming information to contact the technical support employee who will check if the information is really problematic. In the case of a reluctant administrator, lawyers or mediators specialized in online defamation laws have to be commissioned and it is more or less easy depending on the legislation in the country hosting the server. Generally, in countries with clear defamation laws, the administrators prefer deleting the information rather than going into a lengthy and costly legal process. Depending on the mediation and the degree of defamation, the host may have to add an apology in place of the defaming information, pay a fine or more... Fraud protection is also needed against reputation calculation attacks. There are different types of attacks that can be carried out to flaw reputation calculation results [13]. Section 4 presents the state of the art of attack-resistant reputation computation.

4. STATE OF THE ART OF ATTACK—RESISTANT REPUTATION COMPUTATION

In most commercial reputation services surveyed in Section 5, the reputation calculation does not take into account the attack-resistance of their algorithm. It is a pity because there are many different types of attacks that can be carried out, especially at the identity level. In addition, most of these reputation algorithms correspond more to a trust metric algorithm rather than reputation as we have defined it in Section 2 because they aggregate ratings submitted by recommenders or the rater itself rather than rely on evidence whose recommenders are unknown. Based on these ratings that we can consider as either direct observations or recommendations, the services compute a reputation score that we can consider as a trust value, generally represented on a scale from 0 to 100% or from 0 to 5 stars. The exact reputation computation algorithm is not publicly disclosed by all services providers and it is difficult to estimate the attack-resistance of each of these algorithms without their full specification. However, it is clear that many of these algorithms do not provide a high-level of attack-resistance for the following reasons:

- Besides eBay, where each transaction corresponds to a very clear trust context with quite well authenticated users and a real transaction that is confirmed by real money transfers, most services occur in a decentralized environment and allow for the rating of non-confirmed transactions (without any real evidence that the transaction really happened, and even worse by anonymous users).

- Still eBay experiences difficulties with its reputation calculation algorithm. In fact, eBay has recently changed its reputation calculation algorithm: the sellers on eBay are not allowed anymore to leave unfavorable or neutral messages about buyers to diminish the risk that buyers fear to leave negative feedbacks due to retaliatory negative feedback from the sellers. Finally, accounts on eBay, which are protected by passwords, may be usurped. According to Twigg and Dimmock [22], a trust metric is γ-resistant if more than γ nodes must be compromised for the attacker to successfully drive the trust value. For example, Rahman and Hailes' [16] trust metric is not γ-resistant for $\gamma > 1$ (a successful attack needs only one victim).

In contrast to the centralized environment of eBay, in decentralized settings there are a number of specific attacks. First, real-world identities may form an alliance and use their recommendation to undermine the reputation of entities. On one hand, this may be seen as collusion. On the other hand, one may argue that real-world identities are free to vote as they wish. However, the impact is greater online. Even if more and more transactions and interactions are traced online, the majority of transactions and interactions that happen in the real world are not reported online. Due to the limited number of traced transactions and interactions, a few faked transactions and interactions can have a high impact on the computed reputation and it is not fair.

Second, we focus below on attacks based on vulnerabilities in the identity approach and subsequent use of these vulnerabilities (see checklist: "An Agenda For

Action For Implementing A Network Vulnerability Assessment"). The vulnerabilities may have different origins, for example, technical weaknesses in the authentication mechanism. These attacks commonly rely on the possibility of identity multiplicity: meaning that a real-world identity uses many digital pseudonyms. A very well-known identity multiplicity attack in the field of computational trust is Douceur's Sybil attack [23]. Douceur argues that in large scale networks where a centralized identity authority cannot be used to control the creation of pseudonyms, a powerful real-world entity may create as many digital pseudonyms as it wishes and recommend one of these pseudonyms in order to fool the reputation calculation algorithm. This is especially important in scenarios where the possibility to use many pseudonyms is facilitated, for example, in scenarios where pseudonyms creation is provided for better privacy protection.

An Agenda for Action for Implementing a Network Vulnerability Assessment

The key areas examined in this checklist include (Check All Tasks Completed):

_____1. Unique user ID and confidential password required.

_____2. Additional identification required for remote access.

_____3. Help screen access available to logged-on users only.

_____4. Last session date and time message back to user at sign-on time.

_____5. Exception reports for disruptions in either input or output.

_____6. Session numbers for users/processors that are not constantly logged in.

_____7. Notification to users of possible duplicate messages.

_____8. Threshold of errors and consequential retransmission on the network related to management via automatic alarms.

_____9. Encryption requirements.

_____10. Encryption key management controls.

_____11. Message Authentication Code requirements for nonencrypted sensitive data transmission.

_____12. System authentication at session start-up (wiretap controls).

_____13. Confirmation of host log-off to prevent line grabbing.

_____14. Downloading controls for connected intelligent workstations.

_____15. User priority designation process.

_____16. Transaction handling for classified communications.

_____17. Trace and snapshot facilities requirements.

_____18. Log requirements for sensitive messages

_____19. Alternate path requirements between nodes

_____20. Contingency plans for hardware as well as all usual system requirements.

_____21. Storage of critical messages in redundant locations.

_____22. Packet recovery requirements

_____23. Physical access for workstations when units are not in use.

_____24. Control units, hubs, routers, cabinets secured.

_____25. Environmental control critical requirements.

_____26. Segregation for sections of the network that are deemed "untrustworthy."

_____27. Gateway identification for authorized nodes.

_____28. Automatic disable of a user/account, line or port if evidence an attack is underway.

_____29. Naming convention to distinguish test messages from production.

_____30. User switching application controls.

_____31. Time-out reauthorization requirements.

_____32. Password changes (time/length/history) requirements.

_____33. Encryption requirements for passwords, security parameters, encryption keys, tables, etc.

_____34. Shielding requirements for fiber-optic lines.

_____35. Controls to prevent wiretapping

_____36. Reporting procedures for all interrupted telecommunication sessions

_____37. Identification requirements for station/ terminal access connection to network.

_____38. Printer control requirements for classified information.

_____39. Appropriate "welcome" connection screens

_____40. Dial-up access control procedures.

_____41. Anti-daemon dialer controls

_____42. Standards for equipment, applications, protocols, operating environment

_____43. Help desk procedures and telephone numbers.

_____44. Protocol converters and access method converters dynamic change control requirements

_____45. LAN administrator responsibilities

_____46. Control requirements to add nodes to the network

_____47. Telephone number change requirements

_____48. Automatic sign-on controls

_____49. Telephone trace requirements

_____50. FTP access controlled

_____51. Are patches tested and applied?

_____52. Software distribution current

_____53. Employee policy awareness

_____54. Emergency incident response plan/procedure

_____55. Internal applications control

_____56. Proper control of the development environment

_____57. Software licensing compliance review

_____58. Portable device (laptop/notebook/PDA) handling procedures.

_____59. Storage and disposal of sensitive data/information

_____60. Default password controls and settings

_____61. Review of off-site storage for disaster recovery resources

_____62. Unnecessary services disabled

_____63. Client server data transfer analyzed and secured

_____64. Restrict telnet and r-commands (rlogin, rsh, etc.)

_____65. Configuration management procedures

_____66. Tracking port scans

_____67. Review monitoring responsibilities

_____68. Separation between test and production environment

_____69. Strong dial-in authentication

_____70. System administrator training

_____71. Voice system protection procedures

_____72. Tunneling for all remote access (inbound or outbound)

_____73. Encryption of laptops

_____74. Management awareness

_____75. Program and system change control procedures

_____76. Open "inbound" modem access for vendor support

_____77. Modem usage policy

_____78. Incident event coordination (procedures)

_____79. Intrusion detection system (IDS) implementation and monitoring

_____80. Monitoring Web site from attack (internal and external)

_____81. Domain Name Server monitoring

_____82. Hardware maintenance requirements

_____83. Hard drive repair, maintenance, and disposal procedures

_____84. BIOS (Basic Input/Output System) boot order

_____85. E-mail content policy and monitoring

_____86. E-mail forwarding policy (hopping)

_____87. Spamming controls and testing procedures

_____88. Employee termination and credential disablement

_____89. After-hours sign-in logs

_____90. Network sniffer policy, procedures, and monitoring

_____91. Validity of e-mail accounts

_____92. Background checks before hiring

_____93. Administrator accounts and password controls

_____94. Time synchronization procedures

_____95. Establishment of a Security Committee

_____96. Testing process for LAN applications

_____97. Business unit security person designated

_____98. Log and review of all Administrator changes

_____99. Review and resolution of past audit comments

_____100. Audit logs secured

In his PhD thesis, Levien [24] says that a trust metric is attack-resistant if the number of faked pseudonyms, owned by the same real-world identity and that can be introduced, is bounded. Levien argues that to mitigate the problem of Sybil-like attacks it is required to compute "a trust value for all the nodes in the graph at once, rather than calculating independently the trust value independently for each node". Another approach proposed to protect against the Sybil attack is the use of mandatory "entry fees" [25] associated with the creation of each pseudonym. This approach raises some issues about its feasibility in a fully decentralized way and the choice of the minimal fee that guarantees protection. Also, "more generally, the optimal fee will often exclude some players yet still be insufficient to deter the wealthiest players from defecting" [25]. An alternative to entry fees may be the use of once in a lifetime (1L [25]) pseudonyms, where an elected party per "arena" of application is responsible to certify only 1L to any real-world entity, which possesses a key pair bound to this entity's real-world identity. The technique of blind signature [26] is used to keep the link between the real-world identity and its chosen pseudonym in the arena unknown to the elected party. However, there are still two unresolved questions about this approach: how the elected party is chosen and how

much the users would agree to pay for this approach. More importantly, a Sybil attack is possible during the voting phase, so the concept of electing a trusted entity to stop Sybil attacks does not seem practical. However, relying on real money turns the trust mechanism into a type of system trust where the use of reputation becomes almost superfluous. In the real world, tax authorities are likely to require traceability of money transfers, which would completely break privacy. Thus, when using pseudonyms, another means must be present to prevent users from taking advantage of the fact that they can create as many pseudonyms as they wish.

"Trust transfer" [13] has been introduced to encourage self-recommendations without attacks based on the creation and use of a large number of pseudonyms owned by the same real-world identity. In a system where there are pseudonyms that can potentially belong to the same real-world entity, a transitive trust process is open to abuse. Even if there is a high recommendation discounting factor due to recommending trustworthiness, the real-world entity can diminish the impact of this discounting factor by sending a huge number of recommendations from his/her army of pseudonyms in a Sybil attack. When someone recommends another person, he/she has influence over the potential outcome of interaction between this person and the trustor. The inclination of the trustor with regard to this influence "provides a goal-oriented sense of control to attain desirable outcomes" [9]. So, the trustor should also be able to increase/decrease the influence of the recommenders according to his/her goals. Moreover, according to Romano, trust is not multiple constructs that vary in meaning across contexts but a single construct that varies in level across contexts. The overall trustworthiness depends on the complete set of different domains of trustworthiness. This overall trustworthiness must be put in context: it is not sufficient to strictly limit the domain of trustworthiness to the current trust context and the trustee; if recommenders are involved, the decision and the outcome should impact their overall trustworthiness according to the influence they had. Kinateder et al. [27] also take the position that there is a dependence between different trust contexts. For example, a chef known to have both won cooking awards and murdered people may not be a trustworthy chef after all. Trust transfer introduces the possibility of a dependence between trustworthiness and recommending trustworthiness. Trust transfer relies on the following assumptions:

- The trust value is based on direct observations or recommendations of the count of event outcomes from recognized entities (for example, the outcome of an eBay auction transaction with a specific seller from a specific buyer recognized by their eBay account pseudos)
- A pseudonym can neither be compromised nor spoofed; an attacker can neither take control of a pseudonym nor send spoofed recommendations; however, everyone is free to introduce as many pseudonyms as they wish;
- All messages are assumed to be signed and time stamped.

Trust transfer implies that recommendations cause trust on the trustor (T) side to be transferred from the recommender (R) to the subject (S) of the recommendation. A second effect is that the trust on the recommender side for the subject is reduced by the amount of transferred trustworthiness. If it is a self-recommendation, that is, recommendations from pseudonyms belonging to the same real-world identity, then the second effect is moot, as it does not make sense for a real-world entity to reduce trust in his/her own pseudonyms. Even if there are different trust contexts (such as trustworthiness in delivering on time or recommending trustworthiness), each trust context has its impact on the single construct trust value: they cannot be taken separately for the calculation of the single construct trust value. A transfer of trust is carried out if the exchange of communications depicted in Figure 65.5 is successful. A local entity's Recommender Search Policy (RSP) dictates which contacts can be used

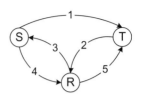

FIGURE 65.5   Trust transfer process.[3]

as potential recommenders. Its Recommendation Policy (RP) decides which of its contacts it is willing to recommend to other entities, and how much trust it is willing to transfer to an entity. Trust Transfer (in its simplest form) can be decomposed into 5 steps:

1. The subject requests an action, requiring a total amount of trustworthiness TA in the subject, in order for the request to be accepted by the trustor; the actual value of TA is contingent upon the risk acceptable to the user, as well as dispositional trust and the context of the request; so the risk module of the trust engine plays a role in the calculation of TA;
2. The trustor queries its contacts, which pass the RSP, in order to find recommenders willing to transfer some of their positive event outcomes count to the subject. Recall that trustworthiness is based on event outcomes count in trust transfer;
3. If the contact has directly interacted with the subject and the contact's RP allows it to permit the trustor to transfer an amount $(A \leq TA)$ of the recommender's trustworthiness to the subject, the contact agrees to recommend the subject. It queries the subject whether it agrees to lose A of trustworthiness on the recommender side;
4. The subject returns a signed statement, indicating whether it agrees or not;
5. The recommender sends back a signed recommendation to the trustor, indicating the trust value it is prepared to transfer to the subject. This message includes the signed agreement of the subject.

Both the RSP and RP can be as simple or complex as the application environment demands. The trust transfer process is illustrated in Figure 65.6 where the subject requests an action, which requires *10* positive outcomes. We represent the trust value as a tree of (s,i,c)-triples, corresponding to a mathematical event structure [28]: an event outcome count is represented as a (s,i,c)-triple, where s is the number of events that supports the

---

3. In this type of figure, the circles represent the different involved entities: S corresponds to the sender, which is the subject of the recommendation and the requester; T is the trustor, which is also the target; and R is the recommender. The directed black arrows indicate a message sent from one entity to another. The arrows are chronologically ordered by their number.

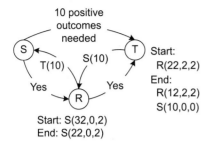

FIGURE 65.6   Trust transfer process example.[4]

outcome, *i* is the number of events that have no information or are inconclusive about the outcome and *c* is the number of events that contradict the expected outcome. This format takes into account the element of uncertainty via *i*.

The *RSP* of the trustor is to query a contact to propose to transfer trust if the *balance (s-i-c)* is strictly greater than *2TA*. This is because it is sensible to require that the recommender remains more trustworthy than the subject after the recommendation. The contact, having a balance passing the *RSP (s-i-c = 32-0-2 = 30)*, is asked by the trustor whether he/she wants to recommend *10* good outcomes. The contact's *RP* is to agree to the transfer if the subject has a trust value greater than *TA*. The balance of the subject on the recommender's side is greater than *10 (s-i-c = 22-2-2 = 18)*. The subject is asked by the recommender whether he/she agrees *10* good outcomes to be transferred. Trustor *T* reduces its trust in recommender *R* by *10* and increases its trust in subject *S* by *10*. Finally, the recommender reduces her/his trust in the subject by *10*.

The recommender could make requests to a number of recommenders until the total amount of trust value is reached (the search requests to find the recommenders are not represented in the figures). For instance, in the previous example, two different recommenders could be contacted, with one recommending *3* good outcomes and the other one *7*.

A recommender chain in trust transfer is not explicitly known to the trustor. The trustor only needs to know his/her contacts who agree to transfer some of their trustworthiness. This is useful from a privacy point of view since the full chain of recommenders is not disclosed. This is in contrast to other recommender chains such as public keys web of trust [29]. Because we assume that the entities cannot be compromised, we leave the issue surrounding the independence of recommender chains in order to increase the attack resistance of the trust metric for future work. The reason for searching more than one path is that it decreases the chance of a faulty path (either due to

malicious intermediaries or unreliable ones). If the full list of recommenders must be detailed in order to be able to check the independence of recommender chains, the privacy protection is lost. This can be an application-specific design decision.

Thanks to trust transfer, although a real-world identity has many pseudonyms, the Sybil attack cannot happen because the number of direct observations (and hence, total amount of trust) remains the same on the trustor side. One may argue that it is unfair for the recommender to lose the same amount of trustworthiness as specified in his/her recommendation, moreover if the outcome is ultimately good. It is envisaged that a more complex sequence of messages can be put in place in order to revise the decrease of trustworthiness after a successful outcome. This has been left for future work, because it can lead to vulnerabilities (for example, based on Sybil attacks with careful cost/benefit analysis). The current trust transfer approach is still limited to scenarios where there are many interactions between the recommenders and where the overall trustworthiness in the network (that is, the global number of good outcomes) is large enough that there is no major impact to entities when they agree to transfer some of their trust (such as in the email application domain [13]). Ultimately, without sacrificing the flexibility and privacy enhancing potential of limitless pseudonym creation, Sybil attacks are guaranteed to be avoided.

5. OVERVIEW OF CURRENT ONLINE REPUTATION SERVICE

As explained in the previous section, most of the current online reputation services surveyed in this section do not really compute reputation as we have defined it in Section 2. Their reputation algorithms correspond more to a trust metric because they aggregate direct observations and recommendations of different users rather than base their assessment on evidence from a group of an unknown number of unknown users. However, one may consider that these services present reputations to their users if we assume that their users do not take the time to understand how it was computed and who made the recommendations.

The remainder of this section starts by surveying the main online reputation services and finishes by a recapitulating table. If not mentioned otherwise, the reputation services do not require the users to pay a fee.

eBay

Founded in 1995, eBay has been a very successful online auction market place where buyers can search for products offered by sellers and buy them either directly or after an auction. After each transaction, the buyers can

---

4. In this figure, an entity *E* associated with a SECURE triple *(s,i,c)* is indicated by *E(s,i,c)*.

rate the transaction with the seller as "positive", "negative" or "neutral". Since May 2008, the sellers have only the choice to rate the buyer experience as "positive" or nothing else. Short comments of maximum 80 characters can be left with the rating. Their reputation is based on the number of positive and negative ratings that are aggregated in the Feedback Score as well as the comments if the user reads them. Buyers or sellers can affect each other's Feedback Score by only one point per week. Each positive rating counts for 1 point and each negative counts for -1 point. The balance of points is calculated at the end of the week and if the Feedback Score is increased by 1 if the balance is positive or decreased by 1 if the balance is negative. Buyers can also leave anonymous "Detailed Seller Ratings" composed of different criteria, such as, "Item as described", "Communication", "Shipping Time"... displayed as a number of stars from 0 to 5 stars. Different image icons are also displayed to quickly estimate the reputation of the user, for example, a star whose color depends on the Feedback Score. After 90 days, detailed item information is removed. From a privacy point of view, on one hand, it is possible to use a pseudonym, on the other hand, a pretty exhaustive list of what has been bought is available, which is quite a privacy concern. There are different "Insertion" and "Final Value" fees depending on the item type. eBay addresses the different reputation service categories as follows:

- Reputation Calculation: As detailed above, reputation is computed based on transactions that are quite well tracked, which is important to avoid faked evidence. However, eBay's reputation calculation has still some problems, for example: as explained above, the algorithm had to be changed recently; the value of the transaction is not taken into account at time of Feedback Score update (a good transaction of 10 Euros should count less than a good transaction of 10 kEuros); it is limited to the e-commerce application domain...
- Monitoring, Analysis and Warnings: eBay does not monitor the reputation of its users outside of its service.
- Influencing, Promotion and Rewards: eBay rewards its users through their public FeedBack Score and their associated icons images. However, eBay does not promote the user reputation outside of its system and does not facilitate this promotion due to a strict access to its full evidence pool although some Feedback Score data can be accessed through eBay software developer Application Programming Interface (API).
- Interaction Facilitation and Follow-up: eBay provides a comprehensive Web-based site to facilitate online auctions between buyers and sellers including a dedicated messaging service and advanced tools to manage the auction. The follow-up based on the Feedback Score is pretty detailed.
- Reputation Certification and Assurance: eBay does not certify a user reputation per se but given its leading position eBay Feedback Score can be considered, to some extent, as some certified reputation evidence.
- Fraud Protection, Mediation, Cleaning and Recovery: eBay facilitates the communication between the buyer and the seller as well as a dispute console with eBay customer support employees. A rating and comment cannot be deleted since the "Mutual Feedback Withdrawal" has been removed. In extreme cases, if the buyer had paid through PayPal, which is now part of eBay, the item might be refunded after some time if the item is covered and depending on the item price. Finally, eBay works with a number of escrow services that act as a third-party who do not deliver the product until the payment is made. Again, if such third-party services are used, the use of reputation is less useful because these third-party services decrease a lot the risk of a negative outcome. eBay does not offer to clean the reputation outside of its own Web site.

Opinity

Founded in 2004, Opinity [30] has been one of the first commercial effort to build decentralized online reputation for users in all contexts beyond eBay's limited e-commerce context. However, at time of writing, that is July 2008, Opinity seems has been inactive for a while. After creating an account, the users had the possibility to specify their login and passwords of other Web sites, especially, eBay, in order to retrieve and consolidate all evidence in the user's Opinity account. Of course, asking the users to provide their passwords was risky and seems not a good security practice. Another safer option was for the users to put hidden text in the HTML pages of their external services, such as, eBay. Opinity was quite advanced at the identity layer as it supported OpenID and Microsoft Cardspace as mentioned in. In addition, Opinity could retrieve professional or education background and verify it to some extent using public listings or for a fee. Opinity users could rate other users in different contexts ("plumbing" or "humor"). Opinity addressed the different reputation service categories as follows:

- Reputation Calculation: The reputation was calculated based on all the above evidence sources and could be accessed by other Opinity partner sites. The reputation could be focused to a specific context called a reputation category.
- Monitoring, Analysis and Warnings: Opinity did not really cover this category of services as most evidence

was pointed out by the users as they were adding the external accounts that they own.

- Influencing, Promotion and Rewards: Opinity had the base "Opinity Reputation Score" and it was possible to include a Web badge representation that reputation on external Web sites.
- Interaction Facilitation and Follow-up: Opinity did not really cover this category of services besides the fact that users could mutually decide to disclose more detail of their profile via the "Exchange Profile" feature.
- Reputation Certification and Assurance: As said above, Opinity certified educational, personal or professional information to some extent via public listings or for a fee to check the information provided by the users.
- Fraud Protection, Mediation, Cleaning and Recovery: One Opinity's relevant feature in this category is its reputation algorithm. However, it is not known how strong this algorithm was resistant to attacks, for example, against a user who creates many Opinity accounts and use them to rate well a main account. Another relevant feature was that users could appeal bad reviews via a formal dispute process. Opinity did not offer to clean the reputation outside of its own Web site.

Rapleaf

Founded in 2006, Rapleaf [31] is the first built reputation about email addresses. Any Rapleaf user was able to rate any other email address, which may open to defamation or other privacy issues because the users behind the email addresses may not have given their consent. If the email address to be rated had never been rated before, Rapleaf was informing the potential rater that it had started crawling the Web to search for information about that email address and that once the crawling would finished it would invite the rater to add a rating. Different contexts were possible "Buyers, Sellers, Swappers and Friends". Once a rating was entered, it could not be removed. However, new comments were possible and users could rate an email address several times. We use the past tense because at time of writing this second edition of this chapter, Rapleaf has changed its service. It does not compute and provide a public reputation score anymore. It now provides marketing data about an email addresses to paying customers willing to carry out emails marketing campaigns, maybe due to the issues depicted below.

Rapleaf was also crawling online social networks and any external profile linked to the searched email address was added to the Rapleaf profile. The email address owners could also add the other email addresses that they own to their profile to provide a unified view of their reputation. Unfortunately, Rapleaf's investors were also involved in two other related services: Upscoop.com that allows users to import their list of social network friends after disclosing their online social networks passwords (which is a risky practice as already mentioned above) and see in which other social networks their friends are subscribed too (at time of writing the first version of this chapter Upscoop had already information about over 400 millions profiles); Trustfuse.com is a third business that retrieves profile information for marketing businesses who submit their lists of email addresses to Trustfuse. Officially, Rapleaf was not selling its base of email addresses. However, according to their August 2007 policy, "information captured via Rapleaf could be used to assist TrustFuse services. Additionally, information collected by TrustFuse during the course of its business could also be displayed on Rapleaf for given profiles searched by e-mail address", which was quite worrisome from a privacy point of view and made a scandal at this time. In its first version, Rapleaf addressed the different reputation service categories as follows:

- Reputation Calculation: There is the "Rapleaf Score" that takes into account ratings evidence in all contexts as well as how the users have rated others and their social network connections. Unfortunately the algorithm is not public and thus its attack-resistance is unknown. In contrast to eBay, the commercial transactions reported in Rapleaf are not substantiated by other facts than the rater rating information. Thus, the chance of faked transactions is higher. Apparently, a user rating may rate several times an email address. However, a user rating only counts for once in the overall reputation of the target email address.
- Monitoring, Analysis and Warnings: Rapleaf warns the target email address when a new rating is added.
- Influencing, Promotion and Rewards: The "Rapleaf Score" can be embedded in a Web badge and displayed on external Web pages.
- Interaction Facilitation and Follow-up: At least, it is possible for the target email address to be warned of a rating and to rate back the rater.
- Reputation Certification and Assurance: There is no real feature in this category.
- Fraud Protection, Mediation, Cleaning and Recovery: There is a form that allows the owner of a particular email address to remove that email address from Rapleaf. For more important issues, such as defamation, a support email address is provided. Rapleaf does not offer to clean the reputation outside of its own Web site.

Venyo

Founded in 2006, Venyo [32] provided a worldwide people reputation index, called the Vindex, based on either direct ratings through the user profile on Venyo Web site or indirect ratings through contributions or profiles on partner Web sites. Venyo was very privacy-friendly because it was not asking the users for their external passwords and it did not crawl the Web to present a user reputation without his or her initial consent. Unfortunately, Venyo got fewer profiles than the other services that were more aggressive and less privacy friendly and was terminated in 2009. Venyo addressed the different reputation service categories as follows:

- Reputation Calculation: Venyo's reputation algorithm is not public and therefore its attack-resistance is unknown. At time of rating, the rater specifies a value between 1 and 5 as well as keywords corresponding to the tags contextualizing the rating as depicted in Figure 65.7. The rating is also contextualized according to where the rating has been done. For example, if the rating is done from a GaultMillau restaurant blog article, the tag "restaurant recommendation" is automatically added to the list of tags.
- Monitoring, Analysis and Warnings: Venyo provides a reputation history chart as depicted in to help the users monitoring the evolution of their reputation on

Venyo's and partner's Web sites. Venyo does not monitor external Web pages or information.

- Influencing, Promotion and Rewards: The Vindex allows the users to search for the most reputable users in different domains specified by tags and it can be tailored to specific locations. In addition, the Venyo Web badge can be embedded in external Web sites. There is also a Facebook plug-in to port Venyo reputation into a Facebook profile.
- Interaction Facilitation and Follow-up: The Vindex facilitates finding the most reputable user for the request context.
- Reputation Certification and Assurance: There is no Venyo feature in this category yet.
- Fraud Protection, Mediation, Cleaning and Recovery: As mentioned above, Venyo's e-reputation algorithm attack-resistance cannot be assessed because Venyo's algorithm is not public. The cleaning feature is less relevant because the users do not know who have rated them. An account may be closed if the user requests it. As said above, Venyo is more privacy-friendly than other services that request passwords or display reputation without their consent.

FIGURE 65.7   Venyo e-reputation user interface.

TrustPlus + Xing + ZoomInfo + SageFire

TrustPlus is another decentralized e-reputation calculation service that existed when writing the first version of this chapter but unfortunately had also to close in April 2012 before finishing the second version of this book chapter due to a business model that did not work. They left a final message on their blog web site that clearly stated that their business model did not work out well enough to be able to continue their service.

Founded in 1999, ZoomInfo is more a people (and company) search directory than a reputation services. However, ZoomInfo, with its 42 millions plus users, 3,8 millions companies and partnership with Xing.com (a business social network similar to LinkedIn.com) had formed an alliance with TrustPlus [33], which was an online reputation service founded in 2006. The main initial feature of TrustPlus was a Web browser plug-in that allowed the user to see the TrustPlus reputation of an online profile appearing on Web pages on different sites, such as, craiglist.org. At the identity layer, TrustPlus asked the users to type their external accounts passwords, for example, eBay's or Facebook's ones, to validate that they own these external accounts as well as to create their list of contacts. This list of contacts could be used to specify who among the contacts could see the detail of which transactions or ratings.

TrustPlus rating user interface and score were pretty complex. There were different contexts: a commercial transaction, a relationship and an interaction, for example, a chat or a date.

Thanks to its partnership with SageFire, which is a trusted eBay Certified Solution Provider who has access to historical archives of eBay reputation data, TrustPlus was able to display and use eBay's reputation evidence when the users agreed to link their TrustPlus account with their eBay account. TrustPlus addressed the different reputation service categories as follows:

- Reputation Calculation: TrustPlus reputation algorithm combines the different sources of reputation evidence reported to TrustPlus by its users and partner sites. However, TrustPlus reputation algorithm is not public and thus again it is difficult to assess its attack-resistance. At time of rating a commercial transaction, it is possible to specify the amount involved in the transaction, which is interesting from a computational trust point of view. Unfortunately, the risk that this transaction is faked is higher than in eBay because there is no other real facts that corroborate the information given by the rating user.
- Monitoring, Analysis and Warnings: TrustPlus warns the user when a new rating has been entered or a new request for rating has been added. However, there is no broader monitoring of the global reputation of the user.
- Influencing, Promotion and Rewards: TrustPlus provides different tools to propagate the user reputation: a Web badge that may include eBay's reputation, visibility once the TrustPlus Web browser plug-in viewer has been installed and link with the ZoomInfo directory.
- Interaction Facilitation and Follow-up: TrustPlus provides an internal messaging service that increases the tracking quality of the interactions between the rated users and the raters.
- Reputation Certification and Assurance: There is no reputation certification done by TrustPlus per se but the certification is a bit more formal when the users have chosen the option to link their eBay reputation evidence.
- Fraud Protection, Mediation, Cleaning and Recovery: As said above, the attack-resistance of TrustPlus reputation algorithm is unknown. In case of defamation or rating disputes, a "Dispute Rating" button is available in the "Explore Reputation" section of the TrustPlus site. When a dispute is initiated, the users have to provide substantiating evidence to the TrustPlus support employees via email. TrustPlus does not offer to clean the reputation outside of its own Web site.

Naymz + Trufina: Visible.Me

Founded in 2006, Naymz [34] has formed an alliance with Trufina.com, which is in charge of certifying identity and background user information. Premium features cost 9,95 $ per month at time of writing the first version of this book chapter. The users are asked for their passwords on external sites such as LinkedIn to invite their list of contacts on these external sites, which is a bad security practice as already mentioned several times above. Unfortunately, it seems that Naymz has been too aggressive concerning its emails policy and a number of users have complained to receive unsolicited emails from Naymz, for example, "I have been spammed several times over the past several weeks by a service called Naymz".[5] In 2011, Naymz has also revised its business model and changed its name to visible.me. Naymz has addressed the different reputation service categories as follows:

- Reputation Calculation: Naymz RepScore combines a surprising set of information: not only the ratings given by other users but also points for the user profile completeness and identity verifications from Trufina. Each rating is qualitative and focused on the

---

5. http://www.igotspam.com/50226711/naymz_sending_spamas_you.php accessed on the 16th of July 2008.

professional contexts of the target user ("Would you like to work on a team with the user)? The answers can be changed at any time. Only users who are part of the target user list of contacts are allowed to rate the user. There is no specific transaction-based rating, for example, for an e-commerce transaction.

- Monitoring, Analysis and Warnings: Naymz has many monitoring features for both inside and outside Naymz reputation evidence. There is a free list of Web sources (Web sites, forum, blogs...) that have mentioned the user's name. A premium monitoring tool allows the user to see on a worldwide map who has accessed the user Naymz profile including the visitor's IP address. It is possible to subscribe to other profiles recent Web activities if they are part of the user's confirmed contacts.

- Influencing, Promotion and Rewards: In addition to the RepScore and Web badges, the users can get ranking in Web search engines for a fee or for free if they maintain a RepScore higher than 9. The users can also get other features for free if they maintain a certain level of RepScore, for example, free detailed monitoring above 10. For a fee of 1 995 $ at time of writing, they also propose to shoot and produce high-quality, professional videos, to improve the user "personal brand".

- Interaction Facilitation and Follow-up: It is possible to search for users based on keywords but the search options and index are not advanced at time of writing.

- Reputation Certification and Assurance: As said above, Trufina is in charge of certifying identity and background user information.

- Fraud Protection, Mediation, Cleaning and Recovery: There are links to report offensive or defaming information to the support employees. The attack-resistance of the RepScore cannot be assessed because the algorithm detail is not public. They have also launched a new service called "Naymz Reputation Repair" whereby a user can indicate the location of external Web pages that contain embarrassing information as well as some information regarding the issues and after analysis Naymz may offer to take actions to remove the embarrassing information for a fee.

The GORB

Founded in 2006, The GORB [35] allowed anybody to rate any email address anonymously. At time of writing the second edition of this book chapter, this service has also been closed, apparently also due to a failing business model. The users could create an account to be allowed to display their GORB score with a Web badge and be notified of their and others reputation evolution. The GORB was very strict regarding their rule of anonymity: the users were not allowed to know who had rated them. The GORB addressed the different reputation service categories as follows:

- Reputation Calculation: They argue that, although they only use anonymous ratings, their reputation algorithm is attack-resistant but it is impossible to assess because it is not public. Apparently, they allow a user to rate several times another email address but they warn that multiple ratings may decrease the GORB score of the rater. The rating has two contexts on a 0 to 10 scale: personal and professional. Keywords called tags can be added to the rating as well as a textual comment.

- Monitoring, Analysis and Warnings: The users can be notified by email when their reputation evolves or when the reputation of user-defined email addresses evolve. However, it does not monitor evidence outside the GORB.

- Influencing, Promotion and Rewards: A Web browser plug-in can be installed to visualize the reputation of email addresses appearing on Web pages in the Web browser. There is a ranking of the users based on the GORB score.

- Interaction Facilitation and Follow-up: There is no follow-up because the ratings are anonymous.

- Reputation Certification and Assurance: There is no feature in this category.

- Fraud Protection, Mediation, Cleaning and Recovery: The GORB does not allow the users to remove their email address from their list of emails. The GORB asks for users passwords to import email addresses from the list of contacts of other Web sites. Thus, one may argue that the GORB, even if the ratings are anonymous, is not very privacy-friendly.

ReputationDefender: Reputation.com

Founded in 2006, ReputationDefender [36] had the following products at time of this writing, during the first version of this book chapter:

- MyReputation and MyPrivacy, that crawl the Web to find reputation information about the users for 9,95 $ a month and allow them to ask for the deletion of embarrassing information for 29,95 $ per item;

- MyChild, which does the same as above, but for 9,95 $ a month and per child;

- MyEdge starting from 99$ to 499$ allows the user with the help of automated and professional copywriters to improve the online presence of a user, for example, in search engines such as Google and with third-person biographies written by professional copywriters.

At time of writing this second version of the book chapter, ReputationDefender has roughly still the same set of reputation services as listed above. It is still very aggressive regarding its marketing claims. Users who create an account have very few free services. The service sends them many "alarming" emails about new reputation threats that have been discovered. However, they can only see those threats if they subscribe to an upgraded account, which is not free. Between the first edition and the second edition of this book chapter, ReputationDefender has been able to acquire the reputation.com URL, which was not owned by them at time of writing the first version of the chapter. ReputationDefender has addressed the different reputation service categories as follows:

- Reputation Calculation: There is no feature in this category.
- Monitoring, Analysis and Warnings: As said above, the whole Web is crawled and synthetic online reports are provided.
- Influencing, Promotion and Rewards: The user reputation may be improved based on expert advices and better positioned in Web search engines.
- Interaction Facilitation and Follow-up: There is no feature in this category.
- Reputation Certification and Assurance: There is no feature in this category.
- Fraud Protection, Mediation, Cleaning and Recovery: There is no reputation algorithm. Cleaning may involve from automated software to real people specialized in legal reputation issues.

Klout

We have seen above different e-reputation calculation services that existed at time of writing the first version of this chapter and disappeared before the second version of this chapter is finalized. Klout [37] is a service that did not exist at time of writing the first version of this chapter. It was created in 2008 by Joé Fernandez in San Francisco when he was injured and could not speak. Klout, instead of computing the reputation of a person mainly based on recommendations from other users as we have seen above in previous reputation calculation services, analyses the Twitter account of that person. Klout score is based on 3 main criterions:

- True Reach: the number of followers of the user's Twitter account and following the user's tweets
- Amplification: the number of people who share a post (who distribute it to other users)
- Network: the influence of the users composing the True Reach themselves

Klout may integrate other evidence such as posts on other social networks (such as Facebook) or other users who recommend the user by adding a + K to the user on specific topics, meaning that they click on a link provided by Klout saying that the user has influenced them regarding that topic. There are similar metrics that have been created since Klout, for example, Twitalizer (which is a very detailed one focusing on Twitter information), Peerindex, Kred, Identified, PROSkore, Jitterater (acquired at time of writing by Meltwater [10])... Unfortunately most of those metrics are not open (it is not really clear how the results have been computed and based on which evidence). Klout initial business models is based on the fact that users with high Klout score in some topic would be rewarded by brands willing to influence that topic. For example, Virgin Airline gave free airline tickets to users with high Klout score. At time of writing the second version of this book chapter, it is still not possible to reward users outside the USA and its business model has still to prove its viability. Anyway, Klout has gained a decent level of visibility compared to earlier e-reputation calculation services, maybe because many more users use social networks than before and e-reputation has become a hot product in traditional marketing companies. Klout has addressed the different reputation service categories as follows:

- Reputation Calculation: Klout calculates a score for the user, mainly based on Twitters performance but information from other social networks is also taken into account.
- Monitoring, Analysis and Warnings: Once the Klout account is linked to a user's social network, it can detect automatically when the user sends a new post and check how much buzz it has generated. If another user gives the user a + K, she is informed by email or a notification on her social networks.
- Influencing, Promotion and Rewards: The Klout users with higher scores may be rewarded by brands willing to influence its network through those users. The Klout rewards are called "perks".
- Interaction Facilitation and Follow-up: Although Klout provides a Web interface and widgets showing the user's Klout score, there is no secure check of the information provided by another user concerning an interaction besides the fact that she can specify that she has been influenced by giving a + K in a specific topic.
- Reputation Certification and Assurance: There is no feature in this category.
- Fraud Protection, Mediation, Cleaning and Recovery: There is no feature in this category, especially because Klout focuses on positive interactions, meaning that it is possible to say that another user has influenced the

current user but not that she has been betrayed by this other user.

e-Reputation Monitoring Services

Since the first version of this book chapter, several online reputation monitoring services have been created. Those services do not focus on computing the reputation score of a specific entity based on transactions but continuously analyse the online posts about the entity and warn this entity if some posts may decrease their reputation. In order to facilitate reacting in case of a potentially harmful post (by commenting on this post, most of these services provide a "engagement" web-based interface where posts authors, content and comments can be easily managed (stored, retrieved, commented, monitored…)). A few of these services allow for the monitoring of many entities based on archived content. However, the more entities and post can be retrieved, the more expensive the service is, at time of writing around several thousands of dollars per month. For example, Sysomos [38] products continuously crawls many sources (public Web sites, social networks, blogs…) and its MAP product allows the user to search for posts about an entity back to up to two years. Sysomos has also a cheaper service that focuses on only entity and provides "engagement" interfaces for this entity. The cheaper services do not give access to archives before the account is created for a specific search entity, e.g., the name of the company to be monitored. A few services argue to make automatic sentiment analysis of posts in different languages, such as Sysomos. Unfortunately most of these services automatic sentiment analysis feature only work well for English so far. A few of these services existed before the term "online reputation" gained popularity, for example, Digimind [39], which is originally a business intelligence service that has added e-reputation services such as engagement in 2012. Another older service that is specialized in newspapers monitoring called Meltwater added a social network influence score to its Meltwater Buzz product in 2012. The main e-reputation monitoring services are: Sysomos, Alterian SM2, Digimind e-reputation, Meltwater Buzz, Ubervu, Brandseye and TrendyBuzz.

e-Reputation Insurances

Although e-reputation insurances did not exist at time of writing the first version of this book chapter, traditional insurance companies have started selling online reputation insurance since June 2011. SwissLife was the first insurance company to propose an insurance to protect a person against e-reputation damages. Axa also proposes such an insurance. However those insurances are quite limited with regard to the e-reputation damages that they cover.

The maximum amount that they guarantee against an online reputation damage is quite limited, up to around ten thousands Euros. They cost around 20 Euros per month. They guarantee to put in place means to mitigate the online reputation damage up to this maximum amount but they do not guarantee to fully recover from the online reputation damage. For example, they will cover the price of using an online reputation protection third-party service, which will try basic means to recover, e.g., creating positive well-referenced Web pages that appear first in Google search results before the Web pages with the reputation issues. Unfortunately, they will stop covering the fees of an external specialized online reputation lawyer as soon as the fees reach the maximum amount of money guaranteed by the insurance.

6. SUMMARY

Online reputation management is an emerging complementary field of computer security whose traditional security mechanisms are challenged by the openness of the World Wide Web where there is no a priori information of who is allowed to do what. There are still remaining technical issues to overcome: the attack-resistance of reputation algorithm is not mature yet; it is difficult to represent in a consistent way reputation built from different contexts (e-commerce, friendship…).

Sustainable business models are still to be found: Opinity seems to have run out of business; Rapleaf had to move from a reputation service to a privacy-risky business of email addresses marketing profiling; TrustPlus had to form an alliance with ZoomInfo, Xing and SageFire but eventually had to close its service in April 2012; the GORB has also had to close; Naymz decreased its own reputation by spamming its base of users in hope to increasing its traffic and has recently changed its name to visibleme.com; new services based on another type of calculation such as Klout have emerged but their business model has still to be confirmed over the next couple of years. Many online reputation monitoring services have also been started. Although their business model seems clearer, as older companies, strong in other domains such as Meltwater or Digimind, have created their own solutions, we might expect that a number of these services will have merged or disappeared in a few years time. Concerning e-reputation insurances services, traditional insurance companies have created them and therefore they are less prone to disappear than the online reputation services launched by startup companies with unproven business models.

It seems that both current technical and commercial issues may be improved by a standardization effort of online reputation management. The attack-resistance of reputation algorithms cannot be certified to the degree it deserves if the reputation algorithms remain private. It has been proven in other security domains that security through obscurity gives lower results, for example, concerning cryptographic algorithms that are now open to review by the whole security research community. Open reputation algorithms will also improve the credibility of the reputation results because it will be possible to clearly explain to the users how the reputation has been calculated. The standardization of the representation of reputation will also diminish the confusion to the eyes of the users. The clearer understanding of which reputation evidence is taken into account in reputation calculation will improve the situation regarding privacy and will open the door for stronger regulation on how reputation information flows.

Finally, let's move on to the real interactive part of this Chapter: review questions/exercises, hands-on projects, case projects and optional team case project. The answers and/or solutions by chapter can be found in the Online Instructor's Solutions Manual.

CHAPTER REVIEW QUESTIONS/EXERCISES

True/False

1. True or False? The state-of-the-art is clearly satisfactory, instead, mobile users and devices need the ability to autonomously authenticate and authorize other parties that they encounter on their way, without relying on a common authentication infrastructure.
2. True or False? The information on the outcomes of the present interactions with the trustee that are used for trust can come from different sources.
3. True or False? Trust engines, based on computational models of the human notion of trust, have been proposed to make security decisions on behalf of their owner.
4. True or False? In most commercial reputation services suveyed, the reputation calculation does take into account the attack-resistance of their algorithm.
5. True or False? Most of the current online reputation services surveyed do really compute reputation.

Multiple Choice

1. What is computed based on transactions that are quite well tracked, which is important to avoid faked evidence?
   A. Reputation
   B. Vulnerabilities
   C. Log
   D. Encrypted
   E. DHS

2. What has been one of the first commercial effort to build decentralized online reputation for users in all contexts beyond eBay's limited e-commerce context?
   A. Opinity
   B. Risk assessment
   C. Scale
   D. Access
   E. Active monitoring

3. What is the first built reputation about email addresses?
   A. Organizations
   B. Rapleaf
   C. Worms
   D. Logs
   E. Security

4. What provided a worldwide people reputation index, called the Vindex, based on either direct ratings through the user profile on Venyo Web site or indirect ratings through contributions or profiles on partner Web sites?
   A. Organizations
   B. Denial of service attack
   C. Venyo
   D. Port traffic
   E. Taps

5. What is another decentralized e-reputation calculation service?
   A. Systems security plan
   B. TrustPlus
   C. Denying service
   D. Decision making
   E. Challenge-Handshake Authentication Protocol (CHAP)

EXERCISE

Problem

Can online e-Reputation management services solve problems overnight?

Hands-On Projects

Project

Can online e-Reputation management services make negative results disappear forever?

Case Projects

Problem

What is a web e-Reputation service?

Optional Team Case Project

Problem

What are the levels that determine if an access to a URL will be blocked or allowed?

BIBLIOGRAPHY

[1] C. Ellison, B. Schneier, Ten Risks of PKI: What you're not being told about Public Key Infrastructure. (2000) Winter 2000 issue of the Computer Security Journal.

[2] R. Housley, T. Polk, Planning for PKI: Best Practices Guide for Deploying Public Key Infrastructure. (2001).

[3] P. Resnick, R. Zeckhauser, J. Swanson, K. Lockwood, The Value of Reputation on eBay: a Controlled Experiment. (2003).

[4] M. Bouvier, Maxims of Law. Law Dictionary. (1856).

[5] K. Kuwabara, Reputation: Signals or incentives? In The annual meeting of the american sociological association. (2003).

[6] The Life and Letters of Benjamin Franklin.

[7] S.R. Covey, The 7 habits of highly effective people. (1989).

[8] J. Seigneur, J. Abendroth, C.D. Jensen, Bank Accounting and Ubiquitous Brokering of Trustos. (2002) 7th Cabernet Radicals Workshop.

[9] D.M. Romano, The Nature of Trust: Conceptual and Operational Clarification. (2003).

[10] D.H. McKnight, N.L. Chervany, What is trust? A Conceptual Analysis and an Interdisciplinary Model. In The americas conference on information systems. (2000).

[11] T. Peters, The brand called you. Fast Company, Mansueto Ventures LLC. (1997).

[12] Execunet. <http://www.execunet.com>.

[13] J.M. Seigneur, Trust, Security and Privacy in Global Computing. (2005).

[14] A.K. Dey, Understanding and Using Context. (2001) Personal and Ubiquitous Computing Journal.

[15] S. Marsh, Formalising Trust as a Computational Concept. (1994).

[16] A. Rahman, S. Hailes, Using Recommendations for Managing Trust in Distributed Systems. (1997).

[17] R. Khare, What's in a Name? Trust. (1999).

[18] Trusted Computing Group. <https://www.trustedcomputinggroup.org/>.

[19] M. Blaze, J. Feigenbaum, J. Lacy, Decentralized Trust Management. In The 17th ieee symposium on security and privacy. (1996).

[20] S. Terzis, W. Wagealla, C. English, A McGettrick, P. Nixon, The SECURE Collaboration Model. (2004).

[21] OpenID. <http://openid.net/>.

[22] A. Twigg, N. Dimmock, Attack-Resistance of Computational Trust Models. (2003) Proceedings of the Twelfth International Workshop on Enabling Technologies: Infrastructure for Collaborative Enterprises.

[23] J.R. Douceur, The Sybil Attack. (2002) Proceedings of the 1st International Workshop on Peer-to-Peer Systems.

[24] R. Levien, Attack Resistant Trust Metrics. (2004).

[25] E. Friedman, P. Resnick, The Social Cost of Cheap Pseudonyms. (2001): pp. 173–199.

[26] D. Chaum, Achieving electronic privacy, Sci. Am. (1992) 96–100.

[27] M. Kinateder, K. Rothermel, Architecture and Algorithms for a Distributed Reputation System. (2003) Proceedings of the First Conference on Trust Management.

[28] M. Nielsen, G. Plotkin, G. Winskel, Petri nets, event structures and domains, Theoritical Comput. Sci. (1981) 85–108.

[29] P.R. Zimmerman, The Official PGP User's Guide. (1995).

[30] Opinity. <http://www.opinity.com>.

[31] Rapleaf. <http://www.rapleaf.com>.

[32] Venyo. <http://www.venyo.org>.

[33] Trustplus. <http://www.trustplus.com>.

[34] Naymz. <http://www.naymz.com>.

[35] The GORB. <http://www.thegorb.com>.

[36] ReputationDefender. <http://www.reputationdefender.com>.

[37] Klout. <http://www.klout.com>.

[38] Sysomos. <http://www.sysomos.com>.

[39] Digimind. <http://www.digimind.com>.

## Chapter 66

Content Filtering

Pete Nicoletti, CISSP, CISA, CCSK
Director of Security Solutions and Compliance at Virtustream, Inc.

Note: This chapter is available in its entirety online at store.elsevier.com/product.jsp?isbn=9780123943972 (click the Resources tab at the bottom of the page).

1. ABSTRACT

Content filtering is a powerful tool that, properly deployed, can offer parents, companies, and local, state, and federal governments protection by classifying Internet-based content. It is disparaged as Orwellian and simultaneously embraced as a positive ROI project, depending on who you are and how it affects your online behavior. In this chapter we examine the many benefits and justifications of Web-based content filtering, such as legal liability, risk reduction, productivity gains, and bandwidth usage. We'll explore the downside and unintended consequences and risks that improperly deployed or misconfigured systems create. We'll also look into methods to subvert and bypass these systems and the reasons behind them. It is important for people who are considering content filtering to be aware of all the legal implications, and we'll also review these. Content filtering is straightforward to deploy, and license costs are so reasonable they can offer extremely fast return on investment while providing a very effective risk reduction strategy. We'll make sure that your project turns out successfully, since we'll look at all the angles: Executives will be happy with the project results and employees won't key your car in the parking lot!

2. CONTENTS

## Chapter 67

Data Loss Protection

Ken Perkins

Blazent Incorporated

IT professionals are tasked with the some of the most complex and daunting tasks in any organization. Some of the roles and responsibilities are paramount to the company's livelihood and profitability and maybe even the ultimate survival of the organization. Some of the most challenging issues facing IT professionals today are securing communications and complying with the vast number of data privacy regulations. Secure communications must protect the organization against spam, viruses, and worms; securing outbound traffic; guaranteeing the availability and continuity of the core business systems (such as corporate email, Internet connectivity, and phone systems), all while facing an increasing workload with the same workforce. In addition, many organizations face

challenges in meeting compliance goals, contingency plans for disasters, detecting and/or preventing data misappropriation, and dealing with hacking, both internally and externally.

Almost every week, IT professionals can open the newspaper or browse online news sites and read stories that would keep most people up at night (see sidebar, "Stealing Trade Secrets From E. I. du Pont de Nemours and Company"). The dollar amounts lost are staggering and growing each year (see sidebar, "Stored Secure Information Intrusions"). Pressures of compliance regulations, brand protection, and corporate intellectual property are all driving organizations to evaluate and/or adopt data loss protection (DLP) solutions.

Stealing Trade Secrets from E. I. du Pont de Nemours and Company

WILMINGTON, DE—Colm F. Connolly, United States Attorney for the District of Delaware; William D. Chase, Special Agent in Charge of the Baltimore Federal Bureau of Investigation (FBI) Field Office; and Darryl W. Jackson, Assistant Secretary of Commerce for Export Enforcement, announced today the unsealing of a one-count Criminal Information charging Gary Min, a.k.a. Yonggang Min, with stealing trade secrets from E. I. du Pont de Nemours and Company ("DuPont"). Min pleaded guilty to the charge on November 13, 2006. The offense carries a maximum prison sentence of 10 years, a fine of up to $250,000, and restitution.

Pursuant to the terms of the plea agreement, Min admitted that he misappropriated DuPont's proprietary trade secrets without the company's consent and agreed to cooperate with the government.

According to facts recited by the government and acknowledged by Min at Min's guilty plea hearing, Min began working for DuPont as a research chemist in November 1995. Throughout his tenure at DuPont, Min's research focused generally on polyimides, a category of heat and chemical resistant polymers, and more specifically on high-performance films. Beginning in July 2005, Min began discussions with Victrex PLC about possible employment opportunities in Asia. Victrex manufactures PEEK,™ a polymer compound that is a

functional competitor with two DuPont products, Vespel® and Kapton®. On October 18, 2005, Min signed an employment agreement with Victrex, with his employment set to begin in January 2006. Min did not tell DuPont that he had accepted a job with Victrex, however, until December 12, 2005.

Between August 2005 and December 12, 2005, Min accessed an unusually high volume of abstracts and full-text. pdf documents off of DuPont's Electronic Data Library ("EDL"). The EDL server, which is located at DuPont's experimental station in Wilmington, is one of DuPont's primary databases for storing confidential and proprietary information. Min downloaded approximately 22,000 abstracts from the EDL and accessed approximately 16,706 documents—fifteen times the number of abstracts and reports accessed by the next highest user of the EDL for that period. The vast majority of Min's EDL searches were unrelated to his research responsibilities and his work on high-performance films. Rather, Min's EDL searches covered most of DuPont's major technologies and product lines, as well as new and emerging technologies in the research and development stage. The fair market value of the technology accessed by Min exceeded $400 million.

After Min gave DuPont notice that he was resigning to take a position at Victrex, DuPont uncovered Min's unusually-high EDL usage. DuPont immediately contacted the FBI in Wilmington, which launched a joint investigation with the United States Attorney's Office and the United States Department of Commerce. Min began working at Victrex on January 1, 2006. On or about February 2, 2006, Min uploaded approximately 180 DuPont documents—including documents containing confidential, trade secret information—to his Victrex-assigned laptop computer. On February 3, 2006, DuPont officials told Victrex officials in London about Min's EDL activities and explained that Min had accessed confidential and proprietary action. Victrex officials seized Min's laptop computer from him on February 8, 2006, and subsequently turned it over to the FBI."[1]

Stored Secure Information Intrusions

Retailer TJX suffered an unauthorized intrusion or intrusions into portions of its computer system that process and store information related to credit and debit card, check and unreceipted merchandise return transactions (the intrusion or intrusions, collectively, the "Computer Intrusion"), which was discovered during the fourth quarter of fiscal 2007. The theft of customer data primarily related to portions of the transactions at its stores (other than Bob's Stores) during the periods 2003 through June 2004 and mid-May 2006 through mid-December 2006.

During the first six months of fiscal 2007 TJX incurred pretax costs of $38 million for costs related to the Computer Intrusion. In addition, in the second quarter ended July 28, 2007, TJX established a pretax reserve for its estimated exposure to potential losses related to the Computer Intrusion and recorded a pretax charge of $178 million. As of January 26, 2008, TJX reduced the reserve by $19 million, primarily due to insurance proceeds with respect to the Computer Intrusion, which had not previously been reflected in the reserve, as well as a reduction in estimated legal and other fees as the Company has continued to resolve outstanding disputes, litigation, and investigations. This reserve reflects the Company's current estimation of probable losses in accordance with generally accepted accounting principles with respect to the Computer Intrusion and includes a current estimation of total potential cash liabilities from pending litigation, proceedings, investigations and other claims, as well as legal and other costs and expenses, arising from the Computer Intrusion. This reduction in the reserve results in a credit to the Provision for Computer Intrusion related costs of $19 million in the fiscal 2007 fourth quarter and a pretax charge of $197 million for the fiscal year ended January 26, 2008.

The Provision for Computer Intrusion related costs increased fiscal 2008 fourth quarter net income by $11 million, or $0.02 per share, and reduced net income from continuing operations for the full fiscal 2008 year by $119 million, or $0.25 per share.[2]

Note: In the June 2007 General Accounting Office article, "GAO-07-737 Personal Information: Data Breaches Are Frequent, But Evidence of Resulting Identity Theft Is Limited; However, the Full Extent Is Unknown," 31 companies that responded to a 2006 survey said they incurred an average of $1.4 million per data breach.[3]

1. PRECURSORS OF DLP

Even before the Internet and all the wonderful benefits it brings to the world, organizations' data were exposed to the outside world. Modems, telex, and fax machines were some of the first enablers of electronic communications. Electronic methods of communications, by default, increase the speed and ease of communication, but they also create inherent security risks. Once IT organizations noticed they were at risk, they immediately started focusing on creating impenetrable moats to surround the "IT castle." As communication protocols standardized and with the mainstream adoption of the Internet, Transmission Control Protocol/Internet Protocol (TCP/IP) became the generally accepted default language of the Internet. This phenomenon brought to light external-facing security technologies and consequently their quick adoption. Some common technologies that protect TCP/IP networks from external threats are:

- *Firewalls.* Inspect network traffic passing through it, and denies or permits passage based on a set of rules.

- *Intrusion detection systems (IDSs).* Sensors log potential suspicious activity and allow for the remediation of the issue.

- *Intrusion prevention systems (IPSs).* React to suspicious activity by automatically performing a reset to the connection or by adjusting the firewall to block network traffic from the suspected malicious source.

- *Antivirus protection.* Attempts to identify, neutralize, or eliminate malicious software.

- *Antispam technology.* Attempts to let in "good" emails and keep out "bad" emails.

The common thread in these technologies: Keep the "bad guys" out while letting normal, efficient business processes occur. These technologies initially offered some very high-level, nongranular features such as blocking a TCP/IP port, allowing communications to and from a certain range of IP addresses, identifying keywords (without context or much flexibility), signatures of

---

1. "Guilty plea in trade secrets case," Department of Justice Press Release, February 15, 2007.

2. "SEC EDGAR filing information form 8-K," TJX Companies, Inc., February 20, 2008.

3. "GAO-07-737 personal information: Data breaches are frequent, but evidence of resulting identity theft is limited; however, the full extent is unknown," General Accounting Office, June 2007.

viruses, and blocking spam that used common techniques used by spammers.

Once IT organizations had a good handle on external-facing services, the next logical thought comes to mind: What happens if the "bad guy," undertrained or undereducated users, already have access to the information contained in an organization? In some circles of IT, this animal is simply known as an employee. Employees, by their default, "inside" nature, have permission to access the company's most sensitive information to accomplish their jobs. Even though the behavior of nonmalicious employees might cause as much damage as an intentional act, the disgruntled employee or insider is a unique threat that needs to be addressed.

The disgruntled insider, working from within an organization, is a principal source of computer crimes. Insiders may not need a great deal of knowledge about computer hacking because their knowledge of a victim's system often allows them to gain unrestricted access to cause damage to the system or to steal system data. With the advent of technology outsourcing, even non-employees have the rights to view/create/delete some of the most sensitive data assets within an organization. The insider threat could also include contractor personnel and even vendors working onsite. To make matters worse, the ease of finding information to help with hacking systems is no harder than typing a search string into popular search engines. The following is an example of how easy it is for non-"black hats" to perform complicated hacks without much technical knowledge:

1. Open a browser that is connected to the Internet.
2. Go to any popular Internet search engine site.
3. Search for the string "cracking WEP How to."

Note: Observe the number of articles, most with step-by-step instructions, on how to find the Wired Equivalent Privacy (WEP) encryption key to "hijack" a Wi-Fi access point.

So, what happens if an inside worker puts the organization at risk through his activity on the network or corporate assets? The next wave of technologies that IT organizations started to address dealt with the "inside man" issue. Some examples of these types of technologies include:

- *Web filtering.* Can allow/deny content to a user, especially when it is used to restrict material delivered over the Web.
- *Proxy servers.* Services the requests of its clients by forwarding requests to other servers and may block entire functionality such as Internet messaging/chat, Web email, and peer-to-peer file sharing programs.
- *Audit systems (both manual and automated).* Technology that records every packet of data that enters/leave the organization's network. Can be thought of as a network "VCR." Automated appliances feature post-event investigative reports. Manual systems might just use open-source packet-capture technologies writing to a disk for a record of network events.
- *Computer forensic systems.* Is a branch of forensic science pertaining to legal evidence found in computers and digital storage media. Computer forensics adheres to standards of evidence admissible in a court of law. Computer forensics experts investigate data storage devices (such as hard drives, USB drives, CD-ROMs, floppy disks, tape drives, etc.), identifying, preserving, and then analyzing sources of documentary or other digital evidence.
- *Data stores* for email governance.
- *IM- and chat-monitoring services.* The adoption of IM across corporate networks outside the control of IT organizations creates risks and liabilities for companies who do not effectively manage and support IM use. Companies implement specialized IM archiving and security products and services to mitigate these risks and provide safe, secure, productive instant-messaging capabilities to their employees.
- *Document management systems.* A computer system (or set of computer programs) used to track and store electronic documents and/or images of paper documents.

Each of these technologies are necessary security measures implemented in [or "by"] IT organizations to address point or niche areas of vulnerabilities in corporate networks and computer assets.

Even before DLP became a concept, IT organizations have been practicing the tenets of DLP for years. Firewalls at the edge of corporate networks can block access to IP addresses, subnets, and Internet sites. One could say this is the first attempt to keep data where it should reside, within the organization. DLP should be looked at nothing more than the natural progression of the IT security life cycle.

2. WHAT IS DLP?

Data loss protection is a term that has percolated up from the alphabet soup of computer security concepts in the past few years. Known in the past as information leak detection and prevention (ILDP), used by IDC; information protection and control (IPC); information leak prevention (ILP), coined by Forrester; content monitoring and filtering (CMF), suggested by Gartner; or extrusion prevention system (EPS), the opposite of intrusion prevention system (IPS), the acronym DLP seems to have won out. No matter what acronym of the day is used,

DLP is an automated system to identify anything that leaves the organization that could harm the organization.

DLP applications try to move away from the point or niche application and give a more holistic approach to coverage, remediation and reporting of data issues. One way of evaluating an organization's level of risk is to look around in an unbiased fashion. The most benign communication technologies could be used against the organization and cause harm.

Before embarking on a DLP project, understanding some example types of harm and/or the corresponding regulations can help with the evaluation. The following sidebar, "Current Data Privacy Legislation and Standards," addresses only a fraction of current data privacy legislation and standards but should give the reader a good understanding of the complexities involved in protecting data.

Current Data Privacy Legislation and Standards

Examples of Harm

Scenario

An administrative assistant confirms a hotel reservation for an upcoming conference by emailing a spreadsheet with employee's credit card numbers with expiration dates; sometimes if they want to make it really easy for the "bad guys," an admin will include the credit card's "secret" PIN, also known as card verification number (CVN).

Problem

Possible violation of GLBA and puts the organization's employees at risk for identity theft and credit card fraud.

Legislation

Gramm-Leach-Bliley Act

GLBA compliance is mandatory; whether a financial institution discloses nonpublic information or not, there must be a policy in place to protect the information from foreseeable threats in security and data integrity.

Major components put into place to govern the collection, disclosure, and protection of consumers' nonpublic personal information; or personally identifiable information:

- Financial Privacy Rule
- Safeguards Rule
- Pretexting Protection

Financial Privacy Rule

(Subtitle A: Disclosure of Nonpublic Personal Information, codified at 15 U.S.C. § 6801–6809)

The Financial Privacy Rule requires financial institutions to provide each consumer with a privacy notice at the time the consumer relationship is established and annually thereafter. The privacy notice must explain the information collected about the consumer, where that information is shared, how that information is used, and how that information is protected. The notice must also identify the consumer's right to opt out of the information being shared with unaffiliated parties per the Fair Credit Reporting Act. Should the privacy policy change at any point in time, the consumer must be notified again for acceptance. Each time the privacy notice is reestablished, the consumer has the right to opt-out again. The unaffiliated parties receiving the nonpublic information are held to the acceptance terms of the consumer under the original relationship agreement. In summary, the financial privacy rule provides for a privacy policy agreement between the company and the consumer pertaining to the protection of the consumer's personal nonpublic information.

Safeguards Rule

(Subtitle A: Disclosure of Nonpublic Personal Information, codified at 15 U.S.C. § 6801–6809)

The Safeguards Rule requires financial institutions to develop a written information security plan that describes how the company is prepared for and plans to continue to protect clients' nonpublic personal information. (The Safeguards Rule also applies to information of those no longer consumers of the financial institution.) This plan must include:

- Denoting at least one employee to manage the safeguards
- Constructing a thorough risk management on each department handling the nonpublic information
- Developing, monitoring, and testing a program to secure the information
- Changing the safeguards as needed with the changes in how information is collected, stored, and used

This rule is intended to do what most businesses should already be doing: *protect their clients*. The Safeguards Rule forces financial institutions to take a closer look at how they manage private data and to do a risk analysis on their current processes. No process is perfect, so this has meant that every financial institution has had to make some effort to comply with the GLBA.

Pretexting Protection

(Subtitle B: Fraudulent Access to Financial Information, codified at 15 U.S.C. § 6821–6827)

Pretexting (sometimes referred to as *social engineering*) occurs when someone tries to gain access to personal nonpublic information without proper authority to do so. This may entail requesting private information while impersonating the account holder, by phone, by mail, by email, or even by phishing (i.e., using a phony Web site or email to collect data). The GLBA encourages the organizations covered by the GLBA to implement safeguards against pretexting. For example, a well-written plan to meet GLBA's Safeguards Rule ("develop, monitor, and test a program to secure the information") ought to include a section on training employees to recognize and deflect inquiries made under pretext. In the United States, pretexting by individuals is punishable as a common law crime of False Pretenses.

Scenario

An HR employee, whose main job function is to process claims, forwards via email an employee's Explanation of

Benefits that contains a variety of Protected Health Information. The email is sent in the clear, unencrypted, to the organization's healthcare provider.

Problem
Could violate the Health Insurance Portability and Accountability Act (HIPAA), depending on the type of organization.

Legislation
The Privacy Rule
The Privacy Rule took effect on April 14, 2003, with a one-year extension for certain "small plans." It establishes regulations for the use and disclosure of Protected Health Information (PHI). PHI is any information about health status, provision of health care, or payment for health care that can be linked to an individual. This is interpreted rather broadly and includes any part of a patient's medical record or payment history.

Covered entities must disclose PHI to the individual within 30 days upon request. They also must disclose PHI when required to do so by law, such as reporting suspected child abuse to state child welfare agencies.

A covered entity may disclose PHI to facilitate treatment, payment, or healthcare operations or if the covered entity has obtained authorization from the individual. However, when a covered entity discloses any PHI, it must make a reasonable effort to disclose only the minimum necessary information required to achieve its purpose.

The Privacy Rule gives individuals the right to request that a covered entity correct any inaccurate PHI. It also requires covered entities to take reasonable steps to ensure the confidentiality of communications with individuals. For example, an individual can ask to be called at his or her work number, instead of home or cell phone number.

The Privacy Rule requires covered entities to notify individuals of uses of their PHI. Covered entities must also keep track of disclosures of PHI and document privacy policies and procedures. They must appoint a Privacy Official and a contact person responsible for receiving complaints and train all members of their workforce in procedures regarding PHI.

An individual who believes that the Privacy Rule is not being upheld can file a complaint with the Department of Health and Human Services Office for Civil Rights (OCR).

Scenario
An employee opens an email whose subject is "25 Reasons Why Beer is Better than Women." The employee finds this joke amusing and forwards the email to other coworkers using the corporate email system.

Problem
Puts the organization in an exposed position for claims of sexual harassment and a hostile workplace environment.

Legislation
In the U.S., the Civil Rights Act of 1964 Title VII prohibits employment discrimination based on race, sex, color, national origin, or religion. The prohibition of sex discrimination covers both females and males. This discrimination occurs when the sex of the worker is made a condition of employment (i.e., all female waitpersons or male carpenters) or where this is a job requirement that does not mention sex but ends up barring many more persons of one sex than the other from the job (such as height and weight limits).

In 1998, Chevron settled, out of court, a lawsuit brought by several female employees after the "25 Reasons" email was widely circulated throughout the organization. Ultimately, Chevron settled out of court for $2.2 million.

Scenario
A retail store server electronically transmits daily point-of-sale (POS) transactions to the main corporate billing server. The POS system records the time, date, register number, employee number, part number, quantity, and if paid for by credit card, the card number. This transaction occurs nightly as part of a batch job and is transmitted over the store's Wi-Fi network.

Problem
PCI DSS stands for Payment Card Industry Data Security Standard. It was developed by the major credit card companies as a guideline to help organizations that process card payments prevent credit-card fraud, cracking, and various other security vulnerabilities and threats. A company processing, storing, or transmitting payment card data must be PCI DSS compliant or risk losing its ability to process credit card payments and being audited and/or fined. Merchants and payment card service providers must validate their compliance periodically. This validation gets conducted by auditors (that is persons who are the PCI DSS Qualified Security Assessors, or QSAs). Although individuals receive QSA status, reports on compliance can only be signed off by an individual QSA on behalf of a PCI council-approved consultancy. Smaller companies, processing *fewer* than about 80,000 transactions a year, are allowed to perform a self-assessment questionnaire. Penalties are often accessed and fines of $25,000 per month are possible for large merchants for noncompliance.

PCI DSS requires 12 requirements to be in compliance:

Requirement 1: Install and maintain a firewall configuration to protect cardholder data

Firewalls are computer devices that control computer traffic allowed into and out of a company's network, as well as traffic into more sensitive areas within a company's internal network. A firewall examines all network traffic and blocks those transmissions that do not meet the specified security criteria.

Requirement 2: Do not use vendor-supplied defaults for system passwords and other security parameters

Hackers (external and internal to a company) often use vendor default passwords and other vendor default settings to compromise systems. These passwords and settings are well known in hacker communities and easily determined via public information.

Requirement 3: Protect stored cardholder data

Encryption is a critical component of cardholder data protection. If an intruder circumvents other network security controls and gains access to encrypted data, without the proper cryptographic keys, the data is unreadable and unusable to that person. Other effective methods of protecting stored data should be considered as potential risk mitigation opportunities. For example, methods for minimizing risk include not storing cardholder data unless absolutely necessary, truncating cardholder data if full PAN is not needed and not sending PAN in unencrypted emails.

Requirement 4: Encrypt transmission of cardholder data across open, public networks

Sensitive information must be encrypted during transmission over networks that are easy and common for a hacker to intercept, modify, and divert data while in transit.

Requirement 5: Use and regularly update anti-virus software or programs

Many vulnerabilities and malicious viruses enter the network via employees' email activities. Antivirus software must be used on all systems commonly affected by viruses to protect systems from malicious software.

Requirement 6: Develop and maintain secure systems and applications

Unscrupulous individuals use security vulnerabilities to gain privileged access to systems. Many of these vulnerabilities are fixed by vendor-provided security patches. All systems must have the most recently released, appropriate software patches to protect against exploitation by employees, external hackers, and viruses. *Note:* Appropriate software patches are those patches that have been evaluated and tested sufficiently to determine that the patches do not conflict with existing security configurations. For in-house developed applications, numerous vulnerabilities can be avoided by using standard system development processes and secure coding techniques.

Requirement 7: Restrict access to cardholder data by business need-to-know

This requirement ensures critical data can only be accessed by authorized personnel.

Requirement 8: Assign a unique ID to each person with computer access

Assigning a unique identification (ID) to each person with access ensures that actions taken on critical data and systems are performed by, and can be traced to, known and authorized users.

Requirement 9: Restrict physical access to cardholder data

Any physical access to data or systems that house cardholder data provides the opportunity for individuals to access devices or data and to remove systems or hardcopies, and should be appropriately restricted.

Requirement 10: Track and monitor all access to network resources and cardholder data

Logging mechanisms and the ability to track user activities are critical. The presence of logs in all environments allows thorough tracking and analysis if something does go wrong. Determining the cause of a compromise is very difficult without system activity logs.

Requirement 11: Regularly test security systems and processes

Vulnerabilities are being discovered continually by hackers and researchers, and being introduced by new software. Systems, processes, and custom software should be tested frequently to ensure security is maintained over time and with any changes in software.

Requirement 12: Maintain a policy that addresses information security for employees and contractors

A strong security policy sets the security tone for the whole company and informs employees what is expected of them. All employees should be aware of the sensitivity of data and their responsibilities for protecting it.[4]

Organizations are facing pressures to become Sarbanes-Oxley compliant.

SOX Section 404: Assessment of internal control

The most contentious aspect of SOX is Section 404, which requires management and the external auditor to report on the adequacy of the company's internal control over financial reporting (ICFR). This is the most costly aspect of the legislation for companies to implement, as documenting and testing important financial manual and automated controls requires enormous effort.

Under Section 404 of the Act, management is required to produce an "internal control report" as part of each annual Exchange Act report. The report must affirm "the responsibility of management for establishing and maintaining an adequate internal control structure and procedures for financial reporting." The report must also "contain an assessment, as of the end of the most recent fiscal year of the Company, of the effectiveness of the internal control structure and procedures of the issuer for financial reporting." To do this, managers are generally adopting an internal control framework such as that described in Committee of Sponsoring Organization of the Treadway Commission (COSO).

Both management and the external auditor are responsible for performing their assessment in the context of a top-down risk assessment, which requires management to base both the scope of its assessment and evidence gathered on risk. Both the Public Company Accounting Oversight Board (PCAOB) and SEC recently issued guidance on this topic to help alleviate the significant costs of compliance and better focus the assessment on the most critical risk areas.

The recently released Auditing Standard No. 5 of the PCAOB, which superseded Auditing Standard No 2. has the following key requirements for the external auditor:

- Assess both the design and operating effectiveness of selected internal controls related to significant accounts and relevant assertions, in the context of material misstatement risks
- Understand the flow of transactions, including IT aspects, sufficiently to identify points at which a misstatement could arise

---

- Evaluate company-level (entity-level) controls, which correspond to the components of the COSO framework
- Perform a fraud risk assessment
- Evaluate controls designed to prevent or detect fraud, including management override of controls
- Evaluate controls over the period-end financial reporting process;
- Scale the assessment based on the size and complexity of the company
- Rely on management's work based on factors such as competency, objectivity, and risk
- Evaluate controls over the safeguarding of assets
- Conclude on the adequacy of internal control over financial reporting

The recently released SEC guidance is generally consistent with the PCAOB's guidance above, only intended for management.

After the release of this guidance, the SEC required smaller public companies to comply with SOX Section 404, companies with year ends after December 15, 2007. Smaller public companies performing their first management assessment under Sarbanes-Oxley Section 404 may find their first year of compliance after December 15, 2007 particularly challenging. To help unravel the maze of uncertainty, Lord & Benoit, a SOX compliance company, issued "10 Threats to Compliance for Smaller Companies" (www.section404.org/pdf/sox_404_10_threats_to_compliance_for_smaller_public_companies.pdf), which gathered historical evidence of material weaknesses from companies with revenues under $100 million. The research was compiled aggregating the results of 148 first-time companies with material weaknesses and revenues under $100 million. The following were the 10 leading material weaknesses in Lord & Benoit's study: accounting and disclosure controls, treasury, competency and training of accounting personnel, control environment, design of controls/lack of effective compensating controls, revenue recognition, financial closing process, inadequate account reconciliations, information technology and consolidations, mergers, intercompany accounts.

Scenario

A guidance counselor at a high school gets a request from a student's prospective college. The college asked for the student's transcripts. The guidance counselor sends the transcript over the schools email system unencrypted.

Problem

FERPA privacy concerns, depending on the age of the student.

Legislation

The Family Educational Rights and Privacy Act (FERPA) (20 U.S.C. § 1232g; 34 CFR Part 99) is a federal law that protects the privacy of student education records. The law applies to all schools that receive funds under an applicable program of the U.S. Department of Education.

FERPA gives parents certain rights with respect to their children's education records. These rights transfer to the student when he or she reaches the age of 18 or attends a school

beyond the high school level. Students to whom the rights have transferred are "eligible students."

Parents or eligible students have the right to inspect and review the student's education records maintained by the school. Schools are not required to provide copies of records unless, for reasons such as great distance, it is impossible for parents or eligible students to review the records. Schools may charge a fee for copies.

Parents or eligible students have the right to request that a school correct records that they believe to be inaccurate or misleading. If the school decides not to amend the record, the parent or eligible student then has the right to a formal hearing. After the hearing, if the school still decides not to amend the record, the parent or eligible student has the right to place a statement with the record setting forth his or her view about the contested information.

Generally, schools must have written permission from the parent or eligible student in order to release any information from a student's education record. However, FERPA allows schools to disclose those records, without consent, to the following parties or under the following conditions (34 CFR § 99.31):

- School officials with legitimate educational interest
- Other schools to which a student is transferring
- Specified officials for audit or evaluation purposes
- Appropriate parties in connection with financial aid to a student
- Organizations conducting certain studies for or on behalf of the school
- Accrediting organizations
- To comply with a judicial order or lawfully issued subpoena
- Appropriate officials in cases of health and safety emergencies
- State and local authorities, within a juvenile justice system, pursuant to specific State law

Schools may disclose, without consent, "directory" information such as a student's name, address, telephone number, date and place of birth, honors and awards, and dates of attendance. However, schools must tell parents and eligible students about directory information and allow parents and eligible students a reasonable amount of time to request that the school not disclose directory information about them. Schools must notify parents and eligible students annually of their rights under FERPA. The actual means of notification (special letter, inclusion in a PTA bulletin, student handbook, or newspaper article) is left to the discretion of each school.

Scenario

Employee job hunting, posting resumes and trying to find another job while working. See Figure 67.1 for an example of a DLP system capturing the full content of a user going through the resignation process.

Problem

Loss of productivity for that employee.

Warning sign for a possible disgruntled employee.

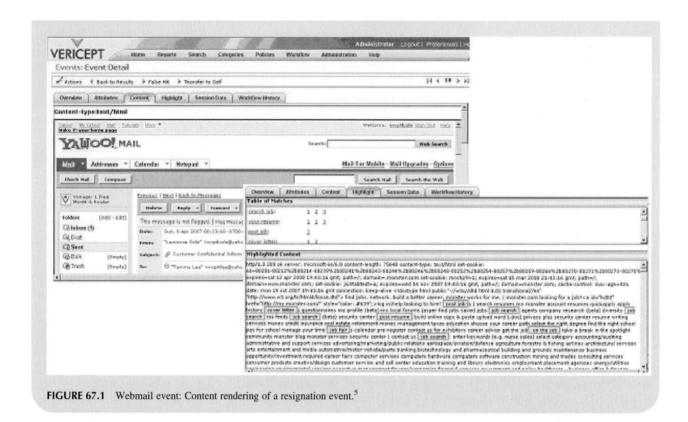

FIGURE 67.1   Webmail event: Content rendering of a resignation event.[5]

3. WHERE TO BEGIN?

A reasonable place to begin talking about DLP is with the department of the organization that handles corporate policy and/or governance (see sidebar, "An Example of an Acceptable Use Policy"). Monitoring employees is at best an interesting proposition. Corporate culture can drive whether monitoring of any kind is even allowed. A good litmus test would be the types of notice that appear in the employee handbook.

Another good indicator that the organization would be a good fit for a DLP application is the sign-on screen that appears before or after a computer user logs on to her workstation (see sidebar, "Accessing a Company's Information System").

Some organizations are more apt to take advantage of the laws and rights that companies have to defend themselves. Simply asking around and performing informal interviews with Human Resources, Security, and Legal can save days and weeks of time down the line.

In summary, implementing a DLP application without the proper Human Resources, Security, and Legal policies could be a waste of time because IT professionals *will*

catch employees violating security standard. The events in a DLP system must be actionable and have "teeth" for changes to take place.

4. DATA IS LIKE WATER

As most anyone who has had a water leak in dwelling knows, water will find a way out of where it is supposed to go. Pipes are meant to direct the proper flow of water both in and out. If a leak happens, the occupant will eventually find a damp spot, a watermark, or a real drip. It might take minutes or days to notice the leak and might take just as long to find the source of the leak.

Much like the water analogy, employees are given data "pipes" to do their jobs with enabling technology provided by the IT organization. Instead of water flowing through, data can ingress/egress the organization in multiple methods.

Corporate email is a powerful efficient time saving tool that speeds communication. A user can attach a 10 megabyte file, personal pictures, a recipe for chili and next quarter's marketing plan or an acquisition target. Chat and IM is the quickest growing form of electronic communication and a great enabler of efficient workflow. Files can be sent as well over these protocols or "pipes." Web mail is usually the "weapon of choice" by users who like to conduct personal business at work. Web mail allows users to attach files of any type.

---

5. Figures 67.1, 67.2 (a–c) and 67.3 (a-b), inclusive of the Vericept trademark and logo, are provided by Vericept Corporation solely for use as screenshots herein and may not be reproduced or used in any other way without the prior written permission of Vericept Corporation. All rights reserved.

An Example of an Acceptable Use Policy

Use of Email and Computer Systems

All information created, accessed or stored using company applications, systems, or resources, including email, is the property of the company. Users do not have a right to privacy regarding any activity conducted using the company's system. The company can review, read, access, or otherwise monitor email and all activities on the company system or any other system accessed by use of the company system. In addition, the Company could be required to allow others to read email or other documents on the company's system in the context of a lawsuit or other legal action.

All users must abide by the rules of network etiquette, which include being polite and using the network and the Internet in a safe and legal manner. The company or authorized company officials will make a good faith judgment as to which materials, files, information, software, communications, and other content and activity are permitted and prohibited based on the following guidelines and under the particular circumstances.

Among the uses that are considered unacceptable and constitute a violation of this policy are the following:

- Using, transmitting, receiving, or seeking inappropriate, offensive, swearing, vulgar, profane, suggestive, obscene, abusive, harassing, belligerent, threatening, defamatory (harming another's reputation by lies), or misleading language or materials; revealing personal information such as another's home address, home telephone number, or Social Security number; making ethnic, sexual-preference, age or gender-related slurs or jokes.
- Users may never harass, intimidate, threaten others, or engage in other illegal activity (including pornography, terrorism, espionage, theft, or drugs) by email or other posting. All such instances should be reported to management for appropriate action. In addition to violating this policy, such behavior may also violate other company policies or civil or criminal laws.
- Among the uses that are considered unacceptable and constitute a violation of this policy are downloading or transmitting copyrighted materials without permission from the owner of the copyright on those materials. Even if materials on the network or the Internet are not marked with the copyright symbol, you should assume that they are protected under copyright laws unless there is explicit permission from the copyright holder on the materials to use them.
- Users must not use email or other communications methods, including but not limited to news group posting, blogs, forums, instant messaging, and chat servers, to send company proprietary or confidential information to any unauthorized party. Such information may be disclosed to authorized persons in encrypted files if sent over publicly accessible media such as the Internet or other broadcast media such as wireless communication. Such information may be sent in unencrypted files only within the company system. Users are responsible for properly labeling such information.

Certain specific policies extend the Company's acceptable use policy by placing further restrictions on that activity. Examples include, but are not limited to: software usage, network usage, shell policy, remote access policy, wireless policy, and the mobile email access policy. These and any additional policies are available from the IT Web site on the intranet.

Your use of the network and the Internet is a privilege, not a right. If you violate this policy, at a minimum you will be subject to having your access to the network and the Internet terminated. You breach this policy not only by affirmatively violating the above provisions but also by failing to report any violations of this policy by other users which come to your attention. Further, you violate this policy if you permit another to use your account or password to access the network or the Internet, including but not limited to someone whose access has been denied or terminated. Sharing your account with anyone is a violation of this policy. It is your responsibility to keep your account secure by choosing a sufficiently complex password and changing it on a regular basis.

Thus, the IT network "plumbing" needs to be monitored, maintained, and evaluated on an ongoing basis. The U.S. government has published a complete and well-rounded standard that organizations can use as a good first step to compare where they are strong and where they can use improvement.

The U.S. Government Federal Information Security Management Act of 2002 (FISMA) offers reasonable guidelines that most organizations could benefit by adopting. Even though FISMA is mandated for government agencies and contractors, it can be applied to the corporate world as well.

FISMA sets forth a comprehensive framework for ensuring the effectiveness of security controls over information resources that support federal operations and assets. FISMA's framework creates a cycle of risk management activities necessary for an effective security program, and these activities are similar to the principles noted in our study of the risk management activities of leading private sector organizations—assessing risk, establishing a central management focal point, implementing appropriate policies and procedures, promoting awareness, and monitoring and evaluating policy and control effectiveness. More specifically, FISMA requires the head of each agency to provide information security protections commensurate with the risk and magnitude of harm resulting from the unauthorized access, use, disclosure, disruption, modification, or destruction of information and information systems used or operated by the agency or on behalf of the agency. In this regard, FISMA requires that agencies implement information security programs that, among other things, include:

- Periodic assessments of the risk
- Risk-based policies and procedures
- Subordinate plans for providing adequate information security for networks, facilities, and systems or groups of information systems, as appropriate
- Security awareness training for agency personnel, including contractors and other users of information systems that support the operations and assets of the agency
- Periodic testing and evaluation of the effectiveness of information security policies, procedures, and practices, performed with a frequency depending on risk, but no less than annually
- A process for planning, implementing, evaluating, and documenting remedial action to address any deficiencies
- Procedures for detecting, reporting, and responding to security incidents
- Plans and procedures to ensure continuity of operations

In addition, agencies must develop and maintain an inventory of major information systems that is updated at least annually and report annually to the Director of OMB and several Congressional Committees on the adequacy and effectiveness of their information security policies, procedures, and practices and compliance with the requirements of the act. An internal risk assessment of what types of "communication," both manual and electronic, that are allowed within the organization can give the DLP evaluator a baseline of the type of transmission that are probably taking place (see checklist: "An Agenda For Action For Evaluating Other Types Of Manual And Electronic Communications").

Accessing a Company's Information System

You are accessing a Company's information system (IS) that is provided for Company-authorized use only. By using this IS, you consent to the following conditions:

- The Company routinely monitors communications occurring on this IS, and any device attached to this IS, for purposes including, but not limited to, penetration testing, monitoring, network defense, quality control, and employee misconduct, law enforcement, and counterintelligence investigations.
- At any time the Company may inspect and/or seize data stored on this IS and any device attached to this IS.
- Communications occurring on or data stored on this IS, or any device attached to this IS, are not private. They are subject to routine monitoring and search.
- Any communications occurring on or data stored on this IS, or any device attached to this IS, may be disclosed or used for any Company-authorized purpose.
- Security protections may be utilized on this IS to protect certain interests that are important to the Company. For example, password, access cards, encryption or biométrie access controls provide security for the benefit of the Company. These protections are not provided for your benefit or privacy and may be modified or eliminated at the Company's discretion.

5. YOU DON'T KNOW WHAT YOU DON'T KNOW

Embarking on a DLP evaluation or implementation can be a straightforward exercise. The IT professional usually has a mandate in mind and a few problems that the DLP application will address. Invariably, many other issues will arise as DLP applications do a very good job at finding most potential security and privacy issues.

An Agenda for Action for Evaluating Other Types of Manual and Electronic Communications

Some types of communications that should be evaluated are not always obvious but could be just as damaging as electronic methods. The following list encompasses some of those obvious and not so obvious methods (Check All Tasks Completed):

_____1. Pencil and paper.
_____2. Photocopier.
_____3. Fax.
_____4. Voicemail.
_____5. Digital camera.
_____6. Jump drive.
_____7. MP3/iPod.
_____8. DVD/CD-ROM/3½ in. floppy.
_____9. Magnetic tape.
_____10. SATA drives.
_____11. IM/chat.
_____12. FTP/FTPS.
_____13. SMTP/POP3/IMAP.
_____14. HTTP post/response.
_____15. HTTPS.
_____16. Telnet.
_____17. SCP.
_____18. P2P
_____19. Rogue ports.
_____20. GoToMyPC.
_____21. Web conferencing systems.

Reports that say that something hasn't happened are always interesting to me, because as we know, there are 'known knowns'; there are things we know we know. We also know there are 'known unknowns'; that is to say we know there are some things we do not know. But there are also 'unknown unknowns'—the ones we don't know we don't know.

—Donald Rumsfeld, U.S. Department of Defense, February 12, 2002

Once the corporate culture has established that DLP is worth investigating or worth implementing, the next logical step would be performing a risk/exposure assessment. Several DLP vendors offer free pilots or proof of concepts and should be leveraged to jumpstart the data risk assessment for a very low monetary cost.

A risk/exposure assessment usually involves placing a server on the edge of the corporate network and sampling/recording the network traffic that is egressing the organization. In addition, the assessment might involve look for high-risk files at rest and the activity of what is happening on the workstation environment. Most if not all DLP applications have predefined risk categories that cover a wide range of risk profiles. Some examples are:

- Regulations: GLBA, HIPAA, PCI-DSS, SOX, FERPA, PHI
- Acceptable use: Violence, gangs, profanity, adult themes, weapons, harassment, racism, pornography
- Productivity: Streaming media, resignation, shopping, Webmail
- Insider hacker activity: Root activity, nmap, stack, smashing code, keyloggers

Deciding what risk categories are most important to your organization can streamline the DLP evaluation. If data categories are turned on but not likely to impact what is truly important to the organization, the test/pilot result will contain a lot of "noise." Focus on the "low-hanging fruit." For example, if the organization's life blood is customer data, focus on the categories that address those types of leaks.

Precision versus Recall

Before the precision versus recall discussion can take place, definitions are necessary:

- *False positive.* A false positive occurs when the DLP application-monitoring or DLP application-blocking techniques wrongly classify a legitimate transmission or event as "uninteresting" and, as a result, the event must be remediated anyway. Remediating an event is a time-consuming process which could involve one to many administrators dispositioning the event. A high number of false positives is normal during an initial

implementation, but the number should fall after the DLP application is tuned.

- *False negative.* A false negative occurs when a transmission is not detected as interesting. The problem with false negatives is usually the DLP administrator does not know these transmissions are happening in the first place. An analogy would be a bank employee who embezzles thousands of dollars and the bank does not notice the theft until it is too late.
- *True positive.* Condition present and the DLP application records the event for remediation.
- *True negative.* Condition not present and the DLP application does not record it.

    DLP application testing and tuning can involve a trade-off:

- The acceptable level of false positives (in which a nonmatch is declared to be a match).
- The acceptable level of false negatives (in which an actual match is not detected).

An evaluator can think of this process as a slider bar concept, with false negatives on the left side and false positives on the right. A properly tuned DLP application minimizes false positives and diminishes the chances of false negatives.

This iterative process of tuning is called *thresholding*. Creating the proper threshold eventually leads to the minimization of acceptable amounts of false positives with no or minimal false negatives.

An easy way to achieve thresholding is to make the test more restrictive or more sensitive. The more restrictive the test is, the higher the risk of rejecting true positives; and, the less sensitive the test is, the higher the risk of accepting false positives.

6. HOW DO DLP APPLICATIONS WORK?

The way that most DLP applications capture interesting events is through different kinds of analysis engines. Most support simple keyword matching. For example, any time you see the phrase "project phoenix" in a data transmission, the network event is stored for later review. Keywords can be grouped and joined. Regular expression (RegEx) support is featured in most of today's DLP applications. Regular expressions provide a concise and flexible means for identifying strings of text of interest, such as particular characters, words, or patterns of characters. Regular expressions are written in a formal language that can be interpreted by a regular expression processor, a program that either serves as a parser generator or examines text and identifies parts that match the provided specification. A real-world example would be the expression:

$$(r|b)?ed$$

Any transmission that contained the word *red, bed*, or even *ed* would be captured for later investigation. Regular expressions can also do pattern matching on credit card number and U.S. Social Security numbers:

$$\wedge \backslash d\{3\} - ?\backslash d\{2\} - ?\backslash d\{4\}$$

which can be read: Any three numbers followed by an optional dash followed by any two numbers followed by an optional dash and then followed by any four numbers. Regular expressions offer a certain level of efficiencies but cannot address all DLP concerns. Weighting of either keyword(s) and/or RegEx's can help. A real-world example might be the word *red* is worth three points and the SSN is worth five points, but for an event to hit the transmission, it must contain 22 points. In this example, four SSNs and the word *red* would trigger an event (4 times 5 plus 3 equals 23, which would trigger the event score rule). Scoring can help address the thresholding issue. To address some of the limitation of simple keyword and RegEx's, DLP applications can also look for data "signatures" or hashes of data. Hashing creates a mathematical representation of the sensitive data and looks for that signature. Sensitive data or representative types of data can be bulk loaded from databases and example files.

7. EAT YOUR VEGETABLES

DLP is like the layers of an onion. Once the first layer of protection is implemented, the next layer should/could be addressed. There are many different forms of DLP applications, depending on the velocity and location of the sensitive data.

Data in Motion

Data in motion is an easy place to start implementing a DLP application because most can function in "passive" mode, meaning it looks at only a copy of the actual data egressing/ingressing the network. One way to look at data-in-motion monitoring is like a very intelligent VCR. Instead of recording every packet of information that passes in and out of an organization, DLP applications only capture, flag, and record the transmissions that fall within the categories/policies that are turned on (see sidebar, "Case Study: DLP Applications"). There are two main types of data-in-motion analysis:

- *Passive monitoring.* Using a Switched Port Analyzer (SPAN) on a router, port mirror on a switch or a network tap(s) that feeds the outbound network traffic to the DLP application for analysis.
- Active (inline) enforcement. Using an active egress port or through a proxy server, some DLP applications can stop the transmission from happening. The port

itself can be reset or the proxy server can show a failure of transmission. The event that keyed off the reset or failure is still recorded.

Case Study: DLP Applications

Background

A Fortune 500 Company has tens of thousands of employees with access to the Internet through an authenticated method. The Company has recently retired a version of laptops with the associated docking station, monitors and mice. New laptops were purchased and given to the employees. The old assets were retired to a storage closet. One manager noticed some docking stations had gone missing. That in and of itself was not concerning as this company had a liberal policy of donating old computer assets to charity. After looking in the company's Asset Management System and talking to the organization's charity manager, the manager found this was not the case. An investigation was launched both electronically and through traditional investigative means.

Action

The organization had a DLP application in use with data-in-motion implemented. This particular DLP application had a strong acceptable use set of categories/policies. One of them was "Shopping," which covered both traditional shopping outlets but also popular online auction sites. The DLP investigator selected the report that returns all transmissions that violated the "Shopping" category and contained the keyword of the model number of the docking station. Within seconds, a user from within their network was found auctioning the exact same model docking stations as the ones the company had just retired.

Result

The Fortune 500 Company was able to remediate a situation quickly that not only stopped the loss of physical assets, but get rid of an employee that was stealing while at work. The real value of this exercise could have been, if an employee is "ok" with stealing assets to make a few extra dollars on the company's dime, one might ask, What else might an employee that thinks it is ok to steal do?

Data at Rest

Static computer files on drives, removable media or even tape can grow to the millions in large multinational organizations. Unless tight controls are implemented, data can spawn out of control. Even though email transmissions account for more than 80% of DLP violations, data-at-rest files that are resting where they are not supposed to be can be a major concern (see sidebar, "Case Study: Data-at-Rest Files").

Data-at-rest risk can occur in other places besides the personal computer's file system. One of the benefits of networked computer systems is the ability to share files. File shares can also pose a risk because the original owner of the file now has no idea what happened to the file after they share it.

The same can be said of many Web-based collaboration and document management platforms that are available in the market today. Collaboration tools can be used to host Web sites that can be used to access shared workspaces and documents, as well as specialized applications such as wikis, blogs, and many other forms of applications, from within a browser. Once again, the wonderful world of shared computing can also put an organization's data at risk.

DLP application can help with databases as well and half the battle is knowing where the organizations most sensitive data resides. The data-at-rest function of DLP applications can definitely help.

Data in Use

DLP applications can also help keep data where it is supposed to stay (see sidebar, "Case Study: Data-in-Use Files"). Agent-based technologies that run resident on the guest operating system can track, monitor, block, report, quarantine or notify the usage of particular kinds of data files and/or the contents of the file itself. Policies can be centrally administered and "pushed" out of the organization's computer assets. Since the agent is resident on the computer, it can also create an inventory of every file on the hard drives, removable media and even music players. Since the agent knows of the file systems down to the operating system level, it can allow or disallow certain types of removable media. For example, an organization might allow a USB storage device if and only if the device supports encryption. The agent will disallow any other types of USB devices such as music players, cameras, removable hard drives, and so on.

Case Study: Data-at-Rest Files

Background
A Fortune 500 Company has multiple customer service centers located throughout the United States. Each customer server representative has a personal computer with a hard drive and Internet access. The representative's job entails taking inbound phone calls to help their customers with account management including auto-pay features. Auto-pay setup information could include taking a credit-card number and expiration date and/or setting up an electronic fund transfer payment which includes an ABA routing number and account number. This sensitive information is supposed to be entered directly into the corporate enterprise resource planning (ERP) system application. Invariably customer service representatives run into issues during this process (connectivity to the ERP system is interrupted, power goes down, computer needs to be rebooted, etc.) and sensitive data finds its way into unapproved places on the personal computer—a note text file, a word-processing document, an electronic spreadsheet, or in an email system. Even though employees went through training for their job that included handling of sensitive data, the management suspected that data was finding a way out of the ERP system. Another issue that the management faced with a very high turnover ratio and that employee training was falling behind.

Action
A DLP data-at-rest pilot was performed and over one thousand files that contained credit-card numbers and other customer personal identifiable information were found.

Result
The Fortune 500 Company was able to cleanse the hard drives of files that contained sensitive data by using the legend the DLP application provided. More important, the systemic cause of the problem had to be readdressed with training and tightening down the security of the representative, personal computers.

Case Study: Data-in-Use Files

Background
An electronics manufacturer has created a revolutionary new design for a cell phone and wants to keep the design and photographs of the prototype under wraps. They have had problems in the past with pictures ending up on blog sites, competitors "borrowing" design ideas, and even other countries creating similar products and launching an imitator within weeks of the initial product launch.

Action
Each document, whether a spreadsheet, document, diagram, or photograph, was secretly watermarked with a special secret code. At the same time, the main security group created an organizational unit within their main LDAP application. This was the only group that had permission to access the watermarked files. At the same time, a DLP application agent was rolled out to the computer assets within the organization. If anyone "found" a marked file and tried to do something with it, unless they were in the privileged group, access was denied *and* an alert (see Figure 67.2c) went back to the main DLP reporting server.

Result
The electronics manufacturer was able to deliver its revolutionary product to market in a secure manner and on time.

Much like the different flavors of DLP that are available (data in motion, data at rest and data in use), conditions of the severity of action that DLP applications take on the event can vary. A good place to diagnose the

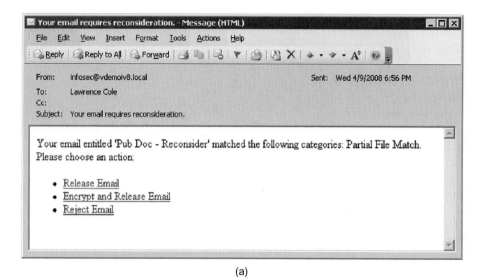

(a)

(b)

(c)

problems organizations are currently facing would be to start with Monitoring (see sidebar, "Case Study in Monitoring"). Monitoring is only capturing the actual event that took place to review at a later time. Most DLP applications offer real-time or near real-time monitoring of events that violated a policy. Monitoring coupled with escalation can help most organizations immediately. Escalation works well with monitoring as when an event happens, rules can be put into place on who should be notified and/or how the notification should take place. Email is the most common form of escalation.

Another action that DLP application supports is notification. Notification can temporarily interrupt that transmission of an event and could require user interaction. See Figure 67.2a for an example of the kind of "bounce"

email a user could receive if she sends an email containing sensitive information. See Figure 67.2b for an example of the type of notification a user could see if he tries to open a sensitive data document. The DLP application could make the user justify why access is needed, deny access, or simply log the attempt back to the main reporting console.

Notification can enhance the current user education program in place and serve as a gentle reminder. The onus of action lies solely on the end user and does not take resources from the already thinly stretched IT organization.

The next level of severity of implementing DLP could be quarantining and then outright blocking. Quarantining events places the transmission in "stasis" for review from published standards on how events should be handled and escalated.

Most DLP applications can segregate duties to allow non-IT personnel to review the disposition of the event captured. One way to address DLP would be to assign certain types of events to administrators in the appropriate department. If a racial email is captured, the most appropriate department might be a Human Resource employee. If a personal information transmission is captured, a compliance officer should be assigned. IT might be tasked if the nature of the event is hacking related.

Users can also have a level of privilege within the DLP application. Reviewers can be assigned to initial investigations of only certain types or all events. If necessary, an event can be escalated to a reviewer's superior. Users can have administrative or reports-only rights.

Each of these functions relates to the concept of workflow within the DLP application. Events need to be prioritized, escalated, reviewed, annotated, ignored and eventually closed. The workflow should be easy to use across the DLP community and reports should be easily assessable and created/tuned. See Figure 67.3a for an example of an Executive Dashboard that allows the user to quickly assess the state of risk and allows for a quick-click drill down for more granular information. Figure 67.3b is the result of a click from the Executive Dashboard to the full content capture of the event.

a DLP administrator. The quarantine administrator can release, release with encryption, block, or send the event back to the offending user for remediation. Blocking is an action that stops the transmission in its entirety based upon the contents.

Both quarantining and blocking should be used sparingly and only after the organization feels comfortable with the policies and procedures. The first time an executive tries to send a transmission and cannot because of the action set forth in the DLP application, the IT professional can potentially lose his job.

8. IT'S A FAMILY AFFAIR, NOT JUST IT SECURITY'S PROBLEM

The IT organization does and most likely maintains the corporate email system; almost everyone across all departments within an organization uses email. The same can be said for the DLP application. Even though IT will implement and maintain the DLP application, the events will most likely come from all different types of users across the entire organization. When concerning events are captured and there will be many captured by the DLP application, most management will turn to IT to resolve the problem. The IT organization should not become the "police and judge." Each business unit should have

9. VENDORS, VENDORS EVERYWHERE! WHO DO YOU BELIEVE?

At the end of the day the DLP market and applications are maturing at an incredible pace. Vendors are releasing new features and functions almost every calendar quarter. In the past, when monitoring seem sufficient to diagnose the central issue of data security, the marketplace was demanding more control, more granularity, easier user interfaces, and more actionable reports, as well as moving the DLP application off the main network egress point and parlaying the same functionality to the desktop/laptops, servers, and their respective end points to document storage repositories and databases.

In evaluating DLP applications, it is important to focus on the type of underlying engine that analyzes the data and then work up from that base. Next rate the ease of configuring the data categories and the ability to pre-load certain documents and document types. Look for a mature product with plenty of industry-specific references. Company stability and financial health should also come into play. Roadmaps of future offerings can give an idea of the features and functions coming in the next release. The relationship with the vendor is an important requirement to make sure that the purchase and

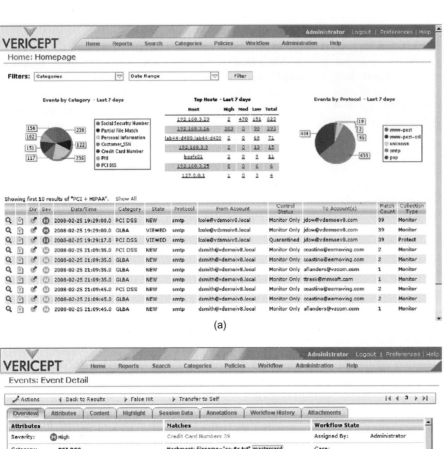

FIGURE 67.3 (a) Dashboard; (b) Email Event Overview.[5]

10. SUMMARY

subsequent implementation goes smoothly. The vendor should offer training that empowers the IT organization to be somewhat self-sustaining instead of having to go back to the vendor every time a configuration needs to be implemented. The vendor should offer best practices that other customers have used to help with quick adoption of policies. This allows for an effective system that will improve and lower the overall risk profile of the organization. Analyst briefings about the DLP space can be found on the Internet for free and can provide an unbiased view from a third party of things that should be evaluated during the selection process.

DLP is an important tool that should at least be evaluated by organizations that are looking to protect their employees, customers, and stakeholders. An effectively implemented DLP application can augment current security safeguards. A well thought out strategy for a DLP application and implementation should be designed first before a purchase. All parts of the organization are likely to be impacted by DLP, and IT should not be the only organization to evaluate and create policies. A holistic approach will help foster a successful implementation that is supported by the DLP vendor and other departments, and ultimately the employees should improve the data risk profile of an organization. The main goal is to keep the brand name and reputation of the organization safe and to continue to operate with minimal data security interruptions. Many types of DLP approaches are available in the market today; picking the right vendor and product with the right features and functions can foster best practices, augment already implemented employee training and policies, and ultimately safeguard the most critical data assets of the organization.

Finally, let's move on to the real interactive part of this Chapter: review questions/exercises, hands-on projects, case projects and optional team case project. The answers and/or solutions by chapter can be found in the Online Instructor's Solutions Manual.

CHAPTER REVIEW QUESTIONS/EXERCISES

True/False

1. True or False? The disgruntled insider, working from within an organization, is a principal source of computer crimes.
2. True or False? Even before DLP became a concept, IT organizations have not been practicing the tenets of DLP for years.
3. True or False? Data loss protection is a term that has percolated up from the alphabet soup of computer security concepts in the past few years.
4. True or False? A unreasonable place to begin talking about DLP is with the department of the organization that handles corporate policy and/or governance.
5. True or False? Employees are given data "pipes" to not do their jobs with enabling technology provided by the IT organization.

Multiple Choice

1. Embarking on a _____ evaluation or implementation can be a straightforward exercise.
   A. Reputation
   B. Internet filters
   C. DLP
   D. Encrypted
   E. Content-control software
2. What occurs when the DLP application-monitoring or DLP application-blocking techniques wrongly classify a legitimate transmission or event as "uninteresting" and, as a result, the event must be remediated anyway?
   A. Opinity
   B. Web content filtering
   C. Scale

   D. False positive
   E. Active monitoring
3. The way that most DLP applications capture interesting events is through different kinds of:
   A. Organizations
   B. Rapleaf
   C. Analysis engines
   D. Content
   E. Security
4. There are many different forms of DLP applications, depending on the velocity and location of the:
   A. Keyword lists
   B. Denial of service attack
   C. Sensitive data
   D. Port traffic
   E. Taps
5. What is an easy place to start implementing a DLP application because most can function in "passive" mode, meaning it looks at only a copy of the actual data egressing/ingressing the network?
   A. Systems security plan
   B. TrustPlus
   C. Denying service
   D. Decision making
   E. Data in motion

EXERCISE

Problem

Data loss protection should be designed to help you improve endpoint security. With implementation, managed security services and software, you should be able to protect sensitive data that is accessed, stored and transmitted on your endpoint devices. In other words, you should be able to do what else to protect your data?

Hands-On Projects

Project

You need to prevent sensitive data loss across your network without introducing complexity to the IT environment. You should also be able to provide a comprehensive solution that helps prevent data loss through enhanced visibility and control of all network ports and internal traffic. In other words, you should be able to do what else to protect your data?

Case Projects

Problem

You need to protect business data at rest, in motion, and in use, even beyond the enterprise network-without increasing complexity in your IT environment. You should also be able to use PGP encryption to provide a comprehensive solution that helps protect sensitive data across endpoints, removable storage media, and e-mail, against loss or unauthorized access. In other words, you should also be able to do what else to protect your data?

Optional Team Case Project

Problem

You need visibility into your information and how it is handled in order to protect sensitive data on endpoints against loss and unauthorized access. You should also be able to provide a comprehensive solution designed to automatically discover and classify sensitive data on desktops and servers, and monitor the data as it is used and exchanged. The solution helps enforce corporate security policies in realtime and reduces the risk of data loss or misuse. In other words, you should also be able to do what else to protect your data?

Satellite Cyber Attack Search and Destroy

Jeffrey Bardin

Treadstone 71 LLC

In the movie *Enemy of the State*, satellites play a vital role in making the viewer believe in the ultimate power of the National Security Agency (NSA). Satellites are repurposed and moved around the sky in moments. They peer down from the heavens tracking the hero's movements, able to determine tiepin logos and license plate expiration dates. Viewers are made to believe that satellites are God-like, roving the atmosphere, seeing everything we do. The NSA does employ satellites for signals and other intelligence; however, it is the National Reconnaissance Office (NRO) that normally owns and operates U.S. spy satellites. The closest Hollywood has come to reality in spy satellites was during the movie *Patriot Games* when Harrison Ford had to look at images through a microscope trying to ascertain the identity, much less the gender of people in the photographs. Grainy images with shadows that look like other images is more in line with reality.

When thinking of satellites, thoughts often drift to Hollywood's images and the surveillance aspects of their capabilities. However, satellites play many roles in society. They provide methods for communication and remote sensing of critical infrastructures, deliver global positioning systems for navigation, keep us occupied with broadband for entertainment, and support mechanisms for videoconferencing and telemedicine. We never see them, but they are essential components in daily human activity. According to the Satellite Industry Association, nearly 37% of all operational satellites are used for business communications. Civil communications accounts for 11%, military communications for 9%, military and surveillance 9%, navigation 8%, remote sensing 9%, and meteorological 4%. The Satellite Industry Association also maintains information on world satellite industry revenue. Satellite growth increased significantly between 2005 and 2011 at an average of 11% per year in growth. The Satellite Industry Association states that satellite services continue to represent the single largest industry sector driven by satellite-TV growth at around 10% [1]. Space launch industry and satellite manufacturing

revenues reflect a history of aggregate growth by yearly fluctuation, while ground equipment revenue growth reflects slight but relatively consistent year-on-year consumer and network equipment sales. It is safe to say that satellites play a prominent role in everyday life.

Very Small Aperture Terminals (VSATs) are prevalent in everyday lives. They consist of a parabolic dish and associated hardware and software. The purpose is to send and receive (uplink and downlink) signals via a satellite. They dot the landscape on homes, recreational vehicles, and boats. Human reliance on satellites is growing at an exponential rate. As with any growing commercial opportunity, security is less than the primary concern. Economics drives the opportunity.

1. HACKS, INTERFERENCE, AND JAMMING

April of 2007 started a series of issues with satellites. Tamil rebels in Sri Lanka were accused of hacking the Intelsat satellite positioned over the Indian Ocean for communicating propaganda [2]. Intelsat responded, indicating this to be a case of signal piracy (not hacking) that would not be tolerated. In a response to the Intelsat press release, the Tamil Tiger rebels indicated that they were not accessing the satellite illegally and that therefore no signal piracy had occurred. The rebels intimated a relationship with the service provider for the satellite but would provide no further explanation [3].

In 2007, the media reported that NASA satellite Landsat-7 used for ground mapping was hacked, experiencing 12 minutes of interference [4]. The same article goes on to state that in 2008, another NASA satellite, Terra AM-1 was hacked for 2 minutes in June and for 9 minutes in October. The problem with the articles and subsequent follow on by the media as well as the NASA Office of Inspector General is the depiction that the satellites were hacked. These two events were not cyber-related events but events characterized by the interference and jamming of radio signals in order to disrupt satellite send and receive transmissions. The point to be made here is that this had nothing to do with cyber security but rather with traditional satellite communication protocols using radio transmissions.

Recently, there have been writings on the Internet of the potential for hacking NASA satellites to access the Curiosity land rover on Mars. Although this is pure speculation, much discussion has occurred due to the subject. The initial topic focused on the pushing of updates to change Curiosity's payload. The idea would be to intercept or to a play man-in-the-middle attack against communications between satellites and the rover. Although highly unlikely, the impact would be significant should such an activity occur. It highlights a renewed focus on satellites as objects for disruption of command, control, communications, and computers. The Jet Propulsion Laboratory (JPL) in Pasadena, California, houses the scientists, engineers, specialists, and mission control center for Curiosity. NASA missions employ a highly compartmentalized framework for computer systems tied to the mission. They are self-contained systems located in self-contained buildings running variations of operating systems or operating systems created specifically for the mission at hand, operated by personnel vetted on several levels. Once a configuration of the operating system, firmware, or other related software is proven to work per the specifications of the designers and engineers, the configuration is locked down as a module ready for execution. It is highly unlikely that a hack or intercept of the encoded transmission between JPL mission control in Pasadena and the Curiosity rover on Mars could occur. Such an unlikely occurrence would have an enormous impact on the mission. But the mission of discovering life on another planet is hardly a target for exploitation that a foreign intelligence service would undertake. It is more likely that a foreign intelligence service would target earth-born operations.

In October 2011, Creech Air Force Base was the subject of a malware attack on the Predator and Reaper drones. It was reported that a keystroke logger infected the ground control stations for drones operating in the Afghanistan theater. The malware proved to be a resilient strain that continued to reoccur after multiple system cleanings. The malware was most likely created by a foreign nation-state intent on learning as much information as possible about the United States' drone activities. What was not stated in the press is the fact that the 30th Reconnaissance Squadron of the United States Air Force operates out of Creech AFB. This is significant since this squadron operates the RQ-170 Sentinel UAV. The same UAV captured by Iran a mere two months after the keystroke logger event at Creech AFB. In what could be termed a coincidence, Iran stated that its Army's electronic warfare unity had downed an RQ-170 violating Iranian airspace by overriding the UAV's controls. An

Iranian engineer later stated that Iran used GPS coordinate spoofing, fooling the UAV into thinking it was landing at an air base in Afghanistan. The Iranian engineer further claimed that it was quite easy to exploit the navigational weakness in the drone system. It is possible that signal jamming of the encrypted channels used by the military forced the UAV to revert to a communications failover process that used unencrypted methods to communicate [5]. Once the failover took place, Iranian engineers were able to manipulate the drone GPS. If the Iranian claim of control override is true, the keystroke logging event at Creech AFB takes on new meaning for cyber security surrounding ground control stations for satellite-based weapons systems. Unsubstantiated claims of Russian or Chinese intelligence services actually executing the keystroke logger and subsequently the downing of the RQ-170 become a potential premise that should be explored further. It demonstrates the need for improved cyber security measures for each component of the satellite command and control ecosystem. It also demonstrates that traditional cyber security countermeasures are not sufficient to prevent penetration or malware infection, or both. In most cases, ground control stations are air-gapped from other networks. Air gapping is a method of security control that delivers network compartmentalization, keeping all networks and devices not required to operate, manage, monitor, and/or control a sensitive system entirely separate. This is usually accompanied by stringent rules related to the use of removable media. It has been intimated that infected nonauthorized hardware was attached to the air-gapped system, providing for the infection of the target ground control stations. Malware of this type with a keystroke logger payload is used for cyber intelligence collection for later disposition and cyber countermeasures to be deployed by the initiating entity. The ability for the malware to communicate data collection efforts back to a collection hub also requires additional review since the methods of cyber security detection are often devised to keep perpetrators out, and not to prevent them from leaving as an additional level of security. It is interesting to note that a 2002 GAO report specifically warned of spoofing as a content-oriented threat for commercial satellites and the unauthorized modification or deliberate corruption of network information, services, and databases, including malicious software implanted into computer systems referencing ground control stations as a target [6]. Just under 10 years later, we have experienced exactly what the GAO warned against.

In June 2012, a group of researchers at the University of Texas at Austin used the spoofing method described by the Iranians to hack the GPS system of a drone. This demonstrates the viability of the claim and presents another issue for concern: Adversaries have the ability to

Chapter | 68   Satellite Cyber Attack Search and Destroy

both commandeer and use the drones as flying missiles whether armed or not. The cost to spoof the drone was reported to be in the range of £700 or about $1100. This ratio of cost to the potential impact is a cornerstone of asymmetric warfare exhibited by Al-Qa'eda on 9/11. Questions over what security controls were or were not in place continue as U.S. military authorities maintain a tight lid on the exact problems and remediation methods employed since the downing of the RQ-170. Additional rumors surfaced that Iran overrode the RQ-170 self-destruct capabilities, while others have claimed no such capabilities exist on the drone.

A few years ago, a $29 program called SkyGrabber (as shown in Figure 68.1) made the news. SkyGrabber allowed interception of packet radio service from a laptop connected to a small satellite. Insurgents in Iraq (as shown in Figure 68.2) were using and training others to use the SkyGrabber software to intercept satellite and small drones communications used to scout positions of enemies prior to special forces or military activities in that particular area. Insurgents were able to intercept these communications with the $29 program largely because of lack of security over the communications between satellite and drone. This flaw was actually well known by the designers of the system. They did not apply the appropriate security controls because applying encryption to the process slowed the communications down to the point where they thought it was not effective. Regardless of their decision, insurgents intercepted this information for quite some time before being discovered. SkyGrabber uses what is called general packet radio

service or GPRS. GPRS is a nonvoice service that is added to networks over 2.5- to 3-gigabit wireless communications. Consumers know this as 3 G or 4 G speeds [7]. The service uses IP transmissions to its advantage. Because Internet Protocol (IP) traffic is made of packets, the network does not need to have continuous data transmission. Each channel is divided eight timeslots, with a maximum data transmission of 13.4 kb per second. One

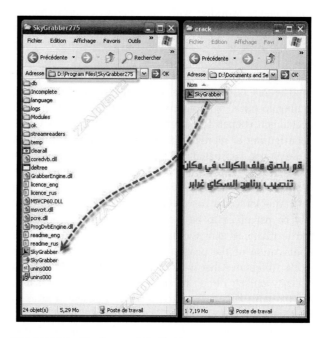

FIGURE 68.1   Jihadist use of SkyGrabber.

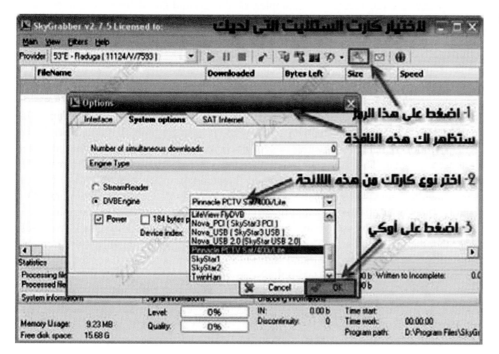

FIGURE 68.2   SkyGrabber .

of these timeslots is used for control, and normal allocation reserves two slots for voice traffic as well. Asymmetric traffic (more downloads and uploads) dictates the distribution of the remaining timeslots.

Requests are sent via the LAN connection, while responses are received from the satellite; since requests are usually small and responses are large, a narrowband connection is quite enough for requests. At the same time, responses were received at a high rate of 4 MB per second, which makes working with the Internet comfortable. If there is no encryption, it is open for interception. When the activity of the insurgents using SkyGrabber was made public, many pundits and even cyber security professionals called this interception hacking. What needs to be understood is that this was not a hack since there was in fact, nothing to hack. Without encryption, the communication mechanism is open for interception. Hacking refers to the reconfiguring or reprogramming of the system to function in ways not facilitated by the owner, administrator, or designer. The term has several related meanings in the information technology industry. A hack may refer to a clever quick fix to a computer program problem or to what may be perceived to be a clumsy solution to a problem. The terms *hack* and *hacking* are also used to refer to a modification of the programmer device to give the user access to features that were otherwise unavailable such as to do-it-yourself circuit bending [8]. It is from this usage that the term *hacking* is often incorrectly used to refer to more nefarious criminal uses such as identity theft, credit-card fraud, or other actions categorized as computer crime. Since there is a distinction between security breaking and hacking, a better term for security breaking would be *cracking* [8]. As we already know, responses are received from the satellite. However, the satellite cannot send data specifically to a particular user and so instead sends data to all dishes that receive a signal from it. Therefore, if you have the proper equipment, the signal is just waiting in the airwaves to be had.

As already surmised, it is not enough to position a small satellite dish, and that dish will also receive a signal with the same data that other satellites receive. The satellite dish may get the signal, but the question remains as to how to extract data from the intercepted signal. That is the purpose of the SkyGrabber program. The program captures what other satellite dishes download and saves the captured information to a laptop. Internet access is not required for this interception. The satellite dish needs to be rotated toward the provider, and the SkyGrabber program, with some configuration, will perform the data extraction. If the transmission is encrypted or encoded, the data extraction is prevented.

As with any information technology, information security and information assurance need to be built in from the beginning. Cyber security professionals have been stating this for years. Regardless, it seems that in the satellite industry as in many others, information security controls will not be built in until such time as a painful breach has occurred. This has been the standard mode of operation for designers, developers, and engineers for years.

Identifying Threats

In 1998 when Presidential Decision Directive 63 was originally issued, satellites were not included in the nation's critical infrastructures. This was seen as a significant oversight in the satellite industry. The General Accounting Office (GAO) report in 2002 referenced issues concerning security around satellites and covered several different areas concerning security. The GAO report covered secure data links and communication ground stations. The report also discussed issues surrounding the use of satellites that have certain security controls especially established to enhance the availability of the satellite. Since the release of that report in 2002, much has been done to bolster the security of satellites. Satellites consist of ground station tracking and control links, which are referred to as a tracking telemetry and control (TT&C) links and data links and satellites. The GAO report examined unintentional threats to commercial satellite systems and divided the threats into three different areas:

1. Ground-based threats
2. Space-based threats
3. Interference-oriented threats [6]

Examples of the ground-based threat could be naturally occurring ones such as acts of God, earthquakes, hurricanes, tornadoes, and floods. Space-based threats could be related to solar activity, different temperature variations, and different types of space debris as more countries launch satellites. Interference-oriented threats to commercial satellite systems focus more on information technology. This deals with unintentional or intentional human interference caused by terrestrial and space-based wireless systems or computer systems intended to cause harm. The interference- and content-oriented threats that are intentional threaten commercial satellite systems with malicious software, denial-of-service attacks, distributed denial-of-service attacks, service moving data interception, and potential man-in-the-middle attack methods. This includes the jamming of communications between ground stations and satellite systems. Over the years, the United States government has worked to ensure the confidentiality, integrity, and availability of satellite systems, although the focus on security is limited based on risk. The likelihood of such an attack has not been high, although attacks are increasing each year as more attention is given to satellites. Since the attacks have not been of paramount concern, satellites related to cyber security controls have been limited in scope and function. It is probable that security controls will increase directly with the increase of threats and validated exploitation.

Communicating with Satellites

There are several methods for communicating with satellites. Many commercial satellites use baseband signals, a method that allows for only one car on the road at a time so to speak. Only one transmission either from the ground station to the satellite or from the satellite to the ground station can occur at a time. Direct broadcast satellites (DBS) is common to consumers. DBS is used by vendors such as DISH and DirecTV. DBS transmissions use various methods to secure the data transfer:

- Basic Interoperable Scrambling System, usually known as BISS, is a satellite signal scrambling system developed by the European Broadcasting Union and a consortium of hardware manufacturers. Prior to its development, "ad-hoc" or "Occasional Use" satellite news feeds were transmitted either using proprietary encryption methods (PowerVu) or without any encryption. Unencrypted satellite feeds allowed anyone with the correct equipment to view the program material.
- PowerVu is a conditional access system for digital television developed by Scientific Atlanta [1]. It is used for professional broadcasting, notably by Retevision, Bloomberg Television, Discovery Channel, AFRTS, and American Forces Network. PowerVu is also used by cable companies to prevent viewing by unauthorized viewers. PowerVu has decoders that decode signals from certain satellites for cable distribution services. These decoders can also be used just like the FTA (Free-To-Air) satellite receivers if properly configured. PowerVu is considered highly secure since it uses a complicated system to authorize each PowerVu receiver and trace its history of ownership and usage. Most PowerVu users are professional cable or satellite companies, using the service and equipment for signal redistribution, because regular users cannot afford it. On March 10, 2010, the hacker called Colibri published after previous work done in 2005 a cryptanalysis of a PowerVU system implementation. The hacker described a flawed design that can be used to gain access to the encryption keys and ultimately decrypt the transmitted content.
- DigiCipher 2, or simply DCII, is a proprietary standard format of digital signal transmission and encryption with MPEG-2 signal video compression used on many communications satellite television and audio signals. The DCII standard was originally developed

in 1997 by General Instrument, which is now the Home and Network Mobility division of Motorola [9]. The original attempt for a North American digital signal encryption and compression standard was DigiCipher 1, which was used most notably in the now-defunct PrimeStar medium-power direct broadcast satellite (DBS) system during the early 1990s. The DCII standard predates wide acceptance of DVB-based digital terrestrial television compression (although not cable or satellite DVB) and therefore is incompatible with the DVB standard [9]. The primary difference between DigiCipher 2 and DVB lies in how each standard handles SI, or System Information. DigiCipher 2 also relies on the fact that its signals must be understood in terms of a virtual channel number in addition to the DCII signal's downlink frequency, whereas DVB signals have no virtual channel number [9]. Approximately 70% of newer first-generation digital cable networks in North America use the 4DTV/DigiCipher 2 format. The use of DCII is most prevalent in North American digital cable television set top boxes. DCII is also used on Motorola's 4DTV digital satellite television tuner and Shaw Direct's DBS receiver [9].

Scrambling and de-scrambling equipment for cable and satellite televisions has been the norm for over 30 years. The solutions have evolved over the years to more advanced solutions for DBS.

There are other encryption methods for DBS such as the use of smart cards allowing a single user to access television shows based on the smart card, receiver hardware, and associated software that securely and accurately identifies the users and their individual subscriptions. This is truly commonplace in the commercial market. Advances have been made to incorporate the Advanced Encryption Standard (AES) in satellite transport networks, providing much greater security using encryption keys. Regardless of the security solution in use, the intent is to protect pay-TV signals enforcing subscription-based access to available programs.

Improving Cyber Security

According to a 2009 report from IGI Global as written by Marlyn Kemper Littman titled "Satellite Network Security," satellite transmissions are subject to lengthy delays, low bandwidth, and high bit-error rates that adversely affect real-time, interactive applications such as videoconferences and lead to data corruption, performance degradation, and cyber incursions [10]. Littman goes on to say that multiple layers of security covering all aspects of the satellite's ecosystem is needed to adequately protect satellite networks. This includes policies and legislation requiring minimum necessary security protocols and standards. The Defense Information Systems Network (DISN) Satellite Transmission Services Global (DSTS-G) Performance Work Statement states that:

DODD 8581.1E requires that commercial satellites used by the Department of Defense employ NSA-approved cryptography to encrypt and authenticate commands to the satellite if supporting Mission Assurance Category (MAC) I or II missions as defined in DoD Directive 8500.1. While NSA approved cryptography is preferred for satellites supporting MAC III missions, cryptography commensurate with commercial best practices is acceptable for encrypting and authenticating commands to satellites that only support MAC III missions.

The change in cryptography requirements is for commercial interoperability with DOD satellite systems. These changes went into effect in 2005 and represent a shift to encrypt using the latest technologies transmitted over higher bandwidth, using mission-specific data networks. The change also calls for continued modifications to the security environment as new threats appear and new solutions are available. The cryptography requirements directly align to the Satellite Internet Protocol Security or SatIPSec initiative from 2004. This protocol provides for encrypted transmissions using a standard symmetric method that clearly identifies the sender and receiver. SatIPSec used in conjunction with the Satellite-Reliable Multicast Transport Protocol (SAT-RMTP), which provides secure transmission methods for audio and video files, enhances the satellite ecosystem security posture.

There are several areas for improvement in satellite cyber security. As with many commercial ventures, the sharing of information is limited due to the potential for leaking intellectual property or proprietary processes, procedures, and methods. The information and cyber security industry is rife with examples of limited information sharing. Most companies are remiss to share information on breaches due to the potential embarrassment public awareness could bring. What is missed is the opportunity to share remediation strategies and information on the attacker. This actionable intelligence could prevent other organizations from suffering the same fate. Methods of remediation that are successful should be shared across the satellite industry and within federal and state governments. The opportunity to share effective security practices could vastly improve satellite cyber defenses. Information sharing coupled with the appropriate education and awareness-raising efforts for the satellite industry is an effective method of propagating actionable intelligence.

Until recently, organizations did not agree on what represented an attack. The underlying issue is the use of a common taxonomy relative to satellite security. Incorporating already defined words, phrases, and concepts from the information security community can and will speed up the adoption of and integration of a common book of knowledge (CBK) surrounding satellite cyber security. Just as Web sites and applications on the Internet are subject to continuous probes, scans, denial of service, and distributed denial-of-service activity, the satellite industry faces continuous intentional interference and jamming. The satellite industry could learn how to adopt methods of interference and jamming prevention by incorporating proven principles and methods achieved over years of parallel activity on the Internet. Additionally, organizations managing satellites need to distinguish between advertent and inadvertent events and events that are intentional and unintentional. The data points gathered by the scores of government and commercial satellite organizations worldwide could be organized into information that is analyzed for links, tendencies, and trends to help devices' ever-changing defenses to transmission penetration and jamming. The underlying premise is information sharing for the benefit of nonhostile entities to improve their defensive, preventive, and even predictive countermeasures through intelligence analysis of satellite-specific data points using proven methods in cyber security. An organization such as the National Council of Information Sharing and Analysis Centers (ISAC) could sponsor or propose an ISAC specific to the satellite industry adopting proven methods across the member ISACs to assist in information-sharing activities. The Communications ISAC could further expand into the satellite industry with very specific goals, emphasizing sharing information used to mitigate and prevent typical satellite-related impacts to confidentiality, integrity, and availability.

Many members of the cyber security industry may overlook the physical security aspects of satellite security. Like any centralized management function, satellite monitoring and maintenance is performed from a ground location. Data centers require hardened perimeters and multiple layers of redundancy. Satellite ground controls stations require the same level of attention to security detail. These facilities should have standardized CCTV and access control methods. Security guards performing 24×7 monitoring and response and employee training and awareness programs must be in place. Many ground control stations are not equipped to withstand electromagnetic plus radiological fallout, or instances of force majeure. They lack what many in the information technology industry would term standard requirements for availability. Furthermore, many ground control stations are within proximity of public areas, providing potentially easy access for those with malicious intent. Standards for the continuity of operations for ground control stations should include conditioned and generated power, as well as backup locations in varied geographic locations with an inventory of equipment available in case of an incident.Ground control centers should also practice disaster recovery and business continuity through regularly scheduled exercises. The points mentioned herein are standard functions of an information technology data center that can and should be applied to the satellite industry. All ground control stations should have centralized and backup network operations, security operations, and satellite operations centers integrated into a cohesive monitoring and data-sharing environment.

Several "anti" solutions should be tested and embedded in each satellite's ecosystem based on risk. Sensitive or military satellites should be required to consistently and continually provide antijamming, antispoofing and antitampering capabilities that can be monitored by the ground control station. Ground control stations need to be outfitted with prevention-based cyber security solutions that either prevent or detect penetrations, prevent malware and data exfiltration, and monitor, record, and analyze malware characteristics.

Another concept for all U.S.-based satellites is the use of all appropriate satellites to act as a sensor while in orbit. The idea is for each satellite to share information on surveilled targets after agreeing to install a government payload or sensor that provides a space-based surveillance and warning network. This concept borrows from cyber security technologies using sensors to monitor network activity across government or commercial entities. The government could offer some type of concession or support to the commercial organization in exchange for carrying the nonintrusive payload.

Although many of the recommendations are already a regular occurrence in military satellite systems, commercial systems do not necessarily require the same level of security or scrutiny. Regardless, recent interference and jamming of satellite-controlled device under the military's purview and the penetration of malware of ground control stations indicate a need for increased attention to security whether it is cyber or of a more traditional need.

A call for all satellite ecosystems to undergo assessment and authorization procedures as defined in the Federal Information Security Management Act (FISMA) and as detailed on the DoD Information Assurance Certification and Accreditation Process (DIACAP) may be warranted based on the role satellites play in critical infrastructures. The use of DIACAP and DSTS-G can help drive cyber security framework standardization for satellites (see checklist: An Agenda for Action for Implementing Cyber Security Framework Standardization Methods for Satellites). They can help drive mitigation measures using onboard satellite radio frequency encryption systems.

When it comes to ground-based network operations centers (NOC) and security operations centers (SOC), traditional cyber security standards and controls apply for both physical and virtual measures. Much the same applies to interference. Interference in the satellite ecosystem comes from several sources such as human error, other satellite interference, terrestrial interference, equipment failure, and intentional interference and jamming [11].

The satellite industry continues to take steps to mitigate and deliver countermeasures to the various types of interference. Use of various types of shielding, filters, and regular training and awareness can help reducemost types of interference. Intentional or purposeful interference (PI) is not remediated through these measures. The satellite industry has created an information technology mirror process and procedure called the Purposeful Interference Response Team or PIRT. Many of the same methods, processes, and procedures used in a computer emergency response team (CERT) program have been adopted for use in the PIRT.Root cause analysis of PIRT incidents is shared back into the process and out to satellite owners to ensure effective security practices and countermeasures are shared across the industry. Communications and transmission security measures are employed using standards such as those defined by the National Institutes of Standards and Technology (NIST) and its Federal Information Process Standard (FIPS) 140−2.

An Agenda for Action for Implementing Cyber Security Framework Standardization Methods for Satellites

Standardization can introduce methods such as carrier lockup, uniqueness, autonomy, diversity, and out-of-band commanding (check all tasks completed):

_____**1.** Carrier lockup is a method used to maintain steady and continuous communication between satellite and the ground control stations ensuring no other transmissions can be inserted from unauthorized ground control stations [11].

_____**2.** Uniqueness provides each satellite with a unique address much like a personal computer's media access control (MAC) address [11].

_____**3.** Autonomy is a predefined protocol of self-operation, giving the satellite the capability to operate autonomously for certain periods should there be some type of interference or jamming [11].

_____**4.** Diversity provides diverse and redundant routes for transmitting data much like the use of multiple Internet connections from different providers in a data center [11].

_____**5.** Out-of-band commanding provides unique frequencies not shared by any other traffic or ground control stations [11].

As the satellite industry continues its move toward traditional information technology-type hybrid networks, satellites will be subjected to the same types of IT vulnerabilities that ground-based systems suffer today. The issues associated with this migration are apparent, but so too are the solutions. Cyber security standards, processes, procedures, and methods are available without the need for creating them anew. Regardless, their application is required in the design phase of the satellite ecosystem in order to be fully effective. Onboard IT systems provide greater features and real-time modifications, but they also introduce traditional IT vulnerabilities and exploits if not managed properly.

2. SUMMARY

Contrary to what is portrayed in Hollywood, satellites cannot be immediately retasked, nor can they see and hear everything humans do. Satellites have progressed substantially over the years, providing society with cell phone services, pay-TV solutions, hand-held global position systems, GPS for automobiles, motorcycles, and boats, telemedicine, and law enforcement. Satellites play roles in society that are now commonplace. The ubiquitous nature of satellites combined with advances in computing power and capabilities is a double-edged sword for satellite ecosystems. The last several years have seen a parallel increase in satellite deployments and efforts to purposefully interfere with satellites, jam satellite transmissions, and penetrate components of the satellite ecosystem with malicious code. In many cases, radio frequency interference and jamming has been confused as hacking. This may change in time as satellites increase the use of onboard computer capabilities with remote updating needs and patching requirements, much like land-based information technology systems. Foreign intelligence services continue to target U.S. satellite ecosystems in particular, with ground control stations as the least path of resistance method of penetration for traditional computer hacking and malware distribution. Once penetrated, the malware can perform various tasks based on its payload. To date, the payload has been intelligence gathering. Future penetrations could result in cyber sabotage or terrorist activities, resulting in the loss of life and disruptions to critical infrastructures.

The need to build cyber security into satellite ecosystems can remediate risk at inception. The risk-based approach, heavily reported to be the best method of cyber security posture management, could in fact be nothing more than a step in developing a cyber security life cycle—a life cycle that could mature appreciably by transparently embedding cyber security into every facet of every process, procedure, method, and component of the satellite ecosystem.

Finally, let's move on to the real interactive part of this chapter: review questions/exercises, hands-on projects, case projects, and optional team case project. The answers and/or solutions by chapter can be found in the Online Instructor's Solutions Manual.

CHAPTER REVIEW QUESTIONS/EXERCISES

True/False

1. True or False? Very Small Aperture Terminals (VSATs) are prevalent in everyday lives.
2. True or False? Recently, there have been writings on the Internet of the potential for hacking NASA satellites to access the Curiosity land rover on Venus.
3. True or False? In October of 2011, Wright Patterson Air Force Base was the subject of a malware attack on the Predator and Reaper drones.
4. True or False? In June of 2012, a group of researchers at the University of Texas at Austin used the spoofing method described by the Iranians to hack the stealth system of a drone.
5. True or False? A few years ago, a $29 program called SkyGrabber made the news. The program allowed interception of packet radio service from a laptop connected to a large satellite.

Multiple Choice

1. Examples of the _____ could be those that are naturally occurring such as acts of God, earthquakes, hurricanes, tornadoes, and floods.
   A. reputation
   B. Internet filters
   C. ground-based threat
   D. encrypted
   E. content-control software
2. There are several methods for communicating with satellites. Many commercial satellites use _____, a method that allows for only one car on the road at a time so to speak?
   A. opinity
   B. Web content filtering
   C. scale
   D. baseband signals
   E. active monitoring
3. What is a satellite signal scrambling system developed by the European Broadcasting Union and a consortium of hardware manufacturers?
   A. Basic Interoperable Scrambling System (BISS)
   B. Rapleaf
   C. Worms
   D. Content
   E. Security

4. What is a conditional access system for digital television developed by Scientific Atlanta?

A. PowerVu

B. Denial-of-service attack

C. Venyo

D. Port traffic

E. Taps

5. What is a proprietary standard format of digital signal transmission and encryption with MPEG-2 signal video compression used on many communications satellite television and audio signals?

A. Systems security plan

B. DigiCipher 2 (DCII)

C. Denying service

D. Decision making

E. URL lists

EXERCISE

Problem

A GAO report examined unintentional threats to commercial satellite systems. The report broke the threats into three different areas. What were those areas?

Hands-On Projects

Project

Please explain in explicit detail the Basic Interoperable Scrambling System.

Case Projects

Problem

Please explain PowerVu in explicit detail.

Optional Team Case Project

Problem

Please explain DigiCipher 2 in explicit detail.

REFERENCES

[1] C. David, State of the Satellite Industry, Washington, DC, November 13, 2006.

[2] D. Morrill, Hack a satellite while it is in orbit. <http://it.toolbox.com/blogs/managing-infosec/hack-a-satellite-while-it-is-in-orbit-15690>, April 13, 2007.

[3] Sri Lankan rebels deny illegal use of US satellite. <http://www.radioaustralia.net.au/international/2007-04-13/sri-lankan-rebels-deny-illegal-use-of-us-satellite/721866>, April 2007.

[4] C. Franzen, Report: Chinese military suspected in hacks of U.S. government satellites. <http://idealab.talkingpointsmemo.com/2011/10/report-chinese-military-suspected-in-hacks-of-us-government-satellites.php>, October 27, 2011.

[5] N. Owano, RQ-170 drone's ambush facts spilled by Iranian engineer. <http://phys.org/news/2011-12-rq-drone-ambush-facts-iranian.html>, December 17, 2011.

[6] Office, United States General Accounting. Critical Infrastructure Protection Commercial Satellite Security Should Be More Fully Addressed. Washington, United States GAO, 2002.

[7] What is meant by gprs connection?. <http://answers.yahoo.com/question/index?qid=20060828085726AAKiqNr>, 9 1, 2006.

[8] Free Engineering Seminar PPT Slides DOC. <http://www.urslides.com/> February 10, 2012.

[9] DigiCipher 2. <http://mp3umax.org/?p=DigiCipher_2>, January 1, 2012.

[10] M.K. Littman, Satellite Network Security. Fort Lauderdale, Nova Southeastern Unniversity, USA, 2009.

[11] Committee, President's National Security Telecommunications Advisory. NSTAC Report to the President on Commercial Satellite Communications Mission Assurance. Washington, DC, NSTAC, 2009.

## Chapter 69

Verifiable Voting Systems

Thea Peacock
University of Luxembourg

Peter Y.A. Ryan
University of Luxembourg

Steve Schneider
University of Surrey

Zhe Xia
Wuhan University of Technology

1. INTRODUCTION

Many general challenges involved in running a voting system securely are common to any complex secure system, and any implementation will need to take account of these. Over and above these challenges, we introduce a particular approach to addressing the challenge of demonstrating trustworthiness, around the key idea of end-to-end verifiability. This means that every step of the processing of the votes, from vote casting through vote tallying, can be independently verified by some agent independent of the voting system itself. In particular, the output of the system can be checked, and so the integrity of the election does not need to rely on the trustworthiness or competence of the system and its programmers, but can be demonstrated independently. *Individual verification* of a step occurs when an individual voter is able to perform some check that his vote was handled correctly. *Universal verifiability* of a step is when any external party is able to check that the step has been carried out correctly. Typically, end-to-end verifiability of a system will include both of these kinds of verifiability. Verifiability provides an assurance that the result of the election is accurate.

This chapter shows how verifiability can be provided within a voting system by introducing several verifiable voting schemes that have been proposed. Section 2 first discusses the many security requirements of voting systems and the relationships between them. As well as verifiability, requirements include ballot secrecy, integrity, coercion-resistance, and usability among others. These requirements are often in tension, and part of the challenge of designing an e-voting system is to find ways of reconciling them. Section 3 then introduces the different kinds of verifiable

voting schemes. Cryptographic mechanisms are used by many schemes in order to achieve particular goals, and this is the topic of Section 4. A simple example would be to provide the voter with a receipt of how they voted in order to allow individual verifiability. In order to maintain the secrecy of the ballot (even if the voter wants to prove how she voted, for example, to sell the vote), the receipt could be encrypted to mask the information. The section introduces more sophisticated cryptographic mechanisms that are used, including secret sharing to distribute trust (no individual party has total access to a critical secret such as the election secret key); zero-knowledge proofs for verification (allowing a check that an operation on a secret has been done correctly without giving away secret information); and mixnets, to shuffle and decrypt a set of votes so that no decrypted vote can be linked to its original encryption. An overview of several noteworthy schemes are then introduced in Section 5, and the development of a particular scheme, Prêt à Voter, is introduced in Section 6 to illustrate in more detail the considerations that go into the design of a verifiable e-voting scheme. We consider threats to such schemes in Section 7 before concluding in Section 8.

2. SECURITY REQUIREMENTS

While e-voting systems often vary widely in design and operation, they generally converge on a standard set of security requirements. These requirements are difficult to capture, and there is no consensus as yet on precise definitions (see checklist: Security Requirements on Electronic Voting Systems).

Security Requirements on Electronic Voting Systems

Intuitive definitions of some important security properties are as follows[1] (check all tasks completed).

____**1.** Ballot secrecy: Only the voter should know how she voted.

____**2.** Legitimacy: Only registered voters may vote.

____**3.** Eligibility: A voter may vote at most once and all votes cast are genuine.

____**4.** Individual verifiability: The voter should be able to check that her vote is accurately recorded for tabulation.

____**5.** Universal verifiability: The final tally should be verifiable by any third party.

____**6.** Accuracy (Integrity): The announced tally should reflect the true count of all legitimate, cast votes.

____**7.** Receipt-freeness: A voter should not be able to prove her vote.

____**8.** Coercion resistance: A voting system is coercion resistant if the voter can vote the way she wishes to, even while appearing to cooperate with the coercer.

____**9.** Robustness: The system should be able to deliver the correct result even in the event of certain, suitably defined, levels of failure of corruption.

____**10.** Availability: Users should be able to access all features of a fully-functioning system during the election.

Interrelationships and Conflicts

These properties are not wholly independent. For example, ballot secrecy and anonymity can be regarded as special cases of confidentiality or privacy; individual and universal verifiability together imply integrity.

Coercion-resistance is a stronger form of receipt-freeness, which can be described as the inability of a voter to prove how she voted. For coercion-resistance to hold, the voter must be able to vote for her chosen candidates even if she appears to cooperate with the adversary during the whole voting process, from the time before the vote is cast until the final result is published.

Observe also that tension exists between certain properties, most markedly ballot secrecy and individual verifiability. While the requirement exists for ballot secrecy, it should also be possible to publicly verify the accuracy of both vote recording and tallying. It is a challenge to reconcile these two requirements.

Achieving System Security

At a high level, any verifiable supervised scheme can be divided into two parts. At the *front-end*, voters interact with the voting client to generate their encrypted votes and then submit their votes to the voting system. At the *back-end*, the received votes are tallied, and the election result is announced. Note that voters only need to be involved in the front-end, while they need not be concerned with the back-end.

Challenges

The privacy, receipt-freeness, and integrity properties need to be considered in both the front-end and the back-end. In the front-end, the voter's intent should not be

leaked, even if the voter wants to prove it to others. This requires the encrypted vote to be generated at some supervised and controlled environment, such as a voting booth. Otherwise, adversaries who see how the encrypted vote is generated will learn the voter's intent. Moreover, the receipt should only contain the encrypted vote, but not the plaintext intent.[2] In the back-end, if each vote is decrypted individually at the end of the tally, the relationships between the received encrypted votes and the decrypted votes have to be kept private using mixnets. Alternatively the homomorphic property can be used to combine received encrypted votes so that no individual vote will be decrypted at the end of the tally.

In the majority of verifiable schemes, the encrypted votes are encoded using encryption algorithms. Although different key lengths can be carefully selected based on different security requirements, this only provides computational privacy. If adversaries have unlimited computational resources, they are able to decrypt the encrypted votes on the Web bulletin board (WBB) directly. Therefore, as the computational power increases and better breaking algorithms are introduced, today's encrypted votes might be decrypted some time later without using the secret key. For this reason, some researchers advocate the *everlasting privacy* property that ensures unconditional privacy that does not depend on the strength of encryption. To achieve this property, the encrypted vote could be encoded using unconditionally hiding bit commitments instead of encryption.

---

1. Further explanation and discussion of these properties can be found in [1].

---

2. Note that the Farnel scheme [2] has introduced another interesting design philosophy for the receipt. Instead of each voter being provided with a receipt that contains her own encrypted vote, the voter will be given a random receipt that contains another voter's vote. Hence the receipt can contain the plaintext intent. However, because some receipts may not be given to any of the voters and they can be removed without being detected, Farnel is not fully verifiable, and we do not discuss it further in this chapter.

Compromises

An e-voting system may only satisfy a subset of the desirable security properties. Similarly, a system may only partially satisfy a certain property, or it may satisfy a weaker form of the property.

For example, a system may be receipt-free but not coercion-resistant: A coercer may be able to obtain a voter's credentials and vote in her place. Therefore, even if the scheme is receipt-free, it is not coercion-resistant. Coercion-resistance is also difficult to achieve in remote e-voting schemes if the entire voting process is unsupervised, as there is no sure way to exclude outside influence during voting. A few solutions to the problem have been devised and are discussed later in the chapter. However, their implementation is not straightforward, and in some cases such as for complex voting methods such as Single Transferrable Vote (STV), they may be computationally infeasible in practice.

If Internet voting is required, the voting administrators may have to accept the possibility of coercion. However, coercion may not be considered a serious threat in the particular voting community. It is a case of balancing system requirements against the achievable level of security, recognizing and accepting the possible threats.

Absolute ballot secrecy is another strong requirement that is not always possible to achieve, for example, when the outcome of voting is unanimous. Likewise, a compromise may need to be reached between ballot secrecy and, for example, introducing human assistance and/or audio/visual aids for disabled voters. The threat then arises of an official and/or device "learning" a vote. If legislation demands increased accessibility, then there is no choice but to implement the (typically) strong safeguards on equipment that becomes necessary.

3. VERIFIABLE VOTING SCHEMES

In the literature, although a large number of verifiable voting schemes have been introduced and various techniques have been used in these schemes, many of them share similar design philosophies. In this section, we review some of the design philosophies for these verifiable voting schemes. Our focus is verifiable supervised schemes, but we will also briefly explain verifiable remote voting and its limitations.

Verifiable Supervised Schemes

The verifiability property consists of three components: cast-as-intended, recorded-as-cast, and counted-as-recorded. The first two components are related to the front-end, ensuring that the voter's encrypted vote is not only correctly generated but also properly recorded by the election system.

The last component is related to the back-end to ensure that all received encrypted votes are correctly tallied. We now explain how these three components can be designed in verifiable supervised schemes.

To achieve the cast-as-intended property, the individual voter needs to verify that the encrypted vote contains her intended vote. One typical strategy is to use the cut-and-choose method. For example, after an encrypted vote is generated by the voting client, the voter randomly decides whether to audit it or cast it. Note that if the encrypted vote is audited, the voter should not be allowed to cast it as her vote. The voter can repeat the audit process as many times as she likes, each time using an independently generated encrypted vote. After she is satisfied, she requests another encrypted vote and submits it without auditing. The cut-and-choose method provides probabilistic assurance that the encrypted vote is correctly generated without cheating on the part of the system. Another typical strategy requires the voting client to generate a cryptographic proof that the encryption is correctly performed, and an honest voter will accept the proof if the encrypted vote is indeed properly generated.[3] This is the approach taken by MarkPledge discussed later in this section. Different from the cut-and-choose method, this direct audit gives a much higher assurance that the voting client is honest, and the voter can cast the vote that has been audited. Auditing is, however, normally more complex than the cut-and-choose method.

The two auditing methods can be illustrated using a simple analogy: Consider the problem of ensuring that an intact fortune cookie contains a fortune. Using cut-and-choose, when given a fortune cookie you can either break it open (but then it cannot be used later as a fortune cookie) and check that it contains a fortune, or you can decide to accept it. If you choose to break open several and confirm that they all contain a fortune, then you can be confident when you decide to accept one that this one will also contain a fortune. Alternatively, to cut-and-choose, you may use high-tech X-ray equipment to scan a cookie. If the result confirms the presence of a fortune, you will have very high assurance that there is a fortune in the cookie. In this way, no cookie needs to be opened, but it needs more advanced technology than the previous method.

To achieve the recorded-as-cast property, two requirements are necessary. First, there needs to be an append-only WBB that can be read by the public but can only be appended by authorized parties. Once some information is written to it, it cannot be altered or removed. In verifiable schemes, after voters submit their encrypted votes to the election system, all these votes will be published on the WBB. Second, each voter will be provided with a

---

3. Note that the voter should not be able to transfer this proof to others. Otherwise, this proof also proves how this voter has voted.

receipt that contains her encrypted vote. To verify that her vote has been recorded by the election system, the voter can later check her receipt against the WBB to verify that her vote has been correctly recorded by the election system. If not, she can use the receipt to support a complaint to the authorities. Note that this check is optional. But since the attackers do not know which votes will be checked, if they remove a few votes before they reach the WBB, this cheating behavior will be caught with high probability.

The counted-as-recorded property is achieved by designing the tally phase so that its entire process is publicly verifiable. In other words, no vote can be added, altered, or removed without being detected. For example, if some invalid votes need to be removed from the tally, it can be verified by the public that all invalid votes have been removed and no valid vote has been removed. Moreover, the election result is calculated using the remaining votes in a publicly verifiable way. Mixnets and homomorphic encryption are two typical techniques used in the tally phase. They not only ensure the counted-as-recorded property, but also protect ballot secrecy.

A similar notion to verifiability is *software independence*[3]: A voting system is software independent when the result it reports does not depend at all on the correctness of its software. In other words, an undetected error or deliberate change in the software cannot cause an undetected error or change to the election result. Hence the software does not need to be trusted in order to have confidence in the election result because its output can be verified for correctness. Since the software is generally the most complex and intricate element of an e-voting system, obtaining software-independence is an important counterbalance to overreliance on the correctness of the software.

Verifiable Remote Schemes

The design philosophy for verifiability is similar in both verifiable supervised and remote voting schemes. However, because voters will cast their votes in an uncontrolled environment (via Internet or post), the receipt-freeness property becomes trickier to achieve. This is because adversaries may observe the voter when she is casting her vote and find out how she has voted.

In a low-coercion environment, (coercion and vote buying are not serious concerns), the verifiable remote scheme can be directly designed based on a verifiable supervised scheme, just ignoring the receipt-freeness property. For example, the voter generates her encrypted vote and then submits it to the election system through a remote channel. She can still check that her vote is correctly generated, but without the receipt-freeness protection, she might be coerced to vote the candidate favored by adversaries. The Helios system [4] is an example of a verifiable remote scheme designed for a low-coercion environment.

The receipt-freeness property can be achieved in verifiable remote schemes, but there needs to be an untappable channel between the voter and the election system, and information transmitted through this channel is kept private from others. A popular design principle is to add a registration phase before the election day. This phase is carried out within some controlled environment, but the voter can participate in it at any convenient time. Here we briefly explain the design philosophy of the JCJ/Civitas scheme [5,6]; its technical details will be further explained later in this chapter. Each voter will register a credential in the registration phase. In the voting phase, the voter should first encrypt her credential and her preferred candidate (as well as some zero-knowledge proofs), and then submit them to the election system. Because adversaries cannot distinguish a fake credential from a real one, when the voter is being coerced, she can use a fake credential to cast a vote. Note that all votes with fake credentials will be removed from the tally in a publicly verifiable way after mixing. Later, she can cast her vote again using her real credential when she is not being coerced. However, this type of scheme also has some limitations. First, voters need to perform complicated cryptographic calculations both in the registration phase and in the voting phase. Either voters need to use some trusted device, or they need to possess special knowledge to perform these tasks. Second, if the credential is learned by any other party (by the voting client or by adversaries using social engineering), this party can cast another vote at a later time to overwrite the voter's vote.

4. BUILDING BLOCKS

In this section, we briefly describe some building blocks that are commonly used to build verifiable voting schemes. These include encryption schemes, secret sharing and threshold techniques, zero knowledge proofs, mixnets, and some other useful techniques, such as blind signature, designated verifier proof, plaintext equivalent test, and proxy re-encryption.

Encryption Schemes

In public key encryption, anyone can encrypt a message using the public key, and the encrypted message can only be decrypted by the party who possesses the corresponding secret key. Moreover, some schemes also enjoy the additive homomorphic property, which is a very handy feature in verifiable voting schemes. It allows the received encrypted votes to be aggregated into a single ciphertext. To tally the election result, only this single ciphertext is decrypted, so that no individual vote will be revealed.

RSA Cipher

The RSA cipher [7] works as follows: let p and q be two large primes, where $n = pq$ and $\phi = (p-1)(q-1)$. We first select a random value e, such that $1 < e < \phi$ and $gcd(e, \phi) = 1$. Then by applying the extended Euclidean algorithm, we can compute a value d such that $1 < d < \phi$ and $ed \equiv 1 \pmod{\phi}$. Now, the RSA public key is (n, e) and the corresponding secret key is d. To encrypt a plaintext $m \in Z_n$, we can compute the ciphertext as $c = m^e \pmod{n}$. To decrypt c, the party who knows the secret key d can compute $c^d = m^{ed} = m^{k\phi+1} = m \pmod{n}$. RSA enjoys the multiplicative homomorphic property. For example, if $E(m_1)$ and $E(m_2)$ are two RSA ciphertexts with plaintexts m_1 and m_2, then we have $E(m_1) \cdot E(m_2) = E(m_1 \cdot m_2)$. RSA is a deterministic public-key encryption scheme,[4] and its security is based on the factoring problem.

ElGamal Cipher

The ElGamal cipher [8] works as follows: Let p, q be two large primes such that $q | p - 1$. We denote G_q as the subgroup of Z_p^* with order q. Let g be a generator of G_q. The secret key is an element $x \in Z_q$ and the corresponding public key is $y = g^x \pmod{p}$. In this chapter, if we apply the ElGamal parameters, we assume all arithmetic to be modulo p where applicable, unless otherwise stated. To encrypt a plaintext $m \in G_q$, we choose a random blinding factor $r \in Z_q$ and compute the ciphertext $E(m, r) = (G, M) = (my^r, g^r)$. Note that an ElGamal ciphertext is a pair of values of G_q. To decrypt the ElGamal ciphertext (G, M), we compute $m = G/M^x$. ElGamal enjoys the multiplicative homomorphic property, and it is a probabilistic public-key encryption scheme, which is semantically secure if the decision Diffie-Hellman assumption holds in the group G_q.

ElGamal re-encryption: Given an ElGamal ciphertext $(G, M) = (my^r, g^r)$, a party can efficiently compute a new ciphertext (G', M') that decrypts to the same plaintext as (G, M). We denote that the ciphertext (G', M') is a re-encryption of (G, M). To re-encrypt a ciphertext, the party chooses a value $s \in Z_q$ uniformly at random and computes $(G', M') = (G \cdot y^s, M \cdot g^s)$. We note that this does not require the knowledge of the secret key x, only the public parameters y and g are needed.

Exponential ElGamal cipher: This is a variant of the ElGamal cipher with an additional parameter h, which is also a generator of the group G_q. To encrypt a plaintext $m \in Z_q$, we randomly choose a blinding factor $r \in Z_q$ and calculate the ciphertext as $E(m, r) = (G, M) = (h^m y^r, g^r)$.

The decryption process is the same as in the ElGamal cipher, but there is no efficient algorithm to retrieve the plaintext m from h^m. Instead, if m is known to be restricted within some field, we can search the field or use precomputed lookup tables to retrieve m.

The exponential ElGamal cipher can be re-encrypted in the same way. But unlike the ElGamal cipher, it enjoys the additive homomorphic property. For example, if $E(m_1)$ and $E(m_2)$ are two exponential ElGamal ciphertexts with plaintexts m_1 and m_2, then we have $E(m_1) \cdot E(m_2) = E(m_1 + m_2)$ and $E(m_1)^k = E(k \cdot m_1)$.

Paillier Cipher

The Paillier cipher [9] works as follows: Let n be an RSA modulus $n = pq$, where p, q are large primes. Let g be an integer of order a multiple of n modulo n^2. The public key is (g, n), and the secret key is $\lambda = lcm((p-1), (q-1))$. To encrypt a message $m \in Z_n$, we randomly choose $x \in Z_n^*$ and compute the ciphertext $c = g^m x^n \pmod{n^2}$. To decrypt c, we compute $m = L(c^\lambda \bmod n^2)/L(g^\lambda \bmod n^2) \pmod{n}$, where the L-function takes input values from the set $S_n = \{u < n^2 | u = 1 \pmod{n}\}$ and computes $L(u) = (u-1)/n$. Clearly, the Paillier cipher also enjoys the additive homomorphic property, but it is superior to the exponential ElGamal cipher in that it is able to retrieve the plaintext directly after the decryption.

Paillier re-encryption: Given a Paillier ciphertext $c = g^m x^n \pmod{n^2}$, we can re-encrypt it without knowledge of the secret key λ. First, we randomly select a value $t \in Z_n^*$, and then we calculate $c' = c \times t^n = g^m \{tx\}^n \pmod{n^2}$. Now, c' is an re-encryption of c.

Secret Sharing and Threshold Techniques

In secret sharing and threshold techniques, the secret information (the secret key) is shared among several parties, and a quorum of these parties can work together to recover the information. Their difference is that in secret sharing, there needs to be a trusted authority to distribute the secret information among all the parties. But in threshold techniques, no trusted authority is needed, and all parties can work together to generate the secret information and distribute it among themselves. Here, we review some basic secret sharing techniques and the threshold ElGamal. Note that the threshold RSA and threshold Paillier are also feasible, but they are more complex. Refer to [10–13] for their technical details.

Shamir's Secret Sharing

Shamir's secret sharing scheme [14] is the fundamental building block for many other secret sharing and threshold techniques. It works as follows: If we want to find out the solution of polynomial $f(z) = f_0 + f_1 z + \cdots + f_{k-1} z^{k-1}$

---

4. In deterministic encryption, the same plaintext will always be encrypted to the same ciphertext. In contrast, the same plaintext can be encrypted to different ciphertexts using probabilistic encryption.

of degree $k-1$, we need to find out every value of $(f_0, f_1, \ldots, f_{k-1})$. Therefore, we need to find out at least k pairs of (z_i, m_i) values such that for each pair, we have $f(z_i) = m_i$. Therefore, if we set f_0 as the secret m, we can generate any number of m_i, such that $m_1 = f(1)$, $m_2 = f(2), \ldots, m_n = f(n)$. Given any subset of k of these m_i values, we can find out all the coefficients of $f(z)$ by interpolation. But on the other hand, knowledge of at most $k-1$ of these values will not enable the calculation of f_0.

By using the Lagrange interpolation, the polynomial can be written as:

$$f(z) = \sum_{i=1}^{k} \left(m_i \prod_{j=1, j \neq i}^{k} \frac{z - z_j}{z_i - z_j} \right)$$

Therefore

$$m = \sum_{i=1}^{k} m_i L_i$$

where

$$L_i = \prod_{j=1, j \neq i}^{k} \frac{j}{j - i}$$

Verifiable Secret Sharing

Verifiable secret sharing [15] is based on Shamir's secret sharing, but it enjoys an additional advantage: All parties can verify that the secret has been properly distributed. The authority first generates the ElGamal secret key $x \in Z_q$, where $y = g^x$ and then distributes x among a number of parties using the Shamir's secret sharing. Let

$$f(z) = f_0 + f_1 z + \cdots + f_{k-1} z^{k-1}$$

where $f_0 = x$. For $i = 0, 1, \ldots, k-1$, the authority also computes each $F_i = g^{f_i}$ and makes these values public. Then the authority can destroy the secret information x. At this moment, any party can check whether her given secret share is correctly constructed. Suppose the j-th party has been assigned the share x_j. She verifies that

$$g^{x_j} = \prod_{l=0}^{k-1} F_j^{j^l}$$

If the share is properly constructed, the above equation will always hold because

$$g^{x_j} = g^{f_0 + f_1 \cdot j + \cdots + f_{k-1} \cdot j^{k-1}} = \prod_{l=0}^{k-1} g^{f_l \cdot j^l} = \prod_{l=0}^{k-1} F_j^{j^l}$$

Threshold ElGamal

The threshold ElGamal [16] works as follows: At the beginning, n parties $(P_1, P_2, \ldots, P_n)$ need to agree on the ElGamal parameters (p, q, g). Recall that p and q are large

primes, where $q | p - 1$, and g is a generator of G_q. Then they work together to implement the following processes:

1. P_i randomly chooses $x_i \in Z_q$ and computes $y_i = g^{x_i}$.
2. The public key y is computed as $y = \prod_{i=1}^{n} y_i$.
   Now all parties know the public key y, but they cannot find the corresponding secret key $x = \sum_{i=1}^{n} x_i \pmod{q}$ unless they all work together. The next step is to learn how to distribute x to all parties in a verifiable way that any subset of k parties can recover it.
3. P_i randomly chooses a polynomial $f_i(z) \in Z_q(z)$ of degree at most $k-1$ such that $f_i(0) = x_i$. Let

$$f_i(z) = f_{(i,0)} + f_{(i,1)}z + \cdots + f_{(i,k-1)}z^{k-1}$$

   where $f_{(i,0)} = x_i$.
4. P_i computes $F_{(i,j)} = g^{f_{(i,j)}}$ for $j = 0, 1, \ldots, k-1$ and broadcasts $(F_{(i,j)})_{j=1,2,\ldots,k-1}$. (Note that $F_{(i,0)} = y_i$ is known beforehand.)
5. After every party broadcasts the $k-1$ values in the previous step, P_i sends $s_{ij} = f_i(j)$ and a signature secretly to every other party P_j where $j = 1, 2, \ldots, n$. (Note that in particular, P_i keeps s_{ii}.)
6. P_i verifies that the share s_{ji} received from P_j is consistent with the previously published values by verifying that

$$g^{s_{ji}} = \prod_{l=0}^{k-1} F_{(j,l)}^{i^l}$$

   This is because

$$g^{s_{ji}} = g^{f_{(j,0)} + f_{(j,1)}i + \cdots + f_{(j,k-1)}i^{k-1}} = \prod_{l=0}^{k-1} g^{f_{(j,l)}i^l} = \prod_{l=0}^{k-1} F_{(j,l)}^{i^l}$$

   If this check fails, P_i broadcasts that an error has been found, publishes s_{ji} and the signature, and then stops.

- P_i computes her share of the secret key as the sum of all shares received in step 5 as

$$s_i = \sum_{j=1}^{n} s_{ji} \pmod{q}$$

As follows, P_i signs the public key y. Finally, after all parties have signed y, anyone can check whether y is agreed among all these parties.

Zero-Knowledge Proofs

A zero-knowledge proof allows the prover to demonstrate some fact to the verifier without revealing the secret details of the fact. According to the definitions in 'Handbook of Applied Cryptography'[17], it should achieve the following three properties:

- **Completeness:** Given an honest prover and an honest verifier, the protocol will succeed with overwhelming probability. The definition of "overwhelming" depends on the application, but generally implies that the probability of failure is not of practical significance.

- **Soundness:** If there exists an expected polynomial-time algorithm with the following property—if a dishonest prover can with nonnegligible probability successfully execute the protocol with the honest verifier—then the same algorithm can be used to extract some knowledge which is essentially equivalent to the honest prover's secret.
- **Zero-knowledge:** There exists an expected polynomial-time algorithm that can produce, upon input of the assertion to be proven but without interacting with the real prover, transcripts indistinguishable from those resulting from interaction with the real prover.

Interactive Proofs and Fiat-Shamir Heuristics

Generally speaking, an interactive zero-knowledge proof works as follows[5]:

- The prover sends a *witness* to the verifier. The witness works as a commitment in the protocol.
- The verifier sends a *challenge* back to the prover. The challenge could be the outcome of fair coin toss.
- The prover sends a *response* to the verifier. The calculation of the response needs to take into account the witness, the challenge, and the secret.

In the interactive zero-knowledge proof, both the prover and the verifier need to be present during the execution of the protocol. Sometimes, it will be more convenient if the prover can generate a transcript of the protocol so that the verifier can verify it at some later time. By using the Fiat-Shamir heuristic [18], this can be achieved by transferring an interactive proof into a noninteractive proof. The noninteractive zero-knowledge proof (NIZKP) normally works as follows:

- The prover generates a *witness*.
- The prover takes the witness as well as some other necessary information as inputs, and outputs the *challenge* using some hash function.
- The prover calculates the *response* and then sends the transcript, which includes the witness, the challenge, and the response to the verifier.

The security of NIZKP, which can be proved using the *Random Oracle Model* [19], is based on the fact that the verifier cannot predict the outcome of the hash function. Otherwise, she can fabricate a proof that will be accepted by the verifier.

In the following paragraphs, we describe several zero-knowledge proofs in the interactive form. They can be transferred into noninteractive zero-knowledge proofs similarly using the Fiat-Shamir heuristics.

Schnorr Identification Algorithm

The Schnorr Identification Algorithm [20] is widely used to prove knowledge of the ElGamal secret key without revealing it. The basic theory is as follows: Suppose p, q are two large primes where $q|p-1$. Let g be a generator of group G_q, which is a subgroup of Z_p^*. Suppose $x \in Z_q$ is the secret key and $y = g^x$ is the corresponding public key. The prover $\boldsymbol{P}$ can prove that she knows x without disclosing it to the verifier $\boldsymbol{V}$.

- $\boldsymbol{P}$ randomly chooses a value $c \in Z_q$ and sends $w = g^c$ to $\boldsymbol{V}$.
- $\boldsymbol{V}$ sends a random challenge $e \in Z_q$ back to $\boldsymbol{P}$.
- $\boldsymbol{P}$ calculates $s = c + xe \pmod{q}$, and sends s to $\boldsymbol{V}$.
- $\boldsymbol{V}$ checks $g^s = wy^e$.

Moreover, for an ElGamal ciphertext $(G, M) = (my^r, g^r)$, the Schnorr Identification Algorithm also can be used to prove knowledge of its plaintext m without revealing it. The protocol first proves that $\boldsymbol{P}$ knows the blinding factor r in g^r. Because y is a public parameter, if $\boldsymbol{P}$ knows r, she can retrieve m by calculating $m = G/y^r$. Therefore, the protocol also proves that $\boldsymbol{P}$ knows the plaintext m.

Chaum-Pedersen Protocol

The Chaum-Pedersen protocol [21] is used to prove the equality of discrete logarithm. Suppose (g, y) is the ElGamal public key pair and the secret key is $x = \log_g y$. By using the Chaum-Pedersen protocol, the prover $\boldsymbol{P}$ can prove to the verifier V that a pair (m, n) achieves the following property: $\log_g y = \log_m n = x$. We denote such a proof as $\boldsymbol{CP}(g, y, m, n)$.

- $\boldsymbol{P}$ randomly chooses a value $c \in Z_q$; then he sends $U = g^c$ and $V = m^c$ to $\boldsymbol{V}$.
- $\boldsymbol{V}$ sends a random challenge $e \in Z_q$ back to $\boldsymbol{P}$.
- $\boldsymbol{P}$ calculates $s = c + xe \pmod{q}$ and sends s to $\boldsymbol{V}$.
- $\boldsymbol{V}$ checks $g^s = Uy^e$ and $m^s = Vn^e$.

The Chaum-Pedersen protocol also can be used to prove that an ElGamal ciphertext $(G', M') = (Gy^s, Mg^s)$ is a re-encryption of $(G, M) = (my^r, g^r)$ without revealing the randomization factor s. The proof is, $\boldsymbol{CP}(y, G'/G, g, M'/M)$ which implies that there exists a value s such that $\log_y(G'/G) = \log_g(M'/M)$. Moreover, the Chaum-Pedersen protocol can be used to prove that an ElGamal ciphertext has been correctly decrypted.

---

5. Here, we only illustrate the technique using examples of three-round interactive proofs. Some proofs may have more rounds, but their concept is similar.

Cramer-Damgård-Schoenmakers Protocol

The witness hiding/indistinguishable protocol was introduced by Cramer, Damgård, and Schoenmakers in [22]; therefore it is also known as the CDS protocol. It can be used to prove that a party knows the solution of k out of n problems without revealing which problems she can solve. This protocol is normally used in verifiable voting schemes to prove that a ciphertext is an encryption of one value within a subset of different values. Here, we only introduce the basic theory of the CDS protocol; for its technical details, please refer to [22].

For example, there exists n different questions $Q_1, Q_2, \ldots, Q_n$. The prover P wants to prove to the verifier V that she knows the solution of one question. But P does not want V to find out which solution she knows. P can execute the CDS protocol with V as follow:

- Suppose P knows the solution δ_i of the i-th question Q_i, P first randomly selects r_i and calculates the genuine witness t_i. P then randomly chooses fake challenges c_j, fake responses s_j and uses them to fabricate the witnesses t_j, where $j \neq i$. P sends all these witnesses $(t_1, t_2, \ldots, t_n)$ to V.
- V randomly selects a challenge c^* and sends it to P.
- P calculates $c_i = c^* - \sum_{j \neq i} c_j$. Then she calculates the real response s_i, using r_i, c_i and her knowledge δ_i. After that, P sends $(c_1, c_2, \ldots, c_n)$ and $(s_1, s_2, \ldots, s_n)$ to V.
- V checks that $c^* = \sum_{k=1}^{n} c_k$ and for all the questions, each of their proofs is satisfied. However, V will be unable to distinguish the real proof from the fake proofs.

Mixnets

A mixnet is a cryptographic building block implemented by a number of mix servers. It takes a list of encrypted values as input, and it outputs a list of values (encrypted or decrypted depending on the type of mixnet) corresponding to the input list, but permuted so that the links between individual inputs and outputs are hidden. When the mixnet receives a number of encrypted values as inputs, each mix server will either partially decrypt (in a decryption mix) or re-encrypt (in a re-encryption mix) each of the encrypted values and output the results to the next mix server in a permuted order. Therefore, if there exists at least one honest mix server, the relationships between the mixnet inputs and outputs will be kept private. However, the main challenge is how to efficiently prove that the mixnet has generated the correct outputs without revealing the input and output relationships.

In the literature, there are two types of mixnets: *decryption mixnets* and *re-encryption mixnets*. Their difference is that in decryption mixnets, each mix server will partially decrypt the received encrypted list and the final mixnets outputs are plaintext values. But in re-

encryption mixnets, each mix server re-encrypts the received encrypted list, and the final mixnets outputs are still encrypted values. In general, re-encryption mixnets are more robust and versatile because their re-encryption phase and the decryption phase are separated. And the mix servers only need public information to carry out the re-encryption phase.

Moreover, there are also two types of methods to verify the correctness of mixnets: *cut-and-choose* and *efficient proofs*. The cut-and-choose method can be used in both decryption mixnets and re-encryption mixnets. For example, we can randomly require half of the links of the mixnet to be opened in order to check whether the partial decryption or re-encryption is done properly. However, the challenge is how to design an architecture so that the opened links still do not reveal the relationships between inputs and outputs—that is, there are no chains of opened links that relate inputs to outputs. Another issue is that if only one value is altered within the mixnets,[6] a single round of the cut-and-choose method only gives 50 percent probability to detect the cheating. To increase the probability of detecting such cheating, we need to run the audit a number of times, but this will make the verification process expensive. Efficient proofs are more complex, and they mainly work for re-encryption mixnets. Each mix server generates a transcript proof for the shuffle she has done. The proof proves that no value is added, removed, or altered during the shuffle, and it can be publicly verified. Otherwise, even if a single value is altered, the proof will fail with overwhelming probability.

In the following paragraphs, we briefly describe two mixnet examples: one decryption mixnet verified using the cut-and-choose method, and one re-encryption mixnet verified using the efficient proofs.

Chaum's Mixnet and Randomized Partial Checking

Chaum's mixnet [23] works as follows: Suppose $\{(K_1, K_1^{-1}), (K_2, K_2^{-1}), \ldots, (K_m, K_m^{-1})\}$ are a number of key pairs, where K_i is the public key and K_i^{-1} is the corresponding secret key (for $i = 1, 2, \ldots, m$). The public keys are all made public, and each secret key is held by an individual mix server. The mixnet inputs are a list of ciphertexts $L_0 = (l_{01}, l_{02}, \ldots l_{0n})$, where the i-th ciphertext is

$$l_{0i} = K_1(K_2(\ldots(K_{m-1}(K_m(m_i, r_m), r_{m-1})\ldots), r_2), r_1)$$

This ciphertext is commonly known as an *onion* due to its layered structure. When receiving the mixnet inputs, the first mix server will use her secret key K_1^{-1} to decrypt each of the onions in L_0, and she then removes the randomization

---

6. Normally, this attack does not aim to dramatically change the election result, but rather to find out how a voter has voted.

values, shuffles the remaining values, and outputs the result list L_1 onto the WBB. At this moment, there should be a value $K_2(\ldots(K_{m-1}(K_m(m_i, r_m), r_{m-1})\ldots), r_2)$ in the list L_1. But because of the shuffle, its index will be changed. As follows, the next mix server downloads the list L_1 from the WBB, decrypts each of the ciphertext using her secret key K_2^{-1}, removes the randomization values, shuffles the remaining values, and outputs the result list L_2 to the WBB. This process is continued until the ciphertext list is decrypted by all the mix servers. Finally, the last mix server will output the list L_m, which contains all the plaintexts.

Chaum's mixnet can be verified using Randomized Partial Checking (RPC) [24]. To enable this, the mixnet needs to be implemented in a slightly different way. Each mix server needs to implement two shuffles, and every two adjacent mix servers are paired together, as shown in Figure 69.1. To audit the mixnet, each pair of the mix servers is verified separately as follows:

1. For the left mix server, the auditor will go down the middle column and randomly assign half units L and the other half units R.

2. For units assigned L, the auditor requires the left mix server to reveal the corresponding links in her first shuffle (incoming links).

3. For units assigned R, the auditor requires the left mix server to reveal the corresponding links in her second shuffle (outgoing links).

4. For the right mix server, for exactly half of the inputs she receives, their incoming links have already been revealed. We denote that these units are in the group G_1 and the other units are in the group G_2. Then the auditor randomly assigns half units in G_1 and half

units in G_2 and requires the right mix server to reveal their outgoing links.

5. In the last shuffle, for the units whose incoming links have not been revealed, the right mix server is required to reveal their outgoing links.

To open a link, the mix server needs to reveal either the source of the link (for incoming links) or the destination of the link (for outgoing links) as well as the randomization value. Therefore, the auditor who has access to the public key can recalculate the link using the revealed information. Thanks to the above architecture, although half of the links have been audited, the remaining links still ensure that the inputs and outputs relationships are kept private if there exists at least one pair of honest mix servers. In other words, a mixnet input can be output at any index with equal probability.

Neff's Mixnet

Neff's mixnet [25,26] works as follows: The original inputs for the mixnet are a list of ElGamal ciphertexts, and each ciphertext is accompanied by a zero-knowledge proof to prove the knowledge of its plaintext.[7] Before the shuffle starts, any input with an invalid proof will be removed, and this process can be publicly verified. After that, the first mix server downloads the remaining ciphertexts from the WBB (ignores their proofs), re-encrypts each of the ciphertexts, and outputs the results to the WBB in a random order. Moreover, the mix server also generates an efficient proof to prove that the re-encryption is correctly performed without revealing the shuffle. Such a proof is also published on the WBB. Then the following mix servers will implement exactly the same processes in sequence. Finally, the mixnet outputs are published onto the WBB by the last mix server.

The key contribution of Neff's mixnet is to demonstrate how to construct an efficient proof. Here, we review the basic ideas. For more technical details, the readers are referred to [25,26].

Iterated Logarithmic Multiplication Proof Protocol (ILMPP): Suppose the vectors $\{X_i\}_{i=1}^k$ and $\{Y_i\}_{i=1}^k$ are publicly known, where $x_i = log_g X_i$ and $y_i = log_g Y_i$ are only known to the prover **P**. Then **P** can use ILMPP to prove to the verifier **V** that $\prod_{i=1}^k x_i = \prod_{i=1}^k y_i$ without revealing any of the x_i and y_i.

The Simple k-Shuffle: Suppose the vectors $\{X_i\}_{i=1}^k$ and $\{Y_i\}_{i=1}^k$ are publicly known, where $x_i = log_g X_i$ and $y_i = log_g Y_i$ are only known to the prover **P**. In addition, constants $c \in Z_q$ and $d \in Z_q$ are only known to **P**, and their commitments $C = g^c$ and $D = g^d$ are made public.

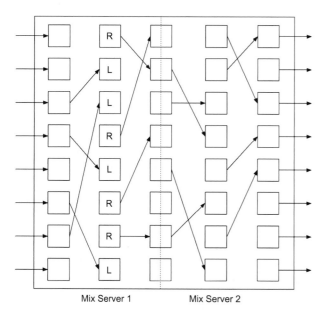

Mix Server 1   Mix Server 2

FIGURE 69.1   Randomized partial checking.

---

7. The proof prevents the adversary from submitting a ciphertext that is related to another ciphertext by an honest party. Otherwise, the adversary may use this attack to find out the honest party's plaintext.

Then P can prove to the verifier V that $Y_i^d = X_{\pi(i)}^c$ for some permutation π, without revealing any of the value x_i, y_i, c, d and π. Note that P actually proves that $y_i/c = x_{\pi(i)}/d$ for $i = 1, 2, \ldots, k$. The protocol works as follows:

- V generates a random challenge $t \in Z_q$ and sends it to P.
- P and V publicly compute $U = D^t = g^{dt}$ and $W = C^t = g^{ct}$.
- Then, for the public inputs

$$(X_1/U, X_2/U, \ldots, X_k/U, \overbrace{C, C, \ldots, C}^{k})$$

and

$$(Y_1/W, Y_2/W, \ldots, Y_k/W, \overbrace{D, D, \ldots, D}^{k})$$

- P can use the ILMPP as a subprotocol to prove to V that $c^k \times \prod_{i=1}^{k}(x_i - dt) = d^k \times \prod_{i=1}^{k}(y_i - ct)$.

Note that if we divide $(cd)^k$ at both sides of the above equation, the equation can be rewritten as:

$$\prod_{i=1}^{k}(x_i/d - t) = \prod_{i=1}^{k}(y_i/c - t)$$

Therefore, because t is a random value chosen by V, P actually proves that for some permutation π and $i = 1, 2, \ldots, k$, we have $y_i/c = x_{\pi(i)}/d$.

ElGamal Shuffle: In a mixnet, if the mix server M is honest, for any output j and some permutation π, we should always have

$$(\alpha_{j'}, \beta_{j'}) = (g^{r_{\pi(j)}}\alpha_{\pi(j)}, y^{r_{\pi(j)}}\beta_{\pi(j)})$$

To prove the shuffle is correctly performed, M first publishes a commitment C and a random vector $\{T_j\}_{j=1}^{k}$, where $c = \log_g C$ and $t_i = \log_g T_j$. Then M can generate $U_j = T_{\pi(j)}^c$ and prove that this is correctly performed using the simple k-shuffle as a subprotocol.[8] Finally, M just demonstrates the knowledge of $\Delta = \sum_{j=1}^{k} r_j t_j$ such that

$$\log_g \frac{\prod_{j=1}^{k}(\alpha_{j'})^{u_i}}{\prod_{j=1}^{k}\alpha_j^{t_i c}} = \log_y \frac{\prod_{j=1}^{k}(\beta_{j'})^{u_i}}{\prod_{j=1}^{k}\beta_j^{t_i c}} = \Delta c$$

If the above equation holds, it proves two facts: first, the same randomization value has been used to re-encrypt both α_j and β_j. And second, because

$$\sum_{j=1}^{k} r_{\pi(j)} t_{\pi(j)} c = \Delta c = \sum_{j=1}^{k} r_j t_j c$$

it proves that the same permutation π has been used both in the simple k-shuffle and the ElGamal shuffle.

---

8. Note that $d = 1$ in this case.

Other Useful Techniques

Some other techniques are also sometimes used in designing verifiable voting schemes. Here we review four of them. The *blind signature* allows the signer to sign a message without learning the message content. The *designated verifier proof* is used to prove some fact to a designated verifier, but the verifier cannot transfer the proof to others. The *plaintext equivalence test* can test whether two ciphertexts are containing the same plaintext without revealing the plaintext. *Proxy re-encryption* is used to transfer a ciphertext encrypted under one public key to a ciphertext encrypted under another public key, where the two ciphertexts contain the same plaintext.

Blind Signature

Blind signature [27] is a kind of digital signature in which the message is blinded before it is signed. Therefore, the signer will not learn the message content. Then the signed message will be unblinded. At this moment, it is similar to a normal digital signature, and it can be publicly checked against the original message. Blind signature can be implemented using a number of public-key encryption schemes. Here, we only introduce the simplest one, which is based on RSA encryption. The signer has a public key (n, e) and a secret key d. Suppose a party A wants to have a message m signed using the blind signature. She should execute the protocol with the signer S as follows:

- A first randomly chooses a value k, which satisfies $0 \le k \le n - 1$ and $gcd(n, k) = 1$.
- For the message m, A computes $m^* = mk^e \pmod{n}$ and sends m^* to S.
- When S receives m^*, S computes $s^* = (m^*)^d \pmod{n}$ and sends s^* back to A.
- A computes $s = s^*/k \pmod{n}$. Now s is S 's signature on the message m.

Designated Verifier Proof

Designated verifier proof (DVP) [28] can be used to prove some fact (e.g., an ElGamal re-encryption is performed correctly) to a designated verifier in a way that the proof cannot be transferred to others.

Let (p, q, g) be the ElGamal parameters. Suppose s_v is the secret key of the verifier V, and the corresponding public key is $y_v = g^{s_v}$. Let $(G, M) = (my^\alpha, g^\alpha)$ be the original message, and $(G', M') = (Gy^\beta, Mg^\beta)$ be a re-encrypted message generated by the prover P. P can prove to V using DVP that the re-encryption is executed properly, but V cannot use the same proof to convince others about this fact. The key point of the proof is to prove that G'/G and M'/M have the same discrete logarithm β under the bases g and y, respectively. A noninteractive proof of the DVP is as follows:

- P chooses $k, r, t \in_R Z_q$.
- P computes $(a, b) = (g^k, y^k)$ and $d = g^r y_v{}^t$.
- P computes $c = H(a, b, d, G', M')$ and $u = k - \beta(c + r)$ (mod q).
- P sends (c, r, t, u) to V.
- V verifies $c = H(g^u(M'/M)^{c+r}, y^u(G'/G)^{c+r}, g^r y_v{}^t, G', M')$.

If P has re-encrypted correctly, the honest V will always accept the proof because:

$$a = g^k = g^{u+\beta(c+r)} = g^u g^{\beta(c+r)} = g^u(M'/M)^{c+r}$$
$$b = y^k = y^{u+\beta(c+r)} = y^u y^{\beta(c+r)} = y^u(G'/G)^{c+r}$$

Therefore

$$c = H(a, b, d, G', M') = H(g^u(M'/M)^{c+r}, y^u(G'/G)^{c+r}, g^r y_v{}^t, G', M')$$

In this protocol, $d = g^r y_v{}^t$ is a trapdoor commitment. If P does not know the secret key s_v, then t and r have been properly committed and P has to calculate u to ensure the proof will be accepted by V. Since P knows β, she can find out such u. But because V knows the secret key s_v, she can reform $d = g^r y_v{}^t$ as $d = g^r \cdot g^{s_v t} = g^{r+s_v t}$, V is able to generate a fake proof for any $(\overline{G}, \overline{M}) = (m'y^\theta, g^\theta)$ that $(G', M') = (my^{\alpha+\beta}, g^{\alpha+\beta})$ is the re-encryption of $(\overline{G}, \overline{M})$. This is because V can generate any pair $(\overline{r}, \overline{t})$, where $r + s_v t \equiv \overline{r} + s_v \overline{t}$ (mod q). In this case, V can work as the prover to fabricate a proof. She first selects $(\overline{\gamma}, \overline{\delta}, \overline{u})$ and computes

$$\overline{c} = H(g^{\overline{u}}(M'/\overline{M})^{\overline{\gamma}}, y^{\overline{u}}(G'/\overline{G})^{\overline{\gamma}}, g^{\overline{\delta}}, G', M')$$

Then V computes $\overline{r}$ as $\overline{r} = \overline{\gamma} - \overline{c}$ (mod q), and $\overline{t}$ to satisfy $\overline{\delta} = s_v \overline{t} + \overline{r}$ (mod q). As a result, the verifier will accept $(\overline{c}, \overline{r}, \overline{t}, \overline{u})$ as the proof because

$$\overline{a} = g^{\overline{u}}(M'/\overline{M})^{\overline{c}+\overline{r}} = g^{\overline{u}}(M'/\overline{M})^{\overline{\gamma}}$$
$$\overline{b} = y^{\overline{u}}(G'/\overline{G})^{\overline{c}+\overline{r}} = y^{\overline{u}}(G'/\overline{G})^{\overline{\gamma}}$$
$$\overline{d} = g^{\overline{r}} y_v{}^{\overline{t}} = g^{\overline{r}+s_v\overline{t}} = g^{\overline{\delta}}$$

Therefore

$$\overline{c} = H(\overline{a}, \overline{b}, \overline{d}, G', M') = H(g^{\overline{u}}(M'/\overline{M})^{\overline{\gamma}}, y^{\overline{u}}(G'/\overline{G})^{\overline{\gamma}}, g^{\overline{\delta}}, G', M')$$

Plaintext Equivalent Test

Suppose (G_1, M_1) and (G_2, M_2) are two ElGamal ciphertexts encrypted under the same public key, where the private key is threshold shared among a set of parties. The plaintext equivalent test (PET) [29] is a function to check whether the two ciphertexts contain the same plaintext, without revealing it. Denote $(\varepsilon, \zeta) = (G_1/G_2, M_1/M_2)$; therefore, if and only if the two ciphertexts contain the same plaintext, (ε, ζ) will represent an encryption of the

plaintext integer 1. Each party P_j randomly selects $z_j \in Z_q$ and commits it using the Pedersen commitment [30]. Then P_j published $(\varepsilon_j, \zeta_j) = (\varepsilon^{z_j}, \zeta^{z_j})$ with the Chaum-Pedersen proof that (ε_j, ζ_j) is well formed. As follows, all parties jointly decrypt $(\gamma, \delta) = (\prod_{j=1}^n \varepsilon_j, \prod_{j=1}^n \zeta_j)$. If and only if the result plaintext is 1, the two ciphertexts (G_1, M_1) and (G_2, M_2) will contain the same plaintext.

Proxy Re-encryption

A proxy re-encryption [31] is a function to transfer an ElGamal encryption from one encryption key to another encryption key. Let $(G_1, M_1) = (m \cdot y_1^r, g^r)$ be an ElGamal encryption of a plaintext m using public key y_1, and let x_1 be the corresponding secret key, which is shared among a number of parties using a threshold scheme. A quorum Q of these parties can transfer (G_1, M_1) to an ElGamal encryption (G_2, M_2), which contains the same plaintext with respect to the public key y_2, without revealing m. First, P_j selects a value δ_j uniformly at random from Z_q, and computes $(\alpha_j, \beta_j) = (M_1^{-x_{1j}L_j} y_2^{\delta_j}, g^{\delta_j})$. Here x_{1j} is P_j's share of the secret key and $L_j = \prod_{i \in Q} \frac{i}{i-j}$. Then (G_2, M_2) can be computed as $(G_2, M_2) = (G_1 \prod_{j \in Q} \alpha_j, \prod_{j \in Q} \beta_j)$.

5. SURVEY OF NOTEWORTHY SCHEMES

In this section, we review a number of noteworthy verifiable voting schemes. Our purpose is not to cover every scheme in the literature, but to divide the existing schemes into several categories; we briefly describe one or two typical schemes in each category. Hopefully, this will give the readers an overview of various research works in developing verifiable voting schemes.

Schemes Based on Blind Signature

Schemes based on blind signature were first introduced by Fujioka, Okamoto, and Ohta in [32], which is normally called the FOO scheme. Although several later papers [33–36] have introduced various further improvements to the FOO scheme, their election procedures are similar, and the FOO scheme is still widely regarded as the milestone in this category.

The FOO scheme works as follows: The involved parties are the voters, the administrator, the counter, and the WBB. At first, a certain voter selects her choice v, encrypting it by bit-commitment $\{v\}_k$ and then by blind signature $\{\{v\}_k\}_{blind}$. After that, she sends it to an administrator. The administrator will only sign the ballot if this voter is eligible and has not applied the signature before. When the voter receives the signed ballot $\{\{\{v\}_k\}_{blind}\}_{sign}$ from the administrator, she will unblind it $\{\{v\}_k\}_{sign}$ and send it to the counter through an anonymous channel. Normally, the anonymous channel is implemented by mixnets. As follows, the counter checks whether the ballot contains the administrator's signature. If yes, the counter will put it onto the WBB. Otherwise, she will reject this ballot. Now, the voter can verify whether her vote $\{v\}_k$ is correctly displayed on the WBB. If not, she can complain to a trusted party. Otherwise, she will send her de-commitment key k to the counter anonymously after some designated time T. Finally, the counter decrypts each ballot v and publishes them on the WBB.

Schemes based on blind signature ensure voter privacy and allow voters to verify that their votes are received by the election system. Furthermore, the fairness property is guaranteed so that no early result can be revealed before the designated time T. However, they also suffer several drawbacks. One issue is that messages must be sent to the election authorities twice, which means that voters have to be involved during the whole election procedures. Another issue is that voter privacy will be violated if a voter discovers an incorrectly recorded receipt and complains to the authority. Moreover, if there exists some mixnet for the anonymous channel, then the blind signature technique is no longer needed to design verifiable voting schemes. Because of these issues, blind signature schemes have not attracted much recent interest.

Schemes Based on Mixnets

Note that the schemes based on mixnets discussed here are early schemes which assume that voters are able to generate their encrypted votes as well as the necessary proofs. So they only focus on the tally phase. Many later voter-verifiable schemes also employ mixnets as building blocks, but they concentrate on a different problem: how to allow ordinary voters to cast their encrypted votes without special knowledge.

Schemes based on mixnets have been developed along with the mixnets. In the first mixnet protocol [23], Chaum suggested that the mixnet can be used in voting schemes to provide voter privacy. And later, many mixnet protocols have used voting as an example of their application. Here, we describe the scheme introduced by Sako and Kilian in [37], and many other schemes share similar ideas.

At first, each voter generates an encrypted vote $(\alpha_i, \beta_i) = (m_i \cdot y^r, g^r)$ that contains her choice m_i. The voter also generates an Σ-proof (e.g., using the Schnorr Identification Algorithm) that she knows m_i without revealing it. Then she publishes (α_i, β_i) as well as the Σ-proof onto the WBB. After receiving all the encrypted votes from every voter, a set of mix servers will re-encrypt and shuffle these votes in sequence. Finally, the mixnet outputs will be decrypted in a threshold fashion.

For a particular mix server, suppose the list $L_{in} = \{(\alpha_1, \beta_1), \ldots, (\alpha_n, \beta_n)\}$ is her inputs and the list $L_{out} = \{(\alpha_{\pi(1)}', \beta_{\pi(1)}'), \ldots, (\alpha_{\pi(n)}', \beta_{\pi(n)}')\}$ is her outputs.

To audit this mix server, she is required to generate another list $L_{mid} = \{(\alpha_{\sigma(1)}'', \beta_{\sigma(1)}''), \ldots, (\alpha_{\sigma(n)}'', \beta_{\sigma(n)}'')\}$, which is also the re-encryption and shuffle of the list L_{in}. Then the verifier can flip a coin. If heads, the mix server needs to reveal σ and all the necessary randomization values to prove that L_{mid} is a shuffle of L_{in}. Otherwise, if tails, the mix server will reveal $\pi \circ \sigma^{-1}$ and all the necessary randomization values to prove that L_{out} is a shuffle of L_{mid}. It is clear that such an audit will not reveal the permutation π, and it gives 50% probability of detecting cheating if one vote has been altered during the shuffle. Moreover, the audit can be repeated for several rounds (each round with an independently generated L_{mid}) to increase the probability of detecting cheating. Hence it can be verified that no vote has been added, altered, or removed within the mixnet.

To design a verifiable voting scheme based on mixnet, another challenge is how to verify that all the mixnet outputs have been correctly decrypted. Normally, the secret key x is shared among a number of tellers in a threshold fashion; and ciphertexts are threshold decrypted by a quorum of tellers.

Schemes Based on Homomorphic Encryption

Schemes based on homomorphic encryption were first introduced by Josh Benaloh in [38−40]. Later, several improved schemes (e.g., [41−45]) were developed. These schemes follow similar election procedures, but they introduce new security properties, such as the receipt-freeness, and they use more efficient building blocks to replace those in Benaloh's schemes. Here, we review a recent scheme introduced by Baudron et al. in [41].

Suppose the maximum number of voters is M and there are k candidates. Those candidates will be assigned the values $\{M^0, M^1, \ldots, M^{k-1}\}$, respectively. Suppose also that a voter wants to vote for the i-th candidate. She first generates a Paillier ciphertext, which encodes M^{i-1} as well as a proof that her ciphertext is valid. The proof is generated using the witness hiding protocol (the CDS protocol), and it proves that her plaintext is within the set $\{M^0, M^1, \ldots, M^{k-1}\}$ without revealing which one it is. Then she submits both the encrypted vote and the proof to the WBB. When the election closes, any vote with invalid proof will be removed from the tally. As follows, the remaining encrypted votes will be multiplied together into a single ciphertext. Thanks to the additive homomorphic property, this single ciphertext will encode a value, R which is the sum of each individual plaintext. Moreover, the R value can be considered to contain a set of counters $\{M^0, M^1, \ldots, M^{k-1}\}$, and each counter records how many votes have been received for the corresponding candidate. For example, if a voter votes for the i-th candidate, when her encrypted vote is aggregated into the single ciphertext, the counter M^{i-1} will add one. Note that the ciphertext aggregation does not require any secret information, so anyone can check whether it is done correctly by performing the calculation again. Finally, the single ciphertext is decrypted in a threshold fashion, and the value R is revealed. At this moment, if R is divided by M^{k-1}, the result is the number of votes received by the k-th candidate. If the remainder of the previous calculation is divided by M^{k-2}, we get the number of votes received by the $(k-1)$-th candidate, and so on.

Compared with schemes based on mixnets, schemes based on homomorphic encryption are much simpler in the tallying phase. However, voters' tasks are more substantial because the witness hiding proof is more complex than the Schnorr Identification proof. Moreover, they are not as versatile as the schemes based on mixnets since they lack the ability to handle information-rich elections such as Single Transferable Vote (STV) elections. Schemes based on mixnets and homomorphic encryption have received much recent interest in the literature.

Specific Voter-Verifiable Schemes

In voter-verifiable schemes, voters are not assumed to have special knowledge to generate their votes as well as to do any necessary proofs themselves. Instead, some novel techniques can help them to generate their verifiable votes, and they can verify that their votes correctly encode their intent. We review three noteworthy schemes in this category: the MarkPledge scheme by Neff [46], a scheme using visual cryptography by Chaum [47], and Scantegrity II [48].

MarkPledge: Suppose there are n candidates $\{C_1, C_2, \ldots, C_n\}$ and κ is a security parameter. The MarkPledge scheme works as follows:

- An authenticated voter in the voting booth will be allowed to use the voting machine. This voter tells her choice C_i to the voting machine, and meanwhile, she gives $n-1$ challenges $\{c_j\}_{j \neq i}$ to the voting machine, where each challenge is a κ bits binary. These challenges are supposed to be generated uniformly random, but if a voter is coerced to vote for the k-th candidate C_k, he can use the value given by the coercer to replace c_k.
- The voting machine generates this voter's ballot, which can be illustrated as follows:

Denote $\boxed{0}$ and $\boxed{1}$ as ElGamal ciphertexts with plaintexts 0 and 1, respectively. If the voting machine is honest, for the i-th candidate C_i, the voting machine generates κ pairs of ElGamal ciphertexts, where the plaintext is the same in each pair. But for all other candidates, it generates κ pairs of ElGamal ciphertexts, where the plaintext is different in each pair.

- For the ballot generated in the previous step, the voting machine commits all pledges on how each ElGamal ciphertext pair will be opened. Because for all candidates except the i-th one, the voting machine has already known how their ElGamal ciphertext pairs will be challenged, it can announce their pledges properly.
- The voter then sends the challenge c_i for the i-th candidate to the voting machine. c_i is also a κ bits binary.
- For all candidates, the voting machine reveals the ElGamal ciphertext pairs according to the challenge values. For example, for any candidate, if the t-th bit of the challenge is 0, the voting machine opens the left part in the t-th ElGamal ciphertext pair. Otherwise, it opens the right part.
- This voter, as well as any party who is interested, can verify whether all opened plaintexts match what the voting machine has committed (the pledges) in the third step.

Later, all the received votes will be tallied using mixnets. An attractive property of this scheme is that the voter does not need knowledge of cryptography to follow the election procedures. Later, whether the encrypted vote is correctly generated can be publicly checked via a cryptographic proof, and this will not reveal how the voter has voted. Moreover, adversaries are unable to coerce the voter to vote for a particular candidate. This is because the voter provides a real proof for her preferred candidate, and decoy proofs are provided for the other candidates; anyone who checks the proofs will not know which one is real.

If the voter follows the correct election procedures in the MarkPledge scheme, the encrypted vote not only can be cast but also can be used to verify that the voting machine is honest. For a dishonest voting machine, its cheating behavior can only go without being detected with probability $2^{-\kappa}$. However, if the voter does not understand the correct election procedures and reveals the challenge for her preferred candidate before the encrypted vote is constructed and how to open the ElGamal ciphertext pairs is pledged, the voting machine can cheat the voter by generating an encrypted vote for a different candidate. Moreover, the MarkPledge scheme lacks the ability to handle ranked elections, and the size of its encrypted votes is much larger compared with that of many other schemes.

Chaum's Visual Cryptography Scheme

To understand this scheme, some basic knowledge of *Visual Cryptography*[49] is necessary. There are two pixel symbols as shown in Figure 69.2. If we randomly choose one pixel symbol as the top layer and one pixel symbol as the bottom layer, and superimpose the two layers, the image can be illustrated in Figure 69.3. Thus, if the same pixel symbol occupies the same position in both layers, the image will be part-transparent. Otherwise, it will be opaque.

As shown in Figure 69.4, visual cryptography can be used to convey information if both layers are superimposed, but given either the top layer or the bottom layer, it contains no useful information. Chaum's visual cryptography scheme works as follows:

1. In the voting booth, an authenticated voter will be allowed to use the voting machine. She first reveals her choice to the voting machine.
2. The machine then prints a ballot image, similar to the one shown in Figure 69.4. In both layers, the information

FIGURE 69.2   Two pixel symbols.

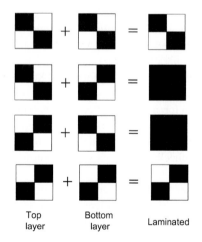

Top layer   Bottom layer   Laminated

FIGURE 69.3   Two pixel symbols are laminated.

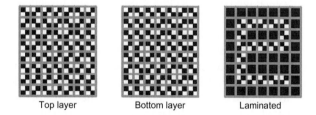

Top layer   Bottom layer   Laminated

FIGURE 69.4   An application of visual cryptography.

(θ_t, θ_b) is printed as well. If θ_t and θ_b are properly decrypted, they can be used to construct the pixel symbols in the top layer and bottom layer, respectively.

3. The voter checks whether the image contains her choice. If yes, she randomly chooses one layer to retain as her receipt, and the other layer needs to be destroyed.
4. Suppose this voter chooses to keep the top layer as her receipt. A copy of this layer will be published on the WBB as her encrypted vote. Later, the voter can check whether the vote in her receipt is displayed on the WBB.[9] If not, she can make a complaint to a trusted party using her receipt.

To tally this vote, the pixel symbols in the top layer and θ_b will enable the election authorities to recover the vote choice. The tallying phase is done using Chaum's mix [23] and incorporating Randomized Partial Checking [24] to ensure that this phase is done properly.

Furthermore, the voter can use her receipt to check whether the ballot has been correctly generated by the voting machine. The voter first sends θ_t to the election authorities. Then they decode it and generate its corresponding pixel symbols. Finally, the voter compares the pixel symbols given by the election authorities and the ones printed on her receipt. As the retained layer is randomly chosen by the voter, this check gives the voter at least a 50 percent chance to detect the cheating if the voting machine is dishonest.

In Chaum's scheme, the voting procedures are straightforward, and it has the potential to handle various election methods (ranked elections). Later we will show that its user interface can be further improved using the Prêt à Voter style ballot forms.

Scantegrity II

This scheme [48] augments existing optical scan voting systems with voter verifiability. Optical scan systems are already in common use in the United States: Voters mark 'bubbles' on a paper ballot against their choices, and the ballot is read by an optical scanner and later tallied. The ballot forms are retained by the system.

Scantegrity II introduces a random secret code (a three-character code) with each bubble. The codes are fixed in advance and precommitted cryptographically so that they cannot be changed during or after the election. The code is revealed only when that bubble is marked. This is achieved using invisible ink for the code and special pens to mark the bubbles, such that the code is revealed. The voter makes a private note of the code and ballot serial number, and the ballot form is scanned and

---

9. Note that she should check that the pixel symbols, θ_t and θ_b are all matching.

retained as before. The codes received are published against the ballot serial numbers, and the voter can verify whether the published code matches her record. If it does not, then she can raise a challenge using her record of the code—a genuine code from the ballot form is considered as evidence of casting that vote, since it is extremely unlikely that a voter will guess a genuine code.

Voters can also audit ballot forms using cut-and-choose to check that the codes printed on them match the precommitted codes, by revealing all of the codes. Hence voters can check that ballot forms are correctly formed and verify that their vote has been captured and recorded correctly.

Non-crypto Schemes

Verifiable voting schemes also can be designed without using cryptography. Here we describe two interesting examples: One was introduced by Randell and Ryan in [50], and the other one is the ThreeBallot scheme by Rivest [51].

Randell and Ryan's Scheme

The Randell and Ryan scheme is a variant of the Prêt à Voter protocol (we will describe Prêt à Voter in more detail in the next section.). The ballot form, as shown in Figure 69.5, has a perforation down the middle. The left-hand side (LHS) lists the candidate names in a random order, and the candidate ordering varies in different ballots. At the bottom of the LHS, there is a unique *voter identification number* (VIN). The voter will use the RHS to mark her choice. At the bottom of the RHS is a number

to record the *order of the candidate names* (OCN), but it is overprinted with a scratch strip, and the same VIN number is printed on top of the scratch strip.

In the polling station, an eligible voter will be given a random ballot. To prevent others from seeing the candidate ordering, each ballot can be distributed within an envelope. The voter takes the ballot into the voting booth, marks the choice against her preferred candidate, and separates the ballot along the perforation. Then she keeps the LHS as her receipt and submits the RHS without removing the scratch surface. Note that the election officials will only accept a ballot if its scratch surface is intact. Later, the VIN values for all the received ballots are published on the WBB. The voter can use her receipt to check whether her VIN number has been correctly recorded. To tally the votes, the election officials first remove the scratch surface of all received ballots. Then for each vote, its selected candidate can be retrieved using the position of the mark and the OCN value.

Apart from casting a ballot, the voter can also audit the ballot. The audit checks that the OCN value correctly represents the candidate ordering, and this will prevent a mark against one candidate being counted as a vote for another candidate. The voter can audit as many ballots as she likes, but she can only use an unaudited ballot to cast her vote. The reason is that once a ballot has been audited, its scratch surface will be removed.

The ThreeBallot scheme: A ballot form, as shown in Figure 69.6, consists of three parts that can be separated along the perforations between them. In each part, the candidate names are listed in the canonical order. But a unique value at the bottom of each part is different. To cast a vote, the voter should proceed row by row through

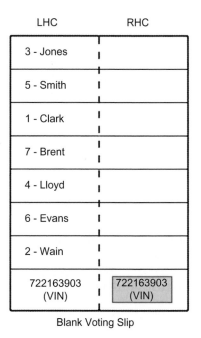

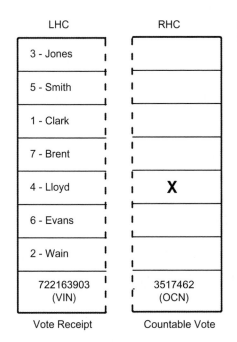

FIGURE 69.5 A ballot form example in the Randell and Ryan scheme.

BALLOT	BALLOT	BALLOT
President	President	President
Alex Jones ○	Alex Jones ○	Alex Jones ○
Bob Smith ○	Bob Smith ○	Bob Smith ○
Carol Wu ○	Carol Wu ○	Carol Wu ○
Senator	Senator	Senator
Dave Yip ○	Dave Yip ○	Dave Yip ○
Ed Zinn ○	Ed Zinn ○	Ed Zinn ○
3147524	7523416	5530219

FIGURE 69.6   A ballot form example in the ThreeBallot scheme.

the ballot form. Each row corresponds to one candidate, and there are three bubbles in each row, one on each part. To vote for a candidate, the voter must fill in exactly two of the bubbles on that candidate row, and exactly one of the bubbles on all the other candidate rows. Then the voter inserts her ballot into some trusted machine that checks whether the ballot is correctly filled in. If yes, the machine prints some marks (e.g., a red line) on the ballot to prove it is valid. Otherwise, it will reject the ballot. Suppose the voter has filled in a valid ballot. Then she separates the ballot along the perforations and submits all three parts to the election officials. At this moment, the voter is allowed to randomly choose one of three parts, make a photocopy of it, and take the photocopy home as her receipt.

Later, all the received ballot parts will be published on the WBB. The voter can then use her receipt to check whether it is correctly displayed. Otherwise, the receipt can be used as the proof to make a complaint. Note that if any part of the voter's ballot has been altered or removed from the WBB, she will have at least 33 percent probability to detect the cheating. Finally, the election result is calculated using the recorded ballot parts on the WBB, and this process can be publicly verified. Suppose there are n voters, and the candidates A, B and C have received a, b, and c marked bubbles, respectively. Then the actual votes received by each voter are calculated by subtracting n from a, b, c, respectively.

Because no complicated crypto technique is used in these non-crypto voting schemes, they are easy to understand and can be used to explain the basic ideas of verifiable voting schemes to ordinary people without special knowledge. However, they normally require much stricter assumptions than their crypto counterparts. For example, in Randell and Ryan's scheme, for any received ballot, it is important that its scratch strip not be removed by dishonest election officials before the tally. Otherwise, this ballot will be treated as invalid, and it will not be

included in the tally. In the ThreeBallot scheme, election integrity relies on the fact that the machine to check the ballot validity is honest. Moreover, the election officials should not know which part of the ballot has been photocopied as the receipt. Otherwise, they can replace the other parts without being detected. Therefore, the non-crypto schemes are normally viewed as academic proposals rather than practical proposals.

Remote Voting schemes

All verifiable voting schemes introduced above require voters to cast their votes in the voting booth. However, this is not convenient for voters who are not able to attend the voting booth on the election day. To solve this issue, several verifiable remote voting schemes have been introduced. However, because voters are not protected from adversaries when they cast their votes, many of these schemes do not ensure the same security level as the supervised voting schemes. Here, we describe a novel remote voting scheme that not only achieves end-to-end verifiability, but also provides very high-level coercion protection to the voters.[10] Because this scheme was introduced by Juels, Catalano, and Jakobsson in [5], it is normally referred to as the JCJ scheme. This scheme works as follows:

1. *Registration phase:* Before the election, every voter needs to register herself in some controlled environment. Once authenticated, the voter V_i will be provided with a credential σ_i, which is generated by some trusted party. After that, the election authorities encrypt this credential using the ElGamal encryption as $E_{pk}(\sigma_i)$, where pk is a public key and its corresponding secret key is threshold shared among a number of tellers. This ciphertext will be published onto the WBB in a list L. Then the authorities prove to V_i that this process is executed properly using the DVP protocol. Note that the voter needs to remember her credential σ_i, and it could be used in many different elections.

2. *Voting phase:* Suppose V_i wants to vote for the candidate m_i; she calculates two encrypted values as

$$c_i^{(1)} = E_{pk}(m_i), \ c_i^{(2)} = E_{pk}(\sigma_i)$$

Then V_i submits her vote $v_i = (c_i^{(1)}, c_i^{(2)}, \delta_i)$ to the WBB through an anonymous channel, where δ_i is a zero-knowledge proof that V_i knows the plaintexts of both ciphertexts.

10. Apart from the privacy and receipt-freeness properties offered by many supervised voting schemes, it also provides protection against three other attacks: the randomization attack, the forced abstention attack, and the simulation attack.

3. *Tallying phase:* After the Election Day, election authorities collect all received votes on the WBB. They first check the proof δ_i of each vote, and any vote with an invalid proof will be eliminated immediately. Then for the remaining votes that form a list L_1, the authorities perform the Plaintext Equivalent Test (PET) between every two votes in L_1. This process ensures that if several received votes use the same credential (either valid or invalid), only the last submitted one will be retained and the others are removed from the list L_1. At this moment, the remaining votes form a list L_2. Then the authorities shuffle the list L_2 using mixnets, resulting in a list $L_{2'}$. As follows, these authorities perform pairwise PET checks between $L_{2'}$ and L. If any vote in $L_{2'}$ cannot be matched with an encrypted credential in L, it means that this vote contains an invalid credential and it will be removed from $L_{2'}$. Finally, the remaining votes form a list L_3, and it will be threshold decrypted by a quorum of tellers to reveal the election result.

To see the ways in which JCJ scheme achieves verifiability, the voter can verify that her encrypted credential $E_{pk}(\sigma_i)$ has been included in the list L and her encrypted vote v_i has reached the WBB. Also, it can be verified by the public that the tallying phase is correctly performed. If adversaries coerce the voter to reveal her credential, she can simply reveal a fake one. This is because adversaries cannot distinguish a fake credential from a real one. Moreover, if adversaries use this fake credential to cast a vote, it will be removed in the tallying phase, but they are unable to find out whether or not their cast vote has been removed.

Prêt à Voter

Prêt à Voter [52] was inspired by Chaum's voting scheme [47], replacing the conceptually and technologically rather complex visual cryptography with a simpler device of permuting the candidate order on each ballot. Each voter is given a ballot form with an independent permutation of candidates printed down the left-hand side and an encryption of the permutation is printed on the right-hand side.

The voting ceremony is as follows. The voter picks a random ballot form at the polling station. The ballot forms will be sealed in envelopes for privacy. A typical ballot form is shown in Figure 69.7. In the privacy of a booth, the voter marks the chosen candidate on the right-hand side of the form. She then separates the two sides and destroys the LHS. Exiting the booth, she takes the RHS to be scanned and recorded by the system. The RHS is validated as cast, for example, by digital signing and franking by the officials. This is retained as a receipt that

Obelix	
Asterix	
Idefix	
Panoramix	
	7rJ94K

FIGURE 69.7 A Prêt à Voter ballot form.

she can later check against a WBB to verify that her vote has been correctly registered.

Note that due to the permutation of candidates, the vote cannot be inferred from the RHS alone without decrypting the onion, thereby ensuring ballot privacy. Receipt-freeness relies on destruction of the LHS, hence eliminating the link between the LHS and RHS of the ballot.

After voting has ended, the receipts posted to the WBB pass through a series of anonymizing mixes. Decrypted votes are then published on the WBB for public verification. Ballot generation and tabulation are discussed in the following.

The way in which the vote is encoded in the receipt has a number of important consequences that distinguish it from previous schemes. First, the voter is not required to communicate her choice to an encryption device. This sidesteps threats arising from the possibility of a corrupt device leaking information about votes via side-channels or subliminal channels. Second, ballot auditing is very clean: Correct encoding of the vote follows from correct construction of the ballot form. Thus, ballot auditing is performed on the ballot forms rather than on the receipts, as would be the case for other verifiable schemes. Whether or not a ballot form is correctly constructed is a simple binary decision and is independent of the vote or indeed the voter. Contrast this with earlier schemes: The voter inputs a choice, and the device produces one or more encryptions of this. Suppose that the voter chooses to audit this: The encryption is opened ,and the plaintext is compared with the claimed input. In the event that the voter claims that the decryption does not match her input, the difficulty lies in how to distinguish the two situations: The device is corrupt and has encrypted the wrong vote; or the voter is mistaken or is lying about her input. A further difficulty is that auditing can undermine ballot privacy. Of course, a voter who intends to audit can input a dummy vote, but this requires a certain level of understanding that not all voters may possess.

Another way of phrasing this is that in Prêt à Voter, what is encrypted is not the vote itself but rather the (randomized) frame of reference in which the vote is encoded. This step can be performed before the ballot form is associated with a vote or voter.

Evolution of Prêt à Voter

Since its inception, Prêt à Voter has undergone a number of changes, and several design options have been identified. We focus here on some of the more important changes and options, highlighting some of the associated issues and challenges. In many cases the driving force behind changes to the system has been to address particular scenarios or contexts and the additional perceived threats that may become relevant in those circumstances. Sometimes enhancements are for practical reasons—for example, to improve the efficiency of the scheme or the availability of new cryptographic primitives.

Tabulation Issues

The original versions of Prêt à Voter used RSA decryption mixes. This has the advantage of allowing the receipts to be transformed as they go through the mixes so that they emerge in the canonical frame of reference. More precisely, the final candidate permutation on the ballot is formed as the product of several permutations, each defined in a layer of the onion. As a receipt moves through the mix, the server reveals the seed value encrypted at the layer in question, computes the inverse permutation, and transforms the index or vector accordingly. The index/rank vector emerges in the canonical frame or reference, that is, in the canonical candidate order. This conveniently removes all information about the permuted candidate order during the mixing.

The downside of decryption mixes is that they lack robustness and flexibility. Mixing and tabulation are intertwined: Each server must hold a decryption key, and the order in which votes are decrypted must be predetermined. Another problem is that the onions grow in size with the number of mixes and the size of the seed space for each layer. These considerations led to the introduction of re-encryption mixes and using ElGamal in place of RSA [53].

With re-encryption mixes, the mixing and decryption phases can be separated. Mix servers do not require secret keys and their ordering does not need to be predetermined, so they can be easily replaced if any one fails. Full mixing of terms in the group is possible, and the onion size is independent of the number of mixes. Perhaps most importantly, many re-encryption mixes can be run in parallel or sequence. Further, if a mix is found to be flawed, it can be rerun and reaudited fairly easily. As decryption mixes are deterministic, they cannot be audited or rerun without compromising privacy.

Permutations of the Candidate Order

A re-encryption mix does not involve (partial) decryption at each stage, so there is no obvious way to mimic the construction above (to transform the index/vector while preserving the meaning). One possibility is to leave the index/vectors invariant. An attacker could partition the mix according to the index values with possible privacy issues, but this is not necessarily a problem if the number of voters greatly outnumbers the number of voting options. In [53], this issue is dealt with by restricting to cyclic shifts of the candidates and exploiting the homomorphic property of ElGamal to absorb the index into the onion, thereby allowing conventional re-encryption mixes to be used. From a secrecy point of view, this is enough to conceal the choice of a single candidate. It is not enough to conceal the choice in more elaborate voting methods such as STV. It is also arguably rather fragile from an integrity point of view: If an adversary has a way to alter ballots in an undetectable way and he wants to shift votes from one candidate to another, he applies the appropriate shift to the index value.

A number of attempts have been made to go beyond cyclic shifts while employing re-encryption mixes in Prêt à Voter. Ryan and Teague [54] propose use of affine permutations of the candidate order while retaining receipt-freeness. The set of possible permutations is defined by a shift and a scaling. This largely eliminates the shift attack described above, while only using one pair of onions.

An obvious approach to handling full permutations is to introduce n onions per ballot (where n is the number of candidates) [55,56]. However, this becomes computationally intensive as the number of candidates grows. Handling full permutations in a re-encryption mix in a more elegant way is an ongoing research problem.

Leakage of Ballot Information

In the case of Prêt à Voter, although no device actually learns the voter's choice, there is still the possibility of a subliminal channel attack: The entity creating the ballot forms secretly encodes information about the permutation in the ciphertext by, for example, selecting the randomization of the encryption in such a way that a secret keyed hash applied to the onion leaks information about the candidate order. These are known as kleptographic attacks [57,58].

A possible counter to such an attack is the use of pseudorandom rather than pure random values. Where ballots are created on demand by a device in the booth, the randomization factor of the encryption could, for example, be derived from a signature applied to a serial number printed on the ballot, or using Verifiable Random Functions [59]. Alternatively, we can use a distributed construction of the ballots in such a way that no single entity knows sensitive information: the final candidate order, the randomization factors, and so on [60,61].

Coercion

"Classic" Prêt à Voter is vulnerable to certain types of coercion such as randomization and "Italian" attacks, particularly with ranked voting methods.

In the randomization attack, the coercer demands that the voter produce a receipt with a mark at a prespecified position, regardless of which candidate this represents. This is tricky to counter in any simple way, but if Benaloh challenges are available, the voter can obtain further receipts until she finds one that allows her to vote as she intends while satisfying the coercer's demands. This works quite well for simple elections with a small number of options on the ballot, but is not feasible for more complex voting methods such as STV.

Chain-voting

This attack, which is also effective against conventional voting systems, is particularly virulent in verifiable schemes. An adversary obtains an unused ballot form, marks it with his chosen candidate, and passes it to a voter, who is required to obtain a fresh ballot at the polling station but to submit the premarked form. The coerced voter smuggles out her unused ballot form, hands it over to the adversary, and so the chain continues.

A possible countermeasure is to use serial numbers on the ballot forms, for officials to note the serial number when the ballot form is issued, and to check it before the vote is cast, similar to the mechanism suggested by Jones [62].

6. THREATS TO VERIFIABLE VOTING SYSTEMS

The failure of voters to verify their receipts against the WBB can impact on the integrity of a system. A possible countermeasure is a Verifiable Encrypted Paper Audit Trail (VEPAT) mechanism [63] in which hard copies of receipts are stored securely and used to perform independent checks against the receipts posted to the WBB. Theoretically, a VEPAT may be useful in the event of a dispute, but in practice, tracing individual receipts in a large election could prove difficult.

In the "Italian" attack, an adversary may demand that the voter fill in the ballot in a very specific way that serves, with high probability as a unique identifier for that ballot. This is potentially very effective where there is a large number of options on the ballot (STV with a significant number of candidates). Such attacks are particularly problematic in verifiable schemes in which decrypted ballots are publicly posted. Countermeasures such as lazy decryption [64] can mitigate this problem by avoiding revealing full ballots at any stage of the tabulation process, but they are computationally intensive and do not eliminate all leakage.

Authentication of Receipts

With receipted schemes, anti-faking mechanisms are important both to prevent dishonest voters from discrediting an election and to help avoid a dishonest system cheating voters. Digital signatures or franking applied to receipts are possibilities but, especially with the former, can be difficult for voters to verify without easily accessible technology.

Ryan has discussed human-verifiable methods such as special printing or paper [65]. In practice, both digital signatures and anticounterfeiting may be necessary: Digital signatures to verify ballot construction and anticounterfeiting to protect the system against fraudulent ballot receipts. Possible mechanisms, practical implementation, and associated issues are important research questions.

Use of Cryptography

Modern cryptography appears to be perfectly suited to solving the apparent conflict between verifiability and privacy in voting systems, but there are obstacles to its deployment.

Establishing understanding and trust in the mechanisms and guarantees provided by cryptographic systems is not straightforward. In addition, proper implementation of cryptography can be complicated and problematic. Because the privacy afforded by cryptographic means is usually computational, there may be concerns about the long-term privacy of votes. Schemes have been devised, however, to provide everlasting privacy [66,67].

An encryption-free, paper-based voting system, conceptually similar to [50], has been described earlier under Randell and Ryan's scheme. The relative simplicity of the system, together with its similarity to lottery card games, may be helpful in gaining voter confidence and trust.

7. SUMMARY

Conducting elections in a way that ensures a demonstrably correct outcome, while at the same time ensuring that all ballots remain secret, has been a challenge to the very foundations of democracy from the outset. The history of democracy is a constant battle between those who seek to guarantee the integrity of elections and those who seek to undermine and corrupt the outcome. Many technologies have been applied to address this challenge, especially in the United States, but none has been wholly successful. More recently, as described in this chapter, cryptographers and security experts have turned their attention to the problem. In many ways, this presents a unique and especially demanding challenge: There is no "god's eye" view to tell us what the correct outcome of an election should be, and consequently a voting system can fail in a nonmanifest fashion. This is in contrast to most other critical systems, for example, Internet banking and avionics, to which voting is sometimes compared. Such comparisons are misleading however, precisely because in these applications failures are manifest and, in the case of banking at least, usually correctable.

A number of cryptographically based schemes have emerged in the last few years which hold out the promise of fully verifiable elections: where the outcome can be proved correct with minimal trust assumptions. In this chapter, we have outlined some of the most notable and promising of these schemes, along with the cryptographic primitives required in their construction. Several of these schemes have been implemented and even subjected to trial. For example, the Scantegrity II scheme has been used in municipal elections in Takoma Park in the United States, and Prêt à Voter is currently being adapted for use in the State of Victoria in Australia.

Despite the significant advances in verifiable voting, we have yet to see significant deployment of such schemes. An interesting question then is: Why has there been so little uptake to date? It appears that the main obstacle is the use of cryptography, which many stakeholders regard with suspicion. Thus, the major challenge now is to present these schemes in a way that will convince the stakeholders of the security properties they afford. It is true that the concepts underlying "modern cryptography" are subtle and the arguments showing that verifiable schemes indeed achieve the claimed security properties are quite sophisticated, so it is unreasonable to expect the average voter to follow all the details. But then, people routinely use cryptography for Internet shopping and the like without understanding all the intricacies. It is to be hoped therefore that, properly presented and after a period of informed debate, verifiable schemes will find their place in supporting democracy. It would seem sensible to initially deploy such schemes for less critical elections: officials of student bodies, professional societies, and so on, before use in real, binding political elections.

Verifiable voting systems remain an active area of research, and doubtless there are further breakthroughs to be made. Various challenges and open questions remain, aside from the previously mentioned challenge of overcoming the natural aversion to cryptography. A prime example is how to perform systematic analysis of a voting system as a sociotechnical system—that is, a system comprising not only technical components such as the cryptographic algorithms and protocols, but also humans and procedures.

In this chapter we have focused on polling station/ supervised elections. There is considerable interest in remote voting, in particular Internet voting. Here the challenges are even more daunting than for supervised voting,

and, in particular, there is no way to ensure that a coercer does not interact with the voter. Some elegant theoretical approaches to countering coercion in the remote context have been proposed, but it seems fair to say that none are sufficiently simple and understandable to be effective in practice.

Finally, let's move on to the real interactive part of this chapter: review questions/ exercises, hands-on projects, case projects, and optional team case project. The answers and/ or solutions by chapter can be found in the Online Instructor's Solutions Manual.

CHAPTER REVIEW QUESTIONS/EXERCISES

True/False

1. True or False? There are many general challenges involved in running a voting system securely, which are common to any complex secure system, and any implementation will need to take account of these.
2. True or False? While e-voting systems often vary widely in design and operation, they generally converge on a standard set of security requirements.
3. True or False? Coercion-resistance is a weaker form of receipt-freeness, which can be described as the inability of a voter to prove how he or she voted.
4. True or False? The privacy, receipt-freeness, and integrity properties need to be considered in only the front-end.
5. True or False? An e-voting system may only satisfy a subset of the desirable security properties.

Multiple Choice

1. The _____ has three components: cast-as-intended, recorded-as-cast, and counted-as-recorded.
   A. reputation
   B. Internet filters
   C. ground-based threat
   D. verifiability property
   E. content-control software
2. To achieve the _____, the individual voter needs to verify that the encrypted vote contains his or her intended vote.
   A. cast-as-intended property
   B. Web content filtering
   C. scale
   D. baseband signals
   E. active monitoring
3. The design philosophy for _____ is similar in both verifiable supervised and remote voting schemes.
   A. the Basic Interoperable Scrambling System (BISS)
   B. Rapleaf
   C. Worms

D. verifiability

E. security

4. In_____, anyone can encrypt a message using the public key, and the encrypted message can only be decrypted by the party who possesses the corresponding ^ secret key

A. PowerVu

B. denial-of-service attack

C. public-key encryption

D. port traffic

E. taps

5. _____ work(s) as follows: Let p, q be two large primes such that $q|p-1$.

A. The ElGamal cipher

B. The DigiCipher 2 (DCII)

C. The denying service

D. Decision making

E. URL lists

EXERCISE

Problem

In secret sharing and threshold techniques, the secret information (the secret key) is shared among several parties, and a quorum of these parties can work together to recover the information. Please expand on this.

Hands-On Projects

Project

A zero-knowledge proof allows the prover to prove some fact to the verifier without revealing the secret details of the fact. Please explain further in explicit detail.

Case Projects

Problem

The witness hiding/indistinguishable protocol was introduced by Cramer, Damgård, and Schoenmakers; therefore, it is also known as the CDS protocol. Please explain further in explicit detail.

Optional Team Case Project

Problem

A mixnet is a cryptographic building block implemented by a number of mix servers. Please explain further in explicit detail.

REFERENCES

[1] P.Y.A. Ryan, D. Bismark, J. Heather, S. Schneider, Z. Xia, Prêt à Voter: a Voter-Verifiable Voting System. In IEEE Transactions on Information Forensics and Security (Special Issue on Electronic Voting), 4(4) (2009) 662–673.

[2] R. Araújo, R.F. Custódio, J. van de Graaf, A verifiable voting protocol based on Farnel. Proceedings of IAVoSS Workshop on Trustworthy Elections (WOTE'2007), Ottawa, Canada, (2007), pp. 57–64.

[3] R.L. Rivest, On the notion of 'software independence' in voting systems, Philos. Trans. R. Soc. A 366 (1881) (2008) 3759–3767.

[4] B. Adida. Helios: Web-based open-audit voting. Proceedings of the 17th Conference on Security Symposium (SS'08), Berkeley, CA, (2008), pp. 335–348.

[5] A. Juels, D. Catalano, M. Jakobsson, Coercion-resistant electronic elections. Proceedings of the 2005 ACM Workshop on Privacy in the Electronic Society (WPES'05), (2005), pp. 61–70.

[6] M.R. Clarkson, S. Chong, A.C. Myers., Civitas: toward a secure voting system, IEEE Symp. Secur. Priv. (2008).

[7] R.L. Rivest, A. Shamir, and L. Adleman, A method for obtaining digital signatures and public-key cryptosystems. Proceedings of the 21st Communication of ACM, 21(2) (1978) 120–126.

[8] T. ElGamal, A public key cryptosystem and a signature scheme based on discrete logarithms, IEEE Trans. IT 31 (4) (1985) 467–472.

[9] P. Paillier, Public-key cryptosystems based on discrete logarithms residues. Advances in EUROCRYPT'99, (LNCS 1592), (1999), pp. 223–238.

[10] D. Boneh, M. Franklin, Efficient generation of shared RSA keys. Advances in CRYPTO'97, (LNCS 1294), (1997), pp. 425–439.

[11] V. Shoup. Practical threshold signature. Advances in EUROCRYPT'00, (LNCS 1807), (2000), pp 207–220.

[12] P.-A. Fouque, G. Poupard, J. Stern, Sharing decryption in the context of voting or lotteries. Proceedings of Financial Cryptography (FC'00), (LNCS 1962), (2000).

[13] I. Damgard, M. Jurik, A generalisation, a simplification and some applications of Paillier's probabilistic public-key system. Proceedings of Public Key Cryptography (PKC'01), (LNCS 1992), (2001).

[14] A. Shamir. How to share a secret. Proceedings of 22nd Communication of ACM, (1979), pp. 612–613.

[15] P. Feldman. A practical scheme for non-interactive verifiable secret sharing. Proceedings of 28th Annual Symposium on the Foundations of Computer Science (FOCS), (1987), pp. 427–437.

[16] T.P. Pedersen. A threshold cryptosystem without a trusted party. Advances in EUROCRYPT'91, (LNCS 547), (1991), pp. 522–526.

[17] A. Menezes, P. van Oorschot, S. Vanstone, Handbook of Applied Cryptography, CRC Press, 1997.

[18] A. Fiat, A Shamir, How to prove yourself: practical solutions to identification and signature problems. Advances in CRYPTO'86, (LNCS 263), (1986), pp. 186–199.

[19] M. Bellare, P. Rogaway, Random oracles are practical: A paradigm for designing efficient protocols. Proceedings of the First ACM Conference on Computing and Communications Society (CCS'93), New York, NY, USA, (1993), pp. 62–73.

[20] C.-P. Schnorr, Efficient signature generation by smart cards, J. Cryptology (1991) 161–174.

[21] D. Chaum, T.P. Pedersen, Wallet databases with observers. Advances in CRYPTO'92, (LNCS 740), (1992), pp. 89–105.

[22] R. Cramer, I. Damgard, B. Schoenmakers, Proofs of partial knowledge and simplified design of witness hiding protocols. Advances in CRYPTO'94, (LNCS 839), (1994), pp. 174–187.

[23] D. Chaum, Untraceable electronic mail, return addresses, and digital pseudonyms, Commun. ACM 24 (2) (1981) 84–88.

[24] M. Jakobsson, A. Juels, R.L Rivest, Making mix nets robust for electronic voting by randomized partial checking. Proceedings of the 11th USENIX Security Symposium, (2002), pp. 339–353.

[25] C. Andrew Neff, A verifiable secret shuffle and its application to e-voting. Proceedings of the 8th ACM Conference on Computer and Communications Security (CSS'01), (2001), pp. 116–125.

[26] C. Andrew Neff, Verifiable mixing (shuffling) of ElGamal pairs. VoteHere document, (2004).

[27] D. Chaum, Blind signature for untraceable payments, Advances in CRYPTO'82 (1982) 199–203.

[28] M. Jakobsson, K. Sako, R. Impagliazzo, Designated verifier proofs and their applications. Advances in EUROCRYPT'96, (LNCS 1070), (1996), pp. 143–154.

[29] M. Jakobsson A. Juels, Mix and match: Secure function evaluation via ciphertexts. Advances in ASIACRYPT'00, (LNCS 1976), (2000), pp. 162–177.

[30] T.P. Pedersen, Non-interactive and information-theoretic secure verifiable secret sharing. Advanced in CRYPTO'91, (LNCS 576), (1991), pp. 129–140.

[31] M. Jakobsson, On quorum controlled asymmetric proxy re-encryption. Proceedings of Public Key Cryptography (PKC'99), (LNCS 1560), (1999), pp. 112–121.

[32] A. Fujioka, T. Okamoto, K. Ohta, A practical secret voting scheme for large scale elections. Workshop on the Theory and Application of Cryptographic Techniques: Advances in Cryptology, LNCS 718:244–251, (1992), (LNCS 817).

[33] S. Canard, M. Gaud, J. Traoré, Defeating malicious servers in a blind signatures based voting system. Proceedings of Financial Cryptography (FC'06), (LNCS 4107), (2006), pp. 148–153.

[34] M. Ohkubo, F. Miura, M. Abe, A. Fujioka, T. Okamoto, An improvement on a practical secret voting scheme. Information Security'99, (LNCS 1729), (1999), pp. 225–234.

[35] T. Okamoto, An electronic voting scheme. Proceedings of IFIP'96, (1996), pp. 21–30.

[36] T. Okamoto. Receipt-free electronic voting schemes for large scale elections. Proceedings of the Fifth International Workshop on Security Protocols, (LNCS 1361), (1997), pp. 25–35.

[37] K. Sako, J. Kilian. Receipt-free mix-type voting scheme. Advances in EUROCRYPT'95, (LNCS 921), (1995), pp. 393–403.

[38] J. Cohen, M. Fisher, A robust and verifiable cryptographically secure election scheme. Proceedings of the 26th IEEE symposium on the Foundations of Computer Science (FOCS'85), (1985), pp. 372–382.

[39] J. Benaloh, Secret sharing homomorphisms: Keeping shares of a secret secret. Advances in CRYPTO'86, (LNCS 263), (1986), pp. 251–260.

[40] J. Benaloh, M. Yung. Distributing the power of a government to enhance the privacy of voters. Proceedings of the Fifth ACM Symposium on Principles of Distributed Computing (PODC'86), pages 52–62, (1986). New York, NY, USA.

[41] O. Baudron, P.-A. Fouque, D. Pointcheval, J. Stern, G. Poupard, Practical multi-candidate election system. Proceedings of the 20th ACM Symposium on Principles of Distributed Computing (PODC'01), New York, NY, USA, (2001), pp. 274–283.

[42] J. Benaloh, D. Tuinstra, Receipt-free secret-ballot elections (extended abstract). Proceedings of the 26th ACM Symposium on Theory of Computing (STOC'94), New York, NY, USA, (1994), pp. 544–553.

[43] R. Cramer, M. Franklin, B. Schoenmakers, M. Yung, Multi-authority secret-ballot elections with linear work. Advances in EUROCRYPT'96, (LNCS 1070), (1996), pp. 72–82.

[44] R. Cramer, R. Gennaro, B. Schoenmakers, A secure and optimally efficient multi-authority election scheme. Advances in EUROCRYPT'97, (LNCS 1233), (1997), pp. 103–118.

[45] E. Magkos, M. Burmester, V. Chrissikopoulos, Receipt-freeness in large-scale elections without untappable channel. The first IFIP Conference on E-commerce/E-business/E-government, Zurich, (2001), pp. 683–693.

[46] C. Andrew Neff, Practical high certainly intent verification for encrypted votes. VoteHere document, (2004).

[47] D. Chaum, Secret ballot receipts: true voter-verifiable elections, IEEE Secur. Priv. Mag. 2 (1) (2004) 38–47.

[48] D. Chaum, R. Carback, J. Clark, A. Essex, S. Popoveniuc, R.L. Rivest, et al., Scantegrity ii: End-to-end verifiability for optical scan election systems using invisible ink confirmation codes. In Electronic Voting Technology Workshop/Workshop on Trustworthy Elections, (2008).

[49] M. Naor, A. Shamir, Visual cryptography. Advances in CRYPTO'94, (LNCS 950), (1994), pp. 1–12.

[50] B. Randell, P.Y.A. Ryan, Voting technologies and trust, IEEE Secur. Priv. 4 (5) (2006) 50–56.

[51] R.L. Rivest. The threeballot voting system. <http://theory.lcs.mit.edu/rivest/Rivest-TheThreeBallotVotingSystem.pdf>, 2006.

[52] D. Chaum, P.Y.A. Ryan, S. Schneider, A practical voter-verifiable election scheme. Proceedings of the 10th European Symposium on Research in Computer Science (ESORICS'05), (LNCS 3679), (2005), pp. 118–139.

[53] P.Y.A. Ryan, S. Schneider, Prêt à Voter with re-encryption mixes. Proceedings of the 11th European Symposium on Research in Computer Science (ESORICS'06), (LNCS 4189), (2006), pp. 313–326.

[54] P.Y.A. Ryan, V. Teague, Ballot permutations in Prêt à Voter. In Proceedings of the 2009 conference on Electronic voting technology/workshop on trustworthy elections, EVT/WOTE'09. USENIX Association, (2009).

[55] Z. Xia, C. Culnane, J. Heather, H. Jonker, P.Y.A. Ryan, S. Schneider, et al., Versatile Prêt à Voter: Handling multiple election methods with a unified interface. In INDOCRYPT, (2010), pp. 98–114.

[56] P.Y.A. Ryan, V. Teague, Pretty good democracy. In Electronic Voting Technology Workshop / Workshop on Trustworthy Elections, (2010).

[57] M. Gogolewski, M. Klonowski, P. Kubiak, M. Kutylowski, A. Lauks, F. Zagórski, Kleptographic attacks on e-election schemes. In International Conference on Emerging trends in Information and Communication Security. <http://www.nesc.ac.uk/talks/639/Day2/workshop-slides2.pdf> 2006.

[58] A.L. Young, M. Yung, The dark side of "black-box" cryptography, or: Should we trust capstone? In CRYPTO, (LNCS 1109), (1996), pp. 89–103.

[59] S. Micali, M. Rabin, S. Vadhan, Verifiable random functions. In Proceedings of the 40th IEEE Symposium on Foundations of Computer Science (FOCS), (IEEE), (1999), pp. 120–130.

[60] C. Burton, C. Culnane, J. Heather, T. Peacock, P.Y.A. Ryan, S. Schneider, et al., Using Prêt à Voter in the Victorian State elections. In the 2012 USENIX/ACCURATE Electronic Voting Technology Workshop (EVT 2012), (2012).

[61] C. Burton, C. Culnane, J. Heather, T. Peacock, P.Y.A. Ryan, S. Schneider, et al., A supervised verifiable voting protocol for the Victorian Electoral Commission. In the Fifth International Conference on Electronic Voting (EVOTE 2012), (2012).

[62] D. Jones. A brief illustrated history of voting. <http://homepage.cs.uiowa.edu/jones/voting/pictures/>.

[63] P.Y.A. Ryan, Technical Report Newcastle Tech Report 966, June 2006 Verified encrypted paper audit trails, University of Newcastle upon Tyne, 2006.

[64] J. Heather, Implementing STV securely in Prêt à Voter. In Proceedings of the 20th IEEE Computer Security Foundations Symposium, CSF '07. IEEE Computer Society, (2007), pp. 157–169.

[65] P.Y.A. Ryan, Prêt à Voter with confirmation codes. In Electronic Voting Technology Workshop/Workshop on Trustworthy Elections, (2011).

[66] J. van de Graaf. Voting with unconditional privacy: CFSY for booth voting. Cryptology ePrint Archive, Report 2009/574, (2009).

[67] T. Moran, M. Naor, Split-ballot voting: Everlasting privacy with distributed trust. In Proceedings of the 14th ACM Conference on Computer and Communications Security, CCS '07, (ACM), (2007), pp. 246–255.

## Chapter 70

Advanced Data Encryption

Pramod Pandya
CSU Fullerton

1. MATHEMATICAL CONCEPTS REVIEWED

In this section we introduce the necessary mathematics of cryptography: Integer and Modular Arithmetic, Fermat's Theorem [1]:

Euler's Phi-Function $\phi(n)$

Euler's totient function finds the number of integers that are both smaller than n and coprime to n:

1. $\phi(1) = 0$
2. $\phi(p) = p-1$ if p is a prime
3. $\phi(m \times n) = \phi(n) \times \phi(m)$ if m, and n are coprime
4. $\phi(p^e) = p^e - p^{e-1}$ if p is a prime

Examples:

$\phi(2) = 1; \phi(3) = 2; \phi(4) = 2; \phi(5) = 4; \phi(6) = 2; \phi(7) = 6;$

$\phi(8) = 4$

Fermat's Little Theorem

In the 1970s, the creators of digital signatures and public-key cryptography realized that the framework for their research was already laid out in the body of work by Fermat and Euler. Generation of a key in public-key cryptography, involves an exponentiation modulo in a given modulus:

$a \equiv b \pmod{m}$ then $a^e \equiv b^e \pmod{m}$ for any positive integer e
$a^{e+d} \equiv a^e \cdot a^d \pmod{m}$
$(ab)^e \equiv a^e \cdot b^e \pmod{m}$
$(a^d)^e \equiv a^{de} \pmod{m}$

Theorem: Let p be a prime number:

1. If a is coprime to p, then $a^{p-1} \equiv 1 \pmod{p}$
2. $a^p \equiv a \pmod{p}$ for any integer a

Theorem: Let p and q be distinct primes:

1. If a is coprime to pq, then

$a^{k(p-1)(q-1)} \equiv 1 \pmod{pq}$, k is any integer

2. For any integer a,

$a^{k(p-1)(q-1)+1} \equiv a \pmod{pq}$, k is any positive integer

Discrete Logarithm

In this section we will deal with multiplicative group $G = <Z_{n*}, x>$. The order of a finite group is the number of elements in the group G. Let us take an example of a group,

$$G = <Z_{21*}, x>$$

$\phi(21) = \phi(3) \times \phi(7) = 2 \times 6 = 12$, that is, 12 elements in the group, and each is coprime to 21.

$$\{1, 2, 4, 5, 8, 10, 11, 13, 16, 17, 19, 20\}$$

The order of an element, ord(a), is the smallest integer i such that

$$a^i \equiv e \pmod{n}, \text{ where } e = 1.$$

Find the order of all elements in $G = <Z_{10*}, x>$

$\phi(10) = \phi(2) \times \phi(5) = 1 \times 4 = 4$

$\{1, 3, 7, 9\}$

Primitive Roots

In the multiplicative group $G = <Z_{n*}, x>$, when the order of an element is the same as $\phi(n)$, then that element is called the primitive root of the group.

$G = <Z_{8*}, x>$ has no primitive roots. The order of this group is, $\phi(8) = 4$

$$Z_{8*} = \{1, 3, 5, 7\}$$

1, 2, 4 each divide the order of the group which is 4:

$$1^1 \equiv 1 \pmod 8 \qquad \rightarrow \mathrm{ord}(1) = 1$$

$$3^1 \equiv 3 \pmod 8; \; 3^2 \equiv 1 \pmod 8 \quad \rightarrow \mathrm{ord}(3) = 2$$

$$5^1 \equiv 5 \pmod 8; \; 5^2 \equiv 1 \pmod 8 \quad \rightarrow \mathrm{ord}(5) = 2$$

$$7^1 \equiv 7 \pmod 8; \; 7^2 \equiv 1 \pmod 8 \quad \rightarrow \mathrm{ord}(7) = 2$$

In the example above, none of the elements have an order of 4; hence this group has no primitive roots. The group $G = <Z_{n*}, x>$ has primitive roots only if n is 2, 4, p^t, or $2p^t$, where p is an odd prime not including 2 and t is an integer.

If the group $G = <Z_{n*}, x>$ has any primitive roots, the number of primitive roots is $\phi(\phi(n))$. If a group, $G = <Z_{n*}, x>$ has primitive roots, then it is cyclic, and each of its primitive root is a generator of the whole group.

Group $G = <Z_{10*}, x>$ has two primitive roots because $\phi(10) = 4$, and $\phi(\phi(10)) = 2$. These two primitive roots are $\{3, 7\}$:

$$3^1 \bmod 10 = 3 \; 3^2 \bmod 10 = 9 \; 3^3 \bmod 10 = 7 \; 3^4 \bmod 10 = 1$$

$$7^1 \bmod 10 = 7 \; 7^2 \bmod 10 = 9 \; 7^3 \bmod 10 = 3 \; 7^4 \bmod 10 = 1$$

Group, $G = <Z_{p*}, x>$ is always cyclic.

The group $G = <Z_{p*}, x>$ has the following properties:

1. Its elements are from 1 to $(p - 1)$ inclusive.
2. It always has primitive roots.
3. It is cyclic, and its elements can be generated using g where x is an integer from 1 to $\phi(n) = p - 1$.
4. The primitive roots can be used as the base of logarithm—discrete logarithm.

Modern encryption algorithms such as DES, AES, RSA, and ElGammal to name a few are based on algebraic structures such as Group Theory and Field Theory as well as Number Theory. We will begin with a set S, with finite number of elements, and a binary operation (*) defined between any two elements of the set:

$$*{:}S \times S \to S$$

that is, if a and $b \in S$, then $a*b \in S$. This is important, for it implies that the set is closed under the binary operation. We have seen that the message space is finite, and we want to make sure that any algebraic operation on the message space satisfies the closure property. Hence, we want to treat the message space as a finite set of elements. We will remind the reader that messages that get encrypted must be finally decrypted by the received party; thus encryption algorithm must run in polynomial time. Furthermore, the algorithm must have the property that it be reversible to recover the original message. The goal of encryption is to confuse and diffuse the hacker

such that it would make it almost impossible for the hacker to break the encrypted message. Therefore, encryption must consist of finite number substitutions and transpositions. The algebraic structure, Classical Group, facilitates the coding of the encryption algorithm. Next we give some relevant definitions and examples before we proceed to introduce the essential concept of a Galois Field, which is central to formulation of the Rijndael algorithm used in the Advanced Encryption Standard (AES).

Definition Group

A group $(G, \bullet)$ is a finite set G together with an operation $\bullet$ satisfying the following conditions:

1. Closure: $\forall$ a, $b \in G$, then $(a \bullet b) \in G$
2. Associatively: $\forall$ a, b, $c \in G$, then $a \bullet (b \bullet c) = (a \bullet b) \bullet c$
3. Existence of Identity: $\exists$ a unique element $e \in G$ such that $\forall$ $a \in G$: $a \bullet e = e \bullet a$
4. $\forall a \in G$: $\exists$ $a^{-1} \in G$: $a^{-1}a = a^{-1} \bullet a = e$

Definition of Finite and Infinite Groups (Order of a Group)

A group G is said to be finite if the number of elements in the set G is finite. Otherwise, the group is infinite.

Definition of Abelian Group

A group G is abelian if for all a, $b \in G$, $a \bullet b = b \bullet a$

The reader should note that in a group, the elements in the set do not have to be a number or objects: They can be mappings, functions, or rules.

Examples of a Group

The set of integers Z is a group under addition (+); that is, (Z, +) is a group with identity $e = 0$, and the inverse of an element a is $(-a)$. This is an additive abelian group, but infinite.

Nonzero elements of Q (rationals), R (reals), and C (complex) form a group under multiplication, with the identity element $e = 1$, and a^{-1} being the multiplicative inverse. For any $n \geq 1$, the set of integers modulo n forms a finite additive group of n elements:

$G = <Z_n, +>$ is an abelian group.

The set of Z_{n*} with multiplication operator, $G = <Z_{n*}, x>$ is also an abelian group. The set Z_{n*}, is a subset of Z_n and includes only integers in Z_n that have a unique multiplicative inverse:

$$Z_{13} = \{0, 1, 2, 3, 4, 5, 6, 7, 8, 9, 10, 11, 12\}$$

$$Z_{13*} = \{1, 2, 3, 4, 5, 6, 7, 8, 9, 10, 11, 12\}$$

Definition Subgroup

A subgroup of a group G is a nonempty subset H of G, which itself is a group under the same operations as that of G. We denote that H is a subgroup of G as H⊆G, and H⊂G is a proper subgroup of G if the set H≠G. Examples of Subgroups:

Under addition, Z⊆Q⊆R⊆C.

H = $<Z_{10}, +>$ is a proper subgroup of G = $<Z_{12}, +>$

Definition of Cyclic Group

A group G is said to be cyclic if there exists an element a∈G such that for any b∈G, and i≥0, b = a^i. Element a is called a generator of G. The group G = $<Z_{10*}, x>$ is a cyclic group with generators g = 3 and g = 7:

$$Z_{10*} = \{1, 3, 7, 9\}$$

The group G = $<Z_6, +>$ is a cyclic group with generators g = 1 and g = 5:

$$Z_6 = \{0, 1, 2, 3, 4, 5\}$$

Rings

Let R be a nonempty set with two binary operations: addition (+) and multiplication (*).

Then R is called a ring if the following axioms are met:

1. Under addition, R is an abelian group with zero as the additive identity.
2. Under multiplication, R satisfies the closure, associative, and identity axiom. 1 is the multiplicative identity, and that 1≠0.
3. For every a, and b that belongs to R, a • b = b • a.
4. For every a, b, and c that belongs to R, then a • (b + c) = a • b + a • c

Examples

Z, Q, R, and C are all rings under addition and multiplication. For any n > 0, Z_n is a ring under addition and multiplication modulo n with 0 as identity under addition, 1 under multiplication.

Definition Field

If the nonzero elements of a ring form a group under multiplication, then the ring is called a field.

Examples

Q, R, and C are all fields under addition and multiplication, with 0 and 1 as identity under addition and multiplication.

[Note that Z under integer addition and multiplication is not a field because any nonzero element does not have a multiplicative inverse in Z.]

Finite Fields GF(2^n)

Construction of finite fields and computations in finite fields are based on polynomial computations. Finite fields play a significant role in cryptography and cryptographic protocols such as the Diffie and Hellman key exchange protocol, ElGamal cryptosystems, and Advanced Encryption Standard (AES):

For a prime number p, the quotient Z/p (or F_p) is a finite field with p number of elements. For any positive integer q, GF(q) = F_q

We define A to be algebraic structure such as a ring or a group or a field.

Definition

A polynomial over A is an expression of the form:

$$f(x) = \sum_{i=0}^{n} a_i x^n$$

where, n is a nonnegative integer, the coefficient $a_i \in A$, $0 \le i \le n$, and x∉A.

Definition

A polynomial f∈A[x] is said to be irreducible in A[x] if f has a positive degree and f = gh for some g, h∈A[x] implies that either g or h is a constant polynomial. The reader should be aware that a given polynomial can be reducible over one structure, but irreducible over another.

Definition

Let f, g, q, and r∈A[x] with g≠0. Then we say that r is remainder of f divided by g:

$$r \equiv f(\text{mod } g)$$

The set of remainders of all the polynomials in A[x] (mod g) denoted as A[x]$_g$.

Theorem

Let F be a field and f be a non-zero polynomial in F[x]. Then F[x]$_f$ is a ring, and is a field iff f is irreducible over F.

Theorem

Let F be field of p elements and f be irreducible polynomial over F. Then the number of elements in the field $F[x]_f$ is p^n.

For every prime p and every positive integer n there exist a finite field of p^n number of elements. For any prime number p, Z_p is a finite field under addition and multiplication modulo p, with 0 and 1 as the identity under addition and multiplication.

Z_p is an additive ring and nonzero elements of Z_p, denoted by Z_{p*} form a multiplicative group. Galois Field, $GF(p^n)$ is a finite field with number of elements p^n, where p is a prime number and n is a positive integer.

Example

Integer representation of Finite Field (Rijnadel) element. Polynomial $f(x) = x^8 + x^4 + x^3 + x + 1$ is irreducible over F_2.

The set of all polynomials (mod f) over F_2 forms a field of 2^8 elements; they are all polynomials over F_2 of degree less than 8. So any element in the field $F_2[x]_f$

$$b_7x^7 + b_6x^6 + b_5x^5 + b_4x^4 + b_3x^3 + b_2x^2 + b_1x^1 + b_0$$

where, $b_7, b_6, b_5, b_4, b_3, b_2, b_1, b_0 \in F_2$ Thus any element in this field can represent a 8-bit binary number.

Data inside a computer is organized in bytes (8 bits) and is processed using Boolean logic; that is, bits are manipulated using binary operation addition and multiplication. These binary operations are implemented using the logical operator XOR, or in the language of finite fields, GF(2). Since the extended ASCII defines 8-bit per byte, an 8-bit byte has a natural representation using a polynomial of degree 8. Polynomial addition would be mod 2, and multiplication would be mod polynomial degree 8. Of course this polynomial degree 8 would have to be irreducible. Hence the Galois Field $GF(2^8)$ would be the most natural tool to implement the encryption algorithm. Furthermore, this would provide a close algebraic formulation. Consider polynomials over GF(2) with p = 2 and n = 1:

$$1, x, x + 1, x^2 + x + 1, x^2 + 1, x^3 + 1$$

Polynomials with negative coefficients, -1 is the same as $+1$ in GF(2). Obviously, the number of such polynomials is infinite. In algebraic operations of addition and multiplication, the coefficients are added and multiplied according to the rules that apply to GF(2). The set of such polynomials forms a ring.

Modular Polynomial Arithmetic over GF(2)

The Galois Field $GF(2^3)$: Construct this field with eight elements that can be represented by polynomials of the form:

$$ax^2 + bx + c \text{ where } a, b, c \in GF(2) = \{0, 1\}$$

Two choices for a, b, c gives $2 \times 2 \times 2 = 8$ polynomials of the form:

$$ax^2 + bx + c \in GF_2[x]$$

What is our choice of the irreducible polynomials for this field?

$$(x^3 + x^2 + x + 1), (x^3 + x^2 + 1), (x^3 + x^2 + x),$$
$$(x^3 + x + 1), (x^3 + x^2)$$

These two polynomials have no factors: $(x^3 + x^2 + 1)$, $(x^3 + x + 1)$. So we choose polynomial $(x^3 + x + 1)$. Hence all polynomial arithmetic multiplication and division is carried out with respect to $(x^3 + x + 1)$. The eight polynomials that belong to $GF(2^3)$:

$$\{0, 1, x, x^2, 1 + x, 1 + x^2, x + x^2, 1 + x + x^2\}$$

You will observe that $GF(8) = \{0,1,2,3,4,5,6,7\}$ is not a field, since every element (excluding zero) does not have a multiplicative inverse such as $\{2, 4, 6\}$ (mod 8).

Using a Generator to Represent the Elements of $GF(2^n)$

It is particularly convenient to represent the elements of a Galois Field with the help of a generator element. If α is a generator element, then every element of $GF(2^n)$, except for the 0 element, can be written down as some power of α. A generator is obtained from the irreducible polynomial that was used to construct a finite field. If $f(\alpha)$ is the irreducible polynomial used, then α is that element that satisfies the equation $f(\alpha) = 0$. You do not actually solve this equation for its roots since an irreducible polynomial cannot have actual roots in the field GF(2). Consider the case of $GF(2^3)$ defined with the irreducible polynomial $x^3 + x + 1$. The generator α is that element which satisfies $\alpha^3 + \alpha + 1 = 0$:

Suppose α is a root in $GF(2^3)$ of the polynomial $p(x) = 1 + x + x^3$

that is, $p(\alpha) = 0$, then $\alpha^3 = -\alpha - 1 \pmod 2 = \alpha + 1$
$\alpha^4 = \alpha(\alpha + 1) = \alpha^2 + \alpha$
$\alpha^5 = \alpha^4 \cdot \alpha = (\alpha^2 + \alpha)\alpha = \alpha^3 + \alpha^2 = (\alpha^2 + \alpha + 1)$
$\alpha^6 = \alpha^5 \cdot \alpha = \alpha \cdot (\alpha^2 + \alpha + 1) = (\alpha^2 + 1)$
$\alpha^7 = (\alpha^2 + 1) \cdot \alpha = (2\alpha + 1) = 1$

All powers of α generate nonzero elements of GF_8.

We will now consider all polynomials defined over $GF(2)$, modulo the irreducible polynomial $x^3 + x + 1$. When an algebraic operation (polynomial multiplication) results in a polynomial whose degree equals or exceeds that of the irreducible polynomial, we will take for our result the remainder modulo the irreducible polynomial. For example,

$$(x^2 + x + 1) * (x^2 + 1) \bmod (x^3 + x + 1)$$

$$= (x^4 + x^3 + x^2) + (x^2 + x + 1) \bmod (x^3 + x + 1)$$

$$= (x^4 + x^3 + x + 1) \bmod (x^3 + x + 1)$$

$$= -x^2 + x$$

$$= x^2 + x$$

Recall that $1 + 1 = 0$ in $GF(2)$. With multiplications modulo $(x^3 + x + 1)$, we have only the following eight polynomials in the set of polynomials over $GF(2)$:

$$\{0, 1, x, x + 1, x^2, x^2 + 1, x^2 + x, x^2 + x + 1\}$$

We will refer to this set as $GF(2^3)$ where the power of 2 is the degree of the modulus polynomial. The eight elements of Z_8 are to be integers modulo 8. Similarly, $GF(2^3)$ maps all of the polynomials over $GF(2)$ to the eight polynomials shown above. But you will note that the crucial difference between $GF(2^3)$ and 2^3: $GF(2^3)$ is a field, whereas Z_8 is NOT.

$GF(2^3)$ is a Finite Field

We know that $GF(2^3)$ is an Abelian group because the operation of polynomial addition satisfies all of the requirements on a group operator and because polynomial addition is commutative. $GF(2^3)$ is also a commutative ring because polynomial multiplication is a distributive over polynomial addition. $GF(2^3)$ is a finite field because it is a finite set and because it contains a unique multiplicative inverse for every nonzero element.

$GF(2^n)$ is a finite field for every n. To find all the polynomials in $GF(2^n)$, we need an irreducible polynomial of degree n. In general, $GF(p^n)$ is a finite field for any prime p. The elements of $GF(p^n)$ are polynomials over $GF(p)$ (which is the same as the set of residues Z_p). Next we show how the multiplicative inverse of a polynomial is calculated using the Extended Euclidean Algorithm:

Multiplicative inverse of $(x^2 + x + 1)$ in $F_2[x]/(x^4 + x + 1)$ is $(x^2 + x)$

$$(x^2 + x)\,(x^2 + x + 1) = 1 \bmod(x^4 + x + 1)$$

Multiplicative inverse of $(x^6 + x + 1)$ in $F_2[x]/(x^8 + x^4 + x^3 + x + 1)$ is $(x^6 + x^5 + x^2 + x + 1)$

$$(x^6 + x + 1) \quad (x^6 + x^5 + x^2 + x + 1) = 1 \quad \bmod (x^8 + x^4 + x^3 + x + 1)\ [1][2]$$

2. THE RSA CRYPTOSYSTEM

Now that we have reviewed the necessary mathematical preliminaries, we will focus on the subject matter of Asymmetric Cryptography, which uses a public and a private key to encrypt and decrypt the plaintext. If Alice wants to send plaintext to Bob, then she will use Bob's public key, which is advertised by Bob, to encrypt the plaintext, and then send it to Bob via an insecured channel. Bob would decrypt the data using his private key, which is known to him only. Of course, this would appear to be an ideal replacement for Symmetric-key cipher, but it is much slower since it has to encrypt each byte; hence it is useful in message authentication and communicating the secret key. See the following Key Generation Algorithm:

1. Select two prime numbers p and q such that $p \neq q$.
2. Construct $m = p \times q$.
3. Set up a commutative ring $R = <Z_m, +, x>$ which is public since m is made public.
4. Set up a multiplicative group $G = <Z^*_{\phi(m)}, x>$ which is used to generate public and private keys. This group is hidden from the public since $\phi(m)$ is kept hidden.
5. $\phi(m) = (p - 1)(q - 1)$
6. Choose an integer e such that $1 < e < \phi(m)$ and e is coprime to $\phi(m)$.
7. Compute the secret exponent d such that, $1 < d < \phi(m)$ and that $ed \equiv 1 \pmod{\phi(m)}$.
8. The public key is "e" and the private key is "d".
9. The value of p, q, and $\phi(m)$ are kept private.

Encryption:

1. Alice obtains Bob's public key (m, e).
2. The plaintext x is treated as a number to lie in the range $1 < x < m - 1$.
3. The ciphertext corresponding to x is $y = x^e \pmod m$.
4. Send the ciphertext y to Bob.

Decryption:

1. Bob uses his private key (m, d).
2. Computes the $x = y^d \pmod m$.

Why RSA works

$$y^d \equiv (x^e \bmod m)^d$$

$$\equiv (x^{ed}) \bmod m$$

$$d \cdot e = 1 + km = 1 + k(p-1)(q-1)$$

$$y^d \equiv x^{ed} \equiv x^{1+k(p-1)(q-1)} \equiv x \pmod m$$

Example:

Choose $p = 7$ and $q = 11$, then $m = p \times q = 7 \times 11 = 77$

$R = <Z_{77}, +, \times>$ and $\phi(77) = \phi(7)\ \phi(11) = 6 \times 10 = 60$

The corresponding multiplicative group $G = <Z_{60}^*, \times>$

Choose $e = 13$ and $d = 37$ from Z_{60}^* such that $e \times d \equiv 1 \pmod{60}$

Plaintext $= 5$ $y = x^e \pmod m = 5^{13} \pmod{77} = 26$

$x = y^d \pmod m = 26^{37} \pmod{77} = 5$

Note: 384-bit primes or larger are deemed sufficient to use RSA securely. The prime number $e = 2^{16} + 1$ is often used in modern RSA implementations.

Factorization Attack

The RSA algorithm relies on the fact that p and q are the distinct prime numbers; and, must be kept secret, even though m = p x q is made public. So if n is an extremely large number, then the problem reduces to finding the factors that make up the number n, which is known as the factorization attack. If the middle man, Eve, can factor n correctly, then she guesses correctly p, q, and $\phi(m)$. Remind yourselves that if the public key e is public, then Eve has to compute the multiplicative inverse of e:

$$d \equiv e^{-1} \pmod m$$

So if the modulus m is chosen to be 1024 bits long, then it would take considerable time to break the RSA system unless an efficient factorization algorithm could be found [1][2].

Chosen-Ciphertext Attack

Z_n is a set of all positive integers from 0 to $(n-1)$.

Z_n^* is a set all integers such that $\gcd(n,a) = 1$, where $a \in Z_n^*$.

$$Z_n^* \subset Z_n$$

$\Phi(n)$ calculates the number of elements in Z_n^* that are smaller than n and coprime to n.

$$\Phi(21) = \Phi(3) \times \Phi(7) = 2 \times 6 = 12$$

Therefore the number of integers in $\in Z_{21}^*$ is 12.

$Z_{21}^* = \{1, 2, 4, 5, 8, 10, 11, 13, 16, 17, 19, 20\}$, each of which is coprime to 21

$Z_{14}^* = \{1, 3, 5, 9, 11, 13\}$, each of which is coprime to 14

$\Phi(14) = \Phi(2) \times \Phi(7) = 1 \times 6 = 6$ number of integers in Z_{14}^*

Example:

Choose $p = 3$ and $q = 7$, then $m = 3 \times 7 = 21$,

Encryption and decryption take place in the ring, $R = <Z_{21}, +, \times>$.

$$\Phi(21) = \Phi(2)\ \Phi(6) = 12$$

Key-Generation Group, $G = <Z_{12}^*, \times>$

$$\Phi(12) = \Phi(4)\Phi(3) = 2 \times 2 = 4 \text{ number in } Z_{12}^*$$

$$Z_{12}^* = \{1, 5, 7, 11\}$$

Alice encrypts the message P using the public key e of Bob and sends the encrypted message C to Bob:

$$C = P^e \bmod m$$

Eve the middle man intercepts the message and manipulates the message before forwarding to Bob:

1. Eve chooses a random integer $X \in Z_m^*$ (since m is public).
2. Eve calculates $Y = C \times X^e \pmod m$.
3. Bob receives Y from Eve, and he decrypts Y using his private key d.
4. $Z = Y^d \pmod m$.
5. Eve can easily discover the plaintext P as follows:
   $Z = Y^d \pmod m = [C \times X^e]^d \pmod m = [C^d \times X^{ed}] \pmod m = [C^d \times X] \pmod m$
   Hence $Z = [P \times X] \pmod m$

Eve, using the Extended Euclidean Algorithm, can then compute the multiplicative inverse of X and thus obtain P:

$$P = Z \times X^{-1} \pmod m$$

The eth Roots Problem

Given:

1. a composite number n, the product of two prime numbers p and q
2. an integer $e \geq 3$
3. $\gcd(e, \Phi(n)) = 1$
4. an integer $c \in Z_{12}^*$
5. Find an integer m such that $m^e \equiv c \bmod n$[1,2].

Discrete Logarithm Problem

Discrete logarithms are perhaps simplest to understand in the group Z_{p*}, where p is the prime number. Let g be the generator of Z_{p*}; then the discrete logarithm problem reduces to computing a, given (g, p, g^a mod p) for a randomly chosen a < (p − 1).

If we want to find the *kth* power of one of the numbers in this group, we can do so by finding its kth power as an integer and then finding the remainder after division by p. This process is called *discrete exponentiation*. For example, consider Z_{23*}

To compute 3^4 in this group, we first compute $3^4 = 81$, and then we divide 81 by 23, obtaining a remainder of 12. Thus $3^4 = 12$ in the group Z_{23*}

Discrete logarithm is just the inverse operation. For example, take the equation $3^k \equiv 12 \pmod{23}$ for k. As shown above $k = 4$ is a solution, but it is not the only solution. Since $3^{22} \equiv 1 \pmod{23}$, it also follows that if *n* is an integer then $3^{4+22n} \equiv 12 \times 1^n \equiv 12 \pmod{23}$. Hence the equation has infinitely many solutions of the form $4 + 22n$. Since 22 is the smallest positive integer *m* satisfying $3^m \equiv 1 \pmod{23}$, that is, 22 is the order of 3 in Z_{23*}, these are all solutions. Equivalently, the solution can be expressed as $k \equiv 4 \pmod{22}$ [1].

In designing public-key cryptosystems, two problems dominate the designs: the integer factorization problem and the discrete logarithm problem. Large instances of these problems are still intractable today.

Discrete logarithms have a natural extension into the realm of elliptic curves and hyperelliptic curves. And Elliptic ElGamal has proved to be a strong cryptosystem using elliptic curves and discrete logarithms. In the next part of the chapter, we will take a look at the discrete logarithm problem and discuss its application to cryptography.

Discrete Logarithm Problem (DLP)

The discrete logarithm problem in group G, given some generator α of a cyclic subgroup G^* of G and an element $\beta \in G^*$, is to find the element x, $0 \le x \le (p − 2)$, such that $\alpha^x = \beta$. The most frequently used cryptosystem utilizing the DLP is ElGamal; we give an elliptic curve variant of ElGamal below [1−3]. For example:

ElGamal Cryptosystem:

Alice wants to talk secretly with Bob.

Setting up: Sometime in the past, Bob has created his keys in the following way:

1. Bob chooses a random large prime p and a generator α of the multiplicative group Z_p^*.
2. Bob chooses a random integer a where $1 \le a \le$ (p − 2).
3. Bob computes α^a mod p.
4. The triple $e_B = (p, \alpha, \alpha^a)$ is the public key, and d_B (p, α, a) is the private key.

Alice obtains Bob's public key from some public key server.

Encryption: Alice wants to encrypt a plaintext M with the cipher $e_B = (e, d, n)$. She starts by choosing a random integer k where $1 \le k \le (p − 2)$ and then encrypting the plaintext M into the cipher-text C:

$$E_{K_B}(M) = C = (\gamma, \delta) = (\alpha^k, M * (\alpha^a)^k \bmod p)$$

Alice then sends Bob the encrypted message C.

Decryption: Bob then decrypts the cipher-text C = (γ, δ) with the cipher $d_B = (e, d, n)$ in the following manner:

$$D_{K_B}(C) = M = (\gamma^{-\alpha}) * \delta \bmod p$$

Lattice-based Cryptography—NTRU

An n-dimensional lattice (see Figure 70.1) is generated using n-linearly independent vectors:

$v_1, \ldots, v_n \varepsilon R^n$; these vectors are known as the basis of the lattice. There are infinite numbers of such bases that can generate the same lattice.

$$L(v_1, \ldots, v_n) = \left\{ \sum_{i=1}^{n} \alpha_i v_i \,\middle|\, \alpha_i \varepsilon Z \right\}$$

In group theory, a lattice in R^n is a discrete subgroup of R^n which spans the real vector space R^n. A lattice is the symmetry group of discrete translational symmetry in n directions. Two NP-hard problems related to lattices are the shortest vector problem (SVP) and the closest vector problem (CVP; see Figure 70.2). Given an arbitrary basis for a lattice, find the SVP in the lattice or find the CVP to an arbitrary nonlattice vector. In both the quantum and classical computational problems, these problems are hard to solve for high-dimensional lattices (see Figure 70.3). There are a number of lattice-based cryptographic schemes, but the NTRU-based cryptographic algorithm appears to be most practical [4,5].

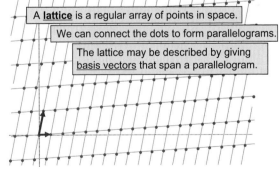

What is a Lattice?

A **lattice** is a regular array of points in space.

We can connect the dots to form parallelograms.

The lattice may be described by giving basis vectors that span a parallelogram.

FIGURE 70.1   Definition of Lattice.

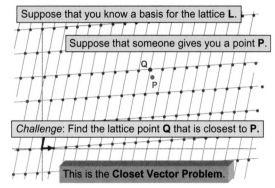

FIGURE 70.2 Closest vector problem (CVP).

Why Is That A Hard Problem?

For lattices in the plane, you're right, it's very easy.
It's not even very hard in dimension 3, or 4, or 5.
However, the Closest Vector Problem is **very hard** in
high dimension, say in dimension 500.

FIGURE 70.3 The hard closest vector problem.

NTRU Cryptosystem

NTRU is not based on factorization or discrete logarithmic problems. Rather, it is a lattice-based alternative to RSA and ECC and is based on the shortest vector problem in a lattice. NTRU was founded in 1996 by three mathematicians: Jeffrey Hoffstein, Joseph H. Silverman, and Jill Pipher. Later on with the addition of yet another member, Daniel Lieman, to the team, NTRU Cryptosystems was incorporated in Boston. NTRU Cryptosystems was acquired by Security Innovation in 2009.

The NTRU cryptosystem was introduced at the rump session of Crypto'96 and was later published in the proceedings of the ANTS-III conference. NTRU is a ring-based public-key cryptosystem and is therefore quite different from the group-based cryptosystems whose security relies on the integer factorization problem or the discrete logarithm problem. This extra structure can be exploited to obtain a very fast cryptosystem: To encrypt/decrypt a message block of length N, NTRU only requires $O(N^2)$ time, whereas the group-based schemes require $O(N^3)$ time. Furthermore, NTRU also has a very short key size of O(N) and very low memory requirements, which makes it ideal for constrained devices such as smart cards.

Truncated Polynomial Rings

Consider a polynomial of degree (N − 1) having integer coefficients:

$$a = a_0 + a_1X + a_2X^2 + a_3X^3 + a_4X^4 \ldots\ldots\ldots\ldots$$
$$+ a_{(N-1)}X^{(N-1)}$$

The set of all such polynomials is denoted by R. The arithmetic on the polynomials in R is as follows. Consider two polynomials a and b:

$$a + b = (a_0 + b_0) + (a_1 + b_1)X + \ldots\ldots + (a_{(N-1)}$$
$$+ b_{(N-1)})X^{(N-1)}$$

Suppose N = 3 and $a = 2 - X + 3X^2$, $b = 1 + 2X - X^2$

$$a + b = 3 + X + 2X^2$$
$$a * b = (2 - X + 3X^2) * (1 + 2X = X^2)$$
$$= 2 + 4X - 2X^2 - X - 2X^2 + X^3 + 3X^2 + 6X^3 - 3X^4$$

N = 3; hence the polynomial cannot have powers of X more than 2, so we have to truncate powers of X higher than 2 with the following rules:

$$X^4 \; by \; X$$
$$X^3 \; by \; X^0 = 1$$

Hence,

$$a * b = 2 + 4X - 2X^2 - X - 2X^2 + 1 + 3X^2 + 6 - 3X$$
$$= (9 - X^2)$$

The distributive law also holds for the polynomials

$$a * (b + c) = a * b + a * c$$

The inclusion of the above law makes the algebraic structure of polynomials into a ring, the Ring of Truncated Polynomials. This ring R is isomorphic to the quotient ring, $Z[X]/(X^{(N-1)})$.

Inverses in Truncated Polynomial Ring

The inverse modulo q of a polynomial a is a polynomial a^{-1} with the property:

$$a * a^{-1} = 1 (mod \; q)$$

Example:

$$N = 7, \quad and \quad q = 11$$
$$a = 3 + 2X^2 - 3X^4 + X^6$$

then,

$$a^{-1} = 2 + 4X + 2X^2 + 4X^3 - 4X^4 + 2X^5 - 2X^6$$
$$= (3 + 2X^2 - 3X^4 + X^6)*$$
$$(2 + 4X + 2X^2 + 4X^3 - 4X^4 + 2X^5 - 2X^6)$$
$$= -10 + 22X - 22X^3 + 22X^6 = 1(mod\ 11)$$

NTRU Parameters and Keys

N—a polynomial in the ring R with degree N − 1, with N being a prime number:

Q—a large modulus to which the coefficient is reduced

P—a small modulus to which each coefficient is reduced

q and p are coprime

f—a polynomial that is a private key

g—a polynomial that is used to generate the public key h from f

NOTE: g (secret) is discarded later on.

H—a polynomial that is a public key

r—a random binding polynomial (discarded later on, but kept secret.

D—coefficient.

Key Generation

Consider a truncated polynomial ring with a degree at most N − 1:

$$a_0 + a_1X + a_2X^2 \ldots \ldots \ldots a_{N-1}X^{(N-1)}$$

1 Choose two small polynomials f and g in the ring R; polynomial f must have an inverse.
2 The inverse of f modulo q and the inverse of f modulo p are computed.
3 $F_q = f^{-1}(mod\ q)$ and $F_p = f^{-1}(mod\ p)$
4 $f*F_q = 1(mod\ q)$ and $f*F_p = 1(mod\ p)$
5 Compute $h = p*(F_q*g)$ mod q.
6 Alice's private key: a pair of polynomials f and F_p
7 Alice's public key: the polynomial h

Public parameters (N, p, q, d) = (7, 3, 41, 2).
Alice chooses: $f(x) = X^6 - X^4 + X^3 + X^2 - 1$

$$g(x) = X^6 + X^4 - X^2 - X$$

$$F_q(x) = f^{-1}(X) - 1(mod\ q) = 8X^6 + 26X^5 + 31X^4 + 21X^3$$
$$+ 40X^2 + 2X + 37\ (mod\ 41)$$

Private Key

$$F_p(x) = f^{-1}(X) - 1(mod\ q)$$
$$= X^6 + 2X^5 + X^3 + X^2 + X + 1\ (mod\ 3)$$

Public Key

$$h(x) = p * (F_q) * g(mod\ q)$$
$$= 20X^6 + 40X^5 + 2X^4 + 38X^3 + 8X^2$$
$$+ 26X + 30\ (mod\ 41)$$

NTRU Encryption

Alice has a message to transmit:

1. Puts the message in the form of polynomial m whose coefficient is chosen modulo p between − p/2 and p/2 (centered lift).
2. Randomly chooses another small polynomial r (to obscure the message).
3. Computes the encrypted message:

$$e = r * h + m(modulo\ q)$$

Example of NTRU Encryption

Alice decides to send Bob the message:

$$m(X) = -X^5 + X^3 + X^2 - X^1 + 1$$

using the random key $r(x) = X^6 - X^5 + X^1 - 1$

$$e = r * h + m\ (modulo\ q)$$

$$e(x) \equiv 31X^6 + 19X^5 + 4X^4 + 2X^3 + 40X^2 + 3X$$
$$+ 25\ (mod\ 41)$$

$$(N, p, q, d) = (7, 3, 41, 2)$$

NTRU Decryption

Bob receives a message e from Alice and would like to decrypt it.

Using his private polynomial f, he computes a polynomial

$$A = f * e(mod\ q).$$

Bob needs to choose coefficients that lie in an interval of length q. He computes the polynomial b = a(mod p). Bob reduces each of the coefficients of a modulo p. Bob uses the other private polynomial F_p to compute c = F_p*b (modulo p), which is the original message of Alice.

Example of NTRU Decryption

$$a = f * e(\mod q)$$

Bob computes $a \equiv X^6 + 10X^5 + 33X^4 + 40X^3 + 40X^2 + X + 40 \ (\mod 41)$

Bob then center lifts modulo q to obtain

$$b = a(\mod p) = X^6 + 10X^5 - 8X^4 - X^3 - X^2 + X - 1 \ (\mod 3)$$

Bob reduces a(x) modulo p and computes

$$c = F_p(x) * b(x) \equiv 2X^5 + X^3 + X^2 + 2X + 1 (\mod 3)$$

Center lifting modulo p retrieves Alice's plaintext

$$m(x) = -X^5 + X^3 + X^2 - X^1 + 1$$

$$(N, p, q, d) = (7, 3, 41, 2)$$

Why Does NTRU Work?

$$a = f * e(\mod q) = f * (r * h + m) \ (\mod q)$$
$$= f * (r * pF_q * g + m)(\mod q) = pr * g + f * m(\mod q)$$

$$b = a = f * m(\mod p)$$

$$c = F_p * b = F_p * f * m = m(\mod p)$$

$$NTRU167 \equiv ECC112 \equiv RSA512$$

$$NTRU263 \equiv ECC168 \equiv RSA1024$$

$$NTRU503 \equiv ECC196 \equiv RSA2048$$

TABLE 70.1 NTRU Parameters.

Security Level	N	q	p
Moderate	167	128	3
Standard	251	128	3
High	347	128	3
Highest	503	256	3

Source: www.ntru.com

Underlying every public-key cryptosystem lurks an extremely difficult mathematical problem waiting to be solved. There is no direct proof that breaking a cryptosystem is equivalent to solving the mathematical problem. Below we list the public-key cryptosystem and the corresponding mathematical problem.

RSA	Integer Factorization Problem
Diffe-Hellman	Discrete Logarithm Problem in F_q^*
Elliptic Curve Cryptography	Discrete Logarithm Problem on an Elliptic Curve
Lattices	SVP and CVP

3. SUMMARY

In this chapter, we reviewed aspects of advanced data encryption security: number theory, group theory, and finite fields relevant to public-key cryptography, as well as advanced data encryption security features (see checklist: An Agenda for Action for Implementing Advanced Data Encryption Security Features). The security of public-key cryptography is determined by what is known as the discrete logarithm problem (DLP), and we gave an example of DLP based on the elliptic curve. In the final section of this chapter, we presented public-key cryptography based on lattice theory—known as the NTRU cryptosystem.

Finally, let's move on to the real interactive part of this chapter: review questions/exercises, hands-on projects, case projects, and optional team case project. The answers and/or solutions by chapter can be found in the Online Instructor's Solutions Manual.

CHAPTER REVIEW QUESTIONS/EXERCISES

True/False

1. True or False? Generation of a key in public-key cryptography involves exponentiation modulo a given modulus.
2. True or False? The order of a finite group is the number of elements in the group H.
3. True or False? In the multiplicative group, H = < Z_{n*}, x >; when the order of an element is the same as $\phi(n)$, then that element is called the primitive root of the group.
4. True or False? A group H is said to be finite if the number of elements in the set H is finite.
5. True or False? The set of integers Z is a group under addition (+); that is (Z, +) is a group with identity e = 0, and inverse of an element a is (−a).

An Agenda for Action for Implementing Advanced Data Encryption Security Features

Please see the following advanced data encryption security features checklist that needs to be implemented in your organization (check all tasks completed):

Core Advanced Data Encryption Security Functionality

_____**1.** Hard Drive Encryption.
_____**2.** Saved Files.
_____**3.** Temporary Files.
_____**4.** Page Files.
_____**5.** Deleted Files.
_____**6.** Secure File Deletion.
_____**7.** Registry or Operating System Boot Files.
_____**8.** Unused Sectors.
_____**9.** Hidden Partitions.
_____**10.** Hibernation Mode.
_____**11.** Logout/Lockout.
_____**12.** Nonmagnetic Drives.
_____**13.** Removable Drives.
_____**14.** Data Recovery by Administrator.

Conformance to Protocol Standards

_____**15.** Password Management/Recovery (Admin).
_____**16.** PKI Authentication.
_____**17.** Multifactor Authentication.
_____**18.** Revocation of Access.

PKI Standards

_____**19.** X.509 Certificates.
_____**20.** LDAP Repository.
_____**21.** Certificate Revocation.
_____**22.** Cryptographic Algorithms.

Cryptographic Standards

Encryption Algorithms

_____**23.** Advanced Encryption Standard (AES).
_____**24.** Triple-Data Encryption Standard (3DES).

Key Establishment Algorithms

_____**25.** Rivest, Shamir, Adleman (RSA).
_____**26.** Other algorithms based on exponentiation of finite fields.
_____**27.** Key Exchange Algorithm (KEA).
_____**28.** Elliptic Curve algorithms.

Digital Signature Algorithms

_____**29.** RSA.
_____**30.** Digital Signature Algorithm (DSA).

_____**31.** Other algorithms based on exponentiation of finite fields.
_____**32.** Elliptic Curve Digital Signature Algorithm (ECDSA).

Hashing Algorithms

_____**33.** SHA-1.
_____**34.** SHA-224.
_____**35.** SHA-256.
_____**36.** SHA-384.
_____**37.** SHA-512.

Assurance Standards

_____**38.** FIPS 140-1.
_____**39.** FIPS 140-2.

Cryptographic Algorithm Validation Program

_____**40.** Cryptographic Module Validated.

Configurability

_____**41.** Changeable Default Values.
_____**42.** Multiple Users.
_____**43.** Different User Access Rights.
_____**44.** Transaction Logging.
_____**45.** Log Integrity.
_____**46.** Log Centralization.
_____**47.** Security Alerts.

Usability

_____**48.** Configuration by Users.
_____**49.** Authentication by Users.
_____**50.** Interruptions during Initial Encryption Process.
_____**51.** Computer use during Initial Encryption Process.
_____**52.** Software/Hardware Compatibility.
_____**53.** Maintenance by Administrators.
_____**54.** Administrator Recovery.
_____**55.** Third Party Recovery.

Manageability

_____**56.** Central Management.
_____**57.** Remote Management.
_____**58.** Unattended Reboot.
_____**59.** Authentication of Management Traffic.
_____**60.** Encryption of Management Traffic.

Scalability

_____**61.** Degree of Scalability.

Multiple Choice

1. A subgroup of a group G is a nonempty subset H of G, which itself is a group under the same operations as that of:
   A. R
   B. I
   C. N
   D. E
   E. G

2. What group is said to be cyclic if there exists an element $a \in G$ such that for any $b \in G$, and $i \geq 0$, $b = a^i$?
   A. O
   B. W

    C. S

    D. G

    E. A

3. Let _____ be a nonempty set with two binary operations addition (+), and multiplication (*).

    A. R

    B. I

    C. W

    D. C

    E. S

4. If the nonzero elements of a ring form a group under multiplication, then the ring is called a:

    A. field

    B. denial-of-service attack

    C. venyo

    D. port traffic

    E. taps

5. Construction of finite fields and computations in finite fields are based on:

    A. systems security plan

    B. polynomial computations

    C. denying service

    D. decision making

    E. URL lists

EXERCISE

Problem

How does advanced data encryption work?

Hands-On Projects

Project

What is a key?

Case Projects

Problem

What is the difference between public and private keys?

Optional Team Case Project

Problem

Which types of data can be encrypted.

REFERENCES

[1] W. Mao, Modern Cryptography, Theory & Practice, Prentice Hall, 2004.

[2] B.A. Forouzan, Cryptography and Network Security, McGraw-Hill, 2008.

[3] P.L. Jensen, Hyperelliptic Curves and Their Application to Cryptography, University of Copenhagen, 2004.

[4] J. Hoffstein, D. Lieman, J. Pipher, J. Silverman, "NTRU": A Public Key Cyrptosystem, NTRU Cryptosystems, Inc. <www.ntru.com>.

[5] J. Hoffstein, J. Pipher, J. Silverman, NTRU—A Ring Based Public Key Cryptosystem.

Index

Note: Page numbers followed by "*f*", "*t*" and "*b*" refers to figures, tables and boxes, respectively.

A

AAA. *See* Authentication, authorization, and accounting (AAA)
Aaditya Corporation, 131
ABAC models. *See* Attribute-based access control (ABAC) models
Abelian group, 670
Abstract model
    network interactions and, 330
        cross-infrastructure cyber cascading attacks, 331–334
        sample cascading attack, 330–331
        vulnerabilities, isolating, 331–334
aCAT. *See* Advanced cellular network vulnerability assessment toolkit (aCAT)
Access
    control, 74–75, 87
        standards, 451
        subsystem, 942–943
    mesh routers, 288
Access confidentiality, 842
Access control entries (ACE), 74, 192
Access control list (ACL), 74, 93, 154, 167–168, 192, 275–276, 411, 531
Access control models, 429–430
Access control policy, 815
Access controls, 1015
    authentication systems, 1018–1020, 1018*b*
    Challenge-Handshake Authentication Protocol (CHAP), 1019–1020
    discretionary access control (DAC), 1015
    Kerberos, 1019–1020
    logical access controls tools, 1017
    mandatory access control (MAC), 1015–1016
    physical access control, 1017
    role-based access control (RBAC), 1016–1017
    wireless security access controls, 1020
Access point (AP) mode, 286
Access-list, 205, 275–276
Accountability, 428
    IT security management, 451
Accounting, user access control, 76
Accurate Background, Inc., 10
ACE. *See* Access control entries (ACE)
ACL. *See* Access control list (ACL)
Action policies, 417
Active probing, 652

Activeworx, 135
Ad-Aware 2008, 135
Ad-Aware 2008 Definition File, 135
Ad hoc networks, wireless
    bootstrapping in, 294–295
    characteristics, 287–288
    internet of things (IoT), 288
    mesh networks, 288
    multimedia sensor networks, 287–288
    sensor networks, 287
Adaptation, 964–965
Additional accounts, 49
Additive cipher, 667
Address Resolution Protocol (ARP), 202, 319, 504–505, 505*f*, 1007
Address space layout randomization (ASLR), 1047–1048
Address-centric communication
    in WSN, 315*f*
Address space layout randomization (ASLR), 1047–1048
Adelman, Leonard, 864
Ad-hoc On-Demand Distance Vector (AODV), 317
Administrative controls, security management system, 411
Adrive, 5*t*
ADSL. *See* Asymmetric Digital Subscriber Line (ADSL)
Advanced cellular network vulnerability assessment toolkit (aCAT), 338–339
    network dependency model, 338
Advanced data encryption, 1127
    mathematical concepts, 1127–1131
        cyclic group, 1129
        Discrete Logarithm, 1127–1129
        Fermat's Little Theorem, 1127
        Primitive Roots, 1127–1128
    RSA cryptosystem, 1131–1136
        Discrete Logarithm Problem (DLP), 1133
        Factorization Attack, 1132–1133
        Key Generation, 1135
        Lattice-based Cryptography, 1133
        NTRU Cryptosystem, 1134
        NTRU Decryption, 1135–1136
        NTRU Encryption, 1135
        NTRU Parameters and Keys, 1135
        Truncated Polynomial Rings, 1134

Advanced Encryption Standard (AES), 40, 290, 320, 354, 669, 863–864, 1037
    bytes, 41–42
    math, 42
    rounds, 43–44
    working of, 41–44
Advanced Encryption System, 1097
Advanced persistent threat (APT), 56
Advent Information Management Ltd, 131
AES. *See* Advanced Encryption Standard (AES)
AF. *See* Application firewalls (AF)
Aggregation switches (AggS), 127–128
Aggregators, instant messaging (IM), 729
Agreement replicas, 133
AH. *See* Authentication Header (AH)
AICPA. *See* American Institute of Certified Public Accountants (AICPA)
Aide, 193
Air Force Research Laboratory, 149
AirDrop, 5
Aladdin Knowledge Systems, 74
Alert policies, 417
Alert.ids file, 268
Algebraic attack, 43
Algebraic Packet Marking (APM), 653–654
Algebraic structure, data encryption, 669–672
Algorithms, 1001, 1037
Alphanumeric symbols, 664–665
Al-Shaer, classification of, 804
Amalgamated preferences, 824
Amazon S3, 5*t*
Amazon VPC, 116
Ambient intelligence (AmI) world
    mobile user-centric identity management in, 480–482
        AmI scenario, 480–481
        requirements for, 481–482
American Institute of Certified Public Accountants (AICPA), 157
American National Standards Institute (ANSI), 860
American Standard Code for Information Interchange (ASCII), 26
AmI. *See* Ambient intelligence (AmI) world
AMPEG Security Lighthouse, 131
Analysis, risk, 906–907
Ancheta, Jeanson James, 232
Angular momentum, 569*b*
Anomaly detection systems, 394
Anomaly-based analysis, 280